WORLD HISTORY
THE HUMAN ODYSSEY

JACKSON J. SPIELVOGEL

**West
Educational
Publishing**

WORLD HISTORY
THE HUMAN ODYSSEY

JACKSON J. SPIELVOGEL
THE PENNSYLVANIA STATE UNIVERSITY

The classic and contemporary world history text, from West Educational Publishing.

It's a STORY

Jack Spielvogel has written several best-selling textbooks and has won numerous teaching awards at Penn State University. So it's not surprising that *World History* is a real story, written by one storyteller—a storyteller who has a gift for engaging students with his exceptionally clear and exciting writing style. Your students will enjoy reading this well told story—the story, filled with drama and action, of the *Human Odyssey*.

Contributions and reviews by more than 70 outstanding high school teachers have helped make *World History* the most interesting and useful text for high school students around the country.

about GLOBAL HISTORY

World History presents a truly balanced history of all the world's cultures. It provides in-depth coverage of the Asian, African, and Latin American cultures—coverage often missing from other world history texts.

TEACHER REVIEWERS

"This is a true World History text—not a Western Civilization text."

"[The author] does a wonderful job of exposing students to various cultures in a positive way."

drawing CONNECTIONS between cultures and time periods

Throughout the text, the author shows your students how one culture connects to another. He also connects the ancient worlds to the modern worlds. Connections are consistently made between past and present events, showing your students how historical events have a direct bearing on their lives.

Connections Around the World

These features illustrate how events in one area of the world are linked to other parts of the world. Feature titles include *Trade and the Silk Road, Feudalism, The Great Flu Epidemic,* and *Female Spies in World War II.*

Connections to Our World

The clash between the Hindus and Muslims, and the relationship between the plagues of the Middle Ages and a children's nursery rhyme are just two examples of the *Connections to Our World* features that show your students how the past reaches across the ages to influence and shape today's world.

CONNECTIONS AROUND THE WORLD

Rulers and Gods All of the world's earliest civilizations believed that there was a close connection between rulers and gods. In Egypt, pharaohs were considered gods whose role was to maintain the order and harmony of the universe in their own kingdoms. In Mesopotamia, India, and China, rulers were thought to rule with divine assistance. Kings were often seen as rulers who derived their power from the gods and who were the agents or representatives of the gods. Many Romans certainly believed that their success in creating an empire was a visible sign of divine favor. As one Roman stated, "We have... all the nations of the world, b... realized that the world is dire... by the gods."

The rulers' supposed conn... also caused them to seek div... of the world. This led to the a... organized method to figure o... the gods. In Mesopotamian a... divination took the form of ex... sacrificed animals or the fligh... mine the will of the gods. The... cle (ORE-eh-cul) bones to re... the gods. The Greeks divine... by use of the oracle, a sacre... a god or goddess who reveal... Underlying all of these practi... supernatural universe; that is... divine forces were in charge... humans were dependent for... on those divine forces. It was... Scientific Revolution of the m... many people began to believ... that was not governed by spi...

CONNECTIONS TO OUR WORLD

Conflict in Palestine In 1948, an independent Jewish state known as Israel was established in an area known as Palestine. The Arab neighbors of the new state were outraged, because 90 percent of the people in Palestine were Arab Muslims. An invasion of the new state of Israel by its Arab neighbors failed. However, conflict between Arabs and Israelis over Palestine continues to this day. In 1964, an Arab organization called the Palestine Liberation Organization was founded. Its goal is to bring about an independent Arab state of Palestine.

Conflict between Jews and other peoples in Palestine has a very long history. When the Hebrews entered Palestine around 1220 B.C., after their enslavement in Egypt, they found other peoples who were already settled there. One of these peoples was the Philistines (FIL-eh-steenz). For over two centuries, Hebrews and Philistines fought over control of much of Palestine.

This struggle made a strong impact on the Hebrews. By 1020 B.C., after a series of defeats, the Hebrews found themselves on the verge of being conquered by the Philistines. In desperation, the Hebrews decided to form a solid united front by giving up their loose tribal organization and choosing one of their members—Saul—as king. At first, Saul was very successful. He organized a small army and went on the offensive against the Philistines. Around 1000 B.C., however, Saul and his army experienced disaster when they dared to meet the Philistines on an open plain. The army was disastrously defeated, Saul's sons were killed, and Saul committed suicide. David, the next king of the Hebrews, was more successful. During his reign, the Hebrews defeated the Philistines and established control over all of Palestine. Although later the Hebrews were conquered and scattered by the Assyrians, Persians, and Romans, for centuries Palestine remained the Promised Land in the minds of many Jews.

using PRIMARY SOURCES

No other world history text comes close to providing as many primary sources within the student text as you'll find in *World History*. No need to photocopy these dramatic, inspiring documents from other sources—they're already accessible to your students, integrated within the textbook narrative and features. Additional primary sources are available—see page 12A.

TEACHER REVIEWERS

"Primary source documents are a must!!! [Having them in the text] will save me from searching for additional information."

"[Primary sources] are often the spark for discussion and questions."

Primary Sources
Where You
Want Them—In The
Student Text!

and HIGH-INTEREST FEATURES

Several text features, such as *You Are There, Young People In...,* and *Sports and Contests,* strive to place your students within the context of a certain culture or time period. Social history, as well as political history, comes alive for your students as they encounter people, places, and events of historical significance.

Focus on Everyday Life

Housing and food in ancient China, castles of the aristocrats, life on slave ships, and many more topics are presented to give your students a close-up look at daily life in different cultures.

Biography

Queen Hatshepsut, Sundiata Keita, Suleyman the Magnificent, Anne Frank, and Aung San Suu Kyi are just a few of the historical figures featured in the text.

TEACHER REVIEWERS

"I liked the special features, especially the ones that feature women in history, the ones on the lives of young people, and the ones with primary sources and literature. They will make history more real to the students."

"[The text features] are all excellent, interesting, chosen with great care."

The Role of Science and Technology

Fire, the wheel, the telescope, the railroad, and the atomic bomb, are featured examples of science and technology's impact on world history.

Our Artistic Heritage

Cave paintings, classical Greek art, traditional Chinese landscape painting, Dadaism and Surrealism, plus much more of the world's greatest art will inspire your students to learn more about distant times and places.

Our Literary Heritage

Excerpts from *Gilgamesh* to Shakespeare to Ibsen provide insights into cultures and time periods as only the world's greatest authors can.

Sports and Contests

Feature titles such as *The Olympic Games of the Greeks, The Deadly Games of Central America, The Growth of Professional Sports,* and more, capture your students' interest and motivate them to learn more about different cultures.

You Are There

With the *You Are There* features, you will be able to transport your students to the very heart of historical events, cultural practices and attitudes, and common experiences of family life—helping your students better appreciate and understand how other people have lived.

Young People In . . .

High-interest stories about the life and times of young people from Greece, the Aztec Empire, Medieval Europe, and other historical periods are presented.

TEACHER'S WRAPAROUND EDITION

Written by experienced classroom teachers, the *World History Teacher's Wraparound Edition* is an extraordinary resource. From planning guides to complete support information for features found in the student text, the *Teacher's Wraparound Edition* is designed to ensure you get the most for your students out of every lesson, every class period, every day.

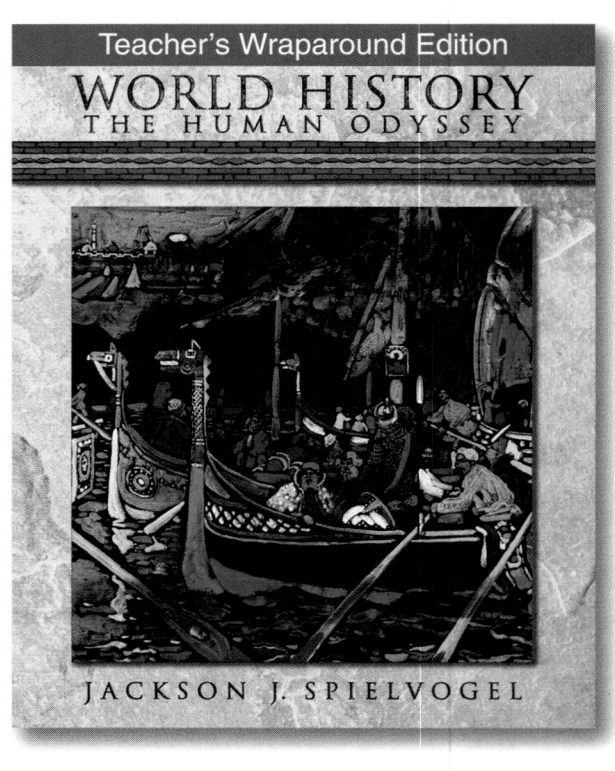

Teacher's Wraparound Edition
WORLD HISTORY
THE HUMAN ODYSSEY

JACKSON J. SPIELVOGEL

Chapter Planning Guide

Provides a complete list of chapter instructional resources, skills and enrichment opportunities, and assessment, multimedia, and Spanish resources. These convenient guides display the many possible choices for structuring your lessons.

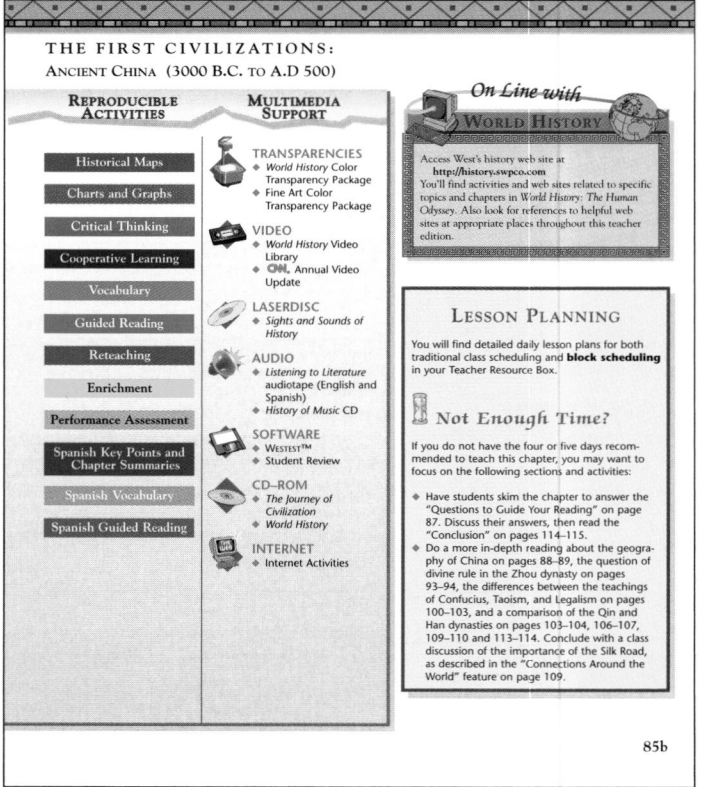

Chapter Introductions

Within the *Teacher's Wraparound Edition* each chapter is introduced with reinforcement opportunities, exercises that prepare your students for the material ahead, and guides for using the additional resources that accompany *World History*.

Chapter 4 — Introducing Chapter

BUILDING ON CHAPTER 3

To prepare students to study Chapter 4 you may use the following questions and activities.

◆ Remind students of the impact that trade on the Silk Road had on civilization in India. Why did it impact Chinese civilization?

◆ Ask students to identify geographic features that influenced the development of civilization in India. Identify similar geographic influences as they study China.

◆ Lead students in a brief discussion of the influence of the Hindu and Buddhist religions on India. Why would it be reasonable for there to be similar religious influences in ancient China?

USING THE OPENING STORY

Depending on the ability levels of your students, select from the following questions and activities to reinforce the reading of the opening story.

◆ Why should food surpluses enable one group of villages to dominate less prosperous people?

◆ Why might a great teacher teach only those who want to learn?

◆ What are several ideas that influence your life today that were developed many years ago?

THE FIRST CIVILIZATIONS:

In the valleys of the two great river systems of East Asia, the Huang (Yellow) and the Yangtze (YANG-SEE), another river valley civilization arose more than four thousand years ago. Like the civilizations of Mesopotamia, Egypt, and India, the civilization of ancient China began with groups of villages that grew crops along major rivers. Changes in farming practices, however, soon led to food surpluses. Food surpluses, in turn, soon led to the growth of an urban civilization. This vibrant new civilization expanded gradually over its neighboring areas and, by the third century B.C., had emerged as a great empire.

The civilization of China is closely tied to Confucius (kun-FYOO-shus), a philosopher who lived in the sixth century B.C. Confucius traveled the

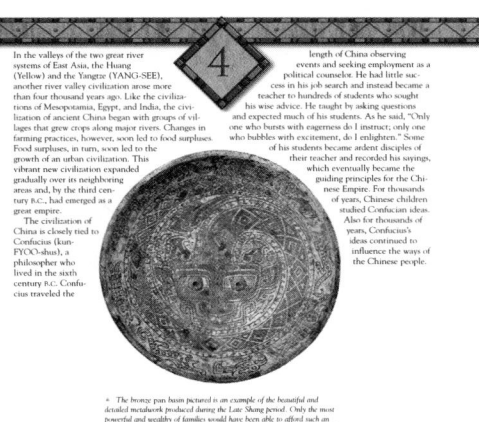

length of China observing events and seeking employment as a political counselor. He had little success in his job search and instead became a teacher to hundreds of students who sought his wise advice. He taught by asking questions and expected much of his students. As he said, "Only one who bursts with eagerness do I instruct; only one who bubbles with excitement, do I enlighten." Some of his students became ardent disciples of their teacher and recorded his sayings, which eventually became the guiding principles for the Chinese Empire. For thousands of years, Chinese children studied Confucian ideas. Also for thousands of years, Confucius's ideas continued to influence the ways of the Chinese people.

The bronze pan basin pictured is an example of the beautiful and detailed metalwork produced during the Late Shang period. Only the most powerful and wealthy of families would have been able to afford such an exquisite piece for use in their cleansing ceremonies. Look carefully to find the dragon lying coiled at the bottom of the basin, perhaps waiting to help the bather communicate with the dead.

ADDITIONAL RESOURCES

The resources below can be used to enrich the lessons in this chapter.

BOOKS FOR STUDENTS
Confucius by Bennett Sins. Franklin Watts.
The Longest Rampart by Robert Silverburg, Chilton.

VIDEOS/FILMS
The First Emperor of China. (CAV laserdisk.) Social Studies School Services. (800) 421-4246

CD-ROM
Religions of the World. Mentarom. Social Studies School Services. (800) 421-4246

Chapter 4 — Right Panel

China was able to avoid destruction at the hands of the invaders and survived intact down through the formation of the Chinese Empire in 221 B.C.

Civilization in China began with the expansion of small farming villages into a more complex society. In a pattern that we have seen elsewhere, civilization gradually spread from these settlements in the valleys of the Huang and Yangtze Rivers to other lowland areas of eastern and central China. Government emerged, along with a writing system. As wealth increased, the societies began to create armies and build walled cities. The process took several thousand years.

Answers to QUESTIONS TO GUIDE YOUR READING

1. civilizations along major rivers; mountains/deserts isolated Chinese; open to attack from the north (pages 87–88)
2. farming economy, large cities, many gods, ancestor worship, bronze casting (pages 89–92)
3. See pages 95–99.
4. See pages 100–103.
5. See pages 104–114.
6. mastered art of fighting on horseback; city walls built to defend against them (pages 104, 106)

FOCUS ON THEMES (Chapter 4)

China and a wide gulf between rich and poor.

The Importance of Cultural Developments Writing literature, Shang bronze ritual vessels and the terracotta army of the First Qin Emperor attest to Chinese cultural achievements.

Religion in History Religion played an important role in China's civilization.

The Role of Individuals Confucius showed the power of an individual to change the course of history.

The Impact of Science and Technology China with remarkable technological achievements led the world until the Industrial Revolution.

The Environment and History China was a river valley civilization. Fierce nomads on China's northern frontier necessitated a strong defense, including building the Great Wall.

Chapter 5 — Introducing Chapter

BUILDING ON CHAPTER 4

To "set the scene" for the study of Chapter 5, have students review Section 4 of Chapter 4. Ask them to describe the scene as the first Chinese Empire, the Qin Dynasty, came to power. Also ask them to give reasons as to why this dynasty and the Han Dynasty achieved so much power. Finally, have them enumerate the reasons why these dynasties ultimately failed. Tell them that in Chapter 5 they will be reading about the rise and fall of another great empire and that they should be on the lookout for differences and similarities between this empire, the Roman Empire, and the Chinese empires.

USING THE OPENING STORY

Select from the following to reinforce the reading of the Pericles Funeral Oration.

◆ How long ago did this story take place? *(approximately 2430 years ago)*

◆ What was the purpose of the ceremony? *(a public funeral to honor the Athenians who had died in the war between Sparta and Athens)*

◆ According to Pericles, why is Athens called a democracy? *(power is in the hands of all the people)*

LEARNING FROM VISUALS

Answer to the caption question: repose and acceptance of death as a natural part of life.

THE CIVILIZATION OF THE GREEKS
(1900 TO 133 B.C.)

In 431 B.C., war erupted in Greece as two very different Greek states—Athens and Sparta—fought for domination of the Greek world. Strengthened by its democratic ideals, Athens felt secure behind its walls. In the first winter of the war, the Athenians held a public funeral to honor those who had died on the war. On the day of the ceremony, the citizens of Athens joined in a procession. The relatives of the dead wailed for their loved ones.

As was the custom in Athens, one leading citizen was asked to address the crowd. On this day it was Pericles (PAIR-ih-KLEEZ) who spoke to the people. This talked about the greatness of Athens and reminded the Athenians of the strength of their political system. "Our constitution," Pericles said, "is called a democracy because power is in the hands not of a minority but of the whole people. When it is a question of settling private disputes, we

one is equal before the law. Just as our political life is free and open, so is our day-to-day life in our relations with each other. . . . Here each individual is interested not only in his own affairs but in the affairs of the state as well."

In this famous Funeral Oration, the citizens of Athens heard about the ideal of democracy and the importance of the individual. The Greeks laid the intellectual foundations of Western civilization. They also asked some basic questions about human life that we still ask today: What is the nature of the universe? What is the purpose of human life? What is our relationship to divine forces? What is a community? What is a state? What is truth itself, and how do we realize it? The Greeks not only gave answers to these questions but also created a system of logical, analytical thought in order to examine the questions. We in the Western world still regard this system of thought as worthwhile.

This gold death mask was initially believed to be the mask of Agamemnon, who led the Greek forces at Troy. The face appears to be sad, but calm. What might this suggest about the Greek view of death?

ADDITIONAL RESOURCES

The resources below can be used to enrich the lessons in this chapter.

BOOKS FOR STUDENTS
Classical Greece by C. M. Boura (Time-Life.) (Great Ages of Man.)
The Last of the Wine by Mary Renault, Pantheon
Alexander the Great by Charles Mercer. Harper and Row (Horizon Caravelle)

VIDEOS/FILMS
Western Civilization: The Greeks: In Search of Meaning. Learning Corp of America. Social Studies School Service (800) 421-4246

CD-ROM
Queue World History: Ancient Greece. Learning Services
East (800) 877-3278
West (800) 877-9378

Chapter 5 — Right Panel

THE BEGINNINGS OF CIVILIZATION

GREEK CIVILIZATION
1900 B.C. — 133 B.C.

OUTLINE

1. EARLY GREEK HISTORY
2. THE WORLD OF THE GREEK CITY-STATES (750 TO 500 B.C.)
3. THE HIGH POINT OF GREEK CIVILIZATION: CLASSICAL GREECE
4. THE CULTURE OF CLASSICAL GREECE
5. THE SPREAD OF GREEK CIVILIZATION: ALEXANDER AND THE HELLENISTIC KINGDOMS

QUESTIONS TO GUIDE YOUR READING

1. How did the geography of Greece affect Greek history?
2. What role did Homer's works play in the lives of the Greeks?
3. What was the polis, or city-state, and how did the major city-states of Athens and Sparta differ?
4. What role did the Persian and Great Peloponnesian (PUL-uh-puh-NEE-shun) Wars play in Greek history?
5. What political and cultural contributions did the Greeks make to Western civilization during the classical period?
6. How did Alexander the Great create an empire?
7. What were the cultural achievements of the Hellenistic world?

EARLY GREEK HISTORY

The story of ancient Greek civilization begins when a group of Greek-speaking Indo-European people moved into Greece from the north around 1900 B.C. By 800 B.C., the basic institution of ancient Greek life, the city-state, had emerged. Greek civilization flourished and reached its height in the classical period of the fifth century B.C.

Greece: The Impact of Geography

Geography played an important role in the development of Greek history. Compared with the landmasses of Mesopotamia and Egypt, Greece occupied a small area. It was a mountainous peninsula that encompassed only forty-five thousand square miles of territory—about the size of the state of Louisiana. The mountains and the sea played especially significant roles in the development of Greek history. Much of Greece consists of small plains and river valleys surrounded by mountain ranges eight thousand to ten thousand feet high. The mountains isolated Greeks from one another, causing Greek communities to develop their

Answers to QUESTIONS TO GUIDE YOUR READING

1. mountains created isolated, independent communities; island geography led to seafaring and creation of colonies (pages 119–120)
2. educational texts, provided heroic ideal (page 122)
3. community with common goals; Athens: "well-rounded" citizens; Sparta: harsh, militaristic, physically fit (pages 125–129)
4. Persian: built military power; Peloponnesian: weakened city-states (pages 129–130, 134)
5. political: male dominance, slavery, free-trade economy, public works projects; cultural: strengthened family unit, importance of religion, physical fitness and sports, love of wisdom, theater, systematic recording of history (pages 133–140)
6. military prowess, destruction of Persian monarchy, global view of the world (page 144)
7. see pages 145–149.

FOCUS ON THEMES (Chapter 5)

Listed below are brief summaries of how the content in this chapter supports the text's key themes.

Politics and History The Greeks developed the following kinds of government: monarchy, aristocracy, tyranny, oligarchy, and democracy. Our word *politics* is derived from the Greek word *polis*.

The Role of Ideas The Greeks contributed two important ideas: the idea that the individual has the ability to use rational thought to gain true wisdom, and the idea that citizens should make the decisions that affect how they are to be governed (the democratic ideal).

Social Life The Greeks had a strong sense of community in their city-states.

The Importance of Cultural Developments The artistic and intellectual achievements of the Greeks (in drama, philosophy, and the writing of history) provided the foundations of Western artistic and intellectual life.

Religion in History Religion was an important element in Greek civilization. Greeks shared a belief in major gods and goddesses and in the importance of appeasing them to maintain a flourishing community. A lack of religious dogma allowed the Greeks to ask questions about the universe and the role of humans in the world.

The Environment and History Mountains and the sea played major roles in Greek history.

Left sample page (16)

COMPARING TIME PERIODS

Guide students in a discussion of the differences in the daily lives of those who lived in or near Lascaux, France; Çatal Hüyük, Turkey; and their own towns. Ask students to compare and contrast daily activities and lifestyles.

CRITICAL THINKING

What features do Europe, India, Egypt, China, and Mesoamerica have in common that permitted the development of Neolithic farming villages? Why would these villages have flourished in the Middle East?

LEARNING FROM VISUALS

Answer to the caption question: Answers will vary but may include gathering berries, sharpening tools, hauling water, etc.

REINFORCING VOCABULARY

Some students may not understand the difference between *artisans* and *artists.* Artisans are craftspeople who make functional items, often that are quite beautiful, but utilitarian. Artists, or painters or sculptors, do not consider useful function foremost in their creations.

CLASS DISCUSSION

The early foodstuffs produced in each of the agricultural regions—beans and maize in the Americas, rice in China, wheat and barley in the Middle East—are still produced and form an important part of the diet in these areas. Ask students why they think primary foodstuffs have not changed since early times.

16

16   UNIT ONE   THE FIRST CIVILIZATIONS AND THE RISE OF EMPIRES (PREHISTORY TO A.D. 500)

walls enclosed thirty-two acres, and its population probably reached six thousand inhabitants during its high point from 6700 to 5700 B.C. People lived in simple mud brick houses that were built so close to one another that there were no streets. To get to their homes, people had to walk along the rooftops and then enter their homes through holes in the roofs.

Archaeologists have found twelve products that were grown in this community, including fruits, nuts, and three kinds of wheat. People grew their own food and kept it in storerooms within their homes. Domesticated animals (animals that had been tamed for human use), especially cattle, yielded meat, milk, and hides. Hunting scenes on the walls indicate that the people of Çatal Hüyük hunted as well. Unlike earlier hunter-gatherers, however, they no longer relied on hunting to survive. Food surpluses made it possible for people to do things other than farming. Some people became artisans. They made weapons and jewelry that were traded with neighboring peoples, thus exposing

This representation of a Neolithic village typifies life for early humans. You can see hunters in the background driving wild horses off a cliff to people waiting at the bottom to slaughter them. Others build more huts or prepare the food. What might the children be doing to help?

the people of Çatal Hüyük to the wider world around them.

Special buildings in Çatal Hüyük were shrines containing figures of gods and goddesses. Female statuettes have also been found there, often of women giving birth or nursing a child. These "earth mothers" may well have been connected with goddess figures. Both the shrines and the statues point to the growing role of religion in the lives of these Neolithic peoples.

The Neolithic agricultural revolution had far-reaching consequences. Once people settled in villages or towns, they built houses for protection and other structures for the storage of goods. The organized communities stored food and a number of material goods, which encouraged the development of trade. In the Middle East, for example, the new communities exchanged such objects as shells, flint, and semiprecious stones, often over long distances. People also began to specialize in certain crafts, and a division of labor developed. Pottery was made from clay and baked in fire to make it hard. The pots were used for cooking and to store grains. Baskets were also made for storage. Stone tools became refined as flint blades were used to make sickles and hoes for use in the fields. Over the course of the Neolithic Age, many of the food plants still in use today began to be cultivated. Moreover, vegetable fibers from such plants as flax and cotton were used to spin yarn that was woven into cloth.

The change to systematic agriculture in the Neolithic Age also had consequences for the relationship between men and women. Men became more active in farming and herding animals, jobs that took them away from the home settlement. Women remained behind, caring for children and taking responsibility for weaving cloth, turning milk into cheese, and other tasks that required much labor in one place. Men came to play a more dominant role, a basic pattern that would remain until our own times.

Other Neolithic patterns were also important in human history. Permanent dwellings, domesticated animals, regular farming, specialized occupations, and men holding power are all part of the human story. Despite all of our scientific and technological progress, human survival still depends on the growing and storing of food, an accomplishment of people in the

---

SPECIAL NEEDS: *Visual/Tactile*

Have students examine the illustrations in this chapter showing the tools of the first humans. Students should bring to class examples of arrowheads, spear points, scrapers, etc. Have students show or explain how these tools may have been used in ancient times. Show modern tools that may correlate to the Stone Age tools and ask students to consider how modern tools are similar to or different from the Stone Age tools. Pass around other artifacts, such as a vase, a spoon, and a coin. Ask students to examine each item and to make inferences about what someone discovering these items in the future might say about the civilization from which they came. Consider asking students to imagine what some of the tools of the future may look like and what their purposes would be.

Right sample page (17)

CHAPTER 1   THE FIRST HUMANS (PREHISTORY TO 3500 B.C.)   17

Neolithic Age. The Neolithic Revolution was truly a turning point in human history.

Between 4000 and 3000 B.C., new developments began to affect the Neolithic towns in some areas. The use of metals marked a new level of human control over the environment and its resources. Even before 4000 B.C., craftspeople had discovered that metal-bearing rocks could be heated to liquefy the metal. The liquid metal could then be cast in molds to make tools and weapons that were more useful than stone instruments. Copper was the first metal to be used in making tools. After 4000 B.C., craftspeople in western Asia discovered that a combination of copper and tin created bronze, a far harder and more durable metal than copper. Its widespread use has led historians to speak of a **Bronze Age** from around 3000 to 1200 B.C. However, few people could afford bronze. Thus, even after the introduction of bronze, people continued to use tools and weapons made of stone.

At first, Neolithic settlements were hardly more than villages. As the inhabitants mastered the art of farming, however, they gradually began to develop more complex human societies. As wealth increased, these societies began to create armies and to build walled cities. By the beginning of the Bronze Age, the concentration of larger numbers of people in the river valleys of Mesopotamia, Egypt, India, and China was leading to a whole new pattern for human life.

◆ SECTION REVIEW ◆

1. **Define:**
(a) Neolithic Revolution, (b) Neolithic Age, (c) Mesolithic Age, (d) Neolithic farming villages, (e) Bronze Age

2. **Identify:**
(a) Mesoamericans, (b) bronze

3. **Recall:**
(a) Name at least three consequences of the agricultural revolution.

(b) What is a Neolithic village or town? What well-known Middle Eastern, Neolithic town is named in your text?

4. **Think Critically:** The word "revolution" is often defined as "an uprising against an established government, or a sudden change." What other definition of revolution would you give based on your understanding of the "agricultural revolution"?

▲ 4
THE EMERGENCE OF CIVILIZATION

As we have seen, early human beings formed small groups that developed a simple culture that enabled them to survive. As human societies grew and developed greater complexity, a new form of human existence—called civilization—came into being. A **civilization** is a complex culture in which large numbers of human beings share a number of common elements. Historians have identified at least six basic characteristics of civilizations. Most of these were present in the early civilizations of Mesopotamia, Egypt, India, and China, which we will examine in Chapters 2, 3, and 4. First, however, we must ask, what are the characteristics of civilizations?

The Rise of Cities

Cities are one of the chief characteristics of civilizations. The first civilizations developed in river valleys that were able to maintain the large-scale farming that was needed to feed a large population. Although farming practices varied from civilization to civilization, in each civilization a significant part of the population lived in cities. These cities were much larger than the Neolithic towns that preceded them, and new patterns of living soon emerged.

The Growth of Governments

Growing numbers of people and the need to maintain the food supply and to build walls for defense soon led

So What?

*If your students question the importance of information on the **agricultural revolution**, tell them . . .*

The domestication of plants and animals may have been the single most revolutionary event in human history. Domesticating plants and animals was responsible for an increase in human life span, the creation of cities, and the formation of laws and government. It

also led to systems of writing, the development of mathematics and science, as well as the establishment of the world's major religions. Once humans began to work cooperatively to grow food, they needed to establish rules for sharing water and dividing crops. And they created a system for establishing and enforcing their laws. All of this was the result of planting the first seed.

ASSESS

Answers to **SECTION REVIEW**

1. (a) shift from hunting and gathering to systematic agriculture
(b) a time when there was a shift from hunting of animals and the gathering of food to the keeping of animals and the growing of food systematically
(c) period when systematic agriculture spread to different areas of the world
(d) permanent settlements
(e) period after 4000 B.C. when bronze was discovered and used widely

2. (a) inhabitants of present-day Mexico and Central America
(b) a combination of copper and tin

3. (a) See page 16, column 2 for answers
(b) town formed by people gathering into an area for purpose of growing crops on a regular basis; Jericho or Çatal Hüyük

4. answers will vary

CLOSE

Emphasize to students the importance of the agricultural revolution. With stable food supply, populations grew, and towns could begin to develop.

FOCUS

OBJECTIVES

After completing this section students should be able to

17

Focus/Teach/Assess/Close

Teaching suggestions for each section of each chapter are organized into a Focus/Teach/Assess/Close lesson-planning format.

Special Needs

Activities for special needs students include suggestions for students with special learning needs and varying ability levels.

Multimedia Support

References to related multimedia resources are provided at appropriate places in the *Teacher's Wraparound Edition.*

Learning From Visuals

Images are wonderful concept anchors for students. They are also invaluable discussion starters. *Learning From Visuals* will help you take advantage of these properties.

Multimedia Support

TRANSPAREN
1–2, Sites of M
Hominid Fossil
Finds

Multimedia Support

LASERDISC
Clay Bison in the Tuc Audoubert Cave, Middle Magdelenian (c. 13,000–10,000 B.C.)

10A

Special Wrap Features

Special features throughout the *Teacher's Wraparound Edition* have been added to ensure all of your students become involved in and intrigued with the study of world history. *More About* and *So What?* features help you show your students how particular events or developments throughout history have impacted their lives. *On Line With World History* features incorporate fun activities with educational World Wide Web sites related to world history.

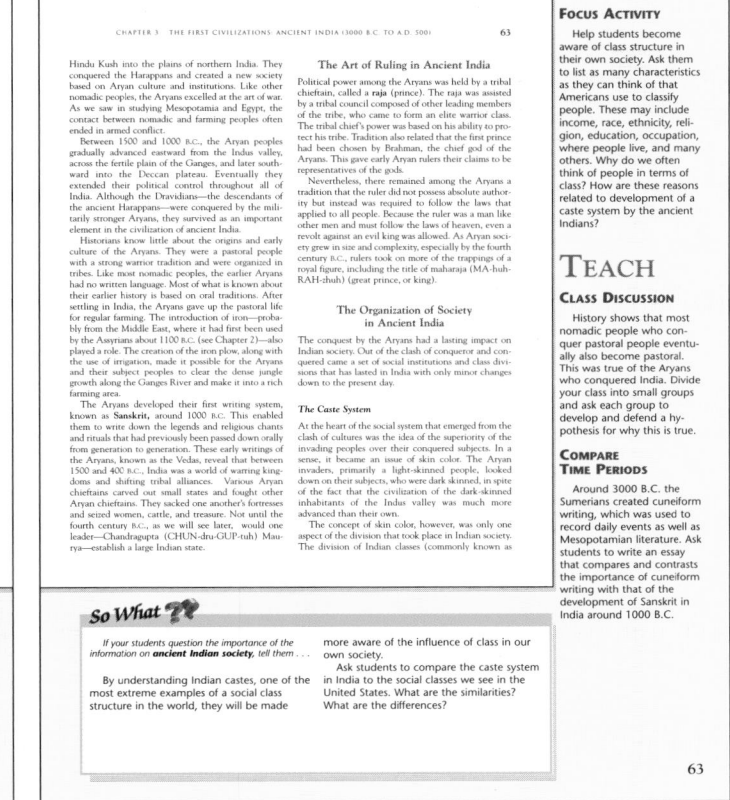

Feature Support

The *Teacher's Wraparound Edition* supports each feature in the student text. The support material consists of an introduction, one or more teaching suggestions, a feature closing or summary, and answers to feature questions.

SPORTS AND CONTESTS

FOCUS ON EVERYDAY LIFE

THE ROLE OF SCIENCE AND TECHNOLOGY

YOUNG PEOPLE IN GREECE

YOU ARE THERE

BIOGRAPHY

OUR LITERARY HERITAGE

OUR ARTISTIC HERITAGE

TEACHER RESOURCES

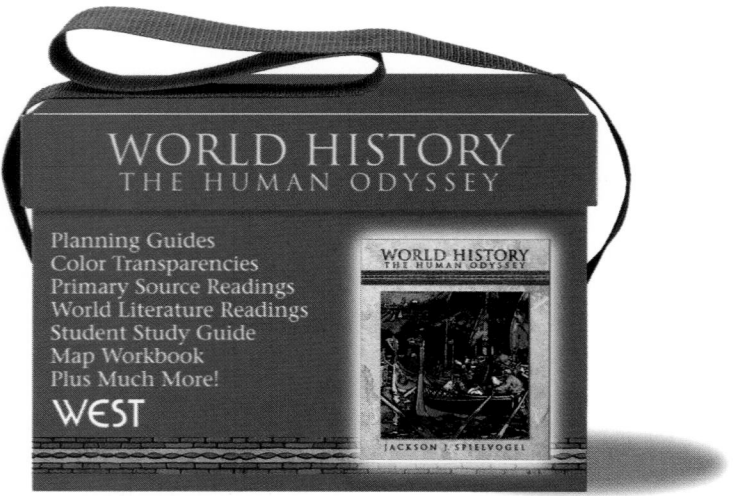

Planning Guides

Daily Lesson Plans

Complete, ready-to-implement lesson plans! Provided for each day are Objectives, Guided and Independent Practice assignments, Enrichment activities, a Closure exercise and an overnight Assignment. Lesson plans also provided for a block scheduling format.

Full-Color Transparency Acetates

World History Transparency Acetates (Binder)

The *World History* transparencies include brilliant, four-color maps, graphs, charts, drawings, and other illustrations from the textbook and supplemental to the text—perfect tools for enhancing your classroom presentations. There are more than 100 transparencies to choose from.

World Art Transparency Package

Your students can discover historical links between the past and present, from all over the world, through art! The *World Art Transparency Package* consists of full-color transparency acetate reproductions of notable works of art. Guided discussion questions are included for each reproduction. Performance-based activities are also included.

Booklets

Primary Source Readings

Chosen from a variety of sources, these documents and excerpts are supplemental to the primary sources already included in the text. The readings will enable your students to better understand events, trends, and issues of major historical significance. Each of the 40 selections includes questions and activities to guide you in promoting critical thinking, historical inquiry, and class discussion.

World Literature Readings

This collection of fine literary works consists of excerpts from a selection of novels, plays, poems, and essays written throughout history. *World Literature Readings* may be used with the *Listening to Literature* audio CD or cassette.

Student Study Guide

This chapter-by-chapter study aid is designed for your students—to reinforce individual understanding of the text and assist in preparation for examinations. Provided are chapter outlines and reviews utilizing concept maps, timelines, self-tests, and more.

History: The Lighter Side
This booklet contains a collection of fun, interesting facts about foods, cultures, and historical events. Written by experienced classroom teachers, this booklet is perfect for enhancing your lessons.

Perspectives: Connecting the Present to the Past
This will prove an invaluable tool as you plan lessons intended to guide your students toward making clear connections between past events and present circumstances. Supplemental materials and support activities provide opportunities for group interactive learning and enrichment.

Exploring the World: A Map Workbook
Reproducible map outlines with related activities will help your students build and practice map skills. They will learn how to read maps, understand keys, and extract valuable information about that time period.

Plus More Than 150 Pages of Worksheets and Materials!
• Critical Thinking Activities
• Vocabulary and Guided Reading Activities
• Chart and Graph Skills Activities
• Cooperative Learning Activities
• Performance Assessment Activities
• Spanish Chapter Key Points and Summaries

• Reteaching Activities
• Enrichment and Extension Activities
• Reading Close

Assessment Materials
• Section Quizzes
• Chapter Tests (A and B Versions)
• Final Examination

MULTIMEDIA RESOURCES

₍ World History Video Update

These exciting video updates consist of short segments covering the year's most important world history related news stories as reported by one of the world's leading news agencies, CNN. For each video segment you will find corresponding teaching material, which includes questions and teaching suggestions to help you prepare for and follow up each segment. You will receive a new videotape, containing the most current coverage and information, each year of your textbook adoption.

World History Video Library

This quality collection of videos covers a range of high-interest topics your students will love. Topics include archaeology in ancient Egypt, treasures of Troy, knighthood and the Crusades, the evolution of China, and immigration and Ellis Island.

Sights and Sounds of History Laserdisc

Short, focused video clips, photos, artwork, animations, music, and dramatic readings add greater depth and meaning to historical topics and events that are most difficult for students to appreciate from a textbook alone. For example, your students will experience the grandeur of Versailles and the devastating effects of defeat as felt by a German soldier at Stalingrad.

World History CD-ROM

With *The Journey of Civilization*, your students will explore history like never before. This dynamic, multimedia experience takes your students on "interactive" journeys to bring history to life. Each journey includes activities that go beyond the limitations of the classroom, allowing your students to hear, see and feel what a time and place in history might have been like. The activities focus on historical analysis, helping your students shape their critical thinking skills.

Available for Macintosh and IBM/PCs/compatibles

CD-ROM

Listening to Literature

Classroom teachers have selected excerpts from the world's greatest literature to support the textbook content.

Available in CD and Audiocassette Formats

History of Music

Especially effective with your auditory learners, these musical selections will help your students become better acquainted with the world's cultures.

Available in CD and Audiocassette Formats

Full-Color Posters

These colorful and informative posters will grab your students' attention and will help you make your classroom the most positive world history learning environment.

Student Review Software

This easy-to-use software contains more than 1,000 questions correlated to the text units and chapters. True/false, multiple-choice, and short answer questions challenge your students' knowledge, helping them prepare for chapter and unit exams.

Available for Macintosh and IBM/PCs/compatibles using Windows

WESTEST™ Computerized Testing

Allows you to create, edit, store and print exams with the touch of a few keys. This handy computerized test bank makes test preparation a snap!

Available for Macintosh and IBM/PCs/compatibles

**West
Educational
Publishing**

Photo Credits:
Black Figure Hydria: *Achilles Dragging the Body of Hector Around the Walls of Troy,* William Francis Warden Fund; Courtesy, Museum of Fine Arts, Boston • Bronze Pan Basin (Late Shang Period): Courtesy of the Freer Gallery of Art, Smithsonian Institution, Washington, D.C. • Dancing Siva: © Royal Smeets Offset, Weert • Gold Death Mask: Scala/Art Resource, NY • Flooded Rice Fields: Courtesy of William J. Duiker • Hindu Brahmins: © Dinodia/Omni-Photo • Giza Pyramids: © Hugh Sitton, Tony Stone World Wide • Earth: © 1997 PhotoDisc, Inc.

WORLD HISTORY

THE HUMAN ODYSSEY

Copyright © 1998 by West Publishing Company
An International Thomson company,
I(T)P® The ITP logo is a registered trademark under license.
All rights reserved
Printed in the United States of America
04 03 02 01 00 99 98   8 7 6 5 4 3

For more information, contact West Publishing Company, 30851 W. Agoura Rd., Suite 105,
Agoura Hills, CA, 91301

Team Leader: Robert Cassel
Project Manager: Theresa O'Dell
Production Manager: John Orr
Production Editor: Mario Rodriguez
Editors: Lynn Bruton, Phyllis Jelinek, Glenda Samples, Pam Starkey, Catherine Wermuth
Interior Wrap Design: Lee Anne Dollison
Interior Wrap Art: Lee Anne Dollison
Cover Design: Janet Bollow Associates
Cover Image: *The Song of the Volga*, Wassily Kandinsky, 1906, Musée National d'Art Moderne, Paris.
            Giraudon/Art Resource, NY
Compositor: Parkwood Composition
Prepress: Clarinda Company
Printing and Binding: West Publishing Company
Proofreading: Suzie DeFazio

Teacher's Wraparound Edition: ISBN 0–314–20562–4
Student Edition: ISBN 0–314–20561–6

JOIN US ON THE INTERNET
WWW: http://www.thomson.com
EMAIL: findit@kiosk.thomson.com   A service of I(T)P®

TEACHER'S WRAPAROUND EDITION

WORLD HISTORY

THE HUMAN ODYSSEY

Jackson J. Spielvogel

The Pennsylvania State University

West Educational Publishing

an International Thomson Publishing company I(T)P®

Cincinnati ✦ Albany, NY ✦ Belmont, CA ✦ Bonn ✦ Boston ✦ Detroit ✦ Johannesburg ✦ London ✦ Los Angeles ✦ Madrid
Melbourne ✦ Mexico City ✦ New York ✦ Paris ✦ Singapore ✦ Tokyo ✦ Toronto ✦ Washington

CLASSROOM CONTRIBUTORS

At West we are committed to involving as many classroom teachers as possible in the development of our middle school and high school textbooks. Teachers who have used West textbook programs tell us that our textbooks are more readable and interesting than other texts. These teachers also tell us that the study material in the student textbooks—the section and lesson review questions, and the Chapter Review exercises and activities—are more appropriate, more varied, and more suitable for use in their classrooms. In addition, users of West materials have found that the Teacher Wraparound editions and accompanying Teacher Resource materials provide them with much more classroom-tested, creative activities and teacher support than is typically found in other teacher editions and resources.

Therefore, we would like to acknowledge the assistance of the classroom teachers who have contributed to *World History, The Human Odyssey*.

Manuscript Reviewing

In addition to the many college-level experts who reviewed the manuscript for accuracy, over seventy high school world history teachers read the manuscript for content appropriateness, student reading level, and interest, as well as currentness and accuracy. The names of these teachers are listed on page xxv.

Textbook Pedagogy

The high school teachers shown and listed on this page and the next wrote the Becoming an Historian skills section that begins on page BH–1, the Section Review question, and the Chapter Review exercises and activities that conclude each chapter.

Teacher Wraparound

The teachers shown and listed on these pages also wrote the teacher support notes and activities for this Teacher Wraparound Edition.

Glenn Anderson
Apopka High School
Apopka, FL
Teacher for eight years; National Honor Society Teacher of the Year; Apopka High Teacher of the Year; Orange County Finalist for Teacher of the Year

Joan Arno
George Washington High School
Philadelphia, PA
Teacher for twenty-five years; contributed to curriculum development for Philadelphia World History Project; assisted development of the National Standards in World History; assisted American Historical Association in development of source materials for World Wide Web

Daniel Blackmon
Coral Gables Senior High School
Coral Gables, FL
Teacher for twenty years; teaches AP American History and International Baccalaureate Contemporary World History

Joseph Lamas
G. Holmes Braddock
Senior High School
Miami, FL
Teacher for twenty years; commendations from Dade County Public School system for contributions to global education; began the Gifted/Honors World History program; co-author of the Global Studies course for Florida

Geoffrey Lillich
Channel Islands High School
Oxnard, CA
*Teacher for twenty-eight years;
Department Chair, Social Science; Score
Teacher on Assignment; Mentor
Technology Teacher; State/Local
Telementor*

John Pearson
Thousand Oaks High School (retired)
Thousand Oaks, CA
*Teacher for thirty years; California
Scholarship Federation advisor; Academic
Decathlon Coach*

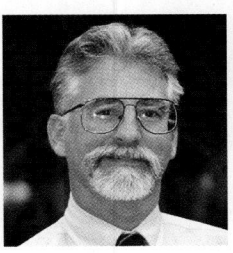

James Lloyd
Bullard High School
Fresno, CA
*Teacher for twenty-three years;
Department Chair, Mentor Teacher,
Master Teacher for the Fresno State
University Education Program; con-
tributed to development of the Social
Studies curriculum for district; revising
Modern World History course of study for
the district*

Matthew Thomas
Santa Clarita Christian High School
Canyon Country, CA
Teacher for three years; listed in Who's
Who in American Colleges and
Universities; *listed in* Who's Who of
American High School Teachers;
*Assistant Principal; developed honors pro-
gram curriculum for Association of
Christian Schools International*

Not Pictured:

Timothy Connell
Laurel High School
Shaker Heights, OH
*Teacher for twenty years; received Woodrow Wilson-Reader's
Digest Fellowship and grant from National Endowment for the
Humanities; editor of the Ohio Council for Social Studies* Review

Alina Diaz
Florida Diagnostic Learning Resource System
Miami, FL
*Former high school teacher for twenty-three years; coordinator,
Florida Diagnostic and Learning Resources System; coordinator,
Child Find Specialist; school psychologist for students with special
needs*

Marilynn Jo Hitchens
Denver, CO
*Teacher for thirty years; Doctorate in Russian, Eastern European,
and Modern European History; taught high school Russian lan-
guage, Western Civilization, and World History; served as presi-
dent, vice president, secretary, and council member of the World
History Association; steering committee member for Rocky
Mountain Regional World History Association*

Richard Holloway
Henry Clay High School
Lexington, KY
*Teacher for twenty-one years; teaches AP European History,
Advanced World Civilization, and is Anthropology Academic
Team Coach*

John Uelman
Newbury Park High School
Newbury Park, CA
*Teacher for twenty-six years; specializes in Modern European
History*

MULTIMEDIA SUPPORT

Our first commitment at West is to the development of the highest quality textbook possible for your Social Studies courses. We know, however, that you are constantly seeking new and improved ways to engage your students and to extend their learning to its fullest potential. Because technology is providing increasingly greater opportunities to support and expand the textbook lessons, we have integrated into the development of *World History, The Human Odyssey* an array of multimedia support materials. Following are brief descriptions of these materials.

The Internet

As you know, your students can explore unlimited world history resources through the Internet. To take advantage of these resources, we have provided you with two basic options:

◆ History Web Page—Please visit West's History Web Page at **http://www.swpco.com**.

At this address you will find web resources and activities organized by chapters of *World History, The Human Odyssey*. The information is updated regularly to ensure that you and your students are receiving the most current and useful links to world history information on the web.

◆ Specific Web References—Where appropriate throughout this Teacher Edition, you will find references to web sites related to the topics being discussed in a particular chapter. These sites were chosen for their superiority to other sites at the time of publication of our Teacher Edition. Please remember, however, that web sites can change quickly and that you can always get the latest, most current information at the West History web page.

Videos

Obviously, world history teachers can draw upon an unlimited supply of videotapes to support their teaching of world history. West is doing its part to help identify and provide high-quality, relevant videos by continually updating its World History Video Library, which supports the textbook.

West also provides an annual World History update in conjunction with CNN®. The CNN® World History Update and accompanying teacher materials are provided free each year.

Color Transparencies

Even though a wide variety of new technologies are becoming increasingly available to the secondary classroom, the vast majority of teachers still rely heavily on overhead transparencies. Therefore, teachers selecting *World History, The Human Odyssey* as their primary World History text will have at their disposal a variety of full-color, overhead transparencies. Included in the various transparency packages are the basic set of chapter-by-chapter transparencies, selected by classroom teachers as the most needed and desirable transparencies for use with the student book; fine art transparencies; and the map overlay transparency package.

Laserdisc

The *Sights and Sounds of History* laserdisc contains hundreds of still images and numerous live-action video segments to support the textbook content. These images and video segments are referenced at the appropriate places throughout your Teacher Edition.

Software

All of the quiz and test questions provided in the Teacher Resource Box are provided in an electronic test bank that you can easily manipulate (add, edit, delete questions) to create your own tests.

Many of your students will also benefit from the Self-Study software, which allows them to study and reinforce the textbook lessons on their own.

CD-ROM

While using it as an independent research tool, your students will both enjoy and learn from the *World History* CD-ROM that accompanies *World History, The Human Odyssey.* Teacher materials are also available to help you implement guided research projects correlated to textbook lessons.

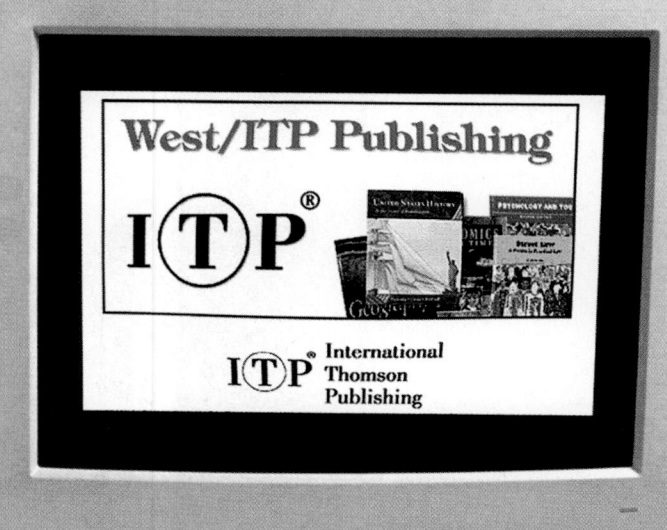

ABILITY LEVELS AND LEARNING STYLES

This Teacher Edition and the Teacher Resource materials accompanying *World History, The Human Odyssey* have been developed for use in classrooms all across the country. This means, of course, that the materials must provide effective teaching and learning for every imaginable student and classroom situation. Consequently, you will find teacher support notes and activity suggestions in the Teacher Edition, handouts and worksheets in the Teacher Resource Box, and a variety of visual materials in the multimedia support package—all to help you teach World History to challenged students, advanced students, and students who learn best through the use of any of the several different kinds of teaching techniques.

Here are just a few representative examples of the variety of activities for different ability levels and learning styles.

Special Needs

At least once or twice per chapter at the bottom of the Teacher Edition pages, you will find suggestions for special needs students, including activities that are especially effective for auditory and kinesthetic learners.

Learning from Visuals

This Teacher Edition contains numerous suggestions for using the hundreds of photographs and drawings in the student text as teaching tools for those students who learn best visually.

Enrichment Activities and More About . . .

Located at the bottom of the Teacher Edition pages are Enrichment Activities and More About . . . . These activities and additional information features are designed primarily for your advanced students, especially the verbal/linguistic learners. Selected activities, however, encourage students to use their visual, spatial, and auditory skills.

Vocabulary Reinforcement

The Teacher Edition includes numerous Vocabulary Reinforcement activities, which will be useful for students reading below grade level and for students with limited English proficiency. You will also find references in the Teacher Edition to handouts and worksheets in the Teacher Resource Box to help Spanish-speaking students master the textbook content.

WORLD HISTORY
THE HUMAN ODYSSEY

WORLD HISTORY
THE HUMAN ODYSSEY

JACKSON J. SPIELVOGEL

The Pennsylvania State University

WEST EDUCATIONAL PUBLISHING

an International Thomson Publishing company I⬡P®

Cincinnati ✦ Albany, NY ✦ Belmont, CA ✦ Bonn ✦ Boston ✦ Detroit ✦ Johannesburg ✦ London ✦ Los Angeles ✦ Madrid
Melbourne ✦ Mexico City ✦ New York ✦ Paris ✦ Singapore ✦ Tokyo ✦ Toronto ✦ Washington

PRODUCTION CREDITS

Team Leader   Robert Cassel
Project Manager   Theresa O'Dell
Production Manager   John Orr
Editors   Lynn Bruton, Phyllis Jelinek,
   Glenda Samples, Pam Starkey
Photo Research   Jan Seidel
Production Editors   Carole Balach, Regan Stilo
Permissions   Elaine Arthur
Illustrators   Lee Anne Dollison, Matthew Thiessen
Copyediting   Mary Berry
Design   Janet Bollow
Composition   Parkwood Composition Service, Inc.
Dummy Artist   José Delgado
Maps   Maryland Cartographics and Magellan GeoGraphix
Index   Terry Casey
Cover Design   Janet Bollow
Proofreader   Suzie De Fazio
Prepress Services   Clarinda Company

COPYRIGHT © 1998 By WEST PUBLISHING COMPANY
An International Thomson Publishing company
I(T)P®The ITP logo is a trademark under license.

05 04 03 02 01 00 99 98   8 7 6 5 4 3 3 1 0

Student edition: ISBN 0-314-20561-6

PHOTO ACKNOWLEDGMENTS

Cover   Kandinsky, Wassily. *The Song of the Volga.* 1906. Musée National d'Art Moderne, Paris, France. Giraudon/Art Resource, NY.

Contents   viii ©The Hulton Getty Picture Collection, Limited/Rischgitz Collection/Tony Stone Images; **ix** Corbis-Bettmann; **x (bottom)** Robert Harding Picture Library, Karachi Museum; **xi (top)** E.T. Archive/Bibliotheque Nationale, Paris; **xi (bottom)** ©Pierre Belzeaux/Photo Researchers, Inc.; **xii (top)** detail, National Museum of American Art, Washington DC/Art Resource, NY; **xii (bottom)** ©N&E Bernheim/Woodfin Camp & Associates; **xiii (top)** ChinaStock; **xiii (bottom)** The Bodleian Library, Oxford; **xiv (top)** The Ancient Art & Architecture Collection Ltd.; **xiv (bottom)** Corbis-Bettmann; **xv (top)** Corbis-Bettmann; **xv (bottom)** Giraudon/Art Resource, NY; **xvi (top)** North Wind Picture Archives; **xvi (bottom)** Mary Evans Picture Library; **xvii (top)** Express News/Archive Photos; **xvii (bottom)** E. T. Archive; **xviii (top)** Corbis-Bettmann; **xviii (bottom)** Julia Waterflow, Eye Ubiquitous/Corbis; **xix (top)** Liba Taylor/Corbis; **xix (bottom)** NASA.

Introduction   **BH1** AP/Wide World Photos; **BH4** © F. Hibon/Sygma; **BH8** ©Dennis Cox/ChinaStock; **BH9** ©The Huntington Library; **BH18** North Wind Picture Archives; **BH22 (top)** Gallery of Prehistoric Art, New York, Scala/Art Resource, NY; **BH22 (bottom)** Musée de Louvre; **BH23** ©Photo 1994 Nippon Television Network Corporation, Tokyo.

Unit Openers   **2** Courtesy of the Arthur M. Sackler Gallery, Smithsonian Institution, Washington, DC; **192** *The Tournament,* FR.2692, f.62v-63. Bibliotheque Nationale, Paris; **416** Private Collection/Explorer/SuperStock; **648** Pablo Picasso, *The Fourteenth of July,* 1901, Solomon R. Guggenheim Museum, New York. Gift, Justin K. Thannhauser, 1964. Photo: David Heald ©The Solomon R. Guggenheim Foundation, New York; **798** Imperial War Museum, London; **940** Jeffrey Dunn/Viesti Associates, Inc.

(continued following index)

ABOUT THE AUTHOR

Jackson J. Spielvogel is associate professor of history at the Pennsylvania State University. He received his Ph.D. from the Ohio State University, where he specialized in Reformation history under Harold J. Grimm. His articles and reviews have appeared in such journals as *Moreana*, *Journal of General Education*, *Archly für Reformationsgeschichte*, and *American Historical Review*. He has also contributed chapters or articles to *The Social History of the Reformation*, *The Holy Roman Empire: A Dictionary Handbook*, *Simon Wiesenthal Center Annual of Holocaust Studies*, and *Utopian Studies*. His work has been supported by fellowships from the Fulbright Foundation and the Foundation for Reformation Research. His book *Hitler and Nazi Germany* was published in 1987 (third edition, 1996). His book *Western Civilization* was published in 1991 (third edition, 1997). He is the co-author (with William Duiker) of *World History*, published in January 1994 (second edition, 1998). Professor Spielvogel has won five major university-wide teaching awards. During the year 1988–1989, he held the Penn State Teaching Fellowship, the university's most prestigious teaching award. In 1996, he won the Dean Arthur Ray Warnock Award for Outstanding Faculty Member. In 1997, he became the first winner of the Schreyer Institute's Student Choice Award for innovative and inspiring teaching.

TO DIANE
whose love and support made it all possible

CONTENTS-IN-BRIEF

CONTENTS-IN-BRIEF

CONTENTS-IN-BRIEF

CONTENTS

UNIT ONE

UNIT TWO

New Patterns of Civilization
(400 to 1500)
192

UNIT TWO

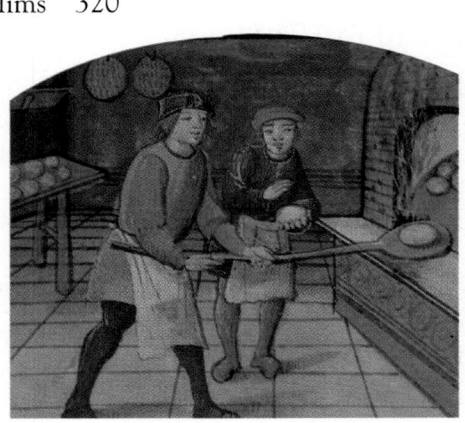

UNIT THREE

The Emergence of New World Patterns
(1400 to 1800)
416

UNIT THREE

UNIT FOUR

Modern Patterns of World History: The Era of European Dominance (1800 to 1914)
648

UNIT FIVE

The Crisis of the Twentieth Century (1914 to 1945)
798

UNIT SIX

Toward a Global Civilization: The World Since 1945
(1945 to Present)
940

UNIT SIX

FEATURES

BIOGRAPHY

FOCUS ON EVERYDAY LIFE

OUR ARTISTIC HERITAGE

FEATURES

OUR LITERARY HERITAGE

THE ROLE OF SCIENCE AND TECHNOLOGY

SPORTS AND CONTESTS

YOU ARE THERE

FEATURES

YOUNG PEOPLE IN . . .

MAPS

MAPS

ACKNOWLEDGMENTS

I began to teach at age five in my family's grape arbor. By the age of ten, I wanted to know and understand everything in the world so I set out to memorize our entire set of encyclopedia volumes. At seventeen, as editor of the high school yearbook, I chose "Patterns" as its theme.

With that as my early history, followed by twenty-five rich years of teaching, writing, and family nurturing, it seemed quite natural to accept the challenge of writing a world history as I entered that period in life often described as the age of wisdom. Although I see this writing adventure as part of the natural unfolding of my life, I gratefully acknowledge that without the generosity of many others, it would not have been possible.

My ability to undertake a project of this magnitude was in part due to the outstanding teachers that I had as both an undergraduate and graduate student. These included Kent Forster at the Pennsylvania State University and William MacDonald and Harold Grimm at the Ohio State University. These teachers provided me with profound insights into history and also taught me by their example that learning only becomes true understanding when it is accompanied by compassion, humility, and open-mindedness. I am especially grateful to William Duiker and his wife Yvonne for their enormous efforts in helping me to understand and put into perspective the history of the non-Western world. My colleague Arthur Goldschmidt also freely gave of his time to review my efforts.

Thanks to West Publishing Company's comprehensive review process, many teachers took time from their busy schedules to evaluate the different drafts of my manuscript. I am grateful to the following for the innumerable suggestions that have greatly improved my work. I am also grateful to those teachers who provided such outstanding review questions and activities.

Bill Anderson
Coeur d'Alene High School
Coeur d'Alene, ID

Glenn Anderson
Apopka High School
Apopka, FL

J. P. Applegate
Oklahoma State Dept. of Education
Oklahoma City, OK

Simone Arias
Cleveland State University
Cleveland, OH

Joan Arno
George Washington High School
Philadelphia, PA

Daniel Berman
Fox Lane High School
Bedford, NY

Marjorie Bingham
St. Louis Park High School
Minnetonka, MN

Henry P. Bitten
Ramapo High School
Franklin Lakes, NJ

Daniel W. Blackmon
Coral Gables Senior High School
Miami, FL

Janna M. Bremer
King Philip Regional High School
Wrentham, MA

James A. (Charlie) Brown
Central Senior High School
Little Rock, AR

Steven L. Buenning
William Fremd High School
Palatine, IL

Frank Burke
St. Louis, MO

Brian Carlson
Dillard High School
Plantation, FL

Anne Chapman
Western Reserve Academy
Hudson, OH

Peter J. Cheoros
Lynwood High School
Lynwood, CA

Timothy C. Connell
Laurel School
Shaker Heights, OH

Scott Crump
Bingham High School
South Jordan, UT

Shirley Cruse
Mayfield High School
Las Cruces, NM

Frank de Varona
Dade County Public Schools
Hialeah, FL

Linda Dennis
Cypress Creek High School
Houston, TX

Suzanne Dillard
Shepton High School
Plano, TX

Robert Doyle
The Community School
Sun Valley, ID

Felicia C. Eppley
Lamar High School
Houston, TX

William R. Everdell
St. Ann's School
Brooklyn, NY

Autumn Farber
Edmonds School District
Lynwood, WA

Maggie Favretti
Scarsdale High School
Bronxville, NY

Helen Crowley Foucault
Deerfield High School
Deerfield, IL

James Grinsel
Wausau West High School
Wausau, WI

Gary L. Hammac
East Central High School
San Antonio, TX

Georgiana Hatch
Upland High School
Upland, CA

Marilynn Jo Hitchens
Wheat Ridge High School
Wheat Ridge, CO

Kathryn Hodgkinson
Berkner High School
Richardson, TX

Richard K. Holloway
Henry Clay High School
Lexington, KY

Paul A. Horne, Jr.
Richland County School Dist. No. One
Columbia, SC

Chris Housel
Centennial High School
Boise, ID

Jean Elliott Johnson
New York University
New York, NY

Rita Johnson
Clear Lake High School
Houston, TX

Larry Jones
Moorpark High School
Moorpark, CA

James T. Jordan
Scotland High School
Laurinburg, NC

Henry G. Kiernan
West Morris Regional High School Dist.
Chester, NJ

Ellen Kottler
Western Senior High School
Las Vegas, NV

Joseph I. Lamas
G. Holmes Braddock Sr. High School
Miami, FL

Samuel J. Lichterman
Armstrong High School
Plymouth, MN

Mary Lindquist
Mercer Island High School
Seattle, WA

Alan Lucibello
Montville Township High School
Montville, NJ

Sally Lyons
Lassiter High School
Marietta, GA

Bobette Manees
Sylvan Hills High School
Sherwood, AR

Silda Mason
Rio Grande High School
Albuquerque, NM

Steven L. McCollum
Thomas Jefferson Independent Day School
Joplin, MO

Carrie H. McIver
San Carlos Summit High School
San Diego, CA

John R. McNamara
Gilbert High School
Gilbert, AZ

R. J. Olivarez
Bloomington High School
Bloomington, TX

Brenda Palmer
Lehigh Senior High School
Ft. Myers, FL

Paul H. Pangrace
Garrett Morgan Middle School
Cleveland, OH

John S. Pearson
Thousand Oaks High School
Thousand Oaks, CA

Susan Philippsen
Simi Valley High School
Simi Valley, CA

Ellen L. Pike
Lancaster Country Day School
Lancaster, PA

Sheila G. Raihl
Gadsden Senior High School
Anthony, NM

Arturo V. Rivera
Cibola High School
Yuma, AZ

Beverly S. Roberts
Brookwood High School
Snellville, GA

Jeri D. Roberts
Green Valley High School
Henderson, NV

Esther M. Robinson
Langham Creek High School
Houston, TX

Heidi Roupp
Aspen High School
Aspen, CO

Denny L. Schillings
Homewood-Flossmoor High School
Flossmoor, IL

Rob T. Sears
Rancho High School
N. Las Vegas, NV

Lawrence A. Spalla
Trinity Senior High School
Washington, PA

Carol K. Thomson
Santa Fe High School, North Campus
Santa Fe, NM

John Turnbull
Chaparral High School
Las Vegas, NV

John Uelmen
Newbury Park High School
Newbury Park, CA

Martha Van Zant
Biloxi High School
Biloxi, MS

Nancy L. Webber
West Charlotte Senior High School
Charlotte, NC

Steve Weiner
Gateway High School
Aurora, CO

Susan Winslow,
Montgomery High School
Montgomery, TX

J. Donald Woodruff, Jr.
Fredericksburg Academy
Fredericksburg, VA

William Zeigler
El Cajon High School
San Diego, CA

The editors at West Publishing Company have been both helpful and congenial at all times. Their flexible policies allowed the creative freedom that a writer cherishes. I especially wish to thank Clyde Perlee, who encouraged me to undertake this project and taught me so much about the world of publishing. In the early stages of this project, Denis Ralling was always helpful with his insightful analyses and organization of many practical details. Members of the current West team who produced this book constitute a remarkable group of people. Bob Cassel, editor in chief, was a soft-spoken but superb leader whose judgment I grew to trust. John Orr, production manager, had a remarkable sense of timing and direction. To the many people—Theresa O'Dell, Project Manager; Jan Seidel; Pam Starkey; Regan Stilo; Lee Anne Dollison; Matt Thiessen; Phyllis Jelinek—I came to know well through telephone conversations and fax messages, and who provided invaluable editorial assistance, I want to express my deepest gratitude for the efforts they have made on behalf of this book. All of them were as cooperative as they were competent. I am also grateful to Mary Berry for her copyediting skills, Elaine Arthur for obtaining permissions, and Janet Bollow for her magnificent design. In an age when the impersonal has become commonplace, I want to express my appreciation for both the professional and personal relationships that I have shared with the West "family" in California.

Above all, I thank my family for their support. The gifts of love, laughter, and patience from my daughters, Jennifer and Kathryn; my sons, Eric and Christian; and my daughters-in-law Liz and Michele, were invaluable. My wife and best friend, Diane, provided me with editorial assistance, wise counsel, and the loving support that made it possible for me to complete a project of this magnitude. I could not have written the book without her.

Jackson J. Spielvogel

INTRODUCTION
BECOMING AN HISTORIAN

On August 19, 1991, a group of Soviet leaders opposed to reform arrested Mikhail Gorbachev, the president of the Soviet Union, and tried to seize control of the government. Hundreds of thousands of Russians, led by Boris Yeltsin, the Russian president, poured into the streets of Moscow and Leningrad to resist the rebels. Some army units, sent out to enforce the wishes of the rebels, went over to Yeltsin's side. Within days, the rebels were forced to surrender. This failed attempt to seize power had unexpected results as Russia and a host of other Soviet states declared their independence from the Soviet Union. By the end of 1991, the Soviet Union—one of the largest empires in world history—had come to an end. Quite unexpectedly, a major turning point in world history had been reached.

The sudden collapse of the Soviet Union has been but one of many important events in world history. However, world history is more than just a series of dramatic events—as important as these events are. World history is the story of the human community. It is the story of all of us. That story is a rich and complex one that not only contains dramatic events but also tells how people were ruled, how they lived on a daily basis, how they fought, how they shared ideas, how they looked for the meaning of life, and how they expressed what they felt about the joys and sorrows of this world. The story of world history is the story of politics, economics, and social change, but it is also the story of everyday life, of ideas, of creative arts, of religious insight, and of dreams fulfilled and unfulfilled.

◄ On August 22, 1991, a crowd of almost 100,000 Russian citizens marched in Red Square, Moscow, to celebrate the collapse of the military coup. Following the attempted coup, who emerged as the president of Russia, and who resigned as president of the USSR?

BH–1

Answer to the caption question: Following the attempted coup, Boris Yeltsin became president of Russia and Mikhail Gorbachev resigned as president of the USSR.

Making History Personal. The history that will be the most meaningful and interesting to your students will be their personal histories. Have your students start by recording the people and events that have been important to them. Discuss with them the best ways for presenting the story of their lives. Does the story break down easily into chapters? Should it be presented chronologically or thematically? Do they see examples of cause-and-effect relationships? How do they determine what to include and what to leave out? The objective is for students to examine their lives with the same critical analysis that professional historians use.

Making History Personal. Have students expand their life stories to include their family and ancestors. Each student should try to create a family tree going back five generations (their genealogy does not have to be of their biological family). Have them interview family members for significant or interesting details about their family history. Where is the family from? For how many generations have they been in the United States? What are the accomplishments and deeds of their family members? The objective is for students to see that they are influenced by, and connected to, a larger world.

WHAT IS HISTORY?

You may think of history as a boring list of names and dates; an irrelevant record of revolutions and battles; or the meaningless stories of kings, queens, and other rulers. The truth is much more basic. History is simply what happens. History is not just what happens to famous and infamous people but what happens to everyone, including yourself.

We could say that history is everything that has happened since the beginning of time. In this sense, we realize that the age of human beings has been a very brief one compared with the geologic age of Earth, which scientists tell us stretches back for billions of years. During the age of humans, people have spent most of their time simply trying to exist, searching for food and shelter as best they could.

The definition of history as everything that has ever happened, however, is so broad that its use would make it impossible to tell our story. History has a more common meaning: a record of the past. To create this record, historians use documents (what has been recorded or written); artifacts, such as pottery, tools, and weapons; and even artworks. History in this sense really began five thousand to six thousand years ago, when people first began to write and keep records. The period before written records we call *prehistory*.

History could also be defined in a third way, as a special field of study. Herodotus, who lived in Greece in the fifth century B.C., is often regarded as the "father of history" in Western civilization. He was one of the first historians. In his history of the Greek and Persian Wars, Herodotus used evidence, tried to tell a good story, and showed a concern for the causes and effects of events.

In modern times, in the nineteenth and twentieth centuries, history became an academic discipline—a formal field of study that is examined in schools and universities. Leopold von Ranke, a German historian who lived in the nineteenth century, is often regarded as the father of this new kind of history. He created techniques for the critical analysis of documents and began to use formal courses in universities to train new historians. In their college courses, people who want to become professional historians learn not only facts but

also methods by which they can analyze those facts critically and make new discoveries that might change our picture of the past. History is based on factual evidence. Historians, however, try to discover both what happened (the factual evidence) and why it happened. In other words, historians use critical thinking to explain the cause-and-effect relationships that exist among the facts.

All of us are involved in the making of history. Abigail Pafford, a student from Apopka, Florida, was talking to her grandmother when she discovered that her great-grandfather had narrowly avoided one of the most tragic shipping disasters of recent times. Because her great-grandfather had fallen in love, he had not used his ticket for the maiden, and only, voyage of the *Titanic*. That ship struck an iceberg shortly before midnight on April 14, 1912, and sank with a loss of over 1,500 lives. At the time, Pafford's great-grandfather was on his way to San Francisco on another ship with her great-grandmother. Thus, a recorded event that might have been just another piece of information in a textbook—the *Titanic* disaster—is, for Pafford, part of family history.

Alex Haley, the editor of *The Autobiography of Malcolm X*, grew up in Henning, Tennessee, listening to his grandmother tell stories of Kunta Kinte, a family ancestor kidnapped in Africa during the 1700s and taken to America as a slave. Haley's search for his family's history led to his famous book *Roots: The Saga of an American Family*. The book was turned into a television miniseries and became one of the most watched shows of all time. Haley's personal family story had a universal appeal.

You will find, with some investigation, that history has been made by your own family and by the families of your friends. These accumulated experiences have become part of who you are. These experiences help to guide your choices and actions, both personal and public. In turn, your choices and actions then become part of your own children's and grandchildren's history. You are an important link in a chain that stretches back into your ancestors' history and forward into your descendants' future.

In this book, you will be asked to read one account of the history of the world. You will also be asked to read some of the documents that historians use to create their pictures of the past. Reading the documents will enable you to develop your critical skills and to be an historian yourself. Historians do what students of all ages seek to do—develop the critical skills that enable them to make some sense of human existence. As Socrates, an ancient Greek philosopher, said, "The unexamined life is not worth living." The study of history will give you the tools to examine not only the lives of others but also your own life.

THEMES FOR UNDERSTANDING WORLD HISTORY

In examining the past, historians often organize their material on the basis of themes that enable them to ask and try to answer basic questions about the past. The following nine themes are especially important. We will meet them again and again in our story.

Politics and History The study of politics seeks to answer certain basic questions that historians have about the structure of a society. These questions include the following: How were people governed? What was the relationship between the ruler and the ruled? What people or groups of people held political power? What rights and liberties did the people have? What actions did people take to change their forms of government? The study of politics also includes the role of conflict. Historians examine the causes and results of wars in order to understand the impact of war on human development.

The Role of Ideas Ideas have great power to move people to action. For example, in the twentieth century, the idea of nationalism, which is based on a belief in loyalty to one's nation, helped lead to two great conflicts—World War I and World War II. Together these wars cost the lives of over fifty million people. At the same time, nationalism has also led people to work together to benefit the lives of a nation's citizens. The spread of ideas from one society to another has also played an important role in world history.

Economics and History A society depends for its existence on meeting certain basic needs. How did the society grow its food? How did it make its goods? How did it provide the services people needed? How did individual people and governments use their limited resources? Did they spend more money on hospitals or on military forces? By answering these questions, historians examine the different economic systems that have played a role in history.

Social Life From a study of social life, we learn about the different social classes that made up a society. We also examine how people dressed and found shelter, how and what they ate, and what they did for fun. The nature of family life and how knowledge was passed from one generation to another through education are also part of the social life of a society.

The Importance of Cultural Developments We cannot understand a society without looking at its culture, or the common ideas, beliefs, and patterns of behavior that are passed on from one generation to another. Culture includes both high culture and popular culture. High culture consists of the writings of a society's thinkers and the works of its artists. A society's popular culture is the world of ideas and experiences of ordinary people. In a historical sense, the term *popular culture* refers to the ideas and experiences of less educated people, such as peasants and artisans. Although many of these people were illiterate, they passed their culture on orally. Today the media have embraced the term *popular culture* to describe the most current trends and fashionable styles.

Religion in History Throughout history, people have sought to find a deeper meaning to human life. How have the world's great religions—such as Hinduism, Buddhism, Judaism, Christianity, and Islam—influenced people's lives? How have those religions spread to create new patterns of culture?

The Role of Individuals In discussing the roles of politics, ideas, economics, social life, cultural developments, and religion, we deal with groups of people and forces that often seem beyond the control of any one person.

Mentioning the names of Cleopatra, Queen Elizabeth I, Napoleon, and Hitler, however, reminds us of the role of individuals in history. Decisive actions by powerful individuals have indeed played a crucial role in the course of history. So, too, have the decisions of ordinary men and women who must figure out every day how to survive, protect their families, and carry on their ways of life.

The Impact of Science and Technology For thousands of years, people around the world have made scientific discoveries and technological innovations that have changed our world. From the creation of stone tools that made farming easier to the advanced computers that guide our airplanes, science and technology have altered how humans have related to their world.

The Environment and History Throughout history, peoples and societies have been affected by the physical world in which they live. They have also made an impact on their world. From the slash-and-burn farming of early societies to the industrial pollution of modern factories, human activities have affected the physical environment and even endangered the very existence of entire societies.

These nine themes will help us to make sense of the past. Of course, these themes do not stand alone. They are connected to one another. Moreover, historians of world history add some special themes that help us to understand our story. In studying world history, we look at the rise, decline, and fall of many civilizations around the world (a civilization, as we will see later, is a complex culture). During much of human history, the most advanced civilizations have been in East Asia or in the Middle East. Only in modern times—in the late nineteenth and early twentieth centuries—did Western civilization dominate the rest of the world. (Western civilization is the civilization of the West—Europe and the Western Hemisphere.) Since the end of World War II, that dominance has gradually faded. In world history, we look at the forces that create civilizations and cause them to fall.

At the same time, world history consists of more than just the study of individual civilizations. From the earliest times, trade served to bring different civilizations into contact with one another. The transmission

of religious and cultural ideas soon followed. *World history can be seen in a broad comparative and global framework,* as peoples and countries come into contact, and often into conflict, with one another. In our own time, people often speak of the world as a global village. They mean that the world can be seen as a single community linked by computers, television, and multinational corporations. (After all, an American who travels abroad can now find a McDonald's restaurant in almost every part of the world.)

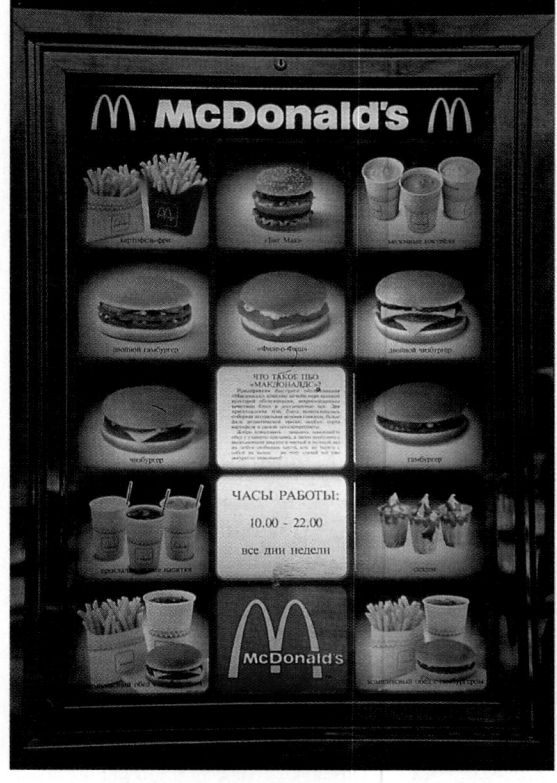

▲ *Thus far, McDonalds in Moscow has been a capitalist success. Why do you think this very American venture is succeeding in a culture far removed from the United States?*

HISTORIANS AND
THE DATING OF TIME

In recording the past, historians try to determine the exact time when events occurred. World War II in Europe, for example, began on September 1, 1939, when Adolf Hitler sent German troops into Poland. The war in Europe ended on May 7, 1945, when Germany surrendered. By using dates, historians can place events in the order they occurred and try to determine the development of patterns over periods of time.

If someone asked you when you were born, you would reply with a number, such as 1984. In the United States, we would all accept that number without question. Why? The number is part of the dating system followed in the Western world (Europe and the Western Hemisphere). This system refers to dates in relation to the assumed date of the birth of Jesus Christ (the year 1). An event that took place four hundred years before the birth of Jesus is dated 400 B.C. ("before Christ"). Dates after the birth of Jesus are labeled as A.D. These letters stand for the Latin words *anno Domini*, which mean "in the year of the Lord" (or the year of the birth of Jesus Christ). Thus, an event that took place 250 years after the birth of Jesus is written A.D. 250, or "in the year of the Lord 250." It can also be written as 250. Similarly, you would give your birth year as simply 1984 rather than A.D. 1984.

Some historians now prefer to use the abbreviations B.C.E. ("before the common era") and C.E. ("common era") instead of B.C. and A.D. This is especially true of historians who prefer to use symbols that are not so Western or Christian oriented. The dates, of course, remain the same. Thus, 1950 B.C.E. and 1950 B.C. are the same year.

Historians make use of other terms to refer to time. A decade is ten years, a century is one hundred years, and a millennium is one thousand years. The fourth century B.C. is the fourth period of one hundred years counting backward from 1, the assumed date of the birth of Jesus. The first century B.C. covers the years 100 to 1 B.C. Therefore, the fourth century B.C. is the years 400 to 301 B.C. We say, then, that an event in 650 B.C. took place in the seventh century B.C.

The fourth century A.D. is the fourth period of one hundred years after the birth of Jesus. The first period of one hundred years is the years 1 to 100, so the fourth hundred-year period, or the fourth century, is the years 301 to 400. For example, we say that an event in 750 took place in the eighth century. Just as the first millennium B.C. is the years 1000 to 1 B.C., the second millennium A.D. is the years 1001 to 2000.

SKILLS FOR BECOMING
A BETTER HISTORIAN

If you are interested in your friends, your family, and yourself, then you are an historian. The more effective we are as historians, the more fully we find out about and understand ourselves and the people with whom we share this planet. The following pages are intended to show how you can better understand the information presented in this text. Even more important, however, you can become a better historian of events relevant to your life.

To be a better historian, you will want to use skills that professional historians use to evaluate historical information. These skills are effective for more than helping you to understand this textbook and get a better grade in world history class. These techniques will allow you to become a better consumer, a more informed citizen, and a more enlightened human being. The table on page BH–6 summarizes the basic skills we will then examine in detail.

1. Understanding Geography
as a Key to History

William Shakespeare said, "All the world's a stage." Historians who seek to truly comprehend the events of the past must know something about the stage upon which the drama was being played out. When meeting people for the first time, we usually soon get around to asking where they are from. That is because the environment in which we live greatly influences our development, opportunities, and even belief systems. A Seminole Indian, told he had to leave his land in North Florida at the beginning of the nineteenth century, said, "If suddenly we tear our hearts from the homes around which they are twined, our heartstrings

Understanding Geography as a Key to History.

Have students apply the themes of geography to their own lives by identifying the location, place, environment, movement, and region of their home.

1. Location—Students should use a map or globe with latitude and longitude lines to find the absolute location of their town or city. Then have them describe their location in relation to significant geographic features and landmarks of the region. You might also have them locate the city where their parents, grandparents, etc. live or were born.

2. Place—Have students describe the place where they live. They should identify climate, landforms, vegetation, people, types of housing and the other characteristics of place.

3. People-Environment Relations—Have students describe the benefits and challenges presented by their environment. How have humans changed their environment?

4. Movement—All of the people in the Western hemisphere migrated here from somewhere else (even native Americans). Have your students describe how the movements of people have affected their town or city. Have them identify the transportation and communication systems which are part of their community.

Skills for Becoming a Better Historian

1. Understanding Geography as a Key to History

Understanding where something happened can help you to understand why it happened.

2. Interpreting Maps

Reading maps is an effective way to understand a great deal of information in a short time.

3. Using Time Lines

Time lines are a simple way of putting information in chronological order.

4. Reading Charts, Graphs, and Tables

Charts, graphs, and tables can condense many facts into a more understandable format.

5. Understanding Cause and Effect

Developing an awareness of the relationship of cause and effect is an essential historical technique.

6. Recognizing and Understanding Bias

All historians bring to their studies bias based upon their backgrounds and life experiences. Learn to recognize bias and account for it.

7. Identifying Primary and Secondary Sources

Primary sources are an essential tool for historians, but both primary and secondary sources are important.

8. Comparing and Contrasting

Almost everything we know can be described in terms of how it is either similar to or different from something else.

9. Recognizing Fact versus Opinion

Facts are information that can be verified as being true or untrue. Opinions are open to dispute.

10. Analyzing Information—Drawing Inferences

The ability to reason and reach conclusions based upon evidence is an advanced skill.

11. Looking at Art as a Key to History

The fullness of history is sometimes better realized through art than through words.

12. Studying Economics as a Key to History

How people distribute and use their resources may be the most powerful indicator of their beliefs, traditions, and actions.

13. Making Hypotheses and Predicting Outcomes

By using other social studies techniques, the advanced student historian should be able to predict outcomes based upon evidence presented.

14. Conducting Research

Conducting thorough research on a topic involves the skills of a detective.

15. Writing Research Papers

The research paper is the culmination of all the social studies skills. It can be the most challenging and rewarding of assignments.

BH–6

will snap." Native Americans have always strongly felt that people and their environments are intimately connected.

Our modern society is more mobile and more distant from the natural world than were the early cultures of North America. However, we are as closely bound to our environment as they were to theirs. Whether we live in a New York City neighborhood, a farm community in Wisconsin, or a small town in Georgia, we are all products of our surroundings.

Geography is the study of Earth and of our interaction with the environment. There are two basic types of geography: human geography and physical geography. Human geography deals with the various people around the world, including their economic, political, and cultural activities. Physical geography is the study of different regions of the world. It focuses on the climate, resources, and other natural features of these regions. Both types of geography use five basic themes: location, place, people-environment relations, movement, and regions.

Location Location refers to where a place is. Absolute location is the exact position of a city, mountain, or river on Earth and is determined by latitudes and longitudes on a map. Latitudes are distances measured by lines drawn on maps or globes to show distance north and south of the equator. Longitudes are distances measured by meridians, or lines drawn on globes or maps to show distances east or west of the prime meridian. The prime meridian is an imaginary line that runs from the North Pole to the South Pole through the Royal Observatory at Greenwich, England. Longitudes and latitudes are both measured in degrees, represented by the symbol °. By using latitudes and longitudes, any place on Earth can be precisely located. For example, look at the world map on page A–7. What city can you find at 39° N latitude and 116° E longitude? Only one city will be found at that specific location.

These absolute locations, however, are probably less helpful to the historian than are relative locations. *Relative location* refers to the location of one place in relation to other places. The absolute location of Beijing, China, which you have just found, does not tell you that Beijing is located on the North China Plain sixty miles from the Yellow Sea and just inside the Great Wall of China. Knowing this relative location helps us to understand why Beijing became an important capital city in Chinese history.

The geographer's theme of location is very useful to the historian. Location helps to show the distribution of climates, vegetation, natural resources, and patterns of human settlement. Where is good farmland? Where are the natural resources that can be used in industries? Answers to these questions help historians to understand where, and even why events take place where they do.

Place A place is a particular city, village, or area with certain physical and human characteristics that make it different from other places. A city such as Beijing, for example, has distinct physical characteristics. It has its own landforms, vegetation, climate, and resources. A city also has distinct human characteristics. What are its different social classes? Where do they live in the city? How are the city's streets laid out? What kinds of dwellings have people built? Together, the physical and human characteristics make up a place's identity. Beijing may be similar to other cities, but it is also its own place. This identity, of course, can change through time. This fact makes the theme of place important to an understanding of history.

People-Environment Relations The study of interactions between humans and their environment helps us to understand why people are where they are, as well as why their cultures developed the way they did. The physical features of a place affect the way people live. A rich soil, for example, means abundant crops and probably a prosperous society. However, people also alter their environments. By cutting down trees, people convert forests into farmlands. By building cities and roads, they change the landscape. The story of how people relate to their environment becomes an important part of a people's history.

Movement The theme of movement encompasses the study of interactions among people located in different places and different environments. Geographers and historians are chiefly concerned with three types of

Map Skills. In order to reinforce map-reading skills you may want to have students practice their map-making skills. A simple exercise is to have students make a map of their home, neighborhood and school. Have them include all of the parts of a map:

1. **title**—puts the information presented in the map into a useful context
2. **key**—tells what the various symbols, lines and colors on the map mean
3. **scale**—depicts distance using either miles or kilometers
4. **directional indicator**—an arrow showing which way north is on the map

▲ *Chinese people still commute on bicycles, but for some the bicycle of choice has become a Western high speed model, and the clothing has become highly fashionable, as well.*

movement: migration, transport, and the spread of ideas.

The movements of people have altered patterns of living and changed environments around the world. Migration has been a constant factor in human history. The migration of Europeans, Africans, Latin Americans, and Asians, for example, brought together a variety of talents and cultures that built the United States into a powerful nation. The movement of goods by transport created trading links that have united many peoples into a global trade network and created a truly global economy. The spread of ideas through communication and trade has been important to the development of world history. The spread of Christianity from the Middle East to Europe, for example, helped create a new society. The movements of peoples and goods and the spread of ideas thus have transformed the world.

Region Regions are parts of Earth's surface that share one or more characteristics that make them different from other areas. Geographers divide the world into regions to show similarities and differences among areas. Both geographers and historians identify culture regions of Earth that share common characteristics and ways of living that distinguish them from other culture regions. Examples of culture regions are the Middle East, Latin America, Africa, and East Asia.

2. Interpreting Maps

Geographers use a number of tools to examine the five basic themes of geography. Their most basic tools are globes and maps. A globe is a spherical representation of Earth. In effect, it is a model of Earth. It is a true map of Earth because it accurately shows both landmasses and bodies of water. Globes are not always practical to use, however. Imagine carrying a globe around with you as a reference tool. Furthermore, the size of a globe limits the amount of detail it can tell us.

More useful to geographers, and to all of us, are maps. Maps are flat representations of Earth. They have a long history. The ancient Egyptians and Babylonians drew maps to show landholdings. The oldest known map is of Mesopotamia around 2300 B.C. It shows an estate in a valley. The Greeks were the first to make a systematic study of the world, which is reflected in the maps they made in the fourth century B.C.

Ptolemy, a Greek man who lived in Egypt around A.D. 150, was the most famous geographer of ancient times. He made a map of the world as it was known at that time, as well as regional maps of Europe, Africa, and Asia. After Ptolemy, the most accurate maps were made by Arab and Chinese scholars until the voyages of Europeans beginning around 1300 enabled Europeans to make more detailed and accurate maps. During the

◄ This beautiful world map was prepared by the Greek astronomer, Ptolemy in the second century A.D. Ptolemy made all of his astronomical observations from Alexandria, Egypt. His Geography was an attempt to map the world, showing latitudes and longitudes of important locations.

TEACHING TIPS

Map Skills. There are two basic types of maps. **General purpose maps** show a wide variety of information about an area. Two examples of general purpose maps are physical maps, which show terrain, elevation, water depth and other physical features, and political maps, which show boundaries, cities and capitals. **Special-purpose maps** focus on a single aspect or idea about an area. Population maps, weather maps, battlefield maps and road maps are all special-purpose maps. Have your students look through the maps in the book and find several examples of each type of map.

last five hundred years, mapmakers, who are also called *cartographers*, have mapped almost every inch of Earth. Beginning in the 1980s, photos of Earth taken from space satellites added to the accuracy of maps.

By their very nature, however, maps can never be exact. The basic problem is this: How can mapmakers draw the round surface of a sphere on a flat piece of paper? They cannot—at least, not exactly. A map cannot show the exact shapes of lands and bodies of water for an obvious reason: a map is flat, and Earth's surface is curved. You cannot flatten the surface of a round globe without distorting shapes and sizes. Try to flatten the rind of an orange, and you will see the problem.

Mapmakers try to limit the amount of distortion by using different kinds of map projections. A map projection is a method by which Earth's curved surface is projected onto a flat piece of paper. Different kinds of projections can show accurately either area, shape, distance, or direction. No one map, however, can show all four of these qualities with equal accuracy at the same time. By looking at a few projections, we can see some of the problems involved in mapmaking.

The most famous map projection in history is the Mercator projection. This projection is the work of a Flemish cartographer, Gerardus Mercator, who lived in the 1500s. The Mercator projection is an example of what mapmakers call a *conformal projection*. It tries to show the true shape of landmasses, but only of limited areas. On the Mercator projection, the shapes of lands near the equator are quite accurate. However, the projection greatly enlarges areas in the polar regions, far away from the equator. Look, for example, at the island of Greenland on the Mercator projection. It appears to be larger than the continent of South America. In fact, Greenland is about one-ninth the size of South America. The Mercator projection, however, was valuable to ship captains. Every straight line on a Mercator projection is a line of true direction, whether north, south, east, or west. Before the age of modern navigational equipment, ship captains were very grateful to Mercator.

Answers to Demonstrating Your Historical Skills.

1. Students should recognize that Poland was situated between two very strong rival nations, Germany and Russia, and that there are no natural barriers (oceans or high mountains) to protect the country. Understanding Poland's location is critical to understanding its history.

2. Map 9.1, "The Geography of Africa" is (*a*) a general-purpose map showing climate and geography. (*b*) No special symbols are used, but the key is color coded.

   Map 13.1, "A Manor" is (*a*) a special-purpose map showing the annual life cycle for an entire medieval manor, including its village site. (*b*) Circles represent trees, and cross-hatching denotes ownership of fields. (*d*) This map gives a picture of medieval farming practices, showing which fields are to be planted, which will lie fallow, and the rotation cycle to be followed.

   Map 30.1, "The States of Eastern Europe and the Former Soviet Union" is (*a*) a general-purpose map showing political boundaries. (*b*) Small squares represent the capitals of each country shown. (*c*) The distance from Moscow to Baku is approximately 1250 miles.

The Mollweide projection is an example of an equal-area projection. As you can see in the Mollweide map, equal-area projections distort the shapes of land areas but show land and water areas in accurate proportions. The size of one body of land or water is true in comparison with that of others.

The Robinson projection was created by cartographer Arthur Robinson. In 1988, the National Geographic Society adopted it as its new map projection to portray more accurately the round Earth on a flat surface. As you can see, on the Robinson projection, countries and continents more closely match their true sizes.

Demonstrating Your Historical Skills

1. Examine the physical map of Poland on page 617. Between 1772 and 1795, Poland was partitioned so often by its neighbors that it ceased to exist as a country until 1919. In 1939 it was again divided, this time by Nazi Germany and the Soviet Union. How can a study of Poland's geography help to explain its recurring problems with its neighbors?

2. Use the following maps to answer questions *a* through *d*: "The Geography of Africa" (Chapter 9, Map 1, page 254), "A Manor" (Chapter 13, Map 1, page 383), and "The States of Eastern Europe and the Former Soviet Union" (Chapter 30, Map 1, page 987).
   (*a*) Identify each of the maps as general-purpose or special-purpose, and describe the focus of each.
   (*b*) What symbols are used on each map? What do these symbols represent?
   (*c*) Use the scale on the map of the former Soviet republics to determine the distance between the capital of Russia and the capital of Azerbaijan.
   (*d*) What does the map of the manor tell you about medieval agricultural practices?

Applying Historical Skills to Your World

1. List the different aspects of your life that are related to the geography of where you live (for example, snow skiing as a hobby for someone from Colorado). How might your life change if you lived in a region of the world that was radically different?

Van Der Grinten

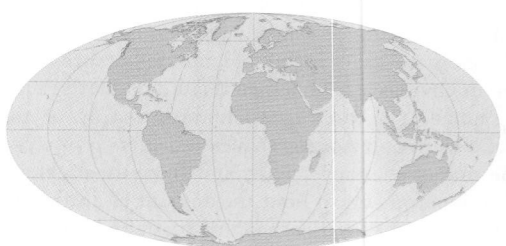

Robinson

Mollweide

2. Make a list of the destinations most frequently visited by you and your family (for example, the grocery store, mall, school, or workplace). Use a road

map to plot the quickest and most efficient way to visit those destinations from your home. Are these the routes you currently use? What factors that are not included on a map do you have to consider when planning a trip?

3. Using Time Lines

In a café in Austin, Texas, the following graffiti can be seen on the wall: "Time is nature's way of keeping everything from happening all at once." If that is true, then time lines are a student's way of avoiding learning everything at once. A time line presents events in chronological order. It is a simple way of comparing events, finding cause-and-effect relationships, and remembering important information.

This text makes frequent use of time lines. Before reading each unit, you should take a few minutes to look at and understand the time lines for that unit. The time line provides a chronological framework that should help to make your reading more understandable. The following are some keys to reading time lines:

1. *Understand the time interval.* Each time line uses its own unit of time, ranging from months to hundreds or even thousands of years. The time interval used can distort your understanding of how closely connected two events were. For example, events might be only a half-inch apart on a time line, but that half-inch could represent five hundred years.

2. *Note the order of events.* Look carefully at the order in which events are presented on the time line. Also make a mental note of the amount of time between each event.

3. *Try to make connections in time.* See if you can make connections between one event on the time line and another. Often a cause-and-effect relationship can be demonstrated between different historical occurrences. Ask yourself what other events also occurred during a particular time period.

Demonstrating Your Historical Skills

Use the following time line to answer these questions:

1. What is the time interval shown on this time line?

2. What time period is covered by this time line?

3. How long was it between the release of *Star Wars: Return of the Jedi* and *Jurassic Park*?

4. Describe the connections you can make among events on this time line.

Michael Jordan begins rookie season with the Chicago Bulls

Challenger shuttle explodes

Jurassic Park most successful film in worldwide box office history

Chicago Bulls win fourth NBA title

1980   1985   1990   1995   2000

Star Wars: Return of the Jedi released—the first time

Oklahoma federal building bombed

First successful cloning of large mammal (sheep)

First successful cloning of a mammal (mouse)

First flight of the Space Shuttle Columbia

U. S. becomes involved in Gulf War—Operation Desert Storm

TEACHING TIPS

Reading Charts, Graphs, and Tables. Have students collect information about a given subject in order to create a chart, graph, or table. You can tailor the information to your needs. It might be something as simple as a class survey of favorite foods, music or sports teams. Or you may have them use information from their math or science class. Once they have their data base, have them select and create the appropriate graphic. Be sure to stress the importance of artistry and eye appeal. The object is for students to use charts, graphs, and tables as a means of communicating information.

Answers to chart questions.

1. Prince Charles is the current successor to the British throne.
2. William of Wales is the nephew of Mark Phillips (who is now divorced from William's aunt, Princess Anne.)

Applying Historical Skills to Your World

Using this time line as a reference, create a time line of your own life. Begin with your birth and end with the present year. Fill in the time segments with the events that have been important in your life. Such a time line depicts a chronology of your life. It allows you to place events in the context of their time periods. Where were you when you heard about the Oklahoma City bombing? Do you remember when *Jurassic Park* opened in theaters? What grade were you in when scientists successfully cloned a sheep?

4. Reading Charts, Graphs, and Tables

Charts, graphs, and tables, like time lines, are graphic aids that communicate a large amount of information in a simple, straightforward manner. Reading these graphic aids is relatively easy, which is what makes them such useful tools.

Use the following steps to make the best use of any chart, graph, or table:

1. *Determine the type and purpose of the graphic aid.* Is it a graph, chart, or table? Read the title to find out what information is being presented.

2. *Identify the various parts of the graphic aid.* Graphs generally have both horizontal and vertical labels explaining the data being presented. Charts often show relationships among items. Tables usually have headings explaining the details found within their rows and columns.

3. *Evaluate the data.* Ask yourself what the comparisons and contrasts are between different facts presented. Are relationships revealed within the chart? Does the graph show trends over time? What comparisons can you make about the information in the table?

Charts

Charts are used to visually display relationships among people, ideas, or organizations. This chart shows the relationships among the four main ideas of the Buddhist religion. The chart is read from the bottom to the

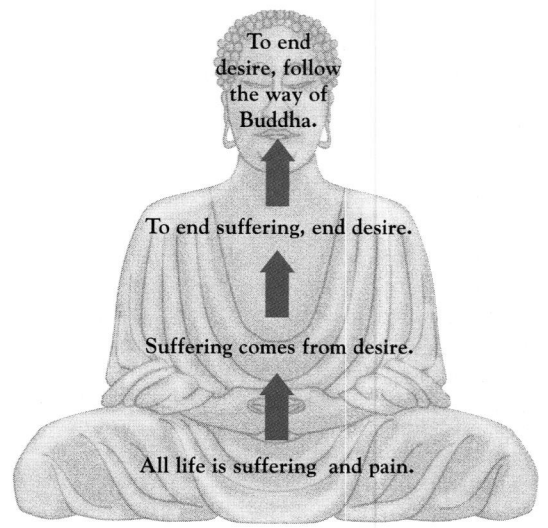

To end desire, follow the way of Buddha.

To end suffering, end desire.

Suffering comes from desire.

All life is suffering and pain.

top. You can see that each idea presented is dependent upon, and is an extension of, the previous one.

The House of Windsor chart is another visual representation of information. In this case, the chart shows the succession of the current royal family in Great Britain. Use the chart to determine the following:

1. Who is the current successor to the British throne?

2. What is the relationship of William of Wales to Mark Phillips?

Graphs

Graphs are a useful way of showing relationships among data, as well as changes over time. The three most common forms of graphs are line graphs, pie graphs, and bar graphs. You have probably used a line graph in math and science classes. It shows changes in information over a period of time.

The pie graph, such as the one on page BH–13 showing the distribution of slaves in the New World, shows proportions relative to the whole. You can see that in this case, a pie graph makes it very easy to identify which regions in the Western Hemisphere had the most and the least percentage of slaves in 1825.

King George VI
(b. 1895, d. 1952, reign: 1936–1952)
m. Lady Elizabeth Bowes-Lyon

Queen Elizabeth II
(b. 1926, reign: 1952–)
m. Philip Mountbatten,
Duke of Edinburgh

Princess Margaret
(b. 1930)
m. Antony, Earl of Snowden
(divorced 1978)

Prince Charles
Prince of Wales (b. 1948)
m. Lady Diana Spencer
(divorced 1996)

Prince Andrew
Duke of York (b. 1960)
m. Sarah Ferguson
(divorced 1996)

David
Viscount Linley
(b. 1961)
m. Serena Stanhope

Lady Sarah
Armstrong-Jones
(b. 1964)
m. Daniel Chatto

Princess Anne
(b. 1950)
m. Cpt. Mark Phillips
(divorced 1992)

Prince Edward
(b. 1964)

Prince William
of Wales (b. 1982)

Peter Phillips
(b. 1977)

Princess Beatrice
of York (b. 1988)

Samuel Chatto
(b. 1996)

Prince Henry
of Wales (b. 1984)

Zara Phillips
(b. 1981)

Princess Eugenie
of York (b. 1990)

House of Windsor
(Mountbatten) Chart

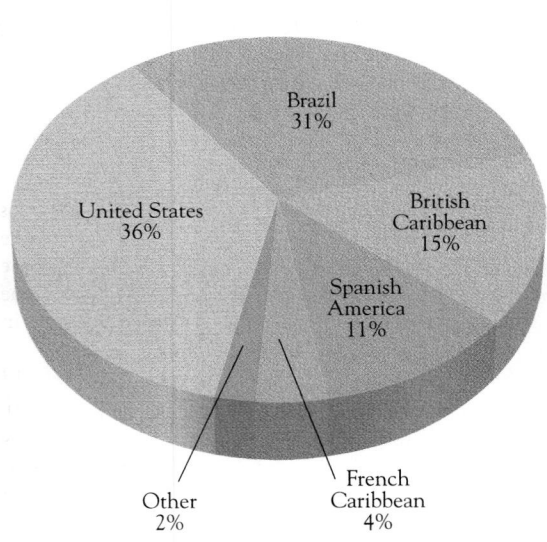

Finally, bar graphs are used for making comparisons among numbers. The bar graph on page BH–14 shows what happened to the Indian population of Central America after the arrival of the Europeans. This bar graph gives a graphic representation of the dramatic drop in the Indian population over a relatively short time.

Tables

Tables are compact lists of details that have been arranged in rows and columns. Tables are particularly effective for making comparisons. For example, the table on page BH–14 compares a few words in English and some of the Romance languages. The purpose of this table is to demonstrate that English, in some ways, is similar to, and has borrowed from, the Romance languages. A comparison of the five words presented here makes that obvious. The table of population growth in the United States is also helpful in making comparisons. Look at this table, and answer the following questions:

Reading Charts, Graphs and Tables. You might wish to have students change the information shown in population table on this page into a pie graph or a bar graph of population distribution among the 15 states in 1995.

Answers to chart questions.

1. The information is arranged in descending order of percentage of growth.
2. California's projected growth rate is 11 percent higher than Texas.
3. Wyoming had the smallest population in 1995.

TEACHING TIPS

Understanding Cause and Effect. Use the front page from your local newspaper to demonstrate cause and effect. Select and read to your students a current news story. Have them identify words that might signal cause and effect relationships. They should determine the primary and secondary causes of the news event. Have them describe the effects of this event. Finally, see if they can imagine how some of the effects of this event might, in the future, become the cause of other events. The object is for students to begin finding the connections between events.

1. How is the information in this table arranged?

2. What is the difference between the growth rates of California and Texas?

3. Which of the states shown here has the smallest population?

Projection of the Fifteen Fastest-Growing States in the United States		
State	**Population in 1995**	**Growth by 2025**
California	31,589,000	56%
New Mexico	1,685,000	55
Hawaii	1,187,000	53
Arizona	4,218,000	52
Nevada	1,530,000	51
Idaho	1,163,000	50
Utah	1,951,000	48
Alaska	604,000	47
Florida	14,166,000	46
Texas	18,724,000	45
Wyoming	480,000	45
Washington	5,431,000	44
Oregon	3,141,000	39
Colorado	3,747,000	39
Georgia	7,201,000	37

Source: U.S. News & World Report, November 4, 1996, p. 14.

5. Understanding Cause and Effect

Understanding why something happened is one of the most important and most difficult tasks of any historian. Without this understanding, history becomes an endless jumble of names and dates, selected at random. The principle of cause and effect enables you to connect actions and ideas with their results. Historians look at an historical event in much the same way as a reporter investigates a story. By asking who, what, why, where, when, and how, the historian begins to understand the actions that resulted in a particular event. What makes this investigative process so complicated is that most events have multiple causes. Historians understand that effects, in turn, can also become causes.

Similarities between English and Some of the Romance Languages				
English	**French**	**Spanish**	**Italian**	**Portuguese**
fraternity	fraternité	fraternidad	fraternità	fraternidade
liberty	liberté	libertad	libertà	liberdade
society	societé	sociedad	società	sociedade
possible	possible	posible	possibile	possível
probable	probable	probable	probabile	probável

Source: Information from Charles Berlitz, *Native Tongues* (New York: Grossett & Dunlap, 1982), p. 28.

For example, in Chapter 29 (Cold War and a New Order in the West), you will read about the Cold War between the United States and the Soviet Union which began in the 1950s. The heightened tension between the two superpowers was one of the *causes* of a "Red Scare" in the United States. Senator Joseph McCarthy exploited and contributed to this fear of communism through a series of government investigations, searching for supposed communist infiltrators. The *effect* of these actions was not only persecution and censorship, but also an increase in conformity and self-censorship by people afraid of appearing suspicious. Censorship was most noticeable in the entertainment and publishing industries, where many writers and actors were "blackballed," or kept from working because of their political beliefs. This *effect* of the Cold War was in turn one of the *causes* of the rise of a non-conformist, counterculture in the 1960s.

When investigating historical events ask yourself how effects may themselves be the causes of further events. During your reading look for some key words and phrases that may help you in making the connection between cause and effect.

During your reading of this text, look for some key words and phrases to help you make the connection between cause and effect. Some examples follow:

Words Showing Cause	Words Showing Effect
contributed to	resulted in
resulting from	as a consequence of
due to	outcome
arising from	product of
developed from	consequently
owing to	therefore
because	leading to
brought about by	dependent upon

Demonstrating Your Historical Skills

Read the following excerpt from Chapter 30 on the changing role of women since 1960:

With early marriage and smaller families, women had more years when they were not raising children. This has contributed to changes in the character of women's employment in both Europe and the United States.

The most important development was the increase in the number of married women working in the workforce. At the beginning of the twentieth century, even working-class wives tended to stay at home if they could afford to do so. In the postwar period, this was no longer the case. In the United States, for example, in 1900, married women made up about 15 percent of the female labor force. By 1990, their number had increased to 70 percent.

1. What was it that changed in the United States and Europe?

2. What brought about that change?

3. How might that change result in other changes in the United States and Europe?

4. The first sentence mentions early marriage and smaller families in the second half of the twentieth century. What might be some possible causes of that trend?

Applying Historical Skills to Your World

Think of an important event or turning point in your life. Make a list of the primary and secondary causes that led up to that point. Describe the effects of that event. Have those effects, in turn, become the causes of other events?

6. Recognizing and Understanding Bias

You, like all historians, have bias. It is impossible for human beings not to be biased. Bias is the inclinations, predispositions, and prejudices we all have as a result of our upbringing, education, and life experiences. There is nothing inherently wrong with being biased, as long as we don't allow it to prevent us from approaching new situations and people with objectivity and tolerance. However, as an historian, you must learn to recognize and understand bias in your studies. All authors have bias. This does not mean that what they are writing is untrue but simply that they have a point of view.

All historical documents are written by people and, as a result, contain the bias of the author. When you approach any source of information, it is appropriate to

---

Answers to Demonstrating Your Historical Skills.

1. The number of married women in the workforce increased significantly.
2. With early marriage and smaller families, women had more years that they could spend working.
3. Answers will vary, but students should realize that as more women work, families have more money for second cars and other luxuries.
4. Answers will vary, but the text suggests that many women can no longer afford to stay home and be full-time homemakers.

Recognizing and Understanding Bias. Have your students examine the reasons why someone would present information to the public. Whether the purpose is for education, entertainment, to make money, or to gain favor and popularity, each document, film, or photograph reflects the bias of its author. Discuss with students the meaning of words such as reactionary, conservative, moderate, liberal and radical. Explain how these political philosophies reflect a certain bias. Describe the role the profit motive plays in determining news coverage. The objective is for students to recognize that every source has an author, and that every author has biases.

TEACHING TIPS

Identifying Primary and Secondary Sources. Explain to your students the importance of primary source materials. It is through primary sources that historians are able to get as close as possible to actual events. The difficulty with primary sources for your students is that they will have to determine for themselves the importance and meaning of the documents. You can guide them by having them answer some basic questions about the document. Who is the author? Is the author a reliable source? Does the information in the document seem representative of the society from which it comes, or are its descriptions an aberration? The objective is for your students to begin to analyze and interpret documents for themselves.

maintain a degree of skepticism. Ask yourself if the statements you are reading are dependable and based upon verifiable evidence. What is the author's interest in the topic? Does the author have a particular philosophy or point of view? How would someone with a different background present the information? Finally, examine not only what the document tells you but also what it leaves out.

The following excerpt is a statement by the Soviet government explaining its military intervention in Hungary in 1956:

> *The Soviet Government and all the Soviet people deeply regret that the development of events in Hungary has led to bloodshed. On the request of the Hungarian People's Government the Soviet Government consented to the entry into Budapest of the Soviet Army units to assist the Hungarian People's Army and the Hungarian authorities to establish order in the town.*

Certainly, the author of this statement, the Soviet government, has a vested interest in the topic as it attempts to justify its military intervention. However, is the statement dependable and based upon an accurate account of events? Since the Hungarian Prime Minister, Imry Nagy, protested the invasion and was arrested shortly after the Soviets took over it would be difficult to conclude that the Hungarian government requested Soviet intervention.

Applying Historical Skills to Your World

Many teenagers feel that the news media portray them only in a negative light. Select one of your local television news programs and watch it for two weeks. Record each story that involves a young person. How does the media characterization of young people compare with what you know about your generation? How might coverage of teenagers be different if teenagers themselves were making editorial decisions for the media?

7. Identifying Primary and Secondary Sources

Primary sources are such things as writings, documents, drawings, and photographs created by participants or observers of an actual historical event. Secondary sources are writings about a historical event after it has occurred, often based upon one or more primary sources. Historians rely on primary sources as the most important tool of their trade. However, both primary and secondary sources serve a useful function.

Primary sources might include diaries, letters, interviews with eyewitnesses, stock inventories, account ledgers, photographs, or any other document that was created by participants of the historical time period in question. Although your textbook includes many primary sources, it is itself a secondary source. It was written after the events described in it occurred, and it was written by someone who did not personally witness these events. Secondary sources, such as textbooks, are useful because they present information in an orderly and understandable context. They are also much more condensed than the primary sources would be. If you were to gather all of the primary sources needed to compile this textbook, you could easily fill your school library.

The following is an example of a primary source. It comes from Chapter 8 and is an account by a twelfth-century Muslim who came to Jerusalem to pray:

> *Whenever I visited Jerusalem I always entered the Aqsa Mosque, beside which stood a small mosque which the Franks had converted into a church. When I used to enter the Aqsa Mosque, which was occupied by the Templars [Christian crusader knights] who were my friends, the Templars would evacuate the little adjoining mosque so that I might pray in it. One day I entered this mosque, repeated the first formula, "Allah is great," and stood up in the act of praying, upon which one of the Franks rushed on me; got hold of me and turned my face eastward, saying, "This is the way you should pray!" A group of Templars hastened to him, seized him and pushed him away from me. I went back to my prayer.*

Notice that the author is speaking in the first person as he describes something that is occurring in his own time.

Here is an example from Chapter 8 that describes an even earlier time period, but is a secondary source:

> *The best expression of Islamic art is to be found in a number of great buildings. Above all, the mosque—a house of worship—represents the spirit of Islam. The*

first great example is the Dome of the Rock. It was built in 691 to proclaim that Islam had arrived. The mosque was placed in the heart of Jerusalem on Muhammad's holy rock (Muslims believe that Muhammad ascended into Paradise from this site). This mosque remains one of the most revered Islamic monuments.

The source of this excerpt is a secondary source, because it was written about the building of the Dome of the Rock by someone who was not there when it was built.

Demonstrating Your Historical Skills

The following are titles or descriptions of discussions found within this text. Identify them as either primary or secondary sources.

1. You Are There: Gautama Buddha Speaks to His Disciples

2. A passage from the *Law of Manu* written in the second century B.C. on the role of women in ancient India

3. A description of everyday life in Aztec society written for this textbook

4. An excerpt about Ibo tribal society from *Things Fall Apart* by Chinya Achebe

5. A description of boy soldiers in Africa, compiled from several sources

8. Comparing and Contrasting

As an historian, one of the most useful ways you have of understanding new information is to compare and contrast it with information with which you are already familiar. Comparing involves examining different events, people, ideas, or facts for similarities. Contrasting is taking those same topics and studying them for differences. You will probably be called upon to compare and contrast frequently in your study of world history.

When comparing and contrasting, it is important first to identify the major characteristics of the two topics you are studying. An effective tool for studying similarities and differences in the Venn diagram. In a Venn diagram of two topics, the overlapping parts of the two circles represent the similarities of both topics. The remaining part of each circle shows the differences, or what is unique to each topic. This example

Characteristics of Aztec Empire
1. Had religion based on struggle between good and evil
2. Was an empire in Central Mexico
3. Had maize and beans as food crops
4. Was destroyed by European invaders
5. Received tribute from surrounding tribes

Similarities
1. Had great warriors
2. Had an authoritarian government
3. Existed in the fourteenth through sixteenth centuries
4. Ended in sixteenth century
5. Studied astronomy

Characteristics of Songhai Empire
1. Followed Muslim religion
2. Was an empire in West Africa
3. Raised cattle
4. Had a slow decline
5. Was a trading empire

Answers to Demonstrating Your Historical Skills.

1. Buddha is a primary source.
2. The *Law of Manu* is a primary source.
3. The description is a secondary source.
4. The passage can be considered a primary source, but students should recognize that it comes from a work of fiction, not a factual document.
5. Information compiled from various sources are secondary sources.

TEACHING TIPS

Comparing and Contrasting. When comparing and contrasting have your students identify characteristics that are important and meaningful. When comparing civilizations or nations they should look at political, economic and social structures. Comparisons of people should focus not only on accomplishments, but also on styles and personalities. Religions, philosophies and ideas should be compared for similarities or differences in their main points, details, causes and effects. By avoiding more superficial characteristics students will have a better understanding of the people, places or things that they are comparing and contrasting. The objective is for students to use comparisons and contrasts to gain insight and meaning.

TEACHING TIPS

Comparing and Contrasting. Draw a large Venn diagram on board, and review its use with students.

compares and contrasts the Aztec Empire of Central America, discussed in Chapter 7, with the Songhai Empire of West Africa, described in Chapter 9.

Demonstrating Your Historical Skills

Read the following biographies of Empress Wu of China (in Chapter 10) and Eleanor of Aquitaine (in Chapter 12). Make a Venn diagram to determine the characteristics of these women that are both the same and different.

Empress Wu

Wu Chao was born in 625, the daughter of a Chinese general. Attracted by her beauty, Emperor Tang Taizong chose her to be his concubine when she was only thirteen years old. After his death in 649, she became concubine to the next emperor, Kao Tsung, and bore him four sons and a daughter. Wu Chao was extremely jealous of the empress and greatly desirous of power. It is said that she strangled her own daughter and then accused the empress, who was childless, of the crime. The emperor chose to accept Wu Chao's story, deposed the empress, and chose Wu Chao as his new empress.

Empress Wu was obsessed with power. After her husband's death in 683, she sent one son into exile and ruled with another son. His weakness, however, gave her supreme power. Empress Wu did not hesitate to get rid of officials and even members of her family who stood in her way.

Although she was known for her ruthlessness, Empress Wu was also a capable ruler. She was the first ruler to select graduates of the civil service examinations for the highest positions in government. She forced Korea to become an ally of China, lowered taxes, and patronized the arts. During her last years, her abilities declined, and she was deposed in 705, at the age of eighty. In a country in which women had a low status, Empress Wu had lived a remarkable life.

Eleanor of Aquitaine

Eleanor of Aquitaine was one of the more remarkable personalities of twelfth-century Europe. Heiress to the duchy of Aquitaine in southwestern France, she was married at the age of fifteen to King Louis VII of France. The marriage was not a happy one. Louis was too pious for Eleanor, and she invited minstrels from southern France to brighten the French court with music, much to her husband's displeasure.

Eleanor went with her husband on the Second Crusade but soon caused a scandal by ignoring her husband and staying with Prince Raymond of Antioch, her tall and handsome uncle. In 1149, Louis and Eleanor returned home, but on separate ships. In 1152, Louis had their marriage annulled. Eleanor promptly created another scandal by marrying again, only eight weeks later. Her choice was Duke Henry of Normandy, who soon became King Henry II of England.

Henry II and Eleanor had a stormy relationship. She spent much time abroad in her native Aquitaine, where she paid special attention to creating a brilliant court dedicated to cultural activities. She and Henry had eight children (five were sons). Eleanor sought to further their careers, even assisting her sons in rebelling against the king (their father) in 1173 and 1174. She was imprisoned by her husband for her activities. After Henry's death, however, Eleanor again assumed an active political life, providing both military and political support for her sons. Two of her sons—Richard and John—became king of England.

◄ *Eleanor of Aquitaine who lived during the twelfth century was queen to both a French and an English king. Two of her sons, Richard and John became kings of England.*

9. Recognizing Fact versus Opinion

Historians create, evaluate, and use historical statements on the basis of evidence. That evidence, however, is often a combination of facts and opinions. As an historian, you must learn to identify both fact and opinion. A fact is information that can be independently verified as true or untrue. Even incorrect facts are still facts. An opinion is an evaluation, impression, or estimation that is open to dispute. Opinions may or may not be true. They simply cannot be verified.

When reading an historical source, attempt to determine if the statements being made can be proved. If the information in a statement can be verified as being either true or untrue by an independent source, then it is probably a fact. However, if the statement contains phrases that are value judgments based upon the writer's impression of the subject, then the information is probably an opinion.

Read this eyewitness account by Bishop Diego de Landa describing examples of the Maya writing system discovered by the Spanish (Chapter 7):

> We found a large number of books in these characters and, as they contained nothing in which there were not to be seen superstition and the lies of the devil, we burned them all, which they regretted to an amazing degree, and which caused them much affliction.

This statement contains a mixture of facts and opinions. That the Spanish found a large number of books and burned them are facts that can be checked for their accuracy. However, Bishop de Landa's statement that the books contained superstition and lies of the devil is an opinion that the Maya who witnessed the burning obviously did not share.

In Chapter 10, Genghis Khan tells of his motivation for conquest:

> Man's highest joy is in victory: to conquer one's enemies, to pursue them, to deprive them of their possessions, to make their beloved weep, to ride on their horses, and to embrace their wives and daughters.

Although Genghis Khan no doubt did these things, his statement is entirely opinion. You would be able to find many people who would disagree that this kind of victory is "man's highest joy." The statement is useful in showing the thinking of the Great Khan but it cannot be taken as being factual.

Demonstrating Your Historical Skills

Create your own comparison chart with three columns: "Fact," "Opinion," and "Uncertain." Analyze the information in the quotation from African writer Cyprian Ekwensi that appears in Chapter 32. List each item of information in the appropriate column of your table. After making your list, explain why you put each item where you did. Discuss the items in the "Uncertain" column, and see if there are any that you could move into the "Fact" or "Opinion" columns.

> We have our pride and must do as our fathers did. You see your mother? I did not pick her in the streets. When I wanted a woman I went to my father and told him about my need of her and he went to her father. . . . Marriage is a family affair. You young people of today may think you are clever. But marriage is still a family affair.

Applying Historical Skills to Your World

Watch ten commercials on television or look at ten advertisements in a magazine. Place the information from those ads on a blank chart similar to the one in the example you just studied. Are you surprised where the bulk of the information gets placed?

Fact	Opinion	Uncertain
1. _____	1. _____	1. _____
2. _____	2. _____	2. _____
3. _____	3. _____	3. _____
4. _____	4. _____	4. _____

Analyzing Information—Drawing Inferences. At the beginning of each chapter in *World History: The Human Odyssey* is a short reading, which serves as an introduction to the material in the chapter. When starting a new chapter have the students read the opening story and analyze the information it contains. They should list the individual facts described, recognize the information as fact or opinion, and identify it as primary or secondary source. Then have students draw inferences about the chapter. An effective brainstorming exercise is to have students list what they definitely know about this chapter's topic, what they think they know, and what they think they will learn.

10. Analyzing Information—Drawing Inferences

Analyzing information and drawing inferences is a skill you began developing as soon as you were old enough to figure out how to use your television's remote control. Analyzing information requires that you examine and investigate the details and relationships of the facts before you. Often it is useful to separate and study the individual parts of what you are analyzing. Drawing inferences is more difficult. An inference is a conclusion you reach after logically studying the facts. A young child looking at the small, rectangular instrument in her hand may analyze it, without knowing that it is a television remote control, by studying its individual components, such as buttons with numbers and other buttons of different colors. She will eventually draw the inference, after some investigation, that pushing the buttons will result in some corresponding action on the television. The ability to analyze information correctly and make accurate inferences is not only important for the study of history but is essential for success and even, at times, for survival.

You can learn more about inferences from studying information about the Johnstown flood. In the nineteenth century, the small working-class factory town of Johnstown, Pennsylvania, experienced frequent flooding. The people of the town would simply move to the upper floors of their homes until the floodwaters receded. In 1852, a group of wealthy factory owners bought a man-made lake as a private fishing retreat. The lake was created by an earthen dam that had discharge pipes and spillways to relieve pressure when the lake waters rose. Hoping to prevent fish from escaping the lake, the owners eventually removed the discharge pipes and blocked the spillways. On May 3, 1889, heavy rains brought flooding to Johnstown and caused the water in the lake to rise at the rate of six inches an hour. Finally, the dam broke, and twenty million gallons of water came roaring down upon the town at forty miles an hour. Houses, factories, and other buildings were washed away by the deadly torrent. The entire town was thoroughly destroyed. A five-month-old baby miraculously survived after floating seventy-five miles downstream on the floor of an uprooted house. Not everyone was so lucky, however. Over 2,200 people were killed, including at least 99 entire families.

The men who hoped to create an ideal vacation resort had incorrectly analyzed the information about the effects their actions would have on the dam, the lake, and Johnstown. Their inferences were limited only to the consequences that blocking off the dam would have on fishing. It is fortunate that your analyses of this information, and of your textbook, have less dire consequences.

In analyzing the Johnstown flood, you should first list the individual facts relevant to the event. These might include Johnstown's previous history of flooding, the man-made lake and earthen dam, the wealthy owners' desire to create a fishing retreat, the blocking off of the spillways and discharge pipes, and the heavy rains. It is easy to infer that the actions of the lake's owners, along with heavy rains, resulted in the Johnstown flood. However, are you able to draw any inferences about environmental and building regulations in the late nineteenth century? The fact that the lake's owners were able to block off the drainage system would suggest that government regulations were lax or nonexistent at the time. Are you able to make any inferences about the source of energy for the town? Because Johnstown was a factory town with a man-made lake, you might reach the conclusion that it, like many nineteenth-century cities, used water as a source of power. What might you infer about the attitude of the factory owners concerning the working-class people of Johnstown? Their actions might suggest that they gave the town's people very little thought, or at least not as much thought as they gave to creating a lake that was well stocked with fish. This might lead you to make some inferences about class divisions in the nineteenth-century United States, although there is probably not enough information here to reach any broad conclusions.

Demonstrating Your Historical Skills

In Chapter 3, you will read about the science and technology of India over a thousand years ago. The following is a description of medical practices in ancient India:

Ancient Indians excelled in the making of surgical instruments. One ancient Hindu medical work describes 20 sharp and 101 blunt medical instruments, including scalpels, razors, probes, needles, forceps, and syringes, all made of iron or steel or other metals. Indian surgeons were skillfully trained in performing operations and also made use of unusual solutions to one difficult problem. Since the intestines are especially subject to infection after surgery, Indian doctors used large ants to stitch them up. The ants were placed side by side along the opening, clamping the wound shut with their jaws. The surgeon then cut away their bodies, leaving the heads behind to decompose after the abdomen was sewn up and the wound healed.

Analyze the facts and draw inferences as follows:

1. Make a list of all of the pertinent facts in the paragraph.

2. Examine these facts, and see if you can find any relationships among them.

3. What can you infer about the state of metallurgy (the preparation, smelting, and refining of metals) in ancient India?

4. Can you make any inferences about the ancient Indians' knowledge of human anatomy?

5. What conclusions might you reach about Indian science and its relation to the natural world?

Applying Historical Skills to Your World

Make a list of the people, places, and things that have played major roles in your life thus far (for example, parents, friends, school, place of worship, television, or books). Analyze the influence each has had on you up to this point. Draw some inferences about the effects those influences will have on you as an adult.

11. Looking at Art as a Key to History

What makes humans distinct from other animals on this planet? Anthropologists, biologists, and theologians may argue vehemently about the answer to that question, but there is little doubt that the urge for artistic creation is a uniquely human trait. No other creature is able to make abstract representations of reality through painting, sculpture, literature, dance, theater, or architecture. All art is abstract art in that it is a human creation, separate from the material world. Marcel Duchamp, a twentieth-century artist, once painted a picture of a pipe, perfect in every detail, and wrote beneath it, "This is not a pipe." His statement is baffling until you realize that he is, indeed, correct that it is not a pipe but rather a *picture* of a pipe. Duchamp's point was that art is a representation of something else. The ability to make those kinds of representations is something all humans possess. Give any six-year-old a box of chalk and a sidewalk, and you will have immediate proof of that shared trait.

Art is a characteristic we all share as humans, but it is also something that defines us as individuals belonging to a distinct society. Probably no other aspect of human culture reveals more about a people than the culture's artistic creations. For that reason, a good historian will look to art as a key to understanding history.

Each society, in every time, has a complex and unique understanding of the world in which its people live. Historians used to speak of "primitive" and "advanced" cultures. The implication was that primitive cultures were childlike and simplistic, whereas advanced cultures were sophisticated and mature. Good historians, however, now acknowledge that every society, through interaction with its environment, develops complex and elaborate systems of economics, government, philosophy, and self-expression. Studying the products of that self-expression can reveal much about people.

The Paleolithic people of Europe who lived twenty thousand years ago were seemingly simple cave dwellers who hunted game and gathered wild fruits and berries. However, the paintings they left behind in the Lascaux caves of France, as well as statues, such as those found in Ain Ghazal in Jordan, reveal them to be quite sophisticated. The intricate attention to detail and realism in the Lascaux paintings have led many art historians to claim them to be masterpieces of naturalistic art. These expressions of Paleolithic culture reveal much about the people who created them. Animals and hunting played a central role in their lives. The paintings might have been their means of instructing

TEACHING TIPS

Looking at Art as a Key to History. Each chapter of this text contains illustrations and pieces or art that are relevant to the cultures and the civilizations being studied. As you read through each chapter, ask students to examine the illustrations carefully, answer the questions that are posed, and have the students discuss why each piece was chosen. Ask them what the art tells about the time period it represents and the culture that produced it.

Answers to Demonstrating Your Historical Skills.

1. Students should recognize that the Mesopotamian artists and artisans who carved this stele were highly trained and creative.
2. Students should recognize the importance of Hammurabi's Code of Law and the importance of justice to the culture.
3. Students should recognize that realistic forms were given to both God and to man. This supports the cultural and religious belief that man (humankind) was created in God's image.
4. Answers will vary, but students should realize that during the Renaissance God was considered an all-powerful being, in complete control over all things on the Earth.

▲ *The caves at Lascaux, France are now closed to the public, but the paintings are world famous.*

young hunters. They could also indicate the development of a system of religious belief. The eight plaster statues found in Jordan are among the oldest human-form sculptures ever found. Scientists and museum curators are working together to piece together the story they represent, an intriguing addition to the human story.

By comparison, a twentieth-century painting by the Spanish artist Pablo Picasso, *The Fourteenth of July*, seems more abstract than the cave paintings of Lascaux. However, it, too, reveals something about the culture and time in which it was created. After the invention of the camera, many artists no longer felt compelled to paint strictly realistic pictures. Artists such as Picasso, influenced by Sigmund Freud's developments in psychology, instead began to paint people's "inner" worlds. Picasso also painted his subjects from many points of view, all at the same time. This approach reflected the influence of Albert Einstein's theories about relativity and perception. Thus, although many of Picasso's works seem simplistic, they are in fact complex expressions of the modern world.

Demonstrating Your Historical Skills

The picture of the Stele of Hammurabi (right) and the detail from Michelangelo's Sistine Chapel ceiling both are representative of the time periods and cultures from which they came. Examine these two pieces of art to see what they reveal about Mesopotamia and Renaissance Italy:

1. What does the artistic workmanship of Hammurabi's Stele tell you about the abilities of Mesopotamian artists and artisans?

2. What can you infer about Mesopotamian society based on the Stele?

3. Michelangelo's painting reveals a realism that did not exist in earlier medieval works of art. What does Michelangelo's style of painting reveal about Renaissance attitudes concerning the human body?

4. Michelangelo makes the human hand weak, but God's arm is forceful. What does this tell us about the European perception of God?

Applying Historical Skills to Your World

You may think that the appreciation of art is limited only to those who regularly attend museums and art shows. However, we are all surrounded by examples of artistic self-expression. Advertisers regularly employ graphic artists to create billboards, television commercials, and magazine ads. Musicians use artists to design compact disc covers or artistic videos. Tee shirts and posters often display examples of popular art. Using the examples cited or more traditional modern-day paintings and sculptures, describe what today's art reveals about modern society.

12. Studying Economics as a Key to History

Economics has been called "the dismal science." Many high school and college students, upon completing an economics course, might wholeheartedly agree that the study of economics is only

▲ *The ceiling frescoes of the Sistine Chapel in Rome painted by Michelangelo are a masterpiece not just of Renaissance art, but of art for all time.*

slightly more interesting than watching toenails grow. Ironically, most of those same students would tell you that getting, keeping, and spending money is of the utmost concern. This attitude is ironic because that is exactly what economics is about.

Of course, economics is about more than just money. It is really about resources. Resources are assets, usually obtained from our environment, that we can use when needed. In the American economic system, the surest way to obtain resources is through the accumulation of money. However, the greatest resource you will ever have is already in your possession. It is you. Your human potential—the ability to do work, to learn, and to adapt—will be your greatest asset in life. In a very real economic sense, your earning capacity is your primary resource.

All societies have resources. How they accumulate, distribute, and use those resources is central to the study of economics. By studying a country's economic system, historians get a sense of the country's priorities, values, governmental policies, philosophies, and even its religion. Economics is one of the major keys to history.

Chapter 14 (Rebirth and Reform in Europe: The Age of the Renaissance and Reformation) deals with the Renaissance, or rebirth of European culture, which began in Italy during the fifteenth and sixteenth century. The artists, writers and scholars of Renaissance Italy became respected and renowned figures in society. Michelangelo's sculptures, Leonardo da Vinci's paintings, and Raphael's frescoes are today considered priceless works of art. However, what would this incredible outburst of artistic creativity have to do with economics?

Because of its geography Italy played a pivotal role in trade between Asia, the Middle East and Europe. Beginning in about the eleventh century Italy experienced an explosion of commercial activity as a result of its role in foreign trade. This in turn gave rise to a wealthy class of merchant families, the most famous of which were the de'Medici.

During the Middle Ages the main patron of artists was the Catholic Church, which commissioned painters and sculptors to create works of art for cathedrals and churches. The subjects of these works, of course, were almost entirely religious. Realism of the human form was not as important as spiritual inspiration. But, with the rise of a new class of wealthy merchants, artists found themselves in demand from new patrons who commissioned works for their elaborate homes and summer villas. The focus of art, while still usually religious, shifted to more earthly beauty. The natural world became a source of inspiration, and the human form was exalted. Patrons wanted portraits of themselves and their families, and artists complied with ever more realistic works.

The world of paint and pallets, so distant from the world of cash and counting houses, experienced one of its most creative periods because of the forces of economics.

Demonstrating Your Historical Skills

In Chapter 12, you will read about the development of the feudal system in Europe. After the fall of the Roman Empire, Europe experienced a time of political

TEACHING TIPS

Economics as a Key to History. As one of the most powerful factors for motivating people and affecting historical events, it is important for your students to recognize and identify the economic influences of the events they study. After each chapter have your students identify the resources of the people, nations, or civilizations they have been studying. Have them describe how those resources, or lack thereof, influenced the course of events. Were there any economic motivations behind the wars, inventions, or cultural developments of these people? The objective is for students to begin to look for the economic factors that influence historical events.

Economics as a Key to History. Students should be aware of the strengths and weaknesses of the various economic philosophies proposed throughout history. Have small groups of students select one of the following economic systems for further study: hunter-gatherer society, barter economy, feudalism, mercantilism, laissez-faire capitalism, zaibatsu (Meiji Japan) economy, modern capitalism, socialism, or communism. Have students report on the philosophy behind the system as well as the economic, political and social pros and cons of that system. The objective is for students to recognize that each economic system has certain benefits and drawbacks for the people who adopt it.

Answers to Demonstrating Your Historical Skills.

1. The fighting men offered to protect the serfs and their families, their homes, and their crops.
2. The main source of wealth was the agricultural products of the land.
3. Answers will vary, but students should recognize the importance of the church in medieval life.
4. The serfs were the most economically valuable, for they worked the land.
5. The nobles and their knights wielded the political power.

TEACHING TIPS

Making Hypotheses and Predicting Outcomes— Educated Guesses. The process of making hypotheses involves formulating questions about the motivations of people and the reasons why events occur. This is a difficult task for many students, who see history as having unfolded along a predetermined path with little or no decision-making by the principals responsible for those events. One exercise to help students see that the future was no clearer for the historical figures they are studying than it is for them, is to imagine alternative outcomes for historical events if other choices had been made. How would history have been different if Admiral Zhenghe and the fifteenth

instability. European peasants faced invasions from Vikings in the north, Magyars in the east, Muslims in the south, and various bandit groups throughout the continent. To provide the basic necessities of life, peasants turned for protection to fighting men. These knights demanded a portion of the peasant's crop for this protection. As these fighting men grew more powerful, they gained control of more land and the peasants who farmed it. Weaker knights gave their allegiance and promises to do battle to stronger nobles, who in turn provided the knights with more land. Soon the peasants found themselves bound to the land, unable to leave without the permission of their lords. These bound peasants were called serfs.

With this background in mind, answer the following questions:

1. What resource did fighting men have to trade for the peasants' crops?

2. What was the main source of wealth in this economic system?

3. What inferences can you draw concerning the effect that this system would have on the development of medieval religion? (Think about the church's need for protection.)

4. Which group was the most economically valuable in this system?

5. Which group had the most political power in this system?

Applying Historical Skills to Your World

An understanding of economics is essential to your world. For one thing, you probably have more disposable income as a teenager than do most adults. The reason for this is that many teenagers have few or no bills. This frees up a great deal of money for luxury items. It also makes teenagers a powerful economic force in the United States. In what ways do advertisers and retailers pursue the teenage dollar?

Furthermore, economics may affect your belief system. For instance, what is your opinion about raising taxes to pay for better schools? Do you think that col-

lege tuition should be lower, or even paid for by state and federal governments? Should the minimum wage be increased? How are your answers influenced by your economic self-interest? In other words, how might someone who is less directly affected by school quality, college tuition, and the minimum wage answer these questions?

13. Making Hypotheses and Predicting Outcomes

When was the last time you were looking for an answer and the teacher said, "Just guess"? School is supposed to be about definite answers to specific questions, right? Actually, the great joy and frustration in the study of history is that there are many questions to which there are no definitive answers. Pablo Picasso once said, "Computers are useless. All they do is give you answers." What he meant is that sometimes a well-thought-out question is more important than pages of factual data. Making hypotheses is the process of formulating questions and then coming up with educated guesses about the answers. Predicting outcomes involves using your educated guesses to try to foresee possible future results based upon your past experience.

In Chapter 32, you will read about the decades-long dispute in the Middle East between Israel and its surrounding Arab neighbors. Beginning in the 1970s, a series of events began that seemed to bode well for peace in the region. Egyptian president Anwar Sadat flew to Israel to meet with Israeli officials. Sadat and Israeli prime minister Menachem Begin met with U.S. president Jimmy Carter and signed a peace treaty. Within the next fifteen years, Israel reached an agreement with the Palestine Liberation Organization, which had previously vowed to destroy Israel. More Arab nations began to normalize relations with Israel. At the same time, however, there have been attacks by both sides upon the other. In 1996, Israeli prime minister Yitzak Rabin was assassinated by an Israeli opposed to peace.

From this information you might hypothesize that both Israel and the Arabs have compelling reasons for making peace after decades of war. Educated guesses about those reasons might include the ideas that war is too costly, that both sides are tired of the killing, or that war is preventing both groups from developing and advancing economically and culturally. You might predict that the outcome of this conflict, based upon past events, will be a gradual movement toward peace and more normal relations, periodically interrupted by times of mistrust and tension.

Demonstrating Your Historical Skills

The following excerpt about popular culture is from Chapter 30:

> Movies and television were the chief vehicles for the spread of American popular culture in the years after World War II. American movies continued to dominate both European and American markets in the next decades. Many American movies make more money in worldwide distribution than they do in the United States. Kevin Costner's Waterworld is but one example of this pattern.
>
> Although developed in the 1930s, television did not become available until the late 1940s. By 1954, there were thirty-two million television sets in the United States as television became the centerpiece of middle-class life. In the 1960s, as television spread around the world, U.S. networks unloaded their products on Europe and the non-Western world at very low prices. Baywatch was the most popular show in Italy in 1996.

See if you can formulate some hypotheses based on the excerpt and predict possible future outcomes:

1. Make a hypothesis, or educated guess, about why American television is so popular in other countries.

2. Hypothesize about the effects that American television has had on the cultures of other countries.

3. Predict the outcome of a continued worldwide demand for American entertainment.

4. Predict the possible future development of television technology.

Applying Historical Skills to Your World

In the last few decades, the U.S. economy has been moving away from industrial, factory-type jobs toward more service and information-dependent jobs. This has meant that nonskilled, direct-entry jobs are being replaced by positions that require more schooling and training. Make a hypothesis about possible reasons for this change. Make a prediction about the future of the American economy, as well as about the types of jobs that will be available when you enter the labor force.

14. Conducting Research

Your textbook contains a great deal of information about a wide variety of topics, but it is not the final word in the study of history. At some point you will be required to go beyond a general discussion of a topic and become more familiar with the specifics of an event. Perhaps there is a subject of particular interest about which you want to know more. In either case, you will need to conduct research.

When you were in fourth grade, a research project was fairly simple and straightforward. You got an encyclopedia, copied down the information about your topic, and put it into your own words. The research project was mostly a matter of rephrasing someone else's words and research. Today, the process is more involved. Not only are you expected to conduct your own research, but the number of sources available is truly staggering. The Information Revolution of the late twentieth century has created a problem that past researchers never would have imagined—too much information. When conducting research, it is helpful to keep a few general questions in mind: Where is the information? How is the information organized? Is the information specific and timely? Is the information credible and reliable?

Where Is the Information?

You have a wide variety of available resources when conducting research. The most traditional, and probably still the most useful, resource is a library. School and public libraries carry a wide variety of books, newspapers, periodicals, and compact discs of general interest. If you live in a town with a university, you have access to a library that will have a collection targeted toward more specific topics. Also, most newspapers, historical

century Chinese had settled the New World instead of Columbus? What would have happened if Hannibal and the Carthaginians had conquered the Roman Empire? What would our world be like if Hitler had been accepted to art school and begun a career as a painter? Once students begin to see historical events as predicated upon many choices and forces, they can begin to make predictions about the outcomes of various choices. The objective is for students to use their skills to hypothesize about motivations and then to attempt to predict outcomes.

Answers to Demonstrating Your Historical Skills. Students can have a lot of fun and still learn valuable principles with this activity. Encourage them to be creative but realistic in their hypotheses. They should support their answers with reason and logic.

TEACHING TIPS

Writing Research Papers. An effective way for showing your students what you expect from their research papers and for making the grading of those papers easier is to provide them with a rubric. A rubric is a detailed list of what should be included in the research paper, along with the points allocated for each item listed. You may wish to break down the assignment into research, rough draft, and final draft and provide a rubric for each. A sample rubric is included as a teaching tip.

TEACHING TIPS

Conducting Research. Conducting research is a highly developed skill which requires, for most students, a great deal of guidance. It is recommended that the process be broken down into easier to manage steps so that students can accomplish one task before going on to the next. The first step involves familiarizing students with the location of available resources. A guided tour of the school or local library, along with a short research assignment requiring the students to use the major, basic resources would help to orient your students. More students are becoming familiar with the Internet and the World Wide Web, but teacher-guided lessons on using this resource effectively will help to keep them on track.

Conducting Research. There are several steps for making student research more organized. Check your students' work at each step of their research project.

1. Have students record bibliographic information first.
2. Have students record each specific piece of information on a separate note card (along with bibliographic information about where the information came from).
3. Have students find information from primary as well as secondary sources (try to avoid using encyclopedias as sources).
4. Have students arrange cards into thematic groups.
5. Have students create an outline based upon the groupings of their note cards.

museums, and large corporations have libraries to which you might be able to gain access with a phone call.

Another possible source of information is the Internet. Using the Internet, you can access libraries, museums, newspapers, and countless home pages from around the world. Even if your school does not yet have Internet access, many copy centers and other businesses offer computers for use by the public on a pay-per-use basis.

You might also try using a computer search service. These services can help find answers to very specific questions, often on a pay-per-use basis. Some examples include the New York Times Index, Educational Resources Information Center (ERIC), and Social Sciences Citation Index (SSCI).

Finally, people might be your greatest resource. Talk to teachers, librarians, parents, and friends about your research topic. You might find that even if they do not have information for you, they might know someone who does. The telephone and computer e-mail also can assist you in your research. If you are doing research about the 1923 Rosewood tragedy, why not send an e-mail message to John Singleton, the director of the movie *Rosewood*, or to the *St. Petersburg Times*, which first printed the story of the destruction of the small Florida town? If you are researching the effect World

▶ *The Internet is an outstanding source of information on myriad subjects. Among the many organizations that have home pages is the Smithsonian Museum in Washington, D.C., "America's Treasure House for Learning."*

Writing Research Papers. The following sample rubric would be for the final draft of a paper. You could change the categories and points to suit your own needs.

Content	Possible Points	Actual
1. Essay has a well thought-out thesis	10	—
2. Information is factual and accurate (opinions are supported with documented data)	15	—
3. Paper demonstrates historical importance of subject	15	—
4. Essay places events in their geographic and chronological context (places and times of		

War II had on professional football, why not write or call the Football Hall of Fame in Canton, Ohio, for a list of football players from that era who are still alive? Interviewing eyewitnesses and experts can be one of the most effective methods of research.

How Is the Information Organized?

Whether you are using a library or the Internet, first you have to determine how the information is organized. Most libraries use the Dewey decimal system to organize their collections. This system divides books into general categories and specific subcategories. Ask your librarian for an explanation of this system so that you can save time when doing further research. You will also want to ask about the organization of the library's collection of newspaper articles and periodicals.

Using the Internet can be more confusing, in part because you generally won't have a librarian to guide you. However, access to the Internet can be made easier by the use of search engines. These are programs that allow you to search the Internet for information based on topic, author, title, or key words. Experimentation is the best method of discovering which search engine is most useful to you.

Is the Information Specific and Timely?

Information is crucial to your research. You want the most specific, up-to-date information available to provide you with the most accurate answers to your questions. General information, such as the type found in encyclopedias, is of little use for the more sophisticated research you are expected to conduct in high school. Whenever possible, you will want to use primary source information. The writings, documents, photographs, and other information produced by actual witnesses and participants of historical events will provide you with the most specific and accurate data. Secondary sources, when used, should come from experts and other reliable sources.

In general, the more up-to-date and recent the information, the better it is for your research. Older information often is proved incorrect by new facts, so it is important that your research be current.

Is the Information Credible and Reliable?

Finally, your research is only as good as the credibility and reliability of your sources. A dependable source is more likely to result in dependable information. For instance, read the following three statements:

1. The United States is in decline.

2. According to *The Rise and Fall of the Great Powers*, the United States is experiencing decline.

3. Paul Kennedy, professor of history at Yale University, wrote in his book *The Rise and Fall of the Great Powers* that the United States is experiencing economic and military decline relative to its world position just after World War II.

Readers are more inclined to believe the last statement than the other two, because some degree of credibility has been established by the citing of a respected source.

Even established and respected researchers are susceptible to unreliable information, however. Pierre Salinger, a noted freelance journalist, reported that a plane crash in 1996 off the coast of Long Island was caused by a missile attack. It was quickly revealed that the source of his information was a hoax story that had appeared earlier on the Internet.

15. Writing Research Papers

Time travel has been a favorite subject of science fiction writers since H. G. Wells wrote *The Time Machine* in the nineteenth century. Although the topic is a favorite with readers and movie audiences, scientists discount the possibility of sending people or objects through time. Historians, however, might disagree with those scientists.

Time travel is as old as human civilization. Through books, music, and art, people have been transporting a treasure trove of ideas, knowledge, and objects of beauty into the future for thousands of years. The information is part of a "Great Conversation" between generations. You are part of that conversation, not only as a recipient but also as a participant. Your creative contribution to the Great Conversation is a well-researched, thoughtfully-written research paper. It is a

	Possible Points	Actual
events are clearly described)	10	—
5. Essay provides a cultural context	10	—
Structure	**Possible Points**	**Actual**
6. Bibliography	10	—
7. Essay has strong introduction	5	—
8. Each paragraph has a topic sentence	5	—
9. Essay uses correct grammar	5	—
10. Spelling	5	—
11. Paragraphs employ smooth transitions	5	—
12. Conclusion summarizes essay and reinforces thesis	5	—
Total Grade	100	—

Writing Research Papers—Creativity. Some students (and teachers) believe that creative writing is reserved for poetry and short stories students write in their English classes. This leads students to approach the process of writing a research paper as a workman-like endeavor of putting large amounts of factual information into prose. Try to encourage your students to see their research and writing process as being akin to the role of a Native American story teller, passing on the legacy of the tribe. The objective is to teach, but also to intrigue, fascinate, and entertain. Students should write papers that will not only please their teacher, but also interest their peers.

way of gathering and presenting your insights and observations as an historian.

What is difficult about writing a research paper is that it requires the use of all, or nearly all, of the social studies skills we have covered in this study guide. There is probably nothing that you will do as a student of history that reveals more about you and your abilities than does your research paper. Writing a research paper is a challenging task, but it is by no means impossible.

Hints for Better Research Papers

When faced with the task of writing a research paper, many students feel like a mountain climber looking up at Mt. Everest. However, follow the example of Edmund Hillary, who was the first man to climb the world's largest mountain: if you divide a task into stages and take it one step at a time, you will find that your goal can be reached. The following are fifteen steps that will help you to create an A+ research paper.

Knowing Your Topic Your first task is to know your topic. The most common problem faced by students writing research papers is selecting a topic that is too vague. This leads to frustration and the wasting of many hours of research. For example, if you decide to research "music," you will find thousands of books, and indeed whole libraries, devoted to the topic. If you narrow the topic to "rock music," you will find it somewhat easier to research your topic, but even that topic is too general. A research paper about "the influence of gospel music on rock and roll" is much more focused and will be immensely easier to research.

Also, make sure that you are researching only one topic. "The influence of gospel music on rock and roll" is a different topic from "the influence of rock and roll on gospel music." Of course, it is possible to narrow your topic too much, but choosing a topic that is too vague is the mistake made by most students.

Knowing Your Purpose What is the purpose of your research paper? Are you writing to find out how to do something (or to describe to others how to do something)? Is your paper a report of events that have occurred in a particular time and place? Are you

explaining an idea or concept to others? Is the purpose of your paper to persuade or influence your readers on a particular point of view using factual information? A "yes" answer to any of these questions will result in a very different type of research paper.

Perhaps your topic deals with the Brazilian rain forest. A how-to paper might be called "Ecologically Responsible Methods of Harvesting the Resources of the Brazilian Rain Forest." An example of a paper dealing with the reporting of events would be "The First Portuguese Missionaries in the Brazilian Rain Forest." If your purpose were to explain an idea, then you could write on "The Life Cycle of Butterflies in the Canopy of the Brazilian Rain Forest." If you were writing a persuasive paper, "The Need to Protect the Endangered Animals of the Brazilian Rain Forest" might be your topic. Knowing your purpose will determine the direction of your research paper and help to narrow your focus.

Creating a Working Outline Once you have chosen a suitably narrow topic and determined your purpose, the next step is to create a working outline. Your outline will help you divide your topic into subtopics and then divide those subtopics into more narrow specifics. The general outline of your paper will include an introduction (where you describe the purpose and topic of your paper), the body (where you write about your topic), and a conclusion (where you summarize the important points of your research paper).

Because you will not have done any research up to this point, your working outline will probably be somewhat vague. You will most likely end up rearranging the order of subtopics, discarding some, and adding others.

As an example, suppose you decide to do a report on the Holocaust during World War II. You have decided to narrow your focus to the fate of children during the Holocaust and have chosen as your purpose to report on the events that occurred at that time. A working outline might look like this:

The Fate of Children in Nazi Concentration Camps
   I.   Children Sent to Camps
       —different groups, transportation to camps

II.   Life in the Camps
    —family life, schooling, religious worship, play, creativity
III.   Slave Labor
    —types of jobs, methods of selection
IV.   Death
    —methods, numbers, escapes

Turning Your Outline into Questions   Once you have a working outline, you can save a great deal of research time by taking the subtopics from that outline and turning them into questions. You will then have a very specific purpose to your research. For example, using the working outline on the fate of children in Nazi concentration camps, you might create the following questions:

▲   What groups were sent to the camps?
▲   When and how were they transported to the camps?
▲   What was life like in the camps?
▲   Did the children attend school?

These and other questions will keep you on track and allow you to make effective use of your research time.

Finding the Right Sources and Resources   At this point, you are ready to begin your research. You have a topic, a purpose, an outline, and a series of questions in need of answers. Where do you begin your search? The previous section on "Conducting Research" goes into more detail about research. You probably will use your school or local library, the Internet, your family's own books and resources, or a combination of these resources.

You must decide what type of sources you will use. Will your research come from primary or secondary sources (see the earlier discussion)? Most professional researchers use primary source material. You should also rely on primary sources whenever possible. Many students are tempted to use encyclopedias when writing reports. However, encyclopedias should be consulted only for general background, not as sources. It is a rare teacher who can't spot the dry, stilted writing of a report based on encyclopedias.

When you have selected your sources of information, be sure that you understand the method of citation required by your school and teacher. Methods vary, so consult your teacher if you are uncertain. It is essential that you give credit for your information.

Organizing Your Data   Many methods of note taking are useful for organizing your information. Whether you are using a notebook, note cards, or some other method, the following guidelines will be useful for organizing your data:

1. Always write the information about the source of your notes first. This will allow you to properly cite your source in your paper. Information that does not have bibliographic information cannot be used.

2. Always write your notes in your own words. Days or weeks after you've written your notes, it is easy to forget whether the wording is yours or is from your source.

3. Create an organizational system that helps you retrieve your information easily. Note cards are useful for this purpose, because they allow you to sort by topic and reshuffle as needed.

Quoting, Paraphrasing, and Plagiarizing   Quoting a source can lend weight and authority to your paper. Using too many quotations, however, implies a lack of confidence in your own words. When quoting, you must use quotation marks and cite the person who made the statement. Sometimes you may want to reword another person's statement or shorten an idea to a few essentials. This is called *paraphrasing*. It is an acceptable practice, as long as you cite the source of the information. What is not acceptable is using other people's words or unique ideas without giving them credit. This practice is both unethical and foolish. Most teachers can tell the difference between the writings of their students and those of established and published authors.

Writing a Thesis Statement   A thesis statement describes in one or two sentences the topic and purpose of your paper. It is often the last sentence in the introduction. Writing a thorough, carefully thought out thesis statement will help keep your essay focused and

---

TEACHING TIPS

Writing Research Papers— Plagiarism. Many students have difficulty with the process of paraphrasing or putting information in their own words. Students wonder how much of another author's ideas they can borrow and how much of it they have to change before it becomes their own. (A common joke is that if you steal from one author, it is plagiarism; but if you steal from many authors, it is research.) Have your students practice paraphrasing by giving them several examples from primary and secondary sources that they must then put into their own words. The objective is for students to learn to use their own words, even when expressing someone else's ideas.

keep you on track in your writing. By constantly checking to see if the information in the report supports your thesis, you will know whether each point is essential or extraneous to the research paper.

Creating a Formal Outline After doing your research and writing a thesis statement, you are ready to make a formal outline. Many students skip this step, thinking that it is simply more work. This is a mistake. A well-organized outline will make the actual writing of your paper much easier. The subheadings of the outline will become the individual paragraphs of the body of the paper. The specific facts listed become the details that support your thesis. Writing an outline allows you to focus on writing technique, because the actual topics and subtopics will already be prepared.

Using Graphics When you pick up a book, newspaper, or magazine, your eyes probably are immediately drawn to the pictures and graphics. The use of pictures, maps, graphs, charts, and other graphics not only enlivens your paper but also helps make your point to the reader. Be sure to give credit to the source of the graphics you use, as you do for other information that was not created by you.

Writing the Body The body of your research paper can be said to be the "meat and potatoes" of the paper. It is where you present the information that supports your thesis statement. Many people find it easier to write the body before they actually create the introduction. When writing the body of your paper, be sure that each paragraph deals with no more than one topic. When changing topics, be sure to change paragraphs. Link your paragraphs together with transitional phrases that let your readers have some idea of what is coming next. Once you have written a paragraph for each of the subtopics in your outline, you will have completed the body of the paper. You then will be ready to go back and write the introduction and conclusion.

Writing the Introduction and Conclusion An introduction to a research paper is no different than an introduction to someone you've never met before. You are giving the reader an idea of the topic and purpose of the paper—in a sense, explaining "who" your paper is. The introduction will contain the thesis statement and will give the reader an idea of the points you will cover in your paper. Save supporting details and factual evidence for the body of the paper.

The conclusion is your summary of the main points of your research paper. You are restating your argument for the benefit of your readers. Do not introduce any new information in the conclusion. The rule is to tell your readers what you are going to tell them (introduction), tell them (body), and tell them what you just told them (conclusion).

Writing with Creativity Writing a research paper is an artistic endeavor that reflects your abilities. You are creating something that did not previously exist. Your paper should be special and unique. It should also be interesting to the reader. If you see the process as a plodding act of boring drudgery, then your writing will be plodding and boring. However, if you are intrigued and excited by your topic, then that sense of enthusiasm will come through in your words.

There are techniques for making your writing more interesting. Try to vary your word choices by using a thesaurus. Use a mixture of sentence lengths so that your writing does not become monotonous. Write in an active voice that avoids the different forms of the verb *to be*. Use vivid, descriptive words and phrases to paint a verbal picture for your readers.

Writing the Rough Draft and Proofreading At this point, you should have before you a written research paper. You might think you are done, but you have one more step to take before you have reached the top of the mountain. You have written only the rough draft. You must now proofread your paper for errors in spelling, grammar, and style. Have someone read your rough draft and give you suggestions. See if you have chosen the best order for the presentation of your facts.

Writing the Final Draft Now you are ready to revise your research paper on the typewriter or word processor. Make all of your final changes. Make sure that the format meets the teacher's requirements. Some students like to use plastic covers or binders for their reports, but many teachers find them cumbersome. You have written a well-researched, creative, and original paper. Let it stand on its own merits.

WORLD HISTORY
THE HUMAN ODYSSEY

THE FIRST CIVILIZATIONS

OVERVIEW OF THE UNIT

The first unit of *World History* is divided into six chapters, spanning 175 pages.

The first chapter, which discusses the first humans, is the shortest chapter (17 pages), and Chapter 6, covering the Romans, is the longest (39 pages). The remaining four chapters, like most of the chapters in the text, average about 30 pages each and can be covered in approximately a week's time, assuming a 36-week course.

Using the
Illustration

Ask each student to write one sentence on a slip of paper describing the illustration on this page. They should describe in their own words what they believe this object is or what it represents. After student volunteers have shared their sentences with the class, tell them that what they see are lifesize plaster statues dating from 6500 B.C. The meaning of these statues is still undetermined. To initiate their thinking about the earliest humans, you may want to continue this discussion by asking what the students' thoughts are concerning early humans.

◄ *These life-size statues made of plaster and bitumen date from 6500 B.C. and were discovered in 1984 in Ain Ghazal, near Amman, Jordan. They are among the oldest statues ever found of the human figure. Archaeologists are studying the sculptures to try to understand their purpose and their meaning.*

	3500 B.C.	3000	2500	2000	1500
Middle East		3000–1800 B.C. Sumerian civilization			
India		3000–1500 B.C. Harappan civilization			1500 B.C. Invasion of Aryans
China					1766–1172 B.C. Shang dynasty
Egypt and the Mediterranean			2700–1085 B.C. Flowering of Egyptian civilization		

UNIT OPENER ACTIVITY

Ask each student to slowly turn through all the pages of this unit, from page 4 to page 191. As they are flipping through the pages, they have two options:

1. They should identify the one illustration from each chapter that they find the most interesting—the one that most quickly grabs their attention—and then pick one of those six illustrations to study more carefully and report to the class its meaning and significance; or,

2. pick one illustration from Chapter 1 and one illustration from Chapters 2 through 6, and then prepare an explanation of how the second illustration, when compared to the first, represents the development of civilization.

AND THE RISE OF EMPIRES
(PREHISTORY TO A.D. 500)

For hundreds of thousands of years, human beings lived in small communities, seeking to survive by hunting, fishing, and gathering food and supplies in an often hostile environment. Then, in the space of a few thousand years, there was an abrupt change of direction. Human beings in a few widely scattered areas of the globe began to master the art of growing food crops. As more food was produced, the population in these areas grew, and people began to live in larger communities. Governments were formed to protect the people and provide other needed services. Cities appeared and became centers for cultural and religious development. Historians call this process the beginnings of civilization. It occurred at about the same time in four different areas of the world —Western Asia, Egypt, India, and China. The ongoing movement toward the creation of larger states reached a high point in the first millennium B.C. The conquests of Alexander the Great, for example, created a large, if short-lived, empire that soon divided into four kingdoms. Later, the western portion of these kingdoms, as well as the Mediterranean world and much of western Europe, fell subject to the mighty empire of the Romans.

UNIT OUTLINE

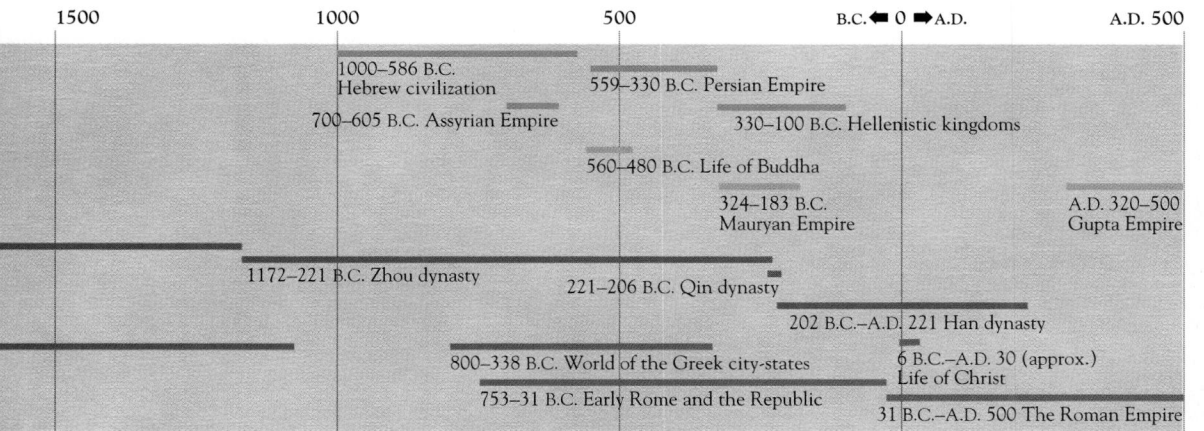

1500 1000 500 B.C. ◀ 0 ▶ A.D. A.D. 500

1000–586 B.C. Hebrew civilization

559–330 B.C. Persian Empire

700–605 B.C. Assyrian Empire

330–100 B.C. Hellenistic kingdoms

560–480 B.C. Life of Buddha

324–183 B.C. Mauryan Empire

A.D. 320–500 Gupta Empire

1172–221 B.C. Zhou dynasty

221–206 B.C. Qin dynasty

202 B.C.–A.D. 221 Han dynasty

800–338 B.C. World of the Greek city-states

6 B.C.–A.D. 30 (approx.) Life of Christ

753–31 B.C. Early Rome and the Republic

31 B.C.–A.D. 500 The Roman Empire

3

PROJECT IDEAS

After determining the amount of time you will be devoting to this unit, you may want to assign one of the following projects to all students, or allow individual students to choose from the list the one project that they will complete during the study of Unit 1.

1. *Creating an Artifact*—Since the ability to work with one's hands was a much more important and common skill in early civilizations than it is today, you may want each student to create a hand-made object. Included in the activity suggestions for each of the chapters are numerous suggestions for producing these objects. Choose one of these activities and enlist the help of industrial, technology, crafts and art teachers in your school.

2. *Using Primary Sources*— The Planner pages for each chapter list the primary sources for each chapter. As a research project, assign students to choose one of the primary sources and develope a class presentation on the source. Students should be prepared to share with the class portions of the source not included in the text. They should also develop and present orally to the class in a minute presentation their view as to why that source is representative of the beginnings of civilization.

STUDYING THE TIME LINE

Ask the students the following questions to help them compare the time periods of the different civilizations they will be studying in this chapter, as well as develop an appreciation for the wide span of years covered in the entire unit.

1. What is the earliest year represented in the timeline? *(3500 B.C.)* the latest? *(A.D. 500)*

2. What is the total amount of time covered in the unit? *(4000 years)*

3. What are the earliest civilizations? *(Sumerian and Harappan)*

4. During which years did Egyptian civilization overlap a Chinese dynasty? *(1766–1500 B.C.)*

1 PLANNING GUIDE

SECTION	KEY TOPICS	PRIMARY SOURCES	ASSESSMENT
1 Prehistory: How Do We Know Its History pages 5–7	◆ Methods used by scientists to uncover early human existence ◆ Differences between archaeologists and anthropologists ◆ Fossil dating		◆ Section Review, page 7 ◆ Section Quiz 1–1, TRB
2 The First Humans: The Old Stone Age pages 7–14	◆ The early stages of human development ◆ Important inventions of Paleolithic peoples ◆ Nomadic lifestyles and their consequences		◆ Section Review, page 14 ◆ Section Quiz 1–2, TRB
3 The Agricultural Revolution (10,000 to 4000 B.C.) pages 14–17	◆ The agricultural revolution ◆ Development of villages and towns ◆ The Neolithic and the Bronze Ages		◆ Section Review, page 17 ◆ Section Quiz 1–3, TRB
4 The Emergence of Civilization pages 17–19	◆ Six basic characteristics of civilization ◆ Early governments ◆ Record keeping in early civilizations		◆ Section Review, page 19 ◆ Section Quiz 1–4, TRB

THE FIRST CIVILIZATIONS:
THE PEOPLE OF WESTERN ASIA AND EGYPT (3500 TO 500)

REPRODUCIBLE ACTIVITIES

- Historical Maps
- Charts and Graphs
- Critical Thinking
- Cooperative Learning
- Vocabulary
- Guided Reading
- Reteaching
- Enrichment
- Performance Assessment
- Spanish Key Points and Chapter Summaries
- Spanish Vocabulary
- Spanish Guided Reading

MULTIMEDIA SUPPORT

TRANSPARENCIES
- ◆ *World History* Color Transparency Package
- ◆ Fine Art Color Transparency Package

VIDEO
- ◆ *World History* Video Library
- ◆ CNN. Annual Video Update

LASERDISC
- ◆ *Sights and Sounds of History*

AUDIO
- ◆ *Listening to Literature* audiotape (English and Spanish)
- ◆ *History of Music* CD

SOFTWARE
- ◆ WESTEST™
- ◆ Student Review

CD–ROM
- ◆ *The Journey of Civilization*
- ◆ *World History*

INTERNET
- ◆ Internet Activities

On Line with WORLD HISTORY

Access West's history web site at
http://history.swpco.com
You'll find activities and web sites related to specific topics and chapters in *World History: The Human Odyssey*. Also look for references to helpful web sites at appropriate places throughout this teacher edition.

LESSON PLANNING

You will find detailed daily lesson plans for both traditional class scheduling and **block scheduling** in your Teacher Resource Box.

Not Enough Time?

If you do not have the four or five days recommended to teach this chapter, you may want to focus on the following sections and activities:

- ◆ Have students skim the chapter to answer the "Questions to Guide Your Reading" on page 5. Discuss their answers, examine the maps on pages 9 and 15, then read the "Conclusion" on page 19. You might also wish to take a few moments to discuss the significance of the illustrations in the chapter.
- ◆ Do a more in-depth reading of pages 8–9 and 17–19. Conclude with a discussion of the beginnings of civilization.

THE FIRST HUMANS
(PREHISTORY TO 3500 B.C.)

SETTING THE SCENE

Ask students to imagine they are embarking on an archaeological expedition to Africa or to China. Have them work in small groups to prepare a list of employees, both scientists and support staff, and supplies they would need for the first six months. When students have finished with their lists and presentations, you might wish to show students the relationship between the work they have done in this activity and the themes of geography, economics and history, social life, culture, the role of individuals, the impact of science and technology, and the environment and history.

USING THE OPENING STORY

Mary Leakey uncovered the skull of Australopithecus boisei in 1959; the skull was more than 1.75 million years old. In 1965 the Leakeys uncovered a skull of Homo erectus, believed to be about one million years old. Discuss the significance of the Leakeys' work with students and then have students create a diary for both Mary and Louis Leakey for the week prior to and following their 1959 discovery. Remind students that living conditions were difficult, supplies had to be brought in from far away, and that the Leakeys had begun their work at Olduvai in 1931, twenty-eight years before discovering the skull.

Louis B. Leakey and his wife, Mary Nicol Leakey, spent most of their lives searching for clues about early human life. Much of their time was spent at Olduvai (OL-duh-vie) Gorge in East Africa, where they dug up many stone tools and a variety of fossils. Evidence of early human beings eluded them for many years. Then one morning, while her husband was back at camp recovering from the flu, Mary Leakey made a remarkable discovery. She jumped into her Land Rover and raced across the African plain back to camp, where she shouted to her startled husband, "I've got him! I've got him!" Despite his illness, Louis jumped into the car, and the Leakeys headed back to where Mary had made her discovery. At the site, they looked at the bones Mary had unearthed. Louis later described the scene: "I turned to look at Mary and we almost cried for sheer joy, each seized by the terrific emotion that comes early in life. After all our hoping and hardship and sacrifice, at last we had reached our goal—we had discovered the world's earliest known human."

Perhaps no people are better known for their work in putting together some of the evidence for early human existence than Louis and Mary Leakey and their son Richard. Like many other scientists, they struggled to find the remains of early humans and to develop a picture of human development. Thanks to their efforts, and to the efforts of many other scientists, we know that for hundreds of thousands of years, early humans struggled to survive by hunting, fishing, and gathering. Eventually, hunting and gathering gave way to regular farming, a dramatic step that in turn led to the emergence of both larger and more complex human communities. This chapter presents the story of that process.

▲ *This reconstructed skull, with its lower jaw intact, is considered to be one of the oldest human skulls ever discovered.*

ADDITIONAL RESOURCES

The resources listed below can be used to enrich the lessons in this chapter.

BOOKS FOR STUDENTS
The Search for Early Man, Charles F. Howell, Harper & Row (Horizon Caravelle)
Cro-Magnum Man, Tom Prideaux, Time-Life (Emergence of Men)

VIDEOS/FILMS
Mysteries of Mankind (National Geographic), Social Studies School Service (800) 421-4246
Lascaux: Prehistoric Cave Art, Social Studies School Service (800) 421-4246

THE BEGINNINGS OF CIVILIZATION

250,000 B.C.	THE FIRST HUMANS	3500 B.C.
250,000 B.C.		1000 B.C.

QUESTIONS TO GUIDE YOUR READING

1. What methods do scientists use to uncover the story of early human existence?

2. What was the nature of human life during the Old Stone Age?

3. What important and dramatic developments took place during the New Stone Age?

4. What is a civilization, and what are the characteristics of civilizations?

PREHISTORY: HOW DO WE KNOW ITS STORY?

Historians rely mostly on documents, or written records, to create their pictures of the past. However, such written records do not exist for the prehistory of humankind. The story of early humans depends upon archaeological (AR-kee-uh-LODG-i-kul) and, more recently, biological information, which archaeologists and anthropologists use to create theories about our early past. What are archaeologists (AR-kee-ALL-uh-justs) and anthropologists, and what kinds of information do they provide?

Archaeology is the study of past societies through an analysis of what people have left behind them. Archaeologists dig up and analyze artifacts—the tools, pottery, paintings, weapons, buildings, and household items—of early people. **Anthropologists** are experts who use these artifacts and the remains of humans—human fossils—to determine how people lived their lives.

Archaeologists and anthropologists have developed scientific methods to carry out their work. Excavations of sites around the globe have uncovered fossil remains of early humans, ancient cities, burial grounds, and other remnants of past peoples. The examination and

5

Answers to QUESTIONS TO GUIDE YOUR READING

1. archaeological, biological (page 5)
2. hunter-gatherers, nomadic, sexual equality (pages 10–11)
3. shift to systematic agriculture; organization of communities; metal tools (pages 14–17)

4. complex culture in which many humans share common elements; rise of cities, growth of governments, role of religion, new social structure, use of writing, artistic activity (pages 17–19)

FOCUS ON THEMES

Listed below are brief summaries of how the content in this chapter supports the text's key themes.

Economics and History The hunting and gathering that provided sustenance for Paleolithic peoples gave way to systematic agriculture in the Neolithic Age. This provided the foundation for surplus food, specialized labor, and new forms of organized living.

Social Life The nomadic way of life of Paleolithic peoples evolved into different forms of social organization with the advent of systematic agriculture. Male and female roles also changed from relationships of rough equality to generally male domination.

The Importance of Cultural Developments Already in prehistory, early humans developed cave paintings as a form of cultural expression and found ways to pass on their knowledge from one generation to another.

The Impact of Science and Technology The development of new technologies—tools and fire—enabled Paleolithic peoples to survive in a hostile environment. The development of agricultural technologies and metals gave humans greater control over their environment.

The Environment and History The hunters and gatherers of the Paleolithic Age developed strategies to survive, especially during the difficult conditions of the Ice Ages. With the systematic agriculture of the Neolithic Age came the ability of human beings to acquire greater control over their environment.

5

FOCUS

OBJECTIVES

After completing this section, students should be able to

1. explain methods used by scientists to uncover early human existence
2. discuss the difference between archaeologists and anthropologists
3. describe various means of dating fossil remains

FOCUS ACTIVITY

Allow five to ten minutes for students to make a list of items archaeologists might find while digging through remains at their school three thousand years hence; then ask them to think as anthropologists to reconstruct the lives of students or city residents based on those remains.

LEARNING FROM VISUALS

Students may not know that the Olduvai Gorge is located on the Serengeti Plains in northern Tanzania. The area was first worked by an entomologist, Wilhelm Kattwinkel in 1911, and following World War I by paleontologist Hans Reck. Reck found the remains of Pleistocene mammals but no human tools. It was the Leakeys who discovered stone tools in the gorge. Ask students to locate Tanzania and the Serengeti Plains on one of the maps in the text and discuss why scientists were attracted to this area.

Answers to the caption questions: Answers will vary.

▲ *Louis and Mary Leakey spent most of their lives searching for early hominids and artifacts at Olduvai Gorge in East Africa. Why are their discoveries important to us today?*

▲ *This is an archaeological excavation site at the Arago cave in France. The person in the center of the photograph is using an aerial grid system to map the location of a newly found artifact. Why is it necessary to carefully document the precise location of archaeological discoveries?*

critical analysis of these remains give archaeologists a better understanding of ancient societies. Artifacts— pottery, tools, and weapons—reveal much about the social and military structures of a society. The analysis of bones, skins, and plant seeds enables scientists to piece together the diet and activities of early people.

Heinrich Schliemann (HINE-rik SHLEE-mon), who lived in the nineteenth century, was an early archaeologist from Germany. Schliemann had always been fascinated by an account by Homer, an ancient Greek poet, of the Greek siege of Troy, in Asia Minor. In Schliemann's time, most people believed that Homer had made up his account. From his early youth, however, Schliemann had believed Homer's story. He became determined to prove it was true. His family was poor, and he could not afford either to get an education or to go off to foreign lands and dig for buried cities. Schliemann persisted, however. He became a wealthy businessman, learned Greek, and went to Asia Minor. After years of digging, he found his beloved Troy and proved that Homer's account was based on actual events. Since Schliemann's time, archaeologists have developed even more scientific techniques to aid their work.

One of the most important and difficult jobs of both archaeologists and anthropologists is dating their finds. Determining the age of human fossils makes it possible to understand when and where the first humans emerged. Likewise, the dating of artifacts left by humans enables these scientists to speculate on the growth of early societies.

How, then, do archaeologists and anthropologists determine the ages of the artifacts and fossils they unearth? One valuable method is **radiocarbon dating.** All living things absorb a small amount of radioactive (RADE-ee-oh-AK-tiv) carbon (C-14) from the atmosphere. After death, there is a gradual loss of C-14. Radiocarbon dating is a method of analysis that calculates the ages of objects by measuring the amount of C-14 left in an object.

MORE ABOUT . . . *Fossil Hunting*

One of the greatest fossil hunters in the world is an African archaeological excavator named Kamoya Kimeu. Working as an assistant to Dr. Louis Leakey, Dr. Mary Leakey, and their son Richard Leakey, he is responsible for finding some of the most important hominid fossils in the later part of the twentieth century. Kimeu jokes that the fossils "speak" to him, accounting for his amazing ability for unearthing the remains of human ancestors. Kemoya Kimeu is currently curator of prehistoric sites for the National Museums of Kenya.

▲ *Accurately dating artifacts and fossils is an important but difficult task. The Berkeley Geochronology Laboratory is set up to help determine an object's age and authenticity by using various scientific methods. What courses in school would be useful in preparing you to work in this laboratory environment?*

Radiocarbon dating, however, is only accurate for dating objects that are no more than about 50,000 years old. Another method—**thermoluminescence dating**—enables scientists to make relatively precise measurements back to 200,000 years. This is a method of analysis that dates an object by measuring the light given off by electrons trapped in the soil surrounding fossils and artifacts.

New microscopic and biological analyses of organic remains—such as blood, hairs, and plant tissues left on rocks, tools, and weapons—have shown that blood molecules may survive millions of years. This recent scientific discovery is especially useful in telling us more about humans, their use of tools, and the animals they killed. Ancient deoxyribonucleic acid (DNA), or genetic material, is providing new information on human evolution. The analysis of plant remains on stone tools yields evidence on the history of farming. All of these new techniques give us insight into the lives of early peoples.

 SECTION REVIEW

1. **Define:**
   (*a*) archaeology,   (*b*) anthropologists,
   (*c*) radiocarbon dating,   (*d*) thermoluminescence dating

2. **Identify:**
   (*a*) Heinrich Schliemann

3. **Recall:**
   (*a*) Explain the difference between an archaeologist and an anthropologist.
   (*b*) How do scientists know the ages of artifacts and human fossils?

4. **Think Critically:** Is the study of prehistory important? Why or why not? Explain your answer.

2

THE FIRST HUMANS: THE OLD STONE AGE

Although modern science has given us more precise methods for examining the prehistory of humankind than we have ever had before, much of our understanding of early humans still depends upon considerable guesswork. Given the rate of new discoveries, the following account of the current theory of early human life might well be changed in a few years. As Louis Leakey reminded us years ago, "Theories on prehistory and early man constantly change as new evidence comes to light."

MORE ABOUT . . . *Mary Leakey*

In 1978 Mary Leakey discovered one of anthropology's most important finds in northern Tanzania. She unearthed a long trail of human-like footprints fossilized in ash from an ancient volcanic eruption. The footprints are evidence of upright walking in remote ancestors of humans. There were two distinct trails of prints, one larger than the other. Within the larger prints Dr. Leakey discovered a smaller, fainter set of prints. It is easy to imagine a family walking across the muddy plain over three-and-a-half million years ago, with the child stepping in the footsteps of its father.

ACROSS THE CURRICULUM

Science. For homework, assign students the task of finding two stones and within 30 minutes grinding a sharp edge on one. Have students bring their finished results and a paragraph summarizing their efforts to class. Display the resulting stone edges with their grinding stones, and have the class decide on which kind of rock makes the best grinder and which the best blade. Lead the class in a discussion of the difficulty in making rudimentary tools, reminding them that the survival of these early people depended upon their abilities to succeed in this task.

Answers to Critical Thinking Questions

1. Tools enabled people to hunt and kill large animals, cultivate the soil, build simple dwellings, prepare food, sew clothing, and make other tools. Before tools were made, humans had to rely on what they could do by hand, with their own strength.
2. Answers will vary.

COMPARING TIME PERIODS

Review with students how modern tools and machinery are made. How much of this work is done by machines, and how much is done by human labor? Remind students of the difference this makes in the definition of labor and the ways in which we spend our time at work and at leisure.

THE ROLE OF SCIENCE AND TECHNOLOGY

Tools

In the broadest sense, the word *technology* refers to the ability of human beings to make things that sustain them and give them some control over their environment. In that sense, technology has played a role in human development from very early times. The technology available at the beginning of human history was quite simple; it consisted primarily of the ability to make tools. By creating tools, humans coped more easily with their environment.

The first tools were made by grinding two stones together to make a sharp edge on one of them. Flint—a very hard stone—was used by early people to make tools. Hand axes of different kinds—made by chipping away flakes to make a pointed tool with one or more cutting edges—were the most common. Eventually axes were set into wooden handles, making them easier to use. By attaching wooden poles to spear points and hardening the tips in fire, humans created spears that gave them the ability to hunt and kill large animals.

Over a period of time, tool technology evolved. Especially noticeable was the movement toward ever smaller stone points and blades. Microliths were tiny stone blades that could be mounted in wooden or bone handles. Damaged blades could then be replaced, prolonging the life of the tool. Bones and antlers were also used for making a great variety of tools. Bones could be used to make harpoons for catching fish. Near the end of the Paleolithic period, there is evidence of even more

▲ *Stone tools, such as spear points, awls, and scrapers from bone and stone, made it easier for early humans to cope with their environment. How might the tools pictured here have been used to improve the lifestyle of these people?*

refined tools, especially bone needles. Needles formed from animal bones could be used for making nets and baskets and even sewing hides together for clothing.

The first tools served a variety of purposes. Humans used stone weapons to kill animals and butcher their meat. Other sharp-edged tools were used for cutting up plants, digging up roots from the soil, and cutting branches for building simple shelters. Scraping tools were used to clean animal hides for clothing and shelter.

1. How did the ability to make simple tools change human life?
2. Describe how your favorite modern tools can give you more control over your environment.

On Line with WORLD HISTORY *Internet Activity*

You may want to have your students visit the following URL, where they will find information and additional web site resources to enhance their study of this chapter.

Flints and Stones: Real Life in Prehistory

http://www.ncl.ac.uk/~nantiq/menu.htm

Explore the world of hunter gatherers.

Due to the ever-changing nature of the World Wide Web, see the West History web site, **http://history.swpco.com** for regular updates of the URLs in this text.

The Earliest Humans

The earliest humanlike creatures—known as **hominids**—lived in Africa as long as three to four million years ago. Called **australopithecines,** or "southern apes" by their discoverer, Donald Johanson, they flourished in eastern and southern Africa. They were the first hominids to make simple stone tools (see "The Role of Science and Technology: Tools"). The oldest known stone tool—a knife blade that is probably 2.6 million years old—was found in Africa.

A second stage in early human development occurred with the appearance of **Homo erectus** ("upright human being"), a species that emerged around 1.5 million years ago. *Homo erectus* made use of larger and more varied tools. These hominids were the first to leave Africa and move into both Europe and Asia. They were able to do so in part because they learned to use fire to keep warm in colder areas.

Around 250,000 years ago, a third—and crucial—stage in human development began with the emergence of a new species, **Homo sapiens** ("wise human being"). By 100,000 B.C., *Homo sapiens* had developed into two groups. One type was the **Neanderthals** (nee-AN-der-thals), who were first found in the Neander Valley in Germany. Their remains have been dated between 100,000 and 30,000 B.C. and have been found in Europe and the Middle East. Neanderthals relied on a variety of stone tools and seem to be the first early people to bury their dead. Some scientists maintain that burial of the dead indicates a belief in an afterlife. Neanderthals in Europe made clothes from the skins of animals that they had killed for food.

The first anatomically modern humans (people who looked like us), known as **Homo sapiens sapiens** ("wise, wise human being"), appeared in Africa between 150,000 and 200,000 years ago. Recent evidence indicates that they began to spread outside Africa around 100,000 years ago. The map below shows probable time periods for different movements. By 30,000 B.C., they had replaced the Neanderthals,

Map 1.1   The Spread of *Homo Sapiens Sapiens*

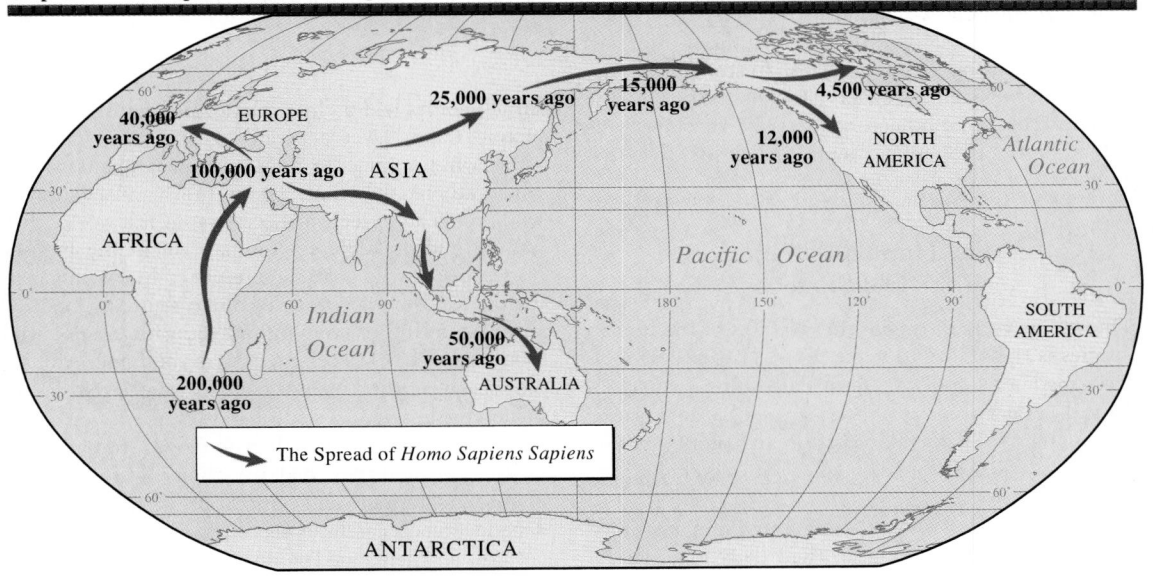

STUDYING MAPS

The following questions will help you guide students through their study of Map 1.1.

1. Did *Homo sapiens sapiens* migrate from northern Africa to southern Africa, or vice versa? *(vice versa)*

2. How long ago did people begin moving toward the area that is now the United States? *(12,000 years ago)*

3. Ask students to show on the map where australopithocenes, *Homo erectus,* Neanderthals, and *Homo sapiens sapiens* lived and flourished. Ask students to explain why no humans are shown living in South America or throughout the United States. *(Students should recognize that the map shows the early migration of Homo sapiens sapiens, and that in time, humans moved throughout North and South America.)*

The First Humans	
Group	**Approximate Dates**
Australopithecines	Flourished approximately 2 million to 4 million years ago
Homo erectus	Flourished approximately 100,000 to 1.5 million years ago
Homo sapiens Neanderthals	Flourished approximately 100,000 to 30,000 B.C.
Homo sapiens sapiens	Began approximately 200,000 B.C.

who had largely died out, possibly as a result of conflict with *Homo sapiens sapiens*.

The movement of the first modern humans was rarely deliberate. Groups of people, probably in search of food, moved beyond their old hunting grounds at a rate of only two to three miles per generation. This was enough, however, to populate the world over tens of thousands of years. By 10,000 B.C., members of the *Homo sapiens sapiens* subspecies of the species *Homo sapiens* could be found throughout the world. All humans today, be they Europeans, Australian Aborigines (ab-uh-RIJ-uh-neez), or Africans, belong to the same subspecies of human being. (The accompanying table shows the approximate dates for the first humans.)

The Hunter-Gatherers of the Old Stone Age

One of the basic distinguishing features of the human species is the ability to make tools. The earliest tools were made of stone. The term **Paleolithic** (pay-lee-o-LI-thik) **Age** (which is Greek for "Old Stone") is used to designate the early period of human history (approximately 2,500,000 to 10,000 B.C.) in which humans used simple stone tools.

For hundreds of thousands of years, humans relied on hunting and gathering for their daily food. Paleo-

▲ *Nomadic Paleolithic people followed the migration of animals in order to provide food and other necessities for their families. Can you imagine hunting mammoths with the primitive tools used by these early humans?*

lithic peoples had a close relationship with the world around them. Over a period of time, they came to know what animals to hunt and what plants to eat. They gathered wild nuts, berries, fruits, and a variety of wild grains and green plants. Around the world, they hunted and ate different animals, including buffalo, horses, bison, wild goats, and reindeer. In coastal areas, various kinds of fish provided a rich source of food.

The hunting of animals and the gathering of wild food no doubt led to certain patterns of living. Archaeologists and anthropologists have speculated that Paleolithic people lived in small bands of twenty or thirty. They were **nomadic** (people who moved from place to place), because they had no choice but to follow animal migrations and vegetation cycles. Hunting depended upon careful observation of animal behavior patterns and demanded group effort for any real chance

MORE ABOUT . . . *Australopithecines*

Donald Johanson named the 3.5 million year old female australopithecine skeleton he found in Ethiopia, Lucy, after a Beatles' song, *Lucy in the Sky with Diamonds,* which was playing on the camp tape player the day of the discovery. The morning of his famous discovery Johanson woke up and recorded in his diary that he was feeling lucky. The hominid skeleton he discovered was the most complete ever found and is evidence of an upright walking human ancestor. The following year Johanson's team found the skeletal remains of an entire band of australopithecines.

of success. Over the years, tools became more refined and more useful. The invention of the spear, and later the bow and arrow, made hunting much easier. Harpoons and fishhooks made of bone increased the catch of fish.

It is probable that both men and women were responsible for finding food—the chief work of Paleolithic peoples. Because women bore and raised the children, they were likely to have stayed close to their camps. However, they played an important role in acquiring food. They gathered berries, nuts, and grains. Men did most of the hunting of large animals, which might take place far from camp. Because both men and women played important roles in providing for the group's survival, some scientists have argued that a rough equality existed between men and women. It is likely that both men and women made decisions that affected the activities of the Paleolithic band. We know that the first small statues of what appear to be religious subjects portray women with exaggerated motherly features.

Groups of Paleolithic people, especially those who lived in cold climates, found shelter in caves. Over a period of time, they created new types of shelter as well. Perhaps most common was a simple structure of wood poles or sticks covered with animal hides. Where wood was scarce, they might use the bones of mammoths to build frames that were then covered by animal hides. The systematic use of fire made it possible to provide a source of both light and heat within both the caves and the handmade structures in which they lived (see "The Role of Science and Technology: Fire").

▶ *Early humans constructed igloo-type dwellings such as you see here from bones, sticks, mud, and animal hides taken from large mammoths.*

The making of tools and the use of fire—two important technological innovations of Paleolithic peoples—remind us how crucial the ability to adapt was to human survival. The Ice Ages especially posed a serious threat to human life. The most recent Ice Age began about 100,000 B.C. and reached its coldest period between 20,000 and 10,000 B.C. Sheets of thick ice covered large parts of Europe, Asia, and North America.

Paleolithic peoples used their technological innovations—such as the making of tools and the use of fire—to change their physical environment. By working together, they found a way to survive. Furthermore, by passing on their common practices, skills, and material products to their children, later generations, too, could survive in a harsh world. Obviously, Paleolithic peoples played a crucial role in human history.

Paleolithic peoples did more than just survive, however. The cave paintings of large animals found at Lascaux (la-SKOE) in southwestern France and Altamira (AL-tuh-MIR-uh) in northern Spain bear witness to the cultural activity of Paleolithic peoples. A cave discovered in southern France in 1994 contained more than three hundred paintings of lions, oxen, owls, panthers, and other animals. Most of these are animals that Paleolithic people did not hunt, which indicates that they were painted for religious or decorative purposes (see "Our Artistic Heritage: The Cave Paintings of Our Paleolithic Ancestors").

 Multimedia Support

 LASERDISC
Venus of Willendorf
(10,000 B.C.)

CRITICAL THINKING

During Paleolithic times equality in relationships between women and men may have been more common than in modern times. Guide students in a discussion of the factors that have led some scientists to believe this, as well as those factors that might work against this theory. What happened in the lives and cultures of these people that gave the male the dominant role in society? *(As men had to move farther away from home camps to hunt, women tended to stay at home and tend to the chores that needed attention there, particularly caring for the children, working in the garden, and sewing clothes.)*

LEARNING FROM VISUALS

Guide students in a discussion of the materials necessary to construct a shelter like the one in the illustration. Small bones, twigs, or sinews might have been used to tie larger bones or tree limbs together to secure the parts. Have students estimate the amount of time necessary to construct this igloo-type dwelling.

MORE ABOUT . . . *Stone Tools*

Nicholas Toth and Kathy Schick conducted an experiment that showed that early hunters could use stone tools effectively for survival. They first demonstrated how to make knives and axes by flaking off chips of stone. Using only stone tools they were able to obtain several hundred pounds of meat by butchering an elephant that had died of natural causes. After preparing elephant steaks, they demonstrated how early humans could obtain protein rich marrow from the bones by using a primitive stone hammer and anvil.

COMPARING TIME PERIODS

Homo erectus may have started fire by rubbing two sticks together until they ignited a spark. Ask students how different is this from modern techniques for starting a fire while camping or when left without modern conveniences? (*Creating sparks through friction still works to start a fire, and there are metal camping tools that are designed to start a fire with a spark.*)

LEARNING FROM VISUALS

Guide students in a discussion of modern uses of fire, including controlled burns in national forests.

Answer to the caption question: Answers will vary but should include that fire was used for warmth as they migrated into colder climates; used for protection to deter wild animals; and, used to prepare and preserve food.

Answers to Critical Thinking Questions

1. As people moved into colder regions, they needed a means to keep warm or they would have died. Fire also protected them from wild animals and enabled people to cook their food.
2. There are no written records or physical remains to use as clues so scholars can only make educated guesses based on their studies of more contemporary, traditional peoples.

THE ROLE OF SCIENCE AND TECHNOLOGY

Fire

As early hominids moved from the tropics into colder regions, they needed to adjust to new, often harsh conditions. Perhaps most important to their ability to adapt was the use of fire.

Early hominids experienced natural fires caused by lightning and learned the benefits of them. It was *homo erectus*, however, who first learned to make fires deliberately. Archaeologists have discovered the piled remains of ashes in caves that prove that Paleolithic people used fire systematically as long ago as 500,000 years. At a *homo erectus* site at Choukoutien, in northern China, archaeologists have discovered hearths, ashes, charcoal, and charred bones. All of these were about 400,000 years old. Because the Choukoutien cave faced northeast, it would have been a dark place without the use of the fire. Fire gave warmth and undoubtedly fostered a sense of community for the groups of people gathered around it. Fire also protected early humans by enabling them to scare away wild animals. Fire might also have enabled early humans to flush animals out of wooded areas or caves and then kill them. In addition, food could be cooked with fire, making it better tasting,

▲ *Ancient peoples were the first to use the friction method for starting fires. Fire became very important to their survival. Why was fire so important to early hominids?*

longer lasting, and easier to chew and digest (in the case of some plants, such as wild grains).

Scholars believe that the discovery of a means for starting fires occurred independently throughout the world. Archaeologists lack concrete evidence on how early peoples started fires. They have been able to examine the methods used by traditional peoples, however, even into the twentieth century. On that basis, archaeologists assume that the earliest methods for starting fires were probably based on friction, such as rubbing two pieces of wood together. Dry grass and leaves could be added as the wood began to smoke. Eventually, Paleolithic peoples devised sturdy, drill-like wooden devices to start fires. Other early humans discovered that a certain stone (iron pyrites), when struck against a hard rock, gave off a spark that could be used to ignite dry grass or leaves.

1. Why was learning to build fires crucial to human survival?

2. Why is it so difficult for archaeologists to determine how early peoples started fires?

On Line with WORLD HISTORY Internet Activity

You may want to have your students visit the following URL, where they will find information and additional web site resources to enhance their study of this chapter.

Virtual Reality Tour of Caves at Lascaux
http://www.earthchannel.com/ gallery/ben/ben01.htm

A tour with description of all the areas. Excellent visuals.

Due to the ever-changing nature of the World Wide Web, see the West History web site, **http://history.swpco.com** for regular updates of the URLs in this text.

OUR ARTISTIC HERITAGE

The Cave Paintings of Our Paleolithic Ancestors

This prehistoric wall painting of a herd of animals was accidently discovered in 1940 by some boys in Lascaux, France. The boys were rescuing their dog who had fallen into a cave. Why do you think these paintings are so well preserved after thousands of years?

The importance of art to human life is evident in one basic fact: art existed even in prehistory, among the hunters and gatherers of the Paleolithic Age. In 1879, the twelve-year-old daughter of a Spanish landowner made a remarkable discovery on her farm in northern Spain. In a cave at Altamira, Paleolithic artists had painted an entire herd of animals—horses, boars, bison, and deer—on the ceiling of the cave. In 1940, four boys in Lascaux in southwest France found a similar group of paintings in a cave. They were trying to rescue their dog, who had fallen through a small hole into the cave. Recent discoveries in other areas of the world have added yet more examples of the artistic achievements of early human beings. According to archaeologists, these cave paintings were done between 25,000 and 12,000 B.C.

All of the caves were underground and in complete darkness, but Paleolithic artists used stone lamps filled with animal fat to light their surroundings. By crushing mineral ores and combining them with animal fat, they could paint in red, yellow, and black. Apparently, they used their fingertips, crushed twigs, and even brushes made with animal hairs to apply these paints to the walls. They also used hollow reeds to blow thin lines of paint on the walls.

Many of these cave paintings show animals in remarkably realistic forms. There are few humans in these paintings. When they are shown, they are not realistic but rather are crude, sticklike figures. The precise rendering of the animal forms has led many historians to believe that they were painted as part of a magical or religious ritual intended to ensure success in hunting. Some believe, however, that the paintings may have been made for their own sake. They beautified the caves and must have been pleasing to the eyes of early humans.

1. Explain two common theories about the purpose of cave paintings.

2. What are some possible reasons that humans are not depicted with as much precision as the animals in cave paintings?

MORE ABOUT . . . *The Domestication of Animals*

One of the unfortunate side effects of civilization and the domestication of animals has been an increase in the number of diseases that afflict humans. Many diseases are the result of humans living in close proximity to animals. Once humans began to domesticate animals, they began to have close daily interaction with animals they had previously only hunted. Influenza is known to originate from pigs and ducks, measles is closely related to canine distemper, and cattle are responsible for anthrax, smallpox and tuberculosis. There are several hundred diseases that now afflict humans which come from other species.

ASSESS

Answers to
SECTION REVIEW

2. (a) earliest humanlike creatures
(b) earliest humanlike creatures living in East and South Africa; first to use simple stone tools
(c) upright human being
(d) wise human being
(e) a type of *Homo sapiens* found in Neander Valley
(f) wise, wise human being
(g) term used to designate that period in human history when the earliest stone tools were made
(h) describes Paleolithic people who moved from place to place
3. Answers will vary; might include that they traveled today, hunted and fished for food, built new shelters of wood poles or sticks covered with hides, created tools from stone
4. Answers will vary.

CLOSE

Remind students of the differences among early humans and the major changes in lifestyles brought about by the abilities of Paleolithic peoples to make tools and use fire to improve their lives. Ask students to name one discovery that has taken place in their lives that has or will change their future.

 SECTION REVIEW

1. Locate:
(a) Africa
2. Define:
(a) hominids,   (b) australopithecines,
(c) *Homo erectus*,   (d) *Homo sapiens*,
(e) Neanderthals,   (f) *Homo sapiens sapiens*,
(g) Paleolithic Age,   (h) nomadic
3. Recall:
(a) What are the three stages of early human development?
(b) What were the two most important technological inventions of the Paleolithic peoples?
4. Think Critically: Imagine that you are a Paleolithic man or woman. What might you have done today?

---

③

THE AGRICULTURAL REVOLUTION (10,000 TO 4000 B.C.)

The end of the last Ice Age, around 10,000 B.C., was followed by what is called the **Neolithic** (nee-o-LIthik) **Revolution;** that is, the revolution that occurred in the **Neolithic Age,** the term used to designate the period of human history from 10,000 to 4000 B.C. (The word Neolithic is Greek for "New Stone.") The name New Stone Age is misleading, however.

The real change in the Neolithic Revolution was the shift from the hunting of animals and the gathering of food to the keeping of animals and the growing of food on a regular basis (what we would call *systematic agriculture*). The planting of grains and vegetables provided a regular supply of food. The taming of animals added a steady source of meat, milk, and fibers. Larger animals could be used as beasts of burden. The growing of crops and the taming of food-producing animals created what historians call an agricultural revo-

lution. Some believe it is the single most important development in human history. Revolutionary change is change that is dramatic and requires great effort. Indeed, the ability to acquire food on a regular basis gave humans greater control over their environment. It also enabled them to give up their nomadic ways of life and begin to live in settled communities.

This shift to food producing from hunting and gathering was not as sudden as was once believed. During the **Mesolithic Age** ("Middle Stone Age," about 10,000 to 7000 B.C.) there was a gradual shift from the old food-gathering and hunting economy to a food-producing one. During this period there was also a gradual taming of animals. Likewise, the movement toward the use of plants and their seeds to create a regular food supply was also not sudden. Archaeological evidence seems to suggest that the Paleolithic hunters and gatherers had already grown some crops to add to their usual sources of food. Moreover, throughout the Neolithic period, hunting and gathering remained a way of life for many people around the world. Even today some people in the world, such as the Inuit (IN-you-wet) peoples of Alaska and northern Canada, still live largely by hunting.

Between 8000 and 5000 B.C., systematic agriculture developed in different areas of the world. People in the Middle East began growing wheat and barley and taming pigs, cows, goats, and sheep by 8000 B.C. From the Middle East, farming spread into the southeastern region of Europe. By 4000 B.C., farming was well established in central Europe and the coastal regions of the Mediterranean (MED-uh-tuh-RAY-nee-un).

The cultivation of wheat and barley also spread from western Asia into the Nile valley of Egypt by 6000 B.C These crops soon spread up the Nile to other areas of Africa, especially the Sudan (Soo-DAN) and Ethiopia (EETH-ee-OH-pee-uh). In the woodlands and tropical forests of central Africa, a separate farming system emerged with the growing of tubers (root crops), such as yams, and tree crops, such as bananas. The farming of wheat and barley also moved eastward into the highlands of northwestern and central India between 7000 and 5000 B.C.

By 5000 B.C., rice was being grown in Southeast Asia, from where it spread into southern China. In northern China, the farming of millet and the taming

---

COOPERATIVE LEARNING ACTIVITY

Ask students to work together in small groups. They should work together in their groups to list the foods they and their families consume each week. They should also identify the sources for the foodstuffs (*sources* does not mean supermarkets, but rather the original sources). When groups have finished, ask them to prepare a similar list of foods they would eat if they had to forage or depend upon the local supply of wild animals for their weekly diets. Relate this to the agricultural revolution and the gradual development of villages and towns.

Map 1.2   The Development of Agriculture

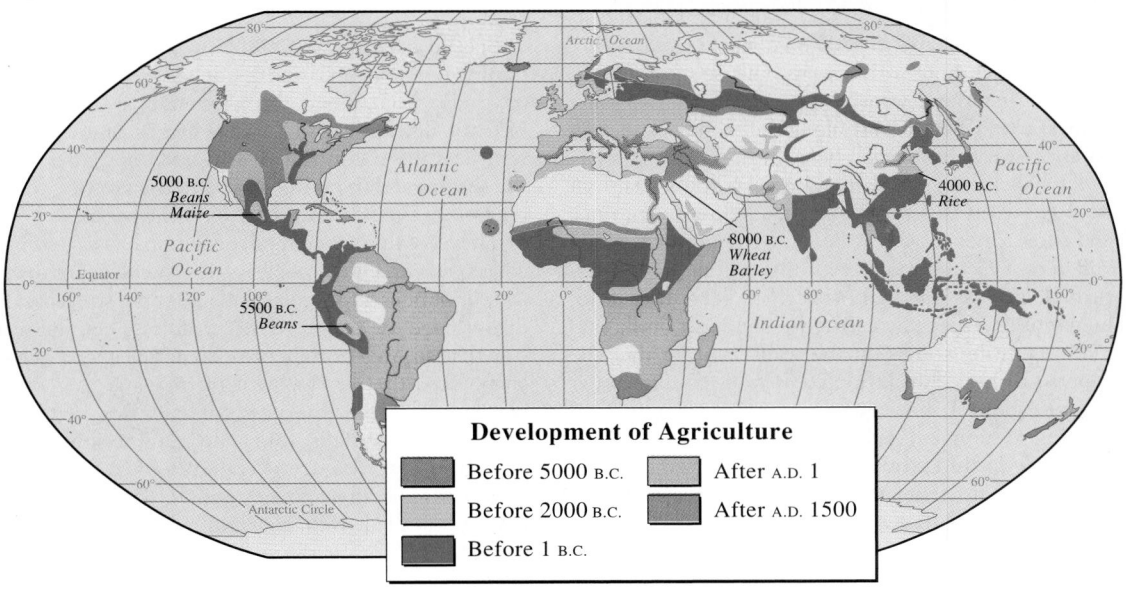

Development of Agriculture

Before 5000 B.C.	After A.D. 1
Before 2000 B.C.	After A.D. 1500
Before 1 B.C.	

of pigs and dogs seem to have been well established by 6000 B.C. In the Western Hemisphere, Mesoamericans (MEZ-oh-uh-MER-i-kuns) (inhabitants of present-day Mexico and Central America) grew beans, squash, and maize (corn) and tamed dogs and fowl between 7000 and 5000 B.C.

The growing of crops on a regular basis made possible the support of larger populations and gave rise to more permanent settlements. Historians refer to these settlements as **Neolithic farming villages.** Neolithic villages appeared in Europe, India, Egypt, China, and Mesoamerica. The oldest and biggest ones, however, were located in the Middle East. Jericho (JER-i-koh), in Palestine near the Dead Sea, was in existence by 8000 B.C. It covered several acres by 7000 B.C. and had a wall several feet thick that enclosed houses made of sun-dried bricks.

Çatal Hüyük (CHAH-tul HOO-YOOK), located in modern-day Turkey, was an even larger community. Its

▼ *This is an artist's drawing of the Neolithic farming town of Çatal Hüyük (located in modern-day Turkey). The houses were constructed of mud bricks and built very close together. How do you think life in this town would be different from life in modern-day towns and cities?*

STUDYING MAPS

The following questions will help you guide students through their study of Map 1.2.

1. Did agriculture develop in the United States before or after A.D. 1? (*after*)
2. Where did agriculture first develop? (*Middle East*)

3. What are the principal foodstuffs of North America, Asia, and Africa. What factors account for the differences? (North America: *beans, corn, squash;* Asia: *rice;* Africa: *barley, wheat, tubers such as yams, and bananas. Climate, native vegetation, and geography account for the major differences.*)

COMPARING
TIME PERIODS

Guide students in a discussion of the differences in the daily lives of those who lived in or near Lascaux, France; Çatal Hüyük, Turkey; and their own towns. Ask students to compare and contrast daily activities and lifestyles.

CRITICAL THINKING

What features do Europe, India, Egypt, China, and Mesoamerica have in common that permitted the development of Neolithic farming villages? Why would these villages have flourished in the Middle East?

LEARNING FROM VISUALS

Answer to the caption question: Answers will vary but may include gathering berries, sharpening tools, hauling water, etc.

REINFORCING VOCABULARY

Some students may not understand the difference between *artisans* and *artists.* Artisans are craftspeople who make functional items, often that are quite beautiful, but utilitarian. Artists, such as painters or sculptors, do not consider useful function foremost in their creations.

CLASS DISCUSSION

The early foodstuffs produced in each of the agricultural regions—beans and maize in the Americas, rice in China, wheat and barley in the Middle East—are still produced and form an important part of the diet in these areas. Ask students why they think primary foodstuffs have not changed since early times.

16

walls enclosed thirty-two acres, and its population probably reached six thousand inhabitants during its high point from 6700 to 5700 B.C. People lived in simple mud brick houses that were built so close to one another that there were few streets. To get to their homes, people had to walk along the rooftops and then enter their homes through holes in the roofs.

Archaeologists have found twelve products that were grown in this community, including fruits, nuts, and three kinds of wheat. People grew their own food and kept it in storerooms within their homes. Domesticated animals (animals that had been tamed for human use), especially cattle, yielded meat, milk, and hides. Hunting scenes on the walls indicate that the people of Çatal Hüyük hunted as well. Unlike earlier hunter-gatherers, however, they no longer relied on hunting to survive. Food surpluses made it possible for people to do things other than farming. Some people became artisans. They made weapons and jewelry that were traded with neighboring peoples, thus exposing

▼ *This representation of a Neolithic village typifies life for early humans. You can see hunters in the background driving wild horses off a cliff to people waiting at the bottom to slaughter them. Others build more huts or prepare the food. What might the children be doing to help?*

the people of Çatal Hüyük to the wider world around them.

Special buildings in Çatal Hüyük were shrines containing figures of gods and goddesses. Female statuettes have also been found there, often of women giving birth or nursing a child. These "earth mothers" may well have been connected with goddess figures. Both the shrines and the statues point to the growing role of religion in the lives of these Neolithic peoples.

The Neolithic agricultural revolution had far-reaching consequences. Once people settled in villages or towns, they built houses for protection and other structures for the storage of goods. The organized communities stored food and a number of material goods, which encouraged the development of trade. In the Middle East, for example, the new communities exchanged such objects as shells, flint, and semiprecious stones, often over long distances. People also began to specialize in certain crafts, and a division of labor developed. Pottery was made from clay and baked in fire to make it hard. The pots were used for cooking and to store grains. Baskets were also made for storage. Stone tools became refined as flint blades were used to make sickles and hoes for use in the fields. Over the course of the Neolithic Age, many of the food plants still in use today began to be cultivated. Moreover, vegetable fibers from such plants as flax and cotton were used to spin yarn that was woven into cloth.

The change to systematic agriculture in the Neolithic Age also had consequences for the relationship between men and women. Men became more active in farming and herding animals, jobs that took them away from the home settlement. Women remained behind, caring for children and taking responsibility for weaving cloth, turning milk into cheese, and other tasks that required much labor in one place. Men came to play a more dominant role, a basic pattern that would remain until our own times.

Other Neolithic patterns were also important in human history. Permanent dwellings, domesticated animals, regular farming, specialized occupations, and men holding power are all part of the human story. Despite all of our scientific and technological progress, human survival still depends on the growing and storing of food, an accomplishment of people in the

SPECIAL NEEDS: *visual/tactile*

Have students examine the illustrations in this chapter showing the tools of the first humans. Students should bring to class examples of arrowheads, spear points, scrapers, etc. Have students show or explain how these tools may have been used in ancient times. Show modern tools that may correlate to the Stone Age tools and ask students to consider how modern tools are similar to or different from the Stone Age tools. Pass around other artifacts, such as a vase, a spoon, and a coin. Ask students to examine each item and to make inferences about what someone discovering these items in the future might say about the civilization from which they came. Consider asking students to imagine what some of the tools of the future may look like and what their purposes would be.

Neolithic Age. The Neolithic Revolution was truly a turning point in human history.

Between 4000 and 3000 B.C., new developments began to affect the Neolithic towns in some areas. The use of metals marked a new level of human control over the environment and its resources. Even before 4000 B.C., craftspeople had discovered that metal-bearing rocks could be heated to liquefy the metal. The liquid metal could then be cast in molds to make tools and weapons that were more useful than stone instruments. Copper was the first metal to be used in making tools. After 4000 B.C., craftspeople in western Asia discovered that a combination of copper and tin created bronze, a far harder and more durable metal than copper. Its widespread use has led historians to speak of a **Bronze Age** from around 3000 to 1200 B.C. However, few people could afford bronze. Thus, even after the introduction of bronze, people continued to use tools and weapons made of stone.

At first, Neolithic settlements were hardly more than villages. As the inhabitants mastered the art of farming, however, they gradually began to develop more complex human societies. As wealth increased, these societies began to create armies and to build walled cities. By the beginning of the Bronze Age, the concentration of larger numbers of people in the river valleys of Mesopotamia, Egypt, India, and China was leading to a whole new pattern for human life.

 SECTION REVIEW

1. **Define:**
   (*a*) Neolithic Revolution,   (*b*) Neolithic Age,
   (*c*) Mesolithic Age,   (*d*) Neolithic farming villages,   (*e*) Bronze Age

2. **Identify:**
   (*a*) Mesoamericans,   (*b*) bronze

3. **Recall:**
   (*a*) Name at least three consequences of the agricultural revolution.

(*b*) What is a Neolithic village or town? What well-known Middle Eastern, Neolithic town is named in your text?

4. **Think Critically:** The word "revolution" is often defined as "an uprising against an established government, or a sudden change." What other definition of revolution would you give based on your understanding of the "agricultural revolution"?

THE EMERGENCE OF CIVILIZATION

As we have seen, early human beings formed small groups that developed a simple culture that enabled them to survive. As human societies grew and developed greater complexity, a new form of human existence—called civilization—came into being. A **civilization** is a complex culture in which large numbers of human beings share a number of common elements. Historians have identified at least six basic characteristics of civilizations. Most of these were present in the early civilizations of Mesopotamia, Egypt, India, and China, which we will examine in Chapters 2, 3, and 4. First, however, we must ask, what are the characteristics of civilizations?

The Rise of Cities

Cities are one of the chief characteristics of civilizations. The first civilizations developed in river valleys that were able to maintain the large-scale farming that was needed to feed a large population. Although farming practices varied from civilization to civilization, in each civilization a significant part of the population lived in cities. These cities were much larger than the Neolithic towns that preceded them, and new patterns of living soon emerged.

The Growth of Governments

Growing numbers of people and the need to maintain the food supply and to build walls for defense soon led

ASSESS

Answers to SECTION REVIEW

1. (a) shift from hunting and gathering to systematic agriculture
   (b) a time when there was a shift from hunting of animals and the gathering of food to the keeping of animals and the growing of food systematically
   (c) period when systematic agriculture spread to different areas of the world
   (d) permanent settlements
   (e) period after 4000 B.C. when bronze was discovered and used widely
2. (a) inhabitants of present-day Mexico and Central America
   (b) a combination of copper and tin
3. (a) See page 16, column 2 for answers
   (b) town formed by people gathering into an area for purpose of growing crops on a regular basis; Jericho or Çatal Hüyük
4. answers will vary

CLOSE

Emphasize to students the importance of the agricultural revolution. With stable food supply, populations grew, and towns could begin to develop.

FOCUS

OBJECTIVES

After completing this section students should be able to

1. list and explain six basic characteristics of civilization
2. describe the purpose of early governments
3. identify means for record keeping in early civilizations

FOCUS ACTIVITY

Have students work in pairs to compile a list of five to ten characteristics they believe define a civilization. Then, compile a class list that can be referred to as students read and discuss this section. Finally, have students write a one-page essay justifying why historians believe the six characteristics outlined in this section are the principal characteristics of a civilization.

TEACH

REINFORCING VOCABULARY

Have students look up the term *culture* in the dictionary and discuss its various meanings. Make sure that students understand that in the general historical context culture refers to the beliefs, attitudes, social manners, and practices of a particular group.

CLASS DISCUSSION

One of the first priorities of governments is to provide for the common defense. In early times, rulers were quick to build walls and fortified cities. Why do students think this was a first priority, even during the Bronze Age? What forces might have been viewed as enemies of these civilizations? *(Villages needed to protect their people, their crops, and their possessions from people from other villages or wandering bands of nomads.)*

to the growth of **governments.** Governments organize and regulate human activity. They also exist to provide for the smooth interaction between individuals and groups. In the first civilizations, governments were led by rulers—usually monarchs (kings or queens who rule a kingdom)—who organized armies to protect their populations and made laws to regulate their subjects' lives. Assisted by the government officials they appointed, these rulers also supervised the construction of important buildings and directed the irrigation projects that kept the fields watered.

The Role of Religion

Important religious developments also characterized the new urban civilizations. All of them developed religions as a means to explain the working of the forces of nature and the fact of their own existence. Gods and goddesses were often deemed crucial to a community's success. To win their favor, priests supervised rituals aimed at keeping good relations with the divine world. This gave the priests special power and made them very important people. Rulers also claimed that their power was based on divine approval, and some rulers claimed to be divine.

A New Social Structure

A new social structure based on economic power also arose. Whereas monarchs and an upper class of priests, government officials, and warriors dominated society, there also existed a large group of free people below this upper class (farmers, artisans, and craftspeople). At the very bottom, socially, was a class of slaves. Abundant food supplies created new opportunities as a surplus of goods enabled some people to work in occupations other than farming. The demand of the upper class for luxury items encouraged artisans and craftspeople to create new products. As urban populations exported finished goods to neighboring populations in exchange for raw materials, organized trade began to grow substantially.

▲ *Religion was important in early civilizations. Ziggurats (stepped towers) like this one were often built in Mesopotamia. Only priests and priestesses were allowed to enter the shrine that was at the top of the staircase.*

The Use of Writing

Writing was an important feature in the life of these new civilizations. Above all, rulers, priests, merchants, and artisans used writing to keep accurate records. Of course, not all civilizations depend on writing to keep records. The Incas in Peru (see Chapter 7), for example, relied on well-trained memory experts to keep track of their important matters. Eventually, all of the first civilizations used writing as a means of creative expression as well as record keeping. This produced the world's first works of literature.

Artistic Activity

Significant artistic activity was another feature of the new urban civilizations. Temples and pyramids (PIR-uh-MIDZ), often monumental in size, were built as places for worship, sacrifice, or burial of kings and other important people. Painting and sculpture were developed as means of portraying the gods and goddesses or other forces in the natural world.

The new urban civilizations also produced new material goods, which encouraged the development of trade. Trade at times brought the new civilizations into

COOPERATIVE LEARNING ACTIVITY

Have students work in groups to make a list of characteristics needed for a successful civilization from 5,000 years ago. Then have them make a list of the characteristics needed for a successful civilization today. They should answer the question, "What do the differences or similarities of these two lists tell you about the changes that have occurred over the past 5,000 years?" Do they think the changes have been for the better or worse? Do they think they would be more successful in one civilization than another? Ask the groups to report their conclusions to the class.

contact with one another. In many cases this contact led to the expansion of new technology from one region to another. By and large, however, the early river valley civilizations developed independently. Each one was based on developments connected to the agricultural revolution of the Neolithic Age and the cities that this revolution helped to produce. Taken together, the civilizations of Mesopotamia, Egypt, India, and China constituted nothing less than a revolutionary stage in the growth of human society. It is to these civilizations that we must now turn.

❀ SECTION REVIEW ❀

1. **Define:**
   (*a*) civilization, (*b*) governments

2. **Recall:**
   (*a*) List six characteristics of a civilization.
   (*b*) What were two methods used to keep accurate records in the new civilizations?

3. **Think Critically:** There are six characteristics of a civilization discussed. Do you feel any one characteristic could be eliminated and the period still be considered "civilized"? Explain your answer.

Conclusion

Historians rely on written documents and artifacts to create their pictures of the past. However, an account of prehistory—the period before written records—depends upon the work of archaeologists and anthropologists. These investigators rely on the scientific analysis of human remains to construct their theories about the development of early human beings.

Humanlike creatures first emerged in Africa more than three or four million years ago. Over a long period of time, Paleolithic people learned how to create more sophisticated tools; how to use fire; and how to adapt to, and even change, their physical environment. Paleolithic people were primarily nomads who hunted animals and gathered wild plants for survival. Nevertheless, they created a human culture that included sophisticated cave paintings.

The agricultural revolution of the Neolithic Age, which began around 10,000 B.C., dramatically changed human patterns of living. The growing of food on a regular basis and the taming of animals made it possible for humans to stop their nomadic ways of living. They began to settle down and form more permanent settlements. These organized communities gradually gave rise to more complex human societies.

These more complex human societies, which we call the first civilizations, emerged around 3000 B.C. in the river valleys of Mesopotamia, Egypt, India, and China. An increase in food production in these regions led to a significant growth in human population and to the rise of cities. Efforts to control the flow of water for farming also led to organized governments in these new urban civilizations. The emergence of civilizations was a dramatic new stage in the story of world history.

So What ❓❓

*If your students question the importance of the information on the **development of cities** tell them . . .*

The establishment of civilizations, and especially cities, allowed for the specialization of labor. No longer did each person have to raise or grow his or her own food. Because of this your students have career options that go beyond being just a hunter or farmer. Ask if any of them have considered careers as hunters or farmers. Would they prefer a civilization in which everyone was responsible for obtaining their own food?

USING KEY TERMS

1. Bronze Age
2. *Homo sapiens*
3. Neolithic Age
4. civilization
5. nomadic
6. thermoluminescence dating
7. *Homo sapiens sapiens*
8. archaeology
9. Neanderthals
10. Neolithic Revolution
11. radiocarbon dating
12. *Homo erectus*
13. Paleolithic Age
14. anthropologists
15. australopithecines
16. Neolithic farming villages
17. Mesolithic Age
18. hominids
19. governments

REVIEWING THE FACTS

1. East Africa
2. dig up and analyze artifacts of early people
3. the study of how people lived their lives based on the artifacts they left
4. Homer's account of the Greek siege of Troy
5. calculates the age of an object based on the amount of C-14 remaining in that object
6. measures the light given off by electrons trapped in the soil surrounding artifacts and fossils; because it can make relatively precise measurements as far back as 200,000 years
7. information about humans, the tools they used, and the animals they killed
8. australopithecenes
9. learned to use fire for warmth in colder climates
10. Neanderthals, Homo sapiens sapiens
11. Africa
12. search for food
13. Answers will vary and could include: use of stone tools; gathered wild plants and hunted wild animals for food; nomadic; lived in small groups; division of labor between the sexes;

CHAPTER 1 REVIEW

USING KEY TERMS

1. People who combined copper and tin to make tools are said to have entered the _____.
2. A crucial stage of human development began with the emergence of _____.
3. The _____, or New Stone Age, arrived after the last Ice Age, following the Mesolithic Age.
4. The rise of cities, the growth of governments, and the development of a priestly class are characteristics of a _____.
5. Paleolithic people were _____, while Neolithic people stayed in one place.
6. For the dating of objects that are older than 50,000 years, scientists use a method called _____.
7. The "modern" type of *Homo sapiens*, people like ourselves, are known as _____.
8. The study of past societies by the analysis of the artifacts they have left behind is called _____.
9. One type of *Homo sapiens*, the _____, appear to be the first to bury their dead.
10. The shift from hunting and gathering to food producing is called the _____.
11. The process that measures the amount of radioactive carbon (C-14) in artifacts and fossils to determine their age is called _____.
12. _____ was able to move into colder climates because he was able to control fire.
13. The earliest part of the Stone Age is known as the _____, or Old Stone Age.
14. _____ focus mainly on the study of human fossils in order to determine how they lived.
15. The _____ were the first hominds to use simple stone tools.
16. The permanent towns called _____ were occupied by people who grew crops.
17. The period between c. 10,000–7,000 B.C. is known as the _____ or Middle Stone Age.
18. The earliest human-like creatures, who inhabited East Africa, are generically called _____.
19. In the first civilizations, _____ were led by rulers who organized armies and made laws.

REVIEWING THE FACTS

1. Many discoveries about early humans were made at Olduvai Gorge. Where is Olduvai Gorge?
2. What do archaeologists do?
3. What is anthropology?
4. What did Schliemann use as a guide to find Troy?
5. How does radiocarbon dating work?
6. How does thermoluminescence dating work, and why is it useful?
7. What kind of data can DNA analysis provide?
8. Who is the earliest hominid to have used tools?
9. Why was *Homo erectus* able to emigrate out of East Africa?
10. What types of *Homo sapiens* are recognized by scientists?
11. Where were *Homo sapiens sapiens* first found?
12. Why did early humans migrate?
13. Give three characteristics of life in the Paleolithic Age.
14. Why were Paleolithic people nomadic?
15. What types of housing did Paleolithic humans use?
16. What do the cave paintings in Lascaux and Altamira indicate about Paleolithic humans?
17. What was the most significant development of the Neolithic Age?
18. When did systematic agriculture appear in:
    (a) the Middle East? (b) the Nile Valley? (c) Northwestern India? (d) Southeast Asia? (e) Europe? (f) China? (g) Mesoamerica?
19. What evidence is there about the role of religion in Çatal Hüyük?
20. Give five outcomes, or results, of the settlement of humans in villages or towns.
21. What is the Bronze Age, and when does it take place?

cave dwellers in colder climates; use of fire; cave paintings
14. had to follow animal migrations and vegetation cycles
15. caves; wood or bone structures covered with animal hides
16. they did more than just survive; they painted for religious and/or decorative purposes
17. shift to systematic agriculture
18. a) 8000 B.C. b) 6000 B.C. c) 7000–5000 B.C. d) 5000 B.C. e) 4000 B.C. f) 6000 B.C. g) 7000– 5000 B.C.
19. shrines and statues

20. permanent dwellings, domesticated animals, regular farming, specialized occupations, men holding power
21. a time when Asian craftspeople discovered that copper and tin created a much more durable metal, bronze; 3000–12,000 B.C.
22. Answers will vary; may include: rise of cities; growth of governments; role of religion; new social structure; use of writing; artistic activity
23. they were able to gain favor with the gods and goddesses
24. Mesopotamia, Egypt, India, and China

CHAPTER 1 REVIEW

22. What are three characteristics of a civilization?

23. How did priests acquire powerful positions in early civilizations?

24. Name the first four major civilizations.

THINKING CRITICALLY

1. The text indicates that "the first statues of what appear to be religious subjects [goddesses] portray women with exaggerated motherly features." Why do you think this is so?

2. If the agricultural revolution had never occurred, what would our lives be like today? Try to be as specific as possible.

3. Imagine you live in a Neolithic farming village. Other than being the chief or ruler, what function or role would you prefer to have, and why? Make a realistic choice based on the real needs of that type of society, as discussed in the text.

4. What kinds of things might a civilization with a well-developed writing system be able to do, that a society without writing could not?

APPLYING SOCIAL STUDIES SKILLS

1. Geography: On a blank outline map, locate and label the following: Africa; Asia; Europe; Oceania; the Americas; Middle East; Nile River Valley; India; Southeast Asia; China; Mesoamerica; Olduvai Gorge; Jericho; Çatal Hüyük.

2. Economics: One of the most basic economics concepts is "specialization of labor." Explain at what point in a society's development this takes place, and what possible consequences follow as a result of this development.

3. Sociology: As a civilization developed a new merchant class with greater economic power than other classes of society, this new class might seek to acquire greater political power as well. What

kinds of conflicts do you visualize as the new merchant class tries to obtain greater political power?

MAKING TIME AND PLACE CONNECTIONS

1. If *Homo erectus* were alive today, do you believe that we (*Homo sapiens sapiens*) would consider him a "human," or an "animal"? Why?

2. Some archaeologists and anthropologists have suggested that Neanderthal man (*Homo sapiens Neanderthalensis*) died out as a result of conflict with our own species. What type(s) of conflict could there have been between the two species?

3. What conditions in modern society contribute to making us more separate and ignorant of nature than early humans probably were?

4. During Neolithic times, according to the text, "men came to play a more dominant role, a basic pattern that would remain until our own time." Consider the conditions that created that change, as indicated in the text. Then, consider today's society. How many of those original conditions for change still are with us? If they are no longer present, how does society today justify a male-dominant role?

5. The text indicates that trade occasionally brought civilizations into contact with one another. Can you speculate on what might be some positive and negative outcomes of this contact?

BECOMING AN HISTORIAN

Art as a Key to History: Analyze carefully the illustration in this chapter of "cave art" drawn by early specimens of *Homo sapiens sapiens*. Develop three inferences about the early societies that created such works, based on your analysis.

MAKING TIME AND PLACE CONNECTIONS

1. Answers will vary; could include discussion of present-day views of apes, chimps, etc.

2. Answers will vary; could include discussion of competition for limited food sources and shelter, etc.

3. Answers will vary; should include permanent dwellings, mass production and sale of food items, modes of transportation that bypass natural barrier, etc.

4. Answers will vary; answers could include traditional male careers are done away from their home; women are better suited for childcare, etc.

5. Answers will vary; benefits could include learning of new technologies, expanding cultural view; negative outcomes might be wars to gain desired territories, loss of original cultural characteristics, etc.

BECOMING AN HISTORIAN

Answers will vary; could include proximity to nature, reverence for nature, worship of nature, fear of nature, etc.

THINKING CRITICALLY

1. Answers will vary; may include reference to ideas of "earth mother"

2. Answers will vary; should refer to nomadic life with no permanent dwellings, different roles of men and women, ways of obtaining food, etc.

3. Answers will vary; should give detailed description of duties of role chosen, i.e., craftsperson or farmer

4. Answers will vary; could include reference to record keeping, recorded history, artistic expression, etc.

APPLYING SOCIAL STUDIES SKILLS

1. see maps

2. Answers will vary; should include discussion of basic needs being met first, role of trade with other communities; social classes and differing gender roles may be possible developments

3. Answers will vary; could include conflict with religious leaders, inherited positions of power, etc.

2 PLANNING GUIDE

SECTION	KEY TOPICS	PRIMARY SOURCES	ASSESSMENT
1 Civilization Begins in Mesopotamia pages 23–33	◆ Geography's impact on the developmnt of civilization ◆ Life in Sumerian city-states ◆ *The Code of Hammurabi* ◆ Cuneiform writing	◆ *The Code of Hammurabi*, page 29 ◆ *The Epic of Gilgamesh*, page 32	◆ Section Review, page 33 ◆ Section Quiz 2–1, TRB
2 Egyptian Civilization: "Gift of the Nile" pages 33–41	◆ Geography's effect on Egyptian civilization ◆ The Three Kingdoms: Old, Middle, and New ◆ Daily life ◆ Writing and education	◆ *The Illustration of the Ptah-hotep,* page 41	◆ Section Review, page 42 ◆ Section Quiz 2–2, TRB
3 New Centers of Civilization pages 43–49	◆ Minoan civilization ◆ Nomadic peoples ◆ Phoenicians ◆ Hebrews	◆ The *Bible*, Isaiah 3:14–17, 24–26; Amos 3:1–2, 48	◆ Section Review, page 49 ◆ Section Quiz 2–3, TRB
4 The Rise of New Empires pages 50–55	◆ The Assyrian Empire ◆ The Persian Empire		◆ Section Review, page 54 ◆ Section Quiz 2–4, TRB

THE FIRST CIVILIZATIONS:
THE PEOPLE OF WESTERN ASIA AND EGYPT (3500 TO 500)

REPRODUCIBLE ACTIVITIES

- Historical Maps
- Charts and Graphs
- Critical Thinking
- Cooperative Learning
- Vocabulary
- Guided Reading
- Reteaching
- Enrichment
- Performance Assessment
- Spanish Key Points and Chapter Summaries
- Spanish Vocabulary
- Spanish Guided Reading

MULTIMEDIA SUPPORT

TRANSPARENCIES
- *World History* Color Transparency Package
- Fine Art Color Transparency Package

VIDEO
- *World History* Video Library
- CNN. Annual Video Update

LASERDISC
- *Sights and Sounds of History*

AUDIO
- *Listening to Literature* audiotape (English and Spanish)
- *History of Music* CD

SOFTWARE
- WESTEST™
- Student Review

CD–ROM
- *The Journey of Civilization*
- *World History*

INTERNET
- Internet Activities

On Line with WORLD HISTORY

Access West's history web site at
http://history.swpco.com
You'll find activities and web sites related to specific topics and chapters in *World History: The Human Odyssey*. Also look for references to helpful web sites at appropriate places throughout this teacher edition.

LESSON PLANNING

You will find detailed daily lesson plans for both traditional class scheduling and **block scheduling** in your Teacher Resource Box.

Not Enough Time?

If you do not have the four or five days recommended to teach this chapter, you may want to focus on the following sections and activities:

- Have students skim the chapter to answer the "Questions to Guide Your Reading" on page 23. Discuss their answers, then read the "Conclusion" on page 55.
- Do a more in-depth reading of pages 23–26, 35–38, and 45–49. Conclude with a class discussion of the "Connections" box on page 46.

THE FIRST CIVILIZATIONS: THE PEOPLES OF

BUILDING ON CHAPTER 1

To "set the scene" for the study of Chapter 2, use the following questions and activities.

◆ Have student volunteers create a time line of human development as traced in Chapter 1.

◆ Ask students to describe the major change in human activity from the Paleolithic to the Neolithic Age. *(the shift from hunting and gathering to keeping animals and growing food on a regular basis)*

◆ Ask students to define civilization and list its six major characteristics. *(pages 17–19)*

◆ Have groups of students prepare charts speculating on the differences between the first simple villages and cities in the first civilizations.

USING THE OPENING STORY

Depending on the ability levels of your students, select from the following questions and activities to reinforce the reading of the William Loftus story.

◆ How long ago does the story take place? *(approximately 150 years ago)*

◆ How hot was it? *(120° Fahrenheit)* Have students ever experienced temperatures this high?

◆ What metaphors are used to indicate that the region Loftus was in was where civilization began? *(roots, cradle)*

In the winter of 1849, a daring young Englishman made a difficult journey into the deserts and swamps of southern Iraq. He moved south down the banks of the river Euphrates (yu-FRATE-eez) while braving high winds and temperatures that reached 120 degrees Fahrenheit. The man, William Loftus, led a small expedition in search of the roots of civilization. As he said, "From our childhood we have been led to regard this place as the cradle of the human race."

Guided by native Arabs into the southernmost reaches of Iraq, Loftus and his small group of explorers were soon overwhelmed by what they saw. He wrote, "I know of nothing more exciting or impressive than the first sight of one of these great piles, looming in solitary grandeur from the surrounding plains and marshes." One of these "piles" was known to the natives as the mound of Warka. The mound contained the ruins of the ancient city of Uruk, one of the first real cities in the world and part of the world's first civilization.

Southern Iraq, known to ancient peoples as Mesopotamia, was one of four areas in the world where civilization began. The other three areas were Egypt, India, and China. In the fertile river valleys of these areas, intensive farming made it possible to support large groups of people. The people in these regions were able to develop the organized societies that we associate with civilization. This chapter examines the early civilizations of western Asia (now commonly referred to as the Middle East) and Egypt. In these cultures were the beginnings of Western civilization.

▲ *These are Sumerian ruins at Uruk, formerly the site of the ziggurat, or stepped tower, of Warka.*

ADDITIONAL RESOURCES

The resources listed below can be used to enrich the lessons in this chapter.

BOOKS FOR STUDENTS
The Illustrated World's Religions by Huston Smith, Social Studies School Service, (800) 421–4246
World History Dates by Jane Chisolm, Social Studies School Service, (800) 421–4246

VIDEOS/FILMS
Pyramid and *Pyramid School Kit*, PBS Video, (800) 344-3337
The Seven Wonders of the Ancient World, Crystal Productions, Box 2159, Glenview, IL 60025

CD-ROMs
Cartopedia, Crystal Productions, Box 2159, Glenview, IL 60025

WESTERN ASIA AND EGYPT

(3500 TO 500 B.C.)

THE BEGINNINGS OF CIVILIZATION

3500 B.C.	WESTERN ASIA AND EGYPT	500 B.C.
3500 B.C.		A.D. 500

QUESTIONS TO GUIDE YOUR READING

1. What effect did geography have on the civilizations that developed in Mesopotamia and Egypt?

2. What contributions did people in Mesopotamia and Egypt make to civilization?

3. Why was religion so important to the people of both Mesopotamia and Egypt?

4. How did nomadic peoples affect the centers of civilization?

5. What contributions did the Phoenicians (fi-NISH-uns) and Hebrews make to Western civilization?

6. What were the common features of the Assyrian (A-SEAR-e-an) and Persian Empires?

OUTLINE

1. CIVILIZATION BEGINS IN MESOPOTAMIA

2. EGYPTIAN CIVILIZATION: "THE GIFT OF THE NILE"

3. NEW CENTERS OF CIVILIZATION

4. THE RISE OF NEW EMPIRES

CIVILIZATION BEGINS IN MESOPOTAMIA

The ancient Greeks spoke of the valley between the Tigris (TIE-grus) and Euphrates Rivers as Mesopotamia, the land "between the rivers." Mesopotamia was at the eastern end of an area known as the Fertile Crescent, an arc of land from the Mediterranean Sea to the Persian Gulf. Because this land had rich soil and abundant crops, it was able to sustain an early civilization.

The Impact of Geography

Mesopotamia was a region with little rain, but its soil was enriched over the years by layers of silt, or sediment, deposited by the two rivers. In late spring, the Tigris and Euphrates often overflowed their banks and deposited their fertile silt. This flooding, however, depended upon the melting of snows in the upland mountains where the rivers began, so it was irregular. Sometimes it was even catastrophic. Too much water created floods that destroyed land, villages, and people. (Even in recent times, the flooding of the Tigris has caused widespread destruction in the modern city of Baghdad.) At other times, the rivers did not flood, and lack of water turned farmland to dust, causing famine.

Because of these circumstances, farming in ancient Mesopotamia could be done only when people controlled the flow of the rivers. Irrigation and drainage

23

FOCUS ON THEMES

Listed below are brief summaries of how the content in this chapter supports the text's key themes.

Politics and History Organized governments were a crucial part of the civilizations that emerged in Mesopotamia and Egypt. Later empires, such as the Assyrian and Persian Empires, developed new techniques for the efficient rule of large numbers of people.

Economics and History Civilized states were possible because of the surplus food produced by systematic agriculture. New economic forms also emerged.

Cultural Developments Civilized communities created writing and literature and built monumental structures to please their gods and preserve their cultures.

Religion in History Religion was a crucial factor in the civilizations that developed in both Mesopotamia and Egypt. The monotheism of the Hebrews was important in the later religions of Christianity and Islam.

The Role of Individuals Individual rulers, such as Hammurabi and Hatshepsut, created important new patterns in law and governing.

The Environment and History Erratic flooding and open plains made civilization in Mesopotamia both insecure and unstable. The regularity of Nile flooding and natural barriers helped make Egyptian civilization both stable and prosperous. In response to these two different sets of conditions, the people in the two areas developed different attitudes toward their gods, who were considered to have power over natural events.

FOCUS

OBJECTIVES

After completing this section students should be able to

1. explain the impact of geography on the development of civilization in Mesopotamia
2. list characteristics of life in Sumerian city-states
3. name the first empires in ancient Mesopotamia
4. list several of the laws included in Hammurabi's code
5. explain the significance of religion for the peoples of ancient Mesopotamia
6. identify and explain the importance of Sumerian inventions

FOCUS ACTIVITY

Make sure students understand the importance of rivers in the development of civilization. Divide students into groups, assigning each group the task of listing all the ways that rivers made possible and facilitated the existence of people who lived in ancient times. To help them develop their lists you might suggest that they try to think of things people do today without the aid of rivers, but for which rivers used to be essential.

ditches—part of a large-scale system of water control—made it possible to grow crops on a regular basis. The resulting abundance of food supplies enabled large numbers of people to live together in cities and to work together to maintain the irrigation system on which their lives depended. At the same time, this complex irrigation system was possible only with a well-organized government to supervise it. Thus, the combination of irrigation, cities, and organized governments in the fertile river valley made possible the emergence of civilization in Mesopotamia.

When we speak of Mesopotamian civilization, we are referring to the achievements of different peoples, beginning with the Sumerians.

Because Mesopotamia was an open plain with no natural barriers, the people who lived there were open to outside attacks. As we will see, neighboring peoples from the hills and deserts would sweep in, destroying houses and taking goods. (The Sumerians called these raiders "people who have never known a city.") Climate and landscape, then, are two long-term patterns that have shaped the history of Mesopotamia.

Map 2.1   Ancient Mesopotamia

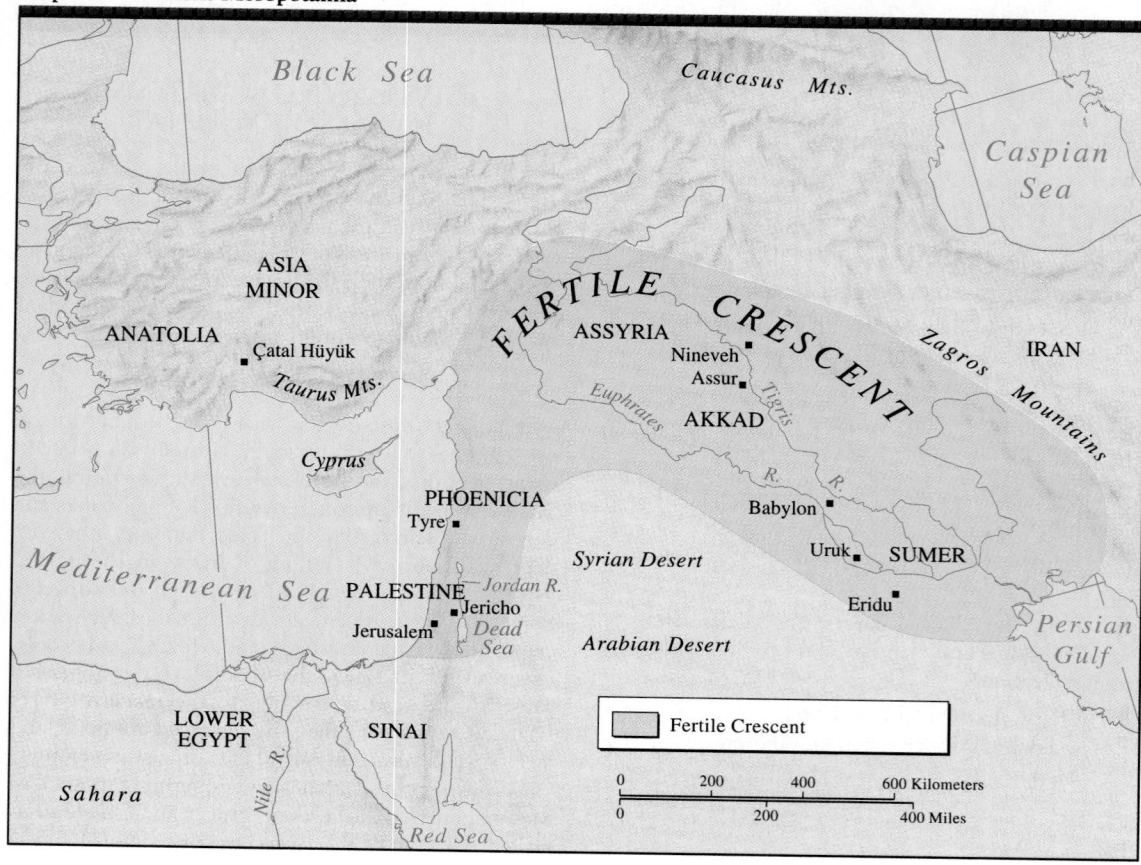

STUDYING MAPS

The following questions will help you guide the students through their study of Map 2.1.

1. What is a crescent? *(a shape with a concave edge)* Trace the crescent in this map with your finger. Why is it called a fertile crescent? (*The soil is rich due to the flooding of rivers.*)
2. Name the Mesopotamian cities shown on the map. (*Nineveh, Assur, Babylon, Uruk, Eridu*)
3. Approximately how far is it from Babylon, on the Euphrates River, to the main channel of the Nile? This distance is the same as from your city to what other city or location? *(approximately 800 miles; Answers will vary.)*

▶ The "Royal Standard" of Ur, a box from c. 2700 B.C. depicts a royal celebration following a military victory. The panels show the king and his court as well as the spoils of victory. How does this method of recording historic events compare to the way events are recorded today?

LEARNING FROM VISUALS

1. Ask students what they are looking at in this illustration. (photo of a Sumerian box) When was the box created (2500 B.C.)
2. Ask each student to pick one of the characters depicted in the artwork and write a paragraph describing what the student imagines that character's lifestyle to be.

Multimedia Support

 LASERDISC
Sumerian Head with Turban
(3000 B.C.)

The City-States of Ancient Mesopotamia

The creators of the first Mesopotamian civilization were the Sumerians, a people whose origins remain a mystery. By 3000 B.C., the Sumerians had established a number of independent cities in southern Mesopotamia, including Eridu, Ur, and Uruk. As the cities expanded, they came to have political and economic control over the surrounding countryside. They formed **city-states,** the basic units of Sumerian civilization.

Sumerian cities were surrounded by walls. Uruk, for example, was encircled by a wall six miles long with defense towers located along the wall every thirty to thirty-five feet. City dwellings, built of sun-dried bricks, included both the small houses of peasants and the larger buildings of the city officials, priests, and priestesses. Although Mesopotamia had little stone or wood for building purposes, it did have plenty of mud. Mud bricks, easily shaped by hand, were left to bake in the hot sun until they were hard enough to use for building. People in Mesopotamia were remarkably creative with mud bricks. They invented the arch and the dome, and they built some of the largest brick buildings in the world. Mud bricks are still used in rural areas of the Middle East today.

The most prominent building in a Sumerian city was the temple dedicated to the chief god or goddess of the city. This temple was often built atop a massive stepped tower called a **ziggurat.** The Sumerians believed that gods and goddesses owned the cities. The people devoted much of their wealth to building temples, as well as elaborate houses for the priests and priestesses who served the gods. Priests and priestesses, who supervised the temples and their property, had much power. The temples owned much of the city land and livestock, and they served as the center of the city physically, economically, and even politically.

In fact, historians believe that in the early stages of the city-states, priests and priestesses played an important role in ruling. The Sumerians believed that the gods ruled the cities, making the state a **theocracy** (a government by divine authority). Eventually, however, ruling power passed into the hands of worldly figures known as kings.

Sumerians viewed kingship as divine in origin. Kings, they believed, derived their power from the gods and were the agents of the gods. Regardless of their origins, kings had power. They led armies, supervised the building of public works, and organized workers for the irrigation projects upon which Mesopotamian farming depended. The army, the government bureaucracy, and the priests and priestesses all aided the kings in their rule. As befitted their power, Sumerian kings, their wives, and their children lived in large palaces.

The economy of the Sumerian city-states was based chiefly on farming, although trade and industry

COMPARING TIME PERIODS

After students have read the description of Sumerian cities, have students list differences between the Sumerian cities and contemporary cities. (Differences might include the following: today's cities have no walls, few buildings are made of mud bricks, religious buildings are not necessarily the most prominent in the city, and religious officials are not the political leaders.) Ask students to explain why these differences exist.

Answer to the caption question: Answers will vary but may include that today we use photography, media technology, and the printed page to record information.

MORE ABOUT . . . Agriculture

Some anthropologists have suggested that the invention of beer might be responsible for humanity's shift from hunting and gathering to agriculture. The domestication of barley began about 10,000 years ago and the gathering of wild barley surely took place earlier than that. Jonathan Sauer of the University of Wisconsin theorizes that too much work was involved in the making of bread for that to be the reason hunters settled down to an agricultural life. Beer, however, might have provided adequate incentive. Hammurabi had stiff penalties for the owners of beer parlors who overcharged (death by drowning) or allowed criminals in their establishments (execution).

THE ROLE OF SCIENCE AND TECHNOLOGY

Make sure students realize the difference between stone and metal. Stone is a hard material that is difficult to shape, cut, or bend. Metals can be more easily worked and, therefore, are more valuable to mankind.

Ask students why gold and silver became such valuable metals. (*Softness made them easy to work.*) Why were gold and silver used less frequently than iron and copper to make weapons and tools? (*Softness caused them to break easily.*)

ACROSS THE CURRICULUM

Industrial Technology. If the facilities are available at your school, have an industrial technology teacher demonstrate casting and forging processes for your class.

Chemistry. Ask for student volunteers who are taking chemistry to prepare overhead transparencies showing various metals and their properties (hardness, melting point, etc.).

LEARNING FROM VISUALS

Answer to the caption question: Answers will vary but may include expensive cars, expensive jewelry, extensive education, holding public office, large homes, etc.

THE ROLE OF SCIENCE AND TECHNOLOGY
The Use of Metals

Sometime around 6000 B.C., people in western Asia began to use metals. They soon realized the advantage of using metal rather than stone to make both tools and weapons. Metal could be shaped more exactly, allowing craftspeople to make more refined tools and weapons with sharp edges and more precise shapes.

Copper, silver, and gold were the first metals to be used. These were relatively soft and could be easily pounded into different shapes. People later made the important discovery that a rock that contained metal could be heated to liquefy the metal (a process called *smelting*).

Being a goldsmith in ancient Egypt was an art form practiced by the finest craftsmen. Intricate jewelry of gold and semiprecious stones was worn as a sign of social status. What do you think are signs of social status today?

The liquid metal then could be poured into molds of clay or stone to make precisely shaped tools and weapons.

Copper was the first metal to be used in making tools. After 4000 B.C., craftspeople in western Asia discovered that when tin is added to copper, it makes bronze. Bronze has a lower melting point, which makes it easier to cast than copper. Bronze is also a harder metal than copper and corrodes less. The widespread use of bronze has led historians to speak of a Bronze Age from around 3000 to 1200 B.C. This is a somewhat misleading term, however, because many people continued to use stone tools and weapons even after bronze became available.

became important as well. The people of Mesopotamia made woolen textiles; pottery; and metalwork, for which they were especially well known (see "The Role of Science and Technology: The Use of Metals"). The Sumerians imported copper, tin, and timber in exchange for dried fish, wool, barley, wheat, and metal goods. Traders traveled by land to the eastern Mediterranean and by sea as far away as India. The invention of the wheel, around 3000 B.C., led to carts with wheels, which made the transport of goods easier.

Sumerian city-states contained three major social groups: nobles, commoners, and slaves. Nobles included royal and priestly officials and their families. Commoners worked for palace and temple estates and as farmers, merchants, fishers, and craftspeople. Probably 90 percent or more of the people were farmers. Slaves belonged to palace officials, who used them mostly in building projects. Temple officials used mostly female slaves to weave cloth and grind grain. Rich landowners also used slaves to farm their lands.

RECOMMENDED READING

General works on ancient Mesopotamia include A. L. Oppenheim, *Ancient Mesopotamia,* 2d ed. (Chicago, 1977); S. Lloyd, *The Archaeology of Mesopotamia,* rev. ed. (London, 1984); and G. Roux, *Ancient Iraq* (Harmondsworth, 1966). The world of the Sumerians has been well described in S. N. Kramer, *The Sumerians* (Chicago, 1963) and *History Begins at Sumer* (New York, 1959). Kramer's book *Sumerian Mythology* (New York, 1961) is a study of Sumer's spiritual and literary achievement in the third millennium B.C. See also the recent summary of the historical and archaeological evidence by H. Crawford, *Sumer and the Sumerians* (Cambridge, 1991). On Ebla, see P. Matthiae, *Ebla: An Empire Rediscovered* (London, 1980).

THE ROLE OF SCIENCE AND TECHNOLOGY

The Use of Metals, continued

After 1200 B.C., bronze was increasingly replaced by iron, which was probably first used in western Asia between 2000 and 1500 B.C. The Hittites, an Indo-European–speaking people who established their own empire in western Asia, were known for making use of iron to develop new weapons. Between 1500 and 600 B.C., iron making spread across Europe, northern Africa, and Asia. Bronze continued to be used, but mostly for jewelry and other domestic purposes. Iron was used to make tools and weapons with sharper edges.

Iron was handled differently than bronze. It was not smelted and cast but instead was heated until it could be beaten into a desired shape. Each ham-

mering produced increased strength for the metal. This wrought iron, as it is called, was typical of iron manufacturing in the West until the Middle Ages. Only in China, as early as the fourth century B.C., did craftspeople develop a method for smelting iron until it too could be cast in a mold.

▲ *Civilized development in every culture reached a major turning point with the discovery of techniques to smelt and temper iron. Iron was used for making weaponry and tools. What effect would iron weaponry have had on an early civilization?*

1. Why were stone tools and weapons still used after metal became available?

2. Describe the relationship between the use of metals and the Sumerian economy.

3. What role do metals play in today's world economy?

Empires in Ancient Mesopotamia

As the number of Sumerian city-states grew and the city-states expanded, new conflicts arose. City-state fought city-state for control of land and water. Located on the flat land of Mesopotamia, the Sumerian city-states were also open to invasion. To the north of the Sumerian city-states were the Akkadians (uh-KADE-ee-unz). We call them a *Semitic people* because they spoke one of the Semitic languages (see the accompa-

nying table). Around 2340 B.C. Sargon, leader of the Akkadians, overran the Sumerian city-states and set up

Some Semitic Languages (Languages in italic are no longer spoken.)		
Arabic	*Akkadian*	Aramaic
Assyrian	*Babylonian*	*Canaanitic*
Hebrew	*Phoenician*	Syriac

SPECIAL NEEDS: *Visual/Auditory*

Have students locate the Nile River in Map 2.2 on Page 34. Describe the uniqueness of the Nile River in terms of length and predictable flooding. Ask students why, in their opinion, the Nile River is of significant importance today and discuss their com-

ments in class. Have students locate the pyramids on the map. Ask them to explain the purposes of the pyramids. Have them locate photographs of the pyramids in the library or via computer programs. Share the findings with the class.

CRITICAL THINKING

Ask students to speculate about reasons why empires are easier to create than maintain. *(Although defeated, groups may not want to be ruled by outside parties and therefore continue to rebel; it was difficult to communicate throughout the empire, especially in ancient times; empire builders often continue to stretch the boundaries of their empires, which weakens their ability to control their existing territories)*

REINFORCING VOCABULARY

Make sure that students know the meaning of *sacking*. *(stealing and looting valuables, destroying property)*

OPPOSING VIEWPOINTS

Divide students into two groups. Have one group defend and the other attack the proposition that empires are superior to city-states as a form of government.

CLASS DISCUSSION

Guide students in a discussion of American laws that may have originated in Hammurabi's law code. Were Hammurabi's laws fair, or were the prescribed punishments unusually cruel?

REINFORCING VOCABULARY

Review the term *patriarchal* with students and discuss its opposite, *matriarchal* *(a society dominated or governed by women).* You might also want to introduce the terms **matrilineal** *(descent traced through the mother's family)* versus **patrilineal** *(descent traced through the father's family).*

the first empire in world history. An **empire** is a large political unit or state, usually under a single leader, that controls many peoples or territories. Empires are often easy to create but difficult to maintain. The rise and fall of empires will be an important part of our story.

Attacks from neighboring hill peoples eventually caused the Akkadian Empire to fall. Its end by 2100 B.C. brought a return to the system of warring city-states. The constant wars, with their burning and sacking of cities, left many Sumerians in deep despair. This mood is evident in the words of a Sumerian poem from the city of Ur: "Ur is destroyed, bitter is its lament. The country's blood now fills its holes like hot bronze in a mould. Bodies dissolve like fat in the sun. Our temple is destroyed, the gods have abandoned us, like migrating birds. Smoke lies on our city like a shroud."[1]

It was not until 1792 B.C. that a new empire came to control much of Mesopotamia. Leadership came from Babylon, a city-state north of Akkad, where Hammurabi (ham-uh-ROB-ee) came to power. He had a well-disciplined army of foot soldiers who carried axes, spears, and copper or bronze daggers. Hammurabi divided his opponents and defeated them one by one. He gained control of Sumer and Akkad, thus creating a new Mesopotamian kingdom. After his conquests, he called himself "the sun of Babylon, the king who has made the four quarters of the world subservient."

Hammurabi, the man of war, was also a man of peace. He built temples, defensive walls, and irrigation canals. He encouraged trade and brought an economic revival. After his death in 1750 B.C., however, a series of weak kings were unable to keep Hammurabi's empire united, and it finally fell to new invaders.

The Code of Hammurabi

Hammurabi is best remembered for his law code, a collection of 282 laws. For centuries, laws had regulated people's relationships with one another in the lands of Mesopotamia. Hammurabi's collection provides considerable insight into social conditions in Mesopotamia and touches on almost every aspect of everyday life there.

The Code of Hammurabi was based on a system of strict justice (see "You Are There: Justice in Mesopotamia"). Penalties for criminal offenses were severe and varied according to the social class of the victim. A crime against a member of the upper class (a noble) by a member of the lower class (a commoner) was punished more severely than the same offense against a member of the lower class. Moreover, the principle of retaliation ("an eye for an eye, tooth for a tooth") was a fundamental part of this system of justice. This and other Mesopotamian ideas would find their way into the Hebrew civilization.

Hammurabi's code took seriously the duties of public officials. Officials were expected to catch burglars. If they failed to do so, the officials in the district where the crime was committed had to replace the lost property. If murderers were not found, the officials had to pay a fine to the relatives of the murdered person.

The law code also encouraged the proper performance of work with what we would call consumer protection laws. Builders were held responsible for the buildings they constructed. If a house collapsed and caused the death of the owner, the builder was put to death. If the collapse caused the death of the son of the owner, the son of the builder was put to death. If goods were destroyed by the collapse, they had to be replaced and the house itself rebuilt at the builder's expense.

The largest category of laws in the Code of Hammurabi focused on marriage and the family. Parents arranged marriages for their children. After marriage, the two parties signed a marriage contract. Without this contract, no one was considered legally married.

Society in Mesopotamia was **patriarchal;** that is, it was dominated by men. Hammurabi's code makes it clear that women had far fewer privileges and rights in marriage than did men. A woman's place was in the home, and failure to fulfill her expected duties was grounds for divorce. If a wife was not able to bear children or tried to leave home to engage in business, her husband could divorce her. Furthermore, a wife who was a "gadabout, . . . neglecting her house [and] humiliating her husband," could be drowned.

Fathers ruled their children as well as their wives. Obedience was expected: "If a son has struck his father, he shall cut off his hand." If a son committed a serious enough offense, his father could disinherit him. Obviously, Hammurabi's law code covered almost every aspect of people's lives.

On Line with WORLD HISTORY Internet Activity

You may want to have your students visit the following URL, where they will find information and additional web site resources to enhance their study of this chapter.

ABZU—Resources for the Study of Ancient Near East

http://www-oi.uchicago.edu:80/

The index for ancient Near East web links.

Due to the ever-changing nature of the World Wide Web, see the West History web site, **http://history.swpco.com** for regular updates of the URLs in this text.

YOU ARE THERE

Justice in Mesopotamia

Although there were earlier Mesopotamian law codes, the Code of Hammurabi is the most complete. The law code emphasizes the principle of retribution ("an eye for an eye") and punishments that vary according to social status. Punishments could be severe, as these examples show.

The Code of Hammurabi

25: If fire broke out in a free man's house and a free man, who went to extinguish it, cast his eye on the goods of the owner of the house and has appropriated the goods of the owner of the house, that free man shall be thrown into that fire.

196: If a free man has destroyed the eye of a member of the aristocracy, they shall destroy his eye.

198: If he has destroyed the eye of a commoner or broken the bone of a commoner, he shall pay one mina of silver.

199: If he has destroyed the eye of a free man's slave or broken the bone of a free man's slave, he shall pay one-half his value.

◁ *The Code of Hammurabi was the most famous, though not the first, early Mesopotamian law code. The upper section of this stone monument shows Hammurabi standing in front of the seated sun god Shamash, who orders the king to record the law. The actual code is inscribed on the lower portion. Do you think the Code of Hammurabi could be enforced today?*

1. Explain the principle of retribution.

2. According to the Code of Hammurabi, what was most highly valued in Mesopotamian society? What was the least valued? Explain your answers.

3. What is the guiding principle in the American criminal justice system? How does this compare with Hammurabi's justice?

COOPERATIVE LEARNING ACTIVITY

Have students work in pairs. Ask them to rewrite, in modern English, the four laws printed in the text. Then have students list the comparable modern-day, American laws and suggest what the possible punishments might be. As a class discussion, ask students to share their lists, then compare and contrast the contents. See how many differences and similarities the students see.

CRITICAL THINKING

Ask students to explain why writing was so important to the development of civilization.

USING PRIMARY SOURCES

Have a student volunteer to read this poem aloud. Ask students when they think the poem was written. Ask them to identify other poems that express despair at the loss of a village, city, or country.

Multimedia Support

LASERDISC
Ziggurat

Ritual at Ziggurat

▲ *This table shows the evolution of eighteen representative signs from c. 3000 B.C. to 600 B.C. Each sign represents an idea or object, such as No. 11, which meant both "water" and "in."*

The Importance of Religion

The physical environment made a strong impact on the way Mesopotamians viewed the world. Ferocious floods, heavy downpours, scorching winds, and oppressive humidity were all part of the Mesopotamian climate. These conditions, as well as famines, easily convinced Mesopotamians that this world was controlled by supernatural forces, which often were not kind or reliable. In the presence of nature, Mesopotamians could easily feel helpless, as this poem relates:

> *The rampant flood which no man can oppose,*
> *Which shakes the heavens and causes earth to tremble,*
> *In an appalling blanket folds mother and child,*
> *And drowns the harvest in its time of ripeness.*[2]

To the Mesopotamians, powerful spiritual beings—gods and goddesses—permeated all aspects of the universe. The Mesopotamians identified almost three thousand gods and goddesses, making Mesopotamian religion **polytheistic** (having many gods). Human beings were supposed to obey and serve the gods. According to Sumerian myth, human beings were created to do the manual labor the gods were unwilling to do for themselves. By their very nature, humans were inferior to the gods and could never be sure what the gods might do to help or hurt them.

The "Cradle of Civilization": The Creativity of the Sumerians

The Sumerians made many inventions that still affect our lives today. The greatest of all was the development of writing. Around 3000 B.C., the Sumerians created a **cuneiform** ("wedge-shaped") system of writing. Using

On Line with WORLD HISTORY Internet Activity

You may want to have your students visit the following URL, where they will find information and additional web site resources to enhance their study of this chapter.
Ancient World Web: Meta Index

http://atlantic.evsc.virginia.edu/julia/aw/meta.html

Hundreds of links to Ancient Civilizations all over Europe and Asia.

Due to the ever-changing nature of the World Wide Web, see the West History web site, **http://history.swpco.com** for regular updates of the URLs in this text.

YOUNG PEOPLE IN MESOPOTAMIA

Sumerian Schools for Scribes

For boys of the upper class in Mesopotamia, becoming a scribe was the key to a successful career. There were thousands of scribes in Sumerian society. They kept the records for palaces and temples, the military, and the government. Men who began their careers as scribes became the leaders of their cities, temples, and armies. Scribes came to hold the most important positions in Sumerian society.

To become scribes, boys from wealthy families, many of them the sons of scribes, attended the new schools that were in operation by 2500 B.C. Young boys seeking to become scribes began school when they were small children and trained until they were young men. School days began at sunrise and ended at sunset. Discipline was harsh. The following essay, written by a teacher as a copying exercise for pupils, shows that punishments—being caned or beaten with a stick—were frequent:

▲ *This tablet contains cuneiform instructions on how to perform a Babylonian marriage ritual.*

> *In the tablet-house, the monitor said to me: "Why are you late?" I was afraid, my heart beat fast. I entered before my teacher, took my place.*
> *My "school-father" read my tablet to me, said, "The word is cut off," caned me.*
> *He who was in charge of drawing said "Why when I was not here did you stand up?" caned me.*

> *He who was in charge of the gate said "Why when I was not here did you go out?" caned me.*
> *My teacher said "Your hand is not good," caned me.*

Scribal students spent most of their school days following the same routine. They were taught by copying and recopying standard works on clay tablets and reciting from them. A Sumerian document reveals the routine.

> *"What did you do in school?"*
> *"I read my tablet, wrote it, finished it; then my prepared lines were prepared for me and in the afternoon, my hand copies were prepared for me."*

Copying prepared texts onto clay tablets day after day became boring. However, this was probably the only way of learning how to form the cuneiform signs neatly and correctly.

1. What skills did scribes possess that enabled them to become leaders in the government, military, and temples?

2. How were wealth and social class factors in the schools for scribes?

3. If you were a Sumerian teenager, would you have wanted to be trained as a scribe? Why or why not?

MORE ABOUT . . . *the Wonders of the World*

Four of the seven Wonders of the Ancient World were to be found in either Egypt or Mesopotamia. The seven Wonders are

1. Statue of Zeus (forty-foot statue of Zeus in ancient Greece)
2. Colossus of Rhodes (Greek statue standing over harbor entrance at Rhodes)
3. Pharos of Alexandria (lighthouse at Egyptian port city of Alexandria)
4. Mausoleum (crypt for King Mausollos of Caria—Turkey)
5. Hanging Gardens (Babylonian terrace gardens)
6. Temple of Artemis at Ephysus (temple in Asia Minor)
7. Great Pyramids (Old Kingdom of Egypt)

YOUNG PEOPLE IN MESOPOTAMIA

CLASS DISCUSSION

After students have read Sumerian School for Scribes, ask them why they think the scribes were the ones who received most of the important government positions. *(they came from wealthy families, became more knowledgeable than others, etc.)* The scribe schools were similar to what institutions in our contemporary society? *(prep schools)*

USING PRIMARY SOURCES

Have student volunteers read the essay, then ask the students their reactions. Would they learn more if this sort of discipline were implemented in their schools today?

Answers to Critical Thinking Questions

1. They knew how to read and write, which were unique and important skills at the time.
2. Only the children of the wealthy and privileged class were given the opportunity to become scribes.
3. Answers will vary. Some students will cite the harsh discipline and the male-only policy of the schools as negatives; others may see the promise of a successful career as positive.

OUR LITERARY HERITAGE

REINFORCING VOCABULARY

You may want to provide students with definitions of the following words:

1. **teemed**—grew out of control; overflowed
2. **babel**—nonsensical talking; gibberish
3. **leagues**—2.4–4.6 miles

USING PRIMARY SOURCES

Assign students this excerpt from *Gilgamesh* and the Noah excerpt from the Bible (Genesis 7:1–8:18). Ask students to compare and contrast the two accounts. How do they differ? How are they similar? Which was written first?

Answers to Critical Thinking Questions

1. They were bothering the gods.
2. Everything was going to be destroyed; by saving living things he could make the process of rebirth possible.
3. They were living at the whims of the gods.

Answer to the caption question: Answers will vary but they may point out the biblical account told of forty days/nights of rain versus six; Noah was not told to tear down his house; Noah was told to warn people; the Ark landed on Mt. Ararat, etc.

OUR LITERARY HERITAGE

The Story of the Great Flood

The great epic poem of Mesopotamian literature, The Epic of Gilgamesh, *includes an account by Utnapishtim, a Mesopotamian version of the later biblical Noah. Utnapishtim had built a ship and survived a flood unleashed by the gods to destroy humankind. In this selection, Utnapishtim tells how the god Ea advised him to build a boat and how he came to land the boat at the end of the flood.*

The Epic of Gilgamesh

"In those days the world teemed, the people multiplied, the world bellowed like a wild bull, and the great god [Enlil] was aroused by the clamour. Enlil heard the clamour and he said to the gods in council, 'The uproar of mankind is intolerable and sleep is no longer possible by reason of the babel.' So the gods agreed to exterminate mankind. Enlil did this, but Ea [Sumerian Enki, god of the waters] warned me in a dream. . . . 'tear down your house and build a boat, abandon possessions and look for life, despise worldly goods and save your soul alive. Tear down your house, I say, and build a boat. . . . then take up into the boat the seed of all

living creatures. . . .' [Utnapishtim did as he was told, and then the destruction came.]

"For six days and six nights the winds blew, torrent and tempest and flood overwhelmed the world, tempest and flood raged together like warring hosts. When the seventh day dawned the storm from the south subsided, the sea grew calm, the flood was stilled; I looked at the face of the world and there was silence, all mankind was turned to clay. The surface of the sea stretched as flat as a roof-top; I opened a hatch and the light fell on my face. Then I bowed low, I sat down and I wept, the tears streamed down my face, for on every side was the waste of water. I looked for land in vain, but fourteen leagues distant there appeared a mountain, and there the boat grounded; on the mountain of Nisir the boat held fast, she held fast and did not budge."

▲ *This is a rendition of Utnapishtim from* The Epic of Gilgamesh, *which tells of a great flood. If you are familiar with the biblical account of Noah and the flood as told in the book of Genesis in the Bible, what are some differences and similarities in the two stories?*

1. Why did the gods want to destroy humankind?

2. What did Enki mean when he told Utnapishtim to "look for life, despise worldly goods and save your soul alive"?

3. What conclusions can you draw about the Mesopotamian view of a person's place in the universe?

ENRICHMENT ACTIVITY

Point out to students that early literature, like the *Epic of Gilgamesh,* had to be painstakingly written on tablets and copied, character by character, when reproduced. Discuss with students how manuscripts are transmitted and prepared today. Very few authors actually pen their works; manuscripts are transmitted electronically, and then printed with highly automated machinery. What impact does this have on our society? *(Students should recognize that information is quickly and easily disseminated, and that books can be written and printed very quickly.)* Have students research printing methods from earliest times to the present and report to the class.

a reed stylus (a tool for writing), they made wedge-shaped impressions on clay tablets, which were then baked or dried in the sun. Once dried, these tablets lasted a very long time. The several hundred thousand tablets that have been found so far have been a valuable source of information for modern scholars.

Mesopotamian peoples used writing primarily for record keeping. Cuneiform tablets recorded tallies of cattle kept by herders for their owners, lists of taxes and wage payments, accounts, contracts, and court decisions affecting business life. Cuneiform texts were also used in schools to train scribes for careers in the temples and palaces, the military, and government service (see "Young People in Mesopotamia: Sumerian Schools for Scribes").

Writing was important because it allowed a society to keep records and maintain knowledge of previous practices and events. Writing also made it possible for people to communicate ideas in new ways. This is especially evident in the most famous piece of Mesopotamian literature, *The Epic of Gilgamesh* (see "Our Literary Heritage: The Story of the Great Flood"). This epic poem records the exploits of a legendary king named Gilgamesh. Gilgamesh is wise, strong, and perfect in body. He is part man and part god. Gilgamesh befriends a hairy beast named Enkidu. Together, they set off to do great deeds. When Enkidu dies, Gilgamesh feels the pain of death and begins a search for the secret of immortality. His efforts fail, however. Gilgamesh remains mortal. The desire for immortality, one of humankind's great searches, ends in complete frustration. "Everlasting life," as this Mesopotamian epic makes clear, is only for the gods.

The Sumerians also made outstanding achievements in mathematics and astronomy. In math, they devised a number system based on 60, using combinations of 6 and 10 for practical solutions. Geometry was used to measure fields and erect buildings. In astronomy, the Sumerians made use of units of 60 and charted the heavenly constellations. A quick glance at your watch and its division into 60 minutes in an hour should remind you of our debt to the Sumerians. Furthermore, their calendar was based on twelve lunar months and was brought into harmony with the solar year by adding an extra month from time to time.

 SECTION REVIEW

1. **Locate:**
   (a) Mesopotamia, (b) the Fertile Crescent,
   (c) Uruk, (d) Babylon

2. **Define:**
   (a) city-states, (b) ziggurat, (c) theocracy,
   (d) empire, (e) patriarchal, (f) polytheistic,
   (g) cuneiform

3. **Identify:**
   (a) Sumerians, (b) Akkadians, (c) Sargon,
   (d) Hammurabi, (e) Code of Hammurabi,
   (f) *The Epic of Gilgamesh*

4. **Recall:**
   (a) What process was necessary to grow crops on a regular basis in Mesopotamia?
   (b) Identify the three major social groups in the Sumerian city-states.
   (c) What conditions convinced the people of Mesopotamia that the world was controlled by supernatural forces?

5. **Think Critically:** Which type of government—separate city-states or an empire—was most advantageous to the people of Mesopotamia? Explain your answer.

EGYPTIAN CIVILIZATION: "THE GIFT OF THE NILE"

"The Egyptian Nile," wrote one Arab traveler, "surpasses all the rivers of the world in sweetness of taste, in length of course and usefulness. No other river in the world can show such a continuous series of towns and villages along its banks." The Nile River was crucial to the development of Egyptian civilization. The Egyptian people certainly knew this, as is apparent in their *Hymn to the Nile:* "The bringer of food, rich in provisions, creator of all good, lord of majesty, sweet of fragrance. . . . [The Nile] . . . makes the granaries wide,

---

So What ⁇

*If your students question the importance of the information on **Sumerian achievements in math**, tell them . . .*

Our modern system of mathematics comes directly from developments in mathematics in ancient Mesopotamia. Four thousand years ago Babylonians were using mul-

tiplication tables, square roots, reciprocals, linear and quadratic equations like those used in our modern system of mathematics. The Babylonians also developed a number system based upon sixty, which we still use today for telling time.

ASSESS

Answers to SECTION REVIEW

2. (a) basic units of Sumerian civilization
   (b) massive stepped tower under a Sumerian temple
   (c) government by divine authority
   (d) large political unit or state, usually under a single leader, that controls many peoples or territories
   (e) society that is dominated by men
   (f) having many gods
   (g) wedge-shaped system of writing

3. (a) creators of the first Mesopotamian civilization
   (b) a Semitic people who lived to the north of the Sumerian city-states
   (c) leader of the Akkadians
   (d) created a new Mesopotamian kingdom; called himself the sun of Babylon; remembered for his law code
   (e) collection of 282 laws based on a system of strict justice
   (f) famous epic poem about legendary King Gilgamesh

4. (a) a large-scale system of water control, including irrigation and drainage ditches
   (b) nobles, commoners, and slaves
   (c) The physical environment (floods, downpours, winds, humidity) plus famines

5. Answers will vary, but should consider that the city-states fought one another for control of land and water and were susceptible to invasion.

FOCUS

OBJECTIVES

After completing this section, students should be able to

1. explain the effect of geography upon Egyptian civilization
2. identify the differences between the Old, Middle, and New Kingdoms
3. describe various aspects of Egyptian daily life
4. describe the significance of writing and education upon Egyptian civilization

FOCUS ACTIVITY

Ask students to list three items or individuals they associate with ancient Egyptian civilization and the significance of each. (*pyramids, the Great Sphinx, mummies, camels, the Nile River, Cleopatra VII, and King Tut*) Discuss the importance of these items and people to Egyptian civilization and culture.

TEACH

Multimedia Support

TRANSPARENCY
2–1, Map of Lower and Upper Egypt
2–2, Egyptian Society

USING PRIMARY SOURCES

Ask students to reread the excerpt from *Hymn to the Nile* and write a brief comparison of this hymn to other songs of thanksgiving that they know. Discuss how they are similar and different.

and gives things to the poor. He who makes every beloved tree to grow."[3] Egypt, like Mesopotamia, was a river valley civilization.

The Importance of Geography

Egypt's geography molded the very character of its civilization. The Nile is a unique river, beginning in the heart of Africa and coursing northward for thousands of miles. It is the longest river in the world. In Egypt, on either side of the river, was an area several miles wide that was fertile and capable of producing abundant harvests. This fertile land was the product of the Nile's "miracle"—its yearly flooding. The river rose in the summer from heavy rains in central Africa, crested in Egypt in September and October, and left a deposit of mud that created an area of rich soil. The Egyptians called this fertile land, which was dark in color from the lush crops that grew on it, the "Black Land." Beyond these narrow strips of fertile fields lay the deserts, the "Red Land."

Unlike the floods of Mesopotamia's rivers, the flooding of the Nile was gradual and predictable. The river itself was seen as life giving, not life threatening. Although some organized irrigation was still necessary, the small villages along the Nile could make the effort without the massive state control that was needed in Mesopotamia. As a result, Egyptian civilization tended to remain more rural. Many small villages were gathered along a narrow band on both sides of the Nile. About one hundred miles from the Mediterranean, the river splits into two major branches before emptying into the sea. This split forms

Map 2.2   Ancient Egypt

the delta, a triangular territory that is called Lower Egypt to distinguish it from Upper Egypt, the land upstream to the south. Egypt's important cities developed at the tip of the delta, where the Nile splits into two branches. Even today, most of Egypt's 58.3 million people are crowded along the banks of the Nile River.

The Nile did more than allow Egyptian farmers to produce surpluses of food in the fertile Nile valley and

STUDYING MAPS

The following activity will help you guide students through their study of Map 2.2.

Ask students to calculate the distance between the first and second cataracts on the Nile River (*approximately 300 kms.*), the length of the delta (*160 kms.*) and its width at its widest point (*approximately 150 kms.*). To ensure that students understand how large this area is, ask them to plot their town in the middle of a hundred mile square. You might also wish to have students calculate the amount of arable land available to Egyptian farmers. In ancient times, how many people could have been supported by this amount of land? Using modern agricultural techniques, how much food might a farmer produce on this same amount of land?

thus make Egypt prosperous. The river also served as a unifying factor in Egyptian history. In ancient times, the Nile was the fastest way to travel through the land, making both transportation and communication easier. Winds from the north pushed sailboats south, and the current of the Nile carried them north. Often when they headed downstream (or north), people used long poles or paddles to move their boats forward.

Unlike Mesopotamia, which was subject to constant invasion, Egypt was blessed by natural barriers that gave it some protection from invasion and a sense of security. These barriers included the deserts to the west and east; the Red Sea to the east; the cataracts (rapids) on the southern part of the Nile, which made defense relatively easy; and the Mediterranean Sea to the north. These barriers, however, did not prevent the development of trade.

The regularity of the Nile floods and the relative isolation of the Egyptians created a feeling of security and changelessness. To the ancient Egyptians, when the Nile flooded each year, "the fields laugh and people's faces light up." Unlike people in Mesopotamia, Egyptians faced life with a spirit of confidence in the stability of things. Ancient Egyptian civilization was marked by a remarkable degree of continuity over thousands of years.

The Importance of Religion

Religion, too, provided a sense of security and timelessness for the Egyptians. Actually, they had no word for religion, because it was an inseparable part of the entire world order to which Egyptian society belonged. The Egyptians were polytheistic. They had a remarkable number of gods associated with heavenly bodies and natural forces. Two groups, sun gods and land gods, came to have special importance. Is that surprising in view of the importance to Egypt's well-being of the sun, the river, and the fertile land along its banks? The sun was the source of life, and thus worthy of worship. The sun god took on different forms and names, depending on his specific role. He was worshiped as Atum in human form and as Re, who had a human body but the head of a falcon. The Egyptian ruler took

the title of "Son of Re," because he was seen as an earthly form of Re.

River and land gods included Osiris (oh-SIE-rus) and Isis (I-sus) with their child Horus, who was related to the Nile and to the sun as well. Osiris became especially important as a symbol of resurrection or rebirth. A famous Egyptian myth told of the struggle between Osiris, who brought civilization to Egypt, and his evil brother Seth, who killed him, cut his body into fourteen parts, and tossed the parts into the Nile River. The pieces were found by Osiris's wife, Isis, who received help from other gods in bringing Osiris back to life. As a symbol of resurrection, Osiris took on an important role for the Egyptians. By identifying with Osiris, people could hope to gain new life, just as Osiris had done. The dead were placed in tombs (in the case of kings, in pyramid tombs); were given the name Osiris; and by a process of magical identification, became Osiris. Like Osiris, they would then be reborn. The flooding of the Nile and its new life for Egypt were symbolized by Isis's bringing all of Osiris's parts together each spring in the festival of the new land.

The Course of Egyptian History: The Old, Middle, and New Kingdoms

Modern historians have divided Egyptian history into three major periods, known as the Old Kingdom, Middle Kingdom, and New Kingdom. These were periods of long-term stability marked by strong leadership, freedom from invasion, the building of temples and pyramids, and considerable intellectual and cultural activity. Between the periods of stability were ages of political chaos and invasion, known as the Intermediate periods.

The history of Egypt begins around 3100 B.C., when King Menes (MEE-NEEZ) united the villages of both Upper (southern) and Lower (northern) Egypt into a single kingdom and created the first Egyptian royal dynasty. A **dynasty** is a family of rulers whose right to rule is passed on within the family. From then on, the Egyptian ruler would be called "King of Upper and Lower Egypt." The royal crown would be a double crown, indicating the unity of all Egypt. Just as the Nile served to unite Upper Egypt and Lower Egypt

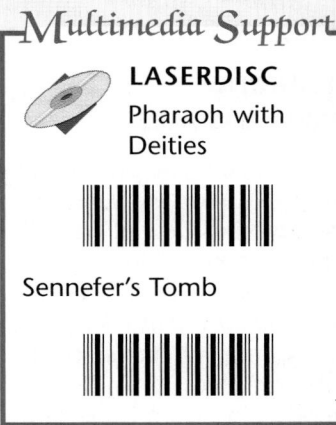
So What ??

USING PRIMARY SOURCES

Reread with the students the passage explaining the role of the king of Egypt. Ask students to review it carefully and write a similar explanation of the role of the president of the United States and another leader, perhaps a European monarch. When students have finished, compare and contrast the roles of the Egyptian kings and their modern counterparts.

LEARNING FROM VISUALS

What does the practice of mummification tell us about the Egyptian view of death? *(They respected both life and death, and the bodies were prepared for the afterlife.)* Today, researchers use computer graphics, CAT scans, bloodtyping from bone samples, and radiocarbon dating to provide information about genetic links and health patterns of ancient peoples.

ACROSS THE CURRICULUM

Science. Assign several students to research the efforts that are currently underway to protect the pyramids and the Great Sphinx from the ravages of pollution. Ask them to present their results to the class.

physically, kingship united the two areas politically.

The Old Kingdom

The Old Kingdom, which lasted from around 2700 to 2200 B.C., was an age of prosperity and splendor. These characteristics were made visible in the building of the greatest and largest pyramids in Egypt's history. Like the kings of the Sumerian city-states, the monarchs of the Old Kingdom were also very powerful rulers over a unified state.

Kingship was a divine institution in ancient Egypt and formed part of a universal cosmic order: "What is the king of Upper and Lower Egypt? He is a god by whose dealings one lives, the father and mother of all men, alone by himself, without an equal."[4] In obeying their king, subjects believed that they were helping to maintain a stable world order. A breakdown in royal power could only mean that citizens were offending the gods and weakening that order. Among the various titles of Egyptian kings, that of **pharaoh** (originally meaning "great house" or "palace"—that is, the royal palace) eventually became the most common.

Egyptian pharaohs possessed absolute power but had help in ruling. At first, members of the pharaoh's family aided the pharaoh in running the country. During the Old Kingdom, however, a government bureaucracy, or administrative organization with officials and regular procedures, developed. Especially important was the office of **vizier,** the "steward of the whole land." Directly responsible to the pharaoh, the vizier was in charge of the government bureaucracy. In time, Egypt was divided into forty-two provinces, which were run by governors appointed by the pharaoh. Each governor was responsible to the pharaoh and vizier.

▲ *The mummified body of Rameses II shows how the pharaohs were preserved and buried in pyramids upon their death.*

Gradually, governors began to build up large holdings of land and power within their provinces, which created problems at times for the pharaohs.

One of the great achievements of Egyptian civilization, the building of pyramids, occurred in the time of the Old Kingdom. In fact, the Old Kingdom is sometimes referred to as the Age of Pyramids. Pyramids were built as part of a larger complex of buildings dedicated to the dead—in effect, a city of the dead. The area included a large pyramid for the pharaoh's burial; smaller pyramids for his family; and several **mastabas,** or rectangular structures with flat roofs, which served as tombs for the pharaoh's noble officials.

The tombs were well prepared for their residents. They contained rooms stocked with supplies, including chairs, boats, chests, weapons, games, dishes, and a variety of food. The Egyptians believed that human beings had two bodies—a physical one and a spiritual one, which they called the *ka*. If the physical body was properly preserved and the tomb furnished with all the various objects of regular life, the *ka* could return. Surrounded by earthly comforts, the *ka* could then continue its life despite the death of the physical body.

To preserve the physical body after death, the Egyptians practiced **mummification,** a process of slowly drying a dead body to prevent it from rotting. This process took place in special workshops that were run by priests, primarily for the wealthy families who could afford it. Workers first removed the liver, lungs, stomach, and intestines and placed them in four special jars that were put in the tomb with the mummy. The priests also removed the brain by extracting it through the nose. They then covered the corpse with a natural salt that absorbed the body's water. Later, they filled the body

RECOMMENDED READING

A. Gardiner, *Egypt of the Pharaohs* (Oxford, 1961) is a good narrative of political and military events in ancient Egypt. Other general surveys include C. Hobson, *The World of the Pharaohs* (New York, 1987); and C. Aldred, *The Egyptians* (London, 1984). For an interesting introduction to Egyptian history, see B. J. Kemp, *Ancient Egypt* (London, 1989). A new approach is attempted in B. G. Trigger, B. J. Kemp, D. O'Connor, and A. B. Lloyd, *Ancient Egypt: A Social History* (Cambridge, 1983). On Akhenaten and his religious revolution, see C. Aldred, *Akhenaten, Pharaoh of Egypt: A New Study* (New York, 1968); and D. Redford, *Akhenaten; the Heretic King* (Princeton, N.J., 1984). Egyptian religion is covered in H. Frankfort, *Ancient Egyptian Religion* (New York, 1948), a brief but superb study; and J. Cerney, *Ancient Egyptian Religion* (New York, 1979).

with spices and wrapped it with layers of linen soaked in resin. At the end of the process, which had taken about seventy days, a lifelike mask was placed over the head and shoulders of the mummy. The mummy was then sealed in a case and placed in its tomb.

Pyramids were tombs for the mummified bodies of pharaohs. The first pyramid—the step pyramid at Saqqara (su-CARE-uh)—was built around 2650 B.C. The first real pyramid, in which each side was filled in to eliminate steps and make an even surface, was built about fifty years later. The largest and most magnificent of all the pyramids, however, was built under King Khufu (KOO-FOO).

Constructed at Giza (GEE-zuh) around 2540 B.C., the famous Great Pyramid of King Khufu covers 13 acres, measures 756 feet at each side of its base, and stands 481 feet high. Its four sides are almost precisely oriented to the four points of the compass. The building of the Great Pyramid was an enormous construction project that used limestone blocks as well as granite from Upper Egypt. The Greek historian Herodotus reported the traditional story that it took 100,000 Egyptians twenty years to build the Great Pyramid.

Herodotus wrote two thousand years after the event, however, and much speculation still surrounds the building of the Great Pyramid. Especially puzzling is how the builders achieved their amazing level of precision. The stone slabs on the outside of the Great Pyramid, for example, fit so closely side by side that even a hair cannot be pushed into the joints between them.

Guarding the Great Pyramid at Giza is a huge statue carved from rock, known as the Great Sphinx. This colossal statue is 240 feet long and 66 feet high. It has the body of a lion and a human head—believed by many to be a likeness of Khufu's son Khafre, who ordered the statue's construction. Historians do not agree on the purpose of the Great Sphinx. Many Egyptians, however, believed that the mythical sphinx was an important guardian of sacred sites.

The Great Pyramid still stands as a visible symbol of the power of the Egyptian pharaohs of the Old Kingdom. No pyramid built later ever matched its size or splendor. The pyramid was not only the pharaoh's tomb but also an important symbol of royal power. It could be seen for miles and served to remind people of the glory, might, and wealth of the ruler who was a living god on Earth.

▶ *The Great Pyramid at Giza is one of a number of pyramids built as repositories for the bodies of pharaohs. The body of the pharaoh would remain in the tomb to await reunification with its soul, or ka. How does the mummification process compare with embalming of bodies in our society?*

LEARNING FROM VISUALS

Answer to the caption question: Answers will vary but may include that the organs are not necessarily removed from bodies today, unless they are being donated; bodies today are not wrapped; embalming is not for the purpose of preventing the rotting process, but to slow down that process.

ACTIVITY

Divide the class into small groups and have each group prepare scaled drawings of the Great Pyramid, using the dimensions given in the text. Each group should also create a set of directions for the construction master to follow to build the pyramid. Ask groups to share their drawings and their instructions with the class.

COOPERATIVE LEARNING ACTIVITY

In this chapter, the students will learn about several civilizations. Divide the students into small groups and have each group research one of the civilizations (Minoans, Hittites, Phoenicians, Hebrews, Assyrians, and Persians). Each team should present either a hyperstudio or poster display of their civilization's time period, geography, major accomplishments and belief system. All students should be prepared to record the information from the other civilizations on a comparison chart. When this assignment is complete, the class should have a better understanding of the early civilizations and how they differed.

38

The Middle Kingdom

The Old Kingdom eventually collapsed, ushering in a period of chaos that lasted about 150 years. Finally, a new royal dynasty managed to gain control of all Egypt and began the Middle Kingdom, a new period of stability lasting from about 2050 to 1652 B.C. Egyptians later portrayed the Middle Kingdom as a golden age—an age of stability.

As evidence of its newfound strength, Egypt began a period of expansion. Lower Nubia, which was located south of Egypt, was conquered. Fortresses were built to protect the new southern frontier. The government also sent armies into Palestine and Syria, although they did not remain there. Pharaohs also sent traders to Kush, Syria, Mesopotamia, and Crete.

One feature of the Middle Kingdom was a new concern of the pharaohs for the people. In the Old Kingdom, the pharaoh had been seen as a god-king far removed from his people. Now he was portrayed as the shepherd of his people who must build public works and provide for the public welfare. Pharaohs of the Middle Kingdom undertook a number of helpful projects. The draining of swampland in the Nile delta provided thousands of acres of new farmland. The digging of a canal to connect the Nile to the Red Sea aided trade and transportation.

Chaos and a New Order: The New Kingdom

The Middle Kingdom came to an end around 1652 B.C. with the invasion of Egypt by a group of people from western Asia known to the Egyptians as the Hyksos. The Hyksos (HIK-sauce) used horse-drawn war chariots and overwhelmed the Egyptian soldiers, who fought from donkey carts. For almost a hundred years, the Hyksos ruled much of Egypt. The conquered took much from their conquerors. From the Hyksos, the Egyptians learned to use bronze in making new farming tools and weapons. They also mastered the military skills of the Hyksos, especially the use of horse-drawn war chariots.

Eventually, a new dynasty of pharaohs used the new weapons to drive out the Hyksos and reunite Egypt. The New Kingdom was established and lasted approximately from 1567 to 1085 B.C. This reunification also launched the Egyptians along a new militaristic path. During the period of the New Kingdom, Egypt created an empire and became the most powerful state in the Middle East.

Massive wealth boosted the power of the New Kingdom pharaohs. The Egyptian rulers showed their wealth by building new temples. In particular, Queen Hatshepsut—the first woman to become pharaoh—built a great temple at Deir el Bahri, near Thebes (see "Biography: Hatshepsut—The First Female Ruler in History").

Hatshepsut was succeeded by her nephew, Thutmose (thoot-MOE-suh) III. He led seventeen military campaigns into Syria and Palestine and even reached the Euphrates River. His forces occupied Palestine and Syria and moved westward into Libya (LIB-ee-uh) as well. Magnificent new buildings and temples were constructed to show the greatness of the empire.

The New Kingdom was not without troubles, however. Amenhotep IV introduced the worship of Aton, god of the sun disk, as the sole god. Amenhotep changed his own name to Akhenaten ("It is well with Aton") and closed the temples of other gods. In a society that had always been polytheistic and tolerant of many gods, Akhenaten's actions were viewed as a religious revolution. To many Egyptians, the destruction of the old gods meant the destruction of Egypt itself. Akhenaten's changes were soon undone after his death by the boy-pharaoh Tutankhamen, who restored the old gods.

The upheavals associated with Amenhotep's religious revolution led to a loss of Egypt's empire. Under Rameses (RAM-uh-seez) II, who reigned from 1279 to 1213 B.C., the Egyptians went back on the offensive. They regained control of Palestine but were unable to reestablish the borders of their earlier empire. Moreover, new invasions in the thirteenth century B.C. by the "Sea Peoples," as Egyptians called them, drove the Egyptians back within their old frontiers and ended the Egyptian empire. The New Kingdom itself collapsed in 1085 B.C.

For the next thousand years, Egypt was dominated by Libyans, Nubians, Persians, and finally Macedonians after the conquest of Alexander the Great (see Chapter 5). In the first century B.C., the pharaoh

MORE ABOUT . . . *the Building of the Pyramids*

The mystery of the pyramids has intrigued historians throughout the ages. Some archaeologists contend that, given the technology of the ancient Egyptians, they could not have moved the blocks required to build the Great Pyramids in one person's lifetime. One of the more intriguing theories about the building of the pyramids is that the giant blocks of stone were not carved at all, but rather were poured from a very sophisticated concrete-like, limestone substance. This would explain the amazing similarity among all of the blocks, their incredibly close fit, and would more realistically fit Herodotus' twenty-year timetable for the completion of the pyramids.

BIOGRAPHY

Hatshepsut—The First Female Ruler in History

In three thousand years of ancient Egyptian history, only four of Egypt's hundreds of rulers were women. The most famous and successful was Hatshepsut, who reigned from about 1473 to 1458 B.C.

Hatshepsut was the daughter of the pharaoh Thutmose I. In keeping with royal tradition, she married her half-brother, who became the pharaoh Thutmose II. When Hatshepsut's husband died, her stepson, Thutmose III, became the next ruler. Because he was only a boy, Hatshepsut ruled in his place (a position known as *regent*). She soon assumed the full power of pharaoh, however. Even when Thutmose III came of age, Hatshepsut continued to rule jointly with her stepson and to exercise the real power. Because pharaohs were almost always male, Hatshepsut in her official statues is shown clothed and bearded as a king would be. She was addressed as "His Majesty."

Hatshepsut's reign was a prosperous one, which is especially evident in her building activity. She is most famous for the temple dedicated to herself at Deir el Bahri on the west bank of the Nile at Thebes. As pharaoh, Hatshepsut sent out military expeditions, encouraged mining, fostered agriculture, and sent a trading expedition to Africa.

◄ *Queen Hatshepsut, one of only four female rulers in Egypt and the first woman pharaoh, was more interested in the welfare of her country than in wars and conquests. She ordered the construction of temples for worship and other public buildings. What famous women of today can you think of who have made an impact on our world?*

We do not know if Hatshepsut died naturally or was removed by force. When Thutmose III became the sole ruler, he reacted angrily against his stepmother by trying to erase her name from all the official records and shattering her stone portraits. Fortunately, the inscriptions Hatshepsut had placed on her temples remained, enabling us to know about the achievements of this remarkable woman. One of her inscriptions read: "Now my heart turns to and fro, in thinking what will the people say, they who shall see my monument in after years, and shall speak of what I have done."

1. Why is Hatshepsut famous?

2. Explain the role of a regent. What complications might arise when a regent actively governs?

3. What do Hatshepsut's words at the end of the selection reveal about her?

MORE ABOUT . . . *Women in Egypt*

Egyptian women probably had more legal, economic, and social equality than women in any other ancient civilization. In addition to business opportunities, Egyptian women could own and manage their own property, even after marriage. They were allowed to initiate lawsuits, engage in con-tracts, and free slaves. When an Egyptian woman's husband died, one-third of his property went to his wife (the other two-thirds being divided among the children). If a husband wished for his wife to receive more property he could legally adopt her so that she would receive a larger share.

Cleopatra VII tried to reestablish Egypt's independence. However, her involvement with Rome led to her suicide and defeat, and Egypt became a province in Rome's mighty empire.

Society and Daily Life in Ancient Egypt

Over a period of thousands of years, Egyptian society managed to maintain a simple structure. It was organized like a pyramid, with the god-king at the top. The pharaoh was surrounded by an upper class of nobles and priests, who joined in the elaborate rituals of the pharaoh's life. This ruling class ran the government and managed its own landed estates, which provided much of its wealth.

Below the upper class was a small class of merchants and artisans. Within Egypt, merchants engaged in an active trade up and down the Nile, as well as in town and village markets. Some merchants also engaged in international trade. They were sent by the pharaoh to Crete and Syria, where they obtained wood and other products. Egyptian artisans made an incredible variety of well-built, beautiful goods: stone dishes; painted boxes made of clay; wooden furniture; gold, silver, and copper tools and containers; paper and rope made of papyrus; and linen clothes.

By far, the largest number of people in Egypt simply worked the land. In theory, the pharaoh owned all the land but granted portions of it to the subjects. Large sections of land were held by nobles and by the priests who supervised the numerous temples. Most of the lower classes were peasants who farmed the land of the estates. They paid taxes in the form of crops to the pharaoh, nobles, and priests; lived in small villages or towns; and provided military service and forced labor for building projects.

Ancient Egyptians had a very positive attitude toward daily life on Earth. They married young (girls at twelve and boys at fourteen) and established a home and family. Monogamy (marriage to one person) was the general rule, although a husband was allowed to keep additional wives if his first wife was childless. Because of their exalted position, pharaohs were entitled to harems. The queen was acknowledged, however, as the Great Wife with a status higher than that of the other wives. The husband was master in the house, but wives were very well respected. They were in charge of the household and the education of the children. From a book of wise sayings (which the Egyptians called "instructions") came this advice: "If you are a man of standing, you should love your wife at home as is fitting. Fill her belly; clothe her back. . . . Make her heart glad as long as you live"[5] (see "You Are There: An Egyptian Father's Advice to His Son").

Although Egypt was a male-dominated society, Egyptian women, unlike Mesopotamian women, had equal legal rights with men in many areas. A woman's property and inheritance stayed in her hands, even in marriage. Although most careers and public offices were closed to women, some did operate businesses. Peasant women worked long hours in the fields and at numerous tasks in the home. Upper-class women could become priestesses, and four queens even became pharaohs.

Parents arranged marriages for their children. Their chief concerns were family and property. Clearly, the chief purpose of marriage was to produce children, especially sons. Only sons could carry on the family name. Daughters were not ignored, however, and numerous tomb paintings show the close and affectionate relationship parents had with both sons and daughters. Although marriages were arranged, the surviving love poems from ancient Egypt suggest that some marriages included an element of romance. In one poem, a lovesick boy laments for his "sister." Lovers referred to each other as "brother" and "sister." However, the practice of brother-sister marriage in the Egyptian royal family probably reached down into the general population as well, so the meaning of *sister* here is unclear:

> Seven days to yesterday I have not seen the sister,
>   and a sickness has invaded me;
> My body has become heavy,
>   And I am forgetful of my own self.
> If the chief physicians come to me,
>   My heart is not content with their remedies. . . .
> What will revive me is to say to me: "Here she is!"
>   Her name is what will lift me up. . . .
> My health is her coming in from outside:
>   When I see her, then I am well.[6]

MORE ABOUT . . . *Recreation*

Recreation, and the need for it, is universal. Like people of all times and places, the ancient Egyptians engaged in different forms of recreation. They had several different types of board games, a variation on the game of darts, and archaeologists have unearthed dice over four thousand years old.

In addition, the Egyptians had many different toys, including simple mechanical devices, such as a snapping crocodile, a baker who kneads dough when a string is pulled, and wooden dolls with movable limbs.

YOU ARE THERE

An Egyptian Father's Advice to His Son

Upper-class Egyptians enjoyed compiling collections of wise sayings to provide guidance for leading an upright and successful life. This excerpt is taken from The Instruction of the Vizier Ptah-hotep *and dates from around 2450 B.C. The vizier was the pharaoh's chief official. In this selection, Ptah-hotep advises his son on how to be a successful official.*

▲ *This rendition of an Egyptian father teaching his son is on the wall of the Tomb of Sennedjem.*

The Instruction of the Vizier Ptah-hotep

Then he said to his son:

If you are a leader commanding the affairs of the many, seek out for yourself every good deed, until it may be that your own affairs are without wrong. Justice is great, and it is lasting; it has been disturbed since the time of him who made it, whereas there is punishment for him who passes over its laws. It is the right path before him who knows nothing. Wrongdoing has never brought its undertaking into port. It may be that it is fraud that gains riches, but the strength of justice is that it lasts. . . .

If you are a man of standing and found a household and produce a son who is pleasing to god, if he is correct and inclines toward your ways and listens to your instruction, while his manners in your house are fitting, and if he takes care of your property as it should be, seek out for him every useful action. He is your son, . . . you should not cut your heart off from him.

But a man's seed [his son] often creates hatred. If he goes astray and does not carry out your instruction, so that his manners in your household are wretched, and he rebels against all that you say, while his mouth runs on in the most wretched talk, quite apart from his experience, while he possesses nothing, you should cast him off: he is not your son at all. He was not really born to you. . . . He is one whom god has condemned in the very womb.

---

1. According to Ptah-hotep, upon what things does a successful father-son relationship depend?

2. Restate "Wrongdoing has never brought its undertaking into port" in your own words. What does it mean? Do you agree?

3. Does any part of the father's advice have value today for sons or daughters? Be specific and support your answer.

ASSESS

Answers to
SECTION REVIEW

2. (a) right to rule is passed on within the family, (b) title of Egyptian kings, (c) "steward of the whole land", (d) rectangular structures with flat roofs, which served as tombs, (e) a process of slowly drying a dead body, (f) Egyptian writing, (g) script used for business transactions, record keeping, and daily life in Egypt, (h) a paper made from the papyrus reed, (i) masters of the art of writing

3. (a) sun god in human form, (b) god with a human body, but the head of a falcon, (c) god who symbolized rebirth, credited with bringing civilization to Egypt, (d) united Upper and Lower Egypt, created first royal dynasty, (e) statue, guards Great Pyramid, (f) people who conquered Egypt around 1652 B.C., (g) the first woman pharaoh, (h) adopted name of Amenhotep IV, who introduced Aton as the sole god of the New Kingdom, (i) the boy-pharaoh who restored Egypt's old gods, (j) pharaoh who regained control of Palestine, (k) unable to reestablish Egypt's independence

Marriages could and did end in divorce. Divorce was allowed, and it included compensation for the wife.

Writing and Education

Writing in Egypt emerged around 3000 B.C., when Egyptian priests developed a system to preserve records of religious rituals. The Greeks later called Egyptian writing **hieroglyphics,** meaning "priest-carvings" or "sacred writings." Hieroglyphics included three elements: drawings that depicted objects or beings, a combination of these drawings to express ideas, and a system of forms to represent sounds. Because drawing hieroglyphs (characters in hieroglyphic script) took much time and skill, another script, known as **hieratic** script, came into being. It used the same principles as hieroglyphic writing, but the drawings were simplified by using dashes, strokes, and curves to represent them. Hieroglyphic script was used for writing on temple walls and in tombs. Hieratic script was used for business transactions, record keeping, and the general needs of daily life.

Egyptian hieroglyphs were at first carved in stone, but later the hieratic script was written on **papyrus,** a paper made from the papyrus reed that grew along the Nile. Papyrus was expensive, however, so limestone and pieces of pottery were used for ordinary writing. Most of the ancient Egyptian literature that has come down to us was written on papyrus rolls.

The Egyptian **scribes** were masters of the art of writing and also its teachers. At the age of ten, boys of the upper classes went to schools run by scribes. Students learned to read and write by copying texts. Discipline was strict, as is evident from the following Egyptian saying: "A boy's ears are on his back. He listens only when he is beaten." Girls remained at home and learned housekeeping skills from their mothers.

▲ *Hieroglyphics was the Egyptian writing form used to express objects, ideas, and sounds. The Egyptians became skilled at using this means of communicating on many varied surface types. Do you think it would be easier to learn the Egyptian form for written communication or the one you use today? Explain.*

❀ SECTION REVIEW ❀

1. **Locate:**
   (a) Nile River,   (b) Egypt,   (c) Giza

2. **Define:**
   (a) dynasty,   (b) pharaoh,   (c) vizier,
   (d) mastabas,   (e) mummification,
   (f) hieroglyphics,   (g) hieratic,   (h) papyrus,
   (i) scribes

3. **Identify:**
   (a) Atum,   (b) Re,   (c) Osiris,   (d) King Menes,
   (e) Great Sphinx,   (f) Hyksos,   (g) Queen
   Hatshepsut,   (h) Akhenaten,   (i) Tutankhamen,
   (j) Rameses II,   (k) Cleopatra VII

4. **Recall:**
   (a) What was the "Black Land"? Why was this land important?

MORE ABOUT . . . *Egyptian Medicine*

The Egyptians have been long renowned for their medical skills. They were one of the first civilizations to record instructions for preparing medicines and prescriptions. One recommendation for a childhood ailment involved swallowing a skinned mouse (several child mummies contain mice in their alimentary tracts). In ancient Egypt the Eye of Horus was the symbol of medicine. By the Middle Ages a "doctor of Egypt" was still respected but the symbol changed ♃. Today the Eye of Horus, in its altered form ℞, is what we look for when seeking out a pharmacy.

(*b*) Give the approximate beginning and ending dates for each of the three Kingdoms of Egyptian history.

(*c*) Why were the pyramids built?

5. **Think Critically:** In what ways were the customs of ancient Egypt similar to the customs in your society today?

NEW CENTERS OF CIVILIZATION

Our story of civilization so far has focused on Mesopotamia and Egypt. These two civilizations, based on cities and settled farming, had at times expanded beyond their own frontiers and made contact with each other before 1500 B.C. By that time, new centers of civilization had also begun to appear in the eastern Mediterranean region. One of them—Minoan Crete—was influenced by Egyptian civilization.

The Minoan Civilization

An English archaeologist, Arthur Evans, first discovered the civilization of Minoan Crete. He named it Minoan after Minos, the legendary king of Crete. At the beginning of the twentieth century, Evans discovered an enormous palace complex on Crete at Knossus (ku-NOSS-us). The remains revealed a rich culture, with Knossus as the center of a far-ranging sea empire based on trade. The ships of the Minoans took them to Egypt as well as southern Greece in search of goods. Egyptian products have been found in Crete and products from Crete, in Egypt.

The Minoan civilization reached its height between 2000 and 1450 B.C. The palace at Knossus, the royal

▼ *Minoan bull games were held on festival days in the great palaces on the island of Crete. Women and men acrobats would somersault over the back of the bull into the arms of another person who waited behind the bull to catch the leapers.*

ENRICHMENT ACTIVITY

Using plaster of paris wrap and newspapers (or dolls of action figures) have students create a mummy. Then have students decorate shoe boxes in the appropriate Egyptian fashion as sarcophaguses. Students should identify their mummy as a specific Egyptian pharaoh and present a short biography of his or her life, complete with a cartouch of his or her name.

---

4. (a) the fertile soil on either side of the Nile; lush crops grew and enabled Egyptian civilization to remain more rural

(b) Old: 2700 B.C.–2200 B.C.; Middle: 2050 B.C.–1652 B.C.; New: 1567 B.C.–1085 B.C.

(c) as tombs for pharaohs and their families

5. Answers will vary.

FOCUS

OBJECTIVES

After completing this section students should be able to

1. explain why historians have few records of the Minoan civilization
2. identify the importance of nomadic peoples
3. list the major cultural contributions of the Phoenicians
4. name special aspects of Hebrew religious traditions.

TEACH

LEARNING FROM VISUALS

Have students examine carefully the fresco of the acrobats and bull and list five assumptions that could be made about Minoan civilization based on this art.

CRITICAL THINKING

Language is generally considered a unifying trait of a particular culture. Have students compile a list, with justifications, of other traits that unify a culture. (*Language is not the only unifying characteristic of a country or culture; for example, in Switzerland, people speak three languages, in Canada, two.*)

ACROSS THE CURRICULUM

Journalism. Have students reread the paragraph about the collapse of the Minoan civilization. Then have them write a first page newspaper feature chronicling the invasion and pillage of Knossos. Have half the class write their articles from the viewpoint of the Minoans; the other half write from the viewpoint of the successful invaders.

seat of the kings, was an elaborate building that included numerous private living rooms for the royal family and workshops for making decorated vases, ivory figurines, and jewelry. Even bathrooms, with elaborate drains, formed part of the complex. The rooms were decorated with brightly colored paintings showing sporting events and nature scenes. Storerooms in the palace held gigantic jars of oil, wine, and grain, items that were paid as taxes to the king.

The centers of Minoan civilization on Crete suffered a sudden and catastrophic collapse around 1450 B.C. The cause of this destruction has been hotly debated. Some historians believe that a tidal wave triggered by a powerful volcanic eruption on the island of Thera (THIR-uh) was responsible for the devastation. Most historians, however, believe that it was the result of invasion and pillage by Indo-European peoples, one of the groups of nomadic peoples that had continued to plague the centers of civilization for centuries.

The Role of Nomadic Peoples

On the fringes of civilization lived nomadic peoples who depended on hunting and gathering, herding, and sometimes a bit of farming for their survival. Most important were the pastoral nomads who on occasion overran settled communities and created their own empires. Pastoral nomads domesticated animals for both food and clothing. They moved along regular migratory routes to provide steady sources of nourishment for their animals.

People who lived in settled communities often viewed nomadic peoples as hostile and barbaric or uncivilized. The two types of groups did interact, however. Nomads traded animals and animal products for grains and vegetables they were unable to grow. Pastoral nomads also aided long-distance trade by carrying products between civilized centers. In this way, nomads often passed on new technological developments, such as the use of bronze and iron, that provided new sources of strength to the old civilizations. However, when the normal patterns of the pastoral nomads were disrupted by drought or overpopulation, they often attacked the civilized communities to obtain relief.

The Indo-Europeans were one of the most important nomadic peoples. *Indo-European* refers to the group of people who used a language derived from a single parent tongue. Indo-European languages include Greek, Latin, Persian, Sanskrit, and the Germanic languages (see the accompanying table). The original Indo-European–speaking peoples were probably based either somewhere in the steppe region north of the Black Sea or in southwestern Asia (in modern Iran or Afghanistan). Around 2000 B.C. they began to move into Europe (including present-day Italy and Greece), India, and western Asia. One group of Indo-Europeans moved into Asia Minor and Anatolia (modern Turkey) around 1750 B.C. and combined with the native peoples to form the Hittite kingdom with its capital at Hattusha (Bogazköy in modern Turkey).

Between 1600 and 1200 B.C., the Hittites created their own empire in western Asia and even threatened the power of the Egyptians. The Hittites were the first of the Indo-European peoples to make use of iron. This technology enabled them to use weapons that were stronger and cheaper to make because of the widespread availability of iron ore. Around 1200 B.C., however, new waves of invaders known to historians only as the "Sea Peoples" destroyed the Hittite Empire. The

Some Indo-European Languages (Languages in italic are no longer spoken.)	
Subfamily	**Languages**
Indo-Iranian	*Sanskrit*, Persian
Balto-Slavic	Russian, Ukranian, Serbo-Croatian, Czech, Polish, Lithuanian
Hellenic	Greek
Latin-Romance	*Latin*; Romance languages (French, Italian, Spanish, Portuguese, Romanian)
Celtic	Irish, Gaelic
Germanic	Swedish, Danish, Norwegian, German, Dutch, English

ENRICHMENT ACTIVITY

Review the table of languages with students and ask them to identify the languages spoken by their ancestors. You might also assign students to identify and chart the writing/alphabets of those languages that do not use the Phoenician alphabet. This activity could be assigned to be either a written or oral report. It could also be used as an optional extra credit assignment.

end of the Hittite kingdom and the weakening of Egypt around 1200 B.C. temporarily left no dominant powers in western Asia. This allowed a number of small kingdoms and city-states to emerge, especially in the area of Syria and Palestine. The Phoenicians were one of these peoples.

The Phoenicians

The Phoenicians lived in the area of Palestine along the Mediterranean coast on a narrow band of land 120 miles long. Their newfound political independence, which resulted from the downfall of Hittite and Egyptian power, helped the Phoenicians expand the trade that was already the basis of their prosperity. The chief cities of Phoenicia—Byblos, Tyre, and Sidon—were ports on the eastern Mediterranean. The Phoenicians produced a number of goods for foreign markets, including purple dye, glass, and lumber from the cedar forests of Lebanon. The Phoenicians improved their ships, became great international sea traders, and thus created a trade empire. They charted new routes, not only in the Mediterranean but also in the Atlantic Ocean, where they reached Britain and sailed south along the west coast of Africa. The Phoenicians set up a number of colonies in the western Mediterranean. Carthage, their most famous colony, was located on the North African coast.

The Phoenician culture is best known for its alphabet. The Phoenicians simplified their writing by using twenty-two different signs to represent the sounds of their speech. These twenty-two characters, or letters, could be used to spell out all the words in the Phoenician language. Although the Phoenicians were not the only people to invent an alphabet, theirs was important because it was eventually passed on to the Greeks. From the Greek alphabet was derived the Roman alphabet that Americans still use today.

The Hebrews

To the south of the Phoenicians lived a group of people known as the Hebrews. Although they were a minor factor in the politics of the region, their religion—known today as Judaism (JU-de-iz-um)—flour-

Map 2.3   Ancient Palestine

A map of ancient Palestine showing the Mediterranean Sea, Cyprus, Syria, cities including Byblos, Sidon, Tyre, Damascus, Samaria, Jerusalem, and features such as the Euphrates R., Jordan R., Dead Sea, Nile R., Sinai, Mt. Sinai, Egypt, and the Red Sea. Legend: Philistines, Kingdom of Judah, Kingdom of Israel, Phoenicians. Scale: 0 100 200 300 Kilometers / 0 100 200 Miles.

ished as a world religion and influenced the later religions of Christianity and Islam. The spiritual heritage of the Hebrews is one of the basic pillars of Western civilization.

The History of the Hebrews

The Hebrews wrote down their history as part of the Hebrew Bible, known to Christians as the Old Testament. According to their own tradition, the Hebrews were descendants of the patriarch Abraham, who had migrated from Mesopotamia to the land of Palestine.

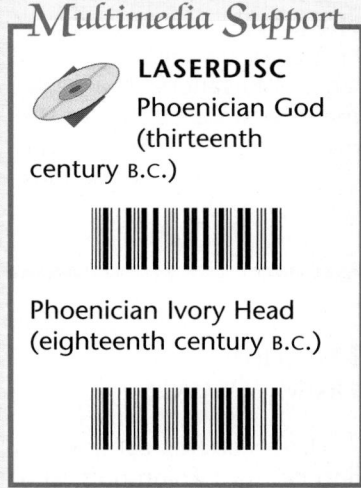
STUDYING MAPS

The following activities will help to guide your students through their study of Map 2.3.

Ask students to examine the maps of the Nile River and the Mediterranean Sea to estimate the distance between Cairo and Jerusalem and Sidon. *(Cairo to Jerusalem, approximately 350 kms; Cairo to Sidon,* *approximately 550 kms; Sidon to Jerusalem, approximately 200 kms)*. Have students estimate how long the journeys between these cities might have taken by boat and by land. *(Students' answers will vary based on their personal opinions.)*

CONNECTIONS
TO OUR WORLD

OPPOSING VIEWPOINTS

Both Palestinian Arabs and Jews have historical claims to the lands of Palestine. You might wish to guide students in a discussion or debate about the Israeli and Arab claims to the lands, their legal justifications, the treatment of Arabs by the Israeli government, and the actions of the PLO and Arab nations toward Israel.

LEARNING FROM VISUALS

Have students compare and contrast Solomon's temple with the ziggurat pictured in Chapter 1 and the pyramids shown earlier in this chapter. How are they similar and different?

Answer to the caption question: Answers will vary but may include that religious practice was the focal point of the Hebrew people's way of life; therefore, the Temple was very important. Much of their history is surrounded by conflicts due, in part, to their desire to worship God.

CONNECTIONS
TO OUR WORLD

Conflict in Palestine   In 1948, an independent Jewish state known as Israel was established in an area known as Palestine. The Arab neighbors of the new state were outraged, because 90 percent of the people in Palestine were Arab Muslims. An invasion of the new state of Israel by its Arab neighbors failed. However, conflict between Arabs and Israelis over Palestine continues to this day. In 1964, an Arab organization called the Palestine Liberation Organization was founded. Its goal is to bring about an independent Arab state of Palestine.

Conflict between Jews and other peoples in Palestine has a very long history. When the Hebrews entered Palestine around 1220 B.C., after their enslavement in Egypt, they found other peoples who were already settled there. One of these peoples was the Philistines (FIL-eh-steenz). For over two centuries, Hebrews and Philistines fought over control of much of Palestine.

This struggle made a strong impact on the Hebrews. By 1020 B.C., after a series of defeats, the Hebrews found themselves on the verge of being conquered by the Philistines. In desperation, the Hebrews decided to form a solid united front by giving up their loose tribal organization and choosing one of their members—Saul—as king. At first, Saul was very successful. He organized a small army and went on the offensive against the Philistines. Around 1000 B.C., however, Saul and his army experienced disaster when they dared to meet the Philistines on an open plain. The army was disastrously defeated, Saul's sons were killed, and Saul committed suicide. David, the next king of the Hebrews, was more successful. During his reign, the Hebrews defeated the Philistines and established control over all of Palestine. Although later the Hebrews were conquered and scattered by the Assyrians, Persians, and Romans, for centuries Palestine remained the Promised Land in the minds of many Jews.

▲ *Solomon's temple, as seen in this artist's rendering, dominated the walled city of ancient Jerusalem. The temple is said to be one of Solomon's greatest accomplishments during his reign. Why was the temple given such a prominent location in the city and why was it such an important part of the Hebrew lifestyle?*

The Hebrews were a nomadic people organized in tribes. They followed a lifestyle based on grazing flocks and herds rather than on farming. According to tradition, because of drought, the Hebrews migrated to Egypt, where they were enslaved until Moses led his people out of Egypt, probably in the first half of the thirteenth century B.C. The Hebrews then wandered for many years in the desert until they entered Palestine (possibly around 1220 B.C.). They became involved in a lengthy conflict with the people who were already settled there. Around 1000 B.C., under the pressure of this ongoing struggle, the Hebrews established a monarchy.

The creation of the monarchy was not easy. However, by the time of King Solomon, who ruled from about 971 to 931 B.C., the Hebrews had established control over all of Palestine and had made Jerusalem into the capital of a united kingdom, known as Israel. Solomon did even more to strengthen royal power. He expanded the government and army and encouraged trade. Solomon is best known for his building projects, of which the most famous was a temple in the city of Jerusalem. The Hebrews viewed the temple as the sym-

On Line with WORLD HISTORY *Internet Activity*

You may want to have your students visit the following URL, where they will find information and additional web site resources to enhance their study of this chapter.

Exploring Ancient World Civilizations—Ancient Egypt

http://eawc.evansville.edu./eqpage.htm

An excellent source for information and links on Egyptian history. Includes chronology, essays, resources and www sites.

Due to the ever-changing nature of the World Wide Web, see the West History web site, **http://history.swpco.com** for regular updates of the URLs in this text.

bolic center of their religion and of the Hebrew kingdom itself. Under Solomon, ancient Israel was at the height of its power.

After Solomon's death, tension between the northern and southern Hebrew tribes led to the creation of two separate kingdoms. The Kingdom of Israel was composed of the ten northern tribes and had its capital at Samaria. The southern Kingdom of Judah consisted of two tribes and had its capital at Jerusalem. In 722 B.C., the Assyrians overran the Kingdom of Israel and sent many Hebrews to other parts of the Assyrian Empire (see "The Assryian Empire" later in the chapter). These scattered Hebrews (the "ten lost tribes") merged with neighboring peoples and gradually lost their identity.

The southern Kingdom of Judah managed to retain its independence for a while, but a new enemy soon appeared on the horizon. The Chaldeans (kal-DEE-unz) defeated Assyria, conquered the Kingdom of Judah, and completely destroyed Jerusalem in 586 B.C. Many upper-class Hebrews were sent as captives to Babylonia. The memory of their exile is still evoked in the words of Psalms 137:

> By the rivers of Babylon, we sat and wept when we
>   remembered Zion. . . .
> How can we sing the songs of the Lord while in a for-
>   eign land?
> If I forget you, O Jerusalem, may my right hand forget
>   its skill.
> May my tongue cling to the roof of my mouth if I do
>   not remember you, if I do not consider Jerusalem
>   my highest joy.[7]

The Babylonian captivity of the Hebrew people did not last. A new set of conquerors, the Persians, destroyed the Chaldean kingdom and allowed the Hebrews to return to Jerusalem and rebuild their city and temple. The revived Kingdom of Judah remained under Persian control until the conquests of Alexander the Great in the fourth century B.C. The people of Judah survived, eventually becoming known as the Jews and giving their name to Judaism, the religion of Yahweh (YAW-WAY), the Jewish God. The Babylonian captivity had changed Judaism. It became a stateless religion based on the belief that God was not fixed to one particular land but instead was Creator and Lord of the whole world.

The Spiritual Dimensions of the Hebrews

According to the Hebrews, there was only one God, called Yahweh, who was the creator of the world and everything in it. God ruled the world; all peoples, whether they knew it or not, were his servants. Moreover, God had created nature but was not in nature. The stars, moon, rivers, wind, and other natural phenomena were not gods, as other ancient peoples believed, but God's handiwork. All of God's creations could be admired for their awesome beauty, but not worshipped as gods.

This powerful creator of the universe, however, was not removed from the life he had created. God was just and good, and he expected goodness from his people. If they did not obey his will, they would be punished. But he was also a God of mercy and love: "The Lord is gracious and compassionate, slow to anger and rich in love. The Lord is good to all; he has compassion on all he has made."[8] Each person could have a personal relationship with this powerful being.

The covenant, law, and prophets were three special aspects of the Hebrew religious tradition. The Hebrews believed that during the exodus from Egypt, when Moses led his people out of bondage into the promised land, a special event occurred. God made a **covenant,** or contract, with the tribes of Israel. The Hebrews promised to obey Yahweh and follow his law. In return, Yahweh promised to take special care of his chosen people, "a peculiar treasure unto me above all people."

This covenant between Yahweh and his chosen people could be fulfilled, however, only by Hebrew obedience to the law of God. Most important were the moral concerns that stood at the center of the law. These commandments spelled out God's ideals of behavior: "You shall not murder. You shall not commit adultery. You shall not steal."[9] God gave the Hebrews true freedom to follow his moral standards voluntarily. If people chose to ignore the good, then suffering and evil would follow.

The Hebrews believed that certain religious teachers, called **prophets,** were sent by God to serve as his

---

Multimedia Support

LASERDISC
Solomon's Temple

[barcode]

CLASS DISCUSSION

Have students compare the three commandments God gave the Jewish people that are listed on page 47 with the laws from Hammurabi's Code of Justice on page 29. In what ways are they similar? In what ways are they different?

REINFORCING VOCABULARY

Some students may not know that Psalms is a book of the Bible composed of poems. They may be unfamiliar with the term *Zion*. Zion is the stronghold in Jerusalem that was captured by David and has become synonymous with Jerusalem and Israel.

So What ??

*If your students question the importance of the information on the **ancient Middle East,** tell them . . .*

Many of the customs and beliefs we have today have filtered into our lives from early civilizations. This is true of our religious heritage. For instance, nearly half of the people on the planet profess a belief in a religious philosophy that had its origins in the Middle East over 5,000 years ago. Judaism, Christianity, and Islam can all trace the beginnings of their religions back to the ancient Hebrews of the Fertile Crescent.

LEARNING FROM VISUALS

Answer to the caption question: Answers will vary but may include the cross for Christianity, the crucifix for Catholicism, the Star of David for Judaism, etc.

Answers to Critical Thinking Questions

1. The elders and leaders ruined the Lord's vineyard, stole from the poor, and crushed His people. The women were haughty and proud.
2. The proud women would lose their beauty and their ornaments; the men would be killed in battle. God wanted a humble and respectful people who cared for the poor.

COMPARING TIME PERIODS

You might wish to invite a parent or knowledgeable student to discuss the significance of each of the items shown in the mosaic and their associated holidays. The menorah, shofar, and grogger are still used today.

CLASS DISCUSSION

Jewish rulers did not claim divine right nor did they ever claim to be descended from God. In what ways did this make their kingdoms and the power of their rulers different from civilizations that believed their rulers to be divine?

OUR LITERARY HERITAGE
The Words of the Prophets

The Hebrew prophets warned the Hebrew people that they must obey God's commandments or face being punished for breaking their covenant with God. These selections from the prophets Isaiah (eye-ZAY-uh) and Amos make clear their belief that God's punishment would fall upon the Hebrews for their sins.

Isaiah 3:14–17, 24–26

The Lord enters into judgment against the elders and leaders of his people: "It is you who have ruined my vineyard; the plunder from the poor is in your houses. What do you mean by crushing my people and grinding the faces of the poor?" declares the Lord, the Lord Almighty. The Lord says, "The women of Zion are haughty, walking along with outstretched necks, flirting with their eyes, tripping along with mincing steps, with ornaments jingling on their ankles. Therefore the Lord will bring sores on the heads of the women of Zion; the Lord will make their scalps bald. . . ." Instead of fragrance there will be a stench; instead of a sash, a rope; instead of well-dressed hair, baldness; instead of fine clothing, sackcloth; instead of beauty, branding. Your men will fall by the sword, your warriors in battle. The gates of Zion will lament and mourn; destitute, she will sit on the ground.

Amos 3:1–2

Hear this word the Lord has spoken against you, O people of Israel—against the whole family I brought you up out of Egypt: "You only have I chosen of all the families of the earth; therefore I will punish you for all your sins."

▲ *The Ark of the Covenant, as depicted in this mosaic, was in Solomon's Temple before it was destroyed and played an important role in Jewish worship. What other symbols do you know of that are important in different religions?*

1. What did Isaiah say were the sins of the Hebrew people?
2. Relate the punishments prophesied by Isaiah to the errors of the people. What kind of people did God desire the Hebrews to be?

COOPERATIVE LEARNING ACTIVITY

Have students work in groups to make lists of the pros and cons of both the Hammurabi system of justice and the Hebrew Ten Commandments. Bring in a newspaper and select a story for the students to analyze. Ask the students to evaluate how the story would be different if either Hammurabi's Code or the Ten Commandments were applied. Have a spokesperson from each group share their group's conclusions with the class.

voice to his people (see "Our Literary Heritage: The Words of the Prophets"). The golden age of prophecy began in the mid-eighth century B.C. and continued during the time when the Hebrews were threatened by Assyrian conquerors. The "men of God," or prophets, went through the land warning the Hebrews that they had failed to keep God's commandments and would be punished for breaking the covenant: "I will punish you for all your iniquities." Amos prophesied the fall of the northern Kingdom of Israel to Assyria. Twenty years later Isaiah said the Kingdom of Judah too would fall.

Out of the words of the prophets came new concepts that enriched the Hebrew tradition. The prophets embraced a concern for all humanity. All nations would someday come to the God of Israel: "all the earth shall worship thee." This vision included the end of war and the establishment of peace for all the nations of the world. In the words of the prophet Isaiah: "He will judge between the nations and will settle disputes for many people. They will beat their swords into plowshares and their spears into pruning hooks. Nation will not take up sword against nation, nor will they train for war anymore."[10]

The prophets also cried out against social injustice. They condemned the rich for causing the poor to suffer. They denounced luxuries as worthless, and they threatened Israel with prophecies of dire punishments for these sins. They said that God's command was to live justly, share with one's neighbors, care for the poor and the unfortunate, and act with compassion. When God's command was not followed, according to the prophets, the community was threatened. These words of the Hebrew prophets became a source for universal ideals of social justice.

The Hebrew religion was unique among the religions of western Asia and Egypt. The most dramatic difference was the Hebrews' belief that there is only one God for all peoples **(monotheism).** Furthermore, in virtually every religion in ancient Mesopotamia and Egypt, only priests (and occasionally rulers) had access to the gods and their desires. In the Hebrew tradition, God's wishes, though communicated to the people through a series of prophets, had all been written down. No Jewish spiritual leader could claim that he

alone knew God's will. This knowledge was open to anyone who could read Hebrew.

Moreover, the demands of the Hebrew religion (the need to obey God) encouraged a separation between Jews and their non-Jewish neighbors. Unlike most other peoples of the Middle East up to that time, Jews would not accept the gods of their conquerors or neighbors and be made part of a community. To remain faithful to the demands of their God, they might even have to refuse loyalty to political leaders. These religious convictions frequently created serious conflicts for Jews.

 SECTION REVIEW

1. **Locate:**
   (*a*) Crete,   (*b*) Palestine,   (*c*) Byblos,   (*d*) Tyre,
   (*e*) Sidon,   (*f*) Jerusalem

2. **Define:**
   (*a*) covenant,   (*b*) prophets,   (*c*) monotheism

3. **Identify:**
   (*a*) Minos,   (*b*) Indo-Europeans,   (*c*) Hittites,
   (*d*) Phoenicians,   (*e*) Hebrews,   (*f*) King
   Solomon,   (*g*) Yahweh,   (*h*) Isaiah

4. **Recall:**
   (*a*) Which civililzation—Egypt or Mesopotamia—
   influenced the development of Minoan civilization?
   (*b*) What is the most popular theory for explaining
   the sudden and catastrophic collapse of Minoan
   civilization?
   (*c*) Who were the first Indo-Europeans to make
   use of iron? In what way was the use of iron
   advantageous to this group of people?
   (*d*) What was the most significant cultural invention of the Phoenicians?
   (*e*) What aspect of the Hebrew culture most
   greatly impacted Western civilization?
   (*f*) Identify the three special aspects of the
   Hebrew religious tradition.

5. **Think Critically:** Explain how nomadic people
   both contributed to and harmed the development
   of civilization.

COOPERATIVE LEARNING ACTIVITY

Have students compare the erratic and sometimes violent flooding of the Tigris and Euphrates rivers, with the more gentle and predictable flooding of the Nile. You may want to have students refer to Maps 2.1 and 2.2 in this chapter, to refamiliarize them with the location of these river valleys. Ask the students how the differences in those two river valleys might account for the stability of their governments and in the different outlooks of their two systems of religious belief.

FOCUS

OBJECTIVES

After completing this section, students should be able to

1. list the contributions made by the Assyrians
2. describe the significance of the Persian Empire

FOCUS ACTIVITY

Guide students in a discussion of the role and responsibilities of the U.S. military. Who is the supreme commander-in-chief? What checks does the United States have in place to keep the military from growing stronger than the civilian government? Point out to students that in the empires to be studied in this section, the military played a major role in establishing and maintaining imperial strength.

TEACH

Multimedia Support

TRANSPARENCY
2–4, Map of Fertile Crescent Civilizations

COMPARING TIME PERIODS

Discuss with students the importance of communication posts and ask them what similar system existed in the United States for mail delivery from the east coast to the west. (*Students should recognize the similarities to stagecoaches and the Pony Express.*)

50

THE RISE OF NEW EMPIRES

A small and independent Hebrew state could exist only as long as no larger state dominated western Asia. New empires soon arose, however, that conquered vast stretches of the ancient world.

The Assyrian Empire

The first of these empires was formed in Assyria, located on the upper Tigris River. The Assyrians were a Semitic-speaking people who exploited the use of iron weapons to establish an empire by 700 B.C. The Assyrian Empire included Mesopotamia, parts of the Iranian plateau, sections of Asia Minor, Syria, Palestine, and Egypt down to Thebes. Within less than a hundred years, however, internal strife and resentment of Assyrian rule began to tear the Assyrian Empire apart. The capital city of Nineveh fell to a coalition of Chaldeans and Medes in 612 B.C. Seven years later, the rest of the empire was finally divided between the two powers.

At its height, the Assyrian Empire was ruled by kings whose power was seen as absolute. Under the leadership of these kings, the Assyrian Empire came to be well organized. Local officials were directly responsible to the king. The Assyrians also developed an efficient system of communication to administer their empire more effectively. A network of staging posts was established throughout the empire that used relays of

Map 2.4   The Assyrian and Persian Empires

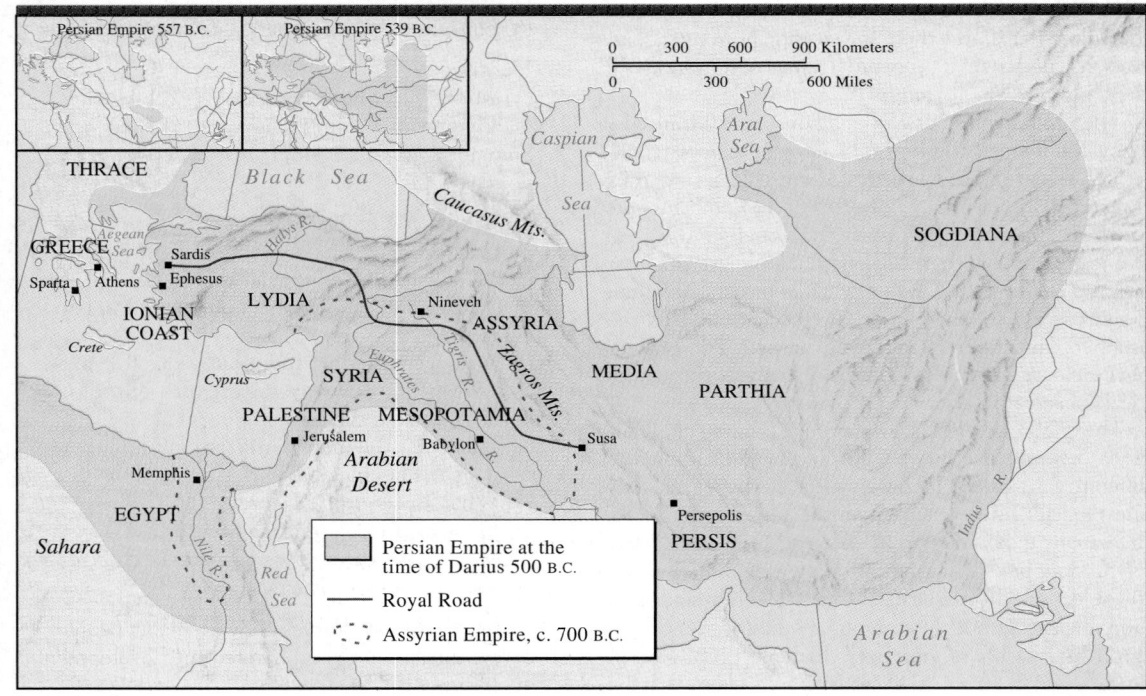

RECOMMENDED READING

A recent detailed account of Assyrian political, economic, social, military, and cultural history is H. W. F. Saggs, *The Might That Was Assyria* (London, 1984). The same author has also written an account of daily life entitled *Everyday Life in Babylonia and Assyria* (London, 1965). A. T. Olmstead, *History of Assyria* (Chicago, 1975) is a basic survey of the Assyrian Empire. Information from the Assyrians themselves can be found in A. Grayson, *Assyrian and Babylonian Chronicles* (New York, 1975); and J. Laessoe, *People of Ancient Assyria: Their Inscriptions and Correspondence*, trans. F. S. Leigh-Browne (London, 1963). On different aspects of Assyrian culture, see R. D. Barnett, *Assyrian Sculpture* (Toronto, 1975); and P. Albenda, *The Palace of Sargon King of Assyria* (Paris, 1986). The Chaldean Empire can be examined in J. Oates, *Babylon* (London, 1979).

▲ *This rendition of one of Ashurnasirpal's military campaigns shows the skill of his warriors as they engaged in close-quarter fighting. Why do you think his army could successfully overwhelm the Elamites in this battle?*

horses (mules or donkeys in the mountains) to carry messages. The system was so effective that a provincial governor (a representative of the king who governed the province) anywhere in the empire could send a question and receive an answer from the king in his palace within a week.

The Assyrians were good at conquering others. Over many years of practice, they developed effective military leaders and fighters. They were able to enlist and deploy troops numbering in the hundreds of thousands, although most campaigns were not on such a large scale. In one case, an Assyrian army of 120,000 men crossed the Euphrates on a campaign. Size alone was not decisive, however. The Assyrian army was well

organized and disciplined. A force of infantrymen was its core, joined by cavalrymen and horse-drawn war chariots that were used as platforms for shooting arrows. Moreover, the Assyrians had the first large armies equipped with iron weapons.

Another factor in the army's success was its ability to use different kinds of military tactics. The Assyrians were capable of waging guerrilla warfare in the mountains and set battles on open ground as well as laying siege to cities. They were especially known for their siege warfare. Some soldiers would hammer a city's walls with heavy, wheeled siege towers and armored battering rams while others dug tunnels to undermine the walls' foundations and cause them to collapse.

The Assyrians used terror as an instrument of warfare. They regularly laid waste the land in which they were fighting. They smashed dams; looted and destroyed towns; set crops on fire; and cut down trees, particularly fruit trees. The Assyrians were especially known for committing atrocities on their captives. King Ashurnasirpal recorded this account of his treatment of prisoners: "3,000 of their combat troops I felled with weapons. . . . Many of the captives taken from them I burned in a fire. Many I took alive; from some of these I cut off their hands to the wrist, from others I cut off their noses, ears and fingers; I put out the eyes of many of the soldiers. . . . I burned their young men and women to death." After conquering another city, the same king wrote: "I fixed up a pile of corpses in front of the city's gate. I flayed the nobles, as many as had rebelled, and spread their skins out on the piles. . . . I flayed many within my land and spread their skins out on the walls."[11] (Obviously, not a king to play games with!)

The Persian Empire

After the collapse of the Assyrian Empire, the Chaldeans, under their king Nebuchadnezzar (NEB-yoo-kud-NEZ-ur) II, made Babylonia the leading state in western Asia. Nebuchadnezzar rebuilt Babylon as the center of his empire and gave it a reputation as one of the great cities of the ancient world. However, the splendor of Chaldean Babylonia proved to be short-lived. Babylon fell to the Persians in 539 B.C.

The classic work on the Persian Empire is A. T. Olmstead, *History of the Persian Empire* (Chicago, 1948), but a recent work by J. M. Cook, *The Persian Empire* (New York, 1983), provides new material and fresh interpretations. Also of value are B. Dicks, *The Ancient Persians* (Newton Abbott, 1979); R. Frye, *The Heritage of Persia* (Cleveland, 1963); and W. Cullican, *The Medes and the Persians* (New York, 1965). On the history of Zoroastrianism, see especially R. C. Zaehner, *The Dawn and Twilight of Zoroastrianism* (London, 1961). Also helpful is M. Boyce, *Zoroastrians: Their Religious Beliefs and Practices* (London, 1979).

Multimedia Support

LASERDISC
Assyrian King
Ashurnasirpal
Dispatching a Lion

Assyrian Priest with
Knotted Whip

REINFORCING VOCABULARY

Discuss the term *guerrilla warfare* with students. The root of guerrilla comes from the German *werra,* which means strife. Students who know Spanish or French will recognize *guerra* or *guerre* (war).

CLASS DISCUSSION

Clearly the Assyrians had a large, effective army, and yet their empire only lasted 100 years. Guide students in a discussion of possible reasons for the quick demise of this once-powerful empire.

LEARNING FROM VISUALS

Students might also be interested to know that relief sculpture, like the one shown here, is the best known form of Assyrian art.

Answer to the caption question: Answers will vary but may include that in close range warfare Ashurnasirpal's army was using axes and crowbars, while Elam's soldiers used bows and arrows, which would be more effective at distance fighting.

ACROSS THE CURRICULUM

Government. Have students compare the responsibilities of Persian satraps with the responsibilities of the governor of their state. What are the differences and the similarities?

COMPARING TIME PERIODS

Discuss with students why Cyrus's policies toward other religious and cultural groups were considered enlightened. Have students identify other rulers who have enforced similar policies and the advantages of these practices.

USING PRIMARY SOURCES

Have students reread Ashurnasirpal's comments on page 51 and those about Cyrus on page 52. Then ask them to write a brief comparison of these rulers from a common citizen's point of view. Encourage students to try their best to consider all the factors that make a leader successful.

LEARNING FROM VISUALS

Have students review the art that has appeared thus far in the chapter. Then have them identify contributions from other empires that can be seen in this wall.

Answer to the caption question: Answers will vary but may include tactical forces such as the Navy Seals, the Green Beret, or honorary groups like the Royal Guard in England.

Rise and Fall of the Persian Empire

The Persians were an Indo-European–speaking people who lived in what is today southwestern Iran. Primarily nomadic, the Persians were organized in tribes until the Achaemenid family managed to unify them. One of the family's members, Cyrus (SIE-rus), who ruled from 559 to 530 B.C., created a powerful Persian state that stretched from Asia Minor in the west to western India in the east. In 539 B.C., Cyrus entered Mesopotamia and captured Babylon. His treatment of Babylonia showed remarkable restraint and wisdom. He made Babylonia into a Persian province but kept many Babylonian government officials in their positions. Cyrus also issued an edict permitting the Jews, who had been brought to Babylon in the sixth century B.C., to return to Jerusalem and rebuild their temple there.

The people of his time called Cyrus "the Great." Indeed, he must have been an unusual ruler for his time, a man who demonstrated much wisdom and compassion in the conquest and organization of his empire. He won approval by using not only Persians but also native peoples as government officials in their own states. Unlike the Assyrian rulers of an earlier empire, Cyrus had a reputation for mercy. Medes, Babylonians, and Jews all accepted him as their ruler. Indeed, the Jews regarded him as one sent by God: "I am the Lord who says of Cyrus, 'He is my shepherd and will accomplish all that I please.'"[12] Cyrus had a genuine respect for ancient civilizations. In building his palaces, he made use of Assyrian, Babylonian, and Egyptian designs and building methods.

Cyrus's successors extended the territory of the Persian Empire. His son Cambyses (kam-BIE-seez) undertook a successful invasion of Egypt. Darius, who ruled from 521 to 486 B.C., added a new Persian province in western India that extended to the Indus River. He then moved into Europe, conquering Thrace and creating the largest empire the world had yet seen. Darius's contact

▲ *A strength of the Persian Empire was the Persian Guard, a band of infantry archers, whose number was never allowed to drop below 10,000. Those killed in battle were replaced immediately. What modern-day military group do you think would be comparable to the Persian Guard?*

with the Greeks led him to undertake an invasion of the Greek mainland, which resulted in the famous Battle of Marathon in 490 B.C. (see Chapter 5).

Darius was responsible for strengthening the basic structure of the Persian government. He divided the empire into twenty provinces, called **satrapies.** Each province was ruled by a governor, or **satrap,** literally a "protector of the Kingdom." Each satrap collected taxes, provided justice and security, and recruited soldiers for the royal army. Darius was generous to those who served him well but harsh to his enemies. One pretender to the throne had his nose and ears cut off and tongue torn out before being impaled.

STUDYING MAPS

The following activity will help you guide students through their study of the maps in this chapter.

Have students use maps within this chapter to estimate the size of the Persian Empire under Darius. Have them compare the size of this empire to the United States so that they have a better idea of the relative size of the empire. Suggest that students select other modern countries they are familiar with to compare to these early empires (a foreign student may want to compare his or her native country).

An efficient system of communication was crucial to sustaining the Persian Empire. Well-maintained roads made it easy for officials to travel through the empire. The Royal Road stretched from Lydia in Asia Minor to Susa (SOO-zuh), the chief capital of the Persian Empire. Like the Assyrians, the Persians set up way stations that provided food and shelter, as well as fresh horses, for the king's messengers.

In this vast administrative system, the Persian king—the "Great King"—occupied an exalted position. All subjects were the king's servants. The Great King was the source of all justice. He held the power of life and death over everyone. At its height, much of the power of the Persian Empire and its rulers depended upon the military. By the time of Darius, the Persian monarchs had created a standing army of professional soldiers. This army was international, composed of people from all over the empire. At its core was a cavalry force of ten thousand and an elite infantry force of ten thousand, known as the Immortals because they were never allowed to fall below ten thousand in number. When one was killed, he was immediately replaced.

After Darius, the Persian kings became more and more isolated at their courts, surrounded by luxuries provided by the immense quantities of gold and silver that flowed into their treasuries. As the Persian kings increased taxes to gain even more wealth, loyalty to the empire began to decline. At the same time, struggles over the throne had the effect of weakening the monarchy.

Persian kings had many wives and many children. Artaxerxes (art-uh-ZERK-seez) II, for example, who ruled in the fourth century B.C., had 115 sons. Of course, the sons had little real power, but that made them even more willing to engage in plots to gain the throne. Of the nine rulers after Darius, six were murdered as a result of court intrigue. Xerxes II, for example, reigned for only forty-five days before being murdered in bed by his half-brother. The assassin was soon killed by another half-brother. Over a period of time, this bloody struggle for the throne weakened the empire. This situation encouraged the Greek ruler Alexander the Great to undertake the conquest of the Persian Empire (see Chapter 5).

▲ *Darius, shown here on his throne, proved to be a capable administrator, establishing civil government, roads, and communication systems throughout the vast Persian Empire. He also was known as a builder of luxurious palaces that were ornamented with copper, silver, and gold.*

Persian Religion

Of all the Persians' cultural contributions, the most original was their religion, especially Zoroastrianism (zor-uh-WAS-tree-u-NIZ-um). According to Persian tradition, Zoroaster was born in 660 B.C. After a period of wandering and solitude, he had visions that caused him to be revered as a prophet of the "true religion." His teachings were eventually written down in the *Zend Avesta*, the sacred book of Zoroastrianism.

LEARNING FROM VISUALS

Discuss the kinds of tribute citizens, wealthy and poor, would have brought to the emperor. What favors might these citizens have asked in return for their gifts?

Answer to the caption question: Answers will vary but may include that the four versions represent different stages of life, or different characteristics of the individual.

ASSESS

You can choose from a variety of assessments to evaluate your students' mastery of the objectives for this section as stated on page 50. Possible assessments include:

1. Section Review questions on this page
2. Section 2–4 Quiz in your Teacher Resource materials
3. Reteaching Worksheets in your Teacher Resource materials
4. Self-Study software

Answers to SECTION REVIEW

2. (a) the 20 provinces of Persia
(b) governor of a Persian province
3. (a) a Semitic-speaking people who built a powerful empire
(b) king of the Chaldeans who rebuilt Babylon as the center of his empire
(c) Indo-European speaking, nomadic people who lived in what is now western Iran

▶ *Persian citizens were expected to pay taxes and to bring gifts, tribute, to their kings. Wealthy citizens loaded their camels with gifts, while others traveled on foot. What kind of favors might citizens have requested in return for these gifts?*

Like that of the Hebrews, the spiritual message of Zoroaster was monotheistic. Ahuramazda was not a new god to the Persians, but to Zoroaster he was the only god, and the religion he preached was the only perfect one. Ahuramazda (the "Wise Lord") was the supreme god who brought all things into being. According to Zoroaster, Ahuramazda also possessed qualities that all humans should aspire to, such as Good Thought, Right, and Piety. Although Ahuramazda was supreme, he was not unopposed. At the beginning of the world, the good spirit of Ahuramazda was opposed by the evil spirit (later identified with Ahriman).

Humans also played a role in the struggle between good and evil. Ahuramazda, the creator, gave all humans the freedom to choose between right and wrong. The good person chooses the right way of Ahuramazda. Zoroaster taught that there would be an end to the struggle between good and evil. Ahuramazda would eventually triumph, and at the last judgment at the end of the world, the final separation of good and evil would occur. Individuals, too, would be judged. Each soul faced a final evaluation of its actions. If a person had performed good deeds, he or she would achieve paradise. If the person had performed evil deeds, the soul would be thrown into an abyss, where it would experience torment and misery.

 SECTION REVIEW

1. **Locate:**
   (*a*) Assyrian Empire,   (*b*) Persian Empire,
   (*c*) Royal Road

2. **Define:**
   (*a*) satrapies,   (*b*) satrap

3. **Identify:**
   (*a*) Assyrians,   (*b*) Nebuchadnezzar,
   (*c*) Persians,   (*d*) Cyrus,   (*e*) Immortals,
   (*f*) Zoroaster,   (*g*) Ahuramazda

4. **Recall:**
   (*a*) Name at least four reasons why the Assyrians were good at conquering others.
   (*b*) Give three reasons why the Persian Empire began to decline after the death of Darius.

5. Think Critically: Compare King Ashurnasirpal to Cyrus. How were they different? Support your answer.

Conclusion

The peoples of Mesopotamia and Egypt built the first civilizations. They developed cities and struggled with the problems of organized states. They invented writing to keep records, and they created literature. They constructed monumental buildings to please their gods, give witness to their power, and preserve their culture for all time. They developed new political, military, social, and religious structures to deal with the basic problems of human existence and organization. These first civilizations left detailed records that allow us to view how they grappled with three of the fundamental problems that humans have thought about: the nature of human relationships, the nature of the universe, and the role of divine forces in that universe. Although later peoples would provide different answers from those of the Mesopotamians and Egyptians, it was they who first posed the questions, gave answers, and wrote them down.

By 1500 B.C., much of the creative impulse of the Mesopotamian and Egyptian civilizations was beginning to decline. By 1200 B.C., the decline of the Hittites and Egyptians had created a power vacuum that allowed a number of small states to emerge and flourish for a short while. All these states were eventually overshadowed by the rise of the great empires of the Assyrians and Persians. The Assyrian Empire was the first to unite almost all of the ancient Middle East. Even larger, however, was the Persian Empire of the "Great Kings" of Persia. Persian rule was not only effi-cient but also tolerant. Conquered peoples were allowed to keep their own religions, customs, and methods of doing business. The many years of peace that the Persian Empire brought to the Middle East aided trade and the general well-being of its peoples. It is no wonder that many peoples expressed their gratitude for being subjects of the Great Kings of Persia. One of these peoples was the Hebrews, who created no empire but nevertheless left an important legacy. In Judaism, the Hebrews developed a world religion that influenced the later religions of Christianity and Islam. Hebrew religious ideas had an important impact on the development of Western civilization.

Notes

1. Quoted in Michael Wood, *Legacy: The Search for Ancient Cultures* (New York, 1992), p. 34.
2. Quoted in Thorkild Jacobsen, "Mesopotamia," in Henri Frankfort et al., *Before Philosophy* (Baltimore, 1949), p. 139.
3. James B. Pritchard, *Ancient Near Eastern Texts*, 3d ed. (Princeton, N.J., 1969), p. 372.
4. Quoted in Milton Covensky, *The Ancient Near Eastern Tradition* (New York, 1966), p. 51.
5. Quoted in B. G. Trigger, B. J. Kemp, D. O'Connor, and A. B. Lloyd, *Ancient Egypt: A Social History* (Cambridge, 1983), p. 413.
6. Quoted in John A. Wilson, *The Culture of Ancient Egypt* (Chicago, 1951), p. 264.
7. Psalms 137:1, 4–6.
8. Psalms 145:8–9.
9. Exodus 20:13–15.
10. Isaiah 2:4.
11. Quoted in H. W. F. Saggs, *The Might That Was Assyria* (London, 1984), pp. 261–262.
12. Isaiah, 44:28; 45:1.

(d) powerful ruler of Persia

(e) elite infantry force of 10,000 professional soldiers

(f) revered as a prophet of the "true religion" by Persians

(g) the "Wise Lord" of Zoroastrianism, considered to be supreme and the creator

4. (a) Students will choose four: Assyrians had developed effective military leaders and fighters; the army was well-organized and disciplined; the forces included infantrymen, cavalrymen, and horse-drawn war chariots; armies were equipped with iron weapons; army was able to use different kinds of military tactics (like guerrilla warfare, battles on open ground, and laying siege to cities); used terror, laid waste to cities, and committed atrocities on their captives

5. Answers will vary, but should consider King Ashurnasirpal's treatment of prisoners, compared with Cyrus's.

CLOSE

Make sure students realize that the Persian Empire was built by military strength, and it was military strength that kept its emperors in power. Like empires before and after, weak leadership and disregard for the common good led to its downfall.

USING KEY TERMS

1. covenant
2. scribes
3. pharaoh
4. theocracy
5. patriarchal
6. polytheistic
7. vizier
8. mastabas
9. empire
10. ziggurat
11. dynasty
12. hieroglyphics
13. satrapies, satrap
14. cuneiform
15. mummification
16. prophets
17. monotheism
18. papyrus
19. hieratic
20. city-states

REVIEWING THE FACTS

1. "between the rivers"
2. beneficial: deposited fertile silt on surrounding farmland; harmful: sometimes did catastrophic damage to land, villages, and people
3. Sumerians
4. mud bricks
5. 300 B.C.
6. land and water
7. 240 years (2340 B.C. to 2100 B.C.)
8. sun gods and land gods
9. as tombs dedicated to the dead, especially the pharaohs
10. nomadic
11. warfare
12. Zoroastrianism; monotheistic

THINKING CRITICALLY

1. the first civilization began here
2. protection from flooding; water supply for crops
3. **city-states:** well-fortified walls; community; open to invasions. **empires:** easy to create; control of many people and territories; difficult to maintain

---

CHAPTER 2 REVIEW

USING KEY TERMS

1. According to the Hebrews, God made a ——— with the tribes of Israel.
2. Egyptian writers and teachers were called ———.
3. An Egyptian king was referred to as a ———.
4. If citizens believe that their city is ruled by gods, they might call their government a ———.
5. In a ——— society women have fewer privileges and rights than men.
6. A person who believes in many gods is ———.
7. In ancient Egypt, the ——— was in charge of the government bureaucracy.
8. Rectangular tombs for the pharaoh's noble officials were called ———.
9. An ———, which included many city-states, was usually easier to create than to maintain.
10. In a Sumerian city the temple was built atop a ———.
11. If ruling power is passed from one generation to the next, the government of a country could be called a ———.
12. The Greeks referred to the Egyptian style of writing as ———.
13. The Persian ruler Darius divided his empire into provinces called ———, which were ruled by ———.
14. The Sumerians invented a system of writing called ———.
15. ——— was a process used by the Egyptians to preserve bodies after death.
16. The Hebrews believed that God communicated through religious teachers called ———.
17. The belief in one god, rather than many gods, is called ———.
18. The Egyptians wrote on ———, not stone.
19. ——— script was used for business transactions and record keeping.
20. The basic units of Sumerian civilization were ———.

REVIEWING THE FACTS

1. What does the word *Mesopotamia* mean?
2. Tell how the spring flooding of the Tigris and Euphrates Rivers was both beneficial and harmful.
3. What peoples created the first Mesopotamian civilization?
4. What was the most important building material in Sumerian cities?
5. When was the wheel invented?
6. What were two primary resources over which the Sumerian city-states fought?
7. How long did the Akkadian empire last?
8. Which two groups of gods were most important to the Egyptians?
9. Why were the pyramids built?
10. Were the Hebrews a sedentary or a nomadic people?
11. Were the Assyrians' greatest accomplishments in the area of art, economics, religion, or warfare?
12. What religion began in the Persian Empire and how was it similar to the Hebrews' religion?

THINKING CRITICALLY

1. Restate in your own words the meaning of William Loftus's phrase "the cradle of civilization."
2. Irrigation played a major role in the development of Mesopotamia. Explain.
3. Compare and contrast the separate city-state system of government with an empire. What are the advantages and disadvantages of both?
4. Describe how the Nile flooded, as compared to the Euphrates and Tigris, and then explain how these flooding patterns caused the two civilizations to develop differently.
5. Explain how the social structure of ancient Egypt resembled a pyramid.
6. Explain how the Hebrew religion was different from religions of other cultures you've studied in this chapter. How did these differences affect the Hebrews' interaction with other peoples?

---

4. Nile flooded gently and predictably, causing Egyptian civilizations to form along river, which differs from the Mesopotamian forming of cities further from their rivers
5. king at the top, supported by upper class, followed by artisans and merchants, with base of large peasant farmers
6. monotheism, prophets, the covenant, the law, separation between Jews and non-Jews, and serious conflicts arising as a result of religious convictions

CHAPTER 2 REVIEW

APPLYING SOCIAL STUDIES SKILLS

1. **Geography:** Through what modern-day countries do the Tigris and Euphrates rivers flow?
2. **Government:** Compare the basic units, or levels, of government in the United States today with the political structure of Sumerian civilization. What advantages or disadvantages can you identify for each type of system?
3. **Government:** Compare the Sumerians' view of the relationship between their gods and their government to the political system in the United States today. How are they fundamentally different?
4. **Economics:** Explain at least one way in which the invention of the wheel affected Mesopotamian economy.
5. **Sociology:** Identify at least five aspects of Mesopotamian society as revealed by the Code of Hammurabi.
6. **Geography:** Explain how the physical environment of Mesopotamia affected the religion of its people.
7. **Economics:** Identify two projects that the pharaohs of the Middle Kingdom undertook that contributed to the economic growth of the kingdom. State how these projects helped the economy.
8. **Geography:** Locate the area in which the Phoenicians lived.

MAKING TIME AND PLACE CONNECTIONS

1. Approximately how many years ago were Sumerian cities such as Uruk established?
2. Why did the Sumerians build walls around their cities? Give two reasons why this is not done today.
3. Compare Mesopotamian laws to the legal system in the U.S. today. What are the differences?
4. How is the number system you learned in elementary school different from the Sumerian number system?

5. What was the major factor leading to the development of both the Mesopotamian and Egyptian civilizations?
6. Compare and contrast the Egyptian process of mummification with burial procedures used today. What basic differences in religious beliefs underlie the differences between Egyptian and modern burial practices?
7. Compare Egyptian and Mesopotamian social life. What are the similarities and differences?
8. Compare the economies of the civilizations studied in this chapter. Identify both similarities and differences.
9. Pastoral nomads aided ancient sedentary peoples by carrying products and passing on technological developments from one city-state to the next. How are these activities performed today in the absence of pastoral nomads?
10. What similarities can you identify in comparing Hammurabi, Solomon, and Cyrus?

BECOMING AN HISTORIAN

Understanding and Interpreting Maps: Examine Map 2.1, Ancient Mesopotamia.

1. What information does the key provide? Can you determine time periods represented from the keys? What symbols are used to represent cities?
2. How far is it from Babylon to Jerusalem? From the Zagros Mountains to the Taurus Mountains?
3. Can you determine the length of the Euphrates and Tigris Rivers from this map? If so, how long are they? Compare this map with the map of ancient Egypt. Are the same distance scales used? If not, why does one have a larger scale?

Reading Tables: Reread the titles of the two tables presented in this chapter. How do these two tables differ? How are they similar? How many languages are listed in the two tables combined? How many of these languages are no longer spoken?

57

MAKING TIME AND PLACE CONNECTIONS

1. 5000
2. protection from invaders; not done today because of limited threat of invasion and because it limits expansion
3. Answers will vary.
4. Based on 6, 10, and 60 rather than our base-ten.
5. the rivers that run through them
6. Religious belief of person living again within their tomb is main difference.
7. both male-dominated, but in Egypt women had more legal rights than in Mesopotamia; had similar hierarchies of citizens; made important but different contributions to education
8. Discussion of similarities should include: traded goods; farmed a great deal. Differences include: Egyptians traded primarily along the Nile while Mesopotamians used land and sea for trade routes.
9. Answers will vary.
10. strong leadership; brought improvements to their people; built significant physical structures

BECOMING AN HISTORIAN

Understanding and Integrating Maps:
1. see map, page 24
2. see map, page 24; Babylon to Jerusalem is about 900 km/560 miles. Zagros Mountains to Taurus Mountains is about 1200 km/744 miles.
3. Euphrates River is about 3600 km/2200 miles long and Tigris River is about 1800 km/1100 miles long. Distance scales are not the same because the maps are presented in different sizes.

Reading Tables: see pages 27 and 44.

APPLYING SOCIAL STUDIES SKILLS

1. Turkey, Syria, and Iraq
2. Discussion of Sumerian should include: monarchy heading up government and army; three main classes of people. Advantages include: efficiency and prosperity when under good king. Disadvantages include: oppression of lower classes and all society suffering under a bad king
3. Sumerians: theocracy
   United States: democracy
4. led to building carts that made transport easier, opening up more trade

5. system of strict justice; "an eye for an eye"; public duties taken seriously; consumer protection laws; family life strictly governed; patriarchal society
6. severe physical elements caused them to believe in supernatural forces
7. draining swampland in Nile delta provided new farmland and canal connecting Nile to Red Sea aided trade transportation
8. in the area of Palestine along Mediterranean Coast. See map, page 47

3 PLANNING GUIDE

SECTION	KEY TOPICS	PRIMARY SOURCES	ASSESSMENT
1 The Emergence of Civilization in India pages 59–62	◆ Geographic features of India ◆ The first civilizations in India ◆ The importance of trade to urban civilizations in India		◆ Section Review, page 62 ◆ Section Quiz 3–1, TRB
2 The Arrival of the Aryans pages 62–68	◆ The impact of Aryan domination on India ◆ The caste system and Indian culture ◆ The family in ancient India	◆ The quotation by Hitler in Aryans in India and Nazi Germany, page 64 ◆ Magathenes, Writing on Brahmins, page 65 ◆ The Law of Manu, page 67	◆ Section Review, page 68 ◆ Section Quiz 3–2, TRB
3 The Religious Heritage of Ancient India pages 68–73	◆ The Hindu religion ◆ The Buddhist religion ◆ Differences between Hindu and Buddhist beliefs	◆ The Eightfold Path, page 71 ◆ Sermon at Benares, page 72 ◆ "How shall we behave before women?" page 73	◆ Section Review, page 73 ◆ Section Quiz 3–3, TRB
4 New Dynasties and New Empires in India pages 73–82	◆ The Mauryan dynasty ◆ The Silk Road and the importance of trade ◆ The Kingdom of the Guptas ◆ The legacy of Indian culture	◆ The Mahabharata, page 80 ◆ The Cloud Messenger, page 81	◆ Section Review, page 82 ◆ Section Quiz 3–4, TRB

THE FIRST CIVILIZATIONS:
ANCIENT INDIA (3000 TO 500)

REPRODUCIBLE ACTIVITIES

- Historical Maps
- Charts and Graphs
- Critical Thinking
- Cooperative Learning
- Vocabulary
- Guided Reading
- Reteaching
- Enrichment
- Performance Assessment
- Spanish Key Points and Chapter Summaries
- Spanish Vocabulary
- Spanish Guided Reading

MULTIMEDIA SUPPORT

TRANSPARENCIES
- *World History* Color Transparency Package
- Fine Art Color Transparency Package

VIDEO
- *World History* Video Library
- **CNN.** Annual Video Update

LASERDISC
- *Sights and Sounds of History*

AUDIO
- *Listening to Literature* audiotape (English and Spanish)
- *History of Music* CD

SOFTWARE
- WESTEST™
- Student Review

CD-ROM
- *The Journey of Civilization*
- *World History*

INTERNET
- Internet Activities

On Line with WORLD HISTORY

Access West's history web site at
http://history.swpco.com
You'll find activities and web sites related to specific topics and chapters in *World History: The Human Odyssey*. Also look for references to helpful web sites at appropriate places throughout this teacher edition.

LESSON PLANNING

You will find detailed daily lesson plans for both traditional class scheduling and **block scheduling** in your Teacher Resource Box.

 Not Enough Time?

If you do not have the four or five days recommended to teach this chapter, you may want to focus on the following sections and activities:

- Have students skim the chapter to answer the "Questions to Guide Your Reading" on page 59. Discuss their answers, then read the "Conclusion" on pages 82–83.
- Do a more in-depth reading about the geography of India on pages 59–62, the caste system on 63–65, differences between Hindu and Buddhist religions on 68–73, and the importance of trade and the Silk Road on pages 75–76. Conclude with a class discussion of the "You Are There" feature, *The Good Life in Gupta India* on page 77.

THE FIRST CIVILIZATIONS:

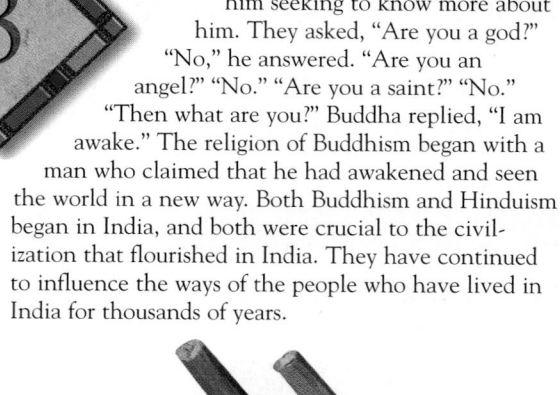

3

BUILDING ON CHAPTER 2

To "set the scene" for the study of Chapter 3, use the following questions and activities.

◆ Ask students to discuss the importance of rivers to civilizations in Egypt and Western Asia and to keep this in mind as they read about ancient India.

◆ Have students list the functions of religion in societies, and discuss why the people in India would also develop religions.

◆ Ask students to explain why the governments of most ancient civilizations were led by one person or family. Would it be realistic to expect early Indian governments to be different?

◆ Remind students why the geography of Egypt made war less likely. Would the same be true of India?

USING THE OPENING STORY

Depending on the ability levels of your students, select from the following questions and activities to reinforce the reading of the opening story.

◆ Why is it correct to say that modern civilization has built on ancient Indian civilization in both literal and figurative ways?

◆ Why do people often fail to recognize the value of preserving artifacts from the past?

◆ Why are people who are thought to be wise often those who listen and watch the best?

After its conquest of India in the 1850s, Great Britain began to build a series of railroads to connect the far-flung lands of its new colony. While building on the floodplain of the Indus River in the 1850s, British engineers realized the need for a strong foundation bed for their railroad tracks. Lacking sufficient quantities of stone, they found another solution. Lying nearby were the ruins of ancient, deserted cities. Why not pull down the walls and use the old bricks? By plundering the old ruins, the British laid the foundation bed for hundreds of miles of railroad tracks. Trains still travel on these tracks today. One of the plundered sites was known as Harappa—the name of a nearby village. In the 1920s, archaeologists discovered that Harappa and a number of other ruins were sites of once-vibrant cities. Indeed, they were all part of a vast civilization in India that had flourished between 3000 and 1500 B.C. and had covered far more territory than the early civilizations of Mesopotamia and Egypt.

One of the great figures of ancient India was Siddhartha Gautama (si-DART-uh GOWT-uh-muh), who was born around 563 B.C. He is better known as the Buddha (BOOD-uh) and in his lifetime gained thousands of devoted followers. People would come to

him seeking to know more about him. They asked, "Are you a god?" "No," he answered. "Are you an angel?" "No." "Are you a saint?" "No." "Then what are you?" Buddha replied, "I am awake." The religion of Buddhism began with a man who claimed that he had awakened and seen the world in a new way. Both Buddhism and Hinduism began in India, and both were crucial to the civilization that flourished in India. They have continued to influence the ways of the people who have lived in India for thousands of years.

▲ *Two miniature oxen pull a tiny cart filled with storage jars in this modern replica of Harappan transportation. Similarly designed carts are still used in India and Pakistan today.*

ADDITIONAL RESOURCES

The resources below can be used to enrich the lessons in this chapter.

BOOKS FOR STUDENTS
The Illustrated World's Religions by Huston Smith. Harper Collins. Social Studies School Service (800) 421-4246
Historic India by Lucille Schulberg. Time-Life (Great Ages of Man).

VIDEOS/FILMS
Hinduism: An Ancient Path in the Modern World. United Learning. Social Studies School Service (800) 421-4246

CD ROMs
Religions of the World. Mentorom. Social Studies School Service (800) 421-4246

ANCIENT INDIA

(3000 B.C. TO A.D. 500)

THE BEGINNINGS OF CIVILIZATION

3000 B.C.	ANCIENT INDIA	A.D. 500
3500 B.C.		A.D. 500

QUESTIONS TO GUIDE YOUR READING

1. How did geography affect the civilization that arose in India?

2. What were the chief features of the Indus (Harappan) civilization?

3. What effect did the Aryans have upon Indian civilization?

4. What are the basic ideas of Hinduism, and how did they influence civilization in India?

5. What are the basic ideas of Buddhism, and how did they influence civilization in India?

6. What was the impact of the Mauryan and Gupta dynasties on Indian history?

OUTLINE

1. THE EMERGENCE OF CIVILIZATION IN INDIA
2. THE ARRIVAL OF THE ARYANS
3. THE RELIGIOUS HERITAGE OF ANCIENT INDIA
4. NEW DYNASTIES AND NEW EMPIRES IN INDIA

THE EMERGENCE OF CIVILIZATION IN INDIA

Civilization first arose in India in the Indus River valley around 3000 B.C. India is a land of diversity, which is perhaps most evident in its languages and cultures. As of the 1990s, people in India spoke eighteen languages, with hundreds of dialects. Like the Middle East, India, too, is known as a cradle of religion. Two of the world's major religions—Hinduism and Buddhism—began in India.

The Land of India

Diversity is also apparent in India's geography. The Indian subcontinent, shaped like a diamond hanging from the southern ridge of Asia, is composed of a number of core regions. In the far north are the Himalayan (HIM-uh-LAY-un) and Karakoram mountain ranges, the highest in the world. Directly south of the Himalayas and the Karakoram range is the rich valley of the Ganges (GAN-JEEZ), one of the chief regions of Indian culture. To the west is the Indus River valley. Today the latter is a relatively dry plateau that forms the backbone of the modern state of Pakistan. In

59

FOCUS ON THEMES

Listed below are brief summaries of how the content in this chapter supports the text's key themes.

Politics and History Organized governments were crucial to the emergence of civilization in India, although it was not until the Mauryan and Gupta dynasties that India had well-organized states with complex administrative systems.

The Role of Ideas The ideas of India's major religions played crucial roles in the civilization of India and also spread to other Asian countries. Today, Buddhism is one of the fastest-growing religions in the United States.

Economics and History Early civilization in India was based on agriculture, but surplus food made possible the growth of crafts and the emergence of trade.

Social Life There were distinct class differences in India. A complex social system was based on castes.

The Importance of Cultural Developments Sanskrit was the language of the government bureaucracy and literary works. It was used for India's great sacred literature and historical epics. Stone pillars, stupas, and rock chambers gave expression to India's religious concerns.

Religion in History Hinduism and Buddhism played major roles in forming the culture of India and eventually spread to other countries.

The Role of Individuals Siddhartha Gautama showed that an individual has the power to change the course of history simply by his or her ideas.

FOCUS

OBJECTIVES

After completing this section, students should be able to

1. explain how geography influenced the development of civilization in India
2. identify characteristics of Harappan civilization
3. explain a variety of reasons for the importance of the Indus River
4. explain why Harappan civilization must have had a well-organized government

FOCUS ACTIVITY

Help students understand that most civilizations have evolved through the mixing of different groups over many years. Ask each student to identify the primary racial, or ethnic group in his or her own heredity. Compile a list of these groups on the board. Lead a discussion concerning how the identified groups have influenced the development of American civilization. Ask students to look for ways that different groups influenced the development of Indian civilization as they read Chapter 3.

ancient times it enjoyed a more balanced climate and served as the cradle of Indian civilization.

South of India's two major river valleys (the valleys of the Ganges and the Indus) lies the Deccan (DEK-un), a region of hills and upland plateau that extends from the Ganges valley to the southern tip of the Indian subcontinent. The interior of the plateau is relatively hilly and dry. The eastern and western coasts are occupied by lush plains, which have historically been among the most densely populated regions of India. Off the southeastern coast of the Indian peninsula is the island known today as Sri Lanka (SREE-LONG-kuh). Although Sri Lanka is now a separate country, the history of the island has been closely linked with that of its larger neighbor.

The primary feature of India's climate is the **monsoon,** a seasonal wind pattern in southern Asia that

blows from the southwest during the summer months and from the northeast during the winter. The southwest monsoon is commonly marked by heavy rains as the moisture-laden winds pass over the Indian landmass. Throughout history many Indian farmers have depended on these rains to grow their crops. If the rains come late, as they frequently do, thousands starve. At the same time, the heavy monsoon rains can also lead to rampaging floods, especially in the lower Ganges valley.

The First Civilization in India

During their excavation of the Indus River valley in the 1920s, archaeologists discovered a number of farming villages that were at least six thousand years old. Those small mud brick villages eventually gave rise to the human communities that historians call Harappan or Indus civilization—the first civilization in India. Between 3000 B.C. and 1500 B.C., the valleys of the Indus River supported a flourishing civilization that extended hundreds of miles from the Himalayas to the

Map 3.1   The Indian Subcontinent

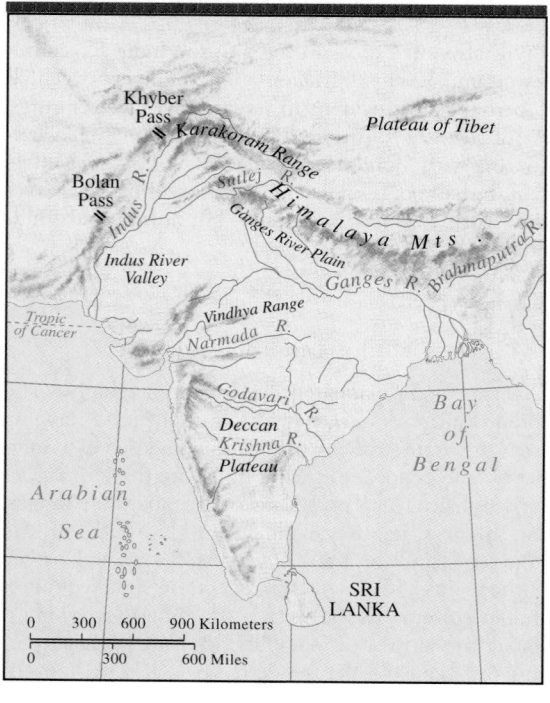

Map 3.2   Ancient Harappan Civilization

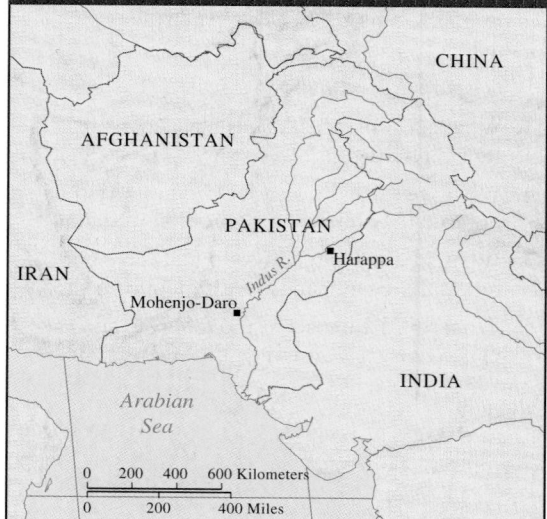

STUDYING MAPS

The following questions will help you guide the students through their study of Map 3.1 and Map 3.2.

1. Locate mountain ranges on Map 3.2. How would they have affected communications, trade, and relations between civilizations in this geographic area? *(They would*

have slowed down communications and made trade and other relations difficult.)

2. Why were the cities of Harappa and Mohenjo-Daro located on major rivers? *(The rivers provided water for the people, animals, and crops and transportation for moving people and trade items.)*

coast of the Arabian Sea. Although more than a thousand settlements have been found, the main archaeological sites were located at two major cities—Harappa and Mohenjo-Daro—that were about 400 miles apart.

Like the cultures of Egypt and Mesopotamia, the Harappan civilization was an urban culture. Harappa,

▲ *Clay seals depicting human figures and animals were probably used by the Harappan peoples to identify the owners of goods for sale. The writings at the top of the seals are rare examples of the Harappan writing system, which has yet to be deciphered.*

the capital city, was surrounded by a brick wall over forty feet thick and three and one-half miles long. Within the wall was a fifty-foot-high citadel or fortress that enclosed the royal palace and a temple. The main streets—some as wide as thirty feet—divided the city into a number of different residential areas. At its height, the city had as many as 35,000 inhabitants.

Much about Harappan civilization is unknown. As is true for Egypt and Mesopotamia, many written records of the Harappan peoples exist. However, the written language used by the Indus valley civilization has not yet been deciphered. The evidence that archaeologists have been able to gather suggests that the Harappan civilization was ruled by a king aided by an **elite** (a small group of powerful people).

As in Egypt and Mesopotamia, the ruling monarchy based its power on a belief in divine assistance. Certainly, religion and state power were closely linked, as is indicated by the combination of the royal palace and the holy temple in the citadel at Harappa. There are signs that religious belief had evolved into a belief in a single god or goddess of fertility. Priests at court probably prayed to this god or goddess to maintain the fertility of the soil and to guarantee the annual harvest.

Like its contemporaries in Mesopotamia and along the Nile, the Harappan civilization had an economy based primarily on farming. The Indus River flooded every year, providing rich soil for the growing of wheat, barley, and peas, the chief crops. Like many other ancient civilizations, the early Harappans probably

lived in tiny farming villages scattered throughout the river valley. These villages grew until a food surplus enabled them to support large populations living in walled cities.

This Indus valley civilization carried on extensive trade with city-states in Mesopotamia. Textiles and foodstuffs were imported from the Sumerian city-states in exchange for copper, lumber, precious stones, cotton, and various types of luxury goods. Much of this trade was carried by ship via the Persian Gulf, although some undoubtedly went by land.

Archaeological excavations make it clear that an advanced urban civilization flourished in the major cities of Harappa and Mohenjo-Daro for hundreds of years. Both cities were carefully planned. The main,

▼ *This aerial photograph of the citadel of Mohenjo-Daro reveals the precision and symmetry with which the city was constructed. What is a citadel? What did the builders do to make it strong?*

MORE ABOUT . . . *Ancient Indian Technology*

The Indus Valley civilization of over 4,000 years ago had modern conveniences that most European nations would not develop until the last few centuries. It was the people of Mohenjo-Daro who developed the world's first sitting toilets. They were made of bricks, with a wooden seat on top. Each toilet had a vertical chute that emptied into a street drain

or cesspit. In addition to toilets the people of Mohenjo-Daro had baths. The "Great Bath" of Mohenjo-Daro measured 39' × 23' and was 10' deep. It was surrounded by rooms (some of which contained smaller baths). Almost all of the hundreds of houses excavated so far in the Indus valley had their own bathrooms.

2. (a) a seasonal wind pattern in southern Asia
   (b) small group of powerful people
3. (a) the capital city of the Harappan civilization
   (b) major city in the Harappan civilization
4. the written language used has not been deciphered
5. Answers will vary. May include: they were well-planned cities with many "modern" conveniences.

CLOSE

Lead students in a discussion of the objectives listed on page 60. Emphasize contributions to civilization made by groups that ruled India.

LEARNING FROM VISUALS

Answer to the caption question: Special attention was paid to the priest's eyes, beard, and garment.

FOCUS

OBJECTIVES

After completing this section, students should be able to

1. describe the impact of the arrival of Aryans on civilization in ancient India
2. identify each caste and explain how the system worked
3. explain the importance of the family in ancient Indian civilization
4. identify characteristics of farming in the Indian economic system

broad streets ran in a north-south direction and were crossed by smaller east-west roads. Both cities were divided into large walled neighborhoods, with narrow lanes separating the rows of houses. Houses differed in size, and some reached as high as three stories. All followed the same general plan based on a square courtyard surrounded by rooms.

Most buildings were constructed of mud bricks baked in ovens and were square, reflecting the grid pattern that formed the basis of both major cities. Public wells provided a regular supply of water for all the inhabitants. Bathrooms featured an advanced drainage system. Wastewater flowed out to drains located under the streets and then was carried to sewage pits beyond the city walls. Household trash was dumped by a system of chutes that took it from houses to street-level garbage bins. Four thousand years later, European cities could not boast of these achievements. However, the cities in the Harappan civilization also had slums. At Harappa, tiny dwellings for workers have been found near metal furnaces and the open areas used for pounding grain. Only a well-organized government could have maintained such carefully structured cities.

 SECTION REVIEW

1. **Locate:**
   (a) Himalaya Mountains,   (b) Ganges River,
   (c) Indus River

2. **Define:**
   (a) monsoon,   (b) elite

3. **Identify:**
   (a) Harappa,   (b) Mohenjo-Daro

4. **Recall:** Why do we know less about Harappan civilization than that of the Middle East?

5. **Think Critically:** The text states that only well-organized governments could have maintained such carefully structured cities as Harappa and Mohenjo-Daro. Do you agree that these cities had well-organized governments? Why? What is some of the evidence that supports your answer?

THE ARRIVAL OF THE ARYANS

One of the most fascinating mysteries of Harappan civilization is how it came to an end. Archaeologists working at Mohenjo-Daro have discovered signs of gradual decay and then a sudden destruction of the city and its inhabitants sometime around 1500 B.C. Most likely, Harappan civilization declined over a period of time. Changes in climate, floods, an earthquake, and even a change in the course of the Indus River all weakened the once-flourishing civilization in the Indus River valley. The invaders—known as the Aryans (AIR-ee-unz)—brought its final end.

Around 2000 B.C., Indo-European–speaking nomadic peoples began to move out of their original homeland in Siberia and the steppes (STEPS) of central Asia. Some of them moved westward and eventually settled in Europe (see Chapter 2). Another group, who called themselves Aryans, moved south across the

▶ *The serenity of the priest-king of Mohenjo-Daro is captured in sculpture here. What details of face and form did the artist emphasize?*

 On Line with

WORLD HISTORY **Internet Activity**

You may want to have your students visit the following URL, where they will find information and additional web site resources to enhance their study of this chapter.

Harappa & Moheno–Daro: Ancient Indus Valley
http://www.harappa.com/har/harl.html

Features sections on geography and Indus Valley sites. Contains well-done descriptions and excellent photographs.

Due to the ever-changing nature of the World Wide Web, see the West History web site, **http://history.swpco.com** for regular updates of the URLs in this text.

Hindu Kush into the plains of northern India. They conquered the Harappans and created a new society based on Aryan culture and institutions. Like other nomadic peoples, the Aryans excelled at the art of war. As we saw in studying Mesopotamia and Egypt, the contact between nomadic and farming peoples often ended in armed conflict.

Between 1500 and 1000 B.C., the Aryan peoples gradually advanced eastward from the Indus valley, across the fertile plain of the Ganges, and later southward into the Deccan plateau. Eventually they extended their political control throughout all of India. Although the Dravidians—the descendants of the ancient Harappans—were conquered by the militarily stronger Aryans, they survived as an important element in the civilization of ancient India.

Historians know little about the origins and early culture of the Aryans. They were a pastoral people with a strong warrior tradition and were organized in tribes. Like most nomadic peoples, the earlier Aryans had no written language. Most of what is known about their earlier history is based on oral traditions. After settling in India, the Aryans gave up the pastoral life for regular farming. The introduction of iron—probably from the Middle East, where it had first been used by the Assyrians about 1100 B.C. (see Chapter 2)—also played a role. The creation of the iron plow, along with the use of irrigation, made it possible for the Aryans and their subject peoples to clear the dense jungle growth along the Ganges River and make it into a rich farming area.

The Aryans developed their first writing system, known as **Sanskrit,** around 1000 B.C. This enabled them to write down the legends and religious chants and rituals that had previously been passed down orally from generation to generation. These early writings of the Aryans, known as the Vedas, reveal that between 1500 and 400 B.C., India was a world of warring kingdoms and shifting tribal alliances. Various Aryan chieftains carved out small states and fought other Aryan chieftains. They sacked one another's fortresses and seized women, cattle, and treasure. Not until the fourth century B.C., as we will see later, would one leader—Chandragupta (CHUN-dru-GUP-tuh) Maurya—establish a large Indian state.

The Art of Ruling in Ancient India

Political power among the Aryans was held by a tribal chieftain, called a **raja** (prince). The raja was assisted by a tribal council composed of other leading members of the tribe, who came to form an elite warrior class. The tribal chief's power was based on his ability to protect his tribe. Tradition also related that the first prince had been chosen by Brahman, the chief god of the Aryans. This gave early Aryan rulers their claims to be representatives of the gods.

Nevertheless, there remained among the Aryans a tradition that the ruler did not possess absolute authority but instead was required to follow the laws that applied to all people. Because the ruler was a man like other men and must follow the laws of heaven, even a revolt against an evil king was allowed. As Aryan society grew in size and complexity, especially by the fourth century B.C., rulers took on more of the trappings of a royal figure, including the title of maharaja (MA-huh-RAH-zhuh) (great prince, or king).

The Organization of Society in Ancient India

The conquest by the Aryans had a lasting impact on Indian society. Out of the clash of conqueror and conquered came a set of social institutions and class divisions that has lasted in India with only minor changes down to the present day.

The Caste System

At the heart of the social system that emerged from the clash of cultures was the idea of the superiority of the invading peoples over their conquered subjects. In a sense, it became an issue of skin color. The Aryan invaders, primarily a light-skinned people, looked down on their subjects, who were dark skinned, in spite of the fact that the civilization of the dark-skinned inhabitants of the Indus valley was much more advanced than their own.

The concept of skin color, however, was only one aspect of the division that took place in Indian society. The division of Indian classes (commonly known as

So What ??

*If your students question the importance of the information on **ancient Indian society**, tell them . . .*

By understanding Indian castes, one of the most extreme examples of a social class structure in the world, they will be made more aware of the influence of class in our own society.

Ask students to compare the caste system in India to the social classes we see in the United States. What are the similarities? What are the differences?

FOCUS ACTIVITY

Help students become aware of class structure in their own society. Ask them to list as many characteristics as they can think of that Americans use to classify people. These may include income, race, ethnicity, religion, education, occupation, where people live, and many others. Why do we often think of people in terms of class? How are these reasons related to development of a caste system by the ancient Indians?

TEACH

CLASS DISCUSSION

History shows that most nomadic people who conquer pastoral people eventually also become pastoral. This was true of the Aryans who conquered India. Divide your class into small groups and ask each group to develop and defend a hypothesis for why this is true.

COMPARE TIME PERIODS

Around 3000 B.C. the Sumerians created cuneiform writing, which was used to record daily events as well as Mesopotamian literature. Ask students to write an essay that compares and contrasts the importance of cuneiform writing with that of the development of Sanskrit in India around 1000 B.C.

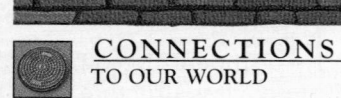

CONNECTIONS
TO OUR WORLD

USING PRIMARY SOURCES

There is a quotation about the Aryan race that is attributed to Adolf Hitler in the "Connections to our World" feature to the right. Ask students to compare and contrast the treatment given to Indian people by their Aryan conquerors around 2000 B.C. with Hitler's treatment of Jewish people before and during World War II. Does the fact that this is a direct quotation from Hitler make it more meaningful to students?

CLASS DISCUSSION

Some people believe that societies always need a group to be at the bottom of a class structure so that most people have someone to feel superior to and who will be forced to do jobs that are distasteful but need to be done. Lead your students in a discussion of this idea. Do they believe there is a class of 'untouchables' in the United States?

CONNECTIONS
TO OUR WORLD

Aryans in India and Nazi Germany   The Aryans were a group of Indo-European–speaking nomadic peoples who moved into the plains of northern India between 2000 and 1500 B.C. In the nineteenth century A.D., linguists (people who study languages) borrowed the term *Aryan* to identify people speaking a common set of languages known as Indo-European.

In the twentieth century, Adolf Hitler and the Nazis used the term *Aryan* in a new way. They identified the Aryans as a race that included the Greeks and Romans of the past and the Germans and Scandinavians of the present. They viewed the Germans as the true descendants and chief leaders of the Aryans.

Hitler believed that the Aryan race, to which all "true Germans" belonged, was the highest race of humanity. According to Hitler, "All the human culture, all the result of art, science, and technology that we see before us today, are almost exclusively the creative product of the Aryan." The Aryans, according to Hitler, were once rulers of the Earth. They are the highest race of humankind. The German people were destined to carry out their higher mission—regaining the former ruling position of the Aryan race and ensuring Aryan world domination. To Hitler, however, one major obstacle stood in the way of Aryan destiny—the Jews. Hitler considered the Jews to be the poisoners of the blood of the Aryan race. The elimination of the Jews became Hitler's special "higher mission." The Holocaust (HO-leh-cost), the deliberate attempt to kill all of Europe's Jews during World War II, was a result of Hitler's twisted ideas of the Aryans as a race.

In our time, the existence of such organizations as the Aryan Nations shows the continuing influence of Hitler's ideas. The Aryan Nations is but one of a number of neo-Nazi and white supremacist groups in the United States that continue to follow Hitler's racial ideals.

castes in English) was also based on economic advantage. Indeed, the **caste system** was a set of rigid social categories that determined not only a person's occupation and economic potential but also his or her position in society.

There were five major castes in Indian society in ancient times. At the top were two castes that were clearly the ruling elites in Aryan society even before their arrival in India: the priests and the warriors. The priestly class, whose members were known as the Brahmins, was usually considered to be at the top of the social scale (see "You Are There: The Training of the Brahmins"). They were in charge of the religious ceremonies that were so important in Indian society.

The second caste was the Kshatriyas (ku-SHA-tree-yuhs), or the warriors. Like the Brahmins, the Kshatriyas were associated with a single occupation—that of fighting. As the character of Aryan society changed, however, the Kshatriyas often acquired new forms of employment. At the same time, new conquering families from other castes were sometimes accepted into the ranks of the warriors.

The third-ranked caste in Indian society was the Vaisyas, or commoners. The Vaisyas were usually the merchants who engaged in commerce. Quite possibly the Vaisyas were originally guardians of the tribal herds of cattle and later moved into trade.

Below these three castes were the Sudras, who made up the great bulk of the Indian population. The Sudras were not Aryans, and the term probably originally referred to the conquered dark-skinned natives (the Dravidians). Most Sudras were peasants, artisans, or people who worked at other forms of manual labor. They had only limited rights in society.

At the lowest level of Indian society, and in fact not even considered a real part of the caste system, were the Untouchables. The Untouchables probably began as a slave class consisting of prisoners of war, criminals, members of minority tribes, and other groups considered outside Indian society. Even after slavery was outlawed, the Untouchables were given menial, degrading tasks that other Indians would not accept, such as collecting trash and handling dead bodies. The Untouchables probably made up about 5 percent of the total population of ancient India.

RETEACHING ACTIVITY

Read the statements below and ask students to identify where each of the individuals would fit in the Indian caste system.

a. I am called Mahadev. I live in a simple hut outside of Pataliputra with other philosophers. I have renounced all worldly pleasures and spend most of my time studying the Vedas and teaching willing pupils. (*Brahman*)

b. My name is Uttamchand. As far back as

can be recalled my family have been retail grocers in Probander province. We are known as very shrewd businessmen. (*Vaisya*)

c. My parents named me Lakshmi. I help my mother and the other women of the ghetto clean the public toilettes. When we walk down the street it is my job to make a loud noise in order to warn others away. (*Untouchable*)

YOU ARE THERE

The Training of the Brahmins

Priests were at the top of ancient India's caste system. They were known as Brahmins and Brahmin meant "one possessed of Brahman." (Brahman was the chief god of the Aryans.) At one time Brahmins had advised the ruler on religious matters in Aryan tribal society. Eventually the Brahmins became an official class. The following selection, written by the Greek ambassador Megathenes around 300 B.C., describes the upbringing of these special people.

Megathenes, Writing on Brahmins

From the time of their conception in the womb they are under the care and guardianship of learned men who go to the mother, and under the pretense of using some incantations for the welfare of herself and her unborn child, in reality give her wise hints and counsels, and the women who listen to them most willingly are thought to be the most fortunate in their offspring. After their birth the children are in the care of one person after another, and as they advance in years their masters are men of superior accomplishments. These philosophers reside in a grove in front of the city within a moderate-sized enclosure. They live in simple style and lie on pallets of straw and [deer] skins. They abstain from animal food and worldly pleasures; and occupy their time in listening to serious discourse and in imparting knowledge to willing ears.

▲ *A Brahmin extends his open hands in prayer. What does the priest's style of dress reveal about his beliefs and lifestyle?*

1. How were Brahmins trained?
2. What was a Brahmin's function in Indian society?
3. Considering the placement of Brahmins at the top of the caste system, what conclusions can you draw about the values of Indian society?

The life of the Untouchables was extremely difficult. They were not considered human, and their very presence was considered harmful to members of the other classes. No Indian would touch or eat food handled by an Untouchable. Untouchables lived in special ghettos and were required to tap two sticks together to announce their presence when they traveled outside their quarters so that others could avoid them.

Technically, these caste divisions were absolute. Individuals supposedly were born, lived, and died in

d. I am Sushma. My mother and father have a small farm in Rajkot. We have a zebu cow that provides us with milk, which my mother makes into ghee (butter), and dung, which we use for cooking fuel and crop fertilizer. (*Sudras*)

e. I am called Sunil and I am a general in Asoka's army. I have fought many battles from the Ganges to the Indus river. As a reward for my bravery I have been made the raj of Wankaner state. (*Kshatriya*)

USING PRIMARY SOURCES

Ask your students to consider the life that Brahmin children in India lead. In what ways does this primary source demonstrate differences between our value system and that of ancient India? Ask your students to write a similar description of the life that may await children of upper class American families.

Answers to Critical Thinking Questions

1. A series of wise masters imparted knowledge and guidance to the chosen person, beginning before his birth.
2. Brahmins were priests and philosophers.
3. Serious discourse, knowledge, priestly functions, and the simple life style were the most highly regarded aspects of Indian life.

LEARNING FROM VISUALS

Answer to the caption question: The Brahmin is dressed very simply, so must not value material things.

REINFORCING VOCABULARY

The word *guru* today has a different connotation than it did in ancient India. Discuss what many people would think if a person said, "I'm going to visit my guru," now with what would have been assumed if a person said the same in ancient India.

TEACHING THEMES

The Importance of Culture. Ask students to write short paragraphs that describe how a new widow would be expected to behave in their families. Have several students read their paragraphs to the class. Discuss differences between cultural values in the United States and those in India when the ritual of sati was required of widows. What does this show about the role of women in ancient Indian culture?

the same caste, and throughout most of Indian history caste divisions remained strict. Members were generally not allowed to marry or share meals outside their castes.

The Family in Ancient India

Life in ancient India centered around the family. The family, not the individual, was the most basic unit in society. The ideal was an extended family, with three generations—grandparents, parents, and children—living under the same roof. It was basically patriarchal, because the oldest male held legal authority over the entire family unit in most of India.

The superiority of males in ancient Indian society was evident in a number of ways. For one thing, women could not serve as priests. In general, only males were educated. The chief goal of learning to read was to carry on family rituals, including family ceremonies to honor the dead and to link the living and the dead. Only the male family head could lead these rituals. In high-class families, young men began their education with a **guru** (teacher). Some then went on to higher studies in one of the major cities. Marriage for such young men was not supposed to occur until after twelve years of study.

In general, only males could inherit property, except in a few cases where there were no sons. According to law, a woman was always considered a minor. Divorce was not allowed, although it sometimes took place. A wife who had been deserted by her husband, for example, could seek a divorce. Husbands could take a second wife if the first was unable to bear children. Children were an important product of marriage, primarily because they were expected to take care of their parents as they grew older. Child marriage, arranged by the parents, was common for young girls, probably because daughters were seen as an economic drain on their parents.

Perhaps the most vivid symbol of women's subjugation to men was the ritual of sati (suh-TEE), which required a wife to throw herself on her dead husband's flaming funeral pyre (PIR). A Greek visitor reported "that he had heard from some persons of wives burning themselves along with their deceased husbands and

doing so gladly; and that those women who refused to burn themselves were held in disgrace." All in all, women had a difficult existence (see "You Are There: The Position of Women in Ancient India").

The subordinate role of women had one major cause. As in most farming societies, in ancient India men did most of the work in the fields. Females were seen as having little usefulness outside the home. Indeed, they were viewed as an economic burden, because parents had to provide a dowry (a gift of money or goods) to get a husband for a daughter. A female child would also offer little help in maintaining the family unit, because she would join the family of her husband after they were married.

The Economy

Like people in other early civilizations, most people in ancient India were primarily concerned with survival. This was certainly true for the vast majority who lived off the land. The Aryan conquest did not dramatically change the economic character of Indian society. Not only did most Aryans take up farming, but it is likely that farming expanded rapidly under Aryan rule with the invention of the iron plow and the spread of North Indian culture into the Deccan plateau. One result of this process was a shift in the focus of Indian culture from the Indus valley further eastward to the Ganges River. Even today this is one of the most densely populated regions on Earth. The flatter areas in the Deccan plateau and in the coastal plains were also turned into cropland.

For most Indian farmers, life was harsh indeed. Most fortunate were those who owned their own land, although they were required to pay taxes. Many others were sharecroppers or landless laborers, who paid high rents to their landlords. The tradition of dividing property among all the sons did limit the amassing of land in large holdings. However, large estates worked by hired laborers or rented out to sharecroppers were not uncommon, particularly in areas where local rajas derived much of their wealth from their property.

Another problem for Indian farmers was the uncertainty of the climate. As we have seen, when the monsoon rains were late, there were shortages of food.

MORE ABOUT . . . *Pepper and the Indian Economy*

One of the primary exports of southern India was pepper. In the ancient world spices, especially pepper corns, were an important commodity because of the difficulty in preserving food. Pepper was often used to cover the flavor of meat which had turned rancid. Once ancient Europeans discovered this flavor enhancer they were willing to pay its weight in gold. Indians received so many gold coins from the Roman Empire that Emperor Nero banned the importation of pepper corns in order to stop the drain on the Roman economy. This same condiment would later play a role in history as the enticement for European traders and explorers of the 15th and 16th centuries.

YOU ARE THERE

The Position of Women in Ancient India

The following passage is from the Law of Manu, *a work on social behavior in ancient India written in the first or second century* B.C. *The passage states that respect for women is the responsibility of men. At the same time, it also makes clear that the place of women is in the home.*

Law of Manu

Women must be honored and adorned by their father, brothers, husbands, and brother-in-law who desire great good fortune.

Where women are honored, there the gods rejoice; where, however, they are not honored, there all sacred rites prove fruitless.

Her father protects her in childhood, her husband protects her in youth, her sons protect her in old age—a woman does not deserve independence.

The father who does not give away his daughter in marriage at the proper time is censurable; censurable is the husband who does not approach his wife in due season; and after the husband is dead, the son is censurable, who does not protect his mother. . . .

The husband should engage his wife in the collection and expenditure of his wealth, in cleanliness, in cooking food for the family, and in looking after the necessities of the household.

▲ *This photograph shows that village life in India has remained essentially unchanged for over 2,000 years. Why are cattle fed and housed with as much consideration as humans in India?*

Women destined to bear children, enjoying great good fortune, deserving of worship, the resplendent lights of homes on the one hand and divinities of good luck who reside in the houses on the other—between these there is no difference whatsoever.

1. How was a woman to be treated by her family in ancient India?

2. Explain what was meant by, "a woman does not deserve independence."

3. What was the relationship between the treatment of women and good fortune?

COOPERATIVE LEARNING ACTIVITY

Divide the class into groups of three or four per group. Each group's assignment is to develop a Venn diagram (overlapping circles) to compare and contrast the role of women in Hindu society with that of women in ancient Egypt.

You may need to remind students that they read about Egyptian civilization in Section 2 of Chapter 2. After each group has developed its diagram, bring students together to present and compare their work.

USING PRIMARY SOURCES

Ask students what was different about the Indian economy that made the Law of Manu acceptable to Indian society when it clearly would not be accepted in American society today? Ask male students to describe how they regard their duty to female members of their family.

Answers to Critical Thinking Questions

1. A woman was to be honored by the men in the family, to make the gods happy. She was to be protected, married off by her father, and engaged in the "collection and expenditure" of her husband's wealth.

2. Independence was something to be avoided because it meant she was not under the protection of the men in her family, and therefore not honored. Students today may interpret the phrase as meaning that a woman wasn't good enough to be independent.

3. Proper treatment of women brought good fortune to the family because the gods were happy and the "divinities of good luck" would reside in the house.

LEARNING FROM VISUALS

Answer to the caption question: Beasts, as living things, are considered to be part of the scale of existence. The cow, in particular, is thought to be sacred.

ASSESS

Possible assessments include:

1. Section Review questions on this page
2. Section 3–2 Quiz in your Teacher Resource materials
3. Reteaching Worksheets in your Teacher Resource materials
4. Self-Study software

Answers to SECTION REVIEW

1. (a) first writing system developed by Aryans,
   (b) prince, Aryan tribal chieftain,
   (c) division of Indian classes,
   (d) teacher
2. (a) invaders in the Indus River Valley,
   (b) dark-skinned natives,
   (c) great prince or king
3. (a) priests—(Brahmins); warriors—(Kshatriyas); commoners—(Vaisyas); Indian population—(Sudras); Untouchables—slave class.
   (b) men served as priests, were educated, lead family rituals, inherited property; women bore children, cared for elderly parents, kept the home.
4. Answers will vary.

CLOSE

Lead students in a discussion of the 'Focus' objectives identified on page 62.

68

Strong governments might deal with this problem by building state-run granaries (storehouses for grain) and maintaining the irrigation works. However, strong governments were rare in India, and famine was probably all too common. The basic crops in the north were wheat, barley, and millet. Rice was common in the fertile river valleys. In the south, grain and vegetables were supplemented by various tropical products, cotton, and spices (such as pepper, ginger, and cinnamon). Later, the Europeans would covet these spices (see Chapter 16).

❀ SECTION REVIEW ❀

1. **Define:**
   (a) Sanskrit, (b) raja, (c) caste system, (d) guru

2. **Identify:**
   (a) Aryans, (b) Dravidians, (c) maharaja

3. **Recall:**
   (a) Name and define the five major castes in the Indian society.
   (b) Discuss the ways male superiority was expressed in ancient Indian society. What were women expected to do?

4. **Think Critically:** Analyze the Indian caste system and compare it to any social structure you see in our country. Identify any parallels and differences you see. If you could, what would you do to change the Indian caste system?

THE RELIGIOUS HERITAGE OF ANCIENT INDIA

Two of the world's great religions, Hinduism and Buddhism, began in India. Both were crucial in shaping the civilization of India. Ancient Aryan beliefs blended with the religious practices of the native peoples (the Dravidians) to form Hinduism. In the sixth century B.C., a new religion, known as Buddhism, emerged to rival Hinduism.

Hinduism

Hinduism had its origins in the religious beliefs of the Aryan peoples who invaded and settled in India after 1500 B.C. Evidence about the religious beliefs of the Aryan peoples comes from the Vedas, which are collections of hymns and religious ceremonies that were passed down orally through the centuries by Aryan priests and then eventually written down.

Early Hindus believed in the existence of a single force in the universe, a form of ultimate reality or God, called **Brahman.** It was the duty of the individual self—called the **Atman**—to seek to know this ultimate reality. By doing so, the self would merge with Brahman after death.

By the sixth century B.C., another new concept—**reincarnation**—had also appeared in Hinduism. Reincarnation is the belief that the individual soul is reborn in a different form after death. As one of the Vedas says, "Worn-out garments are shed by the body/Worn-out bodies are shed by the dweller [the soul]." After a number of existences in the earthly world, the soul reaches its final goal in a union with the Great World Soul, or Brahman. According to Hinduism, all living beings seek to achieve this goal.

Important to this process is the idea of **karma,** or the force of a person's actions in this life in determining his or her rebirth in a next life. What people do in their life determines what they will be in the next life. Hinduism puts all living things on a vast scale of existence that includes the four castes and the Untouchables in human society. The current status of an individual soul, then, is not simply an accident but a result of the actions of the individual in a past existence.

At the top of the scale are the Brahmins (the priestly caste). They are the most advanced souls and the closest to being released from the law of reincarnation. The Brahmins are followed in descending order by the other castes in human society and the world of the animals. Within the animal kingdom, an especially

RECOMMENDED READING

Hinduism, its origins and development, is the subject of S. Radhakrishnan, *The Hindu View of Life* (Oxford, 1926) and B. Walker, *Hindu World,* 2 vols. (London 1969). For a more general treatment, see S. N. Dasgupta, *A History of Indian Philosophy,* 5 vols. (Cambridge, 1922–55) and S. Radhakrishnan, *Indian Philosophy,* revised ed., 2 vols. (London, 1958).

There are also a number of good books on the introduction of Buddhism into Indian society. Buddha's ideals are presented in A. K. Coomaraswamy, *Buddha and the Gospel of Buddhism* (London, 1916; revised, New York, high position is held by the cow. Even today the cow is revered by Hindus as a sacred animal. The sacred position of the cow may have come from the concept of the sacred bull in Dravidian culture.

The concept of karma is ruled by the **dharma,** or the divine law. The law requires different actions from different individuals, depending on their status in society. Those high on the social scale, such as the Brahmins, are held to higher expectations than the lower castes. The Brahmins, for example, are expected not to eat meat. To do so would mean the killing of another living being, thus interrupting its karma.

The system of reincarnation provided a religious basis for the rigid class divisions that had emerged in Indian society. It justified the privileges of those on the higher end of the scale. At the same time, the concept of reincarnation gave hope to those lower on the ladder of life. The poor, for example, could hope that if they behaved properly in this life, they might improve their condition in the next.

How does one become aware of one's spiritual nature? How does one achieve oneness with God? Hindus developed the practice of **yoga** (union), a method of training designed to lead to union with God. Because people are different, Hindus developed four types of yoga to meet different needs. They are the path of knowledge, the path of love, the path of work, and the path of meditation. In following the last path, the follower seeks to still the mind and achieve oneness with God. As one Hindu writing states, "When all the senses are stilled, when the mind is at rest, that, say the wise, is the highest state."

The final goal of any path is to leave behind the cycle of existence and achieve the spiritual union of the individual soul with the Great World Soul, or Brahman, seen as a form of dreamless sleep. Most ordinary Indians, however, could not easily relate to this ideal and needed a more concrete form of heavenly salvation. It was probably for this reason that the Hindu religion came to be peopled with a number of very human gods and goddesses. There are more than 33,000 deities in the Hindu religion, including three chief ones: Brahma the Creator, Vishnu the Preserver, and Siva (SHIV-uh) the Destroyer. There were also many minor gods and goddesses, each having a specific

▲ *Hindu Brahmins chant together for days at a time. What do you notice about where and how the priests are praying?*

role to play. One, for example, might bring good fortune, whereas another might arrange a good marriage.

Many Hindus regard the multitude of gods as simply different expressions of the one ultimate reality, Brahman. However, the various gods and goddesses gave ordinary Indians a way to express their religious feelings. Through devotion at a Hindu temple, they sought not only salvation but also a means of gaining the ordinary things they needed in life. Hinduism became the religion of the vast majority of the Indian people.

Buddhism

In the sixth century B.C., a new doctrine, called Buddhism, appeared in northern India and soon became a rival of Hinduism. The founder of Buddhism was Siddhartha Gautama, who came from a small kingdom in the foothills of the Himalaya Mountains (in what is today southern Nepal). Born around 563 B.C., he was the son of a ruling princely family. The young and very handsome Siddhartha was raised in the lap of luxury. Like others of his class, he was also trained in being a warrior. At the age of sixteen, he married a neighboring princess and began to raise a family.

1964) and E. Conze, *Buddhism: Its Essence and Development* (Oxford, 1951). For a short summary, see E. A. Burtt, *The Teachings of the Compassionate Buddha* (New York, 1955). H. Akira, *A History of Indian Buddhism: From Sakyamuni to Early Mahayana* (Hawaii, 1990) provides a detailed analysis of early activities by Siddhartha Gautama and his followers. The intimate relationship between Buddhism and commerce is discussed in Liu Hsin-ju, *Ancient India and Ancient China: Trades and Religious Exchanges* (Oxford, 1988).

FOCUS

OBJECTIVES

After completing this section, students should be able to

1. identify the central beliefs of Hinduism
2. identify the central beliefs of Buddhism
3. explain differences between Hindu and Buddhist beliefs

FOCUS ACTIVITY

Help students understand that religious differences leading to social conflict is not unique to India. Ask your students to identify other religious conflicts and list them on the board. Can students find similarities among these situations?

TEACH

REINFORCING VOCABULARY

Discuss the relationship between the Hindu belief in reincarnation and the idea of karma.

COMPARING TIME PERIODS

Divide the class into groups and assign each group to compare, contrast, and record their ideas about the Hindu belief in reincarnation and Egyptian beliefs about what happened to people when they died.

LEARNING FROM VISUALS

Answer to the caption question: Answers will vary.

Multimedia Support

LASERDISC
700-year-old Tempera Color Painting of Birth of Buddha

Carving of Queen Maya Asleep Conceiving Buddha

CLASS DISCUSSION

On the previous page the text states that there are more than 33,000 deities in the Hindu religion. Ask your students to identify and explain possible reasons why people might prefer a religion with many deities rather than one with one all-powerful god. Why might other people choose a religion with only one god?

Multimedia Support

TRANSPARENCY
3–2, Comparing the Major Characteristics of Hinduism and Buddhism

TEACHING THEMES

The Role of Individuals. Remind students that the founder of Buddhism was one person, Siddhartha Gautama, who chose to abandon a life of wealth and privilege to spend his life seeking a cure for human suffering. Ask them to identify and discuss other individuals who have given up personal wealth to help less fortunate people.

▲ *The dancing Siva in this bronze statue is a visual reminder to his followers of the Hindu deity's power and compassion. While Siva creates the universe with his right hand, he destroys it by fire with his upper left hand. Eternal blessing is offered with his lower two hands.*

Siddhartha appeared to have everything: wealth, a good appearance, a model wife, a child, and a throne that he would someday inherit. In his late twenties, however, Siddhartha became aware of the pain of illness, the sorrow of death, and the effects of old age on ordinary people. He exclaimed, "Would that sickness, age, and death might be for ever bound!" He decided to spend his life seeking the cure for human suffering. He gave up his royal clothes, shaved his head, abandoned his family, and set off to find the true meaning of life.

At first he tried to follow the example of the **ascetics** (people who practiced self-denial as a means of achieving an understanding of ultimate reality). The abuse of his physical body did not lead him to a greater understanding of life, however. It led to a close brush with death from not eating. He abandoned asceticism and turned instead to an intense period of meditation. (As we have seen, in Hinduism this was a way to find oneness with God.) One evening, while sitting in meditation under a tree (which came to be known as the Bo Tree—short for bodhi [BO-dih], or wisdom), Siddhartha finally reached enlightenment as to the meaning of life. He spent the rest of his life preaching what he had discovered. His teachings became the basic principles of Buddhism.

It is not certain that Siddhartha Gautama ever intended to create a new religion or doctrine (a system of belief). In some ways, his ideas could be seen as an attempt to reform Hinduism. In his day, Hinduism had become complex and dependent on the Brahmins as keepers of religious secrets. Siddhartha challenged people to be responsible for their own lives: "Do not accept what you hear by report. Be lamps unto yourselves." He also advised, "Do not go by what is handed down, nor by the authority of your traditional teachings. When you know of yourselves, 'These teachings are good or not good,' only then accept or reject them."

Siddhartha did, in fact, accept much of the belief system of Hinduism. He followed Hinduism in praising nonviolence and borrowed the idea of living a life of simplicity and self-denial from the Hindu ascetics. Moreover, his vision of Nirvana—or ultimate reality—is close to the Hindu concept of Brahman. Nirvana means the end of the self and a reunion in life with the Great World Soul.

At the same time, the new doctrine differed from Hindu practices in a number of important ways. Siddhartha did not believe in the existence of an individual soul. To him, the Hindu idea of Atman—the individual soul—meant that the soul was subject to rebirth and did not achieve a complete freedom from the cares of this world. Siddhartha, in fact, denied the ultimate reality of the material world. The physical surroundings of humans were simply an illusion. The pain, poverty, and sorrow that afflict human beings are caused by their attachment to things of this world. Once people let go of their worldly cares, pain and sorrow can be forgotten. Then comes *bodhi,* or wisdom. (The word *bodhi* is the root of the word *Buddhism* and of the usual name of Gautama Buddha, or Gautama the Wise.)

So What ??

*If your students question the importance or relevance of the information on **Indian religions,** tell them . . .*

An awareness of the power and influence of religion on the lives of the people of India provides a mirror of those same influences in our own lives. You might use this opportunity to ask students if they can identify any similarities between the religious beliefs and practices that they have been reading about and those in their own culture. Can they see how studying other cultures can help them better understand their own?

Achieving wisdom is a key step to achieving Nirvana. Siddhartha preached this message in a sermon to his followers in the Deer Park at Sarnath (outside India's holy city of Benares). It is a simple message based on the Four Noble Truths: (1) ordinary life is full of suffering; (2) this suffering is caused by our desire to satisfy ourselves; (3) the way to end suffering is to end desire for selfish goals and to see others as extensions of ourselves; and (4) the way to end desire is to follow the Middle Path. (See "You Are There: Gautama Buddha Speaks to His Disciples.")

This Middle Path is also known as the Eightfold Path, because it consists of eight steps:

1. **Right view.** We need to know the Four Noble Truths.

2. **Right intention.** We need to decide what we really want.

3. **Right speech.** We must seek to speak truth and to speak well of others.

4. **Right action.** The Buddha gave five precepts: "Do not kill. Do not steal. Do not lie. Do not be unchaste. Do not take drugs or drink alcohol."

5. **Right livelihood.** We must do work that uplifts our being.

6. **Right effort.** The Buddha said, "Those who follow the Way might well follow the example of an ox that arches through the deep mud carrying a heavy load. He is tired, but his steady, forward-looking gaze will not relax until he comes out of the mud."

7. **Right mindfulness.** We must keep our minds in control of our senses: "All we are is the result of what we have thought."

8. **Right concentration.** We must meditate to see the world in a new way.

Buddhism also differed from Hinduism in another way. Siddhartha accepted the idea of reincarnation.

◀ *Roaring lions proclaim Buddhist teachings to the four corners of the world from the top of this stone pillar, built during the rule of Asoka. Known as the Lions of Sarnath, this is the most famous of all the pillar capitals because of its beauty and Buddhist symbolism. The wheel represents Buddha's law and declares Asoka's position as the enlightened ruler of India.*

He, too, believed that human beings differed as a result of karma from a previous existence, but he rejected the Hindu division of human beings into rigidly defined castes based on previous reincarnations. He taught instead that all human beings could reach Nirvana as a result of their behavior in this life. This made Buddhism appealing to the downtrodden peoples at the lower end of the social scale. In this regard, it had an appeal similar to what Christianity had for ancient Romans (see Chapter 6).

Buddhism also differed from Hinduism in its simplicity. Siddhartha rejected the multitude of gods that had become identified with Hinduism. He forbade his followers to worship either his person or his image after his death. For that reason, many Buddhists see Buddhism as a philosophy rather than as a religion. In fact, if you look for books on Buddhism in an American bookstore, you will usually find them under the subject of philosophy rather than religion.

In one respect, Siddhartha Gautama was unable to move beyond the social outlook of his day. Like many of his fellow Indians, he was unwilling to accept women as being equal to men. In a conversation with his follower Ananda, he remarked: "Women are soon angered, Ananda; women are full of passion, Ananda; women are envious, Ananda; women are stupid, Ananda. That is the reason, Ananda, that the cause, why women have no place in public life, do not carry on a business, and do not earn their living by any profession."

Siddhartha's suspicion toward women was probably based on his belief that they would distract individuals from the search for wisdom. He believed that Buddhist monks—those who follow a solitary life to find

LEARNING FROM VISUALS

Ask students to consider the Lions of Sarnath pictured to the left. What does it tell them about Indian society, abilities, and values beyond the information included in the caption?

TEACHING THEMES

The Role of Ideas. Siddhartha believed that pain, poverty, and sorrow that afflict humans are caused by their attachment to things in this world. Ask students to discuss why leaders in India might have supported such a belief for reasons that had nothing to do with religion.

USING PRIMARY SOURCES

The Eightfold Path was Gautama Buddha's idea of the way to end desire. Ask students to write an essay about the personality they believe Buddha must have had based on this primary source.

How would your students define the concept of "Right mindfulness"? Do they believe his statement that, "All we are is the result of what we have thought?"

ENRICHMENT ACTIVITY

Have students more closely examine the Buddha's Four Noble Truths and the Middle Path. Have each student select one of the four truths or one of the eight steps listed for achieving the Middle Path and either do research to find commentary on that truth or step, or write their own commentary on its meaning. Have the students share their findings or personal thoughts with their classmates. In addition, you may ask the students to explain why this philosophy might be at odds with traditional American consumer society.

YOU·ARE·THERE

USING PRIMARY SOURCES

In his sermon at Benares, Gautama Buddha describes two extremes in words and phrases that are not typically used by most students. Assign your students to rewrite this sermon in a way that keeps its meaning but which would allow their friends to understand its message.

Answers to Critical Thinking Questions

1. Passionate behavior was thought to be vulgar and common; self torture was painful. Following either of these two paths would never produce insight and knowledge, calm, or enlightenment—Nirvana.
2. Any disciple of Siddhartha; anyone seeking enlightenment.

Multimedia Support

TRANSPARENCY
3–3, Spread of Hinduism and Buddhism

YOU ARE THERE
Gautama Buddha Speaks to His Disciples

One of the most famous passages in Buddhist literature is the sermon at Benares, which Siddhartha Gautama delivered to his followers in the Deer Park. Here he set forth the key ideas that would define Buddhist beliefs for centuries to come:

Gautama Buddha, Sermon at Benares

Thus have I heard: at one time the Lord dwelt at Benares in the Deer Park. There the Lord addressed the five monks:

"These two extremes, monks, are not to be practised by one who has gone forth from the world. What are the two? That connected with the passions and luxury, low, vulgar, common, and useless; and that connected with self-torture, painful, and useless. Avoiding these two extremes the seeking one has gained the enlightenment of the Middle Path, which produces insight and knowledge and tends to calm, to higher knowledge, enlightenment, Nirvana.

▲ *Siddhartha, the Buddha, assumes the lotus position called* padmasana *in this fifth-century limestone sculpture. Beneath him, figures representing his first five students gather to hear Buddha's teaching, symbolized by the wheel in the center. The image was found in Sarnath, where Siddhartha preached his first sermon.*

"And what, monks, is the Middle Path, of which the seeking one has gained enlightenment, which produces insight and knowledge, and tends to calm, to higher knowledge, enlightenment, Nirvana? This is the noble Eightfold Way: namely, right view, right intention, right speech, right action, right livelihood, right effort, right mindfulness, right concentration. This, monks, is the Middle Path, of which the seeking one has gained enlightenment, which produces insight and knowledge, and tends to calm, to higher knowledge, enlightenment, Nirvana."

---

1. What are the two extremes of behavior that disciples of Siddhartha Gautama are to avoid? Explain why these paths are called useless.

2. Who is "the seeking one" referred to in these passages?

So What ⁇

If your students question the importance of the information on **Hinduism and Buddhism,** *tell them . . .*

Since two out of every five people in the world is either Chinese or Indian, two cultures strongly influenced by Hindu and Buddhist philosophy, it is essential that students are aware of these very different ways of looking at the world. More and more we will be interacting on a regular basis with people of other cultures. It is especially important to understand diversity as we move toward a more closely joined global community.

wisdom—should be free of desire for women. The presence of women would be a distraction. When Ananda asked Siddhartha, "How shall we behave before women?" their conversation went as follows:

"You should shun their gaze, Ananda."
"But if we see them, master, what then are we to do?"
"Not speak to them, Ananda."
"But if we do speak to them, what then?"
"Then you must watch over yourselves, Ananda."[1]

As time went on, Siddhartha agreed to accept women into the Buddhist monastic order. However, their inferior position within the order had been established. This Buddhist attitude remained the same down to modern times. Nevertheless, the position of women tended to be better in Buddhist societies than it was elsewhere in ancient India.

Siddhartha Gautama died in 480 B.C. at the age of eighty after eating some poisoned mushrooms that had been placed accidentally in his food. After his death, his dedicated followers traveled throughout India, spreading his message. Buddhist monasteries were also established to promote his teaching and provide housing and training for monks dedicated to the simple life and the pursuit of wisdom. Temples and **stupas** (STOO-pahz) (stone towers housing relics of the Buddha) sprang up throughout the countryside. During the next centuries, Buddhism and Hinduism began to compete actively for followers.

 SECTION REVIEW

1. **Define:**
   (*a*) Brahman,   (*b*) Atman,   (*c*) reincarnation,
   (*d*) karma,   (*e*) dharma,   (*f*) yoga,   (*g*) ascetics,
   (*h*) stupas

2. **Identify:**
   (*a*) Siddhartha Gautama

3. **Recall:**
   (*a*) Why were the Brahmins expected not to eat meat?
   (*b*) What are the four types of yoga?

(*c*) One of the Four Noble Truths in Siddhartha's message is to follow the "Middle Path." List the eight steps in the Middle Path.

4. **Think Critically:** As a young man in his twenties, Siddhartha appeared to have everything, but was not content and wanted to find a cure for human suffering. Imagine that you are Siddhartha and you experienced these feelings. What would you have done differently?

NEW DYNASTIES AND NEW EMPIRES IN INDIA

The Aryans brought little unity to India. For hundreds of years after their arrival, warring kingdoms and shifting tribal alliances disturbed the peace. However, India was soon affected by empires to its west. First came Persia, which extended its empire into western India. Then came the Greeks and Macedonians (mass-uh-DON-ee-unz). Alexander the Great had heard of the riches of India, and after conquering Persia, he swept into northwestern India in the summer of 327 B.C. His soldiers refused to continue fighting, however, and they departed almost as quickly as they had come.

The Mauryan Dynasty

Alexander the Great's conquests in western India form only a brief episode in Indian history, but they gave rise to the first dynasty to control much of India. A new Indian state was founded by Chandragupta Maurya, who ruled from 324 to 301 B.C. He drove out the Greek occupation forces and established the capital of his new Mauryan Empire in northern India at Pataliputra (modern Patna [PUTT-nuh]) in the Ganges valley.

This first Indian empire was highly centralized and even despotic. According to the *Arthasastra*, a work on politics written by a Mauryan court official, "It is power and power alone which, only when exercised by the

RECOMMENDED READING

If you are looking for more detailed information on the Mauryan period, see D. D. Kosambi, *The Culture and Civilization of* *Ancient India* (London, 1965) and R. Thapar, *Asoka and the Decline of the Mauryas* (Oxford, 1961).

ASSESS

Possible assessments include:

1. Section Review questions on this page
2. Section 3–3 Quiz in your Teacher Resource materials
3. Reteaching Worksheets in your Teachers Resource materials
4. Self-Study software

Answers to SECTION REVIEW

1. (a) a single force in the universe
   (b) the individual self
   (c) soul is reborn in a different form after death
   (d) a person's actions in this life determines that person's rebirth in a next life
   (e) the divine law that requires different actions from different people
   (f) a method of training designed to lead to union with God
   (g) practicing self-denial to achieve an understanding of ultimate reality
   (h) stone towers housing relics of the Buddha
2. (a) founder of Buddhism
3. (a) it would mean killing another living being, thus interrupting its karma
   (b) the paths of knowledge, love, work, and meditation
   (c) right view, right intention, right speech, right action, right livelihood, right effort, right mindfulness, right concentration
4. Answers will vary.

CLOSE

Lead students in a discussion of the 'Focus' objectives identified on page 69.

FOCUS

OBJECTIVES

After completing this section, students should be able to

1. identify and explain characteristics of the Mauryan dynasty
2. explain the importance of the Silk Road and of trade to India
3. identify and explain events in the growth of the Kingdom of the Guptas
4. explain how Indian culture influenced historical events in other parts of the world

king with impartiality, over his son or his enemy, maintains both this world and the next."[2] The king had a large army and a secret police that followed his orders. According to Megasthenes, the Greek ambassador to the Mauryan court, Chandragupta Maurya was always afraid of assassination. All food was tasted in his presence, and he made a practice of never sleeping twice in the same bed in his large palace.

The Mauryan Empire was divided into provinces that were ruled by governors who were appointed by the ruler. Most of these governors were relatives of the king or military commanders favored by the king. In turn, the provinces were divided into districts, each governed by an official appointed by the governor. At the base of the government structure was the village, where the vast majority of the Indian people lived. Although this system of government was headed by the king, the king's authority outside the capital was often limited.

The Reign of Asoka

According to tradition, Chandragupta Maurya ruled for a quarter-century and then retired and turned over his kingdom to his son Bindusara. Little is known about Bindusara. His son and successor, Asoka (uh-

SOKE-uh), is well known, however. Asoka ruled from 269 to 232 B.C. and is generally considered to be the greatest ruler in the history of India. Asoka began his reign like many others, conquering and killing. However, after a particularly bloody victory and his conversion to Buddhism, which teaches nonviolence, the king began to change and tried to rule kindheartedly. One of his edicts stated: "When the king, Beloved of the Gods, had been consecrated eight years Kalinga was conquered, 150,000 people were deported, 100,000 were killed, and many times that number died. But after the conquest of Kalinga, the Beloved of the Gods began to follow Righteousness, to love righteousness, and to give instruction in Righteousness. . . . The participation of all men in common suffering is grievous to the Beloved of the Gods."[3]

Asoka appears to have lived up to his reputation. He set up hospitals for both people and animals. He ordered that trees and shelters be placed along the road to provide shade and rest for weary travelers. He sent Buddhist missionaries throughout India and ordered the erection of stone pillars with Buddhist writings inscribed on them to instruct people in the proper way. Asoka was more than a kind ruler, however. Trade and industry flourished during his reign, and his kingdom prospered.

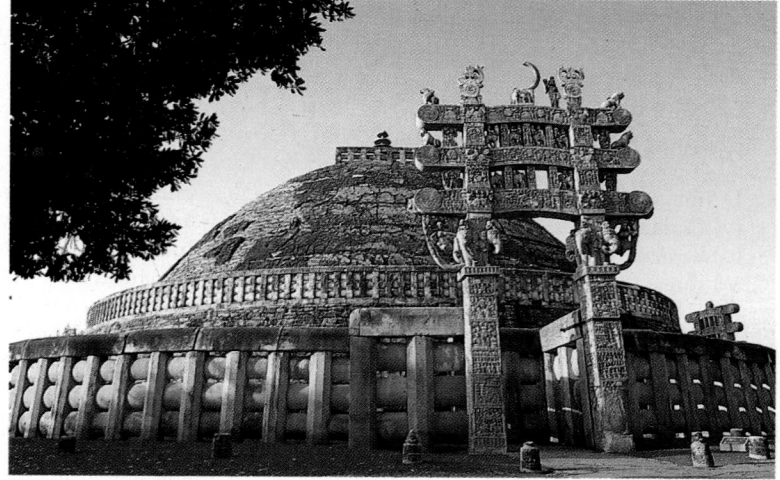

▶ Built in the third century B.C., the Sanchi stupa was originally intended to house a relic of the Buddha. Over time, it was enlarged and has now become the greatest Buddhist monument in India and a holy place of devotion. The Sanchi gate in the foreground is one of four gates, each of which tower over forty feet, their elaborate carvings displaying symbolic Buddhist statues.

After Asoka's death in 232 B.C., the Mauryan Empire began to decline. In 183 B.C., the last Mauryan ruler was killed by one of his military commanders. India then fell back into the disunity that characterizes much of Indian history.

The Importance of Trade

Most, but not all, Indians were farmers. As time passed, India became one of the most advanced trading civilizations in the ancient world. After the rise of the Mauryan Empire, India's role in regional trade began to expand. India became a major crossroads in a vast commercial network that extended from the rim of the Pacific to the Middle East and the Mediterranean Sea.

This regional trade went both by sea and by camel caravan. Maritime trade across the Indian Ocean may have begun as early as the fifth century B.C. It extended eastward from the Red Sea as far as Southeast Asia and China. It went southward as far as the straits between Africa and the island of Madagascar. At first, most ships followed the coastline. Later navigators mastered the monsoon winds and went directly across open sea to their destinations. Westward went spices, salt, perfumes, jewels, textiles, precious stones and ivory, and wild animals. In return, India received gold, tin, lead, and wine.

Map 3.3   The Empire of Asoka

The Kushan Kingdom and the Silk Road

After the collapse of the Mauryan Empire, a number of new kingdoms arose along the fringes of India in Bactria, known today as Afghanistan. In the first century A.D., nomadic warriors seized power in the area and proclaimed the new Kushan kingdom. For the next two centuries, the Kushans spread over northern India as far as the central Ganges valley, while in the rest of India other kingdoms fought for control. Sitting astride the main trade routes across the northern half of India, the Kushans prospered from the trade that passed through the area on its way between the Mediterranean Sea

TEACH

TEACHING THEMES

The Role of Individuals. Assign students to list the actions of Asoka while he was the ruler of the Mauryan Kingdom. Lead a discussion based on these lists that investigates the difference one person can make in the course of history. Do the times make the person? Or, does the person make the times?

TEACHING THEMES

Economics and History. Assign students to write an essay that explains why communities along the Silk Road were likely to prosper and grow. How could social or political unrest in China, the Near East, or Europe harm these communities?

STUDYING MAPS

The following questions will help you guide students through their study of Map 3.3.

1. Using the scale of miles, approximately how far, north to south, did the Asoka Empire extend? *(approximately 2250 miles)*

2. What geographic feature of India tended to speed communication and the exchange of ideas? *(The many rivers and the long coastline tended to speed communication and the exchange of ideas.)*

3. What may the fact that rock and minor rock edicts were more widespread in India than pillar edicts show about the growth and power of the Asoka Empire? *(Answers will vary.)*

and the countries bordering the Pacific Ocean. Most of that trade was between the Roman Empire and China and was shipped along the route known as the Silk Road. One section of the Silk Road passed through the mountains northwest of India.

Trade between India and Europe expanded rapidly in the first century A.D. At that time sailors learned to navigate the Indian Ocean, understanding currents and seasonal monsoon winds. For the first time, goods could be shipped with some certainty from the Mediterranean to seaports on the west coast of India. From there, the goods could be carried overland through the Pamir Mountains and to China. Contacts between India and China had begun as early as 200 B.C.

The connection between the Mediterranean and the Indian Ocean was widespread and often profitable. It even resulted in the establishment of several small Roman settlements along the Indian coast. Rome imported ivory, textiles, precious stones, and pepper from India and silk from China. The Romans sometimes paid cash for these goods, but they also traded in silver, wine, perfume, slaves, glass, and cloth. Overall, Rome imported more than it sold to the Far East, leading one Roman emperor to complain that "the ladies and their baubles are transferring our money to foreigners."

Above all, the Romans wanted silk, which came chiefly from China. The Silk Road ran from the Chinese capital at Chang'an (HONG-on) westward along the northern and southern fringes of the vast Taklamakan (TOK-luh-muh-KON) Desert, through ports on the Arabian Sea. From there, the silk was shipped to Rome through the Persian Gulf or the Red Sea. China remained the main supplier of silk to the Mediterranean world for centuries.

The Kingdom of the Guptas

The Kushan kingdom came to an end in the third century A.D., when invaders from Iran overran it. In 320 a new state was created in the central Ganges valley by a

Map 3.4   The Gupta Empire

YOU ARE THERE

The Good Life in Gupta India

In the fifth century A.D., a Chinese Buddhist monk, Fa Xian, made a visit to the India of the Guptas in search of documents recording the teachings of the Buddha. He provides a description of life in part of India under the Guptas.

Fa Xian, Describing Life under the Guptas

Southward from this is the so-called middle-country. The climate of this country is warm and equable, without frost or snow. The people are very well off, without poll-tax or official restrictions. Only those who farm the royal lands return a portion of profit of the land. If they desire to go, they go; if they like to stop, they stop. The kings govern without corporal punishment; criminals are fined, according to circumstances, lightly or heavily. Even in cases of repeated rebellion they only cut off the right hand. The king's personal attendants, who guard him on the right and left, have fixed salaries. Throughout the country the people kill no living thing nor drink wine, nor do they eat garlic or onions, with the exception of the untouchables only. The untouchables are named "evil men" and dwell apart from others; if they enter a town or market, they sound a piece of wood in order to separate themselves; then men, knowing who they are, avoid coming in contact with them. In this country they do not keep swine nor fowls, and do not deal in cattle; they have no shambles or wine-shops in their market-places. The untouchables only hunt and sell flesh.

▲ *A street musician in Jaipur, India, today carries on a tradition thousands of years old. What kind of instrument is he playing?*

1. What was good about life in Gupta India?

2. Is there anything that the monk viewed as positive about life in Gupta India that you view as negative? Explain your answer.

3. Analyze your high school community (students, teachers, administration, and other staff). Is there a caste system? What is the high school good life? Is school life equally good for everyone? Develop your ideas.

local prince named Chandragupta (no relation to the earlier Chandragupta Maurya). He located his capital at Pataliputra, the site of the decaying palace of the Mauryas. His successor, Samudragupta, expanded his father's empire into surrounding areas. A court official wrote of Samudragupta that he "was skillful in waging hundreds of battles with only the strength of his arms. The beauty of his charming body was enhanced by the number of wounds, caused by the blows of battle axes, arrows, spears, pikes, barbed darts, swords, lances,

YOU ARE THERE

CLASS DISCUSSION

This description of the "Good Life in Gupta India" is told from the point of view of a foreigner. Ask your students to discuss and then work together to create a description of life in Gupta as it would have been told by one of the untouchables.

Answers to Critical Thinking Questions

1. Students may mention the climate, the freedom to come and go as people chose, the prosperity of the people, lack of taxes, and so on.
2. Students may comment on the punishment for rebellion or the people's diet. Students should notice the separation of the untouchables from the rest of the community. Though the monk thought it was nice that local residents could be spared contact with the lowly caste, life certainly wasn't good for the untouchables.
3. Student answers will vary.

LEARNING FROM VISUALS

Answer to the caption question: The instrument appears to be stringed like a lute.

On Line with WORLD HISTORY *Internet Activity*

You may want to have your students visit the following URL, where they will find information and additional web site resources to enhance their study of this chapter.

Exploring Ancient World Cultures— Ancient India
http://eawc.evansville.edu/ inpage.htm

An excellent source for resources and links in Ancient Indian history. Chronology, essays, resources, www sites are included.

Due to the ever-changing nature of the World Wide Web, see the West History web site, **http://history.swpco.com** for regular updates of the URLs in this text.

In Chapter 2, this text states that the decline of Persia was associated with kings who became "more isolated at their courts, surrounded by luxuries provided by the immense quantities of gold and silver that flowed into their treasuries." Ask students to write an essay that compares the Persian experience with the decline of the Guptas.

TEACHING THEMES

The Importance of Culture. Ask students to explain why civilizations that had multiple spoken languages often chose to maintain one written language. How did a universal written language help maintain unity and stability in their cultures?

javelins, iron arrows, and many other weapons." Eventually the new kingdom of the Guptas became the dominant political force throughout northern India. It also established loose control over central India, thus becoming the greatest state in India since the decline of the Mauryan Empire.

Under a series of efficient monarchs—especially Chandragupta II, who reigned from 375 to 415—the Gupta Empire created a new age of Indian civilization. The greatness of its culture was reported by a Chinese traveler, Fa Xian (SHEE-on), who spent several years there in the fifth century. Fa Xian, a Buddhist monk, was not pleased that the Gupta rulers had adopted the Hindu faith. However, he admired the character of their rule, their tolerance of Buddhism, and the prosperity of the country (see "You Are There: The Good Life in Gupta India").

The Gupta Empire actively engaged in trade with China, Southeast Asia, and the Mediterranean and also encouraged domestic trade in cloth, salt, and iron. Cities that were famous for their temples as well as for their prosperity rose along the main trade routes throughout India. Much of their wealth came from the religious trade as pilgrims from across India and as far away as China came to visit the major religious centers.

India's development as a trading center also aided the growth of the state. Although there was a large private sector, much of the trade in the Gupta Empire was managed by the government. The Guptas owned silver and gold mines and vast lands. They earned massive profits from their commercial dealings. They lived in luxury, awakening to the sound of music and spending much time in dining with followers and guests. It was said that "the king and his companions drank wine out of ruby cups while lutes were strummed; there was dance and music."

The good fortunes of the Guptas did not last, however. Beginning in the late fifth century A.D., invasions by nomads (peoples known as the Huns) from the northwest gradually reduced the power of the empire. The military commander Harsa briefly revived the empire in the middle of the seventh century. After his death, however, the empire fell completely apart. North India would not be reunited for many centuries while local and regional governments held control.

The World of Indian Culture

Few cultures in the world are as rich and varied as that of India. The country produced great works in almost all cultural fields, including literature, art and sculpture, and science (see "The Role of Science and Technology: Science in Ancient India"). Indeed, the reign of Chandragupta II is often seen as the high point of Indian culture. Some have called it a Golden Age similar to that of Athens in the time of Pericles (PAIR-uh-KLEEZ) and that of Rome in the time of Augustus.

Literature: A Lasting Legacy

The earliest known Indian literature comes from the Aryan tradition in the form of the four Vedas. These were passed down orally from generation to generation. After the Aryan conquest of India, they were written down. The earliest of the Vedas, the Rigveda, dates from the second millennium B.C. and consists of over a thousand religious hymns used in Aryan tribal society. The other three Vedas were written later and contain instructions for religious ceremonies connected with Aryan religious beliefs.

The language of the Vedas was Sanskrit, a member of the Indo-European family of languages (see the table in Chapter 2). After the Aryan conquest of India, Sanskrit gradually declined as a spoken language, but it continued to be used as the language of the government bureaucracy and literary works for many centuries. Like Latin in Europe during the Middle Ages, Sanskrit served as a common language of written communication among various parts of India.

After the development of a writing system sometime in the first millennium B.C., India's sacred literature was written on palm leaves stitched together into books. Also put into written form for the first time were India's great historical epics, the *Mahabharata* and the *Ramayana*. Like the Homeric epics in Greece, both of these epics were recited orally and recounted the legendary deeds of great warriors.

The *Mahabharata* consists of over ninety thousand stanzas (a series of lines of poetry), making it the longest poem in any written language. Probably written about 100 B.C., it describes a war between cousins in Aryan tribal society for control of the kingdom

RECOMMENDED READING

Many editions of Sanskrit literature are available in English translation. Many are available in the multivolume *Harvard Oriental Series.* For a one-volume annotated anthology of selections from the Indian classics, consult S. N. Hay, ed., *Sources of Indian Tradition,* 2 vols. (New York, 1988), or J. B. Alphonso-Karkala, *An Anthology of Indian Literature,* 2d revised ed. (New Delhi, 1987), put out by the Indian Council for Cultural Relations.

THE ROLE OF SCIENCE AND TECHNOLOGY

Science in Ancient India

Ancient Indians possessed an impressive amount of scientific knowledge. Especially noteworthy was their work in astronomy. They charted the movements of the heavenly bodies and recognized that Earth was a sphere that rotated on its axis and revolved around the sun. Their ideas in physics were similar to those of the Greeks. Matter was divided into the five elements of earth, air, fire, water, and ether.

Ancient Indians excelled in the making of surgical instruments. One ancient Hindu medical work describes 20 sharp and 101 blunt medical instruments, including scalpels, razors, probes, needles, forceps, and syringes, all made of iron, steel, or other metals. Indian surgeons were skillfully trained in performing operations. They also had an unusual solution to one difficult problem. Because the intestines are especially subject to infection after surgery, Indian doctors used large ants to stitch them up. The ants were placed side by side along the opening, clamping the wound shut with their jaws. The surgeon then cut away their bodies, leaving the heads behind to

▲ Surgeons in Ancient India likely used instruments such as these to perform eye surgeries and amputations. The medical practices being used in India, were so far ahead of those in Europe that Indian doctors were often invited to Europe to teach.

decompose after the abdomen was sewn up and as the wound healed. The most important Indian contribution to the world of ancient science was in the field of mathematics. The most famous Indian mathematician of the Gupta Empire was Aryabhata. He devised a decimal system of counting in tens, a method unknown elsewhere in the ancient world. Indian mathematicians also introduced the concept of zero and used a symbol (0) for it. After Arabs conquered parts of India in the eighth century A.D., Arab scholars adopted the Indian system. In turn, European traders borrowed it from the Arabs, and it spread through Europe in the 1200s. Today it is called the Indian-Arabic numerical system.

1. Which scientific advancement described here do you find intriguing? Why?

2. In your opinion, what events and actions prompt scientific investigation?

about 1000 B.C. Above all, the *Mahabharata* is a tale of moral dilemmas. The most famous section of the book is the so-called *Bhagavadgita*, a sermon by Krishna, one of the incarnations of the god Vishnu, on the eve of a major battle. In this sermon Krishna sets forth one of the key points of Indian society. In taking action, one must not worry about success or failure. One should only be aware of the moral rightness of the act itself (see "Our Literary Heritage: The *Mahabharata*, the Great Indian Epic").

MORE ABOUT . . . *Ancient Indian Culture*

Given the tropical and subtropical climate of much of India, cooling food and drink before electricity required ingenuity. Ancient Indians developed a simple but effective form of refrigeration. They would line up shallow clay pots of water, covered with reeds, and expose them to drafts. Evaporation chilled the water, sometimes even producing small amounts of ice. Salt added to the water would raise the freezing point. The clay pots also allowed some of the liquid to seep through and evaporate, further cooling their contents.

OUR LITERARY HERITAGE

USING PRIMARY SOURCES

Divide your class in two. Ask the two groups of students to take the parts in reading the *Mahabharata.* Do this several times until it is read smoothly and with feeling. Ask your students to consider, evaluate, and then discuss their feelings about the Indian people who heard and believed these words.

LEARNING FROM VISUALS

Assign your students to explain the painting of Krishna supporting Mount Govardhana to a younger sibling or friend. Ask them to describe their experience. Did the younger person understand and like the painting? What reasons may explain the person's reaction?

Answer to the caption question: Answers will vary. Notice the elephant in flight over the mountain, with riders on its back, for example.

Answers to Critical Thinking Questions

1. The voice of the dharma asks the question; the hero answers.
2. The hero values the mind, knowledge, and skill, and controlling one's temper. He is honest and compassionate.
3. Answers will vary.

OUR LITERARY HERITAGE

The *Mahabharata,* the Great Indian Epic

The Mahabharata *is one of India's great historical epics. Like all great pieces of literature, it includes bits of simple wisdom that still touch us today. For example, when the voice of the* dharma—*the Hindu law regulating human behavior—tries to find out whether the hero is worthy of becoming a king, it tests his merit by posing riddles about the meaning of life. Those questions are eternal ones that are still asked today:*

Mahabharata

"What is swifter than the wind?"

"The mind is swifter than the wind."

"What is more numerous than the blades of grass in a meadow?"

"Our thoughts number more than that."

"What is the best of all things that are praised?"

"Skill."

"What is the most valuable possession?"

"Knowledge."

"What is not thought of until it departs?"

"Health."

"What is the best happiness?"

"Contentment."

"What enemy cannot be overcome?"

"That is anger."

"What is honesty?"

"That is to look and see every living creature as yourself, bearing your own will to live, and your own fear of death."

▲ *This colorful Indian painting depicts Krishna supporting Mount Govardhana. What fanciful elements are portrayed that give the picture a surreal quality?*

1. In this selection, who is posing the questions and who is answering them?

2. What are the characteristics and beliefs of the hero?

3. How would you answer, "What is the most valuable possession?" and "What is honesty?"

MORE ABOUT . . . *Indian Society*

The ancient Indians developed a manual to guide them in the art of love called the *Kama Sutra*. Many westerners think of it as a pornographic work because of the explicit drawings of various sexual positions. Many people are not aware, however, that it is also a guide for all aspects of relationships between men and women—a sort of *Men Are From Mars, Women Are From Venus* of ancient India. Included in the manual are the recommendation that men kidnap reluctant brides, suggestions that women leave men who were poor, plus twenty-seven different suggestions for getting money from lovers.

The *Ramayana*, written at about the same time, is much shorter than the *Mahabharata*. It is an account of the ruler Rama. As a result of a palace intrigue, he is banished from the kingdom and forced to live as a hermit in the forest. Later, he fights the demon-king of Ceylon, who had kidnapped his beloved wife Sita. Like the *Mahabharata* (and most works of the ancient world), the *Ramayana* is strongly imbued with religious and moral lessons. Rama is seen as the ideal Aryan hero, a perfect ruler and ideal son. Sita projects the supreme duty of wifely loyalty to her husband. The *Ramayana* is a story of the triumph of good over evil, of duty over self-indulgence, and of generosity over selfishness. To this day, the *Mahabharata* and *Ramayana* remain popular favorites among Indians of all age groups. Many Indians know them by heart, and they are often performed publicly.

One of ancient India's most famous authors was Kalidasa (CALL-i-DAH-suh), who lived during the Gupta dynasty. He has been called the Indian Shakespeare. Kalidasa's hundred-verse poem, *The Cloud Messenger*, remains one of the most popular of Sanskrit poems. It tells of an exiled male earth spirit who misses his beautiful wife and shares his grief with a passing cloud. He laments:

> I see your body in the sinuous creeper, your gaze in the
>   startled eyes of deer,
> your cheek in the moon, your hair in the plumage of
>   peacocks,
> and in the tiny ripples of the river I see your sidelong
>   glances,
> but alas, my dearest, nowhere do I find your whole
>   likeness![4]

He tells the cloud what path it must take to reach his beloved to give her his message of love.

Architecture and Sculpture: Devotion to Buddha

After literature, the greatest achievements of early Indian civilization were in architecture and sculpture. Both served religious purposes. Some of the earliest examples of Indian architecture stem from the time of Asoka, when Buddhism became the religion of the state. The desire to spread the ideas of Gautama Buddha inspired the great architecture of the Mauryan dynasty and the period that followed.

There were three main types of religious structures: the pillar, the stupa, and the rock chamber. The pillar is the most famous. During Asoka's reign, many stone pillars were erected alongside roads to mark sites related to events in Buddha's life, as well as pilgrims' routes to holy places. Weighing up to fifty tons each and rising as high as thirty feet, these polished sandstone pillars were topped with a carving, usually depicting lions uttering Buddha's message. Ten remain standing today.

A stupa was originally meant to house a relic of the Buddha, such as a lock of his hair, and was built in the form of a burial mound. Eventually, the stupa became a place for devotion and the most familiar form of Buddhist architecture. It rose to considerable heights and was surrounded with a spire. According to legend, Asoka ordered the construction of eighty-four thousand stupas throughout India to promote Buddha's message.

The final development in early Indian architecture was the rock chamber. This structure was developed by Asoka to provide a series of rooms to house monks and to serve as a hall for religious ceremonies. The rooms were carved out of rock cliffs on the sides of mountains. Both exteriors and interiors were carved from top to bottom as pieces of sculpture.

One of the most famous rock chambers was at Ajanta (uh-JUNT-uh). The twenty-eight caves of Ajanta are known for their sculpture and painting, as well as their architecture. Most of the caves were carved out of solid rock over an incredibly short period of seventeen years, from A.D. 460 to 478. Their rooms were decorated with ornate pillars, beamed ceilings, and statues of the Buddha. Several caves served as monasteries, which by then had been transformed from simple holes in the wall to large complexes with living apartments, halls, and shrines to the Buddha. Here the monks resided and studied the life and teachings of the Buddha.

All the inner surfaces of the caves, including the ceilings, sculptures, walls, door frames, and pillars, were painted in bright colors. The caves of Ajanta are perhaps best known, however, for their wall paintings, which illustrate scenes from the life of the Buddha.

ALTERNATIVE ASSESSMENT

Assign students to draw or paint a picture similar to the one of Krishna supporting Mount Govardhana on page 80. However, require them to use modern people and objects instead of those that were typical to ancient India. They should explain their picture either in writing or orally.

Answers to SECTION REVIEW

2. (a) ruler of the first dynasty to control much of India
   (b) considered to be greatest ruler in India's history
   (c) trade route between the Roman Empire and China
   (d) earliest known Indian literature
   (e) one of ancient India's most famous authors

3. (a) empire divided into provinces like our states; provinces were divided into districts, like our counties; they had villages, like our cities; each had a ruling person or body

▶ *The twenty eight caves of Ajanta are one of the wonders of India and renowned around the world. Most famous for the paintings and sculptures of the Buddha inside, the caves also contain temple halls and monasteries for Buddhist monks. Digging of the caves began in the second century* B.C., *though most of it was done in the fifth century* A.D. *Soldiers on a tiger hunt accidentally rediscovered the caves, hidden under jungle growth, in the 1800s.*

 SECTION REVIEW

1. **Locate:**
   (*a*) Pataliputra,   (*b*) Indian Ocean

2. **Identify:**
   (*a*) Chandragupta Maurya,   (*b*) Asoka,
   (*c*) Silk Road,   (*d*) Vedas,   (*e*) Kalidasa

3. **Recall:**
   (*a*) How does the division and government structure of the Mauryan Empire parallel the division of our country today?
   (*b*) Why do you think Asoka was considered to be the greatest ruler in the history of India?
   (*c*) What is one of the key points of Indian society as set forth in the section of the *Mahabharata* by Krishna?
   (*d*) Name the three types of religious structures.

4. **Think Critically:** India's literature, architecture and sculpture all reflect strong religious sentiments. Based on the country's religious heritage discussed in this section, why do you think this is true?

Conclusion

The first civilization in India arose in the Indus River valley during the fourth millennium B.C. This Harappan civilization was based in two major cities, Harappa and Mohenjo-Daro. Harappan civilization made significant political and social achievements for some two thousand years. Internal decline then weakened the civilization, and the invasion of the Aryans finally brought its end around 1500 B.C.

The Aryans were an Indo-European–speaking people who established political control throughout all of India and created a new Indian civilization. A rigid caste system, in which people were clearly divided into distinct classes, became a chief feature of the new Indian civilization.

Two of the world's great religions, Hinduism and Buddhism, began in India. Hinduism was an outgrowth of the religious beliefs of the Aryan peoples who invaded and settled in India. With its belief in reincarnation, Hinduism provided justification for the rigid caste system of India. Buddhism was the product of one man, Siddhartha Gautama, whose simple message of achieving wisdom created a new spiritual philosophy that came to rival Hinduism.

For most of the time between 325 B.C. and A.D. 500, India was a land of many different states. Two major empires, however, were able to create large, unified Indian states. The Mauryan Empire in northern India lasted from 324 to 183 B.C. The Gupta Empire flourished from A.D. 320 until the invasion of the Huns reduced its power in the late fifth century. Both empires experienced strong central government and a flourishing of the arts. Indian civilization was extensive. Eventually, in the form of Hinduism and Buddhism, it spread to China and Southeast Asia.

Notes

1. Quoted in Ananda K. Coomaraswamy, *Buddha and the Gospel of Buddhism* (New York, 1964), pp. 160–162.
2. Quoted in Richard Lannoy, *The Speaking Tree: A Study of Indian Culture and Society* (London, 1971), p. 319.
3. William Theodore de Bary et al., eds., *Sources of Indian Tradition* (New York, 1966), p. 146.
4. Quoted in A.L. Basham, *The Wonder That Was India* (London, 1964), p. 288.

(b) he ruled kindheartedly; set up hospitals, provided trees and shelters for travelers and sent missionaries throughout India to instruct people in the proper way; trade and industry flourished; the kingdom prospered,
(c) In taking action, one must not worry about success or failure; one should only be aware of the moral rightness of the act itself.
(d) pillars, stupas, rock chambers
4. Answers will vary.

CLOSE

Lead students in a discussion of the 'Focus' objectives identified on page 74. Emphasize the importance of trade to the accumulation of wealth and to the support of religion and the arts.

Answers to CHAPTER REVIEW 3

USING KEY TERMS

1. Brahman
2. raja
3. karma
4. dharma
5. monsoon
6. yoga
7. Atman
8. caste system
9. reincarnation
10. elite
11. stupas
12. guru
13. Sanskrit
14. ascetics

REVIEWING THE FACTS

1. the end of self, reunion with God
2. priests/warriors or *brahmins/kshatriya*
3. Chandragupta Maurya
4. world's longest written poem
5. Indus, Ganges
6. built pillars, stupas, and rock chambers, sent missionaries abroad
7. Brahma with Creator, Vishnu the Preserver, Siva the Destroyer
8. Rome and China
9. Aryans
10. farming
11. wife would kill herself on husband's funeral pyre
12. collected writings of Hindu hymns and religious ceremonies
13. *Sanskrit*
14. 1—life is suffering, 2—suffering is caused by desire, 3—to end suffering, end desire, 4—to end desire follow the Eightfold Path
15. Siddhartha Guatama, Hinduism

THINKING CRITICALLY

1. Buddhism founded by a Hindu, believes in karma, reincarnation, and nirvana, however Buddha rejected the caste system and believed that enlightenment could be achieved in a single lifetime.

USING KEY TERMS

1. _____ is the Hindu word for the ultimate force of the universe.
2. Although he was the tribal chieftan, the _____ was required to follow the same laws that applied to all people.
3. _____, the Hindu belief that all of life's actions have consequences, is similar to the American proverb, "what goes around, comes around."
4. Each caste must follow its own _____, or laws.
5. India's climate is dominated by the _____, which can bring either life-giving rains or devastating floods.
6. The Hindu method of achieving oneness with God is called _____.
7. Hindus believe it is the duty of the individual self, or _____, to seek Brahman.
8. The Aryan invaders of India imposed the _____, which was a rigid system of social categories that determine a person's place in society.
9. According to Hinduism, after death a person's soul experiences _____ and is reborn in a different form.
10. A small group of powerful people called an _____ helped the Harappan king rule.
11. _____ are stone towers that house relics of the Buddha.
12. Young men in high-class Indian families began their education under the instruction of a _____.
13. The development of _____ allowed the Aryans to write down their legends and religious rituals.
14. People who practiced self-denial as a means of understanding ultimate reality were called _____.

REVIEWING THE FACTS

1. Describe the concept of Nirvana.
2. Name the two ruling castes of India.
3. Who was the founder of the first dynasty to control much of India?
4. What is the *Mahabharta?*
5. Name the two major river valleys of India.
6. How did Asoka promote and spread Buddhism throughout India and Asia?
7. List the three chief deities of Hinduism.
8. What two trading empires were on either end of the Silk Road in northern India?
9. Who were the warlike nomads that conquered the Harappans?
10. What was the basis of Harappan economy?
11. Describe the Indian ritual of sati.
12. What are the Vedas?
13. What language was the "Latin" of India?
14. List the Four Noble Truths of Buddhism.
15. What was the Buddha's given name and religion?

THINKING CRITICALLY

1. Explain how Buddhism is both an extension of Hinduism and at the same time different. Give examples of similarities and differences.
2. Five of the six special features (colored boxes) in this chapter contain primary sources. Identify the one that is a secondary source.
3. Asoka is generally considered to be India's greatest ruler. What was the cause of his conversion to Buddhism, and what were the effects of that conversion?
4. Analyze the description of the city of Harappa and give supporting evidence for the inference that this ancient Indian city had a well-organized government.
5. Analyze and explain what the Buddha meant when he said, "Do not go by what is handed

2. See *"What is history, and why do we study it"* from the text's introduction to review the difference between primary and secondary sources.
3. *Cause*—bloody battle; *Effect*—set up hospitals, planted trees, built shelters, sent missionaries throughout India, set up stone pillars with Buddha's message

4. gridded streets, indoor plumbing, waste disposal systems, walled neighborhoods, metal furnaces
5. think for yourself, similar to socrates, *"What is good, Phaedrus, and what is not good—need we ask anyone to tell us these things?"*—Examples will, of course, vary.

CHAPTER 3 REVIEW

down, nor by the authority of your traditional teachings. When you know of yourselves, 'These teachings are good or not good,' only then accept or reject them." Include an example from your own experience that would illustrate the meaning.

APPLYING SOCIAL STUDIES SKILLS

1. **Geography:** List the four primary geographic regions of India.
2. **Sociology:** In spite of the difficulties faced by Untouchables, most did not opt to convert to other religions in order to escape their lot in life. What social pressures would prevent a person from converting from the religion of his or her childhood?
3. **Psychology:** In what way would the belief in karma affect the way a person would view the negative events that have occurred in his or her life?
4. **Government:** Asoka was successful as both a violent, conquering warrior and as a peace-loving convert to Buddhism. Which traits do you consider to be more desirable in a leader: compassion and kindness, or ruthlessness and aggression? Make a list of influential people throughout history who embody these traits and determine which group has had a greater impact on humanity.

MAKING TIME AND PLACE CONNECTIONS

1. In the first half of the twentieth century Mahatma Gandhi fought against untouchability, calling Untouchables "Harijans" (Children of God). In modern day India untouchability is officially illegal, but it is often easier to change laws than to change people's attitudes. How could attitudes about race in the United States today offer a clue to understanding untouchability in modern India?

2. Compare the role of women in ancient India with that of women in ancient Sumeria and Egypt by identifying their rights and responsibilities. How do the roles of women in the present-day United States compare with women's roles in these early civilizations?
3. The four major river valley civilizations discussed in Chapters 2, 3 and 4 all developed at about the same time and in the same general latitudinal location (between 20°N and 40°N). Imagine that there once was a lost continent in either the Pacific or Atlantic Ocean that was home to a civilization contemporary with ancient Egypt, Sumeria, India, and China. The ruins of this civilization have just been discovered by your underwater archaeological team. Write the chapter for your history text that describes this civilization. Your completed project should include maps, a description of the geography, a history of their early civilization, details about their society, culture, economy, government and religion, as well as an analysis of how they compare and contrast with other river valley civilizations. This can be an individual, group, or class project.

BECOMING AN HISTORIAN

Geography as a Key to History: Of the early river valley civilizations you have studied thus far, the Egyptians proved to have the most stable and longest lasting empire. Use your knowledge of the geography of Egypt, Western Asia, and India to explain possible reasons for Egypt's success relative to its neighbors.

Art as a Key to History: Look at examples of the art of each of the civilizations of Egypt, Western Asia, and India from Chapters Two and Three. After having read about each river valley civilization, explain how the art of each civilization reveals something about its culture. How do these examples of art differ from those of early man as shown in Chapter One?

85

MAKING TIME AND PLACE CONNECTIONS

1. Answers will vary
2. Answers will vary
3. Answers wll vary.

BECOMING AN HISTORIAN

Geography as a Key to History: Egypt has more stable river flooding, is better protected from invasion by desert, sea, river cataracts, ability to trade by seas and river; Sumerians subjected to frequent raids by nomads from mountains; Indians subjected to invasion from north west, blocked from trade to east by mountains and desert
Art as a Key to History: Answers will vary.

APPLYING SOCIAL STUDIES SKILLS

1. 1—Himalayan/Karakoram mountains, 2—Indus river plain, 3—Ganges river plain, 4—Deccan plateau
2. Answers will vary.
3. Answers will vary.
4. Answers will vary.

4 PLANNING GUIDE

SECTION	KEY TOPICS	PRIMARY SOURCES	ASSESSMENT
1 **The Dawn of Chinese Civilization** pages 87–92	◆ Geographic features of China ◆ Political and social structure in the Shang dynasty ◆ Religion and culture under the Shang		◆ Section Review, page 91 ◆ Section Quiz 4–1, TRB
2 **The Zhou Dynasty** pages 93–100	◆ Political power in the Zhou dynasty ◆ Life and culture during the Zhou dynasty ◆ The role of the family in ancient China ◆ The importance of China's written language	◆ The importance of the crossbow, page 94 ◆ The "Big Rat," page 95 ◆ A poem about the power of women, page 99	◆ Section Review, page 100 ◆ Section Quiz 4–2, TRB
3 **The Development of the Chinese Traditions** pages 100–103	◆ The influence of Confucius ◆ Taoism in China ◆ The beliefs of Legalism	◆ A description of the Golden Age of China by Confucius, page 101 ◆ Poems concerning Taoist beliefs, page 102	◆ Section Review, page 103 ◆ Section Quiz 4–3, TRB
4 **The Rise and Fall of the Chinese Empires: The Qin and the Han** pages 103–114	◆ Life in the Qin dynasty ◆ Society in the Han dynasty ◆ Differences between Qin and Han China ◆ The fall of the Han Empire	◆ Li Su, on the destruction of books, page 105 ◆ A description of the treatment of farmers, page 109	◆ Section Review, page 114 ◆ Section Quiz 4–4, TRB

THE FIRST CIVILIZATIONS:
ANCIENT CHINA (3000 B.C. TO A.D 500)

REPRODUCIBLE ACTIVITIES

- Historical Maps
- Charts and Graphs
- Critical Thinking
- Cooperative Learning
- Vocabulary
- Guided Reading
- Reteaching
- Enrichment
- Performance Assessment
- Spanish Key Points and Chapter Summaries
- Spanish Vocabulary
- Spanish Guided Reading

MULTIMEDIA SUPPORT

 TRANSPARENCIES
- ◆ *World History* Color Transparency Package
- ◆ Fine Art Color Transparency Package

 VIDEO
- ◆ *World History* Video Library
- ◆ **CNN**® Annual Video Update

 LASERDISC
- ◆ *Sights and Sounds of History*

 AUDIO
- ◆ *Listening to Literature* audiotape (English and Spanish)
- ◆ *History of Music* CD

 SOFTWARE
- ◆ WESTEST™
- ◆ Student Review

 CD–ROM
- ◆ *The Journey of Civilization*
- ◆ *World History*

 INTERNET
- ◆ Internet Activities

 On Line with **WORLD HISTORY**

Access West's history web site at
http://history.swpco.com
You'll find activities and web sites related to specific topics and chapters in *World History: The Human Odyssey*. Also look for references to helpful web sites at appropriate places throughout this teacher edition.

LESSON PLANNING

You will find detailed daily lesson plans for both traditional class scheduling and **block scheduling** in your Teacher Resource Box.

 ## Not Enough Time?

If you do not have the four or five days recommended to teach this chapter, you may want to focus on the following sections and activities:

- ◆ Have students skim the chapter to answer the "Questions to Guide Your Reading" on page 87. Discuss their answers, then read the "Conclusion" on pages 114–115.
- ◆ Do a more in-depth reading about the geography of China on pages 88–89, the question of divine rule in the Zhou dynasty on pages 93–94, the differences between the teachings of Confucius, Taoism, and Legalism on pages 100–103, and a comparison of the Qin and Han dynasties on pages 103–104, 106–107, 109–110 and 113–114. Conclude with a class discussion of the importance of the Silk Road, as described in the "Connections Around the World" feature on page 109.

THE FIRST CIVILIZATIONS:

4

BUILDING ON CHAPTER 3

To prepare students to study Chapter 4 you may use the following questions and activities.

◆ Remind students of the impact that trade on the Silk Road had on civilization in India. Why did it impact Chinese civilization?

◆ Ask students to identify geographic features that influenced the development of civilization in India. Identify similar geographic influences as they study China.

◆ Lead students in a brief discussion of the influence of the Hindu and Buddhist religions on India. Why would it be reasonable for there to be similar religious influences in ancient China?

USING THE OPENING STORY

Depending on the ability levels of your students, select from the following questions and activities to reinforce the reading of the opening story.

◆ Why should food surpluses enable one group of villages to dominate less prosperous people?

◆ Why might a great teacher teach only those who want to learn?

◆ What are several ideas that influence your life today that were developed many years ago?

In the valleys of the two great river systems of East Asia, the Huang (Yellow) and the Yangtze (YANG-SEE), another river valley civilization arose more than four thousand years ago. Like the civilizations of Mesopotamia, Egypt, and India, the civilization of ancient China began with groups of villages that grew crops along major rivers. Changes in farming practices, however, soon led to food surpluses. Food surpluses, in turn, soon led to the growth of an urban civilization. This vibrant new civilization expanded gradually over its neighboring areas and, by the third century B.C., had emerged as a great empire.

The civilization of China is closely tied to Confucius (kun-FYOO-shus), a philosopher who lived in the sixth century B.C. Confucius traveled the length of China observing events and seeking employment as a political counselor. He had little success in his job search and instead became a teacher to hundreds of students who sought his wise advice. He taught by asking questions and expected much of his students. As he said, "Only one who bursts with eagerness do I instruct; only one who bubbles with excitement, do I enlighten." Some of his students became ardent disciples of their teacher and recorded his sayings, which eventually became the guiding principles for the Chinese Empire. For thousands of years, Chinese children studied Confucian ideas. Also for thousands of years, Confucius's ideas continued to influence the ways of the Chinese people.

▲ *The bronze pan basin pictured is an example of the beautiful and detailed metalwork produced during the Late Shang period. Only the most powerful and wealthy of families would have been able to afford such an exquisite piece for use in their cleansing ceremonies. Look carefully to find the dragon lying coiled at the bottom of the basin, perhaps waiting to help the bather communicate with the dead.*

ADDITIONAL RESOURCES

The resources below can be used to enrich the lessons in this chapter.

BOOKS FOR STUDENTS
Confucius by Bennett Sins. Franklin Watts.
The Longest Rampart by Robert Silverburg, Chilton.

VIDEOS/FILMS
The First Emperor of China. (CAV laserdisk.) Social Studies School Services. (800) 421-4246

CD-ROM
Religions of the World. Mentarom. Social Studies School Services. (800) 421-4246

ANCIENT CHINA

(3000 B.C. TO A.D. 500)

THE BEGINNINGS OF CIVILIZATION

3000 B.C.	ANCIENT CHINA	A.D. 500
3500 B.C.		A.D. 500

QUESTIONS TO GUIDE YOUR READING

1. How did geography affect the civilization that arose in China?

2. What basic characteristics of civilization were present in China under the Shang dynasty?

3. What were the political, economic, social, and cultural achievements of the Zhou dynasty in China?

4. What are the major ideas associated with the three different philosophies that emerged in China between 500 and 200 B.C.?

5. What were the basic political, economic, social, and cultural achievements of the Qin and Han dynasties in China?

6. What role did nomadic peoples play in Chinese history?

THE DAWN OF CHINESE CIVILIZATION

Soon after the first great civilizations had appeared in Mesopotamia, Egypt, and the Indus valley, similar developments were beginning further to the east. A new civilization, which we call ancient China, emerged more than four thousand years ago along the two great river systems of East Asia, the Huang (Yellow) and the Yangtze Rivers.

Like the other first civilizations, ancient China faced a threat from pastoral peoples on its borders. Unlike Harappa, Mesopotamia, and Egypt, however, ancient China was able to avoid destruction at the hands of the invaders and survived intact down through the formation of the Chinese Empire in 221 B.C.

Civilization in China began with the expansion of small farming villages into a more complex society. In a pattern that we have seen elsewhere, civilization gradually spread from these settlements in the valleys of the Huang and Yangtze Rivers to other lowland areas of eastern and central China. Government emerged, along with a writing system. As wealth increased, the societies began to create armies and build walled cities. The process took several thousand years.

87

FOCUS ON THEMES

Listed below are brief summaries of how the content in this chapter supports the text's key themes.

Politics and History The Qin and Han dynasties established well-organized states with complex administrative systems.

The Role of Ideas Through their idea of the mandate of Heaven, the Chinese established the basis for a stable monarchical system. The ideas of Confucian philosophy played a major role in China's civilization.

Economics and History Early civilization in China was based on agriculture. Surplus food made possible the growth of crafts and the emergence of trade, which increased in importance.

Social Life There were distinct class differences in China and a wide gulf between rich and poor.

The Importance of Cultural Developments Writing literature, Shang bronze ritual vessels and the terracotta army of the First Qin Emperor attest to Chinese cultural achievements.

Religion in History Religion played an important role in China's civilization.

The Role of Individuals Confucius showed the power of an individual to change the course of history.

The Impact of Science and Technology China with remarkable technological achievements led the world until the Industrial Revolution.

The Environment and History China was a river valley civilization. Fierce nomads on China's northern frontier necessitated a strong defense, including building the Great Wall.

Answers to QUESTIONS TO GUIDE YOUR READING

1. civilizations along major rivers; mountains/deserts isolated Chinese; open to attack from the north (pages 87–88)
2. farming economy, large cities, many gods, ancestor worship, bronze casting (pages 89–92)

3. See pages 95–99.
4. See pages 100–103.
5. See pages 104–114.
6. mastered art of fighting on horseback; city walls built to defend against them (pages 104, 106)

FOCUS

OBJECTIVES

After completing this section, students should be able to

1. explain how geography influenced the development of civilization in China

2. explain why there was a continuing struggle between pastoral and farming people in ancient China

3. describe contributions that are thought to have been made to Chinese civilization during the Xia and Shang dynasties

4. explain relationships between political and social structures, and the role of religion in the Shang dynasty

FOCUS ACTIVITY

Help students understand why the study of religious artifacts, like Chinese oracle bones, tells us much more about ancient people than just their religious beliefs. Ask students to identify and discuss types of information about our civilization that the contents of a local religious building could provide to future generations.

The Geography of China

The Huang (Yellow River) stretches across China for more than 2,900 miles, carrying its rich yellow silt all the way from Mongolia to the Pacific Ocean. The Yangtze is even longer, flowing for 3,400 miles across central China before emptying into the Yellow Sea. It was in the densely cultivated valleys of these two rivers that East Asia began to emerge as one of the great food-producing areas of the ancient world. China, however, is not just a land of fertile fields. In fact, only 12 percent of the total land area is suitable for farming, compared with 23 percent for the United States. Much of the rest of the land in China consists of mountains and deserts, which ring the country on its northern and western frontiers.

This forbidding landscape is a dominant feature of Chinese life and has played an important role in Chinese history. The geographical barriers—mountains and deserts—isolated the Chinese people from peoples in other parts of Asia. Peoples of Mongolian, Indo-European, or Turkish backgrounds lived in the frontier regions in the Gobi (Go-BEE) Desert, central Asia, and the Tibetan (tuh-BET-uhn) plateau. Most lived in pastoral societies. As was the case in the other river valley civilizations, the contacts of these tribal groups with the Chinese were often marked by conflict. Although these tribal peoples were fewer in number than the Chinese, many were fierce warriors and sometimes sought to gain wealth or land in the settled regions of China south of the Gobi Desert. Over the next two thousand years, the northern frontier of China became one of the great areas of conflict in Asia as Chinese armies tried to protect their precious farmlands from invading tribal peoples.

This struggle between pastoral and farming peoples was an ongoing one. The outcome at any given time depended on the ability of the settled peoples to ward off the threats of the invaders. When China was unified and blessed with strong rulers, it could usually defeat the nomadic intruders and even make them subject to Chinese authority. In times of internal weakness, however, China was open to attack from the north. On several occasions, tribal peoples succeeded in defeating native Chinese rulers and then setting up their own regimes.

From other directions, China normally had little to fear. To the east lay the China Sea, a haven for pirates and the source of powerful typhoons that sometimes devastated the Chinese coast. Otherwise, the eastern border was rarely a source of concern. South of the Yangtze River was a hilly region inhab

▼ *The Li River flows through a lush and serene valley in China. Flooded land beyond the river bank would be ideal for growing rice crops.*

ENRICHMENT ACTIVITY

Have students gather from outside sources visual information, such as photos or drawings of artifacts, from the Xia dynasty, as well as any other data available on that dynasty. Students should label each item and provide a brief written description of the item or of what is occurring in the photo. Select a day to allow the students to show and present their findings in class. Follow the presentations with a brief discussion of the achievements of the Xia civilization.

ited by a mixture of peoples of varied language and ethnic backgrounds who lived by farming, fishing, or food gathering. They were gradually absorbed in the expansion of Chinese civilization.

The Shang Dynasty

Historians of China have traditionally dated the beginning of Chinese civilization to the founding of the Xia (SHEE-oh) dynasty over four thousand years ago. Little is known about this dynasty, but legend maintains that the founder was a ruler named Yu. It was said that Yu was a man great in virtue and dedicated to the service of his people. Supposedly, he introduced irrigation and drained the floodwaters that often threatened to cover the North China plain. The Xia dynasty, in turn,

was replaced by a second dynasty, the Shang, which emerged in the eighteenth century B.C.

China under the Shang dynasty (about 1750 to 1122 B.C.) was a mostly farming society ruled by an aristocratic class whose major concern was war. (An aristocracy is an upper class whose wealth is based on land and whose power is passed on from one generation to another.) One ancient writer wrote that "the big affairs of state consist of sacrifice and soldiery."[1] Combat was carried on by means of two-horse chariots, a practice that the Shang may have learned through contact with the peoples of neighboring regions.

Archaeologists have found evidence of impressive cities in Shang China. Shang kings may have had at least five different capital cities before settling at Anyang (ON-YONG), just north of the Huang River

Map 4.1 The Geography of China

TEACH

COMPARING TIME PERIODS

Assign students to write a paragraph that explains how geography has contributed to the many similarities between ancient Indian and Chinese history

CLASS DISCUSSION

Lead students in a discussion of why national boundaries formed by sea coasts, like those of eastern China, were usually not subject to invasions in ancient times. What technological advances have eliminated this type of safety in the modern world?

TEACHING THEMES

Economics and History. Ask students to identify and discuss different values demonstrated by the Xia and Shang dynasties. How can these different values be seen in their economic systems? What economic weaknesses may nations based on war be subject to?

STUDYING MAPS

The following questions will help you guide students through their study of Map 4.1.

1. Trace the courses of the Huang (Yellow) and Yangtze Rivers. What well-known metropolitan city lies at the mouth of the Yangtze River and the Yellow Sea? *(Shanghai)*
2. What other rivers do you see on this map? *(Ganges, Brahmaputra, Mekong, Xi Jiang, Wei He)*
3. What geographical conditions contributed to China becoming known as one of the great food-producing areas of the ancient world? Why? *(fertile valleys of the two major rivers for growing rice; isolated from other parts by geographic barriers; surrounded by water to the east promoted excellent fishing)*

TEACHING THEMES

Politics and History. Ask students to discuss ways in which the leaders of the Shang state may have used the Chinese belief in supernatural forces to help them govern. Do they see any evidence that leaders of modern states use superstition to maintain their power?

Multimedia Support

TRANSPARENCY
4–1, Ideograph for *Crisis*

REINFORCING VOCABULARY

Ask your students if they usually respect people who are old. Discuss how this type of respect is different from the **veneration of ancestors** that was common in Chinese culture.

Multimedia Support

LASERDISC
Oracle Bone (Shang Dynasty, China)

Map 4.2   Shang China

Major regions of the late Shang state

in north-central China. Excavation of some of these urban centers reveals huge city walls, royal palaces, and large royal tombs. Whereas rulers and aristocrats lived within the walls, craftspeople and workers lived outside the walls near their workshop areas.

One archaeological excavation in 1976 led to the discovery of an elaborate royal tomb that had survived for three thousand years. Its splendor indicated that the person buried there had been someone of great renown within the royal family of Shang. It turned out to be Fu Hao, the most influential of the wives of the Shang king Wu Ding, who reigned during the thirteenth century B.C. During his fifty-nine-year reign, Wu Ding sent out a number of important military expeditions, two of which were led by Fu Hao. Inscriptions found in the tomb revealed that this remarkable woman had commanded an army of thirteen thousand soldiers against the Qiang tribes in the west and had led another army against a rebellious northwestern state.

Political and Social Structures

The Shang king ruled with the help of a bureaucracy in the capital city of Anyang. His realm was divided into a number of territories governed by aristocratic chieftains or warlords (military leaders), but the king had

the power to choose these chieftains and could also depose them at will. The king was also responsible for defending the realm and controlled large armies that often fought on the fringes of the kingdom. That the king was important is evident in the ritual sacrifices undertaken at his death. Like rulers in Mesopotamia and Egypt, early Chinese kings were buried with the corpses of their faithful retainers in the royal tombs.

The Chinese rulers believed in the existence of supernatural forces that were beyond the power of human beings. The rulers thought that they could communicate with those forces to obtain divine help in worldly affairs. To communicate with the gods, rulers made use of oracle bones. These were bones on which priests scratched questions asked by the rulers. Heated metal rods were then stuck into the bones, causing them to crack. The priests interpreted the shapes of the cracks as answers to the questions posed to the gods. The questions inscribed on the bones often raised practical concerns: Will it rain? Will the king be victorious in battle? Will the king recover from his illness? The priests wrote down the answers and stored the oracle bones. For later historians, the inscriptions on the bones have become a valuable source of information about the Shang period. Unfortunately, many oracle bones have been destroyed over the centuries when Chinese medical healers ground them into powders that were thought to heal cuts and wounds.

At the top of Shang society were the king and his family, aided by a number of aristocratic families. The aristocrats not only waged war and served as officials but also were the chief landowners. The great majority of people were farmers. However, most peasants did not own their own farms but had to work the land of the aristocratic landowners. In addition to the aristocrats and peasants, the Shang society was also made up of a small number of merchants and artisans, as well as slaves. The latter were either criminals or prisoners captured in battle.

Religion and Culture under the Shang

The early Chinese had a clear sense of life in the hereafter. Some of the human sacrifices discovered in the royal tombs were no doubt meant to win the favor of

STUDYING MAPS

The following questions will help you guide students through their study of Map 4.2.

1. What were the approximate dimensions of the late Shang state? *(approximately 800 miles × 1000 miles)*

2. Why was the late Shang state located in an area with many rivers? *(the fertile valley and water access made it conducive for growth of civilization; provided needed food)*

3. Why may the leaders of the Shang state have chosen to divide their lands into many territories instead of maintaining one large state? *(provided smaller territories for ruling aristocrats to govern; gave the king more control; may have provided larger, better-trained military)*

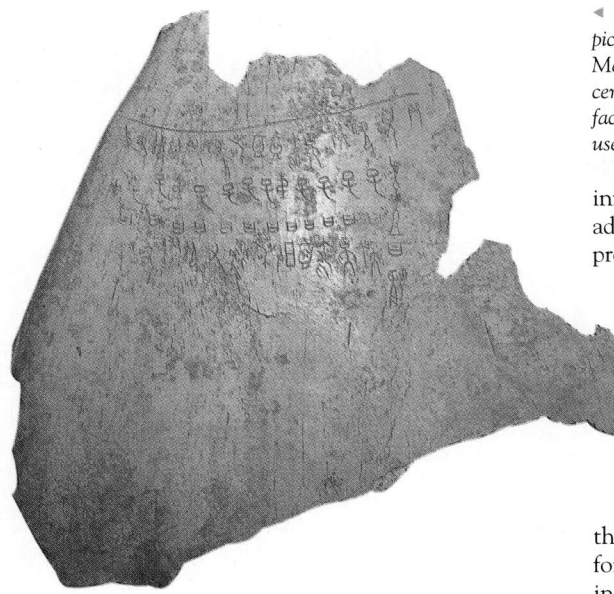

◄ *The earliest known form of Chinese writing was composed of pictographs and ideographs scratched on shells or animal bones. Messages were written to the gods and exposed to fire; then sorcerers interpreted the meaning of the resulting cracks on the surface. What kind of implements do you think might have been used to make these delicate markings over 4,000 years ago?*

influence. These bronze objects are among the most admired creations of Chinese art. Bronze casting was probably first used in making weapons, but the Shang later used the art in making bronze vessels for ritual purposes. The veneration of ancestors played an important part in this art, as the souls of the dead had to be kept alive to protect their descendants. The bronze vessels were used as ceremonial instruments for preparing and serving food and drink in the ancestral rites. Later they were used for decoration or for dining at court.

Bronze casting became a large-scale business. More than ten thousand vessels of an incredible variety of form and design survive today. The art of bronze working continued into later dynasties, but the quality declined. The Shang bronzes represent the high point of creative art in ancient China (see "Our Artistic Heritage: The Shang Bronze Ritual Vessels").

the gods. Others were intended to keep company with the king or members of his family on the journey to the next world. From this belief would come the idea of the **veneration of ancestors** (commonly known in the West as "ancestor worship") and the practice, which continues to this day in many Chinese communities, of burning replicas of physical objects to accompany the departed on their journey to the next world. The early Chinese believed that the spirits of family ancestors could bring good or evil fortune to the living members of the family. It was important to treat them well.

The Chinese also believed that divine forces existed in objects of nature, including a god of the harvest. In fact, spirit worship in various forms has survived in China down to the present century. By the time of the Shang dynasty, the Chinese had already come to believe in the existence of one superior god, known as Shang Di (Supreme Emperor).

The Shang are perhaps best remembered for their mastery of the art of bronze casting. Objects made of bronze have been found in tombs in urban centers throughout the area known to have been under Shang

SECTION REVIEW

1. **Locate:**
   (*a*) Huang River,   (*b*) Yangtze River,   (*c*) Gobi Desert,   (*d*) Tibet,   (*e*) Anyang

2. **Define:**
   (*a*) veneration of ancestors

3. **Identify:**
   (*a*) Yu,   (*b*) Fu Hao,   (*c*) Wu Ding,   (*d*) Shang Dynasty,   (*e*) Shang Di

4. **Recall:**
   (*a*) From which direction was ancient China's civilization most vulnerable to attacks from invaders?
   (*b*) Describe the purpose and use of oracle bones.
   (*c*) For what are the Shang best remembered?

5. **Think Critically:** Why was ancient Chinese civilization, unlike the Mesopotamian civilizations, able to progress steadily century after century?

MORE ABOUT . . . *Ancestor Worship*

Some students might question the logic or wisdom of venerating one's ancestors. If so, point out that this practice allowed the Chinese to "make contact" with the spiritual world by providing a contact point that at one time at least, was a real flesh-and-blood person. The ancestor, now inhabiting the enigmatic world of the beyond, could be visualized or imagined clearly. He or she could be addressed and understood, and through his or her intervention, the living could make contact with the hereafter. Note that in some Christian groups the veneration of saints provides a similar special benefit.

OUR ARTISTIC HERITAGE

TEACHING THEMES

Art and History. Although the Shang bronze vessel pictured to the right is of great artistic interest, it also tells us much about the economy and technical skills of the civilization that produced it. Ask students to list and explain other types of information this vessel provides.

LEARNING FROM VISUALS

Answer to the caption question: The bronze vessels are treasured today because of their age, rarity, and fine workmanship.

Answers to Critical Thinking Questions

1. because of their role in ancestor veneration rituals; were magnificently crafted
2. an established form of a ceremony; families made offerings of food and wine to venerate their ancestors and bring good fortune to the living
3. Answers will vary.

LASERDISC

Gilded Bronze Leopard

Kuang Bronze Ritual Vessels (Shang and Chou Dynasties)

OUR ARTISTIC HERITAGE
The Shang Bronze Ritual Vessels

Shang bronzes are one of the great cultural achievements of the ancient world. Bronze vessels—used to hold food and wine—played a significant role in family ritual ceremonies. Ancestor veneration was important to the Chinese. They believed that the souls of the dead could bring good or evil fortune to the living members of a family. Thus, ancestral rites had to be properly performed. As one poet observed, "Every custom and rite is observed, every smile, every word is in place." As part of the ritual, members of the family knelt before several of these vessels that held offerings of wine and various kinds of food. The quality of the vessels was considered an important part of the ceremony. Well-to-do families, who were the only ones who could afford these vessels, competed to acquire these magnificently crafted pieces.

One reason for the unusual quality of Shang bronze work is the method of casting used. Bronze workers in most ancient civilizations used the lost wax method, in which a model was first produced in wax. Then a clay mold was formed around it. The model was heated so that the wax would melt and drain out. The empty space was

▲ *This bronze vessel was made during the Shang dynasty, during the second or first century B.C. It stands at just under 14½ inches high. Because the dead were often buried with their finest earthly possessions, many ritual vessels found today are discovered in tombs. Why do collectors treasure these bronze pieces so highly?*

then filled with molten metal. In China, clay molds made in several sections were tightly fitted together before the liquid bronze was poured. This technique enabled artisans to apply their designs directly to the mold. In this way they could use intricate motifs in a rich surface decoration.

The most important decorative motif on Shang bronzes was the *taotie* mask. It featured a pair of large eyes, nostrils, and fangs, giving it the look of a fantastic beast. Although fierce in appearance, the *taotie* represented a protective force against evil spirits.

1. Why are the Shang bronzes considered to be great cultural achievements?

2. What is a ritual? Explain how ritual was a part of Chinese family life.

3. Explain what part, if any, rituals or ceremonies play in your life. How are special foods, decorations, tableware, or other things involved in your celebrations and traditions?

If your students question the importance of the information on **mandate of Heaven,** *tell them . . .*

This mandate probably still has an impact on relations between Chinese and Western nations today.

The Chinese political philosophy of the *mandate of Heaven* provides an ethical foundation for the right to rule: a ruler is selected by Heaven to rule for the benefit of his peo-

ple. If he doesn't rule properly, another would-be ruler can overthrow him. During the time of the Zhou dynasty, no other civilization in the world had a more advanced ethical foundation. More than two thousand years later, Machiavelli would propose a different ethic for the Western rule: morality plays no role in governing; if it works, do it. It is interesting to speculate whether Western democracies are still guided by this mandate.

THE ZHOU DYNASTY

In 1122 B.C., an aggressive young state, which was located near the great bend of the Huang River as it begins to flow directly eastward to the sea, overthrew the Shang dynasty. The new dynasty, which called itself the Zhou, lasted for almost nine hundred years (1122 to 256 B.C.). It was the longest-lived dynasty in the history of China.

The Zhou leaders ruled over a frontier region on the western fringes of the Shang state. According to legend, the last of the Shang rulers was a wicked tyrant who oppressed the people, swam in "ponds of wine," and ordered the writing of lustful music that "ruined the morale of the nation." This led the ruler of the state of Zhou to revolt and establish a new dynasty.

The Zhou located their capital in their home territory, near the present-day city of Xian (SHEE-on). Later they established a second capital city at modern-day Luoyang, farther to the east, in order to govern new territories captured from the Shang. This established a pattern of having both western and eastern capital cities that would last off and on in China for nearly two thousand years.

Political Power: Does the Ruler Have the Mandate of Heaven?

The Zhou dynasty continued the political system of the rulers they had overthrown. At the head of the government was the Zhou king, who was served by a bureaucracy of growing size and complexity. It now included several offices responsible for education, law, public works, and rites. The latter office was especially important, because the king was seen as the link between Heaven and Earth, people and nature, and the living and the dead. The performance of correct rituals or ceremonial acts that served to strengthen those links was crucial to a king's duties.

The Shang practice of dividing the kingdom into a number of territories governed by officials appointed by the king was continued under the Zhou. The governing officials of these territories were members of the hereditary aristocracy. They were appointed by the king and were subject to his authority. At least in the beginning, many were members of the royal family. The Zhou king was like the head of a large extended

▼ *This bell chime is from Zhou China.*

*If your students question the importance of information about **early Chinese civilizations**, tell them . . .*

As the text indicates, Chinese historians ordinarily date the first civilization in China (Xia) to over four thousand years ago; but the tendency among Western historians has been to consider the Shang (c. 1750–1122 B.C.) the first civilization. Why? One reason

might be that when Western historians acknowledge that an advanced civilization existed in China prior to the Shang, competition exists for "first place" with the Sumerian civilization. To avoid this possibility the Xia civilization is often not even mentioned in Western textbooks. Yet, wouldn't a civilization that has managed the craft of silk weaving surely deserve at least a mention?

FOCUS

OBJECTIVES

After completing this section, students should be able to

1. identify issues in the debate over whether the leaders of the Zhou dynasty had the mandate of Heaven to rule
2. describe the lives and culture of different groups during the Zhou dynasty
3. identify and explain social institutions and the role of the family during the Zhou dynasty
4. explain how the development of a written language changed Chinese culture

FOCUS ACTIVITY

Help students understand why leaders in history have often claimed the divine right to rule. Ask them to identify and discuss the types of decisions leaders are often forced or choose to make that could erode their popular support. Discuss how much easier it would be for leaders to make these decisions if their subjects believe God gave the leaders the right to rule.

TEACH

COMPARING TIME PERIODS

Remind students that the Egyptian Pharaohs were seen as links to the gods, just as the king in the Zhou dynasty was. Ask students to discuss how a Pharaoh or king might behave differently if he honestly believed himself to be a link to God. Do students think this would make him more arrogant, or would it give him a greater will to serve his people?

CLASS DISCUSSION

Ask students if they believe, as Chinese Tao suggests, that people have a "right to revolution." If there is such a right, how may people exercise it without causing great harm to innocent people and their civilization?

USING PRIMARY SOURCES

Ask students to consider what an advancement in military technology, like the crossbow, which is described in the primary source on this page, can do to the balance of power between groups or nations. What other advancements in weaponry can they identify that have made differences in historical events?

family, with each individual princely official owing a loose allegiance to his lord. Like the Shang rulers, the Zhou king was in charge of defense and controlled armies that served under his command throughout the country.

The Zhou kings also made some changes, however. As described by the *Rites of Zhou*, one of the oldest surviving documents on political power, the Chinese began to develop a theory of government. The document stated that the Zhou house ruled China because it possessed the **mandate of Heaven.** What was the mandate of Heaven? It was believed that Heaven—which was not a god but an impersonal law of nature—kept order in the universe through the Zhou king. Thus, he ruled over all humanity by a mandate or authority to command from Heaven. The king, who was chosen to rule because of his talent and virtue, was then responsible for ruling the people with goodness and efficiency. The concept of the heavenly mandate became a basic principle of Chinese statecraft.

The mandate of Heaven, however, was double edged. The king was expected to rule according to the proper "Way" (called the *Tao* [DOW]). It was his duty to keep the gods pleased in order to protect the people from natural disaster or a bad harvest. Later, this role would be embodied in a ritual ceremony conducted once each year by the Chinese emperor at the Temple of Heaven in Beijing. If the king failed to rule effectively, he could be overthrown and replaced by a new ruler.

This theory has strong political side effects. It sets forth a "right of revolution" to overthrow a corrupt or evil ruler. It also makes clear that the king, though serving as a representative of Heaven, is not a divine being himself. In practice, of course, each founder of a new dynasty would say that he had earned the mandate of Heaven. Who could disprove it except by overthrowing the king? The practical Chinese would later sum up this view in the saying, "He who wins is the king; he who loses is the rebel."

The mandate of Heaven was closely tied to the practice of dynastic cycles. From the beginning of Chinese history to A.D. 1912, China was ruled by a series of dynasties. The Zhou dynasty, as we have seen, lasted for almost nine hundred years, and others, not as long.

Each dynasty ruled with the mandate of Heaven. Each king in each dynasty was the intermediary between Heaven and Earth. No matter how long the dynasties lasted, however, all went through a cycle of change. A new dynasty established its power, ruled successfully for many years, and then eventually began to decline. For a variety of reasons, the power of the central government would begin to collapse, giving rise to rebellions and even invasion. Finally, the dynasty collapsed, a new dynasty took over, and another dynastic cycle began.

The Zhou rulers followed this pattern. The dynasty had centuries of wise and efficient rulers. However, the later rulers of the Zhou royal house began to decline, both intellectually and morally. By the fifth century B.C., the Zhou kings ruled in name only. Several of the small territories into which the Zhou kingdom had been divided began to evolve into powerful states that challenged the Zhou ruler himself. In 403 B.C., civil war broke out, beginning an age known in Chinese historical records as the "Period of the Warring States." Powerful states fought among one another and largely ignored the Zhou court.

By this time, the nature of warfare had also changed in China. Chariots were not useful in hilly land or in the damp Yangtze valley. New forms of warfare emerged with the making of iron weapons that were more powerful than bronze weapons. Foot soldiers (the infantry) and soldiers on horseback (the cavalry) made their first appearance. Members of the cavalry were now armed with the powerful crossbow. According to an ancient Chinese text, the crossbow was invented as early as the seventh century B.C.:

> Ch'in (CHIN) considered . . . that the bow and arrow was no longer sufficient to keep the world in obedience, for in his time all the lords were fighting against one another with weapons, and could not be controlled by ordinary archery. He therefore added at right-angles to the bow a stock and established a trigger-mechanism with a box or housing, thus increasing its strength. In this way all the lords could be subdued. Ch'in transmitted his invention to the Three Lords of Ch'u (JOO). . . . Before their time the men of Ch'u had for several generations guarded their frontiers only with bows of peachwood and arrows of thorn.[2]

ENRICHMENT ACTIVITY

Have students develop written statements of the *mandate of Heaven*. They should write their statements in a way that would make them apply to a contemporary, democratic government such as the one in the U.S. In their statements, have students specify how the people will recognize whether the government is indeed complying with the *mandate of Heaven*. Their statements should conclude with a checklist that the people could refer to that would indicate that the government did comply.

Eventually, one of the warring states—that of Qin (TSIN)—took control. In 221 B.C. it created a new dynasty.

Life and Culture during the Zhou Dynasty

During the Zhou dynasty, the basic features of Chinese economic and social life began to take shape. The Zhou continued the pattern of land ownership that had existed under the Shang. The peasants worked on lands owned by their lord, but they also had land of their own that they farmed for their own use. Each peasant family farmed an outer plot for its own use and then joined with other families to work the inner one for their lord. Life for most farmers was not easy, as the following poem indicates. (The "big rat" probably refers to the high taxes paid by peasants to the government or lord.)

> Big rat, big rat
> Do not eat my millet!
> Three years I have served you.
> But you will not care for me.
> I am going to leave you
> And go to that happy land;
> Happy land, happy land,
> Where I will find my place.

In addition to the nobles and the peasants, there was also a class of artisans and merchants. They lived in walled towns under the direct control of the local lord. At first, trade involved the exchange of local products that were used on an everyday basis. Eventually, trade increased to include goods brought in from distant regions. Among these goods were salt, iron, cloth, and various luxury items. Merchants did not operate freely but were considered the property of the local lord.

Map 4.3   China during the Period of the Warring States

Sometimes they could even be bought and sold. There was also a class of slaves, who performed a variety of humble tasks. Most of them were probably prisoners of war captured during conflicts with the neighboring states. Slaves did not make up a large percentage of the total population.

Economic and Technological Growth

The period from the sixth to the third centuries B.C. was one of rapid change. As we have seen, this period was marked by the growth of large, independent states owing only a loose loyalty to the Zhou ruling house. Along with these political developments, an economic revolution was also taking place. As the states grew in size and power, they began to direct their local economies and impose new taxes for their expanding armies. The period of the later Zhou rulers was an age

Ask students to discuss their own feelings toward taxes. Remind them that Americans, through our political process, have some voice in setting the taxes we pay. Farmers during the Zhou dynasty had no say in setting the taxes they paid. How may this have inspired the author to write this poem?

STUDYING MAPS

The following questions will help you guide students through their study of Map 4.3.

1. How many smaller states were created from lands held by the Zhou dynasty? *(eleven)*

2. What reasons often cause small states to unite to form larger states? *(to gain military strength; to gain a "voice;" to gain economic advantage)*

3. Why is it surprising that Qin would be the state to unite the other lands of the former Zhou dynasty? *(it was already larger than other individual states; could have maintained its own independence)*

LEARNING FROM VISUALS

Divide your students into groups and assign each group to create a description of a typical day in the life of the man in the picture to the right. They should base their descriptions on their knowledge of ancient China and their imagination. What do they believe are his worries and hopes for the future? What brings him sorrow or fills him with joy?

Answer to the caption question: The Han Canal was built for military purposes. The canal connected the Huai and Yangtze rivers to make it easier for the prince of Wu to supply his army.

Multimedia Support

TRANSPARENCY
4–2, Shou Housing

▶ *The Chinese barge floating along the mouth of the Grand Canal at the Yangtze River is both this bargeman's home and his business. He may spend his whole life on the interconnecting canals and streams. What was the main purpose of the Han Canal when it was first built in 486 B.C.?*

of significant economic growth and technological change, especially in farming.

For thousands of years, farmers had been dependent upon rainfall to water their crops. In the Huang River valley and other areas of northern China, for the most part farmers grew millet and other crops that could survive on little moisture. Farther south, in the Yangtze River delta or along the southern coast, farmers grew rice in marshy regions or along the banks of the rivers. Irrigation was probably used in a limited way during the Shang dynasty, but it was in wide use by the sixth century B.C. During that time, large-scale water projects were set in motion to control the flow of rivers and spread water evenly to the fields. Canals were built to make the transport of goods easier from one region to another.

Changes in farming methods also increased food production. By the mid-sixth century B.C., the use of iron had led to the development of iron plowshares. These were more advanced than those used elsewhere and made it possible to plow land that had not yet been used for farming. This development allowed the Chinese to add to the amount of land available for growing crops. The new technique of leaving some land unplanted to renew the nutrients in the soil also increased food production.

These advances in farming enabled the population of China to rise as high as fifty million people during the late Zhou period. The changes were also a major factor in encouraging the growth of trade and manufacturing. During the later Zhou period, economic wealth began to replace noble birth as a prime source of power and influence. Utensils made of iron became more common, and products such as cloth, salt, and various manufactured goods were traded regularly.

One of the most important items of trade in ancient China was silk. Silk cloth was used not only for clothing but also for wrapping the body of the dead before burial. Chinese silk fragments have been found throughout central Asia and as far away as Athens, Greece—a clear indication of a far-reaching trade network.

The Family in Ancient China

Of all the social institutions that have appeared in organized human societies, few have been as closely identified with China as the family. As in most agri-

So What ??

If your students question the importance of the information on **Chinese families,** *tell them . . .*

The emphasis on family loyalty and filial piety during the Zhou years and beyond goes a long way toward explaining the amazing strength of the Chinese family today. Even in foreign countries (such as the U.S.A.), Chinese families often share a stability, strength, and unity that makes a marked contrast with the characteristics of our typical Western family. Greater obedience to and respect for parents often results in sons and daughters who, under the parental influence, study harder and have fewer conflicts. As a result, children from Chinese families often accomplish more academically than their counterparts in school.

cultural societies, in ancient China the family served as the basic economic and social unit. However, the family there took on an almost sacred quality as a symbol of the entire social order.

The concept of family began to grow in importance during the Zhou dynasty. Loyalty to family members was considered even more important than was loyalty to the state. Indeed, one Chinese philosopher remarked that a son should protect his father even if the father had committed a crime against the community. That, he said, is the mark of a civilized society.

At the heart of the concept of family in China was the idea of **filial piety.** *Filial* refers to the duty of a son or daughter. Filial piety, then, meant that all members of the family had to subordinate their needs and desires to those of the male head of the family. More broadly, it created a system in which every family member had his or her place. All Chinese learned the "five relationships" that were the key to a proper social order. The son was subordinate to the father, the wife to her husband, and the younger brother to the older brother. All were subject to their king. The fifth relationship was the proper one between friend and friend. Only if all members of the family and the community as a whole behaved in a proper way would society work well.

What explains the importance of the family in ancient China? Certainly, the need to work together on the land was a significant factor. In ancient times, as today, farming in China required the work of many people. This is especially true in growing rice, which, due to its nutritive qualities, had become the chief crop in the region of the Yangtze River and the provinces to the south.

Growing rice requires hard work. First, rice seedlings are planted in several inches of water in a nursery bed, while the farmer plows the larger paddy fields to prepare them for planting. During the rainy season, the plants are moved one by one by backbreaking labor to the paddy fields after they have flooded. After the transplanting, the irrigation network bringing water into and through the fields must be kept in operation. Moreover, the plants themselves must be protected from insects. When the crop is ripe for harvesting, the stalks must be cut. Then the kernels have to be separated from the stalks and husks and brought to the

▲ *Flooded rice fields are a common site in China. The growing of rice requires the labor of many workers to plant the seedlings and keep them properly watered. Flooding the fields helps to root the seedlings and add nutrients to the soil. Mosquitoes and other insects are controlled by the fish that breed in the fields. After the plants mature, the fields are drained and the rice ripens in dry soil.*

house, where the rice is prepared for sale to the rice miller (see "Focus on Everyday Life: Housing and Food in Ancient China").

Under such circumstances, it is hardly surprising that the overall needs of the family would be more important than the needs of each family member in ancient China. Children, too, were essential to the family's needs. They worked in the fields during their youthful years. Later, sons were expected to take over the burden of physical labor on the family plots and provide for the well-being of their parents.

As we have seen, then, male supremacy was a key element in the social system of ancient China (and in the other civilizations that we have examined). As in many traditional societies, the male was considered so important because he was responsible for providing food for his family or, in the case of farming communities, for actually growing the food. In ancient China, men worked in the fields. They also governed society and

On Line with WORLD HISTORY *Internet Activity*

You may want to have your students visit the following URL, where they will find information and additional web site resources to enhance their study of this chapter.

Exploring Ancient World Cultures— Ancient China

http://eawc.evansville.edu/chpage.htm

This site contains resources and links about Ancient China.

Due to the ever-changing nature of the World Wide Web, see the West History web site, **http://history.swpco.com** for regular updates of the URLs in this text.

Assign students to identify and list information a future archaeologist would be able to ascertain about the life of a typical American family by digging up their family's kitchen 5,000 years from now. What types of information about American family life would they not be able to determine?

LEARNING FROM VISUALS

Answers to the caption questions: Elaborate pieces would have been owned only by the wealthy. Student answers about the bowl's purpose will vary.

Answers to Critical Thinking Questions

1. We learn a lot about people by their homes. Built with sturdy materials, some of the houses of the wealthy survived over time, giving archaeologists clues about the people who lived in them. Common people used mud and other simple materials that did not last.

2. Fruits, fish, and animals need a consistent, accessible water supply to flourish. Water for these foods was not available everywhere.

FOCUS ON EVERYDAY LIFE
Housing and Food in Ancient China

We know much more about the lifestyle of the ruling elite than of the common people in ancient China. According to Chinese tradition, people began to build houses in the late third millennium B.C. Early examples consisted of two rooms, with a main hall in front and living rooms in the back. The first houses were built of wooden planks, but later Chinese used tile and brick. By the first millennium B.C., most public buildings and the houses of the rich were probably built this way.

▲ *Pictured is a large, shallow three-footed bronze bowl made in Ming China. The bowl is 23½ inches in diameter and encrusted with malachite. Who would have owned such a bowl? What might have been its purpose?*

Few examples of the homes of the common people have survived outside of a few archaeological sites, such as Ban Po village in central China. In the beginning, according to one Chinese author, "man dwelt in the cave and lived out in the field. Later on, the wise men substituted houses with ridgepoles and roofs to protect them from the rain." By 200 B.C., most Chinese probably lived in simple houses of mud, wooden planks, or brick with thatch or sometimes tile roofs. In some areas of China, however, people continued to live in caves, even down to modern times. This was especially true in areas of North China, where the yellow soil is soft and provides good protection from the heat and cold.

Chinese houses usually had little furniture. Most people squatted or sat with their legs spread out on the packed mud floor. Chairs were not introduced until the sixth or seventh centuries A.D.

The cooking of food had been introduced in early times. The staple foods were millet or other crops suited to dry weather in the north and rice in the south. Other common vegetables were wheat, barley, mustard greens, and bamboo shoots. In early times, such foods were often eaten in the form of porridge. By the Zhou dynasty, however, stir-frying in a wok (bowl-shaped iron frying pan) was becoming common. Where possible, the Chinese family would vary its diet of grain foods with vegetables, fruit (including pears, peaches, apricots, and plums), and fish or meat. For most people, however, such additions to the daily plate of rice or millet were a rare luxury.

1. Why do we know more about the lifestyle of the Chinese ruling class than that of the common people?

2. Why were fish, meats, and fruits rare additions to the Chinese diet?

MORE ABOUT . . . Crisis and the Chinese Language

The Chinese symbol for *crisis* is, interestingly, composed by the addition of two symbols: "danger" and "opportunity." Portraying crisis in this fashion gives the individual not only a less tragic feeling about the crisis situation itself, but also an expectation that something positive may come out of the present crisis, if handled properly. The world of the individual who perceives a situation as "danger plus opportunity" is likely to be less threatening than the world of one who perceives a crisis as a dramatically negative event. Words allow humans to develop mental concepts. Without the specific word, it may be much harder to have a positive attitude when faced with a real crisis.

were the warriors, scholars, and government ministers. Women raised the children and worked in the home.

In ancient China, although women did not hold positions of authority, some did become a force in politics. This was especially true at the royal court, where wives of the ruler or other female members of the royal family played a part in court affairs. These activities were clearly looked down upon by males, as this Chinese poem indicates:

> A clever man builds a city,
> A clever woman lays one low;
> With all her qualifications, that clever woman
> Is but an ill-omened bird.
> A woman with a long tongue
> Is a flight of steps leading to calamity;
> For disorder does not come from heaven,
> But is brought about by women.[3]

The written Chinese language clearly shows how women and men were viewed in ancient China. The character for *man* (**男**) unites the symbols for *strength* and *rice field*. The character for *woman* (**女**) shows a person in a posture of submission and respect. The character for *peace* (**安**) is a woman under a roof. Male supremacy had deep roots in the Chinese language.

The Chinese Written Language

Perhaps the most important cultural contribution of ancient China to later Chinese society was the creation and development of the Chinese written language. By Shang times, the Chinese had developed a simple script that is the ancestor of the highly complex written language of today. Like many other languages of antiquity, it was primarily **pictographic** and ideographic in form. Pictographs are picture symbols, usually called *characters*, that form a picture of the object to be represented. For example, the Chinese characters for *mountain* (**山**), *sun* (**日**), and *moon* (**月**) were meant to represent the objects themselves. Ideographs are characters that combine two or more pictographs to represent an idea. For example, the word *big* (**大**) is shown as a man with outstretched arms. The word *east* (**東**) symbolizes the sun coming up behind the trees.

Each character, of course, would be given a sound by the speaker when pronounced. In other cultures, this process led to the disuse of pictographs and ideographs and to the adoption of a written language based on phonetic symbols, such as the Roman alphabet. The Chinese, too, eventually began to attach phonetic meaning to some of their symbols. It is sometimes possible for Chinese speakers to guess the pronunciation of a character they have not seen before. However, although the Chinese language has evolved continuously over a period of four thousand years, it has never entirely abandoned its original format. In that sense, the Chinese written language is almost unique in the world today.

Important in shaping the evolution of the Chinese written language was its role as a tool in aiding national unity. If the written language had developed in the direction of a phonetic alphabet, it could no longer have served as the written system for all the peoples of an expanding civilization. Although most people spoke some form of an original Chinese language, the versions spoken in various regions of the country differed from one another in pronunciation. For the most part, they were (and are today) mutually unintelligible. For example, natives of today's capital city of Beijing in North China could not talk in their own language with people from the industrial city of Shanghai in the lower Yangtze valley.

The Chinese answer to this problem was to give all the various spoken versions of the Chinese language the same writing system. Although any character might be pronounced differently in different regions of China, that character would be written the same way everywhere. The development of a single writing system was the cement that helped to create and maintain a sense of unity and common identity throughout China.

This system of written characters could be read by educated Chinese from one end of the country to the other. It became the language of the bureaucracy and literature and the vehicle for spreading Chinese culture to all within Chinese boundaries. The Chinese written language brought together the various peoples of the widespread Chinese empire and transformed what otherwise would have been a highly diverse region of the world into a single culture.

USING PRIMARY SOURCES

Ask students to write a sentence that sums up the meaning of the poem to the left. What does it tell them about women in Chinese society? What may the author's experience with women have been? Have students write a poem as it might have been written by a Chinese woman at that time.

ACTIVITY

Have students devise their own pictographic or ideographic language. It should be extensive enough to communicate at a basic, everyday level. Then, discuss the difficulty of expressing ideas like "satisfaction," "pleasure," or "insistence" using ideographs.

ASSESS

You can choose from a variety of assessments to evaluate your students' mastery of the objectives for this section as stated on page 93. Possible assessments include:

1. Section Review Questions on the next page
2. Section 3–2 Quiz in your Teacher Resource materials
3. Reteaching Worksheets in your Teacher Resource materials
4. Self-Study software

ALTERNATIVE ASSESSMENT

Assign students to list activities that a farming family would have carried out. Identify and explain three of these activities that show how different ancient Chinese society was from our own.

So What ??

*If students question the importance of information on **Chinese language**, tell them . . .*

The pictographic and ideographic aspects of the Chinese language may account, according to some scholars, for the superior math scores that many Chinese students obtain in school (the same is true of other similar languages, such as classic Japanese). The thinking is that pictographs and ideographs may initially be harder to learn, but their more abstract aspects may help the young mind develop its abstract thinking capacity to a greater degree than Western alphabetic languages do. This same abstract ability is what is called into use by much of mathematics, which is itself a type of language (it conveys ideas and meanings). Alphabetic language may be easier to learn, but may not help our minds as much to develop abstract thinking potential.

Answers to SECTION REVIEW

2. (a) authority from Heaven for a king to rule, (b) all members submit to the male head; everyone had a place, (c) referring to characters (picture symbols) of the Chinese written language

3. (a) ancient Chinese document on political power, (b) period of civil war

4. (a) last of the Shang rulers ruined the people's morale, lead Zhou to revolt and establish a new dynasty, (b) sets forth a right of revolution to overthrow a corrupt ruler; the king is not divine, (c) use of iron for plowshares; leaving some land unplanted to renew the nutrients in the soil, (d) son subordinate to father; wife subordinate to husband; younger brother subordinate to older brother; all subordinate to king; proper relationship between friends

5. (a) Chinese character for man unites the symbols for strength and rice field; men were responsible for growing/providing food for the family. Answers will vary. (b) all spoken versions given the same writing system

CLOSE

Lead students in a discussion of the 'Focus' objectives identified on page 93. Stress the importance of the debate over whether Chinese leaders had or did not have the divine right to rule. Explain that this question reappears in other places and times throughout history and that they should expect to discuss it again in this course.

100

❋ SECTION REVIEW ❋

1. Locate:
(a) Luoyang

2. Define:
(a) mandate of Heaven,   (b) filial piety,
(c) pictographic

3. Identify:
(a) *Rites of Zhou*,   (b) Period of the Warring States

4. Recall:
(a) According to legend, what events led to the establishment of the Zhou dynasty?
(b) Describe two political side effects of the theory known as Tao.
(c) Describe the two major developments in farming technology in the later part of the Zhou dynasty that led to population growth.
(d) Name the five relationships that were the basis of social order in ancient China.

5. Think Critically:
(a) Explain how the concept of male supremacy in Chinese culture is related to the importance of China's chief crop, rice.
(b) Explain how the Chinese written language helped to unify China.

THE DEVELOPMENT OF THE CHINESE TRADITIONS

Like people in India, the Chinese tried to understand the nature of the universe and the role of human beings within it. Between 500 and 200 B.C., three major schools of thought emerged in China about the nature of human beings and the universe—Confucianism (kun-FYOO-shun-iz-um), Taoism (DOW-iz-um), and Legalism. The Chinese philosophers took a different approach than did those in India. Hindus and Buddhists focused on freeing the human soul from the cycle of rebirth. Chinese philosophers were more concerned about the immediate world in which people lived and how to create a stable order in that society.

Confucius: The First Teacher

Perhaps no one name is more closely associated with Chinese culture than Confucius, who is known to the Chinese as the First Teacher. (*Confucius* is the Latin form of the title *Kung Fuci,* meaning "Master Kung," as he was called by his followers.) Confucius was born in 551 B.C. He hoped to get a job as a political advisor in one of the many principalities into which China was divided at that time, but he had little success in finding a patron. Upset by the violence and moral decay of his age, he traveled around China in an attempt to persuade political leaders to follow his ideas. Few did at the time, but a faithful band of followers revered him as a great teacher, recorded his sayings in the *Analects,* and spread his message. Until the twentieth century, almost every Chinese pupil studied his sayings. This made **Confucianism,** or the system of Confucian ideas, an important part of Chinese history. What, then, were his ideas, and why were they so powerful?

Confucius lived at a time of great confusion in China. The chaos in China was largely caused by unceasing warfare among numerous Chinese armies that did not hesitate to slaughter opposing soldiers and their families. Men, women, and children were beheaded in mass executions. China was faced with one basic question: How do we restore order to this society? Confucius provided a basic set of ideas that eventually came to be widely accepted.

Confucius's interest in philosophy was political and ethical, not spiritual. He believed that it was useless to speculate on spiritual questions. It was better by far to assume that there was an order in the universe and then focus one's attention on ordering the affairs of this world. The universe was made in such a way that, if humans would act in harmony with its purposes, their own affairs would prosper. Much of his concern was with human behavior. The key to proper behavior was to behave in accordance with the **Tao** (Way).

Two elements stand out in the Confucian view of the Tao: duty and humanity. The concept of duty

So What ⁇

If your students question the importance of information on **tradition,** *tell them . . .*

Tradition has many positive and negative connotations. While it is generally agreed that Chinese society is more traditional than the allegedly more dynamic Western society, there is not much agreement on how much tradition and how much dynamism is optimum for social welfare. Tradition makes it easier to find one's place in his or her society. Too much reliance on tradition, however, may make a society inflexible and unable to adapt to new realities.

Dynamic change helps a society adapt to new challenges, but too much dynamism (too little reliance on tradition) may produce a society of confusing and frustrating standards

▲ *Confucius is represented in a rubbing from the temple in Shantung, his birthplace. Notice the fine details of his scholar's robes and his beard. How has the artist characterized the philosopher?*

meant that all people had to subordinate their own interests to the broader need of the family and the community, and everyone should be governed by the Five Constant Relationships. These included parent and child, husband and wife, older sibling and younger sibling, older friend and younger friend, and ruler and subject. To Confucius, the health of society depended on the careful observation of these relationships. Each person in the relationship had a duty to the other. Parents should be loving. Children should revere their parents. Husbands should be good, and wives obedient. The elder sibling should be kind, and the younger sibling respectful. The older friend should be considerate, and the younger friend deferential. Rulers should be benevolent, and subjects loyal. Three of these five relationships concern the family, which shows its importance to Confucius: "The duty of children to their parents is the foundation from which all virtues spring."

The Confucian concept of duty is often expressed in the form of a "work ethic." If each individual worked

hard to fulfill his or her duties, then the affairs of society as a whole would prosper as well. As Confucius stated, "If there is righteousness in the heart, there will be beauty in the character. If there is beauty in the character, there will be harmony in the home. If there be harmony in the home, there will be order in the nation. If there be order in the nation, there will be peace in the world." Above all, the ruler must set a good example. If the king followed his "kingly way"— the path of goodness and the common good—then subjects would respect him, and society would prosper.

A second key element in the Confucian view of the Tao is the idea of humanity. This consists of a sense of compassion and empathy for others. It is similar in some ways to Christian ideas, but with a twist. Christians are taught, "Do unto others as you would have others do unto you." Confucius would say, "Do not do unto others what you would not wish done to yourself." To many Chinese, this attitude meant that others should be tolerated. Confucius urged people to "measure the feelings of others by one's own," for "within the four seas all men are brothers."

The ideas of Confucius had a strong appeal to his contemporaries. After his death in 479 B.C., his message spread widely throughout China. Confucius was a harsh critic of his own times. He seemed to stress the need to return to the values of an earlier age—the Golden Age of the early Zhou dynasty. He saw it as an age of perfection that no longer existed. In referring to that age, he is quoted as saying the following:

When the Great Way was practiced, the world was shared by all alike. The worthy and the able were promoted to office and practiced good faith and lived in affection. The aged found a fitting close to their lives, the robust their proper employment; the young were provided with an upbringing and the widow and widower, the orphaned and the sick, with proper care. Men had their talks and women their hearths. They hated to see goods lying about in waste, yet they did not hoard them for themselves; they disliked the thought that their energies were not fully used, yet they used them not for private ends. Therefore all evil plotting was prevented and thieves and rebels did not arise, so that people could leave their outer gates unbolted. This was the age of Grand Unity.[4]

and goals. If "today" is considered better than "yesterday," the lack of respect for the past may introduce a lack of direction and a lost sense of purpose. Ask students what they

think is the right blend of tradition and dynamism. Can they identify both the attributes and liabilities of tradition and dynamism?

Confucius was not just living in the past, however. Many of his key ideas looked forward rather than backward. Perhaps his most striking political idea was that the government should not be limited solely to those of noble birth but should be open to all men of superior talent. This concept of rule by merit was, of course, not popular with the aristocrats who held political offices based on their noble birth. Although Confucius's ideas did not have much effect in his lifetime, they opened the door to a new idea of statecraft that would later be put into widespread use.

The Old Master and Taoism

One of the most popular rivals to Confucianism was the philosophy of **Taoism** (a system of ideas based on the teachings of Lao Tzu). According to tradition, it was founded by a contemporary of Confucius known as Lao Tzu (LOUD ZUH), or the Old Master. Scholars do not really know if Lao Tzu actually existed. Nevertheless, the ideas people associate with him became popular in the fifth and fourth centuries B.C., and Taoism became a rival to Confucianism.

The chief ideas of Taoism are discussed in a short work known as *Tao Te Ching* (The Way of the Tao). Legend says that Lao Tzu, seeking solitude in his older years, got on a water buffalo and rode westward to Tibet. A gatekeeper at the Hankao Pass, recognizing him, asked him to turn back and not leave China. Lao Tzu refused, which prompted the gatekeeper to ask him if he would at least make a record of his beliefs before he left civilization. Lao Tzu agreed and returned in three days with *Tao Te Ching*. It is a puzzling book, and

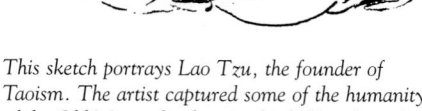

This sketch portrays Lao Tzu, the founder of Taoism. The artist captured some of the humanity of the Old Master by drawing his half smile and long fingernails. What does it appear Lao Tzu is carrying?

scholars have argued for centuries over its real meaning. The opening line, for example, explains less what the Tao (Way) is than what it is not: "The Tao that can be told is not the eternal Tao. The name that can be named is not the eternal name."

Nevertheless, the basic ideas of Taoism, as interpreted by followers of the doctrine, are straightforward. Like Confucianism, Taoism does not concern itself with the underlying meaning of the universe. Rather, it tries to set forth proper forms of behavior for human beings on Earth.

However, Taoism puts forth a point of view of life that is quite different from that of Confucianism. Followers of Confucius believe that it is the duty of human beings to work hard to improve life here on Earth. Taoists believe that the true way to follow the will of Heaven is not action, but inaction:

> *Without going outside, you may know the whole world.*
> *Without looking through the window, you may see the ways of heaven.*
> *The farther you go, the less you know.*
> *Thus the sage [wise man] knows without traveling;*
> *He sees without looking;*
> *He works without doing.*[5]

The best way to act in harmony with the universal order is to act spontaneously and let nature take its course by not interfering with it:

> *Do you think you can take over the universe and improve it?*
> *I do not believe it can be done.*
> *The universe is sacred.*
> *You cannot improve it.*
> *If you try to change it, you will ruin it.*
> *If you try to hold it, you will lose it.*[6]

MORE ABOUT . . . *Confucianism and Taoism*

Can Confucianism and Taoism coexist? Experts on Chinese culture believe that they do, in fact, in most Chinese people. To understand how this happens is to separate public from personal life. While the Chinese tend to pursue Taoist principles in their private lives, the old Western perception of the Chinese as "inscrutable" (not easily understood) may in fact be due to Taoist-style reactions to external events—instead of reacting *against* the environment, one is best served by agreeing and giving in; no amount of emotional outburst will make things better. Only the acceptance of reality is the proper way. In public life, however, Confucian principles have been deeply implanted and over fifty years of communist retraining has been unable to dislodge Confucian ethics from Chinese society—much to the disappointment of party strategists.

The philosophy of Taoism was popular with Chinese intellectuals. There was also a popular Taoism for the common people.

Popular Taoism was less a philosophy than a religion. It consisted of a variety of rituals and forms of behavior that were seen as a means for achieving heavenly salvation. Taoist magicians practiced various types of exercises for mind or body control in the hope of achieving power and long life. It was chiefly in this form that Taoism would survive into a later age.

Legalism

A third philosophy that became popular in China was **Legalism.** Unlike Confucianism or Taoism, Legalism believed that human beings were evil by nature. Human beings could only be brought to follow the correct path by harsh laws and stiff punishments. Legalists were referred to as the "School of Law" because they rejected the Confucian view that government by "superior men" could solve society's problems. Instead, they argued for a system of impersonal laws.

The Legalists disagreed with the Confucian belief that the universe has a moral core. They believed that only firm action by the state could bring social order. Because human nature was corrupt, officials could not be trusted to carry out their duties in a fair and even-handed fashion. Only a strong ruler could create an orderly society. All human actions should be subordinated to the effort to create a strong and prosperous state that was subject to the will of the strong ruler.

Confucius had said, "Lead the people by virtue and restrain them by the rules of good taste, and the people will have a sense of shame, and moreover will become good." The Legalists did not believe this. To them, people were not capable of being good. A ruler and his officials did not have to show a true compassion for the needs of the people. Only fear of harsh punishment would cause the common people to serve the interests of the ruler. Legalists, then, believed in a strong, authoritarian ruler who governed by harsh punishment. Only this system could maintain order and stability in society.

 SECTION REVIEW

1. **Define:**
   (a) Confucianism, (b) Tao, (c) Taoism,
   (d) Legalism

2. **Identify:**
   (a) Confucius, (b) Lao Tzu, (c) *Tao Te Ching*

3. **Recall:**
   (a) What was a basic difference between the Chinese and the Indian explanation of the nature of the universe?
   (b) Was Confucius more concerned with spiritual or worldly questions?
   (c) What were the two major elements of the Confucian view of the Tao?
   (d) Describe one way in which the Taoist view of life differed from the view of Confucianism.

4. **Think Critically:** Which of the three Chinese philosophies most appeals to you? Which is least appealing? Give reasons for your answers.

THE RISE AND FALL OF THE CHINESE EMPIRES: THE QIN AND THE HAN

For almost two hundred years after 400 B.C., China experienced bloody civil war. Powerful states fought one another and ignored the authority of the Zhou kings. One state—that of Qin—gradually defeated its chief rivals. In 221 B.C., the Qin ruler declared the creation of a new dynasty.

The Qin Dynasty (221 to 206 B.C.)

The ruler of Qin was Qin Shi Huangdi (the name means "the First Qin Emperor"). A person of much ambition, Qin Shi Huangdi had come to the throne of

On Line with WORLD HISTORY *Internet Activity*

You may want to have your students visit the following URL, where they will find information and additional web site resources to enhance their study of this chapter.

The Silk Road

http://www.atm.ch.cam.ac.uk/~oliver/silk.html

The story is of one of the world's oldest and most historically important trade routes and its influences on the culture of China, Central Asia, and the West.

Due to the ever-changing nature of the World Wide Web, see the West History web site, **http://history.swpco.com** for regular updates of the URLs in this text.

FOCUS

OBJECTIVES

After completing this section, students should be able to

1. identify and explain the major accomplishments of the Qin dynasty
2. describe differences between the policies of the Qin and Han dynasties
3. identify and explain social and economic problems of peasant farmers during the Han dynasty
4. describe cultural and artistic achievements of the Han dynasty

FOCUS ACTIVITY

Help students understand the relationship between government economic and social policies. Although the policy of the Han dynasty was to allow farmers to own land, taxes and other demands placed on free farmers became so burdensome that some revolted. Ask students to think of examples in their own lives where economic reality was more important than government statements about social policy.

TEACH

LEARNING FROM VISUALS

Answer to the caption question: Answers will vary; he must have feared his journey, wanted an army to protect him.

Qin in 246 B.C. at the age of thirteen. He was described by the famous Chinese historian Sima Qian as having "the chest of a bird of prey, the voice of a jackal, and the heart of a tiger." In 221 B.C., he defeated the last of Qin's rivals and founded a new dynasty, with himself as emperor. Indeed, Qin Shi Huangdi was to be his dynasty's only ruler.

The Qin dynasty dramatically changed Chinese politics. Legalism was adopted as the regime's official ideology. Those who opposed the policies of the new regime were punished or even executed. Books presenting ideas opposed to the official views were publicly burned (see "You Are There: The Burning of Books").

The ideas of Legalism led to a number of important administrative and political developments. Some of them survived the Qin dynasty and served as models for future dynasties. In the first place, unlike the Zhou

▼ *Qin Shi Huangdi's Tomb, an elaborate underground palace complex, was built by order of the powerful First Emperor of Qin. An army of life-sized soldiers and horses made of terra cotta was fashioned to accompany the emperor on his journey to the afterlife. What does this tomb tell you of the emperor's view of death?*

dynasty, the Qin dynasty ruled a highly centralized state. The central bureaucracy was divided into three divisions: the civil division, the military division, and the **censorate.** The censorate had inspectors who checked on government officials to make sure they were doing their jobs. This became standard procedure for future Chinese dynasties.

Below the central government were two levels of administration—provinces and counties. Officials at these levels did not inherit their positions (as was done under the Zhou) but were appointed and dismissed by the emperor. The censors, who reported directly to the throne, kept a close watch over officials. Those found guilty of wrongdoing were executed.

Qin Shi Huangdi unified the Chinese world. He created a single monetary system and ordered the building of a system of roads throughout the entire empire. Many of these roads led out from his capital city of Xianyang (she-ANG-YANG), just north of modern-day Xian. He reduced the powers of the landed aristocrats by dividing their estates among the peasants, who were now taxed directly by the state. In doing so, he eliminated possible rivals and gained tax revenues for the central government.

Qin Shi Huangdi was equally aggressive in foreign affairs. His armies advanced to the south, extending the border of China to the edge of the Red River in modern-day Vietnam. To supply his armies, he had a canal dug from the Yangtze River in central China to what is now the modern city of Guangzhou (GWANG-JO) (Canton).

The Qin emperor's major concern, however, was in the north. In the area south of the Gobi Desert, there resided a nomadic people known to the Chinese as the Xiongnu, who had mastered the art of riding on horseback. Mounted on their horses, these people ranged far and wide in search of pasture for their flocks of cattle, sheep, or goats. Organized loosely into tribes, they moved with the seasons from one pasture to another.

These peoples had also mastered the art of fighting on horseback. They soon became a challenge to Chinese communities near the northern frontier. A number of Chinese states in the area began to build walls to keep them out. Warriors on horseback, however, had definite advantages over the infantry troops of the

RECOMMENDED READING

There are a number of useful books on the Han Dynasty. Zhongshu Wang, *Han Civilization* (New Haven, Conn., 1982) presents new evidence from the mainland on recent excavations from Han tombs and the old imperial capital of Changan. M. Loewe, *Everyday Life in Early Imperial China during the Han Period, 202 BC–220 AD* (London, 1968) contains useful material on religious beliefs and the development of social classes during the Han. Also, see the lavishly illustrated *The Han Civilization of China* (Oxford, 1982) by M. P. Serstevens. For a firsthand view, see B. Watson, *Records of the Grand Historian of China* (New York, 1961), a translation of key passages from Sima Qian's history of the period. For the historian's life, consult *Ssuma Ch'ien: Grand Historian of China* (New York, 1958).

YOU ARE THERE

The Burning of Books

Li Su, the author of the following passage, was a chief minister of the First Qin Emperor. A follower of Legalism, he hoped to eliminate all rival theories of government. His recommendation to the emperor on the subject of book burning was recorded by the Han dynasty historian Sima Qian.

Li Su, On the Destruction of Books

Your servant suggests that all books in the imperial archives, save the memoirs of Qin, be burned. All persons in the empire, except members of the Academy of Learned Scholars, in possession of the Book of Odes, the Book of History, and discourses of the hundred philosophers [including Confucius] should take them to the local governors and have them burned. Those who dare to talk to each other about the Book of Ideas and the Book of History should be executed and their bodies exposed in the market place. Anyone referring to the past to criticize the present should, together with all members of his family, be put to death. Officials who fail to report cases that have come under their attention are equally guilty. After thirty days from the time of issuing the decree, those who have not destroyed their books are to be branded and sent to build the Great Wall. Books not to be destroyed will be those on medicine and pharmacy, agriculture and arboriculture [the cultivation of trees and shrubs]. People wishing to pursue learning should take the officials as their teachers.

▲ *As a Chinese ruler looks on in this painting, books are being burned and scholars are being killed outside the gates of his palace. What school of philosophy must he have followed?*

1. Why did the chief minister think that burning books would eliminate all rival theories of government?

2. Ideas were dangerous during the dynasty of the First Qin Emperor. Explain why it was dangerous to have a new idea.

3. Do you know of any other time in history when book burning and government controls paralleled the Qin Dynasty? Explain your answer.

USING PRIMARY SOURCES

The idea of destroying books to try to destroy ideas or knowledge is not unique to China. Ask students to explain why they support or oppose the position of Li Su. Discuss possible similarities between his opposition to the burning of books and the recent debate over the wisdom of placing limitations on the types of material that can be sent out over the Internet. Do students believe this is an appropriate comparison?

LEARNING FROM VISUALS

Answer to the caption question: The Chinese ruler must have been a Legalist.

Answers to the Critical Thinking Questions

1. The minister reasoned that if the books were gone, the ideas they contained would be gone.
2. The government wanted to control what people learned and thought. People who talked to each other about ideas and history would be executed, as would people who referred to the past to criticize the present or failed to report others.
3. Students may think of Nazi Germany. Other supported answers are acceptable.

SPECIAL NEEDS: *Visual*

Charts can provide much useful information that can be read easily by students who may have learning disabilities and difficulty with reading comprehension. The title provides the main idea of the presented information.

Have students fill in the appropriate spaces for a chart regarding ancient China with the following columns: Government (dynasty), Social Structure (primarily nobles and peasants, also a class of artisans, and merchants), Philosophies (Confucianism, Taoism, and Legalism), Economic and Technological Contributions (farming, paper, silk)

This completed chart can be used for review purposes by the students.

Ask students to compare the efforts of Qin Shi Huangdi's reaction to nomadic invaders with those of the Indian people when the Aryans invaded around 2000 B.C. Which do they feel was worse for native people: to be invaded by nomads, as in India, or to be led by a ruthless government, as in the Qin dynasty?

CLASS DISCUSSION

Lead students in a discussion that evaluates the importance of establishing a civil service system as a means to choose bureaucratic officials. Today civil service employees are accused of being slow and lazy by some people in our society. Can students think of a realistic alternative to this system that would improve the efficiency and fairness of the government?

Multimedia Support

LASERDISC
Painting of Chinese Burial Chamber

CRITICAL THINKING

Tell students that Qin Shi Huangdi became emperor at the age of thirteen and that other rulers have also acquired power while very young. Then have students imagine themselves to be the rulers of a large area in today's world. Have them create a list of their ten priorities or goals while governing that area.

Chinese. Historian Sima Qian remarked about these nomadic invaders that "the little boys start out by learning to ride sheep and shoot birds and rats with a bow and arrow, and when they get a little older they shoot foxes and rabbits, which are used for food. Thus all the young men are able to use a bow and act as armed cavalry in time of war."

Qin Shi Huangdi's answer to the problem was to strengthen the existing system of walls to keep the nomads out. Today we know Qin Shi Huangdi's project as the Great Wall of China. However, the wall that we know today from films and photographs was not built at the order of the First Qin Emperor but 1,500 years later. Some of the walls built by Qin Shi Huangdi do remain standing, but many of them were constructed of loose stone, sand, or piled rubble and disappeared long ago. Moreover, Qin Shi Huangdi did not begin the building of the Great Wall. Defensive walls against nomads had existed in various parts of North China for years. Qin Shi Huangdi only linked these sections of walls together to create "The Wall of Ten Thousand Li" (a *li* is about a third of a mile).

This is not to say, of course, that the wall was not a massive project. It required the efforts of thousands of laborers. Many of them died while working there and, according to legend, are now buried within the wall. With his wall, the First Qin Emperor did enjoy some success in fighting off the threat of the nomads, but the victory was only temporary. Over the next two thousand years, China's northern frontier became one of the great areas of conflict in Asia.

By ruthlessly gathering control over the empire into his own hands, Qin Shi Huangdi had hoped to establish a rule that "would be enjoyed by his sons for ten thousand generations." In fact, the First Qin Emperor had angered many Chinese. Landed aristocrats and Confucian intellectuals, as well as the common people, groaned under the censorship of speech, harsh taxes, and forced labor projects. Sima Qian said of Qin Shi Huangdi, "He killed men as though he thought he could never finish, he punished men as though he were afraid he would never get around to them all, and the whole world revolted against him."[7] The emperor died in 210 B.C. Four years later, his dynasty was overthrown.

The Han Dynasty
(202 B.C. to A.D. 221)

The fall of the Qin dynasty was followed by a period of civil war, but it did not last long. One of the greatest and most long-lasting dynasties in Chinese history—the Han (HAUN) dynasty—emerged in 202 B.C. The founder of the Han dynasty was a man of peasant origin who became known by his title of Han Gaozu (Exalted Emperor of Han). Under his strong rule and that of his successors, the new dynasty quickly established its control over the empire.

The first Han emperor had expressed his desire to discard the harsh policies of the Qin dynasty. He did abandon the use of cruel and unusual punishments that had been part of the Legalistic approach to law enforcement. Confucian principles, rather than Legalism, soon became the basis for the creation of a new state philosophy. However, Han Gaozu and his successors found it convenient to keep some of the practices of the First Qin Emperor, including the division of the central government into three ministries—the military, civil service, and censorate. The Han rulers also kept the system of local government that divided the empire into provinces and counties.

Most important, the Han rulers continued the Qin system of choosing government officials on the basis of merit rather than birth. To create a regular system for new officials, the Han dynasty introduced the civil service examination and established a school to train these candidates. This system for officials influenced Chinese civilization for two thousand years. Students were expected to learn the teachings of Confucius, as well as Chinese history and law. By creating a group of well-trained officials well versed in Confucian thought, the system ensured the influence of Confucianism on government for a long time. (For a discussion of the civil service examination system, see Chapter 10.)

China under the Han dynasty was a vast empire. The population increased rapidly—by some estimates rising from about twenty million to over sixty million at the height of the dynasty. The large size of the population created a growing need for a large and efficient bureaucracy to maintain the state in proper working order.

MORE ABOUT . . . *Chinese Ethnicity*

There are over one hundred different ethnic groups in China, many of which share the same problems as minority groups elsewhere in the world. The Chinese mainstream culture strongly associates itself with the Han dynasty. It is not unusual, for example, to see in a popular film a conflict between "the people of Han" (usually the "good guys") and another Chinese ethnic group (usually the "bad guys"). Although the present government ideology in China is to stress the unity of all Chinese, there are still ethnic differences that rise to the surface when least expected. The diversity in China may be compared to the ethnic diversity in the U.S. Many of the problems we experience regarding ethnic diversity in the U.S. can be compared to our cultures, as well.

In addition to providing a strong central government, the Han emperors also continued to expand the Chinese Empire. Han rulers, especially Han Wudi (HAHN WOO-DEE) (Martial Emperor of Han), added the southern regions below the Yangtze River into the empire. Along the coast of the South China Sea, part of what is today northern Vietnam became part of the empire (see "Biography: The Trung Sisters"). Han armies also went westward into central Asia, extending the Chinese boundary there. Han Wudi also had to deal with the Xiongnu, the nomads beyond the Great Wall to the north. His armies drove the Xiongnu back, and after he died in 87 B.C., China experienced almost another 150 years of relative peace.

Society in the Han Empire

As in the realm of politics, Han rulers saw some value in the economic and social policies of their predecessors. They especially agreed with the benefit of free peasants paying taxes directly to the state. This would limit the power of the great noble families and increase the state's revenues. This policy was not easy on the free peasants. Land taxes on free farmers were fairly light, but there were other demands on them, including military service and forced labor of up to one month annually. Then, too, the tripling of the population under the Han dynasty eventually reduced the average size of the individual farm plot to about one acre per person—barely enough for survival.

Map 4.4   The Han Empire

STUDYING MAPS

The following questions will help you guide students through their study of Map 4.4.

1. About how long was the Great Wall of China in the Han period? *(approximately 1500 miles)*
2. Why would the decision to construct the Great Wall have been the source of controversy in Chinese society? *(not only would it protect against invaders, but it would also limit mobility of the Chinese)*
3. Why was it difficult for China's dynasties to successfully attack the nomadic tribes that lived north of the Great Wall? *(had mastered the art of fighting on horseback; were more difficult for infantry to fight)*

BIOGRAPHY

TEACHING THEMES

The Role of Individuals.
With few exceptions, women have not often been successful military leaders. Ask students to list factors that may have allowed the Trung sisters to organize and lead an army against the Chinese. What other examples of female military leaders can students think of? Were the situations they faced similar to that of the Trung sisters?

Answers to Critical Thinking Questions

1. The sisters are honored as leaders of the first national revolt against the Chinese.
2. Review the meaning of a legend with your students. This story is full of legendary elements: two sisters were able to begin a revolution, they supposedly killed a people-eating tiger, they ruled the country for a while, and drowned themselves to avoid capture when the enemy returned. Answers will vary.

BIOGRAPHY
The Trung Sisters

▲ *Liberation Day celebrations are still held in modern Vietnam. Marchers are parading down the streets of Ho Chi Minh City.*

In 111 B.C., the Han dynasty took control of Vietnam. Although the Chinese imposed their value system on the conquered people, the Vietnamese managed to keep some of their own ways, including greater freedom for women. Women could inherit property and even be political leaders. Two Vietnamese sisters, Trung Trac and Trung Nhi, daughters of a powerful Vietnamese landowner, became especially well known for their leadership.

Over time, the Vietnamese had grown restless under Chinese rule, and some powerful lords carried the banner of rebellion. One of these was Thi Sach, husband of Trung Trac. To crush dissent, the Chinese military commander in 39 B.C. killed a number of prominent Vietnamese lords, including

Thi Sach. After her husband's death, Trung Trac and her sister took up the cause of revolution.

The Trung sisters recruited an army of men and women to fight the Chinese. Thirty-six of the army's leaders were women, including the mother of the two sisters. It is said that to encourage the Vietnamese to fight, the Trung sisters killed a people-eating tiger, cut off its skin, and wrote an appeal on it urging people to rebel.

The defeat of the Chinese forces by the Trung sisters' army led to the creation of a Vietnamese state that stretched from Hue into southern China. The sisters became co-rulers and as queens of Vietnam eliminated the taxes levied by the Chinese.

The rule of the Trung sisters proved to be short lived, however. In 42 B.C., the Han emperor sent fresh troops to restore Chinese control of Vietnam. Although the Vietnamese fought courageously, they were soon overwhelmed by the well-trained Chinese forces. To avoid capture, the Trung sisters took their own lives by drowning—a traditional Vietnamese way of preserving one's honor. The Trung sisters continue to be revered by the Vietnamese people as leaders of the first national revolt against the Chinese. An annual national holiday celebrates their achievements.

1. Why do the Vietnamese revere the Trung sisters?

2. What dramatic events contribute to the legendary nature of the Trung story?

So What ??

*If your students question the importance of information on the **Trung sisters,** tell them . . .*

Almost two thousand years ago, the Trung sisters provided an exceptional example of leadership in Vietnam. The memory of their valor, strength, and accomplishments remained alive through French colonial exploitation, and the American intervention in Vietnam. The fierce resistance of the Viet Cong guerrillas in South Vietnam during the 1960s was supported by a female population that believed in its own power and potential. The Viet Cong received great support from Vietnamese women who had internalized the historical role of the Trung sisters.

As time went on, many poor peasants were forced to sell their land and become tenant farmers, who paid rents ranging up to half of the annual harvest. Land once again came to be held in the hands of the powerful landed aristocrats. These nobles often owned thousands of acres worked by tenants. They gathered their own military forces to bully free farmers into becoming tenants. The following description, written in the second century B.C., gives a picture of the situation:

What with their plowing in the spring and hoeing in the summer, harvesting in the autumn and storing in the winter, with cutting firewood, repairing government offices and rendering labor-services, the peasants will be unable to escape the wind-blown dust of spring, the heat of summer, the heavy rain of autumn, or the chill of winter. In none of the four seasons will they have a day of rest. . . . When the time comes that the levy [to the government] must be met, those who own something sell it off at half price; and those that own nothing borrow at doubled rates of interest. It is for this reason that some dispose of their lands and houses, and sell their children and grandchildren to redeem their debts.[8]

It was not a comforting scene for the peasants. Despite the efforts of reformers, peasants continued to suffer. They grew discontented and in some places became violent in their desire for change.

Although the economic problems in the countryside helped lead to the eventual downfall of the dynasty, in general the Han period was one of great prosperity. There was a major expansion of trade and manufacturing. Much of this activity was directed by the state. The government owned shipyards, manufactured weapons, and controlled mining and the operation of granaries. The government also moved into foreign trade, mostly with neighboring areas in central and Southeast Asia. Trade relations were even established with areas as far away as India and the Mediterranean. Some of the long-distance trade was carried by sea through southern ports, but more was transported by overland caravans on the Silk Road and other similar routes through the vast deserts and plateaus that led westward into central Asia.

New technology added to the economic prosperity of the Han Era. Much progress was made in such areas

as textile manufacturing, water mills for grinding grain, and iron casting. Iron casting technology led to the invention of steel. Paper was developed under the Han dynasty (see "The Role of Science and Technology: Papermaking in Han China"). With the invention of

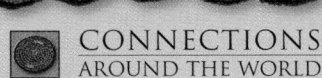

CONNECTIONS
AROUND THE WORLD

Trade and the Silk Road   Throughout history, trade has served as a bridge between peoples and cultures. Religious, intellectual, scientific, and artistic ideas, as well as diseases, have been spread from one part of the world to another by merchants who traveled from one region to another carrying their goods. One of the greatest avenues of cross-cultural trade in the ancient world was the Silk Road, which linked the Chinese and Roman Empires.

Sometime between 200 B.C. and A.D. 100, an organized caravan trade arose between China and the eastern end of the Mediterranean Sea (then part of the Roman Empire). This trade reached from the city of Chang'an in China across central Asia to Mesopotamia. This Silk Road, as it was called because of China's most valuable export, covered a distance of about four thousand miles. Men and camels took their goods westward through mountains and deserts and stopped in Syria at Antioch (AN-tee-ock), a port city on the Mediterranean. At Antioch, luxury goods from the West were traded for luxury goods from the East. The eastern goods were then shipped across the Mediterranean to Greece and Rome. Only luxury goods were carried on the Silk Road, because travel by camel caravan was difficult and dangerous, and thus expensive.

Chinese merchants made large fortunes by sending luxury goods, such as silk, spices, teas, porcelain, and lacquerware. These goods were exchanged for woolen and linen clothes, glass, and precious stones from the Roman Empire. Silk was especially desired by the Romans, who considered it worth its weight in gold. The Romans knew China as Serica, which means "Land of Silk."

CLASS DISCUSSION

Lead students in a discussion of what often happens to government policies that go against the values of the people. Use the decision of the Han rulers to first weaken the family and then to renew the emphasis on the value of family loyalty. Students may want to identify some modern-day situations where they feel government has gone against the values of the people.

the rudder and fore-and-aft rigging, ships could sail into the wind for the first time. This made it possible for Chinese merchant ships carrying heavy cargoes to travel throughout the islands of Southeast Asia and into the Indian Ocean.

Another change during the Han dynasty was an increase in the importance of the family in the Chinese system of life. The First Qin Emperor had tried to weaken the family, seeing family loyalty as a threat to a strong monarch. However, the efforts of the Qin emperor to weaken the family system ran into heavy opposition. Thus, the Han rulers, drawing on the ideas of Confucianism, renewed the emphasis on the family. Under the Han rulers, the family system began to take

Map 4.5   Trade Routes of the Ancient World

Traded goods:

∾ slaves	♓ glassware
◆ precious stones	◗ coinage
⌕ wine	⚔ weapons
◣ metal	⌸ timber
♠ cloth and clothing	◆ silks

tortoiseshell, ivory, spices, incense

STUDYING MAPS

The following questions will help you guide students through their study of Map 4.5.

1. How long was the Silk Road between Antioch and Luoyang? *(approximately 4000 miles)*
2. Why did the invention of ships that could sail against the wind cause the importance of the Silk Road to decline? *(ships could now sail around Southeast Asia, had access to more seaports, no land barriers.)*
3. Why did the importance of the cities of Kashgar, Turfan, and Dunhuang decline after the invention of the rudder? *(less overland traffic; more travel by sea)*

THE ROLE OF SCIENCE AND TECHNOLOGY
Papermaking in Han China

▲ *A modern artisan demonstrates the ancient art of papermaking, invented in the Han dynasty.*

斬竹漂塘

◄ *This drawing shows some of the steps involved in Chinese papermaking. After workers collected bamboo, it was stripped of its leaves and soaked. Later, it was reduced to pulp, formed into sheets on mesh frames, and dried.*

The ancient Chinese were a remarkably inventive people. They were responsible for four inventions that were crucial to the development of modern technology: the magnetic compass, paper, printing, and gunpowder. How to make paper was one of their early discoveries.

The oldest piece of paper found in China dates from the first century B.C. Made from hemp fibers, it was thick, rough, and useless for writing. That was not a problem for the ancient Chinese, however, because they preferred to write on bamboo or silk.

Around A.D. 100 paper that has writing on it began to appear. By this time, the Chinese had figured out how to make paper of better quality. After soaking hemp or linen rags in water, they were mixed with potash and mashed into a pulp. A frame with a fine bamboo mesh was lowered into this vat of pulp. The frame was then removed, together with a thin sheet of pulp. Any extra water was removed. As seen in the illustration, the sheets of paper were then hung up to dry.

The art of papermaking spread eastward from China beginning in the seventh century A.D. First India and then the Arab world developed the technique. The Arab cities of Baghdad, Damascus, and Cairo (KIE-ROE) all had large papermaking industries. Paper was shipped from these centers to the West, but Europeans did not begin their production of paper until the twelfth century.

1. Why was Chinese papermaking called an art?

2. What is remarkable about the beginning of European production of paper?

THE IMPORTANCE OF CULTURE

Assign students to write an essay that explains what the creation of the terra-cotta army shows about the beliefs and culture in China at the time of the Qin Emperor. What might future historians conclude from our memorials to dead leaders, such as the Washington or Lincoln Monuments or the faces carved into Mt. Rushmore?

LEARNING FROM VISUALS

Answer to the caption question: Students may think the warrior's stance resembles martial arts poses.

Answers to Critical Thinking Questions

1. The more than 6,000 stone figures were a recreation of the First Qin Emperor's imperial guard and were meant to be with him on his journey to the next world.

2. Answers will vary. Students may note that no expense was spared to prepare the elaborate tombs. Emperors' lives were very valuable; not so the lives of common people.

OUR ARTISTIC HERITAGE
The Tomb Army of the First Qin Emperor

In 1974, farmers digging a well about thirty-five miles east of Xian discovered a remarkable underground pit about one mile east of the burial mound of the First Qin Emperor. Chinese archaeologists who were then sent to work at the site discovered a vast terra-cotta army. They believed that it was a re-creation of Qin Shi Huangdi's imperial guard and was meant to be with the emperor on his journey to the next world.

One of the astounding features of the terra-cotta army is its size. The army is contained in four pits that were originally enclosed in a wooden framework. The wood has since fallen apart. More than a thousand figures have already been unearthed in the first pit, along with horses, wooden chariots, and seven thousand bronze weapons. Archaeologists estimate that there are more than six thousand figures in that pit alone.

Equally noticeable is the quality of the work. The figures are slightly larger than life-size. They were molded of clay and then fired and painted, apparently in brilliant colors. The detail on the uniforms is realistic. The most striking feature, however, is the individuality of the faces of the soldiers. Ten different head shapes were used, but they were then modeled by hand to reflect the different ethnic types in the army.

This remarkable terra-cotta army shows that the Chinese had come a long way from the human sacrifices that had taken place at the death of the Shang rulers over a thousand years earlier. The project must have been enormously expensive, however. It has been estimated that one-third of the national income may have been spent on preparations for the ruler's afterlife.

Though unarmed, this sculpted warrior from a burial tomb must be an infantryman because bronze arrowheads and parts of wooden bows were found nearby. He was positioned in a row with dozens of others in front of kneeling archers. Is his stance familiar to you? If so, how?

The emperor's underground palace complex, which this army of soldiers was protecting, has not yet been unearthed. According to tradition, traps were set within the massive tomb to prevent intruders. The workers putting on the final touches were buried alive in the tomb, along with its secrets. Qin Shi Huangdi's ambitious effort to provide for his afterlife became a pattern for his successors during the Han dynasty. In 1990, Chinese workers discovered a similar underground army for a Han emperor of the second century B.C. Like the soldiers of the First Qin Emperor, these underground soldiers were buried in parallel pits and possessed their own weapons and individual facial features. However, they were much smaller—only one-third the height of the average human adult—and were armed with wooden weapons. A burial pit nearby indicated that as many as ten thousand workers, probably slaves or prisoners, died in the process of building the emperor's elaborate tomb.

1. What was the purpose of the terra-cotta army?

2. What conclusions can you draw about the value placed on human life during the Qin and Han dynasties?

RECOMMENDED READING

For a comprehensive introduction to Chinese art, consult M. Sullivan, *The Arts of China,* 3d ed. (Berkeley, 1984) with good illustrations in color. Also, see M. Tregear, *Chinese Art* (Oxford, 1980); and L. Sickman and A. Sopor, *Art and Architecture of China,* 3d. ed. (Middlesex, 1968). For a discussion of the ancient art of China, see J. Rawson, *Ancient China: Art and Archeology* (New York, 1980). Many beautifully illustrated volumes on Chinese art in general and several series on ancient Chinese art are available. See the four-volume series entitled *Chinese Art* by the Universe Library of Antique Art (New York, 1960–1965) and the first two volumes of *Art in China* (Tokyo, 1968 and 1969) by Japanese scholars and coordinated by M. Tregear on Neolithic cultures and the arts of the Buddhist cave temples. See also B. Smith and Wan-go Wang, *China: A History of Art* (New York, n. d.), on the character that it would have until the twentieth century. The family was not only the basic economic unit but also the basic social unit for education and training in morals. According to a popular Confucian saying, to make sure of proper behavior, it was necessary to begin in the family and then extend outward to the broader community: "only when families are regulated are states well governed; and only when states are well governed is there peace in the world."

Culture in Qin and Han China

The Qin and Han dynasties were also known for their cultural achievements (see "Our Artistic Heritage: The Tomb Army of the First Qin Emperor"). The key works of the Confucian school were made into a set of so-called Confucian classics, which became required reading for generations of Chinese schoolchildren. These classics introduced them to the forms of behavior that they would need as adults.

During the Han dynasty, the writing of history became the chief form of literary effort. The major histories of the Han period, written by Sima Qian and Ban Gu, set a model for future dynastic histories. These works combined political and social history with biographies of key figures. Like other literary works in China, their primary purpose was moral and political. They were intended to instruct readers on the basic reasons for the rise and fall of individual human beings and dynasties.

Ban Gu's sister Ban Zhao was a prominent female historian of the Han dynasty. Her own career was an exception to the rule that women were primarily mothers and homemakers. Even Ban Zhao wrote, "To behave properly in serving her husband; to be serene and self-possessed, shunning jests and laughter . . . this is called being worthy of continuing the husband's lineage."

No discussion of ancient Chinese culture can be complete without mentioning music. According to an

▲ *This tomb relief portrays a wealthy tax collector receiving rent in the form of grain from a poor peasant. The stamped brick clearly shows the bamboo tally slips held by the taxman, the peasant's simple clothing, and details of the building in the background. Why do you think the peasant's back is stooped?*

ancient Chinese historian, the first musical instrument was a set of bamboo pipes. Other musical instruments invented in ancient China included the flute, various stringed instruments, bells and chimes, and the drum.

From early times, music was seen not just as a pleasure but also as a means of achieving political order and refining the human character. In fact, music may have originated as a means of accompanying sacred ritual at the royal court. Eventually, however, music came to be appreciated for its own sake, as well as for accompaniment to singing and dancing.

The Fall of the Han Empire

Over a period of time, the Han Empire began to fall into decay. As weak rulers amused themselves with the pleasures of court life, the power of the central government began to decline. The great noble families filled the gap, amassing vast landed estates and forcing free farmers to become their tenants. Official corruption and the concentration of land in the hands of the wealthy led to widespread peasant unrest. The population of the empire had been estimated at sixty million in China's first census in the year A.D. 2. Two hundred years later it had declined to less than twenty million.

a beautifully illustrated one-volume survey. Finally, see D. L. Goldschmidt and J. C. Moreau-Gobard, *Chinese Art* (New York, 1962), which presents ancient Chinese art treasures from private collections.

There are a number of useful books on the Han Dynasty. Zhongshu Wang, *Han Civilization* (New Haven, Conn., 1982) presents new evidence from the mainland on recent

excavations from Han tombs and the old imperial capital of Changan. M. Loewe, *Everyday Life in Early Imperial China during the Han Period*, 202 B.C.–220 A.D. (London, 1968) contains useful material on religious beliefs and the development of social classes during the Han.

ASSESS

Answers to SECTION REVIEW

2. (a) a division of the Qin dynasty's central bureaucracy; had inspectors who checked on government officials to make sure they were doing their jobs

3. (a) name means the First Qin Emperor; adapted Legalism as dynasty's official ideology

(b) nomads from beyond the Great Wall to the north

(c) Qin Shi Huangdi's project to keep invaders out by linking existing defensive walls together; not the wall we know today from photographs

(d) peasant who became Exalted Emperor of Han; established one of the greatest dynasties in Chinese history

(e) Martial Emperor of Han; expanded empire south below the Yangtze River, including modern northern Vietnam, and west into central Asia

(f) with Sima Qian, wrote major histories of the Han period

(g) sister of Ban Gu; prominent female historian of Han dynasty

4. (a) angered many Chinese by use of censorship, harsh taxes, forced labor; dynasty overthrown after his death

(b) division of government into three ministries; system of provinces and counties; choosing government officials by merit, not birth

5. tripling of population forced poor peasants to sell land, while nobles owned thousands of

114

▶ *Found in a Han tomb, this painting of dignified Han gentlemen, dressed in elegant robes, brings ancient Chinese customs to life. What activities occupied the time of such gentlemen 2,000 years ago?*

Then, too, nomadic raids on Chinese territory continued in the north. At one point, a group of marauders reached the gates of the capital city at Chang'an, located on the site of modern-day Xian.

By A.D. 170, wars, intrigues at the court, and peasant uprisings brought the virtual collapse of the Han dynasty. In 189, rebel armies sacked the Han capital, Chang'an. The final blow came in 220, when a general seized control. He was unable to maintain his power, however. China again plunged into civil war, made worse by invasions of northern tribal peoples. The next great dynasty did not arise until four hundred years later.

 SECTION REVIEW ❀

1. Locate:
(a) Guangzhou, (b) Chang'an

2. Define:
(a) censorate

3. Identify:
(a) Qin Shi Huangdi, (b) Xiongnu, (c) Great Wall of China, (d) Han Gaozu, (e) Han Wudi, (f) Ban Gu, (g) Ban Zhao

4. Recall:
(a) Why was Qin Shi Huangdi's dynasty so short lived?
(b) List at least three Qin practices continued by the Han.

5. Think Critically: How did the prosperity of the early Han dynasty contribute to its eventual decline?

Conclusion

Of the great civilizations discussed so far, China was the last to come into full flower. By the time the Shang dynasty began to display the first signs of emerging as an organized state, the societies in Mesopotamia, Egypt, and India had already reached an advanced level of civilization. Not enough is known about the early stages of any of these civilizations to allow us to determine why some developed earlier than others. One likely reason for China's late arrival was its virtual isolation from the other emerging centers of culture elsewhere in the world. Basically, China was forced to develop on its own.

The Shang dynasty created the first flourishing Chinese civilization. Under the Shang, China developed organized government, a system of writing, and advanced skills in the making of bronze vessels. During the Zhou dynasty, China began to adopt many of the features that characterized Chinese civilization for centuries. Especially important politically was the "mandate from Heaven," which, it was believed, gave kings a divine right to rule. The family, with its ideal of filial piety, also emerged as a powerful economic and social unit.

Between 500 and 200 B.C., three major schools of thought emerged in China: Confucianism, Taoism, and Legalism. All three sought to spell out the principles that would create a stable order in society. All three came to have an impact on Chinese civilization that lasted until the twentieth century.

After two hundred years of civil war, a new dynasty known as the Qin created a new era of Chinese unity. However, the First Qin Emperor was also the last of his dynasty. A new dynasty—the Han—then established a vast empire that lasted over four hundred years. During the glory years of the Han dynasty, China extended the boundaries of its empire far into the sands of central Asia and southward along the coast of the South China Sea into what is modern-day Vietnam. Chinese culture appeared to be unrivaled, and its scientific and technological achievements were unsurpassed.

One reason for China's striking success was that, unlike other civilizations of its time, it was for long able to fend off the danger from nomadic peoples, the Xiongnu, along the northern frontier. By the end of the second century B.C., however, the presence of the Xiongnu was becoming a threat, and tribal warriors began to nip at the borders of the empire. While the dynasty was strong, the problem was manageable. When internal difficulties began to weaken the unity of the state, however, China became vulnerable to the threat from the north and entered a time of troubles.

Notes

1. *The Book of Changes*, quoted in Chang Chi-yun, *Chinese History of Fifty Centuries*, vol. 1, *Ancient Times* (Taipei, 1962), p. 381.
2. Quoted in Robert Temple, *The Genius of China: 3000 Years of Science, Discovery, and Invention* (New York, 1986), p. 219.
3. Quoted in Herbert A. Giles, *A History of Chinese Literature* (New York, 1923), p. 19.
4. *Ibid.*, p. 192.
5. Lao Tsu, *Tao Te Ching*, trans. Gia-Fu Feng and Jane English (New York, 1972), No. 29.
6. *Ibid.*, No. 47.
7. Burton Watson, *Records of the Grand Historian of China*, vol. 2, (New York, 1961), p. 32.
8. Quoted in Mark Elvin, *The Pattern of the Chinese Past* (Stanford, 1973), p. 28.

acres; weak rulers enjoyed court life, but lost control of government; peasant unrest; attacks by nomads; answers will vary

CLOSE

Lead students in a discussion of the 'Focus' objectives identified on page 104. Emphasize the fact that harsh treatment of common people by China's leaders often led to social, economic, and political upheavals in China's history.

SPANISH SUPPORT

The *Conclusion* has been translated into Spanish for your Spanish-speaking students. Included with this translation (in your Teacher Resource Box) are Section Key Points, which consist of one or two sentences summarizing each section in the chapter. These Key Points have also been translated into Spanish.

TIME LINE

As students conclude the chapter, you may want to refer them to the chapter time line in the *Study Guide*. The time line will help them put key dates in perspective. Supporting questions and activities are also provided.

USING KEY TERMS

1. veneration of ancestors
2. Taoism
3. Legalism
4. Tao
5. mandate of Heaven
6. Confucianism
7. censorate
8. pictographic
9. filial piety

REVIEWING THE FACTS

1. Huang, Yangtze
2. Confucius
3. mountains and deserts
4. Xia; 4000 years ago (c. 2000 B.C.)
5. Zhou
6. Shang had a large, successful army often led by a woman.
7. to find answers to questions posed to the gods
8. to treat the spirits of ancestors well because they could bring good or evil to living family members
9. bronze casting
10. mandate of Heaven
11. If a king did not rule effectively and displeased the gods, he would be replaced.
12. Intellectual and moral decay led to civil wars and eventual loss of power.
13. use of iron weapons, foot soldiers, and soldiers on horseback
14. landowners; peasants who worked their own land and the lord's land; artisans and merchants who worked under control of the lord; class of slaves made up of prisoners of war
15. Changes in flood control and farming methods led to increased food production which led to increased population and economic and trade growth.
16. sacred quality; loyalty to family greater than loyalty to government
17. All family members submit individual needs/desires to male head of household.
18. Intensive labor to grow rice

CHAPTER 4 REVIEW

USING KEY TERMS

1. The idea of the _____ came from the Chinese belief in life after death.
2. The philosophy which stresses an individual's harmony with the universe is called _____.
3. _____ is the philosophy that assumes that humans need strict controls and harsh penalties in order to do the right thing.
4. A prevailing Chinese philosophical view in ancient China (3000 B.C.–A.D. 500) is that life must be lived in accordance with the _____.
5. The Chinese political concept by which a ruler exercises power because of a higher principle, and therefore must govern with wisdom and goodness is called _____.
6. The school of political philosophy that focuses on the proper relationships and proper behavior among humans is called _____.
7. One division of the Qin dynasty bureaucracy was the _____, whose officials checked to be sure government workers did their jobs.
8. Chinese writing is said to be _____, meaning characters symbolize objects.
9. Members of Chinese families knew their place in a system of relationships based on the idea of _____.

REVIEWING THE FACTS

1. What are the two rivers along which civilization first developed in China?
2. What philosopher has been the most influential thinker in Chinese history?
3. What geographical features had the effect of isolating China from other civilizations?
4. Which dynasty marks the beginning of Chinese civilization? When did it rule?
5. Which dynasty followed the Shang?
6. What do recent archaeological findings tell us about the Shang dynasty?

116

7. What were oracle bones used for?
8. Describe the purpose of ancestor worship.
9. What form of art is characteristic of the Shang dynasty?
10. What principle was followed by the Zhou in order to overthrow the Shang?
11. Why was the principle of the mandate of Heaven double edged?
12. How did the Zhou lose power?
13. How did the nature of warfare change during the Zhou period?
14. How was social life structured under the Zhou?
15. Describe the economic revolution that took place under the Zhou.
16. Describe the role of the family in ancient China.
17. What does filial piety mean?
18. What role did rice agriculture have in Chinese life?
19. The Chinese language is pictographic and ideographic in form—what does this mean?
20. What are the key elements of Confucian philosophy?
21. What is the primary goal of Taoist philosophy?
22. What are the main beliefs of the philosophy of Legalism?
23. How did the Qin ruler change Chinese politics?
24. How long did the Han dynasty rule China?
25. How did technology add to the economic prosperity of the Han Era?
26. Why did the Han dynasty fall?

THINKING CRITICALLY

1. How might Chinese society and culture have evolved differently if there had been more contact with other civilizations?
2. The Shou replaced the Shang dynasty using the concept of the mandate of Heaven. Could Qin emperor Shi Huangdi have used the same principle to overthrow the Zhou? Explain.
3. Imagine the following situation taking place in Zhou China: There is a noticeable increase in the crime rate and the emperor has called a group of

led to unity of family and male dominance.
19. pictographic: picture symbols from a picture of objects represented;
ideographic: combination of pictographs to represent ideas
20. duty and humanity
21. to set forth proper forms of behavior through inaction rather than action
22. Humans are evil by nature and can be controlled only through harsh punishment.

23. highly centralized government; created single monetary system; built system of roads; reduced powers of landed aristocrats; aggressive in foreign affairs
24. over 400 years
25. led to increased goods for trade; shipping technology enabled merchant ships to carry goods to many trading partners
26. wars, court intrigue, peasant uprisings

CHAPTER 4 REVIEW

philosophers to advise him regarding a solution. How would Confucian, Taoist, and Legalist philosophers address the issue?
4. Which political philosophy—Confucianism, Taoism, or Legalism—do you believe would work better in today's American society? Why?
5. In modern China, some Chinese call themselves the people of Han. Explain why they may have adopted that term.

APPLYING SOCIAL STUDIES SKILLS

1. **Geography:** Using the concept of relative location, explain why China expanded to the West and South, rather than to the North and East.
2. **Government:** Identify changes in the Chinese style of government from the Shang to the Zhou, Qin, and Han dynasties.
3. **Sociology/Government:** Explain the structure of the Chinese family and explain what effect this type of family structure may have on the structure of government and the stability of the state.
4. **Art History:** What do Chinese art forms tell us about technological development in ancient China?
5. **Economics:** Explain what developments are part of the economic revolution that took place during the Zhou dynasty.
6. **Philosophy:** Prepare a short position paper justifying the philosophy of your choice (Confucianism, Taoism, or Legalism) as being the best for ancient China.

MAKING TIME AND PLACE CONNECTIONS

1. How is today's Chinese language different from that of Shang China?
2. What creations or products of ancient China can still be seen today, in or out of museums?
3. Consider today's crime problem in our society. List five to ten suggestions for solving the problem.

Determine whether you would be likely to get support from a Confucian, Taoist, or Legalist philosopher for each suggestion.
4. The Chinese used oracle bones to try to know what the future held. Do we still have this interest today? What means do we use for the same purpose?
5. The Chinese built the Great Wall to keep the northern nomads off their lands. What means are used today to protect territorial boundaries?
6. How does the ancient Chinese system of writing differ from cuneiform and hieroglyphic writing? Why do you think the Chinese system has survived (with some changes) to the present, while the other two have not?

BECOMING AN HISTORIAN

Charts, Graphs, Tables: One of the historian's most difficult tasks is to maintain a sense of perspective and objectivity in describing and analyzing the past.

Knowing this, those of us who live in a predominantly Western culture have to make a special effort to understand the contribution of non-Western cultures. The following activity will help you develop an appreciation of the earliest, non-Western civilizations covered so far in the text. Develop a table, on an 8-1/2 × 11-inch sheet of paper, showing the following:

Ancient Civilizations	Technological Contributions	Intellectual Contributions	Religious Contributions
Sumarian			
Egyptian			
Indus Valley			
Chinese			

Making Hypotheses and Predicting Outcomes: Develop two hypotheses, not already discussed in the chapter, that you feel apply to ancient China, based on the data presented in this chapter.

117

THINKING CRITICALLY

1. Answers will vary; discussion should include influences of other religions, political systems, languages, art forms, etc.
2. Answers will vary; should include differing political philosophies (mandate of Heaven vs. Legalism), role of gods vs. rules to control human action, etc.
3. Answers will vary; could include the following: Confucian—appeal to sense of duty and honor; Taoist—let "nature run its course" for things to work themselves out in the end; Legalistic—punish criminals harshly
4. Answers will vary; should include discussion of

how Americans might best be motivated based on our political, religious, and humanitarian culture
5. Answers will vary; should include discussion of length of dynasty; the teachings still followed today, success of dynasty, etc.

APPLYING SOCIAL STUDIES SKILLS

1. Answers will vary; should include deserts to the north, Tibetan plateau/water to the south.
2. Answers will vary; should include different philosophies adopted by rulers, favoring landed aristocrats vs. strong central government, etc.
3. Answers will vary; could include discussion of fil-

ial piety, ancestor worship, male/female roles, importance of loyalty, male dominance, role of different philosophies in relation to family structure.
4. Answers will vary; should include discussion of bronze casting, paper making, written language, etc.
5. Answers will vary; should include improvements in agricultural technology, trade expansion, the Silk Road, etc.
6. Answers will vary; should indicate understanding of differing Chinese philosophies.

MAKING TIME AND PLACE CONNECTIONS

1. Pronunciation is different in different regions, but characters are basically unchanged.
2. Answers will vary; should include bronze castings, silks, porcelain
3. Answers will vary; should indicate understanding of differing philosophies and the methods used by each one to gain desired results.
4. Answers will vary; could include horoscopes, psychic hotlines, palm readers, etc.
5. Answers will vary; could include check points, border patrols, fences, international laws, etc.
6. Answers will vary; a) cuneiform and hieroglyphics both had ways to represent sounds while Chinese does not, and both are more like an alphabet than Chinese, b) could include discussion of little outside influence on Chinese, the fact that many different dialects of spoken language can use the same written language, language was passed on from dynasty to dynasty, etc.

BECOMING AN HISTORIAN

Charts, etc. Answers will vary; should discuss major points of the chapter
Making Hypotheses, etc. Answers will vary; should indicate knowledge and understanding of Chinese culture

117

PLANNING GUIDE

SECTION	KEY TOPICS	PRIMARY SOURCES	ASSESSMENT
1 Early Greek History pages 119-122	◆ Impact of geography on Greek history ◆ The Mycenean city-state ◆ The "Dark Age" of Greece		◆ Section Review, page 122 ◆ Section Quiz 5-1, TRB
2 The World of the Greek City States (750 to 500 B.C.) pages 122-129	◆ The city as center of Greek activity ◆ Greek colonization ◆ Rise of tyrants ◆ Sparta ◆ Athens	◆ Plutarch on Spartan youth, page 127	◆ Section Review, page 129 ◆ Section Quiz 5-2, TRB
3 The High Point of Greek Civilization: Classical Greece pages 129-135	◆ Conflict with Persia ◆ Age of Pericles ◆ Peloponnesian War ◆ Daily life in Athens	◆ Illustration of Xerxes, page 130 ◆ Thucydides, *History of the Peloponnesian War*, page 131 ◆ Xenophon, On a Wife's Duties, page 134	◆ Section Review, page 135 ◆ Section Quiz 5-3, TRB
4 The Culture of Classical Greece pages 135-143	◆ Gods and goddesses ◆ Greek drama ◆ Early Greek philosophers ◆ Early Greek historians		◆ Section Review, page 143 ◆ Section Quiz 5-4, TRB
5 The Spread of Greek Civilization: Alexander and the Hellenistic Kingdoms pages 143-149	◆ Alexander the Great ◆ Hellenistic kingdoms ◆ Culture in the Hellenistic era	◆ Diodorus of Sicily on the destruction of Persepolis, page 143	◆ Section Review, page 149 ◆ Section Quiz 5-5, TRB

THE CIVILIZATION OF THE GREEKS (1900 TO 133 B.C.)

REPRODUCIBLE ACTIVITIES

- Historical Maps
- Charts and Graphs
- Critical Thinking
- Cooperative Learning
- Vocabulary
- Guided Reading
- Reteaching
- Enrichment
- Performance Assessment
- Spanish Key Points and Chapter Summaries
- Spanish Vocabulary
- Spanish Guided Reading

MULTIMEDIA SUPPORT

 TRANSPARENCIES
- *World History* Color Transparency Package
- Fine Art Color Transparency Package

 VIDEO
- *World History* Video Library
- **CNN** Annual Video Update

 VIDEODISC
- *Sights and Sounds of History* Videodisc

 AUDIO
- *Listening to Literature* audiotape (English and Spanish)
- *History of Music* CD

 SOFTWARE
- WESTEST™
- Student Review

 CD–ROM
- *The Journey of Civilization*
- *World History*

 INTERNET
- Internet Activities

 On Line with WORLD HISTORY

Access West's history web site at
http://history.swpco.com
You'll find activities and web sites related to specific topics and chapters in *World History: The Human Odyssey*. Also look for references to helpful web sites at appropriate places throughout this teacher edition.

LESSON PLANNING

You will find detailed daily lesson plans for both traditional class scheduling and **block scheduling** in your Teacher Resource Box.

 ## Not Enough Time?

If you do not have the four or five days recommended to teach this chapter, you may want to focus on the following sections and activities:

- Have students skim the chapter to answer the "Questions to Guide Your Reading" on page 119. Discuss their answers, then read the "Conclusion" on page 149.
- Do a more in-depth reading of pages 119-122, 129-132, and 141-145. Conclude with a class discussion of the "Connections" box on page 136.

THE CIVILIZATION OF THE GREEKS

(1900 TO 133 B.C.)

5

5

BUILDING ON CHAPTER 4

To "set the scene" for the study of Chapter 5, have students review Section 4 of Chapter 4. Ask them to describe the scene as the first Chinese Empire, the Qin Dynasty, came to power. Also ask them to give reasons as to why this dynasty and the Han Dynasty achieved so much power. Finally, have them enumerate the reasons why these dynasties ultimately failed. Tell them that in Chapter 5 they will be reading about the rise and fall of another great empire and that they should be on the lookout for differences and similarities between this empire, the Roman Empire, and the Chinese empires.

USING THE OPENING STORY

Select from the following to reinforce the reading of the Pericles Funeral Oration.

◆ How long ago did this story take place? *(approximately 2430 years ago)*
◆ What was the purpose of the ceremony? *(a public funeral to honor the Athenians who had died in the war between Sparta and Athens)*
◆ According to Pericles, why is Athens called a democracy? *(power is in the hands of all the people)*

LEARNING FROM VISUALS

Answer to the caption question: repose and acceptance of death as a natural part of life.

In 431 B.C., war erupted in Greece as two very different Greek states—Athens and Sparta—fought for domination of the Greek world. Strengthened by its democratic ideals, Athens felt secure behind its walls. In the first winter of the war, the Athenians held a public funeral to honor those who had died in the war. On the day of the ceremony, the citizens of Athens joined in a procession. The relatives of the dead wailed for their loved ones.

As was the custom in Athens, one leading citizen was asked to address the crowd. On this day it was Pericles (PAIR-uh-KLEEZ) who spoke to the people. He talked about the greatness of Athens and reminded the Athenians of the strength of their political system. "Our constitution," Pericles said, "is called a democracy because power is in the hands not of a minority but of the whole people. When it is a question of settling private disputes, every one is equal before the law. Just as our political life is free and open, so is our day-to-day life in our relations with each other. . . . Here each individual is interested not only in his own affairs but in the affairs of the state as well."

In this famous Funeral Oration, Pericles gave voice to the ideal of democracy and the importance of the individual. The Greeks laid the intellectual foundations of Western civilization. They asked some basic questions about human life that we still ask today: What is the nature of the universe? What is the purpose of human life? What is our relationship to divine forces? What is a community? What is a state? What is true education? What is truth itself, and how do we realize it? The Greeks not only gave answers to these questions but also created a system of logical, analytical thought in order to examine the questions. We in the Western world still regard this system of thought as worthwhile.

▲ *This gold death mask was initially believed to be the mask of Agamemnon, who led the Greek forces at Troy. The face appears to be sad, but calm. What might this suggest about the Greek view of death?*

ADDITIONAL RESOURCES

The resources below can be used to enrich the lessons in this chapter.

BOOKS FOR STUDENTS

Classical Greece by C. M. Boura (Time-Life.) (Great Ages of Man.)
The Last of the Wine by Mary Renault, Pantheon
Alexander the Great by Charles Mercer. Harper and Row (Horizon Caravelle)

VIDEOS/FILMS

Western Civilization: *The Greeks: In Search of Meaning.* Learning Corp of America. Social Studies School Service (800) 421-4246

CD-ROM

Queve World History: Ancient Greece. Learning Services
East (800) 877-3278
West (800) 877-9378

THE BEGINNINGS OF CIVILIZATION

| GREEK CIVILIZATION |
| 1900 B.C.   133 B.C. |
| 3500 B.C.   A.D. 500 |

QUESTIONS TO GUIDE YOUR READING

1. How did the geography of Greece affect Greek history?

2. What role did Homer's works play in the lives of the Greeks?

3. What was the polis, or city-state, and how did the major city-states of Athens and Sparta differ?

4. What role did the Persian and Great Peloponnesian (PUL-uh-puh-NEE-zhun) Wars play in Greek history?

5. What political and cultural contributions did the Greeks make to Western civilization during the classical period?

6. How did Alexander the Great create an empire?

7. What were the cultural achievements of the Hellenistic world?

OUTLINE

1. EARLY GREEK HISTORY

2. THE WORLD OF THE GREEK CITY-STATES (750 TO 500 B.C.)

3. THE HIGH POINT OF GREEK CIVILIZATION: CLASSICAL GREECE

4. THE CULTURE OF CLASSICAL GREECE

5. THE SPREAD OF GREEK CIVILIZATION: ALEXANDER AND THE HELLENISTIC KINGDOMS

EARLY GREEK HISTORY

The story of ancient Greek civilization begins when a group of Greek-speaking Indo-European people moved into Greece from the north around 1900 B.C. By 800 B.C., the basic institution of ancient Greek life, the city-state, had emerged. Greek civilization flourished and reached its height in the classical period of the fifth century B.C.

Greece: The Impact of Geography

Geography played an important role in the development of Greek history. Compared with the landmasses of Mesopotamia and Egypt, Greece occupied a small area. It was a mountainous peninsula that encompassed only forty-five thousand square miles of territory—about the size of the state of Louisiana. The mountains and the sea played especially significant roles in the development of Greek history. Much of Greece consists of small plains and river valleys surrounded by mountain ranges eight thousand to ten thousand feet high. The mountains isolated Greeks from one another, causing Greek communities to develop their

119

Listed below are brief summaries of how the content in this chapter supports the text's key themes.

Politics and History   The Greeks developed the following kinds of government: monarchy, aristocracy, tyranny, oligarchy, and democracy. Our word *politics* is derived from the Greek word *polis*.

The Role of Ideas   The Greeks contributed two important ideas: the idea that the individual has the ability to use rational thought to gain true wisdom, and the idea that citizens should make the decisions that affect how they are to be governed (the democratic ideal).

Social Life   The Greeks had a strong sense of community in their city-states.

The Importance of Cultural Developments   The artistic and intellectual achievements of the Greeks (in drama, philosophy, and the writing of history) provided the foundations of Western artistic and intellectual life.

Religion in History   Religion was an important element in Greek civilization. Greeks shared a belief in major gods and goddesses and in the importance of appeasing them to maintain a flourishing community. A lack of religious dogma allowed the Greeks to ask questions about the universe and the role of humans in the world.

The Environment and History   Mountains and the sea played major roles in Greek history.

Answers to QUESTIONS TO GUIDE YOUR READING

1. mountains created isolated, independent communities; island geography led to seafaring and creation of colonies (pages 119-120)

2. educational texts, provided heroic ideal (page 122)

3. community with common goals; Athens: "well-rounded" citizens; Sparta: harsh, militaristic, physically fit (pages 125-129)

4. Persian: built military power; Peloponnesian: weakened city-states (pages 129-130, 134)

5. political: male dominance, slavery, free-trade economy, public works projects; cultural: strengthened family unit, importance of religion, physical fitness and sports, love of wisdom, theater, systematic recording of history (pages 133-140)

6. military prowess, destruction of Persian monarchy, global view of the world (page 144)

7. see pages 145-149.

FOCUS

OBJECTIVES

After completing this section, students should be able to

1. explain the influence of geography on the development of the independent city-states
2. describe the social hierarchy of the Mycenean civilization
3. discuss the characteristics and importance of the period called the Dark Age
4. explain the importance of the two great epic poems of Homer as they relate to the development of Greek history and identity

FOCUS ACTIVITY

Share with students the story of how the Trojan war started according to Homer. Paris was asked to judge who was the most beautiful goddess—Aphrodite, Hera, Athena. Paris chose Aphrodite, after she promised him the love of the world's most beautiful woman, Helen of Troy. He persuaded Helen, the wife of the king of Mycenae, to run away with him to Troy.

Then ask students to look again at the map, noting Troy's strategic position. Have them speculate on what they think would be a more likely explanation for war. *(Mycenae was jealous of the power of Troy to control trade in and out of the Propontis.)* Ask students to consider why so many legends and myths might have grown out of this epic event.

own ways of life. Over a period of time, these communities became fiercely independent and only too willing to fight one another to gain advantage.

The sea also influenced the evolution of Greek society. Greece had a long seacoast dotted by bays and inlets that provided many harbors. The Greeks also lived on a number of islands to the west, south, and particularly east of the Greek mainland. It is no accident that the Greeks became seafarers. They sailed out into the Aegean (i-JEE-un) and the Mediterranean Seas, making contact with the outside world. Later they established colonies that spread Greek civilization throughout the Mediterranean world.

The First Greek State: The Mycenaeans

The term *Mycenaean* (mie-see-NEE-un) comes from Mycenae (mie-SEE-nee), a fortified site in Greece first discovered by the German archaeologist Heinrich Schliemann. Mycenae was one center in a Mycenaean Greek civilization that flourished between 1600 and 1100 B.C. The Mycenaean Greeks were part of the Indo-European family of peoples (see Chapter 2) who spread from their original location in the steppe region north of the Black Sea into southern and western Europe, India, and Iran. One group entered the terri-

Map 5.1   Classical Greece

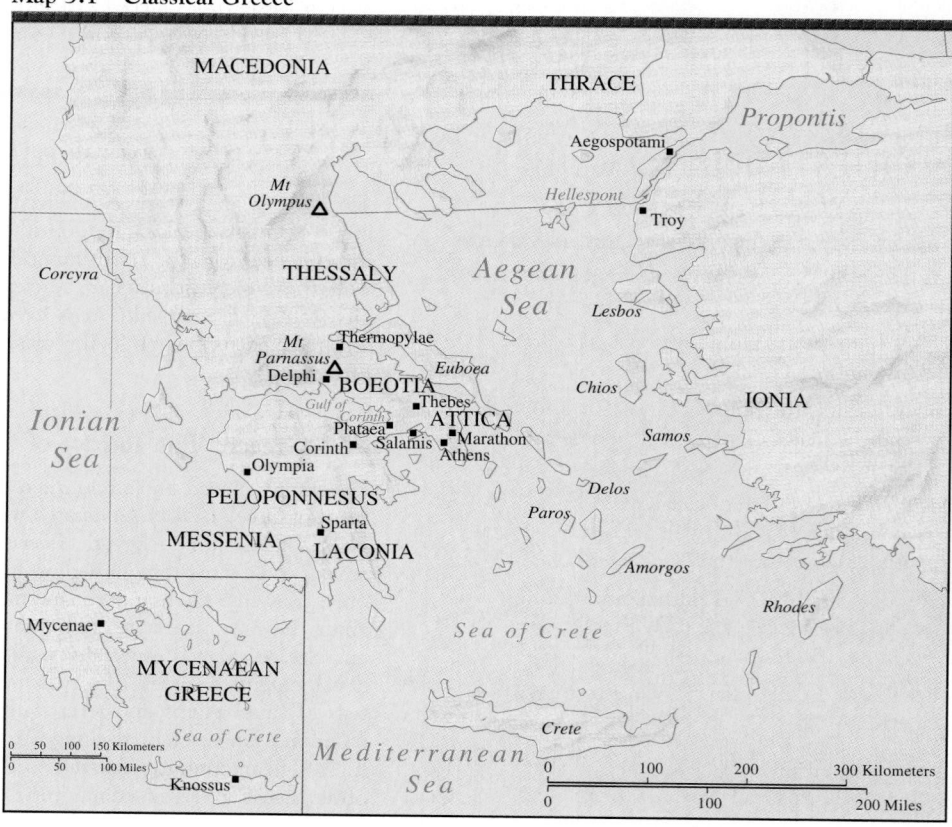

STUDYING MAPS

The following questions will help you guide the students through their study of Map 5.1.

1. What is a peninsula? *(a portion of land nearly surrounded by water and connected to a larger body of land by an isthmus, or narrow strip of land)* Outline the Greek Peninsula with your finger on the map. Is it easy to determine the boundaries of the peninsula?

2. What features of Greek geography caused the city-states to become independent? *(mountains, rivers, rugged topography, and peninsulas)*

3. Why would you expect the Greeks to be great seafarers? *(location of cities on the coasts, long seacoasts with many natural harbors, limited resources made trade necessary)*

tory of Greece from the north around 1900 B.C. Over a period of time, it managed to gain control of the Greek mainland and develop a civilization.

Mycenaean civilization, which reached its high point between 1400 and 1200 B.C., consisted of a number of powerful monarchies that resided in fortified palace centers. Like Mycenae, they were built on hills and surrounded by gigantic stone walls. These various centers of power probably formed a loose alliance of independent states, with Mycenae the strongest. Next in importance to the kings in these states were commanders of the army, the priests, and the bureaucrats who kept careful records. Free citizens included peasants, soldiers, and artisans. The lowest rung of the social ladder consisted of serfs and slaves.

The Mycenaeans were, above all, a warrior people who prided themselves on their heroic deeds in battle. Some scholars believe that the Mycenaeans spread outward and conquered the Minoan civilization in Crete (see Chapter 2). The most famous of all their supposed military adventures has come down to us in the poetry of Homer (see later in this section). Did the Mycenaean Greeks, led by Agamemnon (AG-uh-MEM-non), king of Mycenae, sack the city of Troy on the northwestern coast of Asia Minor around 1250 B.C.?

Ever since the excavations of Schliemann, begun in 1870, scholars have debated this question. Many believe that Homer's account does have a basis in fact.

By the late thirteenth century B.C., Mycenaean Greece was showing signs of serious trouble. Mycenaean states fought one another while major earthquakes caused widespread damage. In the twelfth century B.C., new waves of Greek-speaking invaders moved into Greece from the north. By 1100 B.C., Mycenaean civilization had collapsed.

The Greeks in a Dark Age (1100 to 750 B.C.)

After the collapse of Mycenaean civilization, Greece entered a difficult period in which the population declined and food production dropped. Historians call it the Dark Age, because few records of what happened exist. Not until 850 B.C. did farming revive. At the same time, some developments were forming the basis for a new Greece.

During the Dark Age, large numbers of Greeks left the mainland and sailed across the Aegean Sea to various islands. Many went to the western shores of Asia Minor, a strip of territory that came to be called Ionia

▶ Mountains and the sea, two major geographical features in the Greek landscape, shaped the country into distinct city-states, physically separated and fiercely independent. In what other ways did these features help shape Greek civilization and culture?

MORE ABOUT . . . *Proto-Greek civilizations*

The term *Proto Greek civilizations* means those civilizations that engendered or created the foundation for classical Greek civilization. One such civilization is the Mycenaian civilization mentioned in the text. Another such civilization is the Minoan civilization, discussed in Chapter 2. A major debate has surfaced among the experts regarding the extent to which Egyptian civil-

ization could also be considered *Proto Greek*. Besides the ordinary questions of scholarship and historical proof, there are issues of emotion and politics. Many westerners would be concerned about the idea that Greek civilization could be said to be an offshoot of Egyptian civilization. For further information on this controversy, see Luis Bernal's *Block Athena* (Princeton University).

ASSESS

LEARNING FROM VISUALS

Answer to the caption question: Canvases or other perishable backgrounds for painting have not survived from the Greeks to modern times. Art that has survived was done on sturdy materials—pottery, walls, and stone. As Greek pottery evolved, scenes of human figures replaced geometric shapes, and artists began to decorate their pottery with scenes from mythology, current day events, and daily life.

Answers to THE SECTION REVIEW.

2. (a) long poems that tell the deeds of great heroes
3. (a) a fortified site in Greece that flourished between 1600 and 1100 B.C.
   (b) Homer's epic poem about the Trojan War
   (c) recounts the journeys of Odysseus after the fall of Troy
4. (a) mountains isolated Greeks, causing communities to develop independently and fight one another
   (b) epics taught courage and honor to Greek males; stories were considered true history
5. Answers will vary.

CLOSE

In a class discussion, ask students to name different ways that history is "recorded." Call on individual students until everyone has had an opportunity to contribute.

(or Ionian Greece). Iron came into use for making weapons. In the eighth century B.C., the Greeks adopted the Phoenician alphabet, giving themselves a new system of writing. Near the very end of the Dark Age appeared the work of Homer, one of the truly great poets of all time.

The *Iliad* and the *Odyssey*, the first great **epic poems** of early Greece, were based on stories that had been passed on from generation to generation. An epic poem is a long poem that tells the deeds of a great hero. Homer made use of the stories to compose the *Iliad*, an account of the Trojan War. In the *Iliad*, the war was caused by an act of Paris, a prince of Troy. By kidnapping Helen, the wife of the king of the Greek state of Sparta, Paris outraged all the Greeks. Under the leadership of the Spartan king's brother, King Agamemnon of Mycenae, the Greeks attacked Troy. Ten years later, the Greeks finally won and sacked the city. The *Iliad* is not so much the story of the war itself, however, as it is the tale of the Greek hero Achilles and how the anger of Achilles led to disaster.

The *Odyssey* recounts the journeys of one of the Greek heroes, Odysseus, after the fall of Troy, and his ultimate return to his wife. Although the *Odyssey* has long been considered Homer's other masterpiece, some scholars believe that it was composed later than the *Iliad* and was possibly not the work of Homer.

Homer proved to be of great value to later Greeks. He did not so much record history; he made it. The Greeks looked on the *Iliad* and the *Odyssey* as true history and as the works of one poet, Homer. These master

◄ *This Grecian vase shows a famous scene from the battle of Troy. Here Achilles is dragging Hector's body through city streets. Why might pottery be a vehicle for portraying historical scenes?*

pieces gave the Greeks an ideal past with a cast of heroes. The epics came to be used as basic texts for the education of generations of Greek males. As one ancient Athenian stated, "My father was anxious to see me develop into a good man . . . and as a means to this end he compelled me to memorize all of Homer."[1] The values Homer taught were courage and honor. A hero strives for excellence, which the Greeks called *arete* (ar-uh-TA). In the world of Homer, arete is won in struggle or contest. Through his willingness to fight, the hero protects his family and friends, preserves his own honor and that of his family, and earns his reputation. Homer gave to later generations of Greek males a model of heroism and honor.

 SECTION REVIEW

1. **Locate:**
   (*a*) Aegean Sea, (*b*) Crete, (*c*) Ionia

2. **Define:**
   (*a*) epic poems

3. **Identify:**
   (*a*) Mycenae,   (*b*) The *Iliad*,   (*c*) The *Odyssey*

4. **Recall:**
   (*a*) What was the effect of Greek geography on Greek history?
   (*b*) Why was Homer used as the basis for Greek education?

5. **Think Critically:** Was the so-called Dark Age really "dark"? Why or why not?

 2

THE WORLD OF THE GREEK CITY-STATES (750 TO 500 B.C.)

In the course of the Dark Age, Greek villages gradually expanded and became independent city-states. By the eighth century B.C., the city-state, or what the Greeks called a **polis,** became the central focus of Greek life. Our word *politics* is derived from the Greek word *polis.*

ENRICHMENT ACTIVITY

Give students a choice for an "extra credit" assignment.

(a) Have students compare the *Iliad* and the *Odyssey* with the Roman *Aenead*. Ask students to point out the aspects of the Roman work that are obviously influenced by the Greek masterpieces.

(b) Assign students an essay in which they name the three causes of the decline of the

Mycenean civilization (*internal-fighting between states; external-invaders;* and *natural-earthquakes*) and explain which of the three they feel is most important to the decline of Mycenia and why.

The results of the students' work can be presented in either a written or oral report.

The Polis as the Center of Greek Life

In a physical sense, the polis was a town, city, or even a village, along with its surrounding countryside. The town, city, or village served as the central point where the citizens of the polis could meet for political, social, and religious activities. The central meeting point was usually a hill, such as the Acropolis at Athens. An **acropolis** (usually the upper fortified part of a city or town) served as a place of refuge during an attack and sometimes came to be the religious center on which temples and public buildings were built. Below the acropolis would be an **agora,** an open place that served both as a place where citizens could assemble and as a market.

City-states varied greatly in size, from a few square miles to a few hundred square miles. They also varied in population. Athens had a population of over 300,000 by the fifth century B.C., but most city-states were much smaller, consisting of only a few hundred to several thousand people.

The polis was, above all, a community of citizens who shared a common identity and common goals. As a community, the polis consisted of citizens with political rights (adult males), citizens with no political rights (women and children), and noncitizens (slaves and resident aliens). All citizens of a polis had rights, but these rights were coupled with responsibilities. The Greek philosopher Aristotle argued that a citizen did not belong just to himself or herself: "we must rather regard every citizen as belonging to the state." However, the loyalty that citizens had to their city-states also had a negative side. City-states distrusted one another, and the division of Greece into fiercely patriotic independent units helped to bring about its ruin.

As the polis developed, so too did a new military system. In earlier times, wars in Greece had been fought by aristocratic cavalry soldiers—nobles on horseback. These aristocrats, who were large landowners, also dominated the political life of their city-states. By 700 B.C., however, a new military order came into being that was based on **hoplites,** who were heavily armed infantry soldiers, or foot soldiers. Each carried a round shield, a short sword, and a thrusting spear about nine feet long. Hoplites went into battle as a unit, marching shoulder to shoulder in a rectangular formation known

OBJECTIVES

After completing this section, students should be able to

1. describe the physical elements of a polis and discuss the importance of the social system in establishing a sense of community in a polis
2. list two important factors leading to the establishment of Greek colonies
3. explain the importance of tyrants in the transition to democracy in Greek city-states
4. compare and contrast the characteristics of life in Sparta and Athens

LEARNING FROM VISUALS

1. Ask the students what they are looking at. *(photo of a part of a decorated vase)* What does the vase depict? *(battle between two armies)*
2. Ask each student to write a paragraph describing either a hoplite and his equipment as shown in the illustration, or a phalanx and how it operated in a battle.

Answer to the caption question: In order to maintain their own security, the lightly armed hoplite forces stayed close together, presenting a wall of shields to their opponents.

▶ *This vase, which dates from the seventh century B.C., shows Greek hoplite soldiers in battle. Hoplites, who carried round shields and long spears, were known as skilled, formidable opponents. What is the significance of their close formation?*

So What ⁇

*If your students question the importance of the information on **common identity of Athenians,** tell them . . .*

It seems that humans have traditionally placed more emphasis on what makes them different from one another than on what makes them alike. If you had stopped someone in the Acropolis and asked him what he was, his answer would have been, "I'm an Athenian." Only secondly would he or she have answered, "I'm a Hellene" (a descendant of the goddess Helen, from whom the Greeks believed they came). This provincial self-perception contributed much to the frequent state of warfare that existed among the inhabitants of Hellas (what we call "ancient Greece"). It seems that in today's world, we have not yet lost this provincialism. It is hard for humans to feel like members of the human family.

as a **phalanx.** As long as the hoplites kept their order, were not outflanked, and did not break, they either beat the enemy or, at the very least, suffered no harm. The phalanx was easily routed, however, if it broke its order.

Colonization: Many Greeks Go Abroad

Between 750 and 550 B.C., large numbers of Greeks left their homeland to settle in distant lands. A desire for good farmland and the growth of trade were two important factors in the people's movement abroad to establish colonies. Each colony became a new polis and was usually independent of the polis that had founded it. Greek colonies were not colonies in the sense that we think of the thirteen American colonies that were controlled by Great Britain.

In the western Mediterranean, new Greek colonies were established along the coastline of southern Italy, southern France, eastern Spain, and northern Africa west of Egypt. To the north, the Greeks set up colonies in Thrace, where they sought good farmland to grow grains. Greeks also settled along the shores of the Black Sea and set up cities on the Hellespont (HEL-uh-SPONT) and the Bosphorus (BOSS-fur-us). The most notable of these cities was Byzantium (bu-ZAN-shee-

Map 5.2   Greek Colonies, 750–550 B.C.

TRANSPARENCY

5–2, Example of Greek Trireme.

▶ *The Olympias, shown here, is a trireme that was reconstructed by the Greek navy. These boats, which had metal prows and were known for their speed, were used to ram enemy ships.*

um), the site of what later became Constantinople (Istanbul). In establishing these colonies, the Greeks spread their culture and political ideas throughout the Mediterranean.

Colonization also led to increased trade and industry. The Greeks on the mainland sent their pottery, wine, and olive oil to these areas. In return, they received grains and metals from the west and fish, timber, wheat, metals, and slaves from the Black Sea region. The expansion of trade and industry created a new group of rich men in many city-states who wanted political power but found it impossible to gain because of the power of the ruling aristocrats.

Tyranny in the Greek City-States

The desires of these new groups opened the door to the rise of tyrants in the seventh and sixth centuries B.C. They were not necessarily oppressive or wicked, as our word *tyrant* implies. Greek tyrants were rulers who seized power by force and who were not subject to the law. Support for the tyrants came from the new rich who made their money in trade and industry, as well as from poor peasants who were in debt to landholding aristocrats. Both groups were tired of the domination of their city-states by the aristocrats.

Tyrants gained power and kept it by using hired soldiers. Once in power, they built new marketplaces, temples, and walls. These constructions glorified the city but, more important, increased their own popularity. Tyrants also favored the interests of merchants and traders. Despite these achievements, however, tyrants fell out of favor by the end of the sixth century B.C. Greeks believed in the rule of law, and tyranny made a mockery of that ideal.

Nevertheless, although tyranny did not last, it played an important role in Greek history. The rule of the tyrants had ended the rule of the aristocrats in many city-states. The end of tyranny opened the door to new and more people in government. In some Greek city-states, this led to the development of **democracy** (rule of the many). Other city-states remained committed to rule by an **oligarchy** (rule by the few). We can see the differences in how Greek city-states were governed by examining the two most famous and most powerful Greek city-states, Sparta and Athens.

Sparta

Located in the southeastern Peloponnesus, Sparta, like other Greek states, was faced with the need for more land. Sparta could have solved its problem by sending its people out to new colonies, as other states did. Instead, beginning around 740 B.C., Sparta conquered the neighboring state of Messenia despite that state's larger size and population. After the conquest, Sparta

LEARNING FROM VISUALS

1. Ask students to describe the boat in the illustration. Ask them to estimate how big it is, how many men it carried, how it was propelled, how it was used in battle.

2. In a class discussion, ask students why boats and a navy were important to the Greek military. *(Sea was important for transporting troops, supplies, provision, and orders. By controlling the sea, an army could limit the ability of its enemy to wage war.)*

REINFORCING VOCABULARY

Make sure students understand the distinction between *aristocrat, tyrant, democracy,* and *oligarchy.* Explain that each has to do with how power and authority are established and maintained in a society.

Be certain students are aware of the two different meanings of *tyrant:* a person who rules with absolute authority; or, a cruel, unjust, or harshly oppressive person.

ACTIVITY

Ask students to play the role of citizens (male and female) in Athens and Sparta, explaining the advantages of each society. Afterwards, poll the class to determine how many males and females would have preferred to live in each system.

On Line with WORLD HISTORY *Internet Activity*

You may want to have your students visit the following URL, where they will find information and additional web site resources to enhance their study of this chapter.

Perseus Project

http://www.perseus.tufts.edu/

This is an evolving digital library on Ancient Greece and has its own search engine.

Due to the ever-changing nature of the World Wide Web, see the West History web site, **http://history.swpco.com** for regular updates of the URLs in this text.

CONNECTIONS
TO OUR WORLD

Have students divide into groups and brainstorm situations that exist in our society today involving a balance between order and freedom. Then have students come together to compile a class list. Identify the situations for which there is the greatest difference of opinion and discuss the pros and cons of more governmental control.

ACROSS THE CURRICULUM

Health. Ask a health instructor or school nurse to discuss the effects of the Spartan diet and training on the health of young Spartans.

Government. Have students list the rights guaranteed in the U.S. constitution and discuss which of these rights would be respected in Sparta and Athens.

CRITICAL THINKING

Ask students how the social structure of Sparta and Athens would affect their ability to wage war. *(Spartans were better trained but because they prohibited contact with the outside world they would be unaware of advances in science and technology. Also, because of their treatment of helots, Spartans had to worry constantly about internal revolt and use some of their military resources to guard against it.)*

REINFORCING VOCABULARY

Point out to students different uses of the word *campaign*—a military campaign, a marketing campaign, a political campaign. They all pertain to a planned operation to achieve a goal.

126

CONNECTIONS
TO OUR WORLD

Order and Freedom   In the world of the Greeks, Athens and Sparta represented two different systems of political power and organization. Sparta was a state that symbolized the desire for order. The Spartans developed a well-regulated state. Boys were put under control of the state at age seven and trained to be tough warriors. The Spartans organized a powerful military state that maintained order and stability.

The state of Athens, in contrast, symbolized the desire for freedom. The Athenians believed that the Spartans paid too high a price for their order, because it was achieved at the expense of the freedom of its citizens. Following a different path, the Athenians created a democratic society that fostered an ideal of the freedom of the individual, at least for those individuals who were citizens.

Order and freedom remain two poles of political organization in the twentieth century. Some people viewed the Cold War as a conflict between one state (the United States) that valued freedom through its democratic system and another state (the Soviet Union) that created a totalitarian order that was willing to crush individual rights for the sake of order and stability. Of course, the proper balance of order and freedom remains a problem within democratic states as well. The threat of terrorism in the contemporary world, for example, causes democratic states to consider whether they should pass laws that severely restrict the freedoms of their citizens in order to maintain stability. Finding the balance between order and freedom remains both an international and a national problem. Knowing how states dealt with this problem in the past provides some help in coping with it in the present.

made the Messenians their serfs, although the Spartans were outnumbered by them 7 to 1. Known as helots, these serfs were forced to work the land for the benefit of the Spartans. In the seventh century B.C., the Messenians revolted. Sparta crushed the revolt, but the strug

gle was so long and hard that the Spartans made a decision. They would create a military state so that their warriors could control Messenia for ages to come.

After 600 B.C., the Spartans transformed their state into a military camp. The lives of Spartans were rigidly organized and tightly controlled (thus, our word *spartan*, meaning "highly self-disciplined"). After a childhood of military discipline (see "Young People in Greece: The Spartan and Athenian Models"), Spartan males were enrolled in the army for regular military service at age twenty. Although allowed to marry, they continued to live in the military barracks. All meals were eaten in public dining halls with fellow soldiers. Meals were simple; the famous Spartan black broth consisted of a piece of pork boiled in blood, salt, and vinegar. A visitor who ate the black broth in a public mess once remarked that he now understood why Spartans were not afraid to die. At thirty, Spartan males were allowed to vote in the assembly (to be discussed later) and live at home, but they stayed in the army until the age of sixty.

While their husbands remained in military barracks until age thirty, Spartan women lived at home. Because of this separation, Spartan women had greater freedom of movement and greater power in the household than was common elsewhere in Greece. Spartan women were expected to exercise and remain fit to bear and raise healthy children. Many Spartan women upheld the strict Spartan values, expecting their husbands and sons to be brave in war. The story is told that as a Spartan mother was burying her son, an old woman came up to her and said, "You poor woman, what a misfortune." "No," replied the other, "because I bore him so that he might die for Sparta and that is what has happened, as I wished." Another Spartan woman, as she was handing her son his shield, told him to come back carrying his shield or be carried on it.

The Spartan government was headed by two kings, who led the Spartan army on its campaigns. A group of five men, known as the ephors (EF-urz), were elected each year and were responsible for the education of youth and the conduct of all citizens. A council of elders, composed of the two kings and twenty-eight citizens over the age of sixty, decided on the issues that would be presented to an assembly. This assembly of all

---

MORE ABOUT . . . *Greek ideals*

It is always dangerous to speak of a "Greek personality," or any other group as sharing a "personality." Yet there are traits and characteristics that do vary from culture to culture. Consider the Greek warriors: prior to the development of the hoplites (see page 123), most Greek warriors went to battle with a minimum of protection, other than a shield and leg guards. Essentially, they were

naked! Yet the Greeks believed that hand-to-hand battle, with minimum protection, was the honorable way to engage the enemy. It was also considered somewhat dishonorable to kill at a distance using a bow and arrow. The Greek's were "purists" even when their lives were on the line; certain acts were not honorable, and were just not done.

YOUNG PEOPLE IN GREECE

The Spartan and Athenian Models

Spartans and Athenians were both Greeks, but they had very different political systems. They also differed on how to raise their young people.

In Sparta, boys were trained to be soldiers. At birth, each child was examined by state officials, who decided whether the child was fit to live. Those who were judged unfit were left in the open on a mountainside to die. Boys judged to be fit were taken from their mothers at the age of seven and put under control of the state. They lived in military-style barracks, where they were subjected to harsh discipline to make them tough and mean. Their education stressed military training and obedience to authority. The Greek historian Plutarch (PLOO-tark) gave a vivid description of the handling of young Spartans:

After they were twelve years old, they were no longer allowed to wear any undergarments, they had one coat to serve them a year; their bodies were hard and dry, with but little acquaintance of baths; these human indulgences they were allowed only on some few particular days in the year. They lodged together in little bands upon beds made of the rushes which grew by the banks of the river Eurotas, which they were to break off with their hands with a knife. . . .

[Spartan boys were also encouraged to steal their food.] They stole, too, all other meat they could lay their hands on, looking out and watching all opportunities, when people were asleep or more careless than usual. If they were caught, they were not only punished with whipping, but hunger, too, being reduced to their ordinary allowance, which

◀ *In Sparta girls and boys were trained to be athletes, as is shown in this bronze statue, which was part of a vase lid. How might the lives of girls raised in Athens have differed from those raised in Sparta?*

was but very slender, and so contrived on purpose, that they might set about to help themselves, and be forced to exercise their energy and address. This was the principal design of their hard fare.

Basically, the Spartan system worked. Spartan males were known for their toughness and their meanness. They were also known as the best soldiers in all of Greece.

Spartan girls received an education similar to that of the boys. Girls, too, underwent physical training, including running, wrestling, and throwing the javelin. The purpose was clear: to strengthen the girls for their roles as healthy mothers. Like the boys, they exercised naked in public, an activity considered shocking to other Greeks.

Well-to-do Athenian citizens raised their children very differently. Athenian children were carefully nurtured by their mothers until the age of seven. At seven, a boy of the upper class was turned over to a male servant, known as a pedagogue, who became the child's constant companion until his late teens. The pedagogue, who was usually a slave, accompanied the child to school. He was also responsible for teaching his charge good manners. He could punish the child with a birch rod to impose discipline.

(continued)

SPECIAL NEEDS: Visual/Auditory

Have students work in groups and design maps of ancient Greece using the maps on pages 120 and 124 as guides. The map should include Athens, the Black sea, the Mediterranean Sea, the Ionian Sea, the Aegian Sea, Sparta, Crete, and Macedonia. Have students describe the different political systems of Sparta and Athens as well as how the cultures differed in raising their families.

Have students complete a chart similar to the one sketched below.

	Athens	Sparta
Geography		
Government		
Economy		
Role of Women		

YOUNG PEOPLE IN GREECE

CLASS DISCUSSION

The methods of training in Sparta and Athens relate to issues of the needs of the state versus the rights of the individual. These are questions that are still very important today.

Ask students why the Spartans treated their youth so harshly and whether they were justified to do so. Does it matter that all youth were treated the same? To stimulate discussion, you might ask students if they would rather live in Sparta or Athens in time of peace and in time of war.

USING PRIMARY SOURCES

Ask students what they think the effect of the treatment of the Spartan boys would be on their physical and mental condition. Ask whether this would be an effective training method today for military basic training or athletic conditioning.

LEARNING FROM VISUALS

Answers to the caption question: Girls in Sparta were raised to exercise more freedom, and in some ways their upbringing mirrored the lives of their brothers. In Athens, girls and women were expected to remain in their houses performing traditional work.

YOUNG PEOPLE IN GREECE

Answers to Critical Thinking Questions:

1. Spartan children were raised to be strong and tough. Boys were trained to be soldiers, housed in military-style barracks, harshly disciplined, and deprived of comforts and indulgences. Girls underwent physical training to strengthen them for their roles as healthy mothers.

2. The Spartan child was toughened—a trained soldier. Educated Athenian youths were carefully nurtured at home and at school to become well-rounded citizens. Athenian boys were physically educated, but also knew how to read, write, perform arithmetic, and play music.

3. Student answers will vary.

COMPARING TIME PERIODS

Equal treatment and equal opportunity for men and women is the goal in the United States, but there is also a tradition of different roles for men and women. Ask students to describe the ways in which young women were treated in Sparta and Athens and discuss which was more fair and which was more desirable. You might then make a comparison between the treatment of women in the military in the United States vs. Israel as a current example of two different approaches.

YOUNG PEOPLE IN GREECE

The Spartan and Athenian Models, continued

The purpose of an education for upper-class Athenian boys was to create a well-rounded person. To that end, a boy had three teachers. One taught him reading, writing, and arithmetic. Another taught physical education, a necessity to achieve the ideal of a sound mind in a sound body. A third taught him music, which consisted of playing the lyre (a stringed instrument) and singing. To Greeks, music was considered an important way to create balance and harmony. Education ended at eighteen, when an Athenian male formally became a citizen.

Formal education in ancient Athens was only for boys. Girls of all classes remained at home, as their mothers did. Their mothers taught them how to run a home, which included how to spin and weave—all activities expected of a good wife. Only in some wealthy families did girls learn to read, write, and even play the lyre.

1. Describe a Spartan upbringing.

2. Compare a well-educated Spartan boy with a well-educated Athenian.

3. Does your education today incorporate any Spartan and/or Athenian ideas? Which ones?

---

male citizens did not debate; it only voted on the issues put before it by the council of elders.

To make their new military state secure, the Spartans turned their backs on the outside world. Foreigners, who might bring in new ideas, were discouraged from visiting Sparta. Furthermore, except for military reasons, Spartans were not allowed to travel abroad, where they might pick up new ideas that might be dangerous to the stability of the state. Likewise, Spartan citizens were discouraged from studying philosophy, literature, or the arts—subjects that might encourage new thoughts. The art of war was the Spartan ideal. All other arts were frowned upon.

Athens

By 700 B.C., Athens had become a unified polis on the peninsula of Attica. Early Athens was ruled by a king. By the seventh century B.C., however, Athens had become an oligarchy when it fell under the control of its aristocrats. They owned the best land and controlled political life by means of a council of nobles, assisted by a board of nine **archons** (rulers). Although there was an assembly of all the citizens, it had few powers.

Near the end of the seventh century B.C., Athens faced political turmoil because of serious economic problems. Many Athenian farmers found themselves sold into slavery when they were unable to repay their debts to their aristocratic neighbors. Over and over, there were cries to cancel the debts and give land to the poor. Athens seemed on the verge of civil war.

The ruling Athenian aristocrats reacted to this crisis in 594 B.C. by giving full power to Solon (SO-lun), a reform-minded aristocrat, to make changes. Solon canceled all land debts and freed people who had fallen into slavery for debts. He refused, however, to take land from the rich and give it to the poor.

Solon's reforms, though popular, did not solve the problems of Athens. Aristocrats were still powerful, and poor peasants could not get land. Internal strife

---

MORE ABOUT . . . Athenian Democracy

Athens taught the West, by its example, that democracy was the most desirable form of government. Yet Athens itself adopted democracy only for roughly 100 years. After the Golden Age of Athens and its defeat by Sparta in the Peloponnesian war, Athens lost confidence in its democratic system. After all, it had been defeated by the authoritarian Spartans, the same people who Pericles disdained in his famous funeral oration! None of the great Greek philosophers who taught in Athens—Socrates, Plato, Aristotle—were believers in the virtues of democracy. Socrates and Plato felt it was folly to allow ordinary people to guide the state. Aristotle was a bit more open, allowing for the possibility of a democracy among the landed aristocracy. Although Athens turned its back on democracy, democracy survived and is the backbone of many governments today.

finally led to the very thing Solon had hoped to avoid—tyranny. Pisistratus (pi-SIS-tru-tus), an aristocrat, seized power in 560 B.C. By aiding Athenian trade, Pisistratus remained popular with the merchants. By taking land from the nobles and giving it to the peasants, he gained the favor of poor citizens. The Athenians rebelled against Pisistratus's son, who had succeeded him, and ended the tyranny in 510 B.C. Two years later, with the backing of the Athenian people, Cleisthenes (KLISE-thu-NEEZ), another reformer, gained the upper hand.

Cleisthenes, first of all, created a new council of five hundred that supervised foreign affairs, supervised the treasury, and proposed the laws that would be voted on by the assembly. The Athenian assembly, composed of all male citizens, was given final authority to pass laws after free and open debate. Because the assembly of citizens now had the central role in the Athenian political system, the reforms of Cleisthenes had created the foundations for Athenian democracy.

 SECTION REVIEW

1. **Locate:**
   (*a*) Mediterranean Sea,   (*b*) Thrace,   (*c*) Black Sea,   (*d*) Hellespont,   (*e*) Byzantium

2. **Define:**
   (*a*) polis,   (*b*) acropolis,   (*c*) agora,
   (*d*) hoplites,   (*e*) phalanx,   (*f*) democracy,
   (*g*) oligarchy,   (*h*) archons

3. **Identify:**
   (*a*) helots,   (*b*) ephors,   (*c*) Pisistratus,
   (*d*) Cleisthenes

4. **Recall:**
   (*a*) What is the polis? Why is it considered by many historians to be an important development in the political history of Western civilization?
   (*b*) Compare and contrast the Greek city-states of Sparta and Athens.

5. **Think Critically:** In what way is Athenian democracy similar to American democracy? In what way is it different?

THE HIGH POINT OF GREEK CIVILIZATION: CLASSICAL GREECE

Classical Greece is the name given to the period of Greek history from around 500 B.C. to the conquest of Greece by the Macedonian king Philip II in 338 B.C. Many of the artistic and intellectual contributions of the Greeks occurred during this period. The age began with a mighty struggle between the Greek states and the mammoth Persian Empire.

The Challenge of Persia

As the Greeks spread throughout the Mediterranean, they came into contact with the Persian Empire to the east. The Ionian Greek cities in western Asia Minor had already fallen subject to the Persian Empire by the mid-sixth century B.C. An unsuccessful revolt by the Ionian cities in 499 B.C.—assisted by the Athenian navy—led the Persian ruler Darius to seek revenge. It is said that Darius ordered one of his slaves to say to him at every meal, "Sire, remember the Athenians."

In 490 B.C., the Persians landed an army on the plain of Marathon, only twenty-six miles from Athens. There a mostly Athenian army, though clearly outnumbered, went on the attack and defeated the Persians decisively. The Persians returned to Asia. Legend has it that the runner Pheidippides ran from Marathon to Athens (a distance of twenty-six miles) to announce, "Victory, we win," before dropping dead. (Our modern **marathon**—or footrace—is twenty-six miles.) Although the Battle of Marathon was a minor defeat to the Persians, to the Athenians it had proved that the Persians could be beaten. In preserving their freedom, the Athenians had also gained new confidence in their city-state.

Xerxes (ZURK-SEEZ), who became the new Persian monarch after Darius died in 486 B.C., vowed revenge and planned to invade Greece. In preparation for the attack, some of the Greek states formed a defensive league under the Spartans. The Athenians, however,

COOPERATIVE LEARNING ACTIVITY

Divide the class into two groups by gender. Allow time for each group to discuss and develop a list of reasons for the following: men will list arguments for women staying home and out of politics; women will list arguments for their rights at an equal chance in politics. Bring the class together. Ask a spokesperson from each group to share the group's list. You may want to write the arguments of both groups on the chalkboard to compare in a class discussion. Encourage students to debate the issues.

FOCUS

OBJECTIVES

After completing this section, students should be able to

1. explain the events leading to the creation of the Delian League and the Athenian Empire
2. describe the reforms and system of democracy established in Athens that led to the flourishing of Greek civilization in the Age of Pericles
3. name the three states that sought to dominate Greek affairs after the Peloponnesian War
4. list at least four major functions of women in a classical Athenian household
5. describe the elements of the Athenian economy, including the importance of slavery and trade

FOCUS ACTIVITY

Break students from the class into four groups, each group representing a city-state of ancient Greece. Assign each group to one corner of the room. Explain to each group that they are separated from the others by imaginary mountains or rivers. The goal of each group is to control the area in the middle of the room, which is a pass that allows access to all other groups. Ask each of the groups to select a leader (any method they choose). The leaders are to deal with the other leaders in an attempt to make deals that would allow for the

▲ *Xerxes became king of Persia in 486 and led the Persian army to a decisive, but short-lived, rout of Athens. He is shown seated on his throne, with an advisor and a soldier in attendance.*

followed a new military policy insisted on by Themistocles, one of the Athenian leaders, and built a navy. By the time of the Persian invasion in 480 B.C., the Athenians had a fleet of about two hundred vessels.

Xerxes led a massive invasion force into Greece: close to 150,000 troops, almost 700 naval ships, and hundreds of supply ships to keep their large army fed. The Greeks tried to delay the Persians at the pass of Thermopylae (THUR-MOP-uh-lee), along the main road into central Greece. A Greek force numbering close to nine thousand, under the leadership of a Spartan king and his army of three hundred Spartans, held off the Persian army for two days. The Spartan troops were especially brave. When told that Persian arrows would darken the sky in battle, one Spartan warrior responded, "That is good news. We will fight in the shade!" Unfortunately for the Greeks, a traitor told the Persians how to use a mountain path to outflank the Greek force. The Spartans fought to the last man.

The Athenians, now threatened by the onslaught of the Persian forces, abandoned their city. While the Persians sacked and burned Athens, the Greek fleet remained offshore near the island of Salamis (SAL-uh-mus) and challenged the Persian navy to fight. Although the Greeks were outnumbered, they managed to outmaneuver the Persian fleet and utterly

defeated it. A few months later, early in 479 B.C., the Greeks formed the largest Greek army seen up to that time and defeated the Persian army at Plataea (plu-TEE-uh), northwest of Athens. The Greeks had won the war and were free to pursue their own destiny.

The Growth of an Athenian Empire in the Age of Pericles

After the defeat of the Persians, Athens took over the leadership of the Greek world. In the winter of 478/477 B.C., the Athenians formed a defensive alliance called the Delian League. Its main headquarters was on the island of Delos (DEE-loss). However, its chief officials, including the treasurers and commanders of the fleet, were Athenian. Under the leadership of the Athenians, the Delian League pursued the attack against the Persian Empire. Virtually all of the Greek states in the Aegean were liberated from Persian control, although the rest of the Persian Empire remained intact and quite powerful. Nevertheless, arguing that the Persian threat was now over, some members of the Delian League wished to withdraw. The Athenians, however, forced them to remain in the league and to pay tribute (a financial payment). In 454 B.C., the Athenians moved the treasury of the league from the island of Delos to Athens. By controlling the Delian League, Athens had created an empire.

At home, Athenians favored the new policy. Under Pericles, who was a dominant figure in Athenian politics between 461 and 429 B.C., Athens expanded its new empire abroad. At the same time, democracy flourished at home. This period of Athenian and Greek history, which historians have called the Age of Pericles, saw the height of Athenian power and its brilliance as a civilization.

In the Age of Pericles, the Athenians became deeply attached to their democratic system. The will of the people was expressed in the assembly, which consisted of all male citizens over eighteen years of age. In the mid-fifth century, that was probably a group of about forty-three thousand. Meetings of the assembly were held every ten days on a hillside east of the Acropolis. Not all attended, and the number present seldom reached six thousand. The assembly passed all laws,

STUDYING MAPS

Have students turn to the Map 5.1, Ancient Greece on page 120. Ask them to locate Ionia, Marathon, Thermopylae, and Delos. Ask students if they can explain from the map why Themistocles insisted on building an Athenian navy. *(Themistocles*

knew that the only effective way of invading Athens was by sea. He also knew that the best defense against such an invasion was a strong navy. Without naval resistance, it might not be possible to withstand the Persian attack.)

YOU ARE THERE

Pericles Speaks to the Athenian People

In his History of the Peloponnesian War, *the Greek historian Thucydides presented his account of the speech given by Pericles to honor the Athenians killed in the first campaigns of the Great Peloponnesian War. It is a magnificent, idealized description of the Athenian democracy at its height.*

Thucydides, *History of the Peloponnesian War*

Our constitution is called a democracy because power is in the hands not of a minority but of the whole people. When it is a question of settling private disputes, everyone is equal before the law; when it is a question of putting one person before another in positions of public responsibility, what counts is not membership in a particular class, but the actual ability which the man possesses. No one, so long as he has it in him to be of service to the state, is kept in political obscurity because of poverty. And, just as our political life is free and open, so is our day-to-day life in our relations with each other. We do not get into a state with our next-door neighbor if he enjoys himself in his own way, nor do we give him the kind of black looks which, though they do no real harm, still do hurt people's feelings. We are free and tolerant in our private lives; but in public affairs we keep to the law. This is because it commands our deep respect. . . .

Here each individual is interested not only in his own affairs but in the affairs of the state as

◄ *For Pericles, shown here, the democratic system that prevailed in Athens was of major importance, and he worked diligently to increase participation in civic affairs. During his rule, the Athenian empire flourished and grew. Do you think leaders can be both democratic and imperialistic?*

well: even those who are mostly occupied with their own business are extremely well-informed on general politics—this is a peculiarity of ours: we do not say that a man who takes no interest in politics is a man who minds his own business; we say that he has no business here at all. . . . Taking everything together then, I declare that our city is an education to Greece.

1. How was Athens "an education to Greece"?

2. What does Pericles say are the rights and responsibilities of Athenian citizens?

3. Would an ideal Athenian citizen make a good modern-day American citizen? Why or why not?

---

elected public officials, and made final decisions on war and foreign policy. Anyone could speak, but usually only respected leaders did so.

Pericles also expanded the involvement of Athenians in their democracy. He made lower-class citizens eligible for public offices formerly closed to them. By paying officeholders, including those who served on the large Athenian juries, he made it possible for poor citizens to take part in public affairs. Pericles believed that Athenians should be proud of their democracy (see "You Are There: Pericles Speaks to the Athenian People").

MORE ABOUT . . . *the Athenian challenge to Persia*

It must have seemed like a child's folly to the Persians that the diminutive Greek city-state, Athens, dared to send military help to its Ionian colonies when they were attacked by the Persian army. A look at the map of page 120 graphically shows the extent of the Athenian's daring. Once Darius was sent to teach the Athenians (and other Greek city-states) a lesson, the Athenians had to rise to meet their greatest challenge ever—the invasion of the Persians. Even though the Athenian's had the advantage of home ground, their defeat of the Persians at Marathon must be ranked as one of the greatest military feats ever. The citizen-warriors of Athens had defeated the mighty Persian empire! It is this kind of feat that has given Athens the shining brilliance in the West that it has held until today. It is the epic story of the "little warrior"—defeating the "civil giant."

---

most advantageous trade and protection arrangements. (Two group leaders may decide to come together to defeat a third group, for example.) In short time, it should become obvious that a great deal of tension and conflict is arising both from the secret dealings as well as from the fear of being overrun by a more aggressive city-state. Explain to students that without common laws and basic trust between states of a country, conflict is almost inevitable.

YOU ARE THERE

CLASS DISCUSSION

Emphasize to students that the democracy described by Thucydides was an ideal that has never been realized, not even in Athens.

Ask students how the actual conditions in Athens were different from the ideal described by Thucydides. *(women, slaves and other non-citizens were not included in the democracy)*

Answers to Critical Thinking Questions

1. Pericles means that Athens was a model city—a democratic, free, and open society to be copied by the rest of Greece.
2. Good Athenian citizens were free and tolerant in their private lives, but they also respected and adhered to the law. An ideal Athenian citizen was interested in the affairs of the state, politically well-informed, and involved.
3. Student answers will vary. Athenians valued many of the same rights guaranteed in our Constitution.

TEACH

COMPARING TIME PERIODS

There is a close parallel between the Delian League and NATO. Both were formed as a defensive alliance in order to face a common threat, Persia in the case of the Delian League and the Soviet Union in the case of NATO. In both cases, once this threat was ended members began to question the need for a continued alliance. Athens kept the Delian League together by force and used it to create an empire. Ask students what they think the future of NATO is likely to be.

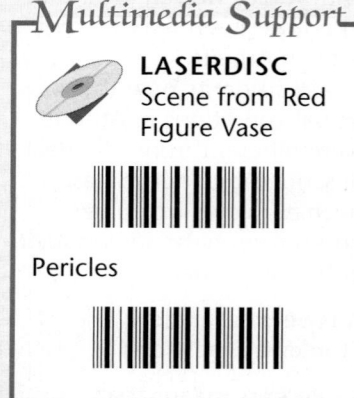

Multimedia Support

LASERDISC
Scene from Red Figure Vase

Pericles

CRITICAL THINKING

Ask students to identify differences between the democracy practiced in Athens and the representative democracy we have in the United States. *(In Athens, important decisions were made by all eligible citizens. In the U.S., we elect representatives who make the decisions on our behalf.)* Ask if the Athenian system could work today. *(It wouldn't work because there are too many people and too great an area.)*

A large body of city officials ran the government on a daily basis. Ten officials known as generals were the overall directors of policy. The generals could be reelected, making it possible for individual leaders to play an important political role. Pericles, for example, was elected to the generalship thirty times between 461 and 429 B.C. The Athenians, however, also devised the practice of **ostracism** to protect themselves against overly ambitious politicians. In this practice, members of the assembly could write on a broken pottery fragment (*ostrakon*) the name of a person they considered harmful to the city. A person who received at least six thousand votes was banned from the city for ten years.

Under Pericles, Athens became the leading center of Greek culture. The Persians had destroyed much of the city during the Persian Wars, but Pericles used the treasury money of the Delian League to set in motion a massive rebuilding program. New temples and statues soon made visible the greatness of Athens. Art, architecture, and philosophy flourished. Pericles broadly boasted that Athens had become the "school of Greece." However, the achievements of Athens alarmed the other Greek states, especially Sparta, and soon all Greece was confronted with a new war.

The Great Peloponnesian War and the Decline of the Greek States

During the forty years after the defeat of the Persians, the Greek world came to be divided into two major camps: Sparta and its supporters and the Athenian empire. Sparta and its allies feared the growing Athenian Empire. Furthermore, Athens and Sparta had built two very different kinds of societies, and neither state was able to tolerate the other's system. A series of disputes finally led to the outbreak of the Great Peloponnesian War in 431 B.C.

At the beginning of the war, both sides believed they had winning strategies. The Athenians planned to remain behind the protective walls of Athens while the overseas empire and the navy would keep them supplied. Pericles knew that the Spartans and their allies could beat the Athenians in open battles, which was the chief aim of the Spartan strategy. The Spartans and their allies surrounded Athens, hoping that the Athenians would send out their army to fight beyond the walls. However, Pericles was convinced that Athens was secure behind its walls, and the Athenians stayed put.

In the second year of the war, however, the plague broke out in the crowded city of Athens and killed over a third of the people. Pericles himself died the following year (429 B.C.), a severe loss to Athens. Despite the losses from the plague, the Athenians fought on in a struggle that dragged on for another twenty-seven years. A crushing blow came in 405 B.C., when the Athenian fleet was destroyed at Aegospotami (EE-guh-SPOT-uh-MEE) on the Hellespont. Within the next year, Athens was besieged, and the city surrendered. Its walls were torn down, the navy disbanded, and the Athenian Empire destroyed. The great war was finally over.

The Great Peloponnesian War weakened the major Greek states and certainly ruined any possibility of cooperation among them. The next seventy years of Greek history are a sorry tale of efforts by Sparta, Athens, and Thebes (a new Greek power) to dominate Greek affairs. In continuing their petty wars, the Greeks ignored the growing power of Macedonia to their north. As we shall see later, this oversight cost them their freedom.

Daily Life in Classical Athens

The polis was above all a male community. Only adult male citizens took part in public life. In Athens, this meant the exclusion of women, slaves, and foreign residents, or roughly 85 percent of the total population. There were probably 150,000 citizens in Athens at its height, of whom about 43,000 were adult males who exercised political power. One social group, the slaves, numbered around 100,000.

Slavery was common in the ancient world. Most people in Athens—except the very poor—owned at least one slave. The very wealthy might own large numbers, but those who did usually employed them in industry. Gangs of slaves worked in the silver mines, often under such pitiful conditions that many did not survive more than three years. Most often, slaves in

So What ??

If your students question the importance of the information on **the greatness of the Persian empire,** *tell them . . .*

The great Persian empire faced by the Greeks thousands of years ago was just the first of several great empires that developed and flourished in the region we today call Iran. In more recent years, the late Shah of Iran tried to recover the greatness of ancient Persia by building a great army, modernizing Iranian society, infusing technology into Iranian culture, and forcing Iranians to become more "Western" in culture and attitude. In the end, Iranians refused his call to contemporary greatness not because they didn't want it; they just didn't want western-style greatness. The Shi'ite theocracy that followed the Shah in power practiced a foreign diplo-

Multimedia Support

TRANSPARENCY
5–3, Male and
Female Dress.

Athens worked in the fields or in the home as cooks and maids. Some slaves were owned by the state and worked on public construction projects.

The Athenian economy was largely based on farming and trade. Athenians grew grains, vegetables, and fruit trees for local use. Grapes and olive trees were cultivated for wine and olive oil, which were used locally and also exported. The Athenians grazed sheep and goats for wool and milk products. Because of the number of people and the lack of fertile land, Athens had to import between 50 and 80 percent of its grain, a basic item in the Athenian diet. Trade was thus highly important to the Athenian economy. The building of

the port at Piraeus (pie-REE-us) and the Long Walls (a series of defensive walls four and one-half miles long connecting Athens and Piraeus) helped Athens become the leading trade center in the fifth-century Greek world.

Craftspeople, although few in number, were important to the economy. Athens was the chief producer of high-quality painted pottery in the fifth century. Through the use of slave labor, some products were made in factories. The shield factory of Lysias, for example, employed 120 slaves. Public works projects also provided jobs for Athenians. The building program of Pericles, paid for from the Delian League trea

▼ *This reconstruction of a farmhouse in the land south of Athens shows the simple, unadorned style typical of Greek housing. Why do you think the houses were so simply constructed compared to public buildings?*

macy that resulted in challenging both the U.S. and the U.S.S.R. at the same time. Few countries would have risked antagonizing both of these powers, but because of the history of great Persian empires, Iran's rulers may

have been more apt to think and act as though they were leading one of the world's great powers. Students should see that the development of the Persian empire does have an impact on their lives today.

REINFORCING VOCABULARY

Students should know that the *economy* refers to the system of producing and providing the goods and services people need in their lives. Trade is a process for obtaining goods that are needed, but which the society (or individual) does not have and cannot produce. Trade can be either cooperative—each party voluntarily exchanges items they have in excess for items they need— or coerced—one party imposes the conditions of trade on the other.

CLASS DISCUSSION

Among the many positive developments that have come to us from ancient Greece, two practices have caused us much difficulty and have been rejected— slavery and the servitude of women.

Ask students why we no longer tolerate slavery (*recognition of universal human rights*) and why women can now take an equal place in society (*men have no special attributes, such as strength, that are particularly valued or needed by our society, which women don't also have*).

LEARNING FROM VISUALS

Answer to the caption question: Religious monuments and public buildings were designed to honor the gods.

CLASS DISCUSSION

Students will probably not be timid about sharing their reactions to this primary source! But to prevent students from making prejudicial and unsupported generalizations, ask them to identify those statements from the reading that they believe are erroneous and then to refute those statements. For example, a student might argue that the statement "For he made the man's body and mind more capable of enduring cold and heat . . ." has been disproved by scientific evidence today. Women live longer than men and can, in fact, endure just as much as men with the same conditioning.

LEARNING FROM VISUALS

Answers to the caption question: Students should recognize the graceful position of the women, as well as the care the artist took to emphasize their long, slender bodies and beauty. At the same time, these women work in isolation at the loom.

Answers to Critical Thinking Questions

1. the servants and the indoor running of the household; she was also largely responsible for the care of the young children
2. Student answers will vary.
3. Student answers will vary. Many women now work outside the home and have careers; however, women are still responsible for a large share of household duties and childcare.

YOU ARE THERE

An Athenian Husband Explains His Wife's Duties

In fifth-century Athens, a woman's place was in the home. She had two major responsibilities: the bearing and raising of children and the care of the household. In his dialogue on estate management, the Greek writer Xenophon (ZEN-u-fun) relates the advice of an Athenian gentleman on how to train a wife:

Xenophon, On a Wife's Duties

[Ischomachus addresses his new wife.] For it seems to me, dear, that the gods have coupled together male and female, as they are called, chiefly in order that they may form a perfect partnership in mutual service. For, in the first place, that the various species of living creatures may not fail, they are joined in wedlock for the production of children. Secondly, offspring to support them in old age is provided by this union, to human beings, at any rate. Thirdly, human beings live not in the open air, like beasts, but obviously need shelter. Nevertheless, those who mean to win stores to fill the covered place, have need of someone to work at the open-air occupations; ploughing, sowing, planting and grazing are all such open-air employments; and these supply the needful food. . . . For he made the man's body and mind more capable of enduring cold and heat, and journeys and campaigns; and therefore imposed on him the outdoor tasks. To the woman, since he had made her body less capable of such endurance, I take it that the gods have assigned the indoor tasks. And knowing that he had created in the woman and had imposed on her the nourishment of the infants, he meted out to her a larger portion of affection for new-born babes than to the man. . . .

◀ *This vase portrays one of the primary duties of Greek women—to make clothes. Look closely at the vase. What does it reveal about Greek ideals of beauty and about women?*

Your duty will be to remain indoors and send out those servants whose work is outside, and supervise those who are to work indoors, and to receive the incomings, and distribute so much of them as must be spent, and watch over so much as is to be kept in store, and take care that the sum laid by for a year be not spent in a month. And when wool is brought to you, you must see that cloaks are made for those that want them. You must see too that the dry corn is in good condition for making food. One of the duties that fall to you, however, will perhaps seem rather thankless: you will have to see that any servant who is ill is cared for.

---

1. Over what areas of life did an Athenian wife have authority?

2. Do you think Ischomachus respected his wife? Why or why not?

3. How are the roles of men and women different in America now compared with their roles in ancient Greece? In what ways have roles remained the same over the centuries?

ENRICHMENT ACTIVITY

The values of courage and honor were important ideas in the stories of Homer. For the Greeks, and for subsequent generations of people throughout the world these values have defined genuine heroism. Ask students to list some of the famous people of today whom they consider to be heroic. Then tell them to be prepared to discuss why they think of these people as heroes. Also ask them to tell why these modern-day heroes would be heroes in ancient Greece, or why not. Allow time for class discussion.

sury, made possible the hiring of both skilled and unskilled laborers.

The family was an important institution in ancient Athens. It was composed of husband, wife, and children (a nuclear family), although other dependent relatives and slaves were regarded as part of the family. The family's primary social function was to produce new citizens.

Women were citizens who could take part in most religious festivals, but they were otherwise excluded from public life. They could not own property beyond personal items and always had a male guardian: if unmarried, a father; if married, a husband; if widowed, a son or male relative. An Athenian woman was expected to be a good wife. Her chief obligation was to bear children, especially male children who would preserve the family line. A wife was next expected to take care of her family and her house. She either did the household work herself or supervised the slaves who did the actual work (see "You Are There: An Athenian Husband Explains His Wife's Duties").

Women were strictly controlled. Because they were married at the age of fourteen or fifteen, they were taught about their responsibilities early. Although many managed to learn to read and play musical instruments, they were not provided any formal education. Women were expected to remain at home out of sight unless attending funerals or festivals. If they left the house, they had to have a companion. A woman did not work alone in public unless she was either poverty stricken or was not a citizen. Given this foundation, it is not surprising that the oppression of women continued to be a feature of Western civilization into the twentieth century.

❀ SECTION REVIEW ❀

1. **Locate:**
   (a) Marathon, (b) Thermopylae, (c) Salamis,
   (d) Delos, (e) Aegospotami

2. **Define:**
   (a) marathon, (b) ostracism

3. **Identify:**
   (a) Battle of Marathon, (b) Xerxes, (c) Delian League, (d) Great Peloponnesian War

4. **Recall:**
   (a) What is meant by the phrase, "The Age of Pericles"?
   (b) What role did each of the following play in the life of Athens: male citizens, women, slaves?

5. **Think Critically:** One historian has remarked that Athenian democracy was ultimately based on imperialism. Explain.

THE CULTURE OF CLASSICAL GREECE

Closely connected to every aspect of Greek life was religion. Greeks considered religion a necessity for the well-being of the state. Temples dedicated to a god or goddess were the major buildings in Greek cities.

Gods and Goddesses

The work of Homer gave an account of the gods that provided a structure to Greek religion. Over a period of time, most Greeks came to accept a common religion based on twelve chief gods and goddesses who were thought to live on Mount Olympus, the highest mountain in Greece. Among the twelve were Zeus (ZUUS), the chief god and father of the gods; Athena, goddess of wisdom and crafts; Apollo, god of the sun and poetry; Aphrodite (af-ruh-DITE-ee), goddess of love; and Poseidon (puh-SIDE-un), brother of Zeus and god of the seas and earthquakes.

Although the twelve Olympian gods and goddesses were common to all Greeks, each polis usually singled out one of the twelve Olympians as the guardian of its community. Athena was the patron goddess of Athens,

---

SPECIAL NEEDS: *Auditory*

Relate stories from Greek mythology to students who have difficulty with reading comprehension. There are several different ways from which you can choose to communicate the stories to your students. You could, for example, share the stories by preparing and delivering short summary readings; or, you could use video or audio tapes. After you have "told" the story, have students write, record, or display the staging of a scene or scenes. Have them share with the class, or each other, the stories they created about the various Greek gods or goddesses and their powers.

FOCUS

OBJECTIVES

After completing this section, students should be able to

1. state the purpose of an oracle
2. describe the roles played by the gods in the everyday lives of the Greeks
3. explain the relationship between religion and Greek drama
4. contrast the basic philosophies of the Sophists, Socrates, and Plato
5. identify the major Greek historians of this period

FOCUS ACTIVITY

Many cultures besides the Greeks believed that supernatural forces controlled or foretold events. The responses of the priestess at Delphi were interpreted by a priest, but even this answer was often ambiguous. This same approach is taken by astrologers and fortune tellers of today who read signs (motion of planets, palms, tea leaves) that are also subject to interpretation. Ask students to discuss reasons that people might have faith in such beliefs. Do they know people who believe in astrology or superstitions?

REINFORCING VOCABULARY

Make sure students understand the meaning of the word *ritual*. Today ritual is also used for any prescribed routine. Ask students to share personal rituals they may have (bedtime routines, good luck motions before important sports events, etc.)

136

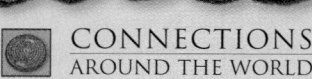

CONNECTIONS
AROUND THE WORLD

Rulers and Gods   All of the world's earliest civilizations believed that there was a close connection between rulers and gods. In Egypt, pharaohs were considered gods whose role was to maintain the order and harmony of the universe in their own kingdoms. In Mesopotamia, India, and China, rulers were thought to rule with divine assistance. Kings were often seen as rulers who derived their power from the gods and who were the agents or representatives of the gods. Many Romans certainly believed that their success in creating an empire was a visible sign of divine favor. As one Roman stated, "We have overcome all the nations of the world, because we have realized that the world is directed and governed by the gods."

The rulers' supposed connection to the divine also caused them to seek divine aid in the affairs of the world. This led to the art of divination, or an organized method to figure out the intentions of the gods. In Mesopotamian and Roman society, divination took the form of examining the livers of sacrificed animals or the flights of birds to determine the will of the gods. The Chinese used oracle (ORE-eh-cul) bones to receive advice from the gods. The Greeks divined the will of the gods by use of the oracle, a sacred shrine dedicated to a god or goddess who revealed the future. Underlying all of these practices was a belief in a supernatural universe; that is, a world in which divine forces were in charge and in which humans were dependent for their own well-being on those divine forces. It was not until the Scientific Revolution of the modern world that many people began to believe in a natural world that was not governed by spiritual forces.

for example. Each polis also had its own local gods, who remained important to the community as a whole.

Greek religion did not have a body of doctrine, nor did it focus on morality. It gave little or no hope of life after death for most people. The spirits of most people,

regardless of what people had done in life, went to a gloomy underworld ruled by the god Hades (HAY-deez). Because the Greeks wanted the gods to look favorably upon their activities, **ritual** became the most important element in their religion. Prayers were often combined with gifts to the gods based on the principle "I give so that you [the gods] will give [in return]." Ritual also meant sacrifices, whether of animals or food. Animals were burned on an altar in front of a temple or on a small altar in front of a home.

Festivals also developed as a way to honor the gods and goddesses. Some of these were important to all Greeks and were held at special locations, such as those dedicated to the worship of Zeus at Olympia or to Apollo at Delphi (DEL-fie). Numerous events were held in honor of the gods at the great festivals, including athletic games to which all Greeks were invited. The first such games were held at the Olympic festival in 776 B.C. (see "Sports and Contests: The Olympic Games of the Greeks").

The Greeks also had a great desire to know the will of the gods. To do so, they made use of the **oracle,** a sacred shrine dedicated to a god or goddess who revealed the future. The most famous was the oracle of Apollo at Delphi, located on the side of Mount Parnassus overlooking the Gulf of Corinth. At Delphi a priestess, thought to be inspired by Apollo, listened to questions. Her responses were then interpreted by priests and given in verse form to the person asking the questions. Representatives of states and individuals traveled to Delphi to consult the oracle of Apollo. States might inquire whether they should undertake a military expedition. Individuals might raise such questions as, "Heracleidas asks the god whether he will have offspring from the wife he has now."

Responses were often puzzling and could be interpreted in more than one way. Croesus (KREE-sus), king of Lydia (LID-ee-uh) in Asia Minor and known for his incredible wealth, sent messengers to the oracle at Delphi asking "whether he shall go to war with the Persians." The oracle replied that if Croesus attacked the Persians, he would destroy a mighty empire. Overjoyed to hear these words, Croesus made war on the Persians but was crushed by his enemy. A mighty empire—that of Croesus—was destroyed!

On Line with
WORLD HISTORY   *Internet Activity*

You may want to have your students visit the following URL, where they will find information and additional web site resources to enhance their study of this chapter.

Exploring Ancient World Cultures— Ancient Greece

http://eawc.evansville.edu/grpage. htm

This is an excellent source for information and links on Greek history which includes chronology, essays, resources, maps, and www sites.

Due to the ever-changing nature of the World Wide Web, see the West History web site, **http://history.swpco.com** for regular updates of the URLs in this text.

SPORTS AND CONTESTS

The Olympic Games of the Greeks

The Olympic games were the greatest of all the ancient Greek sports festivals. They were held at Olympia every four years beginning in 776 B.C. to honor Zeus, father of the gods. At first, the Olympic games consisted only of footraces. Later wrestling, boxing, javelin and discus throwing, long jumping, and chariot races were added. Competitions were always between individuals, not groups. Only young men took part until contests for boys were added in 632 B.C. Beginning in 472 B.C., the games were held over a five-day period.

In the Olympic games, there was only one winner in each event. His prize was simply a wreath made of olive leaves, considered sacred to Zeus. However, the Greeks looked upon winning athletes as great heroes and often rewarded them in other ways. The people of a city in Sicily welcomed home the winner of the two-hundred-meter race with a parade of three hundred chariots pulled by white horses. Some communities rewarded their winners with money and free rents for life.

The long-held belief that athletes in the Olympic games were amateurs is simply not true. City-states supported both athletes and their trainers. This practice freed them to train for long periods of time in the hope that they would bring back victories—and thus glory—to their communities. Larger city-states even bribed winners from other city-states to move to their communities and compete for them in the next games.

This famous statue, Discobolos, pays tribute to the athlete and to the ideals of sound mind in a sound body. This is a Roman copy; the original was made c. 450 B.C. What particular features of the statue show that it represents an ideal?

Olympic games were not without danger to the participants. Athletes competed in the nude, and rules were rather relaxed. Wrestlers, for example, were allowed to gouge eyes and even pick up their competitors and bring them down head first onto a hard surface. Boxers wrapped their hands and forearms with heavy leather thongs, making their blows damaging. Some athletes were killed during the games. Given the hatreds that often existed between city-states in ancient Greece, their deaths were not always accidental.

The Greek Olympic games came to an end in A.D. 393, when a Christian Roman emperor banned them as pagan exercises. Fifteen hundred years later, the games were revived through the efforts of a French baron, Pierre de Coubertin, who was inspired by the ideals of the ancient Greeks. In 1896, the first modern Olympic games were held in Athens, Greece.

1. Why were winning athletes so enthusiastically rewarded by their communities?

2. How were the Greek Olympics influenced by governments and politics?

CLASS DISCUSSION

You may wish to ask students to compare how the Olympic games described in this reading were similar to those held today, and in what ways they were different. Continue the discussion by asking students if they can think of ways the Olympic games today might be improved. For instance, are the games today too politicized? Is too much pressure placed on athletes to win, leading to abuse of drugs, etc.

Answers to Critical Thinking Questions

1. Victorious athletes were looked upon as great heroes who brought glory to their communities.
2. The governments of city-states supported athletes and their trainers, and even bribed athletes from other city-states to compete for them.

Answer to the caption question: Students should note the muscular physical fitness of the body and the alert tension in the figure.

ENRICHMENT ACTIVITY

Ask for student volunteers to take turns delivering in class the entire "funeral Oration," by Pericles. Ask the rest of the students to analyze the speech and point out the basic features of Athenian society, according to Pericles. You may want to write student responses on the chalkboard and use them to promote a class discussion on the comparison of the Athenian society to today's society.

Multimedia Support

LASERDISC
Ruins of Delphi Oracle

OUR ARTISTIC HERITAGE

OUR ARTISTIC HERITAGE

The Classical Ideals of Greek Art

The arts of the Western world have been largely dominated by the standards set by the Greeks of the classical period. Classical Greek art did not aim at experimentation for experiment's sake but was concerned with expressing eternally true ideals. The subject matter of this art was the human being, but presented as an object of great beauty. The classic style, based on the ideals of reason, moderation, balance, and harmony in all things, was meant to civilize the emotions.

In architecture the most important form was the temple dedicated to a god or goddess. At the center of Greek temples were walled rooms that housed both the statues of deities and treasuries in which gifts to the gods and goddesses were safeguarded. These central rooms were surrounded, however, by a screen of columns that made Greek temples open structures rather than closed ones. The columns were originally made of wood. In the fifth century B.C., marble began to be used.

The Greeks used different shapes and sizes in the columns of their temples. The Doric style consisted of thick, fluted columns with simple capitals (the decorated tops of the columns). The Greeks considered the Doric style dignified and masculine. The Ionic style was first developed in western Asia Minor. It consisted of slender columns with spiral-shaped capitals. The Greeks thought of the Ionic order as slender, elegant, and feminine in principle. Corinthian columns, with their more detailed capitals modeled after acanthus leaves, came later, near the end of the fifth century B.C.

Some of the finest examples of Greek classical architecture were built in fifth-century Athens. The most famous building, regarded as the greatest example of the classical Greek temple, was the Parthenon. It was built between 447 and 432 B.C.

▲ The Parthenon, which was built between 447 and 432 B.C., still stands on the Acropolis in Athens. Its classical beauty and symmetry symbolize the power and wealth of the Athenian Empire.

The master builders Ictinus and Callicrates directed the construction of this temple dedicated to Athena, the patron goddess of Athens. The Parthenon, an expression of Athenian enthusiasm, was also dedicated to the glory of Athens and the Athenians. The Parthenon shows the principles of classical architecture: the search for calmness, clarity, and freedom from unnecessary detail.

Greek sculpture also developed a classical style. Statues of the male nude, the favorite subject of Greek sculptors, showed relaxed attitudes. Their faces were self-assured, their bodies flexible and smooth muscled. The figures possessed natural features that made them lifelike. Greek sculptors did not seek to achieve realism, however, but rather a

(continued)

COMPARING TIME PERIODS

Ask students to name buildings in their own community that display features of Greek classical architecture. Or, suggest that they look through history books or photography books in the library that feature government buildings, especially those in Washington, D.C. They should point out the specific features, such as porticos and columns that reflect the Greek style of architecture.

CRITICAL THINKING

Ask students why all the statues from this period of Greek culture are of young, well-proportioned, and beautiful men and women. *(Greeks believed that art should reflect the perfect, ideal form. They did not believe in portraying life as it really was, rather only as the ideal form of life would be.)*

Multimedia Support

LASERDISC
Discobolos

Aesculapius, Greco-Roman God of Medicine

"Thinking Athena" Relief

So What ⁇

*If your students question the importance of the information on **the Greek models in architecture**, tell them . . .*

The Greeks set the classical ideals that future Western cultures tried to emulate. In architecture, the great temples and structures of the Acropolis became models for architects throughout Europe and its cultural descendants in the Americas. If you visit Washington D.C., you will see great monuments (such as the Lincoln and Jefferson memorials) in the Greek style. Even today, when architects and sculptors try to create something grand and "classic" in design, they turn to Greek models.

OUR ARTISTIC HERITAGE

The Classical Ideals of Greek Art, continued

Doric, Ionic, and Corinthian columns were mainstays of Greek temple architecture. The Doric, with plain capitals and no base, gave way to the more slender Ionic column, which had both base and decorated capital. The Corinthian column had leaf-shaped capitals and a graceful base. All three of these architectural columns are often seen today in public buildings throughout the United States.

standard of ideal beauty. Polyclitus (POL-i-KLITE-us), a fifth-century sculptor, wrote down systematic rules for proportions that he illustrated in a work known as the *Doryphoros*. The writing is now lost. However, his theory maintained that the use of ideal proportions, based on mathematical ratios found in nature, could produce an ideal human form, beautiful in its perfected features. This search for ideal beauty was the dominant feature of classical sculpture.

1. How did Greek architecture express eternally true ideals?

2. Describe the classic style of Greek sculpture.

3. Describe a building in your community that contains one or more Greek architectural design elements. If there is no such building, describe the feature(s) you were looking for, but could not find.

MORE ABOUT . . . Greek Art

It is relatively easy to distinguish a Hellenic (pre-Alexander the Great) from a Hellenistic (post-Alexander the Great) sculpture. Ask students to look at the facial characteristics and the body design. Do they show perfection, lack of emotion, and great mobility? *(Hellenic)* Do they show emotion, challenge, or Karma? *(Hellenistic)* As we get to the period c. 700 B.C., Greek sculpture looks Egyptian. The rigidity of form, the nonde-

script expressions—even the arms hanging straight down, with clenched fists, leave no doubt where the early Greek models came from: ancient Egypt. Earlier (see page 121, "More About Proto-Greek civilizations") we discussed the influence that Egypt may have had on Greek civilization; in terms of sculpture it is clear that the early Greeks learned their art from Egyptian masters.

Explain that Greek drama followed very strict rules. One rule limited all speaking parts to three actors. Another "rule" insisted that the actors use masks. Ask students to try to think of reasons why actors would want to wear masks. *(easier for males to assume female characters; easier for the actors to assume well-known characters)* You may wish to find examples of these stylized masks and have students reproduce these in class.

LEARNING FROM VISUALS

Theaters in Greece were built in naturally occurring amphitheaters. The action took place within a level circle called the *orchestra.* On one side of the orchestra the audience sat in naturally tiered seats set into the hillside. On the opposite side of the orchestra a facade (false front) was erected that served two purposes: to provide a changing room for the actors and to provide a backdrop for scenery. Using the visual on this page, ask students to point out the orchestra, the facade, the changing area, and the seating.

Answer to the caption question: Student answers will vary, but they should recognize that many outdoor theaters today are very similar to the Greek amphitheaters.

Greek Drama

Drama as we know it in Western culture was created by the Greeks. Plays were presented in outdoor theaters as part of a religious festival. The form of Greek plays remained rather stable. Three male actors who wore masks acted all the parts. A chorus (also male) spoke the important lines that explained what was going on. Action was very limited, because the emphasis was on the story and its meaning.

The first Greek dramas were tragedies, plays based on the suffering of a hero and usually ending in disaster. Aeschylus (ES-ku-lus) is the first tragedian whose plays are known to us. As was customary in Greek tragedy, his plots are simple. The entire drama focuses on a single tragic event and its meaning. Greek tragedies were supposed to be presented in a **trilogy** (a set of three plays) built around a common theme. The only complete trilogy we possess, called the *Oresteia,* was composed by Aeschylus. This set of three plays related the fate of Agamemnon, a hero in the Trojan War, and his family after he returns from the war. In the plays, evil acts are shown to breed evil acts and suffering. In the end, however, reason triumphs over the forces of evil.

▶ *Greeks were fond of theater and often attended outdoor performances in amphitheaters like this one at Epidarus. The acoustics were excellent, everyone could see the performers, and the settings were usually very dramatic. How does this amphitheater differ from ones in your city or state?*

Another great Athenian playwright was Sophocles (SOF-uh-kleez), whose most famous play was *Oedipus* (ED-uh-pus) *the King.* In this play, the oracle of Apollo foretells how a man (Oedipus) will kill his own father and marry his mother. Despite all attempts at prevention, the tragic events occur. Although it appears that Oedipus suffered the fate determined by the gods, Oedipus also accepts that he himself as a free man must bear responsibility for his actions: "It was Apollo, friends, Apollo, that brought this bitter bitterness, my sorrows to completion. But the hand that struck me was none but my own."[2]

The third outstanding Athenian tragedian, Euripides (yoo-RIP-uh-deez), tried to create more realistic characters. His plots became more complex and showed a greater interest in real-life situations. Euripides was controversial. He questioned traditional values. For example, he was critical of the widely accepted view that war was glorious. He portrayed war as brutal and barbaric and expressed deep compassion for the women and children who suffered as a result of it.

Greek tragedies dealt with universal themes still relevant to our day. They examined such problems as the nature of good and evil, the rights of the individual, the nature of divine forces, and the nature of human

MORE ABOUT . . . *The Transmission of Writing*

The language of the Greeks acquired a written medium when the Greeks came in contact with the Phoenicians, who had developed an alphabetic language. The Greeks added vowel sound to the Phoenician alphabet and made it their own. As Greek colonies settled on the west coast of the Italian peninsula, they took their language with them. It was there that the Greeks first came into contact with the Etrurians of central Italy. The Etrurians, who were masters of the Romans at the time, adopted the Greek alphabet and passed it on to the Romans, who used it to write their Latin language. As the Romans spread throughout Europe, they took their alphabet with them. Romance languages, springing from Latin, all use the Roman alphabet. Germanic tribes, who didn't have an beings. Over and over again, the tragic lesson was repeated: humans were free and yet could work only within limitations imposed by the gods. To strive to do the best may not always gain a person success in human terms but is nevertheless worthy of the endeavor. Greek pride in human accomplishment and independence was real. As the chorus chanted in Sophocles' *Antigone* (an-TIG-uh-NEE), "Is there anything more wonderful on earth, our marvelous planet, than the miracle of man?"[3]

Greek comedy developed later than tragedy. We first see comedies organized at the festival of Dionysus (DIE-uh-NIE-sus) in Athens in 488/487 B.C. The plays of Aristophanes (air-uh-STOF-uh-NEEZ) are examples of Greek comedy, which was used to attack both politicians and intellectuals. Comedy made a point. It jabbed at society and was intended to both entertain and provoke a reaction. In *The Clouds*, for example, Aristophanes portrayed the philosopher Socrates as the boss of a thought factory where people could learn deceitful ways to handle other people.

The Greek Love of Wisdom

Philosophy (an organized system of thought) is a Greek word that means "love of wisdom." Early Greek philosophers were concerned with the development of critical or rational thought about the nature of the universe and the place of divine forces in it. The Sophists (SAW-fists), however, were a group of teachers in fifth-century Athens who rejected such speculation as foolish. They argued that to understand the universe was simply beyond the reach of the human mind. It was more important for individuals to improve themselves. The Sophists sold their services as professional teachers to the young men of Greece, especially those of Athens. The Sophists stressed the importance of rhetoric (the art of persuasive speaking) in winning

▲ *Socrates, shown here, was a master of logic, and his reasoned, questioning method of teaching is still used today. Can you cite examples in your own education of the Socratic method?*

debates and swaying an audience, a skill that was especially valuable in democratic Athens. To the Sophists, there was no absolute right or wrong. What was right for one individual might be wrong for another. True wisdom consisted of being able to perceive and pursue one's own good. Because of these ideas, many people viewed the Sophists as harmful to society and especially dangerous to the values of young people.

One of the critics of the Sophists was Socrates. Because he left no writings, we know about him only from his pupils. Socrates was a stonemason, but his true love was philosophy. He taught a number of pupils, although not for pay, because he believed that the goal of education was only to improve the individual. He made use of a teaching method with his students that is still known by his name. The **Socratic method** of teaching uses a question-and-answer format to lead pupils to see things for themselves by using their own reason. Socrates believed that all real knowledge is already present within each person. Only critical examination is needed to call it forth. This is the real task of philosophy, because "the unexamined life is not worth living." This belief in the individual's ability to reason was an important contribution of the Greeks.

Socrates questioned authority, and this soon led him into trouble. Athens had had a tradition of free thought and inquiry, but defeat in the Peloponnesian War changed the Athenians. They no longer trusted open debate and soul-searching. Socrates was accused and convicted of corrupting the youth of Athens by teaching them to question and think for themselves. An Athenian jury sentenced him to death.

One of Socrates' students was Plato, considered by many the greatest philosopher of Western civilization. Unlike his master Socrates, who did not write down his thoughts, Plato wrote a great deal. He was fascinated with the question of reality. How do we

alphabet of their own, also adopted the Roman alphabet to write their language. As Europeans spread throughout the world in the sixteenth, seventeenth, and eighteenth centuries, the "Roman" alphabet spread throughout the world. All of this was due in part, to the Greek's borrowing of the Phoenician alphabet, and the adding of vowels!

ACTIVITY

Assign a group of students to research Plato's myth of the cave and present this story in skit form to the rest of the class.

CRITICAL THINKING

Ask students to contrast the basic difference between how Plato and Aristotle approached the study of philosophy. *(Plato believed in the idea of an eternal and perfect form for every object and that reality was a "shadow" of this perfect form. Aristotle did not believe in the existence of the perfect ideal, but rather observed all forms of life and analyzed and classified them.)*

REINFORCING VOCABULARY

The term *academy* originally meant a place where Greek philosophers met. It came from the name of the man who owned the estate where the first group of philosophers met. His name was Academus. Remind students that often words become generic that were once proper. Ask them to suggest other words that are now common nouns that used to be proper (for example, Kleenex or Xerox).

know what is real? To Plato, a higher world of eternal, unchanging ideal Forms has always existed. These ideal Forms constitute reality and can be apprehended only by a trained mind—which, of course, is the goal of philosophy. The objects that we perceive with our senses (a tree, for example) are simply reflections of the ideal Forms (treeness). They (the trees) are but shadows, whereas reality is found in the Form (treeness) itself.

Plato set out his ideas of government in his work entitled *The Republic.* Based on his experience in Athens, Plato had come to distrust the workings of democracy. It was obvious to him that individuals could not achieve a good life unless they lived in a just and rational state. Plato's search for the just state led him to construct an ideal state in which people were divided into three basic groups. At the top was an upper class of philosopher-kings: "Unless either philosophers become kings in their countries or those who are now called kings and rulers come to be sufficiently inspired with a genuine desire for wisdom; unless, that is to say, political power and philosophy meet together . . . there can be no rest from troubles . . . for states, nor for all mankind."[4] The second group in Plato's ideal state were those who showed courage. They would be the warriors who protected society. All the rest made up the masses, who were people driven not by wisdom or courage but by desire. They would be the producers of society—the artisans, tradespeople, and farmers. Contrary to common Greek custom, Plato also believed that men and women should have the same education and equal access to all positions.

Plato established a school at Athens known as the Academy. One of his pupils, who studied there for twenty years, was Aristotle (AIR-uh-STOT-ul). He did not accept Plato's theory of ideal Forms. He thought that by examining individual objects (trees), we can perceive their form (treeness). However, they do not exist as a separate higher world of reality beyond material things. They are a part of things themselves (we know what treeness is by examining trees). Aristotle's interests, then, lay in analyzing and classifying things based on observation and investigation. His interests were wide ranging. He wrote works on an enormous number of subjects, including ethics, logic, politics, poetry, astronomy, geology, biology, and physics. Until

the seventeenth century, science in the Western world remained largely based on Aristotle's ideas.

Like Plato, Aristotle wanted an effective form of government that would rationally direct human affairs. Unlike Plato, he did not seek an ideal state but tried to find the best form of government by analyzing existing governments. For his *Politics,* Aristotle looked at the constitutions of 158 states and found three good forms of government: monarchy, aristocracy, and constitutional government. Based on his examination, however, he warned that monarchy can easily turn into tyranny, aristocracy into oligarchy, and constitutional government into radical democracy or anarchy. He favored constitutional government as the best form for most people.

The Writing of History

History as we know it—as a systematic analysis of past events—was created in the Western world by the Greeks. Herodotus, an Ionian Greek from Asia Minor, was the author of *History of the Persian Wars,* a work commonly regarded as the first real history in Western civilization. The central theme of Herodotus's work is the conflict between the Greeks and the Persians, which he viewed as a struggle between Greek freedom and Persian despotism. Herodotus traveled widely and questioned many people for his information. He was a master storyteller and sometimes included very fanciful material, but he was also capable of taking a critical look at the materials he used.

Many historians today consider Thucydides (thoo-SID-uh-DEEZ) the greatest historian of the ancient world. Thucydides was an Athenian general who fought in the Great Peloponnesian War. A defeat in battle led the Athenian assembly to send him into exile. This gave him the opportunity to write his *History of the Peloponnesian War.*

Unlike Herodotus, Thucydides was not concerned with divine forces or gods as causal factors in history. He saw war and politics in purely human terms, as the activities of human beings. He examined the causes and course of the Peloponnesian War in a clear and objective fashion, placing much emphasis on the accu-

Multimedia Support

LASERDISC
Poseidon of Artemision

MORE ABOUT . . . *Dualism*

Dualism—the belief that the mind and the body are two different things—was proposed by Plato and accepted by most European philosophers and theologians for the next two thousand years. The "mind" acquired a mystical nature apart from the "body." As scientists discovered more and more about human anatomy, physiology, and behavior, it became apparent that the "mind" was indeed the "brain," very much a part of the body and of the material world, conforming to the laws of nature. Not mystical at all, the brain is nevertheless a tremendously complex part of our human apparatus.

racy of his facts. As he stated, "And with regard to my factual reporting of the events of the war I have made it a principle not to write down the first story that came my way, and not even to be guided by my own general impressions; either I was present myself at the events which I have described or else I heard of them from eye-witnesses whose reports I have checked with as much thoroughness as possible."5 Thucydides also provided remarkable insight into the human condition. He believed that the study of history is of great value in understanding the present.

 SECTION REVIEW

1. **Locate:**
   (*a*) Mount Olympus,   (*b*) Delphi,   (*c*) Gulf of Corinth

2. **Define:**
   (*a*) ritual,   (*b*) oracle,   (*c*) trilogy,
   (*d*) philosophy,   (*e*) Socratic method

3. **Identify:**
   (*a*) Sophocles,   (*b*) Plato,   (*c*) Aristotle,
   (*d*) Herodotus,   (*e*) Thucydides

4. **Recall:** Describe the major contributions of classical Greece in areas such as the arts, drama, philosophy, and the writing of history and their influence on future civilizations.

5. **Think Critically:** Why are the Greeks considered to be the cornerstone of the Western intellectual tradition?

THE SPREAD OF GREEK CIVILIZATION: ALEXANDER AND THE HELLENISTIC KINGDOMS

While the Greek city-states were busy fighting one another, to their north a powerful kingdom, Macedo-

nia, was emerging in its own right. Although a Greek-speaking people, the Macedonians were viewed as barbarians by their southern neighbors, the Greeks. The Macedonians were mostly rural folk organized in tribes, not city-states. Not until the end of the fifth century B.C. did Macedonia emerge as an important kingdom. After Philip II came to the throne in 359 B.C., he built a powerful army and turned Macedonia into the chief power of the Greek world. He was soon drawn into Greek affairs. A great admirer of Greek culture, he longed to unite all of Greece under Macedonia.

The Greeks had mixed reactions to Philip's growing strength. Some viewed Philip as a savior who would rescue the Greeks from themselves by uniting them. Many Athenians, however, portrayed Philip as a ruthless and treacherous man. Fear of Philip finally spurred the Athenians into action. Allied with a number of other Greek states, Athens fought the Macedonians at the Battle of Chaeronea (CARE-uh-NEE-uh), near Thebes (THEEBZ), in 338 B.C. The Macedonian army crushed the Greeks. Philip quickly gained control of all Greece, bringing an end to the freedom of the Greek city-states. He insisted that the Greek states form a league and then cooperate with him in a war against Persia. Before Philip could undertake his invasion of Asia, however, he was assassinated, leaving the task to his son Alexander.

Alexander the Great

Alexander was only twenty when he became king of Macedonia. Philip had carefully prepared his son for kingship. Alexander received his formal education from the Greek philosopher Aristotle, who served as his tutor. Like his father, Alexander held great admiration for Greek culture, especially as it was expressed in Athens. By taking Alexander along on military campaigns, Philip taught him the fundamentals of military leadership. After his father's assassination, Alexander moved quickly to fulfill his father's dream, the invasion of the Persian Empire. He was motivated by the desire for glory and empire, but also by the desire to avenge the Persian burning of Athens in 480 B.C.

MORE ABOUT . . . *Alexander the Great*

What kind of man was Alexander? While still an adolescent, his father offered him as a gift whatever horse he would select. Alexander noticed a large, powerful horse, full of spirit and energy. He was told that several people, including the king, had tried to tame it, all unsuccessfully. After a couple of failed trials, Alexander noticed that the animal seemed to react not only to the rider, but to the shadow of the rider, as well as to

his own shadow. Believing he had a solution, Alexander headed the horse straight towards the sun, so that no shadows would be visible, and jumped on the horse. The horse galloped at full speed until exhausted— Alexander was still on top. Alexander and his horse Bucephalus became inseparable. When the horse died, he mourned it as a fallen comrade.

FOCUS

OBJECTIVES

After completing this section, students should be able to

1. identify Philip of Macedonia and Alexander the Great
2. explain how Greek ideals were spread throughout the world
3. state the main reasons for the breakup of Alexander's empire
4. identify the major scientific and cultural developments in the Hellenistic era

Multimedia Support

LASERDISC

Animation: Map of the Conquests of Alexander the Great

FOCUS ACTIVITY

Alexander the Great was the first of a line of rulers who dreamed of conquering the world. Ask students to name others who followed. Ask students to discuss what motivations or characteristics these men might have shared, and whether they believe any of these men could have succeeded for long. Finally, ask them if they believe military conquest is still a possibility today, or has it been replaced by economic conquest and empires. Could Bill Gates be considered a modern-day Alexander the Great?

144

Map 5.3   The Conquests of Alexander the Great

There is no doubt that Alexander was taking a chance in attacking the Persian Empire. Although weakened in some respects, it was still a strong state. In the spring of 334 B.C., Alexander entered Asia Minor with an army of some 37,000 men (both Macedonians and Greeks). The cavalry, which would play an important role as a striking force, numbered about five thousand. By the next year, Alexander had freed the Ionian Greek cities of western Asia Minor from the Persians and had defeated a large Persian army at Issus. He then turned south, and by the winter of 332 B.C., Syria, Palestine, and Egypt were under his control. He built the first of a series of cities named after him (Alexandria) as the Greek capital of Egypt. It became, and remains today, one of the most important cities in both Egypt and the Mediterranean world.

In 331 B.C., Alexander turned east and fought the decisive battle with the Persians at Gaugamela, not far from Babylon. After his victory, Alexander took possession of the rest of the Persian Empire (see "You Are There: Alexander Destroys the Persian Palace at Persepolis"). However, he was not content to rest with the spoils of the Persian Empire.

Over the next three years Alexander moved east and northeast, as far as modern Pakistan. By the summer of 327 B.C., he had entered India, where he experienced a number of difficult campaigns. Weary of campaigning year after year, his soldiers refused to go further. Alexander agreed to return. He led his troops through southern Iran across the desert, where conditions were appalling. A blazing sun and lack of water led to thousands of deaths. At one point, when a group

STUDYING MAPS

The following questions will help you guide the students through their study of Map 5.3.

1. Calculate the approximate length of Alexander's empire east-to-west. (*3000 miles*)
2. Name the battle sites indicated on the map. (*Gaugamela, Issus, and Granicus River*)

3. How many continents did Alexander's army enter? Name them. (*three—Africa, Europe, and Asia*)
4. Alexander traveled as far east as what modern-day countries? (*Pakistan and India*)

TEACH

YOU ARE THERE

Alexander Destroys the Persian Palace at Persepolis

After Alexander's decisive victory at Gaugamela, he moved into Persia, where he captured the chief Persian cities. At Persepolis, he burned the Persian grand palace to the ground. The ancient historian Diodorus of Sicily, who lived in the first century B.C., gave the following account of the destruction:

◄ *This bust of Alexander the Great is a Roman copy of just the head of a Greek statue. In what ways does this statue embody classical Greek ideals?*

Diodorus of Sicily, *Library of History*

Alexander held games in honor of his victories. He performed costly sacrifices to the gods and entertained his friends bountifully. While they were feasting and the drinking was far advanced, as they began to be drunken a madness took possession of the minds of the intoxicated guests. At this point one of the women present, Thaïs by name and Athenian by origin, said that for Alexander it would be the finest of all his feats in Asia if he joined them in a triumphal procession, set fire to the palaces, and permitted women's hands in a minute to extinguish the famed accomplishments of the Persians. This was said to men who were still young and giddy with wine, and so, as would be expected someone shouted out to form the procession and light torches, and urged all to take vengeance for the destruction of the Greek temples [by the Persians during the Persian Wars]. Others took up the cry and said that this was a deed worthy of Alexander alone. . . .

Promptly many torches were gathered. Female musicians were present at the banquet, so the king led them all out for the procession to the sound of voices and flutes and pipes, Thaïs the courtesan leading the whole performance. She was the first, after the king, to hurl her blazing torch into the palace. As the others all did the same, immediately the entire palace area was consumed, so great was the conflagration. It was most remarkable that the impious act of Xerxes, king of the Persians, against the acropolis at Athens should have been repaid in kind after many years by one woman, a citizen of the land which had suffered it, and in sport.

1. How were women involved in the destruction of the palace?

2. Explain why the historian, Diodorus of Sicily, thought it "most remarkable that the impious act of Xerxes, king of the Persians, against the acropolis at Athens should have been repaid in kind after many years by one woman, a citizen of the land which had suffered it, and in sport."

YOU ARE THERE

CLASS DISCUSSION

Point out to students that although the event described here took place in 331 B.C., the account was not written until the first century B.C., at least 127 years after. Ask students whether the length of time between the event and the writing of the account is important to historians evaluating primary sources. Why or why not? How much can the details of the account be trusted with such a long time between the actual event and the record? What evidence does the author give for the motivation he assigns to the Greeks?

Answers to Critical Thinking Questions

1. A courtesan, Thaïs, suggested they set fire to the palace and led the procession of drunken men and female musicians, armed with blazing torches.

2. His use of the word remarkable is the same as saying the situation was ironic. The Greeks got their revenge for the burning of Athens in an instant when one woman at a victory party rallied the drunken guests and Alexander himself to set fire to the Persian palace, accompanied by music and song.

Answer to the caption question: Students should recognize the calm, symmetrical beauty of the face; the face is focused, looking directly forward.

On Line with WORLD HISTORY *Internet Activity*

You may want to have your students visit the following URL, where they will find information and additional web site resources to enhance their study of this chapter.

Argos

http://argos.evansville.edu/

Argos provides a limited area search engine of ancient and medieval Internet sources.

Due to the ever-changing nature of the World Wide Web, see the West History web site, **http://history.swpco.com** for regular updates of the URLs in this text.

CRITICAL THINKING

Ask students to evaluate how much Alexander's global view was responsible for his success while he was alive. What might have happened if his generals had also accepted this world view rather than relying only on the Greeks and Macedonians to form the ruling class?

REINFORCING VOCABULARY

Students might wonder about the origin of the term *Hellenistic.* Inform them that the ancient Greek name for the country of Greece was Hellas.

Multimedia Support

LASERDISC

The Greek Amphitheater (Video)

Alexander the Great and Pebble Portrait of Alexander

Ruins of Herat

of Alexander's soldiers found a little water, they scooped it up in a helmet and gave it to him. Then, according to one ancient Greek historian, Alexander, "in full view of his troops, poured the water on the ground. So extraordinary was the effect of this action that the water wasted by Alexander was as good as a drink for every man in the army."[6] Alexander returned to Babylon, where he planned more campaigns. However, in June 323 B.C., exhausted from wounds, fever, and probably too much alcohol, he died at the age of thirty-two.

What explains Alexander's extraordinary military success? No doubt, he was a great military leader—a master of strategy and tactics, fighting in every kind of terrain and facing every kind of opponent. Alexander was a brave and even reckless fighter who was quite willing to lead his men into battle and risk his own life. His example inspired his men to follow him into unknown lands and difficult situations. Alexander sought to imitate Achilles, the warrior-hero of Homer's *Iliad* who was an ideal still important in Greek culture. Alexander kept a copy of the *Iliad*—and a dagger—under his pillow.

Alexander truly created a new age, the **Hellenistic Era.** The word *Hellenistic* is derived from a Greek word meaning "to imitate Greeks." It is an appropriate way, then, to describe an age that saw the expansion of the Greek language and ideas to the non-Greek world of the Middle East and beyond. Alexander's destruction of the Persian monarchy created opportunities for Greek engineers, artists, merchants, administrators, and soldiers. Those who followed Alexander brought their Greek ways with them. As a result of Alexander's conquests, Greek language, art, architecture, and literature spread throughout the Middle East. The cities of the Hellenistic Age, many founded by Alexander and his successors, became centers for the spread of Greek culture.

Unlike many of the Greeks, however, Alexander held a global view of the world. He considered Persians and other non-Greeks to be the equal of Greeks. He envisioned a world in which mixed cultures would live together—under Alexander's control, of course. To this end he encouraged his generals to marry Persian princesses, and he married two himself. His global per-

spective was not shared by many of Alexander's Macedonian troops, who at times became suspicious of their general's broader views.

The World of the Hellenistic Kingdoms

The united empire that Alexander created by his conquests fell apart soon after his death as the most important Macedonian generals engaged in a struggle for power. By 300 B.C., any hope of unity was dead. Eventually four Hellenistic kingdoms emerged as the successors to Alexander: Macedonia, Syria and the east, the kingdom of Pergamum in western Asia Minor, and Egypt. As we shall see in Chapter 6, all were eventually conquered by the Romans.

Alexander the Great had planned to fuse Macedonians, Greeks, and easterners in his new empire by using Persians as officials and encouraging his soldiers to marry native women. The Hellenistic monarchs who succeeded him, however, relied only on Greeks and Macedonians to form the new ruling class. Even those easterners who did advance to important government posts had learned Greek (all government business was transacted in Greek). The Greek ruling class was determined to maintain its privileged position.

In his conquests, Alexander had created a series of new cities and military settlements. Hellenistic kings did likewise. The new population centers varied in size and importance. Military settlements were meant to maintain order and might consist of only a few hundred men. There were also new independent cities with thousands of people. Alexandria in Egypt was the largest city in the Mediterranean region by the first century B.C.

Hellenistic rulers encouraged a massive spread of Greek colonists to the Middle East. Greeks (and Macedonians) provided not only new recruits for the army but also a pool of civilian administrators and workers who contributed to economic development. Architects, engineers, dramatists, and actors were all in demand in the new Greek cities. Many Greeks and Macedonians were quick to see the advantages of moving to the new urban centers and gladly sought their fortunes in the Middle East. The Greek cities of the

MORE ABOUT . . . *Alexander the Great*

Students should remember that as a young boy, Alexander was tutored by the great philosopher, Aristotle. Because of this, Alexander had a great respect and love for philosophy and for philosophers. Students might enjoy hearing the story of how Alexander one day visited the cynic Diogenes (famous for looking for an honest man) as he was sitting beside a barrel enjoying the sun. The emperor asked the poor man if there was anything he could do for him—was there anything he desired. Diogenes replied, "Yes. You can stand to one side. You are blocking my sun." Alexander obliged him and was said to have learned something that day about riches and power.

Map 5.4   The World of the Hellenistic Monarchs

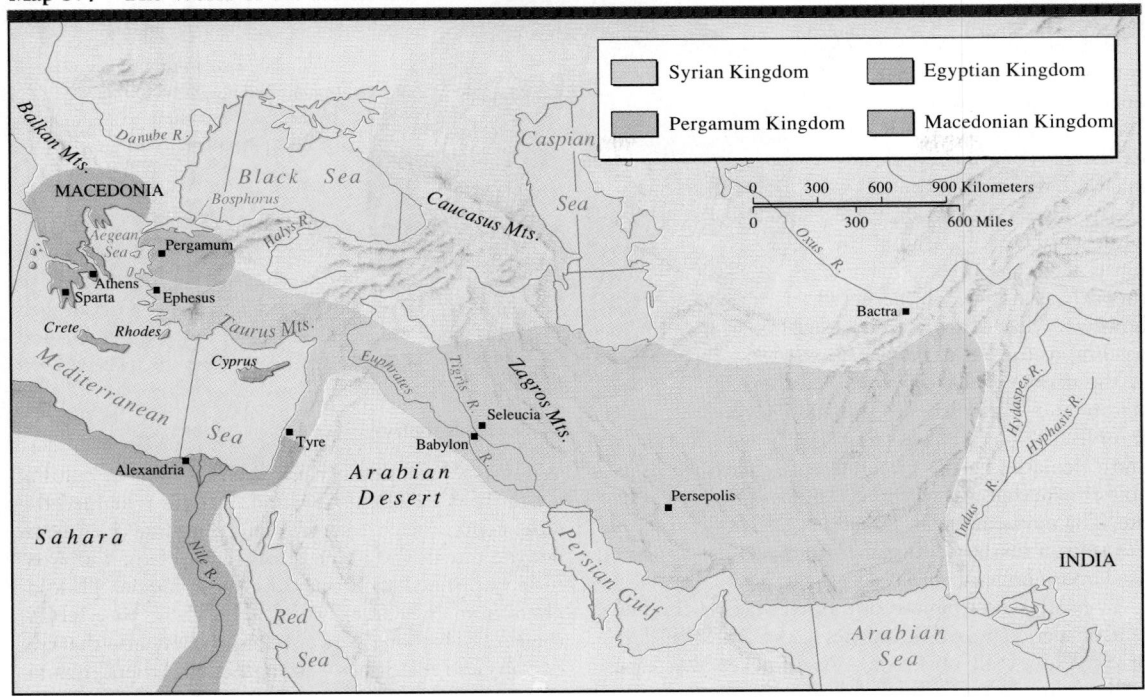

Hellenistic Era became the chief agents in the spread of Greek culture in the Middle East—as far, in fact, as modern Afghanistan and India.

Hellenistic Culture

The Hellenistic kingdoms encompassed vast territories and many different peoples. Only the spread of Greek culture throughout the Hellenistic world provided a sense of unity. The Hellenistic Era was a period of considerable cultural accomplishment in many areas—especially science and philosophy. These achievements occurred throughout the Hellenistic world, although certain centers, especially the great Hellenistic city of Alexandria, stood out. Alexandria became home to poets, writers, philosophers, and scientists—scholars of all kinds. The library there became the largest in ancient times, with over 500,000 scrolls.

The founding of new cities and the rebuilding of old ones presented many opportunities for Greek architects and sculptors. Hellenistic kings were very willing to spend their money to beautify the cities within their states. The buildings characteristic of the Greek homeland—baths, theaters, and temples—lined the streets of these cities.

Both Hellenistic kings and rich citizens patronized sculptors. Thousands of statues were erected in towns and cities all over the Hellenistic world. Hellenistic sculptors maintained the technical skill of the classical period, but they moved away from the idealism of fifth-century classicism to a more emotional and realistic art. This is especially evident in the numerous statues of old women, drunks, and little children at play.

STUDYING MAPS

The following questions will help you guide the students through their study of Map 5.4.

1. Which kingdom covered the largest territory? *(Syria)*
2. Which kingdom controlled the Nile River Valley? *(Egypt)*
3. Which kingdom occupied portions of present-day Turkey? *(Pergamum)*
4. Which kingdom contained the Fertile Crescent *(Syria)*
5. What large modern-day country is entirely within the ancient boundary of Syria? *(Students should answer Iran, but might also suggest Iraq or Syria.)*

COMPARING TIME PERIODS

Students learn on this page that Eratosthenes accurately predicted the circumference of the Earth. Ask students how many of them grew up thinking that before the time of Columbus people believed that the Earth was flat. The fact is, most educated people did believe that the Earth was round. Students might be able to suggest other "myths" that seem to persist in spite of the fact they are obviously false.

ACROSS THE CURRICULUM

Geography. Eratosthenes was the first geographer to combine mathematics with geography. It was his knowledge of angles and geometry that allowed him to measure the circumference of the Earth so successfully—even though this information was not accepted for many centuries—thanks in part to Ptolemy, the father of geography. Ptolemy rejected Eratosthenes' figures completely since they disagreed with his own miscalculated total.

CRITICAL THINKING

Ask students which of the philosophers that they studied earlier in this chapter also talked about "eternally true ideals" and "perfect forms." *(Socrates and Plato believed in the external and ideal perfect form.)*

Science

The Hellenistic Age witnessed considerable progress in the sciences. One astronomer—Aristarchus (AIR-uh-STAR-kus) of Samos (SA-mus)— developed the theory that the sun is at the center of the universe while Earth rotates around the sun in a circular orbit. This new theory was not widely accepted, however. Most scholars continued to cling to the belief that Earth was at the center of the universe. Another astronomer—Eratosthenes (UR-uh-TOSS-thu-NEEZ)—determined that Earth was round and calculated Earth's circumference at 24,675 miles, an estimate that was within 200 miles of the actual figure. The mathematician Euclid (YOO-klud) wrote the *Elements*, a textbook on plane geometry that has been used up to modern times.

By far the most famous of the scientists of the Hellenistic period was Archimedes (ARE-ku-MEE-deez) of Syracuse (SIR-uh-kyooz). Archimedes was especially important for his work on the geometry of spheres and cylinders, as well as for establishing the value of the mathematical constant pi (PIE). Archimedes was also a practical inventor. He may have devised the Archimedes' screw used to pump water out of mines and to lift irrigation water. During the Roman siege of his native city of Syracuse, he built a number of devices to beat off the attackers. According to an ancient Greek's account, the Romans became so frightened "that if they did but see a little rope or a piece of wood from the wall, instantly crying out, that there it was again, Archimedes was about to let fly some engine at them, they turned their backs and fled."[7]

Archimedes' achievements inspired a number of stories. Supposedly, he discovered specific gravity by observing the water he displaced in his bath. He then became so excited by his realization that he jumped out of the water and ran home naked, shouting, "Eureka" ("I have found it"). He is said to have emphasized the importance of levers by proclaiming to the king of

◄ *This plate humorously shows a war elephant and her baby. On the elephant's back is a battle-castle, thought to be an invention of the Greeks.*

Syracuse, "Give me a lever and a place to stand on and I will move the earth." The king was so impressed that he encouraged Archimedes to lower his sights and build defensive weapons instead.

Philosophy

Whereas Alexandria became the most famous cultural center of the Hellenistic world, Athens remained the chief center for philosophy. After the time of Alexander the Great, the home of Socrates, Plato, and Aristotle continued to attract the most famous philosophers from the Greek world, who chose to establish their schools there. New schools of thought—the Epicureans and the Stoics—strengthened Athens' reputation as a philosophical center.

Epicurus, the founder of a philosophy that came to be known as **Epicureanism,** established a school in Athens near the end of the fourth century B.C. Epicurus believed that human beings were free to follow self-interest as a basic motivating force. Happiness was the goal of life, and the means to achieve it was the pursuit of pleasure, the only true good. However, Epicurus did not speak of the pursuit of pleasure in a physical sense (which is what our word *epicurean* has come to mean). Pleasure was not satisfying one's desire in an active, gluttonous fashion. It was freedom from emotional turmoil, freedom from worry, the freedom that comes from a mind at rest. To achieve this kind of pleasure, people had to free themselves from public activity. However, they were not to give up all social life. To Epicurus, a life could only be complete when it was centered on the basic ideal of friendship.

Another school of thought was **Stoicism,** which became the most popular philosophy of the Hellenistic

COOPERATIVE LEARNING ACTIVITY

Ask students to work together to create charts in which they compare and contrast the basic teachings of the Stoics and the Epicureans. Under the headings for each of these philosophies students should write brief, descriptive phrases that obviously correspond to one or the other of these philosophies. Examples of phrases are "takes at least two vacations a year" and "endures discomfort or pain rather than going to the doctor." Bring the groups together to compare their charts. *(The Stoics believed that man should learn to accept everything that happens to him and not complain since it is destiny.) The Epicureans believed that the highest good was pleasure—freedom from emotional upheaval— and the greatest evil was pain.)*

world and later flourished in the Roman Empire as well. It was the product of a teacher named Zeno. Zeno came to Athens and began to teach in a building known as the Painted Portico (the *Stoa Poikile*—hence, the word *Stoicism*). Like Epicureanism, Stoicism was concerned with how people find happiness. However, the Stoics took a very different approach to the problem. To them, happiness, the supreme good, could be found only by living in harmony with the will of God, by which people gained inner peace. Life's problems could not disturb these people. They could bear whatever life offered (hence, our word *stoic*). Unlike Epicureans, Stoics did not believe in the need to separate oneself from the world and politics. Public service was regarded as noble. The real Stoic was a good citizen and could even be a good government official.

 SECTION REVIEW

1. **Locate:**
   (*a*) Macedonia,   (*b*) Issus,   (*c*) Alexandria,
   (*d*) Babylon

2. **Define:**
   (*a*) Hellenistic Era,   (*b*) Epicureanism,
   (*c*) Stoicism

3. **Identify:**
   (*a*) Philip II,   (*b*) Archimedes

4. **Recall:**
   (*a*) What were Epicureanism and Stoicism? Why did they have such a strong appeal to the intellectuals of the Hellenistic age?
   (*b*) Why can it be said that Philip II of Macedonia did for the Greek city-states what they were not able to do for themselves?

5. **Think Critically:** Why is Alexander the Great called "Great"? Do you think this title is justified? Why or why not?

Conclusion

The civilization of the ancient Greeks was the principal source of Western culture. Socrates, Plato, and Aristotle established the foundations of Western philosophy. Western literary forms are largely derived from Greek poetry and drama. The Greek notions of harmony, proportion, and beauty have remained the touchstones for all subsequent Western art and architecture. A rational method of inquiry, so important to modern science, was conceived in ancient Greece. Many political terms are Greek in origin. So are concepts of the rights and duties of citizenship, especially as they were conceived in Athens, the first great democracy the world had seen.

All of these achievements came from a group of small city-states in ancient Greece. However, there remains an element of tragedy about Greek civilization. For all of their brilliant accomplishments, the Greeks were unable to rise above the divisions and rivalries that caused them to fight one another and undermine their own civilization. Of course, their cultural contributions have outlived their political struggles.

Although the independent Greek city-states lost their freedom when they were conquered by the Macedonians, Greek culture did not die. Under the leadership of Alexander the Great, both Macedonians and Greeks invaded and conquered the Persian Empire. In the conquered lands, Greeks and non-Greeks formed a new society in what is known as the Hellenistic Era. As a result of this fusion, Greek culture survived. The culture took on a new form, however, as it mixed with the local cultures conquered by Alexander.

Notes

1. Xenophon, *Symposim*, trans. O. J. Todd (Cambridge, Mass., 1968), III, p. 5.
2. Sophocles, *Oedipus the King*, trans. David Grene (Chicago, 1959), pp. 68–69.
3. Sophocles, *Antigone*, trans. Don Taylor (London, 1986), p. 146.
4. Plato, *The Republic*, trans. F. M. Cornford (New York, 1945), pp. 178–179.
5. Thucydides, *The Peloponnesian War*, trans. Rex Warner (Harmondsworth, 1954), p. 24.
6. Arrian, *The Campaigns of Alexander*, trans. Aubrey de Sélincourt (New York, 1971), p. 339.
7. Plutarch, *Life of Marcellus*, trans. John Dryden (New York, n.d.), p. 378.

ASSESS

ALTERNATE ASSESSMENT

Ask students to do a major idea outline to assess their understandings of the key ideas in this section.

Answers to THE SECTION REVIEW

2. (a) age created by Alexander when Greek language and ideas expanded into the non-Greek world
   (b) philosophy that humans were free to follow self-interest
   (c) philosophy that people gained inner peace by living in harmony with the will of God and bearing whatever life offered
3. (a) Macedonian king
   (b) scientist known for work on geometry of spheres and cylinders, establishing value of pi, and practical inventions
4. (a) Epicurianism held that pursuit of happiness was goal of life; Stoicism emphasized public service, good citizenship; both schools of thought considered the nature of happiness and how to achieve it
   (b) city-states formed an alliance to fight the Macedonians, instead of each other
5. Answers will vary.

CLOSE

Have students work in pairs to complete an outline map that shows the path taken by Alexander on his conquests. Students should include major cities, rivers, and battles.

RETEACHING ACTIVITY

Students may have difficulty understanding the concept of the Socratic method. If so, you may wish to help them understand by telling them the following: Socrates believed that real understanding must come from within and cannot be imparted by someone else. Only understanding that comes from within can lead to true insight. Socrates, whose mother was a midwife, said that his art was like the art of the midwife. She does not herself give birth to the child, but she is there to help during its delivery. Similarly, Socrates saw his task as helping people to "give birth to correct insight." Ask students if they agree with Socrates' belief about true insight.

Answers to CHAPTER REVIEW 5

USING KEY TERMS

1. democracy, oligarchy
2. acropolis
3. hoplites
4. phalanx
5. polis
6. ostracism
7. oracle
8. Epicurianism
9. agora
10. photosophy
11. trilogy
12. archons
13. epic poems
14. Socratic method
15. Stoicism
16. Hellenistic Era
17. ritual
18. marathon

REVIEW ANSWERS

1. small in area; mountains created isolation and independence; sea promoted seafaring
2. 1400 to 1200 B.C.
3. the *Iliad* and the *Odyssey*
4. They became fiercely patriotic independents, eventually leading to the ruin of Greece.
5. Mainland Greece sent pottery, wine and olive oil to the colonies and received back from them grains, metals, fish, timber, and slaves.
6. ended rule of aristocrats; began opening doors that led to democracy
7. a desire to maintain control of Messenia
8. land ownership did not go to the poor; aristocrats stayed in power, leading to tyranny of Pisistratus
9. A traitor told Persians about a mountain path to outflank Spartans.
10. to be able to collect tribute from members
11. height of Athenian power and brilliance; massive rebuilding programs; Athenians became deeply attached to democratic principles
12. causes: disputes between

USING KEY TERMS

1. Some Greek city-states were committed to government by the many, a _____, while others ruled by _____, which means rule by the few.
2. The upper fortified part of a city, the _____, served as a place of refuge during an attack.
3. _____ were a heavily armed military order of infantrymen or foot soldiers.
4. Marching shoulder to shoulder in a rectangular formation was known as a _____.
5. The central focus of ancient Greek life was known as the _____.
6. Athenians devised the practice of _____ to protect themselves against overly ambitious politicians.
7. In order to know the will of the gods the Greeks consulted an _____, a sacred shrine dedicated to a god or goddess who revealed the future.
8. According to the Greek philosophy of _____, human beings are free to follow self-interest as a basic motivating force.
9. Greek citizens assembled in an open area called an _____, that also served as a market.
10. _____ is a Greek word that means "love of wisdom."
11. Greek tragedies were presented in a _____, a set of three plays.
12. Aristocrats in Athens controlled political life, in part, by a board of nine rulers, or _____.
13. Deeds of great heroes in Greece were told in _____.
14. The _____ uses a question and answer format that trains pupils to see things for themselves by using their own reasoning.
15. _____ was a school of thought which encouraged its followers to bear whatever life offered.
16. During the _____ Greek ideas and language spread to the non-Greek world of the Middle East and beyond.

150

17. The most important part of Greek religion was _____.
18. The 26-mile victory run to Athens by Pheidippides is the basis of our modern word for a footrace, the _____.

REVIEWING THE FACTS

1. How did geography play an important role in the development of Greek history?
2. When did the Mycenaean civilization reach its highest point?
3. What was the basic textbook for the education of Greek males?
4. What was the result of the Greek city-states' distrust of each other?
5. What types of goods were exchanged between the Greek city-states and their colonies?
6. What role did tyrants play in the development of Greek history?
7. What caused the Spartans to create a military state?
8. Why didn't Solon's reforms solve Athens' problems?
9. How did the Persians defeat the Spartan forces at Thermopylae?
10. Why did the Athenians refuse to abolish the Delian League?
11. What is significant about the Age of Pericles?
12. What were the causes and results of the Great Peloponnesian War?
13. How were slaves treated in Greek society?
14. How were Greek women kept under strict control?
15. Name five of the twelve chief gods that were worshiped in Ancient Greece.
16. What problems arose from the Greeks' attempts to foresee the future?
17. Describe the simple plot of most Greek tragedies.
18. According to Plato, which three groups composed the ideal state?

Sparta and Athenian empire; results: weakened Greek states; fostered continuing petty wars
13. excluded from public life; sometimes forced to work in very bad conditions (silver mines)
14. married young; taught responsibilities at early age; not formally educated; expected to remain at home
15. Zeus, Athena, Apollo, Aphrodite, Poseidon
16. They sometimes made major, unwise decisions based on oracle replies.
17. focuses on single tragic event and its meaning
18. philosopher kings, warriors, and the masses
19. constitutional government
20. Thucydides
21. They were mostly rural folk organized in tribes.

22. Aristotle
23. to imitate Greeks
24. relied on Greeks and Macedonians to form new ruling class; required all government business to be transacted in Greek language

THINKING CRITICALLY

1. Answers will vary.
2. It was important to be responsible to society, to family, and to one's self.
3. intentional isolation; warring attitude; avoided new/outside ideas; remained very focused and disciplined on their tasks
4. Because of the Delian League, Greek states were

CHAPTER 5 REVIEW

19. Which form of government did Aristotle favor?
20. Who is considered to be the greatest historian of the ancient world?
21. Why were the Macedonians considered to be barbarians by the Greeks?
22. Who was Alexander the Great's teacher?
23. What is the meaning of the term Hellenistic?
24. How did the Greek ruling class manage to maintain its position of privilege after 300 B.C.?

THINKING CRITICALLY

1. What is the meaning of life? How does your answer to this question compare with that of the Greeks?
2. What did the value of responsibility mean to the ancient Greeks?
3. How did the Spartans' distrust of the outside world shape their society?
4. How does the formation of the Delian League give proof to the saying that strength lies in unity?
5. Who had the better battle strategy—the Athenian defense, or the Spartan offense?
6. How did the Sophocles play, *Oedipus the King*, reinforce Greek assumptions about the nature of man?
7. How was Alexander the Great influenced by his father?
8. How did Alexander create the new age known as the Hellenistic Era?

APPLYING SOCIAL STUDIES SKILLS

1. **Geography:** On the map on page 144, trace the extent of Alexander the Great's empire, including the names of the modern nations.
2. **Government:** Choose a partner—one of you will take the role of Pericles, the other the role of Plato. List the major arguments each of you would make in describing the perfect government.

3. **Economics:** Why was trade so important to the Greek city-states? Why is trade so important today to countries like Japan?
4. **Art:** Draw examples of the Doric, Ionic, and Corinthian columns. List any buildings in your community with these columns.
5. **Religion:** What function did the role of sacrifice play in Greek religion?
6. **Sociology:** The Greeks used oracles to predict the future. What are some modern means of trying to find out the future? Are modern efforts any more valid than the oracles' methods?

MAKING TIME AND PLACE CONNECTIONS

1. Compare and contrast your education with that of ancient Greeks.
2. In search of security, Sparta turned its back on the outside world. Does an isolated modern state, such as North Korea, face the same problems? What are the problems?
3. Compare and contrast slavery in ancient Athens to slavery in the United States before the Civil War.
4. How would a person who enjoys modern-day action films feel about sitting through a Greek tragedy?
5. If you could choose a teacher from ancient Greece, who would you choose to study with—Socrates, Plato, or Aristotle? Why?

BECOMING AN HISTORIAN

Art as a Key to History: Carefully explain the reproductions of Greek vases on pages 122, 123, and 134.
1. What information about Greek life is provided by each of these scenes?
2. How do the scenes differ? Do they reflect daily life or special activities? What themes are central to each piece?

151

liberated from Persian control.
5. See page 132.
6. perplexing match-up between fate and responsibility for one's own actions in determining one's destiny
7. provided him with formal education from Aristotle; passed on love of Greek culture; taught him military leadership; gave him dream of invading Persian Empire
8. He created the opportunity for expansion of Greek language and Greek ideas to non-Greek world in Middle East and beyond.

APPLYING SOCIAL STUDIES SKILLS

1. See map, page 142. Names of modern nations may include Egypt, Israel, Jordan, Syria, Turkey, Iraq, Iran, Saudi Arabia, Afghanistan, Pakistan, and India.
2. Discussion will vary but should include knowledge of: Pericles's views (pages 130–132) and Plato's views (pages 139–140).
3. Some needed items could only be obtained through trade.
4. Drawings will vary. See pages 147–148. Community architecture will vary.
5. Greeks believed that by giving to the gods, the gods would give blessings back to them.

6. Answers will vary.

MAKING TIME AND PLACE CONNECTIONS

1. Answers will vary.
2. Answers will vary. Student responses may include: fear of others; fear of change; lack of progress and new ideas; oppression of citizens; lack of allies
3. Answers will vary. Responses may make mention of items on pages 132–133, as well as mention that slavery was common in both societies; that slaves were often treated poorly; and that slaves were owned in larger numbers by the wealthy.
4. Answers will vary.
5. Answers will vary.

BECOMING AN HISTORIAN

Art as a Key to History

1. The vases on pages 122 and 123 depict war scenes that portray the soldiers in an idealized, heroic light. The war elephant on page 146 is treated humorously, without any indication of the damage these elephants were expected to inflict. The ladies at the loom presents a scene of peace and tranquility. The contrast between the action of the men and the women is indicative of the different roles assigned to Greek men and women. Students should recognize that war and soldiers were idealized in Greek society and that women were praised for their domestic abilities.
2. The scenes of the soldiers are tense and convey action and strength. The women at the loom show a gentle beauty and harmony in the design. Students should recognize that the historical scene of Achilles and Hector is a specific, historical occasion, and the other scenes are more reflective of daily life. In each of the first three scenes, the people, or individuals, represent the central focus. In the last scene, the emphasis is on the mother and her baby.

PLANNING GUIDE

SECTION	KEY TOPICS	PRIMARY SOURCES	ASSESSMENT
1 The Roman Republic pages 153–160	◆ Geography's and location's impact on the history of Rome ◆ Peoples who influenced the development of early Rome ◆ The development of Roman government ◆ Rome's gaining control of the lands surrounding the Mediterranean	◆ Livy, *The Early History of Rome*, page 157	◆ Section Review, page 160 ◆ Section Quiz 6–1, TRB
2 The Fall of the Republic and the Emergence of the Empire pages 161–170	◆ The legacy of the Roman general Marius ◆ Circumstances that led to the collapse of the Roman Republic ◆ Problems of the early Roman Empire	◆ Plutarch, *Life of Caesar*, page 163–164	◆ Section Review, page 170 ◆ Section Quiz 6–2, TRB
3 Culture and Society in the Roman World pages 170–180	◆ Writers of the Roman Republic ◆ Roman contributions to architecture ◆ Structure of the Roman family ◆ Slavery during the Roman Republic ◆ Daily life in Rome	◆ Virgil, the *Aeneid*, page 170 ◆ Livy, *The History of Rome*, page 172 ◆ Plutarch, Cato's education of his son, page 176	◆ Section Review, page 180 ◆ Section Quiz 6–3, TRB
4 The Development of Christianity pages 181–186	◆ Roman state religion ◆ The affect of Roman rule on Judaism ◆ Basic beliefs of Christianity ◆ The attraction of Christianity	◆ The *Bible*, Matthew 5:1–11, 38–39, 6:19–21, 26, 31–33, pages 182–183	◆ Section Review, page 186 ◆ Section Quiz 6–4, TRB
5 The Decline and Fall of the Western Roman Empire pages 186–189	◆ Reforms during the times of Diocletian and Constantine ◆ Theories about the decline and fall of the Roman Empire		◆ Section Review, page 189 ◆ Section Quiz 6–5, TRB

THE WORLD OF THE ROMANS (600 B.C. TO A.D. 500)

REPRODUCIBLE ACTIVITIES

- Historical Maps
- Charts and Graphs
- Critical Thinking
- Cooperative Learning
- Vocabulary
- Guided Reading
- Reteaching
- Enrichment
- Performance Assessment
- Spanish Key Points and Chapter Summaries
- Spanish Vocabulary
- Spanish Guided Reading

MULTIMEDIA SUPPORT

 TRANSPARENCIES
- *World History* Color Transparency Package
- Fine Art Color Transparency Package

 VIDEO
- *World History* Video Library
- **CNN**® Annual Video Update

 LASERDISC
- *Sights and Sounds of History*

 AUDIO
- *Listening to Literature* audiotape (English and Spanish)
- *History of Music* CD

 SOFTWARE
- WESTEST™
- Student Review

 CD–ROM
- *The Journey of Civilization*
- *World History*

 INTERNET
- Internet Activities

 On Line with **WORLD HISTORY**

Access West's history web site at
http://history.swpco.com
You'll find activities and web sites related to specific topics and chapters in *World History: The Human Odyssey*. Also look for references to helpful web sites at appropriate places throughout this teacher edition.

LESSON PLANNING

You will find detailed daily lesson plans for both traditional class scheduling and **block scheduling** in your Teacher Resource Box.

 Not Enough Time?

If you do not have the four or five days recommended to teach this chapter, you may want to focus on the following sections and activities:

- Have students skim the chapter to answer the "Questions to Guide Your Reading on page 153. Discuss their answers, then read the conclusion on page 189.
- Do a more in depth reading of pages 161–169, 174–176, and 184–186. Activities on pages 168, 173, and 189 will help pull together major themes from the chapter.

THE WORLD OF THE ROMANS

(600 B.C. TO A.D. 500)

6

Early Roman history is filled with legendary stories that tell of the heroes who made Rome great. One of the best known is the story of Horatius (hu-RAY-shee-us) at the bridge. Threatened by attack from the neighboring Etruscans, Roman farmers abandoned their fields and moved into the city of Rome, protected by the city's walls. One weak point in the Roman defense was a wooden bridge over the Tiber River. On the day of the Etruscan attack, Horatius was on guard at the bridge. A sudden attack by the Etruscans caused many Roman troops to throw down their weapons and run. Horatius acted promptly, urging them to make a stand at the bridge in order to protect Rome. As a last resort, he challenged the Roman troops to destroy the bridge while he made a stand at the outer end to give them more time. At first, the Etruscans held back, astonished at the sight of a single defender. Soon, however, they threw their spears at the lone figure who barred their way. Horatius caught the spears on his shield and held his ground. The Etruscans advanced on foot, ready to overwhelm the sole figure. However, the Roman soldiers had used the extra time to bring down the bridge. When Horatius heard the sound of the bridge crashing into the river behind him, he dove, fully armed, into the water and swam, despite the arrows that fell around him. He safely reached the other side. Rome had been saved by the courageous act of a Roman who knew his duty and was determined to carry it out.

Courage, duty, determination—these were common words to many Romans, who believed that it was their mission to rule nations and peoples. Whereas the Greeks had excelled in philosophy and the arts, the Romans were practical people. Their strength lay in government, law, and engineering. They knew how to govern people, make laws, and build the roads that took them to the ends of the known world. Throughout their empire, they carried their political institutions, their law, their building skills, and their Latin language. Even after the Romans were gone, those same gifts continued to play an important role in the civilizations that came after.

◄ *This bronze figure of a legionnaire shows him in full battle dress at the height of the Roman Empire during the second century A.D. Here, his armor is constructed of metal bands that overlap each other. Roman legionnaires were both courageous and resolute in their duty. What differences are immediately visible between Greek hoplite forces and Roman legionnaires?*

ADDITIONAL RESOURCES

THE BEGINNINGS OF CIVILIZATION

	THE ROMANS
	600 B.C. A.D. 500
3500 B.C.	A.D. 500

QUESTIONS TO GUIDE YOUR READING

1. What impact did geography have on the history of Rome?

2. How did the Roman Republic gain control of the lands of the Mediterranean?

3. Why and how did the Roman Republic collapse?

4. What were the chief political and economic features of the Roman Empire during the first two centuries of its existence?

5. What were the chief features of Roman culture and society?

6. What similarities and differences existed between the Greeks and the Romans?

7. How did Christianity develop, and why did it triumph?

8. What problems led to the decline and fall of the Western Roman Empire?

OUTLINE

THE ROMAN REPUBLIC

In the first millenium B.C., a group of Latin-speaking Indo-European people built a small community on a plain called Latium (LAY-shee-um) on the Italian peninsula. This community, called Rome, was merely one of many Latin-speaking communities in Latium. The Latin speakers, in turn, made up only some of the many peoples in Italy. Roman history is the story of the Romans' conquest of the plain of Latium, then of Italy, and finally of the entire Mediterranean world. Why were the Romans able to do this? Scholars do not really know all the answers. The Romans made the right decisions at the right time. That is, the Romans were a people who had a high degree of political wisdom.

The Land and Peoples of Italy

Italy is a peninsula extending about 750 miles from north to south. It is not very wide, however, averaging about 120 miles across. The Apennine Mountains form a ridge from north to south down the middle of Italy that divides west from east. Italy has some fairly large

153

Answers to QUESTIONS TO GUIDE YOUR READING

1. adequate farmland for population; way to the sea; easily defended; natural crossing point of traffic and trade (page 154)

2. See page 160.

3. growing inequality between Senate and Roman people led to unrest; new military system led to civil war; Caesar defeated Roman government in 47 B.C. (pages 161–163)

4. corrupt emperors during first century (page 166)

5. Greek influence on literature (pages 170–179)

6. differences: structure of family and education of children; similarities: literature, architecture (pages 170–179)

7. See page 185.

8. wars; plagues; economic decline; failure of reforms by Diocletian and Constantine; weakening of armies (pages 186–188)

OBJECTIVES

After completing this section, students should be able to

1. explain the impact geography and location had on the history of Rome
2. tell what peoples influenced the development of early Rome
3. describe the development of Roman government
4. explain how Rome gained control of the lands surrounding the Mediterranean

FOCUS ACTIVITY

Have your class look at the map on page 159. Point out the peninsula that contains Italy. Have students study the location of Italy with respect to the rest of the Mediterranean countries. Then have students brainstorm advantages and disadvantages to Italy's being on a peninsula. You might list students' answers on the board and have them decide whether the advantages outweigh the disadvantages or vice versa.

TEACH

LEARNING FROM VISUALS

Answer to the caption question: Greece and Italy are both peninsular, Mediterranean countries with mountains and valleys. The mountain ranges in Greece are steeper, and the water barriers between islands present stronger physical barriers than exist in Italy.

fertile plains ideal for farming. Most important are the Po River valley in the north; the plain of Latium, on which Rome was located; and Campania to the south of Latium. To the east of the Italian peninsula is the Adriatic Sea. To the west is the Tyrrhenian (tuh-REEN-ee-un) Sea, with the nearby large islands of Corsica and Sardinia (sar-DIN-ee-uh). Sicily lies just west of the toe of the boot-shaped Italian peninsula.

Geography had an impact on Roman history. The Apennines, less rugged than the mountain ranges of Greece, did not divide the peninsula into many small, isolated communities. Italy also had more land for farming than did Greece, enabling it to support a large population. Rome's location was favorable from a geographical point of view. Located eighteen miles inland on the Tiber River, Rome had a way to the sea. However, it was far enough inland to be safe from pirates. Built on seven hills, it was easily defended. Situated where the Tiber could be easily forded, Rome became a natural crossing point for north-south traffic in western Italy. All in all, Rome had a good central location in Italy from which to expand.

Moreover, the Italian peninsula juts into the Mediterranean, making it an important crossroads between the western and eastern Mediterranean. Once Rome had unified Italy, it was easy to become involved in Mediterranean affairs. After the Romans had conquered their Mediterranean empire, governing it was made easier by Italy's central location.

We know little about the Indo-European peoples who moved into Italy during the second half of the second millennium B.C. By the first millennium B.C., other peoples had also settled in Italy—the two most notable being the Greeks and the Etruscans. The Greeks came to Italy in large numbers during the age of Greek colonization (750 to 550 B.C.; see Chapter 5). They settled in southern Italy and then slowly moved around the coast and up the peninsula. The eastern two-thirds of Sicily was also occupied by the Greeks. The Greeks had much influence on Rome. They cultivated the olive and the vine, passed on their alphabet, and gave the Romans artistic and cultural models through their sculpture, architecture, and literature.

The early development of Rome, however, was influenced most by the Etruscans. They were located north of Rome in Etruria. After 650 B.C., they expanded into north-central Italy and came to control Rome and most of Latium. The Etruscans made an impact on Roman civilization, finding Rome a village but leaving it a city. Etruscan dress—the toga and short cloak—was adopted by the Romans. The organization of the Roman army also was borrowed from the Etruscans.

▶ Italy is renowned for its rich, fertile valleys ringed by mountains, as shown here in this photo of the Apennines. How is this landscape similar to and different from that of Greece?

RECOMMENDED READING

General accounts of Rome's expansion in the Mediterranean world are provided by R. M. Errington, *The Dawn of Empire: Rome's Rise to World Power* (Ithaca, N.Y., 1971); and J. Heurgon, *The Rise of Rome to 264 B.C.*, trans. J. Willis (Berkeley, 1973). On Carthage, see B. H. Warmington, *Carthage,* rev. ed. (London, 1969) and the detailed study by J. Lazenby, *Hannibal's War: A Military History of the Second Punic War* (Warminster, 1978). Especially important works on Roman expansion and imperialism include W. V. Harris, *War and Imperialism in Republican Rome* (Oxford, 1979); and *Roman Imperialism in the Late Republic* (Oxford, 1968).

The Expansion of the Roman Republic

According to Roman legend, Rome was founded by the twin brothers Romulus and Remus in 753 B.C. Archae-ologists have found that by the eighth century B.C. there was a settlement consisting of huts on the tops of Rome's hills. The early Romans, who were herders and farmers, spoke Latin. Like Greek, Latin belongs to the

Map 6.1   Ancient Italy and the City of Rome

ACTIVITY

1. Have students prepare a historical map showing the expansion of the Latin tribe throughout Italy.
2. Using this map as a starting point, have students draw a historical map of the Roman conquest of the Mediterranean area, to c. 100 B.C.

Multimedia Support

LASERDISC
Details from Gundestru Cauldron

Gold Tablets Showing Etruscan and Phoenician Alphabet

Etruscan Sea Scene, Tomb of 6th Century B.C.

The Wolf, Romulus and Remus

Multimedia Support

TRANSPARENCY
Transparency 6–1, Map 6.1

Transparency 6–2, Map 6.2

STUDYING MAPS

The inset in the upper right corner of Map 6.1 shows the ancient city of Rome. Your students might be interested in some of the following facts about ancient Rome.

The Via Appia (Appian Way) was the main route from Rome to Greece. Its length was more than 350 miles (560 km).

The Forum was the corporate and admin-istrative headquarters of Rome. Many build-ings such as the Basilica Julia, the temple of

Divus Julius, and the Rostrum were located in the Forum.

The Capitoline Temple was located on the Capitoline Hill, which was one of the Seven Hills of Rome. The Servian Wall (Wall of Servius) was constructed to surround the city and keep out marauding enemies. Fitted with double gates and towers, it was con-structed during the time of Servius Tullius (578–534 B.C.).

ACROSS THE CURRICULUM

Have students read "You Are There: Cincinnatus Saves Rome" on page 157. Discuss how Livy, the author, brought out the popular Roman virtues of duty, courage, and discipline. Have students choose a virtue, one of those listed here, or another one, and write a modern-day or historical story, which shows that virtue in action. Allow volunteers to share their stories with the rest of the class.

LEARNING FROM VISUALS

This sculpture of an Etruscan couple shows the relative equality enjoyed by Etruscan women. In Roman homes, the men reclined during meals while the women sat in chairs. Roman women did offer advice to their husbands and were in charge of running the household.

Multimedia Support

LASERDISC

Hellenistic Dish of Pyrrhus' Elephants

Companion Warriors (detail of a 4th century B.C. fresco)

LEARNING FROM VISUALS

Answer to the caption question: (photo on page 157) The scene is pastoral. Discuss why this ceremony did not take place in a public building with an audience.

156

Indo-European family of languages (see the table in Chapter 2). Roman tradition also held that early Rome (753 to 509 B.C.) had been under the control of seven kings and that two of the last three had been Etruscans. What historians know for certain is that Rome did fall under the influence of the Etruscans for about a hundred years during this time. The Etruscans were responsible for a building program that left Rome a city. In 509 B.C., when the Romans overthrew the last Etruscan king and established a republic, a new Rome had emerged.

At the beginning of the republic, Rome was surrounded by enemies. For the next two hundred years the city was engaged in almost continuous warfare. Later Romans believed that what made their early ancestors successful in these struggles was their sense of duty, courage, and discipline. The Roman historian Livy, writing in the first century B.C., provided a number of stories to teach Romans the virtues that had made Rome great. His account of Cincinnatus, a simple farmer who was chosen as a temporary ruler to save Rome from attack, is one such example (see "You Are There: Cincinnatus Saves Rome").

▼ *This sculpture, which dates from 550 B.C., shows an upper-class Etruscan man and his wife reclining on a couch. The Etruscans played a major role in the development of Rome, particularly in sports, religion, and the military.*

By 340 B.C., Rome had crushed the Latin states in Latium. During the next fifty years, the Romans waged a fierce struggle with the Samnites, a hill people from the central Apennines, some of whom had settled south of Rome. Rome was again victorious. The conquest of the Samnites gave the Romans control over a large part of Italy and brought them into direct contact with the Greek communities of southern Italy. Soon the Romans were at war with these Greek cities and by 267 B.C. had completed their conquest of southern Italy. After defeating the remaining Etruscan states to the north in the next three years, Rome had conquered virtually all of Italy.

To rule Italy, the Romans devised the Roman Confederation. Under this system, Rome allowed some peoples—especially the Latins—to have full Roman citizenship. Most of the remaining communities were made allies. They remained free to run their own local affairs but were required to provide soldiers for Rome. Moreover, the Romans made it clear that loyal allies could improve their status and even have hope of becoming Roman citizens. Thus, the Romans made the conquered peoples feel they had a real stake in Rome's success.

How can we explain Rome's success? First of all, the Romans were good diplomats. They were firm, and even cruel, when necessary. Rebellions were crushed without mercy. The Romans were also shrewd in extending their citizenship and allowing states to run their own internal affairs. They were not only accomplished soldiers but also persistent ones. The loss of an army or a fleet did not cause them to quit but instead spurred them on to build new armies and new fleets. Finally, the Romans were very practical. As they conquered, the Romans built colonies—fortified towns—throughout Italy. By building roads to these towns and thus connecting them, the Romans could move troops quickly throughout their conquered territory. This enabled them to rule effectively and efficiently.

The Roman State

In law and politics, as in conquest, the Romans were practical. They did not try to build an ideal govern-

---

So What ??

*If your students question the importance of the information on **language roots** tell them . . .*

The term "Latin" today, applied to a person, means someone with roots in Latin America. The Spaniards and Portuguese who colonized most of South and Central America naturally introduced their languages to the region. Spanish and Portuguese are "Latin" languages because they derive primarily from the Latin of Ancient Rome. Other languages derived from Latin are French, Italian, and Romanian. The correct term to identify languages derived from Latin is "romance" languages. In contrast, English, German, and the Scandinavian languages are Germanic, since they developed from the German-speaking tribes living north and east of the Roman Empire. Over the years, however, many Latin terms have found their way into English as well.

YOU ARE THERE

Cincinnatus Saves Rome

There is perhaps no better account of how the virtues of duty and simplicity enabled good Roman citizens to succeed during the difficulties of the fifth century B.C. than Livy's account of Cincinnatus. In this account, Cincinnatus did his duty—defeated the enemy—and returned to his simple farm in fifteen days.

Livy, *The Early History of Rome*

The city was thrown into a state of turmoil, and the general alarm was as great as if Rome herself were surrounded. The situation evidently called for a dictator [the position of dictator was a temporary one used only in emergencies], and, with no dissenting voice, Lucius Quinctius Cincinnatus was named for the post.

Now I would solicit the particular attention of those numerous people who imagine that money is everything in this world, and that rank and ability are inseparable from wealth: let them observe that Cincinnatus, the one man in whom Rome reposed all her hope of survival, was at that moment work- ing a little three-acre farm . . . west of the Tiber. A delegation from the city found him at work on his land—digging a ditch, maybe, or ploughing. Greetings were exchanged, and he was asked— with a prayer for divine blessing on himself and his country—to put on his toga and hear the Sen- ate's instructions. This naturally surprised him, and, asking if all were well, he told his wife to run to their cottage and fetch his toga. The toga was brought, and wiping the grimy sweat from his hands and face he put it on; at once the envoys from the city saluted him, with congratulations, as Dictator, invited him to enter Rome, and informed him of the terrible danger of the enemy's army. . . .

▲ *Lucius Quinctius Cincinnatus, Roman statesman and dictator, is shown here receiving his dictatorship. What fea- tures in the picture are at odds with the serious nature of this occasion?*

[Cincinnatus proceeded to raise an army, marched out, and defeated the enemy.]

In Rome the Senate was convened, and a decree was passed inviting Cincinnatus to enter in triumph with his troops. The chariot he rode in was preceded by the enemy commanders and the military flags, and followed by his army loaded with its spoils. . . . Cincinnatus finally resigned after holding office for fifteen days, having origi- nally accepted it for a period of six months. He returned to his farm.

1. Describe the character traits of Cincinnatus.

2. What lesson(s) did Livy hope to teach his readers?

3. Compare the position of dictator in this account with its present-day connotation.

MAKING HISTORY RELEVANT

Cincinnatus was chosen dictator of Rome to defend the city against the Aequi. During this time in Rome, a dictator could be chosen to rule temporarily. The consuls would resign from their posi- tions and the dictator would have unlimited power for up to six months. Not all of the people liked this idea, how- ever. As Cincinnatus was escorted to begin his reign the street was lined with spec- tators, many of whom were common folk. The common folk were not pleased to see the dictator because they felt his power was excessive and they dreaded the ways in which he might use it.

Ask students to discuss how our government is orga- nized so that one person cannot control the country.

Answers to Critical Thinking Questions

1. He was a hard-working farmer, who led a simple life. He accepted his responsibilities, dutifully and humbly and returned to his home when his job was done.

2. The story of Cincinnatus contradicts the view "that money is everything in this world, and that rank and ability are inseparable from wealth."

3. The role of dictator assumed by Cincinnatus was a temporary leader- ship position to which one was appointed in a time of national emer- gency. Students may compare this to a dictator today who takes absolute control of his country and is an oppressive leader.

MORE ABOUT . . . *Roman Imperialism*

The word "imperialism" is used to denote the use of power by one nation to expand at the expense of another. The Romans were imperialistic since their beginnings in central Italy. Conquering first other Latin tribes, then the Gauls and Southern Italy, across the sea to Sicily, Iberia, Macedonia, Greece, Asia Minor, and North Africa. Having surrounded the Mediterranean Sea, they began to call it *Mare Nostrum*—"our sea"! In the end, the imperialistic drive to expand became one of the key factors in the fall of Rome, since the frontiers became too spread out. When Rome could no longer effectively police its own frontiers, Germanic tribes filtered in. Without the communications and transporta- tion technology we have today, Roman terri- tory became too unwieldy for effective administration. Imperialism, in the end, weakened the life of Rome.

CLASS DISCUSSION

Divide the class into two groups, the plebeians and the patricians. Have the groups informally debate whether plebeians should be allowed political equality with the patricians.

COMPARING TIME PERIODS

Ask students what incidents in United States history they are reminded of by the account of the plebeians gaining political equality. *(Answers will likely include Amendment 15—The Right to Vote for all men regardless of race, and Amendment 19—Women's Right to Vote.)*

Multimedia Support

TRANSPARENCY
6–3, Government of the Roman Republic

CRITICAL THINKING

In 451 B.C. the Twelve Tablets, which contained Rome's laws, were constructed. They were made public so that all people had access to them. As the only ones with access to the laws before the Twelve Tablets, magistrates had held arbitrary power, which the people wanted to restrict.

Have students research different codes of law that have been used in the past. (The Code of Hammurabi, the Ten Commandments, the Twelve Tablets, and Napoleon's Civil Code are possible research topics). Have students compare and contrast the different types of laws as well as the content of the laws.

Government of the Roman Republic

Government Officials

- ▲ **Consuls.** Two elected for one year; executive officials; led the armies.
- ▲ **Praetors.** Elected for one year; responsible for administration of the laws.
- ▲ **Quaestors.** Elected for one year; in charge of finances; administered the treasury.
- ▲ **Aediles.** Elected for one year; in charge of maintenance and repair of public buildings.
- ▲ **Tribunes of the plebs.** Ten elected from the plebeians for one year; summoned meetings of the council of the plebs.
- ▲ **Censors.** Two elected to hold office for eighteen months; responsible for censuses of property and citizens.

Legislative Bodies

- ▲ **Senate.** Body of three hundred, enlarged to nine hundred under Julius Caesar; could not make laws, but its decrees came to have the force of law; during the Roman Republic, was the ruling body of Rome.
- ▲ **Popular Assemblies.**
  Centuriate assembly. Decided on war and peace; elected higher officials.
  Council of the plebs. Beginning in 287 B.C., its resolutions were binding on all citizens.

ment but instead fashioned political institutions in response to problems as they arose. The Romans had a distrust of kingship and of one sole ruler as a result of their experience with the Etruscans, so they devised a sophisticated system of government (see the accompanying table).

The chief executive officers of the Roman Republic were the **consuls** and **praetors.** Two consuls, chosen every year, ran the government and led the Roman army into battle. In 366 B.C., a new office, that of the praetor, was created. The praetor was in charge of civil law (law as it applied to Roman citizens). As the Romans' territory expanded, they added another praetor to judge cases in which one or both people were noncitizens. The Romans also had a number of officials who had special duties, such as supervising the treasury.

The Roman **Senate** came to hold an especially important position in the Roman Republic. It was a select group of about three hundred landowning men who served for life. At first, its only role was to advise government officials. However, the advice of the Senate was not taken lightly, and by the third century B.C. it had the force of law.

The Roman Republic had a number of popular assemblies. By far the most important was the **centuriate assembly.** Organized by classes based on wealth, it was fixed in such a way that the wealthiest citizens always had a majority. The centuriate assembly elected the chief officials and passed laws. However, another assembly, the **council of the plebs,** came into being in 471 B.C. as a result of internal struggle.

This struggle arose as a result of the division of early Rome into two groups—the **patricians** and the **plebeians** (pli-BEE-yuns). The patricians were great landowners, who became Rome's ruling class. Only they could be consuls, other officials, and senators. The considerably larger numbers of less wealthy landholders, craftspeople, merchants, and small farmers were called plebeians. They, too, were citizens, but they did not have the same rights as the patricians. Both patricians and plebeians could vote, but only the patricians could be elected to governmental offices. Patricians and plebeians were forbidden to marry each other. Plebeians also fought in the Roman army. As a result, they thought that they deserved both political and social equality with the patricians.

The struggle between the patricians and plebeians dragged on for hundreds of years, but it led to success for the plebeians. A popular assembly for plebeians only, called the council of the plebs, was created in 471 B.C. New officials, known as **tribunes of the plebs,** were given the power to protect the plebeians. A new

MORE ABOUT . . . Roman Government

Ancient Rome has the doubtful distinction of being one of a few great civilizations in history to evolve from a very sophisticated system of government to one of the most primitive types. What accounts for this backward development? We saw earlier how Athens dropped democracy in the frustration and insecurity that followed the Peloponnesian War. The same process was at work in Rome. Republican Rome faced economic problems, instability, and insecurity. The appeal of a simpler, stronger government increases at such times. Leaders promise to cure all the nation's ills if they are given enough power. Once the Roman republic was dismembered, Rome was never the same. Imperial government depended not on a system, but on individuals—and many individual emperors didn't make the grade.

law allowed marriages between patricians and plebeians. In the fourth century B.C., plebeians were permitted to become consuls. Finally, in 287 B.C., the council of the plebs received the right to pass laws for all Romans.

The struggle between the patricians and the plebeians had a significant impact on the development of the Roman state. Plebeians could hold the highest offices of state, they could intermarry with the patricians, and they could pass laws binding on the entire Roman community. By 287 B.C., all Roman citizens were supposedly equal under the law. In reality, however, a select number of wealthy patrician and plebeian families formed a new senatorial ruling class that came to dominate the political offices. The Roman Republic had not become a democracy.

The Roman Conquest of the Mediterranean (264 to 133 B.C.)

After their conquest of Italy, the Romans found themselves face to face with a strong power in the Mediterranean—the state of Carthage. Founded around 800 B.C. on the coast of North Africa by Phoenicians, Carthage had flourished and created an enormous trading empire in the western Mediterranean. By the third century B.C., the Carthaginian Empire included the coast of northern Africa, southern Spain, Sardinia, Corsica, and western Sicily. With its control of western Mediterranean trade, Carthage was the largest and richest state in the area. The presence of Carthaginians in Sicily, an island close to the Italian coast, made the Romans fearful. In 264 B.C., the two powers

Map 6.2   Roman Conquests in the Mediterranean

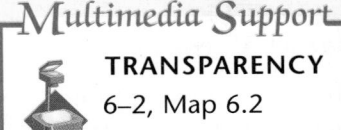
ACTIVITY

Divide the class into two groups, Romans and Carthaginians. Let each group review the development of their people's civilization (refer to chapter 2, page 45 for Phoenicia) and list characteristics and contributions of their group. Guide a discussion or debate between the two groups regarding the reasons for conflict between Rome and Carthage.

CLASS DISCUSSION

Share with students the following information.

At the beginning of the First Punic War, the Romans had no navy with which to fight the Carthaginians. Fortunately for the Romans, a Carthaginian ship washed ashore and they were able to use that as a model for their own warships. However, the Romans added their own innovation to the ships. They added a gangplank with a hook at the end so that when a Roman ship drew alongside a Carthaginian ship, the Romans could drop the gangplank, which would hook into the Carthaginian ship's deck and then the Roman soldiers could board the ship.

Have students brainstorm other innovations or inventions that were brought about because of war.

STUDYING MAPS

The following activities will help you guide the students through their study of Map 6.2.

1. Have students estimate the distance Hannibal traveled from New Carthage to Cannae. Then have them determine obstacles that Hannibal and his army encountered on their journey. *(Pyrenees Mountains, Alps, Ebro and Po Rivers)*

2. As students study the map, have them decide why Rome and Carthage would want to have control of the lands of the Mediterranean area. *(Answers might include trade, riches the lands offered, etc.)*

3. Based on the map, have students discuss why they think Hannibal took his troops through the Alps rather than along the Mediterranean coast. *(The coastal area would have been more heavily settled and was controlled by Roman allies.)*

Answer to the caption question: Answers will vary.

ASSESS

Answers to SECTION REVIEW

2. (a) executive officers of the Roman Republic in charge of the government and army
(b) executive officers of the Roman Republic in charge of civil law as it applied to Roman citizens
(c) a select group of about 300 landowning men who served for life, advised officials; advice had the force of law
(d) most important popular Roman assembly; wealthiest citizens always had a majority
(e) assembly created from struggle between patricians and plebeians
(f) great landowners; became Rome's ruling class
(g) larger part of Roman population, less wealthy than patricians; citizens; could vote but not hold governmental offices
(h) Roman officials who had the power to protect plebeians

3. (a) a Roman historian writing in the 1st century B.C.
(b) a simple farmer who was chosen as a temporary ruler to save Rome from attack
(c) the greatest of the Carthaginian generals
(d) a Roman politician who called for Carthage's destruction

---

began a lengthy struggle for control of the western Mediterranean.

The First Punic War (the Latin word for Phoenician was *punicus* [PYOO-ni-cus]) began in 264 B.C., when the Romans sent an army to Sicily. The Carthaginians, who thought of Sicily as part of their empire, considered this an act of war. Both sides became determined to conquer Sicily. The Romans—a land power—realized that they could not win the war without a navy and promptly created a large naval fleet. After a long struggle, a Roman fleet defeated the Carthaginian navy off Sicily, and the war quickly came to an end. In 241 B.C., Carthage gave up all rights to Sicily and paid a fine to the Romans. Sicily became the first Roman province.

Carthage vowed revenge, however, and added new lands in Spain to make up for the loss of Sicily. The Romans encouraged one of Carthage's Spanish allies to revolt against Carthage. In response, Hannibal, the greatest of the Carthaginian generals, struck back, beginning the Second Punic War (218 to 201 B.C.).

This time the Carthaginians decided to bring the war home to the Romans by fighting them in their own backyard. Hannibal crossed into Spain, moved east, and crossed the Alps with an army of thirty to forty thousand men and six thousand horses and elephants. He began to defeat the Romans. The Alps had taken a toll on the Carthaginian army; most of the elephants did not survive the trip. The remaining army, however, posed a real threat. In 216 B.C., the Romans decided to meet Hannibal head on. It was a serious mistake. At Cannae, the Romans lost an army of almost forty thousand men. Rome was on the brink of disaster but refused to give up and raised yet another army.

Rome gradually recovered. Although Hannibal remained free to roam in Italy, he had neither the men nor the equipment to lay siege to the major cities, including Rome itself. The Romans began to reconquer some of the Italian cities that had been taken by Hannibal. More important, they sent troops to Spain and by 206 B.C. had pushed the Carthaginians out of Spain.

In a brilliant military initiative, Rome decided to invade Carthage rather than fight Hannibal in Italy.

◄ *This coin, which dates from the second century B.C., shows a portrait of Hannibal. What do the engravings on our coins reflect about our culture and our country?*

This strategy forced the Carthaginians to recall Hannibal from Italy. At the Battle of Zama (ZAY-muh) in 202 B.C., the Romans crushed Hannibal's forces, and the war was over. Carthage lost Spain, which became a Roman province. Rome had become the dominant power in the western Mediterranean.

Fifty years later, the Romans fought their third and final struggle with Carthage. For years a number of prominent Romans had called for the complete destruction of Carthage. The politician Cato, for example, ended every speech he made to the Senate with the words, "And I think Carthage must be destroyed." In 146 B.C., it was destroyed. For ten days, Roman soldiers burned and pulled down all of the city's buildings. The inhabitants—fifty thousand men, women, and children—were sold into slavery. The territory of Carthage became a Roman province called Africa.

During its struggle with Carthage, Rome also became involved in problems with the Hellenistic states in the eastern Mediterranean. After the defeat of Carthage, Rome turned its attention there. In 148 B.C., Macedonia was made a Roman province. Two years later, Greece was placed under the control of the Roman governor of Macedonia. In 133 B.C., the king of Pergamum gave his kingdom to Rome, providing Rome with its first province in Asia. Rome was now master of the Mediterranean Sea.

 SECTION REVIEW

1. Locate:
(a) Apennine Mountains, (b) Po River, (c) Corsica, (d) Sardinia, (e) Sicily, (f) Carthage

---

COOPERATIVE LEARNING ACTIVITY

Discuss with students some of the methods of warfare used during this time period. You might cover such tactics as the phalanx used by Roman armies on the open battlefield along with fortification and siege warfare tactics.

Assign students to groups to research the different warfare tactics of Rome. If time and interest allow, you might have students build scale models of some of the weapons used, such as battering rams, catapults, and ballistas.

2. **Define:**
(*a*) consuls, (*b*) praetors, (*c*) Senate, (*d*) centuriate assembly, (*e*) council of the plebs, (*f*) patricians, (*g*) plebeians, (*h*) tribunes of the plebs

3. **Identify:**
(*a*) Livy, (*b*) Cincinnatus, (*c*) Hannibal, (*d*) Cato

4. **Recall:**
(*a*) Briefly describe the Roman Confederation.
(*b*) What are some reasons for Rome's successful expansion?

5. **Think Critically:** Compare and contrast what you know about the government of the Roman Republic with the democratic system of government used in the United States.

THE FALL OF THE REPUBLIC AND THE EMERGENCE OF THE EMPIRE (133 B.C. TO A.D. 180)

By 133 B.C., Roman domination of the Mediterranean Sea was well established. However, the process of creating an empire had weakened the internal stability of Rome. This led to a series of crises that plagued Rome for the next hundred years.

Growing Inequality and Unrest

By the second century B.C., the Senate had become the real governing body of the Roman state. Drawn mostly from the landed aristocracy, members of the Senate remained senators for life and held the chief offices of the republic. The Senate directed the wars of the third and second centuries and took control of both foreign and domestic policy, including financial affairs. Moreover, the Senate and political offices were increasingly controlled by a small circle of wealthy and powerful families.

Of course, these aristocrats formed only a tiny minority of the Roman people. The backbone of the Roman state and army had always been the small farmers. Over a period of time, however, many small farmers had found themselves unable to compete with large, wealthy landowners and had lost their lands. By taking over state-owned land and by buying out small peasant owners, these landed aristocrats had developed large estates that used slave labor. Thus, the rise of large estates led to a decline in the number of small citizen farmers. Many of these small farmers drifted to the cities, especially Rome, forming a large class of landless poor.

Some aristocrats tried to remedy this growing economic and social crisis. Two brothers, Tiberius and Gaius Gracchus (GAY-yus GRAK-us), came to believe that the basic cause of Rome's problems was the decline of the small farmer. To help the landless poor, they had the council of the plebs pass land-reform bills that called for the government to take back public land held by large landowners and to give it to landless Romans. Many senators, themselves large landowners whose estates included large areas of public land, were furious. A group of senators took the law into their own hands and killed Tiberius in 133 B.C. His brother Gaius later suffered the same fate. The attempts of the Gracchus brothers to bring reforms had opened the door to more instability and more violence. Changes in the Roman army soon brought even worse problems.

A New Role for the Roman Army

At the beginning of the first century B.C., a Roman general named Marius began to recruit his armies in a new way. For a long time the Roman army had been an army of small farmers who were landholders. Now generals recruited volunteers from both the urban and rural poor who owned no property. These volunteers swore an oath of loyalty to the general, not to the Roman state, creating a new type of army no longer subject to the state. To recruit these men, a general would promise them land. This strategy forced generals to be involved in politics in order to get laws passed that would provide the land for their veterans. Marius left a powerful legacy. He had created a new system of military recruitment that placed much power in the hands of the individual generals.

RECOMMENDED READING

For a general account of the Roman Empire, see J. Boardman, J. Griffin, and O. Murray, eds., *The Oxford History of the Classical World* (Oxford, 1986), pp. 531–828. Good surveys of the Early Empire include P. Garnsey and R. P. Saller, *The Roman Empire: Economy, Society and Culture* (London, 1987); C. Wells, *The Roman Empire* (Stanford, 1984); J. Wacher, *The Roman Empire* (London, 1987); and F. Millar, *Roman Empire and Its Neighbors,* 2d ed. (London, 1981).

Studies of Roman emperors of the first and second centuries include F. Millar and E. Segal, eds., *Caesar Augustus* (Oxford, 1984); A. Barrett, *Caligula, The Corruption of Power* (New Haven, Conn., 1990), A. Momigliano, *Claudius, the Emperor and His Achievement,* trans. W. D. Hogarth (Cambridge, 1961); and M. Griffin, *Nero: The End of a Dynasty* (London, 1984).

4. (a) a system under which Rome allowed some peoples to have full Roman citizenship. Other communities were made allies. Allies could improve their status and gain citizenship under this system.
(b) crushed rebellions; shrewd; persistent, practical (built colonies and roads)

5. Answers will vary.

CLOSE

Write the following list of words on the board and have students write one-sentence explanations of how each term relates to this period in Roman history.

◆ Etruscans
◆ Greeks
◆ Consuls
◆ Praetors
◆ Plebeians
◆ Patricians
◆ Carthaginians

FOCUS

OBJECTIVES

After completing this section, students should be able to

1. explain the legacy left by the Roman general Marius
2. list the circumstances that led to the collapse of the Roman Republic
3. describe the problems of the early Roman Empire

Refer students to the map of the Roman Empire on page 169.

FOCUS ACTIVITY

Refer students to the map of the Roman Empire on page 169. Explain that the number of days indicated on the map tells how long it took to get places at this time. Ask students how they think the Roman Empire was held together when travel and communication were so slow.

TEACH

COMPARING TIME PERIODS

After reading about Tiberius and Gaius Gracchus and their attempt to gain land for the landless poor, ask students if this account reminds them of any modern-day American reformers. (Answers to the following questions will depend on the people students mention.) Ask students how these modern-day people were similar to and different from the Gracchus brothers. Ask if any of the modern-day Americans received a fate similar to that of the Gracchus brothers. Ask students if they think reformers are received any better today than they were during the time of the Roman Empire. Why do they think the way they do?

Multimedia Support

LASERDISC
Roman Soldier Fighting Gauls (1st century A.D.)

Roman Pottery Shard of Barbaric Bearded Celt

162

Lucius Cornelius Sulla was the next general to take advantage of the new military system. The Senate had given him command of a war in Asia Minor. When the council of the plebs tried to transfer command of this war to Marius, however, a civil war broke out. Sulla won and seized Rome itself in 82 B.C., conducting a reign of terror to wipe out all opposition. Then Sulla restored power to the hands of the Senate and eliminated most of the powers of the popular assemblies. Sulla hoped that he had created a firm foundation for the traditional republic governed by a powerful Senate, but his real legacy was quite different from what he had intended. His example of using an army to seize power would prove most attractive to ambitious men.

The Collapse of the Republic

For the next fifty years, Roman history was characterized by two important features: competition for power by a number of individuals and the civil wars caused by their conflicts. Three powerful individuals—Crassus, Pompey (POM-pee), and Julius Caesar (SEE-zur)—came to hold enormous military and political power. Crassus was known as the richest man in Rome. Pompey had returned from a successful military command in Spain as a military hero. Julius Caesar also had a military command in Spain. In 60 B.C., Caesar joined with Crassus and Pompey to form the **First Triumvirate** (government by three people).

The combined wealth and power of these three men was enormous, enabling them to dominate the political scene and achieve their basic aims. Pompey received a command in Spain, Crassus was given a command in Syria, and Caesar was granted a special military command in Gaul (modern France). When Crassus was killed in battle in 53 B.C., it left two powerful men. During his time in Gaul, Caesar had gained military experience, as well as an army of loyal veterans.

Leading senators seized on Pompey as the least harmful to their cause. They voted for Caesar to lay down his command, but Caesar refused. He chose to keep his army and moved into Italy by illegally crossing the Rubicon, the river that formed the southern boundary of his province. ("Crossing the Rubicon" is a phrase used today to mean being unable to turn back.)

Caesar marched on Rome, starting a civil war between his forces and those of Pompey and his allies. The defeat of Pompey's forces left Caesar in complete control of the Roman government.

Caesar was officially made dictator in 47 B.C. Realizing the need for reforms, he gave land to the poor and increased the Senate to nine hundred members. By filling it with many of his supporters and increasing the number of members, he effectively weakened the power of the Senate. He granted citizenship to a number of people in the provinces who had helped him. He also reformed the calendar by introducing the Egyptian solar year of 365 days. (With later changes in 1582, it became the basis of our own calendar.) Caesar planned much more in the way of building projects and military adventures to the east. However, in 44 B.C., a group of leading senators assassinated him (see "You Are There: The Assassination of Julius Caesar").

A new struggle for power followed Caesar's death. Octavian, Caesar's heir and grandnephew; Antony, Caesar's ally and assistant; and Lepidus, who had been commander of Caesar's cavalry, joined forces to form the Second Triumvirate. Within a few years after Caesar's death, however, only two men divided the Roman world between them. Octavian took the west, and Antony took the east. The empire of the Romans, though, large as it was, was still too small for two masters, and Octavian and Antony came into conflict. Antony allied himself with the Egyptian queen Cleopatra VII, with whom, like Caesar before him, he fell deeply in love. At the Battle of Actium in Greece in 31 B.C., Octavian's forces smashed the army and navy of Antony and Cleopatra. Both fled to Egypt, where they committed suicide a year later:

Antony was the first to commit suicide, by the sword. Cleopatra threw herself at Octavian's feet, and tried her best to attract his gaze: in vain, for his self-control enabled him to ignore her beauty. It was not her life she was after, . . . but a portion of her kingdom. When she realized this was hopeless . . . she took advantage of her guard's carelessness to get herself into the royal tomb. Once there, she put on the royal robes . . . and lay down in a richly perfumed coffin beside her Antony. Then she applied poisonous snakes to her veins and passed into death as though into a sleep.[1]

RETEACHING ACTIVITY

Help students understand the changing government leadership in Rome during the collapse of the republic by having them develop a visual similar to the following.

First Triumvirate

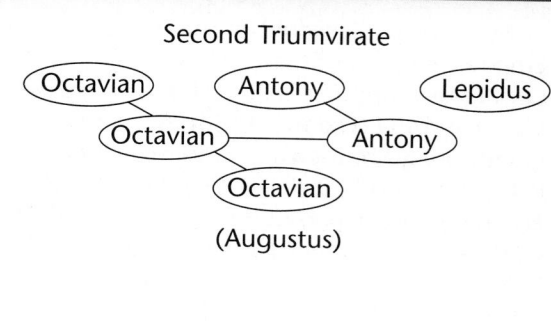

Second Triumvirate

YOU ARE THERE

The Assassination of Julius Caesar

When it became obvious that Julius Caesar had no intention of restoring power to the Senate, about sixty senators, many of them Caesar's friends or pardoned enemies, decided to assassinate the dictator. Led by Gaius Cassius (cash-EE-us) and Marcus Brutus, the conspirators set the Ides of March (March 15), 44 B.C., as the date for the assassination. Although warned about a plot against his life, Caesar chose to ignore it, as seen in this account by Plutarch.

◄ *This noble bust of Julius Caesar was done in marble. Caesar first gained fame as the conqueror of Gaul and is probably the best-known ruler of the late Republic.*

Plutarch, *Life of Caesar*

Fate, however, is to all appearance more unavoidable than unexpected. . . . One finds it related by many that a soothsayer told Caesar to prepare for some great danger on the Ides of March. When this day was come, Caesar, as he went to the senate, met this soothsayer, and said to him, "The Ides of March are come," who answered him calmly, "Yes, they are come, but they are not past. . . ."

When Caesar entered, the senate stood up to show their respect to him, and of Brutus's confederates, some came about his chair and stood behind it, others met him, pretending to add their petitions to those of Tillius Cimber, in behalf of his brother, who was in exile; and they followed him with their joint applications till he came to his seat. When he was sat down, he refused to comply with their requests, and upon their urging him further began to reproach them severely for their importunities, when Tillius, laying hold of his robe with both his hands, pulled it down from his neck, which was the signal for the assault. Casca gave him the first cut in the neck, which was not mortal nor dangerous, as coming from one who at the beginning of such a bold action was probably very much disturbed; Caesar immediately turned about, and laid his hand upon the dagger and kept hold of it. And both of them at the same time cried out, he that received the blow, in Latin, "Vile Casca, what does this mean?" and he that gave it, in Greek to his brother, "Brother, help!" Upon this first onset, those who were not privy to the design were astonished, and their horror and amazement at what they saw were so great that they dared not fly nor assist Caesar, nor so much as speak a word. But those who came prepared for the business enclosed him on every side, with their naked daggers in their hands. Whichever way he turned he met with blows, and saw their swords levelled at his face and eyes, and was encompassed like a wild beast in the toils on every side. For it had been agreed they should each of them make a thrust at him, and flesh themselves with his blood: for which reason Brutus also gave him one stab in the groin. Some say that he fought and resisted all

(continued)

Answers to Critical Thinking Questions

1. Apparently warned by a soothsayer (someone who predicts the future) that he was in danger, Caesar took no precautions. In that way, the event of his death was not unexpected. Because he was killed that day, it would seem that his fate was unavoidable.

2. Caesar's assassins were friends or pardoned enemies, people he knew and with whom he had worked and fought. The attack by Brutus in particular seemed to cause the dictator to give up fighting for his life. He surely was wounded emotionally as well as physically.

3. The murder was carefully planned, the date selected in advance. All participants agreed to strike a blow—they were all equally guilty.

Multimedia Support

LASERDISC
Celtic Helmet

Celtic Fortress Site

CRITICAL THINKING

Octavian was awarded many titles during his reign in Rome. He became *Augustus*—the revered one, *imperator*—commander in chief, *princeps*—first citizen, and *pontifex maximus*—chief pontiff, head of the official state religion.

YOU ARE THERE

The Assassination of Julius Caesar, continued

the rest, shifting his body to avoid the blows, and calling out for help, but that when he saw Brutus's sword drawn, he covered his face with his robe and submitted, letting himself fall, . . . and breathed out his soul through his multitude of wounds, for they say he received three-and-twenty. And the conspirators themselves were many of them wounded by each other, while they all leveled their blows at the same person.

1. Explain what Plutarch meant in writing, "Fate, however, is to all appearance more unavoidable than unexpected."

2. Was Caesar wounded by the physical attack alone?

3. Was the assassination carefully planned or done in the heat of the moment? Explain.

Octavian, at the age of thirty-two, stood supreme over the Roman world. The civil wars had ended. So had the republic.

The Age of Augustus
(31 B.C. to A.D. 14)

In 27 B.C., Octavian proclaimed the "restoration of the Republic." He knew that only traditional republican forms would satisfy the Senate. At the same time, Octavian was aware that the republic could not be fully restored. Although he gave some power to the Senate, Octavian in fact became the first Roman emperor. In 27 B.C., the Senate awarded him the title of Augustus—"the revered one," a fitting title in view of his power, which previously had been reserved for gods. Augustus proved to be highly popular. No doubt, people were glad the civil wars had ended. At the same time, however, his continuing control of the army was the chief source of Augustus's power. The Senate gave Augustus the title of **imperator,** or commander in chief. *Imperator* gave us our word *emperor.*

Augustus maintained a standing army of twenty-eight legions, or about 150,000 men (a legion was a military unit of about 5,000 troops). Only Roman citizens could be legionnaires (members of a legion). Subject peoples could serve as auxiliary forces, which numbered around 130,000 under Augustus. Augustus also set up a praetorian guard of roughly 9,000 men who had the important task of guarding the person of the emperor.

While claiming to have restored the republic, Augustus began a new system for governing the provinces. Under the Roman Republic, the Senate had appointed the governors of the provinces. Now, certain provinces were given to the emperor, who assigned deputies known as *legates* to govern them. The Senate still chose the governors of the remaining provinces. However, the power of Augustus enabled him to overrule the senatorial governors and establish unity in imperial policy.

Augustus also stabilized the frontiers of the Roman Empire. He conquered the central and maritime Alps and then expanded Roman control of the Balkan peninsula up to the Danube (DAN-yoob) River. His attempt to conquer Germany failed when three Roman legions were massacred by a group of German tribes. His defeats in Germany taught Augustus that Rome's power was not unlimited. This knowledge devastated

---

So What ??

*If your students question the importance of the information on **Octavian** tell them that . . .*

In the midst of instability, uncertainty, and insecurity, Octavian offers himself to Rome as its savior. Under normal times, confident governments are not likely to extend the power of the ruler. But in times of crisis, a "savior" becomes tempting. If the savior asks for more power, more he is given. So, Octavian is made "Augustus" by the Senate, and the Roman Republic dies. Was this an isolated example of such an event in history? Napoleon Bonaparte and Adolph Hitler are evidence that such a danger is not isolated, but recurrent. Will we be better prepared when the next would-be "savior" knocks at the door of government? Only if we can learn from history.

▲ *The praetorian guard, an elite group of legionnaires, was established by Augustus to serve as the imperial bodyguard. Their elaborate uniforms and shields are clearly shown in this second-century relief that features five members of the guard. What body in the U.S. government is responsible for the personal safety of the president?*

him; for months he would beat his head on a door, shouting, "Varus [the defeated Roman general in Germany], give me back my legions!"

The Early Empire (A.D. 14 to 180)

Augustus's new political system allowed the emperor to select his successor from his natural or adopted family. The first four emperors after Augustus came from his family. During their reigns, more and more of the responsibilities that Augustus had given to the Senate tended to be taken over by the emperors. At the same

▲ *Octavian, Caesar Augustus, is pictured in this marble statue. Augustus, the first emperor, maintained strong control over the army, guaranteeing no opposition to his regime. He ruled, however, through formal legal procedures, which made him popular with the people.*

time, as the emperors grew more powerful, they also became more corrupt. Nero, for example, had people killed if he wanted them out of the way, including his own mother. Without troops, the senators were unable to oppose his excesses, but the Roman legions finally revolted. Nero committed suicide, and a civil war broke out in A.D. 69. It soon became obvious that the Roman Empire had a major flaw. Without a system for selecting a new emperor, emperors could be made and deposed by the Roman legions.

COOPERATIVE LEARNING ACTIVITY

Nero was one of the most infamous of the Roman emperors, and many historians today consider Nero to have been a psychopath. He seemed to have no conscience when it came to killing people who he perceived were against him. He killed his stepbrother, his mother, two wives, the husband of a woman he wanted to marry, and many political foes.

But, Nero also did several positive things as emperor of Rome. Have your students

research Nero to find the good he did as emperor. You might arrange for students to debate a controversial statement such as "Nero was only a product of his upbringing." Have students who agree stand on one side of the classroom, those who disagree on the other. Have one side, then the other, defend their position, but allow students to migrate between groups as their views change.

REINFORCING VOCABULARY

Some terms students might not fully understand and which you might want to discuss include: *arbitrary executions*—executions committed solely by the choice of the emperor; laws were not considered

domestic policies—government rules and regulations that affected the people of the Roman Empire

tolerance—putting up with people who believe and/or act differently

LEARNING FROM VISUALS

Answer to the caption question: Answers will vary.

ACTIVITY

Identify, from the information in the text, aspects of Roman civilization having a Greek foundation.

Multimedia Support

LASERDISC
Roman Emperors

Some Roman Emperors (unless noted, dates are A.D.)
Julio-Claudian Dynasty
Augustus, 31 B.C.–A.D. 14
Tiberius, 14–37
Caligula, 37–41
Claudius, 41–54
Nero, 54–68
Five Good Emperors
Nerva, 96–98
Trajan, 98–117
Hadrian, 117–138
Antoninus Pius, 138–161
Marcus Aurelius, 161–180
Emperors of the Late Roman Empire
Diocletian, 284–305
Constantine, 306–337
Last Western Emperor
Romulus Augustulus, 475–476

At the beginning of the second century, however, a series of five so-called good emperors created a period of peace and prosperity (known as the Pax Romana—the "Roman Peace") that lasted for almost one hundred years. These rulers treated the ruling classes with respect, ended arbitrary executions, maintained peace in the empire, and supported domestic policies generally helpful to the empire. Although they were absolute monarchs, they were known for their tolerance. By adopting capable men as their sons and successors, the first four good emperors reduced the chances of succession problems.

Under the five good emperors, the powers of the emperor continued to expand at the expense of the Senate. Officials appointed and directed by the emperor took over the running of the government. The good emperors also created new programs to help the people. Trajan, for example, created a program that provided state funds to assist poor parents in the raising and education of their children. The good emperors were widely praised for their building programs.

Trajan and Hadrian were especially active in building public works—aqueducts, bridges, roads, and harbor facilities—throughout the provinces and in Rome.

Frontiers and the Provinces

Trajan extended Roman rule into Dacia (modern Romania), Mesopotamia, and the Sinai (SIE-nie) peninsula. His successors, however, realized that the empire was too large to be easily governed. Hadrian withdrew Roman forces from much of Mesopotamia and also went on the defensive in his frontier policy. He strengthened the fortifications along a line connecting the Rhine and Danube Rivers and built a defensive wall eighty miles long across northern Britain to keep the Scots out of Roman Britain. By the end of the second century, it became apparent that it would be more and more difficult to defend the empire.

▼ *The Pont du Gard, as this Roman aqueduct in southern France is called, stands today as a tribute to the skills of the Roman builders. The Romans were the first to use concrete extensively and to employ curvilinear forms on such a massive scale. What buildings in your community do you think will be standing 2,000 years from now?*

MORE ABOUT . . . *Greco-Roman Civilization*

Romans admired the Greek example. They became extremely effective cultural "sponges," absorbing and romanizing the ideas of the Greeks. The greatest achievements of Roman sculpture were in fact copies of Greek originals. Without the Roman copies, we would not have knowledge of many Greek sculptures. Roman religion is a thinly-disguised version of Greek religion, and Roman literature likewise aims to copy the Greek examples. In some areas, however, the Romans clearly diverge. While the Greeks were speculative philosophers, the Romans were practical people—excelling in engineering. While the Greeks believed in moderation, Rome was the first Western society to be hypnotized by excess. Greed for material wealth, over-eating, and over-drinking, all found a home in Rome.

Map 6.3   The Roman Empire from A.D. 14 to 117

Roman Empire at the end of Augustus's reign, A.D. 14

Roman Empire at the end of Trajan's reign, A.D. 117

ACTIVITY

Hadrian's Wall was built to keep the Scots out of Roman Britain. Have students locate Hadrian's Wall on the map on page 167. Ask students how many realized that Rome's empire extended to Britain.

The wall was about 20 feet high and 8 feet across. You might graphically demonstrate the size of the wall for students by measuring 20 feet up a wall, flagpole, etc. and then measuring 8 feet from the base. Ask students to explain how they think the construction of such a massive structure was accomplished around 122 A.D.

Roman forces were located in permanent bases behind the frontiers. However, when one frontier was attacked, troops had to be drawn from other frontiers, leaving those other frontiers open to attack.

At its height in the second century, the Roman Empire was one of the greatest states the world had ever seen. It covered about three and a half million square miles and had a population that has been estimated at more than 50,000,000. The emperors and the imperial administration provided a degree of unity. At the same time, much leeway was given to local customs, and the privileges of Roman citizenship were granted to many people throughout the empire. In 212, the emperor Caracalla gave Roman citizenship to every free person in the empire. Latin was the language of the western part of the empire, whereas Greek was used in the east (as a result of Alexander the Great's earlier invasion). Roman culture spread to all parts of the empire and freely mixed with Greek culture, creating what has been called Greco-Roman civilization.

The administration and cultural life of the Roman Empire depended greatly upon cities and towns. A provincial governor's staff was not large, so it was left to local city officials to act as Roman agents in carry-

Multimedia Support

 LASERDISC
Gold Bead

Stone Marker (Ireland, A.D. 500–800)

Celtic Mirror

Celtic Jewelry

Multimedia Support

 TRANSPARENCY
6–4, The Roman Empire (Map 6.3)

STUDYING MAPS

The following activities will help you guide the students through their study of Map 6.3.

◆ Have students estimate the length (west to east) of the Roman Empire. (approximately 2,650 mi., 4,275 km)

◆ Then have them estimate the width (north to south) of the Empire. (approximately 1,975 mi., 3,262 km)

◆ Ask students to explain why having control of the Mediterranean Sea would have been important to the Roman Empire. (They would have been in control of all trade, could move military forces easily and relatively quickly, put an end to piracy, etc.)

◆ What are the natural frontiers of the empire? (the ocean to the west, the rivers to the north, and the deserts to the south and east)

LEARNING FROM VISUALS

This photo of the ruins of Timgad in Africa shows how uniformly Roman cities were built throughout the empire. The physical appearance of Rome was recreated in the building of markets, amphitheaters, temples, and other public buildings.

ACTIVITY

Have students compare and contrast three policies or institutions under the Roman Republic and the Roman Empire. Have them discuss how extensively these policies or institutions led toward a stronger government.

ACTIVITY

Have students write an essay comparing and contrasting the Roman and Han Empires.

ACTIVITY

Have students write an essay comparing and contrasting the Early Roman Republic and the Roman Empire at its height. How did the Roman traits of courage, duty, and determination change in their focus?

ACTIVITY

Have each student draw a map of the Roman Empire at its height, then select and locate on the map three major cities in different parts of the Empire (east, west and south). Have the student outline on the map the best routes to each city from Rome. Have them plan both land and sea routes and describe why they selected these and which would be easiest. What are the dangers along each route?

▶ *Pictured are the ruins of Timgad, a Roman city in Algeria that was built by Trajan in A.D. 100. Cities like Timgad began as military forts and developed into bustling communities to meet the soldiers' needs. Over time these cities met all the necessities for Roman civilized life.*

ing out many government duties, especially those related to taxes. Most towns and cities were not large by modern standards. The largest was Rome, but there were also some large cities in the east. Alexandria in Egypt, for example, had over 300,000 inhabitants. In the west, cities were usually small, with only a few thousand inhabitants. Cities were important in the spread of Roman culture, Roman law, and the Latin language. The cities resembled one another with their temples, markets, and other public buildings.

Economic and Social Conditions in the Early Empire

The Early Empire was a period of much prosperity, with internal peace leading to high levels of trade. Merchants from all over the empire came to the chief Italian ports of Puteoli (pyuh-TEE-uh-LIE) on the Bay of

▶ *Although poor people were given grain in Rome, baked bread was generally available only to wealthier people who had ovens or could afford to have grain ground and baked into loaves for them. Nonetheless, by the second century B.C., a baker's stall like this one may have been a common sight. This wall painting comes from the House of the Baker in Pompeii, where loaves have been found with lines incised in the top, probably so that the loaves could be easily broken.*

On Line with WORLD HISTORY   *Internet Activity*

You may want to have your students visit the following URL, where they will find information and additional web site resources to enhance their study of this chapter.

Exploring Ancient World Cultures— Ancient Rome

http://eawc.evansville.edu/ropage.htm

This is an excellent source for information and links on Roman history and includes chronology, essays, resources, maps, and www sites.

Due to the ever-changing nature of the World Wide Web, see the West History web site, **http://history.swpco.com** for regular updates of the URLs in this text.

Map 6.4   Trade Routes and Products in the Roman Empire, c. 200

REINFORCING VOCABULARY

Discuss with students the meaning of the phrase "consumption-oriented society." *(The phrase refers to the desired luxuries that were wanted rather than needed, which the wealthy Romans could afford.)* Have students compare Rome's consumption-oriented society with a society, such as the American Indian tribes, which was more subsistence-oriented.

COMPARING TIME PERIODS

Discuss the differences between the socioeconomic classes in Rome. Then have students compare those differences to the differences they see in U.S. society today. What are the similarities? What are the differences? How were the poor taken care of in Roman society? How are they taken care of in U.S. society? Should the U.S. look at Rome's example for ideas on taking care of the poor? Why or why not?

Naples (NAE-pulz) and Ostia at the mouth of the Tiber. Trade, however, went beyond the Roman frontiers and included even silk goods from China. Large quantities of grain were imported, especially from Egypt, to feed the people of Rome. Luxury items poured in to satisfy the desires of the wealthy upper classes. It could be said that the Roman Empire became the first consumption-oriented society in the West.

Despite the active trade and commerce, however, farming remained the chief occupation of most people and the underlying basis of Roman prosperity. Large landed estates (called *latifundia*) dominated farming in

southern and central Italy. These large estates mostly used slaves to raise sheep and cattle on a large scale. Small peasant farms continued to exist in northern Italy.

There was an enormous gulf between rich and poor in Roman society. The upper classes lived lives of great leisure and luxury in their villas and on their vast estates. Many small farmers became dependent on the huge estates of their wealthy neighbors. In the cities, many poor citizens worked in shops and markets. There were also thousands of unemployed people who depended on the emperor's handouts of grain to survive.

ASSESS

You can choose from a variety of assessments to evaluate your students' mastery of the objectives for this section as stated on page 161. Possible assessments include:

1. Section Review questions on the following page
2. Section 6–2 Quiz in your Teacher Resource materials
3. Reteaching Worksheets in your Teacher Resource materials
4. Self-Study software

STUDYING MAPS

The following questions will help you guide the students through their study of Map 6.4.

◆ Discuss the contents of the legend box. What use would the Romans have made of the different items listed? *(Answers will vary.)*

◆ From what area were slaves provided for the empire? *(the northern part of Africa,*

near Carthage, and from the area north of Greece)

◆ How long would it have taken to ship grain from Carthage to Ostia? *(3–5 days)*

◆ What trade items originated on the Italian peninsula? *(textiles and pottery)*

2. (a) government by Caesar, Crassus, and Pompey
(b) commander in chief

3. (a) Two brothers who believed that the basic cause of Rome's problems was the decline of the small farmer, they were eventually killed by the landowners.
(b) Roman general who used his army to gain control of Rome in 82 B.C. and institute a reign of terror to wipe out opposition
(c) richest man in Rome, part of the First Triumvirate, killed in battle in 53 B.C.
(d) member of First Triumvirate; military hero; defeated by Caesar
(e) surviving member of the First Triumvirate; dictator of Rome; he weakened power of the Senate; reformed the calendar; assassinated by members of the senate
(f) became Augustus, first Roman emperor; ended Civil wars; began a new system of governing provinces; stabilized the frontiers of the Roman Empire
(g) Roman emperor known for his brutality
(h) one of the five good emperors; created a program to assist poor parents in the raising of their children.

4. Marius recruited army volunteers from the landless poor, promising them land in return for their loyalty to him rather than to the state. His legacy was armies loyal to their generals and generals politically active to provide land for their men.

❀ SECTION REVIEW ❀

1. Locate:
(a) Rubicon River,   (b) Danube River,
(c) Dacia,   (d) Mesopotamia,   (e) Sinai peninsula

2. Define:
(a) First Triumvirate,   (b) imperator

3. Identify:
(a) Tiberius and Gaius Gracchus,   (b) Lucius Cornelius Sulla,   (c) Crassus,   (d) Pompey,
(e) Julius Caesar,   (f) Octavian,   (g) Nero,
(h) Trajan

4. Recall: What was the military legacy left by Marius?

5. Think Critically: Why was the military legacy left by Marius important?

CULTURE AND SOCIETY IN THE ROMAN WORLD

One of the most noticeable characteristics of Roman culture and society is the impact of the Greeks. Greek ambassadors, merchants, and artists traveled to Rome and spread Greek thought and practices. After their conquest of the Hellenistic kingdoms, Roman military commanders shipped Greek manuscripts and artwork back to Rome. Large numbers of educated Greek slaves worked in Roman households. Rich Romans hired Greek tutors and sent their sons to Athens to study. As the Roman poet Horace said, "Captive Greece took captive her rude conqueror." Greek thought captivated Roman minds, and the Romans became willing transmitters of Greek culture (see "Our Artistic Heritage: Roman Art and Architecture").

Roman Literature

The Latin literature that first emerged in the third century B.C. was strongly influenced by Greek models. Although there were many talented Roman writers in the Roman Republic, the high point of Latin literature was reached in the age of Augustus. The literary achievements of the Augustan Age were such that the period has been called the golden age of Latin literature.

The most distinguished poet of the Augustan Age was Virgil. The son of a small landholder in northern Italy, he welcomed the rule of Augustus and wrote his greatest work in honor of the ruler. Virgil's masterpiece was the *Aeneid* (i-NEE-ud), an epic poem clearly meant to rival the work of Homer. The connection between Troy and Rome is made in the poem when Aeneas, a hero of Troy, survives the destruction of Troy and eventually settles in Latium. Thus, Roman civilization is linked to Greek history. The character of Aeneas is portrayed as the ideal Roman—his virtues are duty, piety, and faithfulness. Virgil's overall purpose was to show that Aeneas had fulfilled his mission to establish the Romans in Italy and thereby start Rome on its divine mission to rule the world:

> Let others fashion from bronze more lifelike, breathing images—
> For so they shall—and evoke living faces from marble;
> Others excel as orators, others track with their instruments
> The planets circling in heaven and predict when stars will appear.
> But, Romans, never forget that government is your medium!
> Be this your art: to practise men in the habit of peace,
> Generosity to the conquered, and firmness against aggressors.[2]

As Virgil expressed it, ruling was Rome's gift.

Another prominent Augustan poet was Horace, a friend of Virgil's. He was a very sophisticated writer who enjoyed pointing out to his fellow Romans the "follies and vices of his age." In the *Satires*, Horace directed his attacks against job dissatisfaction ("How does it happen, Maecenas, that no man alone is content with his lot?")[3] and greed. Horace mostly laughs at the weaknesses of humans. In his final work, the *Epistles*, he used a Greek form—the imaginary letter in verse—to provide a portrait of the things he held most dear: a simple life, good friends, and his beloved countryside.

RECOMMENDED READING

A good survey of Roman literature can be found in R. M. Ogilvie, *Roman Literature and Society* (Harmondsworth, 1980). A brief survey of Roman art can be found in J. M. C. Toynbee, *Art of the Romans* (London and New York, 1965). Architecture is covered in the standard work by J. B. Ward-Perkins, *Roman Imperial Architecture* (Harmondsworth, 1981).

Studies on Roman women include J. P. V. D. Balsdon, *Roman Women: Their History and Habits* (London, 1969); and S. B. Pomeroy, *Goddesses, Whores, Wives and Slaves: Women in Classical Antiquity* (New York, 1975), pp. 149–226.

General studies of daily life in Rome include F. R. Cowell, *Everyday Life in Ancient Rome* (London, 1961); and J. Balsdon, *Life and Leisure in Ancient Rome* (New York, 1969).

OUR ARTISTIC HERITAGE

Roman Art and Architecture

During the third and second centuries B.C., the Romans adopted many features of the Greek style of art. They developed a taste for Greek statues, which they placed not only in public buildings but also in their private houses. Once demand had outstripped the supply of original works, reproductions of Greek statues became fashionable.

The Romans were also quite different from the Greeks, however. Greek portraits were usually of famous people. Roman portraits, in contrast, were made for anyone who had the money to pay for them. Greek sculptors aimed for an ideal appearance in their figures. The Romans' own portrait sculpture was marked by an intense realism that included even unpleasant physical details. Wall paintings in the houses of the rich realistically depicted landscapes, portraits, and scenes from stories.

The Romans excelled in architecture, a highly practical art. Imitating the Greeks, they made use of rows and columns and rectangular buildings. The Romans also took new approaches. They used curvilinear forms (forms based on curved lines): the arch, vault, and dome. The Romans were also the first people in antiquity to develop the use of concrete on a massive scale. By combining the use of concrete with curvilinear forms, they were able to construct massive buildings undreamed of by

▲ *Wall paintings were popular in the houses of the rich. As is evident in this scene of a Roman villa, Roman paintings reflected the Roman desire for realism and attention to detail.*

▼ *The Colosseum in Rome (shown below) is an immense amphitheater constructed during the reign of Vespasian and Titus, his son. Amphitheaters, where the gladiator contests were held, varied in size from one city to another, but each played an important role in entertaining the masses.*

(continued)

On Line with WORLD HISTORY *Internet Activity*

You may want to have your students visit the following URL, where they will find information and additional web site resources to enhance their study of this chapter.

Rome Project

http://www.nltl.columbia.edu/ Groups/Rome/

This site is from the Dalton Project and contains valuable sources on Roman literature, military, archaeology, politics, philosophy, drama, religion and general topics. A search engine is included.

Due to the ever-changing nature of the World Wide Web, see the West History web site, **http://history.swpco.com** for regular updates of the URLs in this text.

OUR ARTISTIC HERITAGE

Answers to Critical Thinking Questions

1. Greek statues; rows, columns, and rectangular buildings
2. arch, vault, dome; use of concrete on a massive scale to make large public baths and amphitheaters (Colosseum); engineered roads, bridges, and aqueducts

COMPARING TIME PERIODS

We know that the Romans were highly influenced by the Greek culture in art and architecture as well as in other areas. Have students do a comparison of Greek and Roman styles through a study of the photos in this text. (Be sure to include other sources if available.)

Ask students what differences they see in the Greek and Roman styles of art and architecture. Can they see the Greek influence in the Roman style? Are there any buildings in your city that are built in the Greek or Roman architectural styles? If so, call students' attention to them and ask students what they think of the architecture? Do they like it? Why or why not?

If possible, take your students to visit any local buildings that show Greek or Roman influence in their architecture.

LEARNING FROM VISUALS

Answer to the caption question: Students should recognize that Greek plays with traditional Greek forms were used by the Romans.

OUR ARTISTIC HERITAGE

Roman Art and Architecture, continued

the Greeks. These included public baths, such as those of Emperor Caracalla, and amphitheaters, the most famous of which was the Colosseum in Rome. The Colosseum was capable of seating fifty thousand spectators.

These large buildings were a product of the remarkable engineering skills of the Romans. The same skills were put to use in constructing roads. The Romans built a network of fifty thousand miles of roads throughout their empire. They also built bridges and aqueducts. In Rome, almost a dozen aqueducts kept a population of one million supplied with water. The Romans were superb builders. Wherever they went—in Europe, North Africa, and western Asia—there remain the remnants of Roman theaters, amphitheaters, temples, aqueducts, roads, and bridges.

1. What style features of Greek art were adopted by the Romans?

2. What unique contributions did the Romans make to architecture?

◄ *This mosaic, which was found at Pompeii, shows Roman actors rehearsing for a Greek play. The chorus master is seated watching two actors who are dancing to pipe music. How does this reflect Horace's statement that "captive Greece took captive her rude conqueror"?*

The most famous Latin prose work of the golden age was written by the historian Livy, whose masterpiece was the *History of Rome*. In 142 books, Livy traced the time of the foundation of the city to 9 B.C. Only 35 of the books have survived. Livy saw history in terms of moral lessons. He stated in the preface that

> The study of history is the best medicine for a sick mind; for in history you have a record of the infinite variety of human experience plainly set out for all to see; and in that record you can find for yourself and your country both examples and warnings: fine things to take as models, base things, rotten through and through, to avoid.[4]

Livy's history celebrated Rome's greatness. He built scene upon scene that not only revealed the character of the chief figures but also demonstrated the virtues that had made Rome great. Of course, he had a serious

COOPERATIVE LEARNING ACTIVITY

Collect several pieces of Roman literature from the time of the Roman Republic. Distribute these to the class and have volunteers "perform" the pieces.

As students listen, tell them to be aware of the political feelings generated by the literature. Is the author praising the government? Is there a cynical feeling in the writing? Ask students why they think the writers wrote what they did. What events were going on in Rome at the time of the writing? How would these events affect what the authors wrote?

CONNECTIONS
TO OUR WORLD

Roman and American Builders   One need only look at many public buildings in the United States to realize that Roman architectural models played an important role in their design. Thomas Jefferson, for example, believed that architecture could be a means for expressing the ideals of the newly founded United States. He wanted the ideals of classical architecture, especially as put into practice by the Romans, to serve as a model for American buildings. Jefferson copied Roman temples for his designs for the buildings of the University of Virginia at Charlottesville.

The Romans were able to create a number of new architectural forms, such as arches, vaults, and domes, as a result of their use of concrete. Concrete enabled the Romans to build mammoth colosseums (col-eh-SEE-ims) that held tens of thousands of spectators. The Romans also used concrete to erect domed buildings that created new interior spaces for human experience.

American engineers continue to learn from the Romans. For example, all of us are aware of highway potholes, as well as crumbling bridges on American highways. In many cases, these problems are a result of concrete that is not sufficiently hard and dense to survive the ravages of wind, ice, and rain. Recently, however, American engineers have experimented with a form of concrete used by the ancient Romans, which is made with fly ash. Today's engineers have found it to be considerably harder and more durable than the usual concrete. By analyzing Roman concrete, they found that the Romans combined lime with deposits of volcanic ash to form a very hard and durable building material that would set into shape even under water. Almost two thousand years later, American engineers have finally caught up with the Romans.

weakness as a historian: he was not always concerned about the factual accuracy of his stories. He did tell a good tale, however, and his work became the standard history of Rome for a long time.

Roman Law

One of Rome's chief gifts to the Mediterranean world of its day and to later generations was its system of law. The Twelve Tables of 450 B.C. was Rome's first code of laws, but it was a product of a simple farming society and proved inadequate for later Roman needs. Nevertheless, from the Twelve Tables the Romans developed a system of civil law that applied only to Roman citizens. As Rome expanded, Romans became involved in problems involving both Romans and non-Romans, as well as those involving only non-Romans. The Romans found that although some of their rules of civil law could be used in these cases, special rules were often needed. These rules gave rise to a body of law known as the law of nations, defined by the Romans as "that part of the law which we apply both to ourselves and to foreigners." Under the influence of Stoicism (see Chapter 5), the Romans came to identify their law of nations with natural law, or universal law based on reason. This enabled them to establish standards of justice that applied to all people.

These standards of justice included principles that we would immediately recognize. A person was regarded as innocent until proved otherwise. People accused of wrongdoing were allowed to defend themselves before a judge. A judge, in turn, was expected to weigh evidence carefully before arriving at a decision. These principles lived on long after the fall of the Roman Empire.

The Roman Family

At the heart of the Roman social structure stood the family, headed by the **paterfamilias**—the dominant male. The household also included the wife, sons with their wives and children, unmarried daughters, and slaves. Like the Greeks, Roman males believed that the weakness of females made it necessary for women to have male guardians. The paterfamilias had that authority. When he died, his sons or nearest male relatives assumed the role of guardian.

Fathers arranged the marriages of their daughters. Traditionally, Roman marriages were meant to be for life, but divorce was introduced in the third century

Multimedia Support

LASERDISC

Dressing Scene (fresco of the first century)

GROUP PROJECT

Assign different groups to research family life in other countries during the time period of the Roman Republic. Have students compare the different aspects of life mentioned here. Then construct a chart that shows a comparison of the different countries and aspects of family life. You might list the countries across the top and the aspects of family life down the left side. Then descriptions could be inserted in the appropriate boxes. Ask students to identify which country had the most restrictive rules about family. Which had the most lenient?

COMPARING TIME PERIODS

Expand the Group Project described above to include modern-day countries and their family structures. Ask students which country has the most restrictive family rules. Which has the most lenient?

174

▲ *This beautiful carving shows a couple holding a wedding contract, an important part of the marriage ceremony in Roman times. Note the purity of the lines and the simple, highly skillful appearance of cloth draped over the figures. How does the artist convey the feeling of tenderness and love?*

B.C. and became fairly easy to obtain. Either husband or wife could ask for a divorce, and no one needed to prove the breakdown of the marriage. Divorce became especially common in the first century B.C.—a period of political turmoil—when marriages were used to put together political alliances.

Some parents in upper-class families provided education for their daughters by hiring private tutors or sending the girls to primary schools. However, at the age when boys were entering secondary schools, girls were pushed into marriage (see "Young People in Rome"). The legal minimum age for marriage was twelve, although fourteen was a more common age in practice (for males, the legal minimum age was fourteen, although most men married later). Although

some Roman doctors warned that pregnancies could be dangerous for young girls, early marriages continued, because women died at a relatively early age. A good example is Tullia, the daughter of the Roman statesman Cicero (SIS-uh-ROE). She was married at sixteen and widowed at twenty-two. She remarried one year later, divorced at twenty-eight, remarried at twenty-nine, and divorced at thirty-three. She died at thirty-four, which was not unusually young for women in Roman society.

By the second century A.D., important changes were occurring in the Roman family. The paterfamilias no longer had absolute authority over his children. He could not sell his children into slavery or have them put to death. The husband's absolute authority over his wife also disappeared. By the late second century, women were no longer required to have guardians.

Upper-class Roman women in the Early Empire had considerable freedom and independence. They had the right to own, inherit, and sell property. Unlike the Greeks, Roman wives were not segregated from males in the home. They were appreciated as enjoyable company and were at the center of household social life. Upper-class women could attend races, the theater, and events in the amphitheater, although in the latter two places they were forced to sit in separate female sections. Moreover, women of rank were still accompanied by maids and companions when they went out. Some women operated businesses, such as shipping firms. Women could not participate in politics, but in the Early Empire a number of important women influenced politics through their husbands. Examples were Livia, the wife of Augustus, and Plotina, the wife of Trajan.

Slavery

Slavery was common throughout the ancient world, but no people had more slaves or relied so much on slave labor as the Romans did. Before the third century B.C., a small Roman farmer might possess one or two slaves, who would help farm his few acres and work in the house. These slaves would most likely be from Italy and be regarded as part of the family household. Only the very rich would have large numbers of slaves.

◀ *In this mosaic found in the ruins of Pompeii, a wealthy Roman woman is pictured at her dressing table. Several female slaves help her dress, while others carry refreshments in for her. How did the Romans control their large slave population?*

The Roman conquest of the Mediterranean brought a drastic change in the use of slaves. Large numbers of foreign slaves were brought back to Italy as a result of their capture in war. Ambitious generals of the first century, such as Pompey and Caesar, made large fortunes by treating slaves captured by their armies as private property.

Slaves were used in many ways in Roman society. The rich owned the most and the best. In the late Roman Republic, it became a badge of prestige to be attended by many slaves. Greek slaves were in much demand as tutors, musicians, doctors, and artists. Roman businessmen would employ them as shop assistants or craftspeople. Slaves were also used as farm laborers. In fact, huge gangs of slaves worked the large landed estates under pitiful conditions. One Roman writer argued that it was cheaper to work slaves to death and then replace them than to treat them well. Many slaves of all nationalities were used as household workers, such as cooks, valets, waiters, cleaners, and gardeners. Roads, aqueducts, and other public structures were built by contractors using slave labor. The total number of slaves is difficult to judge. Estimates vary from two to four free men to every slave.

The treatment of Roman slaves varied. There are many instances of humane treatment by masters and situations where slaves even protected their owners from danger. Slaves were also subject to severe punishments, torture, abuse, and hard labor that drove some to run away, despite the strict laws Romans had against helping a runaway slave. Some slaves revolted against their owners and even murdered them, causing some Romans to live in great fear of their slaves. The murder of a master by a slave might mean the execution of all the other household slaves.

Near the end of the second century B.C., large-scale slave revolts occurred in Sicily, where enormous gangs of slaves were worked under horrible conditions on large landed estates. Slaves were branded, beaten, fed little, kept in chains, and housed at night in underground prisons. It took three years (from 135 to 132 B.C.) to crush a revolt of 70,000 slaves. The great revolt in Sicily (104 to 101 B.C.) took a Roman army of 17,000 men to suppress. The most famous revolt in

YOUNG PEOPLE IN ROME

YOUNG PEOPLE IN ROME

The Education of Roman Children

In Greece, the state played a crucial role in the development of young people. In Rome, especially during the republic, the family was the center of attention. Unlike the Greeks, the Romans raised their children at home. Every Roman upper-class child (boy or girl) was expected to learn to read. The father was the chief figure in providing for the education of his children. He made the decision to teach his children himself, acquire a teacher for them, or send them to school. Teachers were often Greek slaves, because upper-class Romans had to learn Greek as well as Latin to prosper in the empire. The conservative politician Cato chose to educate his son himself, as we see from this description by the ancient writer Plutarch:

> As soon as the boy showed signs of understanding, his father took him under his own charge and taught him to read, although he had an accomplished slave, Chilo by name, who was a schoolteacher, and taught many boys. Still, Cato thought it not right, as he tells us himself, that his son should be scolded by a slave, or have his ears tweaked when he was slow to learn. . . . Cato himself was therefore not only the boy's reading-teacher, but also his tutor in law and his athletic coach, and he taught his son not merely how to hurl the javelin, fight in armor and ride a horse, but also how to box, to endure heat and cold and to swim lustily through the eddies and billows of the Tiber.

Roman boys learned reading and writing, moral principles and family values, law, and physical training to prepare them to be soldiers. Some upper-class families also educated their children in the fine arts.

Roman children learned by imitating their teachers. Thus, they learned to read by repeating aloud what the teacher read. They learned to write by copying from standard texts. If they made a mistake, they were beaten. Those boys and girls who attended schools were always accompanied by their teachers or nurses.

The end of childhood for Roman males was marked by a special ceremony. At the age of sixteen, a young Roman man exchanged his purple-edged toga for a plain white toga—the toga of

---

Italy occurred in 73 B.C. Led by the gladiator Spartacus, the revolt broke out in southern Italy and involved 70,000 slaves. Spartacus managed to defeat several Roman armies before being trapped and killed in southern Italy in 71 B.C. There were also 6,000 followers of Spartacus who were crucified (put to death by nailing to a cross), the usual form of execution for slaves.

Daily Life in Imperial Rome

At the center of the colossal Roman Empire was the ancient city of Rome. Truly a capital city, Rome had the largest population of any city in the empire, at close to one million by the time of Augustus. For anyone with ambitions, Rome was the place to be. People from all over the empire resided there. Entire sections were inhabited by specific groups, such as Greeks or Syrians.

Rome was an overcrowded and noisy city. Because of the congestion, cart and wagon traffic was banned from the streets during the day. However, the noise from the traffic at night often made sleep difficult. Walking in Rome at night was also dangerous. Although Augustus had organized a police force, people could be assaulted, robbed, or soaked by filth thrown out of the upper-story windows of Rome's massive apartment buildings.

ENRICHMENT ACTIVITY

Divide the class into groups and assign each group the task of writing a short story illustrating daily life in Imperial Rome. Then have each group present its story to the class. A particularly creative class might enjoy presenting their story as a play, song, or video.

Encourage students to make use of the large variety of information in this chapter, including trade items available in Rome, the extent of the Empire, behavior of various emperors, art, architecture, food and the like.

Consider showing portions of *The Robe* or *The Silver Chalice* and have students evaluate the accuracy of these depictions of daily life in Imperial Rome.

YOUNG PEOPLE IN ROME

The Education of Roman Children, continued

▲ *A Roman teacher is shown with his two pupils who are reading from papyrus scrolls. Wealthy Romans tried to prepare their sons for public careers by educating them in rhetoric and philosophy. How does the goal of public education in your state differ from Roman goals of education?*

manhood. The elaborate ceremony in which this occurred was on March 17 and included sacrifices to the household gods. In this way, young Romans entered manhood and soon after began their careers. Young Roman girls ended their education around the age of twelve. They then prepared to be good housewives, which was necessary because the common age for marriage of young girls was fourteen.

1. What subjects were taught to upper-class Roman children?

2. What places in society were educated young people expected to take?

3. What does the involvement of slaves in education reveal about Roman society?

An enormous gulf existed between rich and poor in the city of Rome. The rich had comfortable villas (see "Focus on Everyday Life: The Banquets of the Rich"). The poor lived in apartment blocks called **insulae,** which might be six stories high. Constructed of concrete, they were usually poorly built and often collapsed. The use of wooden beams in the floors and movable stoves, torches, candles, and lamps within the rooms for heat and light made fire a constant threat. Once started, fires were extremely difficult to put out. The famous fire of A.D. 64, which the emperor Nero was falsely accused of starting, destroyed a good part of the city.

Living conditions were poor in Rome. High rents forced entire families to live in one room. There was no plumbing or central heating. These conditions, along with open fireplaces, made homes uncomfortable. As a result, many poor Romans spent most of their time outdoors in the streets.

Fortunately for these people, Rome boasted public buildings unequaled anywhere in the empire. Its temples, markets, baths, theaters, triumphal arches, governmental buildings, and amphitheaters gave parts of the city an appearance of grandeur and magnificence.

Although it was the center of a great empire, Rome had serious problems. Beginning with Augustus, the

LEARNING FROM VISUALS

Answer to the caption question: In the U.S. education is mandatory for both girls and boys, not reserved for the wealthy.

COOPERATIVE LEARNING ACTIVITY

Divide the class into small groups to discuss the conditions of the poor in ancient Rome and the conditions of the poor in different countries today. In preparation for the discussion, have students collect newspaper and magazine articles that describe the conditions of the poor today. They might look for articles on countries such as India and China as well as some western countries. Be sure groups discuss the public buildings, entertainment, and food provided in Rome. Do any countries today provide anything similar for their poor?

ACROSS THE CURRICULUM

Read over the banquet menu with students. Tell them that taste was not as important to the Romans as how expensive and unique a food was.

Have students use their creative writing skills and work singly or in pairs to develop a dinner menu and evening of entertainment for a Roman banquet.

If time allows, you might have students share thoughts on the most exotic food they have tasted. Did they like it? Why or why not?

Answers to Critical Thinking Questions

1. Jellyfish and sea urchins come from the ocean; woods and grazing land support deer and cattle; sun and farm land are needed to grow figs, dates, nuts, and roses.

2. Rich have money and lands to buy or grow a variety of foods, including scarce items. Answers will vary.

$\mathcal{M}$ultimedia $\mathcal{S}$upport

 LASERDISC
Roman Reception on the Nile

FOCUS ON EVERYDAY LIFE
The Banquets of the Rich

Wealthy Roman homes contained a formal dining room, the scene of the dinner parties that were the chief feature of Roman social life. The banquet usually consisted of three courses: the appetizers, main course, and dessert. As the following menu from a cookbook by Apicius illustrates, each course included an enormous variety of unusual foods. Banquets lasted an entire evening. They were accompanied by entertainment provided by acrobats, musicians, dancers, and even poets. People usually ate reclining on couches. It was not considered improper for diners to vomit after each course so they could have room enough for the next course. Naturally, the diet of lower-class Romans was much different. It consisted of the basics: bread, olives, and grapes. Poorer Romans ate little meat.

▲ *This painting gives an idea of how lavish the Roman banquets of the rich could be. The poor in the Roman Empire served, while the rich enjoyed their wealth.*

A Sample Banquet Menu

Appetizers
Jellyfish and eggs
Sow's udders stuffed with salted sea urchins
Patina of brains cooked with milk and eggs
Boiled tree fungi with peppered fish-fat sauce
Sea urchins with spices, honey, oil, and egg sauce

Main Course
Fallow deer roasted with onion sauce and rue
Jericho dates, raisins, oil, and honey
Boiled ostrich with sweet sauce
Turtle dove boiled in its feathers
Roast parrot
Dormice stuffed with pork and pine kernels
Ham boiled with figs and bay leaves, rubbed with honey, baked in pastry crust
Flamingo boiled with dates

Dessert
Fricassee of roses with pastry
Stoned dates stuffed with nuts and pine kernels fried in honey
Hot African sweet-wine cakes with honey

1. What does the wide variety of foods suggest about the geographical location of Rome?

2. Explain the differences in the diets of the rich and the poor. Do those differences still exist today?

ENRICHMENT ACTIVITY

As a class, review the story of Horatius from the chapter's introduction. Now, imagine Horatius sped forward in time to the reign of Nero. What changes would he see in Rome's people, military, culture, even the city? Would he still find courage, duty and determination? If so, where?

Have students be Horatius and write a newspaper article for *The Imperial Times* discussing what is wrong with Rome and how the Empire can be saved. If he were bold enough to discuss Nero, what might he say? How might Nero respond?

Multimedia Support

LASERDISC

The Roman Colosseum, construction completed in A.D. 80

SPORTS AND CONTESTS

The Gladiatorial Shows and the Roman Masses

This fresco portrays a battle of gladiators, a popular spectacle during Roman times. A few gladiators were free men, but most came from the ranks of slaves and condemned prisoners. Occasionally a successful gladiator might win his freedom through victory in these games. Why do you think these fierce spectacles were so popular with the Romans?

Gladiatorial shows were an important part of Roman society. They took place in public arenas known as amphitheaters (similar in appearance to our modern football stadiums) and were free to the public. Most famous was the Colosseum, constructed at Rome to seat 50,000 people.

Gladiatorial games were held from dawn to dusk. Contests to the death between trained fighters formed the central focus of these games. Most gladiators were slaves or condemned criminals who had been trained for combat in special gladiatorial schools.

Gladiatorial games included other forms of entertainment as well. Criminals of all ages and both sexes were sent into the arena without weapons to face certain death from wild animals, who would tear them to pieces. Numerous kinds of animal contests were also held: wild beasts against each other (such as bears against buffalo) and gladiators in the arena with bulls, tigers, and lions. It is recorded that five thousand beasts were killed in one day of games when the Emperor Titus inaugurated the Colosseum in A.D. 80.

Amphitheaters, which varied greatly in size, were built throughout the empire. Many resources and much ingenuity went into building them, especially in the arrangements for moving wild beasts into the arena. In most cities and towns, amphitheaters came to be the biggest buildings, rivaled only by the circuses for races and by the public baths. Where a society invests its money gives an idea of what it considers important. Because the

(continued)

MORE ABOUT . . . *Entertainment, Roman Style*

As Juvenal said, Roman citizens were widely influenced by "bread and circuses." The imperial governments usually exploited this situation effectively, subsidizing the price of bread (so anyone could get at least bread to eat), and generally offering free circus for the masses. Rather than the tragic or comedic theater or the purist athletic events of the Greeks, Romans held mass spectacles that catered to the lowest common denominator of human nature—battle, blood, and gore. The Roman Colosseum and the many circuses all over the empire attest to the Romans' effective manipulation of human emotion. Today, in lieu of chariot races and ships in battle, we have boxers and highly paid teams of athletes who fight it out before loud and approving audiences. We have learned well from the Roman masters of entertainment.

LEARNING FROM VISUALS

Answer to the caption question: Students should remember that entertaining the masses was an important Roman strategy used to divert potential political unrest.

SPORTS AND CONTESTS

CRITICAL THINKING

Use the following questions to guide students in a discussion about this feature.

◆ What were the main reasons for the Roman games? *(fulfilled political and social needs; kept the minds of the people off political unrest; reminded the masses of what could happen if they displeased their masters)*

◆ How would the constant exposure to violence affect the people of Rome? *(Answers might include the fact that constant exposure to violence tends to desensitize people to it.)*

◆ Can students draw any parallels to society today as to how sports events affect our society? *(Students might mention the increased interest in professional sports, the amount of money spent on them, and the increased amount of violence related to sports events.)*

Answers to Critical Thinking Questions

1. entertainment; contest to the death between trained combatants
2. kept the minds of the idle masses off any political unrest; reminded people of what happens to those who fail to please their masters.

ASSESS

Answers to
SECTION REVIEW

2. (a) dominant male in the Roman family
   (b) blocks of apartments in Rome where the poor lived
3. (a) most distinguished poet of the Augustan Age; masterpiece was *Aeneid*
   (b) prominent Augustan poet, friend of Virgil; famous work *satires*
   (c) Roman gladiator who led slave revolt; defeated several Roman armies before being killed
4. a person is innocent until proven guilty; people accused of a crime are allowed to defend themselves before a judge; judge is expected to weigh evidence carefully before arriving at a decision
5. Answers will vary, but might include the following: Horace wrote about the way Greek slaves taught their masters and their master's children, ran their masters' businesses, and had other strong influences on the society that had conquered them.

SPORTS AND CONTESTS
The Gladiatorial Shows and the Roman Masses, continued

amphitheater was the chief location for the gladiatorial games, it is fair to say that public slaughter was an important part of Roman culture.

These bloody spectacles were indeed popular with the Roman people. The Roman historian Tacitus said, "Few indeed are to be found who talk of any other subjects in their homes, and whenever we enter a classroom, what else is the conversation of the youths." To the Romans, the gladiatorial games, as well as the other forms of public entertainment, fulfilled both a political and a social need. Certainly, the games served to keep the minds of the idle masses off any political unrest. The games performed in the amphitheaters also served to remind the masses of what happens to those who fail to please their masters. The masses became accustomed to violence as the rulers used it to strengthen their own positions.

1. What was the appeal of gladiatorial contests?
2. Explain how the games satisfied the ruling class's political purposes.

emperors provided food for the city poor. About 200,000 people received free grain. Even with the free grain, conditions were grim for the poor. Early in the second century A.D., a Roman doctor claimed that rickets (a disease caused by malnutrition that leads to deformed bones) was common among children in the city.

In addition to food, entertainment was also provided on a grand scale for the inhabitants of Rome. The poet Juvenal said of the Roman masses, "But nowadays, with no vote to sell, their motto is 'Couldn't care less.' Time was when their vote elected generals, heads of state, commanders of legions: but now they've pulled in their horns, there's only two things that concern them: Bread and Circuses."[5] Public spectacles were provided by the emperor as part of the great religious festivals celebrated by the state. The festivals included three major types of entertainment. At the Circus Maximus, horse and chariot races attracted hundreds of thousands. Dramatic performances were held in theaters. The most famous of all the public spectacles, however, were the gladiatorial shows (see "Sports and Contests: The Gladiatorial Shows and the Roman Masses").

 SECTION REVIEW

1. **Locate:**
   (*a*) Latium,   (*b*) Rome
2. **Define:**
   (*a*) paterfamilias,   (*b*) insulae
3. **Identify:**
   (*a*) Virgil,   (*b*) Horace,   (*c*) Spartacus
4. **Recall:** List the principles of justice, contributed by the Romans, that are still in use today in our own justice system.
5. **Think Critically:** Explain what the poet Horace meant when he said, "captive Greece took captive her rude conqueror."

COOPERATIVE LEARNING ACTIVITY

Divide the class into two groups—Greeks and Etruscans. Allow each group to work out their group's contributions to Rome, then let them debate the question, "Which culture contributed more to the development of Roman civilization—the Etruscans or the Greeks?"

Have students use examples of art, architecture and literature to back up their arguments. Complete the debate with a vote, allowing students to express why they voted as they did—especially if they "changed groups," so to speak.

THE DEVELOPMENT OF CHRISTIANITY

The rise of Christianity marks an important break with the dominant values of the Greek and Roman worlds. The Christian views on God, human beings, and the world were quite different from those of the Greeks and Romans. To understand the development of Christianity, we must first examine religion in the Roman world, as well as the Jewish background from which Christianity emerged.

The Religious World of the Romans

Augustus had taken a number of steps to revive the Roman state religion, which had declined during the turmoil of the late Roman Republic. The official state religion focused on the worship of a number of gods and goddesses, including Jupiter, Juno, Minerva, and Mars. The Romans believed that the observation of proper ritual by state priests brought them into a right relationship with the gods. This guaranteed peace and prosperity. The Romans believed that their success in creating an empire confirmed the favor of the gods. As the first-century politician Cicero claimed, "We have overcome all the nations of the world, because we have realized that the world is directed and governed by the gods."[6]

The polytheistic Romans were very tolerant of other religions. They allowed the worship of native gods and goddesses throughout their provinces. They even adopted some of the local gods. In addition, beginning with Augustus, emperors were often officially made gods by the Roman Senate, thus bolstering support for the emperors.

In addition to their official state religion, the Romans had household and countryside spirits, whose worship appealed especially to the common people. Here, too, proper ritual was important. The paterfamilias, as head of the family, made offerings to Vesta, goddess of the home, on a daily basis. Although these cults gave the Romans a more direct sense of spiritual con-

tact than they found in the official religion, they, too, failed to satisfy many people.

The desire for a more emotional spiritual experience led many people to the mystery religions of the Hellenistic east. These religions flooded into the western Roman world after the Romans conquered the Hellenistic states. The mystery religions promised their followers an entry into a higher world of reality and the promise of a future life superior to the present one. By participating in their ceremonies, a person could commune with spiritual beings and open the door to life after death.

The Jewish Background

In Hellenistic times, the Jewish people had been given considerable independence. By A.D. 6, however, Judaea (joo-DEE-uh) (which embraced the lands of the old Jewish Kingdom of Judah) had been made a Roman province and been placed under the direction of a Roman official called a **procurator.** Unrest in Judaea continued, made worse by divisions among the Jews themselves. One group—the Sadducees—favored cooperation with the Romans. The Essenes, as revealed in the Dead Sea Scrolls, a collection of documents first discovered in 1947, were a Jewish sect that lived in a religious community near the Dead Sea. They, like many other Jews, awaited a Messiah who would save Israel from oppression, usher in the kingdom of God, and establish a true paradise on Earth. A third group, the Zealots, were extremists who advocated the violent overthrow of Roman rule. A Jewish revolt in 66 was crushed by the Romans four years later. The Jewish temple in Jerusalem was destroyed, and Roman power once more stood supreme in Judaea.

The Rise of Christianity

It was in the midst of the confusion and conflict in Judaea that Jesus of Nazareth began his public preaching. Jesus—a Palestinian Jew—grew up in Galilee, an important center for the militant Zealots. Jesus' message was simple. He told his fellow Jews that he did not plan to harm their traditional religion: "Do not think that I have come to abolish the Law or the Prophets; I

TEACH

ACTIVITY

Have students research some of the Roman gods and goddesses such as those mentioned on this page—Jupiter, Juno, Minerva, and Mars. Let them share their research with the rest of the class.

REINFORCING VOCABULARY

Students may be unfamiliar with some of the words used in the Sermon on the Mount. You might go over the following definitions with them.

disciples—those who accept and help spread the teachings of another

meek—patient; humble; gentle

merciful—those who show kindness and forgiveness

persecuted—harassed or ill-treated

GROUP PROJECT

Divide the class into groups. Assign each group one of the sentences that begins with the word "Blessed," from the Sermon on the Mount. Have the groups determine the meanings of the sentences. As a class discuss how contrary to human nature these teachings are.

Ask if anyone knows how Jesus intended for people to actually accomplish these things. (not through their own power, but through God's power)

ACTIVITY

Have students identify, in a brief essay, at what point (doctrinally) Christianity separates from Judiasm and becomes a distinct religion.

182

OUR LITERARY HERITAGE

The Sermon on the Mount

The four Gospels of the New Testament are sacred books to Christians, but they are also great literature and an important part of the literary heritage of Western civilization. Written originally in Greek, they were later translated into Latin. Jesus' Sermon on the Mount is taken from the Gospel of Saint Matthew. As these excerpts illustrate, in the Sermon Jesus emphasized humility, charity, love for others, and a belief in the inner being and a spiritual kingdom superior to this material world. These values and principles were not those of classical Greco-Roman civilization as seen in the words and deeds of its leaders. Thus, they were an important part of Christianity's appeal to the poor and powerless.

The Gospel According to Saint Matthew

Now when he saw the crowds, he went up on a mountainside and sat down. His disciples came to him, and he began to teach them saying:
Blessed are the poor in spirit: for theirs is the kingdom of heaven.
Blessed are those who mourn: for they will be comforted.
Blessed are the meek: for they will inherit the earth.
Blessed are those who hunger and thirst for righteousness: for they will be filled.

Blessed are the merciful: for they will be shown mercy.
Blessed are the pure in heart: for they will see God.
Blessed are the peacemakers: for they will be called sons of God.
Blessed are those who are persecuted because of righteousness: for theirs is the kingdom of heaven. . . .

You have heard that it was said, "Eye for eye, and tooth for tooth." But I tell you, Do not resist an evil person. If someone strikes you on the right cheek, turn to him the other also. . . .

You have heard that it was said, "Love your neighbor, and hate your enemy." But I tell you, Love your enemies and pray for those who persecute you. . . .

Do not store up for yourselves treasures on earth, where moth and rust destroy, and where thieves break in and steal. But store up for yourselves treasures in heaven, where moth and rust do not destroy, and where thieves do not break in and steal. For where your treasure is, there your heart will be also. . . .

No one can serve two masters. Either he will hate the one and love the other, or he will be devoted to the one and despise the other. You cannot serve both God and money.

---

have not come to abolish them but to fulfill them."[7] According to Jesus, what was important was not strict adherence to the letter of the law but the transformation of the inner person: "So in everything, do to others what you would have them do to you, for this sums up the Law and the Prophets."[8] God's command was a simple one: to love God and one another. Jesus said, "Love the Lord your God with all your heart and with all your soul and with all your mind and with all your

strength. The second is this: Love your neighbor as yourself."[9] In the Sermon on the Mount (see "Our Literary Heritage: The Sermon on the Mount"), Jesus voiced the ethical concepts—humility, charity, and love toward others—that would form the basis for the value system of medieval Western civilization.

Some people welcomed Jesus as the Messiah, who would save Israel from oppression and establish God's kingdom on Earth. However, Jesus spoke of a heavenly

---

MORE ABOUT . . . *Did Jesus Speak Latin?*

For those who search for the historical Jesus, such questions provide keys to understanding. As a carpenter, and son of a carpenter, Jesus spoke the language of the common people in Judaea—Aramaic (a Semitic language related to Hebrew). When Jesus was brought before Pontius Pilate, the Roman authority in the land, how did they communicate? The Bible indicates a direct dialogue between them. Yet, there is no

record that Pontius Pilate spoke Aramaic and it is unlikely that a Jewish carpenter spoke Latin. Did they use translators? Perhaps they spoke in Greek? Greek was a second language to Romans, especially those stationed in the eastern part of the empire. Judaea at the time of Jesus was a Hellenistic area, so this is the most probable answer. And then again . . . ?

OUR LITERARY HERITAGE

The Sermon on the Mount, continued

This illustrated page from an early Bible, c. A.D. 700, shows Saint Matthew. What features indicate that he is considered a saint?

Therefore I tell you, do not worry about your life, what you will eat or drink; or about your body, what you will wear. Is not life more important than food, and the body more important than clothes? Look at the birds of the air; they do not sow or reap or store away in barns, and yet your heavenly Father feeds them. Are you not much more valuable than they? . . . So do not worry, saying, What shall we eat? or What shall we drink? or What shall we wear? For the pagans run after all these things, and your heavenly Father knows that you need them. But seek first his kingdom and his righteousness, and all these things will be given to you as well.

1. What are the ideals of early Christianity?

2. How do Christian values differ from the principles of classical Greco-Roman civilization?

kingdom, not an earthly one: "My kingdom is not of this world."[10] As a result, he disappointed the radicals. He also alienated conservative religious leaders, who believed Jesus was undermining respect for traditional Jewish religion. To the Roman authorities of Palestine, Jesus was a potential revolutionary who might lead Jews into another revolt against Rome. Therefore, Jesus found himself denounced by the leadership on all sides and was given over to the Roman authorities. The

procurator Pontius (PON-chus) Pilate ordered his crucifixion. That did not solve the problem, however. Loyal followers of Jesus believed that he had overcome death and come back to life. He was called *Christos*, or "the anointed one," and hailed as the Savior who had come to reveal the secrets of personal immortality.

Christianity began as a religious movement within Judaism. A prominent figure in early Christianity was

So What ??

If your students question the importance of the information on **Christians** *tell them . . .*

The term "Christian" was not used by the followers of Jesus while he was alive. Even after his death, they were known as followers of "the Way." In Antioch, Syria, c. A.D. 79,

the Greek term *Christianol* is first used to denote a follower of the Christ (the Messiah, in Greek). The term was originally negative in connotation, but followers of Christ embraced it willingly. Christian became their identifying name, spreading with the belief in Jesus as the Christ, the Annointed One.

Answers to Critical Thinking Questions

1. humility, charity, love enemies, turn the other cheek
2. Answers will vary, but may include the Roman consumption or entation, polytheism, violent entertainment, etc.

LEARNING FROM VISUALS

Answer to the caption question: Matthew has a full halo as do the two other figures in the illustration. One is clearly an angel hovering above him.

ACTIVITY

Have students list ways in which ideas of human behavior in Christianity and the Roman concept of rule by a code of laws affect us today.

MAKING HISTORY RELEVANT

Be sure students realize that two holidays we celebrate today—Christmas and Easter—are directly tied to the Christian religion. Christmas commemorates the birth of Jesus and Easter celebrates his resurrection from the dead.

REINFORCING VOCABULARY

Explain to students the Roman form of execution called crucifixion.

During a crucifixion, the subject was either tied or nailed (at wrists and ankles) to a cross. The cross was then stood upright (usually dropped into a hole in the ground) and the subject hung there until dead. It was an extremely painful, torturous death.

LEARNING FROM VISUALS

Tell students that a fresco is a piece of art that is accomplished by painting on fresh plaster that is still moist with water dissolved pigments.

The fresco shown here was found in the catacombs of Rome. Ask students if they know what the catacombs are and why they are important to the Christian religion. *(The catacombs are cemeteries under ground. Early Christians buried their dead in them.)*

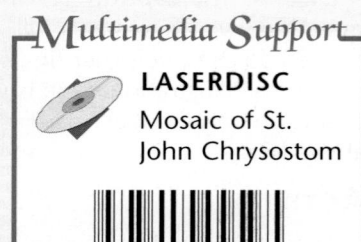

Multimedia Support

LASERDISC
Mosaic of St. John Chrysostom

CRITICAL THINKING

In the last paragraph on this page, the author states, "The basic values of Christianity differed markedly from those of the Greco-Roman world." Have students review the values of the Greeks and Romans and compare and contrast those values with the values of Christianity that are presented on pages 182–183 in Our Literary Heritage: The Sermon on the Mount.

CLASS DISCUSSION

Have students research and prepare for a dialog between Augustus and Paul of Tarsus on the relative importance of political power and human values. They could debate as groups or have a spokesperson from each group to "be" Augustus or Paul.

▶ *This fresco showing Christ and his disciples was found in the catacombs of Rome and then transferred to the Church of San Lorenzo in Milan. Through the work of these disciples, particularly Paul of Tarsus, Christianity grew to be the dominant religion in the Roman Empire and in Europe.*

Paul of Tarsus, who reached out to non-Jews. Paul was a Jewish Roman citizen who followed the command of Christ to preach the gospel to both Jews and Gentiles (non-Jews). Paul founded Christian communities throughout Asia Minor and along the shores of the Aegean.

Paul taught that Jesus was the Christ, the Messiah. He taught that Jesus was the Savior, the Son of God who had come to Earth to save all humans, who were all sinners as a result of Adam's sin of disobedience against God (original sin) and of their own evil acts. Paul taught that by Jesus' death, he had made up for the sins of all humans and thus had made possible their reconciliation with God and hence their salvation. By accepting Jesus as Christ and Savior, they could be saved from the penalty of sin.

After the reports that Jesus had overcome death, Christianity spread slowly. The teachings of early Christianity were passed on mostly by the preaching of convinced Christians. Written materials also appeared, however. Paul and other followers of Christ, had written letters, or epistles, outlining Christian beliefs for different Christian communities they had helped to found around the west-

ern Mediterranean. Also, some of Jesus' disciples (followers) may have preserved some of the sayings of Jesus in writing and would have passed on personal memories that later, between A.D. 40 and 100, became the basis of the written Gospels—the "good news" concerning Christ. These writings gave a record of Jesus' life and teachings, and they formed the core of the New Testament.

Jerusalem was the first center of Christianity, but its destruction by the Romans in A.D. 70 left Christian churches elsewhere with much independence. By 100, Christian churches had been established in most of the major cities of the eastern empire and in some places in the western part of the empire. Most early Christians came from the Jews and the Greek-speaking populations of the east. In the second and third centuries, however, an increasing number of followers were Latin-speaking people.

The basic values of Christianity differed markedly from those of the Greco-Roman world. The Romans, however, did not pay much attention to the Christians, whom they regarded at first as simply another sect of Judaism. The structure of the Roman Empire itself aided the growth of Christianity. Christian missionar-

MORE ABOUT . . . *Becoming a Christian*

Since Christianity is born of Judaism, you may expect a good deal of overlap between the two. Indeed, early Christians believed that you had to be a Jew in order to become a Christian. This involved following the Jewish law and accepting circumcision of males. This was a problem for Gentiles attracted to the teachings of Jesus. Saul of Tarsus (St. Paul), himself a Jew, believed that a Christian was not obligated to be a Jew. In order to

solve this dilemma, a top level meeting was called in Jerusalem in A.D. 50. Peter, James, Paul, and most of the disciples attended. The outcome was a compromise: you didn't have to be a Jew, but you had to respect Jewish law and customs. However, you didn't have to be circumcised! One obstacle was removed (so to speak) from those adult males who wished to become Christian.

ies, including some of Jesus' original twelve disciples or apostles, used Roman roads to travel throughout the empire in spreading the gospel (the "good news").

As time passed, however, the Roman attitude toward Christianity began to change. The Romans tolerated other religions except when they threatened public order or public morals. Many Romans came to view Christians as harmful to the Roman state, especially because Christians held their meetings in secret. Then, too, Christians refused to worship the state gods and emperors. Because the Romans regarded these practices as important to the state, they saw the Christians' refusal as an act of treason, punishable by death. The Christians, however, believed there was only one God. To them, the worship of state gods and the emperors meant worshiping false gods and endangering their own salvation.

The Roman persecution of Christians in the first and second centuries was never done on a regular basis. Persecution began during the reign of Nero. The emperor blamed the Christians for the fire that destroyed much of Rome. He accused them of arson and subjected them to cruel deaths in Rome. In the second century, Christians were largely ignored as harmless. By the end of the reigns of the five good emperors, Christians still represented a small minority, but one of considerable strength.

The Triumph of Christianity

The occasional persecution of Christians by the Romans in the first and second centuries had done nothing to stop the growth of Christianity. It had, in fact, served to strengthen Christianity in the second and third centuries by forcing it to become more organized. Crucial to this change was the emerging role of the bishops, who began to assume more control over church communities. The Christian Church was creating a new structure in which the **clergy** (the bishops and priests) were salaried officers separate from the **laity** (the regular church members).

Christianity grew slowly in the first century, took root in the second, and by the third had spread widely. Why was Christianity able to attract so many follow-

ers? First, the Christian message had much to offer the Roman world. The promise of salvation, which they believed was made possible by Jesus' death, made a strong impact on a world full of suffering and injustice. Christianity gave life a meaning and purpose beyond the simple material things of everyday reality. Second, Christianity seemed familiar. It was viewed by some as another mystery religion, offering immortality as the result of the sacrificial death of a savior-god. At the same time, it offered more than the other mystery religions did. Jesus had been a human figure who was easy to relate to. Moreover, Christianity did not require a painful or expensive initiation rite, as other mystery religions did. Initiation was by baptism—a purification by water—by which one entered into a personal relationship with Christ. In addition, Christianity gave new meaning to life and offered what the Roman state religions could not—a personal relationship with God.

Finally, Christianity fulfilled the human need to belong. Christians formed communities bound to one another, in which people could express their love by helping one another and offering assistance to the poor, the sick, widows, and orphans. Christianity satisfied the need to belong in a way that the huge Roman Empire could never do.

Christianity proved attractive to all classes, but especially to the poor and powerless. The promise of eternal life was for all—rich, poor, aristocrats, slaves, men, and women. As Paul stated in his Epistle to the Colossians, "And [you] have put on the new self. . . . Here there is no Greek nor Jew . . . barbarian, Scythian (SITH-ee-un), slave or free, but Christ is all, and is in all."[11] Although Christianity did not call for revolution, it stressed a sense of spiritual equality for all people.

The Christian Church became more organized in the third century. Some emperors began new persecutions, but their schemes failed to work. The last great persecution was by Diocletian (DIE-uh-KLEE-shun) at the beginning of the fourth century. Even he had to admit, however, what had become obvious in the course of the third century: Christianity was too strong to be blotted out by force.

In the fourth century, Christianity prospered as never before after the Emperor Constantine became the first Christian emperor. Although he was not bap-

RETEACH

Reinforce the reasons Christianity attracted so many followers during the first few centuries A.D.

◆ The Christian message had much to offer the Roman world. The promise of salvation made possible through the death of Jesus gave life meaning and purpose beyond the material things that were affordable only for rich Romans.

◆ Christianity seemed familiar. It did not require a painful or expensive initiation rite, only belief in Jesus the Christ.

◆ Christianity gave new meaning to life through a personal relationship with God.

◆ And, it fulfilled the human need to belong. The Christian communities formed strong bonds that allowed them to help each other and to reach out to those in need who were not Christians.

ASSESS

You can choose from a variety of assessments to evaluate your students' mastery of the objectives for this section as stated on page 181. Possible assessments include:

1. Section Review Questions on page 186.
2. Section 6–4 Quiz in your Teacher Resource materials
3. Reteaching Worksheets in your Teacher Resource materials
4. Self-Study software

MORE ABOUT . . . *Persecution of Christians*

When we think about Christians in Rome being persecuted, we envision them in the Colosseum, huddled in groups, waiting to be mauled by lions while huge crowds cheer and the blood flows. But the Colosseum was not built until A.D. 80, and persecution began under Nero in A.D. 64. He blamed Christians and launched a public campaign against them. Some of those arrested were crucified, others were sewn into the skins of wild beasts

to be torn apart by dogs. Still others were burned at the stake as human torches to light Nero's garden.

You may want to ask your students to research the persecution of Christians under Nero, the five good emperors, and Diocletion. As a class, discuss how useful the persecution was in the long run. Why did persecution strengthen rather than hinder the growth of Christianity?

2. (a) directed Roman province of Judaea
(b) the salaried officers in the Christian Church (bishop and priests)
(c) regular church members

3. (a) first-century Roman politician who claimed, "We have overcome all the nations of the world, because we have realized that the world is directed and governed by the gods"
(b) the "founder" of Christianity
(c) procurator who ordered the crucifixion of Jesus of Nazareth
(d) called the "second founder of Christianity;" carried the message of Christ to non-Jews (Gentiles)
(e) first Christian emperor of Rome
(f) made Christianity the official religion of the Roman Empire

4. (a) The persecution of Christians by the Romans caused Christianity to become stronger rather than wiping it out as the Romans had wanted.
(b) promise of salvation, gave life meaning; seemed familiar; personal relationship to God; filled human need to belong

5. Answers will vary. Roman State Religion: worship of a number of gods and goddesses, observation of ritual, often adopted local gods of conquered peoples, emperors were often made gods; Christianity: worship of one God, observation of rituals not important, ethical concepts—humility, charity, brotherly love—should form the basic value system

tized until the end of his life, in 313 Constantine issued the Edict of Milan, which proclaimed official tolerance of Christianity. Under Theodosius the Great, who ruled from 378 to 395, it was made the official religion of the Roman Empire. Christianity had triumphed.

SECTION REVIEW

1. **Locate:**
   (*a*) Judaea, (*b*) Jerusalem, (*c*) Nazareth,
   (*d*) Tarsus, (*e*) Asia Minor

2. **Define:**
   (*a*) procurator, (*b*) clergy, (*c*) laity

3. **Identify:**
   (*a*) Cicero, (*b*) Jesus of Nazareth, (*c*) Pontius Pilate, (*d*) Paul of Tarsus, (*e*) Constantine, (*f*) Theodosius

4. **Recall:**
   (*a*) How did the persecution of Christians by the Romans actually backfire?
   (*b*) Why did Christianity attract so many followers?

5. **Think Critically:** Compare the Roman state religion with Christianity. What are the similarities? What are the differences?

5

THE DECLINE AND FALL OF THE WESTERN ROMAN EMPIRE

In the course of the third century, the Roman Empire came close to collapsing. A military monarchy under the Severan rulers, who ruled from 193 to 235, restored order after a series of civil wars. However, this monarchy was followed by military anarchy. For a period of almost fifty years, from 235 to 284, the Roman imperial throne was occupied by anyone who had the military strength to seize it. In these almost fifty years, there were twenty-two emperors, only two of whom did not meet a violent death. At the same time, the empire was troubled by a series of invasions. In the east, the Sas-

sanid (su-SAW-nud) Persians made inroads into Roman territory. Germanic tribes also poured into the Balkans, Asia Minor, Gaul, and Spain. It was not until the end of the third century that most of the boundaries were restored.

Invasions, civil wars, and plague came close to causing an economic collapse of the Roman Empire in the third century. There was a noticeable decline in trade and small industry while the labor shortage created by plague affected both military recruiting and the economy. Farm production declined as fields were ravaged by invaders or, even more often, by the defending Roman armies. The monetary system began to show signs of collapse as a result of debased coinage (coins with a reduced amount of precious metal) and the beginnings of serious inflation.

Armies were needed more than ever, but financial strains made it difficult to pay and enlist more soldiers. By the mid-third century, the state had to rely on hiring Germans to fight under Roman commanders. These soldiers did not understand Roman traditions and had no loyalty to either the empire or the emperors.

The Reforms of Diocletian and Constantine

At the end of the third and the beginning of the fourth centuries, the Roman Empire gained a new lease on life through the efforts of two strong emperors, Diocletian and Constantine, who restored order and stabil-

◄ *This immense marble head of Emperor Constantine is 8 feet, 6 inches high and is just part of an enormous statue of the emperor. Following Constantine's conversion to Christianity, Christians were no longer persecuted, and cathedrals were built from Trier, the northern capital of the Empire, to Jerusalem.*

RECOMMENDED READING

The classic work of the Roman Empire is Edward Gibbon, *The Decline and Fall of the Roman Empire,* J. B. Bury edition (London, 1909–14). An excellent survey is P. Brown, *The World of Late Antiquity* (London, 1971). Also valuable are R. MacMullen, *Roman Government's Response to Crisis A.D. 235–337* (New Haven, Conn., 1976), and *Corruption and the Decline of Rome* (New Haven, Conn., 1988). See also, D. Bowder, *The Age of Constantine* and Julian (London, 1978); T. D. Barnes, *The New Empire of Diocletian and Constantine* (Cambridge, Mass., 1982); and S. Williams, *Diocletian and the Roman Recovery* (London, 1985). Recent studies include J. Matthews, *Western Aristocracies and Imperial Court, A.D. 364–425* (Oxford, 1975); E. A. Thompson, *Romans and Barbarians* (Madison, 1982); and A. Ferrill, *The Fall of the Roman Empire: The Military Explanation* (London, 1986).

ity. The Roman Empire was changed into a new state: the so-called Late Empire, which included a new governmental structure, a rigid economic and social system, and a new state religion—Christianity.

Believing that the empire had grown too large for a single ruler, Diocletian, who ruled from 284 to 305, divided it into four units. Despite the four-man rule, however, Diocletian's military power enabled him to claim a higher status and to hold the ultimate authority. Constantine, who ruled from 306 to 337, continued and even expanded the policies of Diocletian. Both rulers greatly strengthened and enlarged the administrative bureaucracies of the Roman Empire. A hierarchy of officials exercised control at the various levels of government. The army was enlarged to 500,000 men, including German units. Mobile units were established that could be quickly moved to support frontier troops where the borders were threatened.

Constantine's biggest project was the construction of a new capital city in the east, on the site of the Greek city of Byzantium on the shores of the Bosphorus. Eventually renamed Constantinople (modern Istanbul in Turkey), the city was developed for defensive reasons and had an excellent strategic location. Calling it his "New Rome," Constantine enriched the city with a forum, large palaces, and a vast amphitheater.

The political and military reforms of Diocletian and Constantine greatly enlarged two institutions—the army and civil service—which drained most of the public funds. More revenues were needed to pay for the army and bureaucracy. The population was not growing, however, so the tax base could not be expanded. Diocletian and Constantine devised new economic and social policies to deal with these financial burdens. Like their political policies, however, the new economic and social policies were all based on coercion and loss of individual freedom. To fight inflation, Diocletian issued a price edict in 301 that set wage and price controls for the entire empire. Despite severe penalties, it failed to work.

To ensure the tax base and keep the empire going despite the shortage of labor, the emperors issued edicts that forced people to remain in their designated vocations. Hence, basic jobs, such as bakers and shippers, became hereditary. The fortunes of free tenant farmers

also declined. Soon they found themselves bound to the land by large landowners who took advantage of depressed agricultural conditions to enlarge their landed estates.

In general, the economic and social policies of Diocletian and Constantine were based on control and coercion. Although temporarily successful, such policies in the long run stifled the very vitality the Late Empire needed to revive its sagging fortunes.

The Fall

The restored empire of Diocletian and Constantine limped along for more than a century. After Constantine, the empire continued to divide into western and eastern parts. The west came under increasing pressure from the invading Germanic tribes. The major breakthrough of invaders into the Roman Empire came in the second half of the fourth century. Ferocious warriors from Asia, known as Huns, moved into eastern Europe and put pressure on the Germanic Visigoths. They, in turn, moved south and west, crossed the Danube into Roman territory, and settled down as Roman allies. However, the Visigoths soon revolted. The Romans' attempt to stop them at Adrianople in 378 led to a crushing defeat for the Romans.

Increasing numbers of Germans now crossed the frontiers. In 410, the Visigoths sacked Rome. Vandals poured into southern Spain and Africa and Visigoths, into Spain and Gaul. Vandals crossed into Italy from northern Africa and sacked Rome in 455. (Our modern word *vandal* is taken from this ruthless tribe.) Twenty-one years later, in 476, the western emperor, Romulus Augustulus, was deposed by the Germanic head of the army. This is usually taken as the date of the fall of the Roman Empire in the west. As we shall see in Chapter 12, a series of German kingdoms replaced the Roman Empire in the west while an Eastern Roman Empire continued with its center at Constantinople.

Many theories try to explain the decline and fall of the Roman Empire. These theories include the following:

▲ Christianity's emphasis on a spiritual kingdom weakened Roman military virtues.

MORE ABOUT . . . *the Fall of Rome*

While most historians have asked, "Why did the Roman Empire fall?" some have suggested that the better question is, "How did the Roman Empire last as long as it did?" If one focuses on the political system of the empire, dependent on the will of one person, and often captive to the army, it is a wonder indeed that the empire lasted as long as it did. One possible explanation,

strangely enough, is Christianity. Early Christians believed the kingdom of God was around the corner. They identified the end of the world with the fall of Rome. As time passed and the world continued, they lost the sense of hourly expectation. With the end of persecution, Christianity became one of the foundations and pillars of the empire, helping perhaps to give it a longer life.

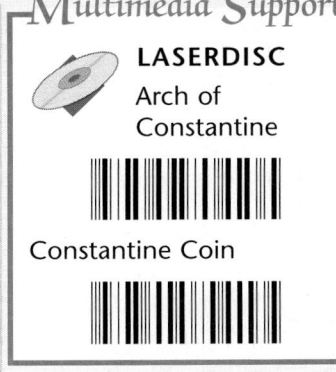

CLASS DISCUSSION

Review the theories used to explain the decline and fall of the Roman Empire as listed on pages 187 and 188. Ask students to determine the merits of each. Then have them discuss the problems with each. Help them see that it was very likely a combination of some or all of the theories that brought about the decline and fall of the Roman Empire.

CLASS DISCUSSION

Have students discuss in class the following question: What needed to have happened in order to avoid the fall of the western Roman Empire?

ASSESS

You can choose from a variety of assessments to evaluate your students' mastery of the objectives for this section as stated on page 187. Possible assessments include:

1. Section Review questions on this page
2. Section 6–5 Quiz in your Teacher Resource materials
3. Reteaching Worksheets in your Teacher Resource materials
4. Self-Study software

▲ Traditional Roman values declined as non-Italians gained prominence in the empire.
▲ Lead poisoning through leaden water pipes and cups caused a mental decline.
▲ The plague wiped out the population.
▲ Rome failed to advance technologically because of slavery.
▲ Rome was unable to put together a workable political system.

There may be an element of truth in each of these theories, but each has also been challenged. History is an intricate web of relationships, causes, and effects. No single explanation will ever suffice to explain historical events. One thing is clear. Weakened by a shortage of men, the Roman army in the west was simply not able to fend off the hordes of people invading Italy and Gaul. In contrast, the Eastern Roman Empire, which would survive for another thousand years, remained largely free of invasion.

Map 6.5   Barbarian Migration and Invasion Routes

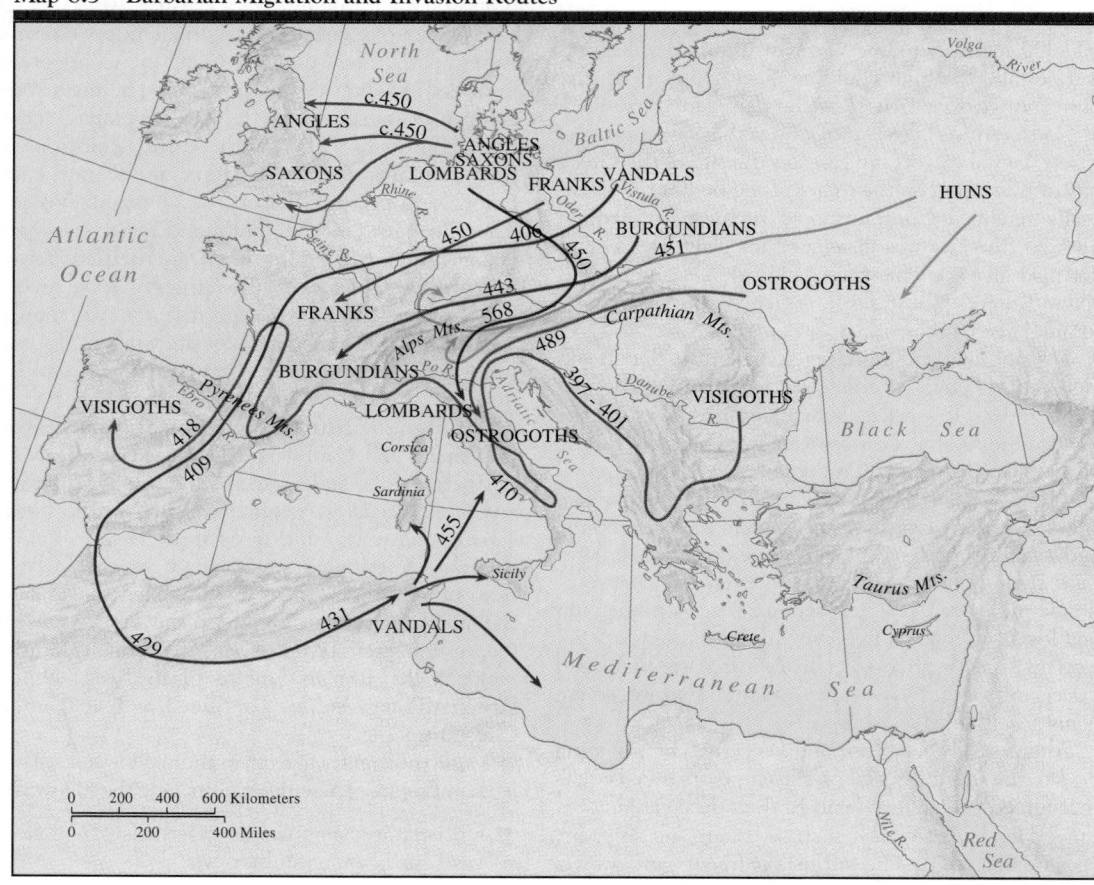

Answers to SECTION REVIEW

2. (a) ferocious warriors from Asia
(b) German tribes that invaded the Roman Empire, eventually settling in Roman territory and becoming Roman allies who then revolted and sacked Rome

STUDYING MAPS

Have students determine how many different peoples invaded the Roman Empire. Use a current political map to help students determine what modern-day countries the invaders were from. Ask students to determine from the dates given on the map, the number of years the Roman Empire fought off the invasions. *(about 162 years)*

1. How many different people groups invaded the Roman Empire? *(9)* What groups were they? *(Angles, Saxons, Lombards, Franks, Vandals, Burgundians, Huns, Ostrogoths, Visigoths)*
2. Trace the route of the vandals. Where did they begin? *(The Vistula River in present-day Poland, across Europe, through France, over the Pyrennes, across Spain and North Africa to Sardinia, Sicily, and Italy)*
3. About how long did the vandals journey take them? *(about fifty years)*

SECTION REVIEW

1. **Locate:**
   (*a*) Byzantium,   (*b*) Spain,   (*c*) Africa,   (*d*) Gaul

2. **Identify:**
   (*a*) Huns,   (*b*) Visigoths,   (*c*) Vandals,
   (*d*) Romulus Augustulus

3. **Recall:** List the many theories that try to explain the fall of the Roman Empire.

4. **Think Critically:** Choose one of the theories you listed in question 3 and explain why you think it did or did not contribute to the fall of the Roman Empire.

Conclusion

Sometime in the eighth century B.C., a group of Latin-speaking people built on the Tiber River a small community called Rome. Between 509 and 264 B.C., the expansion of this city led to the union of almost all of Italy under Rome's control. Even more dramatically, between 264 and 133 B.C., Rome expanded to the west and east and became master of the Mediterranean Sea. Rome's republican institutions failed, however. After a series of bloody civil wars, Augustus created a new order that began the Roman Empire. Between 14 and 180, the Roman Empire experienced a lengthy period of peace and prosperity. Trade flourished, and the provinces were ruled in an orderly fashion.

The Roman Empire was one of the largest empires in antiquity. Using their practical skills, the Romans made achievements in law, government, language, and engineering that were passed on and that became an important part of Western civilization. The Romans also preserved the intellectual heritage of the Greek world.

Although we are justified in praising the empire, it is also important to remember its dark side: the enormous gulf between rich and poor, the dependence upon slaves, the bloodthirsty spectacles in the amphitheaters, and the use of official terror to maintain the order for which the empire is so often praised. As the British chieftain Calgacus is supposed to have said, "To robbery, slaughter, plunder, they [the Romans] give the lying name of empire; they make a solitude and call it peace."[12]

In the last two hundred years of the Roman Empire, Christianity grew, along with its new ideals of spiritual equality and respect for human life. A slow transformation of the Roman world also took place. Germanic invasions hastened this process and brought an end to the Western Roman Empire in 476. Many aspects of the Roman world would continue. However, a new civilization, which we will examine in Chapter 12, was emerging that would carry on yet another stage in the development of human society.

Notes

1. Florus, *Epitome of Roman History*, trans. E. S. Forster (Cambridge, Mass., 1960), II, xxii, p. 327.
2. Virgil, *The Aeneid*, trans. C. Day Lewis (Garden City, N.Y., 1952), p. 154.
3. Horace, *Satires*, in *The Complete Works of Horace*, trans. Lord Dunsany and Michael Oakley (London, 1961), 1.1, p. 139.
4. Livy, *The Early History of Rome*, trans. Aubrey de Selincourt (Harmondsworth, 1960), p. 18.
5. Juvenal, *The Sixteen Satires*, trans. Peter Green (Harmondsworth, 1967), Satire 10, p. 207.
6. Quoted in Chester Starr, *Past and Future in Ancient History* (Lanham, Md., 1987), pp. 38–39.
7. Matthew 5:17.
8. Matthew 7:12.
9. Mark 12: 30–31.
10. John 18:36.
11. Colossians 3:10–11.
12. Tacitus, *The Life of Cnaeus Julius Agricola*, in *The Complete Works of Tacitus*, trans. Alfred Church and William Brodrib (New York, 1942), p. 695.

RETEACHING ACTIVITY

As a class discussion or in smaller groups, help students work through the strengths and weaknesses of the six popular explanations given for the fall of Rome. *(1. Christianity weakened Rome, 2. Roman values declined as non-Italians took over, 3. Lead poisoning, 4. plague, 5. slavery kept Rome technologically backwards, 6. poor political system)* Then think through possible explanations which each of the following might have given: Horatius, Greeks, Germanic tribes, and Christians. Develop a class explanation for Rome's fall.

Finally, discuss with the class how these and similar reasons are given for the "decline" of the United States.

(c) German tribe that attacked the Roman Empire and sacked Rome (d) the emperor of the western Roman Empire who was deposed by the Germanic head of the army

3. The theories include: Christianity's emphasis on a spiritual kingdom weakened Roman military virtues; traditional Roman values declined as non-Italians gained prominence in the empire; lead poisoning from leaden water pipes and cups caused a mental decline; plague wiped out the population; Rome failed to advance technologically because of slavery; Rome was unable to put together a workable political system.

4. Answers will vary.

CLOSE

Have students work in pairs or groups of three to list contributions, both positive and negative, that the Roman Empire made to the world.

TIME LINE

As students conclude the chapter, you may want to refer them to the chapter time line in the *Study Guide*. The time line will help them put key dates in perspective. Supporting questions and activities are also provided.

SPANISH SUPPORT

The *Conclusion* has been translated into Spanish for your Spanish-speaking students. Included with this translation (in your Teacher Resource Box) are Section Key Points, which consist of one or two sentences summarizing each section in the chapter. These Key Points have also been translated into Spanish.

USING KEY TERMS

1. praetors
2. paterfamilias
3. tribunes of the plebs
4. procutator
5. consuls
6. insulae
7. First Triumverate
8. Senate
9. clergy, laity
10. Plebeians, patricians
11. conturiate assembly
12. imperator
13. council of the plebs

REVIEWING THE FACTS

1. Their strength lay in law, government, and engineering.
2. (Students will choose at least three.) Apennines do not divide Italy into many separate sections; fairly flat, good as farm land; Rome eighteen miles inland, safe from pirates, close by river to the Mediterranean; Rome natural crossing point for north-south traffic; Italy, a peninsula, crossroads in the Mediterranean; easy to conquer other regions; could control empire
3. found Rome a village and left it a city; impact on dress and organization of army
4. patricians: landowners, ruling class; plebeians: less wealthy landholders, craftsmen, merchants and small farmers; plebeians wanted social and political power
5. Hannibal was a Carthigian general who crossed the Alps into Italy. He was called back to Carthage to defend the city from the Romans. Hannibal was crushed in battle and Carthage lost the war.
6. Crassus—killed in battle; Pompey—defeated by Caesar; Julius Caesar—became dictator of Rome
7. period of the five good emperors, second century, noted for era of peace and prosperity, policies helpful to the empire

190

CHAPTER 6 REVIEW

USING KEY TERMS

1. Cases of civil law were applied to citizens and later to noncitizens by judges who were called _____.
2. The term _____ refers to the idea in Roman society that males should be dominant because females were too weak.
3. Officials, who were to protect the power of the less wealthy landholders, craftspeople, merchants, and small farmers, were called _____.
4. Judaea became a Roman province under the direction of an official called a _____.
5. During the Roman Republic, two _____ led the army and directed the government.
6. _____, constructed of concrete and usually poorly built, housed the poor in the city of Rome.
7. Caesar, Crassus, and Pompey formed a powerful governmental coalition called the _____.
8. By the third century B.C. the Roman _____ determined the laws of the Republic.
9. The _____ in the Christian Church were salaried officials who were separate from regular church members called the _____.
10. _____ were Roman citizens who wanted political and social equality with the wealthy _____.
11. The _____ was organized in such a way that the wealthiest citizens always had a majority.
12. Augustus was a popular ruler who was given the title of _____, or commander in chief, by the Senate.
13. A popular assembly for the less wealthy Roman citizens was created after hundreds of years of struggle and was named the _____.

REVIEWING THE FACTS

1. Why were the Romans considered practical people?

190

2. List at least three ways in which geography influenced Roman history.
3. Why were the Etruscans considered to be the greatest influence on early Rome?
4. Who were the patricians and plebeians and why were they in conflict with each other?
5. Who was Hannibal, what happened to him, and why was he important?
6. Name the men who formed the First Triumvirate. Describe what happened to each of them.
7. What is meant by Pax Romana? What conditions made it possible?
8. What is meant by Greco-Roman civilization?
9. Why did the Roman emperors resort to "Bread and Circuses"?
10. Name three famous Roman writers. Name their works and explain why these works are important.
11. What rights did women have during the Early Empire?
12. According to Jesus Christ, what was God's simple command?
13. Why was Paul of Tarsus a prominent figure in early Christianity?
14. What reforms did Diocletian and Constantine institute?
15. A.D. 476 is considered the end of the Roman Empire for what reason?

THINKING CRITICALLY

1. Analyze the important beliefs common to Judaism and Christianity and explain why they appealed to those living in the Roman Empire.
2. Research the Jewish revolt in A.D. 66, the crushing of the revolt, and the destruction of the Temple in Jerusalem. Research and analyze the long-term effects of these events on Judaism.

8. Roman and Greek culture mixed and became the basis for Western European traditions
9. entertained the landless and poor, kept them fed and under control
10. Virgil: *Aeneid,* linked Roman and Greek civilizations, established "divine mission to rule the world;" Horace: *Satires, Epistles,* pointed out problems and vices of his time; Livy: *History of Rome,* celebrated Rome's greatness
11. considerable independence; right to own, inherit, and sell property; not segregated, center of family life, could attend races, theater, and amphitheater; some owned businesses
12. God's command according to Jesus: "Love the lord your God with all your heart and with all your soul and with all your mind and with all your strength. The second is this: Love your neighbor as yourself."
13. provided a broad foundation for the spread of Christianity
14. restored order and stability; Diocletian divided the empire into four parts, enlarged Roman army; Constantine established a capital in the eastern part of the empire, enlarged army and civil services, made Christianity legal
15. marks the date that Romulus Augusulus was deposed by a German general

APPLYING SOCIAL STUDIES SKILLS

1. **Politics and History:** Assume the role of Augustus, Nero, or Constantine. Write a speech describing the conditions in the Roman Empire at the time and what you were doing to address those conditions.
2. **The Role of Ideas:** Look up the *Twelve Tables* and write them as they would be written today.
3. **Economics and History:** Identify the ways in which slavery was a detriment and/or a help to the Roman economy. Write a petition to the emperor upholding your position.
4. **Social Life:**
   (a) Pretend you are in a public forum in Rome. In class, debate with another citizen the extent to which the gulf between the patricians and plebeians is straining the Roman Empire versus providing much needed-stability.
   (b) Write a diary describing a day in the life of a poor Roman. (Be sure to read the **You Are There** selections before you write.)
5. **Religion in History:** Explain why the ethical monotheism of Christianity appealed to Romans and why persecution did not stop Christianity's spread. Include ideas from **Our Literary Heritage: The Sermon on the Mount.**
6. **The Role of Individuals:** Write an epitaph for Gaius Gracchus or Julius Caesar.
7. **The Impact of Science and Technology:** Pretend you are a citizen of ancient Rome. Write an article for publication bragging about the superiority of Romans because of their ability as builders and engineers. Support your bragging with examples.

MAKING TIME AND PLACE CONNECTIONS

1. Under the United States Constitution the president is the commander in chief of the army. How is this different than it was in the Roman Empire? What problems arose in the Empire because of this difference?
2. Compare and contrast the lives of young men and women in the Early Empire with the lives of young men and women in the United States today.
3. Read **You Are There: Cincinnatus Saves Rome.** Explain why George Washington is sometimes called a modern Cincinnatus.
4. Photograph or photocopy a picture of the facade of a building in your area which is designed in the Roman tradition. How does it reflect Roman building style and how do the carvings (bas relief) reflect traditions coming from the Romans?

BECOMING AN HISTORIAN

Understanding and Interpreting Maps: Find a blank map of Afroeurasia. Outline the Roman Empire at its height. Trace the trade routes leading into the Empire, including the Silk Road. Analyze how well connected Rome was with other parts of the world. How was this beneficial to the Empire? How might it have caused a trade deficit? What were the areas in which trade was not extensive? Why?

Cause and Effect: Research the effects of lead on humans. Read about the effects of lead during the time of the Roman Empire. Argue the extent to which it was or was not a cause in the decline of the Roman Empire.

Analyzing Information/Drawing Inferences: Read about Benito Mussolini. Why did he call on Italians to recreate the "Glory that was Rome"? Develop other modern examples in which history has been or is used to encourage nationalism. To what extent is this propaganda or simply historical accuracy?

191

6. Students will evaluate the role of the individual in society.
7. Students will appreciate historical perspectives, examine the influence of inventions.

MAKING TIME AND PLACE CONNECTIONS

1. Answers will show that students understand why the military is under civilian control in the United States. (Compare and contrast.)
2. Answers will vary. Students will reconstruct patterns of historical succession and duration, role of the individual in society.
3. Answers will vary.
4. Answers will vary.
5. Students will reconstruct patterns of historical succession and duration; draw comparisons across eras and regions.

BECOMING AN HISTORIAN

Understanding and Interpreting Maps: Maps showing the trade routes connecting the Roman Empire will point out the interdependence within the Empire and the linkages to other parts of Afroeurasia. Students will realize that the empire did not exist in a vacuum.

Cause and Effect: Researching lead and its effects on humans will give students a chance to understand how the historian uses scientific data in interpreting events.

Analyzing Information/ Drawing Inferences: Students can research efforts to increase nationalism through using past glories by studying Benito Mussolini, Adolf Hitler, and Saddam Hussein. Students can read the speeches of Presidents and look for ways in which the past is used to inspire people.

THINKING CRITICALLY

1. Beliefs common to Judaism and Christianity include ethical monotheism, beliefs coming from the Torah and Old Testament such as the Ten Commandments, common founders such as Abraham. The appeal to those living in the Roman Empire can be in part derived from the text.
2. will give the students the opportunity to improve research skills; will provide background in understanding the Diaspora and desire of Jews for a homeland

APPLYING SOCIAL STUDIES SKILLS

1. Students will explore the role of the individual in history, cause and effect, relationships.
2. encourages students to appreciate historical perspectives, reconstruct patterns of historical succession and duration
3. Students will analyze cause and effect relationships: compare and contrast differing sets of ideas, values, and institutions.
4. Students will analyze cause and effect relationships: compare and contrast differing sets of ideas, values, and institutions.
5. Students will analyze the importance of ideas.

UNIT TWO

OVERVIEW OF THE UNIT

The second unit of World History is divided into seven chapters, spanning about 220 pages.

This unit brings students up to about the year A.D. 1500. Chapters 7, 8, 9, and 11 are the shortest (27 to 29 pages) while chapters 10, 12, and 13 run between 33 and 37 pages. Assuming a 36-week course, you may wish to condense these seven chapters into six weeks, including assessment time.

Using the Illustration

Creative Writing. Ask students to suggest adjectives that describe this illustration. Write them on the board. Most likely students will suggest words such as *colorful, busy, action-packed,* and *detailed.* Ask students to write a short story explaining why the knights have gathered in the tourney. Students should use as many of the adjectives on the board as possible. These stories will help give you an idea of the general knowledge base of the class about the legends and traditions (as well as stereotypes).

If you prefer to do an art activity, discuss with students the important role that banners and flags played in an era of widespread literacy. Ask them to design a banner that would represent themselves, their family, or their homeland and to include an explanation for the symbols or icons they use.

▶ *This illustration from* The Book of Tourneys *by King Rene of Anjou, France, shows the formal proceedings of a medieval jousting tournament.*

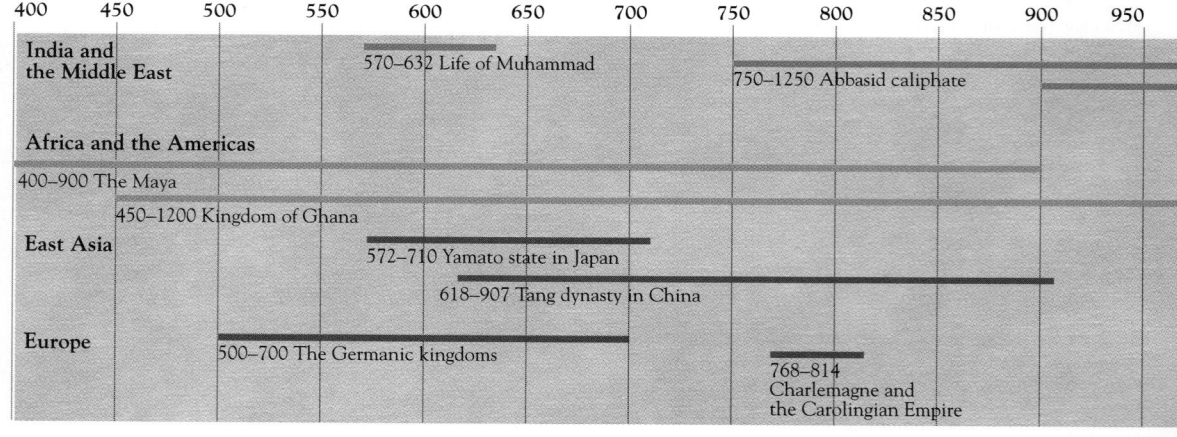

400	450	500	550	600	650	700	750	800	850	900	950

India and the Middle East — 570–632 Life of Muhammad; 750–1250 Abbasid caliphate

Africa and the Americas — 400–900 The Maya; 450–1200 Kingdom of Ghana

East Asia — 572–710 Yamato state in Japan; 618–907 Tang dynasty in China

Europe — 500–700 The Germanic kingdoms; 768–814 Charlemagne and the Carolingian Empire

UNIT OPENER ACTIVITY

Divide the class into eight groups and assign each group one of the following regions: North America, South America, India, China, Southeast Asia, the Middle East, Eastern Europe, and Western Europe. Without looking at their textbooks students in the group should write three questions that they would like answered about the region they have been assigned. The questions should deal with the time period up to A.D. 1500.

Afterwards, switch the questions among the groups so that no group has its own list. Using the index and the table of contents, students should try to find answers (or list page numbers that address these issues). This activity will help students anticipate the direction of the next six weeks.

By the beginning of the first millennium A.D., the great states of the ancient world were mostly in decline. On the ruins of these ancient empires, new patterns of civilization began to take shape between 400 and 1500. In some cases, these new societies were built on the political and cultural foundations of earlier states. In other cases, new states built on elements of earlier civilizations, but embarked in different directions.

In the meantime, new civilizations were also beginning to appear in a number of other parts of the world—in Japan, in Southeast Asia, in Africa, and in the Americas. Like earlier states, most of these new states obtained much of their wealth from agriculture. What is most striking about the period, however, is the growing importance of trade as a factor in national and global development. All of these states were being increasingly linked by trade into what was becoming the first "global civilization."

UNIT OUTLINE

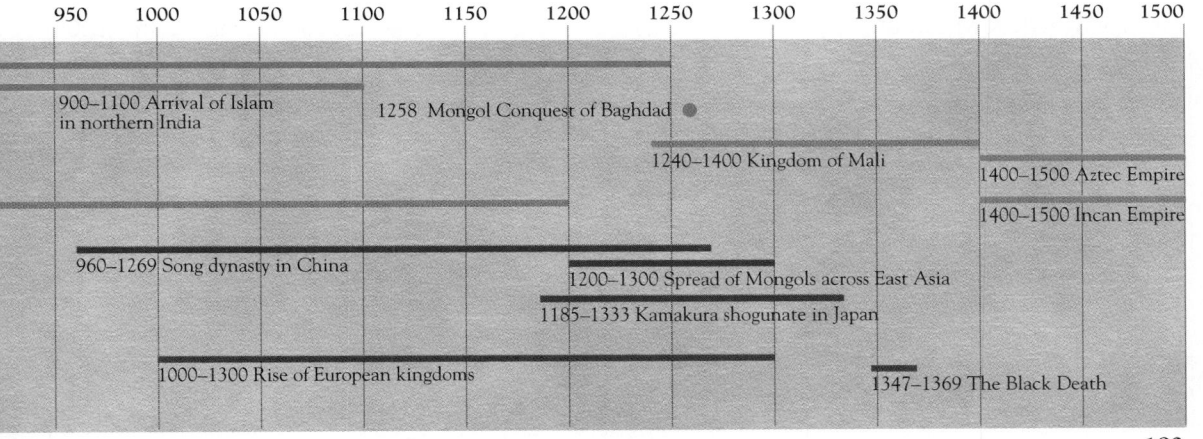

| 950 | 1000 | 1050 | 1100 | 1150 | 1200 | 1250 | 1300 | 1350 | 1400 | 1450 | 1500 |

900–1100 Arrival of Islam in northern India

1258 Mongol Conquest of Baghdad ●

1240–1400 Kingdom of Mali

1400–1500 Aztec Empire

1400–1500 Incan Empire

960–1269 Song dynasty in China

1200–1300 Spread of Mongols across East Asia

1185–1333 Kamakura shogunate in Japan

1000–1300 Rise of European kingdoms

1347–1369 The Black Death

193

STUDYING THE TIME LINE

Ask students the following questions to help them compare the time periods of the different civilizations they will be studying in this unit, as well as develop an appreciation for the wide span of years covered.

1. What is the earliest year represented in the time line? *(A.D. 400)*

2. What is the latest year represented in the time line? *(A.D. 1500)*

3. What is the total amount of time covered in the time line? *(1100 years)*

4. Approximately how long did the Kingdom of Mali exist? *(160 years)*

5. According to the time line, which two empires existed simultaneously? *(Aztec and the Incan)*

6. How is the Mongol conquest of Baghdad indicated on the time line? *(by a dot rather than a line)*

PROJECT IDEAS

After determining the amount of time you will be devoting to this unit, you may want to assign one of the following projects to all students, or allow individual students to choose from the list the one project that they will complete during the study of Unit Two.

1. Scientists have credited the Aztecs with having created an extremely sophisticated calendar based on the solar year. Ask creative and artistic students to research the Aztec calendar and decorate a plaster model for display.

2. Islam was one of the first religions to forbid its followers to create an image of the deity. Because of this taboo, beautiful and complex mosaics were developed. Students should research some of these patterns and re-create them for a border in the classroom.

3. Most students will be somewhat familiar with Roman and Greek mythology through traditional stories, movies, etc. Few students are likely to have been exposed to the interesting mythology of the Hindu religion. Ask students to research one of the Hindu gods. They should use visual aids to present what they learn to the rest of the class.

PLANNING GUIDE

SECTION	KEY TOPICS	PRIMARY SOURCES	ASSESSMENT
1 The First Americans and the Peoples of North America pages 195-201	◆ Geographical Features of the Americas ◆ The First Americans ◆ Amerindians of North America		◆ Section Review, page 201 ◆ Section Quiz 7-1, TRB
2 Early Civilizations in Central America pages 202-214	◆ Early Central American Civilizations ◆ The Mayan and Toltec Civilizations ◆ The Aztec Society	◆ The Ritual of Human Sacrifice, page 212	◆ Section Review, page 214 ◆ Section Quiz 7-2, TRB
3 The First Civilizations in South America pages 214-220	◆ The Moche Civilization ◆ The Inca Empire		◆ Section Review, page 220 ◆ Section Quiz 7-3, TRB

THE WORLD OF THE AMERICAS (1000 B.C. TO 1500 A.C.)

REPRODUCIBLE ACTIVITIES

Historical Maps

Charts and Graphs

Critical Thinking

Cooperative Learning

Vocabulary

Guided Reading

Reteaching

Enrichment

Performance Assessment

Spanish Key Points and Chapter Summaries

Spanish Vocabulary

Spanish Guided Reading

MULTIMEDIA SUPPORT

TRANSPARENCIES
- *World History* Color Transparency Package
- Fine Art Color Transparency Package

VIDEO
- *World History* Video Library
- CNN. Annual Video Update

LASERDISC
- *Sights and Sounds of History*

AUDIO
- *Listening to Literature* audiotape (English and Spanish)
- *History of Music* CD

SOFTWARE
- WESTEST™
- Student Review

CD–ROM
- *The Journey of Civilization*
- *World History*

INTERNET
- Internet Activities

On Line with WORLD HISTORY

Access West's history web site at
http://history.swpco.com
You'll find activities and web sites related to specific topics and chapters in *World History: The Human Odyssey*. Also look for references to helpful web sites at appropriate places throughout this teacher edition.

LESSON PLANNING

You will find detailed daily lesson plans for both traditional class scheduling and **block scheduling** in your Teacher Resource Box.

Not Enough Time?

If you do not have the four or five days recommended to teach this chapter, you may want to focus on the following sections and activities:

- Have students read to find answers to the Questions to Guide Your Reading on page 195.
- Assign students the Cooperative Learning activity on the bottom of page 221.

THE WORLD OF THE AMERICAS
(400 TO 1500)

7

Across the Atlantic Ocean from the great civilizations of the Old World, new civilizations were in the process of being formed. During or at the end of the last Ice Age—more than ten thousand years ago—peoples from Northeast Asia began to move across the Bering Strait into Alaska and then continued down into the plains of North America. Most of these early peoples, today often referred to as Amerindians, lived by hunting and fishing or by food gathering.

By 1200 B.C., the first organized societies began to take root in Central and South America. One key area of societal development was on the plateau of central Mexico. Another was in the lowland regions along the Gulf of Mexico and extending into modern-day Guatemala. A third was in the central Andes (AN-deez) Mountains, adjacent to the Pacific coast. Other societies were just beginning to emerge in the river valleys and great plains of North America.

When the Spanish arrived in Mexico in 1519, they were startled to see the brilliant civilizations existing in lands that they had assumed were occupied by primitive savages. Bernal Díaz (DEE-az), who accompanied Hernán Cortés (kor-TEZ) on his expedition to Mexico in 1519, could not believe his eyes when he saw the Aztec city of Tenochtitlán (tay-NAWCH-teet-LAWN) in central Mexico: "When we beheld so many cities and towns on the water, and other large settlements built on firm ground, and that broad causeway running so straight and perfectly level to the city of Tenochtitlán, we were astonished because of the great stone towers and temples and buildings that rose up out of the water." To some of the soldiers accompanying Cortés, "all these things seemed to be a dream." The Aztecs were equally astonished, but for quite different reasons. One wrote, "They [the Spanish] came in battle array, as conquerors, and the dust rose in whirlwinds on the roads, their spears glinted in the sun, and their flags fluttered like bats. Some of them were dressed in glistening iron from head to foot; they terrified everyone who saw them." Within a short time, the Spanish destroyed the Aztec Empire. Díaz remarked, "I thought that no land like it would ever be discovered in the whole world. But today all that I then saw is overthrown and destroyed; nothing is left standing."

◀ *This Spanish map of Tenochtitlán was published in 1524, not long after the Aztec Empire fell to the Spanish. How does its plan differ from colonial cities in the United States?*

NEW PATTERNS OF CIVILIZATION

400	THE AMERICAS	1500
400		1500

QUESTIONS TO GUIDE YOUR READING

1. Who were the first Americans?

2. What were the major features of the stateless societies developed in North America?

3. What were the main characteristics of the Mayan civilization?

4. What were the major features of the Aztec civilization?

5. What were the most important achievements of the Inca Empire?

OUTLINE

1. THE FIRST AMERICANS AND THE PEOPLES OF NORTH AMERICA

2. EARLY CIVILIZATIONS IN CENTRAL AMERICA

3. THE FIRST CIVILIZATIONS IN SOUTH AMERICA

THE FIRST AMERICANS AND THE PEOPLES OF NORTH AMERICA

As a result of an enormous variety of climates and geographical features, many different and isolated cultures emerged in the Americas. Trade and expansion, however, made it inevitable that many of these peoples would come into contact with one another.

The Lands of the Americas

The Americas make up an enormous land area, stretching about nine thousand miles from the Arctic Ocean in the north to Cape Horn at the tip of South America. Over this vast area are many different landscapes: ice-covered lands; dense forests of pine, spruce, cedar, and fir; fertile river valleys ideal for hunting and farming; lush, tropical forests; and hot, dry deserts.

Along the western coast of the Americas are two major mountain ranges: the Rocky Mountains in North America and the Andes Mountains in South America. Both are actually part of the same mountain chain. On the eastern coasts, the mountains are less awesome, with the Appalachian Mountains in North America and the Brazilian Highlands in South America. Between the mountain ranges of the west and east

195

195

FOCUS

OBJECTIVES

After completing this section, students should be able to

1. describe the characteristics of the major geographical regions in North America

2. name at least five Amerindian peoples and describe major features of their cultures

3. explain the importance of agriculture on the development of Amerindian cultures

4. discuss the main purpose of the League of Iroquois

Multimedia Support

TRANSPARENCY
7–1, Map 7.1
(page 196)

FOCUS ACTIVITY

For early Americans, the environment was composed of natural conditions over which they had no control. Inform students that one criteria used today by geographers to differentiate between "developed" and "developing" countries is the ability to control their environment and use technology to exploit resources.

Divide the class into groups and assign one of the four climatic regions of North America to each group (Arctic/Far North, Eastern Woodlands, Great Plains, Southwest). Have each group prepare a list of the climatic conditions for their region and the impact this might have on the lives of the people living there.

196

coasts are broad valleys with rich land for farming. Through the valleys run great rivers, such as the Mississippi in North America and the Amazon in South America. The Amazon is the world's second longest river, flowing almost 3,900 miles from the Andes Mountains to the Atlantic Ocean.

The First Americans

Between 100,000 and 12,000 years ago, the last Ice Age produced low sea levels that in turn created a land bridge in the Bering Strait between the Asian and North American continents. Scholars believe that small communities of people from Asia crossed this land bridge. Most likely, they were hunters and their families who were pursuing the herds of bison and caribou that moved in search of grazing land into North America as the glaciers receded. These people became the first Americans.

Scholars do not agree on exactly when human beings were living in the Americas. They do know, however, that people gradually spread throughout the North American continent. Scholars also know that by 10,000 B.C., people had penetrated almost to the tip of South America. These first Americans were hunters and food gatherers who lived in small, nomadic communities close to the source of their food supply.

The Peoples of North America

North America is a large continent with varying climates and geographical features. South of the ice of the Arctic is the cold, treeless plain known as the **tundra.** Along the northern Pacific coast are dense forests of fir, spruce, and cedar. In the east, from the Great Lakes down to the

Gulf of Mexico is an area known as the Eastern Woodlands. This area contains lush forests with both evergreens and deciduous trees such as birch and oak. Between the Rocky Mountains and the Mississippi River is the area of the Great Plains. The plains area makes for ideal grazing land for the great buffalo herds that once roamed there. Southwest of the Plains are deep canyons and desert land. These different geographical areas became home to various groups of Amerindians, who created their own unique ways of living.

Most Amerindian communities lived by hunting, fishing, or foraging. It was probably during the third millennium B.C. that people in certain parts of North America began to grow plants for food in a systematic way. As was the case elsewhere, early agriculture was often combined with hunting and food gathering. As the population grew, however, wild game and food

Map 7.1   Peoples and Cultures of North America

STUDYING MAPS

The following activities will help you guide the students through their study of Map 7.1.

1. Locate the Appalachian and Rocky Mountains, the Great Lakes, and the Great Plains on the map.

2. Name the major Amerindian urban settlements shown on the map. *(Mesa Verde, Cahokia, Moundville, and Hopeville)*

3. Approximately how wide, east to west, is the region settled by the Woodland farmers? *(about 1200 miles)*

became scarce, forcing some communities to place more emphasis on regular farming.

The Arctic and Northwest: The Inuit

About 4000 B.C., a group of people popularly known as the Eskimos (now called the Inuit) moved into North America from Asia. They were hunters and fishers who had to learn unique ways to survive in such a cold and harsh environment. Most Inuit settled along the coasts of the tundra region, the treeless land south of the Arctic. With a variety of harpoons and spears, the Inuit became skilled at hunting the seal and caribou that provided both their food and clothing. Sealskins became summer clothes. Inuit women stitched the hides of the caribou together with bone needles and gut thread to make winter clothes. In winter, the Inuit built homes of stones and turf. The traditional igloo, or snow house, made out of cut blocks of hard-packed snow, was only a temporary shelter used for traveling in winter. Until the beginning of the twentieth century, the Inuit continued to live much as they had a thousand years earlier.

The Eastern Woodlands: The Mound Builders and Iroquois

By about 1000 B.C., farming villages were being established in the Eastern Woodlands, the land in eastern North America from the Great Lakes to the Gulf of Mexico. People grew crops but also continued to gather wild plants for food. Perhaps best known are the Hopewell people in the Ohio River valley, who

▲ *The Inuits inhabited northern Canada, Greenland, and Alaska. Although igloos are commonly associated with the Inuit, these huts made of ice blocks were only used as temporary lodging while the Inuits hunted.*

▼ *People of the Adena culture built mounds in the shapes of birds, tortoises, and snakes. This representation of the snake, seen from an aerial view, is a quarter of a mile long, 20 feet wide, and 5 feet high.*

TEACH

LEARNING FROM VISUALS

The harsh climate of the tundra prohibited farming and the Inuit survived primarily by hunting and fishing. While hunting, temporary shelters were built using packed snow and ice. An experienced Inuit could build a snow igloo in one to two hours using a snow knife made of bone. If students wonder how people can survive in shelters made from blocks of ice inform them that ice is a good insulating material and will hold heat well. To make the igloo livable, it has to be "iced." This is done in two stages: First, the igloo is sealed and a small oil fire is lit inside. As the snow melts, moisture is drawn to the outside and freezes to create a hard shell like a turtle. Next, the door is opened and a small hole is bored in the roof. As the cold air rushes in, the inside walls become coated with a thin film of ice. Two layers of ice with the snow in between act as a good insulator. The inside can remain comfortable while outside temperatures plunge to 50° F below zero.

ACTIVITY

Mounds are found throughout the Eastern Woodlands and were built by a number of different peoples over several hundred years. Ask students what the presence of the mounds tells us about the life of the Mound Builders. Was their life likely to have been easier or harder than the inuits?

CRITICAL THINKING

Most of our knowledge of the early peoples of North America comes from archae-ologists—scientists who study ancient cultures through the ruins, artifacts, bones, and other remains that are left from the culture. Ask students if the period of the early Americans can be compared to the Dark Ages of Greece and Rome. Do they think our knowledge of Amerindian culture is more or less accurate than our knowledge of ancient Greece or Rome? What other records do we have of this era?

LEARNING FROM VISUALS

1. Ask students to describe the role of women as shown in the visual. What tasks are women shown doing? What are the men doing? (As common with many cultures, women are engaged in household tasks such as preparing food and clothing, while men are consulting and repairing canoes.)
2. Ask students what this illustration tells us about the life of the Iroquois. (Answers will vary. Students should support their answers with facts from the text.)
3. Compare this Iroquois set-tlement to the Inuit settlement shown on page 197.

Answer to the caption question: Uses of fire include hollowing out logs to make a corn grinder, cook-ing, and perhaps using fire to make wood pliable for use in framework for housing and in bark canoes. The second-growth forest shows that the Algonquin practiced slash-and-burn agriculture.

extended their culture along the Mississippi River. The Hopewell people, also known as the Mound Builders, are especially known for the large and elaborate earth mounds that they built. Some of the mounds were bur-ial mounds and have been found to contain necklaces and bracelets made of gold, silver, copper, and shells. These pieces of jewelry were made by skilled crafters. Many of the precious materials they worked with were obtained by trading with peoples from as far away as the Great Lakes and the Gulf of Mexico.

A shift to full-time farming occurred around A.D. 700. From this shift emerged a prosperous culture that was located in the Mississippi River valley from Ohio, Indi-ana, and Illinois down to the Gulf of Mexico. Among the most commonly grown crops of this Mississippian culture—as it is called—were corn, squash, and beans. As the population in the area increased, people began to live in villages. Communities emerged in the low-lands, where the soil could be farmed for many years at a time because of the nutrients deposited by the river water. As the communities grew, village councils were established to deal with disputes. In a few cases, several villages banded together under the authority of a local chieftain. Such chieftains may have claimed divine powers.

Urban centers began to appear, some of them con-taining as many as ten thousand people or more. At the site of Cahokia (ku-HOE-kee-uh), near the modern city of East St. Louis, Illinois, archaeologists found a burial mound over ninety-eight feet high with a base larger than that of the Great Pyramid in Egypt. A hun-dred smaller mounds were also found nearby. A town at the site covered almost three hundred acres and was surrounded by a wooden stockade. Between 850 and 1150, a flourishing Cahokia was apparently the seat of government for much of the Mississippian culture. Cahokia carried on extensive trade with other commu-nities throughout the region. By the thirteenth cen-tury, for reasons largely unknown, Cahokia was in a state of serious decline and soon collapsed.

▼ This painting reveals many details of daily life for the Iroquois. How many examples of the importance of fire in the daily life of this tribe can you find?

RECOMMENDED READING

For a profusely illustrated and informative overview of the early civilization of the Amer-icas, see M. Coe, D. Snow, and E. Benson, Atlas of Ancient America (New York, 1988). The first arrival of human beings in the New World is discussed in J. D. Jennings, ed., Ancient Native Americans (San Francisco, 1978); and B. Fagan, The Great Journey: The Peopling of Ancient America (London, 1987).

To the northeast of the Mississippian culture were the Amerindians known as the Iroquois (IR-uh-kwoy), who were hunters and farmers. In their world, each person—man or woman—had a separate task. Men were hunters who stalked deer, bear, caribou, and small animals like rabbits and beaver. They were also the warriors who protected the community. Women owned the dwellings; gathered wild plants; planted the seeds; and harvested the crops, the most important of which were the "three sisters"—corn, beans, and squash. The women also cooked, made baskets, and took care of the children.

The Iroquois lived in villages that usually consisted of **longhouses** surrounded by a wooden fence for protection. Each longhouse, built of wooden poles covered with sheets of bark, was 150 to 200 feet in length and housed about a dozen families. Villages varied in size. Some held about a dozen longhouses and others, as many as fifty.

The Iroquois were also traders. They exchanged corn, tobacco, and fishing nets with neighboring Amerindian tribes (groups of related families that share a common language and beliefs) for meat and furs. When Europeans arrived in North America beginning in the sixteenth century, the Iroquois traded their furs for European goods, including beads, cloth, and guns.

Wars were common, especially among the five tribes of the Iroquois who lived in much of the modern states of Pennsylvania and New York, as well as in parts of southern Canada. Legend holds that around 1400, when the Iroquois civilization seemed about to be torn apart by warfare, an elder of the Huron tribe, named Deganawida, appeared and preached the need for peace. One who listened to his wise words was Hiawatha, a member of the Onondaga (awn-AWN-doe-GAH) tribe. From the combined efforts of Deganawida and Hiawatha came the Great Peace, which created a tribal alliance called the League of Iroquois. One of the thirteen laws of the Great Peace made clear its purpose: "In all of your acts, self-interest shall be cast away. Look and listen for the welfare of the whole people, and have always in view not only the present, but also the coming generations . . . the unborn of the future Nation."[1]

A council of representatives (a group of fifty Iroquois chiefs) from each of the five tribes, known as the Grand Council, met regularly to settle differences among its members. They were chosen in a special fashion. In each Iroquois tribe, the women of every **clan** (a clan was a group of related families) singled out a well-respected woman as the clan mother. The clan mothers, in turn, chose the male chiefs who would represent the clans at the Grand Council. The hope was that this system would produce the wisest and best leaders to participate in the Grand Council. Much was expected of them: "With endless patience, they shall carry out their duty. Their firmness shall be tempered with a tenderness for their people. Neither anger nor fury shall find lodging in their minds, and all their words and actions shall be marked by calm deliberation."[2] The Grand Council, an experiment in democracy, was successful and brought a new way for the Iroquois to deal with their problems. In 1754, Benjamin Franklin used the League of Iroquois as a model for a Plan of Union for the British colonies.

The Amerindians of the Great Plains

West of the Mississippi River basin, most early Amerindian peoples lived by hunting or food gathering. During the first millennium A.D., knowledge of agriculture gradually spread up the rivers to the Great Plains, and farming was practiced as far west as southwestern Colorado. Most of the Plains Amerindians cultivated beans, corn, and squash along the river valleys of the eastern Great Plains. The light soil was easily worked by hoes and digging sticks. Every summer, the men left their villages to hunt buffalo, a very important animal to the Plains culture. A group of hunters would work together to frighten a herd of buffalo, causing them to stampede over a cliff.

The buffalo served many uses for Plains Amerindians. The people ate the meat, utilized the skins for clothing, and made tools from the bones and rope from the hair. They used buffalo skins to make **tepees** (circular tents used for shelter) by stretching the skins over wooden poles. Tepees provided excellent shelter; they were warm in winter and cool in summer. They could also be taken apart quickly when it was time to move.

ENRICHMENT ACTIVITY

Have students research examples of Anasazi or Pueblo art, compiling a display for the class. Instruct them to use file cards or cardstock to hold titles and short explanations of the work, as they might actually see in a museum. *Note:* Color is important, so sug- gest that they bring library books into class, or use a color copier, or they may want to try to reproduce the art themselves (in which case they should be careful to label it as a reproduction).

CRITICAL THINKING

Make sure students make the connection between the development of agriculture and the development of permanent villages and political institutions. The practice of agriculture is perhaps the most transformative development in human history and is one of the *parallel developments* that allowed civilizations to develop independently at different places and times across the globe. It allowed people for the first time to exert control over the environment rather than be totally subject to the vagaries of nature. With a more reliable source of food more children survived, people lived longer, and populations grew. Permanent villages were established in locations best suited to growing crops, and these settlements became the center of communal life. Because less time was required to provide food, people were able to produce improvements in both their art and technology. Task specialization developed along with expanded trade and economic activity. People also had a vested interest in protecting and expanding their lands, necessitating governments to resolve conflicts and raise armies for protection. Agriculture is a major catalyst for civilization. Ask students to discuss some of the changes that resulted from the development of agriculture and produce a pyramid of resulting developments, with agriculture at the top, producing changes at the next level, which produce further changes at the next level and so on.

LEARNING FROM VISUALS

1. Ask students to compare the scene of a Comanche village with the Inuit settlement shown on page 197 and the Iroquois settlement on page 198. What similarities and differences can they identify? *(Obvious differences include climate and topographical factors that resulted in different types of food products, housing, and clothing. Similarities would include the roles played by men and women, and the amount of time taken up by providing for the basic needs.)*

2. Ask students to examine the treatment of women, children, and men in the three scenes. How are they different? Can the students think of reasons why different roles may have developed?

Answer to the caption question: Students might suggest that everyone seems to be working, but socializing as well.

LEARNING FROM VISUALS

The bottom scene on this page shows a buffalo hunt.

1. Ask students when and how horses were introduced into North America. *(Horses were introduced into Central America by Spanish explorers in the 16th century.)*

2. Ask students how horses changed the lives of the Amerindian people. Were the Inuit or Iroquois likely to have used horses? *(Students might suggest that the climate of the Inuit and the heavy forested region of the Iroquois would have discouraged the migration of horses to those areas.)*

In this painting of a Texas Comanche village, women are depicted scraping and stretching buffalo hides in order to make new tepees. The Comanche are one of many of the Great Plains Amerindian tribes. What other aspects of daily life can you infer from this painting by George Catlin?

In the western Plains, where a dry climate made farming difficult, Amerindians were nomadic hunters who followed buffalo herds on foot. Buffalo hunting became even more popular with the Plains people (as well as easier) with the introduction of the horse by the Spanish in the sixteenth century.

Amerindians in the Southwest: The Anasazi

The Southwest was home to a number of Amerindians who survived there by growing such crops as corn, beans, and squash. The Southwest covers the territory of the modern American states of New Mexico, Arizona, Utah, and Colorado. Conditions are dry, but there is sufficient rain in some areas for farming. It was there that the Anasazi (AW-nuh-SAW-zee) peoples established an extensive farming society.

Between 500 and 1200, the Anasazi irrigated the desert regions and grew corn and squash. Using canals and

Alfred Jacob Miller, who painted this scene, never actually witnessed Indians driving buffalo over a cliff, but his work captures the intense drama and excitement of such an event. These mass hunts were both arduous and dangerous, and although they were life sustaining, some Amerindians lost their lives during these pursuits.

MORE ABOUT . . . *the Anasazi*

The Anasazi, or "ancient ones," left a rich artistic tradition. Most of what has survived the elements are examples of their pottery, which can be seen in the major museums of the United States and regional museums of the Southwest. On a generally off-white background, the Anasazi drew stylized figures of animals and geometric patterns. The primitive designs are classic in their simplicity and artistic beauty. Their art did not die with their society; it was transmitted to their cultural descendants, the Pueblo Indians of the southwestern United States. Today they are a critically important part of the artistic tradition of the southwestern United States.

▲ *Mesa Verde National Park, located in southwestern Colorado, contains spectacular ruins of Anasazi towns built into the sides of cliffs or in narrow river valleys. Cliff Palace, the group of apartments shown here, once housed as many as 400 people. Why do you think the Anasazi built their homes in such inaccessible sites?*

earthen dams, they turned parts of the desert into fertile gardens. They were skilled at making baskets and beautifully crafted pottery. They used stone and **adobe** (sun-dried brick) to build pueblos, multistoried structures that could house up to 250 people. In the Chaco (CHAW-koe) Canyon in northwestern New Mexico, they built an elaborate center for their civilization. At the heart of Chaco Canyon was Pueblo Bonito, a large complex that contained six hundred rooms housing more than a thousand people. Chaco Canyon was also the main center of a vast trade network in which turquoise tiles were sent south to Mexico in return for other goods. This flourishing center, however, could not survive a fifty-year series of droughts, which led the Anasazi to abandon it.

The Anasazi culture itself, however, did not die. To the north, in southern Colorado, a large community had formed at Mesa Verde (MAY-suh-VURD-ee) (today a U.S. national park). Groups of Anasazi there built a remarkable series of buildings in the recesses of the cliff walls. Perhaps as many as three thousand cliff dwellers lived there. A serious drought in the late thirteenth century made farming impossible. The settlement at Mesa Verde was abandoned in the fourteenth century. The Anasazis lived on, however. When the Spaniards arrived in the area, they labeled the Anasazi descendants the **Pueblos** (Spanish for "town") because of their unique, adobe dwellings.

SECTION REVIEW

1. **Locate:**
   (*a*) Appalachian Mountains,   (*b*) Gulf of Mexico,
   (*c*) Cahokia,   (*d*) Mesa Verde

2. **Define:**
   (*a*) tundra,   (*b*) longhouses,   (*c*) clan,
   (*d*) tepees,   (*e*) adobe,   (*f*) Pueblos

So What ⁉️

*If your students question the importance of the information on **the Anasazi**, tell them . . .*

The art of the Anasazi lives today through its multiple re-births in the different native American "Pueblos" of the Southwest. Few Americans can recognize or are even aware of the artistic achievement of present-day Pueblos. The Hopi, the Navaho, the Acoma, and many more Pueblos today create pottery, weavings, and other specialized products such as Kachina dolls and sand paintings, which are world-class in their artistic expression (as well as in their cost). Unfortunately, such handmade works of art have not made it to all parts of the country due to limited supply. Many Americans today are still unaware of one of their country's greatest artistic traditions.

ASSESS

Have the class prepare a visual display on the daily life and customs of North American peoples. Include religion, government, role of women, sources of food, healing practices, types of shelter, village structure, etc. Because topics overlap students will have to cooperate in producing the materials.

Answers to SECTION REVIEW

2. (a) treeless plain south of the Arctic; (b) homes built of wooden poles covered with bark; (c) a group of related families; (d) shelters made from buffalo skins; (e) sun-dried brick; (f) descendants of the Anasazis
3. (a) people who moved into North America from Asia; (b) lived in the Ohio Valley; (c) early North American culture centered near Cahokia; (d) lived northeast of the Mississippian culture
4. learned to irrigate the desert; built multistoried structures; developed trade network
5. Answers will vary.

CLOSE

Call on individual students to describe the different environmental conditions in North America and how different peoples adapted.

FOCUS

OBJECTIVES

After completing this section, students should be able to

1. name the four major advanced civilizations that developed in Central America
2. discuss the calendar and hieroglyphic writing system of the Maya
3. describe the living conditions in Aztec society
4. compare and contrast the social, religious, and political structures of the Maya and Aztec civilizations
5. explain the influence of the Spanish explorers on Mesoamerican cultures

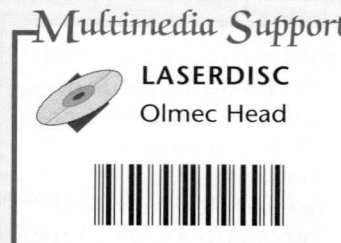

Multimedia Support

LASERDISC
Olmec Head

FOCUS ACTIVITY

Sports and games were an important part of the Mesoamerican cultures and reflect the values and beliefs of that culture.

Divide the class into small groups and assign a modern game to each of the groups. Include sports, video, board and internet games. Have each group discuss how the game is a reflection of the values and beliefs of our culture (For example, individual versus collective accomplishment, winning versus cooperating, physical versus mental requirements, team versus individual games).

3. **Identify:**
   (*a*) Eskimos,   (*b*) Hopewell people,
   (*c*) Mississippian Valley culture,   (*d*) Iroquois

4. **Recall:** Identify the different factors that set the Anasazi apart as an "advanced" Amerindian people.

5. **Think Critically:** Explain why the Iroquois League made a good model for a Plan of Union, which was developed by Benjamin Franklin for the British colonies.

EARLY CIVILIZATIONS IN CENTRAL AMERICA

Around 5000 B.C., in the central plateau of Mexico, people began to grow maize (corn) and other crops. Farming was also under way in the lowland regions near the modern-day city of Veracruz and in the Yucatán peninsula further to the east. There, in the region that archaeologists call Mesoamerica (a name we use for areas of Mexico and Central America that were civilized before the Spaniards arrived), the first civilizations in the New World began to appear.

The first signs of civilization in Central America began around 1200 B.C. with the Olmec. Located in the hot and swampy lowlands along the coast of the Gulf of Mexico south of Veracruz, the Olmec peoples farmed along the muddy riverbanks in the area. They had large cities that were centers for their religious rituals. They carved colossal stone heads, probably to represent their gods. These huge heads are especially remarkable because the Olmec had no metal tools. Carving them with instruments of stone must have taken a great deal of time.

One of the chief political and religious centers of Olmec civilization was La Venta. A thirty-foot-high pyramid towered above the city. Around 400 B.C., La Venta was destroyed when an unknown group of people wrecked many of its buildings and monuments.

Although the Olmec peoples had a flourishing agriculture, they did not have many of the raw materials, such as certain kinds of rocks and iron ore, that they

Map 7.2   The Heartland of Mesoamerica

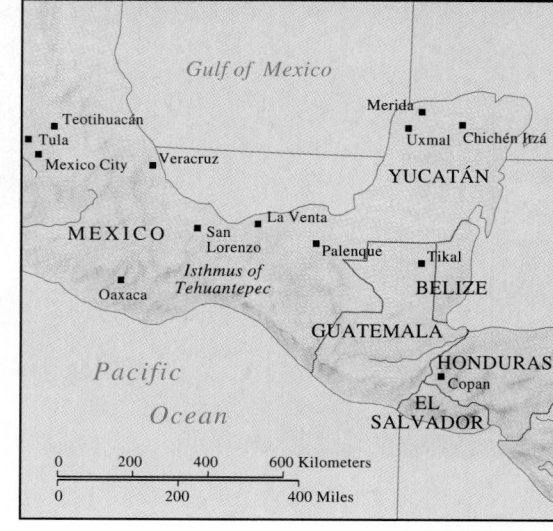

used for making their monuments and jewelry. As a result, the Olmec peoples traded widely in the area. Olmec objects have been found in central Mexico and Central America. Around 400 B.C., for reasons not yet fully understood, the Olmec civilization declined and eventually collapsed.

The first major city in Central America was Teotihuacán (TAY-oh-TEE-wuh-KAWN) ("Place of the Gods"), which was the capital of an early kingdom that arose around 250 B.C. and collapsed about A.D. 800. Located about thirty miles northeast of Mexico City in a fertile valley, Teotihuacán had as many as 150,000 inhabitants at its height. Along its main thoroughfare, known as the Avenue of the Dead, were temples and palaces. All of them, however, were dominated by a massive Pyramid of the Sun rising in four tiers to a height of over two hundred feet.

Most of the people of Teotihuacán were farmers. Fertile soil and a good supply of water made their valley one of the richest farming areas in Central America. Teotihuacán was also a busy center for trade. In scores of workshops throughout the city, skilled arti-

STUDYING MAPS

The following activities will help you guide the students through their study of Map 7.2.

1. Name the major Mesoamerican cities shown on the map. (Help students with pronunciation if required.)

2. Locate the Yucatan Peninsula on the map.
3. What is the approximate length of the Mesoamerica region? *(1000 miles)*

sans made tools, weapons, pottery, and jewelry. These goods were shipped to other parts of Central America, Mexico, and even the southwestern part of North America in return for the raw materials used in their crafts. As we have seen, the Anasazi were a major source for turquoise. Sometime during the eighth century A.D., for reasons yet unknown, the city's power began to decline. Around A.D. 750, large areas of the city were burned. The legends of Teotihuacán, however, continued to inspire and guide future civilizations.

The Maya and the Toltecs

Far to the east of Teotihuacán, another major civilization had arisen in the Yucatán peninsula. This was the civilization of the Maya (MIE-uh), which flourished between A.D. 300 and 900. It was one of the most sophisticated civilizations in the Americas. The Maya built splendid temples and pyramids, were accomplished artists, and developed a sophisticated calendar as accurate as any in existence in the world at that time. The Maya were a farming people who cleared the dense rain forests, developed farming, and built a patchwork of city-states. Mayan civilization came to include much of Central America and southern Mexico.

The Mayan cities were built around a central pyramid topped by a shrine to the gods. Nearby were other temples, palaces, and a sacred ball court (see "Sports and Contests: The Deadly Games of Central America"). Each Mayan city controlled the land surrounding the city, thus forming a city-state. Mayan civilization was composed of a series of city-states, each governed by a hereditary ruling class. These Mayan city-states were often at war with each other; in fact, as one historian has said, "The Maya were obsessed with war."[3] Ordinary soldiers who were captured in battle became slaves, whereas captured nobles and war leaders were used for human sacrifice. Their hearts were ripped out or they were beheaded, which was the Maya's favorite form of sacrifice.

Mayan Writings and Calendar

The Maya created a writing system that was much more sophisticated than the systems used elsewhere in Central America. Unfortunately, the Spanish conquerors in the sixteenth century made no effort to decipher the language or respect the Maya's writings. Instead, the Spaniards assumed the writings were evil or of no value. Bishop Diego de Landa said, "We found a large number of books in these characters and, as they contained nothing in which there were not to be seen superstition and lies of the devil, we burned them all, which they regretted to an amazing degree, and which caused them much affliction."[4] In their colonization of the New World, the Spanish would repeat this behavior over and over. They would apply their own religious views to the native civilizations with which they came in contact. The Spaniards' subsequent destruction of religious objects, and sometimes entire cities, helped to bring an end to these civilizations.

The Maya used hieroglyphs or pictures to express themselves. The Mayan hieroglyphs remained undeciphered until modern scholars discovered that many passages contained symbols that recorded dates in the calendar known as the Long Count. This calendar, which measures time back to August 13, 3114 B.C.,

▼ *Mayan hieroglyphs and priests decorate this stone lid that covered Pacal's sarcophagus found in the Temple of Inscriptions at Palenque. How might Mayan royal tombs have differed from Egyptian tombs?*

MORE ABOUT . . . the Olmecs

The Olmec colossal stone heads are remarkable for reasons beyond the artistic achievement that they clearly reflect. The 10-to-12-foot-high heads picture a type of human face which to most people clearly does not belong in Mesoamerica, but in Africa. The tight-fitting skull caps are of a design not seen elsewhere in the area. Were these heads the representations of African beings? If so, how did Africans make it to Central America? The second question can be partially answered by tracing the trans-Atlantic currents, which flow from West Africa to the Caribbean and Central America. Were Africans considered gods by the Olmec? What influence did they have in the advancement of Olmec civilization? The answers to these questions surround one of the most interesting enigmas in world history.

TEACH

CLASS DISCUSSION

Remind students that they learned the definition of civilization and the six characteristics of civilization in Chapter 1. It might be beneficial to many of the students to review this material now.

REINFORCING VOCABULARY

The prefix *meso* means middle, so Mesoamerica refers to the region in the middle of the Americas, between North and South America. Remind students that they have already studied Mesopotamia, the land between the rivers. Ask students to suggest other terms that use the root for middle in them. (*Mesozoic, mezzanine, mesosoprano*)

COMPARING TIME PERIODS

Unlike the early European and Asian cultures, the Mesoamericans did not use either metals or the wheel for practical uses. This is remarkable because the principle of the wheel was known in Mesoamerica. Small clay models with wheels, have been found dating to the 1st century A.D. The Mayans built broad, flat roads between their cities but the wheel was never put to practical use for pottery-making or for transport.

LEARNING FROM VISUALS

Answer to the caption question: Egyptian tombs were ornately decorated, and both royal Egyptians and Mayans were buried in temples.

REINFORCING VOCABULARY

Students may be interested to know that hieroglyphic means *sacred writing*. The first known use of hieroglyphics was the sacred writings of the Egyptians but it also developed in other regions, including the Americas. Hieroglyphics is a means of writing in which pictures rather than words are used to represent objects.

The Mayan writing system was the most complex of the early American civilizations. It contained more than 850 characters that included phonetic and ideographic as well as hieroglyphic symbols, representing a much more sophisticated form of writing.

Discuss with students why the Spanish explorers were unlikely to have realized the significance of the hieroglyphic records of the Mayans. Would it have made a difference in their treatment of the Mayan books?

SPORTS AND CONTESTS

LEARNING FROM VISUALS

Answer to the caption question: Answers will vary.

SPORTS AND CONTESTS

The Deadly Games of Central America

Most Mayan cities contained a ball court. Each of these courts usually consisted of a rectangular space surrounded by walls with highly decorated stone rings. The contestants tried to drive a solid rubber ball through these rings. Ball players, usually two or three on a team, used their hips to propel the ball (hands and feet were not allowed). Players donned helmets, gloves, and knee and hip protectors made of hide to protect themselves against the hard rubber balls. Because the stone rings were placed twenty-seven feet above the ground, it took considerable skill to score a goal.

The exact rules of the game are unknown, but we do know that it was more than a sport. The ball game had a religious meaning. The ball court was a symbol of the world, and the ball represented the sun and the moon. Apparently, it was also believed that playing the game often would produce better harvests. The results of the game were deadly. The defeated players were sacrificed in ceremonies held after the end of the game. Sim-

◀ Players wore stone yokes like this one on one hip to provide some protection during the ball games. The yoke in this picture was made in the fifth century B.C. near Veracruz, Mexico. Why do you think the yokes were decorated?

ilar courts have been found at sites throughout Central America, as well as present-day Arizona and New Mexico.

1. Why was great skill required of athletes who played the Mayan ball game?

2. Explain the symbolism of the Mayan ball game.

3. What other sporting events that you have read about in this course resulted in death for the losing participant?

was based on a belief in cycles of creation and destruction. According to the Maya, our present world was created in 3114 B.C. and is scheduled to complete its downward cycle on December 23, 2012.

The Maya used two different systems for measuring time. One was based on a solar calendar of 365 days, divided into 18 months of 20 days each, with an extra five days at the end. The other system was based on a sacred calendar of 260 days divided into 13 weeks of 20 days. Only trained priests could read and use this calendar in order to foretell the future and know the omens associated with each day.

As the meaning of the Mayan hieroglyphs was uncovered, it became clear that many of them record important events in Mayan history, especially those in the lives of Mayan rulers. This discovery provided scholars with an important tool for learning more about this fascinating civilization. One of the most

SPECIAL NEEDS: *Visual*

Important collections of Mayan hieroglyphs have told historians invaluable information about Mayan traditions and practices. Have your students think of a few things about themselves, their family, school, or community that they would like explorers 1,000 years from now to know about or discover.

Ask students to create a set of hieroglyphics and write their sentences on paper, or create simple drawings illustrating their message.

For students having trouble creating a message, you can assign them such messages as "Our football team is #1," or "My favorite restuarant is ___ ." Have students guess the messages once everyone is finished. This activity can be adapted using patterns of raised or hole-punched paper for the visually impaired.

SPORTS AND CONTESTS

The Deadly Games of Central America, continued

▲ *Throughout Mesoamerica, a dangerous game was played on courts such as this one from Mayan ruins in modern-day Guatamala. What was the importance of these ball games?*

important collections of Mayan hieroglyphs is at Palenque (pul-LENG-kae), located deep in the jungles in the neck of the Mexican peninsula, considerably to the west of the Yucatán (YOO-kuh-TAN). At Palenque, archaeologists discovered a royal tomb and a massive limestone slab covered with hieroglyphs. By deciphering the message on the slab, archaeologists for the first time identified a historical figure in Mayan history, a ruler named Pacal. It was his body that was buried in the tomb.

Mayan Political and Social Structures

The inscriptions at Palenque reveal much about a Mayan city-state. As a city-state, Palenque had been relatively unimportant until the reign of Pacal. Pacal came to the throne at the age of twelve. During Pacal's long reign (he lived to the age of eighty) and those of his sons, Palenque became a powerful Mayan city-state.

On Line with
WORLD HISTORY *Internet Activity*

You may want to have your students visit the following URL, where they will find information and additional web site resources to enhance their study of this chapter.

The Mayan Temple of Links

http://www.ruf.rice.edu/~jchance/link.html

This is an excellent source for everything about Mayan history.

Due to the ever-changing nature of the World Wide Web, see the West History web site, **http://history.swpco.com** for regular updates of the URLs in this text.

Multimedia Support

LASERDISC

Mayan Painting on a Tomb Vase

Great Funerary Mask (jade, pyrite and shell: Mayan)

Aerial View of Tikal (Mayan)

CLASS DISCUSSION

A *mother culture* is a culture that develops new ideas that are later adopted by other societies. The Olmecs were a mother culture because so much of their way of life was the basis for features of other Mesoamerican peoples. What developments of the Olmec were adopted by other cultures? *(hierarchial society, human sacrifice, calendar, written language, games, architecture)* What innovation did the Toltec introduce that may make them a mother culture? *(metal working)* Ask students to consider the impact of the Spanish explorers on the early Americans. Were the Spanish a mother culture? Does the transfer of American culture and technology make the United States a mother culture? Ask students if there is a difference between voluntary imitation of new ideas and the imposition of cultural and technological change.

206

Like the rulers of the other Mayan city-states and other early civilizations around the world, Pacal claimed to be descended from the gods. The Mayan rulers were helped by nobles and a class of scribes who may also have been priests. Historians once believed that the Maya had only two classes, priests and peasants, but it is now clear that there were also townspeople who were skilled artisans, officials, and merchants. Although the size of the larger cities is difficult to estimate, some scholars believe that urban centers such as Tikal (ti-KAWL) (in present-day Guatemala) may have had as many as 100,000 inhabitants during the height of their power.

Most of the Mayan people were farmers. They lived on tiny plots or on terraced hills in the highlands. Houses were built of adobe and thatch and were probably like the houses of most people living in the area today. There was a fairly clear-cut division of labor. Men were responsible for fighting and hunting, and women for homemaking and raising the children. Women also made cornmeal, the basic food of much of the population.

Crucial to Mayan civilization was its spiritual perspective. For the Maya, all of life was in the hands of divine powers. The name of their supreme god was Itzamna (eet-SAWM-nuh) (Lizard House). Gods were ranked in order of importance. Some, like the jaguar god of night, were evil rather than good. Like other ancient civilizations in Central America, the Maya practiced human sacrifice. They considered it a way to appease the gods, thus benefiting both people and the environment. Human sacrifices were also used for special ceremonial occasions. When a male heir was presented to the throne, war captives were tortured and then beheaded. In A.D. 790, one Mayan ruler took his troops into battle to gain prisoners for a celebration honoring his son as his heir apparent.

Sometime around 800, the Mayan civilization in the central Yucatán peninsula began to decline. Scholars are not sure why. Suggestions include invasion, internal revolt, or a natural disaster such as a volcanic eruption. A more recent theory is that overuse of the land led to reduced crop yields. Whatever the case, cities like Tikal and Palenque were abandoned and covered by dense jungle growth. They were not rediscovered until the nineteenth or twentieth centuries. Newer cities in the northern part of the peninsula, like Uxmal (oosh-MALL) and Chichén Itzá (chuh-CHEN ut-SAW), survived and continued to prosper.

The Toltecs

Around 1000, this latter area was taken over by peoples known as the Toltecs, who had built an empire in central Mexico. The center of the Toltec Empire was at

▼ *This seventh-century palace at Palenque had both religious and worldly functions—the tower was used for astronomy. Palenque was abandoned and remained covered by the dense Yucatan jungle until the mid-nineteenth century, approximately 1300 years.*

COOPERATIVE LEARNING ACTIVITY

Divide the class into cooperative learning groups. Be sure each group has a recorder, facilitator, time keeper, and any other jobs you feel are necessary.

Tell students that geography has a tremendous impact on how people organize their lives. Have each group choose two different societies explained in this chapter and explain how they responded to the geography of their region. Or, ask students to research parallel developments. Irrigation was developed independently by the Egyptians and by the Early Americans. City states developed both in Greece and in Mesoamerica. Ask students to think of reasons that would lead to parallel development and to list other examples of parallel, not borrowed, developments in technology between the civilization of Europe and Asia and the Americas.

Tula, built on a high ridge about forty miles northwest of present-day Mexico City. The Toltecs were a fierce and warlike people who extended their conquests into the Mayan lands of Guatemala and the northern Yucatán. The Toltecs were also builders who constructed pyramids and palaces. They brought metalworking to Mesoamerica and were the first people in Mexico to work in gold, silver, and copper. The Toltecs controlled the upper Yucatán peninsula from their capital at Chichén Itzá for several centuries. Then their civilization, too, declined. When the Spaniards arrived in the sixteenth century, the area was divided into a number of small states. Former cities such as Uxmal and Chichén Itzá had long been abandoned.

The Aztecs

Scholars are not certain about the origins of the Aztecs, but sometime during the early twelfth century A.D., these peoples began a long migration that brought them to the Valley of Mexico late in the century. They established their capital at Tenochtitlán, on an island in the middle of Lake Texcoco (tess-KOE-KOE) (now the location of Mexico City). According to their own legends, the Aztecs had had a difficult time when they arrived in the Valley of Mexico. Other peoples had attacked them and, hoping to get rid of them, had driven them into a snake-infested part of the valley. The Aztecs survived, however, strengthened by their belief that their god of war, Huitzilopochti, had told them that when they saw an eagle perched on a cactus growing out of a rock, their journey would end. There they should stop and build their city. In 1325, under attack by another people, they were driven back into the swamps and islands of Lake Texcoco. On one of the islands, they saw an eagle standing on a prickly pear cactus on a rock. There they built Tenochtitlán (or "place of the prickly pear cactus"): "Now we have found the land promised to us. We have found peace for the weary Mexican people. Now we want for nothing. Be comforted, children, brothers and sisters, because we have obtained the [promise of our god]."

For the next hundred years, the Aztecs built their city. They constructed temples, other public buildings,

▲ *This famous pyramid at Chichén Itzá is part of the Mayan city that survived into the second millennium A.D. In addition to the pyramid, there are four well-preserved temples and a ball court. What do you think was the purpose of this pyramid?*

and houses. They built causeways of stone across Lake Texcoco to the north, south, and west, linking the many islands to the mainland. At the beginning of the fifteenth century, they constructed an **aqueduct** to bring fresh water from a spring four miles away.

The Aztecs were outstanding warriors. While they were building their capital city, they also set out to bring the entire area around the city under their control. By the early fifteenth century, they had become the leading city-state in the lake region. For the remainder of the fifteenth century, the Aztecs consolidated their rule over much of what is modern Mexico, from the Atlantic to the Pacific Oceans and as far south as the Guatemalan border. The new kingdom was not a centralized state but a collection of semi-independent territories governed by local lords. These rulers were confirmed in their authority by the Aztec ruler in return for the payment of tribute (goods or money paid by conquered peoples to their conquerors). Their loose political organization would later be a cause of the downfall of the Aztec Empire.

ENRICHMENT ACTIVITY

1. Have students read *The Broken Spears: The Aztec Account of the Conquest of Mexico,* edited by Miguel Leon-Portilla (Beacon Press, Boston, 1990), and report to the class. Because of the time factor associated with this activity, it could be offered as extra credit.
2. The *Popul Voh* is a sacred book of the ancient Mayans that relates their religious beliefs. It was written in Latin shortly after

the Spanish conquest of the Maya and was later translated into Spanish.

The Popul Voh recounts the Mayan myth of the creation. You may wish to arrange for the English literature teacher (or Spanish language teacher) to visit your class to compare the Mayan myths with those of Greek, Roman, and Norse peoples.

ACROSS THE CURRICULUM

Science. The Aztec built their empire on a remarkable and highly effective system of agriculture. The limited available farm land was intensively cultivated and it was augmented by an elaborate system of reclaimed swampland. This highly effective agricultural system produced abundant food and the population grew and expanded into surrounding mainland areas.

Ask students how the Aztec adapted their agriculture to their environment. What other innovations resulted from the Aztec's agriculture? *(causeways to link the expanding population, aqueducts to provide water for the increasing population)*

CLASS DISCUSSION

It is apparent that class distinctions were important to the Aztecs. Upper and middle-class people benefited from the labors of the lower class and enjoyed luxuries and special foods not available to the masses. Commoners lived in small adobe and mud huts, while the upper and middle-class lived in large palaces that were surrounded by gardens. Ask the class how education and society reinforced this class system.

Political and Social Structures of the Aztecs

Like all great empires in ancient times, the Aztec state was authoritarian. Power was vested in the hands of the monarch, whose authority had both a divine and a secular nature. The Aztec ruler claimed that he was descended from the gods and served as a link between the material and spiritual worlds. The Aztec king, however, did not obtain his position by a rigid law of succession. On the death of the ruler, a small group of senior officials chose his successor from within the royal family.

Once placed on the throne, the Aztec ruler was assisted by a small council of lords and a government bureaucracy. The council was headed by a prime minister, who served as the chief executive of the government. Outside the capital city, the power of the central government was limited. Rulers of territories conquered by, or otherwise made subject to, the Aztecs were allowed considerable independence. In return they paid tribute, either in goods or captives, to the central government.

Only the hereditary nobility held positions in the government bureaucracy. All nobles traced their lineage to the founding family of the Aztec clan. Male children in noble families were educated for careers in either the government or the priesthood (see "Young People in the Aztec Empire"). As a reward for their

services, senior officials in the government were frequently given large estates.

The rest of the population consisted of commoners, **indentured workers,** and slaves. Indentured workers

Map 7.3   The Valley of Mexico under Aztec Rule

STUDYING MAPS

The following questions will help you guide the students through their study of Map 7.3.

1. Locate Lake Texcoco, Tenochtitlán, and Tlaxcala on the map. (Point out to students that Tenochtitlán is the site of Mexico City and is about 200 hundred miles east of Veracruz on the Gulf of Mexico.)

2. About how wide (east to west) is Lake Texcoco? *(approximately 10 miles)*

3. About how long is the longest causeway the Incas built? *(From Tenochtitlán to Iztapalapa via Acachinanco and Xoloc is about 5 miles.)*

YOUNG PEOPLE IN THE AZTEC EMPIRE

Growing Up in Aztec Society

In the Aztec Empire, as soon as a male baby had been born, the midwife who had attended the birth said, "You must understand that your home is not here where you have been born, for you are a warrior." To a female infant, the midwife said, "As the heart stays in the body, so you must stay in the house." From the very beginning of their lives, boys and girls in Aztec society were given very different roles and were brought up accordingly.

A father was held responsible for the education of a son between the ages of three and fifteen. Similarly, a mother was responsible for her daughter's education. This was chiefly true for common people, because the members of the ruling class placed their children in schools at an early age. The education that children received at home was practical. Boys learned to fish, go to the marketplace, and fight. Girls learned to spin, sweep the house, and weave cloth. Discipline was severe. Punishments included scratching children with thorns and holding them over a fire made with chili peppers.

Male children of the ruling classes, who went to temple schools for their education, were trained to be priests or high officials in the state. The girls of the ruling classes who attended school were trained only to be priestesses in the state religion. In the temple schools, students were severely punished for any mistake. They were awakened at night to offer incense to the gods. They had to fast regularly. Sacrifice was a chief theme. As a father said to his son who was about to enter a temple school, "Listen, my son, you are not going to be honored, nor esteemed. You are going to be looked down upon, humiliated and despised. Every day you will cut agave-thorns for penance, and you will draw blood from your body with these spines and you will bathe at night even when it is very

▶ *This young boy wears traditional Aztec headgear at a festival in Guadalajara, Mexico. The plumed serpent seen on the front recurs frequently in Aztec sculpture and art.*

cold. Harden your body to the cold and when the time comes for fasting do not go and break your fast." Students in temple schools received the only intellectual education available in the Aztec system. They were taught the holy songs, how to speak well, how to determine time, and how to interpret dreams.

Boys of common background might also enter schools, but their education was aimed at one chief goal: to prepare them to become warriors. As a result, they spent time with experienced soldiers, lived together in dormitories, and did work for the state, such as building canals. Their education was fairly relaxed. In the evening, young men in these schools were allowed to sing, dance, and even have female companions.

1. How did an Aztec family's social class affect the upbringing of its children?

2. How were discipline and sacrifice part of the Aztec educational system?

3. What was an intellectual education in the Aztec Empire and who received one?

On Line with WORLD HISTORY *Internet Activity*

You may want to have your students visit the following URL, where they will find information and additional web site resources to enhance their study of this chapter.

The Aztecs/Mexicas

http://www.indians.org/welker/aztec.htm

After a brief history of the Aztec, an excellent series of links follow with many brief essay-type descriptions of the culture.

Due to the ever-changing nature of the World Wide Web, see the West History web site, **http://history.swpco.com** for regular updates of the URLs in this text.

USING PRIMARY SOURCES

Students may be interested in this primary source excerpt of a description of the Aztec, "pleasure palaces" as written by Hernan Cortés, the destroyer of the Aztec empire. "[The houses] are as good as the best in Spain; that is, in respect of size and workmanship, both in their masonry and woodwork and their floors, and furnishings for every sort of household task; but they have no reliefs or other rich things which are used in Spain but not found here. They have many upper and lower rooms and cool gardens with many trees and sweet smelling flowers; likewise, there are pools of freshwater, very well made and with steps leading down to the bottom. There is a very large kitchen garden next to the house, and overlooking it a gallery with very beautiful corridors and rooms, and in the garden a large reservoir of fresh water well-built with fine stonework around which runs a well-tiled pavement so wide that four people can walk there abreast. Beyond the pavement, toward the wall of the garden there is a latticework of canes, behind which are all manner of shrubs and scented herbs." Ask students with artistic interests or talents to create a wall mural of an Aztec pleasure palace based on the description above.

LEARNING FROM VISUALS

Answer to the caption question: It is likely that residents went up to the roofs for the cooling breezes and to enjoy the view.

FOCUS ON EVERYDAY LIFE
Housing and Food in Aztec Society

Most houses in the Aztec world were made of sun-dried bricks. Those of the common people consisted of one or two rooms. Each house was separate from its neighbors and had direct access to the surrounding streets and canals.

The houses of both rich and poor were simply furnished. People slept on mats. Speaking of these mats, which he found very uncomfortable, one Spanish visitor said, "However great a lord he might be, no one had any bed other than this kind." A few seats and wicker chests to hold a family's clothes were the only other furniture in an Aztec house, wealthy or poor. Wood fires were used when heating was required.

The houses of the wealthy, however, did differ in some ways from those of the poor. For one thing, they were larger and had many more rooms. They were also surrounded by magnificent gardens. Referring to the garden of one house where he stayed for a night, a Spanish visitor reported, "We went into the garden; it was delightful to walk in it, and I was never weary of observing the variety of the plants and their perfumes, the flower beds, many fruit trees and roses of the country, and a pool of sweet water. There was another extraordinary thing: large boats would come right into this orchard from the lake."

The diet of ordinary Aztecs was simple. The major foods included maize (used to make cakes,

◄ *Aztec homes were distinct from one another and each decorated differently, as shown here. However, the rectangular shape and the building material, adobe brick, were consistent. What was the purpose of the open-roof patios and balconies?*

porridge, and tamales), vegetables such as beans and squash, and amaranth (a plant whose seeds were made into a porridge). There were two meals a day: breakfast in the morning after a few hours of work and a main meal. The latter was usually eaten in the middle of the day, during the hottest hours. Water was the chief beverage.

The rich, of course, ate considerably more. Their meals would include different kinds of maize cakes and tamales; fruits, such as avocados and prickly pears; a variety of vegetables; sweet potato, pimento, and tomato dishes; fish; and meat. Meat came chiefly from two domesticated animals, the turkey and the dog. Various forms of game, such as rabbits, deer, wild pigs, and wild fowl found in the lakes, also graced the tables of the rich. Some unusual items, such as worms, tadpoles, and ants, were also part of the Aztec diet. Cocoa, sweetened with honey and flavored with vanilla, was a favorite drink of the rich.

1. How were the houses of the rich and the poor the same? What elements distinguished homes of the rich?

2. What were the staples of the Aztec diet? What foods do you eat regularly that were luxuries for the Aztecs?

So What ??

If your students question the importance of the information on **the Aztecs,** *tell them . . .*

Few countries have as rich a native background as Mexico. The Olmecs, Mayas, Aztecs, and Toltecs, among many others, created a native foundation to Mexican society that European influences could not erase. Contemporary Mexicans are rightfully proud of their cultural heritage. Descriptive names emanating from the past often make their way to products and institutions that wish to associate themselves with the great Mexican past. Many present-day Mexican groups, primarily in the rural areas of Mexico, proudly trace their ancestry to the great cultures of the past.

were landless laborers who contracted to work on the nobles' estates. Slaves worked in the households of the wealthy. Children of slaves, however, were considered to be free citizens. Both male and female slaves were sold in the markets.

Most of the people were commoners, many of whom were farmers. There was also a large number of commoners who engaged in trade, at least in the densely populated Valley of Mexico, where half of the people lived in cities. Within the families of commoners, male children were trained for war and served in the army upon becoming adults.

Aztec merchants were also active traders. Especially in Tenochtitlán and other large cities, merchants exported and traded goods made by Aztec craftspeople from imported raw materials. In exchange for their goods, the traders obtained tropical feathers, cacao beans, animal skins, and gold. When the Spanish arrived, they were astonished to find city markets that were considerably larger and better stocked than any markets in Spain. Bernal Díaz, who had arrived in Mexico in 1519, wrote:

Let us begin with the dealers in gold, silver, and precious stones, feathers, cloaks, and embroidered goods, and male and female slaves who are also sold there. . . . Next there were those who sold coarser cloth, and cotton goods and fabrics made of twisted thread, and there were chocolate merchants with their chocolate. In this way you could see every kind of merchandise to be found anywhere in Mexico, laid out in the same way as goods are laid out in my own district of Medina del Campo, a center for fairs.[5]

Women in Aztec society possessed some rights but were not equal to men. They were allowed to own and inherit property and to enter into contracts, something not allowed in other world cultures at the time. Women were expected to work in the home, weave textiles, and raise children. However, they were also permitted to become priestesses. Most Aztec men had one wife, although noblemen sometimes had more than one. As in most societies at the time, parents selected their child's spouse, usually to advance their

CONNECTIONS TO OUR WORLD

Using the Past to Create a New Future   In the 1920s, after a successful revolution, a new Mexican government sought to create a new image of the Mexican nation and a new sense of national identity for the Mexican people. The revolutionary government enlisted the support of artists to make Mexicans aware of their glorious past as a way to create a national consciousness in the present. Diego Rivera, one of Mexico's leading artists, accepted the government's challenge. Between 1920 and 1950, he completed a series of massive paintings on the walls of Mexico's schools and government buildings.

In his murals, Rivera used his knowledge of Mexico's past to achieve an imaginative re-creation of the world of the ancient Aztecs. In scene after scene, he showed an idealized version of the wonders and simple life of the Aztecs as well as their betrayal: people engaged in the busy and prosperous markets of the capital city of Tenochtitlán; Aztec doctors performing remarkable operations; Aztec men and women playing instruments and engaged in native arts and crafts; Aztec women grinding corn and preparing tortillas; and Spanish knights armed with guns crushing the Aztec people. Rivera wanted Mexicans to be aware of their past. He also sought, however, to encourage modern Mexicans to create a civilization as pure, simple, and noble as he imagined that of the Aztecs to have been.

families politically or socially. (See "Focus on Everyday Life: Housing and Food in Aztec Society.")

Aztec Religion and Culture

Like other peoples in Central America and around the world, the Aztecs believed in many gods. There were over a hundred. Some of them were nature spirits, like the rain god Tlaloc. There was a supreme god, called Ometeotl, who represented the all-powerful forces of

ENRICHMENT ACTIVITY

Discuss with students the following question: Do children learn best when discipline is severe or when it is lax?

Tell students that the Aztecs thought children learned best under conditions of severe and strict discipline. It is reported that they even held children over fires made of chili peppers as a form of discipline.

Have students write an essay describing the effects of discipline on themselves and how they would discipline and motivate children in an ideal school.

LASERDISC

Aztec Mosaic
Mask

Sculpture of Coatlicue
(Aztec)

Aztec Calendar

YOU ARE THERE

USING PRIMARY SOURCES

Ask students how their earlier understandings about sacrifice compared with this primary source excerpt. According to one source, the Aztecs believed that the sun died every night and needed human blood to give it strength to rise the next day. One account puts at 15,000 the number of men sacrificed yearly to the fearsome sun god. Many of these were prisoners taken in wars started with the sole purpose of gaining sacrificial victims. Another story tells of a yearly sacrifice to the chief Aztec god Tezcatlipoca. For one whole year the victim was allowed every luxury and pleasure. Then, he was led in a great procession to the temple, where his chest was cut open and his heart torn out.

YOU ARE THERE

The Ritual of Human Sacrifice

▶ *The stone that the king stood on in the ritual may have looked much like this one. In the center of the twenty-six ton disc you can see the sun god clutching human hearts with his talon.*

The ritual of human sacrifice was a central part of Aztec religion. The Aztecs believed that only the gift of human hearts would appease their god, Huitzilopochtli. A Spanish observer wrote this description of the ritual.

Spanish Observer Describes Human Sacrifice

The king [Moctezuma] and Tlacaelel now appeared before the assembly and went to stand upon the stone which was the likeness and image of the sun, one having ascended by one staircase and the other by another. The five priests of sacrifice followed them. They were to hold down the feet, hands, and heads of the victims, and they were painted all over with red ochre, even their loincloths and tunics. . . .

The five priests entered and claimed the prisoner who stood first in the line at the skull rack. Each prisoner they took to the place where the king stood and, when they had forced him to stand upon the stone which was the figure and likeness of the sun, they threw him upon his back. One took him by the right arm, another by the left, one by his left foot, another by his right, while the fifth priest tied his neck with a cord and held him down so that he could not move.

The king lifted the knife on high and made a gash in his breast. Having opened it he extracted the heart and raised it high with his hand as an offering to the sun. When the heart had cooled he tossed it into the circular depression, taking some of the blood in his hand and sprinkling it in the direction of the sun. In this way the sacrificers killed four, one by one; then Tlacaelel came and killed another four in his turn. And so, four by four, the prisoners were slain, till every last man that had been brought from the Mixteca had perished.

1. Do you think the prisoners who were sacrificed to the god Huitzilopochtli were willing participants in the ritual? Why or why not?

2. Is it significant that a human heart, and not some other body part, was offered to the god? What did the Aztecs believe their sacrifices would accomplish?

3. What does the practice of human sacrifice tell you about the Aztec civilization?

COOPERATIVE LEARNING ACTIVITY

Divide the class into cooperative learning groups. Be sure to assign each student with a role to play in the group such as recorder, reader or facilitator.

Assign students the task of researching various religions (modern or ancient) to determine how different religions appease the gods. You might have each group research one religion or have each group research several. After students have completed their research, have them share their results with the rest of the class. Then, as a class, discuss the question: Are the Maya and Aztecs to be condemned more than other societies for practicing human sacrifice?

◄ *The Aztec ruler Moctezuma initially welcomed Cortés and his army to his royal court, a decision he came to regret. Why did the Spaniards so completely destroy Aztec cities and vestiges (traces) of their culture?*

the heavens. However, he was remote and had little impact on the lives of the people. The feathered serpent Quetzalcoatl (ket-SAWL-KWAWT-ul) had a more direct impact. He represented the forces of creation, virtue, and learning. According to Aztec tradition, this godlike being had left his homeland in the Valley of Mexico in the tenth century, promising to return in triumph. The story of Quetzalcoatl had become identified with a Toltec legend that said the Toltec people had been led by a man known as Kukulcan (koo-KOOL-kawn) ("feathered serpent"), who migrated to the peninsula from Central Mexico sometime in the tenth century. The story held that Kukulcan was a Toltec prince who was banished and sailed east with a promise that his return would be signaled by a sign made from an arrow through a sapling. This general shape was important when the Spanish sailed out of the east with a similar sign—the cross—on their breastplates. When the Aztecs saw the Spanish with their crosses, they thought that representatives of Quetzalcoatl had returned.

Aztec religion was based on a belief in an unending struggle between the forces of good and evil throughout the universe. This struggle, according to their religion, had led to the creation and destruction of four

worlds, or suns. People were now living in the time of the fifth sun. However, this world, too, was destined to end with the destruction of the Earth by earthquakes. In an effort to postpone the day of reckoning, the Aztecs practiced human sacrifice. They believed that by appeasing the sun god Huitzilopochtli with sacrifices, they could delay the final destruction of their world (see "You Are There: The Ritual of Human Sacrifice").

A chief feature of Aztec culture was its monumental architecture. At the center of the capital city of Tenochtitlán was the sacred district, dominated by a massive pyramid dedicated to Huitzilopochtli. According to a Spanish observer, at its base the pyramid was equal to the plots of six large European town houses and tapered from there to the top. At the top was a platform containing shrines to the gods and an altar for performing human sacrifices. A stairway of 114 steps led from ground level to the platform. At the top the viewer could take in a breathtaking panorama of the entire city. The area surrounding the pyramid was paved with white flagstones and bordered with smaller shrines and dormitories for the priests. The imperial palace and the homes of senior officials were located nearby. The entire scene struck the Spanish visitor with awe.

RETEACHING ACTIVITY

You probably cannot overemphasize to students the role that diseases played in the collision of cultures. Due to the relatively small population, lack of contact between distinct population gene groups, basic hygiene practices, and temperate climates, many areas in the Americas were healthy and relatively disease-free compared to Africa and Europe. It was this good health that made the Amerindians so very vulnerable to European contact. After European contact, smallpox wiped out more people than all the wars combined. One estimate places the decline in population in Mesoamerica from 25 million to 3 million in 150 years.

ASSESS

Divide the class into cooperative groups and assign them the following task: Create a visual that compares and contrasts the most important features of the Maya and Aztec civilizations. Encourage them to be creative, and to draw upon their artistic and theatrical talents if they choose.

Answers to
SECTION REVIEW

2. (a) an artificial channel for carrying water; (b) laborers who contracted to work on estates
3. (a) the first civilization in Central America; (b) a major civilization located on the Yucatán peninsula; (c) a fierce people who extended their conquests into the Mayan lands of Guatemala and northern Yucatán; (d) advanced civilization located in the Valley of Mexico; (e) leader that conquered the Aztecs; (f) Aztec leader defeated by Cortés
4. invasion, internal revolt, natural disaster, overuse of the land
5. enabled the peoples to gain items that were not available in their own areas; social contact

CLOSE

One of the major perceptions that students should obtain from this section is that there were great civilizations in the Americas long before the arrival of Columbus and the Europeans.

The Destruction of Aztec Civilization

For a century, the Aztec kingdom ruled much of central Mexico from the Atlantic to the Pacific coasts. Most local officials accepted the authority of the Aztec king in Tenochtitlán. In the region of Tlaxcala (tlaw-SKAW-luh) to the east, however, the local lords wanted greater independence.

In 1519, a Spanish force under the command of Hernán Cortés landed at Veracruz, on the Gulf of Mexico (see Chapter 16). Cortés marched to Tenochtitlán at the head of a small body of troops (550 soldiers and 16 horses). As he went, he made alliances with city-states that had tired of the oppressive rule of the Aztecs. Especially important was Tlaxcala, a state that the Aztecs had not been able to conquer. In November, Cortés arrived at Tenochtitlán and received a friendly welcome from the Aztec monarch Moctezuma (often called Montezuma). At first, Moctezuma believed that his visitor was a representative of Quetzalcoatl, the god who had departed from his homeland centuries before and had promised that he would return. Riddled with fears, Moctezuma offered gifts of gold to the foreigners and gave them a palace to use while they were in the city.

Eventually, tensions arose between the Spaniards and the Aztecs. The Spanish took Moctezuma hostage and began to pillage the city. In the fall of 1520, one year after Cortés had first arrived, the local population revolted and drove the invaders from the city. Many of the Spanish were killed, but the Aztecs soon experienced new disasters. As one Aztec related, "But at about the time that the Spaniards had fled from Mexico, there came a great sickness, a pestilence, the smallpox." With no natural immunity to the diseases of the Europeans, many Aztecs fell sick. Meanwhile, Cortés received fresh soldiers from his new allies; the state of Tlaxcala alone provided fifty thousand warriors. After four months, the city surrendered. Then the destruction began. The forces led by Cortés leveled pyramids, temples, and palaces. The stones were then used to build Spanish government buildings and churches. The rivers and canals were filled in. The magnificent city of Tenochtitlán was no more. As the Spanish soldier Díaz remarked, "All is overthrown and destroyed, nothing is left standing."

 SECTION REVIEW

1. **Locate:**
   (a) Veracruz,   (b) Yucatán Peninsula,
   (c) Uxmal,   (d) Chichén Itzá,
   (e) Tenochtitlán

2. **Define:**
   (a) aqueduct,   (b) indentured workers

3. **Identify:**
   (a) Olmec peoples,   (b) the Maya,   (c) the Toltecs,   (d) the Aztecs,   (e) Hernán Cortés, (f) Moctezuma

4. **Recall:** What are the reasons scholars suggest for the decline of the Mayan civilization?

5. **Think Critically:** Discuss the importance of trade for the early American civilizations.

THE FIRST CIVILIZATIONS IN SOUTH AMERICA

South America is a vast continent, marked by extremes in climate and geography. The north is dominated by the vast Amazon River, which flows through dense tropical jungles carrying a larger flow of water than any other river system in the world. Further to the south, the jungles are replaced by prairies and steppes stretching westward to the Andes Mountains, which extend the entire length of the continent from the Isthmus of Panama to the Strait of Magellan far to the south. Along the Pacific coast, on the western slopes of the mountains, are some of the driest desert regions in the world.

Human beings have lived in South America for at least twelve thousand years. Early peoples were hunters and food gatherers. On the northern fringes of the Andes Mountains, irrigated farming was being practiced around 2000 B.C. Early civilizations began to emerge during the first millennium B.C.

MORE ABOUT . . . *Moctezuma*

Moctezuma, leader of the Aztecs, may have been the single most important factor why the Aztec empire crumbled before Cortés and the Spaniards. He reacted to a critical challenge in a dogmatic, nonrational manner, allowing the Spaniards to make key advances prior to the final blow, and refusing to strike when the Aztecs could have held a winning position. A primary source account by contemporary Aztecs indicates that

Moctezuma may have been suffering from a clinical depression:

> [Motecuhzoma] wanted to turn away and hide; he thought of evading the 'gods,' of escaping to hide in a cave. . . "But he could not do it. He could not run away, could not go into hiding. He had lost his strength and is spirit, and could do nothing . . . he was weak and listless and too uncertain to make a decision.

The Moche Civilization

Early in the first millennium B.C., an advanced civilization appeared near the Pacific coast not far south of

Map 7.4   Peoples and Cultures of South America

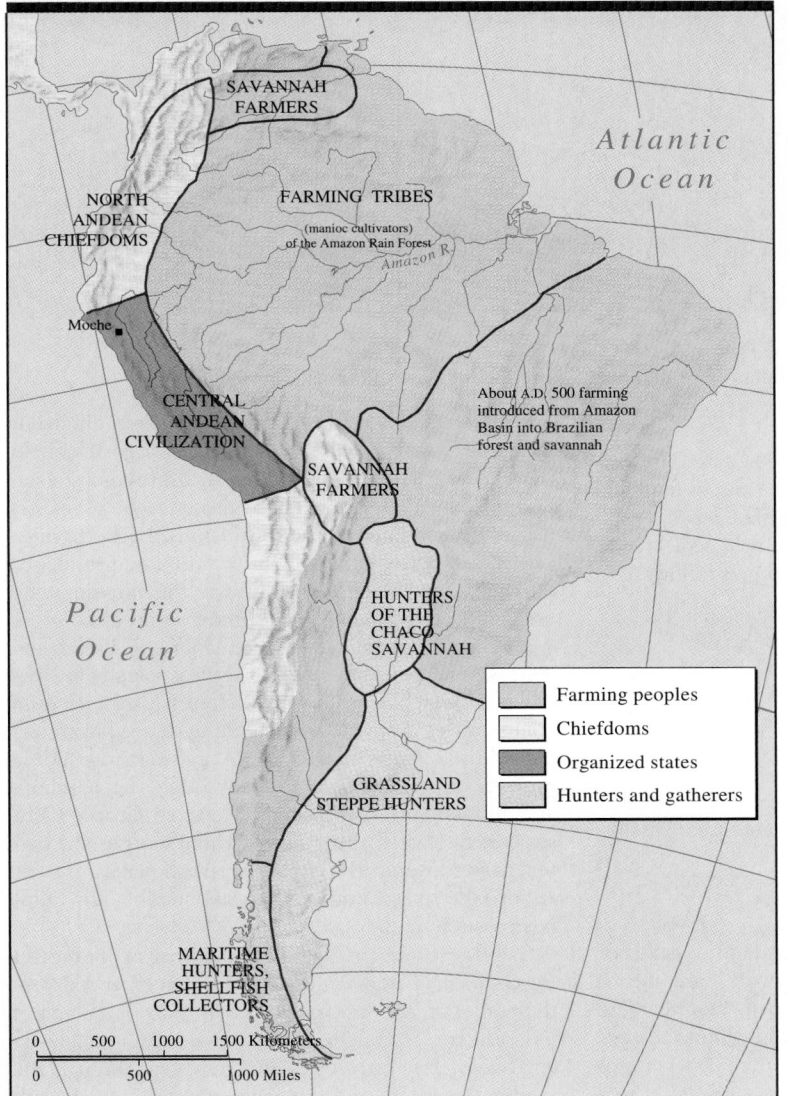

the border of Ecuador. At Moche, a major urban center arose amid irrigated fields in the valley of the Moche River, which flows from the foothills of the Andes Mountains into the Pacific Ocean. Farmers in the area grew maize, peanuts, potatoes, and cotton. They probably supplied much of the food for peoples living throughout the region.

Moche was the capital of a powerful state. The authority of the Moche rulers may have extended as far as four hundred miles along the coast. The people of Moche had no written language, but their pottery gives us some idea of their interests. Among other things, the pottery indicates that the people at Moche, like those in Central America, led lives centered around warfare. Paintings and pottery frequently portray warriors, prisoners, and sacrificial victims.

After the collapse of the Moche civilization in the eighth century, a period of decline set in until the rise of a new power about three hundred years later. The kingdom of Chimor dominated the area for nearly four centuries until it was destroyed by people who created an even more spectacular empire—the Inca.

The Inca

In the late fourteenth century, the Inca (ING-kuh) were only a small community in the area of Cuzco (KOO-SKOE), a city located at an altitude of ten thousand feet in the mountains of southern Peru. In the 1440s, however, under the leadership of their powerful ruler

STUDYING MAPS

The following questions will help you guide the students through their study of Map 7.4.

1. Refer to the map on page 217 which shows the area occupied by the Incan empire. What geographical feature dominates the Inca territory? *(the Andes Mountains)*

2. According to the map on page 215, were the Inca people primarily farmers or hunter-gatherers? *(farmers)*

TEACH

LEARNING FROM VISUALS

Answer to the captain question: The Aztec, Mayan, Egyptian and some African cultures (Zimbabweans) were gifted in masonry.

CRITICAL THINKING

Students by now should realize that the Aztecs, Mayans, and Incas all practiced some form of sun worship. Ask them why they think the sun was such an important image to many early cultures. *(The sun was essential to daily life. It was the source of light and warmth. As cultures became agriculturally dependent, the sun took on an even more important role. The sun determined the growing seasons and the length of the day.)*

CRITICAL THINKING

The text states that the Incan ruler relied on forced labor to build the roads and communities of this vast empire. Ask students to discuss whether they believe the Incan ruler was just to demand this labor. What benefits, gained by this forced labor, were shared among all peoples? What circumstances are mentioned in the text that might lead you to believe the burden was not so terrible? *(The roads, bridges, waystations, and temples added to the general prosperity and health of the whole community. Citizens of the empire were responsible for laboring for several weeks during the year, as opposed to fewer people being enslaved the whole year. Periods of famine that exist today were unknown at that time since surplus food was put into public storehouses and saved for drought years.)*

216

▶ *The Inca built these fifty-foot-high stone walls in Cuzco, Peru, their capital. Built without mortar, the walls protected equally monumental stone altars or thrones made to honor the Inca's sacred mountain. What other civilizations were known for their stonework?*

Pachakuti, the Inca launched a campaign of conquest that eventually brought the entire region under their control.

Pachakuti created a highly centralized state. The capital of Cuzco was transformed from a a city of mud and thatch into an imposing city of stone. The most impressive structure within the city was a temple dedicated to the sun. A Spanish observer described it as follows:

> It is built of smooth masonry, very level and smooth. The roof was of wood and very lofty so that there would be plenty of air. It was covered with thatch: they had no tiles. All four walls of the temple were covered from top to bottom with plates and slabs of gold. Over what we have called the high altar they had the image of the Sun on a gold plate twice the thickness of the rest of the wall-plates. The image showed him with a round face and beams and flames of fire all in one piece, just as he is usually depicted by painters. It was so large that it stretched over the whole of that side of the temple from wall to wall.[6]

Under Pachakuti and his immediate successors, Topa Inca and Huayna Inca (the word *Inca* means "ruler"), the boundaries of the Inca Empire were extended as far as Ecuador, central Chile, and the edge of the Amazon basin. The empire included perhaps twelve million people.

Incan Political and Social Structures

To create a well-organized empire, Pachakuti divided it into four quarters, with each ruled by a governor. In turn, the quarters were divided into provinces, each also ruled by a governor. Those chosen to be governors were usually related to the royal family. Each province was supposed to contain about ten thousand residents. At the top of the entire system was the emperor, who was believed to be descended from the sun god.

The state was built on forced labor. All Incan subjects were responsible for labor service, usually for several weeks each year. Laborers, often with their entire communities, were moved according to need from one part of the country to another to take part in building projects. Forced laborers probably built the buildings and monuments of the capital city of Cuzco. Constructed of close-fitting stones without mortar (the better to withstand the frequent earthquakes in the region), these buildings were the wonder of early European visitors.

The Inca were great builders. Another major project was a system of 24,800 miles of roads that extended from the border of modern-day Colombia to a point south of modern-day Santiago, Chile. Two major roadways extended in a north-south direction, one through the Andes Mountains and the other along the coast, with

So What ⁇

*If your students question the importance of the information on **Incan culture**, tell them . . .*

Incan culture continues to have an impact on modern Peru, as seen in its art and its music. The Andean pipes, an instrument with connections to Incan times, is an instrument often used for popular music in Peru, and is slowly making its way to the rest of the Americas, including the United States.

Descendants of the Incas play music which is airy, spiritual, and sublime in its melody. The descendants of the Incas are also known for their textiles, leatherwork, and pottery. The Incan legacy has made northern Peru one of the most artistically accomplished countries in South America.

Map 7.5 The Inca Empire about 1500

connecting routes between them. Rest houses, located a day's walk apart, and storage depots were placed along the roads. Various types of bridges, including some of the finest examples of suspension bridges in premodern times, were built over ravines and waterways.

The roads were used chiefly for official and military purposes. Government permission was needed to use them. Trained runners carried messages rapidly from one way station to another, enabling information to travel up to 140 miles in a single day. Most people walked the roads, but rulers and other high officials were carried in **litters** (covered couches used for carrying passengers).

Incan society was highly regimented. So, too, were marriage and the lives of women. Men and women were required to select a marriage partner from within their immediate tribal groups. After marriage, women were expected to care for the children and to weave cloth. Spanish visitors noted that women carried their weaving tools wherever they went. For women, there was only one alternative to a life of working in the home. Some young girls were chosen to serve as priestesses in temples throughout the country.

In rural areas, the people lived chiefly by farming. In the mountains, they used terraced farms, watered by irrigation systems that carried precise amounts of water into the fields. These were planted with corn, potatoes, and other crops. The houses of the farmers, built of stone or adobe with thatched roofs, were located near the fields. Villages were connected by roads and paths that snaked through the mountainous terrain, sometimes crossing vast ravines on suspension bridges made of braided fiber. Nothing shows the architectural genius of the Inca more than the ruins of the abandoned city of Machu Picchu (MAW-CHOO PEEK-CHOO) (see "Our Artistic Heritage: The Splendor of Machu Picchu").

Incan Culture and Conquest

Like the civilizations of the Aztecs and the Maya, the Incan state was built on war. All young men were required to serve in the 200,000-person Incan army, the largest and best armed in the region. Military units were moved rapidly along the highway system and resided in the rest houses located along the roads. Because the Inca, like other people in the early Americas, did not make use of the wheel, supplies were carried on the backs of llamas.

Once an area was placed under Inca control, the local inhabitants were instructed in the Quechua (KECH-uh-wuh) language. Control of new territories was carefully regulated. A noble of high rank was sent out to govern the new region. Local leaders could keep their posts as long as they were loyal to the Inca emperor. To encourage loyalty, the children of local leaders were taken as hostages to the Incan capital, where they were educated in Incan ways before returning home.

The Inca had no writing system but instead kept records using a system of knotted strings called the *quipu*

COMPARING TIME PERIODS

The text states on this page that the Incan road system was used chiefly for official and military purposes. (Ironically, the well-developed Incan highway system hastened the defeat of this empire by the Spanish.) During the years 1930–1932, Nazi Germany developed its autobahn system for both economic and military purposes as the Germans prepared for World War II. Students will probably be surprised to learn that the U.S. Congress authorized the large expansion of our own highways system in 1944 after recognizing the military value of highways (as well as the need for improved highways for civilian reasons). Ask students to think of other technological improvements that were originally developed for military purposes *(transistors, communications, satellites, etc.).*

STUDYING MAPS

The following questions will help you guide the students through their study of Map 7.5.

1. What information does this map provide? *(the major transportation routes used by the Incans)*

2. What is the approximate distance (north-south) of the road network? *(approximately 3000 miles)*

3. Why are there so few major east-west roads in the lower half of the map? *(the ruggedness of the terrain prevents anything other than small trails)*

ACROSS THE CURRICULUM

Archaeology   Much of what is known about early peoples is a result of the persistence of individuals like Hiram Bingham—people who achieve because they are skilled in many areas, not just one. Share with students some of these "facts" about Bingham:

◆ He was an accomplished mountaineer who learned the skill from his missionary father.

◆ He was a Yale professor specializing in Latin American history who tried to replicate the journeys of early traders to make history more exciting for his students.

◆ He was elected a governor and senator and eventually worked with the Truman administration to "investigate controversial cases of suspected subversion."

Students interested in this feature may also want to read about Henry Schliemann, Margaret Mead, or the famous Leakey family.

Answers to Critical Thinking Questions

1. No one even knew about Machu Picchu until it was rediscovered in 1911.

2. This poetic phrase refers to the proximity of the stairway at Machu Picchu to the sun, and to the people's desire to keep the sun overhead.

3. Buildings are placed harmoniously in their natural setting.

OUR ARTISTIC HERITAGE
The Splendor of Machu Picchu

Machu Picchu was built on a lofty hilltop surrounded by mountain peaks far above the Urubamba River. Machu Picchu was hardly a city, containing only about 200 buildings. Perhaps 1,200 people lived there, growing crops on agricultural terraces similar to the ones used throughout the mountainous regions of the Incan Empire. At some unknown time the area was deserted by the Incas.

The Spanish conquerors of the Incas did not know of the existence of Machu Picchu. In 1911, it was rediscovered by Hiram Bingham, an archaeologist from Yale University. Bingham was astounded by his discovery. He wrote, "Suddenly I found myself confronted with the walls of ruined houses built of the finest quality of Inca stonework. It seemed like an unbelievable dream."

The buildings of Machu Picchu included temples, residences, storage houses, and public buildings. At the southeastern end of the community was a special building—a semicircular tower. Like the other buildings, it had walls made of stones fitted together without mortar. Awed by their beauty, Bingham spoke of their craftsmanship "as fine as the finest stonework in the world." The tower clearly served a religious purpose.

In another part of Machu Picchu, a long stairway leads to an elegant stone. It was known to the Incas as the "hitching post of the sun." Carved from the mountain, this "hitching post" may have been used as a solar observatory. During the sun festivals held in June and December, the people of Machu Picchu gathered here to chant and say prayers to Inti, the sun god.

Machu Picchu is a place of incredible beauty. The buildings were placed harmoniously in their natural setting. One art historian has said that the terraces and buildings of Machu Picchu resemble

▲ *Machu Picchu was built between the fourteenth and fifteenth centuries A.D. The carefully fitted stones have withstood time and the ravages of weather, an incredible tribute to the Incan people.*

"a patterned blanket thrown over a great rock." At Machu Picchu, architecture and environment became one.

1. What is amazing about the discovery of Machu Picchu?

2. Explain the meaning of the phrase, the "hitching post of the sun."

3. How did architecture and environment become one at Machu Picchu?

On Line with WORLD HISTORY   *Internet Activity*

You may want to have students visit the following URL, where they will find information and additional web site resources to enhance study of this chapter.
The Inca Trail and Machu Picchu

http://www.tardis.ed.ac.uk/~angus/Gallery/Photos/SouthAmerica/Peru/IncaTrail.html

Take this virtual field trip to Machu Picchu, Peru. Walk through fabulous sites learning Incan history and culture.

Due to the ever-changing nature of the World Wide Web, see the West History web site, **http://history.swpco.com** for regular updates of the URLs in this text.

YOU ARE THERE
The *Quipu*

The Inca did not possess a written language. To record events and other aspects of their lives that they wished to remember, they used a system of knotted strings, called the quipu. *This is a description of the process.*

Description of the *Quipu* or System of Knotted Strings

These men recorded on their knots all the tribute brought annually to the Inca, specifying everything by kind, species, and quality. They recorded the number of men who went to the wars, how many died in them, and how many were born and died every year, month by month. In short they may be said to have recorded on their knots everything that could be counted, even mentioning battles and fights, all the embassies that had come to visit the Inca, and all the speeches and arguments the king had uttered. But the purpose of the embassies or the contents of the speeches, or any other descriptive matter could not be recorded on the knots, consisting as it did of continuous spoken or written prose, which cannot be expressed by means of knots, since these can only give numbers and not words. To supply this want they used signs that indicated historical events or facts or the existence of any embassy, speech, or discussion in time of peace or war. Such speeches were committed to memory and taught by tradition to their successors and descendants from father to son. . . . Another method too was used for keeping alive in the memory of the people their deeds and the embassies they sent to the Inca and the replies he [the king] gave them. The philosophers and sages took the trouble to turn them into stories, no longer than fables, suitable for telling to children, young people, and the rustics of the countryside: they were thus passed from hand to hand and age

▲ *Using quipus woven with strands of different-colored yarn like the one in this photo, royal statisticians were able to keep accurate records of many kinds of information. Interpreting the lengths of yarn, however, is denied to us, for there are no "rememberers" left to tell the stories or sing the songs of the ancient Incas. Can you give several reasons why our society relies less and less on oral traditions?*

to age, and preserved in the memories of all. . . . Similarly their poets composed short, compressed poems, embracing a history, or an embassy, or the king's reply. In short, everything that could not be recorded on the knots was included in these poems, which were sung at their triumphs. Thus they remembered their history.

1. What did the *quipu* record? What was it unable to record?

2. In what other ways was Incan history preserved?

RECOMMENDED READING

On the Inca and their predecessors, see R. W. Keatinge, ed., *Peruvian Prehistory: An Overview of Pre-Inca and Inca Society* (Cambridge, 1988); G. Bankes, *Peru before Pizarro* (Oxford, 1977); and E. P. Lanning, *Peru before the Incas* (Englewood Cliffs, N.J., 1967). The arrival of the Spanish is chronicled in C. Howard, *Pizarro and the Conquest*

of Peru (New York, 1967). For an extended account of Inca civilization, see G. de la Vega, El Inca, *Royal Commentaries of the Incas and General History of Peru* (Austin, Tex., 1966).

On the art and culture of the ancient Americas, see E. Henning and J. Raney, *Monuments of the Inca* (Boston, 1982).

ASSESS

You can choose from a variety of assessments to evaluate your students' mastery of the objectives of this section as stated on page 215. Possible assessments include:

1. Section Review questions on this page
2. Section 7-3 Quiz in your Teacher Resource materials
3. Reteaching Worksheets in your Teacher Resource materials
4. Self-Study software

Answers to SECTION REVIEW

2 (a) covered couches used for carrying passengers (b) a system of knotted strings that was used by the Incas to keep records

3. (a) an advanced civilization that appeared near Ecuador early in the first millennium B.C. The people of Moche were farmers, their pottery indicates that they were obsessed with warfare; the civilization collapsed in the eighth century. (b) a fourteenth century civilization in the mountains of Peru that grew to include perhaps 12 million people; built suspension bridges, a road system that was 24,800 miles long, and buildings constructed of close-fitting stones without mortar (c) the leader of the Inca (d) the Spanish conqueror who defeated the Inca

4. by conquering new peoples and making them and their land part of the empire

5. Answers will vary.

220

(see "You Are There: The *Quipu*"). However, the lack of a fully developed writing system did not prevent the Inca from attaining a high level of cultural achievement. The Inca had a well-developed tradition of court theater, consisting of both tragic and comic works. Plays often involved the recounting of valiant deeds and other historical events. Actors were not professionals but rather members of the nobility or senior officials who memorized their parts. Poetry was also recited, often accompanied by music played on reed instruments.

The Incan Empire was still flourishing when the first Spanish expeditions arrived in the central Andes. In December 1530, Francisco Pizarro landed on the Pacific coast of South America with only a small band of about 180 men. However, like Cortés, Pizarro had steel weapons, gunpowder, and horses. The Inca had seen none of these. Furthermore, the Incan Empire had already experienced an epidemic of smallpox. Like the Aztecs, the Incas had no immunities to European diseases. All too soon, smallpox was devastating entire villages. Even the Incan emperor was a victim—more good fortune for Pizarro. Upon the emperor's death, his two sons claimed the throne. This led to a civil war. Pizarro took advantage of the situation by capturing Atahualpa (AWT-uh-WALL-puh), one of the sons, whose forces had just defeated his brother's. Armed only with stones, arrows, and light spears, Incan soldiers provided little challenge to the charging horses of the Spanish, let alone to their guns and cannons. After executing Atahualpa, Pizarro and his soldiers, aided by their Incan allies, marched on Cuzco and captured the Incan capital. By 1535, Pizarro had established a new capital at Lima (LEE-muh) for a new colony of the Spanish Empire.

 SECTION REVIEW

1. **Locate:**
   (*a*) Andes Mountains,   (*b*) Amazon River,
   (*c*) Cuzco,   (*d*) Machu Picchu

2. **Define:**
   (*a*) litters,   (*b*) *quipu*

---

3. **Identify:**
   (*a*) Moche civilization,   (*b*) the Inca,
   (*c*) Pachakuti,   (*d*) Francisco Pizarro

4. **Recall:** How was the size of the Inca Empire increased?

5. **Think Critically**: There is a quote that says, "Those who take up the sword will perish with the sword." How does this saying relate to the rise and fall of the Inca Empire?

Conclusion

Around 5000 B.C., farming settlements began to appear in river valleys and upland areas in both Central and South America. Shortly after, organized communities located along the coast of the Gulf of Mexico and the western slopes of the central Andes Mountains began the long march to civilization. The Maya and Aztecs were especially successful in developing advanced and prosperous civilizations. Both cultures built elaborate cities with pyramids, temples, and palaces. Both were polytheistic and practiced human sacrifice as a major part of their religions. Mayan civilization collapsed in the ninth century, whereas the Aztecs fell to Spanish invaders in the sixteenth century.

In the fifteenth century, another remarkable civilization—that of the Inca—flourished in South America. The Incan Empire was carefully planned and regulated, which is especially evident in the extensive network of roads that connected all parts of the empire. However, the Inca, possessing none of the new weapons of the Spaniards, eventually fell to the foreign conquerors.

While the Maya, Aztecs, and Inca were developing their civilizations, the peoples of North America were creating a remarkable number of different cultures. The Inuits, Mound Builders, Iroquois, Plains Amerindians, and Anasazi all developed flourishing societies that responded in their own unique ways to the environmental conditions that they faced.

All of these societies in the Americas developed in apparently total isolation from their counterparts elsewhere in the world. This lack of contact with other

---

ENRICHMENT ACTIVITY

Have students brainstorm cultural differences that would be created by a civilization that is mountain-based. List their ideas on the board. Then, have them research the Incan civilization to determine whether the differences listed can be identified in the Incan culture. Allow volunteers to share their feelings with the rest of the class.

human beings deprived them of access to developments taking place in Africa, Asia, and Europe. They
did not know of the wheel, for example, and their written languages were not as sophisticated as those in
other parts of the world. In other respects, however,
their cultural achievements were the equal of those
realized elsewhere. When the first European explorers
arrived in the Americas at the beginning of the sixteenth century, they described much that they
observed in glowing terms. One need only point to the
awed comments of early Spanish visitors, who said that
the cities of the Aztecs were the equal of any found in
Spain.

One development that the peoples of the Americas
lacked was the knowledge of firearms. In a few short
years, tiny bands of Spanish explorers were able to conquer the magnificent civilizations of the Americas and
turn them into ruins. Meanwhile, during the heyday of
the Mayan civilization, another new civilization was
emerging in the Middle East that would build an
empire upon some of the ruins of the collapsed Roman
Empire. In the next chapter, we turn to the world of
Islam.

Notes

1. Quoted in Alvin Josephy, Jr., *500 Nations* (New York, 1994), p. 48.
2. *Ibid.*, p. 50.
3. Michael Coe, *The Maya*, 5th ed. (London, 1993), p. 171.
4. Quoted in Sylvanus Morley and George W. Brainerd, *The Ancient Maya* (Stanford, Calif., 1983), p. 513.
5. Bernal Díaz, *The Conquest of New Spain* (Harmondsworth, 1975), p. 232.
6. Garcilaso de la Vega, *Royal Commentaries of the Incas: And General History of Peru*, part 1, trans. Harold V. Livermore (Austin, Tex., 1966), p. 180.

ALTERNATE ASSESSMENT

Ask students to write a short essay describing how the rigid and centralized Incan political system was both its major strength and its major weakness.

CLOSE

The technology available to the Spanish conquerors was both a practical and psychological weapon. Lead a classroom discussion on what usually happens when a technologically superior culture collides with a less technically developed culture. Do students believe that technology will always triumph? Should technology always triumph?

SPANISH SUPPORT

The *Conclusion* has been translated into Spanish for your Spanish-speaking students. Included with this translation (in your Teacher Resource Box) are Section Key Points, which consist of one or two sentences summarizing each section in the chapter. These Key Points have also been translated into Spanish.

TIME LINE

As students conclude the chapter, you may want to refer them to the chapter time line in the *Study Guide*. The time line will help them put key dates in perspective. Supporting questions and activities are also provided.

COOPERATIVE LEARNING ACTIVITY

Divide the class into cooperative learning groups. Assign a particular role to each group member. Roles may include reader, recorder, materials handler, facilitator, etc. Have groups prepare charts that compare the government, social system, family life, educational system of the ancient civilization discussed in this chapter (Amerindians, Incas, Mayans, Aztecs).

ANSWERS TO USING KEY TERMS

1. Pueblos
2. teepees
3. adobe
4. tundra
5. indentured workers
6. quipu
7. longhouses
8. clan
9. aqueduct
10. litters

REVIEWING THE FACTS

1. by hunting and fishing or by food gathering
2. Rocky Mountains and Andes Mts.
3. The Great Peace created a tribal alliance among the Iroquois. Its purpose was to "look and listen for the welfare of the whole people."
4. about 10,000 people
5. necklaces of gold, silver, copper, and shells and artifacts
6. The Great Peace
7. hunters would work together to cause a stampede
8. horses
9. without metal tools
10. They believed that the books contained superstitions and lies of the devil.
11. invasion, internal revolt, natural disasters, or possibly overuse of the land
12. Senior officials chose his successor from within the royal family.
13. the forces of creation, virtue, and learning
14. Cortés had 550 soldiers and 15 horses.
15. Moctezuma
16. an imposing city of stone
17. weaving utensils
18. the llama
19. The court was a symbol of the world and the ball represented the sun and moon.
20. Poor Aztecs ate maize cakes, porridge and tamales; vegetables such as beans and squash supplemented the diet. The rich ate fruits, a greater variety of vegetables, fish, and meat, especially dog and turkey.
21. His/her heart was cut out.
22. the quipi and oral traditions

USING KEY TERMS

1. _____ were Anasazi descendants, named after their unique dwellings.
2. The Plains hunters stretched buffalo skins over wooden poles to make their homes called _____.
3. Sun-dried bricks are called _____.
4. The Inuit lived on cold, treeless plains known as a _____.
5. Landless laborers who contracted to work on the estates of Aztec nobles were called _____.
6. The Inca used knotted strings called _____ to record events that they wished to remember.
7. Iroquois _____ were about 150–200 feet in length and housed about a dozen families.
8. A group of related families is called a _____.
9. The Aztecs constructed a(n) _____ to transport fresh water to Tenochtitlán.
10. Incan rulers did not walk the roads, but were carried over them in _____.

REVIEWING THE FACTS

1. How did the first settlers make a living when they came to America?
2. Name the two major mountain ranges in the western portion of the Americas.
3. Explain the Great Peace of the Iroquois.
4. How many people lived in the Hopewell urban centers?
5. What did the Hopewell burial mounds contain?
6. The phrase "self-interest shall be cast away" comes from which Iroquois document?
7. How did the Plains hunters capture buffalo before they had horses and guns?
8. What did the Spanish bring to America that changed the lives of the Plains Indians?
9. The Olmec stone heads were made without what kinds of tools?
10. Why did the Spanish burn Mayan books?

11. What are the possible explanations for the decline of Mayan civilization?
12. How did the Aztecs choose their rulers?
13. What forces did the Aztec god Quetzalcoatl represent?
14. How large was Cortés' army when he came to Mexico?
15. Who was the leader of the Aztecs at this time?
16. Describe the Incan city of Cuzco.
17. What utensils did the Incan women carry with them wherever they went?
18. What was the main beast of burden used by the Inca?
19. In the Mayan ball game what did the court and ball represent?
20. What were the basic components of the diet of the Aztecs? How did the diet of the rich differ from that of the poor?
21. Describe the Aztec ritual of human sacrifice.
22. How did the Inca remember their history?

THINKING CRITICALLY

1. What were the "three sisters of the Iroquois agriculture"? Why do you think that the feminine is chosen? Would it be appropriate to call them the "three brothers"?
2. Pyramids seem to be a common form of monumental architecture. What is it about this kind of building that seems so appealing?
3. Wars are most often fought to obtain land or booty, and sometimes they are fought over ideas, such as religion. What was different about Mayan warfare? What impact do you think that it had on their society that they "were obsessed with war"?
4. "In all of your acts, self-interest shall be cast away." What does this phrase from the Iroquois Great Peace mean? How do you think it affected Iroquois leaders? Do we ask this of our leaders today?

THINKING CRITICALLY

1. corn, squash, and beans; women were in charge of the agriculture
2. Answers will vary; rising to God or the gods is significant. The symmetry of the pyramids is also pleasing to the eye.
3. The Mayans fought to obtain captives. A society that seeks things such as arable land, precious metals, and agricultural products in war will benefit in a way that the Mayas did not.
4. The Iroquois were asking their leaders to put the interest of the group ahead of their own personal needs. Democracy makes it more difficult for leaders to enrich themselves. Politicians must be re-elected on a regular basis and so must convince the voters of their merits.
5. Gunpowder technology was a significant advantage of the Spanish and without it they would not have been successful.

APPLYING SOCIAL STUDIES SKILLS

1. The 50 chiefs of the Grand Council represented all of the five tribes to settle differences among its members. This experiment in democracy impressed Benjamin Franklin among other American colonists.
2. The Iroquois traded their furs for European beads, cloth, and guns.

5. The strength of a country depends on its military technology. Discuss this statement in the context of the Spanish conquest of the Aztecs and Inca.

7. Compare the hostage system of the Incas to the hostages that were kept at Edo during the Tokugawa shogunate in Japan.

APPLYING SOCIAL STUDIES SKILLS

1. **Government:** Explain how the Grand Council system of the Iroquois worked.
2. **Economics:** How did the Iroquois change their trading habits when the Europeans arrived?
3. **Sociology:** What leadership roles did women take in Iroquois society?
4. **Geography:** Locate the present South American countries where the Inca dominated.

MAKING TIME AND PLACE CONNECTIONS

1. When did the first civilizations appear in Central America? What was happening in the Fertile Crescent at this time?
2. Compare the purpose of the Great Peace to the preamble of the United States Constitution.
3. Compare the Aztec search for what was to become Tenochtitlán to the Hebrews wandering in the desert.
4. It is said that the Maya were obsessed with war and that the Egyptians were obsessed with death. In a thousand years what will historians say twentieth-century Americans are obsessed with?
5. Compare the Incan system of roads to those built by the Romans. How does the purpose of these roads compare with the purpose of our roads today?
6. Compare the value of the llama of the Inca to that of the horse, ox, and camel that were used in Africa and Eurasia.

BECOMING AN HISTORIAN

Geography as a Key to History: *Climate and geography have an important impact on how people order their lives.*

Studying the history of the Americas provides a perfect example of the way in which geography and climate affect historical developments. As noted in the Conclusion, the people of America all developed "flourishing societies that responded in their own unique ways to the environmental conditions that they faced." Geography limits the choices that people can make and how they order their lives. For example, the Inuit could not really farm beca use of the tundra. Because they were nomadic hunters, they lived in small groups. In sharp contrast to this, the fertile lands of the Mississippi river valley led to the development of a wealthy and highly populated society. Greater population meant a more complicated society.

Choose two different societies mentioned in this chapter and explain further how geography affected their lives. Choose one nomadic society (Inuit or Plains Indians) and one sedentary society (Hopewell, Anasazi, Aztec, or Inca) and compare and contrast their development. Consider how geography affected the following: how food was obtained, materials used for homes and monumental structures (if any), need for trade and the goods traded, size of communities, impact of natural boundaries such as mountains and bodies of water, and source of drinking water.

223

7. The Incas appointed nobles of high rank to rule newly conquered areas and they could keep their posts as long as they were loyal to the emperor. The noble's children were kept hostages in the capital to ensure their loyalty. The Tokugawas followed a similar system and required the daimyo to keep their children as hostages in the capital at Edo for the same reasons.

BECOMING AN HISTORIAN— GEOGRAPHY AS A KEY TO HISTORY

Answers will vary. For the nomadic society the governments were less authoritarian and the people had more autonomy. Their lives were likely to be more precarious, and more greatly affected by natural calamities. For the most part, there was more stability in sedentary civilizations although one can find significant exceptions. Nomadic communities were smaller. All societies, no matter what their size, benefited from trade. Natural boundaries were sometimes important as protectors from invaders, although this is not as significant an issue as it was for some Eurasian societies. Little is mentioned in the text directly about drinking water so that is an area that students can pursue in other sources. Note how we take for granted the easy and adequate supply of water in this country.

3. The chiefs were chosen by the clan mothers.
4. See map.

MAKING TIME AND PLACE CONNECTIONS

1. Around 5,000 B.C. people began to grow corn. This was a few thousand years later than in the Fertile Crescent. Civilization began around 1200 B.C., the time of Moses and the Exodus.
2. They had similar purposes. The Great Peace encouraged the Iroquois to consider the welfare of the whole people and not only for the present but also for future generations. The Preamble says that the purpose of the government is to "pro-mote the general welfare, and secure the blessings of liberty to ourselves and our posterity."
3. Both struggled to survive against enemies in a foreign territory. They both survived because of support from their God or gods.
4. Answers will vary. Some will argue that we were obsessed with youth, food, or material wealth.
5. Both the Incans and the Romans used the roads to connect their empire and ensure their political hegemony. The original purpose of the U.S. interstate highway system, begun in the 1950s, was to ensure the rapid transportation of troops in the event of war.
6. The llama is inferior in most ways other than the ability to live at high altitudes.

PLANNING GUIDE

SECTION	KEY TOPICS	PRIMARY SOURCES	ASSESSMENT
1 The Rise of Islam pages 225–230	◆ Muhammad and the beginnings of Islam ◆ the basic tenets of the Islamic faith	◆ *A Pilgrimage to Mecca,* page 229	◆ Section Review, page 230 ◆ Section Quiz, 8–1, TRB
2 The Arab Empire and Its Successors pages 230–239	◆ the growth of Islam following Muhammad's death ◆ Sunni and Shi'ite Muslims ◆ Umayyad and Abassid dynasties	◆ *The Crusaders in Muslim Eyes,* page 237	◆ Section Review, page 239 ◆ Section Quiz 8–2, TRB
3 Islamic Civilization pages 239–243	◆ the caliphate ◆ development of Islamic cities ◆ life and cultural advances in Islamic cities	◆ Chinese Description of the caliphs, pages 239–240 ◆ Chinese description of life along the Nile River, pages 241–242	◆ Section Review, page 243 ◆ Section quiz, 8–3, TRB
4 The Culture of Islam pages 243–249	◆ educational contributions of the Muslims ◆ Arabic literature ◆ Arabic art and architecture	◆ The *Quran,* page 244 ◆ *The Rubaiyat* of Omar Khayyam, pages 245–246 ◆ Poem by Rumi, page 246	◆ Section Review, page 249 ◆ Section Quiz 8–4, TRB

THE WORLD OF ISLAM (600 to 1500)

REPRODUCIBLE ACTIVITIES

- Historical Maps
- Charts and Graphs
- Critical Thinking
- Cooperative Learning
- Vocabulary
- Guided Reading
- Reteaching
- Enrichment
- Performance Assessment
- Spanish Key Points and Chapter Summaries
- Spanish Vocabulary
- Spanish Guided Reading

MULTIMEDIA SUPPORT

TRANSPARENCIES
- *World History* Color Transparency Package
- Fine Art Color Transparency Package

VIDEO
- *World History* Video Library
- CNN. Annual Video Update

LASERDISC
- *Sights and Sounds of History*

AUDIO
- *Listening to Literature* audiotape (English and Spanish)
- *History of Music* CD

SOFTWARE
- WESTEST™
- Student Review

CD–ROM
- *The Journey of Civilization*
- *World History*

INTERNET
- Internet Activities

On Line with WORLD HISTORY

Access West's history web site at
http://history.swpco.com
You'll find activities and web sites related to specific topics and chapters in *World History: The Human Odyssey*. Also look for references to helpful web sites at appropriate places throughout this teacher edition.

LESSON PLANNING

You will find detailed daily lesson plans for both traditional class scheduling and **block scheduling** in your Teacher Resource Box.

 Not Enough Time?

If you do not have the four or five days recommended to teach this chapter, you may want to focus on the following sections and activities:

- Have students read the first two sections about the history of Islam, pages 225–239 and answer the section review questions.
- Have students read the feature, Our Artistic Heritage: The Mosque, on page 247, and discuss it in class.

THE WORLD OF ISLAM

(600 TO 1500)

8

USING THE OPENING STORY

USING THE OPENING STORY

◆ Review this opening story with the students, and have them use the map on page 227 to locate the Arabian Peninsula and Mecca.

◆ Ask students when Muhammad was born *(A.D. 570)* and how old he was when he heard the angel's voice calling to him *(50)*.

◆ What book for Christians is similar to the Quran for the Muslims? *(the Bible)*

◆ How extensive was the Islamic Empire by the mid 600s? *(It extended from Spain to the Indus River Valley.)*

◆ What did Allah promise to those who did good deeds? *(to forgive their sins and ennoble them)* To those who died serving Allah? *(admittance to Heaven)*

◆ How might the belief that death in a holy battle would bring you an after-life in Paradise affect Islamic soldiers? *(Answers will vary.)*

LEARNING FROM VISUALS

Prayer rugs are still used today. Muslims are called to prayer five times each day and kneel on rugs they place on the ground. Today many of these rugs are prized for their design and ornate use of color.

Answer to the caption question: Rectangles, squares, triangles, circles, and spirals, are intertwined.

In Mecca, a small town of about three thousand people located in the desert lands of the Arabian peninsula, a man named Muhammad (MOE-ham-ud) was born in 570. His father died when he was not yet one; and his mother died when he was only five. He was raised by relatives, from whom he learned how to buy, sell, and transport goods. Intelligent and hardworking, he became a capable merchant. He married, had children, and seemed to have a happy and rewarding life. Muhammad, however, was not content. Deeply disturbed by problems in Meccan society, he spent days on end in a nearby cave, as he prayed and meditated. According to tradition, one night in 610, while Muhammad was deep in meditation, an angelic voice called out, "Recite!" A frightened Muhammad replied, "What shall I recite?" The voice responded, "In the name of thy Lord the Creator, who created mankind from a clot of blood, recite!" The voice then began to speak about the nature of God. Over a period of time, Muhammad memorized everything the voice revealed and began to preach these words to others: "Allah will bring to nothing the deeds of those who disbelieve. . . . As for the faithful who do good works and believe in what is revealed to Muhammad—which is the truth from their Lord—He will forgive them their sins and ennoble their state. . . . As for those who are slain in the cause of Allah, . . . He will

▲ *This Turkish prayer rug dates from the early sixteenth century. Turkish rugs were handmade and prized for their rich colors and intricate patterns. What geometric shapes are used in this one?*

admit them to the Paradise He has made known to them." Words such as these would later be gathered together to form the Quran (kuh-RAN) (Koran), the sacred book of Islam, the religion founded by Muhammad.

Muhammad's life changed the course of world history. At the time of his birth, old empires that had once ruled the entire Middle East were only a memory. The region was now divided into many separate states, and the people worshiped many different gods. Within a few decades of Muhammad's death, the Middle East was united once again. Arab armies marched westward across North Africa and eastward into Mesopotamia and Persia, creating a new empire that stretched from Spain to the Indus River valley. Arab rule also brought with it a new religion and a new culture—that of Islam.

Islamic beliefs made a powerful impact in all areas occupied by Arab armies, but the Arab Empire failed to last. Internal struggles led first to its decline and then to its destruction. Still, the Arab conquest left a powerful legacy. The appeal of Islam remained strong throughout the Middle East and extended, as we shall see in Chapters 9 and 11, into areas not occupied by Arab armies, such as Africa, India, and Southeast Asia.

ADDITIONAL RESOURCES

The resources listed below can be used to enrich the lessons in this chapter.

BOOKS FOR STUDENTS
The Illustrated World's Religions by Huston Smith, Harper Collins, Social Studies School Service, (800) 421-4246
Early Islam by Desmond Stuart. Time-Life.

VIDEO/FILMS
Islam and the Sciences, Phoenix, Social Stud-

ies School Service, (800) 421-4246
The Torchbearers: Bridging the Dark Ages, Encyclopedia Britannica, Social Studies School Service, (800) 421-4246

CD-ROM
Religions of the World, Mentorom, Social Studies School Service, (800) 421-4246

NEW PATTERNS OF CIVILIZATION

| 600 | THE WORLD OF ISLAM | 1500 |
| 400 | | 1500 |

QUESTIONS TO GUIDE YOUR READING

1. What was the role of Muhammad in creating the religion of Islam?

2. What are the major characteristics of the religion of Islam?

3. What were the major developments during the Umayyad and the Abbasid dynasties? Why did they fall?

4. How did the Seljuk Turks, Christian crusaders, and Mongols affect Islamic civilization?

5. What was the basic political structure of the Arab Empire in the Middle East?

6. What were the basic characteristics of Islamic society?

7. In what ways are the mosque and the palace both good examples of Islamic art?

THE RISE OF ISLAM

From ancient times, the Middle East has been the site of great empires. Beginning with the Sumerians and continuing with the Assyrians, the Babylonians, the Persians, and the brief conquests of Alexander the Great, the area has given birth to some of the most powerful civilizations in history. In the seventh century, a new force—the Arabs—arose in the Arabian peninsula and spread rapidly throughout the Middle East.

The Arabs

Like the Hebrews and the Assyrians, the Arabs were a Semitic-speaking people of the Middle East with a long history. Eventually, they settled in the Arabian peninsula, a desolate place filled with desert land and sorely lacking in rivers and lakes. The Arabs were nomads who moved constantly to find water and food for their animals.

Survival in such a harsh environment was not easy, and the Arabs organized into tribes to help one another. Each tribe was ruled by a sheikh (SHEEK) who was chosen from one of the leading families by a council of elders. Each tribe was independent, but also

225

FOCUS ON THEMES

Politics and History As successors to Muhammad, caliphs assumed both political and spiritual power over the Muslim Empire of the Arabs. As the Umayyad and Abbasid dynasties developed, the caliph became a more powerful kingly figure.

The Role of Ideas The Quran provided fundamental guidelines for all Muslims, not only in spiritual affairs but also in politics, economics, and social life.

Economics and History Although most people made their living in the Arab Empire by farming, the development of an extensive trade network brought considerable prosperity to the Islamic world.

Social Life The Quran stated that all people were equal in the eyes of Allah. In reality, however, there were wide gaps between rich and poor. Slaves had few rights, and the roles of women were limited.

The Importance of Cultural Developments The translation of Arabic works into Latin was a significant factor in the revival of learning in the West in the High Middle Ages.

Religion in History The rise of Islam created a unified Middle East. The spread of Islam to Africa and Asia enabled Islam to become one of the world's great religions.

The Role of Individuals Muhammad was a powerful figure who created a religion that eventually spread to all of the world.

The Impact of Science and Technology Muslim scholars made significant advances in mathematics, astronomy, and medicine.

225

FOCUS

OBJECTIVES

After studying this section, students should be able to

1. identify groups known as the Arab tribes and describe their living patterns
2. describe the life of Muhammad
3. describe the basic tenets of the Islamic religion

FOCUS ACTIVITY

Have students work in pairs to brainstorm a list of ten to fifteen items they associate with desert living or with Arab peoples. As students read through this section, have them compare the reality of desert life with their lists. As an alternative, you might wish to have students list what they know about Islam.

TEACH

CLASS DISCUSSION

Remind students that the life of the Arab sheiks was not glamorous or luxurious, as has been portrayed in many romantic novels and movies. Guide students in a discussion of stereotypes they may have about the Arab nomadic tribes and contrast those stereotypes with the information provided in the text.

ACTIVITY

Have students work in pairs to create maps showing the trading routes described in this section.

226

▲ *In this fourteenth century miniature, Muhammad is shown restoring the black stone to its rightful place in the wall of the Ka'bah. Before Islamic times, Arabs were polytheistic, and their supreme god was symbolized by a sacred stone. However, all tribes worshiped the black meteorite stone that was kept in the Ka'bah in Mecca.*

loosely connected to all the other tribes in the region. At first, the Arabs supported themselves by sheepherding or by raiding the trading caravans that passed through the desert. After the camel was domesticated in the first millennium B.C., however, the Arabs began to take part in the caravan trade themselves. In fact, they became major carriers of trade between the Persian Gulf and the Mediterranean Sea.

These early Arabs were polytheistic; that is, they believed in many gods. There was, however, a supreme god named Allah (*Allah* is Arabic for "God"), who ruled over the other gods. There was no priesthood. All members of the tribe were involved in the practice of the faith. Allah was symbolized by a sacred stone, and each tribe had its own stone. All tribes, however, worshiped a massive black meteorite, the Black Stone, which had been placed in a central shrine called the Ka'bah (KAW-buh) in the city of Mecca.

In the fifth and sixth centuries A.D., the Arabian peninsula took on a new importance. As a result of political disorder in Mesopotamia and Egypt, the usual trade routes in the region began to change. A new trade route—from the Mediterranean through Mecca to Yemen and then by ship across the Indian Ocean—became more popular. The communities in that part of the Arabian peninsula, such as Mecca, began to prosper from this caravan trade. As a result, tensions arose between the Arabs in the desert, known as Bedouins (BED-uh-wuns), and the increasingly wealthy merchant classes in the towns.

The Life of Muhammad

Into this world of tension stepped Muhammad. Born in Mecca to a merchant family, he became an orphan at the age of five. Muhammad, who lived from 570 to 632, grew up to become a caravan manager. Eventually, he married a rich widow named Khadija, who was also his employer. For several years he lived in Mecca, but he was troubled by the growing gap between the simple honesty and generosity of the Bedouins and the greediness of the rich trading elites in the city. Deeply worried, he began to visit the nearby hills to be alone to meditate.

During one of these visits, he experienced visions and heard a voice that he believed was inspired by Allah. According to tradition, the message had been given by the angel Gabriel, who told Muhammad to recite what he was hearing. Muhammad had a knowledge of Jewish and Christian thought and came to believe that Allah had already revealed himself in part through Moses and Jesus—and thus through the Hebrew and Christian traditions. He believed, however, that the final revelations of Allah were now being given to him. Out of his revelations, which were eventually written down, came the Quran (Koran), the holy scriptures of the religion of **Islam**. (The word *Islam* means "submission to the will of Allah.") The Quran

On Line with WORLD HISTORY *Internet Activity*

You may want to have your students visit the following URL, where they will find information and additional web site resources to enhance their study of this chapter.

Islamic Texts and Resources Metapage

http://wings.buffalo.edu/ student-life/sa/muslim/isl.html

Provides a springboard for exploring texts and resources on Islam and Islamic thought, ideas, and related issues.

Due to the ever-changing nature of the World Wide Web, see the West History web site, **http://history.swpco.com** for regular updates of the URLs in this text.

Map 8.1   The Middle East in the Time of Muhammad

The Middle East, about A.D. 600

—— Approximate boundary of the
Roman and Sassanian Empires

contained the guidelines by which the followers of Allah were to live. Those who practice Islam are called Muslims. Islam has only one God, Allah, and Muhammad is his Prophet.

After receiving the revelations, Muhammad returned home. His wife, Khadija, who urged him to follow Gabriel's message, became the first convert to Islam. Muhammad then set out to convince the people of Mecca of the truth of his revelations. At first, many thought he was insane. Others feared that his attacks on the corrupt society around him would upset the established social and political order. After three years of preaching, he had only thirty followers.

Muhammad became discouraged by the persecution of his followers, as well as by the failure of the Meccans to accept his message. In 622, he and some of his closest supporters left the city and moved north to the rival city of Yathrib, a city later renamed Medina (mu-DEEN-uh) ("city of the prophet"). The journey of Muhammad and his followers to Medina is known in history as the **Hegira.** The year the journey occurred became year 1 in the official calendar of Islam.

Muhammad, who had been invited to Medina by a number of prominent residents, soon began to win support from people there, as well as from members of Bedouin tribes in the surrounding countryside. From these groups, he formed the first Muslim community. Muslims saw no separation between political and religious authority. Submission to the will of Allah meant submission to his prophet Muhammad. Muhammad soon became both a religious and a political leader. His political and military skills enabled him to put together a reliable military force. To support themselves, Muhammad and a number of his followers began to make raids on Meccan caravans. Their successes soon attracted larger numbers of supporters.

In 630, Muhammad returned to Mecca with a force of ten thousand men. The city quickly surrendered, and most of the townspeople converted to the new faith. During a visit to the Ka'bah, Muhammad declared it a sacred shrine of Islam. He removed all tribal idols and kept only the Black Stone there. Two years after his triumphal return to Mecca, Muhammad died, just as Islam was beginning to spread throughout the Arabian peninsula.

ENRICHMENT ACTIVITY

In 1258, the Mongol general Hulegu conquered Baghdad; in 1259, he crossed the Tigris to attack Syria, and in 1260, he conquered Aleppo and Damascus. Many of the forces who fought with him were actually Christians, who hoped he would restore the Holy Land to them. Ask students to enact a meeting between Hulegu and a Jewish rabbi, a Christian monk, and a Muslim imam in Damascus. Hulegu, who is a shamanist, must decide whether to proclaim one religion as the official religion, whether to persecute them all, or to tolerate them all. He knows nothing about any of them. The rabbi, the monk, and the imam must compare and contrast their respective faiths to him. Students should include issues such as (1) monotheism or polytheism, (2) natural or revealed religion, (3) the role of Scriptures, (4) prophets and founders of the faith.

COMPARING TIME PERIODS

Have students compare the year numbering system they are familiar with (B.C./A.D.) with the Islamic calendar. Have students compute the year A.D. 2000 in the Islamic calendar. (It will be 1378.) You might assign some students to determine the year A.D. 2000 in the Hebrew calendar as well. (In September 2000, the Hebrew year will be 5760).

CLASS DISCUSSION

You might wish to have students compare and contrast the life of Muhammad with that of Jesus Christ and Siddhartha Gautama (Buddha) who is also discussed in this text and then have students compare the basic beliefs of these three religions.

ACROSS THE DISCIPLINE

Math. Have students compute the distance between Mecca and Medina (Medina is 300 miles north of Mecca by coastal roadways). Have students estimate how long it might have taken for Muhammad to travel this distance on foot with his family and supporters.

CRITICAL THINKING

Muhammad left Mecca in 622 with only thirty followers that he had gathered after three years. Yet, eight years later, he returned to Mecca with an army of 10,000. Have students propose methods that Muhammad might have used to gain such large support in such a short period of time. (Students need to understand that Muhammad was both a religious and a political leader.)

◄ *The Ka'bah is the holiest shrine of the Islamic faith. All Muslims are encouraged to make a hajj, a pilgrimage to Mecca, at least once in their lifetimes. This pilgrimage is considered the ultimate in spiritual fulfillment for all Muslims.*

The Teachings of Muhammad

Like Christianity and Judaism, Islam is monotheistic. Allah is the all-powerful being who created the universe and everything in it. Islam is also concerned with salvation and offers the hope of an afterlife. Those who hope to achieve life after death must subject themselves to the will of Allah. Unlike Christianity, Islam does not believe that its founder was divine. Muhammad, like Jesus and Moses, is considered a prophet, but he was also a man like other men. Muslims believe that because human beings rejected Allah's earlier messengers, Allah sent his final revelation through Muhammad.

At the heart of Islam is the Quran. Its basic message is that there is no god but Allah, and Muhammad is his prophet. The Quran consists of 114 chapters and is the sacred book of Islam. It is also a guidebook for ethics and a code of law combined.

Early Islam was a direct and simple faith, stressing the need to obey the will of Allah. This meant following a basic ethical code consisting of the "five pillars" of Islam: (1) belief in Allah and in Muhammad as his prophet; (2) standard prayer five times a day and public prayer on Fridays at midday to worship Allah;

► *During Ramadan, the holy month of Islam, Muslims fast from dawn to sunset, and observance of Ramadan is considered one of the "five pillars" of the Islamic faith. This Persian miniature shows a festive group of Muslims celebrating the end of Ramadan.*

On Line with WORLD HISTORY *Internet Activity*

You may want to have your students visit the following URL, where they will find information and additional web site resources to enhance their study of this chapter.

Exploring Ancient World Cultures— Early Islam

http://eawc.evansville.edu/ ispage.htm

An excellent source of information on Islamic history. Includes chronology, essays, resources, maps, and www sites. Islam, Judaism, and Christianity are compared.

Due to the ever-changing nature of the World Wide Web, see the West History web site, **http://history.swpco.com** for regular updates of the URLs in this text.

YOU ARE THERE
A Pilgrimage to Mecca

The pilgrimage to Mecca is one of the "five pillars" of Islam and is the duty of every Muslim. In this selection, Ibn Jubayr, a twelfth-century Spanish Muslim, tells how he reached his final destination in his pilgrimage—the Ka'bah at Mecca, which contains the Black Stone.

Ibn Jubayr Describes His Pilgrimage to Mecca

The blessed Black Stone is encased in the corner [of the Ka'bah] facing east. . . . It has four pieces, joined together. . . . Its edges have been braced with a sheet of silver whose white shines brightly against the black sheen and polished brilliance of the Stone, presenting the observer a striking spectacle which will hold his gaze. The Stone, when kissed, has a softness and moistness which so enchants the mouth that he who puts his lips to it would wish them never to be removed. This is one of the special favors of Divine Providence, and it is enough that the Prophet—may God bless and preserve him—declared it to be a covenant of God on earth. May God profit us by the kissing and touching of it. By His favor may all who yearn fervently for it be brought to it. In the sound piece of the stone, to the right of him who presents himself to kiss it, is a small white spot that shines and appears like a mole on the blessed surface. Concerning this white mole, there is a tradition that he who looks upon it clears his vision, and when kissing it one should direct one's lips as closely as one can to the place of the mole.

▲ *This rare thirteenth-century realistic painting of a hajj shows all the pomp and joy that surrounded the trip to Mecca. Realistic artistic representations were considered sacrilegious, so Islamic art took many other intricate forms.*

1. What are the unique properties of the Black Stone?
2. What is the significance of the Stone?

So What ??

If your students question the importance of the information on **the religion of Islam,** *tell them . . .*

Islam is the most widely practiced religion in the world today. On that basis alone, one ought to become at least generally familiar with its tenets. What happens in the Muslim world directly affects our well-being, and there is, in addition, a growing number of Muslims in this country. Ask students to list ways in which knowing more about Islam could have a direct impact on their lives.

ASSESS

Answers to
SECTION REVIEW

2. (a) submission to the will of Allah
   (b) the journey of Muhammad and his followers to Medina
   (c) pilgrimage to Mecca
3. (a) Arabic ruler
   (b) Arabic name for God
   (c) shrine in Mecca housing Black Stone
   (d) founder of Islam
   (e) Muhammad's wife
   (f) holy scriptures of Islam
   (g) set of law codes
4. (1) belief in Allah and Muhammad as his prophet
   (2) standard prayer five times a day and public prayer on Friday
   (3) observation of the holy month of Ramadan which includes fasting
   (4) making a pilgrimage to Mecca in one's lifetime
   (5) alms to the poor
5. Answers will vary.

CLOSE

Islam is not only a religion, it is a way of life and a system of government whose followers number in the millions. Begun by Muhammad, it quickly spread throughout the West and continues to grow today.

---

(3) observation of the holy month of Ramadan (the ninth month in the Muslim calendar), including fasting (no eating or drinking) from dawn to sunset; (4) making a pilgrimage (known as the **hajj** [HADGE]), if possible, to Mecca in one's lifetime (see "You Are There: A Pilgrimage to Mecca"); and (5) giving alms to the poor and unfortunate. The faithful who followed the law were guaranteed a place in an eternal paradise.

Islam was not just a set of religious beliefs but a way of life as well. After the death of Muhammad, Muslim scholars drew up a law code known as the Shari'ah. It provided believers with a set of practical laws to regulate their daily lives. Much of the Shari'ah was taken from the Quran.

Believers were expected to follow strict guidelines for their behavior. In addition to the guidelines in the "five pillars," Muslims were forbidden to gamble, eat pork, drink alcoholic beverages, or engage in dishonest behavior. Sexual standards were also strict. Marriages were to be arranged by parents, and contacts between unmarried men and women were discouraged. In accordance with Bedouin custom, husbands were allowed to have more than one wife as long as they could adequately provide for them. Muhammad did, however, try to control the practice by limiting men to four wives.

❋ SECTION REVIEW ❋

1. **Locate:**
   (a) Mecca,   (b) Medina

2. **Define:**
   (a) Islam,   (b) Hegira,   (c) hajj

3. **Identify:**
   (a) sheikh,   (b) Allah,   (c) Ka'bah,
   (d) Muhammad,   (e) Khadija,   (f) Quran,
   (g) Shari'ah

4. **Recall:** Name the five pillars of Islam.

5. **Think Critically:** Compare and contrast the Islamic religion to Christianity.

THE ARAB EMPIRE AND ITS SUCCESSORS

The death of Muhammad left his followers with a problem. Muhammad had not claimed to be divine, but Muslims saw no separation between religious and political authority. Submission to the will of Allah was the same thing as submission to the will of his prophet Muhammad. According to the Quran, "Whoever obeys the messenger obeys Allah." Unfortunately, Muhammad had never named a successor. Although he had several daughters, he had left no son. In a male-oriented society, who would lead the community of the faithful?

Shortly after Muhammad's death, some of his closest followers chose Abu Bakr (uh-BOO BACK-ur), a wealthy merchant and Muhammad's father-in-law. He was named **caliph** (KAY-luff), the secular leader of the Islamic community. Under Abu Bakr's leadership, the Islamic movement began to grow. Muhammad had made use of the Arabic tribal custom of making raids against one's enemies, and Muhammad's successor turned to the same custom to expand the movement. The Quran called this activity "struggle in the way of God," or **jihad** (ji-HOD). This word is sometimes translated as *holy war*, but that is not quite accurate. The jihad grew out of the Arabic tradition of tribal raids, which were allowed as a way to channel the warlike energies of the Bedouin tribes.

Once the Arabs had become unified under Abu Bakr, they began to direct the energy they had once directed against one another outward against neighboring peoples. The Byzantine (BIZ-un-TEEN) and the Persian Empires were the first to feel the strength of the Arabs, who were newly united and aroused to a peak of zeal by their faith. At Yarmuk in 636, the Arab army defeated the Byzantine army in the midst of a dust storm that enabled the Arabs to take their enemy by surprise. Four years later, they took control of the Byzantine province of Syria. To the east, the Arabs defeated a Persian force and then went on to conquer the entire Persian Empire (the Sassanids [suh-SAW-nuhdz]) by 650.

MORE ABOUT . . . *The Horse Archer and the Compound Bow*

The Asiatic nomads who repeatedly raided the civilized world, from the Scythians of 700 B.C. to the Golden Horde of the early gunpowder age, used a very sophisticated weapon: the compound, reflex bow. These bows were much shorter than the English longbow (which was approximately as tall as the man who used it), so that they could be used on horseback, but were at least as powerful. The draws on longbows recovered from the wreck Mary Rose ranged from 100 to 172 lbs.; reflex bows used by the Mongols, Turks, and others ranged up to 160 lbs. For comparison, draws on the bows used by the Blackfoot and Cheyenne Indians ranged from 45 to 65 lbs. Mongol bows could cast an arrow 800 yards, with an effective range of 300 yards (the effective range of the heavier longbows).

Map 8.2   The Expansion of Islam

In the meantime, by 642, Egypt and other areas of northern Africa had been added to the new Arab Empire. Some historians have argued that the ongoing conflict between the Byzantines and the Persians had weakened both sides and made the Arab victories easier. This may be true, but the power of the Arab armies should not be overlooked. The Arabs, led by a series of brilliant generals, had put together a large, dedicated army. The courage of the soldiers was enhanced by the belief that Muslim warriors were assured a place in Paradise if they died in battle. As we shall see in Chapter 12, Christian soldiers of the time were also promised the same reward for defending Christianity.

To some, the advance of the Arabs was seen as a religious war in which Muslims were determined to impose their faith on others. However, this was not the case. Arab administrators in the conquered territories were quite tolerant, sometimes even allowing local officials to continue to govern. Moreover, conquered people were not forced to convert to Islam. Conversion to Islam was voluntary. Those who chose not to convert were required only to be loyal to Muslim rule and to pay taxes.

Early caliphs, ruling from Medina, organized the newly conquered territories into taxpaying provinces, but problems soon arose over who should become caliph. In 656, Ali, Muhammad's son-in-law, was chosen for the position, but he was soon assassinated. In 661, the general Mu'awiyah, the governor of Syria and one of Ali's chief rivals, became caliph. He was known for one outstanding virtue: he used force only when absolutely necessary. As he said, "I never use my sword when my whip will do, nor my whip when my tongue will do."[1] Mu'awiyah moved quickly to make the

A compound reflex bow is constructed by laminating layers of wood, horn, sinew, and glue to take advantage of the materials of each. When unstrung, the bow ends, or "ears," pointed in the direction away from the archer. Skilled bowyers, fletchers, and string-makers were greatly prized. Great care was taken with the materials. The Mongols had to import their glue, which was made from fish taken off the coast of China. The horse archer was an opponent against whom the urban world had few satisfactory answers—witness the fate of Crassus when he invaded Parthian Mesopotamia. Only the advent of mobile artillery spelled the end of nomadic military power.

LEARNING FROM VISUALS

The Dome of the Rock is considered to be one of the most magnificent structures built by the Muslims. It is located on Temple Mount, part of the old city in Jerusalem.

Answers to the caption question: Most cities do not have gold-domed churches, nor are most churches as large as the Dome of the Rock. However, student answers will vary.

COMPARING TIME PERIODS

Point out to students that the continual fighting over the caliphate did not stop the expansion or limit the power of the Islamic Empire. Have them compare this phenomenon with the Great Schism that occurred in the Catholic Church over the papacy, which did indeed weaken the influence of the Catholic Church in Europe. Ask students to suggest reasons for this very major difference. *(Students should recognize the difference in government structure, the power of kings and nobles who were often at odds with the pope, and the military forces of the Muslims.)*

CLASS DISCUSSION

Many historians believe that the defeat of the Arabs at the Battle of Tours in 732 marked a critical point in Western European history. Guide students in a discussion of the importance of this battle, which was fought half way between Tours and Poitiers, France. *(If the Franks had not stopped the Muslims, it is possible that Western Europe would have become Islamic, rather than Christian.)*

▲ *This magnificent building, the Dome of the Rock, was built by Muslims during the seventh century. Muslims believe that Muhammad ascended into Paradise from this site. How does this site of worship compare to those in your city?*

caliphate (the office of caliph) hereditary in his own family, thus establishing the Umayyad dynasty. As one of its first actions, the Umayyad dynasty moved the capital of the Arab Empire from Medina to Damascus, in Syria.

The Umayyads

Fighting over the caliphate did not stop the expansion of Islam, however. At the beginning of the eighth century, the Arabs carried out new attacks at both the western and eastern ends of the Mediterranean world. Arab armies moved across North Africa and conquered and converted the Berbers, a pastoral people living along the Mediterranean coast. Then, around 710,

combined Berber and Arab forces crossed the Strait of Gibraltar and occupied southern Spain. By 725, most of Spain had become a Muslim state with its center at Córdoba (CARD-uh-buh). Seven years later, an Arab force, making a foray into southern France, was defeated at the Battle of Tours (TOO-urs) in 732. Arab expansion in Europe came to a halt.

In the meantime, in 717 another Muslim force had launched an attack on Constantinople with the hope of destroying the Byzantine Empire (see Chapter 12). However, the Byzantines destroyed the Muslim fleet and saved the Byzantine Empire. The defeat also saved Christian Europe. The fall of Constantinople would no doubt have opened the door to Muslim expansion into eastern Europe. The Byzantine Empire and the Islamic

ENRICHMENT ACTIVITY

In the 600s people whose lands were conquered by Muslims were not forced to convert to Islam. Ask students to read recent accounts about Iran, Iraq, Saudi Arabia, and Afghanistan, and compare the current attitudes of these governments with the attitudes of Arabs in earlier times. Which was more lenient? What might be some of the reasons for the apparent change? You might also wish to ask students to remember this information for comparison when they study the Inquisition and the Spanish expulsion of Muslims that occurred during the Middle Ages *(Chapter 13)*.

world now established an uneasy frontier in southern Asia Minor.

The Arab advance had finally come to an end, but not before the southern and eastern Mediterranean parts of the old Roman Empire had been conquered. The Mediterranean had become a "Muslim lake." The Umayyad dynasty at Damascus now ruled an enormous empire. Expansion had brought not only great wealth and new ethnic groups into the fold of Islam but also contact with other civilizations. As a result, the new Arab Empire would be influenced by Byzantine culture, as well as the older civilizations of the ancient Middle East, such as that of the Persians. The children of the conquerors would be educated in new ways and produce a brilliant culture that would eventually influence western Europe (see Chapter 12). Arab power also extended to the east in Mesopotamia and Persia and northward into central Asia.

Internal struggles still plagued the empire, however. Many Muslims of non-Arab background did not like how local administrators favored the Arabs. Sometimes, anger led to revolt, as in Iraq. There Ali's second son, Hussein (hoo-SANE), encouraged his followers to rise up against Umayyad rule in 680. Hussein set off to do battle, but many of his soldiers defected, leaving him with an army of seventy-two warriors against ten thousand Umayyad soldiers. Hussein's tiny force fought courageously, but all died. Hussein's head was cut off and sent to Damascus, where it was placed before the feet of the Umayyad caliph.

This struggle led to a split in Islam. The Shi'ites (SHEE-ITES) on the one hand, accepted only the descendants of Ali as the true rulers of Islam. The Sunnites (SUH[oo]-NITES), or Sunni Muslims, on the other hand, claimed that the descendants of the Umayyads were the true caliphs. This seventh-century split in Islam continues to the present. The Sunnites are a majority in the Muslim world, but most of the people in Iraq and neighboring Iran consider themselves to be Shi'ites.

The Rise of the Abbasids

The Umayyad dynasty of caliphs had established Damascus as the center of an Islamic empire created by

CONNECTIONS
TO OUR WORLD

The Conflict between Sunnites and Shi'ites   In 1990, a brutal and bloody war erupted between Iran and Iraq. Border disputes were one cause of the war, but religious differences were another

Both Iranians and Iraqis are Muslims. The Iranians are largely Shi'ites. Although the Iraqi people are mostly Shi'ites, the ruling groups in the country are Sunnites, or Sunni Muslims. During the war, Iran hoped to defeat Iraq by appealing to the Shi'ite majority in Iraq for support. The attempt largely failed, however.

The clash between Shi'ites and Sunnites goes back to the seventh century. The Shi'ites believed that only the descendants of Ali, Muhammad's son-in-law, were the true leaders of Islam. Sunnites, however, were those Muslims who claimed that only descendants of the Umayyad dynasty were the true leaders. Over the years, Shi'ites developed their own body of law, which differed from that of the Sunnite majority. Most Muslims remained Sunnites, although Shi'ites form majorities in both Iran and Iraq. Shi'ite minorities also continue to exist in Turkey, Syria, Lebanon, India, Pakistan, and east Africa. The success of the Iranian Revolution in 1978–1979, led by the Ayatollah Khomeini, resulted in a noticeable revival of Shi'ism in Iran and in parts of the Islamic world adjacent to Iran. In August, 1979, Khomeini established an Islamic Revolutionary Guard Corps. Its job was to train Shi'ite militants from many countries in the methods of terrorism.

Arab expansion in the seventh and eighth centuries. However, Umayyad rule created resentment, not only in Mesopotamia but also in North Africa. The Umayyads also helped bring about their own end by their corrupt behavior. One caliph, for example, supposedly swam in a pool of wine and drank enough of it to lower the wine level considerably. Finally, in 750, Abu al-Abbas, a descendant of Muhammad's uncle,

OPPOSING VIEWPOINTS

Ask students to read the first paragraph on this page. Then divide them into two groups to debate the proposition: *Breaking down the distinctions between the Arab and non-Arab Muslims was beneficial for both groups in the long run.*

LEARNING FROM VISUALS

Answers to the caption question: Camels were the primary source of transportation.

CRITICAL THINKING

Harun al-Rashid was the fifth caliph of Baghdad and was memorialized in *The Arabian Nights*. However, many historians believe he was a corrupt ruler, known more for the opulent luxury of his court than for the quality of his leadership. Ask students why, if this is true, the Abassid culture flourished under his rule. *(The empire was fairly stable, he was a patron of the arts, and was willing to spend vast amounts of money on artistic endeavors.)*

brought an end to the Umayyad dynasty and set up the Abbasid dynasty, which lasted until 1258.

The Abbasid rulers brought much change to the world of Islam. They tried to break down the distinctions between Arab and non-Arab Muslims. All Muslims, regardless of ethnic background, could now hold both civil and military offices. This change opened Islamic culture to the influences of the civilizations that the Arabs had conquered. Many Arabs now began to intermarry with the peoples they had conquered.

In 762, the Abbasids built a new capital city at Baghdad, on the Tigris River far to the east of the Umayyad capital at Damascus. The new capital was well placed. It took advantage of river traffic to the Persian Gulf and at the same time was located on the caravan route from the Mediterranean to central Asia. The move eastward allowed Persian influence to become important and encouraged a new cultural outlook. Under the Umayyads, warriors had been seen as the ideal citizens. Under the Abbasids, judges, merchants, and government officials were the new heroes.

The Abbasid dynasty experienced a period of splendid rule well into the ninth century. Best known of the caliphs of the time was Harun al-Rashid (ha-ROON all ru-SHEED), whose reign is often described as the golden age of the Abbasid caliphate. His son al-Ma'mun was a great patron of learning. He founded an astronomical observatory and created a foundation for translating classical Greek works.

This was also a period of growing economic prosperity. After all, the Arabs had conquered many of the richest provinces of the Roman Empire. They now controlled the trade routes to the East. Baghdad became the center of an enormous trade empire that extended into Asia and Africa and greatly added to the riches of the Islamic world. Not until the revival of trade in western Europe in the eleventh and twelfth centuries did a more extensive trade network arise in the western part of the Mediterranean.

Despite the prosperity, all was not quite well in the empire of the Abbasids. There was much fighting over the succession to the caliphate. When Harun al-Rashid died, his two sons fought to succeed him in a struggle that almost destroyed the city of Baghdad. As the tenth-century Muslim historian al-Mas'udi wrote,

▲ *Arabs gained fame as traders, and their routes extended over half the globe. As they traveled, they also spread the Islamic faith. What was the primary means of transportation as shown in this painting?*

"Mansions were destroyed, most remarkable monuments obliterated; prices soared. . . . Brother turned his sword against brother, son against father, as some fought for Amin, others for Ma'mun. Houses and palaces fuelled the flames; property was put to the sack."[2]

Vast wealth also gave rise to financial corruption. By giving important positions to court favorites, the Abbasid caliphs began to undermine their own power. Members of Harun al-Rashid's clan were given large sums from the state treasury. His wife Zubaida was reported to have spent vast sums while shopping on a pilgrimage to Mecca. One powerful family, the Barmakids, amassed much money and power until Harun al-Rashid wiped out the entire family in a fit of jealous rage.

The life of luxury enjoyed by the caliph and his court in Baghdad was contrary to the strict moral code of Islam. Divorce was common, and caliphs were said

So What ??

*If your students question the importance of the information on **wealth and corruption**, tell them . . .*

There is a recurring pattern in the history of empires. This pattern consists of an early idealism and success, then, a growing wealth and a falling away from earlier standards, which eventually leads to decline. The question to be asked is, "Could this happen to us today?"

Ask students to take a few minutes to recount what they know about the history of the United States. Where in this pattern do they think the U.S. is today? Do they think the pattern will hold for the U.S.? Why or why not?

to have hundreds of concubines in their harems. Alcohol was drunk in public despite Islamic law, which prohibited alcohol.

The process of disintegration was helped along by changes taking place in the military forces and the government bureaucracy. There was a shortage of qualified Arabs for key positions in the army and the civil service. As a result, caliphs began to recruit officials from among the non-Arab peoples within the empire, such as Persians and Turks from central Asia. Of course, these people were trained to serve the caliphs, but gradually they also became a dominant force within the army and the bureaucracy.

Eventually, rulers of the provinces of the empire began to break away from the central authority and establish their own independent dynasties. Spain had established its own caliphate when a prince of the Umayyad dynasty fled there in 750. Morocco became independent, and a new dynasty under the Fatimids (FAT-uh-mids) was established in Egypt in 973. The Muslim Empire was now divided politically. Only two

common bonds held the world of Islam together: the Quran and the use of Arabic as a common language.

By the mid-tenth century, as the Abbasid caliphate in Baghdad continued to decline, the Fatimids tried to create a new Shi'ite caliphate at their capital in Cairo (KIE-ROE). They sent their armies into Syria and Arabia, but they were unable to defeat the Abbasids in Mesopotamia. The Islamic world remained divided.

The Seljuk Turks

The Fatimid dynasty prospered and soon became the dynamic center of Islamic civilization. Benefiting from their position in the heart of the Nile delta, the Fatimids played a major role in the regional trade passing from the Mediterranean to the Red Sea and beyond. They were tolerant in matters of religion. They created a strong army by hiring nonnative peoples to fight for them (we call them mercenaries). One such group, the Seljuk (SELL-JOOK) Turks, came to be a danger to the Fatimids themselves.

Map 8.3   The Abbasid Caliphate at the Height of Its Power

CRITICAL THINKING

The Quran and the Arabic language were the unifying, common bonds of the Islamic world. Discuss with students, or have them write a position paper discussing, whether or not these two factors alone are sufficient to maintain political and religious institutions. You might also wish to have students debate this issue in class.

Multimedia Support

TRANSPARENCY
8–1, Map of The Abbasid Caliphate at the Height of Its Power

REINFORCING VOCABULARY

Make sure students understand the terms *civil service* and *bureaucracy*. Students should realize that *civil* in this context refers to activities of the general public as distinguished from the activities of special groups, such as military and religious groups. *Bureaucracy* refers to all the non-elected people working in government. Explain to students that the term takes on a negative meaning when the system becomes too large, too specialized, and too particular about rules.

STUDYING MAPS

Have students estimate the amount of territory under the influence of the Abbasid dynasty at the end of the eleventh century. *(very rough estimate is approximately three million square miles).* How does this amount of territory compare to the amount of territory held by the Abbasid Caliphate in the late eighth and early ninth centuries? *(The empire was larger, most notably because of the territories in northern Africa that were now under control of the Almohads.)* Ask students to compare these empires to the Greek and Roman Empires that they studied in Chapters 5 and 6. They should gain an understanding of the relative size of each of these, and be able to compare their sizes.

CRITICAL THINKING

Ask students to speculate on why the Seljuk Turks would have allowed the Abbasid Caliph to retain control of religious affairs after they captured Baghdad. *(appease people and thereby increase likelihood of maintaining power)*

CLASS DISCUSSION

Much European literature has been written about the Crusades, with the theme of saving the Holy Lands from the infidels. Guide students in a discussion of the reality of the situation and the success or lack thereof of Europeans who traveled to Palestine.

The Seljuk Turks were a nomadic people from central Asia. They had converted to Islam and prospered as soldiers for the Abbasid caliphate. They were especially known for their ability as mounted archers. Some of them had been given large tracts of land from the caliphate in return for their services. As the Abbasids grew weaker, the Seljuk Turks moved gradually into Iran and Armenia. They grew in number until, by the eleventh century, they had taken over the eastern provinces of the Abbasid Empire.

In 1055, a Turkish leader captured Baghdad and took command of the empire with the title of **sultan** (the word means "holder of power"). The Abbasid caliph was still the chief religious authority, but the Seljuk Turks now held the real military and political power of the state.

By the second half of the eleventh century, the Seljuks were putting military pressure on Egypt and the Byzantine Empire. In 1071, the Byzantines foolishly challenged the Turks, and their army was routed at Manzikert in eastern Turkey. The Turks now took over most of the Anatolian peninsula. In desperation, the Byzantine Empire turned to the West for help, setting in motion the Crusades, which will be discussed more fully in Chapter 12.

In Europe, and within the Muslim world as well, the Turks were viewed as barbarians who destroyed civilizations and oppressed the people. In fact, however, Turkish rule in the Middle East was probably beneficial. As converts to Islam, the Turks brought a temporary end to the fighting between Sunni and Shi'ite Muslims while supporting the Sunnites. They gave much-needed political stability to the Abbasid Empire and helped to restore its prosperity.

The Crusades

The Byzantine emperor Alexius I asked the Christian states of Europe for help against the Turks. To win the support of these states, Alexius said that the Turks were destroying Christian shrines in the Holy Land and molesting Christian pilgrims. In fact, the Muslims had hurt neither the shrines nor the Christian pilgrims. Nevertheless, the Christian states of Europe and the

Map 8.4   The Turkish Occupation of Anatolia

Frontier between Byzantine Empire and Abbasid Caliphate, c. 930

Frontier of Byzantine Empire, c. 1070

——— Frontier between Byzantine Empire and Ottoman Turks, 1371–1453

——— Controlled by Seljuk Turks, c. 1080

- - - - Controlled by Seljuk Turks, early 13th century

world of Islam both feared and disliked each other. Many Europeans gladly responded to the emperor's request, beginning a series of Crusades in 1096.

At first, Muslim rulers were thrown on the defensive by the invading crusaders. The heavily armored European knights were a real challenge to local warriors. At the same time, the Seljuk Turks were busy elsewhere and took no action themselves, enabling the European crusaders to conquer and establish their crusader states. In 1169, however, Sunni Muslims under the leadership of Saladin brought an end to the Fatimid dynasty. Saladin made himself sultan and declared Egypt to be independent of the Seljuk Turks. He also established control over Syria and took the offensive against the Christian states in the area.

In 1187, Saladin's army invaded the kingdom of Jerusalem and destroyed the Christian forces there. Soon the Christians were left with only a handful of fortresses along the coast of Palestine. Unlike the Christians, however, Saladin did not allow a massacre

STUDYING MAPS

The following questions will help you guide your students through their study of Map 8.4.

1. The area labeled Anatolia is part of what country today? *(Turkey)*
2. Approximately how wide was the buffer zone, or frontier (green area), between the Byzantine and Abbasid empires? *(Approximately 200 miles)*

3. Is Baghdad to the east or west of the area students are looking at on this map? *(east)* You may want to refer students back to the map on page 235 after asking this question and as you discuss the conquests of the Seljuk Turks.
4. Did the Seljuk Turks gain or lose territory from 1080 to the early thirteenth century? *(lost territory)*

YOU ARE THERE

The Crusaders in Muslim Eyes

Usamah, an early twelfth-century Muslim warrior, had close ties to the Crusaders. When he was ninety years old, he wrote his memoirs, including his observations on the Franks (the French). Here Usamah expresses his astonishment at the Franks' rudeness to the Muslims.

Usamah, Excerpt from His Memoirs

Everyone who is a fresh emigrant from the Frankish lands is ruder in character than those who have become acclimatized and have held long association with the Muslims. Here is an illustration of their rude character.

Whenever I visited Jerusalem I always entered the Aqsa Mosque, beside which stood a small mosque which the Franks had converted into a church. When I used to enter the Aqsa Mosque, which was occupied by the Templars [Christian crusader knights] who were my friends, the Templars would evacuate the little adjoining mosque so that I might pray in it. One day I entered this mosque, repeated the first formula, "Allah is great," and stood up in the act of praying, upon which one of the Franks rushed on me, got hold of me and turned my face eastward, saying, "This is the way you should pray!" A group of Templars hastened to him, seized him and pushed him away from me. I went back to my prayer. The same man, while the others were otherwise busy, rushed once more on me and turned my face eastward, saying, "This is the way you should pray!" The Templars again came in to him and expelled him. They apologized to me, saying, "This is a stranger who has only recently arrived from the land of the Franks and he has never before seen anyone praying except eastward." Thereupon I said to myself,

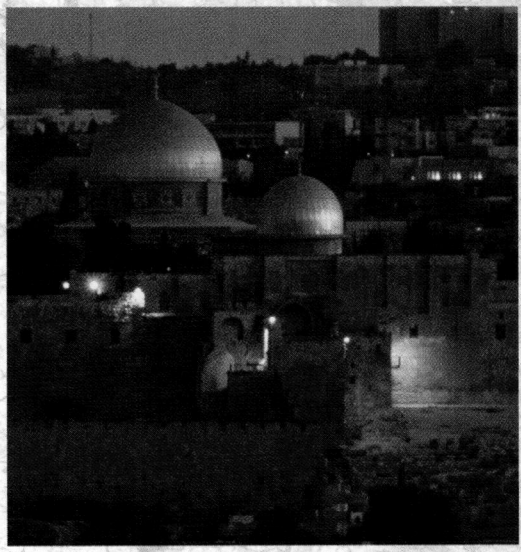

▲ *The silver-domed El Aqsa Mosque stands within the walled city of Jerusalem and appears to be dwarfed by its larger neighbor, the gold-covered Dome of the Rock.*

"I have had enough prayer." So I went out, and have ever been surprised at the conduct of this devil of a man.

1. Identify the Franks and the Templars, then retell the story in your own words.

2. Based on Usamah's account, characterize the city of Jerusalem.

3. How is religious tolerance part of this incident?

ENRICHMENT ACTIVITY

Provide students with an option for an artistic enrichment activity. They can either (1) design and draw the floor plan of a place of worship, or (2) design and create a segment of a decorative wall from a place of worship for either a Byzantine church or a Muslim mosque. Display the resulting pieces. Ask students to explain the inspiration and thinking that led to the development of their designs. Then ask the students as a group to identify the differences and significance of each type of art.

USING PRIMARY SOURCES

Ask students to read this feature carefully and then have them rewrite it from a French or Western European point of view. Have students share their results.

REINFORCING VOCABULARY

The Templars were a religious and military order founded in Jerusalem during the Crusades to protect pilgrims traveling to the Holy Lands. Their full name was the Poor Fellow-Soldiers of Christ and the Temple of Solomon. St. Bernard of Clairvaux, who is discussed in Chapter 13, created the rules for the order. In the thirteenth century, the Templars' principal activity was banking and lending money.

Answers to Critical Thinking Questions

1. The Franks were French; the Templars were Christian crusader knights. Student answers will vary.

2. Jerusalem was a holy city, the destiny of pilgrims of many faiths. It was also an international city and was politically important.

3. The writer, a Muslim, had friends who were Christian; by evacuating the small mosque, they allowed him to worship as he chose and defended his right to do so. By contrast, the newly-arrived Franks insisted that prayer be conducted their way and drove the writer out of the mosque.

ACTIVITY

Have students work in pairs to write directions that a commander might have given to his Mongol warriors before they sacked a city. Have students be specific and use information presented in this section for their imaginary orders.

LEARNING FROM VISUALS

Answer to the caption question: From this photo it is difficult to distinguish between the two, but the Mongols carried long lances and wore plated body armor.

ASSESS

Answers to SECTION REVIEW

2. (a) secular leader of the Islamic community
   (b) "struggle in the way of God," making raids against enemies in order to expand the Islamic movement
   (c) "holder of power," a king or sovereign (especially of Muslim state)
3. (a) the caliph of the Islamic community, chosen after Muhammad's death
   (b) the governor of Syria who became caliph in 661. His chief virtue was that he used force only when absolutely necessary.
   (c) a pastoral people who lived along the Mediterranean coast
   (d) established when Mu'awiyah made caliphate hereditary; moved capitol of Arab Empire from Medina to Damascus

of the civilian population. He even allowed Christian religious services to continue in the territories he had conquered (see "You Are There: The Crusaders in Muslim Eyes"). Although the Christians would retain a toehold on the coast for much of the thirteenth century, they were no longer a significant force in the Middle East. All in all, the Crusades had little lasting impact on the Middle East. Far more important was the threat posed by a new invader—the Mongols.

The Mongols

The Mongols were a pastoral people who swept out of the Gobi Desert in the early thirteenth century to seize control over much of the known world (see Chapter 10). Unlike the Seljuk Turks, the Mongols were not Muslims. As nomadic peoples, they often found it difficult to adapt to the settled conditions they found in the major cities in the Middle East. They were destructive in their conquests. According to one historian, after conquering a city, the Mongols killed not only entire families but also their cats and dogs. They burned cities to the ground, destroyed dams and other irrigation works, and reduced farming villages to mass

starvation. In one city, they stacked the heads of men, women, and children in pyramids. Their goal was to create such terror that people would not fight back.

Beginning with the advances led by Genghis Khan (JENG-gus KAWN) in North China, Mongol armies spread across central Asia. In 1258, under the leadership of Hulegu (hoo-LAY-GOO), brother of the more famous Khubilai Khan (KOO-bluh KAWN), the Mongols seized Persia and Mesopotamia. The Abbasid caliphate at Baghdad was now brought to an end. Hulegu had a strong hatred of Islam, and after his forces captured Baghdad in 1258, he decided to destroy the city. Schools, libraries, mosques, and palaces were burned to the ground. Possibly a million Muslims were killed, and members of the Abbasid dynasty were wrapped in carpets and trampled to death by the horses of the Mongol conquerors.

The Mongols advanced as far as the Red Sea. However, their attempt to seize Egypt failed, in part because of the resistance from the Mamluks. The Mamluks (sometimes spelled Mamelukes) were Turkish slave-soldiers who had overthrown the administration set up by Saladin and seized power themselves.

Over time, the Mongol rulers in the Middle East began to change. They converted to Islam and began to

▶ *This fourteenth-century miniature depicts Mongol troops attacking the soldiers of the Abbasid caliphate in the famous battle in Baghdad in 1258 that ended Abbasid rule. Can you tell which soldiers are Mongols and which are Abbasids?*

ENRICHMENT ACTIVITY

Ask students to trace the rise and fall of the Arab Empire with the Mongol Empire. Factors to be researched and then compared are: (1) the nomadic origin; (2) method of war; (3) the inspirational leader; (4) range of conquest; (5) assimilation of conquered peoples; (6) methods of administration; (7) corruption and decline; (8) political and religious divisions; (9) legacy (in this case, why the Arab legacy is so much more lasting). Give students options as to how they might present their findings. Written reports, oral presentations, and large poster charts are possibilities.

intermarry with local peoples. They began to rebuild the cities. By the fourteenth century, the Mongol Empire began to split into separate kingdoms and then to fall apart. In the meantime, however, the old Islamic empire established by the Arabs in the seventh and eighth centuries had come to an end. As a result of the Mongol destruction of Baghdad, the new center of Islamic civilization was Cairo, now under the Mamluks.

To the north, another new force began to appear: the Ottoman Turks on the Anatolian peninsula. In 1453, they seized the city of Constantinople and brought an end to the Byzantine Empire. As we shall see in Chapter 17, the Ottomans then began to turn their attention to the rest of the Middle East, creating a new Muslim empire.

 SECTION REVIEW

1. **Locate:**
   (*a*) Syria,   (*b*) Damascus,
   (*c*) Baghdad

2. **Define:**
   (*a*) caliph,   (*b*) jihad,
   (*c*) sultan

3. **Identify:**
   (*a*) Abu Bakr,   (*b*) Mu'awiyah,
   (*c*) Berbers,   (*d*) Umayyad dynasty,
   (*e*) Hussein,   (*f*) Abbasid dynasty,
   (*g*) Seljuk Turks,   (*h*) Saladin,
   (*i*) Genghis Khan

4. **Recall:** What were the two common bonds that held the politically divided Islamic world together in the mid-tenth century?

5. **Think Critically:** Muhammad had not named a successor to lead the people in the event of his death. Unrest and a series of wars followed. In your opinion, could Muhammad have better prepared the people of Islam for the future? What steps might he have taken? How would those steps have helped?

ISLAMIC CIVILIZATION

To be a Muslim is not simply to worship Allah. It also means to live one's life according to Allah's teachings as revealed in the Quran. This sacred book of Islam is viewed as basic doctrine not to be revised by human beings. In Islamic society there is no rigid dividing line between church and state, or between the sacred and the secular. As Allah has decreed, so must humans live. Questions concerning politics, economics, and social life are answered by following Islamic teachings.

The Political World of Islam

Creating political institutions for a large empire was not easy for the Arabs. They had been used to living in small pastoral communities, and their own political structures were simple. Muhammad was accepted as both the political and religious leader of the Islamic community, which was known as the **umma.** After his death, however, a problem emerged.

The problem was simple: How should a successor be chosen, and what authority should that person have? As we have seen, the problem was solved at first by choosing a successor for Muhammad who was called the caliph. The authority of the caliphs was purely political, although they were also considered religious leaders in general terms. At first, each new caliph was chosen by leading members of the umma. Soon, succession became hereditary in the Umayyad dynasty.

Under the Abbasids, who seized power in 750, the caliphs began to act in a more regal fashion. More kings than spiritual leaders, they ruled by the same means as kings and emperors did in European civilization. A thirteenth-century Chinese author left the following description of one of the later caliphs:

The king wears a turban of silk brocade and foreign cotton stuff. On each new moon and full moon he puts on an eight-sided flat-topped headdress of pure gold, set with the most precious jewels in the world. His robe is of silk brocade and is bound around him with a jade girdle. On his feet he wears golden shoes. . . . The

CLOSE

The Muslims established their own culture, which flourished for several centuries. They established mosques, libraries, schools, and hospitals. However, like dynasties to come and dynasties that students have already studied, corrupt, weak leadership led to a serious decline.

So What ??

*If your students question the importance of the information on the **transfer of authority**, tell them . . .*

A serious weakness of any system of rule based upon a single person is the transfer of authority upon the death or incapacity of that person—whether a dictator, emperor, general, or caudillo. The tendency is always towards civil war and an internal power struggle, which in turn often invites attack from outside. Constitutional governments, in theory, offer protection against this since power is frequently transferred, and must be transferred, at fixed intervals and according to clearly understood rules.

FOCUS

OBJECTIVES

After completing this section students should be able to

1. explain the authority of the caliphs
2. identify the major Islamic cities
3. describe daily life in the Islamic cities
4. explain the Islamic social structure

FOCUS ACTIVITY

Ask students to imagine they have never been to a city before and suddenly move to a vibrant, growing city of 200,000. What might be some of the first things they notice? What public buildings (libraries, universities), religious buildings, and public monuments might they see? Would they like the city, or would they yearn for simpler life on the farms? Point out that during the Abassid rule, mosques, libraries, universities, and palaces, as well as thriving cities, were developed.

TEACH

CLASS DISCUSSION

According to the text, Muslims must live their lives according to the decrees of Allah. Does this point of view differ from Christianity or any of the other great world religions? Is it possible to reject some of the beliefs or decrees of a particular religion and still be part of that group?

king's throne is set with pearls and precious stones, and the steps of the throne are covered with pure gold. The various vessels and utensils around the throne are of gold or silver, and precious pearls are knotted in the screen behind it. In great court ceremonies the king sits behind this screen, and on either side, protecting him, the ministers of state surround him bearing golden bucklers and helmets and armed with precious swords.[3]

As the caliph took on the trappings of an autocratic king, the bureaucracy assisting him in administering the growing empire grew more complex as well. A council headed by a prime minister known as a vizier (or wazir) advised the caliph, who did not attend meetings of the council but instead sat behind a screen listening to the council's discussions and then communicated his divine will to the vizier. No doubt, the new atmosphere of pomp and circumstance was a natural consequence of the growing power and prosperity of the empire.

In theory, the authority of the caliphs in Baghdad was supreme throughout the Islamic world. In reality, rebellious forces in various parts of the empire opposed the rule of the caliph from the very beginning. Sometimes revolt erupted within the walls of the capital city. As we have seen, after the death of Harun al-Rashid, fighting between his two sons led to a bitter civil war that ended in a lengthy siege of Baghdad. Eventually, several of the major parts of the empire, including Persia, Egypt, North Africa, and Spain, became independent states. Even the efforts of the Seljuk Turks and Mongols were not able to reunite these areas.

Prosperity in the Islamic World

Despite the internal struggles, overall this was one of the most prosperous periods in the history of the Middle East. The Quran encouraged trade and industry, and both flourished. There was an extensive trade, not only within the Islamic world but also with China, the Byzantine Empire, India, and Southeast Asia. Trade was carried both by ship and by camel caravans that traveled from Morocco in the far west to the countries beyond the Caspian Sea. From south of the Sahara came gold and slaves; from China, silk and porcelain; from eastern Africa, gold and ivory; and from the lands of Southeast Asia and India, sandalwood and spices. Within the empire, Egypt contributed grain; Iraq, linens, dates, and precious stones; and western India, various textile goods. The development of banking and the use of coins made it easier to exchange goods.

With flourishing trade came prosperous cities. While the Abbasids were in power, Baghdad, with a population of over 200,000, was probably the greatest city in the empire and one of the greatest cities in the world. After the rise of the Fatimids in Egypt, however, the focus of trade shifted to Cairo. A traveler described it as "one of the greatest and most famous cities in all the whole world, filled with stately and admirable palaces and colleges, and most sumptuous temples."[4] Other great trading cities included Basra at the head of the Persian Gulf, Aden at the southern tip of the Arabian peninsula, Damascus in modern-day Syria, and Marrakech (muh-ROCK-ish) in Morocco.

Baghdad, Damascus, and Cairo were the centers of administrative, cultural, and economic activity for their regions. Aside from these capital cities, Indian and Chinese travelers did not find the cities of the Middle East especially grand by their standards. However, Islamic cities did outshine the towns and cities of mostly rural Christian Europe. This is exemplified by Córdoba, the capital of Umayyad Spain. With a population of 200,000, Córdoba was Europe's largest city after Constantinople.

Islamic cities had a distinctive physical appearance. Usually, the most impressive urban buildings were the palaces for the caliphs or the local governors and the great mosques for worship. There were also public buildings with fountains and secluded courtyards, public baths, and bazaars or marketplaces.

The **bazaar,** or covered market, was a crucial part of every Muslim city or town. The bazaar was an important trading center, where goods from all the known world were for sale. Customers could compare prices and seek the best bargains. To make sure of high standards, bazaars had market inspectors who enforced rules. Counters and containers, for example, had to be washed daily. Food prepared for sale at the market was carefully watched. A rule in one Muslim city stated, "Grilled meats should only be made with fresh meat

---

ENRICHMENT ACTIVITY

Guide students in a discussion of the isolation of the caliph from the governing body if he sat behind a screen and communicated only to his vizier. Over time, how might this affect a caliph's ability to rule? Would it affect his ability to understand the problems of the Empire? If so, in what way? How would it affect his ability to comprehend problems of merchants and common people?

You might erect a screen of some sort in your classroom and ask for a volunteer to spend part of a class period behind the screen. Conduct a normal class while the volunteer is behind the screen. At the end of the given time, have the volunteer share his or her feelings about how "connected" to the rest of the class they felt. How "connected" to the governing body do they think the caliph felt?

◄ This woodcut of Tangiers shows a city that overlooks the sea. The houses, built closely together, have simple exteriors. Many, however, were luxurious inside. How does this neighborhood differ from communities in the United States?

and not with meat coming from a sick animal and bought for its cheapness." The bazaar also housed many craftspeople's shops, as well as services such as laundries and bathhouses.

Merchants, of course, benefited the most from the cities. Wealthy merchants brought in food supplies, animals, and raw materials from the surrounding countryside. Cities were also home to artisans who produced goods such as textiles and pottery for sale locally, as well as high-quality goods, such as fine textiles, for sale abroad. A lower class, including peasants who wandered in from the surrounding countryside, joined officials, scholars, and students in making up the rest of the urban population.

People in the cities were also divided by religion. Jews and Christians were both tolerated by the Muslims, but they did not have the same rights. They paid a special tax to the government and lived in separate areas. Usually a Jewish or Christian community gathered around a church or synagogue—its own place of worship. Of course, all people were equally subject to the most common threats to urban life—fire, flood, and disease.

Although the Arab Empire was more urbanized than most other areas of the known world at the time, a majority of people still lived in the countryside and made their living by farming or herding animals. During the early stages of the empire, most of the farmland was owned by independent peasants. Later, however, wealthy landowners began to amass large estates. Some lands were owned by the state or the court and were farmed by slave labor. In river valleys like the Tigris and Euphrates and the Nile, most farmers were probably independent peasants. A Chinese traveler described life along the Nile:

The peasants work their fields without fear of floods or droughts; a sufficiency of water for irrigation is sup-

MORE ABOUT . . . *Damascus Steel*

A sword of Damascus steel could be bent until the point touched the hilt, but would spring back into shape and hold a keen edge. The process of making Damascus steel requires great skill and considerable time as well. It is made by alternating bars of carbon steel to bars of wrought iron or softer steel. The bars are heated and hammered together. This is called "forge welding." The bar or billet is then folded over, beaten out, and forge welded again. The process is repeated over and over. This process produces a blade that is, in effect, laminated from thousands of layers of steel. Quenching, or dousing the hot blade in liquid, will produce an extremely hard outer surface but the core of the blade will remain more flexible and durable. The result is a blade that can accept a razor sharp edge, but which will not shatter if it strikes a hard object.

COMPARING TIME PERIODS

Ask students to compare and contrast the practice of slavery in the United States with the Islamic practice. *(Students should recognize that the treatment of slaves was different, and that the laws concerning slavery were also very different.)*

CLASS DISCUSSION

Have students write a position paper about the role of women in Islamic society and then debate the rights (or lack thereof) in Muslim countries. Remind students that in some countries, women are forced to wear a veil in public, that their educational opportunities are limited, that they cannot enter certain professions, and in some countries women cannot even drive a car.

ASSESS

You can choose from a variety of assessments to evaluate your students' mastery of the objectives for this section as stated on page 239. Possible assessments include:

1. Section Review Questions on page 243
2. Section 8–3 Quiz in your Teacher Resource materials
3. Reteaching Worksheets in your Teacher Resource materials
4. Self-Study software.

▲ *Although Muslims believed in equality, many owned slaves. These young Africans are probably being marched to a sea port so that they can be shipped to slave markets in the Arab Empire, as well as other parts of the world.*

plied by a river whose source is not known. During the season when no cultivation is in progress, the level of the river remains even with the banks; with the beginning of cultivation it rises day by day. Then it is that an official is appointed to watch the river and to await the highest water level, when he summons the people, who then plough and sow their fields. When they have had enough water, the river returns to its former level.[5]

Despite all the changes since the days of ancient Egypt, peasants along the Nile continued to farm the way their ancient ancestors had.

Islamic Society

The Arab Empire was a society that in theory was based on equality. According to Islam, all people were equal in the eyes of Allah. In reality, this was not strictly the case. There was a fairly well defined upper class that consisted of the ruling families, senior officials, tribal elites, and wealthiest merchants. Even ordinary merchants, however, enjoyed a degree of respect that merchants did not receive in Europe, China, or India.

One group of people in the Islamic world, however, knew little of equality. They were the slaves. As in the other civilizations we have examined so far, slavery was widespread. Because Muslims could not be slaves, most of their slaves came from sub-Saharan Africa or from non-Islamic populations elsewhere in Asia. Many had been captured in war.

Many slaves served in the army, especially those recruited by Abbasid caliphs from the Turks of central Asia. Military slaves were special, however. Many were freed and even came to exercise considerable power. Many slaves, especially women, were used as domestic servants and were sometimes permitted to purchase their freedom. Islamic law made it clear that slaves should be treated fairly. It was also considered a good act to free them.

The Islamic principle of equality was also not true for women. The Quran did instruct men to treat women with respect, and women did have the right to own and inherit property. Nevertheless, the male was dominant in Muslim society. According to Muslims, there were basic differences between men and women. By their nature, men were born to rule states, wage war, and provide for their families. Women, in contrast, were meant to be good mothers and wives by raising their children and caring for their husbands.

Every woman had a male guardian, be it father, brother, or other male relative. Parents or guardians arranged marriages for their children. The Quran allowed Muslim men to have more than one wife, but no more than four. Most men, however, were unable to afford more than one, because they were required to pay a dowry (a gift of money or property) to their brides. Only the rich had the luxury of four wives. Although women had the legal right to divorce under some circumstances, in practice the right of divorce was limited to the husband. Adultery was strictly forbidden.

Islamic custom required that women be secluded in their homes and kept from social contacts with males outside their own families. One jurist wrote that "some of the pious elders (may God be pleased with them) have said that a woman should leave her house on three occasions only: when she is conducted to the house of her bridegroom, on the deaths of her parents,

SPECIAL NEEDS

Create or have more advanced students create a Bingo-type game using words from the chapter. The words would be in squares under the word "Muslim." Numbers from 1 to 5 would be along the left column. Separate the class into groups and, as you read or display the definition of each term on the board or overhead projector, have each group identify the word, Bingo style. For example, if you read "The Arabic word for God" and the word "Allah" is in the square "M-2," then the answer given by the students would be "M-2." Vocabulary words that should be included would be: Sheikh, Allah, Bedouins, Koran (Quran), Hegira, monotheistic, Islam, hajj, caliph, jihad, Cairo, sultan, bazaar, umma, mosque.

Muslim women, following centuries-old traditions, cover their bodies and faces when going out. Pictured here are two women out for a ride. Do you think the Arab custom of isolating women and forcing them to wear veils will continue in the next millennium? Why or why not?

and when she goes to her own grave."[6] The custom of requiring women to cover virtually all parts of their bodies when appearing in public was common in the cities and is still practiced today in many Islamic societies. It should be noted, however, that these customs owed more to traditional Arab practice than to the Quran. Despite the restrictions, the position of women under Islam was better than it had been in former times, when women had often been treated like slaves.

SECTION REVIEW

1. **Locate:**
   (a) Caspian Sea,   (b) Cairo,   (c) Córdoba,
   (d) Constantinople

2. **Define:**
   (a) umma,   (b) bazaar

3. **Recall:**
   (a) Name five popular items used for trading in the Middle East and the region from which they came.
   (b) What are three capital cities that were the centers of administrative, cultural, and economic activity for their regions?

4. **Think Critically:** The Arab empire was a society based in theory on equality. Two groups of citizens knew little of equality—slaves and women. Compare and contrast the existence of these two groups with that of the ruling families, senior officials, tribal elites, and merchants.

THE CULTURE OF ISLAM

From the beginning of their empire, Muslim Arabs had shown a desire to absorb the culture of the people they had conquered. The Arabs were truly heirs to many parts of the remaining Greco-Roman culture of the Roman Empire. Just as readily, they absorbed Byzantine and Persian culture. In the eighth and ninth centuries, many Greek, Syrian, and Persian scientific and philosophical works were translated into Arabic. As the chief language in the southern Mediterranean and Middle East, as well as the required language of Muslims, Arabic became a truly international tongue. From the ninth to the thirteenth centuries, Arabic was also the chief language for scientific work.

Philosophy and Science

During the first few centuries of the Arab Empire, it was the Islamic world that saved and spread the scientific and philosophical works of ancient civilizations. At a time when the ancient Greek philosophers were largely unknown in Europe, key works by Plato and Aristotle were translated into Arabic. They were put in a library called the House of Wisdom in Baghdad, where they were read and studied by Muslim scholars. Texts on mathematics were brought from India. This process was aided by the use of paper. The making of

CNN. WORLD HISTORY UPDATES

You can update your coverage of World History topics, as well as spark lively classroom discussion and deeper understanding, by using the **CNN World History Updates.**

For assistance in using and incorporating the **CNN World History Updates** into your classroom presentations, see the *Classroom Guide.*

Answers to Critical Thinking Questions

1. The faithful do good works and believe in what is revealed to Muhammad; they follow the truth. Believers are tested by their treatment of unbelievers—in battle, believers must punish nonbelievers by killing or capturing them.

2. The righteous will be rewarded in gardens where unpolluted rivers flow, as well as rivers of fresh milk, wine, and honey. Every fruit will be available to eat and all will be forgiven by their Lord.

LEARNING FROM VISUALS

Answer to the caption question: Students should note the beauty of the calligraphy. Few books today show such care in preparation and printing.

FOCUS ACTIVITY

Brainstorm with students what they already know about *The Rubaiyat* of Omar Khayyam and *The Arabian Nights.* Point out to them that in this section they will be learning more about these works and about the rich culture of Islam.

OUR LITERARY HERITAGE
The Quran

The Quran is the sacred book of the Muslims, comparable to the Bible in Christianity. In this selection, taken from Chapter 47 of the Quran, it is apparent that Islam encourages the spreading of the faith. For believers who died for Allah, there awaited a garden of Paradise quite unlike the arid desert homeland of the Arab warriors.

The Quran

Allah will bring to nothing the deeds of those who disbelieve and debar others from His path. As for the faithful who do good works and believe in what is revealed to Muhammad—which is the truth from their Lord—He will forgive them their sins and ennoble their state.

This, because the unbelievers follow falsehood, while the faithful follow the truth from their Lord. Thus Allah coins their sayings for mankind.

When you meet the unbelievers in the battlefield strike off their heads and, when you have laid them low, bind your captives firmly. Then grant them their freedom or take ransom from them, until War shall lay down her armor.

Thus shall you so. Had Allah willed, He could Himself have punished them; but He has ordained it thus that He might test you, the one by the other.

As for those who are slain in the cause of Allah, He will not allow their works to perish. He will vouchsafe them guidance and ennoble their states; He will admit them to the Paradise He has made known to them. . . .

Allah will admit those who embrace the true faith and do good works to gardens watered by running streams. The unbelievers take their fill of pleasure and eat as the beasts eat: but Hell shall be their home. . . .

▲ *The page from the Quran shown in this illustration dates from the fourteenth century. The text is handwritten, and the decorations were made even more ornate by using gold leaf. How does this compare to current religious or art books that you have seen?*

This is the Paradise which the righteous have been promised. There shall flow in it rivers of unpolluted water, and rivers of milk forever fresh; rivers of delectable wine and rivers of clearest honey. They shall eat therein of every fruit and receive forgiveness from their Lord. Is this like the lot of those who shall abide in Hell for ever and drink scalding water which will tear their bowels?

Know that there is no god but Allah. Implore Him to forgive your sins and to forgive the true believers, men and women. Allah knows your busy haunts and resting-places.

---

1. What behavior characterizes a faithful believer in Allah?

2. Describe the Muslim idea of Paradise.

MORE ABOUT . . . *Religion and Slavery*

Ironically, religion can sometimes foster the enslavement of other people. Just as Islam forbade the enslavement of believers, so too did the Catholic Church forbid the enslavement of the faithful. Throughout the Mediterranean world, however, the practice of slavery never entirely died out with the fall of the Roman Empire. Both the Arabs in the Middle Ages and the Spanish and Portuguese turned to sub-Saharan Africa for slaves, since most of the tribes of that region were animist in religion. Religion provided a rationale for an essentially economic activity.

▲ *Shown here is an eleventh-century Persian script, an outstanding example of Arabic calligraphy. Several different styles developed in different places and in different times, but the incredible beauty of the writing remained constant.*

paper was introduced from China (see Chapter 4) in the eighth century, and by the end of the century, paper factories had been established in Baghdad. Booksellers and libraries soon followed. European universities later benefited from this scholarship when these works were translated from Arabic into Latin.

Islamic scholars are rightly praised for preserving much of classical knowledge for the West, but they also made considerable advances of their own. Nowhere is this more evident than in their contributions to mathematics and the natural sciences. The list of Muslim achievements in mathematics and astronomy alone is long. The Muslims took over and passed on the numerical system of India, including the use of the zero. In Europe, it became known as the "Arabic" system. A ninth-century Iranian mathematician created the mathematical discipline of algebra, which is still taught in U.S. schools today. In astronomy, Muslims set up an observatory at Baghdad to study the position of the stars. They were aware that the Earth was round, and they named many stars. They also perfected the astrolabe, an instrument used by sailors to determine their location by observing the positions of heavenly bodies. It was the astrolabe that made it possible for Europeans to sail to the Americas.

Muslim scholars also made many new discoveries in chemistry and developed medicine as a field of scientific study. Especially well known was the scholar Ibn Sina (IB-un SIE-NAY). Known as Avicenna in the West, he wrote a medical encyclopedia that, among other things, stressed the contagious nature of certain diseases. He also showed how diseases could be spread by contaminated water supplies. After it was translated into Latin, Avicenna's work became a basic medical textbook for university students in medieval Europe. Avicenna was only one of many Arabic scholars whose work was translated into Latin and thus helped the development of intellectual life in Europe in the twelfth and thirteenth centuries.

Islamic Literature

Islam brought major changes to the culture of the Middle East, including its literature. Muslims regarded the Quran as their greatest literary work (see "Our Literary Heritage: The Quran"). Nevertheless, pre-Islamic traditions continued to influence writers throughout the region. Sometimes, pre-Islamic traditions were combined with Muslim themes to produce new and original works.

To Western observers, the most famous works of Middle Eastern literature are the *Rubaiyat* (ROO-bee-aught) of Omar Khayyam (KIE-yom) and *The Tales from 1001 Nights* (also called *The Arabian Nights*). Little is known of the life or the poetry of the twelfth-century poet Omar Khayyam, who did not write down his poems but composed them orally with friends. They were recorded later by friends or scribes. His poetry is simple and down to earth. As can be seen in the following lines, Omar Khayyam was skeptical about the meaning of life. It seemed to pass too quickly. He writes,

> *They did not ask me, when they planned my life;*
> *Why then blame me for what is good or bad?*
> *Yesterday and today go on without us;*
> *Tomorrow what's the charge against me, pray?*

In youth I studied for a little while;
Later I boasted of my mastery.
Yet this was all the lesson that I learned:
We come from dust, and with the wind are gone.

Of all the travelers on this endless road
No one returns to tell us where it leads,
There's little in this world but greed and need;
Leave nothing here, for you will not return.[7]

The stories of *The Arabian Nights* are a collection of folktales, fables, and romances that blend the natural with the supernatural. The earliest stories were told orally and then written down later, with many additions, in Arabic and Persian. The famous story of Aladdin and the magic lamp, for example, was an eighteenth-century addition. *The Arabian Nights* has entertained readers for centuries. The stories allow the reader to enter a land of wish fulfillment through unusual plots, comic and tragic situations, and a cast of unforgettable characters.

Some Arabic and Persian literature reflected the deep spiritual and ethical concerns of the Quran. Many writers, however, carried Islamic thought in new directions. The thirteenth-century poet Rumi, for example, embraced Sufism, a form of Sunni religious belief that focused on a close personal relationship between Allah and human beings. Rumi was converted to Sufism by a wandering dervish. (Dervishes try to achieve union with Allah through dancing and chanting.) He then abandoned orthodox Islam to embrace God directly through love. He sought to achieve union with God through a trance attained by the whirling dance of the dervish, set to enchanting music. As he twirled, Rumi composed his poems. These lines reveal his belief in achieving oneness with God:

Come!
But don't join us without music.
We have a celebration here.
Rise and beat the drums….

Hush!
You are made of feeling and thought and passion;
The rest is nothing but flesh and bone.
We are the soul of the world,
Not heavy or sagging like the body.

We are the spirit's treasure,
Not bound to this earth, to time or space

How can they talk to us of prayer rugs and piety?
We are the hunter and the hunted,
Autumn and spring,
Night and day,
Visible and hidden.
Love is our mother.
We were born of Love.[8]

Islamic Art and Architecture

Islamic art is a blend of Arab, Turkish, and Persian traditions. For a long time, Islamic art remained remarkably the same over a wide area. The best expression of Islamic art is found in the magnificent Muslim houses of worship known as **mosques** (see "Our Artistic Heritage: The Mosque"). Because the Muslim religion combines spiritual and political power in one, palaces also reflected the glory of Islam.

▼ *These whirling dervishes, as they are commonly known, observe the anniversary of the death of their founder Celaleddin Rumi in 1273 by presenting this ritual dance every December. The dancers twirl on one foot, with their left hands pointing toward the earth and their right hands pointing toward heaven. Are any of these movements seen in modern dances performed today?*

OUR ARTISTIC HERITAGE
The Mosque

The best expression of Islamic art is to be found in a number of great buildings. Above all, the mosque—a house of worship—represents the spirit of Islam. The first great example is the Dome of the Rock. It was built in 691 to proclaim that Islam had arrived. The mosque was placed in the heart of Jerusalem on Muhammad's holy rock. (Muslims believe that Muhammad ascended into Paradise from this site.) This mosque remains one of the most revered Islamic monuments. Rebuilt several times, this first monument to Islam represents the birth of a new art form.

At first, desert Arabs, whether nomads or conquering armies, prayed in an open court, which was shaded along the *kibla* (the wall facing the holy city of Mecca) by thatched roofs supported by rows of palm trunks. There was also a ditch where the faithful could wash off the dust of the desert prior to prayer. As Islam became better established, enormous mosques were built. They were still modeled, however, on the open court, enclosed on all four sides with pillars supporting a wooden roof over the prayer area and facing the *kibla*. The Great Mosque of Samarra, the largest mosque ever built (848 to 852), covered ten acres and contained 464 pillars in aisles surrounding the open court. Remains of the massive thirty-foot-high outer wall still stand. The most famous section of the

The mosque in Córdoba, Spain is famous for its intricate beauty and the impressive symmetry of its arches. The view through the columnar archways gives the entire building a sense of mass and depth, as well as a sense of light airiness. Which of these architectural features were commonly used in the United States?

Samarra mosque is its minaret. This is the tower accompanying the mosque from which the muezzin (myoo-EZ-un) (crier) calls the faithful to prayer five times a day. The minaret of Samarra, nearly ninety feet in height, was unusual because of its outside spiral staircase.

The Samarra style exerted considerable influence on later Islamic architecture. Cairo's famous Ahmad Ibn Tulun mosque, built in 879, was modeled directly on the Great Mosque of Samarra. Later, the Seljuk Turks were skilled builders, creating masterpieces such as the eleventh-century mosque at Isfahan. The original building consisted of four towering arched gates leading into a central court covered by a high dome.

No discussion of mosques would be complete, however, without mentioning the famous ninth-century mosque at Córdoba in southern Spain. It is still in remarkable condition. Its 514 columns, which support double-horseshoe arches, transform this building into a unique forest of trees pointing upward, giving it a light and airy effect.

1. What architectural elements are characteristic of mosques?

2. How did the Dome of the Rock represent the birth of a new art form?

MORE ABOUT . . . *Church and State*

Since Islam is a revealed religion with scriptures, which one can (and must) study, religious and secular life cannot be separated. One cannot choose to obey God only part of the time. Furthermore, since religion teaches morality and ethics, it has profound implications in politics, art, and society. The same patterns may be seen in the early Puritans, and, in recent years, in orthodox rabbis in Israel, Muslim fundamentalists, and the Christian Coalition.

OUR ARTISTIC HERITAGE

CLASS DISCUSSION

Unlike churches or cathedrals, mosques often contained schools, libraries, and hospitals. Discuss with students the role of the mosques in the daily lives of the Muslim peoples. How was it different and how was it similar to the medieval churches? To churches today?

ACTIVITY

You might wish to divide the class into several groups and ask them to prepare oral and illustrated reports on the mosques listed in the feature.

LEARNING FROM VISUALS

Answer to the caption question: Many towns and buildings, especially in the Southwest, feature colonnaded archways like those in this mosque.

Answers to Critical Thinking Questions

1. Mosques contain open courts, pillars, minarets (towers), arches, and domes.
2. Desert Arabs had prayed in an open court, which was shaded along the wall facing the holy city of Mecca by thatched roofs supported by rows of palm trunks. This design was the model for the enormous mosques built when Islam became better established.

ACTIVITY

Have students read very carefully the paragraphs on prayer rugs and examine the rug that illustrates the first page of this chapter. Have each group create its own paper version of an Islamic prayer rug and present it to the class.

ASSESS

You can choose from a variety of assessments to evaluate your students' mastery of the objectives for this section as stated on page 243. Possible assessments include

1. Section Review Questions on page 249
2. Section 8–4 Quiz in your Teacher Resource materials
3. Reteaching Worksheets in your Teacher Resource materials
4. Self Study software

Beginning in the eighth century with the spectacular castles of Syria, Islamic rulers constructed large brick buildings with protective walls, gates, and baths. Most no longer remain. Designed around a central courtyard surrounded by two-story arcades and massive gate-towers, the buildings resembled fortresses as much as palaces. With their numerous official and residential rooms, in addition to a mosque and a series of courtyards surrounded by fortified walls, many of these Islamic palaces looked like small towns. One feature of these palaces was a gallery over the entrance gate with holes through which boiling oil could be poured down on the heads of attacking forces. This feature was taken over by the crusaders and became part of European castles.

The finest example of the Islamic palace is the fourteenth-century Alhambra in Spain. The extensive succession of courtyards, rooms, gardens, and fountains created a fairy-tale castle perched high above the city of Granada. Every inch of the castle's surface is decorated in floral and abstract patterns. Much of the decoration is carved plasterwork that is so fine that it looks like lace. The Alhambra is considered an excellent expression of Islamic art.

Out of Islamic architecture arose a variety of art forms related to the palace and especially the mosque. Beautiful glass lamps were used when reading the Quran. Detailed wood carvings were made to decorate the staircase leading to the pulpit from which the Quran was recited.

Brought to the Middle East by Turkish tribes in the eighth and ninth centuries, the woolen knotted rug became an important aspect of Islamic art. In trying to imitate the animal skins that were used as floor and wall coverings in tents, weavers knotted their rugs with additional threads that looked like animal hairs. Later, these long, knotted "hairs" were turned from the underside to the topside and then cut, thus creating the thick pile of the carpet.

First and foremost, rugs served as prayer mats, both for individual use and as donations to the mosques by wealthy Muslims. They were also used for wall decorations and warmth in palaces. Rulers even gave them as rewards for political favors. Middle Eastern carpets were (and are) highly prized all over the world. Their

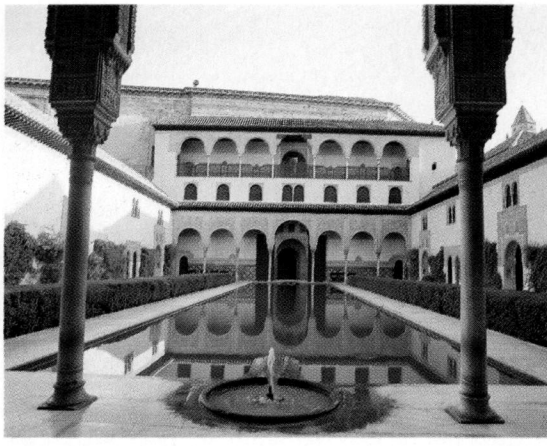

▲ *The Alhambra is an exquisite Moorish palace that overlooks the city of Granada, Spain. The fortified exterior gives way to gardens, courts, and reflecting pools within. The Alhambra was the final royal Islamic palace built in Spain.*

production was extremely time consuming and demanding. A small carpet five feet square, with three hundred knots to the square inch, could take over a year to make. Because of the fine detail, rug knotting was most easily done by the slender fingers of children.

Most decorations on the rugs, as well as on all forms of Islamic art, consisted of Arabic letters, natural plants, and abstract figures. These decorations were repeated over and over in geometric patterns called arabesques and completely covered the surface. No area was left undecorated.

No representation of the prophet Muhammad ever adorned a mosque, in painting or in any other art form. The Quran does not forbid representational painting, but the Hadith, an early collection of the prophet's sayings, warned against any attempt to imitate God through artistic creation or idolatry. As a result, from early on, no representations of figures appeared in Islamic religious art. Human beings could still be shown in secular art, but little survives from the early centuries except for a few wall paintings from the royal palaces.

SECTION REVIEW

1. **Define:**
   (a) mosques

2. **Identify:**
   (a) Arabic,   (b) House of Wisdom,   (c) Ibn Sina
   (Avicenna),   (d) Omar Khayyam,   (e) *The Arabian Nights*,   (f) Alhambra,   (g) Hadith

3. **Recall:**
   (a) What instrument used by sailors was perfected by the Muslims in Baghdad? How did it ultimately aid in the discovery of the Americas?
   (b) What was the primary use of rugs by the Muslims? Why were the rugs highly prized all over the world?

4. **Think Critically:** You are a young Muslim Arab talking with a visiting European friend your age. In a brief paragraph summarize how you would "brag" to the visitor about Arabic accomplishments in *one* of the following areas: philosophy and science; Islamic literature; or Islamic art and architecture.

Conclusion

In the seventh century, a new force arose in the Arabian peninsula and spread rapidly throughout the Middle East. This force was a new religion called Islam, which means "submission to the will of Allah," and it was the work of a man named Muhammad. After Muhammad's death, his successors—known as caliphs—organized the Arabs and set in motion a great expansion. Arab armies moved westward across North Africa and into Spain, as well as eastward into the Persian Empire, conquering Syria and Mesopotamia. Internal struggles, however, soon weakened the empire. The Umayyad dynasty, which began in 661, was replaced by the Abbasid dynasty in 750. The Abbasids were weakened by the Seljuk Turks and in 1258 fell to the Mongols.

Islamic civilization was built upon the teachings of the Quran. Nevertheless, over a period of time, the caliphs came to rule more like kings than spiritual leaders. The teachings of the Quran also had an impact on Islamic society, as is evident in its attitude toward women. Much of the prosperity of the Islamic civilization in the Middle East was based on trade.

Muslim Arabs tended to absorb the culture of the people they conquered. At the same time, they made advances of their own, especially in mathematics and the natural sciences. In literature and art, the Muslim world combined Islamic ideals with pre-Islamic traditions to create original works. Mosques from this period that remain standing today are visible symbols of the greatness of Islamic art and architecture.

Like other empires in the Middle East, however, the Arab Empire did not last. Nevertheless, Islam brought a code of law and a written language to societies that had previously not had them. By creating a flourishing trade network stretching from West Africa to East Asia, Islam also brought untold wealth to thousands and a better life to millions.

By the end of the thirteenth century, the Arab Empire was no more than a memory. However, it left a powerful legacy in Islam, which remains one of the great religions of the world. As we shall see in the next chapter on Africa, the spread of Islam to other continents ensured that it would affect more than just the Middle East.

Notes

1. Quoted in Arthur Goldschmidt, Jr., *A Concise History of the Middle East*, 4th ed. (Boulder, Colo., 1991), p. 56.
2. Mas'udi, *The Meadows of Gold: The Abbasids*, ed. Paul Lunde and Caroline Stone (London, 1989), p. 151.
3. Friedrich Hirth and W. W. Rockhill, trans., *Chau Ju-kua: His Work on the Chinese and Arab Trade in the Twelfth and Thirteenth Centuries, Entitled Chu-fan-chi* (New York, 1966), p. 115.
4. Leo Africanus, *The History and Description of Africa and of the Notable Things Therein Contained* (New York, n. d.), pp. 820–821.
5. Hirth and Rockhill, p. 116.
6. Quoted in Albert Hourani, *A History of the Arab Peoples* (Cambridge, Mass., 1991), p. 120.
7. Ehsan Yarshatar, ed., *Persian Literature* (New York, 1988), pp. 154–155.
8. *Ibid.*, p. 334.

Answers to
SECTION REVIEW

1. houses of worship
2. (a) chief language in southern Mediterranean and Middle East
   (b) library where key works of Plato and Aristotle were placed
   (c) author of a medical encyclopedia
   (d) twelfth-century poet
   (e) a collection of folktales, fables, and romances
   (f) Islamic palace in Spain
   (g) collection of the Prophet Muhammad's sayings
3. (a) astrolabe; used to determine location
   (b) prayer mats; they were time consuming and demanding to produce
4. Answers will vary.

CLOSE

The World of Islam is a complex one, and although the Arab Empire did not last, Islam continues to be a major world religion and its sphere of influence is expanding.

SPANISH SUPPORT

The *Conclusion* has been translated into Spanish for your Spanish-speaking students. Included with this translation (in your Teacher Resource Box) are Section Key Points, which consist of one or two sentences summarizing each section in the chapter. These Key Points have also been translated into Spanish.

TIME LINE

As students conclude the chapter, you may want to refer them to the chapter time line in the *Study Guide*. The time line will help them put key dates in perspective.

Answers to CHAPTER REVIEW

USING KEY TERMS

1. mosques
2. bazaar
3. Hegira
4. Islam
5. caliph
6. umma
7. hajj
8. jihad
9. sultan

REVIEWING THE FACTS

1. Arabs, Hebrews, Assyrians
2. Ka'bah
3. The merchants of Mecca became rich. This divided Arabs into two groups.
4. submission to the will of God
5. the growing gap between merchant and Bedouin
6. persecution and his failure to convert Meccans to Islam
7. Hegira, or flight to Medina from Mecca
8. Muslims see Muhammad as a prophet and not divine
9. 1) belief in Allah and Muhammad as his prophet, 2) standard prayer five times a day and public prayer on Friday, 3) observation of the holy month of Ramadan, 4) making a pilgrimage to Mecca once in one's lifetime, 5) giving alms to the poor and unfortunate
10. Abu Bakr
11. Syria, Persia, Egypt, North Africa
12. Mu'awiyah made the caliphate hereditary
13. Shi'ites accept the descendants of Ali as caliphs. Sunnites claim the Umayyads.
14. *Quran* and use of Arabic
15. nomadic peoples of Central Asia who converted to Islam; they grew in number and power and took over Iran and Armenia
16. a Sunni Muslim who brought an end to the Fatamid dynasty in Egypt; Islamic leader who invaded Jerusalem and destroyed Christian fortresses

250

CHAPTER 8 REVIEW

USING KEY TERMS

1. _____ are Muslim houses of worship.
2. A crucial part of every Muslim city or town was the covered market, called the _____.
3. The journey of Muhammad from Mecca to Medina is known in history as the _____.
4. The sacred book of _____ is called the Quran (Koran).
5. The temporal leader of the Islamic community is called a _____.
6. Muhammad was the religious and political leader of the Islamic community known as the _____.
7. One of the five pillars of Islam is making a pilgrimage, called the _____, to Mecca.
8. According to the Quran, _____ means struggle in the way of God.
9. The secular political and military head of state or "holder of power" under the Turkish Islamic rule is called a _____.

REVIEWING THE FACTS

1. Name three groups of Semitic-speaking people.
2. What central shrine did all early Arabs worship?
3. What caused tensions between Arabs of the desert and those of the town in the fifth and sixth centuries?
4. What does the word Islam mean?
5. What economic and social situation in Arabia caused Muhammad to flee to the hills and meditate?
6. Why did Muhammad move to Medina in 622?
7. What marks year one of the official calendar of Islam?
8. What is the chief difference between the way Christians see Jesus and the way Muslims see Muhammad?
9. What are the five pillars of Islam?
10. Who was the first caliph to unify the Arab tribes and begin an expansionist movement?

250

11. By 650, what conquests had the Arabs made?
12. How did the caliphate become a dynasty?
13. What are the main differences between the Shi'ites and the Sunnites?
14. What were the only two common bonds holding the world of Islam together after 973?
15. Who were the Seljuk Turks and how were they able to gradually replace the Abbasids?
16. Who is Saladin and why is he famous in both Islamic and Christian European history of the twelfth century?
17. Who are the Ottoman Turks?
18. How did Islamic beliefs encourage trade and industry?
19. Identify and describe two important Islamic works of literature.
20. What is Sufism?

THINKING CRITICALLY

1. Explain why Muslims incorporate the angel Gabriel, Moses, and Jesus into their religious tradition.
2. Explain why in the earliest Muslim community there was no separation between political and religious authority.
3. What accounts for the astounding success of the Arabs in conquering foreign territories?
4. What is the significance in world history of the Battle of Tours in 732 and the destruction of the Muslim fleet in 717?
5. Why is 1453 an important date in both Islamic and European history?
6. Analyze the concept of equality in Islamic society, especially as it related to women and slaves.
7. Evaluate the historical viewpoint that expresses the idea of Islamic culture as a preserver and transmitter of culture, rather than as a creator of culture.

---

17. brought down the Byzantine Empire in 1453
18. Muhammad himself had been a merchant and the *Quran* encouraged it.
19. The *Rubaiyat* by Omar Khayyam: poetry reflecting Persian influence; The *Tales from 1001 Nights (Arabian Nights)*: a collection of international folktales.
20. Sunni religious belief that focused on a personal relationship between Allah and humans

THINKING CRITICALLY

1. Allah communicated to Muhammad through each of these.

2. Muhammad was a religious and political leader.
3. the Islamic belief that those involved in spreading the Islamic faith would go to Heaven
4. Islamic expansionism into Europe was stopped until 1453.
5. It signaled the domination of the Islamic world by the Turks; it opened the door for the movement of Islam into Europe.
6. Slaves were to be treated fairly. Women could own property and were to be treated with respect.
7. collected knowledge from Persian, Indian, Roman cultures; made advances of their own

APPLYING SOCIAL STUDIES SKILLS

1. **Sociology:** What social tensions make Arab unity difficult today?
2. **Geography:** How did the harsh environment of Arabia shape the political and economic life of the people?
3. **Geography:** Trace the expansionist movement of the Arabs from 632 to 1055.
4. **Geography:** Why might the Umayyads have moved their capital from Mecca to Damascus? What were the geographical advantages of the move to Baghdad in 762?
5. **Government:** What were some of the weaknesses in Arab political rule as exemplified in Hussein's revolt against the Umayyads in 680?
6. **Sociology:** What social changes did the Abbasid rulers make? Identify the social and cultural results of these changes.
7. **Economics:** Map the trade routes of the Abbasid period of Islamic history. Identify the major cities, items of trade, and modes of transportation used during this period.
8. **Government:** How did caliphs administer their empires?
9. **Sociology:** Describe pictorially and verbally the social structure of the typical Muslim city or town and its surrounding areas. Include all groups of people, including religious communities.

MAKING TIME AND PLACE CONNECTIONS

1. Muhammad lived between 570 and 632. Describe the situation in the eastern and western Roman Empire at the time and how that may have influenced the rise of Islam.

2. Compare the golden age of the Abbasid caliphate with the golden age of one of the following: Greece, China, India, or Rome.
3. Why is the Battle of Manzikert in 1071 and the sultan Saladin so important in the chronicles of western European history?
4. Compare Sufism with Protestantism.

BECOMING AN HISTORIAN

Examining Architecture

1. Examine the picture of the Alhambra, the finest example of an Islamic palace, in this chapter. What conclusions about the nature of Islamic civilization can be drawn from the fortress layout and the abstract patterns of design?
2. How does the mosque incorporate aspects of classical Greek, Roman, and Christian architectural styles as well as Islamic beliefs?

Literature as History

1. In Chapter 47 of the Quran, the peacefulness of Heaven is described. Why might the Arabs have envisioned Heaven in terms of gardens and running streams?
2. What can Rumi's poem tell us about the austere nature of Islamic religious ritual?
3. The *Arabian Nights* incorporate tales from many cultures. What can this tell us about the cosmopolitan nature of Islamic society?

251

1. The western Roman Empire had fallen to the Germanic tribes and was weak and disunited. The eastern Roman Empire or Byzantium had expanded into the Middle East but was weakened in its rivalries with Persia. This disrupted the traditional trade routes to the east and caused merchants to go by way of the Arabian peninsula.
2. Prosperity, cosmopolitanism, encouragement of learning and outpourings of art are the foundations of any golden age.
3. Battle of Manzikert initiated the Crusades; Saladin destroyed the Crusader strongholds in the Middle East.
4. Similarities include the desire to reach God directly and a close personal relationship with God. Protestants were more austere and practical and less mystical than Sufis.

BECOMING AN HISTORIAN

Examining Architecture

1. basic forms are borrowed from the Greek and Roman classical world; fortress style walls bespeak of the fact that Arabs needed to protect themselves; decorations conform to the belief that it should consist of beautifully scripted passages from the Quran and reflect mathematical shapes
2. The mosque incorporates the rectangular style of the Greeks, the dome of the Romans, and the bell tower of Christian churches.

APPLYING SOCIAL STUDIES SKILLS

1. Answers will vary.
2. The harsh desert climate caused Arabs to organize into tribes to help each other.
3. 635, Arab peninsula; 640, Syria; 642, Egypt, northern Africa; 650, Persia; 725 Spain
4. Answers will vary; more centrally located to the trade patterns they were developing
5. struggles for succession; struggles between Arabs/non-Arabs, Muslims/non-Muslims
6. attempted to break down the distinctions between Arab and non-Arab Muslims; opened Islamic society to influences of different civilizations

7. major cities: Baghdad, Damascus and Cairo, by ship and camel caravan, from south of the Sahara, gold and slaves; from China silk and porcelain; from eastern Africa gold and ivory; from Southeast Asia and India sandalwood and spices; from Egypt grain; from Iraq linens, dates and precious stones; from western India cotton textiles
8. assisted by a bureaucracy, and a council headed by a prime minister (vizier)
9. mosques and palaces surrounded by walls in the center; ringed with public buildings; craftsmen and merchant work sites and dwellings; religious communities; independent farmers and later estates

LITERATURE AS HISTORY

1. a place with an abundance of water; Answers will vary.
2. did not incorporate gaiety, love, mysticism, or individualism.
3. reflect influences from the many cultures Arabs conquered, traded with, and learned from

PLANNING GUIDE

	SECTION	KEY TOPICS	PRIMARY SOURCES	ASSESSMENT
1	**The Development of Civilizations in Africa** pages 252–258	◆ Geography's impact on the development of African civilizations ◆ Rise and fall of Kush and Axum empires		◆ Section Review, page 258 ◆ Section Quiz 9–1, TRB
2	**The Royal Kingdoms of West Africa** pages 258–266	◆ Kingdoms of Ghana, Mali, and Songhai ◆ Expansion of trade ◆ Rulers' support of learning	◆ Al-Bakri's account, page 249 ◆ Tenth-century Arabian traveler, page 260 ◆ Ibn Batutta, page 261 ◆ Engraving of Timbuktu, page 262 ◆ Portrait of Sundiata Keita, page 263 ◆ Drawing of Mansa Musa, page 264 ◆ Ibn Batutta, page 264	◆ Section Review, page 266 ◆ Section Quiz 9–2, TRB
3	**States and Stateless Societies in Eastern and Southern Africa** pages 266–270	◆ Bantu society ◆ Stateless societies in southern Africa ◆ Trading ports of Mogadishu, Mombasa, and Kilwa ◆ Great Zimbabwe		◆ Section Review, pages 269–70 ◆ Section Quiz 9–3, TRB
4	**African Society and Culture** pages 270–277	◆ Lineage groups ◆ Roles of women ◆ Slavery ◆ Traditional religious beliefs ◆ Art, music, dance, and storytelling	◆ Ibn Battuta, page 270	◆ Section Review, page 277 ◆ Section Quiz 9–4, TRB

EARLY CIVILIZATIONS IN AFRICA (400 to 1500)

REPRODUCIBLE ACTIVITIES

- Historical Maps
- Charts and Graphs
- Critical Thinking
- Cooperative Learning
- Vocabulary
- Guided Reading
- Reteaching
- Enrichment
- Performance Assessment
- Spanish Key Points and Chapter Summaries
- Spanish Vocabulary
- Spanish Guided Reading

MULTIMEDIA SUPPORT

TRANSPARENCIES
- *World History* Color Transparency Package
- Fine Art Color Transparency Package

VIDEO
- *World History* Video Library
- **CNN.** Annual Video Update

LASERDISC
- *Sights and Sounds of History*

AUDIO
- *Listening to Literature* audiotape (English and Spanish)
- *History of Music* CD

SOFTWARE
- WESTEST™
- Student Review

CD–ROM
- *The Journey of Civilization*
- *World History*

INTERNET
- Internet Activities

On Line with WORLD HISTORY

Access West's history web site at
http://history.swpco.com
You'll find activities and web sites related to specific topics and chapters in *World History: The Human Odyssey*. Also look for references to helpful web sites at appropriate places throughout this teacher edition.

LESSON PLANNING

You will find detailed daily lesson plans for both traditional class scheduling and **block scheduling** in your Teacher Resource Box.

Not Enough Time?

If you do not have the four or five days recommended to teach this chapter, you may want to focus on the following sections and activities:

- Have students skim the chapter to answer the "Questions to Guide Your Reading" on page 253.
- Discuss their answers; then read the "Conclusion" on page 277.
- Do a more in-depth reading of pages 253–255, 259–262, 265–266, 269, 270–273. Conclude with a class discussion of the features on pages 261, 272, 275, and 276.

EARLY CIVILIZATIONS IN AFRICA
(400 TO 1500)

In 1871, the German explorer Karl Mauch began to search South Africa's Central Plateau for the colossal stone ruins of a legendary lost civilization. In late August, he found what he had been looking for. He wrote in his diary, "Presently I stood before it and beheld a wall of a height of about 20 feet of granite bricks. Very close by there was a place where a kind of foot-path led over rubble into the interior. Following this path I stumbled over masses of rubble and parts of walls and dense thickets. I stopped in front of a towerlike structure. Altogether it rose to a height of about 30 feet." Mauch was convinced that "a civilized nation must once have lived here." Like many other nineteenth-century Europeans, however, Mauch was equally convinced that the Africans who had lived there could never have built structures as splendid as the ones he had found at Great Zimbabwe (zim-BOB-way). Mauch and other archaeologists believed that Great Zimbabwe must have been the work of "a northern race closely akin to the Phoenician and Egyptian." It was not until the twentieth century that Europeans could overcome their prejudices and finally admit that Africans south of Egypt had developed advanced civilizations with spectacular achievements.

The continent of Africa has played a central role in the long evolution of humankind. It was in Africa that the first hominids appeared more than three million years ago. It was in Africa that the immediate ancestors of modern human beings—*Homo sapiens sapiens*—emerged between 200,000 and 150,000 years ago (see Chapter 1). Both the growing of crops and the taming of animals may have occurred first in Africa. Certainly, one of the first civilizations appeared in Africa: the kingdom of Egypt in the Nile valley in the northeastern corner of the continent, which we examined in Chapter 2. A number of advanced societies took root in other parts of Africa as well, which we will examine in this chapter.

▲ *The gold pendant shown in this photograph was made by the Akan peoples of the Ivory Coast. What can you infer about their society from this pendant?*

400	AFRICAN CIVILIZATIONS	1500
400		1500

QUESTIONS TO GUIDE YOUR READING

1. What effect did geography have on the history of Africa?

2. What were the accomplishments of the West African kingdoms of Ghana, Mali, and Songhai? Why did each decline?

3. What impact did Islam have on Africa between 700 and 1500?

4. What is the significance of Great Zimbabwe?

5. What were the roles of family relationships, women, and slavery in the society of Africa?

6. What were three major cultural achievements of African society?

OUTLINE

THE DEVELOPMENT OF CIVILIZATIONS IN AFRICA

After the decline of the Egyptian Empire during the first millennium B.C., the focus of social change began to shift from the lower Nile valley to other areas of Africa: to the region of the upper Nile River, where the trading states of Kush and Axum flourished for several centuries; to West Africa, where a series of major trading states developed; and to the eastern coast, where African peoples began to play an active role in the trade of the Indian Ocean.

The Land and Climate of Africa

After Asia, Africa is the largest of the continents. It stretches nearly five thousand miles from the Cape of Good Hope in the south to the Mediterranean in the north. Africa is as diverse as it is vast, and it includes several distinct geographical zones. The northern fringe, on the coast washed by the Mediterranean Sea, is mountainous along much of its length. South of the mountains lies the largest desert on Earth, the Sahara, which stretches from the Atlantic to the Indian Oceans. To the east is the Nile River, heart of the

253

FOCUS ON THEMES

Listed below are brief summaries of how the content in this chapter supports the text's key themes.

Politics and History Strong states based on agriculture and trade flourished. Rule by kings was common in all of these states.

Economics and History Civilizations depended upon farming, hunting, and fishing. They also developed extensive trade networks. Gold and salt were especially valuable commodities.

Social Life Most African societies were organized around extended family units combined into larger communities known as lineage groups. Lineage groups served as the basic building blocks of African society.

The Importance of Cultural Developments The arts played an important role as a means of serving religion. Africans were skilled in wood carving, metalwork, and building monumental structures of stone.

Religion in History Traditional African religions maintained common beliefs in a creator god, the importance of ancestors, the use of ritual, and an afterlife. The spread of Islam added yet another spiritual tradition to Africa.

The Role of Individuals A number of individual rulers played important roles in guiding the development of their states. The griot, a storyteller, who preserved a people's history, was also important.

The Impact of Science and Technology Africans were master builders in stone and were also adept in the smelting of ores.

Answers to QUESTIONS TO GUIDE YOUR READING

1. four distinct climate zones created very different lifestyles of African peoples (pages 253–255)

2. See pages 259–266.

3. Islam affected location of cities and trade routes and architecture in all of Africa; intermarriage of Muslims to others spread religion throughout Africa (pages 266–268)

4. illustration of kingdom's power and influence (page 269)

5. family relationships: gave sense of identity, lineage group was building block of society women: valued for work; in some societies, lineage was matrilineal
   slavery: common; harsh treatment; included prisoners of war, criminals, debtors (pages 270–272)

6. rock paintings, wood carvings, sculpture, music and dance, pyramid, storytelling (pages 273–276)

The Environment and History Distinct geographical and climate zones helped to produce a variety of societies as people responded to the unique conditions.

FOCUS

OBJECTIVES

After completing this section, students should be able to

◆ describe and locate the four major climate zones of Africa
◆ discuss the economy and society of the Kush empire
◆ identify the most distinctive feature of Axumite civilization
◆ discuss the impact of Islam on the African kingdom of Axum

FOCUS ACTIVITY

On the board, list Africa's four major climate zones: 1. mild, temperate; 2. desert; 3. rain forest; 4. savanna. (Be sure students understand that a savanna is grassland having unreliable amounts of rainfall.) Divide the class into four groups, assigning each group one of the four zones. Allow about ten minutes for groups to brainstorm ways each type of climate might affect such areas as housing, food gathering, transportation, and population growth. Have the groups come together and combine their ideas into a class list or poster.

ancient Egyptian civilization. Beyond that lies the Red Sea, separating Africa from Asia.

The Sahara separates the northern coast from the rest of the continent. Africa south of the Sahara (known as sub-Saharan Africa) is itself divided among a number of major regions. In the west is the so-called hump of Africa, which juts like a massive shoulder into the Atlantic Ocean. Here the Sahara gradually gives way to grasslands in the interior and then to tropical jungles along the coast. This region is rich in natural resources.

Far to the east is a very different terrain of snow-capped mountains, upland plateaus, and lakes. Much of this region is grassland populated by wild animals.

Further to the south lies the Congo basin, with its jungles watered by the mighty Zaire (ZIE-ear) (formerly Congo) River. The jungles of equatorial Africa then fade gradually into the hills, plateaus, and deserts of the south. This rich land contains some of the most valuable mineral resources known today.

Africa also includes four distinct climate zones, which help to explain the different lifestyles of the peoples of Africa. A mild climate zone stretches across the northern coast and southern tip of Africa. Moderate rainfall and warm temperatures result in fertile land that produces abundant crops. This crop production can support large numbers of people.

Deserts form another climate zone. The Sahara in the north and the Kalahari in the south are the two largest deserts. Altogether, deserts cover about 40 percent of Africa. Deserts make travel difficult but not impossi-

ble. Around A.D. 300, when the camel was brought to Africa from Arabia, camel caravans began to travel across the Sahara carrying goods.

A third climate zone is the rain forest that stretches along the equator and makes up about 10 percent of the continent. Heavy rains and warm temperatures produce dense forests where little farming and little travel are possible. The rain forest is also home to disease-carrying insects, especially the tsetse ([T]SEET-see) fly, which infects both animals and humans with

Map 9.1   The Geography of Africa

STUDYING MAPS

The following questions will help you guide the students through their study of Map 9.1.

1. What four major bodies of water surround the continent of Africa? (*Atlantic Ocean, Indian Ocean, Mediterranean Sea, Red Sea*)

2. What are the two major deserts in Africa? (*Sahara and Kalahari*)

3. Which are more prevalent in Africa: deserts or mountains? (*deserts*)

4. People often associate Africa with jungles. What part of Africa would you estimate is jungle-like area: ½₂, ⅕, ½, ¾? (*⅟₁₂*)

▲ *Saharan nomads and Arab traders journeyed from North Africa, through the Sahara, to West African kingdoms by camel. The camel served as transportation, a source of fuel, and a food source, all in one.*

sleeping sickness. As a result, people who live in the rain forest do not raise cattle or use animals, hoping in this way to avoid the tsetse fly.

A final climate zone consists of the **savannas,** or broad grasslands dotted with small trees and shrubs. Savannas stretch across Africa both north and south of the rain forest and cover perhaps 40 percent of Africa's land area. The savannas receive enough rainfall to allow for farming and the herding of animals, but the rain is unreliable. Heavy rains one year might be followed by drought the next, making farming difficult at times.

The Emergence of Civilization

About seven or eight thousand years ago, hunters and gatherers in Africa began to tame animals and grow crops. Wheat and barley were grown in the Nile Valley, and sorghum and rice were raised in West Africa. The mastery of farming, which we called the Agricultural Revolution in Chapter 1, gave rise to the first civilizations in Africa: Egypt, Kush, and Axum.

South of Egypt is an area known as Nubia. By 2000 B.C., a busy trade had arisen between Egypt and Nubia. Egyptian merchants traveled to Nubia to obtain ivory, ebony wood, frankincense, and leopard skins. Although Nubia was subject to Egyptian control for many centuries, it freed itself around 1000 B.C. and became the independent state of Kush. In 750 B.C., Kush even conquered Egypt. In 663 B.C., however, the Kushites, who were still using bronze and stone weapons, were overwhelmed by the Assyrians, who were armed with iron spears and swords. The Kushites were driven out of Egypt and returned to their original lands in the upper Nile valley.

The economy of Kush was based at first on farming. Millet and other grain crops were grown along the banks of the river. Kush soon emerged, however, as one of the major trading states in the region, with its cen-

MORE ABOUT . . . *Tsetse flies and the Sleeping Sickness*

The tsetse fly carries the sleeping sickness to humans and the disease nagana to animals. Sleeping sickness has two variants: the Gambian and the Rhodesian. In the Gambian form, the disease attacks the central nervous system, causing severe headaches, apathy, lethargy, and sleepiness. This form will usually be fatal within several years, although some persons develop a level of tolerance and become carriers. The Rhodesian form is more virulent, and usually soon results in death. The tsetse fly has had a major effect in retarding the economic development of large areas of Africa, and also, ironically, in defending Africa from the incursions of Europeans. It was not until European medicine could provide protection against African diseases that Africa ceased to be known as "the White Man's Grave."

CRITICAL THINKING

"The major exports of Kush were ivory, gold, ebony, and slaves." Ask students what they can deduce about Kush, based on this sentence. *(rich in elephants, precious metals, and trees; used people as currency; culture and ethical system included and allowed slavery)*

LEARNING FROM VISUALS

We can learn much about a people from their burial customs. What can we say about Kush, based on their use of pyramids as royal tombs? *(influenced by Egypt; had many laborers; kings were wealthy and venerated, although pyramids were smaller than those of Egyptian pharaohs)*

Answer to the caption question: The Kush pyramids at Meroe were smaller than Egyptian pyramids and unpointed at the top.

▲ *The rulers of Kush borrowed much from their northern Egyptian neighbors, including the building of pyramids as royal tombs. What differences and similarities are visible between these pyramids and those built by the Egyptians?*

ter at the city of Meroe (MER-uh-WEE). Well located at the point where a newly opened land route across the desert to the north crossed the Nile River, Meroe was also blessed with a large supply of iron ore. Having learned iron ore smelting from the Assyrians, the Kushites made iron weapons and tools that were sent abroad.

For the next several hundred years, Kush was a major trading empire with links to other states throughout the region. Kush provided its own quality iron products and goods from central and East Africa to the Roman Empire, as well as to Arabia and India. The major exports of Kush were ivory, gold, ebony, and slaves. In return, the Kushites received luxury goods, including jewelry and silver lamps from India and Arabia.

Not much is known about Kushite society. It seems likely that it was mostly urban. At first, state authorities probably controlled foreign trade. However, the presence of extensive luxury goods in the numerous private tombs in the area indicates that at one time material prosperity was relatively widespread. This suggests that at some point a fairly large merchant class carried on trading activities. Indeed, the merchants of Meroe built large houses with central courtyards. Like the Romans, they also built public baths. Kushite prosperity was also evident in the luxurious palaces of the Kushite kings. Like the Egyptian pharaohs, these kings were buried in pyramids, although theirs were considerably smaller than those of their Egyptian models.

The state of Kush flourished from about 250 B.C. to about A.D. 150 and then began to decline, possibly because of the rise of a new power in the region. Known as Axum, it was located in the highlands of modern-day Ethiopia. Axum was founded as a colony by Arabs from across the Red Sea on the southern tip of the Arabian peninsula. Eventually, Axum emerged as an independent state that combined Arab and African cultures.

So What ??

If your students question the importance of information about **Kush and Axum,** *tell them . . .*

One of the justifications for enslaving Africans used by Europeans was the alleged inability of Africans to build an advanced civilization. Geography and climate (particularly the disease environment) hampered the development of advanced civilizations, but the fact is that Africans did build cities, establish kingdoms, and maintain elaborate trade routes. For African-Americans whose ancestors were brought to the New World by force studying this information can help build confidence and pride as they learn more about their heritage. For students of European ancestry, studying this information will help them gain respect for the cultures and achievements of all peoples.

Map 9.2 Ancient Nubia and Ethiopia

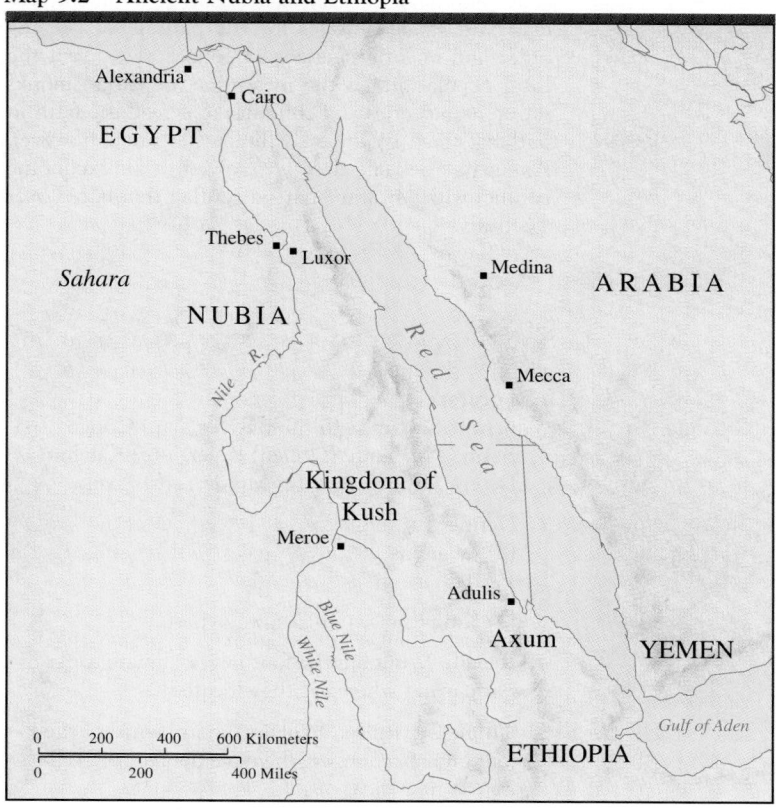

Axum owed much of its prosperity to its location along the Red Sea on the trade route between India and the Mediterranean. Axum exported ivory, frankincense, myrrh, and slaves. It imported textiles, metal goods, wine, and olive oil. For a time, Axum competed with the neighboring state of Kush for control of the ivory trade. Hunters from Axum, armed with imported iron weapons, scoured the entire region for elephants. Probably as a result of this competition for ivory, in the fourth century A.D., King Ezana, the Axumite ruler, claimed that he had been provoked, launched an invasion of Kush, and conquered it.

Perhaps the most distinctive feature of Axumite civilization was its religion. In A.D. 324, King Ezana converted to Christianity, which was first brought by Syrians who were shipwrecked. The king made Christianity the official religion of Axum. When Ezana died, Axum was a flourishing kingdom. Within a few centuries, however, a new religious force—Islam—brought profound challenges to the kingdom of Axum.

The Coming of Islam

The rise of Islam in the Arabian peninsula during the first half of the seventh century A.D., which we examined in Chapter 8, soon had an impact on neighboring areas. In 641, Arab forces seized the delta of the Nile River and took control of Egypt. To guard against attacks, the Arabs eventually built a new capital at Cairo, inland from the old capital of Alexandria. The Arabs then began to consolidate their control over the entire region. From Egypt, they expanded westward across North Africa. By the early eighth century, the entire coastal region as far west as the Strait of Gibraltar was under Arab rule.

Arab expansion in Africa soon brought conflict with the state of Axum. By the eighth century, a number of Muslim trading states had been established on the African coast of the Red Sea. At first, relations between Christian Axum and its Muslim neighbors were relatively peaceful. Beginning in the twelfth century, however, problems arose as the Muslim states along the coast began to move inland to gain control over the growing trade in slaves and ivory. Axum,

LEARNING FROM VISUALS

Besides height, what else do students notice about this example of Axum stelae? *(Ornate carving; intricate designs)* What can they infer about the person whose tomb is being marked? *(probably a king; certainly an extremely important person)*

Answer to the caption question: Many old grave sites had monuments similar to, but much smaller than, these stelae.

ASSESS

Answers to
SECTION REVIEW

2. (a) broad grasslands dotted with small trees and shrubs
3. (a) ruler of Axum
   (b) seized control of Axum in the mid-twelfth century
4. mild climate zone—across the northern coast and southern tip; desert zone—Sahara in the north and Kalahari in the south; rain forest—along the equator; savannas—stretch across Africa north and south of the rain forest
5. Answers will vary, but might include that the mild climate zones and savannas allowed for settlement and farming; the deserts and rain forests made travel difficult and did not allow for farming and settlement.

▲ *During the fourth century, the rulers of Axum built these slender columns, known as stelae, to mark the position of their royal tombs. This photo shows the tallest of the Axum stelae that is still standing in Ethiopia. How do stelae compare to gravestones and vaults found in cemeteries today?*

which had dominated this trade, reacted with force. At first it had some success. In the early fourteenth century, however, the Muslim state of Adal, located at the point where the Indian Ocean meets the Red Sea, launched a new attack on the Christian kingdom.

Axum also underwent much internal change during this period. The Zagwe dynasty, which had seized control of the country in the mid-twelfth century, centralized the government and extended the Christian faith throughout the kingdom, now known as Ethiopia. The rulers also gave military leaders and government officials vast landed estates for the purpose of keeping order and making it easier to collect taxes from the local population. In the meantime, Christian monks set up monasteries and churches to spread the faith in outlying areas. By the early fifteenth century, however, Axum had become deeply involved in an expanding conflict with Muslim Adal—a conflict that lasted over a century.

 SECTION REVIEW

1. **Locate:**
   (a) the Sahara,   (b) Nile River,   (c) Congo Basin,   (d) Zaire (Congo) River,   (e) Kalahari Desert,   (f) Kush,   (g) Meroe,   (h) Axum

2. **Define:**
   (a) savannas

3. **Identify:**
   (a) King Ezana,   (b) Zagwe dynasty

4. **Recall:** What are the four major climate zones of Africa, and where are they located?

5. **Think Critically:** Explain the influence of the four climate zones on the development of civilization in Africa.

2

THE ROYAL KINGDOMS OF WEST AFRICA

During the eighth century, a number of major trading states emerged in the area south of the Sahara in West Africa. Eventually, these states made the Sahara into one of the leading avenues of world trade. A crisscross pattern of caravan routes led to destinations as far away as the Atlantic Ocean, the Mediterranean Sea, and the Red Sea.

ENRICHMENT ACTIVITY

Among the oldest populations of Jews anywhere are the Jews of Ethiopia. Assign students to research the history of this African group, including the recent exodus of many to Israel. They should present their findings to the class.

▲ *The ancient kingdom of Ghana was situated about 500 miles northwest of the modern-day country of Ghana. What can we infer about the lifestyles of the people who lived here from the mixture of grasslands and forest shown in this photo?*

The Kingdom of Ghana

The first of the great trading states south of the Sahara was Ghana (GAWN-uh). This state emerged in the fifth century A.D. in the upper Niger River valley, a grassland region between the Sahara and the tropical forests along the West African coast. The modern state of Ghana, which takes its name from this early state, is located in the forest region to the south. Most of the people in the area were farmers living in villages under the authority of a local chieftain. Gradually, these communities were brought together to form the kingdom of Ghana.

The kings of Ghana were **absolute rulers** (free to govern without any laws) who played active roles in running their kingdom. Their wealth was vast. One Muslim observer wrote that a Ghanaian king called Kanissa'ai was the equal of any Egyptian pharaoh. Supposedly, he owned ten thousand horses, each of which was housed in its own stable with three servants to meet its needs. For their public appearances, the kings of Ghana dressed in resplendent robes, wore gold neck-

laces and rings, and were crowned with turbans trimmed in gold. Al-Bakri, an eleventh-century Muslim traveler, wrote of the Ghanaian king's court:

The king sits in audience or to hear grievances against officials in a domed pavilion around which stand ten horses covered with gold-embroidered materials. Behind the king stand ten pages holding shields and swords decorated with gold, and on his right are the sons of subordinate kings of his country wearing splendid garments and their hair mixed with gold. The governor of the city sits on the ground before the king and around him are ministers seated likewise. At the door of the pavilion are dogs of excellent pedigree who hardly ever leave the place where the king is, guarding him. Round their necks they wear collars of gold and silver studded with a number of balls of the same metals.[1]

To protect their kingdom and enforce their wishes, Ghanaian kings relied on a well-trained regular army of thousands of men.

USING PRIMARY SOURCES

Read aloud the description of Ghana's "silent trade." Ask for student volunteers to portray the process in a pantomime.

CRITICAL THINKING

Ask students what it might have been like to journey from North Africa through the Sahara on camel? Ask students to write a diary entry by a desert-crossing trader enroute to the West African kingdoms.

ACTIVITY

Ask students to take the role of merchants traveling along trade routes. Students should explain which goods they would carry and what mode of travel they would use along each leg of travel. Among the routes they should travel are: (a) Timbuktu to Fez, to Cordoba to Valencia to Marseilles to Paris to Bruges; (b) Gao to Tunis to Naples to Constantinople to Kiev; (c) Mogadishu to Mecca to Bagdad to Bokhara to Samarkand to the Sung Empire; (d) Samarkand to Bagdad to Aleppo to Constantinople to Venice to Nuremberg to Lübeck to Riga.

Although the people of the region had lived off the land for centuries, the kingdom of Ghana prospered from both iron and gold. The region had an abundant supply of iron ore, and the Ghanaians were skilled in making tools and weapons. The blacksmiths of Ghana were highly valued as people who could "magically" use fire to turn ore into tools and weapons. (They knew the process of smelting iron ore.)

Ghana also had an abundance of gold, as a tenth-century Muslim geographer made clear in his travel writings: "There is the kingdom of Ghana, whose king is also very powerful. In his country are the gold mines, and under his authority are a number of kings. . . . Gold is found in the whole of this country."[2] The heartland of the state was located near one of the richest gold-producing areas in all of Africa. Ghana's gold was an important element in making it the center of an enormous trade empire.

Muslim merchants from North Africa brought to Ghana metal goods, textiles, horses, and salt obtained from mines in the Sahara. Salt was an especially valuable trade item for the Ghanaians. It was used to preserve food, as well as to make it more tasty. Salt was also important because the people needed extra salt to replace what their bodies lost in sweat in the hot climate in which they lived. A major source of salt was the salt mines at Taghaza in the Sahara, apparently a very unpleasant place (see "You Are There: The Salt Mines").

Ghanaians traded their abundant gold for salt and other products brought from North Africa. The exchange of goods in Ghana was done by a method of silent trade, as described by a tenth-century Arabian traveler:

The kingdom of Ghana is one of great importance and it adjoins the land of the gold mines. Great people of the Sudan [the Arab name for West Africa] lived there. They had traced a boundary which no one who sets out to them ever crosses. When the merchants reach this boundary, they place their wares and cloth on the ground and then depart, and so the people of the Sudan come bearing gold which they leave besides the merchandise and then depart. The owners of the merchandise then return, and if they were satisfied with what they had found, they take it. If not, they go away again, and the people of the Sudan return and add to the price until the bargain is concluded.[3]

Eventually, other exports from Ghana found their way to the markets of the Mediterranean coast and beyond. These goods included ivory, ostrich feathers, hides, leather goods, and slaves.

Much of the trade across the desert was still carried by the Berbers, the nomadic peoples whose camel caravans became known as the "fleets of the desert." Camels had been brought to Africa from Arabia by A.D. 300 and became a crucial factor in trade across the Sahara. Camels adapted well to conditions in the desert, where temperatures could reach 130 degrees Fahrenheit. They could drink enormous quantities of water at one time and needed little food for days. In a typical caravan trek, as many as a hundred camels would be loaded

Map 9.3   West Africa and the Trans-Saharan Trade Routes

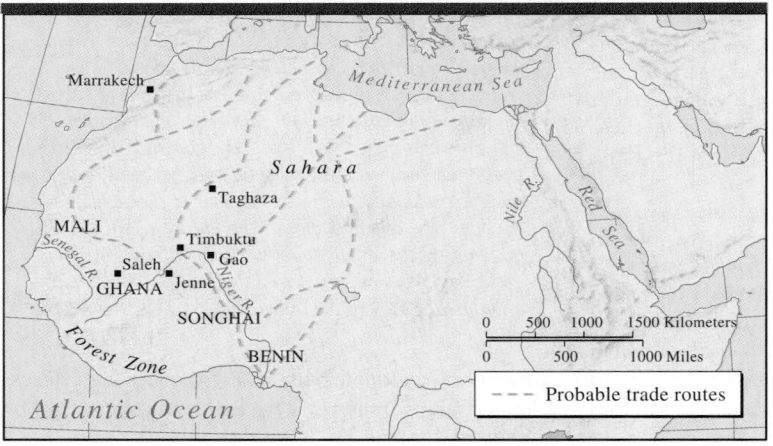

STUDYING MAPS

The following questions and activities will help you guide students through their study of Map 9.3.

1. Point to the four kingdoms shown. What are they? *(Mali, Ghana, Songhai, Benin)*
2. Trace each probable trade route, noting important cities along the way. Where does each route either begin or end? *(coast of Mediterranean Sea)*
3. What desert must be crossed on most of the routes? *(Sahara)*

YOU ARE THERE
The Salt Mines

Ibn Batutta was born in Morocco in 1304. When he was twenty-one years old, he went on a pilgrimage to Mecca. He then began to travel and spent the next twenty-four years wandering throughout Africa and Asia. In writing an account of his travels, he provided modern readers with an accurate description of conditions in the fourteenth century.

Ibn Batutta, Describing Work in the Salt Mines

We arrived after twenty-five days at Taghaza. It is a village with no good in it. Among its curiosities is the fact that the construction of its houses is of rock salt with camel skin roofing and there are no trees in it, the soil is just sand. In it is a salt mine. It is dug out of the ground and is found there in huge slabs, one on top of another as if it had been carved and put under the ground. A camel can carry two slabs of salt. Nobody lives in the village except slaves who dig for the salt and live on dates and on the meat of camels that is brought from the land of the blacks. The blacks arrive from their country and carry away the salt from there. The blacks exchange the salt as money as one would exchange gold and silver. They cut it up and trade with it in pieces. In spite of the insignificance of the village of Taghaza, much trading goes on in it. We stayed in it ten days in miserable con

Working in the salt mines was hard physical labor, but without salt people in Arab countries could not survive. Do you know the source of the table salt you use?

ditions, because its water is bitter and it is of all places the most full of flies. In it water is drawn for the entry into the desert which comes after it. This desert is a traveling distance of ten days and there is no water in it except rarely.

1. Why did Ibn Batutta write that the village of Taghaza was insignificant?

2. Explain the economic value of Taghaza.

with goods and supplies for the journey across the desert wastelands of the Sahara. Accompanied by guards, the caravan moved at a rate of about three miles per hour, stopping at oases, or fertile areas where underground water bubbles to the surface. Three important groups of trails crossed the Sahara from North Africa to West Africa. A caravan traveling on any one of these groups

of trails might take about forty to sixty days to reach its destination.

The merchants of Ghana also played an active role in trade as they exchanged tropical products such as bananas and palm oil from the forest states of Guinea to the south. By the eighth and ninth centuries, however, much of this trade was carried by Muslim mer-

MORE ABOUT . . . *Salt*

Salt is essential to human body chemistry. It has also been widely used for the preservation of food and for flavoring. As a result, salt mining has always been a lucrative trade, even being referred to upon occasion as "white gold." The Tang dynasty derived a large portion of its tax revenues from a salt monopoly. Salt was as important to the economy of central Africa as copper and textiles. As with the Tang, African rulers often

tried to control the trade in salt. Another important location for salt mining is Salzburg, Austria, (Salzburg means "salt mountain") where salt has been mined since prehistoric times. In Salzburg, archaeologists have obtained valuable insight into earlier times from prehistoric workers who died in the mines and were preserved in the salt.

chants, who bought the goods from local traders and then sold them to Berbers, who carried them across the desert. The merchants who carried on this trade often became wealthy and lived in splendor in cities like Saleh, the capital of Ghana.

The Kingdom of Mali

The state of Ghana flourished for several hundred years. Eventually, it was weakened by wars with members of Berber tribes, and it collapsed around 1200. In its place rose a number of new trading societies. The greatest of the states that emerged after the destruction of Ghana was Mali (MALL-ee), established in the mid-thirteenth century by Sundiata Keita. Like George Washington in the United States, Sundiata is often considered the founder of his nation (see "Biography: Sundiata Keita: The George Washington of Mali"). Sundiata defeated the Ghanaians and captured their capital in 1240. This "lion prince," which is what Sundiata means, united the people of Mali and created a strong government.

Extending from the Atlantic coast inland as far as the famous trading city of Timbuktu (TIM-BUCK-TOO), Mali built its wealth and power on the gold and

salt trade. Most of its people, however, were farmers who grew sorghum, millet, and rice. The farmers lived in villages ruled by a local chieftain, who served as both a religious and administrative leader. The chieftain was responsible for sending tax revenues from the village to higher levels of government.

Much of the wealth of the country was accumulated in the cities, where the merchants lived. They were usually local people, and many of them had become Muslims. The king of Mali levied a tax on trading activities but was never able to establish a royal monopoly over key items of foreign trade. The gold trade, in particular, remained largely in the hands of local producers. They paid a tax to the king of Mali but sold their metal directly to private merchants, who then shipped it to buyers beyond the Sahara. Nevertheless, the kings of Mali had little reason to complain.

One of the richest and most powerful kings was Mansa Musa, who ruled from 1307 to 1337 (**mansa** means "king"). Mansa Musa doubled the size of the kingdom of Mali. He created a strong central government and divided the kingdom into provinces ruled by governors that he appointed. Once he felt secure, he decided—as a devout Muslim—to make a pilgrimage to Mecca. (As we saw in Chapter 8, Muslims were

▶ *Timbuktu, shown here in an 1853 engraving, was a major trading center for gold, salt, and agricultural goods. By 1550, it was a prosperous city, with three universities connected to its mosques and 180 religious schools.*

MORE ABOUT . . . *Ibn Battuta*

Ibn Battuta (1304–1368), whose writings are quoted frequently in this chapter, was an astonishing traveler. Unlike Marco Polo, who traveled with trade in mind, Ibn Battuta was chiefly interested in knowledge. His wanderings covered 75,000 miles, from Granada in Spain and the Sudan to the Golden Horde on the Russian steppe, Kilwa in Africa, through the Ottoman Empire to Samarkand, over the Hindu Kush and into India, all the way to Sumatra and China. His accounts have proven to be immensely valuable to scholars for information about the Muslim world, and he has proven to be quite reliable.

BIOGRAPHY

Sundiata Keita: The George Washington of Mali

Sundiata Keita was born with a disability in a family that had ruled Mali for about two centuries. By the age of seven, he still could not walk. With the aid of a blacksmith, however, who made braces for his legs, Sundiata gradually and painfully learned to walk. When his half-brother became ruler, Sundiata and his mother fled the kingdom because they feared they would be killed by the new ruler. In exile in the nearby kingdom of Mema, Sundiata became headman of a village, where he put together a personal army. When Mali was overrun by the kingdom of Susu, Sundiata's brothers were killed by Sumaguru, king of Susu. Sundiata marched on Susu and, supposedly with the aid of magical powers, gained victory. Sumaguru was killed. Having demonstrated his courage and leadership, Sundiata became mansa, or ruler, of Mali, which he governed from 1230 to 1255.

Sundiata went on to defeat Ghana. This conquest enabled Mali to become the chief power in West Africa. Sundiata's people praised him as a wise and strong ruler. His policy of not disturbing the local customs of people in his kingdom gained him much support. His system of justice, however, was swift and even harsh. A man convicted of stealing had his hand cut off. A person who lied had his tongue torn out. Despite the severity of

◄ *This vivid portrait of Sundiata Keita shows him armed as a warrior, dressed as a Muslim. Why do you think he was shown on horseback?*

these judgments, many of his people revered him. When Sundiata returned to his capital from a campaign, people lined the streets and cheered. Children sang:

He has come
And happiness has come
Sundiata is here
And happiness is here.

Although he became a Muslim, Sundiata kept his traditional African religion as well. This enabled him to maintain the support of the common people, who believed that the king had magical powers. As a powerful warrior-king and the creator of the kingdom of Mali, Sundiata Keita became revered as the father of his country.

1. How did Sundiata Keita become mansa of Mali?

2. Evaluate the twenty-five-year rule of Sundiata, including both positive and negative aspects of his reign.

CLASS DISCUSSION

Why might Sundiata Keita also be called "the Franklin Roosevelt of Mali"? *(Both had disabilities that impeded walking; both were from famous families; Sundiata is shown on horseback as Roosevelt was shown appearing to stand, without wheelchair or crutches.)*

CRITICAL THINKING

Besides reverence, what other reasons might Sundiata's people have had for cheering his return and for children singing a song equating his arrival with happiness? *(probably fear and intimidation given his reputation for harsh punishment and for magical powers)*

LEARNING FROM VISUALS

Answer to the caption question: Sundiata Keita's physical problems would not have been noticeable on horseback. Also, it adds to his stature and position as a military leader to be shown on horseback.

Answers to Critical Thinking Questions

1. His family had ruled Mali for two centuries, but Sundiata was forced to live in exile when his half-brother became mansa. After his brothers were killed by the king of Susa, Sundiata returned to Mali with a personal army and defeated the invaders. Because of his courageous leadership, Sundiata Keita became ruler.

SPECIAL NEEDS: *Multi-Modal/Auditory*

For students who benefit from multi-modal methods of presentation of material and also for those whom music may be a motivation for learning:

After reading and discussing the description of the Ghanaian King's court on page 259, assign students a world leader to study. (Could be famous athletes, singers, writers or television/movie stars.)

According to what the students have read or seen on video or TV, have them write, record, or draw a similar description of their subject's typical surroundings when they are in public. Factors to consider are personal protection, jewelry, clothing, significant others, cars and friends. Do these items symbolize anything to the students? What must they symbolize to those who wear or have them?

2. Student answers will vary. Under Sundiata, Mali became the chief power in West Africa. His people praised him as just and strong, even though his system of justice was quite harsh. Many people appreciated that he maintained local and traditional customs. He is revered today as the father of his country.

CLASS DISCUSSION

Guide students in a discussion of Mansa Musa's other legacy: his encouragement of architecture, literacy, and learning. Emphasize the connection between these interests and the king's religious faith.

USING PRIMARY SOURCES

Ask a volunteer to read Ibn Battuta's description of the people of Mali. Compare Battuta's comments on the kingdom's peace and order with the fact that by 1359, Mali was torn by civil war. Why might Ibn Battuta have been unaware of such potential for strife? *(Foreigners often saw only what they were permitted to see, and they interpreted what they saw based on their personal beliefs and perceptions, which were frequently different from Ibn Battuta's.)*

LEARNING FROM VISUALS

Answer to the caption question: He is the largest figure, is distinctly drawn, and the details of the crown and the uplifted arm holding the large nugget pull the eye to him.

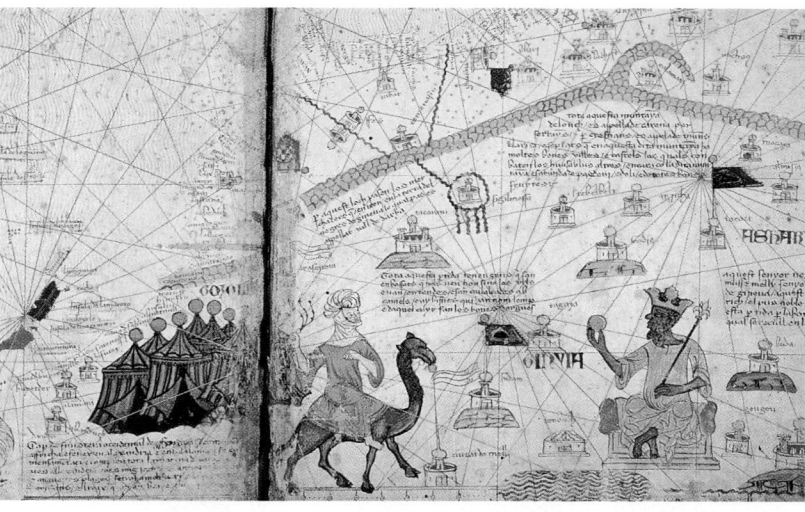

▶ *After Mansa Musa made his famous pilgrimage to Mecca, knowledge of his riches spread as far as Europe. Here he is shown seated on a golden throne holding a giant gold nugget. How does the artist make Mansa Musa the central figure in the picture?*

expected, if possible, to make a pilgrimage to Mecca at least once in their lifetimes.) A king, of course, was no ordinary pilgrim. Mansa Musa was joined by personal servants, porters, and soldiers supposedly numbering sixty thousand people altogether, although the figures are no doubt exaggerated. Accompanying the people were one hundred camels, each carrying three hundred pounds of gold. Another hundred camels bore food, clothing, and other supplies. After eight months of travel, Mansa Musa and his grand caravan reached Cairo. After a stay in Egypt, the group continued to Arabia and its destination of Mecca.

Everywhere he went, Mansa Musa lavished gold gifts on his hosts and made hundreds of purchases from merchants who hounded him along his journey. In fact, by putting so much gold into circulation in such a short time, he caused the value of gold to fall. As one observer reported, "Gold was at a high price in Egypt until they came in that year. Its value fell and it cheapened in price and has remained cheap till now. . . . This has been the state of affairs for about twelve years until this day by reason of the large amount of gold which they brought into Egypt and spent there."[4]

No doubt, Mansa Musa's great pilgrimage left people with an image of him as a great ruler of a powerful and prosperous kingdom. Mansa Musa also left another

legacy as a supporter of the Muslim faith. Earlier rulers of Mali had already converted to Islam, but Mansa Musa strongly encouraged the building of mosques and a palace, as well as the study of the Quran in his kingdom. He imported scholars and books to introduce his subjects to the message of Allah. He brought architects back with him from the Middle East to build mosques like the ones he had seen in Cairo and Arabia. The famous Sankore mosque in Timbuktu was one of the results. Sankore also became an important center of learning.

At its height in the fourteenth century, the kingdom of Mali was both stable and prosperous. Ibn Battuta, the fourteenth-century Arab traveler, was especially impressed by the peace and order in the kingdom. He said of the people of Mali,

> One of their good features is their lack of oppression. They are the farthest removed of people from it and their king does not permit anyone to practice it. Another is the security throughout the entire country, so that neither traveler there nor dweller there has anything to fear from robbers or men of violence.[5]

Mansa Musa proved to be the last powerful ruler of Mali, however. By 1359, Mali had become divided by civil war. Within another hundred years a new king-

RECOMMENDED READING

In few areas of world history is scholarship advancing as rapidly as in African history. New information is constantly forcing archaeologists and historians to revise their assumptions about the early history of the continent. Standard texts therefore quickly become out-of-date as their conclusions are supplanted by new evidence.

Still, there are several worthwhile general surveys that provide a useful overview of the

early period of African history. The dean of African historians, and certainly one of the most readable, is B. Davidson. For a sympathetic portrayal of the African people, see his *African History* (New York, 1968); and *Lost Cities in Africa,* rev. ed. (Boston, 1970). Other respected accounts are R. Oliver and J. D. Fage, *A Short History of Africa* (Middlesex, 1986); and J. M. Harris, *Africans and Their History* (New York, 1972). A more detailed interdom—that of Songhai—was beginning to surpass the kingdom of Mali.

The Kingdom of Songhai

Like the Nile in North Africa, the Niger River in West Africa floods and thus provides a rich soil for raising crops and taking care of cattle. East of Timbuktu, the river makes a wide bend. Along the river south of that bend, a people known as the Songhai established themselves. Neighboring peoples often threatened the Songhai, but they were fiercely determined to maintain their independence. In 1009, a ruler named Kossi converted to Islam and established the Dia dynasty. This first Songhai state benefited from the Muslim trade routes that linked Arabia, North Africa, and West Africa. An era of prosperity ensued with Kukya as the capital city and Gao (GAH-oh) as the chief trade center of Songhai.

Songhai, however, was soon threatened by the growing power of Mali, whose forces captured the city of Gao in 1325. After the death of Mansa Musa in 1337, several neighboring peoples attacked Mali, and it began to decline. Mali's misfortunes were Songhai's good luck. Under the leadership of Sunni Ali, who created a new dynasty—the Sunni—in 1464, Songhai began to expand.

Sunni Ali spent much of his reign on horseback and on the march as he led his army in one military campaign after another. His army had cavalry, both on horses and on camels, armed with spears and swords. It also had foot soldiers who wore padded armor and fought with spears and poisoned arrows. Two of Sunni Ali's conquests, Timbuktu and Jenne, were especially important. They gave Songhai control of the trading empire—especially the trade in salt and gold—that had made Ghana and Mali so prosperous.

In 1468, Sunni Ali conquered Timbuktu. His forces sacked the city and killed many of its inhabitants, especially Muslim leaders and scholars. After the conquest of Timbuktu, Sunni Ali gathered a navy of war canoes and blockaded the city of Jenne, located on the Niger River about 250 miles southwest of Timbuktu. After a lengthy siege, Jenne fell to Ali's forces in 1473. By having gained both Timbuktu and Jenne, Songhai now

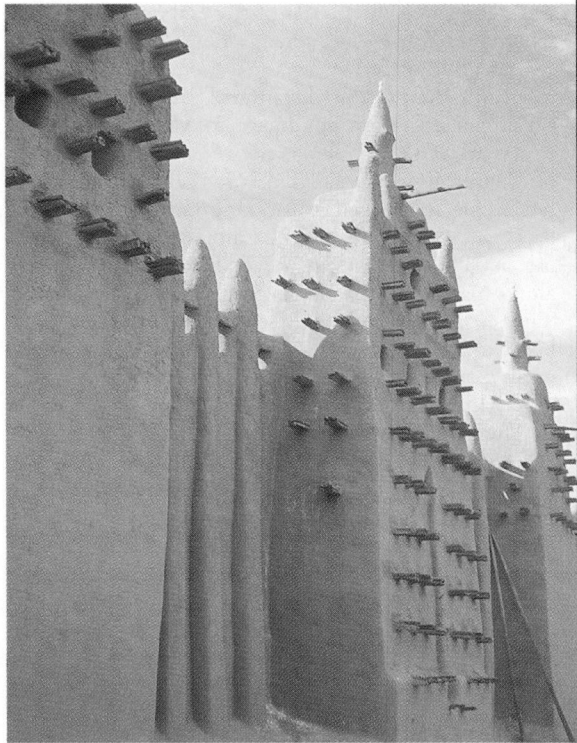

▲ *This fourteenth-century mosque built of mud bricks is located at Jenne, in current-day Mali. It stands as a tribute to Muslim influence in the western Sudan.*

controlled the trading empire that had made Ghana and Mali so prosperous. Sunni Ali died in the midst of an expedition when he was thrown from his horse and drowned in a river.

The Songhai Empire reached the height of its power during the reign of Muhammad Ture. A military commander and devout Muslim, Muhammad Ture overthrew the son of Sunni Ali and seized power in 1493, thus creating a new dynasty, the **Askia** (Askia means "usurper"). Muhammad Ture continued Sunni Ali's policy of expansion, creating an empire that stretched one thousand miles along the Niger River. He was also an able administrator who divided Songhai into provinces and appointed a governor to be in charge of each

pretation, by four respected historians, is P. Curtin, et al., *African History* (Boston, 1978). For a readable treatment embodying recent scholarly evidence, see K. Shillington, *History of Africa* (New York, 1989). For an overview

with maps and illustrations, see J. Barraclough, ed., *The Times Atlas of World History* (Maplewood, N.J., 1978); and *Past Worlds: The Times Atlas of Archaeology* (Maplewood, N.J., 1988).

CRITICAL THINKING

Ask students to explain this sentence about the decline of Mali and the rise of Songhai: "Mali's misfortunes were Songhai's good luck." *(In a competitive world led by warrior-kings, the downfall of a rival state would allow a new state to gain prominence, removing an enemy from the scene.)*

CLASS DISCUSSION

Ask students to explain the importance of Sunni Ali's capture of both Timbuktu and Jenne. *(gave Songhai control of trading empire that had benefitted Ghana and Mali)*

Multimedia Support

 LASERDISC
City of Agadez
Niger

CLASS DISCUSSION

What were the accomplishments of Muhammad Ture? *(expanded empire; was able administrator; devout Muslim who made notable pilgrimage to Mecca; supported learning and scholarship)*

ASSESS

Possible assessments include:

1. Section Review Questions on this page
2. Section 9–2 Quiz in your Teacher Resource materials
3. Reteaching Worksheets in your Teacher Resource materials
4. Self-Study software

Answers to SECTION REVIEW

2. (a) rulers free to govern without any laws
(b) king
(c) "usurper," dynasty of Muhammad Ture

3. (a) nomadic people whose camel caravans became known as the "fleets of the desert"
(b) considered the founder of Mali, which was established in the mid-thirteenth century after a defeat of Ghana
(c) one of the most powerful kings of Mali who did much for the expansion of the Muslim religion
(d) famous mosque in Timbuktu, built during the rule of Mansa Musa
(e) leader of Songhai who greatly expanded the size of his kingdom
(f) ruled the Songhai Empire at the height of its power

4. The cities of Timbuktu and Jenne were important trade centers, especially for gold and salt. Capture of these cities meant that Sunni Ali could control the trading empire.

5. Answers will vary.

CLOSE

Guide students in a discussion of the impact of powerful personalities such as Sundiata Keita, Mansa Musa, Sunni Ali, and Muhammad Ture on a society and culture, and on the history of a region.

---

one. The three chief cities of the empire—Gao, Timbuktu, and Jenne—prospered as never before from the salt and gold trade.

Unlike Sunni Ali, Muhammad Ture was a devout Muslim. He made a pilgrimage to Mecca that lasted two years. Although it was not as extravagant as that of Mansa Musa, Muhammad Ture's pilgrimage made a noticeable impression as the king moved in a stately procession with an armed guard of 1,500 men. Carrying 300,000 gold pieces, he bought and gave freely along his journey. As a devout Muslim, Muhammad Ture also supported Islamic scholars and restored Timbuktu as a center of Islamic learning. At Sankore University, students learned astronomy, medicine, logic, music, literature, and mathematics.

After Muhammad Ture's death in 1538, Songhai entered a period of slow decline. Near the end of the sixteenth century, that decline quickened when the forces of the sultan of Morocco occupied much of Songhai. One observer wrote, "From that moment on, everything changed. Danger took the place of security, poverty of wealth. Peace gave way to distress, disasters, and violence." By 1600, the Songhai Empire was little more than a remnant of its former glorious self.

❁ SECTION REVIEW ❁

1. **Locate:**
   (*a*) Ghana,   (*b*) Mali,   (*c*) Timbuktu,   (*d*) Songhai

2. **Define:**
   (*a*) absolute rulers,   (*b*) mansa,   (*c*) Askia

3. **Identify:**
   (*a*) Berbers,   (*b*) Sundiata Keita,   (*c*) Mansa Musa,   (*d*) Sankore mosque,   (*e*) Sunni Ali,   (*f*) Muhammad Ture

4. **Recall:** Why was the capture of the cities of Timbuktu and Jenne by Sunni Ali so important?

5. **Think Critically:** Do you think African civilizations and peoples would have developed in the same way if the camel had not been brought to Africa from Asia? Explain your answer.

STATES AND STATELESS SOCIETIES IN EASTERN AND SOUTHERN AFRICA

In eastern and southern Africa, a variety of states and small societies took root. Islam strongly influenced many of them. Some became extremely wealthy as a result of trade.

East Africa and the Indian Ocean Trade

South of Axum, along the shores of the Indian Ocean and in the inland plateau that stretches from the mountains of Ethiopia through the lake district of central Africa, lived a mixture of peoples. Some lived by hunting and food gathering, whereas others followed pastoral pursuits. Beginning in the first millennium B.C., new peoples began to migrate into eastern Africa from the west. Farming peoples who spoke dialects of the Bantu (BAN-TOO) family of languages began to move from the region of the Niger River into East Africa and the Zaire River basin. They moved slowly, not as invading hordes but as small communities. Today Bantu-speaking peoples live throughout the entire region of central Africa south of the Sahara.

Recent archaeological work has provided us with a better idea of the nature of Bantu society. The communities that arose as a result of these population movements were based on **subsistence farming** (growing just enough crops for personal use, not for sale). The primary crops were millet and sorghum, along with yams, melons, and beans. The land was farmed with both iron and stone tools; ironworking may have been practiced as early as the seventh century B.C. Some people kept domestic animals such as cattle, sheep, goats, or chickens. Because the population was small and land was abundant, most settlements were small, with each village serving as a self-sufficient political and economic unit.

Within the families in the villages, men and women performed different tasks. Women tilled the fields and cared for the children. Men tended the herds or

---

ENRICHMENT ACTIVITY

Ask students to research the travels and experiences of Marco Polo and Ibn Battuta, using their textbook and outside sources. The information should include excerpts from Polo's and Battuta's writings. Then ask students to compare the travels, motives, experiences, and reliability of the two writers. One source of information on Ibn Battuta might be **http://www.cs.utk.edu/~basoglu/history/battuta.html**

Map 9.4   Early States in Africa

Early states and their spheres of influence

engaged in such tasks as hunting and trade. Most trade was local and involved necessities such as salt and commodities such as animal products, copper, and iron ore.

On the eastern fringe of the continent, the Bantu-speaking peoples gradually began to take part in the regional trade that moved by sea up and down the East African coast. With the growth in regional trade following the rise of Islam during the seventh and eighth centuries A.D., the eastern coast of Africa became an important part of the trading network throughout the Indian Ocean. Beginning in the eighth century, Mus-

lims from the Arabian peninsula and the Persian Gulf began to settle at ports along the coast and on the small islands scattered up and down the coast.

The result was the formation of a string of trading ports that included Mogadishu (MOG-uh-DEE-shoo) (today the capital of Somalia), Mombasa, and Kilwa in the south. Merchants in these cities grew very wealthy, as evidenced by their lavish stone palaces. One of the most magnificent cities of the day was Kilwa. In the fourteenth century, two monumental buildings were constructed in Kilwa of coral cut from the cliffs along the shore. Blocks of coral were joined together with a cement made by burning the coral itself. Far grander than the Great Mosque of Kilwa was the Husuni Kubwa palace, an enormous clifftop building of more than a hundred rooms. Members of Kilwa's wealthy elite built their houses of coral blocks near the palace and Great Mosque. Adorned with the Chinese porcelain they had imported and complete with indoor plumbing, the homes of the rich provided a luxurious lifestyle. The Arab traveler Ibn Battuta called Kilwa, which he visited in 1331, "one of the most beautiful and well-constructed towns in the world."[6] Kilwa's splendor did not last long, however. Even before the Portuguese arrived in 1505, Kilwa had begun to decline. The Portuguese finished the job by sacking the city and destroying its major buildings.

Intermarriage between the Arab immigrants and the local population was common in East African coastal areas. However, a distinct Arab community, made up chiefly of merchants, continued in many areas. The

3

FOCUS

OBJECTIVES

After completing this section, students should be able to

1. list what archaeologists have discovered about Bantu society
2. explain what subsistence farming is
3. name the three important trading ports along the eastern coast of Africa
4. explain what stateless societies were
5. describe Great Zimbabwe and explain its importance

FOCUS ACTIVITY

Be sure students understand what is meant by a stateless society. Ask them to speculate on why states formed somewhat more slowly in the southern half of the African continent than in the north. (*possibly because this area is more remote, less desirable as a focus of conquest, further from established trade routes*) Record class hypotheses on a chart.

Multimedia Support

TRANSPARENCY
9–3, Trade Routes from East Africa to China

STUDYING MAPS

The following questions and activities will help you guide students through their study of Map 9.4.

1. What is a sphere of influence? (*area under the control of a particular ruler or government*) With your finger, trace the spheres of influence of Benin, Ghana, Songhai, Hausa, Kongo, Zimbabwe, Axum, Adal.

Which looks to be the largest? (*Songhai and/or Hausa*)

2. Find the trading ports of Mogadishu, Mombasa, and Kilwa. How did Kilwa exploit its coastal location to build monumental buildings? (*used coral*)

3. Locate the Niger and Zambezi rivers. Which river appears to be longer? (*Niger R.*)

REINFORCING VOCABULARY

Discuss the following terms to be certain students understand them: inter-marriage *(marriage between members of different groups)*, *mixed heritage (family descending from different groups)*, *elites (socially superior or powerful groups)*, *commerce (business)*, *artifacts (a usually hand-made object, such as a tool or ornament, representing a culture)*

LEARNING FROM VISUALS

What clues might historians and archaeologists glean from religious structures such as the Great Mosque at Kilwa? *(a culture's gods and mythology, building materials and methods, use of ornament and decoration, objects of reverence and of scorn, differences and similarities with other cultures, values and moral standards)*

Answer to the caption question: The upturned roof and series of windows resemble Chinese pagodas, not the native buildings.

CLASS DISCUSSION

Discuss with students the mixture of African and Arabian cultures that became known as Swahili.

ACROSS THE CURRICULUM

Language Arts. Assign volunteers to research the structure of the Swahili language. Ask them to teach the class several Swahili words and expressions.

◄ *As Islam spread in Africa, so did the number of mosques, and over time they became as ornate as some in Iran and Iraq. The Great Mosque at Kilwa, shown here, has given historians many clues about the life and prosperity of Africa's east coast.*

► *Wealthy merchants in Mombasa built stone palaces, shown here, some of which are still standing today. Ivory and gold were shipped as far away as China. What evidence do you see in this picture that would support the idea that merchants knew about China?*

ivory, spices, and slaves in return for textiles, manufactured articles, and weapons. The quality of the relations apparently varied, and the coastal merchants sometimes resorted to force to obtain goods from the inland peoples. A Portuguese visitor observed that "the men of [Mombasa] are often at war and but seldom at peace with those of the mainland, and they carry on trade with them."

As time passed, a mixed African-Arabian culture, eventually known as Swahili (swaw-HEE-lee), began to emerge throughout the coastal area. Intermarriage was common among the ruling groups, and the Muslim religion and Middle Eastern architectural styles gradually became part of a society still largely African. The term *Swahili* (from *sahel*, meaning "coast" in Arabic, and thus "peoples of the coast") was also applied to the major language used in the area. Swahili was a mixed language that combined Bantu with a number of Arabic words and phrases. Today it is the national language of Kenya and Tanzania (TAN-zuh-NEE-uh).

members of the ruling class were often of mixed heritage but usually traced their family backgrounds to Arab or Persian ancestors. Goods such as ivory, gold, and rhinoceros horn were exported to countries as far away as China. Imports included Indian glassware and textiles, as well as Chinese porcelain. Trading activities brought considerable prosperity to the area—or at least to the elites.

Most of these coastal city-states were self-governing, although sometimes several towns were grouped together under a single ruler. Government revenue came chiefly from taxes imposed on commerce. Some trade went on between these coastal city-states and the peoples of the interior, who provided gold and iron,

States and Stateless Societies in South Africa

In the southern half of the African continent, from the great basin of the Zaire River to the Cape of Good Hope, states formed somewhat more slowly than in the north. Until the eleventh century A.D., most of the peoples in this region lived in what are sometimes called **stateless societies.** A stateless society was a group of independent villages that were organized by clans and ruled by a local chieftain or clan head. Beginning in the eleventh century, in some parts of southern Africa, these independent villages gradually began to consolidate. Out of these groupings came the first states.

ENRICHMENT ACTIVITY

The modern descendants of the stone sculptors of Great Zimbabwe, the Shona people, are becoming internationally famous for their unique sculptures, developed without reference to Western art movements (due to the former Rhodesia's geographical and political isolation during the 1960s and 1970s) or to their ancestors' sculptures, which have only recently begun to return to Zimbabwe from Europe and other places.

Ask students interested in art to research Shona sculpture and to bring pictures or illustrations for the class to examine. Ask the students also to find pictures of the eight large, hand-carved soapstone birds from Great Zimbabwe that were recently restored to Zimbabwe and that once surrounded the Queen's enclosure. (These birds are the national symbol of Zimbabwe.) Compare these carvings with the contemporary work.

In the grassland regions immediately to the south of the Zambezi (zam-BEE-zee) River, a mixed economy of farming, cattle herding, and trade had begun to develop during the early centuries of the first millennium A.D. Villages in this area were usually built inside walls to protect the domestic animals from wild animals at night. The most famous of these communities was Zimbabwe. It was favorably located on a high plateau that provided fertile land and adequate rainfall for farming. Not far away were the gold fields. From about 1300 to the middle of the fifteenth century, Zimbabwe was the most powerful and prosperous state in the region. It prospered from the gold trade with the Swahili trading communities on the eastern coast. Zimbabwe's gold even ended up in the court of Khubilai Khan, emperor of China.

The ruins of Zimbabwe's capital, known as Great Zimbabwe, provide a good illustration of the kingdom's power and influence. Modern visitors generally agree that the ruins are the most impressive archaeological site in southern Africa. Great Zimbabwe was well placed to benefit from trade between the coast and the interior. The town sits on a hill overlooking the Zambezi River. The Great Enclosure, whose exact purpose is not known, dominated the site. It was an oval space surrounded by a wall eight hundred feet long, seventeen feet thick, and thirty-two feet high. Near the Great Enclosure were smaller walled enclosures that contained round houses built of a mudlike cement on stone foundations. Common people lived in small, unwalled villages in huts made of dried mud with thatched roofs. The entire town may have held ten thousand residents. In the valley below is the royal palace surrounded by a stone wall thirty feet high. Artifacts found at the site include household items and ornaments made of gold and copper, as well as jewelry and even porcelain imported from China.

The massive walls of Great Zimbabwe are unusual. The local people used granite blocks found nearby for building. Like the Inca in South America, they stacked these blocks without mortar to build solid walls.

Most of the king's wealth came from two sources: the ownership of cattle and the king's ability to levy heavy taxes on the gold that passed through the kingdom en route to the coast. By the middle of the

▲ *Great Zimbabwe was once the capital of a prosperous state in southern Africa. Its thirty-foot-high walls, shown here, were the first in Africa to be built without mortar. Why would Europeans have difficulty accepting this proof that advanced civilization existed at Zimbabwe?*

fifteenth century, however, the city was abandoned, possibly because of damage to the land through overgrazing or natural disasters such as droughts and crop failures. With the decline of Zimbabwe, the focus of economic power began to shift northward.

 SECTION REVIEW ❀

1. **Locate:**
   (*a*) Niger River,   (*b*) Arabian peninsula,
   (*c*) Mogadishu,   (*d*) Cape of Good Hope,
   (*e*) Zambezi River,   (*f*) Zimbabwe,   (*g*) Ethiopia

2. **Define:**
   (*a*) subsistence farming,   (*b*) stateless societies

3. **Identify:**
   (*a*) Swahili,   (*b*) Khubilai Khan

On Line with

WORLD HISTORY *Internet Activity*

You may want to have your students visit the following URL, where they will find information and additional web site resources to enhance their study of this chapter.
   The Diaspora
http://www.ubp.com/The_Diaspora/

At this site you will find a set of links to both modern and ancient African culture.
   Due to the ever-changing nature of the World Wide Web, see the West History web site, **http://history.swpco.com** for regular updates of the URLs in this text.

Multimedia Support

 LASERDISC
Video: The Ruins of Great Zimbabwe

CRITICAL THINKING

Why do you think many Europeans persisted in dismissing African achievements such as Great Zimbabwe as either not African or as "primitive," unworthy of serious regard? *(Racism was widespread and ran deep; such attitudes excused the plunder of African artifacts by late-nineteenth century treasure seekers; such attitudes helped justify African slavery in North America.)*

LEARNING FROM VISUALS

Answer to the caption question: Europeans tended to think that their civilization was the only advanced one in the world.

Answers to SECTION REVIEW

2. (a) growing enough crops for personal use, not for sale
   (b) independent villages organized by clans and ruled by a local chieftain or clan head

3. Identify:
   (a) a mixed African-Arabian culture that emerged throughout the coastal area; the language combines Bantu with a number of Arabic words and phrases; national language of Kenya and Tanzania.
   (b) emperor of China

4. farming, cattle herding, and trade

5. Answers will vary but might mention the placement of the city (it benefited from trade between the coast and the interior); the royal palace is surrounded by a 30-feet high stone wall; artifacts include items of gold, copper and imported items from China.

ASSESS

You can choose from a variety of assessments to evaluate your students' mastery of the objectives for this section, as stated on page 267. Possible assessments include:

1. Section Review questions on this page
2. Section 9–3 Quiz in your Teacher Resource materials
3. Reteaching Worksheets in your Teacher Resource materials
4. Self-Study software

CLOSE

Guide students in a discussion of the important connections and contacts between Arab and African cultures in eastern and southern Africa. Note especially the impact on families, language, religion, and architecture.

FOCUS

OBJECTIVES

After completing this section, students should be able to

270

4. Recall: On what was the economy of the grasslands south of the Zambezi River based?

5. Think Critically: How do the ruins of the city of Great Zimbabwe show the power and influence the city once had?

AFRICAN SOCIETY AND CULTURE

It is not easy to make generalizations about society and culture in the early period of African history. Africa was a vast continent with many different cultures and languages; different practices took place in different areas. Moreover, few written records are available, because most African societies did not have written languages. The few records that are available come from the reports of foreign visitors, such as Arab travelers. Those reports provide much information, but the visitors usually saw things from their own perspectives and only came into contact with the wealthy and the powerful. The visitors' accounts do not tell us much about the lives of ordinary people.

Aspects of African Society

African towns often began as fortified walled villages and gradually grew into larger communities serving several purposes. These towns were the centers of government, and the teeming markets were filled with goods from faraway regions. They were also home to artisans skilled in metalworking, woodworking, pottery making, and other crafts, as well as farmers who tilled the soil in the neighboring fields.

The relationship between the ruler and the merchant class in West Africa was different from that in most Asian societies, where the royal family and the aristocracy were largely isolated from the rest of the people. In Africa, the gulf between the king and the common people was not as great. Frequently, the ruler would hold an audience to allow people to voice their complaints.

Nevertheless, the king was still held in a position high above all others. In wealthier states, the walls of the audience chamber would be covered with sheets of beaten silver and gold. The king would be surrounded by hundreds of armed soldiers and some of his trusted advisors. As described by the Arab Ibn Battuta, an audience must have been an awesome experience:

> The blacks are the most humble of men before their king. . . . When he calls one of them while he is in session the man invited takes off his clothes and wears patched clothes, takes off his turban, puts on a dirty cap, and goes in raising his clothes and trousers up his legs half-way to his knees. He advances with humility looking like a beggar. He hits the ground with his elbows, he hits it hard. He stands bowed, listening to what the king says. When one of them speaks to the king and he gives him an answer, he removes his clothes from his back and throws dust on his head and back, as a person does when bathing with water. I used to wonder how they do not blind their eyes.[7]

The close relationship between king and subject in many African states helped both sides. The merchants received honors and favors from the king, and the king's treasury was filled with taxes paid by the merchants. It was certainly to the benefit of the king to maintain law and order in the kingdom so that the merchants could practice their trade.

Lineage and Family

Few Africans, of course, ever had an audience with their kings. Most African people lived in small villages in the countryside. Their sense of identity was determined by their membership in an extended family and a lineage group. At the basic level was the extended family made up of parents, children, grandparents, and other family dependents. They lived in small, round huts made of packed mud and topped with a thatch roof. In most African societies, these extended family units would in turn be combined into larger communities known as **lineage groups.**

The lineage group was similar in many respects to the clan in China or the caste system in India. All members of the group could claim to be descended

RECOMMENDED READING

For more detailed information on East Africa, see D. Nurse and T. Spear, *The Swahili: Reconstituting the History and Language of an African Society, 800–1500* (Philadelphia, 1985). For the larger picture, see K. N. Chaudhuri, *Trade and Civilization in the Indian Ocean: An Economic History from the Rise of Islam to 1750* (Cambridge, 1985). On the early history of Ethiopia, see the classic work by S. H. Sellassie, *Ancient and Medieval Ethiopian History* (1972); and J. D. Fage and R. Oliver, eds., *The Cambridge History of Africa,* vol. 4 (Cambridge, 1977–1985).

For useful general surveys of southern Africa, see N. Parsons, *A New History of Southern Africa* (New York, 1983); and K. Shillington, *A History of Southern Africa* (Essex, 1987), a profusely illustrated account.

◄ *Africans lived in simple round, thatched huts, and family groups and tribes lived in relative isolation. Why do you think the population was so sparse in southern Africa?*

from a real or legendary common ancestor. An important concept of lineage is that it includes generations not yet born, as well as past and present members. Lineage groups, then, served as the basic building blocks of African society. As in China, the elders—the leading members of the lineage group—had much power over the other people in the group. A lineage group provided mutual support for all its members. Members of extended families and lineage groups were expected to take care of one another.

The Role of Women

Women were usually subordinate to men in Africa, as they were in most early societies around the world. In some cases, they were valued for the work they could do or for their role in having children, thus increasing the size of the lineage group. Women often worked in the fields while the men of the village tended the cattle or went on hunting expeditions. In some communities, the women were merchants. In one area in southern Africa, young girls, because of their smaller size, were sent into the mines to extract gold.

There were some key differences between the role of women in Africa and elsewhere, however. In many African societies, lineage was based on the mother rather than the father; in other words, these were **matrilineal societies** (societies in which descent is traced through the mother) rather than **patrilineal societies** (societies in which descent is traced through the father). As one Arab traveler noted, "A man does not pass on inheritance except to the sons of his sister to the exclusion of his own sons." The traveler said he had never encountered this custom before. Women were often permitted to inherit property, and the husband was often expected to move into his wife's house.

Slavery

When we use the term *African slavery*, we usually think of the period after 1500, when European slave ships carried millions of Africans in bondage to Europe or the Americas (see Chapter 16). Slavery, however, did not begin with the coming of the Europeans, and it was not unique to Africa. Like many other societies throughout the world, slavery had been practiced in Africa since ancient times and continued into the early period of state building.

Berber tribes in North Africa regularly raided farming villages south of the Sahara for captives. They were then taken northward and sold throughout the Mediterranean. Some became soldiers, whereas others

---

SPECIAL NEEDS: *Auditory*

Although African music varied from one society to another, much of its purpose remained the same. Discuss with students the characteristics and purposes of African music (page 274). Make a T-chart on the overhead. One column should be African music, and the other should be Modern Popular Music. List the characteristics and purposes of each underneath the appropriate column.

Have students tell you what is the same and what is different between the two societies' music. Are there places where traditional African music still exists? It is possible to find recordings to play for contrast with a popular song of today. How does our society use music 1) to motivate, 2) to excite, 3) to tell a story, 4) to relax? What are the students' favorite songs or types of music? Why?

---

1. discuss the importance of lineage groups in African society
2. describe the various roles assigned to African women
3. discuss slavery in Africa
4. list several religious beliefs in traditional Africa
5. explain the religious and social purposes of African music and dance

LEARNING FROM VISUALS

Answer to the caption question: The land was dry and barren and could not support large populations.

USING PRIMARY SOURCES

Ask students to write their own description of the audience between king and subject (page 270), this time from the point of view of the subject. What might the man have been thinking and feeling as he went through the rituals that showed humility?

CRITICAL THINKING

Ask students to speculate as to why many African societies were matrilineal, rather than patrilineal. What might such a system say about a culture's religion and their view of humans' place in the world?

COMPARING TIME PERIODS

Students may have been surprised to learn that slavery was common in Africa, as it was in many parts of the world. Ask students to list differences they see between African slavery of the period and the institution of African slavery in Europe and the Americas.

TRANSPARENCY
9–4, Religions of
Africa

REINFORCING VOCABULARY

Check students' understanding of vocabulary by asking them to use each of the following terms in a sentence: appease (calm, pacify), derived (have origin in), suppressed (silenced, banned), pacified (appeased, calmed), supernatural (beyond the natural world), bountiful (plentiful, generous).

CONNECTIONS
TO OUR WORLD

REINFORCING VOCABULARY

Ask students if they remember from an earlier chapter the term for religions that teach the worship of one god (monotheism). Many gods? (polytheism) Ask students if they think the Yoruba religion as described would be considered mono- or polytheistic? How would they characterize Catholicism?

CRITICAL THINKING

Ask students to speculate on the reasons why Castro suppressed Santeria. (Answers will vary.)

CLASS DISCUSSION

Tell students that Santeria is very popular in the Caribbean. Ask students what impact they think the Caribbean region has on the U.S. (reggae music).

---

were used as domestic servants in the homes of the well-to-do. The use of captives for forced labor or for sale was also common in African societies further south and along the coast of East Africa. In traditional Africa, slaves included people captured in war, debtors, and some criminals. They were not necessarily seen as inferior but rather might be trusted servants and even be respected for their special knowledge or talents.

Life was difficult for most slaves. Those who worked on plantations owned by the royal family or other wealthy landowners worked hard, long hours. Those enrolled as soldiers were sometimes better off. At least in Muslim societies in the Middle East, slaves might at some point win their freedom. Many slaves were used in the royal household or as domestic servants in private homes. In general, these slaves usually had the best existence. Their living conditions were often decent and sometimes were almost the same as those of the free individuals in the household.

Religious Beliefs in Traditional Africa

Early African religious beliefs varied from place to place. Most African societies shared some common religious ideas. One of these was a belief in a single creator god. The Yoruba (YAR-uh-buh) peoples in Nigeria, for example, believed that their chief god sent his son Oduduwa down from Heaven in a canoe to create the first humans. The Yoruba religion was practiced by many of the slaves transported to the Americas.

Sometimes, the creator god was joined by a whole group of lesser gods. The Ashanti (uh-SHAN-tee) people of Ghana, for example, believed in a supreme being called Nyame, whose sons were lesser gods. Each son served a different purpose: one was the rainmaker, and another brought sunshine. Like the gods of the ancient Greeks, the Ashanti gods could not always be trusted. Humans needed to appease them to avoid their anger. Some peoples believed that the creator god originally lived on Earth but left in disgust at the behavior of human beings. However, he was also merciful and could be pacified by proper behavior.

One way to communicate with the gods was through ritual, a process usually carried out by a special class of diviners (people who believe they have the power to

---

CONNECTIONS
TO OUR WORLD

From Yoruba to Santeria   The religion of the Yoruba people in Africa was based on a belief in one supreme god. Those who followed the Yoruba religion also believed that this one supreme god gave birth to many children, known as *orishas*. Each *orisha* is virtually treated as an independent spirit-being. Those devoted to a particular *orisha* have special songs and prayers they use to worship and honor it.

When many of the Yoruba people were shipped as slaves to the Americas, they brought their religion with them. In Cuba, they encountered the Catholic religion. Soon people began to combine elements of their native Yoruba religion with Catholic practices to form a new religious system called Santeria (Spanish for "saints"). Especially noticeable was the identification of the Yoruba *orishas* with Catholic saints to form new spirit-beings. For example, Shopana, the Yoruba god of smallpox, became associated with Saint Lazarus, who was supposedly raised from the dead by Jesus. In Santeria, followers are taught to sacrifice an animal associated with a spirit-being in order to achieve union with that spirit. Santeria also includes the use of such African practices as drumming, dancing, and singing.

After he seized power in Cuba in 1959, Fidel Castro suppressed the practice of Santeria. Many Cuban refugees took Santeria with them to the United States, where they continue to practice this unique religion that has its roots in traditional African society.

---

foretell events, usually by working with supernatural forces). Many of these diviners were employed by the king to contact the supreme god in order to guarantee a bountiful harvest or otherwise protect the interests of the ruler and his subjects.

Another key element in African religion was the importance of ancestors. Each lineage group could

---

MORE ABOUT . . . *Syncretic Religions*

Santeria is a *syncretic* religion, which means that it is a combination of different forms of belief or practice; a fusion of two or more different forms. Santeria combines elements of African religion with Catholicism. Voudun, or voodoo, which is practiced in Haiti, and Macumba from Brazil are other examples. Both are a response of Africans transported to the Caribbean to the trauma of enslavement. Both Voudun and Macumba represented a form of rebellion against the Europeans, as well as a means of comfort and support under intolerable conditions. Protestant Europeans, such as the Massachusetts Bay Puritans, would regard Santeria as witchcraft; the Salem Witch Trials began when several adolescent girls attempted a seance with the aid of Tituba, a West Indian slave.

▲ *African societies relied on traditional healers for curing the ill. Shown here is a healer trying to cure a sick woman in northern Cameroon. The woman lies on a mat surrounded by family members as the healer works.*

trace itself back to a founding ancestor or group of ancestors. Ritual ceremonies dedicated to ancestors were important because the ancestors were believed to be closer to the gods. They had the power to influence, for good or evil, the lives of their descendants. Because the gods were often seen as being aloof, people needed the dead ancestors to communicate with their deities.

Many African religions shared a belief in an afterlife. Human life, it was thought, consisted of two stages. The first stage was life on Earth. The second stage was an afterlife in which the soul floated in the atmosphere throughout eternity. Ancestral souls would live on in the afterlife as long as the lineage group continued to perform rituals in their names.

Such beliefs were challenged, but not always replaced, by the arrival of Islam. Islam swept rapidly across the northern coast of Africa in the wake of the Arab conquest. It was slower to penetrate the lands south of the Sahara. The process probably began as a result of trade, as merchants introduced Muslim beliefs to the trading states in the areas south of the desert. At first, conversion took place on an individual basis. The rulers at first did not convert to Islam themselves, although they welcomed Muslim merchants and did not try to keep their subjects from adopting the new faith. The first rulers to convert to Islam were the royal family of Gao at the end of the tenth century. By the end of the fifteenth century, much of the population in the grasslands south of the Sahara had accepted Islam.

The process was even more gradual in East Africa. As Islam spread southward, it was adopted by many lowland peoples. It had less success in the mountains of Ethiopia, where, as we have seen, Christianity continued to win adherents. Islam was first brought to the coast of East Africa by Muslim merchants from Arabia, but it did not win many adherents there until the twelfth and thirteenth centuries. At that time, Swahili culture emerged, and many members of the upper class converted to the Muslim faith.

In some ways, of course, the beliefs of Islam were in conflict with traditional African beliefs and customs. Islam's rejection of spirit worship ran counter to the beliefs of many Africans and was often ignored in practice. Likewise, Islam's insistence on the separation of men and women —women were required to cover their bodies to avoid giving temptation to men—was contrary to the relatively informal relationships that prevailed in many African societies. Thus, this practice was slow to take root. As elsewhere, in Africa imported ideas were combined with native beliefs to create a unique brand of Africanized Islam.

African Culture

In early Africa, as in much of the rest of the world at the time, the arts—whether painting, literature, or music—were a means of serving religion. A work of art was meant to express religious convictions.

The earliest art forms in Africa were rock paintings. The most famous examples are in the Tassili Mountains in the central Sahara. These paintings, some of which date back as far as 4000 B.C., show the life of the peoples of the area as they shifted from hunting to cattle herding and eventually to trade. Some of the later

ACROSS THE CURRICULUM

Art. Research the sculpture of the Nok, Ife, or Benin peoples. Explain to the class, for example, how most Benin art was made to glorify the ruler, called the *oba,* who was believed to be divine. Benin also had artists' guilds, whose work was produced largely at the request of the oba or a member of the oba's court.

LEARNING FROM VISUALS

Answer to the caption question: Cave paintings have been found in the Dordogne area of France and in North America.

COMPARING TIME PERIODS

Invite students to compare African music or dance to African American music or dance (or, more broadly, to mainstream American music or dance). What are the similarities? What are the differences?

CLASS DISCUSSION

Guide students in a discussion about how music served to transmit legends and traditions through the generations in Africa, in the absence of written languages. How does this function compare with the uses of, say, American folk music?

▲ *These rock paintings, some of which date from 4000* B.C., *give evidence that early societies existed in the Sahara, supporting themselves by farming, hunting, and herding animals. In what other continents have archaeologists found cave paintings such as these?*

paintings depict the two-horse chariots used to transport goods prior to the introduction of the camel.

More familiar are African wood carvings and sculpture. Wood carvers throughout Africa made remarkable masks and statues. The carvings often represent gods, spirits, or ancestral figures and were believed to embody the spiritual powers of the subject. Terra-cotta and metal figurines served a similar purpose. For example, the impressive terra-cotta human figures and human heads found near the city of Nok in northern Nigeria are believed to have had religious significance. The Nok peoples of the Niger River produced a flourishing culture from 500 B.C. to A.D. 200 In fact, the Nok culture is the oldest known culture in West Africa to have created sculpture.

In the thirteenth and fourteenth centuries, metalworkers at Ife, in what is now southern Nigeria, produced handsome bronze and iron statues. The Ife sculptures, in turn, may have influenced artists in Benin in West Africa, who produced equally impressive works in bronze during the same period. The

Benin sculptures include bronze heads and figures of various types of animals that can be rivaled only by the sculptures of the Chinese (see "Our Artistic Heritage: The Metalwork of Ife and Benin").

Like wood carving and sculpture, African music and dance often served a religious purpose. African dancing, with its heavy rhythmic beat that has strongly influenced modern Western music, was "the great popular art of the African people." The dances, however, were also a means of communicating with the spirits. The frenzied movements that are often seen in African dance were meant to represent spirits expressing themselves through humans.

African music varied from one society to another. A wide variety of instruments was used, including drums, bells, horns, flutes, and stringed instruments such as the fiddle and harp. Nevertheless, music throughout Africa had some common features. A strong rhythmic pattern was an important feature of most African music, although many different means were used to achieve the desired effect. These included gourds, pots, sticks beaten together, and hand clapping, as well as drums.

Another important feature of African music was the combining of voice, dance, and instrument into a total musical experience. Musical instruments and the human voice were often woven together to tell a story. In turn, instruments, such as a "talking drum," were often used to represent the voice. Choral music and individual voices were frequently used in a pattern of repetition (not unlike rap music today). The soloist's part changed while the choral response, uttered by the audience, consisted of a single phrase repeated over and over.

Finally, African music served a social purpose. It was used to pass on to the young people information about the history of the community. In the absence of written languages, music served to transmit folk legends and religious traditions from generation to generation. Storytelling, usually by priests or a special class of storytellers, served the same purpose (see "Our Literary Heritage: The Art of the Griot").

No aspect of African artistic creativity is more varied than its architecture. The earliest surviving architectural form found in Africa, of course, is the pyramid.

ENRICHMENT ACTIVITY

Ask students to point out the ways in which African music has influenced modern music in the United States. Have them bring in examples and be prepared to explain their reasoning to the class. Ask the students if they can trace the ways in which this music tradition traveled from Africa to the United States. Ask students to find and bring examples of Afro-Cuban or Afro-Brazilian music, or other styles from the Caribbean. Have students be prepared to present their findings to the class in brief, oral reports.

OUR ARTISTIC HERITAGE
The Metalwork of Ife and Benin

Ife was the capital of the Yoruba people in what is now southern Nigeria. By the eleventh century A.D., artists in Ife had begun to make portraits of kings and other royal figures in brass and copper. They used the lost wax method. They first carved their subjects in wax. They then covered the wax sculpture with clay and heated the clay to produce a mold. When the heated wax melted and ran out, it was replaced by molten metal. When the metal had cooled, the artist broke the mold and was left with a piece of sculpture. Sculptors in Ife produced realistic portraits that reveal very detailed features of their subjects.

It is probable that the Ife sculptures had an impact on artists in Benin, another kingdom in

This lifelike bronze sculpture of an Ife king was made during the fifteenth–sixteenth century A.D. It is probable that these statues were made for ancestor worship, but it is believed that they were made while the subjects were still alive. What features give this sculpture, which is only 14½ inches tall, a modern appearance?

This delicately carved Benin bronze head of the queen mother dates from the 1500s. The queen mother, who was revered in Benin society, might have ordered several statues like these to be placed on her altar as a memorial following her death.

southern Nigeria. Indeed, according to its own oral history, a king of Benin brought a sculptor by the name of Iguegbae from Ife to Benin to instruct the craftspeople of Benin in the lost wax method. By 1500, the West African state of Benin had expanded into a powerful empire with a highly developed official court art, especially in metalwork. Rulers were commemorated with bronze, brass, and copper sculpture, such as the stunning head of a queen mother shown here. These sculptures were intended as memorial portraits and were placed on the altars of the dead rulers by their successors. The queen mother, who claimed a special position in Benin culture, would have ordered several such pieces of sculpture. The delicate attention to detail and the graceful sense of movement of this head show the technical excellence of Benin bronze casting.

1. What was the purpose of official court art?

2. How were the metalwork artists able to capture fine details in their bronze works?

The kingdom of Kush adopted the pyramidal form from Egypt, although the pyramids at Meroe had their own unique style. They were much smaller and were topped with a flat platform rather than rising to a point. All pyramids served the same purpose, however: they were burial places for kings.

Further to the south, the kingdom of Axum developed its own architectural traditions. The elites at

---

On Line with WORLD HISTORY Internet Activity

You may want to have your students visit the following URL, where they will find information and additional web site resources to enhance their study of this chapter.

African Art: Aesthetics and Meaning
http://www.lib.virginia.edu/dic/exhib/93.ray.aa/African.html

At this site you will find electronic exhibition illustrating and explaining the aesthetics and meaning of African art.

Due to the ever-changing nature of the World Wide Web, see the West History web site, **http://history.swpco.com** for regular updates of the URLs in this text.

OUR LITERARY HERITAGE

CRITICAL THINKING

Since the "sudden and unexpected death of a griot was similar to the burning of an entire library," ask students to speculate on what a griot's normal preparation for death might include. How would a griot prepare for his eventual death? *(for example, by gradually conveying all knowledge to a successor)*

CRITICAL THINKING

Do students think our current Western culture has an oral tradition? Who are our storytellers?

Answers to Critical Thinking Questions

1. Because the early Africans had no written language, much of their early history was, and still is, lost.
2. The griot kept all the history of his village in his head. Unless he had passed everything he remembered on to others, the history would die with the griot.
3. Answers will vary.

LEARNING FROM VISUALS

Answer to the caption question: Students should understand that as stories are passed down from generation to generation, veracity is lost. Some events are emphasized, while others fade from memory.

OUR LITERARY HERITAGE
The Art of the Griot

Without written languages, early Africans used a timeworn method of remembering their traditions and history: telling stories. The griot was a special kind of storyteller, not unlike the ancient Greek poets such as Homer. The griots brought together poetry, music, dance, and drama to amuse, but also to teach, their audiences. They were more than storytellers, however. They were also historians who kept alive a people's history. Villages had griots, but so, too, did kings and noble families, who hired griots to keep a record of their achievements. A griot's tale could also be used to tell the story of a great ruler or person. Much of what we know about Sundiata Keita, for example—the founder of the kingdom of Mali—has come down to us from the oral traditions of the griot.

Griots remembered all important events in the history of a village, a king, or a people, be they battles, coronations, births, deaths, or marriages. The use of griots explains why so much of Africa's early past is unknown. The sudden and unexpected death of a griot was similar to the burning of an entire library. A complete body of knowledge was lost. When that knowledge was a people's history, it was a tragic collective loss that could never be recovered.

▲ *Because early African cultures lacked a written language, the griot was an essential part of tribal life and culture. Here he is surrounded by attentive listeners as he passes down the stories of the children's ancestors and heritage. How accurate do you think the legends passed down by griots are?*

1. Why is so much of Africa's early past unknown?

2. How was the sudden and unexpected death of a griot similar to the burning of an entire library?

3. Do you keep any written records of your personal history? Why or why not?

Axum built palaces, religious monuments, and tombs for the royal family, all made of stone. Most distinctive were the carved stone pillars, known as **stelae,** that were used to mark the tombs of dead kings. Some stood as high as a hundred feet.

In West Africa, buildings constructed in stone were a rarity until the emergence of states. Then the royal palaces, as well as other important buildings, were often built of stone or cement. The most famous stone buildings in sub-Saharan Africa are those at Great

---

CNN WORLD HISTORY UPDATES

You can update your coverage of World History topics, as well as spark lively classroom discussion and deeper understanding, by using the **CNN World History Updates.**

For assistance in using and incorporating the **CNN World History Updates** into your classroom presentations, see the *Classroom Guide.*

Zimbabwe. Built of carefully cut stones that were set in place without mortar, the great wall and the public buildings at Great Zimbabwe are an impressive reminder of the architectural creativity of the peoples of Africa.

 SECTION REVIEW

1. **Locate:**
   (*a*) Ife,   (*b*) Benin

2. **Define:**
   (*a*) lineage groups,   (*b*) matrilineal societies,
   (*c*) patrilineal societies,   (*d*) stelae

3. **Identify:**
   (*a*) Gao

4. **Recall:** What were three of the differences between the role of women in Africa and the role of women elsewhere?

5. **Think Critically:** African music and dance often served religious and social purposes. How do these purposes compare with the purposes of music in our culture? In what ways are the purposes the same? In what ways are they different?

Conclusion

Thanks to the dedicated work of a generation of archaeologists, anthropologists, and historians, we now have a much better understanding of the evolution of human societies in Africa than we did a few decades ago. The mastery of agriculture gave rise to three early civilizations in northern Africa: Egypt, Kush, and Axum. Later, new states emerged in different parts of Africa, some of them strongly influenced by the spread of Islam. Ghana, Mali, and Songhai were three flourishing trading states in West Africa. Zimbabwe, which emerged around 1300, played an important role in the southern half of Africa. The continent was also an active participant in emerging regional and global trade with the Mediterranean world and across the Indian Ocean. Although the state-building process in sub-Saharan Africa was still in its early stages com-

pared with the ancient civilizations of India, China, and Mesopotamia, in many respects the new African states were as impressive and sophisticated as their counterparts elsewhere in the world.

Because of a lack of written records, we know little about early African society and culture. We do know that the relationship between king and subjects was often less rigid in African society than in other civilizations. Family, and especially the lineage group, was the basic unit in African society. Religious beliefs in many African societies focused on various gods, nature spirits, the role of diviners, and the importance of ancestors. Africans produced a distinctive culture in wood carving, sculpture, music, and architecture.

In the fifteenth century, a new factor came to affect Africa. Fleets from Portugal began to probe southward along the coast of West Africa. At first their sponsors were in search of gold and slaves. However, when Portuguese ships rounded the southern coast of Africa by 1500, they began to seek to dominate the trade of the Indian Ocean as well. The new situation posed a threat to the peoples of Africa, whose new states would be severely tested by the demands of the Europeans.

The peoples of Africa were not the only ones to confront a new threat from Europe at the beginning of the sixteenth century. When the Portuguese sailed across the Indian Ocean, they sought to reach India, where a new empire capable of rivaling the great kingdom of the Mauryas was in the throes of creation.

Notes

1. N. Levtzion and J. F. P. Hopkins, *Corpus of Early Arabic Sources for West African History* (Cambridge, 1981), p. 80.
2. *Ibid.*, p. 21.
3. Margaret Shinnie, *Ancient African Kingdoms* (London, 1965), pp. 45–46.
4. N. Levtzion and J. F. P. Hopkins, *Corpus of Early Arabic Sources*, p. 271.
5. Said Hamdun and Noel King, eds., *Ibn Battuta in Black Africa* (London, 1975), p. 47.
6. *Ibid.*, p. 19.
7. *Ibid.*, p. 39.

USING KEY TERMS

1. lineage groups
2. mansa
3. stateless societies
4. savannas
5. Askia
6. stelae
7. patrilineal societies
8. subsistence farming
9. absolute rulers
10. matrilineal societies

REVIEWING THE FACTS

1. mild, desert, rain forest, savanna
2. on farming, then trade with ivory, gold, ebony, and slaves
3. Meroe
4. highlands of Ethiopia
5. Christianity
6. supposedly owned 10,000 horses, housed in stables, three servants for each horse
7. process of smelting iron ore
8. held enormous quantities of water, needed little food for days, could cross the desert
9. trading center and education center of Mali
10. rich, powerful, led pilgrimage to Mecca
11. Kukya and Gao
12. palace in Kilwa, more than 100 rooms
13. invasion by the sultan of Morocco, lack of cannon and gunpowder
14. to honor the king; enhance daily life; preserve a community heritage
15. captives were taken northward and sold throughout the Mediterranean
16. pass on history to young people; transmit folk legends and religious traditions

CHAPTER 9 REVIEW

USING KEY TERMS

1. Extended family units were combined into larger communities forming _____, the basic building blocks of African society.
2. _____ Musa ruled as king of Mali from A.D. 1307 to 1337.
3. Until the eleventh century A.D., most of the people in southern Africa lived in independent villages organized by clans and known as _____.
4. Broad grasslands dotted with small trees and shrubs are called _____.
5. A new dynasty called the _____, or usurper, was formed under Muhammad Ture in 1493.
6. Distinctive carved stone pillars, or _____, were used to mark the tombs of dead kings of Axum.
7. In _____ societies, inheritance and lineage is passed through the father.
8. Bantu farmers grew grains, yams, melons, and beans to feed their local communities by a system called _____.
9. The kings of Ghana were _____ who played active roles in running their kingdom.
10. Many African societies were _____, meaning that descent was traced through the mother.

REVIEWING THE FACTS

1. What are the four climate zones of Africa?
2. On what was the economy of Kush based?
3. Name the capital of Kush.
4. Where were the remains of Axum found?
5. What was the official religion of Axum?
6. In what way was the Ghanian king Kanissa'ai compared to an Egyptian pharaoh?
7. Why were the blacksmiths of Ghana so highly valued?
8. Why was the camel so important to Africa?
9. What was the importance of Timbuktu?

278

10. Why was Mansa Musa so important to Mali?
11. Name two cities of the Songhai that were part of the Muslim trade routes.
12. What was the importance of Husuni Kubwa?
13. What caused the downfall of the Songhai?
14. What purpose did the arts serve in African society?
15. What did Berber tribes in North Africa do with their captives?
16. How did African music serve a social purpose?

THINKING CRITICALLY

1. Explain how land and climate affected settlement patterns in Africa.
2. Explain the effect of Islam on traditional African societies.
3. Compare and contrast the kingdoms of Ghana and Mali.
4. Explain Mansa Musa's impact on the value of gold in the fourteenth century.
5. Compare and contrast the religious beliefs in traditional Africa.
6. How did the lineage group system ensure that African society's values would be continued?
7. Explain the impact of matrilineal and patrilineal societies on the role of women.
8. Explain the role of music and dance in African society.

APPLYING SOCIAL STUDIES SKILLS

1. **Geography:** What modern day nations make up the Sahara?
2. **Economics:** Compare and contrast the economies of Kush, Ghana, Mali, and Songhai.
3. **Geography:** Locate Timbuktu on a map and explain its importance.

THINKING CRITICALLY

1. desert region was sparsely populated while grasslands were highly populated (Songhai and Mali)
2. Answers will be based on effects of Arab expansion and religion.
3. Answers will vary.
4. caused the value of gold to fall
5. Answers will vary. The Yoruba of Nigeria believed in a chief god and his son, which reflects a tie to converted Christianity. The Ashanti believed in a Supreme being and a pantheon of lesser gods.
6. The spirits of departed ancestors were guardians of tradition, values, and laws.

7. matrilineal: allow women to inherit and own property; patrilineal: goods, power, and status are passed down the male side
8. served religious, social, and esthetic purposes

APPLYING SOCIAL STUDIES SKILLS

1. Western Sahara, Mauritania, Mali, Algeria, Niger, Chad, Libya, Sudan, Egypt
2. Kush: agricultural power and trading power; Ghana: gold and salt were traded for metal goods, textiles, and horses; Mali: based on gold; Songhai: based on gold used to restore Timbuktu to an important learning center
3. learning and trading center (see map)

CHAPTER 9 REVIEW

4. **Sociology:** Explain how lineage groups affected the civilization of Africa.
5. **Government:** Explain the relationship between the ruler and the merchant class in West Africa.
6. **Geography:** Trace Muslim trade routes into Africa.
7. **Sociology:** Explain the devastating social impact of the Portuguese on coastal Africa.
8. **Economics:** Identify two trade goods that contributed to the growth of Ghana and explain how these products helped the economy.
9. **Sociology:** Explain the traditional gender roles in African society.
10. **Sociology:** Explain the African belief in the afterlife and its effect on society.

8. Compare and contrast slavery in early Africa with slavery in nineteenth-century America.
9. Compare African music with contemporary rap music in the United States.
10. Compare and contrast African stelae with Trajan's Column in Ancient Rome (see Chapter 6) and the Arc de Triomphe in Paris (see Chapter 20).

MAKING TIME AND PLACE CONNECTIONS

1. Compare the role of geography in site selection for African kingdoms with the location of major cities in the United States today.
2. Compare and contrast the Ghanaian king with an Egyptian pharaoh (see Chapter 2).
3. Compare and contrast the economic activity of Axum and Kush with the United States today.
4. In which ways can Sundiata Keita (the "George Washington" of Mali) be compared to the real George Washington of the United States?
5. Compare the construction techniques of Great Zimbabwe with the Inca (see Chapter 7) and the Egyptians (see Chapter 2).
6. In what ways can the description of Ibn Battuta be compared to your recollection of seeing new and novel things?
7. Compare and contrast the role of women in African society with their role in the United States today.

BECOMING AN HISTORIAN

Understanding and Interpreting Maps: Examine the maps on page 260 and page 267.

1. What information do the keys provide?
2. How far is it from Axum to Songhai? From Mali to Ghana?
3. Can you determine the length of the Zaire (formerly Congo) River from the map? Compare the map on page 267 with the one on page 254. Are they using the same distance scale? If not, why?

Understanding Cause and Effect: Reread the section, **The Land and Climate of Africa.** Why do people settle where they do? How do rainfall, fertile soil, great rivers, and natural resources affect settlement patterns?

Analyzing Primary and Secondary Sources: Reread **You Are There: The Salt Mines.** What insight into historical events can first-person accounts give? How valuable are first-person accounts in understanding how people at that time interpreted the events they witnessed? Under what circumstances might the writer's cultural or national background influence the recording of an event?

between the African interior and the Red Sea; Kush trade based on iron ore, ivory, gold, ebony, and slaves.
4. Answers will vary; Sundiata Keita was a warrior king, creator of the Mali Empire; George Washington was a Revolutionary War General, the first president of the U.S.
5. Answers will vary; all three used construction techniques without mortar.
6. Answers will vary.
7. Answers will vary.
8. Answers will vary.
9. "Rap": a solo backed up by rhythm; African: a solo backed up by strong rhythmic backgrounds.
10. Answers will vary.

BECOMING AN HISTORIAN

1. trade routes, distances, spheres of influence
2. refer to maps
3. refer to maps

Understanding Cause and Effect. Sahara was sparsely populated; grasslands were highly populated; (Songhai and Mali). Population in many African kingdoms was based on the amount of gold or iron ore present.

Analyzing Primary and Secondary Sources. Answers will vary.

4. guardians of tradition, values, and laws; families had to honor the traditions of lineage ancestors
5. trade to enhance their wealth as well as the wealth of the king
6. (see map)
7. Policies were to control seaboard towns, control trade, and exploit for personal gain, destroying Africans that got in the way.
8. Gold was traded for many goods; salt was used to replace bodily fluids and to preserve food stuffs.
9. Women tilled the fields and cared for the children while men tended the herds or engaged in hunting and trade.

10. shared a belief in the afterlife; soul floated in the atmosphere throughout the eternity; would live on as long as lineage group continued rituals in their name

MAKING TIME AND PLACE CONNECTIONS

1. Major cities are located on major rivers or at least at the junction of transportation. African cities were located along rivers or along trade routes.
2. Both were absolute and the Ghanaian king supposedly owned 10,000 horses.
3. Answers will vary; Axum controlled trade

279

279

10 PLANNING GUIDE

SECTION	KEY TOPICS	PRIMARY SOURCES	ASSESSMENT
1 Restoration of a Chinese Empire: The Sui, Tang and Song Dynasties pages 281–292	◆ Accomplishments of the Sui, Tang, and Song dynasties ◆ Structure in government and philosophy ◆ Organization of China's economy and society ◆ The daily life of China's people	◆ A description of preparations for the Emperor's boat, pages 281–282 ◆ A description of sea-going ships, pages 286–287 ◆ A description of the work of Pi Sheng, page 289	◆ Section Review, page 292 ◆ Section Quiz 10–1, TRB
2 The Mongol and Ming Dynasties pages 292–301	◆ Accomplishments of the Mongol dynasty ◆ Changes made during the Ming dynasty ◆ Development of the culture of China	◆ A description of Mongol military tactics, page 292 ◆ Marco Polo's description of the Great Khan, page 295 ◆ A poem about the destruction of a city, page 299	◆ Section Review, page 301 ◆ Section Quiz 10–2, TRB
3 The Emergence of Japan pages 301–307	◆ The Rise of Japan during the Nara and Heian Periods ◆ The impact of the Kamakura Shogunate on Japan ◆ The economic and social systems of early Japan		◆ Section Review, page 307 ◆ Section Quiz 10–3, TRB
4 Religion and Culture in Early Japan Pages 307–311	◆ Religious and cultural practices in Japan ◆ Art and architecture in early Japan	◆ A poem by Jakuren, page 308 ◆ The Tale of Genji, pages 309–310	◆ Section Review, page 311 ◆ Section Quiz 10–4, TRB

GOLDEN AGES IN EAST ASIA (400 TO 1500)

REPRODUCIBLE ACTIVITIES

- Historical Maps
- Charts and Graphs
- Critical Thinking
- Cooperative Learning
- Vocabulary
- Guided Reading
- Reteaching
- Enrichment
- Performance Assessment
- Spanish Key Points and Chapter Summaries
- Spanish Vocabulary
- Spanish Guided Reading

MULTIMEDIA SUPPORT

 TRANSPARENCIES
- *World History* Color Transparency Package
- Fine Art Color Transparency Package

 VIDEO
- *World History* Video Library
- **CNN.** Annual Video Update

 LASERDISC
- *Sights and Sounds of History*

 AUDIO
- *Listening to Literature* audiotape (English and Spanish)
- *History of Music* CD

 SOFTWARE
- WESTEST™
- Student Review

 CD–ROM
- *The Journey of Civilization*
- *World History*

 INTERNET
- Internet Activities

On Line with WORLD HISTORY

Access West's history web site at **http://history.swpco.com**
You'll find activities and web sites related to specific topics and chapters in *World History: The Human Odyssey*. Also look for references to helpful web sites at appropriate places throughout this teacher edition.

LESSON PLANNING

You will find detailed daily lesson plans for both traditional class scheduling and **block scheduling** in your Teacher Resource Box.

 ## Not Enough Time?

If you do not have the four or five days recommended to teach this chapter, you may want to focus on the following sections and activities:

- Have students skim the chapter to answer the "Questions to Guide Your Reading" on page 281. Discuss their answers, then read the "Conclusion" on page 311.
- Do a more in-depth reading about the Sui, Tang, and Song dynasties on pages 281–283, the Mongol and Ming dynasties on pages 292–296, the rise of the Japanese state on pages 301–304 and religion in Japan on pages 307–308. Conclude with a discussion of the importance of printing with movable type included in the "Role of Science and Technology" feature on pages 289–290.

GOLDEN AGES IN EAST ASIA
(400 TO 1500)

BUILDING ON CHAPTER 9

To prepare students to study Chapter 10 you may use the following questions and activities.

◆ Remind students that the African nations of Ghana and Mali gained wealth and power through trade. Trade was an important factor in China.

◆ Inform students that just as African states relied on farming as the backbone of their economy so did China and Japan.

◆ Discuss the fact that the gulf between kings and common people in most African states was not great.

USING THE OPENING STORY

Depending on the ability levels of your students, select from the following questions and activities to reinforce the reading of the opening story.

◆ What reasons might the leaders of China have had to invade the much less developed state of Japan?

◆ How could the relatively poor and weak states in Japan maintain their independence from foreign domination over many years?

LEARNING FROM VISUALS

Answer to the caption question: The arm muscles are knotted, the hands and fists are arranged in a threatening pose; the position of the legs suggests this warrior is ready to move.

280

In 1266, the Mongol emperor of China, Khubilai Khan, demanded that the Japanese pay tribute to China or face invasion. When the Japanese refused, the khan sent a force of thirty thousand warriors to teach the Japanese a lesson. Bad weather forced the emperor's forces to retreat, and it was not until 1281 that the Great Khan was prepared to try again. This time he sent a force of two fleets, consisting of 4,400 ships carrying almost 150,000 warriors. The Japanese appeared to be doomed. On August 15, however, just as the khan's forces were preparing to land, the sky darkened and a massive typhoon struck, battering the Mongol fleet and killing thousands. One Korean observer wrote, "The bodies of men and broken timbers of the vessels were heaped together in a solid mass so that a person could walk across from one point of land to another on the mass of wreckage." Those warriors who made it to shore were cut down by the Japanese defenders. To the Japanese, this was a sign of divine aid. They called the storm a "divine wind" (*kamikaze* [KAWM-i-KAWZ-ee]) and became convinced that they would always be protected from foreign invasion.

This great confrontation between the ancient and well-established civilization of China and the newly emerged Japanese state was but one of the events in East Asia during this period. Between 581 and 1644, five different dynasties ruled China. During each dynasty, Chinese civilization flourished. Between the dynasties, however, China experienced both civil war and disorder. Overall, however, Chinese civilization continued to build upon the political and cultural achievements of previous dynasties, making Chinese civilization one of the greatest in the world during this time.

Along the fringes of Chinese civilization, other societies were emerging. One of these was on the islands of Japan. Although China influenced Japan, the latter was able to develop its own unique civilization. The contrast between China and Japan remains one of the most complex and fascinating issues in the study of East Asian society today.

▲ *This Japanese guard was carved from wood during the Kamakura period, 1185–1333. How do the positions of the arms and legs contribute to the threatening look that we see on the face?*

ADDITIONAL RESOURCES

The resources listed below can be used to enrich the lessons in this chapter.

BOOKS FOR STUDENTS
Early Japan by Jonathan Norton Leonard. Time-Life.
Marco Polo's Adventures in China by Milton Rugoff. Horizon Caravell, Harper and Row.
Japanese Mythology by Juliet Piggott. P. Bedrick.
The Samurai by S. R. Turnbull, Macmillan.

VHS
China in Transition: 581–1279 Series: The World: A Television History, Social Studies School Service, (800) 421-4246.
The Art and Architecture of China (Clearvue) Social Studies School Service, (800) 421-4246.

CD-ROM
Cosmology of Kyoto (Dynaware/Yano Electronic). Educorp Direct. (800) 843-9497

NEW PATTERNS OF CIVILIZATION

| 400 | EAST ASIA | 1500 |
| 400 | | 1500 |

QUESTIONS TO GUIDE YOUR READING

1. What did the Sui, Tang, and Song dynasties contribute to Chinese civilization?

2. What are four significant economic and social changes that occurred during the Sui, Tang, and Song dynasties?

3. What were the major achievements of the Mongol and Ming dynasties?

4. What political practices did the Japanese copy from the Chinese?

5. What was the social structure of early Japan?

6. What were the major developments in Chinese and Japanese literature and art during the period covered in this chapter?

OUTLINE

1. RESTORATION OF A CHINESE EMPIRE: THE SUI, TANG, AND SONG DYNASTIES

2. THE MONGOL AND MING DYNASTIES

3. THE EMERGENCE OF JAPAN

4. RELIGION AND CULTURE IN EARLY JAPAN

RESTORATION OF A CHINESE EMPIRE: THE SUI, TANG, AND SONG DYNASTIES

The Han dynasty came to an end in 220, and China fell into chaos. For the next three hundred years, the Chinese suffered through disorder and civil war until 581, when a new Chinese empire was set up under a dynasty known as the Sui.

The Sui Dynasty

The Sui dynasty (581 to 618) did not last long, but it managed to unify China once again under the emperor's authority. Sui Yangdi, the second emperor of the dynasty, used forced labor to complete the 1,400-mile-long Grand Canal linking the two great rivers of China, the Huang and the Yangtze. Both rivers flowed from west to east. The new canal created a water route that linked north and south and made it easier to ship rice from the south to the north. Sui Yangdi also used the Grand Canal to keep an eye on his empire, as this seventh-century Chinese work describes:

> Moreover, the emperor caused to be built dragon boats, war boats of the "Yellow dragon" style, and multi-

281

281

FOCUS

OBJECTIVES

After completing this section, students should be able to

1. identify and explain differences and similarities among the Sui, Tang, and Song dynasties
2. explain the method and purpose of selecting government bureaucrats in the Tang and Song dynasties
3. describe changes that took place in China's economic system during the Sui, Tang, and Song dynasties
4. describe ways in which trade changed the daily lives of people in China

FOCUS ACTIVITY

Help students understand that important advancements can be made by civilizations in which most people are peasant farmers who never leave the immediate vicinity of their farms. This was the case in China and in most other ancient civilizations. Take a poll of students to find how far they have traveled from their homes. Discuss how people who never travel can still contribute to advancements in civilization.

decked transports. Boatmen hired from all the waterways pulled the vessels by ropes of green silk on the imperial progress to Yangshou. The Emperor rode in the dragon boat, and civil and military officials rode in the multi-decked transports. . . . The districts through which they passed were ordered to prepare to offer provisions. Those who made bountiful arrangements were given an additional office or title; those who fell short were given punishments up to the death penalty.[1]

Imperial processions and the execution of his subjects could not save Sui Yangdi, however. He was a cruel ruler. His use of forced labor, high taxes, an extravagant and luxurious lifestyle, and the failure of his army in Korea caused a rebellion. The emperor was murdered, and his dynasty came to an end.

The Tang Dynasty

One of Sui Yangdi's generals soon established a new dynasty, known as the Tang (TONG). The Tang dynasty lasted for almost three hundred years, from 618 until 907. Many of the Tang rulers were dynamic leaders who made the Tang one of the greatest dynasties in the long history of China.

The first rulers of a new Chinese dynasty often began their reigns by instituting reforms. The early Tang rulers were no exception. They tried to strengthen the central government by streamlining its political institutions. They restored the civil service examination from earlier times to serve as the chief method of recruiting officials for the civilian bureaucracy. The Tang rulers also tried to create a more stable economy by giving land to the peasants and breaking up the power of the owners of the large estates.

Tang rulers worked hard to restore the power of China in East Asia. They brought peace to the northwestern part of China and expanded China's control into the area north of the Himalayan Mountains—known as Tibet—for the first time. China now claimed to be the greatest power in East Asia. Neighboring states, including Korea, offered tribute to China and adopted the Chinese form of government. The Chinese imperial court also set up trade and diplomatic relations with the states of Southeast Asia (see Chapter 11).

Under the Tang, China witnessed a flowering of culture and reached a high point in poetry and painting (to be discussed later in the chapter). The city of Chang'an, now restored to the glory it had known as the capital of the Han dynasty, became the seat of the empire and possibly the greatest city in the world. Chang'an was filled with temples and palaces and had an estimated population of two million. Its markets were filled with goods from all over the known world.

Like the Han, however, the Tang sowed the seeds of their own destruction. Tang rulers were unable to curb intrigues at court and corruption by government officials. One emperor was especially unfortunate. Emperor T'ang Hsüan-tsung (TONG shoo-ON-zung) is remembered for his undying devotion to a commoner's daughter named Tang Kuei-fei (TONG GWAY-fay). It

▲ *This silk painting from the Tang dynasty shows a woman playing chess. Her beautiful silk kimono is similar to those worn by rich women who lived at court. How do you think the life of this woman, and her dress, differed from middle-class or peasant women of the same time period?*

RECOMMENDED READING

For a general history of China, see C. O. Hucker, *China's Imperial Past: An Introduction to Chinese History and Culture* (Stanford, Calif., 1975); and C. Schirokauer, *A Brief History of Chinese and Japanese Civilizations,* revised ed. (San Diego, Calif., 1989).

For the post-Han period, see A. E. Dien, ed., *State and Society in Early Medieval China* (Stanford, Calif., 1990); E. Balazs, *Chinese Civilization and Bureaucracy: Variations on a Theme* (New Haven, Conn.; 1964); and D. Twitchett and M. Loewe, *Cambridge History of China,* vol. 3, *Medieval China* (Cambridge, 1986).

For the brief Sui dynasty, see A. F. Wright, *The Sui Dynasty* (New York, 1978). For a new and exciting interpretation of the Song dynasty, see J. T. C. Liu, *China Turning Inward: Intellectual Changes in the Early Twelfth Century* (Cambridge, Mass., 1988).

TEACH

Map 10.1   China under the Tang

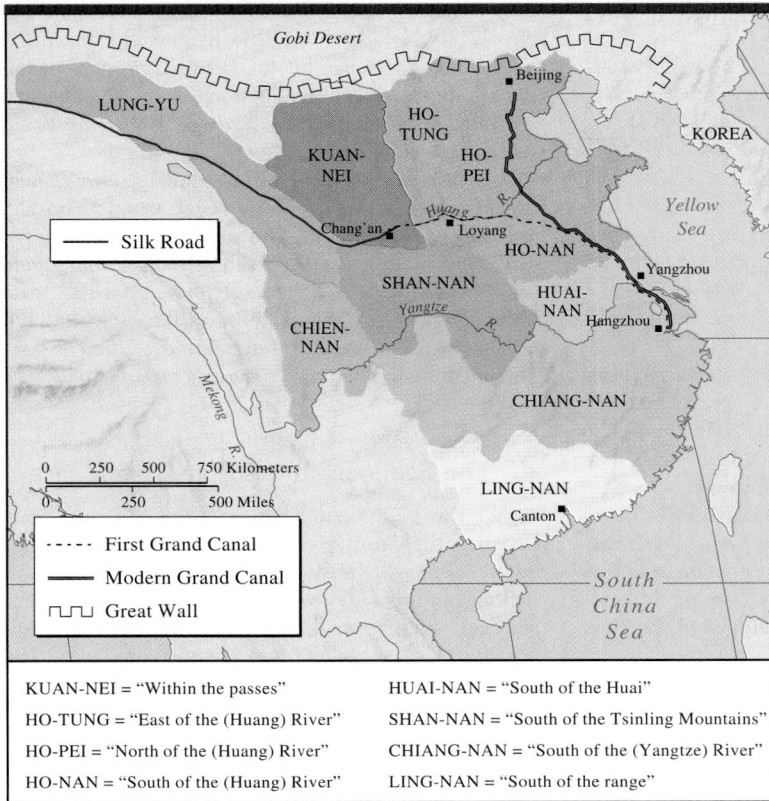

KUAN-NEI = "Within the passes"   HUAI-NAN = "South of the Huai"

HO-TUNG = "East of the (Huang) River"   SHAN-NAN = "South of the Tsinling Mountains"

HO-PEI = "North of the (Huang) River"   CHIANG-NAN = "South of the (Yangtze) River"

HO-NAN = "South of the (Huang) River"   LING-NAN = "South of the range"

Along the northern and western frontiers of China, powerful landed families ruled without even bothering to consult the Tang emperors. The end of the Tang dynasty finally came in the early tenth century. A northern tribal group known as the Uighurs (WEE-goo-urs) (a Turkic-speaking people), who were hired to fight for the Tang dynasty, turned on it instead and overthrew the government in 907. China again slipped into civil war.

The Song Dynasty

In 960, a new dynasty known as the Song (SUNG) (960 to 1269) rose to power. From the start, however, the Song ran into problems, especially from the Uighurs in northern China. The imperial court was forced to move its capital from Chang'an further south to Hangzhou (HONG-JOE), on the coast just south of the Yangtze River delta. The Song also lost control over Tibet. Despite its problems, however, the Song dynasty ruled during a period of economic prosperity and cultural achievement.

The Song dynasty could never overcome the challenge from the north, however. During its last years, the Song rulers were forced to pay tribute to the Jurchen peoples from Manchuria. Then, to stay in power, the Song formed an alliance with the Mongols, a new—and, at that time, little-known—nomadic people from the Gobi Desert. This proved to be a disaster. Within a few years, the Mongols not only defeated the Jurchen but also turned on the Song dynasty. As we shall see later, the Mongols overthrew the Song and then created a new Mongol dynasty.

is reported that in order to please his beloved, he kept hundreds of dancers and musicians at court just to entertain her. He also kept horses and riders traveling back and forth the 1,500 miles from Canton to Chang'an to bring her fresh litchi, her favorite fruit. However, when the emperor's favorite general led a bloody revolt, the army demanded that someone be held accountable for the war and strife in the country. The emperor invited his true love to hang herself from a nearby tree, although it is said that for the rest of his life, the emperor "washed his face everyday with a fountain of tears."

STUDYING MAPS

The following questions will help you guide students through their study of Map 10.1.

1. What did the Silk Road have to do with the location of the first Grand Canal? *(The Silk Road joined the first Grand Canal.)*

2. Is it likely that Beijing would have become an important city if the Great Wall had not been built? *(probably not)*

3. Why is it reasonable to argue that the location of the Modern Grand Canal is at least partially the result of the construction of the Great Wall? *(Answers will vary.)*

USING PRIMARY SOURCES

Ask students to read the description of the Emperor's boat trip to Yanghou. Do they believe that this practice was a waste of China's resources? Might it have served any practical social or political purpose?

LEARNING FROM VISUALS

Answer to the caption question: Peasant women in China worked in the fields and rice paddies; they would not have worn silk kimonos or have their hair done in such elaborate fashions.

CLASS DISCUSSION

Ask students to discuss and evaluate the following statement. Do they believe it is true? Does the experience of the Tang dynasty support it? "Wealth breeds corruption."

CLASS DISCUSSION

Ask students to discuss why states that rely on hired mercenaries to fight for them are often destroyed or, at the least, unsuccessful, in their military confrontations. Use the example of the Mongols who employed the Song rulers to oppose the Jurchen people from Manchuria. The Hessen soldiers who were hired by the British to fight in the American Revolution are another possible example.

TEACHING THEMES

Economics and History.
Assign students to make a list of new products China manufactured during the Sui, Tang, and Song dynasties. Ask them to identify and support their choice of the product they believe was most important to changing the history of China.

Multimedia Support

TRANSPARENCY
10–1, Chinese Rod and Bead Abacus Diagram

CLASS DISCUSSION

Have students think through the workings of a bureaucracy. What are the advantages of such a system? What are some disadvantages? Do they have examples of working with bureaucracies today?

CLASS DISCUSSION

Why is literacy important in a bureaucracy? Have students consider this question. Then discuss why the importance of literacy tended to keep the poor out of government jobs. *(Even with state run schools, candidates needed to be literate before they entered them.)*

The Structure of Government: The Triumph of Confucianism

The era from the Sui to the end of the Song dynasties lasted nearly seven hundred years. During that period, a mature political system based on principles first put into practice during the Qin and Han dynasties gradually emerged in China. As in the Han Era, China was a monarchy that employed what was for its time a relatively large bureaucracy to maintain an orderly government. Beyond the capital, government was based on provinces; districts; and at the lowest level, the village. State Confucianism was still the cement that held the system together.

The Tang and Song dynasties continued the effort begun by the Qin dynasty to base the appointment of officials on merit rather than heredity. A formal civil service examination was set up at several levels to recruit worthy candidates for the government bureaucracy. The court also established schools in the capital city to prepare people for the examinations. Under the Song, the civil service examination system became the chief route to an official career (see "Young People in Traditional China: Preparing for the Civil Service Examination").

Three levels of examinations were given. The first was a qualifying examination given every year. Those who passed it could take a second examination given every three years. Those who passed the second examination could apply for an official position. Some went on to take the final examination, which was also given once every three years. Those who passed it could hold the highest positions in the central government.

The Confucian classics—the works of Confucius and his followers—formed the basis of the civil service examinations. Students had to memorize passages and be able to explain the moral lessons they contained. The system made certain that those people who succeeded and became officials received a full education in Confucian political and social ethics. Whether they followed those ethics, of course, was another matter. Many students complained about a process that involved mostly memorization.

All males except criminals were allowed to take the examinations. Schools were set up to help candidates. Without such schools, only people fortunate enough to receive training in the Confucian classics in family-run schools would have been able to pass the examinations. Thus, most candidates would have come from rich families. Under the new system, families that had not previously been involved in government could participate.

Even the government schools did not always help the poor, however. Only those young people who had been given a basic education in the classics at home were able to enter the state-run schools and compete for a position in the bureaucracy. The poor had little chance. Nevertheless, despite its weaknesses, the civil service examination gave China a more efficient government staffed by a literate bureaucracy.

The Economy and Society of China

During the long period between the Sui and Song dynasties, the Chinese economy grew in size and complexity. China was still primarily a farming society. In the long period of civil war and chaos, aristocratic families had taken control of most of the land, and the majority of peasants had become serfs or slaves. The government, however, worked to weaken the power of the large landholders and to help poor peasants obtain their own land. These efforts, as well as the opening of new lands in the Yangztze valley, led to an abundance of food under the Song.

Changes were also taking place in Chinese cities. Especially dramatic was the growth in trade and manufacturing. Chinese dynasties had always controlled or limited trading activities, but several new technological developments added new products and aided the growth of trade. During the Tang dynasty, the Chinese began to make steel by a process of mixing cast iron and wrought iron. High heat was reached in the blast furnace by the burning of coal, used as a fuel in China from about the fourth century. The new steel was then used to make swords and sickles. The introduction of cotton made it possible to make new kinds of clothes. The Chinese also invented gunpowder during the Tang dynasty and used it to make explosives and a primitive form of flamethrower.

So What ⁇

*If your students question the importance of the information on **Chinese government**, tell them . . .*

The concept of a civil service exam, instituted by the Chinese nearly a thousand years before the United States began a similar system, established the concept of merit, instead of influence, as the chief requirement for a job.

Lead students in a discussion of the merits of a civil service exam. What basic qualifications should such exams establish? What type of questions would be needed to establish these qualifications? If you can obtain an example of questions from a civil service exam, analyze these with the students to determine what qualifications are being tested.

YOUNG PEOPLE IN TRADITIONAL CHINA

Preparing for the Civil Service Examination

By using the civil service examination, Tang and Song rulers sought to recruit a class of civil servants based on merit. This undermined the power of the aristocrats and created a new class of scholar-gentry.

To the sons of the scholar-gentry, the civil service examinations were crucial in gaining a civil service position and hence a government career. Consequently, preparing their sons for these examinations became very important to scholar-gentry families.

Education began at a young age. Boys began to learn to write Chinese characters at the age of four. Within three years, they were able to read a number of characters and were then expected to memorize their first work, *The Thousand Character Classic* by Confucius. This consisted of a thousand different characters, rhymed in four-character lines. Any mistake in recitation was greeted with a blow on the backside by a boy's teacher. Many more years of education consisted of memorizing other Confucian classics. Not until a work was completely memorized was a student given an explanation of the work's meaning. Over a period of many years, students memorized all of the Confucian classics.

Young men who were being educated for the civil service examinations worked hard at their studies and had little time for recreation. They were not allowed to take part in any strenuous physical activities. They could fish, which was considered a scholarly sport; play the lute; write poems; paint landscapes; and look at scenery. Stu-

▲ *From the time of the Ming dynasty, government officials wore large badges sewn onto their coats to show their ranks. There were nine different ranks, and the crane shown here signified the first rank. This badge comes from the Qing dynasty.*

dents were taught never to use their hands except for painting or writing. Manual labor was strictly forbidden.

After many years of education, young men began to take their civil service examinations. If they passed (only one in five did), they could go on to positions in the civil service. Those who failed could teach, assist officials, or hope for

(continued)

Tang and Song rulers recruited civil servants based on merit in part to undermine the power of the aristocrats. Why would they want to do this? *(a weaker aristocracy was less of a threat to the ruler's power)*

How did a bureaucracy based on merit undermine the power of the aristocracy? *(Unless the aristocracy worked as hard as the scholar-gentry to be qualified, they were shut out of the workings of government, where political power and influence lay.)*

Discuss the ingenuity of this plan. What are the political and social benefits to the rulers, the people, the scholar-gentry, and even to the aristocracy?

COOPERATIVE LEARNING ACTIVITY

History is full of governments that appointed people to political office as a reward for loyal support of rulers. A person's training or qualifications for the job had little to do with who was placed in public office. Divide students into groups and ask each group to develop a list of problems which could occur in a nation where training and qualifications are not required for public office. Discuss these lists. Then have the groups develop and support a hypothesis for why Chinese governments awarded public office to people based on civil service examinations.

COMPARING TIME PERIODS

Assign students to write an essay that explains why they believe young men in China were willing to complete the work and follow the rules of their society to prepare to take the civil service examination. Why would few young people today be willing to make the same effort?

YOUNG PEOPLE IN TRADITIONAL CHINA

Answers to Critical Thinking Questions

1. writing and reading Chinese characters; memorizing Confucian classic works; work and discipline
2. Tests were graded without graders knowing who they belonged to. This was accomplished by covering names or grading copies.
3. Government service had traditionally been performed only by sons of aristocrats. This new examination selected boys for government careers, based on their merits instead of on their heredity.

LEARNING FROM VISUALS

Answer to the caption question: Gunpowder was a Chinese invention, and these exploding rockets must have been very frightening to invaders and opponents.

YOUNG PEOPLE IN TRADITIONAL CHINA
Preparing for the Civil Service Examination, continued

family support. Because of their family connections, few starved.

During the Tang period, people complained that the choice of who would pass the test was already predetermined. In response, the Song instituted the policy of "name covering" so that the test graders would not know whose test they had. Later they required that each test be copied so that only the copies would be graded. The examiners thus could not tell from the handwriting whose test they had graded.

1. What skills were Chinese boys required to master in preparation for the civil service exams?

2. What measures were taken to prevent favoritism in the testing process?

3. How was use of the civil service examination a departure from the traditional way of placing young men in government service?

◀ *During the Song dynasty, military rockets like the one shown in this pen-and-ink drawing were developed. What do you think opponents might have thought of the Chinese rocket warfare?*

The nature of trade also changed. State officials had long carried on most long-distance trade. By the time of the Song, however, many private merchants were active in both wholesale and retail trade. Guilds (associations of merchants) began to appear, along with a new money economy (an economic system based on money rather than barter). As merchants found that strings of copper coins were too heavy for their business deals, the use of paper money began in the eighth and ninth centuries. With the increased flow of paper money, banking began to develop.

Long-distance trade, both by land and by sea, expanded. Trade with countries and peoples to the west had been carried on for centuries, but it had declined drastically between the fourth and sixth centuries as a result of the collapse of the Han dynasty and the Roman Empire. Long-distance trade began to revive with the rise of the Tang dynasty and the unification of much of the Middle East under the Arabs. The Silk Road revived and then reached its height. During the Tang, caravans of two-humped camels carried goods back and forth between China and the countries of the Middle East and South Asia.

The Silk Road was often dangerous, however, so goods were often shipped by sea. China had long been engaged in sea trade with other countries, but most of the trade was in the hands of Korean, Japanese, or Southeast Asian merchants. Better ships and the invention of the compass, however, soon increased Chinese sea trade. The Chinese governor of Canton in the early twelfth century remarked:

According to the government regulations concerning sea-going ships, the larger ones can carry several hun-

SPECIAL NEEDS: *Auditory/Tactile/Vision*

Have students read to each other about daily life, the family, and the role of women in early China (pages 287–291). Have them go to the library and look up pictures exemplifying scenes of life in China during this period (7th–8th century); some of these scenes may show the new forms of entertainment (playing cards and board games), farming, dancing, merchants, trading, ship building, villages, etc. They can then share these items with the class by making a presentation, a collage, or create a story to act out.

dred men, and the smaller ones may have more than a hundred men on board. . . . The ship's pilots are acquainted with the layout of the coasts; at night they steer by the stars, and in the day-time by the Sun. In dark weather they look at the south-pointing needle.[2]

Regional trade also increased during the era of the Tang and the Song. The Chinese exported tea, silk, and porcelain to the countries beyond the South China Sea. In return, they received exotic woods, precious stones, and various tropical goods. Along the Silk Road to China came raw hides, furs, and horses. Chinese aristocrats were fascinated by the exotic goods of the desert and the tropical lands of the South Seas. As a result of trade, the city of Chang'an became the wealthiest city in the world during the Tang Era. The major port of exit in southern China was Canton, where an estimated 100,000 merchants lived.

Economic changes, in turn, had an impact on Chinese society. Cities were now important population centers, and city life had changed. Cities were no longer administrative centers dominated by officials and their families. They now included a broader mix of officials, merchants, artisans, and entertainers. For wealthier city dwellers, it was indeed an age of prosperity. There was probably no better example than the Song capital of Hangzhou. Marco Polo described it to unbelieving European readers in the late thirteenth century as one of the largest and wealthiest cities on Earth. "So many pleasures may be found," he said, "that one fancies himself to be in Paradise."

▼ *The colorful camel shown here was made in the early eighth century by Tang potters. Camels were the transportation vehicles for the Silk Road and over time, camels themselves were associated with trading wealth. What advantages were there in using camels rather than horses on the Silk Road?*

Changes were taking place in the countryside as well. Before, there had been a great gulf between wealthy landowners and the mass of poor peasants. A more complex mixture of landowners, free peasants, sharecroppers, and landless laborers now emerged. Most significant was the rise of the landed gentry, a group of people who controlled much of the land in the countryside and at the same time produced most of the candidates for the civil service. The scholar-gentry, as this class was known, replaced the old landed aristocracy as the political and economic elite of Chinese society.

Daily Life

For rich Chinese during this period, life offered many pleasures. There were new forms of entertainment, such as playing cards and chess (brought from India). The paddle-wheel boat and horseback riding (made possible by the introduction of the stirrup) made travel easier. With the invention of block printing in the eighth century, people found new ways to communicate (see "The Role of Science and Technology: The Invention of Printing in Tang China"). There were also new foods brought in from lands beyond the frontier. Tea had been introduced from Burma. Brandy and

MORE ABOUT . . . *Feng Shui*

The literal translation of Feng Shui is "wind and water." It is a 3,000 year old Chinese belief that all things, living or inanimate, contain energy or life force. This life force is called *Ch'i*. Feng Shui is the building and arrangement of a home based upon the principals of manipulating *Ch'i*. The Chinese believe that colors, shapes, plants, rocks, furniture and architecture all have an impact on a person's energy and peace of mind. They also believe that the arrangement of a home and its contents can influence health, stamina, success and personal relationships.

COMPARING TIME PERIODS

Ask students to write an essay that compares the city of Kilwa, described in Chapter 9, with the Song capital of Hangzhou. Why are cities like these most likely to be constructed by people who are involved in trade?

LEARNING FROM VISUALS

Lead students in a discussion of how the pottery camel pictured to the left shows the value Chinese society placed on these animals. Do they believe wooden carvings of burros that are common in Mexico might have a similar purpose in Mexican society?

Answer to the caption question: Camels can travel long distances with little water, they are sure-footed in the desert, their long eyelashes keep desert sand out of their eyes, and their noses are adapted to desert sand storms.

RETEACHING

Retrace with your students the steps from government trade to banking. *(Trade was opened to private merchants. They prospered and organized themselves into guilds. Increased trade led to a shift from barter to money. The first money would be metal, just a step away from barter, followed by paper, representing the metal, and finally banking.)*

LEARNING FROM VISUALS

Ask students to study the Chinese scroll to the right and identify and list as many products and occupations that it shows as possible. What information does this provide about the state of the Chinese economy?

Answer to the caption question: The people in this scroll are exceedingly well dressed and well-fed. There is no sign of poverty in this scroll at all.

COMPARING TIME PERIODS

The text states that in China the "oldest male ruled the family." Ask students to identify other cultures they have studied where this was true. What factors may have caused many societies to be dominated by men?

Compare the structure of the Chinese family to the structure of the Roman family. How were they similar? How was the "ruling male" similar to the Roman paterfamilias?

▲ *This Chinese scroll,* Spring Festival on the River, *is considered a masterpiece of early twelfth-century China. It is almost thirty-three feet long and records in detail a spectrum of Chinese society from the imperial court to the lowliest peasants. What features in this scroll reveal that this was a time of prosperity in China?*

other kinds of alcoholic beverages were invented in the seventh century.

The vast majority of the Chinese people still lived off the land in villages, which ranged in size from a few dozen people to several thousand. A group of villages would be linked to a larger market town nearby and, beyond that, to the district capital. Most peasants never left their villages except for an occasional visit to a nearby market town.

An even more basic unit than the village in the lives of most Chinese, of course, was the family. The

ideal was the joint or extended family—with at least three generations under one roof (grandparents, parents, and children). When a son married, he was expected to bring his new wife back to live in his parents' home. If a woman married, she went to live with her husband. Women who did not marry remained in the home where they grew up.

The oldest male ruled the family. He performed the family's ancestral religious rites at an altar, usually in the main room of the house. He had legal rights over his wife. If she did not provide him with a male heir, he

So What ??

If your students question the importance of the **information on Chinese philosophy,** *tell them . . .*

Some of the Chinese ideas about illness, including the concept of holistic medicine, the Chinese exercise called T'ai Chi, and the practice of acupuncture are not confined to China. These practices are now being accepted and adopted in the United States.

What do they know of each of these? Have students gather information in Chinese medical practices such as acupuncture, then discuss them as a class. Do the students consider them valid medical practices? Why or why not?

THE ROLE OF SCIENCE AND TECHNOLOGY
The Invention of Printing in Tang China

A primitive form of printing was done in China with stone seals, which were stamped on a surface. Later, ink rubbings began to be made from the original stone carvings of text. By the end of the Han dynasty, texts of the main Confucian classics were engraved on forty-six stone tablets.

Woodblock printing on paper began in the seventh century A.D. The first printed text in China (and in the world) was a Buddhist prayer, done sometime between 704 and 751. The first complete book was a Buddhist work printed in 868. Once woodblock printing was developed, it was used to make numerous copies of important works. Thousands of calendars were printed in China in the ninth century. In the tenth century, a printing of the Confucian classics used over 20,000 woodblocks and comprised 130 volumes. Over 400,000 copies still exist of one Buddhist work printed in the tenth century.

In the eleventh century, the Chinese improved upon the art of printing by inventing movable type. An eleventh-century Chinese author described the work of Pi Sheng, who lived from 990 to 1051:

> During the reign of Ch'ing-li, Pi Sheng, a man of unofficial position, made movable type. His method was as follows: he took sticky clay and cut in it characters as thin as the edge of a coin. Each character formed, as it were, a single type. He baked

▲ The Diamond Sutra, *a Buddhist text, is the earliest known printed book. Woodblock printing was used, rather than movable type. Why do you think the Gutenberg Bible is more famous than this work?*

> them in the fire to make them hard. He had previously prepared an iron plate and he had covered his plate with a mixture of pine resin, wax, and paper ashes. When he wished to print, he took an iron frame and set it on the iron plate. In this he placed the type, set close together. When the frame was full, the whole made one solid block of type. If one were to print only one or three copies, this method would be neither simple nor easy. But for printing hundreds of thousands of copies, it was marvelously quick.

(continued)

MORE ABOUT . . . *Chinese Writing*

Chinese classical writing dates back over 2,500 years and is an intricate system of characters that used to be written with a paintbrush. A Chinese typewriter contains a tray of over 2,000 characters, with several thousand more available on other trays. The typist lines up the tray, presses a key which in turn causes an arm to pick up a character and strike it against the paper. The machine can type both vertically and horizontally, but is rather slow. A good typist can type 20 characters a minute.

Answers to Critical Thinking Questions

1. confucian classics, Buddhist works, calendars; engraving on stone tablets, stone seals used as stamps, ink rubbings of stone carvings
2. There were thousands of characters in the Chinese language; hardly be worth it to print only a few copies, but for hundreds of thousands of copies was "marvelously quick."
3. Answers will vary; block printing and movable type technology spread to Europe; written communication to large groups of people possible both within a country and between countries; anything from great works of literature to personal letters could be preserved, studied, and shared.

LEARNING FROM VISUALS

Answer to the caption question: The impassive faces reflect the requirements of Chinese court etiquette. The artist does not concentrate on the individuality of the women, but on this specific moment in their lives.

TEACHING THEMES

Politics and History. Speculate about why the rules of leaders who are obsessed with power, such as Wu Zhao, are often followed by times of weak leadership and political chaos.

THE ROLE OF SCIENCE AND TECHNOLOGY
The Invention of Printing in Tang China, continued

Pi Sheng's movable type was made of fired clay. By the thirteenth century, both metal and wood were used to make movable type. Movable type, however, was not easy to use because of the thousands of characters in the Chinese language. Wang Chen, who published a basic work on agriculture in 1313, used sixty thousand wooden type characters to print his work. By the fifteenth century, printing by woodblock and movable type had also spread to Europe.

1. What works were printed in China before the eleventh century? What methods were used?
2. What were the technical difficulties and benefits of making and using movable type?
3. What did the invention of movable type mean to China and the rest of the world?

◄ In this copy of an eighth-century Tang painting, two royal ladies amuse themselves by playing a form of backgammon, while two others stand and watch. Why do you think their faces are so calm and lacking in excitement or enthusiasm?

was allowed to take a second wife. His first wife, however, could not divorce him. As the old saying went, "Marry a chicken, follow the chicken; marry a dog, follow the dog." In keeping with the teachings of Confucius, children were expected, above all, to obey their parents. Parents chose their children's careers and selected their marriage partners.

As in other parts of the world, female children were considered less desirable than male children, because they could not do heavy work in the fields, and when they married, they became part of their husbands' families. In addition, a girl's parents were expected to provide a dowry to her husband when she married. Poor families often sold their daughters to wealthy villagers to serve as concubines. In times of famine, female infants were often killed to ensure there would be food for the rest of the family. Of course, there were some exceptions to the low status of women in Chinese society. The outstanding example was Wu Zhao, popularly known as Empress Wu (see "Biography: Empress Wu").

So What ??

*If your students question the importance of the **information on Chinese culture**, tell them . . .*

The Chinese invention of printing not only led to the creation of books, but also to the easy expansion and exchange of knowledge which resulted from mass produced books. This practice continues today in the form of e-mail, compact discs and the Internet.

Discuss with the class other aspects of Chinese culture which are part of our lives today. *(tea, silk, porcelain, gunpowder, banking, paper money)*

BIOGRAPHY

Empress Wu

▲ *This painting of Empress Wu was done during the Tang dynasty and shows how powerful the Empress was. How does the artist convey her power in such a simple painting?*

Wu Zhao (WOO CHOW) was born in 625, the daughter of a Chinese general. Attracted by her beauty, Emperor Tang Taizong chose her to be his concubine when she was only thirteen years old. After his death in 649, she became concubine to the next emperor, Kao Tsung, and bore him four sons and a daughter. Wu Zhao was extremely jealous of the empress and greatly desirous of power. It is said that she strangled her own daughter and then accused the empress, who was childless, of the crime. The emperor chose to accept Wu Zhao's story, deposed the empress, and chose Wu Zhao as his new empress.

Empress Wu was obsessed with power. After her husband's death in 683, she sent one son into exile and ruled with another son. His weakness, however, combined with the support of the army, gave her supreme power. Empress Wu did not hesitate to get rid of officials and even members of her family who stood in her way.

Although she was known for her ruthlessness, Empress Wu was also a capable ruler. She was the first ruler to select graduates of the civil service examinations for the highest positions in government. She forced Korea to become an ally of China, lowered taxes, and patronized the arts. During her last years, her abilities declined, and she was deposed in 705, at the age of eighty. In a country in which women had a low status, Empress Wu had lived a remarkable life. She is still known as one of the strongest leaders in China's history.

1. In your own words, tell the story of how Wu Zhao become empress of China.

2. What qualities of character enabled Empress Wu to hold on to her power?

3. What do you find most remarkable about the life of Empress Wu?

4. Empress Wu used many unethical methods to obtain and keep a position of power, and yet she improved the quality of life for many of her subjects. Explain why you would favor either an ethical, ineffective ruler or an unethical, effective ruler.

On Line with WORLD HISTORY   *Internet Activity*

You may want to have your students visit the following URL, where they will find information and additional web site resources to enhance their study of this chapter.

China the Beautiful

http://www.chinapage.com/

This web site presents samples of 5000 years of classical Chinese art, calligraphy, poetry, history, literature, painting, and philosophy. There are an excellent set of links at this site.

Due to the ever-changing nature of the World Wide Web, see the West History web site, **http://history.swpco.com** for regular updates of the URLs in this text.

Answers to SECTION REVIEW

2. (a) ruled China from 581 until 618; unified China under the emperor's authority; built Grand Canal

(b) ruled China from 619 until 907; one of China's greatest dynasties; streamlined political institutions, broke up power of land owners; expanded control into Tibet

(c) ruled China from 960–1269; lost Tibet; ruled during economic prosperity and cultural achievement; overthrown by the Mongols in 1269

3. (a) instituted to ensure more efficient government staffed by literate bureaucracy with a full dose of Confucian political and social ethics philosophy

(b) composed of three levels, a qualifying level, an entry level, and the highest level

4. Answers will vary.

CLOSE

Lead students in a discussion of the 'Focus' objectives identified on page 282. Emphasize the importance of economic prosperity.

FOCUS

OBJECTIVES

After completing this section, students should be able to

❧ SECTION REVIEW ❧

1. **Locate:**
   (*a*) Huang River, (*b*) Yangtze River,
   (*c*) Tibet, (*d*) Chang'an,
   (*e*) Hangzhou, (*f*) Gobi Desert

2. **Identify:**
   (*a*) Sui dynasty, (*b*) Tang dynasty, (*c*) Song dynasty

3. **Recall:**
   (*a*) Describe the purpose of the civil service exam in early China.
   (*b*) Describe the process of the civil service exam system in early China.

4. **Think Critically:** Compare family life in early China with family life in our culture today. What similarities are there? What differences do you find?

THE MONGOL AND MING DYNASTIES

The Mongols rose to power in Asia with stunning speed. They were pastoral people in the region of modern-day Outer Mongolia who were organized loosely in clans and tribes. Rivalry among the various tribes was intense, but this changed with the Mongol chieftain Genghis Khan.

The Mongols' Conquests

Temuchin was a man born during the 1160s who gradually unified the Mongol tribes. In 1206 he was elected Genghis Khan (universal ruler) at a massive tribal meeting somewhere in the Gobi Desert. From that time on, he devoted himself to fighting. "Man's highest joy," Genghis Khan remarked, "is in victory: to conquer one's enemies, to pursue them, to deprive them of their possessions, to make their beloved weep, to

---

ride on their horses, and to embrace their wives and daughters."[3]

The army that Genghis Khan unleashed on the world was not unusually large; it totaled less than 130,000 in 1227. It was the Mongols' mastery of military tactics that set them apart from their enemies. John of Plano Carpini, a Franciscan friar at the time, remarked:

> As soon as they discover the enemy they charge and each one unleashes three or four arrows. If they see that they can't break him, they retreat in order to entice the enemy to pursue, thus luring him into an ambush prepared in advance. If they conclude that the enemy army is stronger, they retire for a day or two and ravage neighboring areas. Or they strike camp in a well chosen position, and when the enemy army begins to pass by, they appear unexpectedly.[4]

Mongol armies traveled both to the west and to the east. Some went as far as central Europe (see Chapter 12). Only the death of Genghis Khan may have kept the Mongols from an attack on western Europe. In 1231 the Mongols attacked Persia and then defeated the Abbasids at Baghdad in 1258 (see Chapter 8). Mongol forces attacked the Song dynasty in China in the 1260s and finally defeated the remnants of the Song navy in 1279.

In their attack on the Chinese, the Mongols encountered the use of gunpowder and a weapon called a fire-lance, an early form of flamethrower that could spit out a mixture of flame and projectiles and could travel as far as thirty or forty yards. Before the end of the thirteenth century, the fire-lance had evolved into the much more effective handgun and cannon. These inventions came too late to save China from the Mongols, however. By the early fourteenth century, foreigners employed by the Mongol rulers of China had introduced the use of gunpowder and firearms in Europe.

The Mongol Dynasty in China

To rule his new empire, Genghis Khan set up a capital city at Karakorum, in present-day Outer Mongolia. The empire changed when he died. Following tribal custom, upon the death of the ruling khan, his heirs

---

RETEACHING ACTIVITY

Assign the students to prepare a chart that compares the Sui, Tang, and Song Dynasties. Their charts should contain the name of the founder of each dynasty, the time period it covered, and any major contribution to Chinese culture that occurred during this time.

You may want to ask for other information that would require further research.

Have students discuss the three dynasties, based on their charts. How do they compare? In which dynasty would students have preferred to live? Why?

Map 10.2   Asia under the Mongols

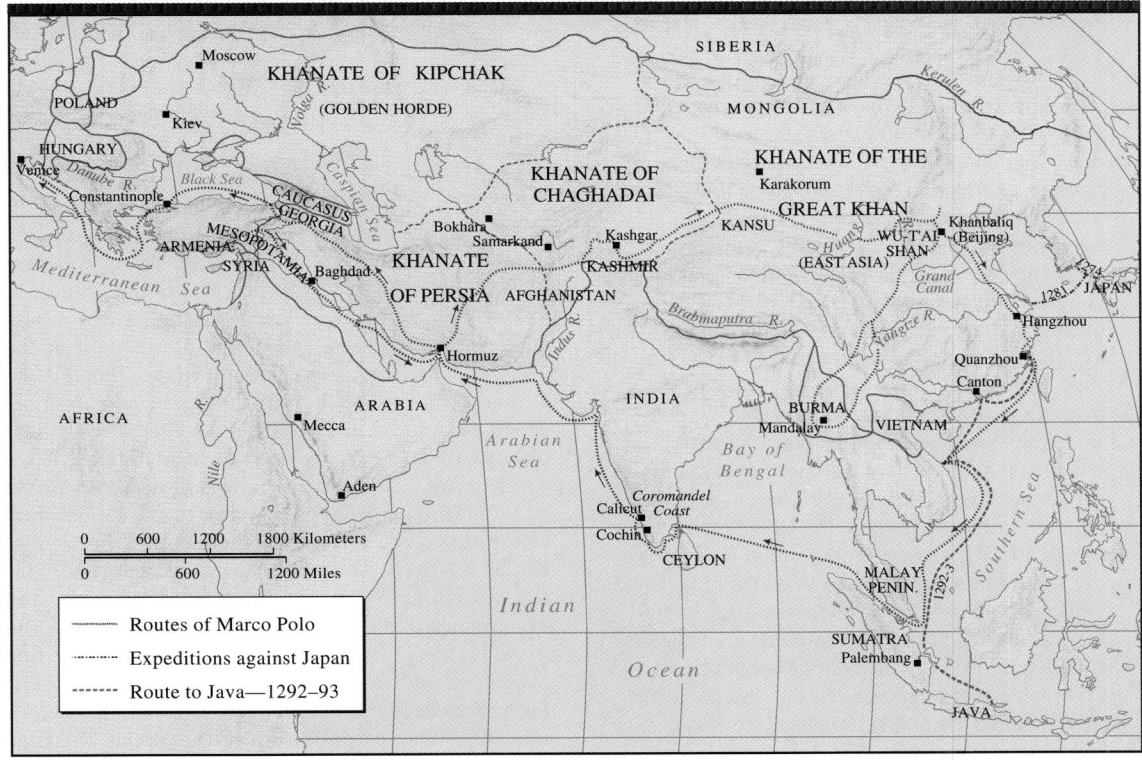

Routes of Marco Polo
Expeditions against Japan
Route to Java—1292–93

1. describe the major accomplishments of the Mongol dynasty
2. identify and describe changes in China that took place during the Ming dynasty
3. identify and explain reasons for the decline of Buddhism and Taoism
4. describe the growth of Chinese culture during the Mongol and Ming dynasties

FOCUS ACTIVITY

Help students understand why civilizations choose to accept foreign ideas at some times and reject them at others. Point out that Buddhism was brought to China from India and eventually became less popular because some people saw it as a foreign intrusion into Chinese culture. Ask students to identify and discuss foreign influences that have been accepted or rejected in American culture.

TEACH

USING PRIMARY SOURCES

Ask students to list and explain advantages of the Mongol tactics of war described at left. Why would an army that used these tactics need strong leadership and tight discipline?

---

divided the territory. The once-united empire of Genghis Khan was thus split into several separate territories called **khanates,** each under the rule of one of his sons. One of his grandsons, named Khubilai Khan, completed the conquest of the Song and established a new Chinese dynasty, called the Yuan (YOO-un) in 1279. Khubilai Khan, who ruled China till his death in 1294, also moved the capital of China northward to Khanbaliq (the city of the Khan). Later the city would be known by the Chinese name Beijing, or Peking (Northern Capital).

The new Chinese dynasty was at first a dynamic one. Under the leadership of the talented Khubilai Khan, the Yuan dynasty continued to expand the

empire. Mongol armies advanced into Vietnam. Mongol fleets were launched against Java, Sumatra, and twice against the islands of Japan. Only Vietnam was conquered—and then only for a while. The other campaigns failed. On one occasion, a massive storm destroyed the Mongol fleet that attacked Japan, killing thousands. After succeeding in China, the Mongols had failed in Japan, Vietnam, and the Indonesian kingdoms. Mongol tactics, such as cavalry charges and siege warfare, were not very effective in tropical and hilly regions.

The Mongols had more success in ruling China. Mongol rulers adapted to the Chinese political system and made use of Chinese bureaucrats. Culturally, how-

---

STUDYING MAPS

The following questions will help you guide students through their study of Map 10.2.

1. Roughly how far was the over-land trip from China to Europe? What was the length of the sea route? Why did many merchants prefer the longer sea route?

2. Why would it be reasonable to expect that the control of Java was less important to China than that of Sumatra and the Malay Peninsula?

3. Why was it easier for China to exert its power over Vietnam than over Japan?

Multimedia Support

LASERDISC
Mongol Scouts Await Invading Russians in 1942

CONNECTIONS
AROUND THE WORLD

The Migration of Peoples   One characteristic of the period between 400 and 1500 was an almost constant migration of peoples. Vast numbers of peoples abandoned their homelands and sought to live elsewhere. Sometimes the migration was peaceful, as was the case with the Bantu-speaking peoples who moved from central to southern Africa. More often than not, however, migration meant invasion and violent conflict. The most active source of migration was in Central Asia. From here, Turkic-speaking peoples spilled over the Hindu Kush into northern India, southwest into Persia, and farther west into the Balkans in southeastern Europe. Later, Mongolian armies from Central Asia rode to the gates of central Europe and conquered China in the thirteenth century. Wherever they went, they left a trail of enormous destruction and loss of life.

There was another side to this age of migrations and invasions, however. Once invaders had completed their conquests, they settled down. The results were often beneficial. The spread of Arabs across the Middle East and North Africa brought a degree of political stability and economic prosperity to the area that it had not had for centuries. German migrations and Viking incursions helped to create dynamic new societies in Europe. Turkish invasions led to the rise of states in the Anatolian Peninsula and north India. The Aztecs created a period of stability in the Valley of Mexico. Even the Mongols, after they settled down, provided an avenue for trade throughout an empire that was greater than anything the world had yet seen.

ever, the Mongols were quite different from the Chinese. The Mongols remained apart as a separate class with their own laws. The highest positions in the bureaucracy were usually staffed by Mongols.

◄ *This painting by an unknown artist captures Khubilai Khan at a calm moment. What do you see in this painting that indicates how powerful or how successful he was?*

Over time, the Mongol dynasty won the support of many Chinese people. Some came to respect the stability and economic prosperity that the Mongols at first brought to China. By bringing the entire Eurasian landmass under a single rule, the Mongols strengthened long-distance trade, especially along the Silk Road.

The capital at Khanbaliq reflected this prosperity. It was a magnificent city. According to the Italian merchant Marco Polo, who lived there during the reign of Khubilai Khan, "The streets are so straight and wide that you can see right along them from end to end and from one gate to the other. And up and down the city there are beautiful palaces, and many great and fine hostelries, and fine houses in great numbers."[5] The magnificence of the empire impressed foreign visitors, including Polo, whose stories of the glories of China were not believed when he returned to Europe (see "You Are There: At the Table of the Great Khan").

The Mongol dynasty, however, eventually fell victim to the same problems of other dynasties: too much spending on foreign conquests, corruption at court and in the bureaucracy, and growing internal instability. By the middle of the fourteenth century, the dynasty had begun to decline rapidly. In 1369, Yuanzhang (YOO-un-JONG), the son of a poor peasant, put together an army, ended the Mongol dynasty, and set up a new dynasty, the Ming dynasty, which would last from 1369 to 1644.

The Ming Dynasty

The founder of the new dynasty took the title of Ming Hongwu (the Ming Martial Emperor). Ming Hongwu,

RECOMMENDED READING

There are a number of recent studies on the Mongol period in Chinese history. See, for example, W. A. Langlois, *China under Mongol Rule* (Princeton, N.J., 1981); and J. W. Dardess, *Conquerors and Confucians: Aspects of Political Change in Late Yuan China* (New York, 1973). M. Rossabi, *Khubilai Khan: His Life and Times* (Berkeley, Calif., 1988) is a recent biography of the dynasty's greatest emperor, while M. Rossabi, ed., *China among Equals: the Middle Kingdom and Its Neighbors* (Berkeley Calif., 1983) deals with foreign affairs. For the rise of the Mongols, see M. Prawdin, *The Mongol Empire: Its Rise and Legacy* (New York, 1966). A more analytic account of the dynamics of nomadic society is A. M. Khazanov, *Nomads and the Outside World* (Cambridge, 1983).

The Ming dynasty will be discussed in part

YOU ARE THERE

At the Table of the Great Khan

The European visitor Marco Polo was clearly impressed by the court of Khubilai Khan. Here he describes the Great Khan at a banquet.

Marco Polo Describes the Great Khan

And when the great Khan sits at table on any great court occasion, it is in this fashion. His table is elevated a good deal above the others, and he sits at the north end of the hall, looking towards the south, with his chief wife beside him on the left. On his right sit his sons and his nephews, and other kinsmen of the blood imperial, but lower, so that their heads are on a level with the emperor's feet. And then the other barons sit at other tables lower still. So also with the women; for all the wives of the lord's sons, and of his nephews and below them again the ladies of the other barons and knights, each in the place assigned by the lord's order. The tables are so arranged that the emperor can see the whole of them from end to end, many as they are. . . .

And you should know that those who wait upon the great Khan with his dishes and his drink are some of the great barons. They have the mouth and nose muffled with fine napkins of silk and gold, so that no breath nor odor from their person should taint the dish or the goblet presented to the lord. And when the emperor is going to drink, all the musical instruments, of which he has a vast store of every kind, begin to play. And when he takes the cup all the barons and the rest of the company drop on their knees and make the deepest obeisance before him, and then the emperor does drink. But each time that he does so the whole ceremony is repeated.

▲ *This painting shows Khubilai Khan dining in a tent, surrounded by guards and servants. How does this scene differ from what might occur during a modern-day military encampment?*

1. What did the arrangement of the banquet tables symbolize about the Great Khan's reign?

2. Who was the center of attention at the banquet—the Great Khan or his guests? Why?

USING PRIMARY SOURCES

Ask students to draw a picture of the hall where the great Khan ate based on the description in the primary source to the left. What does such intricate court life show about the culture, politics, and economics of China at that time?

Answers to Critical Thinking Questions

1. The seating arrangement expressed Khan's desire to exert his power and authority over his subjects in all ways. Students will note that even his family members sat beneath him—their heads level with the emperor's feet.

2. From Marco Polo's description, the banquet revolved around the host. Great care was taken that nothing tainted Khubilai Khan's food or drink, music was played as he commenced to sip, and all the company bowed before him as he did so. Again, this is how the power of his position was reinforced.

LEARNING FROM VISUALS

Answer to the caption question: It is unlikely that modern-day military leaders would camp in such resplendent tents or be attended by so many servants while dining alone.

in a later chapter, but see E.L. Dreyer, *Early Ming China: A Political History, 1355–1435* (Stanford, Calif., 1982) for a readable survey of the early period.

The period from the fall of the Han to the early Ming was an important period in Chinese intellectual history. For developments in Confucianism, see Fung Yu-lan, *A Short History of Chinese Philosophy,* ed. Derk Bodde (New York, 1948); and Carsun Chang, *The Development of Neo-Confucian Thought* 2 vols. (New Haven, Conn., 1963).

The best introduction to Chinese literature is Liu Wu-chi, *An Introduction to Chinese Literature* (Bloomington, Ind., 1966). Also of interest is Ch'en Shou-yi, *Chinese Literature: A Historical Introduction* (New York, 1961).

▲ *Emperor Hongwu, shown here, was born a peasant, gained fame as a military leader, and eventually established the Ming dynasty. He is credited with pushing the Mongols back behind the Great Wall.*

who ruled from 1369 to 1398, was a man of enormous energy. He abolished slavery, launched a land-reform program, strengthened the powers of the central government, and even pacified the border regions.

After his death, his son Yongle moved the imperial capital from Nanjing (NON-JING), where Hongwu had located it, back to Beijing. There it would remain until the end of the dynastic system early in the twentieth century. Yongle also took a more aggressive policy in the south, restoring Chinese rule over Vietnam and sponsoring a series of naval voyages into the Indian Ocean that sailed as far west as the eastern coast of Africa. The voyages pushed Chinese trade far to the west and opened China even more to the wider world.

The voyages sponsored by Emperor Yongle were led by the court official, Zhenghe (JUNG-hee), who made seven voyages of exploration between 1405 and 1431. Zhenghe's voyages were of a grand scale. On the first voyage in 1405, nearly 28,000 men embarked on 62 ships. The largest ship was over 440 feet long. (Columbus's *Santa Maria* was only 88 feet long.) The fleet passed through Southeast Asia and eventually visited ports as far away as the western coast of India and the city-states of East Africa.

Why were the expeditions undertaken? Some assume they were for economic profit. Others point to Yongle's native curiosity about the outside world. The fleet returned not only with goods but also with considerable information about the outside world, as well as with some items unknown in China. The emperor was especially fascinated by the giraffes from Africa, and he placed them in the imperial zoo. Whatever the motivations, the voyages led to enormous profits. This alarmed conservatives within the bureaucracy; some of them viewed trading activities with contempt. Shortly after Yongle's death, the voyages were halted, never to be revived.

To many historians, the decision to stop the expeditions marked an important turning point in Chinese history. The Chinese state turned inward, away from trade and toward a more traditional emphasis on agriculture. The state turned away from the exotic lands to the south and toward the heartland of the country in the Huang River valley. China would not look outward again for four centuries. One can only speculate on the question of what difference it would have made if Zhenghe's fleet had reached the Americas before Columbus did.

The Culture of China

By the time of the Sui and Tang dynasties, Buddhism and Taoism had emerged as major rivals of Confucianism. In the eighth and ninth centuries, however, during the last half of the Tang dynasty, Confucianism revived and once again became dominant at court, a position it retained until the end of the dynastic period in the early twentieth century.

On Line with

WORLD HISTORY   *Internet Activity*

The Rise and Decline of Buddhism and Taoism

Buddhism arrived in China in the first century A.D. with merchants and missionaries from India. At first, only merchants and intellectuals were intrigued by the new ideas. However, as a result of the insecurity that prevailed after the collapse of the Han dynasty, both Buddhism and Taoism became more attractive to many people. Both gained support among the ruling classes.

◄ *Admiral Zhenghe traveled far and wide in an oceangoing junk like the one shown here. How did the Chinese voyages differ from those of European explorers that followed?*

Map 10.3   The Voyages of Zhenghe

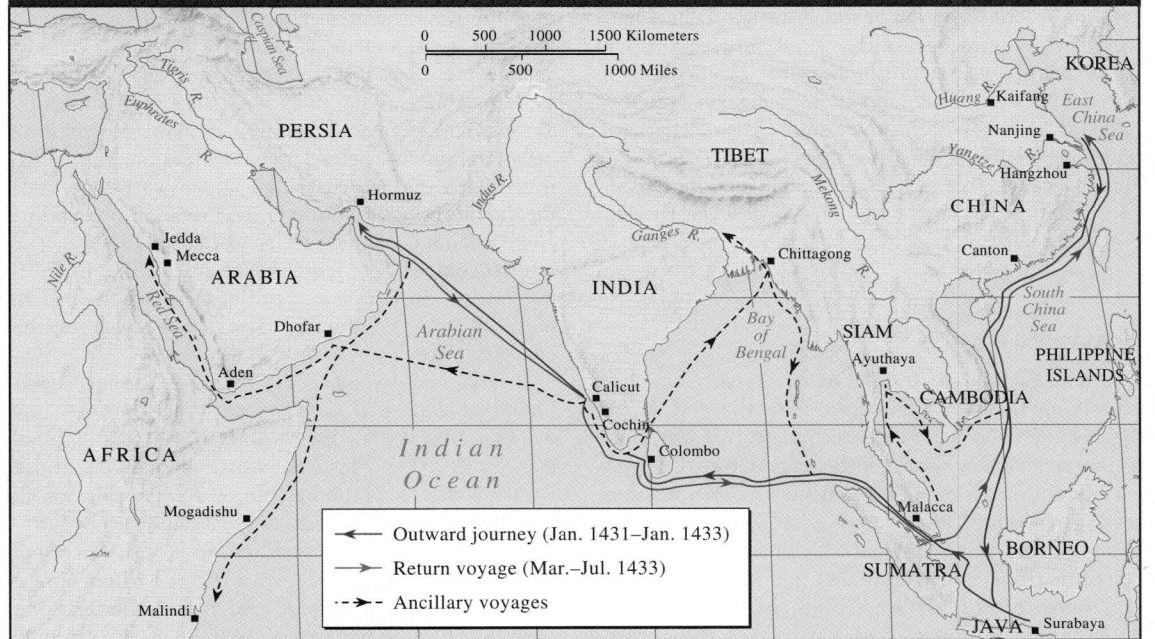

Outward journey (Jan. 1431–Jan. 1433)
Return voyage (Mar.–Jul. 1433)
Ancillary voyages

STUDYING MAPS

The following questions will help you guide students through their study of Map 10.3.

1. Why did many legs of Admiral Zhenghe's voyage reach the end of a gulf or a bay?
2. What meteorological reason might explain why Zhenghe's voyage did not extend far into the Pacific Ocean?
3. Why were the locations of Malacca, Hormuz, and Aden particularly important to sea trade?

The growing popularity of Buddhism continued into the early years of the Tang dynasty. Early Tang rulers lent their support to Buddhist monasteries that were set up throughout the country. Buddhists and Taoists also became advisors at court. Ultimately, however, Buddhism and Taoism lost favor at court and were increasingly subject to attack.

Part of the reason these religions were criticized was a general dislike of foreign ideas. Buddhism was criticized for being a foreign religion. Another reason for the criticism was financial. Like Christian monasteries in Europe during the Middle Ages, Buddhist monasteries had acquired thousands of acres of land and serfs. With land came corruption. The government reacted strongly. During the later Tang period, it destroyed countless Buddhist temples and monasteries and forced more than 100,000 monks to leave the monasteries and return to secular life.

There were other reasons for the state's attack on Buddhism. Buddhists taught that the material world was not real, but an illusion. By teaching this, Buddhism was denying the very essence of Confucian teachings—the need for devotion to family and hard work. These were virtues that the Chinese state had reason to support. Buddhism, however, by encouraging young Chinese to abandon their rice fields and seek refuge in the monasteries, was undermining the basic building blocks of Chinese society—the family unit and the work ethic. Although Buddhism and Taoism continued to win converts at the local level, they no longer received support from the state.

Neo-Confucianism

Official support went instead to a revived Confucianism. From the late Tang dynasty to the end of the dynastic system in the twentieth century, Confucianism served as the bulwark of the state. However, it was a different kind of Confucianism than the system established during the Han dynasty. Confucian doctrine changed as it competed with Buddhist and Taoist teachings.

Confucianism had always been chiefly a system of social ethics and a set of political ideals. Now, challenged by Buddhist and Taoist ideas about the nature of the universe, Confucian thinkers began to speculate on the nature of the universe and humanity's place in it.

Neo-Confucianism, as the new doctrine was called, served as a Confucian response to Buddhism and Taoism. Neo-Confucianism taught that the world is real, not an illusion, and that fulfillment comes not from withdrawal but from participation in the world. Neo-Confucianists divided the world into a material world and a spiritual world. Humans form the link between the two worlds. Although humans live in the material world, each individual is also linked with the Supreme Ultimate. The goal of individuals is to move beyond the material world to reach union with the Supreme Ultimate. Humans do this through a careful examination of the moral principles that rule the universe.

A Golden Age in Chinese Culture: Literature and Art

The period between the Tang and Ming dynasties was in many ways the great age of Chinese literature and art. The development of literature had been encouraged by the invention of paper during the Han dynasty (see Chapter 4). The invention of printing during the Tang dynasty—several hundred years before printing began in Europe—helped to make literature more readily available and more popular. The invention of printing did not bring literature to the masses, however. Literary writing continued to be practiced chiefly by the scholar-gentry. Most Chinese remained illiterate until modern times. However, printing certainly helped to make all forms of literary writing popular among the educated elite.

It was in poetry, above all, that the Chinese of this time best expressed their literary talents. The Tang dynasty is viewed as the great age of poetry in China. At least 48,000 poems were written by 2,200 authors. Poetry was seen as the best form of expression for all educated Chinese. Women of good family and courtesans (prostitutes for the wealthy classes) also cultivated their poetic skills. Poetry was expected to encourage high moral ideals among its readers and also served as a means of self-expression. Chinese poems celebrated

MORE ABOUT . . . *Chinese Dragon Dance*

The Chinese Dragon Dance, usually seen during the New Year's celebration, dates back to the Sung dynasty. The dragon mask is usually gold, green, or a brilliant red. When the dance is performed at night the dragon is preceded by someone carrying a flaming torch. The length of the dragon varies from 9 to 24 sections, with each section being 5–6 feet in length. A similar dance is the Lion Dance, which requires fewer people and is therefore more easily performed. Two people control the lion's head and tail while a third wears a laughing Buddha mask. This laughing Buddha moves ahead of the Lion, teasing him throughout the dance.

the beauty of nature, the changes of the seasons, the joys of friendship, sadness at the shortness of life, and old age and parting.

Li Bo (LEE-BOE) and Du Fu were two of the most popular poets during the Tang Era. Li Bo was a free spirit whose writing often centered on nature. The following is probably the best-known poem in China and has been memorized by schoolchildren for centuries. It is entitled "Quiet Night Thoughts":

> *Beside my bed the bright moonbeams bound*
> *Almost as if there were frost on the ground.*
> *Raising up, I gaze at the Mountain moon;*
> *Lying back, I think of my old home town.*[6]

Where Li Bo was carefree, Du Fu was a sober Confucian. His poems often dealt with ethical themes. Many of his works reflect a concern with social injustice and the plight of the poor. In his poem entitled "Spring Prospect," the poet has returned to his home in the capital after a rebellion against the dynasty has left the city in ruins:

> *The capital is taken. The hills and streams are left,*
> *And with spring in the city the grass and trees*
> *   grown dense.*
> *Mourning the times, the flowers trickle their tears;*
> *Saddened with parting, the birds make my heart flutter.*
> *The army beacons have flamed for three months;*
> *A letter from home would be worth ten thousand in*
> *   gold.*
> *My white hairs have I anxiously scratched ever*
> *   shorter;*
> *But such disarray! Even hairpins will do*
> *   no good.*[7]

The poems of the Tang dynasty were not written for, nor did they reach, most of the Chinese population. By the Song dynasty, China had sixty million people—one million in the city of Hangzhou alone. With the growth of the cities came an increased demand for popular entertainment. City gates and bridges were closed at dark, but food stalls and entertainment continued into the night. Throughout the year, one could find come-

dians, musicians, boxers, wrestlers, acrobats, puppeteers, and especially storytellers. Many of these arts became the favorite forms of amusement of the Chinese people.

In addition, new forms of literary activity began to appear that would bring the written word to a larger audience. During the Mongol and the early Ming dynasties, popular theater, dramas, short stories, and novels first began to appear. Especially significant was the novel. One of the major novels of the Mongol dynasty was *Tale of the Marshes*, which tells of rebellion by bandit heroes who come together to oppose government taxes and oppression. The bandits rob from those in power to share with the poor. *Tale of the Marshes* vividly portrays the suffering of people at the hands of the ruling class. It was the first novel to describe the daily ordeal of ordinary Chinese people in their own language.

During the period from the Tang dynasty to the end of the Ming dynasty, Chinese art also flourished. During the Song and Mongol dynasties, painting reached its high point in traditional China. Best known to modern viewers are the stunning landscape paintings (see "Our Artistic Heritage: Landscape Painting in Traditional China").

Next to painting in creativity was the field of ceramics, especially the making of **porcelain**. Made of fine clay baked at very high temperatures in a kiln, porcelain was first produced during the period after the fall of the Han. It became popular, however, during the Tang Era. As an Arab traveler in 851 described it, "There is in China a very fine clay from which are made vases having the transparency of glass bottles; water in these vases is visible through them, and yet they are made of clay."[8] The technique for making porcelain did not reach Europe until the eighteenth century.

◀ *This blue-and-white porcelain jar dates from the Yuan dynasty. Porcelains like these were exported both to Asia and to Europe. Do you think their use was entirely decorative?*

MORE ABOUT . . . *Chinese Dance*

Chinese dance is older than Chinese writing with evidence of colorful dancing figures appearing on ceramic pots that are 6,000 years old. During the Tang dynasty dance experienced a golden age with the founding of dance academies. One of the popular dances of the time was called the "Ten Movement Music" dance and incorporated elements from China, Korea, Sinkiang, India, Persia and Central Asia (reflecting lands the Chinese either conquered or came into contact with) in one gigantic dance. It involved intricate choreographed body movements, poetry, and a dramatic plot and is considered a forerunner of modern Chinese opera.

OUR ARTISTIC HERITAGE

Ask students to construct a poster or bulletin board that contains a painting or drawing similar to the one in this feature, but of a landscape near their school. Their work may show a reverence for nature or for some other human value which they identify.

Answers to Critical Thinking Questions

1. nature and the search for balance between earth and water emphasized; focus on the essence of nature, instead of realism; believed that people could not know the whole truth, so empty spaces left in paintings; humans were portrayed as insignificant in nature

2. allowed paintings to be unfolded slowly, involving the viewer as each part of the work was revealed

Answers to SECTION REVIEW

2. (a) territories into which Genghis Khan's empire was split
(b) ceramics made from fine clay baked at high temperatures in a kiln

3. (a) unified Mongol tribes; elected universal ruler; devoted to fighting and conquering other peoples
(b) grandson of Genghis Khan; completed conquest of Song dynasty; established Yuan dynasty
(c) in power in China 1369–1644; slavery was abolished; central government strengthened; trade increased

OUR ARTISTIC HERITAGE
Landscape Painting in Traditional China

Influenced by Taoism, Chinese artists went into the mountains to paint and find the Tao, or Way, in nature. This explains in part the emphasis on nature in traditional Chinese painting. The word *landscape* in Chinese means "mountain-water" and reflects the Taoist search for balance between earth and water.

To represent the totality of nature, Chinese artists tried to reveal the hidden forms of the landscape. Rather than depicting the actual realistic shape of a specific mountain, for example, they tried to portray the idea of "mountain." Empty spaces were left in the paintings because in the Taoist vision, one cannot know the whole truth. Taoist influence was also evident in the portrayal of human beings as insignificant in the midst of nature. Chinese artists painted people as tiny figures fishing in small boats or wandering up a hillside trail, living in but not dominating nature.

The Chinese used a special method to display their paintings—the scroll. Paintings were mounted on long sheets of silk or paper, attached to a wooden bar at the bottom. The paintings, which varied in length from three to twenty feet, were unfolded slowly for the viewer. The eye could then enjoy each segment, one after the other, beginning at the bottom with water or a village and moving upward into the hills to the mountain peaks and the sky.

By the tenth century, Chinese painters began to eliminate color from their paintings. They tried to capture the essence of the landscape in brush strokes of black ink on white silk. They created black-and-white landscapes characterized by a serious mood and dominated by overpowering mountains. These black-and-white paintings remained popular until the mid-twelfth century.

▲ *This famous painting was done in the eleventh century and shows Chinese reverence for nature. There are human elements here—two tiny figures driving mules, a bridge, and a temple—but all are dwarfed and overpowered by the mountain.*

1. What influence did Taoism have on traditional Chinese painting?

2. Why did some artists display their paintings on scrolls?

RETEACHING ACTIVITY

Assign students to construct a time line that identifies and explains important events in China's history during times covered in sections one and two of this chapter. Have the students be prepared to discuss the event in class if you have time for class discussion. Base your evaluation of their work on its accuracy, completeness, appearance and overall knowledge of the event.

SECTION REVIEW

1. **Locate:**
   (*a*) Mongolia,   (*b*) Khanbaliq,   (*c*) Vietnam,
   (*d*) Java,   (*e*) Sumatra,   (*f*) Japan

2. **Define:**
   (*a*) khanates,   (*b*) porcelain

3. **Identify:**
   (*a*) Genghis Khan,   (*b*) Khubilai Khan,
   (*c*) Ming dynasty,   (*d*) Yongle

4. **Recall:** What reasons do historians give for Yongle sending out so many naval expeditions?

5. **Think Critically:** Buddhism taught that the material world was not real, but an illusion. Confucian teachings stressed the need for devotion to family and hard work. Explain how these philosophies conflict and what impact that conflict might have had on the way people viewed life.

THE EMERGENCE OF JAPAN

Chinese and Japanese societies have historically been very different. One of the reasons for these differences is geography. Whereas China is on a continent, Japan is a chain of more than three thousand islands cut off from the mainland by 120 miles of ocean. The population is concentrated on four main islands: Hokkaido (haw-KIDE-oh) in the north, the main island of Honshu in the center, and the two smaller islands of Kyushu (kee-OO-shoo) and Shikkoku (shi-KOE-koo) in the southwest. Japan's total land area is about 146,000 square miles—about the size of the state of Montana.

Japan is blessed with a temperate climate. It is slightly warmer on the east coast, which also has a number of natural harbors that provide protection from the winds and high waves of the Pacific Ocean. Like China, much of Japan is mountainous. Only about 20 percent of the total land area can be farmed. The

Map 10.4   Early Japan

mountains are volcanic in origin, because the Japanese islands are located where the Asian and Pacific tectonic plates meet. On the one hand, volcanic soils are very fertile, which has helped Japanese farming. On the other hand, the area is prone to earthquakes. In 1923, an earthquake almost destroyed the entire city of Tokyo.

The fact that Japan is an island nation has also affected its history. Because of their geographical isolation, the Japanese developed a number of unique qualities. These qualities contributed to the Japanese belief that they had a separate destiny from the peoples of the continent.

The Rise of the Japanese State

The early Japanese, who are known as the Yayoi people, lived at first on the southern island of Kyushu. Eventually, they moved northward onto the main island of Honshu and settled in the Yamato plain near the modern-day cities of Osaka (oh-SAW-kuh) and Kyoto (kee-OH-toe). The Yayoi set up a tribal society. The people were divided between a small aristocratic class (who were the chieftains of the different tribes) and the majority of the population, composed of rice farmers, artisans, and household servants of the aristocrats. Tribal chieftains provided protection to the local population in return for a share of the annual harvest.

(d) second of Ming emperors; restored Chinese rule over Vietnam; sponsored naval voyages
4. economic profit; intense curiosity about the outside world
5. Answers will vary.

CLOSE

Lead students in a discussion of the 'Focus' objectives identified on page 293. Emphasize developments in Chinese culture that took place during the Mongol and Ming dynasties.

FOCUS

OBJECTIVES

After completing this section, students should be able to

1. identify and describe important political and social events during the Nara and Heian periods in Japan
2. describe changes in political structures and power that took place during the Kamakura Shogunate
3. describe the economic and social systems of Japan and explain how they influenced Japanese history

STUDYING MAPS

The following questions will help you guide students through their study of Map 10.4.

1. What geographic features tended to protect Japan from invasion? *(surrounded by water)*
2. What are the approximate dimensions of Japan? *(1800 miles long; approximately 300 wide)*

3. What geographic characteristics of Japan encouraged the creation of many small tribal states rather than a single united state? *(extreme length from end to end; some smaller island areas)*

FOCUS ACTIVITY

Help students understand how the threat of invasion from a foreign power can unite many small states who had previously fought among themselves. This was the case in Japan when the Tang dynasty of China attempted to invade. Can students think of other similar examples they know of from history? Consider the ability of German tribes to resist the power of Rome and to ultimately destroy the Roman Empire.

TEACH

Multimedia Support

LASERDISC

Fifty-three-foot-high Bronze Buddha at Podai-ji Temple in Nara (eighth century)

The Samurai Warrior (the feudal period, 1185–1868) (VIDEO)

COMPARING TIME PERIODS

Ask students to compare the idea that the Japanese sovereign is "likened to heaven" with the "Mandate of Heaven" that was enjoyed by rulers in China's Zhou and Shang dynasties. Why is this belief common throughout history?

▲ *Earthquakes are fairly common in Japan. This photo records the devastation that occurred in Tokyo during the 1923 earthquake when entire neighborhoods were leveled.*

Eventually, one powerful chieftain in the Yamato region achieved supremacy over the others.

In the early seventh century, Japan was faced with the threat of attack from Tang China. To meet this threat, Shotoku Taishi, ruler of Yamato, realized that he must try to unify the various tribes so that the Japanese could more effectively resist a possible Chinese invasion. Prince Shotoku sent missions to the Tang capital of China to learn more about Chinese political institutions. He then began a series of reforms to create a new centralized political system based roughly on the Chinese model, which he admired.

In the so-called seventeen-article constitution, Prince Shotoku called for the creation of a centralized government under a supreme ruler. A merit system was to be used for choosing public officials. The prince's objective was to limit the powers of the aristocrats and enhance the authority of the Yamato ruler—namely, himself. This ruler was now portrayed as a divine figure and the symbol of the Japanese nation.

The constitution set up a centralized government subject to the will of the ruler. It read: "When an imperial command is given, obey it with reverence. The sovereign is likened to heaven, and his subjects are likened to earth." However, the new government was also meant to be helpful to its subjects: "The way of the minister is to turn away from private motives and to uphold public good."[9] Evil was to be punished and good, rewarded.

After Shotoku Taishi's death in 622, his successors continued to make reforms based on the Chinese model. The territory of Japan was divided into administrative districts following the Chinese pattern, and the senior official of each district was selected from among the local nobles. As in China, the rural village was the basic unit of government. The village chief was responsible for overseeing the affairs of the village. A law code was introduced, and a new tax system was set up. Now all farmland technically belonged to the state. Taxes were to be paid directly to the central government rather than to local nobles.

The Nara and Heian Periods

At first the Japanese effort to build a new state modeled after the Tang state in China was successful. After Shotoku Taishi's death in 622, political influence fell into the hands of the powerful Fujiwara clan, which managed to marry into the ruling family and continue the reforms Shotoku had begun. In 710, a new capital was established at Nara, on the eastern edge of the Yamato plain. The Yamato ruler began to use the title "son of Heaven" in the Chinese fashion.

Had these reforms succeeded, Japan might have followed the Chinese pattern and developed a centralized bureaucratic government. As time passed, however, the central government was unable to undermine the

SPECIAL NEEDS: *Activity*

Have students develop a time line that would include the following: (1) the Sui Dynasty (581–618); (2) the Tang Dynasty (618–907); (3) Woodblock printing on paper (600–700); (4) the Song Dynasty (960–1269); (5) Movable type invented (1000); (6) Mongol Dynasty (1269–1369); (7) Ming Dynasty (1369–1644).

power of the court aristocracy in the capital, who were able to dominate the ranks of the public officials. Although Japan, like China, used civil service examinations, they were restricted to individuals of noble birth. Only aristocrats became public officials.

In addition, the central government in Japan was not able to undermine the power of the landed nobility in the countryside. Leading officials were awarded large tracts of land. They and other powerful families were able to keep the taxes from the lands for themselves. Unable to gain tax revenues, the central government steadily lost power and influence.

In 794, the emperor moved the capital to his family's original power base at nearby Heian, on the site of present-day Kyoto. At Heian, the emperor continued to rule in name, but actual power was in the hands of the Fujiwara clan. In fact, what was happening was a return to the decentralized political system that had existed before the time of Shotoku Taishi. Attempts to strengthen the power of the central government by imposing taxes directly on the rice lands had failed. Powerful families whose wealth was based on the ownership of tax-exempt farmland dominated the rural areas. To avoid paying taxes, peasants would often surrender their lands to a local aristocrat, who then would allow the peasants to farm the land in return for the payment of rent. This system reminds one of the lord and peasant manorial system in medieval Europe (see Chapter 12). However, unlike European serfs, Japanese peasants were not legally bound to their lords' land.

With the decline of central power at Heian, local aristocrats tended to take justice into their own hands. They turned increasingly to military force as a means of protecting their interests. A new class of military retainers emerged whose purpose it was to protect the security and property of their patrons. Called the **samurai** (those who serve), these warriors resembled the knights of medieval Europe. Like knights, the samurai fought on horseback, clad in helmet and armor, although a samurai carried a sword and a bow and arrow rather than a lance and shield. Like knights, the samurai were supposed to live by a strict warrior code, known in Japan as **Bushido** (the way of the warrior). As time went on, they became a major force in the Japanese countryside. Above all, the samurai's code

During the Kamakura period, painters began to show scenes from the lives of samurai warriors. Here the samurai is mounted on an impressive steed ready to engage in battle for his lord. What differences exist between the samurai and their European counterparts?

was based on loyalty to one's lord. Neither love of wife and children nor duty to one's parents could interfere with this loyalty. Fear of death was also unknown to the samurai. As one samurai expressed in a twelfth-century Japanese tale: "I spurred my horse on, careless of death in the face of the foe. I braved the dangers of wind and wave, not reckoning that my body might sink to the bottom of the sea, and be devoured by monsters of the deep. My pillow was my harness, arms my trade."

The Kamakura Shogunate and Its Aftermath

By the end of the twelfth century, rivalries among noble families had led to almost constant civil war. Finally, a powerful noble named Minamoto Yoritomo defeated several rivals and set up his power base on the Kamakura peninsula, south of the modern city of Tokyo. To strengthen the state, he created a more centralized government under a powerful military leader

RECOMMENDED READING

Some treatments of Japanese civilization appear in textbooks dealing with the early history of East Asia, such as J. K. Fairbank, E. O. Reischauer, and A. M. Craig, *East Asia: Tradition and Transformation* (Boston, 1973); and C. Schirokauer, *A Brief History of Chinese and Japanese Civilizations* (San Diego, Calif., 1989). For the latest scholarship on the early period, see the first three volumes of *The Cambridge History of Japan,* edit. J. W. Hall,

M. B. Jansen, M. Kanai, and D. Twitchett (Cambridge, 1988).

The relationship between disease and state building is analyzed in W. W. Farris, *Population, Disease, and Land in Early Japan, 645–900* (Cambridge, 1985). The Kamakura period is covered in J. P. Mass, ed., *Court and Bakufu in Japan: Essays in Kamakura History* (1982).

CLASS DISCUSSION

Ask your students to discuss why times of chaos and civil war are often followed by the emergence of strong, authoritarian central governments.

COMPARING PERIODS

Can students see any similarity between the relationship of the Japanese emperor to the shogun in Japan and the King or Queen of Britain to the prime minister today?

Multimedia Support

LASERDISC
Nagoya Castle
(Japan)

LEARNING FROM VISUALS

Ask students to consider what the possibility of a burning of a retired emperor's home, like that pictured to the right, might do to an emperor's desire to maintain his power.

▲ *This thirteenth-century* Scroll of the Heiji Period *shows the burning of a retired emperor's home. Confusion and violence reign as servants and ladies try to flee from the flames.*

known as the **shogun** (general). The shogun tried to increase the powers of the central government while reducing the power of rival families. In this new system—called the **shogunate**—the emperor remained ruler in name only, and the shogun exercised the actual power. The shogunate served as the political system in Japan until the last half of the nineteenth century. The Kamakura shogunate, founded by Yoritomo, lasted from 1185 to 1333.

At first the system worked well. The Japanese were fortunate that it did, because the government soon faced its most serious challenge yet from the Mongols. As we have seen, the Mongols conquered China and then began to expand into other areas of Asia. In 1281, Khubilai Khan invaded Japan with an army nearly 150,000 strong. Fortunately for the Japanese, almost the entire fleet was destroyed by a massive typhoon. The Japanese referred to it as a "divine wind" (*kamikaze*) that had protected the Japanese people and their divine emperor from their enemies. Japan would not again face a foreign invader until American forces landed in the summer of 1945.

Fighting the Mongols had put a heavy strain on the political system. In 1333, the Kamakura shogunate was overthrown by a group of powerful families. A new shogun, supplied by the Ashikaga family, arose in Kyoto and tried to continue the shogunate system. However, the Ashikaga were unable to restore any strong centralized power. The power of the local landed nobles continued to grow. Heads of great noble families, now called **daimyo** (great names), controlled vast landed estates that owed no taxes to the government. As family rivalries continued, the daimyo relied on the samurai for protection, and political power came into the hands of a loose coalition of noble families.

By 1500, Japan was close to chaos. A disastrous civil war known as the Onin War, which lasted from 1467 to 1477, led to the virtual destruction of the capital city of Kyoto. Armies passed back and forth through the city, burning temples and palaces. The power of the shogunate collapsed. As central authority disappeared, powerful aristocrats in rural areas seized control over large territories and ruled as independent great lords. Their rivalries led to almost constant warfare.

On Line with
WORLD HISTORY *Internet Activity*

You may want to have your students visit the following URL, where they will find information and additional web site resources to enhance their study of this chapter.
Tokugawa Art Museum
http://www.cjn.or.jp/tokugawa/room0.html

This site has nine different rooms to visit with Japanese treasures and much more to explore.

Due to the ever-changing nature of the World Wide Web, see the West History web site, **http://history.swpco.com** for regular updates of the URLs in this text.

▲ *This thirteenth-century scroll portrays city life in Edo, which is now Tokyo. As trade developed, communities grew into bustling cities.*

Economic and Social Life in Early Japan

Early Japan was mostly a farming society. Its people took advantage of the limited amount of farmland and abundant rainfall to grow wet rice (rice grown in flooded fields). Despite the efforts of Shotoku Taishi and his successors, noble families were able to maintain control over most of the land. When central authority had almost completely disappeared, powerful local lords, assisted by their military retainers, the samurai, were able to control large tracts of land somewhat similar to the manors of medieval Europe.

As in China, trade in Japan was slow to develop. With the rise of the Yamato state, a money economy slowly began to emerge. Most trade, however, was still conducted through barter until the twelfth century, when metal coins introduced from China became more popular.

Trade and manufacturing began to develop more rapidly during the Kamakura period. Markets appeared in the larger towns, and industries such as paper, iron casting, and porcelain emerged. Trade between regions also grew. Goods were carried in horse-drawn carts, by boats on rivers or along the coast, or on human backs. Foreign trade, mainly with Korea and China, began during the eleventh century. Japan shipped raw materials, paintings, swords, and other manufactured items in return for silk, porcelain, books, and copper coins.

Social Structure and Daily Life

There was a sharp division in Japanese society between the aristocrats and the common people. The existence of class differences went back to ancient times. The Japanese aristocracy—the ruling elite—was composed of the hereditary rulers of the various families. The rise

So What ??

▲ *In this pastoral scene we see performers attempting to entertain the people passing by. Can you guess at reasons why the country people seem to be ignoring the performers?*

of the centralized Yamato state in the seventh century also led to the growth of a court aristocracy. In many ways, Japanese aristocrats were like the landed aristocrats in medieval Europe. They enjoyed a life of leisure and elaborate court ritual.

Like the aristocrats of medieval Europe, Japanese aristocrats were most at home in the countryside, on their estates. Many also relished military combat. The samurai, who were considered members of the lesser nobility, were the symbol of the rural aristocracy. A samurai lived by a strict warrior code and was expected to maintain an undying loyalty to his lord.

Below the nobles were the masses of people. Life for the common people probably changed little over hundreds of years. Most were peasants who worked on land owned by their manorial lords or by the state. Not all peasants were equal. Some became well-to-do and emerged as local officials who supervised the mass of the peasants. Some peasants who were unable to pay their taxes fell into the ranks of the **genin,** or landless

laborers, who could be bought and sold like slaves. Some fled to escape such a fate and survived by living in the mountains or becoming bandits.

The bottom of the social scale was occupied by the **eta,** a class of hereditary slaves who carried out such degrading occupations as burying the dead and curing leather (much like the Untouchables in the caste system of India). The eta were probably descendants of prisoners of war or criminals. As we shall later, the eta are still a part of Japanese society. Discrimination against them is still common.

Daily life for ordinary people in early Japan was like that of ordinary people everywhere in Asia. The vast majority lived in small villages. Housing was simple. Most lived in small, two-room houses of timber, mud, or thatch, with dirt floors covered by straw or woven mats. Their diet consisted of rice, wild grasses, millet, roots, and some fish and birds. Festivals, folk dramas, jugglers, and acrobats broke the monotony of the daily routine, but life must have been difficult at best.

ENRICHMENT ACTIVITY

Assign students to write the text of a fictional debate that takes place between two leaders in Japan. One wishes to maintain the independence and power of local nobles while the other wants a strong central government. Tell students that their work will be evaluated on the basis of the logic and reason they build into the statements of the two fictitious leaders.

After students have completed their assignment, hold a class debate on the issue.

The Role of Women

In early Japan, women were said to have a certain level of equality with men. An eighth-century law code, for example, guaranteed the inheritance rights of women. Wives who were abandoned by their husbands were allowed to obtain a divorce and to remarry. However, later practices make it clear that women were also considered subordinate to men. A husband could divorce his wife if she did not produce a male child, committed adultery, disobeyed her parents-in-law, talked too much, was jealous, or had a serious illness.

Although women did not possess the full legal and social rights of men, they played an active role at various levels of Japanese society. Aristocratic women were prominent at court. Some became known for their artistic or literary talents. Women often appear in the paintings of the period along with men. The women are doing the spring planting; threshing and hulling rice; and acting as peddlers, salespersons, and entertainers.

 SECTION REVIEW

1. **Locate:**
   (*a*) Hokkaido,   (*b*) Honshu,
   (*c*) Kyushu,   (*d*) Shikoku,
   (*e*) Osaka,   (*f*) Kyoto

2. **Define:**
   (*a*) samurai,   (*b*) Bushido,
   (*c*) shogun,   (*d*) shogunate,
   (*e*) daimyo,   (*f*) genin,
   (*g*) eta

3. **Identify:**
   (*a*) Prince Shotoku,   (*b*) Kamakura shogunate

4. **Recall:** Why was Japan unable to develop a centralized bureaucratic government as China had developed?

5. **Think Critically:** Explain how the samurai and shogun affected the government of early Japan.

4
RELIGION AND CULTURE IN EARLY JAPAN

As with other parts of Japanese society, religion, writing, art, and architecture were strongly influenced by the Chinese. However, the Japanese also carefully shaped Chinese ideas to fit their own society.

Religion

In Japan, as elsewhere, religious belief began with the worship of nature spirits. Early Japanese worshiped spirits, called *kami*, who they believed resided in trees, rivers, streams, and mountains. They also believed that the spirits of their ancestors were present in the air around them. In Japan, these beliefs evolved into a kind of state religion called Shinto (the Sacred Way or the Way of the Gods), which is still practiced today.

One feature of Shinto is its stress on the beauty of nature and the importance of nature itself. Shinto shrines are usually located in places of great beauty. These beliefs contributed to a common characteristic of the Japanese—their love of nature.

In time, Shinto evolved into a state doctrine that was linked to a belief in the divinity of the emperor and the sacredness of the Japanese nation. A national shrine was established at Ise (EE-SAY), north of the early capital of Nara. At Ise the emperor paid tribute to the sun goddess every year. There is a legend that the first emperor was descended from Amaterasu, the sun goddess. The emperor is therefore above the natural order of humans. It was not until 1945, following Japan's defeat in World War II, that Emperor Hirohito was forced to say that he was not divine.

Shinto, however, did not satisfy the spiritual needs of all the Japanese people. Some turned to Buddhism, which Buddhist monks from China brought to Japan during the sixth century A.D. At first Buddhism was popular only at the royal court, where its rich symbolism appealed to aristocrats. Shinto, a nature religion, had no such symbols. By the eighth century, however, Buddhism began to spread to the rest of the people. Most Japanese saw no problem in worshiping both the

---

(d) political system where emperor ruled in name only; shogun exercised actual power
(e) (great names) heads of great noble families who controlled vast landed estates owing no taxes to the government
(f) peasants, unable to pay their taxes, who became landless laborers and were bought and sold as slaves
(g) hereditary slaves who carried out the most degrading occupations in society

3. (a) regent of Yamato; created a new centralized political system based on Chinese model
(b) most successful of the shogunates; power of the central government increased, power of the rival families was reduced; Mongols successfully turned away during this shogunate

4. central government was unable to undermine the power of court aristocracy in the capital, which dominated the ranks of the public officials

5. The samurai protected local landowners, giving them power, while the shogun, a military leader, controlled the central government and attempted to shift power from landowners to himself.

CLOSE

Lead students in a discussion of the 'Focus' objectives identified on page 300. Stress the difficulty Japan's leaders experienced in establishing and maintaining central control over their lands.

MORE ABOUT . . . *Yin and Yang*

The original meaning of the Chinese words yin and yang was the sunny side and the dark side of the hill. It is a philosophy of complementary opposites which, according to both the Chinese and Japanese, can be found in all aspects of life. These polarities can be seen in male and female, hot and cold, expansion and contraction, just to name a few. Unlike in the Western view of opposites, neither is good or bad. Nor is there conflict between the two. Yin is constantly becoming yang, yang flows into yin. And, as is seen in the familiar yin/yang symbol, each contains a seed of its opposite.

FOCUS

OBJECTIVES

After completing this section, students should be able to

1. describe the importance of religion in Japanese society
2. identify and explain examples of Japanese literature
3. describe and explain examples of Japanese art and architecture

FOCUS ACTIVITY

Help students understand the culture of early Japan by discussing why national leaders encouraged and supported a religion and forms of art that linked the divinity of the emperor to the sacredness of the Japanese nation. Ask students to look for similarities between the Shinto religion and the divine right to rule claimed by leaders in many other states both before and after the spread of Shintoism in Japan.

TEACH

COMPARING TIME PERIODS

Ask students to consider the willingness of the Shinto religion to tolerate the simultaneous worship of other religions and gods. What factors may have caused the leaders of Shintoism to accept this practice? How would leaders of most modern religions react to this idea?

Buddha and their own local nature gods. Great Buddhist monasteries were set up by the noble families that ruled the country.

In China, Buddhism had divided into a number of different schools. Among the aristocrats in Japan, one sect, known as Zen, became the most popular. In Zen teachings, there are different ways to achieve enlightenment (a state of pure being). Some said that it could be achieved suddenly. One monk, for example, was supposed to have achieved enlightenment by carefully watching the opening of peach blossoms in the spring. Others claimed that enlightenment could only be achieved by a strong self-discipline, especially a long process of meditation that cleared the mind of all thoughts.

Literature

Growing contact with China during the rise of the Yamato state stimulated Japanese artists. Missions sent to China during the seventh and eighth centuries returned with examples of Chinese literature and art, all of which influenced the Japanese.

Borrowing from Chinese models was difficult for Japanese authors, however. The early Japanese had no writing system for recording their own spoken language. At first, then, they took over the Chinese written language. Eventually, however, the Japanese began to adapt the Chinese written characters so they could be used for recording the Japanese language. It took many centuries, however, before the Japanese began to create a literature in their own language.

Japanese poetry is unique. For the aristocratic classes, poetry was a symbol of one's breeding and high moral character. Poetry expresses its themes in a simple form, following a general principle of Japanese aesthetics: "less is more." The aim of the Japanese poet was to create a mood by focusing on a single subject, as seen in this twelfth-century poem by Jakuren, on raindrops:

> *The hanging raindrops*
> *Have not dried from the needles*
> *Of the fir forest*
> *Before the evening mist*
> *Of autumn rises.*

During much of the history of traditional Japan, aristocratic men wrote in Chinese. Many also believed that prose fiction was merely "vulgar gossip" and was thus beneath them. Consequently, from the ninth to the twelfth centuries, Japanese women were the most productive writers of prose fiction in Japanese. Females were excluded from school and learned to read and write at home. They wrote diaries, stories, and novels to pass the time. Some of the most talented women were invited to the royal court as authors-in-residence.

From this tradition of female prose appeared one of the world's truly great novels, *The Tale of Genji*. It was written by the court author Murasaki (MYOOR-uh-SOCK-ee) Shikibu around the year 1000. The novel has 430 realistic characters and covers a span of seventy-five years in 2,500 pages.

The novel traces the life of the noble Genji as he tries to remain in favor with those in power. The different aspects of Genji's personality are explored as he moves from youthful adventures to a life of sadness and compassion in his later years. The most important part of the novel is not so much the story as the analysis of the characters (see "Our Literary Heritage: *The Tale of Genji*"). The novel is also a reflection of court life in Japan; because power was in the hands of others, there was nothing much for royals to do.

Between 1100 and 1400, a new form of the novel, that of the heroic war tale, developed out of the new warrior class. These works described the military exploits of warriors, combined with a sense of sadness and loneliness. A classic of this kind, *The Tale of the Heike*, is the twelfth-century story of an assault on Kyoto. It opens with the following words: "The pale hue of the flowers of the teak-tree shows the truth that they who prosper must fall. The proud ones do not last long, but vanish like a spring-night's dream. And the mighty ones too will perish in the end, like dust before the wind."[10]

During this period, the famous Japanese drama known as **No** also emerged. No developed out of a variety of entertainment forms, including dancing and juggling. The plots for No dramas were usually based on stories from Japanese history or legend. Over a period of time, No evolved into a drama in which the performers wore masks and danced to the accompaniment

RECOMMENDED READING

The most comprehensive and helpful anthology of Japanese literature is still D. Keene, *Anthology of Japanese Literature* (New York, 1955). A more recent contribution is J. T. Rimer, ed., *A Reader's Guide to Japanese Literature: From the Eighth Century to the Present* (Tokyo and New York, 1988). Still the best introduction is the concise and insightful D. Keene, *Japanese Literature: An Introduction for*

Western Readers (London, 1953). A good all-round presentation is found in E. Putzar, *Japanese Literature: A Historical Outline* (Tucson, Ariz., 1973).

For the text of *The Tale of Genji,* see A. Waley's translation (New York, 1935), and a more recent one by E. Seidensticker (Tokyo 1977). The best translation for students is the latter's abridged Vintage classical edition of

OUR LITERARY HERITAGE
The Tale of Genji

The Tale of Genji, *written by Murasaki Shikibu around 1000, is Japan's most famous novel. Some consider it one of the world's great novels. In this scene, the author describes the meeting of Genji at the age of seventeen with his foster mother, who had once nursed him, but who had now been ill and become a nun.*

Murasaki Shikibu,
The Tale of Genji

The nun too rose from her couch: "For a long time I had been waiting to give up the world, but one thing held me back: I wanted you to see your old nurse just once again as you used to know her. You never came to see me, and at last I gave up waiting and took my vows. Now, I have got back a little of my health, and having seen my dear young master again, I can wait with a quiet mind for the Lord Amida's Light," and in her weakness she shed a few tears. . . .

People such as old nurses regard even the most blackguardly and ill-favored foster children as prodigies of beauty and virtue. Small wonder then if Genji's nurse, who had played so great a part in his early life, always regarded her office as immensely honorable and important, and tears of pride came into her eyes while he spoke to her.

The old lady's children thought it very improper that their mother, having taken holy orders [and become a nun], should show so lively an interest in a human career. Certain that Genji himself would

▲ *Here you see a closeup view of an ornate wood writing table decorated with gold and silver lacquer. The theme, Palace by the Sea, alludes to* The Tale of Genji.

be very much shocked, they exchanged uneasy glances. He was on the contrary deeply touched. "When I was a child," he said, "those who were dearest to me were early taken away, and although there were many who gave a hand to my upbringing, it was to you only, dear nurse, that I was deeply and tenderly attached. When I grew up I could not any longer be often in your company. I have not even been able to come here and see you as often as I wanted to. But in all the long time which has passed since I was last here, I have

(continued)

1990, which captures the spirit of the original in 360 pages. Of the many works on the novel, a most accessible and stimulating presentation is I. Morris, *The World of the Shining Prince: Court Life in Ancient Japan* (New York, 1964).

For the most comprehensive and accessible introduction to Japanese art, consult "History of Japanese Art" by P. Mason (NY, 1993). Also see the concise J. Stanley-Baker, *Japanese Art* (London, 1984). For a stimulating text with magnificent illustrations, see D. and V. Elisseeff, *Art of Japan* (New York, 1985). Also see J. E. Kidder, Jr., *The Art of Japan* (London, 1985), for an insightful text accompanied by beautiful photographs.

CLASS DISCUSSION

Divide students into groups and ask them to achieve consensus in their opinion of the following statement (discussed on page 308).

The path to enlightenment may only be found through a life of self-discipline and meditation.

Do they feel their position on achieving enlightenment could be extended to other mental or physical conditions such as in education or athletics?

USING PRIMARY SOURCES

Assign students to write a paragraph that describes how the poem on page 308 makes them feel. What do they think the principle of Japanese aesthetics: "less is more" means? Would they consider following this principle in their own lives?

OUR LITERARY HERITAGE

USING PRIMARY SOURCES

Assign students to read the excerpt from the Tale of Genji and list the social values and beliefs it demonstrates. Do students believe that similar feelings may be experienced by those who are or have household servants in our own society?

Answers to Critical Thinking Questions

1. The nun had been his nurse when Genji was young. Even then, the young child was her master. She was proud to have served him and considered her job honorable and important.

2. Answers will vary. The elderly nun rising from the couch, her tears, her pride in the prince, the prince's sentimental speech about his childhood, and his reference to the many bitter partings of life all contribute to the impact of the scene.

3. Genji, who represents Japanese aristocracy, was isolated from the people he loved at an early age. He was held in awe by those who served him, even when he was young. The responsibilities associated with his station in life kept him apart from other people.

LEARNING FROM VISUALS

The Golden Pavilion in Kyoto is a wooden structure that is neither large nor a great feat of engineering achievement. It is covered in gold foil but in other ways is not particularly unique. What is it about it then that makes it so universally recognized as an example of both Japanese art and architecture?

ACTIVITY

Have students do additional research on No drama and Greek tragedy. Compare the two and analyze the values each reveals about the society that produced it.

310

OUR LITERARY HERITAGE

The Tale of Genji, continued

thought a great deal about you and wished that life did not force so many bitter partings upon me."

So he spoke tenderly. The princely scent of the sleeve which he had raised to brush away his tears filled the low and narrow room, and even the young people, who had till now been irritated by their mother's obvious pride at having been the nurse of so splendid a prince, found themselves in tears.

1. What was the relationship between Genji and the nun?

2. What words and actions were most effective in developing the tender mood of this scene?

3. What does this selection reveal about the lifestyle and values of Japanese aristocrats?

---

of instrumental music. In some respects, No reminds us of Greek tragedy. Both use a story, music, dance, a chorus, and masks. In No drama, however, the chorus does not take part in the action on stage. No plays were usually short. Often as many as five were presented in a single evening.

Art and Architecture

In art and architecture, as in literature, the Japanese pursued their interest in beauty, simplicity, and nature. To some degree, Japanese artists and architects were influenced by Chinese forms.

The search for beauty was an outstanding aspect of Japanese painting. Nature themes were important, such as seashore scenes, spring rain, moon and mist, or flowering cherry blossoms. The themes were intended to awaken an emotional response on the part of the viewer. Unlike Chinese painting, Japanese painting suggested the frail beauty of nature by presenting it on a smaller scale. The majestic mountain in a Chinese painting became a more intimate Japanese landscape with rolling hills and a rice field.

During the Kamakura period (1185 to 1333), painters focused more on the exploits of the warrior class. Painting, as a result, became more realistic. Por-

◄ *The Golden Pavilion in Kyoto stands as a monument to the Japanese idea of harmony in nature and architecture. The pavilion was built in the fourteenth century. Because it was covered in gold foil, it was named the Golden Pavilion. The pavilion was destroyed in a fire in 1950 but was rebuilt and reopened in 1987.*

CNN WORLD HISTORY UPDATES

You can update your coverage of World History topics, as well as spark lively classroom discussion and deeper understanding, by using the **CNN World History Updates**.

For assistance in using and incorporating the **CNN World History Updates** into your classroom presentations, see the *Classroom Guide*.

trait art flourished as artists depicted warriors in realistic detail, including crooked teeth and worry lines on foreheads. Japanese sculptors also produced realistic wooden statues of generals and nobles.

Landscape served as an important means of expression in both Japanese art and architecture. Japanese gardens were at first based on Chinese models. The landscape surrounding the fourteenth-century Golden Pavilion in Kyoto displays a harmony of garden, water, and architecture that makes it one of the treasures of the world. Because of the shortage of water in the city, later gardens were made with rocks. White pebbles, for example, were used to represent water. In the Ryoanji Temple, rocks and pebbles are used to suggest mountains emerging from the sea.

 SECTION REVIEW

1. **Locate:**
   (a) Nara

2. **Define:**
   (a) No

3. **Identify:**
   (a) Shinto,   (b) Buddhism

4. **Recall:** Why were Japanese women the most productive writers of Japanese prose fiction from the ninth through the twelfth centuries?

5. **Think Critically:** Why does Chinese and Japanese writing look so similar?

Conclusion

During the Sui, Tang, and Song dynasties, Chinese civilization flourished once again. The Mongols overthrew the Song dynasty and established a new dynasty in 1279. Although Mongol rulers adapted to the Chinese political system, this dynasty, too, failed to last. In 1369, a new Ming dynasty came into power.

During the thousand years of these five dynasties, China advanced in many ways. Industry and trade grew in size and technological capacity. In the countryside a flourishing agriculture bolstered China's economic prosperity. In addition, Chinese society achieved a high level of development and stability. The civil service provided for a stable government bureaucracy and an avenue of upward mobility that was virtually unknown elsewhere in the world. China's achievements were unsurpassed throughout the world and made it a civilization that was the envy of its neighbors and of the world. China also influenced other states in the region, including Japan.

Few societies in Asia historically have been as isolated as Japan. Cut off from the mainland by 120 miles of ocean, the Japanese had little contact with the outside world during most of their early development. However, once the Japanese became acquainted with Chinese culture, they were quick to take advantage of the opportunity. In the space of a few decades, the young state adopted many features of Chinese society and culture and thereby introduced major changes into the Japanese way of life. Nevertheless, while early Japanese rulers tried to create a centralized political system like that of China, the power of landed aristocrats ensured a weak central authority. The result was a society that was able to make use of ideas imported from beyond its borders without endangering customs, beliefs, and institutions inherited from the past.

Notes

1. Quoted in Arthur F. Wright, *The Sui Dynasty* (New York, 1978), p. 180.
2. Quoted in Robert Temple, *The Genius of China: 3,000 Years of Science, Discovery, and Invention* (New York, 1986), p. 150.
3. Quoted in John K. Fairbank, Edwin O. Reischauer, and Albert M. Craig, *East Asia: Tradition and Transformation* (Boston, 1973), p. 164.
4. John of Plano Carpini, quoted in Rene Grousset, *L'Empire des Steppes* (Paris, 1939), p. 285.
5. *The Travels of Marco Polo* (New York, n.d.), p. 119.
6. Charles O. Hucker, *China's Imperial Past* (Stanford, 1975), p. 100.
7. *Ibid.*, p. 150.
8. Temple, *The Genius of China*, p. 91.
9. Quoted in David John Lu, *Sources of Japanese History*, vol. 1 (New York, 1974), p. 33.
10. Donald Keene, *Anthology of Japanese Literature* (New York, 1955), p. 192.

ASSESS

Answers to SECTION REVIEW

2. (a) Japanese drama; the plots were usually based on stories from Japanese history or legend
3. (a) a state religion of Japan, the belief centers around the worship of nature spirits
   (b) another religion in Japan; the sect of Zen became most popular
4. aristocratic men wrote in Chinese; women learned to read and write at home and used their spare time to develop their writing skills
5. because the Japanese first took over the Chinese written language

TIME LINE

As students conclude the chapter, you may want to refer them to the chapter time line in the *Study Guide.* The time line will help them put key dates in perspective.

SPANISH SUPPORT

The *Conclusion* has been translated into Spanish for your Spanish-speaking students. Included with this translation (in your Teacher Resource Box) are Section Key Points, which consist of one or two sentences summarizing each section in the chapter. These Key Points have also been translated into Spanish.

CLOSE

Lead students in a discussion of the 'Focus' objectives identified on page 308.

USING KEY TERMS

1. genin
2. shogunate
3. khanates
4. daimyo
5. Bushido
6. No
7. shogun
8. porcelain
9. eta
10. samurai

REVIEWING THE FACTS

1. The Yangtze and the Huang, it provided a north-south route and allowed the emperor to supervise his empire better.
2. streamlined the operations of the government; restored civil service examinations; gave land to the peasants; broke up the power of the large estate holders
3. the Confucian classics
4. steel, cotton, gunpowder, paper money, and the compass
5. the landed gentry, or scholar-gentry
6. the family, ideally would be an extended or joint family
7. Genghis Khan
8. Khanbaliq; Beijing
9. Buddhism and Taoism
10. Li Bo and Du Fu
11. the Kamikaze
12. Shinto (the Sacred Way)
13. Zen Buddhism

THINKING CRITICALLY

1. The Chinese bureaucracy was staffed by civil servants chosen on the basis of competitive examinations. In Japan, the civil service was open only to the aristocrats.
2. to provide for a more stable economy and to strengthen the power of the central government. The early Ming rulers also wanted to strengthen the central government. In Japan, the same attempt failed because leading officials were awarded large tracts of tax-free land.

312

USING KEY TERMS

1. In Japan, the _____ were landless peasants who could be bought and sold like slaves.
2. The system of government established in Japan by Minamoto Yoritomo was called the _____.
3. The sons of Genghis Khan divided his empire up into separate territories called _____.
4. The _____ were the heads of great noble families in Japan who controlled vast landed estates, paid the emperor no taxes, and controlled the samurai.
5. The "way of the warrior," or _____, strictly governed the behavior of the Japanese military class.
6. A form of Japanese drama where the actors wear masks and dance to instrumental music is known as the _____ play.
7. A powerful Japanese general who exercised actual power while ruling under the emperor's name was called a _____.
8. _____, which became popular in China during the Tang dynasty, is a ceramic made of fine clay fired at very high temperatures in a kiln.
9. Members of the lowest social class in Japan were the _____, hereditary slaves who performed tasks like burying the dead.
10. The class of military retainers who served local aristocrats in Japan was called the _____.

REVIEWING THE FACTS

1. Which two rivers in China did the Great Canal connect? Explain why the canal was important to Emperor Sui Yangdi.
2. How did the early Tang rulers try to strengthen the central government? How did they attempt to provide a more stable economy?
3. What formed the basis of the Chinese civil service examinations?

312

4. Name five new technological developments or new products introduced during the Tang dynasty.
5. Who became the new political and economic elite of Chinese society during the Tang era?
6. What was the most basic unit of Chinese society, and what form would it ideally take?
7. Who was the Mongol chieftain who united the tribes of the steppe and conquered a vast empire in China, Persia, and the Abbasid empire?
8. To what city did Khubilai Khan move the capital of the Yuan dynasty? What is the modern name of that city?
9. What two religions emerged in China to compete with Confucianism?
10. Name two important poets of the Tang period.
11. What prevented the conquest of Japan by the Mongols?
12. What became the state religion in Japan?
13. What form of Buddhism became most popular in Japan?

THINKING CRITICALLY

1. Compare and contrast the Chinese and Japanese civil service systems.
2. Why did the Tang and, later, the Ming rulers in China attempt to institute land reform? Why were similar attempts in Japan unsuccessful? What consequence did that failure in Japan have?
3. Compare Buddhism with Confucianism. Why was Buddhism eventually seen as a threat to the state?
4. What was the economic significance of the Mongol conquest of Eurasia?
5. Why do some historians consider the decision to stop the great trading expeditions as a turning point in Chinese history?
6. In what ways are Chinese and Japanese poetry similar?
7. Compare and contrast the Chinese *Tale of the Marshes* with the Japanese *Tale of the Heike*.
8. Compare Chinese and Japanese painting.

3. The essence of Confucianism was the need for devotion to family and for hard work—qualities that supported the state. Buddhism taught that the material world was an illusion and encouraged young men to withdraw from the world. These qualities tended to undermine the authority of the state.
4. strengthened long distance trade, especially along the Silk Road
5. It turned China inward upon itself, back towards traditional agriculture.
6. Both idealized high moral character.
7. *Tale of the Marshes* portrays rebellion in the face of oppression; represents a form of social criti-

cism. *Tale of the Heike* expresses violence in the form of heroism in war; reinforces the values of the authority. Both have a pessimistic element.
8. Both Chinese and Japanese painting features nature scenes heavily. In Chinese painting, nature is portrayed on a large scale, with human figures small. Japanese painting is smaller in scale. Both forms concentrate on creating a mood.
9. in poetry by creating a mood through focusing on a single subject; in painting, nature themes were represented on a small scale; in landscaping, an emphasis was placed on the harmony of garden, water, and architecture, rather than elaborate designs

CHAPTER 10 REVIEW

9. How is the Japanese aesthetic principle that "less is more" exemplified in poetry, painting, and landscaping?

APPLYING SOCIAL STUDIES SKILLS

1. **Geography:** How did geography lead to historical differences between China and Japan?
2. **Geography:** Consult Map 10.1 on page 283 and identify the extent of the Tang Empire. What modern countries did it include?
3. **Geography:** Consult Map 10.1 and identify the Yangtze River and the Huang River. Locate the first Grand Canal and the modern Grand Canal. Approximately how long is the Yangtze River? The Yellow River? The first Grand Canal? The modern Grand Canal? Why might the Chinese have constructed a modern Grand Canal?
4. **Geography:** Consult Map 10.2 on page 293 and examine the Mongol Empire. What modern-day countries did it include?
5. **Geography:** Consult Map 10.2. How many khanates were formed in the Mongol Empire?
6. **Geography:** Compare the Mongol Empire with the Roman Empire (see Chapter 6). Which empire was larger in size?
7. **Economics:** Consult Map 10.3 on page 297. Speculate on what kind of products Zhenghe might have brought back from the East Indies, from East Africa, from Arabia and Persia, and from India.
8. **Economics:** How did the nature of trade change during the Tang dynasty?
9. **Geography:** Consult Map 10.4 on page 301 and identify at least four major cities in Japan.
10. **Sociology:** Draw a diagram of the social pyramid for China and then for Japan. How are they similar? In what ways do they differ?

MAKING TIME AND PLACE CONNECTIONS

1. Compare the Buddhist monasteries of China with the Christian monasteries of medieval Europe.
2. In what ways was Japan similar to medieval Europe with regard to the central government and landholding?
3. In what ways were the samurai of Japan similar to the knights of medieval Europe?
4. What social and economic conditions in Japan and medieval Europe account for similarities between Japan and Europe?
5. In what ways were the eta of Japan similar to the Untouchables in India?
6. Does the existence of a class such as the eta represent a society that is fundamentally hierarchical or democratic? Why?
7. What modern-day society has a caste system with some classes in the position of the eta or the Untouchables?
8. Compare and contrast Greek tragedy with Japanese No plays.

BECOMING AN HISTORIAN

1. Consult **You Are There: At the Table of the Great Khan** and **Biography: Empress Wu.** Determine whether each is a primary or a secondary source.
2. What might you infer about the purpose of the elaborate court ritual described by Marco Polo?
3. What biases might Marco Polo's account of China under Khubilai Khan have? What might have been his purpose in writing his account?
4. What inference can be made from the fact that in Tang China poor families often sold their daughters as concubines and, in time of famine, female infants were often killed?
5. What common factors are there in the fall of the Tang and Yuan dynasties?

313

11 PLANNING GUIDE

SECTION	KEY TOPICS	PRIMARY SOURCES	ASSESSMENT
1 India after the Guptas pages 315-323	◆ Causes and effects of the decline of Buddhism in India ◆ Expansion of Islam to the East ◆ Impacts of Islam on Indian government and culture	◆ Ala-ud-din outlaws the use of alcohol and gambling, page 321	◆ Section Review, page 323 ◆ Section Quiz 11-1, TRB
2 Life and Culture in India pages 323-327	◆ Developments in the economic system and daily life of Indian people ◆ Growth of Indian culture	◆ Description of merchants in Bengal, pages 324-325 ◆ A poem by Amaru, page 325	◆ Section Review, page 327 ◆ Section Quiz 11-2, TRB
3 The Development of Civilization in Southeast Asia pages 327-332	◆ Geography and population of Southeast Asia ◆ Foundations of civilizations in Southeast Asia ◆ Growth of states in Southeast Asia	◆ Description of Vietnamese resistance to invasion, page 329	◆ Section Review, page 332 ◆ Section Quiz 11-3, TRB
4 Society and Culture in Early Southeast Asia pages 333-338	◆ Developments in social structure and the daily lives of people in Southeast Asia ◆ Religious beliefs in early Southeast Asia ◆ Culture in Southeast Asia	◆ Description of pirates in the Straits of Malacca, page 333	◆ Section Review, page 338 ◆ Section Quiz 11-4, TRB

CIVILIZATION IN SOUTH ASIA AND SOUTHEAST ASIA (500 TO 1500)

REPRODUCIBLE ACTIVITIES

Historical Maps

Charts and Graphs

Critical Thinking

Cooperative Learning

Vocabulary

Guided Reading

Reteaching

Enrichment

Performance Assessment

Spanish Key Points and Chapter Summaries

Spanish Vocabulary

Spanish Guided Reading

MULTIMEDIA SUPPORT

TRANSPARENCIES
- *World History* Color Transparency Package
- Fine Art Color Transparency Package

VIDEO
- *World History* Video Library
- CNN. Annual Video Update

LASERDISC
- *Sights and Sounds of History*

AUDIO
- *Listening to Literature* audiotape (English and Spanish)
- *History of Music* CD

SOFTWARE
- WESTEST™
- Student Review

CD–ROM
- *The Journey of Civilization*
- *World History*

INTERNET
- Internet Activities

On Line with WORLD HISTORY

Access West's history web site at
http://history.swpco.com
You'll find activities and web sites related to specific topics and chapters in *World History: The Human Odyssey*. Also look for references to helpful web sites at appropriate places throughout this teacher edition.

LESSON PLANNING

You will find detailed daily lesson plans for both traditional class scheduling and **block scheduling** in your Teacher Resource Box.

Not Enough Time?

If you do not have the four or five days recommended to teach this chapter, you may want to focus on the following sections and activities:

- Have students skim the chapter to answer the "Questions to Guide Your Reading" on page 315. Discuss their answers, then read the "Conclusion" on page 339.
- Do a more in-depth reading about the decline of Buddhism and the rise of Islam in India on pages 315-318, the development of the Indian economic system on pages 323-325, the formation of political states in Southeast Asia on pages 330-332, and social structure and daily life in Southeast Asia on pages 333-335. Conclude with a class discussion of conflicts between Islam and Hindu religions as demonstrated by the "You Are There" feature on page 321.

CIVILIZATION IN SOUTH ASIA

BUILDING ON CHAPTER 10

To prepare students to study Chapter 11, you may use the following questions and activities.

◆ Remind students that many of China's government officials were chosen through a civil service examination. Ask them to keep this in mind as they learn about the government in India and Southeast Asia.

◆ Students should recall that harsh treatment of Chinese peasants caused them to revolt at times. Were peasants treated differently in India? What factors may have caused them to be more satisfied with their lives?

LEARNING FROM VISUALS

Answer to the caption question: Students should recognize that this elephant is colorfully adorned and seems joyous.

USING THE OPENING STORY

Select from the following questions to reinforce the reading of the opening story.

◆ Why would the effort of Islamic invaders to force their religion on Indian people tend to reduce the number of wars between non-Islamic people?

◆ Why have most small kingdoms in history lasted for relatively short periods of time?

By 500, the Gupta dynasty, which had ruled northern India since 320, had begun to collapse. Northern India fell into chaos. For the next five hundred years, India was divided into a large number of small kingdoms, and fighting among these states became a way of life. Indian poems of the period tell of combat between Indian kings that was carried on by warrior bands seated on elephants and in chariots and armed with lances, swords, and bows and arrows. When a king won, he and his warriors collected their loot, returned to the palace, and celebrated. Colossal banquets were served, according to one poet, "by beautiful women decked in fine jewels and sweet smiles." Eating never seemed to end. One poet described how a participant felt: "By eating flesh day and night, the edges of my teeth became blunt like the plowshare after plowing dry land." When a king lost, his deeds were remembered in poetry and song.

Indian poets gave advice to those who wanted to follow a military career: "When you see a fight, rush to the front, divide your enemy's forces, stand before them,

and get your body scarred by the deep cuts of their swords; thus your fame is pleasant to the ear, not your body to the eye. As for your enemies, when they see you, they turn their backs, and with bodies whole and unscarred, they are pleasant to the eye, not so their shame to the ear." One king, who was injured in the back when he retreated, was so ashamed that he starved himself to death.

Beginning in the eleventh century, much of northern India was conquered by Turkish people from the northwest, who established some sense of order. Turkish dynasties, which were set up in many areas, brought Islamic religion and civilization to India, adding yet another religion to this land of religions. The new faith caused serious conflict between its followers and the Hindu majority.

Meanwhile in Southeast Asia, a number of new civilizations also arose. Between 500 and 1500, organized states developed throughout the mainland and islands of Southeast Asia. Both China and India had an impact on the development of these Southeast Asian states.

▲ *This spirited elephant is decorated with a colorful rug and primed for battle as it carries its warrior off to war. How does this compare to the picture of Greek war elephants in Chapter 5?*

ADDITIONAL RESOURCES

The resources listed below can be used to enrich the lessons in this chapter.

BOOKS FOR STUDENTS
Historic India by Lucille Shulberg, Time-Life
Illustrated World's Religions by Huston Smith, Harper Collins (used earlier)

VIDEOS/FILMS
The Art of Asia, India, Southeast Asia, China, Korea, and Japan by J. Weston Walch,

Social Studies School Service, (800) 421-4246

CD-ROM
Religions of the Worlds, Mentorom, Social Studies School Service (800) 421-4246

AND SOUTHEAST ASIA

(500 TO 1500)

NEW PATTERNS OF CIVILIZATION

500	SOUTH AND SOUTHEAST ASIA	1500
400		1500

QUESTIONS TO GUIDE YOUR READING

1. What were the major steps in the Islamic expansion into India?

2. What impact did Muslim rule have upon Indian society?

3. What was life like for the average Indian peasant between 500 and 1500?

4. Which states emerged in Southeast Asia between 500 and 1500, and what were their major features?

5. What were the major features of the social structures in Southeast Asian societies?

6. How does Southeast Asia reflect Chinese, Indian, and Muslim influences?

INDIA AFTER THE GUPTAS

In the centuries that followed the collapse of the Gupta Empire, the idea of a united Indian state was only a dream. Political power remained in the hands of many people. A seventh-century Chinese traveler reported that India was divided into about seventy states. Fighting among these states plagued the lives of ordinary Indians.

The Decline of Buddhism

For hundreds of years, Buddhism had retained its popularity among the Indian people. However, with popularity came change. Like all great religious and philosophical doctrines, the teachings of the Buddha came to be interpreted in different ways. People did not always agree on the meaning of the original teachings of the Buddha. As a result, a split developed among the followers of Buddhism in India.

One group of Buddhists believed that they were following the original teachings of the Buddha. They called themselves the school of **Theravada** (the teachings of the elders). Followers of Theravada saw Buddhism as a way of life, not a religion that was centered

315

Answers to QUESTIONS TO GUIDE YOUR READING

1. Turkish slaves founded new Islamic state called Ghazni; conquering of Mahmud and then pushed further by Tamerlane (pages 317-319)

2. separation between Muslim ruling class and mass of Hindu population; converted millions to Islam; imposed on some Hindu customs and required tax from non-Muslims; created mutual hostility between Muslims and Hindus (pages 319-323)

3. most farmed tiny plots of land and paid share of harvest to landlord; (pages 323-324)

4. (see pages 330-332)

5. In many locations, hereditary aristocrats held power and wealth and lived in cities; beyond city walls lived rest of population. Some were influenced by Chinese practices and some by Indian practices (pages 333-335)

6. through religion, cultural practices, societal values, and ideas of government (page 339)

FOCUS ON THEMES

Listed below are brief summaries of how the content in this chapter supports the text's key themes.

Politics and History Both India and Southeast Asia were divided into numerous small states. A number of these small states, such as Vietnam and Angkor, experienced long periods of rule by strong monarchs.

The Role of Ideas The introduction of new ideas, especially religious, political, and cultural ideas, led to new ways of life in South Asia and Southeast Asia. Islam had a strong impact on India, whereas Hinduism, Buddhism, and Islam made important inroads in Southeast Asia. Moreover, Indian and Chinese political, social, and cultural ideas influenced developments in Southeast Asia.

The Importance of Cultural Developments Indian and Chinese models in art and architecture were important influences in Southeast Asia.

Religion in History The civilizations of India and Southeast Asia witnessed the flourishing of a variety of religions, including Hinduism, Buddhism, and Islam.

The Role of Individuals Some individual rulers, such as Tamerlane in India and Jayavarman in Angkor, made a strong impact on the region. Religious missionaries were influenced in a quite different way.

The Impact of Science and Technology Their technical skills enabled the peoples of India and Southeast Asia to build a remarkable number of splendid temples and palaces.

315

FOCUS

OBJECTIVES

After completing this section, students should be able to

1. identify and explain the causes and effects of the decline of Buddhism in India
2. describe the events that brought about the introduction of Islam into India
3. describe the impact of the spread of Islam on India's society and culture

FOCUS ACTIVITY

Help students understand why people often fight to avoid religious persecution. When the Muslim leaders, like Mahmud of Ghazni, killed thousands of Hindus and destroyed their places of worship, they sowed the seeds of hatred that still exist today. Students may be assigned to investigate other religious conflicts such as those between Protestants and Catholics in Europe at the time of the reformation (Chapter 14) or of Jewish people in Spain during the inquisition (Chapter 13). In other cases people have been willing to leave their homes to achieve religious freedom. This was the case when the Puritans colonized Massachusetts. Do students believe India would be a more peaceful land today if there had been greater religious toleration in the past?

on individual salvation. They continued to insist that an understanding of one's self was the chief way to gain Nirvana, or release from the wheel of life (see Chapter 3).

Another view of Buddhist doctrine was emerging in northwest India. Here Buddhist believers stressed the view that Nirvana could be achieved through devotion to Buddha and not just through painstaking attention to one's behavior. This school, known as **Mahayana**

Buddhism, said that Theravada teachings were too strict for ordinary people to follow. Only the rich, they said, would have the time and resources to spend weeks or months in meditation and self-reflection. Mahayana thus tried to assure the masses that they, too, could reach Nirvana.

To Mahayana Buddhists, Buddhism was a religion, not a philosophy. Buddha was not just a wise man but

Map 11.1   The Spread of Buddhism

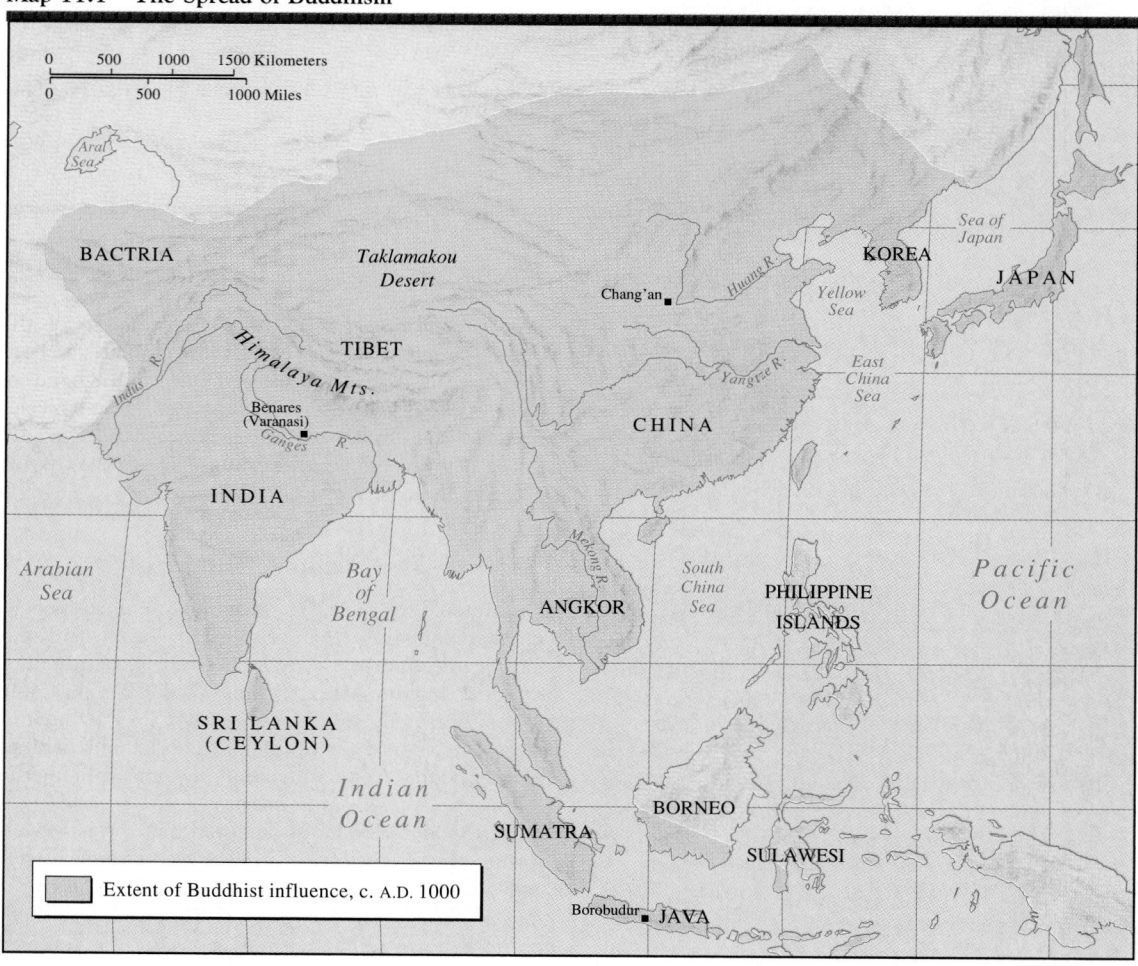

STUDYING MAPS

The following questions will help you guide students through their study of Map 11.1.

1. Have students compare this map wth Map 11.5 on page 336. What areas that are Buddhist on this map, have changed to Islam on Map 11.5? *(part of Borneo, Sumatra, Java, part of Celebes, the end of the Malay peninsula)*

2. Did geographic barriers, such as rivers, oceans, or mountains, seem to prevent Buddhism from spreading? *(no)*

3. Why can religions and philosophic points of view appeal to many groups of people with different languages, cultures, and social values? *(Answers will vary.)*

also a divine figure. Nirvana was not just a release from the wheel of life but a true Heaven. Through devotion to Buddha, the faithful—whether rich or poor—could hope to achieve salvation in this Heaven after death.

In the end, neither the Mahayana nor the Theravada sect of Buddhism was able to remain popular in Indian society. By the seventh century, Theravada had declined rapidly. Although Mahayana prospered in the northwest for centuries, it, too, was absorbed by a revived Hinduism and later by a new arrival, Islam. Despite its decline in India, Buddhism found success abroad. Carried by monks to China, Korea, and Japan, the practice of Buddhism has remained active in all three countries in East Asia to the present.

The Eastward Expansion of Islam

In the seventh century, the entire Middle East was shaken by the birth of a new and dynamic religion. The leader was Muhammad, and the religion was Islam (see Chapter 8). The new faith spread rapidly westward from its origins on the Arabian peninsula, advancing across North Africa and into Spain. Islam also moved eastward across Persia. Finally, in the early eighth century, it moved into the northwestern corner of the Indian subcontinent.

The new religion had a major impact on Indian civilization, which is still evident today in the division of the subcontinent into mostly Hindu India and two Islamic states, Bangladesh and Pakistan. One reason for Islam's success in South Asia is that it arrived at a time when India was in a state of even greater political disunity than usual. The Gupta Empire had collapsed, and no central authority had replaced it.

When the Arab armies reached India in the early eighth century, they did little more than move into the frontier regions. At the end of the tenth century, however, a new phase of Islamic expansion took place when rebellious Turkish slaves founded a new Islamic state—known as Ghazni (GAWZ-nee), located in present-day Afghanistan. When the founder of the new state died in 997, his son, Mahmud of Ghazni, succeeded him. Mahmud, an ambitious man, began to make attacks against neighboring Hindu kingdoms to the southeast. Before his death in 1030, he was able to

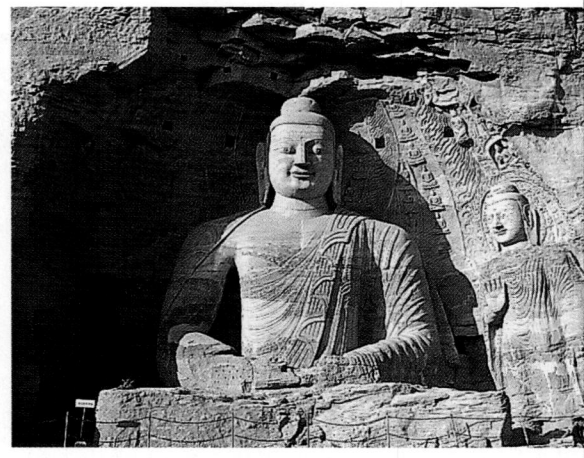

▲ *This colossal Buddha, carved c. A.D. 460, sits in the Yun-Kang caves in China. In what other countries can you find statues of Buddha?*

extend his rule throughout the upper Indus valley and as far south as the Indian Ocean. He also established a brilliant court at Ghazni.

Resistance against the advances of Mahmud and his successors into northern India was led by the **Rajputs,** who were Hindu warriors. They fought bravely, but their military tactics, based on infantry supported by elephants, were no match for the cavalry of the invaders, which struck with lightning speed. Mahmud's successors continued their advances. By 1200, Muslim power had reached over the entire plain of northern India, creating a new Muslim state known as the Sultanate of Delhi.

In the fourteenth century, the Sultanate of Delhi extended its power into the Deccan plateau, but during the latter half of the century it began to decline. Near the end of the century, a new military force crossed the Indus River from the northwest, raided the capital of Delhi, and then withdrew. As many as 100,000 Hindu prisoners were massacred before the gates of the city. It was India's first meeting with Tamerlane.

Tamerlane was the ruler of a Mongol state based in Samarkand, to the north of the Pamir Mountains. Born sometime during the 1330s in Samarkand, Tamerlane

---

TEACH

REINFORCING VOCABULARY

Assign students to review the points of view of the **Theravada** and **Mahayana** Buddhists. Ask students to discuss why divisions in any group are likely to result in a decline in its power and popularity.

LEARNING FROM VISUALS

Answer to the caption question: Statues of Buddha can be found in Japan, India, and Korea.

CLASS DISCUSSION

Lead students in a discussion of the following statement. "The success of Islam in India was primarily the result of the state of India's political disunity in the eighth century." Do they believe it is, or is not, true? What reasons can they give to support their opinions?

COMPARING TIME PERIODS

Ask students to investigate the German blitzkrieg during World War II that is discussed in Chapter 28 and compare it with the tactics used by the forces of Mahmud of Ghazni against the Hindu Rajputs. Why is superior mobility an advantage in any war?

RETEACHING ACTIVITY

Have students draw a map of the Middle East and Asia, showing the extent of Islamic expansion by the 15th century. Then, have them determine where Islam is located today. What conclusions can they draw from the comparison?

Ask students whether geographical barriers tended to slow the spread of Islam. Was the extent of Islamic influence as great as that of Buddhism? (See Map 11.1 on page 316.) Why do students think this is the case?

COMPARING TIME PERIODS

Ask students to write an essay in which they compare the Chinese experiences with invading Mongol forces, discussed in Chapter 10, and that of India when it first fought with Tamerlane. What happened in India to end the Mongol threat that did not occur in China? How might the history of India be different if there had been a permanent Mongol ruler?

ACTIVITY

Refer students to the bottom photo on page 319. Have them examine this and other pictures of architectural monuments in India and the Indianized states of Southeast Asia. Then have them determine the Indian and native features of Southeast Asian buildings.

Map 11.2   India, 1100–1400

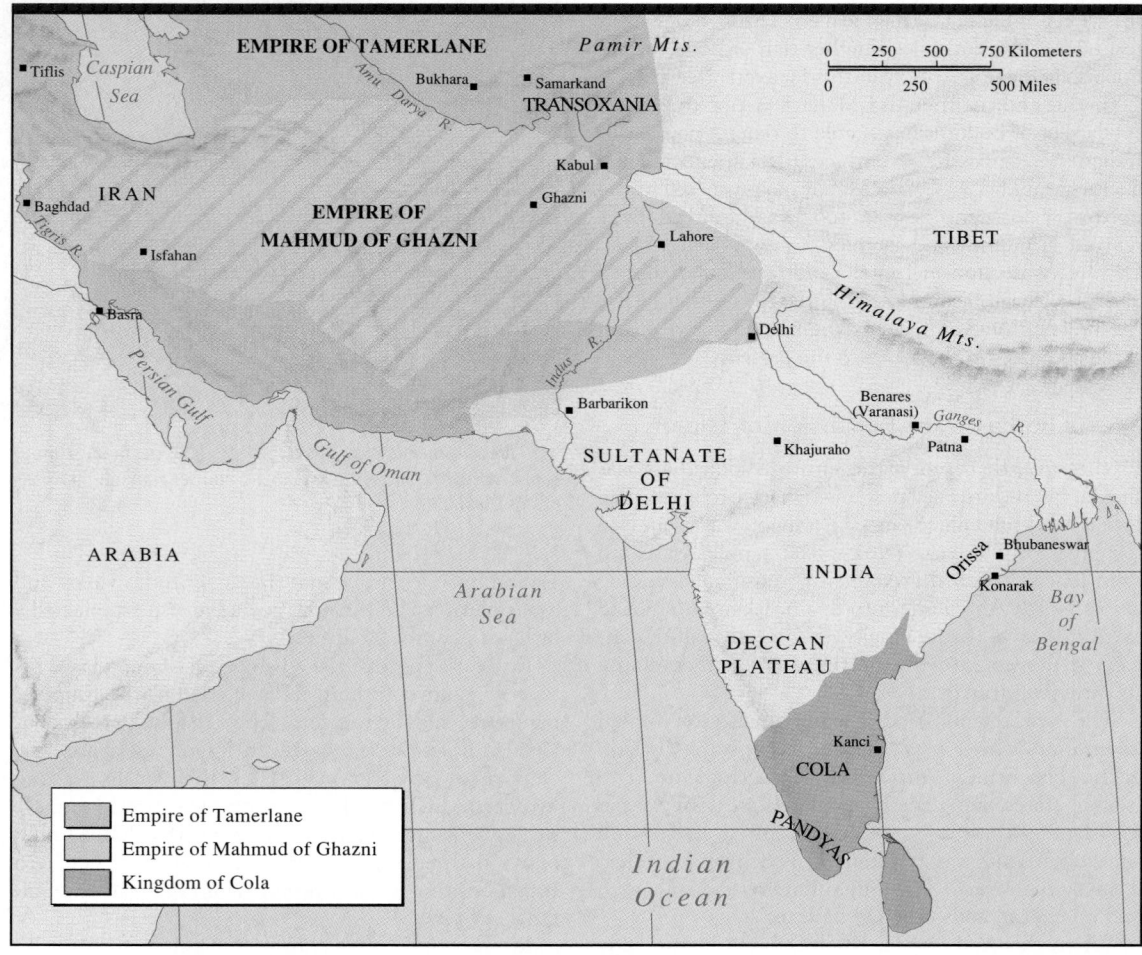

seized power in 1369 and immediately launched a program of conquest. During the 1380s, he placed the entire region east of the Caspian Sea under his authority and then occupied Mesopotamia. After his brief foray into northern India, he turned to the west. He died in 1405 in the midst of a military campaign.

The death of Tamerlane removed a major menace from the different states of the Indian subcontinent, but the calm did not last long. By the end of the fifteenth century, two new challenges had appeared from beyond the horizon. One came from the north in the form of the Mughals, a newly emerging nomadic power. The

STUDYING MAPS

The following questions will help you guide students through their study of Map 11.2.

1. About how many times larger is the Empire of Mahmud of Ghazni than the Kingdom of Cola? *(about 6 times larger)*
2. Why would Tamerlane attack Delhi before other important Indian cities? *(Answers will vary. It was near his empire, located on a major river, etc.)*

3. Consider the vast lands Tamerlane's forces conquered. Why is it unlikely that he really controlled these lands? Why did the Mongol threat to India end after his death? *(Answers will vary. The empire was too large to be controlled by one person. The Mongols focused their efforts in other areas.)*

other came from Europe, from Portuguese traders arriving by sea in search of gold and spices. As we shall see in Chapters 17 and 18, both the Mughals and the Portuguese, in their different ways, would exert a major impact on the later course of Indian civilization.

Islam and the State

At first, the establishment of Islamic power in northern India did not change local methods of government. Muslim rulers simply set up their own states, which became part of the existing state system. The Sultanate of Delhi had few contacts with Muslim rulers in the Middle East.

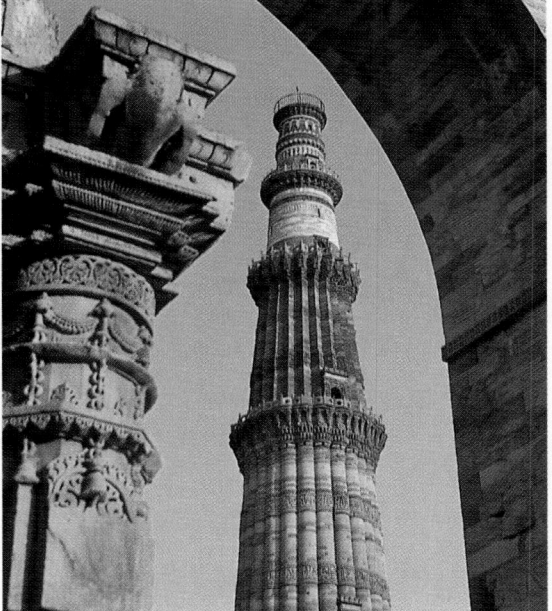

◄ *This miniature taken from an Indian manuscript shows the Mongol Tamerlane. What signs of a courageous warrior and conqueror do you see in the image?*

One major difference, however, between the Muslim and Hindu rulers was that the Muslims continued to view themselves as foreign conquerors. As a result, they maintained a strict separation between the Muslim ruling class and the mass of the Hindu population. In the Muslim states, a few Hindus rose to important positions in the local bureaucracy, but Muslims continued to hold high posts in the central government and the provinces.

Islam and Indian Society

Many Muslim rulers in India were tolerant of other faiths. They used peaceful means, if any, to encourage people to convert to Islam. Some, however, could be fierce when their religious zeal was aroused. Said one, "I forbade the infliction of any severe punishment on the Hindus in general, but I destroyed their idol tem-

ples and raised mosques in their place." Most Muslim rulers realized that there were simply too many Hindus to convert them all. They accepted the need to tolerate what to them was an alien religion. Nevertheless, Muslim rulers did impose many Islamic customs on Hindu society (see "You Are There: A Muslim Ruler Suppresses Hindu Practices").

Although Hindu religious practices were tolerated, non-Muslims were required to pay a tax to the state. Over time, millions of Hindus did turn to the Muslim faith.

► *This ornate tower was originally 238 feet tall. It was built by Muslims on the site of Delhi's largest Hindu temple to commemorate Muslim victory. The inscription on the tower reveals its mission—to cast the shadow of God over the Hindus.*

TEACHING THEMES

Politics and History. Ask student to write a paragraph in which they explain how the separation of Hindus from the Muslim ruling class in India may have contributed to problems between these groups that have lasted to the present day.

LEARNING FROM VISUALS

Ask students to consider how they would feel if an enemy defeated them, tore down their house of worship, and erected a monument to their loss on the same site? How may the tower pictured to the left have contributed to hard feelings between Hindus and Muslims in the past as well as the present?

Answer to the caption question: Tamerlane appears well armed, even as he sits upon his throne.

So What ⁇

*If your students question the importance of the information on the **Hindu-Muslim conflict in India,** tell them . . .*

The Muslim country of Pakistan and the Hindu nation of India are both widely believed to possess nuclear weapons. Ask students to consider this theory with the knowledge that the Hindus and Muslims still continue the ancient antagonisms that began 500 years ago. Ask students how these facts could impact their own lives.

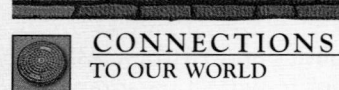

CONNECTIONS
TO OUR WORLD

CLASS DISCUSSION

Lead students in a discussion of the rights of minorities to follow religious beliefs that conflict with the beliefs of those in power. This can be seen in Muslim opposition to the sexual frankness in Hindu art. It can also be seen in American opposition to marriages of children to adults. Although this is an acceptable practice in many cultures it is against the law in this country. In 1996 a marriage was arranged between an adult male and a twelve year old girl in a religious community where this practice was accepted. Do students believe the U.S. government was right to stop this marriage?

LEARNING
FROM VISUALS

Ask students to speculate about where the drawing to the right might have been placed or used. What purpose do drawings of military victories serve for the victor? How may they affect the defeated?

CONNECTIONS
TO OUR WORLD

The Clash Between Hindus and Muslims On December 7, 1992, a mob of Hindu militants in India sacked a Muslim mosque in the town of Ayodhya, in northern India. For years, militant Hindus had demanded that this Muslim mosque, built on a Hindu holy site that had once been occupied by a Hindu temple, should be destroyed. The mosque had been constructed in the seventeenth century, but was no longer used to any great extent.

When the government failed to meet the militants' demands, the Hindu demonstrators pulled down the mosque and began to erect a Hindu temple at the site. These actions in turn led to clashes between Hindus and Muslims throughout the country. In neighboring Pakistan as well, Muslim rioters destroyed a number of Hindu shrines.

Since 1982, the tensions between Hindus and Muslims in India have continued to grow. Recently, a militant Hindu political party led by Balasaheb Thackeray, who calls himself the "Hitler of Bombay," has called for a new Indian state that would only meet the interests of the Hindu majority. This conflict between Hindus and Muslims has been a feature of life in India for over a thousand years.

The invasion of India by Muslim forces began in the eighth century. At the end of the tenth century, however, Muslim invaders became more numerous and more deadly. One Muslim conqueror of northern India, Mahmud of Ghazni, delighted in destroying Hindu places of worship. His army once massacred 50,000 Hindus who had gathered in a Hindu holy city. Other Muslim conquerors after Mahmud continued his destructive example. Stones from demolished Hindu temples were often used to build mosques. The fanaticism of these early Muslim conquerors angered Hindus and helped create the bitter rivalries that have lasted in India to this day.

▲ *Indian elephants were no match for invading Muslim horsemen (shown here). Although Muslims were known as conquerors, they also built libraries and universities in many Muslim cities, a lasting legacy for all.*

Some were people who were employed by the Muslim ruling class, including government officials, artisans, or merchants who served the needs of the court. Many others, however, were peasants from the lowest caste or even Untouchables. In the Hindu social scheme, these people had a low-caste status. In Islam, they were regarded as equal with all other believers in Allah.

Seldom have two religions been so different. Hinduism believed in many manifestations of one god; the Muslims, only one. Hinduism had a priestly caste. Islam did not have priests, because no one was allowed to come between the individual believers and Allah. At the popular level, Muslims were critical of the sexual frankness in Hindu art, whereas the Hindus disliked the Muslim habit of eating beef. Such differences contributed to the mutual hostility that developed between the believers of the two faiths, which has continued until today.

In some cases, however, the two peoples borrowed political and cultural ideas from each other. Some

COOPERATIVE LEARNING ACTIVITY

Have students work together in small groups to prepare charts of the major religions of the Indian subcontinent. The charts should give major doctrines and show where each religion became the dominant religion.

Ask students what lessons they think they should learn about the history of the Indian subcontinent based upon the information in the charts?

YOU ARE THERE

A Muslim Ruler Suppresses Hindu Practices

Muslim rulers in northern India tried to impose Islamic customs on Hindu society. This excerpt, written by a fourteenth-century Muslim historian, describes the attempt of one Muslim ruler, Ala-ud-din, to outlaw alcohol and gambling. Both were forbidden in Muslim society.

A Muslim Ruler Outlaws Alcohol and Gambling

He forbade wine, beer, and intoxicating drugs to be used or sold; dicing, too, was prohibited. Vintners [wine merchants] and beer-sellers were turned out of the city, and the heavy taxes which had been levied from them were abolished. All the china and glass vessels of the Sultan's banqueting room were broken and thrown outside the gate, where they formed a mound. Jars and casks of wine were emptied out there till they made mud as if it were the season of the rains. The Sultan himself entirely gave up wine parties. Self-respecting people at once followed his example; but the ne'er-do-wells went on making wine and spirits and hid the leather bottles in loads of hay or firewood and by various such tricks smuggled it into the city. Inspectors and gatekeepers and spies sought to seize the contraband and the smugglers; and when seized the wine was given to the elephants, and the importers and sellers and drinkers flogged and given short terms of imprisonment. So many were they, however, that holes had to be dug for their imprisonment outside the great thoroughfare of the gate, and many of the wine-drinkers died from the rigor of their confinement and others were taken out half-dead and were long in recovering their health. The terror of these holes kept many from drinking. The prevention of drinking proving very difficult, the Sultan enacted that people might distill and drink privately in

▲ *A banquet at the sultan's palace was indeed a lavish affair, as this copper engraving done in* A.D. *1483 shows. The sultan and his guests wear jeweled turbans and sit upon luxurious handwoven rugs. What does the dress and demeanor of the servants reveal about their lives and about the life of the sultan?*

their own homes, if drinking parties were not held and the liquor not sold. After the prohibition of drinking, conspiracies diminished.

1. Summarize the actions adopted by the Muslim ruler to prohibit consumption of alcohol and gambling.

2. How effective were these measures in outlawing drinking and gambling?

3. Are you aware of any modern parallels to the situation described here?

On Line with

WORLD HISTORY *Internet Activity*

You may want to have your students visit the following URL, where they will find information and additional web site resources to enhance their study of this chapter.

Understanding Islam and the Muslims
**http://darkwing.uoregon.edu/
~kbatarfi/islam.html**

At this site you will find good graphics and links to Islam in Africa, Japan, Middle East, and Asia.

Due to the ever-changing nature of the World Wide Web, see the West History web site, **http://history.swpco.com** for regular updates of the URLs in this text.

YOU ARE THERE

USING PRIMARY SOURCES

Divide the class into groups and ask each group to compare the reported result of the Muslim ruler with prohibition in the United States during the 1920s. Why might the Muslims' law have been more successful than prohibition was in the United States? Could it have had anything to do with the nature or the way punishment was administered?

LEARNING FROM VISUALS

Answer to the caption question: The servants appear to be well fed, well dressed, and healthy. Students might infer that the sultan spent money not only on himself and family, but also on all those who attended him.

Answers to Critical Thinking Questions

1. threw out the sellers of spirits, destroyed drinking glasses, emptied liquor out onto the street, and gave up wine parties himself
2. The prevention of drinking proved difficult.
3. Students may be familiar with Prohibition in 1920s America.

Multimedia Support

TRANSPARENCY 11–1, Comparative Chart of Hindu and Muslim Beliefs

USING PRIMARY SOURCES

Assign students to write a description of life in India as seen from the point of view of an Untouchable. What would lead such a person to deliberately touch women of higher castes?

LEARNING FROM VISUALS

Answer to the caption question: This untouchable woman is stooped under labor, isolated from all other beings. She appears as a tragic figure, worn out by her work and the caste system.

Answers to Critical Thinking Questions:

1. These are scorned folk of a lowly caste, who live where others would never even travel.
2. Nayres women lived in fear of being stalked and touched by a Poleas during certain times of the year.
3. Anyone who would do such a thing must believe that the caste system is more important than the life of a family member.

ASSESS

Possible assessments include:

1. Section Review questions on this page
2. Section 11-1 Quiz in your Teacher Resource materials
3. Reteaching Worksheets in your Teacher Resource materials
4. Self-Study software

YOU ARE THERE
Untouchables in South India

Some of the best descriptions of Indian society came from European merchants. In this passage, the Portuguese traveler Duarte Barbosa describes an Untouchable caste (the Poleas) on the southwestern coast of India in the early sixteenth century. The Nayres were a higher caste in the region.

Duarte Barbosa Describes the Untouchables

And there is yet another caste of Heathen lower than these whom they call Poleas, who among all the rest are held to be accursed; they dwell in the fields and in secret places, where folk of good caste never go save by mischance, and live in huts very strait and mean. They are tillers of rice with buffaloes and oxen. They never speak to the Nayres save from afar off, shouting so that they may hear them, and when they go along the roads they utter loud cries, that they may be let past, and whosoever hears them leaves the road, and stands in the wood till they have passed by; and if anyone, whether man or woman, touches them his kinsfolk slay him forthwith, and in vengeance therefore they slay Poleas until they weary without suffering any punishment. In certain months of the year they do their utmost to touch some Nayre woman by night as secretly as they can, and this only for the sake of doing evil. They go by in order to get into the houses of the Nayres to touch women, and during these months the women guard themselves carefully, and if they touch any woman, even though none have seen it, yet she declares it at once, crying out, and she will stay no longer in her house that her caste may not be destroyed; in general she flees to the house of some other low caste folk, and hides herself, that her kinsfolk may not slay her. And the manner of touching is this,

▲ *The caste system in India continues to this day and has proven to be hard to eradicate. Here an Untouchable woman is shown sweeping the street, isolated and alone. What can you infer about this woman from both her posture and her demeanor?*

even though no words are exchanged, they throw something at her, a stone or a stick, and if it touches her she is touched and ruined.

1. Describe the life of a member of the Poleas caste.

2. Explain the fears of the Nayres women.

3. The passage says that if the Poleas touch a person, that person's relatives kill the person who has been touched. What does this practice say about the importance of the caste system to Indian society?

RECOMMENDED READING

A number of studies of Indian society and culture deal with this period. See, for example, R. Lannoy, *The Speaking Tree,* Oxford, 1971), for a sophisticated interpretation of Indian culture during the medieval period. On Buddhism, see H. Nakamura, *Indian Buddhism: A Survey with Bibliographical Notes* (Delhi, 1987); and H. Akira, *A History of Indian Buddhism from Sakyamuni to Early Mahayana*

(Hawaii, 1990). For an interesting treatment of the Buddhist influence on commercial activities that is reminiscent of the role of Christianity in Europe, see L. Xinru, *Ancient India and Ancient China: Trade and Religious Changes A.D. 1-600* (Delhi, 1988).

The Islamic period in Indian history is treated in S. M. Ikram, *Muslim Civilization in India* (New York, 1964); and C. E. Bosworth,

Muslim rulers took over the Indian idea of divine kingship. Hindu leaders learned by bitter experience that cavalry mounted on horses was superior to cavalry mounted onelephants.Some upper-class Hindu males were attracted to the Muslim tradition of keeping women in seclusion, and this custom entered Indian civilization.

All in all, however, Muslim rule did not have a significant impact on the lives of most Indian women. In many respects Muslim women had more privileges than Hindu women. They had more property rights, and they were legally permitted to divorce under certain conditions and to remarry after the deaths of their husbands. As we saw in Chapter 3, upper-class Hindu women were expected to throw themselves on their dead husbands' funeral pyres.

Overall, the relationship between Muslim and Hindu was that of conqueror and conquered, a relationship marked by suspicion and dislike rather than friendship and understanding. One problem area for both Muslims and Hindus as they tried to come to terms with the existence of a mixed society was the problem of caste. Could non-Hindus form castes? If so, how were these castes related to the Hindu castes? Over a period of time, Muslims did form their own castes that were roughly the same as the Hindu castes. In most of India, then, Muslim rule did not really disrupt the caste system. Early European visitors to India reported on the social distinctions they found in Indian society (see "You Are There: Untouchables in South India").

 SECTION REVIEW

1. **Locate:**
   (a) Ghazni,   (b) Deccan plateau,
   (c) Samarkand,   (d) Pamir Mountains

2. **Define:**
   (a) Theravada,   (b) Mahayana,   (c) Rajputs

3. **Identify:**
   (a) Buddhism,   (b) Islam,
   (c) Muhammad,   (d) Mahmud of Ghazni,

(e) Sultanate of Delhi,
(f) Tamerlane

4. **Recall:** Identify the route that Islam followed from its place of origin to India.

5. **Think Critically:** Did the introduction of Islam into the Indian culture have a positive or negative effect on the culture? Give reasons that support your answer.

LIFE AND CULTURE IN INDIA

Conquerors come, and conquerors go. The life of India between 500 and 1500 seemed to continue as it had for centuries. At the same time, Indian writers and artists built upon the literary and artistic achievements of earlier centuries.

Economy and Daily Life

Between 500 and 1500, most Indians lived on the land and farmed their own tiny plots. In return, peasants paid a share of their harvest each year to a landlord, who in turn sent part of the payment to the local ruler. In effect, the landlord worked somewhat as a tax collector for the king, who in theory owned all the land in his state.

Although the vast majority of Indians were peasants, reports by foreign visitors between 500 and 1500 indicate that a considerable minority of the population lived in the cities. It was here that the landed elites and rich merchants lived, often in conditions of considerable wealth. Rulers, of course, had the most wealth. One maharaja (great king) of a small state in southern India, for example, had over 100,000 soldiers in his pay, along with 900 elephants and 20,000 horses. Another ruler kept a thousand high-caste women to serve as sweepers of his palace. Each carried a broom and a brass basin holding a mixture of cow dung and water, and "when the King goes from one house to another, or to a house of prayer, he goes on foot, and these women go before him with their brooms and

The Later Ghaznavids: Splendour and Decay (New York, 1977). On the career of Tamerlane, see B. F. Manz, *The Rise and Rule of Tamerlane* (Cambridge, 1989).

The most up-to-date treatment of the Indian economy, in particular, the regional trade throughout the Indian Ocean, is K. N. Chaudhuri, *Trade and Civilization in the Indian*

Ocean: An Economic History from the Rise of Islam to 1750 (Cambridge, 1985), a groundbreaking comparative study. See also his more recent and massive *Asia before Europe: Economy and Civilization of the Indian Ocean from the Rise of Islam to 1750* (Cambridge, 1990), which owes a considerable debt to F. Braudel's classical work on the Mediterranean Sea.

Answers to
SECTION REVIEW

2. (a) saw Buddhism as a way of life; (b) said Theravada teachings were too strict for ordinary people to follow; (c) Hindu warriors who resisted Mahmud of Ghazni

3. (a) a religion based on the teachings of the Buddha; (b) a religion begun by Muhammad; (c) the leader of Islam; (d) leader of the Islamic state of Ghanzi; (e) the Muslim state created in 1200 in northern India; (f) ruler of a Mongol state based in Samarkand

4. began in the Middle East, advanced across North Africa and into Spain, moved across Persia and into the Indian subcontinent

5. Answers will vary.

CLOSE

Lead students in a discussion of the 'Focus' objectives identified on page 316.

FOCUS

OBJECTIVES

After completing this section, students should be able to

1. identify and explain developments in the Indian economic system under Muslim rule
2. identify and explain changes in Indian society under Muslim rule
3. describe Indian culture under Muslim rule

FOCUS ACTIVITY

Help students understand that supporting a large military and an opulent life for rulers may be both a stimulus and a danger to a state's economy. Although farmers and merchants may benefit from sales to their government, the state's purchase of goods and services is based on its ability to tax. This may create many jobs, but it is also likely to cause dissatisfaction and poverty among farmers and workers who see production and consumption that they are not allowed to share. Ask students to find evidence of this type of problem in India.

Multimedia Support

TRANSPARENCY
11–2, Comparative Population Maps of South Asia showing Hindu and Muslim population distribution in the 15th century and 20th century.

TEACH

LEARNING FROM VISUALS

Divide the class into groups and ask them what it would take to enable the farmer in the photograph to the right to be as efficient as most American farmers. Point out that he has need for more than a modern tractor. What skills would he have to learn? How would he take his crops to market? What seeds and fertilizers would he use? Why were Indian farmers able to lead a better life in the past even when they used these farming methods?

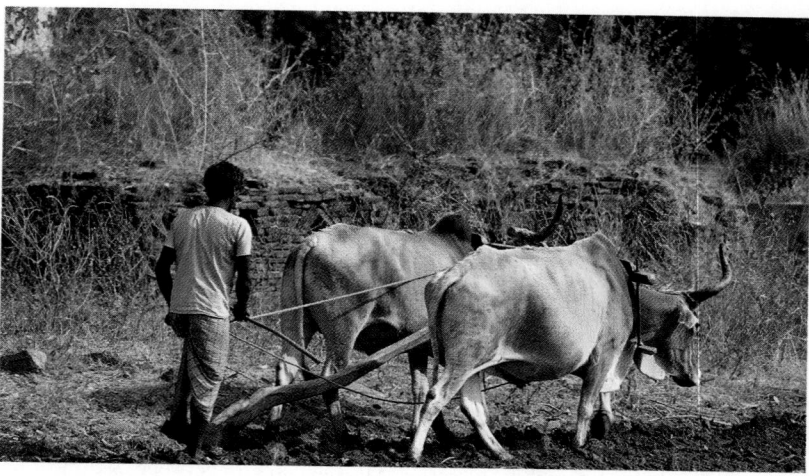

▶ *India has been called the land of wonders and the land of contrasts. Poverty and the hard life of the peasants contrasted sharply with the rich luxury of the sultans and the upper castes. Farmers today still use bull carts for plowing, just as they did centuries ago.*

basins in their hands, plastering the path where he is to tread."

Life for ordinary Indian peasants may not have been as difficult in some respects as it is for Indian peasants today. The population of India was much smaller then than it is now (100 million compared with over 900 million today). Farm plots were therefore larger. The soil was also fertile. Accounts by foreign visitors to India indicate that many farmers were able to harvest two crops a year from their land. In the north and in the upland regions of the Deccan plateau, the primary grain crops were wheat and barley. In the Ganges valley and the southern coastal plains, the main crop was rice.

According to Xuan Zang, a Chinese missionary who visited India in the seventh century, the most common foods were milk and other dairy products, corn bread, fish, mutton, and venison. Eating the meat of cattle, elephants, pigs, and dogs was prohibited, and everyone despised those who did so. Vegetables were grown everywhere, and southern India produced many spices, sugarcane, fruits, and cotton. Tropical products such as cinnamon, pepper, ginger, cardamom, and cumin were mainly shipped abroad.

Still, life was hard for the average Indian peasant. Then, as today, most farmers tilled their small plots of land with a small wooden plow pulled by oxen. They paid a high percentage of the harvest to the landlord.

These rents in turn funded the sumptuous lifestyle, the wars, and the grandiose temples of the rich and high born. At best, most peasants barely scraped by. At worst, they were forced into debt and fell victim to moneylenders who charged high rates of interest.

Agriculture, of course, was not the only source of wealth in India. Since ancient times, India's location had made it a center for trade between the Middle East and the Pacific basin. It had also been a source for other goods shipped throughout the known world. Internal trade within India probably declined during this period, primarily because of the fighting among the many states of India.

The level of foreign trade, however, remained high, especially in the south and along the northwestern coast. Both areas were located along the traditional trade routes to the Middle East and the Mediterranean Sea. Wealthy Hindu castes with close ties to the royal courts carried on much of the foreign trade. Others, including Muslims, also participated in this trade.

According to accounts by early European travelers, merchants often lived quite well. One Portuguese traveler described some merchants in Bengal as follows:

They have girdles of cloth, and over them silk scarves, they carry in their girdles daggers garnished with silver and gold, according to the rank of the person who car-

MORE ABOUT . . . *Indian Medicine*

The Indian practice of medicine is called *Ayurveda*, which means "the science of life and longevity." Ayurvedic medicine is both a system of health medicine and surgical treatment. Unlike medical practices in the West, Indian medicine focuses on treatment of the person rather than the disease. Whereas Western medicine focuses on diagnosing and treating a bacteria or virus, regardless of who has it, Indian medicine is concerned with the total patient. A person's body type, personality, diet, mental state, and family relations are all taken into account. As in Chinese health care, Ayurvedic medicine is concerned with ensuring the correct balance of a person's energy.

ries them; on their fingers many rings set with rich jewels, and cotton turbans on their heads. They are luxurious, eat well and spend freely, and have many other extravagances as well. They bathe often in great tanks which they have in their houses.[1]

Outside the small, specialized trading communities, most manufacturing and trade were in the hands of artisans and petty traders, who were generally limited to local markets. During this period, India failed to build a strong merchant class or to produce an urban revolution similar to the growth of cities that began in Europe during the High Middle Ages. One factor preventing this was the monopoly on foreign trade held by the government in many areas. One Indian observer reported that at Barbarikon, a seaport near the delta of the Indus River, "all the cargoes are taken up the river to the king." By keeping such a tight control over the importation of goods, governments helped to limit the development of a strong merchant class.

The Wonder of Indian Culture

Between 500 and 1500, Indian artists and writers built upon the achievements of their predecessors. At the same time, they made innovations in all fields of creative endeavor.

Before 500, the primary forms of religious architecture were the Buddhist cave temples and monasteries (see Chapter 3). Between 500 and 1500, religious architecture went from caves to new monumental structures, a development that is especially evident in the Hindu temples (see "Our Artistic Heritage: The Hindu Temple").

The delicate bronze statues of Cola are yet another achievement of this period. Cola was a major trading state on the southeastern coast of India. The most famous of the Cola statues is the Nataraja, or Siva as Lord of the Dance, in which the god Siva is shown destroying the universe so that it can be reborn. These Cola bronzes, dating from the tenth to the twelfth centuries, are found today in museums all over the world.

Indian authors produced a large number of written works between 500 and 1500, which were both secular and religious in nature. Unfortunately, many have been lost because of the climate or the destructive force of the Muslim occupation of northern India.

Many Indian religious poems were written, both in Sanskrit (which, like Latin in Europe, was the language of the educated) and in the languages of southern India. As Hinduism became a more devotional religion, its poetry became more passionate and prompted a sense of divine ecstasy. Much of the religious verse praised the lives and heroic acts of the gods Siva, Vishnu, Rama, and Krishna.

The great secular literature of traditional India was also written in Sanskrit in the form of poetry, drama, and prose. Some of the best Indian poetry of the time is found in single-stanza poems, which create an entire emotional scene in just four lines. Witness this poem by the poet Amaru:

> We'll see what comes of it, I thought, and I hardened
>   my heart against her.
> What, won't the villain speak to me? she thought, flying into a rage.
> And there we stood, sedulously refusing to look one
>   another in the face,
> Until at last I managed an unconvincing laugh, and
>   her tears robbed me of my resolution.[2]

The use of prose was well established by the sixth and seventh centuries. This is truly astonishing in light of the fact that the novel did not appear in Japan until the tenth century and in Europe until the seventeenth century. One of the greatest masters of Sanskrit prose was Dandin, a seventh-century author. In *The Ten Princes*, he created a fantastic and exciting world, fusing history and fiction. His keen powers of observation, details of low life, and humor give his writing much vitality.

Another area of creativity that developed in India during this era was music. Ancient Indian music had come from the chanting of the Vedic hymns (see Chapter 3) and thus had a strong spiritual flavor. In fact, Indians believed that the actual physical vibrations of music were related to the spiritual world. A sloppy performance of a sacred text could upset the harmony and balance of the entire universe.

SPECIAL NEEDS: *Visual*

Pair a visually impaired partner with another student. Assign each student to bring a sampling of two or three spices from home. These can be cinnamon, nutmeg, thyme, bay leaves, pepper, curry, tumeric, etc. The non-visually impaired partner is to use library resources to find out where the spices originated. The visually impaired partner is to conduct interviews to find out in which foods/dishes these spices are commonly used. These interviews may be taped for replay to aid the student or to share with the class. They are to present their findings in an oral report to the class or the teacher. Discussion can move toward why spices were valuable trading commodities in India, and why some spices today still cost a great deal more than others.

USING PRIMARY SOURCES

Ask students to discuss what the description of Bengal merchants showed about the importance of trade to India. If so much money was spent on gold, jewels, and fine clothing, could much be spent on improving the methods of production? Was there probably a fair distribution of income among the people who actually produced the goods that were bought and sold?

Multimedia Support

TRANSPARENCY
11–3, Economic Map showing Indian Trade Routes

USING PRIMARY SOURCES

Ask a student to read the poem by Amaru aloud to the class. Ask students how the person makes them feel. Can they picture the situation in their minds? Ask students to write the beginning and end for the story told in the poem. What happened to cause these people to be angry with each other? How did they act after their dispute was ended? Are they different from many people today?

Multimedia Support

LASERDISC
Temple Caves Carved by Buddhist Monks (Hyderabad, A.D. 500)

OUR ARTISTIC HERITAGE

OUR ARTISTIC HERITAGE
The Hindu Temple

From the eighth century on, Indian architects built a number of magnificent Hindu temples. Each temple consisted of a central shrine surrounded by a tower, a hall for worshipers, an entryway, and a porch, all set in a rectangular courtyard. Temples became ever more ornate. The towers became higher and the temple complexes more intricate. Some became walled compounds set one within the other and resembling a town in themselves.

Some of the best examples of temple art are in the eastern Indian state of Orissa. The temples of Bhubaneswar (built between 750 and 1000) have massive, beehive-shaped towers. However, it is the Sun Temple at Konarak, standing at the edge of the sea and covered with intricate carvings, that is generally considered a masterpiece. Although now in ruins, the Sun Temple still boasts some of India's best-known sculptures. Especially renowned are the twelve pairs of carved wheels, each ten feet high and seated on a raised platform. Each represents one of the twelve signs of the zodiac.

The greatest example of medieval Hindu temple art, however, is probably Khajuraho. Of the original eighty temples dating from the tenth century, twenty remain standing today. All of the towers are buttressed (supported by stone walls) at various levels on the sides. This gives the whole a sense of unity and creates an upward movement similar to Mount Kailasa in the Himalayas, which is sacred to Hindus. Everywhere the viewer is entertained by temple dancers frozen in stone. One dancer is removing a thorn from her foot, another is applying eye makeup, and yet another is wringing out her hair.

There was a different temple style in southern India. The southern temple style was marked by

▲ *Khajuraho is one of the greatest examples of Hindu temple art and architecture. The eye is drawn up vertically along the sides of the temple, which creates a sense of soaring height. How is this temple similar to and different from Christian churches and cathedrals?*

the erection of massive stone towers, some as much as two hundred feet high. The towers were often covered with sculpted figures and were visible for miles in the surrounding countryside. Certainly the temple is one of India's most significant contributions to world art.

1. What are the architectural features of Hindu temples?
2. What themes were explored in the temple carvings and sculptures?

RECOMMENDED READING

The early history of Southeast Asia is not as well documented as the history of China or India. Except for Vietnam, where histories written in Chinese appeared shortly after the Chinese conquest, written materials on societies in the region are relatively sparse. Historians have therefore been compelled to rely on stone inscriptions and the accounts of travelers and historians from other countries.

Very useful in this regard is the Chinese port official Chau Ju-kua's *Records of Foreign Nations.* For a translation, see F. Hirth and W. W. Rockhill, *Chau Ju-kua: His Work on the Chinese and Arab Trade in the Twelfth and Thirteenth Centuries, entitled Chu-fan-chi* (New York, 1966). See also *The Travels of Marco Polo* (New York, n.d.); I-tsing, *A Record of the Buddhist Religion as Practiced in India and the*

◄ *The sitar is thought to be the invention of an Indian poet, Amir Khusram, who lived in the late thirteenth century. The modern sitar shown here resembles a lute but has metal strings. What Western instruments resemble the sitar?*

Indian classical music is based on a musical scale, called a **raga.** There are dozens of separate scales, which are grouped into separate categories according to the time of day during which they are to be performed. The performers use a stringed instrument called a **sitar** and various types of wind instruments and drums. The performers select a basic raga and then are free to improvise the melody and rhythm. The music begins slowly at the lower end of the scale. The performers then explore all the notes and combinations in the scale as they move up the register. A good musician never performs any one raga the same way twice. The audience is concerned not so much with faithful reproduction but with the performer's own creativity, as is the case with jazz music in the West.

 SECTION REVIEW

1. **Locate:**
   (*a*) Ganges River,   (*b*) Cola

2. **Define:**
   (*a*) raga,   (*b*) sitar

3. **Identify:**
   (*a*) Sanskrit

4. **Recall:** Why did India fail to develop a strong merchant class and produce an urban revolution such as was seen in Europe during the Middle Ages?

5. **Think Critically:** The author concludes that life for Indian peasants may have been easier between 500 and 1500 than it is today because of population size. Do you agree with his conclusion? Why or why not?

THE DEVELOPMENT OF CIVILIZATION IN SOUTHEAST ASIA

Because Southeast Asia did not produce a major civilization during antiquity, historians have paid it less attention than India, China, Africa, and the Middle East. Nevertheless, the people of Southeast Asia made some remarkable achievements. They were, for example, among the first to master the techniques of rice cultivation, possibly as far back as nine thousand years ago. Around 200 B.C., a small Vietnamese state emerged in the Red River delta. About two hundred years later, the kingdom of Funan arose in the area of modern Cambodia. From that point on, the region began to play a major role in the affairs of Asia. Very important to the development of Southeast Asia was the fact that all the states that emerged in the area were affected to varying degrees by political and cultural influences coming from China, India, and the Middle East.

The Land and People of Southeast Asia

Between China and India lies the region that today is called Southeast Asia. It has two major parts: a mainland region extending southward from the Chinese border down to the tip of the Malay peninsula and an extensive **archipelago,** or chain of islands, most of which is part of present-day Indonesia and the Philippines.

The term *Southeast Asia* is a recent one. It was adopted during World War II to distinguish the region from East Asia to the north and South Asia to the west. Ancient mariners called the area the "golden region" or the "golden islands." Located between India and China, two highly advanced and densely populated regions of the world, Southeast Asia is a melting

Malay Archipelago (Oxford, 1896); and A. Cortesao, ed. and tran., *The Suma Oriental of Tome Pires and the Book of Francisco Rodrigues* (London, 1944).

The role of commerce has recently been highlighted as a key aspect in the development of the region. For two fascinating accounts, see K. R. Hall, *Maritime Trade and State Development in Early Southeast Asia* (Honolulu, 1985); and A. Reid, *Southeast Asia in the Era of Commerce, 1450–1680: The Lands below the Winds* (New Haven, Conn., 1989). For an overview of the region and its role in the Indian Ocean trade, see the early chapters in K. N. Chaudhuri, *Trade and Civilization in the Indian Ocean: An Economic History from the Rise of Islam to 1750* (Cambridge, 1985).

FOCUS ACTIVITY

Help students understand how the geography of Southeast Asia contributed to the many states and cultures that developed in that part of the world. Compare the vast land masses of India and China with the mountainous peninsulas, jungle, rivers, and islands of Southeast Asia. Ask students to imagine that an earthquake opened up a deep, impassable canyon in the middle of their community. How easy would it be for people to maintain friendships, business relationships, or their form of government?

TEACH

COMPARING TIME PERIODS

In Chapter 9 students learned that in many parts of Africa a variety of cultures, societies, religions, and languages developed. What physical similarities in the geography of parts of Africa and Southeast Asia can students identify that may explain why many small independent states also tended to develop in Southeast Asia?

pot of peoples. Like the Middle East, it is a vast mixture of races, cultures, and religions.

Although the soil in some areas is poor, water is plentiful in Southeast Asia, and the climate is conducive to growing rice. Mainland Southeast Asia consists of several mountain ranges, all of them originating in southern China and then extending southward into the Bay of Bengal or the South China Sea. Between these north-south ranges are several river valleys that run in a southerly or southeasterly direction. Many early peoples came down these river valleys from China in search of a new homeland. Once in Southeast Asia, most of these peoples settled in the fertile delta regions created by the rivers—the Irrawaddy and the Salween in Burma, the Chao Phraya (CHOW PRIE-uh) in Thailand, and the Red River and Mekong (MAY-KONG) in Vietnam. Others settled in lowland areas in the islands to the south.

In contrast, movement between east and west on the Southeast Asia mainland was somewhat difficult. The mountains are densely forested and often infested with malaria-bearing mosquitoes. Thus, the lowland peoples in the river valleys were often cut off from one another and had only limited contacts with the upland peoples living in the mountains.

These geographical barriers may help explain why Southeast Asia is one of the few regions in Asia that was never unified under a single government. This division may also explain the region's slow development. Advanced civilizations did not develop in the region until more than two thousand years after similar societies had emerged in India, China, and the Middle East. When advanced civilizations did emerge, the geographical barriers allowed distinctive cultures to develop with diverse cultural practices, such as different clothes, religions, and languages. It has been said that a greater number of different languages are spoken in Southeast Asia than in any area of comparable size on Earth.

Southeast Asia's geography also led to the emergence of two cultures: the lowland peoples, who grew rice, and the upland hill peoples. The lowland river valley peoples began to develop agricultural civilizations. The peoples living in the hills continued to survive by hunting and fishing or by a simple slash-and-

burn agriculture. When the lowland peoples began to establish kingdoms, they expanded up into the hills and imposed their domination over the tribal peoples living there.

The Beginnings of Civilization in Southeast Asia

Two early civilizations emerged in Southeast Asia: Vietnam and Funan. The Vietnamese first appear in history during the first millennium B.C. in the region of the Red River delta, in what is today northern Vietnam. By about 210 B.C., they began to form a state. However, the Chinese under the Qin (see Chapter 4) were in the process of expanding their empire. Chinese armies entered Vietnam but found the Vietnamese a difficult people to conquer (see "You Are There: The Chinese Invade Vietnam"). The Qin failed, but a century later the Han dynasty succeeded. Vietnam fell under Chinese control by 111 B.C.

The Han rulers then set out to make Vietnam a part of the Chinese Empire. For nearly a thousand years, Vietnam was subject to Chinese political institutions and culture. However, Chinese officials were often frustrated by the Vietnamese. As one official said, "The people are like birds and beasts; they wear their hair tied up and go barefoot, while for clothing they simply cut a hole in a piece of cloth for their head or they fasten their garments on the left side [in barbarian style, to the Chinese]. It is useless to try to change them."[3] Chinese rule also brought Buddhism, Taoism, and Confucian ideas to the Vietnamese.

While China was extending its power southward into Vietnam, Indian influence was beginning to enter Southeast Asia from the west. Indian culture was first introduced to mainland Southeast Asia by merchants. The first society to show the effects of Indian influence was the kingdom of Funan.

Funan was located on the lower Mekong River in present-day Cambodia and was first mentioned by a Chinese traveler in the third century A.D. Funan was both a farming and a trading society. It had trading ties with both India to the west and China to the east. The people of Funan were probably ancestors of the modern

MORE ABOUT . . . Vietnamese Origin

The Vietnamese tell a legend about their origin. A Vietnamese prince, Lac Long Quan came to northern Vietnam from the sea (hinting at a Malay-Polynesian origin) and married a princess, Au Co, from the mountains. In the legend Au Co is described as being the former wife of a northern intruder (indicating possible Chinese ancestry). On top of Mt. Tan Vien, Au Co laid one hundred

eggs, from which emerged one hundred sons. Lac Long Quan told Au Co that they could no longer live together because he was a sea dragon and she was a fairy. So the fifty sons she led to the mountains became the ancestors of the Moung people and the fifty sons he led to the coast became the ancestors of the Vietnamese.

YOU ARE THERE

The Chinese Invade Vietnam

◀ ▶ These statues of Chinese soldiers from the Han dynasty, c. 210 B.C., represent Chinese soldiers who successfully defeated the Vietnamese. How did these soldiers differ from warriors and soldiers from other cultures that were flourishing during this time period?

Around 210 B.C., the armies of the Chinese state of Qin invaded the Red River delta to launch an attack on the small Vietnamese state located there. This selection from a Chinese historian shows that the Vietnamese were not easy to conquer.

A Chinese Historian on Fighting the Vietnamese

Qin Shi Huangdi [the Chinese emperor] was interested in the rhinoceros horn, the elephant tusks, the kingfisher plumes, and the pearls of the land of Yueh [Vietnam]; he therefore sent Commissioner T'u Sui at the head of five hundred thousand men divided into five armies. . . . For three years the sword and the crossbow were in constant readiness. Superintendent Lu was sent; there was no means of assuring the transport of supplies so he employed soldiers to dig a canal for sending grain,

thereby making it possible to wage war on the people of Yueh. The lord of Western Qu, I Hsu Sung, was killed; consequently, the Yueh people entered the wilderness and lived there with the animals; none consented to be a slave of Qin, choosing from among themselves men of valor, they made them their leaders and attacked the Qin, by night, inflicting on them a great defeat and killing Commissioner T'u Sui; the dead and wounded were many. After this, the emperor deported convicts to hold the garrisons against the Yueh people.

The Yueh people fled into the depths of the mountains and forests, and it was not possible to fight them. The soldiers were kept in garrisons to watch over abandoned territories. This went on for a long time, and the soldiers grew weary. Then the Yueh came out and attacked; the Qin soldiers suffered a great defeat.

1. Why was the Chinese emperor interested in conquering the Vietnamese?

2. What strategies did the Vietnamese use to avoid defeat?

3. What are guerrilla war tactics? Are they used today?

Cambodian people known as the Khmer. According to local legend, the first king of Funan was an Indian.

Indian ideas and practices also had an impact on Funan. The rulers of Funan worshiped Indian gods. Sanskrit, the formal language of India, was adopted as

the official language of Funan. Indian forms were used in art and architecture. Although Indian culture affected the major towns and the upper classes, we do not know if Indian influence spread into the countryside and affected ordinary people.

YOU ARE THERE

COMPARING TIME PERIODS

Ask your students to write essays or discuss similarities between the military tactics of the Vietnamese when they fought against the Chinese in 210 B.C. and against the United States more than 2000 years later during the 1960s.

LEARNING FROM VISUALS

Answer to the caption question: These soldiers are lightly clad, are on foot, and although they are in a martial stance, the sculptures are not armed. Students might wish to compare these soldiers with the Greek hoplites shown in Chapter 5.

Answers to Critical Thinking Questions

1. He wanted rhinocerous horn, elephant tusks, kingfisher plumes, and pearls.
2. They went to the wilderness and attacked their enemies by night.
3. They are not conventional tactics, not unlike the people of Yueh used, and they are used today.

Lead students in a discussion of how nations influence each other even when they are enemies. Point out that for generations the Chinese and Vietnamese fought each other. For a while China occupied Vietnam only to be thrown out. Still, much of Vietnam's history, beliefs, and culture were shaped by Chinese influence. Ask students to describe differences they believe there might have been in Vietnam's culture and society if China had been 5,000 miles away.

TEACHING THEMES

Economics and History Ask students to label a map of Southeast Asia with the primary types of production or trade that took place in each of the states. Ask them to explain similarities or differences between the economies of these states in terms of their geographic locations.

The Formation of States

Neither Funan nor Vietnam was a great civilization comparable to China or India. Between 500 and 1500, however, several other large and more complex civilizations emerged in Southeast Asia. By 1500, organized states had developed throughout Southeast Asia. One reason for the growth of states was the region's growing role in trade. Especially important was the trade that passed through the area between the Indian Ocean and the South China Sea. As trade increased, local societies began to produce goods for export, such as spices and tropical foods. This new role helped create more complex forms of political and social organization.

In addition, the introduction of foreign ideas also aided the development of civilizations in the region. Chinese armies and government officials brought Chinese ideas with them. Foreign merchants and sailors brought information about Indian institutions and culture to peoples elsewhere in the region. As a result, when the peoples of Southeast Asia began to form states, they used models from China and India. At the same time, they adapted these models to their own needs and created their own unique states.

Vietnam

As we have seen, the Vietnamese were one of the first peoples in Southeast Asia to develop their own state and their own culture. After the Chinese conquered Vietnam, they tried for centuries to make Vietnam part of China. However, the Vietnamese clung to their own identity. In the tenth century, the Vietnamese finally overthrew Chinese rule in the Red River delta.

Chinese influence remained, however. Vietnamese rulers were wise enough to realize the advantages of taking over the Chinese model of centralized government. The new Vietnamese state adopted state Confucianism (see Chapter 4) and called itself Dai Viet (Great Viet). Following the Chinese model, the rulers called themselves emperors and adopted Chinese court rituals. They also introduced the civil service examination as a means of recruiting government officials on the basis of merit. The Vietnamese adopted much of the Chinese administrative structure. This included

Map 11.3   Southeast Asia in the Thirteenth Century

the village at the lowest level. Like its Chinese model, the Vietnamese village was basically independent. As the popular Vietnamese saying put it, "The authority of the emperor stops at the village gate."

The state of Dai Viet (DIE VEE-et) became a dynamic new force on the Southeast Asian mainland. As its population grew, Dai Viet expanded southward. Several centuries of bitter warfare with its southern neighbor, Champa, finally led to Vietnamese victory by 1500. Continuing its "March to the South," by 1600 the Vietnamese reached the Gulf of Siam.

The Vietnamese faced even more serious challenges from the north, however. The Chinese still dreamed of

STUDYING MAPS

The following questions will help you guide students through their study of Map 11.3.

1. What are the approximate dimensions of Southeast Asia? *(about 1,500 miles east to west, and 3,500 miles north to south)*
2. Why was Vietnam the logical Southeast Asian state for China to invade? *(They share a border.)*
3. Why would China's interest in Southeast Asia grow as its trade with other parts of the world increased? *(They would want to profit from the trade.)*

making Vietnam part of the Chinese Empire. The Mongols made the first effort in the late thirteenth century but were driven out after a series of bloody battles. A century later, the Ming dynasty tried again. For twenty years Vietnam was again under Chinese rule. Then in 1428, the Vietnamese once more drove the Chinese out, adding to the already strong sense of Vietnamese identity.

Angkor

Vietnam was not the only powerful state on the Southeast Asian mainland. In the ninth century, the kingdom of Funan collapsed, giving way to the new and more powerful kingdom of Angkor. The kingdom was formed in the ninth century when a powerful figure named Jayavarman united the Khmer (kuh-MEAR) people and established a capital at Angkor Thom. In 802, Jayavarman was crowned as god-king of his people. For several hundred years, Angkor (as it was called because of its capital city, Angkor Thom)—or the Khmer Empire—was the most powerful state in mainland Southeast Asia.

Although Angkor carried on some trade, its wealth was based on farming. This success was the result of an extensive system of irrigation throughout much of what is now Cambodia. Angkor made use of institutions brought from India and also maintained trade relations with China.

Angkor faced enemies on all sides. To the east were the Vietnamese and the kingdom of Champa. To the west was the Burman kingdom of Pagan. With the arrival in the fourteenth century of new peoples from the north—known today as the Thai (TIE)—Angkor began to decline. In 1432 the Thai from the north destroyed the Angkor capital. The Angkor ruling class fled to the southeast, where they set up a new capital near Phnom Penh (pu-NAWM PEN), the capital of present-day Cambodia.

Thailand

The Thai first appeared in the sixth century as a frontier people in China. Beginning in the eleventh or twelfth century, Thai tribes began moving southward.

▲ *These monuments to Buddha remind us of the greatness that existed at Ayuthaya, which was one of the most beautiful cities in Asia. When the Burmese invaded in 1767, most of the city's residents were killed, and all official records were destroyed.*

This process was encouraged by the Mongol invasion of China in the mid-thirteenth century. At first these migrating peoples settled in the mountains just south of the Chinese border. Later they moved further south, into the broad valley of the Chao Phraya River, where they came into conflict with Angkor. As we have seen, the Thai destroyed the Angkor capital in 1432.

The Thai set up their own capital at Ayuthaya, on the Chao Phraya River, where they remained as a major force in the region for the next four hundred years. Although they converted to Buddhism and borrowed Indian political practices as well, they created their own unique blend that evolved into the modern-day culture of Thailand.

Burma

The Thai were also threatened from the west by the Burman peoples, who had formed their own agricultural society in the valleys of the Salween and Irrawaddy Rivers. The Burmans had migrated from the highlands of Tibet beginning in the seventh century A.D., probably to escape advancing Chinese armies.

TEACHING THEMES

Economics and History
Ask students to explain why many nations in Southeast Asia that could not be defeated in a military encounter were eventually subdued by economic forces. For another example consider the United States and Japan in the years following World War II. The United States may have won the war, but we are now a debtor nation to Japan. What did trade have to do with the ability of India and China to exert their influence in Funan?

MORE ABOUT . . . *the Vietnamese War with the Mongols*

Kublai Khan, the Mongol leader of 13th century China, sent an army to conquer Vietnam. The Mongols smashed the Vietnamese capital, but were repulsed by a Vietnamese guerilla counter-offensive. A second Mongol invasion consisted of 500,000 soldiers. The Vietnamese force of 200,000 men was led by Tran Hung Dao, who is today considered to be Vietnam's greatest national hero. According to a legend reminiscent of England's King Arthur tale, a magical turtle arose from a lake and gave Trung a mystical sword. He used this sword to again defeat the Mongols and then returned it to the turtle in the lake.

LEARNING FROM VISUALS

Ask students to discuss differences in the kind of lives people would lead in a city with waterways for streets, like the one pictured to the right, and one that was built on higher ground and used dirt roads. Why might people prefer to live in one city or the other?

ASSESS

Answers to
SECTION REVIEW

2. (a) chain of islands

3. (a) an early farming and trading society in what is now Cambodia; (b) (Great Viet) an early Vietnamese state; (c) a Vietnamese kingdom that took over when Funan collapsed; it was the most powerful state in mainland Southeast Asia; (d) a great Burman kingdom founded in the eleventh century; Mongol attacks in the late thirteenth century weakened Pagan and caused it to decline; (e) founded in the late thirteenth century, Majapahit was the greatest empire the Malay region had ever seen

4. geographical barriers

5. Answers will vary.

▲ *The islands in Malaysia used waterways as others used roads, and boats such as these were the principal means of transportation.*

The Burmans were pastoral peoples, but they adopted farming soon after their arrival in Southeast Asia. In the eleventh century they founded the first great Burman state, the kingdom of Pagan. Like the Thai, they converted to Buddhism and also adopted Indian political institutions and culture. During the next two hundred years, Pagan became a major force in the western part of Southeast Asia. It played an active role in the sea trade throughout the region. Attacks from the Mongols in the late thirteenth century, however, weakened Pagan, causing it to decline.

The Malay World

In the Malay peninsula and the Indonesian archipelago, a different pattern emerged. For centuries, this area had been tied to the trade that passed from East Asia into the Indian Ocean. Much of its wealth had come from the export of tropical products to China, India, and the Middle East. The area had never been united under a single state, however. The vast majority of the people of the region were of Malay background, but the peoples of the area were divided into numerous separate communities.

Two organized states finally emerged in the region. In the eighth century, Sri Vijaya (SREE VIJ-uh-wuh) became a powerful trading state that dominated the trade route passing through the Strait of Malacca. At the same time, the kingdom of Sailendra emerged in eastern Java. Both states were influenced by Indian culture. Sri Vijaya depended on trade, whereas the wealth of Sailendra was based primarily on farming.

Like the mainland states, these island kingdoms were in constant conflict with each other, as well as with the nearby mainland states. In the late thirteenth century, Sri Vijaya was destroyed by Singhasari, a new kingdom formed by the conquest of Sailendra. Singhasari itself was attacked by the Mongols. However, after the Mongols were thrown out, the new kingdom of Majapahit was founded and became the greatest empire the region had yet seen. In the mid-fourteenth century, Majapahit incorporated most of the archipelago and perhaps even parts of the mainland under a single rule.

Majapahit did not have long to enjoy its new status, however. By the fifteenth century, a new state was beginning to emerge in the region. After the Muslim conquest of northern India, Muslim merchants—either Arabs or Indian converts—had settled in port cities in the region and had begun to convert the local population. Around 1400, an Islamic state began to form in Malacca (muh-LACK-uh), a small town on the western coast of the Malay peninsula. It soon became the major trading port in the region and a chief rival to Majapahit. From Malacca, Muslim traders and the Muslim faith moved into the interior. Eventually, almost the entire population of the region was converted to Islam and became part of the Sultanate of Malacca.

 SECTION REVIEW ❀

1. Locate:
(*a*) Vietnam,   (*b*) Red River,   (*c*) Cambodia,
(*d*) Malay peninsula,   (*e*) Philippine Islands,
(*f*) Bay of Bengal,   (*g*) Burma,   (*h*) Thailand,
(*i*) Chao Phraya River

CLOSE

Lead students in a discussion of the 'Focus' objectives identified on page 327. Stress the importance of the physical geography of Southeast Asia on the development of states and cultures in its history.

So What ??

If your students question the importance of the information on **Vietnam**, *tell them . . .*

Vietnam's success against the more powerful Mongols and Chinese invaders foreshadowed their war with the United States in the 20th century. Ask students to tell their classmates what they know about the Vietnam War. Ask them to compare their knowledge of that war with the information they now have about Vietnamese history. Do they think that U.S. military leaders should have been able to predict the outcome of their war with the Vietnamese?

2. **Define:**
   (*a*) archipelago

3. **Identify:**
   (*a*) Funan,   (*b*) Dai Viet,   (*c*) Angkor,
   (*d*) Pagan,   (*e*) Majapahit

4. **Recall:** What explanation is given for the region
   of Southeast Asia never being unified under a
   single government and for its slow development?

5. **Think Critically:** Explain how an increase in
   trade and exporting would cause a region to
   develop more complex forms of political and social
   organization.

SOCIETY AND CULTURE IN EARLY SOUTHEAST ASIA

The traditional states of Southeast Asia can be divided
into two groups: **agricultural societies** (countries with
primarily farming economies) and **trading societies**
(countries depending primarily on trade for income).
Of course, the agricultural states had some trading
activities, and the trading societies had some farming.
Some states, however, such as Vietnam, Angkor,
Pagan, and Sailendra, drew most of their wealth from
the land. Others, such as Sri Vijaya and the Sultanate
of Malacca, supported themselves chiefly through
trade.

The differences between agricultural and trading
societies were a product of the environment. Vietnam,
Angkor, and Pagan were located in rich river deltas
that made it easy to grow rice. None was tempted to
turn to trade as the prime source of income. Moreover,
none was located along the main trade routes that
crisscrossed the region. By the seventh century, the
chief regional trade route was through the Strait of
Malacca, thus allowing the new state of Sri Vijaya to
prosper.

The rulers of Sri Vijaya had strengthened the use of
this trade route by controlling the pirates who had
once played havoc with shipping in the Strait of
Malacca. After Sri Vijaya's decline, piracy again
became a major problem for the ships passing through
the area. One thirteenth-century Muslim traveler
wrote, "Here there are little islands, from which armed
black pirates with poisoned arrows emerge, possessing
armed warships; they plunder people but do not
enslave them."[4] Eventually, Sri Vijaya collapsed, and
the Sultanate of Malacca became the most important
trading power in the area.

Trade through Southeast Asia had expanded after
the emergence of states in the area, but it reached even
greater heights after the Muslim conquest of northern
India. The rise in demand for spices also added to the
growing volume of trade. As the wealth of Europe and
the Middle East increased, there was greater demand for
the tropical products of East Asia. Merchant fleets from
India and the Arabian peninsula sailed to the Indonesian islands to buy the cloves, pepper, nutmeg, cinnamon, and precious woods that the wealthy in China
and Europe wanted. India and Africa provided textile
goods, metals, and such specialty items as rhinoceros
horn. From China came silk, porcelain, and salt.

At first, private merchants living in port cities in
Sumatra, Java, and the Malay peninsula carried on
much of the trade through Southeast Asia. Traders
from outside the area, such as Arab, Indian, and Chinese traders, were restricted to shipping goods between
their home countries and Southeast Asian ports. Eventually, however, the outsiders sought to increase their
profits by taking a more active role in local trade. Muslim merchants from India were especially aggressive in
pursuing this trade and thus increased the strength of
the Sultanate of Malacca. Because of its location on
the western coast of Malaya, the Sultanate of Malacca
offered natural protection from the great storms that
sweep through the straits during the monsoon season—
another factor that contributed to its growth as a trade
center.

Social Structures and Daily Life

At the top of the social ladder in most Southeast Asian
societies were the hereditary aristocrats. They held
both political power and economic wealth. Most aris-

CLASS DISCUSSION

Lead students in a discussion of the following statement. "Restrictions placed on profitable trade are not likely to be either successful or long lived." Do they believe it is true? What examples can they provide from this or other chapters to support their point of view?

COMPARING TIME PERIODS

Ask students to compare the city of Angkor Thom with major cities they learned about in India or China. How were they similar? What differences were there between them?

Map 11.4   Trade Routes in South Asia and Southeast Asia

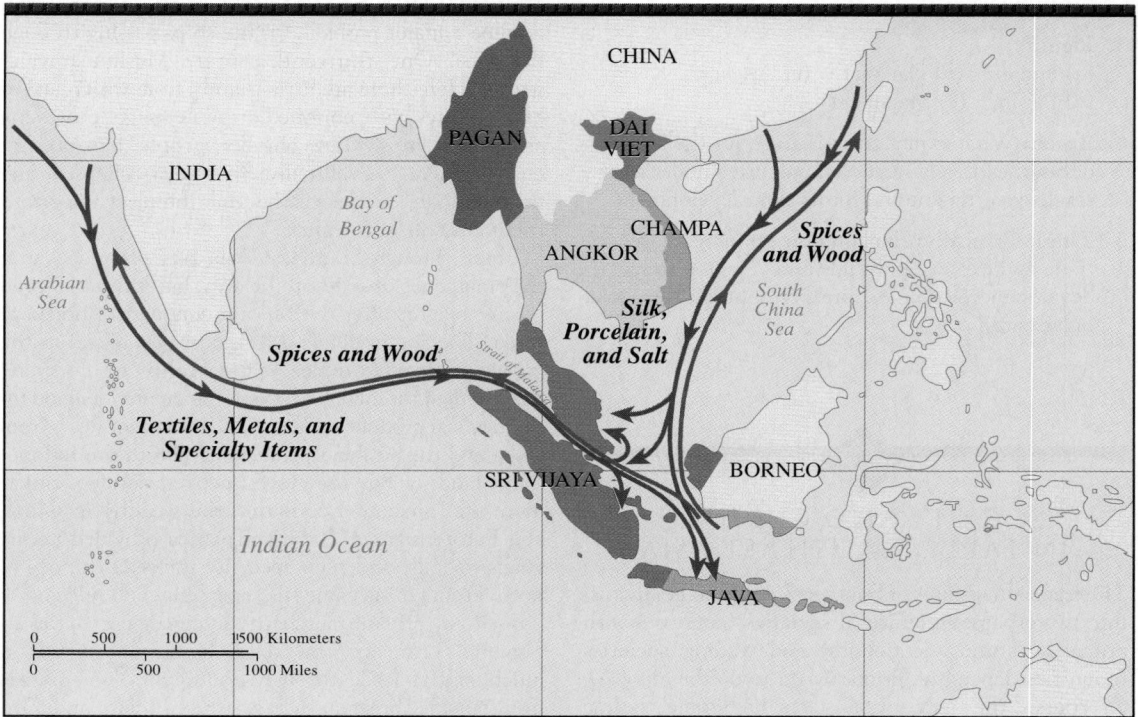

tocrats lived in the major cities, which were the chief source of power and wealth. Angkor Thom, located in northern Cambodia, had royal palaces and parks, a massive parade ground, reservoirs, and numerous temples. The city itself was large enough to hold an immense population. The city was surrounded by a massive stone wall, each side of which was two miles long. The entire city was also surrounded by a moat. Four main gates led into the center of the city.

Beyond the major cities lived the rest of the population, which consisted of farmers, fishers, artisans, and merchants. In most Southeast Asian societies, the majority of people were probably rice farmers who lived at a bare level of subsistence and paid heavy rents or taxes to a landlord or local ruler.

In the Malay world, some peasants were involved in growing or mining products for export, which included tropical food products, precious woods, tin, and precious gems. Most of the trade within the region was carried on by local merchants who bought products from local growers and then carried them to the major port cities. Roads were few and basically primitive. Small boats carried most of the trade down rivers to the major ports along the coast. There the goods were loaded onto larger ships for delivery outside the region.

In a region so diverse, social structures varied a great deal. In Vietnam, social customs were strongly influenced by those of China. As in China, the use of civil service examinations in Vietnam led to the growth of a scholar-gentry ruling class. Below the ruling elite was

STUDYING MAPS

The following questions will help you guide students through their study of Map 11.4.

1. What products were brought from the West for trading in Southeast Asia? *(textiles, metals, and specialty items)*
2. What products came from China and Vietnam to Malacca? *(silk, porcelain and salt)*
3. What products left Southeast Asia for China and the West? *(spices and wood primarily)*
4. Why was control of the Strait of Malacca a great trade advantage? *(It was necessary to pass through this strait in order to trade in Indonesia and then heat out to India and beyond.)*

the mass of the population. Most Vietnamese people were peasants who lived in small villages. Most peasants were small landholders or sharecroppers, who rented their plots from wealthier farmers. Large estates were rare, however. The Vietnamese government limited the size of estates to prevent the rise of a powerful local landed elite.

Family life in Vietnam was similar in many respects to that of China. Chinese rule in Vietnam had led to a Confucian concept of family with its emphasis on obedience to the male head of the family. There was, however, one major difference between family practices in China and Vietnam. Since ancient times, Vietnamese women had possessed more rights than Chinese women. Wives were permitted to own property and could also divorce their husbands.

In the states influenced by Indian practices, the Hindu custom of dividing the population into separate classes was followed. In Angkor and Pagan, for example, the divisions were based on occupation or ethnic background. Each community was under a chieftain, who in turn was subordinate to a higher official responsible for passing on the tax revenues of each group to the central government.

In the kingdoms on the Malay peninsula and the Indonesian archipelago, social relations were generally less formal. Most of the people in the region, whether they were farmers, fishers, or artisans, lived in small villages. Their houses were wooden and were built on stilts to avoid flooding during the monsoon season. Some of the farmers were probably sharecroppers, who paid a part of their harvest to a landlord. In other areas, however, farmers worked their land for themselves.

Like Vietnam, most of the other societies in Southeast Asia gave greater rights to women than did their counterparts in China and India. Women worked side by side with men in the fields and often played an active role in trading activities. Family relations were more informal. The nuclear family (parents and children) was common in Burma and Thailand. In Vietnam and Malaysia, the extended family system (grandparents, parents, and children under the control of the oldest male) was similar to the joint family common in China and India.

▲ Canals were the traditional roads of Thailand and are still used for transportation and trade. Shown here is a floating market in the town of Bangkok.

Religion in Early Southeast Asia

Before the introduction of Indian religious ideas into Southeast Asia early in the first millennium A.D., religious belief in Southeast Asia took the form of the spirit worship that we have seen in other cultures in the area. Like the Japanese, Southeast Asians believed that spirits dwelled in the mountains, rivers, streams, and other sacred places in their environment. Mountains were especially sacred, because they were thought to be the place where the souls of all the departed ancestors retired after death.

Hindu and Buddhist ideas began to move into Southeast Asia in the first millennium A.D. and had an especially strong influence on local elites. Hindu and Buddhist ideas offered a more convincing way to explain the universe, and they also provided local rulers with a means of enhancing their prestige and power.

RECOMMENDED READING

Working with limited resources, modern scholars are bringing out some fascinating interpretations of the early history of the region. An extensive analysis of the "Indianized" states of mainland Southeast Asia is available in G. Coedes, *The Making of Southeast Asia* (Berkeley, Calif., 1966). More recently, some scholars have tended to emphasize the role of indigenous forces in the evolution of the region. See, for example, O. W. Wolters, *Early Indonesian Commerce: A Study of the Origins of Sri Vijaya* (Ithaca, N.Y., 1967); and *The Fall of Srivijaya in Malay History* (Ithaca, N.Y., 1970). See also J. C. Van Leur, *Indonesian Trade and Society: Essays in Asian Social and Economic History* (The Hague, 1955).

COMPARING TIME PERIODS

Ask students to identify other states, in addition to those in Southeast Asia, in which religious orders were able to amass great wealth through their tax-free status. Why does this practice place greater burdens on other groups in society?

ACTIVITY

Assign students to write a hypothetical debate between religious leaders of the Hindu and Buddhist faiths. In their debate they should discuss the merits of their beliefs and explain why they cannot accept the other's point of view. Evaluate students on the clarity and completeness of their work and how well they present opposing religious points of view.

However, the new religions did not entirely replace existing beliefs. In all Southeast Asian societies, as in China and Japan, old beliefs were blended with those of the new faiths. In this process, the king played a central role. The ruler of Angkor, for example, was seen as a living link between the people and the gods. As part of his duties, the king performed the sacred rituals on the mountain (where the gods dwelled) in the capital city. In time, the ritual became a state cult and united the new Hindu gods with the local nature gods.

This state cult, paid for by the royal court, eventually led to the building of temples throughout the country. Many of these temples housed thousands of priests and amassed great wealth, including vast estates farmed by local peasants. It has been estimated that there were as many as 300,000 priests in Angkor at the height of its power. This vast wealth was often exempt from taxes. In any case, it was the upper classes who largely held the new faith. The common people took part in the state cult and helped build the temples, but they did not give up their old beliefs in local gods and ancestral spirits.

Buddhism also spread to Southeast Asia. It made little impact, however, until the introduction of Ther-

Map 11.5   Religions in Southeast Asia

STUDYING MAPS

The following questions will help you guide students through their study of Map 11.5.

1. Which religion(s) appear to be most popular in this area? *(Islam, Buddhism)* Which are least popular? *(Hinduism, Christianity)*

2. This map shows distinct boundaries between religious beliefs. Is this an accurate representation of reality? Explain your answer. *(No. Explanations will vary.)*

3. If this map had been drawn to represent religions in Southeast Asia as they existed in the year 500, how would it be different? *(Answers will vary.)*

avada Buddhism in the eleventh century. These beliefs were introduced to the peoples of Burma by monks returning from the island of Sri Lanka, which had become the chief center of Theravada Buddhism. From Burma, Theravada spread rapidly to other areas of Southeast Asia.

Eventually, Theravada Buddhism became the religion of the masses in much of Southeast Asia. Why did it have such appeal? For one thing, it taught that people could seek Nirvana through their own efforts; they did not need priests or rulers. Moreover, it tolerated local gods and posed no threat to the established faith in spirit worship. Theravada Buddhism gradually undermined the influence of state-supported religions and became the dominant religion in Burma, Thailand, Laos, and Cambodia.

Theravada did not penetrate far into the Malay peninsula or the Indonesian archipelago, however. The Malay world found its own popular alternative to state religions when Islam began to enter the area in the thirteenth and fourteenth centuries. Like Theravada Buddhism, Islam became a religion of the masses. Its supporters, however, soon found that it was not easy to spread the faith into the rural, mountainous areas, where primitive customs continued to exist until recent times. Because Islam's expansion into Southeast Asia took place for the most part after 1500, its emergence as a major force in the region will be discussed in a later chapter.

Culture in Southeast Asia

During the state-building era in Southeast Asia, Indian traders brought their culture with them. Chinese culture, like Chinese political institutions, made an impact on Vietnam. However, cultural ideas imported from abroad were adapted in various ways to the needs and preferences of the local populations, which led to the creation of a variety of Southeast Asian cultures that were as distinctive in their own way as the older cultures of China and India.

Even after Vietnam achieved its independence from China, it remained tied to Chinese culture. Educated

▲ *The Temple of Borobudur on the island of Java is one of the most ornate and famous of all Buddhist monuments. It was buried for one thousand years under the jungle and rediscovered in the nineteenth century. What might account for the differences between this temple and famous national monuments in the United States?*

Vietnamese wrote Chinese poetry and followed Chinese models in sculpture, architecture, and porcelain. Many of the notable buildings, such as the famous One-Pillar Pagoda in Hanoi, are classic examples of Chinese architecture. However, by the tenth century, Vietnamese writers were beginning to write essays and poetry in their own language. Today the Vietnamese no longer use Chinese characters in their writing. They use the Roman alphabet introduced by the French.

In many other areas of Southeast Asia, Indian cultural influence prevailed. The most visible example was in architecture. Temple architecture reflecting South Indian styles began to appear in Southeast Asia during the first century A.D. Although Indian influence was evident, local artists also began to follow their own creative urges and produced religious structures of astonishing size and grace. Most famous is the Buddhist temple at Borobudur, in central Java. Begun in the late eighth century, Borobudur is a massive stupa (see

LEARNING FROM VISUALS

Ask students to compare the photograph of Angkor Wat with a picture of St. Peter's Basilica in Rome. What do such edifices show about the power of religious leaders?

ASSESS

Possible assessments include:

1. Section Review questions on this page
2. Section 11-4 Quiz in your Teacher Resource materials
3. Reteaching Worksheets in your Teacher Resource materials
4. Self-Study software

Answers to SECTION REVIEW

2. (a) countries with primarily farming economies (b) countries depending primarily on trade
3. (a) at one time, the most important trading power in Southeast Asia (b) a massive temple that was built in the city of Angkor Thom in Cambodia
4. (a) Vietnamese women had more rights; wives would own property and divorce their husbands. (b) The people believed the souls of all departed ancestors retired to the mountains after death. (c) taught that people could seek Nirvana through their own efforts, without priests or rulers; tolerated local gods and posed no threat to the established faith in spirit worship
5. Answers will vary.

338

▲ *This enormous temple at Ankgor Wat in Cambodia was built by the Khmer people and then buried under jungle growth for centuries. It was dedicated to Hindu mythology.*

Chapter 3) with nine terraces. The entire structure is more than three miles in circumference and dominates the landscape for miles around.

Second only to Borobudur in technical excellence, and even more massive in size, are the ruins of the old capital city of Angkor Thom in northern Cambodia. Of all the existing structures at Angkor Thom, the temple of Angkor Wat is the most famous and most beautiful. It combines Indian architectural techniques with native inspiration in a structure of impressive grace. Surrounded by walls measuring 1,700 by 1,500 feet, Angkor Wat rises like a 200-foot-high mountain in a series of three great terraces. Each side of the temple is 660 feet long, and all its outside surfaces, including the columns and even the roof, have carvings. Many of the carvings are life-size, and many different subjects are represented: unicorns, winged dragons pulling chariots, warriors, and heavenly dancing girls with elaborate hairstyles and fanciful jewelry. The construction of Angkor Wat, which took forty years to complete, required an enormous quantity of stone—as much as did Egypt's Great Pyramid.

 SECTION REVIEW

1. **Locate:**
   (*a*) Strait of Malacca,   (*b*) Sri Vijaya,
   (*c*) Sri Lanka,   (*d*) Sumatra,   (*e*) Java,
   (*f*) Arabian peninsula

2. **Define:**
   (*a*) agricultural societies,   (*b*) trading societies

3. **Identify:**
   (*a*) Sultanate of Malacca,   (*b*) Angkor Wat

4. **Recall:**
   (*a*) What was the main difference between family practices in China and in Vietnam?

CNN® WORLD HISTORY UPDATES

You can update your coverage of World History topics, as well as spark lively classroom discussion and deeper understanding, by using the **CNN World History Updates.**

For assistance in using and incorporating the **CNN World History Updates** into your classroom presentations, see the *Classroom Guide.*

(b) Why did Southeast Asians early in the first millennium A.D. consider mountains to be especially sacred?

(c) Why was Theravada Buddhism popular with the masses in Southeast Asia?

5. **Think Critically:** Why do you think Vietnam remained tied to Chinese culture after it gained independence from China? Give reasons to support your answer.

Conclusion

Between 500 and 1500, Indian civilization faced a number of severe challenges. One was an ongoing threat from beyond the mountains in the northwest. This challenge, which began in the eleventh century, led to the takeover of all of northern India by Turkish warriors, who were Muslims. A second challenge came from the tradition of internal rivalry that had marked Indian civilization for hundreds of years. After the fall of the Guptas, that tradition continued almost without interruption down to the sixteenth century. The third challenge was the religious divisions between Hindus and Buddhists, and later between Hindus and Muslims, that existed throughout much of this period. Hinduism was able to absorb Buddhism and reassert its dominant position in Indian society. However, that victory was short lived. One result of the Turkish conquest of northern India was the introduction of Islam into the region. As we shall see later, the new religion became a serious rival to the traditional beliefs among the Indian people.

Situated at the crossroads between two oceans and two great civilizations, Southeast Asia has long served as a bridge linking peoples and cultures. Despite the central position that Southeast Asia occupied in the ancient world, complex societies were slow to take form in the region. When they did begin to appear, they were strongly influenced by the older civilizations of neighboring China and India. In Vietnam, the Chinese imposed their culture by conquest. Elsewhere, merchants and missionaries brought Indian influence. Whatever the means, all the young states throughout the region—Vietnam, Angkor, Thailand, the Burmese kingdom of Pagan, and several states on the Malay peninsula and Indonesian archipelago—were heavily affected by foreign ideas and adopted them as a part of their own cultures. At the same time, the Southeast Asian peoples, like the Japanese, put their own unique stamp on the ideas that they adopted. The result was a region marked by cultural richness and diversity, yet rooted in the local culture.

Notes

1. Duarte Barbosa, *The Book of Duarte Barbosa* (Nedeln, 1967), pp. 147–148.
2. A. L. Basham, *The Wonder That Was India* (London, 1954), p. 426.
3. Quoted in Keith W. Taylor, *The Birth of Vietnam* (Berkeley, Calif., 1983), p. 75.
4. Quoted in O. W. Wolters, *Sri Vijaya in Malay History* (Ithaca, N.Y., 1970), p. 11.

USING KEY TERMS

1. sitar
2. Theravada
3. raga
4. archipelago
5. Mahayana
6. trading societies
7. Rajputs
8. agricultural societies

REVIEWING THE FACTS

1. 10th century. Ghazni occupied present-day Afghanistan, the upper Indus valley and south to the Indian Ocean.
   13th century. The Sultantate of Delhi occupied the entire plain of India and the Deccan Plateau.
   15th century. The Mughals occupied the north and the Portuguese came into the south.
2. Muslims believe in one God; Hindus in many. Muslims were against sexual frankness in art. Hindus disliked the Muslim habit of eating beef. Muslims had no priests; Hindus had a priestly class.
3. Students might mention that Hindus borrowed the cavalry or that they acquired the Muslim idea of keeping women secluded.
4. The majority of Indians were non-urban dwellers.
5. in praise of and heroic acts of the gods Siva, Vishnu, Rama, Krishna
6. the peoples of Southeast Asia
7. Vietnam and Funan
8. farming
9. The conquest of Angkor by the Thais in 1432.
10. India
11. agricultural societies (Vietnam, Angkor or Cambodia, Pagan or Burma, Sailendra or Java, and Thailand) and trading societies (Sri Vijaya and Malacca)
12. fusion of indigenous and borrowed culture

CHAPTER 11 REVIEW

USING KEY TERMS

1. The basic instrument of Indian music is the _____.
2. The group of Buddhists that saw Buddhism more as a philosophy and way of life in which understanding oneself would lead to Nirvana was _____.
3. A _____ is the scale on which classical Indian music is based.
4. One of the two major regions of Southeast Asia is a chain of islands called an _____.
5. The group of Buddhists that stressed that Nirvana could be achieved through devotion to Buddha, not through attention to one's behavior was _____.
6. _____ were Southeast Asian countries that depended primarily on trade for income.
7. Hindu warriors who resisted the advances of Mahmud and his successors into northern India were called _____.
8. Vietnam and Angkor, with economies based on farming, were characterized as _____.

REVIEWING THE FACTS

1. What were the key steps in Islamic expansion in India in the tenth, thirteenth, and fifteenth centuries?
2. Describe three major differences between Muslims and Hindus.
3. Name one practice borrowed by Hindus from the Muslims.
4. How urbanized was India between 500 and 1500?
5. What was the subject matter of most religious verse written during the medieval period in Indian history?
6. Who were the first peoples to master the art of rice cultivation?
7. What were the two early civilizations that emerged in Southeast Asia during the first millennium B.C.?

340

8. On what was the wealth of Angkor based?
9. The origins of Phnom Penh are connected with what historical event?
10. Burma, like Thailand, was most influenced by what culture?
11. The traditional states of Southeast Asia were divided into what two economic groups?
12. What is a distinguishing characteristic of culture all over Southeast Asia?

THINKING CRITICALLY

1. Why were the lower classes in India attracted to Mahayana Buddhism?
2. Why was it relatively easy for Islam to penetrate into India in the eleventh century?
3. Why did many in the lower castes convert to Islam?
4. Why did trade along the Indian coast flourish from 500 to 1500?
5. Why is climate a factor in preserving written work?
6. What does the feature **The Chinese Conquest of Vietnam** suggest was the main Chinese motive for invading Vietnam?
7. Why do you find more Indian influences in Funan (Cambodia) than in Vietnam?
8. Why were both the states of Sri Vijaya and Sailendra influenced by Indian culture?
9. Why was Theravada Buddhism appealing to peoples in Southeast Asia?
10. The basis for culture in Southeast Asia can be found in what four traditions?

APPLYING SOCIAL STUDIES SKILLS

1. **Geography:** Consult Map 11.2 on page 318. Why did Muslim invasions of India come from the northwest?

THINKING CRITICALLY

1. Mahayana stressed devotion to Buddha over elaborate codes of behavior.
2. Political disunity made it easy for Muslim armies to invade.
3. In Islam, all were regarded as equals before Allah.
4. Maritime trade along the traditional routes to the Middle East and Mediterranean coast was unaffected by the internal fighting that prevented free trade in the interior.

5. A dry climate slows down decomposition of natural materials. A wet climate speeds it up.
6. economic, for luxury items such as rhinoceros horn, elephant tusks, pearls, and kingfisher plume
7. Vietnam was conquered by China while Funan (Cambodia) traded heavily with India.
8. India was the major trading state in the area at the time.
9. People could achieve Nirvana through their own efforts and local gods were tolerated.
10. Indian, Chinese, Islamic and local traditions

CHAPTER 11 REVIEW

2. **Sociology:** What was the relative position of women in Hindu and Muslim society?

3. **Geography:** Consult Map 11.3 on page 330. How does geography help to explain the fact that east-west movement was difficult in Southeast Asia?

4. **Government:** Describe the political system of independent Vietnam after it overthrew Chinese rule in the tenth century.

5. **Economics:** What economic factors came into play for the growth of trade in Southeast Asia during this time?

MAKING TIME AND PLACE CONNECTIONS

1. How are religious events that took place in India in the eighth century reflected in India today?

2. Why did India fail to develop a strong merchant class as happened in Europe during the High Middle Ages?

3. What kinds of religious architecture were found in Eastern and Western Europe, Mesoamerica, China, and Southeast Asia when Hindu temple architecture was reaching its zenith in India?

4. In what ways is contemporary jazz music of the West similar to Indian classical music?

5. Most early civilizations grew up along rivers. Is this also true in the case of Southeast Asia? Explain and hypothesize as to why civilization came later to this area.

6. How did the Mongol invasion of China in the mid-thirteenth century affect the history of Southeast Asia?

7. What is the major difference between family life in China and Vietnam, though both are Confucian?

8. How does the social structure system of Vietnam reflect Chinese influence, while that of Angkor and Pagan reflect Indian influence?

BECOMING AN HISTORIAN

Analyze Information–Drawing Inferences

1. What generalization can be made with regard to the impact of Islam on Hindu society from the following three facts? 1) Hindu women became more secluded after the pattern of Arab women. 2) The Muslims became another Hindu caste. 3) Some Muslim rulers adopted the Hindu idea of divine kingship.

2. On what evidence does the author base his statement that the life of the Indian peasant in centuries past may not have been as difficult as it is today?

3. Why might the tradition of the nuclear family be common in Burma and Thailand, but the extended family be the rule in Vietnam and Malaysia?

4. In the years between 500 and 1500, the history of Western Europe is known variously as the Middle Ages, Dark Ages, Age of Faith, or Medieval Period. Was this true in the case of India during the same time period?

5. Describe the Mongol impact on India and Southeast Asia.

6. In world trade from 1000 to 1500, certain items were of central importance as was the monopoly of certain states. What states and trade items dominated?

APPLYING SOCIAL STUDIES SKILLS

1. The first wave of invaders originated from Ghanzi, modern day Afghanistan.
2. In Muslim society, women were to be secluded but could own property and allowed to divorce and remarry; in Hindu society, women were less secluded but were expected to throw themselves on their husbands' funeral pyre.
3. The river valleys run north and south and are cut off from each other by mountains.
4. Vietnam adopted the Chinese model of centralized government, State Confucianism, court rituals, civil service examination, and the administrative structure of the village.

5. Strong states like Sri Vijaya and Malacca made trade safe from pirating; with the Muslim conquest of N. India and the revival of trade in Western Europe, the demand for spices of the area grew.

MAKING TIME AND PLACE CONNECTIONS

1. Religious, political, and social conflicts between Hindus and Muslims are still a major source of disunity in India.
2. A monopoly on foreign trade was often held by governments rather than merchants.
3. Maya temples in Mesoameria; Romanesque and then Gothic cathedrals in Western Europe; Byzantine churches in Constantinople; Orthodox churches in Russia; Buddhist temples in China; Hindu/Buddhist temple complexes at Angkor Wat in Cambodia.

4. Performers select a basic raga or scale and then are free to improvise the melody and rhythm.

5. It is true also in Southeast Asia. They were settled by migrating peoples.

6. It encouraged Chinese migration south.

7. Students might answer that Vietnamese women possessed more rights.

8. In Vietnam, the family is central; in Angkor and Pagan, classes based on occupation and ethnic background are common.

BECOMING AN HISTORIAN

1. Both societies influenced each other, but there was never full integration.
2. The population was less, the soil was fertile, and records suggest a rich diet.
3. Coastal states such as Vietnam and Malaysia were more subject to outside influences.
4. Yes, in the sense that the time period for both regions was filled with invasions (mostly Islamic) and the state was divided, and of great temple (church) building. No, in the sense that it was also in India a period of arts and culture and there was a high level of trade.
5. created Islamic states and encouraged trade in Southeast Asia, and India, brought their culture with them.
6. Cotton from India, spices from Southeast Asia, silk and porcelain from China dominated trade.

12 PLANNING GUIDE

SECTION	KEY TOPICS	PRIMARY SOURCES	ASSESSMENT
1 The Transform-ation of the Roman World pages 343–351	◆ Rise of Germanic and Frank Kingdoms ◆ Society of the Germanic peoples ◆ Influences of Christianity ◆ Charlemagne and the Carolingians	◆ A description of an ordeal, pages 347–348	◆ Section Review, page 351 ◆ Section Quiz 12–1, TRB
2 The World of Feudalism pages 351–359	◆ Invasions of Europe in the ninth and tenth centuries ◆ Growth of feudalism ◆ Roles of the nobility in the Middle Ages	◆ A description of feudal practices, page 354 ◆ A poem of war, page 355	◆ Section Review, page 359 ◆ Section Quiz 12–2, TRB
3 The Growth of European Kingdoms pages 359–367	◆ Development of kingdoms in England ◆ Growth of French kingdoms ◆ The Holy Roman Empire ◆ Developments in Eastern Europe and Russia	◆ A description of the Swedish Rus, pages 366–367	◆ Section Review, page 367 ◆ Section Quiz 12–3, TRB
4 The Byzantine Empire and the Crusades pages 367–375	◆ Beginnings of the Byzantine Empire ◆ Daily life in the Byzantine Empire ◆ Impacts of the Crusades	◆ A description of Byzantine architecture, page 371	◆ Section Review, page 375 ◆ Section Quiz 12–4, TRB

THE EMERGENCE OF EUROPEAN CIVILIZATION AND THE WORLD OF THE BYZANTINE EMPIRE (400 TO 1300)

REPRODUCIBLE ACTIVITIES

- Historical Maps
- Charts and Graphs
- Critical Thinking
- Cooperative Learning
- Vocabulary
- Guided Reading
- Reteaching
- Enrichment
- Performance Assessment
- Spanish Key Points and Chapter Summaries
- Spanish Vocabulary
- Spanish Guided Reading

MULTIMEDIA SUPPORT

TRANSPARENCIES
- *World History* Color Transparency Package
- Fine Art Color Transparency Package

VIDEO
- *World History* Video Library
- CNN. Annual Video Update

LASERDISC
- *Sights and Sounds of History*

AUDIO
- *Listening to Literature* audiotape (English and Spanish)
- *History of Music* CD

SOFTWARE
- WESTEST™
- Student Review

CD–ROM
- *The Journey of Civilization*
- *World History*

INTERNET
- Internet Activities

On Line with WORLD HISTORY

Access West's history web site at **http://history.swpco.com** You'll find activities and web sites related to specific topics and chapters in *World History: The Human Odyssey*. Also look for references to helpful web sites at appropriate places throughout this teacher edition.

LESSON PLANNING

You will find detailed daily lesson plans for both traditional class scheduling and **block scheduling** in your Teacher Resource Box.

 Not Enough Time?

If you do not have the four or five days recommended to teach this chapter, you may want to focus on the following sections and activities:

- Have students skim the chapter to answer the "Questions to Guide Your Reading" on page 343. Discuss their answers, then read the "Conclusion" on page 375.
- Do a more in-depth reading about the rise of kingdoms in Western Europe on pages 343–346, feudalism on pages 351–355, the growth of the French Kingdom on pages 362–363, the creation of the Byzantine Empire on pages 368–370, and the Crusades on pages 372–375. Conclude with a class discussion of the importance of the Magna Carta, which is described on page 361.

THE EMERGENCE OF EUROPEAN CIVILIZATION AND THE WORLD

BUILDING ON CHAPTER 11

To prepare students to study Chapter 12 you may use the following questions and activities.

◆ Ask students to list factors that often contributed to the decline and fall of various states in India and Southeast Asia. Have them keep these lists and mark the factors that also contributed to the decline and fall of the Roman Empire.

◆ Remind students of how economic systems worked in India and Southeast Asia. Ask students to look for similarities in the treatment of peasants in Europe under feudalism.

◆ Lead students in a discussion of the role of religion in India. Was it an independent force or an extension of the state?

USING THE OPENING STORY

Depending on the ability levels of your students, select from the following questions and activities to reinforce the reading of the opening story.

◆ Why would a strong king like Charlemagne agree to be crowned by a pope who was the leader of a religion that appeared to be in decline?

◆ Why would the pope agree to crown a king of Rome?

◆ Why did the existence of the Byzantine Empire provide Western Europe with a degree of safety from invasions from the East?

In 800, Charlemagne (SHAR-luh-MANE), the king of the Franks, journeyed to Rome to help Pope Leo III, head of the Catholic Church. The pope was barely clinging to power in the face of rebellious Romans. On Christmas Day, Charlemagne, his family, and a host of visitors crowded into Saint Peter's Basilica to attend mass. All were surprised, according to a Frankish writer, when, "as the king rose from praying before the tomb of the blessed apostle Peter, Pope Leo placed a golden crown on his head." In keeping with ancient tradition, the people in the church shouted, "Long life and victory to Charles Augustus, crowned by God the great and peace-loving Emperor of the Romans." It appeared that the Roman Empire in the West had been reborn, and Charles had become the first Roman emperor since 476. However, this Roman emperor was actually a German king, and he had been crowned by the head of the Western Christian Church. In truth, the coronation of Charlemagne was a sign not of the rebirth of the Roman Empire but of

the emergence of a new European civilization that came into being in western Europe after the collapse of the Western Roman Empire. This new civilization—European civilization—was formed by the coming together of three major elements: the Germanic peoples who moved in and settled the Western Roman Empire, the legacy of the Romans, and the Christian Church. By 800, this new European civilization was taking shape. Increasingly, Europe would become the center of what we call Western civilization. European civilization emerged and developed during a period that historians call the Middle Ages or the medieval period. It lasted from about 500 to 1500. To historians who first used the title, the Middle Ages was a middle period between the ancient world and the modern world.

During the time when European civilization was emerging in the west, the eastern part of the old Roman Empire continued to survive as the Byzantine Empire. While serving as a buffer between Europe and the peoples to the east, the Byzantine Empire also preserved many of the accomplishments of the Greeks and Romans.

◄ Charlemagne, the first emperor of a European civilization, lived to be seventy-two years old and spent many of those years at war, converting conquered people to Catholicism.

ADDITIONAL RESOURCES

The resources listed below can be used to enrich the lessons in this chapter.

BOOKS FOR STUDENTS
Constantinople. The Forgotten Empire by Isaac Asimov. Houghton-Mifflin *Barbarian Europe* by Gerald Simons. Time-Life

VHS
Castle (PBS) SSSS

The Magna Charta (Films for the Humanities: (800) 257-5126

CD–ROM
The Anglo-Saxons (Learning Resources) Social Studies School Service (800) 421-4246

OF THE BYZANTINE EMPIRE
(400 TO 1300)

NEW PATTERNS OF CIVILIZATION

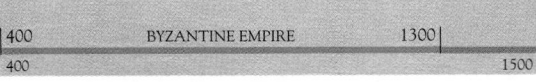

400	BYZANTINE EMPIRE	1300
400		1500

QUESTIONS TO GUIDE YOUR READING

1. What contributions did the Germanic peoples make to the new European civilization?

2. What role did monasticism play in early European civilization?

3. What were the major achievements of Charlemagne?

4. What were the major features of feudalism?

5. In what ways did centralized monarchies develop in Europe in the Middle Ages?

6. What were the major characteristics of the Byzantine Empire?

7. What were the reasons for the Crusades, and what did they accomplish?

OUTLINE

1. THE TRANSFORMATION OF THE ROMAN WORLD
2. THE WORLD OF FEUDALISM
3. THE GROWTH OF EUROPEAN KINGDOMS
4. THE BYZANTINE EMPIRE AND THE CRUSADES

THE TRANSFORMATION OF THE ROMAN WORLD

The Germanic peoples were an important part of the new European civilization. They had begun to move into the lands of the Roman Empire by the third century A.D. As imperial authority vanished in the fifth century, a number of German kings set up new states. By 500, the Western Roman Empire had been replaced by a number of states ruled by German kings.

The New Germanic Kingdoms

The fusion of the Romans and Germans took different forms in the various Germanic kingdoms. The kingdom of the Ostrogoths (AH-struh-GAWTHS) in Italy managed to preserve the Roman tradition of government. After establishing his control over Italy, the Ostrogothic king Theodoric kept the entire structure of imperial Roman government, although he used separate systems of rule for the Ostrogoths and Romans. The native Italian population lived under Roman law and Roman officials. The Ostrogoths were governed by their own customs and their own officials.

Like the kingdom of the Ostrogoths in Italy, the kingdom of the Visigoths in Spain favored coexistence

343

Answers to QUESTIONS TO GUIDE YOUR READING

1. See pages 343–346.
2. Important force; monks new heroes of Christian civilization; provided education and health care for societies; monasteries became community learning centers; converted many pagans to Christianity (pages 346–348)
3. Greatly expanded the Frankish kingdom and created Carolingian Empire (pages 348–351)
4. See pages 353–355.

5. French Normans conquered Anglo-Saxons in England and then combined through marriage and language to form centralized monarchy (page 359)
6. Greek-speaking empire built on profoundly unifying faith in Christ found in majority of its citizens; believed they were called to preserve Christianity (pages 369–370)
7. See pages 372–375.

343

FOCUS

OBJECTIVES

After completing this section, students should be able to

1. identify and describe factors that contributed to the rise of the Germanic and Frank Kingdoms
2. describe the society of Germanic peoples
3. explain how Christianity influenced kingdoms in Western Europe
4. describe the rule of Charlemagne and the Carolingians

FOCUS ACTIVITY

Help students understand why religious and political leaders often cooperate with each other. *(This can be seen in the conversion of Clovis to Christianity and the support he then received from the Catholic Church. Another example was the crowning of Charlemagne by the pope as described in the opening story on page 342. In this exchange the Church gained the support of the strongest king in Western Europe and Charlemagne gained the official sanction of the leader of the prevalent religion for his rule.)* Ask students to identify other examples of religious and political cooperation. *(Several appropriate examples were discussed in Chapters 10 and 11.)*

between the Roman and German populations. Both states had a group of warriors who dominated the considerably larger native population. Both tried to keep much of the Roman structure of government while largely excluding Romans from power. Over a period of time, the Visigoths and native peoples began to fuse.

Roman influence was weaker in Britain. When Roman armies abandoned Britain at the beginning of the fifth century, the Angles and Saxons, Germanic tribes from Denmark and northern Germany, moved in and settled there. Eventually, these peoples succeeded in carving out small kingdoms throughout the island.

The Kingdom of the Franks

Only one of the German states on the European continent proved long lasting—the kingdom of the Franks. The creation of a Frankish kingdom was the work of Clovis, who became a Christian around 500. Prior to this time, Clovis had refused the pleas of his Christian wife to become a Christian. According to Gregory of Tours, a sixth-century historian, Clovis had remarked to his wife, "Your god can do nothing." During a battle with another Germanic tribe, however, when Clovis's army faced certain destruction, he cried out, "Jesus Christ, if you shall grant me victory over these enemies, I will believe in you and be baptized." When he had uttered these words, the enemy began to flee, and Clovis soon became a Christian.

Clovis was not the first German king to convert to Christianity. However, others had joined the Arian sect of Christianity, a group

of Christians who believed that Christ had been human and thus not truly God. The Christian Church in Rome, which had become known as the Roman Catholic Church, regarded the Arians as heretics (people who believed in teachings different from the official beliefs of the church). To Catholics, Christ was human but also truly God, being of the "same substance" as God. Clovis found that his conversion to

Map 12.1   The New Germanic Kingdoms, c. 500

Political Divisions of Britain

- Angles
- Saxons
- Jutes
- Britons

0   200   400   600 Kilometers
0   200   400 Miles

STUDYING MAPS

The following questions will help you guide students through their study of Map 12.1.

1. Which kingdom in Europe occupied the largest physical area? *(Visigoths)*
2. Why may the largest kingdom not have been the most powerful or important kingdom? *(Answers will vary; may include location away from other kingdoms being a disadvantage.)*
3. What may the fact that England is an island have had to do with the greater number of smaller kingdoms that existed there? *(would be difficult to defend all borders from invaders)*

◄ *Bishops and nobles look on while Clovis is baptized. One of the nobles holds a crown while a dove, symbol of the Holy Spirit, comes down from heaven bringing sacred oil for the ceremony.*

Catholic Christianity gained him the support of the Roman Catholic Church, which was only too eager to obtain the friendship of a major ruler in the Germanic states who was a Catholic Christian.

By 510, Clovis had established a powerful new Frankish kingdom stretching from the Pyrenees in the west to German lands in the east (modern-day France and western Germany, respectively). After Clovis's death, however, as was the Frankish custom, his sons divided his newly created kingdom. During the sixth and seventh centuries, the once-united Frankish kingdom came to be divided into three major areas.

The Society of the Germanic Peoples

As Germans and Romans intermarried and began to create a new society, some of the social customs of the Germanic people came to play an important role. The crucial social bond among the Germanic peoples was the family, especially the extended family of husbands, wives, children, brothers, sisters, cousins, and grandparents. This extended family worked the land together and passed it down to future generations. It also provided protection, which was much needed in the violent atmosphere of the time.

The German conception of family affected the way Germanic law treated the problem of crime and punishment. In the Roman system, as in our own, a crime such as murder was considered an offense against society or the state. Thus, a court would hear evidence and arrive at a decision. Germanic law was personal. An injury by one person against another could mean a blood feud in which the family of the injured party took revenge on the family of the wrongdoer. Feuds could lead to savage acts of revenge, such as hacking off hands or feet, gouging out eyes, or slicing off ears and noses. Because this system could easily get out of control, a different system arose that made use of a fine called **wergeld.** This was the amount paid by a wrongdoer to the family of the person he or she had injured or killed. Wergeld, which means "money for a man," was the value of a person in monetary terms. That value varied according to social status. An offense against a member of the nobility, for example, cost considerably more than one against a freeman or a slave.

RECOMMENDED READING

Good general histories of the entire medieval period can be found in B. Tierney and S. Painter, *Western Europe in the Middle Ages, 1300–1475* (New York, 1983); E. Peters, *Europe and the Middle Ages,* 2d ed. (Englewood Cliffs, N.J., 1989); and G. Holmes, ed., *The Oxford Illustrated History of Medieval Europe* (Oxford, 1988). For a good general survey of the social history of the Middle Ages, see C. B. Bouchard, *Life and Society in the West: Antiquity and the Middle Ages* (San Diego, 1988). A brief history of the period covered in this chapter can be found in R. Collin, *Early Medieval Europe, 300–1000* (New York, 1991). Brief histories of the period from 400 to 750 include M. Grant, *Dawn of the Middle Ages* (New York, 1981); P. Brown, I>The World of Late Antiquity (New York, 1971); and J. M. Wallace-Hadrill, *The Barbarian West* (Oxford, 1985).

THE ROLE OF INDIVIDUALS

Have students describe how the history of Western Europe and the Christian religion might have been different if Clovis had not converted to Christianity. Do students believe that the description of divine intervention in his battle is the literal truth or a myth created to explain his conversion? *(Answers will vary.)*

CLASS DISCUSSION

Ask students to discuss whether or not they agree with the following statement:

"Marriage between members of opposing groups is the best way to encourage future cooperation and understanding."

Is this statement true of relations between Roman and German people?

LEARNING FROM VISUALS

What does the drawing tell students about the importance and manner of the baptism ceremony during the rule of Clovis? How might the ceremony have been different if the person being baptized was a common German farmer instead of a king?

ACTIVITY

Have students list the pros and cons of the Germanic justice system. *(wergeld, oath helpers, ordeal).* List some common crimes and punishments from today and have the students apply Germanic law to modern society. What penalties (weregeld) would they establish for each crime? *(Answers will vary.)*

REINFORCING VOCABULARY

Ask students how fair the practice of determining guilt through compurgation could have been. Might this have been as much a measure of one's popularity or power as it was one of justice? How does this practice compare with our jury system?

CLASS DISCUSSION

Have students consider why the monastic movement was successful in spreading the Christian religion. Monks set themselves apart from much of society by living in difficult circumstances, in a basket for example, or in monasteries where they were devoted to worship. How could these acts have encouraged others to become Christians?

Germanic law had two common means of determining guilt: **compurgation** and the **ordeal.** Compurgation was the swearing of an oath by the accused person, backed up by a group of twelve or twenty-five "oath-helpers," who would also swear that the accused was telling the truth. The ordeal was a means of determining a person's guilt based on the idea of divine intervention. Divine forces (whether pagan or Christian) would not allow an innocent person to be harmed, it was believed (see "You Are There: The Ordeal"). Thus, if the accused person was unharmed after a physical trial, or ordeal, he or she was presumed innocent.

The Role of the Christian Church

By the end of the fourth century, Christianity had become the supreme religion of the Roman Empire. As the official Roman state fell apart, the Christian Church played an increasingly important role in the growth of the new European civilization.

The Organization of the Church

By the fourth century, the Christian Church had developed a system of government. The Christian community in each city was headed by a bishop, whose area of authority was known as a bishopric, or **diocese.** The bishoprics of each Roman province were joined together under the direction of an archbishop. The bishops of four great cities—Rome, Jerusalem, Alexandria, and Antioch—held positions of special power in church affairs. The churches in these cities all believed that they had been founded by the original apostles sent out by Christ. Soon, however, one of them—the bishop of Rome—claimed that he was the leader of the western Christian Church. According to church tradition, Christ had given the keys to the kingdom of Heaven to Peter, who was considered the chief apostle and the first bishop of Rome. Later bishops of Rome were viewed as Peter's successors. They came to be known as **popes** (from the Latin word *papa*, meaning father) of the Catholic Church.

Western Christians came to accept the bishop of Rome—the pope—as head of the church in the fourth and fifth centuries, but people did not agree on how much power the pope should have. In the sixth century, a strong pope, Gregory I, known as Gregory the Great, strengthened the power of the papacy and the Roman Catholic Church. Gregory I, who was pope from 590 to 604, took control of Rome and its surrounding territories, thus giving the papacy a source of political power. Gregory also extended papal authority over the Christian Church in the West and was especially active in converting the pagan peoples of Germanic Europe. His chief instrument was the monastic movement.

The Monks and Their Missions

A **monk** was one who sought to live a life cut off from ordinary human society in order to pursue an ideal of total dedication to God. At first, Christian **monasticism** (the practice of living the life of a monk) was based on the model of the solitary hermit who gives up all civilized society to pursue a spiritual life. Saint Simeon the Stylite (stuh-LITE-ee), for example, lived for thirty years in a basket atop a pillar over sixty feet high.

These early monks, however, soon found themselves unable to live by themselves. Their feats of holiness attracted followers on a wide scale. As the monastic ideal spread, a new type of monasticism based upon living together in a community soon became the chief form. The monastic community came to be seen as the ideal Christian society that could provide a moral example to the wider society around it.

Saint Benedict, who founded a monastic house for which he wrote a set of rules, established the basic form of monastic life in the western Christian Church. The Benedictine rule came to be used by other monastic groups and was crucial to the growth of monasticism in the western Christian world.

Benedict's rule divided each day into a series of activities, with primary emphasis upon prayer and manual labor. Physical work of some kind was required of all monks for several hours a day, because idleness was "the enemy of the soul." At the very heart of community practice was prayer, the proper "Work of God." Although this included private meditation and reading, all monks also gathered together seven times dur-

MORE ABOUT . . . *Medieval Music*

Music is probably the most difficult aspect of medieval culture to reproduce. Very little written music has survived to the present day. It is known that a singer or musician was free to improvise during a performance, and, through this improvisation, a performer's reputation was made. In battles minstrels would inspire soldiers. Drummers and pipers would play martial music, both to encourage the troops and to cover up the sounds of screaming. The most well known music to come down to us from the Middle Ages is the Gregorian Chant. It is a single melodic line which was sung in unison and without rhythm by Catholic monks. The timelessness of this music was demonstrated in 1994 when a recording of church hymns by the Benedictine Monks of Santo Domingo de Silos became a best seller.

YOU ARE THERE
The Ordeal

In Germanic law, the ordeal was used as a means by which accused persons might clear themselves. All ordeals involved a physical trial of some sort, such as holding a red-hot iron. It was believed that God would protect the innocent and allow them to come through the ordeal unharmed. This sixth-century account by Gregory of Tours describes an ordeal by hot water.

◁ *The ring shown in this picture is an example of the type of jewelry worn by the rich during the time of the ordeals.*

Gregory of Tours, Describing an Ordeal by Water

An Arian priest disputing with a deacon of our religion [Roman Catholic] spoke harshly against the Son of God and the Holy Ghost, as is the habit of that sect [the Arians]. But when the deacon had spoken a long time concerning the reasonableness of our faith and the heretic, blinded by the fog of unbelief, continued to reject the truth, . . . the deacon said: "Why weary ourselves with long discussions? Let acts approve the truth; let a kettle be heated over the fire and someone's ring be thrown into the boiling water. Let him who shall take it from the heated liquid be approved as a follower of the truth, and afterwards let the other party be converted to the knowledge of the truth. And do you also understand, O heretic, that this our party will fulfill the conditions with the aid of the Holy Ghost, you shall confess that you are wrong." The heretic consented and they separated after appointing the next morning for the trial.

But the fervor of faith in which the deacon had first made this suggestion began to cool through the instigation of the enemy [Satan]. Rising with the dawn he bathed his arm in oil and smeared it with ointment. About the third hour they met in the market place. The people came together to see the show. A fire was lighted, the kettle was placed upon it, and when it grew very hot the ring was thrown into the boiling water. The deacon invited the heretic to take it out of the water first. But he promptly refused, saying, "You who did propose this trial are the one to take it out." The deacon all of a tremble bared his arm. And when the heretic priest saw it smeared with ointment he cried out: "With magic arts you thought to protect yourself, but what you have done will not avail." While they were thus quarreling there came up a deacon from Ravenna named Iacinthus and inquired what the trouble was about. When he learned the truth he drew his arm out from under his robe at once and plunged his right hand into the kettle. Now the ring that had been thrown in was a little thing and very light so that it was thrown about by the water; and searching for it a long time he found it after about an hour. Meanwhile the flame beneath the

(continued)

MORE ABOUT . . . *German influences on Feudalism*

The Germanic tribes of Europe had a profound influence on the creation of a European culture and particularly the system of feudalism that dominated much of the Middle Ages. In addition to trial by ordeal these influences include:

◆ the contractual relationship of protection and obedience that existed between rulers and subjects

◆ the concept of an elective kingship (originally German tribes had no kings, they elected military leaders for battle)
◆ the relationship between lord and vassal based upon personal honor
◆ laws established by custom, not at the whim of a king

Answers to Critical Thinking Questions

1. The Arian priest spoke harshly to the Catholic deacon against the Son of God and the Holy Ghost, in accordance with his beliefs. Though the Catholic tried to convince the "heretic" of the truth, the man rejected it. Surprisingly, the Arian priest did agree to undergo a trial of boiling water to determine who was right. The day of the test the men continued to quarrel about who should put his hand in the kettle first and the deacon's use of ointment.

2. That the deacon from Ravenna was not harmed when he put his arm in the hot water illustrated that he was a man of God, a follower of the truth who was aided by the Holy Ghost. This supported the Catholic view.

3. Student answers will vary.

CLASS DISCUSSION

Have students discuss the meaning and significance of the quotation, "Let all things be common . . ." Why do they believe members of religious orders would reject ownership of worldly goods? Contrast this vow with the fact that the Catholic Church became wealthy and its leaders lived in great luxury. Why did this disparity lead to conflict within the Catholic religion?

YOU ARE THERE

The Ordeal, continued

kettle blazed up mightily so that the greater heat might make it difficult for the ring to be followed by the hand; but the deacon extracted it at length and suffered no harm, saying rather that at the bottom the kettle was cold while at the top it was just pleasantly warm. When the heretic beheld this he was greatly confused and thrust his hand into the kettle saying, "My faith will aid me." As soon as his hand had been thrust in all the flesh was boiled off the bones clear up to the elbow. And so the dispute ended.

1. Describe the dispute between the Arian priest and the Roman Catholic deacon.

2. What truth was illustrated when the deacon from Ravenna plunged his arm into the kettle?

3. Do you think this account is factual? Why or why not?

ing the day for common prayer and the chanting of Psalms. A Benedictine life was a communal one. Monks ate, worked, slept, and worshiped together.

Each Benedictine monastery was strictly ruled by an abbot, or "father" of the monastery, who had complete authority over the monks. Unquestioning obedience to the will of the abbot was expected of each monk. Each Benedictine monastery held lands that enabled it to be a self-sustaining community, isolated from and independent of the world surrounding it. Within the monastery, however, monks were to fulfill their vow of poverty: "Let all things be common to all, as it is written, lest anyone should say that anything is his own."[1] The first monks were men, but women (called *nuns*) also began to withdraw from the world to dedicate themselves to God.

Monasticism was an important force in the new European civilization. Monks became the new heroes of Christian civilization, and their dedication to God became the highest ideal of Christian life. They were the social workers of their communities. Monks provided schools for the young, hospitality for travelers, and hospitals for the sick. Monks also copied Latin works and passed on the legacy of the ancient world to the new European civilization. Monasteries became centers of learning wherever they were located. Moreover, the monks were important in spreading Christianity to the entire European world. English and Irish monks were particularly enthusiastic missionaries who undertook the conversion of pagan peoples, especially in German lands.

Women, too, played an important role in the monastic missionary movement and the conversion of the Germanic kingdoms. Many of the **abbesses** (the heads of convents for nuns) belonged to royal houses, especially in Anglo-Saxon England. In the kingdom of Northumbria, for example, Saint Hilda founded the monastery of Whitby in 657. As abbess, she was responsible for giving learning an important role in the life of the monastery. Five future bishops were educated under her direction.

Charlemagne and the World of the Carolingians

During the seventh and eighth centuries, the kings of the Frankish kingdom had gradually lost their power. The mayors of the palace, who were the chief officers of the king's household, assumed more and more control of the kingdom. One of these mayors, Pepin,

On Line with WORLD HISTORY *Internet Activity*

You may want to have your students visit the following URL, where they will find information and additional web site resources to enhance their study of this chapter.

The Labyrinth

http://www.georgetown.edu:80/labyrinth/

This World Wide Web server for Medieval Studies has a built in search engine and large database of Medieval materials.

Due to the ever-changing nature of the World Wide Web, see the West History web site, **http://history.swpco.com** for regular updates of the URLs in this text.

▲ *This illustration from the eleventh-century manuscript,* Life of Saint Benedict, *written by Pope Gregory, illustrates six scenes from St. Benedict's life. Can you interpret what the six scenes represent?*

▲ *This miniature painting shows Pope Leo III placing a crown on Charlemagne's head while church officials watch. What did this occasion symbolize for the church and the state?*

finally took the logical step of assuming the kingship of the Frankish state for himself and his family. Upon his death in 768, his son came to the throne of the Frankish kingdom.

This new king was the dynamic and powerful ruler known to history as Charles the Great, or Charlemagne (from *Carolus magnus* in Latin). Charlemagne was a determined and decisive man who was highly intelligent and curious. He was a fierce warrior, a strong statesman, and a pious Christian. Although he was unable to read or write, he was nevertheless a wise patron of learning. During his lengthy rule from 768 to 814, Charlemagne greatly expanded the territory of the Frankish kingdom and created what came to be known as the Carolingian (CARE-uh-LIN-jee-un) Empire.

In the tradition of the Germanic kings, Charlemagne was a hardy warrior who undertook fifty-four military campaigns, which took him to many areas of Europe. His most successful campaigns were in Germany, especially the campaigns against the Saxons between the Elbe River and the North Sea. As Einhard, Charlemagne's biographer, recounted, "No war ever undertaken by the Frank nation was carried on with such persistence and bitterness, or cost so much labor, because the Saxons, like almost all the tribes of Germany, were a fierce people."[2] At its height, Charlemagne's empire covered much of western and central Europe. Not until the time of Napoléon Bonaparte in the nineteenth century and Adolf Hitler in the twentieth century would an empire its size be seen again in Europe.

Charlemagne continued the efforts of his father, Pepin, in organizing the Carolingian kingdom. The administration of the empire depended upon both Charlemagne's household staff and the use of counts as the king's chief representatives in local areas. As an

The figures in the illustration to the far left are not particularly life-like. Do students believe this is the result of a lack of artistic ability or of a desire to make them look perfect and holy? Are the figures in the miniature painting more realistic? What might explain differences between these works of art?

Answer to the caption question (left): On the top left of the picture, St. Benedict is shown writing; the right shows his death. The middle left shows St. Benedict's burial, followed by various miracles attributed to him. In the final box, bottom left, Pope Gregory has finished writing the *Life of St. Benedict.*

Answer to the caption question (right): When Pope Leo crowned Charlemagne, the king and the church became linked for centuries to come. This event marked by beginning of modern Europe, and many French kings believed that they ruled through divine right, granted by God through the pope.

POLITICS AND HISTORY

Have students explain why a government based on the administrative ability of the leader's household staff is likely to decline after his or her death. Compare this personal method of choosing government officials with the civil service examinations that were used in China.

So What ⁇

If your students question the importance of the information on **European civilization,** *tell them . . .*

The dominant influences in the formation of American society has been the economic, political and culture traditions which were

created in Medieval Europe. Students should be able to identify areas of life today which reflect the European influence. They should also be able to identify differences.

Map 12.2   The Carolingian Empire, 768–814

important check on the power of the counts, Charlemagne established the *missi dominici* (messengers of the lord king), two men who were sent out to local districts to ensure that the counts were carrying out the king's wishes.

Charlemagne as Emperor

As Charlemagne's power grew, so too did his prestige as the most powerful Christian ruler. One monk even wrote of Charlemagne's empire as the "kingdom of Europe." In 800, Charlemagne acquired a new title—emperor of the Romans. Charlemagne welcomed the new title. After all, he was now an emperor on the same level as the Byzantine emperor (see "The Byzantine Empire and the Crusades" later in this chapter).

Moreover, the papacy now had a defender of great stature. Charlemagne's coronation as Roman Emperor demonstrated the strength of the idea of an enduring Roman Empire. After all, his coronation took place three hundred years after the collapse of the Western Roman Empire. It also symbolized the coming together of those Roman, Christian, and Germanic elements that made up the basis of European civilization. A Germanic king had been crowned emperor of the Romans by the spiritual leader of Western Christendom. A new civilization had emerged.

An Intellectual Renewal

Charlemagne had a strong desire to revive learning in his kingdom, an attitude that stemmed from his own intellectual curiosity as well as from the need to provide educated clergy for the church and literate officials for the government. His efforts led to a revival of learning and culture that some historians have labeled a Carolingian Renaissance, or "rebirth," of learning.

During the Carolingian Era, there was a revival of classical studies (the works of the Greeks and Romans) and an attempt to preserve Latin culture. This attempt was undertaken by the monasteries, many of which had been established by the Irish and English missionaries of the seventh and eighth centuries. By the ninth century, the work asked of Benedictine monks consisted of copying manuscripts. Monasteries established **scriptoria,** or writing rooms, where monks copied not only the works of early Christianity, such as the Bible, but also the works of Latin classical authors. The head of the writing room became one of the important offices of the monastery. The copying of manuscripts in Carolingian monastic scriptoria was a crucial factor in the preservation of the ancient legacy. About eight thousand manuscripts survive from Carolingian times. About 90 percent of the ancient Roman works that we have today exist because they were copied by Carolingian monks.

▲ *Monks who worked in scriptoria, like the one illustrated in this thirteenth-century drawing, would spend months copying a single manuscript.*

SECTION REVIEW

1. **Locate:**
   (*a*) Frankish kingdom,   (*b*) Pyrenees,
   (*c*) Carolingian Empire,   (*d*) Elbe River,
   (*e*) North Sea

2. **Define:**
   (*a*) wergeld,   (*b*) compurgation,   (*c*) ordeal,
   (*d*) diocese,   (*e*) popes,   (*f*) monk,
   (*g*) monasticism,   (*h*) abbesses,   (*i*) scriptoria

3. **Identify:**
   (*a*) Ostrogoths,   (*b*) Visigoths,   (*c*) Angles,
   (*d*) Saxons,   (*e*) Clovis,   (*f*) Gregory I,
   (*g*) Saint Benedict,   (*h*) Charlemagne

4. **Recall:**
   (*a*) How did the beliefs of the Arian sect of Christianity differ from those of the Catholics?
   (*b*) Name one basic difference between the Roman and Germanic legal systems.
   (*c*) Why did the bishop of Rome rather than a bishop from another major city become head of the Catholic Church?
   (*d*) Give at least three reasons why monasticism was an important factor in the development of European civilization.

5. **Think Critically:** Explain in your own words the significance of Charlemagne being crowned by the pope.

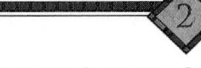

THE WORLD OF FEUDALISM

The Carolingian Empire began to fall apart soon after Charlemagne's death in 814. Less than thirty years later, it had been divided among his grandsons into three major sections. At the same time, powerful nobles gained even more power in their own local territories while the Carolingian rulers fought each other. Invasions in different parts of the old Carolingian world added to the process of disintegration.

Invasions of the Ninth and Tenth Centuries

In the ninth and tenth centuries, western Europe was beset by a wave of invasions. The Muslims raided the southern coasts of Europe and sent raiding parties into

"oath-helpers"; (c) means of determining a person's guilt; (d) Christian bishop's geographical area of authority; (e) heads of the Catholic Church; (f) person who pursued a life of total dedication to God; (g) the practice of living the life of a monk; (h) heads of convents; (i) writing rooms in monasteries

3. (a) Germanic peoples in Italy; (b) Germanic peoples in Spain; (c) Germanic tribes in Britain in the fifth century; (d) Germanic tribes from northern Germany who settled in Britain; (e) German king, converted to Christianity; (f) strengthened political power of the papacy and Roman Catholic Church; (g) wrote a set of rules for monastic life; (h) Charles the Great, greatly expanded Frankish kingdom

4. (a) Arians: Christ was human, not truly God; Catholics: Christ was human and truly God; (b) Answers may include: Germanic law: personal, related to concepts of family; feuds, wergeld, compurgation, ordeal; Roman: crime was offense against society or the state, court made decisions based on evidence; (c) believed to be successors to first bishop of Rome, Peter, who Christ appointed; (d) Answers may include: monks were heroes, modeled ideal Christian life, social workers, copied and preserved Latin works spread Christianity throughout Europe

5. Answers will vary.

FOCUS

OBJECTIVES

After completing this section, students should be able to

1. explain the impacts of invasions on Europe during the ninth and tenth centuries
2. identify and explain forces that contributed to growth of feudalism in Europe during the Middle Ages
3. describe the roles of the nobility in the economic, political, and social systems in Europe during the Middle Ages

FOCUS ACTIVITY

Help students understand the advantages of European society that were derived from the rigid economic, political, and social structures that existed in feudalism. You might have them list the problems European states and peoples faced prior to the Middle Ages. Discuss how feudalism, repressive as it may have been, solved many problems students identified.

TEACH

COMPARING TIME PERIODS

Ask students to compare the settlement and conversion of Viking invaders to Christianity in Europe with the invasion of China by Mongol nomads. What significant difference was there between the Mongol place in China's society and that of the Vikings in Europe?

352

Map 12.3   Invasions of the Ninth and Tenth Centuries

southern France. The Magyars, a people from western Asia, moved into central Europe at the end of the ninth century and settled on the plains of Hungary. From there they made raids into western Europe. The Magyars were finally crushed at the Battle of Lechfeld in Germany in 955. They then converted to Christianity and settled down to create the kingdom of Hungary.

The most far-reaching attacks of the time came from the Northmen or Norsemen of Scandinavia, also known to us as the Vikings. The Vikings were a Germanic people based in Scandinavia. Their great love of adventure and their search for booty and new avenues of trade may have been what led them to invade other areas of Europe.

Two features of Viking society help to explain what the Vikings accomplished. First of all, they were war-

riors. Second, they were superb shipbuilders and sailors. Their ships were the best of the period. Long and narrow with beautifully carved, arched prows, the Viking dragon ships carried about fifty men. Their shallow draft enabled them to sail up European rivers and attack places at some distance inland. In the ninth century, Vikings sacked villages and towns, destroyed churches, and easily defeated small local armies.

Early Viking raids were largely limited to the summer. By the mid-ninth century, however, the Vikings had begun to build winter settlements in different areas of Europe. By 850, groups of Vikings from Norway had settled in Ireland, and the Danes occupied northeast England by 878. Beginning in 911, the ruler of the western Frankish lands gave one band of Vikings land at the mouth of the Seine (SANE) River, forming a

STUDYING MAPS

The following questions will help you guide students through their study of Map 12.3.

1. From how many locations did invasions of Europe in the ninth and tenth centuries originate? *(three)*
2. What parts of Europe were essentially free of foreign invasions in the ninth and

tenth centuries? *(Scandinavia; Kingdom of Hungary; Eastern Europe)*

3. How would people's daily lives and political systems in Europe have been affected by the frequency of invasion? *(Answers will vary.)*

▲ *This picture from an eleventh-century English manuscript shows armed Vikings invading England. Two ships have already reached shore and some Vikings are walking down a gangplank to reach land. How can you tell these are Viking ships?*

section of France that came to be known as Normandy. This Frankish policy of settling the Vikings and converting them to Christianity was a deliberate one; by their conversion to Christianity, the Vikings were soon made a part of European civilization.

The Development of Feudalism

The disintegration of any central authority in the Carolingian world and the invasions by Muslims, Magyars, and Vikings led to the emergence of a new type of

▲ *The knight in this photograph is shown in full dress armor as his horse charges into battle. Can you identify the pieces of armor and equipment on both the knight and the horse?*

political order. When royal governments could no longer defend their subjects, people turned to the local landed aristocrats or nobles to protect them. It became important to find some powerful lord who could offer protection in return for service. This led to a new political and military system known as **feudalism.**

At the heart of feudalism was the idea of **vassalage.** In Germanic society, warriors swore an oath of loyalty to their leaders. They fought for their chiefs, and they in turn took care of the warriors' needs. One who served a lord in a military capacity was known as a *vassal.*

With the breakdown of royal governments, powerful nobles took control of large areas of land. They needed men to fight for them, so the practice arose of giving grants of land to vassals who, in return, would fight for their lords. The Frankish army had originally consisted of foot soldiers who dressed in coats of mail (armor made of metal links or plates) and were armed with swords. In the eighth century, however, a military change began to occur when larger horses and the stirrup were introduced. Earlier, horsemen had been throwers of spears. Now they came to be armored in coats of mail (the larger horse could carry the weight).

RECOMMENDED READING

A good introduction to the problems of the late ninth and tenth centuries can be found in G. Barraclough, *The Crucible of Europe* (Berkeley and Los Angeles, 1976). The Vikings are examined in F. D. Logan, *The Vikings in History,* 2d ed. (New York, 1991); and G. Jones, *A History of the Vikings,* rev. ed. (Oxford, 1984).

Two important introductory works on feudalism are F. L. Ganshof, *Feudalism* (London,

1952); and the classic work by M. Bloch, *Feudal Society* (London, 1961). Military aspects of feudalism are examined in J. Beeler, *Warfare in Feudal Europe* (Ithaca, N.Y., 1954).

For the economic history of the Early Middle Ages, see G. Duby, *The Early Growth of the European Economy: Warriors and Peasants from the Seventh to the Twelfth Century* (Ithaca, N.Y., 1974).

LEARNING FROM VISUALS

Why might lightly armed men on foot, such as the Viking invaders in the drawing to the left, have an advantage over knights in heavy armor? Discuss with students why the Vikings most often invaded during summer.

Answer to the caption question (left): Students should recognize the Viking prows of these ships.

Answer to the caption questions (right): Knights wore heavy armor, including breastplates, coats of chain mail, and helmets, and they carried long lances. Horses were equipped with saddles, stirrups, and sometimes they also wore heavy padding.

REINFORCING VOCABULARY

Ask students to write a contract for an imaginary king and noble that includes all the major parts of an agreement made under the system of vassalage.

ECONOMICS AND HISTORY

Although advancements in weaponry made the knights of Europe more powerful, the cost of supplying these soldiers also increased. Have students explain how this practice and the taxes placed on peasants who supported the knights affected the feudal economy.

ACTIVITY

Have students write an imaginary conversation that might have taken place between a knight from Europe and a Japanese samurai. What experiences would they have shared? How would their experiences and lives have been different?

USING PRIMARY SOURCES

Ask students to read the description of the vow of loyalty. Discuss with the class why it is significant that the vow was given to a particular person rather than a nation, written constitution, or religion. How might the system of vassalage have contributed to political instability in Europe during the Middle Ages?

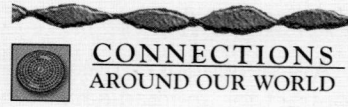

CONNECTIONS
AROUND OUR WORLD

COMPARING TIME PERIODS

Students will be interested in the similarities and differences among the three feudal systems described in the Connections box. Ask them to research these cultures to find additional similarities and differences. Have them report back to class. As an alternative, you may want to make this a group project, dividing the class into three groups, with each group developing a presentation for the class on one of the three cultures.

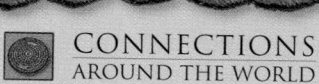

CONNECTIONS
AROUND THE WORLD

Feudalism   When we use the word feudalism, we usually think of European knights on horseback clad in iron coats and armed with swords and lances. However, between 800 and 1500, feudal systems developed in different parts of the world. Feudalism was a decentralized political system in which local lords owed loyalty and provided military service to a king or more powerful lord. In Europe, a feudal system based on lords and vassals arose between 800 and 900 and flourished for the next four hundred years.

In Japan, a feudal system much like that found in Europe developed between 800 and 1500. Powerful nobles in the countryside owed only a loose loyalty to the Japanese emperor. The nobles in turn depended on samurai, or warriors who owed loyalty to the nobles and provided military service for them. Like knights in Europe, the samurai fought on horseback, clad in iron.

In the Valley of Mexico, the Aztecs developed a political system between 1300 and 1500 that bore some similarities to Japanese and European feudalism. Although the Aztec king was a powerful, authoritarian ruler, the local rulers of lands outside the capital city were allowed considerable freedom. However, they did pay tribute to the king and also provided him with military forces. Unlike the knights and samurai of Europe and Japan, however, Aztec warriors were armed with sharp knives made of stone and spears of wood fitted with razor-sharp blades cut from stone.

They wielded long lances that enabled them to act as battering rams (the stirrup kept them on their horses). For almost five hundred years, warfare in Europe was dominated by heavily armored cavalry, or knights, as they came to be called. The knights came to have great social prestige and formed the backbone of the European aristocracy.

Of course, it was expensive to have a horse, armor, and weapons. It also took time and much practice to learn to use these instruments skillfully while riding a horse. Lords who wanted men to fight for them had to grant each vassal a piece of land that provided for the support of the vassal and his family. In return for the land, the vassal provided his lord with one major service, his fighting skills. In the feudal society of the Early Middle Ages (from 400 to 1000), where there was little trade and where wealth was based primarily on land, land became the most important gift a lord could give to a vassal in return for military service.

The relationship between lord and vassal was made official by a public ceremony. To become a vassal, a man performed an act of homage to his lord, as described in this medieval treatise:

> *The man should put his hands together as a sign of humility, and place them between the two hands of his lord as a token that he vows everything to him and promises faith to him; and the lord should receive him and promise to keep faith with him. Then the man should say: "Sir, I enter your homage and faith and become your man by mouth and hands [that is, by taking the oath and placing his hands between those of the lord], and I swear and promise to keep faith and loyalty to you against all others, and to guard your rights with all my strength.*[3]

As in the earlier Germanic band, in the feudal society loyalty to one's lord was the chief virtue.

By the ninth century, the grant of land made to a vassal had become known as a **fief** (FEEF). A fief was a piece of land given to a vassal by a lord in return for military service. Vassals who held such grants of land came to exercise political authority within these fiefs. As the Carolingian world disintegrated politically under the impact of internal dissension and invasions, an increasing number of powerful lords arose. Instead of there being a single government, many people were now responsible for keeping order.

Feudalism also became increasingly complicated with the development of **subinfeudation.** In this system, the vassals of a king, who were themselves great lords, might also have vassals who would owe them military service in return for a grant of land taken from their estates. Those vassals, in turn, might likewise

COOPERATIVE LEARNING ACTIVITY

Divide the class into three groups and have each group research feudalism as it existed in Europe, Medieval Japan and in the fifteenth century Aztec civilization. Each group should report on political, social and economic developments as well as cultural achievements. Have each group work as a team to prepare a presentation which includes political and physical maps, as well as at least one specialty map. Students within each group should have individual as well as group responsibilities. When the assignment is completed, you may want to have the class discuss their findings, and compare similarities and differences.

have vassals, who at such a level would be simple knights with barely enough land to provide income for their equipment. The lord-vassal relationship, then, bound together both greater and lesser landowners.

The lord-vassal relationship at all levels was always an honorable relationship between free men and did not imply any sense of servitude. Because kings could no longer provide security in the midst of the breakdown created by the invasions of the ninth century, the system of feudalism became ever more widespread.

Feudalism was basically a product of the Carolingian world, but it also spread to England, Germany, central Europe, and in some form to Italy. Feudalism came to be characterized by a set of unwritten rules—known as the **feudal contract**—that determined the relationship between a lord and his vassal. The major obligation of a vassal to his lord was to perform military service, usually about 40 days a year. A vassal was also required to appear at his lord's court when summoned to give advice to the lord. He might also be asked to sit in judgment in a legal case, because a lord's important vassals were peers, and only they could judge one another. Vassals were also responsible for making financial payments to the lord on a number of occasions. These included the knighting of the lord's eldest son, the marriage of the lord's eldest daughter, and the ransom of the lord's person if the lord had been captured.

Under the feudal contract, a lord also had responsibilities toward his vassals. Of course, the lord supported a vassal by granting him land. The lord, however, was also required to protect his vassal, either by defending him militarily or by taking his side in a court of law.

The Nobility of the Middle Ages

In the Middle Ages, European society, like that of Japan during the same period, was dominated by men whose chief concern was warfare. Like the Japanese samurai, many nobles loved war. As one nobleman wrote in a poem:

And well I like to hear the call of "Help" and see the wounded fall,
Loudly for mercy praying,

And see the dead, both great and small,
Pierced by sharp spearheads one and all.[4]

The "men of war" were the lords and vassals of medieval society. The lords were the kings, dukes, counts, barons, and even bishops and archbishops who had large landed estates and considerable political power (see "Young People in Medieval Europe: The Way of the Young Aristocrat"). They formed an aristocracy or nobility that consisted of people who held real political, economic, and social power. The great lords and ordinary knights came to form a common group. After all, they were warriors, and the institution of knighthood united them all. However, there were also social divisions among them based on extremes of wealth and landholdings (see "Focus on Everyday Life: The Castles of the Aristocrats").

Many people in the Middle Ages believed that the warlike qualities of the nobility were justified by their role as defenders of society. Knights, however, were also known for fighting one another. Beginning in the eleventh century, the Catholic Church tried to limit the bloodletting by establishing the Peace of God, which asked knights to take an oath to respect churches and not to attack clergy, poor people, merchants, or women. They could, of course, still kill one another. At the same time, the church began the Truce of God, which outlawed fighting on Sundays and on the chief feast days of the church.

In the eleventh and twelfth centuries, under the influence of the church, there gradually evolved among the nobility an ideal of civilized behavior, called **chivalry.** Chivalry was a code of ethics that knights were supposed to uphold. In addition to their oath to defend the church and the defenseless, knights were expected to treat captives as honored guests instead of putting them in dungeons. Chivalry also implied that knights should fight only for glory. However, this account of a group of English knights, by a medieval writer, reveals another motive for battle: "The whole city was plundered to the last farthing, and then they proceeded to rob all the churches throughout the city, . . . and seizing gold and silver, cloth of all colors, women's ornaments, gold rings, goblets, and precious stones. . . . they all returned to their own lords

USING PRIMARY SOURCES

Ask students to write a poem of similar length to the one on this page that expresses their personal feelings toward war. Assign them to write a paragraph that compares the messages and feelings that are evoked by the two poems.

Multimedia Support

LASERDISC
Knights and Chivalry

REINFORCING VOCABULARY

Explain how a pyramid marketing systems works. Ask students if they can see a similarity between these systems and subinfeudation. How much power and wealth do individuals at the bottom of either system obtain? Why do people join these organizations even when they understand that they won't gain much from them?

CLASS DISCUSSION

Have students make and compare lists of relationships that were included in a typical feudal contract and that currently exist between citizens and the government of their local communities. How different is paying property, sales, or income taxes from performing 40 days of service per year for a lord?

SPECIAL NEEDS: *Auditory/Visual*

Have students examine Map 12.3 on page 352, "Ninth- and Tenth-Century Invaders." Points for discussion should include rivers, seas and popular roadway routes. For students with language disorders, stress the use of prepositions such as over, under, above, through, around, on top of, beneath, ahead of, etc. The directional words north, south, east, and west should also be used during this discussion. Then, have students examine

a large scale map of their region or state. It may be helpful to project the map on the wall and have students take turns tracing the major routes available by land or sea. Ask them to describe an escape route, in the event of a natural disaster. They can then pick another region of the United States, or anywhere in the world, to design an escape route using major highways or waterways.

CLASS DISCUSSION

Lead students in a discussion of the type of training and daily activities of the child of a peasant farmer during the Middle Ages. Why were public schools not needed, affordable, or even desirable for maintaining social order?

Answers to Critical Thinking Questions

1. Boys were trained for a religious career or prepared for the life of a nobleman. Young men learned military lessons (jousting, hunting, riding, weapon handling) and some were taught to read and write. Girls married in their teens and were trained in the skills needed for running an estate. Girls were tutored in sewing, weaving, reading and writing, dancing, singing, and playing musical instruments.

2. Tournaments were designed to give bored young knights something to do. Trained as warriors, but with no adult responsibilities, the young men needed a constructive outlet for their urge to fight. The tournaments were an excellent way to prepare for war.

3. Answers will vary.

YOUNG PEOPLE IN MEDIEVAL EUROPE
The Way of the Young Aristocrat

At the age of seven or eight, boys were sent either to a clerical school to pursue a religious career or to another nobleman's castle where they prepared for the life of the nobility. The chief lessons at a castle were military. They learned how to joust, hunt, ride, and handle weapons properly. Occasionally, aristocrats' sons might also learn the fundamentals of reading and writing.

At about the age of twenty-one, a young man formally entered the adult world in a ceremony of knighting. A sponsor put a sword on the young candidate and struck him on the cheek or neck with an open hand. Later the practice arose in which the sponsor touched the candidate three times on the shoulder with the blade of a sword. This probably symbolized the passing of the sponsor's military courage to the new knight.

After his initiation into the world of warriors, a young man returned home to find himself once again subject to his parent's authority. Young men were discouraged from marrying until their fathers died, at which time they could marry and become lords of the castle. Trained to be warriors but with no adult responsibilities, young knights had little to do but fight. This was destructive to their society. In the twelfth century, tournaments began to appear as a way to keep young knights busy. At first, tournaments consisted of the melee, in which warriors on horseback fought with blunted weapons in free-for-all combat. By the late twelfth century, the joust—individual combat between two knights—

◄ *At an early age, knights learned to be skillful horsemen. They could shoot arrows with deadly accuracy and use weapons like this battle-ax with lethal results.*

had become the main part of the tournament. Knights saw tournaments as an excellent way to train for war. As one knight explained: "A knight cannot distinguish himself in war if he has not trained for it in tourneys. He must have seen his blood flow, heard his teeth crack under fist blows, felt his opponent's weight bear down upon him as he lay on the ground."

Young girls took a quite different path. Childhood ended early for the daughters of aristocrats. Aristocratic girls were married in their teens (usually at the age of fifteen or sixteen). Because they were expected by their husbands to assume their responsibilities at once, the training of girls in a large body of practical knowledge could never start too early. Girls were sent at an early age to the castles of other nobles for their upbringing and were trained there as ladies-in-waiting. The lady of the castle taught them sewing, weaving, and all the skills needed for running an estate. They also learned some reading and writing, dancing, singing, and how to play musical instruments.

1. Compare the upbringing of aristocratic young men and women in the High Middle Ages.

2. What was the significance of the tournaments for young knights?

3. What events signify that a young person has entered the adult world in your community?

COOPERATIVE LEARNING ACTIVITY

An ambitious project for the study of the Middle Ages involves having your students stage a Medieval Fair. The students will work to create costumes appropriate to the time period, research Medieval games, make foods from feudal Europe, and stage theatrical skits from the era. The project could be on a small scale, within the classroom, or larger, for the benefit of the entire school. This is an opportunity to involve students of all ability levels and interest levels. You can also build on this assignment each year to develop an annual function that will be anticipated by all students.

FOCUS ON EVERYDAY LIFE
The Castles of the Aristocrats

The growth of the European nobility in the High Middle Ages (1000 to 1300) was made visible by a growing number of castles scattered across the landscape. Castle building varied considerably, but castles did possess two common features: they were permanent residences for the noble family, its retainers, and servants, and they were defensible fortifications.

The earliest castles were made of wood. However, by the eleventh century, they were beginning to be built of stone. At first, the basic castle plan had two parts. The motte was a man-made or natural steep-sided hill. The bailey was an open space next to the motte. Both motte and bailey were then encircled by large stone walls. The keep, the central building of the castle, was built on the motte.

The keep was a large building with a number of stories constructed of massively thick stone walls. On the ground floor were the kitchens and stables. The basement housed storerooms for equipment and foodstuffs. Above the ground floor was the great hall. This very large room served a number of purposes. Here the lord of the castle held court and received visitors. Here, too, the inhabitants of the castle ate and even slept. Smaller rooms might open off the great hall, including bedrooms with huge curtained beds with straw mattresses, latrines, and possibly a chapel.

The growing wealth of the High Middle Ages made it possible for European nobles to improve their standard of living. Nobles sought to buy more luxury goods, such as better clothes, jewelry, and exotic spices. They also built more elaborate castles with thicker walls and more stone buildings and towers. Rooms also became better furnished and more elaborately decorated.

▲ The Tres Riches Heures of the Duke of Berry is one of the most famous illustrated manuscripts of the Middle Ages. The peasants shown here are harvesting grapes on the Duke of Saumur's land. How do you think the duke spent his time?

1. What architectural and design features supported the two basic functions of the castles?

2. Describe the lifestyle of the European nobility in the High Middle Ages.

3. Does a nobility exist today? Where?

MORE ABOUT . . . The Trés Riches Heures

Students might be interested to know that the artists who created the *Très Riches Heures du duc de Berry* were Pol de Limbourg and his two brothers, who had moved from Flanders to France. The work was created for the brother of the king of France. Included in the book is a twelve-month calendar which shows the daily activities of life on a manor and includes both peasants and lords.

BIOGRAPHY

The Role of Individuals

Have students evaluate the life of Eleanor of Aquitaine. Do they believe it is likely that she made any long-term difference in the role of women during the Middle Ages? What may the fact that she was not put to death by any of the men she offended show about the rights and powers of noble women? What might have happened to a commoner who behaved in a similar way?

Answers to Critical Thinking Questions

1. Eleanor married two kings, Louis VII and Henry II. Her influence was felt in attention to cultural activities. She traveled, bore eight children, and provided military and political support for her sons, two of whom became kings of England.
2. Eleanor remained independent and politically active all her life. Because she assisted her sons in rebelling against her husband, Henry II, she was imprisoned.

Learning from Visuals

Answer to the caption question: Answers will vary.

BIOGRAPHY

Eleanor of Aquitaine

Eleanor of Aquitaine was one of the more remarkable personalities of twelfth-century Europe. Heiress to the duchy of Aquitaine in southwestern France, she was married at the age of fifteen to King Louis VII of France. The marriage was not a happy one. Louis was too pious for Eleanor, and she invited minstrels from southern France to brighten the French court with music, much to her husband's displeasure.

Eleanor went with her husband on the Second Crusade but soon caused a scandal by ignoring her husband and staying with Prince Raymond of Antioch (AN-tee-OCK), her tall and handsome uncle. In 1149, Louis and Eleanor returned home, but on separate

► *Eleanor of Aquitaine led an illustrious life. Do you think that her dress in this picture reflects her royal status? Why or why not?*

ships. In 1152, Louis had their marriage annulled. Eleanor promptly created another scandal by marrying again, only eight weeks later. Her choice was Duke Henry of Normandy, who soon became King Henry II of England.

Henry II and Eleanor had a stormy relationship. She spent much time abroad in her native Aquitaine, where she paid special attention to creating a brilliant court dedicated to cultural activities. She and Henry had eight children (five were sons). Eleanor sought to further their careers, even assisting her sons in rebelling against the king (their father) in 1173 and 1174. She was imprisoned by her husband for her activities. After Henry's death, however, Eleanor again assumed an active political life, providing both military and political support for her sons. Two of her sons—Richard and John—became king of England.

1. What were some of Eleanor of Aquitaine's accomplishments?
2. Why was Eleanor's behavior considered scandalous?

rich men."[5] Apparently, not all the ideals of chivalry were taken seriously.

Aristocratic Women

Although women could legally hold property, most remained under the control of men—of their fathers until they married and their husbands after they married. Nevertheless, aristocratic women had many opportunities for playing important roles. Because the lord was often away at war or court, the lady of the castle had to manage the estate. Households could include large numbers of officials and servants, so this was no small responsibility. Care of the financial accounts

On Line with World History *Internet Activity*

You may want to have your students visit the following URL, where they will find information and additional web site resources to enhance their study of this chapter.
Byzantine and Medieval Studies
http://www.fordham.edu/halsall/med/medweb.html

This is a one stop web site that contains a massive set of resources on Byzantine and Early Medieval history.

Due to the ever-changing nature of the World Wide Web, see the West History web site, **http://history.swpco.com** for regular updates of the URLs in this text.

alone took considerable knowledge. The lady of the castle was also responsible on a regular basis for overseeing the food supply and maintaining all the other supplies needed for the smooth operation of the household. Women were expected to be subservient to their husbands, but there were many strong women who advised, and sometimes even dominated, their husbands. Perhaps most famous was Eleanor of Aquitaine (see "Biography: Eleanor of Aquitaine").

 SECTION REVIEW

1. **Locate:**
   (*a*) Hungary,   (*b*) Scandinavia

2. **Define:**
   (*a*) feudalism   (*b*) vassalage,   (*c*) fief,
   (*d*) subinfeudation,   (*e*) feudal contract,
   (*f*) chivalry

3. **Identify:**
   (*a*) Magyars,   (*b*) Vikings,   (*c*) Eleanor of Aquitaine

4. **Recall:**
   (*a*) What was the most important gift a lord could give a vassal?
   (*b*) Name two factors that led to the emergence of feudalism.

5. **Think Critically:** Compare the advantages and disadvantages of feudalism to empires. Under which political system would you prefer to live? Why?

THE GROWTH OF EUROPEAN KINGDOMS

The domination of society by the nobility reached its high point in the High Middle Ages (the period between 1000 and 1300). At the same time, however, kings began the process of extending their power in more effective ways. Out of this growth in the monar-chies would eventually come the European states that dominated much of later European history.

In theory, kings were regarded as the heads of their kingdoms and were expected to lead their vassals and subjects into battle. The king's power, however, was limited. He had to honor the rights and privileges of his vassals. In the case of disputes, he had to resolve them by principles of established law. If the king failed to observe his vassals' rights, they could and did rebel.

Kings, however, did possess some sources of power that other feudal lords did not. War and marriage alliances made it possible for them to increase their power, and their conquests enabled them to reward their followers with grants of land and to bind powerful nobles to them. In the High Middle Ages, kings found ways to extend their powers. The growth of cities, the revival of commerce, and the emergence of a money economy—all of which we will examine in the next chapter—enabled monarchs to hire soldiers and officials and to rely less on their vassals.

England in the High Middle Ages

On October 14, 1066, an army of heavily armed knights under William of Normandy landed on the coast of England and soundly defeated King Harold and the Anglo-Saxon foot soldiers. William was crowned king of England at Christmastime in London and then began the process of combining Anglo-Saxon and Norman institutions to create a new England. Many of the Norman knights were given parcels of land that they held as fiefs from the new English king. William made all nobles swear an oath of loyalty to him as sole ruler of England, and he insisted that all people owed loyalty to the king.

The Norman ruling class spoke French, but the intermarriage of the Norman French with the Anglo-Saxon nobility gradually merged Anglo-Saxon and French into a new English language. The Normans also took over existing Anglo-Saxon institutions, such as the office of sheriff. William took a census and developed more fully the system of taxation and royal courts begun by the Anglo-Saxon kings of the tenth and eleventh centuries. All in all, William of Normandy created a strong, centralized monarchy.

FOCUS

OBJECTIVES

After completing this section, students should be able to

1. describe the development of kingdoms in England
2. describe the development of kingdoms in France
3. identify the role played by the Holy Roman Empire in Europe
4. describe the growth of states in Eastern Europe and Russia

FOCUS ACTIVITY

Help students understand that the rights of individuals were very limited in all kingdoms in Europe. For example, although the Magna Carta assured some rights to nobles it did nothing for the rights of common people. In France most power was held by dukes who were in a position to determine the rights of common people in the lands they controlled. Even when a French parliament was created the townspeople were given only one vote as the third estate.

TEACH

LEARNING FROM VISUALS

Answer to the caption question: The English foot soldiers are armed with battle-axes and spears. The Norman French carry lances and shields.

▲ *The tapestry of Bayeux, a detail of which is shown here, chronicles the invasion of England by the Norman French. How many medieval weapons can you identify in this scene?*

The Norman conquest of England had other effects as well. Because the new king of England was still the duke of Normandy, he was both a king (of England) and a vassal to a king (of France). This vassal, however, was now far more powerful than his lord. This connection with France kept England heavily involved in European affairs throughout the High Middle Ages.

In the twelfth century, the power of the English monarchy was greatly enlarged during the reign of Henry II, from 1154 to 1189. The new king was especially successful in strengthening the power of the royal courts. Henry expanded the number of criminal cases to be tried in the king's court and also devised means for taking property cases from local courts to the royal courts. Henry's goals were clear: expanding the power

of the royal courts expanded the king's power. Moreover, because the royal courts were now found throughout England, a body of common law (law that was common to the whole kingdom) began to replace the different law codes that had often varied from place to place.

Henry was less successful at imposing royal control over the church. He became involved in a famous struggle between church and state in medieval England. Henry claimed the right to punish clergymen in church courts. However, Thomas à Becket, archbishop of Canterbury and the highest-ranking English cleric, claimed that only church courts could try clerics. Attempts at compromise failed, and an angry king publicly expressed the desire to be rid of Becket. "Who will

So What ⁇

If your students question the importance of the information on **Magna Carta** *you may want to tell them . . .*

This document marks a turning point in the relationship between the ruler and the

ruled. The Magna Carta is seen as the starting point on the long road to the democratic rights we enjoy today.

▲ *King Henry II is shown here with Thomas à Becket, archbishop of Canterbury. Do you think the king really meant for his knights to murder the archbishop?*

▲ *King John did not sign the Magna Carta, but he did affix his seal, signifying his approval. This may have been because he was illiterate. Why is the Magna Carta considered to be such a milestone in civil rights?*

free me of this priest?" he screamed. Four knights took the challenge, went to Canterbury, and murdered the archbishop in the cathedral. Faced with public outrage, Henry backed down in his struggle with the English church.

Many English nobles came to resent the ongoing growth of the king's power and rose in rebellion during the reign of King John. At Runnymeade in 1215, John was forced to put his seal on the Magna Carta (the Great Charter) of feudal liberties. The Magna Carta was, above all, a feudal document. It conferred more rights to the nobility than the commoners. Only later would the acknowledgment of the rights of common people make its entry into English law. Feudal custom had always recognized that the relationship between king and vassals was based on mutual rights and obligations. The Magna Carta gave written recognition to that fact and was used in later years to strengthen the idea that a monarch's power was limited, not absolute.

During the reign of Edward I, an important institution in the development of representative government—the English Parliament—also emerged. At first the word *parliament* referred to the king's Great Council, which was made up of the king's officials, nobles, and bishops. However, in his need for money, in 1295 Edward I invited two knights from every county and two residents from each town to meet with the Great Council to consent to new taxes. This was the first official Parliament.

MORE ABOUT . . . *the Magna Carta*

You may wish to inform students that the concept of due process was first enunciated in the MAGNA CARTA in 1215. "No free man shall be arrested or imprisoned . . . except by the lawful judgment of his peers or by the law of the land." The 5TH AMENDMENT to the Constitution of the United States established this protection with the words: "Nor shall {any person} be deprived of life, liberty or property without due process of law."

Due process of law establishes limits to the powers of government, specifically against the arbitrary deprivation of life, liberty, or property.

POLITICS AND HISTORY

362

Have students explain either in writing or orally why the growth of power within the English Parliament was an important development in the history of government for the United States.

Map 12.4   Europe in the High Middle Ages

The English Parliament came to be composed of two knights from every county, two people from every town, the nobles, and bishops. Eventually, nobles and church lords formed the House of Lords; knights and townspeople formed the House of Commons. The Parliaments of Edward I granted taxes, discussed politics, and passed laws. Although it was not yet the important body it would eventually become, the English Parliament nevertheless had clearly emerged as an institution by the end of the thirteenth century. The law of the English kingdom would be determined not by the king alone but by king and Parliament together. Much conflict, and even open war, would ensue before Par-liament gained the primary political power it has today in England.

The Growth of the French Kingdom

In 843, the Carolingian Empire had been divided into three major sections. The west Frankish lands formed the core of the eventual kingdom of France. In 987, after the death of the last Carolingian king, the west Frankish nobles chose Hugh Capet (KAY-puht) as the new king, thus establishing the Capetian (cuh-PAY-shun) dynasty of French kings. Although they carried the title of king, the Capetians had little real power.

STUDYING MAPS

The following questions will help you guide students through their study of Map 12.4.

1. What are three empires identified on this map? *(Seljuk Empire, Holy Roman Empire, and the Byzantine Empire)*
2. Why is a state's size not necessarily a good indication of its power or importance? *(Size is irrelevant to power. Better*

indicators would be location near navigable water, population, climate, and political system.)
3. On which boundary shown on this map would the likelihood of war have been the greatest? Explain the reasons for your answer. *(Answers will vary.)*

They controlled as the royal domain (the lands of the king) only the lands around Paris known as the Ile-de-France. As kings of France, the Capetians were formally the overlords of the great lords of France, such as the dukes of Normandy, Brittany, Burgundy, and Aquitaine. In reality, however, many of the dukes were considerably more powerful than the Capetian kings. All in all, it would take the Capetian dynasty hundreds of years to create a truly centralized monarchical authority in France.

The reign of King Philip II Augustus, who ruled from 1180 to 1223, was an important turning point. Philip II waged war against the rulers of England, who also ruled the French territories of Normandy, Maine, Anjou, and Aquitaine. He was successful in gaining control of most of these territories. Through these conquests, he expanded the income of the French monarchy and greatly enlarged its power. To administer justice and collect royal revenues in his new territories, Philip appointed new royal officials.

Capetian rulers after Philip II continued to add lands to the royal domain. Although Philip had used military force, other kings used both purchase and marriage to achieve the same end. Philip IV the Fair, who ruled from 1285 to 1314, was especially effective in strengthening the French monarchy. French kings had always had a household staff for running their affairs. Over time, however, this household staff was enlarged and divided into three groups to form three major branches of government: a council for advice; a chamber of accounts for finances; and a *Parlement,* or royal court. By the beginning of the fourteenth century, the Capetians had created an effective royal bureaucracy.

Philip IV also brought a French parliament into being by asking representatives of the three estates, or classes—the clergy (first estate), the nobles (second estate), and the townspeople (third estate)—to meet with him. They did so in 1302. Thus began the Estates-General, the first French parliament, although it had little real power. By the end of the thirteenth century, France was the largest, wealthiest, and best-governed monarchical state in Europe.

The Lands of the Holy Roman Empire

In the tenth century, the powerful dukes of the Saxons became kings of the lands of the eastern Frankish kingdom (or Germany, as it came to be known). The best known of the Saxon kings of Germany was Otto I. In return for protecting the pope, he was crowned Emperor of the Romans in 962, a title that had not been used since the time of Charlemagne. Otto's creation of a new "Roman Empire" in the hands of the Germans had long-range consequences. The kings of Germany now had the difficult task of ruling Italy as well.

In the eleventh century, German kings created a strong monarchy and a powerful empire by leading armies into Italy. To strengthen their power, they relied upon their ability to control the church and select bishops whom they could then use as royal administrators. However, the struggle between church and state during the reign of Henry IV weakened the king's ability to use church officials in this way (see Chapter 13). The German kings also tried to bolster their power by using their position as emperor to exploit the resources of Italy, but this tended to backfire. Many a German king lost armies in Italy in pursuit of the dream of an empire. No German dynasty demonstrates this better than the Hohenstaufens (HOE-un-SHTOW-funz).

The two most famous members of the Hohenstaufen dynasty, Frederick I and Frederick II, tried to create a new kind of empire. Previous German kings had focused on building a strong German kingdom, but Frederick I planned to get his chief revenues from

◄ *Otto I, known as Otto the Great, is shown pardoning his brother Henry. Otto was a patron of German culture and brought the church under his control.*

CLASS DISCUSSION

Have students explain how it was possible for the weak control of the Capetian kings to have grown into almost total domination of France over about two hundred years with only a limited use of force.

COMPARING TIME PERIODS

There is such a thing as "biting off more than you can chew" when it comes to military and political domination of other lands. How can this be seen in China's attempt to dominate Vietnam and other states in Southeast Asia? Ask students if they can see evidence of this problem in Otto I's creation of a new Roman Empire that spanned much of Germany and Italy.

MORE ABOUT . . . *the Three Estates*

Beginning in the fourteenth century, France initiated a system of three estates. The first was the clergy, the second was comprised of the nobility, and the third estate was comprised of middle-class commoners. Each estate had equal power, one vote per estate. The French Assembly, usually called the Estates-General, met occasionally between 1302 and 1789, when the monarchy felt a need to summon them or to create a base of support for financial or political policies. It was however, only an advisory body to the king. Sessions held between 1355–1357 briefly controlled the French government following the English victory at Poitiers, following Louis XI's death, and finally in 1789, the year the French Revolution began. At that time, the third estate demanded equal representation (votes equal to their numbers).

Italy as the center of a "holy empire," as he called it (hence the term Holy Roman Empire). However, his attempt to conquer northern Italy led to severe problems. The pope opposed him, fearing that the emperor wanted to include Rome and the Papal States as part of his empire. The cities of northern Italy, which had become used to their freedom, were also not willing to be subjects of Frederick. An alliance of these northern Italian cities and the pope defeated the forces of Emperor Frederick I in 1176.

The main goal of Frederick II was to establish a strong, centralized state in Italy. In attempting to conquer Italy, however, he became involved in a deadly struggle with the popes. They feared that a single ruler of northern and southern Italy would mean the end of papal power in central Italy. The northern Italian cities were also unwilling to give up their freedom. Frederick II waged a bitter struggle in northern Italy, winning many battles but ultimately losing the war.

The struggle between popes and emperors had dire consequences for the Holy Roman Empire. By spending their time fighting in Italy, the German emperors left Germany in the hands of powerful German feudal lords, who ignored the emperor and created their own independent kingdoms. This ensured that the German monarchy would remain weak and incapable of maintaining a centralized monarchical state. Thus, the German Holy Roman Emperor had no real power over either Germany or Italy. Unlike France and England, neither Germany nor Italy created a unified national monarchy in the Middle Ages. Both Germany and Italy consisted of many small, independent states, and both had to wait until the nineteenth century before they formed united states.

The Slavic Peoples of Central and Eastern Europe

East of the Carolingian Empire lay a spacious plain through which a number of Asiatic nomads, such as the Huns, Bulgars, Avars, and Magyars, had pushed their way westward. Eastern Europe was ravaged by these successive waves of invaders, who found it relatively easy to create large empires that, in turn, were overthrown by the next invaders. Over time, the invaders themselves were largely assimilated into the native Slavic peoples of the area.

The Slavic peoples were originally a single people in central Europe, but they were gradually divided into three major groups: the western, southern, and eastern Slavs. The western Slavs eventually formed the Polish and Bohemian kingdoms. German missionaries converted both the Czechs (CHECKS) in Bohemia and the Slavs in Poland by the tenth century. The non-Slavic kingdom of Hungary, which emerged after the Magyars settled down after their defeat in 955, was also converted to Christianity by German missionaries. The Poles, Czechs, and Hungarians all accepted Catholic or western Christianity and became closely tied to the Roman Catholic Church and its Latin culture.

The southern and eastern Slavic populations largely took a different path because of their closeness to the Byzantine Empire (see the next section). The Slavic peoples of Moravia were converted to the Orthodox Christianity of the Byzantine Empire by two Byzantine missionary brothers, Cyril and Methodius, who began their activities in 863. The southern Slavic peoples accepted Christianity, but there was an eventual split between the Croats, who accepted the Roman Catholic Church, and the Serbs, who remained loyal to Orthodox Christianity.

The Bulgars were originally an Asiatic people who conquered much of the Balkan peninsula. They were eventually absorbed by the larger native south Slavic population. Together, they formed a largely Slavic Bulgarian kingdom that embraced the church services developed earlier by Cyril and Methodius. The acceptance of Eastern Orthodoxy by the southern Slavic peoples, the Serbs and Bulgarians, meant that their cultural life was linked to the Byzantine state.

The eastern Slavic peoples, from whom the modern Russians and Ukrainians are descended, had settled in the territory of present-day Ukraine and Russia. There, beginning in the late eighth century, these peoples began to encounter Swedish Vikings, who moved down the extensive network of rivers into the lands of the eastern Slavs in search of booty and new trade routes. These Vikings built trading settlements and eventually came to dominate the native peoples. The native peoples called them "the Rus," from which the

MORE ABOUT . . . *Magna Carta*

Habeas corpus (Latin, "you are to bring the body") is a WRIT issued by a court, requiring a person in custody to be brought before it. Although the writ is issued for various purposes, it is usually issued in criminal cases in order to determine whether a prisoner is lawfully being held by the police, and if so, what the charges are.

There is some debate among jurists whether the Magna Carta actually set forth the principle of habeas corpus. Due process was definitely spelled out, but the origins of the concept of habeas corpus is more accurately traced to principles already established in English common law.

The American colonists viewed habeas corpus as one of the most important protections of personal freedom. It was specifically guaranteed in the U.S. Constitution, Article I, Section 9.

**COMPARING
TIME PERIODS**

Assign students to make a list of lands they have studied that were occupied by Mongol forces. What conclusions can students draw about the society and social values of Mongol peoples from these lists?

Map 12.5   The World of the Slavs

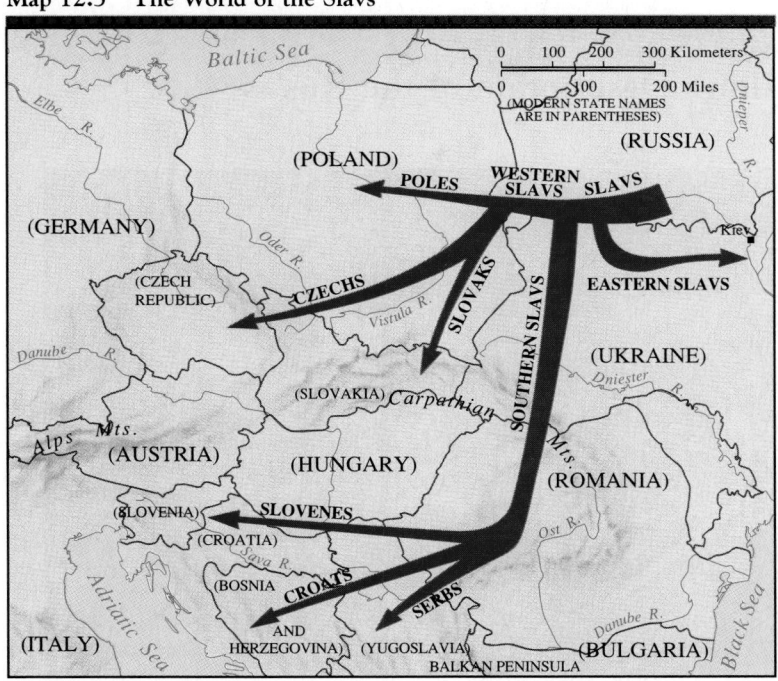

name *Russia* is derived (see "You Are There: A Muslim's Description of the Rus").

The Development of Russia

One Viking leader, Oleg, settled in Kiev (KEE-ev) at the beginning of the tenth century and created the Rus state known as the principality of Kiev. His successors extended their control over the eastern Slavs and expanded the territory of Kiev until it included the territory between the Baltic and Black Seas and the Danube and Volga Rivers. By marrying Slavic wives, the Viking ruling class was gradually assimilated into the Slavic population.

The growth of the principality of Kiev attracted religious missionaries, especially from the Byzantine Empire. One Rus ruler, Vladimir, married the Byzantine emperor's sister and officially accepted Christianity for himself and his people in 987. From the end of the tenth century on, Byzantine Christianity became the model for Russian religious life.

The Kievan Rus state prospered and reached its high point in the first half of the eleventh century. Kievan society was dominated by a noble class of landowners known as the boyars, and Kievan merchants carried on a regular trade with Scandinavia to the north and the Islamic and Byzantine worlds to the south. However, civil wars and new invasions by Asiatic nomads caused the principality of Kiev to collapse. The sack of Kiev by north Russian princes in 1169 brought an end to the first Russian state.

That first Russian state had remained closely tied to the Byzantine Empire, not to the new Europe. Its Christianity had been Orthodox Christianity, not the Catholicism of Europe. In the thirteenth century, the Mongols conquered Russia and cut it off even more from Europe for the next two hundred years.

The Mongols had exploded upon the scene in the thirteenth century, moving east into China and west into the Middle East and central Europe. They conquered Russia but were not numerous enough to settle the vast Russian lands. They occupied only part of Russia, but they required Russian princes to pay tribute to them. One Russian prince soon emerged as more powerful than the others. Alexander Nevsky, prince of Novgorod, defeated a German invading army in northwestern Russia in 1242. His cooperation with the Mongols won him their favor. The khan, leader of the western part of the Mongol Empire, rewarded Alexander Nevsky with the title of grand-prince. This enabled his descendants to become the princes of Moscow and eventually leaders of all Russia.

STUDYING MAPS

The following questions will help you guide students through their study of Map 12.5.

1. What modern states occupy lands settled by Slavic people? *(Poland, the Czech Republic, Slovakia, Hungary, Croatia, Bosnia and Herzegovina, Yugoslavia, Romania, Russia, the Ukraine, and Slovenia)*

2. What possible reasons could there be for the migration of Slavic people to so many different lands? *(Answers will vary.)*

3. What groups formed a sort of human barrier to further expansion of Slavic peoples to the west or south? *(the Germans, the Russians, the Italians and the Turks)*

USING PRIMARY SOURCES

Ask students whether the author of this primary source feared or had only contempt for the Swedish Rus he described? Is it possible that he experienced both of these feelings? Why would a Muslim be particularly upset by the habits of these people?

LEARNING FROM VISUALS

Answer to the caption question: The men have rough clothing, they are bearded and unkempt, and they are crowded together on these boats.

Answers to Critical Thinking Questions

1. The Muslim diplomat thought the men had perfect physiques, but considered them "the filthiest of God's creatures."

2. The Rus did not sympathize with, or care for, the sick. Death was not treated in a spiritual or ceremonial manner. A sick person was left alone in a tent with bread and water and was not spoken to or visited. Dead bodies were burned, unless the person had been a serf, in which case he would be left for the dogs and vultures.

3. Muslims were very concerned with cleanliness and the spread of disease and followed strict guidelines for all aspects of their behavior. Muslims believed in God and an afterlife.

YOU ARE THERE

A Muslim's Description of the Rus

Despite the difficulties that travel presented, early medieval civilization did witness some contact among the various cultures. In this selection, Ibn Fadlan, a Muslim diplomat sent from Baghdad in 921 to a settlement on the Volga River, gives a description of the Swedish Rus. His comments on the filthiness of the Rus reflect the Muslim concern with cleanliness.

▲ *Although the* Song of the Volga *is a modern painting, the Russian artist Wassili Kandinsky captures the rough, barbaric nature of the Volga boatmen and their lives. What features can you see in the painting that support Ibn Fadlan's description?*

A Muslim Diplomat, Describing the Swedish Rus

I saw the Rus folk when they arrived on their trading-mission and settled at the river Atul (Volga). Never had I seen people of more perfect physique. They are tall as date-palms, and reddish in color. They wear neither coat or kaftan, but each man carried a cape which covers one half of his body, leaving one hand free. No one is ever parted from his axe, sword, and knife.

They [the Rus] are the filthiest of God's creatures. They do not wash after discharging their natural functions, neither do they wash their hands after meals. They are as lousy as donkeys. They arrive from their distant lands and lay their ships alongside the banks of the Atul, which is a great river, and there they build big houses on its shores.

Ten or twenty of them may live together in one house, and each of them has a couch of his own where he sits and diverts himself with the pretty slave girls whom he had brought along for sale.

They wash their hands and faces every day in incredibly filthy water. Every morning the girl brings her master a large bowl of water in which he washes his hands and face and hair, then blows his nose into it and spits into it. When he has finished the girl takes the bowl to his neighbor—who repeats the performance. Thus the bowl goes the rounds of the entire household. . . .

YOU ARE THERE

A Muslim's Description of the Rus, continued

If one of the Rus folk falls sick they put him in a tent by himself and leave bread and water for him. They do not visit him, however, or speak to him, especially if he is a serf. Should he recover he rejoins the others; if he dies they burn him. But if he happens to be a serf they leave him for the dogs and vultures to devour. If they catch a robber they hang him to a tree until he is torn to shreds by wind and weather.

1. How did Ibn Fadlan's impression of the physical attributes of the Swedish Rus differ from his impression of their hygiene?

2. What does the way in which the Rus handled sickness and death tell you about their culture?

3. Why would the Rus way of dealing with hygiene and death be especially repulsive to a Muslim?

4. What are the clues in this account that the Rus are self-sufficient and able to protect themselves against dangers of all kinds?

❀ SECTION REVIEW ❀

1. **Locate:**
   (a) England,   (b) Normandy,   (c) Aquitaine,
   (d) Balkan peninsula,   (e) Kiev

2. **Identify:**
   (a) High Middle Ages,   (b) William of Normandy,   (c) Henry II,   (d) Thomas à Becket,
   (e) Magna Carta,   (f) Edward I,   (g) English Parliament,   (h) Capetians,   (i) Philip II,
   (j) Philip IV,   (k) Otto I,   (l) Frederick I,
   (m) Slavs,   (n) Mongols,   (o) Alexander Nevsky

3. **Recall:**
   (a) Name three sources of power kings had that other feudal lords did not have.
   (b) What steps did the Normans take to create a strong, centralized monarchy in England?

(c) Give two reasons why the first Russian state was more closely tied to the Byzantine Empire than to Europe.

4. **Think Critically:** Explain why unified, national monarchies did not develop in Germany and Italy as they did in France and England in the High Middle Ages.

THE BYZANTINE EMPIRE AND THE CRUSADES

In the fourth century, a separation between the western and eastern parts of the Roman Empire began to develop. In the course of the fifth century, Germanic tribes moved into the western part of the empire and

ASSESS

Answers to
SECTION REVIEW

2. (a) period between 1000 and 1300
   (b) king of England in 1066
   (c) king who enlarged power of monarchy
   (d) archbishop of Canterbury
   (e) supported idea of limited power of monarchs
   (f) convened first official Parliament
   (g) English representative government
   (h) French dynasty, named after king
   (i) Capetian king who expanded French monarchy
   (j) created a French parliament of three estates
   (k) first Roman emperor since Charlemagne
   (l) German king who attempted to conquer northern Italy
   (m) peoples originally from central Europe
   (n) 13th century conquerors of Russia
   (o) powerful Russian prince of Novgorod

3. (a) war, marriage alliances, and conquests
   (b) new English language, kept existing institutions, took census, taxation and royal courts
   (c) They were Orthodox Christians, not Catholics; Mongols conquered Russia and cut it off from Europe.

4. Answers will vary.

CLOSE

Lead students in a discussion of the Focus objectives identified on page 359.

FOCUS

OBJECTIVES

After completing this section, students should be able to

1. identify and explain factors that helped create the Byzantine Empire
2. describe the daily lives of the people
3. explain why the Crusades happened and their effect

Multimedia Support

LASERDISC
Mosaic of the Three Wise Men Bearing Gifts to the Virgin Mary

FOCUS ACTIVITY

Help students understand how a split in the Christian religion contributed to the creation of the Byzantine Empire. Remind students that this type of event was not unique to Christianity. In Chapter 8, they learned about the split in Islam between the Shi'ites and Sunnites. Do students believe that hostilities between factions of a religion may be even more serious than conflict between different religions?

▶ *This sixth-century mosaic located in a church in Ravenna, Italy, shows the Emperor Justinian surrounded by his court. What can you infer from their long elaborate robes?*

established their states while the Roman Empire in the east, centered on Constantinople, continued to exist.

The Reign of Justinian (527 to 565)

When he became emperor of the Eastern Roman Empire, Justinian was determined to reestablish the Roman Empire in the entire Mediterranean world. His army, commanded by Belisarius, probably the best general of the late Roman world, sailed into North Africa and then quickly moved into Italy and defeated the Ostrogoths.

By 552, Justinian appeared to have achieved his goals. He had restored the Roman Empire in the Mediterranean. His empire included Italy, part of Spain, North Africa, Asia Minor, Palestine, and Syria. However, the conquest of the western empire proved fleeting. Only three years after Justinian's death, the Lombards had conquered much of Italy, and other areas were soon lost.

Justinian's most important contribution was his codification of Roman law. The eastern empire had inherited a vast quantity of legal materials, which Justinian wished to simplify. The result was *The Body of Civil Law*. This codification of Roman law became the basis of imperial law in the Eastern Roman Empire until its end in 1453. Furthermore, because it was written in Latin (it was, in fact, the last product of eastern Roman culture to be written in Latin, which was soon replaced by Greek), it was also used in the west and became the basis for much of the legal system of Europe.

From Eastern Roman Empire to Byzantine Empire

Justinian's accomplishments had been spectacular, but the Eastern Roman Empire was left with serious problems: too much territory to protect far from Constantinople, an empty treasury, a decline in population after a plague, and renewed threats to its frontiers. In the first half of the seventh century, the empire was faced with attacks from the Persians to the east and the Slavs to the north. The empire survived, only to face a new series of threats.

The most serious challenge to the Eastern Roman Empire came from the rise of Islam, which unified the Arab tribes and created a powerful new force that swept through the eastern empire. The defeat of an army of the Eastern Roman Empire at Yarmuk in 636 meant the loss of the provinces of Syria and Palestine. Problems arose along the northern frontier as well, especially in the Balkans. In 679, the Bulgars defeated the Eastern Roman Empire's forces and took possession

On Line with WORLD HISTORY Internet Activity

You may want to have your students visit the following URL, where they will find information and additional web site resources to enhance their study of this chapter.

Exploring Ancient World Cultures—Medieval Europe

http://eawc.evansville.edu/

mepage.htm

You may wish to use this site for both Chapters 12 and 13. This is an especially good set of www sites.

Due to the ever-changing nature of the World Wide Web, see the West History web site, **http://history.swpco.com** for regular updates of the URLs in this text.

Map 12.6 The Byzantine Empire in the Time of Justinian

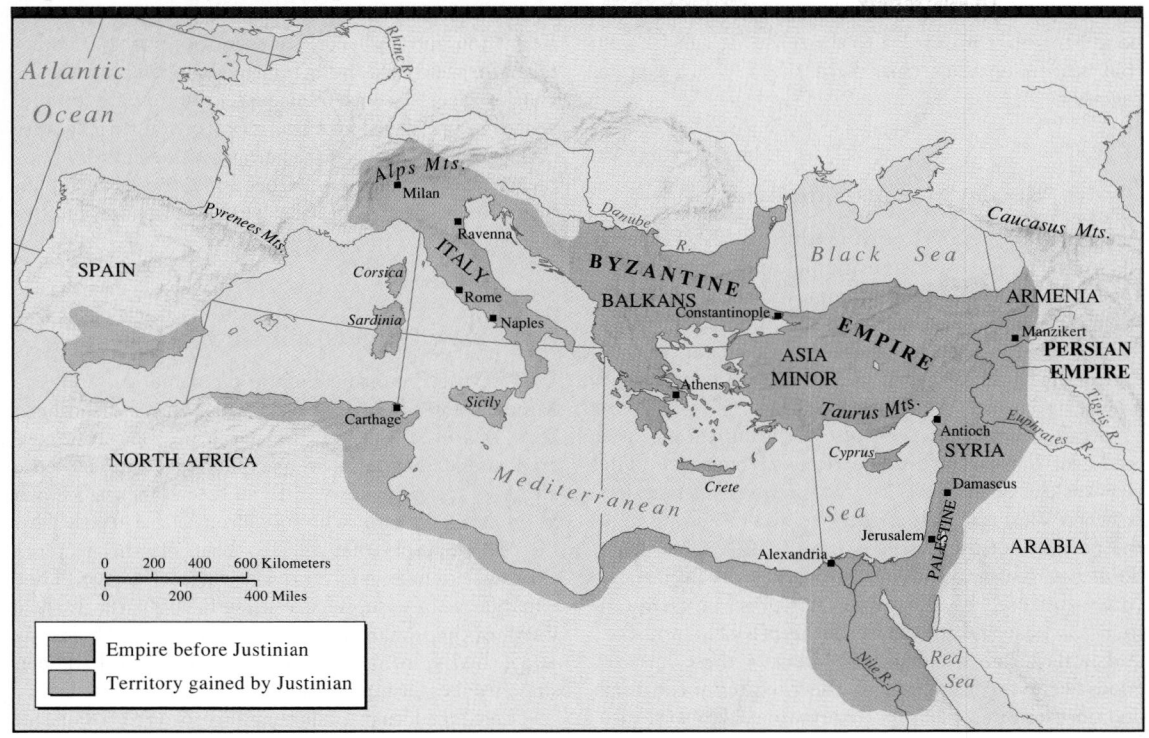

Empire before Justinian
Territory gained by Justinian

TEACH

COMPARING TIME PERIODS

The re-establishment of the Roman Empire ended soon after the death of Justinian. Ask students to identify and compare the fates of other empires they have studied that apparently relied on the personal leadership of one man for their existence. The empires of Alexander the Great the Tamerlane are two examples that could be discussed.

LEARNING FROM VISUALS

Answer to the caption question (page 368): These long elaborate court robes are indicative of the high status of the Emperor and his court. Common people and merchants would not have dressed like this.

Multimedia Support

 LASERDISC
Fleet of the Emperor Michael II Defeating an Enemy with "Byzantinic Fire"

---

of the lower Danube valley, creating a strong Bulgarian kingdom.

By the beginning of the eighth century, the Eastern Roman Empire was much smaller, consisting only of the eastern Balkans and Asia Minor. However, the external challenges had produced important internal changes. By the eighth century, this smaller Eastern Roman Empire had become what historians call the Byzantine Empire, a civilization with its own unique character that lasted until 1453. What were the characteristics of this Byzantine Empire?

The Byzantine Empire was both a Greek and a Christian state. Increasingly, Latin fell into disuse as Greek became both the common language and the official language of the empire. The Byzantine Empire was

also a Christian state. The empire was built on a faith in Christ that was shared in a profound way by almost all its citizens. An enormous amount of artistic talent was poured into the construction of churches, church ceremonies, and church decoration to honor this faith (see "Our Artistic Heritage: Hagia Sophia: Byzantine Architecture in the Service of God").

The emperor occupied a crucial position in the Byzantine state. Portrayed as chosen by God, he was crowned in sacred ceremonies. His subjects were expected to prostrate themselves in his presence. His power was considered absolute. Because the emperor appointed the head of the church (known as the **patriarch**), he also exercised control over both church and state. The Byzantines believed that God had com-

CLASS DISCUSSION

Have students compare the political and religious powers of the Holy Roman Emperor in Western Europe with those of the Byzantine Emperor in Eastern Europe. How might these differences explain some of the hostility between the two branches of the Christian religion?

STUDYING MAPS

The following questions will help you guide students through their study of Map 12.6.

1. Why were most of the lands conquered by Justinian close to the Mediterranean Sea? *(Transportation of supplies was easier by sea than land.)*

2. What economic advantage might Justinian's empire have enjoyed as the result of his control of most of the Mediterranean

Sea? *(Control of important port cities would give the empire a tremendous trade advantage.)*

3. Why is it often easier for an empire to win control over distant lands than to maintain its control over long periods of time? *(Maintenance requires an investment of men and resources over a long period of time.)*

manded their state to preserve the true Christian faith. Emperor, church officials, and state officials were all bound together in service to this ideal. It can be said that spiritual values truly held the Byzantine state together.

Life in Constantinople

After the destruction caused by riots in 532, Emperor Justinian rebuilt Constantinople and gave it the appearance it would keep for almost a thousand years. With a population estimated in the hundreds of thousands, Constantinople was the largest city in Europe during the Middle Ages. It viewed itself as center of an empire and a special Christian city.

Until the twelfth century, Constantinople was medieval Europe's greatest center of commerce. The city was the chief center for the exchange of products between West and East. Highly desired in Europe were the products of the East: silk from China, spices from Southeast Asia and India, jewelry and ivory from India (the latter used by Byzantine craftspeople for church items), wheat and furs from southern Russia, and flax and honey from the Balkans. Many of these Eastern goods were then shipped to the Mediterranean area and northern Europe. Imported raw materials were also used in Constantinople for local industries. In Justinian's reign, silkworms were smuggled from China by two Christian monks to begin a Byzantine silk industry. The state controlled the production of silk cloth. In fact, the workshops themselves were housed in Constantinople's royal palace. European demand for silk cloth made it the city's most lucrative product.

Much of Constantinople's appearance in the Early Middle Ages was due to Justinian's program of rebuilding in the sixth century. The city was dominated by an immense palace complex, hundreds of churches, and a huge arena known as the Hippodrome. No residential district was particularly fashionable because palaces, apartment buildings, and slums existed alongside one another. Justinian added many new buildings. His public works projects included roads, bridges, walls, public baths, law courts, schools, churches, and colossal underground reservoirs to hold the city's water supply.

The Hippodrome was a huge amphitheater constructed of brick covered by marble, holding between forty thousand and sixty thousand spectators. Gladiator fights were held there, but the main events were the chariot races. Twenty-four races would usually be presented in one day. The citizens of Constantinople were passionate fans of chariot racing, and successful charioteers were acclaimed as heroes and honored with public statues. The loss of a race in the Hippodrome frequently resulted in bloody riots.

New Heights and New Problems

By 750, the Byzantine Empire consisted only of Asia Minor, some lands in the Balkans, and the southern coast of Italy. However, the Byzantine Empire recovered and endured. It even expanded because of the efforts of a new dynasty of Byzantine emperors known as the Macedonians, who ruled from 867 to 1081. This line of emperors managed to beat off the empire's external enemies and go over to the offensive. They expanded the empire to include Bulgaria in the Balkans, the islands of Crete and Cyprus, and Syria. By 1025, the Byzantine Empire was the largest it had been since the beginning of the seventh century.

The Macedonian emperors also fostered a burst of economic prosperity by expanding trade relations with western Europe, especially by selling silks and metalworks. Thanks to this prosperity, the city of Constantinople flourished. Foreign visitors continued to be astounded by its size, wealth, and physical surroundings. To western Europeans, it was the stuff of legends and fables.

The Macedonian dynasty of the tenth and eleventh centuries had restored much of the power of the Byzantine Empire, but its incompetent successors soon undid most of the gains. Struggles for power between ambitious military leaders and aristocratic families led to political and social disorder in the late eleventh century. The Byzantine Empire had also been troubled by the growing split between the Catholic Church of the West and the Eastern Orthodox Church of the Byzantine Empire. The Eastern Orthodox Church was unwilling to accept the pope's claim that he was the

MORE ABOUT . . . *Byzantine Marriage*

As with many early civilizations Byzantine marriages were arranged by the family, with primary concern being the economic and political betterment of the family. Initially the age of consent was seven, but was later raised to ten in the 7th century. For practical purposes most marriages were arranged for girls beginning about twelve and boys at age fourteen. The actual betrothal was a legal, notarized document which specified the date of the marriage, the amount of the dowry and any penalties for breaking their engagement. The law required that parents find a spouse for their children, and a young woman still unmarried at twenty-five had the right to insist that her parents find her a husband.

OUR ARTISTIC HERITAGE

Hagia Sophia: Byzantine Architecture in the Service of God

Building churches was the special passion of the Emperor Justinian. In Constantinople alone he built or rebuilt thirty-four churches. His greatest achievement was the famous Hagia Sophia—the church of the Holy Wisdom.

Completed in 537, Hagia Sophia was designed by a Greek architect who did not use the simple, flat-roofed church of Western architecture. The center of Hagia Sophia consisted of four large piers crowned by an enormous dome, which seemed to be floating in space. This effect was stressed by Procopius, the emperor's court historian, who wrote a treatise on the emperor's building projects: "From the lightness of the building, it does not appear to rest upon a solid foundation, but to cover the place beneath as though it were suspended from heaven by the fabled golden chain."

In part, this impression was created by putting forty-two windows around the base of the dome. This allowed an incredible play of light within the cathedral. Light served to remind the worshipers of God. As Procopius commented,

Whoever enters there to worship perceives at once that it is not by human strength or skill, but by the favor of God that this work has been perfected; his mind rises sublime to commune with God, feeling that He cannot be far off, but must especially love to dwell in the place which He had chosen; and this takes place not only when a man sees it for the first time, but it always makes the same impression upon him, as though he had never beheld it before.

As darkness is illuminated by invisible light, so too it was believed that the world is illuminated by an invisible spirit. Hagia Sophia is a visible reminder of the Byzantine faith in a spiritual world.

▲ *Shown here is the interior of the church of the Holy Wisdom, known as Hagia Sophia. In the fifteenth century, the Turks converted this church into a mosque.*

1. What was the special passion of the Emperor Justinian, and how did he indulge it?

2. How was Hagia Sophia different from the churches of Western architecture? How did this influence the worshipers?

3. Can you think of a place of worship that inspires you by its beauty?

USING PRIMARY SOURCES

Assign students to visit a local house of worship that they personally find impressive and to write a description of it that is similar in style to the description of the Hagia Sophia. Have students discuss if they believe an impressive structure makes any difference to people's religious convictions. What reasons do they have for their points of view?

Multimedia Support

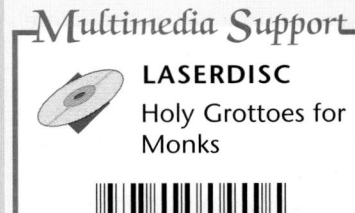

LASERDISC
Holy Grottoes for Monks

Answers to Critical Thinking Questions

1. Building churches was Justinian's passion. He built or rebuilt 34 of them in Constantinople alone. His greatest achievement was the Hagia Sophia.
2. The Greek architect of Hagia Sophia did not use the simple, flat-roofed church of Western architecture prevalent at the time. Instead, the church of the Holy Wisdom had an enormous dome, which appeared to be floating in space. The forty-two windows around the based allowed for an incredible play of light within the cathedral that encouraged a sublime communion of the worshippers with God.
3. Answers will vary.

SPECIAL NEEDS: *Visual and Multi-modal*

Read the description of the Hippodrome on page 370 aloud to students. Make notes on the overhead or chalkboard concerning: 1) number of spectators; 2) construction materials, 3) frequency of events occurring and 4) type of events occurring. Next, have students give examples of nearby football stadiums, basketball arenas, or colliseums. Compare and contrast all examples on the above four areas. Layouts of the buildings can be copied from ticket backs or promotional brochures to aid in visualizing each location. Then, have students discuss how spectatorship and the games themselves have changed. Are there still instances where riots occur? Are certain winners hailed as heroes or heroines? What are the main differences between sports in A.D. 600 and sports today?

sole head of the church. In 1054, Pope Leo IX and the patriarch Michael Cerularius, head of the Byzantine Church, formally excommunicated each other. This began a schism between the two great branches of Christianity that has not been completely healed to this day.

The Byzantine Empire faced threats from abroad as well. The greatest challenge came from the advance of the Seljuk Turks who had moved into Asia Minor—the heartland of the empire and its main source of food and workers. In 1071, a Turkish army disastrously defeated the Byzantine forces under Emperor Romanus IV Diogenes (die-AWJ-uh-neez) at Manzikert. Lacking the resources to undertake new campaigns against the Turks, the new emperor, Alexius I, turned to Europe for military aid. The response of Europeans to the emperor's request led to the Crusades, and the Byzantine Empire lived to regret it.

The Crusades

The **Crusades** (Christian military expeditions) were based upon the idea of a holy war against the **infidel,**

or unbeliever. The wrath of Christians was directed against the Muslims, and at the end of the eleventh century, Christian Europe found itself with a glorious opportunity to attack them. The push for the Crusades came when the Byzantine emperor Alexius I asked Pope Urban II for help against the Seljuk Turks, who were Muslims. The pope saw a golden opportunity to provide papal leadership for a great cause: to rally the warriors of Europe for the liberation of Jerusalem and the Holy Land (Palestine) from the infidel. At the Council of Clermont in southern France near the end of 1095, Urban II challenged Christians to take up their weapons and join in a holy war to recover the Holy Land. The pope promised remission of sins: "All who die by the way, whether by land or by sea, or in battle against the pagans, shall have immediate remission of sins. This I grant them through the power of God with which I am invested."[6] The enthusiastic crowd cried out in response: "It is the will of God, it is the will of God."

The warriors of western Europe, particularly France, formed the first crusading armies. The knights who made up this first crusading host were motivated by

▶ *This medieval illustration shows one of the battles of the Crusades. How do you think the idealistic goals of the Crusades compare with the view shown here?*

MORE ABOUT . . . *Byzantine Families*

The main purpose of the Byzantine family was to produce children. In order to do this, Byzantine family law focused on keeping the family unit together. Divorce was allowed only under very specific instances. A man could seek divorce if his wife was seen at the baths or having expensive dinners with a man who was not from her family or if she made trips to the races at the Hippodrome. Both men and women could seek divorce for adultery, attempts on the life of the spouse, or leprosy. Adulterous spouses had their noses cut off and women were then sent to a convent. If a woman left her husband he had up to six months to win her back. He was to "flatter her with words, to lay on a full table before her, and to do everything in his power to rekindle old feelings, but without violence or assault."

Map 12.7   The Crusades

Crusader kingdom
First Crusade 1096–1099
Second Crusade 1147–1149
Third Crusade 1189–1192
Fourth Crusade 1202–1204
Children's Crusade 1212

religious fervor, but there were other attractions as well. Some sought adventure and welcomed the chance to pursue their favorite pastime—fighting. Others saw an opportunity to gain territory, riches, and possibly a title. From the perspective of the pope and European kings, the Crusades offered a chance to free Europe of young nobles who disturbed the peace and wasted lives and energy fighting one another.

Three organized crusading bands of noble warriors, most of them French, made their way to the East. The crusading army probably numbered several thousand cavalry and as many as ten thousand infantry. After the capture of Antioch in 1098, much of the crusading host proceeded down the Palestinian coast, evading the well-defended coastal cities. The crusaders reached Jerusalem in June 1099. After a five-week siege, the Holy City was taken amid a horrible massacre of the inhabitants—men, women, and children.

After the further conquest of Palestinian lands, the crusaders organized four Latin crusader states there. These crusader kingdoms existed in a world surrounded by Muslims and depended upon Italian cities for supplies from Europe. Some Italian cities, such as Genoa, Pisa, and especially Venice, grew rich and powerful in the process.

It was not easy for the crusader kingdoms to maintain themselves in the East, however. Already by the 1120s, the Muslims had begun to strike back. In 1144, Edessa became the first of the four Latin kingdoms to be recaptured. Its fall led to renewed calls for another crusade, especially from the monastic firebrand Saint Bernard of Clairvaux (KLAIR-voe). He exclaimed: "Now, on account of our sins, the enemies of the cross have begun to show their faces. . . . What are you doing, you servants of the cross? Will you throw to the dogs that which is most holy? Will you cast pearls before swine?"[7] Bernard aimed his message at knights and even managed to enlist two powerful rulers, King Louis (LOO-ee) VII of France and Emperor Conrad III of Germany. This Second Crusade, however, proved to be a total failure.

The Third Crusade came about when the Holy City of Jerusalem fell in 1187 to the Muslim forces under Saladin. Now all of Christendom was ablaze with calls for a new crusade in the East. Three important rulers agreed to lead their forces in person: Emperor Frederick Barbarossa of Germany, Richard I the Lionhearted of England, and Philip II Augustus, King of France. Some of the crusaders finally arrived in the East by 1189, only to encounter problems. Frederick Barbarossa drowned while swimming in a local river, and his army quickly fell apart. The English and French arrived by sea and met with success against the coastal cities, where they had the support of their fleets. However, when they moved inland, they failed miserably. Eventually, after Philip went home, Richard the Lionhearted negotiated a settlement in which Saladin agreed to allow Christian pilgrims free access to Jerusalem.

After the death of Saladin in 1193, Pope Innocent III initiated the Fourth Crusade. On its way to the East, the crusading army became involved in a dispute over the succession to the Byzantine throne. The Venetian leaders of the Fourth Crusade saw an opportunity to neutralize their greatest commercial competitor, the Byzantine Empire. Diverted to Constantinople, the crusaders sacked the great capital city of Byzantium in 1204 and created a new Latin Empire of Constantinople. Thus, a crusade ostensibly against the heathen Muslims attacked instead the Christian city of Constantinople. Not until 1261 did a Byzantine army recapture Constantinople. The Byzantine Empire had been saved, but it was no longer a great Mediterranean power. The restored empire now comprised the city of Constantinople and its surrounding lands, as well as some lands in Asia Minor. In this reduced size, the empire limped along for another 190 years, until its weakened condition finally enabled the Ottoman Turks to conquer it in 1453.

Despite the failures, the crusading ideal was not yet completely lost. In Germany in 1212, a youth known

▲ *This thirteenth-century miniature shows the capture of Constantinople during the Fourth Crusade. Soldiers are hurling stones while knights attack the walls.*

as Nicholas of Cologne (kuh-LONE) announced that God had inspired him to lead a "children's crusade" to the Holy Land. Thousands of young people joined Nicholas and made their way down the Rhine and across the Alps to Italy, where the pope told them to go home. Most tried to do so. At about the same time, a group of about twenty thousand French children made their way to Marseilles (mar-SAY), where two shipowners agreed to transport them to the Holy Land. Seven ships packed with hymn-singing youths soon left the port. Two of the ships perished in a storm near Sardinia. The other five sailed to North Africa, where the children were sold into slavery. The next crusades of adult warriors were hardly more successful.

Did the Crusades have much effect on European civilization? Historians disagree. There is no doubt that the Crusades benefited the Italian port cities, especially Genoa, Pisa, and Venice. Even without the Crusades, however, Italian merchants would have pursued new trade contacts with the Eastern world. The Crusades did have some side effects that were unfortunate for

European society. The first widespread attacks on the Jews began in the Crusades. Some Christians argued that to undertake holy wars against infidel Muslims while the "murderers of Christ," as they called the Jews, ran free at home was unthinkable. The massacre of Jews became a regular feature of medieval European life.

 SECTION REVIEW

1. Locate:
(*a*) Constantinople,   (*b*) Syria,
(*c*) Palestine,   (*d*) Asia Minor

2. Define:
(*a*) patriarch,   (*b*) Crusades,   (*c*) infidel

3. Identify:
(*a*) Justinian,   (*b*) *The Body of Civil Law*,
(*c*) Macedonians,   (*d*) Seljuk Turks,
(*e*) Urban II,   (*f*) Council of Clermont,
(*g*) Saint Bernard of Clairvaux,   (*h*) Saladin

4. Recall:
(*a*) Approximately how long did the Byzantine Empire last?
(*b*) Why was Constantinople the largest and most commercially active city in Europe during the Middle Ages?

5. Think Critically: Why did cities such as Venice flourish as a result of the Crusades?

Conclusion

After the collapse of the Roman Empire and the establishment of the Germanic states, a new European civilization slowly began to emerge in the Early Middle Ages. The coronation of Charlemagne—a descendant of a Germanic tribe who had converted to Christianity—as Roman emperor in 800 symbolized the fusion of the three chief components of the new European civilization: the German tribes, the Roman legacy, and the Christian Church. In the long run, the creation of Charlemagne's empire fostered the idea of a distinct European identity. The lands north of the Alps now became the political center of Europe.

With the disintegration of the Carolingian Empire, new forms of political institutions began to develop in Europe. The feudal system put power into the hands of many different lords, who came to constitute a powerful group of nobles that dominated the political, economic, and social life of Europe. Quietly and surely within this world of castles, however, kings gradually began to extend their powers. Although they could not know it then, their actions laid the foundations for the European kingdoms that have dominated the European political scene ever since.

While a new civilization arose in Europe, the Byzantine Empire created its own unique civilization in the eastern Mediterranean. While Europe struggled in the Early Middle Ages, the Byzantine world continued to prosper and flourish. However, the Crusades to Palestine, supposedly carried out with religious motives, eventually had the result of weakening the Christian power that had initiated the whole process: the Byzantine Empire. Then a revival of trade, the growth of towns and cities, and a dramatic expansion of the population—all of which we will examine in the next chapter—soon gave rise to a new and stronger European world.

Notes

1. Norman F. Cantor, ed., *The Medieval World: 300–1300* (New York, 1963), pp. (in order of quotations) 104, 101, 108, 103.
2. Einhard, *The Life of Charlemagne*, trans. Samuel Turner (Ann Arbor, Mich., 1960), p. 30.
3. Quoted in Oliver Thatcher and Edgar McNeal, eds., *A Source Book for Medieval History* (New York, 1905), p. 363.
4. Quoted in Marvin Perry, Joseph Peden, and Theodore Von Laue, *Sources of the Western Tradition, vol. 1* (Boston, 1987), p. 218.
5. Quoted in Joseph and Frances Gies, *Life in a Medieval Castle* (New York, 1974), p. 175.
6. Oliver J. Thatcher and Edgar H. McNeal, eds., *A Source Book for Mediaeval History*, p. 517.
7. Quoted in Hans E. Mayer, *The Crusades*, trans. John Gillingham (New York, 1972), pp. 99–100.

ASSESS

Assign students to create recruiting literature for a crusade similar to the material that is distributed to high school students by the U.S. military today. Have them include information about what the crusades were expected to accomplish for Christianity and for the individual soldiers who went.

Answers to
SECTION REVIEW

2. (a) head of the Byzantine church
(b) Christian military expeditions
(c) unbeliever
3. (a) emperor of Eastern Roman Empire
(b) codification of Roman law
(c) dynasty of Byzantine emperors who ruled from 867 to 1081
(d) moved into Asia Minor, threatened Byzantine Empire, provoking Crusades
(e) pope who organized first Crusade
(f) meeting where Urbin II challenged Christians to join in a holy war
(g) monastic firebrand of the Second Crusade
(h) leader of Muslim forces who conquered Jerusalem in 1187
4. (a) around 700 years
(b) Answers will vary.
5. Port cities benefitted from increased use and trade.

CLOSE

Lead students in a discussion of the Focus objectives identified on page 367. Emphasize the impact of the division of Christianity on the history of Europe.

USING KEY TERMS

1. monasticism
2. chivalry
3. wergeld
4. diocese
5. fief
6. abbesses
7. feudal contract
8. monk
9. ordeal
10. compurgation
11. popes
12. patriarch
13. feudalism
14. scriptoria
15. subinfeudation
16. infidel
17. vassalage
18. Crusades

REVIEWING THE FACTS

1. the nature of the Germanic peoples, the legacy left by the Romans, and the Christian church
2. compurgation and ordeal
3. good works and feats of holiness carried out by monks
4. The works of early Christianity and Latin classical authors copied there were used as a basis for research.
5. by expanding the power of the royal courts
6. Parliament
7. codification of Roman law in the *Body of Civil Law.*
8. The First Crusade resulted in the capture of Jerusalem in 1099 and the establishment of four crusader states. The Second Crusade failed to liberate the crusader state of Edessa from the Muslims. The Third Crusade allowed Christians access to the Holy city.

THINKING CRITICALLY

1. The ordeal was a Germanic custom being used to solve a Christian question based on faith.
2. work, prayer, poverty
3. disintegration of central authority in the Carolingian world and the invasions of

USING KEY TERMS

1. _____ refers to the practice of living the life of a monk.
2. Under the influence of the church noblemen followed a code of behavior called _____.
3. _____ was the amount paid by a wrongdoer to the family of an injured person.
4. A Christian bishop headed an area called a bishopric, or _____.
5. A _____ was the grant of land from the lord to a vassal in return for military service.
6. The heads of convents are called _____.
7. The _____ determined the relationship between a lord and his vassals.
8. A _____ was a person who wanted to live a life totally dedicated to God.
9. The _____ was based on the idea that divine forces would protect the innocent.
10. _____ involved the swearing of oaths by the accused and a group of "oathhelpers."
11. Bishops of Rome became known as _____ of the Catholic Church.
12. The _____ is the Byzantine counterpart to the pope in Rome.
13. A system of rules in which powerful lords offered protection in return for service was called _____.
14. _____ were writing rooms where Benedictine monks copied manuscripts.
15. _____ complicated feudalism as vassals granted portions of their estates to other vassals who owed them military service.
16. The _____, or unbeliever, was the target for attack in the eleventh-century holy wars.
17. At the heart of the feudal system was the idea of _____, or serving in a military capacity.
18. Christian military expeditions were called the _____.

REVIEWING THE FACTS

1. What were the three major elements in forming the European society in the Middle Ages?
2. What were two means of determining guilt in Germanic law?
3. What attracted followers on a wide scale to the monastic movement?
4. Why are scriptoria so important to the history of Western Europe?
5. How did Henry II enlarge the power of the English monarchy?
6. What important English political institution emerged during the reign of Edward I?
7. What was Emperor Justinian's most important contribution?
8. Summarize the results of the First, Second, and Third Crusades.

THINKING CRITICALLY

1. How does the feature on page 347 illustrate both Roman and Germanic cultures?
2. What were the three cardinal principles prescribing life in a Benedictine monastery?
3. What factors helped feudalism develop in Western Europe in the ninth and tenth centuries?
4. How did European kings enlarge their powers, and how were these powers also limited?
5. Why was Germany unable to create a unified national monarchy in the Middle Ages, as France and England had done?
6. What was the relationship between church and state in the Byzantine Empire? What belief justified the relationship?

Muslims, Magyars and Vikings
4. by wars, marriage alliances, and taxation of commerce
5. The German kings spent precious resources in their efforts to control the church and extend their rule over Italy.
6. was supreme as he appointed the head of the church and exercised control over both

APPLYING SOCIAL STUDIES SKILLS

1. Germanic law was personal whereby crimes were considered family feuds and were handled by a system of determination of guilt and payment for injury. Payment was based on rank in society.
2. Monasteries held tax free lands upon which they worked. Because they took vows of poverty, they created a surplus which they used to help others and further missionary activity.
3. The system provided for military service, taxes, judicial functions, an advisory body to the king, and an executive or enforcement function.
4. The western Slavs formed the Polish and Bohemian (Czech) kingdoms; the eastern Slavs formed Ukraine and Russia; the south Slavs formed Serbia and Croatia.

APPLYING SOCIAL STUDIES SKILLS

1. **Sociology:** How did the bond of extended family affect the way Germanic law treated the problem of crime and punishment?
2. **Economics:** Describe how monasteries were able to carry on welfare activities as well as missionary activity.
3. **Government:** How can feudalism be considered a political system?
4. **Geography:** Consult Map 12.5 on page 365. What were the three branches of Slavic peoples that inhabited central Europe and what countries did each inhabit?

MAKING TIME AND PLACE CONNECTIONS

1. Which system of law, Germanic or Roman, became the basis for contemporary European law?
2. Besides Christianity, what other religious systems taught methods of enlightenment?
3. How can Europe in the Middle Ages be compared to Japan during the same time period?
4. Are there any similarities between European knighthood and the Islamic concept of the jihad?
5. How did the rise of Islam in the seventh century affect the Byzantine Empire?
6. What are the historical origins of the idea of separation of church and state?

BECOMING AN HISTORIAN

Analyzing Information—Drawing Inferences

1. What are two historical interpretations of the meaning of the crowning of Charlemagne by Pope Leo in 800? Which one does the author claim and how does it determine the direction of his narrative?

2. Charlemagne has been viewed as both saint and sinner. What is the evidence for both viewpoints?
3. During the European Renaissance of the fifteenth century, people "rediscovered" the classics. According to the viewpoint of this text, where might these classics have been rediscovered?

Cause and Effect

1. In the view of some historians, feudalism and its style of warfare was closely connected with the invasion of Asian nomads. What evidence is there for this viewpoint?
2. There is a disagreement over how the Crusades affected European civilization. Make a list of as many effects as you can think of and come to some interpretation, based on these facts, as to whether it had a positive or negative impact on or changed the course of European history.

Primary and Secondary Sources

The story of the "ordeal" between the Arian priest and the Christian deacon was written by Gregory of Tours, a Roman Christian. Does the way he records the event serve a missionary purpose?

Conducting Research

1. What was the historical context (reasons) for the successful Christian conversion of Germanic kings?
2. What was the context in which Saint Simeon the Stylite lived for thirty years in a basket on top of a pillar?
3. Given the general trends in Europe at the time, why might the Frankish king have given the Vikings a piece of land (Normandy) in their territory?
4. What was the historical context in which the code of chivalry emerged?
5. What was the political context in Western Europe, Byzantium, and the Middle East in which the Crusades occurred?

377

MAKING TIME AND PLACE CONNECTIONS

1. Roman law became the European model.
2. Buddhists, Sufis and Tao priests
3. In both places, warfare, the culture of knighthood, and the political economic, and social power of the knight dominated society.
4. Both were warrior activities aimed at conquest justified by religious conversion and principles, and promises of rewards in Heaven.
5. It diminished the size of the Empire.
6. In Western Europe, the kings were never able to appoint Catholic clerics or override church law.

BECOMING AN HISTORIAN

Analyzing Information

1. One interpretation is that it marked the rebirth of the Roman Empire; the other is that it reflected the emergence of a new European civilization. The author subscribed to the latter interpretation. The narrative that follows develops the idea of a novel new civilization infused with Germanic and Christian elements, as opposed to Byzantium where Roman customs predominated.
2. Answers will vary.
3. in the Middle Age monasteries

Cause and Effect

1. While the coats of armor were of Frankish origin, the mounted soldier had its origins in two innovations, both of Asiatic steppe origin.
2. Students might mention 1) revival of trade, 2) growth in power of the Italian merchants, 3) attacks on Jews, 4) diminished integrity of Christian principles, 5) continued presence of Christians in the Middle East, 6) death and destruction, 7) extending feudalism.

Primary and Secondary Sources

Students should recognize that a definite bias exists in the writing independent of its truthfulness.

Conducting Research

1. prior conversion of some of the population and the benefit gained by power and support of the church in rule
2. In the early stages of Christian monasticism, monks believed that total dedication to God could be achieved only by withdrawal from society and life as a solitary hermit.
3. Students might suggest as a bribe to prevent further invasions, for conversion purposes, as well as to safeguard Frankish peoples.
4. The influence of Christianity is reflected in chivalry, a code that applied to knights and royalty.
5. In western Europe, there existed a class of knights without a mission or the prospects of gaining territory. In the Middle East, Arab control of the Islamic movement was giving way to Seljuk Turkish control. The Byzantine emperor lost a key battle to the Seljuk Turks at Manzikert in 1071. Momentarily the two Christian churches allied against the "infidel" Muslims or unbelievers.

13 PLANNING GUIDE

SECTION	KEY TOPICS	PRIMARY SOURCES	ASSESSMENT
1 The World of the Peasants pages 379–385	◆ Farming techniques that led to increased food production ◆ the manorial system ◆ daily life for peasants	◆ Cistercian monk on life in the High Middle Ages, page 381	◆ Section Review, page 385 ◆ Section Quiz 13–1, TRB
2 The New World of Trade and Cities pages 385–391	◆ the relationship between trade and a market economy ◆ the growth of towns and cities during the Middle Ages ◆ medieval city life ◆ the guild system		◆ Section Review, page 391 ◆ Section Quiz 13–2, TRB
3 Christianity and Medieval Civilization pages 391–397	◆ papal power and the relationship between the pope and European monarchs ◆ monastic orders formed during the High Middle Ages ◆ the importance of the Catholic Church in the daily lives of Europeans	◆ Miracle from the life of St. Bernard of Clairvaux, page 394	◆ Section Review, page 397 ◆ Section Quiz 13–3, TRB
4 The Culture of the High Middle Ages pages 397–403	◆ development of medieval universities and student life at a university ◆ literature of the High Middle Ages ◆ Gothic and Romanesque architecture	◆ poem by Jaufre Rudel, page 399 ◆ *Song of Roland,* page 400	◆ Section Review, page 403 ◆ Section Quiz 13–4, TRB
5 A Time of Troubles: Europe in the Late Middle Ages pages 403–412	◆ The Black Death ◆ Great Schism of the Catholic Church, 1378–1417 ◆ Hundred Years' War ◆ Monarchical changes in Europe during the 1400s	◆ Black Death, page 405 ◆ A Medieval Holocaust: The Cremation of the Strasbourg Jews, page 407	◆ Section Review, page 412 ◆ Section Quiz 13–5, TRB

EUROPEAN CIVILIZATION IN THE MIDDLE AGES (1000 TO 1500)

REPRODUCIBLE ACTIVITIES

- Historical Maps
- Charts and Graphs
- Critical Thinking
- Cooperative Learning
- Vocabulary
- Guided Reading
- Reteaching
- Enrichment
- Performance Assessment
- Spanish Key Points and Chapter Summaries
- Spanish Vocabulary
- Spanish Guided Reading

MULTIMEDIA SUPPORT

TRANSPARENCIES
- *World History* Color Transparency Package
- Fine Art Color Transparency Package

VIDEO
- *World History* Video Library
- CNN® Annual Video Update

LASERDISC
- *Sights and Sounds of History*

AUDIO
- *Listening to Literature* audiotape (English and Spanish)
- *History of Music* CD

SOFTWARE
- WESTEST™
- Student Review

CD-ROM
- *The Journey of Civilization*
- *World History*

INTERNET
- Internet Activities

On Line with WORLD HISTORY

Access West's history web site at **http://history.swpco.com** You'll find activities and web sites related to specific topics and chapters in *World History: The Human Odyssey*. Also look for references to helpful web sites at appropriate places throughout this teacher edition.

LESSON PLANNING

You will find detailed daily lesson plans for both traditional class scheduling and **block scheduling** in your Teacher Resource Box.

Not Enough Time?

If you do not have the four or five days recommended to teach this chapter, you may want to focus on the following sections and activities:

- Have students read pages 380–383 that detail the manorial system.
- Have students read pages 391–396, and answer the Section Review on page 397.
- Have students read the troubadour poem on page 399 and the excerpt from the *Song of Roland* on page 400.
- Have students read pages 403–405 on the Black Death and answer Section Review question 4a on page 412.
- Have students read pages 405–410. Students should understand the reasons for the Hundred Years' War and its impact.
- It is important that students understand the shape that Europe had adopted by the end of the 1400s. Have them read pages 411–412 and summarize the information.

EUROPEAN CIVILIZATION

BUILDING ON CHAPTER 12

To "set the scene" for the study of Chapter 13, use the following questions and activities.

◆ Lead students in a discussion of how the Germanic kingdoms differed from the Roman Empire.

◆ Have students debate the pros and cons of the feudal system.

◆ Have students work in groups to develop short summaries of the Crusades. Then have them write their impressions of the Crusades. Do they think they were worthwhile? Why or why not?

USING THE OPENING STORY

Have students write a brief paraphrase of William Fitz-Stephen's description of London to describe the largest city in their state. When they have finished, discuss their writings and the accuracy of the views they have presented.

LEARNING FROM VISUALS

You might wish to discuss illuminated manuscripts with students and guide them in a discussion of the beauty and care that was given to each page.

Answer to the caption question: The streets are crowded and there are many buildings.

In the twelfth century, William Fitz-Stephen spoke of London as one of the noble cities of the world: "It is happy in the healthiness of its air, in the Christian religion, in the strength of its defences, the nature of its site, the honor of its citizens, the modesty of its women; pleasant in sports; fruitful of noble men." To Fitz-Stephen, London offered a number of opportunities and pleasures: "practically anything that man may need is brought daily not only into special places but even into the open squares, and all that can be sold is loudly advertised for sale." Any man, according to Fitz-Stephen, "if he is not a good-for-nothing, may earn his living expenses and esteem according to his station." Sporting events and leisure activities were available in every season of the year: "In Easter holidays they fight battles on water." In summer, "the youths are exercised in leaping, dancing, shooting, wrestling, casting the stone; the maidens dance as long as they can well see." In winter, "when the great fen, or moor, which waters the walls of the city on the north side, is frozen, many young men play upon the ice; some, striding as wide as they may, do slide swiftly." To Fitz-

Stephen, "every convenience for human pleasure is known to be at hand" in London. One would hardly know from his cheerful description that medieval cities faced overcrowded conditions, terrible smells from rotting garbage, and the constant threat of epidemics and fires.

The rise of cities was but one aspect of the new burst of energy and growth that characterized European civilization in the High Middle Ages (the period from 1000 to 1300). New farming practices, the growth of trade, and the rise of cities, all accompanied by a growing population, created a vigorous European society. Strong leadership by the popes, combined with new aspects of religious life, made the Catholic Church a forceful presence in every area of life. The new energy of European society was also evident in a burst of intellectual and artistic activity. However, in the fourteenth and early fifteenth centuries (the Late Middle Ages), Europeans experienced a time of troubles, visible in plague, famine, economic crisis, the decline of the Catholic Church, war, and political instability.

▲ This illustrated page from a medieval manuscript shows the Tower of London at the time Henry VIII reigned. What features in this illustration show that London was a growing, bustling city?

ADDITIONAL RESOURCES

The resources listed below can be used to enrich the lessons in this chapter.

BOOKS FOR STUDENTS
The Age of Faith by Anne Freemantle, Time-Life

Women in the Middle Ages by Joseph and Frances Gies, Barnes and Noble

VIDEOS/FILMS
The Black Death: March 27, 1361, Time-Line, Social Studies School Service

Cathedral, David Macauby, PBS, Social Studies School Service (800) 421-4246

IN THE MIDDLE AGES

(1000 TO 1500)

NEW PATTERNS OF CIVILIZATION

QUESTIONS TO GUIDE YOUR READING

1. What changes during the High Middle Ages enabled peasants to grow more food?

2. What were the major features of medieval cities?

3. What role did Christianity play in European civilization during the Middle Ages?

4. What were the major cultural achievements of European civilization in the High Middle Ages?

5. What was the Black Death, and what was its impact?

6. What were the "new monarchies," and what did they accomplish?

OUTLINE

1. THE WORLD OF THE PEASANTS
2. THE NEW WORLD OF TRADE AND CITIES
3. CHRISTIANITY AND MEDIEVAL CIVILIZATION
4. THE CULTURE OF THE HIGH MIDDLE AGES
5. A TIME OF TROUBLES: EUROPE IN THE LATE MIDDLE AGES

THE WORLD OF THE PEASANTS

In the Early Middle Ages, Europe had a relatively small population. In the High Middle Ages, this situation changed. There was a dramatic increase in population as the number of people in Europe almost doubled between 1000 and 1300, from 38 million to 74 million people. What caused this huge increase in population? For one thing, conditions in Europe were more settled and peaceful after the invasions of the Early Middle Ages had stopped. Then, too, there was a dramatic expansion in food production after 1000. Whether this high rise in food supplies was a cause or an effect of the population increase is uncertain, but without it, the growth in population could never have been sustained.

The New Agriculture

During the High Middle Ages, Europeans began to farm in new ways. A change in climate made for better growing conditions. Another important factor in increasing the amount of food grown was the expansion of cultivated, or arable, land. Eager for land, peasants of the eleventh and twelfth centuries found new lands to use for farming by cutting down trees and

379

Answers to QUESTIONS TO GUIDE YOUR READING

1. climate; expansion of arable land; labor saving devices; shift to three-field system (pages 379–381)

2. trade centers; community governments; small compared to ancient and modern cities; walled; crowded and often dirty (pages 386–389)

3. Christian ideas and practices touched lives of all Europeans (pages 391–397)

4. birth of universities; new developments in literature; explosion of building and architecture (pages 397–403)

5. deadly plague (often Bubonic); spread terror; killed between 39–38 million people between 1347–1351; triggered wave of anti-Semitism (pages 403–408)

6. attempt to reestablish centralized power of monarchical governments, especially in France, England, and Spain; were generally successful (pages 411–412)

FOCUS

OBJECTIVES

After completing this section, students should be able to

1. identify the new farming techniques that led to increased food production
2. explain the manorial system, including the role of the lord and the serf
3. describe the daily activities of a serf

FOCUS ACTIVITY

Ask students to work in small groups to list the responsibilities of citizens in a democratic society and the responsibilities of the government toward its citizens. Compile a class list that students can refer to as they discuss the role of peasant and nobles during the medieval period.

TEACH

COMPARING TIME PERIODS

Have students investigate the materials that are used to make tools today. How does their tensile strength compare to iron? Are modern tools more ergonomically designed than early farming tools? Which tools have changed? Which ones have not?

ACROSS THE CURRICULUM

Agriculture. Alternating fields and allowing fields to lie fallow were early soil conservation practices. Have students report on modern-day conservation practices.

---

draining swamps. By the thirteenth century, Europeans had more land for farming than they do today.

Changes in technology also aided the development of farming as the Middle Ages witnessed an explosion of labor-saving devices. Many of them were made from iron, which was now mined in different areas of Europe. Of course, iron was used to make swords and armor. However, it was also used to make scythes, axes, and hoes for use on farms, as well as saws, hammers, and nails for building. Iron was crucial in making the **carruca,** a heavy-wheeled plow with an iron plowshare that could turn over the heavy clay soil north of the Alps.

Because of the weight of the *carruca*, six or eight oxen were needed to pull it. However, oxen were slow. Two new inventions for the horse made it possible to plow even faster. A new horse collar spread the weight around the shoulders and chest rather than the throat. Now a series of horses could be hitched up, enabling them to pull the new, heavy plow faster and turn over more land. The use of the horseshoe, an iron shoe nailed to the horses' hooves, made it easier for horses to pull the heavy plow through the rocky and heavy clay soil of northern Europe.

The use of the heavy-wheeled plow also led to the growth of farming villages, where people had to work together. Because iron was expensive, a heavy-wheeled plow had to be bought by the entire community. Likewise, one family could not afford a team of animals, so villagers shared their beasts. Moreover, the size and weight of the plow made it necessary to plow the land in long strips to minimize the amount of turning that would have to be done. Besides using horsepower, the people of the High Middle Ages harnessed the power of water and wind to do jobs once done by human or animal power (see "The Role of Science and Technology: Harnessing the Power of Water and Wind").

The shift from a two-field to a three-field system also led to an increase in food production. In the Early Middle Ages, it was common to plant one field while another of equal size was allowed to lie fallow, or remain unplanted, to regain its fertility. Now lands were divided into three parts. One field was planted in the fall with winter grains, such as rye and wheat. Spring grains (such as oats and barley) and vegetables (such as peas, beans, or lentils) were planted in the sec-

▲ *The heavy-wheeled iron plow shown here made it possible for peasants to till the heavy clay soil of northern Europe. This illuminated page from a sixteenth-century manuscript also shows a team of draft horses wearing their collars.*

ond field. The third was allowed to lie fallow. By rotating their use, only one-third, rather than one-half, of the land lay fallow at any time. The rotation of crops also kept the soil from being exhausted so quickly, and more crops could then be grown.

The Manorial System

The system of feudalism that we examined in the last chapter rested upon an economic system known as

---

THE ROLE OF SCIENCE AND TECHNOLOGY
Harnessing the Power of Water and Wind

In the High Middle Ages, the powers of water and wind were harnessed to do jobs that humans or animals once did. The watermill, or mill powered by water, was invented as early as the second century B.C. It was not used much in the Roman Empire, however. The Romans had an abundant source of labor from slaves and thus had no need to mechanize. In the High Middle Ages, the use of metals spread and made the watermill easier to build. The watermill then came into widespread use. In 1086, the survey of English land known as the Domesday Book listed 6,000 watermills in England. Located along streams, mills powered by water were used to grind grains for flour. Dams were even built to increase waterpower. The development of the cam enabled mill operators to mechanize entire industries. Waterpower was used in mills for making cloth and in sawmills for cutting wood and stone, as well as to power triphammers for the working of metals.

Cistercian monks especially made use of the new technology surrounding waterpower. The following excerpt from a twelfth-century report describes how one Cistercian monastery made use of a local stream to grind grain and make cloth:

Entering the Abbey under the boundary wall, the stream first hurls itself at the mill where in a flurry of movement it strains itself, first to crush the wheat beneath the weight of the millstones, then to shake the fine sieve which separates flour from bran. . . . The stream does not yet consider itself discharged. The fullers [people who shrank and thickened woolen cloth to finish its manufacture] established near the mill beckon to it. In the mill it had been occupied in preparing food for the brothers; it is therefore only right that it should now look to their clothing. It never shrinks back or refuses to do anything that is asked

▲ *This woodcut shows an elementary water mill like those used during the High Middle Ages. After examining the picture, can you explain exactly how it worked?*

for. One by one it lifts and drops the heavy pestles, the fullers' great wooden hammers . . . and spares, thus, the monks' great fatigues. How many horses would be worn out, how many men would have weary arms if this graceful river, to whom we owe our clothes and food, did not labor for us.

Rivers, however, were not always available or easily dammed. Where this was the case, Europeans developed windmills to harness the power of the wind. Historians are unsure whether windmills were imported into Europe (they were invented in

(continued)

ENRICHMENT ACTIVITY

Have students compare the illustrated manuscript on page 378 with the one on page 380. Compare and contrast the two different views of medieval life that are presented. From the 7th through the 13th centuries, most of the copying and illumination of manuscripts was done by monks, who decorated large initials and created highly ornamented borders. The border ornaments were frequently spirals, knotwork, or intertwined animals.

REINFORCING VOCABULARY

Students may not recall that Cistercian monasteries evolved from the Benedictine order, and that the Cistercians were established in 1098 in Citeaux, France. The name Cistercian is derived from Citeaux.

CRITICAL THINKING

Have students reread the excerpt from the Cistercian monk regarding the role of the stream. Then, have students write a two or three paragraph summary describing daily life in a Cistercian monastery.

LEARNING FROM VISUALS

Answer to the caption question: The water forced the wheel to turn, which in turn powered other mechanisms.

CLASS DISCUSSION

Guide students in a discussion of the materials that might have been used to construct early wind mills. Obviously, they were rudimentary wood and metal structures. You might wish to have students diagram a wind mill showing which parts would have been made of wood and which might have been made of metal. How do these early wind mills compare to modern wind machines?

Answers to Critical Thinking Questions

1. Watermills and windmills were built to perform jobs that humans and animals once did. Water power was used to grind grains for flour, make cloth, and cut wood and stone. Wind power was used to pump water.
2. Dams harness water for hydroelectric power. Windmills are used in the desert of California to supply electricity.

CRITICAL THINKING

Guide students in a discussion of the specific factors that might have led free farmers to attach themselves to a manor. Have them examine the disadvantages and the advantages of the manor system to the farmer.

COMPARING TIME PERIODS

Today citizens do not pay their rents or taxes to a lord, but to local and federal governments. Have students compare and contrast the services received for taxes compared to those services peasants and serfs received for their rents.

ACTIVITY

Divide the class into small groups or pairs and have them write a contract between a serf and his lord, giving specific details of the amount of labor that will be exchanged for particular services. All the labor to be provided by the serf and his family should be listed, and all the noble's responsibilities should also be included.

THE ROLE OF SCIENCE AND TECHNOLOGY
Harnessing the Power of Water and Wind, continued

Persia) or designed independently by Europeans. In either case, by the end of the twelfth century, windmills were beginning to dot the European landscape. Like the watermill, the windmill was first used for grinding grains. Later, however, windmills were used for pumping water and even cutting wood. However, watermills offered a greater range of possible uses.

The watermill and windmill were the most important devices for the harnessing of power before the invention of the steam engine in the eighteenth century. Their spread had revolution ary consequences in enabling Europeans to produce more food and to make the manufacture of a wide array of products easier.

1. How did medieval people harness the power of water and wind? What did harnessing this power enable them to do?
2. How are water and wind power used today?

manorialism. A manor was an agricultural estate run by a lord and worked by peasants. It was the basic unit of rural organization in the Middle Ages.

Manorialism grew out of the chaotic conditions of the Early Middle Ages. Small farmers often needed protection or food in a time of bad harvests. Free peasants gave up their freedom to the lords of large landed estates in return for protection and the use of the lords' lands. Although a large class of free peasants continued to exist, increasing numbers of free peasants became **serfs,** or peasants bound to the land. Serfs had to provide labor services, pay rents, and be subject to the lords' control. By the ninth century, probably 60 percent of the people of western Europe had become serfs.

A serf's labor services consisted of working the lord's land, which might make up one-third to one-half of the cultivated lands scattered throughout the manor. The rest would be used by the peasants for themselves. Building barns and digging ditches were also part of the labor services. Serfs usually worked about three days a week for their lords.

The serfs paid rents by giving the lords a share of every product they raised. Moreover, serfs paid the lords for the use of the manors' common pasturelands, streams, ponds, and surrounding woodlands. If a serf fished in the pond or stream on a manor, he turned over part of the catch to his lord. Peasants were also obliged to pay a tithe (a tenth of their produce) to their local village churches.

Lords possessed a variety of legal rights over their serfs. Serfs were legally bound to the lords' lands. They could not leave without the lords' permission and could not marry anyone outside their manors without the lords' approval. Moreover, lords often had political authority on their lands, which gave them the right to try peasants in their own courts. In fact, the court on a lord's manor provided the only law that most peasants knew. Peasants were also required to pay lords for certain services, such as bringing their grain to the lords' mills and paying a fee to have it ground into flour.

As towns and cities needed more food, food prices tended to rise in the thirteenth century. This led lords to try to grow more food for profit. One way to do so was to rent their own land to serfs. This practice changed labor services into fixed rents or money payments. Thus, it became possible for serfs to be no longer legally tied to the land. Unfree serfs became free peasants. Lords, in turn, became collectors of rents

On Line with WORLD HISTORY Internet Activity

You may want to have your students visit the following URL, where they will find information and additional web site resources to enhance their study of this chapter.

On-line Text Materials for Medieval Studies
http://orb.rhodes.edu/default.html

This is an academic site written and maintained by medieval scholars for the benefit of fellow instructors and serious students.

Due to the ever-changing nature of the World Wide Web, see the West History web site, **http://history.swpco.com** for regular updates of the URLs in this text.

Map 13.1   A Manor

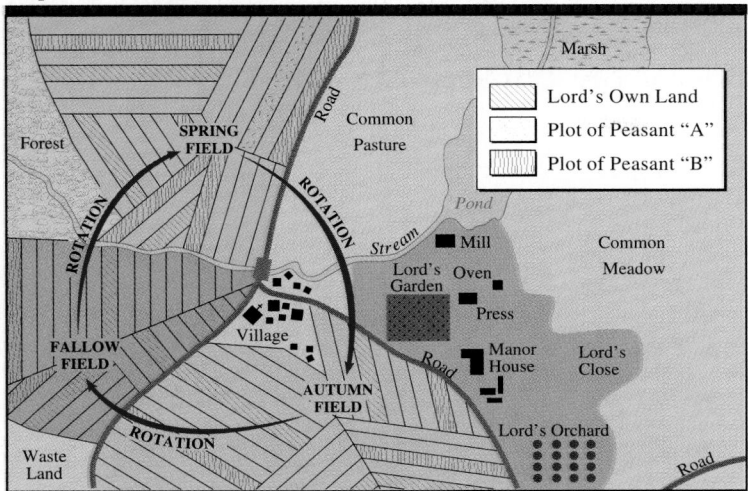

rather than operators of manors with both political and legal privileges. As feudal lords gave up these powers, the emerging monarchical states absorbed them.

Daily Life of the Peasantry

Peasant activities were largely determined by the seasons of the year. Each season brought a new round of tasks appropriate for the time. Some periods, of course, were more hectic than others, especially harvest time in August and September. The basic food of the peasant diet was bread, so a good harvest of grains was crucial to survival in the winter months. A new cycle began in October, when peasants worked the ground for the planting of winter crops. In November came the slaughter of excess livestock, because there was usually not enough fodder (food to be fed to the animals) to keep animals all winter. The meat would be salted to preserve it for winter use. In February and March, the land was plowed for spring crops—oats, barley, peas, beans, and lentils. Early summer was a fairly relaxed time, although there was still weeding and sheepshearing to be done. In every season, the serfs

worked not only their own land but also the lords' lands. They also tended the small gardens next to their dwellings, where they grew the vegetables that made up part of their diet (see "Focus on Everyday Life: The Lifestyle of the European Peasants").

Peasants did not face a life of constant labor, however, thanks to the feast days, or holidays, of the Catholic Church. These feast days celebrated the great events of the Christian faith or the lives of Christian saints or holy persons. The three great feasts of the Catholic Church were Christmas (celebrating the birth of Christ), Easter (celebrating the resurrection of Christ), and Pentecost (celebrating the descent of the Holy Spirit on Christ's disciples fifty days after his resurrection). Other feasts dedicated to saints or the Virgin Mary, the mother of Christ, were also celebrated. A total of more than fifty days were essentially holidays.

Religious feast days, Sunday mass, baptisms, marriages, and funerals all brought peasants into contact with the village church, a crucial part of manorial life. The village priest taught the peasants the basic ideas of Christianity so that they would gain the Christian's final goal—salvation. However, village priests were

STUDYING MAPS

The following questions will help you guide students through their study of Map 13.1.

1. What is a fallow field? *(a field left unplanted so the soil can regain lost minerals, etc.)*
2. Why would the farmers rotate the fields? *(This is another method of allowing the soil to replenish itself.)*
3. Why do you think the lord's demesne and the peasants' plots were alternated in the same fields? *(Answers will vary.)*
4. What is the one identifiable building in the village? *(the church)* How is it identified? *(It has a cross on it.)*

FOCUS ON
EVERYDAY LIFE

REINFORCING VOCABULARY

Some students may not understand what a *thatched roof* is. Generally made of straw matted tightly together, thatched roofs were thick and fairly durable. You might also guide students in a discussion of the term *hearth*.

CRITICAL THINKING

Ask students to list reasons why community ovens for baking bread were used, especially in light of the fact that most peasant huts contained their own fireplace. *(It was an economical and efficient way to conserve fuel.)*

LEARNING FROM VISUALS

Answer to the caption question: The lambs and budding trees indicate that it is spring.

Answers to Critical Thinking Questions

1. Peasant homes were simply constructed with a wooden frame surrounded by sticks with the space filled in with straw and rubble and then plastered over with clay. The roof was thatched. The houses consisted of one to two rooms.
2. Grains were used in making bread and also ale, the most common drink of the poor.
3. Answers will vary.

FOCUS ON EVERYDAY LIFE
The Lifestyle of the European Peasants

The lifestyle of the peasants in Europe was simple. Their cottages had wood frames surrounded by sticks, with the spaces between them filled with straw and rubble and then plastered over with clay. Roofs were simply thatched. The houses of poorer peasants consisted of a single room. Others, however, had at least two rooms—a main room for cooking, eating, and other activities and another room for sleeping. There was little privacy in a medieval household. A hearth in the main room was used for heating and cooking. However, because there were few or no windows and no chimney, the smoke created by fires in the hearth went out through cracks in the walls or, more likely, through the thatched roof.

Though simple, a peasant's daily diet was adequate when food was available. The basic staple of the peasant diet, and of the medieval diet in general, was bread. Women made the dough for the bread. The loaves were usually baked in community ovens, which were owned by the lord of the manor. Peasant bread was highly nutritious because it contained not only wheat and rye but also barley, millet, and oats. These ingredients gave the bread its dark appearance and very heavy, hard texture. Numerous vegetables from the household gardens; cheese from cow's or goat's milk; nuts and berries from woodlands; and fruits, such as apples, pears, and cherries, added to the peasant's diet. Chickens provided eggs and sometimes meat. Peasants usually ate meat only on the great feast days, such as Christmas, Easter, and Pentecost.

Grains were important not only for bread but also for making ale. In northern European coun-

▲ *A peasant's life was one of harsh labor, and the kind of work peasants performed changed each season and month by month. Here a flock of sheep is being taken out to pasture. One woman is milking a cow while another churns butter. What season is shown here? How can you tell?*

(continued)

SPECIAL NEEDS: *Visual*

Draw a spider diagram with the word "farming" in the middle. Elicit responses from students to determine what factors are necessary to successfully farm a piece of land. Responses might include: 1) the availability of the land itself; 2) the condition of the land; 3) equipment available; 4) chemicals; 5) climate; 6) personnel; and 7) political stability.

Then, have students read the section entitled "The New Agriculture" on page 379. Draw another spider diagram with these words in the center. Read the paragraph aloud slowly. Allow students to tell you when to add a leg as you go through conditions that made the agricultural explosion possible. Discuss differences between agriculture then and now.

Have students copy the spider diagrams for study purposes.

FOCUS ON EVERYDAY LIFE
The Lifestyle of the European Peasants, continued

tries, ale was the most common drink of the poor. If records are accurate, enormous quantities of ale were consumed. A monastery in the twelfth century records a daily allotment to the monks of three gallons a day. Peasants in the field probably consumed even more. This high consumption of alcohol might help to explain the large number of accidental deaths recorded in medieval court records.

1. How were the peasants' homes constructed? Do they sound comfortable to you? Compare the construction to that of your home.

2. Why were grains important?

3. Compare your diet with that of medieval peasants.

---

often peasants themselves; most were not able to read. It is difficult to know how much church teaching the peasants actually understood. Very likely, they saw God as an all-powerful force who needed to be appeased by prayer to bring good harvests.

Peasant women had both an important and a difficult position in manorial society. They were expected to work in the fields and at the same time to carry and bear children. Their ability to manage the household might determine whether a peasant family would starve or survive in difficult times.

3. **Recall:**
   (*a*) Give two reasons why the population of Europe almost doubled between 1000 and 1300. (*b*) List four changes that led to greater food production during the High Middle Ages.

4. **Think Critically:** Imagine that you are a peasant in the High Middle Ages. Decide whether you would rather be a free peasant or a serf and then explain your decision.

 SECTION REVIEW

1. **Define:**
   (*a*) *carruca,*
   (*b*) manorialism,
   (*c*) serfs

2. **Identify:**
   (*a*) Christmas,
   (*b*) Easter,
   (*c*) Pentecost

THE NEW WORLD OF TRADE AND CITIES

Medieval Europe was basically an agrarian, or agricultural, society in which most people lived in small villages. In the eleventh and twelfth centuries, however, new elements changed the economic foundation of European civilization. The new features included a revival of trade, the emergence of specialized craftspeople and artisans,

RECOMMENDED READING

For a good introduction to the High Middle Ages, see M. Barber, *The Two Cities: Medieval Europe, 1050–1320* (London and New York, 1992); C. N. L. Brooke, *Europe in the Central Middle Ages, 962–1154,* rev. ed. (New York, 1988); and J. Mundy, *Europe in the High Middle Ages, 1150–1309* (New York, 1973). On economic conditions, see N. J. G. Pounds, *An Economic History of Medieval Europe* (New York, 1974); R. S. Lopez, *The Commercial Revolution of the Middle Ages: 950–1350* (Englewood Cliffs, N.J., 1971); and A. Sapori, *The Italian Merchant in the Middle Ages* (New York, 1970). Urban history is covered in E. Ennen, *The Medieval Town* (Amsterdam, 1978). A good short introduction to medieval society is C. Brooke, *The Structure of Medieval Society* (London, 1971).

ASSESS

Answers to SECTION REVIEW

1. (a) heavy-wheeled plow with iron plowshare used for tilling clay soil; (b) economic system that was basis of feudalism; basic unit of rural organization in the Middle Ages; (c) peasants bound to the land, subject to the lords' control
2. (a) Christian holiday celebrating the birth of Christ; (b) Christian holiday celebrating the resurrection of Christ; (c) Christian holiday celebrating descent of Holy Spirit on Christ's disciples
3. (a) conditions in Europe were more peaceful, dramatic expansion in food production; (b) new farming methods, change in climate, expansion of cultivated land, new technology, shift to a three-field system
4. Answers will vary.

CLOSE

Manorialism was an effective economic system that grew from the need for small farmers to acquire protection for their families and their crops. The system provided a clearly defined societal order for both peasants and the manorial lords. However, the Catholic Church played a major role in establishing and maintaining social order and structure for both the peasants and the lords during the medieval period.

FOCUS

OBJECTIVES

After completing this section, students should be able to

1. explain the relationship between trade and a money economy
2. list reasons for the growth of towns and cities
3. describe problems associated with medieval city life
4. explain the organization of medieval guilds

FOCUS ACTIVITY

Have students work in pairs to compile a list of ten advantages and ten disadvantages of modern-day urban life. Students should then choose and justify whether they prefer living in large cities, small towns, or in rural areas.

TEACH

LEARNING FROM VISUALS

You may wish to point out to students that it was the Cistercians who built the big flocks of sheep in England for export to Flanders.

Answer to the caption question: Answers will vary.

Multimedia Support

LASERDISC
Solid Gold and Gem Stone
(Christ with angels)

and the growth and development of towns and cities. These changes were made possible by new agricultural practices and the subsequent increase in food production. Part of the European population no longer had to grow its own food. Merchants and craftspeople could now buy what they needed to live.

The Revival of Trade

The revival of trade was gradual. During the chaotic conditions of the Early Middle Ages, large-scale trade had declined. By the end of the tenth century, however, people were emerging in Europe with both the skills and products for trade. Cities in Italy took the lead in this revival of trade. Venice, for example, had emerged by the end of the eighth century as a town with close trading ties to the Byzantine Empire. Venice developed a mercantile fleet (a fleet of trading ships) and by the end of the tenth century it had become a major trading center.

While Venice and other northern Italian cities were busy trading in the Mediterranean, the towns of Flanders were doing the same in northern Europe. Flanders, the area along the coast of present-day Belgium and northern France, was known for its much desired, high-quality woolen cloth. The location of Flanders made it an ideal center for the traders of northern Europe. Merchants from England, Scandinavia, France, and Germany met there to trade their goods for woolen cloth. Flanders prospered in the eleventh and twelfth centuries, and such Flemish towns as Bruges (BROOZ-uh) and Ghent became centers for the trade and manufacture of woolen cloth.

▲ *Flanders gained fame for its woolen cloth, handwoven on looms like the one shown here. Wool was shipped from England and made into cloth in Flanders. The cloth was then sold throughout Europe. How does this loom vary from modern looms you may have seen at craft fairs?*

By the twelfth century, then, Italy in southern Europe and Flanders in northern Europe had become centers of a brisk trade. As one would expect, a regular exchange of goods soon developed between these two major centers. To encourage this trade, the counts of Champagne (sham-PANE), in northern France, devised a series of six fairs held every year in the chief towns of their territory. They guaranteed the safety of visiting merchants; supervised the trading activities; and, of course, collected a sales tax on all goods exchanged at the fairs. At the fairs of Champagne, northern merchants brought the furs, woolen cloth, tin, hemp, and honey of northern Europe and in return received the cloth and swords of northern Italy and the silks, sugar, and spices of the East.

As trade increased, both gold and silver coins came to be in demand at fairs and trading markets of all kinds. Slowly, a **money economy,** or an economic system based on money, rather than barter, began to emerge. New trading companies as well as banking firms were set up to manage the exchange and sale of goods. All of these new practices were part of the rise of **commercial capitalism,** or an economic system in which people invested in trade and goods in order to make profits.

The Growth of Cities

The revival of trade led to a revival of cities. Merchants needed places where they could live and build

MORE ABOUT . . . *Medieval Money*

The basis for medieval money was a pound of silver, out of which was minted 240 pennies. Twelve pennies made up a shilling or sous and twenty shillings or sous made up a pound. By the mid-thirteenth century, the closest to a standard unit was the gold florin (from Florence) or ducat (from Venice), each of which was worth one silver pound and was struck from 3.5 grams of gold.

Map 13.2   Medieval Trade Routes

warehouses to store their goods. To meet the needs of merchants, cities were usually located near sources of protection (such as castles) and alongside rivers or roads that provided routes for carrying the goods.

Towns had greatly declined in the Early Middle Ages, especially in Europe north of the Alps. Old Roman cities continued to exist, but their size and population had dwindled. With the revival of trade, merchants began to settle in these old cities and were followed by craftspeople or artisans. These were people who, on manors or elsewhere, had developed skills and

saw a chance to make goods that could be sold by the merchants. In the course of the eleventh and twelfth centuries, the old Roman cities came alive with new populations and growth.

Beginning in the late tenth century, many new cities or towns were also founded, especially in northern Europe. Usually a group of merchants built a settlement near a castle because it would be located along a major route of transportation or at the crossroads of two trade routes. The lords of the castle also offered protection. If the settlement prospered and expanded,

STUDYING MAPS

The following activities will help you guide students through their study of Map 13.2.

1. Ask students to locate Flanders on the map. What are the principal cities in and near to Flanders? *(Bruges, Ghent within Flanders, Paris and the cities of Champagne, in France, London is not far)*

2. Have students compute the distance from

Flanders to Venice. *(approximately 600 miles)*

3. Guide students in a discussion of the similarities and differences in the location of Flanders and Venice. *(both have access to water, sailors could stay close to land for long distances, both are centrally located within Europe)*

TEACHING WITH VISUALS

Carcassonne, which is fairly close to the large city of Toulouse, is now divided into two parts. The lower city is the modern business district, and the Cite, which sits on the hilltop is the recon-structed medieval fortress shown here. Construction on the Cite was initially begun by the Romans in the fifth century, and in the twelfth and thirteenth centuries, Carcassonne was an active city. Its restoration was begun in 1844, and today it is a popular tourist attraction.

Answer to the caption question: Modern skyscrap-ers have many more win-dows, are built of very differ-ent materials, and their purpose is not defensive.

REINFORCING VOCABULARY

Students may not know that a *charter* is a document issued by a recognized gov-erning body that grants spe-cific rights to an individual, to a group of people, or to a corporation. Students should know that the first colonies in the U.S. were founded by charter from the British Crown.

CRITICAL THINKING

In medieval times, only men could be considered cit-izens of a town. Considering the role women played on the farms and occasionally in the guilds, what justification might have been used to exclude women from citizen-ship?

➤ *This picture of Carcassonne, a medieval walled city built on a hill in southern France, clearly shows its thick, fortified walls and defensive towers. Entry into town was con-trolled by the use of gates that could be closed and barred. How does the tower-dotted skyline compare with modern city skylines?*

new walls were built to protect it. The merchants and artisans came to be called *burghers* or *bourgeoisie* from the word *burgus* (BUR-juss), a Latinized version of the German word *burg* meaning "a walled enclosure."

Most towns were closely tied to the land around them because they depended on the food grown there. In addition, they were often part of the territory belonging to a feudal lord and were subject to his authority. Although lords wanted to treat towns and townspeople as they would their vassals and serfs, the townspeople saw things differently.

Townspeople needed freedom to trade. This necessi-tated the creation of their own unique laws. Because the townspeople were making money from the growth of trade and the sale of their products, they were will-ing to pay for the right to make their own laws and to govern themselves. Often, lords and kings in turn saw that they could also make money and were willing to sell to the townspeople the liberties they wanted.

By 1100, townspeople were getting charters of liber-ties from their lords that gave them the rights they wanted. These included the right to buy and sell prop-erty, freedom from military service to the lord, a writ-ten law that guaranteed the freedom of the townspeo-

ple, and the right to become a free person after residing a year and a day in the town. This last right made it possible for a runaway serf who could avoid capture to become a free person in a city. The people in almost all new towns and cities gained these basic liberties, but some also received the right to govern themselves by choosing their own officials and having their own courts of law.

Over a period of time, medieval cities developed their own governments for running the affairs of the community. Only those males born in the city or who had lived there for some time were citizens. In many cities, these citizens elected the members of a city council, who served as judges and city officials and who passed laws. Elections were carefully rigged to make sure that only members of the wealthiest and most powerful families—known as the patricians—were elected.

A city government kept close watch over the activ-ities of its community and provided for the commu-nity's welfare. A government would provide water bar-rels and prepare people in every section of the town to fight fires, which were an ever-present danger. The government built warehouses to store grain in the case

ENRICHMENT ACTIVITY

Ask students to take the role of merchants along trade routes. They should explain which goods they would carry and what mode of travel they would use along each leg of travel. Among the routes should be: London–Bruges–Nuremburg–Budapest–

Belgrade–Constantinople; Bergen–Stock-holm–Danzig–Krakow–Kiev; Lisbon–Bor-deaux–Winchester; Bruges–Paris–Milan–Venice–Tunis–Alexandria–Damascus–Bagdad; Cordoba–Barcelona–Genoa–Constantinople–Budapest–Vienna–Danzig.

of food shortages. It set the standards for the weights and measures used in local goods and industries.

Urban crime was not a big problem in medieval cities, because their relatively small size made it difficult for criminals to operate openly. City governments, however, did hire guards to patrol the streets at night to break up fights and prevent robberies. People caught committing criminal acts were quickly tried. Serious crimes, such as murder, were punished by execution, usually by hanging. Lesser crimes were punished by fines, flogging, or branding.

Medieval cities were small in comparison with either ancient or modern cities. A large trading city would number about 5,000 inhabitants. By 1200, London was the largest city in England, with 30,000 people. Italian cities tended to be larger. Venice, Florence, Genoa (JEN-uh-wuh), Milan, and Naples each had almost 100,000 inhabitants. Even the largest European city, however, seemed small alongside the Byzantine capital of Constantinople or the Arab cities of Damascus, Baghdad, and Cairo. For a long time to come, Europe remained a rural society. In the long run, however, the growth of trade and the rise of towns laid the foundations for the eventual transformation of Europe from a rural agricultural society to an urban industrial one.

Daily Life
in the Medieval City

Medieval towns were surrounded by stone walls. Because the walls were expensive to build, the space within was precious and tightly filled. Thus, medieval cities had narrow, winding streets. Houses were crowded against one another, and the second and third stories of the dwellings were built out over the streets. The danger of fire was great. Dwellings were built mostly of wood before the fourteenth century, and candles and wood fires were used for light and heat. Medieval cities burned rapidly once a fire started.

Most of the people who lived in cities were merchants involved in trade and artisans active in manufacturing of some kind. Generally, merchants and artisans had their own sections within a city. The

▲ *This woodcut of a medieval town shows a sharp contrast in city life. As a woman empties garbage into the street, musicians continue to serenade her, apparently oblivious to the litter.*

merchant area included warehouses, inns, and taverns. Artisan sections were usually divided along craft lines. Each craft had its own street, where its activity was pursued.

The physical environment of medieval cities was not pleasant. The cities were often dirty and smelled from animal and human waste deposited in backyard privies or on the streets. Pigs and other animals roamed the streets, often dining on the by-products of human urban life. Air pollution was also a fact of life. Wood fires, present everywhere, were the usual cause. Even worse pollution, however, came from the burning of cheap grades of coal by brewers, dyers, and people who could not afford to purchase wood.

Cities were also unable to stop water pollution, especially from the tanning and animal-slaughtering industries. Both industries were forced, however, to locate downstream to avoid polluting the water used by the city upstream. Butchers dumped blood and all other waste products from their butchered animals into the rivers. Tanners unloaded tannic acids, dried blood, fat,

MORE ABOUT . . . *Hygiene in Medieval Cities*

Privacy was virtually unknown in Medieval Europe. One chronicler notes an earl and a countess, their daughter and her governess who slept in the same room. A peasant family would sleep in the same bed, and often keep pigs, chickens, and even cows and sheep with them at night. City sanitation was rudimentary. In London, the aristocrats built their privies directly over the river. Poorer people usually emptied their wastes into the middle of the street. The London Assizes records two men in 1347 who emptied their privy into their neighbor's cellar; the neighbor sued them when his cellar overflowed.

ASSESS

hair, and the other waste products of their operations. Tanneries and slaughterhouses existed in almost every medieval town, so rivers rapidly became polluted.

Because of the pollution, cities did not use the rivers for drinking water but relied instead on wells. Some cities repaired the aqueducts left over from Roman times and even built new ones. Private and public baths also existed in medieval towns. Paris, for example, had thirty-two public baths for men and women. City laws did not allow lepers and people with "bad reputations" to use them. This did not, however, keep public baths from being known for permissiveness because of public nudity. City authorities came under increasing pressure to close down the public baths, and the great plague of the fourteenth century (discussed later in this chapter) sealed the fate of the baths.

There were considerably more men than women in medieval cities. Women were expected to supervise the household, prepare meals, raise the children, and manage the family's finances. Often, they were expected to help their husbands in their trades. Some women also developed their own trades to earn extra money. Sometimes, when a master craftsman died, his widow even carried on his trade. Some women in medieval towns were thus able to lead lives of marked independence.

Industry in Medieval Cities

The revival of trade enabled cities and towns to become important centers for manufacturing a wide range of goods, such as cloth, metalwork, shoes, and leather goods. A host of craft activities were carried on in houses located in the narrow streets of the medieval cities. From the twelfth century on, craftspeople began to organize themselves into **guilds** (associations of people with common aims and interests), which came to play a leading role in the economic life of the cities.

By the thirteenth century, there were guilds for almost every craft, such as tanners, carpenters, and bakers. There were also separate guilds for specialized groups of merchants, such as dealers in silk, spices, wool, or money (banking). Craft guilds directed almost every aspect of the production process. They set the

▲ This illustration captures the activity of a French medieval town. Tailors, furriers, a barber, and a grocer are seen working in their shops. Craftspeople worked in ground-level rooms and lived upstairs, above their shops. How does this scene compare to a suburban mall?

standards for the articles produced, specified the actual methods of production to be used, and even fixed the price at which the finished goods could be sold. Guilds also determined the number of people who could enter a specific trade and the procedure they must follow to do so.

A person who wanted to learn a trade first became an apprentice, usually around the age of ten, to a master craftsperson. Apprentices were not paid, but they did receive room and board from their masters. After five to seven years of service, in which they learned their craft, apprentices became journeymen (or journeywomen, although most were male) who then worked for wages for other masters. Journeymen or journeywomen aspired to become masters as well. To do so, they were expected to produce a "masterpiece," a finished piece in their craft that allowed the master craftspeople of the guild to judge whether the journeymen or journeywomen were qualified to become masters and join the guild.

MORE ABOUT . . . Guilds

Guilds did not start out as the organizers and overseers of the production process for the craftspeople and merchants. Originally, guilds were organizations within communities that were developed to meet the common needs of the people. They functioned mainly as religious and social fraternities. The guilds provided needed assistance to widows and orphans and to the elderly. They also financed religious festivals and helped maintain and build local churches.

SECTION REVIEW

1. **Locate:**
   (*a*) Venice,   (*b*) Flanders

2. **Define:**
   (*a*) money economy,   (*b*) commercial capitalism,
   (*c*) guilds

3. **Identify:**
   (*a*) apprentice,   (*b*) masterpiece

4. **Recall:**
   (*a*) Give at least three reasons why medieval cities
   were not pleasant places to live.
   (*b*) Why were fires so common in medieval cities?

5. **Think Critically:** Compare the advantages and
   disadvantages of living and working in a medieval
   city versus living and working on the farmlands.

CHRISTIANITY AND MEDIEVAL CIVILIZATION

Christianity was a crucial element in medieval European society. The tremendous number of churches throughout Europe was only the most obvious visible symbol of the basic role played by Christianity in all levels of European society. Christian ideas and practices touched the lives of all Europeans in ways not so visible.

The Papal Monarchy

Since the fifth century, the popes of the Catholic Church had been supreme over the affairs of the church. They had also come to control the territories in central Italy that came to be known as the Papal States. This control kept the popes involved in political matters, often at the expense of their spiritual duties. At the same time, the church became increasingly involved in the feudal system. Chief officials of the church, such as bishops and abbots, came to hold their offices as fiefs from nobles. As vassals, they were obliged to carry out the usual services, including military duties. Of course, feudal lords assumed the right to choose their vassals, even when these vassals were bishops and abbots. They often chose their vassals from other noble families for political reasons. As a result, these bishops and abbots were often worldly figures who cared little about their spiritual responsibilities. The Catholic Church was in danger of becoming more of a political than a religious institution.

Reform of the Papacy

By the eleventh century, church leaders realized the need to be free from the interference of lords in the appointment of church officials. **Lay investiture** was the practice by which secular rulers both chose nominees to church offices and gave them the symbols of their office. Pope Gregory VII decided to fight this practice.

Elected pope in 1073, Gregory was convinced that he had been chosen by God to reform the church. To pursue this aim, Gregory claimed that he—the pope—was truly God's "vicar on earth" and that the pope's authority extended over all of Christendom, including its rulers. Gregory sought nothing less than the elimination of lay investiture. Only in this way could the church regain its freedom, by which Gregory meant the right of the church to appoint clergy and run its own affairs. If rulers did not accept this, then they would be deposed by the pope.

Gregory VII soon found himself in conflict with the king of Germany over these claims. King Henry IV of Germany was also a determined person. For many years, German kings had appointed high-ranking clerics, especially bishops, as their vassals in order to use them as administrators. Without them, the king could not hope to maintain his own power in the face of the powerful German nobles. In 1075, Pope Gregory issued a decree forbidding high-ranking clerics from receiving their investiture from lay leaders: "We decree that no one of the clergy shall receive the investiture with a bishopric or abbey or church from the hand of an

TEACH

CLASS DISCUSSION

Many students may not comprehend the mingling of religion and state that existed during the Middle Ages. Review the practice of lay investiture and its impact on the government and on the Catholic Church. Remind students that separation of church and state is a basic tenet of the United States constitution.

WORKING WITH VISUALS

You might wish to point out to students that the headpiece Pope Innocent is wearing is called a miter. They are usually made of linen or silk and heavily embroidered with gold thread.

Answer to the caption question: The current pope, although he holds a powerful position, does not exert the same power that popes were able to exert during the Middle Ages.

USING PRIMARY SOURCES

Have students reread the excerpt from Innocent III concerning royal power and papal power. Ask students to compare Innocent's views on papal power to the power of presidents or prime ministers. How do they vary? What might be the difference in scope of influence or in consequences when one's power comes from the people and when it comes from the church or from the pope?

emperor or king or of any lay person."[1] Henry, however, had no intention of obeying a decree that challenged the very heart of his administration.

The struggle between Henry IV and Gregory VII, which is known as the Investiture Controversy, was one of the great conflicts between church and state in the High Middle Ages. It dragged on until a new German king and a new pope reached a compromise in 1122 called the Concordat of Worms. Under this agreement, a bishop in Germany was first elected by church officials. After election, the new bishop paid homage to the king as his feudal lord, who in turn invested him with the symbols of temporal office. A representative of the pope, however, then invested the new bishop with the symbols of his spiritual office.

The Church Supreme

The popes of the twelfth century did not give up the reform ideals of Pope Gregory VII, but they were more inclined to strengthen their power and build a strong administrative system. During the papacy of Pope Innocent III in the thirteenth century, the Catholic Church

▼ *Pope Innocent III was a powerful pope who inaugurated the Fourth Crusade, approved the creation of both the Franciscan and Dominican orders, and frequently intervened in European political affairs. How did his view of the papacy compare to the current pope's work as a worldwide statesman?*

reached the height of its power. At the beginning of his rule in 1198, in a letter to a priest, the pope made a clear statement of his views on papal supremacy:

> As God, the creator of the universe, set two great lights in the firmament of heaven, the greater light to rule the day, and the lesser light to rule the night so He set two great dignities in the firmament of the universal church, . . . the greater to rule the day, that is, souls, and the lesser to rule the night, that is, bodies. These dignities are the papal authority and the royal power. And just as the moon gets her light from the sun, and is inferior to the sun . . . so the royal power gets the splendor of its dignity from the papal authority.[2]

Innocent III's actions were those of a man who believed that he, the pope, was the supreme judge of European affairs. He forced the king of France, Philip Augustus, to take back his wife and queen after Philip had tried to have his marriage annulled. The pope compelled King John of England to accept his choice for the position of archbishop of Canterbury. To achieve his political ends, Innocent used the spiritual weapons at his command. His favorite was the **interdict.** This decree forbade priests to give the sacraments of the church (see "Popular Religion in the High Middle Ages" later in this chapter) in the hope that the people, deprived of the comforts of religion, would exert pressure against their ruler. Pope Innocent's interdict was so effective that it caused Philip to restore his wife to her rightful place as queen of France.

New Religious Orders and New Spiritual Ideals

In the second half of the eleventh century and the first half of the twelfth century, a wave of religious enthusiasm seized Europe and led to a spectacular growth in the number of monasteries and the emergence of new monastic orders. Most important was the Cistercian (sis-TUR-shun) order founded in 1098 by a group of monks unhappy with the lack of strict discipline at their own Benedictine monastery. Cistercian monasticism spread rapidly from southern France into the rest of Europe.

RECOMMENDED READING

Good general studies of the church in the fourteenth century can be found in F. P. Oakley, *The Western Church in the Later Middle Ages* (Ithaca, N.Y., 1980); and S. Ozment, *The Age of Reform, 1250–1550: An Intellectual and Religious History of Late Medieval and Reformation Europe* (New Haven, Conn., 1980). On the Cluniac reform movement, see H. E. J. Cowdrey, *The Cluniacs and the Gregorian Reform* (Oxford, 1970). For a general survey of church life, see R. W. Southern, *Western Society and the Church in the Middle Ages* (Baltimore, 1970). On the papacy in the High Middle Ages, see C. Morris, *The Papal Monarchy* (Oxford, 1989); and I. S. Robinson, *The Papacy* (Cambridge, 1990). The reign of Innocent III is covered in H. Tillmann, *Innocent III* (Amsterdam, 1980). Good works on monasticism include B. Bolton, *The Medieval Reformation* (London, 1983); C. H. Lawrence,

The Cistercians were strict. They ate a simple diet and each had only a single robe. All decorations were eliminated from their churches and monastic buildings. More time for prayer and manual labor was attained by shortening the number of hours spent at religious services.

The Cistercians played a major role in developing a new, activistic spiritual model for twelfth-century Europe. A Benedictine monk often spent hours in prayer to honor God. The Cistercians were different: "Arise, soldier of Christ, arise! Get up off the ground and return to the battle from which you have fled! Fight more boldly after your flight, and triumph in glory!"[3] These were the words of Saint Bernard of Clairvaux. He, more than any other person, was the embodiment of the new spiritual ideal of Cistercian monasticism (see "You Are There: A Miracle of Saint Bernard").

Women were also actively involved in the spiritual movements of the age. The number of women joining religious houses grew dramatically. In the High Middle Ages, most nuns were from the ranks of the landed aristocracy. Convents were convenient for families who were unable or unwilling to find husbands for their daughters and for aristocratic women who did not wish to marry. Female intellectuals found convents a haven for their activities. Most of the learned women of the Middle Ages, especially in Germany, were nuns. This was certainly true of Hildegard of Bingen, who became abbess (head) of a religious house for females in western Germany.

Hildegard shared in the religious enthusiasm of the twelfth century. Soon after becoming abbess, she began to write down an account of the mystical visions she had had for years. "A great flash of light from heaven pierced my brain and . . . in that instant my mind was imbued with the meaning of the sacred books," she wrote. Eventually she produced three books based on her visions. Hildegard gained fame as a mystic and prophetess. Popes, emperors, kings, dukes, bishops, abbots, and abbesses eagerly sought her advice.

In the thirteenth century, two new religious orders emerged that had a strong impact on the lives of ordinary people. Founded by Saint Francis of Assisi (uh-SIS-ee), the Franciscans lived among the people,

▲ Although the medieval church viewed women as inferior to men, many women still joined convents. In this miniature, a group of Flemish nuns are listening to an abbot. Why do you think the nuns have bowed their heads?

preaching repentance and aiding the poor. Their calls for a return to the simplicity and poverty of the early church, reinforced by their own example, were especially effective in providing a more personal religious experience for ordinary people, especially in the cities.

The second new religious order of the thirteenth century—the Dominicans—was founded by a Spanish priest, Dominic de Guzmán (gooz-MAWN). He wanted to defend church teachings from **heresy** (the holding of religious doctrines different from the orthodox teachings of the church). The spiritual revival of the High Middle Ages had led to the emergence of heretical movements, which became especially widespread in southern France. Dominic was an intellectual who was shocked by the growth of heresy within the church and came to believe that a new religious order of men who lived lives of poverty but were capable of preaching effectively would best be able to attack heresy. The Dominicans became especially well known for their roles as the inquisitors of the papal Inquisition.

The church's desire to have a method of discovering and dealing with heretics led to the creation of the **Inquisition.** This court, whose job it was to find and try heretics, developed a regular procedure to deal with

Medieval Monasticism (London, 1984), a good general account; and H. Leyser, *Hermits and the New Monasticism* (London, 1984). On the Cistercians, see L. J. Lekai, *The Cistercians* (Kent, Ohio, 1977). The new monastic orders of the thirteenth century are examined in R. B. Brooke, *The Coming of the Friars* (New York, 1975). For a good introduction to popular religion in the eleventh and twelfth cen-

turies, see R. and C. N. L. Brooke, *Popular Religion in the Middle Ages* (London, 1984). On heresy, see M. Lambert, *Medieval Heresy* (New York, 1977); and W. L. Wakefield, *Heresy, Crusade and Inquisition in Southern France, 1100–1250* (Berkeley, Calif., 1974). On the Inquisition, see B. Hamilton, *The Medieval Inquisition* (New York, 1981).

WORKING WITH VISUALS

Point out to students that the young woman dressed in white is a novice, which means that she has not yet taken her first vows to become a nun. After she takes her first vows, this woman will have to work with the nuns for several years before she will be issued an invitation to take her final vows and become a full member of the convent.

Answer to the caption question: It is probable that the nuns are showing obedience and deference to their abbot by bowing their heads.

Multimedia Support

 LASERDISC
The Spiritual Visions of Hildegard of Bingen (1098–1179) (Video)

COMPARING TIME PERIODS

Review with students the lack of educational opportunities available to women during the Middle Ages. For many, like Hildegard of Bingen, entering a convent was the only means to acquiring an education and to pursuing a life as a writer. You might wish to have students compare Hildegard's story with that of Sor Juana Ines de la Cruz, who joined a convent in Mexico when she was refused admission to the university in the 17th century *(see Chapter 20)* or with early education practices in the United States. Like Hildegard, de la Cruz is known to us from her writings.

YOU·ARE·THERE

CLASS DISCUSSION

The miracles of St. Bernard of Clairvaux were both widely told and illustrated during the High Middle Ages. Guide students in a discussion of why the reports of his miracles were important to church members and how these miracles strengthened the power of the Catholic Church.

WORKING WITH VISUALS

Some students may not understand that certain church pieces, such as the altar box, were designed to hold communion pieces. Communion refers to the sacrament of the Lord's Supper, sharing consecrated bread and wine.

Answer to the caption question: St. Bernard is shown with a halo.

YOU ARE THERE
A Miracle of Saint Bernard

Saint Bernard of Clairvaux has been called "the most widely respected holy man of the twelfth century." He was an outstanding preacher who was completely dedicated to the service of God. His reputation inspired a number of stories dealing with his miracles, one of which follows.

Saint Bernard

A certain monk, departing from his monastery, threw off his habit, and returned to the world at the persuasion of the Devil. And he took a certain parish living; for he was a priest. Because sin is punished with sin, the deserter from his Order lapsed into the vice of lechery [excessive sexual activity]. He took a concubine to live with him, and by her he had children.

But as God is merciful and does not wish anyone to perish, it happened that many years after, the blessed abbot [Saint Bernard] was

passing through the village in which this same monk was living, and went to stay at his house. The renegade monk recognized him, and received him very reverently, and waited on him devoutly; but as yet the abbot did not recognize him.

On the morrow, the holy man said mass and prepared to be off. But as he could not speak to the priest, since he had got up and gone to the church for mass, he said to the priest's son, "Go, give this message to your master." Now the boy had been born dumb. He obeyed the command and feeling in himself the power of him who had given it, he ran to his father and uttered the words of the Holy Father

St. Bernard of Clairvaux is shown in this detail taken from an altar box designed to hold communion pieces. This box, which was made in Germany c. 1330, is covered with silver gilt and enamel. What features show that Bernard is a saint?

them. If an accused heretic confessed, he or she was forced to perform public penance and was subjected to punishment, such as flogging. The heretic's property was then seized and divided between the state and the church. Beginning in 1252, those who did not confess voluntarily were tortured until they did confess. Those who did not confess and were still considered guilty were turned over to the state for execution. So also were relapsed heretics—those who confessed, did penance, and then reverted to heresy again. To the Christians of

the thirteenth century who believed that there was only one path to salvation, heresy was a crime against God and against humanity. In their minds, force should be used to save souls from damnation.

Popular Religion in the High Middle Ages

We have witnessed the actions of popes, bishops, and monks. But what of ordinary people? What were their

ENRICHMENT ACTIVITY

Ask students to name several saints whose history they know, St. Bernard and St. Joan are featured in this chapter. What did they do to be named as saints? What is the significance of achieving sainthood?

Some people believe that Mother Theresa, who has received the Nobel Peace prize for her work in India, will be named a saint. Do students agree or not? Have them support their opinions.

Answers to Critical
Thinking Questions

YOU ARE THERE

A Miracle of Saint Bernard, continued

clearly and exactly. His father, on hearing his son's voice for the first time, wept for joy, and made him repeat the same words; and he asked what the abbot had done to him. "He did nothing to me," said the boy, "except to say 'Go and say this to your father.'"

At so evident a miracle the priest repented, and hastened after the holy man and fell at his feet saying "My Lord and Father, I was your monk, and I ran away from your monastery. I ask you to allow me to return with you to the monastery, for in your coming God has visited my heart." The saint replied unto him, "Wait for me here, and I will come back quickly when I have done my business, and I will take you with me." But the priest, fearing death, answered, "Lord, I am afraid of dying before then." But the saint replied, "Know this for certain, that if you die in this condition, and in this resolve, you will find yourself a monk before God."

The saint [eventually] returned and heard that the priest had recently died and been buried. He ordered the tomb to be opened. And when they asked him what he wanted to do, he said, "I want to see if he is lying as a monk or a clerk in his tomb." "As a clerk," they said; "we buried him in his secular habit." But when they had dug up the earth, they found that he was not in the clothes in which they had buried him; but he appeared in all points, tonsure and habit [hair and clothing], as a monk. And they all praised God.

1. What does the story of Saint Bernard tell us about the reputation of the "holy man"?

2. According to the story, why did the monk leave the monastery? What do you think this means if you read it figuratively, rather than literally?

3. What do you think would have happened if the monk had not died? Would he have returned to the monastery? If so, would he have remained there for life, or would he have once again "returned to the world"? Give rea-

1. The story recounting two miracles attributed to St. Bernard tells us that his reputation of being "the most widely-respected holy man of the twelfth century" was well-deserved.

2. He left the monastery at the persuasion of the Devil. Answers will vary, students may say he wanted to return to the pleasures of the world.

3. Answers will vary.

REINFORCING VOCABULARY

Remind students that the term *apostle* means one who is sent on a mission, and usually refers to the original twelve disciples and Paul. The *sacraments* are Christian rites, such as baptism. (See "More About . . . Sacraments" below.)

religious hopes and fears? What were their religious beliefs?

The sacraments of the Catholic Church ensured that the church was a crucial part of people's lives, from birth to death. There were seven sacraments, administered only by the clergy. Sacraments, such as baptism and the Lord's Supper, were seen as a means for receiving God's grace and were necessary for a Christian's salvation. Therefore, the clergy were seen to have a key role in the attainment of salvation.

Other church practices were also important to ordinary people. One was the role of saints. Saints were seen as men and women who were especially holy and who had achieved a special position in Heaven, which enabled them to ask for favors before the throne of God for people who prayed to them. The saints' ability to protect poor souls enabled them to take on great importance at the popular level. Jesus Christ's apostles, of course, were recognized throughout Europe as saints, but there were also numerous local saints that were of

MORE ABOUT . . . *Sacraments*

Of the seven sacraments defined by the Catholic church, five directly influenced the lives of Christians during medieval times. *Baptism* removed original sin and indicated membership in the church. *Marriage* dignified the union of two people. In the *Eucharist* bread and wine were thought to miraculously become the body and blood of Jesus.

Through *penance* Christians received forgiveness for their sins. *Extreme unction,* or the *last rites,* were administered for the dying. The other two sacraments included *holy orders,* which was reserved for the clergy, and *confirmation* of older children, which did not become a regular practice until the 13th century.

WORKING WITH VISUALS

Answer to the caption question: The celebration of the mass and of holy days was an integral part of their faith and religious practices.

ASSESS

Answers to SECTION REVIEW

1. (a) secular rulers chose nominees to church offices; (b) forbade priests to give the sacraments of the church; (c) holding of religious doctrines different from the church; (d) court created to find and try heretics; (e) bones or other objects connected with saints

2. (a) territories under the control of popes; (b) fought for elimination of lay investiture; (c) king of Germany, wanted to maintain ability to appoint bishops; (d) struggle between Henry IV and Gregory VII; (e) agreement to resolve investiture conflict; (f) believed he was supreme judge of European affairs; (g) monks desiring strict discipline; (h) Catholic saint who embodied ideal of Cistercian monasticism; (i) abbess of women's religious house in Germany; (j) founded Franciscans religious order; (k) religious order founded by Spanish priest

3. (a) only clergy could administer the seven sacraments; (b) holy people, able to approach God

4. Answers will vary.

CONNECTIONS TO OUR WORLD

From Saint Nicholas to Santa Claus   Saint Nicholas was a bishop in Asia Minor who died in 342. He was known as a generous man who was fond of children. During the Middle Ages in Europe, Saint Nicholas became known as the patron saint of children who brought them gifts on his feast day, which was December 6. Saint Nicholas was portrayed as dressed in a red-and-white bishop's robe and sporting a flowing white beard. His gifts to children were quite simple—fruit, nuts and candies.

The Dutch brought the tradition of Saint Nicholas with them to their colonies in the New World. In America, however, changes occurred in the practices associated with Saint Nicholas. In Holland, children placed wooden shoes next to the fireplace to be filled with gifts from Saint Nicholas. In America, stockings were hung by the chimney. The Dutch words for Saint Nicholas were "Sint Nikolass." In America, they became "Sinte Klaas." After the English took control of the Dutch colonies, "Sinte Klaas" became pronounced as Santa Claus. Later in the nineteenth century, the physical appearance of Santa Claus also changed. Saint Nicholas had been a tall and thin man. By the 1880s, Santa Claus had become pictured as the jolly fat man that we still know today.

▲ *Churches that possessed holy relics held special masses to honor their saints. The large picture depicts the celebration of this kind of mass. The relics are displayed on a table to the left, and the small pictures show various parts of the mass. Why were the celebration of the mass and the relics such a large part of medieval life?*

special significance to a single area. New saints emerged rapidly, especially in the intense religious atmosphere of the eleventh and twelfth centuries. The English, for example, had Saint Nicholas, the patron saint of children, who is known today as Santa Claus.

Of all the saints, the Virgin Mary, the mother of Jesus, was the most highly regarded in the High Middle Ages. Mary was seen as the most important mediator between mortals and her son, Jesus Christ, the judge of all sinners. Moreover, from the eleventh century on, a fascination with Mary as Jesus' human mother became more evident. A sign of Mary's importance is the num-

ber of churches all over Europe that were dedicated to her in the twelfth and thirteenth centuries. (These churches were known in France as Notre Dame, or "our lady.")

Emphasis on the role of the saints was closely tied to the use of **relics.** Relics were usually the bones of saints or objects connected with saints that were considered worthy of worship by the faithful. A twelfth-century English monk began his description of an abbey's relics by saying, "There is kept there a thing more precious than gold, . . . the right arm of St. Oswald. . . . This we have seen with our own eyes and have kissed, and have

RECOMMENDED READING

General works on medieval intellectual life are A. Murray, *Reason and Society in the Middle Ages* (Oxford, 1978); and D. Knowles, *The Evolution of Medieval Thought* (New York, 1962). The development of universities is covered in S. Ferruolo, *The Origin of the University* (Stanford, 1985); A. B. Cobban, *The Medieval Universities* (London, 1975); and the brief, older work by C. H. Haskins, *The Rise of Universities* (Ithaca, N.Y., 1957). Various

aspects of the intellectual and literary developments of the High Middle Ages are examined in J. W. Baldwin, *The Scholastic Culture of the Middle Ages, 1000–1300* (Lexington, Mass., 1971); R. W. Southern, *St. Anselm, A Portrait in a Landscape* (Cambridge, 1990); J. Weisheipl, *Friar Thomas d'Aquino: His Life, His Thought and Work* (New York, 1974); and H. Waddell, *The Wandering Scholars* (New York, 1961). A good introduction to handled with our own hands. . . . There are kept here also part of his ribs and of the soil on which he fell."[4] The monk went on to list additional relics possessed by the abbey, which included two pieces of Jesus' swaddling clothes, pieces of his manger, and part of the five loaves of bread with which he fed five thousand people. The holiness of a saint was thought to be present in his or her relics, so these objects were believed to be capable of healing people or producing other miracles.

 SECTION REVIEW

1. **Define:**
   (*a*) lay investiture,   (*b*) interdict,   (*c*) heresy,
   (*d*) Inquisition,   (*e*) relics

2. **Identify:**
   (*a*) Papal States,   (*b*) Pope Gregory VII,
   (*c*) King Henry IV,   (*d*) Investiture Controversy,
   (*e*) Concordat of Worms,   (*f*) Pope Innocent III,
   (*g*) Cistercians,   (*h*) Saint Bernard of Clairvaux,
   (*i*) Hildegard of Bingen,   (*j*) Saint Francis of
   Assisi,   (*k*) Dominicans

3. **Recall:**
   (*a*) Why did the clergy have a key role in attaining salvation for the common people?
   (*b*) Why were saints thought to be so important in the High Middle Ages?

4. **Think Critically:** Explain why the church leaders were often at odds with the leaders of the various European kingdoms.

4

THE CULTURE OF THE HIGH MIDDLE AGES

The High Middle Ages was a time of intellectual and artistic vitality—a time that witnessed the birth of universities and new developments in literature. There was also a building spree that left Europe bedecked with churches and cathedrals.

The Rise of Universities

The university as we know it, with faculty, students, and degrees, was a product of the High Middle Ages. The word *university* comes from the Latin word *universitas*, meaning "corporation" or "guild." Medieval universities were educational guilds or corporations that produced educated and trained individuals.

The first European university appeared in Bologna (buh-LONE-yuh), Italy, where a great teacher named Irnerius, who taught Roman law, attracted students from all over Europe. Most of them were laymen, or nonclerics (women did not attend universities), usually older individuals who were administrators for kings and princes. They were eager to learn more about law in order to apply it in their own jobs. To protect themselves, students at Bologna formed a guild, which was recognized by the ruler of Germany (who also controlled northern Italy) and given a charter in 1158. Although the faculty also organized itself as a group, the guild of students at Bologna was far more influential. It obtained a promise of freedom for students from local authorities; regulated the price of books and lodging; and determined the curriculum, fees, and standards for their masters. Teachers were fined if they missed a class or began their lectures late.

The first university in northern Europe was the University of Paris. In the second half of the twelfth century, a number of students and masters left Paris and started their own university at Oxford, England. In the Late Middle Ages, kings, popes, and princes competed to found new universities. By the end of the Middle Ages, there were eighty universities in Europe, with most of them located in England, France, Italy, and Germany.

Students began their studies at a medieval university with the traditional liberal arts curriculum, which consisted of grammar, rhetoric, logic, arithmetic, geometry, music, and astronomy. Teaching at a medieval university was done by a lecture method. The word *lecture* is derived from Latin and means "to read." Before the development of the printing press in the fifteenth century, books were expensive. Few students could afford them, so teachers read from a basic text and then added their explanations. No exams were given after a series

Romanesque style is G. Künstler, *Romanesque Art in Europe* (New York, 1973). On the Gothic movement, see G. Henderson, *Gothic* (Baltimore, 1967); E. Panofsky, *Gothic Architecture and Scholasticism* (New York, 1957); and J. Bony, *French Gothic Architecture of the Twelfth and Thirteenth Centuries* (Berkeley, Calif., 1983). A good book on the construction of Gothic cathedrals is J. Gimpel, *The Cathedral Builders* (New York, 1961).

CLOSE

The medieval church and the clergy played a dominant role in the lives of common people during the High Middle Ages. The goal for most people was to reach salvation, and the path was the Catholic Church and the clergy. Nobles too, in many cases, owed their power to the church and to the pope, but the struggles that arose from European rulers and the pope would not cease for several centuries to come.

FOCUS

OBJECTIVES

After completing this section, students should be able to

1. describe student life at a medieval university
2. identify troubadour and epic poetry
3. explain the differences between Gothic and Romanesque architecture

FOCUS ACTIVITY

Have students brainstorm a list of those contributions of American civilization or culture that will stand out 500 years from now and that will serve as trademarks of the late 1900s. Compare this list with the cultural contributions of medieval society, particularly in literature and architecture.

TEACH

CLASS DISCUSSION

Compare and contrast the role of teachers and students in modern-day schools with those of the High Middle Ages. How did the students of Bologna acquire so much power? At what period in time did teachers begin to have more authority than students (if they do)?

CLASS DISCUSSION

What are the normal subjects that students must study in order to graduate from high school and to enter universities in their own state? How does this list compare to the liberal arts curriculum offered at universities during the High Middle Ages?

CRITICAL THINKING

How has the role of the university changed since medieval times? What role do graduates play in modern-day society as compared to medieval society? What factors account for the differences?

CRITICAL THINKING

Have students review what they learned about Aristotle in Chapter 5 and then explain why universities taught in an Aristotelian fashion. Remind the students that Aristotle was very interested in analysis and in classification based on thorough research and investigation. Why might this style of learning have been at odds with medieval Christian theology? *(The belief in divine power, creation, and miracles would have been questioned by Aristotle.)*

▶ *This picture shows a university classroom in fourteenth-century Germany. The master teacher reads while students listen and take notes. Boys as young as age twelve or thirteen could attend university classes, and as shown here, the age and attention level of the students varied greatly.*

of lectures. However, when a student applied for a degree, he was given an oral examination by a committee of teachers. These examinations were taken after a four- or six-year period of study. The first degree a student could earn was a bachelor of arts. Later, he might receive a master of arts. All degrees were licenses to teach, but most students receiving them did not become teachers.

After completing the liberal arts curriculum, a student could go on to study law, medicine, or theology. The latter was the most highly regarded subject of the medieval university. The study of law, medicine, or **theology** (the study of religion and God) could take ten years or more. A student who passed his final oral examinations was granted a doctor's degree, which officially enabled him to teach his subject. Students who received degrees from medieval universities could pursue careers that proved to be much more lucrative than teaching. A law degree was necessary for those who wished to serve as advisors to kings and princes. The growing bureaucracies of popes and kings also demanded a supply of people with a university education who could keep records and draw up official documents. Universities thus provided the teachers, administrators, lawyers, and doctors for medieval society.

The Development of Scholasticism

The importance of Christianity in medieval society made it certain that theology would play a central role

in the European intellectual world. Theology was the formal study of religion. In the new universities, theology was queen of the sciences.

Beginning in the eleventh century, the effort to apply reason or logical analysis to the church's basic teachings had a significant impact on the study of theology. The word **scholasticism** is used to refer to the philosophical and theological system of the medieval schools. Scholasticism tried to reconcile faith and reason, to show that what was accepted on faith was in harmony with what could be learned by reason.

The chief task of scholasticism was to harmonize Christian teachings with the work of the Greek philosopher Aristotle. In the twelfth century, largely because of the work of Muslim and Jewish scholars, western Europe was introduced to a large number of Greek works and, above all, to the works of Aristotle. However, Aristotle's works upset many Christian theologians. Aristotle was highly regarded and was, in fact, called "the philosopher." The problem was that he had arrived at his conclusions by rational thought—not by faith—and some of his ideas contradicted the

MORE ABOUT . . . *Scholasticism*

Medieval philosophers sought to apply Christian ethical concepts to every aspect of human life, including economic life. Therefore they evolved the idea of the "just price." The activities pursued by a merchant or artisan should provide a livelihood and a fair living, but no more. Technical innovations, underselling, raising prices in time of dearth, employing extra apprentices or working by

artificial light were all forbidden as being "unjust." Usury, which was defined as charging any interest at all (as opposed to charging excessive interest) for the loan of money was also forbidden. Jews were not bound by Church law, and thus were free to enter into money lending—one of the few avenues of making a living allowed them.

teachings of the church. The most famous attempt to reconcile Aristotle and the doctrines of Christianity was that of Saint Thomas Aquinas (uh-KWINE-us).

While he was teaching in Paris, Thomas Aquinas finished his famous *Summa Theologica* (*A Summa of Theology*; a summa was a book of knowledge that attempted to bring together all the knowledge on a given subject into a single whole). Aquinas's masterpiece was organized according to the dialectical method of the scholastics. In other words, Aquinas first posed a question, then cited sources that offered opposing opinions on the question, and finally reconciled them by arriving at his own conclusions. In this fashion, Aquinas raised and discussed some six hundred questions.

Aquinas's fame is based on his attempt to reconcile faith and reason. He took it for granted that there were truths arrived at by reason and truths arrived at by faith. He was certain, however, that the two kinds of truths could not be in conflict with each other. The natural mind, unaided by faith, could arrive at truths concerning the physical universe. Without the help of God's grace, however, unaided reason alone could not grasp spiritual truths, such as the Trinity or the Incarnation.

Vernacular Literature

Latin was the universal language of medieval civilization. Used in the church and schools, Latin enabled learned people to communicate anywhere in Europe. However, in the twelfth century much new literature was being written in the **vernacular** (the language used in a particular region, such as Spanish, French, English, or German). A new market for vernacular literature appeared in the twelfth century when educated laypeople at courts and in the cities took an interest in new sources of entertainment.

Perhaps the most popular vernacular literature of the twelfth century was troubadour poetry, which was chiefly the product of nobles and knights. This poetry told of the love of a knight for a lady, who inspires him to become a braver knight and a better poet. A good example is found in the laments of the noble Jaufré

Rudel. He cherished a dream woman from afar, whom he feared he would never meet but would always love:

> Most sad, most joyous shall I go away,
> Let me have seen her for a single day,
>   My love afar,
> I shall not see her, for her land and mine
> Are sundered, and the ways are hard to find,
> So many ways, and I shall lose my way,
>   So wills it God.
>
> Yet shall I know no other love but hers,
> And if not hers, no other love at all.
>   She has surpassed all.
> So fair she is, so noble, I would be
> A captive with the hosts of paynimrie [the Muslims]
> In a far land, if so be upon me
>   Her eyes might fall.[5]

Troubadour poetry arose in southern France and spread to northern France, Italy, and Germany.

Another type of vernacular literature was the *chanson de geste* (SHAWN-sone-duh-zhest), or heroic epic. The earliest and finest example is the *Chanson de Roland* (*The Song of Roland*), which appeared around 1100 and was written in French (see "Our Literary Heritage: *The Song of Roland*"). The *chansons de geste* were written for a male-dominated society. The chief events described in these poems are battles and political contests. Their world is one of combat, in which knights fight courageously for their kings and lords. Women play only a small role or no role at all in this literature.

Architecture in the Middle Ages

The eleventh and twelfth centuries witnessed an explosion of building in medieval Europe. The construction of churches and castles absorbed many resources while also reflecting medieval society's basic preoccupations, God and warfare. The churches were by far the most noticeable of the buildings. Hundreds of new cathedrals as well as thousands of parish churches in rural villages were built in the eleventh and twelfth centuries. The building spree was a direct reflection of a revived religious culture. At the same time, it reflected the increased wealth of the period produced by agriculture, trade, and the growth of cities.

USING PRIMARY SOURCES

Have students bring in one love poem that they have studied during the year and compare its tone and theme with the troubadour poem written by Rudel that appears on this page. How is this poem different from more modern ones? From sonnets written by Shakespeare? From the poems of Elizabeth Barrett Browning or of Robert Browning?

CRITICAL THINKING

Have students reread the poem and the information presented about the *Chanson de Roland* on page 400. How were women seen during this time period? Do students think the view presented in troubadour poetry was realistic? Why or why not?

MORE ABOUT . . . *Knightly Culture*

Knights were expected to be men of prowess, generosity, and loyalty. The church expected knights to use their swords to serve the poor and needy.

One aspect of the knightly culture may be illustrated by King John of Bohemia, who enjoyed fighting for its own sake. Even though he was blind, he eagerly sought battle and glory. At Crécy, he demanded that his peers guide him into battle against the English. He was found on the battlefield, entangled with his horse, dead.

CLASS DISCUSSION

Guide students in a discussion of modern heroes who have given their lives for their countries. How are they remembered? Are there poems, novels, and/or legends that commemorate their lives and heroic actions?

LEARNING FROM VISUALS

Answer to caption question: Answers will vary. Some may include World War II stories, other may recount various legends of the West.

CRITICAL THINKING

How does the writer create the image that Roland is a hero? Have students identify certain passages or words that allude to his greatness and his courage.

Answers to Critical Thinking Questions

1. It was a chanson de geste, or heroic epic. The events described fierce battles and political contests.
2. They admired his courage in battle and also his humility in asking for God's forgiveness.

YOU ARE THERE
The Song of Roland

The Song of Roland *is one of the best examples of the medieval heroic epic. Based on a historical event, it tells of the ambush of the rear guard of Charlemagne's Frankish army in the Pyrenees Mountains. It was written three hundred years after the event it supposedly describes, however, and reveals more about the eleventh century than about the age of Charlemagne. The Basques (BASKS) who ambushed Charlemagne's army have been changed into Muslims and the Frankish soldiers, into French knights. These lines describe the death of Roland, Charlemagne's nephew, who was the commander of the rear guard:*

The Song of Roland

*Now Roland feels that he is at death's door;
Out of his ears the brain is running forth.
Now for his peers he prays God call them all,
And for himself St. Gabriel's aid implores,
Then in each hand he takes, lest shame befall,
His Olifant and Durendal his sword.
Far as a quarrel flies from a cross-bow drawn,
Toward land of Spain he goes, to a wide lawn,
And climbs a mound where grows a fair tree tall,
And marble stones beneath it stand by four.
Face downward there on the green grass he falls,
And swoons away, for he is at death's door. . . .*

*Now Roland feels death press upon him hard;
It's creeping down from his head to his heart.
Under a pine-tree he hastens him apart,
There stretches him face down on the green grass,*

This detail from one of the famous stained glass windows at Chartres Cathedral in France shows two scenes from The Song of Roland. *On the left, Roland is trying to destroy his sword, Durendahl, in a rock high in the Pyrenees; on the right Roland calls on his horn for Charlemagne to rescue him from this ambush. What modern-day epics are similar in theme to* The Song of Roland?

*And lays beneath him his sword and Olifant.
He's turned his head to where the Paynims [Muslims] are,
And this he does for the French and for Charles,
Since fain is he that they should say, brave heart,
That he has died a conqueror at the last,
He beats his breast full many a time and fast,
Gives, with his glove, his sins into God's charge.*

*Now Roland feels his time is at an end;
On the steep hill-side, toward Spain he's turned his head,
And with one hand he beats upon his breast;
Says: "Mea culpa; Thy mercy, Lord, I beg
For all the sins, both the great and the less,
That e'er I did since first I drew my breath
Unto this day when I'm struck down by death."
His right-hand glove he unto God extends;
Angels from Heaven now to his side descend.*

1. What type of literature was *The Song of Roland*? What events were described in these poems?

2. From this feature, what qualities do you think medieval men admired in Roland?

So What ??

If your students question the importance of the information on **troubadours,** *tell them . . .*

Medieval literature has given us some of our most enduring and important stories—the Arthurian legends, the Nibelungen Lied, the love stories of Lancelot and Guinevere (Anglo-Norman), Tristan and Isolde (Celtic), and Eloise and Abelard (a true story). They are the beginning of a popular modern literature.

OUR ARTISTIC HERITAGE
The Gothic Cathedral

► *Notre Dame in Paris is one of the largest Gothic cathedrals in Europe and stands as one of the great architectural and artistic triumphs of the High Middle Ages. This view from the east shows the graceful span of the flying buttresses that allow room for the windows set in the stone framework. What other features of Gothic architecture are shown here?*

► *Chartres is an exception among French Gothic cathedrals because most of its windows are original ones, and each of the windows in Chartres has its own story to tell. Some windows present the lives of saints, while others portray the daily activities of medieval town life. This window presents scenes from the life of Christ. Some people believe that the stained glass windows served as teachers for the illiterate. Do you agree or not?*

Begun in the twelfth century and brought to perfection in the thirteenth, the Gothic cathedral remains one of the greatest artistic triumphs of the High Middle Ages. Soaring skyward, almost as if to reach Heaven, it was a fitting symbol for medieval people's preoccupation with God.

Two basic innovations of the twelfth century made Gothic cathedrals possible. The combination of ribbed vaults and pointed arches replaced the barrel vault of Romanesque churches and enabled builders to make Gothic churches higher than Romanesque churches. The use of pointed arches and ribbed vaults created an impression of upward movement, a sense of weightless upward thrust as

if reaching to God. Another technical innovation, the flying buttress—basically a heavy, arched pier (a supporting part) of stone built onto the outside of the walls—made it possible to distribute the weight of the church's vaulted ceilings outward

(continued)

(continued)

MORE ABOUT . . . *Stained Glass*

One of the most beautiful art forms to flourish during the Middle Ages was the craft of painted glass. Between the 12th and 16th centuries, artisans created stained glass for some of the world's most magnificent cathedrals. Its original purpose was to illustrate the stories of the Bible for illiterate peasants and serfs. The sun shining through the many pieces of colored glass, glittering like precious gems, was thought to convey the mystery of God and evoke an emotional, spiritual experience.

Artists would create the colored glass by adding cobalt, silver, iron, or copper oxides to the glass. Details were painted on and then the glass was fired in a kiln. The Chartres Cathedral, one of Europe's most majestic, had over 100 stained glass windows.

Answers to Critical Thinking Questions

1. ribbed vaults and pointed arches
2. The cathedrals used pointed arches and ribbed vaults creating an impression of upward movement. The flying buttress made it possible to distribute the weight of the church's vaulted ceilings outward and down. The use of stained glass windows was done by people who believed that natural light was a symbol of the divine light of God.
3. Money was raised from wealthy townspeople. Master masons who were both architects and engineers designed the cathedrals. Stonemasons and other craftsmen provided skilled labor.
4. dedication to a spiritual ideal

ASSESS

You can choose from a variety of assessments to evaluate your students' mastery of the objectives for this section, as stated on page 397. Possible assessments include

1. Section Review questions on this page
2. Section 13–4 Quiz in your Teacher Resource materials
3. Reteaching Worksheets in your Teacher Resource materials
4. Self-Study software

OUR ARTISTIC HERITAGE

The Gothic Cathedral, continued

and down. This eliminated the heavy walls needed in Romanesque churches to hold the weight of the massive barrel vaults. Gothic cathedrals were built, then, with thin walls that were filled with magnificent stained glass windows, which created a play of light inside that varied with the sun at different times of the day. The preoccupation with colored light in Gothic cathedrals was not accidental. Natural light was believed to be a symbol of the divine light of God.

The Gothic style was a product of northern France. By the mid-thirteenth century, however, French Gothic architecture had spread to England, Spain, and Germany—virtually all of Europe. Its most brilliant examples were the French cathedrals in Paris (Notre Dame), Reims (REEMZ), Amiens (am-YAHN), and Chartres (SHART).

A Gothic cathedral was the work of an entire community. All classes contributed to its construction. Money was raised from wealthy townspeople who had profited from the new trade and industries, as well as from kings and nobles. Master masons, who were both architects and engineers, designed the cathedrals. They drew up the plans and supervised the construction. Stonemasons and

other craftspeople were paid a daily wage and provided the skilled labor to build the cathedrals. The building of cathedrals often became highly competitive as communities vied with one another to build the highest tower. Most important, a Gothic cathedral symbolized the chief preoccupation of a medieval Christian community: its dedication to a spiritual ideal. As we have observed before, the largest buildings of an era reflect the values of its society. The Gothic cathedral, with its towers soaring toward Heaven, bears witness to an age when most people believed in a spiritual world.

1. What innovations made the Gothic cathedrals possible?

2. What does the Gothic cathedral tell us about medieval values and medieval science?

3. How was the entire community involved in building the cathedral?

4. What did the Gothic cathedral symbolize?

The cathedrals of the eleventh and twelfth centuries were built in the Romanesque (ROE-muh-NESK) style, prominent examples of which can be found in Germany, France, and Spain. Romanesque churches were normally built in the basilica shape used in the construction of churches in the late Roman Empire. Basilicas were rectangular buildings with flat wooden roofs. Romanesque builders used this basic plan but made a change. They replaced the flat wooden roof with a long, round stone vault (an arched structure), called a barrel vault, or with a cross vault, in which two barrel vaults intersected. The cross vault was used

when a builder wished to create a church plan in the shape of a cross. Although barrel and cross vaults were technically difficult to create, they were considered more beautiful than the flat wooden roofs and were also less apt to catch fire.

Because stone roofs were extremely heavy, Romanesque churches required massive pillars and walls to hold them up. This left little space for windows, so Romanesque churches were dark on the inside. Their massive walls and pillars made Romanesque churches almost resemble fortresses. Indeed, massive walls and slit windows were also used in castles.

ENRICHMENT ACTIVITY

Read to students this quote from an 11th century writer.

As the year 1003 approached, people all over the world, but especially in Italy and France began to rebuild their churches. Although most of them were well built and in little need of alterations, Christian nations were rivaling each other to have the most beautiful edifices.

(As quoted in John W. Baldwin, *The Scholastic Culture of the Middle Ages, 1000–1300* (Lexington, Mass., 1971, p. 15.)

Have students discuss why they think the Christians of this time competed to have the most beautiful buildings.

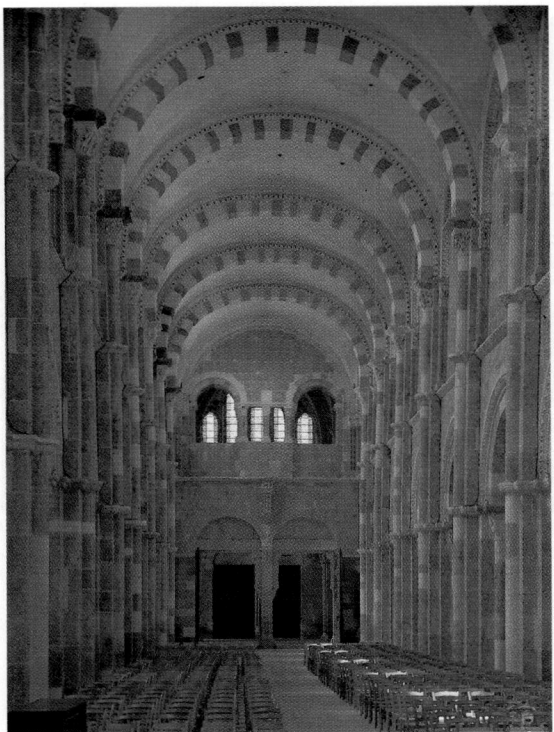

▲ *The interior of this Romanesque church in Vienne, France, is an excellent example of barrel vaulting. Barrel vaults were an improvement over long, flat wooden roofs, but still limited the size of a church. Can you explain why barrel vaults limited both the length of a church and the number and size of its windows?*

❀ SECTION REVIEW ❀

1. **Define:**
   (*a*) theology,   (*b*) scholasticism,   (*c*) vernacular

2. **Identify:**
   (*a*) liberal arts curriculum,
   (*b*) bachelor of arts degree,   (*c*) Aristotle,
   (*d*) Saint Thomas Aquinas,
   (*e*) *Summa Theologica*,   (*f*) *chansons de geste*,
   (*g*) Romanesque

3. **Recall:**
   (*a*) Which group—the administration, the faculty, or the students—had the most influence in regulating the activities of Europe's first university?
   (*b*) Why were most early university courses taught as lecture classes?
   (*c*) Did Thomas Aquinas believe that truths arrived at by reason were in conflict with truths arrived at by faith?

4. **Think Critically:** Compare what you know of modern university courses of study with those of the first European universities. What are the similarities and differences?

A TIME OF TROUBLES: EUROPE IN THE LATE MIDDLE AGES

The Middle Ages in Europe had reached its high point in the thirteenth century. In the fourteenth century, a period of disastrous changes took place, and medieval society began to disintegrate. At the beginning of the fourteenth century, there were noticeable changes in weather patterns as Europe entered a period that has been called a "little Ice Age." Shortened growing seasons and disastrous weather conditions, including heavy storms and constant rain, led to widespread famine and hunger. Soon, an even greater catastrophe struck.

The Black Death

The Black Death of the mid-fourteenth century was the most devastating natural disaster in European history. One observer wrote that "father abandoned child, wife husband, one brother another, for the plague seemed to strike through breath and sight. And so they died. And no one could be found to bury the dead, for money or friendship."[6] People were horrified by the plague, an evil force they could not understand.

1. (a) study of religion
   (b) philosophical and theological system of medieval schools
   (c) language used in a particular region
2. (a) course of study at medieval university that included grammar, rhetoric, logic, arithmetic, geometry, music, and astronomy
   (b) first degree obtained by a university student upon successful completion of oral examination
   (c) Greek philosopher
   (d) saint who attempted to reconcile Aristotle and Christian doctrines
   (e) masterwork of Thomas Aquinas
   (f) vernacular literature, heroic epics, written for male-dominated society
   (g) architectural style of eleventh- and twelfth-century cathedrals
3. (a) students
   (b) books were expensive
   (c) no

CLOSE

Make sure students realize that the High Middle Ages were a time of relative stability, when universities began to flourish and attract many students, when towns grew and prospered, and when countries began to see their own forms of literature and architecture develop.

LEARNING FROM VISUALS

Answer to the caption question: thick walls needed to support roof; very few openings possible

MORE ABOUT . . . *The Little Ice Age*

As stated in the text above, some extremely bad weather at the beginning of the fourteenth century made life very difficult for people living in Europe. You may want to give students some of the following facts about the "little ice age." For example, the Baltic Sea froze over in 1303 and in 1307–1308. The Caspian and Mediterranean Seas rose noticeably, Alpine glaciers advanced, icebergs blocked North Atlantic shipping lanes. The Thames River froze over twelve times. Such poor weather caused very serious problems in a rural economy. Shortages of food led to chronic malnutrition.

FOCUS

OBJECTIVES

After completing this section, students should be able to

1. explain the impact of the Black Death
2. describe the reasons for and the consequences of the Great Schism in the Catholic Church
3. explain the monarchical changes that occurred in Europe during the mid to late 1400s

TEACH

Multimedia Support

LASERDISC
The Black Death
(1347–1350)
(Video)

LEARNING FROM VISUALS

Answer to the caption question: Answers will vary.

CRITICAL THINKING

What might be some of the immediate consequences in the United States if 40 to 50 percent of the people died within a two-year span? Ask students to predict consequences in a variety of areas, not just the economy.

▲ *The Black Death spread quickly through France and by the end of 1348 had reached northern Europe. Mass burials were often held for victims, as shown here in Tournai, a city in modern Belgium. As the plague intensified, victims were no longer buried in coffins but thrown into open pits. Do you believe any current diseases will reach the monstrous, deadly proportions of the plague?*

Bubonic plague was the most common form of plague. We now know that it was spread by black rats infested with fleas who were host to the deadly bacterium *Yersinia pestis*. The plague began in Europe when merchants from Genoa, Italy, brought it from the Middle East to the island of Sicily, off the coast of southern Italy, in October 1347. It quickly spread to southern Italy and southern France and Spain by the end of 1347. Usually, the path of the Black Death followed trade routes. In 1348, the plague spread through France and the Low Countries and into Germany. By the end of that year, it had moved to England, which it ravaged in 1349. By the end of 1349, it had expanded to northern Europe and Scandinavia. Eastern Europe and Russia were affected by 1351.

Overall, death rates were incredibly high. Especially hard hit were Italy's crowded cities where 50 to 60 percent of the people died. One citizen of Florence wrote:

"A great many breathed their last in the public streets, day and night; a large number perished in their homes, and it was only by the stench of their decaying bodies that they proclaimed their death to their neighbors. Everywhere the city was teeming with corpses."[7] In England and Germany, entire villages simply disappeared from history. It has been estimated that out of a total European population of 75 million, 19 million to 38 million people died of the plague between 1347 and 1351. Not until the mid-sixteenth century did Europe begin to regain its thirteenth-century population levels.

Many people at the time believed that the plague had either been sent by God as a punishment for their sins or was caused by the devil. Some reactions became extreme. Groups of **flagellants** (people who beat themselves), both men and women, wandered from town to town. They flogged one another with whips to beg the forgiveness of a God they felt had sent the plague to

MORE ABOUT . . . *the Plague and the Black Death*

There have been three great pandemics of bubonic plague in history. The first was Justinian's Plague (542–662); the second the Black Death (1347–1665); the third began in Yunnan, China in 1892 and spread to India by 1896, killing approximately 6 million people in India alone.

There are three related diseases that make up the Black Death. Bubonic plague is the

most common, and, without antibiotics, is fatal 50–60% of the time. Pneumonic plague is less common, is extremely contagious, and is fatal 95% of the time. Septicaemic plague, which is fortunately very rare, attacks the blood stream and is always fatal.

Map 13.3   Spread of the Black Death

CLASS DISCUSSION

Have students review the information in the chapter concerning the Inquisition and the Black Death, and then hypothesize why Jews were so heavily persecuted during the Middle Ages. Remind students that the persecution of Jews continued in Europe, eventually reaching the point of the incredible atrocities of the Holocaust, which students will study in Chapter 28.

CLASS DISCUSSION

Besides the massive effect on population and society, the Black Death is a reminder of the power of epidemic disease to drastically influence history. In an era when exploitation of natural resources is bringing man in contact with diseases never before encountered, this is another sobering reminder that human beings may not be as completely in control of their fate as we would like to think. Lead a class discussion to gain students' reactions to this statement.

punish humans for their sinful ways. One observer wrote:

> The penitents went about, coming first out of Germany. They were men who did public penance and scourged themselves with whips of hard knotted leather with little iron spikes. Some made themselves bleed very badly between the shoulder blades and some foolish women had cloths ready to catch the blood and smear it on their eyes, saying it was miraculous blood. While they were doing penance, they sang very mourn-

> ful songs about the nativity and the passion of Our Lord. The object of this penance was to put a stop to the mortality, for in that time . . . at least a third of all the people in the world died.[8]

The flagellants created mass hysteria wherever they went, but authorities worked overtime to crush the movement.

An outbreak of anti-Semitism was another result of the Black Death. Jews were accused of causing the plague by poisoning town wells. Jews were persecuted

STUDYING MAPS

The following questions will help you guide your students through their study of Map 13.3.

1. Looking at this map alone, where do you think the Black Death started? *(Sicily)*
2. Did the Black Death move primarily toward the north or south? *(north)*

3. What time span is represented by this map? *(1347 to 1350, or 3 years)*
4. During which two time periods represented did the plaque spread the farthest? *(from October to December of 1347, and from June to December of 1350)*

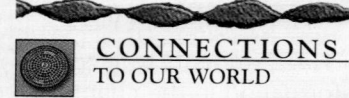

CONNECTIONS
TO OUR WORLD

As an extra credit assignment, ask for student volunteers to research other nursery rhymes and traditional games to discover the origins and their connections to historical events.

ACTIVITY

You might wish to divide the class into small groups and have each report on the various popes who lived at Avignon and in the papal palace that was built in that city.

CLASS DISCUSSION

Brainstorm reasons why having the pope established in the south of France would lead to a gradual decline in the power and prestige of the papacy. Is the pope's location in Rome central to his power? What other reasons contributed to the problems encountered by the popes during this time?

CONNECTIONS
TO OUR WORLD

Plague and a Nursery Rhyme—"Ring around the Rosies"   A common nursery rhyme often sung by children engaged in a child's game is "Ring around the Rosies." It is hardly an innocent children's song, however. It probably arose as a rhyme during the time of plague in Europe, either that of the Black Death of the fourteenth century or the Great Plague that suddenly struck London in 1664–1665, causing the death of one-fifth of the city's population.

The first line, "Ring around the Rosies," is a reference to the rosy-colored ring that appeared on a person's body as the initial symptom of infection. To ward off the plague, people filled their pockets with herbs, or "a pocket full of posies." "Ashes, ashes, we all fall down" refers to a frequent form of death for plague victims. They sneezed ("ashes" is a variation of "a-choo") and then fell over and died, victims of a frightening disease little understood by the people at that time.

in Spain, but the worst attacks were carried out in Germany. Over sixty Jewish communities in Germany were wiped out by 1351 (see "You Are There: A Medieval Holocaust: The Cremation of the Strasbourg Jews"). Many Jews fled eastward, especially to Poland, where the king offered them protection. Eastern Europe thus became home to large Jewish communities.

The death of so many people in the fourteenth century also had severe economic consequences. Trade declined, and some industries suffered greatly. Florence's woolen industry, one of the giants, had produced 70,000 to 80,000 pieces of cloth in 1338; in 1378, it was yielding only 24,000 pieces.

Both peasants and noble landlords were also affected. A shortage of workers caused a dramatic rise in the price of labor. At the same time, the decline in the number of people lowered the demand for food, resulting in falling prices. Landlords were now paying more for labor at the same time that their rents, or income, was declining. Furthermore, the decline in the number of peasants after the Black Death made it easier for some to bargain with their lords and convert their labor services to rent, thus freeing them from serfdom.

The Decline of the Church

The popes of the Roman Catholic Church reached the height of their power in the thirteenth century. Then a series of problems in the fourteenth century led to a serious decline for the church. By that time, the monarchies of Europe were no longer willing to accept papal claims of supremacy. This is evident in the struggle between Pope Boniface (BAWN-uh-fuss) VIII and King Philip IV of France at the end of the thirteenth century. In his desire to gain new revenues, Philip said that he had the right to tax the clergy of France, but Boniface VIII claimed that the clergy of any state could not pay taxes to their ruler without the pope's consent. In no uncertain terms he argued that popes were supreme over both the church and the state.

Philip IV refused to accept the pope's position and sent French forces to Italy to capture Boniface and bring him back to France for trial. The pope escaped but soon died from the shock of his experience. Philip had won a clear victory for the national monarchy over the papacy, because no later pope dared renew the claims of Boniface VIII. To ensure his position, Philip IV engineered the election of a Frenchman, Clement V, in 1305 as pope. The new pope took up residence in Avignon (a-VEEN-YONE), in southern France.

From 1305 to 1378, the popes lived in Avignon, leading to a decline in papal prestige and a growing sentiment against the papacy. The pope was the bishop of Rome, and it was quite unseemly that the head of the Catholic Church should reside in Avignon instead of Rome. Then, too, many people believed that the popes at Avignon were simply stooges of the French kings. The splendor in which the pope and cardinals were living in Avignon also led to strong criticism of

On Line with WORLD HISTORY *Internet Activity*

You may want to have your students visit the following URL, where they will find information and additional web site resources to enhance their study of this chapter.

Internet Medieval Sourcebook

http://www.fordham.edu/halsall/sbook.html

This is an excellent compilation of Internet resources dealing with all aspects of the medieval period.

Due to the ever-changing nature of the World Wide Web, see the West History web site, **http://history.swpco.com** for regular updates of the URLs in this text.

YOU ARE THERE

A Medieval Holocaust—The Cremation of the Strasbourg Jews

◄ In this picture Christian townspeople watch in apparent approval as wood is added to the fire and Jews are burned alive. Although Pope Clement VI opposed these burnings, they continued until the Black Death declined.

In their attempt to explain the widespread horrors of the Black Death, medieval Christian communities looked for scapegoats. The Jews were blamed for spreading the plague by poisoning wells. This selection, written in 1349, gives an account of how Christians in the town of Strasbourg in the Holy Roman Empire dealt with their Jewish community.

Description of the Cremation of the Strasbourg Jews

In the year 1349 there occurred the greatest epidemic that ever happened. Death went from one end of the earth to the other. . . . This epidemic also came to Strasbourg in the summer of the above-mentioned year, and it is estimated that about sixteen thousand people died.

In the matter of this plague the Jews throughout the world were accused in all lands as having caused it through the poison which they are said to have put into the water and the wells—that is what they were accused of—and for this reason the Jews were burned all the way from the Mediterranean into Germany. . . .

[The account then goes on to discuss the situation of the Jews in the city of Strasbourg.]

On Saturday . . . they burned the Jews on a wooden platform in their cemetery. There were about two thousand people of them. Those who wanted to baptize themselves were spared. [Some say that about a thousand accepted baptism.] Many small children were taken out of the fire

(continued)

YOU ARE THERE

WORKING WITH VISUALS

Guide students in a discussion of this woodcut. What do they see? What can they infer from the scene as depicted by the artist? Why do students believe that Pope Clement, or other secular leaders, chose not to intervene to stop the burnings and other persecutions of the Jews?

CLASS DISCUSSION

Guide students in a discussion of the economic situation discussed in the feature. Who benefited most from the loss of property suffered by the Jews? Do students believe that the opportunity to seize property figured into the decision to round up Jews and murder them? Why or why not?

CNN® WORLD HISTORY UPDATES

You can update your coverage of World History topics, as well as spark lively classroom discussion and deeper understanding, by using the **CNN World History Updates.**

For assistance in using and incorporating the **CNN World History Updates** into your classroom presentations, see the *Classroom Guide.*

Answers to Critical Thinking Questions

1. The Jews were accused of causing the plague by poisoning the wells. The Jews were burned because they had money. If the feudal lords had not been in debt to them, the Jews would have been spared.
2. Answers will vary.

ACTIVITY

Have students work in pairs to create a time line of the period beginning with the Black Death and ending with the Great Schism. Students should use the text and their own research to chronicle the events of this period of disruption and change.

REINFORCING VOCABULARY

Some students may not understand the word *schism*. In its simplest form, it simply means a division or separation. It also refers to a formal division within a church or other religious organization.

YOU ARE THERE

A Medieval Holocaust—
The Cremation of the Strasbourg Jews, continued

and baptized against the will of their fathers and mothers. And everything that was owed to the Jews was canceled, and the Jews had to surrender all pledges and notes that they had taken for debts. The council, however, took the cash that the Jews possessed and divided it among the working-men. The money was indeed the thing that killed the Jews. If they had been poor and if the feudal lords had not been in debt to them, they would not have been burnt.

1. Who became scapegoats and were blamed for causing the Black Death? Were these charges economically motivated? Why or why not?
2. Can you show examples of discrimination today that are similar to what the Jews experienced in medieval communities?

the papacy. At last, Pope Gregory XI, perceiving the disastrous decline in papal prestige, returned to Rome in 1377.

Gregory XI died in Rome in the spring of 1378, soon after his return. When the college of cardinals met to elect a new pope, the citizens of Rome warned that the cardinals would not leave Rome alive unless an Italian were elected pope. The terrified cardinals wisely elected an Italian as Pope Urban VI. Five months later, a group of cardinals—the French ones—declared this election invalid and chose a Frenchman as pope, who promptly returned to Avignon. Because Urban remained in Rome, there were now two popes, beginning what has been called the Great Schism of the church.

The Great Schism, which lasted from 1378 to 1417, divided Europe. France and its allies supported the pope in Avignon, whereas France's enemy England and its allies supported the pope in Rome. The Great Schism was also damaging to the church. The pope was widely believed to be the true leader of Christendom. When both lines of popes denounced the other as the Antichrist, people's faith in the papacy and the church were undermined. Finally, a church council met at Constance, Switzerland, and ended the schism in

1417. After the competing popes either resigned or were deposed, a new pope was elected who was acceptable to all parties.

These crises in the Catholic Church led to renewed cries for reform. A group of Czech reformers led by John Hus called for an end to the corruption of the clergy and the excessive power of the papacy within the Catholic Church. Hus was accused of heresy by the Council of Constance and burned at the stake in 1415. This angered the Czechs and led to a revolutionary upheaval in Bohemia that was not crushed until 1436.

By the mid-fifteenth century, as a result of these crises, the church had lost much of its political power. The popes no longer had any hope of asserting supremacy over the state. Even worse, the papacy and the church had also lost much of their moral prestige.

The Hundred Years' War

Plague, economic crisis, and the decline of the Catholic Church were not the only problems of the fourteenth century. War and political instability must also be added to the list. Of all the struggles that took place in the fourteenth century, the Hundred Years' War was the most violent.

MORE ABOUT . . . *The Hussite movement*

The Hussite movement in the 1420s and 1430s provided interesting tactical innovation to defeat the knights. The Hussites were both a religious movement (Jan Hus was burned at the stake as a heretic) and a Czech nationalist movement. Led by Jan Zizka, they built war-wagons armed with heavy muskets and small cannon. They would advance against the enemy, then form a lager. The wagons would be chained together, and defended by pikes and flails as well as the firearms. After defeating the charges of the knights, they would leave the lager and counterattack. Upon his death, Jan Zizka ordered his body flayed, and the skin made into leather to use on a great war drum, which led the Hussites into battle.

In the thirteenth century the English king, Henry III, still held one small possession in France, known as the duchy of Gascony. As duke of Gascony, the English king pledged loyalty as a vassal to the French king. However, when King Philip VI of France seized Gascony in 1337, the duke of Gascony—King Edward III of England—declared war on Philip.

The Hundred Years' War began in a burst of knightly enthusiasm. Trained to be warriors, knights viewed battle as a chance to show their fighting abilities. The Hundred Years' War proved to be an important turning point in the nature of warfare. It was peasant foot soldiers, not knights, who won the chief battles of the Hundred Years' War.

The French army of 1337 still relied largely on its heavily armed noble cavalrymen, who looked with contempt upon foot soldiers, people they viewed as social inferiors. The English, too, used heavily armed cavalry, but they relied even more on large numbers of paid foot soldiers, who were armed not only with pikes but also with the longbow. The longbow had greater striking power, longer range, and more rapid speed of fire than the crossbow (formerly the weapon of choice).

The first major battle of the Hundred Years' War occurred in 1346 at Crécy (kray-SEE), just south of Flanders. The larger French army followed no battle plan but simply attacked the English lines in a disorderly fashion. The arrows of the English archers devastated the French cavalry. As the chronicler Froissart described it, "[with their longbows] the English continued to shoot into the thickest part of the crowd, wasting none of their arrows. They impaled or wounded horses and riders, who fell to the ground in great distress, unable to get up again without the help of several men."[9] It was a stunning victory for the English.

The Battle of Crécy was not decisive, however. The English simply did not have enough resources to conquer all France, but they continued to try. The English king, Henry V, was especially eager to achieve victory. At the Battle of Agincourt in 1415, the heavy, armorplated French knights tried to attack Henry's forces across a field turned to mud by heavy rain. They were disastrously defeated, and 1,500 French nobles died on the battlefield. The English were masters of northern France.

▲ *Joan of Arc was only seventeen years old when she met King Charles VII and just nineteen when she was burned at the stake. The banner she is holding in this portrait shows Christ and two angels. Why do you think the king of France did not intervene to save Joan's life?*

The French cause, now seemingly hopeless, fell into the hands of the French dauphin (eldest son of the king) Charles, the heir to the throne who governed the southern two-thirds of French lands. Charles's cause seemed doomed until a French peasant woman quite unexpectedly saved the timid monarch. Joan of Arc was born in 1412, the daughter of well-to-do peasants. She was a deeply religious person who experienced visions and came to believe that her favorite saints had commanded her to free France. In February 1429, Joan made her way to the dauphin's court, where her sincerity and simplicity persuaded Charles to allow her to

MORE ABOUT . . . *Longbows*

The English longbow is justly famous, although misnamed. The weapon was developed by the Welsh, and adopted first by English living along the Welsh marshes. Many of the professional longbowmen during the Hundred Years' War were Welsh. The bow was as tall as the man who carried it, and was drawn by stooping over with the bow parallel to the ground, and then straightening up, using the leg and back muscles. The arrow was drawn to the ear. Bowmen could drive a thirty-inch "cloth-yard" shaft tipped with an armor piercing bodkin (dagger-like) head through three inches of oak. When the English archers loosed at Crêcy, Poitiers, and Agincourt, the arrow storm literally darkened the sky. Such mastery required big, powerful men and constant practice.

ACROSS TIME PERIODS

Have students compare and contrast the role and social position of European knights with the Japanese samurai and ronin discussed in Chapter 24. How were these groups similar and how were they different?

ACROSS THE CURRICULUM

Journalism Have students write newspaper-type obituaries for Joan of Arc and share their results with the class.

REINFORCING VOCABULARY

Make sure students know the modern use of *heretic (a person who dissents from an accepted belief or doctorine; nonconformist),* as well as the earlier, more specific meaning *(a baptized member of the Roman Catholic Church who disavows a revealed truth).* Ask students to use the word in sentences describing modern-day events.

Map 13.4   The Hundred Years' War

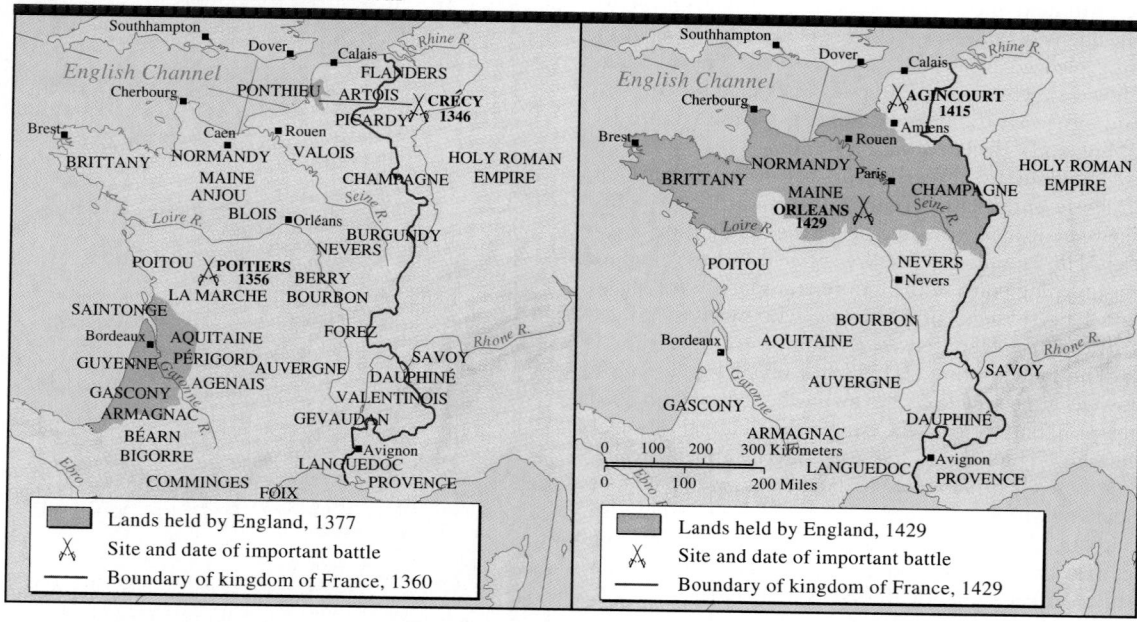

accompany a French army to Orléans. Apparently inspired by the faith of the peasant woman who called herself "the Maid," the French armies found new confidence in themselves and captured Orléans. Within a few weeks, the entire Loire valley had been freed of the English. Joan had brought the war to a decisive turning point.

Joan did not live to see the end of the war, however. She was captured in 1430 and turned over by the English to the Inquisition on charges of witchcraft. In the fifteenth century, spiritual visions were thought to be inspired either by God or the devil. Joan was condemned to death as a heretic and burned at the stake in 1431. To the end, as the flames rose up around her, she declared "that her voices came from God and had not deceived her." Twenty-five years later, a new church court declared her innocent of the charges. Five centuries later, in 1920, she was made a saint of the Roman Catholic Church.

Joan of Arc's achievements were decisive. Although the war dragged on for another two decades, defeats of English armies in Normandy and Aquitaine led to a French victory by 1453. Important to the French success was the use of the cannon, a new weapon made possible by the invention of gunpowder. (The Chinese had invented gunpowder, and the Muslims brought it to Europe.)

Political Instability and Political Recovery

By the fourteenth century, the feudal system had begun to break down. With money from taxes, kings could now hire professional soldiers, who tended to be more reliable than feudal knights anyway. No longer needed as warriors, some nobles banded together, looking for new opportunities to advance their power and wealth at the expense of their monarchs. Others went to the royal courts where they offered to serve the kings.

STUDYING MAPS

The following activities will help you guide your students through their study of Map 13.4.

1. Ask students to trace with their fingers the eastern boundary of France on each map. Ask them to note where the boundary is in relation to landmarks such as Calais and the Rhine River. Then ask them to describe how the boundary changed over the course of the war. *(virtually*

unchanged from 1360 to 1429)

2. Ask students to name and date the important battles noted on the maps. *(Crécy—1346, Poitiers—1356, Agincourt—1415, Orleans—1429).*

3. Have students compare the lands on the continent held by England in 1377 with those held in 1429. *(The English increased their held territories considerably.)*

Fourteenth-century kings had their own problems, however. Many dynasties in Europe were unable to produce male heirs. The founders of new dynasties had to fight for their positions when groups of nobles, trying to gain advantages for themselves, supported opposing candidates for the kingship. Rulers found themselves with financial problems as well. Hiring professional soldiers left monarchs always short on cash, and this situation added yet another element of uncertainty and confusion to fourteenth-century politics.

In the second half of the fifteenth century, however, recovery set in as a number of new rulers attempted to reestablish the centralized power of monarchical governments. Some historians have spoken of them as the **"new monarchies,"** especially those of France, England, and Spain, at the end of the fifteenth century. There were, of course, variations from area to area in the degree to which monarchs were successful in extending their political authority. Unlike rulers in western Europe, rulers in central and eastern Europe were often weak and unable to impose their authority.

Western Europe

The Hundred Years' War left France exhausted. A decline in population, wasted farmlands, ruined trade, and unruly nobles made it difficult for the kings to assert their authority. However, the war had also developed a strong degree of French national feeling toward a common enemy. The kings could use that spirit to reestablish royal power.

The development of a strong French state was greatly advanced by King Louis XI, who ruled from 1461 to 1483. Known as the Spider because of his devious ways, Louis strengthened the use of the **taille**—an annual direct tax, usually on land or property—as a permanent tax imposed by royal authority. The taille gave Louis a sound, regular source of income, which helped him to create the foundations of a strong French monarchy.

The Hundred Years' War had also strongly affected the English. The cost of the war in its final years and the losses in the labor force strained the English economy. Moreover, at the end of the war, England faced even greater turmoil when a civil war—known as the War of the Roses—erupted. Noble factions fought over the monarchy until 1485 when Henry Tudor established a new dynasty.

As the first Tudor king, Henry VII worked to create a strong royal government. Henry ended the wars of the nobles by abolishing their private armies. He was also very thrifty. By using diplomacy to avoid wars, which are always expensive, the king was able to avoid calling Parliament on any regular basis to grant him funds. By not overburdening the nobles and the middle class with taxes, Henry won their favor. They thus provided much support for his monarchy.

Spain, too, experienced the growth of a strong national monarchy by the end of the fifteenth century. During the Middle Ages, several independent Christian kingdoms had emerged in the course of the long reconquest of the Iberian peninsula from the Muslims. Two of the strongest kingdoms were Aragon and Castile (kas-TEE-ul). When Isabella of Castile married Ferdinand of Aragon in 1469, it was a major step toward unifying Spain. The two rulers worked to strengthen royal control of the government. They stripped the royal council of nobles. (The royal council supervised government policies.) They then filled it primarily with loyal middle-class lawyers. They also enlisted townspeople in the policy of state building by getting their help in stopping the nobles from disturbing the peace. Ferdinand and Isabella also took control of the Catholic Church by choosing the most important church officials in Spain. They also pursued a policy of strict conformity to Catholicism.

Spain had two large religious minorities, the Jews and the Muslims. Increased persecution in the fourteenth century led many Spanish Jews to convert to Christianity. The introduction of the Inquisition into Spain in 1478 ensured that these converts remained true to their new Christian faith. Because the Inquisition had no authority over practicing Jews, in 1492 Ferdinand and Isabella took the drastic step of expelling all professed Jews from Spain.

Muslims, too, after their final loss in 1492 to the armies of Ferdinand and Isabella, were "encouraged" to convert to Christianity. In 1502, Isabella issued a decree expelling all professed Muslims from her kingdom. To a very large degree, Ferdinand and Isabella,

CRITICAL THINKING

Following the plague and the Hundred Years' War, western Europe began to take its modern form. Ask students to read this section carefully and then prepare a list of the governmental policies and practices that would remain in place for centuries to come. When students have completed this assignment, have them share their results with the class and have them justify their selections.

REINFORCING VOCABULARY

The *taille* was a direct tax levied against every citizen, no matter how wealthy or poor. It was common for those who were somewhat more wealthy to try to hide any sign of their prosperity from the tax collectors, and over time, strong resentment developed over the methods of the tax collectors and the taxes. The *taille*, however, remained in place.

MORE ABOUT . . . *Pikes*

Of greater importance to weakening chivalry than the longbow was the emergence of Swiss pikemen. Beginning with the Battle of Morgarten in 1315, the Swiss mountaineers not only stopped knightly charges., but even attacked groups of knights. They used twenty-foot pikes with three-foot iron shanks and halberds, or eight- to ten- foot long pikes with heavy ax heads and hooks (for dragging horsemen down). The Swiss were disciplined and ferocious. Unlike the longbow, the pike is a simple weapon, and its use could be readily taught to peasants.

ASSESS

Answers to SECTION REVIEW

2. (a) people who beat themselves
(b) governments of rulers who attempted to reestablish centralized power
(c) annual direct tax, usually on land or property

3. (a) plague, especially Bubonic plague
(b) hatred of Jews
(c) French pope
(d) King of France who successfully maintained power of monarchy over the papacy
(e) separation caused when Italians elected second pope
(f) Czech reformers
(g) English king
(h) French peasant woman who inspired French armies to free Loire valley from English
(i) French king
(j) first Tudor king
(k) Spanish rulers who strengthened royal control of government
(l) dynasty of wealthy rulers in Austrian lands along the Danube
(m) great prince of Russia

4. (a) about 200 years (from 1351 to mid-1500s)
(b) peasant foot soldiers, not knights, won the chief battles
(c) marriage of Isabella of Castile and Ferdinand of Aragon in 1469
(d) The loss of Jewish and Muslim intellectuals caused Spain to lose its place of intellectual prominence in Europe.

5. Answers will vary.

---

the "most Catholic" monarchs, had achieved their goal of religious uniformity. To be Spanish was to be Catholic, a policy of uniformity enforced by the Inquisition. As part of the price for religious uniformity, Spain lost the Jewish and Muslim intellectuals who had kept that country ahead of other European countries during the Middle Ages. After a short period of glory bought with the gold and silver of the Americas, Spain never recovered its prominent intellectual place in Europe.

Central and Eastern Europe

Unlike France, England, and Spain, the Holy Roman Empire failed to develop a strong monarchical authority. The failure of the Hohenstaufens in the thirteenth century had made Germany a land of hundreds of states, and almost all of them acted independently of the German ruler. After 1438, the position of Holy Roman emperor was held in the hands of the Habsburg dynasty. As rulers of the Austrian lands along the Danube, the house of Habsburg had become one of the wealthiest landholders in the empire. By the mid-fifteenth century these rulers began to play an important role in European affairs. Much of their success in the fifteenth century was due not to military success but to a well-executed policy of dynastic marriages.

In eastern Europe, rulers found it difficult to centralize their states. Although the population was mostly Slavic, there were islands of other ethnic groups that caused untold difficulties. Religious differences also troubled the area, as Roman Catholics, Eastern Orthodox Christians, and pagans confronted one another. In Poland, the nobles gained the upper hand and established the right to elect their kings, a policy that drastically weakened royal authority. In Hungary, King Matthias Corvinus broke the power of the wealthy lords and created a well-organized central administration. After his death, however, his work was largely undone.

Since the thirteenth century, Russia had been under the domination of the Mongols. Gradually, the princes of Moscow rose to prominence by using their close relationship to the Mongol khans to increase their wealth and expand their possessions. During the reign of the great prince Ivan III, a new Russian state was born. Ivan III annexed other Russian territories and threw off the yoke of the Mongols by 1480.

Eastern Europe felt increasingly threatened by the steadily advancing Ottoman Turks. The Byzantine Empire had served as a buffer between the Muslim Middle East and the Latin West for centuries, but it had been severely weakened at the beginning of the thirteenth century by the Fourth Crusade. Although the Byzantine Empire limped along for almost another two centuries, the Ottoman Turks finally doomed the long-lasting empire. In 1453, the great city of Constantinople fell to the Turks after a siege of several months.

❁ SECTION REVIEW ❁

1. **Locate:**
   (a) Sicily,   (b) Avignon,   (c) Gascony,
   (d) Crécy,   (e) Agincourt,   (f) Orléans

2. **Define:**
   (a) flagellants,   (b) new monarchies,
   (c) taille

3. **Identify:**
   (a) Black Death,   (b) anti-Semitism
   (c) Pope Boniface VIII,   (d) King Philip IV,
   (e) Great Schism,   (f) John Hus,
   (g) Henry V,   (h) Joan of Arc,   (i) King Louis XI,   (j) King Henry VII,   (k) Ferdinand and Isabella,   (l) Habsburgs,   (m) Ivan III

4. **Recall:**
   (a) Approximately how long did it take for Europe to regain the population levels it had attained prior to the Black Death?
   (b) Why was the Hundred Years' War a turning point in the nature of warfare?
   (c) What event was a major step in unifying Spain?

(*d*) How did expelling the Jews and Muslims have a negative impact on Spain?

5. **Think Critically:** Although the Catholic Church lost much of its power in the fourteenth and fifteenth centuries, religious belief was strong. Why do you think this was the case?

Conclusion

European civilization began to flourish in the High Middle Ages. The revival of trade, the expansion of towns and cities, and the development of a money economy did not mean the end of a mostly rural European society, but these factors did offer new opportunities for people to expand and enrich their lives. The High Middle Ages also gave birth to an intellectual and spiritual revival that transformed European society. The intellectual revival led to new centers of learning in the universities and to the use of reason in theology. Spiritual renewal in the High Middle Ages led to many, and even divergent, paths: strong papal leadership, the crusading "Holy Warrior" who killed for God (see Chapter 12), a dramatic increase in the number and size of churches, and new religious orders. All seemed to reflect a greater concern for salvation. Growth and optimism appeared to characterize the High Middle Ages.

European society in the fourteenth century, however, was challenged by an overwhelming number of disastrous forces. A devastating plague, a decline in trade and industry, seemingly constant warfare, political instability, the decline of the church, and even the spectacle of two popes' condemning each other as the Antichrist all seemed to overpower the Europeans. Not surprisingly, much of the art of the time showed the Four Horsemen of the Apocalypse (uh-POCK-uh-LIPS) described in the New Testament book, The Revelation: Death, Famine, Pestilence, and War. To some people, it no doubt appeared that the last days of the world were at hand.

Notes

1. Ernest F. Henderson, ed., *Select Historical Documents of the Middle Ages* (London, 1892), p. 365.
2. Oliver J. Thatcher and Edgar H. McNeal, eds., *A Source Book for Medieval History* (New York, 1905), p. 208.
3. Quoted in R. H. C. Davis, *A History of Medieval Europe from Constantine to Saint Louis*, 2nd ed. (New York, 1988), p. 252.
4. Quoted in Rosalind and Christopher Brooke, *Popular Religion in the Middle Ages* (London, 1984), p. 19.
5. Helen Waddell, *The Wandering Scholars* (New York, 1961), p. 222.
6. Quoted in Robert Gottfried, *The Black Death* (New York, 1983), p. xiii.
7. Giovanni Boccaccio, *The Decameron*, trans. Frances Winwar (New York, 1955), p. xxviii.
8. Jean Froissart, *Chronicles*, ed. and trans. Geoffrey Brereton (Harmondsworth, 1968), p. 111.
9. *Ibid.*, p. 89.

CLOSE

Emphasize to students that one of the consequences of the plague was the destruction of the stable social order that had existed during the Middle Ages. The deaths of approximately 30 percent of the population in Europe brought about the end of the feudal state, which led to a new social order and the eventual creation of strong European monarchies, particularly in Spain, England, and France.

SPANISH SUPPORT

The *Conclusion* has been translated into Spanish for your Spanish-speaking students. Included with this translation (in your Teacher Resource Box) are Section Key Points, which consist of one or two sentences summarizing each section in the chapter. These Key Points have also been translated into Spanish.

TIME LINE

As students conclude the chapter, you may want to refer them to the chapter time line in the *Study Guide*. The time line will help them put key dates in perspective. Supporting questions and activities are also provided.

CHAPTER 13 REVIEW

Answers column (left)

USING KEY TERMS

1. new monarchies
2. theology
3. interdict
4. *carruca*
5. serfs
6. taille
7. Inquisition
8. flagellants
9. scholasticism
10. manorialism
11. commercial capitalism
12. relics
13. vernacular
14. money economy
15. lay investiture
16. guilds
17. heresy

REVIEWING THE FACTS

1. new farming practices, growth of trade, rise of cities, rising population, strong papal leadership, burst of intellectual and artistic activity
2. better climate, clearing of land, the iron plowshare, use of horses in plowing, horse collar, horseshoe and three-field system
3. rights to control marriage, legal issues, and taxes
4. Most were peasants themselves and could not read.
5. near castles and rivers and older, deserted cities
6. property rights, freedom rights, and self-government rights
7. the Franciscans and the Dominicans
8. troubadour poetry of chivalric love, and chansons de geste or heroic epics
9. the "little ice age"
10. France and its allies supported the pope in Avignon, while France's enemy England and its allies supported the pope in Rome.
11. power range, and speed

THINKING CRITICALLY

1. They allowed more efficient cultivation of the soils of Europe.
2. Besides human and animal

414

USING KEY TERMS (center column)

1. Governments that attempted to reestablish centralized power were called _____.
2. _____ is the study of religion.
3. Pope Innocent's _____ forbade priests from giving the sacraments of the church.
4. A(n) _____ is a heavy-wheeled plow with an iron plowshare.
5. _____ were peasants tied to the land.
6. The _____ was an annual direct French tax on land or property.
7. The religious court whose job it was to find and try heretics was called the _____.
8. People who wandered from town to town, flogging each other with whips to beg forgiveness of God, were called _____.
9. The idea that faith and reason can be reconciled is called _____.
10. The economic system called _____ was the basis of feudalism.
11. People began to invest in trade and goods to make profits, an economic system known as _____
12. _____ were thought to be capable of healing or producing other miracles.
13. The language of a particular region is called the _____.
14. A new economic system called a(n) _____ slowly replaced the barter system as trade increased.
15. The practice by which secular rulers chose and invested their nominees to church offices was called _____.
16. For protection, craftspeople organized themselves into _____.
17. A Spanish priest founded the Dominicans to defend church teachings from _____.

414

REVIEWING THE FACTS (right column)

1. What were four characteristics of European civilization in the High Middle Ages?
2. What explains the increased agricultural output of the High Middle Ages?
3. What legal rights did the lords have over the serfs?
4. How literate were village priests?
5. Where did towns tend to be located and why?
6. What freedoms were townspeople given in the Charters of Liberty?
7. What were two new religious orders that emerged in the thirteenth century?
8. What were the most popular types of vernacular literature in the twelfth century?
9. Besides the plague, what other natural disaster took place in the fourteenth century?
10. How did the Great Schism divide Europe?
11. Why was the longbow superior to the crossbow?

THINKING CRITICALLY

1. Why were the three-field system, iron plowshare, horse collar, and horseshoe so important to increased food production?
2. Besides an agricultural revolution, the High Middle Ages also experienced a power revolution. Explain.
3. How were medieval guilds like monopolies? How were prices and quality kept under control?
4. What did the Concordat of Worms say? Was the Concordat likely to settle the power struggle between church and state? Why or why not?
5. Why was heresy seemingly so prevalent in the thirteenth century?
6. Why was theology considered the "queen of the sciences" in the High Middle Ages?
7. How does the architecture of the eleventh and twelfth centuries reflect the major preoccupations of medieval society?

Bottom answer continuation (center column)

labor, the power of water and wind developed into major new energy sources in the High Middle Ages.
3. Guilds set standards for articles produced, specified production methods, fixed prices, and determined the number of men who could enter the trade. They could not charge more than the market would bear.
4. Under the Concordat, a bishop in Germany was first elected by church officials. History suggests the compromise did not work.
5. Medieval Christians believed that force should be used to save these souls from damnation.
6. Theology reconciled faith and reason by show-

ing that faith was in harmony with what could be learned by reason.
7. Cathedrals reflect the preoccupation with religion, and castles with warfare.
8. The political results include a decline in the power of the church and of the noble class. Social results include an outbreak of anti-Semitism and freedom from serfdom. Economic results include a huge loss of labor and a concomitant rise in labor costs, falling prices because of lowered demand, decline of rent incomes for the nobility, and declining production and trade.
9. Spain lost many of its intellectuals.
10. It failed to create a centralized, unified state.

8. Briefly analyze the political, social, and economic results of the Black Plague in Europe.
9. What was the effect of expelling Jews and Muslims from Spain?
10. Why did the Holy Roman Empire fail to develop strong monarchical authority?

APPLYING SOCIAL STUDIES SKILLS

1. **Economics:** Explain briefly how the manorial economic system of the Middle Ages worked.
2. **Cultural Anthropology:** What was the cultural fabric of a peasant's life?
3. **Government:** Describe the system of governance in medieval towns.
4. **Sociology:** In what role in medieval society might women have had the most chance to become rich and/or powerful?
5. **Geography:** Consult Map 13.3 on page 405. Trace the spread of the plague from the Middle East through Europe.

MAKING TIME AND PLACE CONNECTIONS

1. What is a major difference between European civilization in the High Middle Ages and in the Late Middle Ages?
2. Iron has played a crucial role in world history. What were two new applications of iron in the Middle Ages and why were they important? Were they more important than other historical applications of iron prior to this period? Explain.
3. Why are there so many churches in France known as Notre Dame—"our lady"?
4. From where did the Western idea that education should be separate from politics come?
5. What new weapon, partly of Chinese origin, helped the French win the Hundred Years' War?

BECOMING AN HISTORIAN

Historical Analysis and Decision Making

1. What were the circumstances that motivated lords to begin freeing serfs in the Late Middle Ages?
2. Why did the counts of Champagne devise a series of six annual fairs to be held in the chief towns of their territories?
3. Why did lords and kings make the decision to grant townspeople charters of liberties even though it diminished the Lords' and kings' power? Evaluate their decision given the context of the times.
4. Take on the role of either Pope Gregory VII or King Henry IV of Germany. Argue the question of lay investiture from your point of view and justify the compromise that you reach.
5. Why might kings, popes, and princes have supported the founding of universities?

Document Interpretation

1. How might an historian go about interpreting different views of urban life, such as William Fitz-Stephen's view of London in the twelfth century and the order of the King of England to the town of Bouthham?
2. Medieval court records reflect a large number of accidental deaths. What conclusions have some historians come to about this and what is the basis for their conclusions?
3. Read the excerpt from *The Song of Roland*. What are all the ways an historian might identify this as a piece of work of the eleventh century in Europe?

415

---

weapons provided military superiority.
3. The Virgin Mary became the most revered saint because she was seen as the most important mediator with Christ.
4. The first university in Bologna, Italy was formed by laymen rather than clerics.
5. the cannon

BECOMING AN HISTORIAN

Historical Analysis and Decision Making

1. For lords to become more wealthy, they grew more food for profit. They rented out their land to serfs. The change of labor service to fixed rents no longer tied the serf to the land.
2. to make money by collecting a sales tax on all goods exchanged at the fairs
3. could make money by granting freedom in exchange for taxes, became independent of their vassals and were able to buy weaponry and soldiers
4. Gregory: since the pope was God's "vicar on earth," his authority extended over all Christendom, Henry IV, precedent allowed him to do this and that the church needed to be defended by the state.
5. needed educated people to serve as administrators and bureaucrats

Document Interpretation

1. Factors: who the author was, (status, class and motivation for writing); the relative affluence of the two places; the time each was written; the circumstances and context in which written.
2. Deaths might be due to the high consumption of alcohol
3. Written in the vernacular, identifies the enemy as Muslim rather than Basque, the Frankish soldiers are French knights, it is an heroic epic, it has many references to saints and God, and it mentions a cross-bow

---

APPLYING SOCIAL STUDIES SKILLS

1. A manor was a self-contained economic unit, peasants provided labor and rents
2. The cultural life of the peasants was closely connected with Catholic church ritual and ceremony.
3. Male citizens elected members of a city council who served as judges and city officials and passed laws. The city government built warehouses, set standards of weights and measures, provided water barrels to fight fire, and hired guards to patrol the streets.
4. A woman might likely become rich as a widow, powerful as the wife of a nobleman or king, and powerful in the realm of ideas as a nun.
5. Answers will vary.

MAKING TIME AND PLACE CONNECTIONS

1. In the High Middle Ages there was population growth, intellectual activity, papal authority and the building of cathedrals, growth in trade, and new farming practices. During the Late Middle Ages there was plague, famine, economic crisis, decline in the church, war and political instability.
2. The iron plowshare and the iron horseshoe created an agricultural revolution in Europe. Iron

OVERVIEW OF THE UNIT

The third unit of World History is divided into seven chapters, spanning about 230 pages.

This unit takes students from A.D. 1500 to 1800. Chapters 16 and 18 are the shortest; Chapters 19 and 20 the longest. To maintain the schedule of one unit every six weeks, you may want to spend two weeks on Chapters 14 and 15; two weeks on Chapters 16, 17, and 18; and one week each on Chapters 19 and 20.

Using the Illustration

Ask students to look closely at this elaborate illustration. What mood does the painting suggest? *(pride, expectancy, excitement)* What element of the painting is the least realistic? Ask students why the artist would make the camels all look alike. What purpose is gained in representing animals or people uniformly? *(The artist wants the viewer to feel a particular way or wants the animal to represent a quality or to project an image.)* Ask students what image the artist wants the camels to project in this case. *(aristocratic in bearing, regal, disciplined, heads are held pointing up, forelegs are stretching forward confidently)*

▶ *Well-dressed, prosperous members of a caravan stride out on their equally well-dressed, fanciful camels. This stylized painting is reminiscent of Mughal art.*

	1450	1500	1520	1540	1560	1580	1600	1620	1640
Africa			● 1518 First boatload of African slaves to the New World						
India and the Middle East		1501–1723 Safavid Empire in Persia							
			1520–1566 Suleyman the Magnificent		1556–1605 Reign of Akbar				
East Asia and Southeast Asia			● 1511 Portuguese seize Malacca				1598–1616 Tokugawa Leyasu in Japan		
		1500–1644 Ming dynasty in China							
Europe and the Western Hemisphere			1517–1623 The Protestant and Catholic Reformations						
			1519–1522 Spanish Conquest of Mexico						

UNIT OPENER ACTIVITY

This unit discusses religious strife and intolerance in Europe. As a reminder that people do things in different ways, divide class into three groups. Each group will learn one of the following methods of greeting people. **Method 1:** Cross arms in front of chest with fists closed. (indicates carrying no weapons and are approaching in friendliness) **Method 2:** (use man to man and woman to woman only) Avoid eye contact, hold the person gently by the arms and lightly "air kiss" both sides of the cheek. (more commonly used in Eastern cultures) **Method 3:** Approach the person with one hand firmly extended and open to be shaken by another person (evolved to show that no weapons were hidden). This activity is designed primarily as a lead-in to a discussion of tolerance and the need to respect others' beliefs and customs.

NEW WORLD PATTERNS

(1400 TO 1800)

Beginning in the late fifteenth century, a new force entered the world scene: a revived Europe. After the breakdown of Christian unity in the Reformation period, Europeans engaged in a vigorous period of state building. The result was the creation of independent monarchies in western and central Europe that formed the basis for a new European state system.

Also during this period two great new Islamic empires, the Ottomans in Turkey and the Safavids in Persia, arose in the Middle East. A third Islamic empire—the Mughal Empire—unified the subcontinent of India for the first time in nearly two thousand years. Least affected by the European expansion were the societies of East Asia—China and Japan. In fact, China remained, in the eyes of many, the most sophisticated civilization in the world. Its achievements were imitated by its neighbors and admired by philosophers in Europe.

UNIT OUTLINE

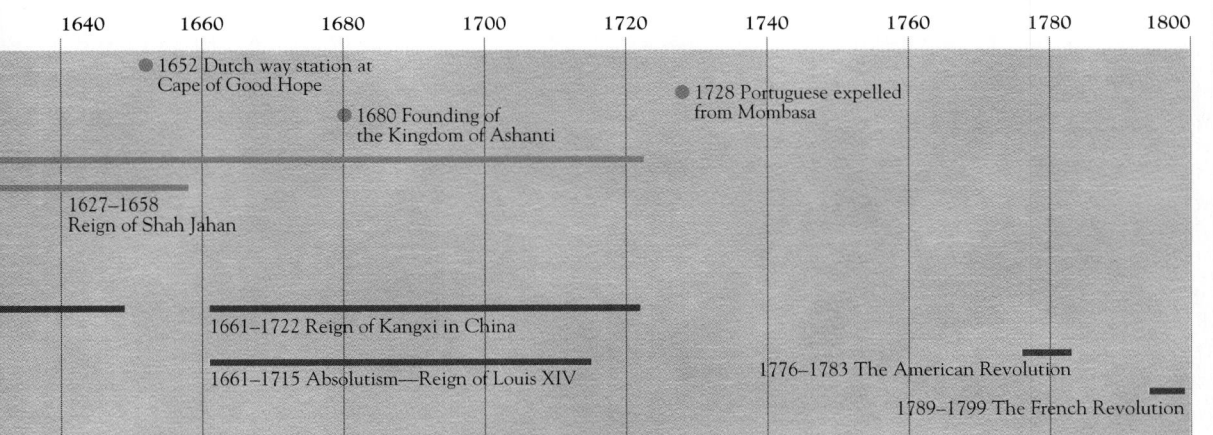

| 1640 | 1660 | 1680 | 1700 | 1720 | 1740 | 1760 | 1780 | 1800 |

● 1652 Dutch way station at Cape of Good Hope

● 1680 Founding of the Kingdom of Ashanti

● 1728 Portuguese expelled from Mombasa

1627–1658 Reign of Shah Jahan

1661–1722 Reign of Kangxi in China

1661–1715 Absolutism—Reign of Louis XIV

1776–1783 The American Revolution

1789–1799 The French Revolution

417

PROJECT IDEAS

After determining the amount of time you will be devoting to this unit, you may want to assign one of the following projects to all students, or allow individual students to choose from the list the one project that they will complete during the study of Unit Three.

1. A fascinating book for young people and adults that supports this period beautifully is *Cathedral: The Story of its Construction* by David MacAulay (Houghton Mifflin, 1973). The book is very popular and readily obtainable at all major book stores and libraries. The black-and-white line drawings can be easily copied by students and will add a wonderfully artistic dimension to the classroom walls.

2. Ask students to start planning now for a "global feast" at the end of this term. There are many delicious dishes that originated in Persia, India, and Europe during this time period that can be prepared by students with a little help from members of the community. Their task is to find the people to provide recipes and guidance as needed.

STUDYING THE TIME LINE

Ask students the following questions to help them compare the time periods of the different civilizations they will be studying in this unit and develop an appreciation for the years covered.

1. What is the earliest year represented in the time line? *(A.D. 1450)*

2. What is the latest year represented in the time line? *(A.D. 1800)*

3. What is the total amount of time covered in the time line? *(350 years)*

4. The time span covered by the time lines has been getting shorter. Why would you expect this to happen? *(Record keeping in modern times has improved and historians have more material to interpret the past.)*

5. Which year appears on all four bars of the time line? *(The year 1680 is represented on all four bars.)*

PLANNING GUIDE

SECTION	KEY TOPICS	PRIMARY SOURCES	ASSESSMENT
1 The Italian Renaissance pages 419–427	◆ Major characteristics of the Italian Renaissance ◆ Contributions of the Italian city-states ◆ Three estates of Renaissance society ◆ Role of women during the Renaissance	◆ *The Book of the Courtier,* page 423 ◆ *The Prince,* page 424 ◆ Letters concerning marriage negotiations in Renaissance Italy, pages 426–427	◆ Section Review, page 427 ◆ Section Quiz, 14–1, TRB
2 The Intellectual and Artistic Renaissance pages 428–435	◆ Renaissance concepts of education ◆ Vernacular language ◆ Artistic masterpieces ◆ Reasons for the Reformation	◆ Description of liberal studies, page 428	◆ Section Review, page 435 ◆ Section Quiz, 14–2, TRB
3 The Protestant Reformation pages 435–440	◆ The humanist movement ◆ Martin Luther and the Reformation ◆ Protestantism in Germany	◆ Erasmus, page 436 ◆ Martin Luther, page 438	◆ Section Review, page 440 ◆ Section Quiz, 14–3
4 The Spread of the Protestant Reformation and the Catholic Response pages 440–448	◆ The Reformation movement in Switzerland ◆ The Catholic Church in England ◆ Anabaptists ◆ Reform in the Catholic Church	◆ A Reformation Debate (Ulrich Zwingli Martin Luther), pages 441–442 ◆ Martin Luther, page 445 ◆ Ignatius Loyola, page 447	◆ Section Review, page 448 ◆ Section Quiz, 14–4

417a

REBIRTH AND REFORM IN EUROPE:
THE AGE OF THE RENAISSANCE AND REFORMATION (1400 TO 1600)

REPRODUCIBLE ACTIVITIES

Historical Maps

Charts and Graphs

Critical Thinking

Cooperative Learning

Vocabulary

Guided Reading

Reteaching

Enrichment

Performance Assessment

Spanish Key Points and Chapter Summaries

Spanish Vocabulary

Spanish Guided Reading

MULTIMEDIA SUPPORT

 TRANSPARENCIES
- *World History* Color Transparency Package
- Fine Art Color Transparency Package

 VIDEO
- *World History* Video Library
- **CNN**. Annual Video Update

 LASERDISC
- *Sights and Sounds of History*

 AUDIO
- *Listening to Literature* audiotape (English and Spanish)
- *History of Music* CD

 SOFTWARE
- WESTEST™
- Student Review

 CD–ROM
- *The Journey of Civilization*
- *World History*

 INTERNET
- Internet Activities

 On Line with **WORLD HISTORY**

Access West's history web site at **http://history.swpco.com** You'll find activities and web sites related to specific topics and chapters in *World History: The Human Odyssey*. Also look for references to helpful web sites at appropriate places throughout this teacher edition.

LESSON PLANNING

You will find detailed daily lesson plans for both traditional class scheduling and **block scheduling** in your Teacher Resource Box.

 ## Not Enough Time?

If you do not have the four or five days recommended to teach this chapter, you may want to focus on the following sections and activities:

- Have students skim the chapter to answer the "Questions to Guide Your Reading" on page 419.
- Do a more in-depth reading of pages 419–426, 430–435, and 436–437. Conclude with a class discussion of "The High Renaissance in Italy" on pages 432–433.

REBIRTH AND REFORM IN EUROPE: THE AGE OF THE

Around 1500, Pope Julius II hired the great Italian artist Michelangelo to paint the ceiling of the Sistine Chapel in Rome. For a man long accustomed to being a sculptor, this was not an easy task. Michelangelo undertook the project but refused for a long time to allow anyone, including the pope, to see his work. Julius grew anxious and pestered Michelangelo on a regular basis about when the ceiling would be finished. Tired of the pope's requests, Michelangelo once replied that the ceiling would be completed "when it satisfies me as an artist." The pope responded, "We want you to finish it soon." He then threatened that if Michelangelo did not "finish the ceiling quickly he would have him thrown down from the scaffolding." Fearing the pope's anger, Michelangelo quickly completed the ceiling, one of the great masterpieces in the history of Western art.

Michelangelo was one of the great artists of the period of European history that we call the Renaissance (REN-uh-SAWNTS). In the fifteenth century, intellectuals in Italy were especially convinced that they had made a decisive break with the Middle Ages and had entered a new age of human achievement. Michelangelo was but one of the great figures who dominated the landscape of their time. Another was Martin Luther, whose break with the Roman Catholic Church at the beginning of the sixteenth century led to the emergence of the Protestant Reformation and a new era in the history of the Christian Church. Taken together, the Renaissance and the Reformation began a new stage in the history of Western civilization.

▲ *Michelangelo Buonarroti began work on this statue, David, when he was just twenty-six years old. Carved from marble and over thirteen feet high, the statue is a masterpiece. With a calm facial expression and tense muscles, David faces his challenge, already a hero.*

RENAISSANCE AND REFORMATION
(1400 TO 1600)

NEW WORLD PATTERNS

	THE RENAISSANCE	
1400	AND REFORMATION	1600

1400   1800

QUESTIONS TO GUIDE YOUR READING

1. What was the Renaissance? What were its chief features?
2. How would you describe the political world that existed in the Italian states? What role did women play in that world?
3. What were the characteristics of Italian Renaissance humanism? How did it differ from Northern Renaissance humanism?
4. What were the chief achievements of Italian and Northern Renaissance painters?
5. What were the chief ideas of Lutheranism, Zwinglianism, Calvinism, and Anabaptism? What did those religions have in common? How were they different from one another and from Catholicism?
6. What role did politics play in the creation and spread of the Protestant Reformation?
7. What were the contributions of the Jesuits, the papacy, and the Council of Trent to the revival of Catholicism?

OUTLINE

1. THE ITALIAN RENAISSANCE
2. THE INTELLECTUAL AND ARTISTIC RENAISSANCE
3. THE PROTESTANT REFORMATION
4. THE SPREAD OF THE PROTESTANT REFORMATION AND THE CATHOLIC RESPONSE

THE ITALIAN RENAISSANCE

The word *Renaissance* means "rebirth." A number of people who lived in Italy between 1350 and 1550 believed that they had witnessed a rebirth of classical antiquity—the world of the Greeks and Romans. To them, this marked a new age, which historians later called the Renaissance and viewed as a distinct period of European history that began in Italy and then spread to the rest of Europe. What, then, are the characteristics of the Italian Renaissance?

First, Renaissance Italy was largely an **urban society** made up of powerful city-states. These city-states became the centers of Italian political, economic, and social life. Within this new urban society, a **secular,** or worldly, spirit emerged as many Italians began to enjoy day-to-day activities and the material products of their prosperous industries and trade.

Second, the Renaissance was an age of recovery from the disasters of the fourteenth century that we examined in Chapter 13. Italy and Europe began to recover from the effects of the Black Death, political disorder, and economic recession. Recovery went hand in hand with rebirth—specifically, a rebirth of classical antiquity. As Italian thinkers became aware of their

419

Answers to QUESTIONS TO GUIDE YOUR READING

1. rebirth of classical antiquity; new age of human achievement; started in Italy; urban and secular in spirit (pages 419–420)
2. strong city-states; women often played important roles (pages 420–422)
3. intellectual movement based on the study of the classics (pages 428–436)
4. Italian: frescoes; mastering of perspective, and anatomy; Northern: realistic paintings (pages 430–434)

5. Lutheranism: (pages 437–440), Zwinglianism: (pages 440–442), Calvinism: (pages 440–442), Anabaptism: (pages 444–445)
6. influenced by political conditions in Germany, France, Switzerland, and England (pages 439–445)
7. See pages 447–448.

Listed below are brief summaries of how the content in this chapter supports the text's key themes.

Politics and History Italy in the Renaissance was a land of independent city-states and principalities in which the practice of secular politics was fostered. Political considerations played a crucial role in the emergence, development, and success of the Protestant Reformation.

The Role of Ideas The Italian Renaissance placed a strong emphasis on human worth and individual achievement. Individualism and secularism first emerged as significant in the Italian Renaissance.

The Importance of Cultural Developments Renaissance humanism was based on the study of the Greek and Roman classics. In northern Europe, humanism sought to correct the ills of the church and society. Renaissance artists such as Michelangelo and Raphael created some of the Western world's greatest art.

Religion in History Protestant reformers created opposition to the Roman Catholic Church. Europe became divided into Protestant and Catholic states.

The Role of Individuals The Renaissance fostered a new ideal of individualism. The era of the Renaissance and Reformation was one of great individuals.

The Environment and History Italy's central location in the Mediterranean fostered the growth of commercial empires by Italy's city-states. This lucrative trade was an important factor in Italy's prosperity.

FOCUS

OBJECTIVES

After completing this section, students should be able to:

1. list three characteristics of the Renaissance
2. describe the importance of the Italian city-states
3. explain the three estates of Renaissance society
4. describe the role of women

FOCUS ACTIVITY

Have students understand that, in general, artistic developments developed during stable, prosperous periods when cities were beginning to thrive. This is the pattern students will see once again as Europe began to recover from the Black Death and its resulting economic problems.

TEACH

Multimedia Support

TRANSPARENCY

14–1, The Italian States (Map 14.1)

REINFORCING VOCABULARY

It is important that students understand the concept of city-states as they begin to read through this section.

Some students may not clearly understand the reference to *antiquity* which generally refers to the historical period before the Middle Ages.

own Roman past, the remains of which were to be seen all around them, they became intensely interested in the culture that had dominated the ancient Mediterranean world. This revival of the world of Rome and Greece affected activities as different as politics and art. It also led some people to see human beings in new ways.

Third, as a result of this new view of human beings, people in the Italian Renaissance began to place an emphasis on individual ability. As one fifteenth-century Italian said, "Men can do all things if they will." A high regard for human worth and a realization of what individuals could achieve created a new social ideal: the well-rounded personality, or universal person who was capable of achievements in many areas of life. Leonardo da Vinci (VIN-chee), for example, was a painter, sculptor, architect, inventor, and mathematician.

Of course, not all parts of Italian society were directly affected by these three general characteristics of the Italian Renaissance. The wealthy upper classes, who made up but a small percentage of the total population, more actively embraced the new ideas and activities. Indirectly, however, the Italian Renaissance did have some impact on ordinary people. Especially in the cities, many of the intellectual and artistic achievements of the period were highly visible and difficult to ignore.

The Italian States

The Renaissance began in Italy. During the Middle Ages, Italy had failed to develop a centralized monarchical state (see Chapter 13). This lack of a single strong ruler had made it possible for a number of city-states in northern and central Italy to remain independent. Three of

them—Milan, Venice, and Florence—expanded and played important roles in Italian politics.

The Italian city-states prospered from a flourishing trade that had expanded in the Middle Ages. Italian cities had taken the lead in establishing mercantile fleets and trading with both the Byzantine and Islamic civilizations to the east. Italian trading ships had also moved into the western Mediterranean and then north along the Atlantic seaboard. These ships exchanged goods with merchants in both England and the Netherlands. Italian merchants had also profited from the Crusades and were able to set up new trading centers in eastern ports. There the Italian merchants obtained silks, sugar, and spices, which they carried back to Italy and the West. At the same time, northern

Map 14.1   The Italian States in the Renaissance

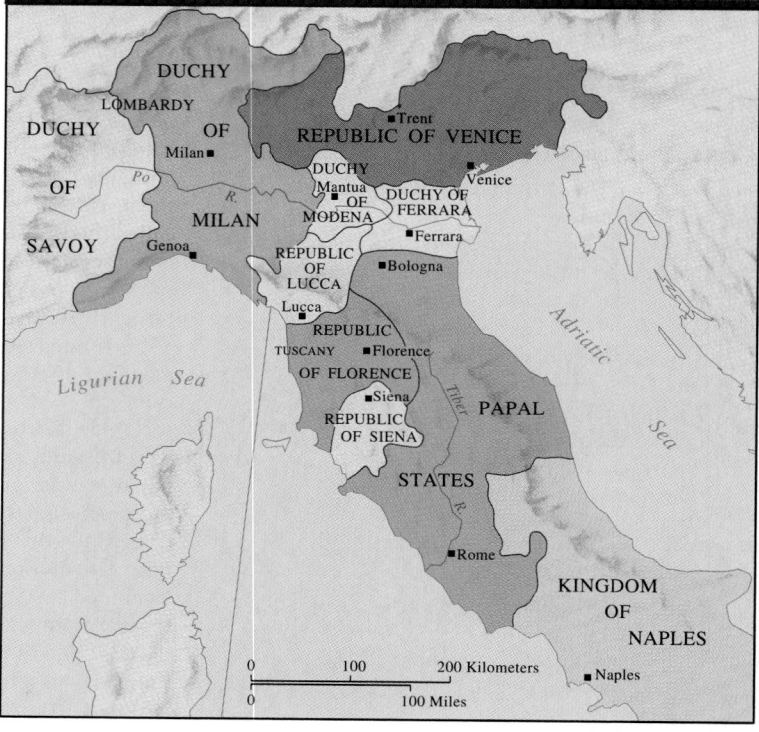

STUDYING MAPS

The following questions will help you guide the students through their study of Map 14.1.

1. Approximately how far is it from Milan to Venice? from Florence to Milan? from Florence to Venice? (*Milan to Venice—160 miles; Florence to Milan—160 miles; Florence to Venice—140 miles*)
2. How far are each of the cities from Rome? (*Milan, 300 miles; Florence, 140 miles;*

Venice, 250 miles)

3. Do these three cities share common geography? If not, how do they differ? (*Venice is coastal; Florence and Milan are on high plateaus; Rome is inland on a low plain and on a river.*)
4. Are there geographic features that might account for their growth and wealth? (*Venice had easy access to the sea which favored trade.*)

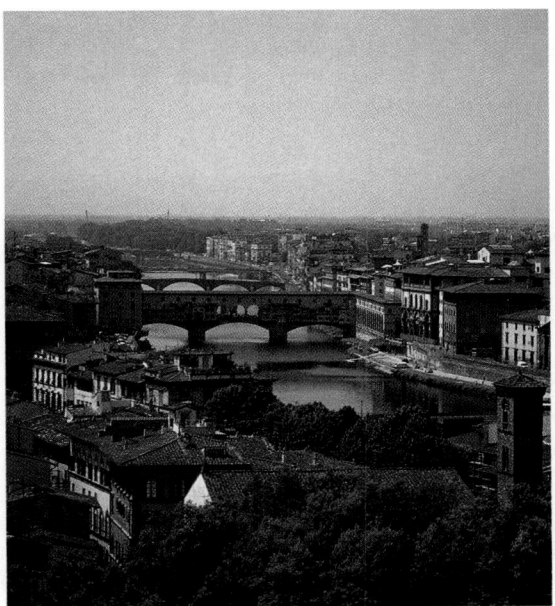

▲ *This graceful bridge over the Arno River is just one of the beauties of Florence. Renaissance art and architecture flourished here, making Florence one of the most beautiful and remarkable Renaissance cities.*

Italy prospered from the making of high-quality woolen cloth, which was also being traded.

Milan, located at the crossroads of the main trade routes from Italian coastal cities to the Alpine passes, was one of the richest city-states in Italy. In the fourteenth century, members of the Visconti family established themselves as dukes of Milan and extended their power over all of Lombardy. The last Visconti ruler of Milan died in 1447. Francesco Sforza, a dynamic **condottiere** (the leader of a band of mercenaries, or soldiers who sold their services to the highest bidder), then conquered the city and became its new duke. Both the Visconti and Sforza rulers worked to build a strongly centralized state. By creating an efficient tax system, they brought in enormous revenues for the government.

The other major northern Italian city-state was the republic of Venice. It had grown rich from trading in the eastern Mediterranean and into northern Europe.

A small group of merchant-aristocrats, who had become wealthy through their trading activities, ran the government of Venice on behalf of their own interests. Venice's trade empire brought in enormous revenues and gave it the status of an international power.

The republic of Florence dominated the region of Tuscany. In the course of the fourteenth century, a small but wealthy group of merchants established control of the Florentine government. They led the Florentines in a series of successful wars against their neighbors and established Florence as a major city-state in northern Italy. In 1434, Cosimo de' Medici (MED-uh-CHEE) took control of the city. The wealthy Medici family kept the republican form of government but ran the government from behind the scenes. Using their wealth and personal influence, both Cosimo and later his grandson Lorenzo selected loyal supporters to fill government posts and carry out their policies. The Medici family dominated the city at a time when Florence was the cultural center of Italy.

Besides Milan, Venice, and Florence, there were other small independent city-states led by powerful ruling families that became brilliant centers of culture in the fifteenth century. One feature of these smaller Italian courts was the important role played by women. The most famous of the Italian ruling women was Isabella d'Este (see "Biography: Isabella d'Este—A Renaissance Woman").

The growth of powerful monarchical states in the rest of Europe led to trouble for the Italian states. Attracted by the riches of Italy, the French king Charles VIII led an army of thirty thousand men into Italy in 1494 and occupied the kingdom of Naples in southern Italy. To protect themselves, other Italian states turned for help to the Spanish, who gladly agreed to send soldiers to Italy. For the next thirty years, the French and Spanish fought to dominate Italy, making Italy their battleground.

A decisive turning point in their war came in 1527. On May 5, thousands of troops of the Spanish king Charles I arrived at the city of Rome. They had not been paid for months. When they yelled, "Money! Money!" their leader responded, "If you have ever dreamed of pillaging a town and laying hold of its treasures, here now is one, the richest of them all, queen of

MORE ABOUT . . . *Diplomacy*

The struggle for political and economic supremacy in northern Italy gave rise to a fundamental diplomatic procedure among the Italian city-states during the Renaissance. It would spread to Europe and eventually the world. The Italians invented the machinery of modern diplomacy, such as placing resident ambassadors in capitals where political and commercial ties could be monitored. Diplomacy enabled rulers to win victories without the expense and risk of military operation. Diplomats from Milan and Florence negotiated the Peace of Lodi (1454).

The role of the ambassador was four-fold, win allies through negotiation, counter the designs of enemies, represent his government at official functions, and report information relevant to aiding the preservation and expansion of his state.

CRITICAL THINKING

The de Medici family was able to dominate Florentine politics for several generations. Ask students to suggest strategies that would have enabled one family to dominate city politics for such a long time. Can students identify American families who have dominated city or state governments for several generations?

CRITICAL THINKING

BIOGRAPHY

Have students compare the actions of Isabella d'Este with those of Eleanor of Aquitaine. (See page 358.) How are these women similar and how are they different? Do students believe Isabella acted as she did to save her son or so that she could retain power? Students should justify their answers.

CLASS DISCUSSION

Guide students in a discussion of the ways Isabella d'Este gained and maintained her power. Why do students think that her husband was unable to send emissaries to take his son and secure his own release?

Answers to Critical Thinking Questions

1. She effectively ruled Mantua both before and after her husband's death.

2. She was known for her intelligence and political wisdom; she attracted artists and intellectuals to the court at Mantua, and put together one of the finest libraries in Italy.

BIOGRAPHY

Isabella d'Este—A Renaissance Woman

Isabella d'Este was the daughter of the duke of Ferrara, a small Italian state. She married the ruler of Mantua (MANCH-uh-wah), and their court joined others as an important center of art and learning in the Italian Renaissance. Educated at the brilliant court of Ferrara, Isabella learned Latin and Greek, as well as such skills as lute playing and dance. She was known for her intelligence and political wisdom. Called by some the "first lady of the world," Isabella attracted artists and intellectuals to the court at Mantua and put together one of the finest libraries in all of Italy. Her numerous letters to friends, family, princes, and artists all over Europe reveal her political knowledge, as well as a good sense of humor.

Both before and after the death of her husband, Francesco, she effectively ruled Mantua. As a result, many Italian and European rulers at the beginning of the sixteenth century regarded Isabella d'Este as an important political figure. After her husband was taken prisoner by the Venetians (vuh-NEE-shunz) in 1509, she refused to accept the condition for his release—namely, that her son be kept as a hostage by the Venetians. When her husband ordered her to send the boy to Venice, she refused and wrote to her husband: "If in this matter Your Excellency were to despise me

◄ *Peter Paul Rubens was a Flemish painter who spent eight years studying in Italy. In this painting of Isabella d'Este, we can easily see why he gained fame throughout Europe, not just in Italy.*

and deprive me of your love and grace, I would rather endure such harsh treatment, I would rather lose our State, than deprive us of our children. . . . Some day I hope I can make you understand."

Isabella's husband was not pleased with her response and exclaimed angrily, "That whore of my wife is the cause of it all. . . . I have lost in one blow my state, my honor and my freedom. If she does not obey, I'll cut her vocal cords." Isabella remained steadfast, however, and the Venetians eventually released her husband without gaining her son. She was then more highly regarded than ever, especially by rulers abroad. The ruler of the Holy Roman Empire said that of all Italian women, she was "the most interesting."

1. Why was Isabella considered to be an important political figure?

2. What do you think people meant when they called Isabella the "first lady of the world"?

---

the world." The next day the forces of Charles smashed down the gates and pushed their way into the city. The troops went berserk in an orgy of bloodshed and looting. One diplomat said, "Hell is nothing to what happened then." Women were raped, church officials sold as slaves, and churches and palaces sacked while drunken soldiers fought over the spoils. The destruction did not end until the stench of corpses forced authorities to establish some order. The terrible sack of Rome in 1527 by the armies of the Spanish king Charles I ended the Italian wars. The Renaissance in Italy, however, was also at an end.

COOPERATIVE LEARNING ACTIVITY

Have students work in small groups to make a visual display of the three major characteristics of the Renaissance. *(emergence of a secular, urban society; a new interest in Greek and Roman remains; and emphasis on individual ability)* They should decide on how to conduct outside research to find specific information or accomplishments that support these three characteristics. Then they should work together on how to best present the results of their research to the class.

Machiavelli and the New Statecraft

No one gave better expression to the Italians' love affair with political power than Niccolò Machiavelli (MAK-ee-uh-VELL-ee). Although he ably served as a diplomat for Florence, he was forced into exile. Embittered by this and compelled by the great love of his life—politics—he wrote *The Prince*, one of the most influential works on political power in the Western world.

Machiavelli's major concern in *The Prince* was political power—how to acquire and keep it. In the Middle Ages, many writers on political power stressed the ethical side of a prince's activity—how a ruler ought to behave based on Christian moral principles. Machiavelli bluntly rejected this approach.

From Machiavelli's point of view, a prince's attitude toward power must be based on an understanding of human nature, which he believed was basically self-centered. He said, "One can make this generalization about men: they are ungrateful, fickle, liars, and deceivers, they shun danger and are greedy for profit." Political activity, therefore, could not be restricted by moral principles. A prince acts on behalf of the state and, for the sake of the state, must be willing to let his conscience sleep. Machiavelli was among the first to abandon morality as the basis for the analysis of political activity (see "You Are There: How Princes Should Honor Their Word"). Machiavelli's views on politics had a profound influence on later political leaders in the Western world.

The Making of Renaissance Society

The Middle Ages had divided society into three estates, or social classes: the clergy (those who prayed), the nobility (those who fought), and the third estate (the peasants and townspeople—those who worked). Although this social order continued into the Renaissance, some changes also became evident. (The clergy will be discussed in "Church and Religion on the Eve of the Reformation" on page 436.)

The Social Classes: The Nobility

Throughout much of Europe, the landholding nobles were faced with declining incomes during the greater part of the fourteenth and fifteenth centuries. Many members of the old nobility survived, however, and new blood also came into its ranks. By 1500, the nobles, old and new, managed to dominate society as they had done in the Middle Ages. Although they made up only between 2 and 3 percent of the population in most countries, the nobles held important political posts and served as advisors to the king.

By 1500, certain ideals came to be expected of the noble, or aristocrat. These were best expressed in *The Book of the Courtier*, written by the Italian Baldassare Castiglione (KAWS-teel-YOE-NAE). First published in 1528, Castiglione's work soon became popular throughout Europe. It remained a basic handbook for European aristocrats for hundreds of years.

In *The Book of the Courtier*, Castiglione described three characteristics of the perfect noble. First, nobles are born, not made, and they should have character, grace, and talent. Second, the perfect noble must develop two basic skills. He should take part in military and bodily exercises, because the chief aim of a noble was being a warrior. However, unlike the medieval knight, who was primarily concerned with military skill, the Renaissance noble must also gain a classical education and adorn his life with the arts. In Castiglione's hands, the Renaissance ideal of the well-developed personality became a social ideal of the aristocracy. Third, the noble is expected to follow a certain standard of conduct. Nobles should not hide their achievements but show them with grace.

What was the purpose of these standards? Castiglione said,

> I think that the aim of the perfect Courtier is so to win for himself the favor and mind of the prince whom he serves that he may be able to tell him, and always will tell him, the truth about everything he needs to know, without fear or risk of displeasing him; and that when he sees the mind of his prince inclined to a wrong action, he may dare to oppose him . . . so as to dissuade him of every evil intent and bring him to the path of virtue.[1]

The aim of the perfect noble, then, was to serve his prince in an effective and honest way. Nobles would adhere to Castiglione's principles for hundreds of years

ACROSS THE CURRICULUM

Have students create a time line of the Italian Renaissance that includes ten to twenty important events, art works, or scientific achievements that were produced during this time.

COMPARING TIME PERIODS

Have students compare the life of Isabella d'Este and the comments of Simone de Beauvoir that appear in Chapter 31. Ask students what they think de Beauvoir would have thought of Isabella.

COMPARING TIME PERIODS

Have students compare the three characteristics of a noble as described by Castiglione to the American idea of a successful businessperson or community leader. How are the two similar and how are they different? You might also wish to have students compare the difference in views between Castiglione and Machiavelli.

RECOMMENDED READING

The classic study of the Italian Renaissance is J. Burckhardt, *The Civilization of the Renaissance in Italy,* trans. S. G. C. Middlemore (London, 1960), first published in 1860. The standard work on the historical interpretation of the Renaissance is W. Ferguson, *The Renaissance in Historical Thought* (Boston, 1948).

A popular biography of Isabella d'Este is G. Marek, *The Bed and the Throne* (New York, 1976). On the *condottieri*, see M. Mallett,

Mercenaries and Their Masters: Warfare in Renaissance Italy (Totowa, 1974). The work by G. Mattingly, *Renaissance Diplomacy* (Boston, 1955) remains the basic one on the subject. Machiavelli's life can be examined in J. R. Hale, *Machiavelli and Renaissance Italy* (New York, 1960); and his thought in F. Gilbert, *Machiavelli and Guicciardini: Politics and History in Sixteenth-Century Florence* (Princeton, N.J., 1965).

CRITICAL THINKING

Have students write their own generalizations about political leaders or mankind in general today. How do those statements compare to Machiavelli's views? If there are differences, have students discuss reasons that account for the change in attitude or in viewpoint.

USING PRIMARY SOURCES

Have students paraphrase Machiavelli's words in modern terms and then have students compare this advice to the oath of office taken by U.S. presidents and other elected officials.

Answers to Critical Thinking Questions

1. According to Machiavelli, princes should not necessarily honor their word, but they should appear to be doing so.
2. Answers will vary according to whether students think achieving great things is more important than one's integrity (in other words, does the end justify the means?).

LEARNING FROM VISUALS

Answer to the caption question: In this portrait, Machiavelli appears kind and compassionate, a vivid contrast to the recommendations in his writing.

YOU ARE THERE
How Princes Should Honor Their Word

In 1513, Niccolò Machiavelli wrote a short work on political power that, justly or unjustly, has given him the reputation of being a political opportunist. In this passage from The Prince, *Machiavelli analyzes whether princes should keep their word.*

Niccolò Machiavelli, *The Prince*

Everyone realizes how praiseworthy it is for a prince to honor his word and to be straightforward rather than crafty in his dealings; nonetheless experience shows that princes who have achieved great things have been those who have given their word lightly, who have known how to trick men with their cunning, and who, in the end, have overcome those abiding by honest principles. . . .

A prince, therefore, need not necessarily have all the good qualities I mentioned above, but he should certainly appear to have them. I would even go so far as to say that if he has these qualities and always behaves accordingly he will find them harmful; if he only appears to have them they will render him service. He should appear to be compassionate, faithful to his word, kind, and devout. And indeed he should do so. But his disposition should be that, if he needs to be the opposite, he knows how. You must realize this: that a prince, and especially a new prince, cannot observe all those things which give men a reputation for virtue, because in order to maintain his state he is often forced to act in defiance of good faith, of charity, of kindness, of religion. And so he should have a flexible disposition, varying as fortune and circumstances dictate. As I said above,

▲ *In this portrait by Santi di Tito, Machiavelli appears kind, compassionate, and calm. How does his appearance compare to his actual beliefs and writings?*

he should not deviate from what is good, if that is possible, but he should know how to do evil, if that is necessary.

---

1. According to Machiavelli, how should princes honor their word?
2. Is the picture Machiavelli paints of princes who have "achieved great things" positive or negative?

On Line with
WORLD HISTORY *Internet Activity*

You may want to have your students visit the following URL, where they will find information and additional web site resources to enhance their study of this chapter.

Leonardo da Vinci—Museum
http://cellini.leonardo.net/ museum/main.htm

At this site you will find award-winning exhibit displays, images and information relating to Leonardo da Vinci.

Due to the ever-changing nature of the World Wide Web, see the West History web site, **http://history.swpco.com** for regular updates of the URLs in this text.

◀ (left) *Piero della Francesca was one of the first artists to recognize and apply perspective in painting the human form, and he is considered to be one of the greatest artists of the early Renaissance. How is his understanding of scientific perspective reflected in this portrait of the Duchess of Urbino?*

◀ (right) *The Duke of Urbino ruled the small central Italian principality of Urbino. These portraits of the duke and the duchess provide historians with a fairly accurate understanding of the dress worn by the rich Italian ruling classes.*

while they continued to dominate European life socially and politically.

The Social Classes: The Third Estate of Peasants and Townspeople

In the Middle Ages, peasants made up the overwhelming mass of the third estate. In the Renaissance, they still constituted as much as 85 to 90 percent of the total European population, except in the highly urbanized areas of northern Italy and Flanders. As the manorial system continued to decline, so too did serfdom. Increasingly, the labor dues owed by a peasant to his lord were converted into rents paid in money. By the end of the fif

teenth century, especially in western Europe, more and more peasants were becoming legally free.

Townspeople made up the rest of the third estate. In the Middle Ages, these were the merchants and artisans, the so-called middle class. The Renaissance town or city of the fifteenth century, however, had become more complex. At the top of urban society were the patricians. Their wealth from trade, industry, and banking enabled them to dominate their communities economically, socially, and politically. Below them

▶ *Despite the care and planning of such elegant menus, banquets during Renaissance times were somewhat rowdy affairs. What table manners are displayed here that would be unacceptable today, especially at a formal banquet?*

SPECIAL NEEDS: *Visual/Auditory*

Read as a class the section entitled "Family and Marriage in Renaissance Italy" beginning on page 426. Have each student make a chart outlining what they feel are the roles that fathers and mothers play in today's society. How are single parents able to perform all responsibilities necessary? How does this differ from society's "norm?" From Renaissance Italy? Various charts can be reproduced on the overhead or copied for the hearing-impaired. Students requiring assistance may list characteristics aloud while a partner constructs the chart.

USING PRIMARY SOURCES

Read aloud the statement from the rich Florentine merchant concerning the poor in the city. Guide students in a discussion of the problems of poverty and homelessness in the United States. What governmental actions and policies provide some margin of protection or assistance to the jobless and the homeless? Do students believe that some Americans would agree with the sentiment of the quote? Why or why not?

YOU-ARE-THERE

CLASS DISCUSSION

Have students compile a list of the advantages and disadvantages of arranged marriages. Why were arranged marriages the normal practice throughout the world until recent times? You might wish to assign students to write a letter to Alessandra explaining and justifying the concept of marriage for love. What do students think her reaction would be to this foreign concept?

Answers to Critical Thinking Questions

1. The fact that he was in exile complicated his family's efforts to find him a wife.
2. She wanted to know whether Marco felt there were other women who should be considered for Filippo's wife. She was still "shopping."
3. Answers will vary.

YOU ARE THERE

Marriage Negotiations in Renaissance Italy

Marriages were so important in maintaining families in Renaissance Italy that much energy was put into arranging them. Parents made the choices for their children, most often for considerations that had little to do with the modern notion of love. This selection is taken from the letters of Alessandra Strozzi to her son Filippo, in Naples. The family's considerations were complicated by the fact that the son was in exile.

▲ *Marriage contracts were considered a normal part of marriage arrangements, as was the banquet that celebrated the wedding and the end of negotiations. This painting by Botticelli illustrates the wedding feast of two wealthy Florentines.*

Alessandra Strozzi to Her Son Filippo in Naples

[April 20, 1464] Concerning the matter of a wife [for Filippo], it appears to me that if Francesco di Messer Tanagli wishes to give his daughter, that it would be a fine marriage. Now I will speak with Marco [Parenti, Alessandra's son-in-law], to see if there are other prospects that would be better, and if there are none, then we will learn if he wishes to give her [in marriage]. Francesco Tanagli has a good reputation, and he

were the petty burghers—the shopkeepers, artisans, guild masters, and guild members who provided the goods and services for their fellow townspeople.

Below the patricians and the burghers were the workers earning pitiful wages and the unemployed, both of whom lived miserable lives. These people made up as much as 30 or 40 percent of the urban population. Everywhere in Europe in the late fourteenth and fifteenth centuries, urban poverty had increased dramatically. One rich merchant of Florence, who had little sympathy for the poor, wrote, "Those that are lazy in a way that does harm to the city, and who can offer no just reason for their condition, should either be forced to work or expelled from the city. The city would thus rid itself of that most harmful part of the poorest class."[2]

Family and Marriage in Renaissance Italy

The family bond was a source of great security in the dangerous urban world of Renaissance Italy. To maintain the family, parents carefully arranged marriages, often to strengthen business or family ties. Details were worked out well in advance, sometimes when children were only two or three years old. A legally binding marriage contract sealed the agreement (see "You Are There: Marriage Negotiations in Renaissance Italy").

ENRICHMENT ACTIVITY

The author refers to the "dangerous urban world of Renaissance Italy" in the text. Have students explain those characteristics of Italy during the Renaissance that made it a dangerous place to live. *(Students may need to refer to this chapter and to Chapters 12 and 13.)* You may want to assign this as a short research project, necessitating a trip to the library. Guide students in a discussion of the role of the family in protecting them from the dangers of growing up in urban America. In what ways can a family assist a young person achieve success as an adult?

YOU ARE THERE

Marriage Negotiations in Renaissance Italy, continued

has held office, not the highest, but still he has been in office.

[July 26, 1465] Francesco is a good friend of Marco and he trusts him. On S. Jacopo's day, he spoke to him discreetly and persuasively, saying that for several months he had heard that we were interested in the girl and . . . that when we had made up our minds, she will come to us willingly. [He said that] you were a worthy man, and that his family had always made good marriages, but that he had only a small dowry to give her. . . . We have information that she is affable and competent. She is responsible for a large family (there are twelve children, six boys and six girls), and the mother is always pregnant and isn't very competent.

[August 31, 1465] I have recently received some very favorable information [about the Tanagli girl] from two individuals. They are in agreement that whoever gets her will be content. Concerning her beauty, they told me what I had already seen, that she is attractive and well-proportioned. Her face is long, but I couldn't look

directly into her face, since she appeared to be aware that I was examining her and so she turned away from me like the wind. She reads quite well and she can dance and sing.

[September 13, 1465] Marco came to me and said that he had met with Francesco Tanagli, who had spoken very coldly, so that I understand that he had changed his mind. [Filippo eventually married Fiametta di Donato Adimari in 1466.]

1. What complicated Filippo Strozzi's family's efforts to find a wife for him?

2. What did Filippo's mother mean when she wrote, "Now I will speak with Marco, to see if there are other prospects that would be better"?

3. How do you think the idea of planned marriages would be received in our society today?

The important aspect of the contract was the size of the **dowry,** a sum of money given by the wife's family to the husband upon marriage. This money was controlled by the husband.

The father-husband was the center of the Italian family. He gave it his name, managed all finances (his wife had no share in his wealth), and made the decisions that determined his children's lives. A father's authority over his children was absolute until he died or formally freed his children. In Renaissance Italy, children did not become adults on reaching a certain age. Instead, adulthood came to children only when their fathers went before a judge and formally freed them. The age varied from the early teens to the late

twenties. The mother's chief role was to supervise the household.

 SECTION REVIEW

1. **Locate:**
   (a) Milan,   (b) Venice,   (c) Florence,
   (d) Rome

2. **Define:**
   (a) urban society,   (b) secular,   (c) condottiere,
   (d) dowry

3. **Identify:**
   (a) Michelangelo,   (b) Francesco Sforza,

ENRICHMENT ACTIVITY

Have students compare the roles of women during Renaissance times with the rights of Greek women (Chapter 5) and with Muslim women (Chapter 7). How are they similar and how are they different? Ask students to suggest reasons for the position and social role assigned to women in these three very different cultures in three different time periods.

CLOSE

Review the legacy of Greek and Roman civilization, their defined societal roles, art, and architecture. Discuss specific ways in which the Renaissance was a rebirth of these ideals, but with a modern interpretation.

FOCUS

OBJECTIVES

After completing this section, students should be able to

1. explain the Renaissance concepts of education
2. describe artistic contributions of the Renaissance
3. identify problems that led to the Reformation

FOCUS ACTIVITY

Have students brainstorm a list of artists or artistic masterpieces. Identify those that were created during the Renaissance. Discuss the factors that contributed to the growth of art and artistic development during this time period.

TEACH

REINFORCING VOCABULARY

Rhetoric refers to the art of speaking persuasively; *prose* refers to ordinary writing (not poetry or drama).

(c) Cosimo dé Medici,   (d) Niccolò Machiavelli,
(e) *The Book of the Courtier*

4. **Recall:**
(a) Explain the three major characteristics of the Renaissance.
(b) What led to the development of the Italian city-states?
(c) Describe the three estates of society during the Middle Ages.

5. **Think Critically:** Why did the Italian city-states of Milan and Florence flourish and grow so quickly during the Renaissance?

THE INTELLECTUAL AND ARTISTIC RENAISSANCE

Individualism and secularism—two characteristics of the Italian Renaissance—are most noticeable in the intellectual and artistic realms. During the fifteenth and sixteenth centuries, Italy was the cultural center of Europe. The most important intellectual movement we associate with the Renaissance is **humanism.**

Italian Renaissance Humanism

Renaissance humanism was an intellectual movement based upon the study of the classics, or the literary works of ancient Greece and Rome. Humanists studied the liberal arts—grammar, rhetoric, poetry, moral philosophy or ethics, and history—all based upon the study of ancient Greek and Roman authors. These subjects are what we call the humanities.

Petrarch, who has often been called the father of Italian Renaissance humanism, did more than any other individual in the fourteenth century to foster the development of humanism. Petrarch sought to find forgotten Latin manuscripts and set in motion a search of monastic libraries throughout Europe. He also began the humanist emphasis on the use of pure classical Latin (Latin as used by Romans). Humanists used the works of Cicero as a model for prose and those of Virgil for poetry. As Petrarch said, "Christ is my God; Cicero is the prince of the language."

In Florence, the humanist movement took a new direction. Fourteenth-century humanists such as Petrarch had described the intellectual life as one of solitude. They rejected family and a life of action in the community. However, the humanists who worked as secretaries for the city council of Florence took a new interest in civic life. They came to believe that it was the duty of an intellectual to live an active life for one's state. This interest of humanists in the life of their communities reflected the values of the urban society of the Italian Renaissance. Humanists came to believe that their study of the humanities should be put to the service of the state. It is no accident that humanists served as secretaries in the Italian city-states or at the courts of princes or popes.

Education in the Renaissance

The humanist movement had a profound effect on education. Renaissance humanists believed that human beings could be dramatically changed by education. They wrote books on education and opened schools based on their ideas (see "The Role of Science and Technology: The Impact of Printing"). At the core of humanist schools were the "liberal studies." Humanists believed that the liberal studies (what we call the liberal arts) were the key to true freedom—that they enabled individuals to reach their full potentials. According to one humanist, "We call those studies liberal which are worthy of a free man; those studies by which we attain and practice virtue and wisdom; that education which calls forth, trains, and develops those highest gifts of body and mind which ennoble men."[3]

What, then, were the liberal studies? According to the humanists, they included history, moral philosophy, eloquence (or rhetoric), letters (grammar and logic), poetry, mathematics, astronomy, and music. In short, the purpose of a liberal education (and thus the purpose of the study of the liberal arts) was to produce individuals who followed a path of virtue and wisdom. They should also possess the rhetorical skills by which they could persuade others to take this path.

MORE ABOUT . . . *Pico della Mirandola*

Giovanni Pico della Mirandola was the wealthy and gifted son of the prince of Mirandola born in 1463. He showed an insatiable thirst for learning. As a teenager, he studied law at Bologna, then at the University of Padua and later at Paris. At twenty-four years of age he went to Rome to write. His most influential book, *Oration on the Dignity of Man,* was intended to introduce his philosophical ideas. Pope Innocent VIII condemned 13 of them as heretical. A subsequent conflict led to Pico's fleeing Italy. He was arrested in France and returned to Italy where he was paroled into the custody of Lorenzo de Medici. Pico died in 1494 at the age of 31. He spoke three languages including Latin, Greek, and Arabic. His *Oration,* printed in 1495–1496 after his death, proclaimed "Man is the most blessed of all living creatures . . ."

THE ROLE OF SCIENCE AND TECHNOLOGY

The Impact of Printing

The Renaissance saw the development of printing in Europe. The art of printing made an immediate impact on European intellectual life and thought. In the fifteenth century, Europeans found out how to print with movable metal type. The development of printing from movable type was a gradual process that occurred about 1450. Johannes (YO-HAWNZ) Gutenberg (GOOT-un-BURG), of Mainz (MINEts), Germany, played a crucial role in completing the process. Gutenberg's Bible, printed about 1455, was the first European book produced from movable type.

By 1500, there were over a thousand printers in Europe who had published almost forty thousand titles (between eight million and ten million copies). More than half were religious books, including Bibles, prayer books, and sermons. Most others were the Latin and Greek classics, legal handbooks, works on philosophy, and an ever-growing number of popular romances.

The effects of printing were soon felt in many areas of European life. The printing of books encouraged scholarly research and the desire to

▲ *This hand-colored woodcut shows the first printing press, like the one Johannes Gutenberg would have used. After examining this picture, can you explain how a manuscript page would have been printed?*

gain knowledge. Printing also stimulated the growth of an ever-expanding lay reading public, which would eventually have an enormous impact on European society. Indeed, the new religious ideas of the Reformation would never have spread as rapidly as they did in the sixteenth century without the printing press.

Printing—and the communication of knowledge that it made possible—allowed European civilization to achieve greater heights and compete for the first time with the civilization of China. The Chinese had invented printing much earlier, as well as printing with movable type. However, their highly structured society made less effort to use printing to increase the knowledge of its citizens.

1. What reason is given for the rapid spread of new religious ideas during the Reformation?

2. Why do you think the printing of books encouraged people's desires to gain knowledge?

Following the Greek precept of a sound mind in a sound body, humanist educators also stressed physical education. Pupils were taught the skills of javelin throwing, archery, and dancing. They were encouraged to run, wrestle, hunt, and swim.

The purpose of the humanist schools was to educate an elite, the ruling classes of their communities. Females were largely absent from such schools. The few female students who did attend humanist schools studied the classics; were encouraged to know some history;

RETEACHING ACTIVITY

Following Gutenberg's development of moveable type, knowledge began to be circulated very quickly throughout Europe. Discuss with students the role of technology in disseminating information. You may want to divide your students into small groups and ask them to compose a list of ways information will be disseminated and to answer the following questions: How do they believe people will receive information in the coming century? Will print materials, like textbooks and newspapers, become obsolete?

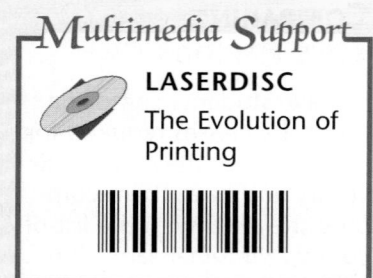

Multimedia Support

LASERDISC
The Evolution of Printing

CRITICAL THINKING

Guide students in a discussion of the humanist view of virtue. Why was this characteristic so central to the humanist education? You might wish to assign students to write a short essay explaining what they feel is the significance of virtue to the Renaissance education.

USING PRIMARY SOURCES

Assign students to read excerpts from *The Canterbury Tales* and present reports or skits based on the stories to the class. Guide students in a discussion of the portrayal of Renaissance life that is gained from this English literary masterpiece.

and were taught to ride, dance, sing, play the lute, and appreciate poetry. However, the female students were told not to learn mathematics or rhetoric. Religion and morals were thought to "hold the first place in the education of Christian ladies" and to help them prepare for their roles as mothers and wives.

Humanist educators thought that humanist education was a practical preparation for life. Its aim was the creation not of a great scholar but of a complete citizen. As one humanist said, "Not everyone is obliged to excel in philosophy, medicine, or the law, nor are all equally favored by nature; but all are destined to live in society and to practice virtue."[4] Humanist schools provided the model for the basic education of the European ruling classes until the twentieth century.

Vernacular Literature

The humanist emphasis on classical Latin led to its widespread use in the Renaissance, especially among scholars, lawyers, and theologians. However, some writers used the vernacular (the language spoken in their own regions, such as Italian, French, or German) to write their works. In the fourteenth century, the works of Dante (DAWN-TAE) and Geoffrey Chaucer (JEFF-ree CHAW-sur) helped make vernacular languages more popular. By the sixteenth century, vernacular languages were beginning to compete with Latin. Eventually, they would replace it.

Dante's masterpiece in the Italian vernacular was the *Divine Comedy*. It is the story of the soul's journey to salvation, a basic concern of people in the Middle Ages. The lengthy poem is divided into three major sections: Hell, Purgatory, and Heaven, or Paradise. Dante is led on an imaginary journey through these three realms of the afterworld until he reaches Paradise, where he beholds God, or "the love that moves the sun and the other stars."

Chaucer made use of the English vernacular in his famous work *The Canterbury Tales*. His beauty of expression and clear, forceful language were important in making his dialect the chief ancestor of the modern English language. *The Canterbury Tales* consists of a collection of stories told by a group of twenty-nine pilgrims journeying to the tomb of Saint Thomas à Becket at Canterbury, England. This format gave Chaucer the chance to portray an entire range of English society, both high and low born. Among others, he presented the Knight, the Monk, the Merchant, the Student, the Lawyer, the Carpenter, the Cook, the Doctor, and the Plowman. Also, of course, "a Good Wife was there from beside the city of Bath—a little deaf, which was a pity." To while away the time, these pilgrims told an enormous variety of stories, some uplifting and others simply anecdotes.

Another writer who used the vernacular was François Rabelais (FRAWN-SWAH RAB-uh-LAE). Rabelais lived at the beginning of the sixteenth century and used French to write his masterpieces, *Pantagruel* and *Gargantua*. Both were comic tales detailing the lusty adventures of the giant Pantagruel and his father Gargantua. In his works, Rabelais moved far beyond Dante's concern with salvation. He made clear his own love of life while pointing out the follies of the society of his day.

The Artistic Renaissance in Italy

The great Italian Renaissance artist Leonardo da Vinci once said, "The painter will produce pictures of small merit if he takes for his standard the pictures of others, but if he will study from natural objects he will bear good fruit . . . those who take for their standard any one but nature . . . weary themselves in vain."[5] Renaissance artists sought to imitate nature in their works of art. They wanted onlookers to see the reality of the object or event they were portraying. At the same time, Renaissance artists had a new attitude of mind as well, one in which human beings became the focus of attention—the "center and measure of all things," as one artist proclaimed.

The **frescoes** painted by Masaccio (muh-ZAWCH-ee-OH) in Florence at the beginning of the fifteenth century have long been regarded as the first masterpieces of Early Renaissance art. (A fresco is a painting done on fresh, wet plaster with water-based paints.) Masaccio's human figures were not flat, as in medieval painting, but rather were three-dimensional. They had depth and came alive. By mastering the laws of perspective, which enabled him to create the illusion of

On Line with WORLD HISTORY *Internet Activity*

You may want to have your students visit the following URL, where they will find information and additional web site resources to enhance their study of this chapter.
Virtual Renaissance: A Journey Through Time
**http://www.twingroves.
district96.k12.il.us/Renaissance/
VirtualRem.html**

This site contains a well done virtual travel back to the Renaissance. It has excellent sources. Invite students to look at the recommended sites.

Due to the ever-changing nature of the World Wide Web, see the West History web site, **http://history.swpco.com** for regular updates of the URLs in this text.

▲ *Masaccio was considered a genius, and during his short life (he died at age twenty-seven), he created a number of masterpieces. This fresco, entitled* Tribute Money, *was one of a series that Masaccio painted in a Florentine church. Like his contemporary Piero della Francesca, Masaccio used perspective to create a realistic relationship between the figures and their background.*

three dimensions, Masaccio had created a new, realistic style of painting. His art appeared to mirror the world of the onlooker—a revolutionary idea at the time.

This new, or Renaissance, style was used and modified by other Florentine painters in the fifteenth century. Especially important were two major developments. One stressed the technical side of painting—the working out of the laws of perspective and the organization of outdoor space and light by geometry and perspective. The second development was the investigation of movement and human anatomy. The realistic portrayal of the individual person, especially the human nude, became one of the chief aims of Italian Renaissance art.

The revolutionary achievements of Florentine painters in the fifteenth century were matched by equally stunning advances in sculpture and architecture. Donato di Niccolo, better known as Donatello, spent time in Rome, studying and copying the statues of the Greeks and Romans. His own work reveals how well he had mastered the essence of what he saw. Among his numerous works was a statue of Saint George, a realistic, freestanding figure. It radiated a

simplicity and strength that reflected the dignity of human beings.

Filippo Brunelleschi was a friend of Donatello who went with him to Rome. Brunelleschi (BROON-ul-ES-kee) drew much inspiration from the buildings of classical Rome. When he returned to Florence, he

▶ *Donato di Donatello, another famous early Renaissance artist, created this bronze statue of Saint George in 1416. The statue is 6 feet, 10 inches high. How does Donatello convey the impression that St. George is confident, relaxed, and ready for battle?*

RECOMMENDED READING

Brief introductions to Renaissance humanism can be found in D. R. Kelley, *Renaissance Humanism* (Boston, 1991); and F. B. Artz, *Renaissance Humanism, 1300–1550* (Oberlin, Ohio, 1966). A more detailed analysis of various aspects of Renaissance humanism is contained in C. Trinkaus, *The Scope of Renaissance Humanism* (Ann Arbor, Mich., 1983). A basic work on the writing of history in the Italian Renaissance is E. Cochrane, *Historians and Historiography in the Italian Renaissance* (Chicago, 1981). On Guicciardini, see M. Philips, *Francesco Guicciardini: The Historian's Craft* (Toronto, 1977). The impact of printing is exhaustively examined in E. Eisenstein, *The Printing Press as an Agent of Change,* 2 vols. (New York, 1978).

CLASS DISCUSSION

Guide students in a discussion comparing the soaring, immense Gothic cathedrals built during the High Middle Ages with the Renaissance concept of smaller churches. How does the smaller size reflect the Renaissance emphasis on the universal person?

USING PRIMARY SOURCES

You may want to point out the similarity between the pointing finger on the hand in *The Creation of Adam* with the finger on the Child's hand in *The Alba Madonna*. Each painting is from a different artist. Could there be any significance between the two?

LEARNING FROM VISUALS

Answer to the caption question: Pope Julius II commissioned the frescoes for the ceiling of the Sistine Chapel; they were done between 1508–1512.

OUR ARTISTIC HERITAGE
The High Renaissance in Italy

The High Renaissance in Italy is associated with three artistic giants, Leonardo da Vinci, Raphael (RAF-ee-ul), and Michelangelo. Leonardo mastered the art of realistic painting and even dissected human bodies in order to better see how nature worked. However, Leonardo also stressed the need to advance beyond such realism. It was Leonardo who began the attempt during the High Renaissance to move beyond realism by painting ideal forms rather than realistic ones.

Raphael blossomed as a painter at an early age. At twenty-five, he was already regarded as one of Italy's best painters. Raphael was well known for his frescoes in the Vatican Palace and was especially admired for his numerous madonnas (paintings of the Virgin Mary). In these he tried to achieve an ideal of beauty far surpassing human standards. His *Alba Madonna* reveals a world of balance, harmony, and order—basically, the underlying principles of the art of the classical world of Greece and Rome.

Michelangelo, an accomplished painter, sculptor, and architect, was another artistic giant of the High Renaissance. Fiercely driven by his desire to create, he worked with great passion and energy on a remarkable number of projects. His figures on the ceiling of the Sistine Chapel in Rome reveal an ideal type of human being with perfect proportions.

The beauty of this idealized human being is meant to be a reflection of divine beauty. The more beautiful the body, the more Godlike the figure.

Another manifestation of Michelangelo's search for ideal beauty was his *David*, a colossal marble statue commissioned by the Florentine government. Michelangelo maintained that the form of a statue already resided in the uncarved piece of stone: "I only take away the surplus, the statue is already there." Out of a piece of marble that had remained unused for fifty years, Michelangelo created a fourteen-foot-high figure, the largest piece of sculpture in Italy since ancient Roman times. Michelangelo's *David* proudly proclaims the beauty of the human body and the glory of human beings.

1. List the three artists associated with the High Renaissance in Italy.

2. For what are each of the three artists best known?

3. What do you think Michelangelo meant when he said, "I only take away the surplus, the statue is already there"?

poured his new insights into the creation of a new architecture. The Medici, the wealthy ruling family of Florence at the time, commissioned Brunelleschi to design the church of San Lorenzo. Inspired by his Roman models, he created a church interior very different from that of the great medieval cathedrals. San Lorenzo's classical columns and rounded arches created an environment that did not overwhelm the worshiper, as Gothic cathedrals did. Instead, it provided comfort as a space created to fit human, not divine, needs. Like painters and sculptors, Renaissance architects sought to reflect a human-centered world.

By the end of the fifteenth century, Italian painters, sculptors, and architects had created a new artistic

ENRICHMENT ACTIVITY

Depending upon the maturity level of your students, you might wish to bring in a color reproduction of the *Creation of Adam* from the Sistine Chapel and discuss it with the class so that they can see how enormous and how beautiful this fresco is. You may also want to bring in copies of other works by Michelangelo to share with the class. Some students may enjoy reading *The Agony and the Ecstasy*, a fictionalized account of Michelangelo's life written by Irving Stone.

Answers to Critical Thinking Questions

1. Leonardo da Vinci, Raphael, and Michelangelo are the three artistic giants of the Italian High Renaissance.
2. Da Vinci is best known for his realistic paintings and for attempting to move beyond realism; Raphael is known for his frescoes in the Vatican palace and his madonnas; Michelangelo is known for the ceiling of the Sistine Chapel and his great sculpture, David.
3. Answers will vary but might include the idea that Michelangelo felt the statue is the creation of the artist. Once conceived in the artist's mind, the real work is done.

OUR ARTISTIC HERITAGE
The High Renaissance in Italy, continued

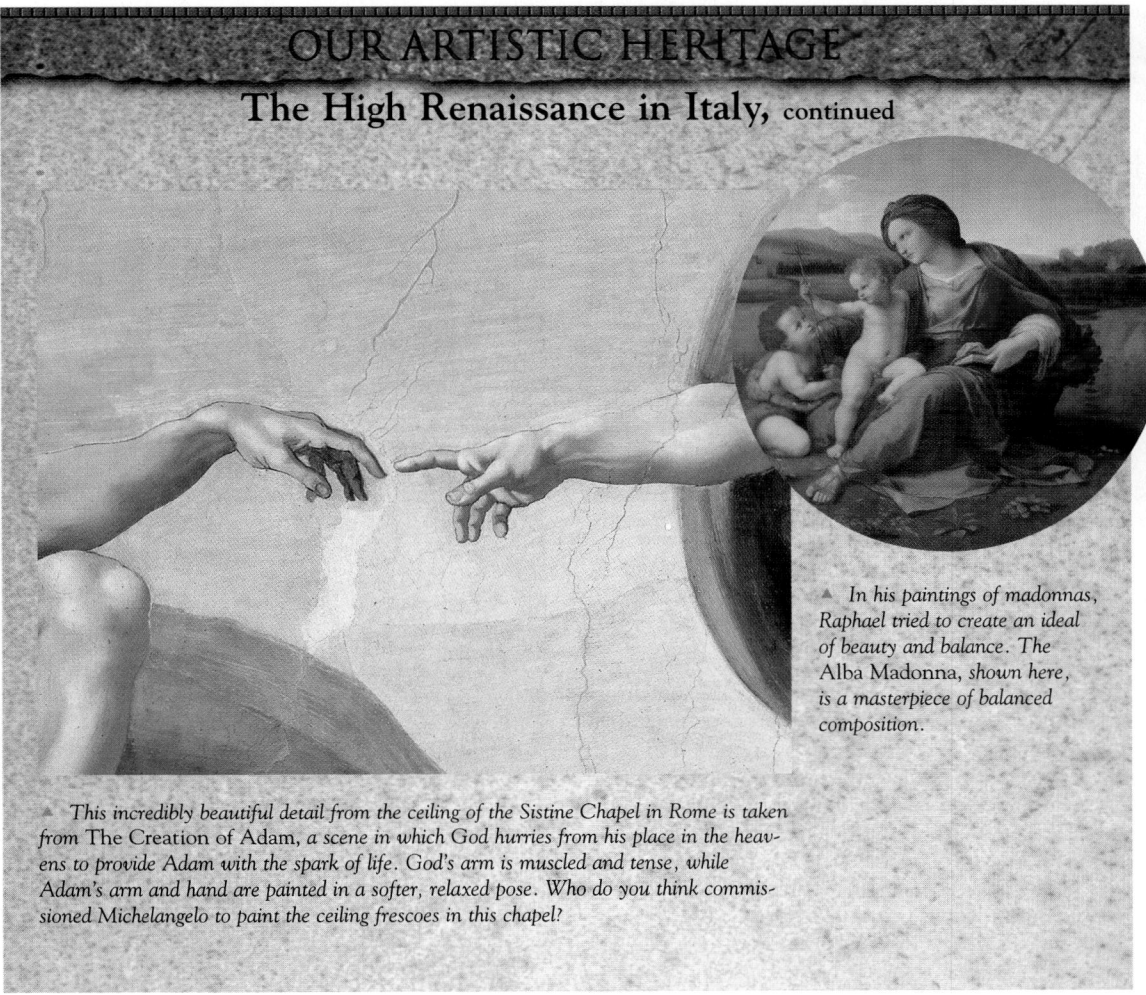

▲ In his paintings of madonnas, Raphael tried to create an ideal of beauty and balance. The Alba Madonna, *shown here*, is a masterpiece of balanced composition.

This incredibly beautiful detail from the ceiling of the Sistine Chapel in Rome is taken from The Creation of Adam, *a scene in which God hurries from his place in the heavens to provide Adam with the spark of life. God's arm is muscled and tense, while Adam's arm and hand are painted in a softer, relaxed pose. Who do you think commissioned Michelangelo to paint the ceiling frescoes in this chapel?*

world. Many artists had mastered the new techniques for a realistic portrayal of the world around them and were now ready to move into new forms of creative expression. This final stage of Renaissance art, which flourished between 1480 and 1520, is called the High Renaissance (see "Our Artistic Heritage: The High Renaissance in Italy").

The Northern Artistic Renaissance

In trying to provide a realistic portrayal of their world, the artists of northern Europe (especially the Low Countries) and those of Italy took different approaches. In Italy, the human form became the chief vehicle of expression. Italian artists mastered the

ENRICHMENT ACTIVITY

Select examples of Renaissance art based on the following Renaissance themes of Individualism, worldliness, learning, antiquity and reform. Study the pictures and write a sentence summary. Have students indicate in writing which of the five themes are represented in each print. Finally, ask students to list evidence of these themes in modern times. Suggested pictures include

Raphael:	"The School of Athens"
Quentin Massy:	"A Money Changer and His Wife"
Leonardo da Vinci:	"Proportional Study of a Man in the Manner of Vitrivius"
Albrecht Durer:	"Erasmus"
Titian:	"Charles V"
Michelangelo:	"The Creation of Adam"

CLASS DISCUSSION

Have students research and bring in examples of Northern European art works from the 1500s. Ask students to compare and contrast these works with the work of the Italian Renaissance artists. Students should be able to see difference in theme, use of color, and in the kinds of details the artists show in their work.

LEARNING FROM VISUALS

Answers to the caption questions: (far right) Students might suggest that it was for the same reasons that families today pay for wedding photographers. Also it was a means of creating a record of events.

(right) Churches were a sign of a city's prosperity and of their faith in God. It is unlikely that the de'Medicis wanted to be seen as poor or as lacking in faith.

▲ *Filippo Brunelleschi designed the interior of this church, San Lorenzo in Florence. Cosimo de' Medici contributed most of the money for the work. Why do you think the de' Medici family was such a strong supporter of the Florentine churches?*

▲ *Jan van Eyck was careful to depict every object in his paintings realistically, as shown here in* Giovanni Arnolfini and His Bride. *Women were often portrayed as pregnant to indicate their willingness to marry and bear children. What does this indicate about the role of women? Why would families have incurred the expense for an artist to record weddings?*

technical skills that allowed them to portray humans in realistic settings. The large wall spaces of Italian churches had given rise to the art of fresco painting. In the north, the Gothic cathedrals with their stained glass windows did not allow for frescoes. Thus, northern artists painted illustrations for books and wooden panels for altarpieces. Great care was needed to depict each object on a small scale. This led northern painters to become masters at painting details.

The most important northern school of art in the fifteenth century was found in Flanders. Jan van Eyck (YAWN van-IKE) was among the first to use oil paint, which enabled the artist to use a wide variety of colors and create fine details. In his *Giovanni Arnolfini and Bride*, van Eyck's attention to detail is staggering. The work includes precise portraits, a glittering chandelier, a mirror reflecting the objects in the room, and the effects of light coming through the window. Each detail was painted as it was seen. Van Eyck, however, did not fully understand the laws of perspective. Like the other Northern Renaissance artists, van Eyck tried to imitate nature not by mastery of the laws of perspective, as the Italians did, but by simply observing reality and portraying details as best he could. By the end of the fifteenth century, however, artists from the north began to study in Italy and were soon influenced by what artists were doing there.

One German artist who was greatly affected by the Italians was Albrecht Dürer. He made two trips to Italy and absorbed most of what the Italians could teach on

MORE ABOUT . . . *Albrecht Dürer*

Albrecht Dürer was perhaps the greatest artist of Renaissance Germany. This Nuremburg goldsmith-illustrator-painter was able to link Italian and Northern art. After spending time studying the Italian Renaissance artists he returned to Germany having grasped the possibilities of printing and engraving as artistic expression.

In 1498, the publication of "The Apocalypse," was the first printed work designed entirely by an artist. It told the story of the biblical work of Revelation in the unique way—fourteen full-page wood cuttings on the right, and the corresponding text (in Latin or German editions) on the left. Because it could be enjoyed by the illiterate and because of the uniqueness of woodcuts and prints together the Apocalypse sold out rapidly and spread Dürer's fame far beyond Nuremburg.

the laws of perspective and Renaissance theories of proportion. At the same time, as can be seen in his famous *Adoration of the Magi*, Dürer did not reject the use of minute details characteristic of northern artists. He did try, however, to fit those details more harmoniously into his works in accordance with Italian artistic theories. Like the Italian artists of the High Renaissance, Dürer tried to achieve a standard of ideal beauty by a careful examination of the human form.

 SECTION REVIEW

1. **Define:**
   (*a*) humanism,   (*b*) frescoes

2. **Identify:**
   (*a*) Petrarch,   (*b*) Dante,   (*c*) Geoffrey Chaucer,
   (*d*) François Rabelais,   (*e*) Masaccio,   (*f*) Filippo Brunelleschi,   (*g*) Jan van Eyck,   (*h*) Albrecht Dürer

3. **Recall:**
   (*a*) How did the humanists change civic life in Italian cities?
   (*b*) What was the purpose of humanist education?
   (*c*) What were the two major developments in art during the Italian Renaissance?

4. **Think Critically:** Compare and contrast the humanist goal and philosophy of education developed during the Renaissance with your high school education.

THE PROTESTANT REFORMATION

The Protestant Reformation began with a typical medieval question: What must I do to be saved? Martin Luther, a deeply religious man in Germany, found an answer that did not fit within the traditional teachings of the late medieval Catholic Church. Ultimately, he split with that church and in so doing destroyed the religious unity of the western Christian world. That other people were concerned with the same question is evident in the rapid spread of the Reformation.

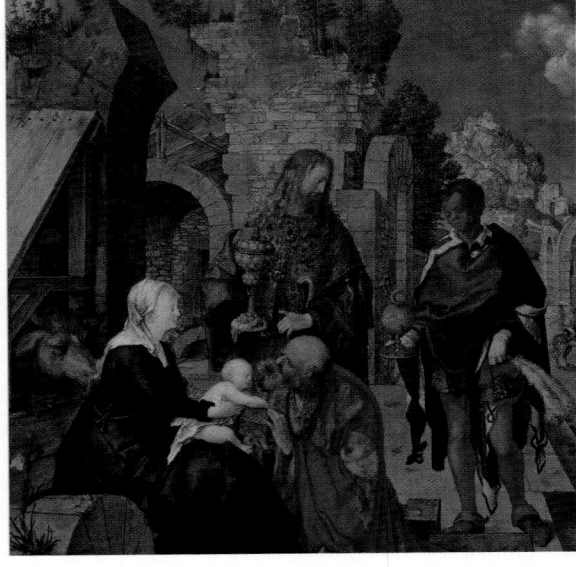

▲ The Adoration of the Magi, *Albrecht Dürer's painting created for a church altarpiece, is a stunning example of northern European work. In this scene, Dürer retains the minute details typical of northern European painting, but he also includes perspective and his ideals of proportion.*

Background to the Reformation

Martin Luther's reform movement was not the first in sixteenth-century Europe. During the second half of the fifteenth century, the new classical learning that was part of Italian Renaissance humanism spread to northern Europe. It spawned a movement called Christian humanism or Northern Renaissance humanism, whose major goal was the reform of Christendom.

The Christian humanists believed in the ability of human beings to reason and improve themselves. They thought that if people would read the classics, and especially the basic works of Christianity, they would become more pious. This inner piety, or inward religious feeling, would bring about a reform of the church and society. For this reason, Christian humanists supported schools, brought out new editions of the classics, and prepared new editions of the Bible. They

RECOMMENDED READING

Basic surveys of the Reformation period include H. J. Grimm, *The Reformation Era, 1500–1650*, 2d ed. (New York, 1973); P. J. Klassen, *Europe in the Reformation* (Englewood Cliffs, N.J., 1979); and D> L. Jensen, *Reformation Europe* (Lexington, Mass., 1981). L. W. Spitz, *The Protestant Reformation, 1517–1559* (New York, 1985), is a sound and up-to-date history.

The classic account of Martin Luther's life is R. Bainton, *Here I Stand: A Life of Martin Luther* (New York and Nashville, 1950). More recent works include H. A. Oberman, *Luther* (New York, 1992); W. von Loewenich, *Martin Luther: The Man and His Work* (Minneapolis, 1986); J. M. Kittelson, *Luther the Reformer: The Story of the Man and His Career* (Minneapolis, 1986); and H. G. Haile, *Luther: An Experiment in Biography* (Garden City, N.Y., 1980).

ASSESS

You can choose from a variety of assessments to evaluate your students' mastery of the objectives as stated on page 428.

Answers to SECTION REVIEW

1. (a) philosophy that emphasizes an individual's dignity and worth
   (b) painting done on fresh, wet plaster
2. (a) the father of the Italian humanist movement
   (b) wrote the *Divine Comedy*
   (c) wrote *The Canterbury Tales*
   (d) French author of comic tales
   (e) fresco painter in Florence
   (f) designer of the church of San Lorenzo
   (g) one of first to paint with oils
   (h) famous painter of *Adoration of the Magi*
3. (a) participated fully in the affairs of the state
   (b) to produce an elite, ruling class who would follow a path of virtue
   (c) ability to create three-dimensional images; investigation of movement and the human figure
4. Answers will vary.

CLOSE

Students should recognize the impact of the art masterpieces that were created during this time and that it was the wealthy Italian families and the Catholic Church who were the primary sponsors of Renaissance art.

3

FOCUS

OBJECTIVES

After studying this section students should be able to
1. describe the humanist movement
2. describe Luther's role in the Reformation
3. explain reasons for state-sponsored Protestantism

FOCUS ACTIVITY

Review the Great Schism in the Catholic Church with students. Earlier disagreements in the Catholic Church had led to a weakening of its power, but until the 1500s it was still the principal religion in Europe.

TEACH

CLASS DISCUSSION

A typical medieval question concerned salvation, which reveals the importance of religion on everyday life. Ask students to compile a list of typical questions about life in the 1990s. What do the questions on students' lists reveal about our civilization?

USING PRIMARY SOURCES

Discuss Erasmus's critiques of monks. Do students believe that Erasmus was accurately reporting the power of monks over the common people? Was Erasmus exaggerating to make his point? You might also assign students to write an essay explaining the statement "Erasmus laid the egg . . ."

436

---

believed that in order to change society, they must first change the human beings who make it up.

The best known of all the Christian humanists was Desiderius Erasmus (i-RAZZ-mus). After giving up being a monk, Erasmus wandered to France, England, Italy, Germany, and Switzerland. He conversed everywhere in the classical Latin that might be called his mother tongue. His *Handbook of the Christian Knight* showed his concern with religion. He called his view of religion "the philosophy of Christ." By this he meant that Christianity should show people how to live good lives on a daily basis rather than provide a system of beliefs that people had to practice to be saved. Erasmus stressed the inwardness of religious feeling. To him, the external forms of religion (such as pilgrimages, fasts, and relics) were not all that important.

To reform the church, Erasmus wanted to spread the philosophy of Christ, provide education in the works of Christianity, and criticize the abuses in the church. In his *Praise of Folly*, written in 1511, Erasmus humorously criticized aspects of his society that he believed were most in need of reform. He was particularly harsh on the abuses in the church and singled out the monks for special treatment. Monks, he said, "insist that everything be done in precise detail. . . . Just so many knots must be on each shoe and the shoelace must be of only one color, . . . and they can sleep only the specified number of hours per day." Because of this attention to detail, he continued, "they think that they are superior to all people" and will be rewarded in heaven.

Erasmus's reform program, however, did not achieve its goal. No doubt, his work helped to prepare the way for the Reformation. As people of his day said, "Erasmus laid the egg that Luther hatched." However, Erasmus turned against Luther and the Protestant reformers. He did not want to destroy the unity of the Catholic Church. His own program was based on reform within the church, not outside it.

Church and Religion on the Eve of the Reformation

Corruption in the Catholic Church was another factor that encouraged people to want reform. Between 1450

and 1520, a series of popes—known as the Renaissance popes—failed to meet the church's spiritual needs. The popes were supposed to be the spiritual leaders of the Catholic Church but, as leaders of the Papal States, were all too often more concerned with Italian politics and worldly interests. Julius II, the fiery "warrior-pope," personally led armies against his enemies. This disgusted the pious Christians who viewed the pope as a spiritual leader. One person wrote, "How, O bishop standing in the room of the Apostles, dare you teach the people the things that pertain to war?"

The Renaissance popes were also great patrons of Renaissance art and architecture. Their efforts made Rome a cultural leader at the beginning of the sixteenth century. However, their building projects, such as the construction of Saint Peter's Basilica, cost money. This led the popes to an unhealthy preoccupation with finances. Raising revenues consumed much of their energy.

The preoccupation of the papal court with finances had an especially strong impact upon the clergy. So, too, did the economic changes of the fourteenth and fifteenth centuries. The highest positions of the clergy were increasingly held by either nobles or wealthy members of the bourgeoisie (BURR-ZWAW-ZEE), who had actually bought their positions. At the same time, to increase their revenues, high church officials (such as bishops, archbishops, and cardinals) took over more than one church office. This practice of **pluralism** (the holding of many church offices) led, in turn, to the problem of **absenteeism.** Absenteeism occurred when church officeholders ignored their duties and paid subordinates to run their offices. The subordinates had little interest in performing their duties. No wonder that so many people complained in the fifteenth century about the ignorance and failure of parish priests!

While the leaders of the church were failing to meet their responsibilities, ordinary people were clamoring for meaningful religious expression and certainty of salvation. As a result, for some the process of salvation became almost mechanical. Collections of relics grew as more and more people sought certainty of salvation through veneration of these relics. Frederick the Wise, elector of Saxony and Luther's prince, had amassed

---

MORE ABOUT . . . the Papacy

The first of the Popes to represent the Renaissance was Nicholas V, who held the post from 1447–1455. He combined humanism with earnest Christian purpose. He is credited with having founded the Vatican Library and as a patron of the arts made Rome a center of the new humanism and art. Nicholas was followed by Callistus III, a Spaniard who was chiefly memorable for his

advancement of his family, the Borgias, including his nephew Rodrigo, who later became the infamous Alexander VI. Alexander VI was elected Pope in 1492, amidst the charges that he obtained the election by wholesale bribery of the cardinals. An able administrator, he is chiefly remembered for the shameless way he sought to further advance his own household. Julius II was 60 years old when elected in over 5,000 relics, to which were attached indulgences that could reduce one's time in purgatory by 1,443 years. (An indulgence is a remission, after death, of all or part of the punishment due to sin.) Other people sought certainty of salvation in the popular mystical movement known as the Modern Devotion. The Modern Devotion downplayed religious dogma and stressed the need to follow the teachings of Christ. Thomas à Kempis, author of *The Imitation of Christ*, wrote, "Truly, at the day of judgment we shall not be examined by what we have read, but what we have done; not how well we have spoken, but how religiously we have lived."

This deepening of religious life was done within the Catholic Church. However, many people soon found that the worldly-wise clergy had little interest in the spiritual needs of their people. It is this environment that helps to explain the tremendous impact of Luther's ideas.

Martin Luther and the Reformation in Germany

Martin Luther was born in Germany on November 10, 1483. His father wanted him to become a lawyer, so Luther enrolled at the University of Erfurt (AIR-furt). However, Luther disliked the study of law. On a hot and muggy summer day in 1505, while returning to Erfurt, he was caught in a ferocious thunderstorm. Terrified when a bolt of lightning knocked him to the ground, he cried out, "St. Anne, help me! I will become a monk." Taking his vow seriously, he entered the monastic order of the Augustinian Hermits in Erfurt. Later, he studied theology at the University of Wittenberg. He received his doctor's degree there and then became a professor, lecturing on the Bible. Through his study of the Bible, Luther arrived at an answer to a problem—the certainty of salvation—that had bothered him since he had become a monk.

Catholic teaching had stressed that both faith and good works were needed if a Christian were to gain personal salvation. In Luther's eyes, human beings, powerless in the sight of an almighty God, could never do enough good works to earn salvation. Through his

▲ *Martin Luther is shown at the far left in this painting, while the prince, Elector John Frederick of Saxony, takes center stage. Other reformers surround the German prince. Why do you think the artist chose to put the prince in the foreground, not Luther?*

study of the Bible, Luther found another way of viewing this problem. To Luther, humans are not saved through their good works but through faith in the promises of God, made possible by the sacrifice of

1503 and ruled until 1513. He was more like an emperor than a bishop and much of his time was devoted to restoring, consolidating, and extending Papal territory. Leo X was Pope from 1513 to 1521. He made Rome a growing center of culture. He was lover of luxury and engaged in political and diplomatic intrigues of the time. This is evident in the

1517 plot to rid Leo by poisoning him. In retaliation, Leo had the leader, a 22 year old dissolute cardinal, tortured and executed, imposed heavy fines on the other cardinals who had been implicated and created 31 new cardinals to ensure his control over the Sacred College. In order to build St. Peter's Leo promoted the sale of indulgences.

CRITICAL THINKING

Much criticism has been directed toward the Catholic Church for lavishly spending on art and church buildings, while neglecting the needs of the poor. Review with students the treasures in Europe and elsewhere that have been sponsored by the Catholic Church in cathedrals, art, and literature. Do students feel that using church resources to build the Gothic cathedrals, for example, was excessive? Have students support their answers with reason and logic.

REINFORCING VOCABULARY

Ensure that students understand the term *veneration*. (reverence or respect).

REINFORCING VOCABULARY

Some students may not understand the terms *indulgences, purgatory, remission,* and *dogma,* but these are critical to understanding the Reform movement begun by Martin Luther. Allow time for students to look these terms up in the dictionary and discuss their meanings with the class.

LEARNING FROM VISUALS

Answer to the caption question: The success of Luther's reform movement depended heavily upon the support provided by the German rulers.

CLASS DISCUSSION

Review the concept of justification by grace through faith alone. This is another key concept in understanding the Reformation.

USING PRIMARY SOURCES

Read Martin Luther's statement to the class and then have them rewrite this paragraph in their own words. Have students add an imaginary response that the local archbishop might have written to Luther.

CLASS DISCUSSION

Guide students in a discussion of the reasons the German rulers would have been motivated as much by politics and economics as by religious reasons for supporting Luther against the Catholic Church and the pope. Use this discussion to refer to the illustration on page 437 that shows the German prince in the foreground. Students should recognize that religion is sometimes just one of many factors that plays a role in social struggles *(such as in Northern Ireland and, arguably, in the Israeli/Palestine disputes).*

ACTIVITY

Have students write a letter from Martin Luther to his father explaining why the path he chose was better than studying law.

Christ on the cross. The doctrine of salvation, or justification by grace through faith alone, became the chief teaching of the Protestant Reformation. Because Luther had arrived at this doctrine from his study of the Bible, the Bible became for Luther, as for all other Protestants, the chief guide to religious truth.

Luther did not see himself as a rebel, but he was greatly upset by the widespread selling of indulgences. Especially offensive in his eyes was the monk Johann Tetzel (YOE-HAWN TET-sul), who hawked indulgences with the following slogan: "As soon as the coin in the coffer [money box] rings, the soul from purgatory springs." People, Luther believed, were simply harming their chances for salvation by buying these pieces of paper. Greatly angered, on October 31, 1517, he posted his Ninety-Five Theses on the door of the Castle Church in Wittenberg. The theses were a stunning attack on the abuses in the sale of indulgences. Luther did not intend any break with the church over the issue of indulgences, but he did want the pope to stop their sale. If the pope had the power to grant indulgences, Luther asked, "Why does the pope not empty purgatory for the sake of most holy love and the supreme need of souls?" The Renaissance pope Leo X, however, did not take the issue seriously and is reported to have said that Luther was simply "some drunken German who will amend his ways when he sobers up." Thousands of copies of the Ninety-Five Theses were printed and quickly spread to all parts of Germany.

Under pressure from both the church and his followers, Luther began to move toward a more definite break with the Catholic Church. He called upon the German princes to overthrow the papacy in Germany and establish a reformed German church. He attacked the system of sacraments as the means by which the pope and church had destroyed the real meaning of the gospel for one thousand years. He kept only two sacraments—baptism and the Lord's Supper—and called for the clergy to marry. Through all these calls for change, Luther expounded more and more on his new doctrine of salvation. It is faith alone, he said, and not good works, that justifies and brings salvation through Christ.

Unable to accept Luther's ideas, the church excommunicated him in January 1521. He was also summoned to appear before the imperial diet, or Reichstag (RIKES-tag)—the legislative assembly—of the Holy Roman Empire, called into session at the city of Worms by the newly elected emperor Charles V. Luther was expected to deny the false teachings he had championed. However, he refused and made the famous reply that became the battle cry of the Reformation:

> Since then Your Majesty and your lordships desire a simple reply, I will answer without horns and without teeth. Unless I am convicted by Scripture and plain reason—I do not accept the authority of popes and councils, for they have contradicted each other—my conscience is captive to the Word of God. I cannot and I will not recant anything, for to go against conscience is neither right nor safe. Here I stand, I cannot do otherwise. God help me. Amen.[6]

The young emperor was outraged. "A single friar who goes counter to all Christianity for a thousand years," he declared, "must be wrong!" By the Edict of Worms, Martin Luther was made an outlaw within the empire. His works were to be burned and Luther himself captured and delivered to the emperor. However, Luther's ruler, Elector Frederick of Saxony, was unwilling to see his famous professor killed. He sent him into hiding and then protected him when he returned to Wittenberg at the beginning of 1522.

During the next few years, Luther's religious movement became a revolution. Luther was able to gain the support of many of the German rulers among the some three hundred states that made up the Holy Roman Empire. These rulers, motivated as much by politics and economics as by any religious feeling, quickly took control of the churches in their territories. The Lutheran churches in Germany (and later in Scandinavia) became state churches in which the state supervised the affairs of the church. The political leaders, not the Roman pope, held the last word. As part of the development of these state-dominated churches, Luther also set up new religious services to replace the Catholic mass. These featured a worship service consisting of Bible reading, preaching of the word of God, and song. Luther also married a former nun, Katherina

So What ??

If your students question the importance of information about **why some German princes supported Luther and others did not,** *tell them . . .*

Some of the princes were motivated by religion while others wanted political and economic benefits. In his tract *Appeal to the Christian Nobility of the German Nation* (1520), Luther appeals to German patriotism. This gained him strong support. This patriotic appeal was also used by Robespierre and the Committee of Public Safety during the French Revolution, when they recruited over one million men for 14 armies. The appeal to patriotism can again be seen both during World Wars I and II. Even in our own day, patriotism has a strong appeal, and one need look no further than the "Yellow Ribbon" and outpouring of flags during the Persian Gulf War for proof.

von Bora, and his marriage provided a model of married and family life for the new Protestant minister.

A series of crises soon made it apparent, however, that spreading the word of God was not as easy as Luther had thought. The Peasant's War was Luther's greatest challenge. In June 1524, peasants in Germany rose in revolt against their lords and looked to Luther for support. However, Luther supported the rulers. To him, the state and its rulers were called by God to maintain the peace and order necessary for the spread of the gospel. It was the duty of princes to stop all revolt. By the following spring, the German princes had crushed the peasants, and Luther found himself even more dependent on state authorities for the growth of his reformed church.

The Influence of Politics and Religion in the German Reformation

From its very beginning, the fate of Luther's movement was closely tied to political affairs. Charles V, the Holy Roman emperor (also known as Charles I as king of Spain), ruled over an immense empire consisting of Spain, the Austrian lands, Bohemia, Hungary, the Low Countries, the kingdom of Naples in southern Italy, and parts of the New World. Politically, Charles wanted to keep control of the rule of his dynasty—the Habsburgs—over his enormous empire. Religiously, he hoped to preserve the unity of his empire in the Catholic faith. However, four major problems—the French, the papacy, the Turks, and Germany's internal situation—kept him busy and cost him both his dream and his health. At the same time, these four factors helped Lutheranism survive. They gave Lutherans time to organize before having to face the armies of the Catholic forces.

The chief political concern of Charles V was his rivalry with the king of France, Francis I. Their conflict over disputed territories in a number of areas led to a series of wars that lasted more than twenty years. At the same time, Charles faced opposition from Pope Clement VII, who, guided by political considerations, joined the side of the French king. The advance of the Ottoman Turks (see Chapter 17) into the eastern part

▲ *This picture shows the coat of arms of Charles V, the Holy Roman emperor and king of Spain. Charles V abdicated in 1555, granting most of the Habsburg lands to his son Philip. What do you think the two-headed eagle in his coat of arms represents?*

of Charles's empire forced the emperor to send forces there as well.

Finally, the internal political situation in the Holy Roman Empire was also not in Charles's favor. Germany was a land of several hundred territorial states. Although all owed loyalty to the emperor, Germany's development in the Middle Ages had enabled these states to free themselves from imperial authority. They had no desire to have a strong emperor. By the time Charles V was able to bring military forces to Germany, the Lutheran princes were well organized. Unable to defeat them, Charles was forced to seek peace. An end to religious warfare in Germany came in 1555 with the Peace of Augsburg. The division of Christianity was formally accepted; Lutheran states were to have the same legal rights as Catholic states. Although the German states were now free to choose between Catholicism and Lutheranism, the peace settlement did not

STUDYING MAPS

The Holy Roman Empire spread over most of Europe and covered an immense amount of territory.

Have students work in pairs to create their own maps of the Holy Roman Empire ruled by Charles V. Students need to understand how large this empire was in relation to the rest of Europe. When students have finished their maps, have them compare the size of the Holy Roman Empire to their state and to the United States. This assignment could be used as optional extra credit.

ASSESS

Answers to
SECTION REVIEW

1. (a) holding many church offices
(b) refers to problem of church officers who ignored their duties

2. (a) led the split with the Catholic Church in Germany
(b) a wandering monk, believed that Christianity should show people how to live good lives
(c) declared Martin Luther an outlaw within the Holy Roman Empire
(d) head of the Habsburg dynasty and of the Holy Roman Empire
(e) signed in 1555, formally ended religious wars in Germany

3. (a) humans attain salvation through their faith in God alone
(b) the state controls the affairs of the church
(c) selling indulgences; the concern of the clergy with political affairs; preoccupation with raising revenues; lack of interest in the common people

4. issued as a reform call to the Catholic Church; gave rise to the spread of separate religious reform movements and to the breakdown of religious unity in Europe

CLOSE

Review Martin Luther's split with the Catholic Church. Do students believe that it led to the destruction of European religious unity?

---

recognize the principle of religious toleration for individuals. The right of each German ruler to determine the religion of his subjects was accepted, but not the right of the subjects to choose their own religion.

 SECTION REVIEW

1. **Define:**
   (a) pluralism,   (b) absenteeism

2. **Identify:**
   (a) Martin Luther,   (b) Desiderius Erasmus,
   (c) Edict of Worms,   (d) Charles V,   (e) The Peace of Augsburg

3. **Recall:**
   (a) Explain what is meant by justification by grace through faith alone.
   (b) What is meant by the term *state church?*
   (c) List three major areas of corruption within the Catholic Church that led to the Reformation.

4. **Think Critically:** Discuss the consequences of Luther's Ninety-Five Theses.

4

THE SPREAD OF THE PROTESTANT REFORMATION AND THE CATHOLIC RESPONSE

The Peace of Augsburg was a victory for the German princes. The freedom of the numerous German states guaranteed the weakness of the Holy Roman Empire. Charles's hope for a united empire had been completely dashed. At the same time, what had at first been merely feared was now certain: the ideal of Christian unity was forever lost. The rapid spread of new Protestant groups made this a certainty.

The Reformation in Switzerland

Switzerland was home to two major Reformation movements, Zwinglianism and Calvinism. Ulrich Zwingli (ZWING-glee) was a priest in Zürich (ZUR-ik), where his preaching of the gospel caused such unrest that the city council in 1523 held a public debate between Zwingli's supporters and the Catholics in the town hall. City leaders declared Zwingli's party the victor. In response, over the next two years the city council, strongly influenced by Zwingli, introduced religious reforms in Zürich. Relics and images were abolished. All paintings and decorations were removed from the churches and replaced by whitewashed walls. The mass was replaced by a new service consisting of scripture reading, prayer, and sermons. Monasticism, pilgrimages, the veneration of saints, and the pope's authority were all abolished.

As his movement began to spread to other cities in Switzerland, Zwingli sought an alliance with Martin Luther and the German reformers. Both the German and Swiss reformers realized the need for unity to defend themselves against Catholic authorities, but they were unable to agree on the meaning of the sacrament of the Lord's Supper (see "You Are There: A Reformation Debate"). Zwingli believed that the Bible's words, "This is my Body, This is my blood" should not be taken literally. He refused to accept Luther's belief in the real presence of the body and blood of Christ in the sacrament of the Lord's Supper.

In October 1531, war broke out between the Protestant and Catholic states in Switzerland. Zürich's army was routed, and Zwingli was found wounded on the battlefield. His enemies killed him; cut up his body; and burned the pieces, scattering the ashes. The leadership of Swiss Protestantism then passed to John Calvin.

Calvin was educated in his native France. After his conversion to Protestantism, however, he was forced to flee Catholic France for the safety of Switzerland. He wrote the *Institutes of the Christian Religion,* a summary of Protestant thought that immediately gave Calvin his reputation as one of the new leaders of Protestantism.

On most important doctrines, Calvin stood very close to Luther. He, too, believed in the doctrine of justification by faith alone to explain how humans achieved salvation. However, Calvin also placed much emphasis on the absolute sovereignty of God or the all-

---

On Line with
WORLD HISTORY *Internet Activity*

You may want to have your students visit the following URL, where they will find information and additional web site resources to enhance their study of this chapter.

Martin Luther—A Biography
http://www.geocities.com/Vienna/1667/luther.htm

This is an interesting site because it also includes Midi files of his music.

Due to the ever-changing nature of the World Wide Web, see the West History web site, **http://history.swpco.com** for regular updates of the URLs in this text.

YOU ARE THERE

A Reformation Debate

◄ *This portrait of Martin Luther was painted in 1529, the same year that the debate with Zwingli occurred. By this time Martin Luther was married and had children, but he was still an active voice in the Reformation.*

Debates played an important role in the Reformation, frequently resolving differences among like-minded Protestant groups.

The following selection contains an excerpt from a debate between Martin Luther and Ulrich Zwingli over the sacrament of the Lord's Supper. This often brutal debate occurred at Marburg, Germany, in 1529. The two opponents in this debate failed to reach agreement.

Excerpt from Martin Luther and Ulrich Zwingli Debate

CHANCELLOR FEIGE: My gracious prince and lord [Landgrave Philip of Hesse] has summoned you for the express and urgent purpose of settling the dispute over the sacrament of the Lord's Supper. . . . And let everyone on both sides present his arguments in a spirit of moderation, as becomes such matters. . . . Now then, Doctor Luther, you may proceed.

LUTHER: Noble prince, gracious lord! Although I have no intention of changing my mind, which is firmly made up, I will nevertheless present the grounds of my belief and show where the others are in error. . . . Your basic contentions are these: In the last analysis you wish to prove that a body cannot be in two places at once, and you produce

◄ *This portrait of Ulrich Zwingli, who began the Reformation in Switzerland, was done in 1531. Why do you think his ideas spread so quickly throughout Switzerland?*

arguments about the unlimited body which are based on natural reason. I do not question how Christ can be God and man and how the two natures can be joined. For God is more powerful than all our ideas, and we must submit to his word.

Prove that Christ's body is not there where the Scripture says, "This is my body!" God is beyond all mathematics and the words of God are to be revered and carried out in awe. It is God who commands, "Take, eat, this is my body." I request, therefore, valid scriptural proof to the contrary.

Luther writes on the table in chalk, "This is my body," and covers the words with a velvet cloth.

ZWINGLI: I insist that the words of the Lord's Supper must be figurative. This is ever apparent, and even required by the article of faith; "taken up into heaven, seated at the right hand of the Father." Otherwise, it would be absurd to look for him in the Lord's Supper at the same time that Christ is telling us that he is in heaven. One and the same body cannot possibly be in different places. . . .

LUTHER: I call upon you as before: your basic contentions are shaky. Give way, and give glory to God!

(continued)

RECOMMENDED READING

The best account of Ulrich Zwingli is G. R. Potter, *Zwingli* (Cambridge, 1976). One aspect of the spread of the Reformation in Switzerland is examined in J. M. Kittelson, *Wolfgang Capito: From Humanist to Reformer* (Leiden, 1975).

The most comprehensive account of the various groups and individuals who are called Anabaptists is G. H. Williams, *The Radical Reformation* (Philadelphia, 1962). Other

valuable studies include C.-P. Clasen, *Anabaptism: A Social History, 1525–1618* (Ithaca, N.Y., 1972); and C. Krahn, *Dutch Anabaptism: Origin, Spread, Life and Thought, 1450–1600* (The Hague, 1968).

Two worthwhile surveys of the English Reformation are A. G. Dickens, *The English Reformation* (New York, 1964); and G. R. Elton, *Reform and Reformation: England, 1509–1558* (Cambridge, Mass., 1977).

FOCUS

OBJECTIVES

After completing this section, students should be able to

1. describe the Reformation movement in Switzerland
2. identify reasons for religious changes in England
3. explain the changes sought by the Anabaptists
4. identify the three reform pillars within the Catholic Church

FOCUS ACTIVITY

Have students brainstorm to compile a list of the religions and religious denominations that exist within their own community. Students may know that each Protestant denomination is slightly different in either its doctrine or organization, but that all the Protestant denominations are rooted in the Reform movement that swept through Europe in the sixteenth century.

TEACH

CLASS DISCUSSION

Guide students in a discussion concerning the debate between Ulrich Zwingli and the Catholic Church officials that took place in Geneva. Could such a debate take place in city council chambers in the United States? Why or why not?

YOU ARE THERE

USING PRIMARY SOURCES

Have students work in pairs to reread this excerpt carefully. At what point do they feel reason gives way to anger or contempt? Compare this exchange to recent political debates. Are current debates more about substantive issues, or are they just about catchy phrases and catching one's opponent off guard?

LEARNING FROM VISUALS

Answer to the caption question: Answers will vary.

ANSWERS TO CRITICAL THINKING QUESTIONS

1. Debates were often used to resolve differences among Protestant groups.
2. No conclusion was reached.

REINFORCING VOCABULARY

Students may not understand the terms *laity* and *doctrine.* Lay church leaders do not belong to the clergy; doctrine are principles that serve as a basis for governing a particular denomination.

CRITICAL THINKING

Have students explain why religious issues could be openly discussed by Swiss citizens. Students should understand that for most Europeans, there was little actual choice in religion; it was what the monarch or state dictated it would be.

YOU ARE THERE

A Reformation Debate, continued

ZWINGLI: And we call upon you to give glory to God and to quit begging the question! The issue at stake is this: Where is the proof of your position? I am willing to consider your words carefully—no harm meant! You're trying to outwit me. I stand by this passage in the sixth chapter of John, verse 63 and shall not be shaken from it. You'll have to sing another tune. . . .

LUTHER: You're trying to dominate things! You insist on passing judgment! Leave that to someone else! . . . It is your point that must be proved, not mine. But let us stop this sort of thing. It serves no purpose.

ZWINGLI: It certainly does! It is for you to prove that the passage in John 6 speaks of a physical meal.

LUTHER: You express yourself poorly and make about as much progress as a cane standing in a corner. You're going nowhere.

ZWINGLI: No, no, no! This is the passage that will break your neck!

LUTHER: Don't be so sure of yourself. Necks don't break this way. You're in Germany, not Switzerland.

1. What was one role the debate played in the Reformation?
2. Was a conclusion arrived at in the debate presented here?

powerful nature of God—what Calvin called the "power, grace, and glory of God."

Calvin's emphasis on the all-powerful nature of God led him to other ideas. One of these ideas was **predestination.** This "eternal decree," as Calvin called it, meant that God had predestined some people to be saved (the elect) and others to be damned (the reprobate). According to Calvin, "He has once for all determined, both whom he would admit to salvation, and whom he would condemn to destruction." Although Calvin stressed that no one could ever be absolutely certain of salvation, his followers did not always heed this warning. The practical effect of the belief in predestination was to give later Calvinists the firm conviction that they were doing God's work on Earth. This conviction, in turn, made them determined to spread their faith to other people. Calvinism became a dynamic and activist faith.

In 1536, Calvin began working to reform the city of Geneva. He created a church government that used both clergy and laity in the service of the church. The Consistory, a special body for enforcing moral discipline, was set up as a court to oversee the moral life and doctrinal purity of Genevans. The Consistory had the right to punish people who deviated from the church's teachings and moral principles. Citizens in Geneva were punished for such varied "crimes" as dancing, singing obscene songs, drunkenness, swearing, and playing cards.

Calvin's success in Geneva made the city a powerful center of Protestantism. John Knox (NOCKS), the Calvinist reformer of Scotland, called Geneva "the most perfect school of Christ on earth." Following Calvin's lead, missionaries trained in Geneva were sent to all parts of Europe. Calvinism became established in France, the Netherlands, Scotland, and central and eastern Europe. By the mid-sixteenth century, Calvinism had replaced Lutheranism as the most important and dynamic form of Protestantism. Calvin's Geneva stood as the fortress of the Protestant Reformation.

CNN WORLD HISTORY UPDATES

You can update your coverage of World History topics, as well as spark lively classroom discussion and deeper understanding, by using the **CNN World History Updates.**

For assistance in using and incorporating the **CNN World History Updates** into your classroom presentations, see the *Classroom Guide.*

▲ *This portrait of John Calvin was done in 1564, almost thirty years after his work had begun in Geneva and shortly before his death. What character attributes does the artist give to Calvin in this painting?*

The Reformation in England

The English Reformation was rooted in politics, not religion. King Henry VIII had a strong desire to divorce his first wife, Catherine of Aragon, with whom the king had a daughter, Mary, but no male heir. He wanted to marry Anne Boleyn (buh-LIN), with whom the king had fallen in love. Normally, church authorities would grant the king an annulment of his marriage. There was a problem in this case, however. The pope was dependent upon the Holy Roman emperor, Charles V, who happened to be the nephew of Queen Catherine. Unhappy with the pope's lack of action, Henry tried to get an annulment of his marriage in England's own church courts. Acting under pressure, the archbishop of Canterbury, head of the highest church court in England, held official hearings on the king's case and ruled in May 1533 that the king's marriage to Catherine was "null and absolutely void." At the beginning of June, Anne was crowned queen. Three months later a child was born. Much to the king's disappointment, the baby was a girl, the future queen Elizabeth I.

In 1534, upon Henry's request, Parliament moved to make final the break of the Church of England with Rome. The Act of Supremacy of 1534 declared that the king was "taken, accepted, and reputed the only supreme head on earth of the Church of England." This position gave the king control of doctrine, clerical appointments, and discipline. Using his new powers, Henry dissolved the monasteries. About four hundred religious houses were closed, and their land and possessions were taken by the king. Many were sold to wealthy landowners and merchants. The king received a great boost to his treasury. He also had a group of supporters who now had a stake in the new order.

Although Henry VIII had broken with the papacy, little change occurred in matters of doctrine, theology, or ceremony. Henry wanted no more changes, and the last ten years of his reign were taken up with his efforts to find the perfect wife. Henry had soon tired of Anne Boleyn and had her beheaded on a charge of adultery. His third wife, Jane Seymour, produced the long-awaited male heir but died during childbirth. His fourth marriage, to a German princess, Anne of Cleves, was arranged for political reasons and on the basis of a painted portrait. Henry was shocked at her actual looks when he first saw her in person and soon divorced her. His fifth wife, Catherine Howard, was more attractive but less moral. When she committed adultery, Henry had her beheaded. His last wife was Catherine Parr, who outlived him. Henry was succeeded by the nine-year-old, sickly Edward VI, the son of his third wife.

So What ??

*If your students question the importance of information about **the English Reformation**, tell them . . .*

the decisions made by King Henry VIII are still affecting Ireland's relations with England. Historically, their relations have not been good. The Irish, most of whom were Catholic, were angered by England's political and commercial domination. In the 17th century Oliver Cromwell identified Catholicism with sedition and savagely crushed a rebellion, leaving a continuing troubled legacy. This, coupled with the 19th century potato famine, led to the death of almost 1.5 million people, and another million emigrated to the U.S. and Great Britain. In the 20th century, Britain granted Ireland full autonomy, but retained Northern Ireland. In the 1990s dialog began between the British government and the Irish Republican Army (IRA), but the problems continue.

CLASS DISCUSSION

Review with students Henry VIII's decision to create a different church in England. Discuss the reasons that his daughter, Mary, intended to restore the Catholic Church as the only church in England. Solicit input from the students on their reaction to Mary's motives.

REINFORCING VOCABULARY

Review with students the prefix "ana," which means *again.* For the Anabaptists, it meant that people should be baptized again, this time when they had reached adulthood, and after they had made a public commitment to Christ.

▲ *Henry VIII, Jane Seymour, and Prince Edward, who became king in 1547, are shown in the center of this painting. On the far left is Princess Mary, who became known as "Bloody Mary," and on the far right is Princess Elizabeth, who later became Queen Elizabeth I.*

During Edward's reign, church officials who favored Protestant doctrines moved the Church of England (or the Anglican Church) in more of a Protestant direction. New acts of Parliament gave the clergy the right to marry and created a new Protestant church service. These rapid changes, however, aroused much opposition. When Mary, Henry's first daughter by Catherine of Aragon, came to the throne, England was ready for a reaction.

There was no doubt that Mary was a Catholic who wanted to restore England to Roman Catholicism. However, the way she went about it aroused much opposition. There was widespread dislike of her husband, Philip II, the son of Charles V and future king of Spain. The burning of over three hundred Protestant heretics caused further anger against "Bloody Mary." As a result of her policies, Mary managed to achieve the opposite of what she had intended. England was even more Protestant by the end of her reign than it had been at the beginning.

The Anabaptists

Reformers such as Luther had allowed the state to play an important, if not dominant, role in church affairs. However, some people strongly disliked giving such power to the state. They favored a far different kind of reform movement. These radicals were known as the Anabaptists. Anabaptism was especially attractive to those peasants, weavers, miners, and artisans who had suffered from the economic changes of the age.

Anabaptists everywhere shared some common ideas. To them, the true Christian Church was a voluntary community of believers who had undergone spiritual rebirth and had then been baptized into the church. Thus, Anabaptists favored adult rather than infant baptism. They also believed in following the practices and the spirit of early Christianity. They considered all believers to be equal, a belief they based on the accounts of early Christian communities in the New Testament. Each church chose its own minister. Any male member

SPECIAL NEEDS: *Visual*

Create a stack of 3 × 5 cards with major events from 1400–1600 written on them. Events should include the Renaissance, humanism, Martin Luther's challenge, the rise of Calvinism, Catholicism and various sub-events and details. Copy the cards, so that you have 1 set for each group of four students in your class.

Ask groups to arrange the cards in sequential order. Mix up the cards again.

Have a race to see which group can place the cards in correct order. The cards can also be used for quizzing in pairs, or for fastening to the desktop for use by physically impaired students. The cards may be used by students who need repetition and for self-study. This activity is helpful for students who benefit from visual aids, practice in sequencing, or have difficulty with reading comprehension.

CONNECTIONS
TO OUR WORLD

The Descendants of the Anabaptists   Because of their belief in the complete separation of church and state, Anabaptists were viewed by other Protestant groups and Catholics as radicals who deserved to be persecuted. Despite the persecution, however, Anabaptists managed to survive. Menno Simons was a popular leader of Anabaptism in the Netherlands. He dedicated his life to the spread of a peaceful Anabaptism that stressed separation from the world in order to live a truly Christ-like life. Because of persecution, the Dutch Mennonites, as Menno Simon's followers were called, spread from the Netherlands into Germany and Russia. In the nineteenth century, many moved to Canada and the United States, where Mennonite communities continue to flourish.

In the 1690s, Jacob Ammann took the lead in encouraging a group of Swiss Mennonites to form their own church. They came to be known as the Amish (after the name Ammann). By the end of the seventeenth century, many of the Amish came to North America in search of a land where they could practice their religion freely. Today, Amish communities exist throughout Canada and the United States. One of the largest groups of Amish can be found in Pennsylvania, where they are known as the Pennsylvania Dutch. The Amish continue to maintain the Anabaptist way of life as it first developed in the sixteenth century. They live simple lives and refuse to make use of any modern devices, including cars and electricity.

of the community was eligible, because all Christians were considered priests (though women were often excluded).

Finally, most Anabaptists believed in the complete separation of church and state. Not only was government to be kept out of the realm of religion, it was not even supposed to have any political authority over real Christians. A ruler of a country might be said to be ordained by God, but true Christians did not accept

that. Anabaptists refused to hold political office or bear arms, because many took literally the biblical commandment "Thou shall not kill." Their political beliefs, as much as their religious beliefs, caused the Anabaptists to be regarded as dangerous radicals who threatened the very fabric of sixteenth-century society. Indeed, the chief thing Protestants and Catholics could agree on was the need to persecute Anabaptists.

The Social Impact of the Protestant Reformation

The Protestants were especially important in developing a new view of the family. Because Protestantism had eliminated any idea of special holiness for celibacy and had abolished both monasticism and a celibate clergy, the family could be placed at the center of human life. The "mutual love between man and wife" could be extolled.

Were idea and reality the same, however? For more radical religious groups, at times they were. One Anabaptist wrote to his wife before his execution: "My faithful helper, my loyal friend. I praise God that he gave you to me, you who have sustained me in all my trial."[7] More often, however, reality reflected the traditional roles of husband as the ruler and wife as the obedient servant whose chief duty was to please her husband. Luther stated it clearly:

The rule remains with the husband, and the wife is compelled to obey him by God's command. He rules the home and the state, wages war, defends his possessions, tills the soil, builds, plants, etc. The woman on the other hand is like a nail driven into the wall . . . so the wife should stay at home and look after the affairs of the household, as one who has been deprived of the ability of administering those affairs that are outside and that concern the state. She does not go beyond her most personal duties.[8]

Obedience to her husband was not a woman's only role. Her other important duty was to bear children. To Calvin and Luther, this function of women was part of the divine plan. Although Protestantism viewed the role of a woman as mother and wife as being a holy vocation, the view left few alternatives for women. Because monasticism had been destroyed, even that

CONNECTIONS
TO OUR WORLD

Encourage students to discuss their thoughts on why people are willing to live today as the Amish in Pennsylvania live (without modern conveniences). Have students make a list of modern conveniences they would have to give up to live as the Amish do *(automobiles, electric hair dryers, television, radio, computers, etc.)* Ask students if they believe as strongly in any cause.

COMPARING TIME PERIODS

Have students read Luther's statement concerning the role of women. Ask them to compare it with the Islamic view of the role of women. Why has the Western view of this role changed, while the Islamic view has remained fairly constant?

MORE ABOUT . . . *the Amish*

The Mennonites, a religious group that includes the Amish, descended from the European Anabaptists. Mennonites refused to serve in state offices, as police officers, or in the military services. Due to persecution in Europe, they emigrated to the American colonies and in 1683 settled in Pennsylvania. There are several branches of Mennonites in the United States and Canada; the Old Mennonite Church is the largest. The Amish, or Mennonites, fasten their clothes with hooks, not buttons, which they consider fanciful adornments. Worship is conducted in private homes, and they still speak a German-English dialect. Most Mennonites live in Pennsylvania, Ohio, Indiana, and Kansas, as well as in Canada.

CLASS DISCUSSION

The author states that for Protestant women, "family life was their only destiny." Were the roles for Catholic women different? If so, in what ways?

Multimedia Support

TRANSPARENCY

14–3, Reformation of Europe c. 1550 (Map 14.2)

ACTIVITY

Ask the students to prepare a chart of religions and Protestant groups that existed in Europe during the Reformation. They should identify either belief, teachings, or actions of each of the religious faiths, then indicate their areas of influence. You may want to provide students with the blank chart contained in your Resource materials.

Map 14.2 Reformation Europe, c. 1550

	Anglican		Roman Catholic
Calvinist		Lutheran
Calvinist influenced		Lutheran influenced
Holy Roman Empire boundary	+	Radical religious sects (Anabaptists)

path was no longer available. For most Protestant women, family life was their only destiny. Overall, the Protestant Reformation did not change women's subordinate place in society.

The attacks of Protestant reformers on the Catholic Church created radical changes in religious practices.

The Protestant Reformation abolished such practices as indulgences, the veneration of relics and saints, pilgrimages, monasticism, and clerical celibacy. The elimination of saints put an end to the many celebrations of religious holy days. In Protestant communities, religious ceremonies, with their processions and statues, were

STUDYING MAPS

The following questions will help you guide the students through their study of Map 14.2.

1. How does this map compare to the map students created earlier of the Holy Roman Empire? What has changed and what has remained the same?

2. If students were to prepare a religious map of Europe today, what might it look

like? Would it be similar to this one? How would it differ?

3. Would it be possible to prepare a religious map of the United States at the present time? Would it have been possible to create a religious map of the colonial period? What would such maps look like? What would they reveal about our culture?

◄ *Ignatius Loyola, founder of the Society of Jesus, is shown here kneeling before Pope Paul III, who officially recognized the Jesuits in 1540. What accomplishments are the Jesuits most known for in the United States?*

replaced by private prayer, family worship, and group prayer and worship at the same time each Sunday.

In addition to abolishing saints' days, some Protestant reformers even tried to eliminate traditional games, plays, and holy days altogether. English Puritans (as English Calvinists were known), for example, attempted to ban card playing, drinking in taverns, and dancing. Dutch Calvinists attacked the tradition of giving small presents to children on the feast of Saint Nicholas, near Christmas. Indeed, the English Puritan leader Oliver Cromwell even tried to outlaw the celebration of Christmas. Some of these Protestant attacks on popular culture failed outright. The importance of taverns in English social life made it impossible to get rid of them. Gift giving and feasting at Christmas continued in both the Dutch Netherlands and England.

The Catholic Reformation

By the mid-sixteenth century, Lutheranism had become rooted in Germany and Scandinavia, and Calvinism had taken hold in Switzerland, France, the Netherlands, and eastern Europe. In England, the split from Rome had resulted in the creation of a national church. The situation in Europe did not look particularly good for the Catholic Church. However, the Catholic Church also had a revitalization in the sixteenth century, giving it new strength and enabling it to regain much that it had lost. There were three chief pillars of this Catholic Reformation: the Jesuits (JEZZ-hu-whutz), a reformed papacy, and the Council of Trent.

The Society of Jesus, whose members are known as the Jesuits, was founded by a Spanish nobleman, Ignatius (ig-NAE-shee-us) of Loyola. Loyola's injuries in battle cut short his military career. He experienced a spiritual struggle similar to Luther's but resolved his problems in a different way. Loyola's solution was not a new doctrine but a decision to submit his will to the will of the church. Indeed, Loyola stressed the need for absolute obedience to the church: "If we wish to proceed securely in all things," he said, "we must hold fast

(continued, page 448)

MORE ABOUT . . . *the Council of Trent*

There arose a party of reforming cardinals who believed that reform of the Catholic Church was so urgent that it must be risked. The Pope summoned a council in 1537, but the wars between France and the Holy Roman Empire forced its abandonment. Then a council was called for 1542 but no one came except a few Italians so it was canceled. Finally in 1545 the council did assemble and begin operations. It met at Trent on the border of Germany and Italy. It met at irregular intervals for almost twenty years in 1545–1547, 1551–1552 and 1562–1563. Attendance at the council was also sporadic. It fell as low as twenty or thirty and on the important decree of "justification," the prime issue raised by Luther, only 60 church leaders were there.

Have students describe the consequence of the reformed papacy and the Council of Trent on the future of the Catholic church throughout the world.

ASSESS

You can choose from a variety of assessments to evaluate your students' mastery of the objectives as stated on page 441.

Answer to
SECTION REVIEW

2. (a) the idea that God has decided who will be saved, who will not

3. (a) a Swiss priest, introduced religious reform in Zurich
   (b) Protestant reformer, believed in predestination and the all-powerful nature of God
   (c) foremost Calvinist reformer in Scotland
   (d) King of England, had himself named head of the Church of England
   (e) founded the Jesuits

4. (a) reform in continental Europe began for spiritual reasons; English reformation was due to the desire of the king to divorce his wife and remarry
   (b) The Anabaptists believed in complete separation of church and state.
   (c) Loyola established a new teaching order, the Jesuits; Pope Paul III took steps to reform the papacy and the clergy; the Council of Trent reestablished traditional Catholic teachings.

5. Answers will vary.

to the following principle: What seems to me white, I will believe black if the Church so defines."

Gradually, Loyola gathered together a small group of people who shared his single-minded devotion. They were eventually recognized as a religious order by the pope in 1540. All Jesuits took a special vow of absolute obedience to the pope, making them an important instrument for papal policy. Jesuits used education to spread their message and were dedicated to engaging in "conflict for God." Jesuit missionaries were very successful in restoring Catholicism to parts of Germany and eastern Europe, as well as in spreading it to other parts of the world.

A reformed papacy was another important factor in the Catholic Reformation. The participation of Renaissance popes in dubious financial transactions and Italian political and military affairs had created many sources of corruption. It took the jolt of the Protestant Reformation to bring about serious reform. Pope Paul III perceived the need for change and took the bold step of appointing a Reform Commission to determine the church's ills. The commission's report in 1537 blamed the church's problems on the corrupt policies of popes and cardinals. It was also Paul III who recognized the Jesuits as a new religious order and who began the Council of Trent, the third major pillar of the Catholic Reformation.

In March 1545, a group of cardinals, archbishops, bishops, abbots, and theologians met in the city of Trent, on the border between Germany and Italy. There they began the Council of Trent, which met off and on for eighteen years in three major sessions. Moderate Catholic reformers hoped that compromises would be made that would encourage Protestants to return to the church. Conservatives, however, wanted only to restate traditional Catholic teachings in strict opposition to Protestant positions.

The conservatives won. The final decrees of the Council of Trent reaffirmed traditional Catholic teachings in opposition to Protestant beliefs. Both faith and good works were declared necessary for salvation. The seven sacraments, the Catholic view of the Lord's Supper, and clerical celibacy were all upheld. Belief in purgatory and in the use of indulgences was strengthened, although the selling of indulgences was forbidden.

After the Council of Trent, the Roman Catholic Church possessed a clear body of doctrine and was a unified church under the supreme leadership of the pope. The Roman Catholic Church had become one Christian group among many. With a new spirit of confidence, the Catholic Church entered a new phase, as well prepared as the Calvinists to do battle for the Lord.

SECTION REVIEW

1. **Locate:**
   (a) Zürich,   (b) Geneva,   (c) Trent

2. **Define:**
   (a) predestination

3. **Identify:**
   (a) Ulrich Zwingli,   (b) John Calvin,   (c) John Knox,   (d) Henry VIII,   (e) Ignatius of Loyola

4. **Recall:**
   (a) How did the English Reformation differ from the reformation movement in continental Europe?
   (b) How did the beliefs of the Anabaptists differ from those of other Protestants and Catholics?
   (c) Discuss three major changes that contributed to the Catholic Reformation.

5. **Think Critically:** During the Reformation, many new Protestant groups came into being. Does this occur today? Explain your answer and provide examples to support your argument.

Conclusion

Between 1350 and 1550, Italian intellectuals believed that they were living in a new age. This new age, based on a rebirth of the culture of the Greeks and Romans, came to be known as the Renaissance. The Renaissance, which began in Italy, was a period of transition as well as a continuation of the economic, political, and social trends that had begun in the High Middle Ages. It was also a new age in which intellectuals and artists proclaimed a new vision of humankind and

MORE ABOUT . . . *the Council of Trent (con't.)*

In addition to its declaration of justification by a combination of works and faith, the Vulgate, a translation of the Bible into Latin was declared to be the only version on which authoritative teaching could be based. In practical matters the council acted against

the abuse of indulgences, ruled that Church leaders should reside in their dioceses, and ordered that a seminary should be set up in each diocese for the education and training of priests.

raised fundamental questions about the value and importance of the individual. Of course, intellectuals and artists wrote and painted for the upper classes. The brilliant intellectual, cultural, and artistic accomplishments of the Renaissance were really products of and for the elite. The ideas of the Renaissance did not have a broad base among the masses of the people.

The Renaissance, however, did raise new questions about medieval traditions. In advocating a return to the early sources of Christianity and criticizing current religious practices, the humanists aroused fundamental concerns about the Catholic Church, which was still an important institution. In the sixteenth century, the intellectual revolution of the fifteenth century gave way to a religious renaissance that touched the lives of people, including the masses, in new and profound ways.

The movement began when Martin Luther challenged the Catholic Church's hawking of indulgences, and his ideas quickly spread across Europe. Within a short time, new Protestant churches were attracting supporters all over Europe. Although seemingly helpless to stop the new churches, the Catholic Church also underwent a religious rebirth and managed to revive its fortunes. By the mid-sixteenth century, the religious division had produced two militant faiths—

Calvinism and Catholicism—that were prepared to do combat for the souls of the faithful. An age of religious passion would soon be followed by an age of religious warfare.

Notes

1. Baldassare Castiglione, *The Book of the Courtier*, trans. Charles S. Singleton (Garden City, New York, 1959), pp. 288–289.
2. Quoted in De Lamar Jensen, *Renaissance Europe* (Lexington, Mass., 1981), p. 94.
3. W. H. Woodward, *Vittorino da Feltre and Other Humanist Educators* (Cambridge, 1897), p. 102.
4. Quoted in Iris Origo, "The Education of Renaissance Man," in *The Light of the Past* (New York, 1959), p. 136.
5. Quoted in Elizabeth G. Holt, ed., *A Documentary History of Art* (Garden City, N.Y., 1957), vol. 1, p. 286.
6. Quoted in Roland Bainton, *Here I Stand: A Life of Martin Luther* (New York, 1950), p. 144.
7. Quoted in Roland Bainton, *Women of the Reformation in Germany and Italy* (Boston, 1971), p. 154.
8. Quoted in Bonnie S. Anderson and Judith P. Zinsser, *A History of Their Own: Women in Europe from Prehistory to the Present* (New York, 1988), vol. 1, p. 259.

Answers to CHAPTER REVIEW   14

USING KEY TERMS

1. absenteeism
2. dowry
3. predestination
4. urban society
5. frescoes
6. condottiere
7. humanism
8. secular
9. pluralism

REVIEWING THE FACTS

1. Greece and Rome
2. silk, sugar, spices
3. the de'Medici family
4. the clergy, the nobility, and the third estate
5. Geoffrey Chaucer
6. in a three-dimensional way with an emphasis on proportion, beauty, and the realistic human form
7. showing people how to lead good lives on a daily basis
8. good works
9. the Bible, not the teachings of popes or church councils
10. Territorial disputes; the pope who joined the French king against Charles; the Turks who were advancing into Austria and Hungary; and Germany's internal situation—there was no united Germany that was easy to control
11. 1455
12. over the meaning of the Eucharist
13. When the pope would not allow Henry to divorce his first wife (Catherine of Aragon, the aunt of Charles V), Henry had Parliament decree the king as head of the church in England.
14. A greater emphasis was put on the family; also a new stress on "mutual love between man and wife;" Luther said "the rule remains with the husband, and the wife is compelled to obey him by God's command." Convents were abolished.
15. It made it easier to spread the views of Protestants; for example, Luther's 95 Theses

gained a wider audience; literacy spread so more people were able to read the Bible for themselves.

THINKING CRITICALLY

1. Some students are likely to say that people are often liars and deceivers. Discussions of politicians are likely to come up. The perceived differences between males and females will be of interest.
2. Americans want many government services but hate taxes. Guide students to an understanding of the difficulty elected officials have in meeting the needs of their various constituencies.
3. Begin by trying to define virtue and wisdom. What value do they have in American society? What is the relation between these things and financial success today? (Probably not much). This is the perfect time to present a defense of a liberal arts education for college bound students. Also, this is a time to present a rationale for the study of the history.
4. Reform from within is usually slow and seldom completely successful to the eye of the reformer. Erasmus failed, Luther succeeded. Reform from without often causes great changes and once started is difficult to stop. War is a frequent result. The American Civil War and the issue of slavery is another situation to consider.
5. Anabaptists challenged the authority of the state. Luther had the German princes on his side; Calvin came close to establishing a theocracy in Geneva. Luther was radical in challenging the church, but had traditional views about government, religion, and just about everything else. The Anabaptists were really calling for a radical reordering of all aspects of society, a completely new way of life. The Anabaptists came the closest to actually practicing equality. Their views on women were centuries ahead of their times. Their refusal to

450

USING KEY TERMS

1. _____ resulted when church leaders ignored their duties and paid subordinates to run their offices.
2. The money and goods given by the wife's family at the time of marriage is a _____.
3. John Calvin emphasized _____, the belief that God chose who would be saved and who would be damned.
4. A(n) _____ is one in which a great many people live in cities.
5. Images painted on fresh, wet plaster are called _____
6. The leader of a band of Renaissance mercenaries was called a _____.
7. The study of grammar, rhetoric, moral philosophy, and history were the basis of the intellectual movement called _____.
8. A(n) _____ society places less emphasis on religion and more emphasis on a worldly spirit.
9. _____ refers to the holding of more than one church office.

REVIEWING THE FACTS

1. The Renaissance was a rebirth in the ideas of which ancient civilizations?
2. What goods did the Europeans import from Asia?
3. Which family dominated Florence during the Renaissance?
4. What were the three major social classes of the European Middle Ages?
5. Who was the author of the *Canterbury Tales*?
6. How did Renaissance artists portray the human body?
7. According to Erasmus, what should be the chief concerns of the Christian Church?
8. According to Catholics, what is necessary for salvation besides faith?

450

9. In his response to Charles V at Worms, what did Luther say was the sole basis for Christian beliefs?
10. What were the four challenges faced by Charles V in keeping his empire strong and united?
11. About when did Gutenberg print his Bible with movable print?
12. Over what issue did Luther and Zwingli disagree?
13. How did politics and religion mix in England under Henry VIII?
14. What impact did the Protestant Reformation have on women?
15. What impact did the printing press have on the Reformation?

THINKING CRITICALLY

1. When do the ends justify the means? For Machiavelli it was simply a matter of doing whatever was expedient, but he believed a ruler had to do so because of human failings. Machiavelli said that in general men are ungrateful, fickle, liars, and deceivers who shun danger and are greedy for profit. Is he correct? If you disagree, choose five characteristics that you think describe people. Do you lump all people together or do you have a different list to describe men and women?
2. Machiavelli said that people were fickle. Are today's American voters fickle?
3. Italian humanists thought that the primary goal of education is to attain and practice virtue and wisdom. What do you see as the primary goal of your high school education?
4. Erasmus believed that reform is best coming from within an institution without overthrowing it. Luther called for more drastic action. How do you think reform is best accomplished?
5. Why were the Anabaptists the most radical of all Christians?
6. Isabella d'Este chose to protect her son rather than risk losing him to free her husband. Why do you

fight in wars was unheard of. All such groups that threaten the established order are likely to come under fire.
6. Basic maternal instinct is one possibility. The historical reason is probably rooted in the fact that her marriage was arranged and not motivated by love.

APPLYING SOCIAL STUDIES SKILLS

1. Basically, the Portuguese cut out the middlemen.
2. A few noblewomen such as Isabelle d'Este had some power, but this situation was rare. There was probably not a "Renaissance" for women, although there is some scholarly debate about

the issue.
3. The Holy Roman Emperor was elected. The seven electors, religious prelates and princes, wanted to choose a weak ruler to ensure their independence. Further, Charles ruled from Spain and did not live within the Empire.
4. Refer to Map 14.2. The generalization is that the north was Protestant (Scandinavia, England, northern Germany, and what was to become Holland). The Catholic areas were Spain, Italy, France, Austria, and Poland (reconverted by the Jesuits). Russia was Orthodox. The Ottoman lands were mostly a mixture of Orthodox, Roman Catholic and a few Muslims.

think that her love was stronger for her son than for her husband?

APPLYING SOCIAL STUDIES SKILLS

1. **Economics:** How were the Portuguese able to sell spices cheaper than the Italian merchants after 1500 even though they had to travel all the way around the tip of Africa?
2. **Sociology:** What power did women have in Renaissance Italy?
3. **Government:** We usually think of an emperor as being strong and mighty. Why was the Holy Roman Emperor Charles V so weak?
4. **Geography:** Consult Map 14.2 on page 446. Which areas of Europe were dominated by the Protestants by about 1560?

MAKING TIME AND PLACE CONNECTIONS

1. The Visconti and Sforza rulers became powerful in part because they created an efficient tax system. Does the United States have an efficient tax system? To what extent is our success based on our tax system? Ask your parents for their thoughts on this.
2. Compare Machiavelli's political views to those of Confucius, who said that rulers must be first and foremost moral and upright.
3. In what way is a bridal shower today similar to the dowry that grooms received in earlier times? How are they different?
4. Compare the conversion experience of Martin Luther to that of Moses and Muhammad.

5. Compare the empire of Charles V to that of Charlemagne and Napoleon.
6. Movable print was the most important invention of the fifteenth century. What do you think is the most important invention of the twentieth century?

BECOMING AN HISTORIAN

Art as a Key to History: How can you communicate to people who are illiterate? The written word will not work. Look at *Giovanni Arnolfini and His Bride* on page 434. Describe what you see in this picture. In order to convey as much information as possible, artists (then and now) use cultural icons or symbols to stand for larger ideas. Van Eyck has not merely painted a picture, he presents us with a marriage certificate. The dog is a symbol of fidelity (think of the name "Fido"). The sandals refer to the biblical command, "Cast off your shoes for this is holy ground." The single candle in the chandelier indicates the coming together of two people as one in marriage. The candle flame is also a sign of the eye of the all-seeing God. Green is a sign of hope; in this case, the hope that the woman will bear a healthy child. The carved figure on the bedpost is of St. Margaret, the patron saint of childbirth. If you look carefully, you will see the painter and another figure reflected in the mirror. They are the witnesses to this marriage.

Find another painting in this book or in your library that also has symbols. Try and determine what they mean. You may need some help, but once you learn more about these symbols the paintings will have much deeper meaning for you, as they did for those who first saw them.

451

5. Charles's base was Spain, and he had weaker control of Germany. He never controlled France, his greatest enemy, and his lands were not contiguous, a serious disadvantage. Charlemagne's empire was centered in France and Germany. Napoleon was emperor of France and set his relatives up as monarchs in Spain, the Netherlands and Italy. His demise was his failure to conquer Russia. (A comparison to Hitler is appropriate). Both Charles V and Charlemagne realized that their empires were too large and divided them on their death, or in the case of Charles V when he abdicated two years before he died. Napoleon's empire was dismantled at the Congress of Vienna.

6. Answers will vary. Divide the possibilities into areas such as transportation, communication, and war. Exploring the rapidity of change in the twentieth century is important. The airplane was invented in 1903 and before then (and until about 25 years later) intercontinental travel was time-consuming and measured in days or weeks. Regarding communication, the cost of books decreased with the printing press and is even less now. Tangential results of technological change such as increased literacy and the growth of the vacation industry because of ease of travel are useful. War technology, especially the atomic bomb, is another avenue to pursue.

MAKING TIME AND PLACE CONNECTIONS

1. In the United States we pay taxes to many agencies of the government at the local, county, state, and federal level. Computers make it easy to keep track of us, and everyone has a social security number. Some people try to evade taxes by way of formal loopholes or by working "under the table."
2. This can be an interesting discussion about how rulers should rule, and how they should be trained. Confucius argued for scholars as government officials. Probity was the highest goal in

China, although it was often more an ideal than the reality. Machiavelli wanted pragmatic rulers and cast aside any notion of the value of honesty.
3. Both provide the new newly married couple some home furnishings. Although the dowry of the wealthy in medieval times was often money or land, the dowry of the poor was more likely to be an animal or some other useful commodity.
4. All three were spoken to by God when they were alone. Moses and Muhammad were reluctant recipients, it seems that Luther was ready to change his life. None of the three immediately began to proselytize. A period of prayer and reflection preceded their more public lives.

BECOMING AN HISTORIAN

Students who enjoy this exercise may want to try their skill at analyzing more modern paintings. Another rich source of cultural icons are the jacket covers from CD-ROMs and older albums. Students might readily understand these more modern icons.

15 PLANNING GUIDE

SECTION	KEY TOPICS	PRIMARY SOURCES	ASSESSMENT
1 Europe in Crisis: The Wars of Religion in the Sixteenth Century pages 453-459	◆ French Wars of Religion ◆ Militant Catholicism of Philip II ◆ England of Elizabeth I	◆ Conversation between papal official and Spanish officer, page 457	◆ Section Review, page 458 ◆ Section Quiz 15–1, TRB
2 Europe in Crisis: Social Disintegration, War, and Revolution (1560 to 1650) pages 459-467	◆ Witchcraft hysteria ◆ The Thirty Years' War ◆ The English Revolution	◆ Excerpts from witchcraft trial, pages 461–462 ◆ Comment from resident of sacked German city, page 463	◆ Section Review, page 467 ◆ Section Quiz 15–2, TRB
3 Response to Crisis: The Practice of Absolutism pages 467-476	◆ Absolutism under Louis XIV ◆ Mercantilism ◆ Rise of Prussia, Austria, and Russia ◆ Peter the Great ◆ England's Glorious Revolution	◆ Words of Louis XIV, page 468	◆ Section Review, page 476 ◆ Section Quiz 15–3, TRB
4 The World of European Culture pages 476-481	◆ Mannerism, Baroque, French late classicism ◆ English and Spanish literature ◆ Political philosophies of Thomas Hobbes and John Locke	◆ Excerpt from *Richard II*, page 480	◆ Section Review, page 481 ◆ Section Quiz 15–4, TRB

CRISIS AND STATE BUILDING IN EUROPE (1550 TO 1715)

REPRODUCIBLE ACTIVITIES

- Historical Maps
- Charts and Graphs
- Critical Thinking
- Cooperative Learning
- Vocabulary
- Guided Reading
- Reteaching
- Enrichment
- Performance Assessment
- Spanish Key Points and Chapter Summaries
- Spanish Vocabulary
- Spanish Guided Reading

MULTIMEDIA SUPPORT

TRANSPARENCIES
- *World History* Color Transparency Package
- Fine Art Color Transparency Package

VIDEO
- *World History* Video Library
- CNN. Annual Video Update

LASERDISC
- *Sights and Sounds of History*

AUDIO
- *Listening to Literature* audiotape (English and Spanish)
- *History of Music* CD

SOFTWARE
- WESTEST™
- Student Review

CD–ROM
- *The Journey of Civilization*
- *World History*

INTERNET
- Internet Activities

On Line with WORLD HISTORY

Access West's history web site at
http://history.swpco.com
You'll find activities and web sites related to specific topics and chapters in *World History: The Human Odyssey.* Also look for references to helpful web sites at appropriate places throughout this teacher edition.

LESSON PLANNING

You will find detailed daily lesson plans for both traditional class scheduling and **block scheduling** in your Teacher Resource Box.

⧗ Not Enough Time?

If you do not have the four or five days recommended to teach this chapter, you may want to focus on the following sections and activities:

- Have students skim the chapter to answer the "Questions to Guide Your Reading" on page 453. Discuss their answers; then read the "Conclusion" on page 481.
- Do a more in-depth reading of pages 454–456, 457, 459–460, 462–464, 466, 468, 470, 472–474, 475, 476, 478–481. Conclude with a class discussion of the features on pages 461–462, 465–466, 469–470, 477, and 480.

CRISIS AND STATE

15

**BUILDING ON
CHAPTER 14**

To "set the scene" for the study of Chapter 15, use the following questions and activities:

◆ Have students create a time line of the major events during the Renaissance.

◆ Have students identify the major causes for the artistic and cultural advances of the Renaissance.

◆ Have students list the problems that led to the Reformation and the impact of the Reformation on European governments.

USING THE OPENING STORY

Depending on the ability levels of your students, select from the following questions and activities to reinforce the reading of the Duc de Saint-Simon story.

◆ Why do you think an absolute monarch like Louis XIV, with limitless, unrestrained vanity, might make "mistakes of judgment"?

◆ Why would such mistaken judgments be particularly serious in a monarch such as Louis XIV?

LEARNING FROM VISUALS

Answer to the caption question: Louis XIV intended to dominate, and he made it clear from the beginning that he alone would rule. Those who opposed him were removed from power or imprisoned.

452

The religious upheavals of the sixteenth century had left Europeans sorely divided and led to a series of wars that dominated much of European history from 1560 to 1650. Wars, revolutions, and economic and social crises all haunted Europe, making the ninety years from 1560 to 1650 an age of crisis in European life.

One of the responses to these crises was a search for order. Many states satisfied this search by extending monarchical power and creating absolutism, or absolute monarchy. Absolutism was most evident in France during the flamboyant reign of Louis XIV, regarded by some as the perfect embodiment of an absolute monarch. In his memoirs, Duc de Saint-Simon (SAN-see-MOE[n]), who had firsthand experience of French court life, said that Louis was "the very figure of a hero, so imbued with a natural majesty that it appeared even in his most insignificant gestures and movements." The king's natural grace gave him a spe-

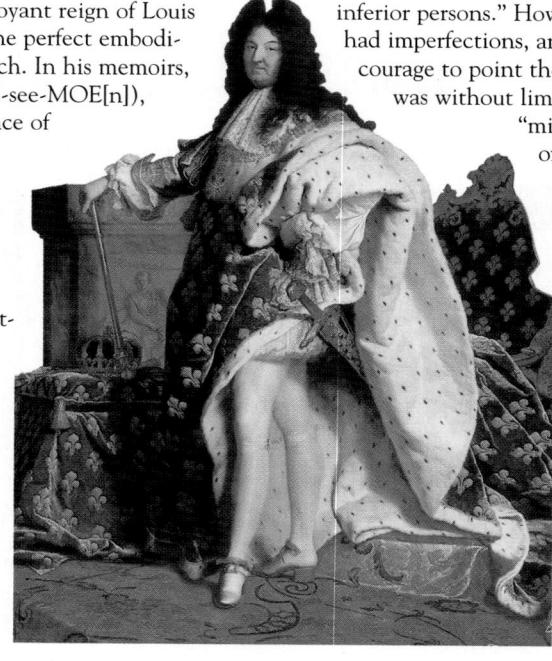

cial charm as well: "He was as dignified and majestic in his dressing gown as when dressed in robes of state, or on horseback at the head of his troops." He excelled at exercise and was never affected by the weather: "Drenched with rain or snow, pierced with cold, bathed in sweat or covered with dust, he was always the same." He spoke well and learned quickly. He was naturally kind, and "he loved truth, justice, order, and reason." His self-control was evident: "He did not lose control of himself ten times in his whole life, and then only with inferior persons." However, even absolute monarchs had imperfections, and Saint-Simon had the courage to point them out: "Louis XIV's vanity was without limit or restraint" and led to his "mistakes of judgment in matters of importance."

Absolutism was not the only response to crisis in the seventeenth century. England, for example, created a system where monarchs were limited by the power of a parliament.

▲ *Louis XIV, shown here, had a clear vision of himself as absolute monarch and had no intention of sharing his power with anyone. What effect do you think his views on monarchical government had on the landed aristocracy and the educated middle class in France?*

ADDITIONAL RESOURCES

The resources listed below can be used to enrich the lessons in this chapter.

BOOKS FOR STUDENTS

The Sun King by Nancy Mitford. Harper and Row

The Spanish Armada by Jay Williams. Horizon Caravell. Harper and Row

The Age of Kings by Charles Blitzer. Time-Life

VIDEOTAPES

"The Puritan Revolution: Cromwell" Social Studies School Service (800) 421-4246

"Europe: State and Power 1453–1700" Series: The World: A Television History Social Studies School Service (800) 421-4246

BUILDING IN EUROPE

(1550 TO 1715)

NEW WORLD PATTERNS

OUTLINE

1. EUROPE IN CRISIS: THE WARS OF RELIGION IN THE SIXTEENTH CENTURY

2. EUROPE IN CRISIS: SOCIAL DISINTEGRATION, WAR, AND REVOLUTION (1560 TO 1650)

3. RESPONSE TO CRISIS: THE PRACTICE OF ABSOLUTISM AND LIMITED MONARCHY

4. THE WORLD OF EUROPEAN CULTURE

EUROPE IN CRISIS: THE WARS OF RELIGION IN THE SIXTEENTH CENTURY

Between 1560 and 1650, Europe experienced religious wars, revolutions, economic and social disintegration, and a witchcraft craze. It was truly an age of crisis, which began with the wars of religion in the sixteenth century.

The wars of religion were a product of the Reformation. By 1560, Calvinism and Catholicism had become highly militant religions dedicated to spreading the word of God as they saw it. Their struggle for the minds and hearts of Europeans was the chief cause of the religious wars of the sixteenth century. Economic, social, and political forces also played an important role in these conflicts. Of the sixteenth-century religious wars, none was more shattering than the French civil wars known as the French Wars of Religion.

The French Wars of Religion (1562 to 1598)

Religion was at the heart of the French civil wars of the sixteenth century. The Calvinists were persecuted by

453

QUESTIONS TO GUIDE YOUR READING

1. What were the causes and results of the wars of religion in the sixteenth century?

2. How would you compare the ruling methods and foreign policies of Elizabeth of England and Philip II of Spain?

3. What were the economic and social problems that troubled Europe from 1560 to 1650?

4. What were the basic issues in the struggle between king and Parliament in seventeenth-century England? How did Parliament put an end to the divine-right theory of kingship in England?

5. What is absolutism, and what were the major features of the practice of absolutism in France?

6. How did the art and political thought of the seventeenth century reflect the political and social life of the period?

FOCUS ON THEMES

Listed below are brief summaries of how the content in this chapter supports the text's key themes.

The Role of Individuals The sixteenth and seventeenth centuries were an age of prominent individuals. In statecraft, Philip II, Elizabeth I, Louis XIV, and Peter the Great played special roles. William Shakespeare and Meguel de Cervantes stand out as men of letters.

The Impact of Science and Technology New developments in the technology of war—especially the ever-increasing use of a variety of firearms—helped lead to armies with better discipline and training, as well as to a tremendous growth in the size of standing armies.

The Role of Ideas A morbid fascination with the ideas of witchcraft led to widespread trials of witches. The political turmoil of the seventeenth century led to new ideas of political order in the thought of Thomas Hobbes and John Locke.

Social Life A series of political, military, and demographic crises resulted in a high degree of social disintegration in the seventeenth century.

Religion in History The divisions in Christianity (especially the emergence of a militant Calvinism and a militant Catholicism) led to a series of devastating religious wars that served to arouse skepticism about Christianity itself and led to a search for a stable, secular order of politics.

Answers to QUESTIONS TO GUIDE YOUR READING

1. Causes: economic, social, and political forces (page 453) Results: France and Spain embraced Catholicism; England remained Protestant (pages 453–458)

2. See pages 456–457.

3. mainly price revolution and increased population, although war, famine, and plague caused trouble as well (page 459)

4. divine right of king versus authority of Parliament; Parliament victorious in civil war, abolished monarchy (pages 463–467)

5. ultimate authority to monarch ruling by divine right, responsible only to God; Louis XIV had complete control of foreign policy, the church, and taxes (page 476)

6. Art reflected suffering, uncertainty, and lack of harmony (page 467); political thought was concerned with order and power, although views differed (pages 479–481)

453

FOCUS

OBJECTIVES

After completing this section, students should be able to

1. describe the religious and political causes of the French Wars of Religion and explain how they were brought to an end
2. explain how the militant Catholicism of Philip II of Spain led to decades of war and, ultimately, to the creation of the Dutch Republic
3. discuss Elizabeth I's policies of moderation
4. describe the defeat of the Spanish Armada and explain its importance

FOCUS ACTIVITY

Divide the class into three groups. Assign each group one of the three major religious wars of the period: French Wars of Religion, Philip II of Spain's battles in the Netherlands, and the Spanish Armada's battles with England. Allow ten minutes for each group to list the religious, social, and political issues involved in these wars. Then, as a class, combine the ideas into a chart or poster. Which of the three wars do students think was the most important?

▶ *The Saint Bartholomew's Day massacre took place in Paris in August 1572. It began with the assassination of Admiral Coligny, a Huguenot, and although the exact number of victims is unknown, historical records indicate that 2,000 to 3,000 Protestants were murdered that night.*

the French kings, but the persecution did little to stop the spread of Calvinism. Huguenots (HYOO-guh-NAWTS), as the French Calvinists were called, came from all levels of society. They included artisans and shopkeepers hurt by rising prices, merchants and lawyers who were fearful of losing their privileges, and members of the nobility. Possibly 40 to 50 percent of the French nobility became Huguenots, including the house of Bourbon, which stood next to the Valois (VAL-WAH) dynasty in the royal line of succession and ruled the southern French kingdom of Navarre (nuh-VAR). The conversion of so many nobles made the Huguenots a powerful political threat to the power of the crown. The Calvinists made up only about 7 percent of the population, but they were a strong-willed and well-organized minority.

The Calvinist minority was greatly outnumbered by the Catholic majority. The Valois monarchy was strongly Catholic, and its control of the Catholic Church gave it little reason to look favorably upon Protestantism. At the same time, an extreme Catholic party—known as the **ultra-Catholics**—favored strict opposition to the Huguenots. Because they possessed the loyalty of Paris and large sections of northern and northwestern France, the ultra-Catholics could recruit and pay for large armies. They also received support

abroad from the popes and Jesuits who favored their extreme Catholic position.

The religious issue was not the only factor that led to the French civil wars. Towns and provinces, which had long resisted the growing power of the French monarchy, were only too willing to join a revolt against that monarchy. This was also true of the nobility, and the fact that so many nobles were Calvinists created an important base of opposition to the king. The French Wars of Religion, then, had political causes as well.

The French Wars of Religion temporarily halted the development of the French centralized monarchical state. The claim of the ruling dynasty of the state to a person's loyalties was temporarily replaced by loyalty to one's religious belief. For thirty years, battles raged in France between the Catholic and Calvinist sides. Both parties obviously thought that the unity of France was less important than religious truth.

Finally, in 1589, Henry of Navarre, the political leader of the Huguenots and a member of the Bourbon dynasty, succeeded to the throne as Henry IV. He realized that he would never be accepted by Catholic France, so he converted to Catholicism. When he was crowned king, the French Wars of Religion had finally come to an end. To solve the religious problem, the king issued the Edict of Nantes (NAN[ts]) in 1598.

RETEACHING ACTIVITY

Have students create a chart as a way of organizing and remembering key facts about the rulers discussed in this chapter. As they complete a section, they can add to their charts. The heading for the first column should be *Rulers.* Students should write Philip II, Elizabeth I, Louis XIV, and Peter the Great in the first column. Headings for the next four columns could be *Country, Religion, Challenge,* and *Accomplishment.* You will find a blackline master of this chart in your Teacher Resource Box.

Map 15.1   Phillip II and the Height of Spanish Power

Legend:
- Spanish possessions
- Holy Roman Empire and Austrian Habsburg possessions
- ← Route of the Armada

TEACH

REINFORCING VOCABULARY

Be sure students can describe what a "centralized monarchical state" is *(government centered around the power of the king or queen)*, and what "crusading fervor" involves. *(A crusade is a proj-ect to fix or remedy something, undertaken with great eagerness; fervor is intensity, passion.)* Also check their understanding of artisan *(craftsperson, skilled worker)*, consolidate *(unite, make secure)*, conformity *(obedience, agreement)*, and heretic *(dissenter from church dogma)*.

Multimedia Support

TRANSPARENCY
15.1, Map of Habsburg Europe

The edict recognized Catholicism as the official religion of France, but it also gave the Huguenots the right to worship and to enjoy all political privileges, such as holding public offices.

Philip II and the Cause of Militant Catholicism

The greatest supporter of militant Catholicism in the second half of the sixteenth century was King Philip II of Spain, the son and heir of Charles V. Philip's reign ushered in an age of Spanish greatness, both politically and culturally.

The first major goal of Philip II was to consolidate the lands he had inherited from his father. These included Spain, the Netherlands, and possessions in Italy and the New World. To strengthen his control, Philip insisted on a strict conformity to Catholicism and a strong, monarchical authority. Achieving the latter was not easy, because each of the states and territories of his empire had its own structure of government. Even in Spain, there was no deep sense of nationhood. Philip did manage, however, to expand royal power by making the monarchy less dependent on the landed aristocrats.

The Catholic faith was crucial to both Philip II and the Spanish people. During the late Middle Ages, Catholic kingdoms in Spain had gradually reconquered most of the land from the Muslims and expelled the Spanish Jews. Driven by this heritage of crusading fervor, it was not difficult for Spain to see itself as a nation of people chosen by God to save Catholic Christianity from the Protestant heretics.

Philip II, the "Most Catholic King," became the champion of Catholicism throughout Europe. This role led to spectacular victories and equally spectacular

STUDYING MAPS

The following questions will help you guide students through their study of Map 15.1.

1. Locate the areas that were under the rule of Philip II.
2. Why was it a difficult undertaking for Philip II to strengthen control in the lands he inherited? *(Philip's lands were spread out from Spain to Italy to the Netherlands.)*
3. Why was it easier for the Spanish Netherlands to fall under the influence of England than that of Philip II? *(close proximity to England; Netherlands had strong Protestant influence)*

▲ *This portrait of Philip II of Spain was done when he was fifty-two. Although Philip tried to make Spain a great power, his military actions, large debts, and the high taxes he imposed on his citizens led to his ultimate failure.*

defeats for the Spanish king. Spain's leadership of a Holy League against the Turks in the Mediterranean led to a stunning victory over the Turkish fleet in the Battle of Lepanto in 1571. Philip's problems with the Netherlands and Queen Elizabeth of England, however, led to his greatest misfortunes.

The Spanish Netherlands, which consisted of seventeen provinces (modern Netherlands and Belgium [BELL-jum]), was one of the richest parts of Philip's empire. Philip's attempt to strengthen his control in the Netherlands soon led to a revolt. The nobles, who stood to lose the most politically if their privileges were weakened, strongly opposed Philip's efforts. When the residents of the Netherlands realized that the taxes they paid were being used for Spanish interests, they

directed their anger against Philip. Finally, religion became a major reason for rebellion when Philip tried to crush Calvinism in the Netherlands. Violence erupted when Calvinists—especially nobles—began to destroy statues in Catholic churches. Philip sent ten thousand troops to crush the rebellion.

The revolt, however, became organized. This was especially true in the northern provinces, where the Dutch, under the leadership of William the Silent of Nassau (NAS-AW), the prince of Orange, offered growing resistance. The struggle dragged on for decades until 1609, when a twelve-year truce ended the war. One result of the war was a growing independence in the northern provinces. They began to call themselves the United Provinces of the Netherlands and became the core of the modern Dutch state that was officially recognized by the Peace of Westphalia (west-FALE-yuh) in 1648.

The seventeenth century has often been called the golden age of the Dutch Republic, because the United Provinces held center stage as one of Europe's great powers. Like France and England, the United Provinces, located on the Atlantic seaboard, prospered from the new worldwide trade.

At the beginning of the seventeenth century, Spain had the most populous empire in the world. It controlled almost all of South America and a number of settlements in Asia and Africa. To most Europeans, Spain still seemed the greatest power of the age, but the reality was quite different. The treasury was empty. Philip II went bankrupt from spending too much on war, and his successor did the same by spending a fortune on his court. The armed forces were out-of-date, and the government was inefficient. Spain continued to play the role of a great power, but the real power had shifted to England.

The England of Elizabeth

When Elizabeth Tudor, the daughter of Henry VIII and Anne Boleyn, ascended the throne in 1558, England had fewer than four million people. During her reign, the small island kingdom became leader of the Protestant nations of Europe and laid the foundations for a world empire.

MORE ABOUT . . .   *The St. Bartholomew's Day Massacre*

Catherine exerted a great deal of diplomatic effort trying to create harmony between Catholic and Protestant leaders. She negotiated a marriage between her daughter Margeurite (Margot) and Henri de Navarre, the ranking Huguenot prince of the blood. Many Catholics felt that the toleration of Huguenots was like a disease in the body of Christ. Nineteen-year-old Henri de Navarre and Margot de Valois were married in Paris on

August 17, 1572. A week later, on the 23rd, which was the feast of St. Bartholomew, the celebration continued. At some point during the night the decision was made to kill the Huguenot leadership in Paris for the wedding. Charles IX was there, as was his mother, Catherine de'Medici. The original plans may not have included a general massacre, but Charles IX, reputedly badgered into this decision by Catherine, finally broke and said,

Ask students to discuss what this picture of Elizabeth I in a ceremonial procession suggests about this queen and the way her subjects viewed her.

USING PRIMARY SOURCES

The conversation between the papal official and the Spanish officer captures the position a "holy war" imposes on people who are called upon to fight. Ask two volunteers to read the dialogue aloud. Then add an English soldier to this encounter. Have students create dialogue for the three characters, illustrating their different opinions on the outcome of battle and the justice of the cause.

CLASS DISCUSSION

Have students discuss the ways in which Elizabeth I of England pursued policies based on moderation. *(She sent secret aid to Huguenots and Calvinists and stayed out of alliances that would force war.)*

◄ *Queen Elizabeth I was intelligent and learned quickly. She knew Latin and Greek and spoke several European languages. She is pictured here in a ceremonial procession surrounded by men and women of her court.*

Intelligent, cautious, and self-confident, Elizabeth moved quickly to solve the difficult religious problem she inherited from her half-sister, Queen Mary Tudor. Elizabeth's religious policy was based on moderation. She repealed the Catholic laws of Mary's reign. A new Act of Supremacy named Elizabeth as "the only supreme governor" of both church and state. The church service used during the reign of Edward VI was revised to make it more acceptable to Catholics. The Church of England under Elizabeth was basically Protestant, but it was a moderate Protestantism that kept most people satisfied in the second half of the sixteenth century.

Elizabeth was also cautious and moderate in her foreign policy. Fearful of other countries, Elizabeth knew that war could be disastrous for England and her own rule. She sent secret aid to French Huguenots and Dutch Calvinists to weaken France and Spain, but she stayed out of alliances that would force her into war with any major power.

Gradually, however, Elizabeth was drawn into war with Spain. Philip II of Spain had toyed for years with the idea of invading England. His advisors assured him that the people of England would rise against their queen when the Spaniards arrived. Moreover, Philip was easily convinced that the revolt in the Netherlands would never be crushed as long as England provided support for the Dutch. In any case, a successful invasion of England would mean the overthrow of the Protestant heresy and the return of England to Catholicism. Philip ordered preparations for an **armada** (fleet of warships) to invade England in 1588.

The Spanish Armada proved to be a disaster. The fleet that finally set sail had neither the ships nor the manpower that Philip had planned to send. A conversation between a papal official and an officer of the Spanish fleet before the Armada left reveals the basic flaw:

> *"And if you meet the English armada in the Channel, do you expect to win the battle?"*
> *"Of course," replied the Spaniard.*
> *"How can you be so sure!" [asked the official].*
> *"It's very simple. It is well known that we fight in*

"Well, then kill them all that no man be left to reproach me."

During the early hours of Sunday morning, a troop of soldiers came to the door of the leading Huguenot prince. They killed the guard and rushed through the house. Admiral Gaspari Coligny was dragged from his bed, stabbed, and thrown out the window to the pavement below. The Catholic leaders announced that this was the king's will.

Rumors spread and somehow the militia and the general population went on a rampage, believing themselves to be fully sanctioned by the king and the church. The killing went on for about three days with the city councilors and the king unable to restore order. The St. Bartholomew's Day Massacre, as it came to be known, destroyed an entire generation of Huguenot leadership.

ASSESS

► *This painting captures the confusion of the Spanish Armada and also shows the massive number of ships, both English and Spanish, that were committed to this decisive battle between the two countries.*

God's cause. So when we meet the English, God will surely arrange matters so that we can grapple and board them, . . . by sending some strange freak of weather. . . . If we can come to close quarters, Spanish steel (and the great masses of soldiers we shall have on board) will make our victory certain. But unless God helps us by a miracle the English, who have faster and handier ships than ours, and many more long-range guns, . . . will never close with us at all, but stand aloof and knock us to pieces with their guns, without our being able to do them any serious hurt. So," concluded the captain, *"we are sailing against England in the confident hope of a miracle."*[1]

The hoped-for miracle never came. The Spanish fleet, battered by a number of encounters with the English, sailed back to Spain by a northward route around Scotland and Ireland, where it was further pounded by storms. The defeat of the Armada guaranteed that England would remain a Protestant country. Although Spain recovered, the defeat was a stunning blow to the Spaniards.

 SECTION REVIEW

1. Locate:
(a) France, (b) Spain, (c) United Provinces of the Netherlands, (d) England

2. Define:
(a) ultra-Catholics, (b) armada

3. Identify:
(a) Huguenots, (b) Henry of Navarre, (c) Valois monarchy, (d) Edict of Nantes, (e) King Philip II, (f) William the Silent of Nassau, (g) Elizabeth Tudor

4. Recall:
(a) Who were the Calvinists? What was their role in the French Wars of Religion?
(b) What were the major reasons for rebellion against King Philip II by the residents of the Netherlands?
(c) How did Queen Elizabeth lay the foundations for her country to become a world power?

MORE ABOUT . . . *Mary, Queen of Scots*

Mary (1542–1587) was the daughter and only child of James V of Scotland by his second wife, Mary of Guise. Mary was sent by her mother to France. There she was brought up at the glittering French court of Henry II, where she excelled at hunting and dancing, and was carefully educated in the manner of a Frenchwoman. She married the Dauphin (1558), later Francis II, but was widowed at 18 (1560), and became the dowager Queen of France with her own estates and a substantial income.

Mary returned to Scotland in 1561 and in 1565 she married her cousin, Henry Stuart, Lord Darnley, a grandson of Margaret Tudor. However, disgusted by his debauchery, she soon became alienated from him. Darnley was mysteriously killed in an explosion (1567). The chief suspect was the Earl of Bothwell, who underwent a mock trial and

5. Think Critically: What comparisons can you draw from the sixteenth-century Wars of Religion and religious wars today?

EUROPE IN CRISIS: SOCIAL DISINTEGRATION, WAR, AND REVOLUTION (1560 TO 1650)

From 1560 to 1650, Europe witnessed severe economic and social crises, as well as political upheaval. The so-called **price revolution** was a dramatic rise in prices (inflation) that was a major economic problem in all of Europe in the sixteenth and early seventeenth centuries. What caused this price revolution? The great influx of gold and silver from the New World (see the next chapter) was one factor. Perhaps even more important was an increase in population in the sixteenth century. A growing population increased the demand for land and food and drove up prices for both.

The price revolution also had benefits, as rising prices and expanding markets led to economic expansion and prosperity. This inflation-fueled prosperity of the sixteenth century, however, showed signs of declining by the beginning of the seventeenth century. An economic slowdown was soon evident in some parts of Europe. As imports of silver from the Americas dwindled, economic decline increased, especially in the Mediterranean area. Spain's economy, which had grown dependent on imported silver, was seriously failing by the decade of the 1640s. Italy, once the financial center of Europe in the age of the Renaissance, was also becoming an economic backwater.

Population figures in the sixteenth and seventeenth centuries reveal Europe's worsening conditions. The sixteenth century was a period of growing population, possibly due to a warmer climate and increased food supplies. The population of Europe probably increased from 60 million in 1500 to 85 million by 1600. However, it leveled off by 1620 and even began to decline by 1650, especially in central and southern Europe.

Only the Dutch, English, and French grew in number in the first half of the seventeenth century.

Europe's longtime enemies—war, famine, and plague—continued to affect population levels. Another "little Ice Age" in Europe after the middle of the sixteenth century brought a fall in average temperatures. This hurt harvests and gave rise to famines. Europe's problems created social tensions that were evident in the witchcraft craze.

The Witchcraft Craze

Hysteria over **witchcraft** affected the lives of many Europeans in the sixteenth and seventeenth centuries, although witchcraft was not new. Its practice had been part of traditional village culture for centuries. However, in the Middle Ages, the Catholic Church had connected witches to the activities of the devil, making witchcraft into a heresy that had to be wiped out. By the thirteenth century, people were being accused of a variety of witchcraft practices. They were often turned over to state authorities for burning at the stake or hanging.

In the sixteenth and seventeenth centuries, many people became hysterical about witchcraft. Neighbors accused neighbors of witchcraft, which led to widespread trials of witches. Perhaps more than 100,000 people were prosecuted throughout Europe on charges of witchcraft. As more and more people were brought to trial, the fear of witches grew, as did the fear of being accused of witchcraft. Larger cities were affected first, but the trials also spread to smaller towns and rural areas as the hysteria lasted well into the seventeenth century (see "You Are There: A Witchcraft Trial in France").

Common people—usually those who were poor and without property—were the ones most often accused of witchcraft. Indeed, where lists are given, those mentioned most often are milkmaids, peasant women, and servant girls. In the witchcraft trials of the sixteenth and seventeenth centuries, over 75 percent of those accused were women. Most of them were single or widowed. Many were over fifty years old.

The accused witches usually confessed to a number of practices, most often after intense torture. Many said

was acquitted. Mary's involvement is unclear, but shortly afterwards she made Bothwell Duke of Orkney, and three months later, married the man most people regarded as Lord Darnley's murderer.

This step united her nobles in arms against her. She fled to England, but Elizabeth placed her in prison. The presence of Mary in England was a constant source of unease to Elizabeth. Mary had a claim to the English throne

through Darnley, and a large Catholic minority naturally looked to Mary as the likely restorer of the old faith. Plot followed plot in England and letters from Mary seemingly approving plans for Elizabeth's death were discovered. Mary was brought to trial in 1586. Early in 1587 Elizabeth signed her death warrant, and she was executed. In 1612 her body was moved to Henry VII's chapel at Westminster, where it still lies.

CLOSE

Ask students to discuss which of the wars of religion they consider the most important, and why.

FOCUS

OBJECTIVES

After completing this section, students should be able to

1. explain the causes and effects of the price revolution of the sixteenth and early seventeenth centuries
2. speculate on the causes of the witchcraft craze
3. list the causes and results of the Thirty Years' War
4. discuss the causes and aftermath of the English Revolution
5. explain the importance of Oliver Cromwell

TEACH

COMPARING TIME PERIODS

Ask students to compare the inflation of the sixteenth and seventeenth centuries with twentieth-century inflation. What are the current views about the causes and remedies of "price revolutions"?

Multimedia Support

 TRANSPARENCY
15–2, European Population

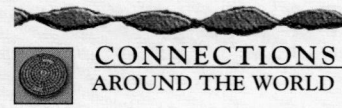

CONNECTIONS
AROUND THE WORLD

After students have read *Natural Disasters in History*, have them describe natural disasters that have occurred recently. Do they need to do research to identify the most damaging disasters of the past fifty years? If so, ask for volunteers to research and report back to class.

REINFORCING VOCABULARY

Check students' comprehension of the following words by asking them to use each in a sentence: turmoil *(extreme confusion, agitation, commotion)*; vulnerable *(open to attack or damage)*; allure *(temptation)*; plausible *(believable)*; susceptible *(impressionable, responsive)*

CRITICAL THINKING

People accused of witchcraft were usually poor, female, single or widowed, and over fifty. What might be reasons why accused witches fit this profile? *(people without power, dependent on charity, without men to defend them; were considered morally weak, easier for the devil to seduce)*

ACROSS THE CURRICULUM

Language Arts Assign students to read *The Crucible* by Arthur Miller, a play that concerns the Salem witch trials. Ask students to present comparisons between the situation described in the play and the European witchcraft hysteria described in this chapter.

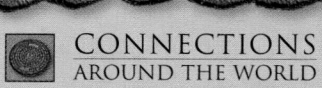

CONNECTIONS
AROUND THE WORLD

Natural Disasters in History   The religious wars in Europe, which led to many deaths, were man-made disasters that created economic, social, and political crises. Between 1500 and 1800, natural disasters around the world also took many lives and led to economic and social crises.

One of the worst disasters occurred in China in 1556. A powerful earthquake in northern China buried alive hundreds of thousands of peasants who had made their homes in cave dwellings carved out of soft clay hills. During the next two hundred years, earthquakes shattered other places around the world. On the last day of 1703, a massive earthquake struck the city of Tokyo. At the same time, enormous tidal waves caused by earthquakes flooded the Japanese coastline, sweeping entire villages and their inhabitants out to sea. An earthquake that struck Persia in 1727 killed 75,000 people in the city of Tabriz. An estimated 600,000 people were killed in Calcutta, India, in 1737 when a cyclone created a forty-foot tidal wave that crashed into the city.

Europe, too, had its share of natural disasters. A massive earthquake leveled the city of Lisbon, Portugal, in 1755, killing over 50,000 people and destroying over 80 percent of the buildings in the city. The massive eruption of Mount Etna on the island of Sicily in 1669 devastated Catania, a port city eighteen miles away.

that they had sworn allegiance to the devil and attended sabbats, or nightly gatherings where they feasted and danced. Others admitted using evil spells and special ointments and powders to bring harm to their neighbors, such as killing their livestock.

Why did the witchcraft craze become so widespread in the sixteenth and seventeenth centuries? Religious uncertainties clearly played some part. Many witchcraft trials took place in areas, such as southwestern Germany, where conflicts between Protestants and Catholics still raged. As hatreds grew, charges of being in league with the devil became common on both sides.

The witchcraft hysteria may also have emerged from the problems of a society in turmoil. This was a time when the old values that stressed working together for the good of the community were declining. Property owners became alarmed at the growing numbers of poor among them and referred to them as agents of the devil. Old women were particularly open to suspicion. Many of them could no longer depend on the local charity found in traditional society and survived by selling herbs, potions, or secret remedies for healing. When problems arose, these same people were the most likely to be accused of being witches.

That women should be the chief victims of witchcraft trials was hardly accidental. Indeed, since the Middle Ages, writers on witchcraft had argued that there was a direct link between witchcraft and women. According to these writers, women were inferior to men both mentally and morally. Women's moral weaknesses made them especially open to temptation and hence especially vulnerable to the allures of Satan. These beliefs were repeated in virtually all of the witchcraft treatises written in the sixteenth and seventeenth centuries. A witchcraft judge in France, for example, found it "not unreasonable that this scum of humanity, i.e., witches, should be drawn chiefly from the feminine sex."[2] Of course, not only witch hunters held these low estimates of women. Most theologians, lawyers, and philosophers in early modern Europe believed in the natural inferiority of women and thus would have found it plausible that women would be more susceptible to witchcraft.

By the mid-seventeenth century, the witchcraft hysteria began to lessen. The destruction caused by the religious wars led many people to become more tolerant. This tolerance, in turn, caused religious passions to subside. Moreover, as governments grew stronger after the period of crisis, fewer officials were willing to disrupt their societies by the trials of witches. Finally, by the end of the seventeenth and the beginning of the eighteenth centuries, as science became more widespread (see Chapter 19), more and more people were questioning their old attitudes toward religion. They

---

SPECIAL NEEDS: *Visual/Auditory*

It is helpful for many students, particularly those with learning disabilities, to relate learning to personal or real life events. Have students read "Natural Disasters in History." Begin a discussion about natural disasters and encourage students to share their experiences. As part of the research activity described above, have them copy magazine pictures in the library, or cut out pictures to make a collage illustrating the disaster.

They then need to record two ways in which this natural disaster forever altered the course of history. Examples would be the destruction of buildings, neighborhoods, or roadways. What would the city have been like if the disaster had not occurred? Focus also on the sounds of natural disasters, the visible warning signs, and how damage might be minimized to a city's infrastructure through proper planning.

YOU ARE THERE
A Witchcraft Trial in France

◄ *Although this young woman is begging for mercy, it is unlikely that she would receive a complete pardon against charges of witchcraft.*

Persecutions for witchcraft reached their high point in the sixteenth and seventeenth centuries, when tens of thousands of people were brought to trial. In this excerpt from the minutes of a trial in France, we can see why the accused witch stood little chance of ridding herself of blame.

The Trial of Suzanne Gaudry

Deliberation of the Court—June 3, 1652

The undersigned members of the Court have seen these interrogations and answers. They say that the aforementioned Suzanne Gaudry confesses that she is a witch, that she had given herself to the devil, that she had renounced God, Lent, and baptism, that she has been marked on the shoulder, that she has cohabited with the devil and that she has been to the dances. . . .

The Torture

On this same day, being at the place of torture.

This prisoner, before being strapped down, was warned to maintain herself in her first confessions and to renounce her lover.

—Says that she denies everything she has said, and that she has no lover. Feeling herself being strapped down, says that she is not a witch, while struggling to cry . . . and upon being asked why she confessed to being one, said that she was forced to say it. Told that she was not forced, that on the contrary she declared herself to be a witch without any threat.

—Says that she confessed it and that she is not a witch, and being a little stretched [on the rack] screams ceaselessly that she is not a witch. . . .

(continued)

CLASS DISCUSSION

Discuss why accused people such as Suzanne Gaudry had little chance of escaping their fate.

CRITICAL THINKING

What reasons might the accusers give for accepting confessions made under torture? *(It was believed that a truly innocent person could withstand torture.)* How do you think people justified such cruel treatment? What is the relevance of the saying, "The means justify the ends" to the treatment of accused witches?

On Line with
WORLD HISTORY *Internet Activity*

You may want to have your students visit the following URL, where they will find information and additional web site resources to enhance their study of this chapter.

Elizabethan England

http://www.springfield.k12.il.us/ schools/springfield/eliz/index.html

This site is an excellent example of a student web project, containing sections on Shakespeare, art and architecture, everyday life, and historical figures and events.

Due to the ever-changing nature of the World Wide Web, see the West History web site, **http://history.swpco.com** for

CLASS DISCUSSION

Have students discuss reasons for the gradual disappearance of witchcraft hysteria.

Answers to Critical Thinking Questions

1. There were more witch trials in France during the sixteenth and seventeenth centuries than at any other time.
2. She was stretched on the rack.
3. Answers will vary but might include the thought that as the torture and pain increased, she might have felt that if she confessed, the torture would end sooner.

CLASS DISCUSSION

Guide students in a discussion of the causes of the Thirty Years' War and the results of this conflict. (*struggle between Catholicism and Calvinism; political motives*)

YOU ARE THERE
A Witchcraft Trial in France, continued

Asked if she did not confess that she had been a witch for twenty-six years.

—Says that she said it, that she retracts it, crying that she is not a witch. . . .

The mark having been probed by the officer, in the presence of Doctor Bouchain, it was adjudged by the aforesaid doctor and officer truly to be the mark of the devil.

Being more tightly stretched upon the torture-rack, urged to maintain her confessions.

—Said that it was true that she is a witch and that she would maintain what she had said.

Asked how long she had been in subjugation to the devil.

—Answers that it was twenty years ago that the devil appeared to her, being in her lodgings in the form of a man dressed in a little cow-hide and black trousers. . . .

Verdict—July 9, 1652

Seeing by her own confessions that she is said to have made a pact with the devil, received the mark from him, . . . and that following this, she had renounced God, Lent, and baptism. . . . Also, seeing that she is said to have been a part of nighttime carols and dances.

The advice of the undersigned is that the office of Rieux can legitimately condemn the aforesaid Suzanne Gaudry to death, tying her to a gallows, and strangling her to death, then burning her body and burying it here in the environs of the woods.

1. During what period of time were the most witch trials held in France?
2. What was the torture that Suzanne Gaudry received?
3. Suzanne retracted her confessions as her torture was beginning. As the torture increased, she maintained her original confession. Why do you think this happened?

found it unreasonable to believe in the old view of a world haunted by evil spirits.

Seventeenth-Century Crises: The Thirty Years' War (1618 to 1648)

Religion, especially the struggle between a militant Catholicism and a militant Calvinism, played an important role in the outbreak of the Thirty Years' War, often called the "last of the religious wars." As the war dragged on, however, it became clear that political motives were extremely important as well.

The Thirty Years' War began in 1618 in the Germanic lands of the Holy Roman Empire. At first it was a struggle between Catholic forces, led by the Habsburg Holy Roman emperors, and Protestant (primarily Calvinist) nobles in Bohemia who rebelled against Habsburg authority. What began as a struggle over religious issues soon became a wider conflict as other European powers—Denmark, Sweden, France, and Spain—entered the war. Especially important was the conflict between France and the rulers of Spain and the Holy Roman Empire for European leadership. Nevertheless, most of the battles were fought on German soil.

MORE ABOUT . . . *The Battle of Breitenfeld and the*

The Thirty Years' War, which began in 1618, was originally a struggle between Roman Catholics and Protestants over the crown of Bohemia. The German States were eventually engulfed in the war. Outside help for the Protestants came from the Danish King Christian in 1624 and later King Adolphus of Sweden in 1630.

When the Catholic army of Count Johannas Tilly (1559–1632) sacked the city of Magdeburg, Protestants everywhere were outraged. The city was razed and 20,000 citizens are alleged to have perished in the fire that followed. For civilians, it was the most terrible massacre in the annals of the Thirty Years' War. Fearing that Tilly and his army would

◄ *This panoramic painting by the Dutch artist Jan Breughel chronicles the horror of the Thirty Years' War. The hired soldiers who made up the professional armies looted and murdered as they wished. The local townspeople and peasants had little protection against them.*

The war in Germany was officially ended by the Peace of Westphalia in 1648. What were the results of this conflict? France emerged as the dominant nation in Europe. The Peace of Westphalia stated that all German states, including the Calvinist ones, were free to determine their own religion. The more than three hundred states that made up the Holy Roman Empire were then recognized as independent states. This brought an end to the Holy Roman Empire as a political entity, but Germany would not be united for another two hundred years. The Peace of Westphalia also made it clear that political motives, not religious convictions, had become the guiding forces in public affairs.

Germany suffered the most from the Thirty Years' War. Some areas of Germany were completely devastated. Many people in Germany would have agreed with this comment by a resident of a city that had been sacked ten times:

Then there was nothing but beating and burning, plundering, torture, and murder. Most especially was every one of the enemy bent on securing much booty. . . . In this frenzied rage, the great and splendid city . . . was now . . . given over to the flames, and thousands of innocent men, women and children, in the midst of a horrible din of heartrending shrieks and cries, were tor-

tured and put to death in so cruel and shameful a manner that no words would suffice to describe, . . . Thus in a single day this noble and famous city, the pride of the whole country, went up in fire and smoke.[3]

The Thirty Years' War was the most destructive conflict the Europeans had yet experienced (see "The Role of Science and Technology: The Changing Face of War"). Unfortunately, it was not the last.

Seventeenth-Century Crises: The English Revolution

Before, during, and after the Thirty Years' War, a series of rebellions and civil wars rocked Europe. To strengthen their power, monarchs tried to extend their authority at the expense of nobles who fought back. At the same time, to fight their battles, governments increased taxes and created such economic burdens that common people also rebelled. By far the most famous struggle was the civil war and rebellion in England, known as the English Revolution.

At the core of the English Revolution of the seventeenth century was a struggle between king and Parliament that turned into an armed conflict to determine what roles each should play in governing England. The

Thirty Years' War

march on Leipzig and repeat the "Horror's of Magdeburg," Protestant lords welcomed Gustavus and the Swedes and allowed them to cross their lands. On the plains near Brentenfeld, 70,000 soldiers met. Tilly and the Catholics lost 13,000 men while the Swede's lost fewer than 3,000 soldiers. King Gustavus Adolphus was applauded as the Protestant

Champion. He also laid the foundation for an increase in Swedish power and prestige that would make that country a leading European power for the next half century. Unfortunately for Sweden and the Protestants, King Gustavus was killed the next year at the battle of Lutzen. France then entered the war, which would last another 18 years.

CLASS DISCUSSION

Have students discuss the political and religious issues at the core of the English Revolution.

COMPARING TIME PERIODS

Ask interested students to research the "divine right of kings." When and where was this theory of government first proclaimed? What is the history of opposition to this idea? You may want to remind them that they have read about this idea earlier in this text.

Map 15.2   Europe in the Seventeenth Century

Kingdom of Denmark and Norway	
Brandenburg – Prussia	
Kingdom of Sweden	
Habsburg – Austrian	
Habsburg – Spanish	
Republic of Venice	

struggle over this political issue was complicated by a deep and profound religious controversy.

With the death of Queen Elizabeth I in 1603, the Tudor dynasty came to an end. The Stuart line of rulers began with the accession to the throne of Elizabeth's cousin, the king of Scotland, who became James I of England. James understood little about the laws and customs of the English. He believed in the **divine right of kings;** that is, he believed that kings receive their power directly from God and are responsible to no one

except God. Parliament, however, did not think much of the divine right of kings. Over time, Parliament had come to assume that the king or queen and Parliament together ruled England.

Then, too, the Puritans (those Protestants in England inspired by Calvinist ideas) did not like the king's strong defense of the Church of England. The Puritans were officially members of the Church of England. However, they were Calvinists by conviction, and they wished to reform the Church of England by

STUDYING MAPS

The following questions will help you guide students through their study of Map 15.2.

1. How many different ruling dynasties and kingdoms are represented? (*six*)

2. Which group encompassed the largest territory? (*students may respond either Habsburg–Spanish or Kingdom of Sweden*)

3. Identify as many states as you can on the map that do not exist today. (*Answers will vary.*)

THE ROLE OF SCIENCE AND TECHNOLOGY

The Changing Face of War

Gunpowder was first invented by the Chinese in the eleventh century and made its appearance in Europe by the fourteenth century, where its chief use was in cannons. Unfortunately, early cannons were unreliable and prone to blowing up. They were probably as dangerous to those firing them as they were to the enemy. During the seventeenth century, however, firearms developed rapidly and increasingly changed the face of war.

By 1600, the flintlock musket had made firearms more deadly on the battlefield. Muskets were loaded from the front with powder and ball. In the flintlock musket, the powder that propelled the ball was ignited by a spark caused by a flint striking on metal. The flintlock musket was easier to fire and more reliable than other muskets. Eight out of twelve shots were successful. Reloading techniques had also improved, to the point where it was possible to make one and even two shots per minute. The addition of the bayonet to the front of the musket made the musket even more deadly as a weapon. It required hand-to-hand combat, which is rare in war today.

One military leader who made effective use of firearms during the Thirty Years' War was Gustavus Adolphus (gu-STAVE-us uh-DOLL-fus), the king of Sweden. The infantry brigades of Gustavus's army, six men deep, were composed of equal numbers of musketeers and pikemen. The musketeers employed the salvo, in which all rows of the infantry fired at once instead of row by row.

This illustration shows a well-armed soldier who served for Prince Moritz of Orange in the early 1600s. Besides his musket, what other weapons does the soldier carry?

These salvos of fire, which cut up the massed ranks of the opposing infantry squadrons, were followed by a pike charge. Despite the use of firearms, pikes—heavy spears eighteen feet long, held by pikemen massed together in square formations—still made effective weapons.

Gustavus also used the cavalry in a more mobile fashion. After shooting a pistol volley, the members of his cavalry charged the enemy with their swords. Gustavus added additional mobility to his forces by using lighter artillery pieces. These were more easily moved during battle than the heavy cannons, which often bogged down in the mud of the battlefield.

The increased use of firearms, combined with greater mobility on the battlefield, demanded armies that were better disciplined and trained. This was the beginning of the end for mercenary troops hired for a single campaigning season. Instead, governments began to fund regularly paid standing armies, based partly on conscription (a draft). In the course of the seventeenth century, these standing armies grew larger and larger. During the Thirty Years' War, armies were never larger than 40,000 to 50,000 men. In 1700, France had a

(continued)

RECOMMENDED READING

Good general works on the period of the Puritan Revolution include G. E. Aylmer, *Rebellion or Revolution? England, 1640–1660* (New York, 1986); L. Stone, *Causes of the English Revolution, 1529–1642* (New York, 1972); and the brief study by R. Howell, Jr., *The Origins of the English Revolution* (St. Louis, 1975). On the war itself, see C. Hill, *God's Englishman: Oliver Cromwell and the English Revolution* (New York, 1970); and R. Ashton, *The English Civil War: Conservatism and Revolution, 1604–1649* (London, 1976). On Oliver Cromwell, see R. Howell, Jr., *Cromwell* (Boston, 1977); and the beautifully written popular account by A. Fraser, *Cromwell: The Lord Protector* (New York, 1974).

THE ROLE OF SCIENCE AND TECHNOLOGY

CRITICAL THINKING

Ask students to speculate about soldiers' experiences in a war featuring hand-to-hand combat. How would such combat differ from more modern warfare, in which weapons are fired from great distances? From warfare in the age of computers and atomic weapons?

CLASS DISCUSSION

Have students discuss why the development of firearms and changing theories of battle marked "the beginning of the end for mercenary troops." What replaced mercenaries? *(standing armies, based partly on conscription)*

ACROSS THE CURRICULUM

Science. Ask interested students to research further the development of firearms. Have them present pictures and diagrams that illustrate how such weapons as the flintlock musket worked.

TEACHING FROM VISUALS

Answer to the caption question: This soldier is armed with a sword and dagger. He also wears a protective helmet and a chain-mail vest.

Answers to Critical Thinking Questions

1. The invention of gunpowder changed the face of war.
2. The increased use of gunpowder (in firearms and artillery) combined with greater mobility on the battlefield, demanded armies that were better disciplined and trained. Governments began to fund regularly-paid standing armes (based partly on conscription) instead of using mercenary troops hired for a single campaigning season. As time went on, more powerful weapons allowed men to fight at ever-greater distances.

OPPOSING VIEWPOINTS

Have students present a debate between the supporters of Charles I (the Cavaliers) and the supporters of Parliament (the Roundheads). What were the arguments used to support each position? Why was compromise so difficult?

CLASS DISCUSSION

Ask students to discuss the connection between the English Revolution and, ultimately, the American Revolution. *(Many Puritans fled England to practice their religion freely in America. They became early settlers in the thirteen original colonies.)*

THE ROLE OF SCIENCE AND TECHNOLOGY
The Changing Face of War, continued

standing army of 400,000. In the seventeenth century, such armies could be maintained only by raising more taxes, making war an economic burden and an ever more important part of the European state. States also needed larger bureaucracies to oversee their military resources.

1. What Chinese invention changed the face of war in the fourteenth century?

2. How did the invention of gunpowder change the way wars were fought?

making it even more Protestant. Many of England's **gentry,** mostly well-to-do landowners below the level of the nobility, had become Puritans. The Puritan gentry formed an important part of the House of Commons, the lower house of Parliament. It was not wise to alienate them.

The conflict that had begun during the reign of James came to a head during the reign of his son Charles I. Charles believed as strongly in divine-right monarchy as his father had. From the first stormy session of Parliament after Charles became king, it became apparent that the problems between this king and Parliament would not be easily solved. In 1628, Parliament passed a Petition of Right, which the king was supposed to accept before being granted any taxes. This petition prohibited taxes without Parliament's consent. At first Charles accepted it. He changed his mind later, realizing that it put limits on the king's power.

Religious differences also added to the hostility between Charles I and Parliament. Charles tried to impose more ritual on the Church of England. To the Puritans, this was a return to Catholic practices. When Charles tried to force the Puritans to accept his religious policies, thousands of them went to the "howling wildernesses" of America instead.

Complaints grew until England finally slipped into a civil war in 1642 between the supporters of the king (known as the Cavaliers or Royalists) and the parliamentary forces (known as Roundheads). Parliament proved victorious, due largely to the New Model Army of Oliver Cromwell, the only real military genius of the war. The New Model Army was made up chiefly of more extreme Puritans, known as the Independents, who believed they were doing battle for God. As Cromwell wrote in one of his military reports, "Sir, this is none other but the hand of God; and to Him alone belongs the glory." We might give some credit to Cromwell as well, because his soldiers were well disciplined and trained in the new military tactics developed in the course of the Thirty Years' War.

The victorious New Model Army lost no time in taking control. Cromwell purged Parliament of any members who had not supported his forces. What was left—the so-called Rump Parliament—then had Charles I executed on January 30, 1649. Parliament next abolished the monarchy and the House of Lords, and it declared England a republic or commonwealth. However, Cromwell and his army found it difficult to work with the Rump Parliament and finally dispersed it by force. As the members of Parliament departed, he shouted after them, "It is you that have forced me to do this, for I have sought the Lord night and day that He would slay me rather than put upon me the doing of this work." With the certainty of one who is convinced he is right, Cromwell had destroyed both king and Parliament. He then set up a military dictatorship.

After Cromwell's death, the army leaders decided that military rule was no longer desirable. They restored the monarchy in the person of Charles II, the

So What ??

If your students question the importance of information about **the sixteenth century,** *tell them . . .*

that people showed a great burst of energy during this century. One cause may have been location. Western Europe stood at the edge of the "known world" and was cut off by the Ottoman Empire from Asia and the "Indies." To the west lay the Atlantic, waiting to be explored.

Another cause was the interest of Europeans in invention and change. Clocks, printing with movable type, gunpowder, new designs for ships and navigation aides—all

◄ *This painting shows the execution of King Charles I. A woman faints at the bottom when the executioner displays the king's head. At the top left is a portrait of the king. Who followed Charles I as England's ruler?*

son of Charles I. With the return of the monarchy, England's time of troubles seemed at an end.

❀ SECTION REVIEW ❀

1. **Locate:**
   (*a*) Holy Roman Empire, (*b*) Bohemia

2. **Define:**
   (*a*) price revolution, (*b*) witchcraft, (*c*) divine right of kings, (*d*) gentry

3. **Identify:**
   (*a*) sabbats, (*b*) the Thirty Years' War, (*c*) Habsburg Holy Roman emperors, (*d*) Peace of Westphalia, (*e*) the Stuart line of rulers, (*f*) Puritans, (*g*) the House of Commons, (*h*) Oliver Cromwell

4. **Recall:**
   (*a*) What caused the dramatic rise in prices during the sixteenth and early seventeenth centuries?
   (*b*) Which people were most commonly accused of witchcraft? How did the witchcraft craze become so widespread during the sixteenth and seventeenth centuries?

(*c*) What was at the core of the English Revolution of the seventeenth century?

5. **Think Critically:** How did social disintegration, war, and revolution put Europe in crisis? Explain your answer.

RESPONSE TO CRISIS: THE PRACTICE OF ABSOLUTISM AND LIMITED MONARCHY

One response to the crises of the seventeenth century was a search for order. Increasing the power of the king became one way to gain more stability. The result was what historians have called **absolutism.** Absolutism meant that the ultimate authority in the state rested in the hands of a monarch who claimed to rule by divine right. Divine right, as we have seen, was the idea that rulers received their power from God and were responsible to no one (including parliaments) except God. With no earthly challenge, absolute monarchs had tremendous powers. They had the ability to make laws, levy taxes, administer justice, control the state's officials, and determine foreign policy.

helped people explore new territories and try to improve the quality of their lives. In western Europe wealth also grew rapidly. And then came the Renaissance—the rebirth of learning and renewed interest in the science and art of human life. Strong national states arose. European states would battle for the

next several centuries over political freedom, absolutism, constitutionalism, and nationalism. These driving forces would make western Europe the leader of the entire world. Today these forces have spread to every continent and have influenced their development.

CLOSE

Ask students to discuss the relevance of the expression "with God on our side" to the witchcraft hysteria, the Thirty Years' War, the doctrine of the "divine right of kings," the rise of Puritanism, the rise and fall of Oliver Cromwell.

◆ 3 ◆

FOCUS

OBJECTIVES

After completing this section, students should be able to

1. discuss the importance of Louis XIV, Cardinal Richelieu, Cardinal Mazarin, Jean-Baptiste Colbert, Ivan the Terrible, Peter the Great, William and Mary
2. list reasons why the reign of Louis XIV is considered the best example of absolute monarchy
3. distinguish between absolute monarchy and constitutional monarchy
4. explain mercantilism
5. discuss the freedoms gained by the English after the Glorious Revolution

FOCUS ACTIVITY

The various crises of the seventeenth century led many Europeans to long for order and stability. Ask students to brainstorm ways governments can respond to (or manipulate) this desire. *(creating a police state, eliminating opposition to the central government, eliminating the monarch, increasing or decreasing government intervention in people's lives)*

468

Absolutism in France under Louis XIV (1661 to 1715)

France during the reign of Louis XIV has long been regarded as the best example of the practice of absolute monarchy in the seventeenth century. French culture, language, and manners reached into all levels of European society. French diplomacy and wars dominated the political affairs of western and central Europe. The court of Louis XIV was imitated throughout Europe.

The fifty years of French history before Louis were a period of struggle as governments fought to avoid the breakdown of the state. The situation was made more difficult because when both Louis XIII and Louis XIV came to the throne, they were only boys. The government was left in the hands of royal ministers. In France, two ministers played important roles in preserving the authority of the monarchy.

Cardinal Richelieu (RISH-uh-LOO), Louis XIII's chief minister, strengthened the power of the monarchy. He took away the political and military rights of the Huguenots while preserving their religious ones. In this way, Richelieu transformed the Huguenots into more reliable subjects. Richelieu also tamed the nobles by setting up a network of spies to uncover plots by nobles against the government. He then crushed the conspiracies and executed the conspirators.

When Louis XIV came to the throne in 1643 at the age of four, Cardinal Mazarin (MAZ-uh-RA[n]), the chief minister, took over control of the government. During Mazarin's rule, a revolt led by nobles unhappy with the growing power of the monarchy broke out. This revolt was crushed. With its end, a vast number of French people concluded that the best hope for stability in France lay with the king.

When Mazarin died in 1661, the greatest of the seventeenth-century monarchs, Louis XIV, took over supreme power. The day after Cardinal Mazarin's death, the new king, at the age of twenty-three, stated his desire to be a real king and the sole ruler of France:

Up to this moment I have been pleased to entrust the government of my affairs to the late Cardinal. It is now time that I govern them myself. You [secretaries and ministers of state] will assist me with your counsels when I ask for them. I request and order you to seal no orders except by my command. I order you not to sign anything, not even a passport without my command; to render account to me personally each day and to favor no one.[4]

The king's mother, who was well aware of her son's love of fun and games and his affairs with the maids in the royal palace, laughed aloud at these words. Louis was serious, however, and was quite willing to pay the price of being a strong ruler. He established a strict routine from which he seldom deviated. He also fostered the myth of himself as the Sun King, the source of light for all of his people.

One of the keys to Louis's power was his control of the central policy-making machinery of government. The royal court at Versailles (VUR-SIE) served three purposes. It was the personal household of the king, or where the king lived. In addition, the machinery of the central government (the chief offices of the state) was located there, so Louis could watch over it. Finally, Versailles was the place where powerful subjects came to find favors and offices for themselves.

The greatest danger to Louis's rule came from the very high nobles and princes of the blood (the royal princes). They believed they should play a role in the government of France. Louis got rid of this threat by removing them from the royal council. This was the chief administrative body of the king, and it supervised the central machinery of government. At the same time, Louis enticed these nobles and royal princes to come to his court, where he could keep them busy with court life and keep them out of politics (see "Focus on Everyday Life: At the Court of Versailles"). For his ministers, Louis chose nobles who came from the new aristocratic families rather than the high nobility or royal princes. His ministers were expected to obey his every wish. Said Louis, "I had no intention of sharing my authority with them."

Louis's control of his ministers gave him control of the central policy-making machinery of government. He had complete authority over the traditional areas of royal power: foreign policy, the church, and taxes. However, Louis had much less success with the internal administration of the kingdom. The traditional

ENRICHMENT ACTIVITY

Assign students to research the court of Louis XIV. Ask them to pay special attention to the development of the powerful cult surrounding Louis. What court ceremonies were involved in creating this cult of power? Could it have been avoided? Why or why not? You might also want students to compare Louis' court with cliques in their school. Do such cliques exist? How are they similar to Louis' court? Ask each student to write a report on his or her findings and observations.

FOCUS ON EVERYDAY LIFE
At the Court of Versailles

▲ *When Versailles was built, it was the largest royal residence in Europe, and it still stands as one of the most lavish. Members of the king's government were housed here, as well as thousands of French nobles and their entire households. Why did Louis insist that his nobles reside in Versailles?*

In 1669, Louis XIV of France decided to build a palace at Versailles, near Paris. Not until untold sums of money had been spent and tens of thousands of workers had labored incessantly was most of the work completed. The enormous palace housed thousands of people.

Life at Versailles became a court ceremony, with Louis XIV at the center of it all. The king had little privacy. Only when he visited his wife, mother, or mistress or met with ministers was he free of the nobles who swarmed about the palace. Most daily ceremonies were carefully staged, such as those attending Louis's rising from bed, dining, praying, attending mass, and going to bed. A mob of nobles

▲ *The Hall of Mirrors in Versailles takes up the center section of the palace and looks out upon beautifully manicured gardens. Lavish in decoration and impressive in size, this room is still used as a meeting place for government officials.*

competed to assist the king in carrying out these solemn activities. It was considered a great honor, for example, for a noble to be chosen to hand the king his shirt while dressing. Why did the nobles

(continued)

FOCUS ON EVERYDAY LIFE

CLASS DISCUSSION

Ask students to discuss the following sentence: "Life at Versailles became a court ceremony, with Louis XIV at the center of it all."

CRITICAL THINKING

Ask students to imagine what it was like to be Louis XIV: surrounded by nobles, servants, and hangers-on; determined to maintain absolute authority over foreign policy, the church, taxation, and the lives of his subjects. Have them write a diary entry in which Louis confides his feelings about his court and reign.

CLASS DISCUSSION

Ask students to discuss why, after the rule of Cardinals Richelieu and Mazarin, many French people "concluded that the best hope for stability in France lay with the king."

LEARNING FROM VISUALS

Answer to the caption question: Louis XIV realized that he could better control his nobles if they were removed from their country-side homes and placed under his watchful eye at Versailles.

CNN® WORLD HISTORY UPDATES

You can update your coverage of World History topics, as well as spark lively classroom discussion and deeper understanding, by using the **CNN World History Updates.**

For assistance in using and incorporating the **CNN World History Updates** into your classroom presentations, see the *Classroom Guide.*

Answers to Critical Thinking Questions

1. Nobles assisted Louis in rising from bed, dining, praying, attending mass, and going to bed. He made it clear that anyone who hoped to obtain an office, title, or pension from him must take part in these activities.
2. Louis felt that having the nobles engaged in gambling kept them busy and out of politics.
3. The system of "who could sit where" indicated who was more important than another in Louis's eyes. Therefore, he could make people feel good or bad, important or not, just by where they were allowed to sit at the dinner table.

TEACH

ACROSS THE CURRICULUM

Art. Ask interested students to research the palace and gardens of Versailles. Have them present details and illustrations that give a flavor of the residence's magnificence.

CLASS DISCUSSION

Guide students in a discussion of the principles of mercantilism, particularly the need for a favorable balance of trade.

FOCUS ON EVERYDAY LIFE

At the Court of Versailles, continued

take part in these ceremonies? Louis had made it clear that anyone who hoped to obtain an office, title, or pension from the king had to participate in these activities. This was Louis's way of controlling their behavior.

Court etiquette became very complex. Nobles and royal princes were expected to follow certain rules. Who could sit where at meals with the king was carefully regulated. Once at dinner, when the wife of a minister sat closer to the king than did a duchess, Louis XIV became so angry that he did not eat for the rest of the evening.

Daily life at Versailles included many forms of entertainment. Louis and his nobles hunted once a week. Walks through the Versailles gardens, boating trips, plays, ballets, and concerts were all sources of pleasure. One form of entertainment—gambling—became an obsession at Versailles. Many nobles gambled regularly and lost enormous sums of money. One princess described the scene: "Here in France as soon as people get together they do nothing but play cards; they play for frightful sums, and the players seem bereft of their senses. One shouts at the top of his voice, another strikes the table with his fist. It is horrible to watch them." Louis did not think so. He was pleased by an activity that kept the Versailles nobles busy and out of politics.

1. How did Louis XIV attempt to control the behavior of his nobles?
2. Why did Louis like the gambling that went on at Versailles?
3. In what way was the system of court etiquette another way Louis controlled his nobles?

---

groups of French society—the nobles, officials, and town councils—were simply too powerful for the king to have direct control over the lives of his subjects. As a result, the king bribed important people in the provinces to see that his policies were carried out.

Maintaining religious harmony had long been a part of monarchical power in France. The desire to keep it led Louis to pursue an anti-Protestant policy aimed at converting the Huguenots to Catholicism. Early in his reign, Louis ordered the destruction of Huguenot churches and the closing of their schools. Although they were officially forbidden to leave France, it is estimated that 200,000 Huguenots left for shelter in England, the United Provinces, and the German states.

The cost of building palaces, maintaining his court, and pursuing his wars made finances a crucial issue for Louis XIV. He was most fortunate in having the services of Jean-Baptiste Colbert (kawl-BARE) as controller-general of finances. Colbert sought to increase the wealth and power of France by following the ideas of **mercantilism**—a set of principles that dominated economic thought in the seventeenth century.

According to the mercantilists, the prosperity of a nation depended upon a large supply of bullion, or gold and silver. For this reason, nations tried to have a **favorable balance of trade** in which the goods they exported were of greater value than those they imported. This would bring in gold and silver payments to increase a country's supply of bullion. To encourage exports, governments stimulated and protected export industries and trade. They granted subsidies to new industries and improved transportation systems by building roads, bridges, and canals. By placing high tariffs on foreign goods, they could be kept out of the

---

MORE ABOUT . . . *Versailles*

Versailles is one of the most famous structures in Western architecture. It was originally built to reflect Louis the 14th's power and grandeur. The armistice that ended World War I was signed at Versailles, and the treaty named after it. Today, the historical building, is in great need of restoration. The Versailles Museum of France (housing 6000 paintings and 2000 sculptures) has been closed for nearly twenty years. Also closed to the public is the Hall of Battles and the magnificent Hall of the Crusades. Funds for restoring buildings and works of art are very scare. A good topic for "Comparing Time Periods" is to ask students to research the problems facing nations trying to cut budgets while maintaining its historical landmarks. Perhaps there is a building or monument in the students' local area that is in the same situation.

country. Colonies were considered important as sources of raw materials and markets for finished goods. Mercantilists believed that the state should play an active role in a nation's economic affairs.

Colbert was a great advocate of mercantilism. To decrease imports and increase exports, he granted subsidies to those who established new industries. To improve communications and the transportation of goods within France, he built roads and canals. To decrease imports directly, Colbert raised tariffs on foreign goods and created a merchant marine to carry French goods.

The increase in royal power that Louis pursued led the king to develop a standing army numbering 400,000 in time of war. Louis made war a constant activity of his reign. He wished to achieve the military glory befitting a Sun King, as well as to ensure the domination of his Bourbon dynasty over European affairs. To achieve these goals, Louis waged four wars between 1667 and 1713. His ambitions roused many European nations to form coalitions to prevent him from dominating Europe. Through his wars, Louis added some territory to France's northeastern frontier and established a member of his own dynasty on the throne of Spain.

Only two years later, in 1715, the Sun King was dead. He left France with great debts and surrounded by enemies. On his deathbed, the seventy-six-year-old monarch seemed remorseful when he told his successor (his great-grandson), "Soon you will be King of a great kingdom. . . . Try to remain at peace with your neighbors. I loved war too much. Do not follow me in that or in overspending. . . . Lighten your people's burden as soon as possible, and do what I have had the misfortune not to do myself."[5] Did Louis mean it? We do not know. In any event, the advice to his successor was probably not remembered; his great-grandson was only five years old.

Absolutism in Central and Eastern Europe

During the seventeenth century, three new powers—Prussia, Austria, and Russia—appeared in central and eastern Europe. All three became great European states.

The Peace of Westphalia, which ended the Thirty Years' War in 1648, left each of the three hundred or more German states making up the Holy Roman Empire virtually independent. Properly speaking, there was no German state, but over three hundred "Germanies." Of these states, two (Prussia and Austria) emerged in the seventeenth and eighteenth centuries as great European powers.

The Emergence of a Powerful Prussia

Frederick William the Great Elector laid the foundation for the Prussian state. Realizing that Prussia was a small, open territory with no natural frontiers for defense, Frederick William built a large and efficient standing army. He had a force of forty thousand men, which made the Prussian army the fourth largest in Europe. To maintain the army and his own power, Frederick William set up the General War Commissariat to levy taxes for the army and oversee its growth. The Commissariat soon became an agency for civil government as well. The new bureaucratic machine became the elector's chief instrument to govern the state. Many of its officials were members of the Prussian landed aristocracy, known as the Junkers, who also served as officers in the all-important army.

In 1701, Frederick William's son Frederick officially gained the title of king. Elector Frederick III became King Frederick I. In the eighteenth century, Prussia emerged as a great power in Europe.

The New Austrian Empire

The Austrian Habsburgs had long played a significant role in European politics as Holy Roman emperors. By the end of the Thirty Years' War, the Habsburg hopes of creating an empire in Germany had been dashed. In the seventeenth century, the Austrian Habsburgs made a difficult transition. They had lost the German empire, but now they created a new empire in eastern and southeastern Europe.

The core of the new Austrian Empire was the traditional Austrian lands in present-day Austria, the Czech Republic, and Hungary. After the defeat of the Turks in 1687 (see Chapter 17), Austria took control

RECOMMENDED READING

For a brief account of seventeenth-century French history, see R. Briggs, *Early Modern France, 1560–1715* (Oxford, 1977). More detailed studies on France during the periods of Henry IV and Cardinals Richelieu and Mazarin are M. Greengrass, *France in the Age of Henri IV and The Struggle for Stability* (London, 1984).

On the creation of an Austrian state, see R. J. W. Evans, *The Making of the Habsburg Monarchy, 1550–1700* (Oxford, 1979).

On Russian history before Peter the Great, see the classic work by V. O. Klyuchevsky, *A Course in Russian History: The Seventeenth Century* (Chicago, 1968); and R. Nellie, *Enserfment and Military Change in Muscovy* (Chicago, 1971). Works on Peter include *Peter the Great* (London, 1978); B. H. Sumner, *Peter the Great and the Emergence of Russia* (New York, 1962).

Map 15.3   The Growth of the Austrian Empire

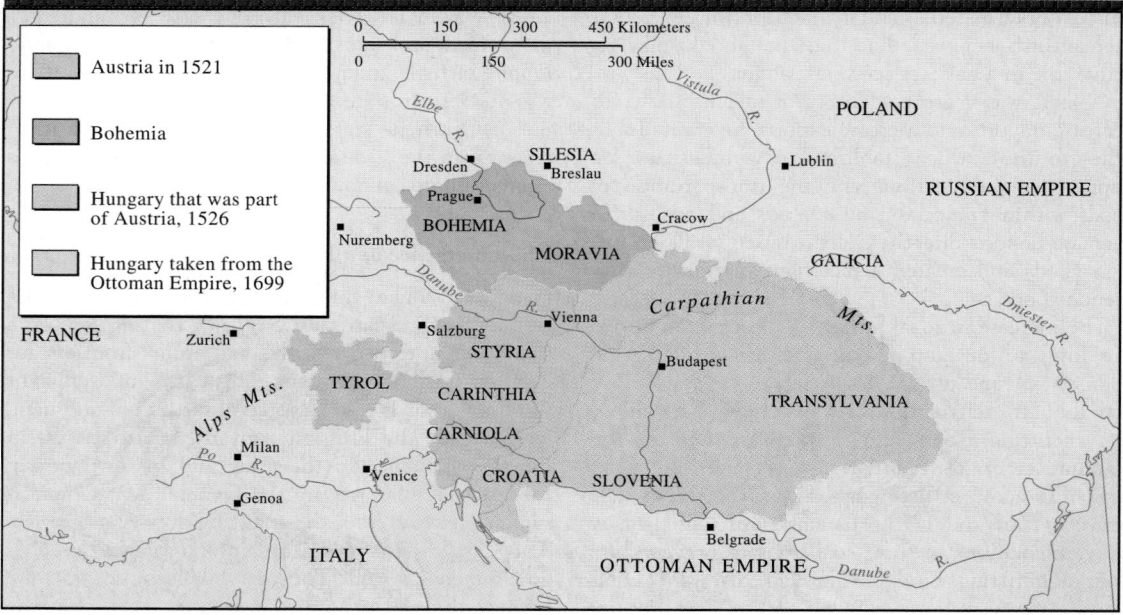

of all of Hungary, Transylvania, Croatia, and Slovenia, thus establishing an Austrian Empire in southeastern Europe. By the beginning of the eighteenth century, the Austrian Habsburgs had gained a new empire.

The Austrian monarchy, however, never became a highly centralized, absolutist state, chiefly because it was made up of so many different national groups. The Austrian Empire remained a collection of territories held together by the Habsburg emperor, who was archduke of Austria, king of Bohemia, and king of Hungary. Each of these areas, however, had its own laws and political life. There was no common sentiment to tie the regions together.

From Muscovy to Russia

A new Russian state had emerged in the fifteenth century under the leadership of the principality of Muscovy and its grand dukes. In the sixteenth century,

Ivan IV became the first ruler to take the title of **tsar,** the Russian word for *Caesar*. Ivan expanded the territories of Russia eastward. He also crushed the power of the Russian nobility, known as the **boyars** (boe-YARZ). He was known as Ivan the Terrible because of his ruthless deeds, among them stabbing his own son to death in a heated argument.

When Ivan's dynasty came to an end, it was followed by a period of anarchy known as the Time of Troubles. This period did not end until the Zemsky Sobor, or national assembly, chose Michael Romanov (roe-MAWN-uf) as the new tsar in 1613, beginning a dynasty that lasted until 1917.

In the seventeenth century, the tsar, who claimed to be divinely ordained, was the absolute ruler of Russia. Russian society was dominated by an upper class of landed aristocrats who, in the course of the seventeenth century, managed to bind their peasants to the land, making them serfs. They also controlled the

STUDYING MAPS

The following questions will help you guide students through their study of Map 15.3.

1. Compare the size of the Austrian Empire before and after the final defeat of the Turks (1699). Approximately how much land was added? (*Austria doubled the size of its territory with the addition of Hungary.*)
2. Give two reasons that would indicate the importance of the Danube River to the

empire. (*The Danube bisects the empire and would be a major transportation route. Secondly, the capital city is located along its banks.*)
3. Look at a contemporary map of this region. What differences do you see? (*Answers will vary, but should acknowledge the many more countries that exist today.*)

Map 15.4   From Muscovy to Russia

Russia in 1584

Acquisitions, 1584–1700

Acquisitions, 1700–1772
(primarily, Peter the Great)

turned to Russia, he was determined to westernize or Europeanize Russia. He was especially eager to borrow European technology. He realized that only this kind of modernization could give him the army and navy he needed to make Russia a great power.

As could be expected, one of his first goals was to reorganize the army. He employed both Russians and Europeans as officers. He drafted peasants for twenty-five year stints of service to build a standing army of 210,000 men. Peter has also been given credit for forming the first Russian navy, which was his overriding passion.

To impose the rule of the central government more effectively throughout the land, Peter divided Russia into provinces. He hoped to create a "police state," by which he meant a well-ordered community governed by law. However, few of his bureaucrats shared his concept of honest service and duty to the state. Peter hoped for a sense of civic duty, but his own personality created an atmosphere of fear that prevented it. He wrote to one administrator, "According to these orders act, act, act. I won't write more, but you will pay with your head if you interpret orders again."[6] Peter wanted his administrators to be slaves and free men at the same time. It did not occur to him that the task was impossible.

To satisfy his need of money for an army and navy that took most of the state revenue, Peter tried to stimulate economic growth by adopting Western mercantilistic policies. He tried to increase exports and develop new industries while exploiting domestic resources, such as the iron mines in the Urals (YUR-ulz). However, his military needs were endless. He came to rely on simply raising taxes, thus placing more burdens upon helpless peasants, who grew ever more oppressed in Peter's Russia.

Peter also sought to gain state control of the Russian Orthodox Church. He abolished the position of patriarch and created a body called the Holy Synod (SIN-ad) to make decisions for the church. At its head stood

townspeople. Many merchants were not allowed to move from their cities without government permission or to sell their businesses to anyone not of their class. In the seventeenth century, merchant and peasant revolts, as well as division in the Russian Orthodox Church, created very unsettled conditions. In the midst of these upheavals, seventeenth-century Russia came into greater contact with Europeans in the West. At the end of the seventeenth century, a new tsar reached out even more to the West.

Peter the Great was an unusual character. A towering, strong man at six feet, nine inches tall, Peter was coarse in his tastes and rude in his behavior. He enjoyed a low kind of humor (belching contests and crude jokes) and vicious punishments (flogging, impalings, and roastings). Peter received a firsthand view of the West when he made a trip there. When he re-

STUDYING MAPS

The following questions will help you guide students through their study of Map 15.4.

1. What geographic feature divides western and eastern Russia? (the Ural Mountains)
2. Find the Baltic Sea. What was Peter the Great's difficulty in establishing a port there? (It was controlled by a foreign power before Peter conquered the land that gave him access.)
3. After defeating Sweden, what city did Peter have built on the Baltic? (St. Petersburg) Find it on the map.

LEARNING FROM VISUALS

Answers to the caption question: (far right) The queen's crown was not edged with fur, nor is there a cross on top.

(near right) Peter the Great had shaved off his beard and abandoned the traditional Russian long-skirted coat.

CLASS DISCUSSION

Ask students to discuss the following sentence: "One group of Russians gained much from Peter's cultural reforms—women." In what ways did Russian women benefit? Which groups did not benefit from westernization? Why was Peter's campaign "a bit of a sham"?

▲ *A Dutch artist painted this portrait of Peter the Great during his first visit to the West in 1697. What Western mannerisms had Peter already adopted when he sat for this portrait?*

◀ *One of Peter the Great's crowns is shown here. The "Cap of Monomach" was made of gold, studded with pearls and other gemstones, and trimmed with sable. How does this compare to the crown worn by Elizabeth I?*

a procurator, a layperson who represented the interests of the tsar. Peter now controlled the church.

After his first trip to the West, Peter began to introduce Western customs, practices, and manners into Russia. He ordered the preparation of the first Russian book of etiquette to teach Western manners. Among other things, it pointed out that it was not polite to spit on the floor or to scratch oneself at dinner. Because westerners did not wear beards or the traditional long-skirted coat, Russian beards had to be shaved and coats shortened. Peter enforced the new look at court by shaving off his nobles' beards and cutting their coats at the knees with his own hands. Outside the court, the edicts were enforced by barbers and tailors planted at town gates with orders to cut the beards and cloaks of those who entered or left.

One group of Russians gained much from Peter's cultural reforms—women. Having watched women mixing freely with men in Western courts, Peter insisted that Russian upper-class women remove the traditional veils that covered their faces and move out into society. Peter also held gatherings in which both sexes could mix for conversation and dancing, a practice Peter had learned in the West. Women were also allowed to marry of their own free will.

The object of Peter's domestic reforms was to make Russia into a great state and military power. An important part of this was to "open a window to the West," meaning an ice-free port with ready year-round access to Europe. This could be achieved only on the Baltic. At that time, however, the Baltic coast was controlled by Sweden, the most important power in northern Europe. A long and hard-fought war with Sweden enabled Peter to acquire the lands he sought. On a marshland on the Baltic, Peter began the construction of a new city, St. Petersburg, his window on the West. Thousands of peasants died during its construction. St. Petersburg was finished during Peter's lifetime and remained the Russian capital until 1917.

Under Peter, Russia became a great military power and, by his death in 1725, an important European state. However, his policies also harmed Russia. His westernization was a bit of a sham, because Western culture reached only the upper classes. The creation of a strong military only added more burdens to the Russian masses. The forceful way in which Peter the Great brought westernization led many Russians to distrust Europe.

MORE ABOUT . . . *St. Petersburg*

Czar Peter the Great launched a war against Sweden to get an access to the Baltic Coast, which came to be known as the Northern War (1700–1721). By 1703, the Neva, from its source to the estuary, was in Russian hands. A pathway to the Baltic Sea and, consequently, to Europe was thus obtained. On May 16, 1703 the cornerstone of the Peter-and-Paul Fortress was laid on the marshy ground of Island Zayachy. This date marks the birth of St. Petersburg.

Czar Peter built the city at unprecedented speed. Thousands of peasants and working men were drafted to work there from all over Russia. Many of the construction workers died from sickness, hunger, and accidents. Peasants hated the forced labor in the capital, and each year between a forth and a third of them ran away. In the forests they cleared passages for the future avenues, drained

Limited Monarchy: The Example of England

Almost everywhere in Europe in the seventeenth century, kings and their ministers were in control of central governments. However, not all European states followed the pattern of absolute monarchy. England was the most prominent example of a state that limited the power of its monarchs.

The Stuart monarchy was restored to England by Parliament in 1660 in the person of Charles II. The restoration of the monarchy did not mean, however, that the work of the English Revolution was undone. Parliament kept much of the power it had won and continued to play an important role in government. The principle that Parliament must give its consent to taxation was also accepted. However, Charles continued to push his own ideas, some of which were clearly out of step with many of the English people.

Charles was sympathetic to Catholicism. Moreover, his brother James, heir to the throne, did not hide the fact that he was a Catholic. Parliament's suspicions about their Catholic leanings were therefore aroused when Charles took the bold step of suspending the laws that Parliament had passed against Catholics and Puritans after the restoration of the monarchy. Parliament would have none of it and forced the king to back down on his action. Driven by a strong anti-Catholic sentiment, Parliament then passed a Test Act, specifying that only Anglicans (as members of the Church of England were called) could hold military and civil offices.

The accession of James II to the crown brought a new constitutional crisis for England. James was an open and devout Catholic. His attempt to promote Catholic interests made religion once more a cause of conflict between king and Parliament. Contrary to the Test Act, James named Catholics to high positions in the government, army, navy, and universities. He issued a Declaration of Indulgence, which suspended all laws excluding Catholics and Puritans from office.

◀ *Peter Hoadley painted this cameo portrait of the new English rulers William of Orange and his wife Mary. How does this painting compare to the portrait of Louis XIV that opens the chapter?*

Parliamentary outcries against James's policies stopped short of rebellion, however. Members knew that James was an old man, and his successors were his Protestant daughters Mary and Anne, born to his first wife. However, when a son was born to James II's second wife, also a Catholic, the possibility of a Catholic hereditary monarchy loomed large. A group of prominent English noblemen invited the Dutch leader, William of Orange, husband of James's daughter Mary, to invade England. William and Mary raised an army and in 1688 "invaded" England while James, his wife, and his infant son fled to France. With almost no bloodshed, England had undergone a "Glorious Revolution"—not over the issue of whether there would be monarchy but rather over who would be monarch.

The events of 1688 were only the first stage of the Glorious Revolution. Early the next year, Parliament offered the throne to William and Mary, who accepted it, along with a Bill of Rights. The Bill of Rights set forth Parliament's right to make laws and levy taxes. It also made it impossible for kings to oppose or to do without Parliament by stating that standing armies could be raised only with the consent of Parliament. The rights of citizens to keep arms and have a jury trial were also confirmed. The Bill of Rights helped to fashion a system of government based on the rule of law and a freely elected Parliament. Thus, it laid the foundation for a limited or constitutional monarchy.

The Bill of Rights, however, did not settle the religious questions that had played such a large role in England's troubles in the seventeenth century. The Toleration Act of 1689 granted Puritans the right of free public worship (Catholics were still excluded). The act did not lead to complete religious freedom and equality. However, it marked a turning point in English

---

swamps, and dug ditches.

St. Petersburg became the capital of the vast Russian empire only nine years after it was created. It grew rapidly and soon developed into a major industrial center. The first foreign ship arrived in 1703. In 1726, the city was already the country's largest center of sea trade. The best sculptors and artists in Europe and Russia created its masterpieces. A naval

academy, a university, a technological institute, and dozens of other higher education establishments appeared to give the country generations of prominent scientists, engineers, and researchers. St. Petersburg is also the city of great Russian writers and poets such as, Alexander Pushkin, Nikolai Gogol, Lev Tolstoy, and Feodor Dostoevsky.

ASSESS

Answers to
SECTION REVIEW

1. (a) rule by divine right
   (b) a nation needs a large supply of gold and silver to be prosperous
   (c) more exports than imports
   (d) Russian ruler
   (e) Russian nobility
3. (a) Louis XIII's chief minister
   (b) Louis XIV's regent
   (c) controller-general of finances under Louis XIV
   (d) laid the foundation for the Prussian state
   (e) Prussian landed aristocracy
   (f) first Russian tsar
   (g) period of anarchy following Ivan the Terrible
   (h) began dynasty that lasted from 1613–1917
   (i) tsar who tried to westernize Russia
   (j) granted Puritans the right of public worship
4. (a) nobles who wanted power
   (b) foreign policy, the church, taxes
   (c) Prussia and Austria
   (d) dress and maners in socializing; liberating women
   (e) gave Parliament right to make laws and levy taxes; keep a standing army; and guaranteed free elections
5. Answers will vary.

CLOSE

Both absolute and limited monarchy were attempts by European nations to restore order and increase stability in their societies. Which do students think succeeded best in reaching this goal?

history: few people would ever again be persecuted for religious reasons.

Many historians have viewed the Glorious Revolution as the end of the seventeenth-century struggle between king and Parliament. By deposing one king and establishing another, Parliament had destroyed the divine-right theory of kingship (William was, after all, king by the grace of Parliament, not God). Parliament had also asserted its right to be part of the government. Parliament did not have complete control of the government, but it now had the right to participate in affairs of state. Over the next century, Parliament would gradually prove to be the real authority in the English system of constitutional monarchy.

SECTION REVIEW

1. **Locate:**
   (a) Versailles, (b) Prussia, (c) Austria, (d) Russia, (e) St. Petersburg

2. **Define:**
   (a) absolutism, (b) mercantilism, (c) favorable balance of trade, (d) tsar, (e) boyars

3. **Identify:**
   (a) Cardinal Richelieu, (b) Cardinal Mazarin, (c) Jean-Baptiste Colbert, (d) Frederick William, (e) Junkers, (f) Ivan IV the Terrible, (g) Time of Troubles, (h) Michael Romanov, (i) Peter the Great, (j) Toleration Act of 1689

4. **Recall:**
   (a) What was the greatest danger to Louis XIV's rule?
   (b) What were the traditional areas of royal power?
   (c) What two German states emerged in the seventeenth and eighteenth centuries as great European powers?
   (d) What customs did Peter the Great use to westernize Russia?
   (e) In England, how did the Bill of Rights establish Parliament's role in government?

5. **Think Critically:** Explain the difference between the results of constitutional monarchy in England and absolute monarchy in France.

THE WORLD OF
EUROPEAN CULTURE

The artistic Renaissance came to an end when a new movement, called Mannerism, emerged in Italy in the decades of the 1520s and 1530s. The Reformation had brought a revival of religious values. With it came much political turmoil. Especially in Italy, the worldly enthusiasm of the Renaissance declined as people grew anxious, uncertain, and desirous of spiritual experience. Mannerism in art reflected this new environment by deliberately breaking down the High Renaissance principles of balance, harmony, and moderation. The rules of proportion were deliberately ignored as elongated figures were used to show suffering, heightened emotions, and religious ecstasy. Unrealistic colors, such as pinkish hues for the color of human skin, heightened a sense of the unusual.

Mannerism spread from Italy to other parts of Europe and perhaps reached its high point in the work of El Greco. He was from the island of Crete. After studying in Venice and Rome, he moved to Spain, where he became a church painter. In his paintings, El Greco used elongated and contorted figures, portraying them in unusual shades of yellow and green against an eerie background of stormy grays. The mood he depicts reflects well the tensions created by the religious upheavals of the Reformation. Mannerism was eventually replaced by a new movement—the Baroque (buh-ROKE)—that dominated the artistic world for another century and a half (see "Our Artistic Heritage: The Splendor of the Baroque").

In the second half of the seventeenth century, France replaced Italy as the cultural center of Europe. Although the French did not entirely reject the new Baroque style, they returned to the classical ideals of the High Renaissance. French late classicism, as it is

RETEACHING ACTIVITY

In the Teacher Resource Box you will find a black line master of a chart that will help students consolidate and recall information about the way in which the limited monarchy in England evolved. Students should complete the chart by filling in the dates and explaining the impact of the different monarchs on the evolution of Parliamentary power in England during the seventeenth century.

OUR ARTISTIC HERITAGE
The Splendor of the Baroque

The Baroque movement began in Italy in the last quarter of the sixteenth century and spread to the rest of Europe. Baroque artists tried to bring together the classical ideals of Renaissance art with the spiritual feelings of the sixteenth-century religious revival. The Baroque style first appeared in Rome in the Jesuit church of Il Gesù, the facade of which was completed in 1575. It was the Catholic reform movement that most wholeheartedly adopted the Baroque style. This can be seen in the buildings at Catholic courts, especially those of the Habsburgs in Madrid, Prague (PRAWG), Vienna, and Brussels. Eventually the Baroque style spread to all of Europe and Latin America.

In large part, Baroque art and architecture reflected the search for power that was such a part of the seventeenth century. Baroque churches and palaces were built with richly detailed facades and magnificent staircases. Kings and princes wanted other kings and princes as well as their subjects to be in awe of their power.

The Baroque painting style was known for its use of dramatic effects to arouse the emotions. Perhaps the greatest figure of the Baroque period was the Italian architect and sculptor Gian Lorenzo Bernini (bur-NEE-NEE), who completed Saint Peter's Basilica in Rome. Action, exuberance, and dramatic effects mark the work of Bernini in the interior of Saint Peter's. His *Throne of Saint Peter* is a highly decorated cover for the pope's medieval wooden throne. The throne seems to hover in midair, held by the hands of the four great theologians of the early Catholic Church. Above the chair, rays of heavenly light drive a mass of clouds and angels toward the spectator.

 Gian Lorenzo Bernini used gilt bronze, marble, and stucco to create this monumental Throne of St. Peter. *It took Bernini eleven years to complete this masterpiece for St. Peter's Basilica.*

1. What did artists attempt to do during the Baroque period?

2. Where did the Baroque style first appear?

3. In what ways did the Baroque style reflect the search for power that was a part of the seventeenth century?

RETEACHING ACTIVITY

Have students study the works of art on pages 477, 478, and 479 by El Greco, Bernini, and Poussin. For each work they should describe the subject matter and then prepare a statement about the ways in which the subject matters compare. Using what they've learned from reading the text, they should then identify the characteristics of each of the representative styles of Mannerism, Baroque, and Classicism. Students should also identify the symbols used by each artist. Finally, students should tell how they are affected by each of the works.

▲ *Mannerism reached one of its highest expressions in the work of El Greco. He moved to Spain in 1577 and spent the rest of his life in Toledo, where he worked as a church painter. In 1597 he painted this* View of Toledo. *Do you think this is a realistic view of the city? Why or why not?*

called, emphasized clarity, simplicity, and balance. Nicholas Poussin (POO-SA[n]) showed these principles in his paintings. His choice of scenes from ancient Greece and Rome, the calmness of his landscapes, the postures of his figures copied from the sculptures of antiquity, and his use of brown tones all reflect the principles of French classicism.

A Golden Age of Literature: England and Spain

In both England and Spain, writing for the theater reached new heights between 1580 and 1640. It was a golden age in English theater, as well as in its cul-

ture in general. The age is often called the Elizabethan (i-LIZ-uh-BEE-thun) Era, because much of the English cultural flowering of the late sixteenth and early seventeenth centuries occurred during the reign of Queen Elizabeth. Of all the forms of Elizabethan literature, none expressed the energy of the era better than drama. Of all the dramatists, none is more famous than William Shakespeare.

When Shakespeare appeared in London, Elizabethans were already addicted to the stage. Elizabethan theater was a very successful business. In or near London, at least four to six theaters were open six afternoons a week. London theaters ranged from the Globe, which was a circular, unroofed structure holding three thousand people, to the Blackfriars, which was roofed and held only five hundred. The Globe's admission charge of one or two pennies enabled even the lower classes to attend. The higher prices of the Blackfriars brought an audience of the well-to-do. Elizabethan audiences varied greatly, which put pressure on playwrights to write works that pleased nobles, lawyers, merchants, and vagabonds alike.

William Shakespeare was a "complete man of the theater." Although best known for writing plays, he was also an actor and shareholder in the chief company of the time, the Lord Chamberlains' Company. Shakespeare has long been viewed as a universal genius. He was a master of the English language. His language skills, however, were matched by an incredible insight into human psychology. Whether in his tragedies or comedies, Shakespeare showed a remarkable understanding of the human condition (see "Our Literary Heritage: The Greatness of Shakespeare").

The theater was one of the most creative forms of expression during Spain's golden century as well. The first professional theaters, created in Seville and Madrid, were run by actors' companies, as they were in England. Soon, every large town had a public playhouse, including Mexico City in the New World. Touring companies brought the latest Spanish plays to all parts of the Spanish Empire.

Beginning in the 1580s, the standard for playwrights was set by Lope de Vega (LOE-PAE de VAE-guh). Like Shakespeare, he was from a middle-class background. He wrote an extraordinary number of plays. Almost

◄ *Nicholas Poussin gained fame for his landscapes and for the beauty of the skies he painted. In this Landscape with the Burial of Phocion, we see a classical theme placed into an ideal landscape. How does this compare to the Baroque style seen in the Throne of St. Peter?*

500 of his 1,500 plays survive. They have been characterized as witty, charming, action packed, and realistic. Lope de Vega made no apologies for the fact that he wrote his plays to please his audiences. He stated that the foremost duty of the playwright was to satisfy public demand. He also remarked once that if anyone thought he had written his plays for fame, "undeceive him and tell him that I wrote them for money."

One of the crowning achievements of the golden age of Spanish literature was the work of Miguel de Cervantes (mi-GELL de sur-VAN-TEEZ). His *Don Quixote* (KEE-HOE-TEE) has been hailed as one of the greatest literary works of all time. In the two main characters of his famous work, Cervantes presented the dual nature of the Spanish character. The knight, Don Quixote from La Mancha, is the visionary who is so involved in his lofty ideals that he does not see the hard realities around him. To him, for example, windmills appear as four-armed giants. In contrast, the knight's fat and earthy squire, Sancho Panza, is the realist who cannot get his master to see the realities in front of him. After adventures that take them to all parts of Spain, each comes to see the value of the other's perspective. We are left with Cervantes's conviction that both visionary dreams and the hard work of reality are necessary to the human condition.

Political Thought: Responses to Revolution

The seventeenth-century concerns with order and power were reflected in the political thought of the time. The English revolutions of the seventeenth century prompted very different responses from two English political thinkers, Thomas Hobbes and John Locke. Hobbes was alarmed by the revolutionary upheavals in seventeenth-century England and wrote a work on political thought—known as the *Leviathan*—that tried to deal with the problem of disorder.

Hobbes claimed that before society was organized, human life was "solitary, poor, nasty, brutish, and short." Humans were guided not by reason and moral ideals but by a ruthless struggle for self-preservation. To save themselves from destroying one another, people made a social contract and agreed to form a state, which Hobbes called "that great Leviathan to which we owe our peace and defense." This state agreed to be governed by an absolute ruler who possessed unlimited power. Subjects may not rebel. If they do, they must be crushed. To Hobbes, such absolute power was needed to preserve order in society.

Locke, who wrote a political work called *Two Treatises of Government*, viewed the exercise of political power quite differently from Hobbes and argued against

USING PRIMARY SOURCES

Have student volunteers read the passage aloud, then discuss Richard's feelings for England. You may also want to discuss Churchill's use of this speech during World War II.

LEARNING FROM VISUALS

Answer to the caption question: Students should recognize the beauty of Shakespeare's writing and the universal themes of his plays.

Answers to Critical Thinking Questions

1. Shakespeare was writing about England.
2. Answers will vary, but should include a comparison with the Eden mentioned in the Bible.

CRITICAL THINKING

Ask students to discern the difference between natural rights and civil rights. *(Natural rights are believed to be innate, part of what it means to be human. Civil rights are granted by nations or governments.)*

TEACHING THEMES

The Role of Ideas   Assign students to read the Declaration of Independence and to find those passages that reflect the political views of John Locke.

OUR LITERARY HERITAGE
The Greatness of Shakespeare

William Shakespeare is one of the most famous playwrights in the Western world. He was a universal genius. His historical plays reflected the patriotic enthusiasm of the English in the age of Queen Elizabeth, as this excerpt from Richard II illustrates.

William Shakespeare, Richard II

This royal throne of kings, this
    sceptered isle,
This earth of majesty, this seat of
    Mars,
This other Eden, demi-Paradise,
This fortress built by Nature for herself
Against infection and the hand of war,
This happy breed of men, this little world,
This precious stone set in the silver sea,
Which serves it in the office of a wall
Or as a moat defensive to a house
Against the envy of less happier lands—
This blessed plot, this earth, this realm, this England,
This nurse, this teeming womb of royal kings,
Feared by their breed and famous by their birth,
Renowned for their deeds as far from home,
For Christian service and true chivalry,
As is the sepulcher in stubborn Jewry [the Holy
    Sepulcher or Tomb in Jerusalem]
Of the world's ransom, blessed Mary's Son—

This portrait of William Shakespeare does not reveal the extraordinary abilities or accomplishments of the actor and playwright. Why do you think his plays were so popular during Elizabethan times, and why do you think they are still popular today?

This land of such dear souls, this
    dear dear land,
    Dear for her reputation through
    the world,
    Is now leased out, I die pro-
    nouncing it,
    Like a tenement or pelting farm.
    England, bound in with the tri-
    umphant sea,
    Whose rocky shore beats back the
    envious siege
Of watery Neptune, is now bound in
    with shame,
    With inky blots and rotten parchment bonds.
That England, that was wont to conquer others,
Hath made a shameful conquest of itself.
Ah, would the scandal vanish with my life,
How happy then were my ensuing death!

1. What country was Shakespeare writing about in this excerpt from *Richard II*?

2. Explain what you think Shakespeare meant by calling England "This other Eden, demi-Paradise."

---

the absolute rule of one person. Unlike Hobbes, Locke believed that before society was organized, humans lived in a state of equality and freedom rather than a state of war. In this state of nature, humans had certain inalienable natural rights—to life, liberty, and property. Like Hobbes, Locke did not believe all was well in the state of nature. People found it difficult to protect these natural rights, so they agreed to establish a government to ensure the protection of their rights. This was a contract of mutual obligations. Government would protect the rights of the people, whereas the people would act reasonably toward government. However, if a govern-

---

So What ??

If your students question the importance of information about **Hobbes and Locke** *tell them . . .*

Thomas Hobbes (1588–1679) was convinced that absolutism was the most desirable and logical form of government. Only the unlimited power of the sovereign, said Hobbes, could contain the human passions that disrupt the social order and threaten civilized life. Only absolute rule could provide an environment secure enough for people to pursue their individual interests. Two significant events influenced Hobbes: the English Civil War and the execution of Charles I in 1649. The *Leviathan* was published in 1652.

Locke's political philosophy was formulated

ment broke this contract—if a monarch, for example, failed to live up to the obligation to protect the natural rights—the people might form a new government. Locke's ideas proved important to both Americans and French in the eighteenth century. They were used to support demands for constitutional government, the rule of law, and the protection of rights. Locke's ideas can be found in the American Declaration of Independence and the U.S. Constitution.

 SECTION REVIEW

1. **Locate:**
   (*a*) Crete,   (*b*) London,   (*c*) Seville,
   (*d*) Madrid

2. **Identify:**
   (*a*) Mannerism,   (*b*) El Greco,   (*c*) Nicholas Poussin,   (*d*) Elizabethan Era,   (*e*) William Shakespeare,   (*f*) Lope de Vega,   (*g*) Miguel de Cervantes,   (*h*) Thomas Hobbes,   (*i*) John Locke

3. **Recall:**
   (*a*) List several artistic styles popular during the sixteenth and seventeenth centuries.
   (*b*) Why was Shakespeare considered a "complete man of the theater"?

4. **Think Critically:** How did Americans in the eighteenth century use John Locke's ideas in forming their own government?

Conclusion

By the mid-sixteenth century, the division of Europe between Catholics and Protestants became a crucial factor in precipitating an age of religious warfare. Europe entered a hundred years of religious warfare—the worst series of international and civil wars in the West since the collapse of the Roman Empire. It took all this warfare, complicated by serious political, economic, and social issues, before Europeans finally admitted that they would have to tolerate different ways to worship God. That people who were disciples of the Apostle of Peace—as they called Jesus—would

kill each other, often in brutal and painful fashion, aroused skepticism about Christianity itself. It is surely no accident that the search for a stable, secular order in politics became so important during the seventeenth century.

The concept of a united Christendom, held as an ideal since the Middle Ages, had been forever destroyed by the religious wars. With the demise of this ideal a system of nation-states in which power politics took on increasing importance emerged. Power became more and more centralized.

In those states called absolutist, strong monarchs provided the leadership needed for greater centralization. The best example of absolutism was the France of Louis XIV. Absolute monarchy was also set up in Austria, Prussia, and Russia. In England, however, Parliament resisted the absolute authority of its kings and created a system of limited or constitutional monarchy. In all the major European states, a growing concern for power and expansion led to larger armies and greater conflict.

In the midst of their internal crises in the sixteenth and seventeenth centuries, Europeans were also engaging in new adventures. The discovery of new trade routes to the East and the accidental discovery of the Americas led Europeans to venture outside the medieval world in which they had been enclosed for virtually a thousand years. As we shall see in the next chapter, a new era of world history was beginning to dawn.

Notes

1. Quoted in Garrett Mattingly, *The Armada* (Boston, 1959), pp. 216–217.
2. Quoted in Joseph Klaits, *Servants of Satan: The Age of the Witch Hunts* (Bloomington, Ind.; 1985), p. 68.
3. Quoted in James Harvey Robinson, *Readings in European History* (Boston, 1934), vol. 2: pp. 211–212.
4. Quoted in John B. Wolf, *Louis XIV* (New York, 1968), p. 134.
5. Quoted in *ibid.*, p. 618.
6. Quoted in B. H. Sumner, *Peter the Great and the Emergence of Russia* (New York, 1962), p. 122.

in *Two Treatises on Government* (1690). He believed that human beings are born with the natural rights of life, liberty, and property, and the state was established to protect these rights. Consequently, no branch of government can deprive the individual of their natural rights. Whereas Hobbes justified absolute monarchy, Locke endorses constitutional government where state authority is limited by agreement. Students should realize that Locke's spirit pervades the American Declaration of Independence, the Constitution, and the Bill of Rights. His ideas form the basis of the liberal tradition that aims to protect individual liberty.

Answers to
SECTION REVIEW

2. (a) artistic movement that ignored rules of proportion
   (b) church painter, work reflected Mannerism and tensions of Reformation
   (c) French classicism painter
   (d) golden age of English theater and culture
   (e) most famous dramatist of the Elizabethan Era
   (f) Spanish playwright
   (g) Spanish writer, author of *Don Quixote*
   (h) English political thinker, wrote the *Leviathan*
   (i) English author whose ideas were used in American Constitution
3. (a) Mannerism, Baroque, French classicism
   (b) Besides writing plays, Shakespeare was an actor and shareholder in the chief theatre company of the time.
4. Answers will vary.

CLOSE

Review with students John Locke's ideas about government and human rights. Then guide them in a discussion of how Locke's ideas influenced both the Americans and the French in the eighteenth century. Why do they think Locke's ideas were more influential than Hobbes' ideas at that point in human history?

CHAPTER 15 REVIEW

USING KEY TERMS

1. mercantilism
2. witchcraft
3. ultra-Catholics
4. divine right of kings
5. boyars
6. favorable balance of trade
7. absolutism
8. armada
9. gentry
10. tsar
11. price revolution

REVIEWING THE FACTS

1. Huguenots
2. The right to worship and political privileges were extended to the Huguenots.
3. the Spanish
4. inferior ships and man-power; the weather did not cooperate
5. harvests were hurt; gave rise to famines
6. Germany from 1618–1648
7. France
8. The monarch needed the permission of Parliament to increase taxes.
9. He took away the political and military rights of the Huguenots, crushed conspiracies, and executed conspirators.
10. to favor peace not war, and to decrease the tax burden on the people
11. different nationality groups; no common sentiment to tie region together
12. European technology
13. Peter abolished the position of patriarch and created the Holy Synod.
14. St. Petersburg
15. It ended the theory of divine right.
16. that visionary dreams and the hard work of human reality are both necessary to the human condition
17. to ensure the protection of rights; government was to be a contract of mutual obligations
18. the French and Americans
19. the flintlock musket, which could shoot about one or

USING KEY TERMS

1. _____ is the economic theory which encourages countries to build up a large supply of gold and silver.
2. _____ refers to the belief in the supernatural and that some people consort with the devil.
3. The _____ were an extreme religious party who favored strict opposition to the Huguenots.
4. The belief that the monarch receives power directly from God is called the _____.
5. The _____ were Russian nobility defeated by Ivan the Terrible.
6. To achieve a _____, nations encouraged exports.
7. _____ refers to the political system in which ultimate authority rests with the monarch.
8. Philip II sent a fleet of warships called a(n) _____ to invade England in 1588.
9. Many of England's well-to-do landowners, known as _____, had become Puritans.
10. The Russian monarch was called a _____, derived from the Russian word for Caesar.
11. A _____ resulted in the sixteenth century due to an increased demand for land and food that drove up prices.

REVIEWING THE FACTS

1. What is the name given to French Calvinists?
2. Why is the Edict of Nantes sometimes called the Edict of Toleration?
3. Who was the winner of the Battle of Lepanto of 1571?
4. What were two reasons for the failure of the Spanish Armada in 1571?
5. What impact did the "Little Ice Age" of the 16th and 17th centuries have on Europe?
6. When and where was the Thirty Years' War fought?

7. After the Thirty Years' War which country dominated Europe?
8. What was the essential feature of the English Petition of Right of 1628?
9. How did Richelieu strengthen the power of the French monarchy?
10. What deathbed advice did Louis XIV give to his great grandson who would succeed him on the throne?
11. What kept Austria from becoming a powerful nation?
12. What did Peter the Great admire most about Western Europe?
13. How did Peter the Great treat the Russian Orthodox Church?
14. What city became Peter the Great's "Window to the West"?
15. What impact did the Glorious Revolution have on the theory of divine right?
16. What is the essential message of Cervantes' _Don Quixote_?
17. According to John Locke, what was the purpose of government?
18. Who in the eighteenth century found Locke's ideas appealing?
19. What new firearm became common for soldiers around 1600? What older style weapon continued to be important?

THINKING CRITICALLY

1. Repression breeds rebellion. Explain how this occurred in the Netherlands when Philip II sent his troops to crush the Dutch Protestants. Did Philip have other options that were likely to work?
2. During times of crisis people turn to extreme solutions. An example of this is the witchcraft hysteria of the sixteenth and seventeenth centuries. What factors led to the hysteria? Why do you think that poor women were so often the targets?

two rounds per minute; pikes

THINKING CRITICALLY

1. Although Philip's actions worsened the problem, there was probably no easy solution.
2. In general, this was a time of great turmoil. The Protestant Reformation had turned the religious world upside down. Economic difficulties in part arising from the price revolution were another factor. The number of poor was growing. People needed scapegoats and women were easy targets. There was also a sense of removing the "marginal" members of society.
3. Answers will vary.

4. The English Parliament had the power of the purse. A further limitation was that standing armies could be raised only by Parliament. After the Glorious Revolution the English monarchs "reigned," they did not "rule."
5. The Palace at Versailles was an enormous structure meant to express the wealth of the French monarch. Louis used Versailles to control the nobles. Catholic Church Baroque painters tended to use dramatic scenes that stand in contrast to the generally sedate and orderly scenes of the Renaissance.
6. Consider having students question this interpretation. Is it really "order" that was sought or

3. Louis XIV was "quite willing to pay the price of being a strong ruler." What did this mean for him? Did he have to make sacrifices in his personal life? How do public figures today have to "pay the price" for their popularity?

4. Absolutism is only a theory. The extent to which rulers are "absolute" depends on the strength of their army and their power to tax. Explain why William and Mary were not truly absolute monarchs in England after the Glorious Revolution.

5. Baroque art and architecture reflected a search for power. How can an art style foster power? Consider especially Louis XIV's Palace at Versailles. How did the Catholic Church use Baroque painting to further its ends during the time of the Counter Reformation?

6. Historically, 1550 to about 1650 is considered to be a period when people were searching for order. Given the frequency and disastrous effects of wars, especially the Thirty Years' War, during this period, how can this be explained?

APPLYING SOCIAL STUDIES SKILLS

1. **Geography:** Consult Map 15.1 on page 455. Identify the areas controlled by Philip II of Spain.

2. **Economics:** Why did Philip II, ruler of the richest country in Europe, go bankrupt?

3. **Economics:** What precious metal from America led to inflation in Europe in the sixteenth century?

4. **Geography:** Consult Map 15.3 on page 472. What geographic dilemma did Prussia face? How did Frederick William deal with this problem?

5. **Geography:** Consult Map 15.4 on page 473. What kept Peter the Great from attaining a warm water port with access to the Mediterranean?

6. **Government:** According to Thomas Hobbes, what was the ideal kind of government? Why was this kind of government needed?

MAKING TIME AND PLACE CONNECTIONS

1. The American playwright Arthur Miller wrote the play about witchcraft, *The Crucible*, in the 1950s. What was going on in America at that time that influenced him to write such a work?

2. Did the Treaty of Westphalia of 1648 change the religious situation that was set forth in the Peace of Augsburg, signed about one hundred years earlier, in 1555?

3. Name a ruler from another period of time who claimed absolute power. Did this ruler also claim power from a god?

4. Who were the absolute rulers of China and India at about the same time that Louis XIV was perfecting European absolutism?

5. In England, the Parliament had the right to propose taxes. In the federal branch of the United States government, who has the power to propose taxes?

6. Compare Versailles to Khufu's pyramids at Giza. What are their essential similarities and differences?

7. What was the extent of gambling at Versailles under Louis XIV? How does it compare to the role of gambling in the United States today?

BECOMING AN HISTORIAN

Comparing and Contrasting: Compare and contrast the methods of ruling and the foreign policies of Elizabeth I of England and Philip II of Spain. Make a chart in which you list their views on the following subjects—areas controlled, religious views, impact of religious views on diplomacy, willingness to compromise, and effective use of military force to accomplish their goals.

pyramid was the final resting place for the pharaoh. Both were massive undertakings that took years to build and employed thousands of workers. The pyramids were a part of the religious cosmology of the Egyptians, while there was little religious about Versailles.

7. Gambling was a great pastime at Versailles and impoverished many nobles. Its goal was not to raise money as it is in the United States today. Many states in particular use lotteries as a way to raise revenue.

BECOMING AN HISTORIAN

Philip ruled Spain and Netherlands, and the Spanish colonies in America; he was a pious Catholic who was consumed by religion; he was driven by a crusading spirit and this led him to make unwise choices, specifically to impose his will on the Netherlands and most foolishly to attack England; he never considered compromise; he attempted to use military force to achieve his goals, but was only successful against the Turks.

Elizabeth ruled Britain and Ireland. She was intelligent, cautious and self-confident; she changed the Anglican service to make it more acceptable to Catholics, a clear indication of her desire for moderation and compromise. Religion did not play much of a role in the diplomacy of Elizabeth. She was willing to compromise; Elizabeth did not choose to fight wars.

483

something else—power, control, religious influence, and others might be better words.

APPLYING SOCIAL STUDIES SKILLS

1. Spain, Netherlands, parts of Italy and America
2. spent too much money on wars
3. silver
4. Prussia had no natural frontiers such as oceans or mountains to serve as protective barriers. Frederick William built a strong army, the fourth largest in Europe, to ensure Prussian security.
5. The Ottoman Empire stood in the way.
6. The essence of Hobbes' message was that absolutism was necessary to preserve order.

MAKING TIME AND PLACE CONNECTIONS

1. Some Hollywood writers were being blacklisted for their alleged Communist views.
2. No. With both treaties the nobles chose the religion for the people, giving individuals no say as to whether or not they wanted to be Catholics or Protestants.
3. Answers will vary.
4. Aurangzeb was the Mogul ruler of India from 1658–1707 and K'ang-hsi rule China from 1661–1722.
5. House of Representatives
6. Versailles was built to house the living king; the

16 PLANNING GUIDE

SECTION	KEY TOPICS	PRIMARY SOURCES	ASSESSMENT
1 An Age of Exploration and Expansion **pages 485–495**	◆ Motives for European exploration ◆ Development of Portugal's trade empire ◆ Voyages of Christopher Columbus ◆ Spanish settlements in Americas ◆ Impact of European expansion ◆ Spain, Netherlands, England, France seek colonial empires	◆ Drawing of Magellan, page 484 ◆ Account of massacre of Arabs by Portuguese, pages 489–490 ◆ Drawing of ship, page 490 ◆ Letter from Columbus, page 491 ◆ Codex showing Indians with smallpox, page 493	◆ Section Review, page 495 ◆ Section Quiz 16–1, TRB
2 Africa in an Age of Transition **pages 495–503**	◆ Slave trade in Africa ◆ Political and social structures of African states	◆ Map of Africa, page 496 ◆ Dutch account of slave ships, page 498 ◆ Painting of slave traders, page 500 ◆ Woodcut, page 502	◆ Section Review, page 503 ◆ Section Quiz 16–2, TRB
3 Southeast Asia in the Era of the Spice Trade **pages 503–510**	◆ Arrival of Europeans in Southeast Asia ◆ Spice trade ◆ Dutch takeover of Indian Ocean trade ◆ Government and politics in Southeast Asia ◆ Economy and daily life in Southeast Asia	◆ Letters of Louis XIV and Vietnamese king, pages 506–507 ◆ Woodcut, page 508 ◆ Woodcut, page 510	◆ Section Review, page 510 ◆ Section Quiz 16–3, TRB

NEW HORIZONS:
THE EMERGENCE OF NEW WORLD PATTERNS (1500 TO 1800)

REPRODUCIBLE ACTIVITIES

Historical Maps

Charts and Graphs

Critical Thinking

Cooperative Learning

Vocabulary

Guided Reading

Reteaching

Enrichment

Performance Assessment

Spanish Key Points and Chapter Summaries

Spanish Vocabulary

Spanish Guided Reading

MULTIMEDIA SUPPORT

 TRANSPARENCIES
- *World History* Color Transparency Package
- Fine Art Color Transparency Package

 VIDEO
- *World History* Video Library
- **CNN** Annual Video Update

 LASERDISC
- *Sights and Sounds of History*

 AUDIO
- *Listening to Literature* audiotape (English and Spanish)
- *History of Music* CD

 SOFTWARE
- WESTEST™
- Student Review

 CD–ROM
- *The Journey of Civilization*
- *World History*

 INTERNET
- Internet Activities

 On Line with **WORLD HISTORY**

Access West's history web site at
http://history.swpco.com
You'll find activities and web sites related to specific topics and chapters in *World History: The Human Odyssey*. Also look for references to helpful web sites at appropriate places throughout this teacher edition.

LESSON PLANNING

You will find detailed daily lesson plans for both traditional class scheduling and **block scheduling** in your Teacher Resource Box.

 Not Enough Time?

If you do not have the four or five days recommended to teach this chapter, you may want to focus on the following sections and activities:

- Have students skim the chapter to answer the "Questions to Guide Your Reading" on page 485. Discuss their answers; then read the "Conclusion" on pages 510–511.
- Do a more in-depth reading of pages 486, 490, 492–494, 495–499, 506–510. Conclude with a class discussion of the features on pages 487–488, 491, 498–499, and 506–507.

NEW HORIZONS: THE EMERGENCE

BUILDING ON
CHAPTER 15

To "set the scene" for the study of Chapter 16, use the following questions and activities.

◆ Review the major causes and effects of the French Wars of Religion and the religious wars of Spain's Philip II.

◆ Discuss the major causes and effects of the Thirty Years' War and the English Revolution.

◆ Have students list important movements and figures in European culture and political thought from about 1520 to about 1640.

USING THE
OPENING STORY

Depending on the ability levels of your students, select from the following questions and activities to reinforce the reading of the Magellan story.

◆ What was Magellan's goal when he set sail on August 10, 1519?

◆ Given the gruesome account of what the crew did to keep from starving, what words would students use to describe this voyage?

◆ Why do students think sailors agreed to such voyages through unknown waters?

LEARNING
FROM VISUALS

Answer to caption question: Answers will vary.

Convinced that he could find a sea passage to Asia through the New World to the west, the Portuguese explorer Ferdinand Magellan persuaded the king of Spain to finance his voyage. On August 10, 1519, Magellan set sail on the Atlantic Ocean with five ships and a Spanish crew of 277 men. After a stormy and difficult crossing of the Atlantic, Magellan's fleet moved down the coast of what is today South America in search of the elusive strait, or sea passage, that would take him through America. His Spanish ship captains thought he was crazy: "The fool is obsessed with his search for a strait," one remarked. "On the flame of his ambition he will crucify us all."

At last, in October 1520, Magellan found an opening in the land. He passed through a narrow waterway (later named the Strait of Magellan) and emerged into an unknown ocean that he called the Pacific Sea. Magellan reckoned that it would then be a short distance to the Spice Islands of the East. He was badly mistaken. Week after week he and his crew sailed on across the Pacific as their food supplies dwindled. According to one account, "When their last biscuit had gone, they scraped the maggots out of the casks, mashed them and served them as gruel. They made cakes out of sawdust soaked with the urine of rats— the rats themselves, as delicacies,

▲ *When Magellan passed by the tip of South America, he and his men had no idea they were entering the 10,000-mile wide Pacific Ocean. Of the 277 men who accompanied Magellan, only eighteen returned to Spain. How do you think they were greeted and treated upon their return?*

had long since been hunted to extinction."

At last they reached the Philippines (named after King Philip of Spain by Magellan's crew), where Magellan was killed by the natives. Although only one of his original fleet of five ships survived and returned to Spain, Magellan is still remembered as the first person to sail around the world.

At the beginning of the sixteenth century, European adventurers such as Magellan had launched their small fleets into the vast reaches of the Atlantic Ocean. They were hardly aware that they were beginning a new era, not only for Europe but also for the peoples of Asia, Africa, and the Americas. Nevertheless, the voyages of these Europeans marked the beginning of a process that led to radical changes in the political, economic, and cultural life of the entire non-Western world. Between 1500 and 1800, European power spread into other parts of the world. In the Americas, Europeans established colonies that spread their laws, religions, and cultures. In the island regions of Southeast Asia, the Europeans firmly established their rule. In Africa and other parts of Asia, their trading activities dramatically affected the local peoples.

ADDITIONAL RESOURCES

BOOKS FOR THE STUDENT
Captain Cook and the South Pacific by Oliver Warner. Horizon Caravell, Harper & Row
The Age of Exploration by John R. Hale. Time-Life
To the Indies by C. S. Forester. Little

VIDEOS/FILMS
"Christopher Columbus and the Great Adventure" (Video Knowledge) Social

Studies School Service (800) 421-4246
"The West and the Wider World" Series: The World: A Television History, Social Studies School Service (800) 421-4246

CD–ROM
Explorers of the New World (Softkey International. Educorp Direct. (800) 843-9497

OF NEW WORLD PATTERNS

(1500 TO 1800)

NEW WORLD PATTERNS

QUESTIONS TO GUIDE YOUR READING

1. What factors contributed to the Europeans' entrance into their age of discovery and expansion?

2. What were the major differences between the overseas empires established by the Portuguese and the Spanish?

3. What were the major features of the African slave trade?

4. What were the general consequences of European expansion into Africa?

5. What were the chief features of the different forms of political systems in Southeast Asia?

6. What were the chief characteristics of the economic and social life of Southeast Asia?

OUTLINE

1. An Age of Exploration and Expansion
2. Africa in an Age of Transition
3. Southeast Asia in the Era of the Spice Trade

AN AGE OF EXPLORATION AND EXPANSION

Nowhere was the dynamic energy of Western civilization betwen 1500 and 1800 more apparent than in this civilization's expansion into the rest of the world. Portugal, Spain, and later the Dutch Republic, England, and France—all states that bordered the Atlantic—rose to new economic heights through their worldwide trading activity.

The Motives

For almost a thousand years, Europeans had mostly remained in one area of the world. At the end of the fifteenth century, however, they set out on a remarkable series of overseas journeys. What caused them to undertake such dangerous voyages to the ends of the Earth?

Europeans had long been attracted to Asia. The most famous medieval travelers to the East were the Polos of Venice. In the late thirteenth century, Marco Polo went with his father and uncle to the Chinese court of the great Mongol ruler Khubilai Khan (see Chapter 10). Marco traveled to Japan as well and did not return to Italy for twenty-five years. His account of his experiences was known as *The Travels*. It was read

485

FOCUS ON THEMES

Listed below are brief summaries of how the content in this chapter supports the text's key themes.

Politics and History The growth of European states made possible European expansion into the rest of the world. Their conquests of the Americas, expansion of the African slave trade, and their establishment of trading enclaves in Africa and Southeast Asia, often destabilized traditional regimes.

The Role of Ideas The European treatment of African slaves had many harmful consequences, one of which was the development of insidious ideas about race. White slave traders and owners developed feelings of superiority over blacks that have continued to the present day.

Economics and History The European desire for new sources of profits led to a search for new trade routes which resulted in trade empires and new worldwide trade patterns.

The Role of Individuals In Western history, explorers such as Magellan and Columbus are heroes, but to people in the Americas and other parts of the world they are exploiters of indigenous peoples.

The Impact of Science and Technology The growth of Europeans' knowledge and technology led to a series of sea voyages that changed the pattern of world history. The use of gunpowder on a massive scale also enabled Europeans to dominate areas of the world that were without such resources.

Answers to QUESTIONS TO GUIDE YOUR READING

1. attraction of Asia; desire for "God, glory, gold"; established monarchies; improved technology (pages 485–486)
2. Portuguese: sailed eastward; empire limited to trading posts on coastal India and China (pages 486–490)
Spanish: sailed westward; grand empire in New World (pages 490–492)
3. See pages 495–499.
4. monarchy became common form of gov-

ernment; some African states united; some assisted in slave trade; Christianity promoted (pages 499–503)
5. See pages 507–508.
6. economic: farming base; barter trade with spice as mainstay; poor but starvation rare (pages 508–509)
social: nuclear family; women subordinate; changing religious beliefs (pages 509–510)

FOCUS

OBJECTIVES

After completing this section, students should be able to

1. explain the three main motives for European exploration
2. discuss the technology that made lengthy sea travel possible
3. trace the development and decline of Portugal's trading empire
4. trace Spanish exploration, particularly the voyages of Columbus and conquests of the conquistadors
5. discuss the impact of European expansion on native populations and on Europeans themselves

FOCUS ACTIVITY

Divide the class into groups. Give the groups about ten minutes to list all the reasons they can think of for average European men to sign on to a voyage of discovery—a trip of uncertain duration, over unknown waters, to an unknown destination. Have the groups come together and share their ideas. Which motives do students think would be most compelling? Why?

by many, including Christopher Columbus, who were fascinated by his adventures in the exotic East. In the fourteenth century, the conquests of the Ottoman Turks and then the breakup of the Mongol Empire drastically reduced the ability of westerners to travel by land to the East. People then spoke of gaining access to the spices and other precious items of Asia by sea.

An economic motive thus looms large in European expansion. Merchants, adventurers, and government officials had high hopes of finding precious metals and expanding the areas of trade, especially for the spices of the East. At that time, spices, which were needed to keep foods from rotting and to add flavor to meals, were shipped to Europe by Arab intermediaries and were outrageously expensive. Some Europeans wanted a larger share of this wealth. As one Spanish adventurer explained, he went to the New World to "serve God and His Majesty, to give light to those who were in darkness, and to grow rich, as all men desire to do."[1]

This statement contains another major reason for the overseas voyages: religious zeal. Both Portugal and Spain had largely driven out the Muslims and Jews in the Middle Ages. Both states had a strong crusading spirit. Many Spaniards and Portuguese shared the belief of the Portuguese prince who said that he was motivated by "his great desire to make increase in the faith of our Lord Jesus Christ and to bring him all the souls that should be saved." Even Hernán Cortés, the Spanish conqueror of Mexico, asked his Spanish rulers if it was not their duty to ensure that the native Mexicans "are introduced into and instructed in the holy Catholic faith."

Spiritual and secular affairs were closely connected in the sixteenth century. Adventurers such as Cortés might have wanted to convert the natives to Christianity, but grandeur, glory, and a spirit of adventure also played a major role in European expansion. Religion provided the moral approval for the more materialistic goals of the explorers.

"God, glory, and gold" seem to have been the chief motives. What, however, made the voyages possible? First of all, European expansion was a government enterprise. By the second half of the fifteenth century, European monarchies had increased their authority and their resources. They could now turn their energies beyond their borders. Second, Europeans had also reached a level of knowledge and technology that enabled them to make a regular series of voyages beyond Europe (see "The Role of Science and Technology: Sea Travel in an Age of Exploration and Expansion"). A new era was about to begin.

The Development of a Portuguese Maritime Empire

Portugal took the lead in European exploration when it began exploring the coast of Africa under the leadership of Prince Henry the Navigator. Prince Henry sought trade opportunities for Portugal and wanted to extend Christianity. In 1419, he founded a school for navigators on the southwestern coast of Portugal. Shortly thereafter, Portuguese fleets began probing southward along the western coast of Africa in search of gold. Soon, Portuguese ships reached the Senegal River, just north of Cape Verde, and brought home a cargo of black Africans. Most of them were sold as slaves to wealthy buyers in Europe. Within a few years, an estimated one thousand slaves were shipped every year from the area back to Lisbon (LIZ-bun).

Through regular voyages, the Portuguese continued their progress southward. They discovered a new source of gold along the southern coast of the hump of West Africa (an area that would henceforth be known to Europeans as the Gold Coast). A few years later, they established contact with the state of Bakongo, near the mouth of the Zaire (Congo) River in central Africa. To make it easier to trade in gold, ivory, and slaves, the Portuguese leased land from local rulers and built stone forts along the coast.

Portuguese sea captains heard reports of a route to India around the southern tip of Africa and continued their probing. In 1487, Bartholomew Diaz rounded the Cape of Good Hope. Vasco da Gama did even more. He rounded the cape, skirted the eastern coast of Africa, and cut across the Indian Ocean to the southwestern coast of India. On May 18, 1498, da Gama arrived off the port of Calicut, where he took on a cargo of ginger and cinnamon. After several skirmishes with Arab mariners who understood the new commer-

RECOMMENDED READING

The best general accounts of European discovery and expansion are G. V. Scammell, *The First Imperial Age* (London, 1989); J. H. Parry, *The Age of Reconnaissance: Discovery, Exploration and Settlement, 1450 to 1650* (New York, 1963); B. Penrose, *Travel and Discovery in the Renaissance, 1420–1620* (New York, 1962); and the brief work by J. H. Parry, *The Establishment of the European Hegemony, 1415–1715* (New York, 1961). On the tech-

nological aspects of the subject, see C. M. Cipolla, *Guns, Sails, and Empires: Technological Innovation and the Early Phases of European Expansion, 1400–1700* (New York, 1965). On the Portuguese expansion, the fundamental work is C. R. Boxer, *The Portuguese Seaborne Empire: 1415–1825* (New York, 1969). The story of the discovery and settlement of America is engagingly portrayed in S. E. Morison, *The European Discovery of America: The*

THE ROLE OF SCIENCE AND TECHNOLOGY

Sea Travel in an Age of Exploration and Expansion

Europeans could not have made their sea voyages without a certain level of knowledge and technology, much of which was acquired from the Arabs. First, they needed to know where they could sail. In the thirteenth and fourteenth centuries, Arab navigators and mathematicians had drawn detailed charts, known as *portolani*. They gave details on the shape of coastlines and distances between

ports. These charts proved to be of great value for voyages in European waters. The *portolani* had a weakness, however: they were drawn on a flat scale and took no account of the curvature of Earth. Thus, they were of little value for longer, overseas voyages. Only as sailors began to move beyond the coasts of Europe did they gain information about the actual shape of Earth. By the

▼ *Long distance voyages were made possible by the development of this ship, the caravel. What special attributes of the caravel made these far-reaching ocean journeys possible?*

The use of multiple masts was pioneered by the Chinese in the fourteenth century.

The triangular lateen sail that allowed the ship to sail into the wind originated in the Muslim world.

The sails were made of different weights of cloth or canvas for different types of winds.

The deep-sea rudder posted on the stern was invented by the Chinese and transmitted to Europe via trade with the Muslims.

(continued)

Northern Voyages, A.D. 500–1600 (New York, 1971) and The Southern Voyages, A.D. 1492–1616 (New York, 1974). On Columbus, see the brief biography by J. S. Collis, Christopher Columbus (London, 1976); and F. Fernandez-Armesto, Columbus (New York, 1991). The standard work on the conquistadors is F. A. Kirkpatrick, The Spanish Conquistadors (Cleveland, 1968). Cortés is examined in W. W. Johnson, Cortés (Boston, 1975). The

impact of expansion on European consciousness is explored in J. H. Elliott, The Old World and the New, 1492–1650 (Cambridge, 1970). The human and ecological effects of the interaction of New World and Old World cultures is examined thoughtfully in A. W. Crosby, The Columbian Exchange, Biological and Cultural Consequences of 1492 (Westport, Conn., 1972).

LEARNING FROM VISUALS

Answer to the caption question: The astrolabe helped sailors determine latitude, but as they traveled further into the oceans they also needed to be able to determine longitude.

Answers to Critical Thinking Questions

1. The Arabs contributed the *portolani,* or detailed charts of the shapes of coastlines, and the astrolabe, which used the sun or a star to ascertain the position of the ship.
2. Cartography, or the science of map-making, and Europe's remarkably seaworthy ships caused exploration to increase by the end of the fifteenth century.
3. Answers will vary.

CLASS DISCUSSION

Have students discuss why spices were especially prized by Europeans. *(Needed to keep food from rotting, desired for adding flavor)*

ACROSS THE CURRICULUM

Science Have students research Europeans' understanding of wind currents, which helped them make long voyages. Ask them to draw or bring in diagrams explaining exactly how the compass and astrolabe work.

THE ROLE OF SCIENCE AND TECHNOLOGY

Sea Travel in an Age of Exploration and Expansion, continued

end of the fifteenth century, cartography— the art and science of mapmaking—had reached the point where Europeans had fairly accurate maps of the known world.

Moreover, Europeans had developed remarkably seaworthy ships. European shipmakers had learned how to build ships large enough and strong enough to sail in any waters. They had also figured out how to combine the use of lateen sails (triangular sails) with a square rig. This enabled them to build ships mobile enough to sail against the wind and to engage in naval warfare. The ships were also large enough to mount heavy cannon and carry a substantial amount of goods over long distances.

Europeans had also learned new navigational techniques from the Arabs. Previously, sailors had used their knowledge of the position of the North Star to figure out their latitude—how far north or south of the equator they were. Below the equator, however, this technique was useless. New naviga-

The Hispano-Moorish astrolabe shown here is from 1068. Why were better navigational aids needed by European sailors in the fifteenth and sixteenth centuries?

tional aids, such as the compass and the astrolabe (also perfected by the Arabs), gave them the confidence to explore the high seas. The compass showed in what direction a ship was moving. The astrolabe used the sun or a star to ascertain a ship's latitude.

1. What two contributions of the Arabs made sailing easier for the Europeans?

2. What two advances made by the end of the fifteenth century caused sea exploration to increase?

3. Which one advance discussed in this feature do you feel was the most important for early explorers? Explain your answer.

---

cial threat, he returned to Portugal and gained a profit of several thousand percent. Is it surprising that da Gama's voyage was the first of many along this route?

Portuguese fleets returned every year to the area to destroy Muslim shipping and to establish their control of the spice trade. In 1509, a Portuguese armada defeated a combined fleet of Turkish and Indian ships off the coast of India. A year later, the Portuguese decided to create a land base in the area. Admiral Alfonso d' Albuquerque (AL-buh-KUR-kee) set up a port at Goa, on the western coast of India. Goa became the headquarters for Portuguese operations throughout the entire area.

The Portuguese then began to range more widely in search of the source of the spice trade. Soon, Albuquerque sailed into Malacca on the Malay peninsula. Malacca was a thriving port and had become a major stopping point for the spice trade. A Portuguese observer described its crucial position: "Men cannot estimate the worth of Malacca, on account of its greatness and profit. Malacca is a city that was made for merchandise, fitter than any other in the world. . . .

SPECIAL NEEDS: *Visual*

Draw a parallel for students between explorers of today and yesterday. Focus on Cortés. Have students construct a chart on which they list two columns: one for Cortés and one for a modern-day explorer of their choice. Underneath each explorer's name, list the motivations for exploration.

Have the students write a few sentences, or present a short oral explanation, of how

this modern explorer has contributed to the advancement of knowledge. Are there any specific, documentable contributions such as charting of unknown land, water or airspace? What area will be explored next, in the students' opinions?

Map 16.1   European Discoveries and Possessions in the Sixteenth and Seventeenth Centuries

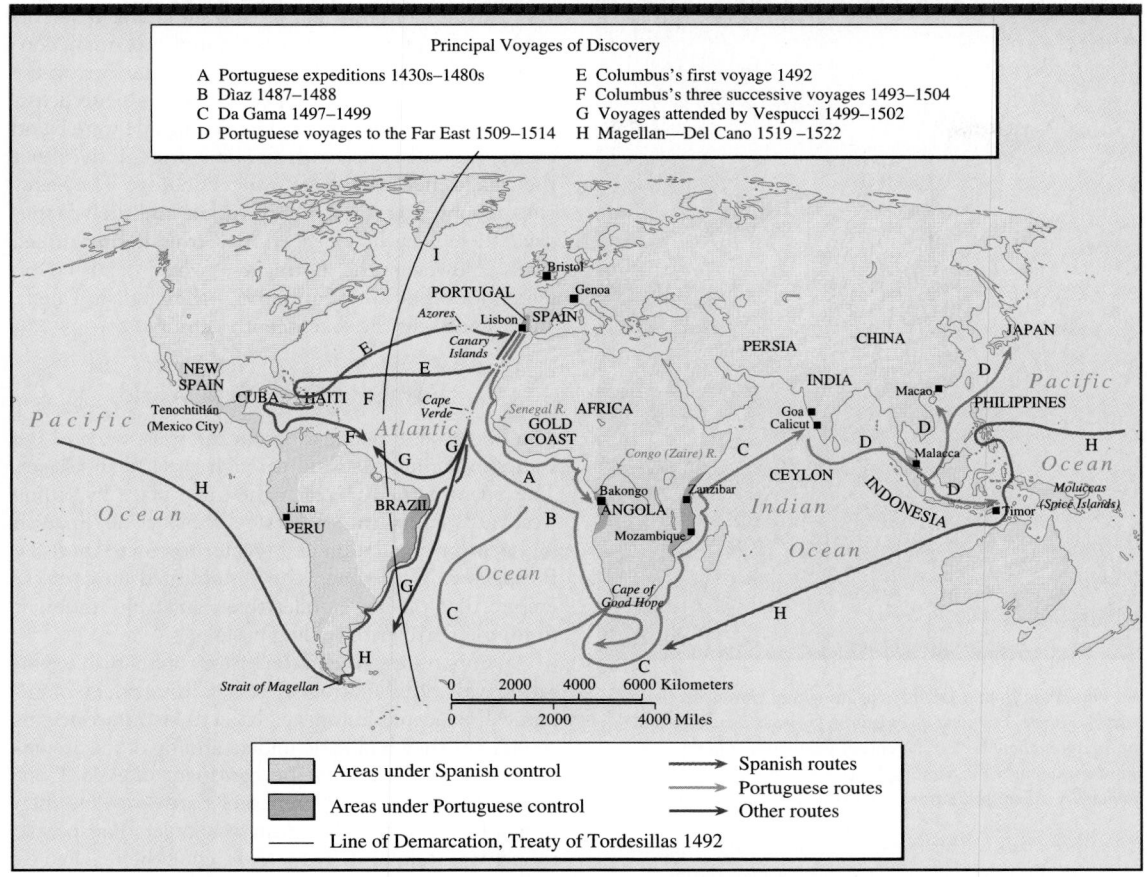

Principal Voyages of Discovery

A Portuguese expeditions 1430s–1480s   E Columbus's first voyage 1492
B Dìaz 1487–1488   F Columbus's three successive voyages 1493–1504
C Da Gama 1497–1499   G Voyages attended by Vespucci 1499–1502
D Portuguese voyages to the Far East 1509–1514   H Magellan—Del Cano 1519 –1522

Areas under Spanish control   → Spanish routes
Areas under Portuguese control   → Portuguese routes
                                     → Other routes
— Line of Demarcation, Treaty of Tordesillas 1492

CLASS DISCUSSION

Have students discuss why Vasco da Gama's voyage to Calicut, in India, encouraged other adventurers to repeat his trip. *(Huge profit for his cargo, was able to win "skirmishes" with Arab mariners)*

Multimedia Support

TRANSPARENCY
16–1, European Discoveries and Possessions, 16th and 17th Centuries (Map 16.1)

CLASS DISCUSSION

Have students discuss the importance to the Portuguese of Malacca, a port on the Malay peninsula. *(Strategically located; control could destroy Arab spice trade and give Portuguese a way station on route to Spice Islands)*

Malacca is surrounded and lies in the middle, and the trade and commerce between the different nations for a thousand leagues on every hand must come to Malacca."[2]

For Albuquerque, control of Malacca would serve two purposes. It could help to destroy the Arab spice trade and also provide the Portuguese with a way station on the route to the Moluccas, then known as the Spice Islands. After a short but bloody battle, the Portuguese seized the city and massacred the local Arab population. This initiated a fierce and brutal struggle between the Portuguese and Arabs. According to one account,

> . . . to enhance the terror of his name he [Albuquerque] always separated Arabs from the other inhabitants of a captured city, and cut off the right hand of the men, and the noses and ears of the women. . . . At Goa he outdid himself in cruelty, ordering the massacre of every Arab man, woman and child, including

STUDYING MAPS

The following questions and activities will help you guide students through their study of Map 16.1.

1. Locate the area of Africa explored by Portugal between the 1430s and 1480s. Trace Diaz's route around the Cape of Good Hope.
2. Trace Da Gama's voyage; locate Calicut.
3. Find Goa, where Albuquerque set up Portuguese headquarters. Trace his route to Malacca. About how far is Malacca from the Moluccas, or Spice Islands? Can you explain Malacca's strategic importance as a way station?
4. Trace further Portuguese voyages to the Far East. About how many miles (or kilometers) did Portugal navigate between 1509 and 1514?

LEARNING FROM VISUALS

Answers to the caption question: Students should recognize the possible bias in the illustration.

USING PRIMARY SOURCES

Do students think the cruelty described in the account of the Portuguese massacres was known to the people of Portugal or to other Europeans? Why, or why not? If it was known, how might it be justified or rationalized? *(Arabs were non-Christians and so fair game for conversion and/or slaughter.)* Ask students to explain why Albuquerque's separation of Arabs from other inhabitants for especially brutal treatment was "to enhance the terror of his name."

CLASS DISCUSSION

Ask students to discuss the key factor that kept the Portuguese Asian empire limited. *(established trading posts but chose not to colonize the region)*

▲ *This detail from a Japanese painting that chronicled the arrival of the Portuguese in Nagasaki provides us with visual information about sixteenth-century Portuguese square-rigged ships. How might the painting have been different if it had been painted by a European artist, rather than a Japanese artist?*

newborn babes. This massacre occupied the Portuguese soldiers for three days of non-stop slaughter, during which they killed more than 8000 people.[3]

From Malacca, the Portuguese launched expeditions further east, to China and the Spice Islands. There they signed a treaty with a local ruler for the purchase and export of cloves to the European market. The Portuguese trading empire was now complete. They had taken control of the spice trade from Muslim traders. However, the Portuguese Empire remained a limited empire that consisted of trading posts on the coasts of India and China. The Portuguese had neither the power, the population, nor the desire to colonize the Asian regions.

Why were the Portuguese so successful? Basically, it was a matter of guns and seamanship. The first Portuguese fleet to arrive in Indian waters was small, consisting of three ships and twenty guns. Later Portuguese fleets were more heavily armed and were able to defeat local naval and land forces. The Portuguese were by no means the only ones with firearms or explosives, but they made effective use of naval technology. The heavy guns mounted on their sturdy vessels and their tactics gave them a military superiority over lightly armed rivals. However, the Portuguese would later be no match for other European forces—the English, Dutch, and French—in the seventeenth century.

Voyages to the New World

The Portuguese sought to attain the spice trade of the Indies by sailing eastward through the Indian Ocean. The Spanish tried to reach the same place by sailing westward across the Atlantic Ocean. The Spanish had a larger population and greater resources than the Portuguese. With these, they established an overseas empire that was far grander than, and quite different from, the Portuguese trading posts.

An important figure in the history of Spanish exploration was an Italian from Genoa, Christopher Columbus. All educated Europeans knew that the world was round, but they had little understanding of its circumference or of the size of the continent of Asia. Convinced that the circumference of Earth was less than others believed and that Asia was larger than people thought, Columbus felt that Asia could be reached by sailing west instead of east around Africa.

Columbus finally persuaded Queen Isabella of Spain to finance an exploratory expedition. He reached the Americas in October 1492, where he explored the coastline of Cuba and the northern shores of Haiti (HAE-tee), or Hispaniola (see "You Are There: Columbus Lands in the New World"). Columbus believed that he had reached Asia, and in three more voyages he sought in vain to find a route through the outer islands to the Asian mainland. In his four voyages, Columbus reached all the major islands of the Caribbean and Honduras in Central America, all of which he called the Indies (IN-deez).

So What ⁇

*If your students question the importance of information about **the Age of Discovery**, tell them . . .*

In ancient times sailors used the constellations and seasonal wind directions to navigate their ships. In the Middle Ages, sailors drew up charts that included sample calculations of wind directions for the different seasons. The invention of both the astrolabe and the compass had a combined impact on ancient civilization that somewhat mirrors the impact of radio on modern civilization. With the development of the astrolabe, sailors at last found an accurate way to measure the angle and movement of stars. Now, if a ship were blown off course by a storm, the astrolabe could show sailors how far they had drifted. A device still used in modern day navigation, the sextant, was developed from the astrolabe.

YOU ARE THERE

Columbus Lands in the New World

On returning from his voyage to the Americas, Christopher Columbus wrote a letter describing his experience. In this passage from the letter, he tells of his arrival on the island of Hispaniola (Haiti).

Columbus, Describing His Arrival on the Island of Hispaniola

The people of this island and of all the other islands which I have found and of which I have information, all go naked, men and women, as their mothers bore them. They have no iron or steel or weapons, nor are they fitted to use them. This is not because they are not well built and of handsome stature, but because they are very marvelously timid. They have no other arms than spears made of canes, cut in seeding time, to the end of which they fix a small sharpened stick. . . . They refuse nothing that they possess, if it be asked of them; on the contrary, they invite any one to share it and display as much love as if they would give their hearts. They are content with whatever trifle of whatever kind they may be given to them, whether it be of value or valueless. I forbade that they should be given things so worthless as fragments of broken crockery, scraps of broken glass and lace tips, although when they were able to get them, they fancied that they possessed the best jewel in the world. So it was found that for a thong a soldier received gold to the weight of two and half castellanos, and others received much more for other things which were worthless. . . . I gave them a thousand handsome good things, which I had brought, in order that they might conceive affection for us and, more than that, might become Christians and be inclined to the love and service of Your Highnesses [king and queen of Spain], and strive to col-

▲ *This painting by Italian painter Sebastiano del Piombo was done in 1519, thirteen years after Columbus's death. To some, Columbus is a hero; to others, he is a villain. Why is there such a difference of opinion concerning his accomplishments?*

lect and give us of the things which they have in abundance and what are necessary to us.

1. Why did Columbus give the natives of Hispaniola "a thousand handsome good things"?

2. How did the explorers take advantage of the natives?

RETEACHING ACTIVITY

After reading the above feature, and to help students who may need additional teaching on the geography of exploration, ask them these further questions based on Map 16.1 on page 489.

1. Ask them to trace Columbus's four voyages. Have them note how far Columbus actually was from Asia.

2. Have students trace the voyages taken by Amerigo Vespucci. What geography would he have described?

3. Have students locate the Strait of Magellan. Have them note the huge distance from the Strait to the Philippines, where Magellan was killed.

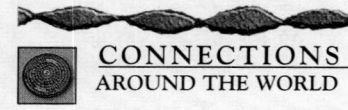

CONNECTIONS
AROUND THE WORLD

Lead students in a discussion of the controversy about firearms in our society. Try to promote balance in the discussion. If time permits, you may want to have two students of different points of view participate in an impromptu debate.

CRITICAL THINKING

Have students do research on the recent controversies surrounding Columbus (see, for example, James W. Loewen's 1992 book, *The Truth about Columbus*). Ask them to weigh the evidence, choose a position on Columbus, and justify their decision.

CRITICAL THINKING

Why might American Indians and other people indigenous to North and South America be offended by the term "New World"? What does the use of the term—and, for another example, the Treaty of Tordesillas dividing the area between Spain and Portugal—suggest about European attitudes toward the rest of the world?

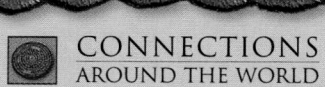

CONNECTIONS
AROUND THE WORLD

Gunpowder and Gunpowder Empires   Gunpowder and guns were invented in China in the thirteenth century and then spread to Europe and the Middle East in the fourteenth century. However, the full impact of gunpowder was not felt until after 1500. Between 1500 and 1650, the world experienced a dramatic increase in the manufacture of weapons based on gunpowder. Large-scale production of cannons was especially evident in Europe, the Ottoman Empire, India, and China. By 1650, guns were also being made in Korea, Japan, Siam and Iran, and to a lesser extent, in Africa. Most cannons were made with bronze barrels, but brass and iron were also being used.

Firearms were a crucial element in the creation of new empires after 1500. Spaniards armed with firearms had devastated the civilizations of the Aztecs and Incas and carved out empires in Central and South America. The Ottoman Empire, the Mughal Empire in India, and the Safavid Empire in Persia, all owed much of their success in creating and maintaining their large empires to the use of the new weapons. Historians have labeled them the "gunpowder empires." Of course, the success of Europeans in creating new trade empires in the East owed much to their use of cannons. Portuguese ships armed with heavy guns that could sink enemy ships at a distance of 100 yards or more easily decimated the lighter fleets of the Muslims in the Indian Ocean.

Although Columbus clung to his belief until his death, other explorers soon realized that he had discovered a new frontier altogether. State-sponsored explorers joined the race to the New World. A Venetian seaman, John Cabot, explored the New England coastline of the Americas for England. The Portuguese sea captain Pedro Cabral landed in South America in 1500. Amerigo Vespucci (ve-SPOO-chee), a Florentine, went along on several voyages and wrote a series

of letters describing the geography of the New World. The publication of these letters led to the use of the name America (after *Amerigo*) for the new lands.

Europeans called their newly discovered territories the New World, but these lands were hardly new. They already had flourishing civilizations made up of millions of people when the Europeans arrived. The Americas were, of course, new to the Europeans, who quickly saw opportunities for conquest and exploitation. The Spanish, in particular, were interested because in 1494 the Treaty of Tordesillas (TAWRD-uh-SEE-yus) had divided up the newly discovered world into separate Portuguese and Spanish spheres of influence. According to the treaty, the route east around Africa was to be reserved for the Portuguese, and the route across the Atlantic (except for the eastern hump of South America) was assigned to Spain.

The Spanish Empire

The Spanish conquerors—known as **conquistadors**—were a hardy lot of individuals motivated by a typical sixteenth-century blend of glory, greed, and religious zeal. Their firearms, organizational skills, and determination brought the conquistadors incredible success. It took Hernán Cortés and a small band of men, beginning in 1519, three years to overthrow the mighty Aztec Empire in Central America (see Chapter 7). By 1550, the Spanish had gained control of northern Mexico. Another expedition led by a hardened soldier, Francisco Pizarro, took control of the Inca Empire high in the Peruvian Andes. The Spanish conquests were aided by the previous arrival of European diseases, which often wiped out the local populations. It took another thirty years before the western part of Latin America was brought under Spanish control (the Portuguese took over Brazil). However, by 1535, the Spanish had already created a system of colonial administration that made the New World an extension of the old.

Queen Isabella declared the natives (called *Indians*, after the Spanish word *Indios*, or "inhabitants of the Indies") to be her subjects and granted the Spanish *encomienda*. This was the right of settlers in the New World to use the natives as laborers. In return, the holders of an *encomienda* were supposed to protect the

MORE ABOUT . . . *Bartolome de Las Casas*

Bartolome de Las Casas (1474–1566) was a Spanish Dominican who strongly supported the distinction between acts performed in accordance with natural law (directly from God) and acts performed in accordance with human law (indirectly from God). The Spaniards concluded that the Indians lived by natural law alone but that they were God's people even without benefit of the church.

Las Casas had gone to the New World in 1502 to convert the heathen and soon became engaged in a struggle to win them better treatment. In 1515 he urged the future Emperor Charles V to end Indian slavery in his American dominions. Las Casas recommended the importation of blacks from Africa, both because church law did not forbid black slavery and because he thought blacks could

▲ *This codex shows Indians suffering from smallpox. Why was this European disease so deadly to the Indians?*

▲ *The Cathedral of Mexico City was built on the same site as the Aztec temple to the sun god at Tenochtitlán, and the materials used to build it came from the destroyed Aztec pyramids. Why did the Spaniards believe that this was acceptable and right?*

Indians. Because they were three thousand miles from Spain, however, the Spanish settlers largely ignored their government. They brutally used the Indians to meet their own economic interests. Indians were put to work on sugar plantations and in the gold and silver mines. Few Spanish settlers worried about protecting the Indians. One exception was Bartolomé de Las Casas, who had helped to conquer Cuba but came to believe that the Spaniards were cruelly mistreating the Indians. He became a monk and spent the remaining years of his life fighting for the Indians. He lived to the age of ninety-two.

Forced labor, starvation, and especially disease took a fearful toll on Indian lives. With little or no natural resistance to European diseases, the Indians of the Americas were ravaged by smallpox, measles, and typhus. These killers came with the explorers and the conquistadors. It has been estimated that 30 to 40 percent of the natives died. On Haiti alone, out of an initial population of 100,000 natives when Columbus arrived in 1493, only 300 Indians survived by 1570. In Mexico, the population dropped from twenty-five million in 1500 to three million in 1570.

By an agreement with the pope, the Catholic rulers of Spain were given extensive rights over church affairs in the New World. They could appoint church officials, collect fees, and supervise the affairs of the vari-

ous religious orders that sought to Christianize the natives. In return, tax money was sent back to the Spanish court. Catholic monks converted and baptized hundreds of thousands of Indians in the early years of the conquest. Soon after the missionaries came the establishment of dioceses (DIE-ah-SEEZ), parishes, schools, and hospitals—all the trappings of a European society.

The Impact of European Expansion

European expansion into the New World made an enormous impact on both the conquerors and the conquered. The native civilizations were virtually destroyed. Old social and political structures were ripped up and replaced by European systems of government, religion, language, and culture.

European expansion also affected the conquerors, especially in the economic arena. Wherever they went, Europeans sought gold and silver. One Aztec commented

better survive under South American conditions. Charles agreed and in 1518 the African slave trade began. When blacks arrived, Las Casas immediately regretted his suggestion. In the early 1520's he took part in a program to found free cities for Christianized Indians. The project failed and he returned to Spain. He retired to a Dominican house and wrote

many works promoting his scheme as well as a *History of the Indian.*

Discuss with students how the interest Las Casas felt in the American Indians affected black Africans. Speculate on the impact one person can have on history. Do students think black slavery would have been as widespread without the influence of Las Casas?

ACROSS THE CURRICULUM

Economics Ask interested students to trace the "new age of commercial capitalism" that began with expanded European trade. What were the characteristics of this capitalism? What were the steps leading to "the world economy that has characterized the modern historical era"?

CLASS DISCUSSION

Discuss with students the threats to the Portuguese trade empire in Southeast Asia from the English and the Dutch.

Multimedia Support

LASERDISC
Slavery (Video)

COMPARING TIME PERIODS

Ask students to research the Dutch East India Company. How did its business strategies compare with similar, more contemporary trading organizations? What are some ways the management of foreign trade has changed since the seventeenth century?

that the Spanish conquerors "longed and lusted for gold. Their bodies swelled with greed, and their hunger was ravenous; they hungered like pigs for that gold."[4] Rich silver deposits were found and exploited in Mexico and southern Peru (modern Bolivia). When the mines in Peru were opened, the value of precious metals imported into Europe increased four times.

Gold and silver were only two of the products sent to Europe from the New World. Into Spain flowed sugar, dyes, cotton, vanilla, and hides from livestock raised in the South American pampas, or plains. Agricultural products native to the Americas, such as potatoes, coffee, corn, and tobacco, were also shipped to Europe. Because of its trading posts in Asia, Portugal soon challenged the Italian states as the chief entry point of the eastern trade in spices, jewels, silk, carpets, ivory, leather, and perfumes. The increase in the volume and area of European trade was a crucial factor in producing a new age of commercial capitalism that was the first step toward the world economy that has characterized the modern historical era.

European expansion also deepened European rivalries and increased the tensions among European states. Bitter conflicts arose over the cargoes coming from the New World and Asia. Although the Spanish and Portuguese were the first in the competition, by the end of the sixteenth century new rivals were entering the scene. The first to arrive were the English and the Dutch.

New Rivals Enter the Scene

The Portuguese were never totally successful in their attempt to dominate the trade of the Indian Ocean. They did not have the resources to colonize the Asian regions. Portugal's empire was too large and Portugal too small to maintain colonies. One Portuguese chronicler lamented, "My country, oh my country. Too heavy is the task that has been laid on your shoulders. Day after day I watch the ships leaving your shores filled always with your best and bravest men. And too many do not return. . . . Who then is left to till the fields, to harvest the grapes, to keep the enemy on our frontiers at bay?"[5]

By the end of the sixteenth century, new European rivals had entered the scene for domination of the Indian Ocean trade. One of them was Spain. The Spanish had established themselves in the region when Ferdinand Magellan had landed in the Philippine Islands. Although Magellan was killed there, the Spanish were able to gain control over the Philippines, which eventually became a major Spanish base in the trade across the Pacific. Spanish ships carried silk and other luxury goods to Mexico in return for silver from the mines of Mexico.

The greatest threat to the Portuguese Empire in Southeast Asia, however, came from the English and the Dutch. At the beginning of the seventeenth century, an English fleet landed on the northwestern coast of India and established trade relations with the Indians. Trade with Southeast Asia soon followed. The first Dutch fleet arrived in India in 1595. Shortly after, the Dutch East India Company was formed under the direction of the government and was soon competing with the English and the Portuguese.

The Dutch also formed the West India Company to compete with the Spanish and Portuguese in the Americas, but they made little headway. Dutch settlements were established on the North American continent. The mainland colony of New Netherlands stretched from the mouth of the Hudson River as far north as Albany, New York. Present-day names such as Manhattan, Staten Island, Harlem, and the Catskills remind us that it was the Dutch who initially settled the Hudson River valley.

In the second half of the seventeenth century, however, rivalry and years of warfare with the English and the French (who had also become active in North America) brought the decline of the Dutch commercial empire in the New World. The English seized the colony of New Netherlands and renamed it New York. The Dutch West India Company soon went bankrupt. Canada became a French colony, although the French failed to provide adequate numbers of people or sufficient money. By the early eighteenth century, the French began to cede some of their American possessions to the English.

The English, meanwhile, had proceeded to create a colonial empire in the New World along the Atlantic

SPECIAL NEEDS: *Spatial/visual*

Have the students make a chart that will include the names, dates, country of origin, and achievement of each of the explorers discussed in pages 488–493. The chart should include the following: (1) Prince Henry the Navigator/1419/Portuguese/Founded school for navigators; (2) Bartholomew Diaz/1487/Portuguese/Discovered southern tip of Africa; (3) Christopher Columbus/1492/Spanish-Italian/discovered the Americas; (4) Vasco da Gama/1498/sailed to India; (5) Pedro Cabral/1500/Portuguese/landed in South America; (6) Admiral Alfonso d'Albuquerque/1510/Portuguese/Set up port on the western coast of India; (7) Magellan/1519/Portuguese/Sailed around the world; (8) Herman Cortés/1519/Spain/conquered the Aztec empire in Central America.

seaboard of North America. The desire to escape from religious oppression, combined with economic interests, made it possible for England to have successful colonies, as the Massachusetts Bay Colony demonstrated. The Massachusetts colony had only four thousand settlers in its early years. Its numbers soon swelled to forty thousand. By the end of the seventeenth century, the English had established control over most of the eastern seaboard of North America.

 SECTION REVIEW

1. **Locate:**
   (*a*) Portugal,   (*b*) Africa,   (*c*) Senegal River,
   (*d*) Cape Verde,   (*e*) Lisbon,   (*f*) Zaire (Congo)
   River,   (*g*) Malacca,   (*h*) Spice Islands,
   (*i*) Cuba,   (*j*) Haiti

2. **Define:**
   (*a*) conquistadors,   (*b*) *encomienda*

3. **Identify:**
   (*a*) Prince Henry the Navigator,
   (*b*) Bartholomew Diaz,   (*c*) Vasco da Gama,
   (*d*) Admiral Alfonso d' Albuquerque,
   (*e*) Christopher Columbus,   (*f*) John Cabot,
   (*g*) Pedro Cabral,   (*h*) Amerigo Vespucci,
   (*i*) Hernán Cortés,   (*j*) Francisco Pizarro

4. **Recall:**
   (*a*) Explain what was meant by "God, glory, and gold" as being the main motives of early explorers.
   (*b*) Which country was the leader in early European exploration?
   (*c*) Why were the Portuguese so successful in their explorations?
   (*d*) Describe the Spanish *encomienda*.

5. **Think Critically:** Some early explorers felt it was their duty to spread their religion around the world. Because of their religious zeal, however, many native peoples died and many civilizations were destroyed. Were the actions of the explorers justified? Why or why not?

AFRICA IN AN AGE OF TRANSITION

At first, the Portuguese sailed around Africa in the hope of finding a sea route to the Spice Islands. They soon discovered, however, that profits could be made in Africa itself. So, too, did other Europeans.

The Portuguese built forts on both the western and eastern coasts of Africa. They tried, above all, to dominate the trade in gold. During the mid-seventeenth century, however, the Dutch seized a number of Portuguese forts along the coast of West Africa. At the same time, they took control of much of the Portuguese trade across the Indian Ocean.

The Dutch East India Company also set up a settlement in southern Africa, at the Cape of Good Hope, which was meant to serve as a base to provide food and other provisions to Dutch ships en route to the Spice Islands. Eventually, however, this settlement developed into a permanent colony. Dutch farmers, known as Boers, began to settle in areas outside the city of Capetown. The area's moderate climate and freedom from tropical diseases made it desirable to European settlers.

The Slave Trade

European exploration of the African coastline did not affect most Africans living in the interior of the continent. For peoples living on or near the coast, however, the impact was great indeed. As the trade in slaves increased, millions of Africans were removed from their homes and shipped to **plantations** (large landed estates) in the New World.

Of course, traffic in slaves was not new. As in other areas of the world, slavery had been practiced in Africa since ancient times. In the fifteenth century, it continued at a fairly steady level. The primary market for African slaves was the Middle East, where most were used as domestic servants. Slavery also existed in many European countries, where some slaves from Africa or war captives from the regions north of the Black Sea were used for domestic purposes.

ASSESS

Answers to SECTION REVIEW

2. (a) Spanish conquerors
   (b) right of settlers to use the natives as laborers
3. (a) leader of Portugal's exploration; sought trade opportunities for Portugal
   (b) first European to round Cape of Good Hope
   (c) sailed to India
   (d) conquered Malacca; known for his brutality
   (e) Italian who explored for Spain; reached the Americas in 1492
   (f) explored North American coast for England
   (g) Portuguese; landed in South America in 1500
   (h) Florentine; wrote letters describing geography of the New World.
   (i) conquistador, conquered the Aztec Empire
   (j) conquistador, conquered the Incas
4. (a) spread their religion (God); fame (glory); wealth (gold)
   (b) Portugal
   (c) their seamanship and weapons
   (d) using natives as laborers; supposed to protect the natives
5. Answers will vary.

CLOSE

Speculate with students how life in Europe might have been changed by exploration in Africa, Asia, and the Americas. How might Europeans look at the wider world differently? What might be the impact of expanded trade on their daily lives?

FOCUS

OBJECTIVES

After completing this section, students should be able to

1. describe the impact of Europeans on the African slave trade
2. list the effects of the slave trade on the peoples of Africa
3. describe traditional African political systems
4. discuss foreign influence on African religious beliefs

Answer to caption question: Cartography became increasingly important as sailors traveled further and further from home. During the first millennium A.D. trade by sea and over land routes had provided explorers with rudimentary knowledge of map-making, and information from these explorations and trading expeditions was eventually gathered together. Students should also know about the school for cartographers established by Prince Henry of Portugal during the fifteenth century.

FOCUS ACTIVITY

As students learned in Chapter 9, slavery had been practiced in Africa, as in other parts of the world, since ancient times. European exploration and expansion, however, greatly changed and increased the traffic in human beings. Ask small groups to take about ten minutes to list differences between slavery in Africa before the Europeans

▲ *This sixteenth-century map of Africa was prepared by Spanish cartographer Juan de la Cosa. How do you think sailors and explorers acquired these maps? How did cartographers gather their information?*

At first, the Portuguese simply replaced their European slaves with African ones. During the last half of the fifteenth century, about a thousand slaves were taken to Portugal each year. Most wound up serving as domestic servants for rich families in Europe. However, the discovery of the Americas in the 1490s and the planting of sugarcane in South America and the islands of the Caribbean changed the situation drastically.

Cane sugar had first been introduced to Europeans from the Middle East during the Crusades. At the end of the fifteenth century, the Portuguese set up sugar plantations worked by African laborers on an island off the central coast of Africa. During the sixteenth century, sugarcane plantations were set up along the eastern coast of Brazil and on several islands in the Caribbean. Growing cane sugar demands both skill and large quantities of labor. The small American Indian population in the New World, many of whom had died of diseases imported from the Old World, could not provide the labor needed. Thus, African slaves were shipped to Brazil and the Caribbean to work on the plantations. The first were sent from Portugal, but in 1518 a Spanish ship carried the first boatload of African slaves directly from Africa to the New World.

During the next two centuries, the trade in slaves grew dramatically. An estimated 275,000 African slaves were exported during the sixteenth century. Two thousand went every year to the Americas alone. In the seventeenth century, the total climbed to over a million. It jumped to six million in the eighteenth century. By then the trade had spread from West Africa and central Africa to East Africa. Even during the nineteenth century, when Great Britain and other European countries tried to end the slave trade, nearly two million slaves were exported. Altogether, as many as ten million African slaves were brought to the Americas between the early sixteenth and the late nineteenth centuries.

One reason for these astonishing numbers, of course, was the high death rate. Many slaves died on the journey before arriving in the New World (see "Focus on Everyday Life: Life in the Slave Ships"). Those who arrived often died from diseases to which they had little or no immunity. Death rates were higher for newly arrived slaves than for those born and raised in the

So What ⁇

*If your students question the importance of information about **the slave trade**, tell them . . .*

slavery in Europe was well entrenched in the later Middle Ages. The bubonic plague, famine, and other epidemics created a severe labor shortage. This encouraged Italian bankers and merchants to buy slaves from Balkan Thrace, Southern Russia and Central Anatolia for sale in the West. Profits were lucrative and papal threats of excommunication failed to stop the slave trade. Genoese traders set up colonial stations in the Crimea and along the Black Sea for the needs of plantation agriculture in the Mediterranean area and the New World. This form of slavery had nothing to do with race; almost all slaves were white. How then, did Black African slavery enter the European picture?

Map 16.2   The Slave Trade

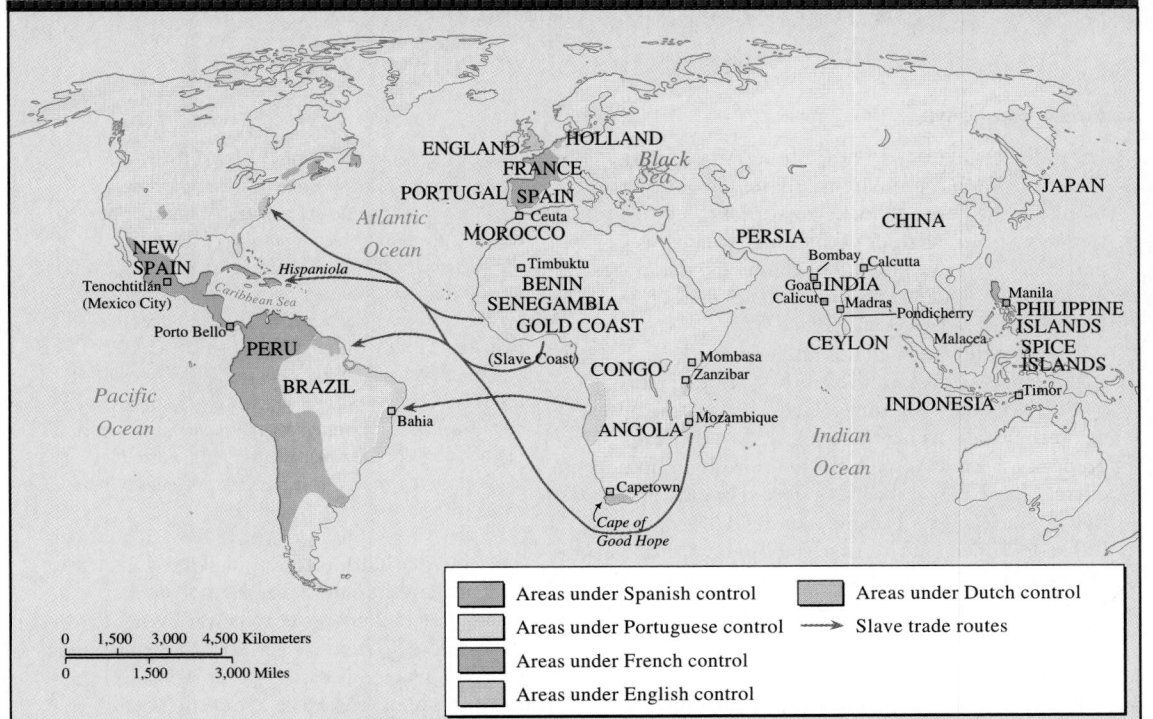

came, and slavery after. As a class, discuss these differences. Was either practice "better," or more humane? Why, or why not?

TEACH

CLASS DISCUSSION

Guide students in a discussion of how the European discovery of the Americas and the planting of sugarcane in South America and the Caribbean changed the face of African slavery.

Multimedia Support

TRANSPARENCY
16–2, Timeline: Legacy, the African Slave Trade

CRITICAL THINKING

What can students surmise from the fact that many slave owners believed it was more economical to buy a new slave than to raise a child to working age? *(may have killed newborns, discouraged or forbade marriage, kept the sexes apart)*

Multimedia Support

TRANSPARENCY
16–3, The Slave Trade (Map 16.2)

New World. The new generation gradually developed at least a partial immunity from childhood to many of the more fatal diseases. Owners, however, rarely encouraged their slaves to have children. Many slave owners, especially in the West Indies, believed that buying a new slave was less expensive than raising a child from birth to working age at adolescence. When the price of slaves rose in the eighteenth century, owners changed their policy.

Before the coming of Europeans in the fifteenth century, most slaves in Africa were prisoners of war. Many served as domestic servants or as wageless workers for the local rulers. When Europeans first began to take part in the slave trade, they bought slaves from local African merchants at slave markets in return for

gold, guns, or other European goods such as textiles or copper or iron utensils.

At first, local slave traders obtained their supply from regions nearby. As demand increased, however, they had to move further inland to find their victims. In a few cases, local rulers became concerned about the impact of the slave trade on the well-being of their societies. In a letter to the king of Portugal in 1526, King Affonso of Congo (Bakongo) said, "so great is the corruption that our country is being completely depopulated."[6] Protests from Africans were generally ignored by Europeans, as well as by other Africans. As a general rule, local rulers viewed the slave trade as a source of income. Many sent raiders into defenseless villages in search of victims. Participation in the slave trade

CRITICAL THINKING

Ask students to debate whether African participation in enslaving other Africans made Europeans engaged in the slave trade any less guilty or reprehensible. Have them consider what factors may have influenced African attitudes toward the trade in human lives.

STUDYING MAPS

The following questions and activities will help you guide students through their study of Map 16.2.

1. Trace the four main slave trade routes. From which areas of Africa were the people taken? *(Atlantic coastal areas; southeastern coast via the Cape of Good Hope)*

2. How far from home did the Africans travel? *(Answers will vary depending on origin of the people in question.)*

3. Locate Capetown, Hispaniola, Congo, Benin, Gold Coast, and Slave Coast.

FOCUS ON EVERYDAY LIFE
Life in the Slave Ships

For African slaves, the voyage from Africa to the Americas was a nightmare that lasted about two months. The desire to make great profits led traders to fill their ships with as many slaves as possible. Overcrowding did have one disadvantage for the slave trader. If too many slaves died on the journey, the trader's profit fell.

Slaves were put in chains and crammed together below deck in the holds of ships. There was little room. Sometimes slaves slept sitting up or on their sides. They were allowed to come up on deck for a few minutes a day for fresh air and exercise. In bad weather, they stayed below. Their living quarters soon became a living hell—dark, filthy, and filled with terrible smells and disease. As seen in this seventeenth-century account, one Dutch trader believed that Dutch ships had somewhat better conditions:

You would really wonder to see how these slaves live on board, for though their number sometimes amounts to six or seven hundred, yet by the careful management of our masters of ships, they are so regulated that it seems incredible. And in this particular our nation exceeds all other Europeans, for the French, Portuguese, and English slave ships are always foul and stinking; on the contrary, ours are for the most part clean and neat. The slaves are fed three times a day with indifferent good victuals, and much better than they eat in their own country. Their lodging place is divided into two parts, one of which is appointed for the men, the other for the women, each sex being kept apart. Here they lie as close together as it is possible for them to be crowded.

The filthy conditions on most slave ships led to high death rates. Some slaves died of "melancholy"—they had no desire to go on living. Diseases, including dysentery and smallpox, also took their toll. On some occasions, sick slaves were simply thrown overboard to avoid the possibility

was also a matter of self-preservation. Even if an African ruler refused to supply slaves, he knew that his neighbor would supply them. Therefore, in order to survive, he felt compelled to participate.

Historians once thought that Europeans controlled the terms of the slave trade and were able to get victims at bargain prices. However, it is now clear that African intermediaries—merchants, members of local elites, or rulers—were very active in the process. They were often able to dictate the prices and numbers of slaves to European buyers. Payment to the slave merchant was often made in various types of imported goods, such as textiles, furniture, and guns.

The effects of the slave trade varied from area to area. Of course, it always had tragic effects on the lives of individual victims and their families. There was also an economic price, as the importation of cheap manufactured goods from Europe undermined local cottage industries and forced countless families into poverty. The slave trade also led to the depopulation of some areas, and it deprived many African communities of their youngest and strongest men and women.

The political effects of the slave trade were also devastating. The need to maintain a constant supply of slaves led to increased warfare and violence. Coastal or near-coastal African chiefs and their followers, armed

On Line with WORLD HISTORY *Internet Activity*

You may want to have your students visit the following URL, where they will find information and additional web site resources to enhance their study of this chapter.
1492: An Ongoing Voyage
http://sunsite.unc.edu/expo/ 1492.exhibit/Intro.html

An exhibit of the Library of Congress. Divided into six main areas it stresses the New World and Mediterranean societies.

Due to the ever-changing nature of the World Wide Web, see the West History web site, **http://history.swpco.com** for regular updates of the URLs in this text.

FOCUS ON EVERYDAY LIFE
Life in the Slave Ships, continued

of an epidemic. In desperation, some slaves committed suicide by throwing themselves overboard and drowning. Others revolted by attacking members of the crew. They were rarely successful, however, and in any case had little effect on the slave trade.

▲ *As this model of a typical slave ship demonstrates, slaves were forced to lie as close to each other as possible. Here you can see representations of 600 slaves crowded into a space designed for 400. It is not surprising that death rates on the ships approached 30 percent. What effect do you think slavery had on traditional ways of life in Africa?*

1. What led slave traders to fill their ships as full as possible with slaves?

2. The passage written by a Dutch trader stated that the conditions on Dutch slave ships were far better than conditions on other slave ships. Do you think this was true?

3. Why do you think some slaves lost their desire for living?

4. Why were the slaves seldom successful when they revolted against crew members on the slave ships?

with guns acquired from the trade in slaves, increased their raids and wars on neighboring peoples. A few Europeans lamented what they were doing to traditional African societies. One Dutch slave trader remarked, "From us they have learned strife, quarrelling, drunkenness, trickery, theft, unbridled desire for what is not one's own, misdeeds unknown to them before, and the accursed lust for gold."[7]

The slave trade continued, however, with devastating effects for some African states. The case of Benin (buh-NIN) in West Africa is a good example. A brilliant and creative society in the sixteenth century, Benin was pulled into the slave trade. As the population declined and warfare increased, the people of Benin lost faith in their gods, their art deteriorated, and human sacrifice became more common. When the British arrived there at the end of the nineteenth century, they found a corrupt and brutal place. It took years to discover the brilliance of the earlier culture destroyed by slavery.

The Political and Social Structures of African States

The slave trade was one of the most noticeable effects of the European presence in Africa between 1500 and

LEARNING FROM VISUALS

Answer to caption question: Slavery destroyed the traditional way of life for many Africans.

Answers to Critical Thinking Questions

1. the desire for profits
2. Answers will vary, but it is doubtful that conditions were much better than on other slave ships.
3. Answers will vary, but may include the following. They probably knew that conditions would not get better. They may have been homesick for family left behind.
4. The crew members probably had weapons, the slaves had none; the slaves were weak from lack of food and the filthy condition on the ships.

CLASS DISCUSSION

Lead students in a discussion of the economic and political effects of the slave trade.

CRITICAL THINKING

Students may recall their study of Benin culture in Chapter 9. Ask them to pretend they are Benin historians, recording the downfall of their culture as a result of slavery. Have them write, draw, sculpt, or in some other way document what they see happening in their society.

COOPERATIVE LEARNING ACTIVITY

By now, students have done a lot of thinking about and discussing the issue of slavery and its impact on the various people involved. Have students work in groups to prepare a one or two page Slavery Issue Report for a Dutch newspaper of this era. Have them write articles covering both sides of the issue. They might have an eyewitness account of a slaveship; a comparison of Dutch slaveships to those of, say, Portugal or Spain; an interview with a slave (where he or she is from, what has happened, how he or she feels); an interview with a ship's captain; and perhaps an "exclusive interview' with Isaac Watts, composer of the hymn "Amazing Grace." Encourage students to be creative in both their writing and newspaper layout. Consider "publishing" the various newspapers for the entire class, or post them somewhere.

LEARNING FROM VISUALS

What can students discern about the two people being bargained over from their postures, gestures, and facial expressions? How does their appearance differ from that of the African leader?

Answer to the caption questions: Answers will vary.

CLASS DISCUSSION

Have students compare and contrast the political systems of the Benin and Yoruba peoples, the state of Ashanti, and the Ibo peoples.

CLASS DISCUSSION

Discuss with students the Yoruba custom of the king's family joining him in death. Do they believe such a custom devalues human life? Would it make the custom of slavery more understandable?

▲ *During the eighteenth century, selling slaves was a profitable commercial enterprise. This painting shows a European slave merchant bargaining with an African leader in Senegal, West Africa. Do you think these were his own tribesmen? Why or why not?*

1800. European influence generally did not penetrate beyond the coastal regions. Only in a few isolated areas, such as South Africa and Mozambique (MOE-zum-BEEK), were there signs that a permanent European presence was being established.

In general, traditional African political systems continued to exist (see "Young People in an African Kingdom: Growing Up in the Kingdom of the Congo"). By the sixteenth century, monarchy had become a common form of government throughout much of the continent. Some states, like the kingdom of Benin in West Africa, were highly centralized, with the king regarded as almost divine. An example of the awesome authority of some African rulers was the Yoruba custom whereby members of the king's family were expected to commit suicide when he died.

Other African states were more like a collection of small principalities knit together by ties of kinship or other loyalties. The state of Ashanti on the Gold Coast was a good example. The kingdom consisted of a number of previously independent small states linked together by kinship ties and subordinated to the king. To provide visible evidence of this unity, each local ruler of a small state was given a ceremonial stool of office to serve as a symbol of the kinship ties linking the rulers together. The king had a golden stool to symbolize the unity of the entire state. It may be that the decision to integrate the various states into a larger state was made in response to the growing challenge of European power.

Many Africans continued to live in small political units in which authority rested in a village or tribal chief. The Ibo (EE-BOE) peoples of eastern Nigeria were an example. Ibo society was based on independent villages linked together only by convenience. The Ibo were active traders, and the area produced more slaves than practically any other in the continent.

Inland areas of Africa were often indirectly affected by events elsewhere. In the western Sahara, for example, the shifting of trade routes toward the coast led to the weakening of the old Songhai trading empire in response to a vigorous new Moroccan dynasty in the late sixteenth century. Morocco had long hoped to expand its influence into the Sahara in order to seize control over the trade in gold and salt. When his advisors warned against taking an army across the desert, the ruler of Morocco replied, "You talk of the perilous desert we have to cross. You talk of the fatal solitudes, barren of water and pasture. But you forget those merchants, mounted or on foot, who regularly cross the wasteland which caravans have never ceased to cross. Far better supplied than they, I can do the same with an army that will inspire terror wherever it appears."[8] In 1590, after a twenty-week trek across the desert, the Moroccan forces defeated the Songhai army and then occupied the great trading center of Timbuktu. Eventually the Moroccans were forced to leave, but Songhai was beyond recovery. Its next two centuries were marked by civil disorder.

MORE ABOUT . . . *The Songhai Empire*

An empire is never easy to maintain, particularly if the real allegiance of the people is to their locality and their own people rather than the larger state and its rulers. In the late 1300s civil war weakened the Mali empire. Over the next century the power of the Songhai replaced the Mali. In 1464, Sonni Ali became the ruthless but able leader of the Songhai. From his capital at Gao he soon extended his control northwards to include the salt mines at Taghaza and reached almost to the borders of Morocco and south to take over the lands and cities of the Hausa. Eastward expansion was stopped by the fierce tribes of the kingdom of Bouni, who controlled much of the Central Sudan and built up a profitable trade in slaves.

Ali created an efficient government. He divided his empire into provinces and appointed trusted officials to regulate com-

YOUNG PEOPLE IN AN AFRICAN KINGDOM

Growing Up in the Kingdom of the Congo

Near the mouth of the Zaire (Congo) River in central Africa was the kingdom of the Congo (Bakongo). By the fifteenth century, it was a large state that quickly came to the attention of the Portuguese. Despite the efforts of the Portugese, it tried to maintain its traditional way of life. Part of that way of life was a process of education that prepared its young people to become part of the community.

Until the age of six, both boys and girls were raised by their mothers. From their mothers, they learned language, their family history, and the songs that gave meaning to their lives. At six, boys and girls went their separate ways. Girls went to live in the "house of the women" and boys, in the "house of the men."

Fathers then took control of their sons' education. Boys learned how to hunt and fish, how to grow plants, and how to clear the fields for planting. By experience, young males learned how to live and survive in the natural world.

Girls continued to learn what they needed to know from their mothers. This included how to take care of the home and how to work in the fields. Girls also learned what they would need in order to be good wives and good mothers. Marriage and motherhood would be the entry into the world of the community for females.

As the children matured, they became a greater part of the community. Boys cleared the fields, built houses, and took part in village discussions and ceremonies. Girls took over more responsibility for household tasks; took care of younger brothers and sisters; and attended village ceremonies, especially those connected with marriages and funerals.

Thus, young people reached a point in their upbringing where they were expected to serve the

▲ *This village scene from Tanzania shows the education of the young by their parents in practical, daily matters. Do you think that teaching by showing and doing works best? Why or why not?*

entire community. This transition—which occurred at the time of puberty—was marked by an initiation ceremony in which young people were kept isolated from the community. They then underwent a ritual ceremony in which they symbolically died and were then reborn. Young females were then fully women; young males were then fully men. Both entered completely into the life of the community at that time.

1. What did children in the kingdom of the Congo learn from their mothers?

2. What did the children learn from their fathers?

3. Why do you think young people symbolically died and were reborn during their initiation ceremonies?

CLASS DISCUSSION

Discuss with students how the education of children in the Congo may have helped the people maintain their traditional way of life, despite the efforts of the Portuguese to intrude. What is the focus of the young people's education? *(Community service)*

Answers to Critical Thinking Questions

1. They learned language, family history, and songs that gave meaning to their lives.
2. The boys learned how to hunt and fish, how to grow plants, and how to clear fields for planting. As far as we know from this information, skills weren't taught to daughters by their fathers.
3. Answers will vary. It may indicate the death of childhood and the birth of adulthood.

LEARNING FROM VISUALS

Answer to the caption question: Student answers will vary, but sociological research shows that teaching by demonstrating behaviors is highly effective and lasting.

merce, agriculture and justice. He established official weights and measures and under his successor, Timbuktu became a great center of learning. In 1590 Sa'dis of Morocco in Northern Africa sent an army across the Sahara to seize the gold mining regions of the Songhai. Only about 2,000 soldiers survived the long desert march, but armed with cannons and muskets, which were unknown to the Songhai, the invaders defeated the Songhai forces.

They sent back over $8,000,000 in gold. The Songhai then broke up into small independent states. Trade continued but political unity ended.

LEARNING FROM VISUALS

Answer to the caption question: Tribal life was usually well-organized, with defined roles for men, women, and children. Dancers and soldiers or warriors were usually well-trained and highly organized.

CLASS DISCUSSION

Have students discuss how African states sometimes allied with one another against the Europeans, and sometimes allied with Europeans against African rivals. Which strategy do students think might have had the better chance of minimizing European disruption of African society?

CRITICAL THINKING

Have students speculate on reasons why Islam, rather than Christianity, made the deepest inroads into the African belief systems.

ASSESS

You can choose from a variety of assessments to evaluate your students' mastery of the objectives for this section, as stated on page 496. Possible assessments include:

1. Section Review questions on this page
2. Section 16–2 Quiz in your Teacher Resource materials
3. Reteaching Worksheets in your Teacher Resource materials
4. Self-Study software

▲ *This hand-colored woodcut shows a tribe performing for their leader while a Western European watches. What does this picture reveal about tribal customs and village life?*

In some instances, African states allied with one another to force Europeans to respect their control of trading operations. At the same time, some African states occasionally relied on the support of European powers against inland rivals. Some, like the powerful Ashanti kingdom established on the Gold Coast at the end of the seventeenth century, profited greatly from their favorable positions to take advantage of the rise in seaborne trade. Some states took an active part in the slave trade. This was particularly true along the so-called Slave Coast in what is now Dahomey and Togo, as well as in the densely populated Niger River delta. The demands of the slave trade and the desire for economic profit, however, also contributed to an increase in conflict among the states in the area.

One area where this conflict was especially pronounced was the region of the Zaire River. Portuguese activities there eventually led to the splintering of the Congo Empire and two centuries of internal strife among the successor states in the area. A similar pattern developed in East Africa, where Portuguese activities led to the decline and eventual collapse of states there. Northward along the coast, in present-day Kenya and Tanzania, African rulers, assisted by Arab forces from the Arabian peninsula, expelled the Portuguese from Fort Jesus in Mombasa in 1728.

A final area where foreign influence began to appear was the realm of religious beliefs. This influence was especially strong in North Africa, where Islam continued to expand. Muslim beliefs had become dominant along the northern coast and had spread southward into the states of West Africa. One way that Islam was able to survive and prosper in its new environment was to come to terms with local beliefs and practices. As in

CNN® WORLD HISTORY UPDATES

You can update your coverage of World History topics, as well as spark lively classroom discussion and deeper understanding, by using the **CNN World History Updates.**

For assistance in using and incorporating the **CNN World History Updates** into your classroom presentations, see the *Classroom Guide.*

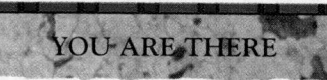

USING PRIMARY SOURCES

In his letter, Louis XIV calls Christian law "the most suitable to have kings reign absolutely over the people." What is he referring to here? *(Divine right of kings)* Discuss why he might make special mention of this virtue of Christianity when writing to the Vietnamese king.

LEARNING FROM VISUALS

Answers to the caption questions: Answers will vary.

CLASS DISCUSSION

Discuss the following sentence: ". . . the Malay states were victims of their own resources." *(Enormous profits from spice trade drove Europeans to seek control)*

YOU ARE THERE

An Exchange of Royal Letters

Economic gain was not the only motivation of Western rulers who wished to establish the presence of Europeans in the East. In 1681, King Louis XIV of France wrote a letter to the Vietnamese king in which he asked permission for Christian missionaries to seek converts in Vietnam. The king politely declined the request.

King Louis XIV of France in a Letter to the Vietnamese King

Most high, most excellent, most mighty and most magnanimous Prince, our very dear and good friend, may it please God to increase your greatness with a happy end! . . .

We have given orders to have brought to you some presents which we believe might be agreeable to you. But the one thing in the world which we desire most, both for you and for your Realm, would be to obtain for your subjects who have already embraced the law of the only true God of heaven and earth, the freedom to profess it, since this law is the highest, the noblest, the most sacred and especially the most suitable to have kings reign absolutely over the people.

▲ *What similarities can you see between the appearance of Louis XIV, as shown here, and his writing style? Do you think that Louis wrote his own letters or had someone write them for him?*

Why were the mainland states better able to resist the European challenge than the states in the Malay world? No doubt, one factor was the cohesive character of these states. The mainland states of Burma, Thailand, and Vietnam had begun to define themselves as distinct political entities. In the Malay states, there was less cohesion. Moreover, the Malay states were victims of their own resources. The spice trade there was enormously profitable. European merchants and rulers were determined to gain control of the sources of the spices. That determination led them to take direct control of the Indonesian archipelago.

State and Society in Southeast Asia

Between 1500 and 1800, Western influence was still relatively limited in most areas of Southeast Asia. Nevertheless, Southeast Asian societies were changing in several small ways—in their means of livelihood, their trade patterns, and their religious beliefs.

Government and Politics

In Southeast Asia, increasingly sophisticated states developed between 1500 and 1800. The political sys-

On Line with WORLD HISTORY Internet Activity

You may want to have your students visit the following URL, where they will find information and additional web site resources to enhance their study of this chapter.

Discoverers Web

http://www.win.tue.nl/cs/fm/engels/discovery/index.html

This site puts in one spot all kinds of information about voyages of discovery and exploration and includes every conceivable country.

Due to the ever-changing nature of the World Wide Web, see the West History web site, **http://history.swpco.com** for regular updates of the URLs in this text.

◄ *Batavia, the capital of the Dutch East Indies, was located on the northern coast of Java. When the canals became breeding areas for malaria-bearing mosquitoes, the Dutch moved their capital south, to the modern-day site of Jakarta.*

CLASS DISCUSSION

Review with students the steps through which the Dutch consolidated control over the spice trade. Read with them the "More About" box below, and discuss the Dutch strategy. Brainstorm reasons why the Dutch were able to exert this high level of control.

CLASS DISCUSSION

Discuss with students why Europeans had less impact on mainland Southeast Asia than they did on the islands along the spice route—the Malay world. *(strong monarchies in Burma, Thailand, and Vietnam; internal cohesion)*

ACROSS THE CURRICULUM

Science Ask students to research the locations of the various spices that Europeans sought. What exactly is a spice? Why were certain spices especially prized? Why were they concentrated in this particular part of Asia?

The shift in power began in the early seventeenth century, when the Dutch seized a Portuguese fort in the Moluccas and then gradually pushed the Portuguese out of the spice trade. During the next fifty years, the Dutch occupied most of the Portuguese coastal forts along the trade routes throughout the Indian Ocean, including the island of Ceylon (today's Sri Lanka) and Malacca. The aggressive Dutch traders also drove the English traders out of the spice market, eventually reducing the English influence to a single port on the southern coast of Sumatra.

The Dutch also began to consolidate their political and military control over the entire area. They tried to dominate the clove trade by limiting cultivation of the crop to one island and forcing others to stop growing and trading the product. Then the Dutch turned their attention to the island of Java, where they had established a fort at Batavia (today's Jakarta) in 1619. The purpose of the fort was to protect Dutch possessions in the East. Gradually the Dutch brought the entire island under their control.

The arrival of the Europeans had less impact on mainland Southeast Asia. Strong monarchies in Burma, Thailand, and Vietnam resisted foreign intrusion. The Portuguese established limited trade relations with several mainland states, including Thailand, Burma, Vietnam, and the remnants of the old Angkor kingdom in Cambodia. By the early seventeenth century, other nations had followed and had begun to compete actively for trade and missionary privileges. To obtain economic advantages, the Europeans soon became involved in local factional disputes. In general, however, these states were able to unite and drive the Europeans out.

In Vietnam, Western merchants and missionaries arrived during a period of internal conflict among ruling groups in the country. Expansion had brought a civil war that temporarily divided the country into two separate states, one in the south and one in the north. After their arrival in the mid-seventeenth century, the European powers began to take sides in local politics. The Portuguese and the Dutch supported rival factions. The Europeans also set up trading posts for their merchants. However, by the end of the seventeenth century, when it became clear that economic opportunities were limited, most of these posts were abandoned. French missionaries tried to stay, but their efforts were blocked by the authorities, who viewed converts to Catholicism as a threat to the prestige of the Vietnamese emperor (see "You Are There: An Exchange of Royal Letters").

MORE ABOUT . . . *Dutch Overseas Trade*

The Dutch adoption of religious toleration stimulated the country's commercial enterprise. As early as 1600, the Dutch had 10,000 ships and throughout the 17th century they owned most of the shipping of Northern Europe. Rounding Cape Horn, which they named after Hoorn in Holland, they entered the Pacific. In 1602 they organized the Dutch East India Company and their merchants increasingly replaced the Portuguese in India and the Far East. The city of Batavia carries the Latin name for Holland. In 1623 the Dutch tortured and killed some English merchants at Amboina in the midst of the Spice Islands. In 1652 the Dutch captured the Cape of Good Hope in South Africa, and Dutch settlers soon appeared. From these settlers and others have come the modern Afrikaner people, whose language and religion still reflect their Dutch origins.

FOCUS

OBJECTIVES

After completing this section, students should be able to

1. discuss the shift in power from Portuguese to Dutch in the control of the spice trade
2. contrast the impact of Europeans on mainland states of Southeast Asia with their impact on the Malay world
3. describe the four main political systems in Southeast Asia
4. discuss features of the economy and daily life of Southeast Asian societies

FOCUS ACTIVITY

Ask students to brainstorm reasons why, unlike in Africa, the destructive effects of European contact in Southeast Asia were only gradually felt.

results as new states arose along the spice route. Islam was accepted first along the coast and then gradually moved inland.

The major impact of Islam, however, came in the fifteenth century, with the rise of the new sultanate at Malacca. Malacca owed its new power to its strategic location astride the strait of the same name, as well as to the rapid growth of the spice trade itself. Within a few years, Malacca had become the leading power in the region.

The Arrival of the West

In 1511, the Portuguese seized Malacca and soon occupied the Moluccas. Known to Europeans as the Spice Islands, the Moluccas were the chief source of the spices that had originally attracted the Portuguese to the Indian Ocean. The Portuguese, however, lacked the military and financial resources to impose their authority in broad areas. Instead, they set up small settlements along the coast, which they used as trading posts or as way stations en route to the Spice Islands.

The situation changed with the arrival of the English and Dutch traders, who were better financed than were the Portuguese. They moved aggressively to take advantage of the traditional trading patterns in the Indian Ocean and began to participate in the regional trade. They shipped Indian cotton goods to Southeast Asia in return for spices. They also shipped precious metals from Japan and the Middle East to India.

Map 16.3   The Patterns of World Trade

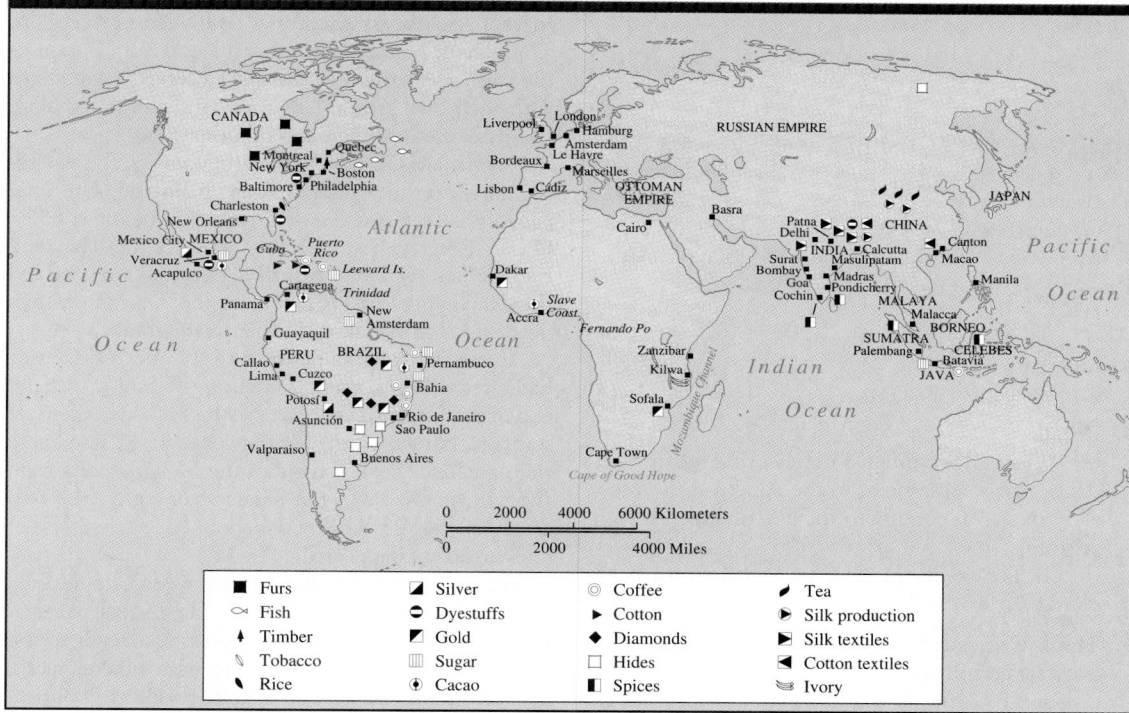

Southeast Asia, as time went on, the original Muslim doctrine took on a number of local practices. This enhanced its appeal to the peoples of West Africa and the Sahara.

The growing European presence in sub-Saharan Africa led to the first appearance of Christianity there. Certainly, a key element in the European voyages of exploration was an effort to destroy the Arab monopoly of trade with the East, but the missionary impulse was by no means absent. During their early years in Africa, the Portuguese had engaged in some missionary activity. When Portuguese authority declined, however, the small Christian communities virtually disappeared. Portugal's European successors, the English, the Dutch, and the French, made little effort to combine their trading activities with the message of the gospel. Except for the tiny European foothold in South Africa and the isolated kingdom of Ethiopia, Christianity was unable to reach its goal of stopping the spread of Islam in Africa.

 SECTION REVIEW

1. **Locate:**
   (a) Capetown,   (b) Brazil,
   (c) Benin,   (d) Mozambique,   (e) Slave Coast

2. **Define:**
   (a) plantations

3. **Identify:**
   (a) Boers,   (b) Ashanti

4. **Recall:**
   (a) What is the estimated number of African slaves that were brought to the Americas from the early sixteenth century to the late nineteenth century?
   (b) List the effects the slave trade had on the peoples of Africa.

5. **Think Critically:** Consider the effects the slave trade had on the peoples of Africa (see Recall question b). How do you think the Europeans and

the local African rulers justified their involvement in the slave trade?

SOUTHEAST ASIA IN THE ERA OF THE SPICE TRADE

In Southeast Asia, the encounter with the West began with the arrival of Portuguese fleets in the Indian Ocean at the end of the fifteenth century. Eventually, this contact led to the breakdown of traditional societies and the advent of colonial rule. In general, however, the process was a gradual one.

Building Stable Political Systems on the Mainland

In 1500, Southeast Asia was a relatively stable region. Throughout mainland Southeast Asia, from Burma in the west to Vietnam in the east, a series of kingdoms with their own ethnic, linguistic, and cultural characteristics were in the process of formation.

Nevertheless, conflicts did erupt among the emerging states on the Southeast Asian mainland. The Thai peoples had secured their control over the lower Chao Phraya River valley. Conflict between the Thai and the Burmese was bitter until a Burmese army sacked the Thai capital in 1767, forcing the Thai to create a new capital at Bangkok, further to the south.

Across the mountains to the east, the Vietnamese had already begun their "March to the South." By the end of the fifteenth century, they had subdued the rival state of Champa on the central coast. The Vietnamese then gradually took control of the Mekong delta from the Khmer. By 1800, the Khmer monarchy (the successor of the old Angkor kingdom—see Chapter 12) had virtually disappeared.

The situation was different in the Malay peninsula and the Indonesian archipelago. The gradual penetration of the area by Muslim merchants, a result of the growing spice trade, had introduced a new element. The creation of an Islamic trade network had political

RECOMMENDED READING

Also, see K. M. Panikkar, *Asia and Western Dominance* (London, 1959); and H. Furber, *Rival Empires of Trade in the Orient, 1600–1800* (Minneapolis, 1976). For an overview on the impact of European expansion in the Indian Ocean, see K. N. Chaudhuri, *Trade and Civilization in the Indian Ocean: An Economic History from the Rise of Islam to 1750* (Cambridge, 1985).

On Portuguese expansion, see C. R. Boxer, *The Portuguese Seaborne Empire, 1415–1825* (New York, 1969); and W. B. Diffie and G. D. Winius, *Foundations of the Portuguese Empire, 1415–1580* (Minneapolis, 1979). On the Dutch, see J. I. Israel, *Dutch Primacy in World Trade, 1585–1740* (Oxford, 1989). The effects of European trade in Southeast Asia are discussed in A. Reid, *Southeast Asia in the Age of Commerce, 1450–1680* (New Haven, Conn., 1989).

YOU ARE THERE

An Exchange of Royal Letters, continued

We are even quite convinced that, if you knew the truths and the maxims which it teaches, you would give first of all to your subjects the glorious example of embracing it. We wish you this incomparable blessing together with a long and happy reign, and we pray God that it may please Him to augment your greatness with the happiest of endings.

Your very dear and good friend,
Louis

**The Vietnamese King's
Response to King Louis XIV**

The King of Tonkin sends to the King of France a letter to express to him his best sentiments, saying that he was happy to learn that fidelity is a durable good of man and that justice is the most important of things. Your communication, which comes from a country which is a thousand leagues away, and which proceeds from the heart as a testimony of your sincerity, merits repeated consideration and infinite praise. Politeness toward strangers is nothing unusual in our country. There

is not a stranger who is not well received by us. How then could we refuse a man from France, which is the most celebrated among the kingdoms of the world and which for love of us wishes to frequent us and bring us merchandise? These feelings of fidelity and justice are truly worthy to be applauded. As regards your wish that we should cooperate in propagating your religion, we do not dare to permit it, for there is an ancient custom, introduced by edicts, which formally forbids it. How could we disdain a well-established custom to satisfy a private friendship? . . .

This letter was written at the beginning of winter and on a beautiful day.

1. What was the purpose of King Louis's letter to the Vietnamese king?

2. Why did the Vietnamese king decline King Louis's request?

3. Why do you suppose the kings were so polite to each other?

---

tems in these states evolved into four main types: Buddhist kings, Javanese kings, Islamic sultans, and Vietnamese emperors, all of whom drew their original inspiration from foreign models. In every case, however, the models were adapted to local circumstances.

The Buddhist style of kingship became the chief form of government in the Buddhist states of mainland Southeast Asia—Burma, Thailand, Laos, and Cambodia. The chief feature of the Buddhist model was the godlike character of the monarch. The king was considered superior to other human beings. The king was, in fact, considered the link between human society and

the universe. Court rituals stressed the sacred character of the monarch.

The sacred quality of the Buddhist ruler enhanced his political authority over his kingdom and his power of life and death over his subjects. A Buddhist king punished his subjects with little regard for legal procedures. Furthermore, his sacred quality often kept him isolated from his subjects and involved in sterile court ritual. The isolation of the king gave immense power to his royal advisors, who often became involved in disputes over the succession to the throne. They appointed high officials outside the capital, most of

COOPERATIVE LEARNING ACTIVITY

Divide the class into four groups. Assign each group one of the four political systems discussed in this section—Buddhist, Javanese, Islamic and Vietnamese. Have each group do outside research and prepare a report on their political system for oral presentation in

class. Their report should include maps, charts, and illustrations of the era's dress, art, and so forth. You might want to follow the oral presentations with a discussion on the similarities and differences of the four systems.

YOU·ARE·THERE

**Answers to Critical
Thinking Questions**

1. Louis asked permission to send Christian missionaries to seek converts in Vietnam.

2. The Vietnamese king told Louis that missionaries could not be allowed to come to Vietnam because of an ancient custom, introduced by edicts, which formally forbade it.

3. King Louis wanted a request to be granted and probably felt he would have a better chance of succeeding if he approached it as politely as possible. The Vietnamese king denied the request and probably felt he should do so politely so as not to encourage any kind of aggression on King Louis' part.

CLASS DISCUSSION

Discuss with students the characteristics of Buddhist kings. What were the practical results of a Buddhist king's godlike nature? *(Isolated from subjects; gave great power to royal advisors; led to independence of territories far from capital)*

ACTIVITY

Comparing Political Systems. Ask students to create a chart that compares Buddhist, Javanese, Islamic, and Vietnamese political systems. Their charts should include the countries, king's role, and chief feature of each system. (You may want to use the blank chart provided in your Teacher Resource materials.)

▲ *This hand-colored woodcut shows the Emperor and Empress of Subakarta. What do their dress and pose reveal about this couple?*

whom were nobles or members of the royal family. In general, these officials ruled their territories as small kingdoms. Those far away from the capital became increasingly independent of the central authority.

The Javanese style of kingship was rooted in the political traditions of India and shared many of the characteristics of the Buddhist system. Like Buddhist rulers, Javanese kings had a sacred quality and maintained the balance between the sacred and the material world. The royal palace was designed to represent the center of the universe. From there, rays radiated outward to the far corners of the realm.

The Javanese kings were not quite the same as the Buddhist kings, however. The Javanese kings did not appoint members of the royal family to serve as officials but instead relied on local officials from the nobility. Then, too, as Muslim influences crept into the Indonesian islands, Javanese kings began to lose their semidivine quality.

Islamic sultans were found on the Malay peninsula and in the small coastal states of the Indonesian archipelago. In the Islamic pattern, the head of state was a sultan. He was viewed as a mortal, although he still possessed some special qualities. He was a defender of the faith and staffed his bureaucracy mainly with aristocrats. He was expected, at least in theory, to rule according to Islamic tradition.

In Vietnam, kingship continued to follow the Chinese model. Like the Chinese emperor, the Vietnamese emperor ruled according to the teachings of Confucius. He was seen as a mortal appointed by Heaven to rule because of his talent and virtue. He also served as the intermediary between Heaven and Earth. The king's powers were extensive but limited in practice by the bureaucracy, which was then generally selected by merit according to the Chinese pattern.

At the bottom of the administrative hierarchy in all Southeast Asia were the villages. They were as different as the styles of kingship were. In some areas, such as the Malay peninsula, the headman inherited his position and was considered a minor noble and the direct representative of the king. In other areas, such as Vietnam, the chief was not the representative of the king but was elected by the village notables. In actuality, he served the council of notables rather than the royal bureaucracy. Vietnamese villages had considerable freedom.

The Economy and Daily Life

Between 1500 and 1800, the economies of virtually all Southeast Asian societies continued to be based on farming, as they had been for thousands of years. Probably 90 percent of the people throughout the region engaged in some form of farming, mostly the cultivation of wet rice. In the upland regions, dry crops were

On Line with WORLD HISTORY *Internet Activity*

You may want to have your students visit the following URL, where they will find information and additional web site resources to enhance their study of this chapter.

India

http://india.indiagov.org/1page.htm

Made by the Ministry of External

Affairs, there is a lot of good informative history under the subtitles Culture and India Perspectives. Major Indian artworks such as Taj Mahal are covered.

Due to the ever-changing nature of the World Wide Web, see the West History web site, **http://history.swpco.com** for regular updates of the URLs in this text.

cultivated by the **slash-and-burn method,** in which farmers cleared an area by chopping down trees and burning off the remaining plants; the ashes provided natural fertilizer for the soil. By the sixteenth century, trade began to affect the daily lives of many Southeast Asians. In part, this was because agriculture was becoming more specialized. Cash crops like sugar and spices, sold to outsiders, replaced subsistence farming in rice or other cereals. (Subsistence farming provides only what a farmer needs for the family's survival.)

By this period, trade was taking place at local, regional, and interregional levels. At the local level, trade consisted chiefly of the exchange of goods made by local artisans and other consumer products such as cloth, iron, and salt. For the most part, local trade was conducted through barter rather than with money. Much of this trade was carried by boat on the rivers or canals, because few countries in Southeast Asia had networks of roads.

Regional and interregional trade were already expanding before the coming of the Europeans. The growing importance of handicrafts contributed to the increase in regional trade. The central geographical location of Southeast Asia enabled it to became a focal point in an interregional trading network. Spices, of course, were the mainstay of the interregional trade, but Southeast Asia exchanged other products as well. The region exported tin (mined in Malaya), copper, gold, tropical fruits and other agricultural products, cloth, gems, and luxury goods in exchange for manufactured goods, ceramics (including Chinese porcelain), and high-quality textiles such as silk from China.

Southeast Asians probably enjoyed a higher standard of living than most of their contemporaries elsewhere in Asia. Most of the population was poor by Western standards, but starvation and even widespread hunger were probably fairly rare. One Portuguese traveler noted that Java was "the most fruitful island in the world; therein is abundance of good rice; fresh meat in great plenty; sheep, cows, hens, goats, swine of great size both tame and wild, all in great numbers."[9]

Several factors explain this relative prosperity. In the first place, most of Southeast Asia has a favorable climate. Uniformly high temperatures, abundant rainfall, and numerous rivers and streams enable as many as two or even three crops to be grown each year. Second, soil in many areas is fertile. Bananas, mangoes, papayas, citrus fruits, and other tropical products thrive throughout the region. Finally, with some exceptions, Southeast Asia was thinly populated.

For most people in Southeast Asia, daily life in the early period of European penetration was not a great deal different from what it had been for hundreds of years. Most people still lived as rice farmers, small traders, hunters, or fishers in the villages that dotted the landscape of rice paddies. Their houses were simple, consisting of a main room, a few smaller ones, and a veranda. Because of the warm climate, the windows had neither panes nor shutters. The houses were built of wood, from palm trees or thatch. Stone was scarce. Generally, houses were raised on stilts, which prevented them from flooding during **monsoon season** (a periodic strong wind). The interiors were simple. Only royalty and the aristocracy would have furniture or rugs. Meals consisted of rice, fruit, and vegetables, with occasionally a little meat or fish. Southeast Asians used no eating utensils and ate on palm leaves.

Social institutions were fairly uniform throughout Southeast Asia. The nuclear family was the norm. In general, women fared better in Southeast Asia than anywhere else in Asia. They were usually limited to specialized work, such as making ceramics, weaving, or transplanting the rice seedlings into the main paddy fields. They rarely possessed legal rights equal to those of men. However, they had a relatively high degree of freedom and status in most societies in the region. Daughters often had the same inheritance rights as sons, and family property was held jointly between husband and wife. Wives were often permitted to divorce their husbands, and monogamy was the rule. In some cases, the family of the groom provided the dowry in marriage. Married couples often went to live in the wife's village.

Religious beliefs were changing during this period. Particularly in the Malay world and the Philippines, Islam and Christianity were beginning to attract converts. Buddhism was advancing on the mainland, where it became dominant from Burma to Vietnam. The spread of these religions often brought changes, but in Southeast Asia, native traditions tended to sur-

---

COOPERATIVE LEARNING ACTIVITY

Divide the class into four groups and assign each group a culture—Greek, Roman, Chinese, or Southeast Asian. Have each group answer the following questions, relying primarily on information in the text.

What was the structure of society? What was the structure of the family? How were women treated?

How were homes and other buildings constructed? What was the diet of the people? Was food generally sufficient?

When the groups have completed their lists, lead them in a discussion of the four cultures. Where and when would they have preferred to live? Why?

COMPARING TIME PERIODS

Have students consider how, in the twentieth century, the "central geographical location of Southeast Asia" made the region strategically important to competing political systems. Ask them to research when trade in the region began taking second place to global politics.

CLASS DISCUSSION

Ask students to list the factors that gave Southeast Asians a higher standard of living than most of their Asian contemporaries. *(favorable climate, fertile soil, small population)*

CRITICAL THINKING

"In general, women fared better in Southeast Asia than anywhere else in Asia." Ask students to speculate on why this was so. Suggest that they consider religious beliefs in the region, particularly the melding of native traditions with Buddhism, Islam, and Christianity.

ASSESS

You can choose from a variety of assessments to evaluate your students' mastery of the objectives for this section, as stated on page 503. Possible assessments include:

1. Section Review questions on this page
2. Section 16–3 Quiz in your Teacher Resource materials
3. Reteaching Worksheets in your Teacher Resource materials
4. Self-Study software

LEARNING FROM VISUALS

Answers to SECTION REVIEW

2. (a) area cleared by chopping down trees and burning off remaining plants; ashes provided natural fertilizer for soil (b) periodic strong wind
3. (a) little cohesion among the independent states; European merchants were determined to gain control. (b) Few countries had a road network. (c) spices
4. (a) Buddhist kings—monarch a godlike character; king considered superior to other humans and the link between human society and the universe; king's sacred quality isolated him from subjects, giving immense power to his royal advisers

   Javanese kings—rooted in Indian traditions; shared characteristics of Buddhist system, i.e. sacred quality of king and balance between sacred and material worlds; kings appointed local officials from nobility to serve as government officials

   Islamic sultans—with defender of Islam faith; staffed bureaucracy with aristocrats; expected to rule according to Islamic theory

   Vietnamese emperors—ruled according to teachings of Confucius; mortal appointed by heaven to rule because of talent and virtue; served as intermediary between heaven and earth; powers extensive, but limited in practice

 This hand-colored woodcut shows a typical home in Khong, Cambodia. The house is raised, and the fishing boats are pulled ashore. What do the other details tell us about the daily lives of this family?

vive and even influence the new religions. For example, Buddhists in Burma and Thailand and Muslims in the Indonesian islands continued to believe in nature spirits while also adhering to their new faiths.

❋ SECTION REVIEW ❋

1. **Locate:**
   (a) India, (b) Japan, (c) Sumatra, (d) Java, (e) Malaya, (f) China, (g) Philippines

2. **Define:**
   (a) slash-and-burn method, (b) monsoon season

3. **Recall:**
   (a) What were the two main factors that caused the Malay world to fall to foreign traders?
   (b) Why was most trade in Southeast Asia carried by boats on the rivers and canals?
   (c) What item was the mainstay of interregional trade in Southeast Asia?

4. **Think Critically:** Compare and contrast the four types of political systems that developed in Southeast Asia between 1500 and 1800.

Conclusion

At the end of the fifteenth century, Europeans burst upon the world scene. The process began with the modest ventures of the Portuguese ships that sailed southward along the West African coast in the mid-fifteenth century. It quickened with the voyages of Columbus to the Americas. Soon a number of other European states had entered the scene. By the end of the eighteenth century, they had created a global trade network dominated by Western ships and Western power.

In less than three hundred years, the European age of exploration changed the world. In some areas, such as the Americas and the Spice Islands, it led to the destruction of local civilizations and the establishment of European colonies. In others, such as Africa and mainland Southeast Asia, it left native regimes intact but had a strong impact on local societies and regional trade patterns. European expansion affected Africa with the dramatic increase of the slave trade. The Dutch built a trade empire based on spices in the Indonesian archipelago. Trade increased in Southeast Asia, but most societies there were still based on farming. One historian has described the period as the beginning of an "age of Western dominance."

The age of European exploration also affected other areas of the world, such as East Asia, South Asia, and the Middle East. South Asia and the Middle East felt the European influence most keenly, because it was the stated objective of many European adventurers to bring an end to Muslim domination of the Indian Ocean trade network. In the next chapter, we turn to the Islamic world to see how it handled that challenge.

Notes

1. Quoted in J. H. Parry, *The Age of Reconnaissance: Discovery, Exploration and Settlement, 1450 to 1650* (New York, 1963), p. 33.
2. J. H. Parry, *The European Reconnaissance: Selected Documents* (New York, 1968), p. 113.
3. Quoted in Ian Cameron, *Explorers and Exploration* (New York, 1991), p. 42.
4. Miguel Leon-Portilla, ed., *The Broken Spears: The Aztec Account of the Conquest of Mexico* (Boston, 1969), p. 51.
5. Quoted in Cameron, *Explorers and Exploration,* p. 42.
6. Quoted in Basil Davidson, *Africa in History: Themes and Outlines,* rev. ed. (New York, 1991), p. 213.
7. Quoted in *ibid.,* p. 198.
8. Quoted in *ibid.,* pp. 198–199.
9. *The Book of Duarte Barbosa* (Nedeln, 1967), 2: p. 191.

CLOSE

Ask students to discuss whether or not they believe that Southeast Asia became part of "the age of Western dominance" during the years covered by this chapter.

TIME LINE

As students conclude the chapter, you may want to refer them to the chapter time line in the *Study Guide.* The time line will help them put key dates in perspective. Supporting questions and activities are also provided.

SPANISH SUPPORT

The *Conclusion* has been translated into Spanish for your Spanish-speaking students. Included with this translation (in your Teacher Resource Box) are Section Key Points, which consist of one or two sentences summarizing each section in the chapter. These Key points have also been translated into Spanish.

USING KEY TERMS

1. *encomienda*
2. monsoon season
3. conquistadors
4. slash-and-burn method
5. plantations

REVIEWING THE FACTS

1. 1519
2. spices
3. ginger and cinnamon; the profit was several thousand per cent
4. Malacca
5. three days of slaughter and the killing of 8,000 Arab men, women, and children
6. naval technology and cannons
7. No. Educated people of the period knew the world was a sphere; the question was calculating the circumference, which Columbus grossly underestimated.
8. Cortés; Pizarro
9. Portugal
10. gold and silver
11. Dutch, then French, then British after the mid-18th century
12. Boers
13. 10 million
14. increased warfare and violence
15. Buddhist and Javanese kings
16. Chinese system where officials were chosen on merit
17. wood; houses built on stilts
18. They had no desire to go on living.
19. calculate latitude; especially necessary in Southern hemisphere
20. prisoners of war; booty of victors

THINKING CRITICALLY

1. Spain and the Portugal were two main players in European exploration; the pope solved dispute between the two; outraged and indignant that Europeans claimed to control the entire world.

512

CHAPTER 16 REVIEW

USING KEY TERMS

1. In the Spanish _____ system natives in America were used as laborers, supposedly in return for protection.
2. The time of great flooding, caused by strong winds, in South Asia and Southeast Asia is called the _____.
3. _____ were Spanish conquerors who were motivated by religious zeal and the desire for glory and riches.
4. When farmers clear an area by chopping down trees and burning off the remaining plants, it is called the _____.
5. Many Africans were removed from their homes and shipped to large landed estates in the New World called _____.

REVIEWING THE FACTS

1. In what year did Ferdinand Magellan begin his voyage to "sail around the world?"
2. What did the Europeans want most from the East?
3. When Vasco da Gama reached India, what cargo did he take back to Portugal? How profitable was his voyage?
4. What was the name of the city located on the Malay peninsula that was the central point in the spice trade?
5. How did the Portuguese deal with the people of Malacca when they captured it?
6. What was the most important Portuguese advantage in securing the trade routes in the Indian Ocean?
7. Did Christopher Columbus think that the world was flat?
8. Who was the conquistador who overthrew the Aztec Empire? Who conquered the Incas?
9. Which European country conquered Brazil?

512

---

10. What did Europeans want more than anything else from America?
11. Who displaced the Portuguese in the Indian Ocean trade?
12. What is the name given to the Dutch who settled in South Africa?
13. Approximately how many Africans came to the Americas as slaves?
14. What political impact did the slave trade have on Africa?
15. Which two of the following rulers were considered divine: Buddhist kings, Japanese kings, Islamic sultans, Vietnamese emperors?
16. What was the model for the Vietnamese bureaucracy?
17. What material was used for most houses in Southeast Asia? How was flooding prevented?
18. What does it mean that some slaves died of "melancholy?"
19. What is the purpose of an astrolabe?
20. How did most Africans become slaves?

THINKING CRITICALLY

1. In the Treaty of Tordesdillas the Spanish and Portuguese divided the world in two with each taking half. Why did they do this? How is this an example of the self-centered attitude of the Europeans? How do you think the Japanese, Chinese, Arabs, and others felt about this?
2. In order for some people to be free, some must be enslaved. Is this a true statement? Explain how the Spanish encomienda system allowed a few Spanish to live a life of leisure while many Indians worked long hours and suffered great casualties. How did the Spanish rationalize this system?
3. Portugal's empire was too large and Portugal too small to maintain its Indian Ocean empires. How was Portugal able to dominate the Arabs in the first place? What led to their demise? What could

---

2. This question essentially deals with the issue of income inequality and why it exists.
3. Portuguese had superior ships carrying cannons, were risk takers; demise result of European rivals, Arab reorganization and lack of gain to crown; work with Arabs, fight fewer wars
4. sale of enemies profitable, groups not engaged in slave trade likely victims; slave trade lasted so long, was a problem plaguing Africa for centuries.
5. both military weapons and unity crucial in fending off Europeans; small, less cohesive countries suffered most
6. Use the question to discuss various map projec-

tions. Also, discuss what is at the center, the focus, of a given map.

APPLYING SOCIAL STUDIES SKILLS

1. **Geography:** New York City area, along Hudson river to Albany.
2. **Economic:** sugar, dyes, cotton, vanilla, hides, potatoes, coffee, corn, tobacco
3. **Economic:** primarily Indian cotton goods
4. **Economic:** favorable climate, high temperatures, abundant rainfall, numerous streams and rivers, fertile soil, lightly populated
5. **Sociology:** women had relatively high degree of

CHAPTER 16 REVIEW

the Portuguese have done differently to sustain their control of the Indian Ocean?

4. Benin is an example of a country that was pulled into the slave trade. What attracted Africans to the slave trade? Did they have a choice? How did slavery lead to Benin becoming "a corrupt and savage place."

5. The strength of a country depends on its military. Evaluate this statement with regard to the greater independence of Southeast Asian mainland countries during the age of European expansion, as opposed to the Malay states. Are there other factors that are more important?

6. All maps lie. This bold statement is a simplification, but it is true that maps, which are flat, cannot precisely convey the Earth, which is spherical. Look at a world map projection. Is the equator placed in the middle of the map? Find other map projections including a "Peter's projection" and see how they differ from one another.

APPLYING SOCIAL STUDIES SKILLS

1. **Geography:** Consult Map 16.2 on page 497. Which areas of the present United States were under Spanish control?

2. **Economic:** Besides gold and silver, what goods were traded from America to Europe?

3. **Economic:** What did the people of Southeast Asia receive when they traded their spices?

4. **Economic:** Why did the people of Southeast Asia have a relatively high standard of living?

5. **Sociology:** Why did women in Southeast Asia generally fare better than other women in Asia?

6. **Geography:** Consult Map 16.3 on page 504. What were the main exports of Canada and Argentina (South of Brazil)?

7. **Government:** How important was the growth of monarchy in European expansion?

8. **Geography:** What are portalans? What was the problem with using them?

MAKING TIME AND PLACE CONNECTIONS

1. From the time that Prince Henry began exploring the West Coast of Africa, how long was it before Portuguese ships reached the tip of Africa? From the time the first American astronaut was launched into space, how long did it take to reach the moon?

2. European diseases were devastating to the natives of America. How did disease affect the Europeans when they traveled to Africa?

3. Explain how the encomienda system is similar to the European feudal system.

4. Based on readings in the chapter, how did Muslims extend their control in Africa from 700 to 1600?

5. What is the most populous Muslim country in Southeast Asia today?

6. Compare the entertainments enjoyed by Sultan Zainal-'Abidis to Roman gladiatorial combat.

BECOMING AN HISTORIAN

Drawing Inferences: Reread the selection entitled **You Are There: Columbus Lands in the New World.** People often make inferences; that is, they try to "read between the lines." This can be risky and lead to false conclusions. What inferences has Columbus made about the lives of the natives? Make a list of purely factual material that he lists and then note his inferences. How accurate do you think he is?

3. Feudalism was the basis for the encomienda system.

4. Muslims moved from Arabia and controlled parts of North Africa by about 700; extended domination to parts of the Sahara and East Africa by 1600

5. Indonesia

6. Both involved the senseless slaughter of innocents for pleasure. Roman combat was a public spectacle, while the Sultan's contests for his pleasure only.

BECOMING AN HISTORIAN—DRAWING INFERENCES

Some possibilities are as follows.

Fact (F), Inference (I)

(F) people scantily clothed
(I) they are inferior
(F) no iron or steel weapons
(I) timid and not fit to use weapons
(F) traded with Spaniards at first
(I) content with whatever given them
(F) Spanish traded broken crockery
(I) Spanish quick to exploit natives
(F) Columbus gave them "a thousand handsome things"
(I) Columbus is generous
(F) Columbus forbade unequal trade
(I) Columbus is fair and just

---

freedom and status; often had some inheritance rights some property held jointly by husband and wife wives permitted to divorce husbands; monogamy was rule; groom might provide dowry; couples often lived in wife's village

6. **Geography:** furs and hides
7. **Government:** significant, but the development of new technology, desire for spices, religious zeal, and European willingness to take risks were other factors
8. **Geography:** Detailed navigational maps commonly used in 13th and 14th centuries, accurately show shape of coastline and distance between ports.

MAKING TIME AND PLACE CONNECTIONS

1. 1419–1498 (79 years); late 1950s
2. The presence of malaria limited European travel to coastal Africa. Few Europeans explored the interior of Africa before the late-nineteenth century when it was realized that drinking quinine could prevent malaria.

17 PLANNING GUIDE

SECTION	KEY TOPICS	PRIMARY SOURCES	ASSESSMENT
1 The Ottoman Empire pages 515–526	◆ Rise and expansion of Ottoman Empire ◆ Janissary corps ◆ Fall of Constantinople ◆ Reign of Suleyman the Magnificent ◆ Nature of Ottoman rule ◆ Ottoman religion and society ◆ Ottoman art	◆ Description of fall of Constantinople, pages 519–520	◆ Section Review, page 526 ◆ Section Quiz 17–1, TRB
2 A New Persian Empire: The Rule of the Safavids pages 526–530	◆ Rise of Safavid Dynasty ◆ Reign of Shah Abbas ◆ Safavid political and social structures ◆ Safavid culture		◆ Section Review, page 530 ◆ Section Quiz 17–2, TRB
3 The Grandeur of the Mughals pages 530–540	◆ Rise and expansion of Mughal Empire ◆ Reign of Akbar ◆ Decline of Mughals ◆ British inroads in India	◆ Painting, page 532 ◆ Babur's memoirs, pages 533–534 ◆ Description of famine, page 534 ◆ Painting of Aurangzeb, page 536 ◆ Words of Haidar Ali, pages 536, 538 ◆ Bernier's account, pages 537–538	◆ Section Review, page 540 ◆ Section Quiz 17–3, TRB
4 Society and Culture under the Mughals pages 540–543	◆ Mughal society and daily life ◆ Mughal culture		◆ Section Review, page 543 ◆ Section Quiz 17–4, TRB

THE MUSLIM EMPIRES (1450 TO 1800)

REPRODUCIBLE ACTIVITIES

- Historical Maps
- Charts and Graphs
- Critical Thinking
- Cooperative Learning
- Vocabulary
- Guided Reading
- Reteaching
- Enrichment
- Performance Assessment
- Spanish Key Points and Chapter Summaries
- Spanish Vocabulary
- Spanish Guided Reading

MULTIMEDIA SUPPORT

TRANSPARENCIES
- *World History* Color Transparency Package
- Fine Art Color Transparency Package

VIDEO
- *World History* Video Library
- CNN® Annual Video Update

LASERDISC
- *Sights and Sounds of History*

AUDIO
- *Listening to Literature* audiotape (English and Spanish)
- *History of Music* CD

SOFTWARE
- WESTEST™
- Student Review

CD–ROM
- *The Journey of Civilization*
- *World History*

INTERNET
- Internet Activities

On Line with WORLD HISTORY

Access West's history web site at
http://history.swpco.com
You'll find activities and web sites related to specific topics and chapters in *World History: The Human Odyssey.* Also look for references to helpful web sites at appropriate places throughout this teacher edition.

LESSON PLANNING

You will find detailed daily lesson plans for both traditional class scheduling and **block scheduling** in your Teacher Resource Box.

Not Enough Time?

If you do not have the four or five days recommended to teach this chapter, you may want to focus on the following sections and activities:

- Have students skim the chapter to answer the "Questions to Guide Your Reading" on page 515. Discuss their answers; then read the "Conclusion" on page 543.
- Do a more in-depth reading of pages 516, 518, 522–525, 526–529, 531, 535–536, 538–539, 540–541. Conclude with a class discussion of the features on pages 517, 519–520, and 542.

THE MUSLIM EMPIRES
(1450 TO 1800)

BUILDING ON CHAPTER 16

To "set the scene" for the study of Chapter 17, use the following questions and activities.

◆ Ask students to list the three major motives for European exploration.

◆ Have students trace the development of Portugal's trade empire.

◆ Have students explain the importance of Columbus's voyages.

◆ Ask students to discuss the effects of the slave trade on African societies.

USING THE OPENING STORY

Select from the following questions and activities to reinforce the reading of the Babur story.

◆ Describe Babur's "pitifully small" first army. *(on foot, wearing sandals and long frocks, armed with clubs)*

◆ What was different about his second army, besides its greatly increased size? *(armed with artillery)*

◆ What were the effects of Babur's words to his troops before the last battle? *(holy war; to fight until death)*

◆ What does it mean to be "flayed"? *(skinned)* Why do you think Babur ordered this dreadful death for the enemy leader? *(as an example to his enemies)*

At the beginning of the sixteenth century, India was still divided into a number of kingdoms. To the north of India, in present-day Afghanistan, lived a military adventurer named Babur (BAWB-ur), a descendant of the great Asian conqueror Tamerlane. Babur began with a pitifully small following. He described them as follows: "The greater part of my followers (about 250 men) were on foot with sandals on their feet, clubs in their hands, and long frocks over their shoulders." After seizing Kabul in 1504, Babur increased his forces, armed them with the new firearms, and expanded his vision to the lands of India. With a force of 8,000, but now armed with artillery, he destroyed the forces of the Lodi (dynasty) ruler of North India (20,000 of the latter's army of 50,000 were left dead on the battlefield). Nine months later, Babur's army faced yet another Indian prince with a considerably larger army. Babur rallied his forces with these words: "Let us, then, with one accord, swear on God's holy word, that none of us will even think of turning his face from this warfare, nor desert from the battle and slaughter that ensues, till his soul separated from his body." Babur's troops responded with enthusiasm and won yet another decisive victory. "Towards evening," he wrote later, "the confusion was complete, and the slaughter was dreadful. The fate of the battle was decided . . . I ordered the [enemy leader] to be flayed alive." With his victories, Babur created a great Muslim empire—the Mughal (MOE-gul) Empire—in India.

Europeans had tried for hundreds of years to weaken the forces of Islam. In the sixteenth century, European fleets had had some success in taking control of the spice trade from Muslim shippers. Even this success, however, did not cripple the power of Islam.

During Europe's age of exploration, between 1500 and 1800, the world of Islam experienced new life with the rise of three great Muslim empires. Known as the Ottomans, the Safavids, and the Mughals, these three powerful Muslim states dominated the Middle East and the South Asia subcontinent. They brought stability to a region that had been in turmoil for centuries. This stability, however, lasted only about two centuries. By 1800, much of India and the Middle East had come under severe European pressure and had returned to a state of anarchy. The Ottoman Empire itself had entered a period of gradual decline.

▲ *The ornament shown here was crafted during the first half of the eighteenth century to decorate a turban. Made of white jade, with rubies, emeralds, and crystals set in gold, it represents the splendor of the Mughal Empire and the wealth of India.*

ADDITIONAL RESOURCES

The resources listed below can be used to enrich the lessons in this chapter.

BOOKS FOR STUDENTS
Historic India by Lucille Shulberg. Time-Life.

VIDEOS/FILMS
The Ottoman Empire: 1280–1683 series: The World: A Television History. Social Studies School Service (800) 421-4246.

India's History: Mogul Empire to European Colonization. Coronet.

NEW WORLD PATTERNS

| 1450 | THE MUSLIM EMPIRES | 1800 |
| 1400 | | 1800 |

QUESTIONS TO GUIDE YOUR READING

1. What were the major stages in the growth of the Ottoman Empire, and how was it ruled?

2. What role did religion play in the Ottoman Empire, and how was its society organized?

3. What were the basic characteristics of Safavid rule in Persia?

4. What contributions did Mughal rulers make to the development of an empire in India?

5. What factors brought about the decline of Mughal power after the death of Akbar?

6. What were the chief characteristics of Mughal society and culture?

7. How did the roles of women compare in the three Muslim empires?

8. What impact did Europeans have on the Ottoman, Safavid, and Mughal dynasties?

OUTLINE

1. THE OTTOMAN EMPIRE

2. A NEW PERSIAN EMPIRE: THE RULE OF THE SAFAVIDS

3. THE GRANDEUR OF THE MUGHALS

4. SOCIETY AND CULTURE UNDER THE MUGHALS

THE OTTOMAN EMPIRE

The Ottoman Turks were among the various Turkic-speaking peoples who had spread westward from central Asia from the ninth to the eleventh centuries. The first to dominate were the Seljuk Turks, who established their power on the peninsula of Anatolia. In the thirteenth century, the advancing Mongols managed to seize and destroy the Seljuk capital. They then withdrew, leaving the Seljuk Turks in control of the area.

In the late thirteenth century, a new group of Turks under the tribal leader Osman began to build up their power in the northwest corner of the Anatolian peninsula. That land had been given to them by the Seljuk rulers as a reward for helping to defend against the Mongols in the late thirteenth century. At first, the Osman Turks were relatively peaceful. However, as the Seljuk Empire began to disintegrate in the early fourteenth century, the Osman Turks began to expand and founded the Ottoman dynasty.

A key advantage for the Ottomans was their location in the northwestern corner of the peninsula. From there they were able to expand westward and eventually control the Bosphorus and the Dardanelles. These

515

FOCUS ON THEMES

Listed below are brief summaries of how the content in this chapter supports the text's key themes.

Economics and History For all three Muslim empires, farming remained the mainstay of life. Trade and manufacturing were also encouraged and produced considerable wealth. The desire of Europeans to extend trade relations also led them to intervene in the affairs of some of these empires, especially the Mughal Empire in India.

The Importance of Cultural Developments All three empires made significant cultural contributions. The Ottomans were famous in architecture, especially for their mosques.

Religion in History Islam was a crucial factor in all three empires. Muslim ideals gave confidence to the rulers and their warriors. In these Muslim empires, rulers often played dual roles as both political and religious leaders. In many cases, Muslim rulers were tolerant of other religions.

The Role of Individuals These three Muslim empires are known for outstanding rulers who were responsible for building their empires. The most prominent rulers include Suleyman the Magnificent, Shah Abbas, Babur, Akbar, and Aurangzeb.

The Impact of Science and Technology These Muslim empires were successful because of their adoption of the new technology in warfare, namely, the use of firearms of different kinds.

Answers to QUESTIONS TO GUIDE YOUR READING

1. spread westward from central Asia; central government appointed local rulers in conquered regions (pages 515–518)

2. Islamic law and customs were supreme but other religions were tolerated. (pages 523–524)

3. Shi'ite political system organized in hierarchical power-structure (pages 526–530)

4. cultural achievement (pages 530–532)

5. See pages 532–535.

6. See pages 531–532.

7. Ottoman: technically like other Muslim societies, actually more tolerant (page 524)
Safavid: initial freedom and influence, later forced into seclusion (page 529)
Mughal: active in most elements of society, sometimes held to Islamic law (page 540)

8. trading ties led to takeovers of vast land-holdings; weakened empires fell quickly (pages 536, 538–539)

FOCUS

OBJECTIVES

After completing this section, students should be able to

1. describe the gradual expansion of the Ottoman Empire
2. discuss the achievements of Mehmet II and Suleyman the Magnificent
3. discuss Ottoman rule, including the division of people by religion and occupation
4. highlight Ottoman achievements in art and architecture
5. describe the signs of decline of the Ottoman Empire

FOCUS ACTIVITY

Ask students to create a time line showing political and cultural events in Europe and in the Islamic world between 1500 and 1800. Have them compare the two parts and speculate on how various events might have affected the common people of the time.

TEACH

Multimedia Support

TRANSPARENCY
17–1, The Ottoman Empire (Map 17.1)

---

two bodies of water, separated by the Sea of Marmara, mark the passage between the Mediterranean and the Black Seas. The Byzantine Empire, of course, had controlled the area for centuries.

In the fourteenth century, the Ottoman Turks expanded into the Balkans and began to put pressure on the Byzantine Empire. Ottoman rulers claimed the title of sultan and began to build up a strong military administration based on the recruitment of Christians into an elite guard. The members of this guard, called **Janissaries,** were recruited from the local Christian population in the Balkans. They were then converted to Islam and trained as foot soldiers or administrators to serve the sultan (see "Young People in the Ottoman Empire: The Sultan's Elite Slaves").

The new Janissary corps was also important because it was a response to changes in warfare. As the knowledge of firearms spread in the late fourteenth century, the Ottomans began to master the new technology, including the use of siege cannons and muskets. The old nomadic technique of cavalry charges became less reliable and was replaced by the use of infantry forces

Map 17.1   The Ottoman Empire

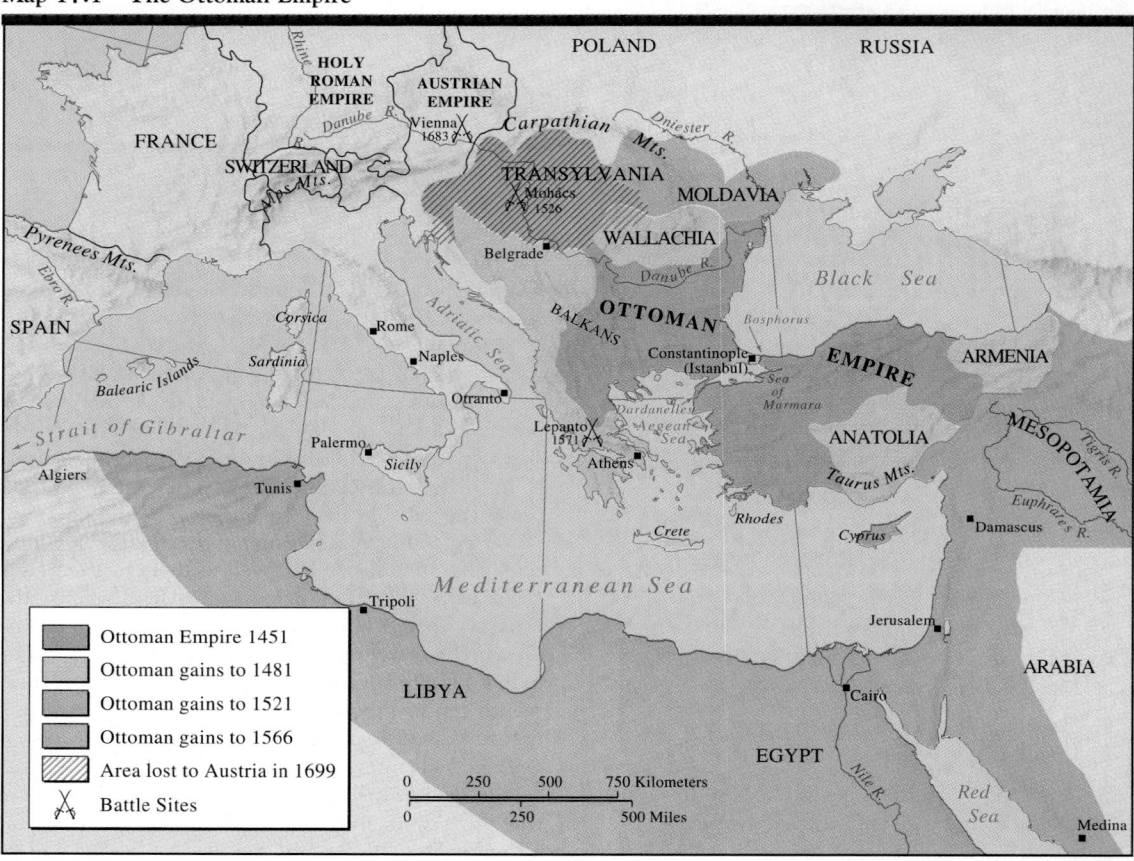

STUDYING MAPS

The following activities will help you guide students through their study of Map 17.1.

1. Locate Anatolia, where the Ottoman Empire began. Find the Bosphorus and Dardanelles and trace the passage between the Mediterranean and Black Seas.
2. Find the Balkans, where the Ottoman Turks moved to pressure the Byzantine Empire.
3. Find Constantinople, now Istanbul, sacked by the Ottomans in 1453.
4. About how much territory did the Ottoman Empire gain between 1451 and 1566? *(Students should realize that the Ottoman Empire more than tripled its size during this period.)*

YOUNG PEOPLE IN THE OTTOMAN EMPIRE

The Sultan's Elite Slaves

Every few years, as need arose, government commissioners went into the provinces of the Ottoman Empire to recruit a special class of slaves. Those chosen were usually Christian boys, because Muslims were not allowed to be made slaves. This collecting of boys was known as the Devshirme—literally, "the boy levy."

The boys who were selected were usually from Christian peasant families in the Balkans. Recruits, usually between the ages of 10 and 20, were selected on the basis of good appearance and good physical build. These boys were brought to Constantinople, where most of them remained for training. They were first converted to Islam. The brightest were then made pages for the sultan and put into palace schools for a special education. Royal servants taught them languages (Turkish, Persian, and Arabic); literature; history; and of course, the Quran. The young boys also received physical and military training.

The boys were strictly disciplined. Sleep, study, and play were all done at very specific times. The boys were told to regard their families as dead and were kept isolated from the outside world. Punishments were severe. Any boy who broke the rules was beaten on the soles of his feet with a thin wooden rod.

At the age of 25, the young men were assigned different roles. Some who were well trained in the use of firearms became Janissaries, or the elite foot soldiers of the Ottoman Empire who also served as guards for the person of the sultan. Some became members of the regular cavalry, and others became government officials. Some of the latter even rose in importance to become chief minister to the sultan.

▲ *The Janissaries were a highly trained, elite group who served the sultan well. How many jobs did the Janissaries perform for the sultan?*

1. Why were Christian boys chosen to be the special class of slaves?

2. The Muslim boys could not be made into slaves, but the Christian slaves could be made into Muslims, so Muslims still ended up being slaves. Do you agree with the logic of this system? Explain your answer.

LEARNING FROM VISUALS

Answer to the caption question: The Janissaries were soldiers and personal bodyguards for the sultan, but they also filled many important government positions.

CLASS DISCUSSION

Discuss with students how the Janissary corps was a response to changes in warfare. *(They became infantry using new firearms.)*

CRITICAL THINKING

Ask students what *recruit* commonly means. *(to fill up an army with new members; to secure the services of)* Do they think slaves can be "recruited"? Why, or why not? Have students speculate on the reaction of Christian peasant families in the Balkans to this forcible recruitment. Remind them that the chosen boys received education and were treated as elite servants of the sultan.

Answers to Critical Thinking Questions

1. Christian boys were chosen because Muslims were not allowed to be made slaves.
2. Answers will vary.

MORE ABOUT . . . *the Janissary corps*

The Janissary corps were the elite soldiers and administrators of the sultan's army. As noted in the text, they were young Christian boys chosen because of their "good appearance and good physical build." This policy of recruiting Janissaries lasted until 1634. After 1634 new recruits came from the sons of Janissaries and the forces became less disciplined. Another problem was paying the soldiers. To minimize the impact on the Ottoman treasury, the Janissaries took jobs in the winter (when they were usually not fighting) as artisans. They became less of an elite fighting force and Ottoman military might correspondingly declined. Still, because they were armed, they were a force to be reckoned with and would not allow the sultan to make changes that threatened their privileges. Their decline corresponds with the demise of the Ottoman Empire.

CRITICAL THINKING

What do students think was more important to the expansion of the Ottoman Empire—a skillful army or strong religious faith?

LEARNING FROM VISUALS

Ask students how they would describe Mehmet II's appearance in this painting. Does he look warlike? Fierce? Peaceful? Determined? Thoughtful? What is the effect of the rose he holds to his nose? What does the inclusion of the rose suggest about the multiple roles of the Ottoman rulers?

Answer to the caption question: The sultan wears an embellished turban, a symbol of nobility.

CLASS DISCUSSION

Despite their ferocity in battle, the Ottomans preferred to administer conquered regions through local rulers, keeping the impact of their rule relatively light. What were the positive and negative aspects of this policy? (*kept conquered peoples from rebelling; freed Ottomans to rule closer to home; weakened links between imperial court and appointed representatives in territories; led to independent territories*)

provided with firearms. Thus, the Janissaries were trained as a well-armed infantry. They served both as an elite guard to protect the sultan and also as a force to spread Ottoman control in the Balkans. With their new forces, the Ottomans defeated the Serbs at the famous Battle of Kossovo in 1389.

Around 1400, the Ottomans advanced northward and annexed Bulgaria. Fifty years later, under the leadership of Mehmet II, they moved to end the Byzantine Empire. With 80,000 troops ranged against only 7,000 defenders, Mehmet laid siege to Constantinople. In their attack on the city, the Ottomans made use of massive cannons with 26-foot barrels that could launch stone balls weighing up to 1,200 pounds each. The Byzantines took their final stand behind their 13-mile city wall along the western edge of the city. The attack began on April 6, 1453, with an Ottoman bombardment. The Byzantines fought desperately to save their city and kept the Ottoman forces at bay for almost two months. Finally, on May 29, the walls were breached, and Ottoman soldiers poured into the city. The Byzantine emperor died in the final battle, and a great three-day sack of the city began (see "You Are There: The Fall of Constantinople"). Mehmet II, standing before the palace of the emperor, paused to reflect on the passing nature of human glory. It was not long, however, before he and the Ottomans were again on the march.

Expansion of the Empire

With their new capital at Constantinople (later renamed Istanbul), the Ottoman Turks were now a dominant force in the Balkans and the Anatolian peninsula. At the beginning of the sixteenth century, Sultan Selim I went on the offensive, taking control of Mesopotamia, Egypt, and Arabia—the original heartland of Islam. Controlling several of the holy cities of Islam, including Jerusalem, Mecca, and Medina, Selim declared himself to be the new caliph (defender of the faith), or successor to Muhammad. During the next few years, Ottoman armies and fleets advanced westward along the African coast, eventually reaching almost to the Strait of Gibraltar.

▲ *In this miniature painting, Mehmet II is shown holding a handkerchief, a symbol of the supreme power held by the Ottoman ruler. In his other hand, he holds a rose, which symbolizes his interest in the arts. What other symbols of his royal status can you identify?*

The Ottomans in North Africa

The impact of Ottoman rule on the peoples of North Africa was relatively light. Like their predecessors, the Ottomans were Muslims. Where possible, they preferred to administer their conquered regions through local rulers. The central government appointed officials, called **pashas,** who collected taxes (a fixed percentage of which was then paid in tribute to the central government), maintained law and order, and were directly responsible to the sultan's court in Constantinople. The Ottomans ruled from coastal cities such as

RETEACHING ACTIVITY

Have the students write a letter from a 15 year-old Balkan Christian boy who had been recruited into the Janissary corps two or three years earlier. Tell them that they must look at both the advantages (a chance to excel, better food, and the excitement of court life, for example) as well as the disadvantages (the strict discipline, instructions to regard their families as dead, and being slaves of the sultan). To help with perspective, ask them to consider how a poor inner city boy would feel if he were given a scholarship to an elite college with the likelihood of getting a high-paying job in the future provided that he entirely give up his family and his former way of life.

YOU ARE THERE
The Fall of Constantinople

Few events in the history of the Ottoman Empire are more dramatic than the conquest of Constantinople in 1453. This is a description by a Greek who later served in the Ottoman administration.

A Greek Describes the Conquest of Constantinople

The heavy infantry were already streaming through the little gate into the City, and others had rushed in through the breach in the great wall. Then all the rest of the army, with a rush and a roar, poured in and scattered all over the City. And the Sultan stood before the great wall . . . and watched the proceeding. The day was already breaking. . . .

The soldiers fell on the citizens with anger and great wrath. For one thing, they were driven by the hardships of the siege. For another, some foolish people had hurled taunts and curses at them from the battlements all through the siege. Now, in general they killed so as to frighten all the City, and to terrorize and enslave all by the slaughter.

When they had had enough of murder, and the City was reduced to slavery, some of the troops turned to the mansions of the mighty, by bands and companies and divisions, for plunder and spoil. Others went to the robbing of churches, and others dispersed to the simple homes of the common people, stealing, robbing, plundering, killing, insulting, taking and enslaving men, women, and children, old and young, priests, monks—in short, every age and class. . . .

After this the Sultan entered the City and looked about to see its great size, its situation, its grandeur and beauty, its teeming population, its loveliness, and the costliness of its churches and

▲ *Mehmet II finally managed to take Constantinople with a surprise attack by Turkish ships that had been dragged overland and placed in water behind enemy lines. Do you think this French miniature painting of the siege of Constantinople is realistic? Why or why not?*

(continued)

MORE ABOUT . . . *the Fall of Constantinople*

According to prophecy, Constantinople would stand as long as the moon waxed. On the night of May 24, 1453, an eclipse brought three hours of darkness, and the moon waned. Another prophecy said that the city would fall when the enemy entered the back gate. Although the gate was supposed to be heavily guarded for this reason, apparently someone accidentally left the gate open. The Ottomans would not have been successful without the use of cannons, but their tactics also included a calculated use of their troops. The first to charge were irregular forces who were poorly armed. They died in great numbers but made their impact felt on the defenders. Next came the well-trained Turkish regulars who breached the walls. The best troops, the elite Janissaries, were saved for the final charge and the Greeks were overwhelmed.

COMPARING TIME PERIODS

Challenge students to find other eyewitness accounts of the destruction of a city by enemy forces. Suggest that they look for one account that preceded the fall of Constantinople and one account that came later in history. Compare the accounts, noting similarities and differences in what was done and the effects of enemy actions.

USING PRIMARY SOURCES

Ask students to discuss how this Greek observer gets such drama into his account. Suggest that they consider his choice of vocabulary and selection of detail. Keep in mind that this person later served in the Ottoman government. You might follow this discussion with an assignment to write a newspaper account of the fall of Constantinople. How might a newspaper account differ in tone and vocabulary?

LEARNING FROM VISUALS

Answer to the caption question: This painting undoubtedly includes many fanciful embellishments but does manage to convey the confusion and activity of the dramatic event.

Answers to Critical Thinking Questions

1. They had gone through great hardships during the siege of the city, and during the siege, many people of the city had insulted and taunted them, so they retaliated.

2. He was filled with compassion because he realized what a large number of people had been killed and what a wonderful city had been destroyed.

USING PRIMARY SOURCES

Ask students to discuss what Mehmet II's reaction to the destruction of Constantinople suggests about his character. Have them look back to Mehmet's portrait on page 518 as they consider their answers.

CLASS DISCUSSION

Ask students to discuss the following sentence: "By the beginning of the seventeenth century, European rulers who sought alliances and trade concessions with the Ottomans were treating the Ottoman Empire like another European power." What does this suggest about European attitudes toward the Ottomans? *(respect, deference, acceptance as equal and worthy rival but above all, pragmatism and a great desire to trade)*

YOU ARE THERE

The Fall of Constantinople, continued

public buildings and of the private houses and community houses and those of the officials. . . . When he saw what a large number had been killed, and the ruin of the buildings, and the wholesale ruin and destruction of the City, he was filled with compassion and repented not a little at the destruction and plundering. Tears fell from his eyes as he groaned deeply and passionately: "What a city we have given over to plunder and destruction."

1. Why did the soldiers destroy the city of Constantinople with such a vengeance?

2. Why was the sultan filled with compassion and repentance when he saw the destruction of the city and people?

Algiers, Tripoli (TRIP-uh-lee), and Tunis and made no attempt to control the interior.

The Ottomans did make a halfhearted effort to extend their control up the Nile River, but they were never able to establish their authority beyond Nubia. They also tried to extend their naval influence into the Indian Ocean in order to take part in the lucrative trade with the East. However, after a major naval defeat by the Portuguese in 1509, they remained in the Red Sea.

By the seventeenth century, the links between the imperial court in Constantinople and its appointed representatives in the Ottoman territories in North Africa had begun to weaken. Some of the pashas were dethroned by local elites, and others became hereditary rulers. Even Egypt gradually became independent.

Ottoman Expansion in Europe

After their conquest of Constantinople in 1453, the Ottoman Turks tried to complete their conquest of the Balkans. They were successful in taking the Romanian territory of Wallachia, but the resistance of the Hungarians kept them from advancing up the Danube valley. From 1480 to 1520, internal problems and the need

to consolidate their eastern frontiers kept the Ottomans from launching any further attacks on Europe.

The reign of Suleyman (SOO-lay-MAWN) I the Magnificent, the greatest of the Ottoman sultans, however, brought the Turks back to Europe's attention. Advancing up the Danube, the Ottomans seized Belgrade. In 1526, at the Battle of Mohács (MOE-HATCH) on the Danube, they won a major victory over the Hungarians. Subsequently, the Ottomans overran most of Hungary, moved into Austria, and advanced as far as Vienna, where they were finally defeated in 1529. At the same time, the Ottoman Turks extended their power into the western Mediterranean, which they threatened to turn into an Ottoman lake until a large Ottoman fleet was destroyed by the Spanish at Lepanto (LEP-un-TOE) in 1571 (see Chapter 15).

By the beginning of the seventeenth century, European rulers who sought alliances and trade concessions with the Ottomans were treating the Ottoman Empire like another European power. During the first half of the seventeenth century, the Ottoman Empire remained a "sleeping giant." Involved in internal problems, the Ottomans were content with the status quo in eastern Europe. However, in the second half of the seventeenth century, they again went on the offensive. By mid-1683, the Ottomans had marched through the

So What ⁉

*If your students question the importance of information on the **Battle of Mohács in 1526**, tell them . . .*

Charles V, who ruled from 1519–1556, was a contemporary of Suleyman the Lawgiver. Charles V viewed the Ottomans as a major threat to his power, and so they were. When Charles presided over the Diet of Worms in 1521 he used the occasion to ask the electors of the Holy Roman Empire for

support against the Turks. He considered Luther an annoyance, but not nearly a problem of the magnitude of the Turkish threat. Had the Turks not been pressing on his western border, Charles might have given more attention to Luther and might have responded differently to the Protestant threat which in retrospect had a much greater impact on Europe than Charles ever imagined.

BIOGRAPHY

Suleyman the Magnificent

Suleyman the Magnificent is known as the greatest ruler of the Ottoman Empire. He became sultan in 1520 and ruled until his death in 1566. Suleyman was one of the great Ottoman military leaders, who led his army on thirteen major military campaigns. His forces completed the conquest of the Balkans, defeated the Hungarians, captured much of the north African coast, and added new possessions in the Middle East. He doubled the size of the Ottoman Empire. Europeans called him the "Grand Turk" and the "Magnificent." One European observer said of him, "His dignity of demeanor and his general physical appearance are worthy of the ruler of so vast an empire."

To his own subjects, however, Suleyman was known as the "Lawgiver." Eager to provide justice for his subjects, he reorganized the government, regulated the laws of the empire, and saw that they were properly enforced.

Suleyman was also a great builder. He was an extremely generous patron of the arts. He lavished funds upon Sinan, his chief architect, who created almost four hundred new buildings throughout the empire. One of Suleyman's works, the elegant bridge linking the two parts of the Bosnian town

▲ *Suleyman I the Magnificent lived in royal splendor at his court in Turkey. He is shown seated on his throne while the son of the king of Hungary kneels before him. What other signs of the sultan's royal power are visible in this picture?*

of Mostar, lasted until it was destroyed by Croatian artillery on November 9, 1993.

For all of his achievements, Suleyman was less fortunate in his personal life. Influenced by his favorite wife Roxalana, Suleyman had Mustafa, his son and heir by an earlier wife, killed. According to one account, "Thereupon (Suleyman's servants) hurled the unhappy Mustafa to the ground, and throwing the bowstring round his neck, strangled him. Then, laying his corpse on a rug, they exposed it in front of the tent, so that the soldiers might look upon the man whom they had wished to make their sultan." After Mustafa's death, the two sons of Roxalana and Suleyman fought over their right to succeed to the throne. After Selim's victory in battle over his brother Bayezid, Suleyman ordered the deaths of Bayezid and his four sons.

---

1. Why do you think Suleyman was able to be "just" with his subjects, but "unjust" with his own sons?

RETEACHING ACTIVITY

Have the students research more about the life of Suleyman. Make a list of the things he did that fall under the category of "Magnificent." Make a list of the reasons why his subjects called him "The Lawgiver."

The list could contain the following: The Europeans called him "magnificent" because they were fascinated with his incredible wealth; he fought yearly military campaigns and his impressive travelling throne was made of gold; he lived a life of incredible luxury; the Europeans were fascinated by his "harem." He is called "lawgiver" not because he revised Muslim laws but because he enforced them fairly; he punished the corrupt and once returned an overpayment of taxes to the Egyptians, an unheard of practice for rulers in any country at any time in history.

Hungarian plain and laid siege to Vienna. Repulsed by a mixed army of Europeans, the Ottomans retreated and were pushed out of Hungary. Although they retained the core of their empire, the Ottoman Turks would never again be a threat to central Europe.

The Nature of Ottoman Rule

Like the other Muslim empires in Persia and India, the Ottoman Empire is often labeled a "gunpowder empire" because its success was based to a considerable extent on its mastery of the technology of firearms. At the head of the Ottoman system was the sultan, who was the supreme authority in both a political and a military sense. The origins of this system can be traced back to the **bey** (BAY), who was only a tribal leader. Considered a first among equals, he could claim loyalty from his chiefs so long as he could provide booty and lands for them.

The rise of the empire brought changes, however, as the Ottomans copied Byzantine traditions of rule. The status and prestige of the sultan increased, and the position took on the trappings of imperial rule. Court rituals were taken over from the Byzantines and Persians. A centralized administrative system was adopted, with the sultan being increasingly isolated in his palace. The position of the sultan was hereditary. A son, although not necessarily the eldest, always succeeded the father. This practice led to succession struggles upon the death of individual sultans. The losers were often executed (strangled with a silk bowstring). Heirs to the throne were trained by being assigned as governors of provinces in order to gain experience.

The heart of the sultan's power was in the Topkapi (meaning "iron gate") Palace, in the heart of Istanbul, built in the fifteenth century by Mehmet II. Like Versailles in France, this palace served as an administrative center as well as the private residence of the ruler and his family.

The private domain of the sultan was called the **harem** (sacred place). Here resided the sultan and his concubines (mistresses). Normally a sultan did not marry but chose four concubines as his favorites, who were so named after they gave birth to sons. When a son became a sultan, his mother became known as the

▲ *The Topkapi Palace is lavish in scale and in its decoration. This photo of the Fruit Room of Ahmet III serves as a beautiful reminder of the splendor of Islamic architecture and painting. How do you think this room acquired its name?*

queen mother and then served as a major advisor to the throne. This tradition often gave considerable power to the queen mother in the affairs of state.

The sultan controlled his bureaucracy through an imperial council that met four days a week. A chief minister, known as the **grand vezir** or **grand wazir** (sometimes known in English as a *vizier*), conducted the meetings of the council. The sultan often attended the meetings from behind a screen, from where he could privately indicate his desires to the grand vezir. The members of the imperial bureaucracy were chosen at least partly by merit from a palace school for training officials. Most officials were Muslims by birth.

The empire was divided into provinces and districts, each governed by officials. These officials, like their

ENRICHMENT ACTIVITY

Have students suppose that Vienna had fallen to the Ottoman armies in 1529. Use a map of Europe in the sixteenth century to consider the next likely Ottoman moves into Europe. What resistance would they have met? What territory do students feel the Ottomans could have conquered and held? Let students discuss how 200 years of Ottoman rule over central Europe would have changed European culture.

tribal predecessors, combined both civil and military functions in their persons. They were assisted by bureaucrats trained in the palace school in Istanbul. Senior officials were given land by the sultan and were then responsible for the collection of taxes and the supplying of armies to the empire from this landed area.

Religion and Society in the Ottoman World

Like most Turkic-speaking peoples in the Anatolian peninsula and throughout the Middle East, the Ottoman ruling elites were Sunni Muslims (see Chapter 8). Ottoman sultans had claimed the title of caliph (defender of the faith) since the early sixteenth century. In theory, they were responsible for guiding the flock and maintaining Islamic law. In practice, the sultans gave these duties to a supreme religious authority known as the **ulema,** which administered the legal system and schools for educating Muslims. Islamic law and customs were applied to all Muslims in the empire.

The Ottoman system was relatively tolerant of non-Muslims, who made up a significant minority within the empire. Non-Muslims were forced to pay a head tax because of their exemption from military service, but they were allowed to practice their religion or to convert to Islam. Muslims, however, were prohibited from adopting another faith. Most of the population in the European areas of the empire remained Christian. In some areas, however, such as the region now called Bosnia, large numbers converted to the Islamic faith.

Non-Muslims were divided by religious faith into a number of "nations." Each religious group had its own leader and own laws. The leaders of the individual nations were responsible to the sultan for the behavior of those subjects under their care. Each nation set up its own local system of justice and schools.

The subjects of the Ottoman Empire were also divided by occupation. In addition to the ruling class, there were four main occupational groups: peasants, artisans, merchants, and pastoral peoples. Peasants farmed land that was leased to them by the state. (Ultimate ownership of all land resided with the sultan.) However, the land was deeded to them, so they were able to pass it along to their heirs. Peasants were not

CONNECTIONS
TO OUR WORLD

Conflict in Yugoslavia In 1919, Yugoslavia was formed as a new state in the Balkans. It consisted of six republics that had little interest in being part of a single nation. From 1945 to 1980, the dictatorial rule of Marshal Tito held the country together. Twelve years after his death, however, Yugoslavia began to disintegrate. By 1992, the republics of Slovenia, Croatia, and Bosnia-Herzegovina had declared their independence. When the republic of Serbia refused to accept the breakup of Yugoslavia, conflict erupted. The war in Bosnia was especially brutal. The Serbians pursued a policy of "ethnic cleansing," in which they killed or forcibly removed Bosnian Muslims from their homes and lands.

This struggle in Yugoslavia had deep roots in the past. In the Middle Ages, the Slavic peoples in the Balkans had accepted Christianity. Nevertheless, while the Croatians and Slovenes became Roman Catholics, the Serbs remained loyal to Eastern Orthodox Christianity. In the fourteenth century, the Ottoman conquest of the Balkans added yet another religious group—the Muslims. Although the Ottomans did not force Christians to convert to Islam, many did, especially in the area of present-day Bosnia. By 1500, the area of Yugoslavia in the Balkans had become a land where Bosnian Muslims, Croatian Catholics, and Eastern Orthodox Serbs maintained an uneasy peace. Their ethnic and religious divisions would remain and continue to scar the region for hundreds of years.

allowed to sell the land and thus, in practice, were forced to remain on the soil.

Artisans were organized according to craft guilds. Each guild was responsible not only for dealing with the governmental authorities but also for providing financial services, social security, and training to their members. Outside the ruling elite, merchants were the most privileged class in Ottoman society. They were

CLASS DISCUSSION

Have students discuss how the subjects of the Ottoman Empire were divided both by religion and by occupation.

ACROSS THE CURRICULUM

Sociology Ask interested students to research the role of women and the family in the Ottoman Empire and compare it to that of Europe during the same time period. Ask them to analyze the role that religion (Christianity and Islam) played in the attitudes toward women.

CLASS DISCUSSION

Have students list the main occupational groups in the Ottoman Empire (rulers, peasants, artisans, merchants, and pastoral peoples). Then compare the list with the European groups studied previously (pages 423–426). As a class, compare and contrast the lives of members of similar occupational groups between the two geographic areas.

MORE ABOUT . . . *Gunpowder Empires*

There have been a number of times when technology has changed war. The 14th and 15th centuries are good examples. Before the 14th century, the advantage in war went to the cavalry with crossbows. Armor was meant to diminish the impact of arrows. Steppe warriors such as the Mongols had a great military advantage with their horses and bows, and these nomadic warriors had plagued sedentary peoples since the earliest of human times. Gunpowder revolutionized warfare, especially with respect to cannons. Cannons came to be the decisive weapons and were most useful in knocking down walls of castles and cities. But cannons required skilled technology and vast sums of money available only to large, wealthy empires. The gunpowder revolution tipped the balance of power away from steppe horsemen.

largely exempt from government regulations and taxes and therefore were able, in many cases, to amass large fortunes.

Pastoral peoples were placed in a separate group and were subject to their own regulations and laws. They were divided into tribes, clans, and "tents" (individual families) and were governed by their hereditary chiefs, the beys. As we have seen, the bey was responsible for administration and providing taxes to the state.

Technically, women in the Ottoman Empire were subject to the same restrictions that affected women in other Muslim societies, but their position was somewhat better. As it was applied in the Ottoman Empire, Islamic law was more tolerant in defining the legal position of women. They were allowed to own and inherit property, including their dowries. They could not be forced into marriage and, in certain cases, were permitted to seek divorce. Women often gained considerable power within the palace. In a few instances women even served as senior officials, such as governors of provinces. This relatively tolerant attitude toward women in Ottoman-held territories was probably due to tribal traditions among the Turkish peoples, which portrayed women as almost equal to men.

Decline of the Ottoman Empire

The Ottoman Empire reached its high point under Suleyman the Magnificent. It was he who had launched the conquest of Hungary, but it was also Suleyman who probably started a period of decline. Having executed his two most able sons on suspicion of treason, Suleyman was succeeded by Selim II (the Sot, or "the drunken sultan"). He was the only surviving son; another had fled and was later executed for treason.

The decline of the Ottoman Empire did not become visible until the Battle of Carlowitz in 1699, when the empire began to lose some of its territory. However, signs of internal disintegration had already appeared at the beginning of the seventeenth century. The training of officials declined, and senior positions were increasingly assigned to the sons or daughters of elites. Members of the elite soon formed a privileged group seeking wealth and power. As the central bureaucracy lost its links with rural areas, local officials grew corrupt, and

taxes rose. Constant wars depleted the imperial treasury. Corruption and palace intrigue grew.

Another sign of change within the empire was a growing wealth and the impact of Western ideas and customs. Sophisticated officials and merchants began to imitate the habits and lifestyles of Europeans. They wore European clothes, bought Western furniture and art objects, and ignored Muslim rules against the drinking of alcohol. During the sixteenth and early seventeenth centuries, both coffee and tobacco were introduced into polite Ottoman society. Cafés, where both were consumed, began to appear in the major cities.

Some sultans and high officials attempted to counter these trends. One sultan in the early seventeenth century issued a decree prohibiting the use of both coffee and tobacco. He even began to wander incognito in the streets of Constantinople at night. If he caught any of his subjects in immoral or illegal acts, they were immediately executed. Their bodies were left on the streets as an example to others.

There were also signs of growing incompetence within the ranks of the ruling family. The first sultans averaged a reign of twenty-seven years, but later ones declined to an average of thirteen years. The oldest surviving male now inherited the throne, and his rivals (his brothers) were kept secluded in the imperial harem. This provided them with no governmental experience in case they succeeded to the throne. Later sultans became less involved in government and allowed their ministers to exercise more power. Earlier, the sultans had regarded members of the ruling class as the "sultan's slaves." Now the sultan became the servant of the ruling class.

Ottoman Art

The Ottoman sultans were enthusiastic patrons of the arts. The period from Mehmet II to the early eighteenth century witnessed the flourishing production of pottery; rugs, silk, and other textiles; jewelry; and arms and armor—all of which adorned the palaces of the new rulers. Artists came from all parts of the realm and beyond. In addition to Turks, there were Persians, Greeks, Armenians, Hungarians, and Italians, all competing for the generous rewards of the sultans.

MORE ABOUT . . . *the Sultan's decree prohibiting coffee*

Coffee was originally drunk at gatherings of people and passed from hand to hand, a sure sign of "loose living" according to an observer of the time. This same observer, Katib Chelebi, a 17th century Turkish author, stated that "drug addicts, in particular, finding it a life-giving thing . . . were willing to die for a cup." Coffeehouses were associated with dissolute living. It was thought that storytellers and musicians who hung around coffeehouses diverted people from their employment and "working for one's living fell into disfavor. Moreover, the people, from prince to beggar, amused themselves with knifing one another." All because of coffee! The coffeehouses were closed in 1633 by imperial edict, and while this had an effect under the government's immediate eye in Istanbul, coffeehouses outside the city flaunted the ban.

▲ *During the reign of Suleyman I the Magnificent, a number of magnificent mosques were built throughout the Ottoman Empire. The Blue Mosque, named for the blue tiles that decorate its interior, still stands as one of the most impressive and graceful in Istanbul.*

By far the greatest contribution of the Ottoman Empire to world art was in architecture, especially the magnificent mosques of the last half of the sixteenth century. The Ottoman Turks modeled their new mosques on the open floor plan of Constantinople's Byzantine church of Hagia Sophia, thus creating a prayer hall with an open central area under one large dome. By the mid-sixteenth century, the greatest of all Ottoman architects, Sinan, began building the first of his eighty-one mosques with open prayer areas. Each was topped by an imposing dome and often the entire building was framed with four narrow towers, known as **minarets.** The minarets gave the building a feeling of incredible lightness.

The lightness of the exterior was reinforced in the mosque's interior by the soaring height of the dome and its many windows. The masterpieces of Sinan, such as the Blue Mosque of Istanbul, were always part of a large complex with a library, school, hospital, and even bazaars (marketplaces).

The sixteenth century also witnessed the flourishing of textiles and rugs. The Byzantine emperor Justinian had introduced silk cultivation to the West in the sixth century. Under the Ottomans the silk industry resurfaced. Factories produced silks for wall hangings, sofa covers, and especially court costumes.

Perhaps even more famous than Ottoman silk are the rugs. Whereas silks were produced under the patronage of the sultans, rugs were a peasant industry. The rugs, made of wool and cotton in villages from different regions, each boasted their own distinctive designs and color schemes.

Ottoman painting was very different from the romantic, almost dreamlike paintings of the Persian school (see "The World of Safavid Culture" later in this chapter). It portrayed, instead, realistic scenes of the sultans, the court, and military exploits. Of special interest are the illustrations for the *Lives of Sultans* and the *Books of Festivals*, which present daily life from sixteenth- to early-eighteenth-century Constantinople.

COOPERATIVE LEARNING ACTIVITY

Divide students into two groups. Have one group list the key feature of a Gothic cathedral (such as Chartres) while the other group lists the key features of a Muslim Mosque (such as the Blue Mosque in Istanbul). Consider building height, building use, building decoration, use of writing, and importance of geometric features. Have the two groups compare their lists.

(1) The exact height is not so important as the idea that both dominated the landscape; (2) both were used as places of worship; (3) windows dominated Gothic cathedrals, while tiled exteriors dominated mosques; (4) calligraphy was used as part of the decorative pattern of mosques, but stories in picture dominated the Gothic cathedrals; (5) Muslim buildings were dominated by geometric patterns; on European buildings, patterns are discernible, but not dominant.

ACROSS THE CURRICULUM

Art. Ask students to bring in examples of the art and architecture of the Ottoman Empire. Have them research and present the major motifs and styles of Ottoman art. How do these reflect religious and political thought?

CRITICAL THINKING

Ask students to speculate on and then to research why mosques were always part of a large complex with a library, school, hospital, and even bazaars (marketplaces). What does this reveal about Islam as practiced in the Ottoman Empire? How do the styles and uses of mosques compare with the styles and uses of Christian churches during this period?

ASSESS

You can choose from a variety of assessments to evaluate your students' mastery of the objectives for this section, as stated on page 516. Possible assessments include

1. Section Review Questions on this page
2. Section 17–1 Quiz in your Teacher Resource materials
3. Reteaching Worksheets in your Teacher Resource materials
4. Self-Study software

ALTERNATIVE ASSESSMENT

Assign students an essay in which they highlight the main achievement of the Ottoman Empire.

Why do students think Ottoman painting emphasized realistic scenes, full of color and energy? What does that suggest about Ottoman culture?

Answers to
SECTION REVIEW

2. (a) an elite guard;
(b) appointed officials who collected taxes;
(c) tribal leader; (d) private residence of the sultan and his concubines;
(e) a chief minister;
(f) supreme religious authority; (g) narrow towers

3. (a) Turkish founder of Ottoman Empire; (b) conquered Constantinople;
(c) greatest Ottoman sultan; (d) central palace of Ottomans; (e) beginning of decline of Ottoman Empire

4. (a) helped expand and manage Ottoman Empire;
(b) based on the mastery of firearm technology;
(c) domes, minarets, light airy spaces

5. Answers should include military expansion, strong, stable government followed by weak leadership, weaker armies, corruption

CLOSE

Ask students to discuss which achievement of the Ottoman Empire they consider the most important and why.

▶ *This illustrated page from the* Book of Festivals *shows a variety of scenes from daily life in the Ottoman Empire. The intricacy of the design and the use of geometric shapes is a principal characteristic of Islamic art.*

 SECTION REVIEW

1. **Locate:**
   (*a*) peninsula of Anatolia,   (*b*) Bosphorus,
   (*c*) Dardanelles,   (*d*) Balkans,   (*e*) Constantinople,   (*f*) Strait of Gibraltar,   (*g*) Danube River,   (*h*) Vienna

2. **Define:**
   (*a*) Janissaries,   (*b*) pashas,   (*c*) bey,   (*d*) harem,
   (*e*) grand vezir (grand wazir),   (*f*) ulema,
   (*g*) minarets

3. **Identify:**
   (*a*) Osman,   (*b*) Mehmet II,   (*c*) Suleyman I the Magnificent,   (*d*) Topkapi Palace,   (*e*) Battle of Carlowitz

4. **Recall:**
   (*a*) Discuss the importance of the Janissaries in the expansion of the Ottoman Empire.
   (*b*) Why is the Ottoman Empire called a "gunpowder" empire?
   (*c*) Describe the architectural features that were developed within the Ottoman Empire.

5. **Think Critically:** Compare the growth and the decline of the Ottoman Empire with one other empire that you have studied thus far. How are they similar and different?

A NEW PERSIAN EMPIRE: THE RULE OF THE SAFAVIDS

After the collapse of the empire of Tamerlane in the early fifteenth century (see Chapter 11), the area extending from Persia into central Asia fell into anarchy. The Uzbeks, a tribal group descended from the Mongols, were the chief political and military force in the area. At the beginning of the sixteenth century, a new dynasty known as the Safavids took control.

The Rise and Fall of the Safavid Dynasty

The Safavid dynasty was founded by Shah Ismail, the descendant of Safi al-Din (thus the name Safavid). Ismail was the leader of a community of Turkish tribespeople in the early fourteenth century in Azerbaijan (Az-ur-BIE-JAWN), near the Caspian Sea. Unlike many of their Islamic neighbors who were Sunni Muslims, the Safavids became ardent Shi'ites (the Sunnites and Shi'ites were the two major groups in Islam—see Chapter 8). The Safavids were known as "red heads" because of their distinctive red cap with twelve folds.

In 1501, Ismail used his forces to seize much of Iran and Iraq and then called himself the **shah** (king) of a new Persian state. Ismail sent Shi'ite preachers into Anatolia to convert members of Turkish tribes in the

---

So What ??

*If your students question the importance of information on the **Sunni Muslims and Shi'ite Muslims** tell them . . .*

This religious division is still seen in Iran and Iraq today. A shah survived as ruler of Iran until 1979 when the Ayatollah Khomeini, a Shi'ite Muslim imam, came to power. Today Iran is the largest Shi'ite Muslim country in the world. Iraq is dominated by Sunni

Muslims. In 1980 Iraq attacked Iran and war dragged on until 1988. There were other reasons for this war (the desire to control oil revenue primary among them), but the religious tension between these two branches of Islam was a primary factor in this conflict that cost hundreds of thousands of lives.

Ottoman Empire. The Ottoman sultan tried to halt this activity, but Ismail refused to stop and ordered the massacre of Sunni Muslims when he conquered Baghdad in 1508. Alarmed by these activities, the new Ottoman sultan, Selim I, advanced against the Safavids in Persia and won a major battle near Tabriz (tuh-BREEZ). However, Selim could not maintain control of the area, and a few years later, Ismail regained Tabriz.

During the next decades, the Safavids tried to consolidate their rule throughout Persia and in areas to the west. Faced with the problem of integrating unruly Turkish tribespeople with the settled Persian-speaking population of the urban areas, the Safavids used the Shi'ite faith as a unifying force. The shah himself claimed to be the spiritual leader of all Islam.

In the 1580s, the Ottomans returned to the attack. They placed Azerbaijan under Ottoman rule, controlled the Caspian Sea with their fleet, and allied with the Uzbeks. This forced the new Safavid shah, Abbas, to sign a peace treaty in which much territory was lost. The capital was moved from Tabriz in the northwest to Isfahan in the south.

Nevertheless, it was under Shah Abbas that the Safavids reached the high point of their glory. A system similar to the use of Janissaries in the Ottoman Empire was created to train administrators to run the kingdom. Shah Abbas also used the period of peace to strengthen his army, which he armed with modern weapons. In the early seventeenth century, he moved against both the Uzbeks and the Ottomans to regain lost territories. In this effort, he was helped by some European states, whose leaders viewed the Safavids as useful allies against their chief enemies, the Ottoman Turks. The Safavids had some initial success, but they could not hold all their territorial gains against the organized force of the Ottoman armies. In 1612, a peace treaty was signed that returned Azerbaijan to the Safavids, although a lasting peace was not achieved for another twenty years.

To his contemporaries, Shah Abbas was known as the "Great." He was beloved by his people for his common touch. He spent many hours walking the streets of his capital and conversing with his subjects. His clothes were simple; as one person observed, "Abbas was clothed in a plain dress of red cloth. He wore no finery about his person; his sabre alone had a gold hilt. . . . It was evident that the shah, surrounded as he was with wealth and grandeur, affected simplicity."[1]

After the death of Shah Abbas in 1629, the Safavid dynasty gradually lost its vigor. In the early eighteenth century, during the reign of Shah Hussein, Afghan tribesmen invaded and seized the capital of Isfahan. The remnants of the Safavid ruling family were forced to retreat to Azerbaijan, their original homeland. The Turks took advantage of the situation to seize territories along the western border. Persia sank into a long period of political and social anarchy.

Political and Social Structures in Safavid Persia

Like the Ottoman Empire, Persia under the Safavids was a mixed society. The Safavids had come to power with the support of nomadic Turkish tribal groups, but the majority of the people were Iranian. Most of them were farmers or townspeople. The combination of Turkish and Iranian elements affected virtually all aspects of Safavid society.

As in most empires, the Safavid political system was organized in the shape of a pyramid. The shah was at the top, the bureaucracy and landed classes were in the middle, and the common people were below. The monarchy had a semidivine character that was eagerly embraced by militant Shi'ite religious elements, who traced the founder of the empire to direct succession from the prophet Muhammad. In return, the Safavids declared Shi'ism to be the state religion. Contemporary visitors reported that the shah was more available to his subjects than were rulers elsewhere. "They show great familiarity to strangers," remarked one visitor, "and even to their own subjects, eating and drinking with them pretty freely." [2] Indeed, the shahs even had their physical features engraved inside drinking cups so that people throughout their empire would know them.

The power of the landed aristocracy was firmly controlled by strong-minded shahs. The shahs seized the large landed estates of the aristocrats and brought them under the control of the crown. Appointment to senior positions in the bureaucracy was by merit rather than

RECOMMENDED READING

A readable account of the Ottoman Empire is by Lord Kinross, *The Ottoman Centuries: The Rise and Fall of the Ottoman Empire* (New York, 1977), which is larded with human interest stories. Also of interest is B. Lewis, *Istanbul and the Civilization of the Ottoman Empire* (Norman, Okla., 1963), written by a veteran Arabist.

For a dramatic account of the conquest of Constantinople in 1453, see S. Runciman, *The Fall of Constantinople, 1453* (Cambridge, 1965). The life of Mehmet II is chronicled in F. Babinger, *Mehmed the Conqueror and His Time,* trans. R. Manheim (Princeton, N.J., 1979). On Suleyman the Magnificent, see R. Merriman, *Suleiman the Magnificent, 1520–1566* (Cambridge, 1944).

FOCUS

OBJECTIVES

After completing this section, students should be able to

1. discuss the importance of Shah Ismail to the rise of the Safavid Empire
2. discuss the achievements of Shah Abbas
3. describe the Safavid political system and social structures
4. name some of the Safavid cultural achievements

FOCUS ACTIVITY

Ask students to return to the time line they created in Section 1. Have them note the political and cultural events involving the Safavid Empire. At what points do these intersect with similar events in the Ottoman Empire? Have students note what was happening in Europe during the years of Safavid prosperity. What similarities do they see?

TEACH

CLASS DISCUSSION

Review with students the main similarities and differences between Sunni Muslims and Shi'ite Muslims. (Refer as necessary to Chapter 8.)

CRITICAL THINKING

Ask students to compare and contrast the Ottoman and Safavid Empires in terms of their governments, military might, and political and social structures.

Multimedia Support

TRANSPARENCY
17–2, The
Ottoman and
Safavid Empires
(Map 17.2)

CLASS DISCUSSION

Compare the activities of the sultan and the shah who traveled their city streets incognito. How were their methods similar? How were they different? How effective does the class think the methods were?

CLASS DISCUSSION

Compare and contrast Safavid Persia at its height with the great Persian empires of the past. In what ways was Safavid Persia a worthy successor to the preceding empires? How was the Safavid Empire limited geographically? *(sea power limited by Europeans, trade routes dictated by Ottoman power)* Do these limits make the Safavid accomplishments more impressive? Or do they prove the weakness of the Safavids? Would the overland trade route have required greater organizational skills or geographic knowledge? What geographic obstacles lay along a trade route through southern Russia?

birth. To avoid competition between Turkish and non-Turkish elements, Shah Abbas hired a number of foreigners from neighboring countries for positions in his government.

The Safavid shahs took a direct interest in the economy. They also played an active part in trade and manufacturing activity, although there was a large and affluent urban middle class. As one of the Ottoman sultans had, one shah regularly traveled the city streets incognito to check on the honesty of his subjects. When he discovered that a baker and butcher were overcharging people for their products, he had the baker cooked in his own oven and the butcher roasted on a spit.

Although the road system was poor, most goods traveled by horse or camel caravans. The government provided resting places for weary travelers and, in times of strong rulers, kept the roads fairly clear of thieves and bandits.

At its height, Safavid Persia was a worthy successor to the great Persian empires of the past. It was probably not as prosperous as its neighbors to the east and west—the Mughals and the Ottomans. Hemmed in by the sea power of the Europeans to the south and by the land power of the Ottomans to the west, the Safavids had no seagoing navy and were forced to divert overland trade with Europe through southern Russia to avoid an Ottoman blockade. Still, the brocades, carpets, and leather goods of Persia were highly prized throughout the world. The knowledge of science, medicine, and mathematics under the Safavids was the equal of other societies in the region.

Map 17.2   The Ottoman and Safavid Empires, c. 1683

STUDYING MAPS

The following questions and activities will help you guide students through their study of Map 17.2.

1. Locate the Uzbeks, Azerbaijan, Caspian Sea, Baghdad, Tabriz, and Isfahan.
2. Compare the size and configuration of the Safavid Empire with that of the Ottoman Empire. What were the geographic factors that limited the growth of the Safavids? *(The Safavids were hemmed in on both the east and west by other empires.)*
3. Compare this map with a contemporary map of the region. What countries now comprise what was the Safavid Empire? *(parts of Saudi Arabia, Iran, Iraq)* The Ottoman Empire? *(Turkey, parts of Saudi Arabia, Iraq, Bulgaria, Greece, Yugoslavia, Romania)*

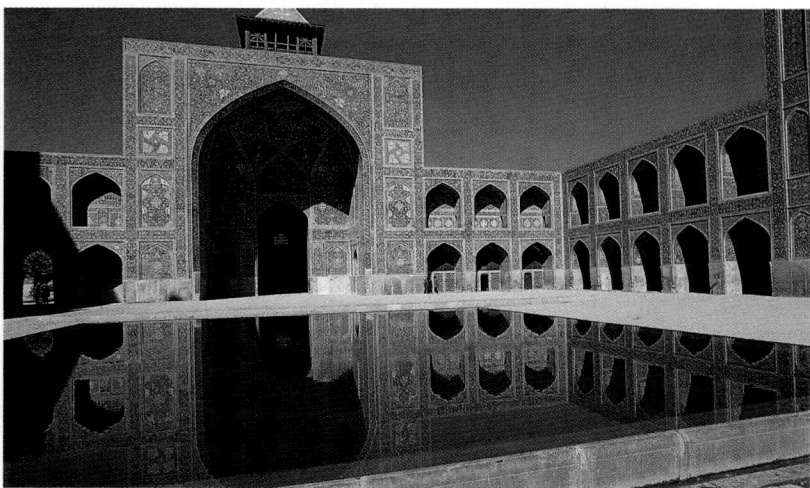

◄ *The Royal Academy of Isfahan was built by the shah of Iran in the early eighteenth century. The large courtyard is surrounded by student rooms. Why would mosques have included schools like this academy?*

Shah Abbas died in 1629. Most of his successors lacked his talent and political skills. As one observer said, "When this great prince ceased to live, Persia ceased to prosper." The power of Shi'ite religious elements began to increase at court and in Safavid society at large. The intellectual freedom that had marked the height of the empire was curtailed under the pressure of religious orthodoxy. Iranian women, who had possessed considerable freedom and influence during the early empire, were forced into seclusion and required to adopt the wearing of the veil.

The World of Safavid Culture

Persia witnessed an extraordinary flowering of the arts during the reign of Shah Abbas. His new capital of Isfahan was a grandiose planned city with wide spaces and a sense of order. The shah ordered his architects to place his palaces, mosques, and bazaars around a massive polo ground. Much of the original city is still in good condition and remains the gem of modern-day Iran. The immense mosques are richly decorated with elaborate blue tiles. The palaces are delicate structures with unusual slender wooden columns. These architectural wonders of Isfahan reflect the grandeur of the Safavid golden age.

To adorn the splendid buildings, Safavid craftspeople created imaginative metalwork, tiles, and delicate glass vessels. The greatest area of productivity, however, was in textiles. Silk weaving based on new techniques flourished throughout the empire. The silks were a brilliant riot of color with silver and gold threads; they portrayed birds, animals, and flowers. Above all, carpet weaving flourished, stimulated by the great demand for Persian carpets in the West. Persian carpets were made primarily of wool with some cotton, and they varied considerably in size. Still highly prized all over the world, these seventeenth-century carpets reflect the grandeur of the Safavid dynasty.

The long tradition of Persian painting continued in the Safavid Era, but it changed from paintings to line drawings and from landscape scenes to portraits, mostly of young women or boys. Although some Persian artists studied in Rome, Safavid art was little influenced by the West. Riza-i-Abbasi, the most famous artist of this period, created exquisite works on simple subjects, such as an ox plowing, hunters, or lovers. Soft colors and flowing movement were the dominant features of the painting of this era.

The artistic excellence of the Safavid Era is clear, but its literature lacked a similar luster. A large amount of poetry was written, but its lack of quality testified to

LEARNING FROM VISUALS

Answer to the caption question: Arabs were expected to welcome others warmly and share their provisions and belongings. The inclusion of Hatam is a reminder of the Arab responsibilities to his fellow man.

Answers to
SECTION REVIEW

2. (a) monarch of the Persian state
3. (a) political and military force in Persia and Central Asia in the 15th century
   (b) founder of the Safavid dynasty
   (c) source of the name Safavid
   (d) sect of Islam
   (e) the Safavids Islamic sect
4. (a) The Safavids used the Shi'ite faith as a unifying force.
   (b) The Safavids were denied access to profitable trade routes by European navies to the south and by the power of the Ottomans on the west.
   (c) brocades, carpets, leather goods
5. Students should recognize the Shah's high moral integrity.

CLOSE

Ask students to compare the Persian painting on page 350 with the page from the Ottoman *Book of Festivals* on page 526. What are the differences in subject matter and style? How does each painting reflect the culture from which it comes?

▲ *This painting done by Riza-i-Abbasi is a fanciful portrayal of an Arab encampment at the tomb of Hātam, a man who had gained fame for his generosity to strangers. Why do you think the artist chose to put this tomb in the painting?*

the decline of Persian poetry. Many Safavid poets, enticed by greater financial rewards, went to India to write for the Mughal emperors.

❋ SECTION REVIEW ❋

1. **Locate:**
   (a) Azerbaijan,   (b) Caspian Sea,   (c) Baghdad,
   (d) Tabriz,   (e) Isfahan

2. **Define:**
   (a) shah

3. **Identify:**
   (a) Uzbeks,   (b) Shah Ismail,   (c) Safi al-Din,
   (d) Sunnis,   (e) Shi'ites

4. **Recall:**
   (a) How were the Safavids able to consolidate Turks and Persians into their empire?
   (b) What political and geographic factors limited the growing wealth of Safavid Persia?
   (c) What were the principal exports from Persia during the Safavid Empire?

5. **Think Critically:** Describe the strategies employed by Shah Abbas to ensure sound, successful government during his reign. Which of these are employed by our government leaders today? Do they still work as well as they worked for Shah Abbas? Why or why not?

THE GRANDEUR OF THE MUGHALS

The period from 1500 to 1800 can be viewed as a high point of traditional culture in India. At the same time, it marked the first stage of its greatest challenge. The age began with the creation of one of India's greatest empires—that of the Mughals. Mughal rulers, although foreigners and Muslims, nonetheless brought India to a peak of political power and cultural achievement. For the first time since the age of the Mauryan dynasty (see Chapter 11), all of India was united under a single government with a common culture.

The Mughal Dynasty: A "Gunpowder Empire"?

When a Portuguese fleet arrived at the port of Calicut in the spring of 1498, the Indian subcontinent was still

---

RECOMMENDED READING

For an overview of the Mughal era, see such standard works as S. Wolpert, *New History of India* (New York, 1989), and the more detailed V. A. Smith, *The Oxford History of India* (Oxford, 1967). A more dramatic account for the general reader is W. Hansen, *The Peacock Throne: The Drama of Mogul India* (New York, 1972).

Personal accounts of the period are numerous, although most are by European visitors. For some examples, see R. C. Temple, ed., *The Travels of Peter Mundy, in Europe and Asia, 1608–1667* (Cambridge, 1907–1936); J. B. Tavernier, *Travels in India* (London, 1925); T. Roe, *The Embassy of Sir Thomas Roe, 1615–1619* (London, 1926); and F. Bernier, *Travels in the Mogul Empire, A.D. 1656–1668* (London, 1968).

divided into a number of Hindu and Muslim kingdoms. However, the land was on the verge of a new era of unity that would be brought about by a foreign dynasty called the Mughals (also known as the Moguls). The founders of the Mughal Empire were not natives of India but came from the mountainous region north of the Ganges River valley. The founder of the dynasty, Babur, had an illustrious background. His father was descended from the great Asian conqueror Tamerlane and his mother, from the Mongol conqueror Genghis Khan.

Babur had inherited a part of Tamerlane's empire in an upland river valley of the Syr Darya (SIR DAR-yuh) River. As a youth, he led a group of warriors who seized Kabul in 1504. Then, thirteen years later, they crossed the Khyber (KIE-bur) Pass to India.

Although his own forces were far smaller than those of his enemies, Babur had advanced weapons, including artillery, and he used them to great effect. His use of swift cavalry tactics was especially successful against the massed forces of his enemy. With only 12,000 troops against an enemy force nearly ten times that size, Babur captured Delhi and established his power in the plains of North India (see "You Are There: The Mughal Conquest of North India"). Over the next several years, he continued his conquests in North India until his early death in 1530 at the age of 47.

Babur's grandson added to the Mughal Empire. Akbar was only 14 when he came to the throne upon his father's death. Highly intelligent and industrious, Akbar set out to extend his domain, then limited to Punjab and the upper Ganges River valley. By the end of his life in 1605, he had brought Mughal rule to most of the subcontinent, from the Himalayan Mountains to the Godavari (guh-DAWV-uh-REE) River in central India, and from Kashmir to the mouths of the Brahmaputra and the Ganges Rivers. Akbar had created the greatest Indian empire since the Mauryan dynasty nearly 2,000 years earlier.

How was Akbar able to place almost the entire subcontinent of India under his rule? One reason was his use of heavy artillery. Akbar's armies were able to besiege and subdue the traditional stone fortresses of their rivals. However, the Mughals did not rely only on heavy artillery. They also used other forms of siege warfare and often offered to negotiate, with much suc-

cess. The Mughals thus created an empire that appeared highly centralized but was actually a collection of semi-independent states held together by the power of the Mughal emperor.

Akbar and Indo-Muslim Civilization

Akbar was probably the greatest of the conquering Mughal monarchs, but he is best known for the humane character of his rule. Although born a Muslim, as all Mughal rulers were, Akbar accepted the diversity of Indian civilization and adopted a policy of religious tolerance. Akbar allowed Hindus to serve at court, although most of the high positions were reserved for Muslims. As emperor, he showed a keen interest in other religions. He tolerated Hindu practices and even welcomed the expression of Christian views by his Jesuit advisors at court. By taking a Hindu princess as one of his wives, Akbar put his policy of religious tolerance into practice. In contrast, in Europe at the same time, Catholics and Protestants were killing one another in a series of religious wars.

Akbar was also tolerant in his administration of the government. The upper ranks of the government bureaucracy were filled with nonnative Muslims, but many of the lower-ranking officials were Hindus. A few Hindus were even given positions of importance. At first, most officials were paid salaries. Later, however, it became common practice to give them plots of farmland for their temporary use. These local officials, known as **zamindars,** kept a portion of the taxes paid by the peasants in lieu of a salary. They were then expected to forward the rest of the taxes from the lands under their control to the central government. Zamindars came to exercise considerable power in their local districts.

Overall, the Akbar Era was a good one, at least by the standards of the day. Although all Indian peasants were required to pay about one-third of their annual harvest to the state through the zamindars, at least the system was applied justly. When bad weather struck in the 1590s, the rate of taxation was reduced, or taxes were even suspended altogether. Thanks to a long period of peace and political stability, trade and manufacturing flourished. The era was an especially prosper

On Line with

WORLD HISTORY   Internet Activity

You may want to have your students visit the following URL, where they will find information and additional web site resources to enhance their study of this chapter.

India

http://india.indiagov.org/1page.htm

Made by the Ministry of External

Affairs, this site has a lot of good informative history under subtitles "culture" and "India perspectives". Major Indian art works such as the Taj Mahal are covered.

Due to the ever-changing nature of the World Wide Web, see the West History web site, **http://history.swpco.com** for regular updates of the URLs in this text.

LEARNING FROM VISUALS

Have students study this painting. Encourage them to note the energy of the figures, the sense of movement, the use of color and line. What details can they point out? What are individuals doing in the painting?

LEARNING FROM VISUALS

Answer to the caption question: The pontoon bridge floats on boats like those shown clearly in the illustration.

Multimedia Support

LASERDISC

Video: The Taj Mahal (video)

CLASS DISCUSSION

Compare Babur and Akbar. How were they similar? How did they differ? Would Akbar have been as successful if his grandfather had not already conquered much of North India?

Allow students to debate the following question: Would you prefer to be Babur or Akbar? Why?

CLASS DISCUSSION

Have students discuss how Shah Jahan's military victories were eclipsed by his failure to address domestic problems, such as the poverty of most of his subjects.

▲ *In this Indian painting, Akbar, Babur's grandson, leads an attack from his war elephant. What was used to construct the bridge that the elephants are using?*

ous one in the area of foreign trade. Indian goods, notably textiles, tropical food products and spices, and precious stones, were exported in exchange for gold and silver. Much of the foreign trade was handled by Arab traders, because the Indians, like their Mughal rulers, did not care for travel by sea.

Twilight of the Mughals

Akbar died in 1605 and was succeeded by his son Jahangir (ju-HAWN-gear). Jahangir was able and ambitious, and during the early years of his reign, he continued to strengthen central control over his vast empire. Eventually, however, his grip began to weaken.

The court fell under the influence of one of his wives, the Persian-born Nur Jahan (ju-HAWN). The empress took advantage of her position to enrich her own family and arranged the marriage of her niece to her husband's third son and ultimate successor, Shah Jahan. When Shah Jahan succeeded to the throne in 1627, he ordered the assassination of all of his rivals in order to secure his own position.

During a reign of thirty years, Shah Jahan maintained the system established by earlier Mughal rulers. He also expanded the boundaries of the empire by successful campaigns in the Deccan plateau and against Samarkand, north of the Hindu Kush. However, Shah Jahan's rule was marred by his failure to deal with the

MORE ABOUT . . . *Akbar*

There were three distinct stages to Akbar's life—an impetuous, dissolute youth, a sober, empire—expanding maturity, religious mysticism later in his life. The foolishness of his youth is shown in a story from the *Akbarnama,* a picture history of his life that he commissioned because he could not read. One day while drinking with his companions he was told how Indian rajput warriors

would charge against a double sided spear and impale themselves. He took this "challenge" and raced towards a sword fixed against a wall. Akbar was saved from senseless death only because someone kicked the sword away. In the scene in the book he is shown trying to strangle the man who saved him. So much for gratitude!

YOU ARE THERE

The Mughal Conquest of North India

In this selection from his memoirs, Babur describes his triumph over the powerful army of his Indian enemy, the sultan Ibrâhim (i-BRAW-him).

Babur, On His Victory over the Sultan Ibrâhim

They made one or two very poor charges on our right and left divisions. My troops making use of their bows, plied them with arrows, and drove them in upon their center. The troops on the right and the left of their center, being huddled together in one place, such confusion ensued, that the enemy, while totally unable to advance, found also no road by which they could flee. The sun had mounted spear-high when the onset of battle began, and the combat lasted till midday, when the enemy were completely broken and routed, and my friends victorious and exulting. By the grace and mercy of Almighty God, this arduous undertaking was rendered easy for me, and this mighty army, in the space of half a day, laid in the dust. Five or six thousand men were discovered lying slain, in one spot, near Ibrâhim. We reckoned that the number lying slain, in different parts of this field of battle, amounted to fifteen or sixteen thousand men. After routing the enemy, we continued the pursuit, slaughtering, and making them prisoners. . . .

(continued)

► *This sixteenth-century Moghul miniature shows Babur, seated on the throne, granting an interview to a nobleman, Bedi Az Zaman Mirza. While there are numerous observers to the scene, not all of them are paying attention to their sultan.*

CLASS DISCUSSION

As a class, list and discuss the examples of Akbar's open attitude toward other religions. Discuss what life in his empire would have been like for a non-Muslim. Discuss how Muslims in his empire may have felt about these policies.

YOU ARE THERE

USING PRIMARY SOURCES

Ask students to compare Babur's language here to the excerpts from his writings at the beginning of this chapter (page 514). What are the similarities? *(assumption of God's favor, huge numbers of dead, use of word* slaughter, *description of cruelty)* In what sense can Babur's campaigns be described as "holy wars"?

Answers to Critical Thinking Questions

1. Babur attributes his success to God.
2. It doesn't sound like he was confident about defeating the sultan.

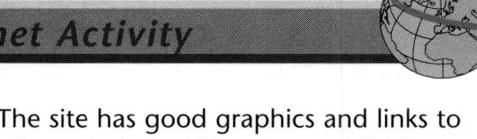

On Line with WORLD HISTORY *Internet Activity*

You may want to have your students visit the following URL, where they will find information and additional web site resources to enhance their study of this chapter.

Understanding Islam and the Muslims

http://darkwing.uoregon.edu/ ~kbatarfi/islam.html

The site has good graphics and links to Muslim culture in Africa, Japan, Middle East, and Asia.

Due to the ever-changing nature of the World Wide Web, see the West History web site, **http://history.swpco.com** for regular updates of the URLs in this text.

COMPARING TIME PERIODS

India in the twentieth century has not been free from scenes of famine much like the one described on this page. Ask students to research modern India's attempts to feed its vast population. How does India prevent famine wherever possible? What factors in India make famine a frequent threat?

CLASS DISCUSSION

Ask students to discuss the positive and negative aspects of Aurangzeb's rule. Have them note how religious intolerance became a factor of the Mughal decline, as it was of the Safavid decline.

RETEACH

Review with the students Akbar's religious policies. Then discuss those of Aurangzeb. You might lead into a class discussion of the two men. Which was more devoted to his religion? What difference did that make in religious toleration?

CLASS DISCUSSION

Compare and contrast Philip II of Spain (Chapter 15) with Aurangzeb. How were they similar? How were they different?

YOU ARE THERE

The Mughal Conquest of North India, continued

Yet, under circumstances, and in spite of this power, placing my trust in God, I advanced to meet so powerful a prince as Sultan Ibrâhim, the lord of numerous armies, and emperor of extensive territories. In consideration of my confidence in Divine aid, the Most High God did not suffer the distress and hardships that I had undergone to be thrown away, but defeated my enemy, and made me the conqueror of the noble country of Hindustân. This success I do not ascribe to my own strength, nor did this good fortune flow from my own efforts, but from the fountain of the favor and mercy of God.

1. To whom does Babur attribute the success of his army over the Sultan Ibrâhim?

2. From the sound of his narrative, do you think Babur felt like he would defeat the Sultan Ibrâhim?

growing domestic problems. He had inherited a nearly empty treasury because of Empress Nur Jahan's love of luxury and ambitious charity projects. While the majority of his subjects lived in grinding poverty, Shah Jahan's military campaigns and expensive building projects put a heavy strain on the imperial finances and compelled him to raise taxes (see "You Are There: An Elephant Fight for the King's Entertainment").

At the same time, the government did little to improve rural conditions. India was a country where drought was frequent and transport was primitive. (For example, it often took three months to travel from Patna, in the middle of the Ganges River valley, to Delhi (DELL-ee), a distance of a little over 600 miles.) However, the dynasty made few efforts to improve farming, the irrigation network, or the roads. A pathetic description of famine conditions in the mid-seventeenth century has been provided by one observer:

As the famine increased, men abandoned towns and villages and wandered helplessly. It was easy to recognize their condition: eyes sunk deep in head, lips pale and covered with slime, the skin hard, with the bones showing through, the belly nothing but a pouch hanging down empty, knuckles and knee-caps showing promi-nently. One would cry and howl for hunger, while another lay stretched on the ground dying in misery; wherever you went, you saw nothing but corpses.[3]

Shah Jahan's troubles soon worsened with his illness in the mid-1650s, which led to a struggle for power between two of his sons. One of them, Aurangzeb, had his brother put to death, imprisoned his father, and had himself crowned emperor in 1658.

Aurangzeb is one of the most controversial rulers in the history of India. A man of high principle, he attempted to eliminate many of what he considered to be India's social evils. He forbade both the Hindu custom of suttee (cremating widows on their husbands' funeral pyres) and the levying of illegal taxes. With less success, he tried to forbid gambling and drinking. Aurangzeb was a devout Muslim and adopted a number of measures that reversed the Mughal policies of religious tolerance. The building of new Hindu temples was prohibited, and Hindus were forced to convert to Islam. Non-Muslims were also driven from the court.

Aurangzeb's policies led to domestic unrest and to a revival of Hindu fervor during the last years of his reign. A number of revolts also broke out against imperial authority. During the eighteenth century, Mughal power was threatened both from within and without.

RETEACHING ACTIVITY

The text calls Aurangzeb "one of the most controversial rulers in the history of India." Discuss with students ways in which Aurangzeb's reign weakened India on the eve of European colonization. Also consider ways in which Mughal rule had already been weakened during the administration of Shah Jahan. Were Akbar able to provide ruling tips to Aurangzeb, what pointers do students think he might have provided his successor? Complete the discussion by dividing the class into two groups, prosecution and defense, and have the students try Aurangzeb for the decline of the Mughal Empire.

Map 17.3   The Mughal Empire

The Empire at Akbar's death, 1605
The Empire, c. 1700
■ Dutch settlement
■ British settlement
□ Portuguese settlement
□ French settlement

Multimedia Support

TRANSPARENCY
17–3, The Mughal
Empire. (Map 17.3)

RETEACH

Review with the students the situation in Britain, Portugal, and Holland at this point in time. Compare these nations' strengths and weaknesses with those of the Mughal Empire. In what ways were the European powers expanding? How was the Mughal Empire at a point of weakness?

CLASS DISCUSSION

How might history have been different had the British encountered the India of Akbar at this point in time? How do students think Akbar would have related to the British? Would he have been able to stand against them? Why or why not?

Rebellious groups in provinces throughout the empire began to reassert local authority and reduce the power of the Mughal emperor. An increasingly divided India was vulnerable to attack from abroad. In 1739, Delhi was sacked by the Persians, who left it in ashes. The arrival of the Europeans also hastened the decline of the empire.

The Impact of Western Power in India

The first Europeans to arrive in India were the Portuguese. At first, Portugal dominated regional trade in the Indian Ocean. At the end of the sixteenth century, however, the British and the Dutch entered the scene. Soon both powers were competing with Portugal, and with each other, for trading privileges in the region.

During the first half of the seventeenth century, the British presence in India steadily increased. By 1650, British trading forts had been established at Surat (a thriving port along the northwestern coast of India), Fort William (now the great city of Calcutta) near the Bay of Bengal, and Madras on the southeastern coast. From Madras, British ships carried Indian-made cotton goods to the East Indies, where they were traded for spices. These in turn were shipped back to Britain.

STUDYING MAPS

The following activities will help you guide students through their study of Map 17.3.

1. Find Calicut, the Ganges River, Kabul, Khyber Pass, Delhi, Himalaya Mountains, Godavari River, Kashmir, Brahmaputra River, Deccan plateau, and Hindu Kush.
2. Trace the route from Patna to Delhi. Recall that because of primitive transport, the trip could take three months.

3. Compare the size of the empire at Akbar's death in 1605 with its size around 1700. Who was responsible for expansion of the Empire between these two periods? *(Shah Jahan)*
4. Note the European presence in India: Dutch, British, Portuguese, and French. Where are they strongest? *(coast, especially in the south)*

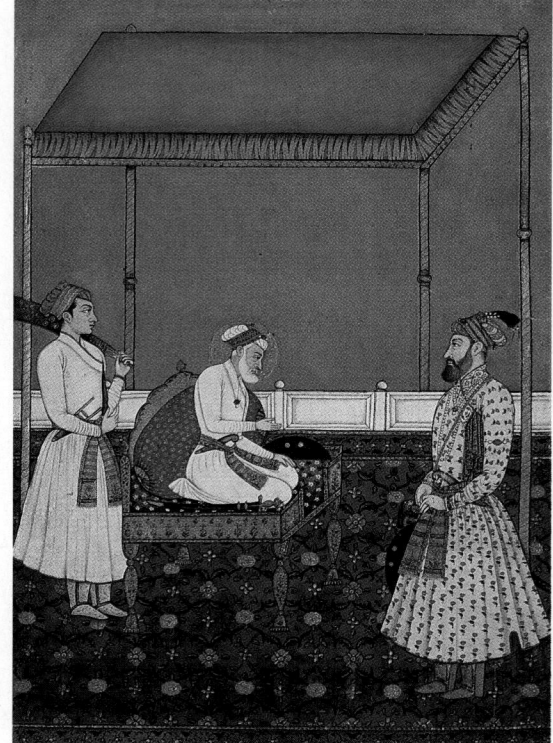

▲ *Aurangzeb, shown here on his knees, ruled for almost 50 years, from 1658 until his death in 1707. Do you believe this painting portrays his power and royal status? Why or why not?*

British success in India attracted rivals, including the Dutch and the French. The Dutch gave up their interests in India to concentrate on the spice trade in the middle of the seventeenth century. The French were more persistent, however, and established their own fort on the east coast at Pondicherry, about one hundred miles south of Madras, as well as at Surat and in the Bay of Bengal. For a brief period, the French competed successfully with the British, even capturing the British fort at Madras.

The British were saved by the military genius of Sir Robert Clive. He was an aggressive British empire builder who eventually became the chief representative of the East India Company (a private company empowered by the British crown to act on its behalf) in the subcontinent. The British were aided as well by the refusal of the French government to provide financial support for French efforts in far-off India. Eventually the French were restricted to the fort at Pondicherry and a handful of small territories on the southeastern coast.

In the meantime, Clive began to consolidate British control in Bengal, where the local ruler had attacked Fort William and imprisoned the local British population in the "Black Hole of Calcutta" (an underground prison for holding the prisoners, many of whom died in captivity). In 1757, a small British force numbering about 3,000 defeated a Mughal-led army more than ten times its size in the Battle of Plassey. As part of the spoils of victory, the British East India Company received from the failing Mughal court the power to collect taxes from lands in the area surrounding Calcutta.

To officials of the East India Company, the expansion of their authority into the interior of the subcontinent probably seemed like a simple economic decision. It made sense to seek regular revenues that would pay for increasingly expensive military operations in India. To historians, it marks a major step in the gradual transfer of all of the Indian subcontinent to the British East India Company and later, in 1858, to the British crown as a colony.

Britain's rise to power in India, however, was not a story of constant success. Officials of the East India Company, from the governor-general on down, often combined arrogance and corruption with incompetence. They offended both their Indian allies and the local population, who were taxed heavily to meet the growing expenses of the East India Company. Intelligent Indian commanders avoided direct pitched battles with well-armed British troops. They preferred to harass and ambush them in the manner of the guerrillas of our time. Said Haidar Ali, one of Britain's chief rivals for control in southern India:

You will in time understand my mode of warfare. Shall I risk my cavalry which cost a thousand rupees each horse, against your cannon ball which cost two pice? No! I will march your troops until their legs swell to

YOU ARE THERE

An Elephant Fight for the King's Entertainment

François Bernier was a well-traveled Frenchman who visited India during the mid-seventeenth century. In this excerpt from his account of the visit, he describes a festival just outside the Red Fort at Delhi for the amusement of the emperor.

A French Traveler Describes an Indian Festival for the Emperor

The festivals generally conclude with an amusement unknown in Europe—a combat between two elephants; which takes place in the presence of all the people on the sandy space near the river: the King, the principal ladies of the court, and the nobles viewing the spectacle from different apartments in the fortress.

A wall of earth is raised three or four feet wide and five or six high. The two ponderous beasts meet one another face to face, on opposite sides of the wall, each having a couple of riders, that the place of the man who sits on the shoulders, for the purpose of guiding the elephant with a large iron hook, may immediately be supplied if he should be thrown down. The riders animate the elephants either by soothing words, or by chiding them as cowards, and urge them on with their heels, until the poor creatures approach the wall and are brought to the attack. The shock is tremendous, and it appears surprising that they ever survive the dreadful wounds and blows inflicted with their teeth, their heads, and their trunks. The stronger or more courageous elephant passes on and attacks his opponent, and, putting him to flight, pursues and fastens upon him with so much obstinacy, that the animals can be separated only by means of fireworks, which are made to explode between them; for they are naturally timid, and have a par-

▲ *This hand-colored woodcut shows the viciousness of elephant fights. How do you think these compared to the Roman games and gladiator fights?*

ticular dread of fire, which is the reason why elephants have been used with so very little advantage in armies since the use of fire-arms.

The fight of these noble creatures is attended with much cruelty. It frequently happens that some of the riders are trodden underfoot; and killed on the spot. . . . So imminent is the danger

(continued)

LEARNING FROM VISUALS

Compare this woodcut to the pictures on page 532. How do the styles differ? Ask students to identify cultural differences between the Europeans in the woodcut and the natives of India.

LEARNING FROM VISUALS

Answer to the caption question: Answers will vary.

USING PRIMARY SOURCES

Ask students to study the woodcut. How do the positions and postures of the onlookers contrast with the violence of what they're watching?

How would students compare these elephant fights with bullfights? With other fights between animals that are engineered by humans for their "amusement"?

Who obviously has the French traveler's sympathy? (the elephants) How can you tell? (use of "poor creatures," "dreadful wounds and blows," "noble creatures")

Why does he describe the riders as unhappy? How do students think these riders were chosen?

So What ??

If your students question the importance of information on the **Dutch departure from India in the middle of the 17th century** *tell them . . .*

This changed the course of Indian history. The Dutch pursued the spice trade and came to dominate the modern country of Indonesia, which they ruled until World War II. India became the crown jewel of the British empire and was ruled by Britain until 1947. Even today, these colonial patterns have significance, since people from former European colonies have migrated to Europe. Many from India and Pakistan live in Britain, and many from Indonesia have settled in Holland.

Answers to Critical Thinking Questions

1. The elephant fights were held for the amusement of the emperor.
2. The elephant riders did not enjoy the sport, as many were killed during the fighting. On the day of the fights, they would take leave of their families as if condemned to death.
3. Answers regarding specific reactions of the ASPCA will vary, but should include the fact that the organization would be totally opposed to such fights.

LEARNING FROM VISUALS

Ask students to study the miniature. How would they interpret the positions and postures of the people shown? Who are the two Indian men behind the Englishman?

LEARNING FROM VISUALS

Answer to the caption question: The Englishman's dress is in sharp contrast to his servants. The wooden verandah is reminiscent of those that were built at English country houses.

CLASS DISCUSSION

Discuss with students the impact, immediate and gradual, of British power in India.

YOU ARE THERE

An Elephant Fight for the King's Entertainment, continued

considered, that on the day of combat the unhappy men take the same formal leave of their wives and children as if condemned to death. . . . The mischief with which this amusement is attended does not always terminate with the death of the rider: it often happens that some of the spectators are knocked down and trampled upon by the elephants.

1. What was the purpose of the elephant fights?
2. Did the elephant riders enjoy the sport? Explain your answer.
3. How do you think the Association for the Prevention of Cruelty to Animals (ASPCA) would react to the elephant fights?

the size of their bodies. You shall not have a blade of grass, nor a drop of water. I will hear of you every time your drum beats, but you shall not know where I am once a month. I will give your army battle, but it must be when I please, and not when you choose.[4]

Unfortunately for India, not all its commanders were as wise as Haidar Ali. When in the late eighteenth century the East India Company came under the capable hands of Lord Cornwallis and his successor Lord Mornington, the stage was set for the consolidation of British rule over the subcontinent.

The immediate impact of these developments was felt mainly along the coast, where Europeans began to establish forts and trading centers to serve their needs in the region. The land around the future city of Madras was leased to the British in 1639. A major city came to surround the original settlement at Fort St. George. A similar process took place at Fort William (the future Calcutta) in the Bay of Bengal, as well as at Bombay on the west coast.

During the eighteenth century, the pattern began to change, as the British moved inland from the great coastal cities. Their original goal was to gain access to tax revenues from the land to pay for the East India Company's military and administrative expenses. However, British expansion brought great riches to individ-

▲ *In this miniature, we see an employee of the British East India Company receiving an Indian visitor. What evidence do you see to support the idea that the British tried to re-create England in India?*

ENRICHMENT ACTIVITY

Have each student decide where he or she would have preferred to live—the Ottoman Empire, the Safavid Empire, or the Mughal Empire—as a Christian in the year 1700. Have them decide why. Then lead the class in an "active debate," with those preferring the Ottoman Empire in one part of the room, those preferring the Safavid Empire in another part of the room, and those preferring the Mughal Empire in a third place in the room. Allow each group to state its case and allow students to migrate between groups.

Map 17.4   India in 1805

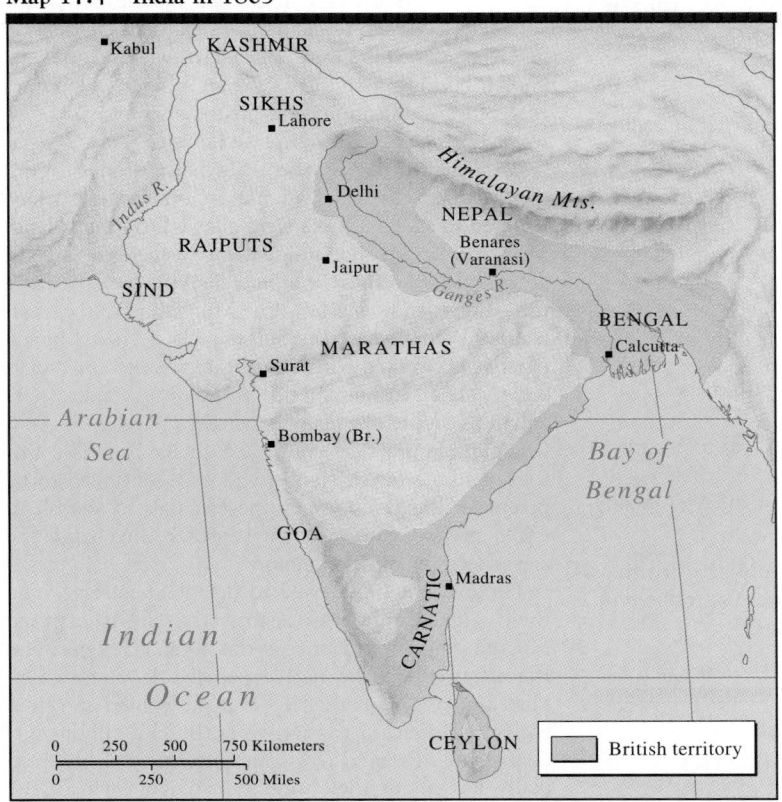

ual merchants and British officials who found they could squeeze money from local rulers by selling trade privileges.

The East India Company's takeover of vast land-holdings, notably in eastern India, may have brought great wealth to British officials, but it was a disaster for the Indian economy. In the first place, the British takeover took money from the hands of the local Indian landowners and put it into the hands of East India Company officials, most of whom sent their profits back to England. Second, it hastened the destruction of once healthy local industries. British goods,

such as machine-made textiles, were imported duty free into India to compete against local products.

Finally, British expansion hurt the peasants. As the British took over the administration of the land tax, they also applied British law. According to the latter, those who were unable to pay taxes could have their lands confiscated. As a result, many peasants became impoverished. In the 1770s, a series of massive famines led to the death of an estimated one-third of the population in the areas under East India Company control. It was hardly a good introduction to "civilized" British rule.

STUDYING MAPS

The following questions will help you guide students through their study of Map 17.4.

1. Compare this map of India in 1805 with a current map of India. What differences do you see? (*Answers will vary, but should include the absence of British territory on the current map, as well as the presence there of Pakistan, Nepal, Bhutan, and*

Bangladesh, they might also note that Ceylon is now called Sri Lanka.)

2. What connection do students note between the location of British territory and water? (*British territory was primarily coastal, but also included The Ganges River valley.*) If students have access to a physical map of India, compare it to Map 17.4.

CLASS DISCUSSION

Have students discuss the ways actions of the East India Company were "a disaster for the Indian economy."

RETEACH

Have students list the weaknesses in the East Indian Company's administration of India.

CLASS DISCUSSION

Drawing from the students' lists, discuss as a class the results of the East India Company's weaknesses. How would various Indians (landowners, merchants, artisans, and peasants) have felt about the British? Why?

ASSESS

You can choose from a variety of assessments to evaluate your students' mastery of the objectives for this section, as stated on page 531. Possible assessments include

1. Section Review questions on this page
2. Section 17–3 Quiz in your Teacher Resource materials
3. Reteaching Worksheets in your Teacher Resource materials
4. Self-Study software

ALTERNATIVE ASSESSMENT

Assign students an essay in which they highlight the main achievements of the Mughal Empire.

Answers to SECTION REVIEW

2. (a) local government officials
3. (a) greatest of conquering Mughal monarchs known for humane rule
(b) Akbar's son, succeeded him as ruler
(c) powerful, Persian-born wife of Jahangir; her extravagance helped impoverish the Mughal empire
(d) expanded the Mughal Empire, but failed to deal with domestic problems
(e) chief agent of the East India Company, expanded and consolidated British control in India
4. (a) Akbar's forces were well trained and courageous, had heavy artillery, and were also skilled negotiators.
(b) Akbar married a Hindu princess, welcomed Jesuit advisers in his court, and appointed non-native Muslims and Hindus to government positions.
(c) heavy taxation, loss of farmland, poverty; taxation policies also destroyed local Indian industries
5. Students should be aware of colonial ideas, particularly that colonies existed only to benefit the mother country.

SECTION REVIEW

1. **Locate:**
(*a*) Ganges River,   (*b*) Godavari River,
(*c*) Brahmaputra River,   (*d*) Kabul,   (*e*) Delhi,
(*f*) Madras

2. **Define:**
(*a*) zamindars

3. **Identify:**
(*a*) Akbar,   (*b*) Jahangir,   (*c*) Nur Jahan,
(*d*) Shah Jahan,   (*e*) Sir Robert Clive

4. **Recall:**
(*a*) How did Akbar gain control of India so quickly?
(*b*) Describe the steps taken by Akbar to ensure religious tolerance.
(*c*) Describe the effects of the East India Company on daily life for most Indians.

5. **Think Critically:** Why do you think the British, under the East India Company, were so indifferent to the plight of the Indian people?

4

SOCIETY AND CULTURE UNDER THE MUGHALS

The Mughals were the last of the great Indian dynasties. Like so many of the ruling dynasties before them, the Mughals were Muslims. To their credit, the best Mughal rulers did not simply impose Islamic institutions and beliefs on a mostly Hindu population. They combined Muslim with Hindu and even Persian cultural values in a unique social and cultural synthesis.

Society and Daily Life in Mughal India

Did Mughal rule affect the lives of ordinary Indians? In some ways, it did. The treatment of women is a good example. Women had long played an active role in Mughal tribal society, and some actually fought on the battlefield alongside the men. Babur and his successors often relied on the women in their families for political advice. Women from aristocratic families frequently received salaries and were allowed to own land and take part in business activities. Women at court sometimes received an education, and aristocratic women often wrote poetry, painted, and played music.

To a certain degree, these Mughal attitudes toward women may have had an impact on Indian society. Women in Mughal India were allowed to inherit land. Moreover, it was not unusual for women to take an active role in business or literary activities. At the same time, however, as Muslims, the Mughals placed certain restrictions on women under Islamic law. These Mughal practices coexisted with existing tendencies in Indian society. The Muslim practice of isolating women (**purdah**) was adopted by many upper-class Hindus. In other ways, Hindu practices continued unchanged. The custom of suttee (cremation of widows) continued to be practiced despite efforts by the Mughals to abolish it. Child marriage (most women were betrothed before the age of ten) remained common.

Hindus sometimes tried to defend themselves and their religious practices against the efforts of some Mughal emperors to impose the Islamic religion and Islamic ways on the native peoples. In some cases, Hindu men forcibly married Muslim women and then converted them to the native faith. The Hindus discouraged conversion to Islam; converts to Islam normally lost all of their inheritance rights within the Indian family. Government orders to destroy Hindu temples were often ignored by local officials. Sometimes Indian practices had an influence on the Mughal elites. Many Mughal leaders married Indian women and adopted Indian forms of dress.

Long-term stability led to the spread of wealth to new groups within Indian society. The Mughal Era saw the emergence of a wealthy landed nobility and a prosperous merchant class. During the late eighteenth century, this economic prosperity was shaken by the decline of the Mughal Empire and the coming of the British. However, many prominent Indians reacted by establishing trading ties with the foreigners, a relationship that for a while worked to the Indians' benefit. Later, as we shall see, they would have cause to regret the arrangement.

CLOSE

Ask students to discuss the following statement: "The period from 1500 to 1800 can be viewed as a high point of traditional culture in India. At the same time, it marked the first stage of its greatest challenge."

RECOMMENDED READING

Standard works on Mughal art and culture include A. L. Basham, *A Cultural History of India* (Oxford, 1975); E. C. Dimock, *The Literature of India: An Introduction* (Chicago, 1974); and R. C. Craven, *Indian Art: A Concise History* (New York, 1976).

▲ *This painting of daily life in Mughal India comes from the Topkapi Palace in Istanbul. Can you identify what the various groups of people are doing?*

Because so little of the daily lives of ordinary Indians is recorded in official documents, most of what we know comes from the observations of foreign visitors. Normally, however, foreigners were more familiar with city life than with rural conditions and generally had little contact with the common people. An occasional foreign visitor has left us a description of Indian life, such as the one that follows:

Their houses are built of mud with thatched roofs. Furniture there is little or none except some earthenware pots to hold water and for cooking and two beds, one for the man, the other for his wife; their bed cloths are scanty, merely a sheet or perhaps two, serving as

under- and over-sheet. This is sufficient for the hot weather, but the bitter cold nights are miserable indeed, and they try to keep warm over little cow-dung fires.[5]

Mughal Culture

The Mughals combined Islamic themes with Persian and native Indian **motifs** (dominant ideas or central themes) in a unique style that enriched Indian art and culture. No doubt, the most visible achievement was in architecture. Here the Mughals brought together Persian and Indian styles in a new and beautiful form best symbolized by the Taj Mahal (TAWZH-mu-HALL) (see "Our Artistic Heritage: The Taj Mahal").

The other major artistic achievement of the Mughal period was in painting. Painting had never been one of the great achievements of Indian culture. This was partly a result of the lack of technology. Paper was not introduced to India from Persia until the fourteenth century. Traditionally, painting had been done on palm leaves, which limited what an artist could do. By the fifteenth century, Indian painting had moved from palm leaf to paper, which led to a rapid development of painting in miniatures, or book illustrations.

As in so many other areas of endeavor, painting in Mughal India resulted from the blending of two cultures. While living in exile, Emperor Humayun had learned to admire Persian miniatures. On his return to India in 1556, he invited two Persian masters to live in his palace and introduce the technique to India. His successor Akbar liked the new style and encouraged artists to imitate it. Akbar established a state workshop for two hundred artists, mostly Hindus, who worked under the guidance of the Persian masters to create the Mughal school of painting.

The "Akbar style" combined Persian with Indian motifs, such as the portrayal of humans in action, a characteristic not usually seen in Persian art. Akbar also encouraged his artists to imitate European art forms, including the use of perspective and lifelike portraits. The depiction of the human figure in Mughal painting angered orthodox Muslims at court, however.

Painting during Akbar's reign followed the trend toward realism and historical narrative as developed in the Ottoman Empire. For example, Akbar had the

542

CROSSING TIME PERIODS

Ask students to research the status of women in today's India. Are Muslim and Hindu women treated differently? Do the customs of *purdah, sati,* and child marriage persist? What inroads has feminism made in today's India?

ACROSS THE CURRICULUM

Religion Ask interested students to research attitudes toward women as expressed in the Quran of Islam and/or in the Upanishads of Hinduism. How have the writings in these sacred books been interpreted by Muslims and Hindus over the years?

OUR ARTISTIC HERITAGE

Answers to Critical Thinking Questions

1. the Indian emperor Shah Jahan (Twenty-thousand workers were employed over a period of 20 years to do the actual labor.)
2. in memory of Shah Jahan's wife who had died during childbirth

CRITICAL THINKING

Ask students to compare the styles, motifs, and subject matter of Mughal, Persian, and Ottoman art and/or architecture. What similarities do they see? What differences? How can paintings and buildings from this era help illuminate these societies' values?

OUR ARTISTIC HERITAGE
The Taj Mahal

The famous Taj Mahal in Agra is widely considered to be the most beautiful building in India, if not in the entire world. It was built by the emperor Shah Jahan in the mid-seventeenth century. The story is romantic: the Taj Mahal was built by the emperor in memory of his wife Mumtaz Mahal, who had died giving birth to her thirteenth child at the age of 39. The emperor employed 20,000 workers in a project that lasted more than twenty years. This forced the government to raise land taxes, thus driving many Indian peasants into complete poverty.

There is no denying the beauty of the Taj Mahal. It evolved from a style that had originated several decades earlier and that combined Persian and Islamic motifs in a square building finished in red sandstone and topped with a dome. The Taj Mahal brought the style to perfection. Working with a model created by his Persian architect, Shah Jahan raised the dome and replaced the red sandstone with brilliant white marble. All the exterior and interior surfaces are decorated with cut stone geometric patterns; delicate black stone tracery, or intricate inlays of colored precious stones in floral mosaics. The effect is one of monumental size, nearly blinding brilliance, and delicate lightness, all at the same time.

Shah Jahan had intended to erect a similar building in black marble across the river for his

▲ *Of all the buildings in India, none is more famous than the Taj Mahal. Its simple symmetry and the placement of the long reflecting pool create a timeless image of beauty.*

own remains. However, the plans were abandoned after he was deposed by his son Aurangzeb. Shah Jahan spent his last years imprisoned in a room in the Red Fort at Agra. From his windows he could see the beautiful memorial to his beloved wife.

---

1. Who built the Taj Mahal?

2. Why was the Taj Mahal built?

---

illustrated *Book of Akbar* made to record his military exploits and court activities. Many of its paintings of Akbar's life portray him in action in his real world. The Mughal emperors were dedicated patrons of the arts, and going to India was the goal of painters, poets, and artisans from as far away as the Mediterranean. Apparently the generosity of the Mughals made it difficult to refuse a trip to India for fame and fortune. It is said that the Mughals would reward a poet with his weight in gold.

The development of literature in India was held back by the absence of printing, which did not come

---

SPECIAL NEEDS: *Visual/spatial*

1. By using the Internet, magazines, and other reference sources, have hearing-impaired or attention-deficit students research the Taj Mahal. They should find pictures and construct a time line depicting all work that has been done to the Taj Mahal.

   Have another student or pair of students make a list of all celebrity events which have occurred at the Taj Mahal. Share this with the class orally, in writing, or as a visual presentation.

   For extension, ask if there is any comparable location in the United States or elsewhere. Compare/contrast orally the date of original construction and size and building materials. Does it really measure up to the Taj Mahal?

until the end of the Mughal Era. Literary works were written by hand; the library at Agra contained over 24,000 volumes. Poetry in particular flourished under the Mughals. Poems were written in the Persian style and in the Persian language. In fact, Persian became the official language of the court until the sack of Delhi in 1739. At the time, Indian anger at the conquerors led India to adopt Urdu as the new language for the court and for poetry. By that time, Indian verse on the Persian model had already lost its original vitality and simplicity and had become more artificial.

 SECTION REVIEW

1. **Define:**
   (*a*) purdah,   (*b*) motifs

2. **Identify:**
   (*a*) Urdu,   (*b*) *Book of Akbar*

3. **Recall:**
   (*a*) Describe the treatment and role of women under Mughal rule.
   (*b*) Why do historians know so little about the daily life of Indian people?
   (*c*) How does the painting of Mughal India reflect a blending of both Persian and Indian influences?

4. **Think Critically:** What factors contributed to the development and appreciation of art and literature during the Mughal Empire?

Conclusion

The three empires discussed in this chapter—the Ottomans, Safavids, and Mughals—were similar in a number of ways. First of all, they were Muslim in their religious affiliation. Moreover, they were formed by conquerors who came from outside the region they conquered. Once they achieved imperial power, all three states showed the ability to govern a large empire and brought stability to peoples who had often been severely divided.

Another similarity is that in all three cases, the mastery of the techniques of modern warfare, including the use of firearms, played a central role in the ability of the empires to overcome their rivals. Some historians have therefore called them "gunpowder empires" in the belief that the skill of these empires in the art of warfare was a key element in their success. That is true, but we should not forget that dynamic leadership, political skills, and a strong following motivated by religious zeal were also important to their success. Weapons by themselves do not make an empire.

These three powerful Muslim states rose at the same time that Europeans were beginning to expand into the rest of the world (the end of the fifteenth century and the beginning of the sixteenth century). The military and political talents of these empires helped to protect much of the Muslim world from the resurgent forces of Christianity—Islam's bitter enemy. In fact, one empire, that of the Ottoman Turks, even carried its armies into the heart of Christian Europe and briefly reached the gates of the great city of Vienna. By the end of the eighteenth century, however, the Safavid dynasty had collapsed, and the powerful Mughal Empire was declining rapidly. Although the Ottoman Empire remained intact, it, too, was beginning to experience internal problems. The weakening of the "gunpowder empires" created a political vacuum into which the dynamic European powers were quick to enter.

The gunpowder empires were not the only states in the Old World that were able to resist the first outward thrust of European expansion. Further to the east, as we shall see in the next chapter, the mature civilizations in China and Japan successfully faced a similar challenge from European merchants and missionaries.

Notes

1. Quoted in Roger Savory, *Iran under the Safavids* (Cambridge, 1980), p. 103.
2. Quoted in *ibid.*, p. 179.
3. Quoted in Michael Edwardes, *A History of India: From the Earliest Times to the Present Day* (London: Thames and Hudson, 1961), p. 188.
4. *Ibid.*, p. 220.
5. *Ibid.*, p. 187.

ASSESS

Answers to
SECTION REVIEW

1. (a) Muslim practice of isolating women
   (b) dominant ideas or central themes
2. (a) after 1739 official language used in royal courts and in Indian poetry
   (b) a pictorial history of Akbar's military and court experiences
3. (a) Women could own land, take part in business activities, be paid salaries, and be educated. Child marriage was common, as was the practice of isolating women and forcing them to practice sati.
   (b) The daily lives of ordinary Indians were rarely recorded, except by visitors, who saw mostly city life.
   (c) Mughal art reflects the Indian concepts of active, realistic scenes but also incorporates Persian miniatures.
4. arts sponsored by an educated court that valued literature and painting

CLOSE

Ask students to give examples that explain the following sentence about the Mughal rulers: "They combined Muslim with Hindu and even Persian cultural values in a unique social and cultural synthesis."

USING KEY TERMS

1. grand vezir or grand wazir
2. minarets
3. motifs
4. pashas
5. purdah
6. shah
7. harem
8. zamindars
9. ulema
10. Janissaries
11. bey

REVIEWING THE FACTS

1. Mughal: India
   Ottoman: Central Asia, into Balkans, Mesopotamia, Egypt, and Arabia
   Safavids: Persia
2. recruited local Christians from Balkan population into an elite guard called Janissaries
3. where possible administered conquered regions through local rulers
4. Romanian territory of Wallachia; Hungary; most of Austria; some Mediterranean areas
5. Ottomans copied Byzantine traditions of rule
6. to conduct the meetings of the sultan's imperial council
7. some loss of territory; training of officials declined; senior positions increasingly assigned to sons or daughters of elites, soon forming a privileged group seeking wealth and power; corruption and high taxes ensued; wars depleted treasury; western ideas and customs began replacing cultural traditions; incompetence in ruling family
8. Shah Ismail used military force to seize much of Iran and Iraq, declaring himself the shah (king) of new Persian state.
9. Ismail sent Shi'ite preachers to Anatolia to convert members of Turkish tribes in Ottoman empire, Ottoman sultan tried to halt, led to massacre of Sunni Muslims and further military conflict

544

CHAPTER 17 REVIEW

USING KEY TERMS

1. The sultan's chief minister, the _____, conducted the meetings of the imperial council.
2. Four narrow towers known as _____ framed the first of Sinan's magnificent mosques.
3. Persian and native Indian _____ contributed to the unique art style of the Mughal period.
4. The regional administrators who reported to the sultan in Constantinople were called _____.
5. Upper-class Hindus adopted the Muslim practice of isolating women called _____.
6. Ismail took the title of _____ after his forces captured much of Iran and Iraq in 1501.
7. The private section of the sultan's palace, where his concubines resided, was called the _____.
8. In India, local officials known as _____ were allowed to keep a portion of the taxes paid by the peasants.
9. Sultans ordinarily gave responsibility for the conduct of religious affairs to the _____.
10. The _____ were an elite guard of Christian youth recruited from the Ottoman Empire.
11. The _____ was a tribal leader whose position was the basis of the Ottoman system of rule.

REVIEWING THE FACTS

1. Between 1500 and 1800, three great Muslim empires flourished. What were they named, and where was each located?
2. What recruitment strategy did the Ottoman Turks use to strengthen the military?
3. What system did the Ottoman Turks use to administer their conquered territories?
4. What European territories fell to the Ottoman Turks after the conquest of Constantinople?
5. What influence did Byzantine civilization have on Ottoman culture?
6. What was the function of the grand vezir?

544

7. What indications of decline appeared in the Ottoman Empire after the reign of Suleyman?
8. How did the Safavids gain control of Persia?
9. Why was there religious friction between the Ottoman Empire and the Safavid Empire?
10. What was the origin of the founders of the Mughal Empire?
11. What things make Akbar's rule a model of government?
12. What impact did the arrival of the Portuguese and British initially have on Mughal India?
13. How did Mughal (Muslim) culture affect daily life among the native Hindus?

THINKING CRITICALLY

1. To what degree did the Ottoman custom of recruiting Christian youth contribute to the stability of the empire?
2. Who holds more personal power over his subjects—a Muslim sultan, or a caliph?
3. Were the hereditary practices of selecting a sultan and the harem system, sources of weakness or strength for the Ottoman Empire? Explain.
4. After the 1453 conquest of Constantinople by the Ottomans, most of the European area remained Christian, but some areas—such as Bosnia—converted to Islam. What present-day consequences have resulted from this development in the area known formerly as Yugoslavia?
5. Review the section, "Religion and Society in the Ottoman World." Identify similarities and differences with the position of women in the U.S. today.
6. Review the reasons that Shah Abbas was given the title "the Great." Is there a ruler in the world today that you feel may have the same characteristics? Who? Explain your answer.
7. The British East India Company was a private, for-profit company. With the support of the British government, it set up a political and military government in parts of India. What are the pros and

10. came from mountainous region north of the Gange River Valley
11. just system of taxation; period of peace and political stability in which trade and manufacturing flourished; prosperous foreign trade
12. increased presences in region used for trading; impact felt mostly along coastal regions
13. Answers will vary. may include: gave Indian women different rights and also required different restrictions than before, based on Islamic law

THINKING CRITICALLY

1. Answers will vary. Student responses should

demonstrate understanding of pages 516–518.
2. Answers will vary. Student responses should refer to page 523.
3. Answers will vary. Student responses should refer to page 522.
4. terrible wars and violence between Muslims and non-Muslims, including "ethnic-cleansing"
5. Answers will vary.
6. Answers will vary. Comparison should be drawn from descriptions on page 527.
7. Answers will vary. Reference should be made to pages 535–539.

cons of allowing private enterprise to engage in that type of activity?

APPLYING SOCIAL STUDIES SKILLS

1. **Government:** Who would present-day American foreign policymakers lean towards supporting—the Sunni, or Shi'ite Muslims in the Middle East? Why?
2. **Anthropology:** Imagine yourself living in the Ottoman Empire, and the Safavid Empire. Compare your life as a Muslim in the two places. If you were a non-Muslim where would you prefer to live and why?
3. **Geography:** Using an outline map, draw from memory the boundaries of the Ottoman Empire, Safavid Empire, and Mughal Empire.
4. **Geography:** Locate a map that shows England and India. Use the map's scale to measure the distance of a voyage from London to Bombay, India, made by sailing around Africa. Now determine the distance traveled by going across the Red Sea and through the present Suez Canal. Compare the two distances to see why England wanted to construct a canal through Suez.

MAKING TIME AND PLACE CONNECTIONS

1. In the 1990s, Christian Serbs moved to destroy the Muslim population of Bosnia. This ethnic cleansing policy led to the present involvement of the United Nations in that area. What events covered in this chapter are the historical links to this contemporary genocide?
2. On any given day, our TV programs may carry news of Muslims in India defacing a Hindu temple, or Hindus protesting against the Muslim presence in their midst. What events reviewed in this chapter explain the present friction between Muslims and Hindus in India?

3. Even though Europe eventually got accustomed to the presence of the Ottoman Empire in the Balkan Peninsula and the Anatolian Peninsula, Europeans never considered the Ottomans "one of us." What factors may have influenced the Europeans to think that way?
4. If the Ottoman Empire still existed today in the Anatolian and Balkan Peninsulas, what present-day countries would not exist as independent entities?

BECOMING AN HISTORIAN

Recognizing and Understanding Bias: Consider the issue of eurocentrism, or looking at the world from a European perspective. The Muslim empires in Persia, India, and the Middle East discussed in this chapter are considered by Europeans to be "gunpowder empires," since the Muslims used firearms in their conquests. Does this label reflect a degree of European prejudice toward Muslims, considering that all European empires around the world were also based on gunpowder? Think of another title that could be given to these empires that would not reflect eurocentrism.

Analyzing Information: Choose three rulers—one from the Ottoman Empire, one from the Safavid Empire, and one from the Mughal Empire—that you feel were the best leaders of their time. List the rulers' similarities and differences. Draw three inferences about what made a successful ruler at this period of history. Do the same characteristics apply to rulers in our time? Why or why not?

Primary and Secondary Sources: Review the list of citations at the end of this chapter, and the information given in this chapter's feature boxes. Which are primary sources? Which are secondary sources?

545

religious groups. Students should make reference to content in "Connections To Our World' on page 523.
2. Answers will vary. Student responses should show understanding of pages 530–534, discussion the Muslim Mughal Empire's reign in Hindu India.
3. Answers will vary. Possible responses may include mention that Europe was mostly Christian rather than Muslim and the Ottomans originally came from Central Asian peoples.
4. Answers may vary some. Students must refer to Map 17.1 on page 516 and compare it to current map of the region.

BECOMING AN HISTORIAN

Recognizing and Understanding Bias Answers will vary. By using ameliorative adjectives in the title of the empire, rather than the simple, crude, relatively pejorative word "gunpowder" the title of the empire may be made to seem less eurocentric. An example may be "The Great Muslim Empires."
Analyzing Information Answers will vary, based on choices among the several rulers listed in chapter.
Primary and Secondary Sources Primary sources are those that are direct, such as any quotations cited. Secondary sources are those which are reports made by compiling primary sources. "The Sultan's Elite Slaves" on page 517 is an example of a secondary source and "The Fall of Constantinople" on page 519 is an example of a primary source.

APPLYING SOCIAL STUDIES SKILLS

1. Answers will vary. Responses should refer to Chapter 8 for more information on the two major Islam groups and to pages 526–527 for more specific information on the Shi'ites. A possible response may include that with the present-day high regard for "tolerance" as a virtue, the Shi'ites may not be viewed as favorably by American policy makers.
2. Answers will vary. Responses should refer to page 523 for Ottoman and 529 for Safavid. As a non-Muslim it may be preferable to have lived in Ottoman Empire as they appeared to have been more tolerant of non-Muslims.

3. Drawings will vary. Student drawings should resemble the following maps:
Ottoman Empire, Map 17.1, page 516
Safavid Empire, Map 17.2, page 528
Mughal Empire, Map 17.3, page 535
4. Answers will vary. Student will need map of Eastern Hemisphere with distance scale; canal through Suez made distance much shorter

MAKING TIME AND PLACE CONNECTIONS

1. Answers will vary. Responses may include: Ottoman conquest of Balkans added Muslims to area, setting eventual stage for conflicts between

PLANNING GUIDE

SECTION	KEY TOPICS	PRIMARY SOURCES	ASSESSMENT
1 China at its Height: The Greatness of the Qing pages 547–556	◆ Decline and fall of the Ming dynasty ◆ Growth and decline of the Qing dynasty ◆ China's political, economic and social structures before contact with Europeans	◆ A description of the Jesuit approach to converting Chinese people to Christianity, page 549 ◆ A proclamation of Confucian commandments, page 555	◆ Section Review, page 556 ◆ Section Quiz 18–1, TRB
2 Changing China: Society and Culture pages 556–564	◆ Economic changes in China that resulted from contact with foreign influences ◆ Social structures and family values in China ◆ Cultural achievements and change in China	◆ A description of housing and food in Qing China, page 559 ◆ A selection from *The Dream of The Red Chamber*, page 562	◆ Section Review, page 564 ◆ Section Quiz 18–2, TRB
3 Tokugawa Japan pages 564–572	◆ Unification of Japan ◆ Japan's contact with the West ◆ Causes and effects of the Tokugawa, "Great Peace" ◆ Japanese economic and social systems during the Tokugawa ◆ Japanese culture during the Tokugawa	◆ A description of the introduction of firearms in Japan, page 567 ◆ Two poems by Basho, page 571	◆ Section Review, page 572 ◆ Section Quiz 18–3, TRB

THE EAST ASIAN WORLD (1500 TO 1800)

REPRODUCIBLE ACTIVITIES

Historical Maps

Charts and Graphs

Critical Thinking

Cooperative Learning

Vocabulary

Guided Reading

Reteaching

Enrichment

Performance Assessment

Spanish Key Points and Chapter Summaries

Spanish Vocabulary

Spanish Guided Reading

MULTIMEDIA SUPPORT

TRANSPARENCIES
◆ *World History* Color Transparency Package
◆ Fine Art Color Transparency Package

VIDEO
◆ *World History* Video Library
◆ **CNN**® Annual Video Update

LASERDISC
◆ *Sights and Sounds of History*

AUDIO
◆ *Listening to Literature* audiotape (English and Spanish)
◆ *History of Music* CD

SOFTWARE
◆ WESTEST™
◆ Student Review

CD–ROM
◆ *The Journey of Civilization*
◆ *World History*

INTERNET
◆ Internet Activities

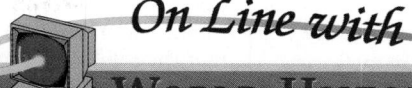

On Line with WORLD HISTORY

Access West's history web site at
http://history.swpco.com
You'll find activities and web sites related to specific topics and chapters in *World History: The Human Odyssey*. Also look for references to helpful web sites at appropriate places throughout this teacher edition.

LESSON PLANNING

You will find detailed daily lesson plans for both traditional class scheduling and **block scheduling** in your Teacher Resource Box.

Not Enough Time?

If you do not have the four or five days recommended to teach this chapter, you may want to focus on the following sections and activities:

◆ Have students skim the chapter to answer the "Questions to Guide Your Reading" on page 547. Discuss their answers, then read the "Conclusion" on page 572.
◆ Do a more in-depth reading about the Ming and Qing dynasties on pages 548–553, economic changes in China on pages 557–558, cultural developments on pages 561–564, the Tokugawa on pages 566–568, and 570–572.

THE EAST ASIAN WORLD
(1500 TO 1800)

18

BUILDING ON CHAPTER 17

To prepare students to study Chapter 18 you may use the following questions and activities.

- Review the poverty situation that contributed to the fall of the Mughals in Persia. Consider the role of poverty in the fall of the Ming dynasty in China.
- Ask students to list ways in which Europeans had an important influence on the course of Indian history. Tell students to expect to find similar impacts resulting from the contact Europeans had with China.
- Trade was an important source of wealth for the Ottoman empire, but it also contributed to corruption within the government. Did trade profits have a similar impact in China?
- In India there was stability under the Mughal Empire during which the lives of many were relatively prosperous. Compare this time in India with the Tokugawa in Japan.

USING THE OPENING STORY

Depending on the ability levels of your students, select from the following questions and activities to reinforce the reading of the opening story.

- Why do many assume that their ideas and products are better than those of foreign peoples?
- Why are attempts to stop change almost certainly doomed to failure?

In 1793, a British official named Lord Macartney led a mission to China. He carried with him British products that he thought would impress the Chinese so much that they would be eager to open their country to trade with Great Britain in order to acquire the products. The Chinese emperor, however, was not impressed: "We possess all things. I set no value on objects strange or clever, and have no use for your country's manufactures." Macartney was shocked. He had believed that the Chinese would recognize, as he said, "that superiority which Englishmen, wherever they go, cannot conceal." An angered Macartney compared the Chinese Empire to "an old, crazy, first-rate man-of-war [naval warship]" that had once awed its neighbors "merely by her bulk and appearance" but was now destined, under poor leadership, to be "dashed to pieces on the shore."

The attitude of the Chinese emperor reflected the Chinese unwillingness to open China to trade with the Euro-

peans. Between 1500 and 1800, China experienced one of its most glorious eras. The empire expanded, and Chinese culture earned the admiration of many European visitors. China seemed unchanging. In reality, however, it was beginning to experience a great deal of change.

Japan, also, was undergoing a period of profound change. Vigorous new leadership at the beginning of the seventeenth century kept the traditional Japanese system alive for almost another 250 years. However, underneath the surface of stability, major changes were taking place in Japanese society.

One of the factors that quickened the pace of change in both China and Japan was contact with the West. At first, both societies opened their doors to Europeans. However, both China and Japan soon closed their doors to foreigners, because they feared the effect of Western ideas. They could not, however, remain closed forever.

◄ *This exquisite vase dates from the Ming dynasty. Its design is typical of the delicate decoration and graceful proportion that made Chinese pottery famous throughout the world.*

ADDITIONAL RESOURCES

The resources listed below can be used to enrich the lessons in this chapter.

BOOKS FOR STUDENTS
The Samurai by S. R. Turnbull. Macmillan.
Shogun by James Clavell, Atheneum.

VIDEOTAPES
"Asia 1600–1800" Series: The World: A Television History Social Studies School Service (800) 421-4246

CD-ROM
"The Silk Road" (DNA Multi-Media) Social Studies School Service (800) 421-4246

QUESTIONS TO GUIDE YOUR READING

1. What caused the downfall of the Ming dynasty?

2. What were the achievements of the emperors Kangxi and Qianlong?

3. How would you describe the major political institutions of the Qing dynasty?

4. What were the major cultural achievements of the Ming and Qing dynasties?

5. Who were the three great unifiers in Japan, and what did they accomplish?

6. How did Tokugawa culture reflect the dynamic changes in Japanese society at the time?

7. How would you compare the role of women in China with the role of women in Japan from 1500 to 1800?

8. How did the Chinese reaction to European contact compare with the Japanese reaction?

OUTLINE

1. CHINA AT ITS HEIGHT: THE GREATNESS OF THE QING

2. CHANGING CHINA: SOCIETY AND CULTURE

3. TOKUGAWA JAPAN

CHINA AT ITS HEIGHT: THE GREATNESS OF THE QING

In 1514, a Portuguese fleet dropped anchor off the coast of China. It was the first direct contact between the Chinese Empire and Europe since the journeys of Marco Polo two hundred years earlier. This event began an era that would eventually change the face of China, and indeed of all Asia.

At the time, the Chinese thought little of the Portuguese arrival. China appeared to be at the height of its power as the most magnificent civilization on the face of the Earth. China's empire stretched from the steppes of Central Asia to the China Sea and from the Gobi Desert to the tropical rain forests of Southeast Asia. From the lofty perspective of the imperial throne in Beijing, the Europeans could be seen as only an unusual form of barbarian. To the Chinese ruler, the rulers of all other countries were simply "younger brothers" of the Chinese emperor, who was viewed as the Son of Heaven.

Marco Polo had first aroused European interest in China in the late thirteenth century. Rumors of a great society in the East also grew as other travelers made their way along the overland Silk Road between China and the West. It was those tales of the riches of the East

547

Answers to QUESTIONS TO GUIDE YOUR READING

1. series of weak rulers, government corruption, inflation, arrival of English and Dutch (pages 549–550)

2. See page 553.

3. flexibility, maintained Ming political system, kept distinct identity devoted to Confucianism (page 553)

4. literature, porcelain, paintings, architecture (pages 561–564).

5. See pages 564–565.

6. See pages 570–572.

7. See page 560 and pages 569–570.

8. See pages 546, 573. China (pages 553–556); Japan (pages 565–566).

FOCUS ON THEMES

Listed below are brief summaries of how the content in this chapter supports the text's key themes.

Politics and History China continued to be ruled by an imperial system. The new ruling dynasty of the Manchus both adopted and adapted the Chinese political system. In Tokugawa Japan, the three unifiers created a somewhat centralized system.

The Role of Ideas Christian missionaries attempted to spread their ideas in both China and Japan. To make these ideas acceptable to the people, the missionaries stressed the similarity between two systems of ideas: Christian morals and Confucian ethics.

Social Life Traditional Chinese society continued, with its strong emphasis on the role of the family. In Japan, rigid class distinctions remained. People were divided into four chief groups: warriors, artisans, peasants, and merchants. Intermarriage between classes was forbidden in theory.

The Importance of Cultural Developments Between 1500 and 1800, both Chinese and Japanese artists kept alive traditional techniques of painting. The rise of the realistic novel was an important literary development.

The Role of Individuals Kangxi and Qianlong were outstanding political leaders who played important roles in the history of the Qing dynasty. The three unifiers in Japan—Oda Nobunaga, Toyotomi Hideyoshi, and Tokugawa Ieyasu—played an important role in creating a centralized government.

FOCUS

OBJECTIVES

After completing this section, students should be able to

1. identify and explain reasons for the decline and fall of the Ming dynasty
2. trace events in the growth and decline of the Qing dynasty
3. describe China's political, economic, and social structures before its contact with Europeans

FOCUS ACTIVITY

Help students understand why a state's decision not to allow the transportation of goods beyond certain boundaries puts its economy at a disadvantage. In 1433 the Chinese government prohibited its ships from sailing beyond the China Sea. Although this policy did prevent Chinese-owned ships from carrying goods to other lands, European captains transported Chinese goods wherever they could be sold. Ask students to discuss why this policy was harmful to China's economy.

LEARNING FROM VISUALS

Answer to the caption question: Students should recognize that this missionary's hair and beard resemble Chinese fashion much more than Western fashion.

548

that spurred Columbus and other adventurers to find a sea route to China.

From the Ming to the Qing

By the time the Portuguese fleet arrived off the coast of China, the Ming dynasty, which ruled from 1369 to 1644, had begun a new era of greatness in Chinese history. Under a series of strong rulers, China extended its rule into Mongolia and central Asia. The Ming even briefly reconquered Vietnam (see Chapter 11). Along the northern frontier, they strengthened the Great Wall and made peace with the nomadic tribes who had troubled China for centuries.

The achievements of the Ming rulers at home were equally impressive. They ran an effective government by making use of the centralized bureaucracy staffed with officials chosen by the civil service examination system (see Chapter 10). Under the Ming rulers, China saw a vast increase in manufactured goods produced in workshops and factories. New crops were introduced, which greatly expanded food production.

At the beginning of the fifteenth century, China seemed ready to open itself up to the wider world. Vast fleets of Chinese ships traveled as far west as the eastern coast of Africa (see Chapter 10). Fighting among people at court undermined the influence of those who favored the project, however, and in 1433 the policy was reversed. Although Chinese junks would continue to sail the South China Sea, they were privately owned and would no longer sail into the open sea. An early European visitor reported that "no one sails the sea from north to south; it is prohibited by the king, in order that the country may not become known."[1]

First Contacts with the West

The Chinese wish to remain unknown was soon shattered when the Portuguese arrived in 1514. However, the Portuguese soon outraged Chinese officials with their behavior and were expelled from Canton. The Chinese called the Portuguese "ocean devils." After negotiations, the Portuguese were allowed to occupy the tiny territory of Macao (muh-COW) as a base of operations. The arrival of the Portuguese had little ini

▲ *This Christian missionary has already adopted Chinese dress. Why would this have made a positive impression upon the Chinese people and government officials? What other evidence do you see in this picture that the missionary has adapted to China?*

tial impact on Chinese society. Direct trade between Europe and China was limited. Portuguese ships became involved in the regional trade network, carrying Chinese silk to Japan in return for Japanese silver.

More important than trade, perhaps, was the exchange of ideas. Christian missionaries had also made the long voyage to China on European merchant ships. The Jesuits were among the most active and the most effective. Many of the early Jesuit missionaries to China were highly educated men who were familiar with scientific developments (see Chapter 19). They brought along clocks and various other instruments

On Line with
WORLD HISTORY *Internet Activity*

Map 18.1   China during the Late Ming Era

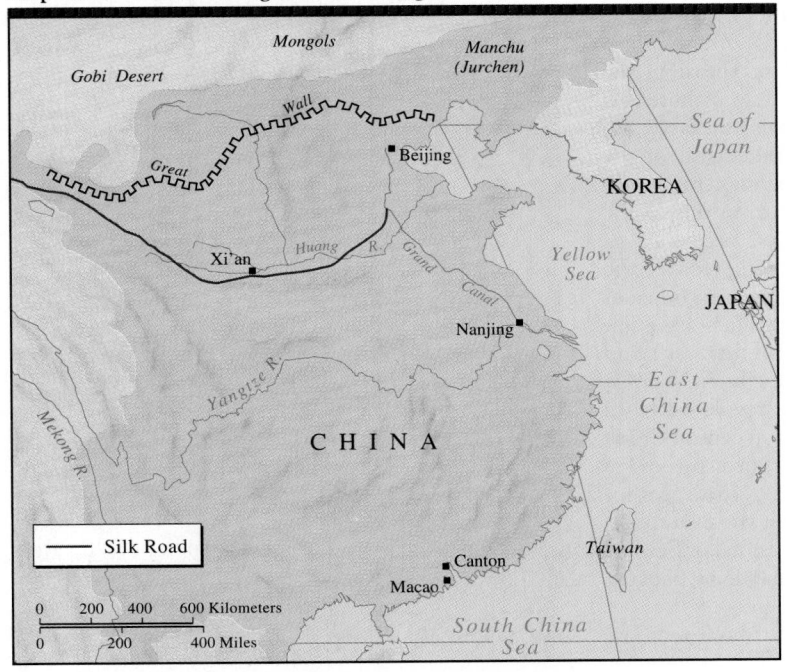

dispose their minds to receive what they could not be persuaded to accept by word of mouth. . . . From the time of their entrance they wore the ordinary Chinese outer garment, which was somewhat similar to their own religious habits; a long robe reaching down to the heels and with very ample sleeves, which are much in favor with the Chinese.[2]

Both sides benefited from this early cultural exchange. Chinese scholars marveled at their ability to read better with European eyeglasses. Christian missionaries were very impressed with many aspects of Chinese civilization, such as the teachings of Confucius, Chinese pottery, and Chinese architecture. Reports back home from these Christian missionaries soon made Europeans even more curious about this great civilization on the other side of the world.

that impressed Chinese officials and made them more open to Western ideas.

The Jesuits used this openness to promote Christianity. To make it easier for the Chinese to accept Christianity, the Jesuits pointed to similarities between Christian morality and Confucian ethics. The Italian priest Matteo (muh-TAY-oh) Ricci described the Jesuit approach:

In order that the appearance of a new religion might not arouse suspicion among the Chinese people, the Jesuit Fathers did not speak openly about religious matters when they began to appear in public. . . . They did, however, try to teach this pagan people in a more direct way, namely, by virtue of their example and by the sanctity of their lives. In this way, they attempted to win the good will of the people and little by little to

The Fall of the Ming

The days of the Ming dynasty were numbered. After a period of prosperity and growth, the Ming gradually began to decline. During the late sixteenth century, a series of weak rulers led to a period of government corruption. The inflow of vast amounts of foreign silver in return for Chinese products led to an alarming increase in inflation. Then the arrival of the English and Dutch disrupted the silver trade. Silver imports dropped, severely straining the Chinese economy. Crop yields declined because of harsh weather. High taxes, caused in part by official corruption, led to peasant unrest and worker violence in urban areas.

As always, internal problems in China went hand in hand with unrest along the northern frontier. The Ming had tried to come to terms with the frontier

STUDYING MAPS

The following questions will help you guide students through their study of Map 18.1.

1. About how long was the Great Wall of China? (approximately 1,000 miles)
2. Why did the Silk Road run immediately to the south of the Great Wall? (Answers will vary; may include that the Wall offered some protection from the frontier tribes in the north.)
3. Would there have been as much need for the Great Wall if there had been no Silk Road? (Answers will vary; some may feel wall was important as protection for cities in southern China.)

tribes by making alliances with them. One of the
alliances was with the Manchus (also known as the
Jurchen). The Manchus (man-CHOOZ), a mixed
farming and hunting people, lived northeast of the
Great Wall in the area known today as Manchuria. At
first the Manchus were content in their own lands and
made little effort to extend their rule south of the
Great Wall. However, as the seventeenth century progressed, the Manchus were tempted to invade as the
problems of the Ming dynasty came to a head.

In the 1630s, a major epidemic greatly reduced the
population in many areas of the country. One observer
in a major city wrote in the summer, "There were few
signs of human life in the streets and all that was heard
was the buzzing of flies."[3] The suffering brought on by
the epidemic helped spark a peasant revolt led by Li
(LEE) Zicheng. Li was a postal worker in central China
who had been fired from his job as part of a cost-saving
measure by the imperial court. In the 1640s, Li enlarged the revolt to extend throughout the country. In
1644, he and his forces occupied the capital of Beijing.
The last Ming emperor committed suicide by hanging
himself from a tree in the palace gardens.

Li was unable to hold his conquest, however. The
overthrow of the Ming dynasty created an opening for
the Manchus. With the help of many military commanders who had deserted from the Ming, the Manchus conquered Beijing. Li Zicheng's army fell apart.
The Manchus then declared the creation of a new
dynasty called the Qing (CHING) (Ch'ing, or Pure).
Once again, China was under foreign rule.

▲ *This scene from Tiangiao, Old Beijing, shows the Manchu
style of dress and hair. What do you think European visitors
thought of the shaved foreheads and braided pigtails?*

The Greatness of the Qing

At first the Chinese resisted the new rulers because of
their ruthless policies and insensitivity to Chinese customs. When rebels seized the island of Taiwan (TIE-
WAWN) 90 miles off the coast of China, the new
Manchu government evacuated the entire coastline
across from the island in preparation for an attack on
the rebels. To make it easier to identify the rebels, the
government also ordered all Chinese males to adopt
Manchu dress and hairstyles. All Chinese males were to

shave their foreheads and braid their hair in pigtails.
Those who refused were to be executed. As a popular
saying put it, "Lose your hair or lose your head."

The Manchus were eventually able to adapt to Chinese conditions, however. They thought it wise to
adopt the Chinese political system and were gradually
accepted by most Chinese as the legitimate rulers of
the country. The Qing were blessed with a series of
strong early rulers. They pacified the country, corrected

Map 18.2   The Qing Empire in the Eighteenth Century

COMPARING
TIME PERIODS

   When Marco Polo
returned from China, few
people believed his stories of
the wealth and grandeur of
the Chinese civilization. Ask
students why the European
merchants were believers
when They returned from
China. *(They had seen the
wealth and returned with Chinese goods.)*

COMPARING
TIME PERIODS

   Ask students to compare
government policies established by Muslims who conquered India in the four-
teenth century (discussed in
Chapter 11) and the policies
of the Manchus in China.
Why might a government
based on native systems be
more effective than one that
brought about radical
change?

Multimedia Support

   TRANSPARENCY
   18–2, Qing Empire
   in the Eighteenth
   Century (Map
   18.2)

the most serious social and economic ills, and restored peace and prosperity.

Two Prominent Rulers

Two Qing monarchs—Kangxi (KANG-SHEE) and Qianlong (chee-UN-LUNG)—ruled China for well over a hundred years, from the middle of the seventeenth century to the end of the eighteenth century. They were responsible for much of the greatness of Manchu China.

Kangxi, who ruled from 1661 to 1722, was perhaps the greatest ruler in Chinese history. He came to the throne at the age of seven. Blessed with diligence, political skill, and a strong character, he took charge of the government while still in his teens and reigned for 61 years. A dedicated ruler, Kangxi rose at dawn and worked until late at night. He wrote, "One act of negligence may cause sorrow all through the country, and one moment of negligence may result in trouble for hundreds and thousands of generations." Kangxi calmed the unrest along the northern and western frontiers by force. As an active patron of the arts and

STUDYING MAPS

   The following questions will help you guide students through their study of Map 18.2.

1. What were the dimensions of the Qing Empire? *(approximately 2,000 miles by 2,500 miles)*
2. How much larger than the empire itself

was the area that paid tributes to the empire? *(approximately another one-fourth its size)*

3. What geographic features may have prevented the Qing Empire from dominating even more land? *(possibly the Himalayan Mts.)*

▲ *Emperor Qianlong is shown here in his dragon robe, which only the emperor or Son of Heaven and the empress were allowed to wear. The dragon robe was usually made of yellow silk and decorated with five-clawed dragons, which represent the emperor. What do you think the waves and rocks represent?*

▲ *The First Empress of Emperor Qianlong is shown here in her dragon robe. These robes were decorated with silver, gold, and pearls, and it took over two years to complete just one robe. All high officials wore necklaces of 108 beads, as shown here.*

letters, he gained the support of scholars throughout the country. All in all, he made the Qing dynasty acceptable to the Chinese people.

During Kangxi's reign, the efforts of the Christian missionaries—Dominicans and Franciscans, as well as Jesuits—reached their height. The emperor was quite tolerant of the Christians. Several hundred officials became Catholics, as did an estimated 300,000 ordinary Chinese. Ultimately, however, the Christian effort was undermined by fighting among the religious orders themselves. To make it easier for the Chinese to convert to Catholicism, the Jesuits had allowed the new Catholics to continue the practice of ancestor worship. Jealous Dominicans and Franciscans (who had fewer converts) complained to the pope, who condemned the practice. After the death of Kangxi, his successor began to suppress Christian activities throughout China.

MORE ABOUT . . . *Kangxi*

A perennial problem for monarchs is choosing a suitable successor, and for an emperor with many wives, and thus many children, the situation is further complicated. Kangxi had thirteen sons who had some claim to the throne. Kangxi, who became emperor at age thirteen amidst some controversy, wanted to prevent a similar situation for his heir. Early in his reign he designated his oldest son, Yin-reng, as his successor. Despite an education that was to provide him with both Confucian virtues and the best Manchu qualities, Kangxi heard rumors that his son was, in the words of one historian "erratic, violent, and cruel." The son was haughty, and even talked of killing his father, and staging a coup. It was difficult for Kangxi to determine the truth since most of his court officials feared punish-

Qianlong, who ruled from 1736 to 1795, was another outstanding Qing ruler. Like Kangxi, Qianlong was known for his diligence, tolerance, and intellectual curiosity. He, too, used vigorous military action against the restless tribes along the frontier. His efforts to promote economic prosperity, administrative efficiency, and artistic excellence won the approval of many Chinese. The result was continued growth for the Manchu Empire throughout much of the eighteenth century.

Qing Political Institutions

Certainly, one reason for the success of the Manchus was their ability to adapt to Chinese conditions. The Qing maintained the Ming political system with very few changes. The most obvious difference, of course, was that the Manchus, like the Mongols earlier, were ethnically and culturally different from their subject population. The Qing dealt with this reality in two ways.

First, the Qing tried to preserve their distinct identity within Chinese society. The Manchus, who made up only 2 percent of the entire population, were defined legally as distinct from everyone else in China. The Manchu nobility kept their aristocratic privileges, and their economic base was protected by large landholdings and revenues provided from the state treasury. Other Manchus were given farmland and were organized into military units, called banners. They were stationed as separate units in various strategic positions throughout China. These "bannermen" were the chief fighting force of the empire. However, a Chinese "green standard" army served as a local police force.

The second way in which the Qing dealt with the problem of ethnic and cultural differences was to bring Chinese into the top ranks of the imperial administration. They created a system, known as a **dyarchy,** in which all important government positions were shared equally by Chinese and Manchus. For example, of the six members of the grand secretariat (see Chapter 10), three were Manchu and three were Chinese. Manchus and Chinese also shared responsibilities at the provincial level. Provincial governors were usually Chinese, but two provinces were often linked under a governor-general who was a Manchu. The willingness of the Manchus to share power won the support of many Chinese. At the same time, many of the Manchus themselves increasingly became part of Chinese civilization.

Members of the Qing dynasty tried to establish that they were China's rightful rulers by stressing their devotion to the principles of Confucianism. Emperor Kangxi, for example, studied the sacred Confucian classics. He issued a "Sacred Edict" that proclaimed to the empire the importance of the moral values established by Confucius (see "You Are There: The Emperor Proclaims the Sixteen Confucian Commandments").

China on the Eve of the Western Onslaught

In some ways, China was at the height of its power and glory in the mid-eighteenth century. However, it was also under Qianlong that the first signs of the internal decay of the Qing dynasty began to appear. Qing military campaigns along the frontier cost much money and placed heavy demands on the treasury. As the emperor grew older, he became less careful in choosing his officials and he fell under the influence of corrupt elements at court. With increasing frequency, these corrupt officials took funds intended for military use, thus angering military officials.

Higher taxes and corrupt officials led to unrest in rural areas. At the same time, growing pressure on the land because of population growth had led to economic hardship for many peasants. The heart of the unrest was located in central China. Here, unhappy peasants who had recently been settled on poor farmland launched a revolt known as the White Lotus Rebellion (1796 to 1804). The revolt was suppressed, but at great expense. It was a warning that the glory years of the Manchus were ending.

Unfortunately for China, the Qing dynasty was declining just as Europe was putting on pressure for more trade. The first conflict had come from the north, where Russian traders sought skins and furs. Formal diplomatic relations between China and Russia were established in 1689 and provided for regular trade between the two countries. Forty years later, a new treaty confirmed Chinese rule over all of Mongolia in

ment if they told the truth about Yinreng. Eventually Kangxi came to believe that Yinreng was guilty of indiscretions and had him thrown in jail. Unfortunately, Kangxi believed that his son was not truly guilty, but bewitched, and so he soon released him from jail, only to have Yinreng return to his evil ways. As Kangxi lay dying, he was in the company of another son, Yongzheng, who said that he was his father's choice as emperor. Conveniently, there were no other witnesses. Yongzheng had the support of the Peking guard so Yinreng and two other brothers were jailed and died shortly thereafter. It is likely that they died either from mistreatment or else they were killed. Yongzheng ruled ably from 1723–1735.

CLASS DISCUSSION

Ask students to discuss whether Chinese people were really being converted to Catholicism if they were allowed to continue the practice of ancestor worship. Might the Jesuits have been more interested in competing with other orders than in actually spreading Catholicism?

REINFORCING VOCABULARY

Ask students to identify potential benefits and problems that might result from creating a government based on *dyarchy,* like the one in Qing China. Although this system worked well in China, is there any guarantee that it would work in other states?

OPPOSING VIEWPOINTS

Ask students to analyze and then debate the following statement. Do they believe it is always true or only true in some situations?

Official toleration of corruption is the first sign of a state's decline.

How does the fall of the Qing dynasty and the Roman Empire tend to support this idea?

LEARNING FROM VISUALS

Ask students to explain why it was unique to find the British, Dutch, and in some cases, French flags flying over the same warehouse in China. Why would it have been unlikely to find this in any other part of the world in the eighteenth century?

Answers to the caption questions: (upper left) Chinese sampans, a type of flat-bottomed skiff, and junks, with their sails aloft, are anchored in the river.

(lower right) The Chinese were undoubtedly stunned at the English lack of respect for their emperor. In turn, the English might have been amazed at the length of this procession and the elaborate preparations taken before the meeting.

CLASS DISCUSSION

Ask students to discuss the extent to which they would follow social expectations in other countries. In some cultures it is bad manners to show the bottom of your foot. In others, young people are expected to back away from their elders rather than turn around and show their backs. There are societies in which men always hold hands if they are having a discussion about business. Would students do these things? Would they kowtow to the emperor?

▲ *The Chinese court strictly limited the movement of Europeans in China. There were, however, warehouses and residences for the foreign community. In this painting, British and Dutch flags fly over the area in Canton where foreigners resided and worked. What kinds of boats are shown in the river?*

return for formal trading rights and permanent residence for Russian merchants in Beijing.

Dealing with the foreigners who arrived by sea was more difficult. By the end of the seventeenth century, the English had replaced the Portuguese as the dominant force in European trade. Operating through the

▶ *This painting depicts the meeting of Emperor Qianlong with Lord Macartney in 1793. Why do you think the Chinese were surprised at Macartney's refusal to kowtow to the emperor? What do you think the English response to the emperor's preparation for this meeting would have been?*

East India Company, which served as both a trading unit and the administrator of English territories in Asia, the English established their first trading post, at Canton, in 1699. Over the next decades, trade with China—and especially the export of tea and silk to England—increased rapidly.

At first the Qing government granted trade privileges to the Europeans in exchange for periodic payments to the government at Beijing. Eventually, however, the Qing rulers adopted a new system. To limit contacts between Europeans and Chinese, the Qing confined all European traders to a small island just outside the city walls of Canton. Moreover, the traders could reside there only from October through March and could deal only with a limited number of Chinese firms licensed by the government.

For a while, the British accepted this system. After all, it brought considerable profit to the East India Company. By the end of the eighteenth century, however, some British traders had begun to demand access to cities other than Canton along the Chinese coast. At the same time, the Chinese government was under pressure from merchants to open China to British manufactured goods.

In 1793, a British mission visited Beijing to press for liberalization of trade restrictions. However, Emperor Qianlong expressed no interest in British products. As

COOPERATIVE LEARNING ACTIVITY

Divide the class into three groups. One group will research Legalism, one Taoism, and the third Confucianism. Their task is to assemble a study guide, one page in length, that outlines the chief ideas of each of these philosophies. The focus should be on each philosophy's view of the family, government, education, art and the individual in society. The material can be presented in a lecture/discussion format or a debate format

in which students argue for their particular philosophy. *(Legalism believed that human nature was evil and that a strong government should demand absolute control. Confucius argued that the family was the basic unit of society and that upright character was a chief goal. Taoism's core is the interplay of Yin and Yang. Government is corrupting according to Taoists, and people should strive to live in harmony with nature.)*

YOU ARE THERE

The Emperor Proclaims the Sixteen Confucian Commandments

Although the Qing dynasty was of foreign origin, its rulers found Confucian maxims (proverbial sayings) convenient for maintaining the social order. In 1670, the great emperor Kangxi issued the Sacred Edict to make known Confucian values among the common people. The following edict was read publicly in every village in the country:

The Sacred Edict

1. Esteem most highly filial piety and brotherly submission, in order to give due importance to the social relations.
2. Behave with generosity toward your family, in order to illustrate harmony.
3. Cultivate peace and concord in your neighborhoods, in order to prevent quarrels.
4. Recognize the importance of farming, in order to ensure a sufficiency of food.
5. Show that you prize moderation and economy, in order to prevent the lavish waste of your means.
6. Encourage schools, in order to make correct the practice of the scholar.
7. Eliminate strange doctrines, in order to exalt the correct doctrine.
8. Lecture on the laws, in order to warn the ignorant.
9. Show courtesy, in order to make manners and customs good.
10. Labor diligently at your proper callings, in order to stabilize the will of the people.
11. Instruct sons and younger brothers, in order to keep them from doing what is wrong.

Emperor Kangxi was a capable and hard-working administrator. Seated on his royal throne, the emperor is pictured wearing his ceremonial dragon robe. What other symbols of royal power do you see in this picture?

(continued)

SPECIAL NEEDS: *Multi-modal: Visual/Auditory*

Answers to SECTION REVIEW

2. (a) all important government positions shared by Chinese and Manchus

3. (a) Dynasty from 1369 to 1644; (b) An Italian priest promoting Christianity; (c) a mixture of farming and hunting people; (d) led a peasant revolt in 1644, led to the downfall of the Ming dynasty (e) Manchu dynasty; (f) Qing monarch, 1661 to 1722; (g) Qing monarch, 1736 to 1795; (h) Manchus, fighting force of the Qing empire; (i) revolt started by unhappy peasants

4. (a) tales of great riches; (b) increase in manufactured goods; new crops introduced; (c) brought clocks and other instruments; pointed to similarities between Christian and Confucian ethics; (d) series of weak rulers; inflow of foreign silver led to inflation; English and Dutch disrupted the silver trade; crop yields declined; high taxes led to peasant unrest, violence; (e) Qing had strong early leaders; pacified country, corrected social and economic problems, restored peace and property

5. Answers will vary.

YOU ARE THERE

The Emperor Proclaims the Sixteen Confucian Commandments,
continued

12. Put a stop to false accusations, in order to preserve the honest and good.
13. Warn against sheltering deserters, in order to avoid being involved in their punishment.
14. Fully remit your taxes, in order to avoid being pressed for payment.
15. Unite in hundreds (territorial units), in order to put an end to thefts and robbery.
16. Remove anger, in order to show the importance due to the person and life.

1. What does the emphasis Confucius placed on the family reveal about Chinese society?

2. Rewrite any two of the sixteen Confucian commandments in simpler language or write a common proverb that has the same meaning. Example: Respect your parents and elder brothers. These are important social laws.

---

the emperor noted in his letter to King George III, China had no need of "your country's manufactures". The Chinese would later pay for their rejection of the British request (see Chapter 25).

 SECTION REVIEW

1. **Locate:**
   (*a*) China,   (*b*) Japan,   (*c*) China Sea,
   (*d*) Gobi Desert,   (*e*) Beijing,   (*f*) Mongolia,
   (*g*) Vietnam,   (*h*) Canton,   (*i*) Macao,
   (*j*) Taiwan

2. **Define:**
   (*a*) dyarchy

3. **Identify:**
   (*a*) Ming dynasty,   (*b*) Matteo Ricci,
   (*c*) Manchus,   (*d*) Li Zicheng,   (*e*) Qing,
   (*f*) Kangxi,   (*g*) Qianlong,   (*h*) bannermen,
   (*i*) White Lotus Rebellion

4. **Recall:**
   (*a*) What spurred Columbus and other adventurers to find a sea route to China?

(*b*) What changes occurred in China during the Ming dynasty?
(*c*) How did the Jesuits promote Christianity without offending the Chinese?
(*d*) What were some of the problems that led to the downfall of the Ming dynasty?
(*e*) What do you think were the main reasons the Qing were able to rule China successfully?

5. **Think Critically:** Compare the Ming and Qing dynasties. Can you think of similarities that caused the fall of their dynasties?

CHANGING CHINA: SOCIETY AND CULTURE

Between 1500 and 1800, during the late Ming and early Qing dynasties, China experienced much change. This was especially evident in the economic sphere.

CLOSE

Lead students in a discussion of the 'Focus' objectives identified on page 548. Emphasize the unsuccessful efforts of the Chinese to resist European influences.

So What ??

*If your students question the importance of information on **population growth in China**, tell them . . .*

China's population in 1993 was estimated at about 1.2 billion. This staggering figure has led to governmental policies that we would consider an invasion of privacy. Policy states that each married couple may have only one child. Couples who break this rule have to pay higher taxes and may have difficulty obtaining better housing. Chinese belief is that the family line is carried on through the male so having only a female child risks ending centuries of a family lineage. This policy also means that there will be no first cousins in China! How would such a policy be received in the United States? Do students think there is a need for population control?

Economic Changes

During the period from 1500 to 1800, China remained the mostly agricultural society it had been throughout recorded history. Nearly 85 percent of the people were farmers. In the south, the main crop was rice, which requires a wet climate and is grown in water. In the north, the main crop was wheat or other crops grown on dry land but dependent on regular rainfall. As they had always been, most Chinese were still small farmers.

Although China was still a country of villages with a few scattered urban centers, the economy was changing. The first change involved a rapid increase in the population. For centuries, China's population had varied within a range of 50 million to 100 million. It was higher in times of peace and lower in periods of foreign invasion and internal chaos. During the late Ming and the early Qing dynasties, the population increased. It went from an estimated 70 million to 80 million in 1390 to more than 300 million at the end of the eighteenth century. (Today China's population is 1.2 billion.)

There were probably several reasons for this population increase. A long period of peace and stability under the early Qing dynasty was one reason. Also, the use of new crops from the Americas, including peanuts, sweet potatoes, and maize, provided more food. The planting of a new species of rice from Southeast Asia also increased the food supply. Because the new kind of rice grew faster than existing varieties, overall production increased.

The population increase meant greater population pressure on the land and led to smaller farms. The imperial court tried to make land available by keeping wealthy landowners from holding too much land. By the eighteenth century, however, almost all the land that could be irrigated was already being farmed. As a result, the problems of rural hunger and lack of land became more and more serious. These hardships, in turn, led to rural unrest and revolts.

Another change that took place during the late Ming and early Qing dynasties was the steady growth of manufacturing and trade. These had existed in China since early times, but they had always been carefully limited by state controls and state monopolies. Now, taking advantage of the long era of peace and prosperity, mer-

CONNECTIONS
AROUND THE WORLD

A Population Explosion   Between 1700 and 1800, many areas in the world experienced a population explosion. In Europe, China, India, and the Muslim world, the number of people grew dramatically. Europe, for example, went from 120 million people to almost 200 million by 1800; China, from less than 200 million to 300 million during the same period.

Four factors were important in causing this population explosion. First, better growing conditions affected wide areas of the world and enabled people to produce more food. Second, by the eighteenth century, people had begun to develop immunities to epidemic diseases. The spread of people by ship after 1500 had led to devastating epidemics. For example, the arrival of Europeans in Mexico led to smallpox, measles, and chicken pox among a native population that had no immunities to European diseases. In 1500, between 11 and 20 million people lived in the area of Mexico; by 1650, only 1.5 million remained. By 1750, however, plagues and epidemic diseases were no longer as devastating in Europe, India, China, and the Middle East.

A third factor in population increase came from new food sources. The use of American food crops, such as sweet potatoes in China, corn in Africa and Europe, and the potato in northern Europe and Russia, provided new sources of nutrition. Finally, the use of new weapons based on gunpowder allowed states to control larger territories and ensure a new degree of order. Less violence led to fewer deaths.

chants and manufacturers began to expand their operations beyond their local provinces. Trade in silk, metal and wood products, porcelain, cotton goods, and cash crops such as cotton and tobacco grew rapidly.

With the expansion of trade came guild organizations on a nationwide basis. Guilds of merchants were set up in cities and market towns throughout the

◆ 2 ◆

FOCUS

OBJECTIVES

After completing this section, students should be able to

1. identify and explain economic changes in China
2. describe the social structure and role of the family
3. identify and evaluate Chinese cultural achievements

Multimedia Support

TRANSPARENCY
18–1, The Most Populous Nations

FOCUS ACTIVITY

Ask students to research past population figures and assemble them in a chart. Begin with the population figures on this page. Students will find that world population grew at a moderate until 1650. Over the last 350 years there has been tremendous growth.

CONNECTIONS
AROUND OUR WORLD

ACROSS THE CURRICULUM

Math Ask students what percentage of population increase occurred in Europe in the eighteenth century. *(66%)* In China? *(approximately 50%)*

On Line with WORLD HISTORY *Internet Activity*

You may want to have your students visit the following URL, where they will find information and additional web site resources to enhance their study of this chapter.
Council on East Asian Libraries
http://darkwing.uoregon.edu/ ~felsing/ceal/welcome.html

This is a huge web site containing links and information guides to East Asian countries. These guides include culture and history, art, and politics.
Due to the ever-changing nature of the World Wide Web, see the West History web site, **http://history.swpco.com** for regular updates of the URLs in this text.

TEACH

REINFORCING VOCABULARY

Ask students to list and explain reasons why commercial capitalism works best when there are few government restrictions on what businesses are able to do. Also ask them to identify areas where government intervention in the economy is needed. Why did the tax structure in China tend to discourage commercial capitalism?

CLASS DISCUSSION

Ask students to write an evaluation of the Confucian concepts of the five relationships. Do they believe these concepts helped or hindered China's ability to deal successfully with Europeans?

---

country. The guilds provided legal protection, as well as food and lodging, for merchants from different provinces. Foreign trade also expanded. Chinese merchants, mainly from the coastal provinces of the south, set up wide-ranging contacts with countries in Southeast Asia.

Despite the growth in trade and manufacturing, China failed to develop the kind of commercial capitalism (a system of private enterprise based on profits from trade) that was emerging in Europe. Some key differences between China and Europe hindered the emergence of capitalism in China. In the first place, middle-class merchants and manufacturers in China were not as independent as they were in Europe. Free cities like those that had long existed in Europe had not emerged in China. In other words, trade and manufacturing remained under the firm control of the state. Moreover, many Chinese, both at court and in society at large, looked down on trade and manufacturing as inferior to the traditional practice of farming. The state reflected this attitude by levying heavy taxes on manufacturing and trade while keeping farming taxes low.

Daily Life in Qing China

For the most part, daily life in China under the Ming and early Qing dynasties was not much different from what it had been in early periods of Chinese history.

The Chinese Family

As in earlier periods, Chinese society under the Qing dynasty was organized around the family. Above all, the family provided room and board. The family was also the chief source of education for the young, of support for unmarried daughters, and of care for the elderly. It was even a focus for religious belief and ritual. At the same time, all family members were expected to sacrifice their individual desires for the benefit of the family as a whole.

The famous Confucian concept of the "five relationships" continued to determine the hierarchical nature of the family. Children were expected to obey

their parents, just as all subjects were expected to obey their rulers. Wives were expected to obey their husbands; younger children, their older brothers and sisters; and friends, the wishes of older friends. Within the family, the oldest male was king. His wishes had to be obeyed by all family members.

For many Chinese, the effects of these values were most apparent in the choice of a marriage partner. Marriages were normally arranged for the benefit of the family, either by the parents or often by a go-between (someone outside the family). The groom and bride were usually not consulted. Frequently, they did not meet until the marriage ceremony. Under such conditions, love was not very important. In fact, love was seen as a distraction that might keep the husband and wife from their chief responsibility to the larger family unit.

Not all obligations were on the side of the children. The husband was expected to provide support for his wife and children. Like the emperor, he was supposed to treat those in his care with respect and compassion. All too often, however, the male head of the family cared mostly about his own privileges rather than his responsibilities.

In many cases, the head of the family would be responsible for more than just his own wife and children. The ideal family unit in Qing China was the extended family, in which as many as three or even four generations lived under the same roof. When sons married, they brought their wives to live with them in the family home. Wealthy families would add a separate section to the house for the new family unit. Unmarried daughters would also remain in the house (see "Focus on Everyday Life: Housing and Food in Qing China"). Those who married left to live with their husbands. Aging parents and grandparents remained under the same roof and were cared for until they died by younger members of the household. This ideal did not always correspond to reality, however. Many families did not have enough land to support a large household. Probably only about 40 percent actually lived in extended families.

Extended families remained important in early Qing China for the same reasons as in earlier times. The Chinese needed large families to help with the growing of rice, which took much labor. These families also

---

MORE ABOUT . . . the Confucian Five Relationships

The text explains the five relationships, a crucial aspect of Confucianism. A related Confucian idea is the three submissions of women. When a woman is young, she should submit to her father; when a wife, to her husband; and, when a widow, to her son. The idea that a woman must submit to someone throughout her life tends to be repugnant to female students, while some

male chauvinists might smugly enjoy the idea. The problem for the male chauvinists is the idea of reciprocity, the system of mutual obligations. Thus while a widow must submit to her son, the son is also required to care for his mother after his father's death. What seems to be a hindrance to women may in fact turn out to have some advantages to her in her older years.

FOCUS ON EVERYDAY LIFE
Housing and Food in Qing China

Housing varied considerably in Qing China according to a family's economic status. Prosperous families lived in larger houses. According to a sixteenth-century Spanish visitor, the houses of the wealthy were often "very large and they occupy a large space, for they have courtyards and more courtyards, and great halls and many chambers and kitchen-gardens." One mansion had "a very fine pond all paved with flagstones, and with arbours and paths above the water, and very fine tables made from single slabs of stone." The houses of the well-to-do might be raised above the ground on stone foundations and have brick floors and tiled ceilings. The houses of the ordinary Chinese were much smaller, consisting of two rooms with a courtyard in between. In urban areas, the side of the house that faced the street might be used as a store.

The Chinese diet remained the same as it had been for centuries. The basic foods continued to be millet or other dry crops in the north and rice in the south. Fruits, vegetables, and occasionally some fish or meat added some variety. For most people, however, such additions to the daily plate of millet or rice were rare. One Spanish diplomat remarked: "The principal food of all Chinese is rice, for although they have wheat and sell bread kneaded therefrom, yet they do not eat it save as if it were a fruit. Their chief bread is cooked rice, and they even make a wine from it."

The same Spanish diplomat was astounded by yet another Chinese eating custom—the use of chopsticks. He said:

They eat seated at tables, but they do not use table-cloths or napkins; for they do not touch with their fingers anything that they are going to eat, but they pick up everything with two long little sticks. They are so expert in this, that they can take any

▲ *This palace scene from China reflects the serene beauty that was revered in court life. Note the simple, elegant beauty of the women's gowns and the symmetry of the outdoor garden. How does this compare to scenes of town or rural life in China and Japan during this time?*

thing, however small, and carry it to their mouth, even if it is round, like plums and other such fruits. . . . Instead of bread they eat three or four dishes of cooked rice, which they likewise eat with their chopsticks, even though somewhat hoggishly.

1. Describe the houses of the average Chinese in the sixteenth century.

2. What did the diet of sixteenth-century Chinese consist of?

3. Compare the diet of sixteenth-century Chinese with your own diet. How are they similar? How are they different?

So What ??

CLASS DISCUSSION

Ask students to discuss the societies they studied in India and Africa that were also based on extended families. Why do students think this sort of family structure was and is still more often found in rural areas than in cities?

COMPARING TIME PERIODS

Ask students to compare how women were treated in China with the treatment they received in Europe under the code of chivalry (discussed in Chapter 12). Although European women were treated differently, do students believe that European women were treated better? Were they considered equal to men? How are women in Europe treated today compared to China? Which group has made the greater gains?

provided security for the parents when they were too old to work in the fields. Sons were especially valuable. They had strong backs and would raise their own families under the parental roof.

The extended family offered benefits to the children as well. Children had few opportunities for employment outside the family, so sons had little choice but to remain with their parents and help on the land. A wealthy family would manage to purchase additional lands. A poorer one would be forced to survive on its existing fields.

Beyond the extended family was the clan. Sometimes called a lineage, a clan consisted of dozens, or even hundreds, of extended and nuclear families. These families were linked by a clan council of elders and a variety of common social and religious activities.

The clan served a number of useful purposes. Because Chinese society did not have welfare or unemployment benefits, individual families had to survive on their own. In bad times family members could go hungry or even starve. The clan system made it possible for wealthier families to help poorer relatives. Sons of poor families might even be invited to study in a school established in the home of a more prosperous relative. If the young man succeeded and became an official, he would be expected to provide favors for the entire clan.

The Role of Women

In traditional China, women were considered to be inferior to men. A sixteenth-century Spanish visitor to South China observed that Chinese women were "very secluded and virtuous, and it was a very rare thing for us to see a woman in the cities and large towns, unless it was an old crone [withered old woman]."[4] Women were more visible, the visitor said, in rural areas, where they frequently could be seen working in the fields.

The concept of female inferiority had deep roots in Chinese history. The Chinese believed that only a male could carry on sacred family rituals and that only males had the ability to govern others. Only males could have a formal education and pursue a career in government or scholarship. Within the family system,

the wife was clearly below the husband. Legally, she could not divorce her husband or inherit property. The husband, in contrast, could divorce his wife if she did not produce male heirs. He could also take a second wife, as well as a concubine for his pleasure.

The lower position of women within the family also involved the children. Female children were less wanted because they were not as physically strong as males. Moreover, the parents of females would have to pay a dowry to the parents of the daughters' future husbands. Female children normally did not receive an education. In times when food was in short supply, daughters might even be put to death.

Although women were clearly held to be inferior to men in theory, this was not always the case in practice. Capable women often played strong roles within the family. Women were often in charge of educating the children and handling the family budget. Some women of the upper class also received training in the Confucian classics, although the length of their schooling was generally shorter than that of males. Women also could not hope for careers as officials, no matter how much schooling they received.

All in all, life for women in traditional China was no doubt difficult. In Chinese novels, women were treated as maids or as love objects. They were usually under the domination of their husbands and mothers-in-law. In some cases the bullying was so brutal that suicide appeared to be the only way out.

An especially painful symbol of women's subordination was the tradition of **foot binding.** The feet of female infants were often deliberately deformed by a binding process that not only was exceedingly painful but also distorted the bones and hindered walking for life. Foot binding was done at first to prevent women from wandering and being unfaithful to their husbands. Over a period of time, however, small feet came to be considered attractive. Poets, for example, compared a woman's foot to a lily. An estimated one-half to two-thirds of the females in China were subjected to the practice. Peasant women were often spared, especially in rice-growing regions, where their labor in the fields was badly needed. The custom was not legally prohibited until the creation of the first Chinese republic, at the beginning of the twentieth century.

SPECIAL NEEDS: *Visual*

Have students recall the role of women in China. Contrast their recollections with the role of men in China. As a class make a time line showing the gradual emergence of the Chinese woman as an "equal" to a Chinese man. Now, have students chart the same information for women of any other culture. Students should support their information by using the encylopedia or other reliable source. Have students cut out pictures of high-ranking women and write a short biography of each. For popular government or business figures, glue the pictures to a card, and write the name and position on the back. Have students practice recognizing famous women and explain what they do or have done.

▲ *The practice of foot binding was a cruel one that continued into the twentieth century. The feet of female children were bound with cloth (silk if the family was wealthy) so that the foot would not develop and grow normally. The small foot was considered beautiful. What do you think about the resulting deformity?*

Cultural Developments

During the late Ming and the early Qing dynasties, traditional culture in China reached new heights of achievement. With the rise of a wealthy urban class, the demand for art, porcelain, textiles, and literature increased.

The Rise of the Chinese Novel

Until the fourteenth century, prose literature (that is, writing other than poetry) was dominated by styles that had been used for centuries and was written by and for an educated audience. As in Europe, popular literature (that is, writing for the masses) consisted primarily of oral traditions, folktales, folk songs, and village theater. During the Ming dynasty, a new form of literature arose that eventually evolved into the modern Chinese novel. Works in this literary form were enormously popular, especially among well-to-do urban dwellers.

The new kind of fiction was characterized by a realism that resulted in vivid portraits of Chinese society.

Many of the stories sympathized with society's poor and often helpless maidens and dealt with such crucial issues as love, money, marriage, and power. Most of these tales had a moral lesson. The bad were punished and the good rewarded.

Two works stand out as examples of the new Chinese novel: *The Golden Lotus* and *The Dream of the Red Chamber*. The late Ming Era witnessed the emergence of realistic novels featuring sharp social comments. *The Golden Lotus* was a cutting look at the decadent, or self-indulgent, aspects of the late Ming society. Considered by many to be the first realistic social novel, *The Golden Lotus* depicts the corrupt life of a wealthy landlord who cruelly manipulates those around him for sex, money, and power. The novel describes the daily lives of an extended Chinese family, including the patriarch, his six wives, and numerous concubines and servants. In this work, the villain is not punished for his evil ways. Justice is served instead by the misfortunes that his descendants experience.

Even today, *The Dream of the Red Chamber* is generally considered to be China's most distinguished popular novel. Published in 1791, it tells of the tragic love between two young people caught in the financial and moral disintegration of a powerful Chinese clan. It is set against the background of daily life in a wealthy eighteenth-century family. The novel weaves together the stories of thirty main characters from a cast of over four hundred. The main characters are seen up close, with all their strengths and weaknesses. The hero and the heroine represent the decline of a family. Their ends are equally tragic: she dies, and he has an unhappy marriage to another. Although the novel is set in a different time, the humanity of the characters still speaks directly to us today (see "Our Literary Heritage: *The Dream of the Red Chamber*").

The Art of the Ming and the Qing

During the Ming and the early Qing dynasties, China produced its last outpouring of traditional artistic brilliance. Most of the creative work was modeled on past examples. Nevertheless, the art of this period is impressive for its technical perfection and breathtaking quality.

CLASS DISCUSSION

Ask students to discuss the following statement. Do they believe it is true? If it is true could the same be said of television programming in the United States? Would this bode well for our future?

A good way to predict the future direction of a society is to look at its popular fiction.

LEARNING FROM VISUALS

Although many Americans are horrified by the idea of foot binding, they are not offended by women or men undergoing cosmetic surgery. Some television and movie stars have gone so far as to have ribs removed to appear thin. Do students believe this represents a double standard? Would they consider having their feet bound? Would they consider plastic surgery?

Answer to the caption question: You might wish to guide students in a discussion of the role women were expected to accept in China, and have students contrast foot-binding with modern day fashion and ideals of beauty. Should women jeopardize their health and well-being, or be forced to do so, in order to be perceived as beautiful?

RECOMMENDED READING

For an excellent introduction to the Chinese literature of this period, consult the classic *An Introduction to Chinese Literature* by Liu Wu-chi (Indiana, 1966). For the best translation of *The Dream of the Red Chamber* see Chi-chen Wang, revised ed. (New York, 1958). For a concise discussion of the novel, see *The Dream of the Red Chamber: A Critical Study*, by Jeanne Knoerle, S.P. (Indiana, 1972). To explore Chinese history through its art, see the beautifully illustrated *China: A History in Art*, by B. Smith and W. Weng, Revised ed. (New York, 1979). For a concise and comprehensive introduction to the Chinese art of this period see *The Arts of China* by M. Sullivan, 3rd ed. (Berkeley, 1984). For a beautifully illustrated text on Chinese Imperial art see *Son of Heaven: Imperial Arts of China* by R. L. Thorp (Seattle, 1988).

OUR LITERARY HERITAGE

USING PRIMARY SOURCES

Ask students to discuss what can be learned about a society from its humor. Is there anything in this selection that could not have happened in Europe or the United States? Can students think of real-life situations or other books or movies that show supposedly sophisticated urbanites ridiculing their "country-bumpkin" relatives? Whom do students think the author was really criticizing—the old Aunt or the proud Matriarch? What might future historians think of our society if they studied our humor?

LEARNING FROM VISUALS

Answers to the caption question: Answers will vary.

Answers to Critical Thinking Questions

1. Old Dame Liu was the country cousin.
2. The text says that Phoenix "plotted to give her a pair of old-fashioned, angular-shaped ivory chopsticks gilded with gold." The fact that Phoenix plotted to give her this unmanageable gift leads one to believe that Old Dame Liu was probably "set up."

OUR LITERARY HERITAGE

The Dream of the Red Chamber

The Dream of the Red Chamber, written in 1791 by Ts'ao Hsüeh-ch'in, is China's best-known popular novel. This passage describes the visit of a country cousin, Old Dame Liu, to the elegant mansion of her city relatives and the comic scene that she provokes by her lack of worldly wisdom.

Ts'ao Hsüeh-ch'in, Excerpt from
The Dream of the Red Chamber

As soon as Old Dame Liu [lee-oo] was seated, she picked up the chopsticks which were uncannily heavy and hard to manage. It was because Phoenix had previously plotted to give her a pair of old-fashioned, angular-shaped ivory chopsticks gilded with gold. Looking at them, Old Dame Liu remarked: "These fork-like things are even heavier than our iron prongs. How can one hold them up?" Everyone laughed. By this time a woman servant had brought in a tiny food box. Inside were two bowls of food. Li Huan took one bowl and placed it on the Matriarch's table as Phoenix picked up a bowl of pigeon eggs to place it on Old Dame Liu's table. . . .

Old Dame Liu lifted up the chopsticks but they were hardly manageable. Looking at the bowl in front of her, she remarked: "Well, well, even your hens are smarter than ours! They lay such tiny delicate eggs, very dainty indeed. Let me try one!" All people had just stopped laughing but they burst out again upon hearing these words. The Matriarch laughed so much that tears dropped down; she just couldn't stop them.

Old Dame Liu was still exclaiming about how tiny and dainty the eggs were when Phoenix said

▲ *This seventeenth-century painting, Pavilion Reflections at Sunset by Tao-chi, provides a view of pavilion-style homes built during this time period. Who do you think might have lived in such houses? Do you think the painting is realistic? Why or why not?*

jokingly to her: "They cost an ounce of silver apiece. You had better hurry up and taste one before they get cold." Old Dame Liu then stretched out her chopsticks to seize the eggs with both ends, but how could she pick them up? After having chased them all over the bowl, she finally

(continued)

MORE ABOUT . . . Chinese Landscape Painting

The Chinese word for painting literally means "to describe a field with a brush." The three common items found in landscape paintings are water, a bridge, and mountains.

Humans are always portrayed small. This is an indication of the power of nature and the relative unimportance of the individual in Chinese society.

Water is a source of life, and an important symbol in most societies. There is a paradox

with water in a stream or river in that in one sense it is always there, yet in another sense it is never the same droplets of water. It is eternal, but always changing.

The bridge is a connector that allows humans to cross the river.

Mountains are dominant structures in China. Their size and majesty make humans seem insignificant.

OUR LITERARY HERITAGE

The Dream of the Red Chamber, continued

captured one with no little effort and was about to crane her neck to eat it when lo! it slipped off and fell on the floor. She was going to pick it up herself when a woman servant got it and took it out. Old Dame Liu sighed: "An ounce of silver. How it disappears without even making a noise."

1. Who was the "country cousin" described in the opening paragraph?

2. Do you think it was planned to make the country cousin look foolish? Explain why you feel the way you do.

In architecture, the most outstanding example is the Imperial City in Beijing. When the third Ming emperor returned the capital to Beijing in 1421, he ordered renovations to begin on the remnants of the palace of the Mongol dynasty. Succeeding emperors continued to add to the palace, called the Imperial City, but the basic design has not changed since the Ming Era. The Imperial City is an immense compound surrounded by six and a half miles of walls. It is divided into a maze of private apartments and offices. An imposing ceremonial quadrangle (an enclosure with buildings on four sides) has a series of stately halls for imperial audiences and banquets. The grandiose scale, richly carved marble, spacious gardens, and graceful upturned roofs contribute to the splendor of the Imperial City. Because it was off-limits to commoners, the compound was known as the Forbidden City.

In the late Ming period, wealthy urban elites throughout the country dedicated their wealth to the arts. They built grand estates with artificial hills, rock gardens, pools, and elaborate interiors. Separate schools of painting were set up to copy different styles from previous dynasties. Court artists were kept busy decorating the numerous rooms in the imperial palace. Court painters fared better than those of the fourteenth century, when the founding Ming

◄ This photograph of the Forbidden City shows the Meridian Gate and the Golden River, with the immense palace in the background. Compare and contrast this view of the Forbidden City with the palace of Versailles, which is discussed in Chapter 15.

So What ??

If your students question the importance of information about **Chinese porcelain** (discussed on the next page) tell them . . .

about the impact that it has had on our eating habits. The Dutch and other Europeans were fascinated by Chinese porcelain when they arrived in China in the early sixteenth century. They viewed with envy the superior quality of this porcelain. The Chinese were reluctant to trade this porcelain, and, anyway, the Europeans had little that the Chinese wanted. The Europeans experimented with replicating the Chinese process for making porcelain, and Delft, Holland became a center of production. The habit of eating one's food on this special porcelain still exists today. People commonly refer to dinnerware plates as "china," a recognition of the origin of this exquisite porcelain.

Answers to SECTION REVIEW

2. (a) wrapping the feet of female Chinese infants
3. (a) a cutting exposé of the decadent aspects of the late Ming society
(b) considered to be China's most distinguished popular novel
(c) another name for the Imperial City
4. (a) long periods of peace and stability and the use of new crops from the Americas
(b) The growing of rice is labor intensive work. The family provided support to all members. It was the chief source of education for the young, supported unmarried daughters, and cared for the elderly.
(c) Women played a strong role in the family. They were often in charge of educating the children and handled the family budget.
(d) These novels dealt with issues such as love, money, marriage, and power.
(e) Art was impressive for its technical perfection and breathtaking quantity; porcelain
5. Answers will vary.

CLOSE

Lead students in a discussion of the 'Focus' objectives identified on page 557. Emphasize the importance of the extended family and the role of women in Chinese society.

564

---

emperor executed four artists because he disliked their works.

The decorative arts flourished in this period. Perhaps the most famous of all the achievements of the Ming Era was the blue-and-white porcelain. Europeans greatly admired its beauty and collected it in great quantities. Styles differed during the reign of each emperor. One variety caused a sensation in Holland and led to the manufacture of blue-and-white porcelain at the Dutch porcelain factory at Delft.

Paintings were also produced in great quantities during the Qing dynasty, mostly for use in homes. The wealthy city of Yangzhou (YONG-JOE) on the Grand Canal emerged as an active artistic center. In Beijing, court painters worked alongside Jesuit artists inside the Forbidden City and experimented with Western techniques. European art, however, did not greatly influence Chinese painting at this time. Many Chinese painters totally rejected foreign techniques and became obsessed with keeping traditional Chinese styles alive. As a result, Qing painting became more and more repetitive.

 SECTION REVIEW

1. **Locate:**
   (a) Yangzhou

2. **Define:**
   (a) foot binding

3. **Identify:**
   (a) *The Golden Lotus,* (b) *The Dream of the Red Chamber,* (c) Forbidden City

4. **Recall:**
   (a) List some of the reasons for the increase in China's population between 1500 and 1800.
   (b) Why were families important in China?
   (c) What were some of women's roles in China during the Ming and Qing dynasties?
   (d) What issues did Chinese fiction deal with?
   (e) What typified the art of this period? What was the most famous decorative art during the Ming dynasty?

---

5. **Think Critically:** Compare and contrast the roles of men and women in early Chinese society.

TOKUGAWA JAPAN

At the end of the fifteenth century, Japan was at a point of near anarchy. As the power of the Ashikaga (AWSH-i-KAWG-uh) shogunate at Kyoto declined (see Chapter 10), clan rivalries had exploded into an era of "warring states." The dream of a united Japan seemed to be at an end. Unexpectedly, however, Japan made a dramatic reversal.

The Three Great Unifiers

The process of unifying Japan began in the mid-sixteenth century with the emergence of three powerful political figures. The first was Oda Nobunaga, the son of a samurai and military commander. Nobunaga seized the imperial capital of Kyoto and placed the reigning shogun under his control. During the next few years, the brutal Nobunaga tried to consolidate his rule throughout the central plains. However, he was killed by one of his generals in 1582 before the process was complete.

Nobunaga was succeeded by Toyotomi Hideyoshi, a farmer's son who had become a military commander. Hideyoshi located his capital at Osaka, where he built a castle to house his headquarters. Gradually, he extended the base of his own power outward to the southern islands of Shikoku and Kyushu. By 1590, he had persuaded most of the *daimyo* (or nobles—see Chapter 10) on the Japanese islands to accept his authority.

Although Nobunaga and Hideyoshi had achieved the unification of Japan, neither was able to eliminate the power of the local *daimyo*. Both were forced to form alliances with some *daimyo* in order to destroy others. Both rulers still depended on local *daimyo* to pacify the territories under their control. The Japanese

---

MORE ABOUT . . . *Oda Nobunaga*

Oda Nobunaga was nicknamed the "great idiot" because he did not show proper respect at his father's funeral. This behavior brought him disdain from many Japanese, but he was a brilliant and ruthless general who began the process of unifying Japan. Nobunaga had the advantage of European muskets. In an important battle he aligned his 3,000 soldiers in three rows, and they could fire a volley every ten seconds. His rival warlord who relied on mounted swordsmen and soldiers with pikes was easy prey. Another enemy with European style weapons was a group of Zen Buddhists. A ten-year battle raged, and when Nobunaga still could not win, he signed a peace treaty. He later surrounded and killed 20,000 of these followers, including men, women, and children. This horrible battle is considered one of the worst in Japanese history.

tradition of decentralized rule had not been completely overcome.

After Hideyoshi's death in 1598, Tokugawa (TOE-koo-GAW-wuh) Ieyasu, the powerful *daimyo* of Edo (modern-day Tokyo), took control of Japan. Ieyasu took the title of shogun in 1603, an act that initiated the most powerful and long lasting of all the Japanese shogunates. The Tokugawa rulers completed the restoration of central authority begun by Nobunaga and Hideyoshi. These rulers remained in power at their capital at Edo until 1868.

Map 18.3   Tokugawa Japan

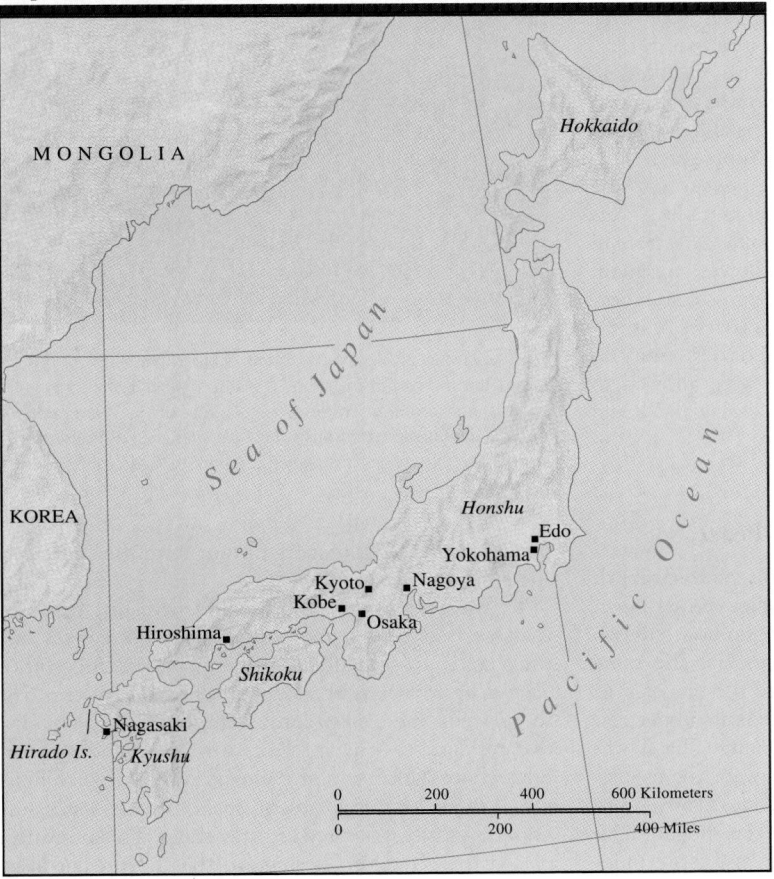

Opening to the West

While the three great commanders were unifying Japan, the first Europeans began to arrive. Portuguese traders had landed on the islands in 1543. In a few years, Portuguese ships began stopping at Japanese ports on a regular basis to take part in the regional trade between Japan, China, and Southeast Asia. The first Jesuit missionary, Francis Xavier, arrived in 1549 and had some success in converting the local population to Christianity.

At first the visitors were welcomed. The curious Japanese were fascinated by tobacco, clocks, eyeglasses, and other European goods. *Daimyo* were interested in buying all types of European weapons (see "You Are There: The Japanese Discover Firearms"). Oda Nobunaga and Toyotomi Hideyoshi found the new firearms helpful in defeating their enemies and unifying the islands. The effect of the Europeans on Japanese military architecture was especially striking. Local lords began to erect castles in stone on the European model. Many of these castles, such as that of Hideyoshi at Osaka, still exist today.

The Jesuits were able to convert a number of local *daimyo*. By the end of the sixteenth century, thousands of Japanese in the southernmost islands of Kyushu and Shikoku had become Christians. However, the Jesuit practice of destroying local idols and shrines and turning some temples into Christian schools or churches caused a severe reaction. At the end of

STUDYING MAPS

The following questions will help you guide students through their study of Map 18.3.

1. What geographic features made Japan a natural sea power? *(the fact that Japan is an island archipelago)*
2. Why was Japan able to keep European powers from dominating its trade? *(Japan*

expelled European traders and closed foreign ports.)
3. Why was Japan interested in controlling Korea and eastern Mongolia? *(By controlling these areas Japan would make itself more secure from foreign attack or invasion.)*

3

FOCUS

OBJECTIVES

After completing this section, students should be able to

1. identify factors that led to Japan's unification
2. describe how Western contact affected Japan
3. describe causes and effects of the Tokugawa
4. explain changes in Japan's economy and society during the Tokugawa

FOCUS ACTIVITY

Help students understand why the introduction of a new religion often results in conflict and social unrest. Leaders of an existing religion have vested interests in maintaining the status quo. Ask students how receptive they would be to a new religion.

Multimedia Support

TRANSPARENCY
18–3, Map of Tokugawa Japan (Map 18.3)

TEACH

COMPARING TIME PERIODS

Divide students into groups and assign each to compare and contrast the rule of kings and nobles in Europe with the rule of Nobunaga and Hideyoshi. These leaders relied on the support of daimyos. Was there a sort of feudal contract in Japan? Bring the groups together to compare results.

the sixteenth century, Hideyoshi issued an edict prohibiting further Christian activities within his lands. Japan, he said, was "the land of the Gods." The destruction of shrines by the foreigners was "something unheard of in previous ages." To "corrupt and stir up the lower classes" to commit such acts, he declared, was "outrageous." The Jesuits were ordered to leave the country within twenty days. Merchants, however, were allowed to continue to operate.

The Jesuits protested, and eventually Hideyoshi backed down. He allowed the Jesuits to continue their activities if they carried them out tactfully and quietly. When a new group of Spanish Franciscans did just the opposite, Hideyoshi ordered the execution of nine missionaries and a number of their Japanese converts. When the missionaries continued to interfere in local politics, the new ruler, Tokugawa Ieyasu, expelled all missionaries. Japanese Christians were now persecuted. When some Christian peasants on the island of Kyushu revolted in 1637, they were violently suppressed.

The European merchants were the next to go. The government closed the two major foreign trading posts on the island of Hirado and at Nagasaki. Only a small Dutch community in Nagasaki was allowed to remain in Japan. The Dutch, unlike the Spanish and Portuguese, had not allowed missionary activities to interfere with their trade interests. However, the conditions for staying were strict. Dutch ships were allowed to dock at Nagasaki harbor only once a year and could remain for only two or three months.

The Tokugawa "Great Peace"

Once in power, the Tokugawa rulers set out to establish control of the feudal system that had governed Japan for over 300 years. The Tokugawa shogun now had two roles. He governed his own lands and, at the same time, set national policy on behalf of the emperor in Kyoto. As before, the state was divided into about 250 separate territories called **hans** (domains). Each was ruled by a *daimyo* lord. The *daimyo* were themselves divided into two types. The **fudai** (inside) *daimyo* were lesser *daimyo* directly subordinate to the shogun. The **tozama** (outside) *daimyo* were greater and more inde-

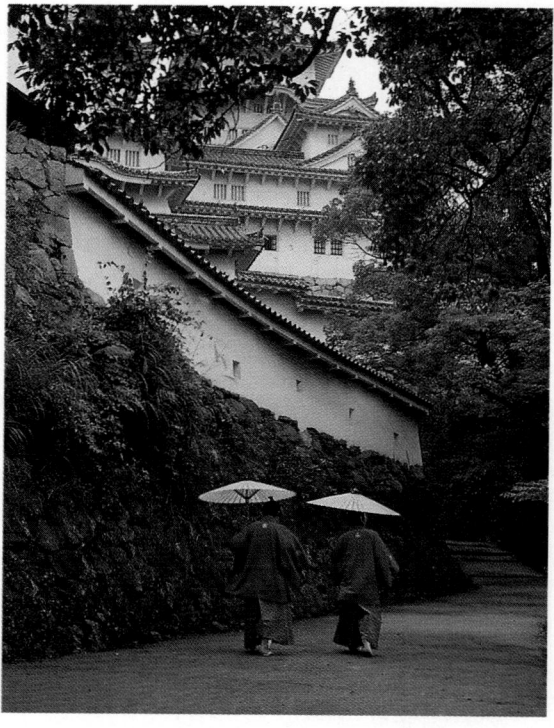

▲ *The Himeji castle, shown in this photograph, is one of the most beautiful castles in Japan. It is also typical of the fortress-palaces that were built in the seventeenth century. What architectural details show that this palace was designed as a military stronghold? How does this palace compare to medieval European castles?*

pendent lords, usually more distant from the center of shogunate power in Edo.

In theory, the *daimyo* were independent, because they were able to support themselves from taxes on their lands. In actuality, the shogunate controlled the *daimyo* by what has been called a **hostage system.** In this system, the *daimyo* lords were forced to maintain two residences—one in their own lands and one in Edo, where the court of the shogun was located. When the *daimyo* lord was absent from his residence in Edo, his family was forced to stay there. This not only placed the *daimyo* in hostage to the shogun but also

MORE ABOUT . . . *Hideyoshi and the Tea Ceremony*

Hideyoshi had a passion for tea so he associated with a tea master, Sen no Rikyu. Because Hideyoshi encouraged people to participate in the tea ceremony, it became even more popular, especially among the elite. Once Hideyoshi had a great tea party with 800 tea masters and others who liked the tea ceremony, including commoners. Relations between Hideyoshi and Sen no Rikyu soon cooled. Rikyu seemed to challenge the political authority of Hideyoshi, whose grip on power was still tenuous. The story has a tragic end in that Hideyoshi had a special wooden statue of Rikyu installed over a symbolic gate. The situation is complicated, but essentially the only honorable choice for Rikyu was to commit ritual suicide. In Hideyoshi's quest to unify Japan, not even a master of the tea ceremony could remain outside Hideyoshi's control.

YOU ARE THERE

The Japanese Discover Firearms

◄ *The first Portuguese traders to Japan landed there by accident. This late sixteenth-century painting is a Japanese account of that first landing at Nagasaki. What features seem out of place or curious to you?*

The Portuguese brought firearms to Japan in the sixteenth century. In this selection, the daimyo of a small island off the southern tip of Japan receives an explanation of how to use the new weapons. Obviously, he is fascinated by the results.

A Daimyo Lord Describes How to Use a Firearm

There are two leaders among the traders. In their hands they carried something two or three feet long, straight on the outside with a passage inside, and made of a heavy substance. The inner passage runs through it although it is closed at the end. At its side, there is an opening which is the passageway for fire. Its shape defies comparison with any thing I know. To use it, fill it with powder and small lead pellets. Set up a small target on a bank. Grip the object in your hand, compose your body, and closing one eye, apply fire to the opening. Then the pellet hits the target squarely. The explosion is like lightning and the report like thunder. Bystanders must cover their ears. This thing with one blow can smash a mountain of silver and a wall of iron. If one sought to do mischief in another man's domain and he was touched by it, he would lose his life instantly. . . . Lord Toki-taka saw it and thought it was the wonder of wonders. He did not know its name at first nor the

(continued)

USING PRIMARY SOURCES

Ask students to write an essay in which they evaluate the reaction of the Japanese daimyo to firearms. Do they believe he was merely intrigued by these weapons, or did he realize how important they would be to the future of Japan. How might Japan's history have been different if the Europeans had not sold western military technology?

LEARNING FROM VISUALS

Answer to the caption question: Answers will vary. Students may think it odd that a tea house pavilion is shown, that the horse seems to have no purpose in the painting, or that a parasol is being held over the head of one of the Portuguese.

ENRICHMENT ACTIVITY

The Tokugawa system of requiring the daimyo to live in Edo (Tokyo) or leave their families there helped keep the peace in Japan for over 250 years. No lord was willing to lose his family to attain political power. Pose the following to students for discussion: all countries with nuclear weapons must have the children of high government and military officials live in their enemy's territory. Thus, the President of the United States' wife and daughter might have to live in Russia, while the Russian president's family might have to live in the United States. China and India might have a similar arrangement. Divide the students into groups and ask them to debate the proposal.

YOU ARE THERE

Answers to Critical Thinking Questions

1. The Portuguese were the first to bring firearms to Japan in the sixteenth century.
2. We would probably call it a rifle, although a very primitive one.
3. *Aliens* refers to the Portuguese. The term is used to describe people from other countries.

ACROSS THE CURRICULUM

Economics. Ask students to evaluate the Japanese policy of placing low taxes on merchants and manufacturers. Although it did contribute to the rapid growth of Japan's productive capacity and over-all wealth, did it also sow the seeds of future problems? Were the economic difficulties of the samurai a cause of the militarism that would plunge Japan into war in the following century?

YOU ARE THERE

The Japanese Discover Firearms, continued

details of its use. Then someone called it "iron-arms. . . ."

Disregarding the high price of the arms, Tokitaka purchased from the aliens two pieces of the firearms for his family treasure. As for the art of grinding, sifting, and mixing of the powder, Tokitaka let his retainer learn it. Tokitaka occupied himself, morning and night, and without rest in handling the arms. As a result, he was able to convert the misses of his early experiments into hits—a hundred hits in a hundred attempts.

1. Who introduced firearms to Japan in the sixteenth century?

2. Considering the description of the firearm the Portuguese brought, what do you think we would call it today?

3. In the last paragraph, what does the term *aliens* refer to?

put the Japanese nobles in a difficult economic position, because they had to keep up with the expenses of two residences.

With the long period of peace—known as the "Great Peace"—brought by Tokugawa rule, the samurai gradually ceased to be a warrior class. Many of them became managers on the lands of the *daimyo* lords. These samurai were still allowed to wear their two swords. At the same time, persons of samurai status were rigidly separated from the rest of the population. The rigid class distinctions within Japanese society were noticed by the Jesuit missionary Francis Xavier. He observed that "on no account would a poverty-stricken gentleman marry with someone outside the gentry, even if he were given great sums to do so." Such a gentleman would lose honor by marrying outside his class.

Economic Changes

The major change that took place in Japanese society under the Tokugawa was a dramatic economic one. Since the fourteenth century, some trade and industry had been carried on in Japan. As in China, however, both had been limited by restrictions from the state

and the social prejudice against them. Many upper-class Japanese considered trade and industry beneath them. Under the Tokugawa, trade and industry began to flourish as never before. By 1800, they had become a significant part of the Japanese economy.

What caused this expansion in trade and industry? For one thing, Japanese merchants were able to benefit from the long period of peace that followed centuries of almost constant civil war. They also benefited from the sale of their goods to the upper classes and from low taxes. Tokugawa shoguns disliked commercial activity and relied chiefly on agricultural taxes for their revenue. Moreover, the hostage system spurred the growth of manufacturing and trade. The *daimyo* were forced to keep residences at the shogun's court as well as in their own lands. In consequence, they promoted the sale of local goods—such as textiles, wood products, sugar, and sake (a Japanese rice wine)—to pay their heavy expenses.

Thus, trade and manufacturing rose dramatically under the Tokugawa, especially in the growing cities of Edo, Kyoto, and Osaka. By 1750, Edo had a population of over one million and was one of the largest cities in the world. With growth came sophistication. Banking flourished, and paper money became the normal

RETEACHING ACTIVITY

Explain the following situation to the class. It's based on an early twentieth century movie, but provides insight into traditional Japanese values. A village schoolmaster collects money from villagers to redeem a young school girl about to be sold into prostitution because her family lives in desperate poverty. The schoolmaster's mother steals the money from her son even though she does not need the money. The son decides to accept blame for his mother because his filial duty to his mother prevents him from even considering telling the truth. A greater complication arises when the schoolmaster's wife, to protect him, leaves a suicide note accepting responsibility, and then drowns herself and young child. As the tragedy unfolds, the mother's role is never revealed. If the schoolmaster had implicated his mother, he could have no longer had any self-respect.

▲ *A bustling commercial city, Edo also had a "floating world" or a pleasure district. This woodblock print portrays courtesans, storytellers, jesters, and others entertaining the city residents. Do you think modern-day amusement parks resemble this floating world? Why or why not?*

medium of exchange in business transactions. Merchants formed guilds to control market conditions. Under the supervision of Japan's noble rulers, a Japanese merchant class gradually began to emerge and to play a significant role in the life of the Japanese nation.

One class that was hard hit by the economic changes of the seventeenth and eighteenth centuries was the samurai. Barred by tradition from commercial activities, the samurai were unable to benefit from the economic change. Most samurai still relied for their incomes on revenues from rice lands, which often failed to cover their rising expenses. Many samurai fell heavily into debt. Others were released from servitude to their lord and became "masterless samurai." Occasionally, these unemployed warriors (known as **ronin,** or "wave men") revolted or plotted against local officials.

What effect did these economic changes have on Japanese peasants, who made up the majority of the population? Some farm families benefited by exploiting the growing demand for cash crops (crops grown for sale), but not all prospered. Most peasants still grew rice and experienced both declining profits and rising costs and taxes. Taxes often took up to 50 percent of the annual harvest. Many peasants were forced to become tenants or to work as wage laborers on the farms of the wealthy or in village industries. When rural conditions became desperate, some peasants revolted. Almost 7,000 peasant revolts took place during the Tokugawa Era, although many were peaceful demonstrations against high taxes.

The Class System and Women

During the Tokugawa Era, Japan's class system became even more rigid than it had been. Tokugawa rulers established strict legal distinctions between the four main classes in Japan: warriors, artisans, peasants, and merchants. Intermarriage between classes was forbidden in theory but sometimes occurred in practice. Below these classes were Japan's outcasts, the *eta.* The Tokugawa enacted severe laws against the *eta* that regulated their places of residence, their dress, and even their hairstyles.

The role of women in Tokugawa society became somewhat more restricted than it had been in the previous era. Especially in the samurai class, where Confucian values were highly prized, the rights of females were restricted. Male heads of households had broad authority over property, marriage, and divorce. Wives were expected to obey their husbands on pain of death. Sons of samurai parents studied the Confucian classics in schools set up by the *daimyo.* Females in these families were raised at home.

Among the common people, women were also restricted. Parents arranged marriages. As in China, a wife in Japan was expected to move in with her husband's family. A wife who did not meet the expectations of her husband or his family was likely to be

CRITICAL THINKING

Ask students why a new set of cultural values appeared in Japan at the same time as the growth of popular literature written by and for common people. What does this timing say about literacy in Japan and about the time people had to participate in leisure activities and the arts?

LEARNING FROM VISUALS

Assign students to find a copy of a picture of idealized beautiful women from a current magazine or newspaper. Ask students to compare the two pictures and draw conclusions about differences in the roles and rights of women in society.

Answer to the caption question: The beautifully colored silk garments these women wear show that they are very wealthy and their activity would indicate that they have leisure time to meet and chat.

▲ *Although Japanese women were viewed as inferior to men during this time, beautiful women like these were commonly portrayed in woodblock prints. This print was made in the late seventeenth-century by a famous artist named Chikanobu. What does the dress of each woman reveal about her status in society?*

divorced. Still, women were probably regarded more highly among the common people than among the nobility. Female commoners were generally valued as childbearers and homemakers. Both sexes worked in the fields, although men did the heavier labor. Schools were set up in villages and market towns, and about one-fourth of the students were female. Poor families, however, frequently put infant daughters to death or sold them into prostitution.

Tokugawa Culture

Two different directions appeared in the culture of the Tokugawa Era. On the one hand, the shogunate continued to patronize the classical culture—influenced by Confucian themes—of an earlier age. On the other hand, a new set of cultural values was beginning to appear, especially in the cities. It included the rise of popular literature written by and for the townspeople. The peace of the Tokugawa Era allowed ordinary Japanese to enjoy entertainment aimed at them both in the theater and in books. With the development of printing in the seventeenth century, literature became available to the common people. The new prose was cheerful, as its primary aim was to amuse.

The Literature of the New Middle Class

The best examples of the new urban fiction in the seventeenth century are the works of Saikaku, considered one of Japan's greatest writers. He began his career as a poet but switched early in life to writing prose. His first novel tells of the financial adventures of its hero, a new self-made merchant. This first novel was very popular and sold over a thousand copies in its first printing.

Saikaku's greatest novel, *Five Women Who Loved Love*, told of the search for love of five women of the merchant class. Based partly on real-life experiences, it broke from the Confucian ethic of a wife's fidelity to her husband. Instead, it portrayed women who were willing to die for love—and all but one eventually did. Because money was of great interest to the merchant class, Saikaku also wrote *The Millionaire's Gospel*, the story of a money-grubbing, self-made merchant. Saikaku was a wise observer of the human condition and a superb storyteller as well. He was immensely popular in his day.

In the theater, the rise of the **Kabuki** form challenged the long dominance of the No play. The new world of entertainment in the cities gave rise to Kabuki, which emphasized violence, music, and dramatic gestures to entertain its viewers. The success of Kabuki, however, led to problems with the government. Early Kabuki dramas dealt with the new world of teahouses and dance halls in the cities. Government officials feared that such activities could corrupt the nation's morals. Thus, the government forbade women to appear on stage. Officials, therefore, created a new professional class of male actors to impersonate female characters.

Much of the popular literature of the Tokugawa Era was lighthearted and intended to please its audiences. Poetry remained the more serious literary form of expression. The most exquisite poetry was written in

So What ??

If your students question the importance of information about **No Drama,** *tell them . . .*

it is still an important art form in Japan today. At the center of a No play there is an encounter between a troubled spirit and a priest, or bystander. The spirit (or *shite*) wears a simple mask that distorts the sounds that come from the mouth. No is danced more than acted. The performers are accompanied by music of the flute and drums. Sometimes the No drama may provide spiritual relief, but often still there is a sense that the encounter could repeat itself.

the seventeenth century by the greatest of all Japanese poets, Basho. He was concerned with the search for the meaning of life and found answers to his quest in nature. His poems are grounded in natural images, as is evident in the following examples, which are among his most famous poems:

> The ancient pond
> A frog leaps in
> The sound of the water.

> On the withered branch
> A crow has alighted—
> The end of autumn.

> Such stillness—
> The cries of the cicadas
> Sink into the rocks.

> The sea darkens,
> The cries of the seagulls
> Are faintly white.

At the age of fifty, in the last year of his life, Basho was ill but still traveling in search of the purpose of life. His last poems express the artist's loneliness:

> Along this road
> There are no travelers—
> Nightfall in autumn.

> This autumn,
> Why do I feel so cold?
> A bird in the clouds.

Like all great artists, Basho made his poems appear effortless and simple. He speaks directly to everyone, everywhere.

Tokugawa Art

Art also reflected the changes in Japanese culture under the Tokugawa regime. The shogun's order that all *daimyo* and their families must live every other year in Edo set off a burst of building. Nobles competed to erect the most magnificent mansion. Furthermore, the shoguns themselves built splendid castles adorned with lavish and beautiful furnishings. Finally, the prosperity

▲ *Kabuki theater, with its ceremonial actions, remains popular in Japan where some people consider it an art form. How would this scene be different from a Shakespearean play performed in the eighteenth century, when this colorful print was made?*

of the newly rising merchant class led to additional support for Japanese painting, architecture, textiles, and ceramics.

Court painters filled magnificent screens with gold foil, which was also used to cover walls and even ceilings. This lavish use of gold foil gave witness to the grandeur of the new Japanese rulers, but it also served a practical purpose. It reflected light in the dark castle rooms, where windows were kept small for defensive purposes.

Although Japan was isolated from the Western world during much of the Tokugawa regime, Japanese

USING PRIMARY SOURCES

Assign students to write critiques of the poems written by Basho. What do the poems mean? Why should people read them? How do they make the reader feel?

LEARNING FROM VISUALS

Assign students to draw or find a picture of a performance they would like to attend. What differences in culture can they identify that are demonstrated by these two pictures or drawings?

Answer to the caption question: Students should recognize that European theater was more ad-lib and impromptu than the highly stylized Japanese kabuki. Both Shakespearean plays and Kabuki theater used only male actors.

ASSESS

Assign students to write a letter describing Japanese politics and culture that might have been sent by a visitor in Japan to his family in Europe in the early nineteenth century.

RECOMMENDED READING

Of specific interest to Japanese literature of the Tokugawa era are D. Keene, *World Within Walls: Japanese Literature of the Pre-Modern Era, 1600–1867* (New York, 1976) and N. Yukihiko, "Modern Period A.D. 1600 to 1868," in *Japanese Literature: A Historical Outline* by E. Putzar (Arizona, 1973) pp. 105–169. Of special value is *Japanese Literature: An Introduction for Western Readers* (London, 1953).

For the most comprehensive and accessible overview of Japanese art see P. Mason, *Japanese Art* (New York, 1993). For a concise introduction to Japanese art of the Tokugawa era see *Japanese Art* by J. Stanley-Baker (London, 1984). For magnificent photographs and stimulating interpretation, consult *Art of Japan* by D. and V. Elisseeff (New York, 1985) and *The Art of Japan* by J. E. Kidder Jr. (London, 1985).

LEARNING FROM VISUALS

Answers to
SECTION REVIEW

2. (a) domains; (b) inside daimyo, directly subordinate to the shogun; (c) outside daimyo, greater, independent lords; (d) system of control over daimyo; (e) unemployed samurai warriors; (f) theater, emphasized violence, music, dramatic gestures
3. (a) Japananese nobles (b) what is now Tokyo (c) first Jesuit missionary to Japan; arrived in 1549 (d) Japanese rice wine (e) outcasts whose behavior was regulated (f) Considered one of Japan's greatest writers (g) greatest of all Japanese poets
4. (a) Oda Nubunaga, Toyotomi Hideyoshi, and Tokugawa Ieyasu. Answers will vary. (b) At first, missionaries were welcomed, but eventually were expelled by Tokugawa Ieyasu. (c) They gradually ceased to be a warrior class (d) The long period of peace after centuries of war, low taxes, patronage of upper classes, and hostage system spurred growth of manufacture and trade (e) As the merchant class became generous patrons of arts
5. Answers will vary.

▶ *The Japanese artist Hokusai created a series of woodblock prints entitled* Thirty-six Views of Mount Fuji. *This famous print,* Mount Fuji across the Water, *shows the mountain in the background while fishermen battle a giant wave. If you were the artist, what name would you have given to this print?*

art was still enriched by ideas from other cultures. Japanese pottery makers borrowed both techniques and designs from Korea to create handsome ceramic pieces. The passion for "Dutch learning" led Japanese to study Western medicine, astronomy, languages, and even painting styles. In turn, Europeans wanted Japanese metalwork and especially ceramics, which were prized as highly as the ceramics of the Chinese.

By the late seventeenth and eighteenth centuries, the merchant class had begun to surpass the nobility in wealth. As a result, the merchants became enthusiastic and generous patrons of the arts. Many schools of painting arose. Some were based on Western styles and others, on Chinese models.

Other artists experimented with new forms, as is evident in the bold work of Korin. His screen with a blue iris and green leaves on gold foil is a departure from the traditional Japanese garden painting of flowers framed with a bridge, water, and clouds. In this screen Korin presents only the iris, inviting the viewer into the picture to be involved directly with the flowers. Korin was a good example of the extravagance of the times. Once, on a picnic, he shocked his friends by unwrapping his food from bamboo leaves lined with gold foil and then casually tossing the leaves into the river.

❊ SECTION REVIEW ❊

1. **Locate:**
   (*a*) Kyoto,   (*b*) Osaka,   (*c*) Shikoku,
   (*d*) Kyushu,   (*e*) Hirado,   (*f*) Nagasaki

2. **Define:**
   (*a*) *hans*,   (*b*) *fudai*,   (*c*) *tozama*,   (*d*) hostage system,   (*e*) *ronin*,   (*f*) Kabuki

3. **Identify:**
   (*a*) *daimyo*,   (*b*) Edo,   (*c*) Francis Xavier,
   (*d*) sake,   (*e*) *eta*,   (*f*) Saikaku,   (*g*) Basho

4. **Recall:**
   (*a*) Who were the three unifiers of Japan? How did they succeed in unifying the country?
   (*b*) How was Christianity tolerated in Japan during this time?
   (*c*) What happened to the samurai during the great peace?
   (*d*) What caused the expansion of trade and industry in Japan under the Tokugawa?
   (*e*) How did the affluence of the late seventeenth and eighteenth centuries affect art in China?

▲ *This six-panel screen of irises was painted over a gold leaf surface by Ogata Korin about 1701. Some art historians believe that Japanese paintings like this one paved the way for the European Impressionist paintings of the late 1800s. Considering the closed nature of Japanese society during the 1700s, do you think that this could be true? Why or why not?*

5. **Think Critically:** How did the closed societies of China and Japan affect the lives of their people? Please explain.

Conclusion

When Christopher Columbus sailed from southern Spain in August 1492, he was seeking a route to China and Japan. He did not find it, but others soon did. In 1514, Portuguese ships arrived on the coast of South China. Thirty years later, a small group of Portuguese merchants became the first Europeans to set foot on the islands of Japan.

At first, the new arrivals were welcomed. Several nations established trade relations with Japan and China. Christian missionaries were active in both countries. However, European success was short lived. During the seventeenth century, most of the merchants and missionaries were forced to leave. From that time until the beginning of the nineteenth century, neither Japan nor China was much affected by events taking place outside the region.

Chinese and Japanese leaders had adopted their "closed country" policy to keep out foreign ideas and protect native values and institutions. In one respect,

the policy worked. Both countries were able to resist the fate of many Asian societies during the period. Both the Japanese and Chinese societies were changing, however, and by the early nineteenth century were quite different from what they had been three hundred years earlier. By the beginning of the nineteenth century, powerful tensions were at work in both Chinese and Japanese society. Under these conditions, both countries were soon forced to face a new challenge from the aggressive power of an industrializing Europe.

Notes

1. Quoted in J. H. Parry, ed., *The European Reconnaissance: Selected Documents* (New York, 1968), p. 129.
2. Louis J. Gallagher, ed. and trans., *China in the Sixteenth Century: The Journals of Matthew Ricci* (New York, 1953), p. 154.
3. Quoted in Jonathan D. Spence, *The Search for Modern China* (New York, 1990), p. 23.
4. Quoted in C. R. Boxer, ed., *South China in the Sixteenth Century* (London, 1953), p. 265.

LEARNING FROM VISUALS

Answer to the caption question: When trade was reopened between France and Japan in 1854, Japanese woodcuts and painting became very popular among French artists.

CLOSE

Lead students in a discussion of the Focus objectives identified on page 565. Emphasize the importance of the progress made in Japan during the "Great Peace."

TIME LINE

As students conclude the chapter, you may want to refer them to the chapter time line in the *Study Guide.* The time line will help them put key dates in perspective. Supporting questions and activities are also provided.

SPANISH SUPPORT

The *Conclusion* has been translated into Spanish for your Spanish-speaking students. Included with this translation (in your Teacher Resource Box) are Section Key Points, which consist of one or two sentences summarizing each section in the chapter. These Key Points have also been translated into Spanish.

CNN. WORLD HISTORY UPDATES

You can update your coverage of World History topics, as well as spark lively classroom discussion and deeper understanding, by using the **CNN World History Updates.**

For assistance in using and incorporating the **CNN World History Updates** into your classroom presentations, see the *Classroom Guide.*

Answers to
CHAPTER REVIEW 18

USING KEY TERMS

1. foot binding
2. *fudai*
3. Kabuki
4. hostage system
5. dyarchy
6. *ronin*
7. *tozama*
8. *hans*

REVIEWING THE FACTS

1. 1514
2. felt they were an unusual form of barbarians
3. brought scientific developments; pointed out similarities between Christian and Confucian ethics; lived virtuous lives
4. series of weak rulers; inflation; disrupted silver trade; harsh winter and poor crop yields; high taxes; government corruption; unrest and instability
5. conquered Beijing and caused Le Zicheng's army to decline, allowing the Manchu to conquer and gain control of country
6. an order for males to shave their foreheads and braid their hair in pigtails
7. They compromised doctrines to win converts.
8. unrest and revolt by peasant farmers in central China who were upset with higher taxes and corrupt officials
9. skins and furs
10. They had no need of European products.
11. It did not develop commercial capitalism.
12. help with labor, such as growing rice; support for young and elderly; support for relatives
13. considered inferior to men; had far fewer privileges, rights, and opportunities than men
14. *The Golden Lotus* and *The Dream of the Red Chamber*
15. blue and white porcelain

16. tobacco, clocks, eyeglasses
17. because of Jesuit practice of destroying local idols and shrines
18. They were barred by tradition from commercial activities and so they were unable to benefit from economic changes.
19. great expansion of trade and industry
20. subordinate to men; arranged marriages; female commoners valued as child bearers and homemakers; poor families sometimes put baby girls to death or sold them into prostitution
21. emphasized violence, music, and dramatic gestures to entertain viewers
22. greatest of all Japanese poets

USING KEY TERMS

1. A painful symbol of Chinese women's subordination was the tradition of _____.
2. The _____ (inside) daimyo were directly subordinate to the shogun and wielded only moderate power.
3. In the seventeenth century, _____ theatre emphasized violence, music, and drama.
4. The shogunate controlled the daimyo with a _____ , by which daimyo lords were forced to keep two residences.
5. The Qing system of sharing important government positions between the Chinese and the Manchu is called a _____.
6. Samurai that had been released from servitude to their lords were called _____.
7. The _____ (outside) daimyo were relatively independent regional lords, not under the direct control of the shogun.
8. During the Tokugawa shoguns, Japan was divided into 250 territories called _____.

REVIEWING THE FACTS

1. What year did the Portuguese make official contact with China?
2. What was the Chinese view of Europeans?
3. How did the Jesuits attempt to promote Christianity to the Chinese?
4. What were the causes of the decline of the Ming dynasty?
5. How did the Manchu acquire control of China?
6. What did "lose your hair or lose your head" mean?
7. How did the infighting among Christian missionaries contribute to the weakening of Christianity in Qing China?
8. What was the White Lotus Rebellion?
9. What did Russia seek to trade with the Chinese?
10. What was the Chinese attitude toward European products?

11. How did the Chinese economic system differ from that of Europe?
12. What were the benefits of the extended family in China?
13. What was the role of women in traditional China?
14. What two works stand out as examples of the Chinese novel during the Ming dynasty?
15. What types of Chinese art were most desired by Europeans?
16. What types of European goods were of interest to the Japanese?
17. Why did Toyotomi Hideyoshi turn against the Jesuit missionaries?
18. Explain how the Samurai gradually ceased to be a warrior class.
19. What economic changes took place under the Tokugawa shoguns?
20. What was the role of women in Tokugawa Japan?
21. Describe the characteristics of Kabuki theatre.
22. Who was Basho?

THINKING CRITICALLY

1. How would you compare the attitudes of Lord Macartney and the Chinese emperor, based on their comments in the opening of this chapter?
2. In 1433, the Ming emperor drastically cut off China's contact with the outside world. In what ways was this isolation positive or negative for China? What different course(s) might Chinese history have taken if this formal isolation had not been enacted?
3. Compare and contrast the policies of the two great Manchu rulers—Kangxi and Qianlong.
4. Is the dyarchy system, as employed in the Qing dynasty, a functional model for today's American society? Why or why not?
5. The strength of the Chinese family is legendary. Can you point to two or three factors discussed in the chapter that, in your opinion, help account for this?

THINKING CRITICALLY

1. Answers will vary. Responses may include that both men thought that his own civilization was superior to the other.
2. Answers will vary. Possible answers may include that China was not entirely sure of the affairs, actions, and accomplishments of the rest of the world and this lack of knowledge may have affected their other decisions regarding the openness (or lack of it) in China for years to come.
3. Answers will vary, but should include mention that both helped establish the greatness of Manchu China.

6. Rephrase the Confucian principles of the five relationships in a manner that they would be acceptable in today's American society.
7. Compare and contrast the social position of women in China and Japan during the years 1500 to 1800.
8. Do you believe that the plots of *The Golden Lotus* and *The Dream of the Red Chamber*, as discussed in the text, could take place in Western society? Why or why not?
9. Compare and contrast the life of the Japanese samurai with that of the European knight.
10. Read Basho's poems on page 571. Explain in prose the meaning of the poems.

APPLYING SOCIAL STUDIES SKILLS

1. **Government:** Under the Ming and Qing dynasties, China had a highly centralized government. In what ways was this good for China? In what ways was it a problem?
2. **Economics:** In what ways were the Chinese attitudes toward commerce different from those of the Europeans?
3. **Economics:** Explain the role that economics played in the collapse of the Ming dynasty.
4. **Art History:** Using the text's description of Chinese and Japanese novels of this time, can you identify themes that could be employed today in contemporary novels?
5. **Economics:** How did the Japanese attitudes toward commerce with Europe compare with those of the Chinese?

MAKING TIME AND PLACE CONNECTIONS

1. "The Chinese believed that only a male could carry on sacred family rituals and that only males had the ability to govern others," according to the text. How is this similar to, or different from, contemporary American attitudes?
2. Based on the text's description of the basic tenets of Kabuki theatre, how similar are its main goals to those of contemporary Western films and television?
3. How does the experience of Christian missionaries in China compare to that in Japan?

BECOMING AN HISTORIAN

1. **Cause and Effect:** What undesired effects came about as a result of the Ming emperors' decisions? Use the following as an example:
Cause: desire of the Ming emperors to keep Chinese culture free from elements of inferior cultures that might weaken Chinese society
Effect: decrees stopping contacts with other culture and isolating China
2. **Art as a Key to History:** Based on the text's relation of artistic achievements in China and Japan from 1500 to 1800, find evidence to support or contradict the following hypothesis: High levels of artistic achievement are found in a civilization only when there is political stability and economic prosperity.
3. **Conducting Research:** Go to a museum with extensive Chinese and Japanese holdings, or visit a major library, and locate as many examples of visual art as possible for this period of history. Ask for help from the reference librarian if you need it. After careful analysis of the objects, develop three or four statements that you believe apply to Chinese or Japanese art or society.

575

---

4. Answers will vary, but may include: not functional in that we do not have two distinct groups among which to divide and share the power. On the other hand, we already do have a system of shared power among the people.
5. Possible answers may include: emphasis on responsibility; caring for others; children being expected to obey their parents.
6. Answers will vary.
7. Answers will vary. Responses should compare and contrast some of the following information between the two groups.
China: inferior to men; not allowed formal education nor careers in government or scholarship; limited legal rights; in times of famine, daughters sometimes put to death; played strong roles within the family; obligated to foot binding
Japan: more restricted than in previous era; subordinate to men; arranged marriages; valued as child bearers and homemakers; one-quarter of students in rural schools were girls; regarded more highly among common people than among nobility; poor families often put baby girls to death or sold them into prostitution
8. Answers will vary.
9. Answers will vary.
10. Interpretations will vary.

PLANNING GUIDE

SECTION	KEY TOPICS	PRIMARY SOURCES	ASSESSMENT
1 Emergence of the Scientific Revolution pages 577–583	◆ Foundations of the Scientific Revolution ◆ A Revolution in astronomy ◆ Advancements in medicine	◆ A description of the telescope, page 581	◆ Section Review, page 583 ◆ Section Quiz 19–1, TRB
2 Aspects of the Scientific Revolution pages 583–587	◆ Women in modern science ◆ Descartes, rationalism and a new view of humankind ◆ The impact of science on religion ◆ The spread of scientific knowledge	◆ A description by Maria Winkelmann of her discovery of a comet, page 584 ◆ Descartes' statement of his own existence, page 585	◆ Section Review, page 587 ◆ Section Quiz 19–2, TRB
3 The Enlightenment pages 588–593	◆ Foundations of the Enlightenment ◆ New philosophies, new ideas ◆ The science of man in the later Enlightenment ◆ Society during the Enlightenment	◆ John Locke's belief that every person is born with a blank mind, page 588	◆ Section Review, page 593 ◆ Section Quiz 19–3, TRB
4 Culture and Society in an Age of Enlightenment pages 593–600	◆ Art, music, and literature during the Enlightenment ◆ Popular cultures in the eighteenth century ◆ Changes in the legal system	◆ A description of criminal punishment, page 599	◆ Section Review, page 600 ◆ Section Quiz 19–4, TRB
5 Religion and the Churches pages 601–604	◆ Toleration of religious minorities ◆ Popular Religion in the eighteenth century	◆ A copy of a father's advice to his son, page 603	◆ Section Review, page 604 ◆ Section Quiz 19–5, TRB

TOWARD A NEW HEAVEN AND A NEW EARTH:
AN INTELLECTUAL REVOLUTION IN THE WEST (1500 TO 1800)

REPRODUCIBLE ACTIVITIES

- Historical Maps
- Charts and Graphs
- Critical Thinking
- Cooperative Learning
- Vocabulary
- Guided Reading
- Reteaching
- Enrichment
- Performance Assessment
- Spanish Key Points and Chapter Summaries
- Spanish Vocabulary
- Spanish Guided Reading

MULTIMEDIA SUPPORT

TRANSPARENCIES
- ◆ *World History* Color Transparency Package
- ◆ Fine Art Color Transparency Package

VIDEO
- ◆ *World History* Video Library
- ◆ CNN® Annual Video Update

LASERDISC
- ◆ *Sights and Sounds of History*

AUDIO
- ◆ *Listening to Literature* audiotape (English and Spanish)
- ◆ *History of Music* CD

SOFTWARE
- ◆ WESTEST™
- ◆ Student Review

CD–ROM
- ◆ *The Journey of Civilization*
- ◆ *World History*

INTERNET
- ◆ Internet Activities

On Line with WORLD HISTORY

Access West's history web site at
http://history.swpco.com
You'll find activities and web sites related to specific topics and chapters in *World History: The Human Odyssey*. Also look for references to helpful web sites at appropriate places throughout this teacher edition.

LESSON PLANNING

You will find detailed daily lesson plans for both traditional class scheduling and **block scheduling** in your Teacher Resource Box.

Not Enough Time?

If you do not have the four or five days recommended to teach this chapter, you may want to focus on the following sections and activities:

- ◆ Have students skim the chapter to answer the "Questions to Guide Your Reading" on page 577. Discuss their answers, then read the "Conclusion" on page 605.
- ◆ Do a more in-depth reading about the background of the Scientific Revolution on pages 577–578, the role of women in the Scientific Revolution on pages 583–584, relations between science and religion on pages 585–586, the Enlightenment on pages 588–591, changes in culture on pages 598–600, and popular religion on pages 602–604. Conclude with a class discussion of why leaders of the Catholic Church forced Galileo to recant his conclusions about the nature of the universe.

TOWARD A NEW HEAVEN AND A NEW EARTH:

19

BUILDING ON CHAPTER 18

To "set the scene" for the study of Chapter 19, use the following questions and activities.

◆ Remind students of economic, political, and social changes that took place in China as a result of contact with Europeans.

◆ Ask students to describe the role of women in Chinese society and be prepared to compare it to the role of women in Europe during the Enlightenment.

LEARNING FROM VISUALS

Answer to the caption question: Until the time of Galileo, most people believed that the moon and stars were made of pure, unblemished, heavenly materials.

USING THE OPENING STORY

Select from the following questions and activities to reinforce the reading of the opening story.

◆ Have students debate the choice between self-respect and self-preservation that Galileo was forced to make by leaders of the Catholic church. What do students believe they would have done in Galileo's situation?

◆ Have students identify religious and ethical conflicts that scientific advancements have forced on society in recent years.

In 1633, the Italian scientist Galileo (GAL-uh-LAE-oh) was put on trial by the Catholic Church for maintaining that the sun was the center of the universe and that the Earth moves around the sun. Galileo, who was 68 years old and in ill health, was kept waiting for two months before he was tried and found guilty of heresy and disobedience. Completely shattered by the experience, Galileo condemned his supposed errors: "With a sincere heart I curse and detest the said errors contrary to the Holy Church, and I swear that I will nevermore in future say or assert anything that may give rise to a similar suspicion of me." Legend holds that when he left the trial room, Galileo muttered to himself, "And yet it does move!" (referring to the Earth). Galileo was but one of the scientists of the seventeenth century who set the Western world on a new path known as the Scientific Revolution. The Scientific Revolution brought to Europeans a new way of viewing the universe and their place in it.

The Scientific Revolution affected only a small number of Europe's educated elite in the seventeenth century. Its effect widened in the eighteenth century, however, as a group of intellectuals used the ideas of the Scientific Revolution to reexamine all aspects of life. The widespread impact of their ideas on European society has caused historians ever since to call the eighteenth century in Europe the Enlightenment.

The great scientists of the seventeenth century believed that their work exalted God. The intellectuals of the eighteenth century, however, saw things differently. Increasingly, intellectuals turned their backs on their Christian heritage. Consequently, European intellectual life in the eighteenth century underwent a revolutionary transition. No longer did thinkers take a Christian outlook on the world.

They began to have the largely secular, rational, and materialistic perspective that has defined modern Western thought in the nineteenth and twentieth centuries.

▶ *By using this telescope, Galileo was able to determine that the moon's surface was pitted and irregular. Why did other people throughout Europe find this so difficult to believe?*

ADDITIONAL RESOURCES

The resources listed below can be used to enrich the lessons in this chapter.

BOOKS FOR STUDENTS
The Age of Enlightenment by Peter Gay, Time Life
Voltaire! Voltaire! by Guy Endore, Simon and Schuster
The Universe of Galileo and Newton by William Bixby, Horizon Caravell,

Harper & Row

VIDEOS/FILMS
The Age of Reason, Chariot Productions, Social Studies School Service (800) 421-4262
Galileo: The Challenge of Reason, Learning Corporation of America, Social Studies School Service (800) 421-4262

AN INTELLECTUAL REVOLUTION IN THE WEST (1550 TO 1800)

NEW WORLD PATTERNS

QUESTIONS TO GUIDE YOUR READING

1. How do you explain the emergence of the Scientific Revolution?

2. What was the old Ptolemaic conception of the universe? What did Copernicus, Kepler, Galileo, and Newton contribute to the development of a new conception of the universe?

3. What was the Enlightenment? What contributions did Montesquieu, Voltaire, Diderot, and Rousseau make to the Enlightenment?

4. What role did women play in the development of the Scientific Revolution and the Enlightenment?

5. What innovations occurred in art, music, and literature during the eighteenth century?

6. What is the difference between high culture and popular culture?

EMERGENCE OF THE SCIENTIFIC REVOLUTION

In one sense, the Scientific Revolution was not a revolution. It was not marked by the rapid change and overthrow of traditional authority that we normally associate with the word *revolution*. The Scientific Revolution did overturn centuries of scientific authority, but only in a gradual and piecemeal fashion.

Background to the Scientific Revolution

To say that the Scientific Revolution brought an end to the medieval worldview is not to say that the Middles Ages was a period of scientific ignorance. Many educated Europeans took an intense interest in the world around them. It was, after all, "God's handiwork" and therefore a fit subject for study. However, medieval "natural philosophers," as medieval scientists were known, did not make observations of the natural world. These scientists relied on a few ancient authorities—especially Aristotle and Galen—for their scientific knowledge. A number of changes in the fifteenth

577

FOCUS ON THEMES

The Role of Ideas The Scientific Revolution and the Enlightenment were important turning points in the history of both Western civilization and world civilization. The ideas of both laid the foundations for a modern worldview based on rationalism and secularism.

Social Life The seventeenth and eighteenth centuries witnessed an increasing separation between the elite and the lower classes.

The Importance of Cultural Developments The seventeenth and eighteenth centuries were brilliant centuries culturally. In art and architecture, Baroque, Rococo, and neoclassical styles were the most prevalent. In music—Bach, Handel, Haydn, and Mozart—dominated the scene.

Religion in History Despite the emergence of new secular perspectives, religion continued to play an important role in European society. In England, Protestantism witnessed a revival of religious enthusiasm in Methodism.

The Role of Individuals Individuals played a crucial role in both the Scientific Revolution and the Enlightenment. We cannot think of the Scientific Revolution without mentioning the names Copernicus, Galileo, Kepler, and Newton. The Enlightenment brings to mind the names Voltaire, Diderot, and Rousseau.

The Impact of Science and Technology The Scientific Revolution was a crucial step in creating a new conception of the universe, as well as a modern civilization based on a secular, rational, and materialistic perspective.

577

FOCUS

OBJECTIVES

After completing this section, students should be able to

1. identify and explain foundations of the Scientific Revolution
2. describe the impact of advancements in astronomy on European civilization
3. describe the impact of advancements in medicine on European civilization

FOCUS ACTIVITY

Help students understand why all parts of society are ultimately affected by scientific advancements. Discuss the root discoveries of many of the products Americans take for granted. Ask students to list and explain ways the invention of the internal combustion engine has changed their lives.

LEARNING FROM VISUALS

Answer to the caption question: Latin was the common, accepted language for scholars and scribes.

and sixteenth centuries, however, played a major role in helping the natural philosophers abandon their old views and develop new ones.

The Renaissance humanists mastered Greek as well as Latin and thus made available new works of Ptolemy and Archimedes, as well as Plato. These writings made it obvious that even some ancient thinkers had disagreed with Aristotle and Galen, the accepted authorities of the Middle Ages. Intellectuals wanted to find out which school of thought was right, and thus they pursued new scientific work. As we shall see, their search for truth sometimes meant a complete rejection of the ideas of both Aristotle and Galen.

Renaissance artists also made an impact on scientific study. Their desire to imitate nature led them to make a close observation of nature. Their accurate paintings of rocks, plants, animals, and human anatomy established new standards for the study of natural objects. At the same time, they studied the problems of perspective and correct anatomical proportions.

Technical problems that required careful observation and accurate measurements, such as calculating the amount of weight that ships could hold, also served to stimulate scientific activity. Then, too, the invention of new instruments and machines, such as the telescope and microscope, often made fresh scientific discoveries possible. Above all, the printing press played a crucial role in spreading new ideas quickly and easily.

Mathematics played a very important role in the scientific achievements of the sixteenth and seventeenth centuries. Mathematics was promoted in the Renaissance by the rediscovery of the works of ancient mathematicians. The works of the Greek philosopher Plato were also influential, because Plato had stressed the importance of mathematics in explaining the universe. Mathematics was seen as the key to navigation, military science, and geography. Renaissance thinkers also believed that mathematics was the key to understanding the nature of things in the universe. Nicolaus Copernicus, Johannes Kepler, Galileo Galilei (GAL-uh-LAY-EE), and Isaac Newton were all great mathematicians of the time who believed that the secrets of nature were written in the language of mathematics. The mention of these names also reminds us that the

Scientific Revolution largely resulted from the work of a handful of great intellectuals.

Toward a New Heaven: A Revolution in Astronomy

The philosophers of the Middle Ages had used the ideas of Aristotle, Ptolemy (the greatest astronomer of antiquity, who lived in the second century A.D.), and Christianity to construct the **Ptolemaic,** or **geocentric** (Earth-centered), conception of the universe. *Ptolemaic* or *geocentric* refers to the view that the universe is a series of concentric (one inside the other) spheres with a fixed or motionless Earth as its center. The Earth, composed of material substance, was seen as being imperfect and constantly changing. The spheres that surrounded the Earth were made of a crystal-like, transparent substance and moved in circular orbits

▲ *This diagram depicts the medieval conception of the universe, with the earth at the center and God and heaven placed outside the tenth sphere. Why do you think the writing is in Latin?*

MORE ABOUT . . . *Copernicus*

The writings of Nicholas Copernicus are said to have triggered what is today known as the Copernican Revolution. However, there are several ironies associated with Copernicus. While he is credited with starting the Copernican Revolution, he himself missed it. Not only did he die shortly after publishing his theories, but his book was largely ignored until the next century.

Furthermore, he thought that he would best be remembered for his theory of circularity, which is that the planets rotate in near-perfect circles. This theory was later proven to be incorrect. Nor was he the first person to suggest that the earth goes around the sun. That honor goes to Nicctas, a philosopher from ancient times.

▲ *The Copernican system shown in this illustration is taken from the first edition of* On the Revolutions of the Heavenly Spheres. *Do you think it represents a direct contrast to the medieval view of the universe?*

around the Earth. The heavenly bodies, seen as pure orbs of light, were embedded in the moving, concentric spheres. In the year 1500 it was believed there were ten of these concentric spheres. Working outward from the Earth, the first eight spheres contained the moon, Mercury, Venus, the sun, Mars, Jupiter, Saturn, and the fixed stars. The ninth sphere gave to the eighth sphere (the sphere of the fixed stars) its daily motion. The tenth sphere was considered the prime mover that moved itself and gave motion to the other spheres.

Beyond the tenth sphere was Heaven, where God and all the saved souls resided. This geocentric conception of the universe, then, was a finite one. The universe had a fixed end. God and the saved souls were at one end of the universe, and humans were at the center. Human beings had been given power over the Earth, but their real purpose was to achieve salvation.

In May 1543, shortly before his death, Nicholas Copernicus, a native of Poland, published his famous book, *On the Revolutions of the Heavenly Spheres*.

Copernicus was a mathematician who felt that the geocentric system was too complicated. He believed that it could not possibly be correct. Copernicus believed that his **heliocentric,** or sun-centered, conception of the universe offered a more accurate explanation.

Copernicus argued that it was the sun, not the Earth, that was at the center of the universe. The planets revolved around the sun in the order of Mercury, Venus, Earth, Mars, Jupiter, and Saturn. The moon, however, revolved around the Earth. Moreover, according to Copernicus, what appeared to be the movement of the sun around the Earth was really explained by the daily rotation of the Earth on its axis and the journey of the Earth around the sun each year. Copernicus, however, did not reject the idea that the heavenly spheres move in circular orbits around the sun.

The ideas of Copernicus had no immediate effect. Most people were not yet ready to accept the theory of Copernicus, but there were growing doubts about the Ptolemaic, or geocentric, system. The next step in destroying the Ptolemaic conception and supporting the Copernican system was taken by the German Johannes Kepler.

Kepler was a brilliant mathematician and astronomer who took a post as imperial mathematician to Emperor Rudolf II of the Holy Roman Empire. Kepler used the detailed astronomical data that his predecessor had collected to arrive at his laws of planetary motion. These confirmed Copernicus's belief that the sun was at the center of the universe. However, Kepler also contradicted Copernicus. In Kepler's first law he showed that the orbits of the planets around the sun were not circular but elliptical (egg-shaped), with the sun toward the end of the ellipse rather than at the center.

Kepler's work destroyed the basic structure of the traditional Ptolemaic system. People were now free to think in new terms of the planets revolving around the sun in elliptical orbits. Important questions remained unanswered, however. What were the planets made of? How does one explain motion in the universe? It was an Italian scientist who answered the first question.

Galileo Galilei taught mathematics. He was the first European to make regular observations of the heavens using a telescope, thereby beginning a new age in

RECOMMENDED READING

Three general surveys of the entire Scientific Revolution are A. G. R. Smith, *Science and Society in the Sixteenth and Seventeenth Centuries* (London, 1972); M. Boas, *The Scientific Renaissance: 1450–1630* (London, 1962); and H. Butterfield, *The Origins of Modern Science* (New York, 1962). A more detailed and technical introduction can be found in A. R. Hall, *The Revolution in Science, 1500–1750* (London, 1983). Also of much

value is A. G. Debus, *Man and Nature in the Renaissance* (Cambridge, 1978), which covers the period from the mid-fifteenth through the mid-seventeenth centuries. The importance of mathematics to the Scientific Revolution is brought out in P. L. Rose, *The Italian Renaissance of Mathematics: Studies on Humanists and Mathematicians from Petrarch to Galileo* (Geneva, 1975).

TEACH

LEARNING FROM VISUALS

Tell students to compare the diagrams of Ptolemaic and Copernican conceptions of the universe. Ask them why a plan with the Earth as the center of the universe was more appealing to religious leaders.

Answer to the caption question: Answers will vary.

THE IMPORTANCE OF INDIVIDUALS

The text states the "Scientific Revolution largely resulted from the work of a handful of great intellectuals." Divide the class into groups and ask each group to evaluate the following alternative statement. "Changes in European civilization encouraged development of new ideas that became the basis for the Scientific Revolution."

The question is, did the men make the times or did the times make the men?

ACROSS THE CURRICULUM

Mathematics Lead students in a discussion of how advancements in mathematics have impacted their lives. For example, the fuel economy of automobiles has improved because of mathematical-based changes in engines and structural design.

THE ROLE OF INDIVIDUALS

Many of the most famous figures in history gained notoriety because of their ability to combine, organize, and apply the work of others. This was the case with Isaac Newton. Assign students to identify a different historical figure they have studied and explain how this person built on the work of others to make his or her contribution to history.

LEARNING FROM VISUALS

Ask students to explain why the saying "one picture is worth a thousand words" is often true. Assign them to identify a scientific concept that they understand but which would have been more difficult to learn without drawings, pictures, or diagrams similar to these that were drawn by Galileo.

astronomy (see "The Role of Science and Technology: The Telescope in the Scientific Revolution"). Galileo turned his telescope to the skies and made a remarkable series of discoveries: mountains on the moon, four moons revolving around Jupiter, the phases of Venus, and sunspots. Galileo's observations seemed to destroy yet another aspect of the geocentric conception. The universe seemed to be composed of material substance similar to that of the Earth rather than some kind of perfect substance (the pure orbs of light).

Galileo's discoveries, published in *The Starry Messenger* in 1610, startled his contemporaries. Galileo did more to make Europeans aware of the new view of the universe than did Copernicus or Kepler. In the midst of his newfound fame, however, Galileo found himself increasingly suspect by the authorities of the Catholic Church.

The Catholic Church condemned the work of Copernicus and ordered Galileo to abandon the Copernican idea. The church attacked the Copernican system because it threatened the church's entire conception of the universe. Under the Copernican view, the heavens were no longer a spiritual world but a world of matter. Humans were no longer at the center of the universe, and God was no longer in a specific place. The church could only condemn a new system that created such uncertainties and seemed to contradict the Bible.

The attack on Galileo by the Catholic Church made further scientific work in Italy almost impossible. Leadership in science now passed from Italy to the northern countries, especially England, France, and the Dutch Netherlands. By the 1630s and 1640s, most astronomers had come to accept the new heliocentric conception of the universe. However, the problem of explaining motion in the universe and tying together the ideas of Copernicus, Galileo, and Kepler had not yet been solved. This was to be the work of an Englishman who has long since been considered the greatest genius of the Scientific Revolution.

Born in 1642, the young Isaac Newton showed few signs of brilliance until he attended Cambridge University. Later, he accepted a chair of mathematics at the university and wrote his major work, *Mathematical Principles of Natural Philosophy* (known simply as the *Principia* by the first word of its Latin title). In this

▲ *Galileo was the first European scientist who used a telescope to make methodical observations of the moon and the night sky. Galileo prepared these drawings of the moon for one of his books.*

work, Newton spelled out the mathematical proofs that supported his universal law of gravitation. Newton's work completed the ideas of Copernicus, Kepler, and Galileo. Each had undermined some part of the Ptolemaic, or geocentric, view of the universe. No one until Newton, however, had put together all the parts of a new conception of the universe.

In the first book of the *Principia*, Newton defined the three laws of motion. First, every object continues in a state of rest or uniform motion in a straight line unless deflected (turned aside) by a force. Second, the

A good introduction to the transformation from the late medieval to the early modern worldview is A. Koyré, *From the Closed World to the Infinite Universe* (New York, 1958). Also still of value are A. Koestler, *The Sleepwalkers: A History of Man's Changing Vision of the Universe* (New York, 1959); and E. A. Burtt, *The Metaphysical Foundations of Modern Physical Science* (London, 1942). On the revolution in astronomy, see E. Rosen, *Copernicus and the Scientific Revolution* (New York, 1984); C. Morphet, *Galileo and Copernican Astronomy* (London 1977); S. Drake, *Galileo* (New York, 1980); M. Casper, *Johannes Kepler,* trans. C. D. Hellman (London, 1959), the standard biography; and F. Manuel, *A Portrait of Isaac Newton* (Cambridge, Mass., 1968). On Newton's relationship to alchemy, see the study by B. J. Dobbs, *The Foundations of Newton's Alchemy* (Cambridge, 1975).

THE ROLE OF SCIENCE AND TECHNOLOGY

The Telescope in the Scientific Revolution

The telescope played an important role in the astronomical discoveries of the Scientific Revolution. The telescope was first invented in Holland by Hans Lippershey in 1608. However, it was the Italian scientist Galileo Galilei who made history with the telescope by focusing it on the heavenly bodies. In his book *The Starry Messenger*, Galileo discussed how he came to make a telescope:

This portrait of Galileo Galilei provides us with some realistic evidence about his appearance. Do you think it is odd that he dressed simply and somberly? Why or why not?

About ten months ago a report reached my ears that a certain Fleming had constructed a spyglass by means of which visible objects, though very distant from the eye of the observer, were distinctly seen as if nearby. Of this truly remarkable effect several experiences were related, to which some persons gave credence while others denied them. This caused me to apply myself wholeheartedly to inquire into the means by which I might arrive at the invention of a similar instrument. This I did shortly afterwards, my basis being the theory of refraction. First I prepared a tube of lead, at the ends of which I fitted two glass lenses, both plane [flat] on one side while on the other side one was spherically convex and the other concave. Then placing my eye near the concave lens I perceived objects satisfactorily large and near, for they appeared three times closer and nine times larger than when seen with the naked eye alone. Next I constructed another one, more accurate, which represented objects as enlarged more than sixty times. Finally, sparing neither labor nor expense, I succeeded in constructing for myself so excellent an instrument that objects seen by means of it appeared nearly one thousand times larger and

over thirty times closer than when regarded with our natural vision.

In the course of the seventeenth century, new and better telescopes were made. Some of them were very long and made use of strong stands to keep them focused on a single object in the sky. Even with these advances, however, color distortion and blurring were regular problems with the early telescopes. The English scientist Isaac Newton solved the problems by developing the reflecting telescope. His telescope used a concave mirror that focused the images from the sky on an eyepiece, thus eliminating any distortion.

1. Who invented the telescope?

2. Who made history with the telescope?

3. What major advance in telescopes is attributed to Isaac Newton?

4. The invention of the telescope allowed scientists to study the stars and planets. In what areas other than science might the telescope have been used?

MORE ABOUT . . . *Galileo*

Galileo traveled to Rome in 1615 to ask Pope Paul V if he could teach the ideas of Copernicus. The Pope, aware of criticism that the Catholic Church wasn't "Biblical enough," said no. Galileo figured he could get around the Pope's ruling by writing a book in which two laymen argued about the two world views, one Copernicus', the other Aristotle's. He himself would take no position on the matter. However, he made the adherent of the old world view an idiot and the believer in Copernicus a wise man. To make matters worse he took some of the arguments supporting Aristotle directly from the writings of the new pope, Urban VIII, and had them spoken by the fool. The new pope felt not only that he was being mocked, but that Galileo had broken his word. In 1992 Pope John Paul II admitted that the Church was wrong in persecuting Galileo.

ASSESS

Answers to
SECTION REVIEW

1. (a) earth-centered conception of the universe
   (b) theory that sun is center of the universe
   (c) Newton's law of motion
2. (a) greatest astronomer of antiquity
   (b) said the sun was at the center of the universe
   (c) showed that the orbits of the planets around the sun were elliptical
   (d) used a telescope to discover many things
   (e) considered the greatest genius of the Scientific Revolution
   (f) professor of surgery, wrote *On the Fabric of the Human Body*
   (g) wrote *On the Motion of the Heart and Blood*
3. (a) Copernicus, Kepler, Galileo, and Newton
   (b) objects continue in a state of rest or uniform motion in a straight line unless deflected by a force; (2) the rate of change of motion of an object is proportional to the force acting upon it; and (3) to every action there is an equal and opposite reaction
4. Answers will vary.

CLOSE

LEARNING FROM VISUALS

Answer to the caption question: National pride, conviction, and political factors made it difficult for the continent to accept the English view.

582

rate of change of motion of an object is proportional to the force acting upon it. Third, to every action there is always an equal and opposite reaction. In Book 3, Newton applied his theories of motion to the problems of astronomy. He showed that his three laws of motion govern the planetary bodies, as well as objects on Earth. Crucial to his whole argument was the **universal law of gravitation,** which explained why the planetary bodies did not go off in straight lines but instead continued in elliptical orbits about the sun. This law explained, in mathematical terms, that every object in the universe is attracted to every other object by a force called gravity.

Newton's ideas had an enormous impact, even if it took another century before they were widely recognized. Newton had shown that one universal law mathematically proved could explain all motion in the universe. The secrets of the natural world could be known by humans working on Earth. At the same time, Newton's ideas created a new picture of the universe. It was now seen as one huge, regulated, and uniform machine that worked according to natural laws in absolute time, space, and motion. Although Newton believed that God was "everywhere present" and acted as the force that moved all bodies on the basis of the laws he had discovered, later generations would drop his spiritual assumptions. Newton's world-machine concept dominated the modern worldview until the twentieth century, when Albert Einstein's concept of relativity created a new picture of the universe (see Chapter 26).

The Breakthrough in Medicine

There was also a Scientific Revolution in medicine. Medicine in the Late Middle Ages was dominated by the teachings of the Greek physician Galen, who had lived in the second century A.D. Galen had relied on animal, rather than human, dissection to arrive at a picture of human anatomy, and he was wrong in many

◄ *Sir Godfrey Kneller painted this portrait of Isaac Newton. Newton's ideas gained rapid acceptance in England, but they were not readily accepted throughout Europe until the late eighteenth century. Why do you think continental Europe was so slow to recognize the brilliance of Newton's work?*

instances. Physiology, or the study of the functioning of the body, was also dominated by the ideas of Galen. These ideas included the belief that there were two separate blood systems. One controlled muscular activities and contained bright red blood moving upward and downward through the arteries. The other blood system governed the digestive functions and contained dark red blood that ebbed and flowed in the veins.

Two major figures are associated with the changes in medicine that took place in the sixteenth and seventeenth centuries: Andreas Vesalius and William Harvey. The new anatomy of the sixteenth century was the work of Andreas Vesalius. In his 1543 book, *On the Fabric of the Human Body*, Vesalius discussed what he had discovered by personally dissecting the human body while he was a professor of surgery at the University of Padua (PAJ-uh-wuh). Vesalius presented a careful examination of the individual organs and general structure of the human body. Vesalius's "hands-on" approach to teaching anatomy enabled him to overthrow some of Galen's most glaring errors. Vesalius did not hesitate, for example, to correct Galen's belief that the great blood vessels originated from the liver, because his own direct observations made it apparent that they came from the heart. Nevertheless, Vesalius still clung to Galen's erroneous ideas on the ebb and flow of two kinds of blood in the veins and arteries. It was William Harvey's work on the circulation of the blood that corrected this view.

Harvey's reputation rests upon his book *On the Motion of the Heart and Blood*, published in 1628. Harvey's work, which was based upon close observations and experiments, led him to destroy the work of Galen.

On Line with WORLD HISTORY Internet Activity

You may want to have your students visit the following URL, where they will find information and additional web site resources to enhance their study of this chapter.

The Galileo Project
http://es.rice.edu/ES/humsoc/ Galileo/index.html

A superior web page done by Rice University. A complete source of almost anything one would want to know about Galileo and his life and works.

Due to the ever-changing nature of the World Wide Web, see the West History web site, **http://history.swpco.com** for regular updates of the URLs in this text.

▶ *Illustrations such as this one from Andreas Vesalius's* On the Fabric of the Human Body *did much to revolutionize the understanding of the human anatomy and the practice of medicine. How accurate is this depiction of the human body?*

Harvey showed that the heart, not the liver, was the beginning point for the circulation of blood in the body. He also proved that the same blood flows in both veins and arteries. Most important, the blood makes a complete circuit as it passes through the body. Harvey's theory of the circulation of the blood laid the foundation for modern physiology.

❁ SECTION REVIEW ❁

1. **Define:**
   (*a*) Ptolemaic or geocentric, (*b*) heliocentric,
   (*c*) universal law of gravitation

2. **Identify:**
   (*a*) Claudius Ptolemy, (*b*) Nicholas Copernicus,
   (*c*) Johannes Kepler, (*d*) Galileo Galilei,
   (*e*) Isaac Newton, (*f*) Andreas Vesalius,
   (*g*) William Harvey

3. **Recall:**
   (*a*) List four great mathematicians who believed that the secrets of nature were written in the language of mathematics.
   (*b*) What are Newton's three laws of motion?

4. **Think Critically:** Why do you think the Catholic Church condemned the work of scientists during the seventeenth and eighteenth centuries? Explain your answer.

ASPECTS OF THE SCIENTIFIC REVOLUTION

A new view of the universe and a new view of the human body were two achievements of the early Scientific Revolution. This revolution also raised other issues that led to new developments.

Women and the Origins of Modern Science

Women as well as men were involved in the Scientific Revolution. However, women were mostly excluded from universities. Thus, to pursue their scientific interests, women were forced to obtain a largely informal education. European nobles had the leisure and resources that gave them easy access to the world of learning. This door was also open to noblewomen, who could take part in the informal scientific networks of their fathers and brothers.

One of the most prominent female scientists of the seventeenth century, Margaret Cavendish, came from an aristocratic family. She took part in the important scientific debates of her time. Despite her achievements, however, she was not allowed to become a member of the English Royal Society (see "The Spread of Scientific Knowledge" later in this section), although she was once allowed to attend a meeting. She wrote a number of works on scientific matters, including

MORE ABOUT . . . *Medicine*

In the 17th century one family created an obstetrical monopoly with the invention of a device to more easily remove a child during birth. Peter Chamberlen invented a pair of metal forceps, which could be inserted into a pregnant woman's vagina, clamp onto her baby's head and then pull the child out. For this he earned the title, "man-midwife"

(obstetrician). His son formed a business, which eventually came to be so powerful that it was not possible to obtain a medical license in Amsterdam without first paying an enormous sum to purchase Chamberlen's forceps. For 130 years the Chamberlen family had a monopoly on the obstetrical forceps.

FOCUS

OBJECTIVES

After completing this section, students should be able to

1. describe the role of women in advancements during the Scientific Revolution
2. explain the ideas of Descartes, rationalism, and the new view of humankind that was developed
3. identify and explain the impact scientific discoveries had on religion
4. describe how scientific knowledge spread through European society

FOCUS ACTIVITY

Lead students in a discussion of why denying a group access to knowledge or the opportunity to make use of their abilities is harmful to all members of society. With the exception of a few individuals, women were excluded from participation in the Scientific Revolution. Ask students if they believe scientific advancements could have been made more rapidly if women had been able to participate. If this is so, why is it reasonable that all of European society suffered from the exclusion of women?

TEACH

LEARNING FROM VISUALS

Answer to the caption question: Considering the information available to Vesalius, this illustration is quite good.

USING PRIMARY SOURCES

Ask students to discuss whether Maria Winkelmann's husband may have been more surprised because his wife found the comet or that he had not found it. Might prejudice explain why early female writers sometimes chose to use a male pseudonym?

TEACHING THEMES

The Role of Individuals. Despite attempts by men to prevent women from participating in the Scientific Revolution, some did. How important do students believe the efforts of women like Margaret Cavendish and Maria Winkelmann were to the ultimate progress of the women's rights movement in the twentieth century?

LEARNING FROM VISUALS

Answer to the caption question: Answers will vary.

Observations upon Experimental Philosophy and *Grounds of Natural Philosophy.* In these works she was especially critical of the growing belief that humans, through science, were the masters of nature: "We have no power at all over natural causes and effects. . . . for man is but a small part, . . . his powers are but particular actions of Nature, and he cannot have a supreme and absolute power."[1]

As an aristocrat, the Duchess of Cavendish was a good example of the women in France and England who worked in science. Women interested in science who lived in Germany came from a different background. There, the tradition of female participation in craft production enabled some women to become involved in observational science, especially astronomy. Between 1650 and 1710, women made up 14 percent of all German astronomers.

The most famous of the female astronomers in Germany was Maria Winkelmann. She was educated by her father and uncle and received training in astronomy from a nearby self-taught astronomer. Her chance to be a practicing astronomer came when she married Gottfried Kirch (GOT-FREED KIRK), Germany's foremost astronomer. She became his assistant at the astronomical observatory operated in Berlin by the Academy of Science. She made some original contributions, including the discovery of a comet. Her husband described the discovery:

> Early in the morning (about 2:00 A.M.) the sky was clear and starry. Some nights before, I had observed a variable star, and my wife (as I slept) wanted to find and see it for herself. In so doing, she found a comet in the sky. At which time she woke me, and I found that it was indeed a comet . . . I was surprised that I had not seen it the night before.[2]

▲ *Margaret Cavendish, the Duchess of Newcastle, is shown in this portrait. Why do you think women were denied access to a university education and to membership in scientific organizations? What connection do you see between these practices and the affirmative action policies in the United States during the last half-century?*

When her husband died, Winkelmann applied for a position as assistant astronomer at the Berlin Academy, for which she was highly qualified. As a woman—with no university degree—she was denied the post. Members of the Berlin Academy feared that they would establish a bad example by hiring a woman. "Mouths would gape," they said.

Winkelmann's problems with the Berlin Academy reflect the obstacles women faced in being accepted in scientific work, which was considered to be chiefly for males only. No woman was invited to join either the Royal Society of England or the French Academy of Sciences until the twentieth century. Most people in the seventeenth century viewed a life devoted to any kind of scholarship as being at odds with the domestic duties women were expected to perform.

Overall, the Scientific Revolution did little to change people's ideas about the nature of women. Male scientists used the new science to spread the view that women were by nature inferior and subordinate to men and suited to play a domestic role as nurturing mothers. The widespread distribution of books ensured the continuation of these ideas. A seventeenth-century French writer spoke for many people when he remarked that an educated woman was like a gun that was a collector's item "which one shows to the curious, but which has no use at all, any more than a carousel horse."

Toward a New Earth: Descartes, Rationalism, and a New View of Humankind

The new conception of the universe brought about by the Scientific Revolution had an impact on the Western view of humankind. Nowhere is this more evident

---

RECOMMENDED READING

On the role of women in the salon, see P. Quennell, ed., *Affairs of the Mind: The Salon in Europe and America from the 18th to the 20th Century* (Washington, D.C., 1980).

The importance of Francis Bacon in the early development of science is underscored in P. Rossi, *Francis Bacon: From Magic to Science* (Chicago, 1968); and C. Webster, *The Great Instauration: Science, Medicine, and Reform, 1620–1660* (London, 1975). A good

introduction to the work of Descartes can be found in A. Kenny, *Descartes* (New York, 1968).

On women and early modern science, see L. Schiebinger, *The Mind Has No Sex? Women in the Origins of Modern Science* (Cambridge, Mass., 1989). The social and political context for the triumph of science is examined in M. Jacobs, *The Cultural Meaning of the Scientific Revolution* (New York, 1988).

▲ *René Descartes is pictured here with Queen Christina of Sweden, who invited Descartes to her court. Throughout his life Descartes never stopped searching for rational explanations for natural phenomena. Why would this have put him at odds with religious teachings of the time?*

than in the work of the seventeenth-century French philosopher René Descartes (ruh-NAY dae-KART). Descartes began by reflecting the doubt and uncertainty that seemed everywhere in the confusion of the seventeenth century. He ended with a philosophy that dominated Western thought until the twentieth century.

The starting point for Descartes's new system was doubt. As he explained in his most famous work, *Discourse on Method*, written in 1637, he decided to set aside all that he had learned and to begin again. One fact seemed to Descartes beyond doubt—his own existence:

> But I immediately became aware that while I was thus disposed to think that all was false, it was absolutely

necessary that I who thus thought should be something; and noting that this truth I think, therefore I am, *was so steadfast and so assured . . . I concluded that I might without scruple accept it as being the first principle of the philosophy I was seeking.*[3]

With this emphasis on the mind, Descartes asserted that he would accept only those things that his reason (a supported conclusion) said were true.

From his first principle—*I think, therefore I am*—Descartes used his reason to arrive at a second principle—the separation of mind and matter. Descartes argued that because "the mind cannot be doubted but the body and material world can, the two must be radically different." From this idea came a separation between mind and matter (and mind and body), or what has been called **Cartesian dualism.** Humans can use their minds or human reason (the path to certain knowledge) to understand the material world.

Descartes's separation of mind and matter allowed scientists to view matter as dead or inert—as something that was totally separate from themselves and that could be investigated independently by reason. The split between mind and body led westerners to equate identity with mind and reason rather than with the whole organism. Descartes has rightly been called the father of modern **rationalism** (a system of thought based on the belief that reason is the chief source of knowledge).

Science and Religion in the Seventeenth Century

In Galileo's struggle with the Catholic Church, we see the beginning of the conflict or split between science and religion that has marked the history of modern Western civilization. For centuries, theology had seemed to be the queen of the sciences. It was natural that the churches would continue to believe that religion was the final measure of everything. The emerging scientists, however, were discovering things about the natural world that were at odds with the teachings of religious leaders.

Many seventeenth-century intellectuals were both religious and scientific. Thus, they feared the consequences of the split between science and religion.

ENRICHMENT ACTIVITY

CLASS DISCUSSION

Divide the class into groups and ask each group to rewrite the quotation from Pascal, "Man is but a reed, the weakest in nature; but he is a thinking reed," in words that would allow other people to understand its meaning. Ask each group to read and discuss their explanations.

ACTIVITY

Assign students to write a letter that might have been written by a Christian leader to his religious superior describing the causes and problems of the continued secularization of European society that resulted from the Scientific Revolution. Ask them to include a suggestion in their letter for how the Church should react to this problem.

LEARNING FROM VISUALS

Ask students to speculate about the significance of the fact that there are no women in the painting on page 587.

Answer to the caption question: Students should realize that royal patrons often dictated the course of research or the kinds of research that would be acceptable.

ASSESS

Possible assessments include:

1. Section Review Questions on this page
2. Section 19–2 Quiz in your Teacher Resource materials
3. Reteaching Worksheets in your Teacher Resource materials
4. Self-Study software

586

Some believed that the split was largely unnecessary. Others felt the need to combine God, humans, and the new view of the universe into a new philosophical system. Blaise Pascal (pass-KAL) illustrates how one European intellectual responded to these problems.

Pascal sought to keep science and religion united. He was a scientist and a brilliant mathematician. After a profound mystical vision one night in 1654, which assured him that God cared for the human soul, he devoted the rest of his life to religious matters. He planned to write an "Apology for the Christian Religion" but died before he could do so. He did leave a set of notes for the larger work, however, which in published form became known as the *Pensées* (pahn-SAEZ) or *The Thoughts*.

In the *Pensées*, Pascal tried to convert rationalists to Christianity by appealing to both their reason and their emotions. Humans, he argued, were weak creatures who were often deceived by their senses, misled by reason, and battered by their emotions. However, they were beings whose very nature involved thinking: "Man is but a reed, the weakest in nature; but he is a thinking reed."[4]

Pascal wanted to show that the Christian religion was not contrary to reason: "If we violate the principles of reason, our religion will be absurd, and it will be laughed at." To a Christian, according to Pascal, a human being is both fallen and at the same time God's special creation. However, it is not necessary to emphasize one aspect of humans at the expense of the other. That is, we need not view humans as only rational or only hopeless. Pascal even had an answer for skeptics in his now-famous wager: God is a reasonable bet. It is worthwhile to assume that God exists. If he does, then we win all; if he does not, we lose nothing.

Despite his own background as a scientist and mathematician, Pascal refused to rely on the scientist's world of reason to attract people to God: "If we submit everything to reason, there will be no mystery and no supernatural element in our religion." A Christian could rely only on a God who cared for human beings. After providing reasonable arguments for Christianity, Pascal came to rest on faith. Reason, he believed, could take people only so far: "The heart has its reasons of which the reason knows nothing." As a Christian, Pas-

cal felt that faith was the final step: "The heart feels God, not the reason."[5]

Pascal failed to achieve his goal of keeping science and religion united. Increasingly, the gap between science and religion would grow wider as Europe continued along its path of **secularization,** or seeing the world in material, not spiritual terms. Of course, Christianity did not die. Nevertheless, more and more people began to act on the basis of secular, or worldly, rather than religious assumptions.

The Spread of Scientific Knowledge

In the course of the seventeenth century, scientific learning began to increase dramatically. Major universities in Europe established new chairs, or professorships, of science, especially in medicine. Kings and princes provided support for individual scientists. Of great importance to the work of science, however, were two developments. One was the creation of a **scientific method.** The other was the emergence of new scientific societies that enabled scientists to communicate their ideas to one another and to spread these ideas to a wider audience.

In the course of the Scientific Revolution, people became concerned about how to go about examining and understanding the physical realm. The result was the creation of a scientific method—or way to examine and understand nature—that was crucial to the evolution of science in the modern world.

The person who developed a scientific method that became widely used was actually not a scientist. Francis Bacon, an English lawyer, believed that a correct scientific method should be built upon **inductive principles,** which means that scientists should proceed from the particular to the general. Carefully organized experiments and systematic, thorough observations would lead to correct general principles.

Bacon was clear about what he believed his scientific method could accomplish. He stated that "the true and lawful goal of the sciences is none other than this: that human life be endowed with new discoveries and power." He wanted science to create devices that would benefit industry, agriculture, and trade. Bacon said, "I am laboring to lay the foundation, not of any

MORE ABOUT . . . *Scientific Methods*

There is no one scientific method used by all scientists. The following list, however, is a good example of the procedure scientists might follow during an investigation.

1. Identify a problem or ask a question.
2. Develop one or more hypotheses or education guesses.
3. Predict what will occur or be observed
4. Devise ways to test the accuracy of the predictions drawn from the hypotheses.

5. Check accuracy of tests.
6. Repeat or devise new tests.
7. Report results and conclusions objectively.

You might want to have a science teacher talk to the class about scientific methods and how they are used in the scientific community. Ask students if they think the scientific method can be used to investigate nonscientific things. If so, what things could be investigated?

◀ *Louis XIV formally recognized the French Academy in 1666, at which time the organization became the French Royal Academy of Sciences. In this painting, Louis is seated and Minister Colbert and members of the academy gather around the king. What advantages and disadvantages might have resulted from the king's patronage?*

sect or doctrine, but of human utility and power." How would this "human power" be used? Bacon believed this power would be able to "conquer nature in action."[6] The control and domination of nature became an important concern of modern science and the technology that accompanied it.

The spread of scientific ideas to a wide public was greatly aided by the new scientific societies. The first scientific societies appeared in Italy, but those of England and France were more significant. The English Royal Society evolved out of informal gatherings of scientists in London and Oxford. It received little government support, and its members simply chose new members. The French Royal Academy of Sciences, in contrast, received state funds and remained under government control. Its members were appointed and paid salaries by the state.

Early on, both the English and French scientific societies stressed the practical value of scientific research. The English Royal Society set up a committee to study how technology could improve industry. The French Academy collected tools and machines.

The concern with the practical benefits of science proved short lived, however. Both societies came to focus on theoretical work in the sciences. The building of observatories in Paris and Greenwich, England, greatly aided research in astronomy by both groups. Both the English and French societies showed that science should proceed along the lines of a cooperative venture.

❀ SECTION REVIEW ❀

1. **Define:**
   (*a*) Cartesian dualism,   (*b*) rationalism,
   (*c*) secularization,   (*d*) scientific method,
   (*e*) inductive principles

2. **Identify:**
   (*a*) Margaret Cavendish,   (*b*) Maria Winkelmann,   (*c*) René Descartes,   (*d*) Blaise Pascal,
   (*e*) Francis Bacon

So What ⁇

If your students question the importance of information about the **Enlightenment** *(see page 588), tell them . . .*

The ideals of reason, natural law, hope, and progress were the philosophical beliefs that led to the American Revolution and the creation of the United States. The Declaration of Independence and American Revolution were signals to Europeans that, for the first time, enlightened ideas were being put into action. Americans wanted the right to think freely, and the right to express their opinions without fear of repression or censorship. Ask students if these ideals are still important to Americans. Have them explain why they think this is or isn't true.

ALTERNATIVE ASSESSMENT

Assign students to identify a famous female scientist from modern times. Have them write an essay that describes how our world might be different if this person had not been allowed to use her skills to make scientific discoveries.

CLOSE

Lead students in a discussion of the "Focus" objectives identified on page 583.

FOCUS

OBJECTIVES

After completing this section, students should be able to

1. identify and describe conditions that led to the Enlightenment
2. explain new philosophies that were created during the Enlightenment
3. explain the meaning of the term "the science of man"
4. describe social changes that took place during the Enlightenment

FOCUS ACTIVITY

Ask students to debate the idea that logic and reason is the best way to approach all problems faced by humankind. Is logic and reason the best way to decide what is right or wrong, good or bad? What do students think of Voltaire's *deism* that is discussed on page 589?

3. **Recall:**
   (*a*) Why were women prevented from pursuing careers in science?
   (*b*) Name and describe the differences and similarities between the two most significant scientific societies in Europe.

4. **Think Critically:** What were Descartes's two principles? Explain in your own words what they mean and how they apply to you.

THE ENLIGHTENMENT

The eighteenth-century Enlightenment was a movement of intellectuals who were greatly impressed with the achievements of the Scientific Revolution. One of the favorite words of these intellectuals was *reason*, by which they meant the application of the scientific method to the understanding of all life. They believed that institutions and all systems of thought were subject to the rational, scientific way of thinking if people would only free themselves from past, worthless traditions, especially religious ones. If Isaac Newton could discover the natural laws regulating the world of nature, these thinkers, too, could use reason to find the laws that governed human society. They hoped that in doing so, they could make progress toward a better society than the one they had inherited. *Reason, natural law, hope, progress*—these were common words to the thinkers of the Enlightenment.

The Path to the Enlightenment

The Enlightenment did not arrive full-blown in the eighteenth century. It was the result of intellectual ideas from the seventeenth century, especially those of two Englishmen, Isaac Newton and John Locke. The intellectuals of the Enlightenment became convinced that by following Newton's methods they could discover the natural laws that governed politics, econom-

ics, justice, religion, and the arts. The world and everything in it was like a giant machine (referred to as the Newtonian world-machine).

John Locke's theory of knowledge also made a great impact on eighteenth-century intellectuals. In his *Essay Concerning Human Understanding,* Locke argued that every person was born with a *tabula rasa,* or blank mind:

> Let us then suppose the mind to be, as we say, white paper, void of all characters, without any ideas. How comes it to be furnished? Whence has it all the materials of reason and knowledge? To this I answer, in one word, from experience. . . . Our observation, employed either about external sensible objects or about the internal operations of our minds perceived and reflected on by ourselves, is that which supplies our understanding with all the materials of thinking.[7]

Locke believed that our knowledge comes from our environment, not from heredity. We learn from reason, not from faith. Locke's ideas suggested that people were molded by their environment, by the experiences that they received through their senses from their surrounding world. By changing the environment and subjecting people to the right influences, people could be changed and a new society created. How should the environment be changed? Newton had already shown how enlightened people could use reason to discover the natural laws that all institutions should follow. No wonder the intellectuals embraced Newton and Locke. Taken together, the ideas of these two men seemed to offer the hope of a "brave new world" built on reason.

The Philosophes and Their Ideas

The intellectuals of the Enlightenment were known by the French term **philosophe.** They were not all French, and few were philosophers in the strict sense of the term. They were literary people, professors, journalists, economists, political scientists, and above all, social reformers. They came from both the nobility and the middle class. A few even had lower-middle-class origins. The Enlightenment was a truly international movement, but most of the leaders of the Enlightenment were French. The French philosophes affected

RECOMMENDED READING

A good, brief introduction to the Enlightenment can be found in N. Hampson, *A Cultural History of the Enlightenment* (New York, 1968). A more detailed synthesis can be found in P. Gay, *The Enlightenment: An Interpretation, 2* vols. (New York, 1966–69). Two older works still of value are by P. Hazard, *The European Mind, 1680–1715* (New York, 1963), and *European Thought in the Eighteenth Century*

(New York, 1963). For a short, popular survey on the French philosophies, see F. Artz, *The Enlightenment in France* (Kent, Ohio, 1968). Studies of the major Enlightenment intellectuals include R. Shackleton, *Montesquieu, A Critical Biography* (London, 1961); T. Besterman, *Voltaire* (London, 1969); A. Wilson, *Diderot* (New York, 1972); P. N. Furbank, *Diderot: A Critical Biography* (New York, 1992); and intellectuals elsewhere and created a movement that touched the entire Western world.

To the philosophes, the role of philosophy was to change the world, not just to discuss it. As one writer said, the philosophe is one who "applies himself to the study of society with the purpose of making his kind better and happier." To the philosophes, reason was scientific method. Reason meant an appeal to facts. A spirit of rational criticism was to be applied to everything, including religion and politics.

The philosophes often disagreed. The Enlightenment spanned almost an entire century, and it evolved over time. Each succeeding generation became more radical as it built upon the contributions of the previous one. A few people, however, dominated the landscape. We might best begin our survey of the ideas of the philosophes by looking at the three French giants—Montesquieu (mawn-TESS-kyoo), Voltaire (vawl-TAIR), and Diderot (DEE-DROE).

The baron de Montesquieu came from the French nobility. His most famous work, *The Spirit of the Laws*, was published in 1748. In this comparative study of governments, Montesquieu tried to apply the scientific method to the social and political arena to find the "natural laws" that governed the social and political relationships of human beings.

Montesquieu found three basic kinds of governments: (1) republics, which are suitable for small states; (2) despotism, which is appropriate for large states; and (3) monarchy, which is appropriate for moderate-size states. Montesquieu used England as an example of monarchy. His analysis of England's constitution led to his most lasting contribution to political thought—the importance of checks and balances created by means of a **separation of powers.** He believed that England's system was based on a separation of the executive, legislative, and judicial powers. Each power limited and controlled the other, which in turn provided the great

◄ *François-Marie Arouet, Voltaire, was well known for his support of religious tolerance. He was also a prolific writer of poetry, history, and plays, both comedies and tragedies.*

est freedom and security for the state. The translation of Montesquieu's work into English made it available to American philosophes, who took its principles and worked them into the U.S. constitution.

The greatest figure of the Enlightenment was a man named François-Marie Arouet, known simply as Voltaire. He was from a prosperous middle-class family in Paris. Although he studied law, he wished to be a writer and achieved his first success as a playwright. Voltaire wrote an almost endless stream of pamphlets, novels, plays, letters, essays, and histories. His writings brought him both fame and wealth.

Voltaire was especially well known for his criticism of Christianity and his strong belief in religious toleration. He fought against religious intolerance in France. In 1763, he penned his *Treatise on Toleration*, in which he reminded governments that "all men are brothers under God."

Throughout his life, Voltaire championed **deism** (a system of thought that denies the interference of the Creator with the laws of the universe), a religious outlook shared by most other philosophes. Deism was built upon the Newtonian world-machine. In this view, a mechanic (God) had created the universe. To Voltaire and most other philosophes, the universe was like a clock. God was the clockmaker who had created it, set it in motion, and allowed it to run according to its own natural laws.

Denis Diderot was the son of a skilled craftsman from eastern France. He went to the University of Paris to fulfill his father's hopes that he would be a lawyer or pursue a career in the church. Diderot did neither. Instead, he became a freelance writer so that he could be free to study and read in many subjects and languages.

TEACH

USING PRIMARY SOURCES

Ask students to evaluate Locke's theory (as stated on page 588) that people are born with a blank mind. Do they believe people are more a product of their nature or nurture, of their genetics or their environment?

CLASS DISCUSSION

Do students believe the contention that a philosopher is one who "applies himself to the study of society with the purpose of making his kind better and happier"? Were Voltaire's and Diderot's criticisms of Christianity, intended to make people happier?

REINFORCING VOCABULARY

Ask students to explain how Voltaire's idea of *deism* conflicted with teachings of the Catholic church that suggested worldly acts of charity could speed one's entry into heaven.

R. Grimsley, *Jean-Jacques Rousseau* (Cardiff, 1961). Specialized studies on various aspects of the Enlightenment include F. Venturi, *Utopia and Reform in the Enlightenment* (Cambridge, 1971); F. Manuel, *The Eighteenth Century Confronts the Gods* (New York, 1967); M. W> Cranston, *Philosophers and Pamphleteers: Political Theorists of the Enlightenment* (London, 1986); M. C. Jacob, *The Radical* *Enlightenment: Pantheists, Freemasons and Republicans* (London, 1981); H. Chisack, *The Limits of Reform in the Enlightenment: Attitudes toward the Education of the Lower Classes in Eighteenth-Century France* (Princeton, N.J., 1980); and R. Darnton, *The Business of Enlightenment: A Publishing History of the Encyclopédie, 1775–1800* (Cambridge, Mass., 1979).

LEARNING FROM VISUALS

Ask students to create a picture similar to the one to the right that shows typical household implements from their lives. What do drawings like these show about the kind of lives people lived at the time of the Scientific Revolution?

Answer to caption questions: Students will recognize the ladders, rakes, shovels, hoes, and wheelbarrow. Most of the tools shown here are still used today, most with only minor modifications.

REINFORCING VOCABULARY

Ask students to identify and list the ways in which their government does not follow a policy of *laissez-faire* but chooses instead to intervene in the economy. Do students believe their lives are better or worse because of government intervention. Ask students to discuss how many young people could afford an education if their families had to pay for their schooling directly from their own funds.

▲ *This illustrated page from Diderot's* Encyclopedia *reveals his preoccupation for precise detail. How many of these gardening tools can you identify? Which are still in use today?*

For the rest of his life, Diderot remained dedicated to new ideas.

One of Diderot's favorite topics was Christianity, which he condemned as fanatical and unreasonable. As he grew older, his literary attacks on Christianity grew more vicious. Of all religions, Christianity, he said, was the worst—"the most absurd and the most atrocious in its dogma."

Diderot's most famous contribution to the Enlightenment was the *Encyclopedia, or Classified Dictionary of the Sciences, Arts, and Trades*. This was a 28-volume collection of knowledge that he edited and referred to as the "great work of his life." The purpose of the *Encyclopedia*, according to Diderot, was to "change the general way of thinking." It became a major weapon in the philosophes' crusade against the old French society. Many articles in the *Encyclopedia* attacked religious superstition and supported religious toleration. Others called for social, legal, and political improvements that would lead to a society that was more tolerant, more humane, and more reasonable. Slavery, for example, was strongly denounced. The *Encyclopedia* was sold to doctors, clergymen, teachers, lawyers, and even military officers, thus spreading the ideas of the Enlightenment.

Toward a New "Science of Man"

The philosophes believed that Newton's methods could be used to discover the natural laws underlying all areas of human life. This led to what the philosophes called a "science of man," or what we would call the social sciences. In a number of areas, such as economics, politics, and education, the philosophes arrived at natural laws that they believed governed human actions. Their efforts laid the foundations for the modern social sciences.

The Physiocrats (FIZZ-ee-uh-KRATS) and Adam Smith have been viewed as the founders of the modern discipline of economics. The leader of the Physiocrats was François Quesnay (kae-NAE), a highly successful French doctor. Quesnay and the Physiocrats claimed they would discover the natural economic laws that governed human society. Their major "natural law" of economics was that individuals should be left free to pursue their own economic self-interest. Through the actions of these individuals, all society would ultimately benefit. Consequently, the Physiocrats argued that the state should in no way interrupt the free play of natural economic forces by imposing government regulations on the economy. The state should leave the economy alone—a doctrine that became known by its French title, **laissez-faire** (to let alone).

The best statement of laissez-faire was made in 1776 by a Scottish philosopher, Adam Smith, in his famous

So What??

If your students question the importance of information about the **natural law economics of laissez-faire,** tell them . . .

The philosophy of Adam Smith is one of the economic supports of the capitalistic system which allows them to own telephones, computers, compact discs and players, and automobiles. Smith believed that competition among merchants could act as a regulator of the economic system. Ask students to explain what Smith meant by that thought. He also felt that private enterprise would stimulate fair distribution of the wealth in a country. Do students think this is true? Why or why not? Have they seen this in the United States?

work known as *The Wealth of Nations*. Like the Physiocrats, Smith believed that the state should not interfere in economic matters. Indeed, Smith gave to government only three basic roles: it should protect society from invasion (the army); defend its citizens from injustice (the police); and keep up certain public works, such as roads and canals, that private individuals could not afford. Thus, in Smith's view, the state should stay out of the lives of individuals.

The Later Enlightenment

By the late 1760s, a new generation of philosophes came to maturity. The most famous of these later philosophes was Jean-Jacques Rousseau (ZHAHN-ZHAWK roo-SOE). The young Rousseau wandered through France and Italy, where he held various jobs. Eventually he made his way to Paris, where he was introduced into the circles of the philosophes. He never really liked the life of the cities, however, and often withdrew into long periods of solitude.

Rousseau's political beliefs were set out in two major works. In his *Discourse on the Origins of the Inequality of Mankind*, Rousseau argued that people had adopted laws and government in order to preserve their private property. In the process, they had become enslaved by government. What, then, should people do to regain their freedom?

In his famous work *The Social Contract*, published in 1762, Rousseau found an answer in the concept of the social contract. In a social contract, an entire society agreed to be governed by its general will. If any individuals wished to follow their own self-interests, they should be forced to abide by the general will. "This means nothing less than that he will be forced to be free," said Rousseau, because the general will represented what was best for the entire community. Thus, liberty was achieved by being forced to follow what was best for each individual.

Another important work by Rousseau was *Emile* (ae-MEEL), one of the Enlightenment's most important works on education. Written in the form of a novel, the work was really a general discussion "on the education of the natural man." Rousseau's basic concern was that education should foster, rather than restrict, children's natural instincts. Rousseau's own experiences had shown him the importance of the emotions. What he sought was a balance between heart and mind, between emotions and reason.

Rousseau did not necessarily practice what he preached, however. His own children were sent to orphanages, where many children died at a young age. Rousseau also viewed women as being "naturally" different from men: "To fulfill her functions, . . . [a woman] needs a soft life to suckle her babies. How much care and tenderness does she need to hold her family together." To Rousseau, women should be educated for their roles as wives and mothers by learning obedience and the nurturing skills that would enable them to provide loving care for their husbands and children. Not everyone in the eighteenth century agreed with Rousseau, however.

The Rights of Women

For centuries, male intellectuals had argued that the nature of women made them inferior to men and made male domination of women necessary. Female thinkers in the eighteenth century, however, provided suggestions for improving the condition of women. The strongest statement for the rights of women in the eighteenth century was advanced by the English writer Mary Wollstonecraft (wool-STUN-kraft). She is seen by many as the founder of modern European **feminism** (the movement for women's rights).

In *Vindication of the Rights of Women*, Wollstonecraft pointed to two problems in the views of women that were held by such Enlightenment thinkers as Rousseau. She noted that the same people who argued that women must obey men also said that a system of government based on the arbitrary power of monarchs over their subjects was wrong. Wollstonecraft pointed out that the power of men over women was equally wrong. Moreover, she argued that the Enlightenment was based on an ideal of reason in all human beings. If women have reason, then they, too, are entitled to the same rights that men have. Women, Wollstonecraft declared, should have equal rights with men in education, as well as in economic and political life.

Learning from Visuals

Answers to
SECTION REVIEW

1. (a) intellectual of the Enlightenment
   (b) Montesquieu's system of checks and balances, in three branches of government
   (c) denying the interference of God with the laws of the universe
   (d) economic theory of nongovernmental interference
   (e) women's rights movement
   (f) elegant drawing rooms where invited guests discussed new ideas
2. (a) applied scientific method to social and political arenas
   (b) a playwright, well known for his criticism of Christianity and his belief in religious toleration
   (c) condemned Christianity as fanatical
   (d) leader of the Physiocrats, founders of modern economics
   (e) founder of modern European feminism.
   (f) hostess of a famous salon
3. (a) reason, natural law, hope, and progress
   (b) Every person is born with *tabule rasa*, knowledge comes from our environment and reason
   (c) republics, despotism, and monarchy
   (d) stay out of the lives of individuals, protect society from invasions, and defend its citizens from injustice
   (e) The *Discourse on the Origins of the Inequality of Mankind*: people had

▲ *The salons of Madame Geoffrin were famous throughout Europe, and it was considered an honor to be invited to her home. She is seated in the front row, third from the right. Do you think these lively evenings of discussion have continued in modern-day society? If not, what has replaced them?*

The Social World of the Enlightenment

Of great importance to the Enlightenment was the spread of its ideas to the upper classes—the literate elite—of European society. The publication and sale of books were important to this process. Equally important in the spread of ideas was the **salon.** The salons were the elegant drawing rooms of the wealthy class's great urban houses. Invited philosophes and guests gathered in these salons and took part in conversations often centered on the new ideas of the philosophes. The salons brought writers and artists together with aristocrats, government officials, and wealthy middle-class people.

The women who hosted the salons found themselves in a position to sway political opinion and influence literary and artistic taste. At her fashionable home in Paris, Marie-Thérèse de Geoffrin (zhoh-FRAN), wife of a wealthy merchant, held sway over gatherings that became the talk of France and even all Europe. Distinguished foreigners, including a future king of Sweden and a future king of Poland, competed to receive invitations. Madame Geoffrin was an amiable but firm hostess who allowed wide-ranging discussions as long as they remained in good taste. When she found that artists and philosophers did not mix well (the artists were high-strung, and the philosophers talked too much), she set up separate meetings. Artists were

ENRICHMENT ACTIVITY

Have students do research on the Parisian salons. Who were the women who organized them and why would they have spent their time and money organizing these evening affairs? Reconstruct an evening of conversation at a salon. You might have students work in groups to write skits or plays of an evening at a salon. Groups could then share their plays with the rest of the class.

invited only on Mondays and philosophers, on Wednesdays. These gatherings were but one of many avenues for the spread of the ideas of the Enlightenment.

 SECTION REVIEW

1. **Define:**
   (*a*) philosophe,   (*b*) separation of powers,
   (*c*) deism,   (*d*) laissez-faire,   (*e*) feminism,
   (*f*) salon

2. **Identify:**
   (*a*) Montesquieu,   (*b*) Voltaire,   (*c*) Denis
   Diderot,   (*d*) François Quesnay,   (*e*) Mary
   Wollstonecraft,   (*f*) Marie-Thérèse de Geoffrin

3. **Recall:**
   (*a*) What were common words to the thinkers of
   the Enlightenment?
   (*b*) In his *Essay Concerning Human Understanding,*
   what ideas did John Locke propose?
   (*c*) What were the three basic kinds of governments that Montesquieu found?
   (*d*) What did Adam Smith believe the role of government should be?
   (*e*) What two major works by Rousseau described
   his political beliefs? Briefly describe.
   (*f*) In *Vindication of the Rights of Women,* what two
   problems did Mary Wollstonecraft point out that
   Enlightenment thinkers believed the roles of
   women should be?

4. **Think Critically:** Can you think of examples that
   show separation of powers in our government
   today? Explain your answer.

CULTURE AND SOCIETY IN AN AGE OF ENLIGHTENMENT

The age of the Enlightenment witnessed both traditional practices and important changes in the world of culture and society.

Innovations in Art, Music, and Literature

The palace of Louis XIV at Versailles, in France, had made an enormous impact on Europe. To keep up with the French king, the Austrian emperor, the Swedish king, German princes, Italian princes, and Russian tsars built grandiose palaces. They were not so much modeled after the French classical style of Versailles as they were after the seventeenth-century Italian Baroque style. In the **Baroque-Rococo** architectural style of the eighteenth century, a building was seen as a total work of art. A building and its sculptures, wall paintings, and ceiling paintings were blended into a harmonious whole. One of the greatest architects of the eighteenth century was Balthasar Neumann (noy-MAWN). Neumann's two masterpieces are the church of the Fourteen Saints in southern Germany and the Residence, the palace of the prince-bishop of Würzburg. In these buildings, secular and spiritual become one as lavish and fanciful ornament, light, bright colors, and elaborate detail greet us. In the church, a pilgrim in search of holiness is struck by an incredible richness of detail. Persuaded by joy rather than fear, the believer is lifted toward heaven on a cloud of rapture.

The eighteenth century was one of the greatest periods in the history of European music. In the first half of the eighteenth century, two composers—George Frederick Handel and Johann Sebastian Bach (BAWK)—stand out as musical geniuses. While Bach was music director at the church of Saint Thomas in Leipzig (LIPE-sig), Germany, he composed his *Mass in B Minor, Saint Matthew's Passion,* and other works that gave him the reputation of being one of the greatest composers of all time. For Bach, music was, above all, a means of worshiping God. In his own words, his task in life was to make "well-ordered music in the honor of God."

Handel, like Bach, was born in Germany in the year 1685. Unlike Bach, however, Handel was a profoundly secular person. He moved to England, where he remained the rest of his life. Handel wrote music for large public audiences, and his pieces were often huge and unusual. The orchestra for his *Fireworks Music,* for example, was supposed to be accompanied by 101 cannons. Handel wrote much secular music, but he is

adopted laws and governors in order to preserve their property and become enslaved by government. *The Social Contract:* society agreed to be governed by its general will.
   (f) The subjection of women to men was wrong, and women are entitled to the same rights as men.
4. Answers will vary.

CLOSE

Lead students in a discussion of the "Focus" objectives identified on page 588. Emphasize the importance of new philosophical ideas about the role of religion in people's lives.

FOCUS

OBJECTIVES

After completing this section, students should be able to

1. identify and describe developments in art, music and literature during the Enlightenment
2. describe the growth of popular culture in the eighteenth century
3. explain changes in European legal systems that took place during the Enlightenment

RECOMMENDED READING

Two general surveys on the arts and literature are M. Levy, *Rococo to Revolution* (London, 1966); and H. Honour, *Neo-classicism* (Harmondsworth, 1968). On the novel in England, see I. Watt, *The Rise of the Novel: Studies in Defoe, Richardson, and Fielding* (Berkeley, 1957). On Gibbon, see W. B. Carnuchan, *Gibbon's Solitude: The Inward World of the Historian* (London, 1987). The development of the attorney and barrister are examined in R. Robson, *The Attorney in Eighteenth Century England* (Cambridge, 1959); and L. Berlanstein, *The Barristers of Toulouse in the Eighteenth Century* (Baltimore, 1975). Different facets of crime and punishment are examined in the important works by M. Foucault, *Discipline and Punish: The Birth of the Prison* (New York, 1977); and J. Langbein, *Torture and the Law of Proof* (Chicago, 1977).

TEACH

ACROSS THE CURRICULUM

Music Have students go to the local library and check out an orchestral selection by each of the following masters of the seventeenth and eighteenth centuries: J. S. Bach, F. Handel, R. J. Haydn, W. A. Mozart. After listening to each composition, have students write down how the music of each composer varies from the others. They should pay attention to the difference between Bach and Handel (Baroque period) and Haydn and Mozart (Classical period).

probably best known for his religious music. He had no problem moving from Italian operas to religious oratorios when they proved to be in greater demand by his English public. An oratorio was a lengthy musical work on a religious subject, usually taken from a biblical story. Handel's oratorio known as the *Messiah* has been called "one of those rare works that appeal immediately to everyone, and yet is indisputably a masterpiece of the highest order."

Bach and Handel perfected the Baroque musical style, with its elaborate musical structures. Two geniuses of the second half of the eighteenth century—Franz Joseph Haydn (HIDE-un) and Wolfgang Amadeus Mozart (AW-muh-DAE-us MOTE-zart)—

Map 19.1   The Age of the Enlightenment in Europe

STUDYING MAPS

The following questions will help you guide students through their study of Map 19.1.

1. In what geographic regions of Europe was the Enlightenment concentrated? *(France, Germany, Italy, Netherlands)*
2. What relationship appears to exist between areas of economic prosperity and the Enlightenment? *(Answers will vary.)*
3. What religious faiths appear to be most closely associated with the Enlightenment? *(Catholicism)*
4. Is this a general-purpose or special-purpose map? Students should explain answers. *(It is a special-purpose map concentrating on the spread of educational institutions.)*

OUR ARTISTIC HERITAGE

Rococo Style

The Baroque and neoclassical styles that had dominated the seventeenth century continued into the eighteenth century. By the 1730s, however, a new artistic style, known as Rococo, had spread all over Europe. Rococo was a French invention and was enormously popular in Germany. However, it truly became an international style.

Unlike the Baroque style, which stressed grandeur, power, and movement, Rococo empha-

Giovanni Battista Tiepolo was born and educated in Venice, and this detail from his ceiling fresco at the Palazzo Sandi in Venice shows the Rococo style at its finest. Tiepolo became famous throughout Europe for his frescoes, and they can be seen in Germany and Spain, as well as in Italy.

Antoine Watteau is one of the most famous painters of eighteenth-century France. This painting, The Pilgrimage to Cythera, *gained him entry into the French Royal Academy. Here we see young couples leaving the island of Cythera, where they have come to pay their respects to Venus, the goddess of love. How can you tell that these couples are wealthy or that they are in love?*

(continued)

TEACHING THEMES

Economics and History. Ask students whether they believe it is appropriate or desirable for governments to support the arts as was the practice during the Enlightenment. On one side of the issue is the cost of artistic endeavors which are often large and difficult for artists or individuals to afford. On the other side is the possibility that the government could control artistic expression through what it chose to support. Do students believe the government of the United States should support artistic activity with public funds? What is their opinion of the National Endowment for the Arts?

OUR ARTISTIC HERITAGE

LEARNING FROM VISUALS

Answer to the caption question: The men and women pictured here are beautifully dressed and coiffed, they are holding hands, walking together, and gazing at each other lovingly.

ENRICHMENT ACTIVITY

Have students take a walking tour of the town in which you live. (You might arrange for a field trip, if that's possible.) Take students to view any buildings that display the Rococo style of architecture. If there are no buildings in the Rococo style, ask students why they think this might be the case. *(It might be because American cities are young in comparison to European cities and the Rococo period was ending by the time buildings were being constructed here.)* What features did students look for to identify a building as Rococo style?

Answers to Critical Thinking Questions

1. Baroque stressed grandeur, power, and movement. Rococo emphasized grace, charm, and gentle action.
2. Answers will vary. The author probably meant that Rococo pursued pleasure, rather than religious themes.

TEACHING THEMES

The Role of Individuals. Play a brief selection of medieval religious music and of Mozart's *The Magic Flute* for your class. Have students describe their reactions to and feelings for each selection. How does Mozart's music reflect the values of the Age of Enlightenment?

OUR ARTISTIC HERITAGE

Rococo Style, continued

sized grace, charm, and gentle action. Rococo rejected strict geometric patterns and had a fondness for curves. It liked to follow the wandering lines of natural objects, such as seashells and flowers. It made much use of interlaced designs colored in gold with delicate contours and graceful curves. The Rococo style was highly secular. Its lightness and charm spoke of the pursuit of pleasure, happiness, and love.

Rococo's appeal is evident in the work of Antoine (an-TWAHN) Watteau (waw-TOE). He painted aristocratic life as refined, sensual, and civilized. Gentlemen and ladies in elegant dress revealed a world of upper-class pleasure and joy. Underneath that exterior, however, was an element of sadness as the artist revealed the fragility and passing nature of pleasure, love, and life.

Another aspect of Rococo was a sense of enchantment and enthusiasm, especially evident in the work of Giovanni Battista Tiepolo (tee-AE-puh-LOE). Much of Tiepolo's painting came to adorn the walls and ceilings of churches and palaces. His masterpiece is the ceiling of the Bishop's Palace at Würzburg, a massive scene representing the four continents.

1. Explain the differences between the Baroque and Rococo styles.

2. Rococo is described as being "highly secular." Secular means that it is not religious but related to worldly things. What do you think the author meant by this description?

were innovators who wrote music called Classical rather than Baroque. Their fame caused the musical center of Europe to shift from Italy to the Austrian Empire.

Haydn spent most of his adult life as musical director for wealthy Hungarian princes. Haydn wrote a great deal, composing 104 symphonies in addition to numerous other works. His visits to England introduced him to a world where musicians wrote for public concerts rather than princely patrons (supporters). This "liberty," as he called it, led him to write his two great oratorios, *The Creation* and *The Seasons*. Both of them were dedicated to the common people.

Mozart was truly a child prodigy. He gave his first harpsichord concert at age 6 and wrote his first opera at 12 (see "Young People in the Age of Enlightenment: Mozart as a Child Prodigy"). He sought a patron, but his discontent with an overly demanding archbishop in Salzburg forced him to move to Vienna. His failure to

get a regular patron made his life miserable. Nevertheless, he wrote music passionately. *The Marriage of Figaro*, *The Magic Flute*, and *Don Giovanni* are three of the world's greatest operas. Mozart composed with an ease of melody and a blend of grace, precision, and emotion that no one, it can be argued, has ever surpassed. Haydn remarked to Mozart's father, "Your son is the greatest composer known to me either in person or by reputation."

The eighteenth century was also decisive in the development of the European novel. The novel was especially attractive to a growing number of middle-class readers. The Englishman Henry Fielding wrote novels about people without scruples (ethical principles) who survived by their wits. His best work was *The History of Tom Jones, a Foundling*, a long novel about the numerous adventures of a young scoundrel. Fielding presented scenes of English life from the slums of London to the country houses of the English aristoc-

CNN. WORLD HISTORY UPDATES

You can update your coverage of World History topics, as well as spark lively classroom discussion and deeper understanding, by using the **CNN World History Updates.**

For assistance in using and incorporating the **CNN World History Updates** into your classroom presentations, see the *Classroom Guide.*

YOUNG PEOPLE IN THE AGE OF ENLIGHTENMENT

Mozart as a Child Prodigy

Wolfgang Amadeus Mozart is often considered the "most complete genius of all composers." His genius was already apparent when he was a young boy. Mozart was not typical of young people in the eighteenth century, or any century, for that matter. He was certainly one of the most unique child prodigies of all time.

Mozart began to play the harpsichord at the age of four. By age six, he could also play the organ and violin. His father, Leopold, was a violinist, music teacher, and composer in Salzburg, where Wolfgang was born. Leopold was astounded by the musical ability of his young son. He called him "the miracle that God let be born in Salzburg." When Wolfgang was only six years old, his father began to take him on concert tours throughout Germany and the rest of Europe. He went first to Vienna. He then went to Paris at age 7, to London at 8, and to Italy at 13. Everywhere he went, Mozart was greeted as a "wonder child."

The young Mozart was often tested. At one concert, a cloth was put over his hands while he played the harpsichord so he could not see the keys. At the Sistine Chapel, Mozart demonstrated one of his remarkable acts of memory. After listening to a nine-voice composition twice, he wrote out the complete score. The rulers of Austria, France, and England greeted him like a king. At Milan, at the age of 14, he conducted his first opera.

In 1771, at the age of 15, Mozart returned to his hometown of Salzburg, where he accepted a position as concertmaster (assistant to the conductor) of the archbishop of Salzburg's orchestra. He soon tired of the job, especially when the archbishop who hired him died and was replaced by a successor who did not appreciate music. On a trip to Vienna in 1773, Mozart heard the string quartets

▲ *Wolfgang Amadeus Mozart is playing the harpsichord, his father is playing the violin, and his sister Nannerl is singing. This painting was done in Paris between 1763 and 1764, when Mozart was only seven years old. Mozart received enthusiastic welcomes and critical acclaim during his three-year tour of northern Europe.*

of Haydn. Deeply moved, he sat down and wrote six quartets of his own. By the age of 17, Mozart was a mature composer who had written two full-scale operas, thirty symphonies, and a large number of shorter pieces.

(continued)

YOUNG PEOPLE IN THE AGE OF ENLIGHTENMENT

LEARNING FROM VISUALS

Ask students to identify and explain what the drawing of Mozart playing the piano tells us about society during the eighteenth century. What must the clothing, furniture, and instruments pictured have cost? What does this tell us about the economy and distribution of wealth in Vienna at that time?

COMPARING TIME PERIODS

Although there is little doubt that Mozart was a musical genius, his abilities were complimented by the spirit of the times in which he lived. Assign students to describe what Mozart's life might have been like if he had been born in 1300 instead of 1756.

SPECIAL NEEDS: *Visual/auditory*

The use of music can be a motivating technique in reinforcing information. It may be particularly appealing to visually impaired students who may often rely on audio recordings.

Have students go to the library and select recordings by Bach, Handel, Haydn, or Mozart. Have them conduct research to see if they can find modern recordings of the above composers—modern songs based on the Classical or Baroque melodies. The students may then prepare a class presentation involving recordings, brief overview of the life of their chosen composer, and a critique of the various musical styles.

Answers to Critical Thinking Questions

1. Mozart was playing the harpsichord, organ, and violin.
2. The test described is that of a cloth put over his hands while he played the harpsichord so he could not see the keys.
3. Answers will vary. Students should support their answers.

CLASS DISCUSSION

Have students identify and explain aspects of current-day high and popular culture. List these on the board and compare them with examples of high and popular culture from the Age of Enlightenment that were identified in the text. Is there more of a blurring or a distinction between the two at the present than in the past? Why might this be true? To what extent is television now the embodiment of our popular culture?

COMPARING TIME PERIODS

Ask students to compare the role of magazines during the Enlightenment with the present. How are news magazines today different from tabloids? Which type of magazine do students believe would have been better received in the eighteenth century?

YOUNG PEOPLE IN THE AGE OF ENLIGHTENMENT

Mozart as a Child Prodigy, continued

1. What instruments was Mozart playing by the time he was six years old?

2. What test of Mozart's abilities is described here?

3. In the last paragraph the author states that Mozart soon tired of his job as concertmaster. Do you think boredom would be a problem for someone of Mozart's genius? Why or why not?

racy. In a number of hilarious episodes, he described characters that reflected real types in English society.

High and Popular Cultures of the Eighteenth Century

A civilization has both a high and a popular culture. High culture is the literary and artistic culture of the educated and wealthy ruling classes. Popular culture is the written and unwritten culture of the masses, most of which is passed down orally. In modern terms, we might say high culture versus popular culture is the difference between the symphony and rock and roll music. By the eighteenth century, European high culture consisted of the work of theologians, scientists, philosophers, intellectuals, poets, and dramatists. Their work was supported by a wealthy and literate group of laypeople, the most important of whom were landed aristocrats and the wealthier upper classes in the cities.

Especially noticeable in the eighteenth century was the growth of both publishing and the reading public. The number of titles issued each year by French publishers rose from 300 titles in 1750 to about 1,600 in the 1780s. Titles had been previously aimed at small groups of the educated elite, but many were now directed at the new reading public of the middle classes, which included women and urban artisans.

An important aspect of the growth of publishing and reading in the eighteenth century was the development of magazines for the general public. Great

Britain, an important center for the new magazines, saw 25 periodicals published in 1700, 103 in 1760, and 158 in 1780. Along with magazines came daily newspapers. The first was printed in London in 1702. By 1780, thirty-seven other English towns had their own newspapers. They were filled with news and special features and were relatively cheap or even provided free in coffeehouses.

Popular culture refers to the often unwritten culture passed down orally that was important to the lives of ordinary people. Popular culture was a regular part of community life. Especially common was the festival, a broad name used to cover a variety of celebrations. In Catholic Europe, Carnival was the most spectacular form of festival. It started in January and lasted until Lent, traditionally the forty-day period of fasting leading up to Easter. Carnival was a time of great indulgence. It was just the reverse of Lent, when people were expected to abstain from meat and most recreations. Heavy eating and heavy drinking were the norm during Carnival.

The sense of community evident in festivals was also present in the chief gathering places of the common people, the local taverns or cabarets (KAB-uh-RAZE). Taverns were a regular gathering place for neighborhood men to talk; play games; conduct small business matters; and, of course, to drink.

Popular culture had always included a vast array of traditional songs and stories that were passed down from generation to generation, but there existed a popular written literature as well. So-called **chapbooks**

MORE ABOUT . . . Carnivals

The word carnival probably comes from the Latin word *carnelevarium,* to remove meat, and the annual modern day Carnival usually begins on Epiphany, January 6, and ends in February with Mardi Gras, the French term for "Fat Tuesday" or Shrove Tuesday. The next day, Ash Wednesday, marks the beginning of Lent.

The first recorded carnival took place in Egypt at the feast of Osiris; and the Romans

had their own carnivals, as well. During the Middle Ages, the Catholic Church tried to limit the celebrations, and over time, carnival became the last festival before Lent. Carnival celebrations continue today in Belgium, Italy, France, West Germany. In the New World, Carnival began in 1840 in Rio de Janeiro where it has become a spectacular festival, and in New Orleans, Louisiana where carnival began in 1857.

YOU ARE THERE

The Punishment of Crime

▲ *This illustration shows one of the harshest punishments of the eighteenth century, breaking on the wheel. What impact do you think pictures and spectacles such as these had on future laws that prohibited cruel and unusual punishment?*

Torture and capital punishment remained common features of European judicial systems well into the eighteenth century. Public spectacles were especially gruesome, as this excerpt from the Nocturnal Spectator *of Restif de la Bretonne demonstrates.*

Restif de la Bretonne, Nocturnal Spectator

I went home by way of rue Saint-Antoine and the Place de Grève. Three murderers had been broken on the wheel there, the day before. I had not expected to see any such spectacle, one that I had never dared to witness. But as I crossed the square I caught sight of a poor wretch, pale, half dead, wracked by the pains of the interrogation inflicted on him twenty hours earlier; he was stumbling down from the Hôtel de Ville supported by the executioner and the confessor. These two men, so completely different, inspired an inexpressible emotion in me! I watched the latter embrace a miserable man consumed by fever, filthy as the dungeons he came from, swarming with vermin! And I said to myself, "O Religion, here is your greatest glory! . . .

I saw a horrible sight, even though the torture had been mitigated. . . . The wretch had revealed his accomplices. He was garroted [strangled] before he was put to the wheel. A winch set under the scaffold tightened a noose around the victim's neck and he was strangled; for a long while the confessor and the hangman felt his heart to see whether the artery still pulsed, and the hideous blows were dealt only after it beat no longer. I left, with my hair standing on end in horror.

1. Of what crime had the "poor wretch" been accused?

2. Why do you think spectacles were made of criminals' punishments?

3. How does the punishment meted out in the eighteenth century compare to the punishment of criminals in our society today?

4. Are you surprised that people would attend and observe the torture and executions that took place in the eighteenth century? Explain why you think most people today would or would not watch these spectacles.

On Line with WORLD HISTORY *Internet Activity*

You may want to have your students visit the following URL, where they will find information and additional web site resources to enhance their study of this chapter.

Modern political Theorists–Machiavelli to Rousseau
http://swift.eng.ox.ac.uk/jdr/moder1.html

Includes the major Enlightenment philosophers.

Due to the ever-changing nature of the World Wide Web, see the West History web site, **http://history.swpco.com** for regular updates of the URLs in this text.

ASSESS

You can choose from a variety of assessments to evaluate your students' mastery of the objectives for this section as stated on page 593.

Answers to
SECTION REVIEW

2. (a) architectural style modeled after the seventeenth-century Italian Baroque
(b) short pamphlets printed on cheap paper

3. (a) architect, masterpieces are the Church of the Fourteen Saints and the Residence
(b) a German Baroque composer
(c) a German Baroque composer of the musical style.
(d) classical composer of many symphonies
(e) a child prodigy who gave his first concert at six and wrote his first opera at twelve
(f) an eighteenth century English writer

4. (a) High culture means the literary and artistic culture of the educated ruling classes. Popular means the written and unwritten culture of the masses.
(b) Book publication increased. Many titles were aimed at the educated elite, but many were directed to the middle class. Magazines and newspapers were developed.
(c) The carnival was the most spectacular form of festival. Chief gathering places of the common people were local taverns.
(d) torture was used to obtain evidence, punishment was often cruel

5. Answers will vary.

600

CONNECTIONS
TO OUR WORLD

Magazines—Then and Now   Today, bookstores and newsstands carry thousands of magazines that appeal to an enormous variety of interests. There are separate magazines on fishing, car racing, fashion styles, politics, television, furniture making, tourism, wrestling, and a host of other subjects.

The first magazines in Europe were a product of a growing reading public in the seventeenth and eighteenth centuries, especially among the middle classes. The first magazine was published in Germany in 1633. It contained poems and articles on religion, the two chief interests of its editor, Johann Rist. Many early magazines had serious goals. Joseph Addison and Richard Steele's *Spectator*, begun in 1711, aimed to "bring Philosophy out of the closets and libraries, schools and colleges, to dwell in clubs and assemblies, at tea-tables and coffeehouses." It did not last long. Some publishers began to broaden the appeal of their magazines, especially to attract a growing number of women readers. *Ladies' Mercury*, published in Britain, provided advice on marriage and child rearing as well as sewing patterns and gossip. Its success brought forth a host of similar magazines.

Many early magazines failed because customers did not always pay on time for them. Isaiah Thomas, editor of the Worcester Magazine, became so desperate that he wrote: "The editor requests all those who are indebted to him for Magazines, to make payment—butter will be received in small sums, if brought within a few days."

were short pamphlets printed on cheap paper and sold by peddlers to the lower classes. The content of the chapbooks varied. Lives of saints and religious stories competed with crude satires and adventure stories.

The chapbooks reflected the growth of literacy in the Enlightenment. Of course, certain groups were more likely to be literate than others. Upper-class elites and the upper middle classes in the cities were mostly literate. However, over the course of the eighteenth century, especially in France, lower-middle-class artisans also learned to read in ever-larger numbers. Peasants, who made up as much as 75 percent of France's population, remained largely illiterate.

Crime and Punishment

By the eighteenth century, most European states had developed a system of courts to deal with the punishment of crime. Except in England, torture remained an important means for obtaining evidence before a trial until the end of the century. Courts used the rack, thumbscrews, and other instruments to obtain confessions in criminal cases. Seventeenth-century legal reforms, however, led to the gradual elimination of torture. In 1780 France was the last European state to abolish it.

Punishments for crimes were often cruel and even spectacular, primarily because of the need to deter crime in an age when a state's police forces were too weak to ensure the capture of criminals. Nobles were executed by simple beheading. Lower-class criminals condemned to death were tortured or broken on the wheel (see "You Are There: The Punishment of Crime"). The death penalty was still commonly used in property cases, as well as criminal cases. By 1800, the English listed over two hundred crimes that would result in the death penalty. In addition to executing criminals, European states put criminals to work in mines, forts, and navies. England also sent criminals to colonies in the New World and, after the American Revolution, to Australia.

   SECTION REVIEW

1. **Locate:**
   (a) Leipzig

2. **Define:**
   (a) Baroque-Rococo, (b) chapbooks

ENRICHMENT ACTIVITY

Have each student conduct outside research to compile a list of 20 current popular magazines, each in a different area of interest (particular sports, fitness, beauty, cooking, literature, etc.). Ask students to attempt not to duplicate magazine lists of other classmates. If possible, students should copy the covers of their chosen magazines. When students have completed their individual assignments, create a class list and a collage of covers of the magazines. Students may be surprised at the number and variety of popular magazines published today.

3. **Identify:**
   (*a*) Balthasar Neumann, (*b*) Johann Sebastian Bach, (*c*) George Frederick Handel, (*d*) Franz Joseph Haydn, (*e*) Wolfgang Amadeus Mozart, (*f*) Henry Fielding

4. **Recall:**
   (*a*) Explain the difference between high and low culture.
   (*b*) With the growth of a reading public, what types of publications were available and to whom were they directed?
   (*c*) Describe some of the types of popular culture in which people participated.
   (*d*) How was crime treated during the eighteenth century?

5. **Think Critically:** What types of cultural festivals are held in your community? Describe them.

RELIGION AND THE CHURCHES

Although much of the great art and music of the eighteenth century was religious, the thinking of the time was antireligious. As life became more secularized, the philosphers attacked the Christian churches. However, most Europeans were still Christians. Except for governments, churches remained the most important institutions in people's lives. Even many of those most critical of the churches accepted that society could not work without religious faith.

In the eighteenth century, the Catholic and Protestant Churches upheld the traditional social order and made few dramatic internal changes. Whether in Catholic or Protestant countries, the parish church run by priest or pastor remained the center of religious life. The parish church held religious services. It also kept records of births, deaths, and marriages; provided charity for the poor; ran schools for children; and cared for orphans—all functions that the government provides today.

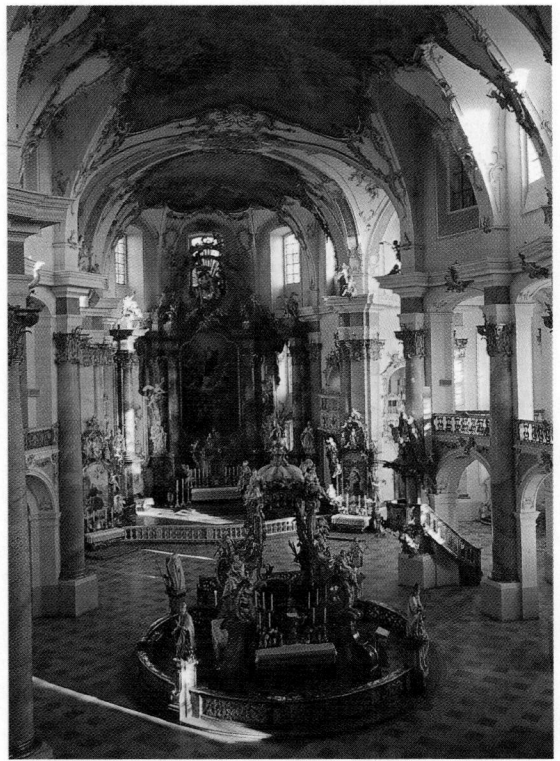

▲ *The interior of Vierzehnheiligen, the church of the Fourteen Saints, is renowned for its lavish detail, rich colors, and opulent decoration. What other characteristics of the Baroque-Rococo style are visible in this church?*

Toleration and Religious Minorities

The philosophes had called loudly for religious toleration. Out of political necessity, a certain level of tolerance of different religions had been reached in the seventeenth century in such places as Germany after the Thirty Years' War and France after the divisive religious wars (see Chapter 15). However, many rulers still found religious toleration difficult to accept. Louis XIV had turned back the clock in France at the end of the seventeenth century by suppressing the rights of the Huguenots. Many devout rulers continued to

RECOMMENDED READING

A good introduction to the religious history of the eighteenth century can be found in G. R. Cragg, *The Church and the Age of Reason, 1648–1789* (London, 1966). A very informative regional study is T. Tacket, *Priest and Parish in Eighteenth-Century France*

(Princeton, N.J., 1977). The problem of religious toleration is examined in C. H. O'Brien, *Ideas of Religious Toleration at the Time of Joseph II* (Philadelphia, 1969); and A. Hertzberg, *The French Enlightenment and the Jews* (New York, 1968).

ALTERNATIVE ASSESSMENT

Assign students to write an article for a seventeenth century magazine that describes an event or person they read about in this section. Tell students that their purpose is to demonstrate knowledge they have gained. Evaluate student work according to its clarity, completeness, and originality.

CLOSE

Lead students in a discussion of the "Focus" objectives identified on page 593. Emphasize the fact that elements of the Baroque style can be seen in the art, music, literature and architecture of the age of Enlightenment.

FOCUS

OBJECTIVES

After completing this section, students should be able to

1. explain reasons for, and results of, religious toleration in Europe
2. describe the development of popular religion in the eighteenth century

FOCUS ACTIVITY

Have students identify and list characteristics a Christian might have been expected to display before and after the Enlightenment. How much of what Christians believe today is a result of changes that took place during the Enlightenment?

CLASS DISCUSSION

Ask students to explain how it was possible for Jewish people to be highly successful in an economic way and at the same time be discriminated against socially and politically. In what ways did nations that expelled Jewish people suffer?

TEACHING THEMES

The Importance of Culture. Assign students to compare the role of parish churches in rural communities at the time of the Enlightenment and at the present. Why was the rate of change in rural communities much slower than in urban areas? Is this difference still apparent today?

TEACHING WITH VISUALS

Answer to the photo caption question: The soaring height of the church and its tall windows provide an idea of the splendor of the interior.

believe that there was only one path to salvation. They thought that it was the true duty of a ruler not to allow subjects to be condemned to hell by being heretics. Thus, the persecution of heretics continued. The last burning of a heretic took place in 1781.

The Jews remained the despised religious minority of Europe. The largest number of Jews (known as the Ashkenazic [ASH-kuh-NAZZ-ik] Jews) lived in eastern Europe. Except in Poland, Jews were restricted in their movements, forbidden to own land or hold many jobs, forced to pay special taxes, and subject to outbursts of popular anger. Jewish communities were often looted and massacred. For Jews, this persecution made existence difficult and dependent upon the favor of their rulers.

Another major group was the Sephardic (suh-FARD-ik) Jews, who had been expelled from Spain in the fifteenth century. Although many had migrated to Turkish lands, some had settled in cities, such as Amsterdam, Venice, London, and Frankfurt. There they could take part in the banking and trading activities that Jews had been allowed to practice since the Middle Ages. Highly successful Jews came to provide valuable services to rulers, especially in central Europe. Even these Jews were insecure, however, because their religion set them apart from the Christian majority.

Some Enlightenment thinkers in the eighteenth century favored a new acceptance of Jews. They argued that Jews and Muslims were all human beings and deserved the full rights of citizenship despite their religions. Other philosophes, especially Voltaire, made no attempt to hide their hatred, and they ridiculed Jewish customs. Many Europeans favored the assimilation of the Jews into the mainstream of society, but only by the conversion of Jews to Christianity. This, of course, was not acceptable to most Jews.

Popular Religion in the Eighteenth Century

Religious devotion remained strong in the eighteenth century for both Catholics and Protestants. It is difficult to assess precisely how religious Europe's Catholics were. The Catholic parish church remained an important center of life for the entire community. How many people went to church regularly cannot be known exactly. However, it has been established that 90 to 95 percent of Catholic populations did go to mass once a year—on Easter Sunday, one of the church's most special celebrations.

After the initial religious fervor that created Protestantism in the sixteenth century, Protestant churches in the seventeenth century had settled down into well-established patterns controlled by state authorities. Many Protestant churches were lacking in religious enthusiasm. Especially in Germany and England, the desire of ordinary Protestant churchgoers for greater depths of religious experience led to new and dynamic religious movements.

Pietism in Germany was one response to this desire for a deeper personal devotion to God. Pietism began

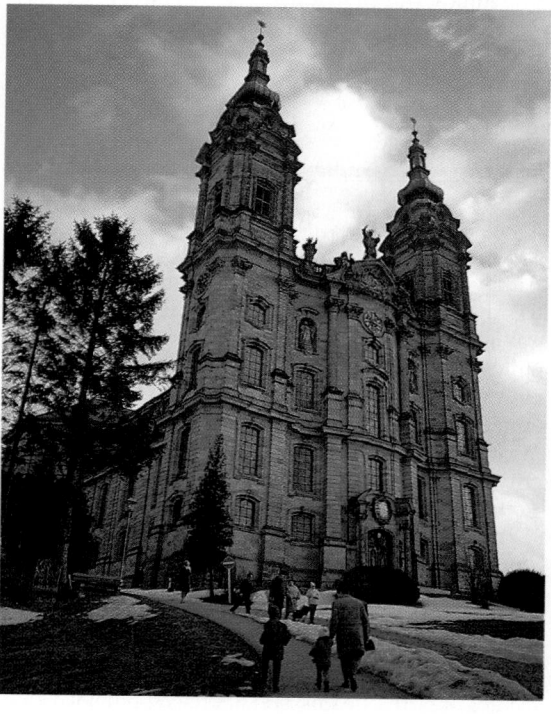

▲ *The exterior of the church of the Fourteen Saints is shown here. How does the exterior facade compare and contrast with the church's interior?*

So What ??

If your students question the importance of the information on the **persecution of Jews in Europe,** *tell them . . .*

They should be aware of the plight of the Strausbourg Jews during the time of the plague and of the Holocaust that occurred during World War II. You might wish to discuss recent attempts of "ethnic cleansing" such as that in Bosnia-Herzegovina and in Rwanda.

TEACH

YOU ARE THERE

A Pietist Writes to His Son

This selection is taken from a letter written by a Pietist religious leader to his son. At the time, his son was an apprentice to a merchant. The father implies that his son's devotion to God would be his most valuable asset in bringing him worldly success.

**Letter of Advice
from a Father to His Son**

Your letter and your wishes for the New Year have pleased me. May God, to whom we direct all our wishes, fulfill them in a way that enhances His glory, benefits my office, and is profitable to all of my family. May He also let you enter a year—or rather all of your years as He has foreordained for you in this world—spent so that the divine light and power in your soul are increased every day through the Holy Spirit. . . .

Always remember that any time spent in this world during which we do not have God before our eyes or do something to His honor is wasted. In order to serve Him faithfully at all times, remember that wherever you are God is with you, seeing and hearing everything you think, say, or do. This thought will often keep you from doing evil and spur you on to do good; it will even be the reason for all the good you do. . . .

Be diligent in your work, pay attention to everything, and remember always that the profession you are learning now will not only be the means of earning a livelihood for the rest of your life but also that of serving God and your fellow man. Remember also that, to a large extent, it

depends on you whether you will be a useless person or whether you will amount to something in the world. Therefore, you must pray to God with all your heart for His Holy Spirit, and also expend all possible effort and care during your years of apprenticeship.

1. What prompted the writing of this letter?

2. After you have read the information in the text on "Popular Religion in the Eighteenth Century" and the father's letter to his son, imagine how the son would have reacted to his father's letter. Consider that the son is a teenager much like you, but living during the eighteenth century.

3. The introduction to this selection states that the son was working for a merchant. As an apprentice to a merchant what could the son do to follow his father's advice? Will he be able to incorporate his father's recommendations on the job, or will he need to do this on his own time? What would the father's answer to the question be?

4. Do you think a father today might write a letter such as this one to his son? Why or why not? If a father did write such a letter, how would it be different from this one?

SPECIAL NEEDS: *Visual/auditory*

At the conclusion of the chapter, ask students to help you make a list of all the improvements that happened between 1550 and 1800. Focus on those changes which made peoples' lives easier.

Next, ask students to think of changes which have occurred during their lifetimes which have made life easier. Especially for the hearing and visually-impaired, there should be a lot of good responses concern-

ing hearing technology, surgery technology and computer technology. Are there improvements that have been made in products that the students have not tried yet? How would these products improve the students' lives?

To extend this activity, have students draw or describe to the class a new invention that would improve peoples' lives.

ASSESS

You can choose from a variety of assessments to evaluate your students' mastery of the objectives for this section as stated on page 601.

LEARNING FROM VISUALS

Answer to the caption question: John Wesley's posture and stance is caring and kind, reaching out to people. The expression on his face, and particularly in his eyes, conveys a welcoming gentleness.

Answers to SECTION REVIEW

2. (a) largest group of Jews, lived in eastern Europe
   (b) expelled from Spain in the fifteenth century
   (c) a missionary to the English people, credited with starting the Methodism movement
3. (a) held religious services, kept records of births, deaths, and marriages, provided charity for the poor, ran schools for children, cared for orphans
   (b) movements were restricted, forbidden to own land or hold many jobs, forced to pay special taxes, subject to outbursts of popular anger
   (c) The desire of ordinary Protestant churchgoers for greater depths of religious experience led to new and dynamic religious movements.
4. Answers will vary.

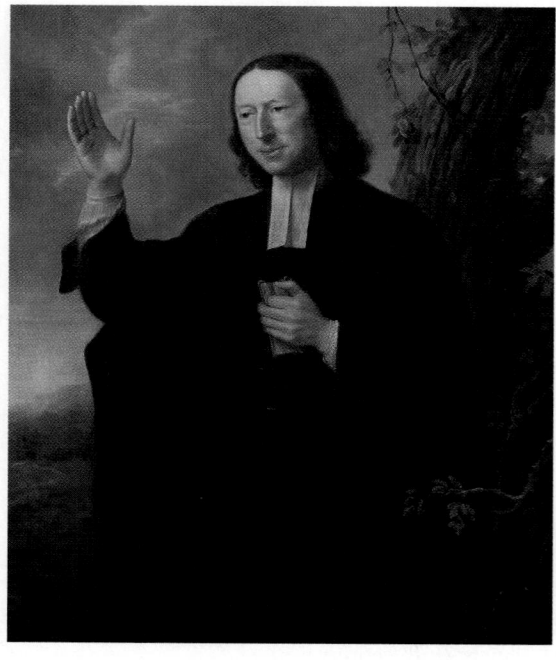

▲ John Wesley, who is shown in this 1766 portrait, led a fervent spiritual revival in England. He enjoyed the opportunity to preach outdoors to large groups of common people. How does the artist convey kindness and compassion in this portrait?

in the seventeenth century when a group of German clergymen sought to make their religion more personal. Most important was Count Niklaus von Zinzendorf, who founded a religious group known as the Moravian Brethren. To Zinzendorf and his followers, it was the personal experience of God that made up a true religious life (see "You Are There: "A Pietist Writes to His Son").

In England, the most famous movement for new religious experience—Methodism—was the work of John Wesley, an Anglican minister. Wesley had a mystical experience in which "the gift of God's grace" assured him of salvation and led him to become a missionary to the English people in order to bring the "glad tidings" of salvation to all people. To Wesley,

everyone could be saved by experiencing God and opening the doors to his grace.

In taking the gospel to the people, Wesley preached to the masses in open fields. He appealed especially to the lower classes neglected by the socially elitist Anglican Church. He tried, he said, "to lower religion to the level of the lowest people's capacities." Wesley's fiery preaching often led to highly charged and even violent conversion experiences. Converts were organized into so-called Methodist societies, in which they could aid one another in doing the good works that Wesley considered a part of salvation. After Wesley's death, Methodism became a separate Protestant group. Methodism proved that the need for spiritual experience had not been eliminated by the eighteenth-century search for reason.

 SECTION REVIEW

1. **Locate:**
   (*a*) Amsterdam, (*b*) Venice, (*c*) London, (*d*) Frankfurt
2. **Identify:**
   (*a*) Ashkenazic Jews, (*b*) Sephardic Jews, (*c*) John Wesley
3. **Recall:**
   (*a*) What important functions did parish churches provide during the eighteenth century?
   (*b*) How were Jews treated during the eighteenth century?
   (*c*) What led to the new dynamic religious movements in the Protestant faith?
4. **Think Critically:** Can you think of religious groups that are persecuted today? How is this different or similar to the persecution of the Jews in the eighteenth century?

Conclusion

The Scientific Revolution was a major turning point in modern civilization. In the Scientific Revolution, the Western world overthrew the medieval, Ptolemaic worldview and arrived at a new conception of the universe. The universe was now seen as having the sun at the center and the planets as material bodies revolving around the sun in elliptical orbits. The world was seen as infinite rather than finite. With the changes in the conception of Heaven came changes in the conception of Earth. The work of René Descartes and Francis Bacon left Europeans with the idea of the separation of mind and matter. Furthermore, it was believed that by using only reason, people could understand and dominate the world of nature. The development of a scientific method furthered the work of scientists. The creation of scientific societies spread the results of the Scientific Revolution. Although churches resisted the new ideas, nothing was able to halt the replacement of the traditional ways of thinking with new ones. This was the time of a fundamental break with the past.

The philosophes of the eighteenth century were highly influenced by the new worldview created by the Scientific Revolution. They hoped that they could create a new society by using reason to discover the natural laws that governed society. The philosophes believed that education could create better human beings and a better human society. They attacked traditional religion as the enemy and created the new "sciences of man" in economics, politics, and education. Together, the Scientific Revolution of the seventeenth century and the Enlightenment of the eighteenth century made up an intellectual revolution that laid the foundations for a modern worldview based on rationalism and secularism.

This was also an age of tradition. Secular thought and rational ideas became part of the mental world of the ruling elites, but most people in eighteenth-century Europe still lived by the old truths and practices—God, religious worship, and farming. However, the forces of secularization were too strong to stop. As we shall see in the next chapter, economic, political, and social changes of great importance were taking shape in the midst of the intellectual change. By the end of the eighteenth century, these changes would lead to both political and industrial revolutions.

Notes

1. Quoted in Londa Schiebinger, *The Mind Has No Sex? Women in the Origins of Modern Science* (Cambridge, Mass., 1989), pp. 52–53.
2. *Ibid.*, p. 85.
3. René Descartes, *Philosophical Writings*, ed. and trans. Norman K. Smith (New York, 1958), pp. 118–119.
4. Blaise Pascal, *The Pensées*, trans. J. M. Cohen (Harmondsworth, 1961), p. 100.
5. *Ibid.*, pp. 31, 165.
6. Francis Bacon, *The Great Instauration,* trans. Jerry Weinberger (Arlington Heights, Ill., 1989), pp. 2, 21.
7. John Locke, *An Essay Concerning Human Understanding* (New York, 1964), pp. 89–90.

ALTERNATIVE ASSESSMENT

Assign students to visit a local house of worship and to ask the religious leader to explain the significance of the structure or its contents. Students should write an essay explaining what they learned.

CLOSE

Lead students in a discussion of the "Focus" objectives on page 601. Emphasize that although religious toleration did become more common in Europe during the Enlightenment, it was not universal or afforded to all religious groups.

TIME LINE

As students conclude the chapter, you may want to refer them to the chapter time line in the *Study Guide.* The time line will help them put key dates in perspective. Supporting questions and activities are also provided.

SPANISH SUPPORT

The *Conclusion* has been translated into Spanish for your Spanish-speaking students. Included with this translation (in your Teacher Resource Box) are Section Key Points, which consist of one or two sentences summarizing each section in the chapter. These Key Points have also been translated into Spanish.

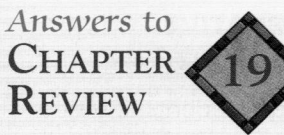

USING KEY TERMS

1. universal law of gravitation
2. feminism
3. secularization
4. separation of powers
5. Ptolemaic or geocentric
6. chapbooks
7. Baroque-Rococo
8. deism
9. rationalism
10. salon
11. Cartesian dualism
12. philosophe
13. laissez-faire
14. scientific method
15. heliocentric
16. inductive principles

REVIEWING THE FACTS

1. a few ancient authorities, mainly Aristotle and Galen
2. telescope, microscope, and printing press
3. Kepler's first law showed that planets orbit the sun in elliptical orbits, destroying the basic structure of Ptolemaic system.
4. their theories threatened the church's basic conception of the universe
5. First, every object continues in a state of rest or uniform motion in a straight line unless deflected by a force. Second, the rate of change of motion of an object is proportional to the force acting upon it. Third, to every action there is always an equal and opposite reaction.
6. His *On the Fabric of the Human Body* provided new understanding of anatomy.
7. showed that the heart, not the liver, was the beginning point for the circulation of blood in the body; also proved that the same blood flows in both veins and arteries and that the blood makes a complete circuit as it passes through the body; laid foundation for modern physiology
8. Margaret Cavendish and Maria Winkelmann

606

USING KEY TERMS

1. Newton's explanation of why heavenly bodies traveled in elliptical orbits around the sun is called the _____.
2. Mary Wollstonecraft is considered by many to be the founder of modern European _____.
3. The _____ of Europe increased as more people acted on the basis of worldly, instead of religious, assumptions.
4. Montesquieu believed that _____ _____ should bring about checks and balances of one branch of government over another.
5. The idea that the earth is at the center of the universe is called the _____ or _____ concept.
6. Short pamphlets of popular literature printed on cheap paper were called _____.
7. The architectural style in which buildings were total works of art is known as _____.
8. _____ is a philosophy that says God does not interfere with the natural laws of the universe.
9. Descartes is called the father of modern _____.
10. The _____ allowed invited guests and philosophes to engage in discussions and introduce new ideas.
11. Descartes' notion that the body and the mind must be radically different led to the idea called _____.
12. The intellectuals, or thinkers, of the Enlightenment were generically called _____.
13. The doctrine that maintains that the state should not intervene in economics is called _____.
14. The _____ is a way to go about examining and understanding the physical realm.
15. The belief that the sun was at the center of the universe is called the _____ theory.
16. _____ should guide scientific investigation according to Francis Bacon.

REVIEWING THE FACTS

1. What did medieval scientists rely on as a means of discovering scientific truth?
2. Name three new technological improvements that assisted in stimulating scientific activity.
3. What was Kepler's contribution to astronomy?
4. Why did the Christian Church attack the Copernican system and Galileo?
5. State the three laws of planetary motion, according to Newton.
6. What role did mathematics play in the intellectual revolution?
7. What was Andreas Vesalius's contribution to the field of medicine?
8. How did William Harvey's work change the ideas of Galen regarding circulation of the blood?
9. Name two women who made significant contributions to the scientific revolution.
10. Name two scientific societies that did much to advance science in Europe.
11. What was the Enlightenment?
12. Generally speaking, who were the philosophes?
13. How did Montesquieu arrive at his idea that a good political system must have a separation of powers?
14. What was Diderot's most lasting contribution to the Enlightenment?
15. What is deism?
16. According to Adam Smith, what is the proper role of government in society?
17. Why is Mary Wollstonecraft often considered the founder of modern European feminism?
18. Name two early eighteenth-century composers who have stood out as musical geniuses of the Baroque style.
19. According to Haydn, who was "the greatest composer known to me either in person or by reputation"?
20. What is the distinction between high and popular cultures?

9. English Royal Society and The French Royal Academy of Sciences
10. a movement of intellectuals who were greatly impressed with achievements of Scientific Revolution
11. the intellectuals of the Enlightenment
12. He analyzed different political systems, especially England's constitution and found that the separation of powers was essential for a good political system.
13. the Encyclopedia or Classified Dictionary of the Sciences, Arts, and Trades
14. a philosophy that believes God does not interfere with the natural laws of the universe
15. the state should not interfere in economic matters; should only have three roles: protect soci-

ety from invasion (the army); defend its citizens (the police); and keep up certain public works, such as roads and canals
16. She made the strongest statement for the rights of women in her book *Vindication of the Rights of Women*.
17. Handel and Bach
18. Mozart
19. High culture is the literary and artistic culture of the educated and wealthy ruling classes; popular culture is the written and unwritten culture of the masses.
20. The messages of Methodism appealed to the lower classes sometimes neglected by the socially elitist Anglicans.

21. How was Methodism, as preached by John Wesley, different from Anglicanism?

THINKING CRITICALLY

1. Without the telescope and printing press, how might the history of this period have developed differently from the way it did?
2. Why did the Ptolemaic or geocentric theory of the universe make sense to Christian theologians?
3. Cite two examples of gross prejudice toward women in science, based on the textbook material.
4. Give an example of finding scientific truth by using inductive reasoning principles.
5. Discuss Rousseau's belief that if any individual is determined to pursue his own self-interests at the expense of the common good, "he will be forced to be free." Do you agree or disagree with Rousseau's ideas? Why?

APPLYING SOCIAL STUDIES SKILLS

1. **Sociology:** How do you think the new ideas of the scientific revolution and the Enlightenment were received by the average person in the seventeenth and eighteenth centuries? How might you react to scientific discoveries that undermine present ideas of life and of the universe? Use a specific example of some recent scientific discovery in your answer.
2. **Economics:** To what extent is American capitalism today the same as that envisioned by the physiocrats? To what extent is it different?
3. **Sociology:** Mary Wollstonecraft, Margaret Cavendish, Maria Einkelmann and many other women of the seventeenth and eighteenth centuries went against the social expectations of the proper role of women. What kind of reactions do women receive today when they press for greater quality in society? Support your ideas, using news articles about women around the world.

4. **Criminology:** After re-reading the text section, "Crime and Punishment," indicate how our present treatment of criminals may be the same or different from that of the era under study, and why.

MAKING TIME AND PLACE CONNECTIONS

1. Galileo was forced by the Catholic Church to recant his views about the universe—even though they were mostly correct. What scientific theories today draw a similar reaction from the established religions? Explain your answer.
2. Adam Smith is considered by many to be the father of capitalism. In his book, *The Wealth of Nations*, he explains that government should not intervene in the economic activity of society. Why do you believe today's capitalist governments frequently intervene in the economy?
3. Anti-Semitism, or hatred of the Jews, has a long history in Europe and America. To what extent is the United States still anti-Semite? How is this anti-Semitism shown? Do you believe religion or economics plays a larger role in anti-Semitism?

BECOMING AN HISTORIAN

1. **Map Interpretation:** On a map of Europe, locate the cities or countries where the major figures in this chapter lived. Write their names and the (approximate) dates of their most important contributions. Then draw arrows connecting each individual, going from the earlier to the later dates to see the dynamic nature of new thinking in different parts of Europe.
2. **Art as a Key to History:** You have been commissioned to write an account of high culture and popular culture for our times. Write an essay that will help people 500 years from now to understand our own time.

607

THINKING CRITICALLY

1. Answers will vary. Possible answers may include that without telescope, many astronomy discoveries would not have been made and without printing press, many scientific discoveries in all fields could not have been as widely published.
2. Answers will vary. Both considered Earth to be in center of universe; world to be made of more than just matter, but of spirit as well; Heaven and God were in specific places.
3. Margaret Cavendish not allowed to become member of English Royal Society; Maria Winkelman denied university teaching position
4. Answers will vary. Possible answers may include

Kepler's first law and Newton's universal law of gravitation
5. Answers will vary. Responses should make reference to and show understanding of Rousseau's ideas.

APPLYING SOCIAL STUDIES SKILLS

1. Answers will vary. Possible answers may include that average people may not have cared much until it impacted their daily lives. All of us tend to feel uncomfortable when our beliefs are shaken, challenged or proved erroneous. An example today could be the debate surrounding genetic engineering and cloning.

2. Answers will vary; similar in many ways in that it is a free-market economy that swings with the "natural law" of supply and demand; different in that American capitalism is somewhat regulated by government, which is not the pure laissez-faire that the physiocrats envisioned
3. Answers will vary. Students will need access to contemporary news articles about women around the world.
4. They are similar in that one goal is to punish criminals and to use them partly as an example to deter other criminals. They differ in several ways, most notably in the degrees of severity and the individual rights of the accused.

MAKING TIME AND PLACE CONNECTIONS

1. Answers will vary. One example could be the conflict of the theory of evolution and religions that believe in a divine Creator of the entire universe.
2. Answers will vary. Possible answers may include to help maintain balance between supply and demand, helping to keep inflation under control and the money in our society flowing
3. Answers will vary.

BECOMING AN HISTORIAN

1. Answers will vary. A map of Europe, ideally a copy upon which the students can write, should be supplied to the students to allow them to complete this project.
2. Answers will vary. Student responses should demonstrate understanding of high and popular culture.

PLANNING GUIDE

SECTION	KEY TOPICS	PRIMARY SOURCES	ASSESSMENT
1 The Old Order and the Emergence of New Patterns pages 609–618	◆ New economic patterns in eighteenth century Europe ◆ Changes in European society ◆ Growth of enlightened absolutism in eighteenth century Europe	◆ The Leeds Woolen Workers' Petition, page 611	◆ Section Review, page 618 ◆ Section Quiz 20–1, TRB
2 Changing Patterns of War: Global Confrontation pages 619–622	◆ The War of Austrian Succession ◆ The Seven Years' War		◆ Section Review, page 622 ◆ Section Quiz 20–2, TRB
3 Colonial Empires and Revolution in the Western Hemisphere pages 622–629	◆ Society and economics in Latin America ◆ British colonies in North America ◆ Revolution and the formation of the United States	◆ A description of an Indian village, page 624	◆ Section Review, page 629 ◆ Section Quiz 20–3, TRB
4 Toward a New Political Order: The French Revolution Begins pages 630–637	◆ Causes of the French Revolution ◆ Destruction of the Old Regime	◆ A declaration of the Rights of Man and the Citizen, page 634 ◆ A declaration of the Rights of Woman and the Female Citizen, page 635	◆ Section Review, page 637 ◆ Section Quiz 20–4, TRB
5 From Radical Revolution to the Age of Napoleon pages 638–643	◆ The Radical Revolution ◆ Causes and results of the Reign of Terror ◆ The Age of Napoleon ◆ The rise and fall of Napoleon's empire	◆ A decree of universal mobilization, page 638 ◆ A description of executions during the Reign of Terror, page 640	◆ Section Review, page 643 ◆ Section Quiz 20–5, TRB

ON THE EVE OF A NEW WORLD ORDER (1700 TO 1815)

REPRODUCIBLE ACTIVITIES

- Historical Maps
- Charts and Graphs
- Critical Thinking
- Cooperative Learning
- Vocabulary
- Guided Reading
- Reteaching
- Enrichment
- Performance Assessment
- Spanish Key Points and Chapter Summaries
- Spanish Vocabulary
- Spanish Guided Reading

MULTIMEDIA SUPPORT

TRANSPARENCIES
- *World History* Color Transparency Package
- Fine Art Color Transparency Package

VIDEO
- *World History* Video Library
- CNN® Annual Video Update

LASERDISC
- *Sights and Sounds of History*

AUDIO
- *Listening to Literature* audiotape (English and Spanish)
- *History of Music* CD

SOFTWARE
- WESTEST™
- Student Review

CD-ROM
- *The Journey of Civilization*
- *World History*

INTERNET
- Internet Activities

On Line with WORLD HISTORY

Access West's history web site at
http://history.swpco.com
You'll find activities and web sites related to specific topics and chapters in *World History: The Human Odyssey*. Also look for references to helpful web sites at appropriate places throughout this teacher edition.

LESSON PLANNING

You will find detailed daily lesson plans for both traditional class scheduling and **block scheduling** in your Teacher Resource Box.

Not Enough Time?

If you do not have the four or five days recommended to teach this chapter, you may want to focus on the following sections and activities:

- Have students skim the chapter to answer the "Questions to Guide Your Reading" on page 608. Discuss their answers, then read the "Conclusion" on pages 644–645.
- Do a more in-depth reading about new economic patterns in Europe on pages 609–612, Enlightened Absolutism on pages 614–618, change in Latin America on pages 622–624, the American Revolution on pages 627–629, destruction of the French Old Regime on pages 632–637, and the age of Napoleon on pages 640–643. Conclude with a discussion of the reason for separate declarations of the rights of men and women on pages 634–636.

ON THE EVE OF A NEW WORLD ORDER
(1700 TO 1815)

BUILDING ON CHAPTER 19

To "set the scene" for the study in Chapter 20, use the following questions and activities.

◆ Ask students to review how the Scientific Revolution changed European civilization.

◆ Assign students to predict how the discrimination against women they studied in Chapter 19 would lead to the growth of feminism.

◆ Ask students why questioning of religious values and leadership might lead people to question the political and social order of a state.

USING THE OPENING STORY

Select from the following questions and activities to reinforce the opening story.

◆ Do you believe the Bastille was stormed to set prisoners free, because it was a symbol of oppression, or as a first step in overthrowing the French monarchy?

◆ What is the difference between a revolt and a revolution? (revolt— *renouncing allegiance; armed uprising; vigorous dissent.* revolution—*a sudden radical, complete change; an overthrow of one government in favor of another.*)

◆ Once the Old Order lost control of the situation in France, why was it so hard to regain power?

On the morning of July 14, 1789, a Parisian mob of some 8,000 men and women in search of weapons streamed toward the Bastille (bah-STEE[uhl]), a royal armory filled with arms and ammunition. The Bastille was also a state prison. Although it contained only seven prisoners at the time, in the eyes of those angry Parisians it was a glaring symbol of the government's despotic policies. The armory was defended by the Marquis de Launay (mar-KEE de loe-NAE) and a small garrison of 114 men. The attack began in earnest in the early afternoon. After three hours of fighting, de Launay and the garrison surrendered. Angered by the loss of 98 of its members, the victorious mob beat de Launay to death, cut off his head, and carried it aloft in triumph through the streets of Paris. When King Louis XVI was told about the fall of the Bastille by the duc de La Rochefoucauld-Liancourt, he exclaimed, "Why, this is a revolt." "No, Sire," replied the duke, "It is a revolution."

The French Revolution began a new age in European political life. The eighteenth century was the final phase of Europe's old order. That old order, still largely based on farming, was dominated by kings and landed aristocrats. We have read about the new intellectual order that emerged in the Scientific Revolution and Enlightenment. At the same time, economic, social, and political patterns were also beginning to change. These changes heralded the emergence of a new order.

A key factor in the emergence of a new world order was the French Revolution. The French Revolution saw the destruction of the old political order in France. The new order that emerged was based on individual rights, representative institutions, and a concept of loyalty to the nation rather than the monarch. The revolutionary upheaval of the era, especially in France, created new political ideals, summarized in the French revolutionary slogan, "Liberty, Equality, and Fraternity." These ideals transformed France and then spread to other European countries and to the rest of the world.

◀ *The guillotine, which was used for the first time in 1792, symbolizes the horror and the reality of the French Revolution. The American Revolution may have served as a model for the French Revolution, but there were many differences between them.*

ADDITIONAL RESOURCES

The resources below can be used to enrich the lessons in this chapter.

BOOKS FOR STUDENTS

The French Revolution by David L. Dowd. Horizon Caravell, Harper & Row.
A Tale of Two Cities by Charles Dickens.
Nelson and the Age of Fighting Sail. Horizon Caravell, Harper & Row.

VIDEOS/FILMS

Eighteenth Century Woman Social Studies School Services (800) 421-4246
Napoleon: The Making of a Dictator (Learning Corporation of America) Social Studies School Services (800) 421-4246
Catherine the Great: A Profile in Power (Learning Corporation of America) Social Studies School Services (800) 421-4246

NEW WORLD PATTERNS

	A NEW WORLD ORDER	
	1700	1815
1400		1815

QUESTIONS TO GUIDE YOUR READING

OUTLINE

THE OLD ORDER AND THE EMERGENCE OF NEW PATTERNS

In the eighteenth century in Europe, economic changes that would have a strong impact on the rest of the world began to occur. The new patterns included rapid population growth, a dramatic increase in food production, the beginnings of an industrial revolution, and an expansion of worldwide trade.

New Economic Patterns

Europe's population began to grow noticeably around 1750. The total European population was probably around 120 million in 1700. It expanded to 140 million by 1750 and grew to 190 million by 1790. A falling death rate was probably the most important cause of population growth. Why did the death rate decline?

609

Answers to QUESTIONS TO GUIDE YOUR READING

1. divided land into the traditional orders, or estates (pages 612–613)
2. concept of monarchs who ruled based on Enlightenment philosophies; in the end made little real difference (pages 614–618).
3. causes: (pages 619–620); results: (pages 620–622)
4. multiracial; controlled by Spanish and Portuguese empires; farming and trade main

parts of economy; Catholic Church very active (pages 622–624)
5. colonists did not want to be taxed by British Parliament; accomplished the birth of new nation (pages 627–629)
6. See pages 630–632
7. destruction of the old regime; time of revolution and Napoleon (pages 632–640)
8. largest-ever French empire; overextended his reach (pages 640–643)

FOCUS

OBJECTIVES

After completing this section, students should be able to

1. identify and explain new economic patterns in Europe
2. describe changes in European society
3. identify enlightened absolutism

Multimedia Support

TRANSPARENCY
20–1, Timeline of Important Historical Events of the Eighteenth Century

FOCUS ACTIVITY

Changes in industrial technology often change social patterns as well. Ask students to identify ways in which the personal computer has changed the way people live and work today. Point out the new technology in the eighteenth century forced production out of the home. Today some work is returning to the home. What might this mean for modern society?

TEACH

LEARNING FROM VISUALS

Answer to the caption question: Dieppe grew and prospered because of trade but did not gain fame for its patronage of the arts.

610

More food and better transportation of available food supplies led to a better diet and relief from the famines that had previously been so common. Also of importance in lowering death rates was the disappearance of bubonic plague.

Agricultural practices and methods improved in the eighteenth century—especially in Britain, parts of France, and the Low Countries. Food production increased as more land was farmed, yields per acre increased, and climate improved. Especially important were the moderate summers that provided more ideal growing conditions. Also important to the increased yields was the spread of new vegetables, including two important American crops, the potato and maize (Indian corn). Both had been brought to Europe from the Americas in the sixteenth century.

In European industry in the eighteenth century, the most important product was textiles. Most were still produced by traditional methods. In the cities, artisans produced finished goods in their guild workshops. In the countryside, peasants added to their incomes by spinning raw materials (mostly wool and flax) into yarn and then weaving it into cloth on simple looms. This was a system known as a **cottage industry,** because spinners and weavers did their work on spinning wheels and looms in their own homes, or cottages. A cottage industry was truly a family enterprise; women and children could spin while men wove on the looms.

In the course of the eighteenth century, the demand for cotton clothes, which were less expensive than woolens and linens, increased dramatically. However, the traditional methods of the cottage industry could not keep up with the growing demand. This situation led British cloth manufacturers to develop new methods and new machines. Richard Arkwright invented a "water frame," powered by horse or water, which spun yarn much faster than cottage spinning wheels could. The resulting abundance of yarn, in turn, led to the development of mechanized looms. These were invented in the 1780s but were not widely adopted until the early nineteenth century (see Chapter 21). Already at the end of the eighteenth century, however, rural workers realized that the new machines meant the end of their cottage industries and began to call for the destruction of the machines (see "You Are There: The Attack on New Machines").

In the eighteenth century, overseas trade boomed. This trade expansion led to the emergence of a global economy. Patterns of trade connected Europe, Africa, the Far East, and North and South America. One trade pattern centered on the gold and silver that went to Spain from the South American part of the Spanish

▶ *During the eighteenth century, Dieppe was a modern port city. Trade was carried on with the French colonies throughout the Americas from this busy commercial center. How does this city compare to Italian city-states made wealthy by trade?*

MORE ABOUT . . . *Disappearance of the Plague*

In 1720 a ship from Syria landed in Marseilles, France. Within weeks nearly half of the city's 90,000 people were dead from Bubonic plague. As Europe braced for another onslaught of the dreaded disease, the epidemic died out. It was the last time plague terrorized the continent. Tighter quarantine methods in Mediterranean ports may have contributed to its disappearance.

The main reason, however, seems to have been a change in rats. The principle carrier of the bubonic plague was the flea of the black rat. For reasons not known to historians, the black rat was driven out of Europe by an Asiatic brown rat. The brown rat's main parasite is a different kind of flea, one that does not carry the plague so readily and is less likely to feed on humans.

YOU ARE THERE

The Attack on New Machines

At the end of the eighteenth century, the use of simple machines brought changes to the traditional cottage industry of cloth making. This selection is taken from a petition of English wool workers to manufacturers. The petition asks that machines (Scribbling-Machines) no longer be used to prepare wool for spinning.

◄ *This illustration of a wool carding, or Scribbling-Machine, shows two men doing the work that had been done by twelve to make the same amount of woolen cloth. Carefully examine this illustration and explain how the machine worked.*

The Leeds Woolen Workers' Petition

The Scribbling-Machines have thrown thousands of your petitioners out of work. . . . We therefore request that you pay attention to the following facts:

The number of Scribbling-Machines extending about seventeen miles south-west of LEEDS, exceed all belief, being no less than *one hundred and seventy!* and as each machine will do as much work in twelve hours, as ten men can in that time do by hand, and they working night and day, one machine will do as much work in one day as would otherwise employ twenty men. . . .

Twelve men are thrown out of work for every single machine used; and as it may be supposed the number of machines in all the other quarters together, nearly equal those in the South-West, full four thousand men are left without work. . . . We wish to propose a few questions to those who would plead for the further use of these machines:

How are those men, thus thrown out of work to provide for their families. . . . Some say, Begin and learn some other business.—Suppose we do, who will maintain our families, while we undertake the difficult task; and when we have learned it, how do we know we shall be any better for all our pains; for by the time we have served our second apprenticeship, another machine may arise, which may take away that business also; . . .

But what are our children to do; are they to be brought up in idleness? Indeed as things are, it is no wonder to hear of so many executions; for our parts, though we may be thought illiterate men, our conceptions are, that bringing children up to industry, and keeping them employed, is the way to keep them from falling into those crimes, which an idle habit naturally leads to.

1. What arguments were used by the English wool workers to get rid of their new Scribbling-Machines?

2. Do these arguments sound familiar? In what ways?

MORE ABOUT . . . the Luddites

Students may have already learned about the first industrial sabotage group in history—although that term would not have been heard then.

In protesting unemployment caused by the Industrial Revolution in the early 19th century, English workers resorted to a campaign of breaking machinery, especially knitting machines. Their name may come from a boy named Ludlam, who, to spite his father, broke a knitting frame. The Luddites often signed their proclamations "General Ludd," "King Ludd," or "Ned Ludd." The movement began in the hosiery and lace industries and spread to the wool and cotton mills of Yorkshire and Lancashire. The government dealt harshly with the Luddites—14 were hanged in 1813. Although sporadic outbreaks of violence continued until 1816, the movement soon died out.

TEACHING THEMES

Economics and History. Ask students to suggest reasons why the power of Spain and Portugal declined while Britain emerged as the world's strongest trading nation in the eighteenth century. If they are unsure ask them to identify the major sources of income for these countries. *(England earned money producing goods that it sold while Spain and Portugal obtained most of their wealth by taking gold and silver from natives of South America.)*

Map 20.1   Global Trade Patterns of the European States in the Eighteenth Century

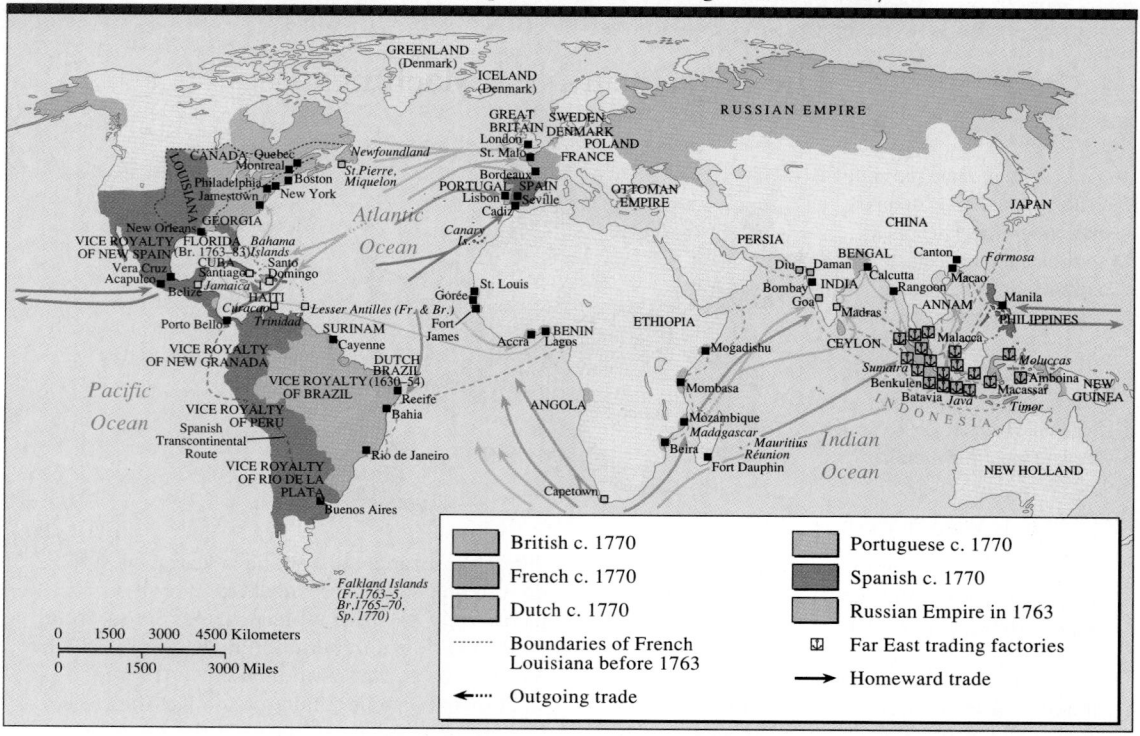

Empire. Much of this gold and silver made its way to Britain, France, and the Dutch Republic, where it was traded for manufactured goods. British, French, and Dutch merchants in turn used their profits to buy tea, spices, silk, and cotton goods from China and India to sell in Europe.

Another important trade pattern involved the plantations of the Americas. The plantations were worked by African slaves and produced tobacco, cotton, coffee, and sugar—all products in demand by Europeans.

In a third pattern of trade, British merchant ships carried British manufactured goods to Africa, where they were traded for a cargo of slaves. The slaves were then shipped to Virginia and paid for by tobacco. The tobacco in turn was shipped back to Britain.

Overseas trade created enormous prosperity for some European countries. By 1700, Spain, Portugal, and the Dutch Republic were increasingly overshadowed by France and England. These two nations built very profitable colonial empires in the course of the eighteenth century. After 1763, however, when France lost much of its overseas empire, Britain emerged as the world's strongest overseas trading nation. London became the world's greatest port.

European Society in the Eighteenth Century

The pattern of Europe's social organization, first established in the Middle Ages, continued well into the

STUDYING MAPS

The following questions will help you guide the students through their study of Map 20.1.

1. Which European state controlled the most colonial territory in 1770? *(From the map and the text reading, students should answer that by 1770, France and Britain were the major trade nations.)*

2. Which European state controlled the largest part of trade in 1770? *(It appears*

that Spain controlled the most territory. The Russian Empire was extensive, but most of it was not a colony.)

3. Why was controlling trade more important than controlling land? *(Land, the source of raw materials, was important, but manufactured goods acquired through trade were more valuable.)*

◄ *This market scene in Turin, Italy, shows the diversity that existed in towns. Communities, then as now, were composed of diverse social groups, with a wide range of incomes and occupations. How many different activities and vendors can you identify in this painting?*

CLASS DISCUSSION

Ask students to identify and discuss reasons why laws against the mixing of social groups are likely to fail in times of dramatic economic change. When new groups obtain wealth, why are they likely to marry members of the old ruling class?

LEARNING FROM VISUALS

Ask students to study the buildings in the background of the scene in the picture. What do the buildings indicate about the skills of Italian craftsmen? What types of structures can students identify? What might a drawing of a poor part of town have looked like?

Answer to the caption question: Fruits, vegetables, and eggs are being sold. Children are playing and fighting, adults are purchasing food, strolling, and chatting.

eighteenth century. Society was still divided into the traditional **orders,** or social groups also known as *estates*. Governments helped to maintain these divisions. In Prussia, for example, a law forbade marriage between noble males and middle-class females. Nevertheless, some forces of change were at work in this traditional society. Enlightenment reformers argued that the idea of an unchanging social order based on special privileges was hostile to the progress of society. Despite these ideas, however, it would not be until the revolutionary upheavals at the end of the eighteenth century that the old order would finally begin to disintegrate.

Because society was still mostly rural in the eighteenth century, the peasantry made up the largest social group, about 85 percent of Europe's population. There were rather wide differences within this group, however, especially between free peasants and serfs. In eastern Germany, eastern Europe, and Russia, serfs remained tied to the lands of their noble landlords. In contrast, peasants in Britain, northern Italy, the Low Countries, Spain, most of France, and some areas of western Germany were largely free. Legally free peas-

ants, however, still had burdens. Many owned little or no land. Peasants who did own land still owed a variety of dues and fees to local aristocrats. All these payments were deeply resented.

The nobles, who made up about two or three percent of the European population, played a dominating role in society. Being born a noble automatically guaranteed a person a place at the top of the social order, with all of the special privileges and rights of that position. Nobles, for example, were exempt from many forms of taxation. Nobles also played important roles in military and government affairs. Since medieval times, landed aristocrats had been military officers. The tradition remained that nobles made the most natural, and thus the best, officers. Eighteenth-century nobles also held most of the important offices in the administrative machinery of state and controlled much of the life of their local districts.

Townspeople were still a distinct minority of the total population except in the Dutch Republic, Britain, and parts of Italy. At the end of the eighteenth century, about one-sixth of the French population lived in towns of 2,000 or more. The biggest city in Europe was

RETEACHING ACTIVITY

You may want to tell your students that the transfer of plants, animals, people, ideas, and diseases between the Old World and the New World has been called the *Columbian Exchange*. Ask them if they can guess why it is called *Columbian* exchange? (named after Columbus) Have your students describe the ways in which Europe benefited from the Columbian Exchange. *(gold and silver to Europe from South America, which provided currency to buy goods from China and India; American plantations produced goods for Europe; overseas trade was, in general, good for European countries)*

London, with its 1,000,000 inhabitants, whereas Paris had about 600,000 people. Altogether, Europe had at least 20 cities in 12 countries with populations over 100,000.

In many cities in western Europe and even central Europe, a small group of very wealthy people known as the patricians continued to control their communities. Just below the patricians stood an upper crust of the middle classes: nonnoble officeholders; bankers; merchants; and important professionals, including lawyers. Another large urban group was the lower middle class, made up of master artisans, shopkeepers, and small traders. Below this group were the laborers, or working classes. Urban communities also had a large group of unskilled workers who were employed as servants, maids, and cooks at pitifully low wages.

Eighteenth-century cities experienced high death rates, especially among children, because of filthy living conditions, polluted water, and a lack of sewers. One observer compared the stench of Hamburg to an open sewer that could be smelled for miles around. Overcrowding became a problem as peasants moved to urban areas in search of work. Because they lacked skills, however, the peasants found few jobs. The result was a serious problem of poverty in the eighteenth century (see "Focus on Everyday Life: The Homeless in Eighteenth-Century Europe").

Political Change: Enlightened Absolutism in the Eighteenth Century

Enlightenment thought had some impact on the political life of European states in the eighteenth century. The philosophes believed in natural rights for all people. These included equality before the law; freedom of religious worship; freedom of speech and press; and the right to assemble, hold property, and pursue happiness. As the American Declaration of Independence expressed, "We hold these truths to be self-evident, that all men are created equal; that they are endowed by their creator with certain unalienable rights; that among these are life, liberty and the pursuit of happiness."

How were these natural rights to be established and preserved? Most philosophes believed that people needed to be ruled by an **enlightened ruler.** What, however, made rulers enlightened? They must allow religious toleration, freedom of speech and press, and the rights of private property. They must nurture the arts, sciences, and education. Above all, enlightened rulers must obey the laws and enforce them fairly for all subjects. Only strong monarchs could bring the enlightened reforms society needed. According to the philosophes, then, reforms should come from above (from absolute rulers) rather than from below (from the people).

Many historians once assumed that a new type of monarchy emerged in the later eighteenth century, which they called **enlightened absolutism.** Did Europe's rulers, however, follow the advice of the philosophes and become enlightened rulers? To answer this question, we can examine three states—Prussia, Austria, and Russia—where philosophes tried to influence rulers to bring enlightened reforms.

Prussia: The Army and the Bureaucracy

Two able Prussian kings, Frederick William I and Frederick II, made Prussia into a major European power in the eighteenth century. Frederick William I strove to maintain a highly efficient bureaucracy of civil service workers. The bureaucracy had its own code, in which the supreme values were obedience, honor, and service to the king as the highest duty. As Frederick William asserted: "One must serve the king with life and limb, and surrender all except salvation. The latter is reserved for God. But everything else must be mine."

Frederick William's other major concern was the army. By the end of his reign, he had doubled the army's size. Although Prussia was tenth in physical size and thirteenth in population in Europe, it had the fourth largest army after France, Russia, and Austria. The nobility or landed aristocracy known as Junkers, who owned large estates with many serfs, were the officers in the Prussian army. These officers, too, had a strong sense of service to the king or state. As Prussian nobles, they believed in duty, obedience, and sacrifice. The Prussian army, because of its size and reputation as one of the best armies in Europe, was the most important institution in the state.

FOCUS ON EVERYDAY LIFE

The Homeless in Eighteenth-Century Europe

Poverty was a highly visible problem in eighteenth-century Europe, both in cities and in the countryside. In Venice, licensed beggars made up three to five percent of the population. Beggars without licenses may have constituted as much as 13 to 15 percent of the population. Beggars in Bologna, Italy, were estimated at 25 percent of the population. In France and Britain by the end of the century, an estimated 10 percent of the people depended on charity or begging for their food.

Earlier in Europe, the homeless poor had been viewed as blessed children of God. Helping them was a Christian duty. By the eighteenth century, however, there had been a drastic change in attitude. Charity to poor beggars, it was argued, simply encouraged their idleness and led to crime. A French official stated, "Beggary is the apprenticeship of crime; it begins by creating a love of idleness which will always be the greatest political and moral evil. In this state the beggar does not long resist the temptation to steal." Private charities, such as the religious Order of Saint Vincent de Paul and the Sisters of Charity, worked hard to help the poor. However, they were soon overwhelmed by the increased numbers of homeless in the eighteenth century.

Some "enlightened" officials argued that the state should become involved in the problem, but in most countries people had mixed feelings about poverty. Since the sixteenth century, homelessness and begging had been considered crimes. In the eighteenth century, French authorities rounded up the homeless and beggars and put them in jail for 18 months as an example to others. The authorities accomplished little by this process, however, because many people had no work. In the 1770s, the French tried to use public works projects, such as road building, to give people jobs, but not enough money was provided to accomplish much.

▲ Homelessness and poverty were serious problems of eighteenth-century Europe. This illustration shows homeless people seeking food at a shelter in London, England. How does the artist convey the difference between those working in the shelter and those seeking help?

(continued)

MORE ABOUT . . . *Les Miserables*

Because of the popularity of the Broadway musical, many students are vaguely familiar with the story of Jean Valjean, Victor Hugo's tragic hero. This novel describes France in the early years of 19th century, and chronicles the social injustice of the time. *Les Miserables* appeared in 1862 after 12 years of composition. Hugo's desire was to denounce "the degradation of man by the proletariat, the downfall of woman through hunger, and the atrophy of children by the night."

Throughout the novel, Valjean remains a symbol of goodness and generosity unshaken by a corrupt world. The novel is well constructed, suspenseful, and at times lyrical in its passionate plea for pity and humanitarianism toward the poor and suffering.

FOCUS ON EVERYDAY LIFE

CLASS DISCUSSION

Ask students to discuss why the problems of poverty were much more serious for all levels of society when poverty occurred in cities rather than in rural areas. What changes in the lives of the wealthy could take place when they were surrounded by many poor people?

OPPOSING VIEWPOINTS

Divide students into teams to debate the proposition that the state should help the disadvantaged and the homeless. Ask them to do some research into the changing opinions on laws on welfare in contemporary United States, and then compare their findings to what they've read about poverty in the eighteenth century.

LEARNING FROM VISUALS

Answer to the caption question: Those distributing the food are well dressed and look comfortable and content. The artist also puts them within the well-lit part of the illustration.

Answers to Critical Thinking Questions

1. It was argued that giving to beggars encouraged their idleness and led to crime.
2. Answers will vary; some people feel the same way today, while others are more sympathetic toward the homeless.

CRITICAL THINKING

Lead students in a discussion of the meaning and significance of Frederick's belief that the king is the "first servant of the state."

COMPARING TIME PERIODS

Ask students to identify and describe other states they have studied that were difficult to rule because of their sprawling empire composed of many different nationalities, languages, religions, and cultures. What similarities and differences do they notice?

LEARNING FROM VISUALS

Ask students to find a photograph of the president at an official retreat, perhaps Camp David. Assign them to compare the kind of relaxation Frederick II was apparently enjoying with what their president does when on vacation. Is relaxation more a function of social values or of the nature of the individual?

FOCUS ON EVERYDAY LIFE
The Homeless in Eighteenth-Century Europe, continued

The problem of poverty remained as a serious blemish on the quality of eighteenth-century life. Societies today are still wrestling with this issue.

1. Describe the attitudes people had toward the homeless in eighteenth-century France.

2. How do those attitudes compare with attitudes toward the homeless in the United States today?

▼ *Frederick II was a well-educated, reform-minded ruler. In this painting, he is shown at his royal retreat Sans-Souci at Potsdam.*

Frederick II, or Frederick the Great, was one of the best educated and most cultured monarchs in the eighteenth century. He was well versed in Enlightenment thought and even invited Voltaire to live at his court for several years. A believer in the king as the "first servant of the state," Frederick the Great was a dedicated ruler. He, too, enlarged the Prussian army (to 200,000 men) and kept a strict watch over the bureaucracy.

For a time, Frederick seemed quite willing to make enlightened reforms. He abolished the use of torture except in treason and murder cases. He also granted a limited freedom of speech and press, as well as complete religious toleration. However, he kept Prussia's rigid social structure intact. He kept serfdom alive and avoided any additional reforms.

The Austrian Empire of the Habsburgs

The Austrian Empire had become one of the great European states by the beginning of the eighteenth century. It was difficult to rule, however, because it was a sprawling empire composed of many different nationalities, languages, religions, and cultures. Empress Maria Theresa worked to centralize the Austrian Empire in order to strengthen the power of the Austrian state. She was not open to the wider reform calls of the philosophes. However, her successor was.

MORE ABOUT . . . *The Habsburgs*

The Habsburg (or Hapsburg) family was one of the oldest and most distinguished royal dynasties in Europe. They were connected to virtually every royal house in Europe, and through marriages and inheritance came to dominate much of Europe. The male line died out in 1740 with Emperor Charles VI, but his daughter Maria Theresa married Francis of Lorraine and began the Habsburg-Lorraine line. After the War of Aus-

trian Succession, the Habsburg fortune was further diminished by the Napoleonic Wars. The Holy Roman Empire was completely dissolved in 1806 and Francis II declared himself Francis I of the Austrian Empire. By 1918 the Austrian empire had been completely broken up into independent republics, although the claim to hereditary titles has been maintained by descendants of the once-great family.

Map 20.2   Europe in 1763

Joseph II was determined to make changes. He believed in the need to sweep away anything standing in the path of reason. As he said, "I have made Philosophy the lawmaker of my empire, her logical applications are going to transform Austria." Joseph's reform program was far reaching. He abolished serfdom, eliminated the death penalty, and established the principle of equality of all before the law. Joseph produced drastic religious reforms as well, including complete religious toleration. Altogether, Joseph II issued 6,000 decrees and 11,000 laws in his effort to change Austria.

Joseph's reform program largely failed, however. He alienated the nobles by freeing the serfs. He alienated the church by his religious reforms. Even the serfs were

unhappy, because they were unable to make sense of the drastic changes in Joseph's policies. Joseph realized his failure when he wrote his own epitaph for his gravestone: "Here lies Joseph II who was unfortunate in everything that he undertook." His successors undid many of his reforms.

Russia under Catherine the Great

In Russia, Peter the Great was followed by six weak successors who were put in power and deposed by the palace guard. After the last of these six successors, Peter III, was murdered by a group of nobles, his

STUDYING MAPS

The following questions will help you guide students through their study of Map 20.2.

1. About how many times larger was the Habsburg Dominions (Austrian Empire) than Prussia in 1763? *(Answers may range from three to four times larger.)*
2. Why was Prussia a stronger military power than the Austrian Empire? *(Students may be able to see from the map that*

Austria covered much of what is today the Balkan and Russian states. The Austrian empire was fragmented even then.)
3. What nations would be affected by conflicts between Prussia and the Austrian Empire? *(Because of the central position of Prussia and Austria, nearly every country in Europe and the countries of western Asia would be affected.)*

▲ *Catherine favored reform, but not at the expense of her own power. This portrait by Dmitry Levitsky shows her in legislative dress in the Temple of Justice. Why might she have preferred this setting, rather than one that shows her wearing a royal gown and crown in her palace?*

German wife emerged as ruler of all the Russians. Catherine II, or Catherine the Great, was an intelligent woman who was familiar with the works of the philosophes and seemed to favor enlightened reforms. She invited the French philosophe Denis Diderot to Russia and, when he arrived, urged him to speak frankly "as man to man." He did so, outlining a far-reaching program of political and financial reform. However, Catherine was skeptical about what she felt were his impractical theories that "would have turned everything in my kingdom upside down." She did consider the idea of a new law code that would recognize the principle of the equality of all people in the eyes of the law. In the end, however, she did nothing because she knew that her success depended upon the support of the Russian nobility. In 1785, she gave the nobles a charter that exempted them from taxes.

Catherine's policy of favoring the landed nobility led to even worse conditions for the Russian peasants, and eventually to rebellion. Led by an illiterate Cossack (a Russian warrior), Emelyan Pugachev, the rebellion spread across southern Russia. The rebellion soon faltered, however. Pugachev was captured, tortured, and executed. The rebellion collapsed completely, and Catherine responded by effecting even greater measures against the peasantry. All rural reform was halted. Serfdom was even expanded into newer parts of the empire.

Above all, Catherine proved to be a worthy successor to Peter the Great in her policies of territorial expansion westward into Poland and southward to the Black Sea. Russia spread southward by defeating the Turks. Russian expansion westward occurred at the expense of neighboring Poland. In three partitions of Poland, Russia gained about 50 percent of the Polish territory.

Of the rulers we have discussed, only Joseph II sought truly radical changes based on Enlightenment ideas. Both Frederick II and Catherine II liked to talk about enlightened reforms, and they even attempted some. However, they never took the reforms seriously. To Frederick II and Catherine II, maintaining the existing system took priority over reform. Actually, all three rulers were chiefly guided by a concern for the power and well-being of their states. In the final analysis, heightened state power in Prussia, Austria, and Russia was not used to undertake enlightened reforms. Rather, it was used to collect more taxes, and thus to create armies, to wage wars, and to gain more power. In the next section, we shall look at the wars.

❀ **SECTION REVIEW** ❀

1. **Locate:**
   (*a*) the Dutch Republic,   (*b*) Prussia,
   (*c*) Russia,   (*d*) Austria,
   (*e*) Black Sea

MORE ABOUT . . . *Catherine the Great*

Although they were betrothed as children, Peter III despised and humiliated his wife Catherine. He openly took a mistress, who one observer said "swore like a trooper, had a squint, stank, and spat when she talked." Peter even had Catherine bestow upon his mistress an insignia reserved only for czarinas—a sign that he intended to repudiate Catherine and make his mistress his new wife. Catherine anticipated her husband, however, and declared herself Russia's czarina. With the help of a group of loyal nobles she forced Peter to sign a note of resignation. Seven days later he was dead, although there is no evidence that she ordered him killed.

2. **Define:**
   (*a*) cottage industry,   (*b*) orders,   (*c*) enlightened ruler,   (*d*) enlightened absolutism

3. **Identify:**
   (*a*) water frame,   (*b*) global economy,   (*c*) the peasantry,   (*d*) patricians,   (*e*) philosophes, (*f*) Junkers

4. **Recall:**
   (*a*) What was the main reason for the rapid growth of population in eighteenth-century Europe?
   (*b*) Name two results of the increased demand for cotton clothing.
   (*c*) What were the three values of the Prussian civil service workers' code during the reign of Frederick William I?
   (*d*) How did Catherine II become ruler of Russia?

5. **Think Critically:** Compare and contrast the reforms of Joseph II of Austria with those of Frederick II of Prussia and Catherine II of Russia.

2
CHANGING PATTERNS OF WAR: GLOBAL CONFRONTATION

The philosophes condemned war as a foolish waste of life and resources in stupid quarrels of no value to humankind. Despite their words, the rivalry among states that led to costly struggles remained unchanged in the European world of the eighteenth century. Europe consisted of a number of self-governing, individual states that were chiefly guided by the self-interest of the ruler.

The eighteenth-century monarchs were concerned with the **balance of power,** the idea that states should have equal power in order to prevent any one from dominating the others. This desire for a balance of power, however, did not imply a desire for peace. Large armies created to defend a state's security were often used to

conquer new lands as well. As Frederick the Great of Prussia remarked, "The fundamental rule of governments is the principle of extending their territories."

War of the Austrian Succession

Between 1715 and 1740, it seemed that Europe did want peace. In 1740, however, a major war broke out over the succession to the Austrian throne. When the Austrian emperor Charles VI died, he was succeeded by his daughter, Maria Theresa. King Frederick II of Prussia took advantage of the succession of a woman to the throne of Austria by invading Austrian Silesia (sie-LEE-zhee-uh). France then entered the war against its traditional enemy Austria. In turn, Maria Theresa made an alliance with Great Britain, which feared that the French were growing too powerful on the European continent. The Austrian succession had rapidly produced a worldwide war.

The War of the Austrian Succession (1740 to 1748) was fought in three areas of the world. In Europe, Prussia seized Silesia while France occupied the Austrian Netherlands. In the Far East, France took Madras in India from the British. In North America, the British captured the French fortress of Louisbourg at the entrance to the St. Lawrence River. By 1748, all parties were exhausted and agreed to stop. The peace treaty guaranteed the return of all occupied territories to their original owners except for Silesia. Prussia's refusal to return Silesia meant another war, at least between the two central European powers of Prussia and Austria.

The Seven Years' War (1756 to 1763): A Global War

Maria Theresa refused to accept the loss of Silesia. She rebuilt her army while working diplomatically to separate Prussia from its chief ally, France. In 1756, Austria achieved what was soon labeled a **diplomatic revolution.** French-Austrian rivalry had been a fact of European diplomacy since the late sixteenth century. However, two new rivalries now replaced the old one: the rivalry of Britain and France over colonial empires, and

On Line with
WORLD HISTORY   *Internet Activity*

You may want to have your students visit the following URL, where they will find information and additional web site resources to enhance their study of this chapter.

http://www.ping.be/napoleon.series/

Interesting because it is an electronic magazine dedicated to the study of

Napoleon and his times. An especially good set of Links to Napoleonic topics and Military History.

Due to the ever-changing nature of the World Wide Web, see the West History web site, **http://history.swpco.com** for regular updates of the URLs in this text.

(b) patterns of trade connecting the world
(c) largest social group in eighteenth century
(d) a small group of very wealthy people
(e) believed in natural rights for all people
(f) the nobility and officers of Prussia

4. (a) falling death rate
(b) development of the water frame and mechanized looms
(c) obedience, honor, and service to the king
(d) When Peter III was murdered

5. Answers will vary. Joseph II: abolished serfdom, eliminated the death penalty, established the principle of equality of all before the law, and supported religious reform, but drastic changes did not last; Frederick II: abolished torture, granted limited freedom of speech and press, allowed complete religious toleration, but kept serfdom and the rigid social order; Catherine II: considered a new code that would have recognized the principle of the equality of all people before the law, but favored the nobility and expanded serfdom

CLOSE

Lead students in a discussion of the Focus objectives identified on page 610. Emphasize the impact of the new wealth and power of the merchant class on political systems in Europe.

FOCUS

OBJECTIVES

After completing this section, students should be able to

1. identify and explain causes and effects of the War of Austrian Succession
2. explain how the Seven Years' War grew out of a realignment of power in Europe

FOCUS ACTIVITY

Help students understand that a balance of power is only likely to prevent war if adversaries believe that there is a balance of power. Tell students that after World War II the world was able to avoid nuclear war at least in part because both superpowers believed they could not win such a conflict. Ask students if they believe Prussia would have invaded Austrian Silesia if it had known England would enter the war against them?

TEACH

REINFORCING VOCABULARY

Assign students to construct a chart that shows which countries were allied with each other before and after the diplomatic revolution. Ask them to explain how these new alliances contributed to the causes of the Seven Years' War.

Map 20.3   The Seven Years' War

the rivalry of Austria and Prussia over Silesia. France abandoned Prussia and allied with Austria. Russia, which saw Prussia as a major threat to Russian goals in central Europe, joined the new alliance with France and Austria. In turn, Britain allied with Prussia. This diplomatic revolution of 1756 led to another worldwide war. The war had three major areas of conflict: Europe, India, and North America.

Europe witnessed the clash of the two major alliances: the British and Prussians against the Austrians, Russians, and French. With his superb army and military skill, Frederick the Great of Prussia was able for some time to defeat the Austrian, French, and Russian armies. His forces were under attack from three different directions, however, and were gradually worn

down. Frederick faced disaster until Peter III, a new Russian tsar who greatly admired Frederick, withdrew Russian troops from the conflict and from the Prussian lands that the Russians had occupied. This withdrawal created a stalemate and led to the desire for peace. The European war ended in 1763. All occupied territories were returned to their original owners, while Austria officially recognized Prussia's permanent control of Silesia.

The struggle between Britain and France in the rest of the world had more decisive results. Known as the Great War for Empire, it was fought in India and North America. The French had returned Madras to Britain after the War of the Austrian Succession, but the struggle in India continued. The British ultimately won out,

STUDYING MAPS

The following questions will help you guide students through their study of Map 20.4.

1. How many regional areas of conflict were there in the Seven Years' War? *(There were three "theaters" of war: North America, Europe, and India.)*
2. How many empires were involved in the Seven Years' War? *(Seven)*
3. Why is it fair to say that the Seven Years'

War was a global conflict? *(Answers will vary, but should show that students realize that seven empires and three continents were involved in the conflict.)*

not because they had better forces but because they were more persistent. With the Treaty of Paris in 1763, the French withdrew and left India to the British.

By far, the greatest conflicts of the Seven Years' War took place in North America. Both the French and British colonial empires in the New World consisted of large parts of the West Indies and the North American continent. On the tropical islands of the West Indies, both the British and the French had set up plantations. These were worked by African slaves and produced tobacco, cotton, coffee, and sugar.

On the North American continent, the French and British colonies were set up in different ways. French North America (Canada and Louisiana) was run by the French government as a vast trading area. It was valuable for its fur, leather, fish, and timber. However, the French state was unable to get its people to move to North America, so its colonies were thinly populated.

British North America had come to consist of 13 colonies on the eastern coast of the present United States. Unlike the French colonies, the British colonies were thickly populated, containing about 1.5 million people by 1750. They were also prosperous. The 13 colonies were supposedly run by the British Board of Trade, the Royal Council, and Parliament, but the colonies actually had legislatures that tended to act independently. Merchants in port cities such as Boston, Philadelphia, New York, and Charleston did not want the British government to run their affairs.

Both the North American and West Indian colonies of Britain and France provided raw materials for the mother countries while buying the latter's manufactured goods. Navigation acts regulated what could be taken from and sold to the colonies. In keeping with the theory of mercantilism (see Chapter 16), the system was supposed to provide a balance of trade favorable to the mother country, at the expense of the colonies.

The British and French fought over two primary areas in North America. One consisted of the waterways of the Gulf of St. Lawrence, which were protected by the fortress of Louisbourg and by forts that guarded French Quebec (kwi-BEK) and French traders. The other area that was fought over was the unsettled Ohio

River valley. The French began to move down from Canada and up from Louisiana to establish forts in the Ohio River valley. This French activity threatened to cut off the British settlers in the 13 colonies from expanding into this vast area. The French were able to gain the support of the Indians. As traders and not settlers, the French were viewed by the Indians with less hostility than the British were viewed.

At first, the French scored a number of victories. However, British fortunes were revived by the efforts of William Pitt the Elder, Britain's prime minister. Pitt was convinced that the French colonial empire would have to be destroyed in order for Britain to create its own colonial empire. Pitt's policy focused on doing little in the European theater of war while putting resources into the colonial war, especially through the use of the British navy. The French had more troops in North America, but not enough naval support. The defeat of French fleets in major naval battles gave the British an advantage, because the French could no longer easily reinforce their garrisons.

A series of British victories soon followed. In 1759, British forces under General Wolfe defeated

▲ *Benjamin West painted this scene of General Wolfe, the British commander who successfully led his troops against the French at the Battle of Quebec. Do you think this is a realistic scene of the general's death?*

CLASS DISCUSSION

Ask students to discuss their opinions of the following statement:

In war the side that is most persistent is most likely to win.

How was this idea supported by events in the Seven Years' War?

TEACHING THEMES

Economics Ask students to form and defend a hypothesis based on economic reasons for why Britain was willing to spend the money necessary to fight the French in North America during the Seven Years' War.

LEARNING FROM VISUALS

Answer to the caption question: This is a heroic, idealized portrayal of the general's death.

ASSESS

Assign students to write a hypothetical newspaper article that might have appeared at the end of the war in Europe in 1763. Tell them to describe the causes of the war and to evaluate its results.

On Line with WORLD HISTORY *Internet Activity*

You may want to have your students visit the following URL, where they will find information and additional web site resources to enhance their study of this chapter.

http://english-www.hss.cmu. edu/18th/

Collection of archives of 18th century

novels, plays, treatises and political writings. Works by Thomas Paine, Montesque, Locke Franklin, French Revolution works are all included. A hardy reference place.

Due to the ever-changing nature of the World Wide Web, see the West History web site, **http://history.swpco.com** for regular updates of the URLs in this text.

Answers to SECTION REVIEW

2. (a) the equality of power so that no one force can dominate
   (b) separation through nonviolent means
3. (a) ruler of Austria after the death of Charles VI
   (b) king of Prussia
   (c) tsar of Russia
   (d) ended the Great War for Empire
   (e) Britain's prime minister
4. (a) Maria Theresa's succession to the throne of Austria prompted Prussia to invade Austrian Silesia.
   (b) France, Austria, and Russia formed an alliance against Great Britain and Prussia.
   (c) part of the Seven Years' War, fought between the French and the British over India and the colonies in North America
   (d) Officially, the 13 colonies were run by the British Board of Trade, the Royal Council, and Parliament.
   (e) the Gulf of St. Lawrence and the unsettled Ohio River valley
5. Answers will vary.

CLOSE

Lead students in a discussion of the Focus objectives identified on page 620. Emphasize the fact that the War of Austrian Succession and Seven Years' War were both global in nature and were aimed at controlling trade.

---

the French under General Montcalm on the Plains of Abraham, outside Quebec. Both generals died in the battle. The British went on to seize Montreal (MAWN-tree-ahl), the Great Lakes area, and the Ohio River valley. The French were forced to make peace. By the Treaty of Paris, they transferred Canada and the lands east of the Mississippi to England. Their ally Spain transferred Spanish Florida to British control. In return, the French gave their Louisiana territory to the Spanish. By 1763, Great Britain had become the world's greatest colonial power.

 SECTION REVIEW

1. **Locate:**
   (a) Silesia,   (b) Madras,   (c) West Indies,
   (d) St. Lawrence River,   (e) Louisiana,
   (f) Ohio River,   (g) Quebec,
   (h) Montreal

2. **Define:**
   (a) balance of power,   (b) diplomatic revolution

3. **Identify:**
   (a) Maria Theresa,   (b) Frederick the Great,
   (c) Peter III,   (d) Treaty of Paris,   (e) William Pitt the Elder

4. **Recall:**
   (a) Summarize the events that caused the War of the Austrian Succession.
   (b) Name the countries in the two major alliances during the Seven Years' War.
   (c) Why was the Great War for Empire fought?
   (d) Name two of the three groups that officially ran the 13 British colonies in North America.
   (e) Over what two geographical areas did the British and French fight in North America?

5. **Think Critically:** How does the conflict between the British and the French in North America illustrate Frederick the Great's remark that "the fundamental rule of governments is the principle of extending their territories"? Why did each country's pursuit of this principle lead to war?

COLONIAL EMPIRES AND REVOLUTION IN THE WESTERN HEMISPHERE

As we have seen, the colonial empires in the Western Hemisphere were an important part of the European economy in the eighteenth century. The colonies had also been involved in the conflicts of the European states. Despite their close ties to their European mother countries, the colonies of Latin America and British North America were developing in ways that sometimes differed significantly from those of Europe.

The Society of Latin America

In the sixteenth century, Portugal came to dominate Brazil while Spain established an enormous colonial empire in the New World that included Central America, most of South America, and parts of North America. Within the lands of Central America and South America, a new civilization arose, which we call Latin America.

Latin America was a multiracial society. Already by 1501, Spanish rulers permitted intermarriage between Europeans and native American Indians, whose offspring became known as the **mestizos.** In addition, another group of people was brought to Latin America—the Africans. Over a period of three centuries, possibly as many as 8 million slaves were brought to Spanish and Portuguese America to work the plantations. Africans also contributed to Latin America's multiracial character. **Mulattoes**—the offspring of Africans and Europeans—joined mestizos and other descendants of Europeans, Africans, and native Indians to produce a unique society in Latin America.

Economic Foundations

Both the Portuguese and the Spanish sought ways to profit from their colonies in Latin America. One source of wealth came from the abundant supplies of gold and silver. Most of the Latin American gold and

---

SPECIAL NEEDS: *Visual*

For students who need additional opportunities to review information, who rely on visual input, and who learn best from material presented in short form, the following activity is suggested. Utilizing the map on page 623 and a map of modern-day Latin America (see this in back of book), have students develop and complete a chart that shows (1) the Portuguese colonies; (2) the Spanish colonies; (3) the French colonies; (4) the Dutch colonies; and (5) the English colonies. In the chart have the students attempt to identify which present-day nations were at one time ruled by the countries named above.

silver wound up being sent to Europe. Little remained in the New World to benefit those whose labor had produced it.

The pursuit of gold and silver offered fantastic financial rewards. However, farming proved to be a more long-lasting and rewarding source of prosperity for Latin America. A noticeable feature of Latin Ameri can agriculture was the dominating role of the large landowner. Both Spanish and Portuguese landowners created immense estates, which left the Indians either to work on the large estates or to work as poor farmers on marginal lands. This system of large landowners and dependent peasants has remained one of the lasting features of Latin American society.

Trade provided another avenue for profit. Latin American colonies became sources of raw materials for Spain and Portugal. Gold, silver, sugar, tobacco, diamonds, animal hides, and a number of other natural products made their way to Europe. In turn, the mother countries supplied their colonists with manufactured goods. Both Spain and Portugal closely regulated the trade of their American colonies to keep others out. By the beginning of the eighteenth century, however, both the British and the French had become too powerful to be kept out of the lucrative Latin American markets.

The State and Church in Colonial Latin America

Portuguese Brazil and Spanish America were colonial empires that lasted over three hundred years. The difficulties of communication and travel between the New World and Europe made the attempts of the Spanish and Portuguese monarchs to provide close regulation of their empires virtually impossible. As a result, colonial officials in Latin America had much freedom in carrying out imperial policies. The most

Map 20.4   Latin America in the Eighteenth Century

Portuguese colonized by 1640	French colonies
Portuguese colonized by 1750	Dutch colonies
Portuguese frontier lands 1750	English colonies
Spanish colonized by 1640	Jesuit mission states
Spanish colonized by 1750	Routes of colonial trade
Spanish frontier lands 1750	Extent of Inca Empire in 1525

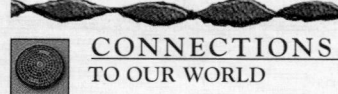

CONNECTIONS
TO OUR WORLD

ACROSS THE CURRICULUM

Economics. Ask students why they believe it was difficult to change the historic basis for land ownership in Brazil. Why are the lives of people in Latin America still influenced by events that took place hundreds of years ago?

USING PRIMARY SOURCES

Ask students to draw a diagram of the village described in the quotation to the right. Did these carefully planned and constructed villages have anything in common with prisons? Ask students if these were places they would have liked to live?

CONNECTIONS
TO OUR WORLD

Large Landowners in Brazil   In April 1997, Brazilian police in the northern state of Pará opened fire on landless peasants who were seeking to settle on land that had not been used for decades. One local landowner admitted that property owners had paid police to clear away the settlers. Although police claimed that the peasants had fired first, a video filmed at the scene revealed that police officers had opened fire as soon as they arrived. Many of the victims were killed by a single shot in the head or back of the neck.

In Brazil, the wealthiest 2 percent of landowners own 20 percent of the land, more than the combined areas of England, France, Germany, and Spain. Almost 65 percent (or hundreds of millions of acres) of that land is not used. At the same time, more than 50 percent of Brazilian peasants farm less than 3 percent of the land. A Landless Workers Movement has emerged, whose goal is to organize peasants to occupy and settle unused lands.

The enormous gap between a small elite of landowners and a mass of peasants who hold very little land has a long history in Brazil. After the creation of a colony in Brazil in the 1500s, Portuguese kings awarded enormous grants of land to Portuguese settlers who became the ruling class. Leading families in Brazil today, many of them descendants of the original landowners, keep their landed estates even though they are so large that they are unable to farm all of the land. Millions of peasants are left without land and with little hope for a decent life.

important posts of the colonial government were kept in the hands of Europeans.

From the beginning of their conquest of the New World, Spanish and Portuguese rulers were determined to Christianize the native peoples. This policy gave the Catholic Church an important role to play in the New World—a role that added considerably to church power. Catholic missionaries—especially the Dominicans, Franciscans, and Jesuits—fanned out to different parts of the Spanish Empire.

To make their efforts easier, missionaries brought Indians together into villages where the natives could be converted, taught trades, and encouraged to grow crops. A German tourist in the eighteenth century commented, "The road leads through plantations of sugar, indigo, cotton, and coffee. The regularity which we observed in the construction of the villages reminded us that they all owe their origin to monks and missions. The streets are straight and parallel; they cross each other at right angles; and the church is erected in the great square situated in the center."[1] Their missions enabled missionaries to control the lives of the Indians. In turn, the missions served to keep the Indians as docile members of the empire.

The Catholic Church built hospitals, orphanages, and schools. Monastic schools taught Indian students the basic rudiments of reading, writing, and arithmetic. The Catholic Church also provided outlets other than marriage for women. One such outlet was the nunnery. Nunneries were places of prayer. Women in religious orders, however—many of them of aristocratic background—often lived well and worked outside their establishments by running schools and hospitals. Indeed, one of these nuns, Sor Juana Inés de la Cruz (WAHN-uh eh-NAZE de la KROOZ), was one of seventeenth-century Latin America's best-known literary figures. She wrote poetry and prose and urged that women be educated.

The legacies left to the church by the rich in their wills enabled the Catholic Church to build the magnificent cathedrals that adorn the cities of Latin America. Even today, the architectural splendor of these cathedrals reminds us of both the wealth and the power that the Catholic Church exercised in some of the colonial empires of the New World.

British North America

In the eighteenth century, Spanish power in the New World was increasingly challenged by the British. (The United Kingdom of Great Britain came into existence in 1707, when the governments of England and Scot

MORE ABOUT . . . *Colonial Life*

In spite of the many hardships of life in North America, colonists, in general, had longer lives, produced more children, and had a higher standard of living than their European counterparts. Food was more plentiful, and famine rare. Many colonists wrote to family members back in England that they ate food every day that English peasants would have only on holidays. Because the population was more scattered and younger than in Europe (the average age in the colonies in 1790 was 16), Americans were less susceptible to disease and epidemics. And, while the average birth rate for European women was 28 per 1,000, the American birth rate was 45 to 50 per 1,000. Life usually improved as soon as a new settler stepped off the boat.

◄ *This sixteenth-century church in Trinidad, Paraguay, was built by Guarani Indians. The two finely hewn stone cherubs carved into this block wall demonstrate the Indians' accomplished skills as stone workers. Why was the church one of the first buildings to be erected when the Spanish created towns in the New World?*

land were united. The term *British* came into use to refer to both the English and the Scots.) In eighteenth-century Britain, the king or queen and the Parliament shared power, with Parliament's gradually gaining the upper hand. The king or queen chose ministers who were responsible to the Crown and who set policy and guided Parliament. Parliament had the power to make laws, levy taxes, pass the budget, and indirectly influence the ministers of the king or queen.

The eighteenth-century British Parliament was dominated by a landed aristocracy divided into two groups: the peers (who sat for life in the House of Lords) and the landed gentry (who were elected to the House of Commons). The two groups had much in common. Both were landowners, and they frequently intermarried. The deputies to the House of Commons were chosen from the towns and counties not by popular voting but by election by holders of property. These

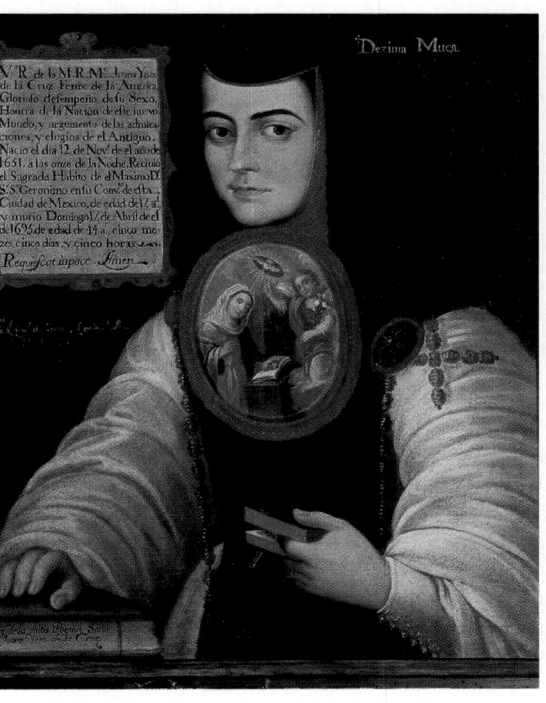

► *Sor Juana Inés de la Cruz was denied admission to the University of Mexico because she was a woman. As a result of this rejection, she chose to enter a convent where she could write poetry and plays. Do you think she would have had different opportunities in England or France? Why or why not?*

ENRICHMENT ACTIVITY

If students are interested in the story of Sor Juana de la Cruz they might also be interested in learning about another woman who wanted her share of civil and political rights. Margaret Brent who was born a Roman Catholic, emigrated to Maryland in 1683 and was the first single woman to own land in her own name. She acted as an attorney for Lord Baltimore and won fame as being "as brave as a man." Feeling she had proved her abilities, she asked for the right to vote. The colony assembly refused her request, so she simply took her assets to Virginia where, still without a vote, she lived out the rest of her life.

CLASS DISCUSSION

Ask students to describe how they would feel if the American presidency was offered to a leader of another nation who did not even speak their language. What does this tell them about the political process in Great Britain during the eighteenth century?

Map 20.5   North America, 1700–1803

landowners tended to elect the same members of the leading landed gentry families over and over again.

In 1714, a new dynasty—the Hanoverians—was established when the last Stuart ruler, Queen Anne, died without an heir. The crown was offered to the nearest relatives, Protestant rulers of the German state of Hanover. Because the first Hanoverian king (George I) did not speak English, and neither the first nor the second George knew the British system very well, their chief ministers were allowed to handle Parliament. Robert Walpole served as prime minister from 1721 to 1742 and pursued a peaceful foreign policy. However, growing trade and industry led to an ever-increasing middle class that favored expansion of trade and world empire. These people found a spokesman in William Pitt the Elder, who became prime minister in 1757. He expanded the British Empire by acquiring Canada and India in the Seven Years' War.

STUDYING MAPS

The following questions will help you guide students through their study of Map 20.5.

1. What part of North America was dominated by the British in 1700? *(Northern Canada and the Atlantic Seaboard)*

2. Which nation lost the most territory between 1700 and 1763? *(France)*

3. What probably accounts for the fact that Florida belonged to Spain in 1700 and England in 1763? *(Spain gave Florida to England in the Treaty of Paris in exchange for French lands West of the Mississippi.)*

The American Revolution

At the end of the Seven Years' War in 1763, Great Britain had become the world's greatest colonial power. In North America, Britain controlled Canada and the lands east of the Mississippi River. After the Seven Years' War, British leaders wanted to get new revenues from the colonies to pay for the expenses the British army had amassed in defending the colonists and to cover war costs. An attempt to levy new taxes by the Stamp Act of 1765 led to riots. The act was quickly repealed.

In the course of the eighteenth century, significant differences had arisen between the Americans and the British. Both peoples shared the same property requirement for voting—voters had to possess a property that could be rented for at least 40 shillings a year. In Britain, this meant that fewer than 20 percent of all adult males had the right to vote. In the colonies, where there was an enormous group of independent farmers, over 50 percent of adult males could vote.

The Americans and British also had different ideas of empire. The British viewed their empire as a single entity, with Parliament as the supreme authority throughout. Only Parliament could make laws for all the people in the empire, including the American colonists. The Americans, in contrast, had their own representative assemblies. To them, neither king nor Parliament should interfere in their internal affairs. American colonists believed strongly that no tax could be levied without the consent of an assembly whose members actually represented the people.

Crisis followed crisis in the 1770s. To counteract British actions, the colonies organized the First Continental Congress, which met in Philadelphia in September 1774. Outspoken members urged colonists to "take up arms and organize militias." When a British army tried to stop rebel mobilization in Massachusetts, fighting erupted in Lexington and Concord between colonists and redcoats in April 1775.

The colonists did not rush headlong into rebellion and war. It was more than a year after the fighting in Lexington and Concord before the decision was made to declare independence from the British Empire. On July 4, 1776, the Second Continental Congress approved a Declaration of Independence written by Thomas Jefferson. A stirring political document, the Declaration of Independence declared the colonies to be "free and independent states absolved from all allegiance to the British Crown." The war for American independence had formally begun.

The war against Great Britain was a great gamble. Britain was a strong European military power with enormous financial resources. The Americans had formed the Continental Army with George Washington as commander in chief. Compared with the British forces, however, it was made up of undisciplined amateurs who agreed to serve for only a short time.

Of great importance to the colonies' cause was support by foreign countries who were eager to gain revenge for earlier defeats at the hands of the British. The French supplied arms and money to the rebels from the beginning of the war. French officers and soldiers also served in Washington's army. The defeat of the British at Saratoga in October 1777 finally led the French to grant diplomatic recognition to the American state. When Spain and the Dutch Republic entered the war against Great Britain, the British were faced with war against much of Europe, as well as against the Americans.

When the army of General Cornwallis was forced to surrender to combined American and French forces under Washington at Yorktown in 1781, the British decided to end the war. The Treaty of Paris, signed in 1783, recognized the independence of the American colonies and granted the Americans control of the western territory from the Appalachians to the Mississippi River.

The Birth of a New Nation

The 13 American colonies had gained their independence, but a fear of concentrated power and concern for their own interests caused them to have little enthusiasm for establishing a united nation with a strong central government. The Articles of Confederation, the American nation's first constitution, were ratified in 1781, but did little to provide for a strong central government. A movement for a different form of national government soon arose. In the summer of 1787, 55 del-

ACROSS THE CURRICULUM

Economics Ask students to identify other conflicts they have studied that were based on heavy taxation. Remind them of the problems of Chinese and Japanese leaders that were described in Chapter 10. Do students believe that the American Revolution would have been avoided if the British had allowed colonists to have a voice in the passage of tax laws?

CLASS DISCUSSION

Ask students to evaluate the following statement. Do they believe it is true? How many other wars may have ended for similar reasons?

The reason the British allowed their American colonies to achieve independence was the cost of continuing to fight the war.

MORE ABOUT . . . *Colonial Life*

A British minister, Andrew Burnaby, who traveled through North America in 1860, recorded his observations of New York City. He described it as a city of 16,000 or 17,000 people. He found it to be very clean, peaceful, and its women "reserved." Among the pastimes New Yorkers enjoyed were balls and sleigh rides in the winter, and boating, fishing, and turtle feasts in the summer. In the evening, gentlemen and ladies enjoyed riding over the Kissing Bridge (now the Bowery in southern Manhattan). Upon crossing, it was "considered polite for the gentleman to salute the lady who has put herself under his protection."

ASSESS

▲ *The* Signing of the Declaration, *painted by John Trumbull, shows John Adams, Roger Sherman, Robert Livingston, Thomas Jefferson, and Benjamin Franklin standing in front of John Hancock, who was president of the Second Continental Congress. Why is this painting so important to American history?*

egates met in Philadelphia to revise the Articles of Confederation. The convention's delegates—who were wealthy, politically experienced, and well educated—decided instead to devise a new Constitution.

The proposed Constitution created a central government that was superior to the governments of the individual states. The national government was given the power to levy taxes, raise a national army, regulate trade, and create a national currency. The central or federal government was divided into three branches, each with some power to check the working of the others. A president would serve as the chief executive with the power to execute laws, veto the legislature's acts, supervise foreign affairs, and direct military forces. The second branch of government would consist of a Senate elected by the state legislatures and a House of Representatives elected directly by the people. A Supreme Court and other courts "as deemed necessary"

by Congress provided the third branch of government. They would enforce the Constitution as the "supreme law of the land."

According to the constitutional convention, the new Constitution would have to be approved by conventions of elected delegates in 9 of the 13 states before it would take effect. The Constitution was approved, but by a slim margin. Important to its success was a promise to add a Bill of Rights to the Constitution. In March 1789, the new Congress enacted the first 10 amendments to the Constitution, which have been known ever since as the Bill of Rights. These amendments guaranteed freedom of religion, speech, press, petition, and assembly. They gave Americans the right to bear arms and to be protected against unreasonable searches and arrests. They guaranteed trial by jury, due process of law, and the protection of property rights. Many of these rights were derived from the

▲ *John Trumbull, an American artist and an aide to George Washington, painted this twelve-by-eighteen-foot scene of Lord Cornwallis (in the center) surrendering to George Washington (just left of the U.S. flag).*

natural rights philosophy of the eighteenth-century philosophes and the American colonists. Is it any wonder that many European intellectuals saw the American Revolution as the embodiment of the Enlightenment's political dreams?

 SECTION REVIEW

1. **Locate:**
   (*a*) Portugal,   (*b*) Brazil,   (*c*) Spain,
   (*d*) Central America,   (*e*) South America,
   (*f*) Mississippi River

2. **Define:**
   (*a*) mestizos,   (*b*) mulattoes

3. **Identify:**
   (*a*) Dominicans,   (*b*) Sor Juana Inés de la Cruz,
   (*c*) House of Commons,   (*d*) Hanoverians,
   (*e*) Robert Walpole,   (*f*) Stamp Act of 1765,
   (*g*) First Continental Congress,   (*h*) Articles of
   Confederation,   (*i*) Federalists

4. **Recall:**
   (*a*) What was the role of Africans in Latin American society?
   (*b*) Name two sources of profit for the Portuguese and the Spanish in Latin America.
   (*c*) What country challenged Spanish power in the New World?
   (*d*) How did the system of representative government in Britain differ from the one in the colonies?

(e) British prime minister who pursued a peaceful foreign policy
(f) passed to help defer costs of the Seven Years' War
(g) met in Philadelphia in 1774 to counteract British interference in American internal affairs.
(h) first document written to organize the new American nation
(i) Americans who favored the proposed Constitution

4. (a) plantation slaves
(b) gold and silver, farming, and trade
(c) Britain (an answer of "France" could also be justified)
(d) indirect in Britain; direct in the colonies
(e) On July 4, 1776, it approved the Declaration of Independence, triggering the American War of Independence
(f) The Constitution created a superior central government.

5. Answers will vary.

CLOSE

Lead students in a discussion of the Focus objectives identified on page 623. Emphasize differences between patterns of land ownership and the distribution of power in Latin American and North American Colonies.

So What ??

*If your students question the importance of the information on the **Constitution** and the **Bill of Rights**, tell them . . .*

These documents still dictate the structure of American government today, and guarantee the freedoms that they enjoy. Ask them to speculate on how their lives would be different if the colonists had not rebelled against English rule, and if the Constitution had never been written. Ask student volunteers to express in their own words how knowing more about the history of the Constitution's creation benefits them.

FOCUS

OBJECTIVES

After completing this section, students should be able to

1. identify and explain causes of the French Revolution
2. explain how the French Revolution brought about the destruction of the Old Regime

FOCUS ACTIVITY

Help students understand the importance of land distribution and ownership in an agrarian economy. Ask students to draw a graph that shows the distribution of the French population and land ownership among the three estates before the French Revolution. Lead them in a discussion of how this inequity contributed to the causes of the revolution.

TEACH

Multimedia Support

TRANSPARENCY
20–2, Members of the Third Estate Chart

REINFORCING VOCABULARY

Ask students to identify and list examples of the relics of feudalism that existed in France in the eighteenth century. Lead students in a discussion of how these relics contributed to the causes of the French Revolution.

630

(e) What was the major accomplishment of the Second Continental Congress?
(f) What was the main difference between the Articles of Confederation and the Constitution?

5. **Think Critically:** Analyze the role of the Catholic Church in colonial Latin America.

TOWARD A NEW POLITICAL ORDER: THE FRENCH REVOLUTION BEGINS

The year 1789 witnessed two far-reaching events: the beginning of a new United States of America and the beginning of the French Revolution. Compared with the American Revolution, the French Revolution was more complex, more violent, and far more radical. It tried to create both a new political order and a new social order.

Background to the French Revolution

The French Revolution has often been seen as a major turning point in European political and social history. The institutions of the Old Regime were destroyed. A new order emerged, which was based on individual rights, representative institutions, and a concept of loyalty to the nation rather than the monarch. The causes of the French Revolution include both long-range problems and immediate, precipitating forces.

The long-range causes of the French Revolution are to be found in the condition of French society. Before the Revolution, French society was based on inequality. France's population of 27 million was divided, as it had been since the Middle Ages, into three orders, or estates.

The First Estate consisted of the clergy and numbered about 130,000 people. These people owned approximately 10 percent of the land. Clergy were exempt from the taille (taw-YEE), France's chief tax. They were also radically divided. The higher clergy,

stemming from aristocratic families, shared the interests of the nobility. The parish priests were often poor and from the class of commoners.

The Second Estate was the nobility, composed of about 350,000 people who nevertheless owned about 25 to 30 percent of the land. The nobility played an important, and even a crucial, role in French society in the eighteenth century. They held many of the leading positions in the government, the military, the law courts, and the higher church offices. The nobles sought to expand their power at the expense of the monarchy. Many nobles said they were defending liberty by resisting the arbitrary actions of the monarchy. They also sought to keep their control over positions in the military, church, and government. Moreover, nobles still possessed privileges, including tax exemptions, especially from the taille.

The Third Estate, or the commoners of society, made up the overwhelming majority of the French population. The Third Estate was divided by vast differences in occupation, level of education, and wealth. The peasants, who alone constituted 75 to 80 percent of the total population, were by far the largest segment of the Third Estate. They owned about 35 to 40 percent of the land. However, their landholdings varied from area to area, and over half of the peasants had little or no land on which to survive. Serfdom no longer existed on any large scale in France, but French peasants still had obligations to their local landlords that they deeply resented. These **relics of feudalism,** or aristocratic privileges, were obligations that survived from an earlier age. They included the payment of fees for the use of village facilities such as the flour mill, community oven, and winepress, as well as tithes (voluntary contributions) to the clergy.

Another part of the Third Estate consisted of skilled craftspeople, shopkeepers, and other wage earners in the cities. In the eighteenth century, a rise in consumer prices that was greater than the increase in wages left these urban groups with a decline in buying power. Simply their struggle for survival led many of these people to play an important role in the Revolution, especially in Paris.

About 8 percent of the population, or 2.3 million people, made up the bourgeoisie, or middle class, who

---

COOPERATIVE LEARNING ACTIVITY

As a way of using literature as a key to understanding history, have your students read Charles Dickens's *A Tale of Two Cities*. Provide students with study guides to help them with the nineteenth-century language and style of writing; or, in cooperation with an English teacher, have students from an English class develop the study guides. Then divide the class into groups making different groups responsible for reading different parts of the novel. Each group is to create a presentation for its part of the book. The presentation can be given as a series.

▲ *This painting by French artist Jacques Louis David captures the drama and tension of the Third Estate meeting held in the tennis court of the Jeu de Paume. Do you think the nobility and clergy believed that the Third Estate would react so vehemently to their actions?*

owned about 20 to 25 percent of the land. This group included merchants, bankers, and industrialists who benefited from the economic prosperity after 1730. The bourgeoisie also included professional people—lawyers, holders of public offices, doctors, and writers. Members of the middle class were unhappy with the privileges held by nobles. At the same time, members of the middle class shared a great deal with the nobility. By obtaining public offices, wealthy middle-class individuals could enter the ranks of the nobility. During the eighteenth century, 6,500 new noble families were created.

Moreover, both aristocrats and members of the bourgeoisie were drawn to the new political ideas of the Enlightenment. Both groups were increasingly upset with a monarchical system resting on privileges and on an old and rigid social order. The opposition of these elites to the old order ultimately led them to drastic action against the monarchical regime.

The French monarchy handled the new social realities and problems poorly. Specific problems in the 1780s made things worse. Despite economic expansion for 50 years, the French economy had periodic crises. Bad harvests in 1787 and 1788 and a slowdown in

ENRICHMENT ACTIVITY

Have students read or see the film version of both *A Tale of Two Cities* and *The Scarlet Pimpernel*. When done, have them analyze the accuracy of these accounts with the information presented in the text concerning the French Revolution. Guide students in a discussion of reasons and ways the French Revolution has been romanticized. You might also wish to have students listen to *The Marseillaise* and compare its lyrics to other national anthems, such as *God Save the Queen* and *The Star-Spangled Banner*. Students may be surprised at the difference in themes.

CLASS DISCUSSION

Lead students in a discussion of the concept of "one man, one vote." Why did the first and second estates in France oppose this concept?

Multimedia Support

TRANSPARENCY
20–3, Governments of France during the Revolution Chart

COMPARING TIME PERIODS

Ask students to prepare a chart that compares the fiscal privileges of the nobles and clergy in France before the revolution with those of the nobles in Japan that were discussed in Chapter 10. Why is it important to political stability that people believe their taxes are fair and used in a reasonable way? What problems have caused "tax revolts" in the United States?

---

manufacturing led to food shortages, rising prices for food, and unemployment in the cities. The number of poor, estimated by some at almost one-third of the population, reached crisis proportions on the eve of the Revolution.

The immediate cause of the French Revolution was the near collapse of government finances. The French government continued to spend enormous sums on costly wars and court luxuries. It had spent large amounts to help the American colonists against Britain. On the verge of a complete financial collapse, the government of Louis XVI was finally forced to call a meeting of the Estates-General. This was the French parliament, and it had not met since 1614. The Estates-General was composed of representatives from the three orders of French society. The First Estate (the clergy) and the Second Estate (the nobility) had about 300 delegates each. The Third Estate had almost 600 delegates, most of whom were lawyers from French towns. In order to fix France's financial problems, most members of the Third Estate wanted to set up a constitutional government that would abolish the fiscal privileges of the church and nobility.

The Destruction of the Old Regime

The meeting of the Estates-General opened at Versailles on May 5, 1789. It was troubled from the start with a problem of voting. Traditionally, each estate would vote as a group and have one vote. That meant that the First and Second Estates could outvote the Third Estate two to one. The Third Estate demanded that each deputy have one vote. With the help of a few nobles and clerics, that would give the Third Estate a majority. When the king declared he was in favor of each estate's having one vote, the Third Estate reacted quickly. On June 17, 1789, it called itself a National Assembly and decided to draw up a constitution. Three days later, on June 20, the deputies of the Third Estate arrived at their meeting place, only to find the doors locked. They then moved to a nearby indoor tennis court and swore (hence, the name **Tennis Court Oath**) that they would continue to meet until they had

produced a French constitution. Louis XVI prepared to use force against the Third Estate.

The common people, however, saved the Third Estate from the king's forces. On July 14, a mob of Parisians (puh-REE-zhunz) stormed the Bastille and proceeded to dismantle it, brick by brick. Paris was abandoned to the rebels. Louis XVI was soon informed that he could no longer trust the royal troops. Royal authority had collapsed. Louis XVI could enforce his will no more. The fall of the Bastille had saved the National Assembly.

At the same time, popular revolutions broke out throughout France, both in the cities and the countryside. A growing hatred of the entire landholding system, with its fees and obligations, led to a popular uprising. Peasants decided to take matters into their own hands. Peasant rebellions took place throughout France and became part of the Great Fear, a vast panic that spread like wildfire through France in the summer of 1789. The fear of invasion by foreign troops that would support the French monarchy encouraged the formation of citizens' militias. The greatest impact of the peasant revolts and the Great Fear was on the National Assembly meeting in Versailles.

One of the first acts of the National Assembly was to destroy the relics of feudalism, or aristocratic privileges. On the night of August 4, 1789, the National Assembly voted to abolish the rights of landlords, as well as the fiscal privileges of nobles and clergy. On August 26, the National Assembly adopted the Declaration of the Rights of Man and the Citizen (see "You Are There: Declaration of the Rights of Man and the Citizen"). This charter of basic liberties began with a ringing affirmation of "the natural and imprescriptible rights of man" to "liberty, property, security, and resistance to oppression." It went on to affirm the destruction of aristocratic privileges by proclaiming freedom and equal rights for all men, access to public office based on talent, and an end to exemptions from taxation. All citizens were to have the right to take part in the making of laws. Freedom of speech and press were coupled with the outlawing of arbitrary arrests.

The declaration also raised another important issue. Did its ideal of equal rights for all men also include women? Many deputies insisted that it did, provided

---

So What ??

*If your students question the importance of the information on the **French Revolution**, tell them . . .*

This was the first of the popular revolts that came to influence much of world history for the next two centuries. The Russian, Chinese, Cuban and countless other revolutions

and revolutionary groups were influenced and inspired by the French Revolution. Have students develop an explanation of an indirect link from their family to a revolution. Can they show how their family might have turned out differently if it had not been for the French Revolution?

▲ With the fall of the Bastille, the French Revolution was truly underway. This prison in Paris, a symbol of royal oppression, was completely dismantled by angry commoners. How does the artist convey the confusion and frenzy of this moment?

that, as one said, "women do not hope to exercise political rights and functions." Olympe de Gouges, a playwright, refused to accept this exclusion of women from political rights. Echoing the words of the official declaration, she penned a Declaration of the Rights of Woman and the Female Citizen, in which she insisted that women should have all the same rights as men (see "You Are There: Declaration of the Rights of Woman and the Female Citizen"). The National Assembly ignored her demands.

In the meantime, Louis XVI had remained quiet at Versailles. He did refuse, however, to accept the decrees on the abolition of feudalism and the Declaration of Rights. On October 5, thousands of Parisian

COOPERATIVE LEARNING ACTIVITY

Have students work in groups to organize a first meeting of the Three Estates after the Estates-General has just been called into session by Louis XVI. Have each estate do a position paper on what it hopes to accomplish at this session to bring about change in France.

You might also wish to organize a debate or mock session meeting of the three Estates.

YOU ARE THERE

USING PRIMARY SOURCES

Provide students with a copy of the American Bill of Rights and have them either discuss or write an essay that identifies and explains similarities between this document and the Declaration of Rights of Man and the Citizen. To what extent do students believe the authors of the Bill of Rights and the Declaration of Rights of Man were influenced by each other?

LEARNING FROM VISUALS

Answer to the caption question: Students should recognize similarities between the figure in this woodcut and the features in the Statue of Liberty.

Answers to Critical Thinking Questions

1. The natural rights of man are liberty, property, security, and resistance to oppression.
2. No.
3. Students should recognize the similarities between the two statements of inalienable rights.

Multimedia Support

LASERDISC

The French Revolution, 1789–1795 (Video)

YOU ARE THERE

Declaration of the Rights of Man and the Citizen

One of the important documents of the French Revolution, the Declaration of the Rights of Man and the Citizen, was adopted in August 1789 by the National Assembly. Here is an excerpt:

Declaration of the Rights of Man and the Citizen

The representatives of the French people, organized as a national assembly, considering that ignorance, neglect, and scorn of the rights of man are the sole causes of public misfortunes and of corruption of governments, have resolved to display in a solemn declaration the natural, inalienable, and sacred rights of man, so that this declaration, constantly in the presence of all members of society, will continually remind them of their rights and their duties; . . . Consequently, the National Assembly recognizes and declares, in the presence and under the auspices of the Supreme Being, the following rights of man and citizen:

1. Men are born and remain free and equal in rights; social distinctions can be established only for the common benefit.
2. The aim of every political association is the conservation of the natural and imprescriptible rights of man; these rights are liberty, property, security, and resistance to oppression. . . .
4. Liberty consists in being able to do anything that does not harm another person. . . .
6. The law is the expression of the general will; all citizens have the right to concur personally or through their representatives in its formation; it must be the same for all, whether it protects or punishes.

◄ *This woodcut shows the figure of Equality holding the Declaration of the Rights of Man and the Citizen. Compare and contrast this figure with the Statue of Liberty which was given to the United States by France.*

7. No man can be accused, arrested, or detained except in cases determined by the law, and according to the forms which it has prescribed. . . .
10. No one may be disturbed because of his opinions, even religious, provided that their public demonstration does not disturb the public order established by law.
11. The free communication of thoughts and opinions is one of the most precious rights of man: every citizen can therefore freely speak, write, and print. . . .
16. Any society in which guarantees of rights are not assured nor the separation of powers determined has no constitution.

---

1. According to this document, what are the natural (or imprescriptible) rights of man?
2. According to this document, can a person be arrested or otherwise "disturbed" because of his religious beliefs?
3. How do the rights listed in number 2 of the document compare to the rights listed in the Bill of Rights?

SPECIAL NEEDS: *Reading Comprehension*

Have students carefully read Pages 620 to 637. Students who have difficulty with reading comprehension may take turns reading to each other. Have students develop and present a newscast on the beginning of the French Revolution. The students should take various roles such as reporters, representatives of the First, Second and Third Estates (clergy, nobility, peasants and commoners, craftpeople, shopkeepers, merchants, bankers, and professionals such as lawyers and doctors), and women. The newscast should include: (1) a reporter sharing some of the long-range problems, as well as some of the precipitating forces that led to the revolution; (2) interviews with different representatives of the

YOU ARE THERE

Declaration of the Rights of Woman and the Female Citizen

Olympe de Gouges (a pen name for Marie Gouze) argued that the Declaration of the Rights of Man and the Citizen did not apply to women. Thus, she composed her own Declaration of the Rights of Woman and the Female Citizen in 1791. Here is an excerpt:

Olympe de Gouges, *Declaration of the Rights of Woman and the Female Citizen*

. . . Believing that ignorance, omission, or scorn for the rights of woman are the only causes of public misfortunes and of the corruption of governments, the women have resolved to set forth in a solemn declaration the natural, inalienable, and sacred rights of woman in order that this declaration, constantly exposed before all the members of the society, will ceaselessly remind them of their rights and duties. . . .

1. Woman is born free and lives equal to man in her rights. Social distinctions can be based only on the common utility.
2. The purpose of any political association is the conservation of the natural and imprescriptible rights of woman and man; these rights are liberty, property, security, and especially resistance to oppression. . . .
4. Liberty and justice consist of restoring all that belongs to others; thus, the only limits on the exercise of the natural rights of woman are perpetual male tyranny; these limits are to be reformed by the laws of nature and reason. . . .
6. The law must be the expression of the general will; all female and male citizens must contribute either personally or through their representatives to its formation; it must be the

▲ *In the days of the French Revolution, women took an active role in the politics of Paris, a role that had previously been denied to them. In this picture a group of women are discussing the decrees of the National Convention. Why do you think it suddenly became possible for women to march in the streets and to conduct their own protests?*

same for all: male and female citizens, being equal in the eyes of the law, must be equally admitted to all honors, positions, and public employment according to their capacity and without other distinctions besides those of their virtues and talents.

7. No woman is an exception; she is accused, arrested, and detained in cases determined by law. Women, like men, obey this rigorous law. . . .

(continued)

YOU-ARE-THERE

USING PRIMARY SOURCES

Ask students to identify and discuss reasons why Olympe de Gouges felt a need to create a separate declaration of rights for women. Why did she apparently regard the use of the word 'men' to refer to males rather than to humans of both sexes?

LEARNING FROM VISUALS

Answer to the caption question: With the revolution many ideas of the past, including the proper role for women, were discarded.

Answers to Critical Thinking Questions

1. Ignorance, omission, or scorn for the rights of women are the "causes of public misfortunes and of the corruption of governments."
2. The rights are "liberty, property, security, and especially resistance to oppression."
3. Answers will vary, and should be supported.

Estates, sharing their concerns, and (3) highlights of events that took place on June 20, 1789 (Tennis Court Oath), July 14, 1789 (Storming of the Bastille) and August 26, 1789 (the Declaration of the Rights of Man and the Citizen).

This "active involvement" type of activity is useful for all students who may need review

of basic concepts, different modalities in the presentation of material, opportunities for students to speak and listen in short question-answer format, and understanding of main ideas. The newscast may be videotaped and/or audiotaped for reinforcement of learning and memorization.

CLASS DISCUSSION

CLASS DISCUSSION

Have students discuss why the practice created during the French Revolution of electing priests and bishops and of paying their salaries from public funds would be unacceptable in the United States.

ASSESS

Assign students to write a letter that might have been sent by King Louis XVI of France to a friend describing his ideas about causes of the revolution.

Answers to
SECTION REVIEW

2. (a) traditions from the days of serfdom
   (b) vow made by the Third Estate to meet until they had produced a French constitution
3. (a) France's chief tax paid by Third Estate only
   (b) merchants, bankers, and industrialists
   (c) the French parliament made up of representatives from the three estates
   (d) prison in Paris, was stormed and dismantled by a mob of common people
   (e) wrote the Declaration of the Rights of Woman and the Female Citizen
   (f) new name of Third Estate when it decided to write a constitution
4. (a) the commoners, 80 percent peasants; the rest were skilled craftsmen, shopkeepers, other wage earners
   (b) Answers will vary. Some causes are based on inequality of rights and other causes are related

YOU ARE THERE

Declaration of the Rights of Woman and the Female Citizen

continued

10. No one is to be disquieted [disturbed] for his very basic opinions; woman has the right to mount the scaffold; she must equally have the right to mount the rostrum, provided that her demonstrations do not disturb the legally established public order.
11. The free communication of thoughts and opinions is one of the most precious rights of woman, since that liberty assured the recognition of children by their fathers. . . .
16. No society has a constitution without the guarantee of rights and the separation of powers; the constitution is null if the majority of individuals comprising the nation have not cooperated in drafting it.

1. What does the author of this document believe to be the "causes of public misfortunes and of the corruption of governments"?

2. What are the rights of women as listed in this document?

3. In point number 11, the document author states that "the free communication of thoughts and opinions is one of the most precious rights of women." Add the word "men" to the statement also. As it reads now, do you agree or disagree with this statement? Explain your answer.

women—described by one eyewitness as "detachments of women coming up from every direction, armed with broomsticks, lances, pitchforks, swords, pistols and muskets"—marched to Versailles and forced the king to accept the new decrees. The crowd now insisted that the royal family return to Paris. On October 6, the king did so. As a goodwill gesture, he brought along wagonloads of flour from the palace stores. The royal family and the supplies were escorted by women armed with pikes, some of which held the severed heads of the king's guards. The women sang, "We are bringing back the baker, the baker's wife, and the baker's boy" (the king, queen, and their son). The king became a virtual prisoner in Paris.

Because the Catholic Church was seen as an important pillar of the old order, it, too, was reformed. Most of the lands of the church were seized. A new Civil Constitution of the Clergy was put into effect. Both bishops and priests were to be elected by the people and paid by the state. The French government now controlled the church. Many Catholics became enemies of the Revolution.

The National Assembly completed a new constitution, the Constitution of 1791, which set up a limited monarchy. There was still a king, but a Legislative Assembly was to make the laws. The Legislative Assembly was to consist of 745 representatives chosen in such a way that only the more affluent members of society would be elected.

By 1791, the old order had been destroyed. However, many people—including Catholic priests, nobles, lower classes hurt by a rise in the cost of living, and radicals who wanted more drastic solutions—opposed the new order. The king also made things difficult for the new government. He sought to flee France in June 1791. He almost succeeded but was recognized, captured, and brought back to Paris. In this unsettled situation, with a seemingly disloyal monarch, the new Leg-

ENRICHMENT ACTIVITY

When students have finished reading Olympe de Gouge's Declaration of the Rights of Women and the Female Citizen, guide them in a discussion of its details. What was the purpose of this document? How did it compare to the Declaration of the Rights of Man and the Citizen? To the U.S. Bill of Rights and Declaration of Independence?

Have students write two responses to this document, one from the viewpoint of a male in a male-dominated society, the other from the viewpoint of a feminist. You might tell students that later in this book they will be reading an excerpt from another ardent feminist, Simone de Beauvoir.

CONNECTIONS
AROUND THE WORLD

A National Holiday The French Revolution gave rise to the concept of the modern nation-state. With the development of the modern state came the celebration of one day a year as a national holiday—usually called Independence Day. The national holiday is a day that has special significance in the history of each nation-state.

In France, the fall of the Bastille on July 14, 1789, has been celebrated ever since as the beginning of the French nation-state. Independence Day in the United States is on July 4. On July 4, 1776, the Second Continental Congress approved the Declaration of Independence. In Norway, people celebrate Constitution Day as a national holiday on May 17. On that day in 1814 Norway received a constitution, even though it did not gain its independence from Sweden until 1905.

Most Latin American countries became independent of Spain or Portugal in the early nineteenth century. Their independence days reflect this. Mexico celebrates its Independence Day on September 16 with a colorful festival. On September 16, 1810, a crowd of local people attacked Spanish authorities in a small village near Mexico City. They were crushed, but that action eventually led to Mexico's independence from Spanish control in 1821.

Most nations in Africa and Asia received their independence from Western colonial powers after World War II. India celebrates Independence Day on August 15. On that day in 1947 India received its independence from the British Empire.

islative Assembly held its first session in October 1791. France's relations with the rest of Europe soon led to the downfall of Louis XVI.

Over time, some European leaders began to fear that revolution would spread to their countries. The kings of Austria and Prussia even threatened to use force to restore Louis XVI to full power. Insulted by this threat,

the Legislative Assembly declared war on Austria in the spring of 1792. The French fared badly in the initial fighting. A frantic search for scapegoats began. One observer noted, "Everywhere you hear the cry that the king is betraying us, the generals are betraying us, that nobody is to be trusted; . . . that Paris will be taken in six weeks by the Austrians . . . we are on a volcano ready to spout flames." [2]

Defeats in war, coupled with economic shortages at home in the spring of 1792, led to new political demonstrations, especially against the king. In August, radical political groups in Paris organized a mob attack on the royal palace and Legislative Assembly. They took the king captive and forced the Legislative Assembly to suspend the monarchy and call for a National Convention, chosen on the basis of universal male suffrage, to decide on the future form of government. (Under a system of universal male suffrage, all adult males had the right to vote.) The French Revolution was about to enter a more radical stage.

 SECTION REVIEW

1. **Locate:**
   (*a*) Paris, (*b*) Versailles

2. **Define:**
   (*a*) relics of feudalism, (*b*) Tennis Court Oath

3. **Identify:**
   (*a*) *taille*, (*b*) bourgeoisie, (*c*) Estates-General, (*d*) Bastille, (*e*) Olympe de Gouges, (*f*) National Assembly

4. **Recall:**
   (*a*) Name and describe the group of people who made up the majority of the French population.
   (*b*) Give two causes of discontent in French society before the revolution.
   (*c*) What prompted Louis XVI to call a meeting of the Estates-General for the first time in 175 years?
   (*d*) What was the Great Fear?
   (*e*) What was one of the main affirmations of the Declaration of the Rights of Man and the Citizen?

to the collapse of the French economy.
(c) The government was on the verge of a complete financial collapse.
(d) a panic that spread through France; included peasant rebellions and fear of invasion by foreign troops
(e) Students will select one. See page 634.
(f) The French government began to control the church, seized its lands, regulated the clergy, and required bishops and priests to be elected by the people and paid by the state.
5. fear that revolution would spread to their countries; if Louis XVI returned to power in France, the old order would prevail

CLOSE

Lead students in a discussion of the 'Focus' objectives identified on page 630. Emphasize the specific actions that brought about the destruction of the Old Regime.

COOPERATIVE LEARNING ACTIVITY

Divide students into small groups and have each group design a page for a revolutionary newspaper. One group could design and write the first page, another the editorials, another letters to the editor, another group could prepare obituaries, another group could act as political columnists and commentators, etc. When each group has finished its page or pages, the class could compile and print its own newspaper.

(*f*) Why did many Catholics become enemies of the Revolution?

5. **Think Critically:** Why did the kings of Austria and Prussia want to restore Louis XVI to full power?

FROM RADICAL REVOLUTION TO THE AGE OF NAPOLEON

In September 1792, the newly elected National Convention began its sessions. It was dominated by lawyers, professionals, and property owners. Two-thirds of its deputies were under age 45. Almost all had had political experience as a result of the Revolution. Almost all distrusted the king. It was therefore no surprise that the National Convention's first major step was to abolish the monarchy and establish a republic. On January 21, 1793, the king was executed, and the destruction of the Old Regime was complete. There could be no turning back. However, the execution of the king created new enemies for the Revolution, both at home and abroad. A new crisis was at hand.

The local government in Paris—known as the Commune—had a number of working-class leaders who wanted radical change. Led by Georges Danton (DAW[n]-TOE[n]), the Commune put constant pressure on the National Convention to adopt ever more radical positions. Moreover, the National Convention itself still did not rule all France. Peasants in western France, as well as many people in France's major cities, refused to accept the authority of the National Convention.

A foreign crisis also loomed large. The execution of the king had outraged the royalty of most of Europe. An informal coalition of Austria, Prussia, Spain, Portugal, Britain, the Dutch Republic, and even Russia took up arms against France. The French armies began to fall back. By late spring of 1793, the coalition was poised for an invasion of France. If successful, both the Revolution and the revolutionaries would be destroyed, and the Old Regime would be reestablished.

▲ *Maximilien Robespierre, shown in this portrait, was executed on July 28, 1794, in the same way that he had ordered thousands of others to their deaths—by guillotine. Many considered France to be the most civilized country in the world at the time. Why do you think its leaders felt it was necessary to conduct a nationwide Reign of Terror?*

The Radical Revolution

To meet these crises, the National Convention gave broad powers to a special committee of twelve known as the Committee of Public Safety. It came to be dominated by Maximilien Robespierre (ROBEZ-PIR), the leader of a political group known as the Jacobins (JACK-uh-bunz). For a twelve-month period, from 1793 to 1794, the Committee of Public Safety took control of France.

A Nation in Arms

To save the republic from its foreign enemies, the Committee of Public Safety decreed a universal mobilization of the nation on August 23, 1793:

Young men will fight, young men are called to conquer. Married men will forge arms, transport military baggage and guns and will prepare food supplies. Women, who at long last are to take their rightful place in the

revolution and follow their true destiny, will forget their futile tasks: their delicate hands will work at making clothes for soldiers; they will make tents and they will extend their tender care to shelters where the defenders of the Patrie will receive the help that their wounds require. Children will make lint of old cloth. It is for them that we are fighting: children, those beings destined to gather all the fruits of the revolution, will raise their pure hands toward the skies. And old men, performing their missions again, as of yore, will be guided to the public squares of the cities where they will kindle the courage of young warriors and preach the doctrines of hate for kings and the unity of the Republic.[3]

In less than a year, the French revolutionary government had raised an army of 650,000; by September 1794, it numbered 1,169,000. The Republic's army was the largest ever seen in European history. It pushed the allies invading France back across the Rhine and even conquered the Austrian Netherlands.

The French revolutionary army was an important step in the creation of modern nationalism (devotion to one's country). Previously, wars had been fought between governments or ruling dynasties by relatively small armies of professional soldiers. The new French army was the creation of a people's government. Its wars were now people's wars. When dynastic wars

became people's wars, however, warfare became more destructive. The wars of the French revolutionary era opened the door to the total war of the modern world (see Chapter 25).

The Reign of Terror

To meet the crisis at home, the National Convention and the Committee of Public Safety set in motion the **Reign of Terror.** Under this system, revolutionary courts were set up to protect the revolutionary Republic from its internal enemies. In the course of 9 months, 16,000 people were killed under the blade of the guillotine—a revolutionary device for the quick and efficient separation of heads from bodies. The true number of the Reign of Terror's victims was probably closer to 30,000. Most executions were held in places that had openly rebelled against the authority of the National Convention. The Committee of Public Safety held that this bloodletting was only temporary. Once the war and domestic crisis were over, the true republic would follow, and the Declaration of the Rights of Man and the Citizen would be fully realized.

Revolutionary Armies were set up to bring rebellious cities back under the control of the National Convention. Lyons had rebelled against the National Convention during a time when the Republic was in peril. The Committee of Public Safety decided to make an example of that city. Soon, 1,880 citizens of Lyons had been executed. When guillotining proved too slow, cannon fire and grapeshot (a cluster of small iron balls) were used to blow condemned men into open graves. A German observed:

◄ *The French National Convention created its own revolutionary army to help protect France from its foreign enemies. In this painting, citizens are enthusiastically signing up at the recruitment table, and they receive money in return for enrolling. Why was it necessary for France to recruit a new army?*

USING PRIMARY SOURCES

Ask students to prepare an example of a recruiting poster that might have been used to encourage young men to join and fight for the French revolutionary army. Ask them to use information from the primary source to this page.

COMPARING TIME PERIODS

Ask students to compare the executions and destruction of property during the Reign of Terror in France with the destruction of cities and killing of native Indians by Spanish and Portuguese forces in Latin America. What might these events have had to do with the respect, or lack of respect people felt for human life? How could the oppressors justify their actions?

LEARNING FROM VISUALS

Answer to the caption question: The French army had been organized to serve the king; following the Revolution, the Royal Army was disbanded, and a new army loyal to the state had to be formed.

MORE ABOUT . . . the Reign of Terror

The Reign of Terror was felt throughout France. In the city of Nantes the prosecutor, Jean-Baptiste Carrier, did not need the guillotine. In a two-month period of time he executed over two thousand people by forcing them into the hulls of boats and having

them capsized in the Loire river. Anyone who attempted to climb out of the water—including children and pregnant women—were hacked with swords. Because of the large number of bodies in the river, disease broke out in the town, killing even more people.

CLASS DISCUSSION

Lead students in a discussion of the following statement. Do they believe it is often true? Does it explain Napoleon's rise to power?

More revolutions fail for economic reasons than because of military defeats.

TEACHING THEMES

Politics and History. Ask students to list and discuss possible reasons for the Catholic Church's decision to give up its claim to lands in France in 1801. How would Napoleon benefit from this agreement? What problems may it have eventually caused him?

USING PRIMARY SOURCES

Guide students in a discussion of the results of the burning of the homes and all the possessions of the aristocrats during the Revolution and the Reign of Terror. Students may not realize that many castles and palaces in France do not have original furniture because it was destroyed during this time.

Whole ranges of houses, always the most handsome, burnt. The churches, convents, and all the dwellings of the former patricians were in ruins. When I came to the guillotine, the blood of those who had been executed a few hours beforehand was still running in the street . . . I said to a group of citizens that it would be decent to clear away all this human blood. Why should it be cleared? one of them said to me. It's the blood of aristocrats and rebels. The dogs should lick it up.[4]

The Reaction

By the summer of 1794, the French had largely defeated their foreign foes. There was less need for the Reign of Terror, but it continued nonetheless. Robespierre, who had become very powerful, was obsessed with ridding France of all the corrupt. Many deputies in the National Convention who feared Robespierre decided to act. They gathered enough votes to condemn him, and Robespierre was guillotined on July 28, 1794.

After the death of Robespierre, a reaction set in as more moderate middle-class leaders took control. The Reign of Terror came to a halt. The National Convention reduced the power of the Committee of Public Safety. Churches were allowed to reopen for public worship. In addition, a new constitution was created in August 1795 that reflected the desire for more stability. Five directors—the Directory—acted as the executive authority.

The period of the Revolution under the government of the Directory (1795 to 1799) was an era of corruption and graft as people reacted against the sufferings and sacrifices that had been demanded in the Reign of Terror. Some people made fortunes in property by taking advantage of the republic's severe money problems. At the same time, the government of the Directory was faced with political enemies. Royalists who desired the restoration of the monarchy continued their plots. The hopes of radicals were revived by continuing economic problems. The Directory, which was unable to find a real solution to the country's economic problems and was still carrying on the wars left from the Committee of Public Safety, increasingly relied on the military to maintain its power. This led to a coup d'etat (KOO-DAE-TAW) (violent overthrow of a government) in 1799 in which the successful and popular military general Napoleon Bonaparte (BOE-nuh-PART) was able to seize power.

The Age of Napoleon

Napoleon dominated both French and European history from 1799 to 1815. He was born in 1769 in Corsica, only a few months after France had annexed the island. The young Napoleon received a royal scholarship to study at a military school in France. When the Revolution broke out in 1789, Napoleon was a lieutenant. The Revolution and the European war that followed gave him new opportunities, and Napoleon rose quickly through the ranks. At the age of only 25, he was made a brigadier general by the Committee of Public Safety. Two years later, he was made commander of the French armies in Italy, where he won a series of victories. He returned to France as a conquering hero. After a disastrous expedition to Egypt, Napoleon returned to Paris, where he took part in the coup d'etat that led to his control of France. He was only 30 years old at the time.

With the coup d'etat of 1799, a new form of the republic—called the **consulate**—was proclaimed. It was hardly a republic. As first consul, Napoleon controlled the entire government. He appointed members of the government bureaucracy, controlled the army, conducted foreign affairs, and influenced the legislature. In 1802, Napoleon was made consul for life. Two years later, he had himself crowned as Emperor Napoleon I.

One of Napoleon's first moves at home was to establish peace with the oldest enemy of the Revolution, the Catholic Church. In 1801, Napoleon made an agreement with the pope. The agreement recognized Catholicism as the religion of a majority of the French people. In return, the pope agreed not to ask for the return of the church lands seized in the Revolution. With this agreement, the Catholic Church was no longer an enemy of the French government. At the same time, those who had bought church lands during the Revolution became avid supporters of the Napoleonic regime.

RECOMMENDED READING

The best, brief biography of Napoleon is F. Markham, *Napoleon* (New York, 1963). Also valuable are J. M. Thompson, *Napoleon Bonaparte* (Oxford, 1963); and P. Geyl, *Napoleon, For and Against* (New Haven, Conn., 1963), a study of biographical writings on the French leader. A good, recent treatment is L. Bergeron, *France under Napoleon* (Princeton, N.J., 1981). On Napoleon's military campaigns, see D. Chandler, *The Campaigns of Napoleon* (London, 1966).

Napoleon's most long-lasting domestic achievement was his codification of the laws. Before the Revolution, France did not have a single set of laws but rather almost 300 different legal systems. During the Revolution, efforts were made to prepare a single code of laws for the entire nation. However, it remained for Napoleon to bring the work to completion in the famous Civil Code (or Code Napoléon). This code preserved most of the revolutionary gains by recognizing the principle of the equality of all citizens before the law, the right of the individual to choose a profession, religious toleration, and the abolition of serfdom and feudalism. Property rights continued to be carefully protected, and the interests of employers were safeguarded by outlawing trade unions and strikes.

The rights of some people were strictly curtailed by the Civil Code, however. During the radical phase of the French Revolution, new laws had made divorce an easy process for both husbands and wives and had allowed all children (including daughters) to inherit property equally. Napoleon's Civil Code undid these laws. Divorce was still allowed, but the Civil Code made it more difficult for women to obtain. Women were now "less equal than men" in other ways as well. When they married, their property was brought under the control of their husbands. In lawsuits they were treated as minors, and their testimony was regarded as less reliable than that of men.

Napoleon also developed a powerful, centralized administrative machine. He worked hard to develop a bureaucracy of capable officials. Early on, the regime showed that it cared little whether the expertise of officials had been gained in royal or revolutionary bureaucracies. Promotion, whether in civil or military offices, was to be based not on rank or birth but on ability only. This principle of a government career open to individual talents was, of course, what the middle class had wanted before the Revolution.

In his domestic policies, then, Napoleon both destroyed and preserved aspects of the Revolution. Liberty had been replaced by Napoleon's despotism, but the Civil Code preserved the equality of all citizens before the law. The concept of careers open to talents was also a gain of the Revolution that he preserved.

▲ *This idealistic portrait of Napoleon was painted by Baron Gros. Napoleon had an amazing ability to seize public attention, and he was a master at political propaganda.*

Napoleon's Empire

When Napoleon became consul in 1799, France was at war with a second European coalition of Russia, Great Britain, and Austria. Napoleon realized the need for a pause in the war and achieved a peace treaty in 1802. However, the peace did not last. War was renewed in 1803 with Britain, which was soon joined by Austria, Russia, and Prussia in the Third Coalition. In a series of battles from 1805 to 1807, Napoleon's Grand Army defeated the Austrian, Prussian, and Russian armies. This gave Napoleon the opportunity to create a new European order.

So What ??

If your students question the importance of the information on **Napoleon,** *tell them . . .*

Napoleon is the archetype for the "great man on a horse," the autocratic, popular leader who will take charge if the people will give him absolute authority. Mussolini, Franco, Hitler, Pinochet, and countless others have followed in Napoleon's footsteps. Can students see how Napoleon's influence on subsequent leaders may have impacted them personally? Were any of their ancestors involved in World War II, for example?

CLASS DISCUSSION

Ask students to discuss the apparent contradiction between Napoleon having himself crowned Emperor and the Code Napoleon that recognized the principle of equality of all citizens.

ACTIVITY

Assign students to research research and write on one of the following two topics. They can either 1.) assess the ways in which Napoleon *fulfilled* the ideals of the Revolution; or 2.) assess the ways in which he *betrayed* the ideals of the Revolution. Have students alternate the reading of their essays between topics 1 and 2.

Map 20.6   Napoleon's Grand Empire

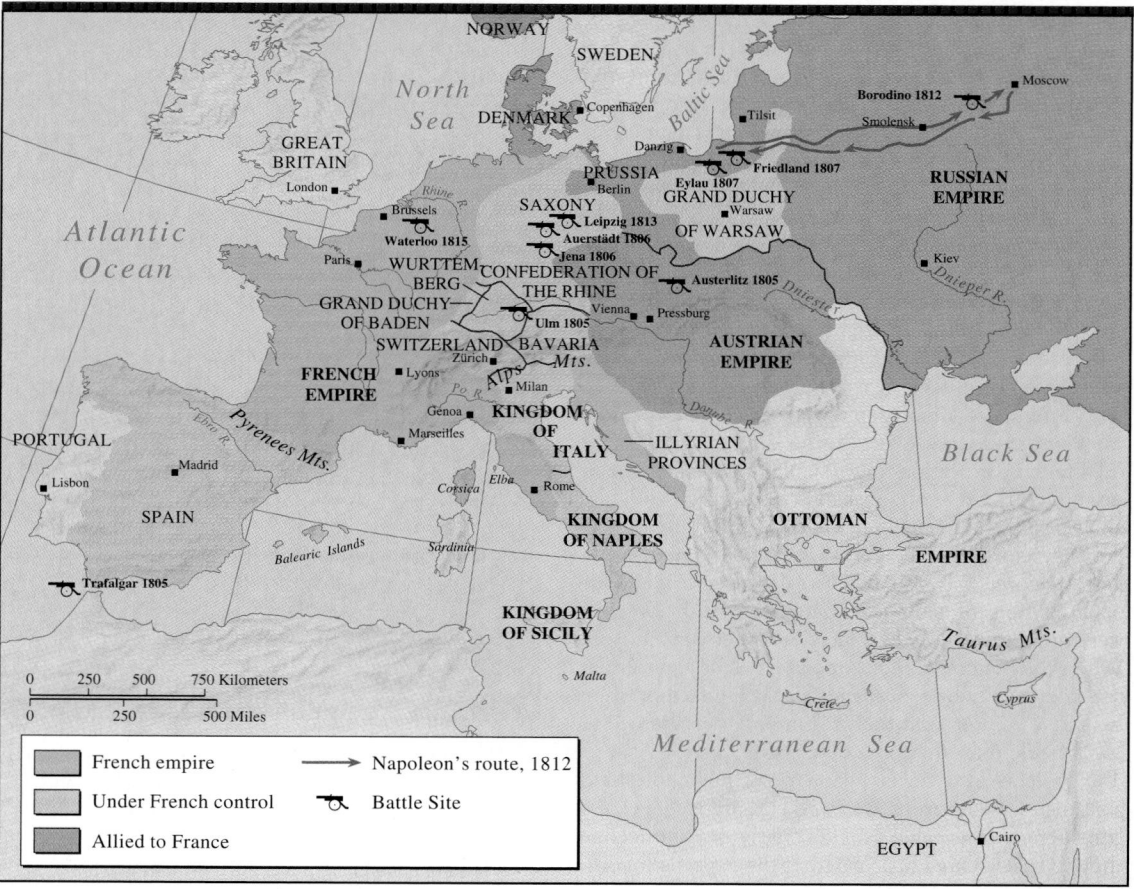

From 1807 to 1812, Napoleon was the master of Europe. His Grand Empire was composed of three major parts: the French Empire, dependent states, and allied states. The French Empire was the inner core of the Grand Empire. The French Empire consisted of an enlarged France extending to the Rhine in the east and including the western half of Italy north of Rome. Dependent states were kingdoms under the rule of Napoleon's relatives. These came to include Spain,

Holland, the kingdom of Italy, the Swiss Republic, the Grand Duchy of Warsaw, and the Confederation of the Rhine (a union of all German states except Austria and Prussia). Allied states were those defeated by Napoleon and forced to join his struggle against Britain. The allied states included Prussia, Austria, Russia, and Sweden.

Within his empire, Napoleon sought to spread some of the principles of the French Revolution, including

STUDYING MAPS

The following questions will help you guide the students through their study of Map 20.6.

1. How many miles is it from Paris to Moscow? From Danzig to Moscow? (*approximately 1750 miles*) Moscow to Friedland? (*approximately 750 miles*)
2. How did this distance make it more and more difficult for Napoleon to succeed in his quest through Russia? (*Severe weather*

conditions in Russia made long travel without supplies very difficult.)

3. How much territory came under French control at the height of Napoleon's Grand Empire? (*French Empire, dependent states, allied states*) How does this compare to the current size of France? (*three to five times larger than current France*)

legal equality, religious toleration, and economic freedom. In the inner core and dependent states of his Grand Empire, Napoleon tried to destroy the old order. The nobility and clergy everywhere in these states lost their special privileges. Napoleon decreed equality of opportunity with offices open to talents, equality before the law, and religious toleration. This spread of French revolutionary principles was an important factor in the development of liberal traditions in these countries.

Napoleon hoped that his Grand Empire would last for centuries, but it collapsed almost as rapidly as it had been formed. Two major reasons help to explain this: the survival of Great Britain and the force of nationalism.

The European Response

Britain's survival was primarily due to its sea power. As long as Britain ruled the waves, it was almost invulnerable to military attack. Napoleon hoped to invade Britain, but he could not overcome the British navy's decisive defeat of a combined French-Spanish fleet at Trafalgar in 1805. To defeat Britain, Napoleon turned to his Continental System, the aim of which was to stop British goods from reaching the European continent to be sold there. By weakening Britain economically, Napoleon would destroy its ability to wage war. However, the Continental System failed. Allied states resented it. Some began to cheat and others, to resist. Then, too, new markets in the Middle East and in Latin America gave Britain new outlets for its goods. Indeed, by 1809–1810, British overseas exports were at near-record highs.

A second important factor in the defeat of Napoleon was **nationalism.** The spirit of French nationalism had made possible the mass armies of the revolutionary and Napoleonic eras. However, Napoleon's spread of the principles of the French Revolution beyond France indirectly brought a spread of nationalism as well. The French aroused nationalism in two ways. First, they were hated as oppressors. This hatred stirred the patriotism of others in opposition to the French. Second, the French showed the people of Europe what nationalism was and what a nation in arms could do. It was a lesson not lost on other peoples and rulers. A Spanish uprising against Napoleon's rule, aided by British support, kept a French force of 200,000 pinned down for years.

The beginning of Napoleon's downfall came in 1812 with his invasion of Russia. The refusal of the Russians to remain in the Continental System left Napoleon with little choice but to invade. He knew the risks in invading such a large country. However, he also knew that if the Russians were allowed to challenge the Continental System unopposed, others would soon follow suit. In June 1812, a Grand Army of more than 600,000 men entered Russia. Napoleon's hopes for victory depended on a quick defeat of the Russian armies. The Russian forces, however, refused to give battle. They retreated for hundreds of miles while burning their own villages and countryside to keep Napoleon's army from finding food. When the troops of the Grand Army arrived in Moscow, they found the city ablaze. Lacking food and supplies, Napoleon abandoned Moscow and made a retreat across Russia in terrible winter conditions. Only 40,000 out of the original army managed to arrive back in Poland in January 1813.

This military disaster led other European states to rise up and attack the crippled French army. Paris was captured in March 1814. Napoleon was soon sent into exile on the island of Elba, off the coast of Italy. Meanwhile, the Bourbon monarchy was restored to France in the person of Louis XVIII, brother of the executed king. Napoleon then escaped from Elba and returned to Paris. He thus had one last period of rule, called the One Hundred Days, from March to June 1815. At the battle of Waterloo, Napoleon's One Hundred Days ended in bloody defeat. He was exiled to St. Helena, a small and forsaken island in the south Atlantic. Only his memory would continue to haunt French political life.

 SECTION REVIEW

1. **Locate:**
   (a) Rhine River,   (b) Lyons, (c) Corsica,
   (d) Trafalgar,   (e) Moscow,   (f) Elba,
   (g) Waterloo

2. **Define:**
   (a) Reign of Terror,   (b) consulate,
   (c) nationalism

ENRICHMENT ACTIVITY

Have students compare and contrast the American and French Revolutions. Why do they think that the French Revolution was so much more violent than the American? It is sometimes said that the Americans had a political revolution but the French Revolution was social and economic, as well as political.

Have the students assess the validity of this comparison and state their views to the class.

You might also wish to have students prepare charts showing the number of deaths that resulted from each of the revolutions, estimates of property damages, and expense.

CLASS DISCUSSION

Ask students to identify and discuss ways in which Napoleon made changes in European civilization that would last even after he was defeated by forces of the Old Order.

ASSESS

You can choose from a variety of assessments to evaluate your students' mastery of the objectives for this section as stated on page 638. Possible assessments include:

1. Section Review questions on this page
2. Section 20–5 Quiz in your Teacher Resource materials
3. Reteaching Worksheets in your Teacher Resource materials
4. Self-Study software

ALTERNATIVE ASSESSMENT

Assign students to create a poster or bulletin board that depicts Napoleon's major accomplishments as emperor of France. Their work should include maps that show his military victories and defeats.

Answers to
SECTION REVIEW

2. (a) program intended to protect the revolutionary Republic from its internal enemies
   (b) a new form of the republic
   (c) devotion to one's country
3. (a) met in 1792, composed of politically experienced, elected delegates
   (b) led the local government in Paris

(c) given broad powers, took control of France for one year it raised the largest army ever seen in European history
(d) device of execution
(e) leader of the Jacobins, continued the Terror in an effort to rid France of corruption
(f) acted as the executive authority in France from 1795–1799; dissolved when Napoleon came to power
(g) military hero, took control of France
(h) the French empire, dependent states, and allied states
(i) Napoleons strategy to stop British goods from reaching Europe
4. (a) abolish the monarchy and establish a republic
(b) Austria, Prussia, Spain, Portugal, Britain, Dutch Republic, Russia; invade France, reestablish Old Regime
(c) rebelled against the National Convention
(d) Reign of Terror ended, reduced power of Committee of Public Safety, churches reopened, new constitution, Directory
(e) through a coup d'etat
(f) codification of the laws (Civil Code)
5. Answers will vary.

CLOSE

Lead students in a discussion of the Focus objectives identified on page 638. Emphasize the conditions in France after the Reign of Terror that allowed Napoleon to gain power.

▲ *Napoleon's defeat in Russia was a disaster for French troops, and it marked the beginning of a new European coalition that joined forces against France.*

3. **Identify:**
(*a*) National Convention,   (*b*) Georges Danton,
(*c*) Committee of Public Safety,   (*d*) guillotine,
(*e*) Robespierre,   (*f*) the Directory,
(*g*) Napoleon Bonaparte,   (*h*) the Grand Empire,
(*i*) the Continental System

4. **Recall:**
(*a*) What was the first action taken by the National Convention in 1792?
(*b*) Name three of the countries in the European coalition in 1793. What was the purpose of this coalition?
(*c*) Why were over 1,800 citizens of Lyons executed?
(*d*) Describe one of the changes in French governmental policy after the death of Robespierre.
(*e*) How did Napoleon gain control of France?
(*f*) What was Napoleon's most long-lasting domestic achievement?

5. **Think Critically:** How was the awakening of nationalism both a benefit and a detriment for France?

Conclusion

At the beginning of the eighteenth century, the old order remained strong everywhere in Europe. Nobles, clerics, towns, and provinces all had privileges. Monarchs sought to enlarge their bureaucracies. In this way, they could raise taxes to support large standing armies. The existence of these armies led to wars on a worldwide scale. Indeed, the Seven Years' War could be viewed as the first world war. The wars changed little in Europe. However, British victories enabled Great Britain to emerge as the world's greatest naval and colonial power.

Everywhere in Europe, increased demands by governments for taxes to support these wars led to attacks

RECOMMENDED READING

A well-written, up-to-date introduction to the French Revolution can be found in W. Doyle, *The Oxford History of the French Revolution* (Oxford, 1989). For the entire revolutionary and Napoleonic eras, see O. Connelly, *The French Revolution and Napoleonic Era,* 2d ed. (Fort Worth, 1991); and D. M. G. Sutherland, *France 1789–1815: Revolution and Counter-Revolution* (New York, 1985). Although controversial, the massive and beau-

tifully written work by S. Schama, *Citizens* (New York, 1989), makes exciting reading. A different approach to the French Revolution can be found in E. Kennedy, *A Cultural History of the French Revolution* (New Haven, Conn., 1989). Three comprehensive reference works are S. F. Scott and B. Rothaus, eds., *Historical Dictionary of the French Revolution,* 2 vols. (Westport, Conn., 1985); F. Furet and M. Ozouf, *A Critical Dictionary of the French Revo-*

on the old order and a desire for change that was not met by the ruling monarchs. At the same time, a growth in population, as well as changes in finance, trade, and industry, created tensions that undermined the foundations of the old order. The inability of the monarchs to deal with these changes led to a revolutionary outburst at the end of the eighteenth century that marked the beginning of the end for the old order.

The revolutionary era of the late eighteenth century brought dramatic political changes. Revolutions, beginning in North America and continuing in France, were movements based on the people as the source of political power and on the principles of liberty and equality. Liberty meant, in theory, freedom from arbitrary power, as well as the freedom to think, write, and worship as one chose. Equality meant equality in rights, although it did not include the equality of men and women.

The French Revolution created a modern revolutionary concept. No one had foreseen or consciously planned the upheaval that began in 1789. After 1789, however, revolutionaries knew that the proper use of mass uprisings could overthrow unwanted governments. The French Revolution became the classic political and social model for revolution in the modern world. A new era had begun, and the world would never again be the same.

Notes

1. Quoted in E. Bradford Burns, *Latin America: A Concise Interpretative History*, 4th ed. (Englewood Cliffs, N.J., 1986), p. 62.
2. Quoted in William Doyle, *The Oxford History of the French Revolution* (Oxford, 1989), p. 184.
3. Quoted in Leo Gershoy, *The Era of the French Revolution* (Princeton, N.J., 1957), p. 157.
4. Quoted in Doyle, *The Oxford History of the French Revolution*, p. 254.

lution, trans. A. Goldhammer (Cambridge, Mass., 1989); and O. Connelly, et al., *Historical Dictionary of Napoleonic France, 1799–1815* (Westport, Conn., 1985).

The origins of the French Revolution are examined in the classic work by G. Lefebvre, *The Coming of the French Revolution* (Princeton, N.J., 1947), although his interpretive framework has been superseded by new work. On the latter, see especially W. Doyle, *Origins of the French Revolution* (Oxford, 1988). See also R. Chartier, *The Cultural Origins of the French Revolution* (Durham, N.C., 1991). On the early years of the Revolution, see J. Egret, *The French Pre-Revolution, 1787–88* (Chicago, 1977); M. Kennedy, *The Jacobin Clubs in the French Revolution: The First Years* (Princeton, N.J., 1982); and N. Hampson, *Prelude to Terror* (Oxford, 1988).

SPANISH SUPPORT

The *Conclusion* has been translated into Spanish for your Spanish-speaking students. Included with this translation (in your Teacher Resource materials) are Section Key Points, which consist of one or two sentences summarizing each section in the chapter. These Key Points have also been translated into Spanish.

TIME LINE

As students conclude the chapter, you may want to refer them to the chapter time line in the *Study Guide*. The time line will help them put key dates in perspective. Supporting questions and activities are also provided.

Answers to CHAPTER REVIEW 20

USING KEY TERMS

1. mestizos
2. balance of power
3. Reign of Terror
4. nationalism
5. enlightened ruler
6. mulattoes
7. enlightened absolutism
8. Tennis Court Oath
9. consulate
10. cottage industry
11. relics of feudalism
12. diplomatic revolution
13. orders

REVIEWING THE FACTS

1. July 14, 1789, when a mob attacked the Bastille
2. Answers may vary, but tobacco, cotton, coffee and sugar were the main items traded.
3. to be in charge of military and government affairs
4. equality before the law; freedom of religious worship; freedom of speech and press; right to assemble, hold property, and pursue happiness
5. Although she believed in the Enlightenment, she did not put any ideas into practice.
6. Prussia's refusal to return Silesia to Austria at the end of the Austrian Succession war
7. Raw materials were sent to Spain and manufactured ones brought back. Spain did not allow trading with other countries.
8. July 4, 1776
9. writing of the Constitution and the French Revolution
10. first estate: clergy; second estate: nobility; third estate: peasants and bourgeoisie
11. The Third Estate took an oath to continue meeting until they had produced a French constitution.
12. It was ignored by the National Assembly.
13. clergy, nobles, radicals, and lower classes
14. The execution of the king outraged the royalty of

646

USING KEY TERMS

1. In the Americas, the offspring of European and American natives were called _____.
2. The _____ theory was an approach to prevent one country from being militarily dominant.
3. An important step in the radicalization of the French Revolution was the development of the _____ by the Committee of Public Safety.
4. French _____ aroused patriotism in nations opposed to France.
5. A(n) _____ allowed religious toleration, freedom of speech and press, and the right to own property.
6. The offspring of Europeans and Africans were referred to as _____.
7. A new type of monarchy called _____ was influenced by reform-minded philosophes.
8. After the members of the Third Estate were locked out of their meeting place, they moved outdoors, where they took the _____.
9. In 1799 Napoleon proclaimed a new form of government called the _____.
10. A _____ was a family enterprise in which spinners and weavers did their work at home.
11. The payment of fees to the local lord in France for the use of village facilities was an example of _____.
12. Empress Maria Theresa of Austria caused a _____ in her successful attempt to separate Russia from its chief ally, France.
13. European society in the eighteenth century was divided into _____ or estates.

REVIEWING THE FACTS

1. What is considered the start of the French Revolution?
2. What was probably the most profitable goods item traded in the New World in the eighteenth century?

646

3. What was the function of the nobility in traditional European society?
4. What rights were considered natural rights by the philosophes?
5. Was Catherine the Great of Russia truly an enlightened monarch? Why or why not?
6. What was the major cause of the Seven Years' War?
7. Explain how Spain benefited from its trading pattern with Latin America.
8. When was the American Declaration of Independence signed by the American colonists?
9. Name two far-reaching events that took place in 1789.
10. Define the three orders or estates that existed in French society prior to the French Revolution.
11. What was the Tennis Court Oath?
12. What happened to the Declaration of the Rights of Woman and the Female Citizen?
13. Who opposed the new order brought about by the Constitution of 1791?
14. How did the French Revolution lead to war with Austria?
15. What is the importance of the Battle of Waterloo?

THINKING CRITICALLY

1. The French revolutionary slogan was "Liberty, Equality, and Fraternity." In a short paragraph, explain what each of these words meant in revolutionary France.
2. What two technological advancements helped to increase productivity in the textile industry? Explain how productivity was increased.
3. Why were the British policies toward North America more likely to establish permanent settlements than the equivalent French policies?
4. Review the section of the chapter that discusses the

---

most of Europe.
15. It was the end of Napoleon's One Hundred Days in Paris.

THINKING CRITICALLY

1. Answers will vary. "Liberty" was a call for freedom; "Equality" was a cry for fair treatment under the law; "Fraternity" speaks of brotherhood.
2. the water frame and mechanized looms; the time it took to spin and weave yarn decreased, allowing more production in less time
3. Answers will vary. When people can rule themselves they take greater ownership and produce a sense of permanency.

4. Answers will vary. Much of the Bill of Rights comes directly from the natural rights philosophies of Enlightenment philosophers, and several governmental structures come from their ideas of government.
5. Answers will vary. The condition of French society was based on inequality with oppressed commoners making up 75–80 percent of population; aristocrats and bourgeoisie, drawn to the Enlightenment, were upset with monarchy and old rigid social order.
6. Answers will vary.
7. The church was the oldest enemy of the Revolution and he wanted to keep the church lands that were seized by the Revolution.

characteristics of the U.S. Constitution. Then, refer to what the textbook says about John Locke, Montesquieu, Rousseau, and Voltaire. How did the ideas of these philosophes influence the Constitution?

5. How could Louis XVI have avoided the initial events of the French Revolution? What could he have done to make things turn out differently?

6. From 1789 to 1812, France was governed by many different types and systems of government. Which is most effective—government of one, a few, or a larger group? Why?

7. Why did Napoleon choose to make peace with the Catholic Church as one of his first moves after taking power?

APPLYING SOCIAL STUDIES SKILLS

1. **Geography:** On a blank map of the world, indicate the three main patterns of worldwide trade activity that developed as a result of the European colonization of the Americas.

2. **Sociology:** Describe the problems of city living in the eighteenth century.

3. **Political Science:** Compare and contrast the Declaration of Independence and the Universal Declaration of the Rights of Man and Citizen.

4. **Political Philosophy:** What characteristics would make a ruler today "enlightened"?

MAKING TIME AND PLACE CONNECTIONS

1. During the sixteenth and seventeenth centuries, transatlantic transportation was slow and uncertain. It often took more than 60 days to get an answer from Spain to a question posed by a local governor in the Americas. What effect could this have on the practice of politics?

2. Read the excerpt from the Untied States Declaration of Independence in the section, "Political Change: Enlightened Absolutism in the Eighteenth Century." Then, develop a statement of your own, indicating your beliefs about the nature of government.

3. Frederick the Great remarked, "the fundamental rule of government is the principle of extending their territories." Do governments today follow this principle? If so, what is the result?

4. Locate a map of the Americas that shows the present location of colonies on the continent. Locate one French colony in North America, and one in South America.

BECOMING AN HISTORIAN

1. **Drawing Inferences:** Write a dialogue that might have taken place between Napoleon and one of the anti-Napoleonic rulers of your choice. Napoleon should take the position of establishing his Grand Empire based on the principles of the French Revolution. His counterpart should be able to point out any contradictions between Napoleon's actions and the principles proclaimed by the French Revolution.

2. **Making Hypotheses:** Napoleon was enormously popular during his time as leader of France. Acting as an historian, based on the information in this chapter and any other information available to you, develop a hypothesis as to why he was so popular.

3. **Writing Research Papers:** Write an essay analyzing the importance of French assistance to the American colonists in their rebellion against Britain.

4. **Making Hypothesis:** The French Revolution has been studied as a model of how a revolution can develop over time. Do your own analysis by developing a time line containing all the events that you feel are of importance. Then form a hypothesis that could apply to other revolutions.

647

APPLYING SOCIAL STUDIES SKILLS

1. 1. gold and silver trade between Spain and South America; 2. Plantation items traded from America to Europe; and 3. British manufactured goods traded to Africa in exchange for slaves then traded to Virginia in exchange for tobacco to be shipped back to Germany via Britain.

2. dirty, crowded, dangerous; not well planned to meet the needs of dense population group

3. Students should note that they are similar to each other, even in wording.

4. Answers will vary. Should mention such characteristics as allows religious toleration, freedom of speech and press, and the rights of private prop-

erty. They must nurture the arts, sciences, and education. Above all, enlightened rulers must obey the laws and enforce them fairly for all subjects.

MAKING TIME AND PLACE CONNECTIONS

1. Answers will vary. Possible answers may include: made for very slow communication and progress on joint decisions; many big issues needed to be discussed at once, rather than little bits at a time; provided for more individual progress and independence because it was so difficult to work together with the delay in communication

2. Answers will vary. Responses should refer to page 614 and 627–629.

3. Possible answers may include that some do, but this usually leads to conflicts and wars; many governments no longer follow this policy of expansion but focus instead upon what land they do have.

4. Responses may vary. Map 20.1 on page 612 may be useful for this project.

BECOMING AN HISTORIAN

1. Students should demonstrate knowledge of page 634 for principles of the French Revolution and pages 640–643 for the reign of Napoleon. Items that may be used as contradictions seen in Napoleon's reign could include liberty replaced by despotism and declaring an official state religion. Items that may be used by Napoleon in his defense should be based on the fact that he set up many individual freedoms that were in line with the philosophies of French Revolution.

2. Students could choose hypothesis from information on pages 640–643. Possible choices could include that he unified nation after time of radical revolution; gave some peace and prosperity; provided good legal code and system; expanded French Empire; upheld many philosophies of French Revolution

3. Students should refer to explanation on page 627 of how beneficial it was to the American colonists to have French assistance against the British.

4. Answers will vary. Time lines should list some of the items found on pages 630–632 under the heading of "Background to the French Revolution".

MODERN PATTERNS
OF WORLD HISTORY:

✿ UNIT FOUR ✿

OVERVIEW OF THE UNIT

The fourth unit of *World History* is divided into four chapters, spanning about 150 pages. Assuming a 36-week course, you may wish to spend three weeks on Chapters 21 and 22, and three weeks on Chapters 23 and 24.

Using the
Illustration

This is probably not a typical "Picasso" for students who are familiar with his work. Ask students to suggest words that come to mind when looking at this painting. *(dynamic, freedom, celebration, liberty, or nationalism).* Ask students to identify the dominant colors of this painting. Inform students that it was the American and French revolutions in the 1700s that ushered in truly national flags. Flags after this time represented governments and citizens. Most people associate red, white, and blue with liberty—because of the U.S. and French flags. Old Austria, czarist Russia, and imperialist Germany used black and gold in their flags, colors now identified with totalitarian regimes. Ask students to work in groups to design a flag for their world history class or for your school. Colors have meanings and are as important as the image.

Another activity is to identify other national flags with red, white, and blue as primary colors. Which of these countries are considered democratic?

▶ *Pablo Picasso's 1901 painting,* The Fourteenth of July *celebrates Bastille Day. Happy crowds gather to celebrate their national holiday, many in red, white, and blue.*

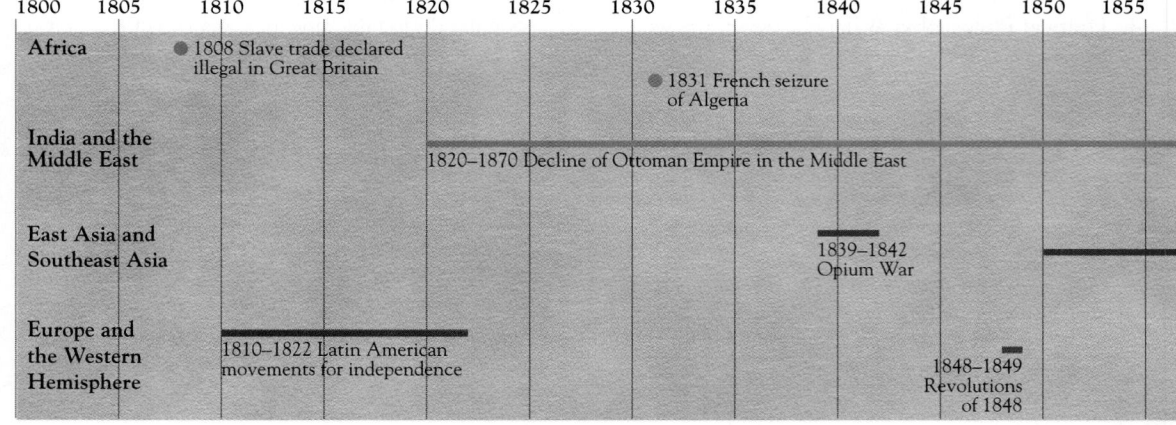

	1800	1805	1810	1815	1820	1825	1830	1835	1840	1845	1850	1855
Africa		● 1808 Slave trade declared illegal in Great Britain					● 1831 French seizure of Algeria					
India and the Middle East					1820–1870 Decline of Ottoman Empire in the Middle East							
East Asia and Southeast Asia									1839–1842 Opium War			
Europe and the Western Hemisphere			1810–1822 Latin American movements for independence							1848–1849 Revolutions of 1848		

📖 UNIT OPENER ACTIVITY

This unit begins by studying the impact of the Industrial Revolution in Europe. Although relatively brief, some very sophisticated concepts are introduced. This unit covers the beginnings of industrialization, the rise of nationalism, and stops just before the outbreak of World War I.

A good review for students would be to ask them to create a montage for the class showing how each of the following changed as a result of industrialization: (1) transportation; (2) communication; and (3) kinds of energy use. Encourage students to use original artwork or to bring in cuttings from newspapers and magazines.

THE ERA OF EUROPEAN DOMINANCE

(1800–1914)

The period of world history from 1800 to 1914 was characterized, above all, by two major developments: the growth of industrialization and Western domination of the world. The two developments were, of course, directly interconnected. The Industrial Revolution became one of the major forces for change in the nineteenth century as it led Western civilization into the industrial era that has characterized the modern world. At the same time, the Industrial Revolution created the technological means, including the new weapons, by which the Western world achieved domination of much of the rest of the world by 1900.

Between 1870 and 1914, Western civilization expanded into all of the Americas, as well as Australia. Most of Africa and Asia was divided into European colonies or spheres of influence. Two major events explain this remarkable expansion: (1) the migration of many Europeans to other parts of the world because of population growth and (2) the revival of imperialism, which was made possible by the West's technological advances.

UNIT OUTLINE

| 1855 | 1860 | 1865 | 1870 | 1875 | 1885 | 1890 | 1895 | 1900 | 1905 | 1910 | 1915 |

1869 Completion of Suez Canal

1899–1902 Boer War

1857–1858 Sepoy Mutiny

1885 Indian National Congress established

Gandhi returns to India

1850–1870 British and French move into Southeast Asia

1868–1890 Meiji reforms in Japan

1900 Boxer Rebellion

Manchu dynasty collapses

1861–1871 Unification of Italy and Germany

1870–1914 Growth of political and social democracy

649

USING PROJECT IDEAS

As students progress through the unit, they will learn about the drive of European nations to obtain colonies. The economic and social effects of colonialism have carried over to this day and are seen in the criteria that geographers and sociologists use to differentiate between developed and developing (often former colonial) countries. Although these are only general guidelines, most developed nations meet at least eight of the ten criteria below. Ask students to work in groups to create visual aids that will illustrate one of these geographical criteria for developed (industrialized) nations:

1. People are relatively well off.
2. People live long lives.
3. People are well educated and highly skilled.
4. Population is growing slowly.
5. Most people live in cities.
6. Few people work in agriculture.
7. Consumption of energy is high.
8. Most people work in manufacturing or service industries.
9. Transportation and communication networks are well developed.
10. Environmental control is high.

STUDYING THE TIME LINE

Ask students the following questions to help them compare the time periods of the different civilizations they will be studying in this unit.

1. What is the earliest year represented in the time line? *(A.D. 1800)*
2. What is the latest year represented in the time line? *(A.D. 1915)*
3. What is the total amount of time covered in the time line? *(115 years)*
4. How many years passed between the

Boxer Rebellion and the collapse of the Manchu dynasty? *(11 years)* Is there a cause-and-effect relationship between these two events? *(Two momentous events so close together will probably have a cause-and-effect relationship.)*

5. What is the focus of the events in the "Europe and the Western Hemisphere" time line? *(They involve the growth of democracy.)*

21 PLANNING GUIDE

SECTION	KEY TOPICS	PRIMARY SOURCES	ASSESSMENT
1 The Industrial Revolution and Its Impact pages 651–661	◆ The impact of the Industrial Revolution in Great Britain ◆ Industrialization's spread through Europe ◆ The growth of cities and new social classes ◆ The birth of socialism	◆ A description of child labor in England, page 660	◆ Section Review, page 661 ◆ Section Quiz 21–1, TRB
2 Reaction and Revolution: The Growth of Nationalism, 1815 to 1848 pages 662–668	◆ Conservatism, liberalism, and nationalism ◆ Revolutionary outbursts in Europe ◆ The revolutions of 1848	◆ A description of the excitement among German liberals at the news of revolution in France, page 666	◆ Section Review, page 668 ◆ Section Quiz 21–2, TRB
3 National Unification and the National State, 1848 to 1871 pages 668–678	◆ Failure of the Concert of Europe ◆ The unification of Italy ◆ The unification of Germany ◆ Nationalism and reform in Europe ◆ Developments in the United States and Canada	◆ Copies of emancipation proclamations from Russia and the United States, page 676	◆ Section Review, page 678 ◆ Section Quiz 21–3, TRB
4 Cultural Life: Romanticism and Realism in the Western World pages 678–684	◆ Characteristics of Romanticism ◆ A New Age of Science ◆ Characteristics of Realism	◆ A poem by William Wordsworth, page 680 ◆ A description of natural selection by Charles Darwin, page 683	◆ Section Review, page 684 ◆ Section Quiz 21–4, TRB

THE BEGINNINGS OF MODERNIZATION:
Industrialization and Nationalism (1800 to 1870)

Reproducible Activities

- Historical Maps
- Charts and Graphs
- Critical Thinking
- Cooperative Learning
- Vocabulary
- Guided Reading
- Reteaching
- Enrichment
- Performance Assessment
- Spanish Key Points and Chapter Summaries
- Spanish Vocabulary
- Spanish Guided Reading

Multimedia Support

TRANSPARENCIES
- *World History* Color Transparency Package
- Fine Art Color Transparency Package

VIDEO
- *World History* Video Library
- **CNN.** Annual Video Update

LASERDISC
- *Sights and Sounds of History*

AUDIO
- *Listening to Literature* audiotape (English and Spanish)
- *History of Music* CD

SOFTWARE
- WESTEST™
- Student Review

CD–ROM
- *The Journey of Civilization*
- *World History*

INTERNET
- Internet Activities

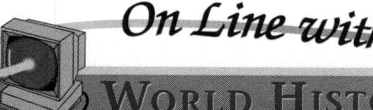

On Line with WORLD HISTORY

Access West's history web site at
http://history.swpco.com
You'll find activities and web sites related to specific topics and chapters in *World History: The Human Odyssey.* Also look for references to helpful web sites at appropriate places throughout this teacher edition.

LESSON PLANNING

You will find detailed daily lesson plans for both traditional class scheduling and **block scheduling** in your Teacher Resource Box.

Not Enough Time?

If you do not have the four or five days recommended to teach this chapter, you may want to focus on the following sections and activities:

- Have students skim the chapter to answer the "Questions to Guide Your Reading" on page 651. Discuss their answers, then read the "Conclusion" on page 685.
- Do a more in-depth reading about the impact of the Industrial Revolution on pages 651–656, revolutions between 1815 and 1848 on pages 662–668, and unification of Italy and Germany on pages 669–675. Conclude with a discussion of how changes in social values can be seen in characteristics of Romanticism and Realism.

THE BEGINNINGS OF MODERNIZATION:

21

BUILDING ON CHAPTER 20

To "set the scene" for the study of Chapter 21 of use the following questions and activities.

◆ Have students identify reasons why cottage industries would become impractical in the Industrial Revolution

◆ Ask students to explain how the growth of cities could encourage revolution

◆ Have students list reasons why many people would not be satisfied with a government of 'enlightened absolutism'

◆ Discuss how the Napoleonic wars might have encouraged national unification of Germany and Italy

USING THE OPENING STORY

Depending on the ability levels of your students, select from the following questions and activities to reinforce the reading of the opening story.

◆ Why would leaders of the Old Order choose to celebrate the defeat of Napoleon with such a display of wealth and pageantry?

◆ Why might this display have been a sign of the need for change in Europe?

◆ Why do some historians believe the Industrial Revolution was as much a cause for the fall of the Old Order as were the revolutions of the early nineteenth century?

In the fall of 1814, hundreds of foreigners began to converge on Vienna, the capital city of the Austrian Empire. Many of these foreigners were members of European royalty—kings, archdukes, princes, and their wives—accompanied by their political advisors and scores of servants. Their congenial host was the Austrian emperor Francis I, who never tired of providing Vienna's guests with concerts, glittering balls, sumptuous feasts, and an endless array of hunting parties. One participant remembered, "Eating, fireworks, public illuminations. For eight or ten days, I haven't been able to work at all. What a life!" Of course, not every waking hour was spent in pleasure during this gathering of notables, known to history as the Congress of Vienna. These people were also representatives of all the states that had fought Napoleon, and their real business was to arrange a final peace settlement after almost 10 years of war.

The French Revolution and the age of Napoleon had unleashed powerful forces for change, which were halted for a while after the defeat of Napoleon. However, the new forces of change had become too powerful to be contained forever. This was especially true of the forces of nationalism and liberalism, products of the revolutionary upheaval

▶ *This painting records a meeting of the Congress of Vienna. In this elegant setting aristocratic negotiators from around Europe gathered to work out the treaties that ensured peace in Europe for almost one hundred years.*

that began in France. The forces of change called forth revolts and revolutions that at times shook Europe in the 1820s and 1830s and led to widespread revolutions in 1848. Some of the revolutions were successful; most were not. Within 25 years, however, many of the goals sought by the liberals and nationalists during the first half of the nineteenth century were achieved.

The Industrial Revolution unleashed yet another set of forces for change at the beginning of the nineteenth century. By transforming the economic and social structure of Europe, the Industrial Revolution led the world into the industrialization that has been such a powerful feature of the modern world. The forces unleashed by two revolutions—the French Revolution and the Industrial Revolution—made it impossible to return to the old Europe and began what historians like to call the modern European world.

ADDITIONAL RESOURCES

The resources listed below can be used to enrich the lessons in this chapter.

BOOKS FOR STUDENTS
Great Ideas of Science by Isaac Asimov, Houghton Mifflin
The Unification of Italy by Christopher Leeds, Putnam
Garibaldi by Nina Baker, Vanguard

VIDEOS/FILMS
Industrial Revolution Series: Western Man and the Modern World, NY Times, Social Studies School Service, (800) 421-4246
The Revolutions of 1848, MultiMedia, Social Studies School Service, (800) 421-4246
Bismarck: Germany from Blood and Iron, Learning Corp of America, Social Studies School Service, (800) 421-4246

INDUSTRIALIZATION AND NATIONALISM

(1800 TO 1870)

ERA OF EUROPEAN DOMINANCE

1800	INDUSTRIALIZATION AND NATIONALISM	1870	
1800			1914

QUESTIONS TO GUIDE YOUR READING

1. What were the basic features of the new industrial system created by the Industrial Revolution?

2. How did the early Industrial Revolution affect the growth of cities, the living and working conditions of industrial workers, the family, and the role of women?

3. What did the Congress of Vienna and the Concert of Europe try to accomplish?

4. What caused the revolutions of 1848, and why did they fail?

5. What were the roles of Count Camillo di Cavour and Count Otto von Bismarck in the unification of their countries? What role did war play in the two unification movements?

6. What were the major features of the cultural movements known as romanticism and realism?

OUTLINE

1. THE INDUSTRIAL REVOLUTION AND ITS IMPACT

2. REACTION AND REVOLUTION: THE GROWTH OF NATIONALISM, 1815 TO 1848

3. NATIONAL UNIFICATION AND THE NATIONAL STATE, 1848 TO 1871

4. CULTURAL LIFE: ROMANTICISM AND REALISM IN THE WESTERN WORLD

THE INDUSTRIAL REVOLUTION AND ITS IMPACT

The Industrial Revolution led to an enormous leap in industrial production. Coal and steam replaced wind and water as new sources of energy and power to drive labor-saving machines. In turn, these machines led to new ways of organizing human labor as factories replaced shop and home workrooms. During the Industrial Revolution, Europe saw a shift from an economy based on farming and handicrafts to an economy based on manufacturing by machines and industrial factories.

It took decades for the Industrial Revolution to spread, but it was truly revolutionary in the way it changed Europeans and the world itself. Large numbers of people moved from the countryside to cities to work in the new factories. Impersonal life in the cities replaced the closeness of life in the country. A revolution in transportation also occurred with the use of railroads and steamboats. New products now moved quickly around the world, and new patterns of living emerged. Finally, the Industrial Revolution changed how people related to nature. This development ultimately created

651

FOCUS ON THEMES

Listed below are brief summaries of how the content in this chapter supports the text's key themes.

Politics and History Three important ideologies that emerged between 1800 and 1870 played important roles in both nineteenth- and twentieth-century history: conservatism, nationalism, and liberalism. All three were by-products of the French revolutionary era, and all three spread widely and made an impact on world history.

The Role of Ideas Political ideas received enormous support. Especially important was nationalism, an idea that encouraged millions of people to seek their own nation-states. Liberal and conservative ideas provided a framework for the political debates of the nineteenth century. The ideas of utopian socialism were a response to some of the problems created by the Industrial Revolution.

Economics and History The Industrial Revolution was responsible for the transformation from an economy based on farming and handicrafts to an economy based on manufacturing by machines and industrial factories. Industrial capitalism dramatically changed where people lived, how they worked, and how they related to the world around them.

Social Life The early Industrial Revolution led to the emergence of two new social classes—the industrial middle class (which soon sought equality with the landowning classes) and the industrial working class.

FOCUS

OBJECTIVES

After completing this section, students should be able to

1. describe the impact of the Industrial Revolution on Great Britain
2. explain how the Industrial Revolution spread to other nations in Europe
3. explain how the Industrial Revolution contributed to the growth of cities and new social classes
4. describe the relationship of the Industrial Revolution to the birth of socialism

FOCUS ACTIVITY

Help students understand how the Industrial Revolution helped cause social revolutions. Ask students to write descriptions of how a typical farmer and an industrial worker would have spent his or her day at the time of the Industrial Revolution. Discuss why their different lives would require different social systems.

TEACH

LEARNING FROM VISUALS

Answer to the caption question: Students should recognize that the gears and the shaft were turned by steam power.

◄ *James Watt's steam engine seems simple compared to modern-day equipment, yet it was revolutionary. Examine this diagram carefully and explain how this machine worked.*

▼ *James Hargreaves's spinning jenny changed the way yarn was made, and this basic machine contributed significantly to the factory system of manufacture. How did this one machine change the way of life for many working-class families in Britain?*

an environmental crisis that in the twentieth century has finally been recognized as a danger to human existence itself.

The Industrial Revolution in Great Britain

The Industrial Revolution began in Great Britain in the 1780s. One important factor in producing the Industrial Revolution was the change in agricultural practices in the eighteenth century (see Chapter 20). These new practices led to a dramatic increase in food production. British agriculture could now feed more people at lower prices with less labor. Even ordinary British families could use some of their income to buy manufactured goods. At the same time, with more abundant food supplies, population grew in the second half of the eighteenth century. This provided a pool of surplus labor for the new factories of the emerging British industry.

As we saw in Chapter 20, the traditional methods of the cottage industry could not keep up with the growing demand for cotton clothes throughout Britain and its vast colonial empire. This problem led British cloth manufacturers to seek new ways to increase production. In so doing, these individuals produced the Industrial Revolution.

Changes in Textile Production

Already in the eighteenth century, Great Britain had surged ahead in the production of cheap cotton goods using the methods of cottage industry. The invention of the flying shuttle by John Kay made weaving on a loom even faster. This invention, however, created shortages of yarn until James Hargreaves's spinning jenny, perfected by 1768, allowed spinners to produce yarn in greater quantities. Edmund Cartwright's loom, powered by water and invented in 1787, then made it possible for the weaving of cloth to catch up with the spinning of yarn. It was now more efficient to bring workers to the machines and have them work in factories placed next to rivers and streams, the sources of power for many of these early machines. Workers and their families came to live in the new towns that rapidly grew up around the factories.

What pushed the cotton industry to even greater heights was the invention of the steam engine. In the 1760s, a Scottish engineer, James Watt, built an engine

RECOMMENDED READING

D. Landes, *The Unbound Prometheus: Technological Change and Industrial Development in Western Europe from 1750 to the Present* (Cambridge, 1969) is the best introduction to the Industrial Revolution. More technical, but also of value are C. Trebilcock, *The Industrialization of the Continental Powers, 1780–1914* (London, 1981); and S. Pollard, *Peaceful Conquest: The Industrialization of Europe, 1760–1970* Oxford, 1981).

G. R. Taylor, *The Transportation Revolution, 1815–60* (New York, 1951) examines the importance of transportation in American industrialization. On the economic ties between Great Britain and the United States, see D. Jeremy, *Transatlantic Industrial Revolution: The Diffusion of Textile Technology between Britain and America, 1790–1830* (Cambridge, Mass., 1981).

powered by steam that could pump water from mines three times as quickly as previous engines had. In 1782, Watt developed a rotary engine that could turn a shaft and thus drive machinery. Steam power could now be used to spin and weave cotton. Before long, cotton mills using steam engines were found all over Britain. Because steam engines were fired by coal, they did not need to be located near rivers.

British cotton cloth production increased dramatically. In 1760, Britain had imported 2.5 million pounds of raw cotton, which was farmed out to cottage industries. In 1787, the British imported 22 million pounds of cotton. Most of it was spun on machines. By 1840, 366 million pounds of cotton were imported annually, much of it from the U.S. South, where it was grown by slaves. By this time, cotton cloth was Britain's most valuable product, and it was produced mainly in factories.

The price of yarn was but one-twentieth of what it had been. Even by using its cheapest labor, India could not compete in quality or quantity with Britain. British cotton goods sold everywhere in the world. In Britain itself, the availability of cheap cotton cloth made it possible for millions of poor people to wear underclothes. These garments had previously been worn only by the rich, who alone could afford underwear made with expensive linen cloth. New cotton work clothing that was tough, comfortable to the skin, and yet inexpensive and easily washable became common. Even the rich liked the colorful patterns of cotton prints and their light weight for summer use.

Other Technological Changes

The steam engine was crucial to Britain's Industrial Revolution. It depended for fuel on coal, a substance that seemed then to be unlimited in quantity. The success of the steam engine led to a need for more coal and, thus, to an expansion in coal production. In turn, new processes using coal aided the development of the iron industry.

The British iron industry changed dramatically during the Industrial Revolution. Britain had always had large resources of iron ore. At the beginning of the eighteenth century, however, the basic process of producing iron had changed little since the Middle Ages.

A better quality of iron came into being in the 1780s, when Henry Cort developed a system called **puddling.** In this process, coke, which was derived from coal, was used to burn away impurities in pig iron (crude iron) and produce an iron of high quality. A boom then ensued in the British iron industry. In 1740, Britain produced 17,000 tons of iron. By 1852, it produced almost 3 million tons—more than the rest of the world combined.

In turn, the new high-quality iron was used to build new machines and new industries. Most noticeable were the new means of transportation—steamboats and railroads (see "The Role of Science and Technology: The Railroad"). The railroad was important to the success of the Industrial Revolution. The needs of railroads for coal and iron led to more growth in those industries. Building railways also created new jobs for farm laborers and peasants. Moreover, less expensive transportation led to lower-priced goods, thus creating larger markets. More sales meant more factories and more machinery. Business owners could reinvest their profits in new equipment, thereby adding to the growth of the economy. This type of regular, ongoing economic growth came to be seen as a basic feature of the new industrial economy.

The New Factories

The factory was also important to the Industrial Revolution. From its beginning, the factory created a new labor system. Factory owners wanted to use their new machines constantly. Thus, workers were forced to work regular hours and in shifts to keep the machines producing at a steady rate. Early factory workers, however, came from rural areas, where they were used to a different pace of life. Peasant farmers worked hard, especially at harvest time, but they were also used to periods of inactivity.

Early factory owners, therefore, had to create a system of work discipline in which employees became used to working regular hours and doing the same work over and over. One early industrialist said that his aim was "to make the men into machines that cannot err." Of course, such work was boring, and factory owners got tough to achieve their goals. They issued detailed

COOPERATIVE LEARNING ACTIVITY

Division of Labor and Mass Production. Select ten students to work together to complete a particular task. It can be as simple as a drawing, or involve a more complicated assembly. Five students will perform the entire task as individuals, the others will divide the work. For example—with a drawing of a person, have five students complete the entire task, while the other five choose a particular part (arm, legs, face, torso) and pass it on to the next person. Both can be timed and judged for quality. Discuss the results as a class. In which way was the task finished most quickly? Who had greatest satisfaction? The best product?

THE ROLE OF SCIENCE AND TECHNOLOGY

The Railroad

▲ *When they were first developed, railroads were used primarily for carrying passengers. Second- and third-class travelers rode in open cars like those shown in this illustration. First-class passengers were transported in covered cars.*

In 1804, Richard Trevithick tested the first steam-powered locomotive on a rail line in southern Wales. The locomotive pulled 10 tons of iron and 70 people at 5 miles per hour. Better locomotives soon followed. The engines built by George Stephenson and his son Robert proved superior, and it was in their workshops in Newcastle upon Tyne that the locomotives for the first modern railways in Britain were built. George Stephenson's locomotive, called the *Rocket*, was used on the first public railway line. The line opened in 1830 and extended 32 miles from Liverpool to Manchester. The *Rocket* sped along at 16 miles per hour while pulling a 40-ton train.

Within 20 years, locomotives were able to reach 50 miles per hour, an incredible speed to passen

regulations. For example, adult workers were fined for being late and were dismissed for more serious misconduct, especially for being drunk. The loss of one's job could be disastrous for adults. Child workers, however, did not care if they were fired, so they were disciplined more directly—often by beating. In one crucial sense the early industrialists were successful. As the nineteenth century wore on, the second and third generations of workers came to view a regular working week as a natural way of life. It was, of course, an attitude that made possible Britain's incredible economic growth in that century.

By the mid-nineteenth century, Great Britain had become the world's first and richest industrial nation. Britain was the "workshop, banker, and trader of the world." It produced one-half of the world's coal and manufactured goods. Its cotton industry alone in 1850 was equal in size to the industries of all other European countries combined.

The Spread of Industrialization

Beginning in Great Britain, the Industrial Revolution spread to the rest of Europe at different times and speeds during the nineteenth century. First to be industrialized on the Continent were Belgium, France, and the German states. In these states, governments were especially active in encouraging the development of industrialization. For example, the governments set up technical schools to train engineers and mechanics. They also bore much of the cost of building roads,

THE ROLE OF SCIENCE AND TECHNOLOGY

ACROSS THE CURRICULUM

Sociology. Construction of railroads not only allowed inexpensive and quick transport of goods but also of people. Ask students how the ability to travel hundreds of miles a day may have affected European society.

Environmental Science. Railroads and other industries relied on burning coal for energy. This often created sulfuric clouds over British cities. Ask students to describe how this would have affected the lives of all British citizens. Why might wealthy people have chosen to spend more time at their country estates?

RETEACHING ACTIVITY

Have students pretend to be George and Robert Stephenson and develop a one-page flyer promoting the business advantages of locomotives. The flyer should be directed to business leaders of the day.

ALTERNATE

Divide class into two groups—the Stephensons and conservative business leaders. Have the Stephenson group attempt to convince the business leaders of the merits of their locomotives, while the business leaders raise appropriate questions and concerns.

THE ROLE OF SCIENCE AND TECHNOLOGY
The Railroad, continued

TRAVELLING ON THE LIVERPOOL AND MANCHESTER RAILWAY. 1831.

gers. During the same period, new companies formed to build additional railroads as the infant industry proved to be not only technically but also financially successful. In 1840, Britain had almost 2,000 miles of railroads. By 1850, 6,000 miles of railroad track crisscrossed much of that country.

The railroad was a perfect symbol of the rapid and dynamic economic growth that came with the Industrial Revolution. The railroad's ability to transport goods and people at dramatic speeds was also a visible reminder of a new sense of power. When railway engineers pierced mountains with tunnels and spanned chasms with breathtaking

bridges, people had a sense of power over nature that had not been felt before in civilization.

1. How fast did the locomotive used on the first public railway travel?

2. Do you think the *Rocket* was worthy of its name by today's standards? By the standards of the 1800s?

3. How do you think the invention of the railroad changed life in England?

canals, and railroads. By 1850, a network of iron rails had spread across Europe.

There was also an Industrial Revolution in North America, in the new nation of the United States. In 1800, six out of every seven American workers were farmers, and there were no cities with more than 100,000 people. By 1860, the population had grown from 5 million in 1800 to 30 million people. Nine U.S. cities had populations over 100,000, and only 50 percent of U.S. workers were farmers. Between 1800 and 1860, the United States had experienced an industrial revolution and the growth of cities that went with it.

Unlike Britain, the United States was a large country. Thousands of miles of roads and canals were built to link east and west. The steamboat made transporta-

tion easier on the Great Lakes, Atlantic coastal waters, and rivers. The steamboat was especially important to the Mississippi River valley; by 1860, a thousand steamboats plied that river.

Most important of all in the development of an American transportation system was the railroad. It began with 100 miles of track in 1830. By 1860, more than 27,000 miles of railroad track covered the United States. This revolution in transportation turned the United States into a single massive market for the manufactured goods of the Northeast.

Labor for the growing number of factories in the Northeast came chiefly from the farm population. Many of the workers in the new textile and shoe factories of New England were women. Indeed, women

---

Answers to Critical Thinking Questions

1. The first public locomotive went 16 miles per hour.
2. By today's standards the *Rocket* was not worthy of its name. By the standards of the 1800s it was worthy.
3. Answers will vary but may include the following ideas: it increased travel; simplified and increased the speed of the transport of goods; made the people more mobile; etc.

COMPARING TIME PERIODS

Ask students to describe what would probably happen to a present day firm that used the methods described on page 654 to maintain control over its workers. What does this indicate about the need for government protection of workers?

CLASS DISCUSSION

In general the working conditions in American industry were better than in Europe until after the 1840s. Ask students to identify and explain possible reasons for this situation. What might it have had to do with the supply of workers?

SPECIAL NEEDS: *Auditory/Visual*

Have the students read pages 658–659 and the Child Labor Section on pages 660 and 661. Divide the class into two groups and designate one group as "The Middle Class and the Industrial Middle Class" and another group as the "Industrial Working Class." Have each group identify the following: (1) Who makes up the group? (*Middle Class: merchants, officials, lawyers, bankers, teachers, doctors, factory builders, marketers;*

Working Class: factory workers, cotton mill workers, coal miners; many women and children) (2) Have each group share how they feel about the employment of children. (*Middle Class: helpful, delicate touch as cotton spinners, more easily trained, cheap labor; Working Class: exploited, abused, dangerous, unhealthy*) Have each group prepare a chart listing the above information and share it with the class.

▶ *This engraving of a cotton factory shows the number of machines that could be tended by just a few workers. In order to maximize production and profitability, work was organized into shifts. Do you think it was easy for workers to adjust to working set hours in factories like this one? Why or why not?*

made up more than 80 percent of the workers in the large textile factories. Factory owners sometimes sought entire families, including children, to work in their mills. One mill owner ran this advertisement in a newspaper in Utica (YOOT-i-kuh), New York: "Wanted: A few sober and industrious families of at least five children each, over the age of eight years, are wanted at the Cotton Factory in Whitestown. Widows with large families would do well to attend this notice."

The Social Impact of the Industrial Revolution

The Industrial Revolution drastically changed the social life of Europe and the entire world in the nineteenth and twentieth centuries. This change was already evident in the first half of the nineteenth century in the growth of cities and the emergence of new social classes.

Growth of Population and Cities

A growth in population had already begun in the eighteenth century, but it became dramatic in the nineteenth century. In 1750, European population stood at an estimated 140 million. By 1800, it had increased to 187 million. By 1850, the population had almost doubled since 1750, to 266 million. The key to this growth was a decline in death rates. Wars and major epidemic diseases, such as smallpox and plague, became less frequent. This led to a drop in the number of deaths. Because of an increase in the food supply, more people were better fed and more resistant to disease. Famine largely disappeared from western Europe, although there were some exceptions. Ireland, for example, experienced a great catastrophe, the Great Potato Famine, caused by overdependence on a single crop—the potato.

Ireland was one of the most oppressed areas in western Europe. Its mostly Catholic peasant population rented land from mostly absentee British Protestant landlords, whose chief concern was collecting their rents. Irish peasants lived in mud huts in desperate poverty. They grew potatoes, a nutritious and relatively easy-to-grow crop that produced three times as much food per acre as grain. The cultivation of the potato gave Irish peasants a basic staple that enabled them to survive and even expand in numbers. Between 1781 and 1845, the Irish population doubled, from four million to eight million. In the summer of 1845, a fungus that turned the potato black devastated the potato

MORE ABOUT . . . *the Molly Maguires*

The secret organization known as the Molly Maguires originated in Ireland during the potato famine in the 1840s. The Mollies had threatened to murder any English landlord who evicted an Irish tenant who was unable to pay his rent. The organization spread to the coal mining regions of Pennsylvania where many Irish immigrated. They found exploitation by mine owners not too different from the landlords at home. The Mollies organized resistance to Civil War conscription in 1862. They were so successful that conscription could never be enforced in the coal regions of Pennsylvania. After the Civil War the Molly Maguires continued violent attacks on mine managers. After their organization was infiltrated by Pinkerton detectives, 20 of the leading Mollies were hanged, which ended the organization's operations.

Map 21.1   The Industrialization of Europe by 1850

Legend:

Manufacturing and industrial areas	▲ Coal mining
No peasant emancipation before 1848	◆ Iron industry
—— Railways by 1850	⬭ Textile industries
◯ Banks	■ Silk industries

Major cities:
▫ 1820
▪ 1850

COMPARING TIME PERIODS

Most European cities did not become large until the Industrial Revolution. This was not true of the Far East where many cities had large populations. Ask students to identify and explain possible reasons for this difference.

Multimedia Support

TRANSPARENCY

21–1, The Industrialization of Europe by 1850 (Map 21.1)

crop in Ireland. Between 1845 and 1851, the Great Famine decimated the Irish population. Over one million people died of starvation and disease, and almost two million emigrated to the United States and Britain. Of all the European nations, only Ireland had a declining population in the nineteenth century.

Elsewhere in Europe, cities and towns grew dramatically in the first half of the nineteenth century. The growth was directly related to industrialization. By 1850, especially in Great Britain and Belgium, cities were rapidly becoming home to many industries. With the steam engine, factory owners did not need water power and could locate their plants in cities, to which people flocked from the country to find work. The workers came on the new railroads.

In 1800, Great Britain had one major city, London, with a population of 1 million, and six cities with populations between 50,000 and 100,000. Fifty years later,

STUDYING MAPS

The following questions will help you guide students through their study of Map 21.1.

1. In which nation was industrialization concentrated? *(Great Britain)*
2. What relationship appears to have existed between industrialization and banking? *(Banks sprang up in industrialized areas.)*
3. What relationship appears to have existed between industrialization and emancipation of the peasants? *(Industrialization closely followed the emancipation of peasants.)*

LEARNING FROM VISUALS

Answer to the caption question: Railroads were noisy, but even worse, they showered neighborhoods with coal dust.

CLASS DISCUSSION

Ask students to explain why the growth of the bourgeoisie shifted political as well as economic power in Europe. Why didn't the masses of factory workers have any effective political power? Why could this situation have contributed to civil unrest and to the creation of new political systems?

TEACHING THEMES

Economics and History. Assign students to draw and label pictures that show working conditions in a British cotton mill. Discuss what their drawings show about British society and class structure.

Multimedia Support

LASERDISC
Industrial Revolution: Work in the Factories, 1800s

▶ *Inner-city housing for the poor was too often overcrowded, filthy, and unhealthy. This drawing of a London slum shows the railroad viaducts that cut through the area. How did the railroad contribute to the pollution that existed in these neighborhoods?*

London's population had swelled to 2,363,000. There were nine cities with populations over 100,000 and eighteen cities with populations between 50,000 and 100,000. Over 50 percent of the British population lived in towns and cities by 1850. Urban populations also grew on the Continent, but less dramatically.

The rapid growth of cities in the first half of the nineteenth century led to pitiful living conditions for many of the inhabitants. Eventually, these conditions led to the rise of urban reformers who called upon city governments to clean up their cities. As we shall see in Chapter 22, their calls would be heeded and produce better living conditions in the second half of the nineteenth century.

New Social Classes: The Industrial Middle Class

The rise of industrial capitalism (a capitalist system based on industrial production rather than trade, as in commercial capitalism) produced a new middle-class group—the industrial middle class. The **bourgeois,** or middle-class person, was not new. The bourgeoisie (middle class) had existed since the emergence of cities in the Middle Ages. Originally, the bourgeois was the burgher or town dweller, who may have been active as a merchant, official, artisan, lawyer, or person of letters. The term *bourgeois* came also to include people involved in industry and banking, as well as professionals, such as lawyers, teachers, doctors, and government officials. At the lower end of the economic scale were master craftspeople and shopkeepers.

The new industrial middle class was made up of the people who built the factories, bought the machines, and figured out where the markets were. Their qualities included initiative; vision; ambition; and often, of course, greed. One cotton manufacturer said, "Getting of money . . . is the main business of the life of men." This was not an easy task, however. The opportunities for making money were great, but the risks were also tremendous.

Members of the industrial middle class sought to separate themselves from the working classes below them. In the first half of the nineteenth century, the industrial working class was actually a mixture of different groups. In the course of the nineteenth century,

RETEACHING ACTIVITY

Have students assume that they are small landowners who lost their lands due to economic changes in the British countryside. In a brief essay, have students explain their changed position and lifestyle as they and their families move to Manchester to gain employment in one of the new factories.

however, factory workers came to form the majority of the working class.

New Social Classes: The Industrial Working Class

Industrial workers faced wretched working conditions. Work hours ranged from 12 to 16 hours a day, 6 days a week, with a half-hour for lunch and dinner. There was no security of employment and no minimum wage. The worst conditions were in the cotton mills, where temperatures were especially harmful. One report noted that "in the cotton-spinning work, these creatures are kept, fourteen hours in each day, locked up, summer and winter, in a heat of from eighty to eighty-four degrees." Mills were also dirty, dusty, dangerous, and unhealthy. Reformers were especially critical of the treatment of married women. One reported, "We have repeatedly seen married females, in the last stage of pregnancy, slaving from morning to night beside these never-tiring machines, and when . . . they were obliged to sit down to take a moment's ease, were fined by the manager."

Conditions in the coal mines were also harsh. Although steam-powered engines were used to lift coal from the mines to the top, inside the mines men still bore the burden of digging the coal out. Horses, mules, women, and children hauled coal carts on rails to the lift. Dangerous conditions, including cave-ins, explosions, and gas fumes (called "bad air"), were a way of life. The cramped conditions in mines—tunnels were often only three or four feet high—and their constant dampness led to deformed bodies and ruined lungs.

Both children and women worked in large numbers in early factories and mines (see "Young People in the Industrial Revolution: Child Labor"). By 1830, women and children made up two-thirds of the cotton industry's workforce. However, the number of children declined under the Factory Act of 1833, which set 9 as the minimum age for employment. Children between 9 and 13 could work only 8 hours a day; those between 13 and 18, could work 12 hours.

As the number of children employed declined, their places were taken by women. Women made up 50 percent of the labor force in textile (cotton and woolen)

▲ *Saltaire, shown here, was considered a model textile town. It was built near Bradford, England, by Titus Salt in 1851. Why would a factory owner have developed an entire town around his mill?*

factories before 1870. They were mostly unskilled labor and were paid half or less than half of what men received. Excessive working hours for women were finally outlawed in 1844.

The employment of children and women was in large part carried over from an earlier pattern. Husband, wife, and children had always worked together in cottage industry. Thus, it seemed perfectly natural to continue this pattern. Men who moved from the countryside to industrial towns and cities took their wives and children with them into the factory or into the mines. The desire for this family work often came from the family itself. The factory owner Jedediah Strutt was opposed to employing children under age 10 but was forced by parents to take children as young as 7.

The Factory Acts that limited the work hours of children and women also led to a new pattern of work. Men were expected to earn most of the family income by working outside the home. Women, in contrast, took over daily care of the family and performed low-paying jobs, such as laundry work, that could be done in the home. Working at home for pay made it possible for women to continue to help with family survival.

COOPERATIVE LEARNING ACTIVITY

Divide the class into groups and provide each group with a selection from such Dickens works as *Oliver Twist, Hard Times,* or *The Old Curiosity Shop.* Let each group use their selection to write an exposé style newspaper article on working class conditions in Britain during the Industrial Revolution. Compile the articles into a newsletter/newspaper for the class. You might want to have students add political cartoons, want ads, etc.

YOUNG PEOPLE IN THE INDUSTRIAL REVOLUTION

LEARNING FROM VISUALS

Answer to the caption question: Initially children were considered a part of the normal family workforce, just as they had been on the farm. Later, to increase profitability, factory owners lobbied to prevent protective child labor laws.

Answers to Critical Thinking Questions

1. Children faced terrible working conditions; worked long hours for little pay and were often physically abused to keep them at work.
2. Owners permitted such conditions and treatment because it was more profitable for them. There was an abundant supply of children, so they were easily replaced.

ASSESS

You can choose from a variety of assessments to evaluate your students' mastery of the objectives for this section as stated on page 652. Possible assessments include:

1. Section Review Questions on this page
2. Section 21–1 Quiz in your Teacher Resource materials
3. Reteaching Worksheets in your Teacher Resource materials
4. Self-Study software

Child Labor

▶ *Small children were often employed in textile mills, and they were carefully supervised to ensure that they worked hard. Why do you think there were no laws to protect children from this kind of exploitation?*

Children had been an important part of the family economy in preindustrial times. They worked in the fields or carded and spun wool at home with the growth of cottage industry. In the Industrial Revolution, however, child labor was exploited. The owners of cotton factories in England found child labor very helpful. Children had a delicate touch as spinners of cotton. Their smaller size

Early Socialism

In the first half of the nineteenth century, the pitiful conditions found in the slums, mines, and factories created by the Industrial Revolution gave rise to a movement known as socialism. Early socialism was largely the product of intellectuals who believed in the equality of all people and who wanted to replace competition with cooperation in industry. To later socialists, especially the followers of Karl Marx, such ideas were merely impractical dreams. The later socialists, in contempt of the earlier theorists, labeled them **utopian socialists.** The term has lasted to this day.

Robert Owen, a British cotton manufacturer, was one utopian socialist. He believed that humans would show their true natural goodness if they lived in a cooperative environment. At New Lanark in Scotland, Owen transformed a squalid factory town into a flourishing, healthy community. He also tried to create a cooperative community at New Harmony, Indiana, in the United States in the 1820s. However, fighting within the community eventually destroyed Owen's dream.

ENRICHMENT ACTIVITY

Assign students to write a hypothetical letter from a British industrialist in 1776 to a potential investor. Include a description of the cotton mill, its efficiency and productive capacity, and the potential this creates for earning profit. How does this show that a policy of laissez-faire may not be the best policy for society?

YOUNG PEOPLE IN THE INDUSTRIAL REVOLUTION

Child Labor, continued

made it easier for them to move under machines to gather loose cotton. Furthermore, they were more easily trained to factory work.

Discipline was often harsh. A report from a British parliamentary inquiry into the condition of child factory workers in 1838 stated:

It is a very frequent thing at Mr. Marshall's [at Shrewsbury] where the least children were employed (for there were plenty working at six years of age), for Mr. Horseman to start the mill earlier in the morning than he formerly did; and provided a child should be drowsy, the overlooker walks round the room with a stick in his hand, and he touches that child on the shoulder, and says, "Come here." In a corner of the room there is an iron cistern; it is filled with water; he takes this boy, and takes him up by the legs, and dips him over head in the cistern, and sends him to work for the remainder of the day. . . .

What means were taken to keep the children to their work?—Sometimes they would tap them over the head, or nip them over the nose, or give them a pinch of snuff, or throw water in their faces, or pull them off where they were, and job them about to keep them waking.

The same inquiry also reported that in some factories, children were often severely flogged (beat with a rod or whip) to keep them at work.

Children represented a cheap supply of labor. In 1821, 49 percent of the British people were under 20 years of age. Hence, children made up a large pool of laborers. They were paid only about one-sixth to one-third of what a man was paid. In the cotton factories in 1838, children under the age of 18 made up 29 percent of the total workforce. In cotton mills, children as young as age 7 worked 12 to 15 hours per day, 6 days a week.

---

1. What kind of working conditions did children face in the factories during the early Industrial Revolution?

2. Why did factory owners permit such conditions and such treatment of children?

 SECTION REVIEW

1. **Define:**
   (*a*) puddling,
   (*b*) bourgeois,
   (*c*) utopian socialists

2. **Identify:**
   (*a*) steam engine,
   (*b*) Great Famine,

   (*c*) Factory Act of 1833,
   (*d*) Karl Marx

3. **Recall:**
   (*a*) What economic shift was experienced in Europe during the Industrial Revolution?
   (*b*) Why were railroads important to the success of the Industrial Revolution?

4. **Think Critically:** In what ways must the growth of the Industrial Revolution have changed the way families lived?

COOPERATIVE LEARNING ACTIVITY

Assign students to one of two groups: factory owners and factory workers. Have the two groups prepare a debate outlining the major differences between them. The owners can research the basic ideas behind Social Darwinism and the capitalist system while the workers can draw on the ideas of Robert Owen. Finish the lesson by assigning the students to write essays in which they must take a side.

Answers to SECTION REVIEW

1. (a) a process for producing better quality pig iron
   (b) an affluent, largely urban middle class that grew in number during the Industrial Revolution
   (c) people who believed in the equality of all people and wanted to replace competition with cooperation in industry
2. (a) machine invented by James Watt in the 1760s
   (b) a series of failures of the potato crop in Ireland between 1845–1851
   (c) law that set minimum standards for hours and age of employment in Great Britain
   (d) a leading utopian socialist
3. (a) a shift from an economy based on farming and handicrafts to one based on manufacturing by machines and industrial factories
   (b) provided cheap transportation, supplied jobs, created a market for industrial products
4. answers will vary but may include: forcing people off the land into cities and factory jobs; making people adhere to a regular schedule, subjecting them to greater poverty, overcrowding and illness; weakening the power of adults to guide the lives of their children

CLOSE

Lead students in a discussion of the 'Focus' objectives identified on page 652. Emphasize the impact of the Industrial Revolution on Europe's social and political systems.

FOCUS

OBJECTIVES

After completing this section, students should be able to

1. explain changes in the popularity and power of conservative, liberal, and nationalist movements
2. identify and explain reasons for revolutionary outbursts in Europe
3. describe causes for and results of the revolutions of 1848

FOCUS ACTIVITY

Help students understand that attempts to maintain the status quo are likely to fail. Discuss an important political or social event from thirty or more years ago. Ask students to explain why this event could no longer happen in the same way. Why do attempts to keep conditions the same fail?

REACTION AND REVOLUTION: THE GROWTH OF NATIONALISM, 1815 TO 1848

After the defeat of Napoleon, European rulers moved to restore much of the old order. This was the goal of the great powers—Great Britain, Austria, Prussia, and Russia—when they met at the Congress of Vienna in September 1814 to arrange a final peace settlement. The leader of the congress was the Austrian foreign minister, Prince Klemens von Metternich (MET-ur-NIK), who claimed that he was guided at Vienna by the **principle of legitimacy.** This meant that the lawful monarchs were restored to their positions of power in order to keep peace and stability in Europe. This had already been done in France with the restoration of the Bourbon monarchy.

In fact, however, the principle of legitimacy was largely ignored elsewhere. At the Congress of Vienna, the great powers all grabbed lands to add to their states. In doing so, they believed that they were forming a new balance of power that would keep any one country from dominating Europe.

The peace arrangements worked out at the Congress of Vienna were a victory for conservative rulers, who wanted to contain the forces of change unleashed by the French Revolution. Those like Metternich believed in the ideology known as **conservatism.** Most conservatives at that time favored obedience to political authority and believed that organized religion was crucial to order in society. Moreover, they hated revolutions and were unwilling to accept the liberal demands for either individual rights or representative

Map 21.2   Europe after the Congress of Vienna

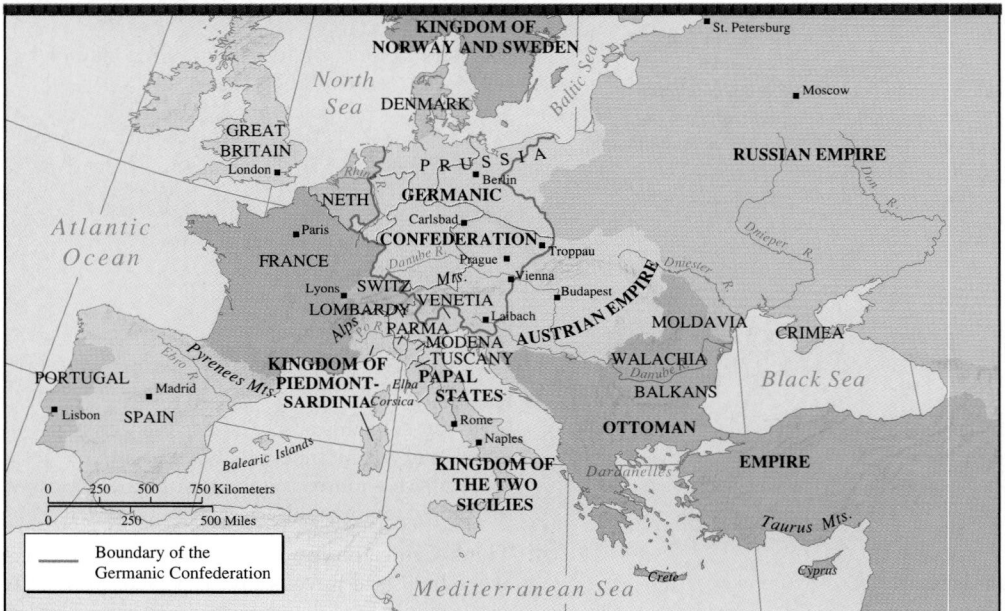

STUDYING MAPS

The following questions will help you guide students through their study of Map 21.2.

1. What changes can you identify from the map of Europe on page 617? (*Answers will vary, but may include Holy Roman Empire has disappeared, Germanic Confederation, Austrian Empire have appeared*)

2. Why did the German Confederation have limited access to the sea? (*Its coastline was limited.*)

3. What states would have been concerned about growth of the German Confederation? (*all of the states surrounding it, as well as states that might eventually feel threatened*)

governments. After 1815, the political philosophy of conservatism was supported by hereditary monarchs, government bureaucracies, landowning aristocracies, and churches, be they Protestant or Catholic. The conservative forces were dominant after 1815.

One method used by the great powers to maintain the new status quo was the Concert of Europe. Great Britain, Russia, Prussia, and Austria (and later France) agreed to meet at times in conferences to discuss their common interests and to take steps that would maintain the peace in Europe. Eventually, the great powers adopted a **principle of intervention.** This was the right of the great powers to send armies into countries where there were revolutions in order to restore legitimate monarchs to their thrones. Britain refused to agree to the principle, arguing that the great powers should not interfere in the internal affairs of other states. Austria, Prussia, Russia, and France ignored the British and used military forces to crush revolutions in Spain and Italy, as well as to restore legitimate (and conservative) monarchs to their thrones.

Revolutionary Outbursts

Between 1815 and 1830, conservative governments throughout Europe worked to maintain the old order. However, powerful forces for change—known as **liberalism** and nationalism—were also at work.

Liberalism owed much to the Enlightenment of the eighteenth century and the American and French Revolutions at the end of that century. Liberals had different opinions at times, but they all agreed that liberalism was the idea that people should be as free from restraint as possible.

Liberals came to hold a common set of political beliefs. Chief among them was the protection of civil liberties, or the basic rights of all people. The civil liberties included equality before the law and freedom of assembly, speech, and press. All of these freedoms

◀ *Prince Klemens von Metternich, shown in this formal portrait, was both a powerful and persuasive politician. He was a dominant member of the Congress of Vienna and one of the main supporters of legitimacy and intervention.*

should be guaranteed by a written document, such as the American Bill of Rights. Most liberals wanted religious toleration for all, as well as separation of church and state. Liberals also demanded the right of peaceful opposition to the government both from within and from outside, and the making of laws by a representative assembly (legislature) elected by qualified voters. Many liberals believed, then, in a constitutional monarchy or constitutional state (rule by a constitution). They believed that written constitutions would guarantee the rights they sought to preserve.

Liberals were not democrats, however. They thought that the right to vote and hold office should be open only to men of property. Liberalism, then, was tied to middle-class men, and especially industrial middle-class men, who wanted voting rights for themselves so that they could share power with the landowning classes. The liberals feared mob rule and had little desire to let the lower classes share that power.

Nationalism was an even more powerful force for change in the nineteenth century than was liberalism. Nationalism arose out of an awareness of being part of a community that has common institutions, traditions, language, and customs. This community is called a *nation*. The chief political loyalty of individuals should be to the nation rather than to a dynasty, city-state, or other political unit.

Nationalism did not become a popular force for change until the French Revolution. From then on, nationalists came to believe that each nationality should have its own government. Thus, the Germans, who were not united, wanted national unity in a Ger-

---

TEACH

─Multimedia Support─

TRANSPARENCY
21–2, Europe after the Congress of Vienna (Map 21.2)

REINFORCING VOCABULARY

Ask students to identify ideas that are representative of conservatism at the present time. Do they believe acceptance of these ideas will last over time?

CLASS DISCUSSION

Have students think through and debate the views of conservatives and liberals. You might have them evaluate the success of the Congress of Vienna based on the two views.

RECOMMENDED READING

For a good, up-to-date survey of the entire nineteenth century, see R. Gildea, *Barricades and Borders: Europe 1800–1914* (Oxford, 1987) in the Short Oxford History of the Modern World series. Also valuable is M. S. Anderson, *The Ascendancy of Europe, 1815–1914*, 2d ed. (London, 1985). For surveys of the period covered in this chapter, see C. Breunig, *The Age of Revolution and Reaction, 1789–1850,* 2d ed, (New York, 1979); and J. Droz, *Europe between Revolutions, 1815–1848* (London, 1967). There are also some useful books on individual countries that cover more than the subject of this chapter. These include R. Magraw, *France, 1815–1914: The Bourgeois Century* (London, 1983); H. Seton-Watson, *The Russian Empire, 1801–1917* (Oxford, 1967); H. Holborn, *A History of Modern Germany* vol. 2, *1648–1840* (New York, 1964).

LEARNING FROM VISUALS

Ask students to describe what they believe caused the man with the sword in the picture to the right to be a leader in the rebellion. What might he have been thinking at this time?

CLASS DISCUSSION

Ask students to discuss their opinions of the following statement. Why do they support or oppose it?

"Acts of civil disobedience, violence, and terrorism have made guaranteeing personal freedoms less desirable for society."

TEACHING THEMES

Politics and History. Ask students to explain why people in Europe would be likely to feel a greater sense of nationalism after the wars in the Napoleonic era.

▶ *On July 25, 1830, Charles X dissolved the French legislative chamber and suspended freedom of the press. The reaction of the Parisians was immediate, and Charles X was overthrown. This painting shows a scene from the July 1830 revolution when students, former soldiers, and middle-class citizens joined together to demand a republic. The attempt to stop these rebels was feeble and short lived.*

man nation-state with one central government. Subject peoples, such as the Hungarians, wanted the right to establish their own governments rather than be subject to the emperor of the Austrian Empire.

Nationalism, then, was a threat to the existing political order. A united Germany, for example, would upset the balance of power set up at Vienna in 1815. At the same time, an independent Hungarian state would mean the breakup of the Austrian Empire. Conservatives feared such change and thus tried hard to repress nationalism.

Beginning in 1830, the forces of change—liberalism and nationalism—began to break through the conservative domination of Europe. In France, liberals overthrew the Bourbon monarch Charles X in 1830 and established a constitutional monarchy. Political support for the new monarch, Louis-Philippe (LOO-ee fi-LEEP), came from the upper middle class.

Liberals played an important role in the 1830 revolution in France, but nationalism was the chief force in three other revolutions the same year. The Belgians, who had been annexed to the Dutch Republic in 1815, rebelled and created an independent state. Revolutions

in Poland and Italy were much less successful. Russian forces crushed the attempt of Poles to free themselves from foreign domination. Austrian troops marched into Italy and crushed revolts in a number of Italian states.

The Revolutions of 1848

Despite the liberal and nationalist successes in France and Belgium, the conservative order still dominated much of Europe. However, the forces of liberalism and nationalism continued to grow. In 1848, these forces of change erupted once more.

As before, revolution in France was once again the spark for revolution in other countries. Severe economic problems beginning in 1846 brought untold hardship in France to the lower middle class, workers, and peasants. At the same time, members of the middle class clamored for the right to vote. As the government of Louis-Philippe refused to make changes, opposition grew. The monarchy was finally overthrown on February 24, 1848. A group of moderate and radical republicans (people who wanted to set up a republic)

So What ⁉️

If your students question the importance of information on **nationalism,** *tell them . . .*

Even today, the most important lever for change in the world comes from the desire for national sovereignty. Nationalism has been the cause for every major war in the twentieth century and will undoubtedly continue to cause problems in the century to follow. Mankind is a territorial animal. Instead

of using scent, we mark our borders with both natural and unnatural barriers. We use religion, skin coloring, and language to separate each other. Modern-day gangs differ very little from Serbs, Croats, and Muslims in their efforts to defend their turf. Even though we are of the same species, the only species of human beings, people insist on seeing only the differences.

set up a provisional (temporary) government. They called for the election by **universal male suffrage** (all adult men could vote) of a Constituent Assembly that would draw up a new constitution.

The provisional government also set up national workshops to provide work for the unemployed. From March to June, the number of unemployed enrolled in the national workshops rose from 6,100 to almost 120,000. This emptied the treasury and frightened the moderates, who reacted by closing the workshops on June 21. The workers refused to accept this decision and poured into the streets. Four days of bitter and bloody fighting by government forces crushed the working-class revolt. Thousands were killed, and 11,000 prisoners were sent to the French colony of Algeria in northern Africa.

The new constitution, ratified on November 4, 1848, set up a republic, called the Second Republic. The Second Republic had a single legislature elected by universal male suffrage. A president, also chosen by universal male suffrage, served for four years. In the elections for the presidency held in December 1848, Charles Louis Napoleon Bonaparte, the nephew of the famous French ruler, won a resounding victory. Within four years, President Napoleon would become Emperor Napoleon (see later in this chapter).

News of the 1848 revolution in France led to upheaval in central Europe as well (see "You Are There: Revolutionary Excitement"). The Vienna settlement in 1815 had recognized the existence of 38 independent German states (called the Germanic Confederation). Austria and Prussia were the two great powers, whereas the other states varied in size. In 1848, cries for change led many German rulers to promise constitutions, a free press, jury trials, and other liberal reforms. In Prussia, King Frederick William IV agreed to establish a new constitution and work for a united Germany.

The governments of all the German states allowed elections by universal male suffrage for deputies to an all-German parliament called the Frankfurt Assembly. Its purpose was to fulfill a liberal and nationalist dream—the preparation of a constitution for a new united Germany. However, the Frankfurt Assembly failed to achieve its goal. The members had no real

CONNECTIONS
TO OUR WORLD

Russian Troops in Hungary   On November 1, 1956, Imry Nagy, leader of Hungary, declared Hungary a free nation and promised new elections. Fearing that these elections would mean the end of Communist rule in Hungary, Nikita Khrushchev, leader of the Soviet Union, reacted dramatically. On November 4, 200,000 Soviet (mostly Russian) troops and 4,000 Soviet tanks invaded Budapest, Hungary's capital city. An estimated 50,000 Hungarians died on that day. Nagy fled but was later arrested and executed. The Hungarian Revolution of 1956 had failed.

To Hungarians who knew their country's history, the use of Russian troops to crush their independence had an all-too-familiar ring. In 1848, Louis Kossuth had led a revolt that forced Hungary's Austrian rulers to grant Hungary its own legislature and a separate national army. Nevertheless, the Austrians remained unwilling to give up their control of Hungary. Austrian armies, however, had little success in defeating Hungarian forces fighting for their country's independence. In April, 1849, the Hungarian legislature declared Hungary a republic. Kossuth was made the new president. Unable to subdue the Hungarians, the Austrian government asked the Russians for help. Tsar Nicholas I of Russia, who feared revolution anywhere, gladly agreed to help. A Russian army of 140,000 men crushed the Hungarian forces, and Kossuth fled abroad. The Hungarian Revolution of 1848–1849 had failed.

means of forcing the German rulers to accept the constitution they had drawn up. German unification was not achieved. The revolution had failed.

The Austrian Empire also had its problems and needed only the news of the revolution in Paris to erupt in flames in March 1848. The Austrian Empire was a **multinational state,** or collection of different peoples, including Germans, Czechs, Magyars (Hungarians), Slovaks, Romanians, Slovenes, Poles, Croats,

TEACHING THEMES

Economics and History. Ask students to evaluate the fact that severe economic problems among the poor of France did not cause a revolt in 1846 but the desire of the middle classes for political rights in 1848 did. What does this tell students about the need for leadership and coordination in a revolution?

COMPARING TIME PERIODS

Ask students to compare the objectives, methods, and results of efforts to help unemployed people in France after the 1848 revolution and in the United States at the present.

CLASS DISCUSSION

Ask students to compare the problems of the former Soviet Union with those of the multinational state of the Austrian Empire.

RETEACHING ACTIVITY

Assign students to create a list of grievances the people of France had against the Old Order and to describe the extent to which each was resolved by the revolution in 1848. Do revolutions often solve people's problems? Why or why not?

TEACHING THEMES

Politics and History. Ask students to write a statement about the possible unification of Germany as it might have been written by the ruler of a small German state in 1848.

YOU ARE THERE

USING PRIMARY SOURCES

Ask students to describe their personal attitude toward political events in other countries. Why do they believe Carl Schurz would be so excited about political events when many young people today seem not to care?

CLASS DISCUSSION

Ask students to discuss their opinions of the following statement. Do they believe it is true or false?

"It is impossible for an oppressive government to give its people just a little freedom."

YOU ARE THERE
Revolutionary Excitement

▶ *In 1848, Austrian students joined the revolutionary civil guard that took control of Vienna and demanded that the emperor call an assembly to draft a constitution. The revolt was short lived. By 1849, the emperor and his powers were restored. This painting depicts students planning the 1848 actions.*

The excitement with which German liberals and nationalists received the news of the revolution in France and their own expectations for Germany are captured well in this selection from the Reminiscences *of Carl Schurz (SHOOurTS). After the failure of the German revolution of 1848, Schurz went to the United States, where he fought in the Civil War and became secretary of the interior.*

Carl Schurz, *Reminiscences*
One morning, toward the end of February, 1848, I sat quietly in my attic-chamber, working hard at my tragedy of "Ulrich von Hutten" [a sixteenth-century German knight], when suddenly a friend rushed breathlessly into the room, exclaiming: "What, you sitting here! Do you not know what has happened?"

Serbians, and Italians. Only the Habsburg emperor provided a common bond. The Germans, though only a quarter of the population, played a leading role in the governing of the Austrian Empire. The Hungarians, however, wanted their own legislature.

In March, demonstrations in the major cities led to the dismissal of Metternich, the Austrian foreign minister, who fled abroad. In Vienna, revolutionary forces took control of the capital and demanded a liberal constitution. Hungary was given its own legislature and a

ENRICHMENT ACTIVITY

Have students study the reminiscences of Carl Schurz on this and the following page, then ask students to consider how an old guard conservative would reply to him. Have students write an essay in which they summarize each position and tell which they agree with. You might wish to organize a class debate as might have transpired between Carl Schurz and a conservative government official.

YOU ARE THERE
Revolutionary Excitement, continued

"No; what?"

"The French have driven away Louis Philippe and proclaimed the republic."

I threw down my pen—and that was the end of "Ulrich von Hutten." I never touched the manuscript again. We tore down the stairs, into the street, to the market-square, the accustomed meeting-place for all the student societies after their midday dinner. Although it was still forenoon, the market was already crowded with young men talking excitedly. . . . We were dominated by a vague feeling as if a great outbreak of elemental forces had begun, as if an earthquake was impending of which we had felt the first shock, and we instinctively crowded together. . . .

The next morning there were the usual lectures to be attended. But how profitless! The voice of the professor sounded like a monotonous drone coming from far away. What he had to say did not seem to concern us. At last we closed with a sigh the notebook and went away, pushed by a feeling that now we had something more important to do—to devote ourselves to the affairs of the fatherland. . . . Certain ideas and catchwords worked themselves to the surface, which expressed more or less the feelings of the people. Now had arrived in Germany the day for the establishment of "German Unity," and the founding of a great, powerful national German Empire. In the first line the meeting of a national parliament. Then the

demands for civil rights and liberties, free speech, free press, the right of free assembly, equality before the law, a freely elected representation of the people with legislative power . . . the word democracy was soon on all tongues, and many, too, thought it a matter of course that if the princes should try to withhold from the people the rights and liberties demanded, force would take the place of mere petition. Of course the regeneration of the fatherland must, if possible, be accomplished by peaceable means. Like many of my friends, I was dominated by the feeling that at last the great opportunity had arrived for giving to the German people the liberty which was their birthright and to the German fatherland its unity and greatness, and that it was now the first duty of every German to do and to sacrifice everything for this sacred object.

---

1. Why were Schurz and other Germans so excited about the revolution in France?

2. Were the German students willing to fight for their freedom?

3. Schurz states that "it was now the first duty of every German to do and to sacrifice everything for this sacred project." The sacred project was freedom and liberty. Would you be willing to sacrifice everything for your freedom and liberty? Why or why not?

separate national army. In Bohemia, the Czechs began to clamor for their own government as well.

Austrian officials had made concessions to appease the revolutionaries, but they were determined to reestablish their firm control. As did officials in France

and the German states, the Austrian officials welcomed the divisions between radical and moderate revolutionaries and played upon the middle-class fear of a working-class social revolution. In June 1848, Austrian military forces crushed the Czech rebels in Prague. By

---

Answers to Critical Thinking Questions:

1. It excited them because they felt that the freedom of the German people could not be far behind. They would demand their own rights and liberties.
2. Yes.
3. Answers will vary.

ASSESS

You can choose from a variety of assessments to evaluate your students' mastery of the objectives for this section as stated on page 662. Possible assessments include:

1. Section Review Questions on this page
2. Section 21–2 Quiz in your Teacher Resource materials
3. Reteaching Worksheets in your Teacher Resource materials
4. Self-Study software

CNN® WORLD HISTORY UPDATES

You can update your coverage of World History topics, as well as spark lively classroom discussion and deeper understanding, by using the **CNN World History Updates.**

For assistance in using and incorporating the **CNN World History Updates** into your classroom presentations, see the *Classroom Guide.*

Answers to SECTION REVIEW

2 (a) a claim made by Prince Kelmens von Metternich at the end of the Napoleonic Wars that stated the families of the former legitimate monarchs should be restored to the power they had before the wars

(b) a resistance to change

(c) an assumed right of great powers to send armies into countries where there were revolutions to restore legitimate monarchs to their thrones

(d) a general willingness to accept change

(e) the right of all adult men to vote

(f) a collection of peoples with different nationalities in one political unit

3. (a) a meeting of the leaders of Europe in 1814 that made final peace settlements at the end of the Napoleonic Wars

(b) a document that guarantees individual civil rights to American citizens

(c) nephew of Napoleon Bonaparte, became president then Emperor of France after 1848

(d) the recognition of thirty-eight independent German states in 1815

4. (a) many monarchies at that time combined people of many nationalities who wanted their own governments

(b) could not agree on their aims, failed to work together to maintain their power

5. Answers should discuss: Industrial Revolution forced people to move, travel to look for work, become more aware of the inequities, changed distribution of wealth and power

the end of October, the rebels had been crushed in Vienna. However, it was only with the help of a Russian army of 140,000 men that the Hungarian revolution was finally crushed in 1849. The revolutions in the Austrian Empire had failed.

So, too, did the revolutions in Italy. The Congress of Vienna had set up nine states in Italy, including the kingdom of Sardinia in the north; the kingdom of the Two Sicilies (Naples and Sicily); the Papal States; a handful of small states; and the northern provinces of Lombardy and Venetia (vi-NEE-shuh), which were now part of the Austrian Empire. In 1848, a revolt broke out against the Austrians in Lombardy and Venetia. Revolutionaries in other Italian states also took up arms and sought to create liberal constitutions. By 1849, however, the Austrians had reestablished complete control over Lombardy and Venetia. The old order also prevailed in the rest of Italy.

Throughout Europe in 1848, popular revolutions had brought about the formation of liberal constitutions and liberal governments. Moderate, middle-class liberals and radical workers were soon divided over their aims, though, and authoritarian regimes were soon reestablished. However, the forces of nationalism and liberalism were by no means dead.

SECTION REVIEW

1. **Locate:**
   (a) Vienna, (b) Prague

2. **Define:**
   (a) principle of legitimacy, (b) conservatism, (c) principle of intervention, (d) liberalism, (e) universal male suffrage, (f) multinational state

3. **Identify:**
   (a) Congress of Vienna, (b) American Bill of Rights, (c) Charles Louis Napoleon Bonaparte, (d) the Germanic Confederation

4. **Recall:**
   (a) Why was nationalism a threat to the existing order in nineteenth-century Europe?

(b) Why did liberal forces who won political rights from the rule of monarchs typically lose their power after a relatively few years?

5. **Think Critically:** How may social and economic changes forced on Europe by the Industrial Revolution have contributed to the spread of liberalism?

NATIONAL UNIFICATION AND THE NATIONAL STATE, 1848 TO 1871

The revolutions of 1848 had failed. Within 25 years, however, many of the goals sought by the liberals and nationalists during the first half of the nineteenth century were achieved. Italy and Germany became nations, and many European states were led by constitutional monarchs.

Breakdown of the Concert of Europe

The growth of nationalism produced dramatic changes in two European countries by 1871: both Italy and Germany became unified. They were able to do so because of the breakdown of the system created by the Concert of Europe. The Crimean (krie-ME-uhn) War played a crucial role in the breakdown.

The Crimean War was the result of a long-standing struggle between Russia and the Ottoman Empire The Ottoman Empire had long been in control of much of southeastern Europe (an area known as the Balkans). By the beginning of the nineteenth century, however, the Ottoman Empire was in decline, and its authority over its territories in southeastern Europe began to weaken. As a result, European states began to take an active interest in the disintegration of the "sick man of Europe," as they called the Ottoman Empire. Russia was especially interested in expanding its power into Ottoman lands in the Balkans and gaining access to the Dardanelles and thus, the Mediterranean Sea.

On Line with WORLD HISTORY *Internet Activity*

You may want to have your students visit the following URL, where they will find information and additional web site resources to enhance their study of this chapter.

Victorian Web

http://www.stg.brown.edu/projects/ hypertext/landow/victorian/victov.html

This is an excellent source on the whole Victorian Era. It covers all areas from literature to economics to politics.

Due to the ever-changing nature of the World Wide Web, see the West History web site, **http://history.swpco.com** for regular updates of the URLs in this text.

Map 21.3 The Unification of Italy

Kingdom of Piedmont, before 1859

To Kingdom of Piedmont, 1859

To Kingdom of Piedmont, 1860

To Kingdom of Italy, 1866; 1870

Such a move would make Russia the major power in eastern Europe and would enable the Russians to challenge British naval control of the eastern Mediterranean. Other European powers feared Russian ambitions and had their own interest in the decline of the Ottoman Empire.

When the Russians invaded the Turkish provinces of Moldavia and Walachia (wah-LAE-kee-uh), the Ottoman Turks declared war on Russia on October 4, 1853. In the following year, on March 28, Great Britain and France, fearful of Russian gains, declared war on Russia. The Crimean War, as the conflict came to be called, was poorly planned and poorly fought. Heavy losses caused the Russians to sue for peace. By the Treaty of Paris, signed in March 1856, Russia

agreed to allow Moldavia and Walachia to be placed under the protection of all the great powers.

The Crimean War destroyed the Concert of Europe. Austria and Russia had been the two chief powers maintaining the status quo in the first half of the nineteenth century. They were now enemies, because Austria, which had its own interests in the Balkans, had refused to support Russia in the Crimean War. A defeated and humiliated Russia withdrew from European affairs for the next 20 years. Austria was now without friends among the great powers. This new international situation opened the door for the unification of both Italy and Germany.

National Unification: Italy

In 1850, Austria was still the dominant power on the Italian peninsula. After the failure of the revolution of 1848 to 1849, more and more Italians saw the northern Italian state of Piedmont, ruled by the royal house of Savoy, as their best hope to achieve the unification of Italy. It was doubtful, however, that the little state could unify Italy, or so it seemed, until King Victor Emmanuel II named Count Camillo di Cavour as his prime minister in 1852.

Cavour was a dedicated political leader. As prime minister, he pursued a policy of economic expansion that increased government revenues and enabled Piedmont to equip a large army. Cavour, however, knew that Piedmont's army was not strong enough to beat the Austrians. He would need help. Consequently, he made an alliance with the French emperor Louis Napoleon and then provoked the Austrians into

CLOSE

Lead students in a discussion of the 'Focus' objectives identified on page 662. Emphasize how conflicts between conservatives and liberals led to nationalism and revolution in Europe.

FOCUS

OBJECTIVES

After completing this section, students should be able to

1. identify and explain reasons for the failure of the Concert of Europe
2. describe events that led to the unification of Italy
3. describe events that led to the unification of Germany
4. explain relationships between nationalism and reforms in Europe
5. describe developments in the United States and Canada

FOCUS ACTIVITY

Help students understand that compromise is generally necessary to achieve lasting unity. Ask students to consider the example of nations in Eastern Europe that were forced into the Soviet bloc after World War II. These nations never fully cooperated with the Soviet Union and took their first opportunity to declare their independence in the 1980s.

STUDYING MAPS

The following questions will help you guide students through their study of Map 21.3.

1. What are the dimensions of Italy? *(about 150 miles across and 675 miles long)*
2. How might the geography of Italy have caused its southern region to be less economically developed than the North? *(The southern region is less accessible by land than the northern region.)*

3. Once it was united, why was most of Italy more difficult to attack than many other European nations? *(because of the length of the country and because troops would have had to be transported by ship or carried overland for many miles)*

TEACH

CLASS DISCUSSION

Ask students to discuss whether they believe the Crimean War (discussed on page 669) destroyed the Concert of Europe or that this agreement was already doomed to failure by other forces.

LEARNING FROM VISUALS

Answer to the caption question: Social changes, as well as the efforts of strong leaders, combined to make unification of Italy possible. Students should recognize that Italy had a strong tradition of self-governed city-states that had fought against each other for power, prestige, and wealth. Only slowly did they band together.

▲ *This painting shows Giuseppe Garibaldi arriving in Sicily on May 11, 1860. Compare and contrast the development of Spain, France, and England with Italy, and explain why it took Italy so long to unify. Was unification due solely to the efforts of leaders such as Garibaldi and Cavour?*

invading Piedmont in 1859. In the early stages of fighting, it was mostly French armies that defeated the Austrians in two major battles. A peace settlement gave the French Nice and Savoy, which they had been promised for making the alliance. Lombardy was given to Piedmont. Cavour's success caused nationalists in some northern Italian states (Parma, Modena, and Tuscany) to overthrow their governments and join their states to Piedmont.

Meanwhile, in southern Italy, a new leader of Italian unification had arisen. Giuseppe Garibaldi (joo-SEP-ee GAR-uh-BAWL-dee), a dedicated Italian patriot,

raised an army of 1,000 volunteers called Red Shirts because of the color of their uniforms. Garibaldi's forces landed in Sicily, where a revolt had broken out against the Bourbon king of the Two Sicilies. By the end of July 1860, most of Sicily was under Garibaldi's control. In August, Garibaldi and his forces crossed over to the mainland and began a victorious march up the Italian peninsula. Naples, and with it the kingdom of the Two Sicilies, fell in early September. Everywhere he went, Garibaldi was hailed by the Italians as a great hero. One reporter wrote: "The people threw themselves forward to kiss his hands, or at least, to touch the hem of his garment. Children were brought up, and mothers asked on their knees for his blessing."

Alarmed by Garibaldi's success, Cavour sent Piedmontese forces to the south. Ever the patriot, Garibaldi chose not to fight another Italian army but to turn over his conquests to Piedmont. On March 17, 1861, a new kingdom of Italy was proclaimed under King Victor Emmanuel II of Piedmont.

The task of unification was not yet complete, however. Venetia in the north was still held by Austria, and Rome was under the control of the pope, supported by French troops. In the Austro-Prussian War of 1866, the new Italian state became an ally of Prussia. The Italian army was defeated by the Austrians, but Prussia's victory left the Italians with Venetia. In 1870, during the Franco-Prussian war (see "National Unification: Germany"), French troops withdrew from Rome. The Italian army then annexed Rome on September 20, 1870. Rome became the new capital of the united Italian state.

National Unification: Germany

After the failure of the Frankfurt Assembly to achieve German unification in 1848 and 1849, German nationalists focused on Austria and Prussia as the only two states powerful enough to unify Germany. Austria was a large multinational empire, however, and it feared the creation of a strong German state in central Europe. Consequently, more and more Germans looked to Prussia for leadership in the cause of German unification.

So What ⁇

*If your students question the importance of information on the **Unification of Germany**, tell them . . .*

World Wars I and II were essentially the same fight—for German hegemony in Europe. The location of the German Republic, and the cultural background of the German people has led to their domination of the entire continent. Even today, the German people enjoy the world's highest standard of living, despite the total destruction of World War II and its subsequent division for over forty years. Germany's influence on the world's stage will become increasingly important as a new generation, a united generation awakens. Hopefully they have learned a lesson that the first part of the twentieth century has taught—that there are other ways besides war to accomplish economic objectives.

Map 21.4   The Unification of Germany

COMPARING TIME PERIODS

Ask students to compare the problems Japan's leaders had to overcome to achieve unification, which were discussed in Chapter 10, with those faced by the Italians. What compromises had to be made by leaders in both states?

TEACHING THEMES

The Role of Individuals. Ask students to write an essay that describes what might have happened in Italy if Garibaldi had chosen to fight the Piedmont for control of Italy. What does this show about the difference individuals can make in history?

Multimedia Support

TRANSPARENCY

21–3, The Unification of Germany, (Map 21.4)

TEACHING THEMES

The Role of Individuals. Ask students to describe what might have happened to the German states if their leader had been less assertive and self-confident than Bismarck.

In the course of the nineteenth century, Prussia had become a strong and prosperous state. Its government was authoritarian. The Prussian king had firm control over both the government and the army. Prussia was also known for its **militarism,** or glorification of the military.

In the 1860s, King William I tried to enlarge the Prussian army. When the Prussian legislature refused to levy new taxes for the proposed military changes, William I appointed a new prime minister, Count Otto von Bismarck (BIZ-MARK). Bismarck ignored the leg-islative opposition to the military reforms. He argued instead that "Germany does not look to Prussia's liberalism but to her power. . . . Not by speeches and majorities will the great questions of the day be decided—that was the mistake of 1848–1849—but by iron and blood."[1] Bismarck proceeded to collect the taxes and strengthen the army. From 1862 to 1866, Bismarck governed Prussia by simply ignoring the parliament. In the meantime, opposition to his domestic policy led Bismarck to follow an active foreign policy, which led to war and German unification. Bismarck has often

STUDYING MAPS

The following questions will help you guide students through their study of Map 21.4.

1. Why did the North German Confederation have such an irregular shape? *(It was put together by Prussia from conquered lands.)*

2. What states suffered loss of lands when Germany was united? *(Denmark, Austria)*

3. Why would Russia be concerned about the unification and growth of Germany? *(Prussia and Russia shared a border. Prussia's increasing strength would be a threat to Russia.)*

▲ *On January 18, 1871, a new German Empire was formally established at a ceremony held in the Hall of Mirrors in Versailles. Bismarck is shown at the foot of the throne as William I is named Emperor William I of the Second German Empire. Why do you think Bismarck is the central figure in the painting, not the emperor?*

been seen as the ultimate realist. He was the foremost nineteenth-century practitioner of **realpolitik**—the "politics of reality," or politics based on practical matters rather than on theory or ethics. Bismarck was also open about his strong dislike of anyone who opposed him. He said one morning to his wife, "I could not sleep the whole night; I hated throughout the whole night."

Bismarck's first war was against Denmark and was fought over the duchies (DUTCH-eez) of Schleswig (SHLESS-WIG) and Holstein (HOLE-STINE). Bismarck persuaded the Austrians to join Prussia in declaring war on Denmark on February 1, 1864. The Danes, who were quickly defeated, surrendered Schleswig and Holstein to the victors. Austria and Prussia then agreed to divide the administration of the two duchies. Prussia took Schleswig, and Austria administered Holstein. However, Bismarck used the

joint administration of the two duchies to create friction with the Austrians and goad them into a war on June 14, 1866.

The Austrians proved to be no match for the well-disciplined Prussian army. The Prussians, with a superior network of railroads, could mass troops quickly. At Königgrätz (kuh-NIK-grats) (or Sadowa [zah-DOE-vuh]) on July 3, the Austrian army was decisively defeated. Prussia now organized the German states north of the Main River into a North German Confederation. The southern German states, which were largely Catholic, feared Protestant Prussia. However, they also feared France, their western neighbor. As a result, they agreed to sign military alliances with Prussia for protection against France.

Bismarck and King William I had achieved a major goal by 1866. Prussia now dominated all of northern

Germany, and Austria had been excluded from any role in German affairs. However, problems with France soon arose. Bismarck realized that France would never be content with a strong German state to its east because of the potential threat to French security. At the same time, Napoleon III, the French ruler, was in need of a diplomatic triumph to offset his serious domestic problems. In 1870, Prussia and France became embroiled in a dispute over the candidacy of a relative of the Prussian king for the throne of Spain. Bismarck took advantage of the misunderstandings between the French and Prussians to goad the French into declaring war on Prussia on July 15, 1870 (the Franco-Prussian War).

The French proved to be no match for the better led and better organized Prussian forces. The southern German states honored their military alliances with Prussia and joined the war effort against the French. The Prussian armies advanced into France. At Sedan, on September 2, 1870, an entire French army and Napoleon III himself were captured. Paris finally surrendered on January 28, 1871, and an official peace treaty was signed in May. France had to pay 5 billion francs (about $1 billion) and give up the provinces of Alsace (al-SASS) and Lorraine (luh-RANE) to the new German state. The loss of these territories left the French burning for revenge.

Even before the war had ended, the southern German states had agreed to enter the North German Confederation. On January 18, 1871, Bismarck and 600 German princes, nobles, and generals filled the Hall of Mirrors in the palace of Versailles, 12 miles outside Paris. The words "Long live His Imperial Majesty, the Emperor William!" rang out, and the assembled guests took up the cry. William I of Prussia had been proclaimed kaiser (KIE-zur), or emperor, of the Second German Empire (the first was the medieval Holy Roman Empire). German unity had been achieved by the Prussian monarchy and the Prussian army. The authoritarian and militaristic values of Prussia were triumphant in the new German state. With its industrial resources and military might, the new state had become the strongest power on the Continent. A new European balance of power was at hand.

Nationalism and Reform: Great Britain, France, the Austrian Empire, and Russia

While Italy and Germany were being unified, other states in Europe were also experiencing changes. Great Britain managed to avoid the revolutionary upheavals of the first half of the nineteenth century. In 1815, Great Britain was governed by the aristocratic landowning classes that dominated both houses of Parliament. However, in 1832, to avoid the revolutionary turmoil on the Continent, Parliament passed a Reform Bill that increased the numbers of male voters, chiefly members of the industrial middle class. By joining the industrial middle class to the landed interest in ruling Britain, Britain avoided revolution in 1848.

In the 1850s and 1860s, the liberal parliamentary system of Britain made both social and political reforms that enabled the country to remain stable. One of the other reasons for Britain's stability was its continuing economic growth. After 1850, middle-class prosperity was at last coupled with some improvements for the working classes as well. Real wages for laborers increased more than 25 percent between 1850 and 1870. The British feeling of national pride was well reflected in Queen Victoria, whose reign from 1837 to 1901 was the longest in English history. Victoria had 9 children and, when she died at age 81, 37 great-grandchildren. Her sense of duty and moral respectability reflected the attitudes of her age, which has ever since been known as the Victorian Age.

In France, events after the revolution of 1848 moved toward the restoration of the monarchy. Four years after his election as president, Louis Napoleon returned to the people to ask for the restoration of the empire. Ninety-seven percent responded with a yes vote. On December 2, 1852, Louis Napoleon assumed the title of Napoleon III. (The first Napoleon had abdicated [renounced the throne] in favor of his son, Napoleon II, on April 6, 1814.) The Second Empire had begun.

The government of Napoleon III was clearly authoritarian. As chief of state, Napoleon III controlled the armed forces, police, and civil service. Only he could introduce legislation and declare war. The Legislative

MORE ABOUT . . . *Queen Victoria the Victorian*

Many of Queen Victoria's ideas about love and marriage were revealed in the letters she wrote to her eldest daughter, Vicky. In a letter written shortly after the seventeen-year-old girl married Fredrick of Prussia in 1858 her mother wrote: "Yes, dearest, it is an awful moment to have to give up one's innocent child to a man, be he ever so kind and good—and to think of all she must go through! I can't say what I suffered, what I felt—what struggles I had to go through—(indeed I have not quite got over it yet). I said to Papa 'After all it is like taking a poor lamb to be sacrificed.'" Victoria could never fathom the design of the Almighty when it came to human reproduction. She told Vicky: "I know that God has willed it so and that these are the trials which we poor women must go through. I must say it is a bad arrangement."

LEARNING FROM VISUALS

Ask students to discuss why Napoleon III would have himself proclaimed emperor. Does his appearance in the painting to the right give them any indication about his character? Why is it easier to be named emperor than to carry out the responsibilities of being emperor?

Answer to the caption question: Following the Revolution, the Reign of Terror, and Napoleon, the French people may have been ready for a more stable government.

REINFORCING VOCABULARY

Ask students to explain why the Ausgleich in the government of Austria-Hungary was unable to satisfy any of the national groups in that empire. What does this show about the difficulty of governing a multinational state?

▲ *Louis Napoleon took the title of Napoleon III on December 2, 1852, and served as an authoritarian monarch until 1870. Why do you think the French people strongly supported an imperial government during these years?*

ter the rapid construction of railroads, as well as harbors, roads, and canals. The major French railway lines were completed during Napoleon's reign. Iron production tripled. In the midst of this economic expansion, Napoleon III also carried out a vast rebuilding of the city of Paris. The old Paris of narrow streets and walls was destroyed and replaced by a modern Paris of broad boulevards, spacious buildings, public squares, an underground sewage system, a new public water supply, and gaslights. The new Paris served a military purpose as well. Broad streets made it more difficult for would-be rebels to throw up barricades and easier for troops to move rapidly through the city in the event of revolts.

In the 1860s, as opposition began to mount, Napoleon III began to liberalize his regime. He gave the Legislative Corps more say in affairs of state, including debate over the budget. In a vote in May 1870, on whether to accept a new constitution that might have begun a parliamentary regime, the French people gave Napoleon another resounding victory. This triumph was short-lived, however. War with Prussia in 1870 brought Napoleon's expulsion, and a republic was proclaimed.

As we have seen, nationalism was a major force in nineteenth-century Europe. However, one of Europe's most powerful states—the Austrian Empire—was a multinational empire that had been able to frustrate the desire of its ethnic groups for independence. After the Habsburg rulers had crushed the revolutions of 1848 and 1849, they restored centralized, autocratic government to the empire. Austria's defeat at the hands of the Prussians in 1866, however, forced the Austrians to make concessions to the fiercely nationalistic Hungarians.

The result was the **Ausgleich,** or Compromise, of 1867. This compromise created the dual monarchy of Austria-Hungary. Each part of the empire now had its own constitution, its own legislature, its own government bureaucracy, and its own capital (Vienna for Austria and Budapest for Hungary). Holding the two states together were a single monarch (Francis Joseph was both Emperor of Austria and King of Hungary) and a common army, foreign policy, and system of finances. In domestic affairs, the Hungarians had become an independent nation. The Ausgleich, however, did not

Corps gave an appearance of representative government, because the members of this group were elected by universal male suffrage for six-year terms. However, they could neither initiate legislation nor affect the budget.

The first five years of Napoleon III's reign were a spectacular success. He took many steps to expand industrial growth. Government subsidies helped to fos-

ENRICHMENT ACTIVITY

Assign students to write an essay comparing the events and outcomes of the rules of Bismarck and Napoleon III. What personal characteristics did each man have that contributed to his accomplishments?

satisfy the other nationalities that made up the multi-national Austro-Hungarian Empire.

At the beginning of the nineteenth century, Russia was overwhelmingly rural, agricultural, and autocratic. The Russian tsar was still regarded as a divine-right monarch with unlimited power. The Russian imperial autocracy, a government based on soldiers, secret police, repression, and censorship, had withstood the revolutionary fervor of the first half of the nineteenth century. The Russian army had even crushed revolutions elsewhere in Europe. However, defeat in the Crimean War in 1856 led even staunch conservatives to realize that Russia was falling hopelessly behind the western European powers. Tsar Alexander II decided to make serious reforms.

Serfdom was the largest problem in tsarist Russia. On March 3, 1861, Alexander issued his **emancipation** (to set free from bondage) edict (see "You Are There: Emancipation—Serfs and Slaves"). Peasants were now free to own property and marry as they chose. However, the new land system was not that helpful to the peasants. The government provided land for the peasants by buying it from the landlords. The landowners, however, often kept the best lands. The Russian peasants soon found that they did not have enough good land to support themselves.

Furthermore, the peasants were not completely free. The state paid the landowners for the land given to the peasants. In turn, the peasants were expected to repay the state in long-term installments. To ensure that the payments were made, peasants were placed in village communes, or communities called **mirs.** The commune was responsible for the land payments to the government. Because the village communes were responsible for the payments, they did not want the peasants to leave their land. Emancipation of the serfs, then, led not to a free, landowning peasantry but to an unhappy, land-starved peasantry that largely followed the old ways of farming.

Alexander II attempted other reforms as well, but he soon found that he could please no one. Reformers wanted more and rapid change. Conservatives thought that the tsar was trying to destroy the basic institutions of Russian society. When a group of radicals assassinated Alexander II in 1881, his son and successor,

Alexander III, turned against reform and returned to the old methods of repression.

The Growth of the United States

The U.S. Constitution, ratified in 1789, committed the United States to two of the major forces of the first half of the nineteenth century, liberalism and nationalism. National unity did not come easy, however. Bitter conflict erupted between the Federalists and the Republicans over the power of the federal government in relation to the states. Led by Alexander Hamilton, the Federalists favored a financial program that would establish a strong central government. The Republicans, guided by Thomas Jefferson and James Madison, feared a strong central government as a danger to popular liberties. These early divisions ended with the War of 1812 against the British. A surge of national feeling at that time served to cover over the nation's divisions.

The election of Andrew Jackson as president in 1828 opened a new era in American politics. Jacksonian democracy introduced mass democratic politics. Property qualifications for voting were dropped. By the 1830s, the right to vote had been extended to almost all adult white males.

By the mid-nineteenth century, the issue of slavery had become a threat to American national unity. Like the North, the South had grown dramatically in population during the first half of the nineteenth century. Unlike the situation in the North, however, the South's economy was based on growing cotton on plantations, chiefly by slave labor. Although the importation of slaves had been banned in 1808, there were four million African American slaves in the South by 1860, compared with one million in 1800. The cotton economy and plantation-based slavery were closely related. The South was determined to maintain them. At the same time, the growth of a movement in the North to end slavery (**abolitionism**) challenged the southern way of life.

As opinions over slavery grew more divided, compromise became less possible. Abraham Lincoln said in a speech in Illinois in 1858 that "this government cannot endure permanently half slave and half free."

ENRICHMENT ACTIVITY

As a class discussion, compare the life of a Russian serf following emancipation with the life of an English factory worker. How were their lives similar and how did they suffer? In which situation would your students have preferred to live? Have the students define freedom from the perspective of the factory worker and of the emancipated serf. What does freedom mean to your students?

YOU·ARE·THERE

USING PRIMARY SOURCES

Ask students to explain why emancipation of serfs or slaves is not the same as creating equality for these people. What other conditions would be needed for true equality?

LEARNING FROM VISUALS

Ask students to find a picture of a family of freed slaves in the United States after the Civil War. Assign them to write an essay that compares their conditions and future with those of the Russian peasants in the photograph to the right. Why would both families have had little reason to be optimistic about their futures?

Answer to the caption question: Like slaves, most serfs lived in one-room cabins or huts with little chance of bettering their living conditions.

YOU ARE THERE
Emancipation—Serfs and Slaves

▶ *Alexander II freed the serfs on March 3, 1861, but this action did little to end their poverty. This photograph taken in 1870 shows a family huddled together in their one-room home. Based on the visual evidence in this photo, how do you think the living conditions of Russian serfs compared to living conditions of slaves in the United States?*

The United States and Russia shared a common feature in the 1860s. Both still had large enslaved populations (the Russian serfs were virtually slaves). The leaders of both countries issued emancipation proclamations within two years of each other.

The Imperial Decree, March 3, 1861

By the grace of God, we, Alexander II, Emperor and Autocrat of all the Russias, King of Poland, Grand Duke of Finland, etc., to all our faithful subjects, make known:

We thus came to the conviction that the work of a serious improvement of the condition of the peasants was a sacred inheritance bequeathed to us by our ancestors, a mission which, in the course of events, Divine Providence called upon us to fulfill. . . .

In virtue of the new dispositions above mentioned, the peasants attached to the soil will be invested within a term fixed by the law with all the rights of free cultivators. . . .

At the same time, they are granted the right of purchasing their close, and, with the consent of the proprietors, they may acquire in full property

When Lincoln was elected president in November 1860, the die was cast. Lincoln carried only 2 of the 1,109 counties in the South. On December 20, 1860, a South Carolina convention voted to repeal ratification

(withdraw formal approval) of the Constitution of the United States. In February 1861, six more southern states did the same, and a rival nation—the Confederate States of America—was formed. In April, fighting

---

SPECIAL NEEDS: *Auditory/Visual/Tactile*

This activity will enhance understanding of the concept of "nation" and "nationalism." Have students review pages 668–673, with particular focus on the map of Italy on page 669 and the map of the German Confederation on page 671. Also, share with the class a map of the United States. Have them review the maps to enhance their understanding of the concept of "nation." Ask students to describe how they feel about the United States being their country. For students from other countries, have them share their feelings about being from their respective countries. Relate their descriptions to the concept of nationalism. Bring to class objects associated with Italian and German traditions (for example, foods, traditional songs, pictures of traditional dress, etc.). Have the students express ideas of how having these traditions in common enhances the feeling of nationalism.

YOU ARE THERE

Emancipation—Serfs and Slaves, continued

the arable lands and other appurtenances [right of ways] which are allotted to them as a permanent holding. By the acquisition in full property of the quantity of land fixed, the peasants are free from their obligations towards the proprietors for land thus purchased, and they enter definitely into the condition of free peasants-landholders.

The Emancipation Proclamation, January 1, 1863

Now therefore, I, Abraham Lincoln, President of the United States, by virtue of the power in me vested as Commander-in-Chief of the Army and Navy of the United States in time of actual armed rebellion against the authority and government of the United States, and as a fit and necessary war measure for suppressing such rebellion, do, on this 1st day of January, A.D. 1863, and in accordance with my purpose to do so, . . . order and designate as the States and parts of States wherein the people thereof, respectively, are this day in rebellion against the United States the following, to wit:

Arkansas, Texas, Louisiana, . . . Mississippi, Alabama, Florida, Georgia, South Carolina, North Carolina, and Virginia. . . .

And by virtue of the power for the purpose aforesaid, I do order and declare that all persons held as slaves within said designated States and parts of States are, and henceforward shall be free; and that the Executive Government of the United States, including the military and naval authorities

▲ *President Lincoln believed that the Emancipation Proclamation was an "act of justice" and a military necessity. Do you think Tsar Alexander II saw the Imperial Decree as an act of justice? As a military necessity? Why or why not?*

thereof, will recognize and maintain the freedom of said persons.

1. Compare and contrast the Emancipation Proclamation of Abraham Lincoln and the Imperial Decree of Alexander II. How are they similar? How are they different?

ASSESS

You can choose from a variety of assessments to evaluate your students' mastery of the objectives for this section as stated on page 669. Possible assessments include:

1. Section Review Questions on this page
2. Section 21–3 Quiz in your Teacher Resource materials
3. Reteaching Worksheets in your Teacher Resource materials
4. Self-Study software

erupted between North and South (the Union and the Confederacy).

The American Civil War (1861 to 1865) was an extraordinarily bloody struggle. Over 600,000 soldiers died, either in battle or from deadly infectious diseases spawned by filthy camp conditions. Over a period of four years, the Union states gradually wore down the South. Moreover, what had begun as a war to save the

So What ??

If your students question the importance of information on **the American Civil War,** *tell them . . .*

The Civil War continues still to this day. The search for full equality for African Americans has yet to be found by any of the generations following the Civil War. The evidence can be found throughout the country in every major city. Despite one hundred and thirty years of "freedom," African Americans are still behind, economically and socially. Fully 25% of young African-American males have had problems with the law. Unemployment in ghetto areas is commonly in the range of 50%. As each succeeding generation of Americans continue to ignore the problem, it only worsens.

Union became a war against slavery. On January 1, 1863, Lincoln's Emancipation Proclamation declared most of the nation's slaves "forever free" (see "You Are There: Emancipation—Serfs and Slaves"). The surrender of Confederate forces on April 9, 1865, meant that the United States would be "one nation, indivisible." National unity had prevailed in the United States.

The Emergence of a Canadian Nation

By the Treaty of Paris in 1763, Canada—or New France, as it was called—passed into the hands of the British. By 1800, most Canadians favored more freedom from British rule. However, there were also serious differences among the colonists. Upper Canada (now Ontario) was mostly English speaking, whereas Lower Canada (now Quebec) was dominated by French Canadians. Increased immigration to Canada after 1815 also fueled the desire for self-government. After two short rebellions against the government broke out in Upper and Lower Canada in 1837 and 1838, the British moved toward change. In 1840, the British Parliament formally joined Upper and Lower Canada into the United Provinces of Canada, but without granting self-government.

The head of Upper Canada's Conservative Party, John Macdonald, became a strong voice for self-government. The British government, fearful of American designs on Canada, finally gave in. In 1867, Parliament passed the British North American Act, which established a Canadian nation—the Dominion of Canada—with its own constitution. John Macdonald became the first prime minister of the Dominion. Although Canada now possessed a parliamentary system and ruled itself, foreign affairs were still in the hands of the British government.

SECTION REVIEW

1. Locate:
(a) Crimean peninsula,   (b) Balkans,
(c) Dardanelles,   (d) Budapest,   (e) Alsace,
(f) Lorraine

2. Define:
(a) militarism,   (b) realpolitik,   (c) Ausgleich,
(d) emancipation,   (e) mirs,   (f) abolitionism

3. Identify:
(a) Count Camillo di Cavour,   (b) Giuseppe Garibaldi,   (c) Franco-Prussian war,   (d) Count Otto von Bismarck,   (e) Queen Victoria,
(f) Legislative Corps,   (g) Francis Joseph,
(h) Tsar Alexander II,   (i) Emancipation Proclamation,   (j) British North American Act

4. Recall:
(a) How did the Crimean War destroy the Concert of Europe?
(b) What action by Giuseppe Garibaldi made him unique among most national leaders?
(c) How was Great Britain able to avoid revolutions that occurred in many parts of Europe in 1848?
(d) Why didn't the distribution of land to the peasants by the Russian government enable them to support themselves?
(e) What was the difference between the basis for the economy of the North and that of the South in the United States before the Civil War?

5. Think Critically: How did the existence of a common enemy help bring about the unification of Germany?

CULTURAL LIFE: ROMANTICISM AND REALISM IN THE WESTERN WORLD

At the end of the eighteenth century, a new intellectual movement, known as romanticism, emerged to challenge the ideas of the Enlightenment. The Enlightenment had stressed reason as the chief means for discovering truth. The romantics emphasized feelings, emotion, and imagination as sources of knowing.

RECOMMENDED READING

G. L. Mosse, *The Culture of Western Europe: The Nineteenth and Twentieth Centuries* (Chicago, 1961), remains a good introduction to the cultural history of Europe. For an interesting analysis of the ideas of the romantics, see H. G. Schenk, *The Mind of the European Romantics* (Garden City, N.Y., 1969). There is an excellent collection of writings by romantics in J. B. Halsted, ed., *Romanticism* (New York, 1969). On German romanticism, see S. Prawer, ed., *The Romantic Period in Germany* (London, 1970). On Wordsworth and English Romanticism, see J. Wordsworth, *William Wordsworth and the Age of English Romanticism* (New Brunswick, N.J., 1987). A beautifully illustrated introduction to the arts can be found in H. Honour, *Romanticism* (New York, 1979).

▲ *The Houses of Parliament in London burned in 1834 and were replaced with new buildings in the neo-Gothic style. What features of Gothic architecture do you see in these tall, graceful buildings that overlook the Thames River?*

The Characteristics of Romanticism

The romantics stressed emotion and sentiment. They believed that these inner feelings were only understandable to the person experiencing them. In their novels, romantic writers created figures who were often misunderstood and rejected by society, but who continued to believe in their own worth through their inner feelings.

Romantics also valued individualism, or the belief in the uniqueness of each person. The desire of romantics to follow their inner drives to know themselves led them to rebel against middle-class conventions. They grew long hair and beards and wore outrageous clothes to express their uniqueness.

Many romantics had a passionate interest in the past. They revived medieval Gothic architecture and adorned European countrysides with pseudomedieval castles. Grandiose neo-Gothic (built in the Gothic style of the Middle Ages) cathedrals, city halls, parliamentary buildings, and even railway stations were built in many European cities. Literature, too, reflected a love of the past. The novels of Walter Scott became European best-sellers in the first half of the nineteenth century. *Ivanhoe*, in which Scott tried to evoke the clash between Saxon and Norman knights in medieval England, became one of his most popular novels. In focusing on their nations' past, romantic writers created national literature and reflected the nineteenth century's fascination with nationalism.

Many romantics had a deep attraction to the exotic and unfamiliar. This attraction gave rise to so-called Gothic literature. Chilling examples are Mary Shelley's *Frankenstein* in Britain and Edgar Allen Poe's short stories of horror in the United States. Some romantics even sought the unusual in their own lives by exploring their dreams and nightmares and seeking altered states of consciousness.

The romantics loved poetry, which they viewed as the direct expression of the soul. Romantic poetry gave full expression to one of the most important characteristics of romanticism—its love of nature. This is especially evident in the poetry of William Wordsworth, the foremost English romantic poet of nature. His

On Line with WORLD HISTORY Internet Activity

You may want to have your students visit the following URL, where they will find information and additional web site resources to enhance their study of this chapter.

Science in the Industrial Era

http://www.Kaiwan.com/ ~lucknow/horus/guide/si10.html

This links to many sources on inventions and works in the field of science without which the Industrial Revolution would not have taken place.

Due to the ever-changing nature of the World Wide Web, see the West History web site, **http://history.swpco.com** for regular updates of the URLs in this text.

CLOSE

Lead students in a discussion of the 'Focus' objectives identified on page 669. Emphasize the fact that in some cases nationalism led to revolution, in others it resulted in political, social, and economic reforms.

FOCUS

OBJECTIVES

After completing this section, students should be able to

1. identify and explain characteristics of Romanticism
2. describe events in the New Age of Science
3. identify and explain characteristics of Realism

FOCUS ACTIVITY

Help students understand that times of harsh reality are often followed by times of materialism and frivolity. This can be seen in the "roaring twenties" after World War I and in the Renaissance that followed the Reformation. Ask students to identify aspects of Romanticism that may have been reactions to wars in preceding years.

TEACH

LEARNING FROM VISUALS

Answer to the caption question: Students should recognize the Gothic arches and tall spires that are basic to Gothic architecture.

USING PRIMARY SOURCES

Ask students to describe the feelings that Wordsworth's poem engenders in their minds. Do they agree with its message?

CLASS DISCUSSION

Have students listen to Beethoven's Sixth and Ninth Symphonies and then describe what they think are the basic characteristics of Romanticism.

▲ *Edgar Allen Poe quickly gained international fame for his short stories, including the* Fall of the House of Usher. *This illustration captures the horror and excitement of the story.*

experience of nature was almost mystical as he claimed to receive "authentic tidings of invisible things":

> One impulse from a vernal wood
> May teach you more of man,
> Of Moral Evil and of good,
> Than all the sages can.[2]

Romantics believed that nature served as a mirror into which humans could look to learn about themselves.

The worship of nature also caused Wordsworth and other romantic poets to be critical of eighteenth-century science, which, they believed, had reduced nature to a cold object of study (see Chapter 20). To Wordsworth, the scientists' dry, mathematical approach left no room for the imagination or for the human soul. The poet who left to the world "one single moral precept," Wordsworth said, did more for the world than did scientists, who were soon forgotten. The monster created by Frankenstein in Mary Shelley's Gothic novel was a symbol of the danger of science's attempt to conquer nature. Many romantics were convinced that the emerging industrialization would cause people to become alienated from their inner selves and the natural world around them.

Like the literary arts, the visual arts and music were also deeply affected by romanticism (see "Our Artistic Heritage: The Romantic Vision"). To many romantics, music was the most romantic of the arts, because it enabled the composer to probe deeply into human emotions. Music historians have called the nineteenth century the age of romanticism. One of the greatest composers of all time, Ludwig van Beethoven (BAE-TOE-vun), was the bridge between the classical and romantic periods in music. At first, Beethoven's work was still largely within the classical framework of the eighteenth century. His style differed little from that of Wolfgang Amadeus Mozart and Franz Joseph Haydn. However, with his Third Symphony, the *Eroica*, Beethoven broke through to the elements of romanticism. His use of powerful melodies to create dramatic intensity led one writer to say that "Beethoven's music opens the flood gates of fear, of terror, of horror, of pain, and arouses that longing for the eternal which is the essence of romanticism."[3]

One of the great figures of the romantic period was Franz Liszt (LIST), who was born in Hungary. Liszt, a child prodigy, established himself as an outstanding concert pianist by the age of 12. Between the ages of 13 and 15, Liszt embarked on a series of concert tours throughout France, England, and Switzerland. His performances and his dazzling personality made him a

MORE ABOUT . . . *the Death of Percy Bysshe Shelly*

Shelly and his friend Lord Byron were enthusiastic sailors who designed their own yachts. In the early 1820s they would vacation in Pisa and plan a Mediterranean cruise. On July 8, 1822 Shelly and Byron's yachts were moored in the harbor at Livorno on the coast of Italy. Although a storm was approaching, Shelly decided to head out to sea. The storm swallowed Shelly and two crew members. Ten days later two corpses washed ashore, both badly decomposed and mutilated by marine animals. Shelly was identified through the jacket he wore. Byron and a friend helped cremate the corpse, but noticed to their surprise that the heart would not burn. Shelly's heart was given to his wife, Mary Wollstonecraft Shelly, the author of the novel *Frankenstein*. She preserved it in a box, which eventually was buried with her remains.

OUR ARTISTIC HERITAGE
The Romantic Vision

Man and Woman Gazing at the Moon shows the romantic, mystical view of nature held by German artist Caspar David Friedrich. Does the artist give more emphasis to the two humans or to the tree? Explain your answer.

Romantic artists shared at least two common features. First, to them, all art was a reflection of the artist's inner feelings. A painting should mirror the artist's vision of the world and be the instrument of the artist's own imagination. Second, romantic artists deliberately rejected classicism. The romantics abandoned classical coldness and reason for warmth and emotion.

The early life experiences of the German painter Caspar David Friedrich (FREE-drik) left him with a lifelong preoccupation with God and nature. Friedrich painted many landscapes, but with an interest that went beyond the mere natural details. His portrayal of mountains shrouded in mist, gnarled trees bathed in moonlight, and the stark ruins of monasteries surrounded by withered trees all conveyed a feeling of mystery. For

Friedrich, nature was a revelation of divine life. As is exemplified in the painting *Man and Woman Gazing at the Moon*, he liked to depict one or two solitary figures gazing upon a natural scene with their backs to the viewer. His human figures were overwhelmed by the grandeur of nature, but they expressed the human desire to lose themselves in the universe. To Friedrich, art depended upon the use of an imagination that could be achieved only through inner vision. He advised artists: "Shut your physical eye and look first at your picture with your spiritual eye, then bring to the light of day what you have seen in the darkness."

Eugène Delacroix (DELL-uh-KrWAW) was one of the most famous French romantic painters. His

(continued)

ENRICHMENT ACTIVITY

Divide class into four groups, and assign each group to conduct research on one of the following topics: The Romantic Movement in
A) Literature,
B) Music,
C) Art,

D) Architecture. Groups should present their reports, which include visual and auditory supplements, to the entire class. All students should take notes on the other reports. Encourage students to bring in pictures and recordings.

OUR ARTISTIC HERITAGE

The Romantic Vision, continued

▲ *Eugène Delacroix often chose the exotic and unknown, North Africa and the Near East, as subjects for his paintings. Women of Algiers, shown here, is typical in that regard. The painting also reflects Delacroix's interest in light and color. Can you tell from which direction the light comes into the room? How did the artist convey that to the viewer?*

paintings showed two chief characteristics: a fascination with the exotic and a passion for color. Both are visible in his *Women of Algiers*. This portrayal of the world of the harem in exotic North Africa is significant for its use of light and its patches of interrelated color. In Delacroix, drama and movememt combined with a daring use of color. Many of his works reflect his own belief that "a painting should be a feast to the eye."

1. What were the two common features shared by romantic artists?

2. How did the artist Friedrich view nature?

3. What do you think the phrase "a painting should be a feast to the eye" means?

famous figure. Liszt has been called the greatest pianist of all time.

A New Age of Science

The Scientific Revolution had created a modern, rational approach to the study of the natural world. For a long time, only the educated elite understood its importance. With the Industrial Revolution, however, came a renewed interest in basic scientific research. By the 1830s, new discoveries in science led to many practical benefits that affected all Europeans. Science came to have a greater and greater impact on European life.

In biology, the Frenchman Louis Pasteur (pass-TUR) discovered the germ theory of disease, which was crucial to the development of modern scientific medical practices. In chemistry, the Russian Dmitri Mendeleev (duh-MEE-tree MEN-duh-LAE-uf) in the 1860s classified all the material elements then known on the basis of their atomic weights. In Great Britain, Michael Faraday (FAR-uh-DAY) put together a primitive generator that laid the foundation for the use of electricity.

The dramatic material benefits often provided by science and technology led Europeans to have a growing faith in science. This faith, in turn, undermined

MORE ABOUT . . . *Louis Pasteur and the Cure for Rabies*

When Louis Pasteur was a child, he witnessed an attack by a mad wolf, which bit anyone who came near, infecting them with the fatal disease of rabies. Throughout his life he would recall the horrible death its victims suffered. He set out to see if he could find a way of immunizing animals against the disease. After months of exhaustive research on dogs, he found that the animals could become immunized over a period of four-teen days through daily injections of dried material from an infected rabbit's spinal cord. On July 6, 1885, the first anti-rabies shot was given to a human being. A nine year old boy whose doctor determined he would die if nothing was done, received fourteen experimental shots. When he returned to his home in Alsace, he never showed a sign of having rabies.

USING PRIMARY SOURCES

Ask students to explain why some religious groups are doubtful of Darwin's theory of natural selection and of the ideas in his publication, *The Descent of Man*.

LEARNING FROM VISUALS

Answer to the caption question: The painting is not an idealized version of work, but rather has a photographic quality showing the hard, wrenching labor that these men dressed in tattered clothing are doing.

RETEACH

Assign students to write an essay about the 'survival of the fittest' in terms of their own lives. Ask them to also identify and explain aspects of their lives that do not support this concept.

▲ The Stonebreakers *by Gustave Courbet, an artist of the realist school, represents a complete break with the mystical and imaginative qualities of the romantic period. These two life-size figures are engaged in hard, manual labor, but the artist does not try to draw the viewer into the painting or gain our sympathy for them. We are simply observers of the scene. Why do you think this work was initially rejected by French art critics as too harsh?*

the religious faith of many people. It is no accident that the nineteenth century was an age of increasing secularization. For many people, truth was now to be found in science and the concrete material existence of humans. No one did more to create a picture of humans as material beings that were simply part of the natural world than Charles Darwin.

In 1859, Charles Darwin published *On the Origin of Species by Means of Natural Selection*. The basic idea of this book was that each kind of plant and animal had evolved over a long period of time from earlier and simpler forms of life. Darwin called this principle **organic evolution.**

How did this natural process work? According to Darwin, in every species, "many more individuals of each species are born than can possibly survive." This results in a "struggle for existence." Darwin believed that some organisms were more adaptable to the environment than others, a process that Darwin called **natural selection.** He describes the natural selection process as follows:

Owing to this struggle [for existence], variations, however slight . . . , if they be in any degree profitable to the individuals of a species, in their infinitely complex relations to other organic beings and to their physical

MORE ABOUT . . . *Charles Darwin Changes the Origin of Man*

As a young man, Charles Darwin became increasingly bored with his studies of medicine. He was then shipped off to Cambridge to become a minister. However, he became preoccupied with natural history. After graduation he got the job of naturalist aboard *H.M.S. Beagle.* Darwin was most impressed by the flora and fauna in the Galapagos Islands. He found it curious that God had created a unique type of finch for each of the Galapagos Islands. Darwin also realized that the population of animals would constantly exceed their food supply. Those most likely to survive were those most skilled in finding food for themselves and their offspring. The most controversial part of his theory pertained to his idea.

CLASS DISCUSSION

Lead students in a discussion of why the writings of Charles Dickens may have done more to make people aware of the plight of the poor in London than any preaching by religious leaders.

ASSESS

You can choose from a variety of assessments to evaluate your students' mastery of the objectives for this section as stated on page 679. Possible assessments include:

1. Section Review Questions on this page
2. Section 21–4 Quiz in your Teacher Resource materials
3. Reteaching Worksheets in your Teacher Resource materials
4. Self-Study software

Answer to
SECTION REVIEW

1. (a) Charles Darwin's principle that all plants, animals evolved over time from earlier, simpler forms of life
   (b) Charles Darwin's theory that most able animals survive, pass on adaptable traits
2. (a) romantic novel by Walter Scott, describes clash between Saxon and Norman knights
   (b) an example of chilling Gothic literature
   (c) by Charles Darwin, suggested all plants and animals evolved over time from earlier and simpler forms of life

---

conditions of life, will tend to the preservation of such individuals, and will generally be inherited by the offspring.[4]

In other words, the organisms that were selected for survival through this natural process—those that had characteristics that favored their preservation—were the organisms that survived. (This is called "survival of the fittest.") The unfit did not survive. The fit, in turn, propagated. In this way they passed on the variations that enabled them to survive until, according to Darwin, a new, separate species emerged.

In *The Descent of Man*, published in 1871, Darwin argued that human beings had animal origins. Humans, he believed, were not an exception to the rule governing other species.

Darwin's ideas raised a storm of controversy. Some people objected that Darwin's theory made human beings ordinary products of nature rather than unique beings. Others were bothered by his idea of life as a mere struggle for survival. "Wasn't there a place in the Darwinian world for moral values?" they asked. Many people also condemned Darwin for denying God's role in creation. Gradually, however, many scientists and other intellectuals came to accept Darwin's theory.

Realism

The belief that the world should be viewed realistically, a view frequently expressed after 1850, was closely related to the scientific outlook. In politics, Bismarck had practiced the "politics of reality." Realism became a movement in the literary and visual arts as well. The literary realists of the mid-nineteenth century rejected romanticism. They wanted to write about ordinary characters from actual life rather than romantic heroes in exotic settings. They also tried to avoid emotional language by using precise description. Thus, they preferred to write novels rather than poems.

The leading novelist of the 1850s and 1860s, the French Gustave Flaubert (floe-BEH[uh]R), perfected the realist novel. His *Madame Bovary* was a straightforward, critical, description of small-town life in France. The British novelist Charles Dickens became very successful with his realistic novels focusing on the lower

and middle classes in Britain's early Industrial Age. In such novels as *Oliver Twist* and *David Copperfield*, Dickens's descriptions of the urban poor and the brutal life they led were vividly realistic.

In art, too, realism became dominant after 1850. Realist artists sought to show the everyday life of ordinary people and the world of nature with photographic realism. The French became leaders in realist painting.

Gustave Courbet was the most famous artist of the realist school. Courbet loved to portray scenes from everyday life. His subjects were factory workers, peasants, and the wives of saloon keepers. "I have never seen either angels or goddesses, so I am not interested in painting them," Courbet said. One of his famous works, *The Stonebreakers*, painted in 1849, shows two roadworkers engaged in the deadening work of breaking stones to build a road. There were those who objected to Courbet's "cult of ugliness" and who found his scenes of human misery scandalous. To Courbet, however, no subject was too ordinary, too harsh, or too ugly to be interesting.

 SECTION REVIEW

1. **Define:**
   (*a*) organic evolution,
   (*b*) natural selection

2. **Identify:**
   (*a*) *Ivanhoe*,   (*b*) *Frankenstein*,
   (*c*) *On the Origin of Species by Means of Natural Selection*,   (*d*) realism

3. **Recall:**
   (*a*) How was romanticism different from the ideas of the Enlightenment?
   (*b*) Why were romantic poets critical of eighteenth-century science?

4. **Think Critically:** Many political, economic, and social injustices existed during the nineteenth century. How do you think this may have contributed to both the ages of romanticism and realism?

RETEACHING ACTIVITY

Provide examples of paintings from both the romantic and realist schools. Discuss these in class and have students use the paintings to analyze the differences in the two schools' art. Have each student state a preference and give a reason for this preference.

Conclusion

In 1815, a conservative order had been reestablished throughout Europe, and the great powers worked to maintain it. However, the waves of revolution in Europe in the first half of the nineteenth century made it clear that the forces of nationalism and liberalism, brought into being by the French Revolution and strengthened by the spread of the Industrial Revolution, were still alive and active.

Between 1850 and 1871, the national state became the focus of people's loyalty. Wars were fought to create unified nation-states, and reforms at home served to make the nation-state the center of attention. Nationalism became a powerful force of change during the first half of the nineteenth century, but its triumph came only after 1850. Tied at first to middle-class liberals, by the end of the nineteenth century nationalism had great appeal to the broad masses as well.

In 1870, however, not all peoples had achieved their national dreams. Large minorities, especially in the empires controlled by the Austrians, Ottoman Turks, and Russians, had not achieved the goal of establishing their own national states. Moreover, nationalism also changed in the course of the nineteenth century. Liberal nationalists had believed that unified nation-states would preserve individual rights and lead to a great community of European peoples. Rather than unifying people, however, the nationalism of the late nineteenth century divided people as the new national states competed bitterly with one another after 1870.

Europeans, however, were hardly aware of nationalism's dangers in 1870. The spread of the Industrial Revolution and the wealth of technological achievements convinced many Europeans that they stood on the verge of a new age of progress.

Notes

1. Louis L. Snyder, ed., *Documents of German History* (New Brunswick, N.J., 1958), p. 202.
2. William Wordsworth, "The Tables Turned," *Poems of Wordsworth*, ed. Matthew Arnold (London, 1963), p. 138.
3. Quoted in Siegbert Prawer, ed., *The Romantic Period in Germany* (London, 1970), p. 285.
4. Charles Darwin, *On the Origin of Species*, vol. 1 (New York, 1872), pp. 77, 79.

(d) the belief that the world should be viewed realistically
3. (a) Romanticism: emotion and sentiment; Enlightenment: reason and logic used to discover truth.
   (b) believed it reduced nature to a cold object of study
4. Answers will vary.

CLOSE

Lead students in a discussion of the 'Focus' objectives identified on page 679. Emphasize how changes in political, economic, and social systems are reflected by Romanticism and Realism.

SPANISH SUPPORT

The *Conclusion* has been translated into Spanish for your Spanish-speaking students. Included with this translation (in your Teacher Resource Box) are Section Key Points, which consist of one or two sentences summarizing each section in the chapter. These Key Points have also been translated into Spanish.

TIME LINE

As students conclude the chapter, you may want to refer them to the chapter time line in the *Study Guide*. The time line will help them put key dates in perspective. Supporting questions and activities are also provided.

ENRICHMENT ACTIVITY

Divide the class into three groups—romantics (represented by Wordsworth), realists (represented by Dickens) and British factory workers. Have each group describe their view of life and nature, then discuss the relative viewpoints of the three. How much appeal would romanticism hold for the factory workers? Why? What about realism?

Answers to CHAPTER REVIEW 21

USING KEY TERMS

1. abolitionism
2. principle of legitimacy
3. universal male suffrage
4. realpolitik
5. puddling
6. organic evolution
7. conservatism
8. bourgeois
9. mirs
10. Ausgleich
11. natural selection
12. multinational state
13. principle of intervention
14. utopian socialists
15. emancipation
16. militarism
17. liberalism

REVIEWING THE FACTS

1. Coal and steam
2. from one based on farming and handicrafts to one based on manufacturing
3. John Kay—the flying shuttle; James Hargreaves—spinning jenny; Edmund Cartwright—loom; James Watt—steam engine
4. A fungus appeared in 1845 which destroyed the potato crop. The result was a devastating famine.
5. Austria, Prussia, Russia and France
6. It involved Russia versus the Ottoman Empire, Great Britain and France. The war broke out over Russian aspirations in the Balkans and desire to take advantage of Turkish weakness.
7. Camillo di Cavour and Giuseppe Garibaldi
8. Otto von Bismarck
9. increased the number of workers
10. to create a Canadian nation chiefly as a result of fears of U.S. desires for Canada

THINKING CRITICALLY

1. Students may focus on the idea that "that government is best which governs the least," or even "that government is best which governs

686

CHAPTER 21 REVIEW

USING KEY TERMS

1. _____ was the movement to end slavery in the United States.
2. At the Congress of Vienna in 1814, the _____ became the guiding political principle for the great powers.
3. _____ means that all adult men have the right to vote.
4. A political philosophy that concentrates on practical matters, rather than on theory or ethics is called _____.
5. The process invented by Henry Cort to produce high quality iron is called _____.
6. The basic idea of Charles Darwin's book, *On the Origin of Species* was the principle of _____.
7. Obedience to political authority, emphasis on organized religion to maintain the social order, and resistance to the ideas of individual rights and representative government are characteristics of _____.
8. The _____ class included merchants, artisans, officials, lawyers, industrialists, bankers, teachers, doctors, and shopkeepers.
9. Traditional Russian peasant communal villages were called _____.
10. The _____, or Compromise, of 1867, created the dual monarchy of Austria-Hungary.
11. Charles Darwin believed that some organisms were able to adapt better to the environment than others, a process he called _____.
12. A state that is made up of many different peoples, such as the Austrian Empire, is called a _____.
13. A(n) _____ justified the use of military forces to crush popular revolts in Spain and Italy.
14. _____ was the name given by Marxists to men who believed that cooperation could replace competition in industry.
15. A(n) _____ edict by Russian Tsar Alexander II allowed peasants to own property and marry as they chose.

686

16. The glorification of war and the military is called _____.
17. _____ is the idea that people should be as free from restraint as possible.

REVIEWING THE FACTS

1. What new sources of energy became important in the early Industrial Revolution?
2. In what ways did the economy of Europe shift during the Industrial Revolution?
3. Name three important inventors in England and their inventions.
4. What was the cause of the famine in Ireland between 1845 to 1851?
5. What four nations were prepared to use military forces to crush revolts in other nations?
6. Which countries were involved in the Crimean War? Why did the war break out?
7. Who are the two men most responsible for the unification of Italy?
8. Who is the man who united Germany?
9. What were the provisions of the British Reform Bill in 1832?
10. Why did Great Britain pass the British North America Act in 1867?

THINKING CRITICALLY

1. Why is liberalism thought to be an outgrowth of the Enlightenment?
2. Describe the importance of the railroads in spurring the Industrial Revolution in Great Britain.
3. Explain why the agricultural revolution in the late eighteenth century led to dramatic population growth in Europe.
4. Who supported the ideology of conservatism? Why would these groups support conservatism?

not at all."
2. created a demand for coal and iron; created jobs to build them; lowered transportation costs and created larger markets.
3. led to an abundant food supply, better nutrition, greater resistance to disease
4. hereditary monarchs, government bureaucracies, landowning aristocracies and churches
5. It led to the breakdown of the Concert of Europe. Piedmont-Sardinia and Prussia needed to defeat Austria to unify their respective countries.
6. Both men worked with a monarch who supported their dream; both men understood that war would have to be an instrument of unifica-

tion. A key difference is that Piedmont-Sardinia was much weaker militarily than Prussia. Cavour had to convince France to do much of the fighting for him. Bismarck had fewer restrictions on his diplomacy since he had more power to work with. Answers will vary.
7. In general, the South held more closely to liberal political philosophies; this was a Jeffersonian heritage. Nationalism is visible in both North and South, with the Northern concept embracing all of the states, and the Southern concept usually embracing just the state.

CHAPTER 21 REVIEW

5. In what way did the Crimean War indirectly contribute to the unification of Italy and Germany?
6. Compare and contrast Cavour and Bismarck. In your opinion, who was the greater statesman?
7. Trace the conflict over national unity in the United States from 1789 to 1865. In what ways were the twin principles of liberalism and nationalism involved?

APPLYING SOCIAL STUDIES SKILLS

1. **Economics:** Consult Map 21.1 on page 657. In 1815, Prussia was the weakest of the great powers. By 1871, Germany was a more powerful nation than France. Does this map provide any clues as to why this was now so? In 1815, Russia was perhaps the most powerful of the great powers; by 1870, it had become the weakest. Does this map provide any clues as to why this had occurred?
2. **Geography:** Consult Map 21.2 on page 662 (Europe After the Congress of Vienna). Which nation dominated the Balkan Peninsula? What is the largest nation in the North German Plain? How many nations occupy the northern portion of Italy?
3. **Government:** Compare the motives for Alexander II's emancipation of the serfs with Abraham Lincoln's motives for the Emancipation Proclamation in 1862.
4. **Government:** Contrast the relationship between the British Prime Minister and Parliament with that of Otto von Bismarck to the Prussian Reichstag.

MAKING TIME AND PLACE CONNECTIONS

1. Why would the Soviet Union name the space station which they sent up to orbit the Earth the *Mir*?

2. How has nationalism influenced the former Yugoslavia? The former Soviet Union? The former Czechoslovakia? Spain? Great Britain? Belgium? Ireland? Refer to at least two countries in your answer. Give examples within your own community, or from recent news, of expressions of nationalism.
3. In what ways are Camilo di Cavour and Giuseppe Garibaldi similar to Simon Bolivar and Jose de San Martin?

BECOMING AN HISTORIAN

1. **Charts, Graphs, Tables:** Construct charts showing (1) British imports from 1760 to 1840; (2) European population growth from 1750 to 1850; and (3) the population of Ireland from 1781 to 1851.
2. **Compare and Contrast:** Compare the portrait of Prince Metternich (p. 663) with that of Emperor Napoleon III (p. 674). How does each portrait reflect the political philosophies of each statesman?
3. **Compare and Contrast:** Compare the photograph of Russian peasants (p. 676) with Courbet's *The Stonebreakers* (p. 683). Decide whether these works are romantic or realist and explain why.
4. What similarities are there between *The July Revolution in Paris* (p. 664), *Austrian Students in the Revolutionary Civil Guard* (p. 666), and *Garibaldi Arrives in Sicily* (p. 670). Why might *Garibaldi Arrives in Sicily* be considered romantic?
5. **Art as a Key to History:** How do Caspar David Friedrich's *Man and Woman Gazing at the Moon* (p. 681) and Eugène Delacroix's *Women of Algiers* (p. 682) represent different facets of romanticism?
6. Compare the view of the world pictured in Caspar David Friedrich's *Man and Woman Gazing at the Moon* (p. 681) with that of Gustave Dore's drawing *Over London By Rail* (p. 658). Would you regard Dore as a romantic or a realist?

687

APPLYING SOCIAL STUDIES SKILLS

1. Germany had greater industrialization. Russia lacked industrial development.
2. the Ottoman Empire; Prussia; six countries in Northern Italy
3. Alexander II was concerned with modernization; Lincoln was interested in saving the Union.
4. The British Prime Minister is elected by Parliament and is answerable to Parliament. Parliament must approve all taxes. Bismarck was not a member of the Reichstag, was answerable only to the monarch, and imposed taxes over the objections of the Reichstag.

MAKING TIME AND PLACE CONNECTIONS

1. Mir was a system where property was held in common and where the good of the village was more important than the good of the individual.
2. The former Yugoslavia has broken up into Slovenia, Croatia, and Serbia. Bosnia is deeply divided ethnically. The bitter civil war has been driven in part, by a desire to create a nation for a single ethnic group by driving out the "alien" ethnic group. The former Soviet Union included ethnic groups who had been nations in earlier times: Ukraine, Latvia, Lithuania, Estonia, Georgia, to

name a few. Czechoslovakia broke into the Czech Republic and Slovakia. Spain has Catalan and Basque independence movements. Great Britain welded together English, Scots, and Welsh, but there are separatist movements. Ireland struggled against English rule. Conflict continues in Northern Ireland.
3. All fulfilled nationalist aspirations. Cavour and Bolivar liberate northern portions of their nations, Garibaldi and San Martin southern. Southern leaders, yielded primacy to northern leaders.

BECOMING AN HISTORIAN

1. (1.) British Cotton Imports (Millions of Pounds) 1760: 2.5; 1787: 22; 1840: 366
   (2.) European Population Growth (in Millions) 1750: 140; 1800: 187; 1850: 266
   (3.) Irish Population (in Millions) 1781: 4; 1845: 8; 1851:5
2. Metternich is confident, arrogant; uniform covered with symbols of power; Napoleon is simply dressed, with fewer marks of obvious power
3. Both portray the lower classes with no attempt to glamorize life.
4. relate to nationalist goals, have political content
5. colors and subject are emotionally evocative; Friedrich portrays two people communing with Nature; mysterious quality to the scene; Delacroix pictures women in an opulent and exotic setting. A yearning for Nature and love of the distant and exotic are important facets of Romanticism.
6. Students will probably regard Dore as a Realist.

687

22 PLANNING GUIDE

SECTION	KEY TOPICS	PRIMARY SOURCES	ASSESSMENT
1 The Growth of Industrial Prosperity pages 689–696	◆ Creation of new products and patterns of production ◆ Development of a world economic system ◆ Organization of the working class	◆ Marx and Engles on the classless society, page 694	◆ Section Review, page 696 ◆ Section Quiz 22–1, TRB
2 The Emergence of Mass Society pages 696–707	◆ Development of a new urban environment ◆ Social structure of mass society ◆ New experiences for women ◆ Changes in education and leisure in mass society	◆ A poem by Alfred Lord Tennyson, page 700	◆ Section Review, page 707 ◆ Section Quiz 22–2, TRB
3 The National State pages 708–715	◆ Developments in the United States and Canada ◆ Growth of political democracy in Western Europe ◆ The Old Order in Central and Eastern Europe ◆ International rivalry and war in the Balkans		◆ Section Review, page 715 ◆ Section Quiz 22–3, TRB
4 Toward the Modern Consciousness: Intellectual and Cultural Developments pages 716–724	◆ Developments in physics and psychology ◆ Social Darwinism and racism ◆ Anti-Semitism in Europe ◆ Growth of Modernism in literature and the arts	◆ One Woman's Cry for Freedom: a selection from Ibsen's, *A Doll's House*, page 719 ◆ A selection from "The Drunken Boat," page 720 ◆ A statement of what Impressionist artists sought, page 721	◆ Section Review, page 724 ◆ Section Quiz 22–4, TRB

MASS SOCIETY AND THE NATIONAL STATE IN THE WESTERN WORLD (1870 TO 1914)

REPRODUCIBLE ACTIVITIES

Historical Maps

Charts and Graphs

Critical Thinking

Cooperative Learning

Vocabulary

Guided Reading

Reteaching

Enrichment

Performance Assessment

Spanish Key Points and Chapter Summaries

Spanish Vocabulary

Spanish Guided Reading

MULTIMEDIA SUPPORT

TRANSPARENCIES
- ◆ *World History* Color Transparency Package
- ◆ Fine Art Color Transparency Package

VIDEO
- ◆ *World History* Video Library
- ◆ CNN. Annual Video Update

LASERDISC
- ◆ *Sights and Sounds of History*

AUDIO
- ◆ *Listening to Literature* audiotape (English and Spanish)
- ◆ *History of Music* CD

SOFTWARE
- ◆ WESTEST™
- ◆ Student Review

CD–ROM
- ◆ *The Journey of Civilization*
- ◆ *World History*

INTERNET
- ◆ Internet Activities

On Line with WORLD HISTORY

Access West's history web site at
http://history.swpco.com
You'll find activities and web sites related to specific topics and chapters in *World History: The Human Odyssey.* Also look for references to helpful web sites at appropriate places throughout this teacher edition.

LESSON PLANNING

You will find detailed daily lesson plans for both traditional class scheduling and **block scheduling** in your Teacher Resource Box.

Not Enough Time?

If you do not have the four or five days recommended to teach this chapter, you may want to focus on the following sections and activities:

- ◆ Have students skim the chapter to answer the "Questions to Guide Your Reading" on page 689. Discuss their answers, then read the "Conclusion" on page 725.
- ◆ Do a more in-depth reading about growth of industrial prosperity on pages 689–692, changes in social structure on pages 698–702, war in the Balkans on pages 712–715, and the idea of Social Darwinism on pages 717–781. Conclude with a discussion of developments in artistic expression that includes Impressionism and Post-Impressionism.

MASS SOCIETY AND THE NATIONAL

BUILDING ON
CHAPTER 21

To "set the scene" for the study of Chapter 22, use the following questions and activities.

1. Ask students to review how production grew during the Industrial Revolution. What impact did increased production have on prosperity in the Western World?
2. Ask students why the Industrial Revolution would have encouraged development of organizations to protect the rights of workers.
3. Ask students to describe changes in the daily lives of women resulting from the Revolution.

USING THE
OPENING STORY

Depending on the ability levels of your students, select from the following questions and activities to reinforce the reading of the opening story.

◆ Why doesn't the growth of prosperity necessarily result in peace and harmony in a nation?
◆ What relationships appear to exist between the growth of mass society and changes in social values?

LEARNING
FROM VISUALS

Answer to the caption question: Parks have more rides that move at a much faster speed.

In the late nineteenth century, Europe witnessed a dynamic age of material prosperity. With new industries, new sources of energy, and new goods, the Second Industrial Revolution dazzled Europeans and led them to believe that their material progress meant human progress. Scientific and technological achievements, many believed, would solve all human problems. The doctrine of progress became widely accepted, and this period has often been labeled an age of progress.

Out of the new urban and industrial world created by the rapid economic changes of the nineteenth century emerged a mass society late in the century. A mass society meant improvements for the lower classes, who benefited from the extension of voting rights, a better standard of living, and mass education.

A mass society also brought mass leisure. New work patterns established the concept of the weekend as a distinct time of recreation and fun. New forms of mass transportation—railroads and streetcars—enabled even workers to make brief trips to amusement parks. Coney Island was only eight miles from central New York City; Blackpool, in England, was a short train ride from nearby industrial towns. With their Ferris wheels and other daring rides that threw young

men and women together, amusement parks offered a whole new world of entertainment. Thanks to the railroad, seaside resorts, once the preserve of the wealthy, became accessible to more people for weekend visits. This accessibility disgusted one upper-class seaside resort regular, who described the new "day-trippers": "They swarm upon the beach, wandering about with apparently no other aim than to get a mouthful of fresh air." Enterprising entrepreneurs in resorts like Blackpool, however, welcomed the masses of new visitors and built for them piers laden with food, drink, and entertainment.

The coming of mass society also created new roles for the governments of the European nation-states, which now fostered national loyalty, created mass armies, and took more responsibility for public health and housing in their cities. By 1870, the national state had become the focus of Europeans' lives. Within the nation-state political democracy grew as the right to vote was extended to all adult males. With political democracy came a new mass politics and a new mass press. Both would become regular features of the twentieth century.

▲ Ferris wheels like this one built for the 1893 Columbian Exposition in the United States were very popular with young people. How have amusement parks changed over the past century?

ADDITIONAL RESOURCES

The resources below can be used to enrich the lessons in this chapter.

BOOKS FOR STUDENTS
Prophet of Revolution: Karl Marx by Alfred Apsler, Messner
Timetables of Women's History by Karen Greenspan, Simon & Schuster

VIDEOS/FILMS
Industry and Empire, 1870–1914, Series: The

World: A Television History, Social Studies School Service (800) 421-4246
La Belle Epoque, 1890–1914, Metropolitan Museum of Art, Social Studies School Service (800) 421-4246

CD-ROMs
The History of Medicine, Flagtower, Social Studies School Service (800) 421-4246

STATE IN THE WESTERN WORLD
(1870 TO 1914)

ERA OF EUROPEAN DOMINANCE

	MASS SOCIETY AND THE NATIONAL STATE	
	1870	1914
1800		1914

QUESTIONS TO GUIDE YOUR READING

1. What was the Second Industrial Revolution? What was its impact on European society?
2. What were the chief ideas of Karl Marx?
3. What do we mean by the phrase *mass society*? What were the chief features of this mass society?
4. How did the position of women change between 1870 and 1914?
5. What domestic problems did the United States, Canada, and the European nations face between 1870 and 1914?
6. What were the issues behind the international crises that occurred in the late nineteenth and early twentieth centuries?
7. What do we mean by the phrase *modern consciousness*? How did the modern consciousness begin to emerge between 1870 and 1914 in the sciences, psychology, and the arts?

OUTLINE

1. THE GROWTH OF INDUSTRIAL PROSPERITY
2. THE EMERGENCE OF MASS SOCIETY
3. THE NATIONAL STATE
4. TOWARD THE MODERN CONSCIOUSNESS: INTELLECTUAL AND CULTURAL DEVELOPMENTS

THE GROWTH OF INDUSTRIAL PROSPERITY

After 1870, Europeans virtually worshiped progress. At the heart of this belief in progress was the stunning material growth produced by what historians have called the Second Industrial Revolution. The first Industrial Revolution had given rise to textiles, railroads, iron, and coal. In the Second Industrial Revolution, steel, chemicals, electricity, and petroleum led the way to new industrial frontiers.

New Products and New Patterns

The first major change in industry between 1870 and 1914 was the substitution of steel for iron. New methods for shaping steel made it useful in the building of lighter, smaller, and faster machines and engines, as well as railways, ships, and weapons. In 1860, Great Britain, France, Germany, and Belgium produced 125,000 tons of steel. By 1913, the total was an astounding 32 million tons.

Electricity was a major new form of energy that proved to be of great value. It could be easily converted into other forms of energy, such as heat, light, and

689

FOCUS ON THEMES

Listed below are summaries of how the content in this chapter supports the text's key themes.

The Role of Ideas The ideas of socialism, as expounded by Karl Marx and Friedrich Engels, had a strong appeal to workers and their leaders. New political parties and mass trade unions were organized to better the living and working conditions.

Economics and History The Second Industrial Revolution, with its growth in steel, chemicals, electricity, and petroleum, created new products and new patterns that led to an era of stunning material prosperity. This revolution, combined with the growth of steamships and railroads, fostered a true world economy.

The Importance of Cultural Developments Between 1870 and 1914, the development of relativity in modern physics, the role of the unconscious in psychology, a new racism, and new art forms that rejected traditional standards created a sense of confusion and anxiety in Western society.

The Role of Individuals This was an age of such inventive geniuses as Guglielmo Marconi, Alexander Graham Bell, and Michael Faraday, whose discoveries created a new way of life. The scientific genius Albert Einstein created a whole new way of viewing the universe.

The Impact of Science and Technology The development of steel, chemicals, electricity, and petroleum—all products of new scientific and technological discoveries and innovations—created a new era of industrial prosperity. New modes of transportation, such as streetcars and automobiles, revolutionized urban patterns of living and helped create new forms of mass leisure.

FOCUS

OBJECTIVES

After completing this section, students should be able to

1. describe the creation of new products and patterns of production
2. outline steps in the creation of a world economic system
3. describe efforts to organize the working class

FOCUS ACTIVITY

Help students understand that growth in production does not necessarily mean all people have better lives. In 1996 national income in the United States grew by more than $340 billion. Ask students to explain why this does not mean that each American received his or her proportionate share (almost $1,300) of this money.

LEARNING FROM VISUALS

Answer to the caption question: Answers will vary.

▲ *This picture from* The Illustrated London News *in 1897 shows the changes in transportation that occurred during the reign of Queen Victoria. Compare the scenes on the left, which date from 1837, with those on the right, which date from 1897. What major changes in transportation do you think will occur between 2000 and 2060?*

in entire areas to be tied into a single, common source of power.

Electricity gave birth to a whole new series of inventions. The creation of the lightbulb by Thomas Edison in the United States and Joseph Swan in Great Britain opened homes and cities to electric lights. A revolution in communications began when Alexander Graham Bell invented the telephone in 1876 and Guglielmo Marconi (mar-KOE-nee) sent the first radio waves across the Atlantic in 1901. Electricity was also put to use in transportation. By the 1880s, streetcars and subways powered by electricity had appeared in major European cities. This development allowed cities to grow even larger, as it enabled workers to get to factories and wealthy people to live in suburbs. Electricity also transformed the factory. Conveyor belts, cranes, and machines could all be powered by electricity and be located anywhere. With electric lights, factories could remain open 24 hours a day. Thanks to electricity, all countries could now enter the Industrial Age.

The development of the internal combustion engine, fired by oil and gasoline, provided a new source of power in transportation. This engine, in which fuel is burned inside the engine itself, gave rise to ocean liners with oil-fired engines, as well as to the airplane and the automobile (see "The Role of Science and Technology: The Automobile"). In 1903, at Kitty Hawk, North Carolina, the Wright brothers made the first flight in a fixed-wing plane powered by a gasoline engine. In 1919, the first regular passenger air service was established.

Industrial production grew at a rapid pace at this time because of the greatly increased sales of manufactured goods. An increase in real wages for workers after 1870, combined with lower prices for manufactured goods because of reduced transportation costs, made it easier for Europeans to buy consumer products. In the cities, the first department stores began to sell a whole new range of consumer goods made possible by the development of the steel and electrical industries. Sewing machines, clocks, bicy-

motion. Also, electricity moved easily through space by means of wires. The British scientist Michael Faraday produced the first electric generator in 1831, but it was not until the 1870s that the first practical generators of electrical current were developed. By 1910, however, hydroelectric power stations and coal-fired steam-generating plants enabled homes and factories

RECOMMENDED READING

Specialized works on the subject matter of this chapter are available in N. Stone, *Europe Transformed, 1878–1919* (London, 1983); and F. Gilbert, *The End of the European Era, 1890 to the Present,* 2d ed. (New York, 1979).

The subject of the Second Industrial Revolution is well covered in D. Landes, *The*

Unbound Prometheus, cited in Chapter 21. For a fundamental survey of European industrialization, see A. S. Milward and S. B. Saul, *The Development of the Economies of Continental Europe, 1850–1914* (Cambridge, Mass., 1977).

THE ROLE OF SCIENCE AND TECHNOLOGY

The Automobile

Of all the new forms of transportation created in the Industrial Revolution, the automobile affected more people on a daily basis than any other. There were early experiments with steam-powered automobiles, but they did not work very well. It was the invention of the internal combustion engine, a unit in which fuel is burned inside the engine itself, that made the automobile possible.

A German engineer, Gottlieb Daimler (GAWT-leeb DIME-lur), invented a light engine in 1886. In 1889, Daimler and Wilhelm Maybach (MIE-bawk) produced an automobile powered by a two-cylinder gasoline engine that reached a speed of 10 miles per hour. However, it was another German, Karl Benz, who went on to design a four-wheeled vehicle that became the basis for the modern automobile. It took time, however, for the automobile to catch on. Early cars, such as the Benz, were handmade and expensive. Only the rich could afford to try one, and only several hundred were sold between 1893 and 1901. Their slow speed, 14 miles per hour, was a problem, too. It prevented early models from being able to climb steep hills.

It was an American, Henry Ford, who revolutionized the car industry. Ford used an assembly line to mass-produce his Model T, beginning in 1908. Before Ford's use of the assembly line, it took a group of workers 12 hours to build a single car. On the assembly line, the same number of workers could build a car in an hour and a half. By cutting production costs, Ford lowered the price of the automobile. A Model T cost $850 in 1908 but only $360 by 1916.

Large numbers of people could now buy an automobile. By 1916, Ford's factories were producing 735,000 cars a year. By 1925, Ford's Model T

▲ *This automobile, a 1914 Ford Model T, was a symbol for the 1920s. Why do you think this car gained popularity so quickly?*

cars made up half of the automobiles in the world. By 1927, when the Ford company decided to discontinue its Model T line, over 18 million of these cars had been built.

1. Who is credited with designing the vehicle that became the basis for our modern-day car?

2. Who revolutionized the car industry? How did he do it?

3. What effect do you think the automobile had on the development of society?

On Line with WORLD HISTORY *Internet Activity*

You may want to have your students visit the following URL, where they will find information and additional web site resources to enhance their study of this chapter.

National Inventors Hall of Fame

http://www.invent.org/book/index.html

This site contains an extensive list of inventors with a short history of the invention. Edison, Bell, Marconi, and the Wright brothers are included.

Due to the ever-changing nature of the World Wide Web, see the West History web site, **http://history.swpco.com** for regular updates of the URLs in this text.

---

cles, electric lights, and typewriters were bought in great quantities.

In the Second Industrial Revolution, manufacturing plants became larger, especially in the iron and steel, machinery, heavy electrical equipment, and chemical industries. Factory owners also streamlined production as much as possible. The development of precision tools enabled manufacturers to produce interchangeable parts, which in turn led to the creation of the assembly line for production. The assembly line was first used in the United States to produce small weapons and clocks. It had moved to Europe by 1850. In the last half of the nineteenth century, it was used in manufacturing sewing machines, typewriters, bicycles, and automobiles.

Not all nations benefited from the Second Industrial Revolution. Between 1870 and 1914, Germany replaced Great Britain as the industrial leader of Europe. Moreover, by 1900, Europe was divided into two economic zones. Great Britain, Belgium, France, the Netherlands, Germany, the western part of the Austro-Hungarian Empire, and northern Italy made up an advanced industrialized core that had a high standard of living, decent systems of transportation, and relatively healthy and educated peoples. Another part of Europe was still largely agricultural. This was the backward and little industrialized area to the south and east, consisting of southern Italy, most of the Austro-Hungarian Empire, Spain, Portugal, the Balkan kingdoms, and Russia. These countries provided food and raw materials for the industrial countries.

Toward a World Economy

The Second Industrial Revolution, combined with the growth of steamships and railroads, fostered a true world economy. By 1900, Europeans were receiving beef and wool from Argentina and Australia, coffee from Brazil, iron ore from Algeria, and sugar from Java. European capital was also invested abroad to develop railways, mines, electrical power plants, and banks. Of course, foreign countries also provided markets for the manufactured goods of Europe. With its capital, industries, and military might, Europe dominated the world economy by the beginning of the twentieth century.

Organizing the Working Classes

Before 1870, capitalist factory owners were largely free to hire workers on their own terms based on market forces. Early efforts by workers to fight for improved working conditions and reasonable wages had largely failed. Real change for the industrial working class came only with the development of **Socialist** parties and Socialist trade unions. These emerged after 1870, but the theory of public ownership of the means of production that made them possible had been developed earlier by Karl Marx.

In 1848, there appeared a short treatise entitled *The Communist Manifesto*, written by two Germans, Karl Marx and Friedrich Engels. Marx and Engels were appalled at the horrible conditions in factories. They blamed the system of industrial capitalism for these conditions and described a new socialist order—a new social system. One form of Marxist socialism was eventually called communism (see Chapter 25).

Marx believed that all of world history was a "history of class struggles." According to Marx, oppressor and oppressed have "stood in constant opposition to one another" throughout history. One group of people—the oppressors—owned the means of production and thus had the power to control government and society. Indeed, government itself was but an instrument of the ruling class. The other group, which depended upon the owners of the means of production, were the oppressed.

In the industrialized societies of Marx's day, the class struggle continued. According to Marx, "society as a whole is more and more splitting up into two great hostile camps, into two great classes directly facing each other: Bourgeoisie and Proletariat." The **bourgeoisie**—the middle class—were the oppressors. The **proletariat**—the working class—were the oppressed. Marx predicted that the struggle between the bourgeoisie and the proletariat would finally break into open revolution with the violent overthrow of the bourgeoisie by the proletariat. For a while the proletariat would form a dictatorship in order to organize the means of production. However, because social classes themselves arose from the economic differences that had been abolished, a classless society would be the end result.

MORE ABOUT . . . *The Self-Starter*

Once started, an automobile engine will run by itself, but it takes a powerful impulse to put all those pistons and shafts in motion. In the early days it was up to the driver to provide that impulse by turning a crank, which could be very dangerous. If left in gear, one could easily end up with broken bones. This made driving a "man's" occupation. In 1911, Charles Kettering figured out how to make a modest size battery deliver a short burst of intense power. His electric starter was introduced on the 1912 Cadillac. Within four years the crank was abandoned on most internal combustion vehicles. Mr. Kettering turned the automobile into a family car, and it became the ordinary household appliance that it is today.

Map 22.1   The Industrial Regions of Europe by 1914

Railroad development		Steel	Oil production	Lowgrade coal
Lines completed by 1848	◆	Engineering	Industrial concentration:	Highgrade coal
Area of main railroad completed by 1870		Chemicals	□ Cities	Iron ore deposits
Other major lines	■	Electrical industry	Areas	Petroleum deposits

ACTIVITY

Have students do additional research on the Second Industrial Revolution, especially world trading patterns. Have them draw a world map that shows the products that were traded, especially foodstuffs, raw materials, and manufactured products. What does the map reveal about industrially developed and industrially underdeveloped nations? How is this information relevant to today?

TEACHING THEMES

Economics and History
Assign students to list reasons why nineteenth century workers might have been dissatisfied with capitalism and, therefore, turned to socialism.

The state—itself an instrument of the bourgeois interests—would wither away (see "You Are There: Marx and Engles Proclaim the Classless Society").

In time, Marx's ideas were picked up by working-class leaders who formed socialist parties. Most important was the German Social Democratic Party (SPD), which emerged in 1875. Under the direction of its two Marxist leaders, Wilhelm Liebknecht (LEEP-next) and August Bebel (BEA-buhl), the SPD spoke of revolution while organizing itself as a mass political party

STUDYING MAPS

The following questions will help you guide students through their study of Map 22.1.

1. Compare this map with the one on page 657. How did the Industrial Revolution spread between the mid- and late-nineteenth century? *(Railroad lines expanded; steel, chemical, electrical industries grew; petroleum played a bigger role)*

2. What parts of Europe still had not progressed through the Industrial Revolution by the late 1800s? *(Eastern Europe)*

3. To what extent had railroad transportation spread beyond the boundaries of industrialization? *(significantly into Eastern Europe and into Spain)*

USING PRIMARY SOURCES

Ask students to write an essay in which they evaluate the final sentences in this selection, "The proletarians have nothing to lose but their chains. They have a world to win." Did the eventual triumph of communism in nations like the Soviet Union or China eliminate all classes? Did their people lose their chains or win the world?

LEARNING FROM VISUALS

Answer to the caption question: Banners with names of the continents join the feet of the workers.

Answers to Critical Thinking Questions

1. Answers will vary.
2. Answers will vary.

YOU ARE THERE
Marx and Engels Proclaim the Classless Society

In The Communist Manifesto, *Karl Marx and Friedrich Engels projected the creation of a classless society as the final end product of the struggle between the bourgeoisie and the proletariat.*

Karl Marx and Friedrich Engels, *The Communist Manifesto*

When, in the course of development, class distinctions have disappeared, and all production has been concentrated in the whole nation, the public power will lose its political character. Political power, properly so called, is merely the organized power of one class for oppressing another. If the proletariat during its contest with the bourgeoisie is compelled, by the force of circumstances, to organize itself as a class, if, by means of a revolution, it makes itself the ruling class, and, as such, sweeps away by force the old conditions of production, then it will, along with these conditions, have swept away the conditions for the existence of class antagonisms and of classes generally, and will thereby have abolished its own supremacy as a class.

In place of the old bourgeois society, with its classes and class antagonisms, we shall have an association, in which the free development of each is the condition for the free development of all. . . .

The Communists disdain to conceal their views and aims. They openly declare that their ends can be attained only by the forcible overthrow of all existing social conditions. Let the ruling classes tremble at a Communist revolution. The proletarians have nothing to lose but their chains. They have a world to win.

Workingmen of all countries, unite!

▲ *Many workers joined working-class parties and socialist groups to try to improve their situations in factories and mines and at home. This German poster proclaims "Proletarians of the World, Unite!" Can you understand the banners that join the feet of the workers?*

---

1. Do you agree with Marx's definition of political power? Why or why not?

2. Do you think Marx's idea of a classless society is realistic? Why or why not?

So What ??

If your students question the importance of information on **Karl Marx,** *tell them . . .*

Marxist thought dominated the world scene for most of the twentieth century. Communism, the antithesis of capitalism, would form the basis for much of the hysteria that drove United States foreign policy during the Cold War. Communism contributed an ideological edge to the existing military threat of the Soviet Union after World War II. After the Revolution of 1917, the United States experienced no less than two "Red Scares," when constitutional freedoms were revoked to protect the country from the "evils" of communism. Most Americans understood the fear, but had little understanding of what communism actually was.

CONNECTIONS
TO OUR WORLD

May Day   On May 1, 1997, parades and demonstrations took place around the world. Mexican workers poured into the streets of Mexico City to denounce the North American Free Trade Agreement (NAFTA). Workers believed it was the cause of the decline in their wages. In Seoul, Korean workers hurled rocks at police to protest government corruption in South Korea. In Berlin and Leipzig, union workers marched to protest high unemployment in Germany. In Beijing, workers filled Tiananmen Square to praise workers at the beginning of a three-day vacation. In Japan, two million workers attended rallies across the country. Fifteen thousand workers marched in the streets of San Salvador to demand that the government pass laws that would benefit the workers of El Salvador.

Why did these marches and demonstrations occur around the world on May 1? In the nineteenth century, the growth of socialist parties in Europe led to a movement to form an international organization. The purpose of this organization was to strengthen the position of socialist parties against international capitalism. In 1889, leaders of various socialist parties formed the Second International, a loose association of national groups. Its first action was to declare May Day (May 1) an international labor day to be marked by strikes and mass labor demonstrations. Although the Second International no longer exists, workers around the world still observe May Day.

competing in elections for the Reichstag (the German parliament). Once in the Reichstag, SPD delegates worked to pass laws that would improve the condition of the working class. Despite government efforts to destroy it, the German Social Democratic Party continued to grow. When it received four million votes in the 1912 elections, it became the largest single party in Germany.

Socialist parties also emerged in other European states. In 1889, leaders of the various socialist parties joined together and formed the Second International, an association of national socialist groups that would fight against capitalism worldwide. (The First International had failed in 1872.) The Second International took some common actions. May Day (May 1), for example, was made an international labor day. However, differences often caused great disorder at its meetings.

One issue that divided international socialism was nationalism. Karl Marx had believed that "the working men have no country" and that workers of all countries would unite against capitalists everywhere. In truth, workers often had strong patriotic feelings. Nationalism remained a much more powerful force than socialism.

Marxist parties were also divided over their goals. Pure Marxists thought that capitalism would be overthrown in a violent revolution. Other Marxists (called **revisionists**) rejected the revolutionary approach and argued that the workers must continue to organize in mass political parties and even work with other parties to gain reforms. As workers received the right to vote, they were in a better position than ever to achieve their aims by working within democratic systems. Revisionists believed that evolution by democratic means, not revolution, would achieve the desired goal of socialism. This idea of evolutionary socialism was especially popular in western Europe, where political rights gave workers the hope of ultimate success.

Another force working for evolutionary rather than revolutionary socialism was the development of trade unions. In Great Britain, unions won the right to strike in the 1870s. Soon after, the masses of workers in factories were organized into trade unions in order to use the instrument of the strike. By 1900, there were two million workers in British trade unions; by 1914, there were almost four million. By 1914, German trade unions, with their three million members, became the second largest group of organized workers in Europe. Trade unions in the rest of Europe had varying degrees of success. By the beginning of World War I, however, they had made considerable progress in bettering both the living and the working conditions of the laboring classes.

MORE ABOUT . . . *Henry George and the Single Tax*

While Marx and Engles advocated state intervention on behalf of the downtrodden workers, a "right wing" argued that the free market was the most efficient and prosperous system. One voice, Henry George, differed from the common left and right wing views. George held that it was society's institutions that were responsible for poverty, and that the institution of land ownership was at the very heart of the problem. Land is owned by the few, while the many are forced to pay the few to make use of it. Taxing land values with a "Single Tax" would have the result of loosening the economic shackles imposed by land owners. Henry George published his ideas in a book called *Progress and Poverty,* and he became one of the most influential reformers of the late nineteenth century.

1. (a) supports public, not private ownership and control over the means of production, (b) the middle class oppressors, per Karl Marx, (c) the working class oppressed, per Karl Marx, (d) Marxists who rejected the revolutionary approach

2. (a) growth in material production after the 1870s
(b) book by Karl Marx and Friedrich Engels, supporting a new social order
(c) Socialist/Marxist political party formed in 1875, (d) a belief that socialism could be brought about gradually, (e) groups of employees organized to bring about better working conditions

3. (a) Answers will vary.
(b) any part could fit in any machine, workers did not need to be skilled

4. (a) Answers will vary.
(b) Answers will vary; students should consider economic, social, ethnic, and educational characteristics.

CLOSE

Discuss the Focus objectives identified on page 690. Emphasize the relationship between progress in the Industrial Revolution and the need workers felt to organize to protect their rights.

SECTION REVIEW

1. **Define:**
   (a) Socialist,   (b) bourgeoisie,   (c) proletariat,
   (d) revisionists

2. **Identify:**
   (a) Second Industrial Revolution,   (b) *The Communist Manifesto*,   (c) German Social Democratic Party (SPD),   (d) evolutionary socialism,   (e) trade unions

3. **Recall:**
   (a) What advantage did electric power and internal combustion engines offer over the steam engine?
   (b) How did interchangeable parts make the assembly line possible?

4. **Think Critically:**
   (a) What similarities can you see between the steamships and railroads that fostered a true world economy in the nineteenth century and the impact the Internet will have on our global economy today?
   (b) For what reasons may people think of society in terms of class structure? What impact may these classifications have on people's lives and society in general?

2

THE EMERGENCE OF MASS SOCIETY

The new urban and industrial world led to the emergence of a mass society by the late nineteenth century. For the lower classes, a mass society brought voting rights, an improved standard of living, and elementary education. Mass society had other features as well. Governments fostered national loyalty and created mass armies. A mass press worked to sway popular opinion. To understand this mass society, we need to examine certain aspects of its structure.

The New Urban Environment

In the course of the nineteenth century, more and more people came to live in cities. In 1800, city dwellers made up 40 percent of the population in Britain, 25 percent in France and Germany, and only 10 percent in eastern Europe. By 1914, urban residents had increased to 80 percent of the population in Britain, 45 percent in France, 60 percent in Germany, and 30 percent in eastern Europe. The size of cities also expanded, especially in industrialized countries. Between 1800 and 1900, London's population grew from 960,000 to 6,500,000. Berlin's population increased from 172,000 to 2,700,000 in the same years.

Urban populations grew so fast mainly because of the vast migration from rural areas to cities. Lack of jobs and lack of land drove people from the countryside to the city. There they found jobs in factories and, later, in service trades and professions. Cities also grew faster in the second half of the nineteenth century because living conditions improved so much that more people could survive there longer.

In the 1840s, a number of urban reformers, such as Edwin Chadwick in England and Rudolf Virchow in Germany, had pointed to filthy living conditions as the chief cause of deadly epidemic diseases in the cities. Cholera (KAW-lur-uh), for example, had ravaged Europe in the early 1830s and 1840s, especially in the overcrowded cities. Following the advice of reformers, city governments created boards of health to improve the quality of housing. City medical officers and building inspectors were authorized to inspect dwellings for public health hazards. New building regulations required running water and an internal drainage system for all new buildings.

Essential to the public health of the modern European city was the ability to bring clean water to it and to expel sewage from it. The need for fresh water was met by a system of dams and reservoirs that stored the water and by aqueducts and tunnels that carried it from the countryside to the city and into individual dwellings. Gas heaters in the 1860s, and later electric heaters, made regular hot baths available to many people. The treatment of sewage was also improved by building mammoth underground pipes that carried raw

---

SPECIAL NEEDS: *Visual*

Have students re-read pages 689–692. Assist them in preparing a chart containing the major achievements that took place in the late 19th and early 20th centuries. The chart should contain three columns: 1) name, 2) country, and 3) achievement. The chart should include Michael Faraday/England/First electric generator; Thomas Edison/U.S./lightbulb; Alexander

Graham Bell/U.S./Telephone; Guglielmo Marconi/Italy/radio waves; Wright Brothers/U.S./airplane; plus others.

Have students prepare a collage or poster of the above inventions along with other inventions that took place during this period; conveyor belts, cranes, sewing machines, etc. They may use the library, internet, or magazines to accomplish this.

Map 22.2   Population Growth in Europe

Inhabitants per square mile

< 20   20–50   50–100   100+

FOCUS

OBJECTIVES

After completing this section, students should be able to

1. describe the development of a new urban environment
2. describe the creation of social structure and mass society
3. identify and explain new opportunities for women
4. identify and describe changes in education and leisure in mass society

FOCUS ACTIVITY

Ask students to make a list of activities in which Americans can participate only if they live in cities. Ask them to explain what the Industrial Revolution had to do with the growth of cities. Finally, ask them to write an essay that describes the relationship between the Industrial Revolution and the growth of urban mass society.

STUDYING MAPS

The following questions will help you guide sutdents through their study of Map 22.2.

1. Where was the heaviest concentration of people per square mile in 1820? *(in the Netherlands between the Seine and Rhine Rivers)*

2. What area had the least inhabitants per square in 1900? *(Russia)*

3. Where is the largest concentration of growth seen in comparing these two maps? *(central part of Western Europe; also, Britain)*

TEACH

COMPARING TIME PERIODS

Ask students to compare the photograph on page 698 with the drawing that appears on page 659. Have them describe how much the life of the poor seems to have changed between the 1870s and 1890s. If they were to find a picture of the same type of neighborhood today what changes would they expect to see? *(Answers will vary based on students' perceptions.)*

▶ *This 1912 photograph shows the grim reality of working-class housing in the East End of London. In most cases these rows of houses had no lawns or trees to break the drab monotony of the streets.*

sewage far from the city for disposal. The city of Frankfurt, Germany, began its program for sewers with a lengthy public campaign featuring the slogan "from the toilet to the river in half an hour."

Middle-class reformers who criticized the unsanitary living conditions of the working class also focused on housing needs. Overcrowded, disease-ridden slums were viewed as dangerous not only to physical health but also to the political and moral health of the entire nation. Early efforts to attack the housing problem followed the middle-class, liberal belief in the power of private, or free, enterprise. Liberal reformers believed that the building of model dwellings that could be rented at a reasonable price would force other private landlords to raise their housing standards. A fine example of this approach was the work of Octavia Hill, a practical-minded British housing reformer who believed that workers and their families were entitled to happy homes.

As the number and size of cities continued to grow, however, governments by the 1880s came to the conclusion that private enterprise could not solve the housing crisis. In 1890, a British Housing Act gave power to local town councils to build inexpensive housing for the working classes. London and Liverpool were the first communities to take advantage of their new powers. Germany was doing the same by 1900. Obviously, the liberal belief that the government that governs least governs best had simply proved untrue in this situation. More and more, governments were moving into new types of activity that they would never have touched earlier.

The Social Structure of Mass Society

At the top of European society stood a wealthy elite that made up only 5 percent of the population while controlling between 30 and 40 percent of the wealth. In the course of the nineteenth century, landed aristocrats had joined with the most successful industrialists, bankers, and merchants (the wealthy upper middle class) to form this new elite. Members of this elite, whether aristocratic or middle class in background, became leaders in the government and military. Marriage also served to unite the two groups. Daughters of business tycoons gained titles, and aristocratic heirs gained new sources of cash. For example, when the

On Line with WORLD HISTORY *Internet Activity*

You may want to have your students visit the following URL, where they will find information and additional web site resources to enhance their study of this chapter.

Edison Internet Museum

http://www.naples.net/~arzone/home.htm

This site includes all aspects of Edison's life and inventions. Other web sight links are included.

Due to the ever-changing nature of the World Wide Web, see the West History web site, **http://history.swpco.com** for regular updates of the URLs in this text.

Ask students to evaluate the following statement. Do they believe it is true? To what extent might it explain social values in different classes of society today?

Middle class values are held by those who can afford them. People who are poor are not likely to be able to afford good conduct or Christian Morality.

American Consuelo Vanderbilt married the British duke of Marlborough, the new duchess brought $10 million to her husband.

The middle classes consisted of a variety of groups. Below the upper middle class was a middle group that included lawyers, doctors, and members of the civil service, as well as the business managers, engineers, architects, accountants, and chemists created by industrial expansion. Beneath this solid and comfortable middle group was a lower middle class of small shopkeepers, traders, and prosperous peasants. The members of this group provided goods and services for the classes above them.

Standing between the lower middle class and the lower classes were new groups of white-collar workers who were the product of the Second Industrial Revolution. They were the traveling salespeople, bookkeepers, telephone operators, department store salespeople, and secretaries. Although they were little better paid than skilled workers, these white-collar workers were often committed to middle-class ideals.

The middle classes shared a certain style of life—one whose values tended to dominate much of nineteenth-century society. The members of the middle class liked to preach their worldview both to their children and to the upper and lower classes of their society. This was especially evident in Victorian Britain, often considered a model of middle-class society. The European middle classes believed in hard work, which was open to everyone and guaranteed to have positive results. They were also regular churchgoers who believed in the good conduct associated with traditional Christian morality. The middle class was concerned with the right way of doing things, which gave rise to such best-selling books as *The Habits of Good Society* and *Don't: A Manual of Mistakes More or Less Prevalent in Conduct and Speech.*

Below the middle classes on the social scale were the working classes of European society, who made up almost 80 percent of the European population. Many of the members of these classes were landholding peasants, farm laborers, and sharecroppers, especially in eastern Europe. The urban working class consisted of many different groups, including skilled artisans and semiskilled laborers. Skilled artisans worked in such trades as cabinetmaking and printing. Semiskilled laborers included carpenters and many factory workers, and they earned wages that were about two-thirds the wages of highly skilled workers. At the bottom of the urban working class were the unskilled laborers. They were the largest group of workers and included day laborers and large numbers of domestic servants. One out of every seven employed persons in Great Britain in 1900 was a domestic servant. Most domestic servants were women.

Urban workers experienced an improvement in the material conditions of their lives after 1870. For one thing, cities created better living conditions. A rise in real wages, accompanied by a decline in many consumer costs, made it possible for workers to buy more than just food and housing. Workers now had money for more clothes and even leisure at the same time that strikes were leading to ten-hour workdays and Saturday afternoons off.

The Experiences of Women

In 1800, women were largely defined by family and household roles. They remained legally inferior and economically dependent. In the course of the nineteenth century, women struggled to change their status.

Women and Work: New Job Opportunities

During much of the nineteenth century, working-class groups upheld the belief that women should remain at home to bear and nurture children and not be allowed in the industrial workforce. Working-class men argued that keeping women out of industrial work would ensure the moral and physical well-being of families. In reality, however, when their husbands were unemployed, women had to do low-wage work at home or labor part-time in sweatshops to support their families.

The Second Industrial Revolution opened the door to new jobs for women. The growth of larger industrial plants and the expansion of government services created a wide number of service and white-collar jobs. The high demand for white-collar workers at relatively low wages coupled with a shortage of male workers led

MORE ABOUT . . . *Thorstein Veblen*

In the late nineteenth century, Thorstein Veblen's ideas about social forces helped to create a new discipline called sociology. Sociology, the study of people living together in society, teaches that institutions mold and shape our thoughts. Institutions form an accepted pattern for the entire group, and are formed by a combination of customs, beliefs, and traditions. Images of success, as shown through advertising and the media, seduce people into buying "status" items. People in the upper and middle classes tend to buy goods that are expensive, useless, or wasteful to impress others with their wealth. Veblen called this type of buying "conspicuous consumption."

USING PRIMARY SOURCES

Have students write an updated version of Tennyson's poem that is appropriate to the economic and social conditions in which they live. Have them explain their work.

LEARNING FROM VISUALS

Assign students to find a photograph that shows a typical location where women employees might work today. Ask students to identify and explain differences between their picture and the picture here. What are several changes in technology and social values that have benefitted women in the past century?

Answer to the caption question: Women may now enter any job market they choose, a major change since the early 1900s.

CLASS DISCUSSION

Ask students to describe changes in the social role of the nuclear family from the beginning of the twentieth century to the present.

employers to hire women. Big businesses and retail shops needed clerks, typists, secretaries, file clerks, and salesclerks. The expansion of government services created opportunities for women to be secretaries and telephone operators, as well as to take jobs in the fields of health and social services. Compulsory (legally required) elementary education created a need for more teachers. The development of hospital services opened the way for an increase in nurses.

Many of the new white-collar jobs were by no means exciting. The work was routine and, except for teaching and nursing, required few skills. However, these jobs had real advantages for the daughters of the middle classes and especially the upward-aspiring working classes. For some middle-class women, the new jobs offered freedom from the domestic patterns expected of them. Most of the new jobs, however, were filled by working-class women who saw their chance to escape from the "dirty" work of the lower-class world.

Marriage and the Family

Many people in the nineteenth century admired the ideal expressed in Alfred, Lord Tennyson's (TENN-i-sun) *The Princess*, published in 1847:

Man for the field and woman for the hearth:
Man for the sword and for the needle she:
Man with the head and woman with the heart:
Man to command and woman to obey.

This view of the sexes was still popular in the nineteenth century, largely because of the impact of the Industrial Revolution on the family. As the chief family wage earners, men worked outside the home. Women were left with the care of the family, work for which they were paid nothing. Of course, the ideal did not always match reality, especially for the lower classes. A need for extra income often drove lower-class women to do low-wage work.

▲ *The Second Industrial Revolution created many new jobs for women. This illustration of a 1904 Paris telephone exchange shows that most of the telephone operators were women, and a woman was employed as a secretary as well. How have jobs for women changed since the early 1900s?*

For most women, marriage was viewed as the only honorable and available career throughout most of the nineteenth century. The middle class glorified the ideal of women in the home. For most women, however, marriage was a matter of economic necessity. The lack of meaningful work and the lower wages paid to women for their work made it difficult for single women to earn a living. Most women chose to marry.

The family was the central institution of middle-class life. Men provided the family income, and women focused on household and child care. At the same time, by reducing the number of children in the family, mothers could devote more time to child care and domestic leisure (see "Young People in Victorian Britain: Middle-Class Children"). The decline in the number of children born to the average woman was the most significant development in the modern family and was already evident in the nineteenth century. This decline in the birthrate was tied to improved economic conditions, the rise of birth control, and abortion. In 1882 in Amsterdam, Dr. Aletta Jacob founded Europe's first birth control clinic.

So What ??

*If your students question the importance of information on "**a rise in real wages**" (see page 699) tell them . . .*

Wages are defined as the payments made to labor for its contribution to the production of wealth. In the United States, wages make up three quarters of all payments to the factors of production. Real wages refer to the purchasing power of money wages—how much real wealth money can buy at current prices. When money wages increase, and inflation increases at the same rate, real wages remain constant.

▲ Many Happy Returns of the Day *depicts a middle-class family celebrating a little girl's birthday. Grandparents, parents, and children are all enjoying the festivities. How does this birthday gathering compare to parties you have attended?*

Women in working-class families were accustomed to hard work. Daughters in working-class families were expected to work until they married. Even after marriage, they often did piecework at home to support the family. For the children of the working classes, childhood was over by the age of nine or ten, when children became apprentices or were employed in odd jobs.

Between 1890 and 1914, however, family patterns among the working class began to change. High-paying jobs in heavy industry and improvements in the standard of living made it possible for working-class families to depend on the income of husbands alone. By the early twentieth century, some working-class mothers could afford to stay at home, following the pattern of middle-class women. At the same time, working-class families also aspired to buy new consumer products, such as sewing machines, clocks, bicycles, and cast-iron stoves.

Working-class families also followed the middle classes in having fewer children. As child labor laws and compulsory education took children out of the workforce and into schools, children were seen as dependents rather than wage earners. At the same time, strikes and labor agitation led to laws that reduced work hours to ten hours per day by 1900 and eliminated work on Saturday afternoons. Working-class parents now had more time to spend with their children and often developed closer emotional ties with them.

The Movement for Women's Rights

Modern European feminism, or the movement for women's rights, had its beginnings during the French Revolution, when some women advocated equality for women based on the doctrine of natural rights. In the 1830s, a number of women in the United States and Europe argued for the right of women to divorce and own property. At the time, it was difficult for women to secure divorces, and property laws gave husbands almost complete control over the property of their wives. The early efforts were not very successful, however. Women did not gain the right to own property until 1870 in Britain, 1900 in Germany, and 1907 in France.

The fight for property rights was only a beginning for the women's movement, however. Some middle- and upper-middle-class women fought for and gained access to universities, and others sought entry into occupations dominated by men. The first occupation to which women gained access was teaching. Medical training was largely closed to women, so they sought alternatives in nursing. A nursing pioneer in Germany was Amalie Sieveking, who founded the Female Association for the Care of the Poor and Sick in Hamburg. Even more famous was the British nurse Florence Nightingale. Her efforts during the Crimean War (1854 to 1856), combined with those of Clara Barton in the U.S. Civil War (1861 to 1865), transformed nursing into a profession of trained, middle-class "women in white."

Answer to the caption question: Answers will vary.

GROUP ACTIVITY

Have students work together in groups to develop biographies on Amalie Sieveking, Florence Nightingale, Clara Barton, and other women who made names for themselves in occupations dominated by men. Assign one woman to be researched by each group. Encourage groups to develop creative ways to present the material they find to the rest of the class.

CLASS DISCUSSION

Why do students believe women were more successful in achieving their demands for more equal rights and opportunities during and after wars?

MORE ABOUT . . . *Margaret Sanger*

Although Margaret Sanger lived in an upper class neighborhood in New York City, she was bored with her existence. Margaret was most interested in what her radical friend, Emma Goldman the anarchist, had to say about the limitation of family size. In the summer of 1912, Margaret met Sadie Sachs, the mother of a number of children, who suffered from blood poisoning caused by a self-induced abortion. Many poverty-stricken women who discovered that they were pregnant tried to abort themselves. Margaret was called back a few months later when Sadie tried the same procedure again. This time, Sadie died a few moments after Margaret's arrival. Later Margaret would say that Sadie Sachs's death would be a turning point in her life. She devoted herself to finding the answer to the last question Sadie and other women asked: "But how can I prevent it?"

YOUNG PEOPLE IN VICTORIAN BRITAIN

Divide students into groups and assign them to develop lists of differences between the lives of Victorian children and their own experiences. Compare and discuss the lists in class. Do students think they would have liked to grow up in Victorian Britain? Ask them to explain their feelings.

LEARNING FROM VISUALS

Answer to the caption question: Students should support their answers with reason and logic.

YOUNG PEOPLE IN VICTORIAN BRITAIN

Middle-Class Children

The new middle-class ideal of the family home had an impact on child raising and children's play in the nineteenth century. People believed that children were entitled to a long childhood in which they were involved in activities with other children their own age. The early environment in which they were raised, it was thought, would determine how they turned out. Mothers were seen as the most important force in protecting children from the harmful influences of the adult world. The father remained the symbol of authority. Children were taught to please their parents, whom they should both love and fear.

New children's games and toys, including mass-produced dolls for girls, appeared in middle-class homes. However, games and toys were not only for fun but also for instruction. One advice manual

▶ *This painting shows well-dressed girls playing a form of picture lotto, a game that continues to be popular with children today. Based on what you have read in your text, do you think boys would have played this game? Why or why not?*

By the 1840s and 1850s, the movement for women's rights had entered the political arena as women called for equal political rights. Many feminists believed that the right to vote was the key to all other reforms to improve the position of women. The British women's movement was the most active in Europe. The Women's Social and Political Union, founded in 1903 by Emmeline Pankhurst and her daughters (see "Biography: The Pankhursts"), used unusual publicity stunts to call attention to its demands. Its members pelted government officials with eggs, chained themselves to lampposts, burned railroad cars, and smashed the win-dows of department stores on fashionable shopping streets. Suffragists had one basic aim: the right of women to full citizenship in the nation-state (see "Our Literary Heritage: *A Doll's House*—One Woman's Cry for Freedom" on p. 719).

Before World War I, the demands for women's rights were being heard throughout Europe and the United States. However, only in Norway and some U.S. states did women actually receive the right to vote before 1914. It would take the dramatic upheaval of World War I before male-dominated governments gave in on this basic issue.

CNN. WORLD HISTORY UPDATES

You can update your coverage of World History topics, as well as spark lively classroom discussion and deeper understanding, by using the **CNN World History Updates**.

For assistance in using and incorporating the **CNN World History Updates** into your classroom presentations, see the *Classroom Guide*.

YOUNG PEOPLE IN VICTORIAN BRITAIN

Middle-Class Children, continued

stated that young children should learn checkers because it "calls forth the resources of the mind in the most gentle, as well as the most successful manner." Puzzles of maps and of the kings of England helped prepare boys for their future careers. Paper patterns for making dolls' clothes prepared girls for their future homemaking roles.

The sons of the middle-class family were expected to follow careers like those of their fathers, so they were kept in school until the age of 16 or 17. Sports were used in the schools to "toughen" boys up. Their leisure activities centered around military concerns and character building. This combination was especially evident in the creation of the Boy Scouts in Great Britain in 1908. The Boy Scouts provided recreation for boys between 12 and 18 years of age. Adventure was combined with the discipline of earning merit badges and ranks. In this way, the Boy Scouts instilled ideals of patriotism and self-sacrifice. Many men viewed activities like those offered by the Boy Scouts as a way of counteracting the possible dangers that female domination of the home posed for boys. As one scout leader wrote, "The REAL Boy Scout is not a sissy. He adores his mother but is not hitched to her apron strings."

There was little organized recreational activity of this kind for girls. Robert Baden-Powell, founder of the Boy Scouts, did encourage his sister to establish a girls' division of the Boy Scouts. Agnes Baden-Powell made clear the goal of the girls' group when she stated that "you do not want to make tomboys of refined girls. The main object is to give them all the ability to be better mothers and guides to the next generation."

1. What were the parents' roles in middle-class Britain?

2. What was the purpose of the Boy Scouts?

3. What was the purpose of the girls' division of the Boy Scouts?

4. Are the ideals stated here for parents, boys, and girls still evident in our society today?

Education in an Age of Mass Society

Mass education was a product of the mass society of the late nineteenth and early twentieth centuries. Being educated in the early nineteenth century had meant attending a secondary school or possibly even a university. In secondary schools, students received a classical education based on the study of Greek and Latin. Secondary and university educations were primarily for the elite or the wealthier middle class.

Between 1870 and 1914, most Western governments began to set up state-financed primary schools that required both boys and girls between the ages of six and twelve to attend. States also took responsibility for training teachers by setting up teacher-training schools.

Why did Western nations make this commitment to mass education? One reason was industrialization. In the first Industrial Revolution, unskilled labor was able to meet factory needs. The new firms of the Second Industrial Revolution, however, needed skilled labor. Mass education gave industrialists the trained workers they needed. Both boys and girls with elementary educations now had new job possibilities beyond their vil-

RETEACHING ACTIVITY

EDUCATION IN AN AGE OF MASS SOCIETY

Review the two goals of Western nations in making a commitment to mass education on pages 703–704. Have students write an essay comparing and contrasting those goals with modern society. Student answers should include comments on the need for a skilled labor force and better educated voters.

CLASS DISCUSSION

Ask students to identify what, for them, constitutes a set of national values. Ask them to discuss whether they have learned national values from attending school. What functions do they believe society expects schools to fulfill. How many of these expectations do students feel can realistically be accomplished in school? What national values are better taught at home?

LEARNING FROM VISUALS

Assign students to find a photograph of a recent gathering of the National Organization for Women (NOW). Have them compare the two pictures. What similarities and differences can they identify between the two groups?

Answer to the caption question: Students should support their answers with reason and logic.

BIOGRAPHY

The Pankhursts

Emmeline Pankhurst recalled that her determination to fight for women's rights stemmed from a childhood memory: "My father bent over me, shielding the candle flame with his big hand and I heard him say, somewhat sadly, 'What a pity she wasn't born a lad.'" Eventually, Pankhurst and her daughters became suffragists; they marched and fought for the right of women to vote.

The struggle was often violent. "They came in bruised, hatless, faces scratched, eyes swollen, noses bleeding," one of the Pankhurst daughters recalled. The women were often arrested for damaging property or disturbing the peace. Once in jail, the Pankhursts, like other suffragists, went on hunger strikes. This was a potentially dangerous action. The government allowed prison authorities to force-feed hunger strikers by pouring liquids

▶ *This black and white photo shows a confident, smiling Emmeline Pankhurst with daughters, Christábel and Adela. They are joined by Mrs. Pethick Lawrence, another suffragist. Why do you think it took so long for women to be granted the right to vote?*

lages or small towns. These included white-collar jobs in railways, post offices, banking firms, and the teaching and nursing fields.

The chief motive for mass education, however, was political. Giving more people the right to vote created a need for better-educated voters. Even more important, however, was the fact that primary schools instilled patriotism. As people lost their ties to local regions and even to religion, nationalism gave them a new faith. Furthermore, children in schools were taught a single national language, which brought greater national unity.

National values, then, determined what was taught in the elementary schools. Reading, writing, arithmetic, national history (especially history geared to a patriotic view), geography, literature, and some singing and drawing were taught in most primary schools. Often, boys and girls were separated. Girls learned domestic skills such as sewing, washing, ironing, and cooking, all necessary for providing a good home for a husband and children. Boys acquired some practical skills, such as carpentry, and even had some military drill. Most of the elementary schools also taught the middle-class virtues of hard work, thrift, cleanliness,

RETEACHING ACTIVITY

Have students construct a chart of the social pyramid in Europe at the turn of the century. Students should include the per-centage of the population at each level, and the groups that belonged at each level.

BIOGRAPHY

The Pankhursts, continued

into their stomachs "through a rubber tube clamped to the nose or mouth."

Neither jail nor abusive treatment could stop the Pankhursts, however. When Emmeline, a strong-willed woman with a flair for public speaking, was arrested and jailed in 1908, she informed her judges, "If you had the power to send us to prison, not for six months, but for six years, or for our lives, the Government must not think they could stop this agitation. It would go on!" It did go on, and women in Britain eventually received the right to vote.

The Pankhursts reacted to their success by taking on new causes. Emmeline became active in moral issues until her death in 1928. Her eldest daughter, Christábel, became an ardent evangelical Christian. She moved to the United States and settled in California, where she died in 1959. Sylvia, Emmeline's second daughter, worked for social reform in London's working-class slums and became one of the founders of Britain's Communist Party. She moved to Ethiopia to fight against the Italian invasion of that African country. At

the time of her death in 1956, she was the editor of the chief English-language newspaper in Ethiopia. Throughout their careers, the Pankhursts remained firmly committed to their ideals.

1. What was Emmeline Pankhurst's early memory that fueled her determination to fight for women's rights?

2. Were the Pankhursts' actions successful?

3. Would you be willing to go through the things the Pankhursts suffered for something you believe in? Why or why not?

4. Can you identify an individual, or individuals, who is fighting today for social causes against strong opposition? Would you be willing to join in the fight? Why or why not?

and respect for the family. For most students, elementary education led to apprenticeship and a job.

Compulsory elementary education created a demand for teachers. Most of them were women. Many men saw the teaching of children as a part of women's "natural role" as nurturers of children. Moreover, females were paid lower salaries, which in itself was a strong incentive for governments to set up teacher-training schools for women. The first female colleges were really teacher-training schools. It was not until the beginning of the twentieth century that women were permitted to enter male-dominated universities.

The most immediate result of mass education was an increase in literacy, or the ability to read. In Germany, Great Britain, France, and the Scandinavian countries, adult illiteracy was almost eliminated by 1900. Where there was less schooling, the story was very different. Adult illiteracy rates were 79 percent in Serbia and Russia, for example.

With the increase in literacy after 1870 came the rise of mass newspapers, such as the *Evening News* (1881) and the *Daily Mail* (1896) in London. Millions of copies were sold each day. Known as the yellow press in the United States, these newspapers were all written

COMPARING TIME PERIODS

Ask students to explain how the growth of organized and professional sports has reduced class distinctions in recent years.

LEARNING FROM VISUALS

Assign students to find a photograph of a recent professional sports event. What similarities and differences can students identify between people in the photograph on this page and the recent photograph? Ask students to describe a family outing to a sporting event that they have experienced. How have technological advancements and economic prosperity made this kind of experience possible?

Answers to Critical Thinking Questions

1. They offered leisure and fun, training in individual and team skills.
2. Answers will vary.
3. Answers will vary.

SPORTS AND CONTESTS
The New Team Sports

Sports were by no means a new activity in the late nineteenth century. Soccer games had been played by peasants and workers, and these games were often bloody or even deadly. In the late nineteenth century, sports became strictly organized. The English Football Association (founded in 1863) and the American Bowling Congress (founded in 1895), for example, provided strict rules and officials to enforce them.

The new sports were not just for leisure or fun. Like other forms of middle-class recreation, they were intended to provide excellent training, especially for youth. The participants not only could develop individual skills but also could acquire a sense of teamwork useful for military service. These characteristics were already evident in the British public schools in the 1850s and 1860s.

▶ *Croquet was especially popular in the 1870s because both men and women could play. Croquet is still played competitively in Britain and in the United States.*

in an easily understood style. They were also sensational, as they provided lurid details of crimes, gossip, and sports news.

Leisure in an Age of Mass Society

With the Industrial Revolution came new forms of leisure. Work and leisure became opposites as leisure came to be viewed as what people do for fun after work. In fact, the new leisure hours created by the industrial system—evening hours after work, weekends, and a week or two in the summer—largely determined the forms of the new mass leisure.

New technology created new experiences for leisure, such as the Ferris wheel at amusement parks. The subways and streetcars of the 1880s meant that even the working classes could make their way to athletic games, amusement parks, and dance halls. Likewise, railroads could take people to the beaches on weekends.

The upper and middle classes had created the first market for tourism. As wages went up and workers were given paid vacations, however, tourism, too, became another form of mass leisure. Thomas Cook was a British pioneer of mass tourism. Cook found that by renting special trains, lowering prices, and increasing the number of passengers, he could make substan-

---

ENRICHMENT ACTIVITY

Have students do some research on how leisure time activities have changed over the years. Students should interview people from their own generation, their parents' generation, and their grandparents' generation. They should ask questions such as: What kinds of leisure activities did you participate in as a child? How much time did you have to spend on leisure activities? What kinds of leisure activities do you participate in now? How much time do you have to spend on leisure activities now? Have students bring their results to class and compile a class analysis of the information collected. Have students discuss why they think leisure activities and the amount of time spent on them has changed over the years.

SPORTS AND CONTESTS

The New Team Sports, continued

Such schools as Harrow and Loretto placed organized sports at the center of education. At Loretto, for example, education was supposed to instill "First—Character. Second—Physique. Third—Intelligence. Fourth—Manners. Fifth—Information."

The new team sports rapidly became professionalized as well. In Britain, soccer had its Football Association in 1863. In the United States, the first national association to recognize professional baseball players was formed in 1863. By 1900, the National League and the American League had complete control over professional baseball. Subways and streetcars made possible the building of stadiums where thousands could attend. Thus, mass spectator sports became a big business. In 1872, 2,000 people watched the British Soccer Cup finals. By 1885, the crowd had increased to 10,000 and by 1901, to 100,000. Spectator sports even reflected class differences. Upper-class soccer teams in Britain viewed working-class teams as vicious and inclined to "money-grubbing, tricks, sensational displays, and utter rottenness."

The sports cult of the late nineteenth century was mostly for men, who believed that females were not particularly suited for "vigorous physical activity." Nevertheless, it was permissible for middle-class women to play such "easy" sports as croquet and lawn tennis. Eventually, some sports began to appear at women's colleges and girls' public schools in England.

1. What did sports offer middle-class men of the late nineteenth century?

2. Why do you think spectator sports became such a big business?

3. Compare the educational goals at your school with those at Loretto. What are the differences? the similarities?

---

tial profits. By the late nineteenth century, team sports had also developed into yet another form of mass leisure (see "Sports and Contests: The New Team Sports").

The new forms of popular leisure drew masses of people and mostly served to provide entertainment and distract people from the realities of their work lives. The new mass leisure was quite different from earlier forms of popular culture. The earlier festivals and fairs had been based on community participation. The new forms of mass leisure were standardized for largely passive mass audiences. Amusement parks and professional sports teams were, after all, big businesses organized to make profits.

 SECTION REVIEW

1. **Identify:**
   (a) white-collar jobs,   (b) the Women's Social and Political Union,   (c) Thomas Cook

2. **Recall:**
   (a) What forces drove people from the countryside to the cities in the nineteenth century?
   (b) What problems did the urban poor encounter in the cities?
   (c) In what way did the Second Industrial Revolution open the door to new jobs for women?

You can choose from a variety of assessments to evaluate your students' mastery of the objectives for this section as stated on page 697. Possible assessments include:

1. Section Review Questions on this page
2. Section 22–2 Quiz in your Teacher Resource Material
3. Reteaching Worksheets in your Teacher Resource material
4. Self-Study software

ALTERNATIVE ASSESSMENT

Assign students to compare the daily life of a typical family in 1880 with their own lives today. Their task is to identify differences and explain why these differences exist.

Answers to SECTION REVIEW

1. (a) traveling salespeople, bookkeepers, telephone operators, etc., held middle-class ideals, (b) founded by Emmeline Pankhurst in 1903, dedicated to promoting equal rights for women in Great Britain, (c) a British pioneer of mass tourism
2. (a) to find jobs, shortage of good farm land. (b) overcrowding, a shortage of good water, sewage treatment, inadequate housing (c) new factories and businesses created demand for workers who would accept low wages; jobs did not require great physical strength (d) did not have the legal right to own property,

receive pay, or enter into contracts
(e) to create an educated work force
3. (a) Answers will vary, some believe government involvement reduces people's freedoms, creates inefficiencies
(b) Answers may involve discussions of people who had no property, opportunity to work, or ability to obtain an education

CLOSE

Lead students in a discussion of the Focus objectives identified on page 697. Stress the importance of changes in society that were made possible through technological advancements.

(d) Why was marriage a matter of economic necessity for most women during the nineteenth century?
(e) Why did many European states provide mass education in the nineteenth century?

3. **Think Critically:**
(a) Why do many people still believe that the "government that governs least governs best"?
(b) Why may it not have been reasonable for European middle classes to believe that hard work was open to everyone and would guarantee positive results?

THE NATIONAL STATE

Throughout much of the Western world by 1870, the national state had become the focus of people's loyalties. Only in Russia, eastern Europe, the Austro-Hungarian Empire, and Ireland did national groups still struggle for independence.

The United States

Four years of bloody civil war had preserved American national unity, but the old South had been destroyed. One-fifth of the adult white male population in the South had been killed, and four million black slaves had been freed. The Thirteenth Amendment to the U.S. Constitution in 1865 abolished slavery. The Fourteenth and Fifteenth Amendments later gave citizenship to blacks and guaranteed black males the right to vote. However, new state laws in southern states soon stripped blacks of their right to vote. By the end of the 1870s, supporters of white supremacy were back in power everywhere in the South.

Between 1860 and 1914, the United States made the shift from an agrarian to an industrial nation. American heavy industry stood unchallenged in 1900. In that year, the Carnegie (KAR-nuh-gee) Steel Com-

pany alone produced more steel than did Great Britain's entire steel industry. As in Europe, industrialization in the United States led to urbanization. Whereas 20 percent of Americans lived in cities in 1860, over 40 percent did in 1900.

By 1900, the United States had become the world's richest nation. Yet serious problems remained. In 1890, the richest 9 percent of Americans owned an incredible 71 percent of all the wealth. Labor unrest over unsafe working conditions and regular cycles of devastating unemployment led workers to organize. By the turn of the century, the American Federation of Labor had emerged as labor's chief voice, but it lacked real power. In 1900, its members were only 8.4 percent of American workers.

During the Progressive Era after 1900, the reform of many features of American life became a key issue. Under President Theodore Roosevelt (ROE-zuh-vult), the federal government began to regulate corrupt industrial practices. President Woodrow Wilson created a graduated federal income tax. Like European states, the United States was slowly adopting policies that increased the power of the central government.

At the end of the nineteenth century, the United States began to expand abroad. The Samoan (suh-MOE-un) Islands in the Pacific became the first important U.S. colony. By 1887, U.S. settlers had gained control of the sugar industry on the Hawaiian Islands. As more Americans settled in Hawaii, they sought to gain political power. When Queen Liliuokalani (li-LEE-uh-WOE-kuh-LAWN-ee) tried to strengthen the power of the monarchy in order to keep the islands for the native peoples, the U.S. government sent U.S. Marines to "protect" American lives. The queen was deposed, and Hawaii was annexed by the United States in 1898.

The defeat of Spain by the United States in the Spanish-American War in 1898 encouraged the United States to extend its empire by acquiring Cuba, Puerto Rico, Guam, and the Philippine Islands. Although the Filipinos (FILL-uh-PEEN-ohz) hoped for independence, the United States refused to grant it. As President William McKinley said, the United States had the duty "to educate the Filipinos and uplift and Christianize them," a remarkable statement in view of

So What ⁇

*If your students question the importance of information on **the Progressive Era**, tell them . . .*

The quality of life for most Americans would be vastly different if it weren't for the many reforms accomplished during this remarkable era. Included among the many

improvements was the Food and Drug Administration for the protection of consumers, the women's right to vote, the direct election of United States Senators, and the Conservation of our forests and natural parks.

the fact that for centuries, most Filipinos had been Roman Catholics. It took 3 years and 60,000 troops to pacify the Philippines and establish U.S. control. By the beginning of the twentieth century, the United States had an empire.

Canada

Canada, too, faced problems of national unity between 1870 and 1914. At the beginning of 1870, the Dominion of Canada had four provinces: Quebec, Ontario, Nova Scotia (SKOE-shuh), and New Brunswick. With the addition of two more provinces in 1871—Manitoba and British Columbia—the Dominion of Canada extended from the Atlantic to the Pacific.

Real unity was difficult to achieve, however, because of the distrust between the English-speaking and French-speaking peoples of Canada. Wilfred Laurier (lor-ee-A), who became the first French-Canadian prime minister in 1896, was able to reconcile Canada's two major groups. During his administration, industrialization boomed and immigrants from Europe helped to populate Canada's vast territories.

Western Europe: The Growth of Political Democracy

By 1871, Great Britain had a working two-party parliamentary system. For the next 50 years, Liberals and Conservatives alternated in power at regular intervals. Both parties were led by a ruling class composed of aristocratic landowners and upper-middle-class businesspeople. The Liberals and Conservatives competed with each other in passing laws that expanded the right to vote. Reform Acts in 1867 and 1884 expanded the number of adult males who could vote. By the end of World War I (1918), all males over age 21 and women over age 30 could vote. At the beginning of World War I (1914), political democracy was well established in Britain. Social welfare measures for the working class soon followed.

The Liberals in Great Britain were disturbed by two developments. First, trade unions grew, and they began to favor a more radical change of the economic system. Second, in 1900 the Labour party, which dedicated itself to the interests of the workers, emerged. The Liberals held the government from 1906 to 1914 and soon perceived that they would have to create a program of social welfare or else lose the support of the workers. Therefore, the Liberals voted for a series of social reforms. The National Insurance Act of 1911 provided benefits for workers in case of sickness and unemployment. Additional laws provided a small pension for those over age 70 and compensation for those injured in accidents while at work.

In France, the collapse of Louis Napoleon's Second Empire left the country in confusion. In 1875, a new constitution created a republic. The new government had an upper house, or Senate, elected indirectly and a lower house, or Chamber of Deputies, chosen by universal male suffrage. The powers of the president, who was chosen by the legislature for seven years, were deliberately left vague. The premier (or prime minister) led the government. He and his ministers were responsible not to the president but to the Chamber of Deputies. This principle of **ministerial responsibility,** or the idea that a prime minister is responsible to the popularly elected legislative body and not to the executive officer, is a crucial one for a democracy.

The French Constitution of 1875 was meant to be temporary, but the republic—France's Third Republic—lasted 65 years. France failed to develop a strong parliamentary system, however. The existence of a dozen political parties forced the premier to depend upon a coalition of parties to stay in power. Regular changes of government plagued the Third Republic. Nevertheless, by 1914, the French Third Republic commanded the loyalty of most French people.

Italy had emerged by 1870 as a united state. It believed that it was now a great power. Its internal weaknesses, however, made that a poor claim. Italy had little sense of community because of the great gulf that separated a poverty-stricken south from an industrializing north. Constant turmoil between labor and industry undermined the social fabric. The Italian government was unable to deal with these problems because of the widespread corruption among government officials. The grant of universal male suffrage in 1912 did little to correct the widespread corruption and weak government.

FOCUS

OBJECTIVES

After completing this section, students should be able to

1. identify and describe developments in the United States and Canada
2. explain the growth of democracy in Western Europe
3. identify and describe reasons for the continued existence of the Old Order in Eastern Europe
4. describe results of international rivalry and war in the Balkans

FOCUS ACTIVITY

Help students understand that a more equal distribution of income and wealth often leads to a more equal distribution of political power. Ask students to explain why poor people are less able to participate in the political process than people who are in the middle or upper economic classes. Assign students to write an essay that explains why the Industrial Revolution resulted in a political revolution in most countries.

ENRICHMENT ACTIVITY

Before discussing the distribution of wealth, pick up a few dozen donut holes, or miniature candy bars. Distribute them to the class as follows: ten percent of the class receives 70 percent of the candy bars, the next ten percent receive 15 percent and the remaining eighty percent receives the last 15 percent of treats. Refer to the distribution of wealth in the United States at the beginning of the twentieth century (p. 708). Then break out some extra candy before your students revolt!

TEACH

CLASS DISCUSSION

By 1918, who could vote in Great Britain? *(All males over age 21, females over age 30.)* Discuss possible reasons for this age difference.

Map 22.3   Europe in 1871

Legend:
- German Empire
- Austria-Hungary
- Italy
- France
- Ottoman Empire

Central and Eastern Europe: Persistence of the Old Order

Germany, Austria-Hungary (or the Austro-Hungarian Empire), and Russia pursued policies that were quite different from those of the western European nations. Germany and Austria-Hungary had legislative bodies and elections by universal male suffrage, but powerful monarchies and conservative social groups remained strong. In Russia, the old system of autocracy was barely touched by the winds of change.

The constitution of the new imperial Germany begun by Bismarck in 1871 provided for a two-house legislature. The lower house of the German parliament, known as the Reichstag, was elected on the basis of universal male suffrage, but it did not have ministerial responsibility. Ministers of government were responsible not to the parliament but to the emperor. The emperor also commanded the armed forces and controlled foreign policy and the government bureaucracy. As chancellor (or prime minister), Bismarck worked to keep Germany from becoming a democracy.

During the reign of Emperor William II, from 1888 to 1918, the new imperial Germany continued as an authoritarian state. By the end of William's reign, Germany had become the strongest military and industrial power on the Continent. Cities had mushroomed in number and size. However, these rapid changes caused divisions in German society. With the expansion of industry and cities came demands for a real democracy. Conservative forces—especially the landowning nobility and big industrialists, two of the powerful ruling groups in imperial Germany—tried to block the movement for democracy by supporting a strong foreign policy. Expansion abroad, they believed, would not only increase their profits but also divert people's attention from democracy.

A new, radical right-wing political movement added to the tensions in German society. Groups such as the Pan-German League stressed strong German patriotism and favored expansion abroad as a way to unite all classes. These groups were also anti-Semitic and blamed Jews for destroying national community.

After the creation of the dual monarchy of Austria-Hungary in 1867, the Austrian part received a constitution that in theory set up a parliamentary system with ministerial responsibility. However, Emperor Francis Joseph largely ignored ministerial responsibility by ruling by decree when the parliament was not in session.

The problem of the various nationalities remained a troublesome one. The German minority that governed Austria felt increasingly threatened by the Czechs, Poles, and other Slavic groups within the empire. Representatives of these groups in the parliament agitated for their freedom, which led the government to ignore the parliament and rely on imperial decrees to govern. Austria-Hungary had not solved its minorities problem.

In Russia, the assassination of Alexander II in 1881 convinced his son and successor, Alexander III, that reform had been a mistake. Alexander III lost no time

▲ *In this political cartoon, Emperor William II relaxes on his throne made of cannonballs and artillery, while Bismarck bids him good-bye. The woman, who represents Germany, watches this scene with serious concern about the future.*

in persecuting both reformers and revolutionaries. When Alexander III died in 1894, his weak son and successor, Nicholas II, began his rule believing that the absolute power of the tsars should be preserved: "I shall maintain the principle of autocracy just as firmly and unflinchingly as did my unforgettable father."[1] Conditions were changing, however, and the tsar's approach was not realistic.

Industrialization progressed rapidly in Russia after 1890. By 1900, Russia had become the fourth largest producer of steel behind the United States, Germany, and Great Britain. With industrialization came factories, an industrial working class, and socialist parties, including the Marxist Social Democratic Party and the Social Revolutionaries. Repression soon forced both parties to go underground and be revolutionary. The Social Revolutionaries worked to overthrow the tsarist autocracy by terrorism. They tried to assassinate government officials and members of the ruling dynasty.

MORE ABOUT . . . *Kaiser William Fires Bismarck*

When twenty-nine year old William II ascended the imperial throne of Germany, a power struggle quickly developed with Prince Otto von Bismarck, national hero and unifier of Germany. Kaiser William wanted to rescind an order requiring Bismarck's permission before ministers conferred with the Kaiser. Rather than discussing this issue with the Kaiser, Bismarck changed the topic to the Kaiser's proposed visit with the Russian tsar. Bismarck produced reports but refused to let the Kaiser read them. William grabbed one and found in it insulting comments about himself. Shortly afterwards, he asked Bismarck to resign. Bismarck later described William as "the man who will certainly ruin Germany."

▶ *Nicholas II, the last tsar of Russia, is shown here with his wife Alexandra. Why do you think all the men in this photograph are wearing military uniforms?*

The growing opposition to the tsarist regime finally exploded into revolution in 1905.

The defeat of the Russians by the Japanese in 1904/1905 (see Chapter 24) brought to Russia severe economic suffering, especially massive food shortages. As a result, on January 9, 1905, a massive procession of workers went to the Winter Palace in St. Petersburg to present a petition of grievances to the tsar. Troops foolishly opened fire on the peaceful demonstration, killing hundreds. This "Bloody Sunday" caused workers to call strikes and forced Nicholas II to grant civil liberties and create a **Duma,** or legislative assembly. Real constitutional monarchy proved short-lived, however. Already by 1907, the tsar had curtailed the power of the Duma, and he fell back on the army and bureaucracy to rule Russia.

International Rivalry and the Coming of War

Between 1871 and 1914, Europeans experienced a long period of peace. There were wars, but none involved the great powers. In Germany, Bismarck had realized that the emergence in 1871 of a unified Germany as the most powerful state on the Continent had upset the balance of power established at Vienna in 1815. Fearing a possible anti-German alliance led by its new enemy, France, Bismarck made a defensive alliance with Austria-Hungary in 1879. In 1882, this German–Austro-Hungarian alliance added a third partner, Italy, which was angry with the French over competing claims in North Africa. The Triple Alliance of 1882—Germany, Austria-Hungary, and Italy—committed the three powers to a defensive alliance against France. At the same time, Bismarck maintained a separate treaty with Russia and tried to remain on good terms with Great Britain.

When Emperor William II fired Bismarck in 1890 and took over direction of Germany's foreign policy, he embarked upon an activist policy dedicated to enhancing German power. He wanted, as he put it, to find Germany's rightful "place in the sun." One of the changes he made in Bismarck's foreign policy was to drop the treaty with Russia. The ending of that alliance brought France and Russia together. In 1894, the two powers concluded a military alliance. During

RECOMMENDED READING

Three general surveys of the mid-century decades are N. Rich, *The Age of Nationalism and Reform, 1850–1890,* 2d ed. (New York, 1979); E. Hobsbawm, *The Age of Capital, 1845–1875* (London, 1975); and J. A. S. Grenville, *Europe Reshaped, 1848–1878* (London, 1976). See also H. Holborn, *A History of Modern Germany* vol. 3, *1840–1945* (New York, 1969); the two detailed volumes of T. Zeldin, *France, 1848–1945* (Oxford,

1973–77); A. J. May, *The Habsburg Monarchy, 1867–1914* (Cambridge, Mass., 1951); and D. Read, *England, 1868–1914* (London, 1979).

A classic on the role of the Prussian military is G. Craig, *The Politics of the Prussian Army* (New York, 1955). On the position of liberals in the unification of Germany, see J. J. Sheehan, *German Liberalism in the Nineteenth Century* (Chicago, 1978).

Map 22.4   The Balkans in 1878

the next ten years, German policies abroad caused the British to draw closer to France. By 1907, an alliance of Great Britain, France, and Russia—known as the Triple Entente (awn-TAWNT)—stood opposed to the Triple Alliance of Germany, Austria-Hungary, and Italy. Europe was dangerously divided into two opposing camps that became more and more unwilling to compromise. A series of crises in the Balkans between 1908 and 1913 set the stage for World War I.

The Ottoman Empire and Nationalism in the Balkans

The Ottoman Empire was severely troubled by the hopes of its subject peoples in the Balkans for their freedom. Corruption and inefficiency had so weakened

the Ottoman Empire that only the efforts of the great European powers, who feared one another's designs on the empire, kept it alive.

In the course of the nineteenth century, the Balkan provinces of the Ottoman Empire gradually gained their freedom, although the rivalry in the region between Austria-Hungary and Russia complicated the process. Greece was made an independent kingdom in 1830 after its successful revolt. In 1875, several peoples in the Balkans revolted. The Ottomans crushed the revolts, but the Russians came to the aid of their fellow Slavs in the Balkans by declaring war on Turkey. After Russia's defeat of the Turks, the great powers met at the Congress of Berlin in 1878 and recognized Romania, Serbia, and Montenegro (MAWN-tuh-NEE-GROE) as independent states. Bulgaria gained autonomous status

STUDYING MAPS

The following questions will help you guide students through their study of Map 22.4.

1. Why were the Bulgarians unhappy with the results of the Congress of Berlin? *(Bulgaria was severely reduced in size.)*
2. How did the Ottoman Empire suffer as a result of the Congress of Berlin? *(The Ottoman Empire lost Romania.)*
3. Why might Austria-Hungary see opportunities in the results of the Congress of Berlin? *(There were territories nearby which might seek Austria-Hungary's help in freeing themselves from the Ottoman Empire.)*

LEARNING FROM VISUALS

Ask students to consider the drawing to the right. Is it likely that either the army of the Ottoman Empire or the Balkan League could have stood up to a major power at that time?

Answer to the caption question: Soldiers are carrying modern guns and evidence can be seen of modern explosives.

CLASS DISCUSSION

Work through with students the various alliances in the Balkans described here. (*Russian protection of Slavs, Serbia's hopes for a large Serbian Kingdom, Austria-Hungary's protection of Bosnia and Herzegovina.*)

What personal goals did the various nations have for their own betterment? Discuss with students how these overlapping territorial goals produced a very unstable political situation in the Balkans.

▲ *This illustration shows the Ottoman army, disorganized and beaten, in a hasty retreat. Well-armed and well-supplied Bulgarian forces continue the pursuit. What modern weaponry do you see in this illustration?*

under Russian protection. The other Balkan territories of Bosnia and Herzegovina (HERT-suh-go-VEE-nuh) were placed under the protection of Austria-Hungary. These gains, however, did not still the forces of Balkan nationalism.

In 1908, Austria-Hungary took the drastic step of annexing the two Slavic-speaking territories of Bosnia and Herzegovina. Serbia was outraged because the annexation dashed the Serbians' hopes of creating a large Serbian kingdom that would include most of the southern Slavs. The Russians, with their mission to protect their fellow Slavs and their own desire to gain access to the eastern Mediterranean through the Bosphorus and Dardanelles (DARD-un-ELZ), sup-

ported the Serbs and opposed the action of Austria-Hungary. Backed by the Russians, the Serbs prepared for war against Austria-Hungary. At this point, Emperor William II demanded that the Russians accept the annexation of Bosnia and Herzegovina by Austria-Hungary or face war with Germany. Weakened from their defeat in the Russo-Japanese War in 1904/1905, the Russians were afraid to risk war, and they backed down. Humiliated, the Russians vowed revenge.

In 1912, Serbia, Bulgaria, Montenegro, and Greece organized the Balkan League and defeated the Ottomans in the First Balkan War. When the victorious allies were unable to agree on how to divide the conquered Ottoman provinces of Macedonia (MASS-uh-DOE-nee-uh) and Albania, a second Balkan War erupted in 1913. Greece, Serbia, Romania, and the Ottoman Empire attacked and defeated Bulgaria. As a result, Bulgaria obtained only a small part of Macedonia. Most of the rest was divided between Serbia and Greece. The two Balkan wars left the inhabitants embittered and created more tensions among the great powers.

Serbia's desire to create a large Serbian kingdom remained unfulfilled. The Serbians blamed Austria-Hungary for their failure. Austria-Hungary was convinced that Serbia was a mortal threat to its empire and must at some point be crushed. As Serbia's chief supporters, the Russians were angry and determined not to back down again in the event of a confrontation with Austria-Hungary or Germany in the Balkans. The allies of Austria-Hungary and Russia were also determined to be more supportive of their respective allies in another crisis.

By the beginning of 1914, two armed camps viewed each other with suspicion. An American in Europe observed: "The whole of Germany is charged with electricity. Everybody's nerves are tense. It needs only a spark to set the whole thing off." The European age of progress was about to come to a bloody end.

On Line with WORLD HISTORY *Internet Activity*

You may want to have your students visit the following URL, where they will find information and additional web site resources to enhance their study of this chapter.

The Marxism-Leninism Project

http://www.idbsu.edu/surveyrc/ Staff/jaynes/marxism/marxism.htm

This site has an extensive examination of the philosophy and history of Marxism.

Due to the ever-changing nature of the World Wide Web, see the West History web site, **http://history.swpco.com** for regular updates of the URLs in this text.

Map 22.5   The Balkans in 1913

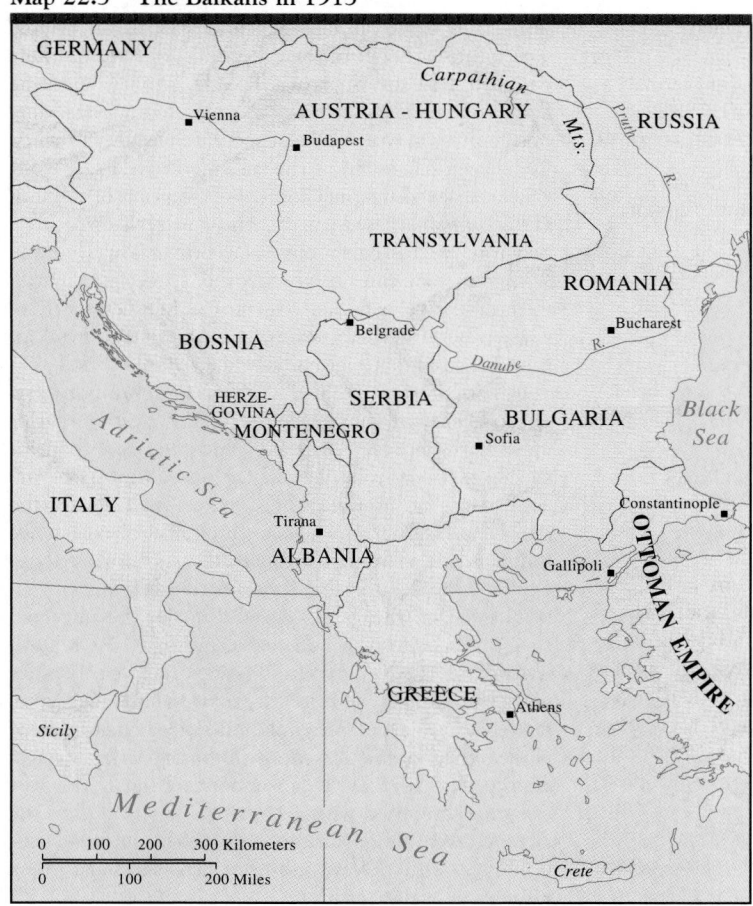

Assign students to prepare a table that compares political, economic, and social conditions in the democracies of Western Europe with those of Germany, Austria-Hungary, and Russia.

Answers to
SECTION REVIEW

2. (a) a policy that makes a prime minister responsible to a popularly elected legislative body, not to an executive officer
(b) a legislative assembly
3. (a) a time of reform and centralization of governmental power in the United States that took place soon after 1900
(b) a war in 1898 which brought about the seizure by the United States of Spanish-held islands in the Caribbean Sea and Pacific Ocean
(c) law passed in 1911, part of a series of social reforms in Britain, that provided benefits for workers in case of sickness and unemployment
(d) a document that provided a strong parliamentary system in France during the 65 years of the Third Republic
(e) the lower house of the German parliament, elected through universal male suffrage after 1871
(f) a radical right-wing political group that stressed German patriotism and expansion
(g) agreement among Germany, Austria, and Italy in 1882 to help each other in opposing France
(h) alliance formed by France, Great Britain and Russia to oppose the Triple Alliance

---

 SECTION REVIEW

1. **Locate:**
   (a) Great Britain,   (b) St. Petersburg,
   (c) Romania,   (d) Serbia,   (e) Montenegro,
   (f) Bosnia, (g) Herzegovina,
   (h) Bulgaria

2. **Define:**
   (a) ministerial responsibility,   (b) Duma

3. **Identify:**
   (a) Progressive Era,   (b) Spanish-American War,
   (c) The National Insurance Act,   (d) the Constitution of 1875,   (e) Reichstag,   (f) Pan-German League,   (g) The Triple Alliance,   (h) The Triple Entente,   (i) The Balkan League

---

STUDYING MAPS

The following questions will help you guide students through their study of Map 22.5.

1. What military and economic advantages would Austria-Hungary gain by taking control of Bosnia? *(access to the Adriatic Sea, and therefore to the Mediterranean)*
2. What geographic limitation did Romania, Serbia, and Austria-Hungary share? *(All lacked ports offering access to the Mediter-*

ranean Sea and world trade. Expansion to these ports was blocked by nations around them.)
3. Why did many nations wish to capture the land around Constantinople and Gallipoli? *(This area controlled access from the Black Sea to the Mediterranean and therefore all trade with those nations on the Black Sea.)*

(i) the group formed in 1921 by Serbia, Bulgaria, Montenegro and Greece; defeated the Ottomans in the First Balkan War

4. (a) division between English- and French-speaking peoples
(b) used as an excuse for expansion of German control over other nations' lands

5. (a) Answers may mention feelings of inequality, possible exploitation, and the burden of creating a more equitable distribution of wealth.
(b) Answers may discuss feelings of frustration and lost opportunities that can exist when costly wars do not produce clear winners or losers.

CLOSE

Lead students in a discussion of the Focus objectives identified on page 709.

4. Recall:
(*a*) What situation made the achievement of true unity in Canada difficult?
(*b*) What problems did the existence of German minorities in many European nations create?

5. Think Critically:
(*a*) Why is it often difficult for people to join together to create a nation when some are poor while others are wealthy?
(*b*) Why may inconclusive wars lead to further conflicts?

TOWARD THE MODERN CONSCIOUSNESS: INTELLECTUAL AND CULTURAL DEVELOPMENTS

Before 1914, many people in the Western world continued to believe in the values and ideals that had been put forth by the Scientific Revolution and the Enlightenment. *Reason, science,* and *progress* were still important words to Europeans. The idea that human beings could improve themselves and build a better society seemed to be proved by a rising standard of living, urban improvements, and mass education. Such products of modern technology as electric lights and automobiles reinforced the popular prestige of science. It was easy to think that the human mind could understand the universe.

Between 1870 and 1914, however, radically new ideas challenged these optimistic views and opened the way to a modern consciousness. The real impact of many of these ideas was not felt until after World War I. Before 1914, however, these ideas created a sense of confusion and anxiety that would become even more pronounced after the war.

The Emergence of a New Physics

Science was one of the chief pillars supporting the optimistic view of the world that many westerners shared in the nineteenth century. Science, which was supposedly based on hard facts and cold reason, offered a certainty of belief in the orderliness of nature. Many believed that by applying already known scientific laws, humans could arrive at a complete understanding of the physical world and an accurate picture of reality.

Throughout much of the nineteenth century, westerners believed in a mechanical conception of the universe that was based on the classical physics of Isaac Newton. In this perspective, the universe was viewed as a giant machine in which time, space, and matter were objective realities that existed independently of those observing them. Matter was thought to be composed of solid material bodies called atoms.

Albert Einstein (INE-STINE), a German-born patent officer working in Switzerland, questioned this view of the universe. In 1905, Einstein published his special theory of relativity, which stated that space and time are not absolute but rather relative to the observer. Neither space nor time had an existence independent of human experience. As Einstein later explained to a journalist, "It was formerly believed that if all material things disappeared out of the universe, time and space would be left. According to the relativity theory, however, time and space disappear together with the things."[2] Moreover, matter and energy reflected the relativity of time and space. Einstein concluded that matter was nothing but another form of energy. This idea led to an understanding of the vast energies contained within the atom. It also led to the Atomic Age and to uncertainty. To some, a relative universe—unlike Newton's universe—seemed to be a universe without certainty.

Sigmund Freud and the Emergence of Psychoanalysis

At the turn of the century, Sigmund Freud (FROID), a Viennese doctor, put forth a series of theories that undermined optimism about the rational nature of the human mind. Freud's thought, like the new physics, added to the uncertainties of the age. His major ideas were published in 1900 in *The Interpretation of Dreams*.

According to Freud, human behavior was strongly determined by the unconscious—by past experiences

RECOMMENDED READING

A well-regarded study of Freud is P. Gay, *Freud: A Life for Our Time* (New York, 1988). Also see R. Clark, *Freud: The Man and the Cause* (New York, 1980).

Very valuable on modern art are J. Rewald, *The History of Impressionism,* 4th ed. (New York, 1973), and *Post-Impressionism,* 3d ed. (New York, 1962). See also D. M. Reynolds, *The Cambridge Introduction to the History of*

Art: The Nineteenth Century (Cambridge, 1985). On literature, see R. Pascal, *From Naturalism to Expressionism: German Literature and Society, 1880–1918* (New York, 1973). The intellectual climate of Vienna is examined in C. E. Schorske, *Fin de Siècle Vienna: Politics and Culture* (New York, 1980).

For an introduction to the intellectual changes of the nineteenth century, see

▲ *Sigmund Freud was a major intellectual leader of the nineteenth century. His theories about the unconscious state and human behavior served as a foundation for much of twentieth-century psychoanalysis.*

and internal forces of which people were largely unaware. For Freud, human behavior was no longer truly rational but rather instinctive or irrational. He argued that painful and unsettling experiences were repressed, or blotted from conscious awareness. They still continued to influence behavior, however, because they had become part of the unconscious. Repression began in childhood. Freud devised a method—known as **psychoanalysis**—by which a psychotherapist and patient could probe deeply into the memory of the patient. In this way, they could retrace the chain of repressed thoughts all the way back to their childhood

origins. If the patient's conscious mind could be made aware of the unconscious and its repressed contents, the patient's conflict could be resolved and the patient healed.

The full importance of Sigmund Freud's thought was not felt until after World War I. In the 1920s, his ideas gained worldwide acceptance. Freudian terms, such as *unconscious* and *repression*, became new standard vocabulary words. Psychoanalysis, pioneered by Freud, developed into a major profession, especially in the United States.

Social Darwinism and Racism

In the second half of the nineteenth century, scientific theories were sometimes applied inappropriately to achieve desired results. For example, Charles Darwin's principle of organic evolution was applied to the social order in what came to be known as **Social Darwinism.** The most popular exponent of Social Darwinism was the British philosopher Herbert Spencer. He argued that societies were organisms that evolved through time from a struggle with their environments. Social progress came from "the struggle for survival" as the "fit"—the strong—advanced while the weak declined. Some prominent businessmen used Social Darwinism to explain their success. To them, the strong and fit—the able and energetic—had risen to the top; the stupid and lazy had fallen by the wayside.

The ideas of Darwin were also applied to human society in a radical way by nationalists and racists. In their pursuit of national greatness, extreme nationalists often insisted that nations, too, were engaged in a "struggle for existence" in which only the fittest (the strongest) survived. The German general Friedrich von Bernhardi (burn-HARD-ee) argued in 1907, "War is a biological necessity of the first importance, . . . since without it an unhealthy development will follow, which excludes every advancement of the race, and therefore all real civilization. War is the father of all things."[3]

Biological arguments were also used to defend racism. Perhaps nowhere was the combination of extreme nationalism and racism more evident and more dangerous than in Germany. One of the chief

---

O. Chadwick, *The Secularization of the European Mind in the Nineteenth Century* (Cambridge, 1975). A detailed biography of Darwin can be found in R. W. Clark, *The Survival of Charles Darwin* (New York, 1984). On the popularization of Darwinism, see A. Kelly, *The Descent of Darwin* (Chapel Hill, N.C., 1981). On Realism, there is a good introduction in L. Nochlin, *Realism* (Harmondsworth,

1971). Also valuable is F. W. J. Hemmings, *Culture and Society in France, 1848–1898* (London, 1971). For an introduction to the transformation of medical practices in the nineteenth century, see the appropriate chapters in E. H. Ackerknecht, *A Short History of Medicine,* rev. ed. (Baltimore, 1982); and A. S. Lyons and R. J. Petrucelli, *Medicine: An Illustrated History* (New York, 1978).

FOCUS

OBJECTIVES

After completing this section, students should be able to

1. describe developments in physics and psychology
2. explain the relationship between the concept of Social Darwinism and racism
3. identify and explain evidence of anti-Semitism in Europe
4. describe the growth of modernism in literature and the arts

FOCUS ACTIVITY

Assign students to write an essay that identifies ways in which people who are less able or lack skills or education are still able to contribute to society. Ask them to discuss the idea that society's willingness to help people who have different abilities makes us human.

TEACH

REINFORCING VOCABULARY

Ask students to write their opinion of the value of *psychoanalysis* on an unsigned piece of paper. Survey their opinions. Discuss why some people have a high regard for this process while others don't. What does this show about our different social values?

CLASS DISCUSSION

Discuss possible relationships between a person's prejudice against any group and his or her personal feelings of inadequacy. Why do so many people need someone else to blame for their problems? What may happen when a nation or its leaders look for someone or some groups to blame? Why are members of these groups often portrayed as being less than human?

REINFORCING VOCABULARY

Ask students to explain why *Zionism* may have grown in Europe as a response to prejudice against Jewish people. Why have some Europeans who are prejudiced against Jewish people supported this movement?

CLASS DISCUSSION

Adolf Hitler (1889–1945) is often viewed as a single, irrational creature who used political power to enforce his personal prejudice and hatred. Discuss how Social Darwinism was applied in Hitler's childhood and youth. Discuss whether Hitler may have become powerful partly because of widespread, or at least influential, agreement with his views.

exponents of German racism was Houston Stewart Chamberlain (CHAME-bur-lun), a Briton who became a German citizen. He believed that modern-day Germans were the only pure successors of the Aryans, who were portrayed as the original creators of Western culture. According to Chamberlain, the Aryan race, under German leadership, must be prepared to fight for Western civilization and save it from the assaults of such lower races as Jews, Negroes, and Orientals. Chamberlain singled out Jews as the racial enemy who wanted to destroy the Aryan race.

Anti-Semitism: Jews within the European Nation-State

Near the end of the nineteenth century, a revival of racism combined with extreme nationalism to produce a new right-wing political movement aimed primarily at the Jews. Of course, anti-Semitism was not new to European civilization. Since the Middle Ages, the Jews had been portrayed as the murderers of Christ and subjected to mob violence. Their rights had been restricted, and they had been physically separated from Christians in areas of cities known as ghettos.

In the nineteenth century, Jews were increasingly granted legal equality in many European countries. Many Jews now left the ghetto and became assimilated into the cultures around them. Many became successful as bankers, lawyers, scientists, scholars, journalists, and stage performers. In 1880, for example, Jews made up 10 percent of the population of Vienna, Austria, but 39 percent of its medical students and 23 percent of its law students.

These achievements were only one side of the picture, however, as is evident from the Dreyfus (DRIE-fus) affair in France. Alfred Dreyfus, a Jew, was a captain in the French general staff. Early in 1895, a secret military court found him guilty of selling army secrets and condemned him to life imprisonment on Devil's Island. During his trial, right-wing mobs yelled, "Death to the Jews." Soon after the trial, however, evidence emerged that pointed to Dreyfus's innocence. Another officer, a Catholic aristocrat, was more obviously the traitor. The army refused a new trial, however. A wave

of public outrage forced the government to hold a new trial and pardon Dreyfus in 1899.

In the 1880s and 1890s in Germany and Austria-Hungary, new parties arose that used anti-Semitism to win the votes of people who felt threatened by the new economic forces of the times. However, the worst treatment of Jews at the turn of the century occurred in eastern Europe, where 72 percent of the entire world Jewish population lived. Russian Jews were forced to live in certain regions of the country. Persecutions and **pogroms** (organized massacres of helpless people) were widespread. Hundreds of thousands of Jews decided to emigrate to escape the persecution.

Many Jews went to the United States. Some (probably about 25,000) moved to Palestine, which became home for a Jewish nationalist movement called **Zionism.** For many Jews, Palestine, the land of ancient Israel, had long been the land of their dreams. A key figure in the growth of political Zionism was Theodor Herzl (HERT-sul), who stated in his book *The Jewish State* (1896), "The Jews who wish it will have their state." Settlement in Palestine was difficult, however, because it was then part of the Ottoman Empire, which was opposed to Jewish immigration. Nevertheless, 1,000 Jews moved to Palestine in 1900. Although 3,000 Jews went annually to Palestine between 1904 and 1914, the Zionist dream of a homeland in Palestine still remained only a dream on the eve of World War I.

Literature and the Arts: Toward Modernism

Between 1870 and 1914, many writers and artists rebelled against the traditional literary and artistic styles that had dominated European cultural life since the Renaissance. The changes that they produced have since been called **modernism.**

Throughout much of the late nineteenth century, literature was dominated by **naturalism.** Naturalists accepted the material world as real and felt that literature should be realistic. They believed that by addressing social problems, writers could contribute to an objective understanding of the world (see "Our Literary Heritage: *A Doll's House*—One Woman's Cry for Freedom"). The naturalists portrayed characters caught in the grip of forces beyond their control.

ENRICHMENT ACTIVITY

Simulate a Congressional hearing in which the class is divided into five groups. Have each group choose from the following list of organizations. The group will prepare an argument and represent that organization before a Congressional hearing convened to discuss the following: What are the causes and possible solutions to the problem of racism? Organizations: Jewish Defense League, National Association for the Advancement of Colored People, National Organization of Women, United Farm Workers, Aryan Nation, and others of their choice.

OUR LITERARY HERITAGE

A Doll's House—One Woman's Cry for Freedom

Henrik Ibsen was a Norwegian writer who took a strong interest in social issues, including a woman's place in the home and society. Most women probably tried to conform to the nineteenth-century middle-class ideal of women as housewives and mothers. However, an increasing number fought for the rights of women. The following selection is taken from Act III of Henrik Ibsen's play A Doll's House *(1879). The character, Nora Helmer, declares her freedom from the control of her husband, Torvald, over her life.*

▲ *This Victorian doll house was made in England in 1889. In what ways do you think it mirrors the lives of middle-class women at this time? Do you think this doll house was a child's toy? Why or why not?*

▲ *This painting by American artist Thomas Eakins symbolizes the lonely, confining role assigned to women during the late nineteenth century. If you were to draw a woman in her modern-day role, what would you include? How would she be dressed?*

Henrik Ibsen, A Doll's House

NORA: Yes, it's true, Torvald. When I was living at home with father, he told me his opinions and mine were the same. If I had different opinions, I said nothing about them, because he would not have liked it. He used to call me his doll-child and played with me as I played with my dolls. Then I came to live in your house.

HELMER: What a way to speak of our marriage!

NORA (*Undisturbed*): I mean that I passed from father's hands into yours. You arranged everything

(continued)

Answers to Critical Thinking Questions

1. Most women still followed the tradition that wife and mother were the most important roles in a woman's life.
2. Answers will vary, but students might suggest that she would have said that you have to be yourself first and the other things second.

CLASS DISCUSSION

Ask students to discuss the symbolist position that the external world is not real but only a collection of symbols that reflect the true reality of the individual human mind? Can they explain what this idea means? Do they believe there is any truth in it?

OUR LITERARY HERITAGE

A Doll's House—One Woman's Cry for Freedom, continued

to your taste and I got the same tastes as you; or pretended to—I don't know which—both, perhaps; sometimes one, sometimes the other. When I look back on it now, I seem to have been living here like a beggar, on hand-outs. I lived by performing tricks for you, Torvald. . . . I must stand quite alone if I am ever to know myself and my surroundings; so I cannot stay with you.

HELMER: You are mad! I shall not allow it! I forbid it!

NORA: It's no use your forbidding me anything now. I shall take with me only what belongs to me; from you I will accept nothing, either now or later. . . .

HELMER: Forsake your home, your husband, your children! And you don't consider what the world will say.

NORA: I can't pay attention to that. I only know that I must do it.

HELMER: This is monstrous! Can you forsake your holiest duties?

NORA: What do you consider my holiest duties?

HELMER: Need I tell you that? Your duties to your husband and children.

NORA: I have other duties equally sacred.

HELMER: Impossible! What do you mean?

NORA: My duties toward myself.

HELMER: Before all else you are a wife and a mother.

NORA: That I no longer believe. Before all else I believe I am a human being, just as much as you are—or at least that I should try to become one. I know that most people agree with you, Torvald, and that they say so in books. But I can no longer be satisfied with what most people say and what is in books. I must think things out for myself and try to get clear about them.

1. Why would many nineteenth-century middle-class women have had a problem with Nora's ideas?

2. What do you think Nora would have said to those women?

The novels of the French writer Émile Zola provide a good example of naturalism. Zola used a backdrop of the urban slums and coalfields of northern France to show how alcoholism and different environments affected people's lives. He wrote *Rougon-Macquart* (ROO-zhawn), a 20-volume series of novels on the history of a family. Zola maintained that the artist must analyze and dissect life as a biologist would a living organism.

At the turn of the century, a new group of writers, known as the **symbolists,** reacted against naturalism. The symbolists were primarily interested in writing poetry and were strongly influenced by the ideas of Freud. They believed that an objective knowledge of the world was impossible. The external world was not real but only a collection of symbols that reflected the true reality of the individual human mind. Art, the symbolists believed, should function for its own sake instead of serving, criticizing, or seeking to understand society.

The period from 1870 to 1914 was one of the most fertile in the history of art. Since the Renaissance, the task of artists had been to represent reality as accurately as possible. By the late nineteenth century,

ENRICHMENT ACTIVITY

Have students look at examples of paintings between 1870 and 1914. Have them compare these to Renaissance paintings and then analyze the basic differences. Have them do the same with examples of modern architecture. Before the activity, have the class brainstorm ideas for the types of criteria they can use for their analyses. After a list has been generated, have students decide on how many criteria they should use. Then have them vote on which items in the list they will use for their criteria. All students should use the same criteria for their analyses. Have volunteers share their analyses with the rest of the class.

artists were seeking new forms of expression. **Impressionism** was a movement that began in France in the 1870s, when a group of artists rejected the studios and went out into the countryside to paint nature directly. Camille Pissarro, one of impressionism's founders, expressed what these artists sought:

> Do not define too closely the outlines of things; it is the brush stroke of the right value and color which should produce the drawing. . . . The eye should not be fixed on one point, but should take in everything, while observing the reflections which the colors produce on their surroundings. Work at the same time upon sky, water, branches, ground, keeping everything going on an equal basis. . . . Don't proceed according to rules and principles, but paint what you observe and feel. Paint generously unhesitatingly, for it is best not to lose the first impression.[4]

Pissarro's suggestions are evident in the work of Claude Monet (moe-NAE). As seen in *Impression, Sunrise*, Monet was especially enchanted with water. He painted many pictures in which he sought to capture the interplay of light, water, and sky.

▲ *Claude Monet had a long, prolific career as an artist. As shown in* Impression, Sunrise, *Monet tried to capture the moment that the sun rose, using light playing on both the water and the atmosphere. How does this compare to* The Stonebreakers, *seen in Chapter 21?*

◄ *This painting of several of France's leading writers of the late nineteenth century shows a serious, thoughtful group. Paul Verlaine and Arthur Rimbaud, the first two on the left, were among the group of symbolist poets. Do you think these poets relied heavily on allusions? Why or why not?*

LEARNING FROM VISUALS

Answer to the caption question: In van Gogh's work form has begun to be nonrepresentational and invokes the viewer's imagination, while the colors startle with their vibrant intensity.

CLASS DISCUSSION

Ask students to identify and discuss differences between the painting by Van Gogh to the right and the work of Monet on the preceding page. Which do they like better? How do the two paintings demonstrate a change in social artistic values?

THE IMPORTANCE OF CULTURE

Do students believe that the statement "by the beginning of the twentieth century, the idea that the task of art was to represent reality had lost much of its meaning," is a reflection on the political and social upheavals that had taken place during the last part of the nineteenth century? Discuss their views on this.

▲ In van Gogh's The Starry Night, *the sky is painted as a series of swirling forms far above and yet dominating the village below. Why do some art critics believe that van Gogh was more interested in color than form?*

By the 1880s, a new movement, known as **post-impressionism,** arose in France but soon spread to other European countries. A famous post-impressionist was the tortured and tragic figure Vincent van Gogh (GOE), who, in a fit of anger, cut off his own ear. For van Gogh, art was a spiritual experience. He was especially interested in color and believed that it could act as its own form of language. Van Gogh maintained that artists should paint what they feel. In his *Starry Night,* he painted a sky alive with whirling stars that overwhelmed the huddled buildings in the village below.

By the beginning of the twentieth century, the idea that the task of art was to represent reality had lost much of its meaning. This was especially true in the visual arts. Perhaps the most important factor in the decline of realism in painting was the spread of photography to the mass markets. Photography had been invented in the 1830s. It became popular and wide

On Line with WORLD HISTORY *Internet Activity*

You may want to have your students visit the following URL, where they will find information and additional web site resources to enhance their study of this chapter.

Women's Net

http://www.igc.org/igc/womensnet/

This site supports women's movements worldwide and has an extensive database of all kinds of women's movements both today and in the past.

Due to the ever-changing nature of the World Wide Web, see the West History web site, **http://history.swpco.com** for regular updates of the URLs in this text.

OUR ARTISTIC HERITAGE
Modern Art and Architecture

Kandinsky used color freely in Painting with White Border, *believing that color would appeal directly to the human soul and heart. He also tried to eliminate representational objects from his paintings. Do you think he was successful? Why or why not?*

One of the most outstanding features of modern art is the attempt of the artist to avoid "visual reality." By 1905, one of the most important figures in modern art was just beginning his career. Pablo Picasso was from Spain but settled in Paris in 1904. He painted in a remarkable variety of styles. He created a new style, called cubism, that used geometric designs as visual stimuli to recreate reality in the viewer's mind. In his paintings, Picasso attempted to view the human form from many sides. In this aspect he seems to have been influenced by the theory of relativity, which was becoming popularized at the time.

The modern artist's flight from visual reality reached a high point in 1910 with the beginning of abstract painting. Vasily Kandinsky, a Russian who worked in Germany, was one of the founders of abstract expressionism. As is evident in his *Painting with White Border*, Kandinsky and the other abstract expressionists sought to avoid visual reality altogether. Kandinsky believed that art should speak directly to the soul. To do so, it must use only line and color.

Modernism in the arts revolutionized architecture and gave rise to a new principle known as functionalism. Functionalism was the idea that buildings, like the products of machines, should be functional or useful; they should fulfill the purpose for which they were built. All unnecessary ornamentation was to be stripped away.

The United States was a leader in the new architecture. The country's rapid urban growth and lack of any architectural tradition allowed for new building methods, especially in the relatively new city of Chicago. The Chicago School of the 1890s, led by Louis H. Sullivan, used reinforced concrete, steel frames, and electric elevators in building skyscrapers virtually free of external ornamentation. One of Sullivan's most successful pupils was Frank Lloyd Wright. Wright's private houses, built chiefly for wealthy patrons, were geometric structures with long lines and overhanging

(continued)

CLASS DISCUSSION

Ask students to discuss characteristics of the work of Pablo Picasso. Some people love his work and find it to be full of meaning. Others think some of his paintings look like deformed people and animals portrayed in unreal situations. What explanations can students suggest for these different points of view?

LEARNING FROM VISUALS

Ask students to compare the painting by Kandinsky to the left with the painting of Prince Klemens von Vetternich on page 663. Why are these works of art so different? What different purposes did they serve? Do students believe one artist shows greater skill than the other?

Answer to the caption question: Most students will concur that Kandinsky's work is nonrepresentational.

COOPERATIVE LEARNING ACTIVITY

Assign students to locate and bring into class samples of impressionist and post-impressionist art. If the class completed the Enrichment Activity on page 720, use the criteria for analysis developed for that project. If not, have student groups develop criteria for analysis of art. Then, working in groups, have students discuss the techniques of impressionist and post-impressionist artists. Have each group identify the individual examples they like best and report to the class the reasons for their choices. Then allow the class, as a whole, to evaluate the samples chosen by the various groups.

LEARNING FROM VISUALS

Answer to the caption question: The long, low rectangular forms are seen in many ranch homes.

Answers to Critical Thinking Questions

1. avoidance of reality; use of line and color, art speaking directly to the soul
2. architectural philosophy that buildings should be useful for their created purpose, without external ornamentation
3. Answers will vary.

ASSESS

Answers to SECTION REVIEW

2. (a) process by which a psychotherapist probes the memory of the patient
(b) principle arguing that society is an organism evolving through struggles between strong and weak
(c) organized massacres of helpless people
(d) belief that there should be a Jewish nation in Palestine
(e) cultural movement rebelling against traditional literary and artistic styles between 1870 and 1914
(f) literary movement accepting the material world as real and striving for realism in literature
(g) poets influenced by Freud, reacting against naturalism
(h) movement founded in France, artists painted nature directly, rejected studios and rules

OUR ARTISTIC HERITAGE
Modern Art and Architecture, continued

Frank Lloyd Wright's homes and buildings quickly won him international fame. The houses he designed seem to be natural extensions of their surroundings. What elements from this house, Fallingwater, do you see in current ranch-house style homes?

roofs. The interiors had large open spaces and included cathedral ceilings, built-in furniture, and built-in lighting features. Wright pioneered the modern American house.

1. Describe *abstract expressionism*.

2. Describe *functionalism*.

3. From the descriptions given here, do you think you would find paintings done in the style of cubism or abstract expressionism more interesting to view? Explain your answer.

spread after George Eastman created the first Kodak camera in 1888. Now anyone could take a photograph that looked exactly like the subject.

Artists came to realize that their strength was not in mirroring reality (which the camera could do) but in creating reality. The visual artists, like the symbolist writers of the time, sought meaning in individual consciousness. Between 1905 and 1914, this search for individual expression created modern art (see "Our Artistic Heritage: Modern Art and Architecture").

At the beginning of the twentieth century, developments in music paralleled those in painting. Expressionism in music was a Russian creation. It was the product of the composer Igor Stravinsky (struh-VIN-skee) and the Ballet Russe (RUSS), the dancing company of Sergei Diaghilev (ser-GAE dee-AWG-uh-LEFF). Together they revolutionized the world of music with Stravinsky's ballet, *The Rites of Spring*. When it was performed in Paris in 1913, the savage and primitive sounds and rhythms of the music and dance caused a near riot from an audience outraged at its audacity.

❀ SECTION REVIEW ❀

1. **Locate:**
   (*a*) Ottoman Empire

2. **Define:**
   (*a*) psychoanalysis,   (*b*) Social Darwinism,
   (*c*) pogroms,   (*d*) Zionism,   (*e*) modernism,
   (*f*) naturalism,   (*g*) symbolists,
   (*h*) impressionism,   (*i*) post-impressionism

3. **Identify:**
(a) theory of relativity,   (b) *The Interpretation of Dreams*,   (c) the Dreyfus affair,   (d) Vincent van Gogh

4. **Recall:**
(a) How did German general Friedrich von Bernhardi support his idea that "War is a biological necessity . . ."?
(b) How have biological arguments been used to defend racism?

5. **Think Critically:** Why are times of political and economic change often associated with a time of artistic change?

Conclusion

The Second Industrial Revolution helped create a new material prosperity that led Europeans to believe they had ushered in a new age of progress. A major feature of this age was the emergence of a mass society. The lower classes in particular benefited from the right to vote, a higher standard of living, and new schools that provided them with some education. New forms of mass transportation, combined with new work patterns, enabled large numbers of people to enjoy weekend trips to amusement parks and seaside resorts, as well as to participate in new mass leisure activities.

By 1870, the national state had become the focus of people's lives. Liberal and democratic reforms made possible greater participation in the political process, although women were still largely excluded from political rights. After 1871, the national state also began to expand its functions beyond all previous limits. The enactment of public health and housing measures, designed to curb the worst ills of urban living, were an example of how state power could be used to benefit the people.

The period between 1870 and 1914 was also a time of great anxiety. International rivalries and the creation of mass armies increased the tensions among the major powers. At the same time, scientists, writers, and artists began to question traditional ideas about the nature of reality and thus frightened many people. By 1914, many people had a sense of unease about the direction society was headed.

Notes

1. Quoted in Shmuel Galai, *The Liberation Movement in Russia, 1900–1905* (Cambridge, 1973), p. 26.
2. Quoted in Arthur E. E. McKenzie, *The Major Achievements of Science*, vol. 1 (New York, 1960), p. 310.
3. Friedrich von Bernhardi, *Germany and the Next War*, trans. Allen H. Powles (New York, 1914), pp. 18–19.
4. Quoted in John Rewald, *History of Impressionism* (New York, 1961), pp. 456–458.

(i)   movement that followed impressionism; use of color as language

3. (a) theory by Albert Einstein that space and time not absolute, but relative to observer
(b) book by Sigmund Freud, undermined optimism about the rational nature of the human mind
(c) case in France, Jewish officer convicted of treason when apparently not guilty
(d) post-impressionist artist, painted *Starry Night*

4. (a) He believed that war brings about advancement of the human race and civilization.
(b) Many people who have held racist views justified them in terms of creating what they believed would be a racially superior society.

5. Answers may discuss how the creation of new nations, wars, economic systems, and international relationship can bring about a need to find new ways of artistic expression.

CLOSE

Lead students in a discussion of the "Focus" objectives identified on page 717. Stress the prevalence in the movement of artistic expression from realism to impressionism as a reflection of changing social values.

TIME LINE

As students conclude the chapter, you may want to refer them to the chapter time line in the *Study Guide*. The time line will help them put key dates in perspective. Supporting questions and activities are also provided.

Answers to CHAPTER REVIEW 22

USING KEY TERMS

1. psychoanalysis
2. revisionists
3. Zionism
4. bourgeoisie
5. Duma
6. Impressionism
7. modernism
8. symbolists
9. Socialist
10. naturalism
11. ministerial responsibility
12. proletariat
13. Social Darwinism
14. post-impressionism
15. pogroms

REVIEWING THE FACTS

1. Faraday: electric generator; Edison: light bulb; Marconi: radio waves
2. capital, industries, military might
3. Karl Marx and Friedrich Engels
4. Wilhelm Liebknecht and August Bebel
5. clerks, typists, secretaries, file clerks, sales clerks, telephone operators, teachers, nurses
6. decline in the average number of children per family, due to increased use of birth control, abortions, and shift toward view of children as dependents rather than wage earners
7. provision of large mass of skilled labor and a means of political and social indoctrination
8. mass newspapers using simple writing style and sensationalist stories to sell papers
9. organization founded by extreme right-wing groups working for German expansion
10. Marxist Social Democratic Party, Social Revolutionaries
11. theories of relativity
12. a French Jew unjustly accused of treason
13. organized massacre of Jews; the Russian Empire
14. founder of Zionism

THINKING CRITICALLY

1. They permit use of assem-

CHAPTER 22 REVIEW

USING KEY TERMS

1. _____ is a method by which a therapist and a patient probe for repressed experiences.
2. Marxists who believed their goals could be achieved by peaceful, democratic evolution were called _____.
3. Palestine became home for the Jewish nationalist movement known as _____.
4. Karl Marx referred to the middle class as the _____.
5. The _____ is the Russian Legislative Assembly.
6. _____ was a movement which attempted to paint both what was observed and what was felt.
7. Literary and artistic styles that rejected traditional styles were called _____.
8. A group of writers who believed that art was for art's sake, not for criticizing society, were the _____.
9. The development of _____ parties and trade unions helped workers in their struggle to achieve better pay and working conditions.
10. A literary style that portrayed individuals caught up in forces beyond their control was _____.
11. The principle by which a prime minister is directly answerable to a popularly elected representative body is _____.
12. Marx called the workers the _____, and predicted their struggles would result in revolution.
13. Herbert Spencer, a believer in _____, argued that social progress came from the advancement of the strong while the weak declined.
14. Vincent van Gogh's painting was a spiritual experience in the style of _____.
15. Russian Jews were massacred in _____ in eastern Europe.

REVIEWING THE FACTS

1. List one invention of Michael Faraday, Thomas Alva Edison, and Guglielmo Marconi.
2. What three factors enabled Europe to dominate the world by 1914?
3. Who wrote *The Communist Manifesto*?
4. Who were the two leaders of the German Social Democratic Party?
5. What new jobs for women were created by the Second Industrial Revolution?
6. What was the most significant development in family life in the nineteenth century? Why did this change occur?
7. What purposes were served by the the institution of compulsory education?
8. What was the yellow press?
9. What was the Pan-German League?
10. Which were the two revolutionary socialist parties of Russia?
11. What was Albert Einstein's greatest contributions to science?
12. Who was Alfred Dreyfus and what was his significance?
13. What was a pogrom? Where did pogroms occur in the early twentieth century?
14. Who was Theodore Herzl?

THINKING CRITICALLY

1. Why are interchangeable parts so important in manufacturing?
2. Describe in your own words Marx' ideas about history and social classes.
3. Why was revisionist, or evolutionary, socialism more powerful in western Europe than in eastern Europe?
4. How did liberals such as Octavia Hill go about reforming urban housing? How is this approach consistent with their liberal philosophy?

---

bly line procedures and lower the price of manufactured goods.
2. Answers should include class struggle, government as an instrument of the ruling class, the proletariat and the bourgeoisie, violent revolution, the dictatorship of the proletariat, and the withering away of the state.
3. Parliamentary democracy gave socialists a role within the political system and allowed them to visualize success in achieving their goals without violent revolution. With more autocratic governments, there was no legal function for political parties of whatever kind. All political parties were therefore revolutionary.
4. believed that private enterprise and private philanthropy could solve urban ills; advocates

minimal government interference with an individual's life, has very optimistic view of ability of individuals to control environment
5. increased use of birth control, abortions, and shift in viewing children as dependents rather than as wage earners
6. Courageous women such as Florence Nightengale and Clara Barton defied current stereotypes to provide nursing care on the battlefields.
7. Teaching was seen as an extension of the woman's role as a nurturer and the job paid relatively little.
8. Answers will vary. Russia converted, technically to a constitutional monarchy; failure, Tsar and his advisers subverted the Duma and the reforms
9. Possible themes are (1) Austrian fear of nationalist

5. Why did the average number of children per family drop during the nineteenth century?
6. In what ways did the Crimean War and American Civil War unintentionally promote feminism?
7. Why did women come to dominate the teaching profession?
8. Was the Revolution of 1905 in Russia a success or a failure? Explain your answer.
9. Explain how the Congress of Berlin helped create conditions which eventually led to the outbreak of World War I in 1914.
10. What was the difference between the approach to manufacturing automobiles between Karl Benz and Henry Ford? Which man had the better approach?

APPLYING SOCIAL STUDIES SKILLS

1. **Sociology:** Proportionately, did London or Berlin grow more in the nineteenth century? How did you reach your conclusion?
2. **Sociology:** Was wealth in the United States more or less evenly distributed in 1890 than in Europe? Please explain your reasoning.
3. **Government:** Draw a diagram showing the structure of the government for the United States, Great Britain, France, and Germany in 1914. In your opinion, which government is the most democratic? The least democratic? Explain.
4. **Geography:** Consult Map 22.3 on page 710 "Europe in 1871." Militarily, what would be Germany's greatest problem in the event of war?

MAKING TIME AND PLACE CONNECTIONS

1. Compare the British Conservative, Liberal, and Labour parties of 1914 with the present U.S. Democratic and Republican parties. Identify their common characteristics.

2. At the turn of the century, how did the United States approach urban problems compared to that of Great Britain and Germany?
3. In what ways have the problems facing Canada not changed since the time of Sir Wilfred Laurier?
4. What is your response to the scene between Helmer and Nora in *A Doll House?*

BECOMING AN HISTORIAN

1. **Charts, Graphs, Tables:** Construct a graph showing urban population growth in Britain, France, Germany, and eastern Europe between 1800 and 1914. Does this graph support or not support the text generalization that Europe had developed two economic zones?
2. **Making Inferences:** Which of the following schools or movements had their roots more in realism than romanticism? Why? (1) Naturalism, (2) Symbolism, (3) Impressionism, (4) Post-Impressionism, (5) Expressionism, (6) Cubism, (7) Abstract Expressionism, (8) The Chicago School of Architecture.
3. **Primary and Secondary Sources:** Classify the following features as either primary or secondary sources, and explain why: (1) The Pankhursts (p. 704), (2) *A Doll's House*—One Woman's Cry for Freedom (p. 719), and (3) Modern Art and Architecture (p. 723).
4. **Analyzing Information:** Interpret the cartoon "Bismarck and William II" (p. 711). What is the message of the cartoon? Why is William portrayed as he is? What is the meaning of the props in his hand?
5. **Art as a Key to History:** Compare Claude Monet's "Impression, Sunrise" (p. 721) with Vincent van Gogh's "The Starry Night" (p. 722). Why is Monet's painting described by art historians as impressionist while van Gogh's painting is described as post-impressionist?
6. Listen to a recording of Igor Stravinsky's "The Rite of Spring." How does Stravinsky try to achieve musically the effect that Kandinsky tried to achieve visually through painting? **727**

aspirations (2) Slavic nationalism, especially Serbian nationalism (3) Russian desire for the Bosporus and Dardanelles (4) Ottoman weakness (5) Germany's sense that it has only Austria to rely upon (6) issues of presuge, which make the Great Powers less and less willing to compromise.
10. autos by Karl Benz handmade, expensive; autos by Ford quickly built and inexpensive

APPLYING SOCIAL STUDIES SKILLS

1. **Sociology:** Berlin grew faster proportionally. London grew 677%; Berlin 1,569%. (6,500,000/960,000 to 2,700,000/172,000)
2. **Sociology:** In Europe, 5% of the population held 30 to 40% of the wealth, while in the U.S.

9% held 71% of the wealth, but the data is inconclusive.
3. **Government:** In theory, the British system is the most democratic, since the executive not only answers to Parliament, but is in fact a member of Parliament.
4. Germany has France on one side and Russia on other, and must therefore divide attention in two directions.

MAKING TIME AND PLACE CONNECTIONS

1. highly monarchist, class conscious and elitist conservative party without U.S. equivalent; Liberal party most resembles U.S. Republican Party,

Labour Party most resembles Democratic Party
2. Both U.S. and Europe moved towards greater government control and regulation of business and society; both originally preferred Liberal approach but were forced to concede voluntarism not capable of solving problems of this magnitude.
3. distrust and misunderstandings between Anglophone and Francophone Canadians probably the most pressing problem facing Canada today
4. Answers will vary.

BECOMING AN HISTORIAN

1. The data for the chart are:

	Urban Population by Percentage	
	1800	1914
Great Britain	40	80
France	25	45
Germany	25	60
Eastern Europe	10	30

2. naturalism focused on realistic objects, conveyed social insights; Chicago School of Architecture stressed function
3. The features on Pankhursts, The Middle Class Home, Modern Art and Architecture are all secondary sources—product of a historian who is summarizing events. The feature on Art for Art's Sake and Ibsen both primary sources—written contemporaneously, by participants in the issues.
4. The cartoon suggests William II is childish and foolish to dismiss Bismarck; cannon balls on the throne suggest William's preoccupation with militarism; the doll might suggest William toying with socialist programs; the worried figure of Germany prefigures fears for future.
5. Monet expresses feelings but colors he uses are "natural;" van Gogh, uses intensity, shapes are stronger colors
6. Answers will vary. The key idea is the expression of intense emotion.

PLANNING GUIDE

SECTION	KEY TOPICS	PRIMARY SOURCES	ASSESSMENT
1 The Spread of Colonial Rule: Southeast Asia pages 729–737	◆ Motives for the new imperialism ◆ European colonization of Southeast Asia ◆ Colonial policies and practices in Southeast Asia ◆ Resistance to the new colonialism	◆ An Appeal to Vietnamese Citizens to Resist the French, page 735	◆ Section Review, page 737 ◆ Section Quiz 23–1, TRB
2 Empire Building in Africa pages 737–747	◆ Increased trade and European colonies in West Africa ◆ The Suez Canal and colonization of North Africa ◆ Exploration and colonization of Central Africa ◆ Competition for East African territories ◆ Conflicting claims and interests in Southern Africa ◆ Policies and practices of colonial rule in Africa ◆ The new class of Africans and the rise of nationalism	◆ King Lo Bengula's Complaint to Queen Victoria, page 743	◆ Section Review, page 747 ◆ Section Quiz 23–2, TRB
3 British Rule in India pages 748–755	◆ Growth of British control over India ◆ Effects of British rule in India ◆ Gandhi and the rise of Indian nationalism ◆ Indian cultural revival	◆ Poetry of Rabindranath Tagore—Gitanjali: Song Offerings, page 755	◆ Section Review, page 755 ◆ Section Quiz 23–3, TRB
4 Nation Building and Imperalism in Latin America pages 756–762	◆ Forces of nationalism and nationalistic revolts in Latin America ◆ Problems in the new nations of Latin America ◆ Economic growth and social instability ◆ Landowners, peasants, and political change	◆ William Wordsworth on Toussaint L'Ouverture, page 757	◆ Section Review, page 762 ◆ Section Quiz 23–4, TRB

THE HIGH TIDE OF IMPERIALISM:
AN AGE OF WESTERN DOMINANCE (1800 TO 1914)

REPRODUCIBLE ACTIVITIES

Historical Maps

Charts and Graphs

Critical Thinking

Cooperative Learning

Vocabulary

Guided Reading

Reteaching

Enrichment

Performance Assessment

Spanish Key Points and Chapter Summaries

Spanish Vocabulary

Spanish Guided Reading

MULTIMEDIA SUPPORT

TRANSPARENCIES
- *World History* Color Transparency Package
- Fine Art Color Transparency Package

VIDEO
- *World History* Video Library
- **CNN**® Annual Video Update

LASERDISC
- *Sights and Sounds of History*

AUDIO
- *Listening to Literature* audiotape (English and Spanish)
- *History of Music* CD

SOFTWARE
- WESTEST™
- Student Review

CD–ROM
- *The Journey of Civilization*
- *World History*

INTERNET
- Internet Activities

On Line with WORLD HISTORY

Access West's history web site at
http://history.swpco.com
You'll find activities and web sites related to specific topics and chapters in *World History: The Human Odyssey*. Also look for references to helpful web sites at appropriate places throughout this teacher edition.

LESSON PLANNING

You will find detailed daily lesson plans for both traditional class scheduling and **block scheduling** in your Teacher Resource Box.

Not Enough Time?

If you do not have the four or five days recommended to teach this chapter, you may want to focus on the following sections and activities:

- Have students skim the chapter to answer the "Questions to Guide Your Reading" on page 729. Discuss their answers and then read the "Conclusion" on page 763.
- Do a more in-depth reading of pages 729–730, 744–747, 750–754, and 760–763. Conclude with a class discussion of imperialism and its lasting effects on the countries that were subjugated to colonial rule.

THE HIGH TIDE OF IMPERIALISM:

23

In 1841, the Scottish doctor and missionary David Livingstone began a series of journeys that took him through much of central and southern Africa. His travels were not easy. Much of his journey was done by foot, canoe, or mule. He suffered at times from rheumatic fever, dysentery, and malaria. He survived an attack by armed warriors and a mutiny by his own servants. Back in Great Britain, his exploits made Livingstone a national hero. People jammed into lecture halls to hear him speak of Africa's beauties. As the *London Journal* reported, "Europe had always heard that the central regions of southern Africa were bleak and barren, heated by poisonous winds, infested by snakes . . . [but Livingstone spoke of] a high country, full of fruit trees, abounding in shade, watered by a perfect network of rivers." Livingstone also tried to persuade his listeners that Britain needed to send both missionaries and merchants to Africa. Combining Christianity and commerce, he said, would achieve civilization for Africa.

During the nineteenth and early twentieth centuries, Western colonialism spread throughout much of the non-Western world. A few powerful Western states—namely, Great Britain, France, Germany, Russia, and the United States—competed for markets and raw materials for their expanding economies. By the end of the nineteenth century, virtually all of the peoples of Asia and Africa were under colonial rule.

Western states sought colonies chiefly to enhance their wealth and power. Some had other goals, such as bringing Western values and institutions to the peoples of Asia and Africa. One result of this colonial process was the beginnings of the westernization of the societies of Asia and Africa. Another result was the rise of nationalism, borrowed from the West. Anticolonist elements in Asia and Africa used the idea of nationalism in their struggles to reassert the rights of native peoples to control their own destinies. By the first quarter of the twentieth century, the revolt against colonial rule had begun to spread throughout much of Asia and Africa. Nowhere, however, had it yet succeeded.

Only in Latin America had resistance to Europeans been successful in the nineteenth century. National movements for independence in South and Central America led to new states by the 1820s and 1830s. However, even these new states found themselves economically dependent on Europe and the United States.

THE LIFE & EXPLORATIONS OF Dr. LIVINGSTONE

◄ *This portrait of David Livingstone shows him in the continent that he grew to love, Africa. Do you think it was difficult for him to convince his fellow Englishmen about the beauties of Africa and of the African people?*

ADDITIONAL RESOURCES

The resources listed below can be used to enrich the lessons in this chapter.

BOOKS FOR STUDENTS
The Last Hero (H. M. Stanley) by Peter Farbath, Simon & Schuster
Fiela's Child by Dalene Mathee, Alfred Knopf
Africa Since 1800 by Roland Oliver and Anthony Atmore, Cambridge University Press

VIDEOS/FILMS
The Bible and the Gun/This Magnificent African Cake, Basil Davidson, Social Studies School Service
Imperialism Series: The World: A Television History, Social Studies School Service (800) 421-4246

AN AGE OF WESTERN DOMINANCE
(1800 TO 1914)

ERA OF EUROPEAN DOMINANCE

1800	HIGH TIDE OF IMPERIALISM	1914
1800		1914

QUESTIONS TO GUIDE YOUR READING

1. What were the major causes of the new imperialism after 1880?

2. What general principles of rule did Europeans follow in their colonial empires?

3. What economic policies were followed by the colonial nations? Who benefited from these policies?

4. How did nationalism affect the colonial peoples of Asia and Africa?

5. What was the nature of British rule in India?

6. How did Latin American nations achieve their independence?

7. What domestic problems did Latin American nations face in the nineteenth century?

OUTLINE

1. THE SPREAD OF COLONIAL RULE: SOUTHEAST ASIA
2. EMPIRE BUILDING IN AFRICA
3. BRITISH RULE IN INDIA
4. NATION BUILDING AND IMPERIALISM IN LATIN AMERICA

THE SPREAD OF COLONIAL RULE: SOUTHEAST ASIA

In the nineteenth century, a new phase of Western expansion into Asia and Africa began. European nations began to view Asian and African societies as a source of industrial raw materials and a market for Western manufactured goods. No longer were Western gold and silver traded for cloves, pepper, tea, and silk. Now the products of European factories were sent to Africa and Asia in return for oil, tin, rubber, and the other resources needed to fuel European industries.

The New Imperialism

Beginning in the 1880s, European states began an intense scramble for overseas territory. **Imperialism,** or the extension of one nation's power over other lands, was not new. Europeans had set up colonies in North and South America and trading posts around Africa and the Indian Ocean by the sixteenth century. However, the imperialism of the late nineteenth century, called the "new imperialism" by some, was different

729

FOCUS ON THEMES

Listed below are brief summaries of how the content in this chapter supports the text's key themes.

Politics and History In their takeover of lands, colonial rulers used both direct and indirect methods of rule in their subject territories. Direct rule was more expensive because it required a large bureaucracy of officials from the mother country for direct control. Indirect rule made use of local elites, thus bypassing the need for a large bureaucracy of colonial officials. Discontent with colonial rule led to nationalistic movements for independence.

The Role of Ideas The new imperialism was based on the idea of the right and duty of Western nations to impose their values and institutions on subject peoples. The idea of nationalism, an idea imported from the West, gave subjects an instrument for seeking their freedom from colonial powers.

Economics and History A major factor in imperialism was the desire on the part of industrialized nations for new sources of raw materials and new markets for the products of their industrial factories. Colonies filled both needs.

Social Life Imperialism tended to create severe social divisions in the colonies between the imperial masters and the subjects, who were often treated as social inferiors. Even the education of native peoples often meant the education of native elites in the languages and ideas of the colonial power in the hope that they would share the outlook of the colonial rulers.

Answers to QUESTIONS TO GUIDE YOUR READING

1. intense scramble for overseas territory motivated by a variety of factors (pages 729–730)
2. either direct or indirect rule (pages 733–734)
3. stressed export of raw materials; benefited colonial masters (page 734)
4. began to unify the people to throw off colonial rule in Asia (page 736) and Africa (page 747)
5. power increased as British became involved with Indian political and military affairs; brought order and stability that helped average Indian citizen (pages 748–751)
6. nationalistic revolts (pages 756–760)
7. losses from the wars for independence; national unity difficult; struggles between Roman catholic Church and the state; destructive caudillos; reverting to old trade patterns; domination of society by landed elites (page 760)

FOCUS

OBJECTIVES

After completing this section, students should be able to

1. explain how the "new imperialism" differed from imperialism of earlier ages and discuss the national motives for establishing colonies under the new imperialism
2. name the three colonial powers that established control of Southeast Asia in the nineteenth century
3. list the differences between direct and indirect colonial rule
4. discuss the impact of colonialism on the economies and cultures of Southeast Asia
5. explain the importance of the rise of nationalism to the revolutionary movements of Southeast Asian countries

FOCUS ACTIVITY

Have students list U.S. territorial possessions that are not states. (the U.S. Virgin Islands, Puerto Rico, numerous Pacific Islands) The U.S. acquired some of these through war, some through colonial-type activities. However, the European nations actively colonized Africa and Asia.

LEARNING FROM VISUALS

Answer to the caption question: Answers will vary.

from the earlier European imperialism. The new imperialism was more rapid and more dominating. Earlier, European states had been content, especially in Africa and Asia, to set up a few trading posts where they could carry on trade and even some missionary activity. Now they sought nothing less than direct control over vast territories.

Why did Westerners begin this mad scramble for colonies after 1880? No doubt, there was a strong economic motive. Capitalist states in the West sought both markets and raw materials such as rubber, oil, and tin for their industries. Moreover, Europeans wanted to be sure they could get these raw materials and set up reliable markets. To do so, they wanted more direct control of the areas where the raw materials and markets were found.

The issue was not simply an economic one, however. As we saw with the new system of alliances described in Chapter 22, European nation-states were involved in heated rivalries. As European affairs grew tense, states sought to gain colonies abroad in order to gain an advantage over their rivals. Colonies were also a source of national prestige. Once the scramble for colonies began, failure to enter the race was seen as a sign of weakness. To some, in fact, a nation could not be great without colonies. One German historian wrote that "all great nations in the fullness of their strength have the desire to set their mark upon barbarian lands and those who fail to participate in this great rivalry will play a pitiable role in time to come."[1]

Then, too, imperialism was tied to Social Darwinism and racism. Social Darwinists believed that in the struggle between nations, the fit are victorious and survive. Superior races must dominate inferior races by military force to show how strong they are. One British professor argued in 1900, "The path of progress is strewn with the wrecks of nations; traces are everywhere to be seen of the [slaughtered remains] of inferior races. Yet these dead people are, in very truth, the stepping stones on which mankind has arisen to the higher intellectual and deeper emotional life of today."[2]

Some Europeans took a more religious and humanitarian approach to imperialism. They argued that Europeans had a moral responsibility to civilize ignorant people, which they called the "white man's bur-

The first step towards lightening

The White Man's Burden

is through teaching the virtues of cleanliness.

Pears' Soap

is a potent factor in brightening the dark corners of the earth as civilization advances, while amongst the cultured of all nations it holds the highest place—it is the ideal toilet soap.

▲ *This advertisement for Pears' Soap clearly communicates the Europeans' view of their responsibility toward other peoples and cultures. To which groups in English society would this ad have appealed?*

den." They believed that the advanced nations of the West should help the backward nations of Asia and Africa. To some, this meant bringing the Christian message to the "heathen masses." To others, it meant bringing the benefits of Western democracy and capitalism to the societies of the East. Either way, many Westerners believed that their governments were bringing civilization to the primitive peoples of the world.

RECOMMENDED READING

Demographic problems are examined in T. McKeown, *The Modern Rise of Population* (New York, 1976). On European emigration, see C. Erickson, *Emigration from Europe, 1815–1914* (Cambridge, 1976). For perspectives on imperialism, see T. Smith, *The Pattern of Imperialism* (Cambridge, 1981); and P. Darby, *Three Faces of Imperialism: British and American Approaches to Asia and Africa, 1870–1970* (New Haven, Conn., 1987).

Imperialism is covered in R. Robinson and J. Gallagher, *Africa and the Victorians,* 2d ed. (New York, 1981); P. Gifford and W. R. Louis, eds., *France and Britain in Africa* (New Haven, Conn., 1971); and W. Baumgart, *Imperialism: The Idea and Reality of British and French Colonial expansion, 1880–1914* (London, 1982). British-Indian relations are examined in J. M. Brown, *Modern India: The Origins of an Asian Democracy* (New York, 1981).

Map 23.1   Colonial Southeast Asia

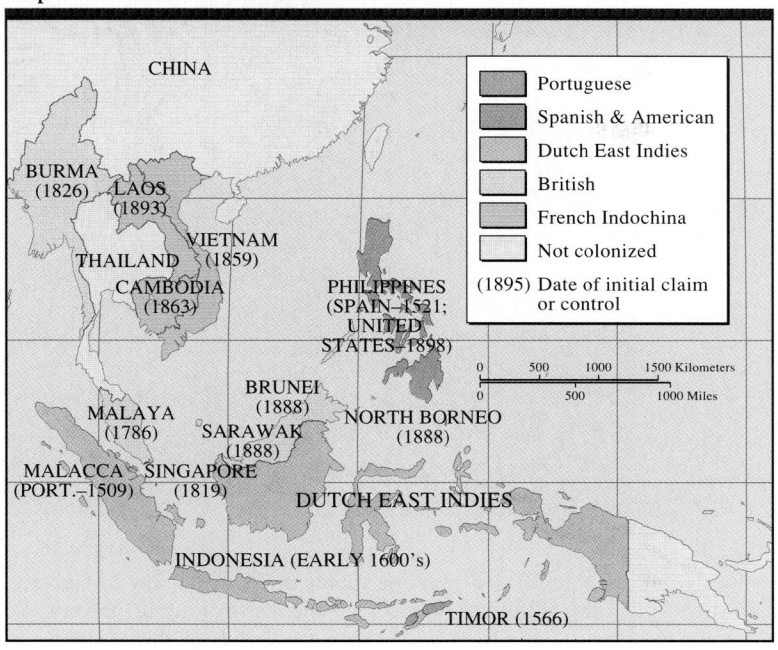

The Colonial Takeover in Southeast Asia

In 1800, only two societies in Southeast Asia were ruled by Europeans: the Spanish Philippines and the Dutch East Indies. By 1900, virtually the entire area was under colonial rule.

The process began with Great Britain. After the Napoleonic Wars (see Chapter 20), the British agreed with the Dutch to abandon British claims to lands in the East Indies in return for a free hand in the Malay peninsula. In 1819, Britain under Sir Stamford Raffles founded a new British colony on a small island at the tip of the peninsula. Called Singapore (city of the lion), it had previously been used by Malay pirates to raid nearby shipping. In the new age of steamships, Singapore soon became a major stopping point for traffic on a route to or from China. Raffles was proud of his new city and wrote to a friend in England, "Here all is

life and activity; and it would be difficult to name a place on the face of the globe with brighter prospects or more present satisfaction."[3]

During the next few decades, the British advance into Southeast Asia continued. At the beginning of the nineteenth century, Great Britain had received the right to trade with the kingdom of Burma (modern Myanmar). A few decades later, Britain sought a more direct presence in the area to protect the eastern flank of its possessions in India. It also sought a land route through Burma into South China. Although the difficult terrain along the frontier between Burma and China caused this effort to fail, British activities in Burma led to the collapse of the Burmese monarchy. Britain soon established control over the entire country.

The British advance into Burma was watched nervously by France, which had some missionaries operating in Vietnam. The French missionaries were persecuted by the local authorities, who viewed Christianity as a threat to Confucian doctrine. However, Vietnam failed to stop the Christian missionaries. Vietnamese internal rivalries divided the country into two separate governments, in the north and the south.

France was especially alarmed at the British attempt to gain a monopoly of trade in South China. To stop this, the French government decided in 1857 to force the Vietnamese to accept French protection. A naval attack launched in 1858 was not a total success, but the French did succeed in forcing the Vietnamese ruler to cede territories in the Mekong River delta. The French occupied the city of Saigon (sie-GAWN) and, during the next 30 years, extended their control over the rest of the country. In 1884, France completed its conquest of Vietnam. It seized the city of Hanoi and made the Vietnamese

STUDYING MAPS

The following questions will help you guide the students through their study of Map 23.1.

1. Ask students to name the countries on the map and to identify the colonizer and date of claim or control of each country.

2. Ask students what they notice about the dates of colonization. *(Except for Malaya [1786], all countries were colonized before*

the early 1600s or after 1800).

3. Ask students what feature of Vietnam might explain its having been divided several times in its history. *(very long and narrow country with north and south connected by a narrow strip)* How long (north to south) is Vietnam? *(about 1200 miles)* How wide (east to west) is it at its narrowest point? *(less than 50 miles)*

TEACH

USING PRIMARY SOURCES

Have students reread the excerpts from the German historian and British professor that appear on page 730. Guide students in a discussion of these two statements and the values they represent. Then have students prepare a written response that might have been composed by an educated Asian or African in response to these two statements.

CLASS DISCUSSION

Guide students in a discussion of how the culture of a city or a country is modified when colonial powers dominate a region. For example, Singapore acquired many British traits, and the official language of Vietnam became French.

CRITICAL THINKING

Social Darwinists seized on the theory of evolution, particularly the idea of the survival of the fittest, to justify racist attitudes toward non-Western peoples. They believed that the white Europeans were more culturally evolved than any other society and were therefore superior. It was the duty of the "superior" European nations to spread Western civilization to the "backward" countries and the loss of culture and tradition was a natural consequence of social evolution.

Ask students how Social Darwinism would have been used by the African slave traders or the Spanish explorers. Does this theory justify their actions? Was it a justification for imperialism in the 19th century? Is it a valid argument for cultural prejudice today?

▶ *This Chinese painting shows the French navy attacking a Vietnamese fort on the Red River. The Manchu court sent forces to help the Vietnamese fight the French, but to no avail.*

Empire a French **protectorate** (a political unit that depends on another state for its protection).

In the 1880s, France extended "protection" over neighboring Cambodia, Annam, Tonkin, and Laos. By 1900, France included all of its new possessions in a new Union of French Indochina.

After the French conquest of Indochina, Thailand was the only remaining free state on the Southeast Asian mainland. During the last quarter of the nineteenth century, British and French rivalry threatened to place Thailand, too, under colonial rule. However, two remarkable rulers, King Mongkut (known to theatergoers as the king in *The King and I*) and his son King Chulalongkorn, acted to prevent colonial rule. Both introduced Western learning and maintained friendly relations with the major European powers. In 1896, Britain and France agreed to maintain Thailand as an independent buffer state between their possessions in Southeast Asia.

One final conquest in Southeast Asia occurred at the end of the nineteenth century. In 1898, during the Spanish-American War, U.S. naval forces under Commodore George Dewey (DOO-ee) defeated the Spanish fleet in Manila Bay. President William McKinley decided that the moral thing to do was to turn the Philippines into an American colony to prevent the area from falling into the hands of the Japanese. In fact, the islands gave the United States a convenient jumping-off point for trade with China.

This mixture of moral idealism and desire for profit was reflected in a speech given in the Senate in January 1900 by Senator Albert Beveridge of Indiana:

> Mr. President, the times call for candor. The Philippines are ours forever. And just beyond the Philippines are China's unlimited markets. We will not retreat from either. We will not abandon an opportunity in the Orient. We will not renounce our part in the mission of our race, trustee, under God, of the civilization of the world. And we will move forward to our work . . . with gratitude for a task worthy of our strength, and thanksgiving to Almighty God that He has marked us as His chosen people, henceforth to lead in the regeneration of the world.[4]

The Filipinos, who had been fighting the Spaniards for their freedom, did not agree with the American senator. Under the leadership of Emilio Aguinaldo (AWG-ee-NAWL-DOE), guerrilla forces fought bit-

MORE ABOUT . . . *Filipinos*

As a result of anti-Chinese immigration laws in the United States in the early 20th century, many sugar, pineapple, and other agricultural planters in Hawaii and California began to recruit cheap Filipino labor. Because the overwhelming proportion of Filipino immigrants were male, and because of racial prejudice, many states prohibited marriage or any other contact between Asian males and Caucasian females. In fact, Filipinos were not even eligible for U.S. citizenship until the late 1940s. Today more immigrants come from the Philippines to the United States than any other Asian nation.

terly against U.S. troops to establish their independence. However, the United States won its first war against guerrilla forces in Asia. Aguinaldo was captured and resistance collapsed in 1901. President McKinley had his stepping-stone to the rich markets of China.

Colonial Regimes in Southeast Asia

Western powers governed their new colonial empires with policies known as either indirect or direct rule. As we have seen, the chief goal of the Western nations was to exploit the natural resources of these lands and open up markets for their own manufactured goods. Sometimes that goal could be realized most easily through cooperation with local political elites. In these cases, **indirect rule** was used. In other words, local rulers were allowed to maintain their positions of authority and status in a new colonial setting. However, indirect rule was not always possible, especially when local elites resisted the foreign conquest. In such cases, the local elites were removed from power and replaced with a new set of officials brought from the mother country. This system is called **direct rule.**

In Southeast Asia, colonial powers, wherever possible, tried to work with local elites. This made it easier to gain access to a region's natural resources. Indirect rule also lowered the cost of government, because Western powers had to train fewer officials. Moreover, indirect rule had less effect on local culture. One example of indirect rule was in the Dutch East Indies. Officials of the Dutch East India Company allowed local landed aristocrats in the Dutch East Indies to control local government. These local elites maintained law and order and collected taxes in return for a payment from the Dutch East India Company.

Indirect rule, then, was convenient and cost less, but it was not always feasible. Local resistance to the colonial conquest made such a policy impossible in some places. In Burma, the staunch opposition by the monarchy caused Great Britain to abolish the monarchy and administer the country directly through its colonial government in India.

In Indochina, France used both direct and indirect rule. It imposed direct rule on the southern provinces in the Mekong delta, which had been ceded to France as a colony after the first war in 1858 to 1860. The northern parts of Vietnam, seized in the 1880s, were governed as a protectorate. The emperor still ruled from his palace in Hue, but he had little power. France adopted a similar policy in Cambodia and Laos, where local rulers were left in charge with French advisors to counsel them.

To justify their conquests, Western powers had spoken of bringing the blessings of advanced Western civilization to their colonial subjects. Many colonial powers, for example, spoke of introducing representative institutions and educating the native peoples in the democratic process. However, many westerners came to fear the idea of native peoples (especially educated ones) being allowed political rights. The westerners were afraid that the native peoples would be too likely to demand full participation in the government, or even want national independence.

Whether they used indirect or direct rule, colonial regimes in Southeast Asia were slow to create democratic institutions. The first legislative bodies were made up almost entirely of European residents in the colonies. When representatives from the local people were allowed to take part, the people chosen were always wealthy and conservative in their political views. When Southeast Asians began to complain, colonial officials gradually extended the right to vote to more people. However, the colonial officials also warned that education in democratic institutions must come before voting rights.

At the same time, colonial officials adopted a cautious attitude toward educational reform. Western powers had said that their civilizing mission included the introduction of Western school systems. However, colonial officials soon discovered that educating the native peoples could backfire. Often there were few jobs for highly trained lawyers, engineers, and architects in colonial societies. Thus, it might be dangerous to have large numbers of educated people without jobs. These people might take out their frustrations on the colonial regime. By the mid-1920s, many colonial governments in Southeast Asia began to limit education to a small elite. As one French official noted, educating the natives meant "one rebel more."

On Line with
WORLD HISTORY *Internet Activity*

You may want to have your students visit the following URL, where they will find information and additional web site resources to enhance their study of this chapter.

The Age of Imperialism

http://www.smplanet.com/ imperialism/toc.html

The Spanish-American War, the Boxer Rebellion and the Panama Canal are covered in this web site.

Due to the ever-changing nature of the World Wide Web, see the West History web site, **http://history.swpco.com** for regular updates of the URLs in this text.

REINFORCING
VOCABULARY

Economic development is the process of transforming the agriculture, industry, and commerce of traditional societies in order to provide a higher living standard for their people.

An *entrepreneur* is a person who organizes and runs a private business, usually using his or her own money. The success of the business depends on the skill and initiative of the entrepreneur and any profits or losses are returned to him or her.

CRITICAL THINKING

The economy for colonies was based on *unequal exchange.* Low value raw materials were exported to Europe and high cost manufactured goods were imported. Local production of manufactured goods was discouraged to assure markets for European industry.

Ask students to list the benefits and harms that would result from this policy. *(Benefits may include job opportunities, infrastructure development [roads, railways, ports, etc.], linking to the world economic system. Harms may include forcing native peoples into low-paying jobs, destroying traditional crafts and industries, preventing growth of local economy, creating class system, creating dependency on Europe for manufactured goods.)*

LEARNING FROM VISUALS

Have students identify the means of restraint used on these prisoners *(stocks).* Why would the French have believed it acceptable to hold prisoners in such harsh, inhumane conditions?

▶ *Resistance against colonial governments was not tolerated, and dissidents were punished harshly. This 1907 photograph shows Vietnamese prisoners awaiting trial for plotting against the French.*

Colonial powers were also not always eager to foster economic development. As we have seen, their chief goals were to gain a source of inexpensive raw materials and to keep markets for manufactured goods. For this reason, the colonial powers did not want their colonists to develop their own industries. Thus, colonial policy stressed the export of raw materials—teak wood from Burma; rubber and tin from Malaya; spices, tea, coffee, and palm oil from the East Indies; and sugar from the Philippines. In many cases, this policy led to some form of plantation agriculture, in which peasants worked as wage laborers on plantations owned by foreign investors.

Some industrial development did take place in Southeast Asia, however, largely to meet the needs of Europeans and local elites. Cities like Rangoon in Burma and Saigon in French Indochina grew rapidly, because they were centers of manufacturing. Textile plants, cement and brick works, and factories for bicycles and automobiles were set up.

Colonial policy was often harmful in urban areas. Most industrial and commercial businesses were owned and managed by Europeans or, in some cases, by Indian or Chinese merchants. In Saigon, for example, even the manufacture of the traditional Vietnamese fish sauce was under Chinese ownership.

In the countryside, these economic changes hurt the natives and benefited their colonial masters. Plantation owners kept the wages of their workers at poverty levels in order to increase profits. Conditions on plantations were often so unhealthy that thousands died. In addition, high taxes levied by colonial governments to pay for their administrative costs were a heavy burden for poor peasants.

Colonial rule did bring some benefits to Southeast Asia. It led to the beginnings of a modern economic system. The development of an export market helped to create an entrepreneurial class in rural areas. In the Dutch East Indies, for example, small growers of rubber, palm oil, coffee, tea, and spices began to share in the profits of the colonial enterprise. Even then, however, most of the profits were taken back to the colonial mother country, and peasants fleeing to cities found few jobs. Many were left with seasonal employment, with one foot on the farm and one in the factory. The old world was being destroyed while the new one had yet to be born.

Resistance to Colonial Rule

Many subject peoples were quite unhappy with being governed by Western powers. At first, resistance came

So What ⁇

If your students question the importance of the information on **colonialism in Southeast Asia,** *tell them . . .*

European colonialism in Vietnam planted the seeds of a conflict that eventually resulted in a war that cost the United States 58,000 lives.

The war also took 1.3 million Vietnamese lives and cost the United States $141 billion in aid. At the end of the war, some 2,500 U.S. soldiers were still listed as missing.

YOU ARE THERE

A Call to Arms

◄ *Vietnamese attempts to regain homelands were not only unsuccessful, they were futile. This drawing shows trained and well-armed French troops in action against their Vietnamese opponents.*

In 1862, the Vietnamese emperor ceded three provinces in southern Vietnam to the French. In outrage, many patriotic Vietnamese military officers and government officials appealed to their fellow Vietnamese to rise up and resist the foreigners. The following lines were written in 1864.

An Appeal to Vietnamese Citizens to Resist the French

This is a general proclamation addressed to the scholars and the people. . . .
Our people are now suffering through a period of anarchy and disorder. . . .
Let us now consider our situation with the French today.

We are separated from them by thousands of mountains and seas.
By hundreds of differences in our daily customs.
Although they were very confident in their copper battleships surmounted by chimneys,
Although they had a large quantity of steel rifles and lead bullets,
These things did not prevent the loss of some of their best generals in these last years, when they attacked our frontier in hundreds of battles. . . .
You, officials of the country,
Do not let your resistance to the enemy be blunted by the peaceful stand of the court,
Do not take the lead from the three subjected provinces and leave hatred unavenged.

(continued)

MORE ABOUT . . . *Vietnam*

Between 1887 and 1893, Vietnam, composed of Cochin China in the south, Tonkin in the north, and Annam in the central part of the country, were joined first with Cambodia and later with Laos into the French ruled Union of Indochina. Many upper-class Vietnamese spoke and wrote in French and joined the Catholic Church, abandoning their native culture and customs. Eventually a nationalist party was formed by Vietnamese patriots who began to protest French rule. By the late 1930s a Communist party led by Ho Chi Minh had become the strongest force in the nationalist movement.

LEARNING FROM VISUALS

This image displays a battle scene from the French invasion of Southeast Asia. Ask students to decide whether they perceive a bias toward one side or the other in the representation. *(Students may note that the Vietnamese forces appear to be in disarray and in retreat while the French are fighting in a well-organized formation.)*

USING PRIMARY SOURCES

Although students may not recognize it as such, this selection may be classified as propaganda. By definition, propaganda is information that is presented with the purpose of persuading people to accept or believe a particular point of view. Only recently—historically speaking—has propaganda been associated with untrue or negative statements. Because it is intended to persuade, however, much propaganda is emotional. Ask students to identify some particularly emotional passages from the writing. Read to students the following quote from *The American Crisis* by Thomas Paine: "Every Tory is a coward; for servile, slavish, self-interested fear is the foundation of Toryism; and a man under such influence, though he may be cruel, never can be brave." Then ask students to create a list of questions that might be used as a guide to determine whether a piece of writing is propaganda. Then ask students to bring in an article, speech or pamphlet that they consider to be propaganda and to explain why.

Answers to Critical Thinking Questions

1. resist the French
2. The writers didn't think too highly of those who collaborated with the French. They called them names: decay, garbage, filth, swine, idiots, fools, lackeys, scoundrels.

Multimedia Support

TRANSPARENCY

23–2, Timeline of Important 19th and Early 20th Century Events in Asia

CLASS DISCUSSION

The resistance to colonial rule points out the inherent contradictions in colonial policy. New governments were established but traditional rulers were excluded. Western education was provided but few opportunities for applying the education were possible. Economic development occurred but the benefits went to a few while the majority were worse off.

In a class discussion or in groups ask students to consider the expected and unintended effects of colonial policies. Under education, for example, an expected result was suppression of traditional culture and values. An unintended result was pride in tradition and resentment of colonial disrespect. Conclude the discussion by pointing out to students that the European's attempts to assure their own dominance, power, and control as well as a lavish life style sowed the seeds for their own downfall.

YOU ARE THERE

A Call to Arms, continued

So many years of labor, of energy, of suffering— shall we now abandon all?

Rather, we should go to the far ends of jungles or to the high peaks of mountains in search of heroes.

Rather, we should go to the shores of the sea in search of talented men.

Do not envy the scholars who now become provincial or district magistrates [in the French administration]. They are decay, garbage, filth, swine.

Do not imitate some who hire themselves out to the enemy. They are idiots, fools, lackeys, scoundrels.

1. What do the writers of these lines want their fellow countrymen to do?
2. What are the writer's feelings toward those who worked with the French administration? How can you tell?

---

from the existing ruling class. In Burma and Vietnam, for example, the resistance to Western domination came from the monarchs themselves. After the emperor in Vietnam had agreed to French control of his country, a number of civilian and military officials set up an organization called Can Vuoug (Save the King). They fought against the French without the emperor's help (see "You Are There: A Call to Arms").

Sometimes resistance to Western control went beyond the elite. When this occurred, it most commonly took the form of peasant revolts. Rural rebellions were not uncommon in traditional Asian societies as a means of expressing peasant discontent with high taxes, official corruption, debt, or famine in the countryside. Under colonial rule, conditions often got worse as peasants were driven off the land to make way for plantation agriculture. Angry peasants then vented their anger at the foreign invaders. For example, in Burma, the Buddhist monk Saya San led a peasant uprising against the British colonial regime many years after the regime had completed its takeover.

These early resistance movements, however, were overcome by Western power, and they failed. At the beginning of the twentieth century, a new kind of resistance began to emerge that was based on the force of nationalism. The leaders were often a new class that had been created by colonial rule: westernized intellectuals in the cities. In many cases, this new urban middle class—composed of merchants, clerks, students, and professionals—had been educated in Western-style schools. A few had spent time in the West. They were the first generation of Asians to understand the institutions and values of the West. Many spoke Western languages, wore Western clothes, and worked in jobs connected with the colonial regimes.

At first, many of the leaders of these movements did not focus clearly on the idea of nationhood but simply tried to defend the economic interests or religious beliefs of the natives. In Burma, for example, the first expression of modern nationalism came from students at the University of Rangoon. They formed an organization to protest against official persecution of the Buddhist religion and British lack of respect for local religious traditions. The students called themselves *Thakin* (meaning "Lord" or "Master," thus showing their demand for the right to rule themselves). They protested against British arrogance and failure to observe local customs in Buddhist temples. Only in the 1930s, however, did these resistance movements begin to demand national independence.

ENRICHMENT ACTIVITY

Have students watch the movie, *The King and I.* Use it as a basis for a class discussion or essay that explains how the movie reflects the historical situation in Southeast Asia in the nineteenth century. In what ways does it oversimplify that situation?

What stereotypes are explored in the film?

SECTION REVIEW

1. Locate:
(a) Indian Ocean,   (b) Dutch East Indies,
(c) Singapore,   (d) Burma,   (e) Vietnam,
(f) Cambodia,   (g) Thailand,   (h) Philippines,
(i) Laos

2. Define:
(a) imperialism,   (b) protectorate,
(c) indirect rule,   (d) direct rule

3. Identify:
(a) new imperialism,   (b) buffer state,
(c) Spanish-American War,   (d) Can Vuoug,
(e) Saya San

4. Recall:
(a) What economic forces drove the movement of European nations to the new imperialism?
(b) How did the ideas of Social Darwinism support the new imperialism?
(c) Why did imperialist nations want to consolidate their control over nations they dominated?
(d) What advantages were provided by indirect rule to imperial nations?
(e) Why did imperial powers often oppose education for dominated peoples?

5. Think Critically: Why did natives of dominated lands, who had been educated and lived in Western nations, often lead their homelands in revolt against imperialist nations?

EMPIRE BUILDING IN AFRICA

Before 1800, Europeans had shown little interest in taking complete control of African territory. The slave trade, the main source of European profit in Africa during the eighteenth century, was carried on by using African rulers and merchants who cooperated for profits. Disease, lack of transportation, and an unhealthy climate all served to keep Europeans out of Africa on any permanent basis.

Gradually, however, Europeans took a greater interest in Africa. Before 1880, they controlled little of the African continent directly. European rule was limited to the fringes of Africa, such as Algeria, the Gold Coast, and South Africa. Between 1880 and 1900, however, a mad scramble for African territory took place. Fed by intense rivalries among themselves, Great Britain, France, Germany, Belgium, and Portugal placed virtually all of Africa under European rule.

The Growing European Presence in West Africa

By 1800, the slave trade, which had particularly affected West Africa, was beginning to decline. One reason was the growing outrage in Western countries over the sale and exploitation of human beings. In 1808, both Great Britain and the United States declared the slave trade illegal. Other European countries eventually followed suit. In the meantime, the demand for slaves began to decline in the Western Hemisphere. Slavery was abolished in the United States in 1865 and in Cuba and Brazil fifteen years later. By the 1880s, slavery had been abolished in all major countries of the world.

The decline of the Atlantic slave trade did not lead to fewer Europeans in West Africa, however. Europe's interest in other forms of trade actually increased as slavery declined. Europeans sold textiles and other manufactured goods in exchange for such West African natural resources as peanuts, timber, hides, and palm oil.

Encouraged by this growing trade, European governments began to push for a more permanent presence along the coast. During the first decades of the nineteenth century, the British set up settlements along the Gold Coast and in Sierra Leone (see-ER-uh lee-OWN). The latter became a haven for freed slaves. When British ships captured illegal slave ships, they freed the slaves and brought them to Sierra Leone. The United States created a homeland for its freed slaves in Liberia. Founded in 1822, Liberia became an independent state in 1850. Its capital city, Monrovia, was named after President James Monroe.

RECOMMENDED READING

On the imperialist age in Africa, above all see R. Robinson and J. Gallagher, *Africa and the Victorians: The Official Mind of Imperialism* (London, 1961). Also see B. Davidson, *Modern Africa: A Social and Political History* (London, 1989); T. Pakenham, *The Scramble for Africa* (New York, 1991), and his *The Boer War* (London, 1979). On South Africa, see J. Guy, *The Destruction of the Zulu Kingdom* (London, 1979); and D. Nenoon and B. Nyeko, *Southern Africa since 1800* (London, 1984).

ASSESS

Answers to SECTION REVIEW

2. (a) the spread of one nation's power over another
(b) political unit that depends on another for protection
(c) control by an imperial power through the use of local rulers
(d) control by an imperial power by replacing local rulers with officials from the imperial nation
3. (a) a more dominating form of imperialism
(b) a political and geographical unit between two greater powers
(c) a war through which the United States gained territories in the Far East
(d) Vietnamese who organized to fight French domination
(e) leader of a peasant uprising in Burma
4. (a) Western nations wanted a reliable supply of raw materials and a market for the goods they produced.
(b) It suggested that strong nations should dominate weak nations.
(c) They could achieve greater economic benefits from trade and try to prevent the incursion of other imperial powers.
(d) Indirect rule was less expensive and often resulted in less resistance.
(e) They feared dissatisfaction and revolt.
5. Answers will vary.

CLOSE

Have students discuss the pros and cons of the new imperialism.

FOCUS

OBJECTIVES

After completing this section, students should be able to

1. discuss the economic and political factors that led to the colonization of Africa by the European countries
2. name the European countries that colonized the different regions of Africa
3. explain how the combination of resources, cultural differences, and location led to the establishment of colonial states in Southern Africa
4. discuss the policies and practices of the colonial governments in Africa
5. explain the importance of the rise of nationalism to Southeast Asian countries

FOCUS ACTIVITY

Be certain students understand why Africa was of interest to the European countries. Divide the class into groups and assign each group to list reasons why Africa was important to European countries.

TEACH

LEARNING FROM VISUALS

Ask students to locate the Suez Canal on Map 23.2 on page 744. Ask students why the Suez Canal was important. *(It provided a more direct route from Europe to India and China than sailing all the way around Africa.)*

▶ *The first ships passed through the Suez Canal in 1869. It is still an important strategic site, and it is Egypt's largest revenue producer.*

The growing European presence in West Africa led to increasing tensions with African governments in the area. British efforts to increase trade with the state of Ashanti, for example, led to conflict in the 1820s. For a long time, most African states were able to maintain their independence. However, by the 1870s, European power had grown too great. In 1874, Great Britain stepped in and annexed the coastal states as the first British colony of Gold Coast. At about the same time, Britain established a protectorate over warring tribal groups in Nigeria. The French also moved into West Africa. By 1900, France had added the huge area of French West Africa to its colonial empire. This left France in control of the largest part of West Africa.

North Africa

Egypt had been part of the Ottoman Empire, but as Ottoman rule declined, the Egyptians sought their independence. In 1805, an officer named Muhammad Ali seized power and established a separate Egyptian state. During the next 30 years, Muhammad Ali introduced a series of reforms to bring Egypt into the modern world. He modernized the army, set up a public school system, and helped to create a small industrial sector. Refined sugar, textiles, munitions, and even ships were among the products manufactured. Muham-

mad Ali's new army also made it possible to extend Egyptian authority southward into the Sudan and across the Sinai peninsula into Arabia.

The growing economic importance of the Nile valley in Egypt, along with the development of steamships, gave Europeans the desire to build a canal east of Cairo to connect the Mediterranean and Red Seas. In 1854, the French entrepreneur Ferdinand de Lesseps (lae-SEPS) signed a contract to begin building the Suez Canal. It was completed in 1869. The project brought little immediate benefit to Egypt, however. The costs of construction gave the Egyptian government a large debt and made the Egyptians more dependent on financial support from European states.

The British took an active interest in Egypt after the Suez (soo-EZ) Canal was opened in 1869. Believing that the canal was its "lifeline to India," Great Britain sought as much control as possible over the canal area. In 1875, Britain bought Egypt's share of stocks in the Suez Canal. When an Egyptian army revolt against foreign influence broke out in 1881, Britain stepped in and set up a protectorate over Egypt.

British interests in the Sudan, south of Egypt, soon brought a confrontation with the French. The British believed that they should control the Sudan in order to protect both Egypt and the Suez Canal. In 1881, the Muslim cleric Muhammad Ahmad, known as the

COOPERATIVE LEARNING ACTIVITY

Divide the class into small groups and have some groups research the development, history, and ownership of the Suez Canal. Groups should prepare a map of the Eastern Hemisphere, using the Suez Canal as the central focus of the map. Students should provide statistical information on the impact of the canal on world trade.

Other groups should prepare similar reports on the Panama Canal.

When all groups have finished their work, organize a class debate over the question of which canal is more important in terms of worldwide economy and strategic location.

Mahdi (MAWD-ee) ("The Rightly Guided One," in Arabic), led a revolt that brought much of the Sudan under his control. Britain sent a military force under General Charles Gordon to restore Egyptian authority over the Sudan. However, Gordon's army was wiped out at Khartoum in 1885 by the Mahdi's troops 36 hours before a British rescue mission arrived. Gordon himself died in the battle.

It was not until 1898 that British troops were able to seize the Sudan. In the meantime, the French had been advancing eastward across the Sahara with the goal of controlling the regions around the upper Nile. French and British forces met unexpectedly at Fashoda, a small town on the Nile River in the Sudan. War between the two great European powers seemed inevitable. However, the French government was preoccupied with the Dreyfus affair, and it backed down. Britain retained control of most of the Sudan, leaving the French to rule in equatorial Africa.

The French were more successful elsewhere in North Africa. In 1879, after 150,000 French people had settled in the region of Algeria, the French government established control there. Two years later, France imposed a protectorate on neighboring Tunisia. In 1912, France established a protectorate over much of Morocco. The rest was left to Spain.

Italy joined in the scramble for North Africa, but it was defeated by Ethiopia in 1896. Italy now was the only European state to lose to an African state. This humiliating defeat led Italy to try again in 1911. Italy invaded and seized Turkish Tripoli, which it renamed Libya (LIB-ee-uh).

Central Africa

Territories in central Africa were also added to the list of European colonies. Popular interest in the dense tropical jungles of central Africa was first aroused in

▲ *This drawing shows the historic meeting of Livingstone and Stanley. Which features in this artist's rendition do you believe are accurate? Which features do you think are inaccurate or imaginative?*

MORE ABOUT . . . *David Livingstone*

David Livingstone began his African explorations in 1849 when he crossed the Kalahari Desert to reach Lake Ngami. From 1853 to 1856, he explored central Africa and was the first non-African to cross the African continent from east to west. In 1871 Livingstone became ill and lost contact with the outside world. It was then that Henry Stanley was sent by the *New York Herald* on his famous search, and he located Livingstone in Ujiji (Tanzania). Livingstone continued his exploration, and died of malaria on May 1, 1873. His books about his experiences in Africa *Missionary Travels* and *The Zambezi and Its Tributaries,* became best sellers, ensuring his fame throughout Europe.

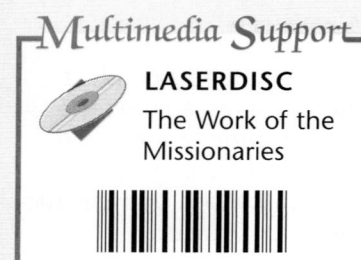

Multimedia Support

LASERDISC
The Work of the Missionaries

ACROSS THE CURRICULUM

Literature Nowhere were the excesses of colonialism more evident than in Africa. Leopold, in spite of his claims of bringing civilization, exemplifies the worst treatment of the African natives. He enslaved the Congolese people to work on his plantations, had forests cut down in order to plant rubber plantations, and had elephant herds slaughtered for ivory. In twenty years of brutal rule, Leopold, "the Civilizer" stripped the Congo of its culture, its people, and its resources.

Ask student volunteers to read aloud from relevant parts of Joseph Conrad's *The Heart of Darkness*. Ask them to discuss how imperialism differed between central Africa and East Asia. Why were the people and cultures treated differently?

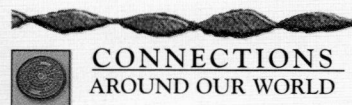

CONNECTIONS
AROUND OUR WORLD

Malaria is still a common disease in Africa, Central America, and Southeast Asia. People who have contracted malaria sometimes suffer relapses years after their first infection.

the 1860s and 1870s by explorers. David Livingstone, as we have seen, first arrived in Africa in 1841. For 30 years he trekked through uncharted regions. He spent much of his time exploring the interior of the continent. When Livingstone disappeared for a while, the *New York Herald* hired a young journalist, Henry Stanley, to find him. Stanley did, on the eastern shore of Lake Tanganyika (TAN-gun-YEE-kuh), and greeted the explorer with the now famous words "Dr. Livingstone, I presume."

After Livingstone's death in 1873, Stanley remained in Africa to carry on the great explorer's work. Unlike Livingstone, however, Stanley had a strong dislike of Africa. He once said, "I detest the land most heartily." In the 1870s, Stanley moved inland from the East African coast. He explored the Congo River and sailed down it to the Atlantic Ocean. Soon he was encouraging the British to send settlers to the Congo River basin. When Britain refused, he turned to King Leopold II of Belgium.

King Leopold II was the real driving force behind the colonization of central Africa. He rushed enthusiastically into the pursuit of an empire in Africa: "To open to civilization," he said, "the only part of our globe where it has not yet penetrated, to pierce the darkness which envelops whole populations, is a crusade, if I may say so, a crusade worthy of this century of progress." Profit, however, was more important to Leopold than progress. In 1876, he hired Henry Stanley to set up Belgian settlements in the Congo.

Leopold's claim to the vast territories of the Congo aroused widespread concern from other European states. France, in particular, rushed to plant its flag in the heart of Africa. Leopold ended up with the territories south of the Congo River, whereas France occupied the areas to the north.

Arab Merchants and European Missionaries in East Africa

Events in East Africa followed their own pattern. The decline in the Atlantic slave trade led to an increase in slavery on the other side of the continent. A sudden growth in plantation agriculture in the region and on the islands off the coast led to a demand for slave labor.

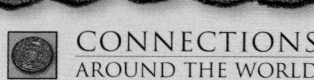

CONNECTIONS
AROUND THE WORLD

The Role of Quinine   Before 1850, the fear of disease was a major factor in keeping many Europeans from moving into Africa. Especially frightening was malaria, an often fatal infection. Malaria is especially devastating in tropical and subtropical regions, which offer good conditions for breeding the mosquitoes that carry and spread the malaria parasites. When the mosquito bites a person, malaria parasites enter the victim's red blood cells. Intense attacks of chills, fevers, and sweats are often followed by death.

By 1850, European doctors had learned how to treat malaria with quinine, a drug that greatly reduced the death rate from malaria. Quinine is a bitter drug obtained from the bark of the cinchona tree, which is native to the slopes of the Andes Mountains in South America. The Indians of Peru were the first people to use the bark of the cinchona tree to treat malaria.

The Dutch, however, took the cinchona tree and began to grow it in the East Indies. The East Indies eventually became the chief source of quinine. With the use of quinine and other medicines, Europeans felt more secure about moving into Africa. By the beginning of the twentieth century, more than 90 percent of African lands were under the control of the European powers. A drug found in the bark of trees in Latin America and then Asia had been used by Europeans to make possible their conquest of Africa.

The French introduced the growing of sugar to the island of Réunion (ree-YOON-yun) early in the century. Clove plantations were set up on the island of Zanzibar. The Arab sultan of Oman established his capital at Zanzibar in 1840. From there, Arab merchants fanned out into Africa in search of slaves, ivory, and other local products. The slave trade in East Africa now made Zanzibar the largest slave market in Africa.

This slave traffic brought East Africa to the attention of the West and its Christian missionaries. David

ENRICHMENT ACTIVITY

Have students work in pairs to create their own maps of Africa, showing the various stages of conquest by the Western powers. How did the colonial policies of the French, British, Germans, and Belgians differ?

◄ *This 1871 sketch shows slave traders murdering Africans during a slave raid on the Lualaba River, west of Lake Tanganyika. What effect might sketches such as these have had on slavery?*

USING PRIMARY SOURCES

Ask students to discuss what Otto von Bismarck meant by his statement "All this colonial business is a sham, but we need it for the elections." What elections would Bismarck be referring to? *(Local towns and burghers sent representatives to a congress where they advised the emperor.)* Ask them to list reasons why a country would feel they needed colonies. What does this statement say about Bismarck's attitude toward the common folk?

CRITICAL THINKING

Remind students that no African delegates were present at the Berlin Conference—the conference that divided up Africa among the European nations. What do they believe would be the reaction today of a nation whose internal affairs were arbitrarily decided by the governments of foreign powers? Tell students that in the near future, Woodrow Wilson would talk to the world about a concept called *self-determination*—the right of a peoples to determine their own fate.

Livingstone, for example, was passionately opposed to slavery. His protests created public outcries, especially in Britain, against the slave trade in East Africa. In 1873, the slave market at Zanzibar was finally closed as the result of pressure from Great Britain.

By that time, Britain and Germany had become the chief rivals in East Africa. Germany came late to the ranks of the imperialist powers. At first, the German chancellor Otto von Bismarck had downplayed the importance of colonies. As more and more Germans called for a German empire, however, Bismarck became a convert to colonialism. As he expressed it, "All this colonial business is a sham, but we need it for the elections." Germany controlled Togo, Cameroons, and Southwest Africa along the west coast of Africa. Germany also sought colonies in East Africa. Most of East Africa had not yet been claimed by any other power. However, the British were also interested, because control of East Africa would connect the British Empire in Africa from South Africa in the south to Egypt in the north. Portugal and Belgium also claimed parts of East Africa.

To settle the conflicting claims in East Africa, Bismarck held a conference in Berlin in 1884. The Berlin Conference, first of all, set basic rules for further annexations of African territory by European nations. Its goal was to avoid war and reduce tensions among European nations competing for the spoils of Africa. Second, the conference gave official recognition to both British and German claims for territory in East Africa. Portugal received a clear claim on Mozambique. No African delegates were present at this conference, which carved up their continent.

Bantus, Boers, and British in South Africa

Nowhere in Africa did the European presence grow more rapidly than in the south. During the eighteenth century, European settlers gradually began to migrate eastward from the Cape Colony (see later in this section) into territory inhabited by Bantu-speaking people. Tribal warfare among the Bantus, however, had largely depopulated the area. This made it easier for

Multimedia Support

TRANSPARENCY
23–3, Africa: Tribal, Ethnic Groupings, Beginning of the 20th Century (Map)

LEARNING FROM VISUALS

Answer to the caption question: Sketches like this one would have helped end the practice of slavery.

MORE ABOUT . . . *David Livingstone*

Although remembered primarily for his explorations in Africa and for his humanitarian work, David Livingstone worked hard to bring Africa into the world community of nations and to alert Europeans to the miserable living conditions of many Africans. His explorations attracted commercial interest in the region near the mouth of the Zambezi River. His writings helped lead to the abolishment of the slave trade in East Africa. He loved the continent so much, that although his body is buried in Westminister Abbey, he gave instructions that his heart was to remain in Africa. It is buried in Blantyre, Malawi—a city named after his birthplace in Scotland.

CLASS DISCUSSION

It is important that students realize that there was already an established civilization in southern Africa before the arrival of the Europeans. Great city-states, such as Greater Zimbabwe, existed and had established trade routes, built elaborate cities with administrative centers, mined precious minerals, and had distinctive cultures and traditions. For many years, white explorers and historians refused to accept evidence of these civilizations and made up fantastic stories of lost white civilizations to explain away the advanced artifacts. Edgar Rice Burrough's Tarzan stories grew out of this tradition. Ask students to discuss what role racism played in the supposedly scientific study of these ruins.

LEARNING FROM VISUALS

In spite of the well-disciplined Zulu army and initial victories, British victory was inevitable. This image provides some clues as to the British advantages. Ask students to name them. (The British had mounted calvary, repeating rifles, and a constant supply of new recruits.)

▲ In 1879, the Zulu king Cetewayo met with British ambassadors who were representing Lord Chelmsford. Cetewayo, who was born c. 1825 and died in 1884, was the last king of independent Zululand. Cetewayo tried to ally himself with the British against the Afrikaners, but the British invaded Zululand and eventually defeated the Zulu forces.

the Boers, or Afrikaners, as the descendants of the original Dutch settlers in the seventeenth century were called, to occupy the land.

In the early nineteenth century, however, another local people, the Zulus (zoo-LOOZ), under a talented ruler named Shaka, had carved out their own empire. A series of wars ensued between the Europeans and the Zulus. Eventually, Shaka was overthrown. The Boers continued their advance northeastward during the so-called Great Trek in the mid-1830s. By 1865, the total white population of the area had risen to nearly 200,000 people.

The Boers' eastward migration was motivated in part by the British. During the Napoleonic Wars, the British had seized Capetown from the Dutch. After the wars, the British encouraged settlers to come to what they called Cape Colony. The British government

seemed to care more about the rights of the local African population than did the Boers. Many Boers saw white superiority as ordained by God. Disgusted with British policies, the Boers fled northward on the Great Trek to the region between the Orange and Vaal (VAWL) Rivers and north of the Vaal River. In these areas, the Boers formed their own independent republics—called the Orange Free State and the Transvaal. The Boers put much of the native population in these areas on reservations.

Hostilities between the British and the Boers continued. In 1877, the British governor of Cape Colony seized the Transvaal. However, a Boer revolt led the British government to recognize the Transvaal as the independent South African Republic. In the 1880s, British policy in South Africa was largely set by Cecil Rhodes. Rhodes had founded both diamond and gold

MORE ABOUT . . . *the Xhosa in South Africa*

The Xhosa were a South African tribe who hated the European settlers and wanted them out of Africa. In 1856 a young girl of the tribe, supposedly speaking with the voice of spirits, foretold that if all of the tribe's livestock and crops were destroyed then the whites would leave Africa and their food supplies would be replaced in abundance. The Xhosas obediently slaughtered their cattle and burned their crops. The famine which ensued is said to have killed more than 60,000 Xhosas.

Map 23.2   The Struggle for South Africa

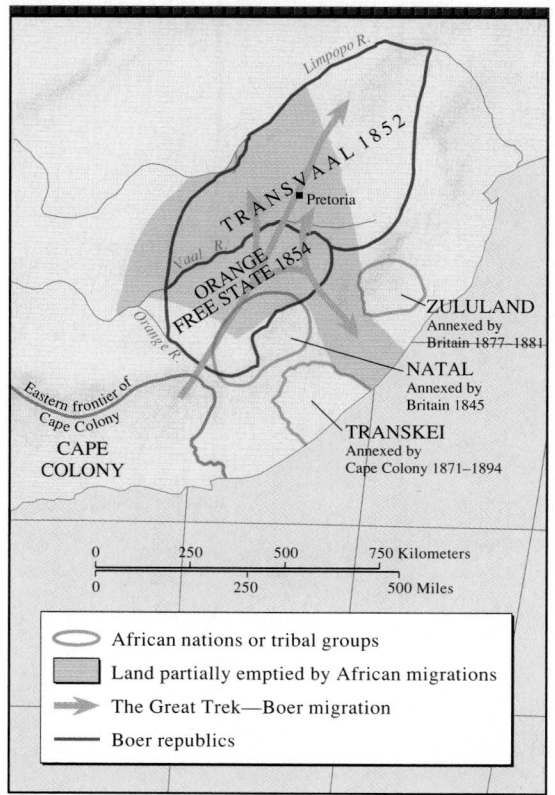

Map legend:
- African nations or tribal groups
- Land partially emptied by African migrations
- The Great Trek—Boer migration
- Boer republics

South African Republic without British approval. Although the British government had hoped to avoid war with the Boers, it could not stop fanatics on both sides from starting a conflict that came to be known as the Boer War.

The Boer War dragged on from 1899 to 1902. Guerrilla resistance by the Boers was fierce. This angered the British. They responded by burning crops and herding more than 150,000 Boer women and children into detention camps, where lack of food caused 26,000 deaths. Eventually, the vastly larger British army won. British policy toward the defeated Boers was generous. In 1910, the British agreed to the creation of an independent Union of South Africa, which combined the old Cape Colony and the Boer republics. To appease the Boers, the British agreed that only whites would vote.

By 1914, Great Britain, France, Germany, Belgium, and Portugal had divided up Africa. Only Liberia and Ethiopia remained free states. Despite the talk about the "white man's burden," Africa had been conquered by European states determined to create colonial empires. Any native peoples who dared to resist (with the exception of the Ethiopians) were simply devastated by the superior military force of the Europeans (see "The Role of Science and Technology: The Machine Gun").

Furthermore, Europeans did not hesitate to deceive the natives in order to gain their way. One southern African king, Lo Bengula (LOE bun-GYOO-luh), informed Queen Victoria about how he had been cheated:

Some time ago a party of men came to my country, the principal one appearing to be a man called Rudd. They asked me for a place to dig for gold, and said they would give me certain things for the right to do so. I told them to bring what they could give and I would show them what I would give. A document was written and presented to me for signature. I asked what it contained, and was told that in it were my words and the words of those men. I put my hand to it. About three months afterwards I heard from other sources that I had given by the document the right to all the minerals of my country.[5]

companies that made him a fortune. He gained control of a territory north of the Transvaal, which he named Rhodesia after himself. He became its prime minister.

Rhodes was a great champion of British expansion. He said once, "If there be a God, I think what he would like me to do is to paint as much of Africa British red as possible." One of Rhodes's goals was to create a series of British colonies "from the Cape to Cairo"—all linked by a railroad. His ambitions, however, led to his downfall in 1896. The British government forced him to resign as prime minister of Rhodesia after he planned to overthrow the Boer government of the

ACROSS THE CURRICULUM

Politics and Government

Students may enjoy hearing the following true story of how three African rulers beat Cecil Rhodes at his own game.

In 1891 Rhodes had very nearly obtained permission to annex the British protectorate of Bechuanaland (now Botswana) to Rhodes's own control. Knowing that this would mean the loss of their land and the forced removal of many of their peoples, three Tswana chieftains (Khama, Sebele, and Bathoen) made up their minds to plead their case in England directly before Queen Victoria. Although Rhodes attempted to use official channels to prevent their leaving, they were able eventually to get to London. Unable to see the queen, they sought the support of the British people. The London Missionary Society organized a publicity campaign (Khama was a strong Christian ruler). Everywhere they went the chiefs emphasized their wish to remain under the protection of the Good Queen and that they wanted to keep liquor and slave-trading out of their country. This appeal was taken up by the temperance and anti-slavery groups. Soon the British prime minister was deluged with letters protesting the proposed handover of the protectorate to Rhodes. Chamberlain had no choice but to back down. Rhodes did receive a corridor of land for his railroad, but the protectorate was spared. It was quite clear that the Botswana chiefs had gotten what they wanted.

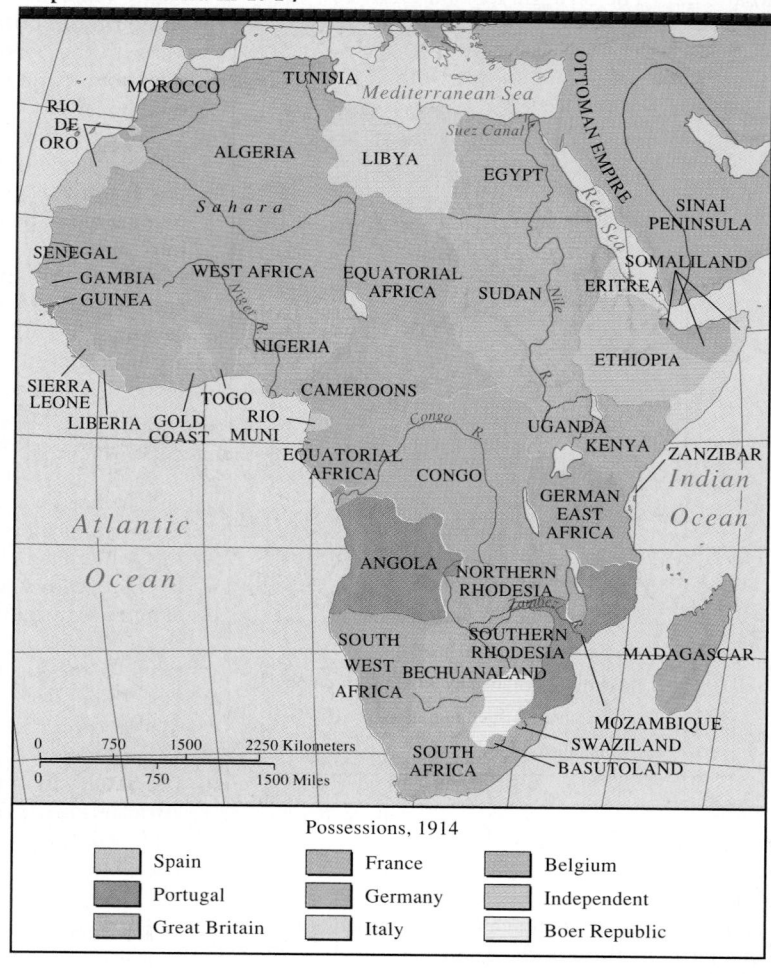

Map 23.3   Africa in 1914

Possessions, 1914

- Spain
- Portugal
- Great Britain
- France
- Germany
- Italy
- Belgium
- Independent
- Boer Republic

Colonialism in Africa

Except in isolated areas like the gold mines in the Transvaal and copper deposits in the Congo, European economic interests in Africa were limited. As a result, European interest in Africa declined once the continent had been conquered. Most European governments ruled their new territories with the least effort and expense possible. In many cases, this led to a form of indirect rule. The British especially followed this approach. Indirect rule meant relying on existing political elites and institutions. At first, in some areas the British simply asked a local ruler to accept British authority and to fly the British flag over official buildings.

The concept of indirect rule was introduced in the Islamic state of Sokoto, in northern Nigeria, in 1900.

STUDYING MAPS

Use the following questions to guide your students as they study Map 23.3.

1. Have students estimate the amount of land colonialized by each European country.

2. Which country had the largest colonial possessions? *(France)*

3. What might account for that country's success in colonization? *(Answers will vary.)*

THE ROLE OF SCIENCE AND TECHNOLOGY
The Machine Gun

▲ *Hiram Maxim invented this lightweight field gun that had a bulletproof shield. What features made this field gun preferable to field cannons?*

The first effective quick-firing gun was invented in 1862 by an American, Richard Gatling. The Gatling gun was made with ten barrels and could fire six hundred shots a minute. This, and models like it, had to be operated by a hand crank.

In 1885, another American, Hiram Maxim, built a gun that used its own recoil energy to load and fire itself and to eject its own empty shells. This eliminated the need for a hand crank and created the first fully automatic machine gun. A soldier had only to hold the trigger, and the gun would keep firing until its ammunition was gone. The gun was supplied with ammunition by a mechanically fed canvas belt easily stored in a box. The belts could be changed rapidly. The gun weighed only 40 pounds and could fire 650 rounds a minute.

Of course, governments were quick to see the advantages of the Maxim machine gun. The British army was using it by 1891. From its beginning, the machine gun played an important role in the ability of Western armies to subdue peoples who were not yet armed with this weapon. At the Battle of Omdurman in 1898, when Sudanese tribespeople tried to stop a British expedition armed with the recently developed machine gun, the Sudanese were massacred. One observer noted: "It was not a battle but an execution. . . . The bodies were not in heaps—bodies hardly ever are; but they spread evenly over acres and acres. Some lay very composedly with their slippers placed under their heads for a last pillow; some knelt, cut short in the middle of a last prayer. Others were torn to pieces." The battle casualties at Omdurman tell the story: twenty-eight British deaths to eleven thousand Sudanese. The machine gun began a new era in deadly warfare.

1. What was revolutionary about the gun invented by Richard Gatling?

2. How did the machine gun affect the Western world's ability to dominate the non-Western world?

ACTIVITY

Have students state how British rule was different from the laws of other European governments. *(The British used indirect method of governing and a dual legal system, preserving African laws for the Africans and British laws for the British.)*

CRITICAL THINKING

Ask students how the rise of nationalism in Africa followed a course similar to that in East Asia. *(In both regions an elite class of educated nationals arose that admired Western technology and wealth/culture but who were determined to assert their own national cultures and destinies. At the same time, a strong discontent and desire to throw off colonial rule was building in the general populace.)*

CRITICAL THINKING

This chapter discusses the aspect of technology in weaponry and how it gave the Western countries an overwhelming military advantage. Ask students how advances in medicine also facilitated European attempts at colonialism. *(The invention of quinine effectively reduced the dangers of malaria.)* Then ask students to explain how advances in travel and communications increased the pace of colonialism. *(The Transatlantic Cable sped international communications; river steamboats and railroads made travel easier.)* For homework, have students copy the following sentence and write a one or two paragraph mini-essay on it: "Technology fostered the growth of worldwide networks through which goods, people, and ideas could be exchanged."

CONNECTIONS TO OUR WORLD

Boundaries and Tribal Rivalries in Africa

Between 1870 and 1910, European states carved up the map of Africa. In drawing the boundaries that separated one colony from another (boundaries that often became the boundaries of the modern countries of Africa), Europeans paid no attention to the political divisions of the tribes of Africa. Europeans often divided a tribe between two colonies, or made two tribes that were hostile to each other, members of the same colony. Most colonies in Africa became collections of different tribes with little or no sense of national identity. This created a problem for many African states after they achieved independence. For example, Ibo tribespeople in the southeastern part of Nigeria became part of the new state of Nigeria. In 1967, they proclaimed a new state of Biafra, plunging Nigeria into civil war. In 1970, after the death of almost one million Ibos, Biafra capitulated. It remains part of Nigeria.

European powers also practiced policies of divide and conquer, as well as divide and rule. To conquer lands in Africa, European states often took advantage of tribal rivalries and allied with one tribe against another. To rule their African colonies, European states often set one tribe against another as a way of maintaining power. In Central Africa, the Belgians allowed the Tutsi to continue their domination of the Hutus as a way of controlling the area. In modern Rwanda, one of the states formed out of Belgian lands, the intense rivalry between Tutsis and Hutus has continued to this day. In 1994, a Hutu massacre of Tutsis in Rwanda led to the death of more than 500,000 Tutsis. Similar ethnic conflicts have occurred in Zimbabwe and Kenya.

At the central level, there was a British government under British officials. Local authority, however, was left in the hands of native chiefs. They were expected to maintain law and order and to collect taxes from the native population. Local customs were left as they had been. There was a dual legal system, with African laws for Africans and British laws for the British.

This system of indirect rule in Sokoto had one good feature: it did not disrupt local customs and institutions. However, it did have some unfortunate consequences. The system was basically a fraud, because British administrators made all major decisions. The native authorities served chiefly to enforce those decisions. Moreover, indirect rule kept the old African elite in power. Such a policy provided few opportunities for ambitious and talented young Africans from outside the old elite. Thus, British indirect rule sowed the seeds for class and tribal tensions, which erupted after independence came in the twentieth century.

The situation was somewhat different in East Africa, especially in Kenya. Kenya had a relatively large European population that had been attracted by the temperate climate in the central highlands. The local government had encouraged white settlers to come to the area as a way of promoting economic development. To attract Europeans, fertile farmlands in the central highlands were reserved for them. Less desirable lands were set aside for Africans. Soon, white settlers sought self-government. Unwilling to run the risk of provoking racial tensions with the African majority, the British agreed only to set up separate government offices for the European and African populations.

Most other European nations governed their African possessions through a form of direct rule. This was true in the French colonies. At the top was a French official, usually known as a governor-general. He was appointed from Paris and governed with the aid of a bureaucracy in the capital city of the colony. French commissioners were assigned to deal with local administrators. These administrators had to be able to speak French and could be sent to a new position to meet the needs of the central government.

Moreover, the French ideal was to assimilate the African subjects into French culture rather than preserve the native traditions. Africans were eligible to run for office and even serve in the French National Assembly in Paris. A few were appointed to high positions in the colonial administration.

COOPERATIVE LEARNING ACTIVITY

Divide the class into groups and assign each group to research a distinct area or country in Africa. Each group should research the dominant languages spoken today in their assigned region. How do areas where European languages are spoken correspond to European conquest of Africa? What countries show an overlap of African languages across their borders? What role did imperialism play in separating people of the same language into different countries? When groups have finished their research, they should present the results (with illustrations and a map) to the entire class.

The Rise of Nationalism in Africa

As in Southeast Asia, in Africa a new class of leaders had emerged by the beginning of the twentieth century. Educated in colonial schools or even in the West, they were the first generation of Africans to know a great deal about the West. Some, like Kwame Nkrumah (KWAN-mee en KROO-muh) in the Gold Coast, even wrote in the language of their colonial masters.

On the one hand, the members of this "new class" admired Western culture and sometimes disliked the ways of their own countries. They were eager to introduce Western ideas and institutions into their own societies. On the other hand, many came to resent the foreigners and their arrogant contempt for colonial peoples. These intellectuals often resented the gap between theory and practice in colonial policy. Westerners had exalted democracy, equality, and political freedom but did not apply these values in the colonies. There were few democratic institutions. Colonial peoples could have only low-paying jobs in the colonial bureaucracy. Also feeding the resentment was the fact that the economic prosperity of the West was never brought to the colonies. To many Africans, colonialism meant the loss of their farmlands or terrible jobs on plantations or in sweatshops and factories run by foreigners.

Normally, middle-class Africans did not suffer as much as poor peasants or workers on plantations. However, members of the middle class also had complaints. They usually qualified only for menial jobs in the government or business. Even when employed, their salaries were lower than those of Europeans in similar jobs. The superiority of the Europeans over the natives was expressed in a variety of other ways. Segregated clubs, schools, and churches were set up as more European officials brought their wives and began to raise families. Europeans also had a habit of addressing natives by their first names or calling an adult male "boy."

Such conditions led many members of the new urban educated class to feel great confusion toward their colonial masters and the civilization the colonists represented. The educated Africans were willing to admit the superiority of many aspects of Western cul

ture. However, these new intellectuals fiercely hated colonial rule and were determined to assert their own nationality and cultural destiny. Out of this mixture of hopes and resentments emerged the first stirrings of modern nationalism in Africa. During the first quarter of the twentieth century, in colonial societies across Africa, educated native peoples began to organize political parties and movements seeking the end of foreign rule.

 SECTION REVIEW

1. **Locate:**
   (a) Algeria,   (b) Gold Coast,
   (c) South Africa,   (d) Sierra Leone,
   (e) Liberia,   (f) Nigeria,
   (g) Sudan,   (h) Sinai peninsula,
   (i) Sahara,
   (j) Tunisia,   (k) Morocco,
   (l) Libya,   (m) Congo River,
   (n) Zanzibar

2. **Identify:**
   (a) Muhammad Ali,   (b) Suez Canal,
   (c) Muhammad Ahmad,   (d) David Livingstone,
   (e) Henry Stanley,   (f) King Leopold II,
   (g) Zulus,   (h) Boers

3. **Recall:**
   (a) Why didn't the decline of the slave trade reduce the number of Europeans in West Africa?
   (b) What did Bismarck mean when he said, "All this colonial business is a sham, but we need it for the elections"?
   (c) What was the new class of Africans that developed in many African nations?
   (d) Why did many educated Africans come to hate colonial rule?

4. **Think Critically:** Why was the fact that no African delegates were invited to the Berlin Conference, which divided territories in Africa among European powers, important to the future of Africa?

COOPERATIVE LEARNING ACTIVITY

Students may not appreciate the vastness and diversity of Africa and the impact of this diversity on African history. Divide the class into groups and assign each group the task of investigating one of the five geographical regions discussed in this section. Each group should produce a display which shows the size of the region (perhaps in comparison to U.S. states or European countries), major geographical features, important resources, and native peoples. Encourage students to use pictures, illustrations, and eye witness reports to illustrate their displays. The individual displays can then be arranged as an "African Montage" to show differences within and between regions.

ASSESS

Answers to SECTION REVIEW

2 (a) an Egyptian officer who seized power in 1805 and brought about a series of reforms
   (b) a canal that connects the Red and Mediterranean Seas
   (c) a Muslim cleric who brought much of the Sudan under his control
   (d) a British explorer who explored central regions of Africa
   (e) an American reporter who found Livingstone
   (f) a king of Belgium who supported colonization of Central Africa
   (g) a tribal group that created their own empire under a ruler named Shaka in South Africa
   (h) descendants of Dutch settlers

3. (a) Europeans increased other types of trade.
   (b) Bismarck thought that there was little of value that could be gained, but it gave voters pride in their nation.
   (c) admired Western culture and sometimes disliked the ways of their own countries
   (d) they were not allowed to participate in the leadership of their nations.

4. many current disputes in Africa have resulted from boundaries that were arbitrarily drawn by Europeans.

CLOSE

Have students discuss the impact of colonization on Africa. What benefits and harm did colonization bring to Africa?

FOCUS

OBJECTIVES

After completing this section, students should be able to

1. list reasons for the expansion of British control over India
2. explain the effect of British rule on the economy, politics, and culture of India
3. discuss the causes of the rise of Indian nationalism and the role of Mohandas Gandhi
4. explain the significance of the renewal of Indian culture in the establishment of a modern Indian identity

FOCUS ACTIVITY

To introduce this section, you may wish to focus on Mohandas Gandhi. David Attenborough's film *Gandhi* is excellent for showing the philosophy of non-violence. You may want to choose relevant sections to show and encourage your students to watch the rest of this film out of class.

TEACH

LEARNING FROM VISUALS

Ask students why they think this form of execution might have been used. *(To be a deterrent to other Sepoys; to make an example of the mutineers)*

Answer to the caption question: Answers will vary.

BRITISH RULE IN INDIA

In the course of the eighteenth century, British power in India had increased while that of the Mughal rulers had declined (see Chapter 17). The British East India Company, a trading company, was given the power by the British government to become actively involved in India's political and military affairs. The British were fortunate to have Sir Robert Clive as the chief representative of the East India Company in India. In 1757, a small British force put together by Clive defeated a much larger Mughal army. As a result, the British East India Company received from the Mughal emperor the right to collect taxes from lands around Calcutta. Less than ten years later, the British captured the Mughal emperor himself. During the next few decades, the British East India Company worked to consolidate its control over India, expanding from its base areas along the coast into the interior.

To rule India, the British East India Company had its own soldiers and forts. It had also hired Indian soldiers, known as **sepoys,** to protect the company's interests in the region. However, a growing Indian distrust of the British led to a revolt in 1857. The major immediate cause of the revolt was the spread of a rumor that

▼ *British punishment of the sepoys was quick and harsh. Why do you think so many troops have been called to witness this execution?*

RECOMMENDED READING

For an overview of the British takeover and administration of India, see S. Wolpert, *A New History of India* (New York, 1989). C. A. Bayly, *Indian Society and the Making of the British Empire* (Cambridge, 1988) is a scholarly analysis of the impact of British conquest on the Indian economy. For a comparative approach, see R. Murphey, *The Outsiders: The Western Experience in China and India* (Ann Arbor, Mich., 1977). For a study of Mahatma Gandhi, see J. M. Brown, *Gandhi: Prisoner of Hope* (New Haven, Conn., 1989); and the psychohistorical study by E. Erikson, *Gandhi's Truth: On the Origins of Militant Nonviolence* (New York, 1969). Also see *All Men Are Brothers: The Life and Thoughts of Mahatma Gandhi as Told in His Own Words* (New York, 1960). For a recent study of Nehru, see S. Gopal, *Jawaharlal Nehru: A Biography,* vol. 1, *1889–1947* (Cambridge, 1976).

Map 23.4   India under British Rule, 1805–1937

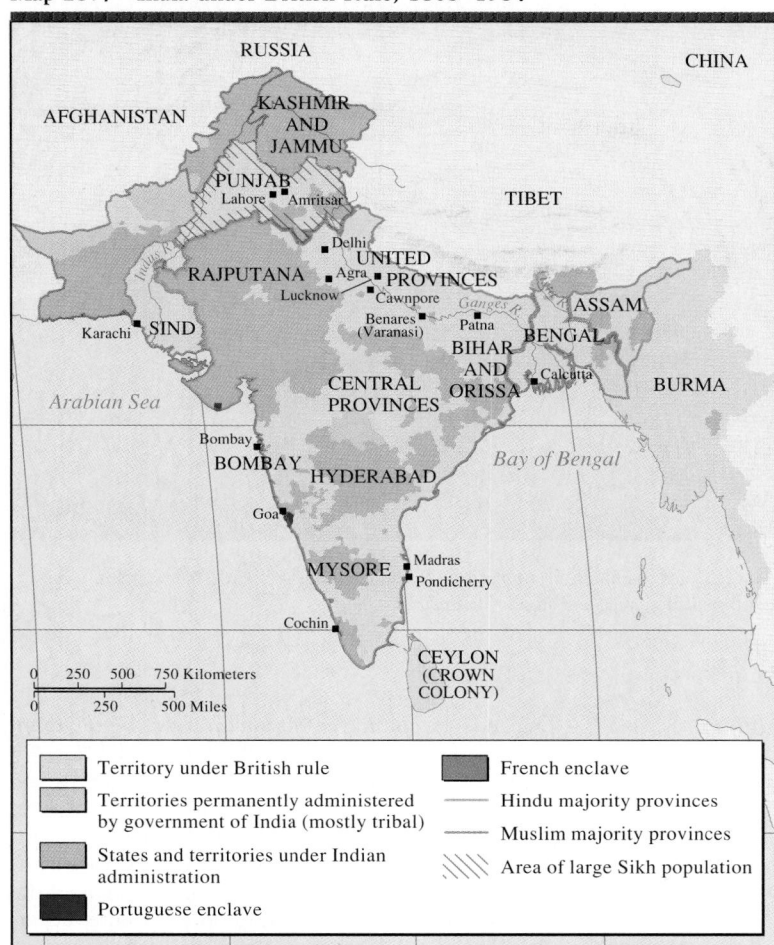

Territory under British rule

Territories permanently administered by government of India (mostly tribal)

States and territories under Indian administration

Portuguese enclave

French enclave

Hindu majority provinces

Muslim majority provinces

Area of large Sikh population

The revolt was known to the British as the Great Rebellion or the Sepoy Mutiny. (Indians call it the First War of Independence.) It quickly spread. Although Indian troops fought bravely and outnumbered the British by 240,000 to 40,000, they were poorly organized. Then, too, rivalries between Hindus and Muslims kept Indians from working together. Within a year, Indian troops loyal to the British and fresh British troops had crushed the revolt. Atrocities were terrible on both sides. At Cawnpore, Indian ruffians armed only with swords and knives massacred two hundred defenseless women and children in a building known as the House of the Ladies. When the British recaptured Cawnpore, they made their Indian captives lick the dried blood off the floor of the House of the Ladies before executing them.

As a result of the uprising, the British Parliament transferred the powers of the East India Company directly to the British government. In 1876, the title of Empress of India was bestowed upon Queen Victoria. The people of India were now her colonial subjects, and India became her "Jewel in the Crown." The British government ruled India directly. Parliament had overall supervision. Parliament's wishes were carried out by a British official known as a **viceroy,** who was assisted by a small British civil service. This civil service staff of about 3,500 officials ruled almost 300 million people, the largest colonial population in the world.

the British were issuing new bullets to their Indian troops that were greased with cow and pig fat. The cow was sacred to Hindus; the pig was taboo to Muslims. A group of sepoys at an army post near Delhi refused to load their rifles with the new bullets. When the British arrested them, the sepoys went on a rampage and killed fifty European men, women, and children.

STUDYING MAPS

The following questions will help you guide the students through their study of Map 23.4.

1. What areas identified on the map were Muslim strongholds? What are these areas called today? *(Pakistan and Bangladesh, or East Pakistan)*

2. Name the regions where Hindus were in the majority. *(Hindus were in the majority in all but the northwestern areas.)*

3. Ask students what the term *enclave* means. *(An enclave is a country or territory that is surrounded by another country. It is derived from the French verb meaning "to lock in.")*

LEARNING FROM VISUALS

Students today will probably think it "weird" or "crazy" that this type of structure was built to impress people with the power of the government. Yet, many buildings operated by one national government in another country are designed to reflect the importance or the culture of the guest country. Ask students what they think might be the more likely approach or focus of a government trying to gain acceptance from the people of another country today. (*economic aid, military assistance, industrialization*)

Answer to the caption question: The railroads served the British, both for transporting people and goods. Few Indians could afford to use the trains.

ACTIVITY

Have students watch the movie, *A Passage to India*. Discuss with students what the movie reveals about the relations between the British and the Indians.

You might wish to have students watch the movie *Gandhi* and use it as the basis for a class discussion.

▲ *The Victoria railway station in Bombay was designed to impress all who saw it. It also glorified the 25,000 miles of British railroads in India. Who do you think the railroads benefited more, the British or the Indians?*

Colonial Rule in India

Not all the effects of British rule in India were bad. British rule brought order and stability to a society that had been badly divided by civil war. British control also led to a fairly honest and efficient government that in many ways operated to the benefit of the average Indian.

One of the benefits of the period was the new attention given to education. Through the efforts of the British administrator and historian Lord Macauley (muh-KAW-lee), a new school system was set up. Its goal was to train upper-class Indian children to serve as trained subordinates in the government and army. Macauley's attitude, however, was strongly pro-British. He argued that "all the historical information which has been collected from all the books written in the Sanskrit language is less valuable than what may be found in short textbooks used at preparatory schools in England." According to Macauley, it was better, then, to teach Indian elites about Western civilization "to form a class who may be interpreters between us and the millions whom we govern; a class of persons, Indian in blood and color, but English in taste, in opinions, in morals, and in intellect."[6] Classes were conducted in the rulers' English language. Moreover, the new system of education served only the elite, upper-class Indians. Ninety percent of the population remained illiterate.

Another benefit of British rule was that it brought an end to some of the more brutal aspects of Indian tradition. The practice of suttee (burning of widows) was outlawed, and widows were legally permitted to remarry. The British also tried to stamp out the religious fanatics (called *thugs*) who strangled their victims according to a ritual dedicated to their goddess Kali (KAW-lee). Railroads, the telegraph, and a postal service were introduced to India shortly after they

MORE ABOUT . . . *Lord Macauley*

Although very influential in India, Lord Macauley is better known as an historian. His five volume *History of England* was a very influential and much imitated work. The attitudes he displayed in India are also reflected in his histories, that English institutions were the best model for the colonies and that English standards of culture and society would be forever the norm for the world.

Macauley stayed in India for only four years, but at an influential time when the British crown was taking over government from the East India Company. He championed liberty of the press and equality before the law for Indians and Europeans. He also established the national education system based on Western principles to train an elite corps of Indians to serve the British crown. Macauley, in his arrogance, could not foresee that the Indians would reject British rule in favor of nationalism.

appeared in Great Britain itself. The first rail network, from Calcutta to Delhi, was begun in 1839 and opened in 1853. By 1900, 25,000 miles of railroads crisscrossed India. Health and sanitation conditions also were improved.

The Indian people, however, paid a high price for the peace and stability brought by British rule. Perhaps the greatest cost was economic. British entrepreneurs and a small number of native Indians attached to the imperial system reaped financial benefits from British rule. However, imperialism brought hardship to millions of others in both the cities and the countryside. British manufactured goods destroyed native industries. Indian wealth was used to pay British officials and a large army. The introduction of British textiles put thousands of women out of work and severely damaged the Indian textile industry.

In rural areas, the British used the zamindar system (a zamindar was a local revenue collector—see Chapter 17). The British believed that this system would make it easier to collect taxes from the peasants. They also hoped that the zamindar system would create a new landed gentry that could become the foundation of imperial Indian rule, just as it had become the foundation of rule in Great Britain itself. However, the local gentry in India took advantage of their new authority. They increased taxes and forced the less fortunate peasants to become tenants or lose their land entirely. Peasant unrest grew. The British also encouraged many farmers to switch from growing food to growing cotton. As a consequence, food supplies could not keep up with the growing population. Between 1800 and 1900, thirty million Indians died of starvation.

The British also worked hard to keep modern industry out of India. Some limited industrialization took place, such as the manufacturing of textiles and jute (used in making rope). The first textile mill opened in 1856. Seventy years later, there were 80 mills in the city of Bombay alone. Nevertheless, by favoring British imports, the British government limited the development of new commercial and manufacturing operations in India itself.

Foreign rule also had a psychological effect on the Indian people. Many British colonial officials sincerely tried to improve the lot of the people in India. However, British arrogance and contempt for native tradition cut deeply into the pride of many Indians. Those of high caste, who were used to a position of superior status in India, were especially disturbed. Educated Indians trained in the Anglo-Indian school system for a career in the civil service wondered where their true cultural loyalties lay. Even for the newly educated upper classes, who benefited the most from their Western-style educations, British rule was degrading. The best jobs and the best housing were reserved for Britons (see "Focus on Everyday Life: The British Official's Home in India"). Despite their education, the Indians were never considered equals of the British.

British racial attitudes were made quite clear by Lord Kitchener, one of Britain's foremost military commanders of India. He said, "It is this consciousness of the inherent superiority of the European which has won for us India. However well educated and clever a native may be, and however brave he may prove himself, I believe that no rank we can bestow on him would cause him to be considered an equal of the British officer."[7] The British also showed disrespect for India's cultural heritage. The Taj Mahal, for example, became a favorite site for English weddings and parties. Many partygoers even brought hammers to chip off souvenirs. British racial attitudes made it difficult for British rulers, no matter how well intentioned, ever to be ultimately accepted. These attitudes also led to the rise of an Indian nationalist movement.

The Rise of an Indian Nationalist Movement

The first Indian nationalists were upper class and educated. Many of them were from urban areas, such as Bombay, Madras, and Calcutta. Some were trained in British law and were members of the civil service. At first, many preferred reform to revolution. They accepted the idea that India needed modernization before it could handle the problems of independence. Gopal Gokhale, an exponent of this view, was a moderate nationalist who hoped that he could convince the British to bring about needed reforms in Indian society. Gokhale and other like-minded reformers did have some

COMPARING
TIME PERIODS

The positive and negative effects of British rule in India may have parallels in economics today. The British instituted improvements in the health, education, infrastructure, and customs of India, but they did so primarily to serve their own interests. Ask students to discuss how these changes benefited England. (The English were attempting to create stable conditions to produce materials for British industry and markets for British goods. Most of the changes were necessary to provide workers, land, and social conditions for British industry, administration, and colonial lifestyle.) Arguments for economic development in the Third World and trade agreements such as NAFTA claim that developing nations will benefit from the activities of Western industry in their economies. Ask students who they believe benefits most from these arrangements, the industrialized countries that establish industry in the Third World, or the Third World countries that accept modern industries.

CLASS DISCUSSION

After the Sepoy rebellion, the British spent immense sums of money on economic development in India. Ask students what the British motives might have been for this investment. (to support the needs of the British Empire while repressing any rebellion or conflict with the Indians) What seems to have been of little concern to the British? (the beliefs and culture of the Indians or their economic security)

MORE ABOUT . . . *English Rule of India*

Over time the British rulers of India became increasingly isolated from India and Indians. The British viceroy of India spent half of the year at his mountain retreat and the other half in Calcutta where most of his dealings were with English gentlemen, merchants and civil service workers. The establishment of an overland telegraph in 1865,

the opening of the Suez Canal in 1869, and a submarine cable in 1870 meant that British officials would often have closer contact with London than with the people of India. As a result they had little understanding of the effects their policies had on the people of the land which they ruled.

FOCUS ON EVERYDAY LIFE

LEARNING FROM VISUALS

In the photograph, very small children are seen in the care of their Indian nurses. Ask students to suppose why they would rarely see European family pictures that included children over the ages of 8 or 10. (*European children, especially English, were sent to boarding school in Europe to prepare them for a successful career. It was a time to start the public school networking that became a mark of the English gentleman.*)

CRITICAL THINKING

Although it may appear to have been a glamorous life on the surface, in reality life for British women in India was very lonely. Husbands were often away on tours of duty and (as was true in most countries at this time) "well-bred" women were very restricted in what was considered proper activities for them. Ask students to consider what life would be like with few amusements, few friends, restricted freedom of movement, and few opportunities for self-development.

Answers to Critical Thinking Questions

1. The wives ran the households. They gave orders to the servants, cooks, etc. They were also responsible for evening entertainment.
2. Answers will vary.

FOCUS ON EVERYDAY LIFE
The British Official's Home in India

During the time that India was a British colony, many British government officials spent a considerable amount of time there in fulfilling their administrative duties. Their families usually came with them during their tours of duty. British officials in India built comfortable bungalows, as they were called (the name comes from the Indian word *bangla*, meaning "Bengali"). Bungalows were elegant and spacious country houses. Many had colonnades (roofs supported by columns) that were open to breezes while protecting the inhabitants from the sun. Surrounding the bungalows were the cottages where dozens of Indian servants lived with their families.

The official's wife was the memsahib, or madam-sahib, queen of the bungalow. Her husband was the sahib—"the master." Wives of British officials generally brought their Victorian lifestyles and many of the furnishings that went with them to their new homes in India. The memsahib was expected to oversee the running of the household on a daily basis. At the beginning of each day, she assigned duties to all the servants. For example, she fixed the menu for the day with the cook. In the evening, the colonial official's wife was expected to entertain. Supper parties with other British families were the usual form of entertainment.

Many British officials had a high standard of living and were expected to have a large number of servants. One woman wrote in 1882, "It is one of the social duties of Indian life that you must keep three servants to do the work of one." A

▲ *This view of an English family enjoying an afternoon together accurately reflects the number of servants assigned to British families during colonial times. However, because children were schooled in England and husbands were often away on official business, family times such as these were infrequent.*

well-to-do family had at least 25 servants; even bachelors had at least a dozen. Indians served as cooks, maids, butlers, gardeners, tailors, and nursemaids for the children. All household servants wore uniforms—usually white with bands on their turbans—and went barefoot in the house.

1. What were the responsibilities of the wife of a British officer in India?

2. What do you learn about British-Indian social relations from this feature?

MORE ABOUT . . . *the British Colonial Family*

The Secret Garden by Frances Hodgson Burnett is a wonderful classic that really has no age limit and would give students a valuable look into the culture of the British colonial family. The introduction describes how disease takes the lives of a little girl's parents and most of the household and guests, as well. The descriptions of the domestic arrangements and relationships are well worth reading with students for their Victorian approach. Other books (for good readers) that deal with British domestic life in India are *A Passage to India* and *Far Pavilions*.

▲ *In spite of British attitudes toward India, it was not uncommon for the English to adopt some local customs. In this painting, an Englishman lives like an Indian prince with his harem, servants, and hookah, an Indian water pipe.*

effect. In the 1880s, the government launched a series of reforms introducing a measure of self-government for the first time. All too often, however, such efforts were sabotaged by local British officials.

The slow pace of reform convinced many Indian nationalists that relying on British goodwill was futile. In 1885, a small group of Indians met in Bombay to form the Indian National Congress (INC). They hoped to speak for all India, but most were high-caste English-trained Hindus. Members of the INC did not demand immediate independence. They accepted the need for reforms to end traditional abuses, such as child marriage. At the same time, they called for an Indian share in the governing process, as well as more spend

ing on economic development and less on military campaigns along the frontier.

The British responded with a few concessions. However, change was slow. As members of the INC became frustrated, radical leaders, such as Balwantrao Tilak, openly criticized the British. Tilak's activities split the INC between moderates and radicals. He and his followers formed the New Party, which called for the use of terrorism and violence to achieve national independence. Eventually, the British jailed Tilak.

The INC also split over religious differences. The goal of the INC was to seek independence for all Indians, regardless of class or religious background. However, many of its leaders were Hindu and reflected

On Line with
WORLD HISTORY   *Internet Activity*

You may want to have your students visit the following URL, where they will find information and additional web site resources to enhance their study of this chapter.

White Man's Burden and Anti-Imperialism

http://rochester.ican.net/~fjzwick/kipling/

Rudyard Kipling's poem caused a great deal of controversy. This page presents both sides of imperialism.

Due to the ever-changing nature of the World Wide Web, see the West History web site, **http://history.swpco.com** for regular updates of the URLs in this text.

Remind students that India faced unique problems when the drive for independence and nationalism became strong. India was very much a polyglot of different peoples—hundreds of dialects were spoken with Hindi and English being the official languages. The other major languages are Telugu, Bengali, Tamil, and Urdu. Religion was a divisive factor in the country as was the ingrained social caste system. As an activity, canvass the class to determine how many different language groups the students come from. (For instance, English, German, Japanese, Vietnamese, Spanish, etc.) Then tell students that 14 languages are recognized in the Indian Constitution. Then ask students if they believe it is necessary for all citizens to speak a common language. This discussion will undoubtedly lead to the issue of bilingual education in the United States.

Hindu concerns. By the first decade of the twentieth century, Muslims began to call for the creation of a separate Muslim League to represent the interests of the millions of Muslims in Indian society.

In 1913, the return of a young Hindu lawyer from South Africa to become active in the INC brought new life to India's struggle for independence. Mohandas Gandhi (GAWN-dee) was born in 1869 in Gujarat (goo-ja-RAWT), in western India, the son of a government minister. In the late nineteenth century, he studied in London and became a lawyer. In 1893, he went to South Africa to work in a law firm serving Indian workers there. He soon became aware of the racial prejudice and exploitation experienced by Indians living in South Africa. He tried to organize them to protect their living conditions.

On his return home to India, Gandhi became active in the independence movement. Using his experience in South Africa, he set up a movement based on nonviolent resistance. Its aim was to force the British to improve the lot of the poor and grant independence to India. Gandhi had two goals: to convert the British to his own views and to strengthen the unity of all Indians. When the British tried to suppress Indian calls for independence, Gandhi called on his followers to refuse to obey British regulations. He began to manufacture his own clothes and dressed in a simple dhoti (DOTE-ee) (loincloth) made of coarse homespun cotton. He adopted the spinning wheel as a symbol of India's resistance to imports of British textiles. Ultimately, as we shall see in Chapter 26, Gandhi's movement would lead to Indian indepen-

▲ *Mohandas Gandhi practiced law in South Africa in the late 1800s. Then, at the age of forty-seven he made the decision to return to India, his native country, to champion the cause of the poor. Ultimately his leadership and dedication to the betterment of the Indian people were major factors in achieving independence from Great Britain.*

Culture and Nationalism in Colonial India

The love-hate tension that arose from British domination led to a cultural, as well as a political, awakening of India. The cultural revival began in the early nineteenth century with the creation of a British college in Calcutta. A local publishing house was opened. It issued textbooks on a variety of subjects, including the sciences, Sanskrit, and Western literature. The publisher also printed grammars and dictionaries in the various Indian languages. This revival soon spread to other regions of India. It led to a search for modern literary expression, as well as for a new national identity. Soon Indian novelists and poets were writing historical romances and epics. Some wrote in English, but most were uncomfortable with a borrowed colonial language. They preferred to use their own regional tongues.

The most illustrious Indian author was Rabindranath Tagore (ru-BIN-dru-NAWT tu GORE). A great poet, novelist, short-story writer, and dramatist, Tagore was also a social reformer, spiritual leader, educator, philosopher, singer, painter, and international spokesperson for the moral concerns of his age. He liked to invite the great thinkers of the time to his country estate where he set up a school that became an international university.

Tagore's life mission was to promote pride in a national Indian consciousness in the face of British domination. He wrote a widely read novel in which he portrayed the love-hate relationship of India toward its colonial mentor. The novel depicted a country that admired and imitated the British model while also ago-

So What ??

*If your students question the importance of the information on **the Indian independence movement** tell them . . .*

The teachings of Mohandas Gandhi directly affected Martin Luther King Jr. and the American Civil Rights movement. King modeled his strategy of nonviolence in the pursuit of African-American civil rights on the methods Ghandi used successfully in India.

OUR LITERARY HERITAGE

The Poetry of Tagore

Rabindranath Tagore considered himself a poet above all. He wrote in Bengali (the language of the Indian state of Bengal) until the age of fifty and then translated some of his verse into English in 1912. Tagore won an international audience and was awarded the Nobel Prize for literature in 1913. The following lines were taken from Gitanjali: Song Offerings, which he wrote in Bengali but then translated into English.

**Rabindranath Tagore,
Gitanjali: Song Offerings**

*Where the mind is without fear
  and the head is held high;
Where knowledge is free;
Where the world has not been
  broken up into fragments
  by narrow domestic walls;*

▲ *This photo of Rabindranath Tagore shows an inner intensity that is reflected in his poetry.*

*Where words come out from
  the depth of truth;
Where tireless striving stretches
  its arms toward perfection;
Where the clear stream of
  reason has not lost its ways
  into the dreary desert sand
  of dead habit;
Where the mind is led forward
  by thee into ever-widening
  thought and action—
Into that heaven of freedom,
  my Father, let my country
  awake.*

1. About what country did Tagore write? How do you know?

2. Put into your own words the line, "Where the clear stream of reason has not lost its ways into the dreary desert sand of dead habit."

---

nizing over how it could establish a modern identity separate from that of Great Britain.

Tagore, however, was more than an Indian nationalist. His life's work was one long prayer for human dignity, world peace, and the mutual understanding and union of East and West. As he once said, "It is my conviction that my countrymen will truly gain their India by fighting against the education that teaches them that a country is greater than the ideals of humanity." In his poetry as well, Tagore spoke of lofty ideals (see "Our Literary Heritage: The Poetry of Tagore").

 SECTION REVIEW

1. **Locate:**
   (a) Delhi,   (b) Bombay,   (c) Madras,
   (d) Calcutta

2. **Define:**
   (a) sepoys,   (b) viceroy

3. **Identify:**
   (a) British East India Tea Company,

MORE ABOUT . . . *Rabindranath Tagore*

Rabindranath Tagore was a Bengali poet and mystic who won the Nobel Prize for Literature in 1913 and who was influential in introducing Indian culture to the West (and vice versa). In the course of managing his father's estates, he developed close working relationships with village folk. His sympathy for their poverty and backwardness formed the basis for much of this later writing. Ask students if they can name writers in the United States at that time (early 1900s) who were also writing about poverty and social injustice. *(Stephen Crane, Theodore Dreiser, Jack London, Sinclair Lewis, John Steinbeck, Lincoln Steffens, Ida Tarbell, William DuBois, Booker T. Washington, etc.)* Point out to students that although the people named above were trying to actively change the social structure, Tagore focused more on describing the beauty and simplicity of the Indian peasant class.

CLOSE

The nonviolent confrontational methods of Gandhi had great influence in India and elsewhere. Lead a class discussion on the reasons nonviolent methods can be effective. Ask students to name examples of nonviolent methods they may be aware of. *(Situations may include examples from the American civil rights movement, environmental protests, picketing, strikes and work slow downs, and student protests.)*

FOCUS

OBJECTIVES

After completing this section, students should be able to

1. explain how developments within Latin America and elsewhere in the world led to revolutions
2. discuss how the domination of the landed elite caused political instability in Latin American nations
3. list the materials and goods that were imported and exported by the Latin American nations and explain how this resulted in the dependency of Latin America on the West
4. discuss the causes of the Mexican revolution

FOCUS ACTIVITY

Have students make a list of primary goods that are exported from the Latin American countries.

756

(*b*) Sepoy Mutiny, (*c*) Gopal Gokhale,
(*d*) Balwantrao Tilak, (*e*) Mohandas Gandhi,
(*f*) Rabindranath Tagore

4. **Recall:**
(*a*) What positive effects may have resulted for the native population from the British rule of India?
(*b*) What economic costs did the Indian people pay for the British occupation?
(*c*) What objectives did the Indian National Congress (INC) have when it started to meet in Bombay in 1885?

5. **Think Critically:** Why do you think Gandhi chose to dress in a simple dhoti and adopt the spinning wheel as a symbol of resistance to British rule?

NATION BUILDING AND IMPERIALISM IN LATIN AMERICA

The force of nationalism also affected the Americas. In both North America and Latin America, nation building became a prominent process. The Spanish and Portuguese colonial empires in Latin America had been part of the old monarchical structure of Europe for centuries. When that structure was challenged by the Napoleonic Wars, Latin America, too, experienced change.

Nationalistic Revolts in Latin America

By the end of the eighteenth century, the new political ideals stemming from the successful revolution in North America against the British (see Chapter 20) were beginning to influence the **creole elites** (locally born descendants of the Europeans who became permanent inhabitants of Latin America). The principles of the equality of all people in the eyes of the law, free trade, and a free press proved very attractive. The Latin American elites, joined by a growing class of merchants, especially disliked the domination of their trade by Spain and Portugal.

The creole elites soon began to use their new ideas to denounce the rule of the Spanish and Portuguese monarchs and the **peninsulars** (Spanish and Portuguese officials who resided temporarily in Latin America for political and economic gain and then returned to their mother countries). The creole elites resented the peninsulars, who dominated Latin America and drained the Americas of their wealth.

At the beginning of the nineteenth century, Napoleon's wars provided the creoles an opportunity for change. When Napoleon overthrew the monarchies of Spain and Portugal, the authority of the Spaniards and Portuguese in their colonial empires was severely weakened. Between 1807 and 1825, a series of revolts enabled most of Latin America to become independent.

An unusual revolution came before the main independence movements. Saint-Domingue (san-doe-MAWNG)—the western third of the island of Hispaniola—was a French sugar colony. Led by François Dominique Toussaint L'Ouverture (too-SAN loo-vur-TOOR) (see "Biography: Toussaint L'Ouverture—Leader of a Slave Revolt"), more than 100,000 black slaves rose in revolt and seized control of all of Hispaniola. An army sent by Napoleon captured Toussaint L'Ouverture. However, the French soldiers, who were weakened by yellow fever, soon fell to the rebel forces. On January 1, 1804, the western part of Hispaniola, now called Haiti, announced its freedom and became the first independent state in Latin America.

Beginning in 1810, Mexico, too, experienced a revolt. It was fueled at first by the desire of the creole elites to overthrow the rule of the peninsulars. The first real hero of Mexican independence was Miguel Hidalgo y Costilla, a parish priest in a small village about 100 miles from Mexico City. Hidalgo had studied the French Revolution and roused the local Indians and mestizos (the offspring of Europeans and native American Indians) to free themselves from the Spanish: "My children, this day comes to us as a new dispensation. Are you ready to receive it? Will you be free? Will you make the effort to recover from the hated Spaniards the lands stolen from your forefathers 300 years ago?"[8] On September 16, 1810, a crowd of Indians and mestizos, armed with clubs, machetes, and a few guns, quickly formed a mob army to attack the Spaniards. Hidalgo was not a good organizer,

---

MORE ABOUT . . . *Central America*

Historians have referred to the late 19th century in Central America as the "Age of Dictatorship." With the backing of a new class of coffee producers, as well as the support of foreign agricultural and mining interests, military commanders repeatedly overthrew the governments of Honduras, Guatemala, El Salvador, Nicaragua and Costa Rica. Revolutions and coups became so common that any president who fulfilled his complete term of office became an exception. While the military in Central America was responsible for many internal improvements and construction projects, they ultimately destabilized the region with their constant intrigues.

BIOGRAPHY

Toussaint L'Ouverture—Leader of a Slave Revolt

François Dominique Toussaint L'Ouverture, the grandson of an African king, was born a slave in Saint-Domingue in 1746. Educated by his godfather, Toussaint was able to amass a small private fortune through his own talents and the generosity of his French master. In 1791, black slaves in Saint-Domingue revolted, inspired by news of the French Revolution. Toussaint became their leader. For years, Toussaint and his ragtag army struck at the French. By 1801, after his army had come to control Saint-Domingue, Toussaint assumed the role of ruler and issued a constitution that freed all slaves.

Napoleon Bonaparte refused to accept Toussaint's control of France's richest colony, however. He sent a French army of 23,000 men under General Leclerc (leh-KLAIR), his brother-in-law, to crush the rebellion. Although yellow fever took its toll on the French army, that army's superior size and arms enabled it to gain the upper hand nevertheless. Toussaint was tricked into surrendering in 1802 because of the following promise by Leclerc: "You will not find a more sincere friend than myself." What a friend he was! Toussaint was arrested, put in chains, and shipped to France, where he died a year later in an obscure dungeon. Haiti, however, became free when Toussaint's lieutenants drove out the French forces in 1804. Toussaint L'Ouverture had been leader of the "only successful slave revolt in history." The romantic English poet William Wordsworth remembered him with a poem:

Toussaint, the most unhappy man of men! . . .
Though fallen thyself, never to rise again,

▲ *Toussaint L'Ouverture led this successful revolt against the better equipped French troops.*

Live, and take comfort. Thou hast left behind
Powers that will work for thee; air, earth, and
* skies;*
There's not a breathing of the common wind
That will forget thee; thou hast great allies;
Thy friends are exultations, agonies,
And love, and man's unconquerable mind. (To
* Toussaint L'Ouverture, 1802)*

1. For what is Toussaint L'Ouverture remembered?

2. Do you think L'Ouverture knew he was successful? Why or why not?

ENRICHMENT ACTIVITY

The division of the productive forces made the Latin American colonies the suppliers of agricultural products and raw materials to the technological world. Extraction of raw materials and agriculture, much like low-skill assembly-line plants, are the low profit points in the production chain. Thus, while the industrialized world was advancing technologically, the less developed countries kept their role as primary producers. Ask students to use the following bolded terms to create a visual teaching aid of this basic production chain: Unskilled, low-paid **labor** produces **raw materials** that are sold cheaply to the **mother country** and used by **industry** to produce **manufactured goods,** some of which are sold back to the **colonies** at high prices for the **elite** of the colony. Display the most creative teaching aids in the classroom.

TEACH

REINFORCING VOCABULARY

Latin American society was stratified by ancestry and place of birth. At the top of the social structure were high government officials from the courts of Europe. Next were the *peninsulars,* temporary immigrants from Europe who ran the economics and became rich but had no interest in the Latin American countries. The *creole* had European parents who lived permanently in Latin America. Although many were wealthy and considered elite, creoles were restricted from high government, church, or economic positions. Finally, at the bottom of the social ladder were the native Indians and the *mestizos,* descendants of mixed Indian and European parents. They formed by far the largest part of the population but had little wealth or resources.

OPPOSING VIEWPOINTS

Organize a class debate on the following topic. "Resolved: Imperialism was a necessary, if sometimes painful, stage in the evolution and modernization of non-European societies." You will need to choose (1) an affirmative team, (2) a negative team, (3) a moderator, and (4) judges. The order of the debate should be: (1) affirmative case, (2) negative case, (3) affirmative rebuttal, (4) negative rebuttal, (5) questions from judges directed to the affirmative team, (6) questions from the judges directed to the negative team, (7) negative summary, and (8) affirmative summary.

758

Map 23.5   Latin America in the First Half of the Nineteenth Century

however, and his forces were soon crushed. A military court sentenced Hidalgo to death, but his memory lived on. In fact, September 16, the first day of the uprising, is Mexico's Independence Day.

The participation of Indians and mestizos in Mexico's revolt against Spanish control frightened both creoles and peninsulars there. Afraid of the masses, they cooperated in defeating the popular revolutionary forces. The conservative elites—both creoles and peninsulars—then decided to overthrow Spanish rule as a way of preserving their own power. They selected a creole military leader, Augustín de Iturbide (ee-tur-BEE-they), as their leader and the first emperor of Mexico in 1821.

Elsewhere in Latin America, independence movements were the work of elites—primarily creoles—who

STUDYING MAPS

The following questions will help you guide the students through their study of Map 23.5.

1. Which country was the first to obtain independence? *(Haiti–1804)*
2. Which country was the last to obtain independence? *(Dominican Republic–1844)*
3. What is ironic about the answers to the above questions? *(both countries share the same island.)*

4. Refer to Map 23.1 on page 731. Look closely at the dates that signify initial claim or control over these areas. Compare this map to Map 23.5 on this page. What generalization can you make about the actions of the European nations. *(The loss of the New World colonies spurred European powers to seek alternative sources for raw materials and markets.)*

◄ *Théodore Géricault painted this heroic image of José de San Martín, one of the most famous of the Latin American liberators. Here San Martín leads his troops at the battle of Chacabuco, Chile.*

ter struggle for independence in Venezuela and then went on to liberate New Granada (Colombia) and Ecuador. In January 1817, San Martín led his forces over the high Andes Mountains, an amazing feat in itself. Two-thirds of the pack mules and horses died during the difficult journey. The soldiers suffered from lack of oxygen and severe cold while crossing mountain passes that were more than two miles above sea level. The arrival of San Martín's forces in Chile completely surprised the Spaniards, who were then badly defeated at the Battle of Chacabuco (CHAW-kaw-VOO-koe) on February 12, 1817. In 1821, San Martín moved on to Lima, Peru, the center of Spanish authority.

Convinced that he was unable to complete the liberation of Peru, San Martín welcomed the arrival of Bolívar and his forces. The "Liberator of Venezuela" took on the task of crushing the last significant Spanish army at Ayacucho on December 9, 1824. By then, Peru, Uruguay, Paraguay, Colombia, Venezuela, Argentina, Bolivia, and Chile had all become free states. In 1823, the Central American states had become independent and in 1838 and 1839 divided into five republics (Guatemala, El Salvador, Honduras, Costa Rica, and Nicaragua). Earlier, in 1822, the prince regent of Brazil had declared Brazil's independence from Portugal.

overthrew Spanish rule and created new governments that they could dominate. The masses of people—Indians, blacks, mestizos, and mulattoes—gained little from the revolts.

José (hoe-ZAE) de San Martín of Argentina, a member of the creole elite, believed that the Spaniards must be removed from all of South America if any nation was to be free. San Martín and Simón Bolívar (see-MONE BAW-lee-VAR) (another member of the creole elite) were hailed as the "Liberators of South America."

By 1810, the forces of San Martín had freed Argentina from Spanish authority. Bolívar led the bit

In the early 1820s, only one major threat remained to the newly won independence of the Latin American states. Members of the Concert of Europe favored the use of troops to restore Spanish control in Latin America. The British, who wished to trade with Latin America, disagreed and proposed joint action with the United States against any European moves in Latin America. Distrustful of British motives, U.S. president

LEARNING FROM VISUALS

Instruct students to study the image on this page of Jose de San Martín leading his troops into battle against the Spanish. Then turn back to page 735 to the picture of the Vietnamese uprising against the French. Ask students for their reactions to these two images.

1. Which is the more sympathetic image to the rebels? Which shows the rebels in a more heroic light? What might that say about the source (artist) of these images? Who do students think of when they look at San Martín? *(Students might suggest he looks like George Washington or the Duke of Wellington. Ask students if they believe this was an intentional imagery on the part of the artist.)*
2. What can you say about the class of the leaders of the Chilean rebellion? How is this different from the general rebellion in Vietnam? *(In Latin America the revolution against the colonial powers was led by the Creole elite and did not affect the status of the peasants.)*

COMPARING TIME PERIODS

The text explains how San Martín surprised the Spanish in Chile by an unexpected attack through the Andes Mountains. Ask students to name two other examples of victories won by soldiers who appeared from an unlikely direction. *(Students might suggest Hannibal descending into Northern Italy by crossing the Alps; or George Washington crossing the Delaware and surprising the British at Trenton.)*

ACTIVITY

Here is a kinesthetic activity that students can act out to reinforce the fact that very little actually changed for most of the population after Latin American independence. Remind students of the production chain (See Enrichment Activity p. 757.) Prepare large cards in the following ratios with this information:

15—"I am Labor. I supply raw materials."

15—"I am Raw Material. I am exported."

(on the back of 3 of these cards write: "I am Finished Goods. I am imported.")

2—"I am Peninsular. I control the economy." (Note: on the back of these cards write "I am Creole Elite. I control the resources.")

A means of attaching cards to the students should be devised.

1. Each student is given one card randomly, but they are instructed not to turn the cards over. Those students with labor cards are either blindfolded or instructed to keep their eyes closed. The point is to make the collection of raw materials a hard task.)

2. Labor has to locate a raw material and bring it to the Peninsular. The Peninsular can give directions. A Labor can bring more than one Raw Material but any Labor who does not bring a Raw Material to a Peninsular is "dead" (out of the game).

3. Peninsulars send the Raw Material out of the room as the Labor brings them up. (After leaving the classroom those Raw Materials with "Finished Goods" on the back of the card return to the Peninsulars as a group.)

James Monroe acted alone in 1823. He guaranteed the independence of the new Latin American nations and warned against any European intervention in the New World in the famous Monroe Doctrine. Actually more important to Latin American independence than American words was Britain's navy. All of the continental powers were afraid of British naval power, which stood between Latin America and any European invasion force.

The Difficulties of Nation Building in Latin America

The new Latin American nations, most of which began their existence as republics, faced a number of serious problems between 1830 and 1870. The wars for independence had resulted in a staggering loss of people, property, and livestock. The new nations, unsure of their precise boundaries, went to war with one another to settle border disputes. Poor roads, a lack of railroads, thick jungles, and mountains made communication, transportation, and national unity difficult.

Severe struggles between church and state were also common in the new nations. The Catholic Church had enormous landholdings in Latin America and exercised great power there. After independence, church officials often took positions in the new governments and wielded much influence. Throughout Latin America, a division arose between liberals, who wished to restrict the political powers of the church, and conservatives, who hoped to maintain all of the church's privileges. In Mexico, this division even led to civil war, the bloody War of Reform fought between 1858 and 1861.

The new nations of Latin America began with republican governments, but they had had no experience in ruling themselves. Soon after independence, strong leaders known as **caudillos** came into power. Caudillos ruled chiefly by military force and were usually supported by the landed elites. Many kept the new national states together. Sometimes they were also modernizers who built roads and canals, ports, and schools. Others, however, were destructive. Antonio

López y Santa Anna, for example, ruled Mexico from 1829 to 1855. He misused state funds, halted reforms, created chaos, and helped lose one-third of Mexico's territory to the United States. Other caudillos were supported by the masses, became extremely popular, and served as instruments for radical change. Juan Manuel de Rosas, for example, who led Argentina from 1829 to 1852, became very popular by favoring Argentine interests against foreigners. In general, the system of caudillos added to the instability in Latin America. The caudillo's authority depended on his personal power. When he died or lost power, civil wars for control of the country often erupted.

Political independence brought economic independence, but old patterns were quickly reestablished. Instead of Spain and Portugal, Great Britain now dominated the Latin American economy. British merchants moved into Latin America in large numbers, and British investors poured in funds. Old trade patterns soon reemerged. Latin America continued to serve as a source of raw materials and foodstuffs for the industrializing nations of Europe and the United States. Exports included wheat, tobacco, wool, sugar, coffee, and hides. At the same time, finished consumer goods, especially textiles, were imported and caused a decline in industrial production in Latin America. The emphasis on exporting raw materials and importing finished products ensured the ongoing domination of the Latin American economy by foreigners.

A fundamental, underlying problem for all of the new Latin American nations was the domination of society by the landed elites. Large estates remained a way of life in Latin America. By 1848, for example, the Sánchez Navarro family in Mexico possessed seventeen estates made up of sixteen million acres. Estates were often so large that they could not be farmed efficiently.

Land remained the basis of wealth, social prestige, and political power throughout the nineteenth century. Landed elites ran governments, controlled courts, and kept a system of inexpensive labor. These landowners made enormous profits growing single, specialized crops for export, such as coffee. The masses, unable to have land to grow basic food crops, experienced dire poverty.

RETEACHING ACTIVITY

Ask students to summarize the main barriers to Latin American national unity. *[(1) The power struggle between the Catholic Church and the emerging governments; (2) the failure of the nationalists to address the unequal class system; and (3) the continued economic dependence on Europe created by the colonial system. The rebel elite continued to profit from the sale of raw materials. Latin America exchanged political colonialism for economic colonialism.]*

Change and Tradition in Latin America

After 1870, Latin America began an age of prosperity based to a large extent on the export of a few basic items, such as wheat and beef from Argentina, coffee from Brazil, coffee and bananas from Central America, and sugar and silver from Peru. These foodstuffs and raw materials were largely exchanged for finished goods—textiles, machines, and luxury items—from Europe and the United States. After 1900, Latin Americans also increased their own industrialization, especially by building textile, food-processing, and construction material factories.

Nevertheless, the growth of the Latin American economy came mostly from the export of raw materials. This simply added to the growing dependency of Latin America on the nations of the West. Old patterns still largely prevailed in society. Rural elites dominated their estates and their workers. Slavery had been abolished by 1888, but former slaves and their descendants were at the bottom of society. The Indians remained poverty stricken, and Latin America remained economically dependent on foreign investment. Despite its economic growth, Latin America was still an underdeveloped region of the world. Latin American countries remained economic colonies of Western nations.

One result of the prosperity that came from increased exports was growth in the middle sectors of Latin American society—lawyers, merchants, shopkeepers, businesspeople, schoolteachers, professors, bureaucrats, and military officers. These middle sectors made up only 5 to 10 percent of the population, hardly enough in numbers to make up a true middle class. Nevertheless, after 1900, the middle sectors of society continued to expand. Regardless of the country in which they lived, they shared some common characteristics. They lived in the cities; sought education and decent incomes; and saw the United States as a model, especially in regard to industrialization. The middle sectors in Latin America sought liberal reform, not revolution. Once they had the right to vote, they generally sided with the landholding elites.

As Latin American export economies boomed, the working class grew. So too did the labor unions, especially after 1914. Radical unions often advocated the use of the general strike as an instrument for change. By and large, the governing elites were able to stifle the political influence of the working class by limiting their right to vote.

As in Europe and the United States, in Latin America industrialization led to urbanization. Buenos Aires (called "the Paris of South America") had 750,000 inhabitants by 1900 and 2 million by 1914. By that time, 53 percent of Argentina's population lived in cities.

Political Change in Latin America

After 1870, large landowners in Latin America began to take a more direct interest in national politics and even in governing. In Argentina and Chile, for example, landholding elites controlled the governments. They wrote constitutions similar to those of the United States and Europe, but they were careful to keep their power by limiting voting rights.

In some countries, large landowners supported dictators who looked out for the interests of the ruling elite. Porfirio Díaz (DEE-az), who ruled Mexico from 1876 to 1910, created a conservative, centralized government with the support of the army, foreign capitalists, large landowners, and the Catholic Church. All these groups benefited from their alliance. However, there were forces for change in Mexico that led to a revolution in 1910.

During Díaz's dictatorial reign, the real wages of workers had declined. Moreover, 95 percent of the rural population owned no land, whereas about 1,000 families owned almost all of Mexico. When a liberal landowner, Francesco Madero, forced Díaz from power, he opened the door to a wider revolution. Madero's ineffectiveness created a demand for agrarian reform led by Emiliano Zapata. He aroused the masses of landless peasants and began to seize the estates of the wealthy landholders.

Between 1910 and 1920, the revolution caused untold damage to the Mexican economy. Finally, a new constitution enacted in 1917 set up a strong presidency, created land-reform policies, established limits on foreign investors, and set an agenda to help the

4. The Peninsulars can distribute or keep the Finished Goods as they please. (Note: Students should pick up on the fact that 10 Raw Materials left the room, but only 3 Finished Goods returned.)
5. Announce that the Revolution has occurred. The Peninsulars turn over their cards which now read "Creole Elite" and the game begins again.
6. Wrap Up: Ask students "What change did the Revolution produce?" *(None)* How does labor benefit from the production chain? *(It doesn't.)* "How do the peninsulars/elite benefit?" *(They make money by selling raw materials and they receive the finished goods.)* "How long could the game go on?" *(As long as labor is willing to play.)*

Multimedia Support

TRANSPARENCY
23–4, Map of American Military Involvement in Latin America

ACROSS THE CURRICULUM

Economics Economists today talk about the theory of Economic Dependency. This basically means that developing countries can never catch up with developed countries. Technological products are valued much more highly than raw materials. Since the developing countries cannot afford to buy the technology, and have only low valued goods to exchange, they are forever dependent on the developed countries for technological products.

ⓒ WORLD HISTORY UPDATES

You can update your coverage of World History topics, as well as spark lively classroom discussion and deeper understanding, by using the **CNN World History Updates.**

For assistance in using and incorporating the **CNN World History Updates** into your classroom presentations, see the *Classroom Guide.*

2. (a) descendants of Europeans who became permanent inhabitants of Latin America
(b) Spanish and Portuguese officials who resided temporarily in Latin America for political and economic gain
(c) strong leaders in Latin America usually supported by landed elite

3. (a) leader of revolt against French in Hispaniola in 1804
(b) a parish priest who roused Indians to revolt against Spanish domination in Mexico in 1810
(c) made first emperor of Mexico in 1821
(d) creole leader of the overthrow of the Spanish at the Battle of Chacabuco in Chile in 1817
(e) a 1823 statement of policy by the U.S. that European powers should not retake control of Latin America
(f) leader who helped lose one-third of Mexico's territory to the U.S.

4. (a) While European attention was diverted to the wars, many of the colonies in Latin America gained their independence.
(b) The British wanted to trade freely with Latin American countries.
(c) a clash between liberals and conservatives over the role of the Catholic Church in Mexico.
(d) American control of trade replaced the former control of other European powers.

▲ *Emiliano Zapata, who led a revolt against wealthy landowners in southern Mexico, is shown in this photograph.*

workers. The revolution also led to an outpouring of patriotism. Intellectuals and artists sought to capture what was unique about Mexico with special emphasis on its Indian past.

By this time, a new power had begun to exert influence over Latin America. By 1900, the United States, which had emerged as a world power, began to interfere in the affairs of its southern neighbors. As a result of the Spanish-American War (1898), Cuba became a U.S. protectorate, and Puerto Rico was annexed outright to the United States. In 1903, the United States supported a rebellion that enabled Panama to separate itself from Colombia and establish a new nation. In return, the United States was granted control of a ten-mile-wide canal zone. There the United States built the Panama Canal, which was opened in 1914.

American investments in Latin America soon followed, as did American resolve to protect those invest-

ments. Between 1898 and 1934, American military forces were sent to Cuba, Mexico, Guatemala, Honduras, Nicaragua, Panama, Colombia, Haiti, and the Dominican Republic to protect American interests. Some expeditions remained for many years. U.S. Marines were in Haiti from 1915 to 1934, and Nicaragua was occupied from 1909 to 1933. Increasing numbers of Latin Americans began to resent this interference from the "big bully" to the north.

    SECTION REVIEW

1. **Locate:**
(*a*) Haiti,   (*b*) Chile,   (*c*) Peru,
(*d*) Uruguay,   (*e*) Paraguay,   (*f*) Colombia,
(*g*) Venezuela,   (*h*) Argentina,   (*i*) Bolivia,
(*j*) Brazil

2. **Define:**
(*a*) creole elites,   (*b*) peninsulars,
(*c*) caudillos

3. **Identify:**
(*a*) Toussaint L'Ouverture,   (*b*) Miguel Hidalgo y Costilla,   (*c*) Augustín de Iturbide,   (*d*) José de San Martín,   (*e*) Monroe Doctrine,
(*f*) Santa Anna

4. **Recall:**
(*a*) How did the Napoleonic wars provide an opportunity for change in Latin America?
(*b*) Why did the British oppose the return of European domination to Latin America?
(*c*) What was the cause of the War of Reform in Mexico that was fought between 1858 and 1861?
(*d*) Why didn't eliminating European domination from Latin America bring about significant economic or social change?

5. **Think Critically:**
(*a*) Why did the ownership of large plots of land prevent economic development and social progress in Latin America?
(*b*) How may the construction of the Panama Canal represent both positive and negative aspects of American involvement in Latin America?

Conclusion

By 1914, virtually all of Africa and a good part of South and Southeast Asia were under some form of colonial rule. In Latin America, colonies of Spain and Portugal had won their independence at the beginning of the nineteenth century, only to become economic colonies of other Western nations during the course of the century. With the coming of the age of imperialism, a world economy was finally established. The domination of Western civilization over much of the world seemed to be complete.

Defenders of colonialism argue that the system was a necessary, if sometimes painful, stage in the evolution of human societies. They believe that Western imperialism was ultimately beneficial to colonial powers and subjects alike, because it created the conditions for world economic development and the spread of democratic institutions. Critics of colonialism, however, charge that the Western colonial powers were driven by a lust for profits. To them, the Western civilizing mission was simply an excuse to hide their greed. Critics of colonialism also reject the notion that imperialism played a helpful role in hastening the adjustment of traditional societies to the demands of industrial civilization. Two recent Western critics of imperialism have argued as follows: "Why is Africa (or for that matter Latin America and much of Asia) so poor? . . . The answer is very brief: we have made it poor."[9] Between these two extreme positions, where does the truth lie?

In one area of Asia, the spreading tide of imperialism did not result in formal Western colonial control. In East Asia, the societies of China and Japan were buffeted by the winds of Western expansionism during the nineteenth century but managed to resist foreign conquest. In the next chapter, we will see how these societies did this and how they fared in their encounter with the West.

Notes

1. Quoted in G. H. Nadel and P. Curtis, eds., *Imperialism and Colonialism* (New York, 1964), p. 94.
2. Karl Pearson, *National Life from the Standpoint of Science* (London, 1905), p. 184.
3. Quoted in C. M. Turnbull, *A History of Singapore, 1819–1975* (Kuala Lumpur, Malaysia, 1977), p. 19.
4. Quoted in Ruth Bartlett, ed., *The Record of American Diplomacy: Documents and Readings in the History of American Foreign Relations* (New York, 1952), p. 385.
5. Quoted in Louis L. Snyder, ed., *The Imperialism Reader* (Princeton, N.J., 1962), p. 220.
6. Quoted in Stanley Wolpert, *A New History of India* (New York, 1977), p. 215.
7. Quoted in K. M. Panikkar, *Asia and Western Dominance* (London, 1959), p. 116.
8. Quoted in Hubert Herring, *A History of Latin America* (New York, 1961), p. 255.
9. Quoted in Tony Smith, *The Pattern of Imperialism: The United States, Great Britain, and the Late-Industrial World since 1815* (Cambridge, 1981), p. 81.

---

5. (a) Answers will vary but students should make reference to the fact that the landed elite were so rich that they did not need to use their land efficiently (b) Answers will vary but students should include mention of the use of force exerted on Colombia to obtain the right to build the canal and the increased trade from which these nations were able to benefit.

CLOSE

Ask students to discuss the causes of instability that led to revolution in Latin America. Students can focus on either internal problems like land distribution, the church, etc., or external events like the American revolution or the Napoleanic wars in Europe. Allow each student the opportunity to participate.

TIME LINE

As students conclude the chapter, you may want to refer them to the chapter time line in the *Study Guide.* The time line will help them put key dates in perspective. Supporting questions and activities are also provided.

SPANISH SUPPORT

The *Conclusion* has been translated into Spanish for your Spanish-speaking students. Included with this translation (in your Teacher Resource Box) are Section Key Points, which consist of one or two sentences summarizing each section in the chapter. These Key Points have also been translated into Spanish.

Answers to CHAPTER REVIEW 23

USING KEY TERMS

1. indirect rule
2. sepoys
3. imperialism
4. peninsulars
5. direct rule
6. protectorate
7. caudillos
8. viceroy
9. creole elites

REVIEWING THE FACTS

1. to secure markets and raw materials, gain commercial advantages and prestige
2. Singapore
3. leader of Philippine guerrillas, first against the Spanish and then the United States
4. Sierra Leone and Liberia
5. Ferdinand de Lesseps
6. The Mahdi was Muhammad Ahmad, led a revolt in the Sudan; Charles Gordon, British soldier who held Khartoum against the Mahdi
7. British and French forces almost clashed over control of the headwaters of the Nile
8. Ethiopia
9. Arabs; based in Zanzibar; David Livingstone and Charles Gordon
10. to get away from the British
11. Britain, France, Belgium, Germany, and Portugal
12. The Sepoy Mutiny in 1857
13. provided education (for the elite), ended *sati,* suppressed the *thugs,* and built railroads, telegraphs, and established a postal service; destroyed native Indian industries, siphoned off wealth to pay for the administration and the army, strengthened a landed gentry at the expense of ordinary peasants, limited economic development
14. convert the British to his views and strengthen the unity of all Indians
15. leader of the Haitian Revolution; only successful slave insurrection of modern

764

USING KEY TERMS

1. The method of colonial government in which local rulers maintain their authority is called _____.
2. Indian soldiers in the service of the East India Company were called _____.
3. The establishment of overseas colonies is called _____.
4. Portuguese and Spanish officials who resided temporarily in Latin America and then returned home were called _____.
5. Control of a colony by the mother country is called _____.
6. A _____ is a political unit that depends on another state for its protection, such as Cambodia in its relationship with France in the 1880s.
7. After independence, strong leaders in Latin America, called _____, gained power and ruled by military force.
8. The _____ was the British representative of Parliament in India, charged with ruling nearly 300 million people.
9. _____ in Latin America denounced the rule of Spanish and Portuguese monarchs.

REVIEWING THE FACTS

1. Why did European states wish to establish colonies?
2. What colony was established by the British on the Malay Peninsula to act as a trading center?
3. Who was Emilio Aguinaldo?
4. What two African nations were founded as refuges for former slaves?
5. Who oversaw the digging of the Suez Canal?
6. Who was the Mahdi? Who was General Charles Gordon?
7. What happened at Fashoda?

764

8. Which African state successfully defeated a European attempt to colonize it in the late nineteenth century?
9. Who came to dominate the East African slave trade? Where was this trade based? Who led the struggle to end this trade?
10. Why did the Boers go on the Great Trek?
11. By 1914, which countries had divided up Africa?
12. What event led to direct imperial control of India?
13. What benefits did British rule bring to India? What harm did British rule bring to India?
14. What were Mohandas Gandhi's goals?
15. Who was Toussaint L'Ouverture? Why was the Haitian Revolution unique?
16. What countries were liberated by Simón Bolivar?
17. What countries were liberated by José de San Martín?
18. What European nation provided important support for the new Latin American republics? Why did it do so?
19. Name two nineteenth-century caudillos and the nation they governed.
20. To what Latin American countries did the United States send troops to protect its interests?

THINKING CRITICALLY

1. Why is the new imperialism called new?
2. What are the advantages and disadvantages of indirect rule of colonies? Use specific examples in your answer.
3. Were French and British education programs in their colonies consistent or inconsistent with moral idealism?
4. Why did the British come to regard control of the Suez Canal as vital to their national interest?
5. Why was David Livingstone significant for the European colonization of Africa?
6. What was Bismarck's purpose for the Berlin Conference of 1884, and how did he try to achieve

times
16. Venezuela, Colombia, Ecuador, and Bolivia
17. Chile and Peru
18. Britain; trade with the former Spanish empire
19. Antonio López y Santa Anna, Mexico; Juan Manuel de Rosas, Argentina
20. Panama, the Dominican Republic, Haiti, Nicaragua, Cuba, Guatemala and Honduras

THINKING CRITICALLY

1. it was more rapid and dominating than earlier imperialism
2. less intrusive of the native culture, less expensive to the colonizer, was not always feasible,

tended to create a local elite with a strong vested interest in the status quo, which inhibited any change and/or development
3. may be argued either way
4. was Britain's lifeline to India and the Far East
5. explored deep into Africa where few Europeans had ever gone; published accounts that attracted other colonists; and created wide spread public interest; struggled against slavery; attempted to introduce modern medicine into the region
6. trying to ease tensions between imperial powers by establishing rules for dividing up Africa; was not interested in colonies, but feared that

that purpose? How did the conference demonstrate European chauvinism?

7. What were Cecil Rhodes's goals in southern Africa? How did he go about achieving those goals? Do you regard him as successful or unsuccessful?

8. What can we infer about British rule in India from the major cause of the Sepoy Mutiny?

9. What led to the War of Reform in Mexico?

10. Explain the significance of Porfirio Díaz, Francisco Madero, and Emiliano Zapata.

APPLYING SOCIAL STUDIES SKILLS

1. **Government:** What was the role and function of native elites given a European education in India, Africa, Asia, and Latin America?

2. **Government:** Why did Napoleon Bonapart's victory over Spain lead to Wars of Liberation in South America?

3. **Government:** What is the weakness of caudillos as a system of government?

4. **Economics:** Compare the Latin American economy under Spanish rule with the Latin American economy as it evolved in the nineteenth century. Could the nineteenth century economy be accurately described as neocolonialism?

5. **Sociology:** Compare the role of landed elites in Latin America under Spanish rule with their role in the young republics of the nineteenth century? What has changed? What has remained the same?

MAKING TIME AND PLACE CONNECTIONS

1. Watch either the movie *Khartoum* (starring Charleton Heston and Lawrence Olivier), or *Zulu* (starring Stanley Baker and Michael Caine). Do you think the film accurately portrays historical events? What is the most striking scene of the

movie? What message (if any) does the movie convey?

2. What do Kwame Nkrumah, Mohandas Gandhi, and Simón Bolivar have in common?

3. The Indian National Congress was composed mostly of high-caste, English-trained Hindus. Does this fact support or undermine the opinion of a French official in Indochina that educating the natives meant "one rebel more"?

4. Simón Bolivar is considered to be the George Washington of South America. Do you think this is a fair comparison? Why? Which man had a more difficult task? Which man was more successful?

5. Why are leaders of recent insurrections in southern Mexico called Zapatistas?

BECOMING AN HISTORIAN

1. **Comparing and Contrasting:** Go back to Unit Three and review European imperialism from 1492 to 1765. Construct a table comparing imperialism with the new imperialism of 1850–1914. Include the following comparisons: (1) Time period of the imperialism, (2) areas colonized and by whom, (3) purpose for colonies, (4) internal conditions permitting imperialist expansion, (5) role of technology in permitting expansion, (6) direct or indirect rule, and (7) reasons the imperialism came to an end.

2. **Primary and Secondary Sources:** Examine the speech by Albert J. Beveridge on p. 732. Where does he reveal moral idealism? Where does he reveal a desire for profit? Make a table classifying each sentence as "Fact," "Opinion," or "Uncertain." Remember that a fact is information that can be verified as true or untrue (even incorrect facts are still facts). An opinion is an evaluation, impression, or estimation that is open to dispute (an opinion may be true, it simply cannot be verified).

765

"new" colonialism since the basic relationship of dependency had not changed

5. **Sociology:** position of dominance in local affairs politically, economically, and socially did not change; economic and political positions previously controlled by peninsulars now fell into creole hands; socially no change

MAKING TIME AND PLACE CONNECTIONS

1. Each student's answer will be highly individual. Try to elicit general discussion, and take advantage of insights students have to illustrate what has been taught with something in the movie.

2. All three men received a Western education and led nationalist movements.

3. Students will probably see this as confirming the French official's point of view.

4. The comparison is fair. Both men were essential military leaders, Constitution writers, and political leaders. Many students will regard Bolivar's task as more difficult, since he was working with a larger area with poor communications, and with regions that were much more divided, and which had much weaker traditions of self-government. The early U.S. was much more successful in solving its problems than most Latin American republics, and in that sense, Washington was more successful.

5. The rebellions are in southern Mexico—Chiapas for instance—and involves mostly Mayan Indians. These are the same people Zapata represented, and their complaint is the same—that the government in Mexico City ignores their needs.

BECOMING AN HISTORIAN

1. See suggested answers (chart) in Teacher Resource materials.

2. See suggested answers (chart) in Teacher Resource materials.

---

imperialism would trigger a European war; Africans were not invited

7. to spread British control in Africa; he plotted to provoke a war with the Boers; successful in that a war was fought resulting in the occupation by the British of the Boer republics

8. the Indians felt that the British ignored or failed to respect their culture

9. fought between liberals and conservatives to determine who would dominate the nation

10. Diaz led Mexico into a period of modernization and economic development; Madero was a Progressive who wanted to institute meaningful reforms; Zapata, a radical whose supporters were the Indians

APPLYING SOCIAL STUDIES SKILLS

1. **Government:** supposed to act as a privileged class that would act as administrators and buffers to the bulk of the population

2. **Government:** weakened the legal basis of Spanish officials to rule

3. **Government:** it is based on the personal power of the caudillo

4. **Economics:** should note the basic similarity; colonial Latin America produced minerals and agricultural resources for export to Spain in exchange for manufactured goods and other products; new republics traded primarily with Great Britain rather than Spain; called "neo" or

SECTION	KEY TOPICS	PRIMARY SOURCES	ASSESSMENT
1 The Decline of the Manchus in China pages 767–776	◆ The decline and fall of the Manchu Dynasty ◆ Opium, revolution, and other forces of change ◆ Internal reforms and Western imperialist penetration ◆ Open Door Policy and the Boxer Rebellion	◆ Zhang Zhidong on introducing democracy to China, page 771	◆ Section Review, page 776 ◆ Section Quiz 24–1, TRB
2 The Collapse of the Old Order in China pages 776–782	◆ Collapse of the Manchu dynasty ◆ Civil war and the decline of central authority ◆ Western influences on society, culture, and the economy	◆ Sun Yat-sen's Program for New China, page 779 ◆ Excerpts from *Family* by Ba Jin, page 783	◆ Section Review, page 782 ◆ Section Quiz 24–2, TRB
3 A Rich Country and a Strong State: The Rise of Modern Japan pages 784–791	◆ Relations with the West and the end of the Shogunate ◆ Transformation into a modern industrial nation	◆ President Filmore writes the Emperor of Japan, page 786–787	◆ Section Review, page 791 ◆ Section Quiz, 24–3, TRB
4 Imperialism and the Move Toward Democracy pages 791–795	◆ Joining the imperialist nations ◆ Experiment in democracy ◆ Japanese culture in an era of transition		◆ Section Review, page 795 ◆ Section Quiz 24–4, TRB

BLACK GUNS IN THE PACIFIC:
EAST ASIA IN AN AGE OF IMPERIALISM (1800 TO 1914)

REPRODUCIBLE ACTIVITIES

- Historical Maps
- Charts and Graphs
- Critical Thinking
- Cooperative Learning
- Vocabulary
- Guided Reading
- Reteaching
- Enrichment
- Performance Assessment
- Spanish Key Points and Chapter Summaries
- Spanish Vocabulary
- Spanish Guided Reading

MULTIMEDIA SUPPORT

TRANSPARENCIES
- *World History* Color Transparency Package
- Fine Art Color Transparency Package

VIDEO
- *World History* Video Library
- **CNN** Annual Video Update

LASERDISC
- *Sights and Sounds of History*

AUDIO
- *Listening to Literature* audiotape (English and Spanish)
- *History of Music* CD

SOFTWARE
- WESTEST™
- Student Review

CD–ROM
- *The Journey of Civilization*
- *World History*

INTERNET
- Internet Activities

On Line with WORLD HISTORY

Access West's history web site at **http://history.swpco.com**
You'll find activities and web sites related to specific topics and chapters in *World History: The Human Odyssey*. Also look for references to helpful web sites at appropriate places throughout this teacher edition.

LESSON PLANNING

You will find detailed daily lesson plans for both traditional class scheduling and **block scheduling** in your Teacher Resource Box.

Not Enough Time?

If you do not have the four or five days recommended to teach this chapter, you may want to focus on the following sections and activities:

- Have students skim the chapter to answer the "Questions to Guide Your Reading" on page 767. Discuss their answers then read the "Conclusion" on page 795.
- Do more in-depth reading of "The Climax of Imperialism in China," on pages 770–774; "Chinese Society in Transition, pages 780–782; "The Rise of Modern Japan," pages 784–785; and "Joining the Imperialist Nations," pages 791–792. Conclude with a study of "A Letter to the Shogun" on pages 786–787.

BLACK GUNS IN THE PACIFIC:

24

BUILDING ON CHAPTER 23

To "set the scene" for the study of Chapter 24 use the following activity.

◆ Have students prepare a color-keyed world map, or a series of world maps, that show the spread of colonialism in the nineteenth century. Use colors to show areas that were controlled by Western countries in 1800, 1825, 1850, and 1900.

USING THE OPENING STORY

Select from the following questions to reinforce the reading of this description of European forces in China and Japan.

◆ Who was trying to carry out activities in China and Japan? *(European merchants and missionaries)*

◆ How did Japan respond to the challenge of western influences? *(by adopting Western institutions and becoming an imperialist power)*

◆ What role did the military play in the opening of China and Japan to European merchants and missionaries? *(a threat of force)*

LEARNING FROM VISUALS

Answer to the caption question: The dragon symbolizes the Emperor of China.

Like the countries of South Asia, Southeast Asia, and Africa, the nations of East Asia faced a growing challenge from the power of the West in the nineteenth century. In East Asia, too, Westerners used their military superiority to pursue their goals. In 1860, for example, Great Britain and France decided to retaliate against Chinese efforts to restrict their activities. In July, an Anglo-French force arrived on the outskirts of Beijing, where it encountered the Summer Palace of the Chinese emperors. The soldiers were astounded by the riches they beheld and could not resist the desire to plunder. Beginning on October 6, British and French troops moved through the palace. They looted anything of value and smashed what they could not cart away. One British observer wrote, "You would see several officers and men of all ranks with their heads and hands brushing and knocking together in the same box." In another room, he said, "a scramble was going on over a collection of handsome state robes . . . others would be amusing themselves by taking shots at chandeliers." Lord Elgin, leader of the British forces in China, soon restored order. After the Chinese murdered twenty European hostages, however, Lord

Elgin ordered the Summer Palace to be burned. Thoroughly intimidated, the Chinese government agreed to Western demands.

The events of 1860 were part of a regular pattern in East Asia in the nineteenth century. Backed by European guns, European merchants and missionaries pressed for the right to carry out their activities in China and Japan. The Chinese and Japanese resisted but were eventually forced to open their doors to the foreigners. Unlike other Asian societies, however, both Japan and China were able to maintain their national independence against the Western onslaught. Japan reacted quickly to the challenge of the West by adopting Western institutions and itself becoming an imperialist power. China, in contrast, fought the Western imperialist influence, which eventually destroyed the Manchu dynasty.

▲ *This detail from the roof of the Summer Palace in Beijing, China, shows the intricate carvings that adorn the palace walls. Why do you think the dragon head is predominant?*

ADDITIONAL RESOURCES

The resources listed below can be used to enrich the lessons in this chapter.

BOOKS FOR STUDENTS
The Horizon History of the British Empire, Ed. Stephen W. Sears. American Heritage.
The Chinese Opium Wars by Jack Beeching. Harcourt Brace Janovich.
Tai Pan, by James Clavell. Attheneum.

VIDEOS/FILMS
"Imperialism" Series: The World: A Television History. Social Studies School Service (800) 421-4246
Colonization: Ogre or Angel? McGraw-Hill.

EAST ASIA IN AN AGE OF IMPERIALISM
(1800 TO 1914)

ERA OF EUROPEAN DOMINANCE

1800	IMPERIALISM IN EAST ASIA	1914
1800		1914

QUESTIONS TO GUIDE YOUR READING

1. Why did Manchu rule decline in nineteenth-century China?

2. In what ways did China become an economic colony of the West in the nineteenth century?

3. How did the Manchu dynasty finally collapse? What role did Sun Yat-sen play?

4. Why did China experience a civil war after the collapse of the Manchu dynasty?

5. What were the major political, economic, social, and military reforms launched by the Meiji rulers in Japan?

6. What steps did Japan take to become an imperialist power? Why did Japan take this route?

7. How did Japan move toward greater democracy during the first quarter of the twentieth century?

OUTLINE

1. THE DECLINE OF THE MANCHUS IN CHINA

2. THE COLLAPSE OF THE OLD ORDER IN CHINA

3. A RICH COUNTRY AND A STRONG STATE: THE RISE OF MODERN JAPAN

4. IMPERIALISM AND THE MOVE TOWARD DEMOCRACY

THE DECLINE OF THE MANCHUS IN CHINA

In 1800, the Manchu dynasty appeared to be at the height of its power. China had had a long period of peace and prosperity. Its borders were secure. A little over a century later, however, humiliated and harassed by the big ships and black guns of the Western powers, the Manchu dynasty collapsed in the dust.

No doubt, one important reason for the rapid decline and fall of the Manchu dynasty was the intense pressure applied to a proud but somewhat complacent society by the modern West. However, internal changes also played a role in the dynasty's collapse.

After an extended period of growth, the Manchu dynasty began to suffer from corruption, peasant unrest, and incompetence at court. These weaknesses were made worse by a rapid growth in the country's population. A long period of peace, the introduction of new crops from the Americas, and the cultivation of new, fast-growing strains of rice enabled the Chinese population to double by the end of the eighteenth century. It continued to grow during the nineteenth century. By 1900 it had reached the unheard-of level of 400 million and created a serious food shortage. One

767

FOCUS

OBJECTIVES

After completing this section, students should be able to

1. describe changes that led to the decline of the Manchu dynasty
2. explain how the Opium Wars and the Taiping Rebellion weakened the Manchus
3. describe the "self-strengthening" reforms of the Manchu
4. list the objectives of the Boxer Rebellion

FOCUS ACTIVITY

Students should understand that the rapid decline of the Manchu dynasty was due to the combination of internal and external causes.

Assign pairs of groups the task of listing factors that force change and how a government may respond to them. One group will list internal factors and the other group will list external factors. Then have the pairs of groups come together and compare their lists. Students should reach the conclusion that the resources the government requires to respond to internal factors are limited by the demands of external forces (military or police intervention, applying funds to alleviate worst symptoms, increasing representation, etc.) and the resources needed to respond to external forces are restricted by internal factors (unified government response, dedicated military, citizen resistance, etc.).

▶ *Tea was a major export for China. This painting shows workers removing leaves from the bushes, packing the leaves into giant crates for shipment, and loading them onto ships bound for England.*

observer wrote in the 1850s, "Not a year passes in which a terrific number of persons do not perish of famine in some part or other of China." The ships, guns, and ideas of the foreigners simply highlighted the growing weakness of the Manchu dynasty and probably hastened its end. In doing so, Western imperialism made a real impact on the history of modern China.

Opium and Rebellion

By 1800, Westerners had been in contact with China for more than 200 years, although Western merchants had been restricted to a small trading outlet at Canton (KAN-TAWN). This arrangement was not acceptable to the British, however. For years, the British had imported tea, silk, and porcelain from the Chinese and sent raw Indian cotton to China to pay for these imports. The raw cotton was not sufficient, however, and the British were forced to pay for their imports with silver. The British sent increasing quantities of silver to China, especially in exchange for tea, which was in great demand by the British.

At first, the British tried negotiations with the Chinese to improve their trade imbalance. When negotiations failed, the British solution was opium. Grown in northern India under the sponsorship of the British East India Company, opium was shipped directly to the Chinese market. Demand for opium—a highly addictive drug—in South China jumped dramatically. Soon, silver was flowing out of China into the pockets of the officials of the British East India Company.

The Chinese reacted strongly. They appealed to the British government on moral grounds to stop the traffic in opium. A government official wrote the following to Queen Victoria: "Suppose there were people from another country who carried opium for sale to England and seduced your people into buying and smoking it; certainly your honorable ruler would deeply hate it and be bitterly aroused." The British refused to halt their activity, however. This refusal led the Chinese government to blockade the foreign area in Canton in order to force traders to hand over their chests of opium. The British responded with force, thus starting the Opium War (1839 to 1842).

On Line with WORLD HISTORY *Internet Activity*

You may want to have your students visit the following URL, where they will find information and additional web site resources to enhance their study of this chapter.
China

http://asnic.utexas.edu/asnic/countries/china/

This site is a compilation of links dealing with many aspects of Chinese history and culture.

Due to the ever-changing nature of the World Wide Web, see the West History web site, **http://history.swpco.com** for regular updates of the URLs in this text.

TEACH

Map 24.1 Canton and Hong Kong

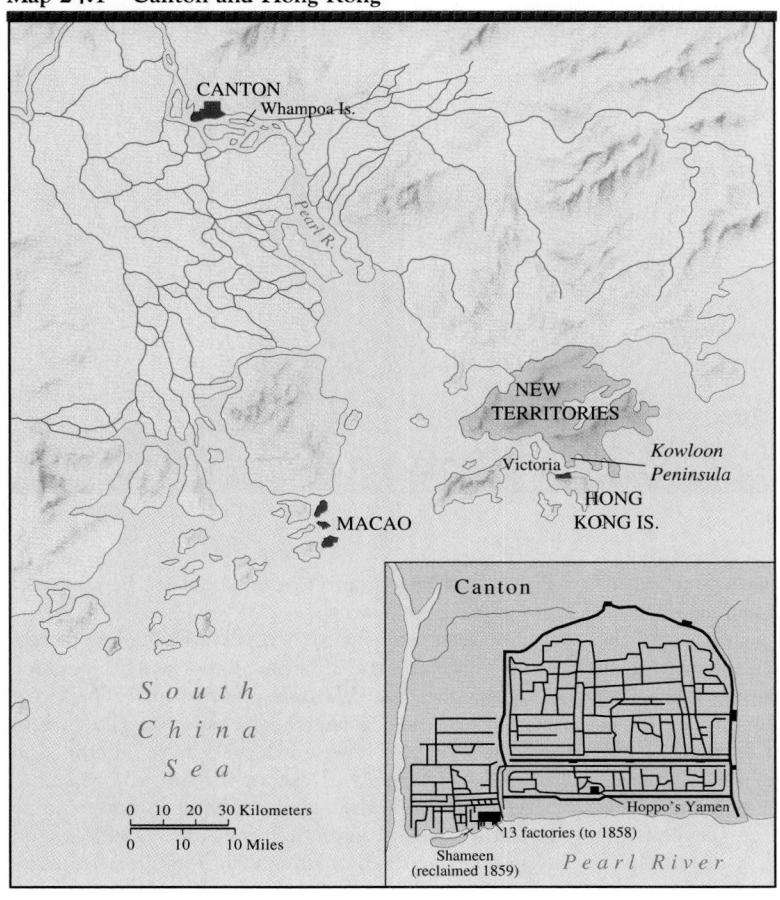

Hong Kong. Nothing was said in the treaty about the opium trade. Moreover, in the five ports, Europeans lived in their own sections and were subject not to Chinese laws but to their own, a practice known as **extraterritoriality**.

The Opium War was the first major stage in the Western penetration of China. For the time being, the Manchus tried to deal with the problem of foreigners by playing them off against one another. Concessions granted to the British were offered to other Western nations, including the United States. Soon thriving foreign areas were operating in the five treaty ports along the southern Chinese coast from Canton in the south to Shanghai, a bustling new port on a tributary of the Yangtze, in the center.

In the meantime, the failure of the Manchus to deal with pressing internal economic problems led to a major peasant revolt, known as the Taiping (TIE-PING) Rebellion (1850 to 1864). It was led by Hong Xiuquan (SHOO-GWAWN), a Christian convert who viewed himself as a younger brother of Jesus Christ. Hong was convinced that God had given him the mission of wiping out the Manchu dynasty. Joined by great crowds of peasants, Hong captured the town of Yongan and proclaimed a new dynasty—the Heavenly Kingdom of Great Peace (Taiping Tianguo in Chinese—hence the name Taiping Rebellion)—with himself as the Heavenly King. His divine mission, he announced, was "to kill all idolaters generally, and to possess the empire as its True Sovereign."

The Chinese were no match for the British. British warships destroyed Chinese coastal and river forts and seized the offshore island of Chusan. When a British fleet sailed virtually unopposed up the Yangtze River to Nanjing, the Manchu dynasty made peace. In the Treaty of Nanjing in 1842, the Chinese agreed to open five coastal ports to British trade, limit taxes on imported British goods, and pay for the costs of the war. China also agreed to give the British the island of

STUDYING MAPS

The following questions and activities will help you guide students through their study of Map 24.1.

1. Have students locate Hong Kong, Canton, the Kowloon Peninsula, Macao, and the New Territories.
2. Ask students why the British may have been dissatisfied with Canton as a center for their trading activities. *(It is isolated by rivers, deltas, and mountains from the rest*

of China; it is indefensible by the British navy; it could be easily blockaded.)

3. Why would the British have desired Hong Kong? *(It has easier access from the sea; it is easier to defend; good port location for British Navy to control shipping in the South China Sea.)*

You may wish to update students on current events in Hong Kong associated with the Chinese taking control in July, 1997.

LEARNING FROM VISUALS

1. Ask students to describe the scene in the picture on page 768. In their opinion, what is the mood of the scene? *(a tea plantation and the countryside surrounding it; peaceful and orderly)*
2. Where are the Europeans in the picture and what are they doing? *(They are all near the port, perhaps barricaded from the rest of the area, and are involved only in buying and loading the tea.)*

Multimedia Support

 LASERDISC Chinese Woodcut of European Steamboat in Canton (c. 1840)

COMPARING TIME PERIODS

You may want to tell students that trade imbalance is still an important issue in international trade and international relations. Ask students why a trade imbalance is regarded as harmful. *(A country pays out more money than it receives.)* What country has a trade imbalance with the United States and what have we done to relieve the imbalance? *(The U.S. has pressured the Japanese to open their markets to American goods.)* How is this similar to the British response to China? *(Both tried to balance trade by increasing exports.)*

Multimedia Support

LASERDISC

Chinese Anti-Foreign Propaganda, "Flogging and Dosing Foreigners" Cartoon from 1850s

COMPARING TIME PERIODS

Make students aware of the very interesting parallel between the drug trade in China in the nineteenth century and in the United States today. The seeds of our drug problem seem to have been sown by the British. In both cases, the exporters (Britain then, Columbia and others today) claim the problem is with the users—if they don't want drugs, don't buy them. The Chinese response was also very much like ours—impose penalties for use, arrest dealers, and seize supplies. Ask students if they think there is a lesson for the United States in the experience of China. *(Responses will vary. Students may feel that drug use signals the decline of society. Or they may feel that where there is demand for a product, it will be made available. Making it illegal and arresting dealers will not stop distribution. Restricting the source may be effective but may also be dangerous.)* Be certain students support their responses with examples from the text and from current events.

LEARNING FROM VISUALS

Answer to the caption question: Answers will vary.

▶ *The Chinese navy was no match for its well-armed British opponent. This painting shows Chinese junks under attack from British steamships. Why do you think the Chinese, who invented gunpowder, had not modernized their military weapons?*

One of the strong appeals of Hong's regime was its call for social reforms. These reforms included a redistribution of land equally among all peasants and the treatment of women as equals of men. Women even served in their own units in the Taiping army. The regime also called for people to give up private possessions and hold all things in common. Hong outlawed alcohol and tobacco and eliminated the practice of foot binding of women. The Chinese Communist Revolution of the twentieth century (see Chapter 33) would have similar social goals.

In March 1853, the rebels seized Nanjing, the second largest city of the empire. They secured their victory by massacring 25,000 men, women, and children. The revolt continued for ten more years but gradually began to fall apart. Europeans came to the aid of the Manchu dynasty when they realized the destructive nature of the Taiping forces. As one British observer noted, there was no hope "of any good ever coming of the rebel movement. They do nothing but burn, murder, and destroy." In 1864, Chinese forces, with European aid, recaptured Nanjing and destroyed the remaining rebel force. The Taiping Rebellion proved to be one of the most devastating civil wars in history.

Probably twenty million people died in the course of the fourteen-year struggle.

One reason for the Manchu dynasty's failure to deal effectively with the internal unrest was its ongoing struggle with the Western powers. In 1856, Great Britain and France launched a new series of attacks against China. They seized the capital, Beijing, in 1860. In the ensuing Treaty of Tianjin, the Manchus agreed to legalize the opium trade, open new ports to foreign trade, and surrender the peninsula of Kowloon (opposite the island of Hong Kong) to Great Britain.

The Climax of Imperialism in China

By the late 1870s, the old dynasty in China was well on the way to disintegrating. In fighting the Taiping Rebellion, the Manchus had been forced to rely for support on armed forces recruited by warlords in each region. The bannermen and Green Standard troops (see Chapter 18) were unable by themselves to restore order. After crushing the revolt, many of these regional commanders or warlords refused to dismiss their units. With the support of the local gentry, they continued to

MORE ABOUT . . . *the Taiping Rebellion*

An American mercenary from Salem, Massachusetts named Frederick Townsend Ward went to China in 1859, and at the age of 28, raised an army of Chinese soldiers commanded by Western officers to fight the Taiping rebels. Using Western weapons and tactics Ward defeated armies much larger than his own *Chang-sheng-chun* ("Ever Victorious Army"). Such was his reputation that the followers of Hong Qiuquan called his men the "devil soldiers." When he was killed three years after coming to China, the Manchu government built a temple and shrine to honor his memory.

◄ *This picture shows French and British troops storming fortified barriers in Canton during the Taiping Rebellion. The rebels eventually occupied the Yangtze Valley before they were crushed.*

collect local taxes for their own use. The old pattern of imperial breakdown was appearing once again.

In its weakened state, the court finally began to listen to the appeals of reform-minded officials. They called for a new policy of "**self-strengthening**." By this they meant that China should adopt Western technology while keeping its Confucian values and institutions. This new policy guided Chinese foreign and domestic policy for the next twenty-five years.

Some reformers even called for changing China's traditional political institutions by introducing democracy. However, such ideas were too radical for most reformers. One of the leading court officials of the day, Zhang Zhidong (CHANG CHI-DONG), argued as follows:

The doctrine of people's rights will bring us not a single benefit but a hundred evils. Are we going to establish a parliament? Among the Chinese scholars and people there are still many today who are content to be vulgar and rustic. They are ignorant of the general situation in the world, they do not understand the basic system of the state. They have not the most elementary idea about foreign countries—about the schools, the politi-

cal systems, military training, and manufacture of armaments. Even supposing the confused and clamorous people are assembled in one house, for every one of them who is clear-sighted, there will be a hundred others whose vision is beclouded; they will converse at random and talk as if in a dream—what use will it be?[1]

For the time being, Zhang Zhidong's arguments prevailed. During the last quarter of the nineteenth century, the Manchus tried to modernize China's military forces and build up an industrial base without touching the basic elements of traditional Chinese civilization. Railroads, weapons factories, and shipyards were built, but the Chinese value system remained unchanged.

In the end, however, the changes did not help. The European advance into China continued during the last two decades of the nineteenth century. In the north and northwest, Russia took advantage of the Manchu dynasty's weakness to force the concession of territories north of the Amur River in Siberia. In Tibet, a struggle between Russia and Great Britain kept either power from seizing the territory outright. This gave Tibetan authorities the chance to free themselves from Chinese influence.

So What ??

*If your students question the importance of the information on **nineteenth-century China**, tell them . . .*

European imperialism in China has contributed to Chinese suspicions of the West in the late twentieth century. The ongoing disputes between the United States and China over such issues as human rights, trade barriers, and environmental concerns have been made worse, in part, by those acts of imperialism. Can students see how the strained relations between the two countries might affect them personally?

LEARNING FROM VISUALS

1. Ask students to describe the scene in the illustration on the opposite page. *(It shows a naval battle between the British and Chinese.)* The students have seen several other battle scenes between the British and native peoples. How is this scene different? *(It involves only ships. No troops are involved.)*

2. Ask students to describe differences between the British and Chinese ships. *(The Chinese ships are boxy, ride high in the water, have only sails for propulsion and maneuvering. The British ships are sleek, low in the water so as to make them harder targets, use steam power and paddle wheels for power and maneuvering, appear to have more powerful canons.)*

USING PRIMARY SOURCES

Have student volunteers read the statement of Zhang Zhidong as a politician would. The argument is against granting democracy to the masses because they "are ignorant of the general situation of the world." Ask students if they feel these are reasonable arguments. Ask if there are preconditions for democracy before "people's rights" should be granted. Could a democratic parliament work effectively in China? Which is more likely to result from democracy, "a single benefit or a hundred evils"?

CONNECTIONS
TO OUR WORLD

Make sure students understand the meaning of the phrase "one country, two systems." *(communism and capitalism in one country, China)* Then ask students to speculate on the long-term results of Hong Kong becoming part of China, as opposed to remaining a British colony.

REINFORCING VOCABULARY

A *sphere of influence* is an area where foreign governments have exclusive trading rights and use of ports but do not have administrative control. By the end of the nineteenth century, large parts of China were claimed as spheres of influence by European countries, Russia, and Japan. Notably, the United States did not claim a sphere of influence in China.

CRITICAL THINKING

The Manchus attempted to implement reforms in order to survive. The "self strengthening" policy was known by the slogan "East for Essence, West for Practical Use." Ask students what this means. *(Self strengthening was a policy of adopting Western technology while retaining Confucian principles.)* Ask students why this policy was not likely to succeed. *(Traditional Confucianism was incompatible with Western technology and the policy did not stop the Western countries from continuing their imperialist policies in China.)* Why were some people opposed to making reforms? *(The elite did not want to give up any control.)*

772

CONNECTIONS
TO OUR WORLD

The Return of Hong Kong to China   In 1984, Great Britain and China signed a Joint Declaration in which Britain agreed to return its colony of Hong Kong to China on July 1, 1997. China promised that Hong Kong would keep its free market, capitalist economy and its way of life. The formula was: "one country, two systems." Many Hong Kong residents, although fearful of Chinese rule, were also delighted.

In 1841, Hong Kong was a small island with a few fishing villages on the southeastern coast of China. A British naval force seized the island and used it as a port for shipping opium into China. A year later, after a humiliating defeat in the Opium War, China agreed to give the island of Hong Kong to Britain. Later, the British took advantage of the declining power of China's Manchu dynasty to gain additional lands next to Hong Kong. In 1861, the Chinese government granted the Kowloon peninsula to Britain. In 1898, the Chinese granted the British a 99-year lease on the nearby New Territories, an area that provided much of the food for the colony of Hong Kong.

In the 1950s and 1960s, Hong Kong was filled with refugees from the new Communist regime in mainland China. The population of Hong Kong swelled to six million. Many of the refugees worked for starvation wages, and the economy of Hong Kong boomed. Today, Hong Kong is the eighth largest trading nation in the world.

Even more ominous changes were taking place in the Chinese heartland. European states began to create so-called **spheres of influence**. After the Taiping Rebellion, warlords in the provinces began to negotiate directly with foreign nations. In return for money, the warlords granted these nations exclusive trading rights or railroad-building and mining privileges. Britain, France, Germany, Russia, and Japan all established spheres of influence in China.

In 1894, one more blow led to further disintegration. The Manchus went to war with Japan over Japanese inroads into Korea, a land that the Chinese had controlled for a long time. The Chinese were roundly defeated. As a reward, Japan demanded and received the island of Taiwan (known to Europeans at the time as Formosa) and the Liaodong (li-OW-DOONG) (Liaotung) peninsula. Fearing Japan's growing power, the European powers forced Japan to give the Liaodong peninsula back to China.

European statesmen, however, were not concerned about the collapse of the Chinese Empire itself. New pressures for Chinese territory soon arose. The process began in 1897. Germany used the pretext of the murder of two German missionaries by Chinese rioters to demand the cession of territories in the Shandong (SHAWN-DOONG) peninsula. When the Chinese government approved the demand, other European nations made new claims on Chinese territory. Russia now demanded the Liaodong peninsula, with its ice-free port at Port Arthur. Great Britain asked for coaling stations in North China.

This latest scramble for territory had taken place at a time of internal crisis in China. In the spring of 1898, a reformer named Kang Youwei (YOE-WAE) had won the support of the young emperor Guangxu (GWAWN-shoo) for a massive reform program based on recent changes in Japan (see the discussion later in this chapter). During the next several weeks (known as the One Hundred Days of reform), the emperor issued edicts calling for major political, administrative, and educational reforms.

Kang's ideas for reform were opposed by many conservatives at court, however, who saw little advantage in copying the West. As one said, "An examination of the causes of success and failure in government reveals that . . . the adoption of foreignism leads to disorder."[2] What was needed, this conservative said, was to reform existing ways rather than give up the tried-and-true rules of the past.

Most important, the new reform program was opposed by the emperor's aunt, Empress Dowager Cixi (see "Biography: The Empress Dowager Cixi"). Cixi had become a dominant force at court and opposed Emperor Guangxu's reforms. With the aid of the impe-

SPECIAL NEEDS: *Visual/Auditory*

After reading pages 767–780, have students find as many of the following words as possible: China, porcelain, Canton, tea, silk, Hong Kong, Nanjing, Beijing, Zhang Zhidong, Russia, Siberia, Tibet, weapons, Great Britain, Japan, Korea, Kang Youwwei, Guangxu, Empress Cixi, John Hay, Sun Yat-sen. Then use an overhead transparency divided into 3 columns: Places, People and Products. Go over each word and ask students to tell under which column the word belongs. As each word comes up and is placed under its appropriate column, have the students share the significance of the place, person or product, according to what they read in the chapter.

BIOGRAPHY

BIOGRAPHY

The Empress Dowager Cixi

Born in 1835, Cixi was educated by her father, a civil servant. At a young age, she became a low-ranking concubine to Emperor Xian Feng (SHEE-AWN FUNG). Cixi proved ambitious. She used her learning and cleverness to rise to the rank of secretary to the emperor, a position that gave her experience in government affairs. Her position became even more influential in 1856, when she gave birth to the emperor's first and only son.

When the emperor died in 1861, Cixi's son, Tong Zhi, became the new emperor. Because he was only five years old, a council of regency under Cixi's direction ruled in his name. Although Tong Zhi came of age (17) in 1873, his mother continued to rule from behind the scenes. Tong Zhi died two years later, a death for which some historians believe his mother was responsible. Cixi then chose her four-year-old nephew Guangxu as the new emperor and continued to rule in his name as regent.

When Guangxu came of age, he and a group of supporters tried to take charge and institute reforms. Cixi thought that Guangxu's reforms were an attempt to reduce her influence at court. With the aid of conservatives at court and the imperial army, she had the emperor jailed in the palace and several of his reformers executed. Guangxu's favorite concubine was also drowned. With Cixi's palace coup, the days of reform had come to an end. The empress continued to rule China until her death in 1908.

Empress Dowager Cixi ruled China for almost 50 years, during a crucial period in the nation's history. She was well aware of her own power. "I have often thought that I am the cleverest woman who ever lived. . . I have 400 million people all dependent on my judgement," she once said.

▲ *Empress Dowager Cixi held power in China until her death in 1908. This photograph, taken in her final years, shows her royal demeanor and dress. What do you think her long fingernails symbolize?*

Many Chinese regard her as the "most powerful woman in China's history." Her rule had some notable accomplishments, especially for women. Among other things, she ended the foot binding of women. However, in some ways her reign was disastrous. She allowed considerable corruption.

(continued)

REINFORCING VOCABULARY

Students may be vaguely familiar with the definition of a concubine as a woman who lives with a man without the full sanctions of legal marriage. They may not realize that concubinage is not strictly an Asian or Middle Eastern custom. The word comes from the Latin *con* ("with") and *cubare* ("to lie"). In Roman law concubinage was the permanent cohabitation of a man and a woman outside of their existing formal marriages. Either a man or a woman could properly be referred to as a concubine. In most cases the children of such a union did have the same legal rights granted the children of legally married couples.

LEARNING FROM VISUALS

Answer to the caption question: Long fingernails were a symbol of the royal, privileged class.

Answers to Critical Thinking Questions

1. Cixi's son was heir to the throne at age five, so she ruled "behind the screen" until he came of age. When he died at an early age, she put her nephew on the throne, and, since he was only four, she ruled for him. She had him arrested when he was old enough to make changes, so she ruled in his place.
2. She reigned during the Manchu dynasty.

RETEACHING ACTIVITY

1. Ask students how Cixi was able to receive an education since schooling was denied to Chinese women. *(She was educated at home by her father.)*
2. Pose the following question to students: Cixi died three years before the Manchu dynasty was overthrown. To what extent was she responsible for the decline and downfall? *(Answers will vary, of course, but students should remember that Cixi nullified the laws put in place during the One Hundred Days. Who knows what course history would have taken otherwise.)*
3. Ask students to hypothesize about the type of personality Cixi must have developed in order to maintain power over the course of five decades. *(Historians write that Cixi, who was nicknamed "The Old Buddha," was autocratic, ruthless, and extravagant.)*

LEARNING FROM VISUALS

The Boxer Rebellion was largely a peasant uprising. It was provoked by a damaging drought and high levels of unemployment, due, at least in part, to European economic activities. The Boxers attacked the foreign residents and Christians they blamed for their problems. This picture shows some of the Boxers captured after the rebellion failed.

1. Ask students to describe the rebels. (*They appeared to be peasants, they are not in uniform, they do not look like soldiers.*)
2. Why are many of the captives holding their heads? (*People around the captives have sticks and appear to be beating them.*)

CRITICAL THINKING

Have students compare and contrast the Taiping Rebellion with the Boxer Rebellion. Be sure they include the motivations, tactics, and outcomes of each.

OPPOSING VIEWPOINTS

Conduct a debate on the issue of foreign trade. Have students assume the roles of Chinese officials and European merchants. The debate topic should be: What should the Chinese trade policy be? Should the Chinese keep foreign merchants out of China?

BIOGRAPHY

The Empress Dowager Cixi, continued

Funds earmarked for the navy in the late 1880s, for example, were used instead to build a summer palace outside Beijing. Also, her unwillingness to make significant reforms no doubt weakened the Manchu dynasty and helped lead to its overthrow only three years after her death.

1. Explain how Cixi came to power in China.
2. During what dynasty did Cixi reign?

rial army, she imprisoned the emperor and ended the days of reform.

Opening the Door to China

As foreign pressure on the Manchu dynasty grew stronger, both Great Britain and the United States came to fear the total collapse of the Manchu Empire. In 1899, U.S. secretary of state John Hay presented the other imperialist powers with a proposal to ensure equal economic access to the China market for all nations. Hay also suggested that all the powers join together to preserve the unity of the Chinese Empire. When none of the other governments flatly opposed the idea, Hay issued a second note. It stated that all major states with economic interests in China had agreed to an "Open Door" policy in China.

In part, the Open Door policy reflected the American concern for the survival of China. It also reflected, however, the interests of some trading companies in the United States. These companies wanted to operate in open markets and disliked the existing division of China into separate spheres of influence dominated by individual states. The Open Door policy did not end the system of spheres of influence. However, it did reduce the number of tariffs or quotas on foreign imports imposed by the dominating power within each sphere of influence.

The Open Door policy also had the practical effect of reducing imperialist hysteria over access to the

▼ Following the Boxer Rebellion, many of the young rebels were rounded up and imprisoned.

MORE ABOUT . . . the Boxer Rebellion

The Empress Dowager Cixi also had a hand in the Boxer Rebellion. Initially the Boxers' objectives were to overthrow the government and to rid China of all foreigners. However, in 1898 conservative, anti-foreign elements in the government persuaded the Boxers to drop their opposition of the government and to join with it to destroy the foreigners. The Empress Dowager and officials in the government supported the Boxers and encouraged their anti-foreigner and anti-Christian campaigns. When the Empress Dowager ordered that all foreigners in Beijing be killed, foreign ministry staff and hundreds of Chinese Christians took refuge in the Roman Catholic cathedral in Beijing for more than two months. It is because of Cixi's participation that the allies were able to claim that the Chinese government should pay heavy reparations.

Map 24.2   Foreign Possessions and Spheres of Influence about 1900

Spheres of Influence

	Russian
	Japanese
	British
	German
	French
	Italian

China market. The Open Door policy reduced fears in Britain, France, Germany, and Russia that other powers would take advantage of China's weakness to dominate the China market for themselves.

The Open Door policy came too late to stop the domestic explosion in China known as the Boxer Rebellion. *Boxers* was the popular name given to members of a secret organization called the Society of Harmonious Fists. Members practiced a system of exercise—a form of shadowboxing, or boxing with an imaginary opponent—that they thought would protect them from bullets. The Boxers were distressed by economic hardships and the foreign takeover of Chinese lands. They wanted to push foreigners out of China.

Their slogan was "destroy the foreigner." They especially disliked Christian missionaries and Chinese converts to Christianity. At the beginning of 1900, Boxer bands roamed the countryside and slaughtered foreign missionaries and Chinese Christians. They then expanded their victims to include railroad workers, foreign businessmen, and even the German envoy to Beijing.

Response to the killings was immediate and overwhelming. An allied army consisting of 20,000 British, French, German, Russian, American, and Japanese troops attacked Beijing in August 1900. The army restored order and demanded more concessions from the Chinese government. The Chinese government

STUDYING MAPS

1. **Which foreign country controlled the largest territory as a sphere of influence?** *(Russia)*
2. **What common geography do most of the areas colored "spheres of influence" share?** *(They are coastal cities or located on large rivers. This makes them more easily accessible than interior cities.)*
3. **What two areas shown on the map are Japanese spheres of influence?** *(the lower part of the Korean peninsula and Formosa)*
4. **What growing imperialist power is missing from the key?** *(Students should notice that the United States did not claim any spheres of influence in this region.)*

CRITICAL THINKING

Ask students what effect the Open Door Policy had on the imperialist countries in China. *(All countries were granted access to all of China. Quotas and tariffs were reduced to allow more equal access within spheres of influence.)* Why would the United States want to allow open access to China? *(The United States did not claim a sphere of influence. Open access would allow them to compete economically with the other powers in China.)* Only twenty-five years after the Open Door Policy was proposed by the United States, the Monroe Doctrine was imposed in Latin America. Ask students to compare the two policies. Are they consistent? *(The Open Door Policy allowed access for all countries to China. The Monroe Doctrine warned against European intervention in the New World.)*

ASSESS

Have students write an essay on one of the following items, describing how the event strengthened the position of the imperialist powers in China. The essay should discuss the background leading up to the event, describe significant elements of the event, and describe the result of the event on China.

◆ The Opium War
◆ The Taiping Rebellion
◆ The Self-Strengthening reforms
◆ The Boxer Rebellion

Answers to
SECTION REVIEW

2. (a) areas in China where European powers enforced their own laws **(b)** adopting Western technology while keeping Confucian values. **(c)** exclusive trading rights or railroad-building and mining privileges in specific areas given to for- eign powers **(d)** large sum of money

3. (a) a drug exported from India to China by the British to build trade **(b)** Chinese Christian opposing the Manchus **(c)** ended the war between the Taiping army and the Manchu dynasty **(d)** Emperor Guangxu's massive reform program **(e)** opened Chinese ports equally to trade from all countries **(f)** revolt against foreign influence in China

4. (a) corruption, peasant unrest, and incompetence **(b)** food shortages and social unrest **(c)** They believed the rebels were destroying China's ability to produce goods for trade.

5. Answers will vary.

CLOSE

In a class discussion, ask students to compare the activities of the European countries in China to their activities in Southeast Asia and India. Ask students to name reasons why the Euro- pean countries did not at- tempt to exert direct control over China the way they did in other countries. Allow all students an opportunity to participate.

was forced to pay a heavy **indemnity** (large sum of money) to the powers that had crushed the uprising. The imperial government was now weaker than ever.

 SECTION REVIEW

1. Locate:
(*a*) Canton,   (*b*) Yangtze River,   (*c*) Hong Kong,
(*d*) Siberia,   (*e*) Tibet,   (*f*) Korea,   (*g*) Taiwan

2. Define:
(*a*) extraterritoriality,   (*b*) self-strengthening,
(*c*) spheres of influence,   (*d*) indemnity

3. Identify:
(*a*) opium,   (*b*) Hong Xiuquan,   (*c*) Treaty of Tianjin,   (*d*) One Hundred Days of reform,
(*e*) Open Door policy,   (*f*) Boxer Rebellion

4. Recall:
(*a*) What internal problems contributed to the decline and fall of the Manchu dynasty in China?
(*b*) What problems did population growth cause in China during the nineteenth century?
(*c*) Why did European powers come to the aid of the Manchu dynasty when it was attacked by the Taiping army in 1853?

5. Think Critically: Why would powerful European nations agree to the Open Door policy suggested by a weaker United States?

THE COLLAPSE OF THE OLD ORDER IN CHINA

During the first few years after the Boxer Rebellion, the old dynasty in China tried desperately to reform itself. Empress Dowager Cixi, who had long resisted change, now embraced a number of reforms in educa- tion, administration, and the legal system. The old civil service examination system was dropped, and a

new educational system based on the Western model was adopted. After 1905, legislative assemblies were set up at the provincial level. Even elections for a national assembly were held in 1910.

The Fall of the Manchus

The reform moves won at least temporary support for the Manchu dynasty among progressive elements in the country. Many were soon disappointed, however. The emerging new provincial elite, composed of mer- chants, professionals, and reform-minded gentry, soon became impatient with the slow pace of political change. They were very angry when they found that the new assemblies were only asked for advice and not allowed to pass laws. In addition, the recent reforms had done nothing for the peasants, artisans, and min- ers, whose living conditions were getting worse as taxes increased. Rising unrest in the countryside was a sign of the deep-seated resentment to which the dynasty seemed unable to respond.

The first signs of revolution appeared during the last decade of the nineteenth century, when the young rad- ical Sun Yat-sen (YAWT-SEN) formed the Revive China Society. Sun was born to a peasant family in a village south of Canton and was educated in Hawaii. He returned to China to practice medicine. Soon he turned his full attention to the ills of Chinese society.

Sun Yat-sen believed that the Manchu dynasty was in a state of decay and could no longer govern the coun- try. Unless the Chinese were united under a strong gov- ernment, they would be at the mercy of other countries. Sun believed that China should follow the pattern of the Western democracies, but he knew that the Chi- nese people were hardly ready for democracy. He called instead for a three-stage process: (1) a military takeover, (2) a transitional phase in which Sun's own revolution- ary party would prepare the people for the final stage, and (3) a constitutional democracy.

Gathering support from radical students, merchants, and secret society members in South China, Sun launched a series of local rebellions to topple the Manchus. At first, his efforts went nowhere. In a con- vention in Tokyo in 1905, however, Sun united radical

MORE ABOUT . . . *the Boxer Rebellion*

The multinational force that put down the Boxer Rebellion included soldiers from Japan, France, Germany, Great Britain, and the United States. The indemnity that the Chi- nese government had to pay to these West- ern nations was $333 million dollars. Of that sum, $24.5 million was to go to the United States. When the U.S. government realized

that this was far more than the expense for its troops and the damages caused from the fighting, it reimbursed the Chinese govern- ment $18 million dollars. This money was then set aside by the Chinese to send stu- dents to study in America. These students would eventually help to bring western ideas to China.

Map 24.3 The Manchu Empire in the Early Twentieth Century

THE MANCHU EMPIRE IN 1775 AND IN 1911
— Area of Chinese sphere of influence about 1775
— Boundary of Chinese Empire, 1911
▢ Sometime tributary states to China

groups from across China in a Revolutionary Alliance (*Tongmenghui*). The program of the new organization was based on Sun's so-called Three People's Principles of Nationalism, Democracy, and People's Livelihood (see "You Are There: A Program for a New China"). The new organization was small and inexperienced. However, it benefited from rising discontent with the failure of Manchu reforms to improve conditions in China.

The Manchu dynasty was near its end. In 1908, Empress Dowager Cixi died. Her nephew Guangxu, a prisoner in the palace, died the day before his aunt. The throne was now occupied by China's "last emperor," the infant Henry Puyi (POO-YEE).

In October 1911, followers of Sun Yat-sen launched yet another uprising in the industrial center of Wuhan, on the Yangtze River in central China. At the time, Sun himself was traveling in the United States. Thus, the **insurrection** (act of revolting against an established government) had no leader, but the government was too weak to react. The dynasty collapsed, opening the way for new political forces.

Sun's party, however, had neither the military nor the political strength to form a new government. The party was forced to turn to a member of the old order, General Yuan Shikai (yoo-AWN SHIR-KIE). Yuan was a prominent figure in military circles, and he had been placed in charge of the imperial army sent to sup-

STUDYING MAPS

The following questions will help you guide students through their study of Map 24.2.

1. What does the term "Chinese sphere of influence" in the key refer to? (*the area over which China had monopoly control for trade and resources but did not necessarily directly govern*)

2. What happened to the Chinese sphere of influence between 1775 and 1911? (*It

was greatly reduced; China lost control over almost all of the off-shore regions.)

3. Why might the southeastern region of the Chinese empire have more states than the rest of the country? (*There are few rivers outside of the southeast and so the population is very sparse.*)

4. What was the maximum extent (east-west) of the Chinese sphere of influence in 1775? (*approximately 4400 miles*)

FOCUS

OBJECTIVES

After completing this section, students should be able to

1. list the three stages Sun Yat-sen proposed to follow to reform China's government

2. name the causes for the period of civil war in China following the collapse of the Manchu Dynasty

3. list the three effects Western influence had on the Chinese economy

FOCUS ACTIVITY

Revolutions frequently fail to bring about the changes that had been hoped for by the revolutionaries. This was the case in Latin America when the European countries were overthrown. This was also the case in China. Sun Yat-sen led a successful revolution to end the rule of the Manchu dynasty, but following the revolt was unable to establish rule over the new government. Ask students to discuss reasons why most revolutions do not bring about intended changes. To focus their discussion, you may want them to list the reasons for a revolution, the characteristics of revolutionaries who are successful in overthrowing a government, and what conditions are likely to be like after the revolution.

TEACH

COMPARING TIME PERIODS

Have students identify characteristics of the collapse of previously studied empires or civilizations (Roman Empire, fifteenth-century Aztecs, French Ancient Regime, etc.). Then have students compare these characteristics with those impacting the decline of China's old order.

There are many parallels with countries today that are trying to modernize their economy while maintaining their culture and tradition. Ask students to name some contemporary examples. (*There are a number of examples from Latin America and Africa. Israel could also be cited.*)

OPPOSING VIEWPOINTS

Have students create a debate by assuming the roles of advisors to the Manchu emperor. One set of advisors favors the making of reforms to modernize China. The other set of advisors favors maintaining the traditional Confucian system. What arguments would each side use to support its position?

LEARNING FROM VISUALS

Answer to the caption question: General Yuan had a much wider base of support than Sun Yat-sen, especially the army. He was, however, disliked by traditionalists.

press the rebellion. He abandoned the Manchus and negotiated with members of Sun Yat-sen's party. Sun Yat-sen himself had arrived in China in January 1912, after reading about the revolution in a Denver, Colorado, newspaper. General Yuan Shikai agreed to serve as president of a new Chinese republic and to allow the election of a legislature.

In the eyes of Sun Yat-sen's party, the events of 1911 were nothing less than a glorious revolution that had ended 2,000 years of imperial rule. However, the 1911 uprising was hardly a revolution. It produced no new political or social order. Sun Yat-sen and his followers had not yet achieved much. Their Revolutionary Alliance was supported mainly by an emerging urban middle class, and its program was based largely on Western liberal democratic principles. However, the urban middle class in China was too small to form the basis for a new political order. Most of the Chinese people still lived on the land, and few peasants supported Sun Yat-sen's party. In effect, then, the events of 1911 were less a revolution than a collapse of the old order. The old dynasty, weakened by its own internal problems and by imperialism, had come to an abrupt end before new political and social forces were ready to take over.

The Era of Civil War

After the collapse of the Manchu dynasty, the military took over. As we have seen, Sun Yat-sen and his colleagues had accepted General Yuan Shikai as president of the new Chinese republic in 1911 because they lacked the military force to compete with his control over the army. Moreover, many feared that if the revolt lapsed into chaos, the Western powers would inter-

▲ *Sun Yat-sen became the founder of the first Chinese republic. This photograph shows Sun in January 1912, shortly after he had returned from the United States. Why did General Yuan Shikai, rather than Sun Yat-sen, become president of the new republic?*

vene. Then the last shreds of Chinese independence would be lost. However, even the general's new allies distrusted his motives.

Yuan understood little of the new ideas sweeping into China from the West. He ruled in a traditional manner and even tried to set up a new imperial dynasty. Yuan was hated by reformers for using murder and terror to destroy the new democratic institutions. He was hated by traditionalists for being disloyal to the dynasty he had served. Yuan's dictatorial efforts rapidly led to clashes with Sun's party, now renamed the Guomindang (GWOE-min TONG) (old spelling, *Kuomintang*), or Nationalist Party. When Yuan dissolved the new parliament, the Nationalists launched a rebellion. When the rebellion failed, Sun Yat-sen fled to Japan.

Yuan was strong enough to brush off the challenge from the revolutionary forces, but he could not turn back the clock of history. He died in 1916 and was succeeded by one of his military officers. For the next several years, China slipped into civil war as the power of the central government disintegrated and military warlords seized power in the provinces. Their soldiers caused massive destruction throughout China. One Chinese observer said, "In China today only cunning, vile, and ruthless people can flourish." Hunger spread throughout the land.

By 1920, central authority had almost ceased to exist in China. Two political forces began to emerge as competitors for the right to rule China. One was Sun Yat-sen's Nationalist Party, which had been driven from the political arena seven years earlier. The Nationalist Party reestablished itself on the mainland of China by making a military alliance with the warlord ruler of Guangdong (GWAWN-DUNG) province in South China. From Canton, Sun sought help from

MORE ABOUT . . . *Self-Strengthening and the*

China maintained its cultural and territorial integrity for over 2000 years due largely to the teachings of Confucius. The teachings and principles of Confucius were adapted as state policy from about 210 B.C. until the 1912 revolution. The teachings can be summarized in three basic concepts. First, the emperor was superior to all others on earth and was considered to be accountable for all events that influenced the welfare of his people—

drought, earthquakes, peace, and prosperity were all the result of the emperor's actions. Second, administrators in the government were to be selected on the basis of merit and competence. As early as 124 B.C. an imperial university was established to train government officials in the practices of Confucian government. This evolved into the civil service examination system, which became a very effective and fair means of testing for high

YOU ARE THERE

A Program for a New China

◄ *Sun Yat-sen, third from left in the light-colored suit, was photographed in Hangzhou, China, with other members of the Revolutionary Alliance. Sun Yat-sen's wife, second from left, is attired in Western clothing. Why do you think both men and women are in the photograph?*

In 1905, Sun Yat-sen united a number of groups into a single patriotic organization called the Revolutionary Alliance (Tongmenghui). The new organization eventually formed the basis of Sun's Nationalist Party. This excerpt is from the organization's program, published in 1905 in Tokyo.

Selection from the Revolutionary Alliance Program

Therefore we proclaim to the world in utmost sincerity the outline of the present revolution and the fundamental plan for the future administration of the nation.

1. Drive out the Tartars: The Manchus of today were originally the eastern barbarians beyond the Great Wall. They frequently caused border troubles during the Ming dynasty; then when China was in a disturbed state they conquered China and enslaved our Chinese people. The extreme cruelties and tyrannies of the Manchu government have now reached their limit. With the righteous army poised against them, we will overthrow that government, and restore our sovereign rights. . . .

(continued)

Confucian Code

government positions. By the nineteenth century, however, it had become more style than substance and was viewed as a means of limiting access to government service. Finally, the Chinese people were taught to value order and social cohesion above personal gain. For farmer peasants this meant submission to authority, respect for tradition, and seeking moderation and harmony in all things.

The self-strengthening policy attempted to reconcile these values with Western technology. The later reforms attempted to modify some aspects of Confucianism while maintaining order. Unfortunately, the Confucian Code leaves little room for compromise, especially as it had come to be practiced in nineteenth century China.

CRITICAL THINKING

Inform students that another translation of "people's livelihood," the third of Sun Yat-sen's principles of the people, is "equalization of land ownership." How does this translation relate to "people's livelihood"?

Answers to Critical Thinking Questions

1. He viewed the Manchus as foreigners because they were originally from beyond the Great Wall, and they had caused trouble along the borders.
2. He believed in democracy. He felt the people were equal and should all be involved in political decisions.
3. Answers will vary, but students will probably say that the ideas would not be well received.

CRITICAL THINKING

Ask students to discuss why Dr. Sun Yat-sen gave up power to General Yuan Shikai in 1911–1912. What was Sun Yat-sen's motivation? *(Students should realize that Sun Yat-sen knew he did not have the power base or support he needed to unite all of China behind his Nationalist Party. Unfortunately, it appears that the General was not the best choice. Perhaps Sun Yat-sen would have been better off trying to stay in power and trying to keep the revolution on track ideologically.)*

YOU ARE THERE

A Program for a New China, continued

2. Restore China: China is the China of the Chinese. The government of China should be in the hands of the Chinese. After driving out the Tartars we must restore our national state. . . .
3. Establish the Republic: Now our revolution is based on equality, in order to establish a republican government. All our people are equal and all enjoy political rights. The president will be publicly chosen by the people of the country. The parliament will be made up of members publicly chosen by the people of the country. A constitution of the Chinese Republic will be enacted, and every person must abide by it. . . .
4. Equalize land ownership: The good fortune of civilization is to be shared equally by all the people of the nation. We should improve our social and economic organization, and assess the value of all the land in the country. Its pres ent price shall be received by the owner, but all increases in value resulting from reform and social improvements after the revolution shall belong to the state, to be shared by all the people, in order to create a socialist state, where each family within the empire can be well supported, each person satisfied, and no one fail to secure employment.

1. Why did Sun Yat-sen view the Manchus as foreigners?
2. Why did Sun Yat-sen want to end the Chinese monarchy?
3. Reread point number 4. How do you think these ideas would be received in the United States today?

abroad to carry out his national revolution. The other political force was the Chinese Communist Party, formed in Shanghai in the summer of 1921. We shall see the outcome of the rivalry between these political forces in Chapter 27.

Chinese Society in Transition

When European traders began to move into China in greater numbers in the mid-nineteenth century, Chinese society was already in a state of transition. The growth of industry and trade was especially noticeable in the cities, where a national market for such commodities as oil, copper, salt, tea, and porcelain had appeared. The growth of faster and more reliable transportation and a better system of money and banking had begun to create the foundation for a money econ-

omy. New crops brought in from abroad increased food production and aided population growth. The Chinese economy had never been more productive.

The coming of westerners to China affected the Chinese economy in three ways. Westerners introduced modern means of production, transportation, and communications; they created an export market; and they integrated the Chinese market into the nineteenth-century world economy. To some, these changes were beneficial. The shaking of China out of its old ways quickened a process of change that had already begun in Chinese society (see "Young People in China: The New Youth"). This forced the Chinese to adopt new ways of thinking and acting. At the same time, however, China paid a heavy price for the new ways. Its local industry was largely destroyed. Also, many of the profits in the new economy flowed abroad.

RETEACHING ACTIVITY

You may want to take the time to ensure that students fully understand the following key statement from the text on this page: The coming of westerners to China affected the Chinese economy in three ways. (1) Westerners introduced modern means of production, transportation, and communications; (2) they created an export market; (3) they integrated the Chinese market into the nineteenth-century world economy. Ask students to create a visual aid (chart, graph, picture, etc.) that illustrates these three important changes. Or, you may wish to break the class into groups and ask each group to work cooperatively to illustrate one of these changes.

YOUNG PEOPLE IN CHINA

The New Youth

In traditional China, children were thought of not as individuals but as members of a family. Indeed, children were valued because they—especially the sons—would help with the work in the fields, carry on the family name, and care for their parents in old age. However, these attitudes had changed by the beginning of the twentieth century.

Some of the changes were the result of the new educational system. After the government abolished the civil service examinations in 1905, a Confucian education was no longer the key to a successful career. New schools based on the Western model were set up. Especially in the cities, both public and private schools educated a new generation of Chinese who began to have less respect for the past.

By 1915, the attack on the old system and old values by educated youth was intense. The main focus of the attack was the Confucian concept of the family. Young people rejected the old family ideas of respect for elders, of supremacy of men over women, and of the sacrifice of individual needs to the demands of the family.

A spirit of individualism emerged out of the revolt of the youth. Young people now saw themselves as important in and for themselves. Sons no longer had to sacrifice their wishes for the concerns of the larger family. Young people demanded the right to choose their own mates and their own careers.

The new individualism and the revolt of the youth also affected the status of women. Young people now demanded that women have rights

◄ The "new youth" in China adopted some Western customs, including dress. What might a peasant farmer think of this smiling young man?

and opportunities equal to those enjoyed by men. They felt that women no longer should be subject to men.

This criticism by the youth had some beneficial results. During the early republic, the tyranny of the old family system began to decline, at least in the cities. Women sought education and jobs alongside men. Free choice in marriage became commonplace among affluent families in the cities. The teenage children of westernized elites copied the clothing and even the music of young people in Europe and America.

As a rule, these changes did not reach the villages, where traditional attitudes and customs persisted. Arranged marriages continued to be the rule rather than the exception. According to a survey taken in the 1930s, well over two-thirds of marriages, even among urban couples, had been arranged by the parents. In one rural area, only 3 villagers out of 170 had even heard of the idea of "modern marriage," or a marriage in which people freely choose their marriage partners.

1. Compare the old way of life for youths in China with the "new youth."

2. How do the "new youth" compare to the young people in the United States today?

COOPERATIVE LEARNING ACTIVITY

The textbook gives several examples of Western influences on Chinese culture. Divide students into groups of three or four. Assign each group the task of listing examples of Asian influences on American culture (food, technology, manufactured goods, etc.) Bring the groups together and compile a class list.

Or, break students into groups to debate the following proposition. *Resolved: Individu-* *als in the United States today have too many rights. Society as a whole is jeopardized by its inability to control individuals.* Ask the groups to appoint a spokesperson to represent their group and allow each group five minutes to present their response to the proposition. Then ask the class to vote on the proposition as a whole.

YOUNG PEOPLE IN CHINA

CLASS DISCUSSION

Students should be very interested in the issues raised in this feature. The rejection of traditional values and cultures by youth is, of course, not a new or even unusual practice. Comparable situations arose in the United States in the 1940s with the Hispanic American youth forming pachuco gangs as a denial of their traditional Hispanic culture, and in the 1960s with the advent of the Hippie and Yippie cultures. Ask students how the youth culture described in this feature was different from the ones mentioned above. *(Students might suggest that the changes among Chinese youth were restricted to the middle and upper classes and that the changes arose in a culture that had very little previous experience with individualism as a cultural value.)*

Answers to Critical Thinking Questions

1. The old ways included sons working in the fields, carrying on the family name, caring for their parents in old age. Respect for elders, supremacy of men over women, and the sacrifice of individual needs to the demands of the family were commonplace. New ways included a spirit of individualism. Sons no longer sacrificed their wishes for the larger family; young people could choose their own mates and careers. The status of women changed as well. They were no longer considered to be subject to men.

2. Answers will vary.

ASSESS

In the text (page 778) it states that "the 1911 revolution was hardly a revolution." Have students write several paragraphs on what this statement means.

Answers to
SECTION REVIEW

1. (a) worked to bring Western democratic rule to China
   (b) radical groups opposed to the Manchu dynasty
   (c) the Chinese nationalist party
2. (a) revolting against government
3. (a) they could only advise
   (b) a military takeover, a transitional phase, and a constitutional democracy
   (c) It produced no new political and social order.
   (d) China slipped into civil war.
   (e) They introduced modern means of production, created an export market, and integrated the Chinese market into the global economy.
4. (a) Answers will vary but should make reference to the lack of Chinese competition and control.
   (b) Answers will vary.

CLOSE

The conflict between tradition and change is never resolved and seems to be repeated, usually with less intensity than in China, every generation. Ask students how they have experienced or witnessed the conflicts between culture, tradition, and change.

During the first quarter of the twentieth century, the pace of change in China began to quicken. Spurred by World War I, which temporarily drew foreign investment out of the country, Chinese businesspeople began to develop new ventures. Shanghai, Wuhan, Tianjin, and Canton became major industrial and commercial centers with a growing middle class and an industrial working class.

Daily Life

In 1800, daily life for most Chinese was not much different from what it had been for centuries. Most were farmers, living in millions of villages in rice fields and on hillsides throughout the countryside. A farmer's life was governed by the harvest cycle, village custom, and family ritual. Male children, at least the more fortunate ones, were educated in the Confucian classics. Females remained in the home or in the fields. All children were expected to obey their parents, and wives were expected to submit to their husbands.

A visitor to China 125 years later would have seen a different society, although it would have still been recognizably Chinese. The changes were most striking in the cities. Here the educated and wealthy had been visibly affected by the growing Western cultural presence. Confucian social ideals were declining rapidly in influence, and those of Europe and North America were on the rise.

China's Changing Culture

Nowhere was the struggle between traditional and modern more visible than in the field of culture. Radical reformers condemned traditional culture as an instrument of oppression. By eliminating it entirely, they hoped to create a new China that could stand on its feet with dignity in the modern world.

The first changes in traditional culture had actually come in the late nineteenth century. Intellectuals began to introduce Western books, paintings, music, and ideas into China. By the first quarter of the twentieth century, Western culture flooded in as intellectuals called for a new culture based on that of the modern West. During the 1920s and 1930s, Western literature and art became popular in China, especially among the urban middle class. Traditional culture, however, remained popular with the more conservative elements of the population, especially in rural areas.

Literature in particular was influenced by foreign ideas. Western novels and short stories began to attract a larger audience. Although most Chinese novels written after World War I dealt with Chinese subjects, they reflected the Western tendency toward a realistic portrayal of society. Often, they dealt with the new Westernized middle class. Mao Dun's *Midnight,* for example, described the changing customs of Shanghai's urban elites. Ba Jin's famous novel *Family* described the disintegration of the traditional Confucian family (see "Our Literary Heritage: Ba Jin and the Chinese Novel"). Most of China's modern authors showed a clear contempt for the past.

❀ SECTION REVIEW ❀

1. **Identify:**
   (*a*) Sun Yat-sen,   (*b*) Revolutionary Alliance (*Tongmenghui*),   (*c*) Guomindang

2. **Define:**
   (*a*) insurrection

3. **Recall:**
   (*a*) Why didn't new legislative assemblies created in China in 1905 satisfy the need for reform?
   (*b*) What were the three stages that Sun Yat-sen believed were necessary for democracy in China?
   (*c*) Why was the 1911 Chinese revolution hardly a real revolution?
   (*d*) What happened to the government of China after the death of President Yuan Shikai in 1916?
   (*e*) What three ways did Western powers use to affect the Chinese economy during the nineteenth century?

4. **Think Critically:**
   (*a*) How may World War I have helped development of China's production and businesses?
   (*b*) What reasons may explain why many modern Chinese authors show a clear contempt for their country's past?

RETEACHING ACTIVITY

Students have been provided with considerable information in this chapter on the daily lives of both urban and rural Chinese. As a reteaching activity, those students with artistic talent should create a wall mural that depicts a typical scene from either a town or village in China during the first quarter of the twentieth century. Encourage them to add as many details and to be as culturally and historically accurate as possible.

Multimedia Support

TRANSPARENCY
24–1, Timeline of Nineteenth and Early Twentieth Century Chinese and Japanese Events

OUR LITERARY HERITAGE

Ba Jin and the Chinese Novel

Ba Jin was one of China's foremost writers at the turn of the century. Shown with his four brothers and his stepmother, Ba Jin (far right) was well attuned to the rigors and expected obedience of Chinese family life. Do you think he was perceived as a radical by traditionalists in China?

Ba Jin, who was born in 1904, wrote many novels and short stories. In his trilogy—Family, Spring, and Autumn—he described how the younger members of a large family tried to break away from their elders. This passage from Family shows how the old patterns still prevailed in the villages.

Ba Jin, *Family*

Brought up with loving care, after studying with a private tutor for a number of years, Chueh-hsin entered middle school. One of the school's best students, he graduated four years later at the top of his class. He was very interested in physics and chemistry and hoped to go on to a university in Shanghai or Peking, or perhaps study abroad, in Germany. His mind was full of beautiful dreams. At the time he was the envy of his classmates.

In his fourth year at middle school, he lost his mother. His father later married again, this time to a younger woman who had been his mother's cousin. Chueh-hsin was aware of his loss, for he knew full well that nothing could replace the love of a mother. But . . . he was able to console himself with rosy dreams of his future. Moreover, he had someone who understood him and could comfort him—his pretty cousin Mei, "mei" for "plum blossom."

But then, one day, his dreams were shattered, cruelly and bitterly shattered. The evening he

(continued)

OUR LITERARY HERITAGE

CLASS DISCUSSION

This Ba Jin feature on this page relates to "The New Youth" feature on page 781 in that there is an issue of individual's vs. society's rights involved. Ask students who felt that individuals in general have too many rights whether they believe that the rights of the family or society should dictate such individual concerns as choosing a mate or a career. For instance, if a state determines there is a shortage of policemen or doctors, is it within the rights of society to offer huge incentives (such as free schooling, or guaranteed low-interest loans) to people who choose those professions? Does this affect unfairly an individual's choice of careers? Should individuals be required to pass a test on child care or demonstrate minimum standards of behavior before they are issued marriage licenses? Does the state's requirement of a blood test before granting a marriage license interfere with an individual's right or protect society? Point out that family issues are often the same as society's, but on a smaller scale.

On Line with WORLD HISTORY *Internet Activity*

You may want to have your students visit the following URL, where they will find information and additional web site resources to enhance their study of this chapter.

China: History in General
http://darkuring.uoregon.edu/ ~felsing/cstuff/history.html

This site includes a compilation of books all dealing with Chinese history.

Due to the ever-changing nature of the World Wide Web, see the West History web site, **http://history.swpco.com** for regular updates of the URLs in this text.

ANSWERS TO CRITICAL THINKING QUESTIONS

1. Chinese tradition dictated that he follow his father's wishes.
2. The son had, obviously, not communicated his feelings or desires to his father.
3. The father was away from home for years as an official, they probably never had time to develop a relationship.
4. Answers will vary.

Multimedia Support

TRANSPARENCY

24–2, Bar Graph Comparing Populations of India, China, and Japan with Major Imperialist Powers at End of Nineteenth Century

FOCUS

OBJECTIVES

After completing this section, students should be able to

1. list events leading to the fall of the shogunate
2. describe the elements of the new political system
3. discuss how government encouraged the development of new industries
4. explain the influence of Western culture on the Japanese social structure

---

OUR LITERARY HERITAGE

Ba Jin and the Chinese Novel, continued

returned home carrying his diploma, his father called him into his room and said:

"Now that you've graduated, I want to arrange your marriage. Your grandfather is looking forward to having a great-grandson, and I, too, would like to be able to hold a grandson in my arms. You're old enough to be married; I won't feel easy until I fulfill my obligation to find you a wife. Although I didn't accumulate much money in my years away from home as an official, still I've put enough for us to get along on. My health isn't what it used to be; I'm thinking of spending my time at home and having you help me run the household affairs. All the more reason you'll be needing a wife. I've already arranged a match with the Li family. The thirteenth of next month is a good day. We'll announce the engagement then. You can be married within the year."

Chueh-hsin did not utter a word of protest, nor did such a thought ever occur to him. He merely nodded to indicate his compliance with his father's wishes. But after he returned to his own room, and shut the door, he threw himself down on his bed, covered his head with the quilt and wept. He wept for his broken dreams. . . . He did not fight back, he never thought of resisting. He only bemoaned his fate. But he accepted it. He complied with his father's will without a trace of resentment. But in his heart he wept for himself.

---

1. How do you explain the willingness of Chueh-hsin to follow his father's wishes?
2. Why is the father so unaware of his son's desires for the future?
3. Why is there so little communication between these two family members?
4. Are there any practices shown in this selection that are evident in American society?

3

A RICH COUNTRY AND A STRONG STATE: THE RISE OF MODERN JAPAN

By the beginning of the nineteenth century, the Tokugawa shogunate had ruled the Japanese islands for 200 years (see Chapter 18). It had driven out foreign traders and missionaries and isolated the country from virtually all contacts with the outside world. The Tokugawa maintained formal relations only with Korea. Informal trading links with Dutch and Chinese merchants continued at Nagasaki.

Isolation, however, did not mean stagnation. Under Tokugawa rule, Japanese society had begun to undergo deep-seated changes. The changes were social and economic, as well as political. Under the centralized system of the Tokugawa, political power was largely concentrated in the hands of the shogunate in Edo. The *daimyo*, at least in theory, were directly subordinated to the shogunate. In the meantime, during the long period of peace and prosperity, both manufacturing and trade began to emerge and grow. Most Japanese were still farmers, but Japanese society was changing.

The Tokugawa system itself was beginning to come apart. There were signs that the shogunate was becoming less effective. Corruption plagued the central bureaucracy. Unrest, fueled by a series of bad harvests

---

MORE ABOUT . . . Ba Jin and Chinese Censorship

Inform students that Ba Jin, the author of the selection in this feature, wrote under a pseudonym. His real name was Li Fei-Kan, and he was born in 1904. His writing was exalted by the Communist regime after 1949, although he lost favor during the time of the Cultural Revolution (1966–1969).

The title Ba Jin gave to the trilogy (Family, Spring, and Autumn) was "Torrent." Ask students what torrent means and what the choice of that term for his novels must have meant to the author. *(The dictionary defines torrent as a rushing, violent, or abundant and unceasing stream of anything; a violent, tumultuous and overwhelming flow. This imagery might refer to the force of destruction exerted by the family on an individual, or perhaps to the revolutionary forces in China.)*

brought about by poor weather, swept the countryside. Farmers fled to the towns, where anger was already rising as a result of declining agricultural incomes for the samurai. Many of the samurai lashed out at the corruption in the government. In response, the shogunate government attacked its critics and tried to force fleeing peasants to return to their lands. In the meantime, the government intensified its efforts to keep the country isolated from the outside world. It drove away foreign ships that were beginning to prowl along the Japanese coast in increasing numbers.

An End to Isolation

Japan, then, was ripe for change at the beginning of the nineteenth century. To the Western powers, the continued isolation of Japanese society was a challenge. Western nations were convinced that the expansion of trade on a global basis would benefit all nations. They now began to approach Japan in the hope of opening it up to foreign economic interests.

The first foreign power to succeed was the United States. American whalers and clipper ships followed a northern route across the Pacific, but they needed a fueling station before completing their long journey to China and other ports in the area. In the summer of 1853, an American fleet of four warships under Commodore Matthew C. Perry arrived in Edo Bay (now Tokyo Bay), seeking, as Perry said, "to bring a singular and isolated people into the family of civilized nations." Perry brought with him a letter from President Millard Fillmore, in which the president asked for better treatment of sailors shipwrecked on the Japanese islands and the opening of foreign relations between the United States and Japan (see "You Are There: A Letter to the Shogun"). Foreign sailors shipwrecked in Japan were treated as criminals and exhibited in public cages.

A few months later, Perry returned with an even larger fleet for an answer. While he was gone, shogunate officials had discussed the issue. Some argued that contacts with the West would hurt Japan. Others pointed to U.S. military superiority and recommended concessions. For the shogunate in Edo, the big black guns of Commodore Perry's ships proved decisive.

Under military pressure, Japan agreed to the Treaty of Kanagawa with the United States. This provided for the return of shipwrecked American sailors, the opening of two ports, and the establishment of a U.S. consulate in Japan. In 1858, U.S. consul Townsend Harris signed a more detailed treaty. It called for the opening of several new ports to U.S. trade and residence, as well as an exchange of ministers. Similar treaties were soon signed by Japan and several European nations.

The decision to open relations with the Western powers was highly unpopular in some quarters. Resistance was especially strong in two *daimyo* territories in the south, Satsuma and Choshu. Both had strong military traditions, and neither was at first exposed to heavy Western military pressure. In 1863, the Sat-Cho alliance (from Satsuma-Choshu) forced the shogun to promise to bring relations with the West to an end.

The rebellious groups soon showed their own weakness, however. When Choshu troops fired on Western ships in the Strait of Shimonoseki, which led into the Sea of Japan, the westerners fired back and destroyed the Choshu fortifications. The incident convinced the rebellious forces of the need to strengthen their military. They also became more determined not to give in to the West. As a result, Sat-Cho leaders continued to urge the shogun to take a stronger position against the foreigners. These leaders now took the initiative.

The Sat-Cho leaders demanded that the shogun resign and restore the power of the emperor. The reigning shogun agreed to resign in favor of a council composed of *daimyo* lords that would work under the emperor, with the shogun as prime minister. However, this arrangement did not please the leading members of the Sat-Cho faction. In January 1868, their armies attacked the shogun's palace in Kyoto and proclaimed that the authority of the emperor had been restored. After a few weeks, resistance collapsed. The shogunate system had come to an end.

The Meiji Restoration

The Sat-Cho leaders had genuinely mistrusted the West, but they soon realized that Japan must change to survive. The new leaders embarked on a policy of

---

MORE ABOUT . . . *the Chinese Literary Tradition*

The Chinese literary tradition is very old and complex, but one twentieth century change involves writing in the vernacular (usually Mandarin) instead of the classic language "wen-yen," which allows more people to enjoy the novels and poetry of these modern writers. For awhile after the Cultural Revolution, the government of China loosened restrictions on writers, and dissenting authors were able to produce what is called "scar literature" and "literature from the ruins" that paints a realistic and critical picture of Chinese society. Since the student uprising in Tienanmen Square, however, the Chinese bureaucracy has again imposed strict literary censorship.

YOU-ARE-THERE

LEARNING FROM VISUALS

Ask students to comment on the dress of Perry and the Japanese officials. In what ways is the dress code similar? In what ways do the uniforms differ? *(They are both obviously dressed in the formal military style, with full swords and headgear. This is a very official meeting. If students don't comment, point out to them the different styles of swords.)* Ask students what is the likely role of the figure on the far left of the picture. *(He is probably an interpreter.)*

Answers to Critical Thinking Questions

1. President Fillmore wanted to open trade with the Japanese.
2. Fillmore was complimentary, direct, and very persuasive in his letter.
3. Answers will vary.
4. Answers will vary.

ACROSS THE CURRICULUM

Geography. In his letter to the Shogun, President Fillmore states "I am desirous that the two countries should trade with each other, for the benefit of both Japan and the United States." Little did he, or the rest of the world, suspect what that wish would result in. Today, Japan is one of the world's leading trade nations.

From a purely geographical standpoint, Japan has relatively few economic advantages. Ask students to identify geographical features that would work against Japan becoming a world

YOU ARE THERE
A Letter to the Shogun

When U.S. commodore Matthew C. Perry arrived in Tokyo Bay on his first visit to Japan in July 1853, he carried a letter from Millard Fillmore, the president of the United States. This excerpt is from Fillmore's letter.

Letter of President Fillmore to the Emperor of Japan

Millard Fillmore, President of the United States of America, To His Imperial Majesty, The Emperor of Japan. Great and Good Friend! . . .

I have directed Commodore Perry to assure your Imperial Majesty that I entertain the kindest feelings towards your Majesty's person and government; and that I have no other object in sending him to Japan, but to propose to your Imperial

▶ *This Japanese painting records Commodore Perry's arrival in Tokyo Bay in July 1853. Why do you think both Perry and his Japanese hosts are dressed in such formal attire?*

reform that transformed Japan into a modern industrial nation.

The symbol of the new era was the young emperor Mutsuhito (moo-TSOO-HEH-TOE). He called his reign the **Meiji** (Enlightened Rule) and began a remarkable transformation of Japan that has since been known as the Meiji Restoration. Of course, the Meiji ruler was controlled by the new leaders, just as earlier emperors had been controlled by the shogunate. In recognition of the real source of political power, the new capital was located at Edo (now renamed Tokyo, or "Eastern Capital"). The imperial court was moved to the shogun's palace in the center of the city.

The Transformation of Japanese Politics

Once in power, the new leaders launched a comprehensive reform of Japanese political, social, economic, and cultural institutions. They moved first to abolish the old order and to strengthen executive power in their hands. To undercut the power of the *daimyo*, the great lords were stripped of the title to their lands in 1871. As compensation, they were given government bonds and were named governors of the territories formerly under their control (the territories were now called **prefectures**). The members of the *eta*, the traditional slave class, were granted legal equality. The

MORE ABOUT . . . *Western Influences in Japan*

As part of the reforms of the Meiji era the Japanese sent fifty men and women to study Western culture. The Iwakura Mission, as it was known, brought back to Japan ideas about government, industry, and culture. One European idea that had a powerful effect on the Japanese was Herbert Spencer's philosophy of "Social Darwinism." This idea, that people and nations are in constant struggle for the "survival of the fittest," mirrored the Japanese nationalist ideology of *fukoku-hyohei* (wealth and strength). Many of the negative results of the Meiji Restoration (the dehumanization of labor, growth of the military, Japan's expansionist policies) came about as a result of the merger of these similar Western and Japanese philosophies.

YOU ARE THERE

A Letter to the Shogun, continued

Majesty that the United States and Japan should live in friendship, and have commercial intercourse with each other. . . .

The United States of America reach from ocean to ocean, and our territory of Oregon and state of California lie directly opposite to the dominions of your Imperial Majesty. Our steamships can go from California to Japan in eighteen days.

Our great state of California produces about sixty millions of dollars in gold, every year, besides silver, quicksilver, precious stones, and many other valuable articles. Japan is also a rich and fertile country, and produces many very valuable articles. . . . I am desirous that our two countries should trade with each other, for the benefit both of Japan and the United States.

We know that the ancient laws of your Imperial Majesty's government do not allow of foreign trade except with the Dutch. But as the state of the world changes, and new governments are formed, it seems to be wise from time to time to make new

laws. . . . If your Imperial Majesty went so far to change the ancient laws, as to allow a free trade between the two countries, it would be extremely beneficial to both.

1. What did President Fillmore want from the Japanese?

2. Why can his letter be seen as a masterful combination of salesmanship, diplomacy, and firmness?

3. What do you think might have happened if the emperor had said "no" to the president's requests?

4. From the perspective of President Fillmore and others in the United States, the emperor's decision may have looked like an easy one. Explain why this would not have been a simple decision for the emperor.

---

samurai, which made up about 8 percent of the total population, received a lump-sum payment to replace their traditional payments. They were forbidden to wear the sword, the symbol of their hereditary status (see Chapter 18).

The Meiji reformers now set out to create a modern political system based on the Western model. In 1868, the new leaders signed a Charter Oath, in which they promised to create a new legislative assembly within the framework of continued imperial rule. Although senior positions in the new government were given to the *daimyo*, the key posts were held by modernizing leaders from the Sat-Cho clique. The country

was divided into seventy-five prefectures. (The number was reduced to forty-five in 1889 and remains at that number today.)

During the next 20 years, the Meiji government undertook a careful study of Western political systems. A commission under Ito Hirobumi (EE-TOE hir-OH-BOO-MEE) traveled to Great Britain, France, Germany, and the United States to study their governments. As the process evolved, a number of factions appeared, each representing different political ideas within the ruling clique. Most prominent were the Liberals. They wanted political reform on the Western liberal democratic model, with supreme authority vested

---

RETEACHING ACTIVITY

Here is an activity for students when they are near to the end of this section. Go back to the list of characteristics of enlightened rulers that the students developed at the beginning of this section. Have students compare the list to the reforms made by the

Meiji. Ask students to identify areas where the reforms matched their list and areas where they are very different. Overall, do they think the Meiji rulers were trying to produce an enlightened rule? Do the students think the Meiji were successful.

---

power. *(Japan is small, made up of hundreds of mountainous islands scattered over 1500 miles. Japan is lacking in natural resources, especially land and oil, Japan has more forested land than any other industrialized nation. Only 15% of Japan's land is arable. Japan is situated on the Ring of Fire—subject to volcanoes, tsunamis, and earthquakes.)*

Then ask students to identify ways Japan has overcome these geographical obstacles. *(Japanese cities are compact, and lifestyles focus on simplicity. The Japanese diet, for instance, does not include large amounts of meat or milk products because cattle require lots of space and must be fed on grain that requires land to grow. Cultural values have developed that reward cooperation, hard work, and the submission of individualism to the needs of the state. The Japanese concept of kazoku, meaning family or harmony, did not change when Western influences affected other areas of Japanese culture. Japanese fidelity and loyalty to authority helped carry the country through many difficult economic times. Japan's island status has forced it to develop international trade as the mainstay of its economy. The Japanese have borrowed technical, agricultural, and architectural expertise from other nations. When the U.S. helped Japan write its constitution after World War II, it was written that not more than 1 percent of Japan's gross national product could be spent on defense or on the military. This freed up a lot of money for investing in business and technology.)*

CRITICAL THINKING

Inform students that many of the Sat-Cho referred to on this page were members of the samurai class and held traditional values that helped them in the drive to industrialize Japan. Although many of the outward trappings of the samurai (such as the samurai sword) were officially banned, the rules of behavior continued. One samurai founder of a large corporation created the following "corporate guidelines." You might want to write some or all of these on the board and ask students to "translate" them into modern-day terms and to state whether they believe that these are values that operate today in the American corporate climate.

1. Do not be preoccupied with small matters but aim at the management of large enterprises.
2. Once you start an enterprise, be sure to succeed.
3. Do not engage in speculative enterprises.
4. Operate all enterprises with the national interest in mind.
5. Never forget the pure spirit of public service and *makoto* (sincerity and fidelity).
6. Be hardworking, frugal, and thoughtful.
7. Utilize proper personnel.
8. Treat your employees well.
9. Be bold in starting an enterprise, but meticulous in its prosecution.

in the parliament as the representative of the people. The Progressives called for a sharing of power between the legislative and executive branches, although with more power for the executive branch. There was also an imperial party that wanted to keep supreme authority in the hands of the emperor.

During the 1870s and 1880s, these factions fought for control. In the end, the Progressives won. The Meiji Constitution, which was adopted in 1890, vested authority in the executive branch. In theory the emperor exercised all executive authority, but in practice he was a figurehead. Real executive authority rested in the hands of a prime minister and his cabinet of ministers, who were handpicked by the Meiji leaders. The upper house of the parliament was to be appointed and have equal legislative powers with the lower house, whose members were to be elected. An interesting feature of the new constitution was that although the **Diet** (the legislature) had the power to appropriate funds, if no agreement was reached, the budget would remain the same as in the previous year. This allowed the executive branch to remain in control.

The final result was a political system that was democratic in form but authoritarian in practice. Although modern in external appearance, it was still traditional, because power remained in the hands of a ruling oligarchy (the Sat-Cho leaders). Although a new set of institutions and values had emerged, the system allowed the traditional ruling class to keep its influence and economic power.

Meiji Economics

With the end of the *daimyo* system, a new system of land ownership came to Japan. A land reform program made the traditional lands of the *daimyo* into the private property of the peasants. The *daimyo* were then compensated with government bonds. One reason for the new policy was that the government needed a regular source of income. To get it, the Meiji leaders levied a new land tax, which was set at an annual rate of 3 percent of the estimated value of the land.

The new tax was an excellent source of revenue for the government. However, it was quite burdensome for

the farmers. Under the old system, farmers had paid a fixed percentage of their harvest to the landowners. In bad harvest years, they had owed little or nothing. Under the new system, the farmers had to pay the land tax every year, regardless of the quality of the harvest. As a result, in bad years, many peasants were unable to pay their taxes. This forced them to sell their lands to wealthy neighbors and become tenant farmers who paid rent to the new owners. By the end of the century, about 40 percent of all farmers were tenants.

With its budget needs met by the land tax, the government turned to the promotion of industry. The chief goal of the reformers was to create a "rich country and a strong state" in order to guarantee Japan's survival against the challenge of Western nations. In a broad sense, the reformers copied the process of industrial development followed by the nations of western Europe. They had an advantage, however, because a small but growing industrial economy already existed. By 1700, for example, manufacturing centers had already developed in Japan's growing cities, such as Tokyo, Kyoto, and Osaka.

Japan's industrial revolution received massive help from the Meiji Restoration. The government gave subsidies to needy industries, provided training and foreign advisors, improved transportation and communications, and started a new educational system that stressed applied science. In contrast to China, Japan was able to achieve results with little reliance on money from abroad. Although the first railroad—built in 1872—was financed by a loan from Great Britain, future projects were all paid for by local funds (primarily the land tax paid by peasants).

By 1900, Japan's industrial sector was beginning to grow. Besides tea and silk, other key industries were weapons, shipbuilding, and sake (SAWK-ee) (Japanese rice wine). From the start, the unique feature of the Meiji model was the close relationship between government and private business. The government encouraged the development of new industries by providing businesspeople with money and privileges. Once an individual enterprise or industry was on its feet, it was turned over entirely to private ownership. Even then, however, the government continued to play some role.

ENRICHMENT ACTIVITY

Have students identify the primary and secondary causes of the Meiji Restoration. Using the historical skills of analyzing information and drawing inferences, students should predict how Chinese history would have been different if they had undergone a similar restoration.

◄ *Workers at this silk mill at Tomioka (photo at left) were mostly women. What resemblance do you see between this mill and the cotton mills in England and the United States?*

The Meiji leaders were determined to improve Japan's military equipment. In photo at right schoolchildren are watching while a naval officer discusses one of the country's new warships.

LEARNING FROM VISUALS

Ask students to examine the drawing of the silk factory. After they describe the scene ask them to identify some contrasts between traditional and modern elements. For instance, the building resembles a factory that might be seen in the early 1900s in the United States, but the women are dressed in their traditional kimonos.

Answer to the caption question: There is little difference between the conditions in the mills. However, no children are shown working in this silk-spinning mill, but they were commonly portrayed in pictures of cotton mills.

The Meiji reforms had a negative impact on rural areas. The new land tax provided the government with funds to subsidize the industrial sector, but it imposed severe hardships on farmers. Many abandoned their farms and fled to the cities in search of jobs. This influx of people, in turn, benefited Japanese industry by providing an abundant source of cheap labor.

Building a Modern Social Structure

The Meiji reformers also transformed other institutions. A key focus of their attention was the army. The Sat-Cho reformers were well aware of the need for a modern military force if they were to compete with the Western powers. Their motto was "Strengthen the Army." A new imperial army based on compulsory military service was formed in 1871. All Japanese men now served for three years. Before, only samurai could carry weapons and be warriors. The new army was well equipped with modern weapons.

Education also changed. The Meiji leaders realized the need for universal education, including instruction in modern technology. A new ministry of education, established in 1871, guided the changes. After a few years of experimentation, it adopted the American model of elementary schools, secondary schools, and universities. In the meantime, it sent bright students to study abroad and brought foreign specialists to Japan to teach in the new schools. Much of the content of the new system was Western in inspiration. However, a great deal of emphasis was still placed on the virtues of loyalty to the family and community. Loyalty to the emperor was especially valued. Both teachers and students were required to bow before a portrait of the emperor each day. In 1890, all students were told, "Should emergency arise, offer yourself courageously to the State; and thus guard and maintain the prosperity of our Imperial Throne."

Daily Life and Women's Rights

Japanese society in the late Tokugawa Era, before the Meiji reforms, could be described by two words: *community* and *hierarchy.* The lives of all Japanese people

COMPARING TIME PERIODS

Life for factory workers in Japan was just as bad as it was in Europe during the early stages of the Industrial Revolution. Twelve-hour shifts in factories meant manufactured goods around the clock. Many teenage women were hired as low-paid workers in textile factories. Low wages for workers produced high profits for factory owners. Crowded slums sprang up near factory districts just as they did in cities in Europe and the United States. However, most citizens accepted the belief that personal sacrifice was necessary to make Japan a more powerful industrial nation.

So What ⁇

*If your students question the importance of the information on **Meiji Restoration,** tell them . . .*

Japan's modernization movement thrust it into the modern era. This movement eventually resulted in Japan's position of economic dominance as we enter the twenty-first century. Ask students to list as many ways as possible in which Japan's economic capabilities have impacted the students' lives either directly or indirectly.

LEARNING FROM VISUALS

During the time of the Meiji Restoration there was a conscious effort made to imitate Western culture. This process was called by the government "civilization and enlightenment." Western culture, from current intellectual trends to clothing and architecture, were widely promoted. Ask students to discuss how the images on this page reflect Western culture. *(Western dress, hairstyles, musical instruments, staging of the choir, use of the piano, the chandeliers, etc.)*

CRITICAL THINKING

The text discusses the Japanese concept of the three obediences: child to father, wife to husband, and widow to son. Ask students to each write their own concept of three obediences. For instance, a student might write: child to parent, friend to friend, citizen to government, or employee to employer. Afterwards, ask volunteers to share their obediences with the class. This activity should lead to some lively discussion of cultural values. Some artistic students may even wish to illustrate the older Japanese obediences and some of the class examples.

▲ *In addition to the Tokyo School of Fine Arts, a music school was begun. At this 1889 recital, the musicians wore Western clothing and played Western music.*

were determined by their membership in a family, village, and social class. At the same time, Japanese society was highly hierarchical. Belonging to a particular social class determined a person's occupation and social relationships with others. Women were especially limited by the "three obediences": child to father, wife to husband, and widow to son. Whereas husbands could easily obtain a divorce, wives could not. Marriages were arranged, and the average marital age of females was sixteen years. Females did not share inheritance rights with males. Few received any education outside the family.

The Meiji Restoration had a marked effect on the traditional social system in Japan. Special privileges for the aristocracy were abolished. For the first time, women were allowed to get an education. As the economy shifted from an agricultural to an industrial base, thousands of Japanese began to get new jobs and establish new social relationships. Western fashions became the rage in elite circles. The ministers of the first Meiji government were known as the "dancing cabinet" because of their addiction to Western-style ballroom dancing. Young people were increasingly influenced by Western culture and values. A new generation of modern boys and girls began to imitate the clothing styles, eating habits, hairstyles, and social practices of European and American young people. Baseball was imported from the United States.

The social changes brought about by the Meiji Restoration also had a less attractive side. Many commoners were ruthlessly exploited in the coal mines and textile mills in the interest of building a "rich country and a strong state." One Japanese official of the time remarked that farmers "are the fertilizer of the nation." Workers labored up to 20 hours a day, often in conditions of incredible hardship. Coal miners who were employed on a small island in the harbor of Nagasaki worked naked in temperatures up to 130 degrees Fahrenheit. When they tried to escape, they were shot.

Popular resistance to such conditions was not unknown. In many areas, villagers were actively

MORE ABOUT . . . *Meiji Baseball*

Before the Meiji Restoration in 1868 the Japanese did not play sports for entertainment. In fact, they had no word for sport, the closest being *undoh,* which means exercise. In 1871 an American named Horace Wilson came to the Tokyo Kaisei School. Within two years he had the students playing baseball. By 1878 Hiroshi Hiraoka formed the first organized baseball team, the Shimbashi Athletic Club Athletics. While in the United States, Hiraoka had become a Boston Red Sox fan and wanted to transplant the American sport to his native country. Today baseball is as popular in Japan as it is in the U.S.

involved in the search for a new political culture. In some cases they demanded increased attention to human rights. Women took part in this process and formed a "Freedom and People's Rights Movement." This movement was demanding voting rights for women as early as 1876.

The transformation of Japan into a "modern society" did not detach the country entirely from its old values, however. Traditional values based on loyalty to the family and community was still an important subject in the new schools. Traditional values were also given a firm legal basis in the Constitution of 1890, which limited the right to vote to men. The Civil Code of 1898 played down individual rights and placed women within the context of their family role.

 SECTION REVIEW

1. **Locate:**
   (a) Nagasaki,   (b) Edo,   (c) Kyoto

2. **Define:**
   (a) Meiji,   (b) prefectures,   (c) Diet

3. **Identify:**
   (a) Matthew C. Perry,   (b) Treaty of Kanagawa,
   (c) Sat-Cho alliance,   (d) Meiji Restoration,
   (e) Charter Oath,   (f) Meiji Constitution,
   (g) three obediences

4. **Recall:**
   (a) Why didn't isolation necessarily mean stagnation in Japan before 1858?
   (b) How did Japan plan its new government during the Meiji Restoration?
   (c) What differences were there between Liberals and Progressives in the Japanese political system of the 1880s?
   (d) How did the Meiji government obtain most of the money it needed?
   (e) What types of help did the Meiji government provide to the process of industrialization?

5. **Think Critically:** Why does the development of a nation's military power often increase the speed and strength of that nation's industrial growth? Use Japan's experience as an example.

IMPERIALISM AND THE MOVE TOWARD DEMOCRACY

The Japanese did not just imitate the domestic policies of their Western teachers. They also copied the Western approach to foreign affairs. This is perhaps not surprising. The Japanese saw themselves as vulnerable in the world economic arena. Their territory was small, lacking in resources, and densely populated. They had no natural room for expansion. To some Japanese, the lessons of history were clear. Western nations had amassed wealth and power not only because of their democratic and economic systems and high level of education but also because of their colonies. Colonies had provided the Western powers with sources of raw materials, inexpensive labor, and markets for their manufactured products.

Joining the Imperialist Nations

Traditionally, Japan had not been an expansionist country. In other words, the Japanese had generally been satisfied to remain on their home islands. They had even deliberately isolated themselves from their neighbors during the Tokugawa Era.

The Japanese began their program of territorial expansion close to home. In 1874, Japan claimed control of the Ryukyu (ree-YOO-KYOO) Islands, which had long been subject to the Chinese Empire. Two years later, Japan's navy forced the Koreans to open their ports to Japanese trade. During the 1880s, Chinese-Japanese rivalry over Korea intensified. In 1894, the two nations went to war. Japanese ships destroyed the Chinese fleet and seized the Manchurian city of Port Arthur. In the Treaty of Shimonoseki (SHIM-uh-noe-SEK-ee), the Manchu rulers of China recognized the independence of Korea. They also ceded Taiwan and the Liaodong peninsula, with its strategic naval base at Port Arthur, to Japan.

So What ??

*If your students question the importance of the information on **Japanese imperialism**, tell them . . .*

Japanese expansionist policies culminated in their conflict with the United States in World War II. Most students should be able to describe a connection from World War II to some member of their family. Ask students to question parents and grandparents about the ways in which World War II affected the family. Challenge students to explain to their family members the history behind the Japanese attacking the U.S.

ASSESS

Have students write a single paragraph summarizing what they feel are the most significant changes implemented by the Meiji Restoration.

Answers to
SECTION REVIEW

2. (a) enlightened rule
   (b) territories governed by the former *daimyo*
   (c) Japanese legislature
3. (a) American commodore who "opened" Japan
   (b) agreement that opened several of Japan's ports to trade
   (c) anti-Western group
   (d) period when Japan adopted Western ways
   (e) promise to continue the imperial rule in Japan
   (f) constitution that gave more power to the executive branch
   (g) child to father, wife to husband, and widow to son
4. (a) There were changes taking place in Japan's society and economic system.
   (b) It sent representatives to many Western nations to study their political systems.
   (c) Liberals wanted Western style democracy while Progressives called for a sharing of power between the legislative and executive branch, but with more power held by the executive.
   (d) taxes on peasant farmers
   (e) subsidies, training, and foreign advisors
5. Answers will vary.

FOCUS

OBJECTIVES

After completing this section, students should be able to

1. trace the path of Japanese expansion in the early twentieth century
2. describe the impact of democracy on the Japanese political system
3. explain the relationship between imperialism and raw materials

FOCUS ACTIVITY

To reinforce geographic and population problems in Japan, try the following demonstration. Let one student represent eight million people. Put five chairs in the front of the room and have four students sit in the chairs, leaving one empty. Tell students that this represents the population and area of the state of California (32 million people). The empty chair represents unpopulated land. Point out that although it is fairly crowded, there is still room for growth. Now call up an additional twelve students so that the population of Japan (approximately 126 million) is represented. Spread out the five chairs to represent the archipelago of Japan. Tell the sixteen students that they must arrange to sit on only 2 of the chairs since 3/5 of Japan's land is uninhabitable, being highly mountainous. They should soon realize that harmony, cooperation, and tolerance were absolute essential characteristics of this small but populous society.

Shortly thereafter, under pressure from the European powers, the Japanese returned the Liaodong peninsula to China. In the early twentieth century, however, the Japanese returned to the offensive. Rivalry with Russia over influence in Korea had led to increasingly strained relations between Japan and Russia. The Russians thought little of the Japanese and even welcomed the possibility of war. Tsar Nicholas II called Japanese diplomats "monkeys." One advisor to the tsar said, "We will only have to throw our caps at them and they will run away."

In 1904, Japan launched a surprise attack on the Russian naval base at Port Arthur, which Russia had taken from China in 1898. When Japanese forces moved into Manchuria and the Liaodong peninsula, Russian troops proved to be no match for them. The Russian commander in chief said, "It is impossible not to admire the bravery and activity of the Japanese. The attack of the Japanese is a continuous succession of waves, and they never relax their efforts by day or by night." In the meantime, Russia had sent its Baltic fleet halfway around the world to East Asia, only to be defeated by the new Japanese navy at Tsushima (tsoo-SHEE-muh) Strait, off the coast of Japan. After their defeat, the Russians agreed to a humiliating peace in 1905. They gave the Liaodong peninsula back to Japan, as well as southern Sakhalin (SACK-uh-LEEN) and the Kurile (CURE-EEL) Islands. Russia also agreed to abandon its political and economic influence in Korea and southern Manchuria, which now came increasingly under Japanese control. The Japanese victory stunned the world. Japan had become one of the Great Powers. The colonial peoples of Southeast Asia began to realize that the West was not unbeatable.

During the next few years, the Japanese consolidated their position in northeastern Asia, annexing Korea in 1908 as a part of Japan. When the Koreans protested, the harsh Japanese response caused thousands of deaths. The United States was the first nation to recognize Japan's annexation of Korea. In return, the United States asked for Japan's declaration of respect for American authority in the Philippines. In 1908, the two countries reached an agreement in which the United States recognized Japanese interests in the region in return for Japanese acceptance of the princi-

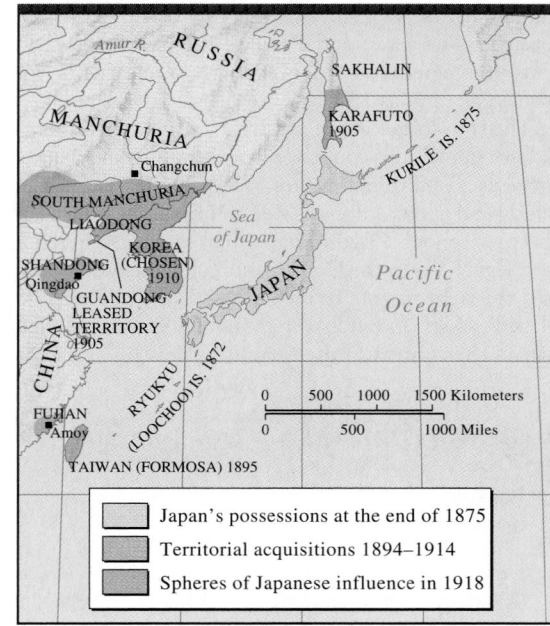

Map 24.4   Japanese Overseas Expansion During the Meiji Era

ples of the Open Door policy in China. However, mutual suspicion between the two countries was growing, sparked in part by U.S. efforts to restrict immigration from all Asian countries. President Theodore Roosevelt's "gentlemen's agreement" with Japan in 1905 resulted in a virtual halt in Japanese immigration to the United States. Moreover, the Japanese were still angry over the way Roosevelt had negotiated the Russo-Japanese peace in 1905. In turn, some Americans began to fear the rise of Japanese power in East Asia.

Experiment in Democracy

During the first two decades of the twentieth century, Japan made remarkable progress toward the creation of an advanced society on the Western model. The economic and social reforms launched during the Meiji Era led to increasing prosperity and the development of a modern industrial and commercial sector. Many

STUDYING MAPS

The following questions and activities will help you guide the students through their study of Map 24.4.

1. Ask students to name those countries and regions that Japan acquired from 1894 to 1914. (Korea, Formosa, Karafuto)

2. Ask students to name the territorial acquisitions from 1915 to 1918. (South Manchuria, Shandong, Liaodong)

帝國艦隊旅順攻撃

▲ *The Japanese surprise attack on Port Arthur was a stunning defeat for the Russians, and it symbolized the growing power of the Japanese military forces.*

believed that Japan was on the road to becoming a full-fledged democracy.

Between 1900 and 1925, the Japanese political system appeared to be moving toward the Western democratic model. Political parties expanded their popular following and became increasingly competitive. Universal male suffrage was instituted in 1925. An independent press and a bill of rights also appeared.

The influence of the old ruling oligarchy, however, still remained strong. Moreover, social turmoil was increasing. Two opposing forces arose to challenge the growth toward democracy. On the left, a Marxist labor movement began to take shape in the early 1920s. It was a response to the increasing unrest among the urban and rural poor. On the right, ultranationalist groups called for a rejection of Western models of development and a more forceful approach to realizing national objectives. The radical nationalist Kita Ikki called for a military takeover and the establishment of

a new system similar to Nazism in Germany (see Chapter 26).

A Zaibatsu Economy

Japan also continued to make impressive progress in economic development. Industrial production increased twelvefold between 1900 and 1930. Much of the increase went into the export market, which caused Western manufacturers to complain about the rising competition for markets from the Japanese.

One characteristic of the Meiji economic model was the concentration of various manufacturing processes within a single enterprise—the so-called **zaibatsu,** or large financial and industrial corporation. These firms gradually developed, often with government help, into vast companies that controlled a major segment of the Japanese industrial sector. By 1937, the four largest zaibatsu (Mitsui, Mitsubishi, Sumitomo, and Yasuda)

MORE ABOUT . . . *the Russo-Japanese War*

Students should realize that the United States had played the diplomatic role very early in its history. The text on the facing page discusses Theodore Roosevelt's role in negotiating the peace at Port Arthur, which ended the Russo-Japanese War. Students should be interested in learning that for this service, Theodore "Rough Rider" Roosevelt

was awarded the Nobel Peace Prize—the first American to ever win that prize. It should also be noted that neither Russia nor Japan were grateful for Roosevelt's efforts. Both countries felt they had received the worst end of the deal and bore a grudge against the United States because of it.

TEACH

CRITICAL THINKING

The concept of the *zaibatsu* might be more easily understood if a parallel is drawn between the *zaibatsu* and the growth of the oil industry in the United States under John D. Rockefeller. Standard Oil gathered smaller oil companies under its management and then concentrated on controlling the companies that provided processing and distribution services. The end result was one giant corporation controlling the vast majority of the market. Unlike in the United States, however, the Japanese government did not try to control the growth of these monopolies or regulate them. In Japan, business and government worked toward a common goal.

CLASS DISCUSSION

Before beginning the section on Shidehara Diplomacy, ask students what would be the inevitable result of Japanese expansion in an area of Western imperialism. Why would the United States fear Japanese expansion into China? *(Remind students about the ever growing American interest in China as a potential market for U.S. goods.)* Also, although the Open Door Policy was created to protect China from Western and Japanese aggression, the policy had had a very negative effect on the Chinese themselves. Ask students why China resented U.S. attempts to guarantee their territorial integrity. *(The Chinese were more than a little suspicious of the motives of the U.S. intervening in what they considered their internal affairs. From the Chinese perspective, the Open Door Policy was an imperialistic call for expanded trade within the existing system for major power spheres of influence.)*

ACROSS THE CURRICULUM

Sociology To illustrate the degree that prejudice and racism affected the climate of world affairs, remind students that the Japanese in America had already suffered discrimination before World War I. Reaction to a wave of Japanese immigration in the late 1890s and early 1900s, Californians had in 1905, organized a Japanese and Korean Exclusion League with the aim of combating the "Japanese menace." In 1906, a San Francisco school board assigned all Asian students to one segregated school. The Japanese government officially protested this intended slur to the government. Regardless of Theodore Roosevelt's private opinion, he knew that the U.S. could not afford to offend Japan. He again played the role of negotiator and fashioned an agreement whereby San Francisco retracted the segregation order in exchange for a promise from Japan to limit immigration of farmers and worders to the U.S. and to Hawaii.

ASSESS

To reinforce the connections between different events and developments, have students make a table showing the major developments described in this section. The table will have five columns, labeled "EXPANSION," "POLITICAL," "ECONOMIC," "DIPLOMATIC," and "CULTURAL." On the right side of the table students are to construct a time line from 1875 to 1925, marked in five-year increments. Students will fill in each column with events that

controlled 21 percent of the banking industry, 26 percent of mining, 35 percent of shipbuilding, and over 60 percent of paper manufacturing and insurance.

The concentration of wealth led to growing economic inequalities. As we have seen, economic growth had been achieved at the expense of the peasants, many of whom fled to the cities to escape rural poverty. Those left on the farms continued to suffer. The labor surplus in the city benefited industry, but city workers were still poorly paid and housed. Rampant inflation in food prices led to food riots shortly after World War I. A rapid increase in population led to food shortages and the threat of rising unemployment. (The total population of the Japanese islands increased from an estimated 43 million in 1900 to 73 million in 1940.)

Shidehara Diplomacy

In the early twentieth century, Japanese leaders began to have difficulty finding sources of raw materials and foreign markets for the nation's manufactured goods. Until World War I, Japan had dealt with the problem by seizing territories—such as Formosa, Korea, and southern Manchuria—and making them part of the growing Japanese Empire. That policy had succeeded brilliantly. However, it had also begun to arouse the concern of the Western nations. China was also becoming suspicious of Japanese intentions.

The United States was especially worried about Japanese aggressiveness. The United States had a strong interest in keeping Asia open for U.S. trading activities. In 1922, in Washington, D.C., the United States held a major conference of nations with interests in the Pacific. The major accomplishment of this Washington Conference was a nine-power treaty that recognized the territorial integrity of China and the maintenance of the Open Door policy. Japan accepted the provisions when the other nations recognized its special position in Manchuria.

During the remainder of the 1920s, the Japanese government tried to play by the rules laid down by the Washington Conference. Known as "Shidehara (SHEE-duh-HAW-rah) diplomacy" from the name of the foreign minister (and later prime minister) who tried to carry it out, this policy sought to use diplomatic and

economic means to realize Japanese interests in Asia. However, this approach came under severe pressure. Japanese industrialists began to move into new areas, such as heavy industry, chemicals, mining, and the manufacturing of appliances and automobiles. These industries desperately needed resources not found in abundance in Japan. The Japanese government came under increasing pressure to find new sources of resources abroad. All too soon, the Japanese would begin to follow a more aggressive approach to solve this problem.

Japanese Culture in an Era of Transition

The wave of Western technology and ideas that entered Japan in the last half of the nineteenth century greatly altered the shape of traditional Japanese culture. Literature was especially affected as European models became popular. Dazzled by this "new" literature, Japanese authors began translating and imitating the imported models.

The novel showed the greatest degree of change. One form that became popular was the naturalistic novel, patterned on the French tradition of Émile Zola. Naturalist Japanese authors tried to present society, the human condition, and the realities of war as objectively as possible.

Japanese victories over China and Russia sparked a great age of creativity in the early twentieth century. Japanese writers wrote novels filled with nostalgia for the old Japan. A well-known example is Junichiro Tanizaki's *Some Prefer Nettles*, published in 1928.

Other aspects of Japanese culture were also affected by the social upheaval that marked the Meiji Restoration. The Japanese invited technicians, engineers, architects, and artists from Europe and the United States to teach their "modern" skills to eager Japanese students. The Meiji Era was a time when the Japanese copied Western artistic techniques and styles. Huge buildings of steel and reinforced concrete, adorned with Greek columns, appeared in many Japanese cities.

A national reaction set in by the end of the nineteenth century, however. Many Japanese artists began to return to older techniques. In 1889, the Tokyo School of Fine Arts was set up to promote traditional

Japanese art. Japanese artists searched for a new but truly Japanese means of expression. Some artists tried to bring together native and foreign techniques. Others returned to past artistic traditions for inspiration.

Cultural exchange also went the other way. Japanese arts and crafts, porcelains, textiles, fans, folding screens, and woodblock prints became fashionable in Europe and North America. Japanese art influenced Western painters. Japanese gardens, with their close attention to the positioning of rocks and falling water, became especially popular in the United States.

 SECTION REVIEW

1. **Locate:**
   (a) Manchuria,   (b) Port Arthur

2. **Define:**
   (a) zaibatsu

3. **Identify:**
   (a) Treaty of Shimonoseki,   (b) gentlemen's agreement,   (c) Shidehara diplomacy,
   (d) *Some Prefer Nettles*

4. **Recall:**
   (a) Why did many Japanese regard their nation as vulnerable in the world economic arena in the late nineteenth century?
   (b) What impact did Japan's defeat of Russia in 1905 have on other European powers in the Far East?
   (c) What situations led to social dissatisfaction and unrest in Japan during the period from 1900 to 1940?

5. **Think Critically:**
   (a) Why didn't the economic development of Japan in the early part of the twentieth century necessarily mean that country would have democracy and social stability?
   (b) Why may the Japanese have been particularly attracted to art forms that were purely Japanese?

Conclusion

Few areas of the world resisted the Western advances as stubbornly and effectively as East Asia. Although military, political, and economic pressures by the European powers were intense during this era, both China and Japan were able to retain their independence. No doubt, one reason was that both had a long history as well-defined states with a strong sense of national community. Geography, too, was in their favor. As a continental nation, China was able to survive partly because of its sheer size. Japan possessed the advantage of an island location.

Even more striking, however, is the different way each state tried to deal with the challenge. The Japanese were practical. They borrowed foreign ideas and institutions that appeared to be of value and at the same time not in conflict with traditional attitudes and customs. China agonized over the issue for half a century. Conservative elements fought a desperate battle to keep intact most of China's traditional heritage.

No doubt the Japanese approach was more effective. Japan made an orderly transition from a traditional to an advanced society. In China, the old system collapsed in disorder. However, the Japanese experiment was by no means a complete success. Ambitious efforts by Japanese leaders to carve out a share in the spoils of the empire led to conflict with China and rival Western powers. Meanwhile in Europe, old rivalries were leading to a bitter conflict that eventually engulfed the entire world.

Notes

1. Quoted in Ssu-yu Teng and John K. Fairbank, eds., *China's Response to the West: A Documentary Survey, 1839–1923* (New York, 1970), p. 140.
2. Quoted in William Theodore de Bary et al., eds., *Sources of Chinese Tradition* (New York, 1963), p. 472.

occurred at specific times or developments that occurred over a period of time.

Answers to SECTION REVIEW

2. (a) large Japanese financial and industrial corporations
3. (a) agreement with China giving Japan the Liaodong peninsula and Taiwan
   (b) agreement whereby Japan slowed emigration of its citizens to the U.S.
   (c) diplomatic pursuit of Japan's goals
   (d) novel written in 1928 by Junichiro Tanizaki
4. (a) Japan was small, lacked many resources and colonies, had little space for expansion.
   (b) They realized European powers were not unbeatable.
   (c) unequal distribution of wealth and income, poor pay and housing, inflation, population growth, food shortages and an apparently insensitive government
5. (a) Answers will vary.
   (b) Answers will vary.

CLOSE

The reform efforts in Japan produced dramatic changes but didn't provide security or stability. Facilitate a class discussion on specific changes and developments in Japan that contributed to instability in the Japanese social and economic system. Call on different students until everybody has had a chance to participate.

SPECIAL NEEDS: *Visual/Auditory*

Have students prepare a visual display of the different Asian countries studied in this chapter during the period from 1800 to 1914. The display may include typical dress, maps, lists of the Japanese colonies, pictures of the Manchu dynasty, Chinese and Japanese products, pictures of daily life, farmers, villages, rice fields, etc. Have the students present their display to the class. Encourage them to look through their homes and find products made in Japan or China. Have them share some of these items with the class. You might wish to play Japanese music during the presentations.

USING KEY TERMS

1. extraterritoriality
2. Meiji
3. zaibatsu
4. spheres of influence
5. self-strengthening
6. prefectures
7. Diet
8. insurrection
9. indemnity

REVIEWING THE FACTS

1. created demand from addicts from which they earned a profit and weakened Chinese society
2. Initiated by the United States, it stated that all nations should be able to trade in China on an equal basis.
3. China was forced to give up additional land and trading rights.
4. It was formed to oppose the Manchu Dynasty in China.
5. the Chinese nationalist party formed by Sun Yat-sen
6. Many groups sought power resulting in a period of general chaos and lack of governmental leadership.
7. He persuaded Japan to open its ports to foreign trade with all nations.
8. to return Japan to its former closed society
9. gave Japan the Liaodong peninsula and Taiwan
10. Japan possessed few natural resources and wanted foreign territories to supply goods to Japan's industries.

CHAPTER 24 REVIEW

USING KEY TERMS

1. A practice in which European colonial power enforced their own laws for their subjects living in Chinese ports was called ——————.
2. Emperor Musuhito of Japan used the term —————— to describe the time of his rule.
3. A —————— is a large financial and industrial business combination in Japan.
4. —————— were areas in China where a particular foreign nation was given exclusive trading rights.
5. The Chinese policy of adopting Western technology while keeping its Confucian values was called ——————
6. Territories given to Japan's lords to govern after 1871 were called ——————.
7. The —————— of the Meiji government had the power to appropriate funds.
8. The act of revolting against an established government is an ——————.
9. The Chinese government was forced to pay a heavy ——————, or payment, to the powers that had crushed the Boxer Rebellion.

REVIEWING THE FACTS

1. How did the British use opium to strengthen their economic and political position in China?
2. What was the Open Door policy?
3. What was the result of the Boxer Rebellion?
4. What was the purpose of the Revolutionary Alliance that was formed under the leadership of Sun Yat-sen?
5. What was the Guomindang?
6. Why did China experience a period of civil war after the death of President Yuan Shikai?
7. What did Matthew Perry achieve in Japan in 1858?
8. What was the goal of the Sat-Cho alliance?
9. What was the result of the Treaty of Shimonoseki?

796

10. Why did Japan feel it needed to gain foreign territories to become an economic success and a military power?

THINKING CRITICALLY

1. Why did European powers choose to establish spheres of influence in China rather than just trading with the Chinese as they did with many other nations?
2. What reasons may explain why the Chinese were not able to successfully resist domination by foreign powers?
3. Why didn't European colonial powers fight each other in China for control over that country's trade?
4. Why do many people believe Sun Yat-sen's three stages for creating democracy were really just a way for him to gain and retain power?
5. What benefits may China have received as a result of its domination by European colonial powers?
6. Why can the influence of western politics, economics, and technology be found in the changes that took place in Japan during the late nineteenth century?
7. Why were many Japanese farmers opposed to the tax policies of the Meiji government?
8. What social conventions caused men to dominate Japanese society?
9. Why was it necessary for Japan to emphasize the construction of a strong navy as it increased its military power?
10. Why didn't the growth of production lead to improved living conditions for most of Japan's people in the early twentieth century?

THINKING CRITICALLY

1. Answers will vary; by setting the rules they were able to get a better deal.
2. A lack of unity within China made it easier for European powers to dominate them. The inefficiencies and corruption of the Chinese government also contributed.
3. The results could have weakened each other's grip on China, lost money from trade, and the great expense to carry out a war so far from their homelands made it too risky.
4. The military take over provided a justification for his domination through force.

5. It acquired new technologies and skills from the Europeans that it used to its own advantage.
6. Japan adapted the technology, economic and political systems of the West.
7. Farmers paid very high taxes to support the government.
8. Children, wives, and widows obeyed the male leader of their families.
9. As an island nation it needed a strong navy to defend itself and impose its will on other lands.
10. Production was not evenly distributed, and used to create a large military and investment in industry.

CHAPTER 24 REVIEW

APPLYING SOCIAL STUDIES SKILLS

1. **Government:** Explain why any political system that automatically passes power from one generation to the next within one family is almost certain to decline over time. Use the experience of China during the nineteenth century as an example.
2. **Economics:** Explain why the economic interests of European colonial powers would not have been served by fighting a war in the Far East.
3. **Geography:** Explain why control of the Malay peninsula and the archipelago of present-day Indonesia was vital to the success of European trade with China but of little importance to the United States.
4. **Geography:** Study Map 24.2 on page 775 that shows the spheres of influence that existed in the Far East. Explain why it would have been foolish for European powers to try to occupy and dominate all of China instead of only taking over areas surrounding major port cities.
5. **Sociology:** Describe social values and frustrations that probably led to the Boxer Rebellion in China and to the Sat-Cho alliance in Japan.
6. **Government:** Explain how Japanese loyalty to the Emperor was apparently used by some people to serve their own interests and gain power.
7. **Economics:** Why was the tax on farm land in Japan really a tax on consumers in that nation as well?

MAKING TIME AND PLACE CONNECTIONS

1. Compare the experiences of people who lived in Britain's American colonies during the 1700s with those of native peoples who lived in European spheres of influence in China in the late nineteenth century.

2. Identify and explain possible reasons why parts of China were occupied and exploited by European powers while Japan was not.
3. Explain why China's vast size and many different people may have made it easier for European powers to dominate its trade and economy.
4. Compare and contrast the economic problems faced by Britain in the 1700s and Japan in the 1800s.
5. Identify similarities between monopolies created by American "robber barons" in the late nineteenth century and the ziabatsus that dominated the Japanese economy at the same time.
6. Compare and contrast the economic, political, and social situations facing Japan after World War I with those of Germany.

BECOMING AN HISTORIAN

1. **Comparing and Contrasting:** Reread the selection "Ba Jin and the Chinese Novel" on pages 783–784. In particular, consider the quotation at the bottom of the first column that begins, "Now that you've graduated, . . ." Write an essay in which you compare and contrast the social values you hold with those held by the young man in this story. Describe conclusions historians might reach about the role of the family in Chinese culture from this passage.
2. **Geography as a Key to History:** Reread the letter from President Fillmore to the Emperor of Japan that appears on page 786. Although the United States may have been sincere in its desire to trade with Japan, identify and explain other geographic objectives this country may have had for the Open Door policy. Remember that the United States had just taken the Philippine Islands and Guam from Spain at the time this policy was initiated.

797

THE CRISIS OF THE

OVERVIEW OF THE UNIT

The fifth unit of World History is divided into four chapters, spanning about 140 pages. Although, like Unit Four, this unit is relatively brief, it deals with two world wars, rising independence movements, the beginnings of communism, and a world-wide depression.

Assuming a 36-week course, you may wish to spend three weeks on Chapters 25 and 26 and three weeks on Chapters 27 and 28.

Charles Cundall's painting The Withdrawal from Dunkirk, 1940 *speaks of the true horror and suffering of war. British soldiers attempt to flee from Dunkirk and escape the heavy German shelling. British Royal aircraft provide some defense for the soldiers.*

Using the Illustration

Students will recognize this painting as contemporary art for more reasons than that it concerns the withdrawal from Dunkirk. Ask them to look back in their textbooks at examples of paintings from much earlier periods. Ask students to identify the elements that, for them, make this painting appear modern. *(Students should note the lack of romantic subjects; lack of the use of symbolism; the overall realism of the image that results from the artist's use of perspective; and the failure of the artist to glorify the content.)* Then ask students if they think that the characteristics that describe this painting are also the characteristics that may be applied to this period between the great world wars.

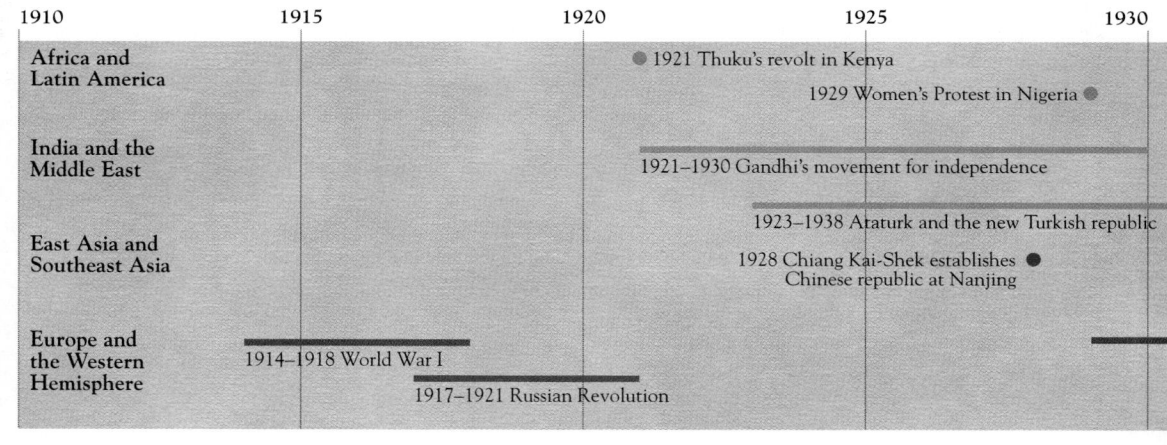

	1910	1915	1920	1925	1930
Africa and Latin America			● 1921 Thuku's revolt in Kenya		
				1929 Women's Protest in Nigeria ●	
India and the Middle East			1921–1930 Gandhi's movement for independence		
				1923–1938 Ataturk and the new Turkish republic	
East Asia and Southeast Asia			1928 Chiang Kai-Shek establishes ● Chinese republic at Nanjing		
Europe and the Western Hemisphere	1914–1918 World War I				
		1917–1921 Russian Revolution			

UNIT OPENER ACTIVITY

An important theme of this unit is how technology changed the way the world waged war. Students will learn about how trench warfare, tanks, machine guns, and the atomic bomb all worked to create a new concept: that of "total war." Ask students to consider the following proposition: *The invention of atomic weapons capable of destroying all life on the planet has made the concept of total war unthinkable for the first time in world history.* Ask students to write short essays agreeing or disagreeing with this statement. They should support their opinions with examples and solid reasoning. When students have finished, ask them to go back and underline in red all statements of fact. They should then underline in blue all statements of opinion. It will surprise students to see how few statements of fact generally accompany this emotional issue.

TWENTIETH CENTURY

(1914–1945)

The period between 1914 and 1945 was one of the most destructive in the history of humankind. Probably sixty million people died as a result of World Wars I and II, the global conflicts that began and ended this era.

The two world wars transformed world history. By 1945, the era of European domination over world affairs was severely shaken. As World War I was followed by revolutions, the Great Depression, the mass-murder machines of totalitarian regimes, and the destructiveness of World War II, it appeared to many that European civilization had become a nightmare. Europeans, who had been accustomed to dominating the world at the beginning of the twentieth century, now watched helplessly at mid-century as the two new superpowers—the United States and the Soviet Union—created by two world wars took control of their destinies. Moreover, the power of the European states had been destroyed by the exhaustive struggles of World War II. The European colonial powers no longer had the energy or wealth to maintain their colonial empires after the war. With the decline of Western power, a new era of global relationships was about to begin.

UNIT OUTLINE

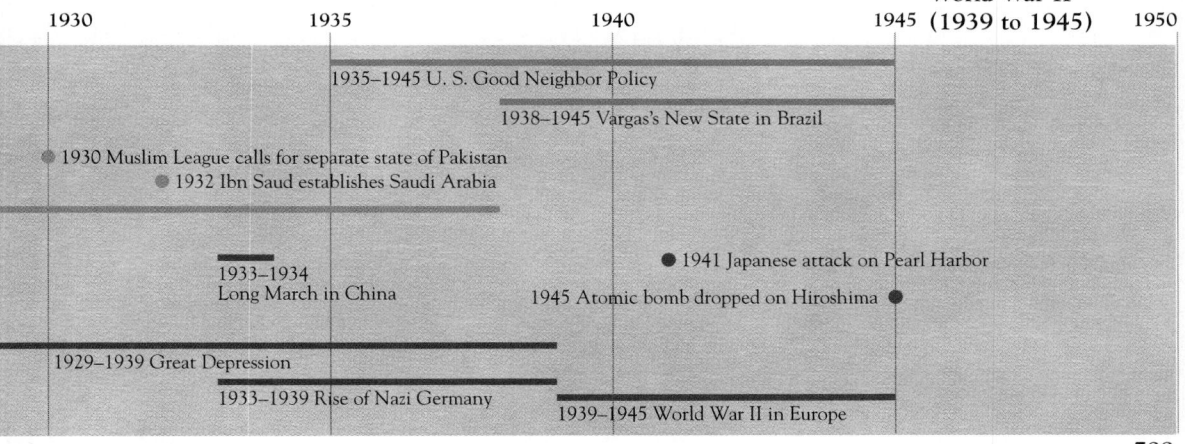

Time line:
1930 — 1935 — 1940 — 1945 — 1950

1935–1945 U. S. Good Neighbor Policy
1938–1945 Vargas's New State in Brazil
1930 Muslim League calls for separate state of Pakistan
1932 Ibn Saud establishes Saudi Arabia
1933–1934 Long March in China
1941 Japanese attack on Pearl Harbor
1945 Atomic bomb dropped on Hiroshima
1929–1939 Great Depression
1933–1939 Rise of Nazi Germany
1939–1945 World War II in Europe

799

STUDYING THE TIME LINE

Ask students the following questions to help them compare the time periods of the different civilizations they will be studying in this unit, as well as develop an appreciation for the wide span of years covered.

1. What is the earliest year represented in the time line? *(1910)*
2. What is the latest year represented in the time line? *(1950)*
3. What is the total amount of time covered in the time line? *(40 years)*
4. The beginning of World War II coincides with the end of what economic event? *(the Great Depression)* How were the two events related? *(The economic stimulus provided by the war ended the depression.)*
5. What two events on the time line covered the same span of time? *(World War I and the Russian Revolution both covered four years.)*

PROJECT IDEAS

To balance the theme of technology and total war (the subject of the Unit Opener activity) and to act as a segue to the next unit, students will benefit from a project focused on civil disobedience and nonviolent protests. Break students into cooperative learning groups to research the following aspects of this. The results may then be presented to the class as visual displays. (Samples of methods include posters, a skit, a student-made videotape, or mock interviews.) When presented in the order suggested below, presentations will give students a overview of nonviolent civil disobedience.

1. **Philosophic base:** Chinese Taoist doctrine of *wu-wei;* the Hindu doctrine of *ahimsa* (nonharming): pacifist doctrines of the Jewish Essenes; and the gospel teachings of the early Christians and the later Albigenses
2. **Political base:** investigate writings of Henry David Thoreau, Mohandas Gandhi, and Martin Luther King.
3. **Nonviolent political movements:** Garrisons's advocacy of nonviolent abolitionism; suffragette movement in Britain; Tolstoi's nonviolent anti-tsarist movement; Gandhi's South African and Indian campaigns; and the civil rights lunch counter protests of the 1960s.

PLANNING GUIDE

SECTION	KEY TOPICS	PRIMARY SOURCES	ASSESSMENT
1 The Road to World War I pages 801–806	◆ Nationalism and alliances ◆ Militarism ◆ Outbreak of war		◆ Section Review, pages 805–806 ◆ Section Quiz 25–1, TRB
2 The War pages 806–817	◆ Stalemate on Western Front ◆ Central Powers' successes on Eastern Front ◆ Trench warfare ◆ Widening of war ◆ Entry of U.S. ◆ Home front	◆ Zweig excerpt, pages 807–808 ◆ Description of mustard gas, page 809 ◆ Remarque excerpt, pages 811–812 ◆ Poster, page 815 ◆ Poem, pages 816–817	◆ Section Review, page 817 ◆ Section Quiz 25–2, TRB
3 Revolution and the End of the War pages 817–827	◆ Background of Russian Revolution ◆ Lenin ◆ Bolschevik seizure of power ◆ Russian Civil War ◆ Last year of war	◆ Police report, page 819 ◆ Ten Days That Shook the World, pages 822–823 ◆ Poster, page 824	◆ Section Review, pages 826–827 ◆ Section Quiz 25–3, TRB
4 The Peace Settlements pages 827–831	◆ Paris Peace Conference ◆ Wilson's Fourteen Points ◆ Treaty of Versailles ◆ Other peace treaties		◆ Section Review, page 831 ◆ Section Quiz 25–4, TRB

THE BEGINNING OF THE TWENTIETH-CENTURY CRISIS:
WAR AND REVOLUTION (1914 TO 1919)

REPRODUCIBLE ACTIVITIES

- Historical Maps
- Charts and Graphs
- Critical Thinking
- Cooperative Learning
- Vocabulary
- Guided Reading
- Reteaching
- Enrichment
- Performance Assessment
- Spanish Key Points and Chapter Summaries
- Spanish Vocabulary
- Spanish Guided Reading

MULTIMEDIA SUPPORT

TRANSPARENCIES
- *World History* Color Transparency Package
- Fine Art Color Transparency Package

VIDEO
- *World History* Video Library
- **CNN**® Annual Video Update

LASERDISC
- *Sights and Sounds of History*

AUDIO
- *Listening to Literature* audiotape (English and Spanish)
- *History of Music* CD

SOFTWARE
- WESTEST™
- Student Review

CD–ROM
- *The Journey of Civilization*
- *World History*

INTERNET
- Internet Activities

On Line with WORLD HISTORY

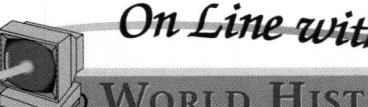

Access West's history web site at
http://history.swpco.com
You'll find activities and web sites related to specific topics and chapters in *World History: The Human Odyssey*. Also look for references to helpful web sites at appropriate places throughout this teacher edition.

LESSON PLANNING

You will find detailed daily lesson plans for both traditional class scheduling and **block scheduling** in your Teacher Resource Box.

Not Enough Time?

If you do not have the four or five days recommended to teach this chapter, you may want to focus on the following sections and activities:

- Have students skim the chapter to answer the "Questions to Guide Your Reading" on page 801. Discuss their answers; then read the "Conclusion" on page 831.
- Do a more in-depth reading of pages 801–805, 808, 813–815, 818–824. Conclude with a class discussion of the features on pages 807–808, 811–812, 822–823.

THE BEGINNING OF
THE TWENTIETH-CENTURY CRISIS:

25

BUILDING ON CHAPTER 24

To "set the scene" for the study of Chapter 25, use the following questions and activities.

◆ Ask students to create a list of conditions that made China an unstable country in the early 20th century. *(breakdown of Confucianism, influence of foreigners, civil war, collapse of central authority, destruction of local industry, conditions of poor)*

◆ Repeat the above exercise for Japan. *(lack of raw materials, resources, markets; concentrated wealth; strained relations with United States and other nations; political uncertainty; conditions of poor.)*

USING THE OPENING STORY

Depending on the ability levels of your students, select from the following questions and activities to reinforce the reading of the story.

◆ When and where did this battle begin? *(July 1, 1916, near Somme River in France)* Who were the opposing forces? *(British and French against German)*

◆ What was "No-Man's Land?" *(Unoccupied area between opposing armies)*

◆ Before World War I, what had convinced people that they were on the verge of creating an "earthly paradise"? *(prosperity, technology)*

On July 1, 1916, British and French infantry forces attacked German defensive lines along a 25-mile front near the Somme River in France. Each soldier carried almost 70 pounds of equipment, which made it "impossible to move much quicker than a slow walk." German machine guns soon opened fire. "We were able to see our comrades move forward in an attempt to cross No-Man's-Land, only to be mown down like meadow grass," recalled one British soldier. "I felt sick at the sight of this carnage and remember weeping." In one day more than 21,000 British soldiers died. After six months of fighting, the British had advanced five miles. One million British, French, and German soldiers had died.

World War I (1914 to 1918) was the defining event of the twentieth century. It devastated the prewar economic, social, and political order of Europe. Its uncertain outcome prepared the way for an even more destructive war. People at the time, overwhelmed by the size of the war's battles and the number of casualties, simply called it the Great War.

The Great War was all the more disturbing to Europeans because it came after a period that many believed to have been an age of progress. There had

▶ *Poison gas, machine guns, and tanks made war more deadly than it had ever been before, particularly because military leaders did not understand the power of the weapons they possessed. This photo shows French soldiers assisting a wounded countryman.*

been international crises before 1914, but somehow Europeans had managed to avoid serious wars. Material prosperity and a strong belief in technological progress had convinced many people that human beings were on the verge of creating an "earthly paradise." The historian Arnold Toynbee expressed what the pre–World War I era had meant to his generation: "[It was expected] that life throughout the World would become more rational, more humane, and more democratic and that, slowly, but surely, political democracy would produce greater social justice. We had also expected that the progress of science and technology would make mankind richer, and that this increasing wealth would gradually spread from a minority to a majority. We had expected that all this would happen peacefully. In fact we thought that mankind's course was set for an earthly paradise."[1]

After 1918, when World War I ended, it was no longer possible to maintain naive illusions about the progress of Western civilization. World War I was followed by revolutions, the mass-murder machines of dictators, and the destructiveness of World War II. It became all too apparent that instead of a paradise, Western civilization had become a nightmare. World War I and the revolutions it spawned can properly be seen as the first stage in the crisis of the twentieth century.

ADDITIONAL RESOURCES

The resources below can be used to enrich the lessons in this chapter.

BOOKS FOR STUDENTS

All Quiet on the Western Front by Enrich Maria von Remarque.

American Heritage History of World War I. (By the editors of American Heritage.) American Heritage

VIDEOS/FILMS

"All Quiet on the Western Front" (1979 TV movie) Social Studies School Service (800) 421-4246

"Prelude to World War I" Series: Western Man and the Modern World (New York Times) Social Studies School Service (800) 421-4246

WAR AND REVOLUTION

(1914 TO 1919)

CRISIS OF THE TWENTIETH CENTURY

WAR AND REVOLUTION
1914 | 1919
1910 | 1945

QUESTIONS TO GUIDE YOUR READING

1. What were the long-range and immediate causes of World War I?

2. Why did World War I become a "war of attrition"?

3. What were the effects of World War I on political life, economic affairs, and women?

4. How did Lenin and the Bolsheviks manage to seize power in Russia despite their small numbers?

5. How did the Bolsheviks win the civil war in Russia?

6. Who were the participants in the 1919 Paris Peace Conference, and what were their objectives?

7. What were the most important results of the Paris Peace Conference?

OUTLINE

1. THE ROAD TO WORLD WAR I

2. THE WAR

3. REVOLUTION AND THE END OF THE WAR

4. THE PEACE SETTLEMENTS

THE ROAD TO WORLD WAR I

On June 28, 1914, the heir to the Austro-Hungarian throne, Archduke Francis Ferdinand, was assassinated in the Bosnian city of Sarajevo (SAWR-ee-YAE-VOE). This event was the immediate cause of World War I. However, long-range, underlying forces had been moving Europeans toward war for some time.

Nationalism, the System of Alliances, and Internal Dissent

In the first half of the nineteenth century, liberals had believed that if European states were organized along national lines, these states would work together and create a peaceful Europe. The liberals had been very wrong. The system of nation-states that emerged in Europe in the last half of the nineteenth century led not to cooperation but to competition. Rivalries over colonies and trade intensified during an age of frenzied nationalism and imperialist expansion. At the same time, Europe's great powers had been divided into two loose alliances. Germany, Austria-Hungary, and Italy had formed the Triple Alliance in 1882. France, Great Britain, and Russia had created the Triple Entente (awn-TAWNT) in 1907 (see Chapter 22).

801

FOCUS

OBJECTIVES

After completing this section, students should be able to

1. name the members of the Triple Alliance and the Triple Entente
2. explain how brinkmanship, extreme nationalism, and militarism made war likely
3. describe the circumstances of the assassination of Francis Ferdinand
4. list the post-assassination events that led to war

FOCUS ACTIVITY

Ask students to consider the differences in attitude and behavior between patriots and extreme nationalists. On the board, write the heading *Attitude.* Underneath, list such topics as: toward own country, toward other countries, toward own armies, toward own expansion, toward others' expansion, toward own leaders, toward other leaders. Beside the list, create a two-column chart of comparison, using the headings *Patriot* and *Nationalist.* Afterward, under the heading *Behavior,* have students brainstorm possible patriotic and nationalistic behaviors stemming from the listed attitudes.

In the early years of the twentieth century, a series of crises had tested these alliances. Especially troublesome were the crises in the Balkans between 1908 and 1913, which taught the European states a dangerous lesson. Those governments that had exercised restraint in order to avoid war wound up being publicly humiliated. Those that went to the brink of war to maintain their national interests had often been praised for having preserved their national honor. By 1914, the major European states had come to believe that their allies were important. They now thought that their security depended on supporting their allies, even when the allies took foolish risks.

Diplomacy was often based on **brinkmanship** (the practice of threatening to go to war to achieve one's goals). This type of diplomacy was especially frightening in view of the nature of the European state system. Each nation-state regarded itself as subject to no higher interest or authority. Each state was guided by its own self-interest and success. Furthermore, most leaders thought that war was an acceptable way to preserve the power of their national states. These attitudes made war an ever-present possibility.

The growth of nationalism in the nineteenth century had yet another serious result. Not all ethnic groups had become nations. Slavic minorities in the Balkans and the Habsburg Empire, for example, still dreamed of creating their own national states. The Irish in the British Empire and the Poles in the Russian Empire had similar dreams.

National desires, however, were not the only source of internal strife at the beginning of the twentieth century. Socialist labor movements (see Chapter 22) had grown more powerful. They were increasingly inclined to use strikes, even

violent ones, to achieve their goals. Some conservative leaders, alarmed at the increase in labor strife and class division, even feared that European nations were on the verge of revolution. Some historians believe that the desire to suppress internal disorder may have encouraged some leaders to take the plunge into war in 1914.

Militarism

The growth of mass armies after 1900 heightened the existing tensions in Europe. These armies also made it obvious that if war did come, it would be highly destructive. **Conscription** (a military draft) had been

Map 25.1   Europe in 1914

STUDYING MAPS

The following questions and activities will help you guide students through their study of Map 25.1.

1. Which was larger, the Triple alliance or the Triple Entente? *(Students may answer the Triple Alliance, but that is because they are not seeing all of Russia in this map.)*
2. Name the countries that were not formally associated with either alliance.

(Neutral countries include Norway, Sweden, Spain, the Netherlands, Denmark and Switzerland.)

3. Find the Balkan states: Serbia, Albania, Bulgaria, Romania, and Greece. Find Sarajevo, the Somme River, and the English Channel.
4. Compare Europe in 1914 with Europe now. What differences do you see?

established as a regular practice in most Western countries before 1914. (The United States and Britain were exceptions.) European armies had doubled in size between 1890 and 1914. With its 1.3 million men, the Russian army had grown to be the largest. The French and German armies were not far behind, with 900,000 each. The British, Italian, and Austro-Hungarian armies numbered between 250,000 and 500,000 soldiers each.

Militarism, or aggressive preparation for war, was growing. As armies grew, so too did the influence of military leaders. They drew up vast and complex plans for quickly mobilizing millions of men and enormous quantities of supplies in the event of war. Military leaders feared that any changes in these plans would cause chaos in the armed forces. Thus, they insisted that their plans could not be altered. In the crises during the summer of 1914, this left European political leaders with little leeway. They were forced to make decisions for military instead of political reasons.

The Outbreak of War:
The Summer of 1914

Militarism, nationalism, the alliance system, and the desire to stifle internal dissent may all have played a role in the coming of World War I. However, it was the decisions made by European leaders in response to another crisis in the Balkans in the summer of 1914 that led directly to the conflict.

As we have seen, states in southeastern Europe had struggled to free themselves of Ottoman rule in the course of the nineteenth and early twentieth centuries. Furthermore, the rivalry between Austria-Hungary and Russia for domination of these new states created serious tensions in the region. By 1914, Serbia, supported

◀ *Russian troops greatly outnumbered the Germans, but the Germans were better trained and far better equipped. What do you think the American reaction would be if 2.5 million soldiers lost their lives in just one year?*

RECOMMENDED READING

A good starting point on causes of World War I is J. Joll, *The Origins of the First World War* (London, 1984). The belief in Germany's responsibility for the war is argued by F. Fischer, *Germany's Aims in the First World War* (New York, 1967); *World Power or Decline: The Controversy over Germany's Aims in World War I* (New York, 1974); and *War of Illustrations: German Policies from 1911 to 1914* (New York, 1975). See also V. R. Berghahn,

Germany and the Approach of War in 1914 (London, 1973); Z. S. Steiner, *Britain and the Origins of the First World War* (New York, 1977); R. Bosworth, *Italy and the Approach of the First World War* (New York, 1983); J. F. Keiger, *France and the Origins of the First World War* (New York, 1984); and D. C. B. Lieven, *Russia and the Origins of the First World War* (New York, 1984).

TEACH

REINFORCING VOCABULARY

Be sure students understand what is meant by "frenzied nationalism" (*hysterical, excessive loyalty to one's own country*), "imperialist expansion" (*extending the power and authority of one nation to other nations or areas*), and "to suppress internal disorder" (*to put down or end a country's own social or political unrest*). Discuss examples illustrating these phrases.

CLASS DISCUSSION

Guide students in a discussion of attitudes and circumstances of early twentieth-century Europe that made war likely.

Multimedia Support

TRANSPARENCY
25–1, Europe by Ethnic Groups Overlaid with 1914 Boundaries (MAP)

LEARNING FROM VISUALS

Answer to the caption question: It is very difficult to grasp numbers of such magnitude, especially when talking about the loss of human life. In order to help them understand what the figure really represents, tell students that during the bloodiest battle ever fought in U.S. history (the Battle of Antietam, Sept. 17, 1862) approximately 4,800 U.S. soldiers died. It would take more than 520 "Battles of Antietam" to equal the 2.5 million lives lost by the Russians in one year.

REINFORCING VOCABULARY

Check students' understanding of the following words by asking them to write a paragraph that uses all of them: restraint *(control, moderation)*, conspirator *(one who plots)*, innocuous *(harmless, without importance)*, sovereignty *(freedom from external control)*.

CRITICAL THINKING

Ask students to explain what a self-fulfilling prophecy is. *(Something that comes true because it has been assumed beforehand.)* Ask them to defend or refute this proposition: Militarism and the growth of mass armies after 1900 made World War I a self-fulfilling prophecy.

CRITICAL THINKING

Ask students to consider the following sentence: "The Austro-Hungarian government did not know whether or not the Serbian government had been directly involved in the archduke's assassination, but it did not care." What does the attitude of Austria-Hungary suggest about the nationalism of this era? Have students speculate on what might have happened if Austria-Hungary had reacted in a less extreme and self-interested way to the Archduke's assassination. Could war have been prevented? If not, why not?

▲ *Hiram Maxim's invention, the machine gun, was used with deadly efficiency during World War I. The old war strategy of sending a mass of men against enemy lines quickly proved to be lethal to both sides.*

by Russia, was determined to create a large, independent Slavic state in the Balkans. Austria-Hungary, which had its own Slavic minorities to contend with, was equally determined to prevent that possibility. Many Europeans saw the potential danger in this explosive situation. The British ambassador to Vienna wrote in 1913:

> Serbia will some day set Europe by the ears, and bring about a universal war on the Continent. . . . I cannot tell you how exasperated people are getting here at the continual worry which that little country causes to Austria under encouragement from Russia. . . . It will be lucky if Europe succeeds in avoiding war as a result of the present crisis. The next time a Serbian crisis arises, . . . I feel sure that Austria-Hungary will refuse to admit of any Russian interference in the dispute and that she will proceed to settle her differences with her little neighbor by herself.[2]

It was against this backdrop of mutual distrust and hatred that the events of the summer of 1914 were played out.

On June 28, 1914, six young conspirators waited in the streets of Sarajevo during the visit of Archduke Francis Ferdinand of Austria-Hungary and his wife Sophia. The conspirators were members of the Black Hand, a Serbian terrorist organization that wanted Bosnia to be free of Austria-Hungary and part of a large Serbian kingdom. The plan was to kill the heir to the throne of Austria-Hungary, along with his wife. One of the six conspirators failed in the morning when the bomb he threw at the archduke's car glanced off and exploded against the car behind him. Later in the day, however, Gavrillo Princip, a nineteen-year-old Bosnian Serb, succeeded in shooting both the archduke and his wife.

The Austro-Hungarian government did not know whether or not the Serbian government had been directly involved in the archduke's assassination, but it did not care. It saw an opportunity to "render Serbia innocuous once and for all by a display of force," as the Austrian foreign minister put it. Austrian leaders, who feared Russian intervention on Serbia's behalf, sought the backing of their German allies. Emperor William II of Germany and his chancellor responded with a "blank check," saying that Austria-Hungary could rely on Germany's "full support," even if "matters went to the length of a war between Austria-Hungary and Russia."

Strengthened by German support, Austrian leaders sent an ultimatum to Serbia on July 23. In it, they made such extreme demands that Serbia had little choice but to reject some of them in order to preserve its sovereignty. Austria-Hungary then declared war on Serbia on July 28. Russia was determined to support Serbia's cause. On July 28, Tsar Nicholas II ordered partial mobilization of the Russian army against Austria-Hungary. (**Mobilization** is the process of assembling and making both troops and supplies ready for war. In 1914, it was considered an act of war.)

At this point, military war plans were at odds with diplomatic and political decisions. Leaders of the Russian army informed the tsar that their mobilization plans were based on a war against both Germany and Austria-Hungary at the same time. They could not par-

COOPERATIVE LEARNING ACTIVITY

An unprecedented number of new machines and devices were first used on a large scale during World War I. These included submarines, airplanes, tanks, motor trucks, machine guns, rapid-fire artillery, barbed wire, and poison gas. Break students into groups and ask them to organize in such as way as to complete a project (paper, visual display, oral report, etc.) that answers the following question: What mistake did military leaders continue to make even though new technology had changed warfare completely? Remind students to define the task thoroughly and to assign roles and responsibilities. After the project is completed, the group should evaluate everyone's contribution, highlighting aspects of the work that went well and suggesting ways the team might have functioned better.

◄ *This photograph records the arrest of Gavrillo Princip shortly after the assassination of Archduke Francis Ferdinand and his wife.*

tially mobilize without creating chaos in the army. As a result, the Russian government ordered full mobilization of the Russian army on July 29, knowing that Germany would consider this an act of war against it. Indeed, Germany reacted quickly. It warned Russia that it must halt its mobilization within twelve hours. When Russia ignored this warning, Germany declared war on Russia on August 1.

At this stage of the conflict, German war plans determined whether or not France would become involved in the war. Under the guidance of General Alfred von Schlieffen (SHLEE-fun), chief of staff from 1891 to 1905, the German General Staff had drawn up a military plan. It was based on the assumption of a two-front war with France and Russia, because the two powers had formed a military alliance in 1894. The Schlieffen Plan called for a small holding action against Russia while most of the German army would make a rapid invasion of France before Russia could become effective in the east or before the British could cross the English Channel to help France. This meant invading France by moving quickly along the level coastal area through Belgium rather than through the rougher terrain to the southeast.

After the planned quick defeat of the French, most of the German army would then move to the east against Russia. Under the Schlieffen Plan, Germany could not mobilize its troops solely against Russia. Therefore, it declared war on France on August 3 after it had issued an ultimatum to Belgium on August 2 demanding the right of German troops to pass through Belgian territory. However, Belgium was a neutral nation. On August 4, Great Britain declared war on Germany, officially for violating Belgian neutrality. In fact, however, Britain was concerned about maintaining its world power. As one British diplomat put it, if Germany and Austria-Hungary would win the war, "what would be the position of a friendless England?" By August 4, all the great powers of Europe were at war.

❀ SECTION REVIEW ❀

1. **Locate:**
   (*a*) Sarajevo,
   (*b*) English Channel

ENRICHMENT ACTIVITY

Have students do additional research on the origins of World War I and then construct a debate. Have them assume the roles of the leaders of Austria-Hungary, Germany, Serbia, Russia, France, and Britain. Debate which country was most responsible for starting World War I and which country bore little or no responsibility for starting the war. Or, have students use a map of 1914 Europe to explain the role geography played in the development of the Schlieffen plan. How did geography effect the war plans of the other World War I participants?

Answers to
SECTION REVIEW

2. (a) threatening to go to war to achieve one's goals
(b) military draft
(c) process of assembling and making troops and supplies ready for war

3. (a) pride of country
(b) Serbian terrorist organization held responsible for assassination of Archduke Ferdinand
(c) chief of staff of German Army; made plans for fighting Eastern and Western front at once

4. (a) Leaders of European nations regarded war as a legitimate way of achieving their goals.
(b) once committed to, plans were difficult to change
(c) conflicts involving only two powers drew in the allied nations

5. Answers will vary. Point out that leaders of nations with internal problems might choose to go to war to distract their citizens by blaming others.

2. **Define:**
(a) brinkmanship,   (b) conscription,
(c) mobilization

3. **Identify:**
(a) national honor,   (b) Black Hand,
(c) General Alfred von Schlieffen

4. **Recall:**
(a) Why was war an ever-present possibility in Europe at the beginning of the twentieth century?
(b) How did the creation of military plans help lead the nations of Europe into World War I?
(c) How did international alliances help to draw nations into World War I?

5. **Think Critically:** Why might the leaders of nations with internal problems be more willing to go to war than those that are economically, politically, and socially successful?

◆ 2 ◆

THE WAR

Before 1914, many political leaders had become convinced that war involved so many political and economic risks that it was not worth fighting. Others had believed that diplomats could easily control any situation and prevent the outbreak of war. At the beginning of August 1914, both these prewar illusions were shattered. However, the new illusions that replaced them soon proved to be equally foolish.

1914 to 1915: Illusions and Stalemate

Europeans went to war in 1914 with remarkable enthusiasm (see "You Are There: The Excitement of War"). Government propaganda had worked in stirring up national hatreds before the war. Now, in August 1914, the urgent pleas of governments for defense against aggressors fell on receptive ears in every nation at war. Most people seemed genuinely convinced that their nation's cause was just.

A new set of illusions also fed the enthusiasm for war. In August 1914, almost everyone believed that the war would be over in a few weeks. People were reminded that all European wars since 1815 had, in fact, ended in a matter of weeks. Of course, they overlooked the U.S. Civil War (1861 to 1865), which was the real model for World War I. Both the soldiers who boarded the trains for the war front in August 1914 and the jubilant citizens who showered them with flowers when they left believed that the warriors would be home by Christmas.

German hopes for a quick end to the war rested upon a military gamble. The Schlieffen Plan had called for the German army to make a vast encircling movement through Belgium into northern France. The army would sweep around Paris and encircle most of the French army. However, the German advance was halted only 20 miles from Paris at the First Battle of the Marne (MARN) (September 6 to 10). In their desperate need to stop the Germans in this battle, French military leaders took control of 2,000 Parisian taxicabs, loaded them with fresh troops, and sent them to the front line.

The war quickly turned into a stalemate, as neither the Germans nor the French could dislodge each other from the trenches they had begun to dig for shelter. Two lines of trenches soon reached from the English Channel to the frontiers of Switzerland. The Western Front had become bogged down in a **trench warfare** (fighting from ditches, protected by barbed wire) that kept both sides in virtually the same positions for four years.

In contrast to the Western Front, the war in the east was marked by much more mobility. The cost in lives, however, was equally enormous. At the beginning of the war, the Russian army moved into eastern Germany but was decisively defeated at the Battle of Tannenberg on August 30 and the Battle of Masurian Lakes on September 15. The Russians were no longer a threat to German territory.

Austria-Hungary, Germany's ally, fared less well at first. The Austrians had been defeated by the Russians in Galicia (ga-LISH-ah) and thrown out of Serbia as well. To make matters worse, the Italians betrayed the Germans and Austrians and entered the war on the Allied side by attacking Austria in May 1915. (France,

---

MORE ABOUT . . . *Trench Warfare*

Trench warfare resulted in a whole new type of injuries to soldiers. Because the soldiers were often standing in water for days and weeks, many developed trench foot. Trench fever was an illness carried by lice, as was trench nephritis which attacked the kidney. In addition, the use of shrapnel shells containing thousands of metal splinters meant that infection was a constant problem. Finally, the use of chlorine, phosgene, and mustard gas left 91,000 dead and 1.3 million soldiers with inflamed lungs or second and third degree burns.

YOU ARE THERE

The Excitement of War

The incredible outpouring of patriotic enthusiasm that greeted the declaration of war at the beginning of August 1914 demonstrated the power that nationalistic feeling had attained at the beginning of the twentieth century. This selection is taken from the autobiography of Stefan Zweig (ZWIGE [hard "g"]), an Austrian writer who captured well the celebration of war in Vienna in 1914.

Stefan Zweig, Selection from His Autobiography

The next morning I was in Austria. In every station placards had been put up announcing general mobilization. The trains were filled with fresh recruits, banners were flying, music sounded, and in Vienna I found the entire city in a tumult. . . . There were parades in the street, flags, ribbons, and music burst forth everywhere, young recruits were marching triumphantly, their faces lighting up at the cheering. . . .

As never before, thousands and hundreds of thousands felt what they should have felt in peace time, that they belonged together. A city of two million, a country of nearly fifty million, in that hour felt that they were participating in world history, in a moment which would never recur, and that each one was called upon to cast his small self into the glowing mass, there to be purified of all selfishness. All differences of class, rank, and language were flooded over at that moment by the rushing feeling of fraternity. Strangers spoke to one another in the streets, people who had avoided each other for years shook hands, everywhere one saw excited faces. Each individual was part of the people, and his person, his hitherto unnoticed person, had been given meaning. . . .

▲ *This photo captures the excitement of the troops as World War I was beginning. Compare and contrast this image with the picture that opens the chapter.*

What did the great mass know of war in 1914, after nearly half a century of peace? They did not know war, they had hardly given it a thought. They still saw it in the perspective of their school readers and of paintings in museums; brilliant cavalry attacks in glittering uniforms, the fatal shot always straight through the heart, the entire campaign a resounding march of victory—"We'll be home at Christmas," the recruits shouted laughingly to their mothers in August of 1914. . . . The young people were honestly afraid that they might

(continued)

RECOMMENDED READING

Two recent accounts of World War I are B. E. Schmitt and H. C. Vedeler, *The World in the Crucible, 1914–1919* (New York, 1984); and J. M. Winter, *The Experience of World War I* (New York, 1989). Trench warfare is examined in T. Ashworth, *Trench Warfare, 1914–1918: The Live and Let-Live System* (London, 1980). Poison gas is examined in L. F. Haber, *The Poisonous Cloud: Chemical Warfare in the First World War* (Oxford, 1985).

Although scholars do not always agree with her conclusions, B. Tuchman's *The Guns of August* (New York, 1962) is a magnificent account of the opening days of the war.

On women in World War I, see G. Braybon, *Women Workers in the First World War: The British Experience* (London, 1981); and J. M. Winter and R. M. Wall, eds., *The Upheaval of War: Family, Work and Welfare in Europe, 1914–1918* (Cambridge, 1988).

2

FOCUS

OBJECTIVES

After completing this section, students should be able to

1. describe how the war on the Western Front quickly turned into a stalemate
2. explain trench warfare
3. summarize major actions on the Eastern Front
4. discuss the widening of the war into "total war"
5. describe the major effects on society at home of World War I

FOCUS ACTIVITY

Can students imagine feeling the intense excitement about going to war that people experienced in August 1914? Ask them to consider if any events closer to their own time engendered such intense feeling.

TEACH

YOU ARE THERE

CRITICAL THINKING

Discuss Stefan Sweig's sentence: "As never before, thousands and hundreds of thousands felt what they should have felt in peace time, that they belonged together."

LEARNING FROM VISUALS

Answer to the caption question: Students should recognize joy, anticipation, excitement in this photo and the sad, depressing reality of war in the first photo.

CRITICAL THINKING

Ask students to imagine the euphoric excitement of August 1914. Have them write a diary entry, a newspaper editorial, or a personal letter describing the scene shown in the photograph on page 807.

Answers to Critical Thinking Questions

1. caused feeling of nationalism, or unity, people had never before felt, people felt they belonged together, were participating in world history
2. It had been 50 years since the Europeans had seen a war. Their "knowledge" came from books that glamorized war.
3. Answers will vary, but students will probably state that having experienced wars throughout much of the century, people in our country today don't like the thought of war.

Multimedia Support

TRANSPARENCY
25–2, Diagram of a Front-Line Trench

ACROSS THE CURRICULUM

Art Ask interested students to bring in examples of visual arts used as propaganda before and during World War I: posters, cartoons, paintings. Who were the artists? How effective was their work?

YOU ARE THERE

The Excitement of War, continued

miss this most wonderful and exciting experience of their lives; that is why they hurried and thronged to the colors, and that is why they shouted and sang in the trains that carried them to the slaughter.

1. Why was war received with such enthusiasm in Europe in 1914?

2. Why were the people ignorant of what war was really about?

3. How do the feelings that people in our country today have about war compare to the feelings described in this feature?

Great Britain, and Russia were called the Allied Powers, or Allies.) By this time, the Germans had come to the aid of the Austrians. A German-Austrian army defeated and routed the Russian army in Galicia and pushed the Russians back 300 miles into their own territory. Russian casualties stood at 2.5 million killed, captured, or wounded. The Russians had almost been knocked out of the war. Buoyed by their success, Germany and Austria-Hungary, joined by Bulgaria in September 1915, attacked and eliminated Serbia from the war.

1916 to 1917: The Great Slaughter

The successes in the east enabled the Germans to move back to the offensive in the west. The early trenches dug in 1914 had by now become elaborate systems of defense. The lines of trenches for both sides were protected by barbed wire entanglements three to five feet high and thirty yards wide, concrete machine-gun nests, and mortar batteries, supported further back by heavy artillery. Troops lived in holes in the ground, separated from each other by a no-man's-land.

The unexpected development of trench warfare baffled military leaders. They had been trained to fight wars of movement and maneuver. The only plan generals could devise was to attempt a breakthrough by throwing masses of men against enemy lines that had first been battered by artillery barrages. Once the decisive breakthrough had been achieved, they thought, they could then return to the war of movement that they knew best. At times, the high command on either side would order an offensive that would begin with an artillery barrage to flatten the enemy's barbed wire and leave the enemy in a state of shock (see "You Are There: The Reality of War—Trench Warfare"). After "softening up" the enemy in this fashion, a mass of soldiers would climb out of their trenches with fixed bayonets and hope to work their way toward the enemy trenches. The attacks rarely worked, however, because the mass of men advancing unprotected across open fields could be fired at by the enemy's machine guns. In 1916 and 1917, millions of young men died in the search for the elusive breakthrough. In ten months at Verdun in 1916, 700,000 men lost their lives over a few miles of land. World War I had turned into a **war of attrition,** or a war based on wearing the other side down by constant attacks and heavy losses.

Warfare in the trenches of the western front produced unimaginable horrors. Battlefields were hellish landscapes of barbed wire, shell holes, mud, and

---

SPECIAL NEEDS: *Visual*

Have the students study Map 25.1 and identify the Triple Alliance and Triple Entente countries on the map. Have them list the countries under their proper category. Then have the students go to the library and find photographs depicting scenes from each of the countries, preferably from the early 1900's. Have the students share their lists and the pictures from the various countries with the class. As a follow-up to aid in memorization and learning, pass out 3×5 cards which identify a country. Have the students categorize each country as part of the Triple Alliance or the Triple Entente. They may do this visually by placing the cards on the correct side of the list they had prepared.

Map 25.2   The Western Front, 1914–1918

Farthest German advance, September 1914 ——   Winter, 1914–1915 ----

German offensive, March–July 1918 ——   Armistice line ——

German advances ←   Allied advances ←

injured and dying men. The introduction of poison gas in 1915 produced new forms of injuries. One British writer described them:

> I wish those people who write so glibly about this being a holy war could see a case of mustard gas . . . could see the poor things burnt and blistered all over with great mustard-coloured suppurating [pus-forming] blisters with blind eyes all sticky . . . and stuck together, and always fighting for breath, with voices a mere whisper, saying that their throats are closing and they know they will choke.[3]

By the end of 1915, the airplane had also appeared on the battlefront for the first time in history. At first, planes were used to spot the enemy's position. However, planes soon began to support offensives by attacking ground targets, especially enemy communications. Fights for control of the air occurred and increased over time. At first, pilots fired shots at each other with handheld pistols. Next, machine guns were mounted on the noses of planes, which made the skies considerably more dangerous. The Germans also used their giant airships—the zeppelins (ZEP-uh-lunz)—to bomb

STUDYING MAPS

The following questions and activities will help you guide students through their study of Map 25.2.

1. Compare this map with the map of the Eastern Front on page 813. Roughly how long was the combined German Front in 1915? *(About 2400 miles)*

2. Locate the Marne River and the Somme River. What is the importance of each in terms of World War I? *(The Marne was where the French stopped the German advance in 1914; the Somme was the location of the British and French offensive described in chapter opener.)*

3. How far did the Germans advance in September 1914? *(nearly to Paris)* Trace the German offensive of 1918.

CLASS DISCUSSION

Discuss with students why the years 1916 to 1917 are referred to as "The Great Slaughter." In what sense did the war turn into a "war of attrition"?

USING PRIMARY SOURCES

Ask a student volunteer to read aloud the description of the effect of poison gas on the soldiers. Then remind students that this weapon has also been used against civilians, including children. Inform students that when Germany first used poison gas in 1915, the effect on Allied lines was so devastating that the Germans were not prepared to exploit their advantage. By the time they were ready, the Allies had been supplied with gas masks and poison gas of their own. Students probably are already aware that the use of poison gas was banned by the Geneva Protocol (1925). During Operation Desert Storm, the raid inside Iraqi territory was justified on the basis that it was directed against a factory suspected of producing chemical weapons.

USING PRIMARY SOURCES

There are many books available in libraries that have photographs from World War I. Have students examine some of the photographs taken of the battle scenes. What can they learn from these photographs about the nature of modern war? What can they predict about the damage to the environment caused by the war?

◄ *The city of Verdun, 125 miles east of Paris, was heavily damaged in a battle that took 700,000 lives and gained the German forces only a few miles of land. Why do you think both sides fought so bitterly over just one town?*

London and eastern England. This caused little damage but frightened many people. Germany's enemies, however, soon found that zeppelins, which were filled with hydrogen gas, quickly became raging infernos when hit by antiaircraft guns.

The Widening of the War

Because of the stalemate on the Western Front, both sides sought to gain new allies who might provide a winning advantage. The Ottoman Empire had already

▲ *This French Breguet bomber plane brought a new kind of warfare to World War I. It was one of the first airplanes to have wing flaps.*

CNN® WORLD HISTORY UPDATES

You can update your coverage of World History topics, as well as spark lively classroom discussion and deeper understanding, by using the **CNN World History Updates.**

For assistance in using and incorporating the **CNN World History Updates** into your classroom presentations, see the *Classroom Guide.*

Multimedia Support

LASERDISC
The United States Enters World War I

YOU ARE THERE

The Reality of War—Trench Warfare

The romantic illusion about the adventure of war that filled the minds of so many young men who marched off to battle quickly fell apart after a short time in the trenches on the Western Front. This description of trench warfare is taken from the most famous novel that emerged from World War I, Erich Maria Remarque's (ruh-MARK['s]) All Quiet on the Western Front. Remarque had fought in the trenches in France.

Erich Maria Remarque,
All Quiet on the Western Front

We wake up in the middle of the night. The earth booms. Heavy fire is falling on us. We crouch into corners. We distinguish shells of every calibre.

Each man lays hold of his things and looks again every minute to reassure himself that they are still there. The dug-out heaves, the night roars and flashes. We look at each other in the momentary flashes of light, and with pale faces and pressed lips shake our heads.

Every man is aware of the heavy shells tearing down the parapet [wall of earth], rooting up the embankment and demolishing the upper layers of concrete. . . . Already by morning a few of the recruits are green and vomiting. They are too inexperienced. . . .

The bombardment does not diminish. It is falling in the rear too. As far as one can see it spouts fountains of mud and iron. A wide belt is being raked.

The attack does not come, but the bombardment continues. Slowly we become mute. Hardly a man speaks. We cannot make ourselves understood.

Our trench is almost gone. At many places it is only eighteen inches high, it is broken by holes,

▲ *A British officer leads a raiding party out of a World War I trench and into the open field. How successful do you think these maneuvers were?*

and craters, and mountains of earth. A shell lands square in front of our post. At once it is dark. We are buried and must dig ourselves out. . . .

Towards morning, while it is still dark, there is some excitement. Through the entrance rushes in a swarm of fleeing rats that try to storm the walls. Torches light up the confusion. Everyone yells and curses and slaughters. The madness and despair of many hours unloads itself in this outburst. Faces are distorted, arms strike out, the beasts scream; we just stop in time to avoid attacking one another. . . .

Suddenly it howls and flashes terrifically, the dugout cracks in all its joints under a direct hit,

(continued)

ENRICHMENT ACTIVITY

Assign Remarque's novel *All Quiet on the Western Front*. Ask students to present the plot, character, and themes of the book using at least two of the following: essay, videotape, painting, sculpture, music, dance, poetry, collage, filmstrip. As a class discussion, compare descriptions of war found in *All Quiet on the Western Front* with accounts of the Gulf War. Consider the viewpoints of both American and Iraqi soldiers.

YOU ARE THERE

LEARNING FROM VISUALS

Answer to the caption question: Death rates from these raids were high.

Remarque was only one of many authors who wrote about World War I. Another was Ernest Hemingway who, despite his many portrayals of battles, never actually fought in any war. He served as a volunteer with the American Red Cross during World War I and was a reporter in the Spanish Civil War and World War II. Remarque was important in that he did not glamorize war the way so many others did.

All Quiet on the Western Front was one of the most influential pieces of fiction to appear in the period between the two world wars. It realistically and compassionately chronicled the hardships and embittering experiences endured by a group of young German soldiers, the most sensitive of whom was killed shortly before the armistice. By exposing the horror, cruelty, and uselessness of war, the novel quickly won worldwide acclaim. The book was banned by the Nazi regime for its antimilitary focus.

ACROSS THE CURRICULUM

Literature. Have students read Erich Maria Remarque's *All Quiet on the Western Front* and then write a letter in which they try to explain to their friends and family back home exactly what they are experiencing in the trenches on the Western Front. What difficulties do they face in trying to describe what they are experiencing?

Answers to Critical Thinking Questions

1. The attack came in the middle of the night.
2. Answers will vary.
3. It became impossible to communicate with one another because of the continuous noise.
4. At the time, the rats were the only things they could lash out against. The enemy was still out of reach.

CLASS DISCUSSION

Have students discuss the widening of the war into the Balkans, the Middle East, Africa, and Asia. Why did military leaders seek to expand the conflict?

YOU ARE THERE

The Reality of War—Trench Warfare, continued

fortunately only a light one that the concrete blocks are able to withstand. It rings metallically, the walls reel, rifles, helmets, earth, mud, and dust fly everywhere. Sulphur fumes poor in. . . . The recruit starts to rave again and two others follow suit. One jumps up and rushes out, we have trouble with the other two. I start after the one who escapes and wonder whether to shoot him in the leg—then it shrieks again. I fling myself down and when I stand up the wall of the trench is plastered with smoking splinters, lumps of flesh, and bits of uniform. I scramble back.

Suddenly the nearer explosions cease. The shelling continues but it has lifted and falls behind us, our trench is free. We seize the hand-grenades, pitch them out in front of the dug-out and jump after them. The bombardment has stopped and a heavy barrage now falls behind us. The attack has come.

No one would believe that in this howling waste there could still be men; but steel helmets now appear on all sides out of the trench, and fifty yards from us a machine-gun is already in position and barking.

The wire-entanglements are torn to pieces. Yet they offer some obstacle. We see the storm-troops

coming. Our artillery opens fire. Machine-guns rattle, rifles crack. The charge works its way across. . . . We recognize the distorted faces, the smooth helmets: they are French. They have already suffered heavily when they reach the remnants of the barbed-wire entanglements. A whole line has gone down before our machine-guns; then we have a lot of stoppages and they come nearer.

I see one of them, his face upturned, fall into a wire cradle. His body collapses, his hands remain suspended as though he were praying. Then his body drops clean away and only his hands with the stumps of his arms, shot off, now hang in the wire.

1. At what time did the attack come?
2. Do you think an attack at night or one during the day would be more frightening? Why?
3. Why did the men "become mute"?
4. Why do you think the men attacked the rats so savagely?

come into the war on Germany's side in August 1914. Russia, Great Britain, and France declared war on the Ottoman Empire in November. The Allies tried to open a Balkan front by landing forces at Gallipoli (guh-LIP-uh-lee), southwest of Constantinople, in April 1915. However, Bulgaria entered into the war on the side of the Central Powers (as Germany, Austria-Hungary, and the Ottoman Empire were called), and a disastrous campaign at Gallipoli caused the Allies to withdraw. Italy, as we have seen, also entered the war

on the Allied side. In return, France and Great Britain promised to let Italy have some Austrian territory. The Italian forces were completely ineffective, however, and the Allies had to come to their rescue.

By 1917, the war that had started in Europe had truly become a world conflict. In the Middle East, a British officer who came to be known as Lawrence of Arabia urged Arab princes to revolt in 1917 against their Ottoman overlords. In 1918, British forces from Egypt destroyed the Ottoman Empire in the Middle

RETEACHING ACTIVITY

Have students do a map of Europe that shows the alliance system and the war plans of Germany and Russia. Why did the alliance system and the war plans guarantee a major war once any two nations went to war? Also, have students construct maps of both the Western and Eastern fronts. What major differences become apparent from the maps? How do they explain the differences?

Map 25.3   The Eastern Front, 1914–1918

-·- Russian advances: 1914–1916   ——— Brest-Litovsk boundary: 1918

····· Deepest German penetration   Battle site, 1914

war dragged on, however, it became more difficult to do so. The immediate cause of U.S. involvement grew out of the naval war between Germany and Great Britain.

Only once did the German and British naval forces actually engage in direct battle—at the Battle of Jutland on May 31, 1916, when the Germans won an inconclusive victory. Britain used its superior naval power to good effect, however, by throwing up a naval blockade of Germany. Germany retaliated by setting up its own blockade of Britain. It enforced its blockade with the use of unrestricted submarine warfare, which included the sinking of passenger liners. On May 7, 1915, the British ship *Lusitania* was sunk by German forces. There were 1,100 civilian casualties, including over 100 Americans. This brought strong U.S. protests. The German government suspended unrestricted submarine warfare in September 1915 to avoid further antagonizing the United States.

By January 1917, however, the Germans were eager to break the deadlock in the war. They decided on another military gamble by returning to unrestricted submarine warfare. German naval officers convinced Emperor William II that the use of unrestricted submarine warfare could starve the British into submission within five months. When the emperor expressed concern about the United States, he was told not to worry; the British would starve before the Americans could act. Even if the Americans did intervene, Admiral Holtzendorff assured the emperor, "I give your Majesty my word as an officer that not one American will land on the continent."

East. For their Middle East campaigns, the British mobilized forces from India, Australia, and New Zealand. The Allies also took advantage of Germany's preoccupations in Europe and lack of naval strength to seize German colonies in the rest of the world. Japan seized a number of German-held islands in the Pacific. Australia seized German New Guinea.

Most important to the Allied cause was the entry of the United States into the war. At first, the United States tried to remain neutral in the Great War. As the

STUDYING MAPS

The following questions and activities will help you guide students through their study of Map 25.3.

1. Find the location of the battles of Tannenberg and Masurian Lakes. What was the significance of those battles? *(Answers will vary.)*

2. Find Galicia, the Ottoman Empire, and Gallipoli. What is the importance of Gallipoli? *(entrance to Constantinople)*

3. Trace German penetration in the East. How far did they get? *(Nearly to St. Petersburg, and well across the Ukraine)*

▶ *The two German military leaders of the war, Paul von Hindenburg (on the left) and Erich Ludendorff, are shown with Emperor William II. Why do you think the emperor gradually lost power during the war?*

The German naval officers were quite wrong, however. The British were not forced to surrender. Furthermore, the return to unrestricted submarine warfare brought the United States into the war on April 6, 1917. U.S. troops did not arrive in large numbers in Europe until 1918. However, the entry of the United States into the war in 1917 not only gave the Allied powers a psychological boost when they needed it but also brought them a major new source of money and war goods.

The year 1917 had not been a good one for the Allies. Allied offensives on the Western Front were badly defeated. The Italian armies were smashed in October. In November 1917, the Russian Revolution led to Russia's withdrawal from the war (see the discussion later in the chapter). Germany was now free to concentrate entirely on the Western Front. The cause of the Central Powers looked favorable, although war weariness in the Ottoman Empire, Bulgaria, Austria-Hungary, and Germany was beginning to take its toll. The home front was rapidly becoming a cause for as much concern as the war front.

The Home Front: The Impact of Total War

As World War I dragged on, it became a **total war** (war involving a complete mobilization of resources and people) that affected the lives of all citizens in the warring countries, however remote they might be from the battlefields. Masses of men and matériel (equipment and supplies) had to be organized for years of combat. (Germany alone had 5.5 million men in uniform in 1916.) This need for organization led to three developments: an increased centralization of government powers, economic controls, and the manipulation of public opinion to keep the war effort going.

The war was expected to be short, so little thought had been given to long-term wartime needs. Governments had to respond quickly, however, when the war machines failed to achieve their knockout blows. More and more men and matériel were needed to continue the war. To meet these needs, governments expanded their powers. Most European countries had already set up some system of mass conscription, or military draft. It was now carried to unheard-of heights as countries

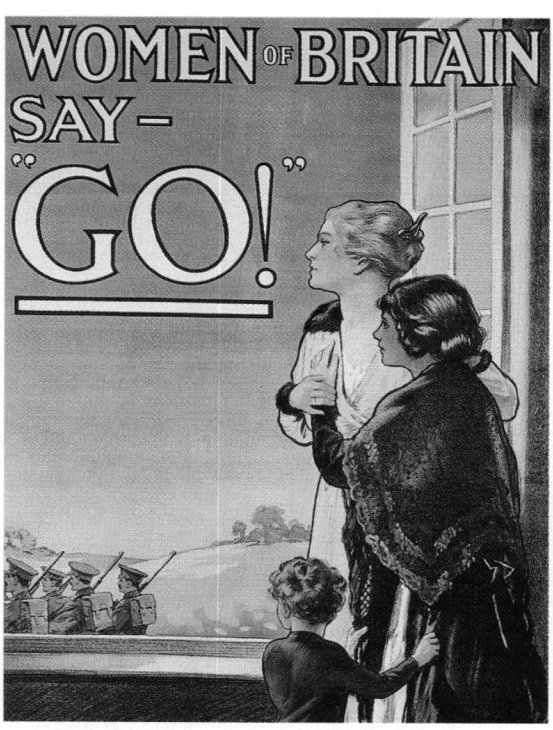

▲ *This patriotic poster was part of an active government campaign to recruit soldiers and create enthusiasm for the war effort. By 1916, even Britain, which had raised the largest volunteer army in modern times, was forced to adopt compulsory military service.*

mobilized tens of millions of young men for final victory. Even countries that continued to rely on volunteers were forced to resort to conscription. In 1916, compulsory military service was introduced in Great Britain. (Great Britain had the largest volunteer army in modern history—one million men—in 1914 and 1915.)

Throughout Europe, wartime governments also expanded their powers over their economies. Free-market capitalistic systems were temporarily put aside. Governments set up price, wage, and rent controls; rationed food supplies and materials; regulated imports and exports; and took over transportation systems and industries. In effect, in order to mobilize the entire resources of their nations for the war effort, European nations set up **planned economies** (systems directed by government agencies). Under conditions of total war mobilization, the differences between soldiers at war and civilians at home were narrowed. In the view of political leaders, all citizens were part of a national army dedicated to victory. As U.S. president Woodrow Wilson said, the men and women "who remain to till the soil and man the factories are no less a part of the army than the men beneath the battle flags."

As the Great War dragged on and casualties grew worse, the patriotic enthusiasm that had marked the early stages of World War I waned. By 1916, there were numerous signs that civilian morale was beginning to crack under the pressure of total war. War governments, however, fought back against the growing opposition to the war. Of course, authoritarian regimes, such as those of Germany, Russia, and Austria-Hungary, had always relied on force to subdue their populations.

Under the pressures of the war, however, even democratic states expanded their police powers to stop internal dissent. The British Parliament passed a Defence of the Realm Act (DORA) at the very beginning of the war. It allowed the government to arrest protestors as traitors. Newspapers were censored, and sometimes their publication was even suspended. In France, government authorities had at first been lenient about public opposition to the war. By 1917, however, the authorities began to fear that open opposition to the war might weaken the French will to fight. When Georges Clemenceau (KLEM-un-SOE) became premier near the end of 1917, the lenient French policies came to an end. Basic civil liberties were suspended for the rest of the war. The editor of an antiwar newspaper was executed on a charge of helping the enemy. Journalists who wrote negative war reports were drafted.

Wartime governments made active use of propaganda to arouse enthusiasm for the war. At the beginning, public officials needed to do little to achieve this goal. The British and French, for example, exaggerated German atrocities in Belgium and found that their citizens were only too willing to believe these accounts. However, as the war progressed and morale sagged, governments were forced to devise new techniques for

MORE ABOUT . . . *War's Vocabulary*

Many words we use today have their roots in World War I. Some examples include:

Ace—originally a pilot who shot down five enemy planes; later came to mean anyone who was good at something

Chow—originally from the Chinese word *ch'ao* (to cook), soldiers used it to describe military food; soldiers themselves were **chowhounds**

Civvies—originally a British soldier's term for non-military (civilian) clothing

Doughboys—a term, the origin of which is unclear, referring to American soldiers

Dud—originally a bomb that didn't go off, later a person who didn't perform

Rookie—from recruit, a new soldier; later used to describe anyone who was inexperienced

COMPARING TIME PERIODS

Compare U.S. government attitudes toward dissent during World War I with its attitudes and actions during another major war; for example, the Revolutionary War, the Civil War, World War II, the Korean conflict, the Vietnam conflict. What were the similarities and differences?

LEARNING FROM VISUALS

Study the British recruiting poster. What exactly is its strategy to pressure men into volunteering for service? Describe the figures inside the window and the figures outside.

CRITICAL THINKING

Have students analyze the language of propaganda during World War I. Why and how was the enemy "demonized"? What words recur often on posters, in newspapers, etc.? What techniques did writers use to keep morale high?

ACROSS THE CURRICULUM

Music Have students listen to the songs (and read their lyrics) sung by soldiers of different nationalities (examples: the German *Watch on the Rhine,* the British *The Old Barbed Wire,* the American *Over There*). What themes emerge in these songs? How do students explain the themes?

▶ *During the war, women were employed in many kinds of jobs that had traditionally been held by men. Here German women work in a munitions factory. How do you think these women were viewed by women who stayed at home or by troops fighting on the front lines?*

motivating the people. In one British recruiting poster, for example, a small daughter asked her father, "Daddy, what did YOU do in the Great War?" while her younger brother played with toy soldiers and cannons.

Total war made a significant impact on European society. For one thing, it brought an end to unemployment. Because millions of men were in the armed services, there were jobs available for everyone who was able to work. World War I also created new roles for women. Because so many men went off to fight at the front, women were called upon to take over jobs that had not been available to them before. The number of women employed in Great Britain who held new jobs or replaced men rose by 1,345,000. Women were also now employed in jobs that had been considered beyond the "capacity of women." These included such occupations as chimney sweeps, truck drivers, farm laborers, and above all, factory workers in heavy industry. Thirty-eight percent of the workers in the Krupp Armaments works in Germany in 1918 were women.

Women were employed at lower wages than men, but they now began to demand equal pay. The French government passed a law in July 1915 that provided a minimum wage for women who worked in the home textile industry. This industry had grown dramatically because of the need for military uniforms. In 1917, the government decreed that men and women should receive equal rates for piecework. Despite the noticeable increase in women's wages that resulted from government regulations, women's industrial wages still were not equal to men's wages by the end of the war.

Even worse, the place of women in the workforce was far from secure. Both men and women seemed to expect that many of the new jobs for women were only temporary. This was evident in the British poem "War Girls," written in 1916:

There's the girl who clips your ticket for the train,
And the girl who speeds the lift from floor to floor,
There's the girl who does a milk-round in the rain,
And the girl who calls for orders at your door.

MORE ABOUT . . . the Home Front

A fad in the United States during World War I was a game which claimed to be able to predict the future. The Ouija board (it gets its name from both the French and German words for yes) is a game actually dating back to the 1880s in which spirits are supposed to move an object around a board with letters on it, spelling out predictions.

Over a million games were sold in 1919, which is not very difficult to explain, as friends and families were anxious to know about their loved ones overseas. In fact, sales for Ouija boards have jumped during every war since, reaching an all time high of 2.3 million games in 1967, during the war in Vietnam.

Strong, sensible, and fit,
They're out to show their grit,
And tackle jobs with energy and knack.
No longer caged and penned up,
They're going to keep their end up
Till the khaki soldier boys come marching back.[4]

At the end of the war, governments quickly removed women from the jobs they had encouraged them to take earlier. By 1919, there were 650,000 unemployed women in Great Britain. Wages for the women who were still employed were lowered. The work benefits for women from World War I seemed to be short-lived as men returned to the job market.

Nevertheless, in some countries the role played by women in the wartime economies did have a positive impact on the women's movement for social and political emancipation. The most obvious gain was the right to vote that was given to women in Germany and Austria immediately after the war. (In Britain, women had obtained this right in January 1918.) Many upper- and middle-class women had also gained new freedoms. In ever-larger numbers, these young women took jobs; had their own apartments; and showed their new independence by smoking in public, wearing shorter dresses, and choosing new hairstyles.

 SECTION REVIEW

1. **Locate:**
   (a) Verdun,   (b) Constantinople

2. **Define:**
   (a) trench warfare,   (b) war of attrition,
   (c) total war,   (d) planned economies

3. **Identify:**
   (a) First Battle of the Marne,   (b) mustard gas,
   (c) zeppelin,   (d) Lawrence of Arabia,
   (e) Woodrow Wilson,   (f) Defence of the Realm Act (DORA)

4. **Recall:**
   (a) What two beliefs were commonly held in Europe that convinced many people that World War I would not take place?

   (b) Why was a "breakthrough" such an important military goal in World War I?
   (c) How did unrestricted submarine warfare draw the United States into World War I?
   (d) What three developments increased centralization of government power during World War I?

5. **Think Critically:** Why do times of war often speed the process of achieving greater rights for women?

3

REVOLUTION AND THE END OF THE WAR

By 1917, total war was creating serious domestic problems in all of the warring European states. Only Russia, however, experienced a complete collapse in that year. Out of Russia's collapse came the Russian Revolution, the impact of which would be widely felt in Europe and the world for decades to come.

Background to the Russian Revolution

Tsar Nicholas II of Russia was an autocratic ruler who relied on the army and bureaucracy to hold up his regime. However, World War I put the tsarist government to a test that it could not meet. Russia was unprepared both militarily and technologically for the total war of World War I. It had no competent military leaders. Even worse, the tsar—and of all European monarchs, only the tsar—insisted on taking personal charge of the armed forces despite his obvious lack of ability and training for such an awesome burden. Russian industry was unable to produce the weapons needed for the army. Many soldiers were trained with broomsticks. Others were sent to the front without rifles and told to pick one up from a dead comrade. Ill led and ill armed, the Russian army suffered incredible losses. Between 1914 and 1916, two million soldiers had been killed, and another four to six million had been wounded or captured. By 1917, the Russian will to fight had vanished.

On Line with

WORLD HISTORY *Internet Activity*

You may want to have your students visit the following URL, where they will find information and additional web site resources to enhance their study of this chapter.

World War I—Trenches on the WEB An Internet History of the Great War

http://www.worldwar1.com/

Comprehensive resource for all aspects of WWI. A good series of graphics on military weapons and political cartoons of the era. A complete reference library included.

Due to the ever-changing nature of the World Wide Web, see the West History web site, **http://history.swpco.com** for regular updates of the URLs in this text.

FOCUS

OBJECTIVES

After completing this section, students should be able to

1. summarize the failure of the tsarist government to cope with World War I
2. explain the significance of Alexandra, Rasputin, Lenin, Trotsky, Kerensky
3. trace the Bolshevik overthrow of the Provisional Government
4. summarize the major reasons for the Bolshevik victory in the civil war
5. summarize the major events of the last year of World War I

FOCUS ACTIVITY

Ask students to imagine the revolutionary fervor and excitement of the early days of Communism. What aspects of the Communist program would have seemed most attractive to people exhausted by the war? What would have been the fascination for people like John Reed, who had become disenchanted with capitalism and angry about continuing social inequalities? Can students imagine their own reactions to Lenin's call for a workers' revolution?

TEACH

CLASS DISCUSSION

Guide students in a discussion of how "World War I put the tsarist government to a test that it could not meet."

818

Map 25.4   The Russian Revolution and Civil War

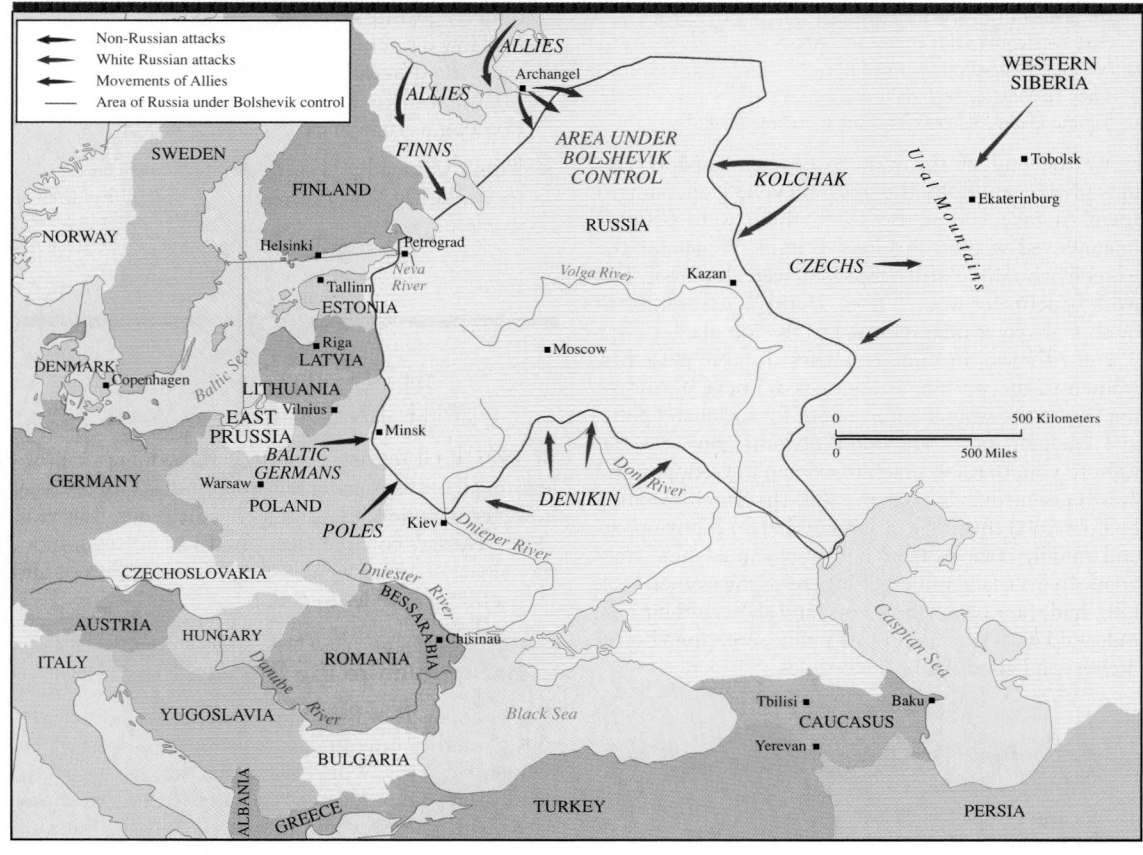

The tsarist government was totally unprepared for the tasks that it faced in 1914. Even conservative aristocrats were appalled by the incompetent and inefficient bureaucracy that controlled the political and military system. In the meantime, Tsar Nicholas II was increasingly cut off from events by his German-born wife, Alexandra. She was a willful and stubborn woman who had fallen under the influence of Rasputin (ra-SPYOOT-un), an uneducated Siberian peasant who claimed to be a holy man. Alexandra believed that Rasputin was holy, for he alone seemed able to

stop the bleeding of her son Alexis. Alexis, the heir to the throne, had hemophilia (a deficiency in the ability of the blood to clot). With the tsar at the front, Alexandra made all important decisions. However, she insisted on first consulting Rasputin, the man she called "her beloved, never-to-be-forgotten teacher, savior, and mentor." Rasputin's influence made him an important power behind the throne. He did not hesitate to interfere in government affairs.

As the leadership at the top stumbled its way through a series of military and economic disasters, the

STUDYING MAPS

The following questions and activities will help you guide students through their study of Map 25.4.

1. Locate Petrograd, Moscow, Siberia, Volga River, Kiev, Caucasus, Bessarabia, and the Ural Mountains.
2. Compare the area of Russia under Bolshevik control in 1919 with the area under anti-Bolshevik control. Which is larger?

(anti-Bolshevikarea) Which contained Russia's main cities? *(Bolshevik area)*
3. Trace the attacks by White Russians and non-Russians during the Russian civil war.
4. Compare this map with a map of the U.S.S.R. and with a map of the current Commonwealth of Independent States. Note the territory of Eastern Russia which does not show on Map 25.4

Russian middle class, aristocrats, peasants, soldiers, and workers grew more and more upset with the tsarist regime. Even conservative aristocrats who supported the monarchy felt the need to do something to save the situation. For a start, they assassinated Rasputin in December 1916. It was not easy to kill this man of incredible physical strength. They shot him three times and then tied him up and threw him into the Neva River. He drowned, but not before he had managed to untie the knots underwater. The assassination of Rasputin, however, proved to be too late to save the monarchy. Its fall came quickly.

At the beginning of March 1917, a series of strikes broke out in the capital city of Petrograd (formerly St. Petersburg). Here the actions of working-class women helped to change the course of Russian history. In February 1917, the government had introduced bread rationing in the capital city after the price of bread had skyrocketed. Many of the women who stood in the lines waiting for bread were also factory workers who worked twelve-hour days. The Russian government had become aware of the situation in the capital from a police report:

▲ *Rasputin was an illiterate Siberian peasant. Why do you think people said that his eyes held hypnotic power?*

> *Mothers of families, exhausted by endless standing in line at stores, distraught over their half-starving and sick children, are today perhaps closer to revolution than [the liberal opposition leaders] and of course they are a great deal more dangerous because they are the combustible material for which only a single spark is needed to burst into flame.*[5]

On March 8, about 10,000 women marched through Petrograd demanding "Peace and Bread" and "Down with Autocracy." Soon the women were joined by other workers. Together they called for a general strike that was able to shut down all the factories in the city on March 10. Alexandra wrote Nicholas II at the battlefront, "This is a hooligan movement. If the weather were very cold they would all probably stay at home." Nicholas ordered the troops to break up the crowds by shooting them if necessary. Soon, however, large numbers of the soldiers joined the demonstrators. The Duma, or legislative body, which the tsar had tried to dissolve, met anyway. On March 12, it established a Provisional Government that urged the tsar to step down. Because he no longer had the support of the army or even the aristocrats, Nicholas II did step down, on March 15.

The Provisional Government headed by Alexander Kerensky decided to carry on the war to preserve Russia's honor. This was a major blunder. It satisfied neither the workers nor the peasants, who wanted above all an end to the war. The Provisional Government was also faced with another authority, the **soviets,** or councils composed of deputies from the workers and soldiers. The soviet of Petrograd had been formed in March 1917. At the same time, soviets sprang up in army units, factory towns, and rural areas. The soviets represented the more radical interests of the lower classes. They were largely made up of socialists of different kinds. One group—the Bolsheviks—came to play a crucial role.

Lenin and the Bolshevik Seizure of Power

The Bolsheviks were a small faction of Russian Social Democrats (a Marxist party) who had come under the leadership of Vladimir Ulianov (ool-YAWN-uf), known to the world as V. I. Lenin. Born in 1870 to a middle-class family, Lenin received a legal education and became a lawyer. In 1887, he turned into a revolutionary—a dedicated enemy of tsarist Russia—when

ADDITIONAL RESOURCES

The resources listed below can be used to enrich the lessons in this chapter.

A good introduction to the Russian Revolution can be found in S. Fitzpatrick, *The Russian Revolution, 1917–1932* (New York, 1982); and R. V. Daniels, *Red October* (New York, 1967). On Lenin, see R. W. Clark, *Lenin* (New York, 1988); and the valuable work by A. B. Ulam, *The Bolsheviks* (New York, 1965). On Allied intervention in the civil war, see M. Kettle, *Russia and the Allies, 1917–1920* (Minneapolis, 1981). On the revolutions in Germany and Austria-Hungary, see F. L. Carsten, *Revolution in Central Europe* (Berkeley, 1972); and A. J. Ryder, *The German Revolution of 1918* (Cambridge, 1967).

▶ *Large crowds gathered in town squares throughout Russia to protest the tsarist governmental actions. Do you think Lenin would have gained power as quickly if the Provisional Government had withdrawn Russian troops from the war?*

his older brother was executed by the tsar's police for planning to assassinate the tsar. Lenin's search for a revolutionary faith led him to Marxism. In 1894, he moved to St. Petersburg, where he organized an illegal working-class group. Lenin was arrested for his revolutionary activity and was shipped to Siberia. After his release, he chose to go into exile in Switzerland. Eventually, he became the leader of the Bolshevik wing of the Russian Social Democratic Party.

Under Lenin's direction, the Bolsheviks became a party dedicated to violent revolution. He believed that only a violent revolution could destroy the capitalist system. A "vanguard" of activists, he said, must form a small party of well-disciplined professional revolutionaries to accomplish the task. Between 1900 and 1917, Lenin spent most of his time in Switzerland. When the Provisional Government was formed in March 1917, he believed that an opportunity for the Bolsheviks to seize power had come. In April 1917, the German military leaders, hoping to create disorder in Russia,

shipped Lenin to Russia in a "sealed train" by way of Finland.

Lenin's arrival in Russia opened a new stage of the Russian Revolution. Lenin maintained that the soviets of soldiers, workers, and peasants were ready-made instruments of power. He believed that the Bolsheviks needed to work toward gaining control of these groups and then use them to overthrow the Provisional Government. At the same time, the Bolsheviks would seek mass support through the use of propaganda by making promises to the people. These promises included an end to the war, the redistribution of all land to the peasants, the transfer of factories and industries from capitalists to committees of workers, and the transfer of government power from the Provisional Government to the soviets. Three simple slogans summed up the Bolshevik program: "Peace, Land, Bread," "Worker Control of Production," and "All Power to the Soviets."

By the end of October, the Bolsheviks had reached a slight majority in the Petrograd and Moscow soviets.

The number of party members had also grown from 50,000 to 240,000. With the close cooperation of Leon Trotsky, a dedicated revolutionary, Lenin organized a Military Revolutionary Committee within the Petrograd soviet. Its task was to plot the overthrow of the government. On the night of November 6, Bolshevik forces seized the Winter Palace, the seat of the Provisional Government. The Provisional Government quickly collapsed with little bloodshed.

This overthrow of the Provisional Government had been timed to coincide with a meeting in Petrograd of the all-Russian Congress of Soviets, which represented local soviets from all over the country. Outwardly, Lenin turned over the power of the Provisional Government to this Congress of Soviets. The real power, however, passed to a Council of People's Commissars, headed by Lenin (see "You Are There: Ten Days That Shook the World").

The Bolsheviks, soon renamed the Communists, still faced enormous obstacles. For one thing, Lenin had promised peace. Fulfilling that promise, he realized, would not be an easy task. It would mean the humiliating loss of much Russian territory. There was no real choice, however. On March 3, 1918, Lenin signed the Treaty of Brest-Litovsk with Germany and gave up eastern Poland, Ukraine, Finland, and the Baltic provinces. To his critics, Lenin argued that it made no difference. The spread of socialist revolution throughout Europe would make the treaty largely irrelevant. In any case, he had promised peace to the Russian people. Real peace did not come, however. The country soon sank into civil war.

Civil War in Russia

Many people were opposed to the new Bolshevik, or Communist, regime. These people included not only groups loyal to the tsar but also liberals and anti-Leninist socialists. These groups were joined by thousands of Allied troops who were sent to different parts of Russia in the hope of bringing Russia back into the war.

Between 1918 and 1921, the Bolshevik (or Red) Army was forced to fight on many fronts. The first serious threat to the Bolsheviks came from Siberia. Here a

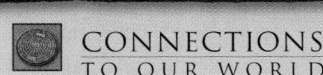

CONNECTIONS
TO OUR WORLD

The Mystery of Anastasia   Soon after the murder of Tsar Nicholas II, his wife Alexandria, and their five children on the night of July 16, 1919, rumors began to circulate that some members of the family had survived. In 1921, a young woman in Dalldorf, Germany, claimed to be the Grand Duchess Anastasia, the youngest daughter of Nicholas II. Some surviving members of the Romanov family became convinced that she was Anastasia. Grand Duke Andrew, Nicholas II's first cousin, said after meeting with her, "For me there is definitely no doubt; it is Anastasia."

Later, the woman claiming to be Anastasia came to the United States. While in New York, she registered at a Long Island hotel as Anna Anderson and soon became known by that name. In 1932, she returned to Germany. During the next thirty years, she pursued a claim in German courts for part of the estate left to Empress Alexandra's German relatives. In the 1960s in the United States, Anna Anderson became even better known as a result of the popular play and film, *Anastasia*.

In 1968, Anna Anderson returned to the United States, where she died in 1984. In 1994, DNA testing of tissues from Anna Anderson revealed that she was not the Grand Duchess Anastasia. In all probability, Anna Anderson was Franziska Schanzkowska, a Polish farmer's daughter who had always dreamed of being an actress.

White (anti-Bolshevik) force attacked westward and advanced almost to the Volga River before being stopped. Attacks also came from the Ukrainians in the southeast and from the Baltic regions. In mid-1919, White forces swept through Ukraine and advanced almost to Moscow. However, they were pushed back. By 1920, the major White forces had been defeated and Ukraine retaken. The next year, the Communist regime regained control over the independent nation

MORE ABOUT . . . *War in Russia*

As if the world war, revolution, and civil war weren't devastating enough to the Russian people, an even greater danger appeared in the form of lice. Lice carry *Rickettsia* bacteria, which cause typhus. During the war years, between 1914 and 1916, the situation on the eastern front was bad (there were no similar outbreaks on the western front due to the use of fumigants), but after the revolution of 1917 Russia experienced the worst typhus epidemics in history. Between 1917 and 1921, over 25 million Russians came down with typhus and over 2.5 million died.

YOU ARE THERE

Ten Days That Shook the World

John Reed was an American journalist who helped found the American Communist Labor party. Accused of treason, he fled the United States and went to Russia. In Ten Days That Shook the World, *Reed left an eyewitness account of the Russian Revolution. He considered V. I. Lenin the great hero of the Bolshevik success.*

John Reed, *Ten Days That Shook the World*

It was just 8:40 when a thundering wave of cheers announced the entrance of the presidium, with Lenin—great Lenin—among them. A short, stocky figure, with a big head set down in his shoulders, bald and bulging. Little eyes, a snubbish nose, wide, generous mouth, and heavy chin. Dressed in shabby clothes, his trousers much too long for him. Unimpressive, to be the idol of a mob, loved and revered as perhaps few leaders in history have been. . . .

Now Lenin, gripping the edge of the reading stand, letting his little winking eyes travel over the crowd as he stood there waiting, apparently oblivious to the long-rolling ovation, which lasted several minutes. When it finished, he said simply, "We shall now proceed to construct the Socialist order!" Again that overwhelming human roar.

"The first thing is the adoption of practical measures to realize peace. . . . We shall offer peace to the peoples of all the warring countries upon the basis of the Soviet terms—no annexations, no indemnities, and the right of self-determination of peoples. . . . This proposal of peace will meet with resistance on the part of the imperialist governments—we don't fool ourselves on that score. But we hope that revolution will soon break out in all the warring countries; that is why we address ourselves especially to the workers of France, England and Germany. . . .

"The revolution of November 6th and 7th," he ended, "has opened the era of the Social Revolution. . . . The labour movement, in the name of peace and Socialism, shall win, and fulfill its destiny. . . ."

---

alist governments in the Caucasus (KAW-ku-sus): Georgia, Russian Armenia, and Azerbaijan (AZ-ur-BIE-JAWN).

The royal family was yet another victim of the civil war. After the tsar had abdicated, he, his wife, and their five children had been taken into captivity. They were moved in August 1917 to Tobolsk, in Siberia. In April 1918, they were moved to Ekaterinburg, a mining town in the Urals. On the night of July 16, members of the local soviet murdered the tsar and his family and burned their bodies in a nearby mine shaft.

How had Lenin and the Communists triumphed in the civil war over what seemed to be overwhelming forces? For one thing, the Red Army was a well-disciplined fighting force. This was largely due to the organizational genius of Leon Trotsky. As commissar of war, Trotsky reinstated the draft and insisted on rigid discipline. Soldiers who deserted or refused to obey orders were executed on the spot.

Furthermore, the disunity of the anti-Communist forces weakened the efforts of the Whites. Political differences created distrust among the Whites and prevented them from cooperating effectively with one another. Some Whites insisted on restoring the tsarist regime. Others believed that only a more liberal and democratic program had any chance of success. These political differences made it virtually impossible for the Whites to achieve military cooperation.

So What ???

YOU ARE THERE

Ten Days That Shook the World, continued

▲ *Lenin may not have been a handsome man, but he was the driving force behind the Bolsheviks as they took control of Russia. In this 1917 photo, Lenin speaks to a crowd in Moscow.*

There was something quiet and powerful in all this, which stirred the souls of men. It was understandable why people believed when Lenin spoke.

1. Did John Reed agree or disagree with Lenin?

2. How do you know that Reed's account of Lenin is biased?

The Whites, then, had no common goal. The Communists, in contrast, had a single-minded sense of purpose. Inspired by their vision of a new socialist order, the Communists had the determination that comes from revolutionary fervor and convictions.

The Communists were also able to translate their revolutionary faith into practical instruments of power. A policy of **war communism**, for example, was used to ensure regular supplies for the Red Army. War communism meant government control of banks and most industries, the seizing of grain from peasants, and the centralization of state administration under Communist control. Another Communist instrument was revolutionary terror. Although the old tsarist secret police had been abolished, a new Red secret police—known as the Cheka (CHAE-kaw)—replaced it. The Cheka began a Red Terror aimed at nothing less than the destruction of all those who opposed the new regime (much like the Reign of Terror in the French Revolution). The Red Terror added an element of fear to the Communist regime.

Finally, the presence of foreign armies on Russian soil enabled the Communists to appeal to the powerful force of Russian patriotism. The Allied powers had originally sent troops to Russia to encourage the Russians to remain in the war. With the end of the war on

ENRICHMENT ACTIVITY

Have students examine the posters depicted on pages 815 and 824. In what ways is art a key to history? What can be learned by studying each poster? What message is each poster trying to convey? How does each poster play on emotions? Design and create a modern American propaganda poster (you pick the topic).

CRITICAL THINKING

Ask students to analyze how and why the presence of Allied troops in Russia served to help the cause they opposed, Communism.

ACROSS THE CURRICULUM

Political Science. Ask students to bring in other examples of Communist "agit-prop." What made these efforts so successful?

CRITICAL THINKING

Ask students to discuss how post-World War I history might have been different had the United States and its allies either supported the Bolsheviks or at least pursued a "hands-off" policy during the Russian civil war.

CRITICAL THINKING

To many, Lenin was a great hero. To others, he was a bloodthirsty tyrant. Which do students feel is correct?

CLASS DISCUSSION

For years, Lenin's embalmed body, displayed in a glass coffin, rested in a mausoleum in Red Square. Russians and foreign visitors waited in line at the shrine to view his remains. Since the breakup of the Soviet Union, what has happened to his body? How does this reflect a changed view of Lenin, the hero?

▲ *Communists used agitational propaganda, such as this vibrant poster, very effectively during the civil war. Brief slogans coupled with stirring images, like the Red Army star, served to educate the Russian people about the Communists.*

November 11, 1918, however, the Allied troops were no longer needed. Nevertheless, they remained, and even more were sent. Allied countries did not hide their anti-Communist feelings. At one point, over 100,000 foreign troops—mostly Japanese, British, American, and French—were stationed on Russian soil. These forces rarely fought, however, nor did they pursue a common strategy. However, they did give material assistance to anti-Communist forces. The Allied troops also made it easy for the Communist government to appeal to patriotic Russians to fight the attempts of foreigners to control their country. Allied troops were never substantial enough to make a military difference in the civil war. They did serve indirectly, however, to help the Bolshevik cause.

By 1921, the Communists were in control of Russia. In the course of the civil war, the Communist regime had transformed Russia into a bureaucratically centralized state dominated by a single party. It was also a state that was largely hostile to the Allied powers that had sought to help the Communists' enemies in the civil war.

The Last Year of the War

For Germany, the withdrawal of the Russians from the war in March 1918 offered new hope for a successful end to the war. The victory over Russia persuaded Erich von Ludendorff, who guided German military operations, to make one final military gamble—a grand offensive in the west to break the military stalemate.

The German attack was launched in March. By April, German troops were within 50 miles of Paris. However, the German advance was stopped at the Second Battle of the Marne, on July 18. French, Moroccan, and American troops (140,000 fresh American troops had just arrived), supported by hundreds of tanks, threw the Germans back over the Marne (see "The Role of Science and Technology: The Beginning of Tank Warfare"). Ludendorff's gamble had failed. With the arrival of two million more American troops, Allied forces began making a steady advance toward Germany.

On September 29, 1918, General Ludendorff informed German leaders that the war was lost. He demanded that the government sue for peace at once. German officials soon discovered, however, that the Allies were unwilling to make peace with the autocratic imperial government of Germany. Reforms were begun to create a liberal government. However, these constitutional reforms came too late for the exhausted and angry German people.

On November 3, sailors in Kiel (KEE-ul), in northern Germany, mutinied. Within days councils of workers and soldiers were forming throughout northern Germany and taking over civilian and military offices. William II gave in to public pressure and left the country on November 9. The Social Democrats under Friedrich Ebert then announced the creation of a democratic republic. Two days later, on November 11, 1918, the new German government agreed to an

MORE ABOUT . . . *Submarine Warfare*

One of the factors which resulted in the United States entering the war was the sinking of the British ocean liner, the *Lusitania.* In May of 1915, carrying 1,959 passengers as well as five thousand cases of war munitions, she left New York for England. Less than a week after she left port, a German U-boat sent two torpedoes into her portside. The ship sank in 18 minutes with a loss of 1,198 lives, including 124 Americans. The American outrage over the sinking resulted in President Wilson taking a tough stand on the issue of freedom of the seas and German attacks on non-belligerents. Discuss whether, with her cargo of war munitions, the *Lusitania* was really non-belligerent.

THE ROLE OF SCIENCE AND TECHNOLOGY
The Beginning of Tank Warfare

▲ *This World War I photo shows British tanks on their way to the front lines. Why do you think the Allies did not use tanks more effectively during the war?*

Trench warfare on the Western Front made World War I a war of stalemate and a defensive slaughter. This state of affairs led some to seek a new way of moving to the offensive. The tank proved to be the answer.

The tank was an armored vehicle that could move across rough ground. A British army officer, Ernest Swinton, first conceived of the idea. The first tank—a British model—appeared in 1916. Its caterpillar tracks enabled it to cross rough terrain. Guns were mounted on its sides. "Male" tanks used two 57-millimeter guns to attack enemy machine gun positions. "Female" tanks carried four machine guns aimed chiefly at enemy infantry.

These first tanks, used in the Battle of the Somme in 1916, were not very effective. A new model, the Mark IV, had more success in November 1917 at the Battle of Cambrai (kam-BRAE).

▲ *This diagram shows the working parts of a French Renault "mosquito" tank. This tank did not travel across rough terrain as well as British ones, but it could turn more quickly.*

Four hundred tanks spearheaded an advance that drove five miles into the enemy lines, and with relatively few casualties.

(continued)

ENRICHMENT ACTIVITY

Some students may be interested in comparing the role that tanks played in World War I with the role they played in Operation Desert Storm. Ask them to trace how the technology of the tanks had developed over the more than 70 years of their use. The sophisticated tank guidance system was brought to the movie screen in the film *Courage Under Fire* which more mature students would appreciate.

1. Britain

2. They felt tanks were a sign of weakness.

3. They enabled armies to conduct lightning attacks using columns of tanks and air power, and virtually did away with trench warfare.

ASSESS

Answers to SECTION REVIEW

2. (a) Russian councils composed of deputies who were workers and soldiers (b) government control of banks and industries, forcible requisition of grain, and centralization of state administration under Communist control

3. (a) wife of Tsar Nicholas (b) Siberian peasant who became a trusted advisor to Alexandra (c) head of the Russian Provisional Government in 1917 (d) Marxist party in Russia (e) Lenin; leader of the Communist take over of Russia (f) Communist leader who helped organize overthrow of the Provisional Government in 1917 (g) Communist secret police (h) battle in 1918 in which a German advance on Paris was stopped with the help of American troops (i) German leader who formed a democratic republic to end the War in 1918

4. (a) Russian economy unable to produce

THE ROLE OF SCIENCE AND TECHNOLOGY
The Beginning of Tank Warfare, continued

The French soon followed with their own tanks. They were less effective, however. The Germans were contemptuous of the new tanks and considered them a sign of weakness. However, they, too, finally got around to producing their own tank—the A7V. It was unstable, required a crew of eighteen, and saw little action, however.

By 1918, the British had developed a Mark V model that had a more powerful engine and could be more easily maneuvered. Tanks, now used in large numbers and coordinated with infantry and artillery, became effective instruments in pushing back the retreating German army.

The tank came too late to have a great effect on the outcome of World War I. The lesson, however, was not lost on those who realized the tank's

potential for creating a whole new kind of warfare. In World War II, lightning attacks that depended on tank columns and massive air power enabled armies to cut quickly across battle lines and encircle entire enemy armies. It was a far cry from the trench warfare of World War I.

1. Which country developed the first tank?

2. Why were the Germans contemptuous of the new tanks?

3. What impact did the development of tanks have on warfare?

armistice (a truce). The war was over, but the revolutionary forces set in motion by the war were not yet exhausted.

The Social Democrats had established a democratic republic in Germany on November 9, 1918. However, a group of radical socialists, unhappy with the moderate policies of the Social Democrats, formed the German Communist Party in December 1918. A month later, the Communists tried to seize power in Berlin. The new Social Democratic government, backed by regular army troops, crushed the rebels and brutally murdered Rosa Luxemburg and Karl Liebknecht (LEEP[kuh]NEKT), leaders of the German Communists. A similar attempt at Communist revolution in the city of Munich (MYOO-nik), in southern Germany, was also crushed. The new German republic had been saved from radical revolution. The attempt at revolution, however, left the German middle class with a deep fear of communism.

Austria-Hungary, too, experienced disintegration and revolution. As war weariness took hold of the em-

pire, ethnic groups increasingly sought to achieve their independence. By the time the war ended, the Austro-Hungarian Empire was no more. It had been replaced by the independent republics of Austria, Hungary, and Czechoslovakia, along with the large monarchical state called Yugoslavia. Rivalries among the nations that succeeded Austria-Hungary would weaken eastern Europe for the next eighty years.

❀ SECTION REVIEW ❀

1. Locate:
(a) Petrograd, (b) Volga River, (c) Ukraine, (d) Caucasus, (e) Ural Mountains

2. Define:
(a) soviets, (b) war communism

3. Identify:
(a) Alexandra, (b) Rasputin, (c) Alexander Kerensky, (d) Russian Social Democrats,

ENRICHMENT ACTIVITY

Ask students to create a chart comparing the American, French, and Russian revolutions for social, economic, and political aims. They should compare changes in the class system, the patterns of wealth distribution, and types of governments instituted. Then discuss the three revolutions. Which brought

about the most lasting government? Which brought about the most significant changes in the class system, wealth distribution, and type of government instituted? Is there any relation between the degree of change and the stability of the resulting government?

(e) Vladimir Ulanov,   (f) Leon Trotsky,
(g) Cheka,   (h) Second Battle of the Marne,
(i) Friedrich Ebert

4. **Recall:**
(a) What factors limited Russia's ability to fight in World War I?
(b) Why did Tsar Nicholas give up power in 1917?
(c) What three promises did the Bolsheviks make to gain popular support in 1917?
(d) What problem of the White Army forces probably kept them from defeating the Red Army?

5. **Think Critically:** Why is the presence of foreign soldiers in a nation likely to stir people to be more willing to fight?

THE PEACE SETTLEMENTS

In January 1919, representatives of 27 victorious Allied nations met in Paris. Their task was to make a final settlement of the Great War. Some delegates believed that this conference would avoid the mistakes made at Vienna in 1815. There, leaders had rearranged the map of Europe to meet the selfish desires of the great powers. Harold Nicolson, one of the British delegates in Paris, expressed what he believed this conference would achieve instead: "We were journeying to Paris not merely to liquidate the war, but to found a New Order in Europe. We were preparing not Peace only, but Eternal Peace. There was about us the halo of some divine mission. . . . For we were bent on doing great, permanent and noble things."[6]

Background to Peacemaking

Nicolson's quest for "Eternal Peace" was a difficult one, however. Over a period of years, the reasons for fighting World War I had changed dramatically. European nations had gone to war in 1914 largely to achieve territorial gains. By the beginning of 1918, some leaders were using more idealistic reasons. No one expressed

these reasons better than the U.S. president, Woodrow Wilson. Wilson outlined "Fourteen Points" to the U.S. Congress—his basis for a peace settlement that he believed justified the enormous military struggle then being waged. Later, Wilson spelled out additional steps for a truly just and lasting peace.

Wilson's proposals included "open covenants (binding agreements) of peace, openly arrived at" instead of secret diplomacy; the reduction of national armaments (military forces or weapons) to a "point consistent with domestic safety"; and the self-determination of people (each people could have its own state) so that "all well-defined national aspirations shall be accorded the utmost satisfaction." Wilson portrayed World War I as a people's war against "absolutism and militarism." These two enemies of liberty, he argued, could be eliminated only by creating democratic governments and a "general association of nations." The latter would guarantee the "political independence and territorial integrity to great and small states alike." Wilson became the spokesperson for a new world order based on democracy and international cooperation. When he arrived in Europe for the peace conference, he was enthusiastically cheered by many Europeans.

Wilson soon found, however, that more practical motives guided other states at the Paris Peace Conference. Secret treaties and agreements that had been made before the war had raised the hopes of European nations for territorial gains. These hopes could not be totally ignored, even if they did conflict with the principle of self-determination put forth by Wilson. National interests also complicated the deliberations of the Paris Peace Conference. For example, David Lloyd George, prime minister of Great Britain, had won a decisive victory in elections in December of 1918. His platform was simple: make the Germans pay for this dreadful war.

France's approach to peace, in contrast, was chiefly guided by its desire for national security. To Georges Clemenceau, the feisty premier of France who had led his country to victory, the French people had suffered the most from German aggression. They deserved revenge, but also security against future German aggression. Clemenceau wanted a Germany stripped of all weapons, vast German payments to cover the costs

enough weapons for soldiers
(b) lost support from the Russian army
(c) They promised peace, land, and bread.
(d) disunity among factions in the White Army
5. Answers will vary but should include the fact that many people feel the presence of foreign soldiers is an offense to their nation's honor and makes them more willing to fight.

CLOSE

Review with students the major events of the last year of the war. Ask them to trace the developments that led to the end of the fighting.

FOCUS

OBJECTIVES

After completing this section, students should be able to

1. compare Wilson's program for peace with the approaches of France and England
2. list the major provisions of the Treaty of Versailles
3. describe the provisions of the other peace treaties

FOCUS ACTIVITY

Ask students to discuss the failure of Wilson's approach to the peace. Since the U.S. entered the war so late and since no battles were fought on U.S. soil, was it reasonable for Wilson to expect the European nations to share his views?

TEACH

LEARNING FROM VISUALS

Answer to the caption questions: Britain, France, and the United States made the major decisions concerning the Treaty of Versailles.

CRITICAL THINKING

Ask students to define an idealist. *(One guided by ideals—lofty, high principles—rather than by practical considerations.)* Have them discuss the ways in which Woodrow Wilson was an idealist. Have them consider how Harold Nicolson's description of the quest for "Eternal Peace" could be called idealistic. Since ideas are usually considered positive and admirable, why weren't Wilson's proposals embraced by European leaders?

CLASS DISCUSSION

Guide students in a discussion of how national interests, desire for revenge, and hopes for territorial gains figured in the 1919 peace talks.

CRITICAL THINKING

Ask students to research and analyze the defeat of the League of Nations proposal in the U.S. Congress. What effect did this defeat have on the career of Woodrow Wilson?

▶ *The Big Four at the Paris Peace Conference were David Lloyd George, Britain; Vittorio Orlando, Italy; Georges Clemenceau, France; and Woodrow Wilson, United States. Which three countries made the major decisions during the conference?*

of the war, and a separate Rhineland as a buffer state between France and Germany. Wilson denounced these demands as contrary to the principle of national self-determination.

Twenty-seven nations met at the Paris Peace Conference, but the most important decisions were made by Wilson, Clemenceau, and Lloyd George. Italy, which was considered one of the so-called Big Four powers, played a much less important role than the other key powers—the United States, France, and Great Britain—called the Big Three. Germany, of course, was not invited to attend, and Russia could not be there because of its civil war.

In view of the many conflicting demands at the peace conference, it was no surprise that the Big Three quarreled. Wilson wanted to create a League of Nations to prevent future wars. Clemenceau and Lloyd George wanted to punish Germany. In the end, only compromise made it possible to achieve a peace settlement.

Wilson's wish that the creation of an international peacekeeping organization be the first order of business was granted. Already on January 25, 1919, the confer-

ence accepted the idea of a League of Nations. In return, Wilson agreed to make compromises on territorial arrangements. He did so because he believed that the League could later fix any unfair settlements. Clemenceau also compromised to get some guarantees for French security. He gave up France's wish for a separate Rhineland and instead accepted a defensive alliance with Great Britain and the United States. Both Great Britain and the United States pledged to help France if it were attacked by Germany.

The Treaty of Versailles

The final peace settlement of Paris consisted of five separate treaties with the defeated nations—Germany, Austria, Hungary, Bulgaria, and Turkey. The Treaty of Versailles with Germany, signed at Versailles near Paris, on June 28, 1919, was by far the most important of the treaties. The Germans considered it a harsh peace. They were especially unhappy with Article 231, the so-called War Guilt Clause, which declared that

ENRICHMENT ACTIVITY

Divide class into three groups, French, British, and U.S. Have each group list the goals of their nation at the Paris Peace Conference. Have them organize the goals in order of priority, from non-negotiable to negotiable. Then have each group elect a spokesperson to play the role of Clemenceau, Lloyd George, and Wilson. Now have these students, backed by their lists and their groups, attempt to draw up a peace treaty.

Germany (and Austria) were responsible for starting the war. Moreover, the treaty ordered Germany to pay **reparations** (financial compensation) for all the damage to which the Allied governments and their people had been subjected as a result of the war "imposed upon them by the aggression of Germany and her allies."

The military and territorial provisions of the Treaty of Versailles also angered the Germans. Germany had to reduce its army to 100,000 men, cut back its navy, and eliminate its air force. Alsace and Lorraine, taken by the Germans from France in 1871, were now returned. Sections of Prussia were awarded to a new Polish state. German land west and as far as 30 miles east of the Rhine was made a demilitarized zone and stripped of all weapons or fortifications. This, it was hoped, would serve as a barrier to any future German military moves westward against France. Outraged by the "dictated peace," the new German government vowed to resist rather than accept the treaty. However, it had no real alternative. Rejection of the treaty would mean a renewal of the war. That, as German army leaders pointed out, was no longer possible.

The Other Peace Treaties

The separate peace treaties made with the other Central Powers (Austria, Hungary, Bulgaria, and Turkey) redrew the map of eastern Europe. Many of these changes had already taken place at the end of the war. Both the German and Russian Empires lost considerable territory in eastern Europe, and the Austro-Hungarian Empire disappeared altogether. New nation-states emerged from the lands of these three empires: Finland, Latvia, Estonia, Lithuania, Poland, Czechoslovakia, Austria, and Hungary. New territorial arrangements were also made in the Balkans. Romania acquired additional lands from Russia, Hungary, and Bulgaria. Serbia formed the nucleus of a new state, called Yugoslavia, which combined Serbs, Croats, and Slovenes.

The Paris Peace Conference was supposedly guided by the principle of self-determination. However, the mixtures of peoples in eastern Europe made it impossible to draw boundaries along neat ethnic lines. Compromises had to be made, sometimes to satisfy the national interests of the victors. France, for example, had lost Russia as its major ally on Germany's eastern border. Thus, France wanted to strengthen and expand Poland, Czechoslovakia, Yugoslavia, and Romania as much as possible. Those states could then serve as barriers against Germany and Communist Russia.

As a result of compromises, almost every eastern European state was left with a minorities problem that had the potential of leading to future conflicts. Germans in Poland; Hungarians, Poles, and Germans in Czechoslovakia; and the combination of Serbs, Croats, Slovenes, Macedonians, and Albanians in Yugoslavia all became sources of later conflict. Moreover, the new map of Eastern Europe was based upon the temporary collapse of power in both Germany and Russia. Neither country, however, accepted the new eastern frontiers. To many, it seemed only a matter of time before Germany or Russia would become strong again and make changes.

Yet another centuries-old empire—the Ottoman Empire—was broken up by the peace settlement after the war. To gain Arab support against the Ottoman Turks during the war, the Western Allies had promised to recognize the independence of Arab states in the Middle Eastern lands of the Ottoman Empire. Once the war was over, however, the Western nations changed their minds. France took control of Lebanon and Syria, whereas Britain received Iraq and Palestine. Both acquisitions were officially called mandates. Woodrow Wilson had opposed the outright annexation of colonial territories by the Allies. As a result, the peace settlement had set up a system of mandates whereby a nation officially governed but did not own a territory on behalf of the League of Nations.

The peace settlement reached at Paris soon came under attack, especially by the defeated Central Powers. There were others who also thought that the peacemakers had been shortsighted. The famous British economist John Maynard Keynes (KAYNZ), for example, condemned the concern with frontiers at the expense of economic issues. He thought that the economic provisions of the treaty would weaken the European economy.

CLASS DISCUSSION

Guide students in summarizing the main provisions of the Treaty of Versailles.

CRITICAL THINKING

Have students research the position of John Maynard Keynes on the peace treaties. What were his arguments to show that the economic provisions of the peace would weaken the European economy?

ACROSS THE CURRICULUM

Political Science Ask students to research and compare the League of Nations and the United Nations.

CRITICAL THINKING

What two key nations were not at the Paris Peace Conference? *(Germany and Russia)* Discuss possible future problems for the peace which could result from their absence.

So What ??

*If your students question the importance or relevance of the information on the **Versailles peace treaty,** tell them . . .*

that the mishandling of the peace of World War I directly led to World War I and the eventual dominant role of the United States in the world. Have them list as many ways as they can in which the Paris Peace Conference and the Versailles peace treaty were mishandled. Then debate the relative importance and possible results of each item on the list.

ACROSS THE CURRICULUM

Political Science Ask students to study isolationism in the U.S. Who were the leaders in the fight against ratification of the Treaty of Versailles? How did the Senate justify its rejection of Wilson's defensive alliance with Great Britain and France?

CLASS DISCUSSION

Guide students in a discussion of the following statement: "Some historians have suggested that perhaps the cause of the failure of the peace of 1919 was its lack of enforcement."

ACROSS THE CURRICULUM

Political Science Ask interested students to research the Treaty of Versailles. What, specifically, were its provisions?

ASSESS

You can choose from a variety of assessments to evaluate your students' mastery of the objectives for this section, as stated on page 827. Possible assessments include:

1. Section Review questions on this page
2. Section 25–4 Quiz in your Teacher Resource materials
3. Reteaching Worksheets in your Teacher Resource materials
4. Self-Study software

ALTERNATIVE ASSESSMENT

Assign students an essay in which they discuss the major results of the 1919 peace negotiations.

830

Map 25.5   Territorial Changes in Europe and the Middle East after World War I

Others, however, thought the peace settlement was the best that could be achieved under the circumstances. Self-determination, they believed, had served reasonably well as a central organizing principle. The creation of the League of Nations, moreover, gave some hope that future conflicts could be resolved peacefully. However, within twenty years of the signing of the peace treaties, Europe was again engaged in war.

Some historians have suggested that perhaps the cause of the failure of the peace of 1919 was its lack of enforcement. To enforce the peace, the chief architects of the treaty needed to be actively involved. This was especially true in helping the new German state

develop into a peaceful and democratic republic. The U.S. Senate was returning to a philosophy of isolationism, however, and thus failed to ratify the Treaty of Versailles. As a result, the United States never even joined the League of Nations. In addition, the U.S. Senate also rejected Wilson's defensive alliance with Great Britain and France. Already by the end of 1919, the United States was limiting its involvement in European affairs.

This retreat by the United States had dire consequences. American withdrawal from the defensive alliance with Britain and France led Britain to withdraw as well. Thus, by removing itself from European

STUDYING MAPS

The following questions and activities will help you guide students through their study of Map 25.5.

1. Trace the territorial losses of Russia, Germany, the Ottoman Empire, Bulgaria, and Austria-Hungary. Rank them from largest to smallest.

2. Find the new countries created from the German and Russian empires.
3. Compare this map of Europe and the Middle East with a current map. What changes do you see?

affairs, the United States forced France to stand alone in facing its old enemy. Frightened by this turn of events, France decided to take strong actions against Germany, and that only made the Germans more resentful. By the end of 1919, it appeared that the peace treaties of 1919 were not going to bring peace. As it turned out, they became the first steps toward World War II.

 SECTION REVIEW

1. **Locate:**
   (*a*) Alsace-Lorraine,   (*b*) Lebanon,
   (*c*) Syria

2. **Define:**
   (*a*) reparations

3. **Identify:**
   (*a*) Fourteen Points,   (*b*) David Lloyd George,
   (*c*) Georges Clemenceau,   (*d*) League of Nations,
   (*e*) Article 231,   (*f*) mandates,   (*g*) John Maynard Keynes

4. **Recall:**
   (*a*) What French demands did the United States denounce as contrary to the principle of self-determination?
   (*b*) What did the creation of a League of Nations have to do with Woodrow Wilson's willingness to sign the Treaty of Versailles?
   (*c*) Why was it impossible to draw state boundaries along ethnic lines in Eastern Europe?
   (*d*) How did the United States leave France to stand alone against Germany after World War I?

5. **Think Critically:** Why may it have been a mistake for Woodrow Wilson to participate directly in the peace talks at the end of World War I?

Conclusion

World War I shattered the liberal, rational society of late-nineteenth- and early-twentieth-century Europe. The incredible destruction and the death of almost ten million people undermined the whole idea of progress.

New propaganda techniques had been successful in leading entire populations to continue to participate in a devastating slaughter.

World War I was a total war—one that involved a complete mobilization of resources and people. The power of governments over the lives of their citizens increased. Civil liberties, such as freedom of the press and speech, were limited in the name of national security. World War I made the practice of strong central authority a way of life.

The turmoil created by World War I seemed to open the door to even greater insecurity. Revolutions broke up old empires and created new states, which led to new problems. The hope that Europe and the rest of the world would return to normalcy was soon dashed by the failure to achieve a lasting peace, economic depression, and the rise of dictatorial regimes that sought even greater control over the lives of their subjects (see Chapters 26 and 27).

Finally, World War I ended the age of European domination over world affairs. By destroying their own civilization on the battlefields of Europe in World War I, Europeans indirectly encouraged the subject peoples of their vast colonial empires to begin movements for national independence. World War II would complete the self-destructive process that Europeans had begun in 1914.

Notes

1. Arnold Toynbee, *Surviving the Future* (New York, 1971), pp. 106–107.
2. Quoted in Joachim Remak, "1914—The Third Balkan War: Origins Reconsidered," *Journal of Modern History* 43 (1971): 364–365.
3. Quoted in J. M. Winter, *The Experience of World War I* (New York, 1989), p. 142.
4. Quoted in Catherine W. Reilly, ed., *Scars upon My Heart: Women's Poetry and Verse of the First World War* (London, 1981), p. 90.
5. Quoted in William M. Mandel, *Soviet Women* (Garden City, New York, 1975), p. 43.
6. Harold Nicolson, *Peacemaking, 1919* (Boston and New York, 1933), pp. 31–32.

Answers to
SECTION REVIEW

2. payments made by the loser to the winner to cover the cost of a war
3. (a) principles upon which Woodrow Wilson wanted to end World War I
   (b) British representative to the peace talks
   (c) French representative to the peace talks
   (d) an international organization designed to settle disputes between nations peacefully
   (e) part of Treaty of Versailles stating Germany had caused the war
   (f) areas assigned to other nations' control by the Treaty of Versailles
   (g) British economist who spoke against the Treaty of Versailles
4. (a) that Germany be stripped of weapons and pay costs of the war, and creation of separate state in Rhineland
   (b) Wilson felt League of Nations could correct mistakes in Treaty.
   (c) Ethnic groups were mixed together throughout Eastern Europe.
   (d) The U.S. Congress refused to ratify the League of Nations treaty.
5. Answers will vary but may include the fact that Wilson was not experienced in negotiating treaties and had alienated many members of Congress.

CLOSE

Review with students the major consequences of World War I on European society. In what sense did the conflict undermine "the whole idea of progress"?

SPECIAL NEEDS: *Auditory*

Have the class read pages 827–831. Assist the students with the reading. Divide the class into three groups representing France, Britain, and the United States. Have the students work in their groups and prepare their country's opinions about how to deal with Germany and make a final settlement of World War I. Once each group is ready, they may come together and discuss their respective concerns in a role-playing activity where each student plays the role of a delegate from the country they represent. Some of the expected responses should be: 1) from the United States: reduction of military forces, and weapons; self determination of people (liberty); 2) Britain: revenge; 3) France: national security, strip Germany of all weapons, make Germany pay.

USING KEY TERMS

1. conscription
2. war of attrition
3. War communism
4. reparations
5. total war
6. mobilization
7. soviets
8. trench warfare
9. planned economies
10. brinkmanship

REVIEWING THE FACTS

1. Germany, Austria, and Italy—the Triple Alliance; France, Great Britain, and Russia—the Triple Entente
2. Serbia
3. mustard gas
4. passed the Defence of the Realm Act
5. Tsar Nicholas spent most of his time away from Moscow leading the Russian army in the war.
6. to provide a method to resolve international conflicts through peaceful means
7. Alsace and Lorraine

THINKING CRITICALLY

1. bound nations to follow into war those nations with whom they were allied
2. new technologies resulted in the death of millions without quick resolution to the war
3. hoped they could win the war before American soldiers could be sent to Europe
4. hoped Lenin would take over the Russian government and withdraw Russia from the war
5. forced them to supply two armies while access to raw materials from other parts of the world was limited
6. peace, food, and land
7. there were many unresolved issues and resentments among nations in the war; no agreement could have satisfied all parties

CHAPTER 25 REVIEW

USING KEY TERMS

1. The practice of requiring young people to join the military, which was followed by many nations before World War I, was called _____.
2. World War I became a _____, or a war based on wearing the other side down by constant attacks and heavy losses.
3. _____ is the term used to describe the Soviet Union's centralization of control over its economy (for example, forcibly taking grain).
4. After World War I Germany was required by the Treaty of Versailles to make payments called _____ to the nations that won the war.
5. World War I involved a complete mobilization of resources and people that affected the lives of all citizens in the warring countries—a situation called _____.
6. Before World War I many European nations completed the _____ of their military by assembling troops and supplies for war.
7. After World War I communist leaders organized Russia by forming councils of workers and soldiers called _____.
8. The development of _____ baffled military leaders who had been trained to fight wars of movement.
9. Nations that have communist governments control their production and distribution of goods and services through _____.
10. The policy of threatening to go to war as a means to achieve national goals has been called _____.

REVIEWING THE FACTS

1. What nations belonged to the Triple Alliance and the Triple Entente before the start of World War I?
2. A nationalist from what nation was accused of the assassination of Archduke Ferdinand?

3. What chemical agent was first used as a weapon in World War I?
4. How did the British government try to eliminate opposition from the people who were opposed to entering World War I?
5. Why were Alexandra and Rasputin able to almost control the Tsar's government during much of World War I?
6. What was the intended purpose of the League of Nations?
7. What territories did Germany give up to France at the end of World War I?

THINKING CRITICALLY

1. How did the creation of the Triple Alliance and the Triple Entente contribute to the causes of World War I?
2. In what ways was the fighting in World War I different from the fighting that took place in earlier wars?
3. Why did the Germans use unrestricted submarine warfare in World War I, even though they realized the policy was likely to bring the United States into the war against them?
4. Why did Germany help Lenin return to Russia from Switzerland in 1917?
5. Why did the fact that Germany was fighting in the East and the West make it more difficult for them to win World War I?
6. What promise did Lenin make to gain the support of the Russian people in 1917?
7. Why do some people feel it is unlikely that a lasting peace could have been created at the end of World War I, no matter what was stated in the Treaty of Versailles?

APPLYING SOCIAL STUDIES SKILLS

1. were not used to having a voice in the political affairs of their nations
2. Wars require the production of both weapons and civilian goods; a shortage of raw materials results in inadequate production of both and ultimately to the loss of the war.
3. people lived in newly created nations or areas where they wished to form nations; brought strong feelings of nationalism that caused people to be willing to fight
4. government in U.S. based on a system of checks and balances between the three branches; quick action difficult to achieve except in situations where there is almost universal agreement on the need to act quickly
5. Maps will vary but should identify major mountain ranges, rivers, seas, and other geographic formations, with importance correctly explained.
6. Leaders were elected by people who were angry and wanted Germany to be punished; political leaders who did not deliver this punishment could have lost their political offices.

APPLYING SOCIAL STUDIES SKILLS

1. **Government:** Why were many people in Europe willing to allow their government leaders to draw them into a war without protest?

2. **Economics:** Why are raw materials of great importance in a war of attrition?

3. **Sociology:** What social values in the years prior to the war contributed to the willingness of many Europeans to go to war?

4. **Government:** What were the differences between the political processes in the United States and in that of many European nations that resulted in the United States being slower to enter World War I?

5. **Geography:** Draw a map of Europe that indicates geographic formations that influenced the course of World War I. Include mountains, rivers, seas, forests, etc. Provide a key that explains the importance of each feature.

6. **Government:** Why was it almost imperative that the leaders of the victorious nations in Europe place the responsibility for the war on Germany?

MAKING TIME AND PLACE CONNECTIONS

1. How might a lack of systems for rapid mass communication (like radio and television) in the early twentieth century have made war more likely then than it is today?

2. Why might military and political leaders during World War I have been more willing than today's leaders to use the weapons of mass destruction?

3. When the United States and North Vietnam negotiated to end the war in Southeast Asia in the early 1970s, it took almost two years for them to agree on the shape of the negotiating table. The Treaty of Versailles that ended World War I,

a much larger war, was completed in only a few months. What made this speedy conclusion possible?

4. Why aren't geographic features like rivers, seas, or mountains likely to have as much importance in fighting a war today as they did in World War I?

BECOMING AN HISTORIAN

1. **Cause and Effect:** What events resulted from each of the causes identified below?
   (*a*) the formation of alliances in Europe before World War I
   (*b*) the use of weapons of mass destruction in World War I
   (*c*) the decision of the Germans to use unrestricted submarine warfare
   (*d*) the decision of the victorious nations to impose unreasonable reparations on Germany
   (*e*) the decision of the United States Senate not to ratify the Treaty of Versailles

2. **Primary and Secondary Sources:** Although the United States Senate chose not to ratify the Treaty of Versailles, a number of U.S. senators stated that the Senate might reconsider its choice if changes were made in the treaty. Part of a specific change suggested by Senator Henry Cabot Lodge appears below. What insights does this primary source give you into the reasons and feelings of the Senate that you may not have found in a secondary source such as this text book?

   > The United States assumes no obligation to preserve the territorial integrity or political independence of any other country or to interfere in controversies between nations. . . or to employ the military or naval forces of the United States under any article of the treaty for any purpose. . . .

ON BECOMING AN HISTORIAN

1. Answers will vary but may involve results similar to those listed below:
   (a) caused nations to be drawn too easily into war
   (b) resulted in the deaths of millions of soldiers and civilians and the widespread destruction of property
   (c) brought the United States into the war and shifted the balance of power to the British and French side
   (d) created such an unfair peace that future war was almost a certainty
   (e) almost guaranteed the failure of the League as a viable method for peacefully resolving international disputes

2. Answers will vary but should discuss why primary sources are able to give a sense of the perceptions and feelings of the time that are often lost in secondary sources.

MAKING TIME AND PLACE CONNECTIONS

1. In 1914 many people in Europe only had access to information provided by their governments. This is no longer true because of the many means of mass communication we have to obtain information.

2. In World War I leaders may not have been aware of the impact their weapons would have on people and the environment. Now we know what the weapons can do and therefore may be more hesitant to use them.

3. When the negotiations to end the War in Vietnam took place neither side was the clear victor. Both sides hoped that achievements on the battlefield could be used to improve their negotiating positions. This was not the case after World War I when it was clear who had won and who had lost.

4. Technology has advanced to the point that modern armies can often cross geographic obstacles with little or no trouble.

PLANNING GUIDE

SECTION	KEY TOPICS	PRIMARY SOURCES	ASSESSMENT
1 The Futile Search for a New Stability pages 835–842	◆ Failure of the League of Nations ◆ German economic collapse ◆ Great Depression ◆ Popular Front and New Deal		◆ Section Review, page 842 ◆ Section Quiz 26–1, TRB
2 The Retreat from Democracy: Dictatorial Regimes pages 842–850	◆ Rise of Mussolini and Italian Fascism ◆ Lenin's New Economic Policy ◆ Rise of Stalin and Stalinist Russia ◆ Spanish Civil War	◆ Belov excerpt, pages 848–849	◆ Section Review, page 850 ◆ Section Quiz 26–2, TRB
3 Hitler and Nazi Germany pages 850–858	◆ Rise of Hitler ◆ The Nazi State ◆ German Anti-Semitism	◆ Young Nazi, page 851 ◆ Hitler excerpts, pages 854–855	◆ Section Review, page 858 ◆ Section Quiz 26–3, TRB
4 Social, Cultural, and Intellectual Trends in the Interwar Years pages 858–865	◆ Mass culture ◆ Mass leisure and professional sports ◆ Dadaism and Surrealism ◆ Schönberg and atonal music ◆ "Stream of consciousness" technique ◆ Uncertainty Principle	◆ Valéry excerpt, page 861 ◆ Tzara excerpt, page 862 ◆ Hitler excerpt, page 863 ◆ Demian excerpt, page 864	◆ Section Review, page 865 ◆ Section Quiz 26–4, TRB

DEPRESSION, DEMOCRACY, AND DICTATORSHIP:
THE WESTERN WORLD BETWEEN WORLD WARS (1919 TO 1939)

REPRODUCIBLE ACTIVITIES

Historical Maps

Charts and Graphs

Critical Thinking

Cooperative Learning

Vocabulary

Guided Reading

Reteaching

Enrichment

Performance Assessment

Spanish Key Points and Chapter Summaries

Spanish Vocabulary

Spanish Guided Reading

MULTIMEDIA SUPPORT

TRANSPARENCIES
- *World History* Color Transparency Package
- Fine Art Color Transparency Package

VIDEO
- *World History* Video Library
- CNN® Annual Video Update

LASERDISC
- *Sights and Sounds of History*

AUDIO
- *Listening to Literature* audiotape (English and Spanish)
- *History of Music* CD

SOFTWARE
- WESTEST™
- Student Review

CD–ROM
- *The Journey of Civilization*
- *World History*

INTERNET
- Internet Activities

On Line with WORLD HISTORY

Access West's history web site at
http://history.swpco.com
You'll find activities and web sites related to specific topics and chapters in *World History: The Human Odyssey*. Also look for references to helpful web sites at appropriate places throughout this teacher edition.

LESSON PLANNING

You will find detailed daily lesson plans for both traditional class scheduling and **block scheduling** in your Teacher Resource Box.

Not Enough Time?

If you do not have the four or five days recommended to teach this chapter, you may want to focus on the following sections and activities:

- Have students skim the chapter to answer the "Questions to Guide Your Reading" on page 835. Discuss their answers; then read the "Conclusion" on page 865.
- Do a more in-depth reading of pages 835–839, 842–847, 850–853, 858–859, 861, 863. Conclude with a class discussion of the features on pages 848–849, 854–855, 856, 857, 862.

DEPRESSION, DEMOCRACY, AND DICTATORSHIP: THE WESTERN

26

BUILDING ON CHAPTER 25

To "set the scene" for the study of Chapter 26, use the following questions and activities.

- Ask students to list the important attributes and major events that led to World War I.
- Have students summarize the widening of the war into "total war."
- Have students name several important effects of the war on life at home.
- Ask students to explain how the Bolsheviks won Russia's civil war.
- Ask students to list the important provisions of the Treaty of Versailles.

USING THE OPENING STORY

Depending on the ability levels of your students, select from the following questions and activities to reinforce the reading of the story.

- What were people's hopes during the 1920s? (*international peace, economic growth, political democracy*)
- Of all the severe economic problems, which was the most devastating? (*The Great Depression*) Why? (*widespread hunger, homelessness, despair*)
- Why do you think social unrest sometimes leads people to follow extremists and demagogues? (*Answers will vary.*)

Only twenty years after the Treaty of Versailles, Europeans were again at war. In the 1920s, however, many people assumed that Europe and the world were about to enter a new era of international peace, economic growth, and political democracy. These hopes of the 1920s were never realized, however. After 1919, most people wanted peace but were unsure how to maintain it. Efforts to find new ways to resolve conflicts, especially through the new League of Nations, failed. Although everyone favored disarmament, few could agree on how to achieve it.

Europe was faced with severe economic problems after World War I. Most devastating of all was the Great Depression that began at the end of 1929. The Great Depression brought untold misery to millions of people. Begging for food on the streets became widespread, especially when soup kitchens were unable to keep up with the demand. Larger and larger numbers of people were homeless and moved from place to place looking for work and shelter. In the United States, the homeless set up

shantytowns they named "Hoovervilles" after the U.S. president, Herbert Hoover. In their misery, some people saw suicide as the only solution. One unemployed person said, "Today, when I am experiencing this for the first time, I think that I should prefer to do away with myself, to take gas, to jump into the river, or leap from some high place. . . . would I really come to such a decision? I do not know." Social unrest spread rapidly. Some of the unemployed staged hunger marches to get attention. In democratic countries, more and more people began to listen to, and vote for, radical voices calling for extreme measures.

According to Woodrow Wilson, World War I had been fought to make the world safe for democracy. For a while after 1919, political democracy did seem well established. The hopes for democracy soon faded, however, as dictatorial regimes spread into Italy and Germany and across eastern Europe.

► *Many middle-class families found themselves unexpectedly homeless during the Great Depression, and some people had to resort to desperate measures for finding food.*

ADDITIONAL RESOURCES

BOOKS FOR STUDENTS
Russia under Stalin by Michael Gibson, Putnam
For Whom the Bell Tolls by Ernest Hemingway, Charles Scribner's Sons

VIDEOS/FILMS
The Russian Revolution, EAV, Social Studies School Service, (800) 421-4262

The Democrat and the Dictator, PBS: Bill Moyers, Social Studies School Service, (800) 421-4262

CD-ROM
Picasso, Grolier Interactive, Educorp Direct, (800) 843-9497

WORLD BETWEEN WORLD WARS

(1919 TO 1939)

CRISIS OF THE TWENTIETH CENTURY

| 1910 | 1919 | BETWEEN THE WORLD WARS | 1939 | 1945 |

QUESTIONS TO GUIDE YOUR READING

1. What were the causes of the Great Depression?

2. How did Great Britain, France, and the United States respond to the Great Depression?

3. To what extent was Fascist Italy a totalitarian state?

4. How did Joseph Stalin establish a totalitarian regime in the Soviet Union?

5. What were Adolf Hitler's basic ideas, and how did he rise to power?

6. What were the chief features of the Nazi total state?

7. What impact did the growth of mass culture and mass leisure have upon European society in the 1920s and 1930s?

OUTLINE

1. THE FUTILE SEARCH FOR A NEW STABILITY

2. THE RETREAT FROM DEMOCRACY: DICTATORIAL REGIMES

3. HITLER AND NAZI GERMANY

4. SOCIAL, CULTURAL, AND INTELLECTUAL TRENDS IN THE INTERWAR YEARS

THE FUTILE SEARCH FOR A NEW STABILITY

The peace settlement at the end of World War I had tried to fulfill the nineteenth-century dream of nationalism by creating new boundaries and new states. From its beginning, however, this peace settlement had left nations unhappy. Conflicts over disputed border regions between Germany and Poland, Poland and Lithuania, Poland and Czechoslovakia, Austria and Hungary, and Italy and Yugoslavia poisoned mutual relations in eastern Europe for years. Many Germans viewed the Treaty of Versailles as a dictated peace and vowed to revise it.

An Uncertain Peace: The Search for Security

The U.S. president Woodrow Wilson had realized that the peace treaties had unwise provisions that could serve as new causes for conflicts. He had placed many of his hopes for the future in the League of Nations.

835

Answers to QUESTIONS TO GUIDE YOUR READING

1. See page 838.

2. See pages 840–842.

3. limited in Fascist Italy due to Mussolini's inability to destroy the old power structure and absorb institutions into the Fascist state (page 845)

4. See pages 846 and 847.

5. Extreme German nationalism, strong anti-Semitism, anti-communism, and a Social Darwinian theory of struggle were Hitler's ideas. See pages 851–853.

6. development of an Aryan racial state, involvement of the people, no individual arbitrary will, economic control (page 853)

7. Mass culture brought in radio and the movies which could be used for propaganda and political purposes. Mass leisure gave totalitarian states new ways to control the people through national recreation efforts. (page 861)

FOCUS

OBJECTIVES

After completing this section, students should be able to

1. explain the weaknesses of the League of Nations
2. identify the Dawes Plan, Treaty of Locarno, and Kellogg-Briand pact
3. list the factors leading to the Great Depression
4. discuss the response to economic hardships by England, France, Germany, and the U.S.

FOCUS ACTIVITY

Divide the class into small groups. Give them about ten minutes to list various results of World War I that made a search for stability doomed from the start. Reunite the class and combine their efforts into one list.

TEACH

CLASS DISCUSSION

Have students discuss why the League of Nations could not maintain peace. What was the major reason? (*U.S. failure to join*)

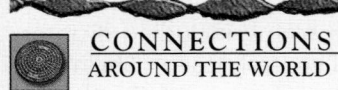

CONNECTIONS
AROUND THE WORLD

Ask students if they have ever thought about more people dying from a flu epidemic than from a major war. Do they think this could happen today?

The league, however, was not very effective in maintaining the peace. The failure of the United States to join the league had weakened its effectiveness from the beginning. Moreover, the league could use only economic sanctions to stop aggression. France wanted to make the league more effective by creating some kind of international army, but other nations feared France's suggestion. They did not want to give up any of their sovereignty to a larger international body.

After both the United States and Great Britain failed to honor their defensive military alliances with France, the French felt dangerously alone. Between 1919 and 1924, their desire for security led them to demand a strict enforcement of the Treaty of Versailles. This tough policy toward Germany began with the issue of reparations. These were the payments that the Germans were supposed to make for the damage they had done in the war.

In April 1921, the Allied Reparations Commission set a sum of 132 billion marks ($33 billion) for German reparations, payable in annual installments of 2.5 billion (gold) marks. Allied threats to occupy the Ruhr valley, Germany's chief industrial and mining center, led the new German republic to make its first payment in 1921. By the following year, however, the German government, faced with financial problems, announced that it was unable to pay any more. France was outraged and sent troops to occupy the Ruhr valley. Because Germany would not pay reparations, France would collect reparations in kind by operating and using the Ruhr mines and factories.

Both Germany and France suffered from the French occupation of the Ruhr. The German government adopted a policy of passive resistance to French occupation. German workers went out on strike, and the government paid their salaries, largely by printing more paper money. This only added to the inflation that had already begun in Germany by the end of the war. The German mark soon became worthless. In 1914, 4.2 marks equaled 1 dollar. By November 1, 1923, the ratio had reached 130 billion marks to 1 dollar. By the end of November, it had increased to an incredible 4.2 trillion to 1. Evidence of runaway inflation was everywhere. Workers used wheelbarrows to carry home their weekly pay. One woman left a basket

---

CONNECTIONS
AROUND THE WORLD

The Great Flu Epidemic   World War I, which cost the lives of ten million people, had a devastating effect on Europe. At the end of the war, a flu epidemic also proved disastrous to people all over the world. Some observers believe that it began among American soldiers in Kansas. When they were sent abroad to fight, they carried the virus to Europe. By the end of 1918, many soldiers in European armies had been stricken with the flu, which then spread quickly throughout Europe. The three chief statesmen at the Versailles peace conference—the American president Woodrow Wilson, the British prime minister David Lloyd George, and the French premier Georges Clemenceau—were all sick with the flu during the negotiations that led to the Treaty of Versailles.

The Spanish flu, as this strain of influenza was called, was known for its swift and deadly action. Many people died within a day of being infected. Complications also arose from bacterial infections in the lungs, causing a deadly form of pneumonia.

In 1918 and 1919, Spanish flu spread around the world with devastating results. Death tolls were enormous: in Russia, 450,000; in India, 5,000,000; in the United States, 550,000. It has been estimated that twenty-two million people, or more than twice the number of people killed in World War I, died from the great flu epidemic of 1918–1919.

---

of money outside while she went into a store. When she came out, the money was there, but the basket had been stolen.

Economic disaster led to political upheavals as Communists staged uprisings in October and Adolf Hitler's band of Nazis (NAWT-seez) tried to seize power in Munich in 1923 (see later in the chapter). Everyone began to seek a way out of the disaster. New governments in Great Britain and France decided to

---

RECOMMENDED READING

For an introduction to the interwar period, see R. J. Sontag, *A Broken World, 1919–39* (New York, 1971); and the general survey by R. Paxton, *Europe in the Twentieth Century*, 2d ed. (New York, 1985). On European security issues, see S. Marks, *The Illusion of Peace: Europe's International Relations, 1918–1933* (New York, 1976). The Locarno agreements have been well examined in J. Jacobson, *Locarno Diplomacy* (Princeton, N.J., 1972).

The role of French diplomacy in the 1920s is analyzed in J. M. Hughes, *To the Maginot Line: The Politics of French Military Preparations in the 1920s.*

On the Great Depression, see C. P. Kindleberger, *The World in Depression, 1929–39*, rev. ed. (Berkeley, 1986). On Keynes and his new economic theories, see R. Skidelsky, *John Maynard Keynes: A Biography* (New York, 1986).

Map 26.1 Europe in 1919

CLASS DISCUSSION

Ask students to explain the following sentence: "Both Germany and France suffered from the French occupation of the Ruhr."

TEACHING THEMES

Economics and History. Have students explain how the economic situation in Europe contributed to the rise of totalitarian governments in Russia, Italy and Germany.

take a more conciliatory approach to Germany and the reparations problem. At the same time, a new German government led by Gustav Stresemann (shTRAE-zuh-MAWN) ended the policy of passive resistance. Germany also began to carry out the provisions of the Treaty of Versailles while seeking a new settlement of the reparations question.

In August 1924, an international commission produced a new plan for reparations. The Dawes (DAWZ) Plan, named after the American banker who chaired the commission, first reduced reparations. Then it tied

Germany's annual payments to its ability to pay. The Dawes Plan also granted an initial $200 million loan for German recovery, which soon opened the door to heavy American investments in Europe. A new era of European prosperity between 1924 and 1929 was the result.

With prosperity came a new age of European diplomacy. A spirit of cooperation was fostered by the foreign ministers of Germany and France, Gustav Stresemann and Aristide Briand (BREE-AW[n]). In 1925, they signed the Treaty of Locarno, which guaranteed

STUDYING MAPS

The following questions and activities will help you guide students through their study of Map 26.1.

1. Find the Ruhr Valley and explain its strategic importance. *(Answers will vary.)*

2. Trace the disputed border regions between Germany and Poland, Poland

and Lithuania, Poland and Czechoslovakia, Austria and Hungary, Italy and Yugoslavia.

3. Compare this map with a map of Europe in 1946 and in 1997. What changes do you see? *(Answers will vary.)*

CRITICAL THINKING

Ask students to speculate about why, given the hopeful signs represented by the Dawes Plan, the Treaty of Locarno, Germany's membership in the League of Nations, and the Kellogg-Briand pack, Europe's economic and political upturn was short-lived.

CLASS DISCUSSION

Guide students in a discussion of the factors leading to the Great Depression. Why was it different from other economic downturns?

LEARNING FROM VISUALS

Answer to the caption questions: Answers will vary.

ACTIVITY

Have students study the maps on pages 802 and 837. Ask them to identify and create a list of the "new" nations of 1919 that did not exist before World War I.

▲ *This German housewife is using her worthless paper money in 1923 to start a fire so that she can cook supper. Do you think the U.S. dollar could ever become this worthless? Why or why not?*

Germany's new western borders with France and Belgium. The Locarno pact was viewed by many as the beginning of a new era of European peace. On the day after the pact was concluded, the headlines in the *New York Times* read "France and Germany Ban War Forever." The *London Times* declared, "Peace at Last."[1]

The new spirit of cooperation grew even stronger when Germany joined the League of Nations in March 1926. Two years later, the Kellogg-Briand pact brought even more hope. Sixty-three nations signed this accord written by U.S. secretary of state Frank B. Kellogg and French foreign minister Aristide Briand. These nations pledged "to renounce war as an instrument of national policy." Nothing was said, however, about what would be done if anyone violated the pact.

Unfortunately, the spirit of Locarno was based on little real substance. Germany did not have the military power to change its western borders even if it wanted to. Promises not to go to war without a way to enforce the promises were worthless. Furthermore, even the spirit of Locarno could not bring nations to cut back on their weapons. The League of Nations Covenant had suggested that nations reduce their military forces to make war less probable. Germany, of course, had been forced to reduce its military forces. At the time, it was thought that other states would later do the same. Numerous disarmament conferences failed to achieve anything, however. States were simply unwilling to trust their security to anyone but their own military forces. When a World Disarmament Conference met in Geneva in 1932, the issue of disarmament was already dead.

The Great Depression

World War I had a devastating effect on the European economy. Recovery was slow. Thanks to U.S. loans, Europeans began to experience a new prosperity after 1924. Because of the Great Depression, however, the new prosperity was short-lived.

One important factor in the coming of the Great Depression was a series of economic problems in the second half of the 1920s. Already in the mid-1920s, prices for farm products, especially wheat, were falling rapidly because of overproduction. In 1925, states in central and eastern Europe began to impose tariffs to close their markets to other countries' goods, thus causing a decline in trade. An increase in the use of oil and hydroelectricity led to a slump in the coal industry even before 1929.

The other factor in the coming of the Great Depression was an international financial crisis created by the collapse of the U.S. stock market in 1929. Much of the European prosperity between 1924 and 1929 had been built upon U.S. bank loans to Germany. The U.S. loans to Germany were needed so that Germany could pay reparations to France and Great Britain. These nations, in turn, were then able to repay the United

---

MORE ABOUT . . . *The Great Depression*

Woody Gutherie was an American balladeer who would ride the railroads during the Great Depression, writing and singing songs about poverty and social justice. His folk music, while written during the depression, was not itself depressing. Rather, he celebrated the indomitable human spirit through more than a thousand ballads. His most popular song is probably, "This Land is Your Land," still sung by countless school children. It is a song of democracy and equality, written at a time when such values were being challenged throughout the world.

"This land is your land, this land is my land
From California to the New York island
From the redwood forest to the gulf stream waters
This land was made for you and me."

◄ France did not suffer from the Great Depression as quickly as some of its European neighbors, but by 1931, unemployed workers were lining up at free-food centers.

States for war loans. Twenty-three billion marks had been invested in German municipal bonds and German industries since 1924. Already in 1928 and 1929, American investors had begun to pull money out of Germany in order to invest in the booming New York stock market. The crash of the U.S. stock market in October 1929 led panicky U.S. investors to withdraw even more of their funds from Germany and other European markets. The withdrawal of funds weakened the banks of Germany and other central European states. The Credit-Anstalt, Vienna's most famous bank, collapsed on May 31, 1931. By that time, trade was slowing down, industrial production was declining, and unemployment was rising.

Economic depression was by no means new to Europe. However, the extent of the economic downturn after 1929 truly made this the Great Depression. During 1932, the worst year of the depression, one British worker in every four was unemployed. Six million Germans, or 40 percent of the German labor force, were out of work at the same time. Between 1929 and 1932, industrial production fell almost 50 percent in the United States and over 40 percent in Germany. The unemployed and homeless filled the streets of the cities.

Governments did not know how to deal with the crisis. The classic liberal remedy for depression was a policy of balanced budgets. This included cutting costs by lowering wages and raising tariffs to exclude other countries' goods from home markets. These measures only made the economic crisis worse, however, and created even greater mass unrest.

One reaction to the Great Depression—even in countries that, like the United States, had a strong laissez-faire tradition, a belief that the government should not interfere in the economy—was the expansion of government activity in the economy. Another reaction was a renewed interest in Marxist doctrines. Hadn't Marx predicted that capitalism would destroy itself through overproduction? Communism thus became more popular, especially among workers and intellectuals. Finally, the Great Depression led masses of people to follow political leaders who offered simple solutions in return for dictatorial power. Everywhere, democracy seemed on the defensive in the 1930s.

The Democratic States

Woodrow Wilson had claimed that World War I had been fought to make the world safe for democracy. In

So What ??

1919, his claim seemed justified. Four major European states and a host of minor ones had democratic governments. Moreover, in a number of states, women could vote. Male political leaders had rewarded women for their contributions to World War I by granting them the right to vote (except in Italy, Switzerland, France, and Spain, where women had to wait until the end of World War II for the right). In the 1920s, Europe seemed to be returning to the political trends of the prewar era—parliamentary regimes and the growth of individual liberties. However, it was not an easy process. Four years of total war and four years of post-war turmoil made a "return to normalcy" difficult.

After World War I, Great Britain went through a period of serious economic difficulties. During the war, Britain had lost many of the markets for its industrial products, especially to the United States and Japan. The decline of such staple industries as coal, steel, and textiles, led to a rise in unemployment. In 1921, 2 million Britons were out of work. Britain soon rebounded, however, and experienced an age of prosperity from 1925 to 1929, although this prosperity was never very widespread. Even in these so-called prosperous years, unemployment remained at a startling level of 10 percent.

By 1929, Britain faced the growing effects of the Great Depression. The Labour Party, which had now become the largest party in Britain, failed to solve the nation's economic problems and fell from power in 1931. A new government, led by the Conservatives, claimed credit for bringing Britain out of the worst stages of the depression. It did so by using the old policies of balanced budgets and protective tariffs.

Political leaders in Britain had largely ignored the new ideas of a British economist, John Maynard Keynes, who published his *General Theory of Employment, Interest, and Money* in 1936. He condemned the traditional view that in a free economy, depressions should be left to work themselves out. Instead, Keynes argued that unemployment came not from overproduction but from a decline in demand. Demand, in turn, could be increased by putting people back to work by building highways and public buildings, even if the government had to go into debt to pay for these works, a concept known as **deficit spending.** These policies, of course, would require direct government intervention in the economy, which was against the principles of laissez-faire. Britain's political leaders were unwilling to go that far in the 1930s.

After the defeat of Germany, France had become the strongest power on the European continent. Its greatest need was to rebuild the areas of northern and eastern France that had been devastated in World War I. However, no French government seemed capable of solving France's financial problems between 1921 and 1926. Like other European countries, though, France did experience a period of relative prosperity between 1926 and 1929.

Because it had a more balanced economy than other nations, France did not begin to feel the full effects of the Great Depression until 1932. Economic instability soon had political repercussions. During a nineteen-month period in 1932 and 1933, six different cabinets were formed as France faced political chaos. Finally, in June 1936, a coalition of leftist parties—Communists, Socialists, and Radicals—formed a Popular Front government.

The Popular Front was able to start a program for workers that some have called the French New Deal. This program was named after President Franklin Delano Roosevelt's New Deal in the United States. The French New Deal consisted of the right of **collective bargaining** (the right of unions to negotiate with employers over wages and hours), a 40-hour workweek, 2-week paid vacations, and minimum wages. The Popular Front's policies, however, failed to solve the problems of the depression. By 1938, the French had little confidence in their political system. This lack of confidence left France unprepared to deal with the new—and aggressive—Nazi German state to the east.

The Imperial Germany of William II had come to an end in 1918, with Germany's defeat in World War I. A German democratic state known as the Weimar (VIE-mur) Republic was then set up. From its beginnings, the Weimar Republic was plagued by a series of problems. The republic had no truly outstanding political leaders. In 1925, Paul von Hindenburg, the World War I military hero, was elected president at the age of 77. Hindenburg was a traditional military man who at heart was not in favor of the republic he had been elected to serve.

So What??

*If your students question the importance of the information on **the New Deal,** tell them . . .*

The debate over government intervention in local affairs and the extent to which the federal government is responsible for social problems (one of today's main political issues) arose out of Franklin Roosevelt's solution to the Depression.

◄ *The Works Progress Administration was one of the back-to-work programs funded by the Roosevelt administration during the Great Depression. This San Francisco mural is just one of the art projects sponsored by the WPA.*

The Weimar Republic also faced serious economic problems. Germany experienced runaway inflation in 1922 and 1923, along with serious social problems. Widows, orphans, retired older people, army officers, teachers, civil servants, and others who lived on fixed incomes all watched their monthly incomes become worthless or their lifetime savings disappear. Their economic losses increasingly pushed the middle class to the rightist parties that were hostile to the republic. To make matters worse, after a period of prosperity from 1924 to 1929, Germany faced the Great Depression. Unemployment increased to 3 million in March 1930 and to 4.38 million by December of the same year. The depression paved the way for social discontent, fear, and the rise of extremist parties. The political, economic, and social problems of the Weimar Republic explain in part why the extremist Adolf Hitler and the Nazis were able to rise to power.

After Germany, no Western nation was more affected by the Great Depression than the United States. By 1932, U.S. industrial production fell to 50 percent of what it had been in 1929. By 1933, there were 15 million unemployed. Under these circumstances, the Democrat Franklin Delano Roosevelt was able to win a landslide electoral victory in the 1932 presidential election. A believer in free enterprise, Roosevelt realized that capitalism would have to be reformed in order to "save it." He pursued a policy of active government intervention in the economy that came to be known as the New Deal.

At first, the New Deal tried to restore prosperity by creating the National Recovery Administration (NRA). The NRA required government, labor, and industrial leaders to work out regulations for each industry. However, the NRA was declared unconstitutional by the United States Supreme Court in 1935.

The NRA was soon replaced by other efforts, known as the Second New Deal. These included a stepped-up program of public works, such as the Works Progress Administration (WPA) established in 1935. The WPA was a government organization that employed between 2 and 3 million people who worked at building bridges, roads, post offices, and airports. The Roosevelt administration was also responsible for new social legislation that began the U.S. welfare system. In 1935, the Social Security Act created a system of old-age pensions and unemployment insurance.

No doubt, the New Deal provided social reform measures that perhaps avoided a social revolution in the United States. However, it did not solve the unem-

On Line with
WORLD HISTORY *Internet Activity*

You may want to have your students visit the following URL, where they will find information and additional web site resources to enhance their study of this chapter.
The Rise of Hitler

http://www.historyplace.com/worldwar2/riseofhitler/index.htm

This site has chronology with extensive descriptions of each important event until March 23, 1933, when Hitler became dictator.

Due to the ever-changing nature of the World Wide Web, see the West History web site, **http://history.swpco.com** for regular updates of the URLs in this text.

Answers to
SECTION REVIEW

2. (a) going into debt to pay for things
(b) union negotiations with employers over wages and hours

3. (a) leader of a new German government that ended the policy of passive resistance to the policies of the Treaty of Versailles
(b) an American plan to help Germany pay its debts
(c) guaranteed German borders
(d) a treaty that renounced war as an instrument of national policy
(e) an unrealistic American desire to return to conditions that had existed before World War I
(f) a series of laws during the Depression that were designed to protect the economic rights of people
(g) the government in Germany created after World War I
(h) an American government agency created to fight the Depression

4. (a) economic sanctions
(b) paid its bills by printing money, which forced prices up
(c) Many American banks stopped making loans to Germany and tried to take money out of that country.
(d) Many people lost their jobs, savings, and security during the Depression. They were willing to listen to extremist groups that promised to help them.

5. Answers will vary.

ployment problems of the Great Depression. In 1938, American unemployment still stood at eleven million. Only World War II and the growth of weapons industries brought U.S. workers back to full employment.

❧ SECTION REVIEW ❧

1. **Locate:**
   (a) Ruhr Valley

2. **Define:**
   (a) deficit spending,
   (b) collective bargaining

3. **Identify:**
   (a) Gustav Stresemann,   (b) Dawes Plan,
   (c) Treaty of Locarno,   (d) Kellogg-Briand Pact,
   (e) return to normalcy,   (f) New Deal,
   (g) Weimar Republic,   (h) National Recovery Administration (NRA)

4. **Recall:**
   (a) What was the only sanction that could be used by the League of Nations against nations that broke international agreements?
   (b) What did Germany do to cause high rates of inflation after World War I?
   (c) How did the collapse of the American stock market in 1929 harm the German economy?
   (d) How did the Great Depression pave the way for social discontent, fear, and extremist political parties throughout the world?

5. **Think Critically:** Why is the following quotation almost certainly true? "Promises not to go to war without a way to enforce them were rather worthless."

◆ 2 ◆

THE RETREAT FROM DEMOCRACY: DICTATORIAL REGIMES

The triumph of democracy in Europe in 1919 was extremely short-lived. By 1939, only two major states

(France and Great Britain) and a number of minor ones remained democratic. Italy, Germany, the Soviet Union under Joseph Stalin, and many other European states adopted dictatorial regimes that took on both old and new forms.

Dictatorship was by no means new, of course, but the modern **totalitarian state** was. The totalitarian regimes, the best examples of which can be found in Stalinist Russia and Nazi Germany, pushed the power of the central state far beyond what it had been in the past. A totalitarian state was a government that aimed to control not only the political side of life but the economic, social, intellectual, and cultural lives of its citizens as well. The immediate origins of the totalitarian state can be found in the total warfare of World War I, when governments used controls over economic, political, and personal freedom in order to achieve victory.

Totalitarian states wanted more than the passive obedience of their subjects. They wanted to conquer the minds and hearts of their subjects, which they did through mass propaganda techniques and high-speed modern communication. Totalitarian states expected the active involvement of the masses in the achievement of the regime's goals, whether they be war, a socialist state, or a thousand-year empire, as Adolf Hitler wanted to establish.

The modern totalitarian state was led by a single leader and a single party. It rejected the liberal ideal of limited government power and guarantees of individual freedoms. Indeed, individual freedom was to be subordinated to the collective will of the masses, which was organized and determined for them by a leader or leaders. Modern technology also gave totalitarian states unheard-of police controls to enforce their wishes on their subjects.

The Birth of Fascism in Italy

In the early 1920s, Benito Mussolini (MOO-suh-LEE-nee) burst upon the Italian scene with the first Fascist movement in Europe. Mussolini began his political career as a socialist. However, he was kicked out of the Socialist Party after supporting Italy's entry into World War I, a position contrary to the socialist position of

ENRICHMENT ACTIVITY

Assign students to research and write an essay in which they discuss how the Great Depression opened the door to extremist political parties throughout the world. Ask them to identify such parties that they feel are active in the U.S.

◄ *Mussolini wanted to be known as a dynamic, strong leader. In this photo, he wears full dress uniform as he jogs with his officers. Do you think this photo was staged, or do you think these exercises were part of Mussolini's daily routine?*

strict neutrality. In 1919, Mussolini created a new political group, the Fascio di Combattimento (FAW-SHO-de-kom-BATT-e-MEN-toe), or League of Combat (hence the name Fascists (FASH-ists). The group received few votes in the elections of 1919, and Mussolini said bitterly that Fascism had "come to a dead end."

Political stalemate in Italy's government, however, soon came to the rescue of Mussolini and the Fascists. The new parliament elected in November 1919 was unable to govern Italy. The three major parties could not form an effective governmental coalition. At the same time, the Socialists, who had now become the largest party, spoke in theory of the need for revolution. This alarmed conservatives, who quickly associated socialists with Bolsheviks or Communists. Thousands of industrial and agricultural strikes in 1919 and 1920 created a climate of class warfare and continual violence.

In 1920 and 1921, Mussolini formed bands of black-shirted, armed Fascists called **squadristi.** These bands were turned loose in attacks on socialist offices and newspapers. They also used violence to break up strikes by trade unionists and socialist workers. A favorite tactic of the squadristi, also known as Blackshirts, was to pour a bottle of castor oil down the throats of their victims. Middle-class industrialists who feared working-class strikes, as well as large landowners who objected to the agricultural strikes, began to support Mussolini's Fascist movement.

Mussolini realized that the Italian people were angry over the failure of Italy to receive more land after World War I. He understood that nationalism was a powerful force. Thus, Mussolini demanded more land for Italy and began to win thousands of converts to Fascism with his patriotic appeals. By 1922, Mussolini's movement began to mushroom. His nationalist rhetoric and the middle-class fear of socialism, Communist revolution, and disorder made the Fascists more and more attractive. On October 29, 1922, Mussolini and the Fascists threatened to march on Rome if they were not given power. Mussolini exclaimed, "Either we are allowed to govern, or we will seize power by marching on Rome." King Victor Emmanuel III gave in and made Mussolini prime minister of Italy.

RECOMMENDED READING

The best biography of Mussolini is now D. Mack Smith, *Mussolini* (New York, 1982). Two brief, but excellent surveys of Fascist Italy are A. Cassels, *Fascist Italy,* 2d ed, (Arlington Heights, Ill., 1985); and A. De Grand, *Italian Fascism* (Lincoln, Neb., 1982). An excellent reference guide for all aspects of Fascist Italy is P. Cannistraro, ed., *Historical Dictionary of Fascist Italy* (Westport, Conn., 1982). The best

work on the rise of fascism is A. Lyttleton, *Seizure of Power* (New York, 1973), which covers the period from 1919 to 1929. Of the recent regional studies, the best is P. Corner, *Fascism in Ferrara, 1915–1925* (London, 1975). On propaganda and other aspects of cultural life in Fascist Italy, see E. R. Tannenbaum, *The Fascist Experience: Italian Society and Culture, 1922–1945* (New York, 1972).

CLOSE

Ask students to suggest examples illustrating the following sentence: "Everywhere, democracy seemed on the defensive in the 1930s."

② FOCUS

OBJECTIVES

After completing this section students should be able to

1. **distinguish between dictatorship and totalitarianism**
2. **discuss Mussolini's rise to power**
3. **describe some of the ways Italian Fascism differed from the German and Russian varieties**
4. **discuss Stalin's rise**
5. **describe conditions in Stalinist Russia**

FOCUS ACTIVITY

Ask students to imagine that they are living in post-World War I Europe. Times are hard, and a charismatic leader is promising to solve all problems if only the people give him total power. Give them about twenty minutes to write letters in which they explain to a relative in the United States how they feel about the new leader and his promises.

LEARNING FROM VISUALS

Answer to caption question: It is likely that this was a staged photo to reinforce the image that Mussolini wished to create.

TEACH

CLASS DISCUSSION

Discuss with students the distinction between dictatorship and totalitarianism. Discuss how the total warfare of World War I led to the beginnings of totalitarianism.

CRITICAL THINKING

Have students research and analyze conditions in Italy that led to Mussolini's rise. What strategies did he use to gain power? In what sense was Italian Fascism uniquely Italian?

LEARNING FROM VISUALS

Answer to the caption question: Children in the United States do not march with weapons, and one must be 18 to join the U.S. military.

CRITICAL THINKING

Ask students to research and speculate about why Mussolini was unable to realize his dream of an ideal Fascist state in Italy. What aspects of Italian history and culture might help to explain his relative failure?

CLASS DISCUSSION

Ask students to discuss how Fascist attitudes toward women reflected traditional Italian attitudes.

▶ *Young Fascists, dressed in military uniforms and bearing rifles, helped celebrate Rome's birthday in 1933. How does this compare to patriotic parades that you have seen?*

Within four years, Mussolini had used his position as prime minister to create a Fascist dictatorship. Press laws gave the government the right to suspend any publications that showed a lack of respect for the Catholic Church, the monarchy, or the state. The prime minister was made "Head of Government" with the power to make laws by decree. The police were given the power to arrest and jail anybody for both nonpolitical and political crimes without a trial. In 1926, all other political parties were outlawed. A secret police, known as the OVRA, was also set up. By the end of 1926, Mussolini ruled Italy as *Il Duce* (DOO-chae), "the leader."

Mussolini conceived of the Fascist state as totalitarian: "Fascism is totalitarian, and the Fascist State, the synthesis and unity of all values, interprets, develops and gives strength to the whole life of the people."[2] Mussolini did try to create a police state, but it was not very effective. Police activities in Italy were never as repressive, efficient, or savage as those of Nazi Germany. The Italian Fascists also tried to exercise control over all forms of mass media, including newspapers, radio, and cinema. In this way, propaganda could serve to integrate the masses into the state. Here, too, Mussolini failed to reach his major goals. Fascist propaganda came to consist chiefly of simple slogans, such as

"Mussolini Is Always Right," plastered on walls all over Italy.

Mussolini and the Fascists also tried to mold Italians into a single-minded community by creating Fascist organizations. Fascist youth groups, known as the Young Fascists, were used to teach Fascist ideals to the young people of the nation. By 1939, about 6.8 million children, teenagers, and young adults of both sexes—or 66 percent of the population between the ages of 8 and 18—were enrolled in some kind of Fascist youth group. Activities for these groups included Saturday afternoon marching drills, mountain summer camps, and youth contests. Underlying all of these activities was the Fascist insistence on military values. The Fascists worshiped war. Beginning in the 1930s, all male youth groups were given premilitary exercises to develop discipline and provide training for war. Results were mixed. Italian teenagers, who liked neither military training nor routine discipline of any kind, simply refused to attend Fascist youth group meetings on a regular basis.

The Fascist organizations hoped to create a new Italian, who would be hardworking, physically fit, disciplined, intellectually sharp, and war loving. In practice, the Fascists largely maintained traditional social attitudes in Italy. This is especially evident in their

RECOMMENDED READING

For a general study of other fascist movements, see F. L. Carsten, *The Rise of Fascism,* 2d ed. (Berkeley, 1980). For a general interpretation of fascism, see S. G. Payne, *Fascism: Comparison and Definition* (Madison, Wis., 1980).

On Russian in the 1920s, see S. F. Cohen, *Bukharin and the Bolshevik Revolution: A Political Biography 1888–1938* (New York, 1973). The collectivization of agriculture is examined

in R. W. Davies, *The Socialist Offensive: The Collectivization of Soviet Agriculture, 1929–30* (Cambridge, Mass., 1980); while the impact of that collectivization on the Russian peasants is discussed in R. W. Davies, *The Soviet Collective Farm, 1929–1930* (Cambridge, Mass., 1980). Industrialization is covered in H. Kuromiya, *Stalin's Industrial Revolution: Politics and Workers, 1928–1932* (New York, 1988).

policies regarding women. The Fascists portrayed the family as the pillar of the state and women as the basic foundation of the family. "Woman into the Home" became the Fascist slogan. Women were to be home-makers and baby producers, which was "their natural and fundamental mission in life," according to Mussolini.

The Fascists viewed population growth as a sign of national strength. Employment outside the home kept women from having babies. Mussolini said the following about such employment: "It forms an independence and consequent physical and moral habits contrary to child bearing."[3] There was another reason for the Fascist attitude toward working women: they would compete with males for jobs. Eliminating women from the market lowered unemployment figures for men in the depression economy of the 1930s.

Despite the instruments of repression, the use of propaganda, and the creation of numerous Fascist organizations, Mussolini did not achieve the degree of totalitarian control accomplished in Hitler's Germany or Stalin's Soviet Union. Mussolini and the Fascist Party never really destroyed the old power structure. Some institutions, including the armed forces and the monarchy, were never absorbed into the Fascist state. They managed to keep most of their independence. Mussolini had boasted that he would help workers and peasants. Instead, he allied himself with the interests of industrialists and large landowners at the expense of the lower classes.

Mussolini's compromise with the traditional institutions of Italy was especially evident in his attempt to gain the support of the Catholic Church. In the Lateran Accords of February 1929, Mussolini's regime recognized the sovereign independence of a small area of 109 acres within Rome, known as Vatican City. This territory had remained in the Catholic Church's hands since Italian unification in 1870. In return, the papacy recognized the Italian state. The Lateran Accords also gave the church a large grant of money and recognized Catholicism as the "sole religion of the state." In return, the Catholic Church urged Italians to support the Fascist regime.

In all areas of Italian life under Mussolini and the Fascists, there was a large gap between Fascist ideals and practice. The Italian Fascists promised much but delivered considerably less. They were soon overshadowed by a much more powerful Fascist movement to the north. Adolf Hitler was a student and great admirer of Mussolini. However, the German pupil soon proved to be far more adept in the use of power than was his Italian teacher.

A New Era in the Soviet Union

The civil war in Russia had taken an enormous number of lives. As we have seen, during the civil war, Lenin had followed a policy of war communism. Once the war was over, however, peasants began to sabotage the program by hoarding food. Added to this problem was the problem of drought, which caused a great famine between 1920 and 1922 that claimed as many as five million lives. With agricultural disaster came industrial collapse. By 1921, industrial output was only 20 percent of its 1913 levels. Russia was exhausted. A peasant banner proclaimed, "Down with Lenin and horseflesh, Bring back the Tsar and pork." As Leon Trotsky said, "The country, and the government with it, were at the very edge of the abyss."

Lenin and the New Communist Order

In March 1921, Lenin pulled Russia back from the abyss. He abandoned war communism in favor of his **New Economic Policy** (NEP). The NEP was a modified version of the old capitalist system. Peasants were now allowed to sell their produce openly. Retail stores, as well as small industries that employed fewer than twenty workers, could be privately owned and operated. Heavy industry, banking, and mines, however, remained in the hands of the government.

In 1922, Lenin and the Communists formally created a new state called the Union of Soviet Socialist Republics, known as the U.S.S.R. by its initials or the Soviet Union by its shortened form. Already by that year, a revived market and a good harvest had brought an end to famine. Soviet agricultural production climbed to 75 percent of its prewar level. Industry, especially state-owned heavy industry, fared less well and continued to stagnate. Only coal production had reached prewar levels by 1926. Overall, the NEP had

CRITICAL THINKING

Ask students to debate the morality of the Lateran Accords. Have them research the position of the Catholic Church on the value of this agreement with the Fascist regime. Suggest that one or two students present the pro-Lateran position, and one or two others present the anti-Lateran position.

CLASS DISCUSSION

Guide students in a discussion of the following sentence: "In March 1921, Lenin pulled Russia back from the abyss."

ACTIVITY

It has been said that Communism is dictatorship of the lower class, Fascism is dictatorship of the middle class, and Monarchy is a dictatorship of the upper class. Have students find examples from history they have studied thus far to support this statement. If they disagree, ask them to be prepared to discuss why.

Learning from Visuals

Ask students to speculate on why Stalin had this photograph taken and circulated. Compare his probable motives with the motives of a U.S. president photographed signing a bill into law.

Class Discussion

Guide students in a discussion of how Stalin—"Comrade Card-Index"—rose to absolute power in the Soviet Union.

Comparing Time Periods

As Stalin's crimes against humanity became more fully known, people sympathetic to Communism had to decide where they stood. Have students research, for example, "destalinization" in the Soviet Union after Stalin's death, and the changing opinions of Stalin held by American Communists.

▶ *In this 1933 photograph, Stalin is shown signing what is supposedly a death warrant. Terror was one strategy Stalin used to maintain an authoritarian system in the U.S.S.R.*

saved the Soviet Union from complete economic disaster. Lenin and other leading Communists, however, intended the NEP to be only a temporary retreat from the goals of communism.

The Rise of Stalin

Lenin died in 1924. A struggle for power among the seven members of the **Politburo** (paw-LIT-byoo-roe), the committee that had become the leading policymaker of the Communist Party, began at once. The Politburo was severely divided over the future direction of the Soviet Union. The Left, led by Leon Trotsky, wanted to end the NEP and launch Russia on a path of rapid industrialization, chiefly at the expense of the peasants. The same group wanted to spread communism abroad and believed that the revolution in Russia would not survive without other Communist states.

Another group in the Politburo, called the Right, rejected the idea of worldwide Communist revolution. It wanted instead to focus on building a socialist state in Russia and to continue Lenin's NEP. Rapid industrialization, it believed, would harm the living standards of the Soviet peasants.

These divisions were underscored by an intense personal rivalry between Leon Trotsky and Joseph Stalin (STAW-lin). In 1924, Trotsky held the post of commissar of war and was the leading spokesperson for the Left in the Politburo. Stalin had joined the Bolsheviks in 1903 and had come to Lenin's attention after staging a daring bank robbery to get funds for the Bolshevik cause. Stalin was neither a dynamic speaker nor a forceful writer. He was a good organizer, however (his fellow Bolsheviks called him "Comrade Card-Index"). He was content to hold the dull bureaucratic job of party general secretary while other Politburo members held party positions that enabled them to display their brilliant oratorical abilities. The other members of the Politburo soon found, however, that the position of general secretary was really the most important in the party. The general secretary appointed the regional, district, city, and town party secretaries. In 1922, for example, Stalin had appointed some ten thousand people, who proved valuable later in his struggle for power.

Stalin used his post as party general secretary to gain complete control of the Communist Party. Expelled from the party in 1927, Trotsky made his way to Mexico. There he was murdered (with a pickax in the

More About . . . *Joseph Stalin*

Joseph Stalin was born Iosif Vissarionovich Dzhugashvili in 1879, but adopted the pseudonym Stalin in about 1910. Stalin means "a man of steel." As a school boy in Gori, which is in the Republic of Georgia, Stalin was forced to learn Russian even though neither of his parents spoke it. Stalin was the best student in the church school he attended and, as such, earned a full scholarship to a theological seminary.

While in seminary, Stalin read literature that was forbidden, especially the works of Karl Marx. It wasn't long before Stalin converted to Russian Marxism. He eventually quit the seminary to become a full-time revolutionary.

Stalin joined the Social-Democratic Party, which was a Marxist revolutionary group. While part of this group, he spread propaganda among railroad workers. He was arrested, spent a year in prison, and then was head) in 1940, no doubt on Stalin's orders. By 1929, Stalin had eliminated from the Politburo the Old Bolsheviks of the revolutionary era and had established a powerful dictatorship.

Stalinist Russia

The Stalinist Era marked the beginning of an economic, social, and political revolution that was more sweeping in its results than were the revolutions of 1917. Stalin made a significant shift in economic policy in 1928. He launched his first five-year plan. Its real goal was nothing less than the virtually overnight transformation of Russia from an agricultural into an industrial country.

Instead of stressing the production of consumer goods, the first five-year plan emphasized maximum production of capital goods (goods devoted to the production of other goods, such as heavy machines) and armaments. The plan quadrupled the production of heavy machinery and doubled oil production. Between 1928 and 1937, during the first two five-year plans, steel production increased from 4 million to 18 million tons per year. Hard coal output went from 36 million to 128 million tons. At the same time, new industrial cities, located near iron ore and coal deposits, sprang up overnight in the Urals and Siberia.

The social and political costs of industrialization were enormous. Little provision was made for caring for the expanded labor force in the cities. The number of workers increased by millions between 1932 and 1940, but total investment in housing actually declined after 1929. The result was that millions of workers and their families lived in pitiful conditions. Real wages in industry also declined by 43 percent between 1928 and 1940. Strict laws even limited where workers could move. To keep workers content, government propaganda stressed the need for sacrifice to create the new socialist state.

With rapid industrialization came an equally rapid **collectivization** of agriculture. Its goal was to eliminate private farms and push people into collective farms (see "You Are There: The Formation of Collective Farms"). Strong resistance to Stalin's plans came from peasants, who responded by hoarding crops and killing

livestock. However, these actions only led Stalin to step up the program. By 1930, 10 million peasant households had been collectivized. By 1934, Russia's 26 million family farms had been collectivized into 250,000 units.

The collectivization of agriculture was done at tremendous cost. The hoarding of food and the slaughter of livestock produced widespread famine. Stalin himself is supposed to have told Winston Churchill during World War II that ten million peasants died in the famines of 1932 and 1933. The only concession Stalin made to the peasants was that each collective farm worker was allowed to have one tiny, privately owned garden plot.

There were other costs to Stalin's program of rapid industrialization as well. To achieve his goals, Stalin strengthened the party bureaucracy under his control. Those who resisted were sent into forced labor camps in Siberia. Stalin's desire for sole control of decision making also led to purges of the Old Bolsheviks. Between 1936 and 1938, the most prominent Old Bolsheviks were put on trial and condemned to death. During this same time, Stalin undertook a purge of army officers, diplomats, union officials, party members, intellectuals, and numerous ordinary citizens. An estimated eight million Russians were arrested. Millions were sent to forced labor camps in Siberia, from which they never returned.

The Stalin Era also undid much of the permissive social legislation of the early 1920s. Believing in complete equality of rights for women, the Communists had made divorce and abortion easy to get. They had also encouraged women to work outside the home and to liberate themselves sexually. After Stalin came to power, the family was praised as a small collective in which parents were responsible for teaching the values of hard work, duty, and discipline. Abortion was outlawed. Divorced fathers who did not support their children were heavily fined.

Authoritarian States in the West

There were a number of states in the Western world that were not totalitarian but that did possess conservative authoritarian governments. These states adopted

CLASS DISCUSSION

Guide students in a discussion of Stalin's programs of rapid industrialization coupled with the collectivization of agriculture. What were three major results of these programs on the lives and fortunes of the Russian people?

CRITICAL THINKING

Ask students to speculate on why ultra-conservative or extremist governments seem to disapprove of such things as women's efforts to secure equal rights, relaxation of laws governing abortion and/or divorce, and expansion of traditional gender roles. How do these conflict with ultra-conservative agendas and programs?

exiled to Siberia. He eventually escaped from Siberia. However, the pattern of arrest, imprisonment, and exile became common to Stalin. Over the next several years he was arrested eight times, exiled seven times, and escaped six times. His last arrest was for helping to organize a bank robbery. This time the government was able to contain him in exile for four years.

Stalin became an important figure in the Social-Democratic party and began writing as editor of the party newspaper, *Pravda*. His first important published work was, *Marxism and the Nationality Question*. HIs organizational skills strengthened his position in the party and, on Lenin's death, Stalin was able to join with Kamenev and Zinovyev to lead the country.

YOU ARE THERE

The Formation of Collective Farms

The collectivization of agriculture transformed Russia's 26 million family farms into 250,000 collective farms (kolkhozes) (kawl-KAWZ-uz). In this firsthand account, we see how the process worked.

Max Belov, *The History of a Collective Farm*

General collectivization in our village was brought about in the following manner: Two representatives of the [Communist] Party arrived in the village. All the inhabitants were summoned by the ringing of the church bell to a meeting at which the policy of general collectivization was announced. . . . The upshot was that although the meeting lasted two days, from the viewpoint of the Party representatives nothing was accomplished.

After this setback the Party representatives divided the village into two sections and worked each one separately. Two more officials were sent to reinforce the first two. A meeting of our section of the village was held in a stable which had previously belonged to a kulak [wealthy peasant]. The meeting dragged on until dark. Suddenly someone threw a brick at the lamp, and in the dark the

▲ *These Russian peasants use scythes to harvest their grain crops. How does their work compare to harvesting practices in Western Europe or the United States in the 1930s?*

some of the features of totalitarian states, especially their wide police powers. However, their greatest concern was not to create a new kind of mass society but only to preserve the existing social order. As a result, the authoritarian states were content with passive obedience rather than active involvement in the goals of the regime.

Nowhere had the map of Europe been more drastically altered by World War I than in eastern Europe. The new states of Austria, Poland, Czechoslovakia, and Yugoslavia (known as the kingdom of the Serbs, Croats, and Slovenes until 1929) adopted parliamentary systems. The kingdoms of Romania and Bulgaria had already gained new parliamentary constitutions in 1920. Greece became a republic in 1924. Hungary's government was parliamentary in form, but it was controlled by its landed aristocrats. At the beginning of the 1920s, political democracy seemed well established in eastern Europe. That situation did not last very long, however.

Several problems threatened political democracy. The eastern European states had little tradition of par-

MORE ABOUT . . . *Russian Culture Between the Wars*

One of the most well known products of pre-war Russian cinema is *Alexander Nevsky*, directed by Sergei Eisenstein, with music by Sergei Prokofiev (probably best known for his symphonic fairy tale, *Peter and the Wolf*). The movie tells the story of a Russian national hero from the 13th century who repelled an invasion of Teutonic (German) invaders. Its significance, beyond its artistic value, is that it helped to encourage patriotic feelings in the Russian people just two years before the Nazi invasion of the Soviet Union.

YOU ARE THERE

The Formation of Collective Farms, continued

peasants began to beat the Party representatives who jumped out the window and escaped from the village barely alive. The following day seven people were arrested. The militia was called in and stayed in the village until the peasants, realizing their helplessness, calmed down. . . .

By the end of 1930 there were two kolkhozes in our village. Though at first these collectives embraced at most only 70 percent of the peasant households, in the months that followed they gradually absorbed more and more of them.

In these kolkhozes the great bulk of the land was held and worked communally, but each peasant household owned a house of some sort, a small plot of ground and perhaps some livestock. All the members of the kolkhoz were required to work on the kolkhoz a certain number of days each month; the rest of the time they were allowed to work on their own holdings. They derived their income partly from what they grew on their garden strips and partly from their work in the kolkhoz.

When the harvest was over, and after the farm had met its obligations to the state and to various special funds and had sold on the market whatever

undesignated produce was left, the remaining produce and the farm's monetary income were divided among the kolkhoz members according to the number of "labor days" each one had contributed to the farm's work. . . . After they had received their earnings, one of them remarked, "You will live, but you will be very, very thin. . . ."

By late 1932 more than 80 percent of the peasant households . . . had been collectivized. . . . That year the peasants harvested a good crop and had hopes that the calculations would work out to their advantage and would help strengthen them economically. These hopes were in vain. The kolkhoz workers received only 200 grams of flour per labor day for the first half of the year; the remaining grain, including the seed fund, was taken by the government. The peasants were told that industrialization of the country, then in full swing, demanded grain and sacrifices from them.

1. What is a collective farm?

2. Why did the peasants resist the collective farms?

---

liamentary politics and no real middle class to support that tradition. Then, too, these states were mostly rural and agrarian. Many of the peasants were illiterate, and much of the land was still dominated by large landowners who feared the peasants. Ethnic conflicts also threatened to tear these countries apart. Powerful landowners, the churches, and even some members of the small middle class feared land reform, Communist upheaval, and ethnic conflict. Thus, they looked to authoritarian governments to maintain the old system. Only Czechoslovakia, with its large middle class, lib-

eral tradition, and strong industrial base, maintained its political democracy.

In Spain, political democracy failed to survive. Led by General Francisco Franco (FRAWNG-KOE), Spanish military forces revolted against the democratic government in 1936. A brutal and bloody civil war began. Foreign intervention complicated the Spanish Civil War. The fascist regimes of Italy and Germany aided Franco's forces with arms, money, and men. Hitler used the Spanish Civil War as an opportunity to test the new weapons of his revived air force. The horrible

---

USING PRIMARY SOURCES

What does Belov's description of the violent end to the village meeting, and the results of that rebellion, suggest about the Soviet government's attitude toward collectivization? Although they held meetings with local people, how did the Party representatives actually get collective farms instituted? Who benefited from these "communal" farms?

Answers to Critical Thinking Questions

1. A collective farm held the land that used to belong to peasants. The peasants were required to work the land a certain number of days each month for a share in the profits. The bulk of the profits went to the government.
2. The peasants made even less on the collective farms than they had made on their own. The government regularly went back on its word and cheated them out of their fair share of things.

ACROSS THE CURRICULUM

Art Ask students to bring in a copy of Picasso's painting, *Guernica* and to lead a discussion of the artist's techniques and the power of the work.

SPECIAL NEEDS: *Visual/Auditory*

Ask students to read pages 839–850. Have groups of students prepare charts comparing the characteristics of a totalitarian state with those of a democracy. Some of the characteristics that may be included are: 1) Government—Democracy: parliamentary, vote, political parties; Totalitarian State: dictatorial, single leader, single party; 2) Citizens—Democracy: individual liberties; Totalitarian State: controlling, no vote, no individual

freedoms; 3) Economy—Democracy: free enterprise, laissez-faire; Totalitarian State: controlled by government.

Students may name the countries that remained democratic (the United States, France and Britain) and those that became totalitarian states (Italy, Germany and the Soviet Union) from 1919–1939. Final presentations may include pictures and/or music of the various countries.

ASSESS

Answers to
SECTION REVIEW

2. (a) almost all power is held by the central government
   (b) Italian fascists
   (c) a policy in the Soviet Union that allowed a return to partial capitalism in most of the 1920s
   (d) the seven-member policy-making committee of the Communist Party
   (e) attempt to eliminate private farms
3. (a) a "League of Combat" to support the Italian fascist movement
   (b) Benito Mussolini
   (c) an agreement between the Catholic church and the government of Benito Mussolini
   (d) leader of the Soviet Union who took power after 1928
   (e) plans to develop the industrial capacity of the Soviet Economy
   (f) dictator of Spain
4. (a) There were too many political groups who could not agree on government policy.
   (b) With only one communist nation it was hard for the Soviet Union to be secure.
   (c) Stalin was an excellent organizer.
   (d) It was an opportunity to test new weapons.
5. Answers will vary.

CLOSE

Ask students to discuss the qualities that brought Mussolini and Stalin to power. How was each representative of his nation and culture?

850

---

destruction of Guernica (gair-NEE-kaw) by German bombers in April 1937 was immortalized in a painting by the Spanish artist Pablo Picasso.

The Spanish republican government was aided by forty-thousand foreign volunteers and trucks, planes, tanks, and military advisors from the Soviet Union. After Franco's forces captured Madrid on March 28, 1939, the Spanish Civil War finally came to an end. Franco then set up a dictatorship that favored large landowners, businesspeople, and the Catholic clergy. It was yet another example of a traditional, conservative, authoritarian regime.

❀ SECTION REVIEW ❀

1. **Locate:**
   (*a*) Madrid,   (*b*) Russia,   (*c*) Czechoslovakia

2. **Define:**
   (*a*) totalitarian state,
   (*b*) squadristi,
   (*c*) New Economic Policy,
   (*d*) Politburo,
   (*e*) collectivization

3. **Identify:**
   (*a*) Fascio di Combattimento,
   (*b*) *Il Duce,*
   (*c*) Lateran Accords,
   (*d*) Joseph Stalin,
   (*e*) Five-Year Plan,
   (*f*) General Francisco Franco

4. **Recall:**
   (*a*) Why couldn't the parliament of Italy form a stable government in 1919?
   (*b*) Why did Trotsky's followers want to spread communism to other nations?
   (*c*) What ability did Stalin possess that helped him gain power?
   (*d*) Why did the Soviet Union and Germany choose to become involved in the Spanish Civil War?

5. **Think Critically:** Why did German and Italian policies of keeping women at home rather than working in factories weaken these countries' ability to prepare for and fight the war?

HITLER AND NAZI GERMANY

In 1923, a small, south German rightist party, known as the Nazis, led by an obscure Austrian rabble-rouser named Adolf Hitler, created a stir when it tried to seize power in southern Germany. Although the attempted takeover failed, it brought Hitler and the Nazis national attention. Within ten years, Hitler and the Nazis had taken over complete power and established another fascist state.

The Rise of Hitler

Born on April 20, 1889, Adolf Hitler was the son of an Austrian customs official. He was a total failure in secondary school and eventually made his way to Vienna to become an artist. He was rejected by the Vienna Academy of Fine Arts and was supported by an inheritance and orphan's pension. Hitler stayed on in Vienna to live the carefree lifestyle of an artist. While there, he established the basic ideas of an ideology from which he never deviated for the rest of his life. At the core of Hitler's ideas was racism, especially his **anti-Semitism** (hostility toward Jews). His hatred of the Jews lasted to the end of his life. Hitler had also become an extreme German nationalist and had learned from the mass politics of Vienna how political parties could effectively use propaganda and terror. Finally, in his Viennese (VEE-uh-NEEZ) years, Hitler came to a firm belief in the need for struggle, which he saw as the "granite foundation of the world."

In 1913, Hitler moved to Munich, still with no real future in sight. He described how World War I then saved him: "Overpowered by stormy enthusiasm, I fell

---

RECOMMENDED READING

Two brief but sound surveys of Nazi Germany are J. Spielvogel, *Hitler and Nazi Germany: A History,* 2d ed. (Englewood Cliffs, N.J., 1992); and J. Bendersky, *A History of Nazi Germany* (Chicago, 1985). The best biographies of Hitler are A. Bullock *Hitler: A Study in Tyranny* (New York, 1964); and J. Fest, *Hitler,* trans. R. and C. Winston (New York, 1974). A good sociological analysis of the Nazi party can be found in M. Kater, *The Nazi Party: A*

Social Profile of Members and Leaders, 1919–1945 (Cambridge, Mass., 1983). A good regional study of the Nazi party's rise to power is W. S. Allen's "classic" *The Nazi Seizure of Power: The Experience of a Single German Town,* rev. ed. (New York, 1984). On the SA, see P. Merkle, *The Making of a Stormtrooper* (Princeton, N.J., 1980). A brief perspective on Germany's economic recovery can be found in R. J. Overy, *The Nazi Eco-*

down on my knees and thanked Heaven . . . for granting me the good fortune of being permitted to live at this time."[4] At the end of World War I, after four years of service as a dispatch runner on the Western Front, Hitler went to Munich and decided to enter politics.

In 1919, Hitler joined the little-known German Worker's Party, one of a number of right-wing extreme nationalist parties in Munich. By the summer of 1921, Hitler had taken over total control of the party, which he renamed the National Socialist German Workers' Party (NSDAP), or Nazi for short. His idea was that the party's name would distinguish the Nazis from the socialist parties. At the same time, it would gain support from both workers and German nationalists.

Hitler worked hard to develop the party into a mass political movement with flags, party badges, uniforms, and its own newspaper. It also had its own police force, or party militia, known as the SA, the Sturmabteilung, or the Storm Troops (also known as the Brownshirts, after the color of their uniforms). The Storm Troops were used to defend the party in meeting halls and to break up the meetings of other parties. Their existence added an element of force and terror to the growing Nazi movement. Hitler's own oratorical skills were largely responsible for attracting an increasing number of followers. By 1923, the party had grown from its early hundreds into a membership of 55,000, with 15,000 SA members.

Overconfident, Hitler staged an armed uprising against the government in Munich in November 1923. The Beer Hall Putsch was quickly crushed, and Hitler was sentenced to prison. During his brief stay in jail, Hitler wrote *Mein Kampf* (MINE KAWMPF) (*My Struggle*), an autobiographical account of his movement and its basic ideas. Extreme German nationalism, a strong anti-Semitism, and anticommunism were linked together by a Social Darwinian theory of struggle. This theory stressed the right of superior nations to *Lebensraum* (LAY-bunz-ROWM)—living space—through expansion, as well as the right of superior individuals to secure authoritarian leadership over the masses. *Mein Kampf* is remarkable. It spelled out a series of ideas that directed Hitler's actions once he took power. That others refused to take Hitler and his extreme ideas seriously was one of his greatest advantages.

The Victory of Nazism

While he was in prison, Hitler came to an important conclusion. He realized that the Nazis would have to come to power by constitutional means, not by a violent overthrow of the Weimar Republic. This meant that the Nazi Party would have to be a mass political party that would compete for votes with the other political parties. After his release from prison, Hitler worked to build such a party. He expanded the Nazi Party to all parts of Germany. By 1929, it had a national party organization. It also grew from 27,000 members in 1925 (it had lost members while Hitler was in jail) to 178,000 by the end of 1929.

Especially noticeable was the youthfulness of the regional, district, and branch leaders of the Nazi organization. Many were between the ages of twenty-five and thirty. They were fiercely committed to Hitler, because he gave them the kind of active politics they sought. Rather than debate, they wanted brawls in beer halls, fiery speeches, and comradeship in the building of a new Germany. One new, young Nazi member expressed his excitement about the party:

> For me this was the start of a completely new life. There was only one thing in the world for me and that was service in the movement. All my thoughts were centred on the movement. I could talk only politics. I was no longer aware of anything else. At the time I was a promising athlete; I was very keen on sport, and it was going to be my career. But I had to give this up too. My only interest was agitation and propaganda.[5]

Such youthful enthusiasm gave the Nazi movement the air of a "young man's movement." The other parties could not match its sense of dynamism.

By 1932, the Nazi Party had 800,000 members and had become the largest party in the **Reichstag** (RYKS-tahg) (the German parliament). No doubt, Germany's economic difficulties were a crucial factor in the Nazi rise to power. Unemployment had risen dramatically, from 4.35 million in 1931 to 6 million by the winter of 1932. The economic and psychological impact of the Great Depression made extremist parties more attractive.

The Nazi rise was also due to the fact that the Nazis developed especially effective modern electioneering

nomic Recovery, 1932–1938 (London, 1982). Basic studies of the SS include R. Koehl, *The Black Corps: The Structure and Power Struggles of the Nazi SS* (Madison, Wis., 1983); and H. Krausnick and M. Broszat, *Anatomy of the SS State* (London, 1970). An insightful book about the responses of ordinary Germans to the Third Reich is D. Peukert, *Inside Nazi Germany: Conformity, Opposition, and Racism in Everyday Life,* trans. R. Deveson (New Haven, Conn., 1987). On women, see J. Stephenson, *Women in Nazi Society* (London, 1975); and C. Koonz, *Mothers in the Fatherland: Women, the Family, and Nazi Politics* (New York, 1987). The Hitler Youth is examined in H. W. Koch, *The Hitler Youth* (New York, 1976). The importance of racial ideology in Nazi Germany is evident in R. Proctor, *Racial Hygiene: Medicine under the Nazis* (Cambridge, Mass., 1988).

FOCUS

OBJECTIVES

After completing this section, students should be able to

1. describe Hitler's rise to power
2. discuss Hitler's main ideas in *Mein Kampf*
3. discuss the major ways the Nazis created their totalitarian state
4. describe life in Hitler's Germany
5. describe the Nazis' anti-Semitic policies and activities

FOCUS ACTIVITY

Ask students to read the words of the new, young Nazi party member on page 851. How would they explain such enthusiasm? Can they imagine themselves feeling this way about a political movement? Why, or why not? Based on their own experience, ask them to write another ending to the sentence, "There was only one thing in the world for me and that was . . ."

TEACH

CRITICAL THINKING

Ask students to speculate on why the young Hitler greeted the outbreak of World War I so ecstatically.

CLASS DISCUSSION

Lead students in a discussion of Hitler's main preoccupations and beliefs, as described in *Mein Kampf.*

CLASS DISCUSSION

Ask students to discuss the following sentence: "The Nazi rise was also due to the fact that the Nazis developed especially effective modern electioneering techniques."

COMPARING TIME PERIODS

How would students compare the Nazis' skill at exploiting the particular fears and hopes of specific audiences with recent U.S. presidential campaigns? How would they compare Nazi use of conservative Germans' fear of Communism to the McCarthy blacklist era of the 1950s in the U.S.?

CLASS DISCUSSION

Ask students to discuss how Hitler became a dictator "appointed by the parliamentary body itself."

▶ *Hitler used a variety of ceremonial actions to strengthen the ties between party members and himself. Here Hitler touches a flag that was supposedly stained with Nazi blood during the Beer Hall Putsch. The man holding the banner makes a "blood oath" of allegiance to Hitler.*

techniques. In their election campaigns, party members pitched their themes to the needs and fears of different social groups. In working-class districts, for example, the Nazis attacked international high finance. In middle-class neighborhoods, they exploited fears of a Communist revolution and its threat to private property. At the same time that the Nazis made blatant appeals to class interests, they were denouncing conflicts of interest. They stood above classes and parties, they proclaimed. Hitler, in particular, claimed to stand above all differences and promised to create a new Germany free of class differences and party infighting. His appeal to national pride, national honor, and traditional militarism struck chords of emotion in his listeners. A schoolteacher in Hamburg said after attending one of Hitler's rallies, "When the speech was over, there was roaring enthusiasm and applause. . . . Then he went.—How many look up to him with touching faith as their helper, their saviour, their deliverer from unbearable distress."[6]

Elections proved to have their limits. In the elections of July 1932, the Nazis won 230 seats, making them the largest party in the Reichstag. Four months later, however, in November, they declined to 196 seats. It became apparent to many Nazis that they would not gain power simply by the ballot box. Hitler saw clearly, however, that the Reichstag after 1930 was not all that important, because the government ruled by decree with the support of President Hindenburg.

More and more, the right-wing elites of Germany—the industrial leaders, landed aristocrats, military officers, and higher bureaucrats—came to see Hitler as the man of the hour. He had the mass support to set up a right-wing, authoritarian regime that would save Germany and people in privileged positions from a Communist takeover. Under pressure, Hindenburg agreed to allow Hitler to become chancellor (on January 30, 1933) and create a new government.

Within two months, Hitler had laid the foundation for the Nazis' complete control over Germany. On February 27, a fire, supposedly caused by the Communists, broke out in the Reichstag building. The next day, Hitler convinced Hindenburg to issue a decree that gave the government emergency powers. The decree

SPECIAL NEEDS: *Auditory*

Have students prepare questions and interview someone they know (it could be a relative, a friend, a teacher, or neighbor) who lived during the period between the World Wars (1919–1939). If they do not know anyone, they may interview a classmate pretending to be someone from that period. The students may choose to ask questions on one or more of the following topics: 1) living during The Great Depression; 2) living in Europe after World War I; 3) Nazi Germany; 4) cultural events: radio, movies, sports, art, music and literature. The interviews may be recorded or videotaped. Have the students share with the class. If video or audiotape is not available, they may prepare a written report, or a presentation for class.

suspended all basic rights of the citizens for the full duration of the emergency. The Nazis could now arrest and jail anyone. The crowning step of Hitler's "legal seizure" of power came on March 23, when a two-thirds vote of the Reichstag passed the Enabling Act. This gave the government the power to ignore the constitution for four years while it issued laws that dealt with the country's problems. The Enabling Act gave Hitler's later acts a legal basis. He no longer needed the Reichstag or President Hindenburg. In effect, Hitler became a dictator appointed by the parliamentary body itself.

With their new source of power, the Nazis acted quickly to bring all institutions under Nazi control. The civil service was purged of Jews and democratic elements. Concentration camps were set up for opponents of the new regime. Trade unions were dissolved. All political parties except the Nazis were abolished. By the end of the summer of 1933, within seven months of being appointed chancellor, Hitler and the Nazis had established the basis for a totalitarian state. When Hindenburg died on August 2, 1934, the office of president was abolished. Hitler became sole ruler of Germany. Public officials and soldiers were all required to take a personal oath of loyalty to Hitler as the "Führer (Leader) of the German Reich and people."

The Nazi State, 1933 to 1939

Hitler now felt the real task was at hand: to develop the "total state." Hitler's aims had not been simply power for power's sake. Hitler had a larger goal—the development of an Aryan racial state that would dominate Europe and possibly the world for generations to come.* To achieve this goal, the German people must be actively involved, not passively cowed by force.

---

*Aryan was a term borrowed from linguists, who used it to identify people speaking a common set of languages known as Indo-European (see Chapter 2). The Nazis misused the term and identified the Aryans with the Greeks and Romans of the past and the Germans and Scandinavians of the present. The Germans were seen by the Nazis as the true descendants and chief leaders of the Aryans.

Hitler stated:

> We must develop organizations in which an individual's entire life can take place. Then every activity and every need of every individual will be regulated by the collectivity represented by the party. There is no longer any arbitrary will, there are no longer any free realms in which the individual belongs to himself. . . . The time of personal happiness is over.[7]

The Nazis pursued the creation of this totalitarian state in a variety of ways. Mass demonstrations and spectacles were used to make the German people an instrument for Hitler's policies (see "You Are There: Mass Meetings in Nazi Germany"). These meetings, especially the Nuremberg party rallies that were held every September, had great appeal. They usually evoked mass enthusiasm and excitement.

The state apparatus of Hitler's "total state" offers some confusing features. One usually thinks of Nazi Germany as having an all-powerful government that maintained absolute control and order. In truth, Nazi Germany was the scene of almost constant personal and institutional conflict. This resulted in administrative chaos. Struggle was a basic feature of relationships within the party, within the state, and between party and state. Hitler, of course, was the ultimate decision maker and absolute ruler.

Hitler and the Nazis also established control in the economic sphere. Hitler made use of public works projects and grants to private construction firms to put people back to work and end the depression. A massive rearmament program, however, provided far more help in solving the unemployment problem. Unemployment, which had stood at 6 million in 1932, dropped to 2.6 million in 1934 and less than 500,000 in 1937. The regime claimed full credit for solving Germany's economic woes. No doubt, the new regime's part in bringing an end to the depression was an important factor in leading many Germans to accept Hitler and the Nazis.

For those who needed coercion, the Nazi total state had its instruments of terror and repression. Especially important were the Schutzstaffeln (guard squadrons), known simply as the SS. The SS was originally created as Hitler's personal bodyguard. Under the direction of

CLASS DISCUSSION

Ask students to discuss the four main ways the Nazis created their totalitarian state. (mass demonstrations, control of economy, terror and repression, control of institutions)

USING PRIMARY SOURCES

Ask students to speculate on the appeal of Hitler's desire to regulate all aspects of people's lives. What is attractive about such total control? (individual freed of responsibility, end to disorder and uncertainty, all-consuming purpose for everyone's life) Are there contemporary, small-scale parallels to Hitler's appeal? (cults; survivalist and other fringe movements with charismatic leaders)

Multimedia Support

TRANSPARENCY
26–1, German Expansion, 1933–1939 (Map)

MORE ABOUT . . . Developing an Aryan State

In its attempt to develop a pure Aryan state, the Nazi regime had to take systematic measures against the Jews. The first problem to be solved, however, was to develop a definition of the word *Jew*.

It didn't matter whether a person actually participated in the Jewish faith, what mattered most was a person's ancestry. If three or four of a person's grandparents were Jews, then that person was considered to be a Jew. Those who were half Jewish (one parent was a Jew) were not considered to be Jewish unless they actually belonged to the Jewish faith or were married to a Jew. Half-Jews who were not Jewish and those with one or two Jewish grandparents were considered half-breeds. Both the Jews and the half-breeds were considered to be non-Aryan.

YOU ARE THERE

Mass Meetings in Nazi Germany

Propaganda and mass rallies were two of the chief instruments that Adolf Hitler used to prepare the German people for the tasks he set before them. In the first excerpt that follows, which is taken from Hitler's book Mein Kampf, *Hitler explains the psychological importance of mass meetings. In the second excerpt, which is taken from Hitler's speech to a crowd at Nuremberg, he describes the mystical bond he hoped to create through his mass rallies.*

Adolf Hitler, *Mein Kampf*

The mass meeting is also necessary for the reason that in it the individual . . . for the first time gets the picture of a larger community. . . . When from his little workshop or big factory, in which he feels very small, he steps for the first time into a mass meeting and has thousands and thousands of people of the same opinions around him, when, as a seeker, he is swept away by three or four thousand others into the mighty effect of suggestive intoxication, when the visible success and agreement of thousands confirm to him the rightness of the new doctrine and for the first time arouse doubt in the truth of his previous conviction—then he himself has succumbed to the magic influence of what we designate as "mass suggestion." The will, the longing, and also the power of thousands are accumulated in every individual. The man who enters such a meeting doubting and wavering leaves it inwardly reinforced: he has become a link in the community.

Hitler's Speech at Nuremberg

Do we not feel once again in this hour the miracle that brought us together? Once you heard the voice of a man, and it struck deep into your hearts; it awakened you, and you followed this voice. Year after year you went after it, though him who had spoken you never even saw. You heard only a voice, and you followed it. When we meet each other here, the wonder of our coming together fills us all. Not everyone of you sees me, and I do not see everyone of you. But I feel you, and you feel me. It is the belief in our people that has made us small men great, that has made us poor men rich, that has made brave and coura-

Heinrich Himmler (see "Biography: Heinrich Himmler—Leader of Terror"), the SS came to control all of the regular and secret police forces. The SS was based on two principles: terror and ideology. Terror included the instruments of repression and murder: the secret police, criminal police, concentration camps, and later the execution squads and death camps for the extermination of the Jews. For Himmler, the SS was a crusading order whose chief goal was to further the Aryan master race.

Other institutions, such as the Catholic and Protestant Churches, primary and secondary schools, and universities, were also brought under the control of the Nazi totalitarian state. Nazi professional organizations and leagues were formed for civil servants, teachers, women, farmers, doctors, and lawyers. Youth organizations, too, were set up to teach young people the Nazi ideals (see "Young People in Nazi Germany: The Hitler Youth").

The creation of the Nazi total state also had an impact on women. Women played a crucial role in the Aryan racial state as bearers of the children who, it was believed, would bring about the triumph of the Aryan race. The Nazis believed there were natural differences

MORE ABOUT . . . *The Berlin Olympics*

The Berlin Olympics in 1936 were so controversial that many nations planned on attending an alternate "People's Olympics" in Barcelona, Spain. However, when the Spanish Civil War broke out those games were canceled. The event that the world attended in Germany was a landmark in Olympic history for several reasons. It was the first Olympics to transmit results immediately throughout Europe, via a telex. The Germans also used zeppelins to quickly send newsreel footage to other countries. Furthermore, the 1936 games were the first televised Olympics. The Germans used a closed circuit to show the games in specially equipped theaters in Berlin. Finally, the Berlin Games mark the beginning of the torch relay, a tradition that has since become synonymous with the Olympics.

YOU ARE THERE

Mass Meetings in Nazi Germany, continued

◄ Hitler and the Nazi Party used mass rallies to create enthusiastic support for their policies. Almost one million people attended this 1937 Harvest Festival near Hamelin. How do you think it would feel to be part of this cheering crowd?

geous men out of us wavering, spiritless, timid folk; this belief made us see our road when we were astray; it joined us together into one whole! . . . You come, that . . . you may, once in a while, gain the feeling that now we are together; we are with him and he with us, and we are now Germany!

1. Why did Hitler say the mass meetings were necessary?

2. How did Hitler try to maximize the effects of the meetings?

between men and women. Men were warriors and political leaders. Women were destined to be wives and mothers. By maintaining this clear distinction, each could best serve to "maintain the whole community."

Nazi ideas determined employment opportunities for women. The Nazis hoped to drive women out of certain areas of the labor market. These included jobs in heavy industry or other jobs that might hinder women from bearing healthy children. Certain professions, including university teaching, medicine, and law, also were considered unsuitable for women, especially married women. The Nazis encouraged women

to pursue professional occupations that had direct practical application, such as social work and nursing. The Nazi regime pushed its campaign against working women with poster slogans such as "Get ahold of pots and pans and broom and you'll sooner find a groom!"

The Nazi total state was intended to be an Aryan racial state. From its beginning, the Nazi Party reflected the strong anti-Semitic beliefs of Adolf Hitler. Once in power, the Nazis translated anti-Semitic ideas into anti-Semitic policies. In September 1935, the Nazis announced new racial laws at the annual party rally in Nuremberg. These "Nuremberg laws" excluded

So What ??

If your students question the importance of the information on **the rise of Nazism,** tell them . . .

Hitler and his followers were elected to power by a cultured and civilized people. They began their reign of slaughter and

extermination with incremental acts of prejudice and persecution. Nazism, at first glance, looked appealing. It's important to study the pattern in the rise of Nazism to ensure it does not surface again in a similar form in our present world.

CRITICAL THINKING

Neither Hitler, Himmler, nor other of Nazism's key figures had "blond hair, blue eyes, and good physique." Why do students suppose this fact was overlooked or explained away? Ask them to look into whether Hitler ever referred to his own physical appearance in any way.

CRITICAL THINKING

Himmler became Hitler's interior minister in 1943 but fell from Hitler's favor in 1945. Ask students to research and analyze Himmler's career during these years.

Answers to Critical Thinking Questions

1. Himmler was the ideal leader because he was totally obedient to Hitler.
2. Gestapo—secret police force that rounded up the regime's enemies
   Security Service—a network of spies
   Death's Head Formations—responsible for running the concentration camps
   Einsatzgruppen—responsible in conquered countries for rounding up and shooting Jews and other racial undesirables
   Waffen-SS—a group of combat soldiers
3. Aryan supremacy was Hitler's and Himmler's idea that the German race should be in control of the world. They felt it was their duty to eliminate all other races or at least reduce them to the level of slaves.

BIOGRAPHY

Heinrich Himmler—Leader of Terror

▲ *Heinrich Himmler quickly rose through the Nazi ranks to lead the Schutzstaffeln.*

Born in 1900, Heinrich Himmler was the son of a middle-class schoolteacher. While a student in agriculture at a technical institute in Munich, he joined the Nazi Party. For a while, he worked as a fertilizer salesperson. He then tried, unsuccessfully, to make a living raising chickens. All the while, he remained in the Nazi Party. In 1929, Adolf Hitler made him leader of the SS.

The SS had been formed in 1925 as Hitler's elite bodyguard. To Hitler, Himmler was an ideal leader, because he was totally obedient to the Führer. Like Hitler, Himmler believed that the racial struggle between Aryans and Jews was the key to world history. To Himmler, the SS should become the elite group of Nazism that would fulfill the dream of Aryan supremacy.

Himmler was a cold, calculating, efficient bureaucrat whose ruthlessness made him an ideal head of the SS. Beginning in 1929, Himmler began to recruit new members for the SS on the basis of his ideas of racial purity. Recruits were pure German types with blond hair, blue eyes, and good physiques. To maintain his racial elite, Himmler insisted that SS men marry only racially pure Aryan women.

As the SS continued to grow, Himmler sought new sources of power through his control of the police. By 1936, he had become chief of the regular police. He then set up new divisions in the SS. The Gestapo was a secret police force that rounded up the regime's enemies. The Security Service was a network of spies. The Death's Head Formations were responsible for running the concentration camps. The Waffen (VAWF-un)-SS was a group of combat soldiers—the SS's own army. The Einsatzgruppen were responsible in conquered countries for rounding up and shooting Jews and other "racial undesirables." Himmler had become leader of a total system of terror. During the war, Hitler made Himmler overseer of Nazi plans for reorganizing Europe along racial lines. Himmler acted ruthlessly. He said: "What happens to the Russians, what happens to the Czechs, is a matter of utter indifference to me. . . . Whether or not 10,000 Russian women collapse from exhaustion while digging a tank ditch interests me only in so far as the tank ditch is completed for Germany."

At the end of the war, with the Nazi Empire in collapse, Himmler sought to escape by taking on a false identity. He was captured by the British and ended his life by swallowing a poison vial he had hidden in his mouth.

1. Why did Hitler consider Himmler to be the ideal leader?

2. Name and explain four of the SS divisions developed by Himmler.

3. What is meant by the term "Aryan supremacy"?

On Line with WORLD HISTORY Internet Activity

You may want to have your students visit the following URL, where they will find information and additional web site resources to enhance their study of this chapter.
The Versailles Treaty
http://ac.acusd.edu/history/text/versaillestreaty/vercontents.htm

This site has complete text and an analysis of why it failed and what this led to in post-war Europe.

Due to the ever-changing nature of the World Wide Web, see the West History web site, **http://history.swpco.com** for regular updates of the URLs in this text.

YOUNG PEOPLE IN NAZI GERMANY

The Hitler Youth

In setting up a total state, the Nazis recognized the importance of winning the youth over to their ideas. The Hitler Youth, an organization for young people between the ages of ten and eighteen, was formed in 1926. By 1939, all German young people were expected to join the Hitler Youth. Upon entering, each took an oath: "In the presence of this blood banner, which represents our Führer, I swear to devote all my energies and my strength to the savior of our country, Adolf Hitler. I am willing and ready to give up my life for him, so help me God."

Members of the Hitler Youth had their own uniforms and took part in a number of activities. For males, these included camping and hiking trips, sports activities, and evenings together in special youth "homes." Almost all activities were competitive and meant to encourage fighting and heroic deeds.

Above all, the Hitler Youth organization worked to foster military values and virtues, such as duty, obedience, strength, and ruthlessness. Uniforms and drilling became a way of life. By 1938, training in the military arts also became part of the routine. Even boys ten to fourteen years old were given small-arms drill and practice with dummy hand grenades. Those who were fourteen to eighteen years old bore army packs and rifles while on camping trips in the countryside.

The Hitler Youth had a female division, known as the League of German Girls, for girls aged ten to eighteen. They, too, had uniforms: white blouses, blue ankle-length skirts, and sturdy hiking shoes. Camping and hiking were also part of the girls' activities. More important, however, girls were taught domestic skills—how to cook, clean houses, and take care of children. In Nazi Ger-

▲ *Many young children were drawn to the Hitler Youth. The children shown here wave their flags, obviously proud to be part of the movement. Do you think youth groups receive strong support in the United States? Why or why not?*

many, women were expected to be faithful wives and dutiful mothers.

1. Explain the ideals and values that Nazi leaders tried to instill in the young people of Germany through the Hitler Youth organization.

2. Use your own perspective to evaluate these virtues and ideals.

ENRICHMENT ACTIVITY

"Holocaust literature" is vast and still growing. Ask interested students to read one or more eyewitness accounts of pre-World War II violence against Jews, particularly the infamous "Kristallnacht." Can they imagine watching such violence? Being a target of it? Being part of it?

ASSESS

2. (a) prejudice against Jewish people
   (b) the German parliament
3. (a) the name of the German Nazi party
   (b) a book written by Hitler while he was in jail
   (c) a demand for living space used by Germany to justify expansion
   (d) a law passed by Hitler's government that it could ignore the constitution for four years
   (e) people of N. European ancestry, Hitler felt were superior to other groups
   (f) mass meetings held to create enthusiasm for the Nazi party and Hitler
   (g) excluded Jewish people from the rights of German citizenship
   (h) Nazis attacked Jewish people and their property; Nov. 9, 1938
4. (a) to build character, strength, and nationalism
   (b) He wrote *Mien Kampf.*
   (c) national pride, national honor, and traditional militarism
   (d) He expanded the German military.
5. Answers will vary.

German Jews from German citizenship and forbade marriages between Jews and German citizens. The "Nuremberg laws" basically separated Jews from the Germans politically, socially, and legally.

A more violent phase of anti-Jewish activity took place in 1938 and 1939. It began on November 9–10, 1938—the Kristallnacht (KRIS-tul-NAWKT), or "night of shattered glass." The assassination of a third secretary in the German embassy in Paris gave Nazis an excuse for a destructive rampage against the Jews. Synagogues were burned, and 7,000 Jewish businesses were destroyed. At least 100 Jews were killed. Moreover, 30,000 Jewish males were rounded up and sent to concentration camps. Kristallnacht also led to further drastic steps. Jews were barred from all public buildings and prohibited from owning, managing, or working in any retail store. Finally, under the direction of the SS, Jews were encouraged to "emigrate from Germany." After the outbreak of World War II, the policy of emigration was replaced by a more gruesome one (see Chapter 28).

❀ SECTION REVIEW ❀

1. **Locate:**
   (*a*) Nuremberg

2. **Define:**
   (*a*) anti-Semitism,   (*b*) Reichstag

3. **Identify:**
   (*a*) National Socialist German Workers' Party,
   (*b*) *Mein Kampf,*   (*c*) Lebensraum,
   (*d*) Enabling Act,   (*e*) Aryan race,
   (*f*) Nuremberg rallies,   (*g*) Nuremberg laws,
   (*h*) Kristallnacht

4. **Recall:**
   (*a*) Why did Hitler feel struggle was important to the growth of nations?
   (*b*) What did Hitler accomplish while he was in prison during the 1920s?
   (*c*) What three appeals did Hitler make to gain popularity in Germany during the 1930s?

(*d*) How did Hitler solve the German unemployment problem during the 1930s?

5. **Think Critically:** Why was it important that Hitler made German soldiers swear allegiance to him personally rather than to the German nation?

SOCIAL, CULTURAL, AND INTELLECTUAL TRENDS IN THE INTERWAR YEARS

Technology continued to have profound effects upon European society. Nowhere is this more evident than in the expansion of mass culture and mass leisure after World War I. Because of technology, popular forms of entertainment could now reach millions of people. No doubt, the new obsession with entertainment and games such as movies, radio, and sporting events was also part of the desire to forget the horrors of the Great War—a "live for today, for tomorrow we may die" mentality.

Mass Culture: Radio and Movies

A series of inventions in the late nineteenth century had led the way for a revolution in mass communications. Especially important was Marconi's discovery of "wireless" radio waves (see Chapter 22). It was not until June 16, 1920, however, that a radio broadcast for a mass audience was tried. The broadcast was a concert by soprano Nellie Melba from London. Broadcasting facilities were then built in the United States, Europe, and Japan during 1921 and 1922. At the same time, the mass production of radios began. In 1926, there were 2.2 million radios in Great Britain. By the end of the 1930s, there were 9 million. Broadcasting networks in the United States were privately owned and financed by advertising. Those in Europe were usually controlled by the government.

Motion pictures had first emerged in the 1890s. However, it was not until shortly before World War I that full-length features appeared. The Italian film *Quo Vadis* (KWOE VAE-dis) and the American film *Birth of*

RETEACHING ACTIVITY

Ask students to create a Venn diagram to compare and contrast Communism and Fascism. Use the diagram to lead students into a discussion of both of these philosophies, asking them why they would or would not prefer either to the form of democracy we have in the United States.

◄ *The classic movie Quo Vadis starred Robert Taylor, Deborah Kerr, and Peter Ustinov in a story of a Roman commander who falls in love with a Christian girl. Does this plot remind you of any movies you have seen in the past year?*

a Nation made it apparent that cinema was a new form of mass entertainment. By 1939, about 40 percent of adults in the more advanced industrial countries were attending a movie once a week. That figure increased to 60 percent by the end of World War II.

Of course, radio and the movies could be used for political purposes. Hitler had said, "Without motorcars, sound films, and wireless, no victory of National Socialism." Radio offered great opportunities for reaching the masses. This became obvious when it was discovered that the fiery speeches of Adolf Hitler made just as great an impact on people when heard on radio as in person. The Nazi regime encouraged radio listening by urging manufacturers to produce inexpensive radios that could be bought on an installment plan.

Film, too, had propaganda potential, a possibility not lost on Joseph Goebbels (GU[r]B-ulz), the propaganda minister of Nazi Germany. Believing that film was one of the "most modern and scientific means of influencing the masses," Goebbels created a special film section in his Propaganda Ministry. He aided the making of both documentaries and popular feature films that carried the Nazi message. *The Triumph of the Will*, for example, was a documentary of the 1934 Nuremberg party rally. This movie was filmed by Leni Riefenstahl, an actress turned director. It forcefully conveyed to viewers the power of National Socialism.

Mass Leisure

Mass leisure activities had developed at the turn of the century (see Chapter 22), but new work patterns after World War I provided people with more free time to take advantage of these activities. By 1920, the eight-hour day had become the norm for many office and factory workers in northern and western Europe.

Professional sporting events for mass audiences were an important aspect of mass leisure (see "Sports and Contests: The Growth of Professional Sports"). Travel opportunities also added new dimensions to mass leisure activities. The military use of aircraft during World War I helped to improve planes and make civilian air travel a reality. The first regular international mail service began in 1919. Regular passenger service

RECOMMENDED READING

The use of cinema for propaganda purposes is well examined in D. Welch, *Propaganda and the German Cinema* (New York, 1985). The organization of leisure time in Fascist Italy is thoughtfully discussed in V. De Grazia, *The Culture of Consent: Mass Organization of Leisure in Fascist Italy* (New York,

1981). On the cultural and intellectual environment of Weimar Germany, see W. Laqueur, *Weimar: A Cultural History* (New York, 1974); and P. Gray, *Weimar Culture: The Outsider as Insider* (New York, 1968). For a study of Carl Jung, see G. Wehr, *Jung: A Biography* (New York, 1987).

SPORTS AND CONTESTS

SPORTS AND CONTESTS

The Growth of Professional Sports

After World War I, sports became an important part of the expansion of mass leisure. Live radio broadcasts of sporting events, especially in the United States, converted sports into a form of mass entertainment. Until the 1920s, sports had been regarded as a pastime of amateurs (people who were not paid). In the 1920s, players began to be paid to play on a regular basis, making them professional athletes. Businesses began to use sports and sports figures as tools to advertise and sell their goods. As the popularity of mass spectator sports grew, so did the amount of money spent on betting.

In Europe, attendance at soccer games grew dramatically. The creation of the World Cup contest in 1930 added to the nationalistic rivalries that had begun to surround soccer and other mass sporting events. Increased attendance at sports events also made the 1920s and 1930s a great era of stadium building. For the 1936 Olympics, Germany built a stadium in Berlin that seated 140,000 people. Strahav Stadium in Prague held 240,000 spectators for gymnastics and track meets, even though these sports remained games chiefly for amateurs.

In the 1930s, sports and politics grew closer together. Benito Mussolini poured lavish sums of money into Italy's soccer team, which enabled it to win the World Cup twice in the 1930s. Even the Olympic Games, played every four years since their initiation in 1896 and intended to bolster the achievements of amateurs, were used for politi-

▲ This soccer final between Italy and Austria took place at the 1936 Olympics in Berlin. Which country do you think was victorious?

cal purposes. Adolf Hitler used the Eleventh Olympic Games, held in Berlin in 1936, to show to the world Germany's physical strength and newfound prestige. The victories of Jesse Owens, an African American, were especially devastating to the Nazi regime, which believed in the superiority of whites over blacks and other races.

1. According to this feature, what "converted sports into a form of mass entertainment"?

2. Why were the Nazis disturbed by Jesse Owens' victories during the 1936 Olympics?

soon followed. Of course, it was mostly the wealthy who used air travel. However, trains, buses, and cars made trips to beaches or holiday resorts more and more popular and affordable. Beaches, such as the one at Brighton in Great Britain, were mobbed by crowds of people from all social classes.

Mass leisure gave totalitarian states new ways to control the people. Mussolini's Italy created the

---

So What ??

*If your students question the importance of the information on **the social trends of the interwar years,** tell them . . .*

The rise of the mass culture society was not just an aberration of totalitarian regimes, but is part of the society we live in today. Radio, movies, sports and other leisure activities are geared toward a mass culture.

Dopolavoro (Afterwork) as a vast national recreation agency. The Dopolavoro set up clubhouses in almost every town and village. They contained libraries, radios, and athletic facilities. In some places, they included travel agencies that arranged tours, cruises, and resort vacations on the Adriatic at reduced rates. Dopolavoro groups gave many Italians their first experience of mass culture and mass leisure with activities such as band concerts, movies, and ballroom dancing. With the Dopolavoro, the Italian government not only provided, but also supervised, recreational activities.

The Nazi regime adopted a program similar to the Dopolavoro in its Kraft durch Freude (Strength through Joy). Strength through Joy offered a variety of leisure activities to fill the free time of the working class. These activities included concerts, operas, films, guided tours, and sporting events. Especially popular were the inexpensive vacations, which were basically modern package tours. A vacation could be a cruise to Scandinavia or the Mediterranean. More likely for workers, it was a shorter trip to different sites in Germany. Only 130,000 workers took cruises in 1938, compared with the 7 million who took short trips.

More and more, mass culture and mass leisure had the effect of giving all the people in a nation similar ideas and similar experiences. Local popular culture was being replaced by a national, and even international, mass culture that brought similar ideas and similar clothing and fashion styles to people throughout Europe.

Artistic and Intellectual Trends

Before World War I, new artistic and intellectual trends had emerged that shocked many Europeans (see Chapter 22). Only a small group of avant-garde artists and intellectuals had been responsible for these new developments. After 1918, however, the new trends became more widespread. In the 1920s and 1930s, artists and intellectuals continued to work out the implications of the ideas developed before 1914. What made the prewar avant-garde culture acceptable in the 1920s and 1930s? Perhaps the most important factor was the impact of World War I.

Four years of devastating war left many Europeans with a profound sense of despair. To many people, World War I could mean only that something was dreadfully wrong with Western values. The experiences of World War I seemed to confirm the prewar avant-garde belief that human beings were really violent animals who were incapable of creating a sane and rational world. The Great Depression, as well as the growth of fascist movements based on violence, only added to the despair created by World War I.

The crisis of confidence in Western civilization indeed ran deep. It was well captured in the words of the French poet Paul Valéry (VAL-uh-REE) in the early 1920s:

> The storm has died away, and still we are restless, uneasy, as if the storm were about to break. Almost all the affairs of men remain in a terrible uncertainty. We think of what has disappeared, and we are almost destroyed by what has been destroyed; we do not know what will be born, and we fear the future,…Doubt and disorder are in us and with us. There is no thinking man, however shrewd or learned he may be, who can hope to dominate this anxiety, to escape from this impression of darkness.[8]

With political, economic, and social uncertainties came intellectual uncertainties. These were evident in the artistic and intellectual achievements of the interwar years.

Nightmares and New Visions: Art and Music

After 1918, artistic trends were largely a working out of the implications of developments before the war. Abstract expressionism, for example, became ever more popular. In addition, the prewar fascination with the absurd and the unconscious content of the mind seemed even more appropriate in light of the nightmare landscapes of World War I battlefronts. "The world does not make sense, so why should art?" was a common response. This gave rise to both the Dada movement and surrealism (see "Our Artistic Heritage: Dadaism and Surrealism").

The move to **functionalism** (a theory of design that places great emphasis on how an object will be used) in

CLASS DISCUSSION

Ask students to discuss the following sentence: "More and more, mass culture and mass leisure had the effect of giving all the people in a nation similar ideas and similar experiences."

CRITICAL THINKING

Ask students to analyze the "crisis of confidence in Western civilization" that followed World War I. Have them discuss the "anxiety" described in the excerpt by Valéry.

ACROSS THE CURRICULUM

Art Ask interested students to bring in examples of functionalist design, particularly from the Bauhaus school. Use the examples to illustrate the precepts of this movement. Has this movement been important beyond the 1920s and 1930s?

MORE ABOUT . . . *Art Between the Wars*

Another influential art form between the world wars was cubism. Developed by artists Georges Braques, Fernand Leger, and Pablo Picasso, cubism changed the art world of the 1920s and 30s. Cubism breaks down the subject and rearranges it in a series of geometric shapes, often viewed from different angles at the same time. With cubism artists no longer were limited to merely creating a visual representation of an object in the conventional sense. One of the most famous cubist pieces of the time is a painting by Pablo Picasso, depicting the horror of the Spanish Civil War, called *Guernica*.

OUR ARTISTIC HERITAGE

USING PRIMARY SOURCES

Ask students to analyze Dalí's famous painting *The Persistence of Memory*. (If possible, bring in a larger copy.) Have students identify the objects they see and the relationships between them. How do Dalí's images relate to memory? What is the mood of the painting?

Answers to Critical Thinking Questions

1. Dadaism held that life had no purpose, it is useless.
2. Surrealism sought to show the "greater reality" that existed beyond the world of physical appearances. Painters portrayed dreams, fantasies, and nightmares.
3. The term implies that Dalí was the leader or the one to whom others looked for inspiration.

LEARNING FROM VISUALS

Answer to the caption question: Students will recognize the elongated, stretched clocks. Their interpretations will vary.

ACTIVITY

Have students examine the Dadaist picture on this page. Using art as a key to history explain what the paintings by Salvador Dalí and Hannah Hoch tell you about the interwar years. How do you think the philosophy of dadaism would apply to today's world?

OUR ARTISTIC HERITAGE
Dadaism and Surrealism

Surrealistic paintings often suggest a dream world, the world of the unconscious. In The Persistence of Memory, 1931, *Dalí painted recognizable objects in contexts that seem out of place. What does this painting suggest to you?*

The Dadaists were artists who were obsessed with the idea that life had no purpose. Tristan Tzara, one of the founders of Dadaism, wrote: "Dada is a state of mind. . . . Dada applies itself to everything, and yet it is nothing. Like everything in life, Dada is useless. Dada is without pretension, as life should be." The Dadaists were revolted by the insanity of life and tried to express that feeling by creating antiart. The 1918 Berlin Dada Manifesto stated, "Dada is the international expression of our times, the great rebellion of artistic movements."

In the hands of Hannah Höch, Dada became an instrument to comment on women's roles in the new mass culture. Höch was the only female member of the Berlin Dada Club, a group of people working in the medium of photomontage. Her work was part of the first Dada show in Berlin in 1920. In her works, Höch created positive images of the modern woman and expressed a keen interest in new freedoms for women.

Perhaps more important than Dada as an artistic movement was surrealism. It sought a reality beyond the material world and found it in the world of the unconscious. By portraying fantasies, dreams, and even nightmares, the surrealists sought to show the "greater reality" that existed beyond the world of physical appearances. The surrealists employed logic to show the illogical and thus created disturbing images.

The Spaniard Salvador Dalí (DAW-lee) was the high priest of surrealism. In *The Persistence of Memory*, as in many of his artistic works, Dalí painted objects that were easily recognizable yet separated from their normal contexts. By placing recognizable objects in unrecognizable relationships, Dalí created a strange world in which the irrational became visible.

---

1. Explain the philosophy behind Dadaism.
2. Explain the philosophy behind surrealism.
3. What does the author mean when he calls Salvador Dalí the "high priest" of surrealism?

MORE ABOUT . . . *Literature Between the Wars*

Literature can sometimes be a more effective barometer of an era's attitudes and feelings than history books. T. S. Eliot, an Anglo-American poet, spoke for many of his generation of the decay of Western culture in his poem, *The Waste Land*. In another poem, *The Hollow Men,* he writes of the despair many felt with the lack of purpose of the "lost generation."

> "We are the hollow men
> We are the stuffed men
> Leaning together
> Headpiece filled with straw. Alas!
> Our dried voices, when

modern architecture also became more widespread in the 1920s and 1930s. Especially important in the spread of functionalism was the Bauhaus school of art, architecture, and design, founded in 1919 at Weimar, Germany, by the Berlin architect Walter Gropius. The Bauhaus teaching staff was made up of architects, artists, and designers. They worked together to combine the study of fine arts (painting and sculpture) with the applied arts (printing, weaving, and furniture making). Gropius urged his followers to foster a new union of arts and crafts in order to create the buildings and objects of the future.

Not everybody accepted modern art forms, however. Many people denounced what they saw as decay in the arts. Nowhere was this more evident than in the totalitarian states of Nazi Germany and the Soviet Union.

In the 1920s, Weimar Germany was one of the chief European centers for modern arts and sciences. Hitler and the Nazis rejected modern art as "degenerate" art. In a speech in July 1937, Hitler proclaimed:

The people regarded this art [modern art] as the outcome of an impudent and shameless arrogance or of a simply shocking lack of skill; it felt that . . . these achievements which might have been produced by untalented children of from eight to ten years old—could never be valued as an expression of our own times or of the German future.[9]

Hitler and the Nazis believed that they were creating a new and genuine German art. It would glorify the strong, the healthy, and the heroic—all of which were supposedly qualities of the Aryan race. The new German art was actually the old nineteenth-century folk art with its emphasis on realistic scenes of everyday life.

Soviet painting, like German painting, was expected to focus on a nineteenth-century realistic style. Both the new German art and the "socialist realism" art of the Soviet Union were meant to instill social values useful to the ruling regimes.

At the beginning of the twentieth century, a revolution had come to music with the work of Igor Stravinsky (see Chapter 22). However, Stravinksy still wrote music in a definite key. In 1924, the Viennese composer Arnold Schönberg (SHU[r]N-BURG) wrote a piano suite in which he used a scale composed of twelve notes free of any tonal key. His atonal music was similar to abstract painting. Abstract painting arranged colors and lines without concrete images. Atonal music organized sounds without any recognizable harmonies. Unlike modern art, however, modern music found little favor until after World War II.

Literature: The Search for the Unconscious

The interest in the unconscious that was evident in art was also a part of new literary techniques. One example was a "stream of consciousness" technique, by which the writer gave a report of the innermost thoughts of each character. The most famous example of this approach was written by the Irish exile James Joyce. His *Ulysses* (yoo-LISS-eez), published in 1922, told the story of one day in the life of ordinary people in Dublin by following the flow of their inner thoughts.

The German writer Hermann Hesse dealt with the unconscious in a quite different fashion. His novels reflected the influence of both Freud's psychology and Eastern religions. The works focused on, among other things, the spiritual loneliness of modern human beings in a mechanized urban society. In both *Siddhartha* (si-DAWR-ta) and *Steppenwolf*, Hesse used Buddhist ideas to show the psychological confusion of modern existence (see "Our Literary Heritage: The Novels of Hermann Hesse"). Hesse's novels had a large impact on German youth in the 1920s. He won the Nobel Prize for literature in 1946.

The "Heroic Age of Physics"

The prewar revolution in physics begun by Albert Einstein continued in the years between the wars. In fact, Ernest Rutherford, one of the physicists who showed that the atom could be split, dubbed the 1920s the "heroic age of physics." By the early 1940s, seven subatomic particles had been identified.

The new picture of the universe that was unfolding from physicists undermined the old certainties of classical physics. A basic belief in physics had been that all phenomena could be completely defined and subject to predictability. Thus, the weather could be predicted if we only knew everything about the wind, sun, and

We whisper together
Are quiet and meaningless . . ."
An Irish poet, W. B. Yeats was prophetic in his poem, *The Second Coming*. In retrospect his images almost provide a warning of the rise of Hitler, as well as the failure of the appeasement of the West to stop fascism.

"Things fall apart; the centre cannot hold;
Mere anarchy is loosed upon the world.
The blood-dimmed tide is loosed, and everywhere
The ceremony of innocence is drowned;
The best lack all conviction, while the worst
Are full of passionate intensity."

OUR LITERARY HERITAGE

USING PRIMARY SOURCES

Challenge students to try and answer the question ending the excerpt from *Demian:* "I wanted only to try to live in accord with the promptings which came from my true self. Why was that so very difficult?"

ACROSS THE CURRICULUM

Literature Assign students one or more of Hesse's novels: *Siddhartha, Steppenwolf, Demian, The Glass Bead Game.* Have them prepare a lesson for the class on Hesse's themes and techniques.

Answers to Critical Thinking Questions

1. Young people were most strongly impacted.
2. His writings described the uncertainty that is often felt during young adulthood.
3. Answers will vary.

ACROSS THE CURRICULUM

Science Ask interested students to research the Uncertainty Principle of physics. In what ways did Heisenberg's work revolutionize physics?

OUR LITERARY HERITAGE
The Novels of Hermann Hesse

The novels of Hermann Hesse made a strong impact on young people, first in Germany in the 1920s and then in the United States in the 1960s (after the novels' translation into English). Many of these young people shared Hesse's fascination with the unconscious and his dislike of modern industrial civilization. This excerpt from Demian *spoke directly to many young people.*

Hermann Hesse, *Demian*

The following spring I was to leave the preparatory school and enter a university. I was still undecided, however, as to where and what I was to study. I had grown a thin mustache, I was a full-grown man, and yet I was completely helpless and without a goal in life. Only one thing was certain: the voice within me, the dream image. I felt the duty to follow this voice blindly wherever it might lead me. But it was difficult and each day I rebelled against it anew. Perhaps I was mad, as I thought at moments; perhaps I was not like other men? But I was able to do the same things the others did; with a little effort and industry I could read Plato, was able to solve problems in trigonometry or follow a chemical analysis. There was only one thing I could not do: wrest the

▲ *Herman Hesse, pictured here, was one of the most influential authors in Europe in the 1920s and early 1930s. His works were especially appealing to young people.*

dark secret goal from myself and keep it before me as others did who knew exactly what they wanted to be— professors, lawyers, doctors, artists, however long this would take them and whatever difficulties and advantages this decision would bear in its wake. This I could not do. Perhaps I would become something similar, but how was I to know? Perhaps I would have to continue my search for years on end and would not become anything, and would not reach a goal. Perhaps I would reach this goal but it would turn out to be an evil, dangerous, horrible one? I wanted only to try to live in accord with the promptings which came from my true self. Why was that so very difficult?

1. Who were most strongly impacted by Hermann Hesse's writings?

2. Why do you think his writings appealed more to a certain age group?

3. Does this passage from *Demian* have any impact on you? Why or why not?

ENRICHMENT ACTIVITY

Ask students to reread the words of French poet Paul Valéry that appear on page 861. Tell them to pretend that they had no idea when he wrote this poem. What might you have been able to conclude about the times in which he lived from this passage? Use this as a tool to discuss uncertainties in life, and ways for coping with them. *(Student responses will vary but should point out that Valéry's poem shows he and other people had experienced some great disaster that was not yet finished and which was likely to bring about additional problems in the future.)*

water. In 1927, the German physicist Werner Heisenberg (HIZE-un-BURG) explained the **Uncertainty Principle.** According to this principle, no one could determine the path of an electron, because the act of observing with light affects the electron's location. The Uncertainty Principle was more than an explanation of the path of an electron, however. It was a new worldview. Heisenberg dared to suggest that at the bottom of all the physical laws was uncertainty. Few nonscientists probably understood the implications of Heisenberg's work, but the principle of uncertainty fit in well with the other uncertainties of the interwar years.

 SECTION REVIEW

1. **Define:**
   (*a*) functionalism, (*b*) Uncertainty Principle

2. **Identify:**
   (*a*) *The Triumph of the Will,* (*b*) Dopolavoro,
   (*c*) surrealism, (*d*) Bauhaus, (*e*) socialist realism, (*f*) Arnold Schönberg, (*g*) James Joyce, (*h*) Herman Hesse

3. **Recall:**
   (*a*) What factors led many people to have similar experiences and ideas during the 1930s?
   (*b*) Why did many more people come to accept the point of view of avant-garde artists after World War I?
   (*c*) Why did Hitler label modern art as "degenerate"?

4. **Think Critically:** Why is the fact that radio stations were owned by governments rather than by private citizens in most of Europe important to bringing about conditions that would lead to World War II?

Conclusion

The devastation wrought by World War I destroyed the liberal optimism of the prewar era. However, many people in the 1920s still hoped that the progress of Western civilization, so evident before 1914, could be restored. These hopes proved largely unfounded as plans for economic revival gave way to inflation and to an even more devastating Great Depression at the end of the 1920s. Likewise, confidence in political democracy was soon shattered by the rise of dictatorial governments. These governments not only restricted individual freedoms but also, in the case of Italy, Germany, and the Soviet Union, sought even greater control over the lives of their subjects in order to guide them to achieve the goals of the totalitarian regimes. To many people, these mass movements, even if they meant the loss of personal freedom, at least offered some sense of security in a world that seemed filled with uncertainties.

When Europeans devastated their civilizations in World War I, they also unexpectedly opened the door to movements for national independence in their colonies around the world. Although those movements would not be successful until after World War II, the next chapter will examine their beginnings.

Notes

1. Quoted in Robert Paxton, *Europe in the Twentieth Century,* 2d ed. (San Diego, 1985), p. 237.
2. Benito Mussolini, "The Doctrine of Fascism," *Italian Fascisms,* ed. Adrian Lyttleton (London, 1973), p. 42.
3. Quoted in Alexander De Grand, "Women under Italian Fascism," *Historical Journal* 19 (1976): 958–959.
4. Adolf Hitler, *Mein Kampf,* trans. Ralph Manheim (Boston, 1943), p. 161.
5. Quoted in Jeremy Noakes and Geoffrey Pridham, eds., *Nazism 1919–1945,* vol. 1 (Exeter, England, 1983), pp. 50–51.
6. Quoted in Jackson Spielvogel, *Hitler and Nazi Germany: A History,* 3rd ed. (Englewood Cliffs, N.J., 1996), p. 58.
7. Quoted in Joachim Fest, *Hitler,* trans. Richard Winston and Clara Winston (New York, 1974), p. 418.
8. Paul Valéry, *Variety,* trans. Malcolm Cowley (New York, 1927), pp. 27–28.
9. Norman H. Baynes, ed., *The Speeches of Adolf Hitler, 1922–1939,* vol. 1 (Oxford, 1942), p. 591.

RETEACHING ACTIVITY

Assign students an essay in which they relate one of the following to the uncertainties and disillusionment of the interwar years: mass entertainment, mass leisure, professional sports, Dadaism, Surrealism, atonal music, "stream of consciousness" technique in literature, Uncertainty Principle. Due to the research and time required for this writing project, you may want to assign this for extra credit.

SPANISH SUPPORT

The *Conclusion* has been translated into Spanish. Included with this translation (in your Teacher Resource Box) are Section Key Points, which consist of one or two sentences summarizing each section in the chapter. These Key Points have also been translated.

TIME LINE

As students conclude the chapter, you may want to refer them to the chapter time line in the *Study Guide.*

ASSESS

Answers to
SECTION REVIEW

1. (a) places emphasis on how an object will be used
   (b) theory that at the bottom of all physical laws is uncertainty
2. (a) Nazi propaganda film
   (b) recreation agency created by Mussolini
   (c) an artistic movement led by Dada
   (d) a school of art and architecture in Germany
   (e) art popular in Stalinist times
   (f) a Viennese composer
   (g) wrote *Ulysses*
   (h) a German writer
3. (a) many countries organized recreation and the arts
   (b) lack of reason and logic in world events
   (c) result of arrogance or a lack of skill
4. Answers will vary.

CLOSE

Review the objectives as listed on page 859.

Answers to CHAPTER REVIEW 26

USING KEY TERMS

1. squadristi
2. anti-Semitism
3. collectivization
4. totalitarian state
5. New Economic Policy
6. deficit spending
7. Uncertainty Principle
8. functionalism
9. Reichstag
10. Politburo
11. collective bargaining

REVIEWING THE FACTS

1. The Treaty of Locarno guaranteed boarders between France, Germany, and Belgium.
2. They renounced the use of war to achieve their national goals.
3. They were called the New Deal.
4. Benito Mussolini took over the Italian government and claimed the power to make laws by himself.
5. Joseph Stalin led the Soviet government to eliminate almost all private business in the Soviet Union.
6. The five year plans in the 1930s were intended to rapidly increase the Soviet Union's industrial capacity.
7. Its official name was the National Socialist German Workers Party.
8. It gave his government the legal right to ignore the German constitution for four years.
9. They were laws that excluded Jewish people from the rights of German citizenship.
10. Avant-guard ideas became more acceptable during the social and political chaos that followed World War I.

THINKING CRITICALLY

1. The only power the League of Nations had to enforce its decision was the threat of economic sanctions.
2. The German government

866

USING KEY TERMS

1. The _____ was a name given to fascists who attacked socialist offices and newspapers in Italy after World War I.
2. _____ is a sense of prejudice against Jewish people.
3. The Soviet government followed a policy of _____ when it took private property after World War I without payments to the former owners.
4. A _____ exists when almost all power in a nation is held by the central government.
5. Lenin abandoned war communism in 1921 in favor of his _____, a modified version of the old capitalist system.
6. The government policy of going into debt to pay for public works projects, such as building highways, is called _____.
7. According to the _____ no one could determine the path of an electron, meaning all physical laws had elements of unpredictability.
8. The Bauhaus school spread the theory of design called _____.
9. The German parliament is known as the _____.
10. The _____ was the leading policymaker of the Communist Party.
11. _____ is the right of unions to negotiate with employers.

REVIEWING THE FACTS

1. What 1925 treaty tried to reduce fears of a new war by guaranteeing national borders between Germany, France, and Belgium?
2. What was promised by the nations that signed the Kellogg-Briand Pact in 1928?
3. What did President Roosevelt call the laws designed to fight the depression in the United States?

4. Who took over the government of Italy in 1922 and created a fascist totalitarian state?
5. What leader ended the New Economic Policy in the Soviet Union and collectivized farms in that nation?
6. What was the purpose of the five-year plans during the 1930s in the Soviet Union?
7. What was the official name of the Nazi party in Germany?
8. Why was the Enabling Act of 1933 important to Hitler's success in controlling Germany?
9. What was the basic purpose of the Nuremberg Laws?
10. How did avant-guarde artistic styles find support in the political and social atmosphere after World War I?

THINKING CRITICALLY

1. Why wasn't the League of Nations an effective organization for enforcing international agreements?
2. Why might the government of Germany have deliberately caused rapid inflation in that country after World War I?
3. How might the depression have helped extremist leaders to gain power in many nations during the 1930s?
4. What abilities, in addition to being a forceful speaker, can help a person gain political power?
5. Why do totalitarian leaders often involve their nations in relatively small wars?
6. What economic problems were resolved in Germany by the military buildup undertaken by Hitler's government?
7. Why did totalitarian leaders like Hitler, Stalin, and Mussolini encourage popular involvement in particular artistic styles?

---

may have hoped this could be used to eliminate their need to make reparation payments.
3. During the depression many people who were in economic distress were willing to listen to any leader who promised improved economic conditions.
4. The experience of Joseph Stalin demonstrates that the ability to keep records and organize people is probably as important as being a good speaker.
5. By involving their nations in small wars they are able to build their military power and create nationalism among their people.
6. The military build-up eliminated most unemployment and created profits for Germany's

businesses and banks.
7. By associating their rule with a proper artistic style they hoped to encourage support for their own political power.

APPLYING SOCIAL STUDIES SKILLS

1. Answers will vary but should discuss the military build-up in Germany. The German military expansion contributed to their ability to follow aggressive policies that led to World War II. The lack of a military build-up in the U.S. and Great Britain made it more difficult for them to respond to German aggression.
2. Answers will vary but should point out that the

APPLYING SOCIAL STUDIES SKILLS

1. **Economics:** In 1932 the unemployment rate in the United States was 33 percent, 31 percent in Great Britain, and 37 percent in Germany. Compare and contrast the ways in which leaders of these nations attempted to deal with their unemployment problem and how their policies contributed to the causes of World War II.
2. **Economics:** The total value of reparations assessed on Germany by the Treaty of Versailles has been estimated to have exceeded $30 billion. In 1928 the total value of all income earned in Germany was measured at a value of $12 billion. Use this information to write a paragraph that explains why it was unrealistic to expect Germany to pay all of its reparations.
3. **Government:** During the 1930s the governments of Great Britain, France, and the United States did almost nothing to discourage Hitler's Germany from rearming and taking over many lands in Europe. Write an essay that discusses why it is difficult for democratic nations to take action quickly when faced by aggression from totalitarian states.
4. **Sociology:** What events and conditions caused a large part of American society to have an isolationist point of view after World War I?

MAKING TIME AND PLACE CONNECTIONS

1. Compare recent military actions of the United Nations in wars in Africa, Eastern Europe, and the Middle East with the inaction of the League of Nations. Why do you believe there has been an apparent difference in the ability of these two organizations to settle international disputes?
2. A reaction of many nations to the start of the depression was to impose high taxes on imported goods. This policy caused a rapid decline in international trade in the 1930s. In recent years most nations have lowered tariffs on imported goods. How might these different policies have affected international relations and the likelihood of war in the 1930s and at the present?
3. Compare the reaction of world powers to Hitler's aggression in the 1930s with actions taken when Iraq invaded Kuwait in 1990.
4. A good deal of American popular art, literature, and music during the 1960s and 1970s focused on anti-establishment ideas and themes. In what way was the art of the 1920s and 1930s in Europe similar?
5. Compare your personal rights and freedoms as an American citizen with those of people who lived in post World War I Germany.

BECOMING AN HISTORIAN

1. **Fact versus Opinion:** The final sentence in Hitler's book, *Mein Kampf* reads, "A state which, in an epoch of race poisoning, dedicates itself to the cherishing of its best racial elements, must some day be master of the world." Discuss how confusion between facts and opinions may have helped Hitler gain power in Germany.
2. **Making Hypotheses and Predicting Outcomes:** The following is a partial contents of the Treaty of Versailles. Pretend you are an historian in 1920 and use this list to form and explain a hypotheses about the likelihood of the treaty's success.
   (*a*) Germany was required to give up almost 25 percent of its land and all of its colonies.
   (*b*) Germany's military forces were limited to 100,000 people.
   (*c*) France was given the right to control and use coal from Germany's Saar river basin for 15 years.
   (*d*) France was given the provinces of Alsace and Lorraine.
   (*e*) Germany was accused of causing the war and was required to pay reparations.
3. **Map Interpretation:** Study map 26.1 on page 837. Use it to evaluate the geographic problems Germany faced after World War I.

867

German reparations were almost three times their entire annual income and they needed to pay the costs of rebuilding their own nation after World War I. They were only able to pay the debt as long as the United States made loans to Germany that covered their debt payments.
3. Answers will vary but should point out that democratic nations require the support of a majority before decisive actions can be taken. In the 1930s many people opposed acting against Germany because they did not feel personally threatened by the German expansion.
4. Answers will vary but may include the idea that Americans felt our nation's soldiers had fought and died to achieve a lasting peace that European powers had made impossible to achieve.

MAKING TIME AND PLACE CONNECTIONS

1. Answers will vary but should involve the United Nations' military intervention into recent disputes and its attempt to protect peace agreements through the threat and use of force. The League of Nations never used force to support any of its resolutions.
2. Answers will vary but may indicate that reduced trade made it easier for them to go to war in the 1930s; increased trade today makes nations interdependent and less likely to go to war.
3. Answers will vary but should point out that world powers were slow to react to Hitler's aggression in the 1930s but acted decisively when Iraq invaded Kuwait in 1990.
4. Answers will vary but should point out that many Americans opposed the establishment in the 1960s and 1970s because of the Vietnam war and lack of progress in the civil rights movement. Frustration was reflected in the art, music, and literature of the time.
5. Answers will vary but should point out that the right to oppose involvement in World War I was guaranteed by our Bill of Rights. Similar rights were generally not guaranteed by European governments (opposition to the war could result in punishment).

BECOMING AN HISTORIAN

1. Answers will vary but may point out the fact that a "Big Lie" told often enough may become perceived as the truth. Hitler presented his opinions as fact and gained support from people who could not (did not) tell it from the truth.
2. Answers will vary but should point out that an agreement that is unbalanced and unfair is likely to result in future conflicts.
3. Answers will vary but should point out that Germany was cut off from trade routes and was forced to send its ships through narrow passages guarded by forces of nations that had been its enemies in World War I.

27 PLANNING GUIDE

SECTION	KEY TOPICS	PRIMARY SOURCES	ASSESSMENT
1 The Nationalist Revolt in the Middle East pages 869–876	◆ Decline of Ottoman Empire ◆ Ataturk's modernization of Turkey ◆ Beginnings of modern Iran ◆ Arab nationalism and Palestine	◆ Account of Armenian deportation, page 871	◆ Section Review, page 876 ◆ Section Quiz 27–1, TRB
2 Nationalism and Revolution in Africa and Asia pages 876–884	◆ Independence movements in Africa ◆ Gandhi's independence campaign in India ◆ Militarism in Japan ◆ Activities of the Comintern in Asia	◆ Jomo Kenyatta, page 879 ◆ Mohandas Gandhi, page 880 ◆ Ho Chi Minh, page 884	◆ Section Review, page 885 ◆ Section Quiz 27–2, TRB
3 Revolutionary Chaos in China pages 885–890	◆ Nationalists versus Communists in China ◆ Nanjing Republic ◆ Shanghai Massacre ◆ Mao's Long March	◆ Mao Zedong, page 887 ◆ Mao Zedong, page 888 ◆ Sun Yat-sen, page 889	◆ Section Review, page 890 ◆ Section Quiz 27–3, TRB
4 Nationalism and Dictatorship in Latin America pages 890–896	◆ U.S. interwar investments in Latin America ◆ Good Neighbor policy ◆ Military dictatorships in Latin America during the 1930s ◆ Influence of modern movements and nationalism on Latin American culture		◆ Section Review, pages 896–897 ◆ Section Quiz 27–4, TRB

NATIONALISM, REVOLUTION, AND DICTATORSHIP:
THE MIDDLE EAST, AFRICA, ASIA, AND LATIN AMERICA (1919 TO 1939)

REPRODUCIBLE ACTIVITIES

Historical Maps

Charts and Graphs

Critical Thinking

Cooperative Learning

Vocabulary

Guided Reading

Reteaching

Enrichment

Performance Assessment

Spanish Key Points and Chapter Summaries

Spanish Vocabulary

Spanish Guided Reading

MULTIMEDIA SUPPORT

TRANSPARENCIES
- *World History* Color Transparency Package
- Fine Art Color Transparency Package

VIDEO
- *World History* Video Library
- CNN. Annual Video Update

LASERDISC
- *Sights and Sounds of History*

AUDIO
- *Listening to Literature* audiotape (English and Spanish)
- *History of Music* CD

SOFTWARE
- WESTEST™
- Student Review

CD–ROM
- *The Journey of Civilization*
- *World History*

INTERNET
- Internet Activities

On Line with WORLD HISTORY

Access West's history web site at
http://history.swpco.com
You'll find activities and web sites related to specific topics and chapters in *World History: The Human Odyssey*. Also look for references to helpful web sites at appropriate places throughout this teacher edition.

LESSON PLANNING

You will find detailed daily lesson plans for both traditional class scheduling and **block scheduling** in your Teacher Resource Box.

Not Enough Time?

If you do not have the four or five days recommended to teach this chapter, you may want to focus on the following sections and activities:

- Have students skim the chapter to answer the "Questions to Guide Your Reading" on page 869. Discuss their answers; then read the "Conclusion" on page 897.
- Do a more in-depth reading of pages 870–875, 878–879, 881–883, 886–887, 889, 892–893. Conclude with a class discussion of the features on pages 879, 880, 884, 888, 895–896.

NATIONALISM, REVOLUTION, AND DICTATORSHIP: THE MIDDLE EAST,

27

BUILDING ON
CHAPTER 26

To "set the scene" for the study of Chapter 27, use the following questions and activities.

◆ Ask students to summarize the causes and effects of the Great Depression.

◆ Have students create a three-column chart comparing the rise of Mussolini, Stalin, and Hitler.

◆ List some important cultural trends and movements of the interwar years.

USING THE
OPENING STORY

Depending on the ability levels of your students, use the following questions to reinforce the reading of the story.

◆ In what year did Gandhi and his 78 followers begin their march to the sea? *(1930)*

◆ What was their destination? *(Dandi)* How far away was it? *(240 miles)* How long did it take them? *(24 days)*

◆ What was the significance of Gandhi and his thousands of followers each picking up a pinch of salt from the sand? *(symbolically broke British law forbidding Indians from making their own salt)*

LEARNING
FROM VISUALS

Answer to the caption question: The British could do little except imprison Gandhi; it is difficult to react against nonviolence.

In 1930, Mohandas Gandhi, the sixty-one-year-old leader of the Indian nonviolent movement for independence from British rule, began a march to the sea with seventy-eight followers. Their destination was Dandi, a little coastal town some 240 miles away. The group covered about 12 miles a day. As they went, Gandhi preached his doctrine of nonviolent resistance to British rule in every village through which he passed: "Civil disobedience is the inherent right of a citizen. He dare not give it up without ceasing to be a man." By the time Gandhi reached Dandi, twenty-four days later, his small group had become a nonviolent army of thousands.

When Gandhi and his followers arrived at Dandi, Gandhi picked up a pinch of crystallized seasalt from the sand. Thousands of people all along the coast did likewise. In so doing, they were openly breaking British laws that prohibited Indians from making their own salt. The British had long profited from their monopoly on the making and sale of salt, an item much in demand in a tropical country. By their simple acts of disobedience, Gandhi and the Indian people had taken yet another step on their long march to independence from the British. The Salt March was but one of many nonviolent activities that Gandhi undertook to win India's goal of national independence from

British rule between World War I and World War II.

World War I not only deeply affected the lives of Europeans but also ended the age of European domination over world affairs. After the Europeans had devastated their own civilization on the battlegrounds of Europe, the people living in the colonies controlled by the European countries began to hope that they might now gain their independence. In Africa and Asia, movements for national independence began to take shape. Some were inspired by the nationalist and liberal movements of the West. Others began to look toward the new Marxist model provided by the victory of the Communists in the Soviet Union, who soon worked to spread their revolutionary vision to African and Asian societies. In the Middle East, World War I ended the rule of the Ottoman Empire and created new states, some of whom adopted Western features in order to modernize their countries. For some Latin American countries, the fascist dictatorships of Italy and Germany provided models for change.

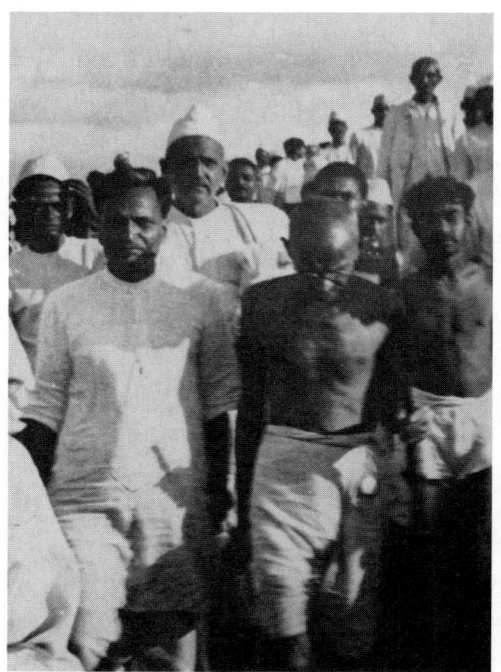

◄ *Mohandas Gandhi's concern for and involvement with the poorer classes in India never ceased. Here he is joined by his followers on the Salt March in 1930. Why do you think Gandhi's nonviolent demonstrations were so successful against the British?*

ADDITIONAL RESOURCES

BOOKS FOR STUDENTS
Things Fall Apart by Achebe Chinua. Fawcett.
The Good Earth by Pearl Buck.
African Firebrand: Kenyatta of Kenya by Jules Archer. Julian Messner.

VIDEOS/FILMS
China Rising: The Epic History of 20th Century

China, Social Studies School Service, (800) 421-4246
Ataturk: The Father of Modern Turkey, McGraw-Hill.

AFRICA, ASIA, AND LATIN AMERICA

(1919 TO 1939)

CRISIS OF THE TWENTIETH CENTURY

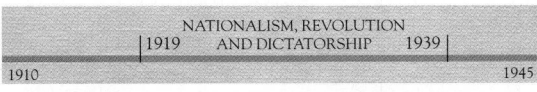

NATIONALISM, REVOLUTION
| 1919 | AND DICTATORSHIP | 1939 |
1910   1945

QUESTIONS TO GUIDE YOUR READING

1. What actions did Kemal Ataturk take to modernize Turkey?

2. What forms did modernization take in Iran?

3. In what ways were the independence movements in the Middle East, Africa, and India similar? In what ways were they different?

4. What role did Mohandas Gandhi play in the Indian movement for independence?

5. What were the major successes and failures of the Nationalists and the Communists in China from 1919 to 1939?

6. What economic and political problems did Latin American countries have in the 1920s and 1930s?

OUTLINE

1. THE NATIONALIST REVOLT IN THE MIDDLE EAST

2. NATIONALISM AND REVOLUTION IN AFRICA AND ASIA

3. REVOLUTIONARY CHAOS IN CHINA

4. NATIONALISM AND DICTATORSHIP IN LATIN AMERICA

THE NATIONALIST REVOLT IN THE MIDDLE EAST

In the Middle East, as in Europe, World War I brought the collapse of old empires. The Ottoman Empire had been growing steadily weaker since the end of the eighteenth century, which led European nations to call it the "sick man of Europe." Government corruption, a decline in the power of the sultans, and the loss of much territory in the Balkans were all visible signs of this decline. In North Africa, Ottoman rule had ended in the nineteenth century when France seized Algeria and Tunisia (too-NEE-zhee-uh) and when Great Britain took control of Egypt.

Decline and Fall of the Ottoman Empire

Reformers in Constantinople had tried to stop the Ottoman Empire's decline. In the eighteenth century, westernizing forces concerned about the shrinking of the empire had tried to modernize the army. However, a modern army could not make up for decaying political and social institutions. One energetic sultan, Selim III, tried at the end of the eighteenth century to estab-

869

Answers to QUESTIONS TO GUIDE YOUR READING

1. established basic democratic framework; stressed nationalism; introduced popular education; modernized economy; provided new laws for women. See pages 872–873.

2. tried to follow example of Turkey. See page 874.

3. similar: saw opportunities for independence
different: influenced by different ideologies. See pages 868–881.

4. great spiritual leader, found success with nonviolent civil disobedience; see pages 878–881.

5. See pages 884–889, 897.

6. Many countries had only one or two products for export. Small groups of church leaders, military leaders, and wealthy landowners led the poverty-stricken peasants. See pages 890–894.

FOCUS

OBJECTIVES

After completing this section, students should be able to

1. discuss the main factors for The Ottoman decline
2. describe the modernization of Turkey by Mustapha Kemal
3. discuss Reza Khan's efforts to modernize Iran
4. explain why Arab nationalism was complicated by Jewish emigration to Palestine

FOCUS ACTIVITY

This chapter concerns, among other things, people who rose to become national heroes. Ask students to brainstorm words they think of when they hear the word "hero." Then divide the class into small groups. Give them about ten minutes to discuss why nationalist feelings *(strong allegiance to one's own country; dislike of foreign presence)* tend to inspire heroic leaders. Reunite the class and have them share the results of their discussions.

lish a "new order" that would update the civilian, as well as the military, bureaucracy. However, the Janissaries (the sultan's special military forces—see Chapter 17), alarmed at the possible loss of their power, revolted and brought the experiment to an end.

Further efforts at reform during the first half of the nineteenth century were somewhat more successful. The government removed the Janissaries from power and began a series of bureaucratic, military, and educational reforms. New roads were built, and the power of local landlords was reduced. An imperial decree issued in 1856 granted equal rights to all subjects of the empire, whatever their religion.

Reforms failed to halt the decline of the empire. Greece declared its independence, and Ottoman power declined steadily in the Middle East. A rising sense of nationality among Serbs, Armenians, and other minority peoples threatened the stability and cohesion of the empire. In the 1870s, a new generation of Ottoman reformers seized power in Constantinople. In 1876 they pushed through a constitution aimed at forming a legislative assembly that would represent all the peoples in the state. However, the sultan they placed on the throne, Sultan Abdulhamid, suspended the new constitution and tried to rule by traditional authoritarian means. Abdulhamid paid a high price for his actions—he lived in constant fear of assassination. He kept a thousand loaded revolvers hidden throughout his guarded estate and insisted that his pets taste his food before he ate it.

By the end of the nineteenth century, the suspended 1876 constitution had become a symbol of change for reformers who now established a group known as the "Young Turks." Leading members of the group set up a Committee of Union and Progress (CUP). It gained support within the Ottoman army and administration, as well as among Turks living in exile. In 1908, Young Turk elements forced the sultan to restore the 1876 constitution and then removed him from power the following year.

The Young Turks had come at a difficult moment for the empire, however. Internal rebellions, combined with new losses of Ottoman territories in the Balkans, undermined the support for the new government and led the army to step in. By this time, most minorities

▲ *The campaigns and adventures of T. E. Lawrence gained him fame throughout the world. Several movies have been made showing him as a dashing, romantic figure.*

from the old empire were no longer under Ottoman authority. Many ethnic Turks began to embrace a new concept of a Turkish state that would encompass all people of Turkish nationality.

The final blow to the old empire came in World War I. The Ottoman government decided to ally with Germany in the hope of driving the British from Egypt and restoring Ottoman rule there. The new sultan called for a holy war by Muslim subjects in Russia and in territories in the Middle East ruled by Britain and France. In response, Great Britain declared an official protectorate over Egypt. To undermine Ottoman rule in the Arabian peninsula, Britain supported Arab Nationalist activities there. The Nationalists were aided by the efforts of the dashing British adventurer T. E. Lawrence, popularly known as "Lawrence of Ara-

RECOMMENDED READING

For a general survey of events in the Middle East, see H. M. Sachar, *The Emergence of the Middle East, 1914–1924* (New York, 1969). On modernization in Iran, see J. M.

Upton, *The History of Modern Iran* (Cambridge, Mass., 1960). The role of Ataturk is examined in J. P. Balfour, *Ataturk: The Rebirth of a Nation* (London, 1964).

Map 27.1   The Middle East, 1919–1939

[Map showing the Middle East with the following labels: SOVIET UNION (RUSSIA), Black Sea, Caspian Sea, Istanbul (Constantinople), Ankara, Anatolian Peninsula, THE CAUCASUS, TURKEY, Tabriz, CRETE, CYPRUS, SYRIA, LEBANON, PALESTINE, Tehran, Baghdad, IRAN (PERSIA), SOVIET UNION (RUSSIA), AFGHANISTAN, CHINA, Tigris R., Euphrates R., IRAQ, TRANS-JORDAN, Cairo, SINAI, KUWAIT, Amritsar, NEPAL, LIBYA, Jordan River, Nile R., EGYPT, Red Sea, Medina, Mecca, Dahran, Persian Gulf, BAHRAIN, QATAR, TRUCIAL STATES, BRITISH HINTERLAND OF ADEN, Strait of Hormuz, OMAN, INDIA, SAUDI ARABIA, Arabian Sea, ANGLO EGYPTIAN SUDAN, YEMEN, HADHRAMAUT, ADEN; scale: 0 500 Kilometers, 0 500 Miles]

TEACH

CLASS DISCUSSION

Guide students in a discussion of reform efforts in the Ottoman Empire before the twentieth century.

CLASS DISCUSSION

Tell students that the term "Young Turk" has entered the language to mean someone who advocates changes within an established group. Who were the original Young Turks, and what did they want for their country?

Multimedia Support

TRANSPARENCY
27–1, The Middle East, 1919–1939 (Map 27.1)

CRITICAL THINKING

Ask students to analyze why the "final blow" to the Ottoman Empire "came in World War I." Why was it disastrous for the Empire to ally itself with Germany and attempt to incite nationalist revolution against Britain, Russia, and France?

---

bia." In 1916, the local governor of Mecca, encouraged by Great Britain, declared Arabia independent from Ottoman rule. British troops, advancing from Egypt, seized Palestine. In October 1918, having suffered more than 300,000 dead during the war, the Ottoman Empire made peace with the Allied Powers.

During the war, the Turks had further alienated the Allies with Turkish policies toward their minority subjects, especially the Armenians. The Christian Armenian minority had pressed the Ottoman government for its independence for some time. In 1915, after an Armenian uprising, the government retaliated with fury by killing Armenian men and expelling women and children. Within seven months, 600,000 Armenians had been killed, and 500,000 had been deported (sent out of the country). Of the latter, 400,000 died

while marching through the deserts and swamps of Syria and Mesopotamia. By September 1915, an estimated 1 million Armenians were dead. They were victims of **genocide,** the deliberate mass murder of a group of people. (The practice was called **ethnic cleansing** in the Bosnian War of 1993 to 1996.) One eyewitness described the 1915 Armenian deportation:

> *She saw vultures hovering over children who had fallen dead by the roadside. She saw beings crawling along, maimed, starving and begging for bread. From time to time she passed soldiers driving before them with whips and rifle-butts whole families, men, women and children, shrieking, pleading, wailing. These were the Armenian people setting out for exile into the desert from which there was no return.*[1]

STUDYING MAPS

The following questions and activities will help you guide students through their study of Map 27.1.

1. Locate Turkey on the map. What is important about its location? *(located in Europe and Asia, controls access to and from the Black Sea)*

2. Study the map to determine how British control of Egypt in 1916 could encourage

Arabian rebellion against the Ottoman Empire *(Britain was in a stronger position to defend Arabia than was the Ottoman Empire.)*

3. If 400,000 Armenians died in the deserts and swamps of Syria and Mesopotamia after expulsion from Turkey, from what part of Turkey do you think the Armenians came? *(southeast)*

CLASS DISCUSSION

Provide students the opportunity to watch the film *Lawrence of Arabia.* Afterward, discuss the portrayal of Lawrence.

ACROSS THE CURRICULUM

Literature. Assign students T. E. Lawrence's book *The Seven Pillars of Wisdom.* Ask them to share Lawrence's philosophy and their sense of his character with the class.

CRITICAL THINKING

Ask students to research the slaughter of the Armenians by the Turks. Why did the Turks respond with such "fury" to Armenian calls for independence? Why did they institute genocide against this particular minority? What has been the post-1918 history of Armenia?

▶ *Kemal Ataturk worked hard to bring modern traditions and reform to Turkey. In this photo taken during the Turko-Greek War, he chats with camel drivers.*

By 1918, another 400,000 Armenians had been massacred. Russia, France, and Britain denounced the Turkish killing of the Armenians as "against humanity and civilization." Because of the war, however, the killings went on.

At the end of World War I, the tottering Ottoman Empire began to fall apart. Great Britain and France made plans to divide up Ottoman territories in the Middle East. At the same time, Greece won Allied approval to seize the western parts of the Anatolian peninsula. Greece dreamed of recreating much of the old Byzantine Empire.

The approaching collapse alarmed key elements in Turkey under the leadership of a war hero, Colonel Mustapha Kemal (moo-staw-FAW kuh-MAWL). Kemal had commanded Turkish forces in their heroic defense of the Dardanelles (the Battle of Gallipoli) against a British invasion during World War I. Now Kemal resigned from the army and summoned a National Congress that called for the creation of an elected government and the preservation of the remaining territories of the old empire in a new Republic of Turkey. Kemal placed his new capital at Ankara. His forces drove the Greeks from the Anatolian peninsula. Kemal then persuaded Great Britain to agree to a new treaty. In 1923, the last of the Ottoman sultans fled the country, which was now declared to be the Turkish Republic. The Ottoman Empire had finally come to an end.

Mustapha Kemal and the Modernization of Turkey

During the next few years, President Kemal (now popularly known as Ataturk [aw-taw-TURK], or "father Turk,") tried to transform Turkey into a modern state. The trappings of a democratic system were put in place with an elected Grand National Assembly. However, the president did not tolerate opposition and harshly suppressed his critics. Turkish nationalism was stressed. The Turkish language, now written in the Roman alphabet, was shorn of many of its Arabic elements. Popular education was introduced, and old aristocratic titles were abolished. All Turkish citizens were forced to adopt family names, in the European style.

MORE ABOUT . . . *Moderization and Islam*

Since its beginnings in the 7th century A.D., Islam has struggled to balance religious and political concerns. Muhammad was both a political/military leader and the religious leader of Islam. The four succeeding Caliphs ("successor of the prophet") held both religious and political leadership. When Islam splintered into various sects, societies developed which combined religion and politics. This is a contrast to the Western hemisphere, where the separation of church and state has been a controlling principle. Mustapha Kemal broke new ground as he secularized an Islamic society. His example was followed later by Egypt, where the tensions between secularization and religion regularly flare-up. Most of Islam, however, continues to blend religious dogma and political principles. In Muslim nations most rulers maintain a public image that politics and religion walk hand-in-hand.

Ataturk also took steps to modernize Turkey's economy. Factories to produce textiles, glass, paper, and cement were established. A five-year plan on the Soviet model was drawn up to provide for state direction over the economy. Ataturk was no fan of Soviet communism, however. The Turkish economy could be better described as a form of state capitalism. Ataturk also tried to modernize farming, but he had little effect on the nation's mostly conservative peasants.

Perhaps the most significant aspect of Ataturk's reform program was his attempt to break the power of the Islamic religion and transform Turkey into a **secular state** (a state that rejects any church influence on its policies). The caliphate was formally abolished in 1924. Ataturk said, "Religion is like a heavy blanket that keeps the people of Turkey asleep." Wearing the **fez** (the brimless cap worn by Turkish Muslims) was forbidden. When Ataturk began wearing a Western panama hat, one of his critics remarked, "You cannot make a Turk into a Westerner by giving him a hat." Women were forbidden to wear the veil, a traditional Islamic custom. New laws gave women equal rights with men in all aspects of marriage and inheritance. In 1934, women received the right to vote. Education and the profes-

sions were now open to citizens of both sexes. Some women even began to take part in politics. All citizens were now given the right to convert to another religion at will.

The legacy of Mustapha Kemal Ataturk was enormous. Not all of his reforms were widely accepted in practice, especially by devout Muslims. However, most of the changes that he introduced were kept after his death in 1938. By and large, the Turkish Republic was the product of Ataturk's determined efforts to create a modern Turkish nation.

Modernization in Persia: The Beginnings of Modern Iran

In the meantime, a similar process of modernization was under way in Persia. Under the Qajar dynasty (1794 to 1925), the country had not been very successful in resisting Russian advances in the Caucasus or in resolving its domestic problems. To secure themselves from foreign influence, the shahs moved the capital from Tabriz (tuh-BREEZ) to Tehran (TAE-RAN), in a mountainous area just south of the Caspian

◄ *Oil discoveries early in the century began to bring wealth to Persia. These workers are developing the fields at Petroleum Springs, Dalaki, in Persia. How do you think Persia used these early revenues?*

On Line with WORLD HISTORY   Internet Activity

You may want to have your students visit the following URL, where they will find information and additional web site resources to enhance their study of this chapter.

Internet Resources on Ethnic Persecution

http://www.arts.mcgill.ca/programs/police/marrett/marrett96r.html

The site contains a list of links addressing issues related to modern-day ethnic persecution.

Due to the ever-changing nature of the World Wide Web, see the West History web site, **http://history.swpco.com** for regular updates of the URLs in this text.

CRITICAL THINKING

Ask students to research and compare the reform efforts of Ataturk in Turkey and Reza Khan in Iran. Which, on balance, would students call more effective in terms of improving people's lives?

TEACHING THEMES

Politics and History. Ask students to research and discuss the history of the Pahlavi dynasty after Mohammed Reza Pahlavi came to power. How and why did foreign influence continue to affect Iran? What happened after the Shah was forced to leave the country in 1979?

Sea. During the mid-nineteenth century, one modernizing shah tried to introduce political and economic reforms, but he was stopped by resistance from tribal and religious forces. Increasingly, the dynasty turned to Russia and Great Britain to protect itself from its own people.

The growing foreign presence, however, led to the rise of a native Persian nationalist movement. Much of it was directed at Russian advances in the northwest. However, the nationalists also condemned the growing European influence within the small, modern industrial sector. The profits from these industries went to foreign investors or found their way into the pockets of the dynasty's ruling elite. Opposition to the regime was supported actively by Islamic religious leaders and rose steadily among both peasants and merchants in the cities. In 1906, popular pressure forced the reigning shah to grant a constitution on the Western model.

The modernizers had moved too soon, however. Their power base was not yet secure. With the support of Russia and Great Britain, the shah was able to retain control. The two foreign powers, however, began to divide the country into separate spheres of influence. One reason for the growing foreign presence in Persia was the discovery of oil in the southern part of the country in 1908. Within a few years, oil exports increased rapidly. Most of the profits went into the pockets of British investors.

In 1921 Reza Khan, an officer in the Persian army, led a military mutiny that seized power in Tehran. The new ruler's original aim had been to declare the establishment of a republic, but resistance from traditional forces stopped his efforts. In 1925 a new Pahlavi (PAL-uh-VEE) dynasty, with Reza Khan as shah, replaced the old dynasty. During the next few years, Reza Khan tried to follow the example of Mustapha Kemal Ataturk in Turkey. He introduced a number of reforms to strengthen the central government, modernize the civilian and military bureaucracy, and establish a modern economic system. Persia had become the modern state of Iran.

Unlike Mustapha Kemal Ataturk, Reza Khan did not try to destroy the power of Islamic beliefs. However, he did encourage the creation of a Western-style educational system and forbade women to wear the veil

in public. Foreign powers, however, continued to harass Iran. To free himself from Great Britain and the Soviet Union, Reza Khan drew closer to Nazi Germany. During World War II, when the shah rejected the demands of Great Britain and the Soviet Union to expel a large number of Germans from Iran, the Soviet Union and Great Britain sent troops into the country. Reza Khan resigned in protest and was replaced by his son, Mohammad Reza Shah.

The Rise of Arab Nationalism and the Problem of Palestine

We have already mentioned the Arab uprising against Ottoman rule during World War I. Unrest against Ottoman rule had existed in the Arabian peninsula since the eighteenth century. At that time, a group of reformers known as the Wahhabis (wuh-HAWB-eez) revolted. They tried to drive out foreigners and cleanse Islam of the outside influences and corrupt practices that had developed in past centuries. The revolt was eventually suppressed, but the influence of the Wahhabi movement continued.

World War I offered an opportunity for Arabs to throw off the shackles of Ottoman rule. However, what would replace that rule? The Arabs were not a nation but an idea, a loose collection of peoples. They often did not see eye to eye on what made up their common sense of community. In fact, disagreement over what makes an Arab has plagued the efforts of generations of political leaders who have sought unsuccessfully to knit together the different peoples of the region into a single Arab nation.

As was noted, in 1916 the local governor of Mecca declared Arabia's independence from Ottoman rule and hoped for British support in the efforts of the Arab nationalists. These nationalists were sorely disappointed, however. At the close of the war, Britain agreed to share with France in the creation of a number of mandates in the area to be placed under the general supervision of the new League of Nations. Iraq and Jordan were assigned to Great Britain. Syria and Lebanon were given to France. (The two areas were separated so that Christian peoples in Lebanon could be placed

So What ??

*If your students question the importance of the information on the **modernization of Persia** tell them . . .*

since the Shah of Iran continued the secularization inroads begun by his father Rega Khan, resentment among the orthodox mullahs grew. This religious resentment was aimed both at the Shah and at the United States. After the overthrow of the Shah, this resentment manifested itself in a policy of open hostility against the United States which continues to this day. Although there are some elements inside Iran that would like to improve relations with the United States, they may have to travel a tricky road through the radical Shi'a majority.

◄ *European Jewish refugees emigrated to Palestine both before and after World War II, but with one goal, to build a new life in a Jewish homeland. Like refugees aboard this ship, they all celebrated as they reached the safety of Palestine. The sign reads "Keep the gates open."*

under Christian administration.) These Middle Eastern states were, for the most part, the creation of Europeans. The Europeans arranged the borders and divided the peoples, but there was no strong identification on the part of most people with their designated countries. There was, however, a sense of Arab nationalism.

In the early 1920s, a leader of the Wahhabi movement, Ibn Saud, united Arab tribes in the northern part of the Arabian peninsula and drove out the remnants of Ottoman rule. Ibn Saud (from whom came the name Saudi Arabia) was a descendant of the family that had led the Wahhabi revolt in the eighteenth century. Devout and gifted, he won broad support among Arab tribal peoples and established the kingdom of Saudi Arabia throughout much of the peninsula in 1932.

At first the new kingdom, consisting mostly of the vast wastes of central Arabia, was desperately poor. Its financial resources were limited to the income from Muslim pilgrims visiting the holy spots in Mecca and Medina. During the 1930s, however, U.S. prospectors began to explore for oil. Standard Oil made a successful strike at Dahran, on the Persian Gulf, in 1938. Soon an Arabian-American oil company, popularly

called Aramco, was set up. The isolated kingdom was suddenly flooded by people in the Western oil industry, along with untold wealth.

Complicating matters in the Middle East was the land of Palestine. In antiquity it had been the home of the Jews. Now under British control, Palestine was inhabited primarily by Muslim Palestinians. According to the Balfour Declaration, issued by British foreign secretary Lord Balfour in November 1917, Palestine was to become a national home for the Jews. It stated: "His Majesty's Government views with favor the establishment in Palestine of a national home for the Jewish people." The declaration promised that the decision would not undermine the rights of the existing non-Jewish peoples currently living in the area. However, Arab nationalists were angered. They questioned how a national home for the Jewish people could be established in a territory in which 98 percent of the population was Muslim.

In the meantime, Jewish settlers began to arrive in Palestine in response to the promises made in the Balfour Declaration. The Zionist movement (see Chapter 22) had long advocated the return of Jews to Palestine

---

COOPERATIVE LEARNING ACTIVITY

Divide students into small groups and have each group construct a time line of Palestine, identifying which group or government has been in control of the area from 1500 B.C. to today. Students should provide documentation and illustrations to support

and complement their efforts. When work is done, have each group present a particular 500 year span of their time line to the class, explaining and defending their input.

TEACHING THEMES

The Impact of Science and Technology. Few substances have affected twentieth-century history more than petroleum. What, exactly, is petroleum? How is it formed? How is it obtained, and what is it used for? What are petrochemicals? Ask students to present their research to the class.

CRITICAL THINKING

Ask students to research and analyze the Balfour Declaration. Why was it issued? What were its effects? What was its relationship to the 1922 mandate in Palestine given to Britain and approved by the League of Nations?

ASSESS

You can choose from a variety of assessments to evaluate your students' mastery of the objectives for this section, as stated on page 870. Possible assessments include:

1. Section Review Questions on this page
2. Section 27–1 Quiz in your Teacher Resource materials
3. Reteaching Worksheets in your Teacher Resource materials
4. Self-Study software

ALTERNATIVE ASSESSMENT

Assign students an essay in which they compare the causes and effects of nationalist revolts in Turkey, Iran, and among Arab peoples.

Answers to SECTION REVIEW

2. (a) deliberately killing members of a particular racial or ethnic group
(b) genocide
(c) state that rejects church influence
(d) brimless cap worn by Turkish Muslims

3. (a) name given to the Ottoman Empire
(b) special forces of the sultan of the Ottoman Empire
(c) forced the sultan to give up power in 1908
(d) military commander who helped create an elected government in Turkey
(e) united Arab tribes to form Saudi Arabia
(f) a 1917 statement by Britain, created a Jewish state in Palestine

4. (a) One million Armenians were killed.
(b) The government provided no real power to the Turkish people.
(c) Oil was discovered.
(d) Tribes refused to cooperate.

5. (a) Answers will vary; forcing people to dress in a particular way is not likely to change beliefs.
(b) Answers will vary; harsh treatment of Jewish people in Europe encouraged many to emigrate.

CLOSE

Discuss with students how the presence and pressures of foreign powers led to nationalist feelings in the Middle East. Do students think this would have occurred if Western powers had been more sensitive and less greedy? Why, or why not?

---

as their homeland. Tensions between the new arrivals and existing Muslim residents began to escalate, especially during the 1930s. At the same time, the increased persecution of Jews with the rise of Nazi Germany led increasing numbers of European Jews to flee to Palestine. By 1939, there were about 450,000 Jews in Palestine. The British, fearing the effect of aroused Arab nationalism, then moved to restrict Jewish immigration into the territory. In 1939, the British government declared that only 75,000 Jewish immigrants would be allowed into Palestine over the next five years. After that, no more Jews could enter Palestine. The stage was set for the conflicts that would take place in the region after World War II.

SECTION REVIEW

1. Locate:
(a) Tunisia, (b) Mecca, (c) Ankara, (d) Anatolian peninsula, (e) Persia, (f) Tehran

2. Define:
(a) genocide, (b) ethnic cleansing, (c) secular state, (d) fez

3. Identify:
(a) "sick man of Europe," (b) Janissaries, (c) Young Turks, (d) Colonel Mustapha Kemal, (e) Wahhabi movement, (f) Balfour Declaration

4. Recall:
(a) How did the Ottoman Empire react to the Armenian uprising in 1915?
(b) Why didn't Turkish efforts to create a democratic government in 1920 succeed?
(c) What happened in 1908 that increased foreign interest in Persia?
(d) Why was it difficult for Arab people to form a nation?

5. Think Critically:
(a) What is the meaning of the following quotation, and why is it true?

"You cannot make a Turk into a Westerner by giving him a hat."

(b) Why did harsh treatment of Jewish people in Europe create problems for Arab people in the Middle East?

NATIONALISM AND REVOLUTION IN AFRICA AND ASIA

Between 1919 and 1939, leaders emerged in Africa and Asia who sought to free their people from the power of the Western imperialists. None of these nationalist movements were successful before World War II, but they were a beginning.

Independence Movements in Africa

Black Africans who fought in World War I in the armies of the British and French hoped for independence after the war. As one newspaper in the Gold Coast put it, if African volunteers who fought on European battlefields were "good enough to fight and die in the Empire's cause, they were good enough to have a share in the government of their countries." This feeling was shared by many. The peace settlement after World War I, then, turned out to be a great disappointment. Germany was stripped of its African colonies, but these colonies were awarded to Great Britain and France to be administered as mandates for the League of Nations. Britain and France now had so much territory in Africa that even they did not know what to do with it all.

After World War I, Africans became more active politically. Those Africans who had fought in World War I had learned new ideas in the West about freedom and nationalism. In Africa itself, missionary schools had often taught their African pupils ideas about liberty and equality. As more Africans became aware of the enormous gulf between Western ideals and practices, they decided to seek reform. Independence, however, remained but a dream.

RECOMMENDED READING

On the imperialistic age in Africa, see R. Robinson and J. Gallagher, *Africa and the Victorians: The Official Mind of Imperialism* (London, 1961). On South Africa, see J. Guy, *The Destruction of the Zulu Kingdom* (London, 1979); and D. Nenoon and B. Nyeko, *Southern Africa since 1800* (London, 1984).

For the British takeover and administration of India, see S. Wolpert, *A New History of India* (New York, 1989).

For Mahatma Gandhi, see J. M. Brown, *Gandhi: Prisoner of Hope* (New Haven, Conn., 1989) and *All Men Are Brothers: The Life and Thoughts of Mahatma Gandhi as Told in His own Words* (New York, 1960).

Map 27.2   Africa, 1919–1939

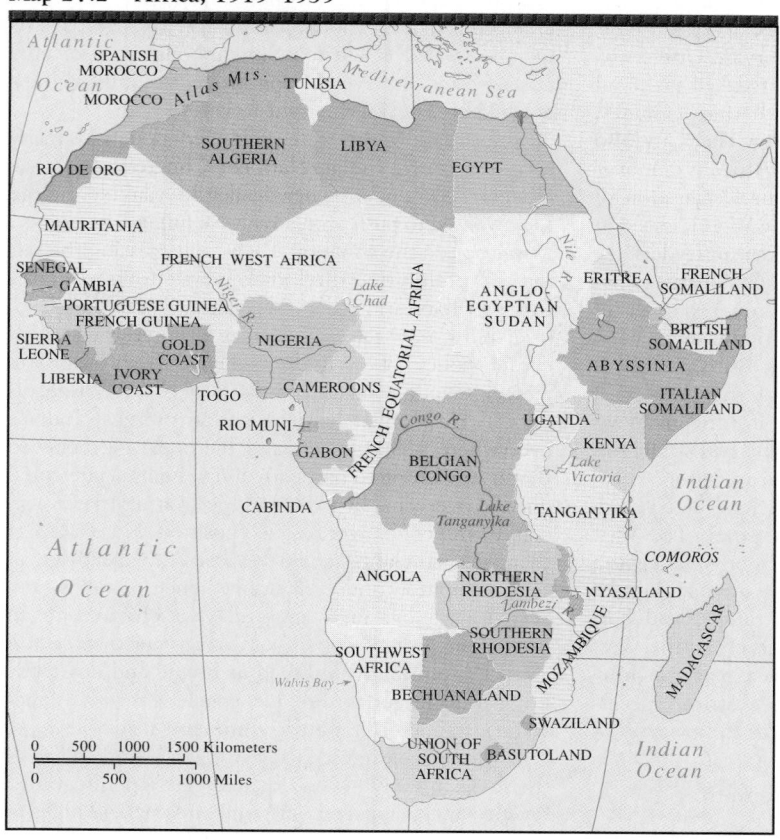

Protest took different forms. In Nigeria and South Africa, workers created trade unions that tried to gain benefits for themselves. There were also cases of violent protest. In British Nigeria in 1929, a group of women protested the high taxes that were levied on the goods they were selling in the markets. During the riot that ensued, women cried for all white men to leave their country. The British killed fifty women and ended the riot.

In 1921, Kenya also witnessed a protest movement. The Young Kikuyu Association, organized by Harry Thuku, a telephone operator, especially protested the high taxes levied by the British rulers. His message was simple: "Hearken, every day you pay hut tax to the Europeans of Government. Where is it sent? It is their task to steal the property of the Kikuyu people." Thuku was arrested. When an angry crowd stormed the jail and demanded his release, government authorities fired into the crowd and killed fifty people. Thuku was sent into exile.

In North Africa, there were also violent attempts at independence. Tribes in the Moroccan mountains, led by Muhammad Abd al-Krim, rebelled against Spanish control in 1921. This led to a lengthy struggle. France, which held the rest of Morocco, then intervened and crushed the revolt. Krim was exiled in 1926.

A struggle against Italian rule in Libya also broke out in the 1920s. Forces led by Omar Mukhtar used guerrilla warfare against the Italians and defeated them a number of times. The Italians reacted ferociously. They established concentration camps and used planes and all available modern weapons to crush the revolt. The death of Mukhtar ended the movement.

Colonial powers responded to these movements with force. However, they also began to make some reforms in the hope of satisfying native peoples. Reforms, however, were too few and too late. By the 1930s, an increasing number of African leaders were calling for independence, not reform.

The clearest calls came from a new generation of young African leaders who had been educated abroad, in Europe and the United States. Those who went to

STUDYING MAPS

The following questions and activities will help you guide students through their study of Map 27.2.

1. Locate countries whose names indicate their colonial status. *(Portuguese Guinea, French Guinea, Belgian Congo, Italian Somaliland, British Somaliland, French Somaliland, Anglo-Egyptian Sudan, French West Africa, French Equatorial Africa)*

2. Why would the Spanish have held territory in Morocco? *(located just a few miles away from Spain)*

3. Find Libya on the map. Where is it in relation to Italy? *(Just south—Italy is the closest European power.)*

CLASS DISCUSSION

Guide students in a discussion of the following statement: "As more Africans became aware of the enormous gulf between Western ideals and practices, they decided to seek reform."

CRITICAL THINKING

Have students research and compare the reaction of colonial powers to nationalist movements in Africa between 1919 and 1939.

ACROSS THE CURRICULUM

Literature. Assign students to read *The Souls of Black Folk* by W. E. B. Du Bois. Ask them to give a class presentation on the ideas of this influential book.

CRITICAL THINKING

Research and analyze the career of Marcus Garvey. Consider the impact of his "back to Africa" movement in the U.S. How and why did Garvey fall from grace in the United States?

CRITICAL THINKING

Was Gandhi, in fact, the opposite of the "secular," "rational," "upper-class," "intellectual" Nehru? Research Gandhi's background. Would you quarrel with any of these descriptors? If so, with which one(s)?

the United States were especially influenced by the ideas of W. E. B. Du Bois and Marcus Garvey. Du Bois, an African American educated at Harvard University, was the leader of a movement that tried to make all Africans aware of their own cultural heritage. Garvey, a Jamaican who lived in Harlem in New York City, also stressed the need for the unity of all Africans, a movement known as **Pan-Africanism.** His Declaration of the Rights of the Negro Peoples of the World, issued in 1920, had a strong impact on later African leaders.

Leaders and movements in individual African nations also appeared. Jomo Kenyatta (kun-YAH-tuh) of Kenya had been educated in Great Britain. In his book *Facing Mount Kenya,* he argued that British rule was destroying the traditional culture of the peoples of black Africa (see "You Are There: If Africans Were Left in Peace"). Léopold Senghor, who had studied in France and written poetry about African culture, organized an independence movement in Senegal. Nnamdi Azikiwe, of Nigeria, began a newspaper, *The West African Pilot,* in 1937 and advocated nonviolence as a method to gain independence. These are but three of the leaders who organized demonstrations and borrowed methods of political organization from the West to gain more followers. All of them were part of a growing movement to end colonial rule in Africa. Success would not come until after World War II, however.

Gandhi and the Movement for Indian Independence

By the time of World War I, the Indian people had already begun to refer to Mohandas Gandhi as India's "Great Soul," or **Mahatma.** He now organized mass protests to achieve his aims. In 1919, the protests got out of hand and led to violence and a strong British reaction. British troops killed hundreds of unarmed protesters in the enclosed square in the city of Amritsar, in northwestern India. Horrified at the violence, Gandhi briefly retreated from active politics. Nevertheless, he was arrested for his role in the protests, and he spent several years in prison.

While Gandhi was in prison, Great Britain passed the Government of India Act. This act expanded the role of Indians in the governing process. What had

been the Legislative Council that only gave advice was changed into a two-house parliament. Two-thirds of its members would be elected. Similar bodies were created at the provincial level. In one stroke, five million Indians had been given the right to vote.

Reforms, however, were no longer enough for many members of the Indian National Congress (INC; see Chapter 23). Under its new leader, Motilal Nehru, the INC wanted to push aggressively for full independence. Britain made the situation worse by increasing the salt tax and prohibiting the Indian people from manufacturing or harvesting their own salt.

Gandhi, now released from prison, returned to his earlier policy of civil disobedience (see "You Are There: Gandhi Takes the Path of Civil Disobedience"). He worked hard to inform ordinary Indians everywhere of his beliefs and methods. He believed that it was wrong to harm any living being. Hate could only be overcome by love, and love, rather than force, could win people over to one's position. Nonviolence, then, was crucial. It could be used in a campaign of noncooperation and civil disobedience. Gandhi said, "Don't pay your taxes or send your children to an English-supported school. . . . Make your own cotton cloth by spinning the thread at home, and don't buy English-made goods. Provide yourselves with homemade salt, and do not buy government-made salt."

In 1930, Gandhi used the British measures on salt as the basis for civil disobedience. He openly joined seventy-eight supporters and walked some 240 miles to the sea. Along the way, thousands of new supporters joined him. When they reached the sea, Gandhi picked up a pinch of salt and urged Indians to do the same and ignore the law. (The British used saltflats along the seashore to collect crystallized seasalt.) When thousands of Indians followed Gandhi's policy of civil disobedience, he and many other members of the INC were arrested.

In the 1930s, a new figure entered the movement. Jawaharlal Nehru, the son of the INC leader Motilal Nehru, was educated in law in Great Britain. The younger Nehru was a good example of the new Anglo-Indian politician. He was secular, rational, upper class, and an intellectual. In fact, he appeared to be everything that Gandhi was not.

MORE ABOUT . . . *Mohandas Gandhi*

Most students would not have recognized Gandhi, the young lawyer in South Africa at the beginning of the 20th century. After emigrating to South Africa in search of professional success, Gandhi set up a legal practice for the "colored" population of the country (i.e., not black African or white European). He enjoyed modest success as a suit-and-tie attorney representing the "colored" minority in an increasingly hostile South Africa. For a

time he became disconnected from the Indian struggle for independence from Britain, but in the end he felt it was his duty to return to India to help the cause. Leaving behind his law practice and his suits and ties, he became the quintessential Indian nationalist hero, wearing clothes that he himself manufactured on his own hand loom, and providing an example that others found impossible to ignore.

YOU ARE THERE

If Africans Were Left in Peace

Jomo Kenyatta was an eloquent spokesper-son for independence for Kenya from British rule. His book Facing Mount Kenya *was a detailed description of the ways of life of his native Kikuyu peo-ple. He ended the book with a plea for African independence.*

Jomo Kenyatta,
Facing Mount Kenya

If Africans were left in peace on their own lands, Europeans would have to offer them the benefits of white civilization in real earnest before they could obtain the African labor which they want so much. They would have to offer the African a way of life which was really superior to the one his fathers lived before him, and a share in the prosperity given them by their command of science. They would have to let the African choose what parts of Euro-pean culture could be beneficially transplanted, and how they could be adapted. He would proba-bly not choose the gas bomb or the armed police force, but he might ask for some other things of which he does not get so much today. As it is, by driving him off his ancestral lands, the Europeans

◀ *Jomo Kenyatta, founder of the Kikuyu Cen-tral Association, was initially interested in improving living conditions for Africans. He became president of Kenya in 1964.*

have robbed him of the material foundations of his culture, and reduced him to a state of serfdom incompatible with human happi-ness. The African is conditioned, by the cultural and social institu-tions of centuries, to a freedom of which Europe has little conception, and it is not in his nature to accept serfdom forever. He realizes that he must fight unceasingly for his own com-plete emancipation; for without this he is doomed to remain the prey of rival imperi-alisms, which in every successive year will drive their fangs more deeply into his vitality and strength.

1. In your own words, describe the appeal that Jomo Kenyatta is making in regard to Africa.

2. How would you, as a westerner, respond to Kenyatta's appeal?

With the emergence of Nehru, the independence movement split into two paths. The one identified with Gandhi was religious, native, and traditional. The other, identified with Nehru, was secular, Western, and modern. Both Gandhi and Nehru were leaders in the INC. Thus, the INC leadership had a duality that probably made the independence movement stronger. After all, the two main impulses behind the desire for independence—nationalism and the primal force of Indian traditionalism—were brought together. How-ever, the existence of two approaches made people uncertain how to define India's future path in the con-temporary world.

In the meantime, another problem arose in the independence movement. Hostility between Hindus and Muslims had existed for centuries. Muslims now

ENRICHMENT ACTIVITY

Have students do additional research on the independence movements of the nations of Africa by focusing on the leaders who emerged in different parts of Africa. What are the common features in the lives of these individuals? How were they different?

ACROSS THE CURRICULUM

Literature/Political Science. Assign students all or part of Jomo Kenyatta's book *Facing Mount Kenya.* What were the "ways of life of his native Kikuyu people"?

CRITICAL THINKING

Have students gather evi-dence to support Kenyatta's belief that foreign interven-tion in Africa drained its "vitality and strength."

Answers to Critical Thinking Questions

1. Kenyatta's appeal is for Westerners to leave Africans alone, not to force themselves upon Africans, but to let them choose what parts of Western culture they would like to adopt. He is also asking for Westerners to leave Africans with their ancestral lands and their independence.

2. Answers will vary.

Multimedia Support

LASERDISC
Mohandas Gandhi
(1869–1948)

CLASS DISCUSSION

Guide students in a dis-cussion of the split in the Indian independence move-ment. How did this "duality" strengthen the movement?

YOU·ARE·THERE

USING PRIMARY SOURCES

Study Gandhi's rhetoric: his effectiveness as a writer and logician. What is the effect of repeating three times that he regards British rule as "a curse"? How does he insist on this point, even as he explains his pacifism? Both Gandhi and Kenyatta (page 879) use the word "serfdom" to describe the effects of foreign rule on native people. Serfdom and servile both come from the Latin word for slave. What, then, is serfdom? Is the word well chosen to make both writers' points? Why does Gandhi use the word "conversion" to describe his goal for England?

Answers to Critical Thinking Questions

1. Gandhi felt that British rule had exploited the people by installing an administration and military that could not be financially supported, reducing them to poverty. He felt the people had been reduced to political serfdom and had been spiritually degraded.
2. Civil disobedience is refusing to obey governmental commands as a nonviolent way of forcing a government to make concessions.
3. Answers will vary.

YOU ARE THERE

Gandhi Takes the Path of Civil Disobedience

Mohandas Gandhi became convinced that only a policy of civil disobedience could free India from British rule. In this letter to a British official, he explains why British rule must end.

Mohandas Gandhi, Letter to a British Official

Before embarking on civil disobedience and taking the risk I have dreaded to take all these years, I would fain approach you and find a way out.

My personal faith is absolutely clear. I cannot intentionally hurt anything that lives, much less fellow human beings, even though they may do the greatest wrong to me and mine. Whilst, therefore, I hold the British rule to be a curse, I do not intend harm to a single Englishman or to any legitimate interest he may have in India.

I must not be misunderstood. Though I hold the British rule in India to be a curse, I do not, therefore, consider Englishmen in general to be worse than any other people on earth. I have the privilege of claiming many Englishmen as dearest friends. Indeed much that I have learned of the evil of British rule is due to the writings of frank and courageous Englishmen who have not hesitated to tell the truth about that rule.

And why do I regard British rule as a curse? It has impoverished the ignorant millions by a system of progressive exploitation and by a ruinously expensive military and civil administration which the country can never afford.

It has reduced us politically to serfdom. It has sapped the foundations of our culture. And, by the policy of cruel disarmament, it has degraded us spiritually. Lacking the inward strength, we have been reduced, by all but universal disarmament, to a state bordering on cowardly helplessness. . . .

▲ *Throughout his life, Gandhi crusaded for rights for both men and women of all classes, from educated professionals to the Untouchables.*

I know that in embarking on non-violence I shall be running what might fairly be termed a mad risk. But the victories of truth have never been won without risks, often of the gravest character. Conversion of a nation that has consciously or unconsciously preyed upon another, far more numerous, far more ancient and no less cultured than itself, is worth any amount of risk.

---

1. According to Gandhi, what had British rule done to India?

2. What is civil disobedience?

3. Why do you think Gandhi believed that non-violent civil disobedience would encourage the British to free India?

So What ??

*If your students question the importance of the information on **Mohandas Gandhi,** tell them . . .*

Mahatma Gandhi led India to independence and showed the world the effectiveness of passive civil disobedience. The disciples of Gandhi forswore aggression, even in self-defense. The outcome was that the aggressors could no longer bear the weight of inflicting pain on peaceful, passive energy.

Gandhi's example was followed by Martin Luther King in the 1960s in the United States. The moral force of passive civil disobedience proved itself—as in Gandhi's India—powerful enough to dismantle institutional discrimination and bring civil rights to millions of Americans. Gandhi and his disciple nation achieved what traditional force might not have.

◄ *By 1932, Japanese forces had occupied the walled city of Manchuria. Why do you think the Chinese were unable to stop the Japanese forces from invading?*

became unhappy with the Hindu dominance of the INC and raised the cry that "Islam is in danger." In 1930, the Muslim League, under the leadership of Muhammad Ali Jinnah, called for the creation of a separate Muslim state of Pakistan (meaning "the land of the pure") in the northwest. Conflict between Muslims and Hindus now began to grow. As it did, many Indians came to realize with sorrow that British rule was all that stood between peace and civil war.

The Rise of a Militarist Japan

As we saw in Chapter 24, during the first two decades of the twentieth century, Japan seemed to be moving toward a more democratic government. The parliament and political parties had grown stronger. Civilian political leaders had been able to control the military. However, appearances were deceiving. The influence of the old ruling oligarchy remained strong. Furthermore, at the end of the 1920s, new problems led to the emergence of militant (aggressive) forces that moved Japan toward an authoritarian and militaristic state.

No doubt, economic crises added to the problem. Japan's economy had already begun to experience problems in the 1920s. The Great Depression made the situation worse. Workers, and especially farmers, suffered the most. With hardships came cries against the West and calls for a return to traditional Japanese values. At the same time, many citizens denounced Japan's attempt to find security through cooperation with the Western powers. Instead, they called upon Japan to use its own strength to dominate Asia in order to meet its needs. Extreme patriotism and a strong militarism marked the Japan of the 1930s.

The rise of militant forces in Japan was not the result of the takeover of power by a new political party, as it was in Fascist Italy and Nazi Germany. The Japanese constitution of 1889 was not abolished. Instead, a new group of militant people was able to control the political system. Some, like the publicist Kita Ikki, were civilians convinced that the parliamentary system had been corrupted by Western values. Others were members of the military who were angered at budget cuts in military expenditures and at the pacifist policies followed by the government during the early 1920s.

On Line with
WORLD HISTORY *Internet Activity*

You may want to have your students visit the following URL, where they will find information and additional web site resources to enhance their study of this chapter.
Mahatma Gandhi Ashram
http://www.news.com/ashram/

The site contains a photo gallery, multimedia video (both downloadable), time lines and a marking list to keep those interested updated on new additions.
Due to the ever-changing nature of the World Wide Web, see the West History web site, **http://history.swpco.com** for regular updates of the URLs in this text.

LEARNING FROM VISUALS

Answer to the caption question: Japan was well on its way to becoming a modern nation, and its military was far better armed and disciplined than the Chinese.

CLASS DISCUSSION

Guide students in a discussion of the following: "Conflict between Muslims and Hindus now began to grow. As it did, many Indians came to realize with sorrow that British rule was all that stood between peace and civil war."

CLASS DISCUSSION

Be sure students know what an oligarchy is *(rule by a small group)*. Discuss the problems in Japan that led to the rise of militant forces in the 1930s.

CRITICAL THINKING

Have students research and analyze the differences between the rise of militant forces in Japan, Germany and Italy between the world wars.

CRITICAL THINKING

Ask students to research the Japanese occupation of Manchuria in 1931. Why was the area of special interest to Japan? How long did Japan occupy Manchuria? What were conditions during the occupation? What happened to end Japanese rule? What is the status of Manchuria now?

CLASS DISCUSSION

Have students discuss why, until the Russian Revolution, Asian intellectuals believed that Marxism had little value for Asia. *(Marxism says that a Communist society arises with the collapse of capitalism. Asia had little capitalism.)*

CONNECTIONS
AROUND THE WORLD

Paths to Modernization   After World War I, new states in the Middle East and Asia sought to modernize their countries. To many people, modernization meant westernization, or the adoption of both political and economic reforms based on Western models. These included the adoption of democratic principles and a free-market, or capitalist, economic system based on industrialization.

After the success of the Communist revolution in Russia, however, a second model for modernization appeared. To some people, a Marxist system seemed to offer a better and quicker way to transform a backward agricultural state into a modern industrial state. The new system would be a socialist model in which an authoritarian state, not private industry, would own and control the economy.

Between World War I and World War II, new republics in Turkey and China tended to combine features of both systems. In Turkey, Kemal Ataturk, creator of the new Turkish republic, set up a National Assembly but ruled with an iron fist. His economic modernization combined private industries with state direction of the economy.

In China, the Nanjing Republic under Jiang Jieshi supported the idea of democracy but maintained the need for dictatorial government as a first stage to prepare the Chinese people for democracy. Economic modernization in the new Chinese republic combined a modern industrial state with the traditional Chinese values of hard work and obedience.

During the early 1930s, extremist patriotic organizations, such as the Black Dragon Society, were formed by civilians, but even more so within the army and the navy. One of these groups, consisting of middle-level officers in the army, waged the takeover of Manchuria in the autumn of 1931. The government opposed the action. The Japanese people received it with great enthusiasm, however, and the government could do nothing to undo the takeover.

Other patriotic military groups terrorized Japanese society by assassinating businessmen and government officials. Moderate elements were forced into silence. Those who were put on trial for their part in assassination attempts were given light sentences while being allowed to portray themselves as selfless patriots. National elections continued to take place, but government cabinets were dominated by the military and other supporters of Japanese expansionism.

In the 1930s, Japanese society was put on a wartime status. A military draft law was passed in 1938. Economic resources were placed under strict government control. All political parties were merged into an Imperial Rule Assistance Association, which served as a mouthpiece for expansionist elements within the government and the military. Labor unions were broken up. Education and culture were purged of all corrupt Western ideas. Militant leaders insisted on the need for stressing traditional Japanese values instead.

Nationalism and Revolution in Asia

Until the outbreak of World War I in 1914, the term **westernization,** to most intellectuals in Asia, had one meaning. It was identified with the capitalist democratic civilization in western Europe and the United States. The intellectuals had little interest in the doctrine of social revolution known as Marxism. That fact is not surprising. Until the Russian Revolution in 1917, Marxism was merely an idea rather than a concrete system of government. To many intellectuals, Marxism had little value for conditions in Asia anyway. Marxist doctrine, after all, declared that a Communist society would arise only with the collapse of an advanced capitalism. Most societies in Asia were still agricultural and were hardly ready for a socialist revolution.

Many patriotic intellectuals in Asia, then, at first found Marxism to have little appeal. That situation began to change after the revolution in Russia in 1917.

COOPERATIVE LEARNING ACTIVITY

Organize a class debate in which students assume that they are Japanese university students of the early 1930s who take opposing sides on the following topic: Expansion in Asia—The Salvation of Japan. Have students work in small groups to conduct outside research, organize theirnotes, and prepare. What positions would the two sides take? Following the debate, discuss with the class whether there might have been a compromise position that would have avoided war?

The rise to power of the Bolsheviks led by Lenin showed that a revolutionary Marxist party could overturn a not fully industrialized, corrupt system and begin a new one. Then, in 1920, Lenin adopted a new revolutionary strategy aimed at the societies outside the Western world.

One of Lenin's reasons for doing so was quite simple. Soviet Russia, surrounded by capitalist powers, desperately needed allies in its struggle to survive in a hostile world. To Lenin, the anticolonial movements now arising in North Africa, Asia, and the Middle East seemed to be the natural allies of the new regime in Moscow. However, there were problems in creating such an alliance. Most nationalist leaders in colonial countries belonged to the urban middle class. Many detested the idea of a Communist revolution.

Lenin sought a compromise. He forged a strategy by which Communist parties could be created among the working class, small as it was in the agricultural societies of Asia and Africa. Such parties would then propose informal alliances with existing middle-class parties to struggle against their Western rulers. Such alliances, of course, would not be permanent. Once the Western imperialists had been overthrown, Communist parties would turn against their nationalist partners and seize power on their own, thus creating the socialist revolution.

Lenin's proposal was adopted as a part of Soviet foreign policy in 1920. Beginning in 1921, Soviet agents fanned out throughout the world to carry the word of Karl Marx beyond the boundaries of Europe. The chief instrument of this effort was the Communist International, or Comintern for short. Formed in 1919 at Lenin's prodding, the Comintern was a worldwide organization of Communist parties dedicated to the advancement of world revolution. At the Comintern's headquarters in Moscow, agents from around the world were trained in the ideas of world communism and then returned to their own countries to form Marxist parties and promote the cause of social revolution. By the end of the 1920s, practically every colonial society in Asia had a Communist party. Moscow had less success in the Middle East or in Africa.

Who joined these early revolutionary parties, and why? According to Marxist doctrine, the members of Communist parties should be urban workers angered by inhuman working conditions in the factories. In practice, most early Marxists were intellectuals. Some were probably drawn into the movement for reasons of patriotism. They saw Marxism as a new means of modernizing their societies and removing the colonial powers (see "You Are There: The Path to Liberation"). Others were attracted by the basic message of communism and its utopian dream of a classless society. The movement gave all who joined a practical strategy for the liberation of their societies from colonial rule.

There were, of course, wide variations in the degree of appeal of the new doctrine in Asian societies. In China and Vietnam, traditional Confucian belief systems had lost favor to a large degree because of their failure to counter the Western challenge. Communism had an almost immediate appeal in these countries and rapidly became a major factor in the anticolonial movement. The situation was different in Malaya, however, where the sense of nationhood was weak. It also differed in Thailand, which, alone in Southeast Asia, had not fallen under colonial rule. In these two countries, the base of the support for the local Communist Party came from minority groups such as the Chinese who lived in the cities.

How successful were these new parties in establishing alliances with existing nationalist parties and in building a solid base of support among the mass of the population? Here again, the answer varied from one society to another. In some instances, the local Communists were briefly able to establish a cooperative relationship with middle-class Nationalist parties in a common struggle against Western imperialism. As we shall see in the next section, this was true in China.

Similar patterns took shape elsewhere. In the Dutch East Indies, the Indonesian Communist Party (known as the PKI) set up an alliance with the middle-class nationalist group Sarekat Islam. Later, the PKI broke loose in an effort to organize its own mass movement among poor peasants. Similar problems occurred in French Indochina. Vietnamese Communists, organized by the Moscow-trained revolutionary Ho Chi Minh (HOE CHEE MIN), sought to cooperate with middle-class nationalist parties against the colonial regime. In 1928, such efforts were abandoned. The Comintern

CRITICAL THINKING

Analyze Lenin's strategy for spreading Marxist ideology. Was his decision to ally temporarily working class parties with middle-class parties realistic? Why, or why not? Was it successful? If so, where and how?

CRITICAL THINKING

Ask students to research and analyze why Communist parties formed fairly easily in Asia, but not in the Middle East or Africa.

CLASS DISCUSSION

Ask students to discuss why communism had great appeal in China and Vietnam, but less appeal in Malaya and Thailand.

CLASS DISCUSSION

Guide students in a discussion of what the Comintern was and what it accomplished before World War II.

On Line with WORLD HISTORY *Internet Activity*

You may want to have your students visit the following URL, where they will find information and additional web site resources to enhance their study of this chapter.

M. K. Gandhi Institute for Nonviolence

http://www.chu.edu/Gandhi

The mission of the Gandhi Institute is to promote and apply the principles of nonviolence. There is a lot of good information on both Gandhi and nonviolence in society today.

Due to the ever-changing nature of the World Wide Web, see the West History web site, **http://history.swpco.com** for regular updates of the URLs in this text.

YOU ARE THERE

USING PRIMARY SOURCES

Notice the words Ho Chi Minh uses to describe his reaction to Lenin's thesis: "emotion," "enthusiasm," "clear-sightedness," "confidence," "overjoyed to tears." Have students ever read anything that affected them this way? Can they describe the personal and political conditions that might lead a person to experience such a "conversion" through the written word?

Answers to Critical Thinking Questions

1. He was in exile.
2. Minh admired Lenin and considered him a great patriot.
3. He joined the French Socialist Party because they had shown sympathy toward him and for the struggle of oppressed peoples.
4. Answers will vary.

ASSESS

You can choose from a variety of assessments to evaluate your students' mastery of the objectives for this section, as stated on page 877. Possible assessments include:

1. Section Review Questions on page 885
2. Section 27–2 Quiz in your Teacher Resource materials
3. Reteaching Worksheets in your Teacher Resource materials
4. Self-Study software

884

YOU ARE THERE
The Path to Liberation

The Vietnamese revolutionary Ho Chi Minh first became acquainted with the revolution in Bolshevik Russia in 1919 while living in France. He became a dedicated follower of V. I. Lenin and eventually became a leader of the Vietnamese Communist movement. In the following passage, Ho Chi Minh talks about his reasons for becoming a Communist.

Ho Chi Minh, On Becoming a Communist

After World War I, I made my living in Paris, now as a retoucher at a photographer's, now as a painter of "Chinese antiquities" (made in France!). I would distribute leaflets denouncing the crimes committed by the French colonialists in Vietnam.

At that time, I supported the Russian Revolution only instinctively, not yet grasping all its historic importance. I loved and admired Lenin because he was a great patriot who liberated his compatriots; until then, I had read none of his books.

The reason for my joining the French Socialist Party was that these "ladies and gentlemen"—as I called my comrades at that moment—had shown their sympathy toward me, toward the struggle of the oppressed peoples. But I understood neither what was a party, a trade-union, nor what was

◄ *This photo of Ho Chi Minh was taken in 1957. Do you think it was difficult for him to return to Vietnam after living in Paris? Why or why not?*

Socialism nor Communism. . . . A comrade gave me Lenin's "Thesis on the National and Colonial Questions" to read.

There were political terms difficult to understand in this thesis. But by dint of reading it again and again, finally I could grasp the main part of it. What emotion, enthusiasm, clear-sightedness, and confidence it instilled in me! I was overjoyed to tears. Though sitting alone in my room, I shouted aloud as if addressing large crowds. "Dear martyrs, compatriots! This is what we need, this is the path to our liberation!"

After that, I had entire confidence in Lenin.

1. Why was Ho Chi Minh living in France?
2. What were Ho Chi Minh's feelings toward Lenin?
3. Why did he join the French Socialist Party?
4. If American foreign policy makers had known of this document after World War II, how might things have gone differently in Vietnam?

declared that Communist parties should recruit only the most revolutionary elements in society; namely, those among urban intellectuals and the working class.

Harassed by colonial authorities, and saddled with directions from Moscow that often had little relevance to local conditions, Communist parties in most colonial societies had little success in the 1930s. They failed to build a secure base of support among the mass of the population. However, this was not entirely the case in China.

On Line with WORLD HISTORY   *Internet Activity*

You may want to have your students visit the following URL, where they will find information and additional web site resources to enhance their study of this chapter.

The Marxism Leninism Project
http://www.idbsu.edu/surveyrc/staff/jaynes/marxism/bios.htm

This site includes biographies, websites, and information on Mao Tse-Tung, Fidel Castro, Ho Chi Minh and Che Guevara, to name a few modern revolutionaries.

Due to the ever-changing nature of the World Wide Web, see the West History web site, **http://history.swpco.com** for regular updates of the URLs in this text.

SECTION REVIEW

1. Locate:
(*a*) Nigeria, (*b*) South Africa,
(*c*) Amritsar, (*d*) Kenya

2. Define:
(*a*) Pan-Africanism, (*b*) Mahatma,
(*c*) westernization

3. Identify:
(*a*) Young Kikuyu Association, (*b*) *Facing Mount Kenya,* (*c*) Government of India Act,
(*d*) Jawaharlal Nehru, (*e*) Kita Ikki,
(*f*) Comintern, (*g*) Ho Chi Minh

4. Recall:
(*a*) Why did many Africans expect to gain independence for their countries after World War I?
(*b*) How did Mohandas Gandhi encourage his followers to work against colonial rule?
(*c*) What was the function of the Imperial Rule Assistance Association in Japan?
(*d*) Why were communists more successful in China than in Siam during the 1920s and 1930s?

5. Think Critically:
(*a*) Why would an act as harmless as picking up a pinch of salt from the sand be seen as worthy of putting a person in jail in India?
(*b*) What did the Japanese army's invasion of Manchuria in 1931 show about the political situation in Japan at that time?

3

REVOLUTIONARY CHAOS IN CHINA

It was in China that revolutionary Marxism had its greatest impact. In 1919, a group of young radicals, including several faculty and staff members from Beijing University, founded the Chinese Communist Party (CCP) in the commercial and industrial city of Shanghai. The new party was soon advised by Com-

intern agents to link up with the more experienced Nationalists.

Nationalists and Communists: Cooperation and Tensions

Sun Yat-sen, leader of the Nationalists (see Chapter 24), welcomed the cooperation. He needed the expertise and the diplomatic support that the Soviet Union could provide. His anti-imperialist words had alienated many Western powers. One English-language newspaper in Shanghai wrote, "All his life, all his influence, are devoted to ideas that keep China in turmoil, and it is utterly undesirable that he should be allowed to prosecute those aims here."[2] In 1923, the two parties—Nationalists and Communists—formed an alliance to oppose the warlords and drive the imperialist powers out of China.

For three years, with the help of a Comintern office set up in Canton, the two parties overlooked their mutual suspicions and worked together. They mobilized and trained a revolutionary army to march north and seize control over China. The so-called Northern Expedition began in the summer of 1926. By the following spring, revolutionary forces had seized control over all of China south of the Yangtze River, including the major river ports of Wuhan and Shanghai.

Internal tensions between the two parties now rose to the surface. Sun Yat-sen had died of cancer in 1925. He was succeeded as head of the Nationalist Party by his military subordinate Jiang Jieshi (jee-ONG jee-AE-SHEE) (Chiang Kai-shek [jee-ONG-KIE-shek]). Jiang pretended to support the alliance with the Communists but actually planned to destroy them. In April 1927, he struck against the Communists and their supporters in Shanghai, killing thousands. The Communists reacted by raising the flag of revolt in central China and Canton. The uprisings were defeated, however, and their leaders were killed or forced into hiding.

The Nanjing Republic

In 1928, Jiang Jieshi founded a new Chinese republic at Nanjing. During the next three years he worked to reunify China. He combined military operations with

RECOMMENDED READING

The rise of the Chinese Communist party is discussed in B. Schwartz, *Chinese Communism and the Rise of Mao* (Cambridge, 1958); and A. Dirlik, *The Origins of Chinese Communism* (Oxford, 1989). There are a number of biographies of Mao Zedong. For a readable and informative version, see S. Schram, *Mao Tse-tung: A Political Biography* (Baltimore, 1966). Also see the same author's *The Politi-*

cal Thought of Mao Tse-tung (New York, 1966). For an inside account of the movement by a sympathetic Western journalist, see E. Snow's *Red Star over China* (New York, 1938). The early Chiang Kai-shek period is dealt with persuasively in L. Eastman's *The Abortive Revolution: China under Nationalist Rule, 1927–1937* (Cambridge, 1974).

Answers to SECTION REVIEW

2. (a) stressed the need for African unity
(b) "Great Soul"; name give to Mohandas Gandhi
(c) capitalist democratic civilization
3. (a) protested high British taxes in Kenya in 1921
(b) book by Kenyatta
(c) expanded the role of Indians in government
(d) leader of the Indian independence movement
(e) Japanese leader, argued government corrupted by Western values
(f) Communist International
(g) Communist leader in Vietnam
4. (a) Africans had fought with colonial powers in the war, felt they had earned independence
(b) ignore British laws, not buy British products
(c) intimidate Japanese who did not favor expansionist policies
(d) China had been dominated by imperial powers, Siam had not.
5. (a) Answers will vary; acts that broke British laws could be regarded as the first step in breaking all British laws.
(b) Answers will vary; Japan opposed the invasion, but the army went ahead.

CLOSE

Ask students to supply evidence that supports the following statement: "Harassed by colonial authorities, and saddled with direction from Moscow that often had little relevance to local conditions, Communist parties in most colonial societies had little success in the 1930s."

FOCUS

OBJECTIVES

After completing this section, students should be able to

1. discuss what happened to the Nationalist and Communist alliance after Jiang Jieshi came to power
2. describe the early efforts of Mao Zedong to defeat Jieshi's Nationalists
3. explain the significance of the "Long March"
4. describe Jieshi's efforts to create a "new China"

FOCUS ACTIVITY

Ask students to consider the following leaders of China's revolutionary movement: Sun Yet-sen, Jiang Jieshi, and Mao Zedong. In what ways would each qualify as a hero, as students discussed earlier? Why do they think it was Mao who emerged as the central figure in twentieth-century China?

Map 27.3   China, 1919–1939

inducements to various northern warlords to join his movement. One of his key targets was the warlord Zhang Zuolin, who controlled Manchuria under the control of Japan. When Zhang agreed to throw in his lot with the Nationalists, the Japanese had him assassinated by placing a bomb under his train as he was returning to Manchuria. The Japanese hoped that Zhang Zuolin's son and successor, Zhang Xueliang, would be more cooperative. However, they had miscalculated. Zhang had been promised a major role in Jiang Jieshi's government, Thus, he began to integrate Manchuria politically and economically into the Nanjing Republic.

Jiang Jieshi saw Japan as a serious threat to the Chinese nation. However, in his mind, Japan was less dangerous than his other enemy, the Communists. He once remarked to an American reporter that "the Japanese are a disease of the skin, but the Communists are a disease of the heart."

The Communist Movement

After the Shanghai Massacre of April 1927, most of the Communist leaders had gone into hiding in the city. There they tried to revive the Communist movement in its traditional urban base among the working class. Shanghai was a rich recruiting ground for the party. It was a city of millionaires, paupers, prostitutes, gamblers, and adventurers. Some party members, however, fled to the hilly areas south of the Yangtze River. They were led by the young Communist organizer Mao Zedong (MOU zuh-DUNG) (Mao Tse-Tung).

Unlike most other leading members of the Communist Party, Mao was convinced that a Chinese revolution must be based on the poverty-stricken peasants in the countryside rather than the urban working class. Mao, the son of a prosperous peasant, had helped to organize a peasant movement in South China during the early 1920s. He had then served as an agitator in

STUDYING MAPS

The following questions and activities will help you guide students through their study of Map 27.3.

1. Locate French Indochina. What modern nations comprise French Indochina? *(Cambodia, Laos, Vietnam)*

2. Locate Manchuria. Why was it a logical site for Japanese militarism? *(located geographically close to Japan)*

3. Locate Jiangxi, Shanghai, Yan'an and Xian.

▲ *Jiang Jieshi was active in the 1911 revolution that ousted the Manchu dynasty. He served as president of China twice, from 1928 to 1931 and from 1943 to 1949.*

rural villages in his native province of Hunan during the Northern Expedition in the fall of 1926. At that time he wrote a famous report to party leaders suggesting that the Communist Party support peasant demands for a land revolution (see "You Are There: A Call for Revolt"). Mao's superiors refused. They feared that adopting such radical policies would destroy the alliance with the Nationalists.

After the spring of 1927, the Communist-Nationalist alliance ceased to exist. Jiang Jieshi tried to root the Communists out of their urban base in Shanghai and their rural base in Jiangxi province. He succeeded in the first task in 1931. Most party leaders were forced to flee Shanghai for Mao's base in South China.

Jiang Jieshi then turned his forces against Mao's stronghold in Jiangxi province. Jiang's forces far outnumbered Mao's, but the latter made effective use of guerrilla tactics. Four slogans by Mao explain his methods:

When the enemy advances, we retreat!
When the enemy halts and camps, we trouble them!
When the enemy tries to avoid battle, we attack!
When the enemy retreats, we pursue!

In 1933 Jiang's troops, using their superior military strength, surrounded the Communist base in Jiangxi. Mao's young People's Liberation Army (PLA), how-

▲ *Mao Zedong, on the left, led his weary troops on the Long March to their new headquarters at Yan'an, just south of the Gobi Desert. Why do you think the men wear padded jackets?*

ever, was able to break through the Nationalist lines. It then began its famous "Long March." Moving on foot through mountains, marshes, and deserts, Mao's army traveled almost six thousand miles to reach the last-surviving Communist base in the northwest of China. His troops had to fight all the way. Many froze or starved. One survivor remembered, "As the days went by, there was less and less to eat. After our grain was finished, we ate the horses, and then we lived on wild vegetables. When even the wild vegetables were finished, we ate our leather belts. After that we had to march on empty stomachs."

One year later, Mao's troops reached safety in the small provincial town of Yan'an (YAWN-an), two hun-

MORE ABOUT . . . *Mao's Communism*

When Marx and Engels envisioned a Communist society along the principles of "scientific socialism," they were exceedingly clear that a Communist society would develop only after capitalism had created an urban working class that would rebel and create a new socialist state, ultimately evolving into a communist society.

Mao Zedong believed that communism could be built on a rural-peasant foundation.

His belief was not shared by Stalin who distrusted the independent tendencies of the rural peasant. As Mao's military achievements brought him closer to power, his Soviet guides decided that rural communism was better than no communism at all. The fundamental differences between Chinese and Soviet communism eventually contributed to the split between China and the U.S.S.R.

USING PRIMARY SOURCES

What words and images does Mao use to convey his excitement about the peasant revolt? *(Images of storm, hurricane, irresistible force; "rise," "smash," "rush forward," "sweep," "hit out," "shattered to pieces," "swept into the dust")* Why would Mao's superiors have considered his ideas "radical"?

LEARNING FROM VISUALS

Have students study the propaganda techniques of the poster. Have them consider Mao's posture, what he's holding, where he's standing. What reaction to the poster did the Party want?

Answer to the caption question: This is a highly idealized portrait, showing Mao in a highly favorable light.

Answers to Critical Thinking Questions

1. the call for a mass peasant revolt against the ruling order
2. The peasants would be unstoppable, and their main targets would be the rich and landed.
3. Answers will vary, the central committee would be giving up its power.

YOU ARE THERE
A Call for Revolt

In the fall of 1926, the young Communist Mao Zedong submitted a report to the Chinese Communist Party Central Committee calling for a massive peasant revolt against the ruling order. The report shows his confidence that peasants could play an active role in a Chinese revolution.

Mao Zedong, Report to the Chinese Communist Party Central Committee

During my recent visit to Hunan I made a firsthand investigation of conditions in five countries. In a very short time, in China's Central, Southern, and Northern provinces, several hundred million peasants will rise like a mighty storm, like a hurricane, a force so swift and violent that no power, however great, will be able to hold it back. They will smash all the trammels [restraints] that bind them and rush forward along the road to liberation. They will sweep all the imperialists, warlords, corrupt officials, local tyrants, and evil gentry into their graves. Every revolutionary party and every revolutionary comrade will be put to the test, to be accepted or rejected as they decide. . . .

The main targets of attack by the peasants are the local tyrants, the evil gentry and the lawless landlords, but in passing they also hit out against patriarchal ideas and institutions, against the corrupt officials in the cities and against bad practices and customs in the rural areas. In force and momentum the attack is tempestuous; those who bow before it survive and those who resist perish. As a result, the privileges which the feudal landlords enjoyed for thousands of years are being shattered to pieces. Every bit of the dignity and prestige built up by the landlords is being swept into the dust. . . .

Every revolutionary comrade should know that the national revolution requires a great change in the countryside. The Revolution of 1911 did not bring about this change, hence its failure. This change is now taking place, and it is an important factor for the completion of the revolution. Every revolutionary comrade must support it.

▲ *This cultural revolution poster shows Mao Zedong as a young man standing high above the world. What do you think the mountaintop setting symbolizes? What caption would you write to accompany this poster?*

1. What did Mao Zedong report to the Chinese Communist Party Central Committee?

2. According to Mao, why should the central committee support the peasant revolt?

3. Why would the committee be opposed to supporting the revolt?

COOPERATIVE LEARNING ACTIVITY

Have student groups research *The Sayings of Chairman Mao* ("The Little Red Book") and locate several sayings that they may agree with, as well as several that they disagree with. End this activity with a class discussion of the power of the press, and of publications to sway public opinion and as a propaganda vehicle.

dred miles north of the modern-day city of Xian in the dusty hills of North China. In the course of the Long March, Mao Zedong had become the sole leader of the Chinese Communist Party. Of the ninety thousand troops who had embarked on the journey in October 1933, only nine thousand arrived in Yan'an a year later. To people who lived at the time, it must have seemed that the Communist threat to the Nanjing regime was over. To the Communists, however, there remained hope for the future.

The New China of Jiang Jieshi

In the meantime, Jiang Jieshi had also been trying to build a new nation. When the Nanjing Republic was set up in 1928, Jiang had publicly declared his commitment to Sun Yat-sen's Three Principles of the People (see Chapter 24). In a program announced in 1918, Sun had written about the all-important second stage of "political tutelage":

> China . . . needs a republican government just as a boy needs school. As a schoolboy must have good teachers and helpful friends, so the Chinese people, being for the first time under republican rule, must have a farsighted revolutionary government for their training. This calls for the period of political tutelage, which is a necessary transitional stage from monarchy to republicanism. Without this, disorder will be unavoidable.[3]

In keeping with Sun's program, Jiang announced a period of political tutelage to prepare the Chinese people for a final stage of constitutional government. In the meantime, the Nationalists would use their dictatorial power to carry out a land-reform program and the modernization of the urban industrial sector.

It would take more than plans on paper to create a new China, however. Years of neglect and civil war had severely weakened the political, economic, and social fabric of the nation. There were faint signs of an impending industrial revolution in the major urban centers. However, most of the people in the countryside were drained by warfare and civil strife. They were still very poor and overwhelmingly illiterate, and they made up 80 percent of China's population.

A westernized middle class had begun to form in the cities. It was there that the new Nanjing government found much of its support. However, the new westernized elite was concerned with the middle-class values of individual advancement and material accumulation. They had few links with the peasants in the countryside or with the **ricksha** (a small two-wheeled cart pulled by a person that carries usually one passenger) driver, "running in this world of suffering," in the words of a Chinese poet. Some critics dismissed Jiang Jieshi and his chief followers as "banana Chinese"—yellow (Chinese) on the outside but white (Western) on the inside.

Jiang Jieshi was aware of the problem of introducing foreign ideas into a population that was still culturally conservative. Thus, while building a modern industrial state, he tried to bring together modern Western ideas with traditional Confucian values of hard work, obedience, and integrity. Jiang and his U.S.–educated wife Mei (MAY)-ling Soong, set up a "New Life Movement." Its goal was to promote traditional Confucian social ethics, such as integrity, propriety, and righteousness. At the same time, it rejected the excessive individualism and material greed of Western capitalist values.

Unfortunately for Jiang Jieshi, Confucian ideas had been widely discredited when the traditional system had failed to provide answers to China's decline. Moreover, Jiang faced a host of other problems. The Nanjing government had total control over only a handful of provinces in the Yangtze valley. As we shall see in the next chapter, the Japanese also threatened to gain control of North China. The Great Depression was also having an ill effect on China's economy. With all of these problems, it was difficult for Jiang to make much progress with his program. He did have some success, however. He undertook a massive road-building project and repaired and extended much of the country's railroad system as well. He also established a national bank and improved the education system.

Fearing Communist influence, Jiang repressed all opposition and censored free expression. In so doing, he alienated many intellectuals and political moderates. Because his support came from the urban middle class and the rural landed gentry, he avoided programs leading to a redistribution of wealth. A land-reform program was enacted in 1930, but it had little effect.

ENRICHMENT ACTIVITY

Discuss with students Jiang Jieshi's efforts to rule and reform China. Then divide class into small groups to brainstorm and propose ways Jiang Jieshi might have successfully established a new government. Following small group work, assign students to write an essay in which they evaluate Jiang Jieshi's efforts to rule and to reform China.

USING PRIMARY SOURCES

What does Jiang mean by "political tutelage"? Why does he compare the Chinese to schoolboys? Was disorder avoided, as Jiang said it would be if China went through this "tutelage"? Why, or why not?

CRITICAL THINKING

Ask students to research and analyze Jiang's "New Life Movement." How exactly did it attempt to merge modern Western ideas with traditional Confucian values? What successes and failures did Jiang have? Why, ultimately, did his efforts fail?

CLASS DISCUSSION

Ask students to supply examples that support the following statement: "The new government . . . had little success in dealing with the deep-seated economic and social problems that affected China during the interwar years."

ASSESS

You can choose from a variety of assessments to evaluate your students' mastery of the objectives for this section, as stated on page 886. Possible assessments include:

1. Section Review Questions on page 890
2. Section 27–3 Quiz in your Teacher Resource materials
3. Reteaching Worksheets in your Teacher Resource materials
4. Self-Study software

Answers to
SECTION REVIEW

2. (a) small two-wheeled cart, pulled by person, carries one passenger
3. (a) Chiang Kai-shek; founded Chinese republic (b) warlord, controlled Manchuria; assassinated by the Japanese (c) Nationalist attack on Communists in 1927 (d) leader of the Chinese Communists (e) almost six thousand mile trip by Mao's army in 1933 to escape Nationalist forces (f) a movement that promoted traditional Chinese social values, rejected Western influences
4. (a) They both wanted to work against foreign rule in China. (b) consolidated his control over the Communist movement in China (c) It was in a state of disorganization that prevented many people from being able to support themselves. (d) attacked the Communists at Shanghai in 1927
5. (a) Answers will vary; Japanese could not change Chinese society or beliefs but Communists could. (b) Answers will vary; European powers faced depression and German expansionism

Jiang Jieshi's government had little more success in promoting industrial development. Between 1927 and 1937, industrial growth averaged only about 1 percent per year. Much of the national wealth was in the hands of the so-called four families, a group of senior officials and close subordinates of the ruling elite. Military expenses took up half the budget. Little was left for social or economic development.

The new government, then, had little success in dealing with the deep-seated economic and social problems that affected China during the interwar years. This was especially true during the Great Depression. China experienced internal disintegration and foreign pressure during this virtual collapse of the global economic order. In addition, militant political forces in Tokyo were determined to extend Japanese influence and power in an unstable China. These forces and the turmoil they unleashed will be examined in the next chapter.

SECTION REVIEW

1. **Locate:**
   (*a*) Wuhan,   (*b*) Shanghai,   (*c*) Hunan province

2. **Define:**
   (*a*) ricksha

3. **Identify:**
   (*a*) Jiang Jieshi,   (*b*) Zhang Xueliang,
   (*c*) Shanghai Massacre,   (*d*) Mao Zedong,
   (*e*) Long March,   (*f*) New Life Movement

4. **Recall:**
   (*a*) Why did the Nationalist and Communist Chinese form an alliance in 1923?
   (*b*) What was Mao able to accomplish during the Long March?
   (*c*) What impact did years of neglect and civil war have on China's economy during the 1920s and 1930s?
   (*d*) What actions did Jiang's fear of communism eventually cause him to take?

5. **Think Critically:**
   (*a*) What did Jiang Jieshi mean when he said,

"The Japanese are a disease of the skin but the Communists are a disease of the heart"?
(*b*) Why didn't the nations of Europe take stronger actions to protect their interests in China during the 1920s and 1930s?

NATIONALISM AND DICTATORSHIP IN LATIN AMERICA

The nations of Latin America played little role in World War I. However, that conflict did have an impact on Latin America, especially on its economy. The Great Depression also had a profound effect on both the economic and political life of the nations of Latin America.

The Latin American Economy and the United States

By the beginning of the twentieth century, the Latin American economy was based largely on the export of foodstuffs and raw materials. Many countries had only one or two products that they relied on for sale abroad. Argentina sent beef and wheat; Chile, nitrates and copper; Brazil, sugar; Central America, bananas; and Cuba and the Caribbean nations, sugar. At the end of the nineteenth and beginning of the twentieth centuries, these exports brought a certain level of prosperity, which varied from country to country. Large landowners in Argentina, for example, grew rich from the sale of beef and wheat abroad.

World War I brought an increased demand from the European states for Latin America's raw materials. For example, the export of Chilean nitrates, a mineral used to make explosives, tripled during the war. However, the war years also saw the beginning of a process in which European nations invested less and the U.S. invested more in Latin America.

Beginning in the 1920s, the United States began to replace Great Britain as the foremost investor in Latin

CLOSE

Ask students to discuss the positive and negative aspects of Jiang's government. What were his major accomplishments? What were his most serious deficiencies or mistakes?

RECOMMENDED READING

On Latin American economic developments, see B. Albert, *South America and the World Economy from Independence to 1930* (London, 1983). For a comprehensive exami-nation of the Mexican Revolution, see A. Knight, *The Mexican Revolution,* 2 vols. (Cambridge, 1986).

Map 27.4   Latin America, 1919–1939

by owning land, packing plants, and railroads there. U.S. companies also gained control of the copper-mining industry in Chile and Peru, as well as of the oil industry in Mexico, Peru, and Bolivia.

The United States has always cast a large shadow over Latin America. It had intervened militarily in Latin American affairs for years. This was especially

STUDYING MAPS

These questions will help you guide students through their study of Map 27.4.

1. What part of South America was colonized by non-Latin-speaking Europeans? *(Northeast coast)* What were these European nations? *(France, Netherlands, Britain)*

2. Look at the inset map of Central America. Where was British influence strong?

(British Honduras) What strategic country was under U.S. control? *(Panama)*

3. What South American nations are landlocked? *(Bolivia, Paraguay)*

4. Locate Sao Paulo and Buenos Aires. What nation is each in? *(Sao Paulo-Brazil; Buenos Aires-Argentina)* Why do you think these major cities are coastal? *(Answers will vary.)*

CRITICAL THINKING

Have students research and analyze the following statement: "It was not difficult for Latin American nationalists to show that profits from U.S. businesses were often used to keep ruthless dictators in power." Suggest that they focus on one or two countries, such as Venezuela.

CLASS DISCUSSION

Ask students to discuss Roosevelt's Good Neighbor policy.

ACROSS THE CURRICULUM

Economics. Ask interested students to study the export-import economy that made the Great Depression such a disaster for Latin America. How, exactly, did Latin American economies function under this system? How did they approach the development of new industries when they lacked the revenues to buy manufactured goods from other countries?

true in Central America and the Caribbean. Many Americans considered both regions their backyard and thus felt they were vital to U.S. security.

The control of many Latin American industries by U.S. investors fueled Latin American hostility toward the United States. A growing Nationalist consciousness led many Latin Americans to view the United States as an imperialist power. It was not difficult for Latin American Nationalists to show that profits from U.S. businesses were often used to keep ruthless dictators in power. In Venezuela, for example, there was no doubt that U.S. oil companies had a close relationship with the dictator Juan Vicente Gómez.

▲ *Chuquicatama, the world's largest copper mine, is now government owned. It is located near the Calama Desert in Chile. Why was the copper-mining industry so important to both U.S. investors and the Chilean government?*

The United States, however, also tried to change its relationship with Latin America. In 1933, Franklin Delano Roosevelt became president of the United States. Two years later, in 1935, the Roosevelt administration announced the Good Neighbor policy. This policy rejected the use of U.S. military force in Latin America. Adhering to his word, the president withdrew the last U.S. Marines from Haiti in 1936. For the first time in thirty years, there were no U.S. troops in Latin American countries.

In the 1930s, the Great Depression underscored a basic weakness in the Latin American economy. As we have seen, Latin Americans exported raw materials while importing the manufactured goods of Europe and the United States. At the beginning of the 1930s, Latin America was still dependent on this **export-import economy.**

The Great Depression, however, was a disaster for this kind of economy. The weakening of U.S. and European economies led to a decreased demand for Latin American foodstuffs and raw materials, especially coffee, sugar, metals, and meat. The total value of Latin American exports in 1930 was almost 50 percent below the figures for the years between 1925 and 1929. The countries that depended on the export of only one product, rather than multiple products, especially faced economic disaster.

The Great Depression had one positive effect on the Latin American economy, however. With a decline in exports, Latin American countries no longer had the revenues to buy manufactured goods. This led many Latin American countries to encourage the development of new industries that would produce the goods that were formerly imported. This process of industrial development was supposed to achieve greater economic independence for Latin America. Because of a shortage of capital in the private sector, governments often invested in the new industries. This led to government-run steel industries in Chile and Brazil, along with government-run oil industries in Argentina and Mexico.

So What ⁇

*If your students question the importance of the information on the **relationship between the United States and Latin America,** tell them that . . .*

American interventionism in Latin America has had mixed results. Often American actions have been rewarded with the "right" general in power, or the "right" political posture (i.e., pro-U.S.). In the long-term, however, most experts today agree that American intervention—whether overtly militaristic or covertly through the C.I.A.—has cost the country more than it has gained. Instead of becoming the leader of the Americas by example, American intervention has created resentment and suspicion of "big brother" to the North. As a result, the United States today has more diplomatic clout in Europe than it has in its own back yard.

The Move to Authoritarianism

Most Latin American countries had begun in the nineteenth century with republican forms of government. In reality, a relatively small group of church officials, military leaders, and large landowners dominated each country. This elite group controlled the masses of people, who were mostly poverty-stricken peasants. Military forces were often crucial in keeping these special-interest groups in power. Indeed, military leaders often took control of the government. Foreign investors, either British or U.S., also supported these oligarchies so that they could maintain order.

The trend toward authoritarianism was increased in the 1930s, largely because of the impact of the Great Depression. Domestic instability from economic crises led to military coups and the creation of military dictatorships at the beginning of the 1930s in Argentina, Brazil, Chile, Peru, Guatemala, El Salvador, and Honduras. These were not totalitarian states but traditional authoritarian regimes. We can examine this trend by looking at three countries: Argentina, Brazil, and Mexico. Together, they possessed over half of the land and wealth of Latin America.

Argentina

Argentina had grown wealthy from the export of beef and wheat. A conservative oligarchy of large landowners basically controlled the country. Their chief emphasis was on continuing Argentina's export economy, which, of course, was the source of their wealth.

The oligarchy, however, failed to realize the growing importance of industry and the cities. This group ignored the growing middle class, which reacted by forming the Radical Party in 1890. In 1916, its leader, Hipólito Irigoyen (ee-PAW-lee-TOE IR-i-GOE-YEN), was chosen to be president of Argentina. The Radical Party achieved little, however. It feared the industrial workers, who were using strikes to improve their conditions, and thus was drawn even closer to the large landowners. The Radical Party also grew more corrupt. By the end of the 1920s, it was no longer able to lead.

In 1930, the Argentine military stepped in. It overthrew President Irigoyen and reestablished the power of the large landowners. By this action, the military hoped to continue the old export economy and thus avoid the growth of working-class power that would come with more industrialization. During World War II, restless military officers formed a new organization, known as the Group of United Officers (GOU). They were unhappy with the civilian oligarchy and overthrew it in June 1943. Three years later, one GOU member, Juan Perón (pae-RONE), established sole power (see Chapter 31).

Brazil

Brazil also followed an authoritarian path. In 1889, the army overthrew the Brazilian monarchy and established a republic. The republic lasted until 1930. It was controlled chiefly by the landed elites, especially those who dominated the growing of coffee. By 1900, three-quarters of the world's coffee was grown in Brazil. As long as coffee prices remained high, the republican oligarchy was able to maintain its power. The oligarchy largely ignored the growth of urban industry and the working class that came with it.

The Great Depression devastated the coffee industry. Already by the end of 1929, coffee prices had hit a record low. In 1930, a military coup made Getúlio Vargas, a wealthy rancher, president of Brazil. Vargas ruled Brazil from 1930 to 1945. Early in his rule, Vargas appeased workers with an eight-hour day and a minimum wage. However, faced with strong opposition in 1937, Vargas established himself as a dictator.

Between 1938 and 1945, Vargas established his New State. This was basically an authoritarian, fascist-like state. It outlawed political parties and restricted civil rights. A secret police that used torture silenced Vargas's opponents. Vargas also pursued a policy of stimulating new industries. The government established the Brazilian steel industry and set up a company to explore for oil. By the end of World War II, Brazil was becoming Latin America's chief industrial power. In 1945, the army, fearing that Vargas might prolong his power illegally after calling for new elections, forced him to resign.

Mexico

Mexico was not an authoritarian state, but neither was it democratic. The Mexican Revolution at the beginning of the twentieth century had been the first significant effort in Latin America to overturn the system of large landed estates and increase the living standards of the masses (see Chapter 23). Out of the political revolution in Mexico emerged a relatively stable political order. It was democratic in form. However, the official political party of the Mexican Revolution, known as the Institutional Revolutionary Party, or PRI, controlled the major groups within Mexican society. Every six years, party bosses of the PRI chose the party's presidential candidate. That candidate was then dutifully elected by the people.

▲ *Getúlio Vargas was a rancher and a lawyer before he turned to politics. How does his background resemble that of recent U.S. presidents?*

A new wave of change began with Lázaro Cárdenas (CARD-un-AWS), who was president of Mexico from 1934 to 1940. He moved to fulfill some of the original goals of the revolution. His major step was to distribute forty-four million acres of land to landless Mexican peasants, an action that made Cárdenas enormously popular with the peasants.

Cárdenas also took a strong stand with the United States, especially over oil. By 1900, it became known that Mexico had enormous oil reserves. Over the next thirty years, foreign oil companies—some British but mostly U.S.—made large investments in Mexico. After a dispute with the foreign-owned oil companies over workers' wages, the Cárdenas government nationalized, or seized control of, the oil fields and property of the oil companies.

The U.S. oil companies were furious and asked President Roosevelt to intervene. He refused, reminding them of his promise in the Good Neighbor policy not to send U.S. troops into Latin America. Mexicans were delighted with Cárdenas, who was cheered as the president who had stood up to the United States. Eventually, the Mexican government did pay the owners for the property it had taken. It then set up PEMEX, a national oil company, to run the oil industry.

Culture in Latin America

Two major factors influenced cultural development in Latin America in the early twentieth century: (1) the influence of the modern artistic and literary movements in Europe that we examined in Chapters 22 and 26 and (2) the growth of nationalism. Symbolism and surrealism were very important in setting new directions in both art and literature. Especially in the cities, such as Buenos Aires in Argentina and Sao Paulo in Brazil, wealthy elites expressed great interest in the work of avant-garde artists. Others became interested in following European models. Latin American artists

MORE ABOUT . . . *Authoritarianism in Latin America*

In Latin America, Spanish colonization left two complementary characteristics that would hinder the road to democracy. One is the Spanish tendency toward personalism over institutionalism: the person, the leader, becomes more important than the system. So, "my leader" continues to be my leader even after he has set aside the constitution. The second legacy from colonial Spain is the preference for a "strong man" with the right answers, rather than the more delicate interplay of opposing ideas, collegiality, and compromise. This second characteristic has been called *caciquismo*—after "Cacique", or Indian chief. Often in Latin American history these two tendencies have combined to create dictators who have ruled with the approval of a sufficient sector of the population to maintain themselves in power up to 30 years.

OUR ARTISTIC HERITAGE
The Mural Art of Mexico

Diego Rivera's mural conveys the complexity and variety of Aztec civilization. When the Spanish arrived, they were amazed at the variety of foods and merchandise for sale in the marketplace in Tenochtitlán. What do you think is symbolized by the figure sitting in the covered chair?

The national art that was created in Mexico in the 1920s and 1930s was also a public art. The Mexican government provided funds for the painting of murals on the walls of public buildings, including schools and government offices. Two artists were especially prominent in the development of Mexico's mural art: Diego Rivera and José Clemente Orozco.

Diego Rivera had studied in Europe, where he was especially influenced by fresco painting in Italy. Upon his return to Mexico, he developed a monumental style that filled wall after wall with murals. Rivera sought to create a national art that would serve two purposes. One was to portray Mexico's past and native traditions. He portrayed Aztec legends, as well as Mexican festivals and folk customs.

Rivera also had a political and social message in his national art. His second purpose was to make the masses aware of the new Mexican political order. Rivera did not want people to forget the Mexican Revolution that had overthrown the large landowners and the foreign interests that supported them. Indeed, his works were not for a

(continued)

LEARNING FROM VISUALS

Answer to the caption question: Seated in the chair is Montezuma, the Aztec emperor. His raised position is intended to convey his authority and power.

CLASS DISCUSSION

Have students examine in detail the murals done by Rivera and Orozco. What themes do they detect in the work of these two painters?

ACROSS THE CURRICULUM

Art. Ask students to bring in examples of the work of Diego Rivera. Have them demonstrate how Rivera both portrayed Mexican traditions and celebrated the Mexican Revolution and the new political order.

Answers to Critical Thinking Questions

1. The art portrayed national events and it was displayed publicly for all to enjoy and learn from.
2. Students might mention Mount Rushmore, statues that depict historic or national events, the war memorials, etc.

SPECIAL NEEDS: *Visual/Auditory/Tactile*

Have students work in groups with each group choosing a Latin American country. Suggested countries are: Argentina, Bolivia, Brazil, Chile, Cuba, Mexico and Peru. Have each group prepare a bulletin board display that includes pictures, maps, drawings of life and culture in each respective country. Foods, traditional dress, housing, arts, crafts, musical instruments, and other products associated with each country may be displayed. Have each group make a presentation of their display to the class. In addition to the bulletin board, the groups may enhance their presentation by bringing to class recordings of Latin American music, particularly the traditional folkloric music, examples of musical instruments that originated in or are associated with the Latin American countries, fruits, foods, or other products from Latin America.

ASSESS

You can choose from a variety of assessments to evaluate your students' mastery of the objectives for this section, as stated on page 891. Possible assessments include:

1. Section Review Questions on this page
2. Section 27–4 Quiz in your Teacher Resource materials
3. Reteaching Worksheets in your Teacher Resource materials
4. Self-Study software

ALTERNATIVE ASSESSMENT

Assign students an essay in which they evaluate the impact of foreign investors on the course of twentieth-century Latin American history.

Answers to SECTION REVIEW

2. (a) small countries dependent on large, wealthy nations
   (b) exporting raw materials while importing manufactured goods
3. (a) policy warning other countries against use of military forces in Latin America
   (b) leader of the Radical Party in Argentina
   (c) sole leader of Argentina in 1946
   (d) president, dictator of Brazil
   (e) president of Mexico
   (f) national oil company of Mexico
4. (a) The economy is too vulnerable to price fluctuations.

OUR ARTISTIC HERITAGE
The Mural Art of Mexico, continued

Orozco's mural of Miguel Hidalgo at the Government Palace in Guadalajara, Mexico pays homage to the priest who led the 1810 Mexican uprising against the Spanish. What do you think the lighted torch represents?

cultivated audience but for the masses of people, many of whom could not even read. His wall paintings can be found in such diverse places as the Ministry of Education, the Chapel of the Agri-culture School at Chapingo, and the Social Security Hospital.

Another leader in the development of Mexican mural art was José Clemente Orozco. Orozco was especially concerned with the cruelty of human beings, as well as their suffering as individuals. His early works showed the brutality imposed on the common people, especially the Indians, by their Spanish masters. In his later work, he became more intrigued with Mexico's native past, especially Aztec religious practices and legends. His murals, like those of Rivera, appeared in diverse places, including the Industrial School at Orizaba, the National Preparatory School, and the Orphanage at Guadalajara.

1. Why would Mexican mural art of the 1920s and 1930s be considered a national art and a public art?

2. Can you think of any examples of art in the United States that might be considered national and public?

---

who went abroad brought back modern techniques, which they often adapted to their own native roots.

In the 1900s, people in the various countries of Latin America began to seek their national essence. By the 1920s, this trend had led intellectuals to a discovery of popular traditions and ethnic lore. For the rest of the twentieth century, the quest for national identity would dominate cultural life in Latin America. Writers and artists took on new importance in this quest. They became the people who helped to define the new national culture that was in the making. The attempt

to create a national art that would combine both new techniques and old traditions was especially evident in the mural art of Mexico (see "Our Artistic Heritage: The Mural Art of Mexico").

❈ SECTION REVIEW ❈

1. **Locate:**
   (*a*) Central America,   (*b*) Cuba

CNN® WORLD HISTORY UPDATES

You can update your coverage of World History topics, as well as spark lively classroom discussion and deeper understanding, by using the **CNN World History Updates.**

For assistance in using and incorporating the **CNN World History Updates** into your classroom presentations, see the *Classroom Guide.*

2. Define:
(*a*) banana republics,   (*b*) export-import economy

3. Identify:
(*a*) Good Neighbor policy,   (*b*) Hipólito Irigoyen,
(*c*) Juan Perón,   (*d*) Getúlio Vargas,   (*e*) Lázaro
Cárdenas,   (*f*) PEMEX

4. Recall:
(*a*) Why is having only a few types of products for
export a danger to a nation's economy?
(*b*) Why did Americans come to own many Latin
American businesses?
(*c*) How did the Great Depression help some Latin
American businesses?
(*d*) How did Brazil encourage its industrial growth
in the 1920s and 1930s?
(*e*) What quest dominated Latin American intellectual and artistic movements after 1920?

5. Think Critically: Why is it unlikely that there
will be rapid progress toward a representative form
of government in nations that have only one
strong political party? Use the Mexican experience
as an example.

Conclusion

The turmoil brought by World War I seemed to open
the door to upheaval throughout the world. In the Middle East, the decline and fall of the Ottoman Empire
led, first of all, to the creation of a new, secular Turkish
Republic. Arab states, too, emerged with the collapse of
Ottoman power, but they were only given mandate status under Great Britain and France. A new state, Saudi
Arabia, emerged in the Arabian peninsula. Palestine
became a source of tension between newly-arrived Jewish settlers and long-time Muslim Palestinians.

Africa and Asia also witnessed movements for
national independence. In Africa these movements
were led by native Africans who were educated in
Europe and the United States. Mohandas Gandhi and
his campaign of civil disobedience played a crucial role

in India's bid to be free of British rule. Communist
movements also began to emerge in Asian societies as
instruments for the overthrow of Western imperialism.
Japan followed its own path to an authoritarian and
militaristic system.

Between 1919 and 1939, China experienced a dramatic struggle to establish a modern nation. Two
forces—the Nationalists and the Communists—first
cooperated and then fought for control of China. The
Nationalists emerged supreme but found it difficult to
control all of China and bring about the kind of modernization they wanted. Japanese interference in Chinese affairs complicated these events.

During the interwar years, the nations of Latin
America faced economic problems because of their
dependence on the export of foodstuffs and raw materials. U.S. investments in Latin America especially led
to hostility against the powerful neighbor to the north.
The Great Depression had two important effects on
Latin Americans. First, it forced them to begin the
development of new industries. Second, it led to military dictatorships and authoritarian governments.

By weakening their own civilization on the battlegrounds of Europe in World War I, Europeans had indirectly helped the subject peoples of the vast colonial
empires to begin their movements for national independence. Once Europeans had again weakened themselves in the even more destructive conflict of the Second World War, the hopes for national freedom could
at last be realized. It is to that devastating world conflict that we now turn.

Notes

1. Quoted in Martin Gilbert, *The First World War* (New York, 1994), p. 213.
2. Quoted in Nicholas Rowland Clifford, *Spoilt Children of Empire: Westerners in Shanghai and the Chinese Revolution of the 1920s* (Hanover, N.H., 1991), p. 93.
3. Quoted in William Theodore de Bary et al., eds., *Sources of Chinese Tradition* (New York, 1963), p. 783.

(b) American investors funded production enter-prises.
(c) People in Latin Amer-ica could not afford to buy as many imported goods.
(d) Steel and oil busi-nesses were started with government funds.
(e) national identity
5. Answers will vary; the Institutional Revolutionary Party dominates Mexican government and politics.

CLOSE

Ask students to offer evi-dence that supports the fol-lowing statement: "The United States has always cast a large shadow over Latin America."

SPANISH SUPPORT

The *Conclusion* has been translated into Spanish for your Spanish-speaking stu-dents. Included with this translation (in your Teacher Resource Box) are Section Key Points, which consist of one or two sentences sum-marizing each section in the chapter. These Key Points have also been translated into Spanish.

TIME LINE

As students conclude the chapter, you may want to refer them to the chapter time line in the *Study Guide*. The time line will help them put key dates in perspective. Supporting questions and activities are also provided.

SPECIAL NEEDS: *Visual*

Have students develop a time line identify-ing main events discussed in the chapter. The time line should begin in the year 1918 and end in 1939. The following events should be identified: 1) the end of World War I; 2) Russian revolution (1917); 3) for-mation of the Comintern (1919); 4) the Chi-nese Communist Party is founded (1919); 5) the end of the Ottoman Empire (1923);

6) women receive the right to vote in Turkey (1934); 7) Reza Khan replaces Qajar dynasty in Persia (1925); 8) Kingdom of Saudi Arabia established (1932); 9) Vargas dictatorship established in Brazil (1937). Provide a world map or refer students to the world map in their texts and have the students study the map and identify the countries noted on their time lines.

USING KEY TERMS

1. Mahatma
2. ricksha
3. Pan-Africanism
4. genocide
5. westernization
6. ethnic cleansing
7. export-import economy
8. secular state
9. banana republics
10. fez

REVIEWING THE FACTS

1. corrupt, making it difficult to govern the lands
2. worked to unite Arab tribes into a single nation
3. It was a British statement that a Jewish State should be created in Palestine.
4. Foreign rule was destroying the traditional culture of native people in Africa.
5. passed the Government of India Act to give people a greater voice in the government
6. It was an international organization dedicated to the spread of communism.
7. attacks by Jiang Jieshi's Nationalist Chinese army
8. He repressed all opposition to his rule and imposed censorship.
9. to improve its relations by promising not to use military force against them
10. The countries are dominated by one political party, and voters have had no choice in their elections.
11. They have nationalized foreign businesses by either buying or taking properties.

THINKING CRITICALLY

1. There is no way for power to be passed to another person or group when leader is old or ill.
2. The internal combustion engine increased demand for petroleum and interest in oil of the Middle East.
3. Answers will vary; Africans served in European armies,

898

CHAPTER 27 REVIEW

USING KEY TERMS

1. A name meaning "great soul" given by his followers to Mohandas Gandhi was _____.
2. A _____ driver pulls a small two-wheel cart.
3. _____ was a movement stressing unity of all Africans.
4. A policy of killing people of a particular ethnic or racial group is called _____.
5. Asian intellectuals identified _____ with the capitalist democratic civilization in western Europe and the United States.
6. Serbian forces in the recent war in Bosnia followed a policy called _____ when they tried to eliminate Muslims from the land.
7. Latin Americans depended on an _____, exporting raw materials while importing manufactured goods.
8. The goal of Ataturk was to break the power of Islamic religion and turn Turkey into a _____.
9. Many central American states became _____ when U.S. companies gained control of export industries.
10. A _____ is a brimless cap worn by Turkish Muslims.

REVIEWING THE FACTS

1. Why was the Ottoman Empire called the "sick man of Europe"?
2. What was the objective of the Wahhabi Movement?
3. Why were many Arabs opposed to the intent of the Balfour Declaration?
4. What message did Jomo Kenyatta use as the basic theme for his book, *Facing Mount Kenya*?
5. What did the British do to try to make Indian people less opposed to their colonial government in 1919?
6. What was the purpose of the Comintern?

7. What happened to cause the Chinese communists to undertake the Long March in 1933?
8. What actions by Jiang Jieshi cost him the support of many intellectuals and political moderates during the 1920s?
9. What did the United States hope to accomplish through its Good Neighbor Policy toward Latin America?
10. Why do people in some apparently democratic Latin American nations have little voice in their country's government?
11. What action has been taken by several Latin American nations to try to eliminate foreign influence from their economies?

THINKING CRITICALLY

1. Why is any government that is dominated by only one person likely to experience decline over time?
2. Why did technological changes tend to also change the relative importance of lands in the Middle East?
3. What events increased opposition to colonial rule in Africa and India after World War I?
4. Why was non-violent opposition to colonial rule often an effective tool for colonies to gain independence?
5. How was opposition to the military's policy of foreign expansion put down in Japan in the 1930s?
6. What is likely to happen to any government that chooses leaders based on political or family relationships instead of according to their qualifications to do a job? What does this have to do with problems experienced by the Nationalist Chinese government of Jiang Jieshi?
7. Why would some Latin American people be more upset by American firms buying their land and businesses than they were by European colonial domination of their governments?
8. Why did the Great Depression cause many Latin American countries to take steps to improve their

---

had gained educations, and became aware of the rights enjoyed by people in other parts of the world.

4. Trying people is time consuming and costly; the government can look ridiculous and ineffective in the eyes of other people.
5. The Black Dragon Society was formed to intimidate people who opposed.
6. Leaders chosen this way, as in China, usually do a poor job.

7. European colonial powers generally left people alone in their daily lives and businesses, while American firms would buy businesses, pay low wages, prevent advancement, and control daily lives.
8. Many Latin Americans could not afford to buy imported goods which increased demand for locally produced products and reduced reliance of foreign economic powers.

economic systems and gain more freedom from foreign economic dominance?

APPLYING SOCIAL STUDIES SKILLS

1. **Geography:** Identify important trade routes in the 1920s and 1930s by drawing them on a map of the world. On the same map circle nations that worked to gain their independence from colonial powers during this time. Does there appear to be any relationship between being on an important trade route and working to gain national independence?

2. **Government:** Although many national groups have been willing to work together to end colonial rule they were less willing to work together to create new governments. What reasons have contributed to this problem?

3. **Sociology:** What social forces may have caused colonial powers to try to maintain their colonies even after they clearly cost more than they were worth?

4. **Economics:** Why were native boycotts of products produced by colonial powers effective tools in many nations' efforts to gain independence?

5. **Geography:** Consider a map of North and South America. Identify geographic reasons for the desire of the United States to dominate Latin America's economic, political, and military conditions.

MAKING TIME AND PLACE CONNECTIONS

1. What relationships can you see between the desire of African nations to gain their independence from colonial powers and the desire of African Americans to achieve equality in the United States?

2. Why are policies of genocide like that of the Turks against the Armenians or the Nazis against the Jews not likely to achieve a government's objectives in the long run?

3. Compare and contrast the Black Dragon Society in Japan with neo-Nazi right wing militia groups in the United States or skin heads in Germany.

4. Why do leaders who seek great personal power, like Jiang Jieshi, Mao Zedong, Stalin, Hitler, or even Richard Nixon, often become paranoid and convinced that someone is out to get them?

5. What similarities and differences can you see between the efforts of the American colonies to gain independence from England in 1776 and India's desire for independence in the 1930s?

BECOMING AN HISTORIAN

1. **Economics as a Key to History:** Use a map of the world to identify important raw material sources that existed in the Middle East, Africa, India, and the Far East over which European colonial powers wanted to maintain their control.

2. **Recognizing and Understanding Bias:** Reread and evaluate the quotation from Sun Yat-sen's writings on page 889. What does the quotation apparently say and what does it really mean? How is there a self-serving bias in the statement from Sun Yat-sen's point of view?

3. **Fact versus Opinion:** When Mao Zedong called for a revolt against the ruling order in China in 1926 he stated,

The main targets of attack by the peasants are the local tyrants, the evil gentry and the lawless landlords, but in passing they also hit out against patriarchal ideas and institutions, against the corrupt officials in the cities and against bad practices and customs in the rural areas.

Underline each word in this quotation that is based on opinion rather than fact. What does this tell you about much of political propaganda?

899

social, and economic system of the United States.

2. Genocide is likely to create an international uproar and governmental opposition from many nations, and those who oppose such policies and efforts to sustain such a policy will impact the government's ability to rule effectively.

3. Answers will vary; the Black Dragon Society included members of the Japanese military and apparently had the sanction of the Japanese government, while the other groups are outside of the political mainstream.

4. They are prone to believe that other people also covet power and often see plots to take their power where none exist.

5. Answers will vary; the American colonies resorted to violence and took their freedom through force, and the Indians gained their freedom through peaceful means.

BECOMING AN HISTORIAN

1. Maps will vary; indicate and explain the raw materials supplied to colonial powers from occupied lands.

2. Answers will vary; Sun Yat-sen did not believe the Chinese people were ready to rule themselves and he had to provide them with leadership. It justified the totalitarian rule he established.

3. Most of the quotation should be identified; shows political propaganda is often based on opinions and half-truths intended to gain the support of people without considering logic or meaning.

APPLYING SOCIAL STUDIES SKILLS

1. Answers will vary; indicate location and importance of passages including the Suez and Panama Canals, the straits of Gilbraltar and Malacca, the Dardanelles, and the English Channel.

2. Answers will vary; it is easier to oppose and eliminate a government than to build and operate a government.

3. People and nations value their status more than they value economic power or profit, and once they established control, they maintained power even when the cost far exceeded the benefit.

4. Boycotting products could remove the colonial power's source of income.

5. Answers will vary; the close proximity of Latin America makes these nations a prime market for American products; the United States would not want any hostile power to establish a power base in Latin America.

MAKING TIME AND PLACE CONNECTIONS

1. Answers will vary; the desire these groups have to their own sense of identity and equality either in their own nations or within the political,

28 PLANNING GUIDE

SECTION	KEY TOPICS	PRIMARY SOURCES	ASSESSMENT
1 The Path to War pages 901–908	◆ Germany prepares for war ◆ Japan prepares for war		◆ Section Review, page 908 ◆ Section Quiz 28–1, TRB
2 The Course of World War II pages 908–918	◆ World War II in Europe ◆ War in the Far East ◆ The turning point in the war ◆ The war's end	◆ A German soldier's description of the Battle of Stalingrad, page 915	◆ Section Review, page 918 ◆ Section Quiz 28–2, TRB
3 The New Order pages 918–925	◆ The new order in Europe ◆ The Holocaust ◆ The new order in Asia	◆ A description of SS death squad activities, page 919 ◆ A description of activities at Auschwitz-Birkenau death camp, page 922 ◆ A description of crematoriums at Auschwitz-Birkenau, page 923	◆ Section Review, page 925 ◆ Section Quiz 28–3, TRB
4 The Home Front and the Aftermath of the War pages 926–936	◆ Mobilization for the war ◆ Civilians in the front line of war ◆ The beginnings of the Cold War		◆ Section Review, page 936 ◆ Section Quiz 28–4, TRB

THE CRISIS DEEPENS:
WORLD WAR II (1939 TO 1945)

REPRODUCIBLE ACTIVITIES

Historical Maps

Charts and Graphs

Critical Thinking

Cooperative Learning

Vocabulary

Guided Reading

Reteaching

Enrichment

Performance Assessment

Spanish Key Points and Chapter Summaries

Spanish Vocabulary

Spanish Guided Reading

MULTIMEDIA SUPPORT

TRANSPARENCIES
- *World History* Color Transparency Package
- Fine Art Color Transparency Package

VIDEO
- *World History* Video Library
- CNN. Annual Video Update

LASERDISC
- *Sights and Sounds of History*

AUDIO
- *Listening to Literature* audiotape (English and Spanish)
- *History of Music* CD

SOFTWARE
- WESTEST™
- Student Review

CD-ROM
- *The Journey of Civilization*
- *World History*

INTERNET
- Internet Activities

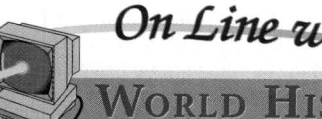
On Line with WORLD HISTORY

Access West's history web site at
http://history.swpco.com
You'll find activities and web sites related to specific topics and chapters in *World History: The Human Odyssey*. Also look for references to helpful web sites at appropriate places throughout this teacher edition.

LESSON PLANNING

You will find detailed daily lesson plans for both traditional class scheduling and **block scheduling** in your Teacher Resource Box.

Not Enough Time?

If you do not have the four or five days recommended to teach this chapter, you may want to focus on the following sections and activities:

- Have students skim the chapter to answer the "Questions to Guide Your Reading" on page 901. Discuss their answers, then read the "Conclusion" on page 937.
- Do a more in-depth reading of the German and Japanese preparation for war on pages 901–907, the final years of the war on pages 914–917, the Holocaust on pages 919–925, and the start of the Cold War on pages 932–936. Conclude with a discussion of the impact World War II had on civilian populations.

THE CRISIS DEEPENS:

BUILDING ON CHAPTER 27

To "set the scene" for the study of Chapter 28, use the following questions and activities.

◆ Have students create a time line of major nationalistic events in the Middle East, Africa, China, and Latin America.

◆ List comparisons between modernization of Turkey and Iran.

◆ Explain how "the problem of Palestine" affected Arab nationalism.

◆ Summarize independence movements in Africa.

◆ Mention important events in India's fight for independence.

◆ Tell how the rise of militarism in Japan differed from its rise in Europe.

◆ Summarize the struggle in China between Nationalists and Communists.

◆ Explain how the depression affected Latin America.

USING THE OPENING STORY

Depending on the ability levels of your students, select from the following questions and activities to reinforce the reading of the opening story.

◆ Why would Hitler regard democracy as a "cancer"?

◆ Could Hitler have come to power in Germany in economic boom times?

◆ How does technology impact total war? How does this concept change over time?

On February 3, 1933, only four days after he had been appointed chancellor of Germany, Adolf Hitler met secretly with Germany's leading generals. He revealed to them his desire to remove the "cancer of democracy," create a new authoritarian leadership, and forge a new domestic unity. All Germans would need to realize that "only a struggle can save us and that everything else must be subordinated to this idea." The youth especially would have to be trained and their wills strengthened "to fight with all means." Because Germany's living space was too small for its people, above all, Hitler said, Germany must rearm and prepare for "the conquest of new living space in the east and its ruthless Germanization."

Even before he had consolidated his power, Hitler had a clear vision of his goals. Reaching these goals meant another European war. World War II was clearly Hitler's war. Although other countries may have helped to make the war possible by not resisting Hitler's Germany earlier, when it was not so strong, it was Nazi Germany's actions that made World War II inevitable.

World War II was more than just Hitler's war, however. World War II consisted of two conflicts. One arose from the ambitions of Germany in Europe. The other arose from the ambitions of Japan in Asia. By 1941, with the involvement of the United States in both conflicts, the two had merged into one global war.

Although World War I has been described as a total war, World War II was even more so. It was fought on a scale unprecedented in history. The entire populations of warring countries were involved. Some were soldiers. Some were workers in wartime industries. Some were innocent civilians who suffered invasion, occupation, and aerial bombing. Some were victims of persecution and mass extermination. The world had never seen such widespread human-made death and destruction.

▲ *High-impact posters such as this helped to glorify the determination and courage needed to fight World War II.*

ADDITIONAL RESOURCES

BOOKS FOR STUDENTS
Diary of a Young Girl by Anne Frank. Doubleday.
Hiroshima by John Hersey. Knopf.

VIDEOS/FILMS
D-Day to Berlin (George Stevens), Social Studies Skills Service, (800) 421-4262
Hiroshima: Why the Bomb Was Dropped (Peter Jennings), Social Studies Skills Service, (800) 421-4262

Why We Fight (Frank Capra, 1942) (MPI Home Video), Social Studies Skills Service, (800) 421-4262

CD-ROMs
World War II: Global Conflict (Mentarom) (SSSS) or Educorp Direct (800) 843-9497
The Holocaust: The Complete Maus: A Survivor's Tale (Voyager) (SSSS) or Educorp Direct (800) 843-9497

WORLD WAR II

(1939 TO 1945)

CRISIS OF THE TWENTIETH CENTURY

	WORLD WAR II
	1939 1945
1910	1945

QUESTIONS TO GUIDE YOUR READING

1. What were the steps taken by Nazi Germany from 1933 to 1939 that led to war?

2. What were the steps taken by Japan from 1931 to 1939 that led to war?

3. What were the early successes of the Germans and the Japanese, from 1939 to 1941? How do you account for these successes?

4. What were the major events in the last years of World War II?

5. What kinds of New Order did Germany and Japan try to establish in Europe and Asia?

6. What was the Final Solution, and how did the Nazis attempt to carry it out?

7. How did the attempt to arrive at a peace settlement after World War II lead to the beginnings of a new conflict, known as the Cold War?

OUTLINE

1. THE PATH TO WAR
2. THE COURSE OF WORLD WAR II
3. THE NEW ORDER
4. THE HOME FRONT AND THE AFTERMATH OF THE WAR

THE PATH TO WAR

Only twenty years after the war to end all wars, the world plunged back into the nightmare of total war. The efforts to end war in the 1920s—the League of Nations, the attempts at disarmament, the pacts and treaties—all proved meaningless in view of the growth of Nazi Germany and the rise of Japan.

The German Path to War

World War II in Europe had its beginnings in the ideas of Adolf Hitler. He believed that only the Aryans were capable of building a great civilization. Hitler also believed that the Germans (the supreme group of Aryans) were threatened from the east by a large mass of inferior peoples, the Slavs, who had learned to use German weapons and technology. Germany needed more land to support a larger population and be a great power. Already in the 1920s, in the second volume of *Mein Kampf*, Hitler had stated where a Nazi regime would find this land: "And so we National Socialists . . . take up where we broke off six hundred years ago. We stop the endless German movement to the south and west, and turn our gaze toward the land in the east.

901

FOCUS ON THEMES

Listed below are brief summaries of how the content in this chapter supports the text's key themes.

Politics and History The war caused the destruction of governments, created political chaos, and led to the emergence of two new superpowers—the United States and the Soviet Union.

The Role of Ideas Adolf Hitler's idea of Aryan racial domination not only brought about World War II in Europe but also led to the Holocaust.

Economics and History Germany and Japan wanted to obtain the material resources that would enable them to be powerful states. World War II led to economic chaos for much of the world.

Social Life The mass civilian destruction in World War II led to the disintegration of the social fabric of many countries. Homeless refugees became a common sight.

The Role of Individuals Adolf Hitler, Joseph Stalin, Franklin Delano Roosevelt, and Winston Churchill were among the leaders who made decisions that affected the lives of hundreds of millions of people.

The Impact of Science and Technology New weapons of mass destruction made World War II the most destructive war in history. New bombers, as well as new bombs (such as the atomic bomb), guaranteed that war had become as deadly for all.

Focus

Objectives

After completing this section, students should be able to

1. describe events in Germany that led to World War II
2. describe events in the Far East that led to Japan's involvement in World War II

Focus Activity

Help students understand that government propaganda and control over what people are able to learn may cause them to support policies that they would normally oppose. Discuss why it is significant that Germany controlled its press before World War I. What information would people of the Soviet Union have had access to? How can informed decisions be made with no information?

. . . If we speak of soil in Europe today, we can primarily have in mind only Russia and her vassal border states."[1]

Once Russia had been conquered, according to Hitler, its land could be resettled by German peasants. The Slavic peoples could be used as slave labor to build the **Aryan racial state** that would dominate Europe for a thousand years. Hitler's conclusion was clear. Germany must prepare for its inevitable war with the Soviet Union. Hitler's ideas were by no means secret. He had spelled them out in *Mein Kampf,* a book readily available to anyone who wished to read it.

When Hitler became chancellor of Germany on January 30, 1933, Germany's situation in Europe seemed weak. The Treaty of Versailles had created a demilitarized zone on Germany's western border that would allow the French to move into the heavily industrialized parts of Germany in the event of war. To Germany's east, the smaller states, such as Poland and Czechoslovakia, had defensive treaties with France. The Treaty of Versailles had also limited Germany's army to 100,000 troops, with no air force and only a small navy.

Hitler posed as a man of peace in his public speeches. He stressed that Germany wished only to revise the unfair provisions of the Treaty of Versailles by peaceful means. Germany, he said, only wanted its rightful place among the European states. On March 9, 1935, Hitler announced the creation of a new air force. One week later, he began a military draft that would expand Germany's army from 100,000 to 550,000 troops. These steps were a direct violation of the Treaty of Versailles. France, Great Britain, and Italy condemned Germany's action and warned against future aggressive steps. Distracted by their own internal problems caused by the Great Depression, however, they did nothing further.

Hitler by now was convinced that the Western states had no intention of using force to maintain the Treaty of Versailles. Hence, on March 7, 1936, Hitler sent German troops into the demilitarized Rhineland. According to the Treaty of Versailles, France had the right to use force against any violation of the demilitarized Rhineland. However, France would not act without British support. Great Britain viewed the occupation of German territory by German troops as another reasonable action by a dissatisfied power. The *London Times* noted that the Germans were only "going into their own back garden." Great Britain was starting a policy of **appeasement.** This policy was based on the belief that if European states satisfied the reasonable demands of dissatisfied powers, the latter would be content, and stability and peace would be achieved in Europe. The British appeasement policy was grounded in large part upon Britain's desire to avoid another war.

Meanwhile, Hitler gained new allies. Benito Mussolini had long dreamed of creating a new Roman Empire in the Mediterranean, and in October 1935, Fascist Italy invaded Ethiopia. Angered by French and British opposition to his invasion, Mussolini welcomed Hitler's support. He began to draw closer to the German dictator he had once called a buffoon. In 1936 both Germany and Italy sent troops to Spain to help General Francisco Franco in the Spanish Civil War. This action brought Italy and Germany closer together. In October 1936, Mussolini and Hitler made an agreement that recognized their common political and economic interests. Only one month later, Mussolini spoke publicly of the new alliance between Italy and Germany, known as the Rome-Berlin Axis. Also in November, Germany and Japan (the rising military power in the Far East) signed the Anti-Comintern Pact, promising to maintain a common front against communism.

By the end of 1936, Hitler and Nazi Germany had achieved a diplomatic revolution in Europe. The Treaty of Versailles had been virtually scrapped. Germany was once more a "World Power," as Hitler proclaimed. Hitler was convinced that neither France nor Great Britain would provide much opposition to his plans. In 1938, he decided to move to achieve one of his longtime goals: **Anschluss** (union) with Austria, his native land.

By threatening Austria with invasion, Hitler forced the Austrian chancellor to put Austrian Nazis in charge of the government. The new government promptly invited German troops to enter Austria and "help" in maintaining law and order. One day later, on March 13, 1938, after his triumphal return to his native land, Hitler annexed Austria to Germany.

CNN World History Updates

You can update your coverage of World History topics, as well as spark lively classroom discussion and deeper understanding, by using the **CNN World History Updates.**

For assistance in using and incorporating the **CNN World History Updates** into your classroom presentations, see the *Classroom Guide.*

Map 28.1   Changes in Central Europe, 1936–1939

Germany

	Reoccupied Rhineland, March 1936
	Annexed Austria, March 1938
	Annexed Sudetenland, October 1938
	Occupied Bohemia and Moravia, March 1939
	Annexed Memel, March 1939

Italy

	Annexed Albania, April 1939

Poland and Hungary

	Annexed Czech territory, 1938 and 1939
( )	Former independent nations: Albania, Austria, and Czechoslovakia

The annexation of Austria improved Germany's strategic position in central Europe and put Germany in position for Hitler's next objective—the destruction of Czechoslovakia. This goal might have seemed unrealistic. Democratic Czechoslovakia, after all, was quite prepared to defend itself. Furthermore, it was well supported by pacts with France and Soviet Russia. Hitler believed, however, that France and Britain would not use force to defend Czechoslovakia.

Hitler was right again. On September 15, 1938, he demanded the cession to Germany of the Sudetenland (soo-DATE-un-LAND), an area in northwestern

STUDYING MAPS

The following questions will help you guide students through their study of Map 28.1.

1. Approximately how much territory did Germany annex between 1936 and 1939, as compared to its size in 1935? *(Students should estimate that Germany increased its size by one-third to one-fourth of its 1935 area.)*

2. Why would supplying raw materials be a problem for Germany in World War II? *(There were few all-year around ports within Germany's territories.)*

3. What territories did Germany annex and occupy in 1938 and 1939? *(Austria, Bohemia, Moravia, and Memel.)*

COMPARING TIME PERIODS

Ask students to discuss what might happen today if another "Hitler-like" individual should surface. Does the time make the man, or does the man make the times?

LEARNING FROM VISUALS

Ask students to identify possible reasons why people might come out to salute Hitler as he entered the Sudetenland. Were they doing it because they wanted to or because they were afraid not to? What might happen to a person who did not participate?

Answer to the caption question: Student answers will vary, but it seems unlikely that U.S. citizens would react favorably to any foreign invasion.

COMPARING TIME PERIODS

The nonaggression agreement between Germany and the Soviet Union was a surprise. Ask students to identify other surprising agreements made between nations during the nineteenth century.

▶ *In October 1938, Hitler entered Eger (now Cheb) in the Sudetenland, an area of Czechoslovakia with a German population of 3.5 million. The crowds who came out to meet Hitler and his entourage cheered him enthusiastically. How do you think Americans would react if their state or area were suddenly annexed to another country?*

Czechoslovakia that was inhabited largely by Germans. He expressed his willingness to risk "world war" to achieve his objective. Instead of objecting, the British, French, Germans, and Italians—at a hastily arranged conference in Munich—reached an agreement that met virtually all of Hitler's demands. German troops were allowed to occupy the Sudetenland. The Czechs, abandoned by their Western allies, stood by helplessly. The Munich Conference was the high point of Western appeasement of Hitler. When Neville Chamberlain, the British prime minister, returned to England from Munich, he boasted that the Munich agreement meant "peace for our time." Hitler had promised Chamberlain that he had made his last demand. Like scores of politicians before him, Chamberlain believed Hitler's promises.

In fact, Hitler believed more than ever that the Western democracies were weak and would not fight. Increasingly, Hitler was convinced that he could not make a mistake, and he had by no means been satisfied at Munich. In March 1939, Hitler occupied the Czech lands (Bohemia and Moravia). The Slovaks, with Hitler's encouragement, declared their independence of the Czechs and became a puppet state (Slovakia) of Nazi Germany. On the evening of March 15, 1939, Hitler triumphantly declared in Prague that he would be known as the greatest German of them all.

At last, the Western states reacted to the Nazi threat. Hitler's naked aggression had made clear that his promises were utterly worthless. Now Hitler began to demand the return to Germany of Danzig (which had been made a free city by the Treaty of Versailles to serve as a seaport for Poland). Great Britain saw the danger at once and offered to protect Poland in the event of war. At the same time, both France and Britain realized that only the Soviet Union was powerful enough to help contain Nazi aggression. They began political and military negotiations with Joseph Stalin and the Soviets. Their distrust of Soviet communism, however, made an alliance unlikely.

Meanwhile, Hitler pressed on in the belief that the West would not really fight over Poland. Hitler now feared, however, that the West and the Soviet Union might make an alliance. To prevent this possibility, which would create the danger of a two-front war, Hitler made his own nonaggression pact with Stalin, the Soviet dictator. Stalin had come to believe that Britain and France were not serious about fighting. He feared they were trying to involve him in a war with Hitler. To get the nonaggression pact, Hitler offered Stalin control of eastern Poland and the Baltic states. Because he expected to fight the Soviet Union anyway, it did not matter to Hitler what he promised—he was accustomed to breaking promises.

RECOMMENDED READING

The basic study of Germany's foreign policy from 1933 to 1939 can be found in G. Weinberg, *The Foreign Policy of Hitler's Germany: Diplomatic Revolution in Europe, 1933–36* (Chicago, 1970) and *The Foreign Policy of Hitler's Germany: Starting World War II, 1937–1939* (Chicago, 1980). Additional works on foreign policy include W. Carr, *Arms, Autarchy and Aggression: A Study in German Foreign Policy, 1933–1939* (New York, 1973); and K. Hildebrandt, *The Foreign Policy of the Third Reich,* trans. A. Fothergill (London, 1973). The ideological background of Nazi imperialism is examined in W. Smith, *The Ideological Origins of Nazi Imperialism* (New York, 1986). For a detailed account of the immediate events leading to World War II, see D. C. Watt, *How War Came: The Immediate Origins of the Second World War, 1938–1939* (New York, 1989).

Hitler shocked the world with the announcement of the nonaggression pact on August 23, 1939. The treaty with the Soviet Union gave Hitler the freedom to attack Poland. He told his generals, "Now Poland is in the position in which I wanted her . . . I am only afraid that at the last moment some swine or other will yet submit to me a plan for mediation."[2] Hitler need not have worried. On September 1, German forces invaded Poland. Two days later, Britain and France declared war on Germany. Europe was again at war.

The Japanese Path to War

In September 1931, Japanese soldiers seized Manchuria, an area of northeastern China that had natural resources Japan needed. Japan used as an excuse the Chinese attack on a Japanese railway near Mukden. (The "Mukden incident" had actually been carried out by Japanese soldiers disguised as Chinese forces.) Japanese officials in Tokyo were divided over the Manchurian issue. The moderates, however, were unable to control the army. Eventually, worldwide protests against the Japanese action led the League of Nations to send investigators to Manchuria. When the investigators issued a report condemning the seizure, Japan withdrew from the league. Over the next several years, Japan strengthened its hold on Manchuria. Japan renamed it Manchukuo (MAN-CHOO-KWOE) and placed it under the authority of the former Chinese emperor and now Japanese puppet Henry Pu Yi. Japan now began to expand into North China.

Not all political leaders in Tokyo agreed with the aggressive policy. However, right-wing terrorists assassinated some of the key critics and intimidated others into silence. By the mid-1930s, militants connected with the government and the armed forces were effectively in control of Japanese politics.

▲ On September 1, 1939, Hitler announced the beginning of war to the German Reichstag. Do you think German people were surprised at Hitler's proclamation? Why or why not?

The United States refused to recognize the Japanese takeover of Manchuria but was unwilling to threaten the use of force. Instead, the United States tried to appease Japan in the hope of encouraging moderate forces in Japanese society. A senior U.S. diplomat warned the president: "Utter defeat of Japan would be no blessing to the Far East or to the world. It would merely create a new set of stresses, and substitute for

COOPERATIVE LEARNING ACTIVITY

Break students into groups to discuss the answer to the following question: Why was it easier for a nation like Germany to take control of a vast area (such as it did in 1939) than it was to maintain control over the same area? *(It is easier to take over a territory through military power than to maintain control and administer an effective government.*

The German effort to occupy vast territories spread its power and people too thin.)

When students have finished their small group discussions, guide class in a general discussion of this question and conclude with a list of other military leaders or empires that experienced the same problems Germany encountered.

USING PRIMARY SOURCES

Guide students in a discussion of reasons why an American official would believe that a defeat of Japan would be "no blessing for the Far East or to the world." Do students believe that the diplomat's apparent fear of the Soviet Union was rational? Might government officials have felt differently if they had been making this judgment in the 1920s instead of the 1940s?

CLASS DISCUSSION

How did Japan's foreign policy aims in the 1930s correspond with Japan's actions during the early years of World War II?

Map 28.2   Japanese Expansion, 1933–1942

Japan the USSR as the successor to Imperial Russia—as a contestant (and at least an equally unscrupulous and dangerous one) for the mastery of the East. Nobody except perhaps Russia would gain from our victory in such a war."[3]

For the moment, the chief victim of Japanese aggression was China. Jiang Jieshi tried to avoid a conflict with Japan so that he could deal with what he considered the greater threat from the Communists. When clashes between Chinese and Japanese troops broke out, he sought to appease Japan by allowing it to govern areas in North China. However, as Japan moved steadily southward, popular protests in Chinese cities against Japanese aggression grew stronger. In December 1936, Jiang was briefly kidnapped by military forces led by General Shang Xueliang. He forced Jiang to end his military efforts against the Communists in Yan'an and to form a new united front against the Japanese. In July

STUDYING MAPS

The following questions will help you guide students through their study of this map.

1. What territories did Japan acquire in 1941? *(South and Central China; French Indochina, which includes modern day Vietnam, Cambodia, and Laos)*

2. How much territory did Japan acquire in 1942? In which year did Japan acquire more land, 1941 or 1942? *(Students should take time to estimate the amount of land Japan acquired; Japan acquired much more land in 1942 than in 1941.)*

3. Why didn't Japan's limit of control in 1942 increase significantly over its 1941 limit of control? *(Without directly attacking Australia, Japan had reached its Pacific limits.)*

4. How far from Tokyo did Japan's limit of control extend? *(Japan controlled lands approximately 1500 miles east of Tokyo and 3,000 miles west of Tokyo.)*

◄ *After seizing Manchuria, Japanese forces moved further into North and East China. By 1939, Japan had taken most of eastern China. Victorious Japanese soldiers celebrated in the ruins of the railway station in Hankow, China's temporary capital after the fall of Nanjing.*

1937, Chinese and Japanese forces clashed at Marco Polo Bridge, south of Beijing. China refused to apologize, and hostilities spread.

Japan had not planned to declare war on China. However, neither side would compromise, and the 1937 incident eventually turned into a major conflict. The Japanese advanced up the Yangtze valley and seized the Chinese capital of Nanjing in December. Jiang Jieshi refused to surrender, however, and moved his government upriver to Hankow. When the Japanese seized that city, Jiang moved on to Chongqing, in remote Sichuan Province.

Japanese military leaders had hoped to force Jiang to agree to join a new Japanese-dominated New Order in East Asia, comprising Japan, Manchuria, and China. This was part of a larger plan to seize Soviet Siberia, with its rich resources, and create a new order in Asia. Japan, it was thought, would guide its Asian neighbors on the path to development and prosperity. After all, who could better teach Asian societies how to modernize than the one Asian country that had already achieved modernization?

During the late 1930s, Japan began to cooperate with Nazi Germany. Japan assumed that the two countries would ultimately launch a joint attack on the Soviet Union and divide up its resources between themselves. When Germany signed a nonaggression pact with the Soviets in August 1939, however, Japanese leaders thought again about their long-term objectives. Japan was not strong enough to defeat the Soviet Union alone. Thus, the Japanese began to shift their eyes south to the vast resources of Southeast Asia—the oil of the Dutch East Indies, the rubber and tin of Malaya, and the rice of Burma and Indochina.

A move southward, of course, would risk war with the European colonial powers and the United States. Japan's attack on China in the summer of 1937 had already aroused strong criticism abroad, especially from the United States. President Franklin Delano Roosevelt threatened to use economic sanctions against the aggressors after Japanese military units bombed a U.S. naval ship operating in China. Public fear of involvement, however, forced the president to draw back. Then, when Japan suddenly demanded the right to exploit economic resources in French Indochina in the summer of 1940, the United States objected. It warned Japan that it would apply economic sanctions unless Japan withdrew from the area and returned to its borders of 1931.

MORE ABOUT . . . *Japan's Geography and Its History*

We often see geography as a study of a region's rivers, lakes, mountains, etc. However, it is much more. Consider Japan and its foreign policy of expansion in the 1930s and 40s. The economic geography of Japan—the economic resources contained within its borders—was a serious limitation to the Japanese aim to become a great power. Japan felt that it had to gain access to the resources for a modern industrial economy. This meant

expansion toward Korea, China, Russia (U.S.S.R.) and adjoining Pacific areas. A weakness in economic geography directly led to the aggression and imperialism. Fortunately, contemporary Japan has found a peaceful way to meet the demands created by a lack of natural resources: export. Through exports, Japan can afford to buy natural resources in the world market, with a few yen to spare.

ASSESS

Ask students to create a table that compares important facts about Germany and Japan before World War II. Have them identify similarities in these nation's social, political, economic, and military areas. Which factors do students believe were most important in leading these states to war? What might the other nations of the world have been able to do to avoid the total war?

CLOSE

Lead students in a discussion of the "Focus" objectives identified on page 902. Most nations of the world followed isolationism or appeasement during the 1930s, allowing Germany and Japan to prepare for war.

Japan viewed the U.S. threat of retaliation as a threat to its long-term objectives. Japan badly needed oil and scrap iron from the United States. Should these resources be cut off, Japan would have to find them elsewhere. Japan was thus caught in a dilemma. To guarantee its access to raw materials in Southeast Asia, which would be necessary to fuel the Japanese military machine, Japan must risk a cutoff of its current source of raw materials (the United States), which would still be needed in case of a conflict. After much debate, Japan decided to launch a surprise attack on U.S. and European colonies in Southeast Asia. It hoped for a quick victory that would push the United States from the region.

❖ SECTION REVIEW ❖

1. **Locate:**
   (a) Austria,   (b) Prague,
   (c) Slovakia,   (d) Danzig

2. **Define:**
   (a) Aryan racial state,
   (b) appeasement,
   (c) Anschluss

3. **Identify:**
   (a) Munich Conference

4. **Recall:**
   (a) Why did Germany say it needed more land?
   (b) How did Germany break the Treaty of Versailles during the 1930s?
   (c) Why did Hitler and Stalin sign a non-aggression pact in 1939?
   (d) Why did Japan withdraw from the League of Nations in 1931?
   (e) Why did Japan shift its expansionary interest to South Asia in 1939?

5. **Think Critically:** Why isn't a policy of appeasement with an aggressive nation likely to result in a lasting peace? Use events that took place in the 1930s as examples in your answer.

②

THE COURSE OF WORLD WAR II

Hitler stunned Europe with the speed and efficiency of the German attack on Poland. His **Blitzkrieg,** or "lightning war," used armored columns or panzer divisions (a panzer division was a strike force of about three hundred tanks and accompanying forces and supplies) supported by airplanes. These forces were used to break quickly through Polish lines and encircle the bewildered Polish troops. Regular infantry units then moved in to hold the newly conquered territory. Within four weeks, Poland had surrendered. On September 28, 1939, Germany and the Soviet Union divided Poland between themselves.

Europe at War

Hitler's hopes to avoid a war with the West were dashed when France and Britain declared war on September 3, 1939. Nevertheless, Hitler was confident that he could still control the situation. After a winter of waiting (called the "phony war"), Hitler resumed the attack on April 9, 1940, with another Blitzkrieg against Denmark and Norway. One month later, on May 10, Germany launched its attack on the Netherlands, Belgium, and France. The main assault through Luxembourg and the Ardennes (awr-DEN) forest was completely unexpected by the French and British forces. German panzer divisions broke through the weak French defensive positions there and raced across northern France, splitting the Allied armies and trapping French troops and the entire British army on the beaches of Dunkirk. Only by heroic efforts did the British manage to evacuate 338,000 Allied (mostly British) troops.

The French surrendered on June 22. German armies occupied about three-fifths of France. An authoritarian regime known as Vichy (VISH-ee) France, led by the aged French hero of World War I, Marshal Henri Pétain (PAE-ta[n]), was set up over the remainder of the country. Germany was now in control of western

On Line with
WORLD HISTORY   *Internet Activity*

You may want to have your students visit the following URL, where they will find information and additional web site resources to enhance their study of this chapter.
Japanese Internment
http://www.geocities.com/Athens/8420/main.html

This is an excellent source presenting all points of view, with pictures, maps, and original primary materials concerning the Japanese internment during World War II.

Due to the ever-changing nature of the World Wide Web, see the West History web site, **http://history.swpco.com** for regular updates of the URLs in this text.

Map 28.3   World War II in Europe and North Africa

OBJECTIVES

After completing this section, students should be able to

1. identify and describe events in the course of World War II in Europe
2. identify and describe events in the course of World War II in the Far East
3. explain the turning point in World War II
4. describe conditions at the end of World War II

FOCUS ACTIVITY

Have students write an essay about or to discuss the following proposition:

It is not possible for one man alone to start or fight a war, but it is possible for one man to lose a war.

How do the experiences of Napoleon and Hitler support this point of view?

and central Europe, but Britain had still not been defeated.

As Hitler realized, an amphibious (land-sea) invasion of Britain would be possible only if Germany gained control of the air. At the beginning of August 1940, the **Luftwaffe** (LOOFT-vah-fuh) (the German air force) launched a major offensive against British air

and naval bases, harbors, communication centers, and war industries. The British fought back with determination. They were supported by an effective radar system that gave them early warning of German attacks.

Nevertheless, by the end of August, the British air force had suffered critical losses. A change of strategy by Hitler, however, came to its rescue. In September, in

STUDYING MAPS

The following questions will help you guide students through their study of Map 28.3.

1. How many major Axis offensives took place between 1939 and 1942? *(nine)*
2. How long was the frontier between Axis and Soviet forces at the farthest Axis advance? *(approximately 2800 miles long)*

3. Why was it a good thing for Allied forces at Normandy that the Soviet Union had not been defeated early in World War II? *(Students should recognize that at the time of the Normandy invasion, Germany was fighting a war on two fronts, a situation their military leaders had hoped to avoid.)*

TEACH

CLASS DISCUSSION

Ask students to identify and discuss possible outcomes that might have happened if Germany had not attacked Great Britain by air in 1940 but had worked instead to consolidate its hold on mainland Europe.

COMPARING TIME PERIODS

Ask students what makes air power effective in war. Germany was not able to use air power to knock Great Britain out of World War II. The United States was not able to defeat the North Vietnamese with air power in the 1970s. However, air power decimated Iraq's forces in 1990. What do students believe made the difference?

LEARNING FROM VISUALS

Ask students to write a hypothetical letter from a resident of London to an American relative that describes how he or she felt after seeing the results of the air raid pictured to the right. How might this destruction change this person's willingness to fight?

Answer to the caption question: It seems highly likely that an attack on Washington D.C. would strengthen American resolve to fight and win a war.

▶ *The bombing of London devastated entire sections of that city. This photograph, taken after the first daylight raid on the English capital on July 1, 1940, shows how far reaching the German attack was. Do you think an enemy attack on Washington D.C. would strengthen or weaken American resolve to fight a war?*

retaliation for a British attack on Berlin, Hitler ordered a shift from bombing military targets to massive bombing of British cities to break British morale. The British rebuilt their air strength quickly and were soon inflicting major losses on Luftwaffe bombers. By the end of September, Germany had lost the Battle of Britain. The invasion of Britain had to be postponed.

At this point, Hitler considered a Mediterranean strategy. This would involve capturing Egypt and the Suez Canal and closing the Mediterranean to British ships, thereby shutting off Britain's supply of oil. However, Hitler was never fully committed to the Mediterranean strategy. His initial plan was to let the Italians decisively defeat the British in North Africa. This strategy failed, however, when the British routed the Italian army. Hitler then sent German troops to the North African theater of war. His chief concern, however, lay elsewhere. He had already reached the decision to fulfill his lifetime obsession with the acquisition of territory to the east of Germany.

Although he had no desire for a two-front war, Hitler became convinced that Britain was remaining in the war only because it expected Soviet support. If the Soviet Union were smashed, Britain's last hope would

be eliminated. Moreover, Hitler had convinced himself that the Soviet Union had a pitiful army and could be defeated quickly.

Hitler's invasion of the Soviet Union was scheduled for the spring of 1941, but the attack was delayed because of problems in the Balkans. Hitler had already gained the political cooperation of Hungary, Bulgaria, and Romania. However, Mussolini's disastrous invasion of Greece in October 1940 exposed Hitler's southern flank to British air bases in Greece. To secure Hitler's Balkan flank, German troops seized both Yugoslavia and Greece in April. Now reassured, Hitler turned to the east and invaded the Soviet Union on June 22, 1941. He believed that the Russians could still be decisively defeated before winter set in.

The massive attack stretched out along an 1,800-mile front. German troops advanced rapidly, capturing 2 million Russian soldiers. By November, one German army group had swept through Ukraine. A second was besieging Leningrad, while a third approached within 25 miles of Moscow, the Russian capital. An early Russian winter and unexpected fierce Russian resistance, however, halted the German advance. Because of their planned spring date for the invasion, the Ger-

RECOMMENDED READING

General works on World War II include M. K. Dziewanowski, *War at Any Price: World War II in Europe, 1939–1945,* 2d ed. (Englewood Cliffs, N.J., 1991); P. Calvocoressi and G. Wint, *Total War: Causes and Courses of the Second World War* (New York, 1979). On Hitler as a military leader, see R. Lewin, *Hitler's Mistakes* (New York, 1986). The Eastern Front is covered in J. Erickson, *Stalin's War with Germany,* vol. 1, *The Road to Stalingrad;* vol. 2, *The Road to Berlin* (London, 1973, 1985). The second front in Europe is examined in C. D'Este, *Decision in Normandy* (London, 1983). The German bombing of Britain is covered in T. Harrisson, *Living through the Blitz* (London, 1985). On Hiroshima, see A. Chisholm, *Faces of Hiroshima* (London, 1985).

◄ *German panzer troops leave their armored tanks to flush out Russian soldiers who have taken refuge in the farmhouse. The initial success of the German Army in Russia led many to believe that Russia would fall within two weeks or a month. What other European army met defeat in the cruel Russian winter?*

COMPARING TIME PERIODS

Ask students to identify differences and similarities between the colonial domination that European powers had imposed on much of China and Southeast Asia before World War I and the Great East-Asia Co-prosperity Sphere Japan created in 1942.

CLASS DISCUSSION

Ask students to identify and discuss reasons why it is less difficult to conquer a state than it is to control that state once it has been conquered. How did Germany and Japan learn this lesson in World War II? Is it true that people fight hardest when they have nothing left to lose?

LEARNING FROM VISUALS

Answer to the caption question: Students should remember that Napoleon Bonaparte suffered a stunning defeat just outside Moscow during the winter of 1812.

mans had no winter uniforms. For the first time in the war, German armies had been stopped. A counterattack in December 1941 by a Soviet army supposedly exhausted by Nazi victories came as an ominous ending to the year for the Germans.

By that time, Hitler had made another fatal decision. When Japan attacked Pearl Harbor, Hitler fulfilled his promises to Japan and declared war on the United States. In doing so, Hitler's eventual defeat appeared more likely. At the same time, another European conflict had been turned into a global war.

Japan at War

On December 7, 1941, Japanese aircraft attacked the U.S. naval base at Pearl Harbor in the Hawaiian Islands. The same day, other Japanese units launched additional assaults on the Philippines and began advancing toward the British colony of Malaya. Soon after, Japanese forces invaded the Dutch East Indies and occupied a number of islands in the Pacific Ocean. In some cases, as on the Bataan peninsula and the island of Corregidor in the Philippines, resistance was fierce. By the spring of 1942, however, almost all of Southeast Asia and much of the western Pacific had fallen into Japanese hands.

A triumphant Japan now declared the creation of a Great East-Asia Co-prosperity Sphere in the entire region under Japanese direction. Japan also announced its intention to liberate the colonial areas of Southeast Asia from Western colonial rule. For the moment, however, Japan needed the resources of the region for its war machine, and it treated the countries under its rule as conquered lands.

Japanese leaders had hoped that their lightning strike at American bases would destroy the U.S. Pacific Fleet. The Roosevelt administration, they thought, would now accept Japanese domination of the Pacific. The American people, in the eyes of Japanese leaders, had been made soft by material indulgence. The Japanese had miscalculated, however. The attack on Pearl Harbor galvanized American opinion and won broad support for Roosevelt's war policy. The United States now joined with European nations and Nationalist China in a combined effort to defeat Japan. Believing the American involvement in the Pacific would make the United States ineffective in the European theater

ENRICHMENT ACTIVITY

Have students research the circumstances surrounding the Japanese "surprise" attack on Pearl Harbor. What validity is there to the claim that the coming of the Japanese was known but Pearl Harbor was not advised either by design or by ineffectiveness? Most historians believe today that by intercepting and decoding messages, the U.S. govern ment knew that Japan was preparing for battle, but did not know specifically where Japan would attack. A message from officials in Washington warning that war with Japan was likely had been carelessly forwarded by commercial channels and was not received in time at Pearl Harbor for the base to go on red alert.

LEARNING FROM VISUALS

By late 1941 there were more than 75 U.S. warships including battleships, destroyers, cruisers, and submarines stationed at Pearl Harbor. During the Japanese attack the battleship *U.S.S. Arizona* was completely destroyed, the *Nevada* heavily damaged, and the *West Virginia* and the *California* were sunk. American losses were staggering, but Japan lost only 29 planes, 5 small submarines, and less than 100 soldiers. A national memorial has been built across the hull of the *U.S.S. Arizona* at Pearl Harbor, just outside Honolulu.

CONNECTIONS AROUND THE WORLD

Ask students to discuss why captured spies have often been treated more harshly than other enemy soldiers who were taken prisoner. What characteristics in enemy spies do we find particularly offensive? Why do we glorify the exploits of our own successful spies?

▲ *The surprise Japanese attack on Pearl Harbor on December 7, 1941, killed nearly 2,400 Americans and wounded 1,200 others. Nineteen American ships were either sunk or disabled, and over 120 U.S. airplanes were destroyed.*

of war, Hitler declared war on the United States four days after Pearl Harbor.

The Turning Point of the War, 1942–1943

The entry of the United States into the war created a coalition (the Grand Alliance) that ultimately defeated the Axis powers (Germany, Italy, and Japan). Nevertheless, the three major Allies—Great Britain, the United States, and the Soviet Union—had to overcome mutual suspicions before they could operate as an effective alliance. Two factors aided that process. First, Hitler's declaration of war on the United States made it easier for the United States to accept the British and Russian argument that the defeat of Ger-

CONNECTIONS AROUND THE WORLD

Female Spies in World War II For thousands of years, governments have relied on spies to gather information about their enemies. Until the twentieth century, most spies were men. During World War II, however, many women became active in the world of espionage.

Yoshiko Kawashima was born in China but raised in Japan. In 1932, she was sent to China by Japanese authorities to gather information for the Japanese invasion of China. Disguised as a young man, Kawashima was an active and effective spy until her arrest by the Chinese in 1945. The Chinese news agency announced that "a long-sought-for beauty in male costume was arrested today in Beijing." She was executed soon after her arrest.

Hekmath Fathmy was an Egyptian dancer. Her hatred of the British, who had occupied Egypt, caused her to become a spy for the Germans. Fathmy sang and danced for British troops in the Kit Kat Club, a nightclub in Cairo. After shows, she took British officers to her houseboat on the banks of the Nile. Any information she was able to obtain from her guests was passed on to John Eppler, a German spy in Cairo. Eventually, she was caught but served only a year in prison for her spying activities.

Violette Szabo became a spy after her husband died fighting the Germans in North Africa. She joined Special Operations Executive, an arm of British Intelligence. In August 1944 she parachuted into France to spy on the Germans. Caught by Gestapo forces at Salon La Tour, she was questioned under torture and then shipped to Ravensbruck, a women's concentration camp near Berlin. She was executed there in April 1945.

many was more important than these countries' differences. For that reason, the United States, under its Lend-Lease program, sent large amounts of military

MORE ABOUT . . . *Hitler the General*

Part of a mythological picture of Adolph Hitler is that he was a great military strategist. The following examples partially show the folly of such thoughts.

Without subduing England, Hitler initiated an attack against the U.S.S.R., creating a two-front war. He seriously underestimated the Soviet capability and paid a huge price for his mistake.

Prior to D-day, Hitler was fooled by the Allies into thinking that the invasion of

Europe would take place at Calais. When the attack came on Normandy, he delayed the redeployment of his forces. By the time his troops became active, it was too late; the Normandy invasion had been a success.

Hitler's decision to use the world's first jet aircraft fighter as a bomber, robbed it of its potential success in the war.

Indeed, it could be said that Hitler was the best general that the allies had on their side.

Map 28.4   World War II in Asia and the Pacific

Multimedia Support

TRANSPARENCY

28–2, World War II in Asia and the Pacific (Map 28.4)

CLASSROOM DISCUSSION

Lead students in a discussion of the costs and benefits of the Allied demand for unconditional surrender of the Axis powers.

aid—including $50 billion worth of trucks, planes, and other arms—to Great Britain and the Soviet Union.

The alliance was also strengthened when the three chief Allies agreed to stress military operations while ignoring political differences. At the beginning of 1943, the Allies agreed to fight until the Axis powers surrendered unconditionally. Some people think that this principle of **unconditional surrender** might have discouraged dissident Germans and Japanese from overthrowing their governments in order to arrange a negotiated peace. In any case, the unconditional surrender principle did cement the Grand Alliance by making it nearly impossible for Hitler to divide his foes.

Defeat, however, was far from Hitler's mind at the beginning of 1942. As Japanese forces advanced into Southeast Asia and the Pacific, Hitler and his European allies continued the war in Europe against Britain and the Soviet Union. Until the fall of 1942, it

STUDYING MAPS

The following questions will help you guide students through their study of Map 28.4.

1. How far was it from the Japanese home islands to the farthest reaches of the land it took over in World War II? *(approximately 3000 miles)*
2. Why was providing adequate supplies for its military forces a problem for Japan in World War II? *(Supplies had to come by ship or by air, and the long distances and hazardous conditions made resupplying troops difficult.)*
3. Was it unrealistic for people in the United States to expect a Japanese invasion of California? *(Answers will vary. Students should recognize that it is a great distance from Japan to California.)*

USING PRIMARY SOURCES

Although it is probably necessary for effective leaders to have a positive attitude about the future and what they can accomplish, Hitler's optimism seems to have had little to do with reality. What reasons can students give for Hitler's boasts being little more than wishful thinking?

COMPARING TIME PERIODS

Ask students to write an essay or prepare a chart that identifies similarities between Napoleon's defeat in Russia in 1812 and the German defeat in the Soviet Union in World War II. What military advantage did the Russians have because of their vast plains and cold winters?

appeared that the Germans might still prevail on the battlefield. Reinforcements in North Africa enabled the Afrika Korps under General Erwin Rommel (RAW-mul) to break through the British defenses in Egypt and advance toward Alexandria. In the spring of 1942, a renewed German offensive in the Soviet Union led to the capture of the entire Crimea. Hitler boasted in August 1942:

> As the next step, we are going to advance south of the Caucasus and then help the rebels in Iran and Iraq against the English. Another thrust will be directed along the Caspian Sea toward Afghanistan and India. Then the English will run out of oil. In two years we'll be on the borders of India. Twenty to thirty elite German divisions will do. Then the British Empire will collapse.[4]

This would be Hitler's last optimistic outburst. By the fall of 1942, the war had turned against the Germans.

In North Africa, British forces had stopped Rommel's troops at El Alamein (EL-AL-uh-MANE) in the summer of 1942. The Germans then retreated back across the desert. In November 1942, British and American forces invaded French North Africa. They forced the German and Italian troops there to surrender in May 1943.

On the eastern front, the turning point of the war in Europe occurred at Stalingrad. After the capture of the Crimea, Hitler's generals wanted him to concentrate on the capture of the Caucasus and its oil fields. Hitler, however, was obsessed by a city named for Stalin and decided that Stalingrad, a major industrial center on the Volga, should be taken first. In perhaps the most terrible battle of the war, between November 1942 and February 2, 1943, German troops were stopped, then encircled, and finally forced to surrender (see "You Are There: A German Soldier at Stalingrad"). The entire German Sixth Army of 300,000 men was lost. By February 1943, German forces in Russia were back to their positions of June 1942. By the spring of 1943, even Hitler knew that the Germans would not defeat the Soviet Union.

In 1942, the tide of battle in the Far East also changed dramatically. In the Battle of the Coral Sea on May 7 and 8, 1942, American naval forces stopped the Japanese advance and temporarily relieved Australia of the threat of invasion. The turning point of the war in Asia came on June 4, at the Battle of Midway Island. U.S. planes destroyed all four of the attacking Japanese aircraft carriers and established American naval superiority in the Pacific.

By the fall of 1942, Allied forces were beginning to gather for two chief operations. One would move into South China from Burma through the islands of Indonesia by a process of "island hopping" by troops commanded by U.S. general Douglas MacArthur. The other operation would move across the Pacific with a combination of U.S. Army, Marine, and Navy attacks on Japanese-held islands. After a series of bitter engagements in the waters of the Solomon Islands from August to November 1942, Japanese fortunes began to fade.

The Last Years of the War

By the beginning of 1943, the tide of battle had turned against Germany, Italy, and Japan. The Axis forces surrendered in Tunisia on May 13, 1943. The Allies then crossed the Mediterranean and carried the war to Italy, an area that Winston Churchill had called the "soft underbelly" of Europe. After taking Sicily, Allied troops began the invasion of mainland Italy in September. In the meantime, after the ouster and arrest of Mussolini, a new Italian government offered to surrender to the Allied forces. However, Mussolini was liberated by the Germans in a daring raid and then set up as the head of a puppet German state in northern Italy. At the same time, German troops moved in and occupied much of Italy.

The new defensive lines set up by the Germans in the hills south of Rome were very effective. The Allied advance up the Italian peninsula turned into a painstaking affair with very heavy casualties. Rome did not fall to the Allies until June 4, 1944. By that time, the Italian war had assumed a secondary role as the Allies opened their long-awaited "second front" in western Europe. Stalin had been pushing for this invasion to relieve the Nazi pressure against the Soviet Union.

Since the autumn of 1943, the Allies had been planning a cross-channel invasion of France from Great

On Line with WORLD HISTORY *Internet Activity*

You may want to have your students visit the following URL, where they will find information and additional web site resources to enhance their study of this chapter.
World War II on the Web
http://www.bunt.com/~mconrad/links.htm

This is a massive one-stop link page with over 450 links to topics on World War II.

Due to the ever-changing nature of the World Wide Web, see the West History web site, **http://history.swpco.com** for regular updates of the URLs in this text.

YOU ARE THERE
A German Soldier at Stalingrad

The Russian victory at Stalingrad was a major turning point in World War II. These words come from the diary of a German soldier who fought and died in the Battle of Stalingrad.

A German Soldier on the Battle of Stalingrad

Today, after we'd had a bath, the company commander told us that if our future operations are as successful, we'll soon reach the Volga, take Stalingrad and then the war will inevitably soon be over. Perhaps we'll be home by Christmas.

July 29. The company commander says the Russian troops are completely broken, and cannot hold out any longer. To reach the Volga and take Stalingrad is not so difficult for us. The Führer knows where the Russians' weak point is. Victory is not far away. . . .

August 10. The Führer's orders were read out to us. He expects victory of us. We are all convinced that they can't stop us. . . .

September 4. We are being sent northward along the front towards Stalingrad. We marched all night and by dawn had reached Voroponovo Station. We can already see the smoking town. It's a happy thought that the end of the war is getting nearer.

September 8. Two days of non-stop fighting. The Russians are defending themselves with insane stubbornness. Our regiment has lost many men. . . .

September 16. Our battalion, plus tanks, is attacking the [grain storage] elevator, from which smoke is pouring—the grain in it is burning, the Russians seem to have set light to it themselves. Barbarism. The battalion is suffering heavy losses. . . .

October 10. The Russians are so close to us that our planes cannot bomb them. We are preparing

▲ *As the war dragged on in Russia, it became more difficult for Nazi troops to conquer their opponents. Here a German soldier is trapped and trying to escape from a dugout in Stalingrad.*

for a decisive attack. The Führer has ordered the whole of Stalingrad to be taken as rapidly as possible. . . .

October 22. Our regiment has failed to break into the factory. We have lost many men; every time you move you have to jump over bodies. . . .

(continued)

ENRICHMENT ACTIVITY

Although women did not serve as soldiers during World War II, they did serve in the military. Have students research the roles of women in all of the warring countries. How did their roles differ from men, and how did their roles differ from country to country? You may also ask some students to address the opportunities that World War II created for women in the military and on the homefront.

COMPARING TIME PERIODS

Ask students to write a comparison of the importance of the breakout of Allied troops through German lines in World War II with that of a breakthrough in the trench warfare of World War I. In what ways were they similar? How were they different?

Multimedia Support

LASERDISC

Diary of a German Soldier at Stalingrad, 1943

YOU ARE THERE

A German Soldier at Stalingrad, continued

November 10. A letter from Elsa today. Everyone expects us home for Christmas. In Germany everyone believes we already hold Stalingrad. How wrong they are. If they could only see what Stalingrad has done to our army. . . .

November 21. The Russians have gone over to the offensive along the whole front. Fierce fighting is going on. So, there it is—the Volga, victory and soon home to our families! We shall obviously be seeing them next in the other world.

November 29. We are encircled. It was announced this morning that the Führer has said: "The army can trust me to do everything necessary to ensure supplies and rapidly break the encirclement."

December 3. We are on hunger rations and waiting for the rescue that the Führer promised. . . .

December 26. The horses have already been eaten. I would eat a cat; they say its meat is also tasty. The soldiers look like corpses or lunatics, They no longer take cover from Russian shells; they haven't the strength to walk, run away and hide. A curse on this war!

1. What city was the German army trying to take?

2. Why was it important for them to take this city?

3. How accurate was the information received by the German soldiers prior to the attack?

4. At what point in the diary does it become obvious that the German soldier knew he would not return home alive?

5. Do you think the German soldiers still trusted the Führer when they knew they would be defeated? Why or why not?

Britain. A series of Allied deceptions caused the Germans to believe that the invasion would come on the flat plains of northern France. Instead, the Allies, under the direction of the U.S. general Dwight D. Eisenhower, landed five assault divisions on the Normandy beaches on June 6 in history's greatest naval invasion. The Germans were not sure this was the real invasion, and their slow response enabled the Allied forces to set up a beachhead. Within three months, the Allies had landed two million men and a half-million vehicles, which pushed inland and broke through German defensive lines.

After the breakout, Allied troops moved south and east. They liberated Paris by the end of August. By March 1945, they had crossed the Rhine River and advanced into Germany. At the end of April 1945, Allied armies in northern Germany moved toward the Elbe (EL-buh) River, where they finally linked up with the Soviets.

The Soviets had come a long way since the Battle of Stalingrad in 1943. In the summer of 1943, Hitler gambled on taking the offensive by making use of newly developed heavy tanks. German forces were soundly defeated by the Soviets at the Battle of Kursk (July 5 to 12), the greatest tank battle of World War II. Soviet forces now began a steady advance westward. They had reoccupied Ukraine by the end of 1943. They had lifted the siege of Leningrad and moved into the Baltic states by the beginning of 1944. Advancing along a northern front, Soviet troops occupied Warsaw in Jan-

COOPERATIVE LEARNING ACTIVITY

Have students put together a world map that shows the major battles of World War II. Based on the battles, analyze the major lines of strategy followed by the Axis powers and by the Allies in their pursuit of the war. Were there other lines of strategy that could have been taken? Would they have been more effective for either side? Why or why not?

Students should work together to define the task, assign the roles (recorder, researcher, map maker, group leader, etc.), and when completed, evaluate the project according to how the members worked together to achieve the task.

◄ *Following the Normandy invasion and the liberation of France, Allied forces began their move toward Germany. Pontoon bridges like this one across the Rhine River made it possible for the Allies to advance into Germany. These troops are part of the 7th United States Army under American General Alexander Patch.*

uary 1945 and entered Berlin in April. Meanwhile, Soviet troops along a southern front swept through Hungary, Romania, and Bulgaria.

In January 1945, Adolf Hitler had moved into a bunker fifty-five feet under Berlin to direct the final stages of the war. In his final political testament, Hitler, consistent to the end in his rabid anti-Semitism, blamed the Jews for the war. He wrote, "Above all I charge the leaders of the nation and those under them to scrupulous observance of the laws of race and to merciless opposition to the universal poisoner of all peoples, international Jewry."[5] Hitler committed suicide on April 30, two days after Mussolini had been shot by partisan Italian forces. On May 7, German commanders surrendered. The war in Europe was over.

The war in Asia continued. Beginning in 1943, U.S. forces had gone on the offensive and advanced their way, slowly at times, across the Pacific. U.S. forces took an increasing toll of enemy resources, especially at sea and in the air. As Allied military power drew closer to

the main Japanese islands in the first months of 1945, President Harry S Truman, who had become president on the death of Roosevelt in April, had a difficult decision to make. Should he use the newly developed atomic weapons to bring the war to an end, thus avoiding an Allied invasion of the Japanese homeland? The Japanese had made extensive preparations to defend their homeland. Truman and his advisors had become convinced that American troops would suffer heavy casualties in an invasion of Japan. At the time, however, only two bombs were available, and no one knew how effective they would be.

As the world knows, Truman decided to use the bombs. The first bomb was dropped on the Japanese city of Hiroshima (HIR-uh-SHEE-muh) on August 6. Three days later, a second bomb was dropped on Nagasaki. Japan surrendered unconditionally on August 14. World War II was finally over. Seventeen million had died in battle. Perhaps twenty million civilians had perished as well (some estimate total losses at fifty million).

So What ??

If your students question the importance of **the outcome of World War II** *tell them . . .*

There is a romantic tendency to think that World War II just had to end the way it did: with the democratic powers victorious and fascism demolished. Somehow, it fits our sense of "rightness," and we quickly jump from that point to "what must be." History shows that rightness has not always won

and good and liberty have not always triumphed.

Recall that Genghis Khan, a ruthless leader, created the world's largest empire. Attila successfully terrorized the world. The Vandals and Visogoths did finish off the Roman Empire, leading Europe into the Dark Ages.

Hitler, Mussolini and Tojo did not have to lose. We owe a huge debt of thanks to those responsible for their defeat.

Answers to
SECTION REVIEW

2. (a) lightning war; rapid advance of German forces over opposition
(b) German air force
(c) absolute surrender
3. (a) puppet government of southern France dominated by Germany during the war
(b) leader of German forces in North Africa
(c) first American victory over Japanese forces
(d) U.S. sank four Japanese aircraft carriers; turning point in the war in the Pacific
(e) commander of American forces in the Pacific
(f) prime minister of Britain during the war
(g) Supreme Allied commander in Europe
4. (a) Britain bombed Berlin
(b) They were expected to defeat the Soviets before winter began.
(c) American people were soft by material indulgence.
(d) The Germans thought the Allied attack would take place elsewhere.
5. Answers will vary. It helped keep the Allied powers working together, may have caused Axis powers to fight harder.

CLOSE

Lead students in a discussion of the Focus objectives identified on page 909. World War II was a global war, which probably decided how the world would be organized and run for generations.

❀ SECTION REVIEW ❀

1. **Locate:**
(a) Ardennes forest,   (b) Dunkirk,
(c) Corregidor,   (d) Alexandria,   (e) El Alamein,
(f) Volga River,   (g) Normandy,   (h) Stalingrad,
(i) Hiroshima,   (j) Nagasaki

2. **Define:**
(a) Blitzkrieg,   (b) Luftwaffe,   (c) unconditional surrender

3. **Identify:**
(a) Vichy France,   (b) Erwin Rommel,
(c) Battle of the Coral Sea,   (d) Battle of Midway,
(e) General Douglas MacArthur,   (f) Winston Churchill,   (g) Dwight D. Eisenhower

4. **Recall:**
(a) Why did Hitler shift his air attacks to British cities in 1940?
(b) Why did German soldiers lack winter uniforms during the winter of 1940 in the Soviet Union?
(c) Why did the Japanese military leadership feel they could attack United States forces without fear of reprisal in 1941?
(d) Why were the Allied forces able to land at Normandy in 1944 with relatively little German opposition?

5. **Think Critically:** In what ways may the Allied forces' demand for unconditional surrender by Germany and Japan have helped and harmed their efforts to win the war?

◆ 3 ◆

THE NEW ORDER

The early victories of Germany and Japan had given these nations the opportunity to create new orders (political systems) in Europe and Asia. Both countries painted positive images of these new orders for public-

ity purposes. In truth, however, both followed policies of ruthless domination of their subject peoples.

The New Order in Europe

After the German victories in Europe, Nazi propagandists created glowing images of a new European order based on "equal chances" for all nations. However, this was not Hitler's conception of a new Europe. He saw the Europe he had conquered simply as being subject to German domination. Only the Germans, he once said, "can really organize Europe."

In 1942, the Nazi Empire stretched across continental Europe from the English Channel in the west to the outskirts of Moscow in the east. In no way was this empire organized in an orderly fashion or governed efficiently. Nazi-occupied Europe was largely organized in one of two ways. Some areas, such as western Poland, were directly annexed by Nazi Germany and made into German provinces. Most of occupied Europe, however, was run by German military or civilian officials with help from local people who were willing to collaborate with the Nazis.

Race played an important role in how conquered peoples were treated. Governments run by German civil officials were set up in Norway, Denmark, and the Netherlands, because the Nazis believed the peoples in these areas to be Aryan, or racially akin to the Germans. These conquered peoples, according to the Nazis, were thus worthy of more lenient treatment. "Inferior" Latin peoples, such as the occupied French, were given military administrations. By 1943, however, as Nazi losses continued to multiply, all the occupied territories of northern and western Europe were ruthlessly exploited to provide the material goods and labor that Germany needed.

Nazi administration in the conquered lands to the east was even more ruthless. These lands were seen as the living space for German expansion. They were populated, in Nazi eyes, by racially inferior Slavic peoples. Hitler's plans for an Aryan racial empire were so important to him that he and the Nazis began to put their racial program into effect soon after the conquest of Poland.

ENRICHMENT ACTIVITY

There is a great deal of new, recent literature on both the Japanese attack on Pearl Harbor and on the dropping of the atomic bomb on Japan. Have students select one of these two issues and then either write a research paper predicting outcomes had the

U.S. Navy been able to anticipate and prepare for the Japanese attack or discussing whether it was a military or political decision, or both. You might also wish to organize a class debate concerning the moral implications of using the atomic bomb.

Heinrich Himmler, a fanatic believer in Nazi racial ideas and the leader of the SS, was put in charge of German resettlement plans in the east. Himmler's task was to move the inferior Slavic peoples out and replace them with Germans. This policy was first applied to the new German provinces created from the lands of western Poland. One million Poles were uprooted and dumped in southern Poland. Hundreds of thousands of ethnic Germans (descendants of Germans who had migrated years ago from Germany to different parts of southern and eastern Europe) were brought in to colonize the German provinces in Poland. By 1942, two million ethnic Germans had been settled in Poland.

The invasion of the Soviet Union made the Nazis even more excited about German colonization in the east. Hitler spoke to his intimate circle of a colossal project of social engineering after the war. Poles, Ukrainians, and Russians would be removed from their lands and become slave labor while German peasants settled on the abandoned lands and germanized them. The Nazis involved in this kind of planning were well aware of the human costs. Himmler told a gathering of SS officers that thirty million Slavs might die in order to achieve German plans in the east. He continued, "Whether nations live in prosperity or starve to death interests me only insofar as we need them as slaves for our culture. Otherwise it is of no interest."[6]

Labor shortages in Germany led to a policy of rounding up foreign workers for Germany. After the invasion of Russia, the four million Russian prisoners of war captured by the Germans became a chief source of heavy labor, although three million of them died because of neglect by their captors.

In 1942, a special office was set up to recruit labor for German farms and industries. By the summer of 1944, seven million foreign workers were laboring in Germany. They made up 20 percent of Germany's labor force. At the same time, another seven million workers were forced to labor for the Nazis in their own countries on farms, in industries, and even in military camps. Forced labor was often counterproductive, however. Sending so many workers to Germany disrupted industrial production in the occupied countries that could have helped Germany. Then, too, the brutal way in which Germany recruited foreign workers

often led more and more people to resist the Nazi occupation forces.

The Holocaust

There was no more terrifying aspect of the Nazi New Order than the deliberate attempt to exterminate the Jewish people of Europe. Racial struggle was a key element in Hitler's world of ideas. To him, racial struggle was a clearly defined conflict of opposites. On one side were the Aryans, creators of human cultural development. On the other side were the Jews, parasites who were trying to destroy the Aryans. By the beginning of 1939, Nazi policy focused on encouraging German Jews to leave Germany. Once the war began in September 1939, the so-called Jewish problem took on new dimensions. For a while there was discussion of the Madagascar Plan, under which Jews would be shipped in large numbers to the African island of Madagascar. When the war made this plan impractical, an even more drastic policy was conceived.

Himmler and the SS closely shared Hitler's racial ideas. The SS was given responsibility for what the Nazis called their Final Solution to the Jewish problem. The **Final Solution** was the physical extermination of the Jewish people. Reinhard Heydrich, head of the SS's Security Service, was given the task of administering the Final Solution. Heydrich created special strike forces (Einsatzgruppen) to carry out Nazi plans. After the defeat of Poland, he ordered these forces to round up all Polish Jews and put them in ghettos set up in a number of Polish cities.

In June 1941, the Einsatzgruppen were given the new job of acting as mobile killing units. These SS death squads followed the regular army's advance into the Soviet Union. Their job was to round up Jews in their villages, execute them, and bury them in mass graves. The graves were often giant pits dug by the victims themselves before they were shot. The leader of one of these death squads described the mode of operation:

The unit selected for this task would enter a village or city and order the prominent Jewish citizens to call together all Jews for the purpose of resettlement. They

So What ⁇

*If your students question the importance of **the Holocaust**, tell them . . .*

The post-war awareness of the realities of the Holocaust had multiple outcomes. For Jews, it intensified the desire for a sovereign nation—Israel—where they would not be the victims of others. World opinion, moved by the huge massacre of the Holocaust, supported the creation of Israel, and the new

state was born with the blessing of the United Nations. Unfortunately, not enough thought was given to the plight of non-Jews living in the area assigned to Israel, creating the Arab-Israeli conflict that persists today.

A second major reaction among Jews (and others) is the "never again" attitude that energizes Jews and non-Jews to ensure that ethnic groups should never again fall victim to such drastic tyranny.

BIOGRAPHY

Anne Frank: A Holocaust Victim

In 1933, after the Nazis had come to power in Germany, Otto Frank and his family moved to the Netherlands. He established a business in Amsterdam. His two daughters, Margot and Anne, soon learned Dutch and became used to their routine in their adopted city. The Franks, a Jewish family, had not really escaped the Nazis, however. The Nazis seized the Netherlands in May 1940. When it became apparent to Hans Frank that the Nazis were beginning to round up Jews, he decided to hide his family. With the help of friends, the Frank family, along with one other family, moved into a secret annex above the family business's warehouse on a street called Prinsengracht. Employees of the Frank family provided food and became their lifeline to the outside world.

Anne and the other refugees established a daily routine for the sake of their survival. During the day, while people were working in the warehouse, they remained very quiet. At night, they had more freedom to move about, but they were still confined to the house itself. Anne's father insisted that his daughters be educated, and he became their teacher. Aspiring to be a writer, Anne was glad to spend much of her time with her studies.

▲ Anne Frank led a normal schoolgirl life until she was forced into hiding. How difficult do you think it might have been for you to spend your teenage years concealed in an attic?

She also began writing in a diary. She recorded her daily routine, as well as her dreams for the future.

At times life in hiding was extremely challenging for the thirteen-year-old girl. Anne wrote this once about her daily routine and the fear of being caught: "My nerves often get the better of me; it is especially on Sundays that I feel rotten. . . . I go and lie on the divan and sleep, to make the time pass more quickly, and the stillness and the terrible fear, because there is no way of killing them." Nevertheless, Anne remained hopeful. In the second-to-last entry in her diary, dated July 15, 1944, she wrote, "It's really a wonder that I haven't dropped all my ideals, because they seem so absurd and impossible to carry out. Yet I keep them, because in spite of everything I still believe that people are really good at heart. I simply can't build up my hopes on a foundation consisting of confusion, misery, and death."

On August 4, 1944, after the Franks had spent two years in hiding, an informant, who was paid five gulden (GOOL-dun) ($1.40) per person, told the Nazis about the secret annex. The Franks were

(continued)

RECOMMENDED READING

The best studies of the Holocaust include R. Hilberg, *The Destruction of the European Jews,* rev. ed., 3 vols. (New York, 1985); L. Dawidowicz, *The War against the Jews* (New York, 1975); L. Yahil, *The Holocaust* (Oxford, 1990); and M. Gilbert, *The Holocaust: The History of the Jews of Europe during the Second World War* (New York, 1985). The role of Hitler in the Holocaust has been well examined in G. Fleming, *Hitler and the Final Solution* (Berkeley, 1984). On the problem of what the Allied countries knew about the Holocaust, see D. Wyman, *The Abandonment of the Jews: America and the Holocaust* (New York, 1984); W. Laqueur, *The Terrible Secret* (Boston, 1980); and M. Gilbert, *Auschwitz and the Allies* (New York, 1981). The other holocaust is examined in R. C. Lukas, *Forgotten Holocaust: The Poles Under German Occupation, 1939–44* (Lexington, Ky., 1986).

Ask students to discuss possible reasons why non-Jewish employees would have risked their lives to hide the Franks. What personal beliefs or values cause some people to forfeit their own security to help others? What do students believe they would have done in a similar situation?

Answers to Critical Thinking Questions

1. They were Jews trying to stay out of the hands of the Germans during World War II.
2. Boredom seemed to be a tremendous problem while she was in hiding.
3. Answers will vary. Reasons might include hatred of Jews, need of money or fear of the Germans.

BIOGRAPHY

Anne Frank: A Holocaust Victim, continued

sent to Auschwitz. Because of the advance of the Allies, theirs was the last train shipped to Auschwitz from the Netherlands. Only Otto Frank survived. Both Anne and her sister had been sent from Auschwitz to Bergen-Belsen in Germany, where they died of typhus shortly before that concentration camp was liberated. Otto Frank later found his daughter's diary and had it published in 1947. *The Diary of Anne Frank* became an international best-seller. For Anne, who wanted to be a writer, it was a fitting tribute.

1. Why did Anne Frank and her family go into hiding?

2. What would you say was Anne's greatest "enemy" while she was in hiding?

3. What do you think would cause someone to "sell" Jews to the Germans for $1.40 per person?

were requested to hand over their valuables to the leaders of the unit, and shortly before the execution to surrender their outer clothing. The men, women, and children were led to a place of execution which in most cases was located next to a more deeply excavated anti-tank ditch. Then they were shot, kneeling or standing, and the corpses thrown into the ditch.[7]

Such constant killing produced morale problems among the SS executioners. During a visit to Minsk in the Soviet Union, SS leader Himmler tried to build morale by pointing out, "I would not like it if Germans did such a thing gladly. But their conscience was in no way impaired, for they were soldiers who had to carry out every order unconditionally. I alone had responsibility before God and Hitler for everything that was happening, . . . and I was acting from a deep understanding of the necessity for this operation."[8]

Probably one million Jews were killed by the Einsatzgruppen. This approach to solving the Jewish problem was soon seen as too slow, however. Instead, the Nazis decided to kill the European Jewish population in specially built death camps. The plan was simple. Jews from countries occupied by Germany (or sympathetic to Germany) would be rounded up, packed like

cattle into freight trains, and shipped to Poland. Six extermination centers were built in Poland for this purpose. The largest and most famous was Auschwitz (OWSH-vits)-Birkenau. Medical technicians chose Zyklon B (the commercial name for hydrogen cyanide) as the most effective gas for quickly killing large numbers of people in gas chambers designed to look like shower rooms. After gassing, the corpses were burned in specially built crematoriums (ovens).

By the spring of 1942, the death camps were in full operation. First priority was given to the elimination of the ghettos in Poland. By the summer of 1942, however, Jews were also being shipped from France, Belgium, and Holland (see "Biography: Anne Frank—A Holocaust Victim"). Even as the Allies were winning the war in 1944, Jews were being shipped from Greece and Hungary. These shipments depended on the cooperation of Germany's Transport Ministry. Indeed, despite desperate military needs, even late in the war when Germany faced utter defeat, the Final Solution had priority in using railroad cars for the shipment of Jews to death camps.

A horrifying experience awaited the Jews when they arrived at one of the six death camps. Rudolf

COMPARING TIME PERIODS

Wars have always involved the killing of innocent civilians. This was true of wars fought between Catholics and Protestants, colonies and colonial powers, conquests by Mongols in India and China, and in many other cases. Ask students to explain what made the killing of the Jewish people by the Nazis different in World War II.

ENRICHMENT ACTIVITY

Students might be interested in the background and writings of Elie Wiesel, one of the few to survive Auschwitz. Wiesel's parents were both killed in concentration camps. He moved to Paris after the war where he studied at the University of Paris and worked as a newspaper correspondent. In 1963 Wiesel became a citizen of the United States, and from 1980–1986 Wiesel was chairman of the

President's Commission on the Holocaust. He received the Congressional Medal of Honor in 1985 and the Nobel Prize in 1986 for his work in promoting human rights. In his book, *Night,* Wiesel describes his experiences at Auschwitz. Other writings include *Dawn, The Accident, The Town Beyond the Wall, A Beggar in Jerusalem, The Testament,* and *The Forgotten.*

USING PRIMARY SOURCES

Why do students believe that Americans have heard more about the atrocities carried out by Nazi forces in Europe than about those inflicted by the Japanese on people of occupied lands? Might racism have anything to do with it as is suggested by some people?

COMPARING TIME PERIODS

Ask students to compare the treatment of people in lands occupied by the Nazi forces of Germany and those of lands conquered by the Japanese. Did either of these powers have any apparent interest in the rights of these people?

CLASS DISCUSSION

Explain to students that the United States might have attacked Japanese positions in South Asia—India and Burma—or might have relied more on fighting in China. However, each of these possibilities had the major drawback of much longer lines of supply. Further, the United States was able to successfully attack Japanese positions when the U.S. massed its strength to have clear advantages in terms of soldiers, air cover, and naval forces.

Höss (HAWSS), commanding officer at Auschwitz-Birkenau, described the experience:

> We had two SS doctors on duty at Auschwitz to examine the incoming transports of prisoners. The prisoners would be marched by one of the doctors who would make spot decisions as they walked by. Those who were fit for work were sent into the camp. Others were sent immediately to the extermination plants. Children of tender years were invariably exterminated since by reason of their youth they were unable to work. . . . at Auschwitz we endeavored to fool the victims into thinking that they were to go through a delousing process. Of course, frequently they realized our true intentions and we sometimes had riots and difficulties due to that fact.[9]

About 30 percent of the arrivals at Auschwitz were sent to a labor camp. The remainder went to the gas chambers (see "You Are There: The Holocaust—The Camp Commandant and the Camp Victims"). After they had been gassed, the bodies were burned in the crematoriums. The victims' goods, and even their bodies, were used for economic gain. Female hair was cut off, collected, and turned into mattresses or cloth. Some inmates were subjected to cruel and painful "medical" experiments. The Germans killed between five and six million Jews, over three million of them in the death camps. Virtually 90 percent of the Jewish populations of Poland, the Baltic countries, and Germany were killed. Overall, the Holocaust was responsible for the death of nearly two out of every three European Jews.

The Nazis were also responsible for the deliberate death by shooting, starvation, or overwork of at least another nine to ten million people. The Nazis considered the Gypsies of Europe, like the Jews, to be a race containing alien blood. The Gypsies, too, were rounded up for mass killing. About 40 percent of Europe's one million Gypsies were killed in the death camps. The leading elements of the "subhuman" Slavic peoples—the clergy, intellectuals, civil leaders, judges, and lawyers—were arrested and killed. Probably an additional four million Poles, Ukrainians, and Belorussians lost their lives as slave laborers for Nazi Germany.

Finally, probably at least three million to four million Soviet prisoners of war were killed in captivity.

The New Order in Asia

Japanese war policy in the areas in Asia occupied by Japan was basically defensive. Japan hoped to use its new possessions to meet its growing needs for raw materials, such as tin, oil, and rubber. The new possessions also would be an outlet for Japanese manufactured goods. To organize Japan's possessions, Japanese leaders set up a so-called Great East-Asia Co-prosperity Sphere. This was an economic community designed to provide mutual benefits to the occupied areas and the home country. A Ministry for Great East Asia, staffed by civilians, was established in Tokyo in October 1942 to handle arrangements between Japan and the conquered territories.

The Japanese conquest of Southeast Asia had been done under the slogan "Asia for the Asiatics." Many Japanese probably sincerely believed that their government was bringing about the liberation of the Southeast Asian peoples from European colonial rule. Local Japanese officials in occupied territories quickly made contact with anticolonialist elements. They promised the people that independent governments would be established under Japanese control. Such governments were eventually set up in Burma, the Dutch East Indies, Vietnam, and the Philippines.

In fact, however, real power rested with Japanese military authorities in each territory. In turn, the local Japanese military command was directly subordinated to the Army General Staff in Tokyo. The economic resources of the colonies were used for the benefit of the Japanese war machine. The native peoples in occupied lands were recruited to serve in local military units or were forced to work on public works projects. In some cases, these policies brought severe hardships to peoples living in the occupied areas. In Indochina, for example, local Japanese authorities forcibly took rice and shipped it abroad. This led directly to a food shortage that caused over a million Vietnamese to starve to death in 1944 and 1945.

Japanese authorities worked to instill a new moral and social, as well as a new political and economic,

---

RETEACHING ACTIVITY

For better understanding, remind students that in 1925 General Jiang Jieshi became leader of the Chinese Nationalist Party; in the 1930s, Mao Zedong emerged as leader of the Chinese Communist Party which had the support of many Chinese peasants. In 1937 when China was invaded by Japan, the two groups joined forces to fight against Japan, and in 1941 the Sino-Japanese War became part of World War II.

YOU ARE THERE

The Holocaust—The Camp Commandant and the Camp Victims

▲ *Polish children whose appearance fit the Nazi idea of a "master race" were often taken from their parents and sent to Germany where they were adopted by German parents. These children, just a few of the 50,000 taken, are being held at Auschwitz en route to new German homes.*

The Holocaust is one of the most horrifying events in history. The first paragraph that follows is taken from an account by Rudolf Höss, commandant of the extermination camp at Auschwitz-Birkenau. The second paragraph contains the words of a French doctor who explains what happened at one of the crematoriums described by Höss.

Rudolf Höss, Describing the Crematoriums at Auschwitz-Birkenau

The two large crematoria, Nos. I and II, were built during the winter of 1942–43. . . . They each could cremate c. 2,000 corpses within twenty-four hours. . . . Crematoria I and II both had under ground undressing and gassing rooms which could be completely ventilated. The corpses were brought up to the ovens on the floor above by lift. The gas chambers could hold c. 3,000 people. The firm of Topf had calculated that the two smaller crematoria, III and IV, would each be able to cremate 1,500 corpses within twenty-four hours. However, owing to the wartime shortage of materials, the builders were obliged to economise and so the undressing rooms and gassing rooms were built above ground and the ovens were of a less solid construction. But it soon became apparent

(continued)

On Line with WORLD HISTORY *Internet Activity*

You may want to have your students visit the following URL, where they will find information and additional web site resources to enhance their study of this chapter.
Nuremberg War Crime Trials
http://www.yale.edu/lawweb/avalon/imt/imt.htm

This site leads to a complete accounting of the trials, how they were run, and who was tried.
Due to the ever-changing nature of the World Wide Web, see the West History web site, **http://history.swpco.com** for regular updates of the URLs in this text.

COMPARING TIME PERIODS

Ask students to make a comparison between the Nazi requirement that Jewish people wear stars like those to the right and the law that was enforced until the 1960s in many parts of the United States that African Americans had to sit in the back of a bus or only used "colored" washrooms.

LEARNING FROM VISUALS

Answer to the caption question: When Jews were forced to wear armbands or yellow stars in public, it provided opportunities for people in public places to discriminate further against the Jews.

Answers to Critical Thinking Questions

1. The Nazis built undressing rooms, gas chambers, and crematoria to use in their extermination attempts.
2. Answers will vary. Students may think it was because they wanted the exterminations to be complete.
3. Answers will vary.

YOU ARE THERE

The Holocaust—The Camp Commandant and the Camp Victims, continued

▲ *In Nazi-controlled territories, Jews were forced to wear identifying star badges like these whenever they went out in public. How do you think others, such as shopkeepers, reacted when they saw the yellow stars?*

that the flimsy construction of these two four-retort ovens was not up to the demands made on it. No. III ceased operating altogether after a short time and later was no longer used. No. IV had to be repeatedly shut down since after a short period in operation of 4–6 weeks, the ovens and chimneys had burnt out. The victims of the gassing were mainly burnt in pits behind crematorium IV.

A French Doctor, Describing the Victims of One of the Crematoriums

It is mid-day, when a long line of women, children, and old people enter the yard. The senior official in charge . . . climbs on a bench to tell them that they are going to have a bath and that afterwards they will get a drink of hot coffee. They all undress in the yard. . . . The doors are opened and an indescribable jostling begins. The first people to enter the gas chamber begin to draw back. They sense the death which awaits them. The SS men put an end to the pushing and shoving with blows from their rifle butts beating the heads of the horrified women who are desperately hugging

their children. The massive oak double doors are shut. For two endless minutes one can hear banging on the walls and screams which are no longer human. And then—not a sound. Five minutes later the doors are opened. The corpses, squashed together and distorted, fall out like a waterfall. The bodies which are still warm pass through the hands of the hairdresser who cuts their hair and the dentist who pulls out their gold teeth . . . One more transport has just been processed through No. IV crematorium.

1. What death camp procedures did the Nazis follow to exterminate the Jews and other so-called undesirables?
2. Why do you think the Nazis were so careful in these procedures?
3. What was your reaction to these two accounts?

ENRICHMENT ACTIVITY

Depending upon the maturity level of your students and the depth in which you wish to study the Holocaust, you might consider the documentary *Night and Fog* and analyze in detail the concentration camp system. What were its goals? How did it work?

What do you think life was like for the inmates? What do you think life was like for the camp commandant and the guards who worked in the camp? Why didn't more people—either the guards or the inmates—rebel against the system?

order in occupied areas. Occupation policy stressed such traditional values as obedience, community spirit, respect for parents, and discipline. These, of course, were the traditional values of Japanese society. At the same time, the Japanese denounced the Western values of liberalism and individualism. To promote the creation of this New Order, as it was called, occupation authorities gave strong support to local religious groups.

At first, many Southeast Asian nationalists took Japanese promises at face value and agreed to cooperate with their new masters. In Burma, for example, an independent government was set up in 1943 and declared war on the Allies. Eventually, the nature of Japanese occupation policies became clear, and sentiment turned against the New Order. Japanese officials sometimes provoked such attitudes by their arrogance and contempt for local customs. In the Dutch East Indies, for example, Indonesians were required to bow in the direction of Tokyo and to recognize the divinity of the Japanese emperor. Such practices, of course, were extremely distasteful to Muslims. In Burma, Buddhist pagodas were sometimes used as military latrines.

Japanese military forces often had little respect for even the lives of their subject peoples. In their conquest of Nanjing, China, in 1937, Japanese soldiers spent several days killing, raping, and looting. After the conquest of Korea, almost 800,000 Koreans were sent to Japan, most of them as forced laborers. Tens of thousands of Korean women were forced to be "comfort women" (prostitutes) for Japanese troops. In construction projects to help their war effort, the Japanese made extensive use of labor forces composed of both prisoners of war and local peoples. In building the Burma-Thailand railway in 1943, for example, the Japanese used 61,000 Australian, British, and Dutch prisoners of war and almost 300,000 workers from Burma, Malaya, Thailand, and the Dutch East Indies. An inadequate diet and appalling work conditions in an unhealthy climate led to the death of 12,000 Allied prisoners of war and 90,000 native workers by the time the railway was completed.

Such Japanese behavior created a dilemma for many nationalists in the occupied lands. They had no desire to see the return of the colonial powers, but they did not like what the Japanese were doing. Some turned against the Japanese. Others simply did nothing. Indonesian patriots tried to have it both ways. They pretended to support Japan while actually sabotaging the Japanese administration. In French Indochina, Ho Chi Minh's Communist Party made contact with U.S. military units in South China. The Communists agreed to provide information on Japanese troop movements and to rescue downed American fliers in the area. In Malaya, where Japanese treatment of ethnic Chinese residents was especially harsh, many joined a guerrilla movement against the occupying forces. By the end of the war, little support remained in the region for the Japanese "liberators."

SECTION REVIEW

1. **Locate:**
   (*a*) Auschwitz-Birkenau

2. **Define:**
   (*a*) Final Solution

3. **Identify:**
   (*a*) Heinrich Himmler,
   (*b*) the Holocaust,
   (*c*) the Madagascar Plan,
   (*d*) Reinhard Heydrich,
   (*e*) Einsatzgruppen,
   (*f*) Rudolf Höss,
   (*g*) Asia for the Asiatics

4. **Recall:**
   (*a*) In what two ways was German occupation of foreign lands organized?
   (*b*) Why did Germans make particular efforts to eliminate leaders of Slavic peoples?
   (*c*) What traditional values did Japan's occupation stress?
   (*d*) Why did Japanese brutality create a dilemma for nationalists in lands they occupied?

5. **Think Critically:** Why was Germany's attempt to solve labor shortages by forcing people from occupied lands to work against their will probably counterproductive?

MORE ABOUT . . . *War Feminism*

The author refers to some of the social disruptions in the United States that were a result of the war. One of these was the manpower shortages caused by the expansion of the U.S. military. Since the men were at war and production was the highest priority, women took jobs of the men who had joined the military. At the time this redeployment of human resources was seen as a wartime need, rather than as a feminist advance. When the men came back, the realities of what transpired could not be ignored. Women had done the jobs of men in a commendable way. No longer could we say the women couldn't do a particular job efficiently. During the 1960s and beyond, when women demanded equal access to economic opportunities, the memory of their war-time counterparts facilitated their move into the economic mainstream.

CLOSE

Lead students in a discussion of the Focus objectives identified on page 919. Emphasize the cost of the "final solution" for Jewish people to the German nation and to all societies in the world.

FOCUS

OBJECTIVES

After completing this section, students should be able to

1. describe efforts taken by states to mobilize for World War II
2. describe the impact of World War II on civilian populations
3. identify and explain the first signs of the Cold War

FOCUS ACTIVITY

Discuss with students the military draft and current military recruitment strategies in the United States.

THE HOME FRONT AND THE AFTERMATH OF THE WAR

World War II was even more of a total war than was World War I. Fighting was much more widespread and covered most of the world. Economic mobilization was more extensive; so, too, was the mobilization of women. The number of civilians killed—almost twenty million—was far higher. Many of these victims were children (see "Young People in World War II: The Other Victims").

The Mobilization of Peoples: Four Examples

The home fronts of the major warring states varied a great deal. World War II had an enormous impact on the Soviet Union, the United States, Germany, and Japan.

The Soviet Union

Known to the Soviets as the Great Patriotic War, the German-Soviet war witnessed the greatest land battles in history, as well as incredible ruthlessness. To Nazi Germany, the war against Russia was a war of oppression and annihilation that called for drastic measures. Two out of every five persons killed in World War II were Soviet citizens.

The initial defeats of the Soviet Union led to drastic emergency measures that affected the lives of the civilian population there. Leningrad, for example, experienced nine hundred days of siege, during which its inhabitants became so desperate for food that they ate dogs, cats, and mice. Probably 1.5 million people died in the city. As the German army made its rapid advance into Soviet territory, Soviet workers dismantled and shipped the factories in the western part of the Soviet Union to the interior—to the Urals, western Siberia, and the Volga regions. Machines were placed on the bare ground. As laborers began their work, walls went up around them.

Stalin called the widespread military and industrial mobilization of the nation a "battle of machines." The Soviets won, producing 78,000 tanks and 98,000 artillery pieces. In 1943, fifty-five percent of the Soviet national income went for war materials, compared with 15 percent in 1940. As a result of the emphasis on military goods, Soviet citizens experienced severe shortages of both food and housing.

Soviet women played a major role in the war effort. Women and girls worked in industries, mines, and railroads. Overall, the number of women working in industry increased almost 60 percent. Soviet women were also expected to dig antitank ditches and work as air raid wardens. In addition, the Soviet Union was the only country in World War II to use women in battle. Soviet women served as snipers and also in aircrews of bomber squadrons. The female pilots who helped to defeat the Germans at Stalingrad were known as the "Night Witches."

The United States

The home front in the United States was quite different from that of the other major powers. The United States faced no threat of war in its own territory. Eventually the United States became the arsenal of the Allied powers; it produced the military equipment the Allies needed. At the height of war production in November 1943, the country was building six ships a day, $6 billion worth of war-related goods a month, and ninety-six thousand planes per year.

The mobilization of the American economy created social problems. The construction of new factories created boom towns where thousands came to work but then faced a shortage of houses and schools. Economic mobilization also led to a widespread movement of people. Sixteen million men and women were enrolled in the military. Another sixteen million, mostly wives and girlfriends of servicemen or workers looking for jobs, also moved around the country. Over one million African Americans moved from the rural South to the cities of the North and West, looking for jobs in industry. The presence of African Americans in areas where they had not lived before led to racial tensions and sometimes even racial riots. In Detroit in June 1943,

---

SPECIAL NEEDS: *Visual/Auditory*

On an overhead transparency, set up a chart with four columns: People, Places, Military Terms and Other Terms Related to World War II. As you read the following terms, have students identify in which column the term should go. Ask the students to share what they have learned about the particular person, place, military or other term. The following terms should be included:

People: Hitler, Franco, Mussolini, Henry Pu Yi, Stalin, Roosevelt, Rommel, MacArthur, Churchill, Eisenhower, Aryans, Jews, Gypsies, Anne Frank, Truman, Oppenheimer.

Places: Czechoslovakia, Ethiopia, Austria, Munich, Poland, Manchuria, Beijing, Denmark, Norway, Hungary, Bulgaria, Pearl Harbor, Midway, Coral Sea, Hiroshima, Nagasaki, Auschwitz, London, Iran.

YOUNG PEOPLE IN WORLD WAR II

The Other Victims

Young people of all ages were also the victims of World War II. They, too, were subject to the same dangers as adults. Jewish children, along with their mothers, were the first ones selected for gas chambers upon their arrival in the death camps of Poland. As Rudolf Höss, commandant at Auschwitz, explained, "Children of tender years were invariably exterminated, since by reason of their youth they were unable to work." Young Jewish males soon learned to look as adult as possible in order to survive. Altogether, 1.2 million Jewish children died in the Holocaust.

Many children on both sides were evacuated from the cities during the war in order to avoid the bombing. The Germans had a program that created about 9,000 camps for children in the countryside. In Japan, 15,000 children were evacuated from Hiroshima before its destruction. The British moved about 6 million children and their mothers in 1939. Some British parents even sent their children to Canada and the United States, although this, too, could be dangerous. When the ocean liner *Arandora Star* was hit by a German torpedo, it had 77 British children on board. They never made it to Canada.

Children evacuated to the countryside did not always see their parents again. Many other children also became orphaned when their parents were killed. In 1945, there were possibly thirteen million orphaned children in Europe. Poland alone had one million orphans.

In eastern Europe, children especially suffered under harsh German occupation policies. All secondary schools in German-occupied eastern

The war left millions of orphans who had neither homes nor any remaining family to help them. These two German-Jewish children on the St. Louis were refused entrance in Cuba and Miami, Florida, and were then returned to Antwerp. Do you think the world reaction to war orphans has changed since World War II? Why or why not?

Europe were closed. Their facilities and equipment were destroyed.

Heinrich Himmler, head of the SS, said of these Slavic children that their education should consist only "in teaching simple arithmetic up to 500, the writing of one's name, and that God has ordered obedience to the Germans, honesty, diligence, and politeness. I do not consider an ability to read as necessary."

At times, young people were expected to carry the burden of fighting the war. In the last year of the war, fanatical Hitler Youth members, often only fourteen or fifteen years old, could be found in the front lines. In the Soviet Union, children as young as thirteen or fourteen spied on German positions and worked with the resistance movement. Some were even given decorations for killing the enemy.

1. In what ways were young people "the other victims" in World War II?

2. What is your reaction to Heinrich Himmler's statement about the education of Slavic children?

3. How would living through a war make a child grow up more quickly?

COMPARING TIME PERIODS

Remind students that during earlier wars it was not uncommon for the entire population of defeated communities to be killed or sold into slavery. Today in Bosnia and Rwanda children are again being made victims. Do students believe there is any way to conduct war without creating innocent victims? Is it necessary at times?

LEARNING FROM VISUALS

Answer to the caption question: The public is better educated about the plight of war orphans. Answers will vary.

Answers to Critical Thinking Questions

1. Many became homeless orphans. Many were killed simply because of their race.
2. Answers will vary.
3. Answers will vary. Children would see death all around them, they might become homeless or orphans, they may have participated in the killing.

Military Terms: Blitzkrieg, panzer divisions, Luftwaffe, unconditional surrender, Einsatzgruppen, Blitz, Superfortresses.

Other Terms: New Order, Final Solution, Cold War, Nazism, appeasement, Allies, Fuhrer, Holocaust, Crematoriums, Manhattan Project, iron curtain, Cold War.

An alternate method of having students complete this activity is to have the class divided into 4 groups and have each group come up with as many people, places, or military terms as they can, based on the chapter. Then, each group may present their lists to the class.

CLASS DISCUSSION

Help students understand how war can change people's willingness to tolerate others with different ethnic heritages. Ask students to explain the fact that during World War I a number of native born American citizens had their names changed from Schultz to Smith. Would students be willing to change their names or lie about their heritage to avoid prejudice? Why couldn't Japanese Americans take similar steps to avoid prejudice?

LEARNING FROM VISUALS

Ask students to write a hypothetical conversation that might have taken place among the workers in the photograph to the right in which they discuss problems they face in their daily lives, with their families, and their work.

▶ *Soviet women were expected to contribute as much to the war effort as Soviet men. Here a group working at a munitions factory put the final touch—grease—on shells.*

for example, white mobs roamed the streets attacking blacks. One million blacks enrolled in the military. There they were segregated in their own battle units. Angered by the way they were treated, some became militant and prepared to fight for their civil rights.

Japanese Americans were treated even worse. On the West Coast, 110,000 Japanese Americans, 65 percent of whom had been born in the United States, were removed to camps surrounded by barbed wire and required to take loyalty oaths. Public officials claimed this policy was necessary for security reasons. However, no similar treatment of German Americans or Italian Americans ever took place. The racism in this treatment of Japanese Americans was evident when the California governor, Culbert Olson, said, "You know, when I look out at a group of Americans of German or Italian descent, I can tell whether they're loyal or not. I can tell how they think and even perhaps what they are thinking. But it is impossible for me to do this with inscrutable orientals, and particularly the Japanese."[10]

Germany

In August 1914, Germans had enthusiastically cheered their soldiers marching off to war. In September 1939, the streets were quiet. Many Germans did not care or, even worse for the Nazi regime, feared disaster. Hitler was well aware of the importance of the home front. He believed that the collapse of the home front in World War I had caused Germany's defeat. In his determination to avoid a repetition of that experience, he adopted economic policies that may indeed have cost Germany the war.

To maintain the morale of the home front during the first two years of the war, Hitler refused to cut consumer goods production or to increase the production of armaments. Blitzkrieg gave the Germans quick victories and enabled them to plunder the food and raw materials of conquered countries. In this way, they could avoid taking resources away from the civilian economy.

After German defeats on the Russian front and the American entry into the war, however, the economic situation in Germany changed. Early in 1942, Hitler finally ordered a massive increase in armaments production and in the size of the army. Hitler's architect, Albert Speer, was made minister for armaments and munitions in 1942. By careful management, Speer was able to triple the production of armaments between 1942 and 1943, despite the intense Allied air raids.

RETEACHING ACTIVITY

Students should understand how heavily cities in Germany were bombed. You may wish to bring in photos or illustrations of Dresden, Hamburg, Kiel, Hannover, or other cities which were almost totally demolished. The British devoted nearly 25 percent of their resources to the bombing campaign, the Americans 9 percent. Later estimates show that the strategic bombing reduced German industrial capacity by less than 8 percent, but it did leave a massive rebuilding effort to be accomplished after the war. Point out the difference between massive attacks on cities, industries, and communication and supply lines and tactical bombing, where certain particular targets are chosen and then destroyed.

Speer's urgent plea for a total mobilization of resources for the war effort went unheeded, however. Hitler, afraid of civilian morale problems that would undermine the home front, refused to make any dramatic cuts in the production of consumer goods. A total mobilization of the economy was not put into effect until July 1944. Schools, theaters, and cafes then were closed. Speer was finally permitted to use all remaining resources for the production of a few basic military items. By that time, it was in vain. Total war mobilization was too little and too late to save Germany from defeat.

Nazi attitudes toward women changed in the course of the war. Before the war, the Nazis had worked to keep women out of the job market. As the war progressed and more and more men were called up for military service, this position no longer made sense. Nazi magazines now proclaimed, "We see the woman as the eternal mother of our people, but also as the working and fighting comrade of the man."[11] However, the number of women working in industry, agriculture, commerce, and domestic service increased only slightly. The total number of employed women in September 1944 was 14.9 million, compared with 14.6 million in May 1939. Many women, especially those of the middle class, did not want jobs, especially in factories.

Japan

Wartime Japan was a highly mobilized society. To guarantee its control over all national resources, the government created a planning board to control prices, wages, labor, and resources. Traditional habits of obedience and hierarchy were used to encourage citizens to sacrifice their resources, and sometimes their lives, for the national cause. The calls for sacrifice reached a high point in the final years of the war. Young Japanese were encouraged to volunteer to serve as pilots (known as **kamikaze,** or "divine wind") in the suicide missions against U.S. fighting ships at sea.

Japan was extremely reluctant to mobilize women on behalf of Japan's war effort. General Hideki Tojo (TOE-JOE), prime minister from 1941 to 1944, opposed female employment. He argued that "the weakening of the family system would be the weakening of the nation . . . we are able to do our duties only because we have wives and mothers at home."[12] In other words, women should remain at home and fulfill their responsibilities by bearing more children. Female employment increased during the war, but only in such areas as the textile industry and farming, where women had traditionally worked. Instead of using women to meet labor shortages, the Japanese government brought in Korean and Chinese laborers.

The Frontline Civilians: The Bombing of Cities

Bombing was used in World War II against a variety of targets, including military targets, enemy troops, and civilian populations. The bombing of civilians made World War II as dangerous on the home front as it was on the battlefield. There had been a small number of bombing raids in the last year of World War I. These bombings had given rise to the argument that the public outcry created by the bombing of civilian populations would be an effective way to force governments into making peace. As a result, European air forces began to develop long-range bombers in the 1930s.

The first sustained use of civilian bombing proved wrong the theory that such bombing would force peace. Beginning in early September 1940, the German air force bombed London and many other British cities and towns nightly. The Blitz, as the British called the German air raids, became a national experience. Londoners took the first heavy blows. Their ability to maintain their morale set the standard for the rest of the British population.

London morale, however, was helped by the fact that the German raids were widely scattered over a very large city. Smaller towns were more directly affected by the air raids. On November 14, 1940, for example, the German air force destroyed hundreds of shops and one hundred acres of the city center of Coventry. The bombings produced morale problems as wild rumors of casualties spread quickly in these smaller communities. Nevertheless, morale was soon restored. War production in these areas, in any case, seems to have been little affected by the raids.

REINFORCING VOCABULARY

Assign students to look up an earlier use of the word kamikaze on page 304 in Chapter 10. Ask students to explain similarities between the "divine wind" that protected Japan in 1281 and what they hoped their pilots would accomplish in 1945.

CLASS DISCUSSION

Some people have compared Allied bombing of German cities and the American use of the Atomic bomb against Hiroshima and Nagasaki with the Nazi death camps where millions of people were killed. Ask students to discuss this proposition. Do they believe it has any merit? What reasons can they give for their points of view?

SPECIAL NEEDS: *Visual/Auditory*

Have students read pages 919–932. Have them form groups according to the following areas of interest: 1) The Holocaust; 2) The Nazis; 3) Anne Frank; 4) Concentration Camps. Have the student groups use the library to study their area of choice more in depth. Have them develop, organize and present an interview or newscast. In each group have students assume the roles of reporters, Nazis, citizens from the various countries affected by the Holocaust, Anne Frank, the Frank family and friends, Holocaust survivors, and prison guards etc. Each person interviewed will relate his or her experiences during World War II.

This active-involvement activity is helpful for all students who may need review of basic concepts, different modalities in the presentation of material, and opportunities for students to speak and listen.

▲ *Clydebank, a city near Glasgow, Scotland, was heavily bombed in March 1941. Only seven homes remained without damage, and 35,000 of the city's 47,000 residents became homeless in just one night. Where would you and your family live if your home and town were suddenly destroyed?*

The British failed to learn from their own experience, however. They soon began to bomb Germany. Churchill and his advisors believed that destroying German communities would break civilian morale and bring victory. Major bombing raids began in 1942 under the direction of Arthur Harris, the wartime leader of the British Air Force's Bomber Command. Britain's four-engine heavy bombers were capable of taking the war into the center of occupied Europe. On May 31, 1942, Cologne became the first German city to be attacked by a thousand bombers.

The entry of the United States into the war produced a new bombing strategy. American planes flew daytime missions aimed at the precise bombing of transportation facilities and wartime industries. The British Bomber Command continued nighttime saturation bombing of all German cities with populations over 100,000.

Bombing raids added an element of terror to circumstances already made difficult by growing shortages of food, clothing, and fuel. Germans especially feared the incendiary bombs, which created firestorms that swept destructive paths through the cities. Four raids on Hamburg in August 1943 produced temperatures of 1,800 degrees Fahrenheit, obliterated half the city's buildings, and killed 50,000 civilians. The ferocious bombing of Dresden from February 13 to 15, 1945, created a firestorm that may have killed as many as 100,000 inhabitants and refugees. Even some Allied leaders began to criticize what they saw as the unnecessary terror bombing of German cities.

Germany suffered enormously from the Allied bombing raids. Millions of buildings were destroyed, and possibly half a million civilians died from the raids (see "Focus on Everyday Life: Homelessness on the Home Front"). Nevertheless, it is highly unlikely that Allied bombing sapped the morale of the German people. Instead, Germans, whether pro-Nazi or anti-Nazi, fought on stubbornly, often driven simply by a desire to live. Nor did the bombing destroy Germany's industrial capacity. The Allied Strategic Bombing Survey revealed that the production of war materials actually increased between 1942 and 1944. Even in 1944 and 1945, Allied raids cut German production of armaments by only 7 percent. Nevertheless, the widespread destruction of transportation systems and fuel supplies made it extremely difficult for the new materials to reach the German military.

In Japan, the bombing of civilians reached a new level with the use of the first atomic bomb. Japan was especially open to air raids, because its air force had been almost destroyed in the course of the war. Moreover, its crowded cities were built of flimsy materials that were especially vulnerable to fire bombing. Attacks on Japanese cities by the new U.S. B-29 Superfortresses, the biggest bombers of the war, had begun on November 24, 1944. By the summer of 1945, many of Japan's industries had been destroyed, along with one-fourth of its dwellings. After the Japanese government decreed the mobilization of all people between the ages of thirteen and sixty into a People's Volunteer Corps, President Truman and his advisors decided that Japanese fanaticism might mean a million U.S. casualties. As we have seen, Truman then decided to drop the atomic bomb on Hiroshima and Nagasaki (see "The Role of Science and Technology: The Atomic Bomb").

MORE ABOUT . . . *Refugees*

Refugees are persons who have fled their country or been expelled from it and who cannot or will not return because they fear persecution. A refugee is not quite the same as a displaced person; the latter term, which came into use during World War II, describes people displaced from home as a result of war or disaster. In many cases, however, the distinction is hard to make. More than 40 million persons have been uprooted since the outbreak of World War II.

The majority of World War II refugees were Europeans; they included a large number of Jews who had escaped from German-occupied territories and other persons who had fled from advancing Soviet armies.

After World War II, Congress passed several acts to admit refugees, who, under U.S. laws, could easily adjust their status to that of immigrant. By the early 1960s it was clear

FOCUS ON EVERYDAY LIFE
Homelessness on the Home Front in Europe

◄ *Families in every country in Europe lost homes, belongings, and the means to make a living. These Russian refugees trudge through the snow to find new shelters, all their household belongings packed onto small carts.*

World War II was the most destructive conflict in history. One of its results was homelessness on a scale never before imagined in history. Air raids virtually turned the home front into another fighting front. Air raids killed people, but they also destroyed dwellings. This created a mass of homeless people who became refugees in search of a safer area. In Germany alone, by 1945 almost twelve million people had become homeless. Many had lost all of their possessions. Even the threat of severe penalties did not keep many from stealing. One historian observed, "Thus on 31 May 1942 Paula W., a seamstress from Cologne, took some clothes, coffee and a suitcase which did not belong to her out of the burning apartment house in which she lived. She was denounced by a neighbor, promptly arrested, hauled in front of a special Court and guillotined on June 3."

Homeless refugees were a major feature of World War II. They were evident from the very beginning of the war. Millions of Polish, Belgian, French, and Soviet citizens fled in all directions when German bombs or gunfire destroyed their homes. In the last year of the war, millions of Germans also became refugees. Most fled westward to escape the advancing Soviet forces.

(continued)

CLASS DISCUSSION

Ask students to discuss their conception of private property. Would they ever consider taking something that was not their own? What would they think of a person who took something of theirs? How would living in a city that had been destroyed in war affect their perspective on what is theirs, what belongs to others, and their ethical perspective on theft?

LEARNING FROM VISUALS

Ask students to compare the photograph to the left with the one of a German soldier near Stalingrad on page 915. What do students imagine these refugees would have to say about the soldier's fate? How much sympathy would the refugees feel? Why does war dehumanize people?

---

that the U.S. national origins quota system of selecting immigrants failed to handle refugee situations and was inconsistent with the growing civil rights consciousness of Americans.

Today, as in the past, a conflict exists between two poles of opinion. One viewpoint states that the United States was founded on the principle of free access to all immigrants and that restrictions on immigration is undemocratic. The opposing viewpoint basically states that there is an economic imperative to protect the employment opportunities of citizens already living in the country. Of course this simplistic summary does not even begin to touch upon the complex arguments on both sides. Encourage your students to do further study on this important and extremely relevant issue.

Answers to Critical Thinking Questions

1. More homes were destroyed during World War II than any other war because of the bombs, artillery, etc. These weapons had not been used in earlier wars.
2. The United Nations Relief and Rehabilitation Administration was set up to take care of the homeless.
3. The refugees also had to face the loss of family members, friends, jobs, and for many of them, their own country.

CLASS DISCUSSION

Ask students to discuss the likelihood of achieving the American objective of providing Europeans with "democratic institutions of their own choice" in light of the military and political situations at the end of World War II.

TEACHING THEMES

The Role of Individuals

Ask students to evaluate each of the three leaders at Yalta. How much difference do students believe these men made in the course of the war as individuals? How much would have happened regardless of who was the leader of the United States, Great Britain, or the Soviet Union?

FOCUS ON EVERYDAY LIFE

Homelessness on the Home Front in Europe, continued

By the end of the war, 30 million homeless refugees clogged the roads of Europe. The newly founded United Nations set up a special organization to deal with them. The United Nations Relief and Rehabilitation Administration (UNRRA) set up camps for displaced persons on the edges of cities all over Western and Central Europe. UNRRA passed out some 25 million tons of food in seventeen countries between 1945 and 1947.

1. Why was there more homelessness as a result of World War II than any other war fought before?
2. What organization was set up to help the homeless in Europe after World War II?
3. In addition to being homeless, what did the refugees also have to face?

The Emergence of the Cold War

The total victory of the Allies in World War II was followed not by a real peace but rather by the beginnings of a new conflict, known as the Cold War. This conflict was to dominate world politics until the end of the 1980s. The Cold War stemmed from the differences between the Soviet Union and the United States. These differences became apparent at the Allied war conferences held in the last years of the war. Allied leaders had different visions of what the world should be like after the war.

Stalin, Roosevelt, and Churchill, the leaders of the Big Three of the Grand Alliance, met at Tehran (the capital of Iran) in November 1943 to decide the future course of the war. Their major tactical decision concerned the final assault on Germany. Stalin and Roosevelt argued successfully for an American-British invasion of the Continent through France. This was scheduled for the spring of 1944. The acceptance of this plan had important consequences. It meant that Soviet and British-American forces would meet in defeated Germany along a north-south dividing line. Most likely, Eastern Europe would be liberated by Soviet forces. The Allies also agreed to a partition of postwar Germany.

By the time of the conference at Yalta in southern Russia in February 1945, the defeat of Germany was obvious. The Western powers, which had earlier believed that the Soviets were in a weak position, were now faced with the reality of eleven million Red Army soldiers taking possession of Eastern and much of Central Europe.

Stalin was deeply suspicious of the Western powers. He wanted a buffer to protect the Soviet Union from possible future Western aggression. At the same time, however, Stalin was eager to gain important resources. Roosevelt, by this time, was moving toward the idea of self-determination for Europe. In other words, the Grand Alliance pledged to help liberated Europe in the creation of "democratic institutions of their own choice." Liberated countries were to hold free elections to determine their political systems.

At Yalta, Roosevelt sought Russian military help against Japan. At that time, the atomic bomb was not yet a certainty. Then, too, American military planners feared the possible loss of as many as one million men in the attacks on the Japanese home islands. Roosevelt therefore agreed to Stalin's price for military aid against Japan: possession of Sakhalin (SACK-uh-LEEN) and the Kurile Islands, as well as two warm-water ports and railroad rights in Manchuria.

MORE ABOUT . . . the Dropping of the "A" Bomb

The war in Europe was over, the Japanese were in retreat, and Americans were advancing on Japan. President Truman said the rationale for using the atomic bomb was based on estimates of huge American losses in the anticipated land invasion of Japan.

Now, after time has allowed for reflection and the facts are more fully known as a result of documents obtained through the Freedom of Information Act, many people have ques-

tioned the wisdom of the president's decision.

It appears today that Truman's estimates of American losses in the event of a land invasion of Japan were greatly overestimated. It also appears that saving American lives was not the only purpose of the bomb; the United States wanted to impress the U.S.S.R., with our power

As we live with the memory of dropping two nuclear bombs on Japan, and the knowl-

THE ROLE OF SCIENCE AND TECHNOLOGY
The Atomic Bomb

▲ *Until August 6, 1945, the world had never experienced the total, mass destruction produced by an atomic bomb. This view of Hiroshima is a commanding visual record of the power of this new weapon.*

The discovery at the beginning of the twentieth century that atoms contained enormous amounts of energy first gave rise to the idea that splitting the atom might be the basis of a devastating weapon. However, it was some time before the idea was taken seriously. In fact, it took the demands of World War II and the fear that the Germans might make an atomic bomb first to convince the U.S. government to try to build an atomic bomb. In 1942, the United States set in motion the Manhattan Project.

The Manhattan Project was a code name for the enormous industrial and technical enterprise that produced the first atomic bomb. The making of the atomic bomb was both complicated and expensive. It cost 2 billion dollars and employed the efforts of 600,000 people. Colonel Leslie Groves had overall supervision. The physicist J. Robert Oppenheimer (AWP-un-HIE-mur) was director of the Los Alamos, New Mexico, center where the bomb was actually built. A successful test explosion on July 16, 1945, near Alamogordo, New Mexico, meant that the bomb could now be used. The war in Europe had already ended, but there was no doubt that the bomb would be used against the Japanese. A committee had already chosen the city of Hiroshima as the first target.

The bomb was dropped on August 6, 1945, by a U.S. B-29 bomber nicknamed "Enola Gay." The destruction was incredible. An area of five square miles was turned to ashes. Of the 76,000 buildings in Hiroshima, 70,000 were flattened. Of the city's 350,000 inhabitants, 140,000 had died by the end of 1945. By the end of 1950, another 50,000 had died from the effects of radiation. A second bomb was dropped on Nagasaki on August 9. The dropping of the first atomic bomb on Hiroshima had introduced the world to the Nuclear Age.

1. Why was the first atomic bomb developed?

2. Why was the atomic bomb dropped on Japan?

3. Imagine yourself in the "Enola Gay" when the first atomic bomb was dropped on Hiroshima. Describe your feelings.

edge that we are the only nation to have actually used such a weapon, other countries try to determine what our actions may mean for them. After World War II, the world entered the period is known as the Cold War. Billions and billions of dollars (and rubles) were spent on bombs, airplanes, missiles, and submarines. Each country acquired enough power to sustain a surprise attack, to retaliate, and to totally destroy the other.

The American people were told of the need to defend themselves from possible Soviet attack, while Soviet citizens were told of the dangers of an American attack. Most Americans were convinced that our country would act in a moral way. Most Soviet citizens saw no reason to doubt that bombs could be dropped on them. Thankfully, no one "pulled the trigger." The world survived the crisis.

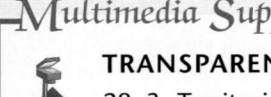

Multimedia Support

TRANSPARENCY

28–3, Territorial Changes in Europe after World War II (Map 28.5)

ACTIVITY

Have students research the opening of the United Nations and have them prepare posters welcoming the organization and its representatives to their new building and home in New York City.

Map 28.5 Territorial Changes in Europe after World War II

The creation of the United Nations was a major American concern at Yalta. Roosevelt wanted the Big Three powers to be part of such a postwar international organization before difficult issues divided them into hostile camps. Both Churchill and Stalin accepted Roosevelt's plans for the establishment of a United Nations organization and set the first meeting for San Francisco in April 1945.

The issues of Germany and eastern Europe were treated less decisively. The Big Three reaffirmed that Germany must surrender unconditionally and be divided into four zones, which would be occupied and governed by the military forces of the United States, Great Britain, France, and the Soviet Union. German reparations were set at $20 billion. A compromise was also worked out in regard to Poland. Stalin agreed to free elections in the future to determine a new government in that country.

STUDYING MAPS

The following questions will help you guide students through their study of Map 28.5.

1. Roughly what share of its territory was lost by Germany after World War II? *(approximately one-quarter to one-third)*

2. Why was the location of the divided city of Berlin certain to be the source of problems between East and West? *(Berlin was close to Soviet-held territory.)*

3. Why might the German people have wished for an earlier successful invasion of Europe from the west? *(Answers will vary.)*

Map 28.6   Territorial Changes in Asia after World War II

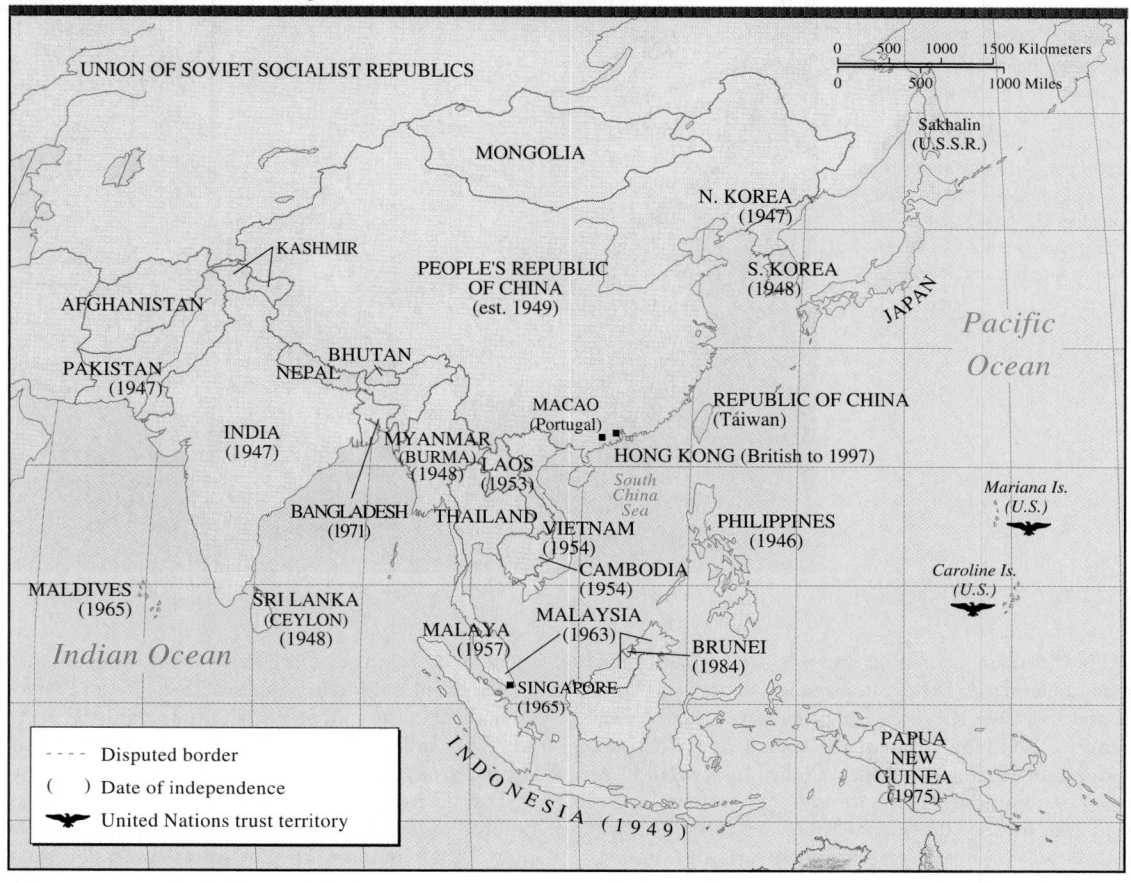

The issue of free elections in Eastern Europe caused a serious split between the Soviets and the Americans, however. The principle was that Eastern European governments would be freely elected, but they were also supposed to be pro-Russian. As Churchill expressed it, "The Poles will have their future in their own hands, with the single limitation that they must honestly follow in harmony with their allies, a policy friendly to Russia."[13] This attempt to reconcile two irreconcilable goals was doomed to failure, as soon became evident at the next conference of the Big Three powers at Potsdam.

Even before the conference at Potsdam took place in July 1945, Western relations with the Soviets were deteriorating rapidly. During the war, the Grand Alliance had been based on the needs of the war. The Allied powers' only common aim was the defeat of Nazism. Once this aim had all but been accomplished, the many differences between the Soviets and the West came to the surface.

CRITICAL THINKING

This chapter introduces the United Nations, the successor to the League of Nations. You may want to review the main weakness of the League—the fact that it had no power to enforce its decisions.

Students have probably grasped the concept that just because nations put their signature to a document it doesn't mean in all cases that they will actually abide by the agreement. The League of Nations is not the only international tribunal that had very little actual power. Ask students to discuss reasons that nations are so unwilling to give up any sovereignty, even though they may be the main beneficiaries of such an arrangement.

COMPARING TIME PERIODS

Ask students to create a chart that compares the end of World War I with the end of World War II. Why was a true and lasting peace unlikely to result from either situation?

STUDYING MAPS

The following questions will help you guide students through their study of Map 28.6.

1. Which countries gained their independence in the late 1940s? *(Burma, India, South Korea, North Korea, Pakistan, Ceylon)*

2. Which islands became United Nations trust territories? *(Marianas and the Carolines)*

3. What is the current political situation in those countries whose borders were in dispute? *(Answers will vary. You might wish to assign this as a research project.)*

ASSESS

Assign students to create a poster that depicts and explains the results of World War II on Germany, Japan, France, Great Britain, the Soviet Union, and the United States.

Answers to SECTION REVIEW

2. (a) Japanese pilots who deliberately crashed into United States ships
3. (a) World War II female Soviet pilots
   (b) German minister of armaments, tripled German war production
   (c) prime minister of Japan during most of war
   (d) 1940 Battle of Britain
   (e) leader of British Air Force's Bomber Command
   (f) nonviolent competition between Communist and non-Communist forces after World War II
   (g) border between Communist and non-Communist nations.
4. (a) lack of transportation to move supplies
   (b) to invade Italy, not northern Europe
   (c) The principle of "self determination" was

936

▶ *During the Yalta conference, February 5–11, 1945, Winston Churchill, Franklin D. Roosevelt, and Joseph Stalin hammered out agreements for postwar Europe and Asia. Roosevelt died two months later. Why do you think each of the Big Three in this photo look so determined and unsmiling? How does this photo compare to current photos of world leaders taken at international meetings?*

The Potsdam conference of July 1945 thus began under a cloud of mistrust. Roosevelt had died on April 12 and had been succeeded as president by Harry Truman. At Potsdam, Truman demanded free elections throughout Eastern Europe. Stalin responded, "A freely elected government in any of these East European countries would be anti-Soviet, and that we cannot allow."[14] After a bitterly fought and devastating war in which the Soviets lost more people than any other country, Stalin sought absolute military security. To him, this security could be gained only by the presence of Communist states in Eastern Europe. Free elections might result in governments hostile to the Soviets. By the middle of 1945, only an invasion by Western forces could undo the developments in eastern Europe. After the world's most destructive conflict had just ended, few people favored such a policy.

As the war slowly receded into the past, a new struggle was already beginning. Many in the West thought Soviet policy was part of a worldwide Communist conspiracy. The Soviets viewed Western, and especially American, policy as nothing less than global capitalist expansionism. In March 1946, in a speech to an American audience, the former British prime minister Winston Churchill declared that "an iron curtain" had "descended across the continent," dividing Germany and Europe into two hostile camps. Stalin branded Churchill's speech a "call to war with the Soviet Union." Only months after the world's most devastating conflict had ended, the world seemed to be bitterly divided once again.

❀ SECTION REVIEW ❀

1. **Locate:**
   (*a*) Leningrad,   (*b*) Coventry,   (*c*) Tehran,   (*d*) Yalta,   (*e*) Potsdam

2. **Define:**
   (*a*) kamikaze

ENRICHMENT ACTIVITY

Divide class into two groups and have them research and then debate the topic of holding free elections in Eastern Europe. Guide students in a discussion of arguments to be used and of the viewpoints of the United States, Great Britain, the Soviet Union. These were the countries who would decide for the East Germans if free elections were not held.

3. **Identify:**
   (a) Night Witches,   (b) Albert Speer,
   (c) General Hideki Tojo,   (d) the Blitz,
   (e) Arthur Harris,   (f) the Cold War,
   (g) the Iron Curtain

4. **Recall:**
   (a) Why didn't increased war production do much to improve Germany's ability to fight the war?
   (b) What important decision was made at the 1943 Tehran conference?
   (c) What important decision was made at the 1945 Yalta conference?
   (d) What events took place at the 1945 Potsdam conference that showed the Cold War had already begun?

5. **Think Critically:** Why were the United States and other Allied powers willing to allow the Soviet Union to place Communist governments in Eastern Europe after World War II?

Conclusion

World War II was the most devastating total war in human history. Germany, Italy, and Japan had been utterly defeated. Perhaps as many as fifty million people—both soldiers and civilians—had been killed in only six years. In Asia and Europe, cities had been reduced to rubble. Millions of people faced starvation as once-fertile lands stood neglected or wasted. Untold millions of people had become refugees.

The Germans, Italians, and Japanese had lost, but only after tremendous sacrifices and costs. Europeans, who had been accustomed to dominating the world at the beginning of the twentieth century, now watched helplessly at mid-century as the two new superpowers created by the two world wars—the United States and the Soviet Union—took control of their destinies. Even before the last battles had been fought, the United States and the Soviet Union had arrived at different visions of the postwar world. No sooner had the war ended than their differences created a new and potentially even more devastating conflict, known as the Cold War. Even though the Europeans seemed merely pawns in the struggle between the two superpowers, they managed to stage a remarkable recovery of their own civilization. In Asia, a defeated Japan made a miraculous economic recovery, and an era of European domination finally came to an end.

Notes

1. Adolf Hitler, *Mein Kampf*, trans. Ralph Manheim (Boston, 1971), p. 654.
2. *Documents on German Foreign Policy*, Series D, vol. 7 (London, 1956), p. 204.
3. Memorandum by John Van Antwerp MacMurray, cited in Arthur Waldron, *How the Peace Was Lost: The 1935 Memorandum* (Stanford, 1992), p. 5.
4. Albert Speer, *Spandau*, trans. Richard Winston and Clara Winston (New York, 1976), p. 50.
5. *Nazi Conspiracy and Aggression*, vol. 6 (Washington, D.C., 1946), p. 262.
6. International Military Tribunal, *Trial of the Major War Criminals*, vol. 22 (Nuremberg, 1947–1949), p. 480.
7. *Nazi Conspiracy and Aggression*, vol. 5 (Washington, D.C., 1946), pp. 341–342.
8. Quoted in Raul Hilberg, *The Destruction of the European Jews*, vol. 1, rev. ed. (New York, 1985), pp. 332–333.
9. *Nazi Conspiracy and Aggression*, vol. 6, p. 789.
10. Quoted in John Campbell, *The Experience of World War II* (New York, 1989), p. 170.
11. Quoted in Claudia Koonz, "Mothers in the Fatherland: Women in Nazi Germany," in *Becoming Visible: Women in European History*, ed. Renate Bridenthal and Claudia Koonz (Boston, 1977), p. 466.
12. Quoted in Campbell, *The Experience of World War II*, p. 143.
13. Quoted in Norman Graebner, *Cold War Diplomacy, 1945–1960* (Princeton, N.J., 1962), p. 117.
14. Quoted in *ibid*.

agreed to but there was no agreement on the means of carrying out this principle.
(d) Stalin refused to hold free elections in Eastern Europe.

5. Answers will vary. The only realistic alternative to Communist domination of Eastern Europe was war with the Soviet Union.

CLOSE

Lead students in a discussion of the Focus objectives identified on page 926. Emphasize the horrendous impact of the war on civilian populations.

TIME LINE

As students conclude the chapter, you may want to refer them to the chapter time line in the *Study Guide*. The time line will help them put key dates in perspective. Supporting questions and activities are also provided.

SPANISH SUPPORT

The *Conclusion* has been translated into Spanish for your Spanish-speaking students. Included with this translation (in your Teacher Resource Box) are Section Key Points, which consist of one or two sentences summarizing each section in the chapter. These Key Points have also been translated into Spanish.

ENRICHMENT ACTIVITY

As a conclusion to the study of World War II and the Holocaust, you might wish to watch, or have students watch on their own time, the movie *Schindler's List,* which was produced in 1993. (Please remember that it is always advisable to preview all films before showing them in class.) Following the viewing, lead students in a discussion of what they learned about the Holocaust and the war from this movie.

USING KEY TERMS

1. appeasement
2. Anschluss
3. kamikaze
4. Blitzkrieg
5. unconditional surrender
6. Aryan racial state
7. Luftwaffe
8. Final Solution

REVIEWING THE FACTS

1. that Germany would be allowed to occupy the Sudetenland in Czechoslovakia
2. a nonaggression pact
3. has almost no raw materials of its own
4. an American program that allowed Allied powers to borrow or rent war materiél from the United States
5. After Berlin was bombed, Hitler concentrated his raids on British cities instead of war industries.
6. By destroying the U.S. navy in the Pacific, the United States would lose its will to fight and make peace.
7. genocide against Jewish people
8. helped remove European domination from much of Asia but replaced it with Japanese domination
9. maintained a high level of production of weapons during the war but its transportation system was damaged, unable to deliver many of these weapons
10. People should be able to determine their own form of government after the war.

THINKING CRITICALLY

1. Answers will vary, a nation that was unwilling to go to war was weak and should not be feared.
2. was possible because of Merman mechanized transport and air power
3. could not unite their forces to fight together but they

USING KEY TERMS

1. The policy of giving in to Hitler's demands before World War II has been called _____.
2. Union with Austria, or _____, was one of Hitler's longtime goals.
3. Toward the end of World War II Japanese _____ pilots crashed their planes into American ships.
4. The German style of attack that called for rapidly overrunning the positions of opposing forces was called a _____.
5. The principle of _____ cemented the Grand Alliance by making it nearly impossible for Hitler to divide his enemies.
6. Hitler wanted to create an _____ in Russia, settled by German peasants and built by slavic slave labor.
7. The German airforce, or _____, inflicted heavy losses on British military targets in 1940.
8. The _____ was the physical extermination of the Jewish people.

REVIEWING THE FACTS

1. What agreement was reached at the Munich Conference?
2. What agreement was reached between Germany and the Soviet Union in 1939?
3. Why did Japan feel a great need to control nations that had significant supplies of natural resources?
4. What was the American Lend Lease policy?
5. What decision by Hitler contributed to Germany's loss of the Battle of Britain in 1940?
6. What hope encouraged Japan to attack United States possessions in the Pacific?
7. To what Nazi policy does the term *Holocaust* refer?
8. Why did Japan's policy of Asia for the Asiatics

create a problem for leaders of nationalist forces in the rest of Asia?
9. Germany's ability to produce many weapons failed to provide the German military with a great advantage in the war? Why?
10. What decisions were made at the Yalta conference in 1945?

THINKING CRITICALLY

1. Restate in your own words what you believe Hitler's attitude was toward nations that were reluctant to go to war.
2. What technological advancements made Hitler's Blitzkrieg possible?
3. What common interest caused Japan and Germany to form an alliance although they were located thousands of miles from each other?
4. Why did Hitler try to defeat the Soviet Union before the Allied powers could open a second front in Western Europe?
5. How might the Allied demand for unconditional surrender have helped Hitler maintain his control over Germany?
6. How did Hitler's effort to eliminate Jewish people from occupied lands harm his ability to win the war?
7. Why was the U.S. policy of island hopping particularly effective in its effort to defeat Japan?
8. What fear may have caused President Truman to order the dropping of atomic weapons on Japan?
9. What were several possible reasons for Stalin's desire to control Eastern European nations after World War II?
10. In what way was Stalin the most secure leader at the Yalta conference? How did this affect his bargaining position?

---

could spread Allied power so neither would fight the Allied power at once
4. so he could redeploy his forces from the east to the west
5. may have caused many Germans to support Hitler because they saw him as the only alternative to national humiliation
6. German resources that were allocated to eliminating the Jewish people could not be used to fight the war.
7. United States was able to cut Japanese supply lines and effectively eliminate these forces from the war.

8. the fear that the U.S. would need to invade Japan costing a million or more American lives
9. Answers will vary, likely to involve Stalin's desire to create buffer states that he controlled between Germany and the Soviet Union; may also have wanted to strip these lands of raw materials and industrial equipment to help rebuild the Soviet Union.
10. Stalin was a totalitarian leader who had no political opposition; Churchill and Roosevelt were required to answer to other leaders of their democratic governments; after Yalta Churchill was voted out of office and Roosevelt died.

APPLYING SOCIAL STUDIES SKILLS

1. **Government:** What effect did the bombing of Pearl Harbor have on United States foreign policy? How did Great Britain benefit from the change in American policy?
2. **Economics:** Make a list and explain the ways that the United States benefitted economically from World War II.
3. **Sociology:** What social values were typically held by Japanese people that made them effective soldiers?
4. **Geography:** Although the Soviet Union dominated Eastern Europe after World War II, many historians believe the Soviets would have been a much more serious threat to the rest of Europe and the United States had they succeeded in taking all of Germany or other nations that were further to the West. Explain the probable logic behind this belief.
5. **Government:** Explain why the United States was concerned about whether or not communist totalitarian governments were created in Eastern Europe by the Soviet Union.

MAKING TIME AND PLACE CONNECTIONS

1. In what ways was the domination of much of Asia by Japanese forces in World War II different from the European colonial domination that came before?
2. How was the decision of the United States to enter World War I different from its decision to enter World War II?
3. During the 1930s the Soviet Union achieved rapid military and industrial growth under a series of five-year plans. Why should the United States, Great Britain, France, and other western nations be pleased Stalin achieved this growth?

4. Why was air power able to destroy Germany's transportation system in World War II but unable to allow the United States to win the war in Vietnam in the 1960s and 1970s?
5. Compare and contrast the leadership styles and military careers of Adolf Hitler and Napoleon Bonaparte.

BECOMING AN HISTORIAN

1. **Fact versus Opinion:** An excerpt from a 1941 speech* given by American aviator Charles A. Lindbergh appears below. Outspoken opposition by many popular Americans may have slowed this nation's entry into the war. How much of what Lindbergh said was fact and what part was opinion?

   It is not only our right but it is our obligation as American citizens to look at this war objectively and to weigh our chances for success if we should enter it. I have attempted to do this, especially from the standpoint of aviation; and I have been forced to the conclusion that we cannot win this war for England, regardless of how much assistance we extend.

2. **Making Hypotheses and Predicting Outcomes:** Some historians believe that President Truman chose to drop atomic weapons on Japan not to end the war in the Pacific but to impress the Soviet Union with United States military power. They believe Truman hoped to prevent further attempts by Stalin to gain territory in other parts of the world. Evaluate this hypothesis in light of what you have learned about Stalin and the United States. In what ways might the history of the last half of the twentieth century have been different if Truman had chosen not to drop the bomb?

*Quoted in *Selected Readings on Great Issues in American History*, Encyclopedia Britannica Educational Corporation, 1969, p. J4. From the Congressional Record of the 77th Congress.

939

1. Japanese took over the nations they defeated while European colonial powers were satisfied to let occupied people run their own lives.
2. There was no one military act that galvanized the U.S. into action such as the bombing of Pearl Harbor which brought about immediate U.S. involvement.
3. If the Soviet Union had not achieved industrial and military growth in the 1930s, it might have been defeated by Hitler's forces in 1941.
4. Germany relied on railroads and highways for transportation, providing easy targets for Allied air power. The North Vietnamese relied on bicycles, people, and oxen to carry most of their war materiél.
5. Answers will vary; wanted to rule vast parts of Europe, lacked an understanding of the limits of their power, were unwilling to delegate authority, they alone could make needed decisions.

BECOMING AN HISTORIAN

1. Answers will vary; Lindbergh was a well known aviator, but he was not a trained military leader or tactician, and his statement was opinion, but taken as fact by many.
2. Answers will vary; students should realize that by the time of the atomic attack on Japan the Soviet Union was shifting forces to Pacific territories. If Truman had not dropped the bomb Japan might have become another Soviet satellite state.

APPLYING SOCIAL STUDIES SKILLS

1. in 1941 leaders of the U.S. vacillating whether to enter the war; bombing ended this indecision, put the U.S. firmly behind the Allied side
2. Answers will vary, may indicate that the war ended U.S. unemployment, increased the profitability of U.S. businesses, increased investment in U.S. industries, encouraged U.S. research and development, and provided this nation with a positive balance of trade.
3. Japanese people value conformity, loyalty, respect for their leaders, hard work, self-sacrifice, and pride in their families and nation.
4. Answers will vary, but areas dominated by the Soviet Union in Eastern Europe did not have easy access to the Atlantic Ocean; would have been more serious if they had ports directly on the Atlantic Ocean so ships did not pass through well guarded channels and straits.
5. Answers will vary, but expansion of Soviet power could improve their economic and military strength that the U.S. might eventually need.

TOWARD A GLOBAL CIVILIZATION:

OVERVIEW OF THE UNIT

The sixth and final unit of World History is divided into six chapters, spanning about 180 pages.

Assuming a 36-week course, you may wish to spend one week each on Chapters 29 and 30; two weeks total on Chapters 31, 32, 33, and 34; and two weeks reviewing, reteaching, and assessing.

Using the
Illustration

This illustration is the first documented example of street art. Its title is "Wall of Respect". Ask students why they think that title is appropriate for the image. It was painted in Chicago in 1967 by William Walker. Soon thereafter, artists all over the country—especially those associated with minority groups and neighbor-hoods—were beautifying their cities with murals like this one. Many schools have also used local talent to paint a mural on the outside of a building that faces a public road, and so identify that school in the public's mind. If your school does not already have a wall mural, have students talk to the chair of the art depart-ment about the possibility of designing and creating one for their school. If the school already possesses a wall mural, take the class out to examine it in detail. Analyze the images and have stu-dents provide an explanation of the theme.

▶ *This wall mural entitled Crosswinds was painted on a wall near Central Square in Cambridge, Massachusetts, in 1992. The first documented example of street art was done in Chicago in 1967, but the style quickly spread to other major cities throughout the United States. A recurring theme is the aspirations, and sometimes the difficulties, faced by ethnic groups that reside within the city.*

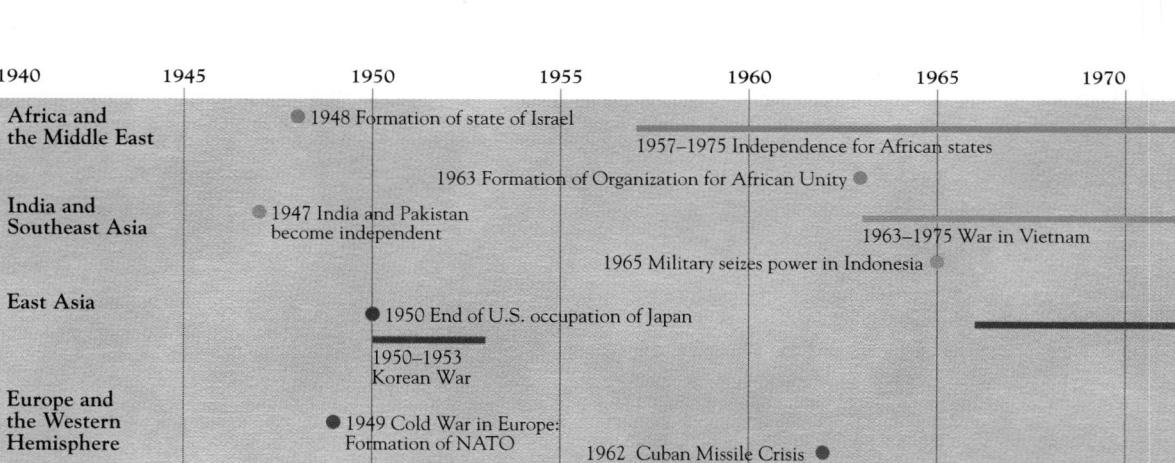

	1940	1945	1950	1955	1960	1965	1970
Africa and the Middle East			● 1948 Formation of state of Israel		1957–1975 Independence for African states		
				1963 Formation of Organization for African Unity ●			
India and Southeast Asia		● 1947 India and Pakistan become independent				1963–1975 War in Vietnam	
				1965 Military seizes power in Indonesia ●			
East Asia			● 1950 End of U.S. occupation of Japan				
			1950–1953 Korean War				
Europe and the Western Hemisphere			● 1949 Cold War in Europe: Formation of NATO				
				1962 Cuban Missile Crisis ●			

UNIT OPENER ACTIVITY

It will be hard for some students to grasp the enormous impact of the collapse of the Soviet Union on world tensions and interrela-tions. Allow two weeks to complete the fol-lowing activity that simulates how the Cold War contest between the superpowers divided the world into two camps. Arrange a method of dividing the class into two by a wall (to sim-ulate the Berlin Wall). If possible, the wall should prevent students from seeing to the other side. In class, spread privileges and rewards to only one side at a time. At the end of the time, ask students how they felt about the people on the "other side." Remind them that the suspicion and doubt raised by this demonstration was nothing compared to the real distrust that grew between peoples of the West and the Soviet world.

THE WORLD SINCE 1945

(1945 TO PRESENT)

World War II can be seen as the end of an era of European domination of the world. At the end of the war, Europe quickly divided into hostile camps as the Cold War rivalry between the United States and the Soviet Union forced the European nations to become dependent on one or the other of the superpowers. In the late 1980s, however, the Soviet Empire began to come apart, and the Cold War quickly came to an end.

In the meantime, the peoples of Africa and Asia had their own reasons for optimism as World War II came to a close. World War II had severely undermined the stability of the colonial order in these lands. By the end of the 1940s, most colonies in Asia had received their independence. Africa followed a decade or two later. In a few instances, such as in Algeria, Indonesia, and Vietnam, the transition to independence was a violent one. For the most part, independence was realized by peaceful means.

UNIT OUTLINE

USING PROJECT IDEAS

The text ends with a discussion of the challenges facing the world today. Areas discussed include: threats to the environment; the widening gap between the rich and poor; the scarcity of needed resources; human and civil rights abuses; and the search for stable and just political systems. Ask each student to identify a topic within one of these broad areas and to trace its development over three distinct time periods. (You may wish to use the time periods established by the units of this text.)

Additionally, students should predict what will happen with this topic in the future. For example, a student may choose the topic of technology. The use of technology in pre-Columbian times, its role in the Industrial Revolution, and finally the social problems arising from uneven access to technology in today's world would be addressed. For the future, the student might consider the effects of advances in medicine, such as the cloning of animals. Encourage students to be concise, original, and creative in their presentations. The important point of the project is for students to make that vital link between the past, present, and the future.

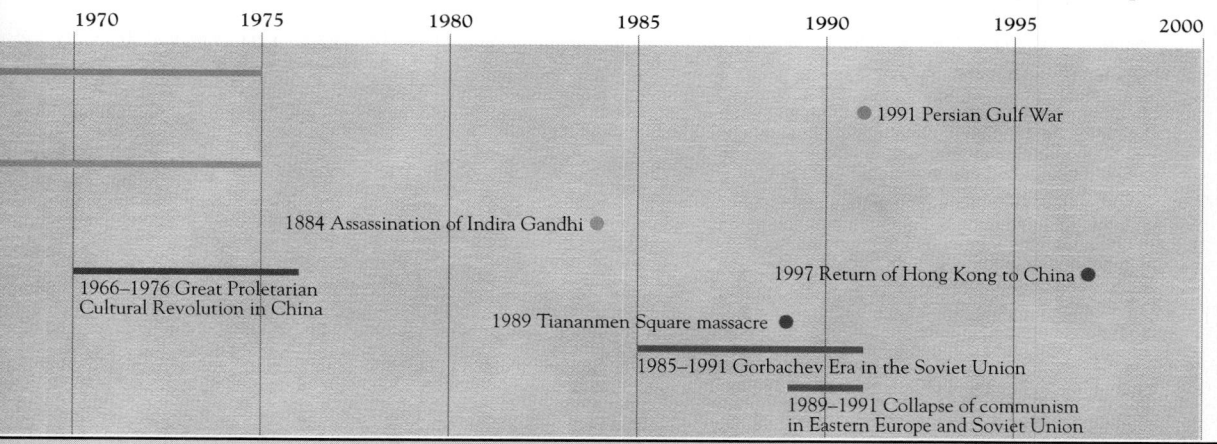

| 1970 | 1975 | 1980 | 1985 | 1990 | 1995 | 2000 |

● 1991 Persian Gulf War

1884 Assassination of Indira Gandhi ●

1966–1976 Great Proletarian Cultural Revolution in China

1997 Return of Hong Kong to China ●

1989 Tiananmen Square massacre ●

1985–1991 Gorbachev Era in the Soviet Union

1989–1991 Collapse of communism in Eastern Europe and Soviet Union

STUDYING THE TIME LINE

Ask students the following questions to help them compare the time periods of the different civilizations.

1. How many of the events on the time line are the direct result of the tension between the political goals represented by the United States and the Soviet Union? *(There is no one right answer; students may respond between four and eight, depending upon how they interpret the question. The important thing is that they can justify or support their opinion including any one event with specifics.)*

2. The time line notes the "Collapse of communism in Eastern Europe and Soviet Union" as falling between 1989 and 1991. Do you think these dates reflect the complete story of the decline of communism? *(Students should realize that the internal collapse had been in process for many decades.)*

PLANNING GUIDE

SECTION	KEY TOPICS	PRIMARY SOURCES	ASSESSMENT
1 The Development of the Cold War (1945 to 1970) pages 943–951	◆ Confrontation between the superpowers ◆ A global Cold War ◆ The Cuban Missile Crisis ◆ The Vietnam War and the domino theory	◆ Dean Acheson on the spread of communism, page 944	◆ Section Review, page 951 ◆ Section Quiz 29–1, TRB
2 The Soviet Union and Its Eastern European Satellites (1945 to 1970) pages 951–957	◆ Stalin's rule of the Soviet Union ◆ Khrushchev's rule of the Soviet Union ◆ Soviet Power and Eastern Europe	◆ A description of Soviet repression in Eastern Europe, page 955	◆ Section Review, page 957 ◆ Section Quiz 29–2, TRB
3 Western Europe: The Revival of Democracy and the Economy pages 958–962	◆ De Gaulle and Changes in France ◆ Economic growth in West Germany ◆ Decline of the British Empire ◆ Movement toward unity in Western Europe		◆ Section Review, page 962 ◆ Section Quiz 29–3, TRB
4 The United States and Canada: A New Era pages 962–967	◆ American politics and society after World War II ◆ Social and political upheaval in the United States ◆ Development in Canada	◆ A selection from a speech by Dr. Martin Luther King, Jr., page 965	◆ Section Review, page 967 ◆ Section Quiz 29–4, TRB
5 The Emergence of a New Society pages 967–973	◆ New structures in European society ◆ Creation of welfare states ◆ Education and student unrest	◆ A student manifesto and student inscriptions from a wall in Paris, page 970 ◆ A selection from Bob Dylan's song, *The Times They are a-Changin'*, page 972	◆ Section Review, page 973 ◆ Section Quiz 29–5, TRB

COLD WAR AND A NEW ORDER IN THE WEST (1945 TO 1970)

REPRODUCIBLE ACTIVITIES

Historical Maps

Charts and Graphs

Critical Thinking

Cooperative Learning

Vocabulary

Guided Reading

Reteaching

Enrichment

Performance Assessment

Spanish Key Points and Chapter Summaries

Spanish Vocabulary

Spanish Guided Reading

MULTIMEDIA SUPPORT

TRANSPARENCIES
◆ *World History* Color Transparency Package
◆ Fine Art Color Transparency Package

VIDEO
◆ *World History* Video Library
◆ CNN® Annual Video Update

LASERDISC
◆ *Sights and Sounds of History*

AUDIO
◆ *Listening to Literature* audiotape (English and Spanish)
◆ *History of Music* CD

SOFTWARE
◆ WESTEST™
◆ Student Review

CD–ROM
◆ *The Journey of Civilization*
◆ *World History*

INTERNET
◆ Internet Activities

On Line with WORLD HISTORY

Access West's history web site at **http://history.swpco.com** You'll find activities and web sites related to specific topics and chapters in *World History: The Human Odyssey*. Also look for references to helpful web sites at appropriate places throughout this teacher edition.

LESSON PLANNING

You will find detailed daily lesson plans for both traditional class scheduling and **block scheduling** in your Teacher Resource Box.

Not Enough Time?

If you do not have the four or five days recommended to teach this chapter, you may want to focus on the following sections and activities:

◆ Have students skim the chapter to answer the "Questions to Guide Your Reading" on page 943. Discuss their answers, then read the "Conclusion" on page 973.
◆ Do a more in-depth reading of development of the Cold War on pages 943–949, developments in Eastern Europe on pages 953–957, changes in American society on pages 962–966, and creation of welfare states on pages 968–969. Conclude with a discussion of the role of students in creating social change.

BUILDING ON CHAPTER 28

To "set the stage" for the study of Chapter 29, use the following questions and activities.

◆ Have students identify and describe political, economic, and social problems that needed resolution at the end of World War II.

◆ Review the beginning of the Cold War.

◆ Explain why the United States and the Soviet Union emerged from World War II as the two superpowers of the world.

◆ Discuss the difference nuclear power would make in world politics.

USING THE OPENING STORY

Depending on the ability levels of your students, select from the following questions and activities to reinforce the reading of the opening story.

◆ Given the existence of weapons of mass destruction, is it possible for any state to win a war?

◆ Why was the loss of 40 million people in World War II made even worse by the fact that many of these people were young men and women?

◆ Why is despair a ready breeding ground for hate and extremism?

The end of World War II in Europe had been met with great joy. One visitor in Moscow reported, "I looked out of the window [at 2 A.M.], almost everywhere there were lights in the window—people were staying awake. Everyone embraced everyone else, someone sobbed aloud."

After the victory parades and celebrations, however, Europeans awoke to a devastating realization: their civilization was in ruins. Almost forty million people (both soldiers and civilians) had been killed over the last six years. Massive air raids had reduced many of the great cities of Europe to heaps of rubble. An American general described Berlin: "Wherever we looked we saw desolation. It was like a city of the dead. Suffering and shock were visible in every face. Dead bodies still remained in canals and lakes and were being dug out from under bomb debris."

Millions of Europeans faced starvation, because grain harvests were only half of what they had been in 1939. Millions were also homeless. In the parts of the Soviet Union that had been occupied by the Germans, almost twenty-five million people were without

homes. The destruction of bridges, roads, and railroads left transportation systems paralyzed. Untold millions of people had been uprooted by the war and became the "displaced persons" who tried to find food and then their way home. Eleven million prisoners of war had to be returned to their native countries. Fifteen million Germans and East Europeans were driven out of countries where they were no longer wanted. Despite the chaos, however, Europe was soon on the road to a remarkable recovery.

World War II had also destroyed European supremacy in world affairs, and from this, Europe did not recover. As the Cold War conflict between the world's two superpowers—the United States and the Soviet Union—grew stronger, the European nations were divided into two armed camps dependent upon one or the other of these two major powers. The United States and the Soviet Union, whose rivalry brought the world to the brink of nuclear war, seemed to hold the survival of Europe and the world in their hands.

▲ In May 1945, joyous crowds took to the streets to celebrate VE Day not only in London, pictured here, but throughout the world.

ADDITIONAL RESOURCES

The resources listed below can be used to enrich the lessons in this chapter.

BOOKS FOR STUDENTS

The Cold War: A Concise History by Charles B. Marshall and Franklin Watts

A Day in the Life of Ivan Denisovitch by Alexander Solzhenitsyn

The Russians by Hedrick Smith, Random House

VHS

"The Cold War" Series: Western Man and the Modern World (NY Times) Social Studies School Service (800) 421-4246

"The Dawn of the Cold War: Setting the Mold, 1945–1983" Brittanica, (800) 554-9862

A NEW ORDER IN THE WEST

(1945 TO 1970)

THE WORLD SINCE 1945

| 1945 | THE COLD WAR | 1970 |
| 1945 | | 2000 |

QUESTIONS TO GUIDE YOUR READING

1. What were the major turning points in the development of the Cold War from 1945 to 1970?

2. What were the major developments in the Soviet Union between 1945 and 1970?

3. How did Soviet policies affect the political and economic history of Eastern Europe from 1945 to 1970?

4. What were the major developments in domestic politics in France, West Germany, and Great Britain between 1945 and 1970?

5. What were the major developments in U.S. and Canadian domestic politics between 1945 and 1970?

6. What were the major social changes in Western society between 1945 and 1970?

THE DEVELOPMENT OF THE COLD WAR (1945 TO 1970)

During World War II, the two major Allied powers—the United States and the Soviet Union—had worked together because of the urgent need to defeat the Axis powers. Once the Axis powers were defeated, however, the differences between the two states came to the front. Stalin had never overcome his fear of the capitalist West, whereas Western leaders still had great fear of communism.

The Confrontation of the Superpowers

There has been much debate about who was more responsible for the beginning of the Cold War. No doubt, both the United States and the Soviet Union took steps at the end of the war that were unwise and that might have been avoided. Both nations, however, were the heirs to the European tradition of power politics. It should not surprise us that two such different

943

FOCUS ON THEMES

Listed below are brief summaries of how the content in this chapter supports the text's key themes.

Politics and History Reflecting the divisions of the Cold War, the Western world became divided politically, toward democratic systems or along totalitarian lines.

The Role of Ideas The Cold War was based on two conflicting systems of ideas, communism and capitalism.

Economics and History The Soviet Union and its satellite states in Eastern Europe developed socialist systems based on government ownership of all industries, collectivization of agriculture, and government management of the economy. The United States and a number of European states pursued free-market, capitalist systems. Some states, such as France and Great Britain, had capitalist economies but also pursued the nationalization of banks, coal and steel industries, and public utilities.

Social Life An increase in real wages enabled workers to become participants in the new consumer society, mass leisure, and mass tourism. Neither the Soviet Union nor its Eastern European satellite states shared in the new prosperity of the west.

The Impact of Science and Technology The period between 1945 and 1970 was the first period in human history when people fully realized the potential of modern weapons to destroy entire civilizations.

Answers to QUESTIONS TO GUIDE YOUR READING

1. Truman doctrine, Marshall Plan, division of Germany, arms race, Korean War, Cuban Missile Crisis, Vietnam (pages 943–950)
2. Stalin and the growth of industrial production, growth of Communist anti-intellectualism and political terrorism, Hungary uprising (pages 951–953)
3. exploitation of Eastern Europe for Soviet gains (pages 953–957)
4. major developments involved the need to rebuild economies and recreate democratic institutions (pages 960–962)
5. (a) growth of the federal government; economic boom times; civil rights struggle, Vietnam; (b) U.S. economic domination; creation of the national welfare state and national health insurance (pages 966–967)
6. urbanization; mobility and fluidity of society; student unrest; growth of social welfare (pages 967–972)

FOCUS

OBJECTIVES

After completing this section, students should be able to

1. identify and explain confrontations between superpowers in the Cold War
2. explain how the Cold War grew to be global in nature
3. identify and describe events in the Cuban Missile Crisis
4. explain the relationship between United States involvement in the Vietnam War and the domino theory

FOCUS ACTIVITY

Assign students to prepare a description of the likely results of a nuclear war. Have them use this as the basis for an explanation of how a balance of power through what is called Mutually Assured Destruction (MAD) has succeeded in preventing such a war from taking place.

LEARNING FROM VISUALS

Answer to the caption question: The Truman Doctrine was put into place following the president's address and subsequent passage of the aid bill to Greece and Turkey.

944

---

systems would become rivals. Because of its need to feel secure on its western border, the Soviet Union was not prepared to give up its control of Eastern Europe after Germany's defeat. American leaders were not willing to give up the power and prestige the United States had gained throughout the world. Suspicious of each other's motives, the United States and the Soviet Union soon became rivals. Between 1945 and 1949, a number of events led the two countries to oppose each other.

Confrontation in Europe

Eastern Europe was the first area of disagreement. The United States and Great Britain believed that the liberated nations of Eastern Europe should freely determine their own governments. Stalin, however, fearful that the Eastern European nations would be anti-Soviet if they were permitted free elections, opposed the West's plans. Having freed Eastern Europe from the Nazis, the Red Army stayed in the conquered areas and set up pro-Soviet regimes in Poland, Romania, Bulgaria, and Hungary. These pro-Soviet governments satisfied Stalin's desire for a buffer zone against the West, but the local populations and the West saw these regimes as an expansion of Stalin's empire. Only another war could change this situation, and few people wanted another armed conflict.

A civil war in Greece created another area of conflict between the superpowers. The Communist People's Liberation Army and the anticommunist forces supported by Great Britain were fighting each other for control of Greece in 1946. However, Britain had its own economic problems, which caused it to withdraw from the active role it had been playing in both Greece and Turkey.

President Harry S Truman of the United States, alarmed by the British weakness and the possibility of Soviet expansion into the eastern Mediterranean,

▲ *On March 12, 1947, President Truman addressed a joint session of Congress asking for money and military assistance for Greece and Turkey. What U.S. policy was enacted as a result of the president's actions?*

responded with the Truman Doctrine. The Truman Doctrine said that the United States would provide money to countries (in this case, Greece and Turkey) that were threatened by Communist expansion. If the Soviets were not stopped in Greece, the Truman argument ran, then the United States would have to face the spread of communism throughout the free world. As Dean Acheson (ATCH-uh-sun), the U.S. secretary of state, explained, "Like apples in a barrel infected by disease, the corruption of Greece would infect Iran and all the East . . . likewise Africa, Italy, France. . . . Not since Rome and Carthage had there been such a polarization of power on this earth."[1]

The Truman Doctrine was soon followed, in June 1947, by the European Recovery Program, better known as the Marshall Plan. This program was intended to rebuild prosperity and stability. It included $13 billion in U.S. loans for the economic recovery of war-torn Europe. Underlying it was the belief that Communist aggression fed off economic turmoil. General George C. Marshall, U.S. secretary of state, noted in a speech at Harvard, "Our policy is not directed against any country or doctrine but against hunger, poverty, desperation and chaos."[2]

From the Soviet perspective, the Marshall Plan was nothing less than a thinly veiled attempt to buy the support of the smaller European countries. In return, these countries would be exploited economically by the United States. The Marshall Plan did not intend to shut out either the Soviet Union or its Eastern European satellite states, but they refused to participate. According to the Soviet view, the Marshall Plan guaranteed "the American loans in return for the relinquishing by the European states of their economic and later also their political independence."[3] The Soviet Union, however, was in no position to compete financially with the United States. In 1949, it founded a

---

MORE ABOUT . . . *the Marshall Plan*

Students might be interested in knowing that it was probably the Soviets themselves who were responsible for the Marshall Plan being approved by the United States Congress. Truman first asked Congress for the $17 billion dollars (over a four-year period) for European recovery in September of 1947. Confident that they could defeat Truman in the upcoming election, the Republican-controlled Congress delayed action on the plan. The Soviets responded to news of the proposed Marshall Plan with their own military and financial aid package. Then, with the Soviet takeover of Czechoslovakia in February of 1948, Truman delivered his blistering speech to Congress demanding immediate passage of the Marshall Plan. Congress acted quickly to meet this request.

Council for Mutual Assistance (COMECON) for the economic cooperation of the Eastern European states. COMECON was intended as a Soviet version of the Marshall Plan, but it largely failed because of the inability of the Soviet Union to provide large amounts of financial aid.

By 1947, the split in Europe between the United States and the Soviet Union had become a fact of life. At the end of World War II, the United States had favored a quick end to its commitments in Europe. American fears of Soviet aims, however, caused the United States to play an increasingly important role in European affairs. In an article in *Foreign Affairs* in July 1947, George Kennan, a well-known U.S. diplomat with much knowledge of Soviet affairs, argued for a **policy of containment** to keep communism within its existing geographical boundaries and prevent further aggressive Soviet moves. After the Soviet blockade of Berlin in 1948 (to be discussed later), containment of the Soviet Union became formal U.S. policy.

The Division of Germany

The fate of Germany also became a source of heated contention between East and West. At the end of the war, the Allied powers had divided Germany (and Berlin) into four zones, each one occupied by one of the Allies. The city of Berlin itself was located deep inside the Soviet zone. Besides dividing Germany (and Berlin) into four occupied zones, the Allied powers had agreed on little else with regard to the conquered nation. The Soviets, hardest hit by the war, took reparations from Germany in the form of industrial materials. The Soviets took apart and removed to the Soviet Union 380 factories from the western zones of Berlin before turning their control over to the Western powers. By the summer of 1946, two hundred chemical, paper, and textile factories in the Soviets' East German zone had likewise been shipped to the Soviet Union. At the same time, the German Communist Party was reestablished and was soon in charge politically of the Soviet zone in eastern Germany.

The foreign ministers of the four occupying powers (the United States, the Soviet Union, Great Britain, and France) met repeatedly in an attempt to arrive at a

▲ *The devastation in Europe led to widespread hunger, and in some cases, famine. Through the Marshall Plan, the U.S. supplied economic aid that made it possible for countries to recover financially and for people to improve their war-torn lives. This photograph, taken in France in 1947, shows new American tractors working together with horses to plow a field. How does this labor combination compare to American agricultural practices in the late 1940s?*

final peace treaty with Germany. However, they only moved further and further apart. At the same time, Great Britain, France, and the United States gradually began to merge their zones economically. By February 1948, they were making plans to unify these three Western sections of Germany and create a West German government. The Soviets reacted with a blockade of West Berlin, which allowed neither trucks, trains, nor barges to enter the three Western zones of Berlin. The Russians hoped to secure economic control of all Berlin and force the Western powers to halt the creation of a separate West German state.

The Western powers were faced with a dilemma. No one wanted to risk World War III. Therefore, an attempt to break through the Soviet blockade with

So What ??

*If your students question the importance of the information on **the Cold War**, tell them . . .*

The deadly product of those years, nuclear weapons, remain a threat to the peace and stability of the world even though the United States and Russia are no longer enemies.

National resources that were directed toward escalating arms productions and military defenses, especially in the Soviet Union, slowed down progress in such areas as health and education.

CLASS DISCUSSION

Have students discuss the following statement. Do they believe it is true? To what extent might it explain why the Soviet Union eventually stopped the blockade of Berlin?

In a Cold War propaganda is a more important weapon than military arms. Nothing is more devastating to a nation's position than looking weak and ineffective to the world.

LEARNING FROM VISUALS

Guide students in a discussion of the difficulties of transporting supplies by air—or by other means over long distances. Supplying troops became a major obstacle for Hannibal, for Napoleon, and for Germany during World War II. Why was the United States able to supply the people of Berlin by air while Germany was unable to do the same for its troops in North Africa?

ACTIVITY

Based on what they know of Soviet history have students explain why many Russians would be mistrustful of the West. What reasons would the Soviet Union have for wanting to control the Eastern European nations? Based upon their understanding of Communist ideology have them explain the reasons for the United States' mistrust of the U.S.S.R. Can they envision how the Cold War might have been avoided?

▶ *Residents of Berlin watch as a U.S. plane arrives loaded with supplies for the city. The fifteen-month-long airlift was directed by the American General Lucius Clay, military governor of Germany.*

tanks and trucks was ruled out. However, how could the 2.5 million people in the three Western zones of Berlin be kept alive, when the whole city was inside the Soviet zone? The solution was the Berlin Air Lift. Berlin would get its supplies by air; they would be flown in by American and British airplanes. For more than 15 months, over 200,000 flights that carried 1.5 million tons of supplies were made. At the height of the Berlin Air Lift, 13,000 tons of supplies were flown daily to Berlin. The Soviets, also not wanting war, gave in and finally lifted the blockade in May 1949.

The blockade of Berlin increased tensions between the United States and the Soviet Union. It also brought the separation of Germany into two states. West Germany, or the Federal Republic of Germany, was formally created in September 1949. A month later, a separate German Democratic Republic, or East Germany, was set up. Berlin remained a divided city, a vivid reminder of the division of West and East.

The Spread of the Cold War

In that same year, the Cold War spread from Europe to the rest of the world. The victory of the Chinese Communists in 1949 in the Chinese civil war (see Chapter 33) created a new Communist regime and strengthened U.S. fears about the spread of communism. The Soviet Union also exploded its first atomic bomb in 1949. All too soon, both the United States and the Soviet Union were involved in a growing arms race that led to the building of ever more destructive nuclear weapons. In 1952, both nations developed the far more destructive hydrogen bomb. Moreover, by the mid-1950s, both powers had built intercontinental ballistic missiles (ICBMs), which enabled the United States and the Soviet Union to send their destructive nuclear warheads to any part of the world.

Soon the search for security took the form of **mutual deterrence.** This was a policy based on the belief that an arsenal of nuclear weapons prevented war by ensuring that even if one nation launched its nuclear weapons in a first strike, the other nation would still be able to respond and devastate the attacker. Mutually assured destruction (MAD), it was believed, would keep either side from risking the use of the massive supply of weapons that had been built up.

The search for security in the new world of the Cold War also led to the formation of military alliances. The North Atlantic Treaty Organization (NATO) was

MORE ABOUT . . . *the Atomic Bomb*

The nuclear age began for the United States in 1945. The first test was part of the Manhattan Project, called operation "Trinity" in Alamagorda, New Mexico. The nuclear device, called "Gadget," was detonated in the *Jornada del Muerto* (Journey of Death) desert in New Mexico. Its explosive yield was between 20 and 22 kilotons. A kiloton is an explosion equal to 1,000 tons of TNT. Between 1945 and 1992 the United States officially conducted 1,054 nuclear tests and two nuclear attacks. In 1962 the United States and the Soviet Union both agreed to stop atmospheric, or above ground, nuclear tests.

◄ *This ominously cloud is the result of a hydrogen bomb explosion from a testing done in 1952. Although the clouds from hydrogen bombs and atomic bombs are very similar, a hydrogen bomb is the fusion of light nuclei.*

formed in April 1949 when Belgium, Luxembourg, the Netherlands, France, Great Britain, Italy, Denmark, Norway, Portugal, and Iceland signed a treaty with the United States and Canada. All the powers agreed to provide mutual help if any one of them was attacked. A few years later, West Germany and Turkey joined NATO.

The Eastern European states soon followed suit with their own military alliance. In 1955, the Soviet Union joined with Albania, Bulgaria, Czechoslovakia, East Germany, Hungary, Poland, and Romania in a formal military alliance, known as the Warsaw Pact. As a result of this agreement Europe was once again divided into hostile alliance systems, just as it had been before World War I.

A system of military alliances also spread to the rest of the world after the United States became involved in the Korean War (see Chapter 33). On June 25, 1950, with the apparent approval of Joseph Stalin, Communist North Korean forces invaded South Korea. The United States, seeing this as yet another example of Communist aggression and expansion, gained the approval of the United Nations (UN) and

sent U.S. troops to turn back the invasion. Several other countries sent troops as well. By September, UN forces had marched northward into North Korea with the aim of unifying Korea. However, Chinese forces then came into the war on the side of North Korea and forced the U.S. and South Korean troops to retreat back to South Korea. In 1953, after two more years of fighting, an uneasy truce was reached. The division of Korea was reaffirmed. To many Americans, the policy of containing communism had succeeded in Asia, just as it had earlier in Europe.

The Korean War confirmed American fears of Communist expansion. The United States was now more determined than ever to contain Soviet power. In the mid-1950s, the administration of President Dwight D. Eisenhower adopted a policy of massive retaliation. Any Soviet advance, even a ground attack in Europe, would be met with the full use of U.S. nuclear bombs. Moreover, U.S. military alliances were extended around the world. As Eisenhower explained, "The freedom we cherish and defend in Europe and in the Americas is no different from the freedom that is imperiled in Asia."

MORE ABOUT . . . *the Atomic Bomb*

The Soviet Union's nuclear weapons program began in 1943, with intelligence information about America's Manhattan Project. The chief source of that information was a refugee German physicist named Klaus Fuchs, who was working at Alamagorda on the U.S. bomb. Fuchs, called the "Atom Spy," passed on all he knew about the American nuclear program through Julius and Ethel Rosenberg and two others. As part of

operation "First Lightning," the Soviets exploded an atomic bomb, modeled from the designs of "Gadget" yielding 20 kilotons, just four years after the U.S. test. Fuchs was arrested in Britain in 1950 and served nine years in prison before being released to East Germany. Julius and Ethel Rosenberg, in one of the most controversial cases of the twentieth century, were executed in 1953.

Ask students to evaluate the following statement. Do they believe it is true? How might it explain the arms race?

It is not important to know whether there was a "missile gap." It is only important that people believed there was a gap.

CLASS DISCUSSION

After World War II what differences developed between the personal freedoms enjoyed by most people in Western Europe and those given to people who lived in the East? How did this impact relations between the West and the United States? Between Eastern European nations of the Soviet block and the West? *(Most people in Western Europe enjoyed personal freedoms and a voice in their government that was much the same as the rights guaranteed by the U.S. Bill of Rights. In Eastern Europe communist dictatorships eliminated most personal freedom and provided ordinary people with little voice in their government. Relations between Western countries generally improved; relations between the Soviet Union and the West deteriorated.)*

Map 29.1   The New European Alliance Systems in the 1950s and 1960s

The Central Treaty Organization (CENTO) of Turkey, Iraq, Iran, Pakistan, Great Britain, and the United States was intended to prevent the Soviet Union from expanding at the expense of its southern neighbors. To stem Soviet aggression in the Far East, the United States, Great Britain, France, Pakistan, Thailand, the Philippines, Australia, and New Zealand formed the Southeast Asia Treaty Organization (SEATO). By the mid-1950s, the United States found itself allied militarily with forty-two states around the world.

A crisis over Berlin added to the tension in the late 1950s. In August 1957, the Soviet Union had launched its first intercontinental ballistic missile (ICBM), capable of reaching the United States from its bases in the U.S.S.R. (The United States had already launched its first.) Shortly afterward, the Soviets sent *Sputnik* I, the first man-made space satellite, to orbit the Earth. New fears seized the American public. Did the Soviet Union have a massive lead in building missiles that was creating a "missile gap" between the United States and the Soviet Union? Could the Soviet Union build a military base in outer space by which it could dominate the world? One American senator said, "It was time for Americans to be prepared to shed blood, sweat and tears if this country and the free world are to survive."

Nikita Khrushchev (nuh-KEET-uh KROOSH-chawf), the new leader of the Soviet Union, tried to take advantage of the American concern over missiles

STUDYING MAPS

These questions will help you guide students through their study of Map 29.1

1. What geographic factors placed NATO forces in a more strategic location than the Warsaw Pact forces? *(NATO forces were in a position to block Soviet Naval access to the Mediterranean and to the Atlantic.)*

2. Which nations along the border between NATO and the Warsaw Pact were neutral? *(Sweden, Finland, Switzerland, Austria and Yugoslavia.)*

3. Why might Warsaw Pact nations have been less loyal than nations of West Europe were to NATO? *(Warsaw Pact nations were not given a choice about belongings.)*

4. Why was the Soviet Union particularly upset by its failure to control Greece, Turkey, Yugoslavia, and Albania? *(These nations would have provided access to the Mediterranean Sea.)*

◄ *During the Cuban Missile Crisis, President Kennedy met frequently with his cabinet. In this October 1962 photograph, Robert McNamara, secretary of defense, sits to the left of the president, and on Kennedy's right is Dean Rusk, secretary of state. What were the international consequences of this crisis?*

to solve the problem of West Berlin. West Berlin had remained a "Western island" of prosperity in the midst of the relatively poverty-stricken East Germany. Many East Germans, tired of Communist repression, managed to escape East Germany by fleeing through West Berlin. In November 1958, Khrushchev announced a new policy. Unless the West removed its forces from West Berlin within six months, he said, he would turn over control of the access routes into Berlin to the East Germans. Unwilling to abandon West Berlin to the Communists, President Eisenhower beefed up American military forces in Europe and stood firm. Khrushchev eventually backed down.

A brief thaw in the Cold War then set in. Eisenhower was invited to visit the Soviet Union. A summit conference on Berlin was arranged. On May 1, 1960, however, Soviet missiles shot down an American U-2 plane over the Soviet Union. Gary Powers, the downed pilot, admitted that the United States had been using U-2 planes to spy on the Soviet Union. An outraged Khrushchev denounced American aggression and cancelled Eisenhower's visit. The summit conference on Berlin also came to an end. American-Soviet relations took a turn for the worse.

The Cuban Missile Crisis and Its Effect

During the administration of John F. Kennedy, the Cold War confrontation between the United States and the Soviet Union reached frightening levels. Kennedy began his presidency with a foreign policy disaster—the Bay of Pigs invasion. In 1959, a left-wing revolutionary named Fidel Castro had overthrown the Cuban dictator Fulgencio Batista (buh-TEE-stuh) and set up a Soviet-supported totalitarian regime in Cuba (see Chapter 31). Kennedy approved a secret plan, first devised by the Eisenhower administration, for an invasion of Cuba by Cuban exiles in the hope of causing a revolt against Castro. The invasion, however, was a disaster. Many of the exiles were killed or captured when they attempted a landing at the Bay of Pigs. The new American president was shaken by the utter failure of the U.S.–supported operation to overthrow Castro.

At a summit meeting in Vienna in 1961, Khrushchev took advantage of the American failure by threatening Kennedy with another six-month ultimatum over West Berlin. Kennedy left Vienna convinced of the need to deal firmly with the Soviet Union. He announced the call-up of U.S. reserve forces

COMPARING TIME PERIODS

Have students compare the decision of the United States to enter the war in Korea with its decision to send military forces to Vietnam. What relation may exist between these decisions? Could events in Europe after World War II have encouraged the U.S. belief in the domino theory?

ASSESS

Assign students to write a hypothetical letter from a leader of the East German forces that surrounded West Berlin during 1947 to his commanding officer. Ask students to include an evaluation of the situation, what the officer had hoped to accomplish, and why he doubted that his objectives would be achieved.

Answers to SECTION REVIEW

2. (a) policy of keeping communism within its 1947 borders
(b) prevention of war based on no one being able to win
(c) if one nation fell to communism, others would follow

3. (a) U.S. support for countries threatened by Communist expansion
(b) Secretary of State who feared Communist takeover in Greece
(c) United States aid to European nations to help them rebuild from World War II
(d) Soviet version of the Marshall plan
(e) 1949 mutual defense pact to oppose communism

and pointed out the U.S. superiority in missiles. Khrushchev was forced once again to lift his six-month ultimatum. He realized, however, the need to stop the flow of refugees from East Germany through West Berlin. In August 1961, the East German government began to build a wall separating West Berlin from East Berlin. Eventually, it became a massive barrier guarded by barbed wire, floodlights, machine-gun towers, minefields, and vicious dog patrols. The Berlin Wall became a striking symbol of the division between the two superpowers.

Stung by reverses and determined to achieve some foreign policy success, Khrushchev soon embarked on a very dangerous adventure in Cuba. Ever since the Bay of Pigs, the Soviet Union had sent arms and military advisors to Cuba. In 1962, Khrushchev began to place medium-range nuclear missiles in Cuba. The United States was not willing to allow nuclear weapons within such close striking distance of the U.S. mainland, despite the fact that the United States had placed nuclear weapons in Turkey within easy range of the Soviet Union. Khrushchev was quick to point out that "your rockets are in Turkey. You are worried by Cuba . . . because it is 90 miles from the American coast. But Turkey is next to us."[4]

In October 1962, the United States found out that Soviet ships carrying missiles were heading to Cuba. Kennedy decided to blockade Cuba and prevent the fleet from reaching its destination. This approach to the problem gave each side time to find a peaceful solution. Khrushchev agreed to turn back the fleet and remove Soviet missiles from Cuba if Kennedy pledged not to invade Cuba. Kennedy quickly agreed.

The Cuban Missile Crisis brought the world frighteningly close to nuclear war. Indeed, in 1992 a high-ranking Soviet officer revealed that short-range rockets armed with nuclear devices would have been used against U.S. troops if the United States had invaded Cuba, an option that Kennedy fortunately had rejected. The realization that the world might have been destroyed in a few days had a profound influence on both sides. A hotline communications system between Moscow and Washington, D.C., was installed in 1963. The two superpowers could now communicate quickly in a time of crisis. In the same year, the two powers agreed to ban nuclear tests in the atmosphere. This step at least served to lessen the tensions between the two nations and keep the Earth's atmosphere free of nuclear pollution.

Vietnam and the Domino Theory

By that time, the United States had also been drawn into a new struggle that had an important impact on the Cold War—the Vietnam War (see Chapter 33). In 1964, under President Lyndon B. Johnson, increasing numbers of U.S. troops were sent to Vietnam. Their purpose was to keep the Communist regime of North Vietnam from gaining control of South Vietnam. U.S. policy makers saw the conflict in terms of a **domino theory** concerning the spread of communism. If the Communists succeeded in South Vietnam, the argument went, all the other countries in the Far East that were freeing themselves from colonial domination would likewise fall (like dominoes) to communism.

Despite the massive superiority in equipment and firepower of the American forces, the United States failed to defeat the determined North Vietnamese, and especially the Vietcong—the South Vietnamese Communist guerrillas who were being supported by North Vietnam. The growing number of American troops sent to Vietnam soon produced a persistent antiwar movement in the United States, especially among college students of draft age. The mounting destruction of the conflict, brought into American homes every evening on television, also turned American public opinion against the war. Finally, President Richard M. Nixon reached an agreement with North Vietnam in 1973 that allowed the United States to withdraw its forces. Within two years after the American withdrawal, Vietnam had been forcibly reunited by Communist armies from the North.

Despite the success of the North Vietnamese Communists, the domino theory proved unfounded. A noisy split between Communist China and the Soviet Union put an end to the theory of a single communism directed by Moscow. Under President Nixon, American relations with China were resumed. New nations in Southeast Asia also managed to avoid Communist governments. Above all, Vietnam helped to show the

---

CNN® WORLD HISTORY UPDATES

You can update your coverage of World History topics, as well as spark lively classroom discussion and deeper understanding, by using the **CNN World History Updates.**

For assistance in using and incorporating the **CNN World History Updates** into your classroom presentations, see the *Classroom Guide.*

limitations of American power. By the end of the Vietnam War, a new era in American-Soviet relations had begun to emerge.

  SECTION REVIEW

1. **Locate:**
   (a) Greece,   (b) Turkey

2. **Define:**
   (a) policy of containment,   (b) mutual deterrence,   (c) domino theory

3. **Identify:**
   (a) Truman Doctrine,   (b) Dean Acheson,
   (c) Marshall Plan,   (d) COMECON,
   (e) NATO,   (f) Warsaw Pact,   (g) CENTO,
   (h) SEATO,   (i) Nikita Khrushchev,
   (j) Vietcong

4. **Recall:**
   (a) What happened to relations between the United States and the Soviet Union after the Axis powers were defeated in World War II?
   (b) How did the Soviets react when the United States, Great Britain, and France made plans to create West Germany in 1948?
   (c) What did the United States believe the invasion of South Korea by North Korea proved about Communist intentions?
   (d) How was the Cuban Missile Crisis resolved?

5. **Think Critically:** Why was it unrealistic for people to think that there was just one united Communist movement in the world after World War II?

THE SOVIET UNION AND ITS EASTERN EUROPEAN SATELLITES (1945 TO 1970)

World War II had left the Soviet Union one of the world's two superpowers. Its leader, Joseph Stalin, was at the height of his power. As a result of the war, Stalin and the Soviet forces were now in control of a vast empire that included Eastern Europe, much of the Balkans, and new territory gained from Japan in the Far East.

The Reign of Stalin

World War II devastated the Soviet Union. Over twenty million citizens had lost their lives. Cities like Kiev and Leningrad lay in ruins. The Soviet people faced incredibly difficult conditions. They worked long hours and ate little. They were badly housed and poorly clothed.

In the immediate postwar years, the Soviet Union removed goods and materials from occupied Germany and took valuable raw materials from its satellite states in Eastern Europe. To create a new industrial base, Stalin returned to the method that he had used in the 1930s. Working hard for little pay, poor housing, and few consumer goods, Soviet workers were expected to produce goods for export with little in return for themselves. The incoming capital from abroad could then be used to buy machinery and Western technology. The loss of millions of men in the war, however, meant that much of this tremendous workload fell upon Soviet women. Almost 40 percent of heavy labor in factories was done by women.

The old methods brought about a spectacular economic recovery in the Soviet Union. By 1947, Russian industrial production had reached prewar levels. Three years later, it had surpassed these levels by 40 percent. New power plants, canals, and giant factories were built, although often with little regard for the environment. Metals plants in Soviet cities, for example, spewed out noxious chemicals that polluted the land and sickened the people. New industrial plants and oil fields were set up in Siberia and Soviet Central Asia. Stalin's newly announced five-year economic plan of 1946 reached its goals in less than five years.

Although Stalin's economic policy led to growth in heavy industry, the results were chiefly for the benefit of the military. Consumer goods were scarce. The development of thermonuclear weapons (hydrogen bombs) in 1952 and the first space satellite (*Sputnik I*) in 1957 enhanced the Soviet state's reputation as a

(f) Communist military alliance
(g) formed to stop Soviet aggression in the Middle East
(h) formed to stop Soviet aggression in Southeast Asia
(i) Soviet leader who had the Berlin wall built
(j) South Vietnamese Communist forces supported by North Vietnam

4. (a) Relations rapidly deteriorated
   (b) blockaded West Berlin
   (c) confirmed that Communist nations intended to expand
   (d) The Soviet Union removed its missiles from Cuba in exchange for a promise from the United States not to invade that country.

5. Answers will vary but should concern the fact that there were very different nationalist, social, cultural, and economic interests that were held by different Communist nations.

CLOSE

Lead students in a discussion of the Focus objectives on page 944. Emphasize the role played by the balance of power.

MORE ABOUT . . . *Russian Casualties*

Students should know that the Soviet Union lost around 20 to 30 million civilian and military people during World War II, and was not eager to see Germany unified and strong, posing a threat once again to Russia. Remind students that past Russian history with Germany played a large part in its actions during the Berlin crisis. Students should also understand that Berlin was the capital of Nazi Germany. It was divided into four spheres of influ-

ence immediately following the war as described in Section 1. During the 1948–1949 crisis in Berlin, the Soviets blocked all entry into West Berlin, but the Allies chose not to give up the city to the Soviets. Instead, they air lifted supplies to the approximately 2 million people living in West Berlin. This airlift continued for almost one year.

FOCUS

OBJECTIVES

After completing this section, students should be able to

1. describe Stalin's rule of the Soviet Union
2. describe changes that took place in the Soviet Union under Khrushchev's leadership
3. explain how the Soviet Union exerted its power over the states of Eastern Europe

FOCUS ACTIVITY

Help students understand that it is easier to dominate a nation through military force than it is to earn the support or cooperation of that nation's people. Have students describe how Hitler and Japan learned this fate in World War II, as well as the United States in the war in Vietnam. You might also wish to include a review of colonialism and nations that struggled for independence in this discussion.

TEACH

LEARNING FROM VISUALS

Remind students that many American citizens felt that the USSR had superior military and scientific capabilities because they were able to launch two successful Sputniks, while the Americans lagged behind in space technology.

▲ *The Soviets launched* Sputnik I *on October 4, 1957. It made a full orbit around the Earth every one and one-half hours, and it stayed up for fifty-seven days.* Sputnik II, *which carried a live dog, was launched in November 1957.*

world power abroad. At home, however, the Soviet people were shortchanged. Heavy industry grew at a rate three times that of consumer goods. Moreover, the housing shortage was severe. An average Russian family lived in a one-room apartment. A British offical in Moscow reported that "all houses, practically without exception, show lights from every window after dark. This seems to indicate that every room is both a living room by day and a bedroom by night. There is no place in overcrowded Moscow for the luxury of eating and sleeping in separate rooms."[5]

When World War II ended in 1945, Stalin had been in power for over fifteen years. During that time, he had removed all opposition to his rule. He remained the undisputed master of the Soviet Union. Other leading members of the Communist Party were completely obedient to his will. Stalin distrusted competitors, and exercised sole power. He pitted his subordinates against one another. Stalin had little respect for other Communist Party leaders. He is reported to have said to members of his inner circle in 1952, "You are as blind as kittens. What would you do without me?"[6]

Stalin's paranoid suspicions added to the constantly increasing repression of the regime. In 1946, government decrees stated that all forms of literary and scientific expression must conform to the political needs of the state and the Communist Party line. An econo-

mist, for example, was condemned for suggesting that the West might have an economic boom. Along with an anti-intellectual campaign came political terror. A new series of purges—like those of the late 1930s—seemed likely in 1953 when a number of Jewish doctors were accused of plotting to kill high-level party officials. A great fear began to spread throughout the country. Only Stalin's death on March 5, 1953, prevented more bloodletting.

The Khrushchev Era

After Stalin's death, power passed into the hands of a group of ten leaders of an executive committee known as the Presidium. A struggle for power soon arose. Lavrenti Beria, head of the secret police, was the first member of the Presidium to fall from power. Others followed as the struggle grew. Gradually, however, the new general secretary of the Communist Party, Nikita Khrushchev, became the chief Soviet leader. Khrushchev had been responsible for ending the system of forced-labor camps, a regular feature of Stalinist Russia. At the Twentieth Congress of the Communist Party in 1956, Khrushchev condemned Stalin for his "administrative violence, mass repression, and terror." Stalin, he said, "often chose the path of repression and annihilation" against both party members and individuals who had committed no crimes whatsoever. The process of eliminating the more ruthless policies of Stalin became known as **de-Stalinization.**

Once in power, Khrushchev extended the policy of de-Stalinization. He stated that "readers should be given the chance to make their own judgements" regarding controversial literature. Police measures, he said, should not be used. He allowed the publication in 1962 of Alexander Solzhenitsyn's (SOLE-zhuh-NEET-sun) *A Day in the Life of Ivan Denisovich,* a grim portrayal of life in a Siberian forced-labor camp. Each day, as Solzhenitsyn related, prisoners were marched from the prison camp to a work project through temperatures of seventeen degrees below zero: "There were escort guards all over the place, . . . their machine guns

---

MORE ABOUT . . . *Stalin and the Cold War*

In 1992 a British expert on the Soviet military released a report indicating that Russia's losses during World War II were even more staggering than previously believed. With the declassification of many Russian records after the fall of communism, John Erickson of Edinburgh University, has estimated that Soviet deaths might have been as high as 49

million, or nearly 30% of its people. If this information proves to be accurate it may hold a key to the beginning of the Cold War. Some historians speculate that Stalin, in an attempt to cover up the Soviet Union's post war weakness, was deliberately hostile to the West, thereby contributing to worsening relations with the United States.

sticking out and pointed right at your face. And there were guards with gray dogs. One dog bared its fangs as if laughing at the prisoners." Many Soviets identified with Ivan as a symbol of the suffering they had endured under Stalin.

There was a limit to de-Stalinization, however. When Khrushchev's revelations about Stalin fed a spirit of rebellion in Soviet satellite countries in Eastern Europe, there was a reaction. Soviet troops crushed an uprising in Hungary in 1956 (see the next section). Khrushchev and the Soviet leaders, afraid of a further undermining of the regime, downplayed their campaign of de-Stalinization.

Khrushchev tried to place more emphasis in the economy on light industry and consumer goods. His attempts to increase agricultural output by growing corn and cultivating vast lands east of the Ural Mountains were not successful and damaged his reputation within the party. These failures, combined with increased military spending, hurt the Soviet economy. The industrial growth rate, which had soared in the early 1950s, now declined dramatically from 13 percent in 1953 to 7.5 percent in 1964.

Khrushchev's personality also did not endear him to the higher Soviet officials. They frowned at his tendency to crack jokes and play the clown. The higher members of the party bureaucracy also were not pleased when Khrushchev tried to curb their privileges. Foreign policy failures further damaged Khrushchev's reputation among his colleagues. His rash plan to place missiles in Cuba was the final straw. While he was away on vacation in 1964, a special meeting of the Soviet leaders voted him out of office (because of "deteriorating health") and forced him into retirement. A group of leaders officially succeeded him, but real power came into the hands of Leonid Brezhnev (BREZH-nef). Supposedly the "trusted" supporter of Khrushchev, it was Brezhnev who had engineered his downfall.

Eastern Europe: Behind the Iron Curtain

At the end of World War II, Soviet military forces had occupied all of Eastern Europe and the Balkans (except for Greece, Albania, and Yugoslavia). All of the occupied states came to be part of the Soviet sphere of influ-

CONNECTIONS
AROUND THE WORLD

Economic Miracles: Germany and Japan   Both Germany and Japan were devastated by World War II. Their economies were in shambles. Their cities lay in ruins. So many German men had been killed or wounded in the war that women had to take on the backbreaking work of clearing the rubble in the cities by hand.

At the end of the twentieth century, Germany and Japan are two of the world's greatest economic powers. What explains their economic miracles?

Because of the destruction of the war, both countries were forced to build new industrial plants. For many years, thanks to American military forces, neither country had to spend much on defense. Their governments could focus on rebuilding the infrastructure (roads, bridges, canals, and buildings) that had been destroyed during the war. Both German and Japanese workers had a long tradition of hard work and basic skills. In both countries, U.S. occupation policy focused on economic recovery, a goal that was made easier by American foreign aid.

Today, Germany and Japan share many similarities in the structure of their economies. Both rely on imports of raw materials for their industries. Both depend for their prosperity on exports of manufactured goods, including machinery, automobiles, steel, textiles, electrical and electronic equipment, and ships. Both nations must import food to feed their populations.

ence. After 1945, they all had similar political developments. Coalitions of all political parties were formed to run the governments in these states. Within a year or two, however, the Communist parties in these coalitions had taken over most of the power. The next step was the creation of one-party Communist governments.

RETEACHING ACTIVITY

On page 787 (Chapter 24, Black Guns in the Pacific: East Asia in an Age of Imperialism) of the Teacher's Wraparound Edition, there is a lengthy explanation of geographical and social obstacles that Japan has over-

come in its rise to an economic super-power. It might be beneficial for some students to cover this material again in light of the topic of the "Connections Around the World" feature above.

CLASS DISCUSSION

Have students identify and discuss changes that took place in the Soviet Union under Khrushchev's leadership. Do students believe that had Stalin lived longer, he would have been able to maintain his absolute hold on power? Was a period of de-stalinization inevitable?

COMPARING TIME PERIODS

Have students write a description of the similarities between the fall of Napoleon III after his defeat in 1871 and Khrushchev's problems after the Cuban Missile Crisis of 1962. Were these defeats the actual reasons for these leaders' fall or were they only an excuse and opportunity for people who already wanted to replace them?

LEARNING FROM VISUALS

Ask students to describe what the Communist leaders in this photograph were really thinking when this picture was taken. Remind them that in 1955 Yugoslavia was the only Communist state that refused to take orders from the Soviet Union. Why was this 'crack' in the solid Communist wall important?

Answer to the caption question: It is highly likely that Krushchev did not wish to be seen as a military dictator, but as a civilian leader of a very powerful nation. Tito, clearly a military leader and dictator, salutes his armed forces as a military leader.

ACROSS THE CURRICULUM

Economics The Soviet emphasis on production of heavy industrial goods resulted in a shortage of consumer goods throughout the Soviet sphere of influence. Do students believe the people of Eastern Europe would have been more tolerant of the Soviet presence in their countries if they had enjoyed a better standard of living?

▶ In 1955, Nikita Khrushchev, on the right, visited Belgrade, Yugoslavia, where he was welcomed by Tito and accorded full military honors. Why do you think Khrushchev is dressed in civilian clothes and Tito is wearing a military uniform?

The timetables of these Communist takeovers varied from country to country. Between 1945 and 1947, Communist governments became firmly entrenched in East Germany, Bulgaria, Romania, Poland, and Hungary. In Czechoslovakia, where there was a strong tradition of democracy, the Communists did not achieve their goals until 1948. In the elections of 1946, the Communist Party of Czechoslovakia had become the largest party, but it was not all-powerful and shared control of the government with the noncommunist parties. When it appeared that the noncommunist parties might win new elections early in 1948, the Communists seized control of the government on February 25. All other parties were dissolved.

Albania and Yugoslavia were exceptions to this pattern of Soviet dominance. Both countries had had strong Communist resistance movements during the war, and yet the Communist parties took control when the war ended. In Albania, local Communists set up a rigidly Stalinist-type regime, but one that grew more and more independent of the Soviet Union.

In Yugoslavia, Josip Broz, known as Tito (TEE-TOE), leader of the Communist resistance movement, seemed to be a loyal Stalinist. After the war, however, he moved toward the creation of an independent Communist state in Yugoslavia. Stalin hoped to take control of Yugoslavia, just as he had done in other Eastern European countries. Tito, however, refused to give in to Stalin's demands. He gained the support of the people by portraying the struggle as one of Yugoslav national freedom. The Yugoslav Communists rejected Stalinism and followed a more decentralized economic system in which workers could manage themselves. Greater social freedom was also part of Yugoslav communism.

Between 1948 and Stalin's death in 1953, the Eastern European satellite states, directed by the Soviet Union, followed a policy of Stalinization. They instituted Soviet-type five-year plans with emphasis on heavy industry rather than consumer goods. They began to collectivize agriculture. They eliminated all noncommunist parties and established the institutions of repression—secret police and military forces.

However, communism—a foreign product—had not developed deep roots among the peoples of Eastern Europe. Moreover, the Soviets exploited Eastern Europe economically for their own benefit and made living conditions harsh for most people. The Soviets had removed factories from their defeated wartime enemies, Bulgaria, Romania, and Hungary, and shipped them to the Soviet Union. The Soviet government

RECOMMENDED READING

Three introductory surveys on postwar Europe are P. Lane, *Europe since 1945: An Introduction* (Totowa, N.J., 1985); J. R. Wegs, *Europe since 1945: A Concise History*, 2d ed. (New York, 1984); and W. Laqueur, *Europe in Our Time* (New York, 1992). The effects of the Cold War on Germany are examined in J. H. Backer, *The Decision to Divide Germany: American Foreign Policy in Transition* (Durham, N.C., 1978). On atomic diplomacy in the Cold War, see G. F. Herken, *The Winning Weapon: The Atomic Bomb in the Cold War, 1945–1950* (New York, 1981). For a good introduction to the arms race, see E. M. Bottome, *The Balance of Terror: A Guide to the Arms Race,* rev. ed. (Boston, 1986). On the Cuban Missile Crisis, ass R. A. Chayes, *The Cuban Missile Crisis* (New York, 1974). For a good account of the Vietnam War, see S. Karrow, *Vietnam: A History* (New York, 1983).

YOU ARE THERE

Soviet Repression in Eastern Europe—Hungary, 1956

◄ *In 1956, Soviet tanks manned by Soviet soldiers traveled freely in Budapest, Hungary. What do you believe were the mood and thoughts of the Hungarians who were watching these tanks move through their capital city?*

The first selection that follows is a statement by the Soviet government justifying the use of Soviet troops in Hungary. The second is a brief and tragic final statement from Imre Nagy, the Hungarian leader.

Statement of the Soviet Government, October 30, 1956

The course of the events has shown that the working people of Hungary, who have achieved great progress on the basis of their people's democratic order, correctly raise the question of the necessity of eliminating serious shortcomings in the field of economic building, the further raising of the material well-being of the population, and the struggle against bureaucratic excesses in the state apparatus.

However, this just and progressive movement of the working people was soon joined by forces of black reaction and counterrevolution, which are trying to take advantage of the discontent of part of the working people to undermine the foundations of the people's democratic order in Hungary and to restore the old landlord and capitalist order.

The Soviet Government and all the Soviet people deeply regret that the development of events in Hungary has led to bloodshed. On the request of the Hungarian People's Government the Soviet Government consented to the entry into Budapest of the Soviet Army units to assist the Hungarian People's Army and the Hungarian authorities to establish order in the town.

(continued)

USING PRIMARY SOURCES

Ask students to imagine a man who lived in Hungary in 1956 who had a family, a job, a few possessions, and a two-room apartment in an old building. His family's life was not wonderful but they were getting by. Assign students to write a description of reasons why such a person would risk all that he had to oppose the Soviet invasion of his country.

LEARNING FROM VISUALS

Tell students to imagine waking up tomorrow morning to find a tank parked in front of their home surrounded by foreign soldiers. What would they feel? What would they do?

Answer to the caption question: The concern and fear of these citizens shows clearly in their faces and in their postures.

On Line with
WORLD HISTORY *Internet Activity*

You may want to have your students visit the following URL, where they will find information and additional web site resources to enhance their study of this chapter.
   Cuban Missile Crisis
http://www.ug.bcc.bilkent.edu.tr/ ~bayer/cmc/main.html

This incident came very close to starting a nuclear war; A well done web page with maps, pictures and links to other sources.
   Due to the ever-changing nature of the World Wide Web, see the West History web site, **http://history.swpco.com** for regular updates of the URLs in this text.

ACTIVITY

After more extensive independent research have students compare and contrast the Soviet invasion of Hungary in 1956 with the attempted Bay of Pigs invasion of Cuba in 1961. How would bias and differing viewpoints affect their analysis of these two events?

Answers to Critical Thinking Questions

1. Answers will vary, but should be supported with reasons.
2. The policy appeared to be to put down any resistance by the people and to make soviet intervention look like a response to a request for help.

Multimedia Support

TRANSPARENCY
29–2, World Map of Countries with Nuclear Weapons (1949, 1965, 1997)

ASSESS

Assign students to pretend they are a Western news reporter in Hungary at the time of the Soviet invasion. They should prepare an article for an American newspaper that describes the events leading up to the Soviet invasion and what possible effect it will have on the Cold War.

YOU ARE THERE

Soviet Repression in Eastern Europe—Hungary, 1956, continued

The Last Message of Imre Nagy, November 4, 1956

This fight is the fight for freedom by the Hungarian people against the Russian intervention, and it is possible that I shall only be able to stay at my post for one or two hours. The whole world will see how the Russian armed forces, contrary to all treaties and conventions, are crushing the resistance of the Hungarian people. They will also see how they are kidnapping the Prime Minister of a country which is a Member of the United Nations, taking him from the capital, and therefore it cannot be doubted at all that this is the most brutal form of intervention. I should like in these last moments to ask the leaders of the revolution, if they can, to leave the country. I ask that all that I have said in my broadcast, and what we have

agreed on with the revolutionary leaders during meetings in parliament, should be put in a memorandum, and the leaders should turn to all the peoples of the world for help and explain that today it is Hungary and tomorrow, or the day after tomorrow, it will be the turn of other countries because the imperialism of Moscow does not know borders, and is only trying to play for time.

---

1. Which of the two accounts do you think is the most accurate description of what actually happened in Hungary? Why do you think this?

2. Based on these selections, what was Soviet policy in the 1950s toward its Eastern European satellite states?

---

also forced all of the Eastern European states to trade with the Soviet Union to the latter's advantage.

After Stalin's death, many Eastern European states began to pursue a new, more nationalistically oriented course. The new Soviet leaders, including Khrushchev, also interfered less in the internal affairs of these states. In the late 1950s and 1960s, however, the Soviet Union also made it clear, especially in Poland, Hungary, and Czechoslovakia, that it would not allow its Eastern European satellites to become independent of Soviet control.

In 1956, after Khrushchev had denounced Stalin, protests—especially by workers—erupted in Poland. In response, the Polish Communist Party adopted a series of reforms in October 1956 and elected Wladyslaw Gomulka as first secretary. Gomulka declared that Poland had the right to follow its own socialist path. Fearful of Soviet armed response, however, the Poles

compromised. Poland pledged to remain loyal to the Warsaw Pact. The Soviets then agreed to allow Poland to follow its own path to socialism. The Catholic Church, an extremely important institution to many Poles, was also allowed to govern its own affairs.

These developments in Poland in 1956 led Hungarian Communists to seek the same kinds of reforms and independence. They chose Imre Nagy as the new Hungarian leader. Internal dissent in Hungary, however, was directed not simply against the Soviets but against communism in general, which was viewed as a creation of the Soviets. The Stalinist secret police had also bred much terror and hatred in Hungary.

The unrest in Hungary, combined with economic difficulties, led to calls for revolt. To quell the rising rebellion, Nagy declared Hungary a free nation on November 1, 1956. He promised free elections. The mood of the country soon made it clear that this could

---

On Line with WORLD HISTORY *Internet Activity*

You may want to have your students visit the following URL, where they will find information and additional web site resources to enhance their study of this chapter.
Cold War Hot Links: Some Cold War Web Resources
http: //www.stmartin.edu/~dprice/

cold.war.html
This site lists links to many topics of the Cold War.
Due to the ever-changing nature of the World Wide Web, see the West History web site, **http://history.swpco.com** for regular updates of the URLs in this text.

mean the end of Communist rule in Hungary. However, Khrushchev was in no position at home to allow a member of the Communist group of nations to leave. Just three days after Nagy's declaration, the Red Army attacked Budapest (see "You Are There: Soviet Repression in Eastern Europe—Hungary, 1956"). The Soviets reestablished control over the country. János Kádár, a reform-minded cabinet minister, replaced Nagy and worked with the Soviet Union to squash the revolt. By collaborating with the Soviet invaders, Kádár saved many of Nagy's economic reforms.

The developments in Poland and Hungary in 1956 did not lead to a revolt in Czechoslovakia. There the "Little Stalin," Antonin Novotny, had been placed in power in 1952 by Stalin himself and remained firmly in control. By the late 1960s, however, Novotny had alienated many members of his own party. He was especially disliked by Czechoslovakia's writers, including the playwright Václav Havel. A writers' rebellion late in 1967, in fact, led to Novotny's resignation. In January 1968, Alexander Dubcek was elected first secretary of the Communist Party. He soon introduced a number of reforms, including freedom of speech and press and freedom to travel abroad. Dubcek hoped to create "communism with a human face." A period of euphoria broke out that came to be known as the "Prague (PRAWG) Spring."

The euphoria proved to be short-lived, however. It had led many to call for more far-reaching reforms, including withdrawal from the Soviet bloc. To forestall the spreading of this "spring" fever, the Red Army invaded Czechoslovakia in August 1968 and crushed the reform movement. Gustav Husák (HYOO-SAWK) replaced Dubcek, crushed his reforms, and reestablished the old order.

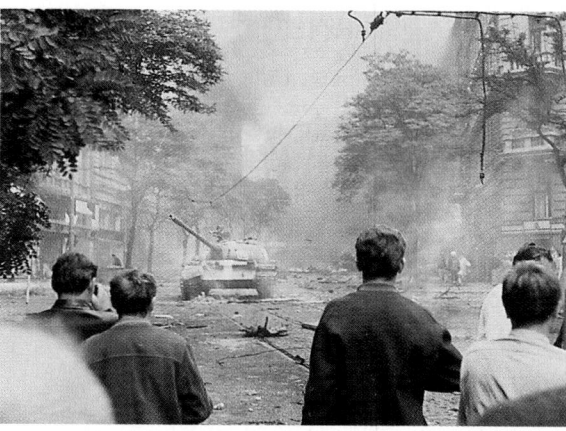

▲ In 1968, the Soviet response to Alexander Dubcek's efforts to reform Communist rule in Czechoslovakia was to send Soviet tanks into Prague to stop any possible changes. Why do you think the Czechs believed they might succeed in liberalizing Communist practices when their neighbors in Hungary had failed to thwart the Soviets?

SECTION REVIEW

1. **Locate:**
   (a) Soviet Union, (b) Hungary

2. **Define:**
   (a) de-Stalinization

3. **Identify:**
   (a) satellite states, (b) Presidium,
   (c) Alexander Solzhenitsyn, (d) Leonid Brezhnev, (e) Tito, (f) "Prague Spring"

4. **Recall:**
   (a) Why did much of the work of rebuilding the Soviet Union after World War II fall on women?
   (b) What prevented even greater repression and terror from taking place in the Soviet Union during the early 1950s?
   (c) What failures did Khrushchev suffer that contributed to his decline from power?
   (d) Why didn't communism develop deep roots among the peoples of Eastern Europe?
   (e) Why did the Soviet Union invade Hungary but not Poland in 1956?

5. **Think Critically:** Both Yugoslavia and Albania had strong Communist parties during World War II but did not come under the direct control of the Soviet Union after the war. Other nations with

On Line with WORLD HISTORY *Internet Activity*

You may want to have your students visit the following URL, where they will find information and additional web site resources to enhance their study of this chapter.
Berlin Airlift, Berlin Wall, Iron Curtain
http://home.cdsnet.net/~howard/ berlin.htm

This site includes pictures and narrative on all three events listed above.

Due to the ever-changing nature of the World Wide Web, see the West History web site, **http://history.swpco.com** for regular updates of the URLs in this text.

CLOSE

Lead students in a discussion of the 'Focus' objective identified on page 952. Emphasize the doubtful nature of unity within the Soviet block.

FOCUS

OBJECTIVES

After completing this section, students should be able to

1. identify and explain changes in French policy toward NATO under de Gaulle
2. describe economic growth in West Germany after World War II
3. identify and explain reasons for the decline of the British Empire after World War II
4. discuss the movement toward unity in Western Europe

FOCUS ACTIVITY

Help students understand ways nations may react to changes in power and influence. After World War II the United States and Soviet Union emerged as superpowers. Have students explain why some nations that were strong before the war fell into economic and political decline while others prospered.

958

weaker Communist parties were quickly dominated by the Soviets. Why was the Soviet Union more successful in controlling nations that had weak Communist movements?

WESTERN EUROPE: THE REVIVAL OF DEMOCRACY AND THE ECONOMY

All the nations of Western Europe faced similar kinds of problems at the end of World War II. Above all, they needed to rebuild their economies and recreate their democratic institutions. Within a few years of the defeat of Germany and Italy, an incredible economic revival brought a renewed growth to European society.

Western Europe: Domestic Politics

The important role that Communists had played in the resistance movements against the Nazis gained them a new strength once the war was over. Communist parties did well in elections in Italy and France in 1946 and 1947, as well as in a few other countries. Communist success was short-lived, however. Once the Cold War was in full swing, Communist support of Soviet policies hurt Communist parties at home. They began to decline.

As part of their election strategies, Communist parties had often joined forces with other left-wing parties, such as the Social Democrats or the Socialists. The Socialist parties had also fared well immediately after the war as people became willing to overthrow the old order. Support for the Socialists soon waned, however. The Cold War also hurt the Socialist parties. Their working together with Communist parties in postwar coalitions cost them dearly.

By 1950, moderate political parties had made a remarkable comeback in Western Europe. Especially important was the rise of Christian Democratic parties.

The new Christian Democrats were sincerely interested in democracy and in significant economic reforms. They were especially strong in Germany and Italy, and they played an important role in achieving Europe's economic recovery.

With the economic aid of the Marshall Plan, the countries of Western Europe recovered relatively rapidly from the devastation of World War II. Between 1947 and 1950, European countries received $9.4 billion for new equipment and raw materials. By 1950, industrial output in Europe was 30 percent above prewar levels. Steel production alone expanded by 70 percent. Furthermore, this economic recovery continued well into the 1950s and 1960s. The decades of the 1950s and 1960s were periods of dramatic economic growth and prosperity in Western Europe. Indeed, Western Europe had virtually full employment during these decades.

France: The Domination of de Gaulle

The history of France for nearly a quarter of a century after the war was dominated by one man—Charles de Gaulle (di-GOLE). He had an unshakable faith in his mission to restore the greatness of the French nation. During the war, de Gaulle had been the leader of French resistance groups. He also played an important role in establishing a French provisional government after the war. The creation of a new government called the Fourth Republic in 1946, with its return to a parliamentary system based on parties that de Gaulle considered weak, led him to withdraw from politics. Eventually, he formed the French Popular Movement, which blamed the parties for France's political mess and called for an even stronger presidency. De Gaulle finally achieved this goal in 1958.

The political stability of the Fourth Republic was badly shaken by the Algerian crisis. After suffering defeat in Vietnam in 1954, the French army was determined to resist the demands of Algerians for independence (see Chapter 32). A strong antiwar movement among French intellectuals and church leaders, however, led to bitter divisions within France. Even the possibility of civil war loomed large. The panic-stricken leaders of the Fourth Republic offered to let

RECOMMENDED READING

For a general view of Soviet society, see D. K. Shipler, *Russia: Broken Idols, Solemn Dreams* (New York, 1983). For a general study of the Soviet satellites in Eastern Europe, see A. Brown and J. Gary, *Culture and Political Changes in Communist States* (London, 1977). On the Soviet Union's actions against Czechoslovakia in 1968, see J. Valenta, *Intervention in Czechoslovakia in 1968* (Baltimore, 1979). The unique path of Yugoslavia is examined in

L. J. Cohen and P. Warwick, *Political Cohesion in a Fragile Mosaic: The Yugoslav Experience* (Boulder, Colo., 1983). On Romania, see L. S. Graham, *Rumania: A Developing Socialist State* (Boulder, Colo., 1978). On Hungary, see B. Kovrig, *The Hungarian People's Republic* (Baltimore, 1970). On East Germany, see C. B. Scharf, *Politics and Change in East Germany* (Boulder, Colo., 1984).

de Gaulle take over the government as president and revise the constitution.

In 1958, de Gaulle drafted a new constitution for the Fifth Republic that greatly enhanced the power of the president. He now had the right to choose the prime minister, dissolve parliament, and supervise both defense and foreign policy. De Gaulle had always believed in strong leadership. The new Fifth Republic under de Gaulle, while preserving the forms of democracy, lacked much of the substance of a democratic system.

As the new president, de Gaulle sought to return France to a position of great power. He did realize, however, that France was only wasting its economic strength by continuing its colonial empire. By 1962, he had granted independence to France's black African colonies and to Algeria. At the same time, the French president believed that playing an important role in the Cold War might enhance France's stature. For that reason, he pulled France out of NATO, arguing that France did not want to be an American "vassal state." With an eye toward achieving the status of a world power, de Gaulle invested heavily in the nuclear arms race. France exploded its first nuclear bomb in 1960. Despite his successes, de Gaulle did not really achieve his ambitious goals of world power. In truth, France was too small for such global ambitions.

Although the cost of the nuclear program increased the defense budget, de Gaulle did not neglect the economy. Between 1958 and 1968, the economy grew at an annual rate of 5.5 percent, faster than that of the United States. By the end of de Gaulle's era, France was a major industrial producer and exporter, especially in automobiles and weapons. However, problems remained. The expansion of traditional industries, such as coal, steel, and railroads, which were now owned by the state, led to large government deficits. The cost of living increased faster in France than in the rest of Europe.

Many French people became unhappy when de Gaulle's government failed to deal with these problems. Some even took violent action. In May 1968, a series of student protests, followed by a general strike by the labor unions, shook de Gaulle's government. Although he managed to restore order, the events of May 1968 had seriously undermined the French peo-

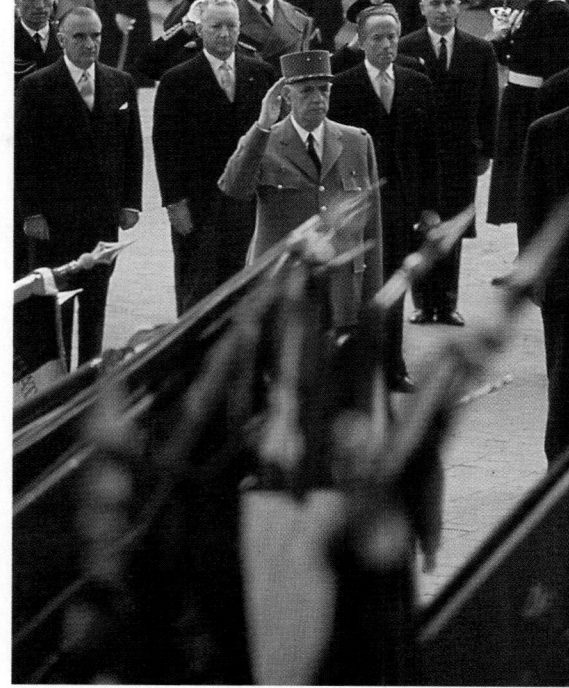

▲ *Charles de Gaulle, shown here in his military uniform, worked to restore France to its previous greatness as a world power. Why do you think the French people turned to a leader of the resistance to restore stability and prosperity to their nation?*

ple's respect for their president. Tired and discouraged, de Gaulle resigned from office in April 1969 and died within a year.

West Germany: The Economic Miracle

As a result of the pressures of the Cold War, the three Western zones of Germany were unified into the Federal Republic of Germany in 1949. Konrad Adenauer (AD-un-OW-ur), the leader of the Christian Democratic Union (CDU), served as chancellor from 1949 to 1963. He became the "founding hero" of the Federal Republic. Adenauer sought respect for West Germany

ENRICHMENT ACTIVITY

Write the following quotation, which is attributed to Charles de Gaulle, on the board or an overhead transparency.

"Only peril can bring the French together. One can't impose unity out of the blue on a country that has 265 different kinds of cheese."

Divide the class into groups and have groups discuss the meaning of the quota

tion. Groups members should work together to write a meaning for the quotation. Once consensus is reached in each group, have groups share their meanings with the rest of the class. The entire class should then reach consensus on the meaning of the quotation.

▲ *Konrad Adenauer, the first chancellor of the Federal Republic of Germany, served as mayor of his hometown, Cologne, following World War I until 1933, when he was removed by the National Socialists. In 1944, he was imprisoned by the Gestapo, but in 1945 he resumed his position as Cologne's mayor. Why is it significant that West Germans elected a Nazi opponent and anticommunist as their first chancellor?*

by cooperating with the United States and the other Western European nations. He especially wanted to work with France—Germany's longtime enemy.

Under Adenauer, West Germany experienced an "economic miracle." This revival of the West German economy was largely guided by the minister of finance, Ludwig Erhard (AIR-hart). The West German economy boomed. Real wages doubled between 1950 and 1965 even though work hours were cut by 20 percent. Unemployment fell from 8 percent in 1950 to 0.4 percent in 1965. To maintain its economic expansion, West Germany even imported hundreds of thousands of guest workers from Italy, Spain, Greece, Turkey, and Yugoslavia.

The beginning of the Korean War in June 1950 had unexpected results for West Germany. The fear that South Korea might fall to Communist forces led many Germans and westerners to worry about the security of West Germany. Calls for West Germany to rearm were now being heard. Many people, afraid of a new German military machine, condemned the proposals for rearmament. Cold War tensions were decisive, however. West Germany rearmed in 1955 and became a member of NATO.

For many years, West Germany remained troubled by its Nazi past. The surviving major Nazi leaders had been tried and condemned as war criminals at the Nuremberg war crimes trials in 1945 and 1946. The victorious Allies continued war crimes trials of lesser officials as well. These declined in frequency, however, as the Cold War produced a shift in attitudes. By 1950, German courts had begun to take over the war crimes trials. Beginning in 1953, the West German government also began to make payments to Israel and to Holocaust survivors and their relatives to atone for the crimes of the Nazi Era. German president Richard von Weizsäcker (VIT-SAW-kur) reminded Germans of their responsibility "for the unspeakable sorrow that occurred in the name of Germany."

Adenauer resigned in 1963, after fourteen years of firmly guiding West Germany through its postwar recovery. Ludwig Erhard succeeded Adenauer as chancellor and largely continued his policies. An economic downturn in the mid-1960s, however, opened the door to the rise of the Social Democrats, who became the leading party in 1969.

Great Britain: The Decline of the Empire

The end of World War II left Great Britain with massive economic problems. In elections held immediately after the war, the Labour Party overwhelmingly defeated Churchill's Conservative Party. The Labour Party had promised far-reaching reforms, especially in the area of social welfare. In a country with a tremendous shortage of consumer goods and housing, the Labour Party's platform was quite appealing. The Labour government under Clement Attlee, the new prime minister, set out to enact the reforms that created a modern **welfare state** in which the government takes responsibility for providing citizens with services and a minimal standard of living.

MORE ABOUT . . . *Clement Attlee*

Clement Richard Attlee was born in to the British middle-class although he was educated at Oxford.

He chose a career as a social worker, until the great war erupted. Attlee served as an officer and then was elected (1919) mayor of Stepney, a London working-class borough. Entering the House of Commons in 1922, he became a minister in the minority Labour Party.

Attlee, headed the cabinet that created Britain's Welfare State. His party nationalized major public utilities and several industries, including coal mining; instituted free medical and hospital care; and established or improved numerous relief programs for the underprivileged.

Map 29.2   The Economic Division of Europe during the Cold War

The establishment of the British welfare state began with the **nationalization** (government ownership) of the Bank of England; the coal and steel industries; public transportation; and public utilities, such as electricity and gas. In the area of social welfare, the new government passed the National Insurance Act and the National Health Service Act, both in 1946. The insurance act provided state funds to help the unemployed, the sick, and the aged. The health act created a system of socialized medicine that forced doctors and dentists to work with state hospitals, although private practices could be maintained. This measure was very costly for the state, but within a few years 90 percent of the medical profession was taking part. The British welfare state became the norm for most European states after the war (see "Creation of the Welfare State" later in the chapter).

The cost of building a welfare state at home forced Britain to reduce expenses abroad. This meant the dismantling of the British Empire and the reduction of military aid to such countries as Greece and Turkey. Economic necessity forced Britain to give in to the demands of its many colonies for national independence.

Continuing economic problems, however, brought the Conservatives back into power from 1951 to 1964. Although they favored private enterprise, the Conservatives accepted the welfare state and even extended it by financing an ambitious building program to improve British housing.

Although the British economy had recovered from the war, it had done so at a slower rate than other European countries. Britain was experiencing a long-term economic decline caused by a variety of factors. For one thing, Britain was not willing or was unable to invest in modern industrial machinery and to adopt new methods. Underlying the immediate problems, however, was a deeper issue. As a result of World War II, Britain had lost much of its revenues from abroad, but it still had a burden of debt from its many international

Answers to SECTION REVIEW

2. (a) the government guarantees a minimum standard of living
(b) government ownership of businesses and services
3. (a) members of political parties that wanted democracy and reform in Europe after World War II
(b) World War II hero and leader of France
(c) the rapid growth of the West German economy after World War II
(d) trade organization for member nations in Europe
4. (a) The socialists became "tainted" by association.
(b) to preserve France's independence
(c) It made many think East Germany might invade West Germany.
(d) shortages of consumer goods
(e) The British were unable or unwilling to invest in new machinery and technology.
5. Answers will vary but should point out that "going it alone" is expensive, requires sacrifice and a unity that is often difficult to achieve.

CLOSE

Lead students in a discussion of the Focus objective identified on page 958. Emphasize the importance of breaks in both the Soviet and American power blocks.

commitments. With the rise of the United States and the Soviet Union, Britain was no longer able to play the role of a world power.

Western Europe: The Move toward Unity

As we have seen, the divisions created by the Cold War led the nations of Western Europe to form the North Atlantic Treaty Organization in 1949. Military unity, however, was not the only kind of unity fostered in Europe after 1945. The destructiveness of two world wars caused many thoughtful Europeans to consider the need for some form of European unity. National feeling was still too powerful, however, for European nations to give up their political sovereignty. As a result, the desire for unity was forced to focus chiefly on the economic arena, not the political one.

In 1951, France, West Germany, the Benelux countries (Belgium, the Netherlands, and Luxembourg), and Italy formed the European Coal and Steel Community (ECSC). It created a common market for coal and steel products among the six nations by getting rid of tariffs and other trade barriers. The success of the ECSC encouraged its members to do more.

In 1957, the same six nations signed the Rome Treaty, which created the European Economic Community (EEC), also known as the Common Market. The EEC eliminated all customs barriers for the six member nations and created a large free-trade area protected from the rest of the world by a common tariff. In this way the EEC encouraged cooperation among the six nations' economies. All the member nations benefited economically. By the 1960s, the EEC nations had become an important trading bloc. With a total population of 165 million, the EEC became the world's largest exporter and purchaser of raw materials.

❀ SECTION REVIEW ❀

1. Locate:
(a) France,   (b) West Germany,   (c) Great Britain

2. Define:
(a) welfare state,   (b) nationalization

3. Identify:
(a) Christian Democrats,   (b) Charles de Gaulle,
(c) the West German "economic miracle",
(d) European Economic Community (EEC)

4. Recall:
(a) How did cooperation with Communist parties hurt Socialist parties in Western Europe after World War II?
(b) Why did de Gaulle pull France out of NATO?
(c) What did the invasion of South Korea have to do with the decision to rearm West Germany?
(d) Why did British voters become dissatisfied with the Conservative Party and Winston Churchill after World War II?
(e) Why did the British experience an economic decline after World War II?

5. Think Critically: Why do nations, such as France under Charles de Gaulle, who try to "go it alone" often suffer economic and social problems that are greater than those of nations that cooperate with each other?

THE UNITED STATES AND CANADA: A NEW ERA

At the end of World War II, the United States emerged as one of the world's two superpowers. Reluctantly, the United States remained involved in European affairs. As the Cold War with the Soviet Union intensified, the United States worked hard to combat the spread of communism throughout the world. American domestic political life after 1945 was played out against a background of American military power abroad.

American Politics and Society in the 1950s

Between 1945 and 1970, the ideals of Franklin Delano Roosevelt's New Deal largely determined the patterns of American domestic politics. The New Deal had brought basic changes to American society. These included a dramatic increase in the role and power of

RECOMMENDED READING

The rebuilding of postwar Europe is examined in A. S. Milward, *The Reconstruction of Western Europe, 1945–51* (Berkeley, 1984). For a general survey, see F. Tipton and R. Aldrich, *An Economic and Social History of Europe from 1939 to the Present* (Baltimore, 1987). On the building of common institutions in Western Europe, see J. Lodge, *Institutions and Policies of the European Community* (New York, 1983). For a survey of West Germany, see M. Balfour, *West Germany: A Contemporary History* (London, 1983). France under de Gaulle is examined in P. Williams and M. Harrison, *Politics and Society in de Gaulle's Republic* (New York, 1971). On Britain, see C. J. Bartlett, *A History of Post-War Britain* (London, 1977); and A. Sampson, *The Changing Anatomy of Britain* (New York, 1982). On Italy, see J. LaPalombara, *Democracy, Italian Style* (New Haven, Conn., 1987).

◀ *Following the war, the United States experienced an unprecedented baby boom and a move to the suburbs. Do scenes like this 1949 photograph of a Levittown shopping center accurately portray postwar America? Why or why not?*

the federal government, the rise of organized labor as a significant force in the economy and politics, the beginning of a welfare state, and a grudging realization of the need to deal fairly with the concerns of minorities.

The New Deal tradition in American politics was reinforced by the election of Democratic presidents—Harry S Truman in 1948, John F. Kennedy in 1960, and Lyndon B. Johnson in 1964. Even the election of a Republican president, Dwight D. Eisenhower, in 1952 and 1956 did not change the basic direction of the New Deal. As Eisenhower stated in 1954, "Should any political party attempt to abolish Social Security and eliminate labor laws and farm programs, you would not hear of that party again in our political history."

No doubt, the economic boom after World War II fueled confidence in the American way of life. A shortage of consumer goods during the war had left Americans with both extra income and the desire to buy consumer goods after the war. Then, too, the growth of labor unions brought higher wages and gave more and more workers the ability to buy consumer goods. Government expenditures also indirectly helped the American private economy. Especially after the Korean War began in 1950, funds spent on defense provided money for scientific research in the universities and markets for weapons industries. After 1955, tax dollars built a massive system of interstate highways. Between 1945 and 1973, **real wages** (actual purchasing power of

income) grew an average of 3 percent a year, the most prolonged advance in American history.

The prosperity of the 1950s and 1960s led to social changes. Work patterns changed. More and more people moved away from work in factories and fields into **white-collar** occupations. These included professional and technical workers, managers, officials, and clerical and sales workers. In 1940, **blue-collar** workers in industrial production occupations made up 52 percent of the labor force; farmers and farm workers, 17 percent; and white-collar workers, 31 percent. By 1970, blue-collar workers constituted 50 percent; farmers and farm workers, 3 percent; and white-collar workers, 47 percent. Many of these white-collar workers now considered themselves middle class.

The growth of this middle class had many repercussions. From rural areas, small towns, and central cities, people moved to the suburbs. In 1940, 19 percent of the American population lived in suburbs, 49 percent in rural areas, and 32 percent in central cities. By 1970, those figures had changed to 38, 31, and 31, respectively. The move to the suburbs also led to an imposing number of shopping malls and automobiles. Americans loved their automobiles, which carried them from suburban home to suburban mall and workplace.

Finally, the search for prosperity led to new migration patterns. The West and South experienced rapid economic growth through the development of new

So What ??

*If your students question the importance of the information on **McCarthyism**, tell them . . .*

Even in a democratic country, with guaranteed freedoms, it is possible for mass hysteria to override personal liberty. Only by

studying events in the past (and not always then) can we learn to recognize the conditions, processes or characteristics of individuals and attitudes that threaten our safety and liberty.

FOCUS

OBJECTIVES

After completing this section, students should be able to

1. identify and explain changes in American politics and society after World War II
2. describe social and political upheavals in the United States
3. identify and explain changes in Canadian politics and society after World War II

FOCUS ACTIVITY

Help students understand why the United States did not take advantage of its status as a superpower to dominate the world. Remind students that the military power and the economic systems of most industrialized nations had been damaged in the war. In 1945 the United States was an economic and military superpower. Have students propose reasons that the United States did not take the opportunity to dominate the world militarily when it had the chance.

LEARNING FROM VISUALS

Answer to the caption question: Student answers will vary, but this is an actual everyday photograph, not a posed scene. Students should also realize, however, that this scene represents only one segment of the postwar population.

TEACH

CRITICAL THINKING

Have students explain why the United States was in a better situation to create a welfare state after World War II than most European nations. Why did the U.S. not move as far along this path as some other nations?

CLASS DISCUSSION

Guide students in a discussion of the 1954 Supreme Court ruling that "separate educational facilities are inherently unequal." Do students believe the court was correct? Why might some members of racial minorities prefer not to attend integrated schools?

ACTIVITY

Using the information provided in the text have students create two pie graphs showing the percent of the American population living in rural, urban, and suburban areas in 1940 and 1970.

industries, especially in the defense field. As a result, massive numbers of people made the exodus from the cities of the Northeast and Midwest to the sunbelt of the South and West. Between 1940 and 1980, cities such as Chicago, Philadelphia, Detroit, and Cleveland lost between 13 and 36 percent of their populations. Los Angeles, Dallas, and San Diego grew between 100 and 300 percent.

A new prosperity was not the only characteristic of the early 1950s. Cold War struggles abroad led to massive fears at home. The takeover of China by Mao Zedong's (MAU zuh-DUNG's) Communist forces in 1949 and Communist North Korea's invasion of South Korea in 1950 led to the widespread fear that communists had infiltrated the United States. President Truman's attorney general warned that communists "are everywhere—in factories, offices, butcher stores, on street corners, in private businesses. And each carried in himself the germ of death for society." For many Americans, proof of this threat to the United States became more evident when thousands of American soldiers were sent to Korea to fight and die in a war against Communist aggression.

This climate of fear produced a dangerous political agitator, Senator Joseph R. McCarthy of Wisconsin. His charges that hundreds of supposed communists were in high government positions helped to create a massive "Red Scare"—fear of communist subversion. When he attacked alleged "Communist conspirators" in the U.S. Army, he was condemned by Congress in 1954. Very quickly, his anticommunist crusade came to an end.

An Age of Upheaval:
The United States from 1960 to 1970

Between 1960 and 1970, the United States experienced a period of upheaval that brought forward problems that had been glossed over in the 1950s. The 1960s began on a youthful and optimistic note. At age forty-three, John F. Kennedy became the youngest elected president in the history of the United States. His administration, cut short by an assassin's bullet on November 22, 1963, focused chiefly on foreign affairs.

Kennedy's successor, Lyndon B. Johnson, won a new term as president in a landslide victory in 1964. (As vice president, Johnson had become president upon Kennedy's assassination.) Johnson used his stunning victory to pursue the growth of the welfare state, first begun in the New Deal. Johnson's programs included health care for the elderly, a War on Poverty to be fought with food stamps and a Job Corps, a new Department of Housing and Urban Development to deal with the problems of the cities, and federal assistance for education.

Johnson's other domestic passion was equal rights for African Americans. The civil rights movement had its beginnings in 1954, when the United States Supreme Court took the dramatic step of striking down the practice of racially segregated public schools. According to Chief Justice Earl Warren, "separate educational facilities are inherently unequal." African Americans in Montgomery, Alabama, boycotted segregated buses. Soon after, the eloquent Martin Luther King, Jr. became the leader of a growing movement for racial equality. King followed the peaceful resistance style of Mohandas Gandhi.

By the early 1960s, a number of groups, including King's Southern Christian Leadership Conference (SCLC), were organizing demonstrations and sit-ins across the South to end racial segregation. In August 1963, King led a March on Washington, D.C., for Jobs and Freedom that dramatized the African American desire for equality. This march and King's impassioned plea for racial equality had an electrifying effect on the American people (see "You Are There: 'I Have a Dream'"). By the end of 1963, 52 percent of the American people called civil rights the most significant national issue. Eight months earlier, only 4 percent had done so.

President Johnson took up the cause of civil rights. As a result of his leadership, Congress passed a Civil Rights Act in 1964. This act created the machinery to end segregation and discrimination in the workplace and all public places. A Voting Rights Act the following year made it easier for African Americans to vote in southern states. Laws alone, however, could not guarantee the Great Society that Johnson talked about creating. He soon faced bitter social unrest from both the civil rights movement and a growing antiwar movement.

MORE ABOUT . . . *American Culture during the Cold War*

The B-grade horror film, a popular fad of the 1950s, offers insight into the paranoia and fears of the early Cold War years. Unlike today's films, such as *Star Wars, Close Encounters of the Third Kind,* and *E.T. The Extraterrestrial,* which are populated by friendly and helpful aliens, 1950s films offered a different view. Movies such as *It Came From Outer Space, The Thing, It Conquered the World* and countless other thrillers, warned of deadly aliens coming to take over and destroy the United States and the world. Many Americans feared that was exactly what the Soviet Union planned to do. *The Invasion of the Body Snatchers* tells the tale of an insidious menace right under the noses of an unsuspecting population. It was the same scenario Sen. Joseph McCarthy and other anticommunists claimed was happening in this country.

YOU ARE THERE
"I Have a Dream"

In the spring of 1963, a bomb attack on a church killed four children and brought the nation's attention to the policies of racial segregation in Birmingham, Alabama. A few months later, on August 28, 1963, Martin Luther King, Jr., led a march on Washington, D.C., and gave an inspired speech that energized the civil rights movement.

Martin Luther King, Jr., A Speech Delivered August 28, 1963, in Washington, D.C.

I am happy to join with you today in what will go down in history as the greatest demonstration for freedom in the history of our nation. . . .

I say to you today, my friends, so even though we face the difficulties of today and tomorrow, I still have a dream. It is a dream deeply rooted in the American dream. I have a dream that one day this nation will rise up and live out the true meaning of its creed, "We hold these truths to be self-evident, that all men are created equal." I have a dream that one day on the red hills of Georgia, sons of former slaves and the sons of former slave owners will be able to sit down together at the table of brotherhood. . . . I have a dream that my four little children will one day live in a nation where they will not be judged by the color of their skin, but by the content of their character. . . .

This is our hope. This is the faith that I go back to the South with. With this faith we will be able to hew out of the mountain of despair a stone of hope. With this faith we will be able to transform the jangling discords of our nation into a beautiful symphony of brotherhood. With this faith we will be able to work together, to pray together, to struggle together, to go to jail together, to stand up for freedom together, knowing that we will be free

▲ *In August 1963, Martin Luther King, Jr., traveled to Washington, D.C., to support civil rights legislation sponsored by President Lyndon B. Johnson. Nearly 200,000 people gathered at the Lincoln Memorial to hear his "I Have a Dream" speech. Despite King's inspiring message, the civil rights legislation was delayed for another year.*

one day. And this will be the day. This will be the day when all of God's children will be able to sing with new meaning, "My country 'tis of thee, sweet land of liberty, of thee I sing. Land where my father died, land of the pilgrims' pride, from every

(continued)

YOU ARE THERE

USING PRIMARY SOURCES

Divide students into groups and ask them to evaluate how far the United States has come toward achieving Dr. King's dream. Have them compare their conclusions in class.

ACTIVITY

Have students watch a videotape of Martin Luther King, Jr.'s entire August 28, 1963 speech. Analyze its basic themes. Why was it such an effective speech? To what extent has king's dream been realized?

So What ⁇

If your students question the importance of the information on **the Civil Rights Movement,** *tell them . . .*

Within the lifetime of their parents and grandparents many Americans had been systematically denied basic rights and free-doms which many of us today take for granted. The repercussions of that time still dominate American race relations today. An interesting, but volatile, discussion question for the class at this time might be "Is there still racism in the United States today?"

Answers to Critical Thinking Questions

1. He was a leader of the civil rights movement in the U.S.
2. His dream was to have men judged by their character rather than by the color of their skin, religious background, economic status, etc.
3. Progress has been made, but there are still discrepancies in treatment and economic status among races.

COMPARING TIME PERIODS

Ask students to list grievances that have caused people to participate in public demonstrations in the past five years in the United States. What changes in U.S. society do their lists indicate?

CLASS DISCUSSION

Have students discuss why relations with the United States are certain to be an important political issue in any Canadian political campaign. Do students believe the two nations will continue cordial relations in the next century? Why or why not?

ASSESS

Assign students to write their own "I Have a Dream" speech on a political or social issue.

YOU ARE THERE

"I Have a Dream," continued

mountainside, let freedom ring." And if America is to be a great nation, this must become true. . . .

And when this happens, and when we allow freedom to ring, when we let it ring from every village and every hamlet, from every state and every city, we will be able to speed up that day when all of God's children, black men and white men, Jews and Gentiles, Protestants and Catholics, will be able to join hands and sing in the words of the old Negro spiritual: "Free at last, Free at last. Thank God Almighty, we are free at last."

1. Who was Martin Luther King, Jr.?
2. What was King's dream?
3. To what extent has his dream been realized?

In the North and West, blacks had had voting rights for many years. However, local patterns of segregation led to higher unemployment rates for blacks than for whites. Blacks often lived in huge urban ghettos. In these ghettos, the calls for action by radical black leaders, such as Malcolm X (MAL-kuh-MECKS) of the Black Muslims, attracted more attention than did the nonviolent appeals of Martin Luther King, Jr. Malcolm X's advice was straightforward: "If someone puts a hand on you, send him to the cemetery."

In the summer of 1965, race riots broke out in the Watts district of Los Angeles. Thirty-four people died, and over one thousand buildings were destroyed. Cleveland, San Francisco, Chicago, Newark, and Detroit likewise exploded in the summers of 1966 and 1967. After the assassination of Martin Luther King, Jr. in 1968, over one hundred cities had riots, including Washington, D.C., the nation's capital. The combination of riots and extremist comments by radical black leaders led to a "white backlash" and a severe division of the United States. In 1964, 34 percent of American whites agreed with the statement that blacks were asking for "too much." By late 1966, that number rose to 85 percent, a figure not lost on politicians eager to achieve political office.

Antiwar protests also divided the American people after President Johnson sent American troops to war in Vietnam (see Chapter 33). As the war progressed and a military draft started, protests grew. There were teach-ins, sit-ins, and the occupations of buildings at universities. More radical demonstrations led to violence. The killing of four student protestors at Kent State University in 1970 by the Ohio National Guard startled the nation. A reaction set in, and the antiwar movement began to decline. By that time, however, antiwar demonstrations had helped to weaken the willingness of many Americans to continue the war.

The combination of antiwar demonstrations and ghetto riots in the cities prepared many people for "law and order." This was the appeal used by Richard Nixon, the Republican presidential candidate in 1968. With Nixon's election in 1968, a shift to the political right in American politics began.

The Development of Canada

Canada experienced many of the same developments that the United States did in the postwar years. For twenty-five years after World War II, a prosperous Canada set out on a new path of industrial development. Canada had always had a strong export economy based on its abundant natural resources. Now it developed electronic, aircraft, nuclear, and chemical engineering industries on a large scale. Much of the Cana-

ENRICHMENT ACTIVITY

Have students analyze the information on the American civil rights movement. Have them draw inferences about the possible reasons why African-Americans in the United States began organizing protests to end racial segregation in the 1950s and 1960s, nearly a century after the end of the Civil War. What events do students see as triggering the civil rights movement during this time period?

dian growth, however, was financed by capital from the United States, which led to U.S. ownership of Canadian businesses. Many Canadians did not care, as they welcomed the economic growth. Others, however, feared American economic domination of Canada.

Canadians also worried about playing a secondary role politically and militarily to its neighboring superpower. Canada agreed to join the North Atlantic Treaty Organization in 1949. It even sent military forces to fight in Korea the following year. To avoid subordination to the United States, however, Canada actively supported the United Nations.

Nevertheless, concerns about the United States did not keep Canada from having a special relationship with its southern neighbor. The North American Air Defense Command (Norad) was formed in 1957. It was based on close cooperation between the air forces of the United States and Canada for the defense of North America against missile attack. As another example of their close cooperation, in 1972, Canada and the United States signed the Great Lakes Water Quality Agreement to regulate pollution of the lakes that border both countries.

The Liberal Party dominated Canadian politics until 1957, when John Diefenbaker (DEEF-fun-BAKE-ur) achieved a Conservative Party victory. Major economic problems, however, returned the Liberals to power. Under Lester Pearson, they created Canada's welfare state by enacting a national social security system (the Canada Pension Plan) and a national health insurance program.

SECTION REVIEW

1. **Define:**
(*a*) real wages,   (*b*) white-collar,   (*c*) blue-collar

2. **Identify:**
(*a*) Senator Joseph R. McCarthy,   (*b*) War on Poverty,   (*c*) John F. Kennedy,   (*d*) Martin Luther King, Jr.,   (*e*) Malcolm X

3. **Recall:**
(*a*) What fueled confidence in the American way of life after World War II?
(*b*) What migration patterns took place in the United States after World War II?
(*c*) What may have caused the "white backlash" that was apparent among many white Americans during the 1960s?
(*d*) Why did rapid growth in the Canadian economy after World War II cause some Canadians to believe the United States had too much power in their nation?

4. **Think Critically:** How may spending for defense both help and harm a nation's economy?

◆ 5 ◆

THE EMERGENCE OF A NEW SOCIETY

After World War II, Western society witnessed rapid change. Such products of new technologies as the computer, television, and jet plane all quickly altered the pace and nature of human life. The rapid changes in postwar society led many to view it as a new society. Called a technocratic society by some and the consumer society by others, postwar Western society was marked by a changing social structure and new movements for change.

The Structure of European Society

The structure of European society was altered after 1945. Especially noticeable were the changes in the middle class. Traditional middle-class groups were made up of businesspeople and professionals in law, medicine, and the universities. Now a new group of managers and technicians, hired by large companies and government agencies, joined the ranks of the middle class. Whether in Eastern or Western Europe, the new managers and experts were very much alike.

CLOSE

Lead students in a discussion of the Focus objective identified on page 963. Emphasize the importance of the strength of the United States economy and its willingness to undertake social challenges of the day.

So What ⁇

*If your students question the importance of the information on **post war society**, tell them . . .*

The creation of an increasingly technological society with rising incomes, increased leisure time, and a government provided social safety net is not only the world which they have grown up in, but the one that they will inherit. They will determine the direction that society will take in the next century.

FOCUS

FOCUS

OBJECTIVES

After completing this section, students should be able to

1. identify and explain new structures in European society
2. describe the creation of welfare states in many European nations
3. identify and describe changes in education and causes of student unrest

FOCUS ACTIVITY

Help students understand that student movements have often led the way toward social change. This was true of protests against American involvement in the war in Vietnam. Ask students to identify and describe issues students are working to resolve today. What progress has been made? What are the chances for future success?

LEARNING FROM VISUALS

Answer to the caption question: Advertising played a major role by influencing traditional values of thrift toward more credit buying and conspicious consumption of goods.

Everywhere their positions depended upon skills gained from some form of higher education. Everywhere they took steps to ensure that their own children would be educated.

Changes also occurred among the lower classes. First, there was a dramatic shift of people from rural to urban areas. The number of people in farming declined drastically. By the 1950s, the number of peasants throughout most of Europe had dropped by 50 percent. Nor did the size of the industrial working class grow. In West Germany, industrial workers made up 48 percent of the labor force throughout the 1950s and 1960s. Thereafter, the number of industrial workers began to decline as the number of white-collar workers increased.

At the same time, a noticeable increase in the real wages of workers made it possible for them to imitate the buying patterns of the middle class. This led to what some observers have called the **consumer society.** Buying on the installment plan, which began in the 1930s, became widespread in the 1950s. Workers could now buy such products as televisions, washing machines, refrigerators, vacuum cleaners, and stereos. The automobile was the most visible symbol of the new mass consumerism. Before World War II, most cars were owned by people in the upper classes. In 1948, there were 5 million cars in all of Europe. By 1957, the number had tripled. By the 1960s, there were almost 45 million cars.

Rising incomes, combined with shorter working hours, created an even greater market for mass leisure activities. Between 1900 and 1960, the workweek was reduced from sixty hours to almost forty hours. The number of paid holidays also increased. All aspects of popular culture—music, sports, the media—now offered opportunities for leisure activities, including concerts, sporting events, and television viewing.

Another very visible symbol of mass leisure was the growth of mass tourism. Before World War II, mostly the upper and middle classes traveled for pleasure. After the war, the combination of more vacation time, higher wages, and package tours with their low-cost rooms enabled millions to travel. By the mid-1960s, 100 million tourists were crossing European boundaries each year. Travel at home was even more widespread.

▲ By 1956, 80 percent of all American families owned a television set. Many families considered a television a necessity, not a luxury. What role do you think advertising played in changing attitudes of Americans in the consumer society?

In Sweden, three out of four people spent a holiday outside their hometowns.

Creation of the Welfare State

One of the most noticeable social developments in postwar Europe was the creation of the welfare state. Supporters of the welfare state believed that eliminating poverty and homelessness, providing medical services for all, providing for the needs of the elderly, and giving education to all who wanted it would free peo-

---

RECOMMENDED READING

For a survey of contemporary Western society, see A. Sampson, *The New Europeans* (New York, 1968). The student revolts of the late 1960s are put into a broader context in L. S. Feuer, *The Conflict of Generations* (New York, 1969).

Ask students how they would react if they were required to dress for school in the way these English students are dressed. Point out that there are only male students in this picture. What social values does this picture presume?

◄ *Many of the primary beneficiaries of the welfare state are children. These students at Holloway Comprehensive School in England received free milk daily as part of government aid to education.*

ple to achieve happiness by satisfying their material needs.

Social welfare schemes were not new, of course. The new postwar social legislation, however, extended earlier benefits and created new ones. In many countries, existing benefits for sickness, accidents, unemployment, and old age were simply extended to cover more people and provide larger payments. Men were generally eligible for old-age pensions at age sixty-five and women, at age sixty.

Affordable health care for all people was another goal of the welfare state. In Great Britain, Italy, and Germany, medical care was free to all people with some kind of insurance. In France, Belgium, and Switzerland, people had to pay toward the cost of their medical care. The amount ranged from 10 to 25 percent of the total cost.

Family allowances were begun in some countries to provide a minimum level of material care for children. Most programs gave a fixed amount per child. In 1964, for example, France granted $60 per month per child. Welfare states also tried to remove class barriers to opportunity by expanding the number of universities

and providing scholarship aid to allow everyone to attend them.

Of course, welfare state benefits cost money. In 1967, spending on social services made up 17 percent of the gross national product of the major European countries. By the 1980s, it absorbed 40 to 50 percent. To critics, this meant that people had become overly dependent on the state. The majority of people, however, favored the benefits. Most leaders were aware that it would be political suicide to cut or lower those benefits.

Higher Education and Student Revolt

Social change was also evident in new educational patterns and student revolts. Before World War II, it was mostly members of Europe's wealthier classes who went to universities. Even in 1950, only 3 or 4 percent of Western European young people were enrolled in a university. In addition, European higher education remained largely centered on the liberal arts, pure science, and preparation for the professions of law and medicine.

MORE ABOUT . . . the Welfare State

From the time following World War II until the recent past, the term welfare state has been used to refer to the decision of governments to assume basic responsibility for the economic and social welfare of its residents. The modern industrial worker, unlike the independent artisan or farmer of the past, largely has no control over conditions that allow him or her to earn a living. Industrial workers, they purport, are dependent on

"far-removed economic forces that influence demand for what they produce and over which they have no control." Critics of the welfare state acknowledge the original causes of its rise, but believe that it has gone too far and created a dependent class of non-employable people who look too much to government for support and not enough to their own initiative.

USING PRIMARY SOURCES

Ask students to evaluate these two selections. How much of what they say is still relevant today? What might students add to these selections to bring them up-to-date? What might a young person in the former Soviet Union say about these selections?

The feature section, "1968—The Year of Student Protests" lists some student inscriptions on the Wall of Paris in 1968. The box section "The Youth Protest Movement" contains the lyrics to a popular protest song by Bob Dylan. Have your students read these inscriptions and lyrics and then identify and summarize the issues that concerned students in the 1960s. Have them then write their own inscriptions (or song) that identifies issues important to students of today.

YOU ARE THERE

1968—The Year of Student Protests

The outburst of student upheavals in the late 1960s reached its high point in 1968. These two very different selections illustrate some of the issues that prompted university students to demand reforms.

A Student Manifesto in Search of a Real and Human Educational Alternative (University of British Columbia), June 1968

Today we as students are witnessing a deepening crisis within our society. We are intensely aware, in a way perhaps not possible for the older generation, that humanity stands on the edge of a new era. Because we are young, we have insights into the present and visions of the future that our parents do not have. Tasks of an immense gravity wait solution in our generation. . . . Much of the burden of solving the problems of the new era rests on the university. We have been taught to look to it for leadership. While we know that part of the reason for the university is to render direct services to the community, we are alarmed at its servility to industry and government as to what and how it teaches. We are scandalized that the university fails to realize its role in renewing and

vivifying those intellectual and moral energies necessary to create a new society—one in which a sense of personal dignity and human community can be preserved.

Student Inscriptions on the Walls of Paris, May and June 1968

May 1968. World revolution is the order of the day.
To be free in 1968 is to take part.
Take the trip every day of your life.
Make love, not war.
No exams.
The mind travels farther than the heart but it doesn't go as far.
Run, comrade, the old are behind you!
Don't make a revolution in the image of your confused and hide-bound university.
Exam = servility, social promotion, hierarchic society.
Love each other.
Are you consumers or participants?
Live in the present.
Revolution, I love you.

Much of this changed after World War II. European states began to encourage more people to gain higher education by eliminating fees. As a result, universities saw an influx of students from the middle and lower classes. Enrollments grew dramatically. In France, 4.5 percent of young people went to a university in 1950. By 1965, the figure had increased to 14.5 percent. The number of students in European universities more than tripled between 1940 and 1960.

There were problems, however. Many European university classrooms had too many students. Many pro-

fessors paid little attention to their students. In addition, students often felt that the universities were not providing an education relevant to the realities of the modern age. Growing discontent led to an outburst of student revolts in the late 1960s (see "You Are There: 1968—The Year of Student Protests").

In part, these protests were an extension of the revolts in U.S. universities in the mid-1960s, which were often sparked by student opposition to the Vietnam War. In West Berlin, university students led a protest against Axel Springer, leader of Germany's

ENRICHMENT ACTIVITY

Students may be interested in putting together a "memory scrapbook" of their parents, relatives, and other community members' recollections of the 1960s and 1970s students protests. Some of the students' parents may have been actively involved and

have interesting stories, anecdotes, or poignant memories that, when written, edited, and illustrated, would make a worthwhile contribution to the oral history of their community.

YOU ARE THERE

1968—The Year of Student Protests, continued

◄ *Student revolt led to extremes in Paris, where daily battles were fought between police and students in the spring of 1968. Streets were barricaded, students threw cobblestones, and police retaliated with tear gas. Why do you think that in the following year these streets were torn up and repaved with asphalt and concrete?*

1. Based on these selections, what were the main issues that generated student unrest in the 1960s?

2. Do you find similar issues today? Why or why not?

largest newspaper. Many German students wanted to destroy what they considered to be the corrupt old order. They were especially influenced by the ideas of the German American philosopher Herbert Marcuse (mar-KOO-suh). In *One-Dimensional Man*, published in 1964, Marcuse argued that a small group of students could free the masses from the control of the capitalist ruling class. However, the German students' attempt at revolutionary violence backfired as angry Berliners supported police repression of the students.

The student protest movement in both Europe and the United States reached its high point in 1968 (see "Young People in the 1960s: The Youth Protest Movement"). There were several reasons for the student radicalism. Some students truly wanted to reform the university system. Others were protesting the Vietnam War, which they viewed as a product of Western imperialism. They also expressed concern about becoming small cogs in the large and impersonal bureaucratic wheels of the modern world. Many students called for democratic decision making within the universities, a

ENRICHMENT ACTIVITY

Guide students in a discussion comparing and contrasting the student riots of the 1960s with the urban ghetto riots of the same time. How were they similar and different? Or, ask them to research a recent disturbance such as the riots that occurred in Los Angeles in April of 1992 following the announcement of the verdict of the Rodney King trial. Ask them to compare this more recent riot with the student disturbances and ghetto riots of the 1960s.

Multimedia Support

TRANSPARENCY

23–3, Chart of Popular Culture of the 1950s, 1960s, and 1970s in the United States

YOUNG PEOPLE IN THE 1960S

LEARNING FROM VISUALS

Answer to the caption question: Answers will vary.

USING PRIMARY SOURCES

Assign students to obtain the lyrics from a modern protest song and compare them with those of Bob Dylan. What social changes does their comparison reveal? Will times ever stop "a-changin'"?

Answers to Critical Thinking Questions

1. The song recognizes that times are changing, and you must either change with the times or get out of the way.
2. The opponents are young people and their parents.
3. Answers will vary, but should reflect the fact that conflict between young people and their parents still exists today.

TIME LINE

As students conclude the chapter, you may want to refer them to the chapter time line in the *Study Guide*. The time line will help them put key dates in perspective. Supporting questions and activities are also provided.

YOUNG PEOPLE IN THE 1960s

The Youth Protest Movement

The decade of the 1960s witnessed a dramatic change in traditional manners and morals. The new standards were evident in the breakdown of the traditional family as divorce rates increased dramatically. Movies, plays, and books broke new ground in the treatment of once-hidden subjects. A growing youth movement also emerged in the 1960s. New attitudes toward sex and the use of drugs were two of its features. Young people also questioned authority and rebelled against the older generation. Spurred on by the Vietnam War, the youth rebellion in the United States became a youth protest movement by the second half of the 1960s. Active participants in the movement were often called "hippies."

In the 1960s, the lyrics of rock music reflected the rebellious mood of many young people. Bob Dylan (DILL-un), a well-known recording artist, expressed the feelings of the younger generation. His song "The Times They Are a-Changin'," released in 1964, has been called an "anthem for the protest movement." Some of its words, which follow, tell us why.

Bob Dylan, "The Times They Are a-Changin'"

Come gather round people
Wherever you roam
And admit that the waters
Around you have grown
And accept it that soon

◄ *This young couple enjoys the sun atop their highly decorated van. Which of the symbols used to embellish this car can you identify?*

You'll be drenched to the bone
If your time to you
Is worth savin'
Then you better start swimmin'
Or you'll sink like a stone
For the times they are a'changin . . .'
Come mothers and fathers
Throughout the land
And don't criticize
What you can't understand
Your sons and your daughters
Are beyond your command
Your old road
Is rapidly agin'
Please get out of the new one
If you can't lend your hand
For the times they are a'changin'

1. How does Bob Dylan's song express the feelings of the young people of the 1960s?

2. Who are the opponents in the song?

3. How relevant is this song today?

MORE ABOUT . . . *Folk Music and Protest Songs*

Strictly speaking, folk music is music that "lives in oral tradition and is learned by ear, without the use of written music, primarily in rural cultures." Today, the concept of folk music has been greatly expanded and includes other forms of music, such as the protest song. These were songs written in the folk music style but for political or social purposes. The most famous folk/protest composers in the United States are probably Bob Dylan, Woodie Guthrie and Pete Seeger. Dylan was arguably the most influential voice of the early 1960s protest era and is still today a leading musician of the folk rock school. He is the author of the well known song "Blowin' in the Wind," the signature song of the sixties and anthem of the civil rights movement.

demand that reflected deeper concerns about the direction in which Western society was headed. Although student revolts fizzled out in the 1970s, the larger issues they raised have been increasingly revived in the 1990s.

 SECTION REVIEW ❀

1. **Define:**
    (*a*) consumer society

2. **Identify:**
    (*a*) Axel Springer, (*b*) Herbert Marcuse

3. **Recall:**
    (*a*) How was the structure of European society altered after 1945?
    (*b*) How did affordable health care become available to most people in Western Europe after World War II?
    (*c*) Why was the rapid increase in the number of students in European universities important?

4. **Think Critically:** Why was it fair to say the following about post–World War II European politicians?

    "Most leaders were aware that it was political suicide to cut or lower those (social) benefits."

Conclusion

At the end of World War II, a new conflict erupted in the Western world as the two new superpowers, the United States and the Soviet Union, competed for political domination of the world. Europeans, whether they wanted to or not, were forced to become supporters of one side or the other. This division also spread to the rest of the world. The United States fought in Korea and Vietnam to prevent the spread of communism, while the Soviet Union used its armies to prop up pro-Soviet regimes in Eastern Europe.

Western Europe also became a new community in the 1950s and 1960s as a remarkable economic recovery fostered a new optimism. Western European states became accustomed to political democracy. With the creation of the European Economic Community, many of them began to move toward economic unity. Although Western Europeans staged a remarkable economic recovery, the Cuban Missile Crisis made it clear that their future still depended on the outcome of the conflict between the two superpowers. In the Western Hemisphere, the two North American countries—the United States and Canada—built prosperous economies and relatively stable communities in the 1950s that were marred by a growing number of problems in the 1960s.

The student protests of the late 1960s caused many people to rethink some of their basic assumptions. Looking back, however, we can see that the student upheavals were not a turning point in the history of postwar Europe, as some people thought at the time. In the 1970s and 1980s, student rebels would become middle-class professionals. The vision of revolutionary politics would remain mostly a memory.

Notes

1. Quoted in Joseph M. Jones, *The Fifteen Weeks (February 21–June 5, 1947)*, 2nd ed. (New York, 1964), pp. 140–141.
2. Quoted in Walter Laqueur, *Europe in Our Time* (New York, 1992), p. 111.
3. Quoted in Wilfried Loth, *The Division of the World, 1941–1955* (New York, 1988), pp. 160–161.
4. Quoted in Peter Lane, *Europe since 1945: An Introduction* (Totowa, N.J., 1985), p. 248.
5. R. Hilton, *Military Attaché in Moscow* (London, 1949), p. 41.
6. Quoted in Laqueur, *op. cit.*, p. 150.

Answers to CHAPTER REVIEW 29

USING KEY TERMS

1. real wages
2. nationalization
3. domino theory
4. de-Stalinization
5. consumer society
6. welfare state
7. mutual deterrence
8. blue-collar
9. policy of containment
10. white-collar

REVIEWING THE FACTS

1. The United States provided European nations with $12.5 billion in financial and economic assistance between 1948 and 1953.
2. After World War II factories were taken apart and large amounts of industrial equipment were shipped from eastern Europe to the Soviet Union to help them rebuild.
3. The Berlin wall was built to stem the flow of people from the East to the West and to make the prosperity in the West less apparent to the people in the East.
4. The Soviet Union invaded Hungary because leaders of that nation threatened to withdraw from the Warsaw Pact and to give up communism.
5. Kennedy demanded that the missile facilities in Cuba be removed. Eventually the Soviets agreed not to send missiles in exchange for an American promise not to invade Cuba.
6. The first break in the united front of NATO took place in 1962 when France withdrew from the organization.
7. The British government nationalized businesses and created a welfare state.
8. the civil rights movement
9. desire to find employment and to achieve a better standard of living

THINKING CRITICALLY

1. Khrushchev had someone to blame for Soviet problems,

974

USING KEY TERMS

1. The value of a person's salary when adjusted for inflation is called ——————.
2. ———— is the act of a government taking over private property either with or without payment.
3. The idea that allowing communist aggressors to take over one country will encourage them to take over other nations as well has been called the ——————.
4. The process of removing Stalin's influence from the Soviet government, economy, and social system was called ——————.
5. A nation that is preoccupied with the desire to provide its people with material goods may be said to have a ——————.
6. Nations with governments that intervene in the economy to assure a minimal standard of living for all people are said to have a ————.
7. The threat of both sides being destroyed during a nuclear war helped discourage such a war, and was known as the policy of ——————.
8. Employees who work in industrial positions are referred to as ———— workers.
9. The attempt of non-communist world powers to prevent a further spread of communism to other states was called a ——————.
10. Employees who have professional, technical, or managerial responsibilities in their jobs are referred to as ———— workers.

REVIEWING THE FACTS

1. How was the Marshall Plan carried out and what was its purpose?
2. How did the Soviet Union make use of factories and tools from Eastern Europe to help them rebuild after World War II?
3. Why did the East Germans build the Berlin Wall?

974

4. What caused the Soviet Union to invade Hungary in 1956?
5. What happened during the Cuban Missile Crisis in 1962?
6. What action resulted in the first break in the united front of NATO nations?
7. What changes were made in the British government's role in their economic system after World War II?
8. What social, political, and economic movement changed the face of American society after World War II?
9. What was the primary reason for many Americans moving north and west during and after World War II?

THINKING CRITICALLY

1. In what ways did the de-Stalinization of the Soviet Union help Nikita Khrushchev gain and maintain his control of the Soviet government?
2. What reasons might the people of Cuba have had for not supporting the Bay of Pigs invasion in 1961?
3. Why did the successful Soviet invasion of Hungary in 1956 make it more difficult for the Soviet Union to influence nations in other parts of the world?
4. How did the formation of the European Economic Community help member nations recover from World War II?
5. What are several reasons for the rapid economic growth that took place in the United States after World War II?
6. Why were many Americans willing to believe Joseph R. McCarthy during the Red Scare?
7. Why have many wealthy people been opposed to the creation of welfare states in their nations?
8. Why do some people believe the creation of welfare states in European nations reduced people's incentive to manage financial affairs carefully?

and at the same time he drew attention to himself and his policies.
2. Cubans probably thought that a foreign power wanted to return Cuba to the control of a corrupt dictatorship.
3. The Soviet Union demonstrated that it would not tolerate any alternative forms of leadership and control in the nations it dominated.
4. By reducing tariffs and increasing trade within the EEC, the member nations were able to increase their rates of economic growth.

5. The United States benefited from a strong demand for manufactured products and machinery from other nations.
6. Many Americans became convinced that there was a Communist plot to take over the world.
7. The costs of welfare states are borne more by wealthy people than by those who are poor.
8. Some people believe that when European governments guaranteed minimum standards of living to their people they destroyed the incentive to work.

APPLYING SOCIAL STUDIES SKILLS

1. **Government:** Identify and explain social and political forces that may have caused the people of France to choose Charles de Gaulle for their president and to approve a constitution that greatly enhanced the power he had in their government.
2. **Sociology:** Identify and describe social forces that caused many Europeans to believe that they were entitled to the benefits of a welfare state after World War II.
3. **Government:** Explain why it is difficult to achieve a smooth transfer of power in a totalitarian form of government. Use the transition of power from Stalin to Khrushchev and from Khrushchev to Brezhnev in the Soviet Union as examples.
4. **Sociology:** Identify and explain social forces that contributed to the growth of the Civil Rights movement in the United States.

MAKING TIME AND PLACE CONNECTIONS

1. In recent years the United States and other developed nations have provided significant amounts of aid to developing nations. In general this assistance has not resulted in rapid economic expansion of these countries. Why was the assistance provided by the United States to European nations after World War II so much more successful in helping them recover from the war?
2. Identify and explain reasons for the different treatments given to Germany at the end of World War I and to West Germany at the end of World War II.
3. Identify and explain possible reasons for the comparatively slow growth of social benefits provided Americans, compared to the rapid growth of these programs in Europe, after World War II.
4. Compare and contrast Hitler's policy of creating fear and blaming problems on Jewish people in Europe with Joseph R. McCarthy's Red Scare tactics in the United States.
5. Explain how recent developments in the means of mass communication may have made it more difficult for the Soviet Union to put down revolts in eastern Europe in the late 1980s than it had been in the mid 1950s.

BECOMING AN HISTORIAN

1. **Economics as a Key to History:** Create a graph that shows trends in American trade with Europe after World War II based on the data in the table below. Explain the probable causes and importance of the information communicated by your graph.

The Value of U.S. Trade With Europe (in millions of dollars)

Year	U.S. Exports	U.S. Imports
1945	$5,515	$ 409
1947	5,187	820
1949	4,118	925
1951	4,044	2,043
1953	2,910	2,335

Source: U.S. Bureau of the Census, *Historical Statistics of the United States; Colonial Times to 1957* (Washington, D.C., 1960), pp. 550, 552.

2. **Making Hypotheses and Predicting Outcomes:** In the past decade revolutions have replaced strong leaders with weak governments that have been unable to stop nationalist groups from creating chaos in many countries. This situation has often led to violence, disruption of economic systems, and a lack of personal security. Form and support a hypothesis about whether these conditions will result in a return to strong central governments in many European nations.

975

30 PLANNING GUIDE

SECTION	KEY TOPICS	PRIMARY SOURCES	ASSESSMENT
1 The Cold War and the Soviet Bloc pages 977–981	◆ Transition from Cold War to a New World Order ◆ Upheaval in the Soviet Union ◆ Brezhnev to Gorbachev ◆ Gorbachev to Yeltsin		◆ Section Review, page 981 ◆ Section Quiz 30–1, TRB
2 Eastern Europe: From Soviet Satellites to Sovereign States pages 981–987	◆ Developments in Soviet satellite states ◆ Reunification of Germany ◆ Disintegration and war in Yugoslavia ◆ Eastern Europe after communism	◆ A speech to the U.S. Congress by Vaclav Havel, page 984	◆ Section Review, page 987 ◆ Section Quiz 30–2, TRB
3 Toward a New Order in Europe and North America pages 988–993	◆ Western Europe and changes in France ◆ Unification's impact on West Germany ◆ Thatcherism in Great Britain ◆ The domestic scene in North America		◆ Section Review, page 993 ◆ Section Quiz 30–3, TRB
4 New Direction and New Problems in Western Society pages 994–1000	◆ Women's changing role in society ◆ The rise of environmentalism ◆ Challenges of guest workers and immigration ◆ A growth of terrorism	◆ A selection from a British Women's Liberation Workshop, page 995 ◆ A selection from *The Second Sex* by Simone de Beauvoir, page 996	◆ Section Review, page 1000 ◆ Section Quiz 30–4, TRB
5 The World of Western Culture pages 1001–1008	◆ Trends in art and literature ◆ Revival of religion ◆ Developments in science and technology ◆ Growth of popular culture	◆ A selection from the work of Albert Camus, page 1001	◆ Section Review, page 1008 ◆ Section Quiz 30–5, TRB

THE CHANGING WORLD OF THE SUPERPOWERS:
THE CONTEMPORARY WESTERN WORLD

REPRODUCIBLE ACTIVITIES

Historical Maps

Charts and Graphs

Critical Thinking

Cooperative Learning

Vocabulary

Guided Reading

Reteaching

Enrichment

Performance Assessment

Spanish Key Points and Chapter Summaries

Spanish Vocabulary

Spanish Guided Reading

MULTIMEDIA SUPPORT

TRANSPARENCIES
- *World History* Color Transparency Package
- Fine Art Color Transparency Package

VIDEO
- *World History* Video Library
- CNN. Annual Video Update

LASERDISC
- *Sights and Sounds of History*

AUDIO
- *Listening to Literature* audiotape (English and Spanish)
- *History of Music* CD

SOFTWARE
- WESTEST™
- Student Review

CD–ROM
- *The Journey of Civilization*
- *World History*

INTERNET
- Internet Activities

On Line with WORLD HISTORY

Access West's history web site at
http://history.swpco.com
You'll find activities and web sites related to specific topics and chapters in *World History: The Human Odyssey*. Also look for references to helpful web sites at appropriate places throughout this teacher edition.

LESSON PLANNING

You will find detailed daily lesson plans for both traditional class scheduling and **block scheduling** in your Teacher Resource Box.

Not Enough Time?

If you do not have the four or five days recommended to teach this chapter, you may want to focus on the following sections and activities:

- Have students skim the chapter to answer the "Questions to Guide Your Reading" on page 977. Discuss their answers, then read the "Conclusion" on page 1009.
- Do a more in-depth reading of the end of the Cold War and fall of the Soviet Union on pages 977–981, events in Eastern Europe after communism on page 986, changes in Western Europe on pages 988–991, and the changing role of women in society on pages 994–996. Conclude with a discussion of the impact of new technological advancements on society.

THE CHANGING WORLD OF THE SUPERPOWERS:

30

BUILDING ON CHAPTER 29

To "set the scene" for the study of Chapter 30, use the following questions and activities.

◆ Have students discuss the effect of military build-ups in the Cold War on consumer needs.

◆ Lead students in a discussion of how advancements in communications technology make it harder to keep people ignorant.

◆ Have students make a list of ways in which the Cold War impacted world culture.

USING THE OPENING STORY

Select from the following questions to reinforce the reading of the opening story.

◆ Why didn't economic progress in West Germany satisfy all German people?

◆ Why didn't physical barriers like the Berlin Wall stop the flow of ideas and information?

◆ What similarities were there between celebrations at the end of World War II and those that took place when the Berlin Wall was destroyed?

LEARNING FROM VISUALS

Answer to the caption question: The Berlin Wall divided East and West Berlin for 28 years.

Between 1945 and 1970, Europe not only recovered from the devastating effects of World War II but also experienced an economic recovery that seemed miraculous. By 1970, after more than two decades of the Cold War, Europeans had become used to a new division of Europe between West and East. A prosperous Western Europe that was allied to the United States stood opposed to a still-struggling Eastern Europe that remained largely subject to the Soviet Union. This new order seemed well established. However, within twenty years, a revolutionary upheaval in the Soviet Union and Eastern Europe would bring an end to the Cold War and would destroy the long-standing division of postwar Europe.

For years, the Berlin Wall had stood as the most visible symbol of the Cold War. In 1988, the American president Ronald Reagan, leader of the Western world, traveled to West Berlin. Facing the Berlin Wall, he challenged Mikhail Gorbachev, leader of the Soviet bloc, to "tear down this wall." During his own visit to West Germany a year later, Gorbachev responded, "The wall could disappear once the conditions that generated the need for it disappear. I do not see much of a

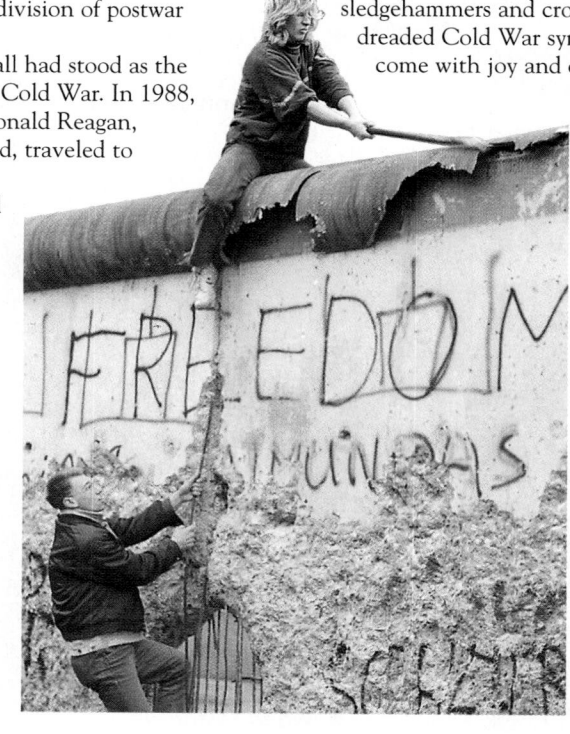

problem here." East Germany's Communist leaders, however, did see a problem, and they refused to remove the wall. In the summer of 1989, tens of thousands of East Germans fled their country while hundreds of thousands took to the streets to demand the resignation of the hardline Communist leader, Erich Honecker (HOE-nuh-kur). Honecker finally caved in. On November 9, 1989, a new East German government opened the wall and allowed its citizens to travel freely between West and East Berlin. The next day, government workers began to knock down the wall. They were soon joined by thousands of West and East Berliners who used sledgehammers and crowbars to rip apart the dreaded Cold War symbol. Germans were overcome with joy and celebrated. Many danced on the wall while orchestras played in the streets. Churches, theaters, and shops remained open day and night in West Germany as East Germans took advantage of their new freedom to travel. In 1990, West and East Germany became a single nation, and Berlin was once again the capital of Germany. With the destruction of the Berlin Wall, the Cold War seemed a thing of the past.

◄ *These two young people are chipping away at the remains of the Berlin Wall, just as many others did in January 1990. For how long did this wall divide East and West Berlin?*

ADDITIONAL RESOURCES

The resources listed below can be used to enrich the lessons in this chapter.

BOOKS FOR STUDENTS

The Soviet Union: Opposing Viewpoints ed. David L. Bender. Greenhaven Press. *American Foreign Policy: Opposing Viewpoints.* eds. Neal Bernards and Lynn Hall.

VHS/FILM

"Vietnam Lessons of a Lost War" (AIMS Multi-Media. (800) 367-2467)

"Struggle of the Superpower: Recasting the Mold, 1959–1975." Britannica (800) 554-9862

"Communism in Retreat: The Mold Broken, Eastern Europe 1989"

THE CONTEMPORARY WESTERN WORLD

(1970 TO PRESENT)

QUESTIONS TO GUIDE YOUR READING

1. How and why did the Cold War end?
2. What reforms did Mikhail Gorbachev make in the Soviet Union?
3. What direction did the Eastern European nations take once Soviet control was gone?
4. What problems have the Western European nations, the United States, and Canada faced since 1970?
5. What have been the major social developments since 1970?
6. What have been the major cultural and intellectual developments since 1970?

THE COLD WAR AND THE SOVIET BLOC

By the 1970s, American-Soviet relations had entered a new phase, known as **détente,** which was marked by a reduction of tensions between the two superpowers. Beginning in 1979, however, the apparent collapse of détente began a new period of East-West confrontation. Then, after Mikhail Gorbachev came to power in 1985, the Soviet Union began to make changes in its foreign policy, and the Cold War rapidly came to an end.

From Cold War to Post-Cold War: Toward a New World Order?

One example of détente in the 1970s was the Helsinki (HEL-SING-kee) Agreements. Signed by the United States, Canada, and all European nations in 1975, these accords recognized all borders in central and Eastern Europe that had been set up since the end of

977

Answers to QUESTIONS TO GUIDE YOUR READING

1. primarily due to the failing Soviet economy (pages 978–979)
2. INF Treaty with U.S.; end of military support of governments in Eastern Europe; market economy, glasnost (pages 980–981)
3. moved to democratic and market systems (page 986)
4. Western Europe: inflation; unemployment; taxation, racism, religious wars;
United States: racism, the deficit, Watergate, inflation and unemployment;
Canada: recession and secession (pages 988–993)
5. role of women in society, environmentalism, increase in immigration, growth of terrorism (pages 994–1000)
6. Theatre of the Absurd and Abstract Expressionism; revival in religion; space exploration; personal computers (pages 1001–1008)

FOCUS

OBJECTIVES

After completing this section, students should be able to

1. identify and describe events in the transition to a New World Order
2. list and explain upheavals in the Soviet Union
3. describe the transition of power in the former Soviet Union from Brezhnev through Yeltsin

FOCUS ACTIVITY

When many nations were afraid of Communist aggression they looked to the United States for leadership and protection. Have students discuss whether they believe many nations will continue to want American leadership after the fall of the Soviet Union and decline of communism throughout the world. Will there be other ways for the United States to provide world leadership?

LEARNING FROM VISUALS

Answer to the caption question: Students might remember that President Reagan was an ardent anti-communist and called the USSR an "evil empire."

TEACH

CLASS DISCUSSION

Have students discuss why Soviet leaders failed to recognize the depth and extent of their problems earlier.

978

World War II. In doing so, they accepted the Soviet sphere of influence in Eastern Europe. The Helsinki Agreements also called for the protection of the human rights of the citizens of the nations signing the agreement.

This protection of human rights became one of the major foreign policy goals of the next U.S. president, Jimmy Carter. Hopes ran high for détente but received a setback in 1979, when the Soviet Union invaded Afghanistan. The Soviet Union wanted to restore a pro-Soviet regime there, but the United States viewed it as another example of Soviet expansion. Carter canceled American participation in the 1980 Olympic Games held in Moscow and placed an embargo on the shipment of American grain to the Soviet Union.

The Cold War intensified when Ronald Reagan was elected president in 1980. Calling the Soviet Union an "evil empire," Reagan began a military buildup and a new arms race. In 1982, the Reagan administration introduced the nuclear-tipped cruise missile, a weapon whose ability to fly at low altitudes made it difficult to detect. Reagan also became an ardent supporter of the Strategic Defense Initiative (SDI), nicknamed "Star Wars." Its purpose was to create a space shield that could destroy incoming missiles. By giving military aid to the Afghan rebels, Reagan helped to maintain a war in Afghanistan that the Soviet Union could not win. Like the Vietnam War for the United States, the war in Afghanistan showed that the power of a superpower was actually limited in the face of strong nationalist opposition. The armed forces of the mighty Soviet Union were not able to defeat rebel armies in Afghanistan, who were armed by an opposing superpower and willing to use guerrilla tactics.

The accession of Mikhail Gorbachev to power in the Soviet Union in 1985 eventually brought a dramatic end to the Cold War. Gorbachev was willing to rethink many of the basic assumptions underlying Soviet foreign policy. His "New Thinking," as it was called, opened the door to a series of stunning changes.

For one, Gorbachev made an agreement with the United States in 1987 to eliminate intermediate-range nuclear weapons (the INF Treaty). Both sides had reasons to dampen the expensive arms race. Gorbachev hoped to make far-reaching economic and internal

▲ *Mikhail Gorbachev, on the right, and Ronald Reagan were photographed in front of St. Basil's Cathedral during President Reagan's 1988 visit to Moscow. The willingness of both leaders to reduce the arms race helped end the Cold War. In light of Reagan's earlier views on the Soviet Union, do you think this meeting was ironic? Why or why not?*

reforms. The United States had its own financial problems. During the Reagan years, as the national debt tripled, the United States had moved from being a creditor nation, exporting more than it imported, to being the world's biggest debtor nation. As its imports

---

SPECIAL NEEDS: *Visual/Auditory*

To help students understand the differences between Soviet leaders, use posterboard and write the names Brezhnev, Gorbachev and Yeltsin across the top. Then give groups of students index cards with characteristics of leadership during each leader's ruling period written on them. The following characteristics/events should be used:

Brezhnev, Emphasized Industry, Complex Bureaucracy, Bad Harvests/Farm Problems, Alcoholism, Poor Working Conditions, Gorbachev, Perestroika, Market Economy, Glasnost, Congress, Begin Complete Independence, Yeltsin, Independent States, Free Market Economy, Organized Crime

Have students use glue sticks to tack index cards under the name of the correct leader. They are then ready to write or say briefly the major characteristics of the time in which each man was in power.

overtook exports, the United States owed money to foreign investors. By 1990, both countries were becoming aware that their large military budgets made it difficult for them to solve their serious domestic social problems.

The years 1989 and 1990 were crucial in the ending of the Cold War. The postwar settlements that had become the norm in central and Eastern Europe came undone as a mostly peaceful revolutionary upheaval swept through Eastern Europe. A new Soviet policy made this upheaval possible. Under Gorbachev, the Soviet Union no longer gave military support to Communist governments in Eastern Europe that were faced with internal revolt.

This unwillingness of the Soviet regime to use force in Eastern Europe opened the door to the overthrow of the Communist regimes there (see "Eastern Europe: From Soviet Satellites to Sovereign States," later in the chapter). The reunification of Germany on October 3, 1990, was a powerful symbol of the end of the Cold War Era. By the end of 1991, the breakup of the Soviet Union made almost impossible any renewal of the global rivalry between the two competing superpowers. Although the United States had emerged as the world's leading military power by 1992, its role in the creation of a "New World Order" that President George Bush called for was not yet clear. After some hesitation, President Bill Clinton began to reassert American power in the world. He sent American troops to Haiti in September 1994 to restore that country's fragile democratic system. In December 1995, the United States took the lead in bringing an end to the war in Bosnia. As part of the agreement signed by the warring parties, twenty thousand U.S. troops were sent to the region as part of a NATO military presence intended to enforce the peace.

Upheaval in the Soviet Union

Between 1964 and 1982, drastic change in the Soviet Union seemed highly unlikely. The man in charge—Leonid Brezhnev—did not want reforms. Nor did he want the states in Eastern Europe to lose their Communist governments. Brezhnev insisted on the right of the Soviet Union to intervene if communism was threatened in another Communist state (known as the **Brezhnev doctrine**).

The Brezhnev Era

Brezhnev benefited from the more relaxed atmosphere associated with détente. The Soviet Union was roughly equal to the United States in nuclear arms. Its leaders felt secure and were willing to relax their authoritarian rule. The regime allowed more access to Western styles of music, dress, and art. Of course, **dissidents**—those who spoke out against the regime—were still punished. Andrei Sakharov (SAW-kuh-RAWF), for example, who had played an important role in the development of the Soviet hydrogen bomb, was placed under house arrest for his defense of human rights.

In his economic policies, Brezhnev continued to emphasize heavy industry. Two problems, however, weakened the Soviet economy. The government's central planning led to a huge, complex bureaucracy that discouraged efficiency and led to apathy. Farm problems added to Soviet economic woes. Collective farmers had no incentive to work hard. Many preferred working their own small private plots to laboring in the collective work brigades. To make matters worse, bad harvests in the mid-1970s, caused by a series of droughts, heavy rains, and early frosts, forced the Soviet government to buy grain from the West, especially the United States.

By the 1970s, the Communist ruling class in the Soviet Union had become complacent and corrupt. Party and state leaders—as well as leaders of the army and secret police (KGB)—received awards and enjoyed a high standard of living. Brezhnev was unwilling to tamper with the party leadership and state bureaucracy, regardless of the inefficiency and corruption that the system encouraged.

By 1980, the Soviet Union was seriously ailing. A declining economy, a rise in infant mortality rates, a dramatic surge in alcoholism, and poor working conditions all gave rise to a feeling that the system was in trouble. Within the Communist Party, a small group of reformers emerged who knew the real condition of the Soviet Union. One member of this group was Mikhail

REINFORCING VOCABULARY

Ask students why they believe Soviet citizens would have a limited interest in Gorbachev's ideas of *perestroika* and *glasnost* at a time when many of them did not have enough to eat or a decent place to live.

CLASS DISCUSSION

Ask students to evaluate the following statement. Do they believe it is true? To what extent do they believe it explains events in the Soviet Union in the late 1980s?

Once oppressed people taste a little freedom they will demand more.

COMPARING TIME PERIODS

Have students compare and contrast the causes for the fall of the Soviet Union with those that led to the disintegration of the Ottoman Empire in the early nineteenth century (Discussed in Chapter 27).

LEARNING FROM VISUALS

Answer to the caption question: It is unlikely that Mikhail Gorbachev foresaw the consequences of his reforms or the direction into which they would carry the USSR.

TEACHING THEMES

Economics and History
Have students explain why Boris Yeltsin could not deliver on the hopes of the Russian people for a rapid improvement in their economic situation.

Gorbachev. A new era began when party leaders chose him in March 1985 to lead the Soviet Union.

▲ *Mikhail Gorbachev was dynamic, outgoing, and determined to improve the daily lives of Soviet citizens. Do you think he initially understood where the reforms he supported would lead?*

The Gorbachev Era

Mikhail Gorbachev had joined the Communist Party in 1952 and worked his way up the ranks. In 1978, Gorbachev was made a member of the party's Central Committee in Moscow. Two years later, he became a full member of the ruling Politburo and secretary of the Central Committee. In March 1985, party leaders elected him general secretary of the party, and he became the new leader of the Soviet Union.

Educated during the reform years of Khrushchev, Gorbachev seemed intent on making new reforms. By the 1980s, Soviet economic problems were obvious. Although the Soviet Union still excelled in space exploration, it fell behind the West in other new technology, especially in the use of computers. Most noticeable to the Soviet people was the actual decline in the standard of living. Ordinary citizens grew tired of standing in line for hours just to buy many basic goods.

From the start, Gorbachev preached the need for radical reforms. The basis of Gorbachev's radical reforms was **perestroika,** or "restructuring." At first, this meant only a restructuring of economic policy. Gorbachev called for the beginning of a market economy (consumers influence what is produced) with limited free enterprise (based on private ownership of businesses) and some private property. He soon realized, however, that in the Soviet system, the economic sphere was closely tied to the social and political spheres. An attempt to reform the economy without political or social reform would be doomed to failure.

One of the most important instruments of perestroika was **glasnost,** or "openness." Soviet citizens and officials were encouraged to discuss openly the strengths and weaknesses of the Soviet Union. *Pravda,* the official newspaper of the Communist Party, now began to report official corruption, sloppy factory work, and protests against government policy. Movies began to show the negative aspects of Soviet life. Music based on Western styles, such as jazz and rock, was performed openly.

Political reforms were equally revolutionary. In June 1987, the principle of two-candidate elections was introduced. Previously, voters had been presented with only one candidate. At the Communist Party conference in 1988, Gorbachev called for the creation of a new Soviet parliament, the Congress of People's Deputies, whose members were to be elected. It met in 1989, the first such meeting in Russia since 1918. Early in 1990, Gorbachev decreed that other political parties could now form. He also struck Article 6, which had guaranteed the "leading role" of the Communist Party, from the Soviet constitution.

At the same time, Gorbachev tried to strengthen his power by creating a new state presidency. Up to this time, the position of first secretary of the party (Gorbachev's position) had been the most important post in the Soviet Union. However, as the Communist Party became less closely tied to the state, the position of first secretary carried less and less power. In March 1990, Gorbachev became the Soviet Union's first president.

One of Gorbachev's most serious problems came from the nature of the Soviet Union. The Union of Soviet Socialist Republics was a truly multiethnic country, containing 92 nationalities and 112 different languages. Before, the iron hand of the Communist Party, centered in Moscow, had kept a lid on the centuries-old ethnic tensions. As Gorbachev released this iron grip, these tensions again came to the forefront. Nationalist movements emerged throughout the republics of the Soviet Union. Between 1988 and 1990, there were calls for independence first in Soviet

---

CNN. WORLD HISTORY UPDATES

You can update your coverage of World History topics, as well as spark lively classroom discussion and deeper understanding, by using the **CNN World History Updates.**

For assistance in using and incorporating the **CNN World History Updates** into your classroom presentations, see the *Classroom Guide.*

Georgia and then in Latvia, Estonia, Moldavia, Uzbekistan, Azerbaijan, and Lithuania.

During 1990 and 1991, Gorbachev struggled to deal with the problems unleashed by his reforms. He especially wanted to work more closely with Boris Yeltsin, who had been elected president of the Russian Republic in June 1991. By 1991, the conservative leaders of the traditional Soviet institutions—the army, government, KGB, and military industries—were worried. The possible breakup of the Soviet Union meant an end to their privileges. On August 19, 1991, a group of these people arrested Gorbachev and tried to seize power. The attempt failed, however, when Yeltsin and thousands of Russians bravely resisted the rebel forces in Moscow. Their actions opened the door to the final disintegration of the Soviet Union.

The Soviet republics now moved for complete independence. Ukraine voted for independence on December 1, 1991. A week later, the leaders of Russia, Ukraine, and Belarus (BELL-uh-ROOS) announced that the Soviet Union had "ceased to exist."

The Yeltsin Era

Gorbachev resigned on December 25, 1991, and turned over his responsibilities as commander in chief to Boris Yeltsin, the president of Russia. By the end of 1991, one of the largest empires in world history had come to an end. A new era had begun in its now-independent states.

Within Russia, a new power struggle soon ensued. Boris Yeltsin was committed to introducing a free-market economy as quickly as possible, but the transition was not easy. Economic hardships and social disarray were made worse by a dramatic rise in the activities of organized crime mobs. This situation led increasing numbers of Russians to support both former Communists and hard-line nationalists who criticized Russia's loss of prestige in world affairs. Yeltsin's brutal use of force against the Chechens (CHET-chunz), who wanted to secede from Russia and create their own independent republic, also undermined his support. Despite the odds against him, however, Yeltsin won reelection as Russian president in 1996.

 SECTION REVIEW

1. **Locate:**
   (*a*) Soviet Georgia,   (*b*) Latvia,
   (*c*) Estonia,   (*d*) Azerbaijan,
   (*e*) Lithuania,   (*f*) Ukraine,
   (*g*) Belarus

2. **Define:**
   (*a*) détente,   (*b*) Brezhnev doctrine,
   (*c*) dissidents,   (*d*) perestroika,   (*e*) glasnost

3. **Identify:**
   (*a*) Strategic Defense Initiative (SDI),
   (*b*) Mikhail Gorbachev,   (*c*) Boris Yeltsin

4. **Recall:**
   (*a*) What was accomplished through the Helsinki Agreements?
   (*b*) What problems did the central planning system create in the former Soviet Union?
   (*c*) Why did Gorbachev need to be elected president to retain much of his power in 1990?
   (*d*) Why did Communist and military leaders try to seize power from Gorbachev in 1991?
   (*e*) What events caused some Russians to wish for a return to Communist leadership in the mid-1990s?

5. **Think Critically:** What benefits did both superpowers receive from the winding down of the Cold War?

EASTERN EUROPE: FROM SOVIET SATELLITES TO SOVEREIGN STATES

As we have seen, Stalin's postwar order had set up Communist regimes throughout Eastern Europe. Few people believed that the new order could ever be undone. People in Eastern Europe, however, were

On Line with WORLD HISTORY *Internet Activity*

You may want to have your students visit the following URL, where they will find information and additional web site resources to enhance their study of this chapter.
Russia on the Web
http://www.valley.net:80/~transat/

This site includes links for topics such as history, philosophy, society, and politics.
Due to the ever-changing nature of the World Wide Web, see the West History web site, **http://history.swpco.com** for regular updates of the URLs in this text.

CLOSE

Lead students in a discussion of the Focus objectives identified on page 978. Emphasize the importance of shortages of consumer goods in bringing about the fall of the Soviet Union.

FOCUS

OBJECTIVES

After completing this section, students should be able to

1. describe developments in Soviet satellite states in Eastern Europe
2. identify and explain events that led to the reunification of Germany
3. describe the disintegration of the government and the course of war in Yugoslavia
4. identify and describe changes that took place in Eastern Europe after the fall of communism

FOCUS ACTIVITY

Provide students with an American news magazine from the mid 1980s. Have them write an essay about how it might have made people in Eastern Europe feel about their lives. Have students explain how access to Western media increased dissatisfaction in Eastern Europe.

never really happy with their Soviet-style regimes. After Gorbachev made it clear that the Soviet Union would not intervene militarily in their states, revolutions broke out throughout Eastern Europe in 1989. In Poland, Hungary, Czechoslovakia, Romania, Bulgaria, East Germany, and Albania, mass protests led to the overthrow of the Communist rulers. By looking at four of these states, we can see how the process worked.

Poland

It was workers' protests that led to demands for change in Poland. In 1980, a worker named Lech Walesa (vaw-LEN-suh) organized a national trade union known as Solidarity. The rise of an independent labor movement soon became a threat to the government's control of power. Solidarity gained the support of the workers and the Roman Catholic Church, now under the leadership of Pope John Paul II, the first Polish pope. The union thus was able to win some concessions from the government. Even a period of military rule in the 1980s, when Walesa was arrested, could not stop the movement.

After new demonstrations in 1988, the Polish regime finally agreed to free parliamentary elections—the first free elections in Eastern Europe in forty years. A newly elected government ended forty-five years of Communist rule in Poland. In December 1990, Walesa was chosen as the new Polish president. Poland's new path, however, was not an easy one. Rapid free-market reforms led to severe unemployment and popular discontent. At the end of 1995, Aleksander Kwasniewski, a former Communist, defeated Walesa and became the new Polish president.

Czechoslovakia

After Soviet troops had crushed the reform movement in Czechoslovakia in 1968 (see Chapter 29), hardline Czech Communists under Gustav Husák used a policy of massive repression to maintain their power. Only writers and other intellectuals provided any real opposition to the government. Even they had little success until the later 1980s. Mass demonstrations took place

throughout Czechoslovakia in 1988 and 1989. When the government tried to suppress them, even larger demonstrations appeared. By November 1989, crowds as large as 500,000 were forming in Prague. In December 1989, the Communist government collapsed. President Husák resigned and at the end of December was replaced by Vaclav Havel, a writer who played an important role in bringing down the Communist government. Havel proved to be an eloquent spokesperson for Czech democracy and a new order in Europe (see "You Are There: Vaclav Havel: The Call for a New Politics").

Within Czechoslovakia, the new government soon faced old problems. The two different national groups, Czechs and Slovaks, did not agree over the makeup of the new state. They were able, however, to agree to a peaceful division of the country. On January 1, 1993, Czechoslovakia split into the Czech Republic and Slovakia. Havel was elected the first president of the new Czech Republic.

Romania

In 1965, the Communist leader Nicolae Ceausescu (NIK-oh-LIE chow-SHES-KOO) and his wife, Elena, set up a rigid and dictatorial regime in Romania. Ceausescu ruled Romania with an iron grip. He used a secret police—the Securitate—to crush all dissent. Nonetheless, opposition to his regime grew. Ceausescu's economic policies led to a sharp drop in living standards, including food shortages and the rationing of bread, flour, and sugar. His plan for rapid urbanization, especially a program that called for the bulldozing of entire villages, further angered the Romanian people.

One incident became the spark that ignited the flames of revolution. In December 1989, the Securitate murdered thousands of men, women, and children who were peacefully demonstrating in the city of Timosoara (TEE-mish-uh-WAWR-uh). News of the massacre soon led to mass demonstrations in the capital city of Bucharest (BYOO-kuh-REST). After the dictator was booed at a mass rally on December 21, the army refused to support any more repression. Ceausescu and his wife were captured on December 22 and executed on Christmas Day. A new government under Ion Iliescu was

RECOMMENDED READING

There is a detailed analysis of American-Soviet relations in the 1970s and 1980s in R. Garthoff, *Détente and Confrontation: American-Soviet Relations from Nixon to Reagan* (Washington, D.C., 1985). See also F. Halliday, *The Making of the Second Cold War,* 2d ed. (New York, 1986). On the end of the Cold War, see B. Denitch, *The End of the Cold War* Minneapolis, Minn., 1990); W. G. Hyland, *The Cold War Is Over* (New York,

1990); and W. Laqueur, *Soviet Union 2000: Reform or Revolution?* (New York, 1990). For important studies of Soviet foreign policy, see A. B. Ulam, *Expansion and Coexistence: Soviet Foreign Policy, 1917–1973,* 2d ed (New York, 1974), and *Dangerous Relations: The Soviet Union in World Politics, 1970–1982* (New York, 1983).

quickly formed. Questions remain, however, about the new government's commitment to democracy.

The Reunification of Germany

After building the Berlin Wall separating West from East Berlin in 1961, East Germany developed the strongest economy among the Soviet Union's Eastern European satellites. Beginning in 1971, Erich Honecker became head of the Communist Party and used the *Stasi*, the secret police, to rule with an iron fist for the next eighteen years.

In 1988, however, popular unrest, fueled by the economic slump of the 1980s and Honecker's harsh regime, led many East Germans to flee their country. Mass demonstrations against the regime broke out in the summer and fall of 1989. By the beginning of November 1989, the Communist government was collapsing. It gave in to popular pressure on November 9, when it opened the entire border with the West. Hundreds of thousands of Germans swarmed across the border, mostly to visit and return. The Berlin Wall, long the symbol of the Cold War, became the sight of massive celebrations as thousands of people used sledgehammers to tear down the wall.

By December, new political parties had emerged. On March 18, 1990, in East Germany's first free elections ever, the Christian Democrats won almost 50 percent of the vote. The Christian Democrats supported political union with West Germany, which took place on October 3, 1990. What had seemed almost impossible at the beginning of 1989 had become a reality by the end of 1990—the country of East Germany had ceased to exist.

The Disintegration of Yugoslavia

Although Yugoslavia had a Communist government, it had never been a Soviet satellite state. It, too, however, was affected by the revolutionary events in Eastern Europe. After World War II, its dictatorial leader, Marshall Joseph (Broz) Tito, had worked to keep together the six republics and two provinces that made up Yugoslavia. After Tito's death in 1980, Tito's responsibilities passed to a collective state presidency

▲ *This young Romanian rebel waves the national flag, but one with the Communist emblem cut from the center. What does her defiant pose suggest she is doing?*

under the leadership of the Communist Party of Yugoslavia. At the end of the 1980s, Yugoslavia was caught up in the reform movements sweeping through Eastern Europe. New parties quickly emerged, and the authority of the Communist Party collapsed.

The Yugoslav political scene was complex. In 1990, the Yugoslav republics of Slovenia, Croatia (kroe-AY-shee-uh), Bosnia-Herzegovina, and Macedonia began to lobby for their independence. Slobodan Milosevic, who became leader of the Yugoslav republic of Serbia in 1987, rejected these efforts. He believed that these republics could only be independent if new borders were drawn up to take care of the Serb minorities in

MORE ABOUT . . . *the Berlin Wall*

Students may need to be reminded that the Berlin Wall was originally built in 1961 (at that time a barbed-wire barricade) in an attempt to control the movement of people from the eastern to the western sectors of Berlin. Before the more famous Berlin Wall was torn down, the government of Hungary began dismantling its own wall that had been erected on its common border with Austria. Because of this, East Berliners were able to travel from East Berlin to Hungary, then on to Austria and back to West Berlin "by way of the West." At that point the Berlin Wall was merely a symbol of Communist oppression and served no practical purpose. The East German government agreed to lift all immigration and traveling restrictions by November of 1989.

USING PRIMARY SOURCES

Have students analyze and evaluate Vaclav Havel's speech. Do they agree that people "don't know how to put morality ahead of politics, science and economics"? To what extent do students believe they are responsible for the values and actions of the society they belong to?

LEARNING FROM VISUALS

Answer to the caption question: Vaclav Havel gives a "V" for victory sign to the U.S. Congress, applauding the fact that he was representing his country in front of the U.S. Congress and the freedoms won by the Czech people.

YOU ARE THERE
Vaclav Havel—The Call for a New Politics

In their attempts to deal with the world's problems, some European leaders have pointed to the need for a new perspective if people are to live in a sane world. This excerpt is taken from a speech that Vaclav Havel gave to the U.S. Congress on February 21, 1990, two months after he had become president of Czechoslovakia.

Vaclav Havel, Speech to the U.S. Congress

For this reason, the salvation of this human world lies nowhere else than in the human heart, in the human power to reflect, in human meekness and in human responsibility.

Without a global revolution in the sphere of human consciousness, nothing will change for the better in the sphere of our being as humans, and

▶ *Vaclav Havel was warmly welcomed when he addressed a joint meeting of the United States Congress in 1990. Standing behind him on the left is Vice President Dan Quayle and on the right is Speaker of the House Thomas Foley. What is the significance of Havel's victory gesture?*

the republics who wanted to live within the boundaries of a Greater Serbian state. Serbs made up 11.6 percent of Croatia's population and 32 percent of Bosnia-Herzegovina's population in 1981.

After negotiations failed, Slovenia and Croatia declared their independence in June 1991. Milosevic's government sent the Yugoslavian army, which it controlled, into Slovenia, but without much success. In September 1991 the Yugoslavian army began a full assault against Croatia. Increasingly, the Yugoslavian army was the Serbian army and was aided by Serbian minorities in Croatia. Before a cease-fire was arranged,

the Serbian forces had captured one-third of Croatia's territory in brutal fighting.

The recognition of Slovenia, Croatia, and Bosnia-Herzegovina by many European countries and the United States early in 1992 did not stop the Serbs from turning their guns on Bosnia-Herzegovina. By mid-1993, Serbian forces had acquired 70 percent of Bosnian territory. The Serbian policy of ethnic cleansing—killing or forcibly removing Bosnian Muslims from their lands—revived memories of Nazi atrocities in World War II. Nevertheless, despite worldwide outrage, European governments failed to take a decisive

So What ⁇

*If your students question the importance or relevance of the information on **the end of the Cold War** tell them . . .*

The events in Eastern Europe and the nations that formerly comprised the Soviet Union will have a direct impact on the future security of the United States. Their successful integration into the world's family of nations, or the lack thereof, may well determine whether they are one day buying sneakers from Bosnia or fighting in Serbia.

Map 30.1   The States of Eastern Europe and the Former Soviet Union

SECTION REVIEW

1. **Locate:**
   (a) Bucharest,
   (b) Yugoslavia,
   (c) Croatia,
   (d) Bosnia,
   (e) Poland

2. **Identify:**
   (a) Solidarity,   (b) Vaclav Havel,
   (c) Nicolae Ceausescu,

(d) Erich Honecker,
(e) Slobodan Milosevic,
(f) Dayton Accords

3. **Recall:**
   (a) What is important about the way Czechoslovakia divided into the Czech Republic and Slovakia in 1993?
   (b) What caused the East German government to open its border with the West in 1989?
   (c) Why didn't European powers and the United States act sooner to end the war in Bosnia?

STUDYING MAPS

The following questions will help you guide students through their study of Map 30.1.

1. With the loss of its satellite nations why was Russia concerned about the intentions of the newly reunified Germany? *(In the past a strong Germany has given Russia reason to fear for her sovereignty.)*

2. Why would trade become both more important and more difficult for Russia?

(Russia will need to negotiate for certain resources and goods from countries that were formerly under her control.)

3. Why would the former satellite nations prefer to form trade relations with Western nations than with Russia? *(The Western nations have solid economies and a long record of successful trade ventures; Russia's credit record is not proven.)*

Answers to SECTION REVIEW

2. (a) trade union organized in Poland by Lech Walesa; helped bring about the overthrow of the Communist government
   (b) writer, played an important role in ending Communist rule in Czechoslovakia
   (c) Communist leader of Romania, killed by anti-Communists in 1989
   (d) head of the Communist Party in East Germany
   (e) leader of Bosnian Serbs, believed responsible for war crimes
   (f) agreement signed in 1995 to end the fighting in Bosnia
3. (a) The division was made peacefully
   (b) The East German leaders could no longer control the population.
   (c) They were probably afraid to become involved in a war that looked like it could go on indefinitely.
   (d) unemployment, inflation, shortages of many consumer goods
4. Many people had vested interests in the former system.

CLOSE

Lead students in a discussion of the Focus objectives identified on page 982. Emphasize the impact of the Soviet Union's internal problems on the ability of states in Eastern Europe to gain their freedom.

FOCUS

OBJECTIVES

After completing this section, students should be able to

1. describe how changes in French policy impacted the solidarity of Europe
2. identify and explain costs and benefits of reunification to Germany
3. explain the meaning and impact of Thatcherism on Great Britain
4. identify and explain domestic events that affected the United States and Canada

FOCUS ACTIVITY

Have students list reasons economic alliances can be both good and bad for a state's national interests. Nations of Europe may benefit from economic union, but they will also give up economic sovereignty. Why are some states hesitant to do this?

(*d*) What difficulties did Russia experience as it changed its economic system to one based on free enterprise?

4. **Think Critically:** Why has it been difficult for most formerly Communist nations to create democratic governments and free-market economies?

TOWARD A NEW ORDER IN EUROPE AND NORTH AMERICA

Between 1945 and the early 1970s, Europe and North America experienced an age of prosperity. Economic growth and virtually full employment continued for so long that when economic problems arose in the 1970s, they came as a shock to many people.

Western Europe: The Winds of Change

Between the early 1950s and late 1970s, Western Europe experienced virtually full employment. Social welfare programs—in the form of affordable health care; housing; family allowances for children; increases in sickness, accident, unemployment, and old-age benefits; and educational opportunities—helped create the modern welfare state. An economic downturn, however, occurred in the mid-1970s and early 1980s. Both inflation and unemployment rose dramatically. No doubt, the dramatic increase in the price of oil that followed the Arab-Israeli conflict in 1973 (see Chapter 32) was a major cause for the downturn. The economies of the Western European states recovered in the course of the 1980s, although problems remained. Unemployment was still high. France had a 10.6 percent unemployment rate in 1993; it reached 11.7 percent by the end of 1995. Despite their economic woes, however, the Western European states seemed quite capable of standing up to economic competition from the United States and Japan.

The Western European nations also moved toward a greater union of their economies after 1970. The European Economic Community expanded in 1973 when Great Britain, Ireland, and Denmark gained membership in what its members now began to call the European Community (EC). By 1986, three additional members—Spain, Portugal, and Greece—had been added.

The European Community was chiefly an economic union, not a political one. By 1992, the EC was comprised of 344 million people and made up the world's largest single trading bloc. It handled almost one-fourth of the world's commerce. In the 1980s and 1990s, the EC moved toward even greater economic integration. The Treaty on European Union (also called the Maastricht [MOSS-TRIKT] Treaty, after the city in the Netherlands where the agreement was reached) was an attempt to create a true economic and monetary union of all EC members. The treaty did not go into effect until all members agreed. Finally, on January 1, 1994, the European Community became the European Union. One of its first goals was to introduce a common currency, called the *euro*, by 2002.

Western Europe became used to political democracy. Even Spain and Portugal, which had kept their prewar dictatorial regimes until the mid-1970s, established democratic systems in the late 1970s. Moderate political parties, especially the Christian Democrats in Italy and Germany, played a particularly important role in achieving Europe's economic recovery. Overall, moderate Socialist parties, such as the Labour Party in Britain and the Social Democrats in West Germany, also continued to share power. Western European Communist parties declined drastically, especially after the collapse of communism in the Soviet Union and Eastern Europe.

Uncertainties in France

The worsening of France's economic situation in the 1970s brought a shift to the left politically. By 1981, the Socialists had become the chief party in the National Assembly. The Socialist leader, François Mitterand (MEE-ter-AW[n]), was elected president. His first concern was with France's economic difficulties. In 1982, Mitterand froze prices and wages in the hope

---

ENRICHMENT ACTIVITY

In light of the terms of the Maastricht Treaty discussed on this page, ask students how they might feel about the European Community's plans to remove tariffs and subsidies if they were (1) an industrialist living in Germany; (2) a factory worker living in Ireland, (3) a factory worker living in Germany, and (4) a farmer living in France.

Map 30.2   The New Europe

ACTIVITY

In many parts of the world today there is increasing fragmentation of nations as ethnic groups break away to form their own countries *(Soviet Union, Yugoslavia, Czech Republic, Slovakia).* However, there is also a trend in other parts of the world toward unification and increased co-operation *(reunited Germany, Western European unity, North American Free Trade Agreement, O.P.E.C.).* Have your students hypothesize about which force is the stronger in the world today, and then predict the outcome of the trend that they see for the world.

of reducing the huge budget deficit and high inflation. Mitterand also passed a number of measures to aid workers: an increased minimum wage, a mandatory fifth week of paid vacation for salaried workers, a thirty-nine-hour workweek, and higher taxes for the rich. The victory of the Socialists had convinced them that they could enact some of their more radical reforms. Consequently, the government nationalized major banks, the steel industry, the space and electronics industries, and important insurance firms.

The Socialist policies, however, largely failed to work. Within three years, a decline in support for the Socialists caused the Mitterand government to return some of the economy to private enterprise. Some economic improvements in the late 1980s enabled Mitterand to win a second seven-year term in the 1988 presidential election. Nevertheless, France's economic decline continued. In 1993, French unemployment stood at 10.6 percent. In the elections in March of that year, the Socialists won only 28 percent of the vote

STUDYING MAPS

These questions will help you guide students through their study of Map 30.2.

1. What has happened to the number of states in Europe since 1980? *(The number has increased due to the break-up of the Soviet Union.)*

2. Although the threat of an all out war has lessened in recent years why may there be greater chance of small wars in Europe? *(Without the fear of involving the superpow-*

ers in a major conflict, small ethnically-based wars, are more likely to erupt.)

3. Why is it important to include the states of the former Soviet Union in economic development plans? *(Answers will vary. Some students may believe that unless the former Soviet states are integrated into the economy they will be a cause of future conflict.)*

CLASS DISCUSSION

Ask students to evaluate the following statement. Why might many Russians believe it is true? What alternative opinions do some people hold?

The reunification of German will lead to new wars in the future. Germany's history is one of aggression. Time will not change its character.

ACTIVITY

Have students do additional research on Margaret Thatcher. What was her background? What events in her early life made her want to pursue a career in politics? Was she a feminist? What was her overall strategy as prime minister? What did she hope to accomplish? In 1997 she became very critical of her successors. Why?

while a coalition of conservative parties gained 80 percent of the seats in the National Assembly. The move to the right in France was strengthened when the conservative mayor of Paris, Jacques Chirac, was elected president in May 1995.

From West Germany to Germany

In 1969, the Social Democrats replaced the Christian Democrats as the leading party in West Germany. The first Social Democratic chancellor in West Germany was Willy Brandt (BRAWNT). He was especially successful with his "opening toward the east" (an attempt to work more closely with East Germany), for which he received the Nobel Peace Prize in 1972. On March 19, 1971, Brandt met with Walter Ulbricht (ul-BRIKT), the East German leader, and worked out the details of a Basic Treaty that was signed in 1972. This agreement called for "good neighborly" relations. As a result, it led to greater cultural, personal, and economic contacts between West and East Germany. Despite this success, Brandt was forced to resign in 1974 after the discovery of an East German spy among his advisors.

Brandt's successor, Helmut Schmidt, concentrated chiefly on the economic problems brought about by high oil prices between 1973 and 1975. Schmidt was successful in eliminating a deficit of ten billion marks in three years. In 1982, the Christian Democrats, under the leadership of Helmut Kohl (KOLE), came back into power.

Kohl was a clever politician who benefited greatly from an economic boom in the mid-1980s. Gradually, however, discontent with the Christian Democrats increased. Then the 1989 revolution in East Germany unexpectedly led to the reunification of the two Germanies, leaving the new Germany, with its seventy-nine million people, the leading power in Europe. Reunification, which was achieved during Kohl's administration, brought rich political benefits as the Christian Democrats remained in power.

However, the joy over reunification soon dissipated as new problems arose. All too soon, it dawned on Germans that the rebuilding of eastern Germany would take far more money than was originally thought. Kohl's government was soon forced to face the politi-

cally undesirable task of raising taxes. Moreover, the virtual collapse of the economy in eastern Germany led to extremely high levels of unemployment and severe discontent.

One of the responses was an attack on foreigners. For years, illegal immigrants and foreigners seeking a place of refuge had found haven in Germany because of its very liberal immigration laws. In 1992, over 440,000 immigrants came to Germany seeking refuge; 123,000 came from former Yugoslavia alone. Attacks against foreigners by right-wing extremists—especially young neo-Nazis who believed in Hitler's idea of a pure Aryan race—became an all-too-frequent part of German life.

Great Britain: Thatcher and Thatcherism

Between 1964 and 1979, the Conservative and Labour Parties alternated in power in Great Britain. Both parties had to face some very difficult problems.

One problem was the intense fighting between Catholics and Protestants in Northern Ireland. When the British government established direct rule over Northern Ireland in 1972, the Irish Republican Army (IRA) staged a series of dramatic terrorist acts. The problems in Northern Ireland have not yet been solved.

Another problem that neither party was able to deal with successfully was Britain's ailing economy. Failure to modernize made British industry less and less competitive. Moreover, Britain was hampered by frequent labor strikes, many of them caused by conflicts between rival labor unions.

In 1979, after Britain's economic problems had appeared to worsen during five years under a Labour government, the Conservatives returned to power under Margaret Thatcher. She became the first female prime minister in British history. Thatcher pledged to lower taxes, reduce government bureaucracy, limit social welfare, restrict union power, and end inflation.

The "Iron Lady," as Thatcher was called, did break the power of the labor unions. Although she did not eliminate the basic parts of the social welfare system, she did control inflation. **Thatcherism,** as her economic policy was termed, improved the British economic situation, but at a price. The south of England, for example, prospered, but old industrial areas else

RECOMMENDED READING

On the recent history of Britain, see P. Riddell, *The Thatcher Decade* (Oxford, 1989); P. Jenkins, *Mrs. Thatcher's Revolution* (London, 1989); P. A. Hall, *Governing the Economy: The Politics of State Intervention in Britain and France* (New York, 1986); G. Ross, S. Hoffmann, and S. Malzacher.

On Nixon and Watergate, see J. Anthony Lukas, *Nightmare: The Underside of the Nixon Years* (New York, 1976). On the 1970s, see

P. N. Carroll, *It Seemed Like Nothing Happened: The Tragedy and Promise of America in the 1970s* (New York, 1982). Works on recent events include B. Glad, *Jimmy Carter: From Plains to the White House* (New York, 1980); and G. Wills, *Reagan's America: Innocents at Home* (New York, 1987). On recent Canadian history, see R. Bothwell, I. Drummond, and J. English, *Canada since 1945* (Toronto, 1981).

where declined and were beset by high unemployment, poverty, and even violence.

In the area of foreign policy, Thatcher, like President Ronald Reagan, her counterpart in the United States, took a hard-line approach against communism. She oversaw a large military buildup aimed at restoring Britain as a world police force. In 1982, Great Britain went to war. Argentina had tried to take control of the Falkland Islands, one of Britain's few remaining colonial outposts, three hundred miles off Argentina's coast. The British victory in the Falklands War brought Thatcher much popular patriotic support.

Thatcher dominated British politics in the 1980s. The Labour Party, beset by divisions between moderate and radical wings, offered little real opposition. Only in 1990 did Labour's fortunes seem to revive when Thatcher's government tried to replace local property taxes with a flat-rate tax payable by every adult. Many argued that this was nothing more than a poll tax (a tax of a fixed amount per person) that would enable the rich to pay the same rate as the poor. In 1990, after antitax riots broke out, Thatcher's once remarkable popularity fell to an all-time low. At the end of November, a revolt within her own party caused Thatcher to resign as prime minister. She was replaced by John Major, whose Conservative Party continued to hold a narrow majority. His government, however, failed to capture the imagination of most Britons. In new elections on May 1, 1997, the Labour Party won a landslide victory.

The United States: The American Domestic Scene (1970 to Present)

With the election of Richard Nixon as president in 1968, American politics made a shift to the right. Nixon ended American involvement in Vietnam by gradually withdrawing U.S. troops. Politically, he followed a "southern strategy." In other words, Nixon

◄ *Margaret Thatcher, Great Britain's first woman prime minister, dominated British politics in the 1980s. She was the first British prime minister in the twentieth century to ever win three consecutive elections. This photo was taken in May 1990, six months before she was forced to resign.*

carefully calculated that "law and order" issues and a slowdown in racial desegregation would appeal to southern whites. The South, which had once been a stronghold for the Democrats, began to form a new allegiance to the Republican Party.

The Republican strategy, however, also gained support among white Democrats in northern cities. Court-mandated busing to achieve racial integration in these cities had led to a white backlash against blacks. Nixon was less conservative on other social issues. Moreover, in a break with his own strong anticommunist past, he visited Communist China in 1972 and

▲ *Zhou Enlai, on the right, and President Richard Nixon relax for a moment over tea during their historic 1972 meeting in Beijing. Why is this trip considered to be a major foreign policy success for President Nixon?*

COOPERATIVE LEARNING ACTIVITY

Break the class into groups to work cooperatively to complete the following task:

Assign the groups to write an essay that explains why Richard Nixon was one of the best and one of the worst presidents the United States ever had. Ask students to evaluate how they believe history will regard him in the next century.

opened the door to the eventual diplomatic recognition of that state (see Chapter 33).

As president, Nixon was afraid of conspiracies. He began to use illegal methods to gain political intelligence on his opponents. One of the president's advisors said that the idea was to "use the available Federal machinery to screw our political enemies." "Anyone who opposes us, we'll destroy," said another aide. Nixon's zeal led to the Watergate scandal—the attempted bugging of the Democratic National Headquarters, located in the Watergate Hotel in Washington, D.C. Nixon repeatedly lied to the American public about his involvement in the affair. Secret tapes of his own conversations in the White House, however, revealed the truth. On August 9, 1974, Nixon resigned the presidency rather than face trial and possible impeachment by the Senate.

After Watergate, American domestic politics focused on economic issues. Vice President Gerald Ford became president when Nixon resigned, only to lose in the 1976 election to the former governor of Georgia, Jimmy Carter. Carter campaigned as an outsider against the Washington establishment. Both Ford and Carter faced severe economic problems. The period from 1973 to the mid-1980s was one of economic stagnation, which came to be known as **stagflation**—a combination of high inflation and high unemployment. In 1984, the median family income was 6 percent below that of 1973.

In part, the economic downturn stemmed from a dramatic change in oil prices. Oil was considered an inexpensive and abundant source of energy in the 1950s, and Americans had grown dependent on its importation from the Middle East. By the late 1970s, 50 percent of the oil used in the United States came from the Middle East. However, an oil embargo and price increases by the Organization of Petroleum Exporting Countries (OPEC) as a result of the Arab-Israeli War in 1973 quadrupled oil prices. Additional price hikes caused oil prices to increase twentyfold by the end of the 1970s. The Carter administration produced a plan for reducing oil consumption at home while spurring domestic production. Neither Congress nor the American people, however, could be persuaded to follow what they considered to be drastic measures.

By 1980, the Carter administration was faced with two devastating problems. First, high rates of inflation and a noticeable decline in average weekly earnings were causing a drop in American living standards. At the same time, a crisis abroad erupted when fifty-three Americans were held hostage by the Iranian government of the Ayatollah Khomeini (EYE-uh-TOLE-uh koe-MAY-nee) (see Chapter 32). Carter had little control over the situation, but his inability to gain the release of the American hostages led to perceptions at home that he was a weak president. His overwhelming loss to Ronald Reagan in the election of 1980 brought forward the chief exponent of right-wing Republican policies and a new political order.

The Reagan Revolution, as it has been called, consisted of a number of new directions. Reversing decades of changes, Reagan cut back on the welfare state by decreasing spending on food stamps, school lunch programs, and job programs. At the same time, his administration oversaw the largest peacetime military buildup in U.S. history. Total federal spending rose from $631 billion in 1981 to over a trillion dollars by 1986. Instead of raising taxes to pay for the new expenditures, which far outweighed the budget cuts in social areas, Reagan convinced Congress to support **supply-side economics.** Massive tax cuts would supposedly stimulate rapid economic growth and produce new revenues. Much of the tax cut went to the wealthy. Between 1980 and 1986, the income of the lower 40 percent of the workforce fell 9 percent, while the income of the highest 20 percent rose by 5 percent.

Reagan's policies seemed to work in the short run. The United States experienced an economic upturn that lasted until the end of the 1980s. The spending policies of the Reagan administration, however, also produced record government deficits, which loomed as an obstacle to long-term growth. In the 1970s, the total deficit was $420 billion. Between 1981 and 1987, Reagan budget deficits were three times that amount.

The inability of George Bush, Reagan's vice president and his elected successor, to deal with the deficit problem, as well as an economic downturn, enabled a Democrat, Bill Clinton, to be elected president in 1992. The new president was a southern Democrat who claimed to be a new Democrat—one who favored a number of the

On Line with WORLD HISTORY *Internet Activity*

You may want to have your students visit the following URL, where they will find information and additional web site resources to enhance their study of this chapter.
Watergate
http://netspace.net.au/~malcolm/wgate.htm

This site is an excellent web source covering one of the biggest scandals in presidential history.
Due to the ever-changing nature of the World Wide Web, see the West History web site, **http://history.swpco.com** for regular updates of the URLs in this text.

Republican policies of the 1980s. This was a clear indication that the rightward drift in American politics was by no means ended by this Democratic victory. In fact, Clinton's reelection in 1996 was partially due to his adoption of Republican ideas and policies.

Canada

In Canada in 1963, during a major economic recession, the Liberals were returned to power. The most prominent Liberal government was that of Pierre Trudeau (TROO-doe), who came to power in 1968. Although French in background, Trudeau was dedicated to Canada's federal union. In 1968, his government passed the Official Languages Act, which allowed both English and French to be used in the federal civil service. The Trudeau government also encouraged the growth of French culture and language in Canada.

Trudeau's government supported a vigorous program of industrialization. However, the problem of inflation, along with Trudeau's efforts to impose the will of the federal government on the powerful provincial governments, alienated voters and weakened his government. Economic recession in the early 1980s brought Brian Mulroney, leader of the Progressive Conservative Party, to power in 1984. Mulroney's government sought to return some of Canada's state-run corporations to private owners. It also made a free-trade agreement with the United States. The agreement, which was bitterly attacked by many Canadians as being too favorable to the United States, cost Mulroney's government much of its popularity. In 1993, the ruling Conservatives were drastically defeated. They received only two seats in the House of Commons.

Mulroney's government also was unable to settle the ongoing crisis over the French-speaking province of Quebec. In the late 1960s, the Parti Québécois (KAY-buh-KWAW), headed by René Lévesque, ran on a platform of Quebec's secession from the Canadian union. In 1970, the party won 24 percent of the popular vote in Quebec's provincial elections. To pursue their dream

◄ *Pierre Trudeau, photographed in June 1977, served twice as prime minister of Canada, first from 1968 to 1979, and again from 1980 until his resignation in 1984.*

of separation, some underground separatist groups used terrorist bombings and kidnapped two government officials. In 1976, the Parti Québécois won Quebec's provincial elections. Four years later, it called for a referendum that would enable the provincial government to gain Quebec's independence from the rest of Canada. In 1995, voters in Quebec narrowly rejected the plan. Debate over Quebec's status continues to divide Canada in the 1990s.

SECTION REVIEW

1. **Define:**
   (*a*) Thatcherism,
   (*b*) stagflation,
   (*c*) supply-side economics

2. **Identify:**
   (*a*) Maastricht Treaty,
   (*b*) the *euro*,
   (*c*) François Mitterand,
   (*d*) Irish Republican Army (IRA),
   (*e*) Organization of Petroleum Exporting Countries (OPEC),
   (*f*) René Lévesque

3. **Recall:**
   (*a*) What caused much of the joy of reunification to dissipate in Germany?
   (*b*) What was the apparent cause for attacks on foreign workers in Germany during the 1990s?
   (*c*) What policy caused Margaret Thatcher's government to lose popularity in 1990?
   (*d*) Why did Richard Nixon's decision to open relations with Communist China represent a change from his traditional point of view?

FOCUS

OBJECTIVES

After completing this section, students should be able to

1. describe changes in women's role in society
2. identify and discuss issues in the environmental movement
3. identify problems that have grown from immigration
4. describe the impact of terrorism on society

FOCUS ACTIVITY

Have students make a list of differences between the role of women in today's society with what they believe it would have been thirty or more years ago. Ask them to make a second list of causes for these changes. Which causes do they believe have been most important? Which changes do they believe have been good for society? Which have been detrimental?

4. Think Critically:

(a) Why is it possible for many nations in Europe to have high rates of unemployment without also having widespread social unrest?

(b) Why is it unlikely that the nations of Europe will completely join together into one political and economic unit in the near future?

NEW DIRECTIONS AND NEW PROBLEMS IN WESTERN SOCIETY

With the political and economic changes since the 1960s have come dramatic social developments. New opportunities for women have emerged, and a women's liberation movement sought to bring new meaning to the principle of women's equality with men. New problems for Western society also arose with a growing awareness of environmental dangers, a reaction against foreign workers, and the growth of terrorism.

A Changing Society:
Women since the 1960s

After World War II, a trend toward earlier marriage continued. In Sweden, the average age of first marriage dropped from twenty-six in the 1940s to twenty-three in 1970. Birthrates declined in most nations as new contraceptive devices and abortion became widely available. It is estimated that mothers need to average 2.1 children to ensure a natural replacement of a country's population. In many European countries, the population has stopped growing. By 1992, among the twelve nations of the European Community, the average number of children per mother was 1.58.

Because of early marriages and smaller families, women since World War II have had more years when they were not raising children. This has contributed to changes in the character of women's employment in both Europe and the United States. The most impor-

tant development has been the increased number of married women in the workforce. At the beginning of the twentieth century, even working-class wives tended to stay at home if they could afford to do so. In the postwar period, this is no longer the case. In the United States, for example, in 1900 married women made up about 15 percent of the female labor force. By 1990, their number had increased to 70 percent.

The increased number of women in the workforce, however, has not changed some old patterns. Working-class women in particular still earn salaries lower than those of men for equal work. Women still tend to enter traditionally female jobs. As one female Swedish guidance counselor remarked in 1975, "Every girl now thinks in terms of a job. This is progress. They want children, but they don't pin their hopes on marriage. They don't intend to be housewives for some future husband. But there has been no change in their vocational choices."[1] A 1980 study of twenty-five European nations revealed that women still made up over 80 percent of the typists, nurses, tailors, and dressmakers in these countries. Many European and American women also still face the double burden of earning income on the one hand and raising a family and maintaining the household on the other. Such inequalities have led increasing numbers of women to rebel.

The participation of women in World Wars I and II helped them achieve one of the major aims of the nineteenth-century feminist movement—the right to vote. After World War I, many governments expressed their thanks to women for their war efforts by granting them the right to vote. Sweden, Great Britain, Germany, Poland, Hungary, Austria, and Czechoslovakia did so in 1918, followed by the United States in 1920. Women in France and Italy, however, did not obtain the right to vote until 1945.

After World War II, European women tended to fall back into the traditional roles expected of them, and little was heard of feminist concerns. By the late 1960s, however, women began to assert their rights again and to speak as feminists. Along with the student upheavals of the late 1960s came renewed interest in feminism, or the **women's liberation movement,** as it came to be called. Increasingly, women argued that political and legal equality had not brought true equality with

RECOMMENDED READING

The changing role of women is examined in E. Sullerot, *Women, Society and Change* (New York, 1971); and A. Cherline, *Marriage, Divorce, Remarriage* (Cambridge, Mass., 1981). On the women's liberation movement, See D. Bouchier, *The Feminist Challenge: The Movement for Women's Liberation in Britain and the United States* (New York, 1983). On terrorism, see the works by

W. Laqueur, *Terrorism,* 2d ed. (New York and London, 1988); and R. Rubenstein, *Alchemists of Revolution: Terrorism in the Modern World* (London, 1987). On the development of the Green parties, see F. Müller-Rommel, ed., *New Politics in Western Europe: The Rise and Success of Green Parties and Alternative Lists* (Boulder, Colo., 1989).

TEACH

▲ *The Second Sex was written in 1949, but it was not until the late 1960s that women began a determined fight for equal rights. At this rally in Washington, D.C., for the equal rights amendment, some young women have climbed the statue of Admiral Farragut to better display their posters. How far do you believe women have come in their struggle for equality with men?*

men. These are the words of the British Women's Liberation Workshop in 1969:

> We are economically oppressed: in jobs we do full work for half pay, in the home we do unpaid work full time. We are commercially exploited by advertisement, television, and the press; legally we often have only the status of children. We are brought up to feel inadequate, educated to narrower horizons than men. This is our specific oppression as women. It is as women that we are, therefore, organizing.[2]

Of great importance to the emergence of the postwar women's liberation movement was the work of Simone de Beauvoir (si-MONE de bove-WAWR). Born into a Catholic middle-class family and educated at the Sorbonne in Paris, de Beauvoir supported herself as a teacher and later as a novelist and writer. She maintained a lifelong relationship (but not marriage) with Jean-Paul Sartre (SAWRTuh).

De Beauvoir believed that she lived a "liberated" life for a twentieth-century European woman. For all her freedom, however, she still came to believe that as a woman she faced limits that men did not. In 1949, she published her highly influential work *The Second Sex*. In it she argued that as a result of male-dominated societies, women had been defined by their differences from men and, as a result, received second-class status. De Beauvoir took an active role in the French women's movement of the 1970s. Her book was a major influence on both the American and European women's movements (see "You Are There: The Voice of the Women's Liberation Movement").

Feminists in the women's liberation movement came to believe that women themselves must change the basic conditions of their lives. They helped women make these changes in a variety of ways. First, in the 1960s and 1970s, they formed "consciousness-raising" groups to make people aware of women's issues. Women also gained a measure of control over their own bodies by seeking to make both contraception and abortion legal. In the 1960s and 1970s, hundreds of thousands of European women worked to repeal the laws that outlawed contraception and abortion. They met with much success. Even in Catholic countries, where the church remained strongly opposed to laws legalizing abortion, laws allowing contraception and abortion were passed in the 1970s and 1980s.

As more women became activists, they also became involved in new issues. In the 1980s and 1990s, female faculty members in universities focused on changing cultural attitudes through the new academic field of women's studies. Other women began to try to affect the political and natural environment by allying with the antinuclear and ecological movements. As one German writer who was concerned with environmental issues said, it is women "who must give birth to children, willingly or unwillingly, in this polluted world of ours."

USING PRIMARY RESOURCES

Ask students to write a selection based on the British Women's Liberation Workshop on page 995 as it might be written today. How much has changed in the economic rights of women in the past thirty years? How different is the message of this selection from the writings of Simone de Beauvoir that were produced in the 1940s?

So What ⁇

If your students question the importance or relevance of the information on the women's movement tell them . . .

that, while few modern students identify themselves as feminists, most agree with the proposition that people of both genders should have equality of opportunity, choice, and rights (which, of course, is the essence of feminism). It is because of the struggles of earlier generations of women that today's students are able to take advantage of career opportunities and lifestyles previously denied them.

ACTIVITY

Have students read selections from Simone de Beauvoir's *The Second Sex*. They should analyze her argument and use examples from the history of the twentieth century to demonstrate the validity of her argument. Why was her book so important to the development of the women's liberation movement?

LEARNING FROM VISUALS

Answer to the caption question: Simone de Beauvoir would have undoubtedly praised the advances made by women in the Western countries, but realized that around the world women are still not treated as equals to their male counterparts.

Answers to Critical Thinking Questions

1. Her basic argument is that men are regarded as the "superior caste" as compared to women who are perceived as being subordinate to men.
2. Answers will vary, but should be supported.

YOU ARE THERE

The Voice of the Women's Liberation Movement

Simone de Beauvoir was an important figure in the emergence of the postwar women's liberation movement. This excerpt is taken from her book The Second Sex, *in which she argued that women have been forced into a position subordinate to men.*

Simone de Beauvoir, *The Second Sex*

Now, woman has always been man's dependent, if not his slave; the two sexes have never shared the world in equality. And even today woman is heavily handicapped, though her situation is beginning to change. Almost nowhere is her legal status the same as man's, and frequently it is much to her disadvantage. Even when her rights are legally recognized in the abstract, long-standing custom prevents their full expression. In the economic sphere men and women can almost be said to make up two castes; other things being equal, the former hold the better jobs, get higher wages, and have more opportunity for success than their new competitors. In industry and politics men have a great many more positions and they monopolize the most important posts. In addition to all this, they enjoy a traditional prestige that the education of children tends in every way to support, for the present enshrines the past—and in the past all history has been made by men. At the present time, when women are beginning to take part in the affairs of the world, it is still a world that belongs to men—they have no doubt of it at all and women have scarcely any. To decline to be the Other, to refuse to be a party to a deal—this would be for women to renounce all the advantages conferred upon them by their alliance with the superior caste. Man-the-sovereign will provide woman-the-liege with material protection and will undertake the moral justification of her existence;

▲ *Simone de Beauvoir, who wrote both essays and novels, was an existentialist and an ardent feminist. She published* The Second Sex *in 1949. What do you think she would have said about the state of women's affairs at the time of her death in 1986?*

thus she can evade at once both economic risk and the metaphysical risk of a liberty in which ends and aims must be contrived without assistance.

1. What is Simone de Beauvoir's basic argument?

2. Do you agree with her argument? Why or why not?

On Line with WORLD HISTORY Internet Activity

You may want to have your students visit the following URL, where they will find information and additional web site resources to enhance their study of this chapter.
Chernobyl
http://www.discovery.com/DCO/doc/1012/world/science/chernobyl/

chernobyl12.html

What actually happened at this plant? Read eyewitness reports and look at some very frightening statistics.

Due to the ever-changing nature of the World Wide Web, see the West History web site, **http://history.swpco.com** for regular updates of the URLs in this text.

The Environment and the Green Movements

Beginning in the 1970s, **environmentalism** (a movement to control the pollution of the Earth) became an important issue. By that time, serious ecological problems had become all too apparent. Air pollution, produced by nitrogen oxide and sulfur dioxide emissions from road vehicles, power plants, and industrial factories, was causing respiratory illnesses and having corrosive effects on buildings and monuments. Many rivers, lakes, and seas had become so polluted that they posed serious health risks. Dying forests and disappearing wildlife alarmed more and more people. The opening of Eastern Europe after the revolutions of 1989 brought to the world's attention the incredible environmental destruction of that region as a result of uncontrolled industrial pollution. In the Bohemian basin in Czechoslovakia, for example, the burning of low-quality brown coals in power stations and industries created a brown chemical haze that destroyed forests and led to high infant mortality rates, ill and malformed children, and high cancer rates.

Environmental concerns forced the major political parties in Europe to favor new regulations for the protection of the environment. In 1986, Europeans became even more aware of environmental hazards when a nuclear power reactor exploded at Chernobyl (chur-NOE-buhl), in the Soviet Union. A radioactive cloud spread over northern Ukraine and across Europe. Hundreds of thousands of people were evacuated from the area, but it was too late to avoid their contamination. Authorities believe that thousands of people will suffer serious or deadly health problems from the Chernobyl disaster. Tragic birth defects are already evident among livestock. Horses, for example, have been born with eight deformed legs.

Growing awareness of the environment also gave rise to Green movements and Green parties. These emerged throughout Europe in the 1970s. The origins of these movements were by no means the same. Some came from the antinuclear movement. Others arose out of such causes as women's liberation and concerns for foreign workers. Most started at the local level and then gradually expanded to include activities at the

▲ *This child was being treated at a hospital in Kiev in 1992 for bone disease that resulted from the Chernobyl disaster. Five years after the explosion at the power plant, children were still being born with bone diseases and tumors. What precautions have been taken at U.S. nuclear power plants to prevent a similar disaster?*

national level, where they became organized as political parties. Most visible was the Green Party in Germany. It was officially organized in 1979, and by 1987 it had elected forty-two delegates to the West German parliament. Green parties also competed successfully in Sweden, Austria, and Switzerland.

The Green movements and parties have played an important role in making people aware of environmental problems, but they have by no means replaced the traditional political parties. For one thing, the coalitions that make up the Greens find it difficult to agree on all issues and tend to divide into factions. Then, too, traditional political parties have taken over the environmental issues of the Greens.   By the early 1990s, more and more European governments were beginning to sponsor projects to safeguard the environment and to clean up the worst sources of pollution.

Guest Workers and Immigrants

As Western European countries made their economic recoveries in the 1950s and 1960s, a severe shortage of

TEACHING THEMES

The Environment and History Ask students to investigate the long term results of the Chernobyl disaster. What has happened to the people and lands that existed near the nuclear plant in 1986? Have any other similar events taken place since? Does it appear that governments and energy agencies have changed their practices following this event?

CLASS DISCUSSION

Ask students whether or not they support the continued use of nuclear power. Remind them that the alternative is for society to use less power or burn more fossil fuel, which might also have a negative impact on the environment. Are there any easy answers to environmental problems?

LEARNING FROM VISUALS

Answer to the caption question: Nuclear power plants in the U.S. are heavily regulated and given regular safety checks by federal agencies. Additionally, the designs provide for automatic shutdown and citizen warnings in case of safety problems.

MORE ABOUT . . . *Modern Medicine*

With the elimination of smallpox in the 1970s many health care professionals believed that we were entering a new era in which all diseases would eventually be conquered. Yet, the last few decades have witnessed the emergence of a whole host of contagions, including Lyme disease, Legionnaire's disease, hantavirus, ebola, and of course, AIDS. To compound the problem, breakdown in world-wide health measures resulted in an upsurge in infections such as cholera and tuberculosis. Antibiotic resistant strains of malaria and pneumococcal disease further strain medical resources. Many doctors claim that part of the problem is that modern medicine is too treatment driven, rather prevention oriented.

Multimedia Support

TRANSPARENCY

30–2, Map of Immigration Trends Around the World

CLASS DISCUSSION

Ask students to evaluate the following statement. Do they believe it is true? What alternative opinions do some people in Europe hold?

Nations have a duty to foreigners who have done work their own people would not do. They should grant guest workers citizenship.

LEARNING FROM VISUALS

Assign students to find and analyze a news article that describes how illegal aliens are treated in the United States. Would students be willing to demonstrate to protect these people? What would they do to resolve the problem of illegal aliens if they had the power?

LEARNING FROM VISUALS

Answer to the caption question: Answers will vary.

▶ *Riot police in France had to force their way through crowds to reach three hundred illegal African immigrants who had occupied a church for two months, protesting their deportation. What do you think public reaction in the United States would be to such a scene?*

workers led them to import foreign workers. Scores of Turks and eastern and southern Europeans went to Germany. North Africans went to France, and people from the Caribbean, India, and Pakistan went to Great Britain. Overall, there were probably fifteen million guest workers in Europe in the 1980s. They constituted 17 percent of the labor force in Switzerland and 10 percent in West Germany.

Although these workers brought economic benefits to their host countries, socially and politically their presence created problems. Many foreign workers complained that they received lower wages. Moreover, their large numbers in certain cities, and even in certain sections of those cities, often created tensions with the local native populations. Foreign workers, many of them nonwhites, made up almost one-fifth of the population in the West German cities of Frankfurt, Munich, and Stuttgart. In the 1970s, as an economic downturn created rising unemployment, many guest workers were unwilling to leave when European countries tried to send the workers home.

In the 1980s, the problem of foreign workers was made worse by an influx of other refugees. This was especially true in West Germany, which allowed people to seek refuge for political persecution. During the 1970s and 1980s, West Germany absorbed over a million refugees from Eastern Europe and East Germany. In 1986 alone, 200,000 political refugees from Pakistan, Bangladesh, and Sri Lanka entered the country.

This great influx of foreigners to Western Europe, many of them nonwhite, strained the patience of many native residents who opposed making their countries ethnically diverse. Especially in a time of growing unemployment, antiforeign sentiment increased and was encouraged by new right-wing political parties that catered to people's complaints. Thus, the National Front in France, which campaigned with the slogan "France for the French," won 10 percent of the vote in the 1986 elections. Even more frightening, however, have been the organized campaigns of violence—especially against African and Asian immigrants—by radical right-wing groups.

The Growth of Terrorism

Acts of terror by those opposed to governments became a regular aspect of modern Western society.

ENRICHMENT ACTIVITY

If you would like to provide a link between the past and present and encourage environmental activism among your students, ask them to review the text discussion about Germany's Green Party. Then ask students to identify an environmental issue in their own community and write a political party platform that would work on finding a solution to this problem. Students may want to work in pairs for this assignment. They may also like to design campaign posters using one of the computer presentation packages available with many recent computer systems.

During the late 1970s and early 1980s in particular, concern about terrorism was widespread in the United States and many European countries. Small bands of terrorists used the killing of civilians (especially by bombing), the taking of hostages, and the hijacking of airplanes to draw attention to their demands or to achieve their political goals. Terrorist acts gained much media attention. When Palestinian terrorists (known as the Black September) kidnapped and killed eleven Israeli (iz-RAY-lee) athletes at the Munich Olympic games in 1972, hundreds of millions of people watched the drama unfold on television. Indeed, some observers believe that media attention has caused some terrorist groups to become even more active.

Why do terrorists commit these acts of violence? Both left- and right-wing terrorist groups flourished in the late 1970s and early 1980s. The major left-wing groups were the Baader-Meinhof (Bayder-MINE-hof) gang (also known as the Red Army Faction) in West Germany and the Red Brigades in Italy. They consisted chiefly of wealthy middle-class young people who denounced capitalism and supported acts of revolutionary terrorism in order to bring down the system. The Red Army killed prominent industrial and financial leaders in West Germany. The Red Brigades were experts in "kneecapping," or crippling their victims by shooting them in the knees. Right-wing terrorist groups, such as the New Order in Italy and the Charles Martel Club in France, used bombings to create disorder and try to bring about authoritarian regimes. These groups received little or no public support, and authorities were able to crush them fairly quickly.

Terrorist acts also came from militant nationalists who wished to create separatist states. These terrorists received much support from local populations who favored their causes. With this support, these terrorist groups could maintain their activities over a long period of time. Most prominent is the Irish Republican Army (IRA), whose goal is to unite Northern Ireland with the Irish Republic. It has resorted to vicious attacks against the ruling government and innocent civilians in Northern Ireland. Over a period of twenty years, IRA terrorists were responsible for the deaths of two thousand people in Northern Ireland.

International terrorism has remained commonplace

CONNECTIONS
AROUND THE WORLD

Global Terrorism   Terrorist acts have become a regular feature of life in the second half of the twentieth century. A growing number of groups have used terrorism as a means to achieve their political goals. Such groups exist around the world: urban guerrilla groups in Latin America; militants dedicated to the liberation of Palestine; Islamic fundamentalists fighting against Western influence in the Middle East; and separatists seeking independent states, such as the Basques in Spain, the Tamils in Sri Lanka, the Québecois in Canada, and the Sikhs in India.

International terrorists, however, did not limit their targets to their own countries. On May 30, 1972, three members of the neo-Marxist Japanese Red Army, who had been hired by the Popular Front for the Liberation of Palestine, opened fire at Tel Aviv's Lod Airport in Israel, killing twenty-four people, chiefly Christian pilgrims from Puerto Rico. The goal of the terrorists was to hurt Israel by discouraging people from visiting there.

International terrorists have been well aware that they can maximize publicity for their cause by appearing on televised newscasts. By killing eleven Israeli athletes at the Munich Olympic Games in 1972, the Palestinian Black September terrorist group gained a television audience of more than 500 million people. In 1975, rebels from the South Moluccas hijacked a Dutch train in order to publicize their demands for independence from Indonesia.

in the 1980s and 1990s. Angered over the loss of their territory to Israel by 1967, some militant Palestinians responded with a policy of terrorist attacks against Israel's supporters. Palestinian terrorists operated throughout European countries, attacking both Europeans and American tourists. In 1983, a Lebanese terrorist blew up U.S. military barracks in Lebanon, killing 241 U.S. Marines and sailors.

MORE ABOUT . . . *the Origin of Terrorism*

Terrorism is not a recent occurrence on the pages of history. It actually dates back to the first century A.D., if not earlier. During the first century, a Jewish religious sect called the Zealots, fought to overthrow the occupation of the Romans in the modern-day country of Israel. Terrorist acts were made against the political and religious leaders of Sunni Islam by the Assassins, a radical group of Shiite Muslims, in Iran during the twelfth century. Before the nineteenth century, terrorist attacks were fueled mainly by religious zeal. However, by the nineteenth century, terrorism became more political and revolutionary oriented.

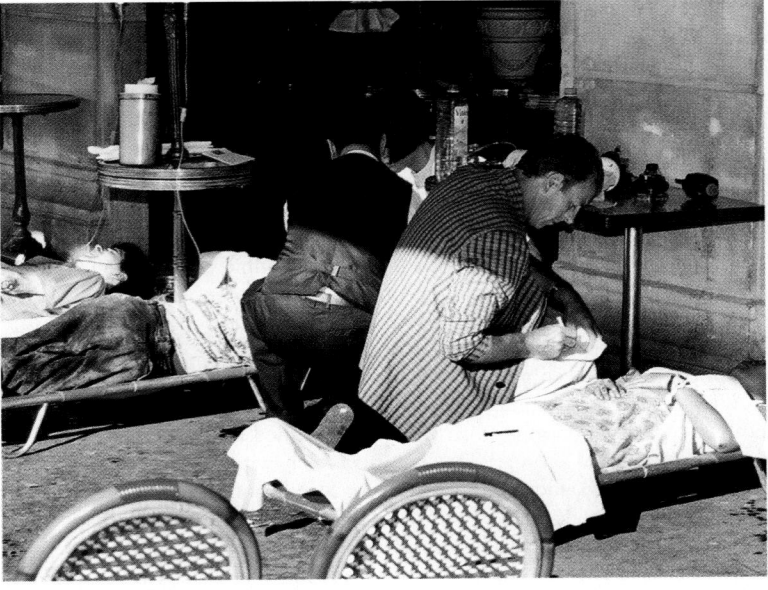

▶ *In July 1995, even the subways in Paris became targets for terrorist activities. A bomb exploded during rush hour, injuring fifty people. What incidents of random terrorism have occurred in the United States during the last decade?*

State-sponsored terrorism was often an important part of international terrorism. Militant governments, especially in Iran, Libya, and Syria, aided terrorist organizations that made attacks on Europeans and Americans. On December 21, 1988, Pan American flight 103 from Frankfurt to New York exploded over Lockerbie (LOCK-ur-bee), Scotland, killing all 259 passengers and crew members. A massive investigation finally revealed that the bomb responsible for the explosion had been planted by two Libyan terrorists. Both were connected to terrorist groups based in Iran and Syria.

Governments fought back by creating special antiterrorist units that became effective in responding to terrorist acts. The German special antiterrorist unit, known as GSG, for example, in 1977 rescued ninety-one hostages from a Lufthansa airplane that had been hijacked to Mogadishu, in Somalia. In a daring raid at Entebbe (en-TEB-uh), Uganda, in 1976, a force of Israeli paratroopers freed a group of Israeli citizens who were being held hostage by a group of Palestinian terrorists. **Counterterrorism,** or a calculated policy of direct retaliation against terrorists, also made states

that sponsored terrorism more cautious. In 1986, the Reagan administration responded to the terrorist bombing of a West German disco club that was popular with American soldiers with an air attack on Libya. Libya had long been suspected as being a major sponsor of terrorist organizations.

❀   **SECTION REVIEW**   ❀

1. **Locate:**
   (*a*) Iran,
   (*b*) Libya

2. **Define:**
   (*a*) women's liberation movement,
   (*b*) environmentalism,
   (*c*) counterterrorism

3. **Identify:**
   (*a*) Simone de Beauvoir,
   (*b*) Chernobyl,

MORE ABOUT . . . *Terrorism in the United States*

It is easy to think that terrorists are from countries other than our own. With the exception of the New York World Trade Center bombing in 1993 by Islamic radicals, though, terrorism in the United States has been of domestic origin. Early in the twentieth century, labor leaders, such as "Big Bill" Haywood promoted a philosophy of revolution and were committed to the violent overthrow of the government. During the 1960s and 1970s the Weather Underground and other left-wing groups bombed buildings on college campuses in opposition to the United States' involvement in the Vietnam War. More recent examples include the Unabomber and the bombing of the Federal Building in Oklahoma City.

(*c*) Green movements,

(*d*) Baader-Meinhof gang,

(*e*) Red Brigades,

(*f*) state-sponsored terrorism

4. Recall:

(*a*) What inequalities led increasing numbers of women to demand more equal treatment in recent years?

(*b*) Why did the fall of communism lead to a greater realization of the need for protection of the environment?

(*c*) Why did many foreigners migrate to Western European nations in the 1950s and 1960s?

(*d*) How have some Europeans reacted to the large number of foreign workers living in their countries?

(*e*) Why do terrorists often act to gain media attention?

5. Think Critically: Why may the decline in birth-rates cause problems in the future as older people live longer lives?

5

THE WORLD OF WESTERN CULTURE

Intellectually and culturally, the Western world during the last half of the twentieth century has been marked by much diversity. Many trends still represent a continuation of prewar modern developments. New directions in the last two decades, however, have led some to speak of a postmodern cultural world.

Recent Trends in Art and Literature

For the most part, the United States has dominated the art world in the second half of this century. American art, often vibrantly colored and filled with activity, reflected the energy of the postwar United States. After 1945, New York City became the artistic center of the Western world. The Guggenheim (GOO-gun-HIME) Museum, the Museum of Modern Art, and the Whitney Museum of American Art, together with New York City's numerous art galleries, promoted modern art. They helped determine artistic taste not only in New York City and the United States but also throughout much of the world (see "Our Artistic Heritage: Modern and Postmodern Art in the Western World").

The most significant trend in postwar literature was the Theater of the Absurd. This new form of drama began in France in the 1950s. Its most famous example is *Waiting for Godot* (1952), a play written by Samuel Beckett, an Irish author who lived in France. In *Waiting for Godot*, it is at once apparent that the action on the stage is not realistic. Two men wait for the appearance of someone, with whom they may or may not have an appointment. No background information on the two men is provided. During the course of the play, nothing seems to be happening. Unlike in traditional theater, suspense is maintained not by having the audience wonder, "What is going to happen next?" but by having it wonder, "What is happening now?"

The Theater of the Absurd reflected its time. After the experience of World War II, many people felt that the world was absurd or even meaningless. This belief gave rise to a new philosophy, called **existentialism.** This philosophy was chiefly the work of two French writers, Albert Camus (KA-M[oo]UH) and Jean-Paul Sartre. The beginning point of the existentialism of Sartre and Camus was the absence of God in the universe. The absence of God meant that humans had no fixed destiny. They were utterly alone in the universe, with no future and no hope. As Camus expressed it:

> *A world that can be explained even with bad reasons is a familiar world. But, on the other hand, in a universe suddenly divested of illusions and lights, man feels an alien, a stranger. His exile is without remedy since he is deprived of the memory of a lost home or the hope of a promised land. This divorce between man and his life, the actor and his setting, is properly the feeling of absurdity.*[3]

According to Camus, then, the world is absurd and without meaning. Humans, too, are without meaning

---

(c) to find work

(d) increase in antiforeign sentiments

(e) to draw attention to demands

5. fewer young people to produce goods and services

CLOSE

Lead students in a discussion of the Focus objectives identified on page 994. Emphasize the growth of conflicts in societies throughout the world in recent years.

FOCUS

OBJECTIVES

After completing this section, students should be able to

1. identify and describe recent trends in art and literature
2. discuss issues in the revival of religion
3. identify important developments in science and technology
4. describe the growth of popular culture

FOCUS ACTIVITY

Assign students to survey their homes and list items that reflect technological changes over the past thirty years.

RECOMMENDED READING

For a general view of postwar thought, see R. N. Stromberg, *European Intellectual History since 1789,* 5th ed. (Englewood Cliffs, N.J., 1990). On contemporary art, see R. Lambert, *Cambridge Introduction to the History of Art: The Twentieth Century* (Cambridge, 1981); and the general work by B. Cole and A. Gealt, *Art of the Western World* (New York, 1989). A physicist's view of science is contained in J. Ziman, *The Force of Knowledge: The Scientific Dimension of Society* (Cambridge, 1976). The space race is examined in W. A. McDougall, *The Heavens and the Earth: A Political History of the Space Age* (New York, 1984). There is an excellent survey of twentieth-century popular culture in R. Maltby, ed., *Passing Parade: A History of Popular Culture in the Twentieth Century* (Oxford, 1989).

OUR ARTISTIC HERITAGE

LEARNING FROM VISUALS

Have students write their own definitions of art descriptions of what an artist does. They should then evaluate the photographs on pages 1002 and 1003. Do they believe this is art? Is Jackson Pollock doing what artists do?

Answer to the caption question: Answers will vary.

LEARNING FROM VISUALS

Answer to the caption question: Answers will vary.

Answers to Critical Thinking Question

1. Modern art included abstractionism in which paintings broke all the usual conventions of form and structure. It also included pop art, which took images from commercial art. Postmodern art uses tradition in both styles of painting and craftsmanship.
2. Answers will vary.
3. Answers will vary.

OUR ARTISTIC HERITAGE

Modern and Postmodern Art in the Western World

Abstractionism, especially abstract expressionism, was the most popular form of modern art after

Jackson Pollock found it easier to work with his huge canvases spread out on the ground. Here a photographer catches Jackson Pollock at work in his studio in Long Island, New York. Do you believe Pollock's paintings will be as famous two hundred years from now as those done by the impressionist painters or Picasso? Why or why not?

World War II. The excitement of American artists with abstract expressionism is evident in the enormous canvases of Jackson Pollock (PAWL-uk). In such works as Pollock's *Lavender Mist* (1950), paint seems to explode, assaulting the viewer with emotion and movement. Pollock's swirling forms and seemingly chaotic patterns broke all the usual conventions of form and structure. His drip paintings, with their total abstraction, were extremely influential to other artists. The public, however, was at first hostile to his work.

The early 1960s saw the emergence of pop art, which took images of popular culture and transformed them into works of fine art. Andy Warhol (WAWR-HAWL) was the most famous of the pop artists. Warhol took as his subject matter images from commercial art, such as Campbell soup cans, and photographs of such celebrities as Marilyn Monroe. Derived from mass culture, these works were mass produced and deliberately "of the moment," expressing the fleeting whims of popular

and purpose. Reduced to despair and depression, humans have but one ground of hope—themselves.

The Revival of Religion

Existentialism was one response to the despair created by the apparent collapse of civilized values in the twentieth century. The revival of religion has been another. Ever since the Enlightenment of the eighteenth century, Christianity, as well as religion in general, had been on the defensive. A number of religious thinkers and leaders, however, tried to bring new life to Christianity in the twentieth century. Despite the attempts of the Communist world to build an atheistic society

---

MORE ABOUT . . . *The Americanization of the World*

The twentieth century is often called the "American century" because of the United States dominant position as a military and economic superpower. Many people from other parts of the world have concerns that U.S. cultural dominance will one day Americanize the world, overwhelming their own society's traditions. Professor Benjamin Barber, of Rutgers University, wrote that in the modern world, "fast food, fast computers, and fast food—MTV, MacIntosh, and McDonalds . . . are pressing nations into one commercially homogenous global theme park, one McWorld tied together by communications, by information, by entertainment, by commerce." His fear for this new "McWorld" is that it may become one where democratically-minded citizens are replaced by dollar-oriented consumers.

OUR ARTISTIC HERITAGE

Modern and Postmodern Art in the Western World, continued

Andy Warhol's painting 100 Cans *was done in 1962. It is a large painting, 72" × 52", and is photographic in nature. What does it reveal about American culture and civilization?*

culture.

In the 1980s, styles emerged that some have referred to as postmodern. Postmodern artists believe in using tradition, whether that includes other styles of painting or raising traditional craftsmanship to the level of fine art. Weavers, potters, glassmakers, metalsmiths, and furniture makers gained respect as postmodern artists.

Another response to modernism has been a return to realism in the arts. Some extreme realists paint with such close attention to realistic detail that their paintings appear to be photographs. Their subjects are often ordinary people stuck in ordinary lives.

1. Describe the characteristics of modern and postmodern art.

2. How do modern art and postmodern art reflect the times in which they were created?

3. What is your reaction to the Warhol painting? Give specific reasons for your opinion of this work of art.

and the attempts of the West to build a secular society, religion continued to play an important role in the lives of many people.

One expression of this religious revival was the attempt by Christian thinkers, such as the Protestant Karl Barth (BART), to breathe new life into traditional Christian teachings. In his numerous writings,

Barth tried to show how the religious insights of the Reformation were still relevant for the modern world. To Barth, the imperfect nature of human beings meant that humans could know religious truth not through reason but only through the grace of God.

In the Catholic Church, attempts at religious renewal came from two popes—John XXIII and John

COMPARING TIME PERIODS

Some people believe that the technological revolution is currently having as dramatic an effect on society as the industrial revolution had in the nineteenth century. Assign students to write an essay in which they evaluate this proposition.

CLASS DISCUSSION

Lead students in a discussion of the following statement. Do they believe it is true? To what extent might it explain the technological advancements that have taken place in recent years?

The Cold War and the arms race have helped society by supporting basic research that led to better technology and consumer products.

ACTIVITY

Have students read selections from E. F. Schumacher's *Small is Beautiful* and suggest ways this book contributed to the modern environmental movement.

▲ *Pope John Paul II is a popular world traveler. In 1987, he visited Chile where he was greeted by this young girl at a Catholic church just outside Santiago.*

Paul II. Pope John XXIII reigned as pope for only a short time (1958 to 1963). Nevertheless, he sparked a dramatic revival of Catholicism when he summoned the twenty-first ecumenical council of the Catholic Church. Known as Vatican Council II, it liberalized a number of Catholic practices. For example, the mass could now be celebrated in the vernacular languages as well as Latin. New avenues of communication with other Christian faiths were also opened for the first time since the Reformation.

John Paul II, who had been the archbishop of Cracow in Poland before he became pope in 1978, was the first non-Italian pope since the sixteenth century. Pope John Paul's numerous travels around the world helped strengthen the Catholic Church throughout the non-Western world. Although he alienated a number of people by reasserting traditional Catholic teaching on such issues as birth control and a ban on women in the priesthood, John Paul II has been a powerful figure in reminding Catholics of the need to temper the pursuit of materialism with spiritual concerns.

The New World of Science and Technology

Since the Scientific Revolution of the seventeenth century and the Industrial Revolution of the nineteenth century, science and technology have played increasingly important roles in world history. Many of the scientific and technological achievements since World War II have revolutionized people's lives. When American astronaut Neil Armstrong walked on the moon on July 20, 1969, for example, millions watched the event on their televisions in the privacy of their living rooms.

Before World War II, science and technology were largely separated. Pure science was the domain of university professors, who were far removed from the practical matters of technicians and engineers. During World War II, however, university scientists were recruited to work for their governments and to develop new weapons and practical instruments of war. British physicists played a crucial role in the development of an improved radar system in 1940 that helped to defeat the German air force in the Battle of Britain. German scientists converted coal to gasoline to keep the German war machine moving. They created self-propelled rockets, as well as jet airplanes, to keep Hitler's hopes alive for a miraculous turnaround in the war.

The computer, too, was a wartime creation (see "The Role of Science and Technology: The Computer"). An equally famous product of wartime scientific research was the atomic bomb, created by a team of American and European scientists under the guidance of the physicist J. Robert Oppenheimer. Obvi-

So What ??

If your students question the importance or relevance of the information on **modern science and technology,** *tell them . . .*

Many people believe that more than any single factor, developments in the sciences will dramatically alter the world in which they live. Advancements in genetics, computers, weapons technology, medicine and chemistry, among others, might result in their children's world being as different from the one in which they are growing up as today is from the sixteenth century.

THE ROLE OF SCIENCE AND TECHNOLOGY
The Computer

▲ *Apple's first computer was a simple machine built in a box; the factory was a garage, not a high-tech, clean laboratory.*

▲ *The computer industry quickly developed into a highly competitive, billion-dollar business. The IBM ThinkPad, shown here, is just one of many laptop computers on the market. What do you believe will be the next major improvement in computer technology?*

▲ *Pentium microprocessor chips, like this one, have made it possible for computers to be both smaller and more powerful.*

The computer may yet prove to be the most revolutionary of all the technological inventions of the twentieth century. The first computer was really a product of World War II. Designed by the British mathematician Alan Turing, the first electronic computer was used to crack enemy codes by doing mathematical calculations faster than any human could do them.

The first electronic computer with stored memory was made in the United States by the IBM Corporation in 1948. The IBM 1401, marketed in 1959, was the first computer used in large numbers in business and industry.

All of these early computers, which used thousands of vacuum tubes to function, were large and took up considerable room space. The development of the transistor and then the silicon chip produced a revolutionary new approach to computers. With the invention in 1971 of the microprocessor, a machine that combines the equivalent of thousands of transistors on a single, tiny silicon chip, the road was open for the development of the personal computer. It was both small and powerful.

The first personal computer was made by Steve Jobs (JOEBZ) and Steve Wozniak. They worked in a family garage to make and market their Apple computer. By the end of 1978, Apple had become one of the fastest-growing companies in the United States. Apple dominated the personal computer market until the IBM Corporation introduced its own personal computer in August 1981.

(continued)

THE ROLE OF SCIENCE AND TECHNOLOGY

ACROSS THE CURRICULUM

Science. Have students investigate and suggest ways in which the development of computer technology has changed each of the following fields of study:

◆ engineering
◆ architecture
◆ physics
◆ drafting/design
◆ medical research

COMPARING TIME PERIODS

Assign students to ask an adult to describe how he or she would have gone about writing a research paper for a history class thirty or more years ago. Ask the student to explain how advances in technology have changed this process.

LEARNING FROM VISUALS

Answer to the caption question: Student answers will vary.

MORE ABOUT . . . *The Cold War and the Internet*

In the 1960s the RAND corporation, a cold war think-tank, was trying to solve the problem of how authorities would communicate in the event of a nuclear attack. Their solution was to create a computerized network with no central authority, designed to operate even if major parts of it were destroyed. They created the Advanced Research Projects Agency, ARPNET, to link together universities, research labs and military labs. Because it was required that members have ties to military research, other nonmilitary sites started their own networks in the 1980s. Eventually, the National Science Foundation (NSFNET) began linking together university supercomputers using the ARPNET ideas. By 1989 there were 100,000 sites and by the 1990s sites from all around the world were linked to the NSFNET, which became known as the INTERNET.

Answers to Critical Thinking Questions

1. The computer is a machine with a function of manipulating, storing, and retrieving information at a pace faster than humanly possible.
2. Answers will vary.

TEACHING THEMES

Economics and History

Remind students that the space race did not just involve scientific research and accomplishment. It was also dependent on the ability of nations to fund their space programs. Discuss with students why the initial Soviet successes were almost certain to be quickly surpassed by those of the United States.

THE ROLE OF SCIENCE AND TECHNOLOGY
The Computer, continued

The computer is a new kind of machine. Its chief function is to store and produce information, which is now considered a basic feature of our fast-paced civilization. By the 1990s, the personal computer had become a regular fixture in businesses, schools, and homes. The Internet—the world's largest computer network—provides millions of people around the world with quick access to immense quantities of information. By 2000, an estimated 500 million people will be using the Internet.

The computer not only makes a whole host of tasks much easier, such as writing this book, but it has also become an important tool in virtually every area of modern life. Indeed, other tools and machines now depend for their functioning on computers. Many of the minute-by-minute decisions used in flying an airplane, for example, are done by a computer.

1. What is the computer and what is its purpose?
2. What problems might the computer create for our civilization?

ously, most wartime devices were created for destructive purposes. Merely the mention of computers or jet airplanes, however, shows how wartime technology could easily be adapted for peacetime uses.

In sponsoring research, governments and the military during World War II created a new scientific model. Science had become very complex. Only large organizations with teams of scientists, huge laboratories, and complex equipment could undertake the large-scale projects that were being funded. Such facilities were so expensive, however, that they could be provided only by governments and large corporations.

Because of its postwar prosperity, the United States was able to take the lead in the development of the new science. Almost 75 percent of all scientific research funds in the United States came from the government in 1965. Unwilling to lag behind, especially in military development, the Soviet Union was forced to provide large outlays for scientific and technological research and development. In fact, the defense needs of the United States and the Soviet Union generated much of the postwar scientific research. One-fourth of the trained scientists and engineers after 1945 worked at creating new weapons systems. Universities found

their research agendas increasingly set by government funding for military-related projects.

There was no more stunning example of how the new scientific establishment operated than the space race of the 1960s. When the Soviet Union announced in 1957 that it had sent the first space satellite—*Sputnik I*—into orbit around the Earth, winning the first stage of the space race, Americans were shocked. President John F. Kennedy led the United States in a gigantic project to land astronauts and their spacecraft on the moon within a decade. Massive government funds financed the scientific research and technological creations that enabled the United States to attain this goal in 1969.

The postwar alliance of science and technology led to a fast rate of change that became a fact of life in Western society. The underlying assumption of this alliance—that scientific knowledge gave human beings the ability and right to manipulate the environment for their benefit—was questioned by some in the 1960s and 1970s. These questioners noted that some technological advances had far-reaching side effects that were damaging to the environment. The chemical fertilizers, for example, that were used for growing

ENRICHMENT ACTIVITY

In order to test the theory that the world is undergoing a homogenization and Americanization of culture, have the students create a series of questions to test knowledge of the current popular culture in the United States. Questions should focus on fashion, television shows, popular movies, sports stars, celebrities, etc. As a long-term project, you might want to arrange to have students e-mail these questions to a variety of schools around the world to test knowledge of U.S. culture. As a reverse experiment you may want to encourage students in other countries to similarly test your students about their culture.

◄ *Rock and roll may have originated in the United States, but its most famous band was certainly the Beatles. Television audiences throughout the United States watched the group's American debut on the* Ed Sullivan Show *in 1964.*

larger crops destroyed the ecological balance of streams, rivers, and woodlands. *Small is Beautiful,* written by the British economist E. F. Schumacher, warned about the dangers of the new science and technology. As we have seen, the spread of fouled beaches and dying forests and lakes made environmentalism one of the important issues of the 1990s.

Popular Culture

Popular culture in the twentieth century, especially since World War II, has played an important role in helping Western people define themselves. The history of popular culture is also the history of the economic system that supports it, for it is this system that makes and sells the images that people buy as popular culture. Modern popular culture, therefore, is closely tied to the mass consumer society from which it has emerged.

The United States has been the most powerful force in shaping popular culture in the West and, to a lesser degree, in the entire world. Through movies, music, advertising, and television, the United States has spread its particular form of the American Dream to millions around the world. Already in 1923, the *New York Morning Post* noted that "the film is to America

what the flag was once to Britain. By its means Uncle Sam may hope some day . . . to Americanize the world."[4] In movies, television, and popular music, the impact of American popular culture on the Western world is obvious.

Movies and television were the chief vehicles for the spread of American popular culture in the years after World War II. American movies continued to dominate both European and American markets in the next decades. Many American movies make more money in worldwide distribution than they do in the United States. Kevin Costner's *Waterworld* is but one example of this pattern.

Although developed in the 1930s, television did not become readily available until the late 1940s. By 1954, there were thirty-two million television sets in the United States as television became the centerpiece of middle-class life. In the 1960s, as television spread around the world, U.S. networks unloaded their products on Europe and the non-Western world at very low prices. *Baywatch* was the most popular show in Italy in 1996.

The United States has also dominated popular music since the end of World War II. Jazz, blues, rhythm and blues, rap, and rock and roll have been by far the most popular music forms in the Western world—and in much of the non-Western world—during this time. All

---

MORE ABOUT . . . *Rap Music*

One of the most influential trends in modern music has been the popularity of rap music. Rap began in the 1960s by jailed black inmates who would pound out a beat while reciting free flowing, angry poetry, often aimed at white society. By the 1970s New York's inner-city clubs began playing music from alternating turntables, sometimes "scratching" the records, while the M.C. (master of ceremony) rapped out to the audience. Originally an expression of black anger and frustration, by the 1990s rap artists toned down their music for mass consumption with the result that rap's largest audience became the white society it had once condemned.

ASSESS

You can choose from a variety of assessments to evaluate your students' mastery of the objectives for this section as stated on page 1001. Possible assessments include:

1. Section Review Questions on this page
2. Section 30–4 Quiz in your Teachers Resource materials
3. Reteaching Worksheets in your Teachers Resource materials
4. Self-Study software

ALTERNATIVE ASSESSMENT

Assign students to draw a picture of a room in their home and to label each item in that room that represents a technological advancement that has taken place in the past thirty years. Have them write an explanation of how these advancements have improved the quality of their lives and at the same time made their lives more complicated.

Answers to SECTION REVIEW

1. (a) a belief that humans are alone in the universe with no future or hope
2. (a) Irish writer of *Waiting of Godot*
   (b) developed existentialist philosophy with Satre
   (c) a leading French existentialist
   (d) A Protestant thinker on religious insights of the Reformation
   (e) American physicist, led scientific team in creating atomic bomb
   (f) a British economist, warned about dangers to the environment

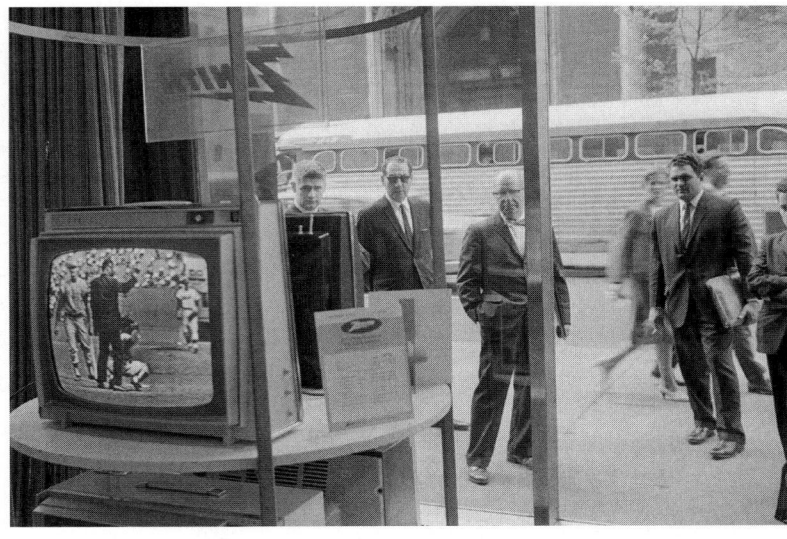

► *These New York businessmen take a moment to check on the New York Mets baseball game against the Philadelphia Phillies in May, 1963. The Mets won the game 3–2, but that year the Los Angeles Dodgers went on to win the World Series against the New York Yankees.*

of these music forms began in the United States, and all are rooted in African American musical forms. American popular music later spread to the rest of the world, inspiring local artists who then transformed the music in their own way. For example, through the 1950s, American figures such as Chuck Berry and Elvis Presley inspired the Beatles and other British performers. The Beatles in turn led an "invasion" of the United States in the 1960s, sparking new American rockers.

In the postwar years, sports have become a major product of both popular culture and the leisure industry. Through television, sports became a worldwide phenomenon. Olympic games could now be broadcast across the globe from anywhere in the world. The World Cup soccer championship is the most-watched event on television. Sports became an inexpensive form of entertainment for consumers, as fans did not have to leave their homes to enjoy sporting events. In fact, some sports organizations at first resisted television because they feared that it would hurt ticket sales. Enormous revenues from television contracts, however, helped change their minds. Many sports organizations came to receive most of their yearly revenues from television contracts.

SECTION REVIEW

1. **Define:**
   (a) existentialism

2. **Identify:**
   (a) Samuel Beckett, (b) Albert Camus,
   (c) Jean-Paul Sartre, (d) Karl Barth,
   (e) J. Robert Oppenheimer, (f) E. F. Schumacher

3. **Recall:**
   (a) What was Theater of the Absurd intended to force the audience to do?
   (b) What action did Vatican Council II take to make Catholic religious services more appealing to many people?
   (c) What inventions were created during World War II that also changed people's lives after the war?
   (d) What event caused John F. Kennedy to set a goal of landing an American on the moon before 1970?
   (e) What did the *New York Morning Post* mean when it printed "the film is to America what the flag was once to Britain"?

SPECIAL NEEDS: *Visual/Auditory*

Create together with students an outline of the section "Popular Culture." Main headings should be 1) Movies and television, 2) popular music and 3) sports. This can be done using the overhead projector or chalkboard. Create discussion as to what trends students think will occur over the next several years in each category. Examples could be the Latin influence on music, and the emergence of soccer in the United States while American football is catching on in Europe. How has the media helped the borders of the world collapse where entertainment and culture are concerned? This is an excellent activity to foster critical thinking and synthesis skills for hard-to-motivate students.

4. Think Critically:
(*a*) Why was the United States able to lead the world in technological advancements after World War II?
(*b*) What facts support the idea that the television has become the "centerpiece of the middle-class life"?

Conclusion

By the end of the 1980s and the beginning of the 1990s, profound changes in the Soviet Union had brought an end to the Cold War. Mikhail Gorbachev began a new Soviet policy in which there would be no military intervention to prop up Communist regimes elsewhere. As a result, revolutions against Communist governments broke out in almost all the Eastern European satellite states at the end of 1989. Quite unexpectedly, the forces of change that had enabled Communist regimes in Eastern Europe to collapse also spread to the Soviet Union and led to its demise as well. The Soviet Union soon broke up into a number of independent states.

After 1970, the nations of Western Europe and North America faced economic challenges stemming from a dramatic increase in the price of oil in the 1970s. They also faced problems unique to each country. Great Britain, for example, had its crisis in Northern Ireland. Germany had problems connected with reunification. Canada had its problems with the desire of French Quebec to separate from the Canadian union.

A number of social and cultural developments have accompanied the political and economic changes since 1970. A women's liberation movement tried to provide new opportunities for women to achieve equality with men. Concerns about planetary pollution gave rise to environmental movements and even new political parties (the Green parties). Terrorist groups used violence to reach their goals. The United States has continued to dominate Western culture in both the arts and popular culture. Through movies and television programs, American popular culture has, in fact, spread to the rest of the world.

Western societies have also been participants in an era of rapidly changing international relationships. Between 1947 and 1962, virtually every colony of European states achieved independence and attained statehood. This process was not easy. However, as we shall see in the next three chapters, it created a new world as the non-Western states put an end to the long-held ascendancy of the Western nations.

Notes

1. Quoted in Hilda Scott, *Sweden's "Right to Be Human"—Sex-Role Equality: The Goal and the Reality* (London, 1982), p. 125.
2. Quoted in Marsha Rowe et al., *Spare Rib Reader* (Harmondsworth, 1982), p. 574.
3. Quoted in Henry Grosshans, *The Search for Modern Europe* (Boson, 1970), p. 421.
4. Quoted in Richard Maltby, ed., *Passing Parade: A History of Popular Culture in the Twentieth Century* (New York, 1989), p. 8.

ENRICHMENT ACTIVITY

Have students prepare a montage, or collection of pictures from around the world that demonstrate how American popular culture has made an impact on other civilizations. What aspects of American popular culture, in particular, seem to stand out? Why?

3. (a) make people think about what is happening now instead of wondering what will happen next
(b) allowed masses to be conducted in vernacular
(c) jet airplanes, computers, radar, rockets
(d) orbit of Soviet Union's Sputnik I around Earth
(e) had power to Americanize the world
4. (a) had money for research and development
(b) amount of time people spend watching

CLOSE

Lead students in a discussion of the Focus objectives identified on page 1001. Emphasize the importance of technological advancements on the lives of all people in the world.

SPANISH SUPPORT

The *Conclusion* has been translated into Spanish for your Spanish-speaking students. Included with this translation (in your Teacher Resource Box) are Section Key Points, which consist of one or two sentences summarizing each section in the chapter. These Key Points have also been translated into Spanish.

TIME LINE

As students conclude the chapter, you may want to refer them to the chapter time line in the *Study Guide*. The time line will help them put key dates in perspective. Supporting questions and activities are also provided.

Answers to CHAPTER REVIEW 30

USING KEY TERMS

1. extentialism
2. dissidents
3. women's liberation movement
4. stagflation
5. Brezhnev doctrine
6. détente
7. environmentalism
8. glasnost
9. supply-side economics
10. counterterrorism
11. perestroika
12. Thatcherism

REVIEWING THE FACTS

1. In the late 1960s attempts had been made in several east European nations to break away from communism and Soviet domination.
2. The Western powers recognized borders in Eastern Europe in exchange for a Soviet promise to respect human rights.
3. Solidarity was a labor union in the Polish shipyards that led the fight for greater rights and eventually the effort to bring down the Polish Communist government.
4. The fighting in Bosnia was at least partially stopped as a result of the Dayton Accords.
5. Richard Nixon began the process of reopening relations when he visited China in 1972.
6. OPEC produces most of the oil that is traded internationally and was able to control the price of crude oil during the 1970s and 1980s.
7. A nuclear accident at Chernobyl sent a radioactive cloud over much of the Soviet Union and Europe.
8. Iraq, Iran, Syria, and Libya are among the nations that have been accused of using state-sponsored terrorism.
9. Schumacher warned that uncontrolled development was likely to cause irreparable damage to the environment.

USING KEY TERMS

1. _____ is the philosophical belief that humans are utterly alone in the universe.
2. People who protest against an existing power structure are called _____.
3. The _____ is a force that is working for greater equality and rights for women.
4. An economic condition that combines high rates of inflation and unemployment is called _____.
5. The _____ asserted that the Soviet Union had the right to intervene in any state where Communist power was threatened.
6. _____ is the period marked by a reduction of tensions between the U.S. and Russia.
7. Efforts to support the protection and preservation of the world's environment have been called _____.
8. _____ is a Russian term used to describe the open discussion of Russia's government and economic systems.
9. The theory that economic growth can be achieved through lowering tax rates to encourage greater production is called _____.
10. _____ is the organized effort to thwart the work of terrorist groups.
11. The restructuring of the Soviet economy in the late 1980s to allow limited free enterprise and greater use of the market is called _____.
12. Efforts of the British government to fight inflation during the 1980s were called _____.

REVIEWING THE FACTS

1. What caused the leaders of the Soviet Union to establish the Brezhnev doctrine?
2. What compromise was reached between the Soviet Union and Western powers through the Helsinki Agreements?
3. What was the Solidarity organization and how did it help achieve independence for Poland?

1010

4. What conflict was stopped, although not entirely settled, by the Dayton Accords?
5. What American president reopened relations between the United States and China?
6. Why was the Organization of Petroleum Exporting Countries an important force in world economics, particularly in the 1970s and 1980s?
7. What happened at Chernobyl that increased support for the anti-nuclear movement?
8. What nations have been accused of using state-sponsored terrorism to achieve their goals?
9. What warning did E. F. Schumacher make about the impact of development on the environment?

THINKING CRITICALLY

1. Why does the military might of the former Soviet Union still represent a threat to global survival?
2. Why is any complex system that is centrally controlled likely to suffer from a difficulty in changing or adjusting to new circumstances?
3. Why couldn't the leaders of East Germany reasonably expect much support from the Soviet Union in the late 1980s?
4. What problems did nations in Eastern Europe experience when they converted their economies from government ownership and control to market economies with private business ownership?
5. Why has the return of many industries to private ownership in Western Europe resulted in widespread dissatisfaction among workers and labor organizations?
6. What reasons could explain why the former leaders of communist governments in Eastern Europe apparently had little or no regard for the environmental impact of their policies?
7. Why are women demanding and to an extent achieving, a greater voice in the political and economic systems of Europe?

THINKING CRITICALLY

1. Although the Soviet Union has been broken into many smaller and weaker nations the weapons it once had, to a large extent, still exist and could be used to start wars.
2. Any system that relies on a limited number of people to make important decisions will experience bureaucratic problems and an inability to change quickly.
3. By the late 1980s the Soviet Union was experiencing such internal turmoil that it could not help Communist governments in other parts of the world.

4. Answers will vary but may concern the lack of experience people in formerly communist nations had in running private businesses.
5. The privatization of industries in Western Europe has resulted in layoffs and reduced benefits for many workers.
6. These people tended to measure their success in terms of their ability to maintain power and produce products. They had little to gain by protecting the environment.
7. Answers will vary but may involve the facts that a greater number of women are alive and better educated and have an increased amount of wealth

APPLYING SOCIAL STUDIES SKILLS

1. **Psychology:** After the Soviet Union fell, Russian soldiers who had lived in Eastern Europe were expected to return to their homeland. Some went, while others refused to go. Why did soldiers from both of these groups experience severe psychological and emotional problems in adjusting to their new living situations?
2. **Economics:** What historical reasons might there be for Germany, Poland, the Czech Republic, and Hungary having been relatively successful in converting their economic systems to capitalism while Romania, Bulgaria, Serbia, and Albania have been much less successful?
3. **Government:** Why is it difficult to exclude former communist leaders from the new governments in Eastern Europe?
4. **Sociology:** Make a list of the social problems that need to be solved to create a lasting peace in the former Yugoslavia. Why is it impossible for the United States or any other power to impose peace on these people?

MAKING TIME AND PLACE CONNECTIONS

1. The unemployment rate in the United States was 5.2 percent in the spring of 1997. At the same time, it was over 10 percent in many western European nations. Why were the Europeans willing to tolerate such high rates? What is likely to happen to these nations if high unemployment rates persist for many years?
2. Some people believe that the nuclear disaster at Chernobyl was also a political disaster for the leaders of the Soviet Union. It showed that they were not in control of their economy or its nuclear facilities, and it cost the nation many billions of rubles. If this is true, why was the nuclear leak at Three Mile Island in Pennsylvania less of a political problem for U.S. leaders?
3. Compare the role of women in Western society in the past decade with their role before World War II. Identify and explain several important events that have contributed to these changes.

BECOMING AN HISTORIAN

1. **Making Hypotheses and Predicting Outcomes:** The North Atlantic Treaty Organization has considered inviting some nations in Eastern Europe to join their organization. Russia's leaders have strongly opposed this idea. If these nations do join NATO how might Russia react? Form and explain a hypothesis of what you think might happen.
2. **Time Lines:** Create a time line of events that contributed to the decline and fall of communism in Eastern Europe and the former Soviet Union. Identify how these events were related to policies of the United States and other Western powers.
3. **Economics as a Key to History:** The table below shows the percent of national income allocated to military spending by the United States and the Soviet Union during the 1980s. At this time the value of production in the United States was roughly twice that of the Soviet Union. Study the data and use it to explain why the Soviet Union found it difficult to maintain its position in the arms race and provide sufficient consumer goods.

Military Spending of the U.S. & U.S.S.R. as a Percent of Production

Year	U.S.	U.S.S.R.
1980	5.3%	12.9%
1982	5.7%	12.9%
1984	5.6%	12.8%
1986	5.4%	12.6%
1988	5.0%	11.9%

1011

MAKING TIME AND PLACE CONNECTIONS

1. Answers will vary; should involve and more extensive social services available to unemployed people in most European nations than those that are available for people in the United States. However, these benefits cost money, and if they are paid in large quantities over extended periods of time they are likely to create large debts, higher taxes, and reduced rates of economic growth.
2. Answers will vary but should put these disasters into an economic and political context. The U.S. has the ability and will to impose higher standards on nuclear facilities. For the most part this was not the case in the Soviet Union. This reflected badly on their leadership.
3. Answers will vary but should be based on the technical, social, political, and economic changes that have taken place since World War II that led to women's changing roles in society.

ON BECOMING AN HISTORIAN

1. Answers will vary; likely to involve a greater Russian feeling of being threatened if nations in Eastern Europe join NATO.
2. Time lines will vary but should include events that took place in the Soviet Union during the 1980s.
3. Answers will vary; should point out that the Soviet Union's choice to allocate a larger part of its smaller production to military spending prevented it from being able to produce sufficient quantities of consumer goods; keeping up with the military expenditures of the U.S. contributed to a dissatisfaction with the Communist leadership, helped bring end to communism.

APPLYING SOCIAL STUDIES SKILLS

1. When people are given a little freedom they are likely to use that freedom to try to achieve more. It is possible that Gorbachev's policy of encouraging people to discuss problems in the Soviet system led them to do more than talk about their problems.
2. Answers will vary but should discuss the fact that these soldiers had been in control of the places where they lived. After the fall of the Soviet Union they were no longer in charge regardless of whether they returned to Russia or stayed in lands they once occupied.
3. The nations in the northern part of East Europe had a history of enjoying at least a degree of self-rule and control of their own businesses. Those in the South had been dominated by the Ottoman Empire and had little history of self determination or economic freedom.
4. Former communist leaders are likely to be the most politically able people, they may have material wealth to use, they are used to cooperating with each other, and, in many cases, are difficult to identify.
5. Answers may include differences in religion and language, historical enmities, and feelings of racial or ethnic pride.

PLANNING GUIDE

SECTION	KEY TOPICS	PRIMARY SOURCES	ASSESSMENT
1 Latin America Since 1945: General Trends pages 1013–1020	◆ Economic and political developments in Latin America ◆ Changes in society in Latin America ◆ The role of the Catholic Church in Latin America ◆ Relations between the United States and Latin America		◆ Section Review, page 1020 ◆ Section Quiz 31–1, TRB
2 The Caribbean Basin: Revolution and Economic Change pages 1020–1028	◆ Developments in Mexico ◆ The Cuban Revolution ◆ Upheavals in Central America	◆ A selection from a account of events by a Mexican student National Strike Council, page 1022 ◆ A selection from a 1953 speech by Fidel Castro, page 1024	◆ Section Review, page 1028 ◆ Section Quiz 31–2, TRB
3 The Nations of South America: Nationalism, Marxism, and the Military pages 1028–1035	◆ Developments in Argentina ◆ Changes in Brazil ◆ Challenges in Chile ◆ Instability in Colombia and Peru		◆ Section Review, page 1035 ◆ Section Quiz 31–3, TRB
4 Culture in Latin America Since 1945 pages 1035–1039	◆ Education in Latin America ◆ Culture in Latin America	◆ A poem by Gabriela Mistral, page 1037	◆ Section Review, page 1039 ◆ Section Quiz 31–4, TRB

REPRODUCIBLE ACTIVITIES

- Historical Maps
- Charts and Graphs
- Critical Thinking
- Cooperative Learning
- Vocabulary
- Guided Reading
- Reteaching
- Enrichment
- Performance Assessment
- Spanish Key Points and Chapter Summaries
- Spanish Vocabulary
- Spanish Guided Reading

MULTIMEDIA SUPPORT

TRANSPARENCIES
- *World History* Color Transparency Package
- Fine Art Color Transparency Package

VIDEO
- *World History* Video Library
- **CNN.** Annual Video Update

LASERDISC
- *Sights and Sounds of History*

AUDIO
- *Listening to Literature* audiotape (English and Spanish)
- *History of Music* CD

SOFTWARE
- WESTEST™
- Student Review

CD–ROM
- *The Journey of Civilization*
- *World History*

INTERNET
- Internet Activities

On Line with WORLD HISTORY

Access West's history web site at
http://history.swpco.com
You'll find activities and web sites related to specific topics and chapters in *World History: The Human Odyssey*. Also look for references to helpful web sites at appropriate places throughout this teacher edition.

LESSON PLANNING

You will find detailed daily lesson plans for both traditional class scheduling and **block scheduling** in your Teacher Resource Box.

Not Enough Time?

If you do not have the four or five days recommended to teach this chapter, you may want to focus on the following sections and activities:

- Have students skim the chapter to answer the "Questions to Guide Your Reading" on page 1013. Discuss their answers, then read the "Conclusion" on page 1039.
- Do a more in-depth reading of economic and political developments in Latin America on pages 1013–1015, the Cuban revolution on pages 1022–1025, and nationalism in Brazil and Argentina on pages 1028–1032. Conclude with a discussion of trends in Latin American culture.

CONFLICT AND CHALLENGE

BUILDING ON CHAPTER 30

To prepare students to study Chapter 31 you may use the following questions and activities.

◆ Ask students to review major international events of the Cold War. Ask them how these events could represent opportunities for Latin American states.

◆ Ask students to discuss how the decline of Communism might have affected Latin American states.

◆ Assign students to list ways in which scientific developments might have impacted Latin American states in recent years.

◆ Ask students to explain how social unrest that took place in Europe and North America in the 1960s and 1970s would be likely to impact society in Latin America.

USING THE OPENING STORY

Depending on the ability levels of your students, select from the following questions and activities to reinforce the reading of the opening story.

◆ What other public figures have been sent to jail only to emerge later as national leaders?

◆ How might nations in Latin America have benefited from the competition between the United States and the Soviet Union?

On July 26, 1953, two brothers, Fidel and Raúl Castro, led a band of 165 young people in an attack on an army camp at Moncada, near Santiago de Cuba. While a law student at the University of Havana, Fidel Castro had become a revolutionary. He was determined to overthrow the government of Fulgencio Batista, the dictator of Cuba. The attack on Moncada, however, was a disaster. Many of the troops led by the Castro brothers were killed, wounded, or arrested. Fidel and Raúl Castro escaped but were later captured and sent to prison with a sentence of fifteen years. The Castro brothers were lucky. They could easily have died in a prison where political prisoners were routinely tortured. Instead, they were released after eleven months. By freeing political prisoners, Batista hoped to win the favor of the Cuban people. He certainly did not gain the favor of the Castros, however. After his release, Fidel Castro fled to Mexico and built a new revolutionary army. Six years later, on January 1, 1959, Fidel Castro and his forces finally seized control of Cuba. Hundreds of thousands of Cubans swept into the streets, overcome with joy. One person remarked, "We were walking on a

cloud." To the many Latin Americans who wanted major social and economic changes, Castro soon became a powerful model and source of hope.

Since 1945, the nations of Latin America have followed different paths of change. Many have relied on military dictators to maintain political stability while undergoing economic change. A few, like Cuba, used Marxist revolutions to create a new political, economic, and social order. Many Latin American nations have struggled to build democratic systems, especially since the late 1980s.

The Cold War also had an impact on Latin America. The two superpowers—the United States and the Soviet Union—carried on their conflicts there as well as in the rest of the world. In the process, many Latin American nations became dependent on American loans and subsidies. A few came to depend on financial support from the Soviet Union. However, the nations of Latin America also sought to free themselves from dependence on other nations, although it was not easy to do so.

◄ On January 1, 1959, Fidel Castro and his band of revolutionary followers successfully overthrew the government of Cuban dictator Fulgencio Batista. This photo of Castro was taken at one of his hidden bases in 1957.

ADDITIONAL RESOURCES

The resources listed below can be used to enrich the lessons in this chapter.

BOOKS FOR STUDENTS
The Cuban Revolution by Robert Golston, Bobbs-Merrill
Central America: Opposing Viewpoints, Ed. by David L. Bender & Bruno Leone (Series Editors) Greenhaven Press
The Cuban Missile Crisis by Fred Cook, Franklin Watts

VIDEOS/FILMS
Latin American Overview (Contemporary Films) Social Studies School Service (800) 421-4246
Latin America in Transition (Southern Center for International Studies) Social Studies School Service (800) 421-4246
Women in Latin America (Upper Midwest Women's History Center) Social Studies School Service (800) 421-4246

IN LATIN AMERICA

(1945 TO PRESENT)

THE WORLD SINCE 1945

QUESTIONS TO GUIDE YOUR READING

1. What economic and political changes did Latin America experience after 1945?

2. How did the roles of women and the Catholic Church change in Latin America after 1945?

3. What problems did Mexico and the nations of Central America face after 1945?

4. What were the chief features and impact of the Cuban Revolution?

5. What role have the military and wealthy elites played in the history of Argentina, Brazil, Chile, Colombia, and Peru since 1945?

6. What have been the major educational and cultural trends in Latin America since 1945?

LATIN AMERICA SINCE 1945: GENERAL TRENDS

Latin America contains many nations with very different outlooks and ways of life. Despite the differences, however, some general economic, political, social, and religious trends have been noticeable throughout this region of the world since 1945.

Economic and Political Developments

As we saw in Chapter 27, the Great Depression of the 1930s forced many Latin American countries to move to a modern economic structure. From the nineteenth century to the 1930s, Latin Americans had been dependent on an export-import economy. In other words, they had exported raw materials, especially minerals and foodstuffs, while buying the manufactured goods of the industrialized countries, particularly Europe and the United States. As a result of the Great Depression, however, the exports from Latin America

1013

FOCUS ON THEMES

Listed below are brief summaries of how the content in this chapter supports the text's key themes.

Economics and History Latin American nations have struggled with the shift from an export-import economy to a more modern economy based on industrial development. Failure to achieve economic stability often led to military takeovers and military regimes. However, the failure of these regimes to establish economic stability has led, beginning in the 1980s, to a movement toward democracy.

Social Life In Latin America, the gap between the rich and the poor is enormous. Landholding and urban elites control huge estates and businesses. This gulf adds to the political and economic instability of many Latin American countries.

The Importance of Cultural Developments Latin America has a large number of outstanding writers. Gabriela Mistral, Jorge Luis Borges, Mario Vargas Llosa, Gabriel García Márquez, and Pablo Neruda have al! won the Nobel Prize for literature.

Religion in History The Catholic Church has continued to play an important role in Latin America. In the 1960s, some members of the church espoused a theology of liberation, or a belief in the need to fight to help the oppressed. In the 1970s and 1980s, the Catholic Church became an important voice for human rights against authoritarian regimes.

The Role of Individuals Among the individuals who have played significant roles in Latin American history since 1945 are Fidel Castro in Cuba, Juan and Eva Perón in Argentina, and Salvador Allende in Chile.

The Environment and History Industrial development in some Latin American countries has led to concern. Environmentalists around the world have mounted considerable opposition to cutting down rain forests in the Amazon region to open up new farmland.

FOCUS

OBJECTIVES

After completing this section, students should be able to

1. describe recent economic and political developments in Latin America
2. identify and explain recent changes in Latin American society
3. describe the role of the Catholic Church in Latin America
4. describe relations between the United States and Latin America in recent years

FOCUS ACTIVITY

Help students understand the relationship between economic difficulties and political change. Remind them that virtually every revolution in nineteenth century Europe was preceded by economic problems. Assign students to review and report on the causes of the revolutions between 1815 and 1848. Identify, worldwide economic problems that Latin American states had to deal with in relation to political change there.

were cut in half. Thus, the revenues that had been used to buy manufactured goods declined. The decline in revenues led many Latin American countries to develop new industries that now made the goods they previously had imported. This process of industrial development was known as **import-substituting industrialization (ISI).**

Import-substituting industrialization was supposed to achieve greater economic independence for Latin America. By the 1960s, however, this process had begun to fail. Latin American countries were still dependent on the United States, Europe, and now Japan, especially for the advanced technology needed for modern industries. Moreover, because of the great poverty in many Latin American countries, many peo-

ple could not buy the products of their own industries. Then, too, many Latin American countries often failed to find markets abroad for their products.

The failure of import-substituting industrialization led to instability and a new reliance on military regimes. These military governments sought to curb the power of the new industrial middle class and working class—classes that had increased in size and power as a result of industrialization. Beginning in the 1960s, almost all economically advanced Latin American countries experienced domestic wars and military despotism. Repressive military regimes in Chile, Brazil, and Argentina abolished political parties.

These military regimes often returned to export-import economies financed by foreigners. They also

▼ *Argentina was one of the Latin American nations that developed a strong industrial base. The Ducilo rayon plant in Berazategui made use of modern technology, as shown in this view of a spinning bay. The company also produced cellophane and nylon.*

CNN. WORLD HISTORY UPDATES

You can update your coverage of World History topics, as well as spark lively classroom discussion and deeper understanding, by using the **CNN World History Updates.**

For assistance in using and incorporating the **CNN World History Updates** into your classroom presentations, see the *Classroom Guide.*

encouraged **multinational corporations** (companies that had divisions in more than two countries) to come into their countries. Those companies that did so wanted chiefly to take advantage of Latin America's raw materials and large supply of inexpensive labor. This, of course, made Latin America even more dependent on the industrially developed nations.

As their economies began to fail in the 1970s, Latin American regimes reacted by borrowing from abroad, especially from banks in Europe and the United States. Between 1970 and 1982, debt to foreigners grew from $27 billion to $315.3 billion. By 1982, a number of governments said that they could no longer pay interest on their debts to foreign banks. Their economies began to crumble. Wages fell, and unemployment and inflation skyrocketed.

To get new loans, Latin American governments were now forced to make basic reforms. Many came to believe that government had taken control of too many industries. Too fast a pace for industrialization had led to the decline of the economy in the countryside as well. Many hoped that encouraging peasants to grow food for home consumption rather than export would stop the flow of people from the countryside to the cities. At the same time, they believed that more people could now buy the products from Latin American industries.

With the debt crisis in the 1980s came a movement toward democracy. Some military leaders were simply unwilling to deal with the monstrous debt problems. At the same time, many people realized that military power without popular consent could not maintain a strong state. Then, too, there was a swelling of popular support for basic rights, as well as for free and fair elections.

The movement toward democracy was the most noticeable trend of the 1980s and early 1990s in Latin America. In the mid-1970s, only Colombia, Venezuela, and Costa Rica had democratic governments. In the mid-1980s, democratic regimes were everywhere except Cuba, some of the Central American states, Chile, and Paraguay. This revival of democracy, however, is fragile. In 1992, for example, President Alberto Fujimori (FOO-ji-MORE-ee) undermined democracy and returned Peru to an authoritarian system (see "Peru" later in the chapter).

Society in Latin America

Latin America's economic problems were made worse by a dramatic growth in the population. Both Latin America and North America (the United States and Canada) had the same population in 1950—about 165 million people. By the mid-1980s, however, Latin America's population had exploded to 400 million. That of North America was about 270 million. Both a decline in death rates and an increase in birth rates in Latin America led to this population explosion.

With the increase in population came a rapid rise in the number and size of cities. In 1930, only one Latin American city had more than one million people. By 1990, there were twenty-nine cities with over a million people, including Mexico City, with sixteen million inhabitants, and Buenos Aires, with eight million. By the 1980s, one-half of Latin America's population lived in cities of over twenty thousand people.

Cities grew in large part because peasants fled their rural poverty to seek a better life. Rarely did they find it, however. Population growth far outstripped economic growth, and millions were left without jobs. Cities could not cope with the needs of the people, and slums, or shantytowns, became part of virtually every Latin American city (see "Young People in Latin America: The Street Kids").

The gap between the poor and the rich had always been enormous in Latin America. It remained so after 1945. Landholding and urban elites still owned huge estates and businesses. These elites were largely descendants of the Europeans who had colonized Latin America centuries before. A small but growing middle class consisted of businesspeople and office and government workers. Peasants and the urban poor, struggling just to survive, became more vocal. The peasants called for reforms that would give them more land. Urban workers joined trade unions and demanded better wages and better working conditions.

The enormous gulf between rich and poor often undermined the stability of Latin American countries. So, too, did the international drug trade. Latin America's northern neighbor, the United States, was one of the world's largest consumers of drugs. Eighty percent of the cocaine and 90 percent of the marijuana used in

▶ *This photo of a favela, or shantytown, documents the misery of Brazil's urban poor. Why do you think the government has not done more to alleviate the housing and health problems of its poverty-stricken people?*

the United States came from Latin America. Bolivia, Peru, and Colombia were especially big producers. Peasants in these countries found that the growing of coca leaves and marijuana plants, from which these drugs were produced, was an important part of their economic survival.

Drug traffickers in Colombia became especially wealthy. Their leaders formed **drug cartels** (groups of drug businesses whose purpose is to eliminate competition) that bribed and intimidated government officials and police officers into protecting their activities. The United States has long sought to work with the governments of Colombia, Bolivia, and Peru to lessen the problem of drug cartels. It has had little success, however. Even when one large cartel is broken up, new ones emerge to continue the business.

The roles of women, too, have changed in Latin American society. Throughout much of Latin American history, women were expected only to be homemakers for their husbands and children. This role continues for many millions of Latin American women.

However, women have also moved into new kinds of jobs. In addition to doing farm labor, lower-class women have found jobs in industry, especially in textile mills. Women, however, are frequently paid less than men in these jobs. Women from the middle and upper classes have found even greater opportunities, and have become teachers, professors, dentists, doctors, and lawyers.

As in many other areas of the world, women have usually not played important roles in the political life of Latin America. Most countries in Latin America did not grant women the right to vote until the 1930s and 1940s. In some countries, such as Mexico and Argentina, women entered the political arena by taking part in demonstrations. In the Cuban and Nicaraguan Revolutions (see later in the chapter), women played an active role. Nevertheless, even now, only 2 or 3 percent of important political posts are held by women. The first female president in Latin America was Isabel Perón, but she came to office as a result of her husband's death.

RECOMMENDED READING

For general surveys of Latin American history, see E. B. Burns, *Latin America: A Concise Interpretive Survey,* 4th ed. (Englewood Cliffs, N.J., 1986); and E. Williamson, *The Penguin History of Latin America* (London, 1992). The twentieth century is the focus of T. E. Skidmore and P. H. Smith, *Modern Latin America,* 3d ed. (New York, 1992). On the role of the military, see A. Rouquié, *The Military and the State in Latin America* (Berkeley, Calif., 1987). Recent United States-Latin American relations are examined in B. Wood, *The Dismantling of the Good Neighbor Policy* (Austin, Tex., 1985).

YOUNG PEOPLE IN LATIN AMERICA

The Street Kids

According to the United Nations, there are 100 million young people living on the streets of the world's cities. Probably half of them live in Latin America. High birth rates have left large numbers of young people living in the shanty-towns that surround Latin America's cities. Many of these young people—from families often torn by poverty, alcoholism, and despair—flee their slum homes and become street kids, or *meninos de rua* (muh-NEEN-yose day ROO-uh).

Those who live on the streets survive as best they can. They work by shining shoes, washing windshields, selling gum, and collecting cardboard. Some beg. Others pick pockets and steal purses and goods. Some work in gangs and are recruited by drug dealers to be couriers. Some kids even kill.

Meninos de rua have been on the streets of Brazil for decades. Beginning in the early 1990s, however, these children were increasingly blamed for rising crime rates. Death squads, often made up of police officers who seek extra work because of their low salaries, have begun to kill the street kids in ever larger numbers. According to a Brazilian congressional investigation, 4,611 children were murdered in Brazil between 1992 and 1995. The investigation also revealed that at least 180 death squads are at work in Rio de Janeiro alone. These death squads, often hired by businesspeople who

◄ *Street kids like these suffer from disease, hunger, exposure, and lack even the most basic amenities associated with family life.*

worry about trade, are supposed to "clean up" commercial districts.

Some people welcome the killings. One Brazilian said of the street kids, "Everyone is making them out to be heroes, but they were not sweet flowers." Another said, "Many of these 13-year-old kids have killed. They deserve to die."

Others are alarmed at the killings. Private groups, many of them run by churches, have organized aid societies. They try to provide jobs, housing, and education for street kids. Their funds are limited, however, and government promises to provide more money for the street kids have usually turned out to be just promises.

1. Why are so many young people living on the streets of Latin America?

2. What dangers do street kids face?

3. How would you solve this enormous social problem?

YOUNG PEOPLE IN LATIN AMERICA

COMPARING TIME PERIODS

Review the description of children in middle class Britain in Chapter 22 on pages 702–703 of the textbook. Ask students how their lives were different from the lives of children described in this feature. Would the lives of lower class British children have been more similar to these children's lives?

Answers to Critical Thinking Questions

1. High birth rates have driven many young people to the streets. Poverty and alcoholism contribute to the problem.
2. Street kids face the dangers of the streets—crime, abuse, starvation—as well as "death squads," or groups that have been hired to kill street kids to clean up the streets.
3. Answers will vary.

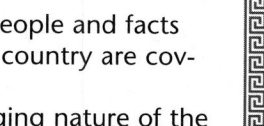

On Line with WORLD HISTORY Internet Activity

You may want to have your students visit the following URL, where they will find information and additional web site resources to enhance their study of this chapter.

Argentina

http://www.middlebury.edu/~leparc/htm/argent2.htm

Geography, culture, people and facts about the history of this country are covered here.

Due to the ever-changing nature of the World Wide Web, see the West History web site, **http://history.swpco.com** for regular updates of the URLs in this text.

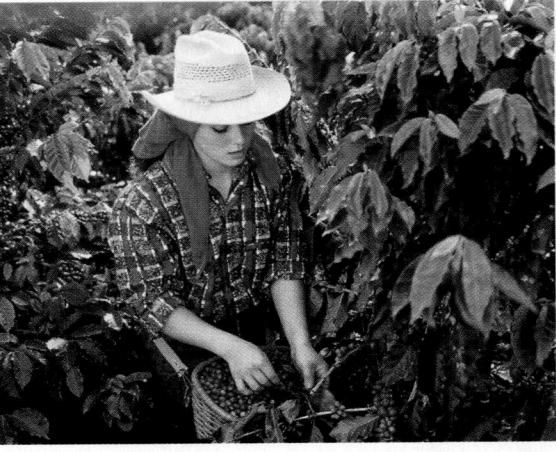

▲ *Working women often find employment in the fields, just as their ancestors did. Here a Colombian woman picks coffee beans. Who do you think will profit most from this crop?*

The Role of the Catholic Church

The Catholic Church had been a powerful force in Latin America for centuries. However, its hold over people declined as cities and industrial societies grew. By the beginning of the twentieth century, most Latin American governments had separated church and state. Nevertheless, the church remained a powerful social and cultural force.

Eventually, the Catholic Church pursued a middle way for Latin American society. It called for a moderate capitalist system that respected workers' rights, brought about land reform, and provided for the welfare of the poor. This policy led to the formation of Christian Democratic parties that had some successes in the 1960s and 1970s.

In the 1960s, however, some Catholics in Latin America took a more radical path to change. Influenced by Marxist ideas, they called for a **theology of liberation.** Supporters of liberation theology believed that Christians must fight to free the oppressed, even if it meant the use of violence. Some members of the Catholic clergy even teamed up with Marxist guerrillas in rural areas. Other radical priests worked in factories

CONNECTIONS
AROUND THE WORLD

International Women's Conferences   As women around the world organized movements to change the conditions of their lives, an international women's movement emerged. Especially in the 1970s, much attention was paid to a series of international conferences on women's issues. Between 1975 and 1985, the United Nations celebrated the Decade for Women by holding conferences in such cities as Mexico City, Copenhagen, and Nairobi. These meetings made it clear how women in both developed and developing nations were organizing to make people aware of women's issues.

The conferences also made clear the differences between women from Western and non-Western countries. While women from Western countries spoke about political, economic, cultural, and sexual rights, women from developing countries in Latin America, Africa, and Asia focused their attention on bringing an end to the violence, hunger, and disease that haunt their lives. At the International Women's Year Tribunal in Mexico in 1974, sponsored by the United Nations, Dimitila Barrios de Chungara, a miner's wife from Bolivia, expressed her lack of patience with professional women at the conference. She said, "So, I went up and spoke. I made them see that they don't live in our world. I made them see that in Bolivia human rights aren't respected. . . Women like us, housewives, who get organized to better our people well, they [the Bolivian police] beat us up and persecute us."

alongside workers or carried on social work among the poor in the slums. Liberation theology attracted much attention, but most church leaders rejected it.

In the 1970s and 1980s, the Catholic Church continued to play a significant role in Latin America by becoming an important voice for human rights against authoritarian regimes. Priests, nuns, and archbishops spoke out against injustice and crimes of the military regimes. To speak out was dangerous. Military regimes did not hesitate to murder members of the Catholic clergy. For example, Archbishop Oscar Romero was a fierce critic of El Salvador's military regime. On March 30, 1980, right-wing assassins murdered him while he was saying mass in a hospital chapel.

The United States and Latin America

The United States has always played a large role in Latin America. For years, the United States had sent troops into Latin American countries to protect U.S. interests and bolster friendly dictators. Eventually, the United States also sought a new relationship with Latin America. In 1933, President Franklin Delano Roosevelt announced the Good Neighbor policy. This policy promised to treat Latin American states as sovereign nations and to stop the use of U.S. military action in the Western Hemisphere. In 1948, the states of the Western Hemisphere formed the Organization of American States (OAS), which called for an end to military action by one state in the affairs of any other state. The OAS encouraged regional cooperation and allowed for group action to maintain peace.

The formation of the Organization of American States, however, did not end the interference of the United States in Latin American affairs. As the Cold War between the United States and the Soviet Union developed, so, too, did the anxiety of American policy makers about the possibility of Communist regimes in Central America and the Caribbean. As a result, the United States returned to a policy of taking action when it believed that Soviet agents were trying to use local communists or radical reformers to set up governments hostile to U.S. interests.

After Fidel Castro created a Marxist state in Cuba (see later in the chapter), the desire of the United States to prevent "another Cuba" largely determined U.S. policy toward Latin America. In the 1960s, President John F. Kennedy's Alliance for Progress encouraged social reform and economic development in Latin America. It was hoped that economic growth would keep ordinary people happy and less inclined to follow radical leaders. The United States provided over $10 billion in aid to those elected governments whose reform programs it deemed acceptable.

The Alliance for Progress failed to work, however. Much of the money intended for economic development ended up in the pockets of the rich. When Cuba began to start guerrilla wars in other Latin American countries, the United States reacted by providing massive military aid to anticommunist regimes, regardless of their nature. By 1979, 83,000 soldiers from 21 Latin American countries had received military training from the United States. Special emphasis was placed

MORE ABOUT . . . *The Cuban Missile Crisis*

Debates concerning the Cuban missile crisis diverge in their points of emphasis. Thomas Patterson, in his article "Fixation with Cuba: The Bay of Pigs, Missile Crisis, an Covert War Against Castro" (1989), for example, argues that the Kennedy administration's unrelenting attempts to overthrow Castro's government in Cuba were the primary reason why Soviet missiles were in Cuba in the first place. Second, he questions how well Kennedy handled the crisis when it occurred. Another historian, Arthur Schlesinger Jr., who worked in the Kennedy administration, argues in *A Thousand Days* (1965) and in *Robert Kennedy and His Times* (1978) that the CIA made mistakes in trying to destabilize Castro's regime, but John Kennedy and his brother Robert were masterful statesmen in handling the missile crisis.

1. Section Review Questions on this page
2. Section 31–1 Quiz in your Teacher Resource materials
3. Reteaching Worksheets in your Teacher Resource materials
4. Self-Study software

Answers to SECTION REVIEW

2. (a) development of industries to produce imported products
(b) firms with divisions in two or more countries
(c) drug businesses working to eliminate competition
(d) fighting to free the oppressed

3. (a) resulted when Latin American nations could not make debt payments
(b) president of Peru
(c) archbishop in El Salvador
(d) formed to end military actions by one state in the affairs of other states
(e) U.S. program for Latin American social reform, economic development

4. (a) instability led to reliance on military
(b) borrowed money from developed nations
(c) escape rural poverty
(d) undermines social, political, economic stability
(e) feared Communists would take over Latin American countries

5. positive: greater stability, progress, protection of human rights; negative: less self-determination, possible armed conflict with U.S.

on antiguerrilla activity so that Latin American countries could fight social revolutionaries.

In the 1980s and 1990s, the United States returned to a policy of direct intervention in Latin American affairs. In 1983, President Ronald Reagan sent U.S. Marines to the tiny island of Grenada (gruh-NADE-uh), where the United States claimed that "a brutal group of leftist thugs had violently seized power." In 1989 and 1990, during the presidency of George Bush, U.S. military forces overthrew the government of Panama. The new government was supported by U.S. troops. President Bill Clinton used U.S. forces to oust a military regime and restore democracy to Haiti in 1994 and 1995.

❀ SECTION REVIEW ❀

1. **Locate:**
(a) Colombia,   (b) Venezuela,   (c) Costa Rica,   (d) Chile,   (e) Paraguay,   (f) Bolivia,   (g) Peru,   (h) El Salvador

2. **Define:**
(a) import-substituting industrialization,
(b) multinational corporations,
(c) drug cartels,
(d) theology of liberation

3. **Identify:**
(a) debt crisis,   (b) Alberto Fujimori,   (c) Oscar Romero,   (d) Organization of American States (OAS),   (e) Alliance for Progress

4. **Recall:**
(a) Why did the attempt of many Latin American countries to industrialize contribute to an emergence of new military regimes?
(b) How did many Latin American countries deal with the declining value of their exports in the 1970s?
(c) What is probably the most important reason for the migration of Latin American people from rural areas to cities?
(d) What effect does the wide gap between the rich and poor have in Latin American countries?

(e) What did the Cold War have to do with American concerns about Latin America?

5. **Think Critically:** What positive and negative events may result for the people of Latin America from a renewed United States policy of direct intervention in their affairs?

THE CARIBBEAN BASIN: REVOLUTION AND ECONOMIC CHANGE

The Caribbean Basin includes Mexico, the states of Central America, and the Caribbean islands. Since 1945, this area has witnessed revolutionary upheavals and considerable economic and political change.

The Mexican Way

The Mexican Revolution at the beginning of the twentieth century created a political order that has remained the most stable in Latin America. The official political party of the Mexican Revolution (known as the Institutional Revolutionary Party, or PRI) came to dominate Mexico. Every six years, party bosses of the PRI chose the party's presidential candidate. He was then dutifully elected by the people, who had no other party to choose from.

During the 1950s and 1960s, Mexico's ruling party focused on a balanced program of industrial growth. Fifteen years of steady economic growth led to real gains in wages for more and more people. To many people, those years appeared to be a golden age in Mexico's economic development.

At the end of the 1960s, however, the true nature of Mexico's domination by a one-party system became apparent in the student protest movement. On October 2, 1968, university students filled Tlatelolco Square in Mexico City to protest government policies. Police forces opened fire and killed hundreds of students (see "You Are There: Student Revolt in Mexico"). Leaders

COOPERATIVE LEARNING ACTIVITY

Divide students into small groups. First, have them debate whether or not the United States should help a faction within a small Latin American country remove its leader in order to protect U.S. interests. Second, have students develop a viable plan for assisting a country in this way. Students should use their understanding of economics, political diplomacy, and knowledge of past history to develop their plan. Ask students to share their results with the entire class.

Map 31.1   The Caribbean Basin

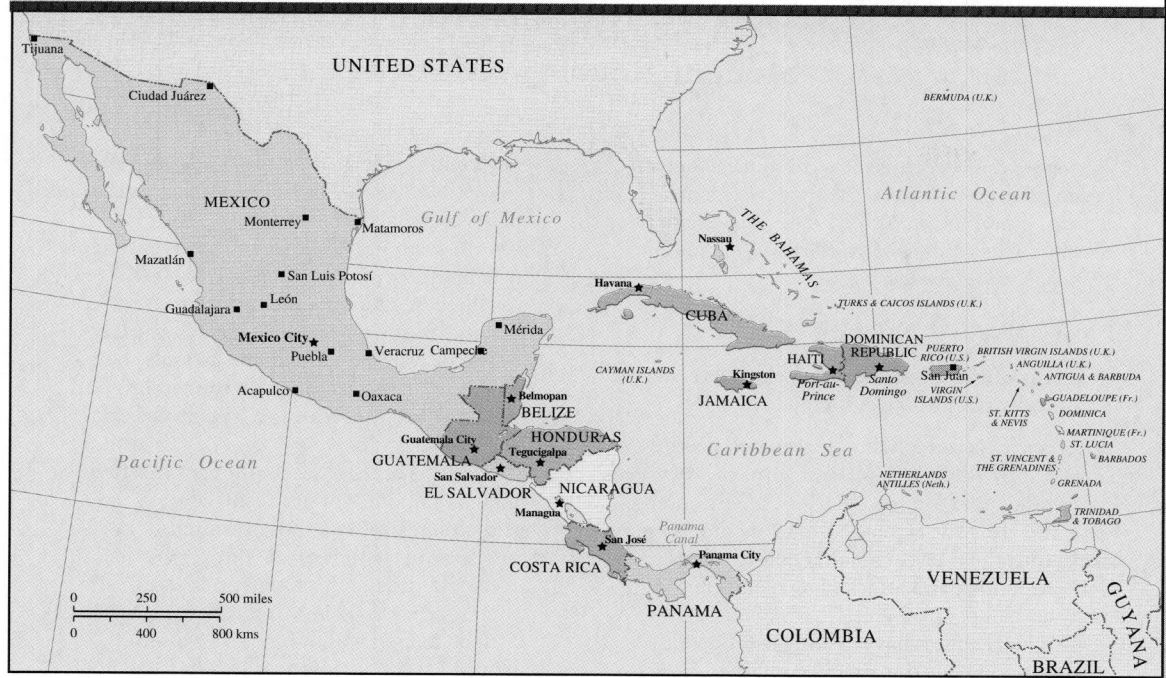

CLOSE

Lead students in a discussion of the 'Focus' objectives identified on page 1014. Emphasize the relationship between economic success and the growth of democracy in Latin America.

FOCUS

OBJECTIVES

After completing this section, students should be able to

1. identify and describe recent developments in Mexico
2. describe causes and results of the Cuban revolution
3. identify and describe recent upheavals in Central America

FOCUS ACTIVITY

Help students understand that nations almost always react negatively to foreign economic domination. This can be seen in India, China, Africa, and Latin America. It can even be seen in American resentment of Japanese economic success after World War II. Assign students to list different ways that people have used to resist foreign economic domination.

of the PRI now became concerned about the need for change in the system.

The next two presidents, Luis Echeverría (AY-chuh-vuh-REE-uh) and José López Portillo, made political reforms. New rules opened the door to the emergence of new political parties. Greater freedom of debate in the press and universities was also allowed. Economic problems, however, continued to haunt Mexico. In the late 1970s, vast new reserves of oil were discovered in Mexico. The sale of oil abroad increased dramatically, which made the government more and more dependent on oil revenues. When world oil prices dropped in the mid-1980s, Mexico was no longer able to make payments on its foreign debt, which had reached $80 billion in 1982. The government was forced to adopt new economic policies. These included the sale of companies owned by the state to private companies (a policy known as **privatization**).

The debt crisis and rising unemployment left many people unhappy with the government. This was especially evident in the 1988 election. The PRI's choice for president was Carlos Salinas. Normally, he would have been expected to win in a landslide. However, he gained only 50.3 percent, a bare majority. The new president continued the economic reforms of the previous presidents. He went even further by making a free-trade agreement with the United States and Canada, known as the North American Free Trade Agreement (NAFTA). The success or failure of these economic policies will no doubt determine the continuing ability of the PRI to dominate Mexico politically. In 1995, a new challenge appeared when a group of rebels in the extreme south of Mexico led an armed revolt against the government. Although the revolt failed, peasant unrest in the area remains a challenge to the government.

STUDYING MAPS

The following questions will help you guide students through their study of Map 31.1.

1. Ask students to examine the area and identify the many countries that make up the Caribbean Basin.
2. Have students speculate on why there is so much unrest within these countries. *(Answers will vary; may include that there are so many ruling governments represented and the countries are all in such* close proximity, they all want to be in control.)*

3. What are reasons for concern in the U.S. when there is unrest in these countries? *(Answers will vary; should include the connecting borders from Mexico makes an easy access for drug trafficking and illegal aliens; Cuba in such close proximity to Florida)*

TEACH

USING PRIMARY SOURCES

Ask students to consider the account of student riots in Mexico. If the information given is true and they had been students in Mexico at that time, do the students believe they would have joined the conflict? What would cause them to risk their lives and freedom?

LEARNING FROM VISUALS

Answer to the caption question: There were student demonstrations in France in 1968, which were discussed in Chapter 29.

Answers to Critical Thinking Questions

1. There had been a growing conflict between students and government. The attack was an attempt to put down the conflict.
2. Answers will vary, but might include the fact that the Olympics were just a few days away and the government probably didn't want any problems during the time.
3. Answers will vary.
4. Answers will vary.

YOU ARE THERE

Student Revolt in Mexico

A growing conflict between the government and university students in Mexico came to a violent and bloody climax on October 2, 1968. This excerpt is taken from an account of the events by the student National Strike Council.

Account of the Clash Between the Government and Students in Mexico, October 2, 1968

After an hour and a half of a peaceful meeting attended by 10,000 people and witnessed by scores of domestic and foreign reporters, a helicopter gave the army the signal to attack by dropping flares into the crowd. Simultaneously, the plaza was surrounded and attacked by members of the army and all police forces.

The local papers have given the following information about the attack, confirmed by first-hand witnesses:

1. Numerous secret policemen had infiltrated the meeting in order to attack it from within, with orders to kill. They were known to each other by the use of a white handkerchief tied around their right hands. . . .
2. High-caliber weapons and expansion bullets were used. Seven hours after the massacre

began, tanks cleaned up the residential buildings of Nonoalco-Tlatelolco with short cannon blasts and machine-gun fire.

3. On the morning of October 3, the apartments of supposedly guilty individuals were still being searched, without a search warrant.
4. Doctors in the emergency wards of the city hospitals were under extreme pressure, being forced to forego attention to the victims until they had been interrogated and placed under guard. . . .
5. The results of this brutal military operation include hundreds of dead (including women and children), thousands of wounded, an unwarranted search of all the apartments in the area, and thousands of violent arrests. . . . It should be added that members of the National Strike Council who were captured were stripped and herded into a small archaeological excavation at Tlatelolco, converted for the moment into a dungeon. Some of them were put up against a wall and shot.

All this has occurred only ten days before the start of the Olympics. The repression is expected to become even greater after the Games. . . .
WE ARE NOT AGAINST THE OLYMPIC GAMES. WELCOME TO MEXICO.

The Cuban Revolution

Until the 1960s, Marxism played little role in the politics of Latin America. The success of Fidel Castro in Cuba and his support of Marxism, however, changed that situation. Other Marxist movements then arose that aimed to gain the support of peasants and industrial workers and to bring radical change to Latin

America. The United States saw these movements as communist threats and provided substantial military aid to fight them.

An authoritarian regime, headed by Fulgencio Batista, had ruled Cuba since 1934. The regime was closely tied economically to U.S. investors. A strong opposition movement to Batista's government developed, led by Fidel Castro. He was assisted by Ernesto

---

SPECIAL NEEDS: *Auditory/Verbal*

Read with students "Student Revolt in Mexico." Separate students into the following groups: Secret police, tank-operators, apartment landlords, doctors at the hospitals where students were treated, interns, students, and journalists. One student should be a television reporter who is doing an interview with those at the campus, while

another student is interviewing people at the hospital, and another is interviewing organizers of the attack (secret police) at their headquarters. Have them design a few questions together and take turns doing the interviews for the whole class. This activity should be used to involve low-interest students in a discussion on government control.

YOU ARE THERE

Student Revolt in Mexico, continued

◄ *This woman was wounded by armed federal troops during the student protest in Tlatelolco Plaza on October 2, 1968. The official government report said that Mexican authorities were fired upon, and they returned the gunfire. What other country experienced student demonstrations and riots in 1968?*

1. What was the reason for the military attack on the students?

2. Why do you think the government reacted with such violence?

3. Do you think the government handled the situation well? Why or why not?

4. What was the result of this incident? What other tragic events in history helped bring about needed changes?

Ché Guevara (gay-VAH-ruh), an Argentinian who believed in the need for revolutionary upheaval to change Latin America. Castro thought that only armed force could overthrow Batista. Castro's first direct attacks on Batista's regime brought little success. Castro, whose forces were based in the Sierra Maestra (MIE-struh) Mountains, then went over to guerrilla warfare (see "You Are There: Castro's Revolutionary Ideals"). As the rebels gained more support, Batista's regime reacted with such brutality that it even alienated its own supporters. The dictator fled in December 1958. Castro's revolutionaries seized Havana on January 1, 1959.

The new government moved cautiously, but relations between Cuba and the United States quickly deteriorated. A land-reform law in May 1959 national

So What ??

*If your students question the importance of the information on **Mexico**, tell them. . .*

After Canada, Mexico is the largest trading partner with the United States. There are millions of U.S. jobs tied directly or indirectly to foreign trade. Because Mexico shares a border with the U.S., it is vitally important to our national security to maintain friendly relations. Also, events in Mexico could easily have an immediate economic impact in this country.

LEARNING FROM VISUALS

Most political leaders wear suits or other formal clothing when they appear in public. Ask students what they believe Castro intended to accomplish by appearing in army fatigues.

Answer to the caption question: Early supporters of Castro could not have ignored his Marxist-Leninist beliefs, and in his self-defense following an unsuccessful coup attempt in 1953, Castro spelled out his beliefs.

Answers to Critical Thinking Questions

1. Wording will vary. (1) return power to the people, (2) grant property to all who hold little or no land, (3) grant workers the right to share in the profit of their companies, (4) grant all planters the right to share 55% of the sugar production, (5) order the confiscation of all holdings and ill-gotten gains of those who had committed fraud during previous regimes.

2. He was trying to help the poor and working class people.

3. Answers will vary.

YOU ARE THERE
Castro's Revolutionary Ideals

On July 26, 1953, Fidel Castro was arrested and put on trial after he and a small band of followers failed to capture the Moncada barracks, near Santiago de Cuba. This excerpt is taken from his defense speech, in which he discussed the goals of the revolutionaries.

Fidel Castro, From His 1953 Defense Speech

I stated that the second consideration on which we based our chances for success was one of social order because we were assured of the people's support. When we speak of the people we do not mean the comfortable ones, the conservative elements of the nation, who welcome any regime of oppression, any dictatorship, and despotism, prostrating themselves before the master of the moment until they grind their foreheads into the ground. When we speak of struggle, the people means the vast unredeemed masses, to whom all make promises and whom all deceive; we mean the people who yearn for a better, more dignified

▲ *Fidel Castro addressed the Cuban nation by radio after the ouster of Fulgencio Batista. Do you think that the Cuban people initially believed Castro would turn Cuba into a Marxist dictatorship? Why or why not?*

ized all landholdings of more than one thousand acres. This irritated the United States. Then the Soviet Union, the Cold War enemy of the United States, agreed early in 1960 to buy Cuban sugar and provide $100 million in credits to Cuba.

On March 17, 1960, President Dwight Eisenhower directed the Central Intelligence Agency (CIA) to "organize the training of Cuban exiles, mainly in Guatemala, against a possible future day when they might return to their homeland."[1] Arms from Eastern Europe began to arrive in Cuba. The United States cut its purchase of Cuban sugar. In response, the Cuban government nationalized U.S. companies and banks. In October 1960, the United States declared a trade embargo of Cuba, thus driving Castro closer to the Soviet Union. In December 1961, Castro declared himself a Marxist.

On January 3, 1961, the United States broke off diplomatic relations with Cuba. The new American president, John F. Kennedy, supported an attempt to overthrow Castro's government. The landing in Cuba of 1,400 Cubans, assisted by the CIA, on April 17, 1961, turned into a total military disaster (the Bay of Pigs invasion). The Soviets were now encouraged to make an even greater commitment to Cuban independence by placing nuclear missiles in the country. This act led to a showdown with the United States—the Cuban Missile Crisis (see Chapter 29). As its part of

---

RETEACHING ACTIVITY

Tell students that world leaders monitored the Bay of Pigs fiasco, and many leaders felt the result mirrored Kennedy's youth and inexperience in foreign affairs. With this dramatic loss of face for the United States, it was a difficult time for the Western allies.

Ask students how they decide who to listen to when they are given conflicting advice, perhaps from two different teachers, from their school counselors, from their friends or family members. Remind them that ultimately the decisions they make are their own, and they will be the ones who must take responsibility for them, just as President Kennedy did in the Bay of Pigs fiasco.

YOU ARE THERE

Castro's Revolutionary Ideals, continued

and more just nation; who are moved by ancestral aspirations of justice, for they have suffered injustice and mockery, generation after generation; who long for great and wise changes in all aspects of their life; people, who, to attain these changes, are ready to give even the very last breath of their lives—when they believe in something or in someone, especially when they believe in themselves.

In the brief of this cause there must be recorded the five revolutionary laws that would have been proclaimed immediately after the capture of the Moncada barracks. . . .

The First Revolutionary Law would have returned power to the people. . . .

The Second Revolutionary Law would have granted property to all planters, sub-planters, lessees, partners and squatters who hold parcels of five or less "caballerias" [tract of land, about 33 acres] of land. . . .

The Third Revolutionary Law would have granted workers and employees the right to share

30 percent of the profits of all the large enterprises, including the sugar mills. . . .

The Fourth Revolutionary Law would have granted all planters the right to share 55 percent of the sugar production. . . .

The Fifth Revolutionary Law would have ordered the confiscation of all holdings and ill-gotten gains of those who had committed frauds during previous regimes. . . .

1. List in your own words the revolutionary laws stated here.

2. Considering the revolutionary laws, who was Castro trying to help?

3. Do you think communism was a basic ingredient of Castro's revolution, or did it become part of his regime after the revolution? Explain your answer.

---

the bargain to end the crisis, the United States agreed not to invade Cuba.

The Cuban Missile Crisis affected Cuba in another way as well. Castro realized that the Soviet Union had been unreliable. If the Cuban Revolution was to be secure, Cuba could no longer be surrounded by hostile states tied to U.S. interests. The Cubans would have to start social revolution in the rest of Latin America. Castro thought that Bolivia, Haiti, Venezuela, Colombia, Paraguay, and a number of Central American states were especially open to radical revolution. By launching guerrilla wars, peasants would flock to the movement and overthrow the old regimes. Guevara began a guerrilla war in Bolivia but was caught and

killed by the Bolivian army in the fall of 1967. The Cuban strategy had failed.

Nevertheless, within Cuba, Castro's Marxist revolution went on, although with mixed results. The Cuban Revolution did secure some social gains for its people, especially in health care and education. The regime provided free medical services for all citizens, and the country's health did improve. Illiteracy was nearly eliminated as new schools and teacher-training institutes that tripled the number of teachers within ten years were set up. The theoretical equality of women in Marxist thought was put into practice in Cuba by new laws. One such law was the family code, which stated that husband and wife were equally responsible for the

---

MORE ABOUT . . . *Kennedy's Foreign Policy*

In his inaugural address, Kennedy spoke exclusively of foreign affairs. He said that the United States was at a crossroads, and that Americans were "defending freedom in its hour of maximum danger." In part, JFK's inaugural address was a response to Soviet Premier Khrushchev's boasting of Soviet technological superiority and his country's rate of economic growth. Khrushchev said that a world war would be too destructive in

the nuclear age. Yet he approved of wars of national liberation by which people in developing nations would gain their freedom from their colonial overlords. What Khrushchev saw as liberation from colonialism, Kennedy saw as Communist "ambitions for world domination." "Our task," Kennedy affirmed, "is to convince them that aggression and subversion will not be profitable routes to pursue these ends."

POLITICS AND HISTORY

When John Kennedy gave his approval for the invasion of Cuba, he had been president of the United States for less than three months. In his presidential campaign Richard Nixon had accused him of being soft on communism. Ask students if they believe this may have had anything to do with his ill-fated decision to sponsor the invasion.

CLASS DISCUSSION

Ask students to identify and discuss possible messages the United States may have sent to other Latin American states when it forced the Soviet Union to withdraw its missiles from Cuba. How did this relate to the American Good Neighbor Policy? Ask students if they feel that most Latin American leaders were pleased with the actions of the United States or upset by them. What do the students feel about this action by the United States?

LEARNING FROM VISUALS

What information does the photograph to the right provide about the state of the Cuban Economy? Do students believe these workers would care whether they were working for the Cuban government or for a private land owner?

Answer to the caption question: In 1960 the Soviet Union agreed to purchase Cuban sugar, and at that time the USSR also pledged $100 million in aid to Cuba. It continued to support Cuba until the breakup of the Soviet Union.

CLASS DISCUSSION

Ask students to discuss the statement below. Do they believe it is true? What light do their opinions cast on American foreign policy in the 1980s?

It is unreasonable to believe that the people of a poor nation will be helped by sending weapons to their government.

▶ *Sugar was one of Cuba's primary exports, but working in the cane fields was hard manual labor, as evidenced by this illustration. How did Cuba replace the income from U.S. sugar imports?*

economic support of the family and household, as well as for child care. Such laws led to improvements but were far from creating full equality for women.

Castro rejected a path of rapid industrialization and encouraged the development of mixed farming. The Cuban economy, however, continued to rely on the production and sale of sugar. Economic problems forced the Castro regime to depend on Soviet aid and the purchase of Cuban sugar by Soviet bloc countries. After the collapse of these Communist regimes in 1989, Cuba lost their support. Without the Soviet subsidies, economic conditions in Cuba have steadily declined. Nevertheless, despite the poor economy and increasing isolation from other countries, Castro manages to remain in power.

Upheaval in Central America

There are six states in Central America: Costa Rica, Nicaragua, Honduras, El Salvador, Panama, and Guatemala. Economically, these states have depended on the export of bananas, coffee, and cotton. Prices for these products vary at times, however, which creates economic crises. An enormous gulf between a wealthy elite and a mass of poor peasants also created a climate of instability. Fear in the United States of the spread of communism often led to American support for repressive regimes in the area. American involvement was especially evident in El Salvador, Nicaragua, and Panama.

El Salvador

El Salvador is the smallest state in Central America. By the beginning of the twentieth century, about forty families owned most of the coffee plantations and controlled both banking and trade. The gulf between this wealthy elite and the mass of poor peasants was enormous.

After World War II, the United States supported the rule of the wealthy elite and the military. The rise of an urban middle class led to some hopes for a more democratic government. This group supported the Christian Democratic Party, led by José Napoleon Duarte (DWAR-tay). The army, however, refused to allow the free elections that were planned for 1972.

In the late 1970s and the 1980s, El Salvador was rocked by a bitter civil war. Both Marxist-led guerrillas and right-wing groups used savage terror to win the struggle. During the presidency of Ronald Reagan, the United States provided weapons and training to the Salvadoran army to defeat the guerrillas. At the same

MORE ABOUT . . . the "futbol war" of 1969

In 1969 El Salvador and Honduras fought a two week war, the spark of which was a series of World Cup soccer games between the two countries. Because of overcrowding and little farmland, El Salvadorans had been moving to Honduras for several decades. In 1968 Honduras passed a law forbidding El Salvadorans from owning land, and a long standing boundary dispute between the two countries heated up. When they played each other in the World Cup playoffs in 1969, the violence surrounding the games forced the teams to play the deciding game in Mexico. When El Salvador won, Hondurans began to savagely attack El Salvadorans living in Honduras. After an invasion by El Salvador and a bombing attack by Honduras, both countries turned to the Organization of American States for mediation.

time, the United States urged land reform and free elections. Even the election of the moderate José Duarte as president in 1984, however, failed to stop the killing. By the early 1990s, this brutal civil war had led to the deaths of at least 75,000 people. Finally in 1992, a peace settlement was reached that brought an end to the civil war.

Nicaragua

The United States had intervened in Nicaraguan domestic affairs in the early twentieth century. U.S. Marines even remained there for long periods of time. The leader of the U.S.–supported National Guard, Anastasio Somoza, seized control of the Nicaraguan government in 1937. The Somoza family ruled Nicaragua for the next forty-three years. U.S. support for the Somoza family's military regime enabled the Somozas to overcome any opponents while enriching themselves at the expense of the state. Here, too, there existed a wealthy elite while most people lived in extreme poverty.

Opposition to the regime finally arose. The Somoza family and the National Guard it controlled used murder and torture to stop the opposition. At the same time, corruption was rampant in the government. By 1979, even the United States, under President Jimmy Carter, was unwilling to support the corrupt, dictatorial family. In that same year, military victories by the Marxist guerrilla forces known as the Sandinista (SAN-duh-NEES-tuh) National Liberation Front left them in virtual control of the country. They now set up a provisional government.

The Sandinistas inherited a poverty-stricken nation. Their alignment with the Soviet Union caused the Reagan and Bush administrations to believe that Central America faced the danger of another Communist state. American money was used to finance rebels, known as **Contras,** to wage a guerrilla war against the Sandinista government. The Contra war and a U.S. economic embargo damaged the Nicaraguan economy and undermined support for the Sandinistas. In 1990, the Sandinistas agreed to free elections, and they lost to a coalition headed by Violeta Barrios de Chamorro. Nevertheless, the Sandinistas remained the strongest

▲ *The Sandinistas celebrate their victory that led to the overthrow of the Somoza dictatorship in Nicaragua. Why is it symbolic that these soldiers are standing on a tank and waving guns?*

single party in Nicaragua. Nicaragua itself remained devastated by these years of bloodshed.

Panama

A revolution in 1903 enabled Panama to free itself from Colombia and form a separate nation. However, this was done with help from the United States. The price for American aid was control of the Panama Canal, which Colombia had refused to give, and extensive influence over the government and economy of Panama. A wealthy oligarchy ruled, with American support.

After 1968, power in Panama came into the hands of the military leaders of Panama's National Guard. One of the most ruthless leaders was Manuel Noriega (NOR-ee-AY-guh), who took control of Panama in 1983. At first, Noriega was supported by the United States. His corruption, brutality, and involvement with the drug trade, however, turned American leaders

ASSESS

You can choose from a variety of assessments to evaluate your students' mastery of the objectives for this section as stated on page 1021. Possible assessments include:

1. Section Review Questions on this page
2. Section 31–2 Quiz in your Teacher Resource materials
3. Reteaching Worksheets in your Teacher Resource materials
4. Self-Study software

Answers to SECTION REVIEW

2. (a) returning government businesses to private ownership
   (b) Nicaraguan rebels
3. (a) PRI president in Mexico in 1988, signed NAFTA
   (b) free-trade agreement signed by U.S., Canada, Mexico in 1995
   (c) Cuban Marxist, overthrew Batista in 1959
   (d) with his family controlled Nicaragua from 1937–1979
   (e) ruthless leader of Panama, jailed by U.S. for drug trafficking
4. (a) only one party nominates candidates
   (b) cut off one of Castro's last sources of economic assistance
5. Answers will vary; only leader many Cubans have ever known, improved health care and education, fear of foreign domination

1028

---

against him. On December 20, 1989, President George Bush sent 24,000 U.S. troops to Panama. Noriega was arrested and sent to prison in the United States on charges of drug trafficking. Guillermo Endara, who had opposed Noriega, then became president of Panama.

 SECTION REVIEW

1. **Locate:**
   (a) Havana,   (b) Haiti,   (c) Nicaragua,
   (d) Honduras,   (e) Panama

2. **Define:**
   (a) privatization,   (b) Contras

3. **Identify:**
   (a) Carlos Salinas,   (b) North American Free Trade Agreement (NAFTA),   (c) Fidel Castro,
   (d) Anastasio Somoza,   (e) Manuel Noriega

4. **Recall:**
   (a) Why haven't the people of Mexico had much choice in the past in determining the political leadership of their country?
   (b) How was Castro's Cuba affected by the collapse of communist governments in Eastern Europe?

5. **Think Critically:** Why was Castro able to maintain control of Cuba even after he lost his foreign support?

THE NATIONS OF SOUTH AMERICA: NATIONALISM, MARXISM, AND THE MILITARY

The countries of South America shared in the political, economic, and social problems that plagued Latin America after 1945. The military in particular became the power brokers of twentieth-century South America. Especially in the 1960s and 1970s, South American armies portrayed themselves as the guardians of national honor and orderly progress, while maintaining dictatorial and often ruthless regimes.

Argentina

Argentina is Latin America's second largest country. For years, it had been ruled by a powerful oligarchy whose wealth was based on growing wheat and raising cattle. Support from the army was crucial to the continuing power of the oligarchy. In 1943, in the midst of World War II, a group of army officers overthrew the oligarchy. The new military regime, however, was unsure of how to deal with the working classes until one of its members, Juan Perón, devised a new strategy.

Using his position as labor secretary in the military government, Perón sought to win over the workers, known as the *descamisados* (the shirtless ones). He encouraged them to join labor unions. Moreover, he increased job benefits, as well as the number of paid holidays and vacations. In 1944, Perón became vice president of the military government and made sure that people knew he was responsible for the better conditions for workers. As Perón grew more popular, however, other army officers began to fear his power, and they arrested him. An uprising by workers forced the officers to back down. In 1946, Perón was elected president, with 54 percent of the vote.

Perón followed a policy of increased industrialization in order to please his chief supporters—labor and the urban middle class. At the same time, he sought to free Argentina from foreign investors. The government bought the railways and took over the banking, insurance, shipping, and communications industries.

Perón's regime was also authoritarian. His wife, Eva Perón, organized women's organizations to support the government (see "Biography: Evita"). She also used state funds to set up foundations that helped orphans and the poor. Juan Perón, meanwhile, created Fascist gangs modeled after Hitler's Brownshirts. They used violent means to terrify Perón's opponents. More and

---

ENRICHMENT ACTIVITY

Assign students to prepare a speech that might have been given by a leader in the Cuban refugee community of Little Havana in Miami after the Bay of Pigs invasion. Students should answer these questions in their speech. What would be said about Castro and Cuba? How would the defeat of the invasion be described? What future actions would be asked of the U.S. government. Have students be prepared to read their speeches to the class. You may want to have the class decide whether or not the speech was informative and persuasive.

Map 31.2   South American Countries

Map 31.2 South American Countries

more people were alienated, however, by the regime's methods and its corruption. After the death of the popular Eva Perón in 1953, the regime's support dropped even further. Fearing Perón's power over the masses, the military overthrew the Argentinian leader in September 1955. Perón went into exile in Spain.

ACTIVITY

Have students use the information in this chapter and in other related chapters to create a time line. The time line should indicate significant events in the relationship between the United States and Cuba. Have students be prepared to provide a brief account of each event appearing on his or her time line.

CLOSE

Lead students in a discussion of the 'Focus' objectives identified on page 1021. Emphasize the importance of the Soviet presence in Cuba to relations between Latin American states and the United States.

STUDYING MAPS

The following questions will help you guide students through their study of Map 31.2.

1. Which is the largest country in land mass in South America? *(Brazil)*

2. What are the dimensions of this continent at its tallest and widest points? *(approxi-mately 5200 miles × 3200 miles)*

3. What does the information in the key tell you about the political climate of this continent? *(one of political unrest, terrorism)*

FOCUS

OBJECTIVES

After completing this section, students should be able to

1. identify and describe developments in Argentina in recent years
2. identify and explain changes in the economic and political system in Brazil
3. identify and explain challenges faced by Chile
4. discuss reasons for instability in Colombia and Peru

FOCUS ACTIVITY

Help students understand that governments which are permeated by corruption are not likely to last very long. This was true of the Ottoman Empire and to an extent of the Holy Roman Empire. Ask students to explain how they feel when they read about a public official who has been found guilty of corruption. How can the governed work to change their national leadership?

TEACH

ACROSS THE CURRICULUM

Economics Ask students to identify and discuss how Brazil's vast size has been both an advantage and a disadvantage in its economic development. How has the exploitation of natural resources in the Amazon basin created political and ecological problems?

BIOGRAPHY

Evita

Eva Perón, known as "Evita" to her followers, was one of five children born to a seamstress who lived in poverty in the small town of Los Toldos. As a child, Eva dreamed of being an actress. At age fifteen, she moved to Buenos Aires, Argentina's largest city, where she tried to get some kind of acting job. She worked in a few theaters and eventually gained fame as a radio soap opera actress.

On January 15, 1944, during a concert to benefit victims of an earthquake, Eva met Juan Perón, one of the army officers then running the government. She later described the meeting: "I put myself at his side . . . I spoke up as best I could: 'If, as you say, the cause of the people is your own cause, however great the sacrifice I will never leave your side until I die.' " Eva became Juan Perón's mistress and a year later, his wife.

Eva Perón was an important force in her husband's rise to power. Together, they courted the working-class poor with promises of higher wages and better working conditions. Juan Perón, who was elected president in 1946, owed much to the people's adoration of his wife.

▲ *Evita Perón was adored by the masses, but shunned by Argentina's upper classes. This photograph was taken in 1952, when Perón celebrated the inauguration of his second term as president. Eva Perón died less than one year after this photo was taken.*

It had been easy for the military to seize power, but it was harder for it to rule. Argentina now had a party of Perón supporters (called Peronistas), who clamored for the return of the exiled leader. In the 1960s and 1970s, military and civilian governments (the latter closely watched by the military) alternated in power. Neither was able to do much to provide economic stability. Thus, the military leaders allowed Juan Perón to come back from exile in Spain.

Perón was again elected president in September 1973. He died one year later before he could accomplish very much. His third wife, Isabel, who had run as vice president, succeeded him, but she was not effective in dealing with the country's problems. In 1976, the military once again took over power. This new military regime was brutal. It tolerated no opposition, and the military leaders encouraged the "disappearance" of its opponents. Perhaps 36,000 people, including 600 leftists, were killed as a result.

Economic problems remained. To divert people's attention, the military regime invaded the Falkland Islands, off the coast of Argentina, in April 1982. Great Britain, which had controlled the islands since the nineteenth century, sent ships and troops to take

On Line with WORLD HISTORY *Internet Activity*

You may want to have your students visit the following URL, where they will find information and additional web site resources to enhance their study of this chapter.

The World Wide Web Virtual Library—Latin American Studies

http://lanic.utexas.edu/las.html

A gateway to a large number of Latin American countries with subjects from agriculture to sociology. Excellent beginning research site.

Due to the ever-changing nature of the World Wide Web, see the West History web site, **http://history.swpco.com** for regular updates of the URLs in this text.

BIOGRAPHY

Evita, continued

As the wife of President Juan Perón, Eva was the first lady of Argentina from 1946 to 1952. Juan and Eva Perón made regular appearances on the balcony of the Presidential Palace, where they spoke to the adoring crowds of workers. Eva Perón became a tireless champion of the people. She went to the slums of the poor and gave them gifts. She formed a charitable foundation that built hospitals, schools, and orphanages, thus providing many services for Argentina's poor. Eva Perón also worked to benefit Argentinian women. She campaigned for women's right to vote and equal pay for equal work.

Eva Perón was also ambitious. She enjoyed her newfound power and loved to appear publicly, adorned in a new gown or jewelry. In 1951, she wanted to be her husband's vice presidential candidate. She backed down, however, after army leaders made it clear that they would never accept Eva Perón in office. Less than a year later, on July 26, 1952, she died of cancer. Her coffin was carried in a mile-long funeral procession, accompanied by government officials and hundreds of thousands of grieving Argentinians. During her illness, she promised the people she would always be with them. To this day, monuments, street names, and even the American musical and movie *Evita* continue to keep her memory alive.

1. Who was Evita, and what was her claim to fame?

2. Do you think Evita was driven to accomplish what she did by a desire to help the people or a desire for personal power? Explain your answer.

3. Why do you think the army leaders opposed Evita's desire to run for the office of vice-president?

4. Can you think of a person, either male or female, who is admired by people today in the way that Evita was? Describe the similarities between this person and Evita.

them back. When the Argentinian forces surrendered to the British in July, angry Argentinians denounced the military regime. The loss discredited the military and opened the door to civilian rule. In 1983, Raúl Alfonsín (al-fawn-SEEN), a member of the Radical Party, was elected president and tried to restore democratic practices. The Perónist Carlos Saúl Menem won the presidential elections of 1989. This peaceful transfer of power gave rise to hope that Argentina was moving on a democratic path. Reelected in 1995, President Menem has pushed to control inflation and government spending.

Brazil

Brazil is the largest country in Latin America. As we saw in Chapter 27, the authoritarian regime of Getúlio Vargas, from 1930 to 1945, brought the first strong industrialization to Brazil. The army, fearing Vargas's power, forced him to resign in 1945.

A second Brazilian republic came into being in 1946. Four years later, Vargas himself won the election to the presidency. However, he was unable to solve Brazil's economic problems, especially its soaring inflation. In 1954, after the armed forces called upon him

ENRICHMENT ACTIVITY

Have students read the four boxed features in this chapter ("The Street Kids," "Student Revolt in Mexico," "Castro's Revolutionary Ideas," and "Evita"). Students should develop a chart in which they list each feature. Then, have them identify the feature as a primary or secondary source. Next, ask students to characterize each article as mainly fact, opinion, or a combination of both.

LEARNING FROM VISUALS

Ask students to identify social and economic problems faced by Brazil that are indicated by the photographs to the right. What could the fact that Brazil has one of the highest birth rates in the world have on these problems? Why do some people believe it will be difficult to solve these problems unless the birth rate can be controlled?

Answer to the caption question: (photo on right) Students should be aware of the many problems caused by deforestation, the loss of many endangered species and of wildlife habitat, depletion of natural resources, insufficient soil conservation techniques, air and water pollution, and the greenhouse effect caused by wide scale deforestation in the Amazon River basin. If deforestation continues, many scientists believe that the ecological balance of the earth will be irrevocably upset.

TEACHING THEMES

Politics and History. Assign students to make a list of economic, political, and social problems faced by Brazil. Ask them to evaluate the probability that any political leader will be able to develop satisfactory solutions to all of these problems. Why do many people believe political stability will be difficult to achieve in Brazil as well as in many other Latin American states?

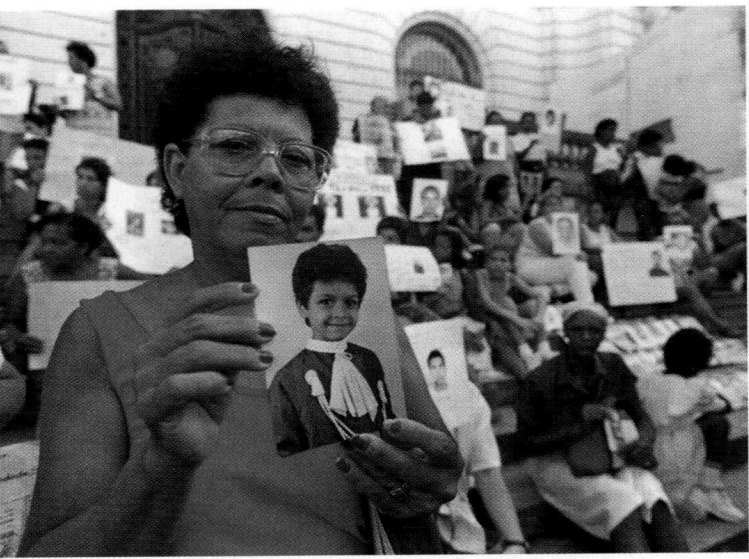

▲ *This mother holds a photo of her ten-year-old son, who disappeared in January 1995 while playing near his home in Rio de Janeiro, Brazil. Every week this woman and the other Mothers of Cinelandia, named after a plaza in the city, march to draw attention to their missing children.*

▲ *Clear-cutting in the Amazon forest is causing worldwide concern. This photo shows the destruction left when a forest is clear-cut. What worldwide environmental problems are caused by clear-cutting in the South American rain forests?*

to resign, Vargas killed himself. The democratically elected presidents who followed Vargas had no more success in controlling inflation while trying to push rapid industrialization. In the spring of 1964, the military stepped in and took over the government.

This time the armed forces remained in direct control of the country—for the next twenty years. The military set course on a new economic direction. It cut back somewhat on state control of the economy and stressed free-market forces. Beginning in 1968, the new policies seemed to work. Brazil experienced an "economic miracle" as its economy grew spectacularly. Women began to participate in the labor force.

Economic growth, however, had its drawbacks and problems. Economic growth included the exploitation of the Amazon basin. The regime opened it to farming by cutting down its extensive rain forests. Some saw this as a serious threat to the ecological balance not only of Brazil but of the Earth itself. Moreover, ordi-

nary Brazilians benefited little from economic growth as the gulf between rich and poor, which had always been wide, grew even wider. In 1960, the wealthiest 10 percent of Brazil's population received 40 percent of the nation's income. In 1980, they received 51 percent. Then, too, rapid development led to an inflation rate of 100 percent a year. Combined with an enormous foreign debt, the economic miracle by the early 1980s was turning into an economic nightmare. Overwhelmed, the generals retreated and opened the door for a return to democracy in 1985.

The new democratic government faced enormous obstacles—a massive foreign debt, almost runaway inflation (it was 800 percent in 1987), and the lack of any real social unity. Presidential elections in 1990 brought a newcomer, Fernando Collor de Mello, into office. He promised to end inflation with a drastic

So What ??

If your students question the importance of the information on **Brazil,** *tell them . . .*

The Brazilian rain forest has been called the "lungs of the earth," producing much of the oxygen that we all breathe. The need for Brazil to find jobs and opportunities for their people, while at the same time conserving

the rain forest becomes a concern for the entire planet. Since the continued good health of the rain forest is a matter of not just national, but international importance, what obligations do the nations of the world have toward helping Brazil reach economic stability?

reform program. Based on strict control of wages and prices, large reductions in public spending, and cuts in the number of government employees, his program soon led to high unemployment and a recession. Collor de Mello's efforts were also undermined by corruption in his own administration. He resigned from office at the end of 1992 after having been impeached. In new elections in 1994, Fernando Cardoso was elected president by an overwhelming majority of the popular vote.

Chile

Another challenge to U.S. influence in Latin America came from Chile. Chile had suffered from a series of economic problems. Much wealth was held by large landowners and a select number of large corporations. Inflation, foreign debts, and a decline in the mining industry (the export of copper made up 80 percent of Chile's export income) caused untold difficulties. Right-wing control of the government failed to achieve any solutions. There was already a strong resentment against American corporations—especially Anaconda and Kennecott, which owned the copper industries.

In elections held in 1970, a split in the moderate forces enabled Salvador Allende (ah-YEN-dae), a Marxist, to become president of Chile with 36 percent of the vote. Allende tried to create a Marxian socialist society by constitutional means. A number of labor leaders, who represented the interests of the working classes, were made the ministers of labor, finance, public works, and interior in the new government. Allende increased the wages of industrial workers. He began to move toward socialism by nationalizing the largest domestic and foreign-owned corporations. Nationalization of the copper industry—which was basically carried out without paying the owners—angered the American owners and Richard Nixon, the American president. Nixon cut off all aid to Chile, which created problems for the Chilean economy. At the same time, radical workers were beginning to take control of the landed estates of the wealthy. The government made little effort to stop them.

These activities brought growing opposition from the upper and middle classes, including many women

▲ This black-and-white photo of Salvador Allende was taken in March 1973 during a press conference. The congressional elections held two days after this photo was taken increased his hold over the country, but his victory was short lived.

who were organized to back the conservative cause. The forces of opposition began to organize strikes against the government (with support from the American CIA). Allende tried to stop the disorder by bringing military officers into his government. This did end the strikes. In March 1973, however, new elections increased the number of Allende's supporters in the Chilean congress. Afraid of Allende's growing strength, the Chilean army, under the direction of General Augusto Pinochet (PEE-noe-shay), decided to overthrow the government. On September 11, 1973, military forces seized the presidential palace. Allende was shot to death. His wife publicly denounced the

▶ *A small group of Shining Path guerrillas was photographed when they came across members of the press who were working in the Andes. How does this group differ from Castro's revolutionary followers or the Sandinistas?*

takeover and maintained that the United States had financed it. Contrary to the expectations of many right-wing politicians, the military remained in power and set up a dictatorship.

The Pinochet regime was one of the most brutal in Chile's history. Thousands of opponents were imprisoned. Thousands more were cruelly tortured and murdered. The regime also moved quickly to outlaw all political parties and remove the congress. It then restored many nationalized industries and landowners' estates to their original owners. The copper industries, however, remained in government hands. The regime's horrible abuse of human rights led to growing unrest against the government in the mid-1980s. In 1989, free presidential elections led to the defeat of Pinochet. A Christian Democrat, Patricio Azócur, became president and restored a somewhat democratic system.

Colombia

On paper, Colombia has long had a democratic political system. In truth, however, a conservative elite—led by the owners of coffee plantations—has dominated the government. When Jorge Eliécer Gaitán led a movement of workers and landless peasants for land

reform in the 1940s, he was assassinated. After 1950, the conservative elite ruled alone. When Marxist guerrilla groups organized the peasants and fought back, the government responded with violence. More than 200,000 peasants had lost their lives in the struggle by the mid-1960s.

Violence remained a constant feature of Colombian life in the 1980s and 1990s. Peasants who lived in poverty turned to a new cash crop—coca leaves—to satisfy the U.S. thirst for cocaine. As the drug trade increased, so, too, did the number of drug lords. They used bribes and violence to get government cooperation in the drug traffic. Despite government attempts to stop the drug traffic, both large and small drug lords continued their trade. The drug trade and the violence that goes with it continue to haunt Colombian life. Many Colombians, however, argue that they are only fulfilling a need and did not create the market for drugs in the United States.

Peru

The history of Peru has been marked by much instability. Peru's dependence on the sale abroad of its products—such as sugar, cotton, fish meal, and copper—has

---

MORE ABOUT . . . *The Drug Trade*

The multibillion dollar, illicit drug trade has continued to be a source of international problems to the United States and many Latin American countries. The U.S. is sometimes critical of countries such as Colombia and Mexico for not doing enough to stop the illegal flow of cocaine and marijuana into this country. These countries respond that until the huge American demand is elimi-

nated drugs will continue to find their way north. It is estimated that agents seize one-third of the cocaine produced every year and still the supply to the United States exceeds the demand by 60 to 100 tons. Unless this surplus is eliminated, the price of cocaine will continue to remain low, thereby making it more accessible.

led to extreme ups and downs in the economy. With these have come the rise and fall of governments. A large, poor, and landless Indian peasant population created an additional source of continual unrest.

A military takeover in 1968 led to some change. General Juan Velasco Alvarado realized the need to help the oppressed Indians. His government seized almost 75 percent of the nation's large landed estates. Ownership of the land was then put into the hands of peasant cooperatives. The government took control of foreign-owned companies and established its own form of socialism. The government also provided low food prices to help urban workers. Economic problems continued, however, and Peruvian military leaders removed General Alvarado from power in 1975. Five years later, unable to cope with Peru's economic problems, the military returned Peru to civilian rule.

New problems made the task of the new civilian governments even more difficult. A radical guerrilla group with ties to Communist China, known as **Shining Path,** waged a ruthless war by killing mayors, missionaries, priests, and peasants. Shining Path members followed the ideas of the Chinese Communist leader Mao Zedong (see Chapter 33). Their goal is to smash all authority and create a classless society. Peruvian drug traffickers, who made enormous profits from the sale of cocaine to the United States, financed Shining Path rebels in return for protection.

In 1990, fed up with their problems, Peruvians chose a political newcomer, Alberto Fujimoro, as their new president. Fujimoro, the son of a Japanese immigrant, promised reforms. Two years later, he suspended the constitution and congress, became a dictator, and began a ruthless campaign against Shining Path guerrillas. It remains to be seen whether Fujimoro's dictatorial powers will help him solve Peru's growing problems.

❈ SECTION REVIEW ❈

1. **Define:**
   (a) *descamisados,*
   (b) Shining Path

2. **Identify:**
   (a) Evita Perón,   (b) Carlos Saúl Menem,
   (c) Fernando Collor de Mello,   (d) Salvador Allende,   (e) General Augusto Pinochet,
   (f) General Juan Velasco Alvarado

3. **Recall:**
   (a) How did Juan Perón seek to free Argentina from foreign investors?
   (b) Why did Argentina invade the Falkland Islands in 1982?
   (c) What is the most apparent environmental cost Brazil has paid for its economic growth?
   (d) What two economic problems did the new democratic government of Brazil face in the late 1980s?
   (e) Why have many poor Latin American farmers turned to the production of coca leaves?

4. **Think Critically:** Why is it often easier for the military to seize power in a nation than it is for the military to rule that nation effectively?

CULTURE IN LATIN AMERICA SINCE 1945

It is difficult to speak of a single Latin American culture. Many different nations make up Latin America. Many different peoples and cultural heritages make up those nations. Mexico and Peru, for example, have rich Indian heritages (that of the Aztecs and Incas). In contrast, Argentina has no Indians, and most of its people are descendants of European immigrants. However, Latin American culture does have some common features. In this section, we will look at a few of them.

Education

All countries in Latin America have compulsory (required by law) education for children. The number of years required varies from five to twelve. Dropout rates, however, are high. In Brazil, for example, less than 60 percent of students advanced from grade 1 to

MORE ABOUT . . . *Peru*

Another Peruvian guerilla group unaligned with the Shining Path is the MRTA, a "Guevarist" group modeled after Cuban Communists. In 1996 Japan's ambassador to Peru was giving a party when a group of MRTA, disguised as waiters, took over the residence and held all 400 guests hostage. The crisis went on for months, with the hostage takers periodically releasing statements via their own Web page on the Internet. Finally, as the captors were playing a game of indoor soccer, Peruvian commandos stormed the building and killed all of the guerrillas. None of the hostages were injured directly—one suffered a heart attack.

ASSESS

You can choose from a variety of assessments to evaluate your students' mastery of the objectives for this section as stated on page 1030. Possible assessments include:

1. Section Review Questions on this page
2. Section 31–3 Quiz in your Teacher Resource materials
3. Reteaching Worksheets in your Teacher Resource materials
4. Self-Study software

ALTERNATIVE ASSESSMENT

Assign students to write a speech that might be given by a politician running for office in a rural area of Brazil. Tell them to include specific promises that would be welcomed by small farmers. In a second part of their assignment, ask students to evaluate the speech they wrote from the point of view of a wealthy land owner. Finally, ask students to explain why political unity is hard to achieve in much of Latin America.

Answers to SECTION REVIEW

1. (a) "shirtless ones;" workers in Argentina
   (b) radical guerrilla group in Peru
2. (a) popular wife of Juan Peron, used state funds to help the poor
   (b) Perónist president of Argentina; monitors inflation, government spending
   (c) president of Brazil, drastic economic reforms caused recession; impeached
   (d) Marxist president of

Chile, nationalized corporations, angered U.S.
(e) Chilean general, overthrew Allende in 1973
(f) led Peruvian government, aided oppressed Indians, lowered food prices

3. (a) bought Argentina's railways, banks, insurance, shipping, and communications industries
(b) divert attention from domestic problems
(c) destruction of the Amazon River basin
(d) enormous foreign debt, runaway inflation
(e) to produce cocaine for sale in the illegal drug market

4. Answers will vary; difficult to achieve cooperation

CLOSE

Lead students in a discussion of the 'Focus' objectives identified on page 1030. Emphasize the importance of the unequal distribution of wealth and power in most Latin American nations.

grade 2. The major reason is poverty. In many countries, parents often need their children to work for survival or cannot afford to send them to school. Those who can afford it often go to private Catholic schools. Children in some Latin American countries also miss many school days. In four countries, for example, illnesses, caused chiefly by the lack of nourishing food, caused children to miss as many as fifty days of school a year. Because many Latin American children are not receiving much education, illiteracy remains a problem in many Latin American countries.

There has been rapid growth in higher education in Latin America, however. In part, this reflects a greater investment of state funds in universities, often at the expense of primary or secondary schools. Also noticeable has been the growth in private universities. As an example, in Brazil, 63 percent of university students are enrolled at eleven Catholic universities and nine private secular schools. The remaining 37 percent of the university students attend 37 state-funded institutions.

The situation is quite different elsewhere, however. In Mexico, for example, 85 percent of university students attend state-funded schools. At the same time, the number of students in Mexican universities and colleges has risen dramatically. In 1965/1966, there were 256,000 university students. Only ten years later, the number had increased to 970,000. Unfortunately, jobs are often not available for the large numbers of university graduates.

The military regimes in Latin America have greatly affected universities. In Chile, for example, the military regime that came into power in 1973 fired 30 to 35 percent of the professors. Military governments have also hired their supporters to run the universities. These changes have led to a decline in the quality of education in many Latin American institutions of higher learning.

Cultural Life

One constant theme in Latin American culture is the desire for a return to a lost past. To many Latin American intellectuals, the European conquest destroyed a world in which native peoples were an organic part of nature. Both artists and writers have sought to recapture this lost natural world. To them, nature frees people of the destructive habits imposed by civilized life.

Another tradition has also developed among some Latin American intellectuals—a civilizing tradition. These intellectuals believe in progress. To them, nature reduces people to primitive habits (to barbarians). Culture gives people their sensitivity and their compassion. The civilizers want a modern Latin America that includes industries and cities. They represent the majority in Latin America today.

Regardless of how they view their world, artists and writers have played important roles in Latin American society. They have been given a public status that few writers and artists have had in other countries. The poet Pablo Neruda, for example, was a Marxist presidential candidate in Chile in 1970. Another novelist and poet, José Sarney, was elected president of Brazil in 1985. Peru's greatest novelist, Mario Vargas Llosa (HOH-suh), ran for the presidency of Peru in 1990. In Latin America, writers and artists are seen as people who can express the hopes and desires of the people.

The Arts

Before World War II, modern forms of art had been brought to Latin America by artists who had studied in Europe. Latin American artists, however, responded to modern art in their own way. For a long time, modern art was closely identified with nationalism, or a search for national identity. As we saw in Chapter 27, for many artists, this search included the desire to incorporate native traditions in their artworks. The painting of nationalist and worker-inspired murals in Mexico in the 1920s and 1930s had a strong impact on artists elsewhere in Latin America. Especially in Ecuador, Peru, and Bolivia, artists followed the Mexican artists in including elements of their native traditions in their murals.

After World War II, Latin American painting moved in new directions that were strongly influenced by international styles. Especially important was abstract painting—the most radical form of modern art. Abstract art was especially important in Argentina and Venezuela.

So What ??

If your students question the importance of the information on **Latin America,** *tell them . . .*

By the 21st century, Latino residents will surpass African-Americans in the United States as this country's largest minority group. As part of the fabric of American society, their history, culture, and traditions continue to increasingly contribute to and benefit society. The Latino influence can be clearly seen in art, music, foods, etc. today.

Modern art in Latin America was also helped by the development of a whole new set of art institutions. In the 1950s, a number of major cities built national museums, as well as museums of modern art. Large corporations also became important patrons of artists. International art exhibits, held in São Paulo, Buenos Aires, and Mexico City, came to be held regularly. These exhibitions set new standards for world art.

The use of modern international styles was also evident in architecture. Brazil, Venezuela, and Mexico led this movement, because these were the richest countries in Latin America at the time and thus were able to provide funds for buildings. Perhaps the most notable example of modern architecture can be seen in Brazil in the building of Brasília, the new capital city, in the 1950s and 1960s. Latin America's greatest modern architect, Oscar Niemeyer (NEE-mie-ur), designed some of the major buildings.

▲ *Lucila Godoy Alcayaga used the pen name Gabriela Mistral. She won her first poetry contest in 1914. Many of her poems have been translated into English by American poet Langston Hughes. Why do you think a well-known poet such as Langston Hughes would commit the time and energy needed to translate Lucila's poems into English?*

Literature

In literature, Latin Americans developed a unique form of expression, which some have called **magic realism.** Magic realism brings together realistic events with dreamlike or fantastic backgrounds. This kind of fiction reflects reality, but with an element of fantasy. Magic realism is evident in the works of many of Latin America's great writers.

Since 1945, Latin American writers have received worldwide recognition. Indeed, a number of them have been awarded the Nobel Prize for literature. Among the great writers were Gabriela Mistral (mee-STRAWL), Jorge Luis Borges (BAW r-hess), Mario Vargas Llosa, Gabriel García Márquez (mahr-KEZ), and Pablo Neruda (nay-ROO-thuh).

Gabriela Mistral was a Chilean poet and teacher. She was trained to be a teacher and became director of a secondary school for girls in 1918. She was soon asked to be the director of a new school for girls in Santiago. In 1922, she was invited by the Mexican government to introduce educational programs for the poor in that country. Later she took up residence in the United States and taught at Middlebury and Barnard Colleges. In 1945, she became the first Latin American author to win the Nobel Prize for literature.

The suicide of her fiancé when Mistral was 21 had a profound effect on her life and her poems. Her poems explored the many dimensions of love but were usually tinged with an element of sadness. Her first book of poetry was published in 1922. Her second collection, *Ternura (Tenderness)*, included a number of children's poems that captured the sweetness of childhood:

Stars are circles of children
Looking at the earth as they play . . .
Wheat stalks are bodies of children
swaying and swaying as they play . . .
Rivers are circles of children
running off to the sea as they play
Waves are circlets of little girls
embracing this world…as they play.[2]

Jorge Luis Borges was born in Argentina, where he spent most of his life. However, he was educated to a great extent in Europe. He wrote numerous poems and a large number of short stories. The latter contain

ENRICHMENT ACTIVITY

A uniquely Latin American literary form is magic realism, combining realistic events with elements of magic and fantasy. In addition to the novels mentioned, there have been several magic-realist movies made such as *Like Water for Chocolate.* Have your students do further research into the elements of magic realism and then write a short story in that style.

USING PRIMARY SOURCES

Ask students to write an essay or discuss differences between the reality that many children in Latin America face and the message of the poem by Gabriela Mistral on page 1037. What might street children of Rio de Janeiro have to say about this poem?

LEARNING FROM VISUALS

Answer to the caption question: Answers may include that he wrote in magic realism.

CLASS DISCUSSION

Ask students to identify and discuss possible reasons why much of Latin American literature is centered on changes in social values or political commentary. Do they believe this is representative of actual events and problems in many Latin American states?

SPANISH SUPPORT

The *Conclusion* has been translated into Spanish for your Spanish-speaking students. Included with this translation (in your Teacher Resource Box) are Section Key Points, which consist of one or two sentences summarizing each section in the chapter. These Key Points have also been translated into Spanish.

TIME LINE

As students conclude the chapter, you may want to refer them to the chapter time line in the *Study Guide.* The time line will help them put key dates in perspective. Supporting questions and activities are also provided.

many of the themes that make his work such a good example of magic realism. In *Fictions*, *The Aleph*, and *Labyrinths*, Borges created a fantastic world in which what seems absurd might well be true. However, who can really know? Borges chooses to stress that we know so little about the world that anything can happen.

Mario Vargas Llosa was born in Peru and educated in both Spain and France. His novels are realistic but also contain an element of fantasy. They mix time, space, and identity into a profound puzzle. His first novel, *Time of the Hero*, takes place in a military school. Here students deny the sensitive sides of their beings in order to appear tough, as society dictates. Many of Vargas Llosa's later works focus on the incredible corruption that he found in all levels of Peruvian society and government. In the 1980s, he began a search for new political values for Latin America. In *The War of the End of the World*, he gave a realistic portrayal of the crushing of a rebellion in Brazil in 1897. His message was clear: he supported the liberal principles of progress and modernization.

In the 1960s, Gabriel García Márquez was the most famous of the Latin American novelists. He was born and brought up in poverty in Colombia. Much of his early career was spent in journalism. He worked as a foreign reporter in Paris, Rome, Havana, and New York City. By the late 1950s and early 1960s, he was becoming known as a novelist. He won the Nobel Prize for literature in 1982.

The best known of his novels is *One Hundred Years of Solitude*. One critic, in fact, has called it one of the greatest novels ever written. It is the story of the development of the fictional town of Macondo as witnessed

▲ *Gabriel García Márquez continues to write. In 1996, he published a new novel,* News of a Kidnapping, *about drug-related kidnappings in Colombia. What is the most unique aspect of his writing style?*

by several generations of the Buendias, its founding family. Macondo is much like García Márquez's own hometown of Aracataca, near the Caribbean coast of Colombia. This novel is the foremost example of magic realism. The author slips back and forth between fact and fantasy. Villagers are not surprised when a local priest rises into the air and floats. However, when wandering gypsies introduce these villagers to magnets, telescopes, and magnifying glasses, the villagers are dumbfounded by what they see as magic. According to the author, fantasy and fact simply depend on one's point of view.

Pablo Neruda was a Chilean poet who won the Nobel Prize for literature in 1971. He was born in Chile but lived for a while in both Spain and Mexico. When he returned home, he entered political life, serving as a Communist deputy in the Chilean senate. In 1948, a new government forced him to leave Chile. He was not able to return until 1952. Neruda was a poet of great power. Through his poetry, he became a voice for the common people. He died in 1973, soon after the military coup that killed his friend, the Chilean president Salvador Allende.

Female writers also achieved new levels of success in Latin America. As we have seen, it was a woman—Gabriela Mistral—who was the first Latin American to win the Nobel Prize for literature, in 1945. In the 1980s, the work of Isabel Allende (niece of Salvador Allende) also achieved worldwide recognition. *The House of the Spirits* was a novel in the tradition of magic realism. It tells the history of twentieth-century Chile through four generations of women.

SECTION REVIEW

1. **Locate:**
   (a) Brasília

2. **Define:**
   (a) magic realism

3. **Identify:**
   (a) Pablo Neruda, (b) José Sarney, (c) Mario Vargas Llosa, (d) Gabriela Mistral, (e) *The War of the End of the World*

4. **Recall:**
   (a) Why is it difficult to speak of a single Latin American culture?
   (b) Although many more Latin American people are completing university degrees, why do they not always benefit materially from their education?
   (c) What is one constant theme in Latin American culture?

5. **Think Critically:** What factors combine to make it difficult to provide adequate education for most children in many Latin American nations?

Conclusion

Since 1945, the nations of Latin America have experienced a number of common trends. Especially troublesome were economic problems. Although some Latin American nations shared in the economic growth of the 1950s and 1960s, this growth was not matched by any real political stability. Often armies overthrew democratic governments and established military regimes. Staggering debts owed to foreign banks made conditions even worse. With the debt crisis in the 1980s, however, came a movement toward democracy.

Democratic governments began to replace oppressive military regimes, and the trend continued into the 1990s.

Since 1945, a population explosion has magnified Latin America's economic and political problems. An enormous gulf between rich and poor has been a key factor in maintaining considerable social upheaval. Then, too, despite attempts to form a new relationship with Latin America, the United States continued to intervene in Latin American affairs, especially in the Caribbean Basin.

The nations of the Caribbean Basin experienced considerable upheaval after 1945. Mexico's economic problems magnified discontent with the nation's sole political party, the PRI. Successful Marxist revolutions in Cuba and Nicaragua fed U.S. fears of the spread of communism and led to active American involvement in the affairs of Caribbean Basin nations.

The nations of South America also experienced economic, social, and political problems. Strong military regimes alternated with civilian regimes in Argentina, Brazil, Chile, Colombia, and Peru. Recently, political democracy has made great strides. However, the vast gulf between rich and poor, along with the drug trade, has added to both the social and economic instability of the region.

Notes

1. Dwight Eisenhower, *The White House Years: Waging Peace, 1956–1961* (Garden City, N.Y., 1965), p. 533.
2. Quoted in Ruth Ashby and Deborah Gore Ohrn, *Herstory: Women Who Changed the World* (New York, 1995), p. 204.

ASSESS

Possible assessments include:

1. Section Review Questions on this page
2. Section 31–4 Quiz in your Teacher Resource materials
3. Reteaching Worksheets in your Teacher Resource materials
4. Self-Study software

Answers to SECTION REVIEW

2. (a) literary expression that combines realistic events with dreamlike backgrounds
3. (a) poet, Marxist presidential candidate in Chile
   (b) novelist and poet, president of Brazil
   (c) Peru's greatest novelist, ran for president in Peru
   (d) Chilean poet, created educational programs in Mexico, won Nobel Prize
   (e) book by Llosa, portrayed a rebellion in Brazil, expressed liberal principles
4. (a) Many different ethnic, racial, religious, and social groups live there.
   (b) not enough jobs
   (c) desire to return to a lost past
5. rapid population growth, unequal distribution of wealth, need for children to help produce income, shortage of funding

CLOSE

Lead students in a discussion of the 'Focus' objectives identified on page 1037. Emphasize the prevalence of social change as a theme in much of the art and literature in Latin America.

Answers to CHAPTER 31 REVIEW

USING KEY TERMS

1. privatization
2. theology of liberation
3. magic realism
4. multinational corporations
5. *descamisados*
6. Contras
7. Shining Path
8. import-substituting industrialization (ISI)
9. drug cartels

REVIEWING THE FACTS

1. to peacefully resolve disputes in the western hemisphere
2. Poverty and rapid population growth in rural areas have caused many people to move to Latin American cities.
3. price of exports fell during the 1980s making it difficult to earn the money
4. a free trade agreement between the United States, Canada, and Mexico
5. nationalized American businesses in 1960
6. The United States military invaded Panama and arrested him.
7. Falkland Islands
8. Allende was a Communist who was progressively taking property and power from wealthy people who supported the military.
9. gave land to the peasants in Peru
10. ran for the presidency of Chile in 1970

THINKING CRITICALLY

1. production is consumed by growing population, little left over to invest in new public facilities, businesses, or industries
2. When Castro led Cuba into communism it may have caused the United States to extend aid to other Latin American countries to try to prevent them from also becoming communist.
3. Answers will vary but should

USING KEY TERMS

1. The process of returning government owned businesses to private ownership is called

   _____.

2. The support given by some religious leaders in Latin America for violence to bring about political change has been called the _____.

3. A style of literature that combines elements of the real world with imaginary events is called

   _____.

4. Businesses that have divisions in two or more countries are called _____.

5. _____ was the name given to workers who supported Juan Perón in Argentina.

6. The anti-Communist forces that fought the Sandinistas in Nicaragua were called _____.

7. The Communist guerrilla movement in Peru is called the _____.

8. When a nation takes steps to encourage the production of products it buys from other countries is has undertaken _____.

9. _____ are organizations that work to eliminate competition for their illegal drug businesses.

REVIEWING THE FACTS

1. What is the purpose of the Organization of American States?

2. Why have many Latin American cities experienced rapid population growth?

3. Why did many Latin American nations have difficulties in making payments on their international debts during the 1980s?

4. What is the North American Free Trade Agreement?

5. What did Fidel Castro do in 1960 that probably contributed to the decision of the United States to sponsor an invasion of Cuba at the Bay of Pigs in 1961?

---

6. What happened that ended Manuel Noriega's control of Panama in 1989?

7. What islands did Argentina invade in 1982?

8. Why did the armed forces of Chile overthrow and apparently kill Salvador Allende in 1973?

9. What did General Juan Velasco Alvarado do in the early 1970s that earned him the support of many of Peru's peasants?

10. What two career goals did Pablo Neruda pursue that made him famous?

THINKING CRITICALLY

1. Why is the rapid rate of population growth in many Latin American countries a problem for their economic and political systems?

2. How may the creation of the Alliance for Progress in 1961 been related to the conversion of Cuba to communism in the same year?

3. What caused the United States to use its military power to arrest Manuel Noriega after ignoring many other dishonest and corrupt leaders in Latin America?

4. Why did relations between the Soviet Union and Cuba become more difficult after 1962?

5. Why was the very close presidential election in Mexico in 1990 such a surprise?

6. Many Latin American nations have attempted to pay the costs of running their governments by printing money instead of collecting taxes. What problems has this policy caused?

7. Why was Evita Perón's use of government funds to help the poor probably bad for that country's political system in the long run?

8. Latin American nations have developed many high quality colleges and universities. Why hasn't this solved their problems of illiteracy and inequality?

---

address the economic and strategic importance of the Panama Canal.

4. Soviet Union backed down in the 1962 Cuban Missile Crisis.

5. The political process in Mexico had been dominated by the Mexican Institutional Revolutionary Party for many years. Any close election was a surprise.

6. Any country that pays its bill by printing money will increase the amount of money in circulation and therefore decrease its value. This is inflation.

7. Although Evita Perón's efforts may have helped some poor people they were not well-organized or efficient, they were outside the law, and undermined the legal and political processes in Argentina.

8. Many of the people who graduate from their institutions of higher learning cannot find employment and these schools do little to help the masses of poor people achieve greater education.

APPLYING SOCIAL STUDIES SKILLS

1. **Sociology:** Identify and explain several possible ways in which the social values of Latin American countries may be influenced by those of the United States.
2. **Geography/Economics:** Draw a map that indicates significant resources and products traded between the United States and Latin American nations. Identify and explain economic advantages each side has in this trade relationship.
3. **Government:** Explain why economic conditions encouraged the growth of dictatorial governments in Latin America during the 1980s.
4. **Geography/Ecology/Economics:** Study a map of the Amazon river valley and investigate the resources and uses of this region. What uses can you suggest that would preserve the Amazon's environment and at the same time provide a means of earning a living for the people of Brazil?

MAKING TIME AND PLACE CONNECTIONS

1. Compare and contrast conditions that existed during the rapid growth of industries in Europe and the United States in the nineteenth century with those that have existed while Latin American nations have worked to industrialize.
2. Some people have compared the policies of the United States toward Latin American countries to those of the Soviet Union toward countries in eastern Europe after World War II. Explain why you feel this is, or is not, a valid comparison.
3. What are the reasons for class distinctions that exist in the United States and in Latin American society? Explain the similarities and differences between the situations in the two countries.
4. Explain why many Latin American nations are more concerned with the influence of multinational corporations than are the United States or developed countries in Europe.

BECOMING AN HISTORIAN

1. **Analyzing Information/Drawing Inferences:** The table below measures and projects the population of Latin America between 1940 and 2025. It also shows what percentage this population was or will be of total world population. Identify and explain the trend demonstrated by this data and what it is likely to mean for the future of Latin America.
2. **Art as a Key to History:** Ask a Spanish teacher in your school to help you identify writings by a well-known current Latin American poet or author. Write an essay that relates his or her point of view with social, political, or economic trends in Latin America.
3. **Conducting Research:** On April 22, 1997 anti-terrorist forces stormed the Japanese embassy in Lima, Peru where 71 hostages were held captive by members of a leftist group called Tupac Amaru. Although initial evaluations of the action were positive some people said it would only encourage reprisals from the guerrilla movement. Conduct research and write a report that describes the long-term results of this action by the Peruvian government.

Latin American Population and Percentages of World Population (in millions of people)

Year	1940	1960	1980	2000	2025
Population	131	213	364	566 *	865 *
% of World	5.7%	7.1%	8.2%	9.2%*	10.6%*

*projections
Source: United Nations, *Long Range Global Population Projections* (New York, 1992), pp. 16–17.

1041

APPLYING SOCIAL STUDIES SKILLS

1. Answers will vary but may identify the transfer of social values through exchanges of media and entertainment, or of travel and tourism.
2. Maps will vary but should identify a significant number of resources and products that are traded between the United States and Latin America. Advantages should include the large labor force that is willing to work at low wages and the greater technological and financial strength of the U.S. economy.
3. Answers will vary; difficult economic conditions in many Latin American countries forced their leaders to make decisions that were often unpopular.
4. Answers will vary; but should demonstrate the economic and ecological issues involved.

MAKING TIME AND PLACE CONNECTIONS

1. Answers will vary; the United States and European powers did not have to compete with other nations that were more developed or provide for the needs of rapidly expanding populations.
2. Answers will vary but may indicate that the

Soviet control of eastern European nations was much more comprehensive than the influence the United States has exerted on Latin American nations. With few exceptions the U.S. has avoided using its military to occupy Latin American nations and to a great extent has not controlled their governments. The U.S. has also generally been more tolerant of different political philosophies than the Soviet Union.

3. Answers will vary but may state that class differences in the U.S. are primarily based on economic or racial distinctions. In Latin America differences may depend on these factors as well as ethnic heritage, educational attainment, where people are from, and in some cases on political or religious affiliations.

4. Answers will vary but are likely to point out that most multinational corporations are controlled by people who live in the United States or the developed nations of Europe.

ON BECOMING AN HISTORIAN

1. Answers will vary but should indicate that the rapid growth of population in Latin America will create a need for more consumer goods, schools, social services, and employment opportunities that their economic systems are likely to have difficulty in providing.
2. Essays will vary but should demonstrate that an appropriate selection was read, studied, and understood, and that its contents were meaningfully related to events in Latin America.
3. Answers will vary but should demonstrate a reasonable effort to find and understand relevant information about events in Peru since 1997, and to evaluate how they were affected by the assault on the Japanese embassy.

PLANNING GUIDE

SECTION	KEY TOPICS	PRIMARY SOURCES	ASSESSMENT
1 The Era of Independence in Africa pages 1043–1050	◆ African struggles for independence ◆ Pan-Africanism and nationalism ◆ Economic, political and social reality in Africa		◆ Section Review, page 1050 ◆ Section Quiz 32–1, TRB
2 Continuity and Change in Modern African Societies pages 1051–1057	◆ Urban and Rural Africa ◆ Women in modern Africa ◆ Recent developments in African culture	◆ A selection from Cyprian Ekwensi's, *Iska,* page 1053 ◆ A selection from Chinua Achebe's, *Things Fall Apart,* page 1056	◆ Section Review, page 1057 ◆ Section Quiz 32–2, TRB
3 Conflict in the Middle East pages 1057–1067	◆ The Question of Palestine ◆ Abdul Nasser, Egypt, and Pan-Arabism ◆ The Arab-Israeli dispute ◆ Revolution in Iran	◆ A speech by Abdul Nasser regarding the Suez Canal Company, page 1059 ◆ A plea for peace by Golda Meir, page 1061	◆ Section Review, page 1067 ◆ Section Quiz 32–3, TRB
4 Society and Culture in the Contemporary Middle East pages 1067–1071	◆ Revival of Islamic fundamentalism ◆ Economics of oil and land ◆ Women's rights in Middle Eastern societies ◆ Recent trends in Middle Eastern art and literature		◆ Section Review, page 1071 ◆ Section Quiz 32–4, TRB

CHALLENGES OF NATION BUILDING IN AFRICA AND THE MIDDLE EAST (1945 TO PRESENT)

REPRODUCIBLE ACTIVITIES

Historical Maps

Charts and Graphs

Critical Thinking

Cooperative Learning

Vocabulary

Guided Reading

Reteaching

Enrichment

Performance Assessment

Spanish Key Points and Chapter Summaries

Spanish Vocabulary

Spanish Guided Reading

MULTIMEDIA SUPPORT

TRANSPARENCIES
- *World History* Color Transparency Package
- Fine Art Color Transparency Package

VIDEO
- *World History* Video Library
- **CNN** Annual Video Update

LASERDISC
- *Sights and Sounds of History*

AUDIO
- *Listening to Literature* audiotape (English and Spanish)
- *History of Music* CD

SOFTWARE
- WESTEST™
- Student Review

CD–ROM
- *The Journey of Civilization*
- *World History*

INTERNET
- Internet Activities

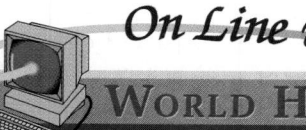

On Line with WORLD HISTORY

Access West's history web site at **http://history.swpco.com** You'll find activities and web sites related to specific topics and chapters in *World History: The Human Odyssey*. Also look for references to helpful web sites at appropriate places throughout this teacher edition.

LESSON PLANNING

You will find detailed daily lesson plans for both traditional class scheduling and **block scheduling** in your Teacher Resource Box.

Not Enough Time?

If you do not have the four or five days recommended to teach this chapter, you may want to focus on the following sections and activities:

- Have students skim the chapter to answer the "Questions to Guide Your Reading" on page 1043. Discuss their answers, then read the "Conclusion" on page 1071.
- Do a more in-depth reading of the growth of nationalism in Africa on pages 1045–1050, the dispute between Arab states and Israel on pages 1062–1064, and the growth of fundamentalism in the Middle East on pages 1067–1069. Conclude with a discussion of the importance of art and literature as a means of studying changing values in Africa and the Middle East.

CHALLENGES OF NATION BUILDING

BUILDING ON CHAPTER 31

To prepare students to study Chapter 32 you may use the following questions and activities.

◆ Ask students to review recent changes in Latin American society, politics, and economic systems. Ask them to identify reasons why they should expect to find similar changes in Africa.

◆ There are three primary languages used in Latin America: Spanish, Portuguese, and English. Ask students to explain why differences in language represent a much greater problem to unity in Africa.

USING THE OPENING STORY

Select from the following questions and activities to reinforce the reading of the opening story.

◆ Why do many people in developing nations blame foreign powers for their problems?

◆ Why is it possible for small bands of poorly equipped guerrilla soldiers to defeat larger, better equipped armies?

◆ What may past colonial domination have to do with the difficulty of finding capable leadership in Africa today?

◆ In what ways are problems of African refugees also problems of developed nations?

In the 1970s, many Iranians began to grow dissatisfied with their ruler, Muhammad Reza Pahlavi, the shah of Iran. An opposition movement, led by the Muslim clergy under the guidance of the Ayatollah (IE-uh-TOE-luh) Ruholla Khomeini (KOE-MAE-nee), grew in strength. (An ayatollah is a major religious leader. The word means "the sign of God.") One observer described a political rally in the capital city of Tehran in 1978: "On Sunday, December 11, hundreds of thousands of people held a procession in the center of Tehran. . . . Slogans against the shah rippled in the wind—'Death to the Shah!' 'Death to the Americans!' 'Khomeini is our leader,' and so on. People from all walks of life could be found in the crowd." In January 1979, the shah left Iran, officially for a "period of rest and holiday." Three weeks later, the Ayatollah Khomeini returned to Iran from exile in Paris. On April 1, his forces seized control and proclaimed Iran to be an Islamic republic. Included in the new government's program was an attack on Western culture and, above all, on the United States, viewed by Khomeini as the "Great Satan." On November 4, after the shah had gone to the United States for medical help, Iranian revolutionaries seized the U.S. Embassy in Tehran, taking fifty-two Americans hostage. Not until the inauguration of a new American president in January 1981 did the Iranians free their American captives.

These revolutionary events in Iran were but one example of the upheavals that changed both the Middle East and Africa after 1945. In both these areas of the world, Europeans were forced to give up their control and allow independent states to emerge. The change from colony to free nation in both regions has not been easy, however. In Africa, the legacy of colonialism left arbitrary boundaries, political inexperience, and continued European economic domination. Combined with overpopulation and climatic disasters, this colonial legacy has made it difficult for the new states to achieve political stability and economic prosperity. In the Middle East, the problems are deep-seated ethnic and religious disputes, superpower involvement, and a gross inequality in the distribution of oil resources throughout the region. All these problems have led to a high level of tension and conflict, as well as a strong anti-Western sentiment. These two regions—Africa and the Middle East—remain among the most conflict ridden in the world.

◀ *This young Iranian armed with a machine gun stands in front of a revolutionary poster, a fitting symbol of the changes that occurred in Iran in the 1980s.*

ADDITIONAL RESOURCES

BOOKS FOR STUDENTS
African Heroes by Naomi Mitchison, Farrar, Strauss, and Giroux
The Palestinians by Jonathan Dimbleb, Quartet Books
Nkrumah by Robin McKown, Doubleday

VIDEOS/FILMS
Africa: Tribalism to Independence, Series: Western Man and the Modern World, Social

Studies School Service, (800) 421-4246
A Chance for Peace in the Middle East, CNN Special Report, 1993, Social Studies School Service, (800) 421-4246

CD-ROM
Lines in the Sand: Pursuit of Peace in the Middle East, Tiger Media, Social Studies School Service, (800) 421-4246

IN AFRICA AND THE MIDDLE EAST

(1945 TO PRESENT)

THE WORLD SINCE 1945

| 1945 | AFRICA AND THE MIDDLE EAST | 2000 |
| 1945 | | 2000 |

QUESTIONS TO GUIDE YOUR READING

1. What were the backgrounds and ideas of the new African political leaders?

2. How have dreams clashed with realities in the independent nations of Africa?

3. What significant tensions exist in contemporary African society?

4. How have the tensions in contemporary African society affected African culture?

5. What political and economic problems have Middle Eastern states faced since 1945?

6. What are the major social and cultural developments in the Middle East since 1945?

THE ERA OF INDEPENDENCE IN AFRICA

European colonial rule had been imposed on almost the entire continent of Africa by 1900. During the 1960s and 1970s, the Europeans finally retreated. Independent states with governments patterned after the Western model emerged across the continent.

The process of nation building has not been easy. The peoples of Africa were not well prepared for democracy. Even with political independence, they remained economically dependent upon their former European masters. The geographical shape of the new states reflected colonial interests rather than African realities. Most of the colonial boundaries had been drawn for the convenience of the European imperialists. Only rarely did the boundaries reflect the ethnic, cultural, or linguistic divisions of Africa.

African societies and their leaders have struggled for a generation to overcome these difficulties, but with only modest success. Many of the poorest nations in the world are in Africa. Several are threatened by mass starvation, and others, by the spread of AIDS. If unchecked, AIDS will devastate the populations

1043

FOCUS ON THEMES

Listed below are brief summaries of how the content in this chapter supports the text's key themes.

Politics and History The new states of Africa and the Middle East have found it difficult to create stable political systems. In Africa, problems left from years of colonial rule, overpopulation, and climatic disasters have left political instability. In the Middle East, ethnic and religious disputes have served to make conflict a regular feature of political life.

Economics and History Economic problems continue to plague both Africa and the Middle East. After independence, African states remained economically dependent upon European states. Dependence on oil in the Middle East and the export of a single crop or natural resource in Africa left areas vulnerable to economic pressures. States in both Africa and the Middle East have experimented with either capitalism or socialism, or with unique combinations of the two.

Social Life Enormous gaps remain between rich and poor in both Africa and the Middle East. Poverty is especially widespread in rural areas of Africa. In the Middle East, there is a wide gap between countries with large oil reserves and those with few or no oil reserves.

Religion in History Islamic fundamentalism, or the attempt to impose the strict teachings of Islam on all facets of life, plays a major role in the Middle East today.

1043

FOCUS

OBJECTIVES

After completing this section, students should be able to

1. describe the struggle for freedom by a variety of African states
2. describe impacts of Pan-African and nationalist movements on African states
3. identify and describe social, political, and economic problems faced by African states

FOCUS ACTIVITY

Help students understand how problems in developed nations made it easier for African states to achieve independence. Ask students to list problems faced by European nations after World War II. Where might controlling African colonies have ranked on their list of priorities? Why didn't many African states become free immediately after World War II?

of these states early in the next century. Political stability is rare, and civil wars often erupt throughout the continent.

Background: The Struggle for Independence

After World War II, Europeans realized that colonial rule in Africa would have to come to an end. Little had been done, however, to prepare Africans for self-rule. The political organizations that had been formed by Africans before the war to gain their rights became formal political parties. Independence was now their goal. In the Gold Coast, Kwame Nkrumah (en-KROO-

▼ *Kwame Nkrumah served as the first president of Ghana (formerly the Gold Coast) after the country gained its independence from Great Britain in 1957. Nkrumah was educated in the United States and became a strong voice in leading African opposition against colonialism.*

muh) formed the Convention People's Party, the first African political party in black Africa. In the late 1940s, Jomo Kenyatta founded the Kenya African National Union. It focused on economic issues but also sought independence or self-rule for Kenya.

For the most part, these political activities were nonviolent. They were led by Western-educated African intellectuals. The members of these parties were chiefly merchants, urban professionals, and members of labor unions. However, the demand for independence was not limited to the cities. In Kenya, for example, the **Mau Mau movement** among the Kikuyu peoples used terrorism to demand *uhuru* (freedom) from the British. Mau Mau terrorism alarmed the European population and caused the British in 1959 to promise eventual independence.

A similar process was occurring in Egypt, which had been a protectorate of Great Britain since the 1880s. In 1918, a formal political party called the Wafd was formed to promote Egyptian independence. Egyptian intellectuals, however, were opposed as much to the Egyptian monarchy as to the British. In 1952, an army coup overthrew King Farouk (fah-ROOK) and set up an independent republic.

In areas such as South Africa, where the political system was dominated by European settlers, the transition to independence was more complicated. In South Africa, political activity by local blacks began with the formation of the African National Congress (ANC) in 1912. At first, it was a group of intellectuals and had little mass support. Its goal was to gain economic and political reforms, including full equality for educated Africans, within the framework of the existing system. The ANC's efforts, however, met with little success. At the same time, by the 1950s, South African whites (descendants of the Dutch, or Afrikaans) were strengthening the laws separating whites and blacks. This activity created a system of racial segregation in South Africa known as **apartheid.** When blacks demonstrated against the apartheid laws, the white government brutally repressed the demonstrators. On March 21, 1960, for example, police opened fire on people who were leading a peaceful march in Sharpeville and killed sixty-nine. Two-thirds of the dead were found to be shot in the back. After the arrest

RECOMMENDED READING

For general surveys of contemporary African history, see R. Oliver and J. D. Fage, *A Short History of Africa* (Harmondsworth, 1986); R. Oliver, *The African Experience* (New York, 1992), which contains interesting essays on a variety of themes; and K. Shillington, *History of Africa* (New York, 1989), which takes a chronological and geographical approach and includes excellent maps and illustrations.

On nationalist movements, see P. Gifford and W. R. Louis, eds., *The Transfer of Power in Africa* (New Haven, Conn., 1982); and J. D. Hargreaves, *Decolonisation in Africa* (London, 1988). For an African perspective, see K. Nkrumah, *Ghana* (London, 1959).

Political events in Africa are often examined on a regional basis. For an overview, see A. Mazrui and M. Tidy, *Nationalism and New States in Africa* (Portsmouth, 1984).

of ANC leader Nelson Mandela in 1962, members of the ANC called for armed resistance to the white government.

In Algeria, some resistance to French rule by Arabs in rural areas had never ceased. However, a widespread rebellion broke out in the mid-1950s. At first, the French government tried to maintain its authority in Algeria. When Charles de Gaulle became president in 1958, however, he reversed French policy. Algeria was given its independence in 1962. The armed struggle in Algeria affected its neighbors as well. Both Tunisia and Morocco won their independence from France in 1956.

When both Great Britain and France decided to let go of their colonial empires in the late 1950s and 1960s, most black African nations achieved their independence. The Gold Coast, now renamed Ghana and under the guidance of Kwame Nkrumah, was first, in 1957. Nigeria, the Belgian Congo (renamed Zaire), Kenya, Tanganyika (TAN-gun-YEE-kuh) (later, when joined with Zanzibar, renamed Tanzania), and others soon followed. Seventeen new African nations emerged in 1960. Another eleven nations soon followed between 1961 and 1965. By the late 1960s, only parts of southern Africa and the Portuguese possessions of Mozambique and Angola remained under European rule. After a series of brutal guerrilla wars, the Portuguese finally gave up their colonies in the 1970s.

Pan-Africanism and Nationalism: The Destiny of Africa

The newly independent African states faced many challenges. Most of them were chiefly traditional, agrarian societies (societies based on farming). Most African leaders, however, came from the urban middle class and had studied in either Europe or the United States. They spoke and read European languages. Most were very critical of colonial policies, but they still believed in using the Western democratic model in Africa.

The views of these African leaders on economics, however, were somewhat more diverse. Some, such as Jomo Kenyatta of Kenya and General Mobutu Sese Seko (moe-BOO-too SAY-SAY SAE-KOE) of Zaire, believed in Western-style capitalism. Others, such as

▲ *South African women unsuccessfully demonstrated in the streets of the Cato Manor Township to protest apartheid policies in 1959. They were outnumbered by the police, who prevented their entry into what had become a "whites-only" building.*

Julius Nyerere (nie-RAIR-ay) of Tanzania, Kwame Nkrumah of Ghana, and Sékou Touré of Guinea, preferred an "African form of socialism." This socialism was not like that practiced in the Soviet Union or Eastern Europe. Instead, it was based on African traditions of community in which ownership of the country's wealth would be put into the hands of the people. As Nyerere declared in 1967, "The basis of socialism is a belief in the oneness of man and the common historical destiny of mankind. Its basis, in other words, is human equality."[1]

The new political leaders in Africa were highly nationalistic. In general, they accepted the boundaries of their states, even though these had been drawn up arbitrarily by the colonial powers. Virtually all of the new states included widely different ethnic, linguistic, and territorial groups. In Zaire, for example, there were over two hundred different territorial groups speaking seventy-five different languages. In Uganda, the state radio station broadcast in twenty-four languages.

On Line with WORLD HISTORY *Internet Activity*

You may want to have your students visit the following URL, where they will find information and additional web site resources to enhance their study of this chapter.

History of South Africa—Beginnings to Overthrow of Apartheid

http://www.sacs.org.za/level2/

history.htm

This site is a good resource for quick reference.

Due to the ever-changing nature of the World Wide Web, see the West History web site, **http://history.swpco.com** for regular updates of the URLs in this text.

Some African leaders themselves helped to undermine the fragile sense of common identity that was needed to knit together these diverse groups in their countries. A number of them, including Nkrumah of Ghana, Touré of Guinea, and Kenyatta of Kenya, believed in the dream of pan-Africanism. This was a belief in the unity of all black Africans, regardless of national boundaries. The Organization of African Unity, founded by the leaders of thirty-two African states in 1963, was a concrete result of this belief.

Pan-Africanists believed in negritude (blackness), meaning that there was a distinctive "African personality." In their view, all black African peoples had a common identity and a common sense of destiny. Pan-Africanism was shared by several of the new African leaders, including Léopold Senghor of Senegal, Nkrumah of Ghana, and Kenyatta of Kenya. Nkrumah in particular hoped that a pan-African union could be established that would unite all of the new countries of the continent in a broader community. His dream never became a reality.

Map 32.1   Modern Africa

Dreams and Realities

Other dreams failed as well in Africa. Many people had hoped that independence would lead to stable political structures based on "one person, one vote." They were soon disappointed as democratic governments gave way to a series of military regimes and one-party states. Between 1957 and 1982, over seventy leaders of African countries were overthrown by violence. In 1984, only seven of the forty-one major African states allowed opposition parties to operate legally. The rest were under single-party regimes or were ruled by the military.

Some of these military regimes were especially brutal. In 1966, President Milton Obote (oh-BOH-tay) had named Idi Amin (ee-DEE ah-MEEN) commander in chief of the Ugandan army. Five years later, Amin seized control of the country. He ruled with an iron fist and gave free rein to his secret police. Political oppo-

STUDYING MAPS

The following questions will help you guide students through their study of Map 32.1.

1. How many nations exist in Africa? (Students should arrive at a figure of 47 depending on how the African free states are counted.)

2. How many of these states are landlocked? (Nine of these states have no access to the sea.)

3. What special problems would landlocked states have? (They must import goods over land through other countries or resort to expensive air shipments.)

nents were shot, bludgeoned to death, and run over by tanks. Probably 150,000 people were murdered. Then, too, Amin ruined Uganda's economy with his lavish expenditures on luxuries and pleasures during his eight years of rule.

Hopes that independence would bring economic prosperity and equality were also crushed. Some of the problems were left over from colonial days. Most newly independent countries in Africa still relied on the export of a single crop or natural resource. Liberia, for example, depended on the export of rubber; Nigeria, on oil. When prices dropped, their economies suffered. To make matters worse, most African states had to import technology and manufactured goods from the West. The prices of those goods usually rose more rapidly than did prices of the export products.

The new states also created their own problems. Scarce national resources were spent on military equipment or expensive consumer goods rather than on building the foundations for an industrial economy. Corruption became almost a way of life in Africa. Bribery was needed to get even the most basic services.

Finally, population growth crippled efforts to create modern economies. By the 1980s, population growth averaged nearly 3 percent throughout Africa, the highest rate of any continent. Drought conditions have led to widespread hunger and starvation, first in West African countries such as Niger and Mali and then in Ethiopia, Somalia, and the Sudan. Millions are in danger of starvation and malnutrition. Countless others have fled to neighboring countries in search of food. In recent years, the spread of AIDS in Africa has caused the disease to reach epidemic proportions. According to one estimate, one-third of the entire population of sub-Saharan Africa is infected with the virus that causes AIDS.

As a result of all these problems, poverty is widespread in Africa, especially among the three-quarters of the population still living off the land. Cities have grown tremendously. In much of Africa, cities are surrounded by massive slums populated by rural people who fled to the cities to find a better life. The growth of the cities has overwhelmed transportation and sanitation systems. Pollution and perpetual traffic jams are the result. Millions are forced to live without water and

▲ Two very wealthy Nigerian aristocrats emerge from their new Mercedes. What is the probable source of their wealth?

electricity in their homes. In the meantime, the fortunate few (usually government officials willing to take bribes in return for favors) have lavish lifestyles. The rich in many East African countries are known as the *wabenzi*, or Mercedes Benz people.

Concern over the dangers of economic inequality (the wide gap between rich and poor) inspired a number of African leaders to limit foreign investment and nationalize the major industries and utilities. Nyerere promoted the ideals of socialism and self-reliance in Tanzania. He placed limits on income and set up village collectives to avoid government corruption. Many observers noted that levels of corruption and political instability were lower in Tanzania than in many other African countries.

The countries that opted for capitalism faced their own problems. Kenya has a strong current of African capitalism and a substantial middle class, mostly based in the capital of Nairobi. However, landlessness, unemployment, and income differences are high. Eighty percent of the population lives in the countryside. Forty percent lives below the poverty line. The result has

TEACHING THEMES

Economics and History. Ask students to evaluate the following statement in an essay or a class discussion.

"It was easier for new states to invest in their economic systems in the past because there were fewer consumer goods for people to buy."

When a wealthy person in a developing nation buys an expensive foreign car, what does it do to that nation's ability to have economic growth?

COMPARING TIME PERIODS

Many African states suffer from corruption among their government officials. This problem is common in many other developing nations. Ask students to identify and explain factors that tend to encourage corruption in these nations.

LEARNING FROM VISUALS

Answer to the caption question: Nigeria has become a wealthy nation due to its oil exports and is the largest exporter of petroleum products in Africa.

MORE ABOUT . . . *Solving the Problem of Famine*

Because of the fighting in Rwanda, half of the country's people were either killed or displaced from their land. When they did return to their farms, and were in such dire need of food that they ate the seeds that were to be used for the next year's crop. Forty-two percent of Rwandans get their protein from various beans. The other important food crops are maize, potatoes, sweet potatoes,

sorghum and cassava. The Center for Tropical Agriculture realized that some of these crops were in danger of being lost forever so they began to collect, multiply and distribute native seeds.

In 1996, twelve African nations formed an alliance to bank one another's seeds for use in the event of famine or other disasters.

TEACHING THEMES

Politics and History. Ask students to imagine a leader of an African state with severe economic and social problems. This person's control over government is being challenged by other groups. Assign students to identify and explain reasons why such a person would be likely to blame his or her nation's problems on European Nations or the United States.

TEACHING THEMES

The Role of Individuals. Ask students to evaluate the efforts of F. W. de Klerk to facilitate a peaceful transition of power in South Africa. Do they believe this transfer would have taken place in more or less the same way no matter who was the President of white South Africa, or did de Klerk make a unique contribution to history? What reasons can they give for their point of view?

been widespread unrest in a country formerly admired for its successful development.

Beginning in the mid-1970s, a few African nations decided to adopt Soviet-style Marxism-Leninism. In Angola and Ethiopia, Marxist parties followed the Soviet model. Economically, the results were disappointing, and both countries faced severe internal opposition. In Ethiopia, the revolt by Muslim tribal peoples in the province of Eritrea (AIR-i-TREE-uh) led to the fall of the Marxist leader Mengistu (MING-jist-oo) and his regime in 1990. A similar revolt erupted against the government in Angola.

Neither capitalism nor socialism could reverse Africa's downward spiral. According to recent statistics, eighteen of the world's twenty poorest countries are in Africa. Excluding South Africa, the gross national product in 1991 for all countries south of the Sahara, representing almost 600 million people, was roughly equivalent to that of Belgium, with a population of about 10 million.

Furthermore, Africans have been disappointed that the dream of a united Africa has not been realized. Some continue to blame the West for their problems and resent any Western interference in their affairs. One reason for the formation of the Organization of African Unity was to reduce Western influence. However, African states have had difficulty achieving a united position on many issues. Their disagreements have left the region open to outsiders and have even led to conflict. During the late 1980s and early 1990s, border disputes festered in many areas of the continent and, in some cases, flared into outright war.

Even within many African nations, the concept of nationhood was undermined by warring tribes. During the late 1960s, civil war tore Nigeria apart. When northerners began to kill the Ibo (EE-boe) peoples, thousands of Ibos fled to their home region in the eastern part of Nigeria. There, Colonel Odumegu-Ojukwu organized the Ibos in a rebellion and declared the eastern region of Nigeria an independent state called Biafra. After three years of bloody civil war, Biafra finally surrendered and accepted the authority of the central government of Nigeria.

Ethnic conflicts also broke out among hostile tribal groups in Zimbabwe (zim-BOB-way). In central Africa,

fighting between the Hutus (HOO-TOOZ) and Tutsis (TOOT-seez) has created unstable governments in both Burundi (buh-ROON-dee) and Rwanda (roo-WAWN-duh). In 1994, a Hutu rampage left 500,000 Tutsis dead in Rwanda. Many of them, including women and children, were hacked to death with machetes. Even those who sought refuge in churches were massacred. As hostilities have grown in many African nations, so too have new ways to put together armies, including the use of children as soldiers (see "Young People in Africa: The Boy Soldiers").

Not all the news in Africa has been bad, however. In recent years, popular demonstrations have led to the collapse of one-party regimes and the emergence of fragile democracies in several countries. The most notorious case was that of Idi Amin of Uganda. After ruling by terror and brutal repression, Amin was finally deposed in 1979. Dictatorships were also brought to an end in Ethiopia, Liberia, and Somalia. However, in each case, the fall of the regime was later followed by bloody civil war.

The election of Nelson Mandela to the presidency of the Republic of South Africa is one of the more remarkable events of recent African history. Mandela was sentenced to life imprisonment in 1962. However, in 1990, he was released because of the efforts of F. W. de Klerk, head of the National Party, and massive world pressure. As head of the African National Congress, Mandela continued to campaign against apartheid. In 1993, the government of President F. W. de Klerk agreed with ANC leader Nelson Mandela to hold democratic national elections—the first in South Africa's history. In 1994, Mandela became South Africa's first black president and expressed his hopes for unity. He declared in his presidential inaugural address, "We shall build a society in which all South Africans, both black and white, will be able to walk tall, without any fear in their hearts, assured of their inalienable right to human dignity—a rainbow nation at peace with itself and the world."

As Africa evolves, it is useful to remember that economic and political change is often a slow and painful process. As one African writer observed, it is easy to be cynical in Africa. Changes in political regimes have had little effect on people's livelihoods. "Still," he said,

So What ??

If your students question the importance of the information on **Africa** *tell them . . .*

that in spite of the many problems facing Africa in this century, the continent remains one of the richest in terms of minerals and other natural resources. Most of the countries in Africa have been independent for less than 50 years and will most likely play a prominent role in the 21st century.

YOUNG PEOPLE IN AFRICA

The Boy Soldiers

Throughout the world, wherever extreme poverty and civil strife have torn apart the normal fabric of society, young boys are being used as full-time soldiers. Between 50,000 and 200,000 are currently fighting in twenty-four conflicts. A number of these conflicts are in Africa.

In Liberia, the rebel leader Charles Taylor made regular use of boy soldiers. In fact, he gave them their own regiment, the Small Boy Unit. Their survival depended upon the ability to steal the supplies they needed on a daily basis. Boy soldiers have also been recruited in other African states, including Mozambique, Angola, the Sudan, Rwanda, and Sierra Leone.

Different methods are used to recruit and keep boys in military units. In Mozambique, the rebel movement known as Renamo recruited boys whose average age was eleven years. The group used terror to recruit the boys, including hanging them upside down from trees. Many were forced to kill their own parents. One recruit, who is now in school, said, "I killed and I robbed and I feel ashamed." Unfortunately, many no longer even feel his kind of remorse.

Other methods also are used to encourage boys to fight. In African bush wars, military leaders used drugs to keep their troops excited for battle. In Liberia, children were given Valium (a tranquilizer used to relieve anxiety and tension) before they went into combat.

What impact does being a soldier have on young children? For some, becoming a soldier is a matter of survival. One gets a uniform, shoes, reg-

▲ *This child, armed with an AK-47 assault rifle, rides his bicycle through the streets of Monrovia, Liberia. Although in 1995 to 1996 a program was established to help change the lives of these "child soldiers," the program collapsed, and half of the children involved returned to the streets, armed with high-powered weapons. What do you think the future holds for these children and for Liberia?*

(continued)

COMPARING TIME PERIODS

Assign students to compare the photograph of boy soldiers to the left with the photograph of street children on page 1017. What do students believe makes the difference between children being homeless victims in Latin American or soldiers to be feared in Africa?

CLASS DISCUSSION

Ask students to discuss the following statement.

"In times of sickness, famine, and death a lesser value is placed on human life."

Do they believe it is true? How might this idea explain the existence of boy soldiers in Africa?

LEARNING FROM VISUALS

Answer to the caption question: It is difficult to imagine a peaceful future with so many children armed with assault rifles and with the lives of violence and death these young people have led.

COOPERATIVE LEARNING ACTIVITY

Working in groups, have your students identify and list the problems facing Africa described in Section 1 "The Era of Independence in Africa." Have them recall their past studies about Africa to find the causes of those problems. What are possible effects resulting from these problems?

YOUNG PEOPLE IN AFRICA

Answers to Critical Thinking Questions

1. Terror and drugs are used to recruit and keep boys in military units.

2. The impact is strong. On the one hand, it gives them regular meals and clothing. On the other hand, they lose the innocence of childhood by killing and fighting.

3. Answers will vary, but might include such things as children are not valued as children, the society will become very brutal because the children are conditioned to kill or be killed, etc.

ASSESS

You can choose from a variety of assessments to evaluate your students' mastery of the objectives for this section as stated on page 1044. Possible assessments include:

1. Section Review Question on this page
2. Section 32–1 Quiz in your Teacher Resource materials
3. Reteaching Worksheets in your Teacher Resource materials
4. Self-Study software

Answers to SECTION REVIEW

2. (a) Kenyan terrorists demanding freedom from British control
(b) policy of racial segregation in South Africa

YOUNG PEOPLE IN AFRICA

The Boy Soldiers, continued

ular meals, and a gun—a symbol of power. In Uganda, hundreds of war orphans recruited into the regular army are now fed and housed.

Of course, the violence that many young people encounter can also ruin their lives. Some fully admit that they enjoy the killing. As one United Nations worker in Liberia observed, "Kids make more brutal fighters because they haven't developed a sense of judgment."

1. How are young boys recruited and kept in military units in many African nations?

2. What impact does being a soldier have on such young people?

3. What does the use of children as soldiers tell about a society?

"let us welcome the wind of change. This, after all, is a continent of winds. The trick is to keep hope burning, like a candle protected from the wind."[2]

SECTION REVIEW

1. **Locate:**
   (a) Algeria,   (b) Tunisia,   (c) Morroco,
   (d) Ghana,   (e) Nigeria,   (f) Zaire,
   (g) Kenya,   (h) Tanzania,   (i) Mozambique,
   (j) Angola,   (k) Niger,   (l) Mali,
   (m) Ethiopia,   (n) Somalia,   (o) Sudan,
   (p) Zimbabwe,   (q) Rwanda

2. **Define:**
   (a) Mau Mau movement,
   (b) apartheid

3. **Identify:**
   (a) Kenya African National Union,   (b) King Farouk,   (c) African National Congress (ANC),
   (d) Nelson Mandela,   (e) Kwame Nkrumah,
   (f) Organization of African Unity,   (g) Hutus,
   (h) Tutsis

4. **Recall:**
   (a) What difficulties have African societies struggled to overcome for generations?
   (b) What challenges did newly independent African states face?
   (c) What dreams of African nationalists have not been achieved?
   (d) What problems resulted from the migration of Africans from rural areas into cities?
   (e) Why are African countries that are regarded as successful, like Kenya, still experiencing many economic and social problems?

5. **Think Critically:**
   (a) Why weren't European powers able to maintain their control over their African colonies after World War II?
   (b) Why has population growth made it almost impossible for many African nations to achieve economic improvements?

COOPERATIVE LEARNING ACTIVITY

Assign student groups to list as many problems as they can identify that have caused political and social upheavals in African states. Discuss the lists as a class.

Each group should then choose the single problem that they feel is most important and explain what they believe should be done to resolve that problem.

CONTINUITY AND CHANGE IN MODERN AFRICAN SOCIETIES

Africa is a study in contrasts. Old and new and native and foreign live side by side. The tension between traditional ways and Western culture is felt especially strongly by many African intellectuals. They are torn between their admiration for things Western and their desire to retain an African identity.

The City and the Countryside

In general, the impact of the West has been greater on the urban and educated and more limited on the rural and illiterate. After all, the colonial presence was first and most firmly established in the cities. Many cities, including Dakar, Lagos, Capetown, Johannesburg, Brazzaville, and Nairobi, are direct products of colonial rule. Most African cities today look like cities elsewhere in the world. They have high-rise buildings, blocks of apartments, wide boulevards, neon lights, movie theaters, and, of course, traffic jams.

The cities are also where the African elites live and work. Wealthy Africans have been strongly attracted to the glittering consumer products of Western culture. They live in Western-style homes or apartments and eat Western foods stored in Western refrigerators. Those who can afford it drive Western cars. It has been said that there are more Mercedes Benz automobiles in Nigeria than in Germany, where they are made.

The minds of the elite have also become Western. In part, this is due to the educational system. In the precolonial era, public schools as we know them did not really exist in Africa. For the average African, education took place in the home or in the village courtyard. It stressed basic skills and being part of a community. This traditional education in Africa provided what the people needed in their communities. Society's values and customs were passed on to the young by the storytellers, often the village elders. One scholar has described the practice among the Luo people in Kenya: "Traditionally, Luo stories were told in *siwindhe*, or the house of a widowed grandmother, a circular building with a thatched cone-shaped roof. Here in *siwindhe*, in the home of a woman who could talk freely about all subjects, Luo boys and girls gathered together to be taught the ways and thinking of their people. Its basic medium of instruction was the story."[3]

◄ *Nairobi, Kenya, is located in the southern part of the country, and its population is close to two million. Nairobi serves as the East African headquarters for many multinational corporations. This modern city, whose skyline is dotted with skyscrapers, was begun in the 1890s as a railroad construction camp.*

3. (a) founded by Jomo Kenyatta; focused on economy, self-rule
(b) king of Egypt, overthrown in army coup in 1952
(c) group of black intellectuals working for economic and political reforms in South Africa
(d) ANC leader, jailed in 1962, South African president in 1994
(e) led Ghana to independence
(f) supported pan-Africanism
(g) killed 500,000 Tutsis in Rwanda
(h) tribal group hostile to Hutus in central Africa
4. (a) boundaries, lack of preparation for democracy, economic dependence
(b) poor economies, scarce resources, corruption, population growth, drought, AIDS, poverty
(c) stable political structures, economic independence
(d) overwhelmed transportation and sanitation systems
(e) differences between rich and landlessness, unemployment, income differences, unrest
5. (a) increased awareness of Africans of how they were being exploited
(b) resources used for increased population, not investments

RECOMMENDED READING

For an up-to-date survey of economic conditions in Africa, see *Sub-Saharan Africa: From Crisis to Sustainable Growth* (Washington, D.C., 1989), issued by the World Bank. Also see A. O'Connor, *The African City* (London, 1983); and J. Illiffe, *The African Poor* (Cambridge, 1983).

For a country-by-country survey of African literature, se L. S. Klein, ed., *African Literatures in the Twentieth Century: A Guide* (New York, 1986). On art, see F. Willett, *African Art: An Introduction* (New York, 1985).

CLOSE

Lead students in a discussion of the Focus objectives identified on page 1044. Emphasize the importance of the many ethnic and tribal groups on Africa and their impact on the creation of unity and stability in African states.

FOCUS

OBJECTIVES

After completing this section, students should be able to

1. identify and describe differences between life in rural and urban Africa
2. discuss changes in the role of women in African society
3. identify and describe recent developments in African culture

FOCUS ACTIVITY

Help students understand that a difference between social values in rural and urban areas can be found in all societies. Ask students who have lived in both city and rural neighborhoods to describe difference in their lives in these places. What differences exist between rural and urban China or Latin America? Ask students to write an essay that discusses why these differences can cause revolutions.

TEACH

LEARNING FROM VISUALS

Answer to the caption question: Teaching is one of the professions open to women, and many elementary school teachers throughout African are women.

Modern Western education was introduced into Africa in the nineteenth century by the Europeans. The French colonists set up the first state-run schools in Senegal in 1818. In British colonies, the earliest schools were set up by missionaries. At first, these schools stressed vocational training with some classes in European languages and Western civilization. Eventually, pressure from Africans led to the introduction of professional training. The first schools of higher learning were established in the early twentieth century. Most college-educated Africans, however, received their higher education abroad.

With independence, African countries set up their own state-run schools. The emphasis was on primary schools, but high schools and universities were established in major cities. The basic objectives have been to introduce vocational training and improve literacy rates. Unfortunately, both trained teachers and funding are scarce in most countries. Few rural areas have schools. As a result, illiteracy rates remain high, estimated at about 70 percent of the population across the continent.

Christianity has also been an avenue for the introduction of Western ideas. Christian missionaries spread their faith rapidly during the nineteenth century among the urban elites and in rural areas as well. By 1950, an estimated fifty million Africans were Christians.

Outside the major cities, where about three-quarters of the inhabitants of Africa live, Western influence has had less of an impact. Millions of people throughout Africa live much as their ancestors did, in thatched huts without modern plumbing and electricity. They farm or hunt by traditional methods. They practice time-honored family rituals and believe in the traditional gods.

Even in the countryside, however, change is taking place. Economic need has brought a massive movement of people. Some leave to work on plantations. Some move to the cities, and others flee to refugee camps to escape starvation. Migration is a wrenching experience, because it disrupts family and village ties.

Nowhere, in fact, is the split between the old and the new, or the rural and the urban, so clear and painful as in Africa. On the one hand, urban dwellers view the

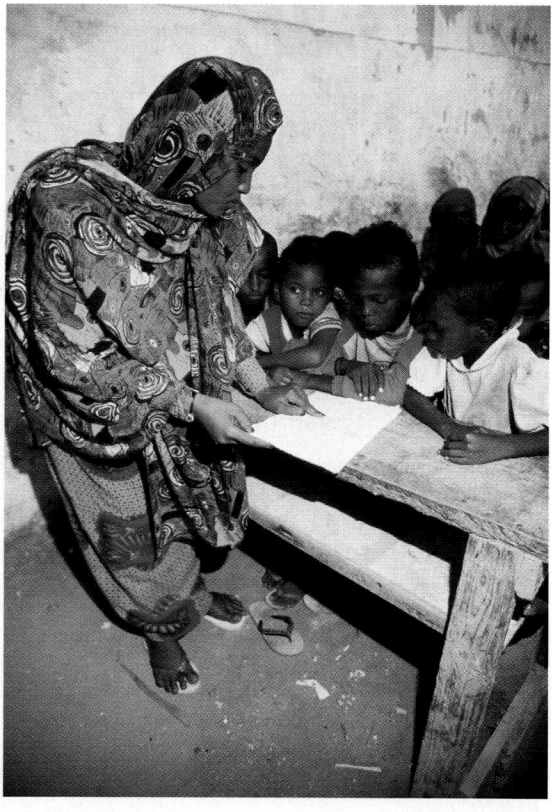

▲ *In Mogadishu, Somalia, students gather around their teacher. List the differences between this makeshift classroom and an elementary school classroom that you remember. Do you think it surprising that the teacher is a woman? Why or why not?*

village as the storehouse of all that is backward in the African past. Rural peoples, on the other hand, view the growing urban areas as a source of corruption and of the destruction of time-honored customs and values.

Women in Modern Africa

Independence from colonial powers had a significant impact on women's roles in African society. Almost without exception, the new governments established the principle of sexual equality. Women were allowed to vote and run for political office. However, as elsewhere, legislation was not enough to make women equals in a world dominated by men. Politics remains a world of men. A few professions, such as teaching, child care, and clerical work, are dominated by women. Most African women, however, are employed in menial positions such as farm laborers, factory workers, workers in retail trade, and servants. Education is open to all at the elementary level. However, women make up less than 20 percent of upper-level students in most African societies today.

Women have made the greatest strides in the cities. Most urban women, like men, now marry on the basis of personal choice. A significant minority, however, are still willing to accept as their spouses the choices of their parents. After marriage, African women appear to occupy a more equal position than married women in most Asian countries. In Africa, each marriage partner usually maintains a separate income. Women often have the right to possess property separate from their husbands.

Nevertheless, many wives still defer to their husbands in the traditional manner. Others, however, are like the woman in Abioseh Nicol's story "A Truly Married Woman" who, after years of living as a common-law wife with her husband, is finally able to provide the price and finalize the marriage. After the wedding, the wife declares, "For twelve years I have got up every morning at five to make tea for you and breakfast. Now I am a truly married woman and you must treat me with a little more respect. You are now my husband and not a lover. Get up and make yourself a cup of tea."[4]

In general, women in cities in contemporary Africa are sometimes held to different standards than men. African men often expect their wives to be both modern and traditional—both wage earners and housekeepers. Furthermore, women do not possess the full range of career opportunities that men do.

In rural areas, traditional attitudes toward women still prevail. In the village, polygamy is not uncommon. Arranged marriages are still the rule rather than the exception. As a father tells his son in Cyprian Ekwensi's *Iska*:

We have our pride and must do as our fathers did. You see your mother? I did not pick her in the streets. When I wanted a woman I went to my father and told him about my need of her and he went to her father. . . . Marriage is a family affair. You young people of today may think you are clever. But marriage is still a family affair.[5]

To villagers in Africa, African cities often look like founts of evil and corruption. Women in particular have suffered from the tension created by the conflict between the lure of the city and their village roots. As men are drawn to the cities in search of employment and excitement, their wives and girlfriends may be left behind in the native villages.

African Culture

The tension between traditional and modern and native and foreign that has played such a large part in modern African society also affects African culture (see "Our Artistic Heritage: Art in Contemporary Africa"). Africans have kept their native traditions while also being affected by foreign influences. Wood carving, metalwork, painting, and sculpture, for example, have kept their old forms, but they are increasingly adapted to please tourists. Some African art retains its traditional purpose, however, including serving as the objects of worship.

Similar developments have taken place in music and dance, which have retained their traditional vigor. The earlier emphasis on religious ritual, however, has been replaced to some degree by a new interest in the spectator. To take advantage of the growing popularity of African dancing, several governments have sponsored traveling folk dance companies. African music has been exported to Europe, North America, and Latin America. It then has returned to Africa in a new synthesis with foreign styles, such as the samba.

No area of African culture has been so strongly affected by political and social events as literature. The most common form of fiction writing in contemporary Africa is the novel. Novels began to appear in British colonies in the decade after World War II. By the

USING PRIMARY SOURCES

Ask students to discuss how they would react if their parents told them what the father tells his son in the selection from Cyprian Ekwensi's *Iska*. Can they think of any friends or relatives who might have been better off allowing their parents to choose their spouse?

CLASS DISCUSSION

Have your students compare and contrast the role of women in 20th century Africa with women's roles in other parts of the world studied thus far.

ENRICHMENT ACTIVITY

There are 56 nations that make up the African continent. Have each of your students research one of those nations and create a database of languages, customs, government types, resources, foods, geography and any other information you might think would be interesting and useful. Have your class compile the information in a notebook, of if your school has a web page on the Internet you may want to add their data as a resource.

OUR ARTISTIC HERITAGE

LEARNING FROM VISUALS

Ask students to explain how the scene in the photograph to the right could indicate progress for women and children in Africa. Do they believe that any school is better than no school at all?

Answer to the caption question: (right) The geometric designs may remind students of Islamic art that is featured in this text.

Answer to the caption question: (far right) The art features the water spirits of the artist's Yoruba culture, but the theme is worked in a very modern medium.

COMPARING TIME PERIODS

Assign students to write a comparison of the figure that appears to the far right and the painting of soup cans on page 1003. How do students believe such different styles of artistic expression can both be representative of changing social values? What do students think makes art?

CLASS DISCUSSION

Discuss the following statement.

"People who move to urban areas often long for the life and values of their rural heritage. This causes them to buy and prize traditional forms of art."

OUR ARTISTIC HERITAGE
Art in Contemporary Africa

One common theme in the work of many contemporary African artists is the need to find a balance between Western techniques and training on the one hand and the rich heritage of traditional African art forms on the other. For some artists who rely on government support for their work,

These two young women are decorating the door to their home compound. What designs are they creating for the door that you have seen in other art?

Sokari Douglas Camp created this 91-inch-tall sculpture, Masquerader with Boat Headdress, in 1987 from steel, pieces of mirror, wood, bells, and cloth. It is just one composition from a full set of huge pieces she made, entitled Echoes of the Kalabari. Douglas Camp was born in Kalabari, and most of her work celebrates her Yoruba culture. In what ways does the artist combine ancient and modern ideas?

the governments have decided which of the two elements is more important. In Senegal under President Léopold Senghor and in Zaire under President Mobutu Sese Soso, artists were told to depict tribal masks, carvings, and scenes of traditional African life. These works are often designed to serve the tourist industry and the export market.

Some African artists have taken their own approaches to this problem. The South African artist David Koloane has argued that artists should be able to use any style they want. Others, however, have chosen to combine new forms with traditional ones. Bruce Onobrakpeya is one of Nigeria's best-known artists. He uses his own unique techniques in making prints. However, the subject

(continued)

MORE ABOUT . . . Art

Mike Bugara, a Kenyan artist and conservationist, has found a way to merge his two passions. Using a recipe inspired from ancient Egyptian papyrus-making techniques, Bugara makes paper from elephant dung. He first boils the dung balls and washes out the brown color. Then he pounds the fibers into a paste-like mixture and soaks it. Later he spreads it on a screen and lets it bake in the sun. Bugara finds the "elephant paper" works quite well for his wildlife paintings. The Kenyan Wildlife Service is so impressed that they have commissioned Bugara to make "elephant paper" for the invitations to their 50th anniversary celebration.

OUR ARTISTIC HERITAGE

Art in Contemporary Africa, continued

matter or content of his prints comes from the history of his own Urhobo people and other Nigerian cultures. Sokari Douglas Camp is another Nigerian artist who has received worldwide attention for her work. Her sculptures in welded metal combine a Western approach to modern sculpture with African traditions.

A second theme in contemporary African art is the continuation of divisions between men and women. Men have traditionally created art using stone, bronze, and wood. Women, in contrast, have expressed themselves through textiles, clay, woven fiber, paint, or other material readily available in the home. The art of women is used to celebrate the gods, beautify their surroundings, and introduce their children to color and design. As seen in the illustration, two young women engage in the annual repainting of the carved door to their family meeting place in Nigeria.

1. What are the two main themes in contemporary African art?

2. What are two purposes of African art?

3. Do you think that artists who are paid and supported by a government should be required to produce art that meets the approval of that government? Why or why not?

4. There are definite differences between the art created by African men and African women. Do you think there are similar differences between the art of men and women in other cultures? If so, what are some general differences? Can you support your claim with examples?

Answers to Critical Thinking Questions

1. One theme is to find a balance between Western techniques and training and the rich heritage of traditional African art forms. The second theme is the continuation of divisions between men and women in certain forms of art.
2. Purposes include: to celebrate the gods, beautify their surroundings, introduce children to color and design, and serve the tourist industry and export market.
3. Answers will vary.
4. Answers will vary.

1960s, they had become increasingly popular, especially in West and East Africa. To appeal to educated English-speaking readers, most of the early novels appeared in English.

African writers, perhaps more than any other group in African society, have been tortured by the tensions and dilemmas that modern Africans face. The conflicting demands of town versus country and native versus foreign were the themes of most of the best-known works of the 1960s and 1970s. These themes certainly characterize the work of Chinua Achebe (A-chay-bay), a Nigerian novelist and winner of the Nobel Prize for literature in 1989. In the 1950s and 1960s, Achebe wrote four novels that won him international acclaim. All four show the problems of Africans caught up in the conflict between traditional and Western values. Most famous of Achebe's four novels is *Things Fall Apart* (see "Our Literary Heritage: *Things Fall Apart*").

Another African author who has received world acclaim is the Nigerian Wole Soyinka. Like many other African writers, Soyinka has expressed his frustration over the failures of many of Africa's new leaders. His novel *The Interpreters* condemned corruption in Nigerian politics. Soyinka also focused on the problems of daily life in Africa, especially the great gap between the traditional rural village and the impersonal modern city. He won the Nobel Prize for literature in 1986.

In Africa, novels are read chiefly by an educated minority in the cities. Some novels have found a larger audience by being serialized in newspapers and magazines. However, they have not entirely replaced the traditional oral literature. Illiteracy rates are still high. Thus, professional storytellers entertain village audiences by telling stories about the past, much as their ancestors did before the colonial era. Even in the villages, however, modern technology has had an impact through radio and television.

On Line with WORLD HISTORY *Internet Activity*

You may want to have your students visit the following URL, where they will find information and additional web site resources to enhance their study of this chapter.

The Mandela Page

http://www.anc.org.za/people/nrmpage.html

This page contains links to speeches, pictures, and an autobiography of President Mandela.

Due to the ever-changing nature of the World Wide Web, see the West History web site, **http://history.swpco.com** for regular updates of the URLs in this text.

COMPARING
TIME PERIODS

Ask students to investigate and then write a description of a Native American village before the arrival of Europeans in North America. What similarities and differences between Native American and African cultures can students identify?

Answers to Critical Thinking Questions

1. The Ibo tribal society was based on long days of work. Children were not allowed to be children. Men had multiple wives and worshipped many different gods. Prosperity was shown by material possessions.
2. Answers will vary.

ASSESS

You can choose from a variety of assessments to evaluate your students' mastery of the objectives for this section as stated on page 1052. Possible assessments include:

1. Section Review Question on this page
2. Section 32–2 Quiz in your Teacher Resource materials
3. Reteaching Worksheets in your Teacher Resource materials
4. Self-Study software

OUR LITERARY HERITAGE
Things Fall Apart

In Things Fall Apart, *Chinua Achebe portrayed the complex society of the Ibo people as it came into contact with Westerners. As seen in this excerpt, Achebe sought to portray the simple dignity of traditional African village life.*

Chinua Achebe, *Things Fall Apart*

During the planting season Okonkwo worked daily on his farms from cock-crow until the chickens went to roost. He was a very strong man and rarely felt fatigue. But his wives and young children were not as strong, and so they suffered. But they dared not complain openly. Okonkwo's first son, Nwoye, was then twelve years old but was already causing his father great anxiety for his incipient laziness. At any rate, that was how it looked to his father, and he sought to correct him by constant nagging and beating. And so Nwoye was developing into a sad-faced youth.

Okonkwo's prosperity was visible in his household. He had a large compound enclosed by a thick wall of red earth. His own hut, or *obi*, stood immediately behind the only gate in the red walls. Each of his three wives had her own hut, which together formed a half moon behind the *obi*. The barn was built against one end of the red walls, and long stacks of yarn stood out prosperously in it. At the opposite end of the compound was a shed for the goats, and each wife built a small attachment to her hut for the hens. Near the barn was a small house, the "medicine house" or shrine where Okonkwo kept the wooden symbols of his personal god and of his ancestral spirits. He wor-

▲ *The family scene described by Achebe could take place in many different areas in Africa. This 1978 photo of an African family was taken in rural Nigeria.*

shipped them with sacrifices of kola nut, food and palm-wine, and offered prayers to them on behalf of himself, his three wives and eight children.

1. What does this excerpt tell about the Ibo tribal society in Nigeria?
2. Put yourself in the place of Nwoye, the son. How would you describe your life?

RETEACHING ACTIVITY

Assign students to draw a picture of the household described by Chinua Achebe on this page. Ask them to write an essay that explains why such households could not continue to exist after the arrival of Europeans in Africa.

SECTION REVIEW

1. **Identify:**
   (*a*) Abioshe Nicol,   (*b*) Chinua Achebe

2. **Recall:**
   (*a*) Why has it been difficult to build an educational system in most African countries?
   (*b*) What signs in African culture demonstrate the conflict between traditional and modern values?

3. **Think Critically:** Why doesn't the fact that many African cities look much like cities in Europe necessarily mean they are as prosperous, successful, or as stable as European cities?

3

CONFLICT IN THE MIDDLE EAST

For the countries of the Middle East, the period between the two world wars was an age of transition. With the fall of the Ottoman and Persian Empires, new, modernizing regimes emerged in Turkey and Iran (see Chapter 27). A fiercely independent government was established in Saudi Arabia in 1932. Iraq gained its independence from Great Britain in the same year. Elsewhere in the Middle East, European influence remained strong. Great Britain and France had mandates in Syria, Lebanon, Jordan, and Palestine (see Chapter 27).

The Question of Palestine

In the Middle East, as in other areas of Asia, World War II led to the emergence of new independent states. Syria and Lebanon had already received their independence near the end of World War II. Jordan achieved complete self-rule soon after the war. Although Egypt had gained its independence in 1922, it still remained under British control. Sympathy for the idea of Arab unity led to the formation of an Arab League in 1945, but its members could not agree on much.

The one issue on which all Muslim states in the area could agree was Palestine. As tensions between Jews

▲ *Local Arabs living in Jerusalem were stopped and searched by British soldiers in the years prior to the declaration of the Israeli state in 1948. How has the treatment of Arab residents changed since this time?*

and Arabs intensified during the 1930s, Great Britain, which had a mandate in Palestine, began to limit Jewish immigration into the area. Moreover, Great Britain firmly rejected Jewish proposals for an independent state in Palestine (see Chapter 27).

The Zionists who wanted Palestine as a home for Jews were not to be denied, however. Many people had been shocked at the end of World War II when they learned about the Holocaust, the deliberate killing of six million European Jews in Nazi death camps. Sympathy for the Jewish cause grew dramatically. As a result, when Zionists turned for support to the United States, they were well received. In March 1948, the Truman administration approved the concept of an independent Jewish state in Palestine, despite the fact that only about one-third of the local population was Jewish. When a United Nations resolution divided Palestine into a Jewish state and an Arab state, the Jews in Palestine acted. On May 14, 1948, they proclaimed the state of Israel.

RECOMMENDED READING

Good general surveys of the modern Middle East include A. Goldschmidt, Jr., *A Concise History of the Middle East* (Boulder, Colo., 1991); and G. E. Perry, *The Middle East: Fourteen Islamic Centuries* (Elizabeth City, N.J., 1992).

On Israel and the Palestinian question, see B. Reich, *Israel: Land of Tradition and Conflict* (Boulder, Colo., 1985); C. C. O'Brien, *The Siege: The Saga of Israel and Zionism* (New York, 1986). On U.S.-Israeli relations, see S. Green, *Living by the Sword: America and Israel in the Middle East, 1968–1987* (London, 1988). Israeli politics are analyzed in D. Peretz, *The Government and Politics of Israel* (Boulder, Colo., 1983).

On the Iranian Revolution, see S. Bakash, *The Reign of the Ayatollahs* (New York, 1984); and B. Rubin, *Iran since the Revolution* (Boulder, Colo., 1985).

Answers to SECTION REVIEW

1. (a) author of "A Truly Married Woman"
   (b) Nigerian novelist
2. (a) shortage of trained teachers and funding
   (b) arts and crafts have kept old forms, but are adapted to please tourists.
3. Answers will vary.

CLOSE

Lead students in a discussion of the Focus objectives identified on page 1052.

FOCUS

OBJECTIVES

After completing this section, students should be able to

1. outline basic issues in determining the future of Palestine
2. describe Nasser's efforts to create Pan-Arabism
3. identify and describe events in the dispute between Israel and its Arab neighbors
4. describe causes and events in the Iranian revolution

FOCUS ACTIVITY

Ask students to identify nations that surround Israel. What is the dominant religion in each of these nations? Has the presence of Israel helped to increase solidarity among the Arab nations, as some people have suggested?

TEACH

LEARNING FROM VISUALS

Answer to the caption question: The Palestinian people are still subject to routine searches and stops by Israeli police.

TEACHING THEMES

Economics and History. Ask students if they believe many nations would have cared when Nasser nationalized the Suez Canal if there was no oil in the Middle East. What other products flowed through this canal that were important to Europe?

Multimedia Support

TRANSPARENCY
32–2, Middle East Oil Map

Map 32.2   The Modern Middle East

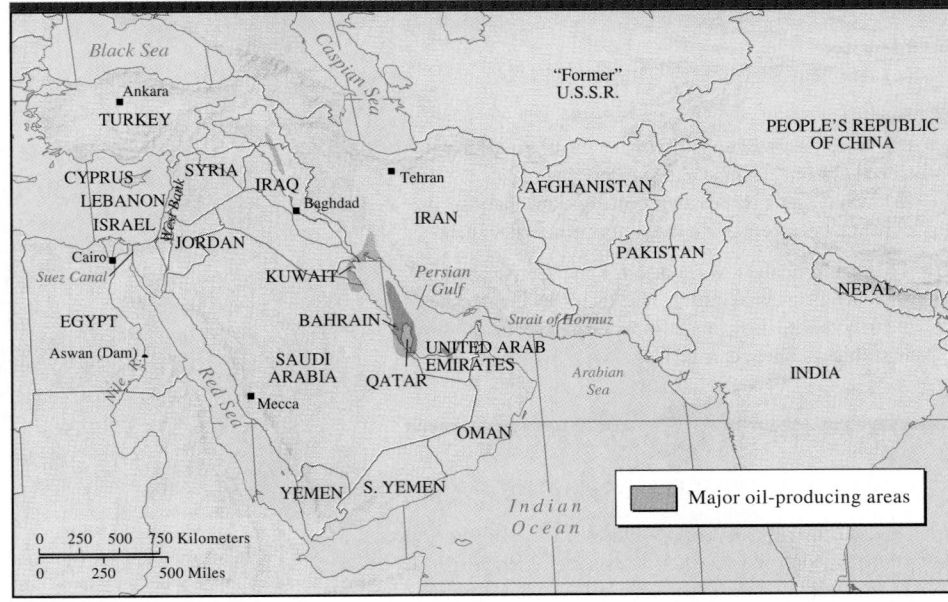

Its Arab neighbors saw the new state as a betrayal of the Palestinian people, 90 percent of whom were Muslim. Outraged at the lack of Western support for Muslim interests in the area, several Arab countries invaded the new Jewish state. The invasion failed, but both sides remained bitter. The Arab states refused to recognize the existence of Israel.

The war in 1948 had other results as well. Thousands of Palestinian refugees fled from Israel into neighboring Muslim states. Jordan, a country occupied by half a million bedouins (BED-oh-winz) (nomads), was now flooded by the arrival of almost one million urban Palestinians. To the north, the state of Lebanon had been created to provide the local Christian community with a country of its own. The arrival of Palestinian refugees, however, upset the delicate balance there between Christians and Muslims. Moreover, the creation of Lebanon had angered the Syrians, who had lost it as a result of European decisions after the war.

Nasser and Pan-Arabism

The dispute over Palestine placed Egypt in a difficult position. Technically, Egypt was not an Arab state. However, King Farouk, who had come to power in 1936, had often declared support for the Arab cause. Farouk, in fact, had committed Egyptian armies to the disastrous war against Israel in 1948.

In 1952, King Farouk was overthrown by a military coup led by young military officers. The real force behind the scenes was Colonel Gamal Abdul Nasser, son of a minor government official. In 1953, Nasser replaced the monarchy with a republic.

One year later, Nasser took control of Egypt. His first act was to begin a land-reform program to help the peasants. While adopting a policy of neutrality in foreign affairs, he expressed sympathy for the Arab cause. Nasser was especially upset with Great Britain. Even after it had granted Egypt independence in 1922,

---

STUDYING MAPS

The following questions will help you guide students through their study of Map 32.2.

1. How evenly are oil producing areas distributed among nations in the Middle East? *(not evenly at all)*

2. Why is the Strait of Hormuz important to events in the Middle East? *(It is the mouth of the Persian Gulf.)*

3. What strategic value is there in the location of Israel? *(almost none)*

YOU ARE THERE

The Suez Canal Belongs to Egypt

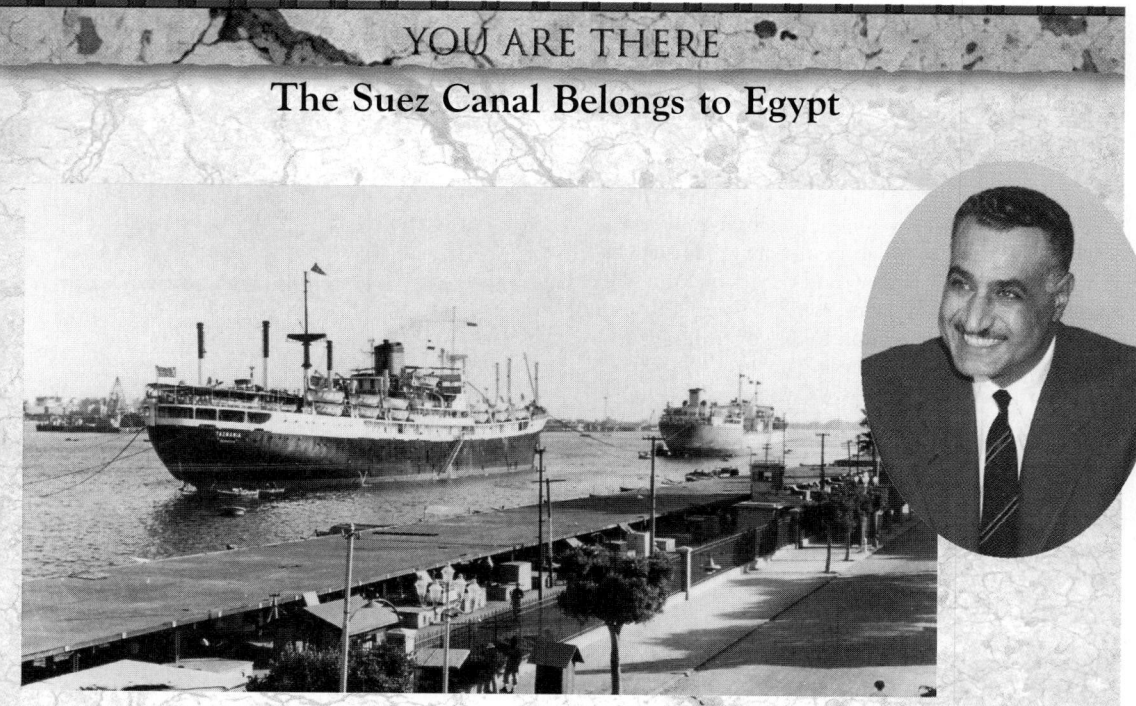

▲ *Gamal Abdul Nasser, shown here, presented an eloquent defense for the Arab cause in the Middle East. He is respected for his integrity and for his attempts to improve the lives of the poor in Egypt.*

The Suez Canal was built between 1854 and 1869, using mainly French money and Egyptian labor. It was managed by a Paris-based corporation, called the Suez Canal Company. In this excerpt from a speech, Egyptian president Gamal Abdul Nasser declared that it was time for the canal to be owned and managed by Egyptians.

Nasser's Speech Nationalizing the Suez Canal Company

The Suez Canal is an Egyptian canal built as a result of great sacrifices. The Suez Canal Company is an Egyptian company that was expropriated [taken away] from Egypt by the British who, since the canal was dug, have been obtaining the profits of the Company. . . . And yet the Suez Canal Company is an Egyptian limited liability company. The annual Canal revenue is 35 million Egyptian pounds. From this sum Egypt—which lost 120,000 workers in digging the Canal—takes one million pounds from the Company.

It is a shame when the blood of people is sucked, and it is no shame that we should borrow for construction. We will not allow the past to be repeated again, but we will cancel the past by restoring our rights in the Suez Canal. . . .

(continued)

YOU ARE THERE

LEARNING FROM VISUALS

What may the photograph of Abdul Nasser show about the westernization of Egypt? Can students be sure that Nasser has accepted Western values because he is wearing a Western suit?

COMPARING TIME PERIODS

Assign students to write an essay that compares the decision of Nasser to nationalize the Suez Canal with the decision of Chile to nationalize foreign businesses under Salvadore Allende in the 1970s. Why do students believe nations of the world were willing to go to war to protect the Suez Canal but not the copper mines in Chile?

CNN. WORLD HISTORY UPDATES

You can update your coverage of World History topics, as well as spark lively classroom discussion and deeper understanding, by using the **CNN World History Updates.**

For assistance in using and incorporating the **CNN World History Updates** into your classroom presentations, see the *Classroom Guide.*

Answers to Critical Thinking Questions

1. Nasser addressed the fact that Egypt was being taken advantage of by the people who ran the canal. They were not getting a fair share of the profits.
2. Egypt was entitled to the canal, according to Nasser, because it was bought with the sacrifices of the people. Many people died and much money was borrowed and spent during the construction of the canal.

REINFORCING VOCABULARY

Although Nasser thought his idea of scientific socialism made good sense for the future of the Arab world few other leaders shared his belief. Ask students why this was particularly true of Arab states having significant oil reserves.

YOU ARE THERE

The Suez Canal Belongs to Egypt, continued

The people will stand united as one man to resist imperialist acts of treachery. We shall do whatever we like. When we restore all our rights, we shall become stronger and our production will increase. At this moment, some of your brethren, the sons of Egypt, are now taking over the Egyptian Suez Canal and directing it. We have taken this decision to restore part of the glories of the past and to safeguard our national dignity and pride. May God bless you and guide you in the path of righteousness.

1. What was the problem President Nasser was addressing?
2. According to Nasser, why does the Suez Canal rightfully belong to Egypt?

Britain had kept control over the Suez Canal in order to protect its sea route to the Indian Ocean. On July 26, 1956, Nasser suddenly nationalized the Suez Canal Company, which had been under British and French administration (see "You Are There: The Suez Canal Belongs to Egypt").

Concerned over the threat to their route to the Indian Ocean, Great Britain and France decided to strike back. They were quickly joined by Israel. The forces of the three nations launched a joint attack on Egypt, starting the Suez War of 1956. Both the United States and the Soviet Union supported Nasser and forced Britain, France, and Israel to withdraw their troops from Egypt (see "You Are There: A Plea for Peace in the Middle East").

Nasser now turned to **pan-Arabism,** or a belief in Arab unity. In 1957, the Ba'ath (BATH) Party, which advocated a union of all Arab states in a new socialist society, assumed power in Syria. It opened talks with Egypt on a union between Syria and Egypt. In March 1958, Egypt formally united with Syria in the United Arab Republic (UAR). Nasser was named the first president of the new state.

Egypt and Syria hoped that the union would eventually include all the Arab states. Other Arab leaders, however, including young King Hussein of Jordan and the kings of Iraq and Saudi Arabia, were suspicious.

The kings of Iraq and Saudi Arabia particularly feared pan-Arabism. They thought that they would be asked to share their vast oil revenues with the poorer states of the Middle East.

Nasser certainly had dreams of a new kind of Middle East. Much of the wealth of the Middle East, he thought, now flowed into the treasuries of a few states or to foreign oil interests. In Nasser's view, through Arab unity, this wealth could be used to improve the standard of living throughout the Middle East. To achieve this, natural resources (including oil) and major industries would have to be nationalized. Central planning could then guarantee that these resources would be utilized efficiently, creating a new economic policy that Nasser called **scientific socialism.**

In the end, however, Nasser's desire to extend state control over the economy brought an end to the UAR. When his government announced the nationalization of a large number of industries and utilities in 1961, a military coup overthrew the Ba'ath leaders in Syria. The new leaders then withdrew Syria from its union with Egypt.

The breakup of the UAR did not end Nasser's dream of pan-Arabism. During the mid-1960s, Egypt was active in promoting Arab unity against Israel. At a meeting of Arab leaders held in Jerusalem in 1964, the Egyptians took the lead in forming the Palestine Liber-

COOPERATIVE LEARNING ACTIVITY

Place students into three groups and divide the following map project among the groups, one date per group.

Have groups draw maps of Palestine in 1945, 1950, and 1995. On each map, show the distribution of Palestinians and Israelis. Discuss, as a class, what conclusions can be drawn from the series of maps. What are the major problems that prevent any easy solution to the Israeli-Palestinian conflict?

YOU ARE THERE

A Plea for Peace in the Middle East

During the Suez War in 1956, Israel quickly captured the Sinai peninsula. The United Nations, however, pressured Israel to withdraw its troops. At first, Israel refused. In March 1957, however, Golda Meir, Israel's foreign minister, announced that Israel had agreed to withdraw from the Sinai. This excerpt is taken from her statement.

Golda Meir Announces the Israeli Withdrawal from the Sinai

May I now add these few words to the states in the Middle East area and, more specifically, to the neighbors of Israel. We all come from an area which is a very ancient one. The hills and the valleys have been witnesses to many wars and many conflicts. But this is not the only thing which characterizes the part of the world from which we come. It is also a part of the world which is of an ancient culture. It is that part of the world which has given to humanity three great religions [Judaism, Christianity, and Islam]. It is also that part of the world which has given a code of ethics to all humanity. In our countries, in the entire region, all our peoples are anxious for and in need of a higher standard of living, of great programs of development and progress. Can we, from now on—all of us—turn a new leaf and, instead of fighting with each other, can we all, united, fight poverty and disease and illiteracy? Is it possible for us to put all our efforts and all our energy into one single purpose, the betterment and progress and development of all our lands and all our peoples? I can here pledge the government and the people of Israel to do their part in this united effort. There is

▲ *Golda Meir served as Israeli minister of foreign affairs from 1956 to 1966 and as prime minister of Israel from 1969 to 1974. Do you believe it unusual that someone born in Kiev, Ukraine, and educated in the United States could become prime minister of Israel?*

no limit to what we are prepared to contribute so that all of us, together, can live to see a day of happiness for our peoples and can see again from that region a great contribution to peace and happiness for all humanity.

1. What is the single purpose Golda Meir wanted to work toward?

2. How did she suggest that the countries of the Middle East achieve that purpose?

3. Has that purpose been achieved in the Middle East?

COOPERATIVE LEARNING ACTIVITY

Working in groups, have students prepare a chart of all the new states in the Middle East since 1945. Have them list the form of government and type of economic system followed in each country, and the number of leaders overthrown by military force or violence. What conclusions do they draw from the chart?

CLASS DISCUSSION

Ask students to discuss the following statement.

"Peace can only exist in an atmosphere of trust."

Do they believe it is true? If it is true, what policies should Israel follow to achieve peace?

CLASS DISCUSSION

Research and debate the Israeli-Palestinian conflict in groups. One group should research and defend the Palestinian position, while the other group takes the Israeli point of view. After they debate the causes of the conflict, have them brainstorm possible resolutions.

ation Organization (PLO) to represent the interests of the Palestinians. The PLO believed that only the Palestinian peoples (and not Jewish immigrants from abroad) had the right to form a state in Palestine. A guerrilla movement called al-Fatah (al-fat-AW), led by the PLO political leader Yasir Arafat, began to launch terrorist attacks on Israeli territory. In retaliation, the Israeli government began to raid PLO bases in Jordan in 1966.

The Arab-Israeli Dispute

The growing Arab hostility was a constant threat to the security of Israel. In the years after independence, Israeli leaders dedicated themselves to creating a Jewish homeland. The government tried to build a modern democratic state that would attract Jews from throughout the world.

It was not easy for such a tiny state to survive in the midst of hostile neighbors. Divisions among the Israeli

Map 32.3   Israel and Its Neighbors

CONNECTIONS
AROUND THE WORLD

Global Migrations   Since 1945, tens of millions of people have migrated from one part of the world to another. There are many reasons for these migrations. Persecution for political reasons caused many people from Pakistan, Bangladesh, Sri Lanka, Eastern Europe, and East Germany to seek refuge in Western European countries. Brutal civil wars in Asia, Africa, the Middle East, and Europe have led to millions of refugees seeking safety in neighboring countries. A devastating famine in Africa in 1984–1985 caused hundreds of thousands of Africans to move to relief camps throughout the continent to find food.

Most people who have migrated, however, have done so to find jobs. Guest workers from Turkey, southern and eastern Europe, North Africa, India, and Pakistan, for example, flooded into prosperous Western European countries. Overall, there were probably fifteen million guest workers in Europe in the 1980s. Many countries adopted policies that allowed guest workers to remain in the host countries for a few years. In the 1980s and 1990s, however, foreign workers often became scapegoats when countries had economic problems. New political parties in France and Norway, for example, called for the removal of blacks and Arabs in order to protect the ethnic purity of their nations. In Asian countries, there is often a backlash against other ethnic Asian groups.

people made it even more difficult. Some Israelis were immigrants from Europe. Others came from the countries of the Middle East. Some were secular and even socialist in their views. Others were politically conservative and stressed religious orthodoxy, or a strict adherence to the traditional practices of Judaism. Israel was also home to many Muslim Palestinians who had not fled to other countries.

To balance these different interests, Israel established a parliament, called the Knesset, on the European model. Each political party received a number of

STUDYING MAPS

The following questions will help guide students through their study of Map 32.3.

1. Why is the gulf of Aqaba important to Israel? *(It is a way to the Red Sea.)*
2. Why is Israel's control of the West Bank important to its ability to defend itself

from possible attack? *(It creates a natural boundary at the Dead Sea.)*
3. What does Israel's control of the Golan Heights have to do with Syria's desire to occupy southern Lebanon? *(It is a way to Israel by going around the Golan Heights.)*

◄ *During the Six-Day War, Israeli forces destroyed oil refineries at Port Suez in Egypt. An Israeli soldier watches the fires burn from the safety of the other side of the Suez Canal.*

representatives based on how many votes each party received in the general election (a system called **proportional representation**). This system created a parliament with so many parties that no one party ever received a majority of the votes. All governments had to be formed from a coalition of several parties. As a result, moderate leaders, such as longtime prime minister David Ben Gurion, had to cater to the wishes of small parties to stay in power.

During the late 1950s and 1960s, the dispute between Israel and other states in the Middle East became more heated. Israel was basically alone except for the sympathy of the United States and a few Western European countries. It adopted a policy of quick and strong response to any hostile act by its Arab neighbors and the PLO. By the spring of 1967, Nasser had stepped up his military activities and imposed a blockade against Israeli shipping through the Gulf of Aqaba (AW-kee-bee). He declared: "Now we are ready to confront Israel. We are ready to deal with the entire Palestine question." When Nasser asked the commander in chief of the Egyptian forces if they were ready for war, the commander replied, "On my own head be it, boss! Everything is in tiptop shape."

Fearing that it was going to be attacked, on June 5, 1967, Israel suddenly launched air strikes against Egypt and several of its Arab neighbors. Israeli warplanes bombed seventeen Egyptian airfields and wiped out most of the Egyptian air force. Israeli armies then broke the blockade at the head of the Gulf of Aqaba and occupied the Sinai peninsula. Other Israeli forces seized Jordanian territory on the West Bank of the Jordan River, occupied the whole of Jerusalem, and attacked Syrian military positions in the Golan Heights area along the Israeli-Syrian border.

In this brief Six-Day War, as it is called, Israel devastated Nasser's forces and tripled the size of its territory. The new Israel aroused even more bitter hatred among the Arabs. Furthermore, another million Palestinians now lived inside Israel's new borders, most of them on the West Bank.

During the next few years, Arab states demanded the return of the occupied territories. Many Israelis, however, argued that the new lands improved their security and should be retained. In 1970, Nasser died of a heart attack and was succeeded by his vice president, Anwar al-Sadat (suh-DAWT). Sadat was more moderate than Nasser and sought to sign a peace treaty with Israel on the condition that the latter retire to its pre-1967 frontiers.

REINFORCING VOCABULARY

Ask students to identify and discuss similarities between the *intifada* in Palestine and guerrilla wars that have taken place in other parts of the world. Why is this type of action used by groups with little real military power? Why is it often effective?

TEACHING THEMES

Economics and History. Ask students to explain why the increase in the price of crude oil in the 1970s may have led to increased disunity within the Arab world. What may the greater difference between have and have-not Arab states have had to do with it? What happened due to their greater ability to purchase modern weapons of war?

When Israel refused, Sadat tried once again to renew Arab unity through war with Israel. On October 6, 1973, Egyptian forces suddenly attacked Israeli positions in the Sinai just east of the Suez Canal. At the same time, Syrian armies attacked Israeli positions in the Golan Heights. Early Arab successes in this October War left the Israelis reeling. Golda Meir (MIE-ear), the prime minister of Israel, remarked: "The circumstances could not have been worse. In the first two or three days of the war, only a thin line of brave young men stood between us and disaster. They fought, and fell, like lions, but at the start they had no chance. What those days were like for me I shall not even try to describe." The Israelis stormed back, and a cease-fire was finally reached on October 24.

In the next few years, a fragile peace was maintained. Negotiations continued but with little success. The conflict spread to Lebanon, where many Palestinians had found refuge. The PLO now set up its headquarters in Lebanon. Heated disputes between Christians and Muslims over control of the capital city, Beirut, added to the rising tension along the border between Israel and Lebanon.

In 1976, the American president Jimmy Carter began to press for a compromise peace. He asked the Israelis to return the occupied Arab territories in exchange for Arab recognition of the state of Israel. President Sadat of Egypt, who wanted to reduce his military expenses, announced his willingness to seek peace.

In September 1978, President Sadat met with Menachem Begin (muh-NAWK-um BAE-gin [hard "g"]), Israel's prime minister, and President Carter at Camp David in the United States. Both sides agreed to the **Camp David Accords,** an agreement to sign an Israeli-Egypt peace treaty on March 26, 1979. The treaty ended the state of war between Egypt and Israel. Israel also agreed to withdraw from the Sinai, but not from other occupied territories until it was recognized by other Arab countries. Many Arab countries refused to recognize Israel, however.

During the early 1980s, Palestinian Arabs became more militant. This militancy led to rising unrest, popularly called the *intifada* (uprising), among PLO supporters living inside Israel. As the 1990s began, U.S.-sponsored peace talks opened between Israel and a number of its Arab neighbors. The first major breakthrough did not come until 1993. Israel and the PLO reached an agreement calling for Palestinian autonomy in certain areas of Israel. In return, the PLO recognized the Israeli state. Yasir Arafat became the head of the semi-independent area known as the Palestinian Authority.

Progress in making the agreement work, however, has been slow. Terrorist attacks by Palestinian militants who are opposed to the agreement have resulted in heavy casualties and have shaken the confidence of many Jewish citizens that their security needs can be protected under the agreement. At the same time, Jewish residents in the Left Bank have resisted the extension of Palestinian authority in the area. In November 1995, Prime Minister Yitzhak Rabin (ruh-BEEN) was assassinated by an Israeli opponent of the accords. National elections held a few months later led to the formation of a new government under Benjamin Netanyahu. This administration has adopted a tougher stance in negotiations with the Palestinian authority under Yasir Arafat. For the moment, future progress in implementing the agreement is in doubt.

Revolution in Iran

The Arab-Israeli dispute also caused an international oil crisis. The Arab states had formed the Organization of Petroleum Exporting Countries (OPEC) in 1960 to gain control over oil prices. In the 1970s they used oil prices as a weapon to force Western governments to abandon their support of Israel. During the 1973 war, some OPEC nations announced large increases in the price of oil to foreign countries. The price hikes, coupled with cuts in oil production, led to an oil shortage and serious economic problems in the United States and Europe. The price increases also brought new riches to oil-exporting countries, such as Libya, now under Colonel Muammar Qadhafi (gah-DAH-fee). Qadhafi used his country's newfound oil riches to build roads, schools, and hospitals. However, he also used these resources to finance terrorist activities against Western nations and to overthrow governments he disliked. President Sadat of Egypt referred to Qadhafi as "that madman of the Mediterranean."

RETEACHING ACTIVITY

Assign students to write a hypothetical letter from a young Palestinian, arrested for being in the *intifada,* to his parents. The letter should trace the causes for this uprising and what the young man hopes to accomplish through his actions.

One of the key oil-exporting countries was Iran. Under the leadership of Shah Mohammad Reza Pahlavi, who occupied his position with the help of the American CIA, Iran had become one of the richest countries in the Middle East. During the 1950s and 1960s, Iran had become a chief ally of the United States in the Middle East. With American encouragement, the shah had tried to carry through a series of reforms to transform Iran into the most advanced country in the region.

The shah's efforts seemed to be succeeding. Per capita income increased dramatically. Literacy rates improved, and an affluent middle class emerged in the capital of Tehran. However, trouble was brewing under the surface. Many peasants were still landless, many people did not have jobs, and the urban middle class felt squeezed by high inflation. Housing costs had skyrocketed.

Some of the unrest that developed took the form of religious discontent. Millions of devout Muslims looked with distaste at the new Iranian civilization. In their eyes, it was based on greed and materialism, which they identified with Western, and especially American, influence. They opposed governmental corruption and the extension of voting rights to women. Some opposition elements used terrorism against wealthy Iranians or foreigners to provoke political disorder. In response, the shah's security police, the *Savak,* imprisoned and sometimes tortured thousands of dissidents.

Leading the opposition was the Ayatollah Ruholla Khomeini, an Iranian cleric who had been exiled to Paris because of his outspoken opposition to the shah's regime. From Paris, Khomeini continued his attacks in print, on television, and in radio broadcasts. By the late 1970s, large numbers of Iranians—students, peasants, and townspeople—began to respond to Khomeini's words.

▶ *The Ayatollah Khomeini who served as leader of Iran from 1979 until his death in 1988 turned Iran into an Islamic state. What is Iran's current relationship with the United States?*

When workers' strikes grew in intensity in 1979, the shah left the country.

With rising public unrest, the shah's government collapsed and was replaced by a hastily formed Islamic republic. The new government, under the guidance of the Ayatollah Khomeini, immediately began to rid the country of Western influence and restore traditional Islamic law. At the same time, a new reign of terror began. Supporters of the shah were rounded up and executed.

Much of the attention of the outside world focused on the American Embassy in Tehran, where militant Iranians held a number of Americans hostage. In the eyes of the ayatollah and his followers, the United States was the "Great Satan," the protector of Israel and enemy of Muslim people everywhere. Furthermore, the United States was held responsible for the corruption of Iranian society under the shah. Now Khomeini demanded that the shah be returned to Iran for trial and that the United States apologize for acts against the Iranian people. In response, the U.S. government stopped buying Iranian oil and froze Iranian assets in the United States.

The effects of the disturbances in Iran quickly spread beyond its borders. Islamic militants called for similar revolutions in Islamic countries around the world. In July 1980, the shah died of cancer in Cairo. With economic conditions in Iran deteriorating, the Islamic revolutionary government finally agreed to free the U.S. hostages in return for the release of Iranian assets in the United States. During the next few years, the intensity of the Iranian Revolution moderated somewhat.

After the death of Khomeini in 1989, a new government, under President Hashemi Rafsanjani (RAWF-san-JAW-nee), began to loosen clerical control over freedom of expression and social activities. Rising criticism of rampant official corruption and a high rate of

CLASS DISCUSSION

Ask students to discuss the following statement.

"Taking hostages is a way for weak powers to exert their will on stronger powers. With the decline of the superpowers and increase in the number of small national states we should expect more hostage situations in the future."

Do they believe it is true? How may it explain the hostage situations in Iran in 1979 or in Peru in the spring of 1997?

COMPARING TIME PERIODS

Ask students to compare events in Iran during the leadership of the Ayatollah Khomeini with the Spanish Inquisition. Were both of these situations a case of a group trying to gain total control over a state? Were they motivated by religious zeal or secular aspirations?

LEARNING FROM VISUALS

Answer to the caption question: Answers will vary.

On Line with WORLD HISTORY *Internet Activity*

You may want to have your students visit the following URL, where they will find information and additional web site resources to enhance their study of this chapter.
Gulf War

http://www.netwizards.net/~cryan/war.html

This site includes material on all of the coalition countries that fought in the war, a war summary, and links to other materials on the Gulf War.

Due to the ever-changing nature of the World Wide Web, see the West History web site, **http://history.swpco.com** for regular updates of the URLs in this text.

▲ *Soldiers of the French Foreign Legion undertook the dangerous task of clearing land mines the Iraqis had placed along Kuwait City beaches. The Kuwait Towers, a modern landmark of this oil-rich city, loom in the background. Why did the Iraqis place land mines along Kuwait City beaches?*

inflation, however, sparked a new wave of government repression in the mid-1990s. Newspapers were censored, the universities were purged of "un-Islamic" elements, and self-appointed religious militants raided private homes in search of treasonous activities. One Iranian journalist remarked, "There is deep fear and absolutely no freedom of expression."

Crisis in the Persian Gulf

During the early phases of the revolution in Iran, the Iranians directed their anger toward the United States. However, Iran also had enemies closer to home. To the

north was the Soviet Union, long considered a threat to Iran. To the west was a militant and hostile Iraq, now under the leadership of the ambitious and ruthless Saddam Hussein. Problems from both directions appeared shortly after Khomeini's rise to power. Soviet military forces moved into Afghanistan in 1979 to prop up a weak Soviet-supported regime there. The following year, Iraqi forces suddenly attacked along the Iranian border.

Iraq and Iran had long had an uneasy relationship, fueled by religious differences. Both were Muslim nations. The Iranians, however, were largely Shi'ites, whereas the members of the ruling caste in Iraq were Sunnites (see Chapter 17). Also, Iran and Iraq had argued for years over borderlands next to the Persian Gulf, the vital waterway for the export of oil for both countries. Like several of its neighbors, Iraq had long dreamed of unifying the Arabs. Suspicion among its neighbors, however, kept Iraq from doing so.

During the 1970s, Iran had given some support to a Kurdish rebellion in the mountains of Iraq. In 1975, the Iranian government agreed to stop aiding the rebels in return for some land at the head of the Persian Gulf. Five years later, Iraq had crushed the Kurdish revolt. President Saddam Hussein now accused Iran of violating the earlier agreement and launched an attack on his neighbor.

The war was a brutal one. Poison gas was used against civilians, and children were used to clear minefields. The Khomeini government told young boys that if they died for their country, they were sure of gaining an afterlife. The war lasted for nearly ten years. The two superpowers—the United States and the Soviet Union—watched nervously in case the conflict would spread throughout the region. With both sides virtually exhausted, a cease-fire was finally arranged in the fall of 1988.

Hussein's appetite for land had not been satisfied, however. In early August 1990, Iraqi troops suddenly moved across the border and occupied the small neighboring country of Kuwait, at the head of the Persian Gulf. Iraq argued, without much cause, that Kuwait was legally a part of Iraq.

The Iraqi invasion of Kuwait in 1990 sparked an international outcry. The United States, under President George Bush, took the lead in amassing an international force that freed Kuwait and destroyed a large part of Iraq's armed forces. However, the allied forces did not occupy the capital city of Baghdad at the end of the war. They feared that doing so would cause the total breakup of the country, and that would only benefit Iran. American casualties would have only increased, and U.S. troops would have had to stay in Iraq longer than the Bush administration was willing to allow. The allies hoped instead that an internal revolt would overthrow Hussein. In the meantime, harsh economic sanctions were imposed on the Iraqi government. The hoped-for overthrow of Hussein, however, did not happen. Hussein's tireless efforts to evade the conditions of the cease-fire continued to vex the administration of President Bill Clinton.

SECTION REVIEW

1. **Locate:**
   (*a*) Iran,   (*b*) Saudi Arabia,   (*c*) Iraq,
   (*d*) Syria,   (*e*) Lebanon,   (*f*) Jordan,   (*g*) Suez Canal,   (*h*) Gulf of Aqaba,   (*i*) Sinai peninsula,   (*j*) West Bank of the Jordan River,   (*k*) Golan Heights,   (*l*) Persian Gulf

2. **Define:**
   (*a*) pan-Arabism,   (*b*) scientific socialism,
   (*c*) proportional representation,   (*d*) Camp David Accords,   (*e*) *intifada*

3. **Identify:**
   (*a*) Arab League,   (*b*) Gamal Abdul Nasser,
   (*c*) Palestine Liberation Organization (PLO),
   (*d*) Yasir Arafat,   (*e*) Anwar al-Sadat,
   (*f*) Golda Meir,   (*g*) Yitzhak Rabin,
   (*h*) Benjamin Netanyahu,   (*i*) Muammar Qadhafi,
   (*j*) Shah Mohammed Reza Pahlavi,
   (*k*) Ayatollah Ruholla Khomeini,   (*l*) Saddam Hussein

4. **Recall:**
   (*a*) How did Jewish and Arab people in Palestine react to the United Nations resolution that divided Palestine in 1948?
   (*b*) In addition to the military defeat of Arab

forces, what resulted from the war in Palestine in 1948?
(*c*) Why did the creation of Lebanon anger the Syrians?
(*d*) Why did Israel launch air strikes against Egypt and its Arab neighbors in 1967?
(*e*) Why did many Iranians oppose the shah even when their average standard of living was improving?

5. **Think Critically:**
   (*a*) Why did the United States and the Soviet Union stand together against Israel, France, and Great Britain when they tried to recover the Suez Canal from Egypt in 1956?
   (*b*) Why do some people believe it was a mistake for the United Nations and the United States not to occupy Iraq after the Persian Gulf War?

SOCIETY AND CULTURE IN THE CONTEMPORARY MIDDLE EAST

In recent years, many developments in the Middle East have been seen in terms of a revival of traditional values in response to Western influence. Indeed, some conservative religious forces in the area have tried to replace foreign culture and values with supposedly "pure" Islamic forms of belief and behavior. This movement to apply the strict religious teachings of Islam to all aspects of political and social life is called **Islamic fundamentalism.**

The Islamic Revival

The revival of Islam that has taken place in the contemporary Middle East has a long history. For quite some time, many devout Muslims have believed that the attempt to follow Western ways in the major cities has given birth to many evils, including the use of alcohol, pornography, and drugs.

This negative response to the West began early in the twentieth century. It grew stronger after World

RECOMMENDED READING

The issue of oil is examined in G. Luciani, *The Oil Companies and the Arab World* (New York, 1984); and P. Odell, *Oil and World Power* (New York, 1986); M. H. Kerr and El Sayed Yassin, eds., *Rich and Poor States in the Middle East: Egypt and the New Arab Order* (Boulder, Colo., 1985). On Egypt, see A. Goldschmidt, Jr., *Modern Egypt: The Formation of a Nation-State* (Boulder, Colo., 1988). For a general overview of Middle Eastern

literature, see J. Kritzeck, *Modern Islamic Literature from 1800 to the Present* (New York, 1970). For a more up-to-date introduction to the various national literatures, consult L. S. Klein, *The Encyclopedia of World Literature of the 20th Century* (New York, 1981). For Iranian literature, see M. Southgate, *Modern Persian Short Stories* (Washington, D.C., 1980); and S. Sullivan and F. Milani, *Iranian Women since the Revolution* (Austin, Tex., 1991)

(b) leader who in 1952 took over Egypt and led that country through several unsuccessful conflicts with Israel
(c) formed to represent interests of Palestinians
(d) leader of the PLO
(e) Egyptian president
(f) prime minister of Israel
(g) prime minister of Israel
(h) prime minister of Israel after Rabin
(i) leader of Libya
(j) Shah of Iran
(k) anti-American leader of Islamic republic
(l) ruthless leader of Iraq

4. (a) The Jewish people proclaimed the state of Israel, which Arab forces attacked.
(b) Millions of refugees flooded into surrounding Arab states.
(c) Lebanon was created as a result of a European decision from land Syria claimed for itself.
(d) Israel was convinced that these countries were determined to attack them so they struck first.
(e) The Shah did not share power with most Iranians, the improvements were not equally shared, and many Iranians felt the Shah was too closely tied to the West.

5. (a) The U.S. was worried about political unrest in the Middle East and an interruption of the flow of oil through the canal; the Soviet Union hoped to increase its influence in that part of the world.
(b) Answers will vary.

CLOSE

Lead students in a discussion of the Focus objectives identified on page 1057.

FOCUS

OBJECTIVES

After completing this section, students should be able to

1. describe the revival of Islamic fundamentalism
2. discuss the economics of oil and land in the Middle East
3. describe changes in the rights of women in the Middle East
4. identify and describe recent developments in art and literature in the Middle East

FOCUS ACTIVITY

Help students understand that there is often a link between feelings of frustration and a turn to fundamentalism. When people feel ineffective and dominated by others they may return to what they regard as the pure lives of fundamentalism. Ask students if they can see a relationship between the Chinese who carried out the Boxer Rebellion in 1900 and Muslim fundamentalists in the Middle East today.

▶ Oil and its by-products have created the modern-day wealth in the Middle East. The Al-Jubail Petrochemical Company plant is a joint venture between a Saudi Arabian company and Exxon. This plant produces low-density polyethylene.

War I, when the Western presence increased. In 1928, devout Muslims in Egypt formed the Muslim Brotherhood. Its goal was to create a new order based on a strict following of the Quran and Islamic law. Later the movement became more radical and made use of terrorism to pursue its goals.

The movement to return to the pure ideals of Islam reached its high point in Iran under the Ayatollah Khomeini. In revolutionary Iran, traditional Muslim beliefs reached into clothing styles, social practices, and the legal system. Divorce was outlawed. Women were expected to wear veils and were fined or even flogged for violating the dress code. Non-Muslims were fired from government jobs. Ancient Islamic punishments were also introduced, including stoning for adultery and cutting off hands for theft.

In turn, these Iranian ideas and practices have spread to other Muslim countries. In Algeria, the political influence of fundamentalist Islamic groups enabled them to win a stunning victory in the national elections in 1992. In Egypt, militant groups such as the Muslim Brotherhood have engaged in terrorism. Militant Muslims assassinated President Sadat. More

recently, they have attacked foreign tourists, who are considered to be carriers of corrupt Western ideas.

Throughout the Middle East, even governments and individuals who do not support the efforts to return to pure Muslim beliefs have changed the way they behave. In Egypt, for example, the government now encourages television programs on religion instead of comedies and adventure shows imported from the West. Middle-class women in Cairo tend to dress more modestly than in the past. The use of alcohol is also discouraged in Egypt.

The Economics of Oil and Land

Millions live in poverty in the Middle East, but a fortunate few rank among the most wealthy people in the world. The annual per capita income in Egypt is about $710, but it is nearly $20,000 in the tiny state of Kuwait. The chief reason, of course, is oil. Oil reserves are distributed unevenly. All too often they are located in areas where the population density is low. Egypt and Turkey, for example, with more than fifty million people apiece, have almost no oil reserves. In contrast, the

MORE ABOUT . . . *Islamic Fundamentalism*

An Islamic poet from the 1930s spoke for many of those growing dissatisfied with the West when he wrote:

"The Westerners have lost the vision of heaven,
they go hunting for the pure spirit in the belly . . .
Communism has nothing to do save with the body,

The religion of that prophet (Marx) who knew not truth . . .
Capitalism too is a fattening of the body, its unenlightened bosom houses no heart . . .
One lives by production, the other by taxation
and man is a glass caught between these two stones."

combined population of the oil-rich states of Kuwait, the United Arab Emirates (i-MIR-its), and Saudi Arabia is well under ten million people.

The growing importance of oil has been a benefit to several of the states in the region. However, oil has been an unreliable basis for an economy. The price of oil has varied dramatically in the last twenty years. So, too, has the income of the oil-producing states. During the 1970s, members of OPEC were able to raise the price of a barrel of oil from about $3 to $42. This has not happened again, however, forcing a number of oil-producing countries to scale back their economic development plans. Prices in the 1990s have varied between $15 and $25 per barrel.

The amount of land that can be farmed in the Middle East is relatively small. Nevertheless, most countries rely to a certain extent on farming to supply food for their growing populations. In some cases—for example, Egypt, Iran, Iraq, and Turkey—farmers until recently have been a majority of the population. Often, much of the fertile land was owned by wealthy landlords. Land-reform programs in several countries, especially in Egypt, have given land to more small farmers.

Lack of water, however, has been the biggest obstacle to farming, and it is reaching crisis proportions. With populations growing at high rates, several governments have tried to increase the amount of water available for irrigation. Many attempts, however, have been ruined by government mistakes or political disagreements. The best-known example is the Aswan Dam, begun in Egypt by Soviet engineers in the 1950s and completed in 1970. The project was designed to control the flow of water throughout the Nile River valley, but it has had unforeseen consequences. Because the dam does not allow the annual flooding of the Nile, farmers no longer get rich silt for growing their crops but must rely on chemical fertilizers. Then, too, if irrigation water is not drained properly, salt deposits can poison the land.

Middle Eastern Societies and Women's Rights

At the beginning of the twentieth century, a woman's place in Middle Eastern society had changed little for

▲ *Many women in Egypt now wear veils when in public. For what reasons might this mother and her daughters have decided to dress so traditionally?*

hundreds of years. Women were secluded in their homes and had few legal, political, or social rights.

Early in the twentieth century, a modernist movement arose in several countries in the Middle East. Supporters of modernist views believed that Islamic doctrine was not inherently opposed to women's rights. During the first decades of the twentieth century, these views had a significant impact on a number of Middle Eastern societies, including Turkey and Iran. In both countries, rulers allowed greater rights for women and encouraged their education.

Modernist views had somewhat less effect in other Islamic states, such as Iraq, Jordan, Morocco, and Algeria. In these countries, traditional views of women prevailed, especially in rural areas. Most conservative by far was Saudi Arabia, where women were segregated and expected to wear veils in public. They were also restricted in education and forbidden to drive automobiles.

CLASS DISCUSSION

If education is more pervasive in Middle Eastern society, how long do students believe fundamentalism will last. Will educated people tolerate being told how to live their lives by these fundamentalists or will they find a way to gain greater freedom?

ASSESS

You can choose from a variety of assessments to evaluate your students' mastery of the objectives for this section as stated on page 1068. Possible assessments include:

1. Section Review Question on this page
2. Section 32–4 Quiz in your Teacher Resource materials
3. Reteaching Worksheets in your Teacher Resource materials
4. Self-Study software

Until recently, the general trend in urban areas of the Middle East was toward a greater role for women. This was especially true in Israel, the most westernized state in the Middle East. Women in Israel, for example, have achieved substantial equality with men. They are active in politics, the professions, and even the armed forces. Golda Meir, prime minister of Israel from 1968 to 1974, became an important symbol of the ability of women to be world leaders.

Beginning in the 1970s, however, there was a shift toward a more traditional approach to women in many Middle Eastern societies. This shift was accompanied by attacks on the growing Western influence within the media and on the social habits of young people. The reactions were especially strong in Iran during the revolution of 1979.

The revolution caused Iranian women to return to more traditional forms of behavior. They were told to wear veils and to dress modestly in public. Films produced in the new Iran expressed the new morality. They rarely featured women. When they did, physical contact between men and women was prohibited. Still, Iranian women have many freedoms that women lacked before the twentieth century. For example, they can attend a university, receive military training, practice birth control, and write novels.

The Iranian Revolution helped to promote a revival of traditional attitudes toward women in other Islamic societies. Women in secular countries such as Egypt, Turkey, and Malaysia have begun to dress more modestly in public. Moreover, public attacks on open sexuality in the media have become more frequent.

Contemporary Literature and Art in the Middle East

The contemporary literature of the Middle East deals with a number of new themes. The rise in national awareness has encouraged interest in historical traditions. Writers also have switched from religious to secular themes. They now discuss the problems of this world and how to fix them. Moreover, literature is no longer the preserve of the elite but is increasingly written for the broader mass of the people.

Iran has produced some of the best-known national literature in the contemporary Middle East. Perhaps the most outstanding Iranian author of the twentieth century was the short story writer Sadeq Hedayat (hay-DAW-yat). Hedayat was obsessed with the frailty and absurdity of life. He wrote with compassion about the problems of ordinary human beings. Frustrated at the government's suppression of individual liberties, he committed suicide in 1951.

Like Iran, Egypt has had a flowering of literature in the twentieth century. The most famous contemporary Egyptian writer is Naguib Mahfouz (ma-FOOZ). He was the first writer in Arabic to win the Nobel Prize for literature (in 1988). His *Cairo Trilogy*, published in 1952, is considered the finest writing in Arabic since World War II. The novel tells the story of a merchant family in Cairo during the years between the two world wars. Mahfouz is especially good at blending historical events with the personal lives of ordinary human beings. Unlike many other modern writers, his message is basically positive and reflects his hope that religion and science can work together for the betterment of humankind.

Although Israeli literature arises from a totally different tradition than that of its neighbors, it shares a concern for ordinary human beings. Israeli writers have inherited not only a long tradition of Hebrew literature but also the various traditions of the many nationalities that make up its population. As Israeli writers identify with the goals of their new nation, many try to find a sense of order in the new reality. They voice both terrors from the past and hopes for the future.

Some Israeli authors are also speaking out on sensitive national issues. The well-known novelist Amos Oz has examined problems in the **kibbutz** (a collective, or commune, in which farmers share property and work together, adults eat together, and children are raised in a separate children's home), one of Israel's most valued institutions. Other novels by Oz examine the psychological complexities of his characters, such as the emotional collapse of a housewife in *My Michael* or the collapse of a marriage in *To Know a Woman*. Oz is a strong supporter of peace with the Palestinians.

Like literature, the art of the modern Middle East has been strongly influenced by Western culture. At

ENRICHMENT ACTIVITY

Assign students to write a news article that might have appeared in an Iranian newspaper at the time of the return of the Ayatollah Khomeini from exile in France.

What hopes and fears might be expressed? Why might the reporter be afraid to say anything negative about the Ayatollah?

first, artists tended to imitate Western models. Later, however, they began to experiment with national styles and returned to earlier forms for inspiration. Some returned to the village to paint peasants and shepherds. Others followed international trends and tried to express the alienation that marks so much of modern life.

Reflecting their hopes for the new nation, Israeli painters sought to bring to life the feelings of pioneers arriving in a promised land. Many tried to capture the longing for community expressed in the Israeli kibbutz. Others searched for the roots of Israeli culture in the history of the Jewish people or in the horrors of the Holocaust. The experience of the Holocaust has attracted special attention from sculptors, who work in wood, metal, and stone.

❊ SECTION REVIEW ❊

1. **Define:**
   (*a*) Islamic fundamentalism,   (*b*) kibbutz

2. **Identify:**
   (*a*) Muslim Brotherhood,   (*b*) modernist movement,   (*c*) Sadeq Hedayat,   (*d*) Naguib Mahfouz,   (*e*) Amos Oz

3. **Recall:**
   (*a*) What do many devout Muslims believe has resulted from attempts to follow Western ways?
   (*b*) What is the greatest obstacle to farming in most Middle East countries?
   (*c*) What freedoms do Iranian women have that they lacked before the twentieth century?
   (*d*) What themes are common in the contemporary literature of the Middle East?

4. **Think Critically:** Why may attempts to return Muslims to strict Islamic lives fail in the long run?

Conclusion

After World War II, colonial rulers began to grant independence to their African states. Many of the new African states emerged on an optimistic note. Problems, however, are rampant. Military regimes, economic problems, climatic disasters, and civil strife all

have made it difficult to create stable governments and prosperous societies in Africa. Contemporary Africa is a land of contrasts between city and country and modern and traditional ways.

Nowhere in the developing world is the dilemma of continuity and change more agonizing than in contemporary Africa. What is the destiny of Africa? Some African political leaders still yearn for the dreams embodied in the program of the Organization of African Unity. Some believe that African states need democracy to survive. Other African political leaders, however, have rejected the democratic ideal and favor subordination of the individual to the community as the guiding principle of national development. Like all peoples, Africans must ultimately find their solutions within the context of their own traditions, not by seeking to imitate the example of others.

Like Africa, the Middle East is one of the most unstable regions in the world today. In part, this turbulence is due to the continued interference of outsiders attracted by the massive oil reserves of the Middle East. Oil is indeed both a blessing and a curse to the peoples of the region. Another factor contributing to the conflict in the Middle East is the tug-of-war between the sense of ethnic identity in the form of nationalism and the intense longing to be part of a broader Islamic community, a dream that dates back to the time of the Prophet Muhammad. The desire to create that broader community inspired Gamal Abdul Nasser in the 1950s and the Ayatollah Ruholla Khomeini in the 1970s and 1980s. Until the peoples of the Middle East are able to reconcile their desire for nationhood with their sense of common religious experience, it seems unlikely that they will find true peace and political stability.

Notes

1. Julius Nyerere, "The Arusha Declaration," *Freedomways* (1970), p. 124.
2. Quoted in *World Press Review*, August 1991, p. 16.
3. Adrian Roscoe, *Uhuru's Fire: African Literature East to South* (Cambridge, 1977), p. 103.
4. Abioseh Nicol, *A Truly Married Woman and Other Stories* (London, 1965), p. 12.
5. Cyprian Ekwensi, *Iska* (London, 1966), p. 21.

SPECIAL NEEDS: *Visual/Tactile*

Have students trace Map 32.2 and locate areas listed under question 1 in the Section review on page 1067. Borrow or bring in colored pencils, and have students shade the map in colors of their choice.

Next, ask students to write labels or place the appropriate letters in the proper locations on the map, according to the key.

Additionally, they should place the initials of those people they are asked to identify in the Locate section of this chapter's section review, on the map in their respective countries. This map can be used as a take home study aid on politics and geography in the Middle East.

CLOSE

Lead students in a discussion of the Focus objectives identified on page 1068.

SPANISH SUPPORT

The *Conclusion* has been translated into Spanish for your Spanish-speaking students. Included with this translation (in your Teacher Resource Box) are Section Key Points, which have also been translated into Spanish.

TIME LINE

As students conclude the chapter, you may want to refer them to the chapter time line in the *Study Guide.*

USING KEY TERMS

1. kibbutz
2. Mau Mau movement
3. *intifada*
4. Camp David Accords
5. apartheid
6. pan-Arabism
7. Islamic fundamentalism
8. proportional representation
9. scientific socialism

REVIEWING THE FACTS

1. The nations of Europe were occupied with rebuilding from World War II, resisting the spread of communism, and creating various forms of welfare states that consumed most of their time, money and energy.
2. Black South Africans were most opposed to their government's policy of apartheid.
3. Mandela supported the use of force to achieve equality for black South Africans.
4. African boundaries were drawn by Europeans in colonial times.
5. In 1994 Nelson Mandela was the first truly democratically-elected president of South Africa.
6. Most people in Africa support themselves by farming.
7. Israel is surrounded by Arab nations most of which are or have been opposed to the very existence of Israel.
8. He was unwilling to share power and he was seen as taking directions from western nations.
9. Saddam Hussein's army was fighting Iran which the United States was even more opposed to at that time.

THINKING CRITICALLY

1. Answers will vary but should mention the many African tribal groups that historically have not cooperated with each other.
2. They were used as official languages in many African

CHAPTER 32 REVIEW

USING KEY TERMS

1. A collective farming community in Israel is called a ——————.
2. The —————— was a native terrorist group dedicated to the elimination of British control from Kenya.
3. The mob violence to protest Israeli domination of Palestine was called the ——————.
4. The peace agreement between Egypt and Israel signed in 1979 was called the ——————.
5. The former South African policy of separating races was called ——————.
6. The belief in Arab unity has been called ——————————.
7. —————— is a movement to enforce strict religious teaching of Islam on all aspects of political and social life in some Arab nations.
8. There is —————— when members of an elective body are chosen based on the share of popular vote received by each political party.
9. President Nassar of Egypt called his objective of uniting and sharing resources of all Arab lands ——————————.

REVIEWING THE FACTS

1. What problems in Europe after World War II contributed to the willingness of colonial powers to grant independence to their African colonies?
2. What aspect of white rule in South Africa did many native Africans find most offensive?
3. Why was Nelson Mandela jailed by the white South African government?
4. Why are many national boundaries in Africa drawn without regard to where different tribal groups live?
5. What did Nelson Mandela achieve in 1994?
6. How do most African people earn their living?

7. Why has Israel allocated a large part of its national production to maintaining one of the most highly trained and best equipped military forces in the world?
8. Why did Shah Mohammed Reza Pahlavi of Iran lose the support of his people despite rapid growth in Iran's economy and standard of living?
9. Why did the United States support the government of Saddam Hussein through much of the 1980s?

THINKING CRITICALLY

1. What are several reasons that have made it difficult for the people of Africa to achieve the dream of pan-Africanism?
2. Why have English and French been used as official languages of government in many African nations?
3. Why might Nelson Mandela have had a greater impact on the lives of South African blacks after he was put in jail than before?
4. Why have many well-educated Africans chosen to leave their native lands to live in Europe or the United States?
5. Although the Israelis have won every war they fought with their Arab neighbors, they must negotiate to acheive a lasting peace. Why is this statement true?
6. Why is it unlikely that a lasting peace could have been established in Iraq even if the United Nations had captured or killed Saddam Hussein?
7. Why is it possible for the Untied States to have good relations with some nations that are strongly Islamic and not with others?
8. Why do all Arab nations rely on imported goods to satisfy the needs of their people? Does this make them vulnerable to pressures from foreign nations? Explain your answer.

---

nations because there was often no one native language that all people spoke.
3. While jailed, Mandela became a living martyr for his cause. People who might not have cared about his ideas became angry because of the treatment he received.
4. Answers will vary but are likely to mention opportunities, freedom, and safety.
5. The Israelis may have won the wars but there are still millions of Arab people who are opposed to the existence of Israel and willing to fight to destroy that state.
6. If Saddam Hussein had been eliminated from

Iraq it would not have changed the fact that this land is occupied by many groups who do not trust each other and are willing to fight.
7. Not all Islamic people have the same beliefs and values and some leaders of Islamic nations want the help of the United States to maintain their positions of power.
8. All Arab nations need products they are unable to produce for themselves. Answers will vary.

APPLYING SOCIAL STUDIES SKILLS

1. Political parties representing a particular tribal group are unlikely to make compromises

CHAPTER 32 REVIEW

APPLYING SOCIAL STUDIES SKILLS

1. **Government:** Often political parties in Africa are associated with a particular tribal group instead of a philosophy. Explain why this makes it difficult for African governments to be efficient, effective, fair, or widely supported.
2. **Economics:** Most African governments generate most of their revenues by taxing businesses and imported goods. Income and property taxes don't exist for most people. Why might this discourage industrialization of these states?
3. **Government:** Explain why the new government of South Africa has difficulty satisfying the desires of its black citizens, who are a majority and now hold the bulk of governmental power.
4. **Geography:** Draw a resource map of the Middle East that shows where major deposits of oil exist. Consider transportation routes used for oil exports from that part of the world. Explain why the western nations should be concerned about maintaining a steady flow of petroleum from the Middle East.
5. **Sociology:** Identify and explain conflicting social values that are likely to cause future disputes within Islamic nations.

MAKING TIME AND PLACE CONNECTIONS

1. Many African Americans who have returned to Africa to visit or live have experienced difficulty in communicating their ideas and values to native African blacks. What situations in the United States and Africa might explain this situation?
2. The United States placed embargoes on trade with Cuba after Cuba became communist, and on South Africa to protest its policy of apartheid. Identify and explain possible reasons why the embargo against South Africa was apparently more effective than the one against Cuba.

3. Compare and contrast conflicts between Catholic and Protestant groups during the reformation in Europe with the conflicts that have taken place between Islamic fundamentalists and more liberal Moslems in the Middle East during recent years.
4. The United States and European nations did little while massacres of civilians took place during the war in Bosnia, but many did intervene when Iraq invaded Kuwait. Explain why this involvement in the Middle East may have been more than a matter of Western powers protecting their supply of oil.

BECOMING AN HISTORIAN

1. **Charts, Graphs, and Tables:** The table below indicates the average value of production per person in various nations in 1994. Explain what this data shows you about the greater difficulty many African nations will experience in achieving economic growth than the United States or countries in Europe.

Gross National Product per person 1994

Nation	GNP	Nation	GNP
United States	$25,810	S. Africa	$2,720
Germany	25,220	Egypt	689
Canada	18,600	Ghana	309
United Kingdom	17,670	Kenya	232
Italy	17,330	Zaire	133

Source: U.S. Government Printing Office, *Statistical Abstract of the United States* (Washington, D.C., 1996), p. 835.

2. **Geography as a Key to History:** Study map 32.3 on page 1062 that shows the boundaries of Israel when it was originally formed and after the wars in 1948 and 1967. Explain why it is unlikely that a lasting peace can be achieved in the Middle East unless the issue of ownership of conquered lands is resolved.

1073

blacks reflect their experiences in the United States. It is possible that their ideas will not be seen as appropriate or desirable by black Africans.
2. Answers will vary but may concern the greater dependence of South Africa on international trade and the fact that the United States stood alone in maintaining its embargo against Cuba while most developed nations participated in the embargo against South Africa.
3. Answers will vary but should involve discussions of the use of violence and intimidation that was common to both events. Differences mentioned may include the influence of foreign powers in the confrontation between Moslems today.
4. Answers will vary but should point out that the situation in Bosnia was limited in scope and did not endanger world health or peace. Iraq, on the other hand, was developing chemical, biological, and nuclear weapons that could have killed millions of people.

ON BECOMING AN HISTORIAN

1. Answers will vary but should indicate that nations which have very low production per person are not likely to be able to make investments in their economies or educational systems to provide tools or trained workers to increase future production.
2. Answers will vary but should indicate that most of the territory Israel controls was taken from their Arab neighbors during various wars. This has made millions of Palestinians into refugees who want a homeland of their own in the land occupied by Israel. To achieve lasting peace an agreement must be reached between the interested parties that is acceptable to all. It is unlikely that such a settlement can be achieved through force.

needed to achieve a stable government that has the support of all groups of people.
2. Any activity that is taxed is less likely to take place. Taxes on industry discourage people from investing in new productive facilities.
3. The black community in South Africa is not one united group. There are many tribal groups that seek power and are not likely to be satisfied with compromise.
4. Maps will vary but should clearly indicate that the bulk of petroleum exports must pass through narrow straits and canals that could easily be blocked.

5. Answers will vary but should contrast the social values of Islamic fundamentalists with those of people who have experienced and accepted the need for greater freedoms similar to those that exist in western nations.

MAKING TIME AND PLACE CONNECTIONS

1. Answers will vary but may discuss the fact that although black Americans and Africans share a common heritage they do not live in nations with similar cultures. Values held by American

33 PLANNING GUIDE

SECTION	KEY TOPICS	PRIMARY SOURCES	ASSESSMENT
1 China Under Communism pages 1075–1080	◆ The Great Leap Forward ◆ The Cultural Revolution ◆ China after Mao	◆ A selection from the writings of a member of the Red Guard, page 1078	◆ Section Review, page 1080 ◆ Section Quiz 33–1, TRB
2 Serve the People: Chinese Society Under Communism pages 1080–1085	◆ Economic priorities in China ◆ Daily life and women's rights in modern China ◆ China's role in the Cold War and Korean War ◆ A shifting balance of power in Asia	◆ A description of the ideal socialist marriage in China, page 1082	◆ Section Review, page 1085 ◆ Section Quiz 33–2, TRB
3 The Emergence of Independent States in South Asia pages 1086–1093	◆ Democratic Socialism in India ◆ India after Nehru ◆ Daily Life in modern India ◆ Pakistan since independence	◆ A speech by Jawaharlal Nehru and a reply by Mohandas Gandhi, pages 1087–1088 ◆ A description of poverty in an Indian village, page 1091	◆ Section Review, page 1093 ◆ Section Quiz 33–3, TRB
4 Independence and Nationalism in Southeast Asia pages 1093–1099	◆ Independent states in Southeast Asia ◆ The Vietnam War ◆ Regional integration in Southeast Asia ◆ Daily Life in modern Southeast Asia		◆ Section Review, pages 1099–1100 ◆ Section Quiz 33–4, TRB
5 Japan and the Little Tigers pages 1100–1106	◆ Allied occupation of Japan ◆ The transformation of society in modern Japan ◆ Social changes, culture, and the role of women in modern Japan ◆ The "little tigers," South Korea, Taiwan, Singapore, and Hong Kong	◆ Rules from a middle school in Japan, page 1105	◆ Section Review, pages 1106–1107 ◆ Section Quiz 33–5, TRB

TOWARD THE PACIFIC CENTURY:
DEVELOPMENT OF THE ASIAN NATIONS (1945 TO PRESENT)

REPRODUCIBLE ACTIVITIES

Historical Maps

Charts and Graphs

Critical Thinking

Cooperative Learning

Vocabulary

Guided Reading

Reteaching

Enrichment

Performance Assessment

Spanish Key Points and Chapter Summaries

Spanish Vocabulary

Spanish Guided Reading

MULTIMEDIA SUPPORT

TRANSPARENCIES
◆ *World History* Color Transparency Package
◆ Fine Art Color Transparency Package

VIDEO
◆ *World History* Video Library
◆ CNN. Annual Video Update

LASERDISC
◆ *Sights and Sounds of History*

AUDIO
◆ *Listening to Literature* audiotape (English and Spanish)
◆ *History of Music* CD

SOFTWARE
◆ WESTEST™
◆ Student Review

CD–ROM
◆ *The Journey of Civilization*
◆ *World History*

INTERNET
◆ Internet Activities

On Line with WORLD HISTORY

Access West's history web site at
http://history.swpco.com
You'll find activities and web sites related to specific topics and chapters in *World History: The Human Odyssey*. Also look for references to helpful web sites at appropriate places throughout this teacher edition.

LESSON PLANNING

You will find detailed daily lesson plans for both traditional class scheduling and **block scheduling** in your Teacher Resource Box.

Not Enough Time?

If you do not have the four or five days recommended to teach this chapter, you may want to focus on the following sections and activities:

◆ Have students skim the chapter to answer the "Questions to Guide Your Reading" on page 1075. Discuss their answers, then read the "Conclusion" on page 1107.
◆ Do a more in-depth reading of the Cultural Revolution in China on pages 1077–1079, changes in China's economic and social systems on pages 1081–1083, problems of independence in India on pages 1085–1090, the Vietnam War on pages 1095–1097 and the transformation of Japan on pages 1101–1103. Conclude with a discussion of the advantages that enabled Japan and the little tigers to prosper after World War II.

TOWARD THE PACIFIC CENTURY:

33

To prepare students to study Chapter 33 you may use the following questions and activities.

◆ Have students list of major events after World War II that impacted economics, politics, and social values in Europe.

◆ Ask students to explain how the end of the Cold War might have impacted events in the Far East in recent years.

USING THE
OPENING STORY

Depending on the ability levels of your students, select from the following questions and activities to reinforce the reading of the opening story.

◆ How worried must a nation's leaders be to oppose unarmed civilians with an army?

◆ Why couldn't forty years of Communist rule erase historical values and beliefs of the Chinese people?

LEARNING
FROM VISUALS

Answer to the caption question: The Chinese students probably were aware of the risks they were taking, but they may not have believed the government would react as it did.

In the spring of 1989, China began to experience a remarkable series of events. Crowds of students, joined by workers and journalists, filled Tiananmen (tee-EN-uh-muhn) Square in Beijing day after day. Some students waged a hunger strike, and others carried posters calling for democracy. To China's elderly rulers, calls for democracy were a threat to the dominating role that the Communist Party had played in China since 1949. Some leaders interested in reform advised restraint in handling the protestors. Most of the Communist leaders, however, wanted to repress the movement. When students erected a thirty-foot-high statue entitled "The Goddess of Democracy" that looked similar to the American Statue of Liberty, party leaders became especially incensed.

On June 3, 1989, the Chinese army moved into action. Soldiers carrying automatic rifles fired into the unarmed crowds. Tanks and troops moved in and surrounded the remaining students in the square. At 5:30 in the morning on June 4, the mayor of Beijing announced that Tiananmen Square had been "handed back to the people." Even then the random killing of unarmed citizens continued. In all, more than five hundred

civilians died in the streets of Beijing. The movement for democracy in China had come to an abrupt end.

This movement for democracy was but one of many tumultuous events that made Asia a continent in ferment after World War II. In China, a violent civil war gave way to a new China under the control of the Communists. Japan not only recovered from the devastation of World War II but went on to build an economic powerhouse. In South Asia and Southeast Asia, nations that had been dominated by Western colonial powers struggled to gain their freedom.

Throughout all of Asia, nations worked to move out of their old ways and develop modern industrialized states. Building modern industrial states was not always easy, however. Old hatreds among different ethnic groups reemerged and led to new sources of conflict. Nevertheless, the success of the Asian states in building strong economies has led many observers to see the next one hundred years as the Pacific Century—a century dominated by the Asian nations bordering the Pacific Ocean.

▶ *Students marched in the streets of Beijing asking for democratic freedom, an end to the corruption in government, and the resignation of China's leadership. The gathering in Tiananmen Square with this* plaster "Goddess of Democracy" proved to be too much for the government to bear. Do you believe the students understood the risks they were taking when they openly opposed the government?

ADDITIONAL RESOURCES

BOOKS FOR STUDENTS

The Japanese by Edwin Reischauer, Belknap Press

The Life and Death of Mahatma Gandhi by Robert Payne, Simon and Schuster

Through Indian Eyes: The Living Tradition by Donald J. and Jean E. Johnson, (Center for International Training and Education) Social Studies School Service (800) 421-4246

VIDEOS/FILMS

Japan: Miracle in Asia, EBE, Social Studies School Service (800) 421-4246

Assignment: Southeast Asia, Christian Science Monitor Video, Social Studies School Service (800) 421-4246

CD-ROM

War in Vietnam, Simon & Schuster, Educorp Direct, (800) 843-9497 ◄

DEVELOPMENT OF THE ASIAN NATIONS

(1945 TO PRESENT)

THE WORLD SINCE 1945

1945	THE ASIAN NATIONS	2000
1945		2000

QUESTIONS TO GUIDE YOUR READING

1. How did the Great Leap Forward and the Great Proletarian Cultural Revolution affect China?
2. What were the major economic, social, and political developments in China after the death of Mao Zedong?
3. What was the impact of Communist rule on women, marriage, and family in China?
4. What policies did Jawaharlal Nehru put into effect in India, both domestically and in foreign policy? What changes occurred after Nehru's death?
5. What problems did Pakistan face after it achieved independence?
6. What internal and external problems did the Southeast Asian nations face after 1945?
7. What important political, economic, and social changes have occurred in Japan and the "little tigers" since 1945?

CHINA UNDER COMMUNISM

At the end of World War II, two Chinese governments existed side by side. The Nationalist government of Jiang Jieshi (see Chapter 27), based in southern and central China, was supported by the United States. The Communists, under the leadership of Mao Zedong, had built a strong base in North China. By the end of World War II, twenty to thirty million Chinese were living under Communist rule. The People's Liberation Army of the Communists included nearly one million troops.

When efforts to form a coalition government in 1946 failed, full-scale war between the Nationalists and the Communists broke out. In the countryside, millions of peasants were attracted to the Communists by promises of land. Many joined Mao's People's Liberation Army. In the cities, even middle-class Chinese, who were alienated by Jiang's repressive policies, supported the Communists. Jiang's troops began to defect

1075

Answers to QUESTIONS TO GUIDE YOUR READING

1. Both resulted in great loss of life and property. (pages 1076–1079)
2. sought foreign capital and ideas, inflation and discontent, democracy held at bay (pages 1079–1080)
3. legal position of women improved, strength of marriage and family undermined (pages 1081–1083)
4. See pages 1085–1090.
5. cultural and geographic divisions, internal conflict between moderate and extremist Muslims, tensions between East and West Pakistan (pages 1092–1093)
6. weakened by internal and external disputes, military and autocratic regimes, economic failures (pages 1094–1095)
7. Japan become world's second greatest industrial power, solidly democratic, stable economy (pages 1101–1106)

FOCUS ON THEMES

Listed below are brief summaries of how the content in this chapter supports the text's key themes.

Politics and History Different kinds of political regimes have emerged in Asia since 1945. China established a rigid Communist system. Democracy has taken hold in Japan, India, and a number of small countries. Military regimes continue to hold power in Myanmar (formerly Burma), Pakistan, and a host of small states.

The Role of Ideas Although the United States feared the spread of Communist political and economic ideas in Asia, the ideas of both democracy and a free-market economy have continued to be both fashionable and widespread.

Social Life Social problems, especially those derived from the gap between rich and poor and from the gap between town and countryside, continue in many countries in Asia. In South Asia and Southeast Asia, the growth of a stable middle class has been a prominent social development.

Religion in History Religious differences, such as those between Hindus and Muslims in India, have continued to play important roles in some areas of Asia. In China, despite the official Communist belief in atheism, there has been a revival of traditional religious beliefs.

The Impact of Science and Technology By adopting the latest technological developments, Asian countries such as South Korea, Japan, and China have created flourishing industrial economies.

FOCUS

OBJECTIVES

After completing this section, students should be able to:

1. identify and describe events in the Great Leap Forward
2. identify and describe events in the Cultural Revolution
3. describe changes that took place in China after Mao's death

FOCUS ACTIVITY

Help students understand that social upheavals are often associated with a decline in production and economic hardship. Ask students to describe what a day of demonstrating in favor of democracy did for China's standard of living. While people are fighting or demonstrating how much are they able to produce? Why do some people believe that political demonstrations are like a luxury good?

TEACH

Multimedia Support

TRANSPARENCY
33–1, The People's Republic of China (Map 33.1)

to the Communists. Sometimes whole divisions—officers as well as ordinary soldiers—changed sides.

By 1948, the People's Liberation Army had surrounded Beijing. The following spring it crossed the Yangtze (YANG-SEE) and occupied Shanghai (SHANG-HIE). During the next few months, Jiang's government and two million of his followers fled to Taiwan (see later in the chapter). On October 1, 1949, Mao Zedong mounted the rostrum of the Gate of Heavenly Peace in Beijing and made a victory statement to the thousands gathered in the square before him. We, the Chinese people, have stood up, he said, and no one will be able to humiliate us again.

The Great Leap Forward

In the fall of 1949, China was at peace. The newly victorious Communist Party, under the leadership of its chairman, Mao Zedong, turned its attention to ruling the country. Its long-term goal was to build a socialist society. Its leaders realized, however, that popular support for the revolution had been based on the party's platform of honest government and land reform, not the socialist goal of a classless society. Thus, the new regime moved slowly, having adopted a program known as the New Democracy.

Like Lenin's New Economic Policy, the **New Democracy** was a program of modified capitalism. Major industries were placed under state ownership, but most trading and manufacturing companies remained in private hands. To win the support of the peasants, lands were taken from wealthy landlords and given to poor peasants. About two-thirds of the peasant households in China received land under the new program.

The New Democracy worked as the economy began to grow. However, there was a darker side to the picture. Thousands, if not millions, of landlords and rich farmers lost their lands, and sometimes their lives. Many of those who died had been tried and convicted of "crimes against the people" in people's courts set up in towns and villages around the country. Some were innocent of any crime. In the eyes of the Communist Party, however, their deaths were necessary to destroy the power of large landowners in the countryside.

The New Democracy was never meant to be permanent. In 1955, the Chinese government launched a new program to build a socialist society. Virtually all private farmland was collectivized. Peasant families were allowed to keep small plots for their private use, but they worked chiefly in large collective farms. In addition, most industry and commerce was nationalized.

The Chinese leaders had hoped that collective farms would increase food production, which would allow more people to work in industry. Food production, however, did not increase. In 1958, Mao began a

Map 33.1   The People's Republic of China

STUDYING MAPS

The following questions and activities will help you guide students through their study of Map 33.1.

1. Locate Beijing on the map. Now find Han Kou, Congqing, and Urumchi. Roughly how far is Urumchi from Beijing? *(approximately 1600 miles.)*

2. Why is it difficult for the central government in Beijing to control events in all

parts of China? *(China is large, with much territory remote from Beijing.)*

3. Why was there resentment of edicts from Beijing in many parts of China? *(Many people thought of themselves as ethnically different from those who lived in Beijing.)*

more radical program, known as the **Great Leap Forward.** Existing collective farms, normally the size of the traditional village, were combined into vast **people's communes.** Each contained more than thirty thousand people.

Mao Zedong hoped this program would mobilize the people for a massive effort to speed up economic growth and reach the final stage of communism—the classless society—before the end of the twentieth century. The party's official slogan promised the following: "Hard work for a few years, happiness for a thousand." However, the Great Leap Forward was a disaster. Bad weather and the peasants' hatred of the new system combined to drive food production downward. Over the next few years, as many as fifteen million people may have died of starvation. Many peasants were reportedly reduced to eating the bark off trees and, in some cases, to allowing infants to starve. In 1960, the people's communes were abandoned and a return was made to the collective farms.

▲ *Mao Zedong was born in 1893 in the Hunan province. He helped found the Chinese Communist Party in 1921 and became its leader in 1936. He was the dominant leader in China until his death in 1976.*

and universities were closed for six months to prepare for a new system of education based on Mao's ideas. Supported by his wife Jiang Qing (jee-ONG SHING) and other radicals in the party, Mao launched China on a new forced march toward communism.

Mao's so-called Great Proletarian Cultural Revolution (the Chinese name literally meant "great revolution to create a proletarian culture") lasted for ten years, from 1966 to 1976. Mao was convinced that Communist Party and government officials had lost their revolutionary zeal. Only an atmosphere of constant revolutionary fervor **(permanent revolution)** could enable the Chinese to overcome the past and achieve the final stage of communism.

Mao's supporters were now in power, and the party carried out vast reforms. A new school system stressed "Maozedong Thought." Mao's famous *Little Red Book*, a collection of his thoughts, was hailed as the most important source of knowledge in all areas. Red Guards set out across the nation to eliminate the **"four olds"** (old ideas, old culture, old customs, and old habits). The Red Guards destroyed temples, books written by foreigners, and jazz records. They tore down street signs and replaced them with ones carrying revolutionary names. At one point the city of Shanghai even ordered that the meaning of colors in stoplights be changed. Red (the revolutionary color) would indicate that traffic could move, not stop.

Destruction of property was matched by vicious attacks on individuals who had supposedly deviated from Mao's thought. Those so accused were humiliated at public meetings, where they were forced to admit their "crimes." Many were brutally beaten, often to death. Intellectuals and artists, who were accused of being pro-Western, were especially open to attack. Red Guards broke the fingers of one pianist for the "crime" of playing the works of Frédéric Chopin, the nineteenth-century European composer.

The Great Proletarian Cultural Revolution

Despite his failures, Mao was not yet ready to abandon his dream of a totally classless society. In 1966, he returned to the attack and unleashed the **Red Guards.** These were revolutionary units composed of unhappy party members and discontented young people (see "Young People in Communist China: The Red Guards"). They were urged to take to the streets to cleanse Chinese society of impure elements guilty of taking the capitalist road. Schools, universities, factories, and even government ministries were all subject to the scrutiny of the Red Guards. In June 1966, all schools

MORE ABOUT . . . *The Great Leap Forward*

The Great Leap Forward is similar to Stalin's collectivization and his first Five Year Plan, but both enacted at the same time. Mao believed that by combining collectivization with crash industrial programs, he could avoid Stalin's disaster. Some 5,376 agricultural collectives were merged into 208 communes, averaging over 8,000 households apiece. The resulting dislocations appalled the Soviets, who withdrew their aid rather than see it wasted. The result of the Great Leap Forward was starvation from 1959–1962. No one knows how many people died of hunger, but the figure is in the millions.

CLASS DISCUSSION

Ask students to discuss whether they believe Chairman Mao understood what he was starting with the Cultural Revolution, or if its results were a surprise to him.

LEARNING FROM VISUALS

Ask students if the photograph of the Red Guard to the right reminds them of pictures they have seen of Nazi demonstrations in Germany during World War II. Do they believe there is more to the similarity than just the appearance?

Answer to the caption question: Young people in China wanted to advance their own careers, be held in a good light by the government, and be seen as loyal and patriotic to the Cultural Revolution.

Answers to Critical Thinking Questions

1. The Red Guards were revolutionary units formed by Mao Zedong. Many of the members were young people between the ages of 15 and 20.
2. The purpose of the Red Guards was to root out all aspects of the old system.
3. They raided homes, burned items, tortured and beat people, and stole items to fulfill their purpose.
4. Answers will vary but may include such groups as the Nazi SS during World War II.

YOUNG PEOPLE IN COMMUNIST CHINA

The Red Guards

The Red Guards were revolutionary units formed by Mao Zedong, beginning in 1966. Many of the Red Guards were young people between the ages of fifteen and twenty, often without any job opportunities. The task of the Red Guards was to root out all aspects of the former capitalist system.

With the energy of the young, the Red Guards carried out their activities with great zeal. They believed Mao's message and even were devoted to him as a god. Liang Heng (LEE-un HUNG), who wrote an account of his activities called *Son of the Chinese Revolution*, describes the ecstasy he felt when he first saw the Chinese leader:

> *Chairman Mao's car was first, a Beijing-brand army jeep. As in a dream, I saw him. He seemed very tall to me, magnificent, truly larger than life. He waved his hat as the jeep drove slowly through the throng. The soldiers forming the passageway stood at attention, but the tears poured down their faces. . . . I was bawling like a baby, crying again and again: "You are our hearts' reddest sun." My tears blocked my vision, but I could do nothing to control myself.*

In his enthusiasm, Liang Heng at first helped friends organize groups of Red Guards: "I thought it was a great idea. We would be following Chairman Mao just like the grownups, and Father would be proud of me. I suppose I too resented the teachers who had controlled me and criticized me for so long, and I looked forward to a little revenge."

Later, Liang Heng had reason to repent. His sister ran off to join the local group of Red Guards. Before she left, she denounced her mother and the rest of her family as enemies of the revolution. Their home was regularly raided by the Red Guards. Their father was beaten and tortured for having three neckties and "Western shirts." Books,

▲ *Chinese Red Guards gather in Beijing to see Mao Zedong. The little red book they are waving is* Thought of Chairman Mao, *which describes his views of the Chinese way to attain a Marxist society. Why do you think so many young men and women eagerly joined this group, whose primary goal was to change the Chinese view of tradition and obedience?*

paintings, and writings were piled in the center of the floor and burned before his eyes. On leaving, a few of the Red Guards helped themselves to his monthly salary and his transistor radio.

---

1. Who were the Red Guards?
2. What was the purpose of the Red Guards?
3. What kind of activities did they carry out in order to fulfill their purpose?
4. What groups in other countries in the twentieth century carried out similar activities?

MORE ABOUT . . . *The Red Guards*

Mao's wife, Jiang Qing announced the slogan, "With hammer in hand, I set out to destroy all the old conventions." The Red Guards took her literally, which is why they smashed the hands of the pianist who played the works of Chopin. The Red Guards also cut girls' braided hair, changed restaurant menus, forbade the sale of cosmetics and sunglasses, burned chess sets, mahjong sets, jazz records, shut tea and coffee shops, closed private restaurants, and forbade wedding, funerals, holding hands, and kite flying.

Mao found that it is not easy to maintain a permanent revolution, or constant mood of revolutionary enthusiasm. Key groups, including Communist Party members, urban professionals, and many military officers, did not share Mao's desire for permanent revolution. Many people were disgusted with the actions of the Red Guards. People began to turn against the movement.

China after Mao

In September 1976, Mao Zedong died at the age of eighty-three. A group of practical-minded reformers, led by Deng Xiaoping (DUNG SHOU-PING) (who had himself been in prison during the Cultural Revolution), seized power from the radicals and brought the Cultural Revolution to an end. Mao's widow, Jiang Qing, and three other radicals (called the **gang of four**) were placed on trial and sent to prison for life. The policies of the last ten years were halted, and a new program was put in place.

Under the leadership of Deng Xiaoping, the government created a new policy called the **four modernizations**—in industry, agriculture, technology, and national defense. Deng had opposed Mao's Cultural Revolution and had been punished for his beliefs. Deng, however, took a practical approach to change. He once said, "Black cat, white cat, what does it matter so long as it catches the mice?" Under the program of four modernizations, people were encouraged to work hard to benefit both themselves and Chinese society.

Crucial to the success of the new program was the government's ability to attract foreign technology and capital. For over twenty years, China had been isolated from the technological advances taking place elsewhere in the world. To make up for lost time, the government now invited foreign investors to China. Moreover, thousands of students were sent abroad to study science and technology, as well as modern business techniques.

By adopting this practical approach, China began to make great strides in ending its problems of poverty and underdevelopment. Per capita income doubled during the 1980s. Housing, education, and sanitation

▲ *During the Cultural Revolution, many professional people lost their jobs and were subjected to constant harassment. Red Guards seem to enjoy humiliating one of their public enemies by placing a tall dunce cap on his head and marching him through the crowded streets.*

improved. Both agriculture and industrial output skyrocketed. Clearly, China had begun to enter the Industrial Age.

However, many people, both inside and outside China, complained that Deng Xiaoping's program had failed to achieve a fifth modernization—that of democracy. It soon became clear that the new leaders would not allow any direct criticism of the Communist Party. Those who called for democracy were suppressed. Some were sentenced to long terms in prison.

RECOMMENDED READING

A number of useful surveys deal with China after World War II. The most comprehensive treatment of the Communist period is M. Meisner, *Mao's China, and After, A History of the People's Republic* (New York, 1986). For shorter accounts of the period, see J. Grasso, et al., *Modernization and Revolution in China* (Armonk, N.Y., 1991); and C. Dietrich, *People's China: A Brief History* (New York, 1986). The Cultural Revolution is treated dramatically in S. Karnow, *Mao and China: Inside China's Cultural Revolution* (New York, 1972). For individual accounts of the impact of the revolution on people's lives, see the celebrated book by Nien Cheng, *Life and Death in Shanghai* (New York, 1986); and Liang Heng and J. Shapiro, *After the Revolution* (New York, 1986).

For a treatment of Mao's famous wife see R. Witke, *Comrade Chiang Ching* (Boston, 1972).

THE ROLE OF INDIVIDUALS

Ask students to discuss the following question. If Mao was the personification of Communist China, what happened as a result of his death? Can the absence of a powerful leader be an important factor in the course of history? What happened after Alexander the Great and Charlemagne died?

REVIEWING VOCABULARY

Point out that reforming the Chinese government was not one of the *four modernizations* Den Xiaoping wanted to achieve. Ask students to explain its absence from this list.

ASSESS

You can choose from a variety of assessments to evaluate your students' mastery of the objectives for this section as stated on page 1076. Possible assessments include:

1. Section Review Questions on this page
2. Section 33–1 Quiz in your Teacher Resource materials
3. Reteaching Worksheets in your Teacher Resource materials
4. Self-Study software

ALTERNATIVE ASSESSMENT

Assign students to create several days worth of entries in a hypothetical diary that might have been carried by a member of the Red Guard. These entries should describe key events and what the writer believes they accomplished.

2. (a) program of modified capitalism allowing most trading and manufacturing firms to remain in private ownership
(b) program to combine small land holdings into collective farms
(c) massive collective farms
(d) revolutionary units
(e) a constant state of revolution to maintain fervor and achieve final stage of communism
(f) old values to be eliminated in China during the Cultural Revolution
(g) leaders of the Cultural Revolution placed on trial and sent to prison for life
(h) policy created by Deng Xiaoping to improve China's industry, agriculture, technology, and national defense

3. (a) 1966–1976 attempt by Red Guard to reform society
(b) Mao's sayings
(c) leader of China, ended Cultural Revolution
(d) location of 1989 demonstration in support of democracy; forcefully put down by the Chinese government

4. (a) Communists promised them land.
(b) Peasants hated the system; bad weather reduced production and caused mass starvation.
(c) foreign technology and capital
(d) greater freedom to control their own lives

5. Answers will vary.

The problem began to intensify in the late 1980s. More Chinese began to study abroad. More information about Western society reached educated people inside the country. The economic improvements of the early 1980s led to pressure from students and other city residents for better living conditions and more freedom to choose jobs after graduation.

In the late 1980s, rising inflation led to growing discontent among salaried workers, especially in the cities. At the same time, corruption and special treatment for senior officials and party members led to increasing criticism. In May 1989, student protestors carried signs calling for an end to official corruption and the resignation of China's aging Communist Party leadership. These demands received widespread support from people in the cities. They also led to massive demonstrations in Tiananmen Square in Beijing.

Chinese leaders were divided over how to respond. Some, led by Communist Party general secretary Zhao Ziyang (JOO ZEE-YANG), were sympathetic to the protestors. Older leaders, such as Deng Xiaoping, however, saw the student demands for democracy as a call for an end to the Communist Party. The government sent tanks and troops into Tiananmen Square to crush the demonstrators. Chinese leaders insisted that economic reforms could take place only with political stability. Democracy remained a dream.

❀ SECTION REVIEW ❀

1. Locate:
 (*a*) Taiwan

2. Define:
 (*a*) New Democracy,   (*b*) Great Leap Forward,
 (*c*) people's communes,   (*d*) Red Guards,
 (*e*) permanent revolution,   (*f*) four olds,
 (*g*) gang of four,   (*h*) four modernizations

3. Identify:
 (*a*) Great Proletarian Cultural Revolution,
 (*b*) *Little Red Book*,   (*c*) Deng Xiaoping,
 (*d*) Tiananmen Square

4. Recall:
 (*a*) What caused many peasants to support the Communist side when war broke out in China in 1946?
 (*b*) Why was the Great Leap Forward an economic disaster for China?
 (*c*) What help did China require to improve its economy after the Cultural Revolution?
 (*d*) What did economic improvements in China lead many students and urban residents to demand?

5. Think Critically: Why has it not been easy to maintain a constant mood of revolutionary enthusiasm in China or any other nation?

SERVE THE PEOPLE: CHINESE SOCIETY UNDER COMMUNISM

Enormous changes have taken place in Chinese society since the Communist rise to power in 1949. No longer an agrarian society, China today is in the midst of its own Industrial Revolution. Beneath the surface of rapid change, however, there are hints of the survival of elements of the old China.

Economics in Command

During the late 1950s, Mao Zedong began to maintain that political considerations were more important than economic ones in building a socialist society. After 1976, in contrast, Deng Xiaoping and other party leaders were hoping that rapid economic growth would satisfy the Chinese people and prevent them from demanding political reforms.

To stimulate the growth of industry, the new leaders allowed local managers in the state-owned factories to have more say over prices, salaries, and quality control. Bonuses could now be paid to workers for extra effort. The regime also permitted a small private sector to emerge. People could set up restaurants or handicraft

---

So What ??

If your students question the importance of the information on the **Four Modernizations** *tell them . . .*

A dominating issue for Third World countries has been how to modernize their societies along the technological European model. Today, the tendency is that traditional societies which cannot modernize become poor and subservient. Discuss this tendency. What examples can students think of to support or disprove it?

shops on their own. Foreign firms were also now invited to build factories in China.

The new leaders abandoned the system of education begun during the Cultural Revolution. They opened new schools that were based on the Western model. Merit examinations determined who could go to universities. Courses in science and mathematics were now given priority.

Under Deng Xiaoping, a new agricultural policy also came into being. Collective farms could now lease land to peasant families. The families paid a rent (in the form of a percentage of their goods) to the collective. Anything produced on the land above the amount of that payment could be sold on the private market. Sideline industries were also allowed. For example, peasants raised fish and made consumer goods they could sell to others.

The reform program had a striking effect on farm production. Farm income doubled during the 1980s. However, the reforms also caused problems. By 1970, the government had launched a strict family planning program. All families were supposed to limit themselves to one child. Those with more than one child would be fined. The new farm program led many peasant families to pay the penalties for having more than one child. They believed that the labor of these extra children would increase family income and make it worthwhile to pay the penalties. Sons, however, continued to be valued more highly than daughters. Thus, female infanticide did not entirely disappear.

Overall, economic modernization worked well for many people in China. The standard of living improved for most people. The average Chinese citizen in the early 1980s had struggled to earn enough to buy a bicycle, radio, or watch. By the 1990s, however, many were beginning to buy refrigerators and color television sets. The government stressed the idea that all Chinese would prosper, although not at the same rate.

Daily Life and Women's Rights

From the start, the Chinese Communist Party intended to create a new citizen free from the ideas of the past. These new citizens would have racial and sexual equality. They would also be expected to contribute their utmost for the good of all. In the words of Mao Zedong, the people "should be resolute, fear no sacrifice, and surmount every difficulty to win victory."

During the 1950s, the government took a number of steps to end the old system in China. Women were allowed to take part in politics. At the local level, an increasing number of women became active in the Communist Party. In 1950, a new Marriage Law was passed, guaranteeing women equal rights with men (see "You Are There: The Correct Viewpoint toward Marriage"). The law also allowed women to initiate divorce proceedings against their husbands. Within a year, nearly one million divorces had been granted.

The new regime also tried to destroy the influence of the traditional family system. To the Communists, loyalty to the family, an important element in the Confucian social order, undercut loyalty to the state. For Communist leaders, family loyalty was against the basic principle of Marxism—dedication to society at large.

During the Great Leap Forward, children were encouraged for the first time to report to the authorities any comments by their parents that criticized the system. These practices continued during the Cultural Revolution. Red Guards expected children to report on their parents, students on their teachers, and employees on their superiors.

At the time, many foreign observers feared that the Cultural Revolution would transform the Chinese people into robots spouting the slogans fed to them by their leaders. However, this did not happen. After the death of Mao Zedong, there was a noticeable shift away from revolutionary fervor and a return to a practical approach to nation building. For most people, the shift meant better living conditions and a return to family traditions. Married couples who had been given patriotic names such as "Protect Mao Zedong" and "Build the Country" by their parents chose more elegant names for their own children.

The new attitudes were also reflected in people's physical appearances. For a generation after the civil war, clothing had been restricted to a baggy "Mao suit" in olive drab or dark blue. Today, young Chinese people crave such Western items as jeans, sneakers, and sweat suits. Cosmetic surgery to create a more Western

CLOSE

Lead students in a discussion of the 'Focus' objectives identified on page 1076. Emphasize the importance of Mao's failed attempts to rule all parts of China's economy, political structure, and society.

FOCUS

OBJECTIVES

After completing this section, students should be able to:

1. identify and describe recent changes in China's economic system and priorities
2. describe daily life and women's rights in modern China
3. describe China's role in the Cold War and the Korean War
4. identify and explain events that demonstrate a shift in power in Asia

FOCUS ACTIVITY

Help students understand the relationship between economic and political freedom. Assign students to list rights people need to run a successful business. These would include freedoms to advertise, buy resources, set prices, determine quality standards, etc. Ask students to discuss why people who were given these rights would also desire a voice in their political system. How do American business people use political rights to protect their economic interests?

TEACH

YOU ARE THERE

USING PRIMARY SOURCES

Ask students to discuss the reading on this page. How would they feel, and what they would do if their government set standards for who should be married and how they should behave in their married lives?

LEARNING WITH VISUALS

Answer to the caption question: The couple is wearing Western dress, the flowers appear to be a Western-style bouquet.

Answers to Critical Thinking Questions

1. The ideal marriage is based on equal rights for men and women, mutual consent of the partners, common political understanding, comradeship in work, mutual help, mutual respect, solemnity, and fidelity.
2. In capitalist countries common political understanding and comradeship in work are usually not issues. Money, position, and "prettiness," which are not to be taken into consideration in a socialist marriage, are often considered in a marriage in a capitalist country.
3. Answers will vary.

YOU ARE THERE

The Correct Viewpoint toward Marriage

One of the major goals of the Communist government in China was to reform the tradition of marriage. In this excerpt, a writer with the magazine China Youth Daily *describes the ideal socialist marriage.*

A Chinese Writer Describes the Perfect Socialist Marriage

Now then, what is our viewpoint? Is it different from that of the exploiting bourgeois class?

For one thing, our basic concept on marriage is and must be that we build our happiness upon the premise that happiness should be shared by all. We advocate equal rights for man and woman, equal rights for husband and wife. We oppose the idea that man is superior to woman or that the husband has special prerogatives over his wife. We also oppose any discrimination against or ill treatment of the wife.

We believe that marriage should be based solely upon mutual consent. We oppose the so-called arranged marriage, or the use of any deceitful or compulsory method by one of the parties in this matter. We uphold the system of monogamy. Hus-

A happy bride and groom celebrate their wedding vows in Lanzhou, China, in 1994. As weddings grow more and more lavish, it is not uncommon for weddings to cost up to four or five times a family's monthly income. What signs of Westernization do you see in this photo?

band and wife ought to have pure and exclusive love toward each other.

We believe that the very basic foundations for love between man and woman are common political understanding, comradeship in work, mutual help, and mutual respect. Money, position, or the so-called prettiness should not be taken into consideration for a right marriage, because they are not reliable foundations for love.

We also believe that solemnity and fidelity are important elements for a correct relationship between husband and wife, and for a happy family life. To abandon one's partner by any improper means is to be opposed. In our society, those who intend to pursue their happiness at the expense of others run contradictory to the moral principle of Communism and will never be happy.

1. What is the ideal marriage according to the Chinese Communist Party?

2. How is this "socialist" ideal of marriage different from marriage in capitalist countries?

3. Is the "socialist" ideal of marriage a realistic one? Why or why not?

On Line with WORLD HISTORY Internet Activity

You may want to have your students visit the following URL, where they will find information and additional web site resources to enhance their study of this chapter.

Korean War—50th Anniversary

http://www.tcsaz.com/korean war.html

Korean War Project

http://biz.onramp.net/~hbarker/

Both these sites are excellent sources for the Korean War.

Due to the ever-changing nature of the World Wide Web, see the West History web site, **http://history.swpco.com** for regular updates of the URLs in this text.

facial look is increasingly common among wealthy young women in the cities.

Religious practices and beliefs have also changed since the Cultural Revolution, when the official belief was atheism. Some Chinese have been returning to the traditional Buddhist faith. Buddhist and Taoist temples are once again crowded with worshipers. Christianity has also become increasingly popular, because many view it as a symbol of success.

Such changes are much more common among urban dwellers and China's small middle class than among rural folk, who still make up more than half of the population. Most peasants have been little affected by the events that have occurred since Mao's death. The gap that has always divided town and country in China still remains. Such practices as arranged marriages and mistreatment of females continue in rural areas. Many parents in the countryside reportedly have killed female infants in the hope of having a son to fulfill the expectation of only one child per family.

China and the World: The Cold War in Asia

In 1949, the Cold War spread from Europe to Asia when the Chinese Communists won the Chinese civil war and set up a new Communist regime. American fears about the spread of communism intensified, especially when the new Chinese Communist leaders made it clear that they supported "national wars of liberation"—or movements for revolution—in Africa, Asia, and Latin America. When Communist China signed a pact of friendship and cooperation with the Soviet Union in 1950, some Americans began to speak of a Communist desire for world domination.

The Korean War

The outbreak of war in Korea helped bring the Cold War to Asia. Korea had once been under the control of China. In 1905, however, Korea became a part of the Japanese Empire and remained so until 1945. In August 1945, the Soviet Union and the United States agreed to divide Korea into two zones at the thirty-eighth parallel. The plan was to hold elections after

Map 33.2   The Korean Peninsula

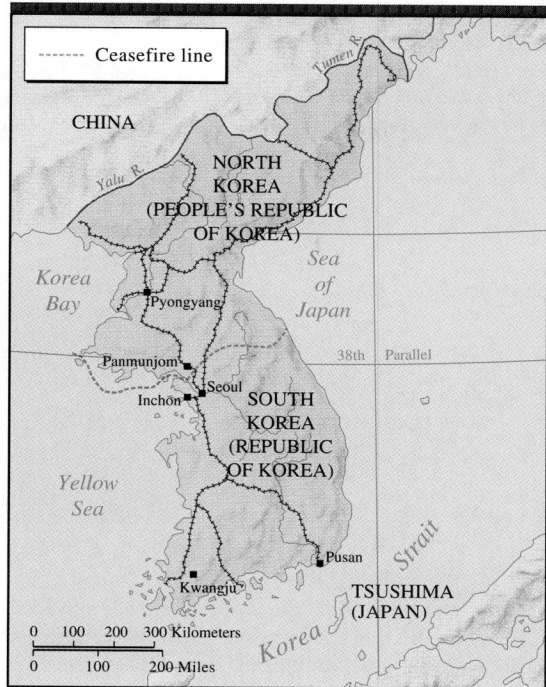

the war to reunify Korea under an independent government. As American-Soviet relations grew worse, however, two separate governments emerged in Korea—a Communist one in the north and an anti-Communist one in the south.

Tensions between the two governments ran high. On June 25, 1950, with the approval of Joseph Stalin, North Korean troops invaded South Korea. U.S. president Harry Truman, seeing this as yet another example of Communist aggression, gained the support of the United Nations and sent American troops to turn back the invasion. By September 1950, UN forces (mostly American soldiers) marched northward across the thirty-eighth parallel with the aim of unifying Korea.

The Chinese, greatly alarmed as U.S. forces approached the Yalu (YAW-LOO) River border with

STUDYING MAPS

The following questions will help you guide students through their study of Map 33.2.

1. Where is Korea in relation to the United States and China? *(about 3,500 miles from the U.S.; just south of China)*

2. What strategic value does Korea have to the United States and China? *(little for the United States, it is attached to Asia and on China's trade routes)*

3. Why was Korea difficult for the U.S. to defend? *(it had to be supplied by sea)*

► A U.S. Tandem helicopter delivers battle-ready American troops in Korea. The U.S. entered the war as part of a UN police action and fought it as a limited war. What were the worldwide consequences of this war?

China, then came into the war on the side of North Korea. Hundreds of thousands of Chinese "volunteers" swarmed into North Korea and pushed UN forces back across the thirty-eighth parallel. When three more years of fighting produced no final victory, an armistice was finally signed in 1953. The thirty-eighth parallel remained the boundary line between North and South Korea. Western fears of China now led to China's isolation from the major Western powers. China was forced to rely almost entirely on the Soviet Union for both technological and economic aid. Even that became more difficult as relations between China and the Soviet Union began to deteriorate in the late 1950s.

The Shifting Power Balance in Asia

Several issues divided China and the Soviet Union in the 1950s. For one thing, the Chinese were not happy with the economic aid provided by the Soviet Union. More important, however, was their disagreement over the Cold War. The Chinese wanted the Soviets to go on the offensive to promote world revolution. Specifi-

cally, China wanted Soviet aid in retaking Taiwan from Jiang Jieshi. The Soviet Union, however, was trying to improve its relations with the West and thus rejected the Chinese demands.

By the end of the 1950s, the Soviet Union had begun to remove its advisors from China. In the 1960s, the dispute between China and the Soviet Union broke into the open. Military units on both sides of the frontier clashed on a number of occasions. Faced with internal problems and a serious security threat on its northern frontier from the Soviet Union, some Chinese leaders decided to improve relations with the United States. In 1972, President Richard Nixon made a state visit to China. The two sides agreed to improve relations. China's long isolation from the West was coming to an end.

After the Cultural Revolution, China further sought to improve relations with the Western states. Diplomatic ties were established with the United States in 1979. In the 1980s, Chinese relations with the Soviet Union also gradually improved. By the 1990s, China emerged as an independent power and was playing an increasingly active role in Asian affairs.

On Line with WORLD HISTORY Internet Activity

You may want to have your students visit the following URL, where they will find information and additional web site resources to enhance their study of this chapter.

The Gate of Heavenly Peace—Tiananmen Square

http://www.nmis.org/gate/

This site highlights Frontline production based on the movie, *The Gate of Heavenly Peace.* It contains good discussions, and links dealing with the events of 1989 in China.

Due to the ever-changing nature of the World Wide Web, see the West History web site, **http://history.swpco.com** for regular updates of the URLs in this text.

SECTION REVIEW ❀

1. **Locate:**
   (a) Yalu River

2. **Identify:**
   (a) Richard Nixon

3. **Recall:**
   (a) How did Deng Xiaoping hope to prevent the Chinese people from demanding political reforms?
   (b) What changes led to a rapid increase in farm production in China during the 1980s?
   (c) Why did the early Communists attempt to weaken the traditionally strong Chinese family structure?
   (d) What event apparently caused Chinese "volunteers" to participate in the Korean War?
   (e) What were the different positions of China and the Soviet Union toward the Cold War in the 1950s?

4. **Think Critically:** Why were urban Chinese more likely to abide by their government's call for only one child per family than rural Chinese?

THE EMERGENCE OF INDEPENDENT STATES IN SOUTH ASIA

For over a century, the peoples of the Indian subcontinent had been ruled by Great Britain. After World War II, they finally gained their independence. Ethnic and religious differences, however, made the process both difficult and violent.

Independence for India

At the end of World War II, Great Britain negotiated with both the Indian National Congress, which was mostly Hindu, and the Muslim League. British India's Muslims and Hindus were bitterly divided and unwilling to accept a single Indian state. Great Britain soon realized that British India would have to be divided into two countries, one Hindu (India) and one Muslim (Pakistan). Pakistan would actually consist of two regions separated by over a thousand miles. One part was to the northwest of India (West Pakistan) and the other (East Pakistan), to the northeast.

Among Congress leaders, only Mohandas Gandhi objected to the division of India. A Muslim woman criticized him for opposition to partition, asking him, "If two brothers were living together in the same house and wanted to separate and live in two different houses, would you object?" "Ah," Gandhi replied, "if only we could separate as two brothers. But we will not. It will be an orgy of blood. We shall tear ourselves asunder in the womb of the mother who bears us."[1]

On August 15, 1947, India and Pakistan became independent. However, Gandhi had been right. The flight of millions of Hindus and Muslims across the new borders led to violence, and more than a million people were killed. One of the dead was especially well known. On January 30, 1948, a Hindu militant assassinated Gandhi as he was going to morning prayer. India's new beginning had not been easy.

Independent India: An Experiment in Democratic Socialism

With independence, the Indian National Congress was renamed the Congress Party, and it began to rule India. It was not an easy task. Most of India's nearly 400 million people were poor and illiterate. There were many religions, ethnic groups, and languages. In fact, fourteen major languages were spoken throughout the country. Congress leaders spoke bravely of building a new nation, but Indian society was badly divided.

The new nation did have one advantage. The Congress Party had some experience in government. The leaders of the party were self-confident and fairly united. Jawaharlal Nehru (ju-WAW-hur-LAWL NAE-roo), the new prime minister, was a popular figure who was respected and even revered by millions of Indians.

India's new leaders had strong ideas about the future of Indian society. Nehru admired Great Britain's political institutions, but he had also been influenced by the socialist ideals of the British Labour Party. Nehru's

---

RECOMMENDED READING

For a recent survey of contemporary Indian history, see S. Wolpert, *A New History of India,* rev. ed. (New York, 1989), and V. S. Naipaul, *India: A Wounded Civilization* (New York, 1977).

On the period surrounding independence, see the dramatic account by L. Collins and D. Lapierre, *Freedom at Midnight* (New York, 1975).

Social issues are examined in a number of recent studies. For an overview, see K. Bhatia, *The Ordeal of Nationhood: A Social Study of India since Independence, 1947–1970* (New York, 1971). See also J. M. Freeman, *Untouchable: An Indian Life History* (Stanford, Calif., 1979); R. G. Revankar, *The Indian Constitution: A Case Study of Backward Classes* (Rutherford, N.J., 1971); and K. Nair's classic *Blossoms in the Dust: The Human Factor in Indian development* (New York, 1961).

Answers to SECTION REVIEW

2. (a) American president who opened relations between the United States and Communist China

3. (a) He hoped that economic improvements would satisfy them.
   (b) Farmers were allowed to produce and sell agricultural products for their own profit after they had paid a tax to the government.
   (c) They thought that people who were loyal to their family would not also be loyal to their Communist leadership.
   (d) Chinese "volunteers" entered the war when U.N. forces approached the border with China at the Yalu River.
   (e) China wanted to actively spread communism while the Soviet Union hoped to build better relations with the West.

4. Answers will vary but should include the fact that more children would often reduce a family's standard of living in a city but could increase their standard in rural areas by contributing to agricultural production.

CLOSE

Lead students in a discussion of the 'Focus' objectives identified on page 1081. Emphasize the importance of changes that took place in China after the death of Mao.

FOCUS

OBJECTIVES

After completing this section, students should be able to:

1. describe the system of Democratic Socialism in India
2. identify and describe events in India after Nehru
3. describe daily life in modern India
4. identify and describe events in Pakistan since it gained independence

FOCUS ACTIVITY

Help students understand why it is difficult to create a welfare state in a developing nation. In India the value of production per person in 1980 was $240. India's budget was about $80 per person to cover the costs of all government programs. Ask students to identify ways they believe the Indian government could have best spent this limited amount.

vision of the new India combined democratic political institutions with a moderate socialist economic structure.

Under Nehru's leadership, the new Republic of India adopted a political system based on the British model. There was a figurehead president and a parliamentary form of government led by a prime minister. There were many political parties, but the Congress Party, with its enormous prestige, was dominant at both the national and the local levels. The Congress Party claimed to represent all Indians, from rich to poor, from Hindus to Muslims and other minority religious groups.

Economic policy was modeled roughly after the program of the British Labour Party (see Chapter 29). The state took over the ownership of major industries, transportation, and utilities. Private enterprise was permitted at the local levels. Farmland remained in private hands. The Indian government also sought to avoid dependence on foreign investment and technological aid. All business enterprises were required by law to be owned primarily by Indians.

Nehru was fully convinced that in order to succeed, India must industrialize. In this respect, he departed sharply from Gandhi. Gandhi had believed that material wealth was morally corrupting. Only simplicity and nonviolence, he said, could save India, and the world itself, from self-destruction. Nehru, however, had little fear of material wealth (see "You Are There: Gandhi and Nehru—Two Visions of India"). He complained that Gandhi "just wants to spin and weave," referring

Map 33.3   Modern South Asia

to Gandhi's practice of making his own cloth and garments.

Nehru actively pursued a policy of industrialization. He set up a series of five-year plans, which achieved some success. India developed a large industrial sector centered on steel, vehicles, and textiles. Industrial production almost tripled between 1950 and 1965.

Nehru also tried to bring about reforms in agriculture. In 1948, farming techniques were still primitive.

STUDYING MAPS

The following questions will help you guide students through their study of Map 33.3.

1. Why did it make little sense to have a nation made up of East and West Pakistan? *(They were 1500 miles apart.)*

2. Why are there relatively few large cities in central India? *(It is a mountainous, arid area.)*

3. Why are the states of Nepal and Bhutan important to India? *(They lie between India and China.)*

YOU ARE THERE

Gandhi and Nehru: Two Visions of India

Whereas Jawaharlal Nehru saw socialism as the answer for India's ills, Mohandas Gandhi found the answer in the traditional village. Nehru favored industrialization to achieve material wealth, whereas Gandhi praised the simple virtues of manual labor. The first excerpt is from a speech by Nehru; the second is from a letter written by Gandhi to Nehru.

Nehru's Speech to the Indian National Congress

I am convinced that the only key to the solution of the world's problems and of India's problems lies in socialism. Socialism is, however, something even more than an economic doctrine; it is a philosophy of life and as such also it appeals to me. I see no way of ending the poverty, the vast unemployment, the degradation and the subjection of the Indian people except through socialism. That involves vast and revolutionary changes in our social structure, the ending of vested interests in land and industry. That means the ending of private property, except in a restricted sense, and the replacement of the present profit system by a higher ideal of cooperative service. In short, it means a new civilization, radically different from the present capitalist order. Some glimpse we can have of this new civilization in the territories of the U.S.S.R. Much has happened there which has pained me greatly, but I look upon that great and fascinating unfolding of a new order and a new civilization as the most promising feature of our dismal age.

Gandhi's Letter to Nehru

I believe that if India, and through India the world, is to achieve real freedom, then sooner or

▲ *Mahatma Gandhi, on the right, shares a happy moment with Jawaharlal Nehru, on the left. The differences in their dress serve as a reminder of their sharply contrasting views for the future of India. Why was it particularly tragic that Gandhi was assassinated?*

later we shall have to go and live in the villages— in huts, not in palaces. Millions of people can never live in cities and palaces in comfort and peace. Nor can they do so by killing one another, that is, by resorting to violence and untruth. I have not the slightest doubt that, but for the pair, truth and non-violence, mankind will be doomed. We can have the vision of that truth and non-violence only in the simplicity of the villages. . . . The sum and substance of what I want to say is that the individual person should have control

(continued)

YOU ARE THERE

USING PRIMARY SOURCES

Assign students to write an essay that compares the ideas of Nehru and Gandhi. They should identify the position they believe is most reasonable and explain the reasons for their choice.

LEARNING FROM VISUALS

Answer to the caption question. Mahatma Gandhi was a pacifist who believed in nonviolence.

ENRICHMENT ACTIVITY

Have students read more of the materials by Gandhi and Nehru to learn about their visions of India's future. Discuss these visions as a class. Then allow students to choose the leader whose visions they most nearly share.

(Or, for students who do well with challenges, have them take the leader with whom they agree least.) Have the two groups of students hold a Gandhi vs. Nehru debate.

Answers to Critical Thinking Questions

1. Nehru felt that socialism was the answer to India's future. He believed that socialism would end India's poverty, unemployment, and the degradation and subjection of the Indian people. He saw "the ending of private property, except in a restricted sense, and the replacement of the present profit system by a higher ideal of cooperative service."

2. Gandhi believed in the village system. He felt that only when people lived in the simplicity of the village could the vision of truth and nonviolence exist.

3. Answers will vary, but should include ideas similar to the following. Gandhi believed that only without the burden of possessions could a person really be free.

4. Answers will vary.

TEACHING THEMES

Politics and History. Divide the class into three groups. Assign one group to represent the United States and to explain why India should join them in opposing communism. The second group should represent Communist powers and explain why India ought to join them in opposing capitalist powers. The third group should represent India and explain why India did not choose to join either side.

YOU ARE THERE

Gandhi and Nehru: Two Visions of India, continued

over the things that are necessary for the sustenance of life. . . . You will not understand me if you think that I am talking about the villages of today. . . . In the villages of my dreams the villager will not be dull—he will be all awareness. . . . Men and women will live in freedom, prepared to face the whole world. . . . Nobody will be allowed to be idle or to wallow in luxury. Everyone will have to do body labour.

1. What vision did Nehru have for the future of India?

2. What vision did Gandhi have for the future of India?

3. What did Gandhi mean when he said "to achieve real freedom . . . we shall have to go and live in the villages—in huts, not in palaces"? How could living in huts make people free?

4. Gandhi says "Nobody will be allowed to be idle or to wallow in luxury. Everyone will have to do body labour." How do you think this statement would be received if it were made by a politician in the United States? Explain.

India had few tractors, and fertilizer was rarely used. Most farms were small because of the Hindu tradition of dividing the land equally among all male children. Nehru realized that a more efficient farming system was needed if industrial growth were to continue.

First, the government tried to limit the size of landholdings, thereby forcing a redistribution of land to the poor. Second, it encouraged farmers to form voluntary cooperatives. Both programs, however, ran into severe opposition. Landlords simply evaded the new laws, and farmers refused to form cooperatives. As one farmer said, many feared that "everyone will leave it to the others to do the work and shirk his own responsibility."

Under Nehru's guidance, India adopted a neutral posture in the Cold War. It also sought to provide leadership to all newly independent nations in Asia, Africa, and Latin America. This neutral and independent stance quickly placed India in opposition to the United States. During the 1950s, the United States was trying to mobilize all nations against what it viewed as the menace of international communism. India tried to remain friendly with both the United States and the

Soviet Union. The country also worked to maintain good relations with the new People's Republic of China, although the two nations did have border disputes.

India did not hesitate, however, to fight for what it considered its own self-interests. Tension between India and Pakistan increased during the early 1960s, which led to war in 1965. India won a quick victory, but hostilities remained. When riots against the Pakistani government broke out in East Pakistan in 1971, India intervened on the side of East Pakistan. The latter declared its independence as the new nation of Bangladesh (see later in the chapter).

The Post-Nehru Era in India

The death of Nehru in 1964 caused widespread concern about India's future. In 1966, the leaders of the Congress Party selected Nehru's daughter, Indira Gandhi (who was not related to Mohandas Gandhi), as the new prime minister. Indira Gandhi had had lit

MORE ABOUT . . . The Green Revolution

The Green Revolution in the 1960s combined new hybrids with pesticides and better fertilizers to dramatically increase crop yield per acre. Population growth has caught up with that gain, and there are economic and ecological costs to the heavy use of pesticides and fertilizers. In 1994, a new strain of "super rice" was introduced that will provide 25% higher yields than strains used today in Asia, and which will require less water and fertilizer. Population growth remains the most serious problem facing both India and China.

tle experience in politics, but she quickly showed that she could lead her nation.

Indira Gandhi basically followed her father's policies, continuing democratic socialism and maintaining neutrality in foreign affairs. In some ways she took an even more active stance than her father. She was especially worried about poverty in the countryside and launched a major program to reduce it. The government nationalized the banks, provided loans to peasants on easy terms, built low-cost housing, and distributed land to the landless.

Indira Gandhi was especially worried by India's growing population. Even in 1948, the country was not able to support its population of nearly 400 million. In the 1950s and 1960s, the population increased at a rate of more than 2 percent per year. To curb the rate of population growth, Gandhi adopted a policy of monetary rewards and enforced sterilization. Males who had fathered too many children were sometimes forced to have vasectomies. Despite these efforts, India has made little progress in holding down its growing population, now estimated at over 900 million.

The Green Revolution of the 1970s at least made the population problem more bearable. The **Green Revolution** was the work of researchers who introduced new strains of rice and wheat that were more productive and resistant to disease, but which required more fertilizer and water. Grain production increased from about 50 million tons per year in 1950 to 100 million in 1970.

India paid a price for the Green Revolution, however. Only wealthy peasants could afford to buy the necessary fertilizer. Therefore, even more poor peasants were now driven off the land. Millions fled to the cities, where they lived in vast slums. They worked at menial jobs or even begged for a living. Almost 40 percent of Calcutta's 8.4 million people live in slum dwellings, while hundreds of thousands remain homeless and sleep in the city's streets every night. Open sewers that drain into the water system have been a major factor in making Calcutta the "cholera capital of the world."

Indira Gandhi's population policy made her unpopular. Growing corruption in her government, as well as her censorship of the press and restriction of civil lib-

▲ *Indira Gandhi tried to help India's poor by providing low-cost loans, building low-cost housing, and giving land to those who owned none. She also helped extend voting rights. In what ways did she carry on her father's legacy?*

erties (begun in 1975), also turned Indians against her. As a result, she was defeated in the general elections in 1977. It was the first time the Congress Party had failed to win a majority at the national level since independence. Three years later, however, Gandhi was back in power after the Congress Party won new national elections. She soon faced a new challenge in the rise of ethnic and religious strife.

The most dangerous situation was in the Punjab (PUHN-JAWB), a province of India that was heavily populated by Sikhs (SEEKS). The Sikhs are followers of a religion founded in the fifteenth century that is based on both Hindu and Muslim ideas. Militant Sikhs

MORE ABOUT . . . Sikhs

The center of the Sikh religion is the Punjab, which is very important to India agriculturally. Sikhs also provide a disproportionate number of professional people in India. Sikh males are distinguished by their beards and turbans (which cover their hair, which they do not cut), and they must carry a knife upon them for religious reasons (which can lead to difficulties with U.S. school authorities). They are renowned as warriors, which is why Indira Gandhi used them for her bodyguard. An attack on the Sikh's holiest shrine, the Golden Temple at Amritsar, to clear out Sikh extremists, resulted in 1,200 deaths and led to her assassination by her own bodyguard.

COMPARING TIME PERIODS

Ask students to compare the description of the "City of Joy" in Calcutta with Latin American cities described on page 1015. What similarities and differences are there among these cities? Why do poor people choose to live near cities instead of in rural areas?

CLASS DISCUSSION

Ask students to discuss whether they believe the election of Indira Gandhi to the office of prime minister in 1966 was an important sign of change in the rights of women or a result of who her father was. Do they see "tokenism" or real change in the role of women in the world?

demanded independence for their province from India. Gandhi refused and used military force against Sikh rebels hiding in Amritsar (um-RIT-sur) in their Golden Temple, one of the Sikhs' most revered shrines. More than 450 Sikhs were killed. In revenge in 1984, two Sikh members of Gandhi's personal bodyguard assassinated her in her garden.

Indira Gandhi's son Rajiv (raw-JEEV), an airline pilot with little interest in politics, was now persuaded to replace his mother as prime minister. Rajiv Gandhi was not an effective leader, however. His government was criticized for inefficiency and corruption, as well as for not caring for the poor.

Rajiv Gandhi's government, however, did move in new directions. Foreign investment was encouraged. So, too, was private enterprise. Moreover, since Rajiv Gandhi's assassination in 1991, his successors have continued to transfer state-run industries into private hands and to rely on the free market. This has led to a noticeable growth in India's new prosperous middle class, now estimated at more than 100 million, or 11 percent of the population.

In the years after the assassination of Rajiv Gandhi, the Congress Party remained the leading political party. However, its powerful hold over the Indian people was now gone. Rising new parties competed with the Congress Party for control of the national and state governments. At the same time, rising tensions between Hindus and Muslims continued to disturb India's stability.

Further problems came from economic growth. For one thing, India has experienced incredible environmental damage. Water and air pollution, as well as the leakage of chemicals, have led to illness and death for many people. Not all the environmental damage is due to industrialization, however. The river Ganges (GAN-JEEZ) is so polluted by human overuse that it is risky for Hindu believers to bathe in it. (Hindus believe the sacred water of the Ganges washes away evil.)

Moreover, not all Indians have benefited from the new prosperity. Nearly one-third of the Indian people live below the national poverty line. Millions continue to live in rural slums, such as the "City of Joy" in Calcutta. Thousands of families there live in primitive shacks and lean-tos, sharing water and toilet facilities.

Indeed, India has been described as two nations: an educated urban India of 100 million people surrounded by 800 million poverty-stricken peasants living in the countryside.

Daily Life in India

One of the major changes introduced in the newly independent India was the official elimination of caste distinctions. The constitution of 1950 guaranteed equal treatment and opportunity for all people, regardless of caste. Discrimination against the Untouchables was specifically outlawed. Of course, prejudice is hard to eliminate. Especially in the villages, the Untouchables are still denied basic human rights (see "Focus on Everyday Life: The Indian Village"). In the cities, however, material wealth rather than caste is increasingly beginning to define status. The days when upper-class Indians refused to eat in a restaurant unless they knew the caste of the cook are gone.

The position of women has also improved. In few societies was the life of women more restricted than in traditional India. Males were dominant in virtually all aspects of life. Females received no education and had no inheritance rights. They were expected to remain at home and were tied to their husbands for life.

After independence, India's leaders sought to give women equality with men. The constitution of 1950 forbade discrimination based on sex and called for equal pay for equal work. Child marriage and the payment of a dowry by the bride's family were outlawed. Women were encouraged to attend school and enter the labor market.

The lives of many Indian women have changed. Middle-class women in urban areas are much more likely to have jobs outside the home. Many hold managerial and professional positions. However, many, if not most, young Indians still accept the idea of arranged marriages. Moreover, an Indian woman is often expected to be a professional executive at work and a dutiful wife and mother at home.

In the countryside, the changes are not as noticeable. Female children are much less likely to receive an education or even to survive. According to a recent study, one-quarter of the female children born in India

MORE ABOUT . . . *Ethnic Conflict*

Ethnic conflict between Tamil separatists and the Sinhalese majority in Sri Lanka has taken over 50,000 lives, of whom Rajiv Gandhi is the most prominent. The roots of the dispute are language. Under British rule, the civil service was dominated by English speakers, many of whom were Tamils. Upon independence, a Sinhalese-only movement began, and in 1956, Sinhalese became the official language. This violence is centered in Sri Lanka, but spills over into India. Rajiv Gandhi was blown up by a suicide terrorist who strapped plastic explosives to her body, got close to him, and detonated herself. The explosion was so violent that virtually nothing was left of either the terrorist or the victim.

FOCUS ON EVERYDAY LIFE
The Indian Village

In the cities in India, the rise of a middle class has changed many of the traditional ways of life. This is not necessarily true in the villages of India. The rural poor appear to live in conditions little changed from past generations. Nearly 80 percent of the Indian people still live in traditional rural villages.

Although some progress in education has been made in India, in the countryside education has been neglected. Thousands of villages remain without schools. The graduation rate from primary school is only 37 percent, compared with more than 60 percent for all Asia.

In Indian villages, housing styles, customs, and methods of farming have changed little since they were first described by Portuguese travelers in the sixteenth century. According to recent statistics, nearly 40 percent of people in rural areas live below the poverty level. The vast majority live in mud-and-thatch dwellings without running water or electricity, without education, and often without hope. Their lives have been affected only slightly by the changes taking place in the cities or in the world beyond.

A visitor described one such village in the state of Uttar Pradesh (prah-DESH) in the upper Ganges valley:

I went inside every single cottage in the village. They are small mud huts with tiled roofs. The entrance is very low and many have no doors. Inside is a small walled-in yard, lined on one side with a little verandah, and one or at the most two rooms. In each room lives a whole family. Inside the room there is usually an earthen silo for storing grain, but no other furniture. The chula [a brick or earthen stove used for cooking] is in the verandah; straw lies scattered in the yard; in some a little

▲ *Despite some improvements and attempted reforms, almost 80 percent of India's population continues to live in primitive villages without running water, paved roads, or electricity.*

grain is drying on the floor. In the corner near the chula are piled neatly, face downward, the cooking utensils, earthen pots and a rare piece of brass.

That description was written in 1961, but could easily apply to thousands of Indian villages today.

1. What do the majority of the rural population in India live without?

2. What percentage of Indians in villages graduate from primary school?

3. Compare your home to the home described here. How are they similar? How are they different?

MORE ABOUT . . . *Disadvantages Women Face*

Added to the usual disadvantages women face in Asian societies is the burden of the dowry. The government of India banned dowries, but the law is simply ignored. There are, in addition, other Hindu ceremonies for women which add to the cost of a girl, such as naming and ear-boring, attaining puberty, marriage, setting up a new home, and first child delivery. Many poor families simply cannot afford to pay a dowry, so they abort female fetuses. An advertising campaign urges parents to "Spend 700 rupees now [for a sonogram to determine sex], save 700,000 rupees later."

Have students compare
the way in which Indira
Gandhi came to power in
India in 1966 and the rise to
power of Benazir Bhutto in
Pakistan. Did both of these
women serve in the shadow
of their fathers?

LEARNING
FROM VISUALS

Answers to the caption
question: Student answers
will vary.

ASSESS

You can choose from a
variety of assessments to
evaluate your students' mastery of the objectives for this
section as stated on page
1086. Possible assessments
include:

1. Section Review Questions
   on the next page
2. Section 33–3 Quiz in your
   Teacher Resource materials
3. Reteaching Worksheets in
   your Teacher Resource
   materials
4. Self-Study software

Answers to
SECTION REVIEW

2. (a) agricultural advancements which doubled
   food production
3. (a) prime minister after
   Gandhi's assassination in
   1947
   (b) daughter of Jawaharlal Nehru; became prime
   minister in 1966
   (c) followers of a religion
   based on Hindu and Muslim ideas
   (d) son of Indira Gandhi;
   who became prime minister after her death

die before the age of fifteen because of neglect or even
infanticide by their parents.

Pakistan since Independence

Unlike its neighbor India, Pakistan was in all respects
a new nation when it attained independence in 1947.
Pakistan, which consisted of two separate territories
over a thousand miles apart, was unique. West Pakistan
was always short of water. East Pakistan, comprising
the eastern parts of the old Indian province of Bengal,
was made up of the marshy deltas of two rivers and was
densely populated with rice farmers. People in East and
West Pakistan spoke different languages.

From its beginnings, the new state was a product of
the Muslims' wish to have their own state. However,
from the start, Pakistan's leaders made it clear that they
were not extremists. Muhammed Ali Jinnah, leader of
the Muslim League, which had been the chief force for
a separate Muslim state, had a broad vision. A united
India, he said, would have been a "terrific disaster." Jinnah also insisted that now that Pakistan was independent, it must put aside its past grievances with the new
India. Pakistan, he said, must assure freedom of religion
and equal treatment for all.

However, there were Muslim extremists who wanted
a state based solely on Islamic principles. As a result,
Muhammed Ali Jinnah's vision of a democratic society
based on equal treatment for all citizens was only partly
realized. His death in 1948 left his nation without a
strong leader. The constitution of 1956 described Pakistan as an "Islamic Republic, under the sovereignty of
Allah." Even though Pakistan was an essentially Muslim society, its first years were marked by intense internal conflicts. Most dangerous was the growing division
between East and West Pakistan.

Many people in East Pakistan felt that the government, based in West Pakistan, ignored the needs of the
eastern section of the country. In 1958, a military coup
led by General Ayub Khan overthrew the civilian government. Khan believed that Pakistan was a badly
divided nation. The only answer to the disunity, he
thought, lay in a greater emphasis on law and order and
less on democracy. His regime dissolved the constitu-

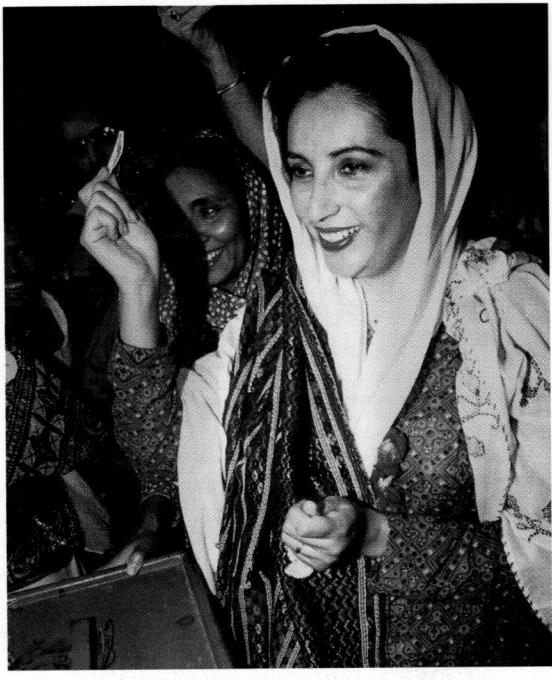

▲ Benazir Bhutto, shown here, proved to be a dynamic leader.
Why do you think both India and Pakistan have had women
prime ministers, but the United States has never had a woman
president?

tion and set up a strong central government with a
small group of 100,000 voters. His military government, however, was unable to curb the growing division between the eastern and western parts of the
country. In March 1971, negotiations between representatives of East and West Pakistan broke down. East
Pakistan now declared its independence as the new
nation of Bangladesh. After a brief struggle, the Pakistan government gave in and recognized Bangladesh.

The breakup of the union between East and West
Pakistan also led to the collapse of the military regime
in West Pakistan. A new civilian government under
Zulfikar Ali Bhutto (BOO-toe) took over, but the mil-

RECOMMENDED READING

There are a number of standard surveys of
the history of modern Southeast Asia. For an
introduction with a strong emphasis on
recent events, see D. R. SarDesai, *Southeast
Asia: Past and Present,* 2d ed. (Boulder, Colo.,
1989).

The best way to approach modern South-
east Asia is through individual country studies.
On Burma, see J. Silverstein, *Burmese Politics:
The Dilemma of National Unity* (New

Brunswick, N.J., 1980). On Thailand, see
D. Wyatt, *Thailand* (New Haven, Conn.,
1982). On the Philippines, the best overall
survey is D. J. Steinberg, *The Philippines: A Singular and a Plural Place* (Boulder, Colo., 1971).
On Malaya and Singapore, see K. von Vorys,
Democracy without Consensus (Princeton, N.J.,
1975); and C. M. Turnbull, *A History of Singapore, 1819–1975* (Kuala Lumpur, 1977).

itary was not yet ready to give up power. In 1977, a new military government under General Zia Ul Ha'q (ZEE-uh ul HAWK) seized power. It was committed to making Pakistan a truly Islamic state. Islamic law became the basis for the legal system and social behavior. Laws based on strict Muslim beliefs outlawed alcohol and governed the position of women. Also introduced was the practice of publicly whipping people with a cane, leather whip, or tree branch for breaking the law.

General Zia's death in a plane crash led to a restoration of democracy in 1988. Benazir Bhutto, educated in the United States and daughter of Zulfikar Ali Bhutto, was elected prime minister. She, too, was removed from power by the military in 1990 on charges of corruption. Reelected in 1993, she tried to crack down on opposition forces but was removed once again by the military on renewed charges of official corruption.

 SECTION REVIEW

1. **Locate:**
   (a) Bangladesh,   (b) Punjab,   (c) Ganges River

2. **Define:**
   (a) Green Revolution

3. **Identify:**
   (a) Jawaharlal Nehru,   (b) Indira Gandhi,
   (c) Sikhs,   (d) Rajiv Gandhi,   (e) Muhammed Ali Jinnah,   (f) General Ayub Khan,
   (g) Zulfikar Ali Bhutto,   (h) Benazir Bhutto

4. **Recall:**
   (a) Why was the former British colony of India divided into two new nations when it achieved its freedom?
   (b) What two programs were begun in India in 1948 that slowed the growth of agricultural production?
   (c) What position did India try to maintain in relation to Communist and non-Communist powers in the Cold War?
   (d) Why was Indira Gandhi particularly concerned with the rapid rate of population growth in India?
   (e) What price did India pay for the Green Revolution?

(f) Why did Pakistan separate into two nations?

5. **Think Critically:**
   (a) Why may the decision to require all businesses in India to be more than half owned by Indians have slowed economic growth in that nation?
   (b) Why didn't the legal elimination of the caste system in India eliminate prejudice and discrimination?

INDEPENDENCE AND NATIONALISM IN SOUTHEAST ASIA

The Japanese occupation of Southeast Asia during World War II had shown that an Asian power could defeat Europeans. Moreover, the Allied governments themselves had promised self-determination for all peoples at the end of the war. After 1945, those promises began to become a reality. The United States was the first to act when, in July 1946, it granted total independence to the Philippines.

Great Britain, too, was willing to end its colonial rule in Southeast Asia. The Labour government under Clement Attlee moved rapidly to grant independence to those colonies prepared to accept it. In 1948, Burma became independent. Malaya's turn came in 1957, after a Communist guerrilla movement had been crushed.

Other European nations—particularly France and the Netherlands—were less willing to abandon their colonial empires in Southeast Asia. Both regarded their colonies as symbols of national grandeur. The Dutch returned to the East Indies and tried to suppress a new Indonesian republic that had been set up by Sukarno, leader of the Indonesian Nationalist Party. When the Indonesian Communist Party began its own attempt to seize power, the United States pressured the Netherlands to grant independence to Sukarno and his non-Communist forces. In 1949, the Netherlands recognized the new Republic of Indonesia.

The situation was different in Vietnam. The leading force in the movement against the colonial French rule

There is a rich selection of materials on modern Indonesia. On the Sukarno era, see J. Legge, *Sukarno* (New York, 1972); and H. Johes, *Indonesia: The Possible Dream* (New York, 1971). On the Suharto era and its origins, see H. Crouch, *The Army in Indonesian Politics* (Ithaca, N.Y., 1978).

For an excellent overall history on Vietnam, see S. Karnow, *Vietnam: A History* (New York, 1983, a companion volume for the PBS series

on the war.) F. Fitzgerald's *Fire in the Lake* (New York, 1970) won a Pulitzer Prize for its discussion of the reasons for the strength of the Viet Cong. On the brutal reign of the Khmer Rouge in Cambodia, see F. Ponchaud, *Cambodia Year Zero* (New York 1977). On conditions in Vietnam since the end of the war, see R. Shaplen, *Bitter Victory* (New York, 1986), a study by a veteran journalist.

(e) leader of Pakistan who believed in making peace with India
(f) a military leader of Pakistan who overthrew the elected government
(g) leader of civilian government in West Pakistan overthrown by General Aiz Ul Ha'f in 1977
(h) daughter of Zulfikar Ali Bhutto, was elected prime minister of Pakistan

4. (a) The Hindus and Muslims who inhabited the former British colony were not able to agree to unite under a single government.
   (b) limiting the size of landholdings, encouraging formation of cooperatives
   (c) neutrality
   (d) India's population almost doubled between the 1960s and the 1990s making the job of feeding and caring for the people very difficult.
   (e) poor peasants driven off land
   (f) The two parts were divided by distance and language.

5. (a) Foreigners may have been less willing to invest in firms that they could not control.
   (b) cannot legislate people's values or feelings

CLOSE

Lead students in a discussion of the Focus objectives identified on page 1086. Emphasize the importance of differences between various ethnic and religious groups in India and Pakistan and the problem of population growth.

FOCUS

OBJECTIVES

After completing this section, students should be able to:

1. identify and describe the independent states of Southeast Asia
2. trace the course of the Vietnam War
3. describe movements in the regional integration of Southeast Asia
4. describe daily life in modern Southeast Asia

FOCUS ACTIVITY

Help students understand that economic forces often make former enemies into friends. Ask students to create a table that identified the opponents in World War II and indicates which former enemies are now friends. What role has economics played in these changes? Why does Vietnam want better relations with the United States?

▲ *Sukarno led the movement for Indonesian independence and became president of the new republic in 1950. Sukarno was a charismatic leader, but his ambitious policies led to his political downfall in 1966.*

there was the local Indochinese Communist Party led by Ho Chi Minh (HOE CHEE MIN). In August 1945, following the collapse of the Japanese occupation, an alliance of patriotic forces (the Vietminh) under Communist leadership seized power throughout most of Vietnam. Ho Chi Minh was elected president of a new provisional republic in Hanoi (ha-NOY). France, however, refused to accept the new government and seized the southern part of the country. War between France and Ho Chi Minh's forces broke out in 1946.

The Era of Independent States

Many of the leaders of the newly independent states in Southeast Asia admired Western political principles and economic practices. They, too, hoped to form democratic, capitalist states like those in the West. Only in Vietnam, where the Communist Party came to

power, did local leaders choose the Soviet Leninist model.

By the end of the 1950s, hopes for rapid economic growth had failed. Internal disputes within the new countries weakened the new democratic governments. Ethnic conflicts were especially troublesome. In Burma, for example, one-third of the population was made up of ethnic groups not related to the majority Burmese people. Some of these ethnic groups launched a rebellion against the government. In Malaysia, the majority Malays—most of whom were farmers—feared domination by the local Chinese minority, who were much more active in industry and commerce. In 1969, tensions between Malays and Chinese erupted into violent battles on the streets of Malaysian cities.

As the experiments in democracy failed, both military and one-party autocratic regimes appeared. In Burma, a modern parliamentary government gave way to a military government. In Thailand, too, a constitutional monarchy was replaced by military rule. In the Philippines, an American-style two-party presidential system survived, but the power of a strong landed elite undermined democratic practices.

The most serious threat to democracy in the region arose in Indonesia. President Sukarno dissolved the democratic political system and tried to rule on his own through what he called **Guided Democracy.** Highly suspicious of the West, Sukarno nationalized foreign-owned enterprises and sought economic aid from China and the Soviet Union. However, Sukarno faced opposition to his rule, especially from the army and from Muslims. The Muslims were especially upset by Sukarno's refusal to make Indonesia an Islamic state. Sukarno was forced into retirement after a military coup in 1966. The new military government also found it difficult to placate the Muslims.

In recent years, some Southeast Asian societies have shown signs of moving again toward more democratic forms. Malaysia, for example, is a practicing democracy. The most spectacular example, however, is the Philippines. The regime of Ferdinand Marcos was overthrown by a massive public uprising in the 1980s. After the assassination of her husband by government forces in 1983, Corazon Aquino (uh-KEE-noe) became leader of the opposition to the Marcos government. After Marcos fled the country, Aquino became presi-

MORE ABOUT . . . *the Vietminh*

In 1945, Franklin D. Roosevelt was sympathetic to the Vietminh and unsympathetic to French hopes to re-establish their Indochinese empire. However, the French understood that Europe was the U.S.'s top priority, and demanded U.S. support as the price of their cooperation in the reconstruction of a devastated Europe. You may wish to discuss with students the steps leading to U.S. involvement in Vietnam.

Map 33.4   Modern Southeast Asia

TEACH

CLASS DISCUSSION

Using Map 33.4, review with students the governments of Burma, Malaysia, Thailand, the Philippines, and Indonesia. What factors within each nation hindered the development of democracy?

Discuss possible prerequisites required for a successful establishment of democracy.

CLASS DISCUSSION

Ask students to discuss why the fall of Vietnam made the Philippine Islands less important to the United States.

dent of a government that tried to establish democratic procedures and improve conditions for the poor.

In addition to their internal problems, Southeast Asian states also became involved in conflicts with each other. Cambodia, for example, fought with both Thailand and Vietnam over mutual frontiers—disputes that have not yet been resolved. Sukarno of Indonesia unleashed a policy of confrontation against Malaysia, arguing that the Malay peoples were part of Indonesia. The people of the Malay peninsula, however, had no desire to be part of Indonesia. In the end, Indonesia dropped its claim.

The Vietnam War

The most important conflict in Southeast Asia immediately after independence was the war in Vietnam. The struggle of Ho Chi Minh's Vietminh Front against the French after World War II had begun as an anticolonial struggle. In the 1950s it became part of the Cold War. China began to provide military aid to the Vietminh to protect its own borders. The Americans supported the French.

At the Geneva Conference in 1954, France agreed to a peace settlement with Ho Chi Minh's Vietminh.

STUDYING MAPS

The following questions will help you guide students through their study of Map 33.4.

1. Why were the Philippine Islands an important military base for the United States during the Vietnam war? *(They were within easy flying distance of Vietnam.)*

2. Why did North Vietnam get much of its help from the Soviet Union instead of

China? *(The USSR was not a threat to Vietnam's independence.)*

3. Why did the domino theory appear to make geographic sense to the United States? *(Many non-Communist states were next to Vietnam, and China and North Korea had become Communist.)*

▲ *The war in Vietnam inflicted heavy civilian damages and destroyed many villages and homes. A fire is spreading quickly through this village market along the Saigon River. The boys quickly gather up their baskets in their attempts to save their meager belongings.*

Vietnam was divided into a northern Communist half based in Hanoi and a non-Communist southern half based in Saigon. Both sides agreed to hold elections in two years to create a single government. Cambodia and Laos were both declared independent states under neutral governments.

The United States, opposed to any further spread of communism, then began to provide aid to South Vietnam. Under the leadership of Ngo Dinh Diem (NYOE DIN DEE-em) and with the support of the United States, South Vietnam refused to hold the national elections called for by the Geneva Conference. It was widely expected that the Communists would win such elections. Disappointed, Ho Chi Minh in 1959 returned to a policy of revolutionary war in the south.

By 1963, South Vietnam was on the verge of collapse. Diem's autocratic methods and widespread corruption in his government had caused him to lose the support of most of the people. Revolutionary forces known as the National Liberation Front, or the **Viet Cong** (Vietnamese Communists), expanded their influence throughout much of the country. In November 1963, the American government supported a military coup that killed Diem and established a military regime. However, the new military leaders were able to do no better than Diem's regime. The situation in South Vietnam grew worse.

By early 1965, the Viet Cong, supported by military units from North Vietnam, were on the verge of seizing control of the entire country. In March, President Lyndon Johnson decided to send U.S. troops to South Vietnam to prevent a total victory for the Communists. The Communist government in North Vietnam responded by sending more of its forces into the south. By the end of the 1960s, the war had reached a stalemate. With American public opinion sharply divided on the issue, President Richard Nixon reached an agreement with North Vietnam in 1973 that allowed the United States to withdraw its forces. Within two years, Vietnam had been forcibly reunited by Communist armies from the north.

ASEAN and the Issue of Regional Integration

The reunification of Vietnam under Communist rule had an immediate impact on the region. By the end of the year, both Laos and Cambodia had Communist governments. In Cambodia, a brutal revolutionary regime under the leadership of the Khmer Rouge (ku-ME[uh]R ROOZH) (Red Khmer) dictator Pol Pot carried out the massacre of more than one million Cambodians. However, the Communist triumph in Indochina did not lead to the "falling dominoes" that many U.S. policy makers had feared.

One reason was that the political and economic situation in Indochina had gradually stabilized during the 1960s and early 1970s. In Indonesia, Sukarno was forced from office in 1966 and replaced by a military government under General Suharto. The new government restored good relations with the West and sought foreign investment to repair the country's ravaged economy. Meanwhile, other countries in the region, such as Malaysia, Thailand, and the island state of Singapore, were experiencing relative political stability and rapid economic growth.

With political stability and improving economies came mutual cooperation. A new regional organization, known as the Association of Southeast Asian Nations (ASEAN), was formed in 1967. Composed of Indonesia, Malaysia, Thailand, Singapore, and the Philippines, ASEAN worked to resist further Communist growth in the region. When Vietnam invaded Cambodia in December 1978 supported resistance troops. This action forced Vietnam to withdraw its forces.

Although some countries today, such as Myanmar (formerly Burma), the Indochinese states (Vietnam, Laos, and Cambodia), and the Philippines, continue to face serious political and economic problems, most of the members of ASEAN have entered a stage of steady economic growth. For the first time, the people of Southeast Asia are trying to control their own destinies.

Daily Life: Town and Country in Contemporary Southeast Asia

Like much of the non-Western world, most Southeast Asian countries today can still be seen as dual societies. Their modern cities are often congested and polluted. Their villages in the countryside are peaceful rural scenes of palm trees and rice paddies. In Bangkok, Manila, and Jakarta, broad boulevards lined with skyscrapers mingle with muddy lanes passing through neighborhoods packed with wooden shacks.

Millions of Southeast Asians in recent years have fled from the peaceful rice fields to the urban slums. To many Southeast Asians, villages mean boredom and poverty. Cities mean jobs that, even if they are menial, pay more than people can earn in the villages.

Perhaps the greatest changes in lifestyle have taken place within the middle class and the small financial and professional elites. Western values, tastes, and customs are common in the lives of the wealthy urban minority. Western films, novels, food, alcohol, and

CONNECTIONS
AROUND THE WORLD

Cities and Cars   Since the beginning of the Industrial Revolution in the nineteenth century, the growth of industrialization has been accompanied by the growth of cities. In both the developed and developing countries, congested and polluted cities have become a way of life. In recent years, as more people have been able to afford to buy cars, traffic jams have also become a regular feature of life.

In São Paulo, Brazil, for example, traffic jams in which nobody moves last for hours. There are 4.5 million cars in São Paulo, twice the number as in New York City, although the cities have about the same population (sixteen million people). Workers in auto factories in Brazil work around the clock to meet the demand for cars.

São Paulo's situation is also evident in other cities around the world. In Cairo, a city of fourteen million people, pollution from stalled traffic erodes the surface of the Sphinx outside the city. In Bangkok, the capital city of Thailand, it can take six hours to reach the airport. (Clever merchants sell small personal toilets for car use.) In many cities in developing nations around the world, it is reported that the use of leaded gasoline is already affecting children's mental development.

A major cause of traffic congestion is a lack of roads. As more and more poor people have fled the countryside for the city, many cities have tripled in population in just twenty years. At the same time, few new roads have been built.

such luxury goods as expensive automobiles have become common among the wealthy. Most speak English, and many have been educated abroad.

Less wealthy urban dwellers are less affected by Western values. However, their lifestyles are changing, too. Television programs (including American programs such as *Dallas*, *Kojak*, and *Baywatch*) and the spread of literacy are having an impact. The literacy rate is well above 80 percent in Singapore, Thailand,

MORE ABOUT . . . *Ngo Dinh Diem*

Diem and his wife, although Vietnamese, where French-speaking Catholics. Discuss with your students why this would be the case with the educated elite in 1950s Vietnam. Would they have been representative of the majority of Vietnam's people? Buddhist monks began protesting Diem's persecution of Buddhist monasteries by setting themselves on fire in public (self-immolation). His wife exhibited a particularly unsympathetic attitude toward these Buddhist monks. It became very clear that Diem did not have the confidence of his country's population.

Discuss with the students why U.S. leadership in the early 1960s would have sympathized with Diem.

BIOGRAPHY

THE ROLE OF INDIVIDUALS

Ask students to compare the life of Aung San Suu Kyi with that of Mohandas Gandhi. How were their beliefs and policies similar? Assign students to investigate and report on the state of democracy in Burma today.

Answers to Critical Thinking Questions

1. Aung San, leader of the movement that led to Burma's independence from British rule

2. Suu Kyi became the leader of a movement for democracy and helped organize the National League for Democracy, which threatened the military regime of General Ne Win.

3. Both led Burmese people toward freedom from oppressive rulers.

ASSESS

You can choose from a variety of assessments to evaluate your students' mastery of the objectives for this section as stated on page 1094. Possible assessments include:

1. Section Review Questions
2. Section 33–4 Quiz in your Teacher Resource materials
3. Reteaching Worksheets in your Teacher Resource materials
4. Self-Study software

BIOGRAPHY

Aung San Suu Kyi: A Study in Courage

Suu Kyi was born in 1945 to Khin Kyi and Aung San. Her father—Aung San—was leader of the movement that led to Burma's independence from British rule on January 4, 1948. In 1989, the country's name was changed to Myanmar.

Suu Kyi barely knew her father, because he was assassinated when she was three years old. Only later did she learn more about the man who was called the Father of Modern Burma. She said: "It was only when I grew older that I conceived an admiration for him as a patriot and statesman. . . . It is perhaps because of this strong bond that I came to feel such a deep sense of responsibility for the welfare of my country."

Aung San Suu Kyi was educated abroad. She first studied in India, where she was influenced by the nonviolent teachings of Mahatma Gandhi. She then studied in Great Britain. She married a British educator and settled in Britain.

In 1988, Suu Kyi returned to Burma to take care of her ailing mother. Soon, she became aware of the repressive tactics used by the military government of General Ne Win. She was appalled by the regime's brutal murder of political opponents. She said, "As my father's daughter, I felt I had a duty to get involved." Suu Kyi became leader of a movement for democracy and helped to organize the National League for Democracy.

Despite the military repression, Suu Kyi toured her country. Everywhere she went, this champion of democracy was received with great joy and respect. Fearing her growing popularity, General

◄ Aung San Suu Kyi first left Burma when she was just fifteen years old and did not return to live there until she was forty-three. One year later, the name of the country was changed to Myanmar.

Ne Win ordered her assassination, an attempt that just barely failed.

Thanks to the efforts of Suu Kyi, General Ne Win resigned in 1988. However, another military regime took power. The new regime agreed to national elections in 1990. The National League for Democracy emerged as the clear winner. Nevertheless, the military government refused to step down. Suu Kyi was arrested and confined to her house, where she remained until July 10, 1995. In 1991, she won the Nobel Peace Prize for her efforts to end military rule in Myanmar by nonviolent methods. Her courageous efforts to bring democracy to her people continue to this day.

1. Who was Aung San Suu Kyi's father, and why was he important?

2. Why did General Ne Win order the assassination of Suu Kyi?

3. How would the phrase "like father, like daughter" apply to Suu Kyi?

On Line with WORLD HISTORY   Internet Activity

You may want to have your students visit the following URL, where they will find information and additional web site resources to enhance their study of this chapter.

Vietnam: Yesterday and Today

http://www.oakton.edu/~wittman/

This is an excellent site with materials for studying and teaching, links, and other topics dealing with the war.

Due to the ever-changing nature of the World Wide Web, see the West History web site, **http://history.swpco.com** for regular updates of the URLs in this text.

LEARNING
FROM VISUALS

◄ *Modern skyscrapers loom over an historic mosque in downtown Kuala Lumpur, the capital of Malaysia. Do you think it is possible to retain a cultural heritage in face of such modern advances?*

and the Philippines. Although the Western way of life is less noticeable in Vietnam, Laos, and Cambodia, even here one can find Coca-Cola, Western sneakers, and sweatshirts for sale in the shops.

In contrast, little has changed in rural areas. Most peasants still live in traditional housing and live their lives according to the annual harvest cycle. Travel is by cart or bicycle or on foot. Telephones are rare. Through the spread of electricity, radio, and television, however, changes are coming to the countryside as well.

In general, women in Southeast Asia traditionally have enjoyed a higher status than women elsewhere in Asia. Nevertheless, they were not the equal of men in every respect. After independence, the trend toward liberating Southeast Asian women continued. Virtually all of the newly independent states granted women full legal and political rights with men, including the right to work. In some respects, that promise has been fulfilled. Women have new opportunities for education and have entered new careers previously reserved for men. Women also have become more active in politics. In the Philippines in 1986, Corazon Aquino was the first woman to be elected president of a country in Southeast Asia.

Women are not truly equal to men in any country in Southeast Asia, however. In Vietnam, where women are legally equal to men, no woman has served on the Communist Party's ruling committee. In Thailand, Malaysia, and Indonesia, women rarely hold senior positions in government or in major corporations. Similar limitations apply in Myanmar (formerly Burma), although Aung San Suu Kyi, the daughter of one of the country's heroes in its struggle for liberation, is the leading figure in the democratic opposition movement. (See "Biography: Aung San Suu Kyi: A Study in Courage.")

❀ SECTION REVIEW ❀

1. **Locate:**
   (*a*) Philippines,   (*b*) Burma,   (*c*) Malaysia,
   (*d*) Indonesia,   (*e*) Cambodia

MORE ABOUT . . . *Women in Asia*

Female infanticide is a very serious problem in Asia, especially in China and India. The population distribution in a developed country is 106 females to 100 males. In a developing nation, demographers expect ratios to be roughly equal, as in Latin America and Africa. But in Asia, the ratios are much lower: China 94.3, India 93.5, Pakistan 92.1 females per 100 males. Reasons include outright female infanticide at birth, and unequal nutrition and medical care of female infants. Selective abortion of female fetuses is also a factor. Demographers estimate there are between 60 and 100,000,000 "missing" girls in Asia. This trend will be very disruptive in future years as an acute shortage of women develops.

(g) Communist military and political movement in Cambodia, responsible for the massacre of more than one million people (h) leader of the Khmer Rouge

4. (a) hopes for rapid economic growth failed, internal disputes, ethnic conflicts
(b) Westernized residents of cities, traditional people in rural areas
(c) American publications, movies, television

5. government of South Vietnam was corrupt, the U.S. could not tell who was Viet Cong, the U.S. never used its total military strength, Americans not committed to a long and costly war

CLOSE

Lead students in a discussion of the Focus objectives identified on page 1094. Emphasize the importance of economic forces in the creation of independent nations in Southeast Asia.

LEARNING FROM VISUALS

Answer to the caption question: Emperor Hirohito is in very formal attire and is stiffly posed. General MacArthur is not wearing a dress uniform, but khakis, looks relaxed, has his hands in his pockets, and gives the impression of a working man.

2. **Define:**
(a) Guided Democracy, (b) Viet Cong

3. **Identify:**
(a) Clement Attlee, (b) Sukarno, (c) Vietminh, (d) Ferdinand Marcos, (e) Corazon Aquino, (f) Ngo Dinh Diem, (g) Khmer Rouge, (h) Pol Pot

4. **Recall:**
(a) What problems emerged in the newly free countries of Southeast Asia in the 1950s?
(b) What population groups show the dual societies that exist in Southeast Asian countries?
(c) How have Western values begun to reach into even the most rural areas of Southeast Asia?

5. **Think Critically:** What factors contributed to the United States' lack of success in defeating the Viet Cong?

JAPAN AND THE LITTLE TIGERS

In August 1945, Japan was in ruins. Its cities were destroyed, its vast Asian empire was in ashes, and its land was occupied by a foreign army. Half a century later, Japan was the second greatest industrial power in the world, democratic in form and content. How did it happen?

The Allied Occupation

For five years after the end of the war in the Pacific, Japan was governed by an Allied administration under the command of U.S. general Douglas MacArthur. The occupation regime was controlled by the United States. As commander of the occupation administration, MacArthur was responsible for destroying the Japanese war machine, trying Japanese civilian and military officials charged with war crimes, and laying the foundations of postwar Japanese society.

Under MacArthur's firm direction, Japanese society was remodeled along Western lines. A new constitution replaced the Meiji (MAE-jee) Constitution of

▲ *General Douglas MacArthur, on the left, posed for a formal photograph with Emperor Hirohito, on the right. What differences do you think are expressed by their body language and by their dress?*

1889. It was designed to change Japan into a peaceful society that would no longer be capable of waging war. The constitution renounced war as a national policy. Japan agreed to maintain armed forces at levels that were only sufficient for self-defense. The constitution also established a parliamentary system, reduced the power of the emperor (the emperor was forced to announce that he was not a god), guaranteed human rights, and gave women the right to vote.

The rise of the Cold War in the late 1940s had an impact on American foreign relations with Japan. On September 8, 1951, the United States and other nations (but not the Soviet Union) signed a peace

RECOMMENDED READING

Perhaps best known treatment of postwar Japan is J. K. Fairbank, E. O. Reischauer, and A. M. Craig, *East Asia: Tradition and Transformation* (Boston, 1976). For a more culture-oriented approach, see C. Schirokauer, *Modern China and Japan: A Brief History* (New York, 1982). For a more contemporary view, see R. Buckley, *Japan Today* (Cambridge, 1985).

C. Nakane, *Japanese Society* (Harmondsworth, 1979) provides a scholarly treatment, while R. J. Hendry, *Understanding Japanese Society* (Beckenham, 1987) is more accessible. For a more local treatment, see R. P. Dore, *Shinohata: A Portrait of a Japanese Village* (New York, 1978); and T. C. Bestor, *Neighborhood Tokyo* (Stanford, Calif., 1989).

On the four little tigers and their economic development, see E. F. Vogel, *The Four Little Dragons: The Spread of Industrialization in East Asia* (Cambridge, Mass., 1991).

Map 33.5   Modern Japan

one of the most stable and advanced democracies in the world today. It has also become the second largest economy in the world.

Japan's achievements in the area of human services are especially noteworthy. The infant mortality rate is only five per thousand, the lowest in the world. The literacy rate is almost 100 percent. Crime rates are low. On an average day, according to a recent statistic, 4,584 crimes are committed in Japan, compared with 93,474 in the United States.

Japan's rapid emergence as an economic giant has often been described as the "Japanese miracle." Whether or not this description is accurate, Japan has made a dramatic recovery from the war. To understand modern Japan fully, we must examine not just the economy but also the changes that have occurred in recent years throughout Japanese society.

Politics and Government

The concepts of universal suffrage and a balance of power among the executive, legislative, and judicial branches of government that were embodied in Japan's new constitution have held firm. Japan today is a stable and mature democratic society. However, the current Japanese political system carries over some of Japan's traditional political culture. Japan has a multiparty system with two major parties—the Liberal Democrats and the Socialists. In practice, however, there was a "government party" and a permanent opposition. The Liberal Democrats were not voted out

treaty restoring Japanese independence. On the same day, Japan and the United States signed a defensive alliance and agreed that the United States could maintain military bases on the Japanese islands.

The Japanese Miracle: The Transformation of Society in Modern Japan

As the world would soon discover, the Japanese quickly adapted to the new conditions. It has developed into

FOCUS

OBJECTIVES

After completing this section, students should be able to:

1. describe the allied occupation of Japan
2. describe the transformation of Japan since the end of World War II
3. describe changes in the role of women in Japan
4. identify and describe accomplishments of the little tigers in the Far East

FOCUS ACTIVITY

Help students to understand that it is easier to follow a new trend or technology than it is to lead one. Ask students to identify political and technological accomplishments that were first created in the United States or in Europe but which were adopted and built in the Far East to create political and economic growth.

STUDYING MAPS

The following questions will help you guide students through their study of Map 33.5.

1. Why was the Soviet Union interested in gaining control over islands in northern Japan at the end of World War II? *(They gave access to Japan and Southeast Asia.)*

2. How far is Korea from Japan at their closest point? *(about 100 miles)*
3. Why have the histories of Japan and Korea often been mixed with each other? *(They are very close geographically.)*

THE IMPORTANCE OF CULTURE

Assign students to describe their own conception of the work ethic. Do they believe American workers always do their best? Will they stay late at work if a job is not finished? Do they take the success of the firm they work for as a sign of their own success? In what ways do firms encourage their workers? Ask students to explain how social or cultural values like these have helped Japan be an economic success. Can students identify and explain any "down side" to these values? Do they believe these values are likely to last in the long run?

of office for thirty years. Decisions on key issues, such as who should become prime minister, were decided by a small group within the party. A dramatic change, however, did occur in 1993, when the Liberal Democrats were defeated on charges of government corruption. Mirohiro Hosokawa was elected prime minister and promised to clean up the political system.

The current political system also continues the centralizing tendencies of the Meiji period. The central government plays an active role in the economy. It establishes price and wage policies and subsidizes vital industries. This government role in the economy is widely accepted in Japan. Indeed, it is often cited as a key reason for the efficiency of Japanese industry and the emergence of the country as an industrial giant. Japan's economic system has been described as "state capitalism."

Some problems remain, however. Corruption in government has shaken Japanese self-confidence in recent years. Two recent prime ministers have been forced to resign over improper financial dealings with business associates. Japan is also experiencing a rise in nationalist sentiment. Especially noticeable are the growing demands for a more assertive stance toward the United States. Moreover, critics at home and abroad have charged that the textbooks used in Japanese schools do not adequately discuss the crimes committed by the Japanese government and armed forces during World War II.

The issue of Japan's behavior during World War II has been especially sensitive. A U.S. professor teaching for a year in Japan reports that many of his students said they had learned about Pearl Harbor and the massacre of Chinese civilians in World War II "from my uncle, from my grandfather, from TV, from books, from family talk," but not from their classes. Asked why such things were not taught in school, the students always say, "Because the Government, or the Education Ministry, does not want us to know."[2]

The Economy

Nowhere are the changes in postwar Japan so visible as in the economic sector. Japan has developed into a major industrial and technological power in the space of a century.

During their occupation of Japan, Allied officials had planned to break up the large conglomerations known as the *zaibatsu* (see Chapter 24). With the rise of the Cold War, however, the policy was scaled back. Only the nineteen largest companies were affected. In addition, the new policy did not keep Japanese companies from forming looser ties, which basically gave rise to another *zaibatsu* system.

The occupation administration had more success with its land-reform program. Half of the population lived on farms, and half of all farmers were tenants of large landowners. Under the reform program, lands were sold on easy credit terms to the tenants. The reform program created a strong class of independent farmers.

At the end of the Allied occupation in 1950, the Japanese gross national product was one-third that of Great Britain or France. Today, it is larger than both put together and well over half that of the United States. Japan is the greatest exporting nation in the world. Its per capita income equals or surpasses that of most advanced Western states.

What explains the Japanese success? Some analysts point to cultural factors. The Japanese are naturally group oriented and find it easy to cooperate with one another. Hardworking and frugal, they are more inclined to save than to buy. This boosts the savings rate and labor productivity. Because the Japanese value education, the labor force is highly skilled. Finally, Japan is a homogeneous society. People share common values and respond in similar ways to the challenges of the modern world.

Other analysts have cited more practical reasons for the Japanese economic success. Because its industries were destroyed in World War II, Japan was forced to build entirely new factories. Japan spends little on defense. Japanese workers spend a substantially longer period of time at their jobs than do workers in other advanced societies. Corporations reward innovation and maintain good management-labor relations. Finally, some charge that Japan uses unfair trade practices—that it dumps goods at prices below cost to break into a foreign market and restricts imports from other countries.

ENRICHMENT ACTIVITY

Ask students to role play the problems of a developing nation, using as examples China, India, Egypt, Singapore, Korea, and/or Argentina. Students should take the roles of premier, minister of economics, minister of agriculture, minister of industry, minister of labor, minister of education and culture, army chief of staff, and spokesperson for a large ethnic minority. Divide the class into groups as required and allow them to work out individual goals and strategies before gathering to prepare overall goals and a direction for their country.

Social Changes and the Role of Women

Allied planners during the occupation tried to change Japanese society. They thought they could eliminate the aggressiveness that had characterized Japanese behavior before and during the war. The new educational system removed all references to patriotism and loyalty to the emperor. At the same time, it stressed individual values. The new constitution gave women the right to get a divorce and hold a job. Women were guaranteed the right to vote and were encouraged to enter politics.

Such efforts to remake Japanese behavior through laws were only partly successful. Many of the distinctive characteristics of traditional Japanese society have persisted into the present day, although in altered form. Emphasis on the work ethic, for example, remains strong. The tradition of hard work is stressed at a young age within the educational system (see "Young People in Japan: Education and Growing Up").

The subordinate role of women in Japanese society has also not been entirely eliminated. Women are now legally protected against discrimination in employment, yet very few have reached senior levels in business, education, or politics. Japan has had no female prime ministers and few female cabinet ministers. Women now make up nearly 50 percent of the workforce, but most are in retail or service occupations. Their average salary is only about half that of males. Most women in Japan consider being a homemaker the ideal position. Only 15 percent of the women surveyed in a poll taken during the 1980s wanted a full-time job.

In the home, however, a Japanese woman has considerable responsibility. She is expected to be a "good wife and wise mother." She manages the family finances and raises the children with intense interest in their performance at school. Japanese husbands do little housework and share few leisure activities with their wives. Both in and out of the family, differences in gender roles and power remain much greater than in the West.

Haruki Murakami, whose novels have become best-sellers, is known for his contemporary style, characters, and his irreverent attitude toward traditional social conventions.

Culture

After the Japanese defeat in World War II, many of the writers who had been active before the war resurfaced. However, their writing was now more sober. This "lost generation" described its anguish and piercing despair. Several writers committed suicide. For them, defeat was made worse by fear of the Americanization of postwar Japan.

Since the 1970s, increasing wealth and a high literacy rate have led to a massive outpouring of books. In 1975, Japan already produced twice as much fiction as the United States. This trend has continued into the 1990s. Much of this new literature deals with the common concerns of all the wealthy industrialized nations. Many current Japanese authors were raised in the crowded cities of postwar Japan, where they soaked up movies, television, and rock music. These writers speak the universal language of today's world.

Haruki Murakami (MUR-uh-KAWM-ee) is one of Japan's most popular authors today. He was one of the first to discard the somber style of the earlier postwar period and to speak the contemporary language. *A Wild Sheep Chase*, published in 1982, is an excellent example of his gripping, yet humorous, writing.

The "Little Tigers"

A number of Asian nations have imitated Japan in creating successful industrial societies. Known as the "little tigers," they are South Korea, Taiwan, Singapore, and Hong Kong. Along with Japan, they have become economic powerhouses. These four states rank among the world's top seventeen trading nations.

YOUNG PEOPLE IN
JAPAN

USING PRIMARY SOURCES

Ask students to describe how they would react if the standards for American students were changed to be the same as those in Japan. Can students think of any negative results that these rules might cause for Japanese society or its economic system?

LEARNING FROM VISUALS

Ask students to compare the photograph to the left with the way students in the United States look and act when they go to school. What differences can they identify? How important are the differences?

Answer to the caption question: Answers will vary. Students will undoubtedly hold strong opinions on the topic of school uniforms and single-gender schools.

YOUNG PEOPLE IN JAPAN
Education and Growing Up

▲ *The emphasis on conformity is clearly mirrored in this photograph of middle school students who are on a field trip with their teacher. In what ways is such conformity an advantage and a disadvantage?*

Young people in Japan grow up in a much stricter environment than do children in the United States. The Japanese school year runs for 240 days, compared with 180 days in the United States. Work assignments outside class are more demanding. A Japanese student averages about five hours of homework per day. Competition for acceptance into universities is intense. Many young Japanese students take cram courses to prepare for the "examination hell" that lies ahead. The results are impressive: The literacy rate in Japanese schools is almost 100 percent. Japanese schoolchildren earn higher scores on achievement tests than do children in other advanced countries.

At the same time, this devotion to success has often been due to bullying by teachers. One Japanese writer has observed: "Many Japanese incorrectly believe that our education has been a success because there aren't as many dropouts as in

South Korea

While the world was focused on the economic miracle in Japan, another miracle of sorts was taking place in South Korea. In 1953, the Korean peninsula was exhausted from three years of bitter war. Two heavily armed countries now faced each other across the thirty-eighth parallel.

North of this line was the People's Republic of Korea (North Korea), a police state under the dictatorial rule of the Communist leader Kim Il-sung. To the south was the Republic of Korea (South Korea), under the dictatorial president Syngman Rhee. South Korea was now under American military protection, but the

U.S. troops there could not save Rhee from the anger of the South Koreans. After several years of harsh rule and government corruption, demonstrations broke out in the capital city of Seoul in the spring of 1960. Rhee was forced to retire.

A coup d'etat in 1961 put General Chung Hee Park in power in South Korea. Two years later, Park was elected president and began to strengthen the South Korean economy. The government played an active role in the process by putting in motion a series of five-year plans. Land reform provided land for ordinary peasants, and new industries were promoted.

South Korea gradually emerged as a major industrial power in East Asia. The key areas for industrial devel-

MORE ABOUT . . . *Korea's Geographic Position*

Korea's geographic position with respect to China and Japan is analogous to Poland's toward Germany and Russia. It is the gateway between the two great Asian powers. For this reason, although the U.S. had not anticipated defending Korea, our interests in Japan forced us to fight in Korea. For the same reason, the approach of the U.N., predominately U.S. troops, towards the Yalu left Mao with little choice but to intervene.

YOUNG PEOPLE IN JAPAN

Education and Growing Up, continued

the United States. But in fact Japanese schools are akin to prisons ruled by fear, where kids must constantly be looking around to make sure they're behaving exactly like everyone else."

This sense of conformity is reinforced by strict rules of behavior. Most Japanese schoolchildren, for example, wear black and white uniforms to school. The following rules were adopted by middle school systems in various parts of Japan:

1. *Boys' hair should not touch the eyebrows, the ears, or the top of the collar.*
2. *No one should have a permanent wave, or dye his or her hair. Girls should not wear ribbons or accessories in their hair. Hair dryers should not be used.*
3. *Wear your school badge at all times. It should be positioned exactly.*
4. *Going to school in the morning, wear your book bag strap on the right shoulder, in the afternoon on the way home, wear it on the left shoulder.*
5. *When you raise your hand to be called on, your arm should extend forward and up at the angle prescribed in your handbook.*
6. *After school you are to go directly home.*
7. *Before and after school, no matter where you are, you represent our school, so you should behave in ways we can all be proud of.*

Parental pride often becomes a factor in the motivation to succeed. Mothers pressure their children to work hard and succeed for the honor of the family.

1. In your own words, describe the Japanese system of education for young people.

2. Compare the Japanese system of education to the American system with which you are familiar. How are they similar? How are they different?

---

opment were chemicals, textiles, and shipbuilding. By the 1980s, South Korea was moving into automobile production. The largest Korean corporations, such as Samsung, Daewoo (DA-WOO), and Hyundai (HUN-DAY), became massive conglomerates. Taking advantage of low wages and a high rate of saving, South Korean businesses began to compete actively with Japanese businesses for export markets throughout the world.

Like many other countries in the region, South Korea was slow to develop democratic principles. Park ruled by autocratic means and suppressed any opposition. Park was assassinated in 1979, and another military government seized power in 1980. However, opposition to military rule began to develop under the leadership of Kim Dae Jung. College and high school students, as well as many people in the cities, protested government policies. Finally, new elections in 1992 brought Kim Young Sam to the presidency. He selected several women for his cabinet and promised that he would make South Korea "a freer and more mature democracy."

Taiwan: The Other China

South Korea is not the only rising industrial power besides Japan in East Asia. To the south, on the island of Taiwan, the Republic of China is joining the other industrial forces.

Answers to Critical Thinking Questions

1. Japanese students attend school 240 days a year, have an average of five hours of homework each day. Discipline is very strict and classes are very structured. Students are encouraged to conform and strict rules of behavior are enforced.

2. Answers will vary but should include some of the following ideas. The Japanese system is more disciplined than the American system. American students are not encouraged to conform, rather they are encouraged to develop their individualism. Americans do not go to school as much as the Japanese, 180 days as compared to 240 days per year. The literacy rate in Japanese schools is higher than in American schools. American students have more freedom and less competition getting into colleges.

SPECIAL NEEDS: *Visual*

Have students pick one of the countries discussed in Chapter 33: China, Taiwan, Korea, India, Pakistan, Japan, Vietnam, Malaysia, Thailand, Cambodia, Philippines or Indonesia. Using library resources such as almanacs, encyclopedias, or the Internet, have the students identify the following for the chosen country: population, form of government, literacy rate, major industries/products, and climate. The students may then report their findings to the class verbally or as a display. As a class, compare the findings presented for each country. The same statistics for the United States may also be presented, as a point of comparison/contrast.

ASSESS

You can choose from a variety of assessments to evaluate your students' mastery of the objectives for this section as stated on page 1101. Possible assessments include:

1. Section Review Questions on this and the following page
2. Section 33–5 Quiz in your Teacher Resource materials
3. Reteaching Worksheets in your Teacher Resource materials
4. Self-Study software

ALTERNATIVE ASSESSMENT

Have students imagine that they are a Japanese business person visiting the United States in 1946. Each student should make a list of things about the United States economy that this person would want to copy and use in his or her own firm in Japan.

Answers to SECTION REVIEW

2. (a) United States commander in the Pacific, occupied Japan, destroyed Japanese war machine
(b) emergence of Japan as an economic giant from the destruction it suffered in World War II
(c) elected prime minister in 1993, promised to clean up corruption in the Japanese political system
(d) conglomerations of businesses in Japan
(e) a value of many workers that they are bound by personal honor to work and produce to the best of their abilities

---

After retreating to Taiwan after their defeat by the Communists, Jiang Jieshi and his followers established a capital at Taipei (TIE-PAY). They then set out to build a strong and prosperous nation based on Chinese traditions. The government continued to call itself the Republic of China. It maintained that it was the legitimate government of the Chinese people and would eventually return in triumph to the mainland.

Protection by American military forces enabled the new regime to concentrate on economic growth without worrying about a Communist invasion. Making good use of foreign aid and the efforts of its own energetic people, the Republic of China built a modern industrialized society.

A land-reform program, which put farmland in the hands of working tenants, doubled food production. With government help, local manufacturing and commerce expanded. At first, relatively small firms engaged in exporting textiles and food products. The 1960s, however, saw a shift to heavy industry—including shipbuilding, steel, and machinery—with a growing emphasis on exports. During the 1960s and 1970s, industrial growth averaged well over 10 percent a year. By the mid-1980s, over three-quarters of the population lived in urban areas. Throughout the industrializing process, the Republic of China actively maintained Chinese tradition.

Prosperity, however, did not lead to democracy. Under Jiang Jieshi, the Nationalists ruled by emergency decree and refused to allow the formation of new political parties. After the death of Jiang in 1975, the Republic of China slowly began to evolve toward a more representative form of government. By the end of the 1980s, democratic elections and opposition parties had come into being. A national election in 1992 resulted in a bare majority for the Nationalists.

A major issue for Taiwan is whether it will become an independent state or be united with mainland China. The United States continues to provide military aid to the Taiwanese military forces and clearly supports self-determination for the people of Taiwan. The United States also believes that any final decision on Taiwan's future must be by peaceful means. Meanwhile, the People's Republic of China remains committed to eventual unification.

Singapore and Hong Kong

The smallest, but by no means the least successful, of the little tigers are Singapore and Hong Kong. Both are city-states with large populations densely packed into small territories.

Singapore, once a British colony and briefly a part of the state of Malaysia, is now an independent state. Under the leadership of Prime Minister Lee Kuan-yew (GWAWN-yoo), Singapore developed an industrial economy based on shipbuilding, oil refineries, tourism, electronics, and finance. Singapore has become the banking center of the entire region.

As in the other little tigers, in Singapore an authoritarian political system has created a stable environment for economic growth. The prime minister once stated that the Western model of democracy was not appropriate for Singapore. Its citizens, however, are beginning to demand more political freedoms. There is reason to believe that a more democratic political system will gradually emerge.

Like Singapore, Hong Kong, too, has become an industrial powerhouse with standards of living well above the levels of its neighbors. The future of Hong Kong is not so clear-cut, however. In negotiations with China, Great Britain returned control of Hong Kong to mainland China in 1997. China, in turn, promised that for fifty years, the people of Hong Kong would live under a capitalist system and be self-governing. Recent statements by Chinese leaders, however, have raised questions about the degree of freedom Hong Kong will receive under Chinese rule. The shape of Hong Kong's future remains in doubt.

 SECTION REVIEW

1. **Locate:**
   (a) Singapore

2. **Identify:**
   (a) General Douglas MacArthur,   (b) Japanese miracle,   (c) Mirohiro Hosokawa,   (d) *zaibatsu* system,   (e) work ethic,   (f) Haruki Murakami,   (g) Kim Il-sung,   (h) Syngman Rhee

---

ENRICHMENT ACTIVITY

Have students do additional research on Japan and the "little tigers" by analyzing the sources of their economic growth. Construct a chart that illustrates the various branches of the economy and the kinds of profits that companies realize. Why have these states been so successful in their economic growth?

3. Recall:

(a) What impact did the beginning of the Cold War have on United States relations with Japan?

(b) Why do many people believe the Japanese political system was not particularly democratic after the war?

(c) Why are the writers in Japan at the time of the war sometimes referred to as the "lost generation"?

(d) Why do some people believe the "little tigers" of Asia owe a debt of gratitude to Japan?

(e) How did promises of military protection from the United States help Taiwan develop its economy?

(f) What happened to Hong Kong in 1997?

4. Think Critically:

(a) One way Japan has maintained its homogeneous society is by accepting few immigrants from other countries. In what ways has this policy probably helped and harmed Japan?

(b) Both North and South Korea were governed by dictators for many years. What made the two countries develop so differently?

Conclusion

Since 1945, Asia has witnessed the growth of two world powers—Communist China and capitalist Japan. The two nations were enemies in World War II and took sharply different paths after the war. Today, both nations play significant roles in world affairs: China for political and military reasons; Japan, for economic reasons.

In 1949, the Chinese Communists took control of all of China. During the next thirty years, Mao Zedong and the Chinese government tried a number of radical programs to bring about a socialist society. They mostly failed. After Mao's death, more moderate party leaders took control and used modified capitalist techniques to encourage growth in industry and farming. These moderates met with considerable success in economic modernization but so far have refused to allow any significant political changes. By crushing the movement for democracy in 1989, China's aging leaders signaled their unwillingness to give up the Communist Party's rigid control of China.

Japan's history after 1945 is a remarkable success story. Under American occupation, Japan's economy and society were modernized. Subsequently, Japan developed a stable and mature democratic society. At the same time, it emerged as one of the world's economic giants.

Elsewhere in Asia, nations have struggled to build stable societies. The people of British India were given their independence on August 15, 1947, when two states—the largely Hindu India and the largely Muslim Pakistan—were formed. India tried to create a system of democratic socialism. However, ethnic and religious divisions, as well as overpopulation and rural poverty, continue to plague Indian society. Pakistan began with a democracy but has been ruled largely by military regimes.

After World War II, most of the states of Southeast Asia received independence from their colonial rulers. Many began with democratic regimes, but military regimes often replaced them. France's refusal to let go of Indochina led to a long war in Vietnam that ultimately involved other Southeast Asian nations in a widening spiral of conflict. After more than thirty years of violence and war, however, there are promising signs of increasing political stability. A number of states in Southeast Asia have joined the steadily growing ranks of flourishing Asian industrial societies, including Japan and the "little tigers" (South Korea, Taiwan, Singapore, and Hong Kong). Indeed, the growing economic strength of Asian nations bordering the Pacific Ocean has led many observers to speak of the next century as the Pacific Century.

Notes

1. Quoted in Larry Collins and Dominique Lapierre, *Freedom at Midnight* (New York, 1975), p. 252.
2. Bernard K. Gordon, "Japan's Universities," *Far Eastern Economic Review*, January 14, 1993.

ENRICHMENT ACTIVITY

Have students do a chart in which they list the breakthroughs made by women in the different countries in Asia. What countries treated women as equals with men? What countries did not? How do they explain the differences? Have students then do a comparison of the position of women in Asia with the position of women in the industrialized countries of Europe and North America. What do students learn from the comparison?

(f) one of the first Japanese authors to discard the somber style of the postwar period

(g) Communist dictator of North Korea

(h) American-supported dictator of South Korea

3. (a) The United States and other nations signed a treaty restoring Japanese independence and the U.S. was given the right to maintain military bases in Japan.

(b) The Liberal democrats held office for over thirty consecutive years.

(c) Many writers were upset by the loss of the war and afraid of Americanization; several committed suicide.

(d) achieved success by following the path first charted by Japan

(e) could use its resources to build its economy instead of using them for defense spending

(f) returned to China with promise of capitalist system

4. (a) helped: less likelihood of social differences and unrest; harmed: less chance for new ideas and change

(b) The economy of the North was controlled by the government, while a system of relatively free enterprise led to greater productivity in the South.

CLOSE

Lead students in a discussion of the Focus objectives identified on page 1101. Emphasize the advantage that people in Japan and other Asian nations had in being able to copy established technologies and political institutions from other parts of the world.

Answers to CHAPTER REVIEW 33

USING KEY TERMS

1. New Democracy
2. four olds
3. Guided Democracy
4. Green Revolution
5. Red Guards
6. people's communes
7. gang of four
8. four modernizations
9. Great Leap Forward
10. permanent revolution
11. Viet Cong

REVIEWING THE FACTS

1. China's peasants were opposed to the reforms and refused to farm the land efficiently.
2. contained quotations from Chairman Mao, used to justify virtually any act or excess by the Red Guard during the Cultural Revolution
3. With 1.3 trillion people, it will be very difficult for China to feed its people if it cannot control its population growth.
4. A demonstration for democracy was broken up by the Chinese military.
5. People who lived in East Pakistan broke away from dominant West Pakistan because they felt their interests were not adequately represented or respected by the government.
6. India includes many national groups who speak more than 100 different languages. It is doubtful that all these groups can agree to support a single government.
7. France
8. killed thousands of people they believed had supported their opposition
9. The United States military made unnecessary for Japan to spend money on defense and it purchased many products produced by Japan.
10. South Korea, Taiwan, Singapore, Hong Kong

1108

USING KEY TERMS

1. The program of modified capitalism used in the first years that Communists controlled China was called _____.
2. The _____ were values Communists tried to eliminate from China's society that included old ideas, culture, customs, and habits.
3. President Sukarno dissolved Indonesia's democratic political system in order to rule on his own through a policy called _____.
4. _____ refers to the development of new seeds and farming methods to increase the amount of food that can be grown.
5. The _____ were units of young Communists who tried to cleanse Chinese society of impure elements.
6. Massive collective farms created in China's Great Leap Forward were called _____.
7. The _____ were leaders of the Cultural Revolution in China who were eventually jailed for their political excesses.
8. The policy created to improve China's industry, agriculture, technology, and national defense during the 1980s was called the _____.
9. The _____ was a plan to combine small land holdings into massive collective farms in China.
10. An idea supported by Mao that a constant state of revolution could create perfect communism was called _____.
11. Vietnamese Communists were revolutionary forces also known as the National Liberation Front, or the _____.

REVIEWING THE FACTS

1. Why was the Great Leap Forward an economic disaster for China?

1108

---

2. What was the *Little Red Book* that was carried by most people in China during the Cultural Revolution?
3. Why has the government of China tried to limit each family to having only one child?
4. What happened in Tiananmen Square in 1989?
5. What events led to the creation of the nation of Bangladesh?
6. Why is it difficult to create a stable government in India?
7. What nations fought for control of Vietnam before the United States became involved in fighting there?
8. What policy did the Khmer Rouge follow toward the people they regarded as enemies after they gained control of Cambodia?
9. Why was United States military presence in the Far East helpful to the Japanese in rebuilding their nation?
10. What nations are called the little tigers?

THINKING CRITICALLY

1. How does the fact that the average Chinese citizen is less than thirty years old make it more difficult for China's leaders to maintain their people's revolutionary enthusiasm?
2. Why is it difficult to wipe out values people have held for generations in only a few years?
3. Although the people of China are not all satisfied with their government, they appear to be willing to tolerate the political situation in their nation because their standard of living has been improving. Why might they not tolerate the political situation in the long run?
4. Why will there continue to be rapid population growth in China for many years even if each family has only one child?
5. Why do some people believe the efforts to provide a minimum standard of living and health care to all people in India are doomed to failure?

THINKING CRITICALLY

1. Answers will vary but may point out that a majority of the Chinese people were not alive when the communist revolution took place.
2. Answers will vary but are likely to state that values are reflected in all parts of people's lives. It is difficult to change values without totally changing how people live.
3. Material goods and an improved standard of living are most important to people who lack them; over time people in China are likely to take these for granted and demand personal freedom as well.
4. The death rate in China has fallen so that even if many young couples only have one child each there will still be rapid population growth.
5. There are so many people being born in India that it is unlikely that any effort will provide them with an adequate standard of living.
6. The increased food production led to a lower death rate and increased population that consumes the additional food.
7. In the 1940s the communist Vietnamese were fighting the Japanese so the U.S. supported them. Later the U.S. fought the Vietnamese to try to prevent the spread of communism.
8. The Japanese economy still needs imported raw materials to keep it running.

6. Why didn't the increased ability of India to produce food as a result of the Green Revolution permanently eliminate its food shortages?
7. Why did the United States support the Vietnamese Communists in the 1940s, only to fight them in the 1960s?
8. Why do the Japanese still feel vulnerable to foreign pressures even when they have one of the richest economies in the world?
9. Why have many wealthy people left Hong Kong in recent years?

APPLYING SOCIAL STUDIES SKILLS

1. **Ecology:** During the Great Leap Forward the leaders of China instituted a program in the countryside that had the slogan, "get the birds." Birds seemed to be eating lots of grain in the fields so they thought that killing the birds would increase harvests. Write an essay that describes the ultimate result of this program in terms of China's environment and harvests.
2. **Geography:** Explain why India's geographic location almost forced it to remain neutral in international politics.
3. **Economics:** Recently Vietnam has aggressively sought political recognition by the United States. Identify and explain reasons why this former enemy may be so interested in establishing diplomatic relations with the United States.
4. **Geography:** Consider the location of the Philippine Islands. Explain why the United States absolutely insisted on maintaining its right to use military bases on these islands until the late 1980s.

MAKING TIME AND PLACE CONNECTIONS

1. Compare the decline of the Ottoman Empire with the fall of the Nationalist Chinese government.

How was the new government that came to power in China different from the political systems that emerged from the Ottoman Empire?
2. In 1959 differences between China and the Soviet Union became apparent to the world. Three years later France withdrew from NATO. Identify and explain ways in which these events were similar and how they were different.
3. Explain why it is unlikely that there will ever be a two-party system in India as there is in the United States.
4. Compare and contrast social, economic, and political problems facing Vietnam after it was united under Communist rule in 1975 with those of former colonies of European nations that have gained their independence in Africa.
5. Explain why Japan didn't need to create an extensive welfare state after World War II similar to those established in many western European countries at that time.

BECOMING AN HISTORIAN

1. **Conducting Research:** Investigate the status of individual rights in Singapore. Compare these with the rights guaranteed to American citizens by the Bill of Rights. Identify and explain possible reasons why the people of Singapore are willing to be regimented by their government. What would probably happen if the government of the United States attempted to impose similar requirements on U.S. citizens?
2. **Map Interpretation:** Consider Map 33.4 on page 1095. Identify and explain reasons why this region is vital to world trade and why the physical geography of the area makes it difficult for foreign nations to dominate these island and peninsular nations.

1109

1109

PLANNING GUIDE

SECTION	KEY TOPICS	PRIMARY SOURCES	ASSESSMENT
1 The Challenges of Our World pages 1111–1116	◆ The environmental crisis ◆ The technological revolution ◆ Economic and social challenges of our world ◆ Political challenges and possibilities	◆ A selection from Dimitila Barrios de Chungara page 1115	◆ Section Review page 1116 ◆ Section Quiz 34–1, TRB
2 The Emergence of New Global Visions pages 1117–1119	◆ The United Nations ◆ New global visions		◆ Section Review page 1119 ◆ Section Quiz 34–2, TRB

EPILOGUE:
TOWARD A GLOBAL CIVILIZATION—CHALLENGES AND HOPES

REPRODUCIBLE ACTIVITIES

Historical Maps

Charts and Graphs

Critical Thinking

Cooperative Learning

Vocabulary

Guided Reading

Reteaching

Enrichment

Performance Assessment

Spanish Key Points and Chapter Summaries

Spanish Vocabulary

Spanish Guided Reading

MULTIMEDIA SUPPORT

 TRANSPARENCIES
◆ *World History* Color Transparency Package
◆ Fine Art Color Transparency Package

 VIDEO
◆ *World History* Video Library
◆ **CNN**® Annual Video Update

 LASERDISC
◆ *Sights and Sounds of History*

 AUDIO
◆ *Listening to Literature* audiotape (English and Spanish)
◆ *History of Music* CD

 SOFTWARE
◆ WESTEST™
◆ Student Review

 CD–ROM
◆ *The Journey of Civilization*
◆ *World History*

 INTERNET
◆ Internet Activities

 On Line with
WORLD HISTORY

Access West's history web site at
http://history.swpco.com
You'll find activities and web sites related to specific topics and chapters in *World History: The Human Odyssey*. Also look for references to helpful web sites at appropriate places throughout this teacher edition.

LESSON PLANNING

You will find detailed daily lesson plans for both traditional class scheduling and **block scheduling** in your Teacher Resource Box.

 ## Not Enough Time?

If you do not have the three or four days recommended to teach this chapter, you may want to focus on the following sections and activities:

◆ Have students skim the chapter to answer the "Questions to Guide Your Reading" on page 1111. Discuss their answers and ask them to explain how most problems we face are interrelated.
◆ Do a more in-depth reading of the environmental crisis on pages 1111–1112, economic and social challenges on pages 1114–1115, and the role of the United Nations on pages 1117–1118. Conclude with a discussion of possible global visions of the future.

1109b

EPILOGUE: TOWARD A GLOBAL CIVILIZATION—

34

BUILDING ON CHAPTER 33

To "set the scene" for the study of Chapter 34, use the following questions and activities.

- ◆ Discuss how economic developments in the Far East and in other parts of the world represent an environmental challenge to our future.
- ◆ What do events in the Far East suggest about the importance of technological revolutions?
- ◆ How are gaps between the rich and the poor in the Far East indicative of global problems of inequality?
- ◆ Is there a difference between the Pacific and global visions of the future?

USING THE OPENING STORY

Depending on the ability levels of your students, select from the following questions and activities to reinforce the reading of the opening story.

- ◆ What dangers are associated with the development and use of new technologies in addition to those related to possible nuclear accidents?
- ◆ What ethical issues may result from advancements in medicine?
- ◆ What weapons of mass destruction threaten the world besides nuclear weapons?
- ◆ Will humankind's desire to delve deeper into scientific knowledge lead to new problems in the future?

On Friday, April 25, 1986, plant managers at the nuclear power plant at Chernobyl (chur-NOE-bul) in Ukraine, ordered a series of tests to determine the capability of Reactor Four. A series of bad decisions quickly led to disaster. At 1:24 the next morning, a massive explosion rocked the site. Clouds of radioactive material raced into the sky and quickly began to spread over the Soviet Union and across Europe. In Sweden, scientists detected radiation levels that were 20 percent above normal. In Reactor Four, a radioactive fire burned out of control. Workers in the immediate vicinity of the explosion died quickly and painfully from the intense radiation.

For thirty-six hours, nothing was done to warn people nearby of the danger. Finally, more than 300,000 people were ordered to leave the area while firefighters dumped tons of concrete on the radioactive inferno. Deadly radiation, however, had immediate effects. More than three hundred people died within a short time in hospitals in the nearby city of Kiev. Many of the workers who fought the blaze, including the pilots of the planes that dropped load after load of concrete onto the fire, died within a year. It is estimated that thousands of people in all will experience physical problems from the disaster. Birth defects are common among people and animals

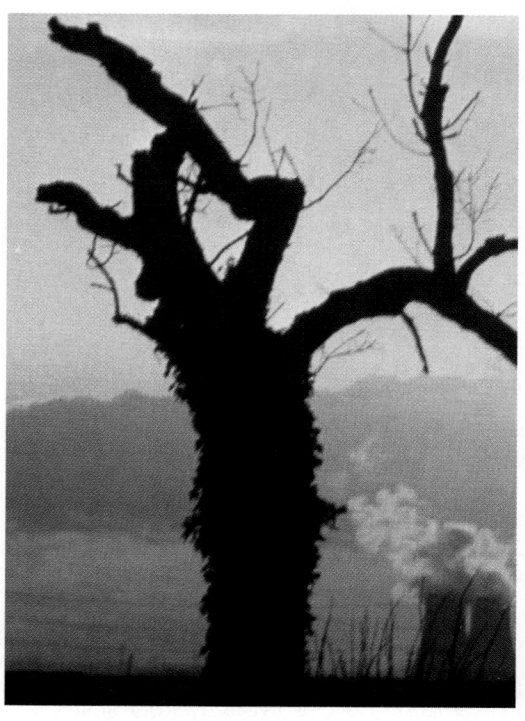

who lived in the surrounding area. Even in other European countries, meat products were found to be contaminated with radiation.

On the eve of the twenty-first century, human beings are coming to understand that destructive forces unleashed in one part of the world soon affect the entire world. Increasingly, more and more people are becoming aware of the political and economic interdependence of the world's nations, as well as of the global nature of our current problems. The spread of nuclear weapons makes nuclear war an ever-present possibility. Nuclear war would mean radioactive fallout and widespread destruction for the entire planet. Pollution from factories in one nation can produce acid rain in another. Oil spills and dumping of wastes in the ocean have an impact on the shores of many nations. The consumption of drugs in the world's wealthy nations affects the stability of both developed and developing nations. As food, water, energy, and natural resources crises increase, solutions by one nation often affect other nations.

◄ *This stunted tree has been killed by acid rain, a combination of sulfuric and nitric acids mixed with moisture in the air. Entire forests of trees killed by acid rain are becoming common sights in Canada, the United States, and Northern Europe.*

ADDITIONAL RESOURCES

The resources listed below can be used to enrich the lessons in this Chapter.

VHS/FILM

"Bosnia: Children of War" (Ted Koppel/Nightline) (MPI Home Video), Social Studies School Service, (800) 421-4246)

"Europe on the Brink" (CNN Special Report), Social Studies School Service, (800) 421-4246)

"Tragedy and Triumph (World Food)" (Journal)

CHALLENGES AND HOPES

THE CHALLENGES OF OUR WORLD

The challenges that seem to threaten human existence itself at the end of the twentieth century and the beginning of the twenty-first century are global challenges. As a Soviet physicist and an American engineer jointly concluded in 1988, "The emergence of global problems and the recognition of their importance is perhaps the greatest accomplishment of contemporary thought."

The Crisis of the Environment

In 1962, the American scientist Rachel Carson published a book entitled *Silent Spring*. Carson argued that the use of pesticides, or chemicals sprayed on crops to kill insects, was having deadly, unforeseen results. Not only insects, but also birds, fish, and other wild animals were being killed by the buildup of these pesticides in the environment. Moreover, the pesticide residue on food, Carson maintained, was harmful to human beings as well. Carson's warnings alarmed many scientists and gave rise to a new field of science called **ecology,** the study of the relationship between living things and their environments. Many people became more aware of the dangers to the environment on which they depended for their survival.

The dangers to the environment had many different sources. A rapid increase in world population led to

1111

QUESTIONS TO GUIDE YOUR READING

1. What environmental challenges does the world now face?

2. What are the promises and perils of the Technological Revolution?

3. What economic, social, and political challenges does the world now face?

4. What new global visions have arisen since World War II to deal with the world's problems?

Answers to QUESTIONS TO GUIDE YOUR READING

1. increased population, deforestation, greenhouse effects, ecological disasters (Chernobyl, Exxon Valdez), pages 1111–1112
2. promises: movement of people worldwide, global communications, space exploration, new medicines, genetic engineering, Green Revolution; perils: super germs, overuse of pesticides, nuclear weapons, pages 1113–1114

3. gap between rich and poor nations, gender gap, establishing national identities in new African and Asian countries, fragility of democracy, problems caused by disintegration of Soviet Union, pages 1115–1116
4. United Nations; non-governmental organizations to deal with everything from environmental to religious issues; "think global, act local," pages 1118–1119

FOCUS ON THEMES

Listed below are brief summaries of how the content in this chapter supports the text's key themes.

Politics and History In recent years there have been many signs of emerging democratic traditions especially in Africa, Asia, Latin America, and in the former satellite states of the Soviet Union.

The Role of Ideas Grassroots social movements in areas of the environment, women's rights, and nonviolence are becoming an increasingly important force in global justice and unity.

Economics and History As economic policy and trends become increasingly multinational, there is an increasing disparity between rich and poor nations. Developing nations are finding it difficult to raise capital to establish a competitive industrial base.

Social Life Distinct lifestyle differences exist between residents of developing nations and those living in developed nations.

The Importance of Cultural Developments The spread of Western culture and ideas throughout the world has undermined many traditional customs and religious beliefs.

The Impact of Science and Technology Advances in technology have advanced medicine, space exploration, and changed the way people communicate and learn. These technological advances, however, have created new concerns and global problems.

FOCUS

OBJECTIVES

After completing this section, students should be able to

1. describe factors in the environmental crisis faced by all nations of the world
2. identify and explain costs and benefits of the technological revolution
3. identify and describe new social challenges
4. identify and describe new political challenges

FOCUS ACTIVITY

Help students understand that most important challenges faced by the world are interrelated. Have students describe relationships among the following issues.

◆ dangers of nuclear power and the greenhouse effect
◆ advancements in computer technology and people's right to privacy
◆ our desire for personal freedom and the need to fight terrorism
◆ our desire to keep people alive and healthy and the need to bring medical costs under control

TEACH

ACTIVITY

Have students investigate the ecological impact of the Soviet Union in Eastern Europe. The emphasis should be on the connections among politics, industrialization, and ecology. Students should search news magazines or the Internet.

new fears that Earth's resources simply could not keep up with the number of human beings. By the early 1990s, there were more than five billion people on Earth. An estimated 1.3 billion are so poor that their basic needs for food and water cannot be met. Many people in less developed nations flee the countryside and move to cities in search of jobs. In 1950, the city of Cairo, Egypt, had one million people; today, it has more than thirteen million. Cities such as Cairo simply cannot keep up with basic needs such as food, water, and garbage disposal.

Deforestation is also a by-product of the growing population. Large forests and jungles have been cut down to provide new farmland and firewood for the growing number of people on Earth. The cutting of the tropical rain forest in the Amazon region of South America has raised fears of drastic worldwide changes in climate. An alarming number of species of plants and animals have become extinct or barely survive because of deforestation.

Another danger to the environment stems from chemical wastes. Many scientists warn that the release of chlorofluorocarbons (gases used in aerosol cans, refrigerators, and automobile air conditioners) are destroying the **ozone layer,** a thin layer of gas in the upper atmosphere that shields Earth from the sun's ultraviolet rays. Other scientists fear the **greenhouse effect,** or Earth's warming because of the buildup of carbon dioxide in the atmosphere. If this warming were sufficient, sea levels could rise and cause flooding of coastal areas. The amount of desert land could increase, which would make it even more difficult to grow enough food for the world's people. Some scientists have wondered whether recent extreme weather patterns, including the heat wave that claimed almost five hundred lives in Chicago in the summer of 1995, are the result of the greenhouse effect. Finally, **acid**

◄ *This view of the Earth shows the Mediterranean Sea, Africa, and Antarctica. Seen from space, Earth is an incredibly beautiful planet; however, recent satellite views show the man-made problems that Earth is facing.*

rain, the rainfall that results when sulfur spewed out by industrial factories mixes with moisture in the air, has been held responsible for killing large forested areas in North America and Europe.

Major ecological disasters also have occurred during the last twenty years. As we have seen, a 1986 explosion at a nuclear power plant at Chernobyl, in Ukraine, spread enormous quantities of radioactive gases over large areas of Europe. In 1984, a chemical plant at Bhopal, India, released toxic fumes into the air, killing 2,000 people and injuring another 150,000. In 1989, the oil tanker *Exxon Valdez* (val-DEEZ), ran aground in Alaska. Thousands of birds were killed, fishing grounds were polluted, and the local environment was devastated.

These ecological disasters made people more aware of the need to deal with environmental problems. In 1987, forty-six nations met in Montreal and agreed to protect Earth's ozone layer by reducing the use of chlorofluorocarbons. In 1992, an Earth Summit in Rio de Janeiro examined the challenges to the environment and proposed new solutions. Individual nations have reacted to environmental problems with the enactment of recycling programs, the curbing of dumping toxic materials, and salt and water conservation measures. Whether these global and national efforts will be sufficient to save the environment and keep Earth habitable will no doubt be one of the major questions of the early twenty-first century.

WORLD HISTORY UPDATES

You can update your coverage of World History topics, as well as spark lively classroom discussion and deeper understanding, by using the **CNN World History Updates.**

For assistance in using and incorporating the **CNN World History Updates** into your classroom presentations, see the *Classroom Guide.*

The Technological Revolution: Promises and Perils

Since World War II, a stunning array of technological changes have transformed the world in which we live. Although the lives of people in highly industrialized societies have been most affected by these developments, developing nations, too, continue to feel their impact. Especially spectacular changes have occurred in transportation, communication, space, medicine, and agriculture.

Since the 1970s, jumbo jet airliners have moved millions of people around the world each year. In 1945, a flight from London to New York took at least fifteen hours. Now a jet airplane takes between five and six hours to fly the route. The development of the Concorde has reduced the time even more—to three hours—but it has also raised issues about damage to the atmosphere.

Global communication systems are transforming the world community. The use of satellites, cable television, facsimile (fax) machines, cellular telephones, and computers (including the Internet and E-mail) make it possible for people to communicate with other people anywhere in the world in minutes. Events happening in one part of the globe are seen a few hours later on news reports in other parts of the world.

Ever since Neil Armstrong and Buzz Aldrin landed on the moon in 1969, the exploration of space has continued. Space stations and **space shuttles,** or reusable spacecraft that return to Earth under their own power, are first steps in developing space-based manufacturing. Space probes have increased our understanding of distant planets. Satellites in orbit provide information about weather on Earth. Other satellites transmit signals for radio, television, and telephone communications.

New medicines enable doctors to treat both physical and mental illnesses. New technologies that include the use of computer-aided imaging have enabled doctors to provide better health care and to perform "miracle" operations. Mechanical valves for the heart, as well as new organ transplants, such as heart and kidney transplants, have allowed people to live longer and more productive lives. **Genetic engineering** is a new scientific field that alters the genetic information of

▲ *Takeoffs and landings of the U.S. space shuttles have become common events, making us forget how fantastic these flights really are. Here, the space shuttle* Columbia *lifts off from the Kennedy Space Center in Florida. What do you think the future holds for the U.S. space program?*

cells to produce new variations—from cells as simple as yeast cells to those as complex as mammal cells.

Technological changes have raised new questions and concerns and have had some unexpected results. For example, some scientists have questioned whether genetic engineering might accidentally create new strains of deadly bacteria that cannot be controlled outside the laboratory. The overuse of antibiotics has created "supergerms" that no longer respond to treatment with the available antibiotics. New diseases, such

MORE ABOUT . . . *Exploration of Space*

Among the products developed as a result of the space race are super glue, velcro, and a new form of glass (which is currently not commercially available, since all of it is purchased by the U.S. government for use in spy satellites). You might wish to have students conduct outside research to compile a more extensive list of commercial contributions derived from the space program.

as AIDS—a disease that destroys the body's immune system and leaves it unable to fight disease—have spread rapidly and have not yet been controlled.

In agriculture, the Green Revolution has promised immense returns. The Green Revolution refers to the development by scientists of new strains of rice, corn, and other grains that have greater yields. It was touted as the technological solution to feeding the world's ever-growing population. However, immense quantities of chemical fertilizers are needed to grow the new strains, which many farmers cannot afford. The new crops have also been subject to insect infestation. Thus, they require the use of pesticides and create additional environmental problems. Then, too, it has been the larger agricultural producers, rather than poor peasants, who often have been the chief beneficiaries of the Green Revolution. These producers often use the new seeds and fertilizers to grow sunflower seeds, cotton, and peanuts for export rather than foods to help feed poor peasants in their own countries.

The Technological Revolution has also led to the development of more advanced methods of destruction. Most frightening have been nuclear weapons. The end of the Cold War in the late 1980s reduced the chances of a major nuclear war. However, nuclear weapons continue to spread, making a regional nuclear war even more likely. At the present time, twelve nations have nuclear weapons, and another fifteen are close to making their own. Another concern is whether any nuclear materials—bombs or radioactive matter—can end up in terrorist hands.

The Economic and Social Challenges of Our World

Since World War II, the nations of the world have developed a **global economy,** or an economy in which the production, distribution, and sale of goods are done on a worldwide scale. About 20 percent of the food and goods produced in the United States, for example, are sold abroad. Almost 40 percent of the profits of American businesses come from the sale of goods abroad or from investments in foreign nations.

The Gap between Rich and Poor Nations

One of the most noticeable features of the global or world economy is the wide gap between rich and poor nations. The rich nations are the **developed nations.** They are mainly in the Northern Hemisphere and include countries such as the United States, Canada, Germany, and Japan. Developed nations have well-organized industrial and agricultural systems, make use of advanced technologies, and have strong educational systems. The poor nations are **developing nations,** which are located mainly in the Southern Hemisphere and include many nations in Africa, Asia, and Latin America. Developing nations are primarily farming nations with little technology or education. In developing nations, students on average attend school for only three years. For many young people, the school experience may last only a few months.

One goal of developing nations is to establish industrial economies. These nations have not found this goal easy to reach, however. Rapidly growing populations place enormous burdens on the economies of developing nations and make it difficult or even impossible to create a new industrial order. The populations of developing nations such as Kenya, for example, double every eighteen years. Overused soil, lack of water, and diseases add to the economic problems.

Another problem in the developing nations is raising capital, or money, to industrialize. Many developing nations rely on the sale of raw materials to raise money. They often find, however, that developed nations pay low prices for raw materials while charging high prices for their own manufactured goods. Many developing nations have tried to raise capital by borrowing, either from the World Bank and the International Monetary Fund (financial organizations whose goal is to provide funds for international trade) or from private banks. These loans, often at high interest rates, can lead to incredible burdens of debt for developing nations. For example, in the 1980s, Brazil owed almost $110 billion to foreign lenders. These massive debts have often made economic development impossible and have even led to declining living standards.

Some developing countries, however, have had remarkable success in creating industrial economies and in joining the ranks of the developed nations. Some nations along the Asian Pacific Rim—including South Korea, Taiwan, Hong Kong, and Singapore, for example—have created prosperous export industries and built nations with high standards of living. Some observers have even spoken of the twenty-first century as the Pacific Century, proving that industrial capitalism is by no means a monopoly of the West.

It should also be kept in mind that the global economy today is highly dependent upon the continued economic prosperity of the industrialized countries. A global economic downturn could put a serious dent in the pace of economic development in many parts of the world. That, in turn, could lead to serious political instability and a crisis in the global economy.

No matter how the current economic situation evolves, it has clearly taken on a truly global character. In fact, today we live not only in a world economy but also in a world society. An economic downturn in the United States can create stagnant conditions in Europe and Asia. A revolution in Iran can cause a rise in the price of oil in the United States. The collapse of an empire in Russia can send shock waves as far as Hanoi and Havana. We live in an interdependent world.

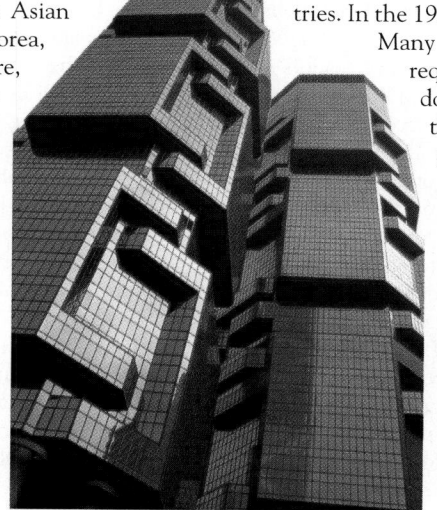

▲ *These two futuristic skyscrapers in Hong Kong city stand as proof that this modern metropolis is ready for the coming millennium. What products used by you and your family indicate that the industrial strength of Hong Kong and the other Pacific Rim nations is increasing?*

half of the university graduates in Western countries. In the 1950s, they made up only 20 percent. Many countries have passed laws that require equal pay for women and men doing the same work, as well as laws that prohibit promotions based on gender. Nevertheless, in most Western countries, women still have not been elected to the top political offices nor do they hold the top positions in business and industry.

Women continue to face considerable difficulties in developing nations. Women usually remain bound to their homes and families and subordinate to their fathers and husbands. Women in poor nations often are unable to obtain education, property rights, or decent jobs. The difficult conditions women face were described well by Dimitila Barrios de Chungara, a miner's wife from Bolivia, in an interview in 1981: "But women like us, housewives, who get organized to better our people, well, they beat us up and persecute us. . . . [People do not know] what it's like to get up at four in the morning and go to bed at eleven or twelve at night, just to be able to get all the housework done, because of the lousy conditions we live in." De Chungara's words remind us of the global problems of poverty and the struggles for equality that go on throughout the world.

The Gender Gap

The gap between rich and poor nations is also reflected in the gap between men and women. In the social and economic spheres of the Western world, the gap that once stood between men and women has been steadily declining. The number of women in the workforce continues to increase. In the 1990s, women make up

Political Challenges and Possibilities

The leaders of African and Asian countries after World War II were concerned with creating a new political culture that met the needs of their citizens. For the most part, they accepted the concept of democracy as the defining theme of that culture. Within a decade,

---

MORE ABOUT . . . *Raising Capital and National Debt*

For many developing nations, obtaining capital for economic growth raises issues of national sovereignty. If the capital comes from a developed nation, that nation or the corporations in that nation may obtain an enormous influence over the economy and the politics of that nation. United Fruit in Guatemala in 1954 and ITT in Chile in the 1970s were both involved in the overthrow of elected governments because the govern-

ments threatened their economic privileges. What is economically necessary may be politically unpopular, putting the governments of developing nations into a quandary.

The oil crisis of the 1970s contributed massively to the indebtedness of developing nations. Industrialized nations of the West were hard hit, and poor nations of the world were devastated, since oil had to be imported.

Answers to
SECTION REVIEW

1. (a) relationship between living things and their environment
(b) destruction of large forests and jungles
(c) thin layer of gas in the upper atmosphere that shields Earth from the sun's ultraviolet rays
(d) gradual warming of the Earth
(e) acidic rain caused by sulphur spewed into the atmosphere
(f) reusable spacecraft
(g) altering cells to produce new life forms
(h) interdependency of worldwide businesses and economies
(i) countries with strong industrial and agricultural systems
(j) countries that rely mostly on farming, limited technology and education

2. (a) author of *Silent Spring*
(b) a town in India, release of toxic fumes killed 2,000 people
(c) oil tanker, ran aground in Alaska
(d) provide funds for international trade

3. (a) lack of resources to satisfy needs
(b) to reduce the use of chlorofluorocarbons
(c) examined challenges to the environment, proposed new solutions
(d) Many are too poor to afford new seeds and fertilizers.
(e) to buy their products

1116

however, democratic systems throughout the developing nations of Africa, Asia, and Latin America were replaced by military dictatorships or one-party governments. It was clear that many of these leaders had underestimated the difficulties of building democratic political institutions in developing societies.

Establishing a common national identity has in some ways been the most difficult of all the challenges facing the new nations of Asia and Africa. Many of these new states were composed of a wide variety of ethnic, religious, and linguistic groups that found it difficult to agree on common symbols of nationalism. Establishing an official language and determining territorial boundaries after the colonial era were difficult in many countries. In some cases, these problems were made worse by political and economic changes. The introduction of the concept of democracy sharpened the desire for a separate identity for individual groups within larger nations. Furthermore, economic development often favored some people or groups at the expense of others.

The introduction of Western ideas and customs has also had a destabilizing effect in many areas. Such ideas often are welcomed by some groups and resisted by others. When Western influence undermines traditional customs and religious beliefs, it sparks tension and even conflict within individual societies. To some people, Western customs and values represent the wave of the future and are to be welcomed as a sign of progress. Others see the Western influences as being destructive of native traditions and as a barrier to the growth of a genuine national identity based on history and culture.

In recent years, there have been signs of a revival of interest in the democratic model in various parts of Asia, Africa, and Latin America. The best examples have been the free elections in South Korea, Taiwan, and the Philippines. Similar developments have taken place in a number of African countries and throughout Latin America. It is clear that in many areas, democratic institutions are fragile. Many political leaders in Asia and Africa are convinced that such democratic practices as free elections and freedom of the press can destroy other national objectives. A good example is China, where official tolerance of free means of expression led ultimately to the demonstrations in Tianan-men Square and the bloody crackdown that brought them to an end. Many people still do not believe that democracy and economic development necessarily go hand in hand.

The collapse of the Soviet Union and its satellite states in Eastern Europe between 1989 and 1991 brought new hopes for democracy and for international cooperation on global issues. In fact, the collapse of the Soviet empire has had almost the opposite effect. The disintegration of the Soviet Union has led to the emergence of several new, squabbling nations and a general atmosphere of conflict and tension throughout much of Eastern Europe. Nationalist sentiment among various ethnic and religious groups is rising not only in Eastern Europe but worldwide, and this sentiment is growing in importance. This nationalism can be seen as a natural result of the rising thirst for group identity in a vast and rapidly changing world.

 SECTION REVIEW

1. Define:
(a) ecology, (b) deforestation, (c) ozone layer, (d) greenhouse effect, (e) acid rain, (f) space shuttles, (g) genetic engineering, (h) global economy, (i) developed nations, (j) developing nations

2. Identify:
(a) Rachel Carson, (b) Bhopal, (c) *Exxon Valdez*, (d) World Bank and the International Monetary Fund

3. Recall:
(a) What fear has the rapid increase in the world's population created?
(b) What international agreement was reached in Montreal in 1987?
(c) What did the Earth Summit in Rio de Janeiro accomplish in 1992?
(d) Why hasn't the Green Revolution benefited all people?
(e) Why do developing nations rely on the success of developed nations?

MORE ABOUT . . . *One-Party Governments*

One of the chief attractions of military dictatorships or one-party governments for developing nations is the promise of a rational or scientific use of limited resources in the drive to modernize. This is especially important since modernization often requires a massive re-education of the population as a whole. Lenin was therefore very attractive to many Third World countries. The difficulty is that the world is too complex for central management, and human beings are not entirely rational.

(*f*) What has happened to the difference between opportunities available to men and women in the developed Western world relative to the gap in developing nations?

(*g*) What problem appears to be the most difficult challenge facing new nations of Asia and Africa?

(*h*) What new threats to world peace have emerged from the fall of the former Soviet Union?

4. Think Critically:

(*a*) Why is it unlikely that any country will be able to keep and use technological advances just for itself?

(*b*) Why will advances in genetic engineering force people to make new ethical and moral decisions in the future?

THE EMERGENCE OF NEW GLOBAL VISIONS

As people have become aware that the problems humans face are global—not national—they have responded to this challenge in different ways. The United Nations has been one of the most visible symbols of the new globalism of the last half of the twentieth century.

The United Nations

The United Nations was founded in 1945 in San Francisco, when representatives of the Allied forces worked out a plan for a new organization. U.S. President Franklin Delano Roosevelt had been especially eager to create a new international organization to help maintain the peace after the war. At the Yalta Conference in February 1945, Joseph Stalin of the Soviet Union had agreed to join the new organization. In the original charter, the members pledged "to save succeeding generations from the scourge of war, which twice in our lifetime had brought untold sorrow to mankind, and to reaffirm faith in fundamental human rights, in the dignity and worth of the human person, in the equal rights of men and women and of nations large and small, and to promote social progress and better standards of life in larger freedom." The United Nations, then, has two chief goals: peace and human dignity.

The General Assembly of the United Nations is composed of representatives of all member nations. It

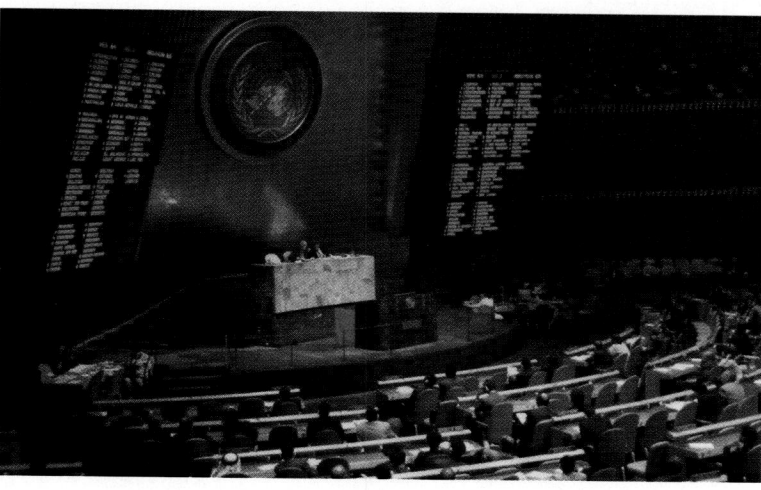

◄ *At the UN headquarters in New York City, votes are recorded on an overhead electronic board so that all can see the results. How effective do you believe the UN has been in establishing worldwide peace?*

On Line with WORLD HISTORY *Internet Activity*

You may want to have your students visit the following URL, where they will find information and additional web site resources to enhance their study of this chapter.

United Nations

http://www.un.org/

The homepage for the United Nations contains all kinds of information about international issues, from human rights to international law.

Due to the ever-changing nature of the World Wide Web, see the West History web site, **http://history.swpco.com** for regular updates of the URLs in this text.

(f) gap smaller in developed nations, little change in developing countries

(g) establishing a common national identity

(h) squabbling new nations, atmosphere of conflict and tension

4. (a) Answers will vary.
   (b) Answers will vary.

CLOSE

Lead students in a discussion of the Focus objectives identified on page 1112. Emphasize the interrelated nature of the problems faced by the world today.

FOCUS

OBJECTIVES

After completing this section, students should be able to

1. identify and describe the purpose and accomplishments of the United Nations
2. identify and describe alternative global visions for the future

FOCUS ACTIVITY

Ask students to write an essay that identifies and describes their global visions for the future.

TEACH

LEARNING FROM VISUALS

Answer to the caption question: Although there have been some notable exceptions, the United Nations has not been particularly effective in ending wars or in maintaining worldwide peace.

was given the power to discuss any question of importance to the organization and to recommend action to be taken. The day-to-day administrative business of the United Nations is supervised by the secretary-general, whose offices are located at the permanent headquarters in New York City.

The most important organ of the United Nations is the Security Council. It is composed of five permanent members—the United States, the Soviet Union (now Russia), Great Britain, France, and China—and ten members chosen by the General Assembly. The Security Council decides what actions the United Nations should take to settle international disputes. Because each of the permanent members can veto the council's decision, a stalemate has frequently resulted.

A number of specialized agencies function under the direction of the United Nations. These include the United Nations Educational, Scientific, and Cultural Organization (UNESCO), the World Health Organization (WHO), and the United Nations International Children's Emergency Fund (UNICEF). All these agencies have been successful in providing aid to help lessen the world's economic and social problems. The United Nations has also performed a valuable service in organizing international conferences on important issues such as population growth and the environment.

The United Nations has also managed to provide peacekeeping military forces drawn from neutral member states to settle conflicts. Until recently, however, the basic weakness of the United Nations was that throughout its history, it had been subject to the whims of the two superpowers. The rivalry of the United States and the Soviet Union in the Cold War was often played out at the expense of the United Nations. The United Nations had little success, for example, in reducing the arms race between the two superpowers. With the end of the Cold War, the United Nations has played a more active role in keeping alive a vision of international order and peace. Missions in Somalia and Bosnia, however, have raised questions about the effectiveness of the United Nations in peacekeeping.

The United Nations also took the lead in affirming the basic **human rights** of all people. On December 10, 1948, the UN General Assembly adopted the Universal Declaration of Human Rights. According to the

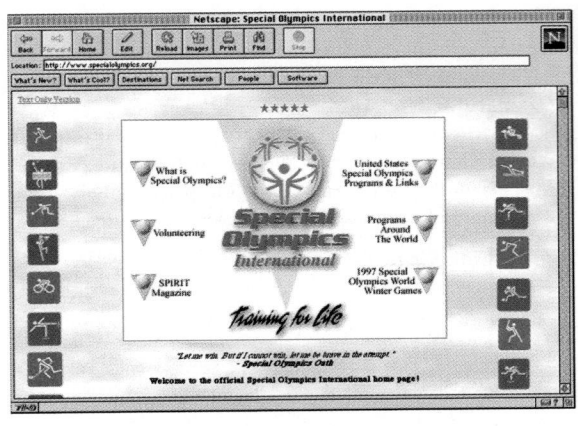

▲ *The Special Olympics International is just one of the 18,000 nongovernmental organizations that maintain offices at the UN. Those interested in their programs in the United States or around the world can contact them on-line. Why might an NGO maintain a Web site?*

declaration, "All human beings are born free and equal in dignity and rights. . . . Everyone is entitled to all the rights and freedoms set forth in this Declaration, without distinction of any kind, such as race, color, sex, language, religion, political or other opinion, national or social origin, property, birth or other status. . . . Everyone has the right to life, liberty, and security of person."

New Global Visions

One approach to the global problems we face has been the development of grassroots social movements, including environmental, women's and men's liberation, human potential, appropriate-technology, and nonviolence movements. Hazel Henderson, a British-born economist, has been especially active in founding public interest groups. She believes that citizen groups can be an important force for greater global unity and justice. In *Creating Alternative Futures*, Henderson explained: "These aroused citizens are by no means all mindless young radicals. Well-dressed, clean-shaven, middle-class businessmen and their suburban wives comprise the major forces in California fighting against

On Line with WORLD HISTORY Internet Activity

You may want to have your students visit the following URL, where they will find information and additional web site resources to enhance their study of this chapter.

United Nations Environment Program

http://www.unep.ch/

The U.N. oversees international treaties and major programs dealing with the environment. A set of links sends you to major sites dealing with the environment.

Due to the ever-changing nature of the World Wide Web, see the West History web site, **http://history.swpco.com** for regular updates of the URLs in this text.

nuclear power. Hundreds of thousands of middle-class mothers are bringing massive pressure to ban commercials and violent programs from children's television."[1] "Think globally, act locally" is frequently the slogan of these grassroots groups.

Related to the emergence of these social movements is the growth of **nongovernmental organizations (NGOs)**. NGOs are often represented at the United Nations and include professional, business, and cooperative organizations; foundations; religious, peace, and disarmament groups; youth and women's organizations; environmental and human rights groups; and research institutes. According to the American educator Elise Boulding, who has been active in encouraging the existence of these groups, NGOs are an important instrument in the cultivation of global perspectives. Boulding states, "Since NGOs by definition are identified with interests that transcend national boundaries, we expect all NGOs to define problems in global terms, to take account of human interests and needs as they are found in all parts of the planet."[2] The number of international NGOs increased from 176 in 1910 to 18,000 in 1990.

Global approaches to global problems, however, have been hindered by political, ethnic, and religious disputes. Pollution of the Rhine River by factories along its banks provokes angry disputes among European nations. The United States and Canada have argued about the effects of acid rain on Canadian forests. The collapse of the Soviet Union and its satellite system between 1989 and 1991 greatly increased the potential for international cooperation on global issues. In fact, however, the collapse of the Soviet empire has had almost the opposite effect. The disintegration of the Soviet Union has led to the emergence of new nations in conflict and a general atmosphere of friction and tension throughout much of Eastern Europe. The bloody conflict in the lands of the former Yugoslavia clearly indicates the dangers in the rise of nationalist sentiment among various ethnic and religious groups in Eastern Europe. Even as the world becomes more global in culture and more interdependent in its mutual relations, disruptive forces are still at work that can work against efforts to enhance our human destiny.

Many lessons can be learned from the study of world history. One of them is especially clear. A lack of involvement in the affairs of one's society can easily lead to a sense of powerlessness. An understanding of our world heritage and its lessons might well give us the opportunity to make wise choices in an age that is often crisis laden and chaotic. We are all creators of history, and upon us depends the future of world civilization.

❧ SECTION REVIEW ❧

1. **Define:**
   (*a*) human rights,   (*b*) nongovernmental organizations (NGOs)

2. **Identify:**
   (*a*) United Nations Educational, Scientific, and Cultural Organization (UNESCO),   (*b*) World Health Organization (WHO),   (*c*) United Nations Children's Emergency Fund (UNICEF),   (*d*) Hazel Henderson

3. **Recall:**
   (*a*) What are the two chief goals of the United Nations?
   (*b*) What position is responsible for the day-to-day administration of United Nations activities?
   (*c*) What is required for the Security Council to approve a resolution?

4. **Think Critically:**
   (*a*) Why is it difficult for the United Nations to intervene with military force?
   (*b*) What lessons have you learned from studying this text that will help you make wise choices and help create a better future for the world?

Notes

1. Hazel Henderson, *Creating Alternative Futures* (New York, 1978), p. 356.
2. Elise Boulding, *Women in the Twentieth Century World* (New York, 1977), p. 186.

So What ❓❗

If students question the role of the **United Nations in human rights,** tell them . . .

that the Declaration of Human Rights appears to be honored more in the breach than in deed. Nevertheless, it represents a statement of what human beings believe and the ideals to which they aspire. It provides a means by which current societies may judge themselves and attempt to improve the quality of life both for themselves and their posterity.

CHAPTER 34 REVIEW

USING KEY TERMS

1. nongovernmental organizations (NGOs)
2. developing nations
3. space shuttles
4. ecology
5. developed nations
6. human rights
7. deforestation
8. global economy
9. genetic engineering
10. acid rain
11. greenhouse effect
12. ozone layer

REVIEWING THE FACTS

1. The message in *Silent Spring* was that the use of pesticides was harming the world's environment by killing the birds and other animals.
2. Chlorofluorocarbons have been identified as a group of chemicals that may damage the ozone layer.
3. The economies of developing nations rely on developed nations to buy their products and to sell them technological products they cannot make themselves.
4. Representatives from many nations met in Rio de Janeiro to discuss the world's environment.
5. Many nations have reduced their spending for environmental protection and monitoring. Some of these responsibilities have been taken over by nongovernmental organizations.
6. The five permanent members each have veto power over Security Council resolutions.
7. The World Health Organization promotes medical research and efforts to help people lead healthier lives.
8. UNICEF exists to help in situations where children's lives or health are in danger.

THINKING CRITICALLY

1. A large part of the damage to the world's environment takes place in developing nations.

1120

USING KEY TERMS

1. When people join in groups that work to define and/or support a particular cause they form _____.
2. _____ are countries that rely primarily on farming to support their people and that have a limited industrial and technological base.
3. The United States sends astronauts on missions in reusable vehicles called _____.
4. _____ is the study of the relationship between living things and their environment.
5. Countries with well-organized, technologically advanced industries and agriculture are called _____.
6. The basic individual rights that were affirmed by the United Nations in 1948 are called _____.
7. _____ is the destruction of large forests and jungles that may result in changes in the world's climate.
8. The interdependency of all nations' economic systems shows that there is a _____ in our world.
9. The ability of scientists to alter cells to produce new life forms is _____.
10. Sulfuric emissions mixing with moisture in the atmosphere results in _____ that may kill fish and vegetation where it falls.
11. The warming of the atmosphere that results from the accumulation of carbon dioxide in the air is called the _____.
12. The _____ is a thin layer of gas in the upper atmosphere that protects the earth from ultraviolet rays from the sun.

REVIEWING THE FACTS

1. What environmental message was the theme of *Silent Spring?*

1120

2. What chemical has been identified as a danger to the Earth's ozone layer?
3. In what ways are economies of developing nations dependent on those of developed nations?
4. When and where did nations of the world meet to discuss environmental issues?
5. Why are nongovernmental organizations (NGOs) taking greater responsibilities in the fight to protect the world's environment?
6. Why is it often difficult for the United Nations Security Council to make decisions?
7. What is the purpose of the World Health Organization?
8. What is the purpose of the United Nations Children's Emergency Fund?

THINKING CRITICALLY

1. Why isn't an agreement among developed nations to protect the world's environment likely to be effective by itself?
2. What possible benefits and ethical problems may result from developments in genetic engineering?
3. Explain why it may be hypocritical for people in developed nations to condemn developing nations for abusing their environments by gathering raw materials to sell to earn money to pay debts and buy imported goods.
4. In the early 1990s, developed nations took a series of steps through a program called the Brady Plan to help developing nations make payments on their international debts. How did the developed nations benefit from providing this help?
5. Why must the United Nations have a respected military capacity if it is to be effective in maintaining the peace in many parts of the world?
6. Why might the fall of the Soviet Union have decreased the likelihood of a major nuclear war between super powers while increasing the potential for relatively small regional wars?

2. Answers will vary but should demonstrate that students have seriously considered the potential costs and benefits of genetic engineering.
3. People in developed nations buy products that were produced in developing nations in ways that damaged the environment.
4. Without help, developing nations could not have paid their bills to developed nations and could not have continued to buy products from developed nations.
5. Answers will vary but should state that leaders in many countries only respect force.
6. Although the United States is now the only true superpower there are many smaller nations that have emerged from the Soviet Union that are

bellicose and may start conflicts.

APPLYING SOCIAL STUDIES SKILLS

1. Answers will vary but should demonstrate that students have seriously considered the impact they have on the environment and ways they could lessen this impact.
2. Answers will vary but may mention the fact that damage done to the environment in developing nations is likely to have an impact on the environment in developed nations. There is some justification then for having developed nations help pay the costs that developing nations cannot afford.

CHAPTER 34 REVIEW

APPLYING SOCIAL STUDIES SKILLS

1. **Ecology:** Identify several activities in your life that are harmful to the environment. Describe steps you could take as an individual to help protect the world's environment.
2. **Economics:** A suggestion was made in the late 1980s to have each developed nation contribute a share of its annual income to developing nations to be used to protect their environments because they could not afford to do this on their own. State whether you would have supported this idea and explain the reasons for your point of view.
3. **Government:** Identify and explain several reasons why it is unlikely that there will be a true world government at any time in the near future.

MAKING TIME AND PLACE CONNECTIONS

1. Why does the birth of another American baby have a greater impact on the world's environment than does the birth of a baby in a developing nation?
2. In the nineteenth century, vast forests in North America were cut for lumber and other products. What right then does the United States or other developed nations have to tell developing nations that they should protect their forests?
3. What events in Africa have increased the need for services of the United Nations Children's Emergency Fund? Why should Americans care what happens to people who are poor in developing nations?

BECOMING AN HISTORIAN

Charts, Graphs, Tables: Study the data below and use it to explain why population density is not a good indicator of a nation's prosperity. What would probably be a better way of predicting what makes a nation's people prosperous?

Population Density and Production Per Person

Country	People per square mile (1990)	Annual production per person (1989)
U.S.A.	69	$20,910
France	267	17,000
Switzerland	424	27,510
Germany (West)	570	19,520
India	669	321
Philippines	570	697
Bangladesh	2,130	180
Zaire	40	258

Source: Statistical Abstract of the United States, U.S. Government Printing Office (Washington, D.C., 1993), p. 840.

Writing Research Papers: Write a thesis statement about your opinion of the ability of the United Nations to resolve international disputes. Choose a recent example and explain what happened that caused the United Nations to become involved. Describe the actions the United Nations took and the results. Explain the impact the situation had on the people who were directly involved, and on the world in general. Finally, explain how these events support the thesis of your report. Be sure to provide appropriate documentation for your statements.

1121

BECOMING AN HISTORIAN

1. Answers will vary but may point out that measurements of the value of tools, education, and training that people have to use to be productive may be a better measure than population density.
2. Research papers and thesis statements will vary but the final product should show that the students have used the knowledge and skill they have acquired in this and other relevant courses to produce an acceptable and appropriately documented research paper.

3. Answers will vary but should include mention of the wide variety of cultures, economic and political systems, and social values that are held by the people of the world. It is doubtful that the world's citizens will soon agree to one government for all nations or people.

MAKING TIME AND PLACE CONNECTIONS

1. Answers will vary but should point out that the higher standard of living enjoyed by Americans means that they will consume more raw materials and have a greater impact on the world's environment.
2. Answers will vary but may point out that we know more about the impact of deforestation on the world's environment than we did a hundred or more years ago.
3. There has been widespread famine in much of Africa in recent years. Children have suffered the most.

HISTORICAL ATLAS

CONTENTS

World Political Map
(Inset: Western Europe)

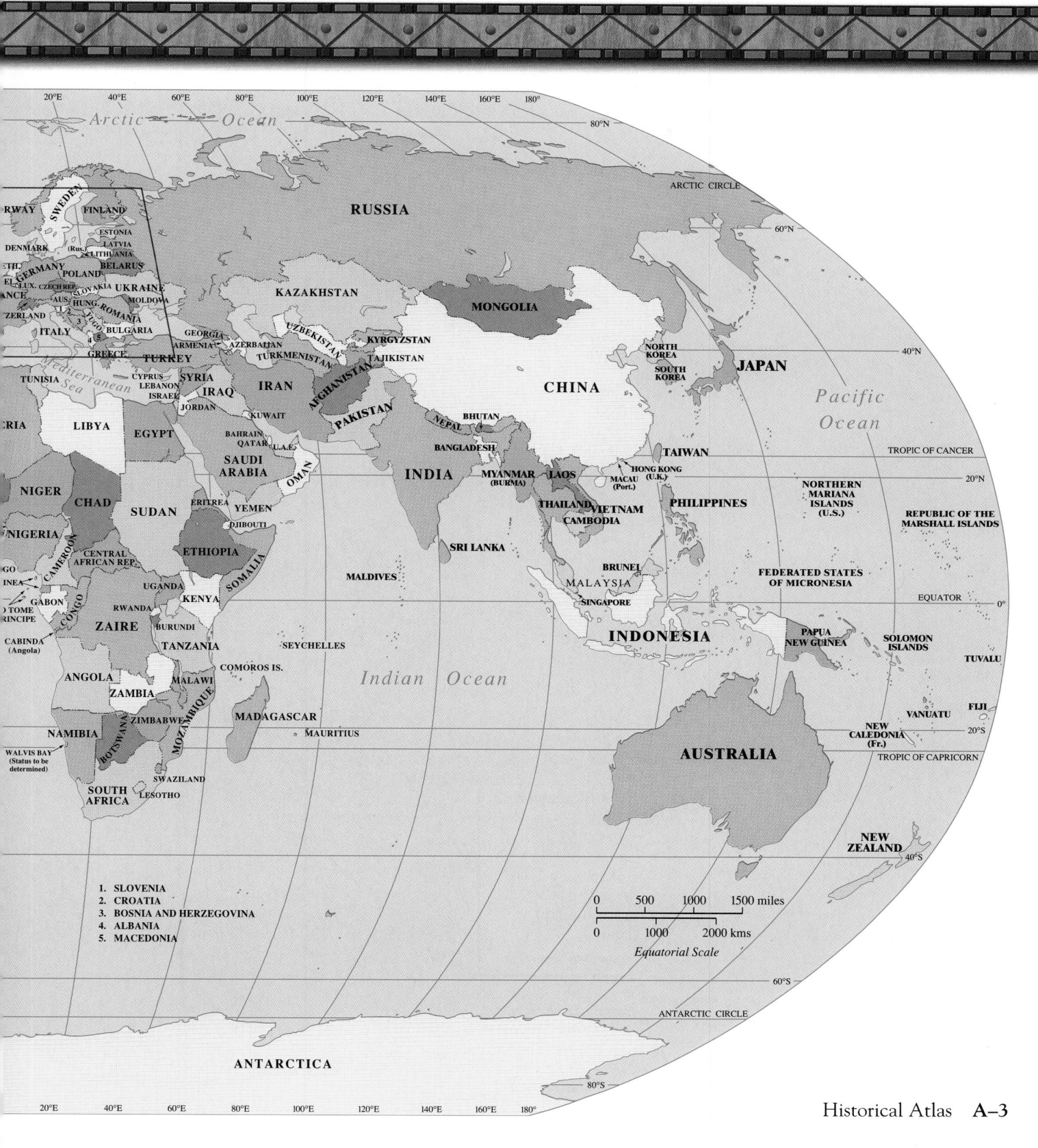

20°E 40°E 60°E 80°E 100°E 120°E 140°E 160°E 180°

Arctic Ocean

80°N

RUSSIA

ARCTIC CIRCLE

60°N

RWAY SWEDEN FINLAND

ESTONIA

DENMARK (Rus.) LATVIA

TH. LITHUANIA

GERMANY POLAND BELARUS

EL LUX. CZECH REP.

ANCE SLOVAKIA UKRAINE

ZERLAND AUS. HUNG. ROMANIA MOLDOVA

ITALY YUGO. BULGARIA

GREECE TURKEY

GEORGIA

ARMENIA AZERBAIJAN

UZBEKISTAN KYRGYZSTAN

TURKMENISTAN TAJIKISTAN

KAZAKHSTAN

MONGOLIA

NORTH KOREA

SOUTH KOREA

JAPAN

40°N

Pacific Ocean

TUNISIA

Mediterranean Sea

CYPRUS

LEBANON

ISRAEL

SYRIA

IRAQ

JORDAN

IRAN

AFGHANISTAN

PAKISTAN

CHINA

20°N

RIA LIBYA EGYPT

KUWAIT

BAHRAIN

QATAR U.A.E.

SAUDI ARABIA

OMAN

NEPAL BHUTAN

BANGLADESH

INDIA

MYANMAR (BURMA)

LAOS

TAIWAN

HONG KONG (U.K.)

MACAU (Port.)

TROPIC OF CANCER

NORTHERN MARIANA ISLANDS (U.S.)

20°N

REPUBLIC OF THE MARSHALL ISLANDS

NIGER CHAD SUDAN

ERITREA YEMEN

DJIBOUTI

THAILAND VIETNAM

CAMBODIA

PHILIPPINES

NIGERIA CAMEROON

CENTRAL AFRICAN REP.

ETHIOPIA

SOMALIA

SRI LANKA

GO

NEA GABON

CONGO

TOME RINCIPE

UGANDA

RWANDA

KENYA

MALDIVES

BRUNEI

MALAYSIA

SINGAPORE

FEDERATED STATES OF MICRONESIA

EQUATOR 0°

ZAIRE BURUNDI

CABINDA (Angola)

TANZANIA

SEYCHELLES

INDONESIA

PAPUA NEW GUINEA

SOLOMON ISLANDS

TUVALU

ANGOLA

ZAMBIA MALAWI

MOZAMBIQUE

COMOROS IS.

Indian Ocean

VANUATU FIJI

NAMIBIA ZIMBABWE

BOTSWANA

MADAGASCAR

MAURITIUS

NEW CALEDONIA (Fr.)

20°S

WALVIS BAY (Status to be determined)

SWAZILAND

SOUTH AFRICA LESOTHO

AUSTRALIA

TROPIC OF CAPRICORN

NEW ZEALAND

40°S

1. SLOVENIA
2. CROATIA
3. BOSNIA AND HERZEGOVINA
4. ALBANIA
5. MACEDONIA

0   500   1000   1500 miles

0   1000   2000 kms

Equatorial Scale

60°S

ANTARCTIC CIRCLE

ANTARCTICA

80°S

20°E 40°E 60°E 80°E 100°E 120°E 140°E 160°E 180°

Historical Atlas   **A–3**

World Physical Map

ARCTIC CIRCLE Brooks Range

Mt. McKinley
20,320 ft.

Aleutian Islands

Rocky Mountains

Great Basin

Great Plains

Sierra Madres

Missouri R.

Mississippi R.

Appalachians

Canadian

Shield

Hudson Bay

Great Lakes

Newfoundland

Greenland

Iceland

British Isles

Azore Islands

Canary Islands

Cape Verde Islands

Atlantic Ocean

Hawaiian Islands

Gulf of Mexico

Cuba

Bahamas

Hispaniola

Caribbean Sea

Isthmus of Panama

Galapagos Islands

Pacific Ocean

Samoa Islands

Tonga Islands

Tahiti

Society Islands

Tuamotu Archip.

Pitcairn Island

Easter Island

Llanos

Amazon R.

Amazon Basin

Andes Mountains

Parana R.

Paraguay R.

Brazilian Highlands

Mt. Aconcagua
22,887 ft.

Pampas

Patagonia

Falkland Islands

Tierra del Fuego

Atlantic Ocean

Vinson Massif
16,864 ft.

ARCTIC CIRCLE

80°N

60°N

40°N

TROPIC OF CANCER

20°N

EQUATOR 0°

20°S

TROPIC OF CAPRICORN

40°S

60°S

80°S

180° 160°W 140°W 120°W 100°W 80°W 60°W 40°W 20°W

Elevation Key

Feet		Meters
9,840		3,000
4,920		1,500
1,968		600
492		150
0		0

Below Sea Level

▲ Mountain peak

0   500   1000   1500 miles

0   1000   2000 kms

Equatorial Scale

Arctic Ocean
Norwegian Sea
Scandinavian Peninsula
North Sea
Baltic Sea
North European Plain
Alps
Volga R.
Ural Mountains
Ob River
West Siberian Plain
Central Siberian Plateau
Lena R.
ARCTIC CIRCLE
80°N
60°N
Lake Baikal
Sea of Okhotsk
Kamchatka Peninsula
Aral Sea
Caspian Sea
Mt. Elbrus 18,510 ft.
Black Sea
Tian Shan
Gobi Desert
Huang He
Sea of Japan
40°N
Mediterranean Sea
Central Plateau of Iran
Hindu Kush
Tibetan Plateau
Mt. Everest 29,028 ft.
Himalaya Mtns.
Yangtze R.
Japanese Archipelago
Pacific Ocean
Sahara
Nile R.
Arabian Peninsula
Red Sea
Ganges R.
Indus R.
Bay of Bengal
Mekong R.
TROPIC OF CANCER
20°N
Lake Chad
African Horn
Arabian Sea
Sri Lanka
Maldive Islands
South China Sea
Philippine Islands
Mariana Islands
Marshall Islands
Zaire R.
Congo Basin
Lake Victoria
Mt. Kilimanjaro 19,340 ft.
Seychelles
Borneo
Sumatra
New Guinea
Mt. Puncak Jaya 16,500 ft.
Caroline Islands
EQUATOR 0°
Solomon Islands
Tuvalu
Comoros Islands
Indian Ocean
Java
Madagascar
Mauritius
Great Sandy Desert
Great Dividing Range
AUSTRALIA
Vanatu
New Caledonia
Fiji Islands
20°S
Kalahari Desert
TROPIC OF CAPRICORN
Cape of Good Hope
New Zealand
40°S
Tasmania
60°S
ANTARCTIC CIRCLE
ANTARCTICA
80°S

20°E 40°E 60°E 80°E 100°E 120°E 140°E 160°E 180°

World Population Density Map

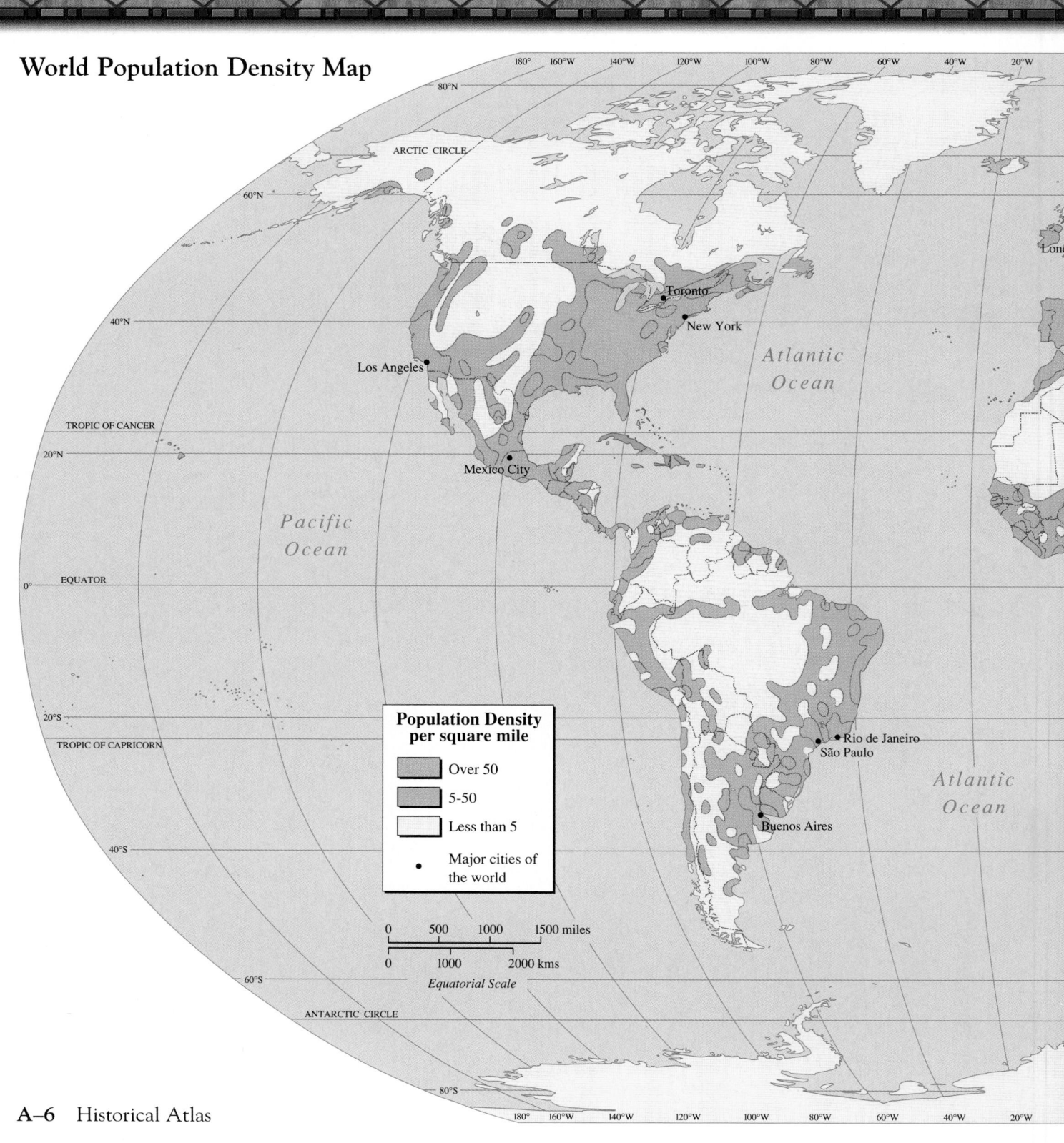

ARCTIC CIRCLE

60°N

40°N

TROPIC OF CANCER

20°N

Pacific
Ocean

EQUATOR
0°

20°S

TROPIC OF CAPRICORN

40°S

60°S

ANTARCTIC CIRCLE

80°S

Toronto
New York
Los Angeles
Atlantic
Ocean
Mexico City

London

Rio de Janeiro
São Paulo
Atlantic
Ocean
Buenos Aires

**Population Density
per square mile**

Over 50

5-50

Less than 5

• Major cities of
the world

| 0 | 500 | 1000 | 1500 miles |

| 0 | 1000 | 2000 kms |

Equatorial Scale

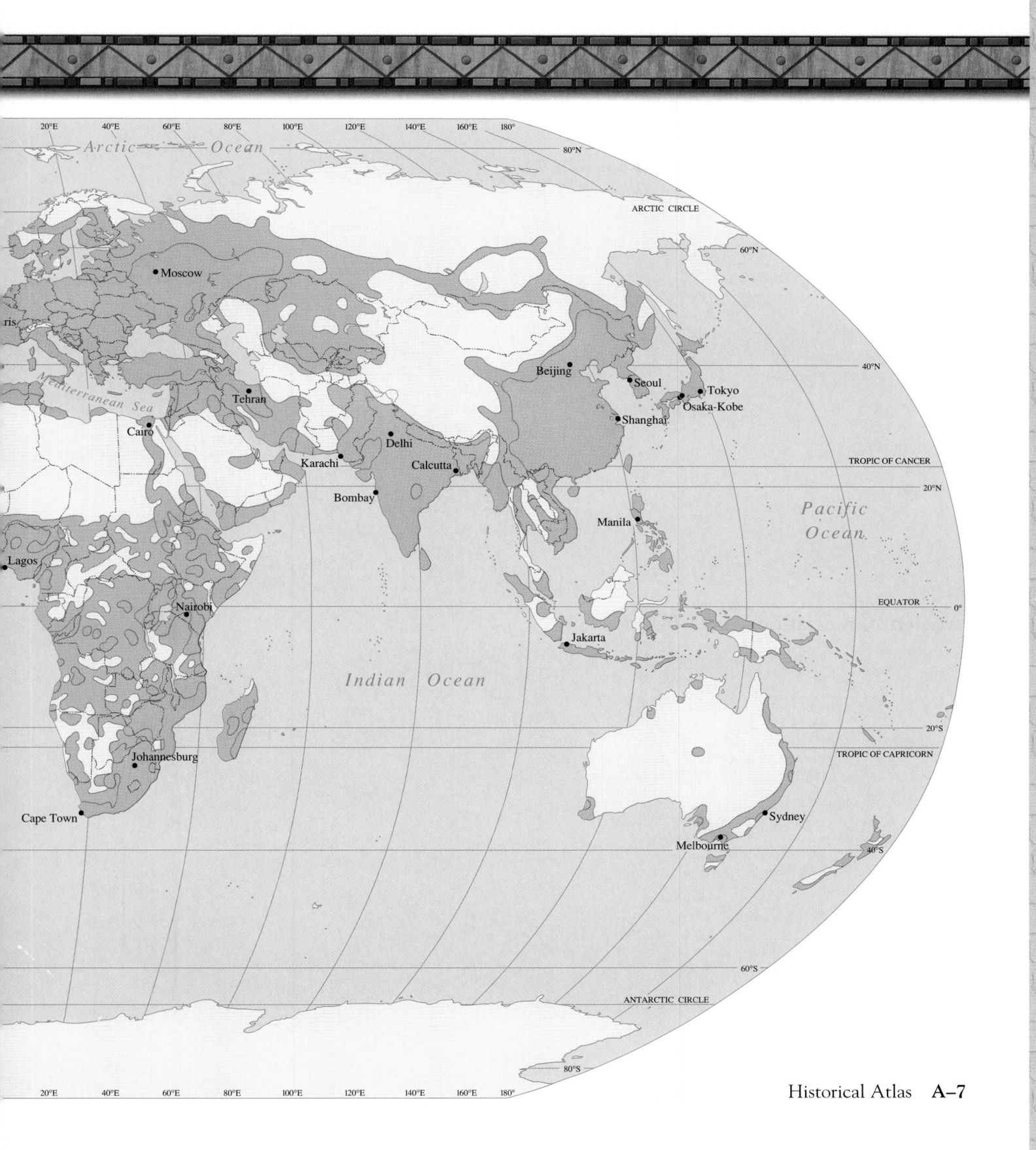

The Beginnings of Civilization

Ancient Civilizations, 100–500

New Patterns of Civilization, 500–1500

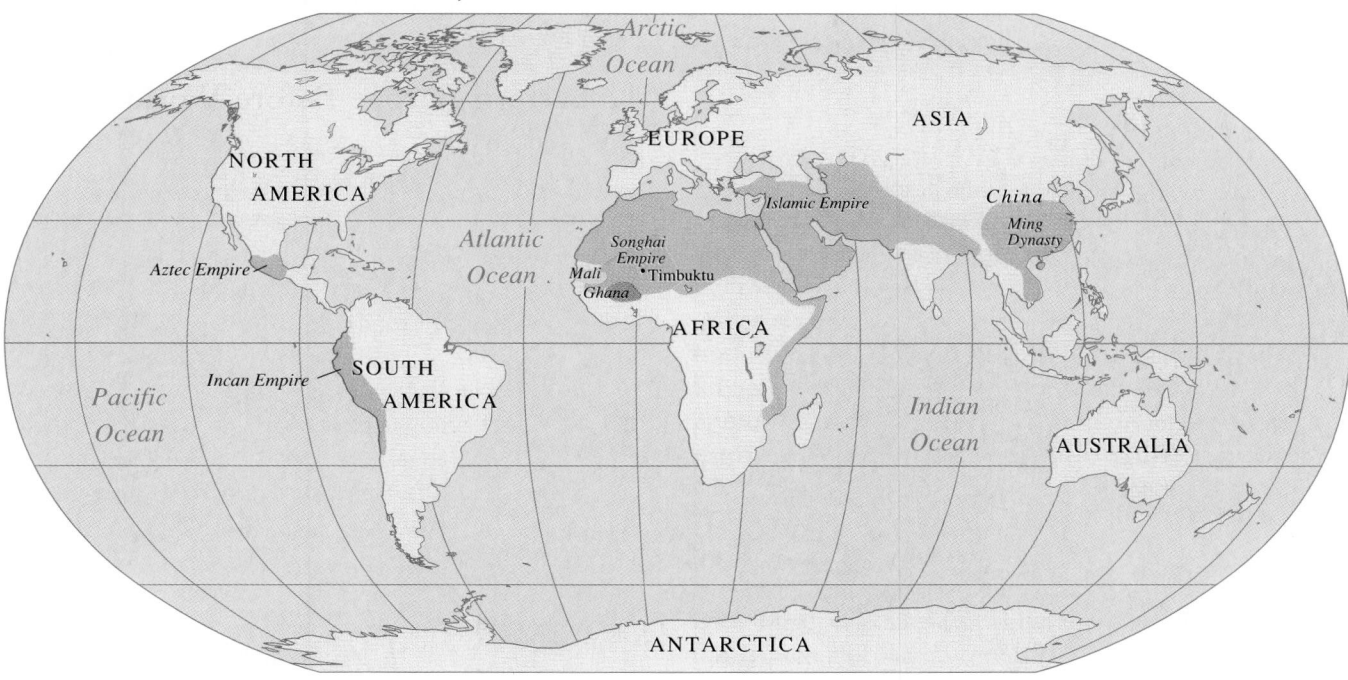

Modern Patterns of World History, 1900

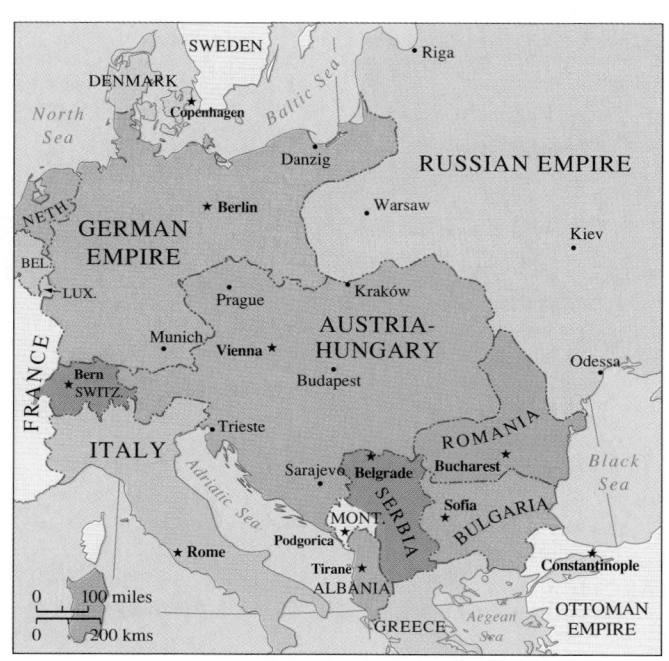

1. Eastern Europe Before World War I

2. Eastern Europe After World War I

3. Eastern Europe After World War II

4. Modern Eastern Europe

GLOSSARY

A

abbesses the heads of convents (348)

abolitionism a movement to end slavery (675)

absenteeism chronic absence from one's duties; this practice of church officeholders who ignored their duties and paid subordinates to run their offices (often badly), contributed to the dissatisfaction that led to the Reformation (436)

absolute rulers rulers who were free to govern without any laws (259)

absolutism a form of rule where ultimate authority was in the hands of a monarch who claimed to rule by divine right (467)

acid rain rainfall that results when sulfur spewed out by industrial factories mixes with the moisture in the air (responsible for killing large forested areas in North America and Europe) (1112)

acropolis usually the upper fortified part of a city or town, which served as a refuge during attack and sometimes as the religious center for temples and public buildings (123)

adobe sun-dried brick used in building shelters (201)

agora an open space below an acropolis that was used for citizen assembly and a market (123)

agricultural societies countries with primarily farming economies (333)

Anschluss refers to Hitler's union of Germany and Austria (902)

anthropologists experts who use artifacts and human fossils to determine how people lived their lives (5)

anti-Semitism hostility toward or discrimination against Jews as a religious group (850)

apartheid a system of racial segregation in South Africa (1044)

appeasement Great Britain's policy (prior to World War II) based on the belief that if European states satisfied the reasonable demands of dissatisfied powers, the latter would be content, and stability and peace would be achieved in Europe (902)

aqueduct an artificial channel through which water is conveyed (the Aztecs in Mexico built an aqueduct in the fifteenth century) (207)

archaeology the study of past societies through an analysis of what people have left behind them (5)

archipelago a chain of islands (327)

archons rulers who assisted the council of nobles in ancient Athens (128)

armada a fleet of warships (457)

Aryan racial state a nation consisting solely of a hypothetical homogeneous ethnic type descended from early Indo-European peoples (Hitler considered Germans the supreme group of Aryans) (902)

ascetics people who practiced self-denial as a means of achieving an understanding of ultimate reality (70)

Askia the name of the dynasty (it means "usurper") created when Muhammad Ture overthrew the son of Sunni Ali in 1493; during his reign, the Songhai Empire reached its height (265)

Atman according to Hindu belief, the individual self whose duty it was to seek to know Brahman (68)

Ausgleich the Compromise of 1867, which created the dual monarchy of Austria-Hungary (674)

australopithecines "southern apes," they flourished in eastern and southern Africa and were the first hominids to make stone tools (9)

B

balance of power the idea that states should have equal power in order to prevent any one state from dominating the others (619)

banana republics small countries dependent on large, wealthy nations (891)

Baroque-Rococo an architectural style of the eighteenth century in which a building was seen as a total work of art—a harmonious whole (593)

bazaar a covered market (the bazaar was a crucial part of every Muslim city or town) (240)

bey   a tribal leader, considered first among equals; he could claim loyalty among his chiefs by providing them with booty and lands (also the origin of the sultan system of governing in Persia and India) (522)

Blitzkrieg   "lightning war," a war conducted with great speed and force (908)

blue-collar   of, relating to, or constituting the class of wage-earners whose duties call for the wearing of work clothes or protective clothing—industrial production occupations (963)

bourgeois   a person of the middle class (658)

bourgeoisie   the middle class (692)

boyars   the Russian nobility (472)

Brahman   according to Hindu belief, a force in the universe, a form of ultimate reality or God (68)

Brezhnev doctrine   Leonid Brezhnev's insistence on the right of the Soviet Union to intervene if communism was threatened in another Communist state (979)

brinkmanship   threatening to go to war to achieve one's goals (802)

Bronze Age   from around 3000 to 1200 B.C., characterized by the widespread use of bronze for tools and weapons (17)

Bushido   "the way of the warrior," the strict warrior code of Japan's samurai (303)

C

caliph   the secular leader of the Islamic community (230)

Camp David Accords   an agreement to sign an Israeli-Egyptian peace treaty on March 26, 1979 (the meeting was held at Camp David, Maryland, and attended by Jimmy Carter, Menachim Begin, and Anwar al-Sadat) (1064)

carruca   a heavy-wheeled plow with an iron plowshare invented during the Middle Ages and used for turning over the heavy clay soil of northern Europe (380)

Cartesian dualism   Descartes's principle of the separation of mind and matter (and mind and body) (585)

caste system   a set of rigid social categories that determined a person's occupation and economic potential and also his or her position in society (a division of classes in India based on economic advantage) (64)

caudillos   strong leaders who ruled the new independent nations of Latin America chiefly by military force; they were usually supported by the landed elites (760)

censorate   a branch of the central bureaucracy of China's Qin dynasty that was made up of inspectors who checked on government officials (104)

centuriate assembly   the most important assembly of the Roman Republic; it was organized by classes based on wealth, where the wealthiest citizens always had the majority (158)

chapbooks   short pamphlets printed on cheap paper and sold by peddlers to the lower classes; they consisted of everything from religious stories to adventure stories and crude satires (598)

chivalry   an ideal of civilized behavior that evolved among the nobility in the eleventh and twelfth centuries under the influence of the church; it became the code of ethics that knights were to uphold (355)

city-states   cities with political and economic control over the surrounding countryside (the basic units of Sumerian civilization) (25)

civilization   a complex culture in which large numbers of people share a number of common elements (17)

clan   a group of related families (199)

clergy   bishops and priests of the Christian Church (185)

collective bargaining   the right of unions to negotiate with employers over wages and hours (840)

collectivization   many small holdings brought together into a single unit for joint operation under governmental supervision (847)

commercial capitalism   an economic system in which people invested in trade or goods in order to make profits (386)

compurgation   a means of determining guilt under Germanic law; the accused swore an oath of innocence and was backed up by a group of twelve or twenty-five "oath-helpers" (346)

condottiere   the leader of a band of mercenaries, or soldiers who sold their services to the highest bidder (421)

Confucianism   a philosophy based on the teachings of Confucius, China's "First Teacher"; the main concepts were the "work ethic" (duty) and a sense of compassion and empathy for others (humanity) (100)

conquistadors   sixteenth-century Spanish conquerors motivated by glory, greed, and religious zeal (492)

conscription   a military draft (802)

conservatism   an ideology that favored obedience to political authority and the belief that organized religion was crucial to order in society (662)

consulate   a new form of French republic proclaimed in 1799, which was entirely controlled by Napoleon Bonaparte (640)

consuls   chief executive officers of the Roman Republic, two of which were chosen every year; they ran the government and led the army into battle (158)

consumer society a preoccupation with and the inclination toward the buying of goods that directly satisfy human wants (968)

Contras American-financed rebels who waged a guerrilla war against the Sandinista provisional government in Nicaragua (1027)

cottage industry the production of goods from one's home (610)

council of the plebs a popular assembly of the Roman Republic created for plebeians only, founded in 471 B.C. (158)

counterterrorism a calculated policy of direct retaliation against terrorists (radicals who commit violent acts, such as killing civilians, taking hostages, and hijacking planes, in order to achieve their goals) (1000)

creole elites locally born descendants of the Europeans who became permanent inhabitants of Latin America (756)

cuneiform "wedge-shaped" (a system of writing developed by the Sumerians with wedge-shaped impressions made by using a reed stylus on clay tablets) (30)

D

daimyo "great names," heads of noble families who controlled vast landed estates in Japan that owed no taxes to the government (304)

deficit spending the spending of government funds raised by borrowing rather than taxation (840)

deforestation the process of cutting down trees in forests and jungles to provide wood products and new farmland (1112)

deism a system of thought that denies the interference of the Creator with the laws of the universe (589)

democracy rule of the many (125)

descamisados "the shirtless ones," the working classes in Argentina (1028)

de-Stalinization Nikita Khrushchev's process of eliminating the more ruthless policies of Stalin (952)

détente a relaxation of strained relations or tensions (as between the United States and the Soviet Union in the 1970s) (977)

developed nations rich nations, located mainly in the Northern Hemisphere, which have well-organized industrial and agricultural systems, make use of advanced technologies, and have strong educational systems (1114)

developing nations poor nations, located mainly in the Southern Hemisphere, which are primarily farming nations with little technology or education (1114)

dharma divine law (the concept of karma is ruled by dharma) (69)

Diet the Japanese legislature (788)

diocese a Christian bishop's area of authority (346)

diplomatic revolution the forming of new alliances without resorting to war (619)

direct rule the form of rule that occurred when local elites were removed from power and replaced with a new set of officials brought from the mother country (733)

dissidents those who speak out against or disagree with the status quo (for example, those who opposed the regime in the Soviet Union) (979)

divine right of kings the belief that kings receive their power directly from God and are responsible to no one except God (464)

domino theory the argument that if the Communists succeeded in one country (that is, South Vietnam), the neighboring countries would likewise fall to communism (950)

dowry a sum of money given by the wife's family to the husband upon marriage (427)

drug cartels groups of drug businesses whose purpose is to eliminate competition (1016)

Duma a legislative assembly, or representative council, in Russia (712)

dyarchy a system created by the Qing dynasty (as a way to deal with ethnic and cultural differences) in which all important government positions were shared equally by Chinese and Manchus (553)

dynasty a family of rulers whose right to rule is passed on within the family (35)

E

ecology the study of the relationship between living things and their environments (1111)

elite a small group of powerful people (61)

emancipation the act of setting free from bondage (675)

empire a large political unit or state, usually under a single leader, that controls many peoples or territories (28)

encomienda the right given to settlers of the New World, by Queen Isabella, to use natives as laborers (492)

enlightened ruler according to the philosophes, a ruler who allowed basic human rights; nurtured arts, sciences, and education; and obeyed the laws and enforced them fairly (614)

environmentalism a movement begun in the 1970s to control the pollution of the Earth (997)

epic poems long poems that tell the deeds of great heroes (the *Iliad* and the *Odyssey* were the first great epic poems of Greece) (122)

Epicureanism a philosophy founded by a teacher, Epicurus, in Athens in the fourth century B.C. based on the concept that happiness through the pursuit of pleasure (freedom that comes from a mind at rest) was the goal of life (146)

eta the lowest class in Japanese society—hereditary slaves (probably descendants of prisoners of war or criminals) whose occupations included burying the dead and curing leather (306)

ethnic cleansing the practice of genocide during the Bosnian War (1993–96) (871)

existentialism a twentieth-century philosophy based on the concept of the absence of God in the universe—meaning that humans were utterly alone and responsible for their actions with no certain knowledge of right or wrong; reduced to despair and depression, their only ground of hope was themselves (1001)

export-import economy an economic system based on exporting raw materials while importing manufactured goods (892)

extraterritoriality a practice (during the 1800s) whereby Europeans lived in their own sections in Chinese ports and were subject not to Chinese laws but to their own (769)

F

favorable balance of trade a practice whereby a nation's exported goods are of greater value than those they import (thereby bringing in gold and silver) (470)

feminism the movement for women's rights (591)

feudal contract a set of unwritten rules that determined the relationship between a lord and his vassal (355)

feudalism the practice of landed aristocrats or nobles providing protection in return for service (353)

fez the brimless cap worn by Turkish Muslims (873)

fief a grant of land made to a vassal (354)

filial piety the concept that all members of a family should subordinate their needs to those of the male head of the family (97)

Final Solution the physical extermination of the Jewish people by the Nazis during World War II (919)

First Triumvirate a coalition formed in 60 B.C. when Caesar joined forces with Crassus and Pompey (162)

flagellants people who beat themselves to beg the forgiveness of God (404)

foot binding a Chinese practice of binding the feet of young females with cloth or silk, which deformed the feet and hindered walking (binding made the feet appear smaller, which was considered attractive) (560)

four modernizations modernization in regard to industry, agriculture, technology, and national defense—a policy set up by Deng Xiaoping in which people were encouraged to work hard to benefit both themselves and Chinese society (1079)

four olds old ideas, old culture, old customs, and old habits—which the Red Guards set out to eliminate by violent means during China's Cultural Revolution (1077)

frescoes paintings done on fresh, wet plaster with water-based paints (430)

fudai inside or lesser daimyo who were directly subordinate to the shogun (566)

functionalism a theory of design that places great emphasis on how an object will be used (861)

G

gang of four Jiang Qing—the widow of Mao Zedong—and three other radicals of the Cultural Revolution who were put on trial and sent to prison for life by reformers led by Deng Xiaoping (1079)

genetic engineering a new scientific field that alters the genetic information of cells to produce new variations—from cells as simple as yeast cells to as complex as mammal cells (1113)

genin one of Japan's lower classes—landless laborers who could be bought and sold like slaves (306)

genocide the deliberate mass murder of a group of people (871)

gentry well-to-do landowners below the level of the nobility (466)

glasnost "openness," an important instrument of Mikhail Gorbachev's perestroika—Soviet citizens were encouraged to discuss openly the strengths and weaknesses of the Soviet Union (980)

global economy an economy, developed by the nations of the world since World War II, in which the production, distribution, and sale of goods are done on a worldwide scale (1114)

governments institutions that organize and regulate human activity (18)

grand vezir, grand wazir the chief minister who conducted the sultan's imperial council meetings during the Ottoman Empire (522)

Great Leap Forward a program begun by Mao Zedong in China in 1958 in the hopes of speeding up economic growth and obtaining a classless society; existing collective farms, normally the size of the traditional village, were combined into vast people's communes (1077)

greenhouse effect Earth's warming because of the buildup of carbon dioxide in the atmosphere (1112)

Green Revolution the work of researchers in India in the 1970s who introduced new strains of rice and wheat that were more productive and resistant to disease but that required more fertilizer and water (1089)

Guided Democracy the government of President Sukarno, who dissolved Indonesia's democratic political system in order to rule on his own; he nationalized foreign-owned enterprises and sought economic aid from China and the Soviet Union (1095)

guilds associations of people with common aims and interests (390)

guru a teacher (66)

H

hajj a pilgrimage to Mecca, believed to be one of the "five pillars," or parts of the ethical code, of Islam (230)

hans domains in Japan, each ruled by a daimyo lord (566)

harem the private domain of a sultan, where he resided with his concubines (522)

Hegira the journey of Muhammad and his followers from Mecca to Medina in the year 622—this year became year 1 in the official calendar of Islam (227)

heliocentric the view that the sun (not the Earth) is at the center of the universe (579)

Hellenistic Era literally, "to imitate Greeks," this era was an age of expansion of Greek language and ideas into the Middle East and beyond (144)

heresy the holding of religious doctrines different from the orthodox teachings of the church (393)

hominids the earliest humanlike creatures (9)

Homo erectus "upright human being," a species that emerged about 1.5 million years ago; they learned to use tools and fire, and were the first hominids to leave Africa for Europe and Asia (9)

Home sapiens "wise human being," a species that emerged around 250,000 years ago and marked the third stage of human development (9)

Homo sapiens sapiens "wise, wise human being," a species that appeared in Africa between 150,000 and 200,000 years ago; they were the first anatomically modern humans (9)

hoplites heavily armed infantry soldiers or foot soldiers (123)

hostage system a practice by which the shogunate controlled the daimyo by forcing the family of a daimyo lord to stay at the lord's government residence (in Edo) when he was absent from it (566)

humanism an intellectual movement—the most important associated with the Renaissance—based upon the study of the classics, or the literary works of ancient Greece and Rome (428)

human rights the just claims of all people, outlined in the Declaration of Human Rights, which was adopted by the UN General Assembly in 1948 (1118)

I

imperator a commander-in-chief of the Roman army (164)

imperialism the extension of one nation's power over other lands (729)

import-substituting industrialization the development of new industries to make goods that previously had been imported (as was done in Latin America after the Great Depression because of a decline in revenues) (1014)

impressionism a theory or practice of painting (which began in France in the 1870s) in which the natural appearances of objects were depicted by dabs and strokes of primary unmixed colors in order to simulate actual reflected light (721)

indemnity a large sum of money (776)

indentured workers landless laborers who contracted to work on the estates of nobles (208)

indirect rule rule that occurred when local rulers were allowed to maintain their positions of authority and status in a new colonial setting (733)

inductive principles a doctrine based on proceeding from the particular to the general through mathematics or logic (586)

Inquisition a court created by the church in the thirteenth century to find and try heretics; it used punishment, torture, and sometimes execution to achieve its goals (393)

insulae apartment blocks as many as six stories high, poorly constructed of concrete, where the poor of Imperial Rome resided (177)

insurrection the act of revolting against an established government (777)

interdict a decree used by Pope Innocent II to achieve his political ends, which forbade priests to give sacraments of the church in the hope that the people, deprived of the comforts of religion, would exert pressure against their ruler (392)

intifada "uprising," a rising unrest created by Palestinian Arab militancy (1064)

Islam "submission to the will of Allah," a religion begun by Muhammad, who believed he had received the final revelations of Allah (226)

Islamic fundamentalism a movement by conservative religious forces in the Middle East to replace foreign culture and values with supposedly "pure" Islamic forms of belief and behavior (1067)

J

Janissaries elite foot soldiers of the Ottoman Empire who also served as guards for the sultan (516)

jihad "struggle in the way of God," the custom of making raids against Islam's enemies in order to expand the Islamic movement (230)

K

Kabuki a theater form in Japan that emphasized violence, music, and dramatic gestures to entertain its viewers (570)

kamikaze "divine wind," a member of the Japanese air attack corps that was assigned to make suicidal attacks on targets (that is, U.S. ships) during World War II (929)

karma the force of a person's actions in this life in determining rebirth in a next life (68)

khanates several separate territories, made from Genghis Khan's united empire after his death, each under the rule of one of Genghis Khan's sons (293)

kibbutz a collective, or commune, in Israel in which farmers share property and work together; adults eat together, and children are raised in a separate children's home (1070)

L

laissez-faire "to let alone," free of government regulations (590)

laity nonclergy members of the Christian Church (185)

lay investiture the practice by which secular rulers chose nominees to church offices and also invested them with the symbols of their office (the disagreement over this practice between Pope Gregory II [against] and King Henry IV [for] in the Middle Ages was known as the Investiture Controversy) (391)

Legalism a philosophy with the main belief that human beings were evil by nature and could be brought to follow the correct path only by harsh laws and stiff punishments (103)

liberalism the idea that people should be as free from restraint as possible; a belief in the protection of civil liberties, or the basic rights of all people (663)

lineage groups African communities formed by combining extended family units (270)

litters covered couches used for carrying passengers (217)

longhouses structures built of wooden poles covered with sheets of bark, 150 to 200 feet in length, built by the Iroquois of North America, and which housed about a dozen families (199)

Luftwaffe the German air force (909)

M

magic realism a form of Latin American literature that brings together realistic events with dreamlike or fantastic backgrounds (1037)

Mahatma "Great Soul," the name Indians used to refer to Mohandas Gandhi (878)

Mahayana a school of Buddhism whose followers saw it as a religion, not a philosophy; they believed Buddha was a divine figure and that through devotion to him, rich and poor could achieve salvation in Nirvana (a true Heaven) after death (316)

mandate of Heaven the authority to command or rule given by heavenly right (it became a basic principle of Chinese statecraft) (94)

manorialism an economic system consisting of "manors," which were agricultural estates run by lords and worked by peasants; the manor was the basic unit of rural organization in the Middle Ages (382)

mansa "king" (262)

marathon a footrace of 26 miles (129)

matrilineal societies societies in which descent is traced through the mother (271)

Mau Mau movement an organized effort among the Kikuyu peoples of Kenya who used terrorism to demand uhuru (freedom) from the British (1044)

Meiji "Enlightened Rule," the reign of the Japanese emperor Mutsuhito (786)

mercantilism a set of principles that dominated economic thought in the seventeenth century, in which the prosperity of a nation depended on a large supply of gold and silver (470)

Mesolithic Age "Middle Stone Age," the period from 10,000 to 7,000 B.C. characterized by a gradual shift from a food-gathering/hunting economy to a food-producing one (14)

mestizos the offspring of Europeans and native American Indians (622)

militarism glorification of the military (671)

minarets four narrow towers framing a mosque (525)

ministerial responsibility the idea that the prime minister is responsible to the popularly elected legislative body and not to the executive officer (a crucial principle of democracy) (709)

mirs village communes or communities of peasants in tsarist Russia that were responsible for land payments to the government (675)

mobilization the process of assembling and making both troops and supplies ready for war (804)

modernism changes produced by writers and artists (between 1870 and 1914) rebelling against the traditional literary and artistic styles dominating European cultural life since the Renaissance (718)

monasticism the practice of living the life of a monk (346)

money economy an economic system based on money rather than barter (386)

monk one who sought to live a life cut off from ordinary human society in order to pursue an ideal of total dedication to God (346)

monsoon a seasonal wind pattern in southern Asia that blows from the southwest during the summer months and from the northeast during the winter (60)

monsoon season a periodic strong wind characterized by very heavy rainfall (509)

mosques Muslim houses of worship (246)

motifs dominant ideas or central themes (541)

mulattoes the offspring of Africans and Europeans (622)

multinational corporations companies that have divisions in more than two countries (1015)

multinational state a collection of different peoples (665)

mutual deterrence the policy based on the belief that an arsenal of nuclear weapons prevents war by ensuring that even if one nation launched its weapons in a first strike, the other nation would still be able to respond and devastate the attacker (946)

N

nationalism loyalty and devotion to a nation (643)

nationalization government ownership (961)

naturalism a literary style where the material world is accepted as real, and therefore, literature is written in a realistic manner (718)

natural selection "survival of the fittest"— organisms most adaptable to their environment pass on the variations that enabled them to survive until a new, separate species emerges (683)

Neanderthals a type of *Homo sapiens* that made clothes from animal skins and seem to have been the first to bury their dead (9)

Neolithic Age Greek for "New Stone" Age, the time from 10,000 to 4000 B.C. (14)

Neolithic farming villages settlements that were more permanent and able to support larger populations due to the growing of crops on a regular basis (15)

Neolithic Revolution the shift from the hunting of animals and the gathering of food to the keeping of animals and the growing of food on a regular basis during the Neolithic Age (14)

New Democracy a modified version of capitalism put into effect by Mao Zedong in China in 1958; major industries were placed under state ownership, but most trading and manufacturing companies remained in private hands (1076)

New Economic Policy a modified version of capitalism put into effect by Vladimir Lenin in Russia in 1921; heavy industry, banking, and mines remained in government hands, but peasants could sell their produce openly, and retail stores and small industries (less than twenty employees) could be privately owned and operated (845)

new monarchies countries such as France, England, and Spain (at the end of the fifteenth century) where new rulers attempted to reestablish the centralized power of monarchical governments (411)

No Japanese drama that developed out of a variety of entertainment forms, including dancing and juggling (308)

nomadic moving from place to place (10)

nongovernmental organizations (NGOs) interest groups (related to the emergence of grass-roots social movements) that transcend national boundaries; they are often represented at the United Nations (1119)

O

oligarchy rule by the few (125)

oracle a sacred shrine dedicated to a god or goddess who revealed the future (136)

ordeal a means of determining guilt under Germanic law; it was believed that if, through divine intervention, the accused was unharmed after a physical trial, then he or she was innocent (346)

orders social groups, also known as *estates* (divisions of society in Europe, first established in the Middle Ages and continuing well into the eighteenth century) (613)

organic evolution Charles Darwin's principle that each kind of plant and animal evolved over a long period of time from earlier and simpler forms of life (683)

ostracism a practice devised in ancient Athens whereby members of the assembly wrote the name of a person who was considered harmful on a pottery fragment (*ostrakon*);

if 6,000 votes were recorded, the person was banned from the city for ten years (132)

ozone layer   a thin layer of gas in the upper atmosphere that shields Earth from the sun's ultraviolet rays (1112)

P

Paleolithic Age   Greek for "Old Stone," the early period of human history in which humans used simple stone tools (10)

pan-Africanism   a movement that stressed the need for the unity of all Africans (878)

pan-Arabism   a belief in Arab unity (1060)

pashas   local rulers in North Africa—appointed by the conquering Ottomans—who collected taxes, maintained law and order, and were directly responsible to the sultan's court in Constantinople (518)

paterfamilias   the dominant male of a family (173)

patriarchal   a society dominated by men (28)

patricians   great landowners who became Rome's ruling class (158)

patrilineal societies   societies in which descent is traced through the father (271)

peninsulars   Spanish and Portuguese officials who resided temporarily in Latin America for political and economic gain and then returned to their mother countries (756)

people's communes   the result of collective farms being combined during the Great Leap Forward in China (1077)

perestroika   "restructuring," a term applied to Mikhail Gorbachev's radical economic, political, and social reforms in the Soviet Union (980)

permanent revolution   constant revolutionary fervor (1077)

phalanx   soldiers marching shoulder to shoulder in a rectangular formation (124)

pharaoh   one of the various titles of Egyptian kings (the word *pharaoh* originally meant "great house" or "palace") (36)

philosophe   a member of the Enlightenment, an eighteenth-century movement of intellectuals who believed in reason, or the application of the scientific method to the understanding of life (588)

philosophy   an organized system of thought (139)

pictographic   the use of pictographs—picture symbols, usually called *characters*—to form a picture of the object to be represented; a type of written communication (99)

planned economies   systems directed by government agencies (815)

plantations   large landed estates (495)

plebeians   Rome's less wealthy landholders, craftspeople, merchants, and small farmers (158)

pluralism   the holding of two or more offices or positions at the same time (436)

pogroms   organized massacres of helpless people (718)

policy of containment   U.S. diplomat George Kennan's plan to keep communism within its geographical boundaries and prevent further aggressive moves (945)

polis   a Greek city-state (122)

Politburo   a committee that was the leading policymaker of the Communist Party (846)

polytheistic   having many gods (30)

popes   heads of the Catholic Church (bishops of Rome who were viewed as Peter's successors) (346)

porcelain   translucent ceramic ware made of fine clay baked at very high temperatures in a kiln; it became popular during China's Tang Era (299)

post-impressionism   an artistic movement (which began in France in the 1880s) where artists were especially interested in color, believing it could act as its own form of language (722)

praetors   chief executives of the Roman Republic; they were in charge of civil law as it applied to Roman citizens (158)

predestination   the belief that God, as a consequence of his foreknowledge of all events, has predetermined those who will be saved (the elect) and those who will be damned (442)

prefectures   Japanese territories, governed by the former daimyo owners (786)

price revolution   a dramatic rise in prices (inflation), which was a major economic problem in all of Europe in the sixteenth and early seventeenth centuries (459)

principle of intervention   the right of great powers to send armies into countries where there were revolutions in order to restore legitimate monarchs to their thrones (663)

principle of legitimacy   a guideline used by Prince Klemens von Metternich during the Congress of Vienna in 1814, which meant that lawful monarchs were restored to their positions of power in order to keep peace and stability in Europe (662)

privatization   the act of changing state-owned (or public-owned) companies to private control or ownership (1021)

procurator   a person who acts on behalf of someone in authority (181)

proletariat   the working class (692)

proportional representation a system where the number of representatives assigned per political party is based on the number of votes each party received during the general election (1063)

protectorate a political unit that depends on another state for its protection (732)

psychoanalysis a method devised by Sigmund Freud by which a psychotherapist and patient could probe deeply into the memory of the patient in order to retrace the chain of repressed thoughts (717)

Ptolemaic or geocentric having the view that the universe is a series of concentric (one inside the other) spheres with a fixed or motionless Earth as its center (578)

puddling a process developed by Henry Cort where coke, derived from coal, was used to burn away impurities in pig iron (crude iron) to make high-quality iron (653)

Pueblos descendants of the Anasazis named after the Spanish word for "town" because of their unique adobe dwellings (201)

purdah the religious practice among Muslims and some Hindus of isolating women (540)

Q

quipu a system of knotted strings used by the Incas for keeping records (217)

R

radiocarbon dating a method of analysis that calculates the age of artifacts and fossils by measuring the amount of C-14 left in them (6)

raga one of dozens of musical scales on which Indian classical music is based; these scales are grouped into separate categories according to the time of day during which they are to be performed (327)

raja the title of the tribal chieftain (prince) who held political power among the Aryans (63)

Rajputs Indian warriors whose military tactics were based on infantry supported by elephants (317)

rationalism a system of thought based on the belief that reason is the chief source of knowledge (585)

realpolitik the "politics of reality," or politics based on practical matters rather than theory or ethics (672)

real wages the actual purchasing power of income (963)

Red Guards Mao Zedong's revolutionary units organized during the Cultural Revolution to cleanse Chinese society of impure elements guilty of taking the capitalist road (1077)

Reichstag the German parliament (851)

Reign of Terror a system devised by the National Convention and the Committee of Public Safety in France (1793–94) whereby revolutionary courts were set up to protect the revolutionary republic from its internal enemies by conducting mass executions (639)

reincarnation the belief that the individual soul is reborn in a different form after death (68)

relics the bones of, or objects connected with, saints considered worthy of worship by the faithful (396)

relics of feudalism obligations of peasants to local landlords (or the privileges of aristocrats) that had survived from an earlier age (for example, the payment of fees by peasants for the use of local facilities) (630)

reparations financial compensation (829)

revisionists Marxists who rejected the revolutionary approach and instead argued for workers to organize in mass political parties (and work with other parties) to gain reforms (695)

ricksha a small, covered, two-wheeled vehicle, usually for one passenger, that is pulled by one man (used originally in Japan) (889)

ritual prayers combined with gifts and sacrifices to gain the favor of the gods in religious ceremonies (136)

ronin "wave men," or samurai who had been released from servitude (masterless samurai) (569)

S

salon a gathering of notables (including writers, artists, aristocrats, government officials, and wealthy middle-class people) who met in fashionable drawing rooms (called "salons") to discuss new ideas (592)

samurai "those who serve," a class of military retainers in Japan whose purpose was to protect the security and property of their patrons (303)

Sanskrit the first writing system of the Aryans, developed around 1000 B.C. (63)

savannas broad grasslands dotted with small trees and shrubs (255)

scholasticism the philosophical and theological system of medieval schools, which tried to reconcile faith and reason (398)

scientific method a way to examine and understand nature built upon inductive principles; the use of carefully organized experiments and systematic, thorough observations to lead to correct general principles (586)

scientific socialism Gamal Abdul Nasser's plan to improve the standard of living throughout the Middle East by nationalizing major industries and using central planning to guarantee that resources would be used efficiently (1060)

scriptoria writing rooms in monasteries where monks copied the works of early Christianity (such as the Bible) and Latin classical authors (351)

secular worldly (419)

secularization seeing the world in material, not spiritual, terms (586)

secular state a state that rejects any church influence on its policies (873)

self-strengthening the idea that China should adopt Western technology while keeping its Confucian values and institutions (771)

Senate a select group of about 300 landowning Roman males who served for life, and whose advice to government officials had the force of law by the third century B.C. (158)

separation of powers a system of government in which the executive, legislative, and judicial powers are separate (thereby providing checks and balances among the powers) (589)

sepoys Indian soldiers hired by the British East India Company in the 1800s to protect its interests in India (748)

serfs peasants bound to the land; they provided labor services, paid rents, and were subject to the lords' control (382)

shah king (526)

Shining Path a radical guerrilla group in Peru with ties to Communist China (1035)

shogun "general," a powerful Japanese military leader who ruled the centralized government; the first one was appointed by Minamoto Yoritomo near the end of the twelfth century (304)

shogunate a centralized governing system in which a Japanese emperor remained ruler in name only, and the shogun exercised the actual power (304)

sitar a stringed instrument (327)

slash-and-burn method a method of farming whereby an area is cleared by chopping down trees and burning off the remaining plants, which provide natural fertilizer for the soil (509)

Social Darwinism a social order that was based on Charles Darwin's principle of organic evolution (717)

Socialist a member of the Socialist Party; an advocate of collective or governmental ownership and administration of the means of production and distribution of goods (692)

Socratic method a form of teaching that uses a question-and-answer format to lead pupils to conclusions by using their own reasoning (139)

soviets Russian councils composed of deputies from workers and soldiers (819)

space shuttles reusable spacecraft that return to Earth under their own power (1113)

spheres of influence areas in China where foreign nations were granted exclusive trading rights or railroad and mining privileges by warlords in exchange for money (772)

squadristi bands of black-shirted armed Fascists organized by Benito Mussolini to attack Socialist offices and newspapers and break up Socialist strikes (843)

stagflation the economic stagnation that occurred from 1973 to the mid-1980s in the United States (it was characterized by high inflation and high unemployment) (992)

stateless societies a group of independent villages that were organized by clans and ruled by a local chieftain or clan head (268)

stelae carved stone pillars (sometimes a hundred feet tall) that were used to mark the tombs of dead kings or religious leaders (276)

Stoicism the most popular philosophy of the Hellenistic world, founded by a teacher, Zeno, based on the concept that happiness, the supreme good, could be obtained only by living in harmony with the will of God, thereby obtaining inner peace (146)

stupas stone towers housing relics of the Buddha (73)

subinfeudation a lord-vassal relationship that bound together both greater and lesser landowners: a system where vassals of a king (also landowners) had vassals owing them military service in return for a grant of land; these vassals might also have vassals who were knights with small landholdings (354)

subsistence farming growing just enough crops for personal use, not for sale (266)

sultan "holder of power," a king or sovereign, especially of a Muslim state (236)

supply-side economics Ronald Reagan's policy of massive tax cuts that would supposedly stimulate rapid economic growth and produce new revenues (992)

symbolists a group of French writers and artists (after the 1880s) who believed an objective knowledge of the world was impossible since the external world was made up of only symbols; they dealt in general truths instead of actualities, exalting the metaphysical and mysterious; they believed that art should exist for art itself (720)

T

taille an annual direct tax, usually on land or property (the use of which was strengthened by King Louis XI as a permanent tax imposed by royal authority) (411)

Tao "Way," or the key to proper behavior (that is, regarding the view of duty and humanity in Confucianism or the noninterference philosophy of Taoism) (100)

Taoism a system of teachings based on the ideas of Lao Tzu; the main belief was that the true way to follow the will of Heaven is inaction—letting nature take its course by not interfering with it (102)

Tennis Court Oath a promise made by the Third Estate in 1789 to meet until they produced a French constitution (the oath was sworn during a meeting that took place at a tennis court) (632)

tepees circular tents used for shelter (199)

Thatcherism the economic policy of Margaret Thatcher, Britain's first female prime minister (990)

theocracy a government ruled by divine authority (25)

theology the study of religion and God (398)

theology of liberation Latin American Catholics in the 1960s who were influenced by Marxist ideas and believed that Christians must fight to free the oppressed, even if it meant the use of violence (1018)

Theravada "the teachings of the elders," a school of Buddhism where followers saw Buddhism as a way of life instead of a religion that was centered on individual salvation (315)

thermoluminescence dating a method of analysis that dates an object by measuring the light given off by electrons trapped in the soil surrounding it (7)

totalitarian state a government that aims to control the political, economic, social, intellectual, and cultural lives of its citizens (842)

total war war involving a complete mobilization of resources and people (814)

tozama outside or greater; more independent lords, usually more distant from the center of the shogunate (566)

trading societies countries depending primarily on trade for income (333)

trench warfare fighting from ditches protected by barbed wire (as in World War I) (806)

tribunes of the plebs Roman officials who were given the power to protect the plebeians (158)

trilogy a set of three plays (140)

tsar the Russian word for *Caesar*; in the sixteenth century, Ivan IV became the first Russian ruler to take this title (472)

tundra a cold, treeless plain located south of the Arctic (196)

U

ulema a supreme religious authority that administered the legal system and a system of schools for educating Muslims in the Islamic world (523)

ultra-Catholics an extreme Catholic party favoring strict opposition to the Huguenots during the French Wars of Religion in the latter half of the sixteenth century (454)

umma the Islamic community; Muhammad was its first political and religious leader (239)

Uncertainty Principle German physicist Werner Heisenberg's statement that one cannot determine the path of an electron because the act of observing with light affects the electron's location (in a larger sense, he suggested that at the bottom of all physical laws was uncertainty) (865)

unconditional surrender absolute, unqualified surrender (913)

universal law of gravitation a law that explains in mathematical terms that every object in the universe is attracted to every other object by a force called gravity (which explains why planets orbit the sun instead of going off in straight lines) (582)

universal male suffrage the right of all adult men to vote (665)

urban society city dwellers; the urban society of Renaissance Italy was made up of powerful city-states (419)

utopian socialists a movement of idealistic intellectuals—begun in the first half of the nineteenth century—who believed in the equality of all people and in replacing competition with cooperation in industry (labeled as such by later socialists) (660)

V

vassalage the practice by which nobles gave grants of land to vassals (those who served a lord in a military capacity) who, in return, would fight for their lords (353)

veneration of ancestors the idea of treating family ancestors well due to the belief that their spirits could bring good or evil fortune to the living family members; it led to the Chinese practice of burning replicas of physical objects to accompany the departed on their journey to the next world (91)

vernacular the language used in a particular region (399)

viceroy the governor of a country or province who rules as a representative of his king or sovereign (British viceroys carried out Parliament's wishes in India in the 1800s) (749)

Viet Cong Vietnamese Communists—also known as the National Liberation Front (1096)

vizier "steward of the whole land," the holder of this office was directly responsible to the pharaoh and was in charge of the government bureaucracy (36)

W

war of attrition   war based on wearing the other side down by constant attacks and heavy losses (808)

war communism   a policy used to ensure regular supplies for the Red Army during the Russian Civil War (1918–21), which included government control of banks and most industries, seizing grain from peasants, and the centralization of state administration under Communist control (823)

welfare state   a nation in which the government takes responsibility for providing citizens with services and a minimal standard of living (960)

wergeld   "money for a man"—in Germanic law, a fine paid by a wrongdoer to the family of the person who was injured or killed, the amount of which varied according to social status (345)

westernization   conversion to or adoption of western traditions or techniques (882)

white-collar   of, relating to, or constituting the class of employees whose duties do not require the wearing of work clothes or protective clothing—such as professional and technical workers, managers, officials, and clerical and sales workers (963)

witchcraft   the practice of sorcery or magic, that was once a part of traditional village culture but was denounced as heresy by the Catholic Church in the Middle Ages (459)

women's liberation movement   a renewed interest in feminism in the late 1960s that called for political and legal equality with men (994)

Y

yoga   "union," a practice developed by the Hindus that is a method of training designed to lead to union with God (69)

Z

zaibatsu   in Japan, a concentration of various manufacturing processes within a single enterprise—a large financial and industrial corporation (793)

zamindars   local officials in India who kept a portion of the taxes paid by peasants in lieu of salary (531)

ziggurat   a massive stepped tower upon which the temple dedicated to the chief god or goddess of a Sumerian city was built (25)

Zionism   an international movement originally for the establishment of a Jewish national or religious community in Palestine and later for the support of modern Israel (718)

SPANISH GLOSSARY

A

abbesses/abadesas   los líderes de conventos (348)

absolitionism/abolicionismo   un movimiento para poner a un fin la esclavitud (675)

absenteeism/ausentismo   ausencia crónica de los deberes de uno; esta práctica de funcionarios de la iglesia sus deberes y pagaron a subordinados para hacer sus funciones (frecuentemente sin éxito), que ignoraron contribuyó a la insatisfacción que causó la Reformación (436)

absolute rulers/gobernantes absolutos   gobernantes que tenían la libertad de gobernar sin leyes (259)

absolutism/absolutismo   una forma de regla donde la autoridad última estaba en las manos de una monarca que sostuvo gobernar por derecho divino (467)

acid rain/lluvia ácida   lluvia que resulta cuando azufre arrojado de fábricas industriales se mezcla con la humedad en el aire (responsable por la matanza de grandes áreas selváticas en Norteamérica y Europa) (1112)

acropolis/acropolis   usualmente la parte de arriba, fortificada de una ciudad o pueblo que sirvió como un refugio durante ataques y a veces como el centro religioso para templos y edificios públicos (123)

adobe/adobe   ladrillo secado en el sol usado en la construcción de asilos (201)

agora/ágora   un espacio abierto debajo de un acropolis que fue usado para la asamblea de la ciudad y para un mercado (123)

agricultural societies/sociedades agrícolas   países con economías primordialmente de agricultura (333)

Anschluss/Unión política de Austria con Alemania en 1938   se refiere a la unión de Hitler de Alemania y Austria (902)

anthropologists/antropólogos   expertos que usan artefactos y fósiles humanos para determinar cómo gente vivía (5)

anti-Semitism/antisemitismo   hostilidad hacia los judíos o discriminación contra los judíos como un grupo religioso (850)

apartheid/segregación racial   un sistema de segregación racial en Sudáfrica (1044)

appeasement/apaciguamiento   la póliza de Gran Bretaña (antes de la Segunda Guerra Mundial) basada en la creencia que si estados europeos satisficieron las demandas razonables de poderes no satisfechos, el segundo sería contento, y se lograría estabilidad y paz en Europa (902)

aqueduct/acueducto   un canal artificial donde pasa el agua (los aztecas en México construyeron un acueducto en el siglo quince (207)

archaeology/arqueología   el estudio de sociedades pasadas a través de un análisis de lo que gente ha dejado (5)

archipelago/archipiélago   una cadena de islas (327)

archons/arcontes   líderes que ayudaron el consejo de nobles en Atenas antigua (128)

armada/armada   una armada de buques de guerra (457)

Aryan racial state/estado racial ario   una nación que consiste sólo de tipo étnico homogéneo hipotético descendido de antiguos indo-europeos (Hitler consideró que los alemanes eran el grupo supremo de los arios) (902)

ascetics/asceta   personas que practican abnegación como una manera de lograr un entendimiento de realidad última (70)

Askia/Askia   el nombre de la dinastía (significa "usurpador") creado cuando Mahoma Ture destronó el hijo de Sunni Ali en 1493; durante su reino, el Imperio Songhai alcanzó su cumbre (265)

Atman/Atmn   según la creencia hindú, el individuo mismo cuyo deber era buscar y conocer a Brahmán (68)

Ausgleich/Ausgleich   el Compromiso de 1867 que creó la monarquía dual de Austria-Hungría (674)

australopithecines/australopithecines   "monos del sur", florecieron en el este y el sur de África y eran los primeros homínidos que hicieron herramientas de piedra (9)

B

balance of power/equilibrio de poder   la idea que los estados deben tener poder igual para prevenir que un estado domine los otros (619)

banana republics/país de la América Latina que está bajo la excesiva influencia económica de los Estados Unidos   países pequeños dependientes de naciones grandes y ricas (891)

Baroque-Rococo/barroco-rococó   un estilo arquitectónico del siglo dieciocho donde uno vio un edificio como una obra de arte total—una totalidad armoniosa (593)

bazaar/bazar   un mercado cubierto (el bazar era una parte crucial de cada ciudad o pueblo musulmán) (240)

bey/bey   un líder tribal, considerado el primer entre iguales; puede exigir lealtad entre sus jefes proveyéndolos con recompensa y terrenos (también el origen del sistema del sultán de gobernar en Persia y la India) (522)

Blitzkrieg/Guerra Relámpago   una guerra conducida con gran rapidez y fuerza (908)

blue-collar/obrero   relacionando a, o constituyendo de la clase de ganadores de sueldos cuyos deberes requieren que usen ropa de trabajo o ropa protector—ocupaciones de producción industrial (963)

bourgeois/burgués   una persona de la clase media (658)

bourgeoisie/burguesía   la clase media (692)

boyars/boyars   la nobleza rusa (472)

Brahman/Brahmán   según la creencia hindú, un fuerza en el universo, una forma de realidad última o Dios (68)

Breshnev doctrine/doctrina de Breshnev   la insistencia de Leonid Breshnev sobre el derecho de la Unión Soviética de intervenir si el comunismo fue amenazado en otro estado comunista (979)

brinkmanship/práctica de llevar las cosas muy cerca de la línea fronteriza de peligro o al borde de una guerra   amenaza de empezar una guerra para lograr las metas de alguien (802)

Bronze Age/Edad de Bronce   desde alrededor de 3000 a 1200 a. de J.C., caracterizada por el uso general de bronce para herramientas y armas (17)

Bushido/bushido   "el código del guerrero", el código del guerrero del samurai de Japón (303)

C

caliph/califa   el líder secular de la comunidad islámica (230)

Camp David Accords/Acuerdos de Camp David   un acuerdo para firmar un convenio de paz entre Israel y Egipto en 26 de Marzo, 1979 (la reunión ocurrió en Camp David, Maryland, y fue asistido por Jimmy Carter, Menachim Begin, y Anwar al-Sadat) (1064)

carruca/*carruca*   un arado con ruedas pesadas con una reja de arado inventado durante la Edad Media y usado para voltear la tierra de arcilla densa de Europa del norte (380)

Cartesian dualism/dualismo cartesiano   el principio de Descartes de la separación de la mente y la materia (y la mente y el cuerpo) (585)

caste system/sistema de casta   una serie de categorías rígidas sociales que determinó la potencial de ocupación y economía de una persona y también su posición en la sociedad (una división de clases en la India basada en la ventaja económica) (64)

caudillos/caudillos   líderes fuertes que dominaron las nuevas naciones independientes de Latinoamérica principalmente por fuerzas militares; usualmente fueron apoyados por la nobleza provinciana (760)

censorate/censorate   una rama de la burocracia central de la dinastía Qin de China que fue hecha de inspectores que miraron a los oficiales gubernamentales (104)

centuriate assembly/asamblea centurión   la asamblea más importante del República Romano; fue organizado por clases basadas sobre la riqueza, donde los ciudadanos más ricos siempre tenían la mayoría (158)

chapbooks/libros de cordeles   folletos cortos imprimidos en papel barato y vendidos por buhoneros a las clases bajas; consistieron de todo de cuentos religiosos a cuentos de aventura y sátiras toscas (598)

chivalry/caballerosidad   un ideal de conducta civilizada que desarrolló entre la nobleza durante los siglos once y doce, bajo la influencia de la iglesia; llegó a ser el código de ética que los caballeros tuvieron que mantener (355)

city-states/ciudad-estados   ciudades con control político y económico sobre el campo alrededor (las unidades básicas de una civilización sumeria (25)

civilization/civilización   una cultura compleja donde grandes números de gente comparten varios elementos comunes (17)

clan/clan   un grupo de familias que son parientes (199)

clergy/clero   obispos y sacerdotes de la Iglesia Cristiana (185)

collective bargaining/contrato colectivo   el derecho de sindicatos de negociar con empleadores sobre sueldos y horas (840)

collectivization/colectivización   muchas pequeñas posesiones unidas en una sola unidad para operación conjunta bajo supervisión gubernamental (847)

commercial capitalism/capitalismo comercial   un sistema económico donde personas invirtieron en intercambio o bienes para hacer ganancias (386)

compurgation/compurgación   una manera para determinar culpabilidad bajo la ley germánica; el acusado juró un juramento de inocencia y fue apoyado por un grupo de doce o veinticinco "ayudantes de juramentos" (346)

condottiere/condotiero   el líder de una banda de mercenarios, o soldados que vendieron sus servicios al mejor postor (421)

Confucianism/Confucianismo   una filosofía basada en las enseñanzas de Confucius, el "Primer Maestro" de China; los conceptos principales eran la "ética del trabajo" (deber) y un sentido de compasión y empatía hacia otros (la humanidad) (100)

conquistadores/conquistadores   conquistadores españoles del siglo dieciséis motivados por gloria, codicia, y celo religioso (492)

conscription/conscripción   reclutamiento militar (802)

conservatism/conservatismo   una ideología que favoreció obediencia a la autoridad política y la creencia que religión organizada era crucial para la orden en la sociedad (662)

consulate/consulado   una nueva forma de república francesa proclamada en 1799, que fue totalmente controlada por Napoleón Bonaparte (640)

consuls/cónsules   los directores ejecutivos oficiales del Repúblic Romano, dos que eran elegidos cada año; dirigieron el gobierno y guió el ejército en batalla (158)

consumer society/sociedad del consumidor   una preocupación con, y la inclinación hacia la compra de bienes que directamente satisfacen los deseos humanos (968)

Contras/Contras   rebeldes financiados por los Estados Unidos que empezaron una guerra guerrillera contra el gobierno provisional sandinista en Nicaragua (1027)

cottage industry/industria de casa de campo   la producción de bienes en el hogar de uno (610)

council of the plebs/consejo de los plebeyos   una asamblea popular del Repúblic Romano creada solamente para los plebeyos, fundada en 471 a. de J.C. (158)

counterterrorism/contraterrorismo   una política calculada de venganza directa contra terroristas (radicales que comiten actos violentos, como matar a civiles, tener como rehenes, y asaltar aviones, para lograr sus metas) (1000)

creole elites/élites criollos   descendentes localmente nacidos de los europeos que llegaron a ser habitantes permanentes de Latinoamérica (756)

cuneiform/cuneiforme   "en forma de cuña" (un sistema de escribir desarrollado por los sumerios con impresiones en forma de cuñas hechas usando punzones de lengüetas en tablas de arcilla) (30)

D

daimyo/daimyo   "grandes nombres", líderes de familias nobles que controlaron propiedades vastas en Japón que no debieron impuestos al gobierno (304)

deficit spending/gastos deficitarios   los gastos de fondos gubernamentales ganados prestando en vez de por impuestos (840)

deforestation/desforestación   el proceso de cortar árboles en bosques y selvas para proveer productos de madera y nuevos terrenos para cultivo (1112)

deism/deísmo   un sistema de pensamiento que deniega la interferencia del Creador con las leyes del universo (589)

democracy/democracia   poder de la mayoría (125)

descamisados/descamisados   "los sin camisas", las clases obreras en Argentina (1028)

de-Stalinization/de-Estalinización   el proceso de Nikita Khrushchev de eliminar las políticas más crueles de Stalin (952)

détente/disminución   un relajamientop de relaciones o tensiones tenas (como entre los Estados Unidos y la Unión Soviética durante la década de 1970) (977)

developed nations/naciones desarrolladas   naciones ricas, localizadas primordialmente en el Hemisferio Norte, que tienen sistemas industriales y agrícolas bien organizados, usan tecnologías avances, y tienen sistemas educativos fuertes (1114)

developing nations/naciones desarrollándose   naciones pobres, localizadas primordialmente en el Hemisferio Austral, que son primordialmente naciones agrícolas con poca tecnología o educación (1114)

dharma/dharma   ley divina (el concepto de karma está gobernado por dharma) (69)

Diet/Diet   la legislatura japonesa (788)

diocese/diócesis   el área de autoridad de un obispo cristiano (346)

diplomatic revolution/revolución diplomática   la formación de nuevas alianzas sin recurrir a guerra (619)

direct rule/dominio directo   la forma de regla que ocurrió cuando élites locales fueron removidos de poder y reemplazados con una nueva serie de oficiales traídas de la madre patria (733)

dissidents/disidentes   aquellos que dan su opinión contra el statu quo o no están de acuerdo con él (por ejemplo, aquellos que opusieron el régimen en la Unión Soviética) (979)

divine right of kings/derecho divino de reyes   la creencia que los reyes reciben sus poderes directamente de Dios y están responsable a nadie sino Dios (464)

domino theory/teoría dominó   el argumento que si los comunistas sucedieron en un país (es decir, Vietnam del Sur), los países vecinos también caerían al comunismo (950)

dowry/dote   una cantidad de dinero dada por la familia del esposo al casarse (427)

drug cartels/carteles de drogas   grupos de negocios de drogas cuyo propósito es eliminar la competencia (1016)

Duma/Duma   una asamblea legislativa, o consejo representativo, en Rusia (712)

dyarchy/diarquía   un sistema creado por la dinastía Qing (como una manera para tratar con diferencias étnicas y culturales) donde todas las posiciones gubernamentales importantes eran compartidas igualmente por los Chinos y los Manchus (553)

dynasty/dinastía   una familia de gobernantes cuyo derecho para gobernar está pasado dentro de la familia (35)

E

ecology/ecología   el estudio de la relación entre cosas vivas y sus ambientes (1111)

elite/élite   un grupo pequeño de gente poderosa (61)

emancipation/emancipación   liberar de cautiverio (675)

empire/imperio   una grande unidad o un estado político, usualmente bajo un solo líder, que controla a mucha gente o territorios (28)

***encomienda*/encomienda**   el derecho dado a los colonizadores del Nuevo Mundo, por la Reina Isabela, para usar a la gente nativa como laboradores (492)

enlightened ruler/gobernante ilustrado   según los filosofes, un gobernante que permitió derechos básicos; las artes fomentadas, las ciencias, y la educación; y obedeció las leyes y las obligó justamente (614)

environmentalism/ambientalismo   el movimiento empezado durante la década de 1970 para controlar la polución de la Tierra (997)

epic poems/poemas épicos   poemas largos que cuentan las acciones de grandes héroes (el *Iliad* y el *Odyssey* eran los primeros grandes poemas épicos de Grecia) (122)

Epicureanism/Epicureanism   una filosofía fundada por un maestro, Epicurus, en Atenas durante el cuarto siglo a. de J.C., basada en el concepto de que la felicidad a través de la búsqueda de placer (libertad que viene de una mente en descanso) era la meta de la vida (146)

eta/eta   la clase más baja en la sociedad japonesa—esclavos de herencia (probablemente descendentes de prisioneros de guerra o criminales) cuyas ocupaciones incluyeron enterrar a los muertos y curar pieles (306)

ethnic cleansing/purificación étnica   la práctica de genocidio durante la Guerra de Bosnia (1993–1996) (871)

existentialsim/existencialismo   una filosofía del siglo veinte basada en el concepto de la ausencia de Dios en el universo—que significa que humanos eran completamente solos y responsables por sus acciones sin cierto conocimiento de lo correcto y lo malo; reducidos a desesperación y depresión, la única base de esperanza era sí mismos (1001)

export-import economy/economía de exportación-importación   un sistema económico basado en la exportación de materias primas mientras importando bienes manufacturados (892)

extraterritoriality/extraterritorialidad   la práctica (durante los años de 1800) donde los europeos vivieron en sus propias secciones en puertos chinos y no eran sujetos a las leyes chinas sino a sus propias leyes (769)

F

favorable balance of trade/la balanza comercial favorable   una práctica donde los bienes exportados de una nación son de más valor de aquellos bienes que están importados (entonces importando oro y plata) (470)

feminism/feminismo   el movimiento para los derechos de mujeres (591)

feudal contract/contrato feudal   una serie de reglas no escritas que determinó la relación entre un lord y su vasallo (355)

feudalism/feudalismo   la práctica de aristócratas o nobleza provinciana que proveen protección a cambio de servicio (353)

fez/fez   el gorro sin ala usado por musulmanes turcos (873)

fief/feudo   una división territorial dada a un vasallo (354)

filial piety/piedad filial   el concepto que todos los miembros de una familia deben subordinar sus necesidades a aquellas de la cabeza masculina de la familia (97)

Final Solution/Solución Final   la exterminación física de la gente judía por los Nazis durante la Segunda Guerra Mundial (919)

First Triumvirate/Primer Triunvirato   una coalición formada en 60 a. de J.C. cuando César unió fuerzas con Crassus y Pompey (162)

flagellants/flagelantes   personas que golpearon a sí mismos para suplicar perdón de Dios (404)

foot binding/atadura de los pies   una práctica china de atar los pies de mujeres jóvenes con tela o seda, que deformó a los pies e impidió que las mujeres caminaran bien (atadura hizo aparecer más pequeños los pies, que fue considerado atractivo) (560)

four modernizations/cuatro modernizaciones   modernización tocante a industria, agricultura, tecnología, y defensa nacional—una política desarrollada por Deng Xiaoping donde se animaron que la gente trabajara duro para beneficiar tanto sí mismos como la sociedad china (1079)

four olds/cuatro antiguos   ideas antiguas, cultura antigua, costumbres antiguas, y hábitos antiguos—que las Guardias Rojas trataron de eliminar usando maneras violentas durante la Revolución Cultural en China (1077)

frescoes/pintar al fresco retratos hechos donde se aplica la pintura al temple a la superficie del yeso mojado (430)

fudai/fudai dentro de o menor; daimyo que era directamente subordinado a los shogún (566)

functionalism/funcionalismo una teoría de diseño que pone gran énfasis en cómo se usará un objeto (861)

G

gang of four/banda de cuatro Jiang Qing—la viuda de Mao Zedong—y tres otros radicales de la Revolución Cultural que fueron enjuiciados y mandados a la cárcel por reformadores guíados por Deng Xiaoping (1079)

genetic engineering/ingeniería genética un nuevo campo científico que cambia la información genética de células para producir nuevas variaciones —de células de tan simples como células de gérmenes a tan complejos como células de mamíferos (1113)

genin/genin una de las clases menores de Japón—laboradores sin tierras que se podían comprar y vender como esclavos (306)

genocide/genocidio la matanza deliberada de un grupo de gente (871)

gentry/gente bien nacida terratenientes prósperos bajo el nivel de la nobleza (466)

glasnost/glasnost "franqueza", un instrumento importante de la perestroika de Mikhail Gorbachev—los ciudadanos soviéticos fueron animaron para discutir francamente las fuerzas y debilidades de la Unión Soviética (980)

global economy/economía global una economía, desarrollada por las naciones del mundo desde la Segunda Guerra Mundial, donde la producción, distribución, y venta de bienes están hechas en una escala mundial (1114)

governments/gobiernos instituciones que organizan y regulan actividad humana (18)

grand vezir, grand wazir/gran visir el ministerio jefe que condujo las reuniones del consejo imperial del sultán durante el Imperio Otomano (522)

Great Leap Forward/Gran Avance Adelante un programa empezado por Mao Zedong en China en 1958 con la esperanza de adelantar rápidamente el crecimiento económico y obtener una sociedad sin clase; combinaron granjas colectivas existentes, normalmente el tamaño del pueblo tradicional, con vastas comunidades de la gente (1077)

greenhouse effect/efecto invernadero la calentura de la Tierra a causa del aumento de bióxido de carbono en la atmósfera (1112)

Green Revolution/Revolución Verde el trabajo de investigadores en la India durante la década de 1970 que introdujeron nuevos estilos de arroz y trigo que eran más productivos y resistentes a enfermedades pero que requisieron más fertilizante y agua (1089)

Guided Democracy/Democracia Guiada el gobierno de Presidente Sukarno, que disolvió el sistema político democrático de Indonesia para dominar él solo; nacionalizó empresas poseídas por extranjeros y buscó ayuda económica de China y la Unión Soviética (1095)

guilds/gremios asociaciones de gente con metas e intereses comunes (390)

guru/guía un maestro (66)

H

hajj/peregrinación un peregrinaje a Meca, creído ser uno de los "cinco suportes principales", o portes del códigos éticos, de Islam (230)

hans/hans dominios en Japón, cada uno gobernado por un lord daimyo (566)

harem/harem el dominio privado de un sultán, donde residió con sus concubinas (522)

Hegira/Hégira el viaje de Mahoma y sus seguidores de Meca a Medina en el año 622—este año llegó a ser el año 1 en el calendario oficial de Islam (227)

heliocentric/heliocéntrico la vista que el sol (no la Tierra) está en el centro del universo (579)

Hellenistic Era/Era Helenística literalmente, "imitar griegos", esta época era una edad de expansión del idioma e ideas griegos al Oriente Medio y más allá de él (144)

heresy/herejía el mantenimiento de doctrina religiosa diferente de las enseñanzas ortodoxas de la iglesia (393)

hominids/homínidos las primeras criaturas que parecían humanas (9)

Homo erectus/Homo erectus "ser humano vertical", una especie que emergió hace alrededor de 1.5 millones de años; aprendió cómo usar herramientas y fuego, y eran los primeros homínidos que salieron de África para ir a Europa y Asia (9)

Homo sapiens/Homo sapiens "seres humanos sabios", una especie que emergió hace alrededor de 250.000 años y marcó la tercera etapa del desarrollo humano (9)

Homo sapiens sapiens/Homo sapiens sapiens "seres humanos re-sabios", una especie que apareció en África entre 150.000 y 200.00 años pasados; eran los primeros humanos anatómicamente modernos (9)

hoplites/hoplitas soldados de infantería excesivamente armados (123)

hostage system/sistema de rehén una práctica donde el shogunado controló el daimyo forzando que la familia de un lord daimyo se quedara en su residencia gubernamental del lord (en Edo) cuando él estaba ausente de la residencia (566)

humanism/humanismo un movimiento intelectual—el más importante asociado con el Renacimiento—basada sobre el estudio de las clásicas, o las obras literarias de Grecia y Roma antigua (428)

human rights/derechos humanos los derechos justos de todo el mundo, delineados en la Declaración de Derechos Humanos, que fue adaptada por la Asamblea General de las Naciones Unidas en 1948 (1118)

I

imperator/imperator un comandante en jefe del ejército romano (164)

imperialism/imperialismo la extensión del poder de una nación sobre otras tierras (729)

import-substituting industrialization/industrialización por substitución de importaciones el desarrollo de nuevas industrias para hacer bienes que previamente habían sido importados (como fue hecho en Latinoamérica después de la Gran Depresión a causa de una reducción de ingresos) (1014)

impressionism/impresionismo una teoría o práctica de pintar (que empezó en Francia en la década de 1870) donde se retrataron las apariencias naturales de objetos por toques suaves y rasgos de colores primarios no mezclados para estimular luz reflejada actual (721)

indemnity/indemnidad una gran cantidad de dinero (776)

indentured workers/trabajadores ligados por contrato laboradores sin tierra que contrataron trabajo en las propiedades de los nobles (208)

indirect rule/dominio indirecto domino que ocurrió cuando fue permitido que gobernantes locales mantuvieran sus posiciones de autoridad y nivel social en una nueva colocación colonial (733)

inductive principles/principios inductivos una doctrina basada en el procedimiento del particular al general a través de matemáticas o lógica (586)

inquisition/inquisición una corte creada por la iglesia durante el siglo trece para encontrar y someter a juicio herejes; usó castigo, tortura, y a veces ejecución para lograr sus metas (393)

insulae/insulae bloques de apartamentos hasta seis pisos de altura, pobremente construidos de concreto, donde la gente pobre de Roma Imperial residió (177)

insurrection/insurrección el hecho de rebelarse contra un gobierno establecido (777)

interdict/interdicción un decreto usado por el Papa Inocente II para alcanzar sus fines políticos que prohibió que los sacerdotes dieran sacramentos de la iglesia con la esperanza que la gente, privada de las comodidades de religión, ejerciera presión contra su líder (392)

intifada/intifada "insurrección", una intranquilidad aumentada creada por la militancia palestino árabe (1064)

Islam/Islam "sumisión a la voluntad de Alá", una religión empezada por Mahoma, que creyó que él había recibido las revelaciones finales de Alá (226)

Islamic fundamentalism/fundamentalismo islámico un movimiento por fuerzas religiosas conservadoras en el Oriente Medio para reemplazar cultura y valores extranjeros con, de modo supuesto, formas "puras" islámicas de creencia y conducta (1067)

J

Janissaries/jenízaros soldados de a pie élites del Imperio Otomano que también sirvieron como guardias para el sultán (516)

jihad/jihad "lucha en el camino de Dios", la costumbre de hacer ataques contra los enemigos de Islam para expandir el movimiento islámico (230)

K

Kabuki/Kabuki una forma de teatro en Japón que enfatizó la violencia, música, y gestos dramáticos para entretener a sus veedores (570)

kamikaze/kamikaze "viento divino", un miembro del cuerpo japonés de ataques por aire que fue asignado para hacer ataques suicidas en objetos (es decir, barcos de EE.UU.) durante la Segunda Guerra Mundial (929)

karma/karma la fuerza de las acciones de una persona en esta vida que determina el renacimiento en una próxima vida (68)

khanates/kanato varios territorios separados, hechos del imperio unido de Genghis Khan después de su muerte, cada uno bajo la jurisdicción de uno de los hijos de Genghis Khan (293)

kibbutz/kibbutz una comunidad, o colectiva, en Israel donde los granjeros comparten propiedad y trabajan juntos, los adultos comen juntos y los niños están criados en hogares de niños separados (1070)

L

laissez-faire/doctrina de no intervención "dejar solo", libre de regulaciones gubernamentales (590)

laity/laicos miembros no cleros de la Iglesia Cristiana (185)

lay investiture/investidura secular la práctica donde líderes seculares eligieron nóminos a oficios de la iglesia y también los invirtieron con el símbolo de su cargo (el desacuerdo sobre esta práctica entre el Papa Gregorio II [contra] y el Rey Henry IV [para] en la Edad Media era conocido como la Controversia de Investidura) (391)

Legalism/Legalismo una filosofía con la creencia principal que seres humanos eran malos por naturaleza y podrían llegar a seguir el sendero correcto sólo por leyes fuertes y castigos rígidos (103)

liberalism/liberalismo la idea que gente deben estar tan libre de restricción como sea posible; una creencia en la protección de libertades civiles, o los derechos básicos de todo la gente (663)

lineage groups/grupos de lineage comunidades africanas formadas combinando unidades familiares extendidas (270)

litters/literas lechos cubiertos usados para llevar pasajeros (217)

Long March/Marcha Larga una caminata de 6.000 millas (a pie) hecha por el Ejército de Liberación de la Gente de Mao (PLO) a través de terreno hostil para alcanzar la dltima base comunista sobreviviendo en el nordeste de China en 1933–34 (887)

longhouses/vivienda comunal de los indios iroqueses estructuras construidas de postes de madera cubiertas con hojas de corteza, 150 a 200 pies de largo, construidas por los iroqueses de Norteamérica, y que alojaron alrededor de una docena de familias (199)

Luftwaffe/Fuerza Aérea alemana (Nazi) durante la Segunda Guerra Mundial la fuerza aérea alemana (909)

magic realism/realismo mágico una forma de literatura latinoamericana que une eventos realísticos con fondos como sueños o fantásticos (1037)

Mahatma/Mahatma "Gran Alma", el nombre que los indios usaron refiriéndose a Mohandas Gandhi (878)

Mahayana/Mahayana una escuela del budismo donde los seguidores lo vieron como una religión, no una filosofía; creyeron que Buda era una figura divina, y que a través de devoción hacia él, los ricos y los pobres podrían alcanzar la salvación en Nirvana (un Cielo verdadero) después de la muerte (316)

mandate of Heaven/mandato del cielo la autoridad de mandar o gobernar por derecho celestial (llegó a ser un principio básico del arte de gobernar de China) (94)

manorialism/señorialismo un sistema económico que consiste de "fincas solariegas" que eran territorios agrícolas manejados por lores y trabajados por campesinos; la finca solariega era la unidad básica de organización rural durante la Edad Media (382)

mansa/mansa "rey" (262)

marathon/maratón una carrera pedestre de 26 millas (129)

matrilineal societies/sociedades por línea materna sociedades donde la descendencia está derivada a través de la madre (271)

Mau Mau movement/movimiento Mau Mau un esfuerzo organizado entre la gente Kikuyu de Kenya que usó terrorismo para demandar uhuru (liberación) de los británicos (1044)

Meiji/Meiji "Dominio Iluminado", el reino del emperador japonés Mutsuhito (786)

mercantilism/mercantilismo una serie de principios que dominó el pensamiento económico en el siglo diecisiete donde la prosperidad de una nación dependió de una oferta grande de oro y plata (470)

Mesolithic Age/Edad Mesolítica "Medio de la Edad de Piedra", el período desde 10.000 a 7.000 a. de J.C. caracterizado por un cambio gradual de una economía de coger y cazar comida a una economía que produce comida (14)

mestizos/mestizos la progenie de europeos e indios americanos nativos (622)

militarism/militarismo glorificación de las fuerzas armadas (671)

minarets/alminares cuatro torres angostos que forman una mezquita (525)

ministerial responsibility/responsabilidad ministerial la idea que el primer ministro está responsable al elegido cuerpo legislativo popular y no al oficial ejecutivo (un principio crucial de democracia) (709)

mirs/mires comunes o comunidades de pueblos de campesinos en Rusia zarista que eran responsables por pagos de tierras al gobierno (675)

mobilization/movilización el proceso de asemblar y hacer tanto las tropas como las ofertas listas para la guerra (804)

modernism/modernismo cambios producidos por escritores y artistas (entre 1870 y 1914) rebelándose contra los estilos literarios y artísticas tradicionales dominando la vida cultural europea desde el Renacimiento (718)

monasticism/monaquismo la práctica de vivir la vida de un monje (346)

money economy/economía monetaria un sistema económico basado en dinero en vez de en la permuta (386)

monk/monje uno que buscó vivir la vida aislada de la sociedad humana ordinaria para perseguir un ideal de dedicación total a Dios (346)

monsoon/monzón   una norma de viento estacional en el sur de Asia que sopla desde el suroeste durante los meses del verano y desde el nordeste durante el invierno (60)

monsoon season/estación de monzón   un viento fuerte regular caracterizado por lluvia muy fuerte (509)

mosques/mezquitas   casas de adoración musulmanes (246)

motifs/motivos   ideas dominante o temas centrales (541)

mulattoes/mulatos   la progenie de africanos y europeos (622)

multinational corporations/corporaciones multinacionales   compañías que tienen divisiones en más de dos países (1015)

multinational state/estado multinacional   una colección de diferentes personas (665)

mutual deterrence/refrenamiento mutual   la póliza basada en la creencia que un arsenal de armas nucleares previene guerra asegurando que si aun una nación lanzara sus armas en un primer ataque, que la otra nación todavía podría responder y devastar él que atacó (946)

N

nationalism/nacionalismo   lealtad y devoción a una nación (643)

nationalization/nacionalización   posesión gubernamental (961)

naturalism/naturalismo   un estilo literario donde se acepta el mundo material como verdadero y, entonces, la literatura está escrita en una manera realista (718)

natural selection/selección natural   "supervivencia del más apto"—organismos más adaptables a sus ambientes pasan las variaciones que les encapaticen sobrevivir hasta que una nueva especie separada emerge (683)

Neanderthals/Neandertales   un tipo de *Homo sapiens* que hizo ropa de pieles de animales y parece haber sido el primer grupo que enterró a los muertos (9)

Neolithic Age/Edad Neolítica   griego para edad de "Piedra Nueva", la época desde 10.000 hasta 4.000 a. de J.C. (14)

Neolithic farming villages/pueblos de cultivación neolíticos   poblaciones que eran más permanentes y capaces de apoyar poblaciones más grandes debido a la cultivación de cosechas en una base regular (15)

Neolithic Revolution/Revolución Neolítica   el cambio del cazar animales y el coger comida al mantenimiento de animales y la cultivación de cosechas en una base regular durante la Edad Neolítica (14)

New Democracy/Democracia Nueva   una versión modificada de capitalismo puesto en efecto por Mao Zedong en China en 1958; industrias mayores fueron puestos bajo la posesión del estado, pero la mayoría de compañías manufactureras y de intercambio permanecieron en las manos privadas (1076)

New Economic Policy/Política Económica Nueva   una versión modificada de capitalismo puesto en efecto por Vladimir Lenin en Rusia en 1921; industria pesadas, bancario, y minería permanecieron en las manos del gobierno, pero los campesinos podrían vender sus productos agrícolas sin restricciones, y las tiendas de ventas al por menor e industrias pequeñas (menos de veinte empleados) podrían ser privadamente poseídas y operadas (845)

new monarchies/monarquías nuevas   países como Francia, la Inglaterra, y España (al final del siglo quince) donde nuevos gobernantes intentaron restablecer el poder centralizado de gobiernos monárquicos (411)

No/No   dramas japonesas que desarrollaron de una variedad de formas de entretenimiento, incluyendo bailes y malabarismos (308)

nomadic/nómada   el mover de un lugar a otro (10)

nongovernmental organizations (NGOs)/organizaciones no gubernamentales   grupos de interés (relacionados a la emergencia de movimientos sociales de orígenes populares) que transcienden fronteras nacionales; frecuentemente están representados en las Naciones Unidas (1119)

O

oligarchy/oligarquía   control por la minoría (125)

oracle/oráculo   un sepulcro sagrado dedicado a un dios o diosa que reveló el futuro (136)

ordeal/ordalía   una manera para determinar culpabilidad bajo la ley germánica; fue creído que si por intervención divina, el acusado fue indemne después de un juicio físico, era inocente (346)

orders/órdenes   grupos sociales, también conocidos como *estados* (divisiones de la sociedad en Europa, establecidas durante la Edad Media y continuando hasta más que la mitad del siglo dieciocho) (613)

organic evolution/evolución orgánica   el principio de Charles Darwin que cada tipo de planta y animal evolucionó sobre un período de tiempo largo de formas de vida simples y más antiguas (683)

ostracism/ostracismo   una costumbre concebida en Atenas antigua donde los miembros de la asamblea escribieron los nombre de una persona que se consideran dañosa en un fragmento de alfarería (*ostrakon*); si habían 6.000 votos registrados, la persona fue proscrita de la ciudad por diez años (132)

ozone layer/ozonosfera   una capa delgada de gas en la parte de arriba de la atmósfera que protege la Tierra de los rayos ultravioletos del sol (1112)

P

Paleolithic Age/Edad Paleolítica griego para "Piedra Vieja", el período antiguo de la historia humana donde los humanos usaron herramientas de piedra simples (10)

pan-Africanism/pan-africanismo un movimiento que enfatizó la necesidad para la unidad de todos los africanos (878)

pan-Arabism/pan-Arabismo una creencia en la unidad árabe (1060)

pashas/bajás gobernantes locales en África del Norte—nombrados por los otomanos conquistadores—que coleccionaron impuestos, mantuvieron la ley y orden, y eran directamente responsables a la corte del sultán en Constantinopla (518)

paterfamilias/paterfamilias el varón dominante de una familia (173)

patriarchal/patriarcal una sociedad dominada por hombres (28)

patricians/patricios grandes propietarios que llegaron a ser la clase gobernadora de Roma (158)

patrilineal societies/sociedades por línea paterna sociedades donde la descendencia está derivada a través del padre (271)

peninsulars/peninsulares oficiales españolas y portugueses que vivieron temporariamente en Latinoamérica para la ganancia política y económica y luego volvieron a su madre patria (756)

people's communes/comunidades de la gente la resulta de la combinación de granjas colectivas durante el Gran Avance Adelante en China (1077)

perestroika/perestroika "reestructurar", un término puesto a las reformas económicas, políticas, y sociales radicales de Mikhail Gorbachev en la Unión Soviética (980)

permanent revolution/revolución permanente fervor revolucionario constante (1077)

phalanx/falange soldados marchando hombro a hombro en una formación rectangular (124)

pharaoh/faraón uno de los varios títulos de reyes egipcios (la palabra *faraón* originalmente significaba "gran casa" o "palacio" (36)

philosophe/filosofe un miembro de la Ilustración, un movimiento de intelectuales del siglo dieciocho que creyó en razón, o la aplicación del método científico al entendimiento de la vida (588)

philosophy/filosofía un sistema de pensamiento organizado (139)

pictographic/pictográfico el uso de pictografías—símbolos de la ilustración, usualmente llamados *caracteres*—para formar una ilustración del objeto representado; un tipo de comunicación escrita (99)

planned economies/economías planeadas sistemas dirigidos por agencias gubernamentales (815)

plantations/plantaciones grandes propiedades terratenientes (495)

plebeians/plebeyos los terratenientes, artesanos, comerciantes, y pequeños granjeros menos ricos de Roma (158)

pluralism/pluralismo el mantenimiento de dos o más cargos o posiciones al mismo tiempo (436)

pogroms/pogromos masacres organizados de gente indefensa (718)

policy of containment/política de contención el plan de diplomático EE.UU. George Kennan de mantener comunismo dentro de sus bordes geográficos y prevenir futuros movimientos agresivos (945)

polis/polis una ciudad-estado griego (122)

Politburo/Politburó un comité que era el constructor principal de las pólizas del Partido Comunista (846)

polytheistic/politeístico el tener muchos dioses (30)

popes/papas líderes de la Iglesia Católica (obispos de Roma que se vieron como los sucesores de Pedro) (346)

porcelain/porcelana artículos cerámicos translúcidos hechos de arcilla fina endurecidas en temperaturas muy altas en un horno; llegó a ser popular durante la Era China de Tang (299)

post-impressionism/post-impresionismo un movimiento artístico (que empezó en Francia en la década de 1880) donde los artistas eran especialmente interesados en colores, creyendo que podría servir como su propia forma de idioma (722)

praetors/pretores directores ejecutivos del Repúblico Romano; se encargaron de la ley civil como fue aplicada a los ciudadanos romanos (158)

predestination/predestinación la creencia que Dios, como consecuencia de su presciencia de todos eventos, ha predeterminado aquellos que serían salvados (los elegidos) y aquellos que serían condenados (442)

prefectures/prefecturas territorios japoneses, gobernados por los antiguos dueños daimyo (786)

price revolution/revolución de precio un aumento drástico en precios (inflación), que era un problema económico mayor en toda Europa durante el siglo dieciséis y el principio del siglo diecisiete (459)

principle of intervention/principio de intervención el derecho de grandes poderes para mandar ejércitos a países donde habían revoluciones para restaurar monarcas legítimas a sus tronos (663)

principle of legitimacy/principio de legitimidad   una guía usada por el Príncipe Klemens von Metternich durante el Congreso de Viena en 1814, que significó que monarcas legítimas eran restauradas a sus posiciones de poder para mantener la paz y estabilidad en Europa (662)

privatization/privatización   el acto de cambiar compañías poseídas por el estado (o el público) a control o posesión privada (1021)

procurator/procurador   una persona que actúa en nombre de alguien en autoridad (181)

proletariat/proletariado   la clase obrera (692)

proportional representation/representación proporcional un sistema donde el número de representativos asignados por partido político está basada en el número de votos que cada partido recibió durante la elección general (1063)

protectorate/protectorado   una unidad política que depende de otro estado para su protección (732)

psychoanalysis/psicoanálisis   un método desarrollado por Sigmund Freud donde el psicoterapista y paciente podrían inquirir profundamente en la memoria del paciente para retrasar la cadena de pensamientos reprimidos (717)

Ptolemaic or geocentric/ptolemaico o geocéntrico   tener la vista que el universo es una serie de esféricos concéntricos (uno dentro del otro) con una Tierra fija o sin moción como el centro (578)

puddling/pudelación   un proceso desarrollado por Henry Cort donde el coque, derivado de carbón, fue usado para quemar las impurezas en hierro en bruto (hierro crudo) para hacer un hierro de alta calidad (653)

Pueblos/Pueblos   descendentes de los Anasazis nombrados por la palabra "pueblo" a causa de sus residencias de adobe únicas (201)

purdah/sistema de reclusión de las mujeres   la práctica religiosa entre musulmanes y algunos hindúes de aislar a las mujeres (540)

Q

quipu/quipu   un sistema de cuerdas con nudos usado para por los incas mantener registros (217)

R

radiocarbon dating/fijar la fecha por carbono radiactivo un método de análisis que calcula la edad de artefactos y fósiles midiendo la cantidad de carbono 14 en ellos (6)

raga/raga   el una de docenas de escalas músicas que la música clásica de la India está basada; estas escalas están agrupadas en categorías separadas según la hora del día en que se las representarían (327)

raja/rajá   título del cacique tribal (príncipe) que tuvo poder politico entre los arios (63)

Rajputs/Rajputs   guerreros indios cuyas tácticas militares fueron basadas sobre infantería apoyada por elefantes (317)

rationalism/racionalismo   un sistema de pensamiento basada en la creencia que la razón es la fuente principal de conocimiento (585)

realpolitik/realpolitik   las "políticas de realidad", o las políticas basadas en asuntos prácticos en vez de en teoría o ética (672)

real wages/salarios reales   el poder adquisitivo actual de ingresos (963)

Red Guards/Guardias Rojas   las unidades revolucionarias de Mao Zedong organizadas durante la Revolución Cultural para purificar la sociedad china de los elementos impuros culpables de tomar el sendero capitalista (1077)

Reichstag/Reichstag   el parlamento alemán (851)

Reign of Terror/reinado de terror   un sistema concebido por la Convención Nacional y el Comité de Seguridad del Público en Francia (1793–1794) donde las cortes revolucionarias fueron establecidas para proteger el república revolucionario de sus enemigos internos conduciendo ejecuciones en muchedumbre (639)

reincarnation/reencarnación   la creencia que el alma del individuo se vuelve a nacer en una forma diferente después de la muerte (68)

relics/restos mortales   los huesos de, u objetos conectados con, santos considerados merecedores de adoración por los fieles (396)

relics of feudalism/reliquia de feudalismo   obligaciones de campesinos a propietarios locales (o los privilegios de aristócratas) que han sobrevividas de una edad antigua (por ejemplo, el pago de honorarios por los campesinos para el uso de facilidades locales) (630)

reparations/reparaciones   compensación financiera (829)

revisionists/revisionistas   Marxistas que rechazaron el método revolucionario y en su lugar argumentaron que los trabajadores organizaran en partidos políticos en grupo (y trabajara con otros partidos) para ganar reformas (695)

ricksha/ricksha   un pequeño vehículo cubierto de dos ruedas, usualmente para un pasajero, halado por un hombre (usado originalmente en Japón) (889)

ritual/ritual   oraciones combinadas con regalos y sacrificios para ganar el favor de los dioses en ceremonias religiosas (136)

ronin/ronin   "hombres de ondas", o samurai que habían sido libertados de servidumbre (samurai sin dueño) (569)

U

ulema/ulema una autoridad religiosa suprema que administró el sistema legal y un sistema de escuelas para educar a los musulmanes en el mundo islámico (523)

ultra-Catholics/ultra-católicos un grupo católico extremo en favor de oposición estricta a los Huguinots durante las Guerras Francesas de Religión en la última mitad del siglo dieciséis (454)

umma/umma la comunidad islámica; Mahoma era el primer líder político y religioso (239)

Uncertainty Principle/Principio de Incertidumbre la declaración de físico alemán Werner Heisenberg que uno no puede determinar el sendero de un electrón porque el acto de observar con luz afecta la localidad del electrón (en un sentido más grande, sugirió que en la base de todas leyes físicas era incertidumbre (865)

unconditional surrender/rendición incondicional rendición absoluta, ilimitada (913)

universal law of gravitation/ley universal de gravitación una ley que explica en términos matemáticos que cada objeto en el universo está atraído a cada otro objeto por una fuerza que se llama gravedad (que explica porque los planetas giran alrededor del sol en vez de ir en líneas rectas) (582)

universal male suffrage/derecho al voto masculino universal el derecho de todos los hombres adultos al voto (665)

urban society/sociedad urbana habitantes de una ciudad; la sociedad urbana de Italia durante el Renacimiento fue hecha de ciudad-estados poderosos (419)

utopian socialists/socialistas utópicas un movimiento de intelectuales idealistas—que empezó en la primera mitad del siglo diecinueve—que creyó en la igualdad de toda la gente y en el reemplazo de la competencia con la cooperación en industrias (nombrado así por futuras socialistas) (660)

V

vassalage/vasallaje la práctica donde los nobles dieron divisiones territoriales (de tierra) a vasallos (aquellos que sirvieron un lord en una capacidad militar) quienes, a cambio, pelearían para sus lores (353)

veneration of ancestors/veneración de antepasados la idea de tratar a antepasados familiares bien debido a la creencia que sus espíritus pueden traer fortuna buena o mala a los miembros vivos de la familia; resultó en la práctica china de quemar réplicas de objetos físicos para acompañar los difuntos en su viaje al mundo venidero (91)

vernacular/lengua vernácula el idioma usado en una región particular (399)

viceroy/virrey el gobernador de un país y provincia que domina como representativo de su rey o soberanía (los virreyes bretañas cumplieron los deseos del Parlamento en India en los años de 1800) (749)

Viet Cong/Vietcong comunistas vietnamitas—también conocidos como el Ejército de Liberación Nacional (1096)

vizier/visir administrador de la tierra entera", el ocupador de esta carga era directamente responsable al faraón y se cargo de la burocracia del gobierno (36)

W

war of attrition/guerra de agotamiento guerra basada en el agotamiento del otro lado por ataques constantes y demasiadas pérdidas (808)

war communism/comunismo de guerra una política usada para asegurar ofertas regulares para el Ejército Rojo durante la Guerra Civil Rusa (1918–1921), que incluyó control gubernamental de bancos y la mayoría de las industrias, tomando granos de campesinos, y la centralización de administsración estatal bajo el control comunista (823)

welfare state/estado benefactor una nación donde el gobierno toma la responsabilidad de proveer a los ciudadanos con servicios y un nivel de vida mínimo (960)

wergeld/indemnización que debían pagar los parientes de un asesino a los parientes de la víctima "dinero por un hombre"—en la ley germánico, una multa pagada por un malhechor a la familia de la persona que fue herida o matada, la cantidad la cual varió según el nivel social (345)

westernization/hacerse occidental conversión a, o adopción de tradiciones o técnicas occidentales (882)

white-collar/oficinista relacionando a, o constituyendo de la clase de empleados cuyos deberes no requieren que usen ropa de labor o ropa protector—como trabajadores profesionales y técnicos, gerentes, oficiales, y trabajadores clericales y de ventas (963)

witchcraft/brujería la práctica de hechicería o májica, las cuales eran una vez parte de la cultura aldeana tradicional pero fue denunciada como herejía por la Iglesia Católica durante la Edad Media (459)

women's liberation movement/movimiento de liberación de mujeres el interés renovado en feminismo al final de la década de 1960 que insistió en igualdad política y legal con hombres (994)

Y

yoga/yoga   "unión", una prática desarrollada por los hindúes que es un método de preparación diseñado para resultar en la unión con Dios (69)

Z

zaibatsu/zaibatsu   en Japón, una concentración de varios procesos manufactureros dentro de una sola empresa—una grande corporación financiera e industrial (793)

zamindars/terratenientes   oficiales locales en la India que guardaron una porción de los impuestos pagados por los campesinos en lugar de sueldos (531)

ziggurat/zigurat   un torre masivo arreglado en filas sobre el cual el templo dedicado al dios o diosa principal de una ciudad sumeria fue construido (25)

Zionism/sionismo   un movimiento internacional originalmente para el establecimiento de una comunidad judía nacional o religiosa en Palestino y luego para el apoyo de Israel moderno (718)

INDEX

H

graphic Society; **357** Giraudon/Art Resource, NY; **358** North Wind Picture Archives; **360** Victor R. Boswell, Jr. ©National Geographic Society; **361 (left)** Cotton Ms. Claud. D.II 70, f.70; reproduced by permission of the British Library, London; **361 (right)** Bridgeman/Art Resource, NY; **363** North Wind Picture Archives; **366** Giraudon/Art Resource, NY; **368** Scala/Art Resource, NY; **371** ©Erich Lessing/Art Resource, NY; **372** Scala/Art Resource, NY; **374** Bibliotheque Nationale, Paris.

Chapter 13   **378** ©SuperStock/British Library, London; **380** Bridgeman Art Library/Art Resource, NY; **381** Ancient Art & Architecture Collection, Ltd.; **384** The Pierpont Morgan Library/Art Resource, MS399, f.5v, c. 1515, Bruges; **386** North Wind Picture Archives; **388** ©Wysocki/Explorer/Photo Researchers, Inc.; **389** Corbis-Bettmann; **390** Bibliothèque Nationale, Paris; **392** Scala/Art Resource, NY; **393** Bibliotheque Royale Ier Albert; Royale MS IV 119, fol.72 verso; **394** Detail from Lichtenthal Altar Tabernacle, Germany. The Pierpont Morgan Library/Art Resource, NY; **396** Bibliotheque Nationale, Paris; **398** Staatliche Museen, Berlin, Photo ©Bildarchiv Preussicher Kulturbesitz; **400** Corbis-Bettmann; **401 (left)** ©Sylvain Grandadam/Photo Researchers, Inc.; **401 (right)** Sonia Halliday Photographs; **403** ©Gianni Dagli Orti, Paris; **404** ©Bibliotheque Royale Albert ier, Bruxelles (Ms. 13076-77, f. 12v); **407** ©Bibliothéque Royale Albert Ier, Brussels; **409** Giraudon/Art Resource, NY.

Chapter 14   **418** Images from Ideas; **421** Images from Ideas; **422** Erich Lessing/Art Resource; **424** ©ARCHIV/Photo Researchers, Inc.; **425 (left)** Scala/Art Resource, NY; **425 (right)** Scala/Art Resource, NY; **425 (bottom)** The Ancient Art & Architecture Collection Ltd.; **426** Private Collection/The Bridgeman Art Library; **429** North Wind Picture Archives; **431 (top)** Scala/Art Resource, NY; **431 (bottom)** Scala/Art Resource, NY; **433 (left)** ©Photo 1994 Nippon Television Network Corporation, Tokyo; **433 (right)** *The Alba Madonna*, Raphael, National Gallery of Art, Washington, Andrew W. Mellon Collection; **434 (left)** Scala/Art Resource, NY; **434 (right)** Reproduced by Courtesy of the Trustees, The National Gallery, London; **435** Alinari/Art Resource, NY; **437** Cranach the Younger, *Martin Luther and the Wittenberg Reformers*, The Toledo Museum of Art, Toledo, Ohio: Gift of Edward Drummond Libbey; **439** Kunsthistorisches Museum, Vienna; **441 (left)** Scala/Art Resource, NY; **441 (right)** Hans Asper, Zwingli, Kunstmuseum Winterthur; **443** ©Bibliotheque Publique et Universitaire, Geneva; **444** The Royal Collection, ©Her Magesty Queen Elizabeth II; **447** Scala/Art Resource, NY.

Chapter 15   **451** Hyacinthe Rigaud, *Louis XIV*, Musee du Louvre, Photo R.M.N.; **454** Francois Dubois D'Amiens, *The St. Bartholomew's Day Massacre*, Museee Cantonal des Beaux-Arts, Lausanne; **456** Derechos Reservados, Museo del Prado, Madrid; **457** Private Collection; **458** Corbis-Bettmann; **461** North Wind Picture Archives; **463** ©Photo by Erich Lessing/Art Resource, NY; **465** Corbis-Bettmann; **467** The National Galleries of Scotland, By permission of the Earl of Rosebery; **469 (left)** Giraudon/Art Resource, NY; **469 (right)** Giraudon/Art Resource, NY; **474 (left)** Russian School, *Czar Peter the Great*, Rijksmuseum, Amsterdam; **474 (right)** Sovfoto/Eastfoto; **475** Peter Hoadley, *William III and Mary Stuart*, Rijksmuseum, Amsterdam; **477** Scala/Art Resource, NY; **478** Metropolitan Museum of Art, Bequest of Mrs. H.O. Havemeyer, 1929. H.O. Havemeyer Collection (29.100.6); **479** Nicholas Poussin, *Landscape with the Burial of Phocion*, Musee du Louvre, ©Photo R.M.N.; **480** John Taylor, *William Shakespeare*, by Courtesy of the National Portrait Gallery, London, England.

Chapter 16   **484** North Wind Picture Archives; **488** Corbis-Bettmann; **490** Giraudon/Art Resource, NY; **491** The Metropolitan Museum of Art, Gift of J. Pierpont Morgan, 1900(00.18.2); **493 (left)** Biblioteca Medicea Laurenziana; **493 (right)** Courtesy of William J. Duiker; **496** Jomard, *Les Monuments de la Geographie*, Paris, 1862. Photo courtesy of the New York Public Library; **499** Wilberforce House, Kingston upon Hull City Museums, Art Gallery and Archives; **500** Bibliotheque des Arts Decoratifs, Photo ©J.L. Charmet; **501** ©Ann Purcell/The Purcell Team; **502** North Wind Picture Archives; **505** E.T. Archive, London; **506** North Wind Picture Archives; **508** North Wind Picture Archives; **510** North Wind Picture Archives.

Chapter 17   **514** Victoria and Albert Picture Library; **517** Corbis-Bettmann; **518** Courtesy of the Topkapi Sarayi Musezi, Istanbul; **519** MS Fr. 9087, Bibliotheque Nationale, Paris; Photo ©Sonia Halliday Photographs; **521** Compliments of the Turkish Government Tourism Office; **522** ©Robert Frerck/Tony Stone Images; **525** Giraudon/Art Resource, NY; **526** Bibliotheque Nationale, Paris/Lauros-Giraudon, Paris/SuperStock; **529** George Holton/Photo Researchers, Inc.; **530** Courtesy of the Arthur M. Sackler Gallery, Smithsonian Institution, Washington, DC; **532** By courtesy of the Board of Trustees of the Victoria and Albert Museum; **533** Giraudon/Art Resource, NY; **536** Giraudon/Art Resource, NY; **537** North Wind Picture Archives; **538** Victoria & Albert Museum, London/Art Resource/NY; **541** Compliments of the Turkish Government Tourism Office; **542** ©Tony Stone Worldwide.

Chapter 18   **546** ©Wang Lu/ChinaStock; **548** ChinaStock; **550** ChinaStock; **552 (left)** The Palace Museum, Beijing; **552**

Vasily Kandinsky, *Painting with White Border*, May 1913; Collection, the Solomon R. Guggenheim Museum, New York; **724** Photo ©E. Louis Lankford.

Chapter 23   **728** Image Select/Art Resource, NY; **730** North Wind Picture Archives; **732** Collections of the Bibliotheque Nationale, Paris, Photo: ©Giraudon/Art Resource, NY; **734** Sipahioglu, Gamma-Liaison; **735** North Wind Picture Archives; **738** The Opening of the Suez Canal, Photo ©Bildarchv Preussischer Kulturbesitz, Berlin; **739** North Wind Picture Archives; **741** Aberdeen University Library; **742** Hulton Deutsch Collection/Corbis; **745** North Wind Picture Archives; **748** North Wind Picture Archives; **750** By permission of the British Library, London, Oriental and India Office Collections, WD.2443; **752** ©The Hulton Getty Picture Collection, Limited/Rischgitz Collection/Tony Stone Images; **753** Reproduced by Courtesy of the British Library, Oriental and India Office Collections; **754** Brown Brothers; **755** Brown Brothers; **757** Corbis-Bettmann; **759** ©G. Dagli Orti; **762** Brown Brothers.

Chapter 24   **766** James P. Blair, ©National Geographic Image Collection; **768** Peabody Essex Museum, Salem, Mass. Photo by Mark Sexton; **770** National Maritime Museum, London; **771** Harper's Weekly/Corbis; **773** Courtesy of the Freer Gallery of Art, Smithsonian Institution, Washington, DC; **774** Corbis-Bettmann; **778** Camera Press/Globe Photos; **779** ChinaStock; **781** Corbis-Bettmann; **783** ChinaStock; **786** Courtesy of the United States Naval Academy Museum; **789 (left)** Corbis-Bettmann; **789 (right)** Mary Evans Picture Library; **790** The Metropolitan Museum of Art, Gift of Lincoln Kirstein, 1959 (JP 3276), photograph by Otto E. Nelson; **793** Culver Pictures, Inc.

Chapter 25   **800** Tony Stone Images; **803** Archive Photos; **804** Bilderdienst Suddeutscher Verlag, Munich; **805** Corbis-Bettmann; **807** ©Roger-Viollet, Paris; **810 (top)** Librairie Larousse, Paris; **810 (bottom)** Express News/Archive Photos; **811** Archive Photos/American Stock; **814** Corbis-Bettmann; **815** E.T. Archive, London; **816** ©Ullstein Bilderdienst; **818** Archive Photos; **819** Archive Photos; **823** Brown Brothers; **824** David King Collection, London; **825** Corbis-Bettmann; **828** Bettmann/Hulton.

Chapter 26   **834** Archive Photos; **838** Corbis-Bettmann; **839** ©Roger-Violett; **841** Ellis Herwig/Stock Boston; **843** ©Popperfoto; **844** Corbis-Bettmann; **846** David King Collection, London; **848** ©The Hulton Getty Picture Collection, Limited/Tony Stone Images; **852** Hugo Jaeger, Life Magazine, ©Time Warner, Inc.; **855** Hugo Jaeger, Life Magazine, ©Time Warner, Inc.; **856** The National Archives/Corbis; **857** Snark/Art Resource, NY; **859** ©The Hulton Getty Picture Collection, Limited/Tony Stone

Images; **860** Archive Photos/Popperfoto; **862** Salvador Dali, *The Persistence of Memory*, 1931, Oil on canvas, 9 1/2 × 13:, Collection, The Museum of Modern Art, New York, Given Anonymously; **864** Corbis-Bettmann.

Chapter 27   **868** Hulton Deutsch Collection/Corbis; **870** Tate Gallery, London/Art Resource, NY; **872** ©The Hulton Getty Picture Collection, Limited/Tony Stone Images; **873** ©The Hulton Getty Picture Collection, Limited/Tony Stone Images; **875** Corbis-Bettmann; **879** ©The Hulton Getty Picture Collection, Limited/Tony Stone Images; **880** Hulton Deutsch Collection/Corbis; **881** Archive Photos; **884** Corbis-Bettmann; **887 (left)** ©The Hulton Getty Picture Collection, Limited/Tony Stone Images; **887 (right)** ©Earl Leaf/Rapho; **888** ChinaStock; **892** Charles O'Rear/©Corbis; **894** ©The Hulton Getty Picture Collection, Limited/Tony Stone Images; **895** Schalkwijk/Art Resource, NY; **896** Nik Wheeler/Corbis.

Chapter 28   **900** Corbis-Bettmann; **902** Paul Dorsey, Life Magazine ©1938 Time Inc.; **904** Hugo Jaeger, Life Magazine, © Time Warner Inc.; **905** National Archives (#306-NT-1222E); **910** Archive Photos/Imperial War Museum; **911** © The Hulton Getty Picture Collection, Limited/Tony Stone Images; **912** The National Archives/Corbis; **915** ©The Hulton Getty Picture Collection, Limited/Tony Stone Images; **917** National Archives (#111-C-273); **920** UPI/Corbis-Bettmann; **923** Main Commission for the Investigation of Nazi War Crimes, courtesy of the United States Holocaust Memorial Museum; **924** Courtesy of the Simon Wiesenthal Center Beit HaShoah Museum of Tolerance Library/Archives, Los Angeles, CA; **927** ©The Hulton Getty Picture Collection, Limited/Tony Stone Images; **928** ©The Hulton Getty Picture Collection, Limited/Tony Stone Images; **930** The Herald & Evening Times Picture Library ©Caledonian Newspapers Ltd.; **931** Snark/Art Resource, NY; **933** J. R. Eyerman, Life Magazine, ©Time Warner Inc.; **936** E. T. Archive.

Chapter 29   **942** Hulton Deutsch Collection/Corbis; **944** AP/Wide World Photos; **945** Corbis-Bettmann; **946** Corbis-Bettmann; **947** Hulton Deutsch Collection/Corbis; **949** Corbis-Bettmann; **954** UPI/Corbis-Bettmann; **955** Corbis-Bettmann; **957** ©Prache-Lewin/Sygma; **959** ©1990 Pierre Boulat-Cosos/Woodfin Camp and Associates; **960** Hulton Deutsch Collection/Corbis; **963** Corbis-Bettmann; **965** ©Bob Adelman/Magnum Photos; **968** Corbis-Bettmann; **969** ©The Hulton Getty Picture Collection, Limited/Tony Stone Images; **971** ©C. Raimond-Dityvon/Viva, Woodfin Camp and Associates; **972** AP/Wide World Photos.

Chapter 30   **976** AP/Wide World Photos; **978** Courtesy Ronald

TEXT CREDITS

GAUTAMA BUDDHA SPEAKS TO HIS DISCIPLES 72
From *The Teachings of the Compassionate Buddha*, E. A. Burtt, ed. Copyright 1955 by Mentor. Used by permission of the E. A. Burtt Estate.

THE GOOD LIFE IN GUPTA INDIA 77
"Fu-kwo-ki," in Hiuen Tsang, Si-Yu Ki: *Buddhist Records of the Western World*, translated by Samuel Beal (London: Routledge and Kegan, Paul), pp. xx, xii. Used with permission.

THE MAHABHARATA, THE GREAT INDIAN EPIC 80
Excerpt from *Sources of Indian Tradition*, Stephen Hay, ed. Copyright 1988, © Columbia University Press. Reprinted with permission of the publisher.

Chapter 4
THE BURNING OF THE BOOKS 105
Excerpt from *Sources of Chinese Tradition* by William Theodore de Bary. Copyright © 1960 by Columbia University Press. Reprinted with permission of the publisher.

Chapter 5
THE SPARTAN AND ATHENIAN MODELS 127
From *Plutarch: The Lives of the Noble Grecians and Romans*, trans. by John Dryden and rev. by Arthur Clough. Reprinted with permission of The Modern Library, Random House.

PERICLES SPEAKS TO THE ATHENIAN PEOPLE 131
From *The History of the Peloponnesian War* by Thucydides, translated by Rex Warner (Penguin Classics, 1954) copyright © Rex Warner, 1954. Reproduced by permission of Penguin Books Ltd.

AN ATHENIAN HUSBAND EXPLAINS HIS WIFE'S DUTIES 134
Reprinted by permission of the publishers and the Loeb Classical Library from *Xenophon: Memorabelia and Oeconomicus, Volume IV*, translated by E. C. Marchant, Cambridge, Mass.: Harvard University Press, 1923.

ALEXANDER DESTROYS THE PERSIAN PALACE AT PERSEPOLIS 145
Reprinted by permission of the publishers and the Loeb Classical Library from *Diodorus Siculus: Library of History*, translated by C. H. Oldfather, Cambridge, Mass.: Harvard University Press, 1923–1967.

Chapter 6
THE SERMON ON THE MOUNT 154
Reprinted from the Holy Bible, New International Version.

CINCINNATUS SAVES ROME 157
From *The Early History of Rome* by Livy, translated by Aubrey de Sel incourt (Penguin Classics, 1960) copyright © the Estate of Aubrey de Selincourt, 1960. Reproduced by permission of Penguin Books, Ltd.

THE ASSASSINATION OF JULIUS CAESAR 163
From *Plutarch: The Lives of the Noble Grecians and Romans*, translated by John Dryden and revised by Arthur Clough. Reprinted with permission The Modern Library, Random House.

THE BANQUETS OF THE RICH 178
Credit Line: from *Great Ages of Man: Imperial Rome*, by Moses Hadas and the Editors of Time-Life Books. © 1965 Time-Life Books, Inc.

Chapter 7
THE RITUAL OF HUMAN SACRIFICE 212
from Diego Duran, *The Aztecs: The History of the Indies of New Spain*, Doris Heydon and Fernando Horcasitas, trans. (New York: Orion Press, 1964), pp. 120–121.

THE QUIPU 219
From *Royal Commentaries of the Incas and General History Of Peru* by Garcilaso de la Vega, translated by Harold V. Livermore, Copyright © 1966. By permission of the University of Texas Press

Chapter 8
A PILGRIMAGE TO MECCA 229
Excerpt from *The Travels of Ibn Jubayr*, J. R.C. Broadhurst, trans. (London: Jonathan Cape, Ltd., 1952). Used with permission of the estate of J. R. C. Broadhurst and Jonathan Cape, Publishers.

THE CRUSADERS IN MUSLIM EYES 237
From *An Arab-Syrian Gentleman and Warrior in the Period of the Crusades* by Usamah ibn Murshid ibn Munqidh. Copyright © 1929 by Columbia University Press. Reprinted with permission of the Publisher.

THE QURAN 244
From *The Koran*, translated by N. J. Dawood (Penguin Classics, Fifth revised edition 1990) copyright © N. J. Dawood, 1956, 1959, 1966, 1968, 1974, 1990. Reproduced by permission of Penguin Books, Ltd.

Chapter 9
THE SALT MINES 261
From The Salt Mines from Said Hamdun and Noel King, eds., *Ibn Battuta in Black Africa* (London, 1975), p. 23

THE MUGHAL CONQUEST OF NORTH INDIA 533
From *The Memoirs of Zehir-ed-Din Muhammed Baber*, translated by John Leyden and William Erskine (Lone: Longman and Cadell, 1826). Reprinted with permission.

AN ELEPHANT FIGHT FOR THE KING'S ENTERTAIN-MENT 537
Excerpt from *Travels in the Mogul Empire*, A.D. *1656–1668* by Francois Bernier (Delhi: S. Chand & Co., 1968).

Chapter 18
THE EMPEROR PROCLAIMS THE SIXTEEN CONFUCIAN COMMANDMENTS 555
From *Popular Culture in Late Imperial China* by David Johnson et al. Copyright © 1985 The Regents of the University of California. Used with permission.

THE DREAM OF THE RED CHAMBER 562
From *Liu Wu-chi, An Introduction to Chinese Literature*, Chi-Chan, trans. Copyright © 1966 by Indiana University Press. Used with permission.

THE JAPANESE DISCOVER FIREARMS 567
From *Sources of Japanese Tradition* by William de Bary. Copyright © 1958 by Columbia University Press, New York. Reprinted with permission of the publisher.

Chapter 19
THE PUNISHMENT OF CRIME 599
Excerpt from *European Society in the Eighteenth Century* by Robert and Elborg Forster. Copyright © 1969 by Robert and Elborg Forster. Reprinted by permission of HarperCollins Publishers, Inc.

THE CONVERSION EXPERIENCE 602
Excerpt from *European Society in the Eighteenth Century* by Robert and Elborg Forster. Copyright © 1969 by Robert and Elborg Forster. Reprinted by permission of HarperCollins Publishers, Inc.

Chapter 20
THE ATTACK ON NEW MACHINES 611
Excerpt from *Society and Politics in England 1780–1960* by J. F. C. Harrison. Copyright © 1965 by J. F. C. Harrison. Reprinted by permission of Harper & Row, Publishers, Inc.

DECLARATION OF THE RIGHTS OF MAN AND THE CITIZEN 634
Excerpt from *The French Revolution* edited by Paul Beik. Copyright © 1971 by Paul Beik. Reprinted by permission of HarperCollins Publishers, Inc.

DECLARATION OF THE RIGHTS OF WOMAN AND THE FEMALE CITIZEN 635
From *Women in Revolutionary Paris 1789–1795* by Darleen Gay Levy, Harriet Branson Applewhite, and Mary Durham Johnson. Copyright © 1979 by University of Illinois Press. Used with permission of the publisher.

Chapter 21
REVOLUTIONARY EXCITEMENT 666
From *The Reminiscences of Carl Schurz* by Carl Schurz (New York: The McClure Co. 1907), vol. 1, pp. 112–113

EMANCIPATION—Serfs and Slaves 676
From *U.S. Statutes at Large* (Washington, D.C., Government Printing Office, 1875), vol. 12, pp. 1268–1269

Chapter 22
MARX AND ENGELS PROCLAIM THE CLASSLESS SOCIETY 694
From *The Communist Manifesto* by Karl Marx and Friedrich Engels (Penguin Classics, 1985) pp. 105, 120–121.

A DOLL'S HOUSE—ONE WOMAN'S CRY FOR FREEDOM 719
From *Roots of Western Civilization* by Wesley D. Camp. Copyright © 1983 by John Wiley & Sons. Reproduced with permission of McGraw-Hill, Inc.

Chapter 23
A CALL TO ARMS 735
from *The Vietnamese Response to Foreign Intervention*, Truong Buu Lam, ed., (New Haven, Conn.: Yale University Southeast Asian Series, 12967), pp. 76–78.

THE POETRY OF TAGORE 755
From *The Poetry of Tagore from Amiya Chakravarty*, ed. A Tagore Reader (Boston, 1961), p. 300

Chapter 24
A PROGRAM FOR A NEW CHINA 779
Excerpt from *Sources of Chinese Tradition* by William Theodore de Bary, Copyright © 1960 by Columbia University Press. Reprinted with permission of the publisher.

BA JIN AND THE CHINESE NOVEL 783
Excerpt from *Family* by Ba Jin. Copyright © 1964 Foreign Language Press, 24 Baiwanzhuang Road, Beijing 100037, P.R. China. Used with permission.

A LETTER TO THE SHOGUN 786
Excerpt from *Commodore Perry in Japan*, Robert L. Reynolds (New York: Harper & Row, 1963), p. 68.

Chapter 30
VACLAV HAVEL — THE CALL FOR NEW POLITICS 984
From Vaclav Havel, *The Washington Post,* February 22, 1990, page A28d

THE VOICE OF THE WOMEN'S LIBERATION MOVEMENT 996
From Simone de Beauvoir, *The Second Sex,* trans. H. M. Parshley (New York: Alfred A. Knopf, Inc., 1962, renewed 1980)

Chapter 31
STUDENT REVOLT IN MEXICO 1022
From Benjamin Keen, ed., *Latin American Civilization* (Boston: Houghton Mifflin, 1974), pp. 226–227)

CASTRO'S REVOLUTIONARY IDEALS 1024
From Benjamin Keen, ed., *Latin American Civilization* (Boston: Houghton Mifflin, 1974), pp. 226–227)

Chapter 32
THINGS FALL APART 1056
From Chinua Achebe, *Things Fall Apart* (NY: Anchor Books: Doubleday, 1959, pp. 13–14)

THE SUEZ CANAL BELONGS TO EGYPT 1059
From a speech nationalizing the Suez canal, Gamal Abdul Nasser, in *The Egyptian Gazette* (July 27, 1956), p. 5

A PLEA FOR PEACE IN THE MIDDLE EAST 1061
From The United Nations: Official Records of the Eleventh Session of the General Assembly, 666th Plenary Meeting, New York, 1 March 1957 (A/PV.666), II, 1275 f.

Chapter 33
THE CORRECT VIEWPOINT TOWARD MARRIAGE 1082
From *Communist China* (The China Reader, Vol. 3) by F. Schurman and O. Schell, eds., Copyright 1966 by Franz Schurman. Copyright 1967 by Franz Schurman and Orville Schell. Reprinted by permission of Random House, Inc.

GANDHI AND NEHRU: TWO VISIONS OF INDIA 1087
From Stephen Hay, *Sources of Indian Tradition* (New York: Columbia University Press, 1988)

GANDHI AND NEHRU: TWO VISIONS OF INDIA 1087
Gandhi in India: In His Own Words, "Letter to Jawaharlal Nehru" p. 329 ed. by Martin Green © 1987 by Navjivan Trust, by permission of University Press of New England.